Official 2001
National Football League

Record & Fact Book

A National Football League Book
Workman Publishing Co., New York

National Football League
280 Park Avenue, New York, N.Y. 10017 (212) 450-2000. NFL Internet Address: http://www.NFL.com

Printed in the United States of America.

A National Football League Book.

Compiled by the NFL Communications Department and Seymour Siwoff, Elias Sports Bureau.

Edited by Randall Liu, NFL Communications Department, and Matt Marini, NFL Publishing Group. Layout by William Tham. Proofread by Joe Velazquez and John Fawaz. Print managing by Dick Falk, Tina Dahl, and Lawson Desrochers. Cover design by Bill Madrid. Typesetting by Jim Gigliotti.
Statistics by Elias Sports Bureau.
Produced by the Publishing Group of the National Football League, Los Angeles.

Cover photograph of the Super Bowl XXXV champion Baltimore Ravens' defense by Phil Hoffmann.

Workman Publishing Co.
708 Broadway, New York, N.Y. 10003
Manufactured in the United States of America.
First printing, July 2001.
10 9 8 7 6 5 4 3 2 1

INDEX

2001 SCHEDULE AND NOTE CALENDAR

(All times local except American Bowl games, which are EDT.)
Nationally televised games indicated by network in parentheses.

	Friday, August 3	Pittsburgh ____ at Atlanta ____	7:30
	Saturday, August 4	Dallas ____ at Oakland ____	6:00
		Cincinnati ____ at Chicago ____	7:00
	Monday, August 6	AFC-NFC Pro Football Hall of Fame Game at Canton, Ohio	
		Miami ____ vs. St. Louis ____	(ABC) 8:00
PRESEASON/FIRST WEEK	**Friday, August 10**	Carolina ____ at Jacksonville ____	7:30
Open Date:		Cincinnati ____ at Detroit ____	7:30
Pittsburgh		New York Giants ____ at New England ____	8:00
	Saturday, August 11	Atlanta ____ at New York Jets ____	8:00
		Chicago ____ at Tennessee ____	7:00
		Denver ____ at Dallas ____	8:00
		Green Bay ____ at Cleveland ____	8:00
		Minnesota ____ vs. New Orleans ____	
		at San Antonio, Texas	(ESPN) 7:00
		Oakland ____ at Arizona ____	8:00
		San Francisco ____ at San Diego ____	7:30
		Seattle ____ at Indianapolis ____	7:00
	Sunday, August 12	St. Louis ____ at Buffalo ____	7:30
		Washington ____ at Kansas City ____	7:30
	Monday, August 13	Baltimore ____ at Philadelphia ____	7:30
		Miami ____ at Tampa Bay ____	(ESPN) 8:00
PRESEASON/SECOND WEEK	**Thursday, August 16**	Jacksonville ____ at New York Giants ____	(ESPN) 8:00
Open Date:		Pittsburgh ____ at Minnesota ____	7:00
Cincinnati	**Friday, August 17**	Atlanta ____ at Washington ____	8:00
		Tennessee ____ at St. Louis ____	(FOX) 7:00
	Saturday, August 18	Arizona ____ at Seattle ____	6:30
		Baltimore ____ at New York Jets ____	(CBS) 8:00
		Chicago ____ at Kansas City ____	7:30
		Dallas ____ at New Orleans ____	7:00
		Detroit ____ at Indianapolis ____	7:00
		New England ____ at Carolina ____	7:30
		Philadelphia ____ at Buffalo ____	7:30
		San Diego ____ at Miami ____	7:00
		Tampa Bay ____ at Cleveland ____	8:00
	Sunday, August 19	Oakland ____ at San Francisco ____	4:00
	Monday, August 20	Denver ____ at Green Bay ____	(ABC) 7:00
PRESEASON/THIRD WEEK	**Thursday, August 23**	Carolina ____ at Baltimore ____	7:30
Open Date:		Kansas City ____ at Jacksonville ____	7:30
Atlanta		Philadelphia ____ at Tennessee ____	(CBS) 7:00
	Friday, August 24	Cleveland ____ at Washington ____	8:00
		Indianapolis ____ at Minnesota ____	(FOX) 7:00
	Saturday, August 25	Arizona ____ at Chicago ____	7:00
		Buffalo ____ at Cincinnati ____	7:30
		Detroit ____ at Pittsburgh ____	1:00
		Miami ____ at Green Bay ____	7:00
		New England ____ at Tampa Bay ____	7:30
		New Orleans ____ at Denver ____	7:00
		New York Jets ____ at New York Giants ____	8:00
		St. Louis ____ at San Diego ____	7:00
		Seattle ____ at San Francisco ____	6:00
	Monday, August 27	American Bowl at Mexico City, Mexico	
		Dallas ____ vs. Oakland ____	(ABC) 7:00

PRESEASON/FOURTH WEEK
Open Date:
Chicago

Thursday, August 30	Buffalo _____ at Pittsburgh _____	7:30
	Indianapolis _____ at Cincinnati _____	7:30
	Jacksonville _____ at Dallas _____	7:30
	New York Jets _____ at Philadelphia _____	7:30
	Tennessee _____ at Detroit _____	7:30
	Washington _____ at New England _____	8:00
Friday, August 31	Cleveland _____ at Carolina _____	8:00
	Green Bay _____ at Oakland _____	6:00
	Kansas City _____ at St. Louis _____	(ESPN) 7:00
	Minnesota _____ at Miami _____	7:00
	New York Giants _____ at Baltimore _____	12:00
	San Diego _____ at Arizona _____	7:00
	San Francisco _____ at Denver _____	7:00
	Tampa Bay _____ at Atlanta _____	7:30
Saturday, September 1	New Orleans _____ at Seattle _____	1:00

FIRST WEEKEND
Open Date:
Arizona

Sunday, September 9	Atlanta _____ at San Francisco _____	1:15
(FOX-TV National Weekend)	Carolina _____ at Minnesota _____	12:00
	Chicago _____ at Baltimore _____	1:00
	Detroit _____ at Green Bay _____	12:00
	Indianapolis _____ at New York Jets _____	1:00
	New England _____ at Cincinnati _____	1:00
	New Orleans _____ at Buffalo _____	1:00
	Oakland _____ at Kansas City _____	12:00
	Pittsburgh _____ at Jacksonville _____	1:00
	St. Louis _____ at Philadelphia _____	4:15
	Seattle _____ at Cleveland _____	1:00
	Tampa Bay _____ at Dallas _____	12:00
	Washington _____ at San Diego _____	1:15
	Miami _____ at Tennessee _____	(ESPN) 7:30
Monday, September 10	New York Giants _____ at Denver _____	(ABC) 7:00

SECOND WEEKEND
Open Date:
San Diego

Sunday, September 16	Arizona _____ at Washington _____	1:00
(CBS-TV National Weekend)	Atlanta _____ at St. Louis _____	3:05
	Buffalo _____ at Miami _____	1:00
	Cincinnati _____ at Tennessee _____	12:00
	Dallas _____ at Detroit _____	1:00
	Denver _____ at Indianapolis _____	12:00
	Green Bay _____ at New York Giants _____	1:00
	Jacksonville _____ at Chicago _____	3:15
	Kansas City _____ at Seattle _____	1:15
	New England _____ at Carolina _____	1:00
	New York Jets _____ at Oakland _____	1:15
	Philadelphia _____ at Tampa Bay _____	1:00
	San Francisco _____ at New Orleans _____	12:00
	Cleveland _____ at Pittsburgh _____	(ESPN) 8:30
Monday, September 17	Minnesota _____ at Baltimore _____	(ABC) 9:00

THIRD WEEKEND
Open Dates:
New Orleans, Pittsburgh, Tampa Bay

Sunday, September 23	Baltimore _____ at Cincinnati _____	1:00
(FOX-TV National Weekend)	Buffalo _____ at Indianapolis _____	12:00
	Carolina _____ at Atlanta _____	1:00
	Detroit _____ at Cleveland _____	1:00
	Minnesota _____ at Chicago _____	12:00
	New York Giants _____ at Kansas City _____	12:00
	New York Jets _____ at New England _____	4:05
	Oakland _____ at Miami _____	1:00
	Philadelphia _____ at Seattle _____	1:15
	St. Louis _____ at San Francisco _____	1:15
	San Diego _____ at Dallas _____	12:00
	Tennessee _____ at Jacksonville _____	1:00
	Denver _____ at Arizona _____	(ESPN) 5:30
Monday, September 24	Washington _____ at Green Bay _____	(ABC) 8:00

2001 SCHEDULE AND NOTE CALENDAR

FOURTH WEEKEND **Sunday, September 30**
Open Dates: **(CBS-TV National Weekend)**
Chicago, Detroit, Tennessee

Atlanta _____ at Arizona _____	1:05
Baltimore _____ at Denver _____	2:15
Cincinnati _____ at San Diego _____	1:15
Cleveland _____ at Jacksonville _____	4:15
Green Bay _____ at Carolina _____	1:00
Indianapolis _____ at New England _____	1:00
Kansas City _____ at Washington _____	1:00
Miami _____ at St. Louis _____	12:00
New Orleans _____ at New York Giants _____	1:00
Pittsburgh _____ at Buffalo _____	1:00
Seattle _____ at Oakland _____	1:15
Tampa Bay _____ at Minnesota _____	12:00
Dallas _____ at Philadelphia _____	(ESPN) 8:30
Monday, October 1 San Francisco _____ at New York Jets _____	(ABC) 9:00

FIFTH WEEKEND **Sunday, October 7**
Open Dates: **(FOX-TV National Weekend)**
Dallas, Indianapolis, Oakland

Arizona _____ at Philadelphia _____	1:00
Chicago _____ at Atlanta _____	1:00
Cincinnati _____ at Pittsburgh _____	1:00
Green Bay _____ at Tampa Bay _____	4:15
Jacksonville _____ at Seattle _____	1:05
Kansas City _____ at Denver _____	2:05
Minnesota _____ at New Orleans _____	12:00
New England _____ at Miami _____	1:00
New York Jets _____ at Buffalo _____	4:05
San Diego _____ at Cleveland _____	1:00
Tennessee _____ at Baltimore _____	1:00
Washington _____ at New York Giants _____	1:00
Carolina _____ at San Francisco _____	(ESPN) 5:30
Monday, October 8 St. Louis _____ at Detroit _____	(ABC) 9:00

SIXTH WEEKEND **Sunday, October 14**
Open Dates: **(CBS-TV National Weekend)**
Buffalo, Jacksonville, Philadelphia

Arizona _____ at Chicago _____	12:00
Baltimore _____ at Green Bay _____	12:00
Cleveland _____ at Cincinnati _____	1:00
Denver _____ at Seattle _____	1:15
Detroit _____ at Minnesota _____	12:00
Miami _____ at New York Jets _____	4:15
New Orleans _____ at Carolina _____	1:00
New York Giants _____ at St. Louis _____	12:00
Pittsburgh _____ at Kansas City _____	12:00
San Diego _____ at New England _____	1:00
San Francisco _____ at Atlanta _____	1:00
Tampa Bay _____ at Tennessee _____	12:00
Oakland _____ at Indianapolis _____	(ESPN) 7:30
Monday, October 15 Washington _____ at Dallas _____	(ABC) 8:00

SEVENTH WEEKEND **Thursday, October 18**
Open Dates: **Sunday, October 21**
Miami, San Francisco, Seattle **(FOX-TV National Weekend)**

Buffalo _____ at Jacksonville _____	(ESPN) 8:30
Atlanta _____ at New Orleans _____	12:00
Baltimore _____ at Cleveland _____	1:00
Carolina _____ at Washington _____	1:00
Chicago _____ at Cincinnati _____	1:00
Dallas _____ at Oakland _____	1:15
Denver _____ at San Diego _____	1:05
Green Bay _____ at Minnesota _____	3:15
Kansas City _____ at Arizona _____	1:05
New England _____ at Indianapolis _____	12:00
Pittsburgh _____ at Tampa Bay _____	1:00
St. Louis _____ at New York Jets _____	1:00
Tennessee _____ at Detroit _____	1:00
Monday, October 22 Philadelphia _____ at New York Giants _____	(ABC) 9:00

EIGHTH WEEKEND
Open Dates:
Atlanta, Cleveland, Green Bay

Sunday, October 28 (CBS-TV National Weekend)	Arizona ____ at Dallas ____	3:05
	Buffalo ____ at San Diego ____	1:15
	Cincinnati ____ at Detroit ____	1:00
	Indianapolis ____ at Kansas City ____	12:00
	Jacksonville ____ at Baltimore ____	1:00
	Miami ____ at Seattle ____	1:15
	Minnesota ____ at Tampa Bay ____	1:00
	New England ____ at Denver ____	2:15
	New Orleans ____ at St. Louis ____	12:00
	New York Jets ____ at Carolina ____	1:00
	Oakland ____ at Philadelphia ____	4:15
	San Francisco ____ at Chicago ____	12:00
	New York Giants ____ at Washington ____	(ESPN) 8:30
Monday, October 29	Tennessee ____ at Pittsburgh ____	(ABC) 9:00

NINTH WEEKEND
Open Dates:
Cincinnati, Minnesota, St. Louis

Sunday, November 4 (CBS-TV National Weekend)	Baltimore ____ at Pittsburgh ____	1:00
	Carolina ____ at Miami ____	1:00
	Cleveland ____ at Chicago ____	12:00
	Dallas ____ at New York Giants ____	1:00
	Detroit ____ at San Francisco ____	1:05
	Indianapolis ____ at Buffalo ____	4:15
	Jacksonville ____ at Tennessee ____	12:00
	Kansas City ____ at San Diego ____	1:15
	New England ____ at Atlanta ____	1:00
	Philadelphia ____ at Arizona ____	2:05
	Seattle ____ at Washington ____	4:15
	Tampa Bay ____ at Green Bay ____	12:00
	New York Jets ____ at New Orleans ____	(ESPN) 7:30
Monday, November 5	Denver ____ at Oakland ____	(ABC) 6:00

TENTH WEEKEND
Open Date:
Washington

Sunday, November 11 (FOX-TV National Weekend)	Buffalo ____ at New England ____	1:00
	Carolina ____ at St. Louis ____	12:00
	Cincinnati ____ at Jacksonville ____	1:00
	Dallas ____ at Atlanta ____	1:00
	Green Bay ____ at Chicago ____	12:00
	Kansas City ____ at New York Jets ____	1:00
	Miami ____ at Indianapolis ____	1:00
	Minnesota ____ at Philadelphia ____	4:15
	New Orleans ____ at San Francisco ____	1:15
	New York Giants ____ at Arizona ____	2:15
	Pittsburgh ____ at Cleveland ____	1:00
	San Diego ____ at Denver ____	2:05
	Tampa Bay ____ at Detroit ____	1:00
	Oakland ____ at Seattle ____	(ESPN) 5:30
Monday, November 12	Baltimore ____ at Tennessee ____	(ABC) 8:00

ELEVENTH WEEKEND
Open Date:
Kansas City

Sunday, November 18 (FOX-TV National Weekend)	Atlanta ____ at Green Bay ____	12:00
	Chicago ____ at Tampa Bay ____	1:00
	Cleveland ____ at Baltimore ____	1:00
	Detroit ____ at Arizona ____	2:15
	Indianapolis ____ at New Orleans ____	12:00
	Jacksonville ____ at Pittsburgh ____	4:05
	New York Jets ____ at Miami ____	1:00
	Philadelphia ____ at Dallas ____	12:00
	San Diego ____ at Oakland ____	1:05
	San Francisco ____ at Carolina ____	1:00
	Seattle ____ at Buffalo ____	1:00
	Tennessee ____ at Cincinnati ____	1:00
	Washington ____ at Denver ____	2:15
	St. Louis ____ at New England ____	(ESPN) 8:30
Monday, November 19	New York Giants ____ at Minnesota ____	(ABC) 8:00

2001 SCHEDULE AND NOTE CALENDAR

TWELFTH WEEKEND	**Thursday, November 22**	Green Bay ____ at Detroit ____	12:30
Open Date:		Denver ____ at Dallas ____	3:05
N.Y. Jets	**Sunday, November 25**	Arizona ____ at San Diego ____	1:05
	(CBS-TV National Weekend)	Atlanta ____ at Carolina ____	1:00
		Baltimore ____ at Jacksonville ____	1:00
		Cincinnati ____ at Cleveland ____	1:00
		Miami ____ at Buffalo ____	1:00
		New Orleans ____ at New England ____	4:05
		Oakland ____ at New York Giants ____	4:15
		Pittsburgh ____ at Tennessee ____	12:00
		San Francisco ____ at Indianapolis ____	1:00
		Seattle ____ at Kansas City ____	12:00
		Washington ____ at Philadelphia ____	1:00
		Chicago ____ at Minnesota ____	(ESPN) 7:30
	Monday, November 26	Tampa Bay ____ at St. Louis ____	(ABC) 8:00
THIRTEENTH WEEKEND	**Thursday, November 29**	Philadelphia ____ at Kansas City ____	(ESPN) 7:30
Open Date:	**Sunday, December 2**	Arizona ____ at Oakland ____	1:15
N.Y. Giants	**(FOX-TV National Weekend)**	Carolina ____ at New Orleans ____	12:00
		Dallas ____ at Washington ____	4:15
		Denver ____ at Miami ____	1:00
		Detroit ____ at Chicago ____	12:00
		Indianapolis ____ at Baltimore ____	1:00
		Minnesota ____ at Pittsburgh ____	1:00
		New England ____ at New York Jets ____	1:00
		St. Louis ____ at Atlanta ____	1:00
		San Diego ____ at Seattle ____	1:05
		Tampa Bay ____ at Cincinnati ____	1:00
		Tennessee ____ at Cleveland ____	1:00
		Buffalo ____ at San Francisco ____	(ESPN) 5:30
	Monday, December 3	Green Bay ____ at Jacksonville ____	(ABC) 9:00
FOURTEENTH WEEKEND	**Sunday, December 9**	Carolina ____ at Buffalo ____	1:00
Open Date:	**(CBS-TV National Weekend)**	Chicago ____ at Green Bay ____	12:00
Baltimore		Cleveland ____ at New England ____	1:00
		Detroit ____ at Tampa Bay ____	1:00
		Jacksonville ____ at Cincinnati ____	1:00
		Kansas City ____ at Oakland ____	1:15
		New Orleans ____ at Atlanta ____	1:00
		New York Giants ____ at Dallas ____	12:00
		New York Jets ____ at Pittsburgh ____	4:15
		San Diego ____ at Philadelphia ____	1:00
		San Francisco ____ at St. Louis ____	12:00
		Tennessee ____ at Minnesota ____	12:00
		Washington ____ at Arizona ____	2:05
		Seattle ____ at Denver ____	(ESPN) 6:30
	Monday, December 10	Indianapolis ____ at Miami ____	(ABC) 9:00
FIFTEENTH WEEKEND	**Saturday, December 15**	Arizona ____ at New York Giants ____	(FOX) 1:30
Open Date:		Oakland ____ at San Diego ____	(CBS) 2:00
Carolina	**Sunday, December 16**	Atlanta ____ at Indianapolis ____	1:00
	(FOX-TV National Weekend)	Cincinnati ____ at New York Jets ____	1:00
		Dallas ____ at Seattle ____	1:15
		Denver ____ at Kansas City ____	12:00
		Green Bay ____ at Tennessee ____	3:15
		Jacksonville ____ at Cleveland ____	1:00
		Miami ____ at San Francisco ____	1:05
		Minnesota ____ at Detroit ____	1:00
		New England ____ at Buffalo ____	1:00
		Philadelphia ____ at Washington ____	1:00
		Tampa Bay ____ at Chicago ____	12:00
		Pittsburgh ____ at Baltimore ____	(ESPN) 8:30
	Monday, December 17	St. Louis ____ at New Orleans ____	(ABC) 8:00

SIXTEENTH WEEKEND
Open Date:
Denver

Saturday, December 22

Miami ____ at New England ____ (CBS) 1:30
Philadelphia ____ at San Francisco ____ (FOX) 2:00
Tennessee ____ at Oakland ____ (ABC) 6:00

Sunday, December 23
(CBS-TV National Weekend)

Buffalo ____ at Atlanta ____ 1:00
Chicago ____ at Washington ____ 1:00
Cincinnati ____ at Baltimore ____ 1:00
Cleveland ____ at Green Bay ____ 12:00
Dallas ____ at Arizona ____ 2:05
Detroit ____ at Pittsburgh ____ 1:00
Jacksonville ____ at Minnesota ____ 3:15
New Orleans ____ at Tampa Bay ____ 1:00
St. Louis ____ at Carolina ____ 1:00
San Diego ____ at Kansas City ____ 12:00
Seattle ____ at New York Giants ____ 1:00
New York Jets ____ at Indianapolis ____ (ESPN) 8:30

SEVENTEENTH WEEKEND
Open Date:
New England

Saturday, December 29

Baltimore ____ at Tampa Bay ____ (ABC) 9:00

Sunday, December 30
(CBS-TV National Weekend)

Arizona ____ at Carolina ____ 1:00
Atlanta ____ at Miami ____ 1:00
Buffalo ____ at New York Jets ____ 1:00
Chicago ____ at Detroit ____ 1:00
Cleveland ____ at Tennessee ____ 12:00
Indianapolis ____ at St. Louis ____ 12:00
Kansas City ____ at Jacksonville ____ 1:00
Minnesota ____ at Green Bay ____ 12:00
New York Giants ____ at Philadelphia ____ 4:05
Oakland ____ at Denver ____ 2:15
Pittsburgh ____ at Cincinnati ____ 1:00
San Francisco ____ at Dallas ____ 12:00
Seattle ____ at San Diego ____ 1:15
Washington ____ at New Orleans ____ (ESPN) 7:30

Wild Card Playoff Games
Site Priorities
Three Wild Card teams (division non-champions with best three records) from each conference and the division champion with the third-best record in each conference will enter the first round of the playoffs. The division champion with the third-best record will play host to the Wild Card team with the third-best record. The Wild Card team with the best record will play host to the Wild Card team with the second-best record. There are no restrictions on intra-division games.

Saturday, January 5, 2002

American Football Conference
____________ at ____________ (ABC)

National Football Conference
____________ at ____________ (ABC)

Sunday, January 6, 2002

American Football Conference
____________ at ____________ (CBS)

National Football Conference
____________ at ____________ (FOX)

Divisional Playoff Games
Site Priorities
In each conference, the two division champions with the highest won-lost-tied percentage during the regular season will play host to the Wild Card winners. The division champion with the best record in each conference is assured of playing the lowest seeded Wild Card survivor. There are no restrictions on intra-division games.

Saturday, January 12, 2002

American Football Conference
____________ at ____________ (CBS)

National Football Conference
____________ at ____________ (FOX)

Sunday, January 13, 2002

American Football Conference
____________ at ____________ (CBS)

National Football Conference
____________ at ____________ (FOX)

2001 SCHEDULE AND NOTE CALENDAR

Championship Games **Site Priorities for Championship Games** The home teams will be the surviving playoff winners with the best won-lost-tied percentage during the regular season. A Wild Card team cannot play host unless two Wild Card teams are in the game, in which case the Wild Card team that was seeded highest in the first round of the playoffs will be the home team.	**Sunday, January 20, 2002**	American Football Conference __________ at __________ (CBS) National Football Conference __________ at __________ (FOX)
Super Bowl XXXVI	**Sunday, January 27, 2002**	Super Bowl XXXVI at Louisiana Superdome, New Orleans, Louisiana __________ vs. __________ (FOX)
AFC-NFC Pro Bowl	**Sunday, February 3, 2002**	AFC-NFC Pro Bowl at Honolulu, Hawaii AFC __________ vs. NFC __________ (ABC)

POSTSEASON AND NATIONALLY TELEVISED GAMES

POSTSEASON GAMES

Saturday, January 5	AFC and NFC Wild Card Playoffs (ABC)
Sunday, January 6	AFC and NFC Wild Card Playoffs (CBS and FOX)
Saturday, January 12	AFC and NFC Divisional Playoffs (CBS and FOX)
Sunday, January 13	AFC and NFC Divisional Playoffs (CBS and FOX)
Sunday, January 20	AFC and NFC Championship Games (CBS and FOX)
Sunday, January 27	Super Bowl XXXVI, Louisiana Superdome in New Orleans (FOX)
Sunday, February 3	AFC-NFC Pro Bowl at Honolulu, Hawaii (ABC)

2001 NATIONALLY TELEVISED GAMES

Regular Season

Sunday, September 9	St. Louis at Philadelphia (day, FOX) Miami at Tennessee (night, ESPN)
Monday, September 10	New York Giants at Denver (night, ABC)
Sunday, September 16	New York Jets at Oakland (day, CBS) Cleveland at Pittsburgh (night, ESPN)
Monday, September 17	Minnesota at Baltimore (night, ABC)
Sunday, September 23	St. Louis at San Francisco (day, FOX) Denver at Arizona (night, ESPN)
Monday, September 24	Washington at Green Bay (night, ABC)
Sunday, September 30	Baltimore at Denver (day, CBS) Dallas at Philadelphia (night, ESPN)
Monday, October 1	San Francisco at New York Jets (night, ABC)
Sunday, October 7	Green Bay at Tampa Bay (day, FOX) Carolina at San Francisco (night, ESPN)
Monday, October 8	St. Louis at Detroit (night, ABC)
Sunday, October 14	Miami at New York Jets (day, CBS) Oakland at Indianapolis (night, ESPN)
Monday, October 15	Washington at Dallas (night, ABC)
Thursday, October 18	Buffalo at Jacksonville (night, ESPN)
Sunday, October 21	Dallas at Oakland (day, FOX)
Monday, October 22	Philadelphia at New York Giants (night, ABC)
Sunday, October 28	Oakland at Philadelphia (day, CBS) New York Giants at Washington (night, ESPN)
Monday, October 29	Tennessee at Pittsburgh (night, ABC)
Sunday, November 4	Seattle at Washington (day, CBS) New York Jets at New Orleans (night, ESPN)
Monday, November 5	Denver at Oakland (night, ABC)
Sunday, November 11	Minnesota at Philadelphia (day, FOX) Oakland at Seattle (night, ESPN)
Monday, November 12	Baltimore at Tennessee (night, ABC)
Sunday, November 18	Washington at Denver (day, FOX) St. Louis at New England (night, ESPN)
Monday, November 19	New York Giants at Minnesota (night, ABC)
Thursday, November 22	Green Bay at Detroit (day, FOX) Denver at Dallas (day, CBS)
Sunday, November 25	Oakland at New York Giants (day, CBS) Chicago at Minnesota (night, ESPN)
Monday, November 26	Tampa Bay at St. Louis (night, ABC)
Thursday, November 29	Philadelphia at Kansas City (night, ESPN)
Sunday, December 2	Dallas at Washington (day, FOX) Buffalo at San Francisco (night, ESPN)
Monday, December 3	Green Bay at Jacksonville (night, ABC)
Sunday, December 9	Kansas City at Oakland (day, CBS) Seattle at Denver (night, ESPN)
Monday, December 10	Indianapolis at Miami (night, ABC)
Saturday, December 15	Arizona at New York Giants (day, FOX) Oakland at San Diego (day, CBS)
Sunday, December 16	Green Bay at Tennessee (day, FOX) Pittsburgh at Baltimore (night, ESPN)
Monday, December 17	St. Louis at New Orleans (night, ABC)
Saturday, December 22	Miami at New England (day, CBS) Philadelphia at San Francisco (day, FOX) Tennessee at Oakland (night, ABC)
Sunday, December 23	Jacksonville at Minnesota (day, CBS) New York Jets at Indianapolis (night, ESPN)
Saturday, December 29	Baltimore at Tampa Bay (night, ABC)
Sunday, December 30	Oakland at Denver (day, CBS) Washington at New Orleans (night, ESPN)

NATIONAL PRIMETIME TELEVISION GAMES AT A GLANCE

(All times local; Sunday on ESPN, Monday on ABC; also on CBS Radio)

Sunday, September 9	Miami at Tennessee (ESPN)	7:30
Monday, September 10	New York Giants at Denver (ABC)	7:00
Sunday, September 16	Cleveland at Pittsburgh (ESPN)	8:30
Monday, September 17	Minnesota at Baltimore (ABC)	9:00
Sunday, September 23	Denver at Arizona (ESPN)	5:30
Monday, September 24	Washington at Green Bay (ABC)	8:00
Sunday, September 30	Dallas at Philadelphia (ESPN)	8:30
Monday, October 1	San Francisco at New York Jets (ABC)	9:00
Sunday, October 7	Carolina at San Francisco (ESPN)	5:30
Monday, October 8	St. Louis at Detroit (ABC)	9:00
Sunday, October 14	Oakland at Indianapolis (ESPN)	7:30
Monday, October 15	Washington at Dallas (ABC)	8:00
Thursday, October 18	Buffalo at Jacksonville (ESPN)	8:30
Monday, October 22	Philadelphia at New York Giants (ABC)	9:00
Sunday, October 28	New York Giants at Washington (ESPN)	8:30
Monday, October 29	Tennessee at Pittsburgh (ABC)	9:00
Sunday, November 4	New York Jets at New Orleans (ESPN)	7:30
Monday, November 5	Denver at Oakland (ABC)	6:00
Sunday, November 11	Oakland at Seattle (ESPN)	5:30
Monday, November 12	Baltimore at Tennessee (ABC)	8:00
Sunday, November 18	St. Louis at New England (ESPN)	8:30
Monday, November 19	New York Giants at Minnesota (ABC)	8:00
Sunday, November 25	Chicago at Minnesota (ESPN)	7:30
Monday, November 26	Tampa Bay at St. Louis (ABC)	8:00
Thursday, November 29	Philadelphia at Kansas City (ESPN)	7:30
Sunday, December 2	Buffalo at San Francisco (ESPN)	5:30
Monday, December 3	Green Bay at Jacksonville (ABC)	9:00
Sunday, December 9	Seattle at Denver (ESPN)	6:30
Monday, December 10	Indianapolis at Miami (ABC)	9:00
Sunday, December 16	Pittsburgh at Baltimore (ESPN)	8:30
Monday, December 17	St. Louis at New Orleans (ABC)	8:00
Saturday, December 22	Tennessee at Oakland (ABC)	6:00
Sunday, December 23	New York Jets at Indianapolis (ESPN)	8:30
Saturday, December 29	Baltimore at Tampa Bay (ABC)	9:00
Sunday, December 30	Washington at New Orleans (ESPN)	7:30

IMPORTANT DATES

2001

July 5	Claiming period of 24 hours begins in waiver system.
Mid-July	Preseason training camps open. Veteran players cannot be required to report earlier than 15 days prior to club's first preseason game or July 15, whichever is later.
July 22	Signing period ends at 4 P.M., Eastern Daylight Time, for Unrestricted Free Agents to whom June 1 tender was made by Old Club, and for Transition Players and Franchise Players who are eligible to receive Offer Sheets. After this date, and through 4 P.M., Eastern Standard Time, on November 13, Old Club has exclusive negotiating rights to these players.
August 6	Hall of Fame Game, Canton, Ohio: Miami vs. St. Louis.
August 10	If a Drafted Rookie has not signed with his club by this date, he may not be traded to any other club in 2001.
August 27	American Bowl, Mexico City, Mexico: Dallas vs. Oakland.
August 28	Roster cutdown to maximum of 65 players on Active List by 4 P.M., Eastern Daylight Time.
September 2	Roster cutdown to maximum of 53 players on Active/Inactive List by 4 P.M., Eastern Daylight Time. NFL Europe League exemptions expire. Clubs may dress minimum of 42 and maximum of 45 players and third quarterback for each regular-season and postseason game.
September 3	After 4 P.M., Eastern Daylight Time, clubs may establish a Practice Squad of five players by signing free agents who do not have an accrued season of free agency credit or who were on the 45-player Active List for less than nine regular-season games during their only Accrued Season(s).
September 9-10	Regular season opens.
September 25	Priority on multiple waiver claims is now based on the current season's standing.
October 16	All trading ends at 4 P.M., Eastern Daylight Time.
October 17	Players with at least four previous pension-credited seasons are subject to the waiver system for the remainder of the regular season and postseason.
November 13	Deadline for clubs to sign by 4 P.M., Eastern Standard Time, their unsigned Franchise and Transition players. If still unsigned after this date, such players are prohibited from playing in NFL in 2001.
November 13	Deadline for clubs to sign by 4 P.M., Eastern Standard Time, their Unrestricted and Restricted Free Agents to whom June 1 tender was made. If still unsigned after this date, such players are prohibited from playing in NFL in 2001.
November 13	Deadline for clubs to sign Drafted players by 4 P.M., Eastern Standard Time. If such players remain unsigned, they are prohibited from playing in NFL in 2001.
November 30	Deadline for reinstatement of players in Reserve List categories of Retired, Did Not Report, and Exclusive Rights, and of players who were placed on Reserve/Left Squad in a previous season.
December 28	Deadline for waiver requests in 2001, except for "special waiver requests" which have a 10-day claiming period, with termination or assignment delayed until after the Super Bowl.
December 31	Clubs may begin signing free-agent players for the 2002 season.

2002

January 5-6	Wild Card Playoff Games.
January 12-13	Divisional Playoff Games.
January 20	AFC and NFC Championship Games.
January 27	Super Bowl XXXVI, Louisiana Superdome, New Orleans, Louisiana.
February 3	AFC-NFC Pro Bowl, Honolulu, Hawaii.
*February 21	Waiver system begins for 2002. Players with at least four previous pension-credited seasons that a club desires to terminate are not subject to the waiver system until after the trading deadline.
*February 21	Deadline at 4 P.M., Eastern Standard Time, for clubs to designate Franchise and Transition players.
Feb. 28-March 4	Combine Timing and Testing, RCA Dome, Indianapolis, Indiana.
February 28	Expiration date of all player contracts due to expire after the 2001 season.
*March 1	Free Agency period begins.
*March 1	Trading period begins for 2002 after expiration of all 2001 contracts.
April 15	Deadline for signing of Offer Sheets by Restricted Free Agents.
April 20-21	Annual Player Selection Meeting, New York, N.Y.
June 1	Deadline for Old Club to send tender to its unsigned Restricted Free Agents or to extend Qualifying Offer, whichever is greater, in order to retain rights.
June 1	Deadline for Old Club to send tender to its unsigned Unrestricted Free Agents to retain rights if player is not signed by another club by July 22.

2003

*January 26	Super Bowl XXXVII, Qualcomm Stadium, San Diego, California.

2004

*February 1	Super Bowl XXXVIII, Reliant Stadium, Houston, Texas.

2005

*February 6	Super Bowl XXXIX, ALLTEL Stadium, Jacksonville, Florida.

2006

*February 5	Super Bowl XL, Ford Field, Detroit, Michigan.

*Tentatively scheduled

The NFL is online to provide fans and media quick and easy access to all the latest professional football information.

NFL.COM—(http://www.NFL.com)

NFL.com, the league's year-round home page on the Internet, enters its fifth season in cyberspace. The site provides NFL information during the regular season, postseason, and offseason, including:

NEWS/STATS: Up-to-the-minute news from around the league, plus game previews, injury reports, and player and team stats.

TEAM AREAS: Customized areas for all 32 clubs, including the Houston Texans, featuring updated rosters, depth carts, and all the latest news from the teams.

GAMEDAY COVERAGE: Live game coverage with play-by-play, scores, and statistics, including graphical drive charts and comprehensive Java scoreboard that does not require reloading to get the latest information. Also includes "Player Tracker," which instantaneously updates individual player statistics.

VIDEO HIGHLIGHTS: The site will showcase NFL Films video highlights of the previous week's games as well as upcoming matchups. Video will also support feature stories and team highlight clips from every game last season.

SUPERBOWL.COM—(http://SuperBowl.com)

Look for SuperBowl.com in late December for complete coverage of the playoffs and Super Bowl XXXVI. The multimedia site follows all postseason action and features audio and video clips of past Super Bowls.

During the week leading up to Super Bowl XXXVI, the site will go 'live' from New Orleans, providing coverage of events, press conferences, and chats with Super Bowl players and coaches.

On Super Bowl Sunday, SuperBowl.com will showcase a live Internet cybercast, complete with online commentators calling the action. The site also features digital photos from the game, live public address audio and press-box announcements, and live audio from foreign broadcasts.

NFLEUROPE.COM—(http://NFLEurope.com)

The official site of NFL Europe League provides in-depth information on the six teams and their players, streaming video of one game each weekend, live audio broadcasts of all games, and weekly video highlights of game action. In addition, the site includes collectible online player trading cards of the league's Players of the Week, weekly player diaries from NFL allocated players, as well as a complete league stats package.

PLAYFOOTBALL.COM—(http://www.playfootball.com)

Play Football.com is the NFL's official web site for kids. It offers boys and girls an interactive sports destination where kids and their families can get actively involved with the NFL, including information on national youth football programs such as Punt, Pass & Kick, and NFL Flag. Youths also can find profiles on NFL players and people behind the scenes of the NFL, vote on weekly MVPs and Plays of the Week, play challenging games, and learn about football strategy and skill.

NFLHS.COM—(http://NFLHS.com)

The League's web site dedicated to high school and youth football. NFLHS.com covers high school football on a nation-wide basis and also looks into the high school careers of current and former NFL players and coaches. NFLHS.com goes behind the scenes at major NFL events, such as the Super Bowl and the Draft, and provides coverage from a high school perspective. The site is packed with tips and drills, health and safety information, academic tips and news on the NFL's and its teams' efforts in the community. Whatever you are looking for regarding high school football, we've got it!

PROFOOTBALLHOF.com—(http://www.profootballhof.com)

Profootballhof.com is the official site of the Pro Football Hall of Fame in Canton, Ohio. In addition to a complete visitor's guide to the Hall, the site features bios, stories and live chats with Hall of Famers, a detailed archive of football history and information on appearances by members of the Hall.

OFFICIAL NFL TEAM SITES

In addition to a dedicated area on NFL.COM, all 32 teams, including the Houston Texans, have created their own Web sites, which have separate URLs, and are linked from NFL.COM.

Arizona Cardinals (www.azcardinals.com)
Atlanta Falcons (www.atlantafalcons.com)
Baltimore Ravens (www.ravenszone.net)
Buffalo Bills (www.buffalobills.com)
Carolina Panthers (www.panthers.com)
Cincinnati Bengals (www.bengals.com)
Chicago Bears (www.chicagobears.com)
Cleveland Browns (www.clevelandbrowns.com)
Dallas Cowboys (www.dallascowboys.com)
Denver Broncos (www.denverbroncos.com)
Detroit Lions (www.detroitlions.com)
Green Bay Packers (www.packers.com)
Houston Texans (www.houstontexans.com)
Indianapolis Colts (www.colts.com)
Jacksonville Jaguars (www.jaguars.com)
Kansas City Chiefs (www.kcchiefs.com)
Miami Dolphins (www.miamidolphins.com)
Minnesota Vikings (www.vikings.com)
New England Patriots (www.patriots.com)
New Orleans Saints (www.neworleanssaints.com)
New York Giants (www.giants.com)
New York Jets (www.newyorkjets.com)
Oakland Raiders (www.raiders.com)
Philadelphia Eagles (www.philadelphiaeagles.com)
Pittsburgh Steelers (www.steelers.com)
San Diego Chargers (www.chargers.com)
St. Louis Rams (www.stlouisrams.com)
San Francisco 49ers (www.sf49ers.com)
Seattle Seahawks (www.seahawks.com)
Tampa Bay Buccaneers (www.buccaneers.com)
Tennessee Titans (www.titansonline.com)
Washington Redskins (www.redskins.com)

2001 SCHEDULING FORMULA

Each 2001 team schedule is based on a "common-opponent" formula initiated for the 1978 season, modified in 1995, and again in 1999 with the addition of Cleveland. Under the common-opponent format, all teams in a division play at least nine of their 16 games the following season against common opponents. It is not a position scheduling format in which the strong play the strong and the weak play the weak.

In creating a schedule, the NFL seeks an easily understood and balanced formula that provides both competitive equality and a variety of opponents. Under the rotation scheduling system in effect from 1970-77, nondivision opponents were determined by a pre-set formula. This often resulted in competitive imbalances.

With common opponents as the basis for scheduling, a more competitive and equitable method of determining division champions and postseason playoff representatives has developed. Teams battling for a division title are playing approximately two-thirds of their games against common opponents.

In 1987, NFL owners passed a bylaw proposal designed to modify the common-opponent scheduling format and create greater equity. And in 1995, with the addition of two expansion teams, the 1987 changes were modified to include fifth-place teams in the common-opponent scheduling format for each division. The following chart shows a history of the pairings in non-division games within the conference since the change to a common-opponent format in 1978:

Prior Year's Finish in Division	Current Pairings in Non-Division Games Within Conference	Previous Pairings 1987-94	Previous Pairings 1978-86
1	1-1-2-3	1-1-2-3	1-1-4-4
2	1-2-2-4	1-2-2-4	2-2-3-3
3	1-3-3-5	1-3-3-4	2-2-3-3
4	2-4-4-5	2-3-4-4	1-1-4-4
5	3-4-5-5		

With the addition of Cleveland as the League's thirty-first franchise, some modifications to the scheduling formula were necessary to accomodate a new six-team division (AFC Central).

Under the common-opponent format, schedules of all NFL teams are figured according to the following formula. (The reference point for the figuring is the team's final division standing. Ties in divisions are broken according to the tie-breaking procedures outlined on page 25.)

A. Divisional Games

Each team will play home-and-home with the other teams in its division (8 games for all divisions except for teams in the AFC Central, which will each have 10 divisional games).

B. Intraconference Games

1. Each team in all divisions except the AFC Central will play four nondivision conference opponents based on the previous season's standings, as shown below.

2. Teams that finished first and second in the AFC Central in the previous season's standings will play two nondivision conference opponents, and teams that finished third, fourth, fifth, and sixth will each play three nondivision conference opponents, as shown below:

Prior Year's Finish in Division	NFC Teams	AFC East/West (alternating years)	AFC Central
1	1-1-2-3	1-1-2-3/1-1-2-4	1-1
2	1-2-2-4	1-2-2-5/1-2-2-3	2-2
3	1-3-3-5	2-3-3-4/1-3-3-5	3-3-4
4	2-4-4-5	1-4-4-6/3-4-4-5	3-4-4
5	3-4-5-5	4-5-5-6/2-5-5-6	3-5-5
6			4-5-5

C. Interconference Games

1. Continuing the current rotation, teams from each division of one conference will play teams from a division of the other conference, as follows:

1999	NFC-E vs. AFC-E	NFC-C vs. AFC-W	NFC-W vs. AFC-C
2000	NFC-E vs. AFC-C	NFC-C vs. AFC-E	NFC-W vs. AFC-W
2001	NFC-E vs. AFC-W	NFC-C vs. AFC-C	NFC-W vs. AFC-E

2. Each team in all divisions except the AFC Central will play four games against teams of a division of the other conference, as is done currently. The NFL will continue the rotation of interconference opponents, including rotation of home and away sites, for games between teams of the NFC and teams from the AFC East and AFC West that provides for all teams from NFC divisions to play all teams from the AFC East and AFC West four times in 15 years, two home and two away.

3. Teams that finish first and second in the AFC Central in the previous season will play four games against teams of a division of the other conference, and teams that finish third, fourth, fifth, and sixth will each play three games against teams of a division of the other conference, based on the standings from the previous season as shown below.

Prior Year's Finish In Division	AFC Central Schedule vs. NFC Division	NFC Division Schedule vs. AFC Central
1	1-2-3-4	1-2-3-4
2	1-2-3-5	1-2-3-5
3	1-2-4	1-2-4-6
4	1-3-5	1-3-5-6
5	2-4-5	2-4-5-6
6	3-4-5	

NFL REALIGNMENT FOR 2002

At the NFL Spring Meeting on May 22, 2001, in Rosemont, Illinois, NFL owners unanimously approved the following realignment for 2002 when the Houston Texans begin play:

AFC

EAST	NORTH	SOUTH	WEST
Buffalo	Baltimore	Houston	Denver
Miami	Cincinnati	Indianapolis	Kansas City
New England	Cleveland	Jacksonville	Oakland
N.Y. Jets	Pittsburgh	Tennessee	San Diego

NFC

EAST	NORTH	SOUTH	WEST
Dallas	Chicago	Atlanta	Arizona
N.Y. Giants	Detroit	Carolina	St. Louis
Philadelphia	Green Bay	New Orleans	San Francisco
Washington	Minnesota	Tampa Bay	Seattle

SCHEDULING FORMULA

Each team within a division will play 14 common opponents as follows:

- Each team will play home and away against its three division opponents (6 games).
- Each team will play the four teams from another division within its conference on a rotating three-year cycle (4 games).
- Each team will play the four teams from a division in the other conference on a rotating four-year cycle (4 games).
- Each team will play a pair of intraconference games based on the prior year's standings (2 games), i.e. first-place teams in a division will play against the first-place teams from another division within the same conference, etc.

NFL PASSER RATING SYSTEM

The NFL rates its passers for statistical purposes against a fixed performance standard based on statistical achievements of all qualified pro passers since 1960. The current system replaced one that rated passers in relation to their position in a total group based on various criteria. The current system, which was adopted in 1973, removes inequities that existed in the former method and, at the same time, provides a means of comparing passing performances from one season to the next.

It is important to remember that the system is used to rate **passers,** not **quarterbacks.** Statistics do not reflect leadership, play-calling, and other intangible factors that go into making a successful professional quarterback. Four categories are used as a basis for compiling a rating:

—Percentage of completions per attempt
—Average yards gained per attempt
—Percentage of touchdown passes per attempt
—Percentage of interceptions per attempt

The **average** standard, is 1.000. The bottom is .000. To earn a 2.000 rating, a passer must perform at exceptional levels, i.e., 70 percent in completions, 10 percent in touchdowns, 1.5 percent in interceptions, and 11 yards average gain per pass attempt. The **maximum** a passer can receive in any category is 2.375.

For example, to gain a 2.375 in completion percentage, a passer would have to complete 77.5 percent of his passes. The NFL record is 70.55 by Ken Anderson (Cincinnati, 1982). To earn a 2.375 in percentage of touchdowns, a passer would have to achieve a percentage of 11.9. The record is 13.9 by Sid Luckman (Chicago, 1943). To gain 2.375 in percentage of interceptions, a passer would have to go the entire season without an interception. The 2.375 figure in average yards is 12.50, compared with the NFL record of 11.17 by Tommy O'Connell (Cleveland, 1957).

In order to make the rating more understandable, the point rating is then converted into a scale of 100. In rare cases, where statistical performance has been superior, it is possible for a passer to surpass a 100 rating. For example, take Steve Young's record-setting season in 1994 when he completed 324 of 461 passes for 3,969 yards, 35 touchdowns, and 10 interceptions. The four calculations would be:

—**Percentage of Completions**—324 of 461 is 70.28 percent. Subtract 30 from the completion percentage (40.28) and multiply the result by 0.05. The result is a point rating of **2.014**.
Note: If the result is less than zero (Comp. Pct. less than 30.0), award zero points. If the results are greater than 2.375 (Comp. Pct. greater than 77.5), award 2.375.

—**Average Yards Gained Per Attempt**—3,969 yards divided by 461 attempts is 8.61. Subtract three yards from yards-per-attempt (5.61) and multiply the result by 0.25. The result is **1.403**.
Note: If the result is less than zero (yards per attempt less than 3.0), award zero points. If the result is greater than 2.375 (yards per attempt greater than 12.5), award 2.375 points.

—**Percentage of Touchdown Passes**—35 touchdowns in 461 attempts is 7.59 percent. Multiply the touchdown percentage by 0.2. The result is **1.518**.
Note: If the result is greater than 2.375 (touchdown percentage greater than 11.875), award 2.375.

—**Percentage of Interceptions**—10 interceptions in 461 attempts is 2.17 percent. Multiply the interception percentage by 0.25 (0.542) and subtract the number from 2.375. The result is **1.833**.
Note: If the result is less than zero (interception percentage greater than 9.5), award zero points.

The sum of the four steps is (2.014 + 1.403 + 1.518 + 1.833) **6.768**. The sum is then divided by six (1.128) and multiplied by 100. In this case, the result is **112.8**. This same formula can be used to determine a passer rating for any player who attempts at least one pass.

The following is a list of qualifying passers who had a single-season passer rating of 100 or higher:

Player, Team	Season	Rating	Att.	Comp.	Pct.	Yds.	Avg.	TD	TD Pct.	Int.	Int. Pct.
Steve Young, San Francisco	1994	112.8	461	324	70.2	3,969	8.61	35	7.6	10	2.2
Joe Montana, San Francisco	1989	112.4	386	271	70.2	3,521	9.12	26	6.7	8	2.1
Milt Plum, Cleveland	1960	110.4	250	151	60.4	2,297	9.19	21	8.4	5	2.0
Sammy Baugh, Washington	1945	109.9	182	128	70.3	1,669	9.17	11	6.0	4	2.2
Kurt Warner, St. Louis	1999	109.2	499	325	65.1	4,353	8.72	41	8.2	13	2.6
Dan Marino, Miami	1984	108.9	564	362	64.2	5,084	9.01	48	8.5	17	3.0
Sid Luckman, Chicago Bears	1943	107.5	202	110	54.5	2,194	10.86	28	13.9	12	5.9
Steve Young, San Francisco	1992	107.0	402	268	66.7	3,465	8.62	25	6.2	7	1.7
Randall Cunningham, Minnesota	1998	106.0	425	259	60.9	3,704	8.72	34	8.0	10	2.4
Bart Starr, Green Bay	1966	105.0	251	156	62.2	2,257	8.99	14	5.6	3	1.2
Roger Staubach, Dallas	1971	104.8	211	126	59.7	1,882	8.92	15	7.1	4	1.9
Y.A. Tittle, N.Y. Giants	1963	104.8	367	221	60.2	3,145	8.57	36	9.8	14	3.8
Steve Young, San Francisco	1997	104.7	356	241	67.7	3,029	8.51	19	5.3	6	1.7
Bart Starr, Green Bay	1968	104.3	171	109	63.7	1,617	9.46	15	8.8	8	4.7
Ken Stabler, Oakland	1976	103.4	291	194	66.7	2,737	9.41	27	9.3	17	5.8
Brian Griese, Denver	2000	102.9	336	216	64.3	2,688	8.00	19	5.7	4	1.2
Joe Montana, San Francisco	1984	102.9	432	279	64.6	3,630	8.40	28	6.5	10	2.3
Charlie Conerly, N.Y. Giants	1959	102.7	194	113	58.2	1,706	8.79	14	7.2	4	2.1
Bert Jones, Baltimore	1976	102.5	343	207	60.3	3,104	9.05	24	7.0	9	2.6
Joe Montana, San Francisco	1987	102.1	398	266	66.8	3,054	7.67	31	7.8	13	3.3
Trent Green, St. Louis	2000	101.8	240	145	60.4	2,063	8.60	16	6.7	5	2.1
Steve Young, San Francisco	1991	101.8	279	180	64.5	2,517	9.02	17	6.1	8	2.9
Len Dawson, Kansas City	1966	101.7	284	159	56.0	2,527	8.90	26	9.2	10	3.5
Vinny Testaverde, N.Y. Jets	1998	101.6	421	259	61.5	3,256	7.73	29	6.9	7	1.7
Steve Young, San Francisco	1993	101.5	462	314	68.0	4,023	8.71	29	6.3	16	3.5
Jim Kelly, Buffalo	1990	101.2	346	219	63.3	2,829	8.18	24	6.9	9	2.6
Steve Young, San Francisco	1998	101.1	517	322	62.3	4,170	8.07	36	7.0	12	2.3
Chris Chandler, Atlanta	1998	100.9	327	190	58.1	3,154	9.65	25	7.6	12	3.7
Jim Harbaugh, Indianapolis	1995	100.7	314	200	63.7	2,575	8.20	17	5.4	5	1.6

WAIVERS

The waiver system is a procedure by which player contracts or NFL rights to players are made available by a club to other clubs in the League. During the procedure, the 30 other clubs either file claims to obtain the players or waive the opportunity to do so—thus the term "waiver." Claiming clubs are assigned players on a priority based on the inverse of won-and-lost standing. The claiming period is three business days from the beginning of the League Year through April 30, 10 calendar days from May 1 through the last business day before July 4, and 24 hours after July 4 through the conclusion of the regular season. If a player passes through waivers unclaimed, he becomes a free agent. All waivers are no recall and no withdrawal. Under the Collective Bargaining Agreement, from the beginning of the waiver system each year through the trading deadline (October 16, 2001), any veteran who has acquired four years of pension credit is not subject to the waiver system if the club desires to release him. After the trading deadline, such players are subject to the waiver system.

ACTIVE/INACTIVE LIST

The Active/Inactive List is the principal status for players participating for a club. It consists of all players under contract who are eligible for preseason, regular-season, and postseason games. Teams are permitted to open training camp with no more than 80 players under contract and thereafter must meet two mandatory roster reductions prior to the season opener. Teams will be permitted an Active List of 45 players and an Inactive List of eight players for each regular-season and postseason game. Provided that a club has two quarterbacks on its 45-player Active List, a third quarterback from its Inactive List is permitted to dress for the game, but if he enters the game during the first three quarters, the other two quarterbacks are thereafter prohibited from playing. Teams also are permitted to establish Practice Squads of up to five players who are eligible to participate in practice, but these players remain free agents and are eligible to sign with any other team in the league.

August 28 ....Roster reduction to 65 players
September 2........Roster reduction to 53 players
September 3........Teams establish a Practice Squad of up to five players

In addition to the squad limits described above, the overall roster limit of 80 players remains in effect throughout the regular season and postseason. The overall limit is applicable to players on a team's Active, Inactive, and Exempt Lists, players on the Practice Squad, and players on the Reserve List as Injured, Physically Unable to Perform, Non-Football Illness/Injury, and Suspended by Club.

RESERVE LIST

The Reserve List is a status for players who, for reasons of injury, retirement, military service, or other circumstances, are not immediately available for participation with a club. Players on Reserve/Injured are not eligible to practice or return to the Active/Inactive List in the same season that they are placed on Reserve. Players in the category of Reserve/Retired, Reserve/Did Not Report, Reserve/Exclusive Rights, and players who were placed in the category of Reserve/Left Squad in a previous season may not be reinstated during the period from 30 days before the end of the regular season through the postseason.

TRADES

Unrestricted trading between the AFC and NFC is allowed in 2001 through October 16, after which trading will end until 2002.

ANNUAL ACTIVE PLAYER LIMITS

NFL

Year(s)	Limit
1991-2001	45**
1985-90	45
1983-84	49
1982	45†-49
1978-81	45
1975-77	43
1974	47
1964-73	40
1963	37
1961-62	36
1960	38
1959	36
1957-58	35
1951-56	33
1949-50	32
1948	35
1947	35*-34
1945-46	33
1943-44	28
1940-42	33
1938-39	30
1936-37	25
1935	24
1930-34	20
1926-29	18
1925	16

**45 plus a third quarterback
† 45 for first two games
* 35 for first three games

AFL

Year(s)	Limit
1966-69	40
1965	38
1964	34
1962-63	33
1960-61	35

NFL FREE AGENCY MOVEMENT

The following chart details veteran free agents who signed with new teams:

	Unrestricted	Restricted	Transition	Franchise	TOTALS
1993	100	8	4	1	113
1994	104	7	4	0	115
1995	154	6	2	0	162
1996	100	4	2	0	106
1997	86	2	2	0	90
1998	112	4	1	2	119
1999	115	2	1	0	118
2000	107	4	0	0	111

NFL ACTIVE STATISTICAL LEADERS

TOP ACTIVE PASSERS

1,000 or more attempts

	Yrs.	Att.	Comp.	Pct. Comp.	Yards	TD	Pct. TD	Had Int.	Pct. Int.	Rating Pts.
1. Brett Favre, G.B.	10	4,932	2,997	60.8	34,706	255	5.2	157	3.2	86.0
2. Peyton Manning, Ind.	3	1,679	1,014	60.4	12,287	85	5.1	58	3.5	85.4
3. Mark Brunell, Jax.	7	2,672	1,608	60.2	19,212	106	4.0	66	2.5	85.1
4. Brad Johnson, T.B.	7	1,821	1,126	61.8	12,973	79	4.3	57	3.1	84.7
5. Neil O'Donnell, Tenn.	10	3,121	1,802	57.7	20,938	116	3.7	65	2.1	81.9
6. Elvis Grbac, Balt.	7	1,978	1,181	59.7	13,741	84	4.2	63	3.2	81.7
7. Randall Cunningham, Balt.	15	4,200	2,375	56.5	29,406	204	4.9	132	3.1	81.5
8. Jeff George, Wash.	11	3,925	2,275	58.0	27,434	154	3.9	110	2.8	80.9
9. Steve Beuerlein, Den.	12	3,148	1,793	57.0	22,732	139	4.4	102	3.2	80.9
10. Rich Gannon, Oak.	12	2,746	1,588	57.8	18,428	118	4.3	79	2.9	80.6
11. Chris Chandler, Atl.	13	3,225	1,860	57.7	23,101	145	4.5	113	3.5	80.4
12. Jeff Blake, N.O.	8	2,532	1,428	56.4	17,199	106	4.2	72	2.8	79.5
13. Steve McNair, Tenn.	6	1,857	1,069	57.6	12,685	65	3.5	49	2.6	79.2
14. Jim Harbaugh, Det.	14	3,918	2,305	58.8	26,288	129	3.3	117	3.0	77.6
15. Doug Flutie, S.D.	7	1,404	764	54.4	9,785	61	4.3	46	3.3	77.3
16. Jon Kitna, Cin.	4	1,130	658	58.2	7,552	49	4.3	45	4.0	76.3
17. Scott Mitchell, Cin.	10	2,334	1,297	55.6	15,654	95	4.1	78	3.3	76.0
18. Drew Bledsoe, N.E.	8	4,452	2,504	56.2	29,257	164	3.7	136	3.1	75.9
19. Gus Frerotte, Den.	7	1,942	1,057	54.4	13,662	66	3.4	59	3.0	75.4
20. Vinny Testaverde, NYJ	14	5,203	2,897	55.7	36,307	226	4.3	216	4.2	74.7
21. Rodney Peete, Oak.	12	1,954	1,116	57.1	13,686	61	3.1	78	4.0	72.6
22. John Friesz, *	10	1,364	745	54.6	8,699	45	3.3	42	3.1	72.3
23. Bubby Brister, K.C.	14	2,212	1,207	54.6	14,445	81	3.7	78	3.5	72.3
24. Tony Banks, Dall.	5	1,857	1,004	54.1	12,047	61	3.3	58	3.1	72.1
25. Trent Dilfer, *	7	2,264	1,251	55.3	14,471	82	3.6	91	4.0	70.1
26. Kerry Collins, NYG	6	2,391	1,289	53.9	15,436	81	3.4	88	3.7	69.9
27. Mike Tomczak, *	16	2,337	1,248	53.4	16,079	88	3.8	106	4.5	68.9
28. Kordell Stewart, Pitt.	6	1,499	815	54.4	9,064	50	3.3	55	3.7	68.4
29. Kent Graham, Pitt.	8	1,320	681	51.6	7,670	37	2.8	33	2.5	68.2
30. Dave Brown, Ariz.	9	1,634	892	54.6	10,248	44	2.7	58	3.5	67.9

TOP ACTIVE SCORERS

(number in parentheses represents 2-point conversions scored)

	Yrs.	TD	FG	PAT	TP
1. Gary Anderson, Minn.	19	0	461	476	2,059
2. Morten Andersen, *	19	0	441	615	1,938
3. Eddie Murray, *	19	0	352	538	1,594
4. Al Del Greco, *	17	0	347	543	1,584
5. Steve Christie, Buff.	11	0	272	358	1,174
6. Jerry Rice, Oak.	16	187	0	(4)	1,130
7. John Carney, *	13	0	263	299	1,088
8. Matt Stover, Balt.	10	0	237	308	1,019
9. Jason Hanson, Det.	9	0	218	304	958
10. Jason Elam, Den.	8	0	204	337	949
11. Emmitt Smith, Dall.	11	156	0	(1)	938
12. John Kasay, Car.	10	0	208	249	873
13. Cris Carter, Minn.	14	124	0	(5)	754
14. Cary Blanchard, Ariz.	7	0	165	188	683
15. Mike Hollis, Jax.	6	0	157	210	681
16. Doug Brien, N.O.	7	0	145	223	658
17. Todd Peterson, K.C.	7	0	143	206	635
18. Jeff Wilkins, St.L.	7	0	124	226	598
19. Adam Vinatieri, N.E.	5	0	136	165(1)	575
20. Tim Brown, Oak.	13	90	0	(1)	542
Ricky Watters, Sea.	9	90	0	(1)	542
22. Marshall Faulk, St.L.	7	89	0	(3)	540
23. Brad Daluiso, *	10	0	125	159	534
24. Irving Fryar, *	17	88	0	(2)	532
25. Andre Reed, *	16	88	0	0	528
26. Andre Rison, *	12	84	0	(1)	506
27. Ryan Longwell, G.B.	4	0	111	159	492
28. Olindo Mare, Mia.	4	0	117	126	477
29. Terry Allen, *	9	76	0	(2)	460
30. John Hall, NYJ	4	0	101	138	441

TOP ACTIVE RUSHERS

	Yrs.	Att.	Yards	TD
1. Emmitt Smith, Dall.	11	3,537	15,166	145
2. Ricky Watters, Sea.	9	2,550	10,325	77
3. Jerome Bettis, Pitt.	8	2,461	9,804	49
4. Marshall Faulk, St.L.	7	1,895	8,060	67
5. Terry Allen, *	9	1,984	7,956	70
6. Curtis Martin, NYJ	6	2,010	7,754	54
7. Chris Warren, *	11	1,791	7,696	52
8. Terrell Davis, Den.	6	1,488	6,906	60
9. Eddie George, Tenn.	5	1,763	6,874	42
10. Jamal Anderson, Atl.	7	1,274	5,146	33
11. Adrian Murrell, Car.	8	1,347	5,092	23
12. Garrison Hearst, S.F.	8	1,166	4,939	14
13. Corey Dillon, Cin.	4	1,073	4,894	26
14. Randall Cunningham, Balt.	15	761	4,888	34
15. Charlie Garner, Oak.	7	994	4,632	28
16. Errict Rhett, Cle.	7	1,174	4,143	29
17. James Stewart, Det.	6	1,104	4,135	43
18. Dorsey Levens, G.B.	7	962	3,772	28
19. Warrick Dunn, T.B.	4	912	3,753	14
20. Stephen Davis, Wash.	5	820	3,538	33
21. Fred Taylor, Jax.	3	715	3,354	32
22. Mike Alstott, T.B.	5	860	3,302	30
23. Edgerrin James, Ind.	2	756	3,262	26
Tyrone Wheatley, Oak.	6	830	3,262	25
25. Lamar Smith, Mia.	7	789	3,087	25
26. Mario Bates, *	7	841	3,048	38
27. Anthony Johnson, *	11	816	2,966	9
28. Antowain Smith, *	4	760	2,932	26
29. Jim Harbaugh, Det.	14	561	2,787	18
30. Terry Kirby, *	8	735	2,775	27

TOP ACTIVE PASS RECEIVERS

	Yrs.	No.	Yards	TD
1. Jerry Rice, Oak.	16	1,281	19,247	176
2. Cris Carter, Minn.	14	1,020	12,962	123
3. Andre Reed, *	16	951	13,198	87
4. Irving Fryar, *	17	851	12,785	84
5. Tim Brown, Oak.	13	846	12,072	86
6. Andre Rison, *	12	743	10,205	84
7. Larry Centers, Buff.	11	685	5,683	25
8. Herman Moore, Det.	10	666	9,098	62
9. Rob Moore, Ariz.	11	628	9,368	49
10. Shannon Sharpe, Balt.	11	619	7,793	49
11. Terance Mathis, Atl.	11	615	8,027	59
12. Tony Martin, *	11	556	8,517	53
13. Eric Metcalf, Oak.	12	537	5,553	31
14. Ben Coates, *	10	499	5,555	50
15. Ricky Proehl, St.L.	11	497	6,492	37
16. Jeff Graham, S.D.	10	490	7,361	25
17. Keenan McCardell, Jax.	9	486	6,416	32
18. Isaac Bruce, St.L.	7	476	7,299	50
19. Jimmy Smith, Jax.	7	472	6,887	36
20. Ed McCaffrey, Den.	10	471	6,230	52
21. Marshall Faulk, St.L.	7	465	4,682	22
22. Ricky Watters, Sea.	9	456	4,141	13
23. Emmitt Smith, Dall.	11	453	2,807	11
24. Sean Dawkins, Jax.	8	425	6,057	25
25. Frank Sanders, Ariz.	6	418	5,561	20
26. O.J. McDuffie, Mia.	8	415	5,074	29
27. Marvin Harrison, Ind.	5	413	5,554	47
28. Jake Reed, Minn.	10	402	6,330	32
29. Wayne Chrebet, NYJ	6	400	5,085	29
Shawn Jefferson, Atl.	10	400	6,044	26

TOP ACTIVE INTERCEPTORS

	Yrs.	No.	Yards	TD
1. Rod Woodson, Balt.	14	58	1,183	9
2. Eugene Robinson, *	16	57	762	1
3. Eric Allen, Oak.	13	53	807	8
Darrell Green, Wash.	18	53	621	6
5. Deion Sanders, Wash.	12	48	1,187	8
6. Aeneas Williams, St.L.	10	46	653	6
7. James Hasty, *	13	45	555	4
8. Ray Buchanan, *	8	38	704	4
Terrell Buckley, Den.	9	38	562	4
LeRoy Butler, G.B.	11	38	533	1
11. Eric Davis, *	11	37	428	4
12. Darren Perry, *	9	35	577	1
13. Troy Vincent, Phil.	9	34	596	3
14. Ray Crockett, Den.	12	33	452	3
15. Darryll Lewis, Den.	10	32	555	5
Mark Carrier, *	11	32	370	1
Greg Jackson, *	12	32	329	2
18. Todd Lyght, Det.	10	31	359	3
19. Darryl Williams, Cin.	9	30	675	4
20. Ashley Ambrose, Atl.	9	28	347	2
Keith Lyle, *	7	28	336	0
Kurt Schulz, Det.	9	28	222	1
23. Tom Carter, Cin.	8	27	360	1
Phillippi Sparks, Dall.	9	27	222	0
25. Donnie Abraham, T.B.	5	25	243	2
26. Dewayne Washington, Pitt.	7	24	496	5
William Thomas, Oak.	10	24	301	2
28. Dale Carter, Den.	8	23	231	1
Jimmy Spencer, Den.	9	23	184	2
30. Marcus Robertson, Sea.	10	22	428	0
Ty Law, N.E.	6	22	347	3
Rodney Harrison, S.D.	7	22	292	2
Ryan McNeil, S.D.	8	22	241	2

TOP ACTIVE PUNT RETURNERS

40 or more punt returns

	Yrs.	No.	Yards	Avg.	TD
1. Charlie Rogers, Sea.	2	48	681	14.2	1
2. Az-Zahir Hakim, St.L.	3	76	950	12.5	2
3. Desmond Howard, Det.	9	213	2,646	12.4	8
4. Darrien Gordon, *	7	248	2,984	12.0	6
5. Jacquez Green, T.B.	3	55	658	12.0	1
6. Jermaine Lewis, Balt.	5	189	2,211	11.7	6
7. Karl Williams, T.B.	5	120	1,393	11.6	3
8. Darrell Green, Wash.	18	51	576	11.3	0
9. Iheanyi Uwaezuoke, *	5	62	696	11.2	1
10. Brian Mitchell, Phil.	11	349	3,811	10.9	8
11. Troy Brown, N.E.	8	143	1,560	10.9	1
12. Reggie Barlow, Oak.	5	146	1,581	10.8	2
13. Winslow Oliver, Atl.	5	126	1,364	10.8	2
14. Jeff Burris, Ind.	7	100	1,045	10.5	0
15. Deion Sanders, Wash.	12	207	2,158	10.4	6
16. Joey Galloway, Dall.	6	80	825	10.3	4
17. Tim Brown, Oak.	13	304	3,106	10.2	2
18. Tiki Barber, NYG	4	83	838	10.1	1
19. Amani Toomer, NYG	5	101	1,019	10.1	3
20. Derrick Mason, Tenn.	4	121	1,210	10.0	2
21. Irving Fryar, *	17	206	2,055	10.0	3
22. David Palmer, Minn.	7	162	1,610	9.9	2
23. Glyn Milburn, Chi.	8	283	2,812	9.9	1
24. Kevin Williams, *	8	231	2,295	9.9	3
25. Craig Yeast, Cin.	2	44	434	9.9	2
26. Leon Johnson, NYJ	4	91	890	9.8	1
27. Eddie Kennison, Den.	5	138	1,343	9.7	3
28. Eric Metcalf, Oak.	12	315	3,042	9.7	9
29. Terrell Buckley, Den.	9	78	746	9.6	1
30. Dale Carter, Den.	9	83	787	9.5	2

TOP ACTIVE KICKOFF RETURNERS

40 or more kickoff returns

	Yrs.	No.	Yards	Avg.	TD
1. MarTay Jenkins, Ariz.	2	82	2,186	26.7	1
2. Terry Fair, Det.	3	91	2,329	25.6	2
3. Tim Brown, Oak.	13	49	1,235	25.2	1
4. Allen Rossum, G.B.	3	148	3,715	25.1	2
5. Tony Horne, K.C.	3	143	3,577	25.0	4
6. Charlie Rogers, Sea.	2	84	2,094	24.9	1
7. Kevin Williams, Mia.	3	41	1,011	24.7	1
8. Tremain Mack, Cin.	4	146	3,583	24.5	2
9. Michael Bates, *	8	298	7,274	24.4	5
10. Brock Marion, *	8	106	2,580	24.3	0
11. Duce Staley, Phil.	4	48	1,158	24.1	0
12. Glyn Milburn, Chi.	8	401	9,636	24.0	2
13. Deltha O'Neal, Den.	1	46	1,102	24.0	1
14. Kevin Mathis, N.O.	4	51	1,216	23.8	0
15. Mario Bates, *	8	53	1,251	23.6	0
16. Reidel Anthony, T.B.	4	95	2,232	23.5	0
17. Jason Tucker, Dall.	2	73	1,712	23.5	0
18. Chad Morton, N.O.	1	44	1,029	23.4	0
19. Reggie Barlow, Oak.	5	70	1,634	23.3	1
20. Corey Harris, Balt.	9	227	5,293	23.3	1
21. David Dunn, Oak.	6	178	4,139	23.3	2
22. Aaron Glenn, NYJ	7	111	2,578	23.2	1
23. Tim Dwight, S.D.	3	112	2,597	23.2	1
24. Karl Williams, T.B.	5	49	1,128	23.0	0
25. Brian Mitchell, Phil.	11	468	10,710	22.9	3
26. O.J. McDuffie, Mia.	8	92	2,103	22.9	0
27. Ronney Jenkins, S.D.	1	67	1,531	22.9	1
28. Kevin Faulk, N.E.	2	77	1,759	22.8	0
29. Will Blackwell, Pitt.	4	76	1,736	22.8	2
30. James Thrash, Phil.	4	65	1,484	22.8	1

TOP ACTIVE QUARTERBACK SACKERS

	Yrs.	No.
1. Bruce Smith, Wash.	16	181.0
2. Clyde Simmons, Chi.	15	121.5
3. John Randle, Sea.	11	114.0
4. Neil Smith, S.D.	13	104.5
5. Trace Armstrong, Oak.	12	98.5
6. Henry Thomas, *	14	93.5
7. Bryce Paup, *	11	75.0
8. Robert Porcher, Det.	9	74.5
9. Cornelius Bennett, *	14	71.5
10. Michael Sinclair, Sea.	9	70.0
11. Rob Burnett, Balt.	11	67.0
12. Kevin Carter, Tenn.	6	62.5
13. Michael Strahan, NYG	8	62.0
14. Michael McCrary, Balt.	8	61.5
15. Phil Hansen, Buff.	10	58.5
Warren Sapp, T.B.	6	58.5
Tracy Scroggins, Det.	9	58.5
Chuck Smith, Car.	9	58.5
19. Cortez Kennedy, *	11	58.0
20. Bryant Young, S.F.	7	57.5
21. Chad Brown, Sea.	8	55.5
Keith Hamilton, NYG	9	55.5
23. Marco Coleman, Wash.	9	52.0
24. Bryan Cox, *	10	51.5
Hugh Douglas, Phil.	6	51.5
Simeon Rice, T.B.	5	51.5
27. Chris Slade, N.E.	8	51.0
28. Jason Gildon, Pitt.	7	50.0
29. Mo Lewis, NYJ	10	49.0
30. Anthony Pleasant, N.E.	11	48.0

TOP ACTIVE PUNTERS

50 or more punts

	Yrs.	No.	Avg.	LG
1. Shane Lechler, Oak.	1	65	45.9	69
2. Darren Bennett, S.D.	5	524	44.8	66
3. Tom Tupa, NYJ	12	530	44.0	73
4. Tom Rouen, Den.	8	531	43.8	76
5. Hunter Smith, Ind.	2	123	43.7	65
6. Josh Miller, Pitt.	5	374	43.5	75
7. Matt Turk, Mia.	6	480	43.4	70
8. Sean Landeta, Phil.	16	1,119	43.4	74
9. Mitch Berger, Minn.	6	364	43.1	75
10. Chris Gardocki, Cle.	10	726	43.1	72
11. Craig Hentrich, Tenn.	7	524	43.0	78
12. Micah Knorr, Dall.	1	58	42.8	60
13. Todd Sauerbrun, Car.	6	410	42.7	72
14. Bryan Barker, Wash.	11	794	42.6	83
15. John Jett, Det.	8	582	42.5	62
16. Lee Johnson, N.E.	16	1,163	42.5	70
17. Mark Royals, T.B.	11	903	42.5	69
18. Scott Player, Ariz.	3	240	42.5	67
19. Toby Gowin, N.O.	4	318	42.4	72
20. Kyle Richardson, Balt.	4	298	42.2	67
21. Tommy Barnhardt, *	14	890	42.1	65
22. Brad Maynard, Chi.	4	380	42.0	64
23. Jeff Feagles, Sea.	13	1,054	41.5	77
24. Will Brice, Car.	3	101	41.5	72
25. Louie Aguiar, *	10	758	41.2	71
26. Daniel Pope, Cin.	2	195	41.0	64
27. Chris Mohr, Atl.	11	853	40.5	80
28. Ken Walter, Car.	4	291	40.4	66
29. Dan Stryzinski, K.C.	11	847	40.2	64
30. Chad Stanley, S.F.	2	138	39.6	70

** Free agent; subject to developments.*

COACHES RECORDS

ACTIVE COACHES' CAREER RECORDS (Order Based on Career Victories)

Start of 2001 Season			Regular Season				Postseason				Career			
Coach	**Team(s)**	**Yrs.**	**Won**	**Lost**	**Tied**	**Pct.**	**Won**	**Lost**	**Tied**	**Pct.**	**Won**	**Lost**	**Tied**	**Pct.**
Dan Reeves	Denver Broncos, New York Giants, Atlanta Falcons	20	171	140	1	.550	10	8	0	.556	181	148	1	.550
Marty Schottenheimer	Cleveland Browns, Kansas City Chiefs, Washington Redskins	15	145	85	1	.630	5	11	0	.313	150	96	1	.609
George Seifert	San Francisco 49ers, Carolina Panthers	10	113	47	0	.706	10	5	0	.667	123	52	0	.703
Jim Mora	New Orleans Saints, Indianapolis Colts	14	119	96	0	.553	0	6	0	.000	119	102	0	.538
Mike Holmgren	Green Bay Packers, Seattle Seahawks	9	90	54	0	.625	9	6	0	.600	99	60	0	.623
Dennis Green	Minnesota Vikings	9	92	52	0	.639	4	8	0	.333	96	60	0	.615
Bill Cowher	Pittsburgh Steelers	9	86	58	0	.597	5	6	0	.455	91	64	0	.587
Dick Vermeil	Philadelphia Eagles, St. Louis Rams, Kansas City Chiefs	10	76	73	0	.510	6	4	0	.600	82	77	0	.516
Mike Shanahan	Los Angeles Raiders, Denver Broncos	8	72	44	0	.621	7	2	0	.778	79	46	0	.632
Jeff Fisher	Tennessee Titans	6	58	44	0	.569	3	2	0	.600	61	46	0	.570
Tom Coughlin	Jacksonville Jaguars	6	56	40	0	.583	4	4	0	.500	60	44	0	.577
Dave Wannstedt	Chicago Bears, Miami Dolphins	7	51	61	0	.455	2	2	0	.500	53	63	0	.457
Tony Dungy	Tampa Bay Buccaneers	5	45	35	0	.563	2	3	0	.400	47	38	0	.553
Bill Belichick	Cleveland Browns, New England Patriots	6	41	55	0	.427	1	1	0	.500	42	56	0	.429
Jim Fassel	New York Giants	4	37	26	1	.586	2	2	0	.500	39	28	1	.581
Steve Mariucci	San Francisco 49ers	4	35	29	0	.547	2	2	0	.500	37	31	0	.544
Jon Gruden	Oakland Raiders	3	28	20	0	.583	1	1	0	.500	29	21	0	.580
Brian Billick	Baltimore Ravens	2	20	12	0	.625	4	0	0	1.000	24	12	0	.667
Andy Reid	Philadelphia Eagles	2	16	16	0	.500	1	1	0	.500	17	17	0	.500
Jim Haslett	New Orleans Saints	1	10	6	0	.625	1	1	0	.500	11	7	0	.611
Dick Jauron	Chicago Bears	2	11	21	0	.344	0	0	0	.000	11	21	0	.344
Mike Martz	St. Louis Rams	1	10	6	0	.625	0	1	0	.000	10	7	0	.588
Mike Sherman	Green Bay Packers	1	9	7	0	.563	0	0	0	.000	9	7	0	.563
Mike Riley	San Diego Chargers	2	9	23	0	.290	0	0	0	.000	9	23	0	.290
Dave Campo	Dallas Cowboys	1	5	11	0	.313	0	0	0	.000	5	11	0	.313
Dick LeBeau	Cincinnati Bengals	1	4	9	0	.308	0	0	0	.000	4	9	0	.308
Dave McGinnis	Arizona Cardinals	1	1	8	0	.111	0	0	0	.000	1	8	0	.111
Butch Davis	Cleveland Browns	0	0	0	0	.000	0	0	0	.000	0	0	0	.000
Herman Edwards	New York Jets	0	0	0	0	.000	0	0	0	.000	0	0	0	.000
Marty Mornhinweg	Detroit Lions	0	0	0	0	.000	0	0	0	.000	0	0	0	.000
Gregg Williams	Buffalo Bills	0	0	0	0	.000	0	0	0	.000	0	0	0	.000

COACHES WITH 100 CAREER VICTORIES (Order Based on Career Victories)

Start of 2001 Season			Regular Season				Postseason				Career			
Coach	**Team(s)**	**Yrs.**	**Won**	**Lost**	**Tied**	**Pct.**	**Won**	**Lost**	**Tied**	**Pct.**	**Won**	**Lost**	**Tied**	**Pct.**
Don Shula	Baltimore Colts, Miami Dolphins	33	328	156	6	.676	19	17	0	.528	347	173	6	.665
George Halas	Chicago Bears	40	318	148	31	.671	6	3	0	.667	324	151	31	.671
Tom Landry	Dallas Cowboys	29	250	162	6	.605	20	16	0	.556	270	178	6	.601
Earl (Curly) Lambeau	Green Bay Packers, Chicago Cardinals, Washington Redskins	33	226	132	22	.624	3	2	0	.600	229	134	22	.623
Chuck Noll	Pittsburgh Steelers	23	193	148	1	.566	16	8	0	.667	209	156	1	.572
Chuck Knox	Los Angeles Rams, Buffalo Bills, Seattle Seahawks	22	186	147	1	.558	7	11	0	.389	193	158	1	.550
Dan Reeves	Denver Broncos, New York Giants, Atlanta Falcons	20	171	140	1	.550	10	8	0	.556	181	148	1	.550
Paul Brown	Cleveland Browns, Cincinnati Bengals	21	166	100	6	.621	4	8	0	.333	170	108	6	.609
Bud Grant	Minnesota Vikings	18	158	96	5	.620	10	12	0	.455	168	108	5	.607
Marv Levy	Kansas City Chiefs, Buffalo Bills	17	143	112	0	.561	11	8	0	.579	154	120	0	.562
Steve Owen	New York Giants	23	151	100	17	.595	2	8	0	.200	153	108	17	.581
Marty Schottenheimer	Cleveland Browns, Kansas City Chiefs, Washington Redskins	15	145	85	1	.630	5	11	0	.313	150	96	1	.609
Bill Parcells	New York Giants, New England Patriots New York Jets	15	138	100	1	.579	11	6	0	.647	149	106	1	.584
Joe Gibbs	Washington Redskins	12	124	60	0	.674	16	5	0	.762	140	65	0	.683
Hank Stram	Kansas City Chiefs, New Orleans Saints	17	131	97	10	.571	5	3	0	.625	136	100	10	.573
Weeb Ewbank	Baltimore Colts, New York Jets	20	130	129	7	.502	4	1	0	.800	134	130	7	.507
Mike Ditka	Chicago Bears, New Orleans Saints	14	121	95	0	.560	6	6	0	.500	127	101	0	.557
George Seifert	San Francisco 49ers, Carolina Panthers	10	113	47	0	.706	10	5	0	.667	123	52	0	.703
Sid Gillman	Los Angeles Rams, Los Angeles-San Diego Chargers, Houston Oilers	18	122	99	7	.550	1	5	0	.167	123	104	7	.541
Jim Mora	New Orleans Saints, Indianapolis Colts	14	119	96	0	.553	0	6	0	.000	119	102	0	.538
George Allen	Los Angeles Rams, Washington Redskins	12	116	47	5	.705	2	7	0	.222	118	54	5	.681
Don Coryell	St. Louis Cardinals, San Diego Chargers	14	111	83	1	.572	3	6	0	.333	114	89	1	.561
John Madden	Oakland Raiders	10	103	32	7	.750	9	7	0	.563	112	39	7	.731
Ray (Buddy) Parker	Chicago Cardinals, Detroit Lions, Pittsburgh Steelers	15	104	75	9	.577	3	1	0	.750	107	76	9	.581
Vince Lombardi	Green Bay Packers, Washington Redskins	10	96	34	6	.728	9	1	0	.900	105	35	6	.740
Tom Flores	Oakland-Los Angeles Raiders, Seattle Seahawks	12	97	87	0	.527	8	3	0	.727	105	90	0	.538
Bill Walsh	San Francisco 49ers	10	92	59	1	.609	10	4	0	.714	102	63	1	.617

Active coaches in bold.

WHAT TO LOOK FOR IN 2001

Marty Schottenheimer, Washington, needs five victories to pass Steve Owen (153) and Marv Levy (154) for tenth all-time in career victories, and five regular-season victories to become the eleventh coach to reach 150 regular-season victories. In 15 seasons, Schottenheimer has 150 career wins and 145 regular-season victories.

Mike Holmgren, Seattle, needs one victory to reach 100 career victories and 10 regular-season victories to reach 100 regular-season victories. In nine seasons, Holmgren has 99 career wins and 90 regular-season victories.

Dennis Green, Minnesota, needs four victories to reach 100 career victories and eight regular-season victories to reach 100 regular-season victories. In nine seasons, Green has 96 career victories and 92 regular-season victories.

Brett Favre, Green Bay, needs to pass for 3,000 yards to become the first player in NFL history with 10 consecutive 3,000-yard seasons. Favre and Dan Marino currently share the league mark of nine consecutive seasons.

Favre needs 301 completions to pass Dave Krieg (3,105) and Dan Fouts (3,297) to move into sixth all-time in pass completions. In 10 seasons, Favre has completed 2,997 passes.

Favre needs 3,442 passing yards to pass Jim Everett (34,837), Jim Kelly (35,467), Vinny Testaverde (36,307), Boomer Esiason (37,920), and Dave Krieg (38,147) and move into eighth place all-time. Favre has passed for 34,706 yards in 10 seasons (see Testaverde note).

Favre has 255 career touchdown passes, tied for eighth all-time with Sonny Jurgensen, and needs 7 to pass Dave Krieg (261) for seventh all-time and 19 to pass Joe Montana (273) for sixth all-time.

Peyton Manning, Indianapolis, needs to pass for 4,000 yards to become only the third quarterback in NFL history (Dan Fouts and Dan Marino) to pass for 4,000 yards in three consecutive seasons.

Vinny Testaverde, New York Jets, needs 4,245 passing yards to pass Boomer Esiason (37,920), Dave Krieg (38,147), Johnny Unitas (40,239), and Joe Montana (40,551) to move into fifth place. In 14 seasons, Testaverde has 36,307 career passing yards.

Testaverde needs 103 completions to become the eighth player all-time with 3,000 completed passes. In 14 seasons, Testaverde has completed 2,897 passes (see Favre note).

Emmitt Smith, Dallas, needs 104 rushing yards to pass Barry Sanders (15,269) for second all-time and 1,561 rushing yards to pass Walter Payton (16,726) to become the NFL's all-time leading rusher. In 11 seasons, Smith has rushed for 15,166 yards.

Smith needs 1,027 combined yards to join Walter Payton (21,803) and Jerry Rice (19,878) as the only players in NFL history with 19,000 combined yards. Smith has gained 17,973 combined yards in his career (see Mitchell note).

Edgerrin James, Indianapolis, can become only the third running back in NFL history (Jim Brown and Earl Campbell) to win the rushing title in each of his first three seasons.

Curtis Martin, New York Jets, needs 1,000 rushing yards to become the third player in NFL history (Barry Sanders and Eric Dickerson) to rush for 1,000 yards in each of his first seven seasons.

Eddie George, Tennessee, needs 1,200 rushing yards to become the first player in NFL history to rush for 1,200 yards in each of his first six seasons. George and Eric Dickerson are the only running backs to have rushed for 1,200 yards in each of their first five seasons.

Corey Dillon, Cincinnati, needs 1,000 rushing yards to become the sixth player in NFL history (Barry Sanders, Eric Dickerson, Curtis Martin, Tony Dorsett, and Eddie George) to rush for 1,000 yards in each of his first five seasons.

Ricky Watters, Seattle, needs 1,028 rushing yards to pass O.J. Simpson (11,236) and John Riggins (11,352) and move into tenth place all-time in rushing yardage. Watters has 10,325 career rushing yards in nine seasons.

Jerry Rice, Oakland, needs 122 yards to join Walter Payton (21,803) as the only players with 20,000 combined yards. In 16 seasons, Rice has 19,878 combined yards (see Mitchell and Smith note).

Cris Carter, Minnesota, needs 80 catches to become the second player in NFL history (Jerry Rice, 1,281) with 1,100 receptions. In 14 seasons, Carter has 1,020 career receptions.

Carter needs 1,043 yards to pass Steve Largent (13,089), Andre Reed (13,198), Henry Ellard (13,777), and James Lofton (14,004) and move into second place all-time in receiving yards. Carter has 12,962 career receiving yards in 14 seasons.

Carter has had eight seasons with 1,000 receiving yards and needs another to move into sole possession of second place all-time. He is currently tied with Tim Brown and Steve Largent (see Brown note).

Carter has scored 124 career touchdowns, sixth all-time, and needs three to pass Walter Payton (125) and Jim Brown (126) into fourth place all-time.

Tim Brown, Oakland, has 846 career receptions and needs six to move into fifth place all-time, and 54 receptions to become the fifth player with 900 catches.

Brown has 12,072 receiving yards in 13 seasons, tenth all-time, and needs 1,127 yards to pass Charlie Joiner (12,146), Art Monk (12,721), Irving Fryar (12,785), Cris Carter (12,962), Steve Largent (13,089), and Andre Reed (13,198) and move into fourth place (see Carter note).

Brown needs 1,452 combined yards to become the sixth player in NFL history to reach 18,000. In 13 seasons, Brown has 16,548 combined yards (see Mitchell and Smith note).

Brown needs 14 receiving touchdowns to become the fourth player with 100 receiving touchdowns.

Brown has eight seasons of 1,000 receiving yards and needs another such season to move into sole possession of second place all-time in the category. He is currently tied with Cris Carter and Steve Largent (see Carter note).

Randy Moss, Minnesota, needs 1,000 receiving yards to become the first player in NFL history with 1,000 receiving yards in each of his first four seasons. Moss is currently tied with John Jefferson with three consecutive 1,000-yard seasons to start a career.

Shannon Sharpe, Baltimore, has 619 career receptions for 7,793 yards and needs 44 catches and 188 yards to pass Ozzie Newsome (662 & 7,980) as the NFL's all-time leading tight end in receptions and yards.

Brian Mitchell, Philadelphia, has 18,640 combined yards in 11 seasons. Mitchell needs 1,360 yards to join Walter Payton (21,803) as the only players in NFL history to attain 20,000 combined yards (see Rice and Smith note).

Mitchell needs one kick return touchdown (kickoff or punt) for sole possession of the all-time lead. Mitchell has 11 in his career, tied with Eric Metcalf for the most in league history (see Metcalf note).

Mitchell needs one punt return for a touchdown to move into a tie with Metcalf (9) for first all-time. In 11 seasons, Mitchell has 8, tied with Jack Christiansen, Desmond Howard, and Rick Upchurch (see Howard note).

Desmond Howard, Detroit, needs one punt return touchdown to move into a tie with Eric Metcalf (9) for first all-time. In nine seasons, Howard has 8 and is tied for second all-time with Jack Christiansen, Brian Mitchell (see Mitchell note), and Rick Upchurch.

Eric Metcalf, Oakland, needs one kick return touchdown (kickoff or punt) for sole possession of the all-time lead. Metcalf has 11 in his career, tied with Brian Mitchell for the most in league history (see Mitchell note).

Jevon Kearse, Tennessee, needs 10 sacks to become only the third defensive player in NFL history (Reggie White and Derrick Thomas) to record double-digit sacks in each of his first three seasons.

Rod Woodson, Baltimore, needs one interception return for a touchdown to take sole possession of the all-time NFL lead. In 14 seasons, Woodson has 9 interception returns for touchdowns, tied with Ken Houston for first all-time.

Morten Andersen needs 65 points to pass George Blanda (2,002) for second all-time in points scored. In 19 seasons, Andersen has scored 1,938 points.

Lee Johnson, New England, needs 44 yards to pass Rohn Stark (49,471) to become the NFL's all-time leader in punting yardage. In 16 seasons, Johnson has 49,428 career yards.

Bruce Matthews, Tennessee, needs to play in three regular season games to pass Jim Marshall (282) to move into second place all-time in most games played among non-kickers. In 18 seasons, Matthews has played in 280 games.

Matthews can move into a tie for second all-time (Jim Marshall) for most seasons with one club with 19 (see Green note).

Darrell Green, Washington, can move into a tie for second all-time (Jim Marshall) for most seasons with one club (19) (see Matthews note).

DRAFT LIST FOR 2001

66th Annual NFL Draft, April 21-22, 2001
*Denotes Compensatory Selection

ARIZONA CARDINALS
1. Leonard Davis—2, T, Texas
2. Kyle Vanden Bosch—34, DE, Nebraska
   Michael Stone—54, DB, Memphis, from St. Louis
3. Adrian Wilson—64, DB, North Carolina State
4. Bill Gramatica—98, K, South Florida
   Marcus Bell—123, DT, Memphis, from Oakland through St. Louis
5. Mario Fatafehi—133, DT, Kansas State
6. Bobby Newcombe—166, WR, Nebraska
7. Renaldo Hill—202, DB, Michigan State
   *Tevita Ofahengaue—246, TE, Brigham Young

ATLANTA FALCONS
1. Michael Vick—1, QB, Virginia Tech, from San Diego
2. Alge Crumpler—35, TE, North Carolina
4. Roberto Garza—99, C, Texas A&M-Kingsville
   Matt Stewart—102, LB, Vanderbilt, from Dallas
5. Vinny Sutherland—136, WR, Purdue
6. Randy Garner—167, DE, Arkansas
7. Corey Hall—215, DB, Appalachian State, from Washington through Denver
   Kynan Forney—219, T, Hawaii, from Green Bay through Denver
   Ronald Flemons—226, DE, Texas A&M, from Denver
   *Quentin McCord—236, WR, Kentucky

BALTIMORE RAVENS
1. Todd Heap—31, TE, Arizona State
2. Gary Baxter—62, DB, Baylor
3. Casey Rabach—92, C, Wisconsin
4. Edgerton Hartwell—126, LB, Western Illinois
5. Chris Barnes—161, RB, New Mexico State
6. Joe Maese—194, C, New Mexico
7. Dwayne Missouri—231, DE, Northwestern

BUFFALO BILLS
1. Nate Clements—21, DB, Ohio State, from Tampa Bay
2. Aaron Schobel—46, DE, Texas Christian
   Travis Henry—58, RB, Tennessee, from Denver
3. Ron Edwards—76, DT, Texas A&M
   *Jonas Jennings—95, T, Georgia
4. Brandon Spoon—110, LB, North Carolina, Reaquired own selection through Denver
5. Marques Sullivan—144, T, Illinois
6. Tony Driver—178, DB, Notre Dame
   *Dan O'Leary—195, TE, Notre Dame
   *Jimmy Williams—196, DB, Vanderbilt
7. Reggie Germany—214, WR, Ohio State
   *Tyrone Robertson—238, DT, Hinds (Miss.) C.C.

CAROLINA PANTHERS
1. Dan Morgan—11, LB, Miami
2. Kris Jenkins—44, DT, Maryland
3. Steve Smith—74, WR, Utah
4. Chris Weinke—106, QB, Florida State
5. Jarrod Cooper—143, DB, Kansas State
6. Dee Brown—175, RB, Syracuse
7. Louis Williams—211, C, Louisiana State
   Mike Roberg—227, TE, Idaho, from Philadelphia

CHICAGO BEARS
1. David Terrell—8, WR, Michigan
2. Anthony Thomas—38, RB, Michigan
3. Mike Gandy—68, G, Notre Dame
4. Karon Riley—103, DE, Minnesota
5. Bernard Robertson—138, C, Tulane
7. John Capel—208, WR, Florida

CINCINNATI BENGALS
1. Justin Smith—4, DE, Missouri
2. Chad Johnson—36, WR, Oregon State
3. Sean Brewer—66, TE, San Jose State
4. Rudi Johnson—100, RB, Auburn
5. Victor Leyva—135, G, Arizona State
6. Riall Johnson—168, LB, Stanford
7. T.J. Houshmandzadeh—204, WR, Oregon State

CLEVELAND BROWNS
1. Gerard Warren—3, DT, Florida
2. Quincy Morgan—33, WR, Kansas State
3. James Jackson—65, RB, Miami
4. Anthony Henry—97, DB, South Florida
5. Jeremiah Pharms—134, LB, Washington
6. Michael Jameson—165, DB, Texas A&M
7. Paul Zukauskas—203, G, Boston College
   *Andre King—245, WR, Miami

DALLAS COWBOYS
2. Quincy Carter—53, QB, Georgia, from New Orleans
   Tony Dixon—56, DB, Alabama, from Miami
3. *Willie Blade—93, DT, Mississippi State
4. Markus Steele—122, LB, Southern California, from Miami
5. Matt Lehr—137, C, Virginia Tech
6. Daleroy Stewart—171, DT, Southern Mississippi
7. Colston Weatherington—207, DE, Central Missouri
   *John Nix—240, DT, Southern Mississippi
   *Char-ron Dorsey—242, T, Florida State

DENVER BRONCOS
1. Willie Middlebrooks—24, DB, Minnesota
2. Paul Toviessi—51, DE, Marshall, from Tampa Bay through Buffalo
3. Reggie Hayward—87, DE, Iowa State
4. Ben Hamilton—113, C, Minnesota, from Green Bay
   Nick Harris—120, P, California
6. Kevin Kasper—190, WR, Iowa

DETROIT LIONS
1. Jeff Backus—18, T, Michigan
2. Dominic Raiola—50, C, Nebraska, from Pittsburgh through New England
   Shaun Rogers—61, DT, Texas, from New York Giants
5. Scotty Anderson—148, WR, Grambling State
   Mike McMahon—149, QB, Rutgers, from New York Jets through New England
6. Jason Glenn—173, LB, Texas A&M, from San Francisco through New England

GREEN BAY PACKERS
1. Jamal Reynolds—10, DE, Florida State, from Seattle
2. Robert Ferguson—41, WR, Texas A&M, from San Francisco
3. Bhawoh Jue—71, DB, Penn State, from San Francisco
   Torrance Marshall—72, LB, Oklahoma, from Seattle
4. Bill Ferrario—105, G, Wisconsin, from San Francisco
6. *David Martin—198, TE, Tennessee

INDIANAPOLIS COLTS
1. Reggie Wayne—30, WR, Miami, from New York Giants
2. Idrees Bashir—37, DB, Memphis, from Dallas
3. Cory Bird—91, DB, Virginia Tech, from New York Giants
4. Ryan Diem—118, G, Northern Illinois
5. Raymond Walls—152, DB, Southern Mississippi
6. Jason Doering—193, DB, Wisconsin, from New York Giants
7. Rick DeMulling—220, G, Idaho

JACKSONVILLE JAGUARS
1. Marcus Stroud—13, DT, Georgia
2. Maurice Williams—43, T, Michigan
3. Eric Westmoreland—73, LB, Tennessee
   *James Boyd—94, DB, Penn State
5. David Leaverton—142, P, Tennessee
6. Chad Ward—170, G, Washington, from New England
7. Anthony Denman—213, LB, Notre Dame
   *Marlon McCree—233, DB, Kentucky
   *Richmond Flowers—235, WR, Tennessee-Chattanooga
   *Randy Chevrier—241, DT, McGill (Canada)

KANSAS CITY CHIEFS
3. Eric Downing—75, DT, Syracuse
   Marvin Minnis—77, WR, Florida State, from Washington
4. Monty Beisel—107, DE, Kansas State
   George Layne—108, RB, Texas Christian, from Jacksonville
5. Billy Baber—141, TE, Virginia
   Derrick Blaylock—150, RB, Stephen F. Austin, from St. Louis
6. Alex Sulfsted—176, G, Miami (Ohio)
7. Shaunard Harts—212, DB, Boise State
   *Terdell Sands—243, DT, Tennessee-Chattanooga

MIAMI DOLPHINS
1. Jamar Fletcher—26, DB, Wisconsin
2. Chris Chambers—52, WR, Wisconsin, from Indianapolis through Dallas
3. Travis Minor—85, RB, Florida State
   Morlon Greenwood—88, LB, Syracuse, from Philadelphia
5. Shawn Draper—156, T, Alabama
6. Brandon Winey—164, T, Louisiana State, from San Diego
   Josh Heupel—177, QB, Oklahoma, from Washington
   Otis Leverette—187, DE, Alabama-Birmingham, from Philadelphia
   Rick Crowell—188, LB, Colorado State

MINNESOTA VIKINGS
1. Michael Bennett—27, RB, Wisconsin
2. Willie Howard—57, DE, Stanford
3. Eric Kelly—69, DB, Kentucky, from New England
4. *Shawn Worthen—130, DT, Texas Christian
   *Cedric James—131, WR, Texas Christian
5. Patrick Chukwurah—157, LB, Wyoming
6. Carey Scott—189, DB, Kentucky State
7. Brian Crawford—225, T, Western Oregon

NEW ENGLAND PATRIOTS
1. Richard Seymour—6, DT, Georgia
2. Matt Light—48, G, Purdue, from Detroit
3. Brock Williams—86, DB, Notre Dame, from Minnesota
4. Kenyatta Jones—96, G, South Florida, from San Diego
   Jabari Holloway—119, TE, Notre Dame, from Minnesota
5. *Hakim Akbar—163, DB, Washington
6. Arther Love—180, TE, South Carolina State, from Detroit
   *Leonard Myers—200, DB, Miami
7. Owen Pochman—216, K, Brigham Young, from Detroit
   *T.J. Turner—239, LB, Michigan State

NEW ORLEANS SAINTS
1. Deuce McAllister—23, RB, Mississippi
3. Sedrick Hodge—70, LB, North Carolina, from Dallas
   Kenny Smith—81, DT, Alabama, from Indianapolis through Dallas
4. Moran Norris—115, RB, Kansas
5. Onome Ojo—153, WR, California-Davis
6. Mitch White—185, T, Oregon State
7. Ennis Davis—221, DT, Southern California

NEW YORK GIANTS
1. Will Allen—22, DB, Syracuse, from Indianapolis
3. William Peterson—78, DB, Western Illinois, from Detroit
4. Cedric Scott—114, DE, Southern Mississippi, from Detroit
   Jesse Palmer—125, QB, Florida
5. John Markham—160, K, Vanderbilt
   *Jonathan Carter—162, WR, Troy State
7. Ross Kolodziej—230, DT, Wisconsin

NEW YORK JETS
1. Santana Moss—16, WR, Miami, from Pittsburgh
2. LaMont Jordan—49, RB, Maryland
3. Kareem McKenzie—79, T, Penn State
4. Jamie Henderson—101, DB, Georgia, from New England
7. James Reed—206, DT, Iowa State, from New England
   Siitupe Peko—217, G, Michigan State

OAKLAND RAIDERS
1. Derrick Gibson—28, DB, Florida State
2. Marques Tuiasosopo—59, QB, Washington
3. DeLawrence Grant—89, DE, Oregon State
5. Raymond Perryman—158, DB, Northern Arizona
6. Chris Cooper—184, DT, Nebraska-Omaha, from Indianapolis
7. Derek Combs—228, RB, Ohio State
   Ken-Yon Rambo—229, WR, Ohio State, from Tennessee

PHILADELPHIA EAGLES
1. Freddie Mitchell—25, WR, UCLA
2. Quinton Caver—55, LB, Arkansas
3. Derrick Burgess—63, DE, Mississippi, from San Diego
4. Correll Buckhalter—121, RB, Nebraska
5. Tony Stewart—147, TE, Penn State, from Green Bay
   A.J. Feeley—155, QB, Oregon

PITTSBURGH STEELERS
1. Casey Hampton—19, DT, Texas, from New York Jets
2. Kendrell Bell—39, LB, Georgia, from New England
3. Choice Forfeited
4. Mathias Nkwenti—111, T, Temple, from New York Jets
5. Chukky Okobi—146, C, Purdue
6. Rodney Bailey—181, DE, Ohio State, from New York Jets
   Roger Knight—182, LB, Wisconsin
7. Chris Taylor—218, WR, Texas A&M

ST. LOUIS RAMS
1. Damione Lewis—12, DT, Miami, from Kansas City
   Adam Archuleta—20, DB, Arizona State
   Ryan Pickett—29, DT, Ohio State, from Tennessee
2. Tommy Polley—42, LB, Florida State, from Kansas City
3. Brian Allen—83, LB, Florida State
4. Milton Wynn—116, WR, Washington State
   *Brandon Manumaleuna—129, TE, Arizona
5. Jerametrius Butler—145, DB, Kansas State, from Washington
6. *Francis St. Paul—197, WR, Northern Arizona

SAN DIEGO CHARGERS
1. LaDainian Tomlinson—5, RB, Texas Christian, from Atlanta
2. Drew Brees—32, QB, Purdue
3. Tay Cody—67, DB, Florida State, from Atlanta
4. Carlos Polk—112, LB, Nebraska, from Pittsburgh through New England
5. Elliot Silvers—132, T, Washington
   Zeke Moreno—139, LB, Southern California, from New England
7. Brandon Gorin—201, T, Purdue
   *Robert Carswell—244, DB, Clemson

SAN FRANCISCO 49ERS
1. Andre Carter—7, DE, California, from Dallas through Seattle
2. Jamie Winborn—47, LB, Vanderbilt, from Green Bay
3. Kevan Barlow—80, RB, Pittsburgh, from Green Bay
5. Choice Forfeited
6. Cedrick Wilson—169, WR, Tennessee, from Chicago
   Rashad Holman—179, DB, Louisville, from Green Bay
   Menson Holloway—191, DE, Texas-El Paso, from Oakland through Seattle
7. Alex Lincoln—209, LB, Auburn
   Eric Johnson—224, TE, Yale, from Miami through Washington

SEATTLE SEAHAWKS
1. Koren Robinson—9, WR, North Carolina State, from San Francisco
   Steve Hutchinson—17, G, Michigan, from Green Bay
2. Ken Lucas—40, DB, Mississippi
3. Heath Evans—82, RB, Auburn, from New Orleans through Green Bay and San Francisco
4. Orlando Huff—104, LB, Fresno State
   *Curtis Fuller—127, DB, Texas Christian
   *Floyd Womack—128, T, Mississippi State
5. Alex Bannister—140, WR, Eastern Kentucky
6. Josh Booty—172, QB, Louisiana State
7. Harold Blackmon—210, DB, Northwestern
   Dennis Norman—222, T, Princeton, from St. Louis through Green Bay and San Francisco
   *Kris Kocurek—237, DT, Texas Tech

TAMPA BAY BUCCANEERS
1. Kenyatta Walker—14, T, Florida, from Buffalo
3. Dwight Smith—84, DB, Akron
4. John Howell—117, DB, Colorado State
5. Russ Hochstein—151, G, Nebraska
6. Jameel Cook—174, RB, Illinois, from Jacksonville
   Ellis Wyms—183, DT, Mississippi State
7. Dauntae' Finger—205, TE, North Carolina, from Atlanta
   Than Merrill—223, DB, Yale
   *Joe Tafoya—234, DE, Arizona

TENNESSEE TITANS
2. Andre Dyson—60, DB, Utah
3. Shad Meier—90, TE, Kansas State
4. Justin McCareins—124, WR, Northern Illinois
5. Eddie Berlin—159, WR, Northern Iowa
6. Dan Alexander—192, RB, Nebraska
   *Adam Haayer—199, T, Minnesota
7. *Keith Adams—232, LB, Clemson

WASHINGTON REDSKINS
1. Rod Gardner—15, WR, Clemson
2. Fred Smoot—45, DB, Mississippi State
4. Sage Rosenfels—109, QB, Iowa State
5. Darnerien McCants—154, WR, Delaware State, from Denver through St. Louis
6. Mario Monds—186, DT, Cincinnati, from St. Louis

DRAFT LIST

NUMBER OF PLAYERS DRAFTED—2001

BY POSITION:

Position	Number
Defensive Backs	45
Wide Receivers	34
Defensive Tackles	27
Linebackers	27
Defensive Ends	21
Running Backs	20
Tackles	19
Tight Ends	15
Guards	13
Quarterbacks	11
Centers	9
Kickers	3
Punters	2

BY COLLEGE:

Florida State	9
Wisconsin	8
Miami	7
Nebraska	7
Georgia	6
Kansas State	6
Notre Dame	6
Ohio State	6
Texas A&M	6
Texas Christian	6
Michigan	5
Purdue	5
Tennessee	5
Washington	5
Florida	4
Minnesota	4
Mississippi State	4
North Carolina	4
Oregon State	4
Penn State	4
Southern Mississippi	4
Syracuse	4
Vanderbilt	4
Alabama	3
Arizona State	3
Auburn	3
Clemson	3
Iowa State	3
Kentucky	3
Louisiana State	3
Memphis	3
Michigan State	3
Mississippi	3
South Florida	3
Southern California	3
Texas	3
Virginia Tech	3
Arizona	2
Arkansas	2
Brigham Young	2
California	2
Colorado State	2
Idaho	2
Illinois	2
Maryland	2
North Carolina State	2
Northern Arizona	2
Northern Illinois	2
Northwestern	2
Oklahoma	2
Stanford	2
Tennessee-Chattanooga	2
Utah	2
Western Illinois	2
Yale	2
Akron	1
Alabama-Birmingham	1
Appalachian State	1
Baylor	1
Boise State	1
Boston College	1
California-Davis	1
Central Missouri	1
Cincinnati	1
Delaware State	1
Eastern Kentucky	1
Fresno State	1
Grambling State	1
Hawaii	1
Hinds (Miss.) C.C.	1
Iowa	1
Kansas	1
Kentucky State	1
Louisville	1
Marshall	1
McGill	1
Miami (Ohio)	1
Missouri	1
Nebraska-Omaha	1
New Mexico	1
New Mexico State	1
Northern Iowa	1
Oregon	1
Pittsburgh	1
Princeton	1
Rutgers	1
San Jose State	1
South Carolina State	1
Stephen F. Austin	1
Temple	1
Texas-El Paso	1
Texas A&M-Kingsville	1
Texas Tech	1
Troy State	1
Tulane	1
UCLA	1
Virginia	1
Washington State	1
Western Oregon	1
Wyoming	1

BY CONFERENCE:

Big 10	40
SEC	40
Big 12	31
Pac 10	24
ACC	21
Big East	18
Conference USA	17
Independent	12
Mountain West	8
MAC	5
WAC	5
Gateway	3
Ivy	3
Southern	3
Sun Belt	3
Big Sky	2
MEAC	2
Southland	2
Columbia Football Association	1
Lone Star	1
Mid-America Intercollegiate Athletic	1
North Central Intercollegiate Athletic	1
Ohio Valley	1
Southern Intercollegiate Athletic	1
SWAC	1

UNDERCLASSMEN AND THE DRAFT

Year	Entered	Drafted	In Top 10
1989	25	12	3
1990	38	18	5
1991	33	22	2
1992	48	25	5
1993	46	24	5
1994	42	26	6
1995	42	22	2
1996	47	21	4
1997	44	27	7
1998	41	20	3
1999	35	27	5
2000	31	20	4
2001	36	31	5

The following procedures will be used to break standings ties for postseason playoffs and to determine regular-season schedules. NOTE: Tie games count as one-half win and one-half loss for both clubs.

TO BREAK A TIE WITHIN A DIVISION

If, at the end of the regular season, two or more clubs in the same division finish with identical won-lost-tied percentages, the following steps will be taken until a champion is determined.

TWO CLUBS

1. Head-to-head (best won-lost-tied percentage in games between the clubs).
2. Best won-lost-tied percentage in games played within the division.
3. Best won-lost-tied percentage in games played within the conference.
4. Best won-lost-tied percentage in common games, if applicable.
5. Best net points in division games.
6. Best net points in all games.
7. Strength of schedule.
8. Best net touchdowns in all games.
9. Coin toss.

THREE OR MORE CLUBS

(Note: If two clubs remain tied after third or other clubs are eliminated during any step, tie breaker reverts to step 1 of the two-club format).

1. Head-to-head (best won-lost-tied percentage in games among the clubs).
2. Best won-lost-tied percentage in games played within the division.
3. Best won-lost-tied percentage in games played within the conference.
4. Best won-lost-tied percentage in common games.
5. Best net points in division games.
6. Best net points in all games.
7. Strength of schedule.
8. Best net touchdowns in all games.
9. Coin toss.

TO BREAK A TIE FOR THE WILD-CARD TEAM

If it is necessary to break ties to determine the three Wild-Card clubs from each conference, the following steps will be taken.

1. If the tied clubs are from the same division, apply division tie breaker.
2. If the tied clubs are from different divisions, apply the following steps.

TWO CLUBS

1. Head-to-head, if applicable.
2. Best won-lost-tied percentage in games played within the conference.
3. Best won-lost-tied percentage in common games, minimum of four.
4. Best average net points in conference games.
5. Best net points in all games.
6. Strength of schedule.
7. Best net touchdowns in all games.
8. Coin toss.

THREE OR MORE CLUBS

(Note: If two clubs remain tied after third or other clubs are eliminated, tie breaker reverts to step 1 of applicable two-club format.)

1. Apply division tie breaker to eliminate all but the highest ranked club in each division prior to proceeding to step 2. The original seeding within a division upon application of the division tie breaker remains the same for all subsequent applications of the procedure that are necessary to identify the three Wild-Card participants.
2. Head-to-head sweep. (Applicable only if one club has defeated each of the others or if one club has lost to each of the others.)
3. Best won-lost-tied percentage in games played within the conference.
4. Best won-lost-tied percentage in common games, minimum of four.
5. Best average net points in conference games.
6. Best net points in all games.
7. Strength of schedule.
8. Best net touchdowns in all games.
9. Coin toss.

When the first Wild-Card team has been identified, the procedure is repeated to name the second Wild-Card, i.e., eliminate all but the highest-ranked club in each division prior to proceeding to step 2, and repeated a third time, if necessary, to identify the third Wild Card. In situations where three or more teams from the same division are involved in the procedure, the original seeding of the teams remains the same for subsequent applications of the tie breaker if the top-ranked team in that division qualifies for a Wild-Card berth.

OTHER TIE-BREAKING PROCEDURES

1. Only one club advances to the playoffs in any tie-breaking step. Remaining tied clubs revert to the first step of the applicable division or Wild-Card tie breakers. As an example, if two clubs remain tied in any tie-breaker step after all other clubs have been eliminated, the procedure reverts to step one of the two-club format to determine the winner. When one club wins the tie breaker, all other clubs revert to step 1 of the applicable two-club or three-club format.
2. In comparing division and conference records or records against common opponents among tied teams, the best won-lost-tied percentage is the deciding factor since teams may have played an unequal number of games.
3. To determine home-field priority among division titlists, apply Wild-Card tie breakers.
4. To determine home-field priority for Wild-Card qualifiers, apply division tie breakers (if teams are from the same division) or Wild-Card tie breakers (if teams are from different divisions).

TIE-BREAKING PROCEDURE FOR SELECTION MEETING

If two or more clubs are tied in the selection order, the strength-of-schedule tie breaker is applied, subject to the following exceptions for playoff clubs:

1. The Super Bowl winner is last and the Super Bowl loser next-to-last.
2. Any non-Super Bowl playoff club involved in a tie shall be assigned priority within its segment below that of non-playoff clubs and in the order that the playoff clubs exited from the playoffs. Thus, within a tied segment a playoff club that loses in the Wild-Card game will have priority over a playoff club that loses in the Divisional playoff game, which in turn will have priority over a club that loses in the Conference Championship game. If two tied clubs exited the playoffs in the same round, the tie is broken by strength of schedule.

If any ties cannot be broken by strength of schedule, the divisional or conference tie breakers, whichever are applicable, are applied. Any ties that still exist are broken by a coin flip.

INSTANT REPLAY

For the 2001-03 seasons, the NFL will continue to employ a system of Referee Replay Review to aid officiating.

Prior to the two-minute warning of each half, a Coaches' Challenge System will be in effect. After the two-minute warning, and throughout any overtime period, a Referee Review will be initiated by a Replay Assistant from a Replay Booth.

The following procedures will be used:

REVIEWS BY REFEREE: All Replay Reviews will be conducted by the Referee on a field-level monitor after consultation with the other covering official(s), prior to review. A decision will be reversed only when the Referee has *indisputable visual evidence* available to him that warrants the change.

COACHES' CHALLENGE: In each game, a team will be permitted a maximum of two challenges that will initiate Referee Replay reviews. Each challenge will require the use of a team time out. If a challenge is upheld, the time out will be restored to the challenging team. A challenge will never be restored. No challenges will be recognized from a team that has exhausted its time outs.

REPLAY ASSISTANT'S REQUEST FOR REVIEW: After the two-minute warning of each half, and throughout any overtime period, any review will be initiated by a Replay Assistant. There is no limit to the number of reviews that may be initiated by the Replay Assistant. His ability to initiate a review will be unrelated to the number of time outs that either team has remaining, and no time out will be charged for any review initiated by the Replay Assistant.

TIME LIMIT: Each review will be a maximum of 90 seconds in length, timed from when the Referee begins his review of the replay at the field-level monitor.

REVIEWABLE PLAYS: The Replay System will cover the following play situations only:

A) PLAYS GOVERNED BY SIDELINE, GOAL LINE, END ZONE, AND END LINE:

1. Scoring plays, including a runner breaking the plane of the goal line.
2. Pass complete/incomplete/intercepted at sideline, goal line, end zone, and end line.
3. Runner/receiver in or out of bounds.
4. Recovery of loose ball in or out of bounds.

B) PASSING PLAYS:

1. Pass ruled complete/incomplete/intercepted in the field of play.
2. Touching of a forward pass by an ineligible receiver.
3. Touching of a forward pass by a defensive player.
4. Quarterback (Passer) forward pass or fumble.
5. Illegal forward pass beyond line of scrimmage.
6. Illegal forward pass after change of possession.
7. Forward or backward pass thrown from behind line of scrimmage.

C) OTHER DETECTABLE INFRACTIONS:

1. Runner ruled not down by defensive contact.
2. Forward progress with respect to first down.
3. Touching of a kick.
4. Number of players on the field.

INSTANT REPLAY HISTORY

From 1986-1991, a limited system of Instant Replay was used on a year-by-year basis. Replay also was experimented with during the 1986 and 1998 preseasons. For the 1999 season, the NFL introduced a system of Referee Replay Review to aid officiating. That system was extended on a one-year basis for the 2000 season and was approved in March 2001 for the next three years through 2003.

Following are the results of the different systems:

REGULAR SEASON, 1986-1991

Year	Games	Reversals	Plays Closely Reviewed
1986	224	38	374
1987	210	57	490
1988	224	53	537
1989	224	65	492
1990	224	73	504
1991	224	90	570
TOTAL	1,330	376	2,967

PRESEASON, 1996, 1998

Year	Games	Reversals	Challenges
1996	10	3	13
1998	10	3	10
TOTAL	20	6	23

REGULAR SEASON, 1999-2000

Year	Games	Total Replay Reviews	Challenges	Reversals
1999	248	195	133	57
2000	248	247	179	83
TOTAL	496	442	312	140

The AFC

BALTIMORE RAVENS

American Football Conference
Central Division
Team Colors: Black, Purple, and Metallic Gold
11001 Owings Mills Boulevard
Owings Mills, Maryland 21117
Telephone: (410) 654-6200

CLUB OFFICIALS

Owner: Arthur B. Modell
President: David Modell
Vice President/Public Relations: Kevin Byrne
Vice President/Business Development and Marketing: Dennis Mannion
Vice President/CFO: Luis Perez
Vice President/Player Personnel: Ozzie Newsome
Director of Football Administration: Pat Moriarty
Senior Director of Broadcast and Corporate Partnerships: Mark Burdett
Senior Director of Ticket Sales and Operations: Roy Sommerhof
Senior Director of Broadcasting and Video Production: Larry Rosen
Director of Operations/Information: Bob Eller
Director of Publications/Assistant Director of Public Relations: Francine Lubera
Director of Player Development: Earnest Byner
Director of Pro Personnel: James Harris
Director of College Scouting: Phil Savage
Assistant Director of Pro Personnel: George Kokinis
Scouts: Eric DeCosta, Ron Marciniak, T.J. McCreight, Terry McDonough, Vince Newsome, Art Perkins
Head Trainer: Bill Tessendorf
Equipment Manager: Ed Carroll
Video Director: Jon Dubé
Stadium: PSINet Stadium (built in 1997)
 • **Capacity:** 69,084
 1101 Russell Street
 Baltimore, Maryland 21230
Playing Surface: Natural Grass
Training Camp: Western Maryland College
 2 College Hill
 Westminster, Maryland 21157

RECORD HOLDERS

INDIVIDUAL RECORDS—CAREER

Category	Name	Performance
Rushing (Yds.)	Byron (Bam) Morris, 1996-97	1,511
Passing (Yds.)	Vinny Testaverde, 1996-97	7,148
Passing (TDs)	Vinny Testaverde, 1996-97	51
Receiving (No.)	Michael Jackson, 1996-98	183
Receiving (Yds.)	Michael Jackson, 1996-98	2,596
Interceptions	Rod Woodson, 1998-2000	17
Punting (Avg.)	Greg Montgomery, 1996-97	43.2
Punt Return (Avg.)	Jermaine Lewis, 1996-2000	13.4
Kickoff Return (Avg.)	Corey Harris, 1998-2000	24.0
Field Goals	Matt Stover, 1996-2000	129
Touchdowns (Tot.)	Michael Jackson, 1996-98	18
	Derrick Alexander, 1996-97	18
Points	Matt Stover, 1996-2000	539

INDIVIDUAL RECORDS—SINGLE SEASON

Category	Name	Performance
Rushing (Yds.)	Jamal Lewis, 2000	1,364
Passing (Yds.)	Vinny Testaverde, 1996	4,177
Passing (TDs)	Vinny Testaverde, 1996	33
Receiving (No.)	Michael Jackson, 1996	76
Receiving (Yds.)	Michael Jackson, 1996	1,201
Interceptions	Rod Woodson, 1999	7
Punting (Avg.)	Kyle Richardson, 1998	43.9
Punt Return (Avg.)	Jermaine Lewis, 2000	16.1
Kickoff Return (Avg.)	Corey Harris, 1998	27.6
Field Goals	Matt Stover, 2000	35
Touchdowns (Tot.)	Michael Jackson, 1996	14
Points	Matt Stover, 2000	135

INDIVIDUAL RECORDS—SINGLE GAME

Category	Name	Performance
Rushing (Yds.)	Priest Holmes, 11-22-98	227
Passing (Yds.)	Vinny Testaverde, 10-27-96	429
Passing (TDs)	Vinny Testaverde, 10-20-96	4
	Tony Banks, 12-5-99	4
Receiving (No.)	Priest Holmes, 10-11-98	13
Receiving (Yds.)	Qadry Ismail, 12-12-99	268
Interceptions	Many times	2
	Last time by Duane Starks, 12-24-00	
Field Goals	Matt Stover, 9-21-97, 12-26-99, 10-28-00	5
Touchdowns (Tot.)	Michael Jackson, 12-22-96	3
	Jermaine Lewis, 12-7-97	3
	Qadry Ismail, 12-12-99	3
Points	Michael Jackson, 12-22-96	18
	Matt Stover, 9-21-97	18
	Jermaine Lewis, 12-7-97	18
	Qadry Ismail, 12-12-99	18

2001 SCHEDULE

PRESEASON

Aug. 13	at Philadelphia	7:30
Aug. 18	at New York Jets	8:00
Aug. 23	**Carolina**	7:30
Aug. 31	**New York Giants**	12:00

REGULAR SEASON

Sept. 9	**Chicago**	1:00
Sept. 17	**Minnesota** (Mon.)	9:00
Sept. 23	at Cincinnati	1:00
Sept. 30	at Denver	2:15
Oct. 7	**Tennessee**	1:00
Oct. 14	at Green Bay	12:00
Oct. 21	at Cleveland	1:00
Oct. 28	**Jacksonville**	1:00
Nov. 4	at Pittsburgh	1:00
Nov. 12	at Tennessee (Mon.)	8:00
Nov. 18	**Cleveland**	1:00
Nov. 25	at Jacksonville	1:00
Dec. 2	**Indianapolis**	1:00
Dec. 9	Open Date	
Dec. 16	**Pittsburgh**	8:30
Dec. 23	**Cincinnati**	1:00
Dec. 29	at Tampa Bay (Sat.)	9:00

PSINet STADIUM

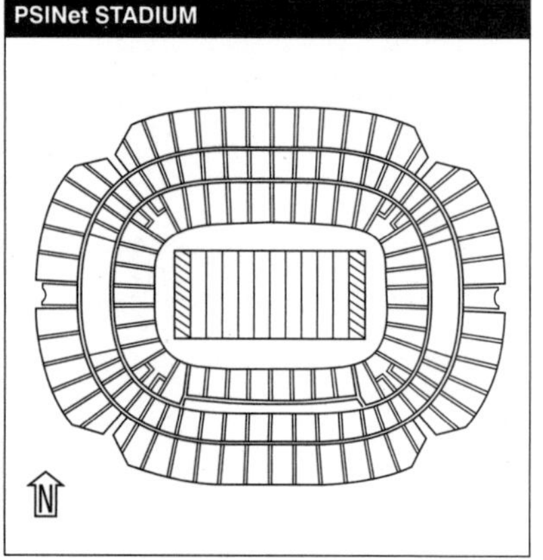

COACHING HISTORY

(40-43-1)

1996-98	Ted Marchibroda	16-31-1
1999-2000	Brian Billick	24-12-0

BALTIMORE RAVENS

2000 TEAM RECORD

PRESEASON (4-0)

Date	Result		Opponent
8/5	W	16-13	Philadelphia
8/12	W	10-0	New York Jets
8/18	W	24-13	at Carolina
8/25	W	24-17	at New York Giants

REGULAR SEASON (12-4)

Date	Result		Opponent	Att.
9/3	W	16-0	at Pittsburgh	55,049
9/10	W	39-36	Jacksonville	68,843
9/17	L	6-19	at Miami	73,464
9/24	W	37-0	Cincinnati	68,481
10/1	W	12-0	at Cleveland	73,018
10/8	W	15-10	at Jacksonville	65,194
10/15	L	3-10	at Washington	83,252
10/22	L	6-14	Tennessee	69,200
10/29	L	6-9	Pittsburgh	69,405
11/5	W	27-7	at Cincinnati	54,759
11/12	W	24-23	at Tennessee	68,490
11/19	W	27-0	Dallas	69,416
11/26	W	44-7	Cleveland	68,361
12/10	W	24-3	San Diego	68,805
12/17	W	13-7	at Arizona	37,452
12/24	W	34-20	New York Jets	69,184

POSTSEASON (4-0)

Date	Result		Opponent	Att.
12/31	W	21-3	Denver	69,638
1/7	W	24-10	at Tennessee	68,527
1/14	W	16-3	at Oakland	62,784
1/28	W	34-7	vs. N.Y. Giants, at Tampa	71,921

SCORE BY PERIODS

Ravens	62	134	67	70	0	—	333
Opponents	44	36	43	42	0	—	165

ATTENDANCE

Home 543,909 Away 511,727 Total 1,055,636
Single-game home record, 69,416 (11/19/00)
Single-season home record, 549,531 (1998)

2000 TEAM STATISTICS

	Ravens	Opp.
Total First Downs	288	216
Rushing	116	59
Passing	156	135
Penalty	16	22
Third Down:Made/Att	95/236	72/211
Third Down Pct.	40.3	34.1
Fourth Down: Made/Att	1/6	4/19
Fourth Down Pct.	16.7	21.1
Total Net Yards	5,014	3,967
Avg. Per Game	313.4	247.9
Total Plays	1,058	924
Avg. Per Play	4.7	4.3
Net Yards Rushing	2,199	970
Avg. Per Game	137.4	60.6
Total Rushes	511	361
Net Yards Passing	2,815	2,997
Avg. Per Game	175.9	187.3
Sacked/Yards Lost	43/287	35/178
Gross Yards	3,102	3,175
Att./Completions	504/287	528/295
Completion Pct.	56.9	55.9
Had Intercepted	19	23
Punts/Average	86/40.2	87/44.5
Net Punting Avg.	86/33.9	87/33.1
Penalties/Yards	95/730	84/535
Fumbles/Ball Lost	26/7	45/26
Touchdowns	32	18
Rushing	9	5
Passing	20	11
Returns	3	2
Avg. Time of Possession	33:19	26:41

2000 INDIVIDUAL STATISTICS

Passing	Att.	Comp.	Yds.	Pct.	TD	Int.	Tkld.	Rate
Banks	274	150	1,578	54.7	8	8	20/152	69.3
Dilfer	226	134	1,502	59.3	12	11	23/135	76.6
Redman	3	2	19	66.7	0	0	0/0	84.0
Je. Lewis	1	1	3	100.0	0	0	0/0	79.2
Ravens	504	287	3,102	56.9	20	19	43/287	72.7
Opponents	528	295	3,175	55.9	11	23	35/178	62.5

SCORING	TD R	TD P	TD Rt	PAT	FG	Saf	PTS
Stover	0	0	0	30/30	35/39	0	135
Ja. Lewis	6	0	0	0/0	0/0	0	38
Ismail	0	5	0	0/0	0/0	0	30
Sharpe	0	5	0	0/0	0/0	0	30
Je. Lewis	0	1	2	0/0	0/0	0	18
Taylor	0	3	0	0/0	0/0	0	18
Ayanbadejo	1	1	0	0/0	0/0	0	12
Holmes	2	0	0	0/0	0/0	0	12
Johnson	0	2	0	0/0	0/0	0	12
Stokley	0	2	0	0/0	0/0	0	12
Gash	0	1	0	0/0	0/0	0	6
McAlister	0	0	1	0/0	0/0	0	6
Coates	0	0	0	0/0	0/0	0	2
McCrary	0	0	0	0/0	0/0	1	2
Ravens	9	20	3	30/30	35/39	1	333
Opponents	5	11	2	15/18	14/19	0	165

2-Pt. Conversions: Coates, Ja. Lewis.
Ravens 2-2, Opponents 0-0.

RUSHING	Att.	Yds.	Avg.	LG	TD
Ja. Lewis	309	1,364	4.4	45	6
Holmes	137	588	4.3	21	2
Dilfer	20	75	3.8	19	0
Banks	19	57	3.0	10	0
Je. Lewis	3	38	12.7	23	0
Ayanbadejo	15	37	2.5	8	1
Johnson	2	21	10.5	19	0
Taylor	2	11	5.5	12	0
Stokley	1	6	6.0	6	0
Gash	2	2	1.0	1	0
Redman	1	0	0.0	0	0
Ravens	511	2,199	4.3	45	9
Opponents	361	970	2.7	33t	5

RECEIVING	No.	Yds.	Avg.	LG	TD
Sharpe	67	810	12.1	59t	5
Ismail	49	655	13.4	53t	5
Holmes	32	221	6.9	27	0
Taylor	28	276	9.9	40	3
Ja. Lewis	27	296	11.0	45	0
Ayanbadejo	23	168	7.3	26	1
Je. Lewis	19	161	8.5	26	1
Johnson	12	156	13.0	46t	2
Stokley	11	184	16.7	32	2
Coates	9	84	9.3	28	0
Gash	6	30	5.0	9	1
B. Davis	3	62	20.7	28	0
Dilfer	1	-1	-1.0	-1	0
Ravens	287	3,102	10.8	59t	20
Opponents	295	3,175	10.8	67	11

INTERCEPTIONS	No.	Yds.	Avg.	LG	TD
Starks	6	125	20.8	64	0
McAlister	4	165	41.3	98t	1
Woodson	4	20	5.0	18	0
Herring	3	74	24.7	30	0
Harris	2	44	22.0	42	0
R. Lewis	2	1	0.5	1	0
Sharper	1	45	45.0	45	0
Burnett	1	3	3.0	3	0
Ravens	23	477	20.7	98t	1
Opponents	19	234	12.3	87t	2

PUNTING	No.	Yds.	Avg.	In 20	LG
Richardson	86	3,457	40.2	35	55
Ravens	86	3,457	40.2	35	55
Opponents	87	3,872	44.5	17	67

PUNT RETURNS	No.	FC	Yds.	Avg.	LG	TD
Je. Lewis	36	9	578	16.1	89t	2
Starks	9	1	135	15.0	47	0
Ravens	45	10	713	15.8	89t	2
Opponents	41	23	382	9.3	31	0

KICKOFF RETURNS	No.	Yds.	Avg.	LG	TD
Harris	39	907	23.3	41	0
Ismail	2	51	25.5	38	0
Brown	1	0	0.0	0	0
Holmes	1	7	7.0	7	0
Je. Lewis	1	23	23.0	23	0
Washington	1	17	17.0	17	0
Ravens	45	1,005	22.3	41	0
Opponents	73	1,558	21.3	52	0

FIELD GOALS	1-19	20-29	30-39	40-49	50+
Stover	2/2	9/9	12/13	10/12	2/3
Ravens	2/2	9/9	12/13	10/12	2/3
Opponents	1/1	2/2	3/4	8/12	0/0

SACKS	No.
Burnett	10.5
Boulware	7.0
McCrary	6.5
Brown	3.0
R. Lewis	3.0
Adams	2.0
Trapp	2.0
Herring	1.0
Ravens	35.0
Opponents	43.0

2001 DRAFT CHOICES

Round	Name	Pos.	College
1	Todd Heap	TE	Arizona State
2	Gary Baxter	DB	Baylor
3	Casey Rabach	C	Wisconsin
4	Edgerton Hartwell	LB	Western Illinois
5	Chris Barnes	RB	New Mexico State
6	Joe Maese	C	New Mexico
7	Dwayne Missouri	DE	Northwestern

BALTIMORE RAVENS

2001 VETERAN ROSTER

No.	Name	Pos.	Ht.	Wt.	Birthdate	NFL Exp.	College	Hometown	How Acq.	'00 Games/ Starts
95	Adams, Sam	DT	6-3	330	6/13/73	8	Texas A&M	Houston, Texas	UFA(Sea)-'00	16/16
30	Ayanbadejo, Obafemi	FB	6-2	235	3/5/75	3	San Diego State	Santa Cruz, Calif.	FA-'99	8/4
74	Bobo, Orlando	G	6-3	320	2/9/74	5	Northeast Louisiana	West Point, Miss.	FA-'00	7/0
58	Boulware, Peter	LB	6-4	255	12/18/74	5	Florida State	Columbia, S.C.	D1-'97	16/15
51	Brown, Cornell	LB	6-0	245	3/15/75	5	Virginia Tech	Lynchburg, Va.	D6-'97	15/1
90	Burnett, Rob	DE	6-4	270	8/27/67	12	Syracuse	Selden, N.Y.	D5-'90	16/16
1	Cunningham, Randall	QB	6-4	215	3/27/63	16	Nevada-Las Vegas	Santa Barbara, Calif.	FA-'00	6/3*
91	Dalton, Lional	DT	6-1	309	2/21/75	4	Eastern Michigan	Detroit, Mich.	FA-'98	16/1
62	Flynn, Mike	G-C	6-3	300	6/15/74	4	Maine	Springfield, Mass.	FA-'97	16/16
18	Grbac, Elvis	QB	6-5	240	8/13/70	9	Michigan	Cleveland, Ohio	UFA(KC)-'01	15/15*
73	Gregg, Kelly	DT	6-0	285	11/1/76	3	Oklahoma	Edmond, Okla.	FA-'00	0*
45	Harris, Corey	S	5-11	200	10/25/69	10	Vanderbilt	Indianapolis, Ind.	FA-'98	16/0
87	Ismail, Qadry	WR	6-0	200	11/8/70	9	Syracuse	Wilkes-Barre, Pa.	FA'99	15/13
50	Jackson, Brad	LB	6-0	230	1/11/75	3	Cincinnati	Akron, Ohio	FA-'98	10/0
83	† Johnson, Patrick	WR	5-10	180	8/10/76	4	Oregon	Redlands, Calif.	D2-'98	12/9
85	Jones, John	TE	6-4	255	4/4/75	2	Indiana (Penn.)	Philadelphia, Pa.	FA-'00	8/0
31	Lewis, Jamal	RB	5-11	231	8/29/79	2	Tennessee	Atlanta, Ga.	D1a-'00	16/13
84	Lewis, Jermaine	WR-KR	5-7	180	10/16/74	6	Maryland	Lanham, Md.	D5-'96	15/1
52	Lewis, Ray	LB	6-1	245	5/15/75	6	Miami	Lakeland, Fla.	D1b-'96	16/16
25	Love, Clarence	CB	5-10	181	6/16/76	3	Toledo	Jackson, Mich.	FA-'99	1/0
21	McAlister, Chris	CB	6-1	206	6/14/77	3	Arizona	Pasadena, Calif.	D1-'99	16/16
99	McCrary, Michael	DE	6-4	260	7/7/70	9	Wake Forest	Falls Church, Va.	UFA(Sea)-'97	16/16
42	Mitchell, Anthony	S	6-1	211	12/13/74	2	Tuskegee	Atlanta, Ga.	FA-'99	16/0
64	Mulitalo, Edwin	G	6-3	340	9/1/74	3	Arizona	Daly City, Calif.	D4b-'99	16/16
75	Ogden, Jonathan	T	6-8	340	7/31/74	6	UCLA	Washington, D.C.	D1a-'96	15/15
43	Poindexter, Anthony	S	6-0	220	7/28/76	3	Virginia	Jefferson Forest, Va.	D7-'99	12/0
7	Redman, Chris	QB	6-3	223	7/7/77	2	Louisville	Louisville, Ky.	D3-'00	2/0
5	Richardson, Kyle	P	6-2	210	3/2/73	5	Arkansas State	Farmington, Mo.	FA-'98	16/0
72	Searcy, Leon	T	6-4	320	12/21/69	9	Miami	Orlando, Fla.	UFA(Jax)-'01	0*
82	Sharpe, Shannon	TE	6-2	232	6/26/68	12	Savannah State	Glennville, Ga.	UFA(Den)-'00	16/15
55	Sharper, Jamie	LB	6-3	240	11/23/74	5	Virginia	Richmond, Va.	D2a-'97	16/16
98	Siragusa, Tony	DT	6-3	340	5/14/67	12	Pittsburgh	Kenilworth, N.J.	UFA(Ind)-'97	15/15
22	Starks, Duane	CB	5-10	170	5/23/74	4	Miami	Miami Beach, Fla.	D1-'98	15/15
80	Stokley, Brandon	WR	5-11	197	6/23/76	3	Southwestern Louisiana	Comeaux, La.	D4a-'99	7/1
3	Stover, Matt	K	5-11	178	1/27/68	12	Louisiana Tech	Dallas, Texas	PB(NYG)-'91	16/0
70	Swayne, Harry	T	6-5	300	2/2/65	15	Rutgers	Philadelphia, Pa.	UFA(Den)-'99	13/13
89	Taylor, Travis	WR	6-1	200	3/30/78	2	Florida	Jacksonville, Fla.	D1b-'00	9/8
96	Thomas, Adalius	DE	6-2	270	8/17/77	2	Southern Mississippi	Equality, Ala.	D6a-'00	3/0
16	Thompson, Germany	WR	6-2	208	1/31/76	2	New Mexico	Greenville, S.C.	FA-'00	0*
38	Trapp, James	CB	6-0	190	12/28/69	9	Clemson	Lawton, Okla.	UFA(Oak)-'99	16/1
77	Vickers, Kipp	G-T	6-2	300	8/27/69	7	Miami	Holiday, Fla.	UFA(Wash)-'00	11/2
79	Webster, Larry	DT	6-5	288	1/18/69	10	Maryland	Elkton, Md.	FA-'95	5/0
54	Wilkinson, Calvin	LB	6-3	230	5/5/77	2	Temple	Vineland, N.J.	FA-'00	0*
78	† Williams, Sammy	T-G	6-5	318	12/14/74	4	Oklahoma	Harvey, Ill.	FA-'99	0*
26	Woodson, Rod	S	6-0	205	3/10/65	15	Purdue	Fort Wayne, Ind.	FA-'98	16/16

* Cunningham played 6 games with Dallas in '00; Grbac played 15 games with Kansas City; Gregg last active with Philadelphia in '99; Searcy missed '00 season because of injury with Jacksonville; Thompson spent '00 season on practice squad; Wilkinson missed '00 season because of injury; Williams was inactive for 15 games.

† Restricted free agent; subject to developments.

Players lost through free agency (4): LB O.J. Brigance (StL; 16 games in '00), S Kim Herring (StL; 16), RB Priest Holmes (KC; 16), C Jeff Mitchell (Car; 14).

Also played with Ravens in '00—CB Robert Bailey (16 games), TE Ben Coates (16), LB Anthony Davis (16), WR Billy Davis (16), QB Trent Dilfer (9), FB Chuck Evans (1), T Spencer Folau (11), FB Sam Gash (15), LS John Hudson (8), TE Frank Wainright (8), DE Keith Washington (16).

COACHING STAFF

Head Coach,
Brian Billick

Pro Career: In only his second year as head coach, Brian Billick guided the Super Bowl XXXV-champion Ravens to a 16-4 record last season following an 8-8 mark in 1999. On the way to the World Championship, the Ravens set numerous records, including fewest points allowed (165) in a 16-game schedule since 1978 and fewest rushing yards allowed (970). The Ravens' defense also established itself as the first team since 1978 to allow fewer than 1,000 rushing yards in a regular season. Baltimore posted its eleventh consecutive victory with a 34-7 win over the New York Giants in Super Bowl XXXV, despite a five-game touchdown drought in October. Even so, the team stayed the course by winning two of those five games on Matt Stover field goals, while struggling with injuries to the offensive line. The Ravens finished the 2000 season ranked first in six categories, including four shutouts and 49 takeaways, and second in three others. The defense has not allowed a 100-yard rusher for two consecutive seasons. In 1999, Baltimore finished 4-0 in December and was in contention for the postseason until week 16. Billick was the Minnesota offensive coordinator for five years (1994-98), orchestrating a Vikings' attack that set a variety of NFL and club records. Minnesota's offense set the NFL record for most points scored in a season (556), surpassing the old mark (541) set by the 1983 Washington Redskins. Career record: 24-12.

Background: Prior to his appointment with the Vikings, Billick was a Stanford assistant from 1989-1991 under Vikings head coach Dennis Green. He spent three seasons as offensive coordinator at Utah State (1986-88). Billick coached receivers, tight ends, and quarterbacks at San Diego State from 1981-85 and held a dual responsibility as recruiting coordinator. He began his coaching career as an assistant at Redlands in 1977 and spent the following year (1978) as a graduate assistant at Brigham Young working with tight ends and the offensive line. Billick was assistant director of public relations for the San Francisco 49ers in 1979-1980.

Personal: Born February 28, 1954 in Fairborne, Ohio, Billick earned All-Western Athletic Conference honors and was a honorable mention All-America in 1976 as a tight end at Brigham Young. Played linebacker at Air Force as a freshman before transferring to Brigham Young. In 1977, Billick was drafted by the 49ers in the eleventh round, was released, and had a brief stint with the Dallas Cowboys, but did not play. He and his wife Kim have two daughters—Aubree and Keegan.

ASSISTANT COACHES

Matt Cavanaugh, offensive coordinator; born October 27, 1956, Youngstown, Ohio, lives in Owings Mills, Md. Quarterback Pittsburgh 1974-77. Pro quarterback New England Patriots 1978-1982, San Francisco 49ers 1983-85, Philadelphia Eagles 1986-89, New York Giants 1990-91. College coach: Pittsburgh 1993. Pro coach: Arizona Cardinals 1994-95, San Francisco 49ers 1996, Chicago Bears 1997-98, joined Ravens in 1999.

Jim Colletto, offensive line; born October 2, 1944, San Francisco, lives in Finksburg, Md. Fullback-linebacker UCLA 1964-67. No pro playing experience. College coach: UCLA 1967-68, Brown 1969, Xavier 1970-71, Pacific 1972-74, Cal State-Fullerton 1975-79 (head coach), UCLA 1980-1981, Purdue 1982-84, Arizona State 1985-87, Ohio State 1988-1990, Purdue 1991-96 (head coach), Notre Dame 1997-98. Pro coach: Joined Ravens in 1999.

Jack Del Rio, Jr., linebackers; born April 4, 1963, Castro Valley, Calif., lives in Reisterstown, Md. Linebacker Southern California 1981-84. Pro linebacker New Orleans Saints 1985-86, Kansas City Chiefs 1987-88, Dallas Cowboys 1989-1991, Minnesota Vikings 1992-95. Pro coach: New Orleans Saints 1997-98, joined Ravens in 1999.

Jeff Friday, strength and conditioning; born October 11, 1966, Milwaukee, Wis., lives in Ellicott City, Md. Attended Wisconsin-Milwaukee. No college or pro playing experience. College coach: Illinois State 1991-92, Northwestern 1992-95. Pro coach: Minnesota Vikings 1996-98, joined Ravens in 1999.

Wade Harman, tight ends-asst. offensive line; born October 1, 1963, Corydon, Iowa, lives in Reisterstown, Md. Linebacker Drake 1985, Utah State 1986. No pro playing experience. College coach: Utah State 1987-1991, Pacific 1992-95, Morningside 1996. Pro coach: Minnesota Vikings 1997-98, joined Ravens in 1999.

Donnie Henderson, secondary; born May 17, 1957, Baltimore, lives in Owings Mills, Md. Defensive back Utah State 1978-79. No pro playing experience. College coach: Utah State 1983-88, Idaho 1989-1990, California 1992-97, Houston 1998. Pro coach: Joined Ravens in 1999.

Milt Jackson, offensive assistant; born October 16, 1943, Groesbeck, Texas, lives in Owings Mills, Md. Free safety Tulsa 1965-66. Pro defensive back San Francisco 49ers 1967. College coach: Oregon State 1973, Rice 1974, Califronia 1975-76, Oregon 1977-78, UCLA 1979. Pro coach: San Francisco 49ers 1980-82, Buffalo Bills 1983-84, Philadelphia Eagles 1985, Houston Oilers 1986-88, Indianapolis Colts 1989-1991, Los Angeles Rams 1992-93, Atlanta Falcons 1994-96, New York Giants 1997, Seattle Seahawks 1998, joined Ravens in 1999.

Marvin Lewis, defensive coordinator; born September 23, 1958, McDonald, Pa., lives in Finksburg, Md. Linebacker Idaho State 1977-1980. No pro playing experience. College coach: Idaho State 1981-84, Long Beach State 1985-86, New Mexico 1987-89, Pittsburgh 1990-91. Pro coach: Pittsburgh Steelers 1992-95, joined Ravens in 1996.

Chip Morton, asst. strength and conditioning; born November 27, 1962, Hamden, Conn., lives in Owings Mills, Md. Attended North Carolina. No college or pro playing experience. College coach: Ohio State 1985-86, Penn State 1987-1992. Pro coach: San Diego Chargers 1992-94, Carolina Panthers 1995-98, joined Ravens in 1999.

Mike Nolan, wide receivers; born March 7, 1959, Baltimore, lives in Baltimore. Safety Oregon 1978-1980. No pro playing experience. College coach: Oregon 1981, Stanford 1982-83, Rice 1984-85, Louisiana State 1986. Pro coach: Denver Broncos 1987-1992, New York Giants 1993-96, Washington Redskins 1997-99, New York Jets 2000, joined Ravens in 2001.

Russ Purnell, special teams; born June 12, 1948, Chicago, lives in Ellicott City, Md. Center Orange Coast (Calif.) J.C. 1966-67, Whittier College 1968-69. No pro playing experience. College coach: Whittier College 1970-71, Southern California 1982-84. Pro coach: Seattle Seahawks 1986-1994, Tennessee Oilers 1995, joined Ravens in 1999.

Rex Ryan, defensive line; born December 13, 1962, Ardmore, Okla., lives in Ellicott City, Md. Defensive end Southwest Oklahoma State 1983-86. No pro playing experience. College coach: Eastern Kentucky 1987-88, New Mexico Highlands 1989, Morehead State 1990-93, Cincinnati 1996-97, Oklahoma 1998. Pro coach: Arizona Cardinals 1994-95, joined Ravens in 1999.

Steve Shafer, secondary, asst. to the head coach; born December 8, 1940, Glendale, Calif., lives in Owings Mills, Md. Quarterback-defensive back Utah State 1961-62. Pro defensive back British Columbia Lions (CFL) 1963-67. College coach: San Mateo (Calif.) J.C. 1968-1974 (head coach 1973-74), San Diego State 1975-1982, 1994. Pro coach: Los Angeles Rams 1983-1990, Tampa Bay Buccaneers 1991-93, Oakland Raiders 1995-97, Carolina Panthers 1998, joined Ravens in 1999.

Matt Simon, running backs; born December 6, 1953, Akron, Ohio, lives in Columbia, Md. Linebacker Eastern New Mexico 1972-75. No pro playing experience. College coach: Washington 1982-1991, New Mexico 1992-94, North Texas 1994-97 (head coach). Pro coach: Denver Broncos 1998, joined Ravens in 1999.

Mike Smith, defensive assistant-defensive line; born June 13, 1959, Chicago, lives in Eldersburg, Md. Linebacker East Tennessee 1977-1980. No pro playing experience. College coach: San Diego State 1982-85, Morehead State 1986, Tennessee Tech 1987-1998. Pro coach: Joined Ravens in 1999.

Bennie Thompson, asst. special teams; born February 10, 1963, New Orleans, lives in Pikesville, Md. Defensive back Grambling State 1981-85. Pro defensive back Winnipeg Blue Bombers (CFL) 1986-88, New Orleans Saints 1989-1991, Kansas City Chiefs 1991-93, Cleveland Browns/Baltimore Ravens 1994-99. Pro coach: Joined Ravens in 2000.

2001 FIRST-YEAR ROSTER

Name	Pos.	Ht.	Wt.	Birthdate	College	Hometown	How Acq.
Ayanbadejo, Brendon (1)	LB	6-0	229	9/6/76	UCLA	Santa Cruz, Calif.	FA
Barnes, Chris	RB	6-0	210	7/31/78	New Mexico State	Wauchula, Fla.	D5
Baxter, Gary	DB	6-2	204	11/24/78	Baylor	Tyler, Texas	D2
Bland, Mike	DT	6-3	298	11/20/77	Hampton	Jackson, Mich.	FA
Brookins, Jason (1)	RB	6-0	235	1/5/76	Lane College	Mexico, Mo.	FA
Callens, Corey	DE	6-2	253	2/25/78	Oklahoma	Tulsa, Okla.	FA
Cook, Damion	T	6-5	316	4/16/79	Bethune-Cookman	Fort Lauderdale, Fla.	FA
Destefano, Pete (1)	DB	6-1	215	4/16/76	California	San Jose, Calif.	FA
Fisher, Ryan	DT	6-1	295	8/6/77	Oklahoma	Arlington, Texas	FA
Harper, Scott	T	6-5	295	12/13/77	Marshall	Grand Bay, Ala.	FA
Hartwell, Edgerton	LB	6-1	250	5/27/78	Western Illinois	Las Vegas, Nev.	D4
Heap, Todd	TE	6-5	252	3/16/80	Arizona State	Mesa, Ariz.	D1
Holland, Richard	CB	5-10	172	2/26/78	Virginia Military Institute	Virginia Beach, Va.	FA
Homer, Derek	RB	5-11	200	11/29/77	Kentucky	Fort Knox, Ky.	FA
Horsey, Albert	WR	6-0	185	1/2/79	Delaware State	Wilmington, Del.	FA
Howell, Evan (1)	DB	5-11	186	10/14/77	Oklahoma State	Monroe, La.	FA
Hughley, Delvin	DB	5-10	202	4/18/78	Jacksonville State	Anniston, Ala.	FA
Jackson, Kenny	LB	6-2	253	9/30/76	Nevada	Los Angeles, Calif.	FA
Jenkins, Ortege	QB	6-1	227	2/1/78	Arizona	Long Beach, Calif.	FA
Johnson, Tim	LB	6-2	219	2/7/78	Youngstown State	Fairfield, Ala.	FA
Jones, Jim	G	6-2	310	1/27/78	Notre Dame	Chicago Ridge, Ill.	FA
Kendall, Billy	TE	6-5	237	1/6/78	Memphis State	Bowie, Md.	FA
Kerneck, Aaron	RB	6-2	225	4/11/79	Austin College	Bowie, Texas	FA
Kopka, Brian	K	5-7	166	11/27/78	Maryland	Hollywood Hills, Fla.	FA
Lambo, Anthony	G	6-2	291	1/4/78	Virginia Tech	Bloomfield, N.J.	FA
Maese, Joe	LS	6-0	241	12/2/78	New Mexico	Cortez, Ariz.	D6
Missouri, Dwayne	DE	6-5	260	12/23/78	Northwestern	San Antonio, Texas	D7
Porter, Alvin	DB	5-11	175	5/10/77	Oklahoma State	Dallas, Texas	FA
Pruce, Dave	T	6-8	295	6/1/78	New York State-Buffalo	Cardon, Ohio	FA
Rabach, Casey	C	6-4	301	9/24/77	Wisconsin	Sturgeon Bay, Wis.	D3
Ricard, Alan (1)	FB	5-11	237	1/17/77	Northeast Louisiana	Amite, La.	FA-'00
Swain, Damian	DB	6-1	175	7/23/77	Alabama State	Jacksonville, Fla.	FA
Waddell, Reggie	DB	6-0	185	11/14/77	Western Illinois	Houston, Texas	FA
Wilson, Adrian	DT	6-2	315	11/10/78	Miami	Jacksonville, Ark.	FA

The term NFL Rookie is defined as a player who is in his first season of professional football and has not been on the roster of another professional football team for any regular-season or postseason games. A Rookie is designated by an "R" on NFL rosters. Players who have been active in another professional football league or players who have NFL experience, including either preseason training camp or being on an Active List or Inactive List, or on Reserve/Injured or Reserve/Physically Unable to Perform for fewer than six regular-season games, are termed NFL First-Year Players. An NFL First-Year Player is designated by a "1" on NFL rosters. Thereafter, a player is credited with an additional year of experience for each season in which he accumulates six games on the Active List or Inactive List, or on Reserve/Injured or Reserve/Physically Unable to Perform.

BUFFALO BILLS

American Football Conference
Eastern Division
Team Colors: Royal Blue, Scarlet Red, and White
One Bills Drive
Orchard Park, New York 14127-2296
Telephone: (716) 648-1800

CLUB OFFICIALS

Owner: Ralph C. Wilson, Jr.
President/General Manager: Tom Donahoe
Corporate V.P.: Linda Bogdan
Treasurer: Jeffrey C. Littmann
Vice President/Player Personnel: Dwight Adams
Vice President/Communications: Scott Berchtold
Vice President/Business Development and Marketing: Russ Brandon
Vice President/Operations: Bill Munson
Vice President/Business Administration: Jim Overdorf
Director of Football Operations: Tom Modrak
Director of Pro Personnel: John Guy
Consultant: Christy Wilson Hofmann
Executive Director/Marketing: Marc Honan
Director of Marketing Partnerships: Jeff Fernandez
Director of Sales: Pete Guelli
Director of Merchandising: Julie Regan
Director of Ticket Sales: Jerry Foran
Director of Archives: Denny Lynch
Director of Guest Services & Event Management: Jan Eberle
Director of Stadium Operations: Joseph Frandina
Director of Security: Bill Bambach
Ticket Director: June Foran
Media Relations Coordinator: Mark Dalton
Business Manager: Don Purdy
Equipment Manager: Dave Hojnowski
Asst. Equipment Manager: Randy Ribbeck
Strength/Conditioning Coordinator: Rusty Jones
Conditioning Assistant: Rich Gray
Trainers: Bud Carpenter, Corey Bennett, Greg McMillen
Video Director: Henry Kunttu
Asst. Video Director: Greg Estes, Matt Smith
Scouts: Brad Forsyth, Tom Gibbons, Joe Haering, Doug Majeski, Bob Ryan, George (Chink) Sengel, David G. Smith, David W. Smith, Bob Williams
Stadium: Ralph Wilson Stadium (built in 1973)
• **Capacity:** 73,967
One Bills Drive
Orchard Park, New York 14127-2296
Playing Surface: AstroTurf
Training Camp: St. John Fisher College
Rochester, New York 14618

RECORD HOLDERS

INDIVIDUAL RECORDS—CAREER

Category	Name	Performance
Rushing (Yds.)	Thurman Thomas, 1988-1999	11,938
Passing (Yds.)	Jim Kelly, 1986-1996	35,467
Passing (TDs)	Jim Kelly, 1986-1996	237
Receiving (No.)	Andre Reed, 1985-1999	941
Receiving (Yds.)	Andre Reed, 1985-1999	13,095
Interceptions	George (Butch) Byrd, 1964-1970	40
Punting (Avg.)	Paul Maguire, 1964-1970	42.1
Punt Return (Avg.)	Clifford Hicks, 1990-92	12.2
Kickoff Return (Avg.)	O.J. Simpson, 1969-1977	30.0
Field Goals	Steve Christie, 1992-2000	234
Touchdowns (Tot.)	Andre Reed, 1985-1999	87
	Thurman Thomas, 1988-1999	87
Points	Steve Christie, 1992-2000	1,011

INDIVIDUAL RECORDS—SINGLE SEASON

Category	Name	Performance
Rushing (Yds.)	O.J. Simpson, 1973	2,003
Passing (Yds.)	Jim Kelly, 1991	3,844
Passing (TDs)	Jim Kelly, 1991	33
Receiving (No.)	Eric Moulds, 2000	94
Receiving (Yds.)	Eric Moulds, 1998	1,368
Interceptions	Billy Atkins, 1961	10
	Tom Janik, 1967	10
Punting (Avg.)	Billy Atkins, 1961	44.5
Punt Return (Avg.)	Keith Moody, 1977	13.1
Kickoff Return (Avg.)	Ed Rutkowski, 1963	30.2
Field Goals	Steve Christie, 1998	33
Touchdowns (Tot.)	O.J. Simpson, 1975	23
Points	Steve Christie, 1998	140

INDIVIDUAL RECORDS—SINGLE GAME

Category	Name	Performance
Rushing (Yds.)	O.J. Simpson, 11-25-76	273
Passing (Yds.)	Joe Ferguson, 10-9-83	419
Passing (TDs)	Jim Kelly, 9-8-91	6
Receiving (No.)	Andre Reed, 11-20-94	15
Receiving (Yds.)	Jerry Butler, 9-23-79	255
Interceptions	Many times	3
	Last time by Jeff Nixon, 9-7-80	
Field Goals	Steve Christie, 10-20-96	6
Touchdowns (Tot.)	Cookie Gilchrist, 12-8-63	5
Points	Cookie Gilchrist, 12-8-63	30

2001 SCHEDULE

PRESEASON

Aug. 12	**St. Louis**	7:30
Aug. 18	**Philadelphia**	7:30
Aug. 25	at Cincinnati	7:30
Aug. 30	at Pittsburgh	7:30

REGULAR SEASON

Sept. 9	**New Orleans**	1:00
Sept. 16	at Miami	1:00
Sept. 23	at Indianapolis	12:00
Sept. 30	**Pittsburgh**	1:00
Oct. 7	**New York Jets**	4:05
Oct. 14	Open Date	
Oct. 18	at Jacksonville (Thurs.)	8:30
Oct. 28	at San Diego	1:15
Nov. 4	**Indianapolis**	4:15
Nov. 11	at New England	1:00
Nov. 18	**Seattle**	1:00
Nov. 25	**Miami**	1:00
Dec. 2	at San Francisco	5:30
Dec. 9	**Carolina**	1:00
Dec. 16	**New England**	1:00
Dec. 23	at Atlanta	1:00
Dec. 30	at New York Jets	1:00

COACHING HISTORY

(310-323-8)

1960-61	Buster Ramsey	11-16-1
1962-65	Lou Saban	38-18-3
1966-68	Joe Collier*	13-17-1
1968	Harvey Johnson	1-10-1
1969-1970	John Rauch	7-20-1
1971	Harvey Johnson	1-13-0
1972-76	Lou Saban**	32-29-1
1976-77	Jim Ringo	3-20-0
1978-1982	Chuck Knox	38-38-0
1983-85	Kay Stephenson***	10-26-0
1985-86	Hank Bullough****	4-17-0
1986-1997	Marv Levy	123-78-0
1998-2000	Wade Phillips	29-21-0

*Released after two games in 1968
**Resigned after five games in 1976
***Released after four games in 1985
****Released after nine games in 1986

RALPH WILSON STADIUM

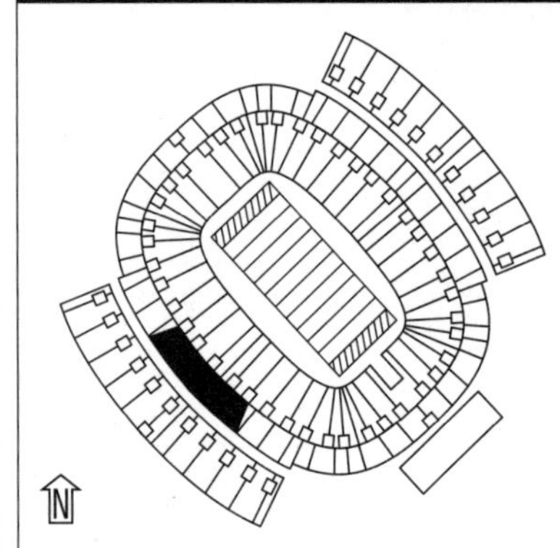

2000 TEAM RECORD

PRESEASON (3-1)

Date	Result		Opponent
8/4	W	21-20	Cincinnati
8/12	L	13-15	at Detroit
8/19	W	31-27	at St. Louis
8/24	W	16-12	at Philadelphia

REGULAR SEASON (8-8)

Date	Result		Opponent	Att.
9/3	W	16-13	Tennessee	77,492
9/10	W	27-18	Green Bay	72,722
9/17	L	14-27	at New York Jets	77,884
10/1	L	16-18	Indianapolis	72,617
10/8	L	13-22	at Miami	73,901
10/15	W	27-24	San Diego (OT)	72,351
10/22	L	27-31	at Minnesota	64,116
10/29	W	23-20	New York Jets	72,861
11/5	W	16-13	at New England (OT)	60,292
11/12	W	20-3	Chicago	72,420
11/19	W	21-17	at Kansas City	78,457
11/26	L	17-31	at Tampa Bay	65,546
12/3	L	6-33	Miami	73,002
12/11	L	20-44	at Indianapolis	56,671
12/17	L	10-13	New England (OT)	47,230
12/23	W	42-23	at Seattle	61,025

(OT) Overtime

SCORE BY PERIODS

Bills	54	97	40	118	6	—	315
Opponents	46	93	76	132	3	—	350

ATTENDANCE

Home 560,413 Away 530,437 Total 1,090,850
Single-game home record, 80,368 (10/4/92)
Single-season home record, 635,889 (1991)

2000 TEAM STATISTICS

	Bills	Opp.
Total First Downs	309	252
Rushing	111	76
Passing	174	153
Penalty	24	23
Third Down: Made/Att	92/247	81/219
Third Down Pct.	37.2	37.0
Fourth Down: Made/Att	9/12	7/11
Fourth Down Pct.	75.0	63.6
Total Net Yards	5,498	4,426
Avg. Per Game	343.6	276.6
Total Plays	1,080	966
Avg. Per Play	5.1	4.6
Net Yards Rushing	1,922	1,559
Avg. Per Game	120.1	97.4
Total Rushes	475	444
Net Yards Passing	3,576	2,867
Avg. Per Game	223.5	179.2
Sacked/Yards Lost	59/360	42/308
Gross Yards	3,936	3,175
Att./Completions	546/312	480/283
Completion Pct.	57.1	59.0
Had Intercepted	10	16
Punts/Average	96/38.1	92/42.0
Net Punting Avg.	96/31.4	92/38.4
Penalties/Yards	101/913	103/905
Fumbles/Ball Lost	28/13	30/13
Touchdowns	34	37
Rushing	11	13
Passing	20	18
Returns	3	6
Avg. Time of Possession	31:25	28:35

2000 INDIVIDUAL STATISTICS

Passing	Att.	Comp.	Yds.	Pct.	TD	Int.	Tkld.	Rate
Johnson	306	175	2,125	57.2	12	7	49/292	82.2
Flutie	231	132	1,700	57.1	8	3	10/68	86.5
Van Pelt	8	4	67	50.0	0	0	0/0	78.6
Mohr	1	1	44	100.0	0	0	0/0	118.8
Bills	546	312	3,936	57.1	20	10	59/360	84.3
Opponents	480	283	3,175	59.0	18	16	42/308	77.4

SCORING	TD R	TD P	TD Rt	PAT	FG	Saf	PTS
Christie	0	0	0	31/31	26/35	0	109
Morris	5	1	0	0/0	0/0	0	36
Moulds	0	5	0	0/0	0/0	0	30
Riemersma	0	5	0	0/0	0/0	0	30
Smith	4	0	0	0/0	0/0	0	24
P. Price	0	3	0	0/0	0/0	0	18
Bryson	0	2	0	0/0	0/0	0	14
McDaniel	0	2	0	0/0	0/0	0	12
Flutie	1	0	0	0/0	0/0	0	6
S. Jackson	0	1	0	0/0	0/0	0	6
Johnson	1	0	0	0/0	0/0	0	6
H. Jones	0	0	1	0/0	0/0	0	6
Linton	0	1	0	0/0	0/0	0	6
Ostroski	0	0	1	0/0	0/0	0	6
Porter	0	0	1	0/0	0/0	0	6
Bills	11	20	3	31/31	26/35	0	315
Opponents	13	18	6	33/33	29/33	1	350

2-Pt. Conversions: Bryson. Bills 1-3, Opponents 3-4.

RUSHING	Att.	Yds.	Avg.	LG	TD
Bryson	161	591	3.7	24	0
Smith	101	354	3.5	59	4
Morris	93	341	3.7	32t	5
Johnson	42	307	7.3	23	1
Flutie	36	161	4.5	32	1
Linton	38	112	2.9	12	0
P. Price	2	32	16.0	27	0
Moulds	2	24	12.0	20	0
Bills	475	1,922	4.0	59	11
Opponents	444	1,559	3.5	39t	13

RECEIVING	No.	Yds.	Avg.	LG	TD
Moulds	94	1,326	14.1	52	5
P. Price	52	762	14.7	42	3
McDaniel	43	697	16.2	74t	2
Morris	37	268	7.2	24	1
Bryson	32	271	8.5	32	2
Riemersma	31	372	12.0	35	5
Collins	6	72	12.0	23	0
S. Jackson	5	36	7.2	12	1
Cavil	4	66	16.5	39	0
Smith	3	20	6.7	9	0
Linton	3	8	2.7	4t	1
Porter	1	44	44.0	44	0
Johnson	1	-6	-6.0	-6	0
Bills	312	3,936	12.6	74t	20
Opponents	283	3,175	11.2	63	18

INTERCEPTIONS	No.	Yds.	Avg.	LG	TD
Carpenter	5	63	12.6	22	0
H. Jones	2	45	22.5	45t	1
Cowart	2	4	2.0	2	0
Irvin	2	1	0.5	1	0
Rogers	1	10	10.0	10	0
Winfield	1	8	8.0	8	0
Flowers	1	0	0.0	0	0
Holecek	1	0	0.0	0	0
Porter	1	0	0.0	0	0
Bills	16	131	8.2	45t	1
Opponents	10	112	11.2	40t	1

PUNTING	No.	Yds.	Avg.	In 20	LG
Mohr	95	3,661	38.5	19	57
Bills	96	3,661	38.1	19	57
Opponents	92	3,865	42.0	37	70

PUNT RETURNS	No.	FC	Yds.	Avg.	LG	TD
Watson	33	18	163	4.9	20	0
P. Price	5	5	27	5.4	12	0
Bills	38	23	190	5.0	20	0
Opponents	51	21	544	10.7	73t	1

KICKOFF RETURNS	No.	Yds.	Avg.	LG	TD
Watson	44	894	20.3	37	0
Black	9	165	18.3	26	0
Bryson	8	122	15.3	26	0
Linton	3	40	13.3	17	0
Cavil	1	1	1.0	1	0
Foreman	1	19	19.0	19	0
H. Jones	1	4	4.0	4	0
Morris	1	17	17.0	17	0
Smith	1	0	0.0	0	0
Bills	69	1,262	18.3	37	0
Opponents	70	1,524	21.8	97t	2

FIELD GOALS	1-19	20-29	30-39	40-49	50+
Christie	2/2	11/13	4/6	9/13	0/1
Bills	2/2	11/13	4/6	9/13	0/1
Opponents	1/1	11/12	11/13	5/5	1/2

SACKS	No.
Wiley	10.5
Newman	8.0
Cowart	5.5
Rogers	5.0
Washington	2.5
Williams	2.5
Flowers	2.0
Hansen	2.0
F. Jones	1.0
Larsen	1.0
Moore	1.0
S. Price	1.0
Bills	42.0
Opponents	59.0

2001 DRAFT CHOICES

Round	Name	Pos.	College
1	Nate Clements	DB	Ohio State
2	Aaron Schobel	DE	Texas Christian
	Travis Henry	RB	Tennessee
3	Ron Edwards	DT	Texas A&M
	Jonas Jennings	T	Georgia
4	Brandon Spoon	LB	North Carolina
5	Marques Sullivan	T	Illinois
6	Tony Driver	DB	Notre Dame
	Dan O'Leary	TE	Notre Dame
	Jimmy Williams	DB	Vanderbilt
7	Reggie Germany	WR	Ohio State
	Tyrone Robertson	DT	Hinds (Miss.) C.C.

BUFFALO BILLS

2001 VETERAN ROSTER

No.	Name	Pos.	Ht.	Wt.	Birthdate	NFL Exp.	College	Hometown	How Acq.	'00 Games/ Starts
89	Black, Avion	WR	5-11	181	4/24/77	2	Tennessee State	Nashville, Tenn.	D4-'00	2/0
31	Brown, Lance	CB-S	6-1	203	2/2/72	5	Indiana	Jacksonville, Fla.	FA-'01	0*
79	Brown, Ruben	G	6-3	304	2/13/72	8	Pittsburgh	Lynchburg, Va.	D1-'95	16/16
38	Bryson, Shawn	RB	6-1	233	8/26/76	2	Tennessee	Franklin, N.C.	D3-'99	16/7
65	Carman, Jon	T	6-7	335	1/14/76	2	Georgia Tech	Waldorf, Md.	FA-'00	3/0
29	Carpenter, Keion	S	5-11	205	10/31/77	3	Virginia Tech	Baltimore, Md.	FA-'99	12/12
82	Cavil, Kwame	WR	6-2	203	5/3/79	2	Texas	Waco, Texas	FA-'00	16/0
37	Centers, Larry	FB	6-0	225	6/1/68	12	Stephen F. Austin	Tatum, Texas	FA-'01	15/5*
2	Christie, Steve	K	6-0	195	11/13/67	12	William & Mary	Oakville, Ontario, Canada	FA-'92	16/0
84	Collins, Bobby	TE	6-4	248	8/20/76	3	North Alabama	York, Ala.	D4b-'99	12/2
63	Conaty, Bill	C-LS	6-2	300	3/8/73	5	Virginia Tech	Pennsauken, N.J.	FA-'97	16/0
56	Cowart, Sam	LB	6-2	245	2/26/75	4	Florida State	Jacksonville, Fla.	D2-'98	12/12
70	Fina, John	T	6-5	300	3/11/69	10	Arizona	Tucson, Ariz.	D1-'92	14/14
96	Flowers, Erik	DE	6-4	270	3/1/78	2	Arizona State	San Antonio, Texas	D1-'00	16/0
55	Foreman, Jay	LB	6-1	240	12/18/76	3	Nebraska	Eden Prairie, Minn.	D5-'99	15/3
90	Hansen, Phil	DE	6-5	273	5/20/68	11	North Dakota State	Oakes, N.D.	D2-'91	10/8
77	Hicks, Robert	T	6-7	330	11/17/74	4	Mississippi State	Atlanta, Ga.	D3-'98	14/7
39	Hill, Raion	S	6-0	200	9/2/76	2	Louisiana State	Marrero, La.	FA-'99	16/0
52	Holecek, John	LB	6-2	242	5/7/72	7	Illinois	Steger, Ill.	D5-'95	16/16
27	Irvin, Ken	CB	5-11	186	7/11/72	7	Memphis	Rome, Ga.	D4a-'95	16/16
88	Jackson, Sheldon	TE	6-3	250	7/24/76	3	Nebraska	Diamond Bar, Calif.	D7a-'99	16/8
11	Johnson, Rob	QB	6-4	212	3/18/73	7	Southern California	Newport Beach, Calif.	T(Jax)-'98	12/11
99	Jones, Fred	LB	6-2	246	10/18/77	2	Colorado	San Diego, Calif.	FA-'00	15/0
20	Jones, Henry	S	6-0	200	12/29/67	11	Illinois	St. Louis, Mo.	D1-'91	16/16
97	Larsen, Leif	DT	6-4	295	4/3/75	2	Texas-El Paso	Tofte, Norway	D6-'00	7/0
86	McDaniel, Jeremy	WR	6-0	197	5/2/76	2	Arizona	New Bern, N.C.	FA-'99	16/6
54	Moore, Corey	LB	5-11	225	3/20/77	2	Virginia Tech	Brownsville, Tenn.	D3-'00	9/4
33	Morris, Sammy	RB	6-0	228	3/23/77	2	Texas Tech	San Antonio, Texas	D5-'00	12/8
80	Moulds, Eric	WR	6-2	204	7/17/73	6	Mississippi State	Lucedale, Miss.	D1-'96	16/16
53	Newman, Keith	LB	6-2	245	1/19/77	3	North Carolina	Tampa, Fla.	D4a-'99	16/16
60	Ostroski, Jerry	G	6-3	327	7/12/70	8	Tulsa	Collegeville, Pa.	FA-'93	16/16
51	Polk, DaShon	LB	6-2	235	3/13/77	2	Arizona	Pacoima, Calif.	D7b-'00	5/0
81	Price, Peerless	WR	6-0	190	10/27/76	3	Tennessee	Dayton, Ohio	D2-'99	16/16
91	Price, Shawn	DE	6-4	290	3/28/70	9	Pacific	Van Nuys, Calif.	FA-'96	13/6
85	Riemersma, Jay	TE	6-5	254	5/17/73	5	Michigan	Zeeland, Mich.	D7b-'96	12/12
28	Tillman, Travares	S	6-1	190	10/8/77	2	Georgia Tech	Lyons, Ga.	D2-'00	15/4
10	Van Pelt, Alex	QB	6-1	220	5/1/70	7	Pittsburgh	Pittsburgh, Pa.	FA-'00	1/0
21	Watson, Chris	CB	6-1	192	6/30/77	3	Eastern Illinois	Chicago, Ill.	T(Den)-'00	16/5
93	Williams, Pat	DT	6-3	310	10/24/72	4	Texas A&M	Monroe, La.	FA-'97	16/4
26	Winfield, Antoine	CB	5-9	180	6/24/77	3	Ohio State	Akron, Ohio	D1-'99	11/11
57	Wright, Kenyatta	LB	6-0	238	2/19/78	2	Oklahoma State	Vian, Okla.	FA-'00	16/1

* L. Brown last active with Pittsburgh in '99; Centers played 15 games with Washington in '00.

Retired—Thurman Thomas, 13-year running back, 9 games in '00 with Miami.

Players lost through free agency (3): CB Donovan Greer (Wash; 13 games in '00), T Marcus Spriggs (Mia; 16), DE Marcellus Wiley (SD; 16).

Also played with Bills in '00—LS Ethan Albright (16 games), QB Doug Flutie (11), CB Ray Hill (5), FB Jonathan Linton (14), P Chris Mohr (16), G Jamie Nails (16), G Joe Panos (13), CB Daryl Porter (16), LB Sam Rogers (11), RB Antowain Smith (11), NT Ted Washington (16).

COACHING STAFF

Head Coach,
Gregg Williams

Pro Career: Became the twelfth head coach in franchise history on February 1, 2001. Spent the previous 11 seasons with the Tennessee organization, including the last four as the Titans' defensive coordinator. Under his leadership in 2000, the Titans' defensive unit led the league in total defense for the first time since joining the NFL, and the 191 points allowed were the third fewest in the NFL since the league adopted a 16-game schedule in 1978. The Tennessee defense also led the league in third-down efficiency (30.8%), fourth-down efficiency (8.3%), and fewest first downs allowed (215). In 2000, the team also established the franchise's single-season records for sacks (55), fewest passing yards allowed (2,424), and fewest offensive touchdowns allowed (17). Williams spent three seasons (1994-96) overseeing the Oilers' linebackers after spending the 1993 campaign as the team's special teams coach. In 1993, Williams's special teams unit had the top-rated punting game and rated sixth in kickoff return defense. From 1990-92, Williams served as the club's first quality control coordinator.

Background: Williams played football (quarterback) and baseball at Northeast Missouri State from 1976-79 where he received his B.S. degree. He later earned his master's degree in education from Central Missouri State. Began his coaching career in the high school ranks as an assistant coach at his hometown of Excelsior Springs (Mo.) High School from 1980-83. He served as head coach at Belton (Mo.) High School from 1984-87. Spent the 1988-89 seasons working with the linebackers as a graduate assistant at the University of Houston for former Oilers head coach Jack Pardee.

Personal: Born July 15, 1958 in Excelsior Springs, Mo. Gregg and his wife Leigh Ann have two sons, Blake (16) and Chase (9), and a daughter, Amy (11).

2001 FIRST-YEAR ROSTER

Name	Pos.	Ht.	Wt.	Birthdate	College	Hometown	How Acq.
Campbell, Stephen	WR	6-2	210	2/25/78	Brown	Kent, Wash.	FA
Clements, Nate	CB	5-11	191	12/12/79	Ohio State	Shaker Heights, Ohio	D1
Crosby, Phillip (1)	FB	6-0	243	11/5/76	Tennessee	Bessemer City, N.C.	FA
Cummins, Randall	C	6-2	276	4/28/78	Kansas State	Cedar Hill, Texas	FA
Davison, Matt	WR	6-0	180	10/24/78	Nebraska	Tecumseh, Neb.	FA
Diepenbrock, Ryan	LS	6-1	245	1/5/78	Bowling Green	Lima, Ohio	FA
Dinkins, David	CB	6-3	206	8/15/78	Morehead State	Pittsburgh, Pa.	FA
Driver, Tony	S	6-1	211	8/4/77	Notre Dame	Louisville, Ky.	D6a
Edwards, Ron	DT	6-2	298	7/12/79	Texas A&M	Houston, Texas	D3a
Farris, Kris (1)	T	6-8	322	3/26/77	UCLA	Mission Viejo, Calif.	FA
Fisher, Bryce (1)	DT	6-2	251	5/12/77	Air Force	Renton, Wash.	D7b-'99
Germany, Reggie	WR	6-1	196	3/19/78	Ohio State	St. Louis, Mo.	D7a
Green, Donny	LB	6-2	233	9/18/77	Virginia	Hampton, Va.	FA
Gonzalez, Pete (1)	QB	6-1	220	7/4/74	Pittsburgh	Miami, Fla.	FA
Hasselbeck, Tim	QB	6-1	211	4/6/78	Boston College	Norfolk, Mass.	FA
Heimburger, Craig (1)	G	6-2	312	2/3/77	Missouri	Belleville, Ill.	FA
Henry, Travis	RB	5-9	221	10/29/78	Tennessee	Frostproof, Fla.	D2b
Hulsey, Corey (1)	G	6-5	358	7/26/77	Clemson	Lula, Ga.	FA-'00
Jennings, Jonas	T	6-3	320	11/21/77	Georgia	College Park, Ga.	D3b
Johnson, Teddy	WR	5-10	193	6/21/79	Northwestern	Elgin, Ill.	FA
Lind, Josh	T	6-5	305	6/3/78	Oklahoma State	St. Charles, Mo.	FA
Nesmith, Carl	S	6-2	223	3/19/79	Kansas	Jacksonville, Fla.	FA
Office, Kendrick	DE	6-4	248	8/2/78	West Alabama	Butler, Ala.	FA
O'Leary, Dan	TE	6-3	260	9/1/77	Notre Dame	Westlake, Ohio	D6b
Peterson, DeVonte	DT	6-2	280	4/1/78	Catawba	Clinton, N.C.	FA
Pidgeon, Pat (1)	P	5-11	200	6/9/77	Penn State	Mayfield, Pa.	FA
Pittman, Jonathan	WR	5-11	177	3/3/78	Brigham Young	Lakewood, Calif.	FA
Procell, Jarrett (1)	DE	6-2	275	11/4/77	Louisiana Tech	Bossier City, La.	FA-'00
Robertson, Tyrone	DT	6-4	277	8/15/79	Hinds (Miss.) C.C.	Danville, Va.	D7b
Roosendaal, Clark	T	6-5	300	12/7/77	Nevada	San Diego, Calif.	FA
Roth, Josh (1)	FB	6-0	235	3/15/78	Buffalo	Conewango Valley, N.Y.	FA-'00
Schobel, Aaron	DE	6-3	261	4/1/77	Texas Christian	Columbus, Texas	D2a
Spoon, Brandon	LB	6-2	244	7/5/78	North Carolina	Burlington, N.C.	D4
Sullivan, Marques	T	6-5	323	2/2/78	Illinois	Oak Park, Ill.	D5
Taylor, Jay (1)	K-P	6-1	191	10/23/76	West Virginia	Hershey, Pa.	FA
Whitman, Josh	TE	6-3	247	8/5/78	Illinois	West Lafayette, Ind.	FA
Williams, Jimmy	CB	5-10	184	3/10/79	Vanderbilt	Baton Rouge, La.	D6c

The term NFL Rookie is defined as a player who is in his first season of professional football and has not been on the roster of another professional football team for any regular-season or postseason games. A Rookie is designated by an "R" on NFL rosters. Players who have been active in another professional football league or players who have NFL experience, including either preseason training camp or being on an Active List or Inactive List, or on Reserve/Injured or Reserve/Physically Unable to Perform for fewer than six regular-season games, are termed NFL First-Year Players. An NFL First-Year Player is designated by a "1" on NFL rosters. Thereafter, a player is credited with an additional year of experience for each season in which he accumulates six games on the Active List or Inactive List, or on Reserve/Injured or Reserve/Physically Unable to Perform.

ASSISTANT COACHES

Miles Aldridge, linebackers; born January 25, 1949, Columbia, S.C., lives in Orchard Park, N.Y. Gardner-Webb 1969-1971. No pro playing experience. College coach: East Tennessee 1973-77, Wichita State 1978, Tulsa 1979, Mississippi 1980-82, Duke 1983-84, Clemson 1985-89, North Carolina State 1990, South Carolina 1991-93, Clemson 1994-95, Arkansas 1996-97, Southwest Louisiana 1998, Middle Tennessee State 1999-2000. Pro coach: Joined Bills in 2001.

Steve Fairchild, running backs; born June 21, 1958 Decatur, Ill., lives in Orchard Park, N.Y. Quarterback Colorado State 1980-81. No pro playing experience. College coach: Mesa (Colo.) J.C. 1982-83, Ferris State 1984-85, San Diego State 1986, New Mexico 1987-89, San Diego State 1991-92, Colorado State 1997-2000. Pro coach: Joined Bills in 2001.

Fred Graves, wide receivers; born March 2, 1950, Los Angeles, lives in Orchard Park, N.Y. Halfback-split end Utah 1968-1970. Pro wide receiver Chicago Bears 1971. College coach: Northeast Missouri State 1975-76, Western Illinois 1977-78, New Mexico State 1979-1981, Utah 1982-2000. Pro coach: Joined Bills in 2001.

Jerry Gray, defensive coordinator; born December 16, 1962, Lubbock, Texas, lives in Orchard Park, N.Y. Safety Texas 1981-84. Pro defensive back Los Angeles Rams 1985-1991, Houston Oilers 1992, Tampa Bay Buccaneers 1993. College coach: Southern Methodist 1995-96. Pro coach: Tennessee Titans 1997-2000, joined Bills in 2001.

Steve Jackson, asst. defensive backs-third down specialist; born April 8, 1969, Houston, lives in Orchard Park, N.Y. Defensive back Purdue 1988-1991. Pro defensive back Houston/Tennessee Oilers 1991-98. Pro coach: Joined Bills in 2001.

Rusty Jones, strength and conditioning; born August 14, 1953, Berwick, Maine, lives in Hamburg, N.Y. Attended Springfield College. No college or pro playing experience. College coach: Springfield College 1978-79. Pro coach: Pittsburgh Maulers (USFL) 1983-84, joined Bills in 1985.

Tommy Kaiser, offensive assistant-special teams assistant; born April 9, 1952, lives in Orchard Park, N.Y. Defensive back Houston 1971-73. No pro playing experience. College coach: Houston 1987-1992, Texas Tech 1993, Oklahoma State 1994-2000. Pro coach: Joined Bills in 2001.

Steve Kragthorpe, quarterbacks; born April 28, 1965, Missoula, Mont., lives in Orchard Park, N.Y. Quarterback Eastern New Mexico 1983-84, West Texas A&M 1985-86. No pro playing experience. College coach: Northern Arizona 1990-93, North Texas 1994-95, Boston College 1996, Texas A&M 1997-2000. Pro coach: Joined Bills in 2001.

Chuck Lester, administrative assistant to the head coach-defensive assistant; born May 18, 1955, Chicago, lives in Orchard Park, N.Y. Linebacker Oklahoma 1974. No pro playing experience. College coach: Iowa State 1980-81, Oklahoma 1982-84. Pro coach: Kansas City Chiefs 1984-86 (scout), joined Bills in 1987.

John Levra, defensive line; born October 2, 1937, Arma, Kan., lives in Hamburg, N.Y. Guard-linebacker Pittsburg State 1963-65. No pro playing experience. College coach: New Mexico Highlands 1966-1970, Stephen F. Austin 1971-74, Kansas 1975-78, North Texas State 1979. Pro coach: British Columbia (CFL) 1980, New Orleans Saints 1981-85, Chicago Bears 1986-1992, Denver Broncos 1993-94, Minnesota Vikings 1995-97, joined Bills in 1998.

Dan Neal, tight ends; born August 30, 1949, Corbin, Ky., lives in Orchard Park, N.Y. Offensive line Kentucky 1970-72. Pro offensive lineman Baltimore Colts 1973-74, Chicago Bears 1975-1983. Pro coach: Philadelphia Eagles 1986-1991, Arizona Cardinals 1994-95, New Orleans Saints 1997-99, Tennessee Titans 2000, joined Bills in 2001.

Mike Sheppard, offensive coordinator; born October 29, 1951, Tulsa, Okla., lives in Orchard Park, N.Y. Wide receiver Cal Lutheran 1969-1972. No college or pro playing experience. College coach: Cal Lutheran 1974-76, Brigham Young 1977-78, U.S. International 1979, Idaho State 1980-81, Long Beach State 1982, 1984-86, Kansas 1983, New Mexico 1987-1991, California 1992. Pro coach: Cleveland Browns 1993-95, Baltimore Ravens 1996, San Diego Chargers 1997-98, Seattle Seahawks 1999-2000, joined Bills in 2001.

Danny Smith, special teams coordinator; born September 7, 1953, Pittsburgh, lives in Orchard Park, N.Y. Defensive back Edinboro State 1972-75. No pro playing experience. College coach: Edinboro State 1976, Clemson 1979, William & Mary 1980-83, The Citadel 1984-86, Georgia Tech 1987-1994. Pro coach: Philadelphia Eagles 1995-98, Detroit Lions 1999-2000, joined Bills in 2001.

Pat Thomas, defensive backs; born September 1, 1954, Plano, Texas, lives in Orchard Park, N.Y. Defensive back Texas A&M 1972-75. Pro defensive back Los Angeles Rams 1976-1982. College coach: Houston 1985-89. Pro coach: Houston Gamblers (USFL) 1983-84, Houston Oilers 1990-92, Dallas Texans (Arena League) 1993, Indianapolis Colts 1994-97, joined Bills in 2001.

Ronnie Vinklarek, offensive line; born January 21, 1959, Weimer, Texas, lives in Orchard Park, N.Y. Attended Southwest Texas State. No college or pro playing experience. College coach: Houston 1988-1993, Valdosta State 1997, Oklahoma State 1998-99. Pro coach: Birmingham Barracudas (CFL) 1995, Tennessee Titans 2000, joined Bills in 2001.

CINCINNATI BENGALS

American Football Conference
Central Division
Team Colors: Black, Orange, and White
One Paul Brown Stadium
Cincinnati, Ohio 45202-3492
Telephone: (513) 621-3550
Ticket Office (513) 621-TDTD (8383)

CLUB OFFICIALS

President: Mike Brown
Senior Vice President: Pete Brown
Executive Vice President: Katie Blackburn
Vice President: Paul Brown
Vice President: John Sawyer
Business Development: Troy Blackburn
Business Manager: Bill Connelly
Chief Financial Officer: Bill Scanlon
Controller: Johanna Kappner
Managing Director of Paul Brown Stadium: Eric Brown
Director of Technology: Jo Ann Ralstin
Director of Sales and Public Affairs: Jeff Berding
Director of Corporate Sales and Marketing: Vince Cicero
Ticket Manager: Paul Kelly
Corporate Sales Executive: Brian Sells
Director of Ticket Sales: Kevin Lane
Merchandise Manager: Monty Montague
Public Relations Director: Jack Brennan
Internet Editor/Writer: Geoff Hobson
Directors of Pro/College Personnel: Jim Lippincott, Duke Tobin
Director of Player Relations: Eric Ball
Athletic Trainer: Paul Sparling
Equipment Manager: Rob Recker
Video Director: Travis Brammer
Stadium: Paul Brown Stadium (built in 2000)
•**Capacity:** 65,393
One Paul Brown Stadium
Cincinnati, Ohio 45202-3492
Playing Surface: Grass
Training Camp: Georgetown College
Georgetown, Kentucky 40324

2001 SCHEDULE

PRESEASON

Aug. 4	at Chicago	7:00
Aug. 10	at Detroit	7:30
Aug. 25	**Buffalo**	7:30
Aug. 30	**Indianapolis**	7:30

REGULAR SEASON

Sept. 9	**New England**	1:00
Sept. 16	at Tennessee	12:00
Sept. 23	**Baltimore**	1:00
Sept. 30	at San Diego	1:15
Oct. 7	at Pittsburgh	1:00
Oct. 14	**Cleveland**	1:00
Oct. 21	**Chicago**	1:00
Oct. 28	at Detroit	1:00
Nov. 4	Open Date	
Nov. 11	at Jacksonville	1:00
Nov. 18	**Tennessee**	1:00
Nov. 25	at Cleveland	1:00
Dec. 2	**Tampa Bay**	1:00
Dec. 9	**Jacksonville**	1:00
Dec. 16	at New York Jets	1:00
Dec. 23	at Baltimore	1:00
Dec. 30	**Pittsburgh**	1:00

RECORD HOLDERS

INDIVIDUAL RECORDS—CAREER

Category	Name	Performance
Rushing (Yds.)	James Brooks, 1984-1991	6,447
Passing (Yds.)	Ken Anderson, 1971-1986	32,838
Passing (TDs)	Ken Anderson, 1971-1986	197
Receiving (No.)	Carl Pickens, 1992-99	530
Receiving (Yds.)	Isaac Curtis, 1973-1984	7,101
Interceptions	Ken Riley, 1969-1983	65
Punting (Avg.)	Dave Lewis, 1970-73	43.8
Punt Return (Avg.)	Mitchell Price, 1990-93	10.4
Kickoff Return (Avg.)	Lemar Parrish, 1970-77	24.7
Field Goals	Jim Breech, 1980-1992	225
Touchdowns (Tot.)	Pete Johnson, 1977-1983	70
Points	Jim Breech, 1980-1992	1,151

INDIVIDUAL RECORDS—SINGLE SEASON

Category	Name	Performance
Rushing (Yds.)	Corey Dillon, 2000	1,435
Passing (Yds.)	Boomer Esiason, 1986	3,959
Passing (TDs)	Ken Anderson, 1981	29
Receiving (No.)	Carl Pickens, 1996	100
Receiving (Yds.)	Eddie Brown, 1988	1,273
Interceptions	Ken Riley, 1976	9
Punting (Avg.)	Dave Lewis, 1970	46.2
Punt Return (Avg.)	Lemar Parrish, 1974	18.8
Kickoff Return (Avg.)	Tremain Mack, 1999	27.1
Field Goals	Doug Pelfrey, 1995	29
Touchdowns (Tot.)	Carl Pickens, 1995	17
Points	Doug Pelfrey, 1995	121

INDIVIDUAL RECORDS—SINGLE GAME

Category	Name	Performance
Rushing (Yds.)	Corey Dillon, 10-22-00	*278
Passing (Yds.)	Boomer Esiason, 10-7-90	490
Passing (TDs)	Boomer Esiason, 12-21-86	5
	Boomer Esiason, 10-29-89	5
Receiving (No.)	Carl Pickens, 10-11-98	13
Receiving (Yds.)	Eddie Brown, 11-6-88	216
Interceptions	Many times	3
	Last time by David Fulcher, 12-17-89	
Field Goals	Doug Pelfrey, 11-6-94	6
Touchdowns (Tot.)	Larry Kinnebrew, 10-28-84	4
	Corey Dillon, 12-4-97	4
Points	Larry Kinnebrew, 10-28-84	24
	Corey Dillon, 12-4-97	24

*NFL Record

COACHING HISTORY

(219-276-1)

1968-1975	Paul Brown	55-59-1
1976-78	Bill Johnson*	18-15-0
1978-79	Homer Rice	8-19-0
1980-83	Forrest Gregg	34-27-0
1984-1991	Sam Wyche	64-68-0
1992-96	Dave Shula**	19-52-0
1996-2000	Bruce Coslet***	21-39-0
2000	Dick LeBeau	4-9-0

* Resigned after five games in 1978
** Released after seven games in 1996
*** Resigned after three games in 2000

PAUL BROWN STADIUM

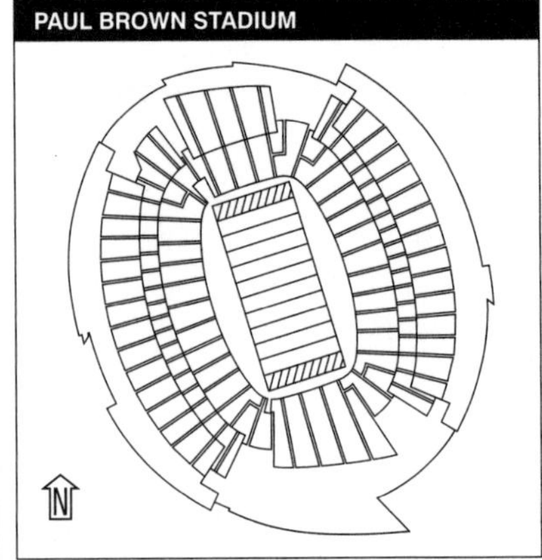

2000 TEAM RECORD

PRESEASON (1-3)

Date	Result		Opponent
8/4	L	20-21	at Buffalo
8/11	L	16-31	at Atlanta
8/19	W	24-20	Chicago
8/25	L	13-21	Detroit

REGULAR SEASON (4-12)

Date	Result		Opponent	Att.
9/10	L	7-24	Cleveland	64,006
9/17	L	0-13	at Jacksonville	45,653
9/24	L	0-37	at Baltimore	68,481
10/1	L	16-31	Miami	61,535
10/8	L	14-23	Tennessee	63,406
10/15	L	0-15	at Pittsburgh	54,328
10/22	W	31-21	Denver	61,603
10/29	W	12-3	at Cleveland	73,118
11/5	L	7-27	Baltimore	54,759
11/12	L	6-23	at Dallas	62,170
11/19	L	13-16	at New England	60,292
11/26	L	28-48	Pittsburgh	63,925
12/3	W	24-13	Arizona	50,289
12/10	L	3-35	at Tennessee	68,498
12/17	W	17-14	Jacksonville	50,469
12/24	L	7-16	at Philadelphia	64,902

SCORE BY PERIODS

Bengals	24	74	41	46	0	—	185
Opponents	92	106	91	70	0	—	359

ATTENDANCE

Home 461,403 Away 517,223 Total 978,626
Single-game home record, 64,006 (9/10/00)
Single-season home record, 473,288 (1990)

2000 TEAM STATISTICS

	Bengals	Opp.
Total First Downs	254	307
Rushing	119	101
Passing	109	182
Penalty	26	24
Third Down: Made/Att	77/227	102/239
Third Down Pct.	33.9	42.7
Fourth Down: Made/Att	10/25	4/13
Fourth Down Pct.	40.0	30.8
Total Net Yards	4,260	5,487
Avg. Per Game	266.3	342.9
Total Plays	1,001	1,068
Avg. Per Play	4.3	5.1
Net Yards Rushing	2,314	1,925
Avg. Per Game	144.6	120.3
Total Rushes	495	504
Net Yards Passing	1,946	3,562
Avg. Per Game	121.6	222.6
Sacked/Yards Lost	52/273	26/168
Gross Yards	2,219	3,730
Att./Completions	454/207	538/318
Completion Pct.	45.6	59.1
Had Intercepted	14	9
Punts/Average	94/40.2	80/41.7
Net Punting Avg.	94/33.1	80/35.5
Penalties/Yards	99/878	115/924
Fumbles/Ball Lost	37/21	22/12
Touchdowns	21	40
Rushing	13	12
Passing	6	26
Returns	2	2
Avg. Time of Possession	27:13	32:47

2000 INDIVIDUAL STATISTICS

Passing	Att.	Comp.	Yds.	Pct.	TD	Int.	Tkld.	Rate
Smith	267	118	1,253	44.2	3	6	36/191	52.8
Mitchell	187	89	966	47.6	3	8	16/82	50.8
Bengals	454	207	2,219	45.6	6	14	52/273	52.0
Opponents	538	318	3,730	59.1	26	9	26/168	89.4

SCORING	TD R	TD P	TD Rt	PAT	FG	Saf	PTS
Rackers	0	0	0	21/21	12/21	0	57
Dillon	7	0	0	0/0	0/0	0	42
Warrick	2	4	1	0/0	0/0	0	42
Bennett	3	0	0	0/0	0/0	0	18
Dugans	0	1	0	0/0	0/0	0	6
McGee	0	1	0	0/0	0/0	0	6
Mitchell	1	0	0	0/0	0/0	0	6
D. Williams	0	0	1	0/0	0/0	0	6
Bengals	13	6	2	21/21	12/21	1	185
Opponents	12	26	2	39/40	26/36	1	359

2-Pt. Conversions: None.
Bengals 0-0, Opponents 0-0.

RUSHING	Att.	Yds.	Avg.	LG	TD
Dillon	315	1,435	4.6	80t	7
Bennett	90	324	3.6	37t	3
Smith	41	232	5.7	21	0
Warrick	16	148	9.3	77t	2
Mitchell	10	61	6.1	12t	1
N. Williams	10	54	5.4	13	0
Keaton	6	24	4.0	8	0
Pope	2	22	11.0	22	0
Yeast	1	15	15.0	15	0
Groce	3	4	1.3	5	0
Rackers	1	-5	-5.0	-5	0
Bengals	495	2,314	4.7	80t	13
Opponents	504	1,925	3.8	30	12

RECEIVING	No.	Yds.	Avg.	LG	TD
Warrick	51	592	11.6	46	4
McGee	26	309	11.9	39	1
Yeast	24	301	12.5	27	0
Farmer	19	268	14.1	38	0
Bennett	19	168	8.8	25	0
Dillon	18	158	8.8	31	0
Dugans	14	125	8.9	17	1
Battaglia	13	105	8.1	15	0
Groce	11	45	4.1	14	0
N. Williams	7	84	12.0	20	0
Bush	3	39	13.0	18	0
Griffin	2	25	12.5	16	0
Bengals	207	2,219	10.7	46	6
Opponents	318	3,730	11.7	77t	26

INTERCEPTIONS	No.	Yds.	Avg.	LG	TD
T. Carter	2	40	20.0	30	0
Spikes	2	12	6.0	7	0
D. Williams	1	36	36.0	36t	1
Hall	1	12	12.0	12	0
C. Carter	1	6	6.0	6	0
Foley	1	1	1.0	1	0
Bean	1	0	0.0	0	0
Bengals	9	107	11.9	36t	1
Opponents	14	138	9.9	39	0

PUNTING	No.	Yds.	Avg.	In 20	LG
Pope	94	3,775	40.2	18	57
Bengals	94	3,775	40.2	18	57
Opponents	80	3,338	41.7	30	70

PUNT RETURNS	No.	FC	Yds.	Avg.	LG	TD
Yeast	34	14	225	6.6	27	0
Warrick	7	1	123	17.6	82t	1
Griffin	1	0	9	9.0	9	0
Bengals	42	15	357	8.5	82t	1
Opponents	40	17	387	9.7	39	0

KICKOFF RETURNS	No.	Yds.	Avg.	LG	TD
Mack	50	1,036	20.7	50	0
Griffin	8	129	16.1	29	0
Yeast	7	106	15.1	29	0
Keaton	6	100	16.7	25	0
Bush	3	18	6.0	8	0
N. Williams	2	12	6.0	12	0
Heath	1	22	22.0	22	0
Battaglia	0f	0	—	—	0
Bengals	77	1,423	18.5	50	0
Opponents	42	898	21.4	37	0

f=fair catch

FIELD GOALS	1-19	20-29	30-39	40-49	50+
Rackers	0/0	5/5	5/9	2/7	0/0
Bengals	0/0	5/5	5/9	2/7	0/0
Opponents	3/3	5/6	12/16	6/10	0/1

SACKS	No.
Foley	4.0
Gibson	4.0
Hall	4.0
Wilson	3.0
Curtis	2.0
Spikes	2.0
Steele	2.0
C. Carter	1.0
Copeland	1.0
Ross	1.0
Simmons	1.0
Spearman	1.0
Bengals	26.0
Opponents	52.0

2001 DRAFT CHOICES

Round	Name	Pos.	College
1	Justin Smith	DE	Missouri
2	Chad Johnson	WR	Oregon State
3	Sean Brewer	TE	San Jose State
4	Rudi Johnson	RB	Auburn
5	Victor Leyva	G	Arizona State
6	Riall Johnson	LB	Stanford
7	T.J. Houshmandzadeh	WR	Oregon State

CINCINNATI BENGALS

2001 VETERAN ROSTER

No.		Name	Pos.	Ht.	Wt.	Birthdate	NFL Exp.	College	Hometown	How Acq.	'00 Games/ Starts
71		Anderson, Willie	T	6-5	340	7/11/75	6	Auburn	Whistler, Ala.	D1-'96	16/16
33		Armour, JoJuan	S	5-11	220	7/10/76	3	Miami (Ohio)	Toledo, Ohio	FA-'00	4/0
90	#	Bankston, Michael	DE	6-5	285	3/12/70	10	Sam Houston State	Elm Grove, Texas	UFA(Ariz)-'98	16/14
93		Barndt, Tom	DT	6-3	300	3/14/72	6	Pittsburgh	Mentor, Ohio	UFA(KC)-'00	14/5
35		Basnight, Michael	RB	6-1	235	9/3/77	3	North Carolina A&T	Norfolk, Va.	FA-'99	0*
89		Battaglia, Marco	TE	6-3	249	1/25/73	6	Rutgers	Queens, N.Y.	D2-'96	16/10
23		Bean, Robert	CB	5-11	178	1/6/78	2	Mississippi State	Atlanta, Ga.	D5-'00	12/4
36		Bennett, Brandon	RB	5-11	220	2/3/73	3	South Carolina	Taylors, S.C.	FA-'99	16/0
96		Booker, Vaughn	DE	6-5	300	2/24/68	8	Cincinnati	Cincinnati, Ohio	UFA(GB)-'00	9/9
74		Braham, Rich	C	6-4	309	11/6/70	8	West Virginia	Morgantown, W. Va.	W(Ariz)-'94	9/9
88	#	Bush, Steve	TE-LS	6-3	258	7/4/74	5	Arizona State	Paradise Valley, Ariz.	FA-'97	16/0
42		Carter, Chris	S	6-2	212	9/27/74	5	Texas	Tyler, Texas	W(NE)-'00	16/10
21		Carter, Tom	CB	6-0	187	9/5/72	9	Notre Dame	St. Petersburg, Fla.	FA-'01	16/11
92		Copeland, John	DE	6-3	287	9/20/70	9	Alabama	Lanett, Ala.	D1-'93	16/16
4		Covington, Scott	QB	6-2	217	1/17/76	3	Miami	Laguna Niguel, Calif.	D7b-'99	0*
8		Cunningham, Richie	K	5-10	167	8/18/70	4	Southwestern Louisiana	Terrebonne, La.	FA-'01	4/0*
98		Curtis, Canute	LB	6-2	257	8/4/74	5	West Virginia	Amityville, N.Y.	FA-'98	15/0
28		Dillon, Corey	RB	6-1	225	10/24/74	5	Washington	Seattle, Wash.	D2-'97	16/16
76		Doughty, Mike	T	6-7	308	2/18/75	2	Notre Dame	Lakeville, Minn.	FA-'00	0*
81		Dugans, Ron	WR	6-2	205	4/27/77	2	Florida State	Tallahassee, Fla.	D3-'00	14/5
83		Farmer, Danny	WR	6-3	215	5/21/77	2	UCLA	Los Angeles, Calif.	W(Pitt)-'00	13/2
95		Foley, Steve	LB	6-3	260	9/9/75	4	Northeast Louisiana	Little Rock, Ark.	D3a-'98	16/16
99		Gibson, Oliver	DT	6-2	315	3/15/72	7	Notre Dame	Chicago, Ill.	UFA(Pitt)-'99	16/16
63		Goff, Mike	G	6-5	311	1/6/76	4	Iowa	Peru, Ill.	D3b-'98	16/16
52	#	Granville, Billy	LB	6-3	246	3/11/74	5	Duke	Trenton, N.J.	FA-'97	14/0
87		Griffin, Damon	WR-KR	5-9	186	6/14/76	3	Oregon	Monrovia, Calif.	W(SF)-'99	8/0
46		Groce, Clif	FB	5-11	240	7/30/72	5	Texas A&M	College Station, Texas	FA-'99	8/6
62		Gutierrez, Brock	C	6-3	304	9/25/73	5	Central Michigan	Charlotte, Mich.	FA-'98	16/7
26		Hall, Cory	S	6-0	210	12/5/76	3	Fresno State	Bakersfield, Calif.	D3-'99	16/6
27		Hawkins, Artrell	CB	5-10	190	11/24/75	4	Cincinnati	Johnstown, Pa.	D2-'98	16/6
22		Heath, Rodney	CB	5-10	177	10/29/74	3	Minnesota	Cincinnati, Ohio	FA-'99	13/9
97		Henry, Kevin	DE	6-4	285	10/23/68	9	Mississippi State	Mound Bayou, Miss.	UFA(Pitt)-'01	15/15*
65		Jackson, John	T	6-6	300	1/4/65	14	Eastern Kentucky	Cincinnati, Ohio	FA-'00	8/5
29		Keaton, Curtis	RB	5-10	219	10/18/76	2	James Madison	Columbus, Ohio	D4-'00	6/0
3		Kitna, Jon	QB	6-2	217	9/21/72	5	Central Washington	Tacoma, Wash.	UFA(Sea)-'01	15/12*
94		Langford, Jevon	DE	6-3	293	2/16/74	6	Oklahoma State	Washington, D.C.	D4-'96	11/3
34		Mack, Tremain	S-KR	6-0	193	11/21/74	5	Miami	Tyler, Texas	D4-'97	16/0
82		McGee, Tony	TE	6-4	248	4/21/71	9	Michigan	Terre Haute, Ind.	D2-'93	14/14
19		Mitchell, Scott	QB	6-6	240	1/2/68	12	Utah	Springville, Utah	UFA(Balt)-'00	8/5
41		Neal, Lorenzo	FB	5-11	240	12/27/70	9	Fresno State	Fresno, Calif.	FA-'01	16/5*
72		O'Dwyer, Matt	G	6-5	313	9/1/72	7	Northwestern	Lincolnshire, Ill.	UFA(NYJ)-'99	10/10
18		Plummer, Chad	WR	6-3	212	11/30/75	2	Cincinnati	Tallahassee, Fla.	FA-'00	3/0*
17		Pope, Daniel	P	5-10	203	3/28/75	3	Alabama	Alpharetta, Ga.	W(KC)-'00	16/0
5		Rackers, Neil	K	6-0	205	8/16/76	2	Illinois	Florissant, Mo.	D6-'00	16/0
79		Rehberg, Scott	G	6-8	315	11/17/73	5	Central Michigan	Kalamazoo, Mich.	FA-'00	10/6
20		Roman, Mark	CB	5-11	184	3/26/77	2	Louisiana State	New Iberia, La.	D2-'00	8/2
57		Ross, Adrian	LB	6-2	256	2/19/75	4	Colorado State	Elk Grove, Calif.	FA-'98	13/4
48		St. Louis, Brad	LS-TE	6-3	247	8/19/76	2	Southwest Missouri State	Belton, Mo.	D7-'00	16/0
86		Scott, Darnay	WR	6-1	204	7/7/72	8	San Diego State	St. Louis, Mo.	D2-'94	0*
56		Simmons, Brian	LB	6-3	248	6/21/75	4	North Carolina	New Bern, N.C.	D1b-'98	1/1
11		Smith, Akili	QB	6-3	220	8/21/75	3	Oregon	San Diego, Calif.	D1-'99	12/11
59		Spearman, Armegis	LB	6-1	258	4/5/78	2	Mississippi	Bruce, Miss.	FA-'00	15/11
51		Spikes, Takeo	LB	6-2	245	12/17/76	4	Auburn	Sandersville, Ga.	D1a-'98	16/16
70		Steele, Glen	DT	6-4	300	10/4/74	4	Michigan	Ligonier, Ind.	D4-'98	16/1
75		Stephens, Jamain	T	6-6	340	1/9/74	6	North Carolina A&T	Lumberton, N.C.	W(Pitt)-'99	5/0
80		Warrick, Peter	WR	5-11	195	6/19/77	2	Florida State	Bradenton, Fla.	D1-'00	16/16
73		Webb, Richmond	T	6-6	325	1/11/67	12	Texas A&M	Dallas, Texas	UFA(Mia)-'01	14/14*
31		Williams, Darryl	S	6-0	205	1/8/70	10	Miami	Miami, Fla.	FA-'00	16/16
30		Williams, Nick	FB	6-2	267	3/30/77	3	Miami	Farmington Hills, Mich.	D5-'99	14/4
91		Williams, Tony	DT	6-1	292	7/9/75	5	Memphis	Germantown, Tenn.	UFA(Minn)-'01	16/15*
55		Wilson, Reinard	DE	6-2	272	12/17/73	5	Florida State	Lake City, Fla.	D1-'97	14/0
84		Yeast, Craig	WR-KR	5-7	167	11/20/76	3	Kentucky	Harrodsburg, Ky.	D4-'99	15/7

* Basnight and Scott missed '00 season because of injury; Covington was inactive for 15 games; Cunningham played 4 games with Carolina; Doughty was on the practice squad for 11 games, inactive for 4 games, and did not play in 1 game with Cincinnati; Henry played 15 games with Pittsburgh; Kitna played 15 games with Seattle; Neal played 16 games with Tennessee; Plummer played 3 games with Indianapolis; Webb played 14 games with Miami; T. Williams played 16 games with Minnesota.

Unrestricted free agent; subject to developments.

Players lost through free agency (0): None.

Also played with Bengals in '00—T Rod Jones (16 games), LB Marc Megna (2), RB Sirr Parker (2).

COACHING STAFF

Head Coach,
Dick LeBeau

Pro Career: LeBeau is entering his second season, and first full season, as head coach of the Bengals. He was named the franchise's eighth head coach on September 25, 2000, following the resignation of Bruce Coslet. He had begun the 2000 season in the role of Bengals assistant head coach/defensive coordinator. A former All-Pro cornerback, LeBeau is in his forty-second NFL season, including twenty-eighth as a coach. Upon his promotion to replace Coslet last season, he became, at age 63, the NFL's oldest rookie head coach since the 1970 merger. The Bengals finished 4-9 under LeBeau last season after starting 0-3 under Coslet. The club showed improvement under LeBeau with a 4-6 record over the last 10 games and a 2-2 mark in the last four. LeBeau began his coaching career as an assistant with the Philadelphia Eagles from 1973-75. He was on the Green Bay Packers staff from 1976-79, and he began the first of two stints with the Bengals in 1980. He was defensive backfield coach through 1983 and was defensive coordinator for eight seasons (1984-1991). LeBeau went to the Pittsburgh Steelers as defensive backs coach in 1992 and was promoted and named Steelers' defensive coordinator for the 1995-96 seasons, when his zone blitz defensive scheme helped power Pittsburgh to Super Bowl XXX. LeBeau left the Steelers in 1997, returning to Cincinnati as assistant head coach/defensive coordinator under Coslet. Career record: 4-9.

Background: LeBeau is a native of London, Ohio, and attended London H.S. He played defensive back at Ohio State from 1955-58, and was a member of OSU's 1957 national championship team.

Personal: Born September 9, 1937. LeBeau and his wife Nancy live in Cincinnati and have a son, Brandon Grant.

ASSISTANT COACHES

Paul Alexander, offensive line; born February 12, 1960, Rochester, N.Y., lives in Cincinnati. Tackle Cortland State 1979-1981. No pro playing experience. College coach: Penn State 1982-84, Michigan 1985-86, Central Michigan 1987-1991. Pro coach: New York Jets 1992-93, joined Bengals in 1994.

Jim Anderson, running backs; born March 27, 1948, Harrisburg, Pa., lives in Cincinnati. Linebacker-defensive end California Western 1967-1970. No pro playing experience. College coach: California Western 1970-71, Scottsdale (Ariz.) C.C. 1973, Nevada-Las Vegas 1974-75, Southern Methodist 1976-1980, Stanford 1981-83. Pro coach: Joined Bengals in 1984.

Ken Anderson, quarterbacks; born February 15, 1949, Batavia, Ill., lives in Fort Mitchell, Ky. Quarterback Augustana (Ill.) 1967-1970. Pro quarterback Cincinnati Bengals 1971-1986. Pro coach: Joined Bengals in 1992.

Bob Bratkowski, offensive coordinator; born December 22, 1995, San Angelo, Texas, lives in Cincinnati. Wide receiver Washington State. No pro playing experience. College coach: Missouri 1978-1980, Weber State 1981-85, Wyoming 1986, Washington State 1987-88, Miami 1989-1991. Pro coach: Seattle Seahawks 1992-98, Pittsburgh Steelers 1999-2000, joined Bengals in 2001.

Louie Cioffi, defensive assistant; born September 21, 1973, Greenlawn, N.Y., lives in Cincinnati. Attended SUNY-Stony Brook. No college or pro playing experience. College coach: C.W. Post 1995-96. Pro coach: New York Jets 1993-94, joined Bengals in 1997.

Kevin Coyle, cornerbacks; born January 14, 1956, Staten Island, N.Y., lives in Cincinnati. Defensive back Massachusetts 1975-77. No pro playing experience. College coach: Cincinnati 1978-79, Arkansas 1980, U.S. Merchant Marine Academy 1981, Holy Cross 1982-1990, Syracuse 1991-93, Maryland 1994-96, Fresno State 1997-2000. Pro coach: Joined Bengals in 2001.

Mark Duffner, defensive coordinator; born July 19, 1953, Annandale, Va., lives in Cincinnati. Defensive lineman William & Mary 1973-74. No pro playing experience. College coach: Ohio State 1975-76, Cincinnati 1977-1980, Holy Cross 1981-1991 (head coach 1986-1991), Maryland 1992-96 (head coach). Pro coach: Joined Bengals in 1997.

John Garrett, offensive assistant; born March 2, 1965, Danville, Pa., lives in Cincinnati. Wide reciever Columbia 1983-84, Princeton 1987. Pro wide receiver Cincinnati Bengals 1989, San Antonio Riders (World League) 1991. Pro coach: Cincinnati Bengals 1995-98, Arizona Cardinals 1999-2000, joined Bengals in 2001.

Rodney Holman, assistant strength & conditioning; born April 20, 1960, Ypsilanti, Mich., lives in Cincinnati. Tight end Tulane 1978-81. Pro tight end Cincinnati Bengals 1982-92, Detroit Lions 1993-95. Pro coach: New Orleans Saints 1998-99, joined Bengals in 2001.

Ray Horton, safeties; born April 12, 1960, Tacoma, Wash., lives in Cincinnati. Defensive back Washington 1979-1982. Pro defensive back Cincinnati Bengals 1983-88, Dallas Cowboys 1989-1992. Pro coach: Washington Redskins 1994-96, joined Bengals in 1997.

Tim Krumrie, defensive line; born May 20, 1960, Menomonie, Wis., lives in Cincinnati. Defensive tackle Wisconsin 1979-1982. Pro defensive tackle Cincinnati Bengals 1983-1994. Pro coach: Joined Bengals in 1995.

Steve Mooshagian, wide receivers; born March 27, 1959, Downey, Calif., lives in Cincinnati. Wide receiver Cerritos College 1978-79, Fresno State 1980-81. No pro playing experience. College coach: Fresno State 1985-1994, Fresno City College 1995 (head coach), Nevada 1996, Pittsburgh 1997-98. Pro coach: Joined Bengals in 1999.

Al Roberts, special teams; born January 6, 1944, Fresno, Calif., lives in Cincinnati. Running back Washington 1964-65, Puget Sound 1967-68. No pro playing experience. College coach: Washington 1977-1982, 1996, Purdue 1986-87. Pro coach: Los Angeles Express (USFL) 1983-84, Houston Oilers 1984-85, Philadelphia Eagles 1988-1990, New York Jets 1991-93, Arizona Cardinals 1994-95, joined Bengals in 1997.

Frank Verducci, tight ends; born March 17, 1957, Glen Ridge, N.J., lives in Cincinnati. Tight end-fullback U.S. Merchant Marine Academy-Kings Port 1975. No pro playing experience. College coach: Colorado State 1980, Maryland 1981-83, Northern Illinois 1984, Iowa 1985-86, 1989-1998, Northwestern 1987-88. Pro coach: Joined Bengals in 1999.

Kim Wood, strength; born July 12, 1945, Barrington, Ill., lives in Cincinnati. Running back Wisconsin 1965-68. No pro playing experience. Pro coach: Joined Bengals in 1975.

2001 FIRST-YEAR ROSTER

Name	Pos.	Ht.	Wt.	Birthdate	College	Hometown	How Acq.
Boyd, LaVell (1)	WR	6-3	215	9/12/76	Louisville	Louisville, Ky.	FA-'00
Boyle, Jeff	DT	6-1	290	5/17/78	Wyoming	Norton, Kan.	FA
Brewer, Sean	TE	6-4	255	10/5/77	San Jose State	Riverside, Calif.	D3
Brown, Ricky (1)	FB	5-11	225	12/6/76	Texas	Arlington, Texas	FA-'00
Bryant, Kenny	CB	5-11	186	3/9/78	Jackson State	Jackson, Miss.	FA
Byrd, Anthony (1)	G	6-5	300	8/12/77	Louisville	Bedford, Ohio	FA
Chase, Jeff	G	6-4	303	3/23/76	Texas A&M-Kingsville	Rowland Heights, Calif.	FA
Edmonds, Chris	LB	6-3	250	1/1/78	West Virginia	Pittsburgh, Pa.	FA
Gavadza, Jason (1)	TE	6-3	258	1/31/76	Kent State	Toronto, Ontario, Canada	FA
Harris, Rashad	LB	6-1	241	9/27/79	Louisville	Huntsville, Ala.	FA
Houshmandzadeh, T.J.	WR	6-1	197	9/26/77	Oregon State	Barstow, Calif.	D7
Johnson, Chad	WR	6-1	192	1/9/78	Oregon State	Miami, Fla.	D2
Johnson, Riall	LB	6-3	243	4/20/78	Stanford	Lynnwood, Wash.	D6
Johnson, Rudi	RB	5-10	233	10/1/79	Auburn	Ettrick, Va.	D4
Lee, Jared	S	5-11	200	4/14/77	Brigham Young	Rexburg, Idaho	FA
Lewis, Calvin	DT	6-4	283	12/6/77	Memphis	Riverdale, Ga.	FA
Leyva, Victor	G	6-3	315	12/18/77	Arizona State	Porterville, Calif.	D5
McCullough, Kent	P	6-1	208	6/8/78	Miami (Ohio)	Coraopolis, Pa.	FA
McMullen, Kirk (1)	LS-TE	6-4	255	7/19/77	Pittsburgh	Imperial, Pa.	FA-'00
Moore, Freddie	T	6-5	304	8/27/77	Florida A&M	Tallahassee, Fla.	FA
North, Ramondo	WR	6-0	180	3/30/77	North Carolina A&T	Charlotte, N.C.	FA
Pettijohn, Duke	LB	6-1	249	6/7/77	Syracuse	Mattapan, Mass.	FA
Puloka, Dave	LB	6-1	258	1/12/79	Holy Cross	Arlington, Mass.	FA
Roesler, Roger (1)	C	6-5	307	10/5/77	Texas	Round Rock, Texas	FA-'00
Rosier, Chris	WR	6-1	205	12/31/77	William & Mary	Great Falls, Va.	FA
Shakir, Kamal	LB	6-1	238	4/17/78	Memphis	Norcross, Ga.	FA
Smith, Justin	DE	6-4	270	9/30/79	Missouri	Jefferson City, Mo.	D1
Thompkins, Gary (1)	S	5-11	200	1/29/77	West Virginia	Miami, Fla.	FA-'00

The term NFL Rookie is defined as a player who is in his first season of professional football and has not been on the roster of another professional football team for any regular-season or postseason games. A Rookie is designated by an "R" on NFL rosters. Players who have been active in another professional football league or players who have NFL experience, including either preseason training camp or being on an Active List or Inactive List, or on Reserve/Injured or Reserve/Physically Unable to Perform for fewer than six regular-season games, are termed NFL First-Year Players. An NFL First-Year Player is designated by a "1" on NFL rosters. Thereafter, a player is credited with an additional year of experience for each season in which he accumulates six games on the Active List or Inactive List, or on Reserve/Injured or Reserve/Physically Unable to Perform.

NOTES

CLEVELAND BROWNS

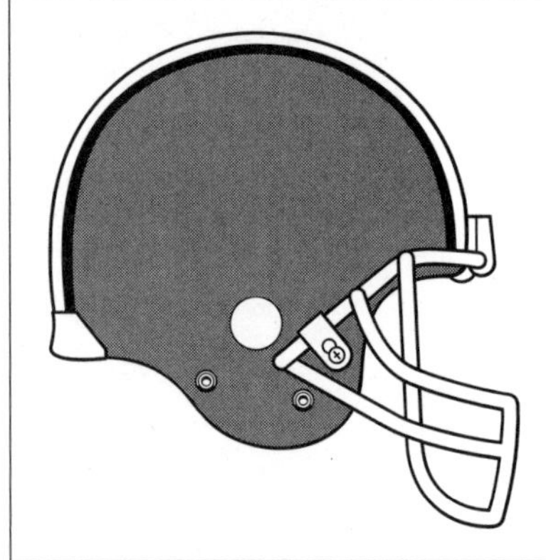

American Football Conference
Central Division
Team Colors: Brown, Orange, and White
76 Lou Groza Blvd.
Berea, Ohio 44017
Telephone: (440) 891-5000

CLUB OFFICIALS

Owner and Chairman: Alfred Lerner
President and Chief Executive Officer: Carmen Policy
Vice President, Director of Football Operations: Dwight Clark
Vice President, Business Operations and Chief Administrative Officer: Kofi Bonner
Vice President of Finance & Treasurer: Doug Jacobs
Vice President, Director of Stadium Operations and Security: Lew Merletti
Vice President, Assistant Director of Football Operations & General Counsel: Lal Heneghan
Vice President, Operations: Bill Hampton
Vice President of Marketing and Development: Bruce Popko
Director of Player Personnel: Joe Collins
College Personnel Coordinator: Phil Neri
Pro Personnel Coordinator: Keith Kidd
Director of Ticket Operations: Mike Jennings
Director of Stadium Operations: Diane Downing
Director, Cleveland Browns Foundation: Judge George White
Director of Publicity/Media Relations: Todd Stewart
Director of New Media: Dan Arthur
Director of Community Relations: Hillary Johnson
Manager of Publicity/Media Relations: Ken Mather
Manager of New Media: Amy Gretsinger
Browns Backers Coordinator: Molly Smith
Facilities Manager: Greg Hipp
Head Athletic Trainer: Mike Colello
Equipment Manager: Bobby Monica
Video Director: Pat Dolan
Head Groundskeeper: Chris Powell
Stadium: Cleveland Browns Stadium (built in 1999)
•**Capacity:** 73,300
1085 West 3rd Street
Cleveland, Ohio 44114
Playing Surface: Grass
Headquarters/Training Camp:
76 Lou Groza Boulevard
Berea, Ohio 44017

2001 SCHEDULE

PRESEASON

Aug. 11	**Green Bay**	8:00
Aug. 18	**Tampa Bay**	8:00
Aug. 24	at Washington	8:00
Aug. 31	at Carolina	8:00

REGULAR SEASON

Sept. 9	**Seattle**	1:00
Sept. 16	at Pittsburgh	8:30
Sept. 23	**Detroit**	1:00
Sept. 30	at Jacksonville	4:15
Oct. 7	**San Diego**	1:00
Oct. 14	at Cincinnati	1:00
Oct. 21	**Baltimore**	1:00
Oct. 28	Open Date	
Nov. 4	at Chicago	12:00
Nov. 11	**Pittsburgh**	1:00
Nov. 18	at Baltimore	1:00
Nov. 25	**Cincinnati**	1:00
Dec. 2	**Tennessee**	1:00
Dec. 9	at New England	1:00
Dec. 16	**Jacksonville**	1:00
Dec. 23	at Green Bay	12:00
Dec. 30	at Tennessee	12:00

RECORD HOLDERS

INDIVIDUAL RECORDS—CAREER

Category	Name	Performance
Rushing (Yds.)	Jim Brown, 1957-1965	12,312
Passing (Yds.)	Brian Sipe, 1974-1983	23,713
Passing (TDs)	Brian Sipe, 1974-1983	154
Receiving (No.)	Ozzie Newsome, 1978-1990	662
Receiving (Yds.)	Ozzie Newsome, 1978-1990	7,980
Interceptions	Thom Darden, 1972-74, 1976-1981	45
Punting (Avg.)	Chris Gardocki, 1999-2000	44.7
Punt Return (Avg.)	Greg Pruitt, 1973-1981	11.8
Kickoff Return (Avg.)	Greg Pruitt, 1973-1981	26.3
Field Goals	Lou Groza, 1950-59, 1961-67	234
Touchdowns (Tot.)	Jim Brown, 1957-1965	126
Points	Lou Groza, 1950-59, 1961-67	1,349

INDIVIDUAL RECORDS—SINGLE SEASON

Category	Name	Performance
Rushing (Yds.)	Jim Brown, 1963	1,863
Passing (Yds.)	Brian Sipe, 1980	4,132
Passing (TDs)	Brian Sipe, 1980	30
Receiving (No.)	Ozzie Newsome, 1983	89
	Ozzie Newsome, 1984	89
Receiving (Yds.)	Webster Slaughter, 1989	1,236
Interceptions	Thom Darden, 1978	10
Punting (Avg.)	Gary Collins, 1965	46.7
Punt Return (Avg.)	Leroy Kelly, 1965	15.6
Kickoff Return (Avg.)	Billy Lefear, 1975	31.7
Field Goals	Matt Stover, 1995	29
Touchdowns (Tot.)	Jim Brown, 1965	21
Points	Jim Brown, 1965	126

INDIVIDUAL RECORDS—SINGLE GAME

Category	Name	Performance
Rushing (Yds.)	Jim Brown, 11-24-57	237
	Jim Brown, 11-19-61	237
Passing (Yds.)	Bernie Kosar, 1-3-87	489
Passing (TDs)	Frank Ryan, 12-12-64	5
	Bill Nelsen, 11-2-69	5
	Brian Sipe, 10-7-79	5
Receiving (No.)	Ozzie Newsome, 10-14-84	14
Receiving (Yds.)	Ozzie Newsome, 10-14-84	191
Interceptions	Many times	3
	Last time by Stevon Moore, 9-17-95	
Field Goals	Don Cockroft, 10-19-75	5
	Matt Stover, 10-29-95	5
Touchdowns (Tot.)	Dub Jones, 11-25-51	*6
Points	Dub Jones, 11-25-51	36

*NFL Record

CLEVELAND BROWNS STADIUM

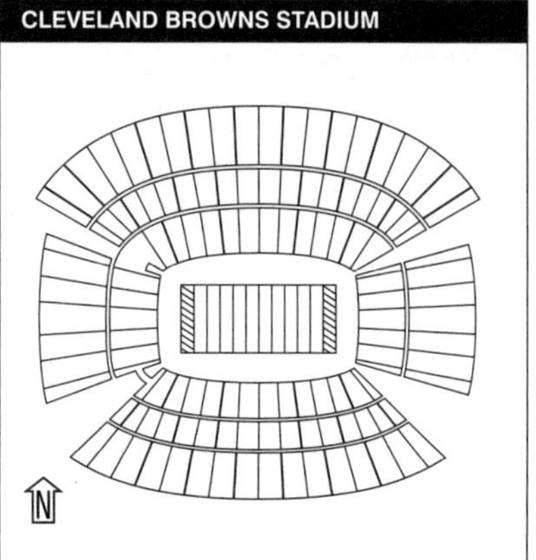

COACHING HISTORY

(390-312-10)

Years	Coach	Record
1950-1962	Paul Brown	115-49-5
1963-1970	Blanton Collier	79-38-2
1971-74	Nick Skorich	30-26-2
1975-77	Forrest Gregg*	18-23-0
1977	Dick Modzelewski	0-1-0
1978-1984	Sam Rutigliano**	47-52-0
1984-88	Marty Schottenheimer	46-31-0
1989-1990	Bud Carson***	12-14-1
1990	Jim Shofner	1-6-0
1991-95	Bill Belichick	37-45-0
1999-2000	Chris Palmer	5-27-0

*Resigned after 13 games in 1977
**Released after eight games in 1984
***Released after nine games in 1990

2000 TEAM RECORD

PRESEASON (1-3)

Date	Result		Opponent
7/30	W	33-22	Philadelphia
8/12	L	6-19	at Chicago
8/19	L	0-24	Washington
8/26	L	33-34	at Green Bay

REGULAR SEASON (3-13)

Date	Result		Opponent	Att.
9/3	L	7-27	Jacksonville	72,418
9/10	W	24-7	at Cincinnati	64,006
9/17	W	23-20	Pittsburgh	73,018
9/24	L	10-36	at Oakland	45,702
10/1	L	0-12	Baltimore	73,018
10/8	L	21-29	at Arizona	39,148
10/15	L	10-44	at Denver	75,811
10/22	L	0-22	at Pittsburgh	57,659
10/29	L	3-12	Cincinnati	73,118
11/5	L	3-24	New York Giants	72,718
11/12	W	19-11	New England	72,618
11/19	L	10-24	at Tennessee	68,498
11/26	L	7-44	at Baltimore	68,361
12/3	L	0-48	at Jacksonville	51,262
12/10	L	24-35	Philadelphia	72,318
12/17	L	0-24	Tennessee	72,318

SCORE BY PERIODS

Browns	51	45	32	33	0	—	161
Opponents	46	176	115	82	0	—	419

ATTENDANCE

Home 569,128 Away 485,630 Total 1,054,758
Single-game home record, 85,073 (9/21/70)
Single-season home record, 620,496 (1980)

2000 TEAM STATISTICS

	Browns	Opp.
Total First Downs	176	343
Rushing	53	147
Passing	110	169
Penalty	13	27
Third Down: Made/Att	58/210	98/227
Third Down Pct.	27.6	43.2
Fouth Down: Made/Att	6/19	11/17
Fouth Down Pct.	31.6	64.7
Total Net Yards	3,530	5,643
Avg. Per Game	220.6	352.7
Total Plays	859	1,122
Avg. Per Play	4.1	5.0
Net Yards Rushing	1,085	2,505
Avg. Per Game	67.8	156.6
Total Rushes	336	594
Net Yards Passing	2,445	3,138
Avg. Per Game	152.8	196.1
Sacked/Yards Lost	40/283	42/270
Gross Yards	2,728	3,408
Att./Completions	483/278	486/262
Completion Pct.	57.6	53.9
Had Intercepted	19	12
Punts/Average	108/45.5	68/42.2
Net Punting Avg.	108/37.3	68/35.8
Penalties/Yards	103/925	71/626
Fumbles/Ball Lost	21/9	27/13
Touchdowns	17	46
Rushing	7	26
Passing	9	18
Returns	1	2
Avg. Time of Possession	25:59	34:01

2000 INDIVIDUAL STATISTICS

Passing	Att.	Comp.	Yds.	Pct.	TD	Int.	Tkld.	Rate
Couch	215	137	1,483	63.7	7	9	10/78	77.3
Pederson	210	117	1,047	55.7	2	8	17/116	56.6
Wynn	54	22	167	40.7	0	1	13/89	41.2
Johnson	3	1	23	33.3	0	1	0/0	22.2
K. Thompson	1	1	8	100.0	0	0	0/0	100.0
Browns	483	278	2,728	57.6	9	19	40/283	63.4
Opponents	486	262	3,408	53.9	18	12	42/270	78.3

SCORING	TD R	TD P	TD Rt	PAT	FG	Saf	PTS
P. Dawson	0	0	0	17/17	14/17	0	59
Prentice	7	1	0	0/0	0/0	0	48
Edwards	0	2	0	0/0	0/0	0	12
Shea	0	2	0	0/0	0/0	0	12
Campbell	0	1	0	0/0	0/0	0	6
Chiaverini	0	1	0	0/0	0/0	0	6
J. Dawson	0	1	0	0/0	0/0	0	6
Ellsworth	0	0	1	0/0	0/0	0	6
Patten	0	1	0	0/0	0/0	0	6
Browns	7	9	1	17/17	14/17	0	161
Opponents	26	18	2	44/44	31/34	2	419

2-Pt. Conversions: None.
Browns 0-0, Opponents 1-2.

RUSHING	Att.	Yds.	Avg.	LG	TD
Prentice	173	512	3.0	17	7
Rhett	71	258	3.6	42	0
White	47	145	3.1	14	0
Pederson	18	68	3.8	15	0
Couch	12	45	3.8	31	0
Northcutt	9	33	3.7	13	0
Wynn	3	15	5.0	11	0
Edwards	2	9	4.5	6	0
K. Thompson	1	0	0.0	0	0
Browns	336	1,085	3.2	42	7
Opponents	594	2,505	4.2	36t	26

RECEIVING	No.	Yds.	Avg.	LG	TD
Johnson	57	669	11.7	79	0
Northcutt	39	422	10.8	37	0
Patten	38	546	14.4	65	1
Prentice	37	191	5.2	13	1
Shea	30	302	10.1	37	2
Edwards	16	128	8.0	21t	2
Rhett	14	78	5.6	16	0
White	13	100	7.7	25	0
Campbell	12	80	6.7	17	1
J. Dawson	9	97	10.8	26	1
Chiaverini	8	68	8.5	18	1
B. Brown	2	14	7.0	8	0
Saleh	1	22	22.0	22	0
Dunn	1	6	6.0	6	0
L. Jackson	1	5	5.0	5	0
Browns	278	2,728	9.8	79	9
Opponents	262	3,408	13.0	61	18

INTERCEPTIONS	No.	Yds.	Avg.	LG	TD
Fuller	3	0	0.0	0	0
Ellsworth	1	33	33.0	33t	1
McCutcheon	1	20	20.0	20	0
Little	1	7	7.0	7	0
Rainer	1	5	5.0	5	0
Moore	1	3	3.0	3	0
Chapman	1	0	0.0	0	0
Holland	1	0	0.0	0	0
J. Miller	1	0	0.0	0	0
Sanders	1	0	0.0	0	0
Browns	12	68	5.7	33t	1
Opponents	19	228	12.0	46t	2

PUNTING	No.	Yds.	Avg.	In 20	LG
Gardocki	108	4,919	45.5	25	67
Browns	108	4,919	45.5	25	67
Opponents	68	2,868	42.2	18	69

PUNT RETURNS	No.	FC	Yds.	Avg.	LG	TD
Northcutt	27	12	289	10.7	30	0
Barnes	1	0	0	0.0	0	0
Chapman	1	2	5	5.0	5	0
Browns	29	14	294	10.1	30	0
Opponents	69	10	793	11.5	54	0

KICKOFF RETURNS	No.	Yds.	Avg.	LG	TD
White	43	935	21.7	40	0
Patten	22	469	21.3	62	0
L. Jackson	9	168	18.7	30	0
Saleh	4	46	11.5	15	0
Campbell	3	30	10.0	13	0
Little	2	20	10.0	12	0
Edwards	1	24	24.0	24	0
Burnett	1	18	18.0	18	0
Browns	85	1,710	20.1	62	0
Opponents	42	1,012	24.1	62	0

FIELD GOALS	1-19	20-29	30-39	40-49	50+
P. Dawson	3/3	4/4	5/5	2/5	0/0
Browns	3/3	4/4	5/5	2/5	0/0
Opponents	0/0	9/9	13/13	8/10	1/2

SACKS	No.
McKenzie	8.0
J. Miller	5.0
C. Brown	4.5
McCutcheon	4.0
Colinet	3.5
Jones	2.5
Abdullah	2.0
Rogers	2.0
Roye	2.0
Spriggs	2.0
A. Miller	1.5
Holland	1.0
Moore	1.0
Rainer	1.0
Smith	1.0
M. Thompson	1.0
Browns	42.0
Opponents	40.0

2001 DRAFT CHOICES

Round	Name	Pos.	College
1	Gerard Warren	DT	Florida
2	Quincy Morgan	WR	Kansas State
3	James Jackson	RB	Miami
4	Anthony Henry	DB	South Florida
5	Jeremiah Pharms	LB	Washington
6	Michael Jameson	DB	Texas A&M
7	Paul Zukauskas	G	Boston College
	Andre King	WR	Miami

CLEVELAND BROWNS

2001 VETERAN ROSTER

No.	Name	Pos.	Ht.	Wt.	Birthdate	NFL Exp.	College	Hometown	How Acq.	'00 Games/ Starts
53	Abdullah, Rahim	LB	6-5	251	3/22/76	3	Clemson	Jacksonville, Fla.	D2b-'99	13/4
28	Barnes, Rashidi	CB-S	5-11	205	6/26/78	2	Colorado	Berkeley, Calif.	D7c-'00	14/0
63	Bedell, Brad	G-T	6-4	299	2/12/77	2	Colorado	Arcadia, Calif.	D6b-'00	12/0
52	Boyer, Brant	LB	6-1	230	6/27/71	8	Arizona	Ogden, Utah	UFA(Jax)-'01	12/5*
89	Brown, Bobby	WR	6-2	197	3/26/77	2	Notre Dame	Ft. Lauderdale, Fla.	FA-'00	6/0
92	Brown, Courtney	DE	6-4	266	2/14/78	2	Penn State	Alvin, S.C.	D1-'00	16/16
65	Bundren, Jim	C	6-3	303	10/6/74	3	Clemson	Wilmington, Del.	ED(NYJ)-'99	11/9
54	Burnett, Chester	LB	5-10	230	4/15/75	2	Arizona	Denver, Colo.	FA-'00	7/0
83	Campbell, Mark	TE	6-6	253	12/6/75	3	Michigan	Clawson, Mich.	FA-'99	16/10
69	Chanoine, Roger	T	6-4	295	8/11/76	2	Temple	Lenden, N.J.	FA-'99	7/0
27	Chapman, Lamar	CB-S	6-0	186	11/6/76	2	Kansas State	Liberal, Kan.	D5b-'00	7/0
84	Chiaverini, Darrin	WR	6-2	210	10/12/77	3	Colorado	Orange County, Calif.	D5-'99	10/2
93	Colinet, Stalin	DT	6-6	288	7/17/74	5	Boston College	New York, N.Y.	T(Minn)-'99	16/16
2	Couch, Tim	QB	6-4	227	7/31/77	3	Kentucky	Hyden, Ky.	D1-'99	7/7
88	Dawson, JaJuan	WR	6-1	197	11/5/77	2	Tulane	Houston, Texas	D3b-'00	2/2
4	Dawson, Phil	K	5-11	190	1/23/75	3	Texas	Dallas, Texas	FA-'99	16/0
11	Detmer, Ty	QB	6-0	194	10/30/67	10	Brigham Young	San Antonio, Texas	T(SF)-'99	0*
82	Dudley, Rickey	TE	6-6	255	7/15/72	6	Ohio State	Henderson, Texas	UFA(Oak)-'01	16/16*
43	Ellsworth, Percy	S	6-2	225	10/19/74	6	Virginia	Drewryville, Va.	UFA(NYG)-'00	16/16
34	Floyd, Chris	FB	6-2	235	6/23/75	4	Michigan	Detroit, Mich.	FA-'00	13/0
24	Fuller, Corey	CB	5-10	205	5/1/71	7	Florida State	Tallahassee, Fla.	UFA(Minn)-'99	15/15
17	Gardocki, Chris	P	6-1	200	2/7/70	11	Clemson	Stone Mountain, Ga.	UFA(Ind)-'99	16/0
10	Holcomb, Kelly	QB	6-2	212	7/9/73	5	Middle Tennessee State	Fayetteville, Tenn.	FA-'01	0*
73	Holland, Darius	DT	6-5	330	11/10/73	7	Colorado	Las Cruces, N.M.	UFA(Det)-'99	16/1
81	Jackson, Lenzie	WR	6-0	184	6/17/77	3	Arizona State	Milpitas, Calif.	FA-'00	5/0
31	Jackson, Raymond	CB-S	5-10	189	2/17/73	6	Colorado State	Denver, Colo.	ED(Buff)-'99	9/1
85	Johnson, Kevin	WR	5-11	195	7/15/76	3	Syracuse	Hamilton Township, N.J.	D2a-'99	16/16
67	Johnson, Tré	G	6-2	326	8/30/71	8	Temple	Peekskill, N.Y.	FA-'01	4/4*
51	Jones, Lenoy	LB	6-1	235	9/25/74	6	Texas Christian	Marlin, Texas	ED(Tenn)-'99	8/1
97	Kuehl, Ryan	DT	6-5	290	1/18/72	5	Virginia	Bethesda, Md.	FA-'99	16/0
79	LaMontagne, Noel	T-G	6-4	301	3/9/77	2	Virginia	Coopersburg, Pa.	FA-'00	2/0
61	Lindsay, Everett	C-G	6-4	302	9/18/70	8	Mississippi	Burlington, Iowa	UFA(Balt)-'00	16/16
20	Little, Earl	S	6-0	198	3/10/73	4	Miami	Miami, Fla.	W(NO)-'99	16/0
26	Malbrough, Anthony	CB	5-10	185	12/9/76	2	Texas Tech	Beaumont, Texas	D5a-'00	9/1
33	McCutcheon, Daylon	CB	5-10	180	12/9/76	3	Southern California	La Puente, Calif.	D3a-'99	15/15
90	McKenzie, Keith	DE	6-3	273	10/17/73	6	Ball State	Detroit, Mich.	UFA(GB)-'00	16/16
98	Miller, Arnold	DE	6-3	239	1/3/75	3	Louisiana State	New Orleans, La.	FA-'99	13/0
95	Miller, Jamir	LB	6-5	266	11/19/73	8	UCLA	Oakland, Calif.	UFA(Ariz)-'99	16/16
48	Monroe, Rod	TE	6-5	254	7/30/75	2	Cincinnati	Hearne, Texas	FA-'00	0*
55	Moore, Marty	LB	6-1	245	3/19/71	8	Kentucky	Phoenix, Ariz.	UFA(NE)-'00	16/9
86	Northcutt, Dennis	WR	5-11	175	12/22/77	2	Arizona	Los Angeles, Calif.	D2-'00	15/8
72	Oben, Roman	T	6-4	305	10/9/72	6	Louisville	Washington, D.C.	UFA(NYG)-'00	16/16
60	O'Hara, Shaun	C	6-3	287	6/23/77	2	Rutgers	Hillsborough, N.J.	FA-'00	8/4
41	Prentice, Travis	RB	5-11	221	12/8/76	2	Miami (Ohio)	Louisville, Ky.	D3a-'00	16/11
71	Pyne, Jim	C-G	6-2	297	11/23/71	8	Virginia Tech	Wallingford, Conn.	ED(Det)-'99	2/2
58	Rainer, Wali	LB	6-2	245	4/19/77	3	Virginia	Charlotte, N.C.	D4-'99	16/16
23	Rhett, Errict	RB	5-11	211	12/11/70	8	Florida	West Hollywood, Fla.	UFA(Balt)-'00	5/4
78	Rogers, Tyrone	DT-DE	6-5	236	10/11/76	2	Alabama State	Montgomery, Ala.	FA-'99	16/0
99	Roye, Orpheus	DT-DE	6-4	288	1/21/74	6	Florida State	Miami, Fla.	UFA(Pitt)-'00	16/16
57	Rudd, Dwayne	LB	6-2	237	2/3/76	5	Alabama	Batesville, Miss.	UFA(Minn)-'01	14/13*
50	Saleh, Tarek	LB	6-0	240	11/7/74	5	Wisconsin	Fairfield, Conn.	ED(Car)-'99	16/0
25	Sanders, Lewis	CB-S	6-0	200	6/22/78	2	Maryland	Staten Island, N.Y.	D4a-'00	11/1
87	Santiago, O.J.	TE	6-7	264	3/4/74	5	Kent State	Toronto, Ontario, Canada	W(Dall)-'00	10/0
44	Sellers, Mike	HB	6-3	260	7/21/75	4	Walla Walla (Wash.) C.C.	North Thurston, Wash.	RFA(Wash)-'01	14/6*
80	Shea, Aaron	TE	6-3	244	12/5/76	2	Michigan	Ottawa, Ill.	D4b-'00	15/8
94	Smith, Mark	DT	6-4	294	8/28/74	5	Auburn	Vicksburg, Miss.	UFA(Ariz)-'01	14/7*
21	Smith, Marquis	S	6-2	213	1/13/75	3	California	San Diego, Calif.	D3b-'99	16/16
91	Spriggs, Marcus	DT	6-4	314	7/26/76	3	Troy State	Washington, D.C.	D6a-'99	8/0
16	Thompson, Kevin	QB	6-5	236	7/27/77	2	Penn State	Damascus, Md.	FA-'00	1/0
96	# Thompson, Mike	DT	6-4	295	12/22/71	5	Wisconsin	Portage, Wis.	ED(Cin)-'99	12/0
77	Verba, Ross	T	6-4	308	10/31/73	5	Iowa	Des Moines, Iowa	UFA(GB)-'01	16/16*
30	White, Jamel	RB	5-9	208	2/11/77	2	South Dakota	Los Angeles, Calif.	W(Ind)-'00	13/0
64	Wohlabaugh, Dave	C	6-3	292	4/13/72	7	Syracuse	Hamburg, N.Y.	UFA(NE)-'99	12/12
13	Wynn, Spergon	QB	6-3	226	8/10/78	2	Southwest Texas State	Houston, Texas	D6a-'00	7/1
75	Zahursky, Steve	G	6-6	305	9/2/76	3	Kent State	Euclid, Ohio	FA-'99	16/16

* Boyer played 12 games with Jacksonville in '00; Detmer missed '00 season because of injury; Dudley played 16 games with Oakland; Holcomb was inactive for 16 games with Indianapolis; T. Johnson played 4 games with Washington; Monroe last active with Atlanta in '99; Rudd played 14 games with Minnesota; Sellers played 14 games with Washington; Mark Smith played 14 games with Arizona; Verba played 16 games with Green Bay.

\# Unrestricted free agent; subject to developments.

Retired—Curtis Enis, 3-year running back, 12 games in '00 with Chicago.

Players lost through free agency (2): FB Marc Edwards (NE; 16 games in '00), WR David Patten (NE; 14).

Also played with Browns in '00—T-G James Brown (7 games), LB Doug Colman (5), WR Damon Dunn (3), LB Michael Hamilton (1), QB Doug Pederson (11), LB Ryan Taylor (4).

COACHING STAFF

Head Coach,
Butch Davis

Pro Career: Named head coach of the Browns on January 30, 2001, coming to Cleveland from the University of Miami where Davis rebuilt the Hurricanes program. Davis officially returned the program back to the college football elite status as Miami handily defeated Florida, 37-20, in the 2001 Nokia Sugar Bowl, and finished second in both the *Associated Press* and ESPN/*USA Today* rankings. The tenth full-time head coach in franchise history, Davis has been successful at every previous stop in his coaching career. He has won two Super Bowl championships with the Dallas Cowboys (1992 and 1993) and, at the collegiate level, he won a national championship with the University of Miami (1987). He boasts more than 20 years of coaching experience, including the past six seasons as the head coach of the University of Miami, where he compiled a 51-20 record, including a 4-0 mark in bowl games. Prior to his tenure as head coach at the University of Miami, Davis spent six years (1989-1994) with the Dallas Cowboys, the last two seasons as the Cowboys' defensive coordinator. Davis was the defensive coordinator on Dallas's 1993 squad that defeated the Buffalo Bills, 30-13, in Super Bowl XXVIII. Davis's 1993 defensive squad helped the Cowboys capture their second consecutive Super Bowl and allowed just one offensive touchdown or less in 12 of 16 games. Prior to being named to the defensive coordinator's post, Davis coached the Dallas defensive line for four seasons.

Background: Davis spent five seasons (1984-88) as the defensive line coach for the University of Miami, including the Hurricanes' 1987 national championship team. Davis entered the collegiate coaching ranks on the offensive side of the ball as an assistant on Jimmy Johnson's Oklahoma State teams from 1979-1983. At Oklahoma State, Davis was responsible for coaching the receivers and tight ends and serving as the recruiting coordinator. Prior to his tenure at Oklahoma State, Davis was the head coach at Rogers High School in Tulsa, Okla., for one season (1978) after spending time as an assistant at two high schools in Oklahoma and one in Arkansas where he taught biology, anatomy, and physiology. Davis played defensive end for Arkansas (1971-74).

Personal: Born Paul Hilton Davis in Tahlequah, Okla., on November 17, 1951. Earned his bachelor's degree in biology and life science from Arkansas. Davis and his wife Tammy have one son, Andrew, 8.

ASSISTANT COACHES

Bruce Arians, offensive coordinator; born October 3, 1952, Paterson, N.J., lives in Cleveland. Quarterback Virginia Tech 1970-74. No pro playing experience. College coach: Virginia Tech 1975-77, Mississippi State 1978-1980, Alabama 1981-82, Temple (head coach) 1983-88, Mississippi State 1993-95, Alabama 1997. Pro coach: Kansas City Chiefs 1989-1992, New Orleans Saints 1996, Indianapolis 1998-2000, joined Browns in 2001.

Phil Banko, defensive assistant; born August 9, 1964, Jacksonville, lives in Cleveland. Attended Southern. No college or pro playing experience. College coach: Miami 1998-2000. Pro coach: Joined Browns in 2001.

Todd Bowles, defensive assistant; born November 18, 1963, Elizabeth, N.J., lives in Cleveland. Defensive back Temple 1982-85. Pro defensive back Washington 1986-1990, 1991-93, San Francisco 1990. College coach: Morehouse College 1997, Grambling State 1998-99. Pro coach: New York Jets 2000, joined Browns in 2001.

Keith Butler, linebackers; born May 16, 1956, Anniston, Ala., lives in Cleveland. Linebacker Memphis 1974-77. Pro linebacker Seattle 1978-1987. College coach: Memphis 1990-97, Arkansas State 1998. Pro coach: Joined Browns in 1999.

Foge Fazio, defensive coordinator; born February 28, 1939, Dawmont, W. Va., lives in Cleveland. Linebacker-center Pittsburgh 1957-1960. No pro playing experience. College coach: Boston University 1966-67, Harvard 1968, Pittsburgh 1969-1972, 1977-1985 (head coach 1982-85), Cincinnati 1973-76, Notre Dame 1986-87. Pro coach: Atlanta Falcons 1988-89, New York Jets 1990-94, Minnesota Vikings 1995-98, Washington Redskins 2000, joined Browns in 2001.

Pete Garcia, football development; born September 18, 1961, Havana, Cuba, lives in Cleveland. Attended Miami. No college or pro playing experience. College coach: Miami 1990-2000. Pro coach: Miami Dolphins 1989-1990, joined Browns in 2001.

Steve Hagen, tight ends; born September 15, 1961, lives in Cleveland. Tight end Cal Lutheran 1979-1982. Pro tight end Boston Breakers (USFL) 1983. College coach: Northern Arizona 1987-88, Notre Dame 1989-1990, Kent State 1991, Nevada 1992-93, Nevada-Las Vegas 1994-95, Wartburg (Iowa) 1996, San Jose State 1997-98, California 1999-2000. Pro coach: Joined Browns in 2001.

Ray Hamilton, defensive line; born January 1, 1951, Omaha, Neb., lives in Cleveland. Nose tackle Oklahoma 1969-1972. Pro defensive lineman New England 1973-1981. College coach: Tennessee 1992. Pro coach: New England Patriots 1985-89, Tampa Bay Buccaneers 1991, Los Angeles Raiders 1993-94, New York Jets 1995-96, New England Patriots 1997-99, New York Jets 2000, joined Browns in 2001.

Tim Jorgensen, head strength and conditioning; born April 21, 1955, St. Louis, Mo., lives in Cleveland. Guard Southwest Missouri State 1974-76. No pro playing experience. College coach: Southwest Missouri State 1977-78, Alabama 1979, Louisiana State 1980-83. Pro coach: Philadelphia Eagles 1984-86, Atlanta Falcons 1987-1998, joined Browns in 1999.

Todd McNair, running backs; born October 7, 1965, Camden, N.J. lives in Cleveland. Running back Temple 1985-88. Pro running back Kansas City 1989-1993, 1996, Houston 1994-95. Pro coach: Joined the Browns in 2001.

Chuck Pagano, defensive backs; born October 2, 1960, Boulder, Colo., lives in Cleveland. Safety Wyoming 1980-83. No pro playing experience. College coach: Southern California 1984-85, Miami 1986, Boise State 1987-88, East Carolina 1989, Nevada-Las Vegas 1990-91, East Carolina 1992-94, Miami 1995-2000. Pro coach: Joined Browns in 2001.

Rob Phillips, asst. strength and conditioning; born December 3, 1971, Ft. Wayne, Ind., lives in Cleveland. Attended Tennessee. No college or pro playing experience. College coach: Western Carolina 1997-98, Miami 1999-2000. Pro coach: Joined Browns in 2001.

Terry Robiskie, wide receivers; born November 12, 1954, New Orleans, lives in Cleveland. Running back Louisiana State 1973-76. Pro running back Oakland Raiders 1977-79, Miami Dolphins 1980-81. Pro coach: Los Angeles Raiders 1982-1993, Washington Redskins 1994-2000 (head coach 2000), joined Browns in 2001.

Jerry Rosburg, special teams; born November 24, 1955, Fairmont, Minn., lives in Cleveland. No college or pro playing experience. College coach: Northern Michigan 1981-86, Western Michigan 1987-91, Cincinnati 1992-95, Minnesota 1996, Boston College 1997-98, Notre Dame 1999-2000. Pro coach: Joined Browns in 2001.

Carl Smith, quarterbacks; born April 26, 1948, Wasco, Calif., lives in Cleveland. Quarterback Bakersfield College 1966-67, defensive back Cal Poly-San Luis Obispo 1969-1970. No pro playing experience. College coach: Colorado 1972-73, Southwestern Louisiana 1974-78, Lamar 1979-1981, North Carolina State 1982. Pro coach: Philadelphia/Baltimore Stars (USFL) 1983-85, New Orleans Saints 1986-1996, New England Patriots 1997-2000, joined Browns in 2001.

Larry Zierlein, offensive line; born July 12, 1945, Lenora, Kan., lives in Cleveland. No college or pro playing experience. College coach: Fort Hays (Kan.) State College 1970-71, Houston 1978-1986, Tulane 1988-1990, 1995-96, Louisiana State 1993-94, Cincinnati 1997-2000. Pro coach: Washington Commandos (Arena League) 1987, New York/New Jersey Knights (WLAF) 1991-92, joined Browns in 2001.

2001 FIRST-YEAR ROSTER

Name	Pos.	Ht.	Wt.	Birthdate	College	Hometown	How Acq.
Allamon, Kyle (1)	TE	6-2	247	12/22/76	Texas Tech	Lubbock, Texas	FA-'00
Caldwell, Cecil	DE-DT	6-1	268	2/23/77	South Carolina	Newberry, S.C.	FA
Carroll, Daymon (Bo)	WR	5-9	165	4/27/77	Florida	Norristown, Pa.	FA
Clare, Mike	G-T	6-3	322	1/9/79	Harvard	Rutherford, N.J.	FA
Davis, Brandon	S	6-4	215	10/3/78	Arkansas	Camden, Ark.	FA
Fair, Carl	RB	6-1	219	6/8/79	Alabama-Birmingham	Starkville, Miss.	FA
Franz, Todd (1)	CB-S	6-0	194	4/12/76	Tulsa	Enid, Okla.	FA-'00
Henry, Anthony	CB-S	6-0	198	11/3/76	South Florida	Fort Myers, Fla.	D4
Jackson, James	RB	5-10	209	8/4/76	Miami	Belle Glade, Fla.	D3
Jameson, Michael	CB-S	5-11	186	7/14/79	Texas A&M	Killeen, Texas	D6
King, Andre	WR	5-11	195	11/26/73	Miami	Fort Lauderdale, Fla.	D7b
Lindstrom, Gabe (1)	P	6-4	225	5/22/76	Toledo	Bisbee, Ariz.	FA
Linnear, Kerry	DE	6-5	259	2/20/77	Texas A&M-Kingsville	DeSoto, Texas	FA
McKinney, Jeremy (1)	G-T	6-6	301	1/6/76	Iowa	Huntington Park, Colo.	FA-'99
Morgan, Quincy	WR	6-1	209	9/23/77	Kansas State	Garland, Texas	D2
O'Connor, Drew (1)	WR	6-3	211	2/2/76	Maine	New Brunswick, N.J.	FA-'00
Rosfeld, Doug	C	6-4	281	5/28/79	Cincinnati	Cincinnati, Ohio	FA
Schorejs, Derek (1)	K	6-0	220	5/14/73	Bowling Green	Westerville, Ohio	FA
Smith, Michael (1)	LB	6-3	240	10/29/77	Miami	Riviera Beach, Fla.	FA
Spikes, Rahshon (1)	RB	5-10	206	10/16/77	North Carolina State	Meriden, N.C.	FA-'00
Warren, Gerard	DT	6-4	322	7/25/78	Florida	Raiford, Fla.	D1
Zukauskas, Paul	G-T	6-5	306	7/12/79	Boston College	Weymouth, Mass.	D7a

The term NFL Rookie is defined as a player who is in his first season of professional football and has not been on the roster of another professional football team for any regular-season or postseason games. A Rookie is designated by an "R" on NFL rosters. Players who have been active in another professional football league or players who have NFL experience, including either preseason training camp or being on an Active List or Inactive List, or on Reserve/Injured or Reserve/Physically Unable to Perform for fewer than six regular-season games, are termed NFL First-Year Players. An NFL First-Year Player is designated by a "1" on NFL rosters. Thereafter, a player is credited with an additional year of experience for each season in which he accumulates six games on the Active List or Inactive List, or on Reserve/Injured or Reserve/Physically Unable to Perform.

DENVER BRONCOS

American Football Conference
Western Division
Team Colors: Orange, Broncos Navy Blue, and White
13655 Broncos Parkway
Englewood, Colorado 80112
Telephone: (303) 649-9000

CLUB OFFICIALS

President-Chief Executive Officer: Pat Bowlen
Vice President of Football Operations/Head Coach: Mike Shanahan
Vice President of Business Operations: Joe Ellis
General Manager: Neal Dahlen
Director of Pro Scouting: Rick Smith
Director of College Scouting: Ted Sundquist
Chief Financial Officer: Allen Fears
Senior Director of Ticket Operations/Business Development: Rick Nichols
Assistant to the President: Yolanda Saltus
Senior Director of Media Relations: Jim Saccomano
Vice President of Stadium Operations: Mac Freeman
Director of Stadium Operations: Gail Stuckey
Senior Director of Operations: Bill Harpole
Senior Director of Marketing: Greg Carney
Senior Director of Community Development: Cindy Walters
Director of Special Services: Fred Fleming
Director of Alumni Relations: Bill Thompson
Director of Community Outreach: Steve Sewell
Trainer: Steve Antonopulos
Equipment Manager: Doug West
Video Director: Kent Erickson
Stadium: INVESCO Field at Mile High (built in 2001)
•**Capacity:** 70,125
1701 Bryant Street
Denver, Colorado 80204
Playing Surface: Grass (fiber-reinforced)
Training Camp: University of Northern Colorado
Greeley, Colorado 80639

2001 SCHEDULE

PRESEASON

Aug. 11	at Dallas	8:00
Aug. 20	at Green Bay	7:00
Aug. 25	**New Orleans**	7:00
Aug. 31	**San Francisco**	7:00

REGULAR SEASON

Sept. 10	**New York Giants** (Mon.)	7:00
Sept. 16	at Indianapolis	12:00
Sept. 23	at Arizona	5:30
Sept. 30	**Baltimore**	2:15
Oct. 7	**Kansas City**	2:05
Oct. 14	at Seattle	1:15
Oct. 21	at San Diego	1:05
Oct. 28	**New England**	2:15
Nov. 5	at Oakland (Mon.)	6:00
Nov. 11	**San Diego**	2:05
Nov. 18	**Washington**	2:15
Nov. 22	at Dallas (Thurs.)	3:05
Dec. 2	at Miami	1:00
Dec. 9	**Seattle**	6:30
Dec. 16	at Kansas City	12:00
Dec. 23	Open Date	
Dec. 30	**Oakland**	2:15

RECORD HOLDERS

INDIVIDUAL RECORDS—CAREER

Category	Name	Performance
Rushing (Yds.)	Terrell Davis, 1995-2000	6,906
Passing (Yds.)	John Elway, 1983-1998	51,475
Passing (TDs)	John Elway, 1983-1998	300
Receiving (No.)	Shannon Sharpe, 1990-99	552
Receiving (Yds.)	Shannon Sharpe, 1990-99	6,983
Interceptions	Steve Foley, 1976-1986	44
Punting (Avg.)	Jim Fraser, 1962-64	45.2
Punt Return (Avg.)	Darrien Gordon, 1997-98	12.5
Kickoff Return (Avg.)	Abner Haynes, 1965-66	26.3
Field Goals	Jason Elam, 1993-2000	204
Touchdowns (Tot.)	Terrell Davis, 1995-2000	65
Points	Jason Elam, 1993-2000	949

INDIVIDUAL RECORDS—SINGLE SEASON

Category	Name	Performance
Rushing (Yds.)	Terrell Davis, 1998	2,008
Passing (Yds.)	John Elway, 1993	4,030
Passing (TDs)	John Elway, 1997	27
Receiving (No.)	Ed McCaffrey, 2000	101
Receiving (Yds.)	Red Smith, 2000	1,602
Interceptions	Goose Gonsoulin, 1960	11
Punting (Avg.)	Tom Rouen, 1998	46.9
Punt Return (Avg.)	Floyd Little, 1967	16.9
Kickoff Return (Avg.)	Bill Thompson, 1969	28.5
Field Goals	Jason Elam, 1995	31
Touchdowns (Tot.)	Terrell Davis, 1998	23
Points	Terrell Davis, 1998	138

INDIVIDUAL RECORDS—SINGLE GAME

Category	Name	Performance
Rushing (Yds.)	Mike Anderson, 12-3-00	251
Passing (Yds.)	Gus Frerotte, 11-19-00	462
Passing (TDs)	Frank Tripucka, 10-28-62	5
	John Elway, 11-18-84	5
	Gus Frerotte, 11-19-00	5
Receiving (No.)	Lionel Taylor, 11-29-64	13
	Bobby Anderson, 9-30-73	13
	Rod Smith, 10-1-00	13
Receiving (Yds.)	Lionel Taylor, 11-27-60	199
Interceptions	Goose Gonsoulin, 9-18-60	*4
	Willie Brown, 11-15-64	*4
Field Goals	Gene Mingo, 10-6-63	5
	Rich Karlis, 11-20-83	5
	Jason Elam, 9-3-95	5
Touchdowns (Tot.)	Mike Anderson, 12-3-00	4
Points	Mike Anderson, 12-3-00	24

*NFL Record

COACHING HISTORY

(328-302-10)

1960-61	Frank Filchock	7-20-1
1962-64	Jack Faulkner*	9-22-1
1964-66	Mac Speedie**	6-19-1
1966	Ray Malavasi	4-8-0
1967-1971	Lou Saban***	20-42-3
1971	Jerry Smith	2-3-0
1972-76	John Ralston	34-33-3
1977-1980	Robert (Red) Miller	42-25-0
1981-1992	Dan Reeves	117-79-1
1993-94	Wade Phillips	16-17-0
1995-2000	Mike Shanahan	71-34-0

*Released after four games in 1964
**Resigned after two games in 1966
***Resigned after nine games in 1971

INVESCO FIELD AT MILE HIGH

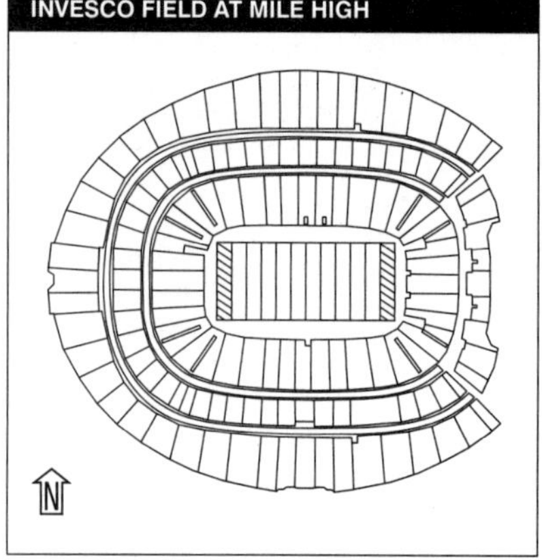

2000 TEAM RECORD

PRESEASON (3-2)

Date	Result		Opponent
8/5	W	31-17	at Arizona
8/13	W	26-20	Green Bay
8/19	W	36-23	Dallas
8/25	W	28-24	at San Francisco

REGULAR SEASON (11-5)

Date	Result		Opponent	Att.
9/4	L	36-41	at St. Louis	65,956
9/10	W	42-14	Atlanta	75,466
9/17	W	33-24	at Oakland	62,078
9/24	L	22-23	Kansas City	74,596
10/1	L	19-28	New England	75,684
10/8	W	21-7	at San Diego	56,079
10/15	W	44-10	Cleveland	75,811
10/22	L	21-31	at Cincinnati	61,603
11/5	W	30-23	at New York Jets	78,305
11/13	W	27-24	Oakland	75,951
11/19	W	38-37	San Diego	75,218
11/26	W	38-31	at Seattle	68,661
12/3	W	38-23	at New Orleans	64,900
12/10	W	31-24	Seattle	75,218
12/17	L	7-20	at Kansas City	78,406
12/23	W	38-9	San Francisco	76,098

POSTSEASON (0-1)

Date	Result		Opponent	Att.
12/31	L	3-21	at Baltimore	69,638

SCORE BY PERIODS

Broncos	88	156	121	120	0	—	485
Opponents	57	120	96	96	0	—	369

ATTENDANCE

Home 594,813 Away 543,302 Total 1,138,115
Single-game home record, 76,098 (12/23/00)
Single-season home record, 594,813 (2000)

2000 TEAM STATISTICS

	Broncos	Opp.
Total First Downs	383	294
Rushing	124	80
Passing	223	189
Penalty	36	25
Third Down: Made/Att	97/218	66/191
Third Down Pct.	44.5	34.6
Fourth Down: Made/Att	9/17	6/18
Fourth Down Pct.	52.9	33.3
Total Net Yards	6,554	5,544
Avg. Per Game	409.6	346.5
Total Plays	1,115	962
Avg. Per Play	5.9	5.8
Net Yards Rushing	2,311	1,598
Avg. Per Game	144.4	99.9
Total Rushes	516	344
Net Yards Passing	4,243	3,946
Avg. Per Game	265.2	246.6
Sacked/Yards Lost	30/221	44/251
Gross Yards	4,464	4,197
Att./Completions	569/354	574/310
Completion Pct.	62.2	54.0
Had Intercepted	12	27
Punts/Average	62/39.6	73/43.8
Net Punting Avg.	62/32.3	73/37.4
Penalties/Yards	89/792	109/898
Fumbles/Ball Lost	26/13	31/17
Touchdowns	58	45
Rushing	21	13
Passing	28	26
Returns	9	6
Avg. Time of Possession	33:15	26:45

2000 INDIVIDUAL STATISTICS

Passing	Att.	Comp.	Yds.	Pct.	TD	Int.	Tkld.	Rate
Griese	336	216	2,688	64.3	19	4	17/139	102.9
Frerotte	232	138	1,776	59.5	9	8	12/77	82.1
Jackson	1	0	0	0.0	0	0	1/5	39.6
Broncos	569	354	4,464	62.2	28	12	30/221	94.2
Opponents	574	310	4,197	54.0	26	27	44/251	73.1

SCORING	TD R	TD P	TD Rt	PAT	FG	Saf	PTS
Elam	0	0	0	49/49	18/24	0	103
Anderson	15	0	0	0/0	0/0	0	92
McCaffrey	0	9	0	0/0	0/0	0	56
R. Smith	1	8	0	0/0	0/0	0	54
Nedney	0	0	0	4/4	8/10	0	28
Carswell	0	3	0	0/0	0/0	0	18
De. Clark	0	3	0	0/0	0/0	0	18
Davis	2	0	0	0/0	0/0	0	12
Griffith	0	2	0	0/0	0/0	0	12
Spencer	0	0	2	0/0	0/0	0	12
Buckley	0	0	1	0/0	0/0	0	6
Chamberlain	0	1	0	0/0	0/0	0	6
Coleman	1	0	0	0/0	0/0	0	6
Crockett	0	0	1	0/0	0/0	0	6
Frerotte	1	0	0	0/0	0/0	0	6
Gold	0	0	1	0/0	0/0	0	6
Griese	1	0	0	0/0	0/0	0	6
Jenkins	0	0	1	0/0	0/0	0	6
McGriff	0	1	0	0/0	0/0	0	6
O'Neal	0	0	1	0/0	0/0	0	6
Pryce	0	0	1	0/0	0/0	0	6
D. Smith	0	1	0	0/0	0/0	0	6
Suttle	0	0	1	0/0	0/0	0	6
Broncos	21	28	9	53/53	26/34	1	485
Opponents	13	26	6	42/43	19/23	0	369

2-Pt. Conversions: Anderson, McCaffrey. Broncos 2-5, Opponents 0-2.

RUSHING	Att.	Yds.	Avg.	LG	TD
Anderson	297	1,487	5.0	80t	15
Davis	78	282	3.6	24	2
Coleman	54	183	3.4	24t	1
Griese	29	102	3.5	18	1
R. Smith	6	99	16.5	50t	1
Gary	13	80	6.2	25	0
Frerotte	22	64	2.9	13t	1
Harris	10	22	2.2	6	0
Griffith	5	4	0.8	3	0
Jackson	1	-1	-1.0	-1	0
Rouen	1	-11	-11.0	-11	0
Broncos	516	2,311	4.5	80t	21
Opponents	344	1,598	4.6	77t	13

RECEIVING	No.	Yds.	Avg.	LG	TD
McCaffrey	101	1,317	13.0	61	9
R. Smith	100	1,602	16.0	49	8
Carswell	49	495	10.1	43t	3
De. Clark	27	339	12.6	44	3
Anderson	23	169	7.3	18	0
Chamberlain	22	283	12.9	38	1
Griffith	16	101	6.3	16	2
Brooks	3	51	17.0	25	0
Gary	3	10	3.3	7	0
McGriff	2	51	25.5	43t	1
Harris	2	19	9.5	16	0
Davis	2	4	2.0	5	0
Montgomery	1	10	10.0	10	0
Miller	1	7	7.0	7	0
Coleman	1	5	5.0	5	0
D. Smith	1	1	1.0	1t	1
Broncos	354	4,464	12.6	61	28
Opponents	310	4,197	13.5	83t	26

INTERCEPTIONS	No.	Yds.	Avg.	LG	TD
Buckley	6	110	18.3	33	1
Jenkins	4	61	15.3	36t	1
Crockett	4	31	7.8	26t	1
Spencer	3	102	34.0	79t	2
Wilson	3	21	7.0	20	0
E. Brown	3	9	3.0	9	0
Romanowski	2	0	0.0	3	0
Mobley	1	9	9.0	9	0
Kennedy	1	0	0.0	0	0
Broncos	27	343	12.7	79t	5
Opponents	12	144	12.0	75t	1

PUNTING	No.	Yds.	Avg.	In 20	LG
Rouen	61	2,455	40.2	18	62
Broncos	62	2,455	39.6	18	62
Opponents	73	3,196	43.8	25	69

PUNT RETURNS	No.	FC	Yds.	Avg.	LG	TD
O'Neal	34	11	354	10.4	64	0
Buckley	2	1	10	5.0	11	0
Broncos	36	12	364	10.1	64	0
Opponents	23	9	270	11.7	86t	1

KICKOFF RETURNS	No.	Yds.	Avg.	LG	TD
O'Neal	46	1,102	24.0	87t	1
Cole	11	264	24.0	37	0
D. Smith	5	73	14.6	17	0
Chamberlain	2	25	12.5	13	0
Carswell	1	0	0.0	0	0
Miller	1	13	13.0	13	0
Broncos	66	1,477	22.4	87t	1
Opponents	90	1,934	21.5	100t	1

FIELD GOALS	1-19	20-29	30-39	40-49	50+
Elam	0/0	7/7	6/7	4/9	1/1
Nedney	0/0	6/6	1/1	1/2	0/1
Broncos	0/0	13/13	7/8	5/11	1/2
Opponents	3/3	5/5	3/4	8/11	0/0

SACKS	No.
Pryce	12.0
Pittman	7.0
Wilson	5.0
Tanuvasa	4.0
Romanowski	3.5
Hasselbach	2.5
Gold	2.0
Mobley	2.0
Reagor	2.0
E. Brown	1.0
Crockett	1.0
Spencer	1.0
Traylor	1.0
Broncos	44.0
Opponents	30.0

2001 DRAFT CHOICES

Round	Name	Pos.	College
1	Willie Middlebrooks	DB	Minnesota
2	Paul Toviessi	DE	Marshall
3	Reggie Hayward	DE	Iowa State
4	Ben Hamilton	C	Minnesota
	Nick Harris	P	California
6	Kevin Kasper	WR	Iowa

DENVER BRONCOS

2001 VETERAN ROSTER

No.		Name	Pos.	Ht.	Wt.	Birthdate	NFL Exp.	College	Hometown	How Acq.	'00 Games/ Starts
38		Anderson, Mike	RB	6-0	230	9/21/73	2	Utah	Winnsboro, S.C.	D6-'00	16/12
79		Berry, Bertrand	DE	6-3	250	8/15/75	4	Notre Dame	Humble, Texas	FA-'01	0*
11		Beuerlein, Steve	QB	6-3	220	3/7/65	15	Notre Dame	Anaheim, Calif.	FA-'01	16/16*
76		Brooks, Ethan	T	6-6	297	4/27/72	5	Williams College	Westminster, Conn.	UFA(Ariz)-'01	15/2*
43		Brown, DeAuntae	CB	5-10	195	4/28/74	2	Central State (Ohio)	Detroit, Mich.	FA-'00	0*
26		Brown, Eric	S	6-0	210	3/20/75	4	Mississippi State	San Antonio, Texas	D2-'98	16/16
27	#	Buckley, Terrell	CB	5-9	176	6/7/71	10	Florida State	Pascagoula, Miss.	FA-'00	16/16
55		Burns, Keith	LB	6-2	235	5/16/72	8	Oklahoma State	Greeleyville, S.C.	FA-'00	13/0
65		Carlisle, Cooper	G-T	6-5	295	8/11/77	2	Florida	McComb, Miss.	D4b-'00	14/0
89		Carswell, Dwayne	TE	6-3	260	1/18/72	8	Liberty	Jacksonville, Fla.	CFA-'94	16/16
37		Carter, Tony	FB	6-0	235	8/23/72	8	Minnesota	Columbus, Ohio	UFA(NE)-'01	16/6*
47		Clark, Darius	S	5-10	204	4/13/77	2	Duke	Tampa, Fla.	CFA-'00	0*
88		Clark, Desmond	TE	6-3	255	4/20/77	3	Wake Forest	Lakeland, Fla.	D6a-'99	16/2
48		Coghill, George	S	6-0	210	3/30/70	5	Wake Forest	Fredericksburg, Va.	FA-'97	16/0
84		Cole, Chris	WR	6-0	195	11/12/77	2	Texas A&M	Orange, Texas	D3-'00	8/0
21		Coleman, KaRon	RB	5-7	198	5/22/78	2	Stephen F. Austin	Missouri City, Texas	CFA-'00	9/0
59		Crockett, Henri	LB	6-2	238	10/28/74	5	Florida State	Pompano Beach, Fla.	UFA(Atl)-'01	15/12*
30		Davis, Terrell	RB	5-11	210	10/28/72	7	Georgia	San Diego, Calif.	D6b-'95	5/4
1		Elam, Jason	K	5-11	200	3/8/70	9	Hawaii	Ft. Walton Beach, Fla.	D3b-'93	13/0
85		Fields, Chafie	WR	6-1	200	2/4/77	2	Penn State	Philadelphia, Pa.	FA-'00	0*
67		Fordham, Todd	T	6-5	308	10/9/73	5	Florida State	Tifton, Ga.	UFA(Jax)-'01	16/8*
12		Frerotte, Gus	QB	6-3	230	7/31/71	8	Tulsa	Ford City, Pa.	UFA(Det)-'00	10/6
64		Friedman, Lennie	G	6-3	285	10/13/76	3	Duke	West Milford, N.J.	D2b-'99	16/8
22		Gary, Olandis	RB	5-11	218	5/18/75	3	Georgia	Washington, D.C.	D4-'99	1/0
52		Gold, Ian	LB	6-0	223	8/23/78	2	Michigan	Ann Arbor, Mich.	D2a-'00	16/0
14	†	Griese, Brian	QB	6-3	215	3/18/75	4	Michigan	Miami, Fla.	D3-'98	10/10
29	#	Griffith, Howard	FB	6-0	240	11/17/67	9	Illinois	Chicago, Ill.	UFA(Car)-'97	14/14
86		Hape, Patrick	TE	6-4	262	6/6/74	5	Alabama	Killen, Ala.	UFA(TB)-'01	16/2*
96		Hasselbach, Harald	DE	6-6	285	9/22/67	8	Washington	Tsawassen, B.C., Canada	FA-'94	16/1
17		Jackson, Jarious	QB	6-0	228	5/3/77	2	Notre Dame	Tupelo, Miss.	D7a-'00	2/0
32		Jenkins, Billy	S	5-10	205	7/8/74	4	Howard	Albuquerque, N.M.	T(StL)-'00	16/16
90		Johnson, Jerry	DT	6-0	290	7/11/77	2	Florida State	Ft. Pierce, Fla.	D4a-'00	0*
60	#	Jones, K.C.	C	6-1	275	3/28/74	5	Miami	Midland, Texas	CFA-'97	16/0
28		Kennedy, Kenoy	S	6-1	215	11/15/77	2	Arkansas	Terrell, Texas	D2b-'00	13/0
10		Kennison, Eddie	WR	6-1	190	1/20/73	6	Louisiana State	Lake Charles, La.	UFA(Chi)-'01	16/10*
78		Lepsis, Matt	T	6-4	290	1/13/74	5	Colorado	Conroe, Texas	CFA-'97	16/16
94		Lett, Leon	DT	6-6	290	10/12/68	11	Emporia State	Mobile, Ala.	UFA(Dall)-'01	9/7*
2		Lindsey, Steve	K	6-1	185	11/25/74	3	Mississippi	Hattiesburg, Miss.	FA-'00	16/0*
97	#	Lodish, Mike	DT	6-3	270	8/11/67	12	UCLA	Birmingham, Mich.	UFA(Buff)-'95	16/0
58		London, Antonio	LB	6-2	238	4/14/71	7	Alabama	Tullahoma, Tenn.	FA-'01	0*
87		McCaffrey, Ed	WR	6-5	215	8/17/68	11	Stanford	Allentown, Pa.	UFA(SF)-'95	16/16
57		McDonald, Ricardo	LB	6-2	252	11/8/69	9	Pittsburgh	Paterson, N.J.	FA-'01	0*
91		McGlockton, Chester	DT	6-4	334	9/16/69	10	Clemson	Whiteville, N.C.	FA-'01	15/15*
83		McGriff, Travis	WR	5-8	185	6/24/76	3	Florida	Gainesville, Fla.	D3b-'99	15/0
82		Miller, Billy	TE	6-3	230	4/24/77	3	Southern California	Westlake Village, Calif.	D7a-'99	12/0
36		Mitchell, Basil	RB	5-10	207	9/7/75	2	Texas Christian	Mt. Pleasant, Texas	FA-'01	0*
51		Mobley, John	LB	6-1	236	10/10/73	6	Kutztown	Chester, Pa.	D1-'96	15/14
81		Montgomery, Scottie	WR	6-1	195	5/26/78	2	Duke	Cherryville, N.C.	FA-'00	4/0
19		Moore, Muneer	WR	6-1	200	3/15/77	2	Richmond	Eastville, Va.	D5-'00	0*
66		Nalen, Tom	C	6-3	286	5/13/71	8	Boston College	Foxboro, Mass.	D7c-'94	16/16
62		Neil, Dan	G	6-2	285	10/21/73	5	Texas	Cypress Creek, Texas	D3-'97	16/16
72		Neujahr, Quentin	C	6-4	302	1/30/71	7	Kansas State	Utica, Neb.	FA-'01	16/2*
24		O'Neal, Deltha	CB	5-10	196	1/30/77	2	California	Milpitas, Calif.	D1-'00	16/0
63		Ostrowski, Phil	G	6-4	291	9/23/75	4	Penn State	Wilkes-Barre, Pa.	FA-'01	13/0*
95		Pittman, Kavika	DE	6-6	273	10/9/74	6	McNeese State	Leesville, La.	UFA(Dall)-'00	15/15
20		Poole, Tyrone	CB	5-8	188	2/3/72	7	Fort Valley State	La Grange, Ga.	FA-'01	15/12*
31		Pounds, Darryl	CB	5-10	189	7/21/72	7	Nicholls State	Magnolia, Miss.	UFA(Wash)-'00	9/0
93		Pryce, Trevor	DT	6-5	295	8/3/75	5	Clemson	Winter Park, Fla.	D1-'97	16/16
99		Reagor, Montae	DT	6-2	280	6/29/77	3	Texas Tech	Waxahachie, Texas	D2a-'99	13/0
53		Romanowski, Bill	LB	6-4	245	4/2/66	14	Boston College	Vernon, Conn.	UFA(Phil)-'96	16/16
16		Rouen, Tom	P	6-3	225	6/9/68	9	Colorado	Hinsdale, Ill.	FA-'93	16/0
71		Ruhman, Chris	T	6-5	321	12/19/74	3	Texas A&M	Houston, Texas	FA-'01	0*
42		Smith, Detron	FB	5-10	230	2/25/74	6	Texas A&M	Dallas, Texas	D3a-'96	16/0
80		Smith, Rod	WR	6-0	200	5/15/70	7	Missouri Southern	Texarkana, Ark.	CFA-'94	16/16
33		Spencer, Jimmy	CB	5-9	188	3/29/69	10	Florida	Belle Glade, Fla.	FA-'00	16/6
35		Suttle, Jason	CB	5-10	182	12/2/74	2	Wisconsin	Burnsville, Minn.	FA-'00	5/0
98		Tanuvasa, Maa	DE	6-2	270	11/6/70	8	Hawaii	Mililani, Hawaii	FA-'95	16/16
41		Taylor, Cordell	CB	6-0	188	12/22/73	3	Hampton	Norfolk, Va.	FA-'01	0*
70	†	Teague, Trey	T	6-5	292	12/27/74	4	Tennessee	Jackson, Tenn.	D7a-'98	2/0
25		Walker, Denard	CB	6-1	190	8/9/73	5	Louisiana State	Garland, Texas	UFA(Tenn)-'01	15/15*
97		Washington, Keith	DE	6-4	275	12/18/72	7	Nevada-Las Vegas	Dallas, Texas	FA-'01	16/0*
56		Wilson, Al	LB	6-0	240	6/21/77	3	Tennessee	Jackson, Tenn.	D1-'99	15/14
54		Woodall, Lee	LB	6-1	230	10/31/69	8	West Chester	Carlislie, Pa.	FA-'01	16/16*

* Berry last active with Indianapolis in '99; Beuerlein and Woodall played 16 games with Carolina in '00; Brooks played 15 games with Arizona; D. Brown last active with Philadlelphia in '97; Carter played 16 games with New England; Da. Clark was on the practice squad for 14 games; Crockett played 15 games with Atlanta; Fields was inactive for 6 games; Fordham played 16 games with Jacksonville; Hape played 16 games with Tampa Bay; Johnson was inactive for 16 games; Kennison played 16 games with Chicago; Lett played 9 games with Dallas; Lindsey played 10 games with Jacksonville; London last active with Green Bay in '98; McDonald and Taylor last active with Chicago in '99; McGlockton played 15 games with Kansas City; Mitchell played 1 game with Green Bay; Moore missed '00 season because of injury; Neujahr played 16 games with Jacksonville; Ostrowski played 13 games with San Francisco; Poole played 15 games with Indianapolis; Ruhman last active with San Francisco in '99; Walker played 15 games with Tennessee; Washington played 16 games with Baltimore.

† Restricted free agent; subject to developments.

Unrestricted free agent; subject to developments.

Retired—Mark Schlereth, 12-year guard, 8 games in '00.

Players lost through free agency (2): TE Byron Chamberlain (Minn; 15 games in '00), CB Ray Crockett (KC; 13).

Also played with Broncos in '00—DE Lester Archambeau (3 games), LB Glenn Cadrez (16), RB Raymont Harris (3), T Tony Jones (16), DT Keith Traylor (16).

COACHING STAFF

Head Coach,
Mike Shanahan

Pro Career: Became the eleventh head coach in Broncos history on January 31, 1995, coming to Denver from the 1994 world champion San Francisco 49ers, where he served as offensive coordinator from 1992-94. Mike Shanahan led the Broncos to back-to-back Super Bowl championships in 1997 and 1998, becoming just the fifth head coach to accomplish that feat. Shanahan led Denver to seven postseason wins in those two seasons, the highest two-year total in history. His 1997 Broncos became just the second Wild Card team to win the Super Bowl, and they became the first AFC team to capture the NFL crown in 14 years. In 1996 Shanahan led the Broncos to a 13-3 record and the AFC Western Division title, tying the club record for wins in a season and leading the NFL in total offense. In 1995 he improved the Broncos to an 8-8 mark. During his NFL career, Shanahan has been a part of teams that have played in nine AFC or NFC Championship Games, in addition to his six Super Bowl appearances, five with Denver and Super Bowl XXIX with San Francisco. In his 25 seasons coaching in the NFL and at the college level, Shanahan's teams have participated in postseason playoffs or bowl games 18 times. A driving force behind the Broncos' offense for all three of the team's Super Bowl appearances in the 1980s (following the '86, '87, and '89 seasons), he first came to Denver in 1984 as wide receivers coach. Shanahan was Broncos' offensive coordinator from 1985-87, and returned to Denver as quarterbacks coach on October 16, 1989, after serving as the Los Angeles Raiders' head coach in 1988 and through the first four games of 1989. His record with the Raiders was 8-12. Career record: 79-46.

Background: Shanahan began his coaching career at Oklahoma in 1975-76, also coaching at Northern Arizona (1977), Eastern Illinois (1978), Minnesota (1979), and Florida (1980-83). During his tenure on the college level, Shanahan's teams had a 77-29-3 (.720) record, including national championship seasons at Oklahoma in 1975 and at Eastern Illinois.

Personal: Shanahan was born in Oak Park, Illinois, on August 24, 1952. He was a wishbone quarterback-defensive back at Eastern Illinois, graduating in 1974 with a degree in physical education and a master's degree in 1975. Mike and his wife, Peggy, have two children, son Kyle and daughter Krystal.

ASSISTANT COACHES

Frank Bush, special teams; born January 10, 1963, Athens, Ga., lives in Englewood, Colo. Linebacker North Carolina State 1981-84. Pro linebacker Houston Oilers 1985-86. Pro coach: Houston Oilers 1992-94, joined Broncos in 1995.

Larry Coyer, linebackers; born April 19, 1943, Huntington, W. Va., lives in Englewood, Colo. Linebacker Marshall 1962-64. No pro playing experience. College coach: Marshall 1965-67, Iowa 1974-77, Oklahoma State 1978, Iowa State 1979-1983, 1995-96, UCLA 1987-89, Houston 1990, Ohio State 1991-92, East Carolina 1993, Pittsburgh 1997-99. Pro coach: Michigan Panthers (USFL) 1984-85, Memphis Showboats (USFL) 1986, New York Jets 1994, joined Broncos in 2000.

Rick Dennison, offensive line; born June 22, 1958, in Kalispell, Mont., lives in Englewood, Colo. Tight end Colorado State 1976-79. Pro linebacker Denver Broncos 1982-1990. Pro coach: Joined Broncos in 1995.

Karl Dorrell, wide receivers; born December 18, 1968, Alameda, Calif., lives in Englewood, Colo. Wide receiver UCLA 1982-86. No pro playing experience. College coach: UCLA 1988, Central Florida 1989, Northern Arizona 1990-91, Colorado 1992-93, 1995-98, Arizona State 1994. Pro coach: Joined Broncos in 2000.

George Dyer, defensive line; born May 4, 1940, Alhambra, Calif., lives in Aurora, Colo. Center-linebacker U.C. Santa Barbara 1961-63. No pro playing experience. College coach: Humboldt State 1964-66, Coalinga (Calif.) J.C. 1967 (head coach), Portland State 1968-1971, Idaho 1972, San Jose State 1973, Michigan State 1977-79, Arizona State 1980-81. Pro coach: Winnipeg Blue Bombers (CFL) 1974-76, Buffalo Bills 1982, Seattle Seahawks 1983-1991, Los Angeles Rams 1992-94, joined Broncos in 1995.

Alex Gibbs, asst. head coach-offensive line; born February 11, 1941, Morganton, N.C., lives in Greenwood Village, Colo. Running back-defensive back Davidson College 1959-1963. No pro playing experience. College coach: Duke 1969-1970, Kentucky 1971-72, West Virginia 1973-74, Ohio State 1975-78, Auburn 1979-1981, Georgia 1982-83. Pro coach: Denver Broncos 1984-87, Los Angeles Raiders 1988-89, San Diego Chargers 1990-91, Indianapolis Colts 1992, Kansas City Chiefs 1993-94, rejoined Broncos in 1995.

David Gibbs, safeties; born January 10, 1968, Mount Airy, N.C., lives in Castle Pines, Colo. Defensive back Colorado 1986-1990. No pro playing experience. College coach: Oklahoma 1991-92, Colorado 1993-94, Kansas 1995-96, Minnesota 1997-2000. Pro coach: Joined Broncos in 2001.

Gary Kubiak, offensive coordinator-quarterbacks; born August 15, 1961, Houston, Texas, lives in Englewood, Colo. Quarterback Texas A&M 1979-1982. Pro quarterback Denver Broncos 1983-1991. College coach: Texas A&M 1992-93. Pro coach: San Francisco 49ers 1994, joined Broncos in 1995.

Anthony Lynn, special teams assistant; born December 21, 1968, McKinney, Texas, lives in Centennial, Colo. Fullback Texas Tech 1987-1990. Pro fullback Denver Broncos 1993, 1997-99, San Francisco 49ers 1995-96. Pro coach: Joined Broncos in 2000.

Pat McPherson, offensive assistant; born April 15, 1969, Santa Clara, Calif., live in Englewood, Colo. Linebacker Santa Clara 1991-92. No pro playing experience. Pro coach: Joined Broncos in 1998.

Ron Milus, defensive backs; born November 25, 1963, Tacoma, Wash., lives in Englewood, Colo. Defensive back Washington 1982-85. No pro playing experience. College coach: Washington 1991-98, Texas A&M 1999. Pro coach: Joined Broncos in 2000.

Brian Pariani, tight ends; born July 2, 1965, San Francisco, lives in Castle Pines, Colo. No college or pro playing experience. College coach: UCLA 1989. Pro coach: San Francisco 49ers 1991-94, joined Broncos in 1995.

Ray Rhodes, defensive coordinator; born October 20, 1950, Mexia, Texas, lives in Englewood, Colo. Running back Texas Christian 1969-1970, wide receiver, defensive back, and kick returner Tulsa 1972-73. Pro wide receiver-defensive back New York Giants 1974-79, San Francisco 49ers 1980. Pro coach: San Francisco 49ers 1981-1991, 1994, Green Bay Packers 1992-93, 1999, Philadelphia Eagles 1995-98, Washington Redskins 2000, joined Broncos in 2001.

Greg Saporta, asst. strength and conditioning; born February 2, 1957, New York, N.Y., lives in Englewood, Colo. Wide receiver Buffalo State 1977-79. No pro playing experience. College coach: Florida 1981-88, 1993-94, North Carolina 1989-1992. Pro coach: Joined Broncos in 1995.

Cedric Smith, asst. strength and conditioning; born May 27, 1968, Enterprise, Ala., lives in Englewood, Colo. Running back Florida 1986-89. Pro fullback Minnesota Vikings 1990, New Orleans Saints 1991, Washington Redskins 1994-95, Arizona Cardinals 1996-98. Pro coach: Joined Broncos in 2001.

John Teerlinck, pass rush specialist; born April 9, 1951, Rochester, N.Y., lives in Englewood, Colo. Defensive lineman Western Illinois 1970-73. Pro defensive tackle San Diego Chargers 1974-76. College coach: Iowa Lakes J.C. 1977, Eastern Illinois 1978-79, Illinois 1980-82. Pro coach: Chicago Blitz (USFL) 1983, Arizona Wranglers/Outlaws (USFL) 1984-85, Cleveland Browns 1989-1990, Los Angeles Rams 1991, Minnesota Vikings 1992-94, Detroit Lions 1995-96, joined Broncos in 1997.

Bobby Turner, running backs; born May 6, 1949, East Chicago, Ind., lives in Englewood, Colo. Defensive back Indiana State 1968-1971. No pro playing experience. College coach: Indiana State 1975-1982, Fresno State 1983-88, Ohio State 1989-1990, Purdue 1991-94. Pro coach: Joined Broncos in 1995.

Rich Tuten, strength and conditioning; born December 30, 1953, Columbia, S.C., lives in Englewood, Colo. Nose guard Clemson 1976-78. No pro playing experience. College coach: Florida 1979-1988, 1993-94, North Carolina 1989-1992. Pro coach: Joined Broncos in 1995.

Steve Watson, defensive assistant; born May 28, 1957, Baltimore, lives in Aurora, Colo. Wide receiver Temple 1975-78. Pro wide receiver Denver 1979-1987. Pro coach: Joined Broncos in 2001.

Zaven Yaralian, head coach's assistant; born February 5, 1952, Syria, lives in Englewood, Colo. Cornerback Nebraska 1972-73. Pro cornerback Green Bay Packers 1974. College coach: Nebraska 1975, Washington State 1976-77, Missouri 1978-1982, Florida 1983-1987, Colorado 1988-89. Pro coach: Chicago Bears 1990-1992, New York Giants 1993-96, New Orleans Saints 1997-99, joined Broncos in 2001.

2001 FIRST-YEAR ROSTER

Name	Pos.	Ht.	Wt.	Birthdate	College	Hometown	How Acq.
Brannon, Robert (1)	DT	6-5	305	9/9/78	Iowa State	Rialto, Calif.	FA
Dominguez, Matt	TE	6-2	219	6/27/78	Sam Houston State	Georgetown, Texas	FA
Feugill, John (1)	T	6-7	309	12/20/75	Maryland	Lawrence, Mass.	FA-'00
Hamilton, Ben	C	6-4	283	8/18/77	Minnesota	Minneapolis, Minn.	D4a
Harris, Nick	P	6-2	220	7/23/78	California	Phoenix, Ariz.	D4b
Hayward, Reggie	DE	6-5	255	3/14/79	Iowa State	Dolton, Ill.	D3
Herndon, Steve (1)	G	6-4	305	5/25/77	Georgia	La Grange, Ga.	FA-'00
Kasper, Kevin	WR	6-0	193	12/23/77	Iowa	Burr Ridge, Ill.	D6
Krick, Jon (1)	DT	6-2	283	11/24/72	Purdue	Mount Morris, Ill.	FA
Marshall, Lemar (1)	S	6-2	208	12/17/76	Michigan State	Cincinnati, Ohio	FA
McAda, Ronnie (1)	QB	6-3	205	12/6/73	Army	Mesquite, Texas	FA
McCaffrey, Brent	T	6-5	275	5/12/77	Southern California	Fresno, Calif.	FA
Middlebrooks, Willie	CB	6-1	200	2/12/79	Minnesota	Homestead, Fla.	D1
Stack, Mike (1)	FB	6-2	253	4/2/78	Northern Illinois	Taylor, Mich.	FA
Toviessi, Paul	DE	6-6	260	2/26/78	Marshall	Alexandria, Va.	D2
Young, Donnie (1)	G	6-4	312	11/17/73	Florida	Venice, Fla.	FA-'00

The term NFL Rookie is defined as a player who is in his first season of professional football and has not been on the roster of another professional football team for any regular-season or postseason games. A Rookie is designated by an "R" on NFL rosters. Players who have been active in another professional football league or players who have NFL experience, including either preseason training camp or being on an Active List or Inactive List, or on Reserve/Injured or Reserve/Physically Unable to Perform for fewer than six regular-season games, are termed NFL First-Year Players. An NFL First-Year Player is designated by a "1" on NFL rosters. Thereafter, a player is credited with an additional year of experience for each season in which he accumulates six games on the Active List or Inactive List, or on Reserve/Injured or Reserve/Physically Unable to Perform.

NOTES

INDIANAPOLIS COLTS

American Football Conference
Eastern Division
Team Colors: Royal Blue and White
P.O. Box 535000
Indianapolis, Indiana 46253
Telephone: (317) 297-2658

CLUB OFFICIALS

Owner and CEO: Jim Irsay
President: Bill Polian
Senior Executive Vice President: Pete Ward
Executive Vice President: Bob Terpening
General Counsel: Dan Luther
Senior Vice President-Sales and Marketing: Ray Compton
Vice President-Finance: Kurt Humphrey
Vice President-Ticket Operations: Larry Hall
Vice President-Public Relations: Craig Kelley
Vice President-Business Development: Tom Zupancic
Director of Football Operations: Dom Anile
Director of Pro Player Personnel: Clyde Powers
Director of College Scouting: Mike Butler
Director of Pro Scouting: Chris Polian
Director of Player Development: Steve Champlin
Executive Director of Sponsorship Sales: Jay Souers
Director of Ticket Sales/Marketing: Greg Hylton
Director of Community Development/Player Relations: Bill Brooks
Director of Community Relations/Marketing: Nicole Duncan
Assistant Director of Public Relations: Ryan Robinson
Equipment Manager: Jon Scott
Video Director: Marty Heckscher
Head Trainer: Hunter Smith
Assistant Equipment Manager: Mike Mays
Assistant Trainers: Dave Hammer, Dave Walston
Assistant Video Director: John Starliper
Purchasing Administrator: Dave Filar
Stadium: RCA Dome (built in 1983)
•**Capacity:** 56,127
100 South Capitol Avenue
Indianapolis, Indiana 46225
Playing Surface: AstroTurf
Training Camp: Rose-Hulman Institute
5500 Wabash Avenue
Terre Haute, Indiana 47803

2001 SCHEDULE

PRESEASON

Aug. 11	**Seattle**	7:00
Aug. 18	**Detroit**	7:00
Aug. 24	at Minnesota	7:00
Aug. 30	at Cincinnati	7:30

REGULAR SEASON

Sept. 9	at New York Jets	1:00
Sept. 16	**Denver**	12:00
Sept. 23	**Buffalo**	12:00
Sept. 30	at New England	1:00
Oct. 7	Open Date	
Oct. 14	**Oakland**	7:30
Oct. 21	**New England**	12:00
Oct. 28	at Kansas City	12:00
Nov. 4	at Buffalo	4:15
Nov. 11	**Miami**	1:00
Nov. 18	at New Orleans	12:00
Nov. 25	**San Francisco**	1:00
Dec. 2	at Baltimore	1:00
Dec. 10	at Miami (Mon.)	9:00
Dec. 16	**Atlanta**	1:00
Dec. 23	**New York Jets**	8:30
Dec. 30	at St. Louis	12:00

RECORD HOLDERS

INDIVIDUAL RECORDS—CAREER

Category	Name	Performance
Rushing (Yds.)	Lydell Mitchell, 1972-77	5,487
Passing (Yds.)	Johnny Unitas, 1956-1972	39,768
Passing (TDs)	Johnny Unitas, 1956-1972	287
Receiving (No.)	Raymond Berry, 1955-1967	631
Receiving (Yds.)	Raymond Berry, 1955-1967	9,275
Interceptions	Bob Boyd, 1960-68	57
Punting (Avg.)	Chris Gardocki, 1994-98	44.8
Punt Return (Avg.)	Ron Gardin, 1970-71	13.5
Kickoff Return (Avg.)	Jim Duncan, 1969-1971	32.5
Field Goals	Dean Biasucci 1984, 1986-1994	176
Touchdowns (Tot.)	Lenny Moore, 1956-1967	113
Points	Dean Biasucci, 1984, 1986-1994	783

INDIVIDUAL RECORDS—SINGLE SEASON

Category	Name	Performance
Rushing (Yds.)	Edgerrin James, 2000	1,709
Passing (Yds.)	Peyton Manning, 2000	4,413
Passing (TDs)	Peyton Manning, 2000	33
Receiving (No.)	Marvin Harrison, 1999	115
Receiving (Yds.)	Marvin Harrison, 1999	1,663
Interceptions	Tom Keane, 1953	11
Punting (Avg.)	Rohn Stark, 1985	45.9
Punt Return (Avg.)	Clarence Verdin, 1989	12.9
Kickoff Return (Avg.)	Jim Duncan, 1970	35.4
Field Goals	Cary Blanchard, 1996	36
Touchdowns (Tot.)	Lenny Moore, 1964	20
Points	Mike Vanderjagt, 1999	145

INDIVIDUAL RECORDS—SINGLE GAME

Category	Name	Performance
Rushing (Yds.)	Edgerrin James, 10-15-00	219
Passing (Yds.)	Peyton Manning, 9-25-00	440
Passing (TDs)	Gary Cuozzo, 11-14-65	5
	Gary Hogeboom, 10-4-87	5
Receiving (No.)	Marvin Harrison, 12-26-99	14
Receiving (Yds.)	Raymond Berry, 11-10-57	224
Interceptions	Many times	3
	Last time by Mike Prior, 12-20-92	
Field Goals	Many times	5
	Last time by Cary Blanchard, 9-21-97	
Touchdowns (Tot.)	Many times	4
	Last time by Eric Dickerson, 10-31-88	
Points	Many times	24
	Last time by Eric Dickerson, 10-31-88	

RCA DOME

N

COACHING HISTORY

BALTIMORE 1953-1983
(346-363-7)

1953	Keith Molesworth	3-9-0
1954-1962	Weeb Ewbank	61-52-1
1963-69	Don Shula	73-26-4
1970-72	Don McCafferty*	26-11-1
1972	John Sandusky	4-5-0
1973-74	Howard Schnellenberger**	4-13-0
1974	Joe Thomas	2-9-0
1975-79	Ted Marchibroda	41-36-0
1980-81	Mike McCormack	9-23-0
1982-84	Frank Kush***	11-28-1
1984	Hal Hunter	0-1-0
1985-86	Rod Dowhower****	5-24-0
1986-1991	Ron Meyer#	36-36-0
1991	Rick Venturi	1-10-0
1992-95	Ted Marchibroda	32-35-0
1996-97	Lindy Infante	12-21-0
1998-2000	Jim Mora	26-24-0

*Released after five games in 1972
**Released after three games in 1974
***Resigned after 15 games in 1984
****Released after 13 games in 1986
#Released after five games in 1991

2000 TEAM RECORD

PRESEASON (3-2)

Date	Result		Opponent
7/29	L	13-20	Atlanta
8/5	L	16-28	at Seattle
8/12	W	17-0	at New Orleans at West Lafayette, Ind.
8/19	W	24-23	vs. Pittsburgh, at Mexico City
8/24	W	32-30	Minnesota

REGULAR SEASON (10-6)

Date	Result		Opponent	Att.
9/3	W	27-14	at Kansas City	78,357
9/10	L	31-38	Oakland	56,769
9/25	W	43-14	Jacksonville	56,816
10/1	W	18-16	at Buffalo	72,617
10/8	L	16-24	at New England	60,292
10/15	W	37-24	at Seattle	63,593
10/22	W	30-23	New England	56,828
10/29	W	30-18	Detroit	56,971
11/5	L	24-27	at Chicago	66,944
11/12	W	23-15	New York Jets	56,657
11/19	L	24-26	at Green Bay	59,869
11/26	L	14-17	Miami	56,935
12/3	L	17-27	at New York Jets	78,138
12/11	W	44-20	Buffalo	56,671
12/17	W	20-13	at Miami	73,884
12/24	W	31-10	Minnesota	56,672

POSTSEASON (0-1)

Date	Result		Opponent	Att.
12/30	L	17-23	at Miami (OT)	73,193

SCORE BY PERIODS

Colts	73	117	84	155	0	— 429
Opponents	52	106	86	82	0	— 326

ATTENDANCE

Home 432,899 Away 550,274 Total 983,173
Single-game home record, 61,139 (10/20/97)
Single-season home record, 481,305 (1984)

2000 TEAM STATISTICS

	Colts	Opp.
Total First Downs	357	310
Rushing	111	109
Passing	213	177
Penalty	33	24
Third Down: Made/Att	94/201	84/217
Third Down Pct.	46.8	38.7
Fourth Down: Made/Att	9/10	10/14
Fourth Down Pct.	90.0	71.4
Total Net Yards	6,141	5,357
Avg. Per Game	383.8	334.8
Total Plays	1,026	1,018
Avg. Per Play	6.0	5.3
Net Yards Rushing	1,859	1,935
Avg. Per Game	116.2	120.9
Total Rushes	435	446
Net Yards Passing	4,282	3,422
Avg. Per Game	267.6	213.9
Sacked/Yards Lost	20/131	42/252
Gross Yards	4413	3674
Att./Completions	571/357	530/317
Completion Pct.	62.5	59.8
Had Intercepted	15	14
Punts/Average	65/44.7	82/42.7
Net Punting Avg.	65/36.4	82/36.2
Penalties/Yards	89/866	103/820
Fumbles/Ball Lost	20/14	16/8
Touchdowns	50	37
Rushing	14	13
Passing	33	22
Returns	3	2
Avg. Time of Possession	29:33	30:27

2000 INDIVIDUAL STATISTICS

Passing	Att.	Comp.	Yds.	Pct.	TD	Int.	Tkld.	Rate
Manning	571	357	4,413	62.5	33	15	20/131	94.7
Colts	571	357	4,413	62.5	33	15	20/131	94.7
Opponents	530	317	3,674	59.8	22	14	42/252	83.6

SCORING	TD R	TD P	TD Rt	PAT	FG	Saf	PTS
Vanderjagt	0	0	0	46/46	25/27	0	121
James	13	5	0	0/0	0/0	0	110
Harrison	0	14	0	0/0	0/0	0	84
Pollard	0	3	0	0/0	0/0	0	20
Dilger	0	3	0	0/0	0/0	0	18
Pathon	0	3	0	0/0	0/0	0	18
Wilkins	0	3	0	0/0	0/0	0	18
Burris	0	0	1	0/0	0/0	0	6
Finn	0	1	0	0/0	0/0	0	6
Green	0	1	0	0/0	0/0	0	6
Holsey	0	0	1	0/0	0/0	0	6
Manning	1	0	0	0/0	0/0	0	6
Muhammad	0	0	1	0/0	0/0	0	6
Bratzke	0	0	0	0/0	0/0	1	2
J. Williams	0	0	0	0/0	0/0	1	2
Colts	14	33	3	46/46	25/27	2	429
Opponents	13	22	2	33/33	21/28	1	326

2-Pt. Conversions: James, Pollard.
Colts 2-4, Opponents 3-4.

RUSHING	Att.	Yds.	Avg.	LG	TD
James	387	1,709	4.4	30	13
Manning	37	116	3.1	14	1
Gordon	4	13	3.3	6	0
Smith	1	11	11.0	11	0
Wilkins	3	8	2.7	6	0
Pathon	1	3	3.0	3	0
Finn	1	1	1.0	1	0
al-Jabbar	1	-2	-2.0	-2	0
Colts	435	1,859	4.3	30	14
Opponents	446	1,935	4.3	55	13

RECEIVING	No.	Yds.	Avg.	LG	TD
Harrison	102	1,413	13.9	78t	14
James	63	594	9.4	60	5
Pathon	50	646	12.9	38	3
Dilger	47	538	11.4	32	3
Wilkins	43	569	13.2	43t	3
Pollard	30	439	14.6	50t	3
Green	18	201	11.2	34t	1
Finn	4	13	3.3	6	1
Colts	357	4,413	12.4	78t	33
Opponents	317	3,674	11.6	50	22

INTERCEPTIONS	No.	Yds.	Avg.	LG	TD
Burris	4	38	9.5	27t	1
Macklin	2	35	17.5	35	0
Peterson	2	8	4.0	5	0
Cota	2	3	1.5	3	0
Muhammad	1	40	40.0	40t	1
Poole	1	1	1.0	1	0
Washington	1	1	1.0	1	0
Johnson	1	-1	-1.0	-1	0
Colts	14	125	8.9	40t	2
Opponents	15	212	14.1	43	1

PUNTING	No.	Yds.	Avg.	In 20	LG
Smith	65	2,906	44.7	20	65
Colts	65	2,906	44.7	20	65
Opponents	82	3,503	42.7	20	70

PUNT RETURNS	No.	FC	Yds.	Avg.	LG	TD
Wilkins	29	13	240	8.3	36	0
P. Williams	7	1	108	15.4	40	0
Muhammad	2	0	4	2.0	4	0
Colts	38	14	352	9.3	40	0
Opponents	28	21	357	12.8	80	0

KICKOFF RETURNS	No.	Yds.	Avg.	LG	TD
Pathon	26	583	22.4	48	0
Wilkins	15	279	18.6	30	0
P. Williams	12	238	19.8	29	0
Muhammad	2	45	22.5	26	0
Dilger	1	0	0.0	0	0
Holsey	1	10	10.0	10	0
Macklin	1	0	0.0	0	0
Colts	58	1,155	19.9	48	0
Opponents	73	1,736	23.8	92t	1

FIELD GOALS	1-19	20-29	30-39	40-49	50+
Vanderjagt	1/1	6/6	13/13	5/6	0/1
Colts	1/1	6/6	13/13	5/6	0/1
Opponents	1/1	11/14	4/4	4/6	1/3

SACKS	No.
Bratzke	7.5
Belser	5.0
Johnson	5.0
M. Thomas	5.0
Bennett	3.0
Burris	3.0
J. Williams	3.0
Chester	2.5
Holsey	2.0
Scioli	2.0
Washington	2.0
Hollier	1.0
Whittington	1.0
Colts	42.0
Opponents	20.0

2001 DRAFT CHOICES

Round	Name	Pos.	College
1	Reggie Wayne	WR	Miami
2	Idrees Bashir	DB	Memphis
3	Cory Bird	DB	Virginia Tech
4	Ryan Diem	G	Northern Illinois
5	Raymond Walls	DB	Southern Mississippi
6	Jason Doering	DB	Wisconsin
7	Rick DeMulling	G	Idaho

INDIANAPOLIS COLTS

2001 VETERAN ROSTER

No.	Name	Pos.	Ht.	Wt.	Birthdate	NFL Exp.	College	Hometown	How Acq.	'00 Games/ Starts
93	Barnes, Lionel	DE	6-5	274	4/19/76	3	Louisiana-Monroe	Suffolk, England	W(StL)-'00	1/0*
92	Bratzke, Chad	DE	6-5	272	9/15/71	8	Eastern Kentucky	Brandon, Fla.	UFA(NYG)-'99	16/16
26	Brooks, Rodregis	CB-S	5-9	184	8/30/78	2	Alabama-Birmingham	Alexander City, Ala.	D7b-'00	0*
20	Burris, Jeff	S	6-0	190	6/7/72	8	Notre Dame	Rock Hill, S.C.	UFA(Buff)-'98	16/16
37	Cota, Chad	S	6-0	196	8/8/71	7	Oregon	Ashland, Ore.	UFA(NO)-'99	16/16
31	Crosby, Clifton	CB-S	5-10	172	9/17/74	2	Maryland	Erie, Pa.	FA-'00	0*
85	Dilger, Ken	TE	6-5	253	2/2/71	7	Illinois	Mariah Hill, Ind.	D2-'95	16/16
36	Finn, Jim	RB	6-0	235	12/9/76	2	Penn	Teaneck, N.J.	FA-'00	16/1
69	Gilbert, Ben	G	6-4	310	6/6/78	2	Ohio State	Lancaster, Ohio	FA-'00	0*
78	Glenn, Tarik	T	6-5	332	5/25/76	5	California	Oakland, Calif.	D1-'97	16/16
30	Gordon, Lennox	RB	6-0	201	9/9/78	3	New Mexico	Highley, Ariz.	FA-'00	9/0
84	Green, E.G.	WR	5-11	188	6/28/75	4	Florida State	Ft. Walton Beach, Fla.	D3-'98	7/0
88	Harrison, Marvin	WR	6-0	178	8/25/72	6	Syracuse	Philadelphia, Pa.	D1-'96	16/16
14	Hobert, Billy Joe	QB	6-3	235	1/8/71	9	Washington	Puyallup, Wash.	FA-'00	0*
79	Holsey, Bernard	DE-DT	6-2	286	10/10/73	6	Duke	Cave Spring, Ga.	UFA(NYG)-'00	16/13
1	Insley, Trevor	WR	6-0	190	12/25/77	2	Nevada	San Clemente, Calif.	FA-'00	0*
74	Jackson, Waverly	G	6-2	315	12/19/72	4	Virginia Tech	South Hill, Va.	FA-'98	16/0
32	James, Edgerrin	RB	6-0	214	8/1/78	3	Miami	Immokalee, Fla.	D1-'99	16/16
62	Johnson, Ellis	DT	6-2	288	10/30/73	7	Florida	Wildwood, Fla.	D1-'95	13/13
83	Keur, Josh	TE	6-4	270	9/4/76	2	Michigan State	Muskegon, Mich.	FA-'00	1/0*
7	Kight, Danny	K	6-1	214	8/18/71	3	Augusta State	Atlanta, Ga.	FA-'99	16/0
95	King, Shawn	DE	6-3	275	6/24/72	6	Northeast Louisiana	West Monroe, La.	UFA(Car)-'00	0*
27	Macklin, David	CB-S	5-9	193	7/14/78	2	Penn State	Newport News, Va.	D3-'00	16/2
18	Manning, Peyton	QB	6-5	225	3/24/76	4	Tennessee	New Orleans, La.	D1-'98	16/16
43	McDougal, Kevin	RB	5-11	203	5/18/77	2	Colorado State	Denver, Colo.	FA-'00	6/0
76	McKinney, Steve	G	6-4	295	10/15/75	4	Texas A&M	Houston, Tex.	D4-'98	16/16
73	Meadows, Adam	T	6-5	295	1/25/74	5	Georgia	Powder Springs, Ga.	D2-'97	16/16
65	Miller, Brandon	DT	6-0	299	11/27/75	2	Georgia	Greensboro, Ga.	FA-'00	0*
50	Moore, Larry	G	6-2	296	6/1/75	4	Brigham Young	San Diego, Calif.	FA-'98	16/16
94	Morris, Rob	LB	6-2	238	1/18/75	2	Brigham Young	Nampa, Idaho	D1-'00	7/0
21	Muhammad, Mustafah	CB	5-9	180	10/19/73	3	Fresno State	Los Angeles, Calif.	FA-'99	13/3
91	Nwokorie, Chukie	DE	6-3	280	7/10/75	3	Purdue	Lafayette, Ind.	FA-'00	2/0
86	Pathon, Jerome	WR	6-0	182	12/16/75	4	Washington	Capetown, South Africa	D2-'98	16/10
97	Peter, Christian	DT	6-3	292	10/5/72	5	Nebraska	Locust, N.J.	UFA(NYG)-'01	16/15*
52	Peterson, Mike	LB	6-2	232	6/17/76	3	Florida	Gainesville, Fla.	D2-'99	16/16
81	Pollard, Marcus	TE	6-3	248	2/8/72	7	Bradley	Valley, Ala.	FA-'95	16/14
61	Renes, Rob	DT	6-1	295	3/28/77	2	Michigan	Holland, Mich.	D7a-'00	0*
63	Saturday, Jeff	C	6-2	293	6/8/75	3	North Carolina	Tucker, Ga.	FA-'99	16/16
99	Scioli, Brad	DE	6-3	274	9/6/76	3	Penn State	Bridgeport, Pa.	D5-'99	16/2
17	Smith, Hunter	P	6-2	212	8/9/77	3	Notre Dame	Sherman, Tex.	D7a-'99	16/0
48	Snow, Justin	TE	6-3	234	12/21/76	2	Baylor	Abilene, Tex.	FA-'00	16/0
98	Sword, Sam	LB	6-1	245	12/4/74	3	Michigan	Saginaw, Mich.	FA-'00	3/0
12	Vanderjagt, Mike	K	6-5	210	3/24/70	4	West Virginia	Oakville, Ontario, Canada	FA-'98	16/0
53	Washington, Marcus	LB	6-3	255	10/17/77	2	Auburn	Auburn, Ala.	D2-'00	16/0
80	Wilkins, Terrence	WR	5-8	178	7/29/75	3	Virginia	Washington, D.C.	FA-'99	14/7
96	Williams, Josh	DT	6-3	284	8/9/76	2	Michigan	Houston, Tex.	D4-'00	14/7

* Barnes played in 1 game with St. Louis in '00; Brooks, Insley, and Rense missed '00 season because of injury; Crosby, Hobert, and Gilbert were inactive for 16 games; King last active with Indianapolis in '99; Miller was inactive for 14 games; Peter played 16 games with N.Y. Giants.

Players lost through free agency (0): None.

Also played with Colts in '00—RB Abdul-Karim al-Jabbar (1 game), C Phillip Armour (3), CB-S Billy Austin (16), S Jason Belser (16), LB Cornelius Bennett (16), CB-S Tony Blevins (16), DT Larry Chester (16), LB Phillip Glover (16), LB Dwight Hollier (16), WR Isaac Jones (1), CB Tyrone Poole (15), RB Paul Shields (8), DE Mark Thomas (14), LB Ratcliff Thomas (12), DE Bernard Whittington (15), CB Payton Williams (7).

COACHING STAFF

Head Coach,
Jim Mora

Pro Career: Jim Mora joined the Colts as their seventeenth head coach on January 12, 1998. Mora led the Colts to 10-6 and 13-3 records during the past two years, including the AFC Easton Division title in 1999. Under Mora, the Colts' 23 regular-season victories equal the most in the NFL during the past two seasons, and marks the club's first consecutive double-digit victory seasons since 1976-77. Mora has a 26-24 record with the Colts. He joined the Colts after producing a 93-74 regular-season record with New Orleans from 1986-1996. Mora won more games than the previous nine Saints coaches combined. Mora is one of only 20 head coaches in NFL history who has had 10 or more consecutive seasons of service with the same team. Mora produced 91 victories during his first 10 seasons, a total exceeded by only eight other coaches in NFL history. Mora's 109 career wins rank third among active coaches, and he was the twenty-seventh coach to produce 100 career victories. Mora stands as the twenty-third-winningest coach in NFL history. His 1991 Saints squad went 11-5, earning the only division title in club history. Prior to his stint with New Orleans, Mora directed the Philadelphia/Baltimore Stars of the USFL from 1983-85. Mora forged a 48-13-1 record and led the Stars to two titles in three league-championship-game appearances. Mora began his pro coaching career in 1978 as defensive line coach with Seattle. In 1982, he was defensive coordinator at New England. Career record: 119-102.

Background: Played tight end and defensive end at Occidental College. Assistant coach at Occidental from 1960-63 and head coach from 1964-66. Linebacker coach at Stanford in 1967. Defensive assistant at Colorado from 1968-1973. Linebackers coach at UCLA in 1974. Defensive coordinator at Washington from 1975-77. Received bachelor's degree in physical education from Occidental in 1957. Also holds master's degree in education from Southern California.

Personal: Born May 24, 1935 in Glendale, Calif. Jim lives in Indianapolis and has three sons—Michael, Stephen, and Jim (defensive coordinator with San Francisco 49ers).

ASSISTANT COACHES

George Catavolos, asst. head coach-defensive backs; born May 8, 1945, Chicago, lives in Indianapolis. Defensive back Purdue 1964-67. No pro playing experience. College coach: Purdue 1967-68, 1971-76, Middle Tennessee State 1969, Louisville 1970, Kentucky 1977-1981, Tennessee 1982-83. Pro coach: Indianapolis Colts 1984-1993, Carolina Panthers 1995-97, rejoined Colts in 1998.

Vic Fangio, defensive coordinator; born August 22, 1958, Dunmore, Pa., lives in Indianapolis. Attended East Stroudsburg. No pro playing experience. College coach: North Carolina 1993. Pro coach: Philadelphia/Baltimore Stars (USFL) 1984-85, New Orleans Saints 1986-1994, Carolina Panthers 1995-98, joined Colts 1999.

Todd Grantham, defensive line; born September 13, 1966, Pulaski, Va., lives in Indianapolis. Attended Virginia Tech. No college or pro playing experience. College coach: Virginia Tech 1990-95, Michigan State 1996-98. Pro coach: Joined Colts in 1999.

Richard Howell, asst. strength and conditioning; born February 19, 1972, Bladenboro, N.C., lives in Indianapolis. Quarterback Davidson 1990-93. No pro playing experience. College coach: Davidson 1994-98, North Carolina 1998-99. Pro coach: Barcelona Dragons (NFL Europe) 1999, joined Colts in 2000.

Gene Huey, running backs; born July 20, 1947, Uniontown, Pa., lives in Indianapolis. Defensive back-wide receiver Wyoming 1966-69. No pro playing experience. College coach: Wyoming 1970-74, New Mexico 1975-77, Nebraska 1978-1986, Arizona State 1987, Ohio State 1988-1991. Pro coach: Joined Colts in 1992.

John Hufnagel, quarterbacks; born September 13, 1951, Pittsburgh, lives in Indianapolis. Quarterback Penn State 1969-1972. Pro quarterback Denver Broncos 1973-75, Calgary Stampeders (CFL) 1976-79, Saskatchewan Roughriders (CFL) 1980-83, 1987, Winnipeg Blue Bombers (CFL) 1984-85. Pro coach: Saskatchewan Roughriders (CFL) 1988, Calgary Stampeders (CFL) 1989-1995, New Jersey Red Dogs (Arena League) 1997-98, Cleveland Browns 1999-2000, joined Colts in 2001.

Tony Marciano, tight ends; born June 14, 1956, Scranton, Pa., lives in Indianapolis. Attended Indiana (Pa.) No college or pro playing experience. College coach: Texas Christian 1978-1980, Southern Methodist 1981-86, Brown 1987-88, Richmond 1989-1990, Kent State 1991-92. Pro coach: Toronto Argonauts (CFL) 1994, Calgary Stampeders (CFL) 1995-97, joined Colts in 1998.

Tom Moore, offensive coordinator; born November 7, 1938, Owatanna, Minn., lives in Indianapolis. Quarterback Iowa 1957-1960. No pro playing experience. College coach: Iowa 1961-62, Dayton 1965-68, Wake Forest 1969, Georgia Tech 1970-71, Minnesota 1972-73, 1975-76. Pro coach: New York Stars (WFL) 1974, Pittsburgh Steelers 1977-1989, Minnesota Vikings 1990-93, Detroit Lions 1994-96, New Orleans Saints 1997, joined Colts in 1998.

Howard Mudd, offensive line; born February 10, 1942, Midland, Mich., lives in Indianapolis. Guard Hillsdale (Mich.) College 1960-63. Pro offensive lineman San Francisco 49ers 1964-69, Chicago Bears 1969-1970. College coach: California 1972-73. Pro coach: San Diego Chargers 1974-76, San Francisco 49ers 1977, Seattle Seahawks 1978-1982, 1993-97, Cleveland Browns 1983-88, Kansas City Chiefs 1989-1992, joined Colts in 1998.

Mike Murphy, linebackers; born September 25, 1944, New York, N.Y., lives in Indianapolis. Guard-linebacker Huron (S.D.) 1963-66. No pro playing experience. College coach: Vermont 1970-73, Idaho State 1974-76, Western Illinois 1977-78. Pro coach: Saskatchewan Roughriders (CFL) 1979-1983, Chicago Blitz (USFL) 1984, Detroit Lions 1985-89, Arizona Cardinals 1990-93, Seattle Seahawks 1995-97, joined Colts in 1998.

Jay Norvell, receivers; born March 28, 1963, Madison, Wis., lives in Indianapolis. Defensive back Iowa 1982-85. Pro defensive back Chicago Bears 1987. College coach: Iowa 1986, Northern Iowa 1988, Wisconsin 1989-1993, Iowa State 1995-97. Pro coach: Joined Colts in 1998.

John Pagano, defensive assistant; born March 30, 1967, Boulder, Colo., lives in Indianapolis. Linebacker Mesa State College 1985-88. No pro playing experience. College coach: Mesa State College 1989, Nevada-Las Vegas 1990-91, Louisiana Tech 1994, Mississippi 1995. Pro coach: New Orleans Saints 1996-97, joined Colts in 1998.

Kevin Spencer, special teams; born November 2, 1953, Queens, N.Y., lives in Indianapolis. Attended Springfield (Mass.) College. No college or pro playing experience. College coach: SUNY 1975-76, Cornell 1979-1980, Ithaca 1981-86, Wesleyan 1987-1990. Pro coach: Cleveland Browns 1991-94, Oakland Raiders 1995-97, joined Colts in 1998.

Jon Torine, strength and conditioning; born November 16, 1973, Livingston, N.J., lives in Indianapolis. Linebacker Springfield (Mass.) College 1991. No pro playing experience. Pro coach: Buffalo Bills 1995-97, joined Colts in 1998.

2001 FIRST-YEAR ROSTER

Name	Pos.	Ht.	Wt.	Birthdate	College	Hometown	How Acq.
Albea, Troy	WR	5-11	218	4/30/78	Appalachian State	Lincolnton, Ga.	FA
Bashir, Idrees	DB	6-2	206	12/7/78	Memphis	Decatur, Ga.	D2a
Bird, Cory	DB	5-10	216	8/10/78	Virginia Tech	Atlantic City, N.J.	D3b
Brown, Kevin	RB	6-1	230	6/26/78	Nevada-Las Vegas	Moss Point, Miss.	FA
Colbert, Nick	LB	6-2	238	10/17/77	Troy State	Fort Rucker, Ala.	FA
Davenport, Joe Dean (1)	TE	6-6	273	10/29/76	Arkansas	Springdale, Ark.	FA
Dees, Dempsy	DB	5-10	177	10/22/77	Boise State	Yuma, Ariz.	FA
DeMulling, Rick	G	6-4	304	7/21/77	Idaho	Cheney, Wash.	D7
Diem, Ryan	G	6-6	332	7/1/79	Northern Illinois	Carol Stream, Ill.	D4
Doering, Jason	DB	6-0	205	8/22/78	Wisconsin	Rhinelander, Wis.	D6b
Fox, Derek (1)	DB	5-11	200	12/27/77	Penn State	Canton, Ohio	FA
Freeman, Brad (1)	DB	6-1	210	9/13/75	Mississippi State	Memphis, Tenn.	FA
Gentry, Josh (1)	LB	6-1	240	6/3/78	Indianapolis	Remington, Ind.	FA
Guazzo, Mike	TE	6-3	247	10/17/77	Boston College	Oakland, N.J.	FA
Haddad, Drew (1)	WR	5-11	190	8/15/78	Buffalo	Westlake, Ohio	FA
Hampton, Jermaine	DB	6-0	205	6/12/79	Northern Illinois	Riverdale, Ill.	FA
Harper, Nick (1)	DB	5-10	184	9/10/74	Fort Valley State	Baldwin, Ga.	FA
Hartsell, Mark (1)	LB	6-4	225	12/7/73	Boston College	Brockton, Mass.	FA
Hogan, De'wayne	RB	6-0	226	5/19/78	Indiana	Indianapolis, Ind.	FA
Jones, Aaron	WR	5-11	185	8/22/77	Utah State	Casa Grande, Ariz.	FA
Jones, Ontei	DB	5-9	190	5/10/79	Oklahoma	Homestead, Fla.	FA
LaQuerre, Paul	G	6-2	294	10/26/77	Boston College	West Barnstable, Mass.	FA
Merandi, John	T-G	6-3	296	2/23/78	Notre Dame	Fontana, Calif.	FA
Meyer, Dave	QB	6-3	200	11/14/77	Virginia Tech	Ramsey, N.J.	FA
Millican, Brett	RB	5-10	202	10/30/77	Georgia	Lilburn, Ga.	FA
Murphy, Rob (1)	G	6-5	310	1/18/77	Ohio State	Cincinnati, Ohio	FA
Nwamuo, Enyi	TE	6-4	255	8/7/78	Oregon	Richmond, Calif.	FA
Olsen, Eric (1)	K	5-9	192	4/12/77	Army	Fort Lauderdale, Fla.	FA-'00
Olsen, Hans	DT	6-4	304	7/31/77	Brigham Young	Weiser, Idaho	FA
Ours, Wes	RB	6-0	284	12/30/77	West Virginia	Rawlings, Md.	FA
Pinkney, Cleveland	DT	6-0	290	9/14/77	South Carolina	Sumpter, S.C.	FA
Redding, Josh	T	6-4	312	12/25/77	Virginia Tech	Hanover, Pa.	FA
Reid, Ike (1)	DE	6-4	250	12/21/75	Ohio Wesleyan	Hartford, Conn.	FA
Rhine, Alan	P	5-11	187	3/11/78	Florida	Sebring, Fla.	FA
Rhodes, Dominic	RB	5-9	208	1/17/79	Midwestern Texas State	Abilene, Texas	FA
Richmond, Akim (1)	WR	6-1	200	10/22/75	Mississippi Valley State	Greenwood, Miss.	FA
Ridder, Tim (1)	T-G	6-7	301	12/17/76	Notre Dame	Omaha, Neb.	FA
Robinson, Roderick (1)	QB	6-3	235	5/17/76	Arkansas-Pine Bluff	Memphis, Tenn.	FA
Sims, Teddy	LB	6-0	234	11/16/77	Southern Illinois	Belle Glade, Fla.	FA
Smith, Matt	LB	6-3	242	6/2/76	Oregon	Grass Pass, Ore.	FA
Stockbauer, Marc (1)	LB	6-3	230	9/25/77	Stanford	Baton Rouge, La.	FA
Walls, Raymond	DB	5-10	175	7/24/79	Southern Mississippi	Kentwood, La.	D5
Warren, David	DE	6-2	253	10/14/78	Florida State	Tyler, Texas	FA
Wayne, Reggie	WR	6-0	197	11/17/78	Miami	Marrero, La.	D1b
Williams, Marcus	WR	6-5	225	12/12/77	Washington State	Oakland, Calif.	FA
Wilmot, Dwayne	WR	5-10	204	2/8/79	Maine	Freeport, N.Y.	FA
Wilturner, Daniel	DB	5-7	172	11/30/76	Baylor	Houston, Texas	FA

The term NFL Rookie is defined as a player who is in his first season of professional football and has not been on the roster of another professional football team for any regular-season or postseason games. A Rookie is designated by an "R" on NFL rosters. Players who have been active in another professional football league or players who have NFL experience, including either preseason training camp or being on an Active List or Inactive List, or on Reserve/Injured or Reserve/Physically Unable to Perform for fewer than six regular-season games, are termed NFL First-Year Players. An NFL First-Year Player is designated by a "1" on NFL rosters. Thereafter, a player is credited with an additional year of experience for each season in which he accumulates six games on the Active List or Inactive List, or on Reserve/Injured or Reserve/Physically Unable to Perform.

JACKSONVILLE JAGUARS

American Football Conference
Central Division
Team Colors: Teal, Black, and Gold
ALLTEL Stadium
One ALLTEL Stadium Place
Jacksonville, Florida 32202
Telephone: (904) 633-6000

CLUB OFFICIALS

Chairman and Chief Executive Officer: Wayne Weaver
Senior Vice President/Football Operations: Michael Huyghue
Senior Vice President/Marketing: Dan Connell
Vice President/Chief Financial Officer: Bill Prescott
Vice President, Administration/General Counsel: Paul Vance
Executive Director of Communications and Broadcasting: Dan Edwards
Director of Player Personnel: Rick Reiprish
Director of Pro Scouting: Fran Foley
Director of College Scouting: Gene Smith
Director of Finance: Kim Dodson
Director of Football Operations: Skip Richardson
Director of Information Technology: Bruce Swindell
Director of Corporate Sponsorship: Macky Weaver
Director of Ticket Sales: Steve Swetoha
Director of Ticket Operations: Tim Bishko
Director of Special Events and Promotions: Bo Reed
Head Athletic Trainer: Michael Ryan
Video Director: Mike Perkins
Equipment Manager: Drew Hampton

Chair & Chief Executive Officer, Jaguars Foundation: Delores Barr Weaver
Executive Director: Peter Racine
Stadium: ALLTEL Stadium (built in 1995)
• **Capacity:** 73,000
One ALLTEL Stadium Place
Jacksonville, Florida 32202
Playing Surface: Grass
Training Camp: ALLTEL Stadium
One ALLTEL Stadium Place
Jacksonville, Florida 32202

RECORD HOLDERS

INDIVIDUAL RECORDS—CAREER

Category	Name	Performance
Rushing (Yds.)	Fred Taylor, 1998-2000	3,354
Passing (Yds.)	Mark Brunell, 1995-2000	19,117
Passing (TDs)	Mark Brunell, 1995-2000	106
Receiving (No.)	Jimmy Smith, 1995-2000	472
Receiving (Yds.)	Jimmy Smith, 1995-2000	6,887
Interceptions	Aaron Beasley, 1996-2000	12
Punting (Avg.)	Bryan Barker, 1995-2000	43.5
Punt Return (Avg.)	Chris Hudson, 1995-98	10.9
Kickoff Return (Avg.)	Reggie Barlow, 1997-2000	23.3
Field Goals	Mike Hollis, 1995-2000	157
Touchdowns (Tot.)	James Stewart, 1995-99	38
	Jimmy Smith, 1995-2000	38
Points	Mike Hollis, 1995-2000	681

INDIVIDUAL RECORDS—SINGLE SEASON

Category	Name	Performance
Rushing (Yds.)	Fred Taylor, 2000	1,399
Passing (Yds.)	Mark Brunell, 1996	4,367
Passing (TDs)	Mark Brunell, 1998, 2000	20
Receiving (No.)	Jimmy Smith, 1999	116
Receiving (Yds.)	Jimmy Smith, 1999	1,636
Interceptions	Aaron Beasley, 1999	6
Punting (Avg.)	Bryan Barker, 1998	45.0
Punt Return (Avg.)	Reggie Barlow, 1998	12.9
Kickoff Return (Avg.)	Reggie Barlow, 1998	24.9
Field Goals	Mike Hollis, 1997, 1999	31
Touchdowns (Tot.)	Fred Taylor, 1998	17
Points	Mike Hollis, 1997	134

INDIVIDUAL RECORDS—SINGLE GAME

Category	Name	Performance
Rushing (Yds.)	Fred Taylor, 11-19-00	234
Passing (Yds.)	Mark Brunell, 9-22-96	432
Passing (TDs)	Mark Brunell, 11-29-98	4
Receiving (No.)	Keenan McCardell, 10-20-96	16
Receiving (Yds.)	Jimmy Smith, 9-10-00	291
Interceptions	Deon Figures, 8-31-97	2
	Aaron Beasley, 9-12-99	2
	Rayna Stewart, 9-10-00	2
Field Goals	Mike Hollis, 12-1-96, 11-30-97, 9-10-00	5
Touchdowns (Tot.)	James Stewart, 10-12-97	5
Points	James Stewart, 10-12-97	30

2001 SCHEDULE

PRESEASON

Aug. 10	**Carolina**	7:30
Aug. 16	at New York Giants	8:00
Aug. 23	**Kansas City**	7:30
Aug. 30	at Dallas	7:30

REGULAR SEASON

Sept. 9	**Pittsburgh**	1:00
Sept. 16	at Chicago	3:15
Sept. 23	**Tennessee**	1:00
Sept. 30	**Cleveland**	4:15
Oct. 7	at Seattle	1:05
Oct. 14	Open Date	
Oct. 18	**Buffalo** (Thurs.)	8:30
Oct. 28	at Baltimore	1:00
Nov. 4	at Tennessee	12:00
Nov. 11	**Cincinnati**	1:00
Nov. 18	at Pittsburgh	4:05
Nov. 25	**Baltimore**	1:00
Dec. 3	**Green Bay** (Mon.)	9:00
Dec. 9	at Cincinnati	1:00
Dec. 16	at Cleveland	1:00
Dec. 23	at Minnesota	3:15
Dec. 30	**Kansas City**	1:00

COACHING HISTORY

(60-44-0)

1995-2000 Tom Coughlin 60-44-0

ALLTEL STADIUM

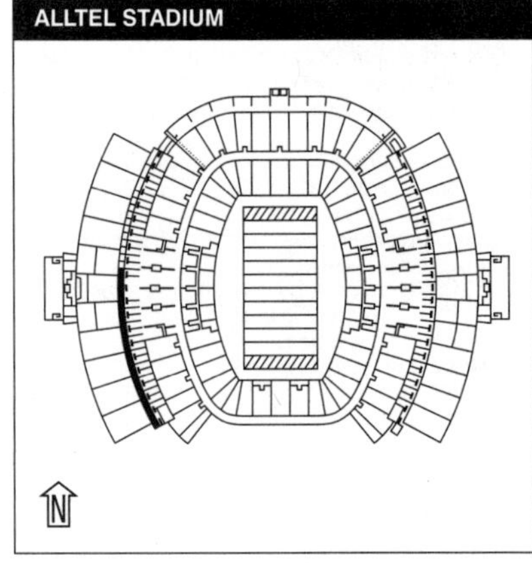

2000 TEAM RECORD

PRESEASON (3-1)

Date	Result		Opponent
8/4	W	34-14	at Carolina
8/11	W	16-13	New York Giants
8/19	W	26-22	at Kansas City
8/24	L	20-31	Atlanta

REGULAR SEASON (7-9)

Date	Result		Opponent	Att.
9/3	W	27-7	at Cleveland	72,418
9/10	L	36-39	at Baltimore	68,843
9/17	W	13-0	Cincinnati	45,653
9/25	L	14-43	at Indianapolis	56,816
10/1	L	13-24	Pittsburgh	64,351
10/8	L	10-15	Baltimore	65,194
10/16	L	13-27	at Tennessee	68,498
10/22	L	16-35	Washington	69,061
10/29	W	23-17	at Dallas (OT)	63,554
11/12	L	21-28	Seattle	68,063
11/19	W	34-24	at Pittsburgh	50,925
11/26	W	16-13	Tennessee	65,454
12/3	W	48-0	Cleveland	51,262
12/10	W	44-10	Arizona	53,472
12/17	L	14-17	at Cincinnati	50,469
12/23	L	25-28	at New York Giants	77,924

(OT) Overtime

SCORE BY PERIODS

Jaguars	69	142	74	76	6	—	367
Opponents	59	88	61	119	0	—	327

ATTENDANCE

Home 543,113 Away 508,028 Total 1,051,141
Single-game home record, 74,143 (12/28/98)
Single-season home record, 561,472 (1998)

2000 TEAM STATISTICS

	Jaguars	Opp.
Total First Downs	318	252
Rushing	109	85
Passing	193	144
Penalty	16	23
Third Down: Made/Att	100/235	74/203
Third Down Pct.	42.6	36.5
Fourth Down: Made/Att	5/14	4/8
Fourth Down Pct.	35.7	50.0
Total Net Yards	5,690	4,845
Avg. Per Game	355.6	302.8
Total Plays	1,080	934
Avg. Per Play	5.3	5.2
Net Yards Rushing	2,032	1,685
Avg. Per Game	127.0	105.3
Total Rushes	481	436
Net Yards Passing	3,658	3,160
Avg. Per Game	228.6	197.5
Sacked/Yards Lost	54/289	40/247
Gross Yards	3,947	3,407
Att./Completions	545/333	458/258
Completion Pct.	61.1	56.3
Had Intercepted	15	12
Punts/Average	79/41.9	90/42.5
Net Punting Avg.	79/34.3	90/37.0
Penalties/Yards	95/703	96/814
Fumbles/Ball Lost	27/14	26/18
Touchdowns	40	39
Rushing	18	14
Passing	22	23
Returns	0	2
Avg. Time of Possession	31:32	28:28

2000 INDIVIDUAL STATISTICS

Passing	Att.	Comp.	Yds.	Pct.	TD	Int.	Tkld.	Rate
Brunell	512	311	3,640	60.7	20	14	54/289	84.0
Martin	33	22	307	66.7	2	1	0/0	104.0
Jaguars	545	333	3,947	61.1	22	15	54/289	85.2
Opponents	458	258	3,407	56.3	23	12	40/247	85.8

SCORING	TD R	TD P	TD Rt	PAT	FG	Saf	PTS
Hollis	0	0	0	33/33	24/26	0	105
Taylor	12	2	0	0/0	0/0	0	84
Ji. Smith	0	8	0	0/0	0/0	0	48
McCardell	0	5	0	0/0	0/0	0	30
Brady	0	3	0	0/0	0/0	0	20
Lindsey	0	0	0	5/5	5/7	0	20
Whitted	0	3	0	0/0	0/0	0	18
Brunell	2	0	0	0/0	0/0	0	12
Howard	1	0	0	0/0	0/0	0	6
Johnson	1	0	0	0/0	0/0	0	6
Mack	1	0	0	0/0	0/0	0	6
Soward	0	1	0	0/0	0/0	0	6
Stith	1	0	0	0/0	0/0	0	6
Jaguars	18	22	0	38/38	29/33	0	367
Opponents	14	23	2	36/36	17/24	1	327

2-Pt. Conversions: Brady.
Jaguars 1-1, Opponents 2-3.

RUSHING	Att.	Yds.	Avg.	LG	TD
Taylor	292	1,399	4.8	71	12
Brunell	48	236	4.9	16	2
Mack	54	145	2.7	14	1
Johnson	28	112	4.0	19	1
Stith	20	55	2.8	12	1
Howard	21	52	2.5	9t	1
Soward	3	28	9.3	20	0
Williams	2	8	4.0	4	0
Shelton	2	3	1.5	2	0
Dukes	2	2	1.0	2	0
Quinn	2	-2	-1.0	-1	0
Martin	7	-6	-.9	2	0
Jaguars	481	2,032	4.2	71	18
Opponents	436	1,685	3.9	45t	14

RECEIVING	No.	Yds.	Avg.	LG	TD
McCardell	94	1,207	12.8	67t	5
Ji. Smith	91	1,213	13.3	65t	8
Brady	64	729	11.4	36	3
Taylor	36	240	6.7	19	2
Soward	14	154	11.0	45	1
Whitted	13	137	10.5	37t	3
Johnson	12	153	12.8	48	0
Shelton	4	48	12.0	16	0
Howard	3	26	8.7	13	0
Barlow	1	28	28.0	28	0
Jones	1	12	12.0	12	0
Jaguars	333	3,947	11.9	67t	22
Opponents	258	3,407	13.2	77t	23

INTERCEPTIONS	No.	Yds.	Avg.	LG	TD
Stewart	2	37	18.5	24	0
Darius	2	26	13.0	21	0
Logan	2	14	7.0	14	0
Beasley	1	39	39.0	39	0
Boyer	1	12	12.0	12	0
Nickerson	1	10	10.0	10	0
Brackens	1	7	7.0	7	0
Bryant	1	0	0.0	0	0
Hardy	1	0	0.0	0	0
Jaguars	12	145	12.1	39	0
Opponents	15	168	11.2	44	0

PUNTING	No.	Yds.	Avg.	In 20	LG
Barker	76	3,194	42.0	29	65
Lindsey	3	117	39.0	0	46
Jaguars	79	3,311	41.9	29	65
Opponents	90	3,822	42.5	25	67

PUNT RETURNS	No.	FC	Yds.	Avg.	LG	TD
Barlow	29	14	200	6.9	21	0
Soward	14	5	108	7.7	18	0
McCardell	3	0	25	8.3	22	0
Jaguars	46	19	333	7.2	22	0
Opponents	38	7	478	12.6	82t	1

KICKOFF RETURNS	No.	Yds.	Avg.	LG	TD
Stith	33	785	23.8	47	0
Barlow	11	224	20.4	27	0
Mack	6	104	17.3	35	0
Soward	4	93	23.3	28	0
Whitted	4	67	16.8	20	0
Williams	2	50	25.0	30	0
Fordham	1	0	0.0	0	0
Leroy	1	0	0.0	0	0
Jaguars	62	1,323	21.3	47	0
Opponents	73	1,523	20.9	66	1

FIELD GOALS	1-19	20-29	30-39	40-49	50+
Hollis	0/0	6/7	8/8	7/8	3/3
Lindsey	2/2	0/0	1/3	2/2	0/0
Jaguars	2/2	6/7	9/11	9/10	3/3
Opponents	2/2	6/7	4/5	5/10	0/0

SACKS	No.
Brackens	7.5
Smeenge	6.0
Beasley	5.0
Walker	5.0
Boyer	3.5
Wynn	3.5
Hardy	3.0
Payne	2.0
Darius	1.0
Logan	1.0
Nickerson	1.0
Spicer	1.0
Meier	0.5
Jaguars	40.0
Opponents	54.0

2001 DRAFT CHOICES

Round	Name	Pos.	College
1	Marcus Stroud	DT	Georgia
2	Maurice Williams	T	Michigan
3	Eric Westmoreland	LB	Tennessee
	James Boyd	DB	Penn State
5	David Leaverton	P	Tennessee
6	Chad Ward	G	Washington
7	Anthony Denman	LB	Notre Dame
	Marlon McCree	DB	Kentucky
	Richmond Flowers	WR	Tennessee-Chattanooga
	Randy Chevrier	LS	McGill (Canada)

JACKSONVILLE JAGUARS

2001 VETERAN ROSTER

No.	Name	Pos.	Ht.	Wt.	Birthdate	NFL Exp.	College	Hometown	How Acq.	'00 Games/ Starts
69	Baniewicz, Mark	T	6-6	304	3/24/77	2	Syracuse	Fairport, N.Y.	D7e-'00	0*
21	Beasley, Aaron	CB	6-0	195	7/7/73	6	West Virginia	Pottstown, Pa.	D3-'96	14/14
71	Boselli, Tony	T	6-7	318	4/17/72	7	Southern California	Boulder, Colo.	D1a-'95	16/16
90	Brackens, Tony	DE	6-4	271	12/26/74	6	Texas	Fairfield, Texas	D2a-'96	16/16
80	Brady, Kyle	TE	6-6	277	1/14/72	7	Penn State	New Cumberland, Pa.	UFA(NYJ)-'99	16/15
8	Brunell, Mark	QB	6-1	217	9/17/70	9	Washington	Santa Maria, Calif.	T(GB)-'95	16/16
25	Bryant, Fernando	CB	5-10	176	3/26/77	3	Alabama	Murfreesboro, Tenn.	D1-'99	14/14
55	Clark, Danny	LB	6-2	240	5/9/77	2	Illinois	Country Club Hills, Ill.	D7d-'00	16/0
29	Craft, Jason	CB	5-10	178	2/13/76	3	Colorado State	Denver, Colo.	D5-'99	16/3
27	Criss, Shad	CB	5-11	184	1/11/76	2	Missouri	Sherman, Texas	FA-'00	3/0
20	Darius, Donovin	S	6-1	216	8/12/75	4	Syracuse	Camden, N.J.	D1b-'98	16/16
85	Dawkins, Sean	WR	6-4	218	2/3/71	9	California	Sunnyvale, Calif.	FA-'01	16/16*
51	Hardy, Kevin	LB	6-4	248	7/24/73	6	Illinois	Evansville, Ind.	D1-'96	16/16
1	Hollis, Mike	K	5-7	174	5/22/72	7	Idaho	Spokane, Wash.	FA-'95	12/0
88	Jones, Damon	TE	6-5	271	9/18/74	5	Southern Illinois	Evanston, Ill.	D5-'97	1/0
64	Koch, Aaron	G-T	6-3	300	2/21/78	2	Oregon State	Keizer, Ore.	FA(Tenn)-'00	8/0
37	Lake, Carnell	S	6-1	213	7/15/67	13	UCLA	Inglewood, Calif.	UFA(Pitt)-'99	0*
34	Mack, Stacey	RB	6-1	237	6/26/75	3	Temple	Orlando, Fla.	FA-'99	6/2
10	Martin, Jamie	QB	6-2	208	2/8/70	7	Weber State	Arroyo Grande, Calif.	FA-'01	5/0
87	McCardell, Keenan	WR	6-1	190	1/6/70	10	Nevada-Las Vegas	Houston, Texas	UFA(Balt)-'96	16/16
63	Meester, Brad	G-C	6-3	300	3/23/77	2	Northern Iowa	Parkersburg, Iowa	D2-'00	16/16
92	Meier, Rob	DE	6-5	270	8/29/77	2	Washington State	West Vancouver, B.C., Canada	D7b-'00	16/0
79	Nelson, Reggie	T	6-3	321	6/23/76	2	McNeese State	Alexandria, La.	FA-'00	1/0
83	Neufeld, Ryan	TE	6-4	240	11/22/75	3	UCLA	Morgan Hill, Calif.	FA-'00	3/0
56	Nickerson, Hardy	LB	6-2	235	9/1/65	15	California	Compton, Calif.	UFA(TB)-'00	6/6
45	Olson, Erik	S	6-1	210	1/4/77	2	Colorado State	Ventura, Calif.	D7a-'00	14/0
91	Payne, Seth	DT	6-4	290	2/12/75	5	Cornell	Victor, N.Y.	D4-'97	16/14
54	Pelshak, Troy	LB	6-2	242	3/6/77	3	North Carolina A&T	Garringer, N.C.	FA-'00	4/0
12	Quinn, Jonathan	QB	6-6	239	2/27/75	4	Middle Tennessee State	Nashville, Tenn.	D3-'98	1/0
53	Slaughter, T.J.	LB	6-0	239	2/20/77	2	Southern Mississippi	Birmingham, Ala.	D3-'00	16/7
73	Smith, Jeff	C-G	6-3	316	5/25/73	6	Tennessee	Decatur, Tenn.	FA-'00	14/12
82	Smith, Jimmy	WR	6-1	204	2/9/69	9	Jackson State	Jackson, Miss.	FA-'95	15/14
94	Smith, Larry	DT	6-5	284	12/4/74	3	Florida State	Folkston, Ga.	D2-'99	14/4
81	Soward, R. Jay	WR	5-11	178	1/16/78	2	Southern California	Rialto, Calif.	D1-'00	13/2
95	Spicer, Paul	DE	6-4	271	8/18/75	2	Saginaw Valley St.	Indianapolis, Ind.	FA-'00	3/0
33	Stith, Shyrone	RB	5-7	206	4/2/78	2	Virginia Tech	Chesapeake, Va.	D7c-'00	14/0
5	Tarle, Jim	K	6-0	221	12/27/72	2	Arkansas State	Jacksonville, Fla.	FA-'00	6/0
28	Taylor, Fred	RB	6-1	231	1/27/76	4	Florida	Belle Glade, Fla.	D1a-'98	13/13
59	Thomas, Edward	LB	6-0	235	9/27/74	2	Georgia Southern	Thomasville, Ga.	FA-'00	8/0
41	Thomas, Kiwaukee	CB	5-11	183	6/19/77	2	Georgia Southern	Perry, Ga.	D5-'00	16/3
66	Wade, John	C	6-5	296	1/25/75	4	Marshall	Harrisonburg, Va.	D5-'98	2/2
96	Walker, Gary	DT	6-2	300	2/28/73	7	Auburn	Lavonia, Ga.	UFA(Tenn)-'99	15/14
13	White, Ted	QB	6-2	225	5/29/76	2	Howard	Baton Rouge, La.	W(TB)-'01	0*
86	Whitted, Alvis	WR	6-0	185	9/4/74	4	North Carolina State	Hillsborough, N.C.	D7a-'98	16/3
77	Wiegert, Zach	T-G	6-5	311	8/16/72	7	Nebraska	Fremont, Neb.	FA-'99	8/8
97	Wynn, Renaldo	DE	6-3	288	9/3/74	5	Notre Dame	Chicago, Ill.	D1-'97	14/14

* Baniewicz was active for 10 games but did not play in '00; Dawkins played in 16 games with Seattle; Lake missed '00 season because of injury; White last active with Kansas City in '99.

Players lost through free agency (6): P Bryan Barker (Wash; 16 games in '00), LB Brant Boyer (Cle; 12), G-T Todd Fordham (Den; 16), S Mike Logan (Pitt; 15), T Leon Searcy (Balt; 0), FB Daimon Shelton (Chi; 16).

Also played with Jaguars in '00—WR Reggie Barlow (16 games), TE Greg DeLong (4), TE Rich Griffith (16), RB Chris Howard (2), RB Anthony Johnson (12), DT Emarlos Leroy (9), K Steve Lindsey (10), LB Lonnie Marts (7), C Quentin Neujahr (16), DE David Richie (1), DE Joel Smeenge (12), G Brenden Stai (16), S Rayna Stewart (12), LB Erik Storz (10), CB Michael Swift (1), FB Jermaine Williams (7).

COACHING STAFF

Head Coach,
Tom Coughlin

Pro Career: Under Tom Coughlin, who has the third-longest tenure with his team among NFL head coaches, the Jaguars became the only expansion team in NFL history to advance to the playoffs four times in their first five seasons. After a 4-12 inaugural season, Coughlin's team went 9-7 in year two on the way to the AFC Championship Game, and 11-5 and into the playoffs in both 1997 and 1998. In 1999, Coughlin posted an NFL-best 14-2 mark in the regular season and a second AFC Championship Game appearance. Last year, the Jaguars finished 7-9. Coughlin became the first head coach of the Jaguars on February 21, 1994, following a successful three seasons as head coach at Boston College. A veteran of 30 years in coaching, including 17 at the collegiate level and seven as an NFL assistant, Coughlin previously coached wide receivers for the Philadelphia Eagles (1984-85), Green Bay Packers (1986-87), and New York Giants (1988-1990). He was a member of the Giants' Super Bowl XXV champion coaching staff prior to being named head coach at Boston College in 1991. In three seasons at Boston College, he turned a struggling program into a top-20 team, posting a 21-13-1 record. Coughlin's previous 14 seasons as a college coach were at Rochester Institute of Technology 1970-73 (head coach), Syracuse 1974-1980, and Boston College 1981-83. Career record: 60-44.

Background: Played wingback for Syracuse from 1965-67 under coach Ben Schwartzwalder, along with teammates Larry Csonka and Floyd Little. Received Syracuse 1967 Orange Key Award as outstanding scholar athlete, and graduated with bachelor's degree in education (1968). Received master's degree in education from Syracuse (1969).

Personal: Born August 31, 1947, Waterloo, N.Y. Was star for Waterloo Central High School. Tom and his wife, Judy, reside in Jacksonville, and have two daughters, Keli and Katie, and two sons, Tim and Brian.

ASSISTANT COACHES

John Bonamego, asst. special teams, born August 14, 1963, Waynesboro, Pa., lives in Jacksonville. Wide reciever-quarterback Central Michigan 1985-86. No pro playing experience. College coach: Maine 1988-1991, Lehigh 1992, Army 1993-98. Pro coach: Joined Jaguars in 1999.

Perry Fewell, secondary; born November 7, 1962, Gastonia, N.C., lives in Jacksonville. Defensive back Lenoir-Rhyne 1981-84. No pro playing experience. College coach: Army 1987, 1992-94, Kent State 1988-1991, Vanderbilt 1995-97. Pro coach: Joined Jaguars in 1998.

Greg Finnegan, asst. strength and conditioning; born February 21, 1969, Toledo, Ohio, lives in Jacksonville. Center Cornell 1988-1992. No pro playing experience. College coach: Kansas State 1993, Boston College 1994-97. Pro coach: Joined Jaguars in 1998.

Frank Gansz, special teams coordinator; born November 22, 1938, Altoona, Pa., lives in Jacksonville. Guard-linebacker Navy 1957-59. No pro playing experience. College coach: Air Force 1964-66, Colgate 1968, Navy 1969-1972, Oklahoma State 1973, 1975, Army 1974, UCLA 1976-77. Pro coach: San Francisco 49ers 1978, Cincinnati Bengals 1979-1980, Kansas City Chiefs 1981-82, 1986-88 (head coach 1987-88), Philadelphia Eagles 1983-85, Detroit Lions 1989-1993, Atlanta Falcons 1994-96, St. Louis Rams 1997-99, joined Jaguars in 2000.

Paul Haynes, defensive quality control; born July 11, 1969, Columbus, Ohio, lives in Jacksonville. Safety Kent State 1987-1990. No pro playing experience. College coach: Bowling Green 1994, Fresno State 1995-96, Northern Iowa 1997-98, Kent State 1999-2000. Pro coach: Joined Jaguars in 2001.

Fred Hoaglin, tight ends; born January 28, 1944, Alliance, Ohio, lives in Jacksonville. Center Pittsburgh 1962-65. Pro center Cleveland Browns 1966-1972, Baltimore Colts 1973, Houston Oilers 1974-75, Seattle Seahawks 1976. Pro coach: Detroit Lions 1978-1984, New York Giants 1985-1992, New England Patriots 1993-96, joined Jaguars in 1997.

Jerald Ingram, running backs; born December 24, 1960, Beaver, Pa., lives in Jacksonville. Fullback Michigan 1979-1984. No pro playing experience. College coach: Ball State 1985-1990, Boston College 1991-93. Pro coach: Joined Jaguars in 1995.

Mike Maser, offensive line; born March 2, 1947, Clayton, N.Y., lives in Jacksonville. Guard Buffalo 1967-1970. No pro playing experience. College coach: Marshall 1973, Bluefield State College 1974-78, Maine 1979-1980, Boston College 1981-1993. Pro coach: Joined Jaguars in 1995.

Garrick McGee, offensive quality control; born April 6, 1973, Kansas City, Mo., lives in Jacksonville. Quarterback Arizona State 1992, Northeast Oklahoma A&M 1993, Oklahoma 1994-95. No pro playing experience. College coach: Langston 1996-98, Northern Iowa 1999. Pro coach: Joined Jaguars in 2000.

John McNulty, wide receivers; born May 29, 1968, Scranton, Pa., lives in Jacksonville. Safety Penn State 1987-1990. No pro playing experience. College coach: Michigan 1991-94, Connecticut 1995-97. Pro coach: Joined Jaguars in 1998.

Gary Moeller, defensive coordinator; born January 26, 1941, Lima, Ohio, lives in Jacksonville. Center Ohio State 1960-62. No pro playing experience. College coach: Miami (Ohio) 1967, Michigan 1969-1976, 1980-1994 (head coach 1990-94), Illinois 1977-79 (head coach). Pro coach: Cincinnati Bengals 1995-96, Detroit Lions 1997-2000 (interim head coach in 2000), joined Jaguars in 2001.

Jerry Palmieri, strength and conditioning; born October 30, 1958, Englewood, N.J., lives in Jacksonville. No college or pro playing experience. College coach: Oklahoma State 1984-87, Kansas State 1988-1992, Boston College 1993-94. Pro coach: Joined Jaguars in 1995.

John Pease, assistant head coach-defensive line; born October 14, 1943, Pittsburgh, lives in Jacksonville. Wingback Utah 1963-64. No pro playing experience. College coach: Fullerton (Calif.) J.C. 1970-73, Long Beach State 1974-76, Utah 1977, Washington 1978-1983. Pro coach: Philadelphia/Baltimore Stars (USFL) 1983-85, New Orleans Saints 1986-1994, joined Jaguars in 1995.

Bob Petrino, offensive coordinator; born March 10, 1961, Lewiston, Mont., lives in Jacksonville. Quarterback Carroll College 1979-1982. No pro playing experience. College coach: Carroll College 1983, 1985-86, Weber State 1984, 1987-88, Idaho 1989-1991, Arizona State 1992-93, Nevada 1994, Utah State 1995-97, Louisville 1998. Pro coach: Joined Jaguars in 1999.

Lucious Selmon, outside linebackers; born March 15, 1951, Muskogee, Okla., lives in Jacksonville. Defensive tackle Oklahoma 1970-73. Pro defensive tackle Memphis Southmen (WFL) 1974-75. College coach: Oklahoma 1976-1994. Pro coach: Joined Jaguars in 1995.

Steve Szabo, inside linebackers; born September 11, 1943, Chicago, lives in Jacksonville. Halfback/defensive back Navy 1961-64. No pro playing experience. College coach: Johns Hopkins 1969, Toledo 1970, Iowa 1971-73, Syracuse 1974-76, Iowa State 1977-78, Ohio State 1979-1981, Western Michigan 1982-84, Edinboro 1985-87 (head coach), Northern Iowa 1988, Colorado State 1989-1990, Boston College 1991-93. Pro coach: Joined Jaguars in 1995.

2001 FIRST-YEAR ROSTER

Name	Pos.	Ht.	Wt.	Birthdate	College	Hometown	How Acq.
Boyd, James	S	5-11	208	10/17/77	Penn State	Chesapeake, Va.	D3b
Brown, Delvin	S	5-11	202	9/17/79	Miami	Carol City, Fla.	FA
Chevrier, Randy	LS-DT	6-2	293	6/6/76	McGill (Canada)	Quebec, Ontario, Canada	D7d
Clemens, Kevin (1)	FB	6-1	275	6/20/76	Grand Valley State	Kankakee, Ill.	FA
Collins, McAllister	C	6-2	307	4/23/79	Northern Illinois	Richton Park, Ill.	FA
Cooks, Kerry (1)	S	5-11	202	3/28/74	Iowa	Irving, Texas	FA
Denman, Anthony	LB	6-1	239	10/30/79	Notre Dame	Rusk, Texas	D7a
Flowers, Richmond	WR	5-11	195	5/4/78	Tennessee-Chattanooga	Birmingham, Ala.	D7c
Gates, Nate	CB	5-11	188	3/29/78	Georgia Southern	Sarasota, Fla.	FA
Goven, Ryan	LB	6-4	258	4/13/78	North Dakota	Turtle Lake, N.D.	FA
Harklau, Ryan	DT	6-3	280	10/1/77	Iowa State	Humboldt, Iowa	FA
Harris, Marcellus	WR	5-10	181	2/15/78	East Carolina	Newport News, Va.	FA
Hart, Lawrence	TE	6-4	260	9/19/76	Southern	Shreveport, La.	FA
Hlavacek, Evan (1)	CB	5-10	185	11/27/74	San Diego	San Diego, Calif.	FA
Hogans, Richard (1)	LB	6-2	253	7/8/75	Memphis	Columbus, Ga.	FA
Johnson, Brent	DE	6-2	262	12/7/76	Ohio State	Kingston, Ontario, Canada	FA
Joseph, Elvis	RB	6-1	217	8/30/78	Southern	New Orleans, La.	FA
Langley, Aron (1)	P	6-0	191	5/31/76	Wyoming	Longwood, Colo.	FA
Leaverton, David	P	6-4	215	4/1/78	Tennessee	Midland, Texas	D5
Ledford, Dwayne (1)	G	6-3	295	11/2/76	East Carolina	Marion, N.C.	FA
Lockhart, Radell	DE	6-2	258	5/11/79	Catawba	Charlotte, N.C.	FA
Long, Jeff	T	6-8	320	10/10/78	Utah State	Thornton, Colo.	FA
Mays, Antonio	DT	6-2	288	1/6/78	Southern	Waterloo, Iowa	FA
McClintock, Dustin	FB	6-2	261	9/10/77	Alabama	Quinlan, Texas	FA
McCree, Marlon	S	5-11	197	3/17/77	Kentucky	Daytona Beach, Fla.	D7b
Miller, Craig (1)	S	5-11	199	10/4/77	Utah State	Bakersfield, Calif.	W(Ind)-'00
Nikolao, Jason	DT	6-2	309	8/3/79	Oregon	Tacoma, Wash.	FA
Prince, Ryan	TE	6-4	252	5/16/77	Weber State	Farmington, Utah	FA
Shepherd, Gannon (1)	T	6-8	301	1/4/77	Duke	Atlanta, Ga.	W(Chi)-'00
Smith, Chandler	DB	6-2	200	3/29/76	Southern Mississippi	Vicksburg, Miss.	FA
Smith, Emanuel (1)	WR	6-1	210	2/3/76	Arkansas	Clinton, Miss.	D6-'00
Stanley, Antonio	WR	5-9	169	9/27/78	Bethune-Cookman	Miami, Fla.	FA
Stroud, Marcus	DT	6-6	317	6/25/78	Georgia	Barney, Ga.	D1
Tuipala, Joseph (1)	LB	6-1	240	9/13/76	San Diego State	Ridgecrest, Calif.	FA
Venzke, Patrick	T	6-6	317	4/6/75	Idaho	Essen, Germany	FA
Ward, Chad	G	6-5	321	1/12/77	Washington	Kennewick, Wash.	D6
Washington, Patrick	FB	6-2	240	3/4/78	Virginia	Washington D.C.	FA
Watkins, James	S	6-4	210	9/22/77	Tennessee State	Hillsboro, Ala.	FA
Westbrooks, Jerry	RB	6-2	230	8/27/77	Ohio State	Boca Raton, Fla.	FA
Westmoreland, Eric	LB	5-11	236	3/11/77	Tennessee	Jasper, Tenn.	D3a
Williams, Brian	LB	6-1	257	7/8/78	Northwest Missouri State	Kansas City, Mo.	FA
Williams, Maurice	T	6-5	307	1/26/79	Michigan	Detroit, Mich.	D2
Williams, Randal	WR	6-3	219	5/24/78	New Hampshire	Bronx, N.Y.	FA
Young, Bill	G	6-4	313	11/11/77	Appalachian State	Browns Summit, N.C.	FA

The term NFL Rookie is defined as a player who is in his first season of professional football and has not been on the roster of another professional football team for any regular-season or postseason games. A Rookie is designated by an "R" on NFL rosters. Players who have been active in another professional football league or players who have NFL experience, including either preseason training camp or being on an Active List or Inactive List, or on Reserve/Injured or Reserve/Physically Unable to Perform for fewer than six regular-season games, are termed NFL First-Year Players. An NFL First-Year Player is designated by a "1" on NFL rosters. Thereafter, a player is credited with an additional year of experience for each season in which he accumulates six games on the Active List or Inactive List, or on Reserve/Injured or Reserve/Physically Unable to Perform.

KANSAS CITY CHIEFS

American Football Conference
Western Division
Team Colors: Red, Gold, and White
One Arrowhead Drive
Kansas City, Missouri 64129
Telephone: (816) 920-9300

CLUB OFFICIALS

Founder: Lamar Hunt
Chairman of the Board: Jack Steadman
President: Carl Peterson
Executive Vice President, Assistant General Manager: Dennis Thum
Senior Vice President: Dennis Watley
Vice President of Football Operations/Player Personnel: Lynn Stiles
Secretary: Jim Seigfreid
Director of Finance/Treasurer: Dale Young
Director of Public Relations: Bob Moore
Vice President of Sales and Marketing: Wallace Bennett
Director of Pro Personnel: Bill Kuharich
Director of College Scouting: Chuck Cook
Director of Operations: Steve Schneider
Director of Development: Ken Blume
Associate Director of Public Relations: Pete Moris
Director of Corporate Sales: Anita Bailey
Director of Sales: Gary Spani
Director of Community Relations: Brenda Sniezek
Director of Ticket Operations: Doug Hopkins
Equipment Manager: Mike Davidson
Asst. Equipment Managers: Allen Wright, Chris Shropshire
Head Athletic Trainer: Dave Kendall
Assistant Trainers: Bud Epps, Don Sherwood
Director of Video Operations: Mike Portz
Video Assistants: Todd Weger, Andrew Hearne
Stadium: Arrowhead Stadium (built in 1972)
•**Capacity:** 79,451
One Arrowhead Drive
Kansas City, Missouri 64129
Playing Surface: Grass
Training Camp: University of Wisconsin-River Falls
River Falls, Wisconsin 54022

2001 SCHEDULE

PRESEASON

Aug. 12	**Washington**	7:30
Aug. 18	**Chicago**	7:30
Aug. 23	at Jacksonville	7:30
Aug. 31	at St. Louis	7:00

REGULAR SEASON

Sept. 9	**Oakland**	12:00
Sept. 16	at Seattle	1:15
Sept. 23	**New York Giants**	12:00
Sept. 30	at Washington	1:00
Oct. 7	at Denver	2:05
Oct. 14	**Pittsburgh**	12:00
Oct. 21	at Arizona	1:00
Oct. 28	**Indianapolis**	12:00
Nov. 4	at San Diego	1:15
Nov. 11	at New York Jets	1:00
Nov. 18	Open Date	
Nov. 25	**Seattle**	12:00
Nov. 29	**Philadelphia** (Thurs.)	7:30
Dec. 9	at Oakland	1:15
Dec. 16	**Denver**	12:00
Dec. 23	**San Diego**	12:00
Dec. 30	at Jacksonville	1:00

RECORD HOLDERS

INDIVIDUAL RECORDS—CAREER

Category	Name	Performance
Rushing (Yds.)	Christian Okoye, 1987-1992	4,897
Passing (Yds.)	Len Dawson, 1962-1975	28,507
Passing (TDs)	Len Dawson, 1962-1975	237
Receiving (No.)	Henry Marshall, 1976-1987	416
Receiving (Yds.)	Otis Taylor, 1965-1975	7,306
Interceptions	Emmitt Thomas, 1966-1978	58
Punting (Avg.)	Jerrel Wilson, 1963-1977	43.5
Punt Return (Avg.)	Noland Smith, 1967-69	11.1
Kickoff Return (Avg.)	Noland Smith, 1967-69	26.8
Field Goals	Nick Lowery, 1980-1993	329
Touchdowns (Tot.)	Otis Taylor, 1965-1975	60
Points	Nick Lowery, 1980-1993	1,466

INDIVIDUAL RECORDS—SINGLE SEASON

Category	Name	Performance
Rushing (Yds.)	Christian Okoye, 1989	1,480
Passing (Yds.)	Bill Kenney, 1983	4,348
Passing (TDs)	Len Dawson, 1964	30
Receiving (No.)	Carlos Carson, 1983	80
Receiving (Yds.)	Carlos Carson, 1983	1,351
Interceptions	Emmitt Thomas, 1974	12
Punting (Avg.)	Jerrel Wilson, 1965	46.0
Punt Return (Avg.)	Abner Haynes, 1960	15.4
Kickoff Return (Avg.)	Dave Grayson, 1962	29.7
Field Goals	Nick Lowery, 1990	34
Touchdowns (Tot.)	Abner Haynes, 1962	19
Points	Nick Lowery, 1990	139

INDIVIDUAL RECORDS—SINGLE GAME

Category	Name	Performance
Rushing (Yds.)	Barry Word, 10-14-90	200
Passing (Yds.)	Len Dawson, 11-1-64	435
Passing (TDs)	Len Dawson, 11-1-64	6
Receiving (No.)	Ed Podolak, 10-7-73	12
Receiving (Yds.)	Stephone Paige, 12-22-85	309
Interceptions	Bobby Ply, 10-16-62	*4
	Bobby Hunt, 12-4-64	*4
	Deron Cherry, 9-29-85	*4
Field Goals	Many times	5
	Last time by Nick Lowery, 9-21-93	
Touchdowns (Tot.)	Abner Haynes, 11-26-61	5
Points	Abner Haynes, 11-26-61	30

*NFL Record

COACHING HISTORY

DALLAS TEXANS 1960-62
(330-289-12)

1960-1974	Hank Stram	129-79-10
1975-77	Paul Wiggin*	11-24-0
1977	Tom Bettis	1-6-0
1978-1982	Marv Levy	31-42-0
1983-86	John Mackovic	30-35-0
1987-88	Frank Gansz	8-22-1
1989-1998	Marty Schottenheimer	104-65-1
1999-2000	Gunther Cunningham	16-16-0

*Released after seven games in 1977

ARROWHEAD STADIUM

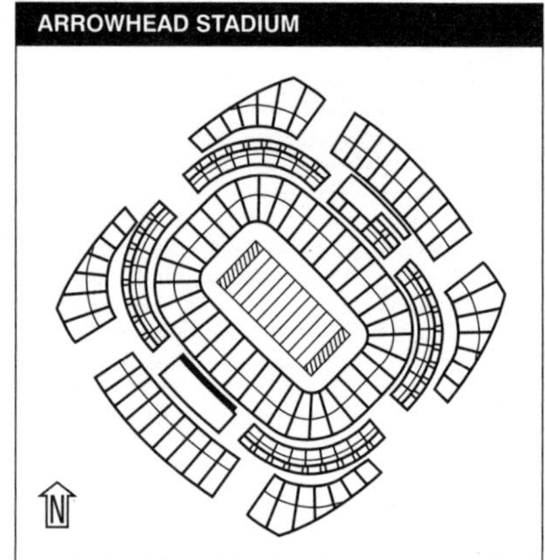

2000 TEAM RECORD

PRESEASON (0-4)

Date	Result		Opponent
8/5	L	10-14	at Tennessee
8/13	L	10-33	San Francisco
8/19	L	22-26	Jacksonville
8/25	L	14-37	at Tampa Bay

REGULAR SEASON (7-9)

Date	Result		Opponent	Att.
9/3	L	14-27	Indianapolis	78,357
9/10	L	14-17	at Tennessee (OT)	68,203
9/17	W	42-10	San Diego	77,604
9/24	W	23-22	at Denver	74,596
10/2	W	24-17	Seattle	82,893
10/15	L	17-20	Oakland	79,025
10/22	W	54-34	St. Louis	79,142
10/29	W	24-19	at Seattle	62,141
11/5	L	31-49	at Oakland	62,428
11/12	L	7-21	at San Francisco	68,002
11/19	L	17-21	Buffalo	78,457
11/26	L	16-17	at San Diego	47,228
12/4	L	24-30	at New England	60,292
12/10	W	15-14	Carolina	77,481
12/17	W	20-7	Denver	78,406
12/24	L	13-29	at Atlanta	41,017

(OT) Overtime

SCORE BY PERIODS

Chiefs	50	99	82	124	0	—	355
Opponents	75	123	64	89	3	—	354

ATTENDANCE

Home 627,093 Away 499,064 Total 1,126,157
Single-game home record, 82,893 (10/2/00)
Single-season home record, 629,569 (1999)

2000 TEAM STATISTICS

	Chiefs	Opp.
Total First Downs	321	330
Rushing	84	103
Passing	207	201
Penalty	30	26
Third Down: Made/Att	75/204	84/207
Third Down Pct.	36.8	40.6
Fourth Down: Made/Att	4/13	8/11
Fourth Down Pct.	30.8	72.7
Total Net Yards	5,614	5,280
Avg. Per Game	350.9	330.0
Total Plays	999	1,041
Avg. Per Play	5.6	5.1
Net Yards Rushing	1,465	1,809
Avg. Per Game	91.6	113.1
Total Rushes	383	441
Net Yards Passing	4,149	3,471
Avg. Per Game	259.3	216.9
Sacked/Yards Lost	34/259	51/266
Gross Yards	4,408	3,737
Att./Completions	582/342	549/358
Completion Pct.	58.8	65.2
Had Intercepted	15	15
Punts/Average	82/44.6	78/43.1
Net Punting Avg.	82/35.8	78/36.8
Penalties/Yards	118/848	108/1,020
Fumbles/Ball Lost	23/11	19/14
Touchdowns	44	42
Rushing	12	13
Passing	29	25
Returns	3	4
Avg. Time of Possession	27:36	32:24

2000 INDIVIDUAL STATISTICS

Passing	Att.	Comp.	Yds.	Pct.	TD	Int.	Tkld.	Rate
Grbac	547	326	4,169	59.6	28	14	29/213	89.9
Moon	34	15	208	44.1	1	1	5/46	61.9
Morris	1	1	31	100.0	0	0	0/0	118.8
Chiefs	582	342	4,408	58.8	29	15	34/259	88.5
Opponents	549	358	3,737	65.2	25	15	51/266	88.6

SCORING	TD R	TD P	TD Rt	PAT	FG	Saf	PTS
Peterson	0	0	0	25/25	15/20	0	70
Alexander	0	10	0	0/0	0/0	0	60
Gonzalez	0	9	0	0/0	0/0	0	54
Richardson	3	3	0	0/0	0/0	0	36
Moreau	4	0	0	0/0	0/0	0	24
Stoyanovich	0	0	0	15/15	2/4	0	21
Morris	0	3	0	0/0	0/0	0	18
Anders	2	0	0	0/0	0/0	0	12
Cloud	1	0	1	0/0	0/0	0	12
Drayton	0	2	0	0/0	0/0	0	12
Lockett	0	2	0	0/0	0/0	0	12
Bennett	1	0	0	0/0	0/0	0	6
Edwards	0	0	1	0/0	0/0	0	6
Grbac	1	0	0	0/0	0/0	0	6
Patton	0	0	1	0/0	0/0	0	6
Chiefs	12	29	3	40/40	17/24	0	355
Opponents	13	25	4	39/39	21/30	0	354

2-Pt. Conversions: None.
Chiefs 0-4, Opponents 0-3.

RUSHING	Att.	Yds.	Avg.	LG	TD
Richardson	147	697	4.7	33	3
Anders	76	331	4.4	69	2
Moreau	67	179	2.7	22	4
Grbac	30	110	3.7	22	1
Cloud	30	84	2.8	15t	1
Alexander	3	45	15.0	26	0
Bennett	27	24	0.9	6	1
Moon	2	2	1.0	2	0
Parker	1	-7	-7.0	-7	0
Chiefs	383	1,465	3.8	69	12
Opponents	441	1,809	4.1	50	13

RECEIVING	No.	Yds.	Avg.	LG	TD
Gonzalez	93	1,203	12.9	39	9
Alexander	78	1,391	17.8	81t	10
Richardson	58	468	8.1	24	3
Morris	48	678	14.1	47	3
Lockett	33	422	12.8	34t	2
Anders	15	76	5.1	12	0
Drayton	8	70	8.8	21	2
Parker	3	41	13.7	27	0
Dunn	2	26	13.0	20	0
Bennett	2	17	8.5	13	0
Cloud	2	16	8.0	13	0
Chiefs	342	4,408	12.9	81t	29
Opponents	358	3,737	10.4	47	25

INTERCEPTIONS	No.	Yds.	Avg.	LG	TD
Hasty	4	53	13.3	38	0
Edwards	2	45	22.5	42t	1
Patton	2	39	19.5	24t	1
Wesley	2	28	14.0	28	0
Woods	2	0	0.0	0	0
Bush	1	33	33.0	33	0
Browning	1	0	0.0	0	0
Dennis	1	0	0.0	0	0
Chiefs	15	198	13.2	42t	2
Opponents	15	295	19.7	56t	3

PUNTING	No.	Yds.	Avg.	In 20	LG
Sauerbrun	82	3,656	44.6	28	68
Chiefs	82	3,656	44.6	28	68
Opponents	78	3,363	43.1	18	64

PUNT RETURNS	No.	FC	Yds.	Avg.	LG	TD
Lockett	26	6	208	8.0	26	0
Hall	6	5	37	6.2	22	0
Parker	5	1	50	10.0	17	0
Chiefs	37	12	295	8.0	26	0
Opponents	43	18	559	13.0	41	0

KICKOFF RETURNS	No.	Yds.	Avg.	LG	TD
Cloud	36	779	21.6	38	0
Hall	17	358	21.1	36	0
Parker	14	279	19.9	27	0
Anders	1	14	14.0	14	0
Lockett	1	25	25.0	25	0
Spears	1	11	11.0	11	0
Chiefs	70	1,466	20.9	38	0
Opponents	70	1,679	24.0	66	0

FIELD GOALS	1-19	20-29	30-39	40-49	50+
Peterson	1/1	5/5	7/9	2/5	0/0
Stoyanovich	0/0	1/1	0/2	1/1	0/0
Chiefs	1/1	6/6	7/11	3/6	0/0
Opponents	0/0	8/8	2/5	7/10	4/7

SACKS	No.
Hicks	14.0
Clemons	7.5
D. Williams	7.5
Browning	6.0
McGlockton	4.0
Maslowski	2.0
T. Williams	2.0
Woods	2.0
Bartee	1.0
Bush	1.0
Edwards	1.0
Hasty	1.0
Patton	1.0
Wesley	1.0
Chiefs	51.0
Opponents	34.0

2001 DRAFT CHOICES

Round	Name	Pos.	College
3	Eric Downing	DT	Syracuse
	Marvin Minnis	WR	Florida State
4	Monty Beisel	DE	Kansas State
	George Layne	RB	Texas Christian
5	Billy Baber	TE	Virginia
	Derrick Blaylock	RB	Stephen F. Austin
6	Alex Sulfsted	G	Miami (Ohio)
7	Shaunard Harts	DB	Boise State
	Terdell Sands	DT	Tennessee-Chattanooga

KANSAS CITY CHIEFS

2001 VETERAN ROSTER

No.	Name	Pos.	Ht.	Wt.	Birthdate	NFL Exp.	College	Hometown	How Acq.	'00 Games/ Starts
82	Alexander, Derrick	WR	6-2	200	11/6/71	8	Michigan	Detroit, Mich.	UFA(Balt)-'98	16/16
72	Alford, Darnel	T	6-4	328	6/11/77	2	Boston College	Fredericksburg, Va.	D6-'00	1/0
26	Allen, Taje	CB	5-11	185	11/6/73	5	Texas	Lubbock, Texas	UFA(StL)-'01	16/16*
35	Atkins, Larry	S	6-3	225	7/21/75	3	UCLA	Venice, Calif.	D3b-'99	15/0
24	Bartee, William	CB	6-1	196	6/25/77	2	Oklahoma	Daytona Beach, Fla.	D2-'00	16/3
69	Blackshear, Jeff	G	6-6	316	3/29/69	8	Northeast Louisiana	Fort Pierce, Fla.	FA-'00	16/15
6	Brister, Bubby	QB	6-3	215	8/15/62	15	Northeast Louisiana	Fort Pierce, Fla.	FA-'01	2/0*
93	Browning, John	DT	6-4	289	9/30/73	6	West Virginia	Miami, Fla.	D3-'96	16/16
56	Bush, Lew	LB	6-2	247	12/2/69	7	Washington State	Atlanta, Ga.	UFA(Minn)-'00	16/8
99	Clemons, Duane	DE	6-5	277	5/23/74	6	California	Riverside, Calif.	FA-'00	12/12
34	Cloud, Mike	RB	5-10	205	7/1/75	3	Boston College	Portsmouth, R.I.	D2-'99	16/4
15	Collins, Todd	QB	6-4	227	11/5/71	7	Michigan	Walpole, Mass.	W(Buff)-'98	0*
39	Crockett, Ray	CB	5-10	184	1/5/67	13	Baylor	Dallas, Texas	UFA(Den)-'01	13/11*
41	Dennis, Pat	CB	6-0	207	6/3/78	2	Louisiana-Monroe	Shreveport, La	D5b-'00	16/13
89	Dunn, Jason	TE	6-4	260	11/15/73	5	Eastern Kentucky	Harrodsburg, Ky.	FA-'00	14/2
59	Edwards, Donnie	LB	6-2	227	4/6/73	6	UCLA	Chula Vista, Calif.	D4-'96	16/16
83	Gammon, Kendall	TE	6-4	258	10/23/68	10	Pittsburg State	Wichita, Kan.	UFA(NO)-'00	16/0
88	Gonzalez, Tony	TE	6-4	249	2/27/76	5	California	Huntington Beach, Calif.	D1-'97	16/16
10	t- Green, Trent	QB	6-3	215	7/9/70	8	Indiana	Cedar Rapids, Iowa	T(StL)-'01	8/5*
20	Hall, Dante	RB	5-8	193	9/1/78	2	Texas A&M	Lufkin, Texas	D5a-'00	5/0
98	Hicks, Eric	DE	6-6	286	6/17/76	4	Maryland	Erie, Pa.	FA-'98	13/11
31	Holmes, Priest	RB	5-9	205	10/7/73	5	Texas	Fort Smith, Ark.	UFA(Balt)-'01	16/2*
81	Horne, Tony	WR	5-9	173	3/21/76	4	Clemson	Rockingham, N.C.	RFA(StL)-'01	11/0*
73	Jones, Willie	T	6-7	365	12/17/75	2	Grambling State	Pahokee, Fla.	FA-'00	0*
91	Jordan, Richard	LB	6-1	255	12/1/74	5	Missouri Southern	Hillsboro, Texas	FA-'01	0*
54	Kazadi, Muadianvita	LB	6-2	236	12/20/73	2	Tulsa	Zaire, Africa	FA-'01	0*
67	Kubik, Brad	G	6-3	299	3/31/75	3	Southwest Missouri St.	Springfield, Mo.	FA-'98	0/0
90	Martin, Steve	DT	6-4	312	5/31/74	6	Missouri	Jefferson City, Mo.	UFA(Phil)-'00	16/0
57	Maslowski, Mike	LB	6-1	251	7/11/74	3	Wisconsin-La Crosse	Thorp, Wis.	FA-'99	16/5
47	McCullough, George	CB	5-10	187	2/18/75	4	Baylor	Galveston, Texas	FA-'01	10/0*
22	Moreau, Frank	RB	6-0	223	9/9/76	2	Louisville	Elizabethtown, Ky.	D4-'00	11/0
84	Morris, Sylvester	WR	6-3	206	10/6/77	2	Jackson State	New Orleans, La.	D1-'00	15/14
52	O'Neal, Andre	LB	6-1	235	12/12/75	2	Marshall	Decatur, Ga.	FA-'00	10/0
97	Owens, Rich	DE	6-6	275	5/22/72	7	Lehigh	Philadelphia, Pa.	UFA(Mia)-'01	12/3*
80	Parker, Larry	WR	6-1	205	7/14/76	3	Southern California	Bakersfield, Calif.	D4-'99	16/0
53	Patton, Marvcus	LB	6-2	237	5/1/67	12	UCLA	Lawndale, Calif.	UFA(Wash)-'99	16/15
2	Peterson, Todd	K	5-10	177	2/4/70	7	Georgia	Washington, D.C.	FA-'00	11/0
95	Ransom, Derrick	DT	6-3	310	9/13/76	4	Cincinnati	Indianapolis, Ind.	D6-'98	10/0
49	Richardson, Tony	FB	6-1	233	12/17/71	7	Auburn	Daleville, Ala.	FA-'95	16/16
85	Ricks, Mikhael	WR	6-5	237	11/14/74	4	Stephen F. Austin	Anahuac, Texas	FA-'00	1/0*
66	Riley, Victor	T	6-5	328	11/4/74	4	Auburn	Swansea, S.C.	D1-'98	16/16
68	Shields, Will	G	6-3	311	9/15/71	9	Nebraska	Lawton, Okla.	D3-'93	16/16
70	Spears, Marcus	T	6-4	312	9/28/71	8	Northwestern State (La.)	Scotlandville, La.	FA-'97	13/0
55	Stills, Gary	LB	6-2	235	7/11/74	3	West Virginia	Trenton, N.J.	D3a-'99	12/0
4	Stryzinski, Dan	P	6-2	200	5/15/65	12	Indiana	Vincennes, Ind.	UFA(Atl)-'01	16/0*
76	Tait, John	T	6-6	305	1/26/75	3	Brigham Young	Phoenix, Ariz.	D1-'99P	15/15
87	Thomas, Chris	WR	6-0	190	7/16/71	5	Cal Poly-San Luis Obispo	Ventura, Calif.	UFA(StL)-'01	16/0*
65	Threats, Jabbar	DE	6-5	268	4/26/75	3	Michigan State	Springfield, Ohio	FA-'01	0*
27	Walker, Bracy	S	6-0	206	10/28/70	8	North Carolina	Fayetteville, N.C.	FA-'98	15/0
44	Warfield, Eric	CB	6-0	198	3/3/76	4	Nebraska	Texarkana, Ark.	D7a-'98	13/3
54	Waters, Brian	C	6-3	293	2/18/77	2	North Texas	Waxahachie, Texas	FA-'00	6/0
25	Wesley, Greg	S	6-2	208	3/19/78	2	Arkansas-Pine Bluff	England, Ark.	D3-'00	16/16
62	Wiegmann, Casey	C	6-3	285	7/20/75	5	Iowa	Parkersburg, Iowa	UFA(Chi)-'01	16/0*
92	Williams, Dan	DT	6-4	288	12/15/69	8	Toledo	Ypsilanti, Mich.	FA-'97	12/0
43	Williams, Jermaine	FB	5-11	235	7/3/72	3	Houston	Greenville, N.C.	FA-'01	0*
96	Williams, Tyrone	DE	6-4	292	10/22/72	4	Wyoming	Papillion, Neb.	FA-'00	10/0
60	Willis, Donald	G	6-3	330	7/15/73	4	North Carolina A&T	Goleta, Calif.	FA-'00	16/2
21	Woods, Jerome	S	6-2	207	3/17/73	6	Memphis	Memphis, Tenn.	D1-'96	16/16

* Allen and Thomas played 16 games with St. Louis in '00; Brister played 2 games with Minnesota; Collins was inactive for 16 games; Crockett played 13 games with Denver; Green played 8 games with St. Louis; Holmes played 16 games with Baltimore; Horne played 11 games with St. Louis; Jones last active with St. Louis in '99; Jordan last active with Detroit in '99; Kazadi last active with St. Louis in '97; McCullough played 10 games with Tennessee; Owens played 12 games with Miami; Stryzinski played 16 games with Atlanta; Threats last active with Jacksonville in '98; Wiegmann played 16 games with Chicago; J. Williams played 7 games with Jacksonville.

t- Chiefs traded for Green (St. Louis).

Retired—Warren Moon, 17-year quarterback, 2 games in '00.

Players lost through free agency (3): RB Donnell Bennett (Wash; 7 games in '00), QB Elvis Grbac (Balt; 15), WR Kevin Lockett (Wash; 16).

Also played with Chiefs in '00—RB Kimble Anders (15), TE Troy Drayton (16), LB Ron George (16), CB Carlton Gray (4), C Tim Grunhard (16), DT Norris McCleary (3), DT Chester McGlockton (15), DE Ty Parten (2), P Todd Sauerbrun (16), K Pete Stoyanovich (5), G Dave Szott (1).

COACHING STAFF

Head Coach,
Dick Vermeil

Pro Career: Dick Vermeil was named the ninth head coach in Chiefs franchise history on January 12, 2001. Vermeil joins Bill Parcells, Dan Reeves, and Don Shula as the only four coaches in NFL history to guide two different teams to the Super Bowl. He led St. Louis to a win in Super Bowl XXXIV following the 1999 season and guided Philadelphia to an appearance in Super Bowl XV after the 1980 season. He is just one of four active NFL head coaches (Mike Shanahan, Mike Holmgren, and George Seifert) who own a Super Bowl victory as a head coach. In 1976, Vermeil inherited a Philadelphia squad that had not produced a winning season since 1966. In 1978, he landed the Eagles in the playoffs for the first time since 1961. After leading Philadelphia to a franchise-best 12-4 record and a Super Bowl trip, he was named NFL coach of the year. In 1997, Vermeil took over a St. Louis team that had suffered seven consecutive losing seasons and hadn't been to the postseason since 1989. In just his third season as head coach of that club, he guided the Rams to a franchise-best regular season 13-3 record and the lone Super Bowl victory in that club's history. Vermeil was again honored as the NFL's coach of the year. Vermeil enters his eleventh season as an NFL head coach in 2001. Vermeil entered the league as the first special-teams coach in NFL history with the L.A. Rams in 1969. After one season at UCLA in 1970, he returned to the Rams where he served as offensive coordinator/quarterbacks coach from 1971-72. He then coached running backs and special teams for Rams head coach Chuck Knox in 1973 before becoming head coach at UCLA. Career record: 82-77.
Background: Vermeil played quarterback at San Jose State from 1956-57 after transferring from Napa (Calif.) Junior College. He owns the distinction of being named "Coach of the Year" on four levels: high school, junior college, NCAA Division I, and the NFL. He earned the first two honors at San Mateo's (Calif.) Hillsdale High School and Napa Junior College before entering the Division I ranks at Stanford from 1965-68. He served a one-year stint on Tommy Prothro's staff as offensive coordinator at UCLA in 1970. He then took over the head coaching reigns at UCLA from 1974-75 where his clubs compiled a 15-5-3 overall record. In 1975, the Bruins capped off an improbable season by upsetting top-ranked Ohio State in the Rose Bowl. He is the only coach to have guided a team to a victory in both the Rose Bowl and the Super Bowl.
Personal: Born October 30, 1936 in Calistoga, Calif. Graduated from San Jose State with degrees in physical education (B.S. 1958, M.A. 1959). Vermeil and his wife Carol reside in Kansas City, Mo. They have three children and 11 grandchildren.

ASSISTANT COACHES

Irv Eatman, assistant offensive line; born January 1, 1961, Birmingham, Ala., lives in Lee's Summitt, Mo. Defensive end-offensive tackle UCLA 1979-1982. Pro offensive tackle Philadelphia/Baltimore Stars (USFL) 1983-85, Kansas City Chiefs 1986-1990, New York Jets 1991-92, L.A. Rams 1993, Atlanta Falcons 1994, Houston Oilers 1995-96. Pro coach: Green Bay Packers 1999, Pittsburgh Steelers 2000, joined Chiefs in 2001.
Frank Gansz, Jr., special teams; born August 8, 1962, Houston, lives in Overland Park, Kan. Defensive back The Citadel 1981-84. No pro playing experience. College coach: Kansas 1987, Pittsburgh 1988-89, Army 1990-91, Houston 1993-97. Pro coach: New York-New Jersey Knights (WLAF) 1992, Oakland Raiders 1998-99, joined Chiefs in 2001.
Peter Giunta, defensive backs; born August 11, 1956, Salem, Mass., lives in Leawood, Kan. Running back-defensive back Northeastern 1974-77. No pro playing experience. College coach: Penn State 1981-83, Brown 1984-87, Lehigh 1988-1990. Pro coach: Philadelphia Eagles 1991-94, N.Y. Jets 1995-96, St. Louis Rams 1997-2000, joined Chiefs in 2001.
Carl Hairston, defensive line; born December 15, 1952, Martinsville, Va., lives in Independence, Mo. Defensive end Maryland-Eastern Shore 1972-75. Pro defensive end Philadelphia Eagles 1976-1983, Cleveland Browns 1984-89, Phoenix Cardinals 1990. Pro coach: Kansas City Chiefs 1995-96, St. Louis Rams 1997-2000, rejoined Chiefs in 2001.
Jeff Hurd, strength and conditioning; born April 24, 1958, Pomona, Calif., lives in Overland Park, Kan. Attended Fort Hays State. No college or pro playing experience. College coach: Fort Hays State 1984, Delta State 1985, Clemson 1986, Western Michigan 1987-1993, Tulsa 1994. Pro coach: Jacksonville Jaguars 1995-97, joined Chiefs in 1998.
Charlie Joiner, receivers; born October 14, 1947, Many, La., lives in Overland Park, Kan. Wide receiver Grambling State 1965-68. Pro defensive back-wide receiver Houston Oilers 1969-1972, Cincinnati Bengals 1972-75, San Diego Chargers 1976-1986. Inducted into Pro Football Hall of Fame 1996. Pro coach: San Diego Chargers 1987-1991, Buffalo Bills 1992-2000, joined the Chiefs in 2001.
Bob Karmelowicz, defensive line; born July 22, 1949, New Britain, Conn., lives in Lenexa, Kan. Nose tackle Bridgeport 1968-1971. No pro playing experience. College coach: Arizona State 1974-79, Massachusetts 1980, Texas-El Paso 1981, Illinois 1982-86, Washington State 1987-88, Miami 1989-1991. Pro coach: Cincinnati Bengals 1992-93, Washington Redskins 1994-96, joined Chiefs in 1997.
Billy Long, asst. strength and conditioning coach; born June 23, 1959, Phenix City, Ala., lives in Lee's Summit, Mo. College coach: Alabama State 1981-86, Arkansas-Pine Bluff 1987-1991, Southern 1992-2000. Pro coach: Joined Chiefs in 2001.
Greg Robinson, defensive coordinator; born October 9, 1951, Los Angeles, Calif., lives in Leawood, Kan. Linebacker-tight end Pacific 1973-74. No pro playing experience. College coach: Pacific 1975-76, Cal State-Fullerton 1977-79, North Carolina State 1980-81, UCLA 1982-89. Pro coach: New York Jets 1990-94, Denver Broncos 1995-2000, joined Chiefs in 2001.
Keith Rowen, tight ends; born September 2, 1952, New York, N.Y., lives in Overland Park, Kan. Offensive tackle Stanford 1972-74. No pro playing experience. College coach: Stanford 1974-75, Long Beach State 1977-78, Arizona 1979-1982. Pro coach: Boston/New Orleans Breakers (USFL) 1983-84, Cleveland Browns 1984, Indianapolis Colts 1985-88, New England Patriots 1989, Atlanta Falcons 1990-93, Minnesota Vikings 1994-96, Oakland Raiders 1997-98, joined Chiefs in 1999.
Al Saunders, offensive coordinator; born February 1, 1947, London, England, lives in Overland Park, Kan. Wide receiver-defensive back San Jose State 1966-68. No pro playing experience. College coach: Southern California 1970-71, Missouri 1972, Utah State 1973-75, California 1976-1981, Tennessee 1982. Pro coach: San Diego Chargers 1983-88 (head coach 1986-88), Kansas City Chiefs 1989-1998, St. Louis Rams 1999-2000, rejoined Chiefs in 2001.
James Saxon, running backs; born March 23, 1966, Beaufort, S.C., lives in Independence, Mo. Running back American River J.C. (S.C.) 1985, San Jose State 1986-87. Pro running back Kansas City Chiefs 1988-1991, Miami Dolphins 1992-94, Philadelphia Eagles 1995. College coach: Rutgers 1997-98, Menlo College 1999. Pro coach: Buffalo Bills 2000, joined Chiefs in 2001.
Terry Shea, quarterbacks; born June 12, 1946, San Mateo, Calif., lives in Leawood, Kan. Quarterback Oregon 1965-67. No pro playing experience. College coach: Oregon 1968-69; Mt. Hood J.C. (Ore.) 1970-75, Utah State 1976-1981, San Jose State 1984-86, 1990-91 (head coach 1990-91), California 1987-89, Stanford 1992-94, Rutgers 1996-2000 (head coach 1996-2000). Pro coach: British Columbia Lions 1995 (CFL), joined Chiefs in 2001.
Mike Solari, offensive line; born January 16, 1955, Daly City, Calif., lives in Leawood, Kan. Offensive lineman San Diego State 1975-76. No pro playing experience. College coach: Mira Vista (Calif.) J.C. 1977-78, U.S. International 1979, Boise State 1980, Cincinnati 1990-91. Pro coach: Dallas Cowboys 1987-88, Phoenix Cardinals 1989, San Francisco 49ers 1992-96, joined Chiefs in 1997.
Jason Verduzco, offensive assistant-quality control; born April 3, 1970, Walnut Creek, Calif., lives in Leawood, Kan. Quarterback Illinois 1989-1993. Pro quarterback: British Columbia Lions (CFL) 1993. College coach: Hamilton College (N.Y.) 1994-96, Illinois 1997-99. Pro coach: Washington Redskins 2000, joined Chiefs in 2001.

2001 FIRST-YEAR ROSTER

Name	Pos.	Ht.	Wt.	Birthdate	College	Hometown	How Acq.
Allen, Ian	G	6-4	305	7/22/78	Purdue	Fairburn, Ga.	FA
Baber, Billy	TE	6-3	255	1/17/79	Virginia	Charlottesville, Va.	D5a
Beisel, Monty	DE	6-3	270	8/20/78	Kansas State	Douglass, Kan.	D4a
Blaylock, Derrick	RB	5-9	188	8/23/79	Stephen F. Austin	Atlanta, Texas	D5b
Blick, John (1)	T	6-6	315	2/10/78	Penn. State	Saylorsburg, Pa.	FA-'00
Carter, Dyshod	CB	5-10	186	6/18/78	Kansas State	Denver, Colo.	FA
Downing, Eric	DT	6-3	302	9/16/78	Syracuse	Ahoskie, N.C.	D3a
Gholston, Kendrick (1)	DE	6-4	279	4/30/75	Louisville	Chicago, Ill.	FA-'00
Hall, Ricky (1)	WR	6-2	207	1/17/76	Virginia Tech	Blacksburg, Va.	FA
Harts, Shaunard	S	5-11	195	8/4/78	Boise State	Pittsburg, Calif.	D7a
Helming, Ryan	QB	6-2	220	12/14/77	Northern Iowa	Springfield, Mo.	FA
Hunt, Robert (1)	G	6-3	307	7/22/75	Virginia	Newport News, Va.	FA
Jacobs, John (1)	G	6-5	335	12/1/72	Baker	Baldwin City, Kan.	FA
Klemic, Dave	WR	5-11	185	6/16/78	Northeastern	Somers Point, N.J.	FA
Layne, George	FB	5-11	243	10/9/78	Texas Christian	Alvin, Texas	D4b
McCleary, Norris (1)	DT	6-4	305	5/10/77	East Carolina	Shelby, N.C.	FA-'00
Minnis, Marvin	WR	6-1	171	2/6/77	Florida State	Miami, Fla.	D3b
Moses, J.J.	WR	5-6	175	9/12/79	Iowa State	Waterloo, Iowa	FA
Muther, Pete (1)	TE	6-3	238	6/9/77	Tulsa	Kansas City, Mo.	FA
Ornstein, Gus (1)	QB	6-5	215	11/23/74	Rowan	New York, N.Y.	FA
Perez, Joe (1)	WR	6-0	202	5/21/77	Murray State	Overland Park, Kan.	FA-'00
Robertson, Wes	LB	6-2	225	11/19/78	Rutgers	Camden, N.J.	FA
Sands, Terdell	DT	6-7	330	10/31/79	Tennessee-Chattanooga	Chattanooga, Tenn.	D7b
Simon, Geroy (1)	WR	6-1	188	9/11/75	Maryland	Johnstown, Pa.	FA
Sulfsted, Alex	G	6-3	317	12/21/77	Miami (Ohio)	Lebanon, Ohio	D6
Thomas, Mark (1)	TE	6-4	248	4/26/76	North Carolina State	Kinston, N.C.	FA
Tisdale, Casey (1)	LB	6-4	256	6/18/76	New Mexico	Oakland, Calif.	FA
Trout, Brad (1)	S	6-0	185	1/22/75	Valdosta State	Miami, Fla.	FA
Tynes, Lawrence	K	6-0	188	5/3/78	Troy State	Milton, Fla.	FA
Warren, Jesse (1)	DE	6-3	263	3/21/78	Colorado	Dallas, Texas	W(Tenn)
Washington, Thomas (1)	DT	6-3	332	12/12/76	Winston-Salem State	Charleston, S.C.	FA-'00

The term NFL Rookie is defined as a player who is in his first season of professional football and has not been on the roster of another professional football team for any regular-season or postseason games. A Rookie is designated by an "R" on NFL rosters. Players who have been active in another professional football league or players who have NFL experience, including either preseason training camp or being on an Active List or Inactive List, or on Reserve/Injured or Reserve/Physically Unable to Perform for fewer than six regular-season games, are termed NFL First-Year Players. An NFL First-Year Player is designated by a "1" on NFL rosters. Thereafter, a player is credited with an additional year of experience for each season in which he accumulates six games on the Active List or Inactive List, or on Reserve/Injured or Reserve/Physically Unable to Perform.

MIAMI DOLPHINS

American Football Conference
Eastern Division
Team Colors: Aqua, Coral, Blue, and White
7500 S.W. 30th Street
Davie, Florida 33314
Telephone: (954) 452-7000

CLUB OFFICIALS

Owner/Chairman of the Board: H. Wayne Huizenga
President/Chief Operating Officer: Eddie J. Jones
Head Coach: Dave Wannstedt
Senior Vice President-Business Operations: Bryan Wiedmeier
Senior Vice President-Finance & Administration: Jill R. Strafaci
Vice President-Player Personnel: Rick Spielman
Director of College Scouting: Ron Labadie
Director of Pro Personnel: George Paton
Vice President-Media Relations: Harvey Greene
Director of Media Relations: Neal Gulkis
Media Relations Coordinator: Seth Levit
Director of Publications & Internet: Scott Stone
Senior Vice President-Sales and Marketing: Bill Galante
Vice President-Sales & Marketing: Jim Ross
Senior Director of Community & Alumni Relations: Fudge Browne
Director of Operations: Rhett Ticconi
Head Athletic Trainer: Kevin O'Neill
Equipment Manager: Tony Egues
Video Director: Dave Hack
Stadium: Pro Player Stadium (built in 1987)
• **Capacity:** 75,192
2269 N.W. 199th Street
Miami, Florida 33056
Playing Surface: Grass (PAT)
Training Camp: Nova University
7500 S.W. 30th Street
Davie, Florida 33314

RECORD HOLDERS

INDIVIDUAL RECORDS—CAREER

Category	Name	Performance
Rushing (Yds.)	Larry Csonka, 1968-1974, 1979	6,737
Passing (Yds.)	Dan Marino, 1983-1999	*61,361
Passing (TDs)	Dan Marino, 1983-1999	*420
Receiving (No.)	Mark Clayton, 1983-1992	550
Receiving (Yds.)	Mark Duper, 1982-1992	8,869
Interceptions	Jake Scott, 1970-75	35
Punting (Avg.)	John Kidd, 1994-97	44.2
Punt Return (Avg.)	Freddie Solomon, 1975-77	11.4
Kickoff Return (Avg.)	Mercury Morris, 1969-1975	26.5
Field Goals	Pete Stoyanovich, 1989-1995	176
Touchdowns (Tot.)	Mark Clayton, 1983-1992	82
Points	Garo Yepremian, 1970-78	830

INDIVIDUAL RECORDS—SINGLE SEASON

Category	Name	Performance
Rushing (Yds.)	Delvin Williams, 1978	1,258
Passing (Yds.)	Dan Marino, 1984	*5,084
Passing (TDs)	Dan Marino, 1984	*48
Receiving (No.)	O.J. McDuffie, 1998	90
Receiving (Yds.)	Mark Clayton, 1984	1,389
Interceptions	Dick Westmoreland, 1967	10
Punting (Avg.)	John Kidd, 1996	46.3
Punt Return (Avg.)	Jeff Ogden, 2000	17.0
Kickoff Return (Avg.)	Duriel Harris, 1976	32.9
Field Goals	Olindo Mare, 1999	*39
Touchdowns (Tot.)	Mark Clayton, 1984	18
Points	Olindo Mare, 1999	144

INDIVIDUAL RECORDS—SINGLE GAME

Category	Name	Performance
Rushing (Yds.)	Mercury Morris, 9-30-73	197
Passing (Yds.)	Dan Marino, 10-23-88	521
Passing (TDs)	Bob Griese, 11-24-77	6
	Dan Marino, 9-21-86	6
Receiving (No.)	Jim Jensen, 11-6-88	12
Receiving (Yds.)	Mark Duper, 11-10-85	217
Interceptions	Dick Anderson, 12-3-73	*4
Field Goals	Olindo Mare, 10-17-99	6
Touchdowns (Tot.)	Paul Warfield, 12-15-73	4
	Mark Ingram, 11-27-94	4
Points	Paul Warfield, 12-15-73	24
	Mark Ingram, 11-27-94	24

*NFL Record

2001 SCHEDULE

PRESEASON

Aug. 6	vs. St. Louis at Canton, Ohio	8:00
Aug. 13	at Tampa Bay	8:00
Aug. 18	**San Diego**	7:00
Aug. 25	at Green Bay	7:00
Aug. 31	**Minnesota**	7:00

REGULAR SEASON

Sept. 9	at Tennessee	7:30
Sept. 16	**Buffalo**	1:00
Sept. 23	**Oakland**	1:00
Sept. 30	at St. Louis	12:00
Oct. 7	**New England**	1:00
Oct. 14	at New York Jets	4:15
Oct. 21	Open Date	
Oct. 28	at Seattle	1:15
Nov. 4	**Carolina**	1:00
Nov. 11	at Indianapolis	1:00
Nov. 18	**New York Jets**	1:00
Nov. 25	at Buffalo	1:00
Dec. 2	**Denver**	1:00
Dec. 10	**Indianapolis** (Mon.)	9:00
Dec. 16	at San Francisco	1:05
Dec. 22	at New England (Sat.)	1:30
Dec. 30	**Atlanta**	1:00

PRO PLAYER STADIUM

COACHING HISTORY

(339-223-4)

Years	Coach	Record
1966-69	George Wilson	15-39-2
1970-1995	Don Shula	274-147-2
1996-99	Jimmy Johnson	38-31-0
2000	Dave Wannstedt	12-6-0

2000 TEAM RECORD

PRESEASON (3-1)

Date	Result		Opponent
8/5	L	10-13	at Pittsburgh
8/10	W	15-13	Tampa Bay
8/21	W	17-14	Green Bay
8/25	W	22-17	at New Orleans

REGULAR SEASON (11-5)

Date	Result		Opponent	Att.
9/3	W	23-0	Seattle	72,949
9/10	L	7-13	at Minnesota	64,112
9/17	W	19-6	Baltimore	73,464
9/24	W	10-3	New England	73,344
10/1	W	31-16	at Cincinnati	61,535
10/8	W	22-13	Buffalo	73,901
10/23	L	37-40	at New York Jets (OT)	78,389
10/29	W	28-20	Green Bay	73,740
11/5	W	23-8	at Detroit	77,813
11/12	W	17-7	at San Diego	56,896
11/19	L	3-20	New York Jets	74,320
11/26	W	17-14	at Indianapolis	56,935
12/3	W	33-6	at Buffalo	73,002
12/10	L	13-16	Tampa Bay	74,307
12/17	L	13-20	Indianapolis	73,884
12/24	W	27-24	at New England	60,292

POSTSEASON (1-1)

Date	Result		Opponent	Att.
12/30	W	23-17	Indianapolis (OT)	73,193
1/6	L	0-27	at Oakland	61,998

(OT) Overtime

SCORE BY PERIODS

Dolphins	67	109	90	57	0	—	323
Opponents	50	57	9	107	3	—	226

ATTENDANCE

Home 589,909 Away 532,673 Total 1,122,582
Single-game home record, 75,283 (10/27/96)
Single-season home record, 592,161 (1999)

2000 TEAM STATISTICS

	Dolphins	Opp.
Total First Downs	251	289
Rushing	104	92
Passing	122	156
Penalty	25	41
Third Down: Made/Att	75/214	70/211
Third Down Pct.	35.0	33.2
Fourth Down: Made/Att	4/6	8/15
Fourth Down Pct.	66.7	53.3
Total Net Yards	4,461	4,636
Avg. Per Game	278.8	289.8
Total Plays	945	995
Avg. Per Play	4.7	4.7
Net Yards Rushing	1,894	1,736
Avg. Per Game	118.4	108.5
Total Rushes	496	417
Net Yards Passing	2,567	2,900
Avg. Per Game	160.4	181.3
Sacked/Yards Lost	28/153	48/270
Gross Yards	2,720	3,170
Att./Completions	421/243	530/282
Completion Pct.	57.7	53.2
Had Intercepted	17	28
Punts/Average	92/42.1	87/40.6
Net Punting Avg.	92/36.2	87/33.3
Penalties/Yards	115/920	86/793
Fumbles/Ball Lost	12/9	30/13
Touchdowns	34	23
Rushing	16	9
Passing	15	13
Returns	3	1
Avg. Time of Possession	30:43	29:17

2000 INDIVIDUAL STATISTICS

Passing	Att.	Comp.	Yds.	Pct.	TD	Int.	Tkld.	Rate
Fiedler	357	204	2,402	57.1	14	14	23/129	74.5
Huard	63	39	318	61.9	1	3	4/22	60.2
L. Smith	1	0	0	0.0	0	0	0/0	39.6
T. Thomas	0	0	0	—	0	0	1/2	—
Dolphins	421	243	2,720	57.7	15	17	28/153	72.2
Opponents	530	282	3,170	53.2	13	28	48/270	57.5

SCORING	TD R	TD P	TD Rt	PAT	FG	Saf	PTS
Mare	0	0	0	33/34	28/31	0	117
L. Smith	14	2	0	0/0	0/0	0	96
Gadsden	0	6	0	0/0	0/0	0	36
Shepherd	0	4	0	0/0	0/0	0	24
Emanuel	0	1	0	0/0	0/0	0	6
Fiedler	1	0	0	0/0	0/0	0	6
Goodwin	0	1	0	0/0	0/0	0	6
Johnson	1	0	0	0/0	0/0	0	6
Madison	0	0	1	0/0	0/0	0	6
Ogden	0	0	1	0/0	0/0	0	6
Taylor	0	0	1	0/0	0/0	0	6
T. Thomas	0	1	0	0/0	0/0	0	6
Haley	0	0	0	0/0	0/0	1	2
Dolphins	16	15	3	33/34	28/31	1	323
Opponents	9	13	1	20/20	22/30	0	226

2-Pt. Conversions: None.
Dolphins 0-0, Opponents 1-3.

RUSHING	Att.	Yds.	Avg.	LG	TD
L. Smith	309	1,139	3.7	68t	14
Fiedler	54	267	4.9	30	1
Johnson	50	168	3.4	16	1
T. Thomas	28	136	4.9	25	0
Denson	31	108	3.5	12	0
Izzo	1	39	39.0	39	0
Konrad	15	39	2.6	5	0
Shepherd	4	3	0.8	14	0
Emanuel	3	-2	-0.7	0	0
McDuffie	1	-3	-3.0	-3	0
Dolphins	496	1,894	3.8	68t	16
Opponents	417	1,736	4.2	45	9

RECEIVING	No.	Yds.	Avg.	LG	TD
Gadsden	56	786	14.0	61	6
Shepherd	35	446	12.7	46t	4
L. Smith	31	201	6.5	28	2
Martin	26	393	15.1	44	0
T. Thomas	16	117	7.3	15	1
McDuffie	14	143	10.2	24	0
Denson	14	105	7.5	28	0
Konrad	14	83	5.9	18	0
Weaver	10	179	17.9	41	0
Johnson	10	61	6.1	11	0
Emanuel	7	132	18.9	53t	1
Goodwin	6	36	6.0	9t	1
Ogden	2	24	12.0	12	0
Dyer	2	14	7.0	13	0
Dolphins	243	2,720	11.2	61	15
Opponents	282	3,170	11.2	59	13

INTERCEPTIONS	No.	Yds.	Avg.	LG	TD
Walker	7	80	11.4	31	0
Madison	5	80	16.0	34	0
Marion	5	72	14.4	24	0
Surtain	5	55	11.0	43	0
Wilson	1	19	19.0	19	0
Jeffries	1	3	3.0	3	0
Taylor	1	2	2.0	2	0
Bowens	1	0	0.0	0	0
Shaw	1	0	0.0	0	0
Z. Thomas	1	0	0.0	0	0
Dolphins	28	311	11.1	43	0
Opponents	17	102	6.0	32	1

PUNTING	No.	Yds.	Avg.	In 20	LG
Turk	92	3,870	42.1	25	70
Dolphins	92	3,870	42.1	25	70
Opponents	87	3,532	40.6	21	65

PUNT RETURNS	No.	FC	Yds.	Avg.	LG	TD
Ogden	19	11	323	17.0	81t	1
Shepherd	15	7	164	10.9	32	0
Kelly	5	0	31	6.2	10	0
McDuffie	0	1	0	—	—	0
Dolphins	39	19	518	13.3	81t	1
Opponents	36	21	258	7.2	40	0

KICKOFF RETURNS	No.	Yds.	Avg.	LG	TD
Marion	22	513	23.3	47	0
Denson	20	495	24.8	56	0
Williams	3	64	21.3	24	0
Goodwin	2	6	3.0	6	0
Johnson	2	26	13.0	26	0
Shepherd	1	14	14.0	14	0
Weaver	1	15	15.0	15	0
Dolphins	51	1,133	22.2	56	0
Opponents	68	1,260	18.5	37	0

FIELD GOALS	1-19	20-29	30-39	40-49	50+
Mare	0/0	7/8	9/10	12/13	0/0
Dolphins	0/0	7/8	9/10	12/13	0/0
Opponents	0/0	4/4	10/12	7/9	1/5

SACKS	No.
Armstrong	16.5
Taylor	14.5
Bowens	2.5
Gardener	2.5
Mixon	2.5
Bromell	2.0
Walker	2.0
Haley	1.5
Z. Thomas	1.5
Surtain	1.0
Owens	0.5
Rodgers	0.5
Wilson	0.5
Dolphins	48.0
Opponents	28.0

2001 DRAFT CHOICES

Round	Name	Pos.	College
1	Jamar Fletcher	DB	Wisconsin
2	Chris Chambers	WR	Wisconsin
3	Travis Minor	RB	Florida State
	Morlon Greenwood	LB	Syracuse
5	Shawn Draper	T	Alabama
6	Brandon Winey	T	Louisiana State
	Josh Heupel	QB	Oklahoma
	Otis Leverette	DE	Alabama-Birmingham
	Rick Crowell	LB	Colorado State

MIAMI DOLPHINS

2001 VETERAN ROSTER

No.		Name	Pos.	Ht.	Wt.	Birthdate	NFL Exp.	College	Hometown	How Acq.	'00 Games/ Starts
62		Andersen, Jason	G	6-6	315	9/3/75	4	Brigham Young	San Jose, Calif.	FA-'00	7/0*
60	#	Bock, John	G	6-3	295	2/11/71	7	Indiana State	Crystal Lake, Ill.	FA-'96	6/1
95		Bowens, Tim	DT	6-4	320	2/7/73	8	Mississippi	Okolona, Miss.	D1-'94	15/15
91		Bromell, Lorenzo	DE	6-6	275	9/23/75	4	Clemson	Georgetown, S.C.	D4-'98	8/0
64		Cesario, Anthony	G	6-5	310	7/19/76	3	Colorado State	Pueblo, Colo.	FA-'00	0*
25		Cousin, Terry	CB	5-9	190	3/11/75	5	South Carolina	Miami, Fla.	UFA(Atl)-'01	15/0*
21		Denson, Autry	RB	5-10	195	12/8/76	3	Notre Dame	Davie, Fla.	FA-'99	11/0
63		Dixon, Mark	G	6-4	300	11/26/70	3	Virginia	Jamestown, N.C.	FA-'98	15/15
33		Dyer, Deon	FB	5-11	255	10/2/77	2	North Carolina	Tidewater, Va.	D4-'00	16/0
9		Fiedler, Jay	QB	6-2	225	12/29/71	6	Dartmouth	Oceanside, N.Y.	UFA(Jax)-'00	15/15
27		Freeman, Arturo	S	6-0	195	10/27/76	2	South Carolina	Orangeburg, S.C.	D5-'00	8/0
86		Gadsden, Oronde	WR	6-2	215	8/20/71	4	Winston-Salem State	Charleston, S.C.	FA-'98	16/16
58		Galyon, Scott	LB	6-2	245	3/23/74	6	Tennessee	Seymour, Tenn.	UFA(NYG)-'00	6/1
42		Gamble, Trent	CB	5-9	195	7/24/77	2	Wyoming	Parker, Colo.	FA-'00	16/0
92		Gardener, Daryl	DT	6-6	315	2/25/73	6	Baylor	Lawton, Okla.	D1-'96	10/10
83		Goodwin, Hunter	TE	6-5	270	10/10/72	6	Texas A&M	Bellville, Texas	RFA(Minn)-'99	16/16
97		Grant, Ernest	DT	6-5	310	5/17/76	2	Arkansas-Pine Bluff	Atlanta, Ga.	D6-'00	2/0
75		Gregory, Damian	DT	6-2	315	1/21/77	2	Illinois State	Lansing, Mich.	FA-'00	0*
94		Haley, Jermaine	DT	6-4	270	2/23/73	2	Butte College	Fresno, Calif.	D7a-'99	15/4
5		Hanson, Chris	P	6-1	217	10/25/76	2	Marshall	East Coweta, Ga.	FA-'00	0*
30		Harris, Jeff	CB	5-11	192	7/19/77	2	Georgia	Jacksonville, Fla.	D7-'00	0*
48		Heffner-Liddiard, Brody	TE	6-4	235	6/12/77	2	Colorado	San Diego, Calif.	FA-'00	5/0
50		Hemsley, Nate	LB	6-1	220	5/5/74	3	Syracuse	Delran, N.J.	FA-'00	0*
51		Hendricks, Tommy	LB	6-2	231	10/23/78	2	Michigan	Houston, Texas	FA-'00	8/0
66		Irwin, Heath	G	6-4	300	6/27/73	6	Colorado	Boulder, Colo.	UFA(NE)-'00	13/0
32		Johnson, J.J.	RB	6-1	232	4/20/74	3	Mississippi State	Mobile, Ala.	D2a-'99	13/1
49		Johnson, Paris	S	6-3	220	1/18/76	2	Miami (Ohio)	Chicago, Ill.	FA-'01	0*
20		Kelly, Ben	CB	5-9	185	9/15/78	2	Colorado	Cleveland, Ohio	D3-'00	2/0
44		Konrad, Rob	FB	6-3	255	11/12/76	3	Syracuse	Andover, Mass.	D2b-'99	15/13
6		Lucas, Ray	QB	6-3	215	8/6/72	4	Rutgers	Harrison, N.J.	UFA(NYJ)-'01	7/0*
29		Madison, Sam	CB	5-11	185	4/23/74	5	Louisville	Monticello, Fla.	D2-'97	16/16
10		Mare, Olindo	K	5-10	195	6/6/73	5	Syracuse	Cooper City, Fla.	FA-'97	16/0
31	#	Marion, Brock	S	5-11	200	6/11/70	9	Nevada	Bakersfield, Calif.	UFA(Dall)-'98	16/16
46	t-	Mayes, Alonzo	TE	6-4	265	6/4/75	4	Oklahoma State	Oklahoma City, Okla.	T(Chi)-'00	5/3*
81		McDuffie, O.J.	WR	5-10	195	12/2/69	9	Penn State	Gate Mills, Ohio	D1-'93	9/1
80		McKnight, James	WR	6-1	200	6/17/72	9	Liberty	Apopka, Fla.	UFA(Dall)-'01	16/15*
79		Mixon, Kenny	DE	6-4	285	5/31/75	4	Louisiana State	Pineville, La.	D2b-'98	16/16
88		Ogden, Jeff	WR	6-0	190	2/22/75	4	Eastern Washington	Snohomish, Wash.	T(Dall)-'00	16/0
90		Ogunleye, Adewale	DE	6-4	278	8/9/77	2	Indiana	Staten Island, N.Y.	FA-'00	0*
72		Palmer, Dan	TE	6-4	290	8/9/77	2	Air Force	Anderson, S.C.	FA-'00	0*
89		Perry, Ed	TE	6-4	270	9/1/74	5	James Madison	Richmond, Va.	D6d-'97	9/0
75		Perry, Todd	G	6-5	308	11/28/70	9	Kentucky	Elizabethtown, Ky.	UFA(Chi)-'01	16/16*
22		Porter, Daryl	CB	5-9	190	1/16/74	4	Boston College	Ft. Lauderdale, Fla.	FA-'01	16/0*
4		Quinn, Mike	QB	6-4	215	4/15/74	5	Stephen F. Austin	Houston, Texas	FA-'00	0*
59		Rodgers, Derrick	LB	6-1	230	10/14/71	5	Arizona State	New Orleans, La.	D3b-'97	16/14
61		Ruddy, Tim	C	6-3	305	4/27/72	8	Notre Dame	Dunmore, Pa.	D2b-'94	16/16
56		Russell, Twan	LB	6-1	228	4/25/74	5	Miami	Ft. Lauderdale, Fla.	FA-'00	16/2
84	#	Shepherd, Leslie	WR	5-11	185	11/3/69	8	Temple	Forestville, Md.	FA-'00	13/11
74		Smith, Brent	T	6-5	315	11/21/73	5	Mississippi State	Pontotoc, Miss.	D3d-'97	16/2
26		Smith, Lamar	RB	5-11	229	11/29/70	8	Houston	Ft. Wayne, Ind.	FA-'00	15/15
76		Spriggs, Marcus	T	6-3	315	5/30/74	5	Houston	Jackson, Miss.	UFA(Buff)-'01	16/11*
23		Surtain, Patrick	CB	5-11	192	6/19/76	4	Southern Mississippi	New Orleans, La.	D2a-'98	16/16
99		Taylor, Jason	DE	6-6	260	9/1/74	5	Akron	Woodland Hills, Pa.	D3a-'97	16/16
85	#	Thomas, Lamar	WR	6-1	175	2/12/70	9	Miami	Gainesville, Fla.	FA-'96	0*
54		Thomas, Zach	LB	5-11	235	9/1/73	6	Texas Tech	Pampa, Texas	D5c-'96	11/11
1		Turk, Matt	P	6-5	235	6/16/68	7	Wisconsin-Whitewater	Greenfield, Wis.	T(Wash)-'00	16/0
71		Wade, Todd	T	6-8	325	10/30/76	2	Mississippi	Jackson, Miss.	D2-'00	16/16
45		Walker, Brian	S	6-1	205	5/31/72	6	Washington State	Colorado Springs, Colo.	UFA(Sea)-'00	16/16
87		Ward, Dedric	WR	5-9	185	9/29/74	5	Northern Iowa	Cedar Rapids, Iowa	UFA(NYJ)-'01	16/16*
82		Weaver, Jed	TE	6-4	246	8/11/76	3	Oregon	Redmond, Ore.	W(Phil)-'00	16/0
38		Williams, Kevin	S	6-0	190	8/4/75	4	Oklahoma State	Pine Bluff, Ark.	FA-'00	11/7*
24	#	Wilson, Jerry	CB	5-10	190	7/17/73	7	Southern	Lake Charles, La.	FA-'96	16/1

* Andersen played 7 games with New England in '00; Cesario inactive for 9 games; Cousin played 15 games with Atlanta; Gregory, Hanson, Harris, Ogunleye, Palmer, and L. Thomas missed '00 season because of injury; Hemsley last active with Dallas in '99; P. Johnson last active with Arizona in '99; Lucas played 7 games with N.Y. Jets; Mayes played 5 games with Chicago; McKnight played 16 games with Dallas; Perry played 16 games with Chicago; Porter played 16 games with Buffalo; Quinn inactive for 14 games; Spriggs played 16 games with Buffalo; Ward played 16 games with N.Y. Jets; Williams played 9 games with N.Y. Jets.

Unrestricted free agent; subject to developments.

t- Dolphins traded for Mayes (Chicago).

Players lost through free agency (7): DE Trace Armstrong (Oak; 16 games in '00), G Kevin Donnalley (Car; 16), WR Bert Emanuel (NE; 11), LB Larry Izzo (NE; 16), DE Rich Owens (KC; 12), CB Terrance Shaw (NE; 11), T Richmond Webb (Cin; 14).

Also played with Dolphins in '00—LB Michael Hamilton (1 game), CB Ray Hill (3), QB Damon Huard (16), S Greg Jeffries (11), LB Robert Jones (16), WR Tony Martin (10), RB Thurman Thomas (9).

COACHING STAFF

Head Coach,
Dave Wannstedt

Pro Career: Was named the fourth head coach in Miami history on January 16, 2000. Begins his eighth season as an NFL head coach and his second with the Dolphins. In 2000, Wannstedt guided the Dolphins to a regular-season record of 11-5 and the team's first AFC East title since 1994. It marked Miami's best regular-season record since 1992. Under Wannstedt last year, the Dolphins defeated the Indianapolis Colts in an AFC Wild-Card playoff and reached the divisional round for the third straight season. Led the Chicago Bears to a regular-season record of 40-56 and a playoff mark of 1-1 in six seasons (1993-98) as head coach. Served as the Dolphins' assistant head coach in 1999. Began his NFL coaching career as linebackers coach with the Dolphins in 1989. Spent seven weeks in that post during the offseason before joining Jimmy Johnson in Dallas as the Cowboys' defensive coordinator prior to the 1989 season, and kept that spot through 1992. In Dallas, Wannstedt took over a defense that had ranked twentieth in the NFL the year prior to his arrival. By 1992, the Cowboys led the league in total defense as they went on to capture the first of two straight Super Bowl titles. Wannstedt took over the head coaching position with the Bears in 1993, and in his second year, he led Chicago to a 9-7 record and the team's first playoff win since the 1990 season as they advanced to the divisional round. In that 1994 playoff victory, the Bears defeated the NFC Central Division champion Minnesota Vikings at the Metrodome, the first road playoff win by Chicago since 1984. Wannstedt was named NFC coach of the year following the 1994 season. Career record: 53-63.

Background: Wannstedt began his coaching career in 1975 as defensive line coach at the University of Pittsburgh. He then served as defensive line coach at Oklahoma State for the 1979-1980 seasons before being promoted to defensive coordinator in 1981, a spot he held for two seasons. He moved on to Southern California in 1983 and was the Trojans' defensive line coach for the next three years. In 1986, Wannstedt took over as defensive coordinator at the University of Miami. In his three seasons in that post (1986-88), the Hurricanes' defense held opponents to a 2.2-yard average per carry, yielded an average of 10.9 points per game, and averaged 48 sacks a season. At Miami, Wannstedt's defenses produced 11 players who were drafted by the NFL, including five in the first two rounds. Wannstedt lettered three seasons (1971-73) as an offensive lineman at the University of Pittsburgh and was the team captain his senior season in 1973 on a club that featured future Heisman Trophy winning running back Tony Dorsett, then a freshman at Pitt. Following his collegiate career, Wannstedt was selected by Green Bay in the fifteenth round of the 1974 NFL draft. He spent the 1974 season on the Packers' injured reserve list with a neck injury.

Personal: Wannstedt was born in Pittsburgh, on May 21, 1952. He attended Baldwin High School in Pittsburgh. He and his wife, Jan, have two daughters, Keri and Jami.

ASSISTANT COACHES

Keith Armstrong, special teams; born December 15, 1963, Trenton, N.J., lives in Miami. Running back-defensive back Temple 1983-86. No pro playing experience. College coach: Temple 1986, Miami 1987-88, Oklahoma State 1990-92, Notre Dame 1993. Pro coach: Atlanta Falcons 1994-96, Chicago Bears 1997-2000, joined Dolphins in 2001.

Jim Bates, defensive coordinator; born May 31, 1946, Pontiac, Mich., lives in Miami. Linebacker Tennessee 1964-67. No pro playing experience. College coach: Tennessee 1968, Southern Mississippi 1972, Villanova 1973-74, Kansas State 1975-76, West Virginia 1977, Texas Tech 1978-1983, Tennessee 1989, Florida 1990. Pro coach: San Antonio Gunslingers (USFL) 1984-85 (head coach 1985), Arizona Outlaws (USFL) 1986, Detroit Drive (AFL) 1988, Cleveland Browns 1991-93, 1995, Atlanta Falcons 1994, Dallas Cowboys 1996-99, joined Dolphins in 2000.

Doug Blevins, kicking; born August 3, 1963, Abingdon, Va., lives in Vero Beach, Fla. No college or pro playing experience. College coach: Tennessee 1982-83, Emory & Henry College 1984-85, East Tennessee State 1986-87. Pro coach: World League kicking coordinator 1995-97, joined Dolphins in 1997.

Clarence Brooks, defensive line; born May 20, 1951, New York, N.Y., lives in Miami. Guard Massachusetts 1970-73. No pro playing experience. College coach: Massachusetts 1976-1980, Syracuse 1981-89, Arizona 1990-92. Pro coach: Chicago Bears 1993-98, Cleveland Browns 1999, joined Dolphins in 2000.

Joel Collier, running backs; born December 25, 1963, Buffalo, lives in Plantation, Fla. Linebacker Northern Colorado 1984-87. No pro playing experience. College coach: Syracuse 1988-89. Pro coach: Tampa Bay Buccaneers 1990, New England Patriots 1991-93, joined Dolphins in 1994.

Robert Ford, wide receivers; born June 21, 1951, Belton, Texas, lives in Pembroke Pines, Fla. Wide receiver Houston 1970-72. No pro playing experience. College coach: Western Illinois 1974-76, New Mexico 1977-79, Oregon State 1980-1981, Mississippi State 1982-83, Kansas 1986, Texas Tech 1987-88, Texas A&M 1989-1990. Pro coach: Houston Gamblers (USFL) 1985, Dallas Cowboys 1991-97, joined Dolphins in 1998.

Chan Gailey, offensive coordinator; born January 5, 1952, Gainesville, Ga., lives in Miami. Quarterback Florida 1970-73. No pro playing experience. College coach: Florida 1974-75, Troy State 1976-78, 1983-84 (head coach), Air Force Academy 1979-1982, Samford 1993 (head coach). Pro coach: Denver Broncos 1985-1990, Birmingham Fire (World League) 1991-92 (head coach), Pittsburgh Steelers 1994-97, Dallas Cowboys 1998-99 (head coach), joined Dolphins in 2000.

John Gamble, strength and conditioning; born June 26, 1957, Richmond, Va., lives in Weston, Fla. Linebacker Hampton Institute 1975-78. No pro playing experience. College coach: Virginia 1982-1993. Pro coach: Joined Dolphins in 1994.

Judd Garrett, offensive quality control; born June 25, 1967, Abington, Pa., lives in Miami. Running back Princeton 1987-89. Pro running back London Monarchs (WLAF) 1991-92, Dallas Cowboys 1993, Las Vegas Posse (CFL) 1994, San Antonio Texans (CFL) 1995. College coach: Princeton 1990. Pro coach: New Orleans Saints 1997-99, joined Dolphins in 2000.

Pat Jones, tight ends; born November 4, 1947, Memphis, Tenn., lives in Ft. Lauderdale, Fla. Nose guard Arkansas Tech 1965, linebacker-nose guard Arkansas 1966-67. No pro playing experience. College coach: Arkansas 1974-75, Southern Methodist 1976-77, Pittsburgh 1978, Oklahoma State 1979-1994 (head coach 1984-1994). Pro coach: Joined Dolphins in 1996.

Bill Lewis, defensive nickel package; born August 5, 1941, Bristol, Pa., lives in Ft. Lauderdale, Fla. Quarterback East Stroudsburg State 1959-1962. No pro playing experience. College coach: East Stroudsburg State 1963-65, Pittsburgh 1966-68, Wake Forest 1969-1970, Georgia Tech 1971-72, 1992-94 (head coach), Arkansas 1973-76, Wyoming 1977-79, Georgia 1980-88, East Carolina 1989-1991 (head coach). Pro coach: Joined Dolphins in 1996.

Robert Nunn, asst. defensive line-defensive quality control; born June 10, 1965, Apache, Okla., lives in Miami. Linebacker Oklahoma State 1983-84 and 1986-87. No pro playing experience. College coach: Northeastern Oklahoma 1988, Tennessee 1989-1990, Georgia Military College 1991-99 (head coach 1992-99). Pro coach: Joined Dolphins in 2000.

Mel Phillips, secondary; born January 6, 1942, Shelby, N.C., lives in Miami Lakes, Fla. Defensive back-running back North Carolina A&T 1964-65. Pro defensive back San Francisco 49ers 1966-1977. Pro coach: Detroit Lions 1980-84, joined Dolphins in 1985.

Brad Roll, asst. strength and conditioning; born July 4, 1958, Houston, lives in Ft. Lauderdale, Fla. Center Blinn (Tex.) J.C. 1976-77, Stephen F. Austin 1978-79. No pro playing experience. College coach: Stephen F. Austin 1980, Southwestern Louisiana 1981-86, Kansas 1987-88, Miami 1989-1992. Pro coach: Tampa Bay Buccaneers 1993-95, joined Dolphins in 1996.

Bob Sanders, linebackers; born December 5, 1953, Jacksonville, N.C., lives in Miami. Linebacker Davidson College 1973-75. No pro playing experience. College coach: Georgia Tech 1978, East Carolina 1980-82, Richmond 1983-84, Duke 1985-89, Florida 1990-2000. Pro coach: Joined Dolphins in 2001.

Mike Shula, quarterbacks; born June 3, 1965, Baltimore, lives in Miami. Quarterback Alabama 1983-86. No pro playing experience. Pro coach: Tampa Bay Buccaneers 1988-1990, 1996-99, Miami Dolphins 1991-92, Chicago Bears 1993-95, rejoined Dolphins in 2000.

Tony Wise, offensive line; born December 28, 1951, Albany, N.Y., lives in Miami. Offensive lineman Ithaca College 1971-72. No pro playing experience. College coach: Albany State 1973, Bridgeport 1974, Central Connecticut State 1975, Washington State 1976, Pittsburgh 1977-78, Oklahoma State 1979-1983, Syracuse 1984, Miami 1985-88. Pro coach: Dallas Cowboys 1989-1992, Chicago Bears 1993-98, Carolina Panthers 1999-2000, joined Dolphins in 2001.

2001 FIRST-YEAR ROSTER

Name	Pos.	Ht.	Wt.	Birthdate	College	Hometown	How Acq.
Adams, Ben (1)	G	6-5	315	12/27/75	Texas	La Mirada, Calif.	FA-'99
Alford, Brian (1)	WR	6-1	190	6/7/75	Purdue	Oak Park, Mich.	FA-'00
Andrew, Troy	C	6-4	297	12/12/77	Duke	Klein, Texas	FA
Chambers, Chris	WR	5-11	212	8/12/78	Wisconsin	Bedford, Ohio	D2
Connor, Rameel (1)	DE	6-3	276	6/26/77	Illinois	Hillside, Ill.	FA
Crowell, Rick	LB	6-2	238	5/21/77	Colorado State	Chula Vista, Calif.	D6d
Draper, Shawn	T	6-3	294	7/5/79	Alabama	Huntsville, Ala.	D5
Finn, Devon	DE	6-5	265	5/6/78	Illinois State	Wheaton, Ill.	FA
Fletcher, Jamar	CB	5-9	177	8/28/79	Wisconsin	Hazelwood, Mo.	D1
Forte, Shawn	S	6-1	204	1/20/77	Maryland	Poughkeepsie, N.Y.	FA
Foye, David	WR	6-1	202	6/24/78	Marshall	Charleston, W. Va.	FA
Gatten, Aaron	LB	6-1	226	2/23/78	Penn State	Washington, Pa.	FA
Greenwood, Morlon	LB	6-0	239	7/17/78	Syracuse	Freeport, N.Y.	D3b
Gurley, Buck	DT	6-2	288	4/7/78	Florida	Tallahassee, Fla.	FA
Harding, Jim	T	6-5	305	7/11/78	Toledo	Maumee, Ohio	FA
Heupel, Josh	QB	6-1	216	3/22/78	Oklahoma	Aberdeen, S.D.	D6b
Johnson, Albert (1)	WR	5-9	184	11/11/77	Southern Methodist	Houston, Texas	FA
Jonsson, Eric	FB	6-1	240	9/8/78	Florida	Seminole, Fla.	FA
Lethridge, Zebbie (1)	CB	6-0	202	1/31/75	Texas Tech	Lubbock, Texas	FA
Leverette, Otis	DE	6-6	285	5/31/78	Alabama-Birmingham	Americus, Ga.	D6c
Mallard, Deshone (1)	CB	5-10	188	1/22/76	Southern Mississippi	Jackson, Miss.	FA
Minor, Travis	RB	5-10	194	6/30/79	Florida State	Baton Rouge, La.	D3a
Sanders, Vaughn (1)	RB	5-10	210	3/19/77	Hofstra	Cedarhurst, N.Y.	FA-'00
Savage, Damon (1)	WR	5-10	185	2/1/76	Tulsa	Tulsa, Okla.	FA-'00
Sorensen, Nick	S	6-2	207	7/31/78	Virginia Tech	Vienna, Va.	FA

The term NFL Rookie is defined as a player who is in his first season of professional football and has not been on the roster of another professional football team for any regular-season or postseason games. A Rookie is designated by an "R" on NFL rosters. Players who have been active in another professional football league or players who have NFL experience, including either preseason training camp or being on an Active List or Inactive List, or on Reserve/Injured or Reserve/Physically Unable to Perform for fewer than six regular-season games, are termed NFL First-Year Players. An NFL First-Year Player is designated by a "1" on NFL rosters. Thereafter, a player is credited with an additional year of experience for each season in which he accumulates six games on the Active List or Inactive List, or on Reserve/Injured or Reserve/Physically Unable to Perform.

NEW ENGLAND PATRIOTS

American Football Conference
Eastern Division
Team Colors: Blue, Red, Silver, and White
Foxboro Stadium
60 Washington Street
Foxboro, Massachusetts 02035
Telephone: (508) 543-8200

CLUB OFFICIALS

Chairman & Owner: Robert K. Kraft
Vice Chairman: Jonathan A. Kraft
Senior Vice President & Chief Operating Officer: Andrew Wasynczuk
Vice President-Finance: James Hausmann
Vice President of Player Development and Community Affairs: Donald Lowery
Vice President of Marketing & Special Events: Lou Imbriano
Director of Player Personnel: Scott Pioli
Director of Operations: Nick Carparelli
Director of Media Relations: Stacey James
Controller: Jim Nolan
Director of Ticketing: John Traverse
General Manager of Foxboro Stadium: Dan Murphy
Building Services Manager: Bernie Reinhart
Head Trainer: Ron O'Neil
Equipment Manager: Don Brocher
Video Director: Jimmy Dee
Stadium: Foxboro Stadium (built in 1971)
•**Capacity:** 60,292
60 Washington Street
Foxboro, Massachusetts 02035
Playing Surface: Grass
Training Camp: Bryant College
Route 7
Smithfield, Rhode Island 02917

2001 SCHEDULE

PRESEASON

Aug. 10	**New York Giants**	8:00
Aug. 18	at Carolina	7:30
Aug. 25	at Tampa Bay	7:30
Aug. 30	**Washington**	8:00

REGULAR SEASON

Sept. 9	at Cincinnati	1:00
Sept. 16	at Carolina	1:00
Sept. 23	**New York Jets**	4:05
Sept. 30	**Indianapolis**	1:00
Oct. 7	at Miami	1:00
Oct. 14	**San Diego**	1:00
Oct. 21	at Indianapolis	12:00
Oct. 28	at Denver	2:15
Nov. 4	at Atlanta	1:00
Nov. 11	**Buffalo**	1:00
Nov. 18	**St. Louis**	8:30
Nov. 25	**New Orleans**	4:05
Dec. 2	at New York Jets	1:00
Dec. 9	**Cleveland**	1:00
Dec. 16	at Buffalo	1:00
Dec. 22	**Miami** (Sat.)	1:30
Dec. 30	Open Date	

RECORD HOLDERS

INDIVIDUAL RECORDS—CAREER

Category	Name	Performance
Rushing (Yds.)	Sam Cunningham, 1973-79, 1981-82	5,453
Passing (Yds.)	Drew Bledsoe, 1993-2000	29,257
Passing (TDs)	Steve Grogan, 1975-1990	182
Receiving (No.)	Stanley Morgan, 1977-1989	534
Receiving (Yds.)	Stanley Morgan, 1977-1989	10,352
Interceptions	Raymond Clayborn, 1977-1989	36
Punting (Avg.)	Tom Tupa, 1996-97	44.7
Punt Return (Avg.)	Mack Herron, 1973-75	12.0
Kickoff Return (Avg.)	Allen Carter, 1975-76	27.2
Field Goals	Gino Cappelletti, 1960-1970	176
Touchdowns (Tot.)	Stanley Morgan, 1977-1989	68
Points	Gino Cappelletti, 1960-1970	1,130

INDIVIDUAL RECORDS—SINGLE SEASON

Category	Name	Performance
Rushing (Yds.)	Curtis Martin, 1995	1,487
Passing (Yds.)	Drew Bledsoe, 1994	4,555
Passing (TDs)	Vito (Babe) Parilli, 1964	31
Receiving (No.)	Ben Coates, 1994	96
Receiving (Yds.)	Stanley Morgan, 1986	1,491
Interceptions	Ron Hall, 1964	11
Punting (Avg.)	Tom Tupa, 1997	45.8
Punt Return (Avg.)	Mack Herron, 1974	14.8
Kickoff Return (Avg.)	Raymond Clayborn, 1977	31.0
Field Goals	Tony Franklin, 1986	32
Touchdowns (Tot.)	Curtis Martin, 1996	17
Points	Gino Cappelletti, 1964	155

INDIVIDUAL RECORDS—SINGLE GAME

Category	Name	Performance
Rushing (Yds.)	Tony Collins, 9-18-83	212
Passing (Yds.)	Drew Bledsoe, 11-13-94	426
Passing (TDs)	Vito (Babe) Parilli, 11-15-64	5
	Vito (Babe) Parilli, 10-15-67	5
	Steve Grogan, 9-9-79	5
Receiving (No.)	Terry Glenn, 10-3-99	13
Receiving (Yds.)	Terry Glenn, 10-3-99	214
Interceptions	Many times	3
	Last time by Roland James, 10-23-83	
Field Goals	Gino Cappelletti, 10-4-64	6
Touchdowns (Tot.)	Many times	3
	Last time by Curtis Martin, 11-3-96	
Points	Gino Cappelletti, 12-18-65	28

COACHING HISTORY

BOSTON 1960-1970
(287-333-9)

1960-61	Lou Saban*	7-12-0
1961-68	Mike Holovak	53-47-9
1969-1970	Clive Rush**	5-16-0
1970-72	John Mazur***	9-21-0
1972	Phil Bengtson	1-4-0
1973-78	Chuck Fairbanks****	46-41-0
1978	Hank Bullough-Ron Erhardt#	0-1-0
1979-1981	Ron Erhardt	21-27-0
1982-84	Ron Meyer##	18-16-0
1984-89	Raymond Berry	51-41-0
1990	Rod Rust	1-15-0
1991-92	Dick MacPherson	8-24-0
1993-96	Bill Parcells	34-34-0
1997-99	Pete Carroll	28-23-0
2000	Bill Belichick	5-11-0

*Released after five games in 1961
**Released after seven games in 1970
***Resigned after nine games in 1972
****Suspended for final regular-season game in 1978
#Co-coaches
##Released after eight games in 1984

FOXBORO STADIUM

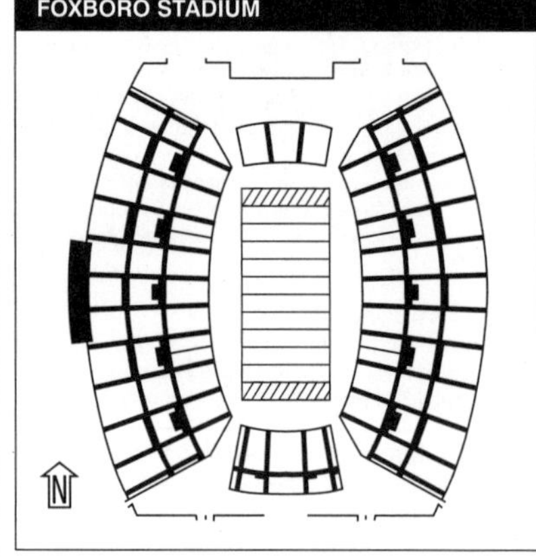

2000 TEAM RECORD

PRESEASON (3-2)

Date	Result		Opponent
7/31	W	20-0	vs. San Francisco, Canton, Ohio
8/4	W	13-10	at Detroit
8/11	L	20-30	at Washington
8/20	L	21-31	Tampa Bay
8/24	W	29-21	Carolina

REGULAR SEASON (5-11)

Date	Result		Opponent	Att.
9/3	L	16-21	Tampa Bay	60,292
9/11	L	19-20	at New York Jets	77,687
9/17	L	13-21	Minnesota	60,292
9/24	L	3-10	at Miami	73,344
10/1	W	28-19	at Denver	75,684
10/8	W	24-16	Indianapolis	60,292
10/15	L	17-34	New York Jets	60,292
10/22	L	23-30	at Indianapolis	56,828
11/5	L	13-16	Buffalo (OT)	60,292
11/12	L	11-19	at Cleveland	72,618
11/19	W	16-13	Cincinnati	60,292
11/23	L	9-34	at Detroit	77,923
12/4	W	30-24	Kansas City	60,292
12/10	L	17-24	at Chicago	66,944
12/17	W	13-10	at Buffalo (OT)	47,230
12/24	L	24-27	Miami	60,292

(OT) Overtime

SCORE BY PERIODS

Patriots	76	86	30	81	3	—	276
Opponents	53	122	52	108	3	—	338

ATTENDANCE

Home 478,816 Away 552,384 Total 1,031,200
Single-game home record, 61,457 (12/5/71)
Single-season home record, 482,572 (1986)

2000 TEAM STATISTICS

	Patriots	Opp.
Total First Downs	283	326
Rushing	80	108
Passing	172	184
Penalty	31	34
Third Down: Made/Att	82/234	103/237
Third Down Pct.	35.0	43.5
Fourth Down: Made/Att	13/26	9/10
Fourth Down Pct.	50.0	90.0
Total Net Yards	4,571	5,353
Avg. Per Game	285.7	334.6
Total Plays	1,037	1,068
Avg. Per Play	4.4	5.0
Net Yards Rushing	1,390	1,831
Avg. Per Game	86.9	114.4
Total Rushes	424	495
Net Yards Passing	3,181	3,522
Avg. Per Game	198.8	220.1
Sacked/Yards Lost	48/280	29/172
Gross Yards	3,461	3,694
Att./Completions	565/328	544/321
Completion Pct.	58.1	59.0
Had Intercepted	15	10
Punts/Average	90/42.2	87/40.4
Net Punting Avg.	90/36.8	87/31.9
Penalties/Yards	99/815	95/897
Fumbles/Ball Lost	23/10	27/13
Touchdowns	28	38
Rushing	9	12
Passing	18	23
Returns	1	3
Avg. Time of Possession	28:56	31:04

2000 INDIVIDUAL STATISTICS

Passing	Att.	Comp.	Yds.	Pct.	TD	Int.	Tkld.	Rate
Bledsoe	531	312	3,291	58.8	17	13	45/264	77.3
Friesz	21	11	66	52.4	0	1	3/16	39.0
Bishop	9	3	80	33.3	1	1	0/0	64.4
Brady	3	1	6	33.3	0	0	0/0	42.4
L. Johnson	1	1	18	100.0	0	0	0/0	118.8
Patriots	565	328	3,461	58.1	18	15	48/280	75.5
Opponents	544	321	3,694	59.0	23	10	29/172	86.0

SCORING	TD R	TD P	TD Rt	PAT	FG	Saf	PTS
Vinatieri	0	0	0	25/25	27/33	0	106
Glenn	0	6	0	0/0	0/0	0	36
Faulk	4	1	0	0/0	0/0	0	32
Brown	0	4	1	0/0	0/0	0	30
Redmond	1	2	0	0/0	0/0	0	18
Bjornson	0	2	0	0/0	0/0	0	12
Bledsoe	2	0	0	0/0	0/0	0	12
Carter	2	0	0	0/0	0/0	0	12
Rutledge	0	1	0	0/0	0/0	0	6
Simmons	0	1	0	0/0	0/0	0	6
Wiggins	0	1	0	0/0	0/0	0	6
Patriots	9	18	1	25/25	27/33	0	276
Opponents	12	23	3	34/34	24/32	1	338

2-Pt. Conversions: Faulk.
Patriots 1-3, Opponents 1-4.

RUSHING	Att.	Yds.	Avg.	LG	TD
Faulk	164	570	3.5	18	4
Redmond	125	406	3.2	20	1
Bledsoe	47	158	3.4	16	2
Carter	37	90	2.4	9	2
Pass	18	58	3.2	11	0
Brown	6	46	7.7	35	0
Glenn	4	39	9.8	35	0
R. Harris	3	14	4.7	7	0
Shaw	9	12	1.3	5	0
Bishop	7	-1	-0.1	2	0
Floyd	2	-1	-0.5	0	0
L. Johnson	2	-1	-0.5	0	0
Patriots	424	1,390	3.3	35	9
Opponents	495	1,831	3.7	32	12

RECEIVING	No.	Yds.	Avg.	LG	TD
Brown	83	944	11.4	44t	4
Glenn	79	963	12.2	39t	6
Faulk	51	465	9.1	52t	1
Bjornson	20	152	7.6	19	2
Redmond	20	126	6.3	20	2
Wiggins	16	203	12.7	59	1
Rutledge	15	103	6.9	16	1
Simmons	14	231	16.5	46	1
Carter	9	73	8.1	21	0
Calloway	5	95	19.0	28	0
Jackson	5	44	8.8	13	0
Pass	4	17	4.3	15	0
S. Davis	2	12	6.0	9	0
Shaw	2	11	5.5	8	0
R. Harris	2	1	0.5	2	0
Floyd	1	21	21.0	21	0
Patriots	328	3,461	10.6	59	18
Opponents	321	3,694	11.5	81t	23

INTERCEPTIONS	No.	Yds.	Avg.	LG	TD
Law	2	32	16.0	32	0
Jones	2	20	10.0	20	0
Milloy	2	2	1.0	2	0
Smith	1	56	56.0	56	0
Langham	1	24	24.0	24	0
Thomas	1	16	16.0	16	0
A. Harris	1	11	11.0	11	0
Patriots	10	161	16.1	56	0
Opponents	15	208	13.9	101t	2

PUNTING	No.	Yds.	Avg.	In 20	LG
L. Johnson	89	3,798	42.7	31	62
Patriots	90	3,798	42.2	31	62
Opponents	87	3,513	40.4	23	62

PUNT RETURNS	No.	FC	Yds.	Avg.	LG	TD
Brown	39	19	504	12.9	66t	1
Faulk	6	3	58	9.7	35	0
Patriots	45	22	562	12.5	66t	1
Opponents	43	21	384	8.9	56	0

KICKOFF RETURNS	No.	Yds.	Avg.	LG	TD
Faulk	38	816	21.5	40	0
Jackson	13	323	24.8	47	0
Simmons	4	82	20.5	39	0
Brown	2	15	7.5	9	0
Bruschi	2	13	6.5	7	0
S. Davis	2	45	22.5	32	0
Carter	1	16	16.0	16	0
Hamilton	1	0	0.0	0	0
Redmond	1	25	25.0	25	0
Patriots	64	1,335	20.9	47	0
Opponents	62	1,350	21.8	87t	1

FIELD GOALS	1-19	20-29	30-39	40-49	50+
Vinatieri	0/0	11/13	8/9	7/8	1/3
Patriots	0/0	11/13	8/9	7/8	1/3
Opponents	1/1	5/7	11/13	7/11	0/0

SACKS	No.
McGinest	6.0
Spires	6.0
Thomas	4.5
Slade	4.0
Eaton	2.5
Serwanga	2.0
Hamilton	1.5
Bruschi	1.0
A. Harris	1.0
T. Johnson	0.5
Patriots	29.0
Opponents	48.0

2001 DRAFT CHOICES

Round	Name	Pos.	College
1	Richard Seymour	DT	Georgia
2	Matt Light	G	Purdue
3	Brock Williams	DB	Notre Dame
4	Kenyatta Jones	G	South Florida
	Jabari Holloway	TE	Notre Dame
5	Hakim Akbar	DB	Washington
6	Arther Love	TE	South Carolina State
	Leonard Myers	DB	Miami
7	Owen Pochman	K	Brigham Young
	T.J. Turner	LB	Michigan State

NEW ENGLAND PATRIOTS

2001 VETERAN ROSTER

No.	Name	Pos.	Ht.	Wt.	Birthdate	NFL Exp.	College	Hometown	How Acq.	'00 Games/ Starts
63	Andruzzi, Joe	G	6-3	315	8/3/75	5	Southern Connecticut St.	Staten Island, N.Y.	FA-'00	11/11
75	Beadles, Terrance	G	6-3	300	4/27/76	2	Arkansas-Pine Bluff	Atlanta, Ga.	FA-'00	0*
7	Bishop, Michael	QB	6-2	215	5/15/76	3	Kansas State	Willis, Texas	D7a-'99	8/0
11	Bledsoe, Drew	QB	6-5	240	2/14/72	9	Washington State	Walla Walla, Wash.	D1-'93	16/16
42	Bowie, Larry	FB	6-0	250	3/21/73	5	Georgia	Anniston, Ala.	FA-'01	0*
12	Brady, Tom	QB	6-4	210	8/3/77	2	Michigan	San Mateo, Calif.	D6b-'00	1/0
80	Brown, Troy	WR	5-10	190	7/2/71	9	Marshall	Blackville, S.C.	D8-'93	16/15
54	Bruschi, Tedy	LB	6-1	245	6/9/73	6	Arizona	Roseville, Calif.	D3-'96	16/16
58	Chatham, Matt	LB	6-4	240	6/28/77	2	South Dakota	Sioux City, Iowa	W(StL)-'00	6/0
77	Compton, Mike	T-G	6-6	300	9/18/70	9	West Virginia	Richlands, Va.	UFA(Det)-'01	16/16*
84	Davis, Shockmain	WR	6-0	205	8/20/77	2	Angelo State	Port Arthur, Texas	FA-'00	12/1
44	Edwards, Marc	FB	6-0	240	11/17/74	5	Notre Dame	Cincinnati, Ohio	UFA(Cle)-'01	16/8*
47	Edwards, Robert	RB	5-11	220	10/2/74	3	Georgia	Tennille, Ga.	D1a-'98	0*
86	Eitzmann, Chris	TE	6-5	255	4/1/77	2	Harvard	Hardy, Neb.	FA-'00	5/1
17	Emanuel, Bert	WR	5-10	185	10/26/70	8	Rice	Langham Creek, Texas	UFA(Mia)-'01	11/0*
33	Faulk, Kevin	RB	5-8	200	6/5/76	3	Louisiana State	Carencro, La.	D2-'99	16/9
41	George, Tony	S	5-11	205	8/10/75	3	Florida	Cincinnati, Ohio	D3-'99	15/0
88	Glenn, Terry	WR	5-11	195	7/23/74	6	Ohio State	Columbus, Ohio	D1-'96	16/16
97	Grimes, Reggie	DE	6-4	290	11/7/76	2	Alabama	Nashville, Tenn.	FA-'00	8/0
91	Hamilton, Bobby	DE	6-5	280	7/1/71	7	Southern Mississippi	Columbia, Miss.	UFA(NYJ)-'00	16/16
23	Harris, Antwan	CB	5-9	190	5/29/77	2	Virginia	Raleigh, N.C.	D6a-'00	14/0
50	Holmberg, Rob	LB	6-3	240	5/6/71	8	Penn State	McKeesport, Pa.	FA-'00	16/5
19	Huard, Damon	QB	6-3	215	7/9/73	5	Washington	Puyallup, Wash.	FA-'01	16/1*
53	Izzo, Larry	LB	5-10	228	9/26/74	5	Rice	Houston, Texas	UFA(Mia)-'01	16/0*
82	Jackson, Curtis	WR	5-10	190	9/22/73	2	Texas	Plano, Texas	FA-'00	5/2
1	Johnson, Charles	WR	6-0	200	1/3/72	8	Colorado	San Bernardino, Calif.	FA-'01	16/15*
60	Johnson, Garrett	NT	6-3	295	12/31/75	2	Illinois	Belleville, Ill.	FA-'00	9/2
10	Johnson, Lee	P	6-2	200	11/27/61	17	Brigham Young	Conroe, Texas	FA-'99	16/0
52	Johnson, Ted	LB	6-4	255	12/4/72	7	Colorado	Alameda, Calif.	D2-'95	13/11
34	Jones, Tebucky	S	6-2	220	10/6/74	4	Syracuse	New Britain, Conn.	D1b-'98	15/9
59	Katzenmoyer, Andy	LB	6-3	255	12/2/77	3	Ohio State	Westerville, Ohio	D1b-'99	8/3
70	Klemm, Adrian	T	6-3	310	5/21/77	2	Hawaii	Los Angeles, Calif.	D2-'00	5/4
24	Law, Ty	CB	5-11	200	2/10/74	7	Michigan	Aliquippa, Pa.	D1-'95	15/15
87	Looker, Dane	WR	6-0	193	5/5/76	2	Washington	Puyallup, Wash.	T(StL)-'00	0*
55	McGinest, Willie	DE	6-5	270	12/11/71	8	Southern California	Long Beach, Calif.	D1-'94	14/14
43	McWilliams, Johnny	TE	6-4	267	12/14/72	6	Southern California	Pomona, Calif.	UFA(Minn)-'01	15/7*
36	Milloy, Lawyer	S	6-0	210	11/14/73	6	Washington	Tacoma, Wash.	D2-'96	16/16
99	Mitchell, Brandon	DE	6-3	285	6/19/75	5	Texas A&M	Abbeville, La.	D2-'97	11/9
19	Morey, Sean	WR	5-11	190	2/26/76	2	Brown	Marshfield, Mass.	D7b-'99	0*
92	Nugent, David	DE	6-4	300	10/27/77	2	Purdue	Collierville, Tenn.	D6c-'00	6/0
71	Osborne, Chuck	DT	6-2	290	11/2/73	6	Arizona	Canyon Country, Calif.	FA-'00	0*
74	Panos, Joe	G	6-3	300	1/24/71	7	Wisconsin	Brookfield, Wis.	FA-'01	13/0*
61	Parker, Riddick	DT	6-3	275	11/20/72	5	North Carolina	Emporia, Va.	UFA(Sea)-'01	16/16*
35	Pass, Patrick	RB	5-10	215	12/31/75	2	Georgia	Tucker, Ga.	D7b-'00	5/2
15	Patten, David	WR	5-10	195	8/19/74	5	Western Carolina	Hopkins, S.C.	UFA(Cle)-'01	14/10*
46	Paulk, Jeff	FB	6-0	240	4/26/76	3	Arizona State	Phoenix, Ariz.	FA-'00	1/0
66	Paxton, Lonie	LS	6-2	260	3/13/78	2	Sacramento State	Corona, Calif.	FA-'00	16/0
98	Pleasant, Anthony	DE	6-5	280	1/27/68	12	Tennessee State	Century, Fla.	UFA(SF)-'01	16/16*
21	Redmond, J.R.	RB	5-11	210	9/28/77	2	Arizona State	Carson, Calif.	D3-'00	12/5
64	Robinson-Randall, Greg	T	6-5	315	6/23/78	2	Michigan State	La Marque, Texas	D4-'00	12/4
67	Ruegamer, Grey	C-G	6-5	310	6/1/76	2	Arizona State	Las Vegas, Nev.	FA-'00	6/0
83	Rutledge, Rod	TE	6-5	270	8/12/75	4	Alabama	Birmingham, Ala.	D2b-'98	16/11
31	Serwanga, Kato	CB	6-0	200	7/23/76	3	California	Sacramento, Calif.	FA-'98	15/0
22	Shaw, Terrance	CB	5-11	190	11/11/73	7	Stephen F. Austin	Marshall, Texas	UFA(Mia)-'01	11/3*
81	Simmons, Tony	WR	6-1	210	12/8/74	4	Wisconsin	Chicago, Ill.	D2a-'98	12/2
13	Small, Torrance	WR	6-3	209	9/4/70	10	Alcorn State	Tampa, Fla.	FA-'01	14/14*
45	Smith, Otis	CB	5-11	195	10/22/65	12	Missouri	Metairie, La.	FA-'00	16/14
94	Spires, Greg	DE	6-1	265	8/12/74	4	Florida State	Cape Coral, Fla.	D3b-'98	16/2
26	Stevens, Matt	S	6-0	206	6/15/73	5	Appalachian State	Chapel Hill, N.C.	W(Wash)-'00	1/0
4	Vinatieri, Adam	K	6-0	200	12/28/72	6	South Dakota State	Rapid City, S.D.	FA-'96	16/0
51	Vrabel, Mike	LB	6-4	250	8/14/75	5	Ohio State	Akron, Ohio	UFA(Pitt)-'01	15/0*
85	Wiggins, Jermaine	TE	6-2	255	1/18/75	2	Georgia	East Boston, Mass.	W(NYJ)-'00	15/2*
76	Williams, Grant	T	6-7	325	5/10/74	6	Louisiana Tech	Clinton, Miss.	FA-'01	15/8
65	Woody, Damien	C	6-3	315	11/3/77	3	Boston College	Beaverdam, Va.	D1a-'99	16/16

* Beadles and R. Edwards missed '00 season because of injury; Bowie last active with Washington in '99; Compton played 16 games with Detroit in '00; M. Edwards played 16 games with Cleveland; Emanuel played 11 games with Miami; Huard and Izzo played 16 games with Miami; C.Johnson played 16 games with Philadelphia; Looker was inactive for 10 games; McWilliams played 15 games for Minnesota; Morey last active with New England in '99; Osborne was inactive for 2 games; Panos played 13 games with Buffalo; Parker played 16 games with Seattle; Patten played 14 games with Cleveland; Pleasant played 16 games with San Francisco; Shaw played 11 games with Miami; Small played 14 games with Philadelphia; Vrabel played 15 games with Pittsburgh; Wiggins played 11 games with N.Y. Jets and 4 games with New England.

Players lost through free agency (2): RB Tony Carter (Den; 16 games in '00), DE Chad Eaton (Sea; 14).

Also played with Patriots in '00—C Jason Andersen (7 games), T Bruce Armstrong (16), TE Eric Bjornson (8), WR Chris Calloway (7), G-T Derrick Fletcher (2), RB Chris Floyd (11), QB John Friesz (1), RB Raymont Harris (1), G Sale Isaia (16), LB Olrick Johnson (12), T-G Max Lane (6), CB Antonio Langham (15), LB Marc Megna (4), RB Harold Shaw (16), LB Chris Slade (16), DT Henry Thomas (16), S Larry Whigham (14).

COACHING STAFF

Head Coach,
Bill Belichick

Pro Career: Bill Belichick returned to New England to be named the fourteenth head coach in Patriots history on January 27, 2000. Recognized as one of the NFL's premier game strategists, Belichick's defensive schemes have contributed to winning two Super Bowl championships, three conference championships, and five division titles during the last 15 years, including a conference title in his only season as a defensive assistant with the Patriots in 1996. A 26-year NFL coaching veteran, Belichick launched his career in 1975 as a special assistant with the Baltimore Colts. He was an assistant special teams coach with Detroit (1976-77) and Denver (1978). In 1979, he joined the New York Giants as the special teams coach. In 1981-82, he took on the dual responsibilities of coaching both special teams and linebackers. By 1985, he was named defensive coordinator. Throughout the next six seasons, he was credited with creating one of the greatest defensive units of all-time. Their success as a unit contributed to the Giants winning two Super Bowl titles in four seasons, in 1986 and again in 1990. Following Super Bowl XXV, Belichick was named head coach of the Cleveland Browns in 1991. At the age of 37, he became the youngest head coach in the league and inherited an aging squad the 3-13 record of which in 1990 was the worst in franchise history. In his first year as head coach, the Browns set a franchise record by committing only 18 turnovers, a 28-turnover improvement from 1990, when the Browns surrendered 46 turnovers. By 1994, Belichick had assembled one of the league's most dominant defenses. That year, the Browns finished 11-5 after the team allowed a league-low 204 total points. The Browns qualified for the playoffs and eliminated the Patriots in the first round. In 1996, Belichick joined New England and was a key contributor to the team's rebound from a 6-10 season in 1995 to an 11-5 division championship season. It was the team's first division title in 10 years. The Patriots hosted two playoff games in which the defense allowed just nine total points. The unit's dominance propelled the Patriots to victories over Pittsburgh (28-3) and Jacksonville (20-6) en route to Super Bowl XXXI against Green Bay. He spent three seasons with the New York Jets from 1997 to 1999. In his first season in New York, the Jets defense played a key factor in the Jets rise from 1-15 in 1996 to 9-7. In 1998, the defense was a critical factor in the team's ability to claim its first AFC East title with a franchise-best 12-4 regular-season record. The Jets advanced to the AFC Championship Game, but lost to the eventual Super Bowl champion Denver Broncos. In 1999, the Jets won seven of their final nine games, allowing only 18.4 points per game during that span. Career record: 42-56.

Background: Belichick was a center/tight end at Wesleyan 1971-74.

Personal: Born April 16, 1952, Nashville. Bill and his wife, Debby, have three children—Amanda, Stephen, and Brian.

ASSISTANT COACHES

Romeo Crennel, defensive coordinator; born June 18, 1947, Lynchburgh, Va., lives in Foxboro. Offensive-defensive tackle, linebacker Western Kentucky 1966-69. No pro playing experience. College coach: Western Kentucky 1970-74, Texas Tech 1975-77, Mississippi 1978-79, Georgia Tech 1980. Pro coach: New York Giants 1981-1992, New England Patriots 1993-96, New York Jets 1997-99, Cleveland Browns 2000, rejoined Patriots in 2001.

Jeff Davidson, asst. offensive line; born October 3, 1967, Akron, Ohio, lives in Franklin, Mass. Offensive lineman Ohio State 1986-89. Pro offensive lineman Denver Broncos 1990-92, New Orleans Saints 1994. Pro coach: New Orleans Saints 1995-96, joined the Patriots in 1997.

Ivan Fears, wide receivers; born November 15, 1954, Portsmouth, Va., lives in Foxboro, Mass. Running back William & Mary 1973-75. No pro playing experience. College coach: William & Mary 1977-1980, Syracuse 1981-1990. Pro coach: New England Patriots 1991-92, Chicago Bears 1993-98, rejoined Patriots in 1999.

Pepper Johnson, inside linebackers, born July 29, 1964, Detroit, lives in Providence, R.I. Linebacker Ohio State 1982-85. Pro linebacker New York Giants 1986-1992, Cleveland Browns 1993-95, Detroit 1996, New York Jets 1997-98. Pro coach: Joined the Patriots in 2000.

Eric Mangini, defensive backs; born January 10, 1971, Hartford, Conn., lives in Medfield, Mass. Nose tackle Wesleyan (Conn.) 1989-1990, 1992-93. No pro playing experience. Pro coach: Cleveland Browns 1995, Baltimore Ravens 1996, New York Jets 1997-99, joined Patriots in 2000.

Randy Melvin, defensive line; born April 3, 1959, Aurora, Ill., lives in Foxboro, Mass. Defensive line Eastern Illinois 1978-1981. No pro playing experience. College coach: Eastern Illinois 1988-1994, Wyoming 1995-96, Purdue 1997-99. Pro coach: Joined Patriots in 2000.

Markus Paul, asst. strength and conditioning; born April 1, 1966, Orlando, Fla., lives in Plainville, Mass. Safety Syracuse 1984-88. Pro safety Chicago Bears 1989-1993, Tampa Bay Buccaneers 1993. Pro coach: New Orleans 1998-99, joined Patriots in 2000.

Dick Rehbein, quarterbacks; born November 22, 1955, Green Bay, lives in North Attleboro, Mass. Center Ripon College 1974-77. No pro playing experience. Pro coach: Green Bay Packers 1979-1983, Los Angeles Express (USFL) 1984, Minnesota Vikings 1984-1991, New York Giants 1992-99, joined Patriots in 2000.

Rob Ryan, outside linebackers; born December 13, 1962, Ardmore, Okla., lives in Franklin, Mass. Linebacker Oklahoma State 1984, Southwestern Oklahoma State 1985-86. No pro playing experience. College coach: Western Kentucky 1987, Ohio State 1988, Tennessee State 1989-1993, Hutchinson (Kan.) C.C. 1996, Oklahoma State 1997-99. Pro coach: Arizona Cardinals 1994-95, joined Patriots in 2000.

Dante Scarnecchia, asst. head coach-offensive line; born February 15, 1948, Los Angeles, lives in Wrentham, Mass. Center-guard California Western (now U.S. International) 1968-1970. No pro playing experience. College coach: California Western 1970-72, Iowa State 1973-74, Southern Methodist 1975-76, 1980-81, Pacific 1977-78, Northern Arizona 1979. Pro coach: New England Patriots 1982-88, Indianapolis Colts 1989-1990, rejoined the Patriots in 1991.

Brad Seely, special teams; born September 6, 1956, Vinton, Iowa, lives in Wrentham, Mass. Tackle-guard South Dakota State 1974-77. No pro playing experience. College coach: Colorado State 1980, Southern Methodist 1981, North Carolina State 1982, Pacific 1983, Oklahoma State 1984-88. Pro coach: Indianapolis Colts 1989-1993, New York Jets 1994, Carolina Panthers 1995-98, joined Patriots in 1999.

Charlie Weis, offensive coordinator-running backs; born March 30, 1956, Trenton, N.J., lives in Cumberland, R.I. Attended Notre Dame. No college or pro playing experience. College coach: South Carolina 1985-88. Pro coach: New York Giants 1988-1992, New England Patriots 1993-96, New York Jets 1997-99, rejoined Patriots in 2000.

Mike Woicik, strength and conditioning; born September 26, 1956, Baltimore, lives in Foxboro, Mass. Attended Boston College. No college or pro playing experience. College coach: Springfield College 1978-79, Syracuse 1980-89. Pro coach: Dallas Cowboys 1990-96, New Orleans Saints 1997-99, joined Patriots in 2000.

2001 FIRST-YEAR ROSTER

Name	Pos.	Ht.	Wt.	Birthdate	College	Hometown	How Acq.
Akbar, Hakim	S	6-0	210	8/11/80	Washington	Riverside, Calif.	D5
Costello, Brad (1)	P	6-1	230	12/24/74	Boston University	Moorestown, N.J.	FA-'00
Dalton, Antico (1)	LB	6-1	240	12/31/75	Hampton	Eden, N.C.	FA-'00
Daniels, Ronney	WR	6-1	210	9/17/76	Auburn	Lake Wales, Fla.	FA
Davis, Adam (1)	G	6-4	300	1/11/77	Oklahoma State	Hobart, Okla.	FA-'00
Gatrell, Rob (1)	C	6-5	300	3/14/77	Fresno State	Brentwood, Calif.	FA-'00
Hadenfeldt, Dan	P	5-10	190	8/7/76	Nebraska	Des Moines, Iowa	FA
Holloway, Jabari	TE	6-2	255	12/18/78	Notre Dame	Riverdale, Ga.	D4b
Inzer, Drew	T-G	6-4	315	12/5/79	Brown	North Smithfield, R.I.	FA
Isabelle, Yubrenal	LB	6-0	230	8/4/79	Virginia	Bluefield, W. Va.	FA
Jones, Kenyatta	G-T	6-3	315	1/18/79	South Florida	Gainesville, Fla.	D4a
Leard, Ben	QB	6-3	220	2/24/78	Auburn	Hartwell, Ga.	FA
Light, Matt	G-T	6-4	305	6/23/78	Purdue	Greenville, Ohio	D2
Love, Arther	TE	6-4	250	9/18/77	South Carolina State	Soperton, Ga.	D6a
McCready, Scott	WR	6-0	200	2/1/77	South Florida	Tampa, Fla.	FA
Myers, Leonard	CB	5-10	190	12/18/78	Miami	Fort Lauderdale, Fla.	D6b
Pochman, Owen	K	5-11	180	8/2/77	Brigham Young	Mercer Island, Wash.	D7a
Rawlings, Josh	T-G	6-3	305	4/11/77	Minnesota	Fort Gratiot, Mich.	FA-'00
Sayler, Jace	DE-DT	6-5	295	2/27/79	Michigan State	McHenry, Ill.	FA
Seymour, Richard	DT-DE	6-6	300	10/6/79	Georgia	Gadsden, S.C.	D1
Tuitele, Maugaula (1)	LB	6-2	255	5/26/78	Colorado State	Torrance, Calif.	FA-'00
Turner, T.J.	LB	6-3	260	10/1/78	Michigan State	Hillsboro, Ohio	D7b
Williams, Brock	CB	5-10	185	8/12/79	Notre Dame	Hammond, La.	D3
Williams, Walter	WR	6-0	205	9/8/77	Grambling State	Baton Rouge, La.	FA

The term NFL Rookie is defined as a player who is in his first season of professional football and has not been on the roster of another professional football team for any regular-season or postseason games. A Rookie is designated by an "R" on NFL rosters. Players who have been active in another professional football league or players who have NFL experience, including either preseason training camp or being on an Active List or Inactive List, or on Reserve/Injured or Reserve/Physically Unable to Perform for fewer than six regular-season games, are termed NFL First-Year Players. An NFL First-Year Player is designated by a "1" on NFL rosters. Thereafter, a player is credited with an additional year of experience for each season in which he accumulates six games on the Active List or Inactive List, or on Reserve/Injured or Reserve/Physically Unable to Perform.

NOTES

NEW YORK JETS

American Football Conference
Eastern Division
Team Colors: Green and White
1000 Fulton Avenue
Hempstead, New York 11550
Telephone: (516) 560-8100

CLUB OFFICIALS

Owner and CEO: Robert Wood Johnson IV
President: Jay Cross
General Manager: Terry Bradway
Principal Advisor: Steve Gutman
Vice President of Finance: Mike Gerstle
Vice President of Operations: Mike Kensil
Vice President of Business Operations: Robert Parente
Vice President of Public Relations: Frank Ramos
Vice President of Stadium Development: Thad Sheely
Assistant General Manager/Director of Pro Personnel: Mike Tannenbaum
Director of Player Personnel: Dick Haley
Head Athletic Trainer: David Price
Director of Player Development: Kevin Winston
Director of Security: Steve Yarnell
Equipment Manager: Clay Hampton
Video Director: John Seiter
Director of Ticket Operations: John Buschhorn
Controller: Mike Minarczyk
Director of Information Technology: Thomas Murphy
Senior Director of Marketing & Business Development: Marc Riccio
Senior Manager Pro Player Development: JoJo Wooden
Scout of other Pro Football Leagues: Brian Gaine
Pro Personnel Assistant: Chris Shea
Talent Scouts: Trent Baalke, Ron Brockington, Joey Clinkscales, Jim Cochran, Michael Davis, Sid Hall, Jesse Kaye, Gary Smith, Bob Schmitz
College Scouting Coordinator: John Griffin
Salary Cap Analyst/Pro Personnel Assistant: Dawn Aponte
Senior Manager of Internet & Special Projects: Ken Ilchuk
Payroll/Human Resource Administrator: Janet Yu
Director of Team Travel: Kevin Coyle
Asst. Director of Public Relations: Douglas Miller
Assistant Director of Operations: Kathy Reade
Assistant Athletic Trainer: John Melody
Assistant Director of Ticket Operations: Carol Anne Coppola
Assistant Video Director: Jim Space
Community Relations Manager: Kimberlee Fields
Public Relations Assistant: Sharon Czark, Jared Winley
Assistant Equipment Manager: Gus Granneman
User Support Specialist: Steve Piazza
Stadium: Giants Stadium (built in 1976)
•**Capacity:** 79,466
East Rutherford, New Jersey 07073
Playing Surface: Natural Grass
Training Center: 1000 Fulton Avenue
Hempstead, New York 11550

RECORD HOLDERS

INDIVIDUAL RECORDS—CAREER

Category	Name	Performance
Rushing (Yds.)	Freeman McNeil, 1981-1992	8,074
Passing (Yds.)	Joe Namath, 1965-1976	27,057
Passing (TDs)	Joe Namath, 1965-1976	170
Receiving (No.)	Don Maynard, 1960-1972	627
Receiving (Yds.)	Don Maynard, 1960-1972	11,732
Interceptions	Bill Baird, 1963-69	34
Punting (Avg.)	Curley Johnson, 1961-68	42.8
Punt Return (Avg.)	Dick Christy, 1961-63	16.2
Kickoff Return (Avg.)	Bobby Humphery, 1984-89	22.8
Field Goals	Pat Leahy, 1974-1991	304
Touchdowns (Tot.)	Don Maynard, 1960-1972	88
Points	Pat Leahy, 1974-1991	1,470

INDIVIDUAL RECORDS—SINGLE SEASON

Category	Name	Performance
Rushing (Yds.)	Curtis Martin, 1999	1,464
Passing (Yds.)	Joe Namath, 1967	4,007
Passing (TDs)	Vinny Testaverde, 1998	29
Receiving (No.)	Al Toon, 1988	93
Receiving (Yds.)	Don Maynard, 1967	1,434
Interceptions	Dainard Paulson, 1964	12
Punting (Avg.)	Curley Johnson, 1965	45.3
Punt Return (Avg.)	Dick Christy, 1961	21.3
Kickoff Return (Avg.)	Bobby Humphery, 1984	30.7
Field Goals	Jim Turner, 1968	34
Touchdowns (Tot.)	Art Powell, 1960	14
	Don Maynard, 1965	14
	Emerson Boozer, 1972	14
Points	Jim Turner, 1968	145

INDIVIDUAL RECORDS—SINGLE GAME

Category	Name	Performance
Rushing (Yds.)	Curtis Martin, 12-3-00	203
Passing (Yds.)	Joe Namath, 9-24-72	496
Passing (TDs)	Joe Namath, 9-24-72	6
Receiving (No.)	Clark Gaines, 9-21-80	17
Receiving (Yds.)	Don Maynard, 11-17-68	228
Interceptions	Many times	3
	Last time by Marcus Coleman, 10-23-00	
Field Goals	Jim Turner, 11-3-68	6
	Bobby Howfield, 12-3-72	6
Touchdowns (Tot.)	Wesley Walker, 9-21-86	4
Points	Wesley Walker, 9-21-86	24

2001 SCHEDULE

PRESEASON

Aug. 11	**Atlanta**	8:00
Aug. 18	**Baltimore**	8:00
Aug. 25	at New York Giants	8:00
Aug. 30	at Philadelphia	7:30

REGULAR SEASON

Sept. 9	**Indianapolis**	1:00
Sept. 16	at Oakland	1:15
Sept. 23	at New England	4:05
Oct. 1	**San Francisco** (Mon.)	9:00
Oct. 7	at Buffalo	4:05
Oct. 14	**Miami**	4:15
Oct. 21	**St. Louis**	1:00
Oct. 28	at Carolina	1:00
Nov. 4	at New Orleans	7:30
Nov. 11	**Kansas City**	1:00
Nov. 18	at Miami	1:00
Nov. 25	Open Date	
Dec. 2	**New England**	1:00
Dec. 9	at Pittsburgh	4:15
Dec. 16	**Cincinnati**	1:00
Dec. 23	at Indianapolis	8:30
Dec. 30	**Buffalo**	1:00

GIANTS STADIUM

N

COACHING HISTORY

New York Titans 1960-62
(275-342-8)

1960-61	Sammy Baugh	14-14-0
1962	Clyde (Bulldog) Turner	5-9-0
1963-1973	Weeb Ewbank	73-78-6
1974-75	Charley Winner*	9-14-0
1975	Ken Shipp	1-4-0
1976	Lou Holtz**	3-10-0
1976	Mike Holovak	0-1-0
1977-1982	Walt Michaels	41-49-1
1983-89	Joe Walton	54-59-1
1990-93	Bruce Coslet	26-39-0
1994	Pete Carroll	6-10-0
1995-96	Rich Kotite	4-28-0
1997-99	Bill Parcells	30-20-0
2000	Al Groh	9-7-0

*Released after nine games in 1975
**Resigned after 13 games in 1976

2000 TEAM RECORD

PRESEASON (2-2)

Date	Result		Opponent
7/29	W	24-20	New Orleans
8/4	L	24-37	at Green Bay
8/12	L	0-10	at Baltimore
8/18	W	27-24	New York Giants

REGULAR SEASON (9-7)

Date	Result		Opponent	Att.
9/3	W	20-16	at Green Bay	59,870
9/11	W	20-19	New England	77,687
9/17	W	27-14	Buffalo	77,884
9/24	W	21-17	at Tampa Bay	65,619
10/8	L	3-20	Pittsburgh	78,441
10/15	W	34-17	at New England	60,292
10/23	W	40-37	Miami (OT)	78,389
10/29	L	20-23	at Buffalo	72,861
11/5	L	23-30	Denver	78,305
11/12	L	15-23	at Indianapolis	56,657
11/19	W	20-3	at Miami	74,320
11/26	W	17-10	Chicago	77,354
12/3	W	27-17	Indianapolis	78,138
12/10	L	7-31	at Oakland	62,632
12/17	L	7-10	Detroit	77,513
12/24	L	20-34	at Baltimore	69,184

(OT) Overtime

SCORE BY PERIODS

Jets	90	69	40	119	3	—	321
Opponents	67	120	46	88	0	—	321

ATTENDANCE

Home 623,948 Away 513,445 Total 1,137,393
Single-game home record, 78,389 (10/23/00)
Single-season home record, 624,847 (1999)

2000 TEAM STATISTICS

	Jets	Opp.
Total First Downs	308	267
Rushing	84	98
Passing	192	152
Penalty	32	17
Third Down: Made/Att	89/233	93/238
Third Down Pct.	38.2	39.1
Fourth Down: Made/Att	11/17	7/16
Fourth Down Pct.	64.7	43.8
Total Net Yards	5,395	4,820
Avg. Per Game	337.2	301.3
Total Plays	1,075	1,033
Avg. Per Play	5.0	4.7
Net Yards Rushing	1,471	1,888
Avg. Per Game	91.9	118.0
Total Rushes	418	476
Net Yards Passing	3,924	2,932
Avg. Per Game	245.3	183.3
Sacked/Yards Lost	20/99	40/234
Gross Yards	4,023	3,166
Att./Completions	637/352	517/265
Completion Pct.	55.3	51.3
Had Intercepted	29	21
Punts/Average	83/44.7	88/40.0
Net Punting Avg.	83/33.2	88/35.3
Penalties/Yards	76/626	100/832
Fumbles/Ball Lost	18/11	21/14
Touchdowns	36	33
Rushing	11	9
Passing	23	17
Returns	2	7
Avg. Time of Possession	30:20	29:40

2000 INDIVIDUAL STATISTICS

Passing	Att.	Comp.	Yds.	Pct.	TD	Int.	Tkld.	Rate
Testaverde	590	328	3,732	55.6	21	25	13/71	69.0
Lucas	41	21	206	51.2	0	4	6/24	26.1
Pennington	5	2	67	40.0	1	0	1/4	127.1
Martin	1	1	18	100.0	1	0	0/0	158.3
Jets	637	352	4,023	55.3	23	29	20/99	67.5
Opponents	517	265	3,166	51.3	17	21	40/234	64.3

SCORING	TD R	TD P	TD Rt	PAT	FG	Saf	PTS
Hall	0	0	0	30/30	21/32	0	93
Martin	9	2	0	0/0	0/0	0	66
Chrebet	0	8	0	0/0	0/0	0	48
Ward	0	3	0	0/0	0/0	0	18
R. Anderson	0	2	0	0/0	0/0	0	12
Baxter	0	2	0	0/0	0/0	0	12
Becht	0	2	0	0/0	0/0	0	12
Parmalee	2	0	0	0/0	0/0	0	12
Coleman	0	1	0	0/0	0/0	0	8
Coles	0	1	0	0/0	0/0	0	8
Conway	0	0	0	2/2	2/2	0	8
Elliott	0	1	0	0/0	0/0	0	6
V. Green	0	0	1	0/0	0/0	0	6
Wiggins	0	1	0	0/0	0/0	0	6
Williams	0	0	1	0/0	0/0	0	6
Jets	11	23	2	32/32	23/34	0	321
Opponents	9	17	7	32/32	29/34	1	321

2-Pt. Conversions: Coleman, Coles.
Jets 2-4, Opponents 1-1.

RUSHING	Att.	Yds.	Avg.	LG	TD
Martin	316	1,204	3.8	55	9
Parmalee	27	87	3.2	18t	2
R. Anderson	27	63	2.3	9	0
Lucas	6	42	7.0	17	0
Testaverde	25	32	1.3	15	0
Ward	4	23	5.8	12	0
Coles	2	15	7.5	8	0
Lewis	1	3	3.0	3	0
Stone	3	3	1.0	9	0
W. Hayes	1	2	2.0	2	0
Pennington	1	0	0.0	0	0
Sowell	2	0	0.0	1	0
Chrebet	3	-3	-1.0	8	0
Jets	418	1,471	3.5	55	11
Opponents	476	1,888	4.0	68t	9

RECEIVING	No.	Yds.	Avg.	LG	TD
R. Anderson	88	853	9.7	41	2
Martin	70	508	7.3	31	2
Chrebet	69	937	13.6	50	8
Ward	54	801	14.8	61	3
Coles	22	370	16.8	63	1
Becht	16	144	9.0	30	2
Parmalee	9	66	7.3	18	0
W. Hayes	6	126	21.0	32	0
Sowell	6	84	14.0	62	0
Brisby	4	60	15.0	19	0
Baxter	4	22	5.5	12t	2
Wiggins	2	4	2.0	3	1
Coleman	1	45	45.0	45t	1
Elliott	1	3	3.0	3t	1
Jets	352	4,023	11.4	63	23
Opponents	265	3,166	11.9	75	17

INTERCEPTIONS	No.	Yds.	Avg.	LG	TD
V. Green	6	144	24.0	43	1
Glenn	4	34	8.5	34	0
Coleman	4	6	1.5	7	0
Lewis	1	23	23.0	23	0
N. Ferguson	1	20	20.0	20	0
Ellis	1	1	1.0	1	0
Frost	1	1	1.0	1	0
Farrior	1	0	0.0	0	0
C. Hayes	1	0	0.0	0	0
Scott	1	0	0.0	0	0
Jets	21	229	10.9	43	1
Opponents	29	545	18.8	98t	4

PUNTING	No.	Yds.	Avg.	In 20	LG
Tupa	83	3,714	44.7	18	70
Jets	83	3,714	44.7	18	70
Opponents	88	3,523	40.0	19	57

PUNT RETURNS	No.	FC	Yds.	Avg.	LG	TD
Ward	27	19	214	7.9	19	0
L. Johnson	10	0	62	6.2	16	0
Dunn	1	0	0	0.0	0	0
Jets	38	19	276	7.3	19	0
Opponents	42	9	660	15.7	89t	2

KICKOFF RETURNS	No.	Yds.	Avg.	LG	TD
Stone	25	555	22.2	43	0
Williams	21	551	26.2	97t	1
Coles	11	207	18.8	24	0
L. Johnson	6	117	19.5	27	0
Glenn	3	51	17.0	22	0
Becht	2	0	0.0	0	0
Dunn	2	35	17.5	21	0
Baxter	1	15	15.0	15	0
Scott	1	0	0.0	0	0
Sowell	1	9	9.0	9	0
Wiggins	1	12	12.0	12	0
Jets	74	1,552	21.0	97t	1
Opponents	62	1,424	23.0	47	0

FIELD GOALS	1-19	20-29	30-39	40-49	50+
Hall	0/0	8/9	6/8	6/12	1/3
Conway	1/1	0/0	0/0	1/1	0/0
Jets	1/1	8/9	6/8	7/13	1/3
Opponents	0/0	8/9	12/13	9/12	0/0

SACKS	No.
Lewis	10.0
Ellis	8.5
Cox	6.0
Abraham	4.5
Phifer	4.0
Burton	1.0
Farrior	1.0
J. Ferguson	1.0
Frost	1.0
Jones	1.0
Lyle	1.0
Wiltz	1.0
Jets	40.0
Opponents	20.0

2001 DRAFT CHOICES

Round	Name	Pos.	College
1	Santana Moss	WR	Miami
2	LaMont Jordan	RB	Maryland
3	Kareem McKenzie	T	Penn State
4	Jamie Henderson	DB	Georgia
7	James Reed	DT	Iowa State
	Siitupe Peko	G	Michigan State

NEW YORK JETS

2001 VETERAN ROSTER

No.	Name	Pos.	Ht.	Wt.	Birthdate	NFL Exp.	College	Hometown	How Acq.	'00 Games/ Starts
94	Abraham, John	DE	6-3	265	5/6/78	2	South Carolina	Lamar, S.C.	D1b-'00	6/0
73	Anderson, Maurice	DT	6-3	280	1/19/75	2	Virginia	Nottoway, Va.	W(NE)-'00	0*
20	Anderson, Richie	FB	6-2	230	9/13/71	9	Penn State	Sandy Spring, Md.	D6-'93	16/15
88	Becht, Anthony	TE	6-5	267	8/8/77	2	West Virginia	Drexel Hill, Pa.	D1d-'00	14/10
98	Burton, Shane	DE-DT	6-6	305	1/18/74	6	Tennessee	Catawba, N.C.	UFA(Chi)-'00	16/16
80	Chrebet, Wayne	WR	5-10	188	8/14/73	7	Hofstra	Garfield, N.J.	FA-'95	16/16
42	Coleman, Marcus	CB	6-2	210	5/24/74	6	Texas Tech	Dallas, Texas	D5-'96	16/16
52	Colman, Doug	LB	6-2	250	6/4/73	6	Nebraska	Ocean City, N.J.	FA-'01	5/0*
87	Coles, Laveranues	WR-KR	5-11	190	12/29/77	2	Florida State	Jacksonville, Fla.	D3-'00	13/0
51	Darling, James	LB	6-0	250	12/29/74	5	Washington State	Kettle Falls, Tenn.	UFA(Phil)-'01	16/0*
76	Elliott, John (Jumbo)	T	6-7	305	4/1/65	14	Michigan	Lake Ronkonkoma, N.Y.	UFA(NYG)-'96	9/0
92	Ellis, Shaun	DE-DT	6-5	280	6/24/77	2	Tennessee	Anderson, S.C.	D1a-'00	16/3
69	Fabini, Jason	T	6-7	312	8/25/74	4	Cincinnati	Fort Wayne, Ind.	D4-'98	16/16
58	Farrior, James	LB	6-2	244	1/6/75	5	Virginia	Ettrick, Va.	D1-'97	16/6
72	Ferguson, Jason	DT	6-3	305	11/28/74	5	Georgia	Nettleton, Miss.	D7b-'97	15/11
25	Ferguson, Nick	S	5-11	201	11/27/74	2	Georgia Tech	Miami, Fla.	FA-'00	7/0
47	Frost, Scott	S	6-3	219	1/4/75	4	Nebraska	Lincoln, Neb.	D3a-'98	16/1
31	Glenn, Aaron	CB-KR	5-9	185	7/16/72	8	Texas A&M	Aldine, Texas	D1-'94	16/16
78	Green, Cornell	T	6-6	320	8/25/76	2	Central Florida	St. Petersburg, Fla.	W(Wash)-'00	0*
21	Green, Victor	S	5-11	210	12/8/69	9	Akron	Americus, Ga.	FA-'93	16/16
9	Hall, John	K	6-3	228	3/17/74	5	Wisconsin	Port Charlotte, Fla.	FA-'97	15/0
83	Hatchette, Matthew	WR	6-2	201	5/1/74	5	Langston	Cleveland, Ohio	FA-'01	14/1*
30	Hayes, Chris	S	6-0	206	5/7/72	5	Washington State	San Bernardino, Calif.	T(GB)-'97	16/8
86	Hayes, Windrell	WR-KR	5-11	198	12/14/76	2	Southern California	Stockton, Calif.	D5-'00	8/0
71	Jenkins, Kerry	G-T	6-5	305	9/6/73	4	Troy State	Tuscaloosa, Ala.	FA-'97	16/16
32	Johnson, Leon	RB-KR	6-0	218	7/13/74	4	North Carolina	Morganton, N.C.	FA-'00	3/0
55	Jones, Marvin	LB	6-2	250	6/28/72	9	Florida State	Miami, Fla.	D1-'93	16/16
53	Ledyard, Courtney	LB	6-2	250	3/9/77	2	Michigan State	Cleveland, Ohio	FA-'00	4/0
57	Lewis, Mo	LB	6-3	258	10/21/69	11	Georgia	Peachtree, Ga.	D3-'91	16/16
79	Loverne, David	G	6-3	299	5/22/76	3	San Jose State	Concord, Calif.	D3-'99	16/0
95	Lyle, Rick	DE	6-5	290	2/26/71	8	Missouri	Hickman Mills, Mo.	FA-'97	14/14
63	Machado, J.P.	C-G	6-4	300	1/6/76	3	Illinois	Monmouth, Ill.	D6b-'99	15/0
28	Martin, Curtis	RB	5-11	210	5/1/73	7	Pittsburgh	Pittsburgh, Pa.	RFA(NE)-'98	16/16
68	Mawae, Kevin	C	6-4	305	1/23/71	8	Louisiana State	Leesville, La.	UFA(Sea)-'98	16/16
24	Mickens, Ray	CB	5-8	184	1/4/73	6	Texas A&M	El Paso, Texas	D3-'96	16/0
38	Moreland, Earthwind	CB	5-11	185	6/13/77	2	Georgia Southern	Atlanta, Ga.	W(TB)-'00	1/0
89	Moreland, Jake	FB-TE	6-3	255	1/18/77	2	Western Michigan	Milwaukee, Wis.	FA-'00	7/1
99	Ogbogu, Eric	DE	6-4	285	7/18/75	4	Maryland	Irvington, N.Y.	D6a-'98	0*
10	Pennington, Chad	QB	6-3	225	6/26/76	2	Marshall	Knoxville, Tenn.	D1c-'00	1/0
22	Robinson, Damien	S	6-2	214	12/23/73	5	Iowa	Dallas, Texas	UFA(TB)-'01	16/16*
27	Scott, Tony	CB	5-10	193	10/3/76	2	North Carolina State	Lawndale, N.C.	D6-'00	16/0
70	Slaughter, Chad	T	6-7	344	6/4/78	2	Alcorn State	Dallas, Texas	W(Dall)-'00	0*
84	Slutzker, Scott	TE	6-4	240	12/20/72	5	Iowa	Hasbrouck Heights, N.J.	FA-'01	0*
33	Sowell, Jerald	FB	6-0	245	1/21/74	5	Tulane	Baker, La.	W(GB)-'97	16/0
16	Testaverde, Vinny	QB	6-5	235	11/13/63	15	Miami	Floral Park, N.Y.	FA-'98	16/16
77	Thomas, Randy	G	6-4	301	1/19/76	3	Mississippi State	East Point, Ga.	D2-'99	16/16
7	Tupa, Tom	P-QB	6-4	225	2/6/66	13	Ohio State	Cleveland, Ohio	UFA(NE)-'99	16/0
91	Wiltz, Jason	DT-DE	6-4	300	11/23/76	3	Nebraska	New Orleans, La.	D4-'99	15/1
74	Young, Ryan	T	6-5	320	6/28/76	3	Kansas State	St. Louis, Mo.	D7a-'99	16/16

* M. Anderson and Slaughter were inactive for 16 games in '00; Colman played 5 games with Cleveland; Darling played 16 games with Philadelphia; C. Green was inactive for 7 games; Hatchette played 14 games with Minnesota; Ogbogu missed '00 season because of injury; Robinson played 16 games with Tampa Bay; Slutzker last active with New Orleans in '99.

Players lost through free agency (4): TE Bradford Banta (Det; 16 games in '00), K Brett Conway (Wash; 1), QB Ray Lucas (Mia; 7), WR Dedric Ward (Mia; 16).

Also played with Jets in '00—TE Fred Baxter (9 games), DE Dorian Boose (9), WR Vincent Brisby (3), LB Bryan Cox (15), WR Damon Dunn (1), LB Dwayne Gordon (15), WR Malcolm Johnson (1), DT-DE Ernie Logan (16), RB Bernie Parmalee (14), LB Roman Phifer (16), WR Jermaine Wiggins (11), CB Kevin Williams (9).

COACHING STAFF

Head Coach,
Herman Edwards

Pro Career: Edwards was named the Jets' thirteenth full-time head coach on January 28, 2001. Edwards took control of the Jets after having served as the assistant head coach-defensive backs coach for Tampa Bay the past five seasons. The 1999 Buccaneers faced eventual Super Bowl XXXIV champion St. Louis Rams in the NFC Championship Game and held the prolific Rams offense to 11 points. Before joining Tampa Bay, Edwards worked for the Kansas City Chiefs for six seasons in several different roles. In 1995 he worked as a scout in the pro personnel department. During the 1992-94 seasons he worked as the team's defensive backs coach. In 1990-91, Edwards was a talent scout for the Chiefs while assisting the defensive backs coach. Edwards began his pro coaching career as a participant of the NFL's Minority Coaching Fellowship program with the Kansas City Chiefs in the summer of 1989.

Background: Played cornerback collegiately for California (1972), (1974), Monterrey Peninsula (Calif.) J.C. 1973, and San Diego State (1975-76). Professionally, Edwards played for the Philadelphia Eagles (1977-1985), Los Angeles Rams (1986), and Atlanta Falcons (1986). He was the defensive backs coach at San Jose State (1987-89).

Personal: Born April 27, 1954, Monmouth, N.J. Edwards and his wife Lia have one son, Marcus.

ASSISTANT COACHES

Bill Bradley, secondary; born January 24, 1947, Palestine, Texas, lives on Long Island, N.Y. Quarterback-defensive back-punter-kicker-returner-holder Texas 1966-68. Pro safety-punter-returner-holder Philadelphia Eagles 1969-1977, St. Louis Cardinals 1978. College coach: Texas 1987. Pro coach: San Antonio Gunslingers (USFL) 1983-84, Memphis Showboats (USFL) 1985, Cagary Stampeders (CFL) 1988-1990, San Antonio Riders (WLAF) 1991-92, Sacramento Gold Miners (CFL) 1993-94, San Antonio Texans (CFL) 1995, Toronto Argonauts (CFL) 1996-97, Buffalo Bills 1998-2000, joined Jets in 2001.

Rubin Carter, defensive line; born December 12, 1952, Ft. Lauderdale, Fla., lives on Long Island, N.Y. Defensive tackle Miami 1970-74. Pro defensive tackle Denver Broncos 1975-1986. College coach: Howard 1989-1993, San Jose State 1995-96, Maryland 1997-98. Pro coach: Denver Broncos 1987-88, Washington Redskins 1999-2000, joined Jets in 2001.

Ted Cottrell, defensive coordinator-asst. head coach; born June 13, 1947, Chester, Pa., lives on Long Island, N.Y. Linebacker Delaware Valley College 1966-68. Pro linebacker Atlanta Falcons 1969-1970, Winnipeg Blue Bombers (CFL) 1971. College coach: Rutgers 1973-1980, 1983. Pro coach: Kansas City Chiefs 1981-82, New Jersey Generals (USFL) 1983-84, Buffalo Bills 1986-89, 1995-2000, Arizona Cardinals 1990-94, joined Jets in 2001.

Paul Hackett, offensive coordinator; born July 5, 1947, Burlington, Vt., lives in Garden City, N.Y. Quarterback Cal-Davis 1965-68. No pro playing experience. College coach: Cal-Davis 1970-71, California 1972-75, Southern California 1976-1980, Pittsburgh 1989-1992 (head coach 1990-92), Southern California 1998-2000 (head coach). Pro coach: Cleveland Browns 1981-82, San Francisco 49ers 1983-85, Dallas Cowboys 1986-88, Kansas City Chiefs 1993-97, joined Jets in 2001.

Bishop Harris, running backs; born November 23, 1941, Phenix City, Ala., lives in Douglaston, N.Y. Running back-defensive back North Carolina College 1960-63. No pro playing experience. College coach: Duke 1972-75, North Carolina State 1977-79, Louisiana State 1980-83, Notre Dame 1984-85, Minnesota 1986-1990, North Carolina Central 1991-92 (head coach). Pro coach: Denver Broncos 1993-94, Oakland Raiders 1995-97, Buffalo Bills 1998-99, joined Jets in 2001.

Mike Henning, quality control-offensive assistant; born January 30, 1973, Houston, lives in Garden City, N.Y. Quarterback Cal Poly 1991-94. No pro playing experience. College coach: C.W. Post 1998-99. Pro coach: Joined Jets in 2001.

Lou Hernandez, asst. strength and conditioning; born June 16, 1967, Alice, Texas, lives on Long Island, N.Y. Attended Houston. No college or pro playing experience. College coach: Houston 1992-2000. Pro coach: Joined Jets in 2001.

John Lott, strength and conditioning; born May 9, 1964, Denton, Texas, lives in Merrick, N.Y. Offensive lineman North Texas 1983-86. Offensive lineman Pittsburgh Steelers 1987. College coach: North Texas 1989, Houston 1990-96. Pro coach: Joined Jets in 1997.

David Merritt, defensive assistant; born September 8, 1971, Raleigh, N.C., lives in East Meadow, N.Y. Linebacker North Carolina State 1989-1992. Pro linebacker Miami Dolphins 1993, Arizona Cardinals 1993-96, Rhein Fire (NFLE) 1997. College coach: Chattanooga 1997, Virginia Military Institute 1998-2000. Pro coach: Joined Jets in 2001.

Bill Muir, offensive line; born October 26, 1942, Pittsburgh, lives in Fort Salonga, N.Y. Tackle Susquehanna 1962-64. No pro playing experience. College coach: Susquehanna 1965, Delaware Valley 1966-67, Rhode Island 1970-71, Idaho State 1972-73, Southern Methodist 1976-77. Pro coach: Orlando (Continental Football League) 1968-69, Houston Shreveport Steamer (WFL) 1975, New England Patriots 1982-88, Indianapolis Colts 1989-1991, Philadelphia Eagles 1992-94, joined Jets in 1995.

Phil Pettey, tight ends; born April 17, 1961, Kenosha, Wis., lives in North Merrick, N.Y. Guard Missouri 1984-86. Pro guard Washington Redskins 1987. College coach: Louisiana State 1990, Pittsburgh 1991, Southern California 1999. Pro coach: New Orleans Saints 2000, joined Jets in 2001.

Eric Price, quality control-offensive assistant; born September 12, 1966, Pullman, Wash., lives in Bellmore, N.Y. Wide receiver Dixie (Utah) J.C. 1986-87, Weber State 1988-89. No pro playing experience. College coach: Weber State 1990, Washington State 1991, Hawaii 1991, Miami 1992-93, Cal Poly-San Luis Obispo 1994-95, Northern Arizona 1996-97, Washington State 1998-2000. Pro coach: Joined Jets in 2001.

Mose Rison, wide receiver; born July 22, 1956, Flint, Mich., lives on Long Island, N.Y. Running back Central Michigan 1974-77. No pro playing experience. College coach: Central Michigan 1981-87, U.S. Naval Academy 1988-89, Rutgers 1990-94, Stanford 1995-2000. Pro coach: Joined Jets in 2001.

Bob Sutton, linebackers; born January 23, 1951, Ypsilanti, Mich., lives on Long Island, N.Y. Attended Eastern Michigan. No college or pro playing experience. College coach: Michigan 1972-73, Syracuse 1974, Western Michigan 1975-76, Illinois 1977-79, North Carolina State 1982, Army 1983-1999 (head coach 1991-99). Pro coach: Joined Jets in 2000.

Mike Westhoff, special teams; born January 10, 1948, Pittsburgh, lives in Garden City, N.Y. Center-linebacker Wichita State 1967-69. No pro playing experience. College coach: Indiana 1974-75, Dayton 1976, Indiana State 1977, Northwestern 1978-1980, Texas Christian 1981. Pro coach: Baltimore/Indianapolis Colts 1982-84, Arizona Outlaws (USFL) 1985, Miami Dolphins 1986-2000, joined Jets in 2001.

2001 FIRST-YEAR ROSTER

Name	Pos.	Ht.	Wt.	Birthdate	College	Hometown	How Acq.
Alston, Corey	WR	6-1	213	8/26/79	Western Michigan	Camden, N.J.	FA
Bonito, Matt	G	6-7	294	7/17/77	Michigan State	Lima, Ohio	FA
Burroughs, Noah	S	6-0	203	6/11/76	Buffalo	Hempstead, N.Y.	FA
Bristol, Mark (1)	T	6-6	305	1/12/78	Mansfield	Philadelphia, Pa.	FA-'00
Comella, Matt	FB	5-11	235	4/24/77	Northeastern	Wellesley, Mass.	FA
Dearth, James (1)	TE	6-4	270	1/22/76	Tarleton State	Scurrey, Texas	FA
Farmer, Matt (1)	WR	6-0	190	6/2/77	Air Force	Pella, Iowa	FA-'00
Henderson, Jamie	CB	6-2	202	1/1/79	Georgia	Carrollton, Ga.	D4
Humphrey, Aaron (1)	LB	6-2	260	9/22/77	Texas	Lubbock, Texas	FA
Jackson, Marlion (1)	RB	6-2	240	10/11/77	Saginaw Valley State	Detroit, Mich.	FA-'00
Jordan, Lamont	RB	5-10	230	11/11/78	Maryland	Forestville, Md.	D2
Keith, Dustin	G	6-5	292	8/8/77	Virginia	Yorktown, Va.	FA
McGeoghan, Phil	WR	6-2	224	7/8/79	Maine	Feeding Hills, N.J.	D3
Kitchings, Desmond (1)	WR-KR	5-9	179	7/19/78	Furman	Columbia, S.C.	FA-'00
McKenzie, Kareem	T	6-6	327	5/24/79	Penn State	Willingboro, N.J.	D3
Michals, Jon (1)	DE	6-4	282	6/29/77	Minnesota	Oak Creek, Wis.	FA-'00
Moses, Kelvin (1)	LB	6-0	234	9/3/76	Wake Forest	Heartsville, S.C.	FA
Moss, Santana	WR	5-10	185	6/1/79	Miami	Miami, Fla.	D1
Myers, Shannon (1)	WR	6-1	194	6/12/73	Lenoir-Rhyne	Salisbury, N.C.	FA
O'Sullivan, Dennis (1)	C	6-3	300	1/28/76	Tulane	Stony Point, N.Y.	FA-'00
Parks, Thomas (1)	P	6-2	225	10/14/71	Mississippi State	Houston, Miss.	FA
Patu, Saul	DE	6-3	272	6/8/78	Oregon	Seattle, Wash.	FA
Peko, Siitupe	G	6-4	298	9/19/78	Michigan State	Whittier, Calif.	D7b
Reed, James	DT	6-0	286	2/3/77	Iowa State	Saginaw, Mich.	D7a
Rooths, James	CB	5-11	210	9/3/76	Shepherd	Baltimore, Md.	FA
Strohmeyer, Dax (1)	LB	6-4	235	1/31/77	Rutgers	Upper Saddle River, N.J.	FA-'00
Syvrud, J.J. (1)	LB	6-3	255	5/10/77	Jamestown (N.D.)	Rock Springs, Wyo.	D7b-'99
Szokola, Ryan	S	6-1	203	12/26/78	Illinois State	Trenton, Mich.	FA
Todd, Joe	LB	6-0	225	4/14/79	Hofstra	Mansfield, Mass.	FA
Viger, David	DE	6-4	281	5/13/75	Navy	Vista, Calif.	FA
White, Reggie	RB	6-0	228	7/11/79	Oklahoma State	Liberty, Texas	FA
Wilcox, Daniel	TE	6-1	229	3/23/77	Appalachian State	Atlanta, Ga.	FA
Woodbury, Tory	QB	6-2	208	7/12/78	Winston-Salem State	Winston-Salem, N.C.	FA

The term NFL Rookie is defined as a player who is in his first season of professional football and has not been on the roster of another professional football team for any regular-season or postseason games. A Rookie is designated by an "R" on NFL rosters. Players who have been active in another professional football league or players who have NFL experience, including either preseason training camp or being on an Active List or Inactive List, or on Reserve/Injured or Reserve/Physically Unable to Perform for fewer than six regular-season games, are termed NFL First-Year Players. An NFL First-Year Player is designated by a "1" on NFL rosters. Thereafter, a player is credited with an additional year of experience for each season in which he accumulates six games on the Active List or Inactive List, or on Reserve/Injured or Reserve/Physically Unable to Perform.

NOTES

OAKLAND RAIDERS

American Football Conference
Western Division
Team Colors: Silver and Black
1220 Harbor Bay Parkway
Alameda, California 94502
Telephone: (510) 864-5000

CLUB OFFICIALS

President of the General Partner: Al Davis
Chief Executive: Amy Trask
Executive Assistant: Al LoCasale
General Counsel: Jeff Birren
Senior Assistant: Bruce Allen
Personnel Executive: Mike Lombardi
Personnel Executive: Chet Franklin
Legal Affairs: Jeff Birren, Roxanne Kosarzycki
Finance: Marc Badain, Tom Blanda, Ron LaVelle, Derek Person
Special Projects: Jim Otto
Senior Administrator: Morris Bradshaw
Senior Executive: John Herrera
Public Relations Director: Mike Taylor
Player Development and Community Relations: Terry Burton
Public Relations: Craig Long
Broadcast and Multimedia: Billy Zagger
Ticket Operations: Peter Eiges
Head Trainer: H. Rod Martin
Assistant Trainer: Scott Touchet
Assistant Trainer: Mark Mayer
Equipment Manager: Bob Romanski
Video Director: Dave Nash
Stadium: Network Associates Coliseum (built in 1966) • **Capacity:** 63,132
Playing Surface: Grass
Training Camp: Napa Valley Marriott, Napa, California 94558

2001 SCHEDULE

PRESEASON

Aug. 4	**Dallas**	6:00
Aug. 11	at Arizona	8:00
Aug. 19	at San Francisco	4:00
Aug. 27	vs. Dallas at Mexico City	7:00
Aug. 31	**Green Bay**	6:00

REGULAR SEASON

Sept. 9	at Kansas City	12:00
Sept. 16	**New York Jets**	1:15
Sept. 23	at Miami	1:00
Sept. 30	**Seattle**	1:15
Oct. 7	Open Date	
Oct. 14	at Indianapolis	7:30
Oct. 21	**Dallas**	1:15
Oct. 28	at Philadelphia	4:15
Nov. 5	**Denver** (Mon.)	6:00
Nov. 11	at Seattle	5:30
Nov. 18	**San Diego**	1:05
Nov. 25	at New York Giants	4:15
Dec. 2	**Arizona**	1:15
Dec. 9	**Kansas City**	1:15
Dec. 15	at San Diego (Sat.)	2:00
Dec. 22	**Tennessee** (Sat.)	6:00
Dec. 30	at Denver	2:15

RECORD HOLDERS

INDIVIDUAL RECORDS—CAREER

Category	Name	Performance
Rushing (Yds.)	Marcus Allen, 1982-1992	8,545
Passing (Yds.)	Ken Stabler, 1970-79	19,078
Passing (TDs)	Ken Stabler, 1970-79	150
Receiving (No.)	Tim Brown, 1988-2000	846
Receiving (Yds.)	Tim Brown, 1988-2000	12,072
Interceptions	Willie Brown, 1967-1978	39
	Lester Hayes, 1977-1986	39
Punting (Avg.)	Shane Lechler, 2000	45.9
Punt Return (Avg.)	Claude Gibson, 1963-65	12.6
Kickoff Return (Avg.)	Jack Larscheid, 1960-61	28.4
Field Goals	Chris Bahr, 1980-88	162
Touchdowns (Tot.)	Marcus Allen, 1982-1992	98
Points	George Blanda, 1967-1975	863

INDIVIDUAL RECORDS—SINGLE SEASON

Category	Name	Performance
Rushing (Yds.)	Marcus Allen, 1985	1,759
Passing (Yds.)	Jeff George, 1997	3,917
Passing (TDs)	Daryle Lamonica, 1969	34
Receiving (No.)	Tim Brown 1997	104
Receiving (Yds.)	Tim Brown, 1997	1,408
Interceptions	Lester Hayes, 1980	13
Punting (Avg.)	Shane Lechler, 2000	45.9
Punt Return (Avg.)	Claude Gibson, 1964	14.4
Kickoff Return (Avg.)	Harold Hart, 1975	30.5
Field Goals	Jeff Jaeger, 1993	35
Touchdowns (Tot.)	Marcus Allen, 1984	18
Points	Jeff Jaeger, 1993	132

INDIVIDUAL RECORDS—SINGLE GAME

Category	Name	Performance
Rushing (Yds.)	Napoleon Kaufman, 10-19-97	227
Passing (Yds.)	Jeff Hostetler, 10-31-93	424
Passing (TDs)	Tom Flores, 12-22-63	6
	Daryle Lamonica, 10-19-69	6
Receiving (No.)	Tim Brown, 12-21-97	14
Receiving (Yds.)	Art Powell, 12-22-63	247
Interceptions	Many times. Last time by Terry McDaniel, 10-9-94	3
Field Goals	Jeff Jaeger, 12-11-94	5
	Sebastian Janikowski, 10-29-00	5
Touchdowns (Tot.)	Art Powell, 12-22-63	4
	Marcus Allen, 9-24-84	4
	Harvey Williams, 11-16-97	4
Points	Art Powell, 12-22-63	24
	Marcus Allen, 9-24-84	24
	Harvey Williams, 11-16-97	24

COACHING HISTORY

OAKLAND 1960-1981
LOS ANGELES 1982-1994
(382-257-11)

1960-61	Eddie Erdelatz*	6-10-0
1961-62	Marty Feldman**	2-15-0
1962	Red Conkright	1-8-0
1963-65	Al Davis	23-16-3
1966-68	John Rauch	35-10-1
1969-1978	John Madden	112-39-7
1979-1987	Tom Flores	91-56-0
1988-89	Mike Shanahan***	8-12-0
1989-1994	Art Shell	57-44-0
1995-96	Mike White	15-17-0
1997	Joe Bugel	4-12-0
1998-2000	Jon Gruden	29-21-0

*Released after two games in 1961
**Released after five games in 1962
***Released after four games in 1989

NETWORK ASSOCIATES COLISEUM

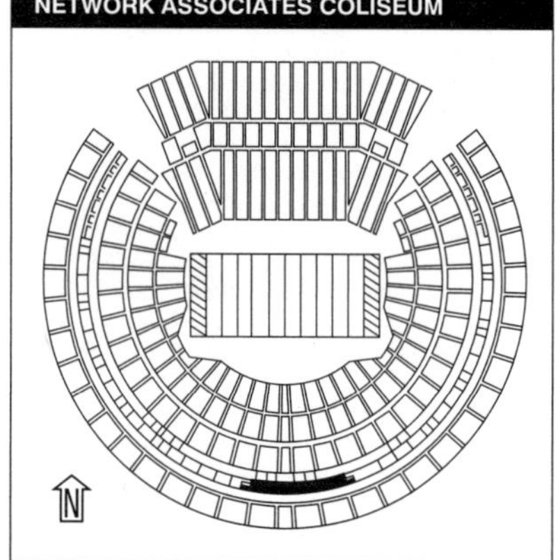

2000 TEAM RECORD

PRESEASON (3-1)

Date	Result		Opponent
8/5	L	17-31	at St. Louis
8/13	W	21-20	at Dallas
8/18	W	23-17	Detroit
8/24	W	20-0	Seattle

REGULAR SEASON (12-4)

Date	Result		Opponent	Att.
9/3	W	9-6	San Diego	56,373
9/10	W	38-31	at Indianapolis	56,769
9/17	L	24-33	Denver	62,078
9/24	W	36-10	Cleveland	45,702
10/8	W	34-28	at San Francisco (OT)	68,344
10/15	W	20-17	at Kansas City	79,025
10/22	W	31-3	Seattle	57,490
10/29	W	15-13	at San Diego	66,659
11/5	W	49-31	Kansas City	62,428
11/13	L	24-27	at Denver	75,951
11/19	W	31-22	at New Orleans	64,900
11/26	W	41-14	Atlanta	55,175
12/3	L	20-21	at Pittsburgh	55,811
12/10	W	31-7	New York Jets	62,632
12/16	L	24-27	at Seattle	68,681
12/24	W	52-9	Carolina	60,637

(OT) Overtime

POSTSEASON (1-1)

Date	Result		Opponent	Att.
1/6	W	27-0	Miami	61,998
1/14	L	3-16	Baltimore	62,784

SCORE BY PERIODS

Raiders	77	179	86	131	6	— 479
Opponents	75	74	43	107	0	— 299

ATTENDANCE

Home 449,948 Away 538,559 Total 988,507
Single-game home record, 62,632 (12/10/00)
Single-season home record, 449,948 (2000)

2000 TEAM STATISTICS

	Raiders	Opp.
Total First Downs	337	320
Rushing	128	85
Passing	177	202
Penalty	32	33
Third Down: Made/Att	89/206	81/205
Third Down Pct.	43.2	39.5
Fourth Down: Made/Att	3/8	4/14
Fourth Down Pct.	37.5	28.6
Total Net Yards	5,776	5,249
Avg. Per Game	361.0	328.1
Total Plays	1,023	1,014
Avg. Per Play	5.6	5.2
Net Yards Rushing	2,470	1,551
Avg. Per Game	154.4	96.9
Total Rushes	520	383
Net Yards Passing	3,306	3,698
Avg. Per Game	206.6	231.1
Sacked/Yards Lost	28/124	43/278
Gross Yards	3,430	3,976
Att./Completions	475/284	588/359
Completion Pct.	59.8	61.1
Had Intercepted	11	21
Punts/Average	66/45.2	79/41.6
Net Punting Avg.	66/38.0	79/35.1
Penalties/Yards	118/940	117/912
Fumbles/Ball Lost	18/9	29/16
Touchdowns	58	35
Rushing	23	8
Passing	28	25
Returns	7	2
Avg. Time of Possession	31:53	28:07

2000 INDIVIDUAL STATISTICS

Passing	Att.	Comp.	Yds.	Pct.	TD	Int.	Tkld.	Rate
Gannon	473	284	3,430	60.0	28	11	28/124	92.4
Hoying	2	0	0	0.0	0	0	0/0	39.6
Raiders	475	284	3,430	59.8	28	11	28/124	92.0
Opponents	588	359	3,976	61.1	25	21	43/278	80.4

SCORING	TD R	TD P	TD Rt	PAT	FG	Saf	PTS
Janikowski	0	0	0	46/46	22/32	0	112
Brown	0	11	0	0/0	0/0	0	66
Wheatley	9	1	0	0/0	0/0	0	60
Crockett	7	0	0	0/0	0/0	0	42
Rison	0	6	0	0/0	0/0	0	36
Jordan	3	1	1	0/0	0/0	0	30
Gannon	4	0	0	0/0	0/0	0	26
Dudley	0	4	0	0/0	0/0	0	24
Allen	0	0	3	0/0	0/0	0	18
Brigham	0	2	0	0/0	0/0	0	12
Jett	0	2	0	0/0	0/0	0	12
Lechler	0	0	0	7/7	0/1	0	7
Conway	0	0	0	3/3	1/1	0	6
Dunn	0	0	1	0/0	0/0	0	6
Gordon	0	0	1	0/0	0/0	0	6
Kaufman	0	1	0	0/0	0/0	0	6
Thomas	0	0	1	0/0	0/0	0	6
Russell	0	0	0	0/0	0/0	1	2
Raiders	23	28	7	56/56	23/34	2	479
Opponents	8	25	2	30/30	19/25	1	299

2-Pt. Conversions: Gannon.
Raiders 1-1, Opponents 0-5.

RUSHING	Att.	Yds.	Avg.	LG	TD
Wheatley	232	1,046	4.5	80t	9
Gannon	89	529	5.9	23	4
Kaufman	93	499	5.4	60	0
Jordan	46	213	4.6	43t	3
Crockett	43	130	3.0	11	7
Kirby	11	51	4.6	28	0
Brown	3	12	4.0	7	0
Hoying	2	-3	-1.5	-1	0
Dudley	1	-7	-7.0	-7	0
Raiders	520	2,470	4.8	80t	23
Opponents	383	1,551	4.0	53	8

RECEIVING	No.	Yds.	Avg.	LG	TD
Brown	76	1,128	14.8	45	11
Rison	41	606	14.8	49	6
Dudley	29	350	12.1	30	4
Jordan	27	299	11.1	55	1
Ritchie	26	173	6.7	17	0
Jett	20	356	17.8	84t	2
Wheatley	20	156	7.8	17	1
Kaufman	13	127	9.8	25	1
Brigham	13	107	8.2	19	2
Crockett	10	62	6.2	15	0
Dunn	4	33	8.3	14	0
Kirby	3	19	6.3	9	0
Woodson	1	8	8.0	8	0
Porter	1	6	6.0	6	0
Raiders	284	3,430	12.1	84t	28
Opponents	359	3,976	11.1	62	25

INTERCEPTIONS	No.	Yds.	Avg.	LG	TD
Allen	6	145	24.2	50t	3
Thomas	6	68	11.3	46t	1
Woodson	4	36	9.0	23	0
James	2	25	12.5	25	0
Pope	2	25	12.5	25	0
Taves	1	24	24.0	24	0
Raiders	21	323	15.4	50t	4
Opponents	11	93	8.5	34	0

PUNTING	No.	Yds.	Avg.	In 20	LG
Lechler	65	2,984	45.9	24	69
Raiders	66	2,984	45.2	24	69
Opponents	79	3,289	41.6	22	66

PUNT RETURNS	No.	FC	Yds.	Avg.	LG	TD
Gordon	29	10	258	8.9	36	0
Dunn	8	3	99	12.4	25	0
Raiders	37	13	357	9.6	36	0
Opponents	30	12	279	9.3	19	0

KICKOFF RETURNS	No.	Yds.	Avg.	LG	TD
Dunn	44	1,073	24.4	88t	1
Kaufman	9	198	22.0	31	0
Branch	2	48	24.0	24	0
Gordon	1	17	17.0	17	0
Raiders	56	1,336	23.9	88t	1
Opponents	80	1,689	21.1	68	0

FIELD GOALS	1-19	20-29	30-39	40-49	50+
Janikowski	1/1	6/6	6/7	8/14	1/4
Conway	1/1	0/0	0/0	0/0	0/0
Lechler	0/0	0/0	0/1	0/0	0/0
Raiders	2/2	6/6	6/8	8/14	1/4
Opponents	0/0	8/9	3/3	6/11	2/2

SACKS	No.
Jackson	8.0
Coleman	6.0
Upshaw	6.0
Bryant	5.5
Johnstone	3.5
Russell	3.0
Taves	3.0
Alexander	2.0
Biekert	2.0
Allen	1.0
Dorsett	1.0
Pope	1.0
Thomas	1.0
Raiders	43.0
Opponents	28.0

2001 DRAFT CHOICES

Round	Name	Pos.	College
1	Derrick Gibson	DB	Florida State
2	Marques Tuiasosopo	QB	Washington
3	DeLawrence Grant	DE	Oregon State
5	Raymond Perryman	DB	Northern Arizona
6	Chris Cooper	DT	Nebraska-Omaha
7	Derek Combs	RB	Ohio State
	Ken-Yon Rambo	WR	Ohio State

OAKLAND RAIDERS

2001 VETERAN ROSTER

No.	Name	Pos.	Ht.	Wt.	Birthdate	NFL Exp.	College	Hometown	How Acq.	'00 Games/ Starts
58	Alexander, Elijah	LB	6-2	235	8/2/70	9	Kansas State	Fort Worth, Texas	FA-'00	16/16
21	Allen, Eric	CB	5-10	185	11/22/65	14	Arizona State	San Diego, Calif.	T(NO)-'98	16/16
93	Armstrong, Trace	DE	6-4	275	10/5/65	13	Florida	Birmingham, Ala.	UFA(Mia)-'01	16/0*
73	Ashmore, Darryl	G-T	6-7	310	11/1/69	10	Northwestern	Peoria, Ill.	FA-'98	16/2
85	Barlow, Reggie	WR	6-0	190	1/22/73	5	Alabama State	Montgomery, Ala.	FA-'01	16/0*
50	Barton, Eric	LB	6-2	245	9/29/77	3	Maryland	Alexandria, Va.	D5-'99	16/3
54	Biekert, Greg	LB	6-2	255	3/14/69	9	Colorado	Longmont, Colo.	D7-'93	16/16
49	Bjornson, Eric	TE	6-4	240	12/15/71	6	Washington	San Francisco, Calif.	FA-'01	8/6*
27	Branch, Calvin	S	5-11	195	5/8/74	5	Colorado State	Spring, Texas	D6-'97	16/0
87	Brigham, Jeremy	TE	6-6	255	3/22/75	4	Washington	Scottdale, Ariz.	D5-'98	16/2
55	Brooks, Bobby	LB	6-2	240	3/3/76	2	Fresno State	Vallejo, Calif.	FA-'00	16/0
81	Brown, Tim	WR	6-0	195	7/22/66	13	Notre Dame	Dallas, Texas	D1-'88	16/16
94	Bryant, Tony	DE	6-6	275	9/3/76	3	Florida State	Marathon, Fla.	D2-'99	16/16
48	Chryplewicz, Pete	TE	6-5	250	4/27/74	4	Notre Dame	Sterling Heights, Mich.	FA-'01	0*
57	Coleman, Rod	DE	6-2	265	8/16/76	3	East Carolina	Philadelphia, Pa.	D5-'99	12/0
79	Collins, Mo	G	6-4	325	9/22/76	4	Florida	Charlotte, N.C.	D1-'98	13/12
32	Crockett, Zack	RB	6-2	240	12/2/72	7	Florida State	Pompano Beach, Fla.	UFA(Jax)-'99	13/1
33	Dorsett, Anthony	S	5-11	200	9/14/73	6	Pittsburgh	Aliquippa, Pa.	UFA(Tenn)-'00	16/16
88	Dunn, David	WR	6-3	210	6/10/72	7	Fresno State	San Diego, Calif.	UFA(Cle)-'00	16/0
89	Fulcher, Mondriel	TE	6-3	250	10/15/76	2	Miami	Coffeyville, Kan.	D7-'00	10/0
12	Gannon, Rich	QB	6-3	210	12/20/65	14	Delaware	Philadelphia, Pa.	UFA(KC)-'99	16/16
25	Garner, Charlie	RB	5-9	190	2/13/72	8	Tennessee	Fairfax, Va.	UFA(SF)-'01	16/15*
37	Harris, Johnnie	S	6-2	210	8/21/72	2	Mississippi State	Chicago, Ill.	FA-'99	15/1
97	Harris, Jon	DE	6-7	270	6/9/74	3	Virginia	Inwood, N.Y.	FA-'01	0*
30	Howard, Chris	RB	5-11	235	5/2/75	4	Michigan	River Ridge, La.	FA-'01	2/1*
14	Hoying, Bobby	QB	6-3	220	9/20/72	6	Ohio State	St. Henry, Ohio	T(Phil)-'99	4/0
68	Hutson, Tony	DE	6-3	320	3/13/74	5	Northeastern State (Okla.)	Houston, Texas	FA-'01	3/0*
90	Jackson, Grady	DT	6-2	325	1/21/73	5	Knoxville	Greensboro, Ala.	D6-'97	15/0
20	James, Tory	CB	6-2	185	5/18/73	6	Louisiana State	Marrero, La.	UFA(Den)-'00	16/16
11	Janikowski, Sebastian	K	6-1	255	3/2/78	2	Florida State	Daytona Beach, Fla.	D1-'00	15/0
82	Jett, James	WR	5-10	170	12/28/70	9	West Virginia	Kearneysville, W. Va.	FA-'93	16/11
41	Johnson, Eric	S	6-0	210	4/30/76	2	Nebraska	Phoenix, Ariz.	FA-'00	16/0
28	Jordan, Randy	RB	5-11	215	6/6/70	8	North Carolina	Manson, N.C.	FA-'98	16/0
72	Kennedy, Lincoln	T	6-6	335	2/12/71	9	Washington	San Diego, Calif.	T(Atl)-'96	15/15
42	Kirby, Terry	RB	6-1	215	1/20/70	9	Virginia	Tabb, Va.	FA-'00	2/0
9	Lechler, Shane	P	6-2	225	8/7/76	2	Texas A&M	Channelview, Texas	D5-'00	16/0
19	McCullough, Andy	WR	6-3	205	11/11/75	2	Tennessee	Dayton, Ohio	FA-'01	0*
31	McDonald, Ramos	CB	6-0	200	4/30/76	5	New Mexico	Texarkana, Texas	FA-'01	3/0*
22	Metcalf, Eric	WR	5-10	190	1/23/68	11	Texas	Seattle, Wash.	FA-'01	0*
	Mickell, Darren	DE	6-5	285	8/3/70	9	Florida	Miami, Fla.	UFA(SD)-'01	16/16*
78	Middleton, Frank	G	6-3	335	10/25/74	6	Arizona	Beaumont, Texas	FA-'01	16/16*
77	Myles, Toby	T	6-5	320	7/23/75	3	Jackson State	Jackson, Miss.	FA-'00	0*
16	Peete, Rodney	QB	6-0	230	3/16/66	13	Southern California	Shawnee Mission, Kan.	FA-'00	0*
51	Phillips, Ryan	LB	6-4	250	2/7/74	6	Idaho	Auburn, Wash.	UFA(NYG)-'01	16/15*
23	Pope, Marquez	S	5-11	205	10/29/70	10	Fresno State	Long Beach, Calif.	FA-'00	15/15
84	Porter, Jerry	WR	6-2	220	7/14/78	2	West Virginia	Washington, D.C.	D2-'00	13/0
67	Pourdanesh, Shar	T	6-6	325	7/19/70	7	Nevada	Irvine, Calif.	UFA(Pitt)-'01	5/2*
80	Rice, Jerry	WR	6-2	196	10/13/62	16	Mississippi Valley State	Crawford, Miss.	FA-'01	16/16*
#	Rison, Andre	WR	6-0	185	3/18/67	14	Michigan State	Flint, Mich.	FA-'00	16/1
40	Ritchie, Jon	RB	6-1	250	9/4/74	4	Stanford	Mechanicsburgh, Pa.	D3-'98	13/11
63	Robbins, Barret	C	6-3	320	8/26/73	7	Texas Christian	Houston, Texas	D2-'95	16/16
96	Russell, Darrell	DT	6-5	325	5/27/76	5	Southern California	San Diego, Calif.	D1-'97	16/16
65	Sims, Barry	G-T	6-5	295	12/1/74	3	Utah	Park City, Utah	FA-'99	16/9
53	Smith, Travian	LB	6-4	240	8/26/75	4	Oklahoma	Tatum, Texas	D5-'98	16/1
74	Stinchcomb, Matt	T	6-6	310	6/3/77	3	Georgia	Lilburn, Ga.	D1-'99	15/8
99	Taves, Josh	DE	6-7	285	5/13/72	2	Northeastern	Yarmouth, Mass.	FA-'00	16/0
59	Thomas, William	LB	6-2	225	8/13/68	11	Texas A&M	Amarillo, Texas	FA-'00	16/16
62	Treu, Adam	C	6-5	300	6/24/74	5	Nebraska	Lincoln, Neb.	D3-'97	16/0
91	Upshaw, Regan	DE	6-4	260	8/12/75	6	California	Pittsburg, Calif.	UFA(Jax)-'00	16/8
17	Van Dyke, Alex	WR	6-0	205	7/24/74	6	Nevada	Sacramento, Calif.	FA-'01	4/0*
47	Wheatley, Tyrone	RB	6-0	235	1/19/72	7	Michigan	Inkster, Mich.	FA-'99	15/15
86	t- Williams, Roland	TE	6-5	265	7/27/75	4	Syracuse	Rochester, N.Y.	T(StL)-'01	16/11*
76	Wisniewski, Steve	G	6-4	305	4/7/67	13	Penn State	Houston, Texas	D2-'89	16/16
24	Woodson, Charles	CB	6-1	205	10/7/76	4	Michigan	Fremont, Ohio	D1-'98	16/16

* Armstrong played 16 games for Miami in '00; Barlow played 16 games with Jacksonville; Bjornson played 8 games with New England; Chryplewicz last active with Detroit in '99; Garner played 16 games with San Francisco; Harris last active with Green Bay in '99; Howard played 2 games with Jacksonville; Hutson played 3 games with Washington; McCullough and Metcalf last active with Arizona in '99; McDonald played 3 games with N.Y. Giants; Mickell played 16 games with San Diego; Middleton played 16 games with Tampa Bay; Myles was inactive for 15 games; Peete was inactive for 16 games; Phillips played 16 games with N.Y. Giants; Pourdanesh played 5 games with Pittsburgh; Rice played 16 games with San Francisco; Van Dyke played 4 games with Philadelphia; Williams played 16 games with St. Louis.

\# Unrestricted free agent; subject to developments.

t- Raiders traded for Williams (StL).

Retired—Napoleon Kaufman, 6-year running back, 16 games in '00.

Players lost through free agency (1): TE Rickey Dudley (Cle; 16 games in '00).

Also played with Raiders in '00—K Brett Conway (1 game), TE Rickey Dudley (16), CB Darrien Gordon (14), DE Lance Johnstone (15), DE Austin Robbins (2).

COACHING STAFF

Head Coach,
Jon Gruden

Pro career: Became the twelfth head coach in Raiders history on January 22, 1998, after seven seasons as an NFL assistant coach. Guided Raiders to a 12-4 record and the AFC Western Division title in his third season as head coach. Led AFC to 38-17 victory in 2001 Pro Bowl. Gruden's teams reached the postseason five times during his assistant coaching tenure. Spent the last three years as offensive coordinator for the Philadelphia Eagles on Ray Rhodes's staff. The Eagles were 26-21-1 during this 1995-97 period, including playoff appearances after both the 1995 and 1996 seasons. In 1997, the Eagles ranked second in passing, fifth in rushing and third in total offense in the NFC. In 1996, they led the NFC in passing, were second in rushing and led the NFC in total offense. In 1995—his first season as an NFL offensive coordinator—the Eagles finished fourth in the league in rushing. He served as an offensive assistant to Green Bay Packers head coach Mike Holmgren in 1992, then spent the 1993 and 1994 campaigns as Green Bay's receivers coach. Gruden spent the 1991 season as wide receivers coach at the University of Pittsburgh under coach Paul Hackett. In 1990, he was an offensive assistant to head coach George Seifert with the San Francisco 49ers, working with offensive coordinator Holmgren. The 49ers were an NFL best 14-2 that season. Career record: 29-21.

Background: Quarterback at Dayton 1983-85, while earning bachelor's degree in communications. Won the prestigious Lt. Andy Zulli Memorial Award given annually "to the senior player who best exemplifies the qualities of sportsmanship and character." Dayton had a 24-7 record in Gruden's three varsity seasons there.

Personal: Born August 17, 1963, in Sandusky, Ohio. Gruden and his wife Cindy have three sons, Jon II, 7, Michael, 4, and Jayson, 1. His father, Jim, is a scout for the San Francisco 49ers and formerly served as an assistant coach under John McKay with the Tampa Bay Buccaneers from 1982-83. His brother Jay, who played in the Arena Football League, served as offensive coordinator of that league's Nashville team and is presently head coach of the Arena League's 1998 champion Orlando Predators.

ASSISTANT COACHES

Fred Biletnikoff, wide receivers; born February 23, 1943, Erie, Pa., lives in San Ramon, Calif. Wide receiver Florida State 1962-64. Pro wide receiver Oakland Raiders 1965-1978, Montreal Alouettes (CFL) 1980. Inducted into Pro Football Hall of Fame in 1988. College coach: Palomar (Calif.) J.C. 1983, Diablo Valley (Calif.) J.C. 1984, 1986. Pro coach: Oakland Invaders (USFL) 1985, Calgary Stampeders (CFL) 1987-88, joined Raiders in 1989.

Chuck Bresnahan, defensive coordinator; born September 8, 1960, Springfield, Mass., lives in Alameda, Calif. Linebacker Navy 1979-1982. No pro playing experience. College coach: Navy 1983, 1986, Georgia Tech 1987-1991, Maine 1992-93. Pro coach: Cleveland Browns 1994-95, Indianapolis Colts 1996-97, joined Raiders in 1998.

Willie Brown, squad development; born December 2, 1940, Yazoo City, Miss., lives in Tracy, Calif. Defensive back Grambling 1959-1962. Pro defensive back Denver Broncos 1963-66, Oakland Raiders 1967-78. Inducted into Pro Football Hall of Fame in 1984. College coach: Long Beach State 1990-91 (head coach 1991). Pro coach: Oakland/Los Angeles Raiders 1979-1988, rejoined Raiders in 1995.

Bill Callahan, offensive coordinator-offensive line; born July 31, 1956, Chicago, lives in Danville, Calif. Quarterback Illinois-Benedictine 1975-77. No pro playing experience. College coach: Illinois 1980-86, Northern Arizona 1987-88, Southern Illinois 1989, Wisconsin 1990-94. Pro coach: Philadelphia Eagles 1995-97, joined Raiders in 1998.

Bob Casullo, special teams; born March 24, 1951, Little Falls, N.Y., lives in Alameda, Calif. Running back Brockport State College 1970-73. No pro playing experience. College coach: Syracuse 1985-1994, Georgia Tech 1995-98, Michigan State 1999. Pro coach: Joined Raiders in 2000.

Jim Erkenbeck, tight ends; born September 10, 1933, Los Angeles, lives in Alameda, Calif. Linebacker-end San Diego State 1949-1951. No pro playing experience. College coach: San Diego State 1961-63, Grossmont (Calif.) J.C. 1964-67 (head coach), Utah State 1968, Washington State 1969-1971, California 1972-76. Pro coach: Winnipeg Blue Bombers (CFL) 1977, Montreal Alouettes (CFL) 1978-1981, Calgary Stampeders (CFL) 1982, Philadelphia/Baltimore Stars (USFL) 1983-85, New Orleans Saints 1986, Dallas Cowboys 1987-88, Kansas City Chiefs 1989-1991, 1995-98, Los Angeles Rams 1992-94, joined Raiders in 1999.

Garrett Giemont, strength and conditioning; born August 31, 1957, Fullerton, Calif., lives in San Francisco. Attended Fullerton College. No college or pro playing experience. Pro coach: Los Angeles Rams 1990-91, joined Raiders in 1995.

Aaron Kromer, asst. offensive line; born April 30, 1967, Sandusky, Ohio, lives in Alameda, Calif. Offensive tackle Miami (Ohio) 1986-89. No pro playing experience. College coach: Miami (Ohio) 1990-98, Northwestern 1999-2000. Pro coach: Joined Raiders in 2001.

Ron Lynn, defensive backs; born December 6, 1944, Youngstown, Ohio, lives in Pleasanton, Calif. Quarterback Mount Union College 1963-66. No pro playing experience. Pro coach: Oakland Invaders (USFL) 1983-85, San Diego Chargers 1986-1991, Cincinnati Bengals 1992-93, Washington Redskins 1994-96, New England Patriots 1997-99, joined Raiders in 2000.

Don Martin, quality control-defense; born September 17, 1949, Carrollton, Mo., lives Oakland. Running back Yale 1968-1970. Pro defensive back New England Patriots 1973, Kansas City Chiefs 1975, Tampa Bay Buccaneers 1976. College coach: Yale 1981-1996. Pro coach: Joined Raiders in 1998.

John Morton, quality control-offense; born September 24, 1969, Pontiac, Mich., lives in Castro Valley, Calif. Wide receiver Western Michigan 1991-92, Grand Rapids (Mich.) C.C. 1989-1990. Pro wide receiver Los Angeles Raiders 1993-94, Toronto Argonauts (CFL) 1995-96, Frankfurt Galaxy (WLAF) 1997. Pro coach: Joined Raiders in 1998.

Fred Pagac, linebackers; born April 26, 1952, Richeyville, Pa., lives in Alameda, Calif. Tight end Ohio State 1971-73. Pro tight end Chicago Bears 1974-75, Tampa Bay Buccaneers 1976-77. College coach: Ohio State 1982-2000. Pro coach: Joined Raiders in 2001.

Skip Peete, running backs, born January 30, 1963, Mesa, Ariz., lives in Alameda, Calif. Wide receiver Arizona 1981-82, Kansas 1984-85. Pro wide receiver New York Jets 1987. College coach: Pittsburgh 1988-92, Michigan State 1993-94, Rutgers 1995, UCLA 1996-97. Pro coach: Joined Raiders in 1998.

David Shaw, quarterbacks; born July 31, 1972, San Diego, lives in Alameda, Calif. Wide receiver Stanford 1990-94. No pro playing experience. College coach: Western Washington 1995-96. Pro coach: Philadelphia Eagles 1997, joined Raiders in 1998.

Marc Trestman, senior assistant; born January 15, 1956, Minneapolis, lives in Alameda, Calif. Quarterback Minnesota 1974-75, Moorhead (Minn.) State 1977. No pro playing experience. College coach: Miami 1981-84. Pro coach: Minnesota Vikings 1985-86, 1990-91, Tampa Bay Buccaneers 1987, Cleveland Browns 1988-89, San Francisco 49ers 1995-96, Detroit Lions 1997, Arizona Cardinals 1998-2000, joined Raiders in 2001.

Mike Waufle, defensive line; born June 27, 1954, Hornell, N.Y., lives in Oakland. Defensive lineman Bakersfield J.C. 1975-76, Utah State 1977-78. No pro playing experience. College coach: Alfred 1979, Utah State 1980-84, Fresno State 1985-88, UCLA 1989, Oregon State 1990-91, California 1992-97. Pro coach: Joined Raiders in 1998.

2001 FIRST-YEAR ROSTER

Name	Pos.	Ht.	Wt.	Birthdate	College	Hometown	How Acq.
Barrett, Michael	LB	6-1	240	1/13/78	New Mexico	Covina, Calif.	FA
Clark, Michael	K	6-1	195	2/14/76	Houston	Bountiful, Utah	FA
Combs, Derrick	RB	6-0	195	2/28/79	Ohio State	Urbancrest, Ohio	D7
Cooper, Chris	DT	6-5	275	12/27/77	Nebraska-Omaha	Lincoln, Neb.	D6
Ekiyor, Emil (1)	DE	6-4	250	12/25/74	Central Florida	Daytona Beach, Fla.	FA
Gibson, Derrick	S	6-2	215	3/22/79	Florida State	Miami, Fla.	D1
Grant, DeLawrence	DE	6-3	280	11/18/79	Oregon State	Compton, Calif.	D3
Green, Javon	WR	6-2	200	5/10/78	Colorado	Inglewood, Calif.	FA
Green, Yatil (1)	WR	6-2	205	11/25/73	Miami	Lake City, Fla.	FA-'00
Hogan, Paul	C	6-3	290	8/9/77	Alabama	Valdosta, Ga.	FA
Huston, Terrance	TE	6-4	255	8/24/76	Butte College	Bakersfield, Calif.	FA
Ioane, Junior (1)	DT	6-4	320	7/21/77	Arizona State	Mt. Pleasant, Utah	D4-'00
Jackson, Jabari	RB	6-2	225	7/29/77	Southern California	San Francisco, Calif.	FA-'00
Jennings, Brandon (1)	S	6-0	195	7/15/78	Texas A&M	Channelview, Texas	FA-'00
Knight, Marcus	WR	6-1	180	6/19/78	Michigan	Sylacauga, Ala.	FA-'00
McGrew, Broderick	WR	6-2	210	5/17/78	North Texas	Hearne, Texas	FA-'00
Parks, Nate (1)	G-T	6-5	305	10/24/74	Stanford	Durham, Calif.	FA-'99
Perryman, Raymond	S	5-11	195	11/27/78	Northern Arizona	Phoenix, Ariz.	D4
Posey, Carlos	CB	5-10	215	3/19/78	Missouri	Baton Rouge, La.	FA
Rambo, Ken-Yon	WR	6-1	195	10/4/78	Ohio State	Cerritos, Calif.	D7
Reed, Robert	WR	6-1	205	1/14/75	Arkansas	Oxford, Miss.	FA
Taylor, Ryan (1)	LB	6-1	240	12/11/76	Auburn	Dublin, Calif.	FA
Tuiasosopo, Marques	QB	6-1	220	3/22/79	Washington	Woodinville, Wash.	D2

The term NFL Rookie is defined as a player who is in his first season of professional football and has not been on the roster of another professional football team for any regular-season or postseason games. A Rookie is designated by an "R" on NFL rosters. Players who have been active in another professional football league or players who have NFL experience, including either preseason training camp or being on an Active List or Inactive List, or on Reserve/Injured or Reserve/Physically Unable to Perform for fewer than six regular-season games, are termed NFL First-Year Players. An NFL First-Year Player is designated by a "1" on NFL rosters. Thereafter, a player is credited with an additional year of experience for each season in which he accumulates six games on the Active List or Inactive List, or on Reserve/Injured or Reserve/Physically Unable to Perform.

NOTES

PITTSBURGH STEELERS

American Football Conference
Central Division
Team Colors: Black and Gold
3400 South Water Street
Pittsburgh, Pennsylvania 15203
Telephone: (412) 432-7800

CLUB OFFICIALS

President: Daniel M. Rooney
Vice President/General Counsel: Arthur J. Rooney II
Vice President: John R. McGinley
Vice President: Arthur J. Rooney, Jr.
Administration Advisor: Charles H. Noll
Communications Coordinator: Ron Wahl
Public Relations/Media Manager: David Lockett
Director of Business: Mark Hart
Business Coordinator/Contract Negotiator: Omar Khan
Business Accounting Coordinator: Jim Ellenberger
Director of Football Operations: Kevin Colbert
College Personnel Coordinator: Bill Baker
Pro Personnel Coordinator: Doug Whaley
College Scouts: Kelvin Fisher, Mark Gorscak, Phil Kreidler, Bob Lane, Bruce McNorton, Dan Rooney
Office/Ticket Coordinator: Geraldine R. Glenn
Ticket Manager: Brian Bonifate
Director of Marketing: Tony Quatrini
Player Development Coordinator: Anthony Griggs
Trainers: John Norwig, Ryan Grove
Equipment Manager: Rodgers Freyvogel
Stadium: TBA (built in 2001)
• **Capacity:** 65,000
TBA
Pittsburgh, Pennsylvania 15212
Playing Surface: Grass
Training Camp: St. Vincent College
Latrobe, Pennsylvania 15650

2001 SCHEDULE

PRESEASON

Aug. 3	at Atlanta	7:30
Aug. 16	at Minnesota	7:00
Aug. 25	**Detroit**	1:00
Aug. 30	**Buffalo**	7:30

REGULAR SEASON

Sept. 9	at Jacksonville	1:00
Sept. 16	**Cleveland**	8:30
Sept. 23	Open Date	
Sept. 30	at Buffalo	1:00
Oct. 7	**Cincinnati**	1:00
Oct. 14	at Kansas City	12:00
Oct. 21	at Tampa Bay	1:00
Oct. 29	**Tennessee** (Mon.)	9:00
Nov. 4	**Baltimore**	1:00
Nov. 11	at Cleveland	1:00
Nov. 18	**Jacksonville**	4:05
Nov. 25	at Tennessee	12:00
Dec. 2	**Minnesota**	1:00
Dec. 9	**New York Jets**	4:15
Dec. 16	at Baltimore	8:30
Dec. 23	**Detroit**	1:00
Dec. 30	at Cincinnati	1:00

RECORD HOLDERS

INDIVIDUAL RECORDS—CAREER

Category	Name	Performance
Rushing (Yds.)	Franco Harris, 1972-1983	11,950
Passing (Yds.)	Terry Bradshaw, 1970-1983	27,989
Passing (TDs)	Terry Bradshaw, 1970-1983	212
Receiving (No.)	John Stallworth, 1974-1987	537
Receiving (Yds.)	John Stallworth, 1974-1987	8,723
Interceptions	Mel Blount, 1970-1983	57
Punting (Avg.)	Bobby Joe Green, 1960-61	45.7
Punt Return (Avg.)	Bobby Gage, 1949-1950	14.9
Kickoff Return (Avg.)	Lynn Chandnois, 1950-56	29.6
Field Goals	Gary Anderson, 1982-1994	309
Touchdowns (Tot.)	Franco Harris, 1972-1983	100
Points	Gary Anderson, 1982-1994	1,343

INDIVIDUAL RECORDS—SINGLE SEASON

Category	Name	Performance
Rushing (Yds.)	Barry Foster, 1992	1,690
Passing (Yds.)	Terry Bradshaw, 1979	3,724
Passing (TDs)	Terry Bradshaw, 1978	28
Receiving (No.)	Yancey Thigpen, 1995	85
Receiving (Yds.)	Yancey Thigpen, 1997	1,398
Interceptions	Mel Blount, 1975	11
Punting (Avg.)	Bobby Joe Green, 1961	47.0
Punt Return (Avg.)	Bobby Gage, 1949	16.0
Kickoff Return (Avg.)	Lynn Chandnois, 1952	35.2
Field Goals	Norm Johnson, 1995	34
Touchdowns (Tot.)	Louis Lipps, 1985	15
Points	Norm Johnson, 1995	141

INDIVIDUAL RECORDS—SINGLE GAME

Category	Name	Performance
Rushing (Yds.)	John Fuqua, 12-20-70	218
Passing (Yds.)	Bobby Layne, 12-3-58	409
Passing (TDs)	Terry Bradshaw, 11-15-81	5
	Mark Malone, 9-8-85	5
Receiving (No.)	Courtney Hawkins, 11-1-98	14
Receiving (Yds.)	Buddy Dial, 10-22-61	235
Interceptions	Jack Butler, 12-13-53	*4
Field Goals	Gary Anderson, 10-23-88	6
Touchdowns (Tot.)	Ray Mathews, 10-17-54	4
	Roy Jefferson, 11-3-68	4
Points	Ray Mathews, 10-17-54	24
	Roy Jefferson, 11-3-68	24

*NFL Record

COACHING HISTORY

Pittsburgh Pirates 1933-1940
(461-486-20)

1933	Forrest (Jap) Douds	3-6-2
1934	Luby DiMelio	2-10-0
1935-36	Joe Bach	10-14-0
1937-39	Johnny (Blood) McNally*	6-19-0
1939-1940	Walt Kiesling	3-13-3
1941	Bert Bell**	0-2-0
	Aldo (Buff) Donelli***	0-5-0
1941-44	Walt Kiesling****	13-20-2
1945	Jim Leonard	2-8-0
1946-47	Jock Sutherland	13-10-1
1948-1951	Johnny Michelosen	20-26-2
1952-53	Joe Bach	11-13-0
1954-56	Walt Kiesling	14-22-0
1957-1964	Raymond (Buddy) Parker	51-48-6
1965	Mike Nixon	2-12-0
1966-68	Bill Austin	11-28-3
1969-1991	Chuck Noll	209-156-1
1992-2000	Bill Cowher	91-64-0

*Released after three games in 1939
**Resigned after two games in 1941
***Released after five games in 1941
****Co-coach with Earle (Greasy) Neale in Philadelphia-Pittsburgh merger in 1943 and with Phil Handler in Chicago Cardinals-Pittsburgh merger in 1944

TBA

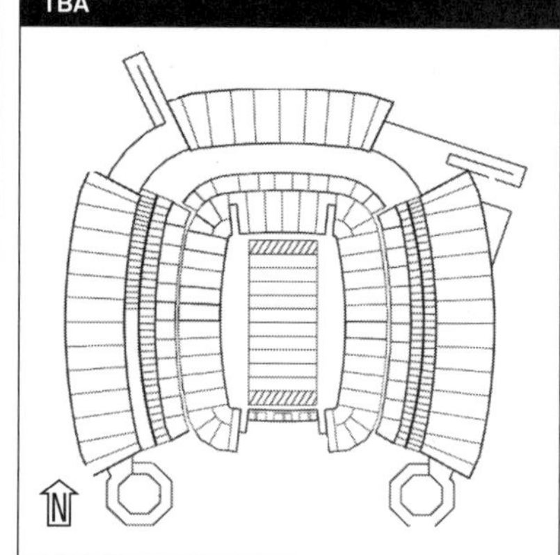

2000 TEAM RECORD

PRESEASON (3-2)

Date	Result		Opponent
7/30	W	38-10	at Dallas
8/5	W	13-10	Miami
8/10	W	13-0	Carolina
8/19	L	23-24	vs. Indianapolis at Mexico City, Mexico
8/25	L	10-17	at Washington

REGULAR SEASON (9-7)

Date	Result		Opponent	Att.
9/3	L	0-16	Baltimore	55,049
9/17	L	20-23	at Cleveland	73,018
9/24	L	20-23	Tennessee	51,769
10/1	W	24-13	at Jacksonville	64,351
10/8	W	20-3	at New York Jets	78,441
10/15	W	15-0	Cincinnati	54,328
10/22	W	22-0	Cleveland	57,659
10/29	W	9-6	at Baltimore	69,405
11/5	L	7-9	at Tennessee	68,498
11/12	L	23-26	Philadelphia (OT)	56,702
11/19	L	24-34	Jacksonville	50,925
11/26	W	48-28	at Cincinnati	63,925
12/3	W	21-20	Oakland	55,811
12/10	L	10-30	at New York Giants	78,164
12/16	W	24-3	Washington	58,183
12/24	W	34-21	at San Diego	50,809

(OT) Overtime

SCORE BY PERIODS

Steelers	58	99	67	97	0	—	321
Opponents	67	76	50	59	3	—	255

ATTENDANCE

Home 471,910 Away 563,101 Total 1,035,011
Single-game home record, 60,608 (12/18/94)
Single-season home record, 471,910 (2000)

2000 TEAM STATISTICS

	Steelers	Opp.
Total First Downs	283	252
Rushing	124	82
Passing	128	153
Penalty	31	17
Third Down: Made/Att	86/229	78/222
Third Down Pct.	37.6	35.1
Fourth Down: Made/Att	5/10	8/17
Fourth Down Pct.	50.0	47.1
Total Net Yards	4,766	4,713
Avg. Per Game	297.9	294.6
Total Plays	1,009	985
Avg. Per Play	4.7	4.8
Net Yards Rushing	2,248	1,693
Avg. Per Game	140.5	105.8
Total Rushes	527	425
Net Yards Passing	2,518	3,020
Avg. Per Game	157.4	188.8
Sacked/Yards Lost	43/220	39/229
Gross Yards	2,738	3,249
Att./Completions	439/217	521/280
Completion Pct.	49.4	53.7
Had Intercepted	10	17
Punts/Average	91/43.3	84/43.3
Net Punting Avg.	91/37.5	84/35.5
Penalties/Yards	81/667	105/876
Fumbles/Ball Lost	24/11	25/18
Touchdowns	35	24
Rushing	19	9
Passing	12	13
Returns	4	2
Avg. Time of Possession	31:27	28:33

2000 INDIVIDUAL STATISTICS

Passing	Att.	Comp.	Yds.	Pct.	TD	Int.	Tkld.	Rate
Stewart	289	151	1,860	52.2	11	8	30/150	73.6
Graham	148	66	878	44.6	1	1	13/70	63.4
Bettis	2	0	0	0.0	0	1	0/0	0.0
Steelers	439	217	2,738	49.4	12	10	43/220	68.9
Opponents	521	280	3,249	53.7	13	17	39/229	67.6

SCORING	TD R	TD P	TD Rt	PAT	FG	Saf	PTS
Brown	0	0	0	32/33	25/30	0	107
Bettis	8	0	0	0/0	0/0	0	48
Stewart	7	0	0	0/0	0/0	0	42
Shaw	0	4	0	0/0	0/0	0	24
Ward	0	4	0	0/0	0/0	0	24
Huntley	3	0	0	0/0	0/0	0	20
Bruener	0	3	0	0/0	0/0	0	18
Porter	0	0	1	0/0	0/0	1	8
Blackwell	0	0	1	0/0	0/0	0	6
Fuamatu-Ma'afala	1	0	0	0/0	0/0	0	6
Gildon	0	0	1	0/0	0/0	0	6
Hawkins	0	1	0	0/0	0/0	0	6
Poteat	0	0	1	0/0	0/0	0	6
Steelers	19	12	4	32/33	25/30	1	321
Opponents	9	13	2	24/24	29/34	0	255

2-Pt. Conversions: Huntley.
Steelers 1-2, Opponents 0-0.

RUSHING	Att.	Yds.	Avg.	LG	TD
Bettis	355	1,341	3.8	30	8
Stewart	78	436	5.6	45t	7
Huntley	46	215	4.7	30t	3
Fuamatu-Ma'afala	21	149	7.1	23	1
Ward	4	53	13.3	23	0
Kreider	2	24	12.0	22	0
Zereoue	6	14	2.3	11	0
Graham	8	7	0.9	7	0
Witman	3	5	1.7	2	0
Edwards	3	4	1.3	15	0
Miller	1	0	0.0	0	0
Steelers	527	2,248	4.3	45t	19
Opponents	425	1,693	4.0	46	9

RECEIVING	No.	Yds.	Avg.	LG	TD
Ward	48	672	14.0	77t	4
Shaw	40	672	16.8	45t	4
Burress	22	273	12.4	39	0
Hawkins	19	238	12.5	33	1
Edwards	18	215	11.9	27	0
Bruener	17	192	11.3	30t	3
Bettis	13	97	7.5	25	0
Fuamatu-Ma'afala	11	107	9.7	25	0
Huntley	10	91	9.1	19	0
Kreider	5	42	8.4	14	0
Witman	5	33	6.6	11	0
Cushing	4	17	4.3	5	0
Geason	3	66	22.0	36	0
Blackwell	2	23	11.5	14	0
Steelers	217	2,738	12.6	77t	12
Opponents	280	3,249	11.6	79	13

INTERCEPTIONS	No.	Yds.	Avg.	LG	TD
Washington	5	59	11.8	31	0
Scott	5	49	9.8	33	0
Alexander	3	31	10.3	15	0
Codie	1	14	14.0	14	0
Kirkland	1	1	1.0	1	0
Flowers	1	0	0.0	0	0
Porter	1	0	0.0	0	0
Steelers	17	154	9.1	33	0
Opponents	10	150	15.0	63t	2

PUNTING	No.	Yds.	Avg.	In 20	LG
Miller	90	3,944	43.8	34	67
Steelers	91	3,944	43.3	34	67
Opponents	84	3,641	43.3	29	65

PUNT RETURNS	No.	FC	Yds.	Avg.	LG	TD
Poteat	36	7	467	13.0	54	1
Hawkins	4	11	15	3.8	9	0
Shaw	2	1	17	8.5	10	0
Edwards	0	1	0	—	—	0
Steelers	42	20	499	11.9	54	1
Opponents	44	14	371	8.4	27	0

KICKOFF RETURNS	No.	Yds.	Avg.	LG	TD
Poteat	24	465	19.4	31	0
Edwards	15	298	19.9	37	0
Blackwell	10	281	28.1	98t	1
Ward	7	186	26.6	57	0
Kreider	1	0	0.0	0	0
Tuman	1	-1	-1.0	-1	0
Shaw	0	-8	—	-8	0
Steelers	58	1,221	21.1	98t	1
Opponents	69	1,496	21.7	62	0

FIELD GOALS	1-19	20-29	30-39	40-49	50+
Brown	1/1	8/8	9/10	6/9	1/2
Steelers	1/1	8/8	9/10	6/9	1/2
Opponents	2/2	9/11	6/7	11/13	1/1

SACKS	No.
Gildon	13.5
Porter	10.5
A. Smith	4.0
Townsend	3.5
Alexander	1.5
Battles	1.0
Flowers	1.0
Holmes	1.0
von Oelhoffen	1.0
Vrabel	1.0
Steelers	39.0
Opponents	43.0

2001 DRAFT CHOICES

Round	Name	Pos.	College
1	Casey Hampton	DT	Texas
2	Kendrell Bell	LB	Georgia
4	Mathias Nkwenti	T	Temple
5	Chukky Okobi	C	Purdue
6	Rodney Bailey	DE	Ohio State
	Roger Knight	LB	Wisconsin
7	Chris Taylor	WR	Texas A&M

PITTSBURGH STEELERS

2001 VETERAN ROSTER

No.	Name	Pos.	Ht.	Wt.	Birthdate	NFL Exp.	College	Hometown	How Acq.	'00 Games/ Starts
27	Alexander, Brent	S	5-11	196	7/10/71	8	Tennessee State	Gallatin, Tenn.	UFA(Car)-'00	16/16
28	Battles, Ainsley	S	5-10	190	11/6/77	2	Vanderbilt	Lilburn, Ga.	FA-'00	16/2
42	Bell, Myron	S	5-11	203	9/15/71	8	Michigan State	Toledo, Ohio	FA-'00	1/0
36	Bettis, Jerome	RB	5-11	250	2/16/72	9	Notre Dame	Detroit, Mich.	T(StL)-'96	16/16
89	Blackwell, Will	WR	6-0	190	7/6/75	5	San Diego State	Texarkana, Tex.	D2-'97	5/0
3	Brown, Kris	K	5-10	204	12/23/76	3	Nebraska	Southlake, Tex.	D7c-'99	16/0
87	Bruener, Mark	TE	6-4	261	9/16/72	7	Washington	Aberdeen, Wash.	D1-'95	16/16
80	Burress, Plaxico	WR	6-5½	229	8/12/77	2	Michigan State	Virginia Beach, Va.	D1-'00	12/8
96	Clancy, Kendrick	NT	6-1	280	9/17/78	2	Mississippi	Tuscaloosa, Ala.	D3a-'00	9/0
24	Codie, Nakia	CB-S	6-2	208	1/20/76	2	Baylor	Cleburne, Tex.	FA-'00	6/0
73	Combs, Chris	DE	6-4	284	12/15/76	2	Duke	Roanoke, Va.	D6a-'00	6/0
48	Cushing, Matt	TE	6-3	258	7/2/75	3	Illinois	Fullerton, Calif.	FA-'99	7/1
62	Duffy, Roger	G-C	6-3	299	7/16/67	12	Penn State	Canton, Ohio	UFA(NYJ)-'98	16/7
81	Edwards, Troy	WR	5-9	192	4/7/77	3	Louisiana Tech	Shreveport, La.	D1-'99	14/1
66	Faneca, Alan	G	6-4	315	12/7/76	4	Louisiana State	New Orleans, La.	D1-'98	16/16
57	† Fiala, John	LB	6-2	235	11/25/73	4	Washington	Kirkland, Wash.	FA-'98	16/0
41	Flowers, Lee	S	6-0	211	1/14/73	7	Georgia Tech	Columbia, S.C.	D5a-'95	13/13
45	Fuamatu-Ma'afala, Chris	RB	5-11	252	3/4/77	4	Utah	Honolulu, Hawaii	D6a-'98	7/1
72	Gandy, Wayne	T	6-5	310	2/10/71	8	Auburn	Haines City, Fla.	UFA(StL)-'99	16/16
85	Geason, Cory	TE	6-3	255	8/12/75	2	Tulane	St. James, La.	FA-'99	9/3
92	Gildon, Jason	LB	6-3	255	7/31/72	8	Oklahoma State	Altus, Okla.	D3a-'99	16/16
11	Graham, Kent	QB	6-5	245	11/1/68	10	Ohio State	Wheaton, Ill.	UFA(NYG)-'00	14/5
53	Haggans, Clark	LB	6-3	250	1/10/77	2	Colorado State	Torrance, Calif.	D5a-'00	3/0
64	Hartings, Jeff	C-G	6-3	295	9/7/72	6	Penn State	St. Henry, Ohio	UFA(Det)-'01	16/16*
50	Holmes, Earl	LB	6-2	250	4/28/73	6	Florida A&M	Tallahassee, Fla.	D4a'-96	16/16
51	Jones, Mike	LB	6-1	240	4/15/69	11	Missouri	Kansas City, Mo.	UFA(StL)-'01	16/16*
35	Kreider, Dan	FB	5-11	242	3/11/77	2	New Hampshire	Mount Joy, Pa.	FA-'00	10/7
31	Logan, Mike	S	6-0	209	9/15/74	5	West Virginia	McKeesport, Pa.	UFA(Jax)-'01	16/11*
83	Loud, Kamil	WR	6-0	190	6/25/76	3	Cal Poly-San Luis Obispo	El Cerrito, Calif.	FA-'00	0*
17	Martin, Tee	QB	6-1	221	7/25/78	2	Tennessee	Mobile, Ala.	D5b-'00	0*
4	Miller, Josh	P	6-3	219	7/14/70	6	Arizona	East Brunswick, N.J.	FA-'96	16/0
61	Myslinski, Tom	G	6-3	293	12/7/68	9	Tennessee	Rome, N.Y.	FA-'00	6/0
55	Porter, Joey	LB	6-2	240	3/22/77	3	Colorado State	Bakersfield, Calif.	D3a-'99	16/16
22	Poteat, Hank	CB	5-10	190	8/30/77	2	Pittsburgh	Harrisburg, Pa.	D3b-'00	15/0
25	Rivers, Ron	RB	5-8	207	11/13/71	7	Fresno State	Elizabeth City, N.J.	UFA(Atl)-'01	6/0*
60	Ross, Oliver	G-T	6-4	310	9/27/74	2	Iowa State	Culver City, Calif.	FA-'00	0*
54	Schneck, Mike	LS	6-0	242	8/4/77	3	Wisconsin	Whitefish Bay, Wis.	FA-'99	16/0
30	Scott, Chad	CB	6-1	192	9/6/74	5	Maryland	Capitol Heights, Md.	D1-'97	16/16
82	† Shaw, Bobby	WR	6-0	186	4/23/75	4	California	San Francisco, Calif.	UFA(Sea)-'98	16/0
23	Simmons, Jason	CB	5-8	186	3/30/76	4	Arizona State	Inglewood, Calif.	D5-'98	15/0
91	Smith, Aaron	DE	6-5	281	4/9/76	3	Northern Colorado	Colorado Springs, Colo.	D4-'99	16/15
77	Smith, Marvel	T	6-5	320	8/6/78	2	Arizona State	Oakland, Calif.	D2-'00	12/9
10	Stewart, Kordell	QB	6-1	211	10/16/72	7	Colorado	Marrero, La.	D2-'95	16/11
74	Sullivan, Chris	NT	6-4	285	3/14/73	6	Boston College	North Attleboro, Mass.	UFA(NE)-'00	15/2
71	Tharpe, Larry	T	6-4	305	11/19/70	9	Tennessee State	Macon, Ga.	FA-'00	12/5
90	Thompson, Donnel	LB	5-11	234	2/17/78	2	Wisconsin	Madison, Wis.	FA-'00	8/0
26	† Townsend, Deshea	CB	5-10	175	9/8/75	4	Alabama	Batesville, Miss.	D4a-'98	16/0
84	Tuman, Jerame	TE	6-3	250	3/24/76	3	Michigan	Liberal, Kan.	D5a-'99	16/1
65	Tylski, Rich	G	6-5	308	2/27/71	6	Utah State	San Diego, Calif.	UFA(Jax)-'00	16/16
67	von Oelhoffen, Kimo	NT	6-4	305	1/30/71	8	Boise State	Kaunakakai, Hawaii	UFA(Cin)-'00	16/16
86	† Ward, Hines	WR	6-0	197	3/8/76	4	Georgia	Rex, Ga.	D3b-'98	16/15
20	Washington, Dewayne	CB	6-0	193	12/27/72	8	North Carolina State	Durham, N.C.	UFA(Minn)-'98	16/16
38	Witman, Jon	FB	6-1	240	6/1/72	6	Penn State	Wrightsville, Pa.	D3b-'96	6/5
21	Zereoue, Amos	RB	5-8	202	10/8/76	3	West Virginia	Hempstead, N.Y.	D3c-'99	12/0

* Hartings played 16 games with Detroit in '00; Jones played 16 games with St. Louis; Logan played 16 games with Jacksonville; Loud last active with Buffalo in '99; Martin was inactive for 15 games; Rivers played 6 games with Atlanta; Ross missed '00 season because of injury.

† Restricted free agent; subject to developments.

Players lost through free agency (2): T Shar Pourdanesh (Oak; 5 games in '00); LB Mike Vrabel (NE; 15).

Also played with Steelers in '00—C Dermontti Dawson (9), WR Courtney Hawkins (14), DE Kevin Henry (15), RB Richard Huntley (13), WR Malcolm Johnson (4), LB Levon Kirkland (16), S Scott Shields (10), DE-DT Jeremy Staat (7).

COACHING STAFF

Head Coach,
Bill Cowher

Pro Career: Became the fifteenth head coach in Steelers history when he replaced Chuck Noll on January 21, 1992. In 1995, at age 38, he became the youngest coach to lead his team to a Super Bowl. Cowher is only the second coach in NFL history to lead his team to the playoffs in each of his first six seasons as head coach, joining Pro Football Hall of Fame member Paul Brown. During Cowher's 15-year coaching career, teams he has been associated with have made the postseason 12 times. Began his NFL career as a free-agent linebacker with the Philadelphia Eagles in 1979, and then signed with the Cleveland Browns the following year. Cowher played three seasons (1980-82) in Cleveland before being traded back to the Eagles, where he played two more years (1983-84). Cowher began his coaching career in 1985 at age 28 under Marty Schottenheimer with the Browns. He was the Browns' special teams coach in 1985-86 and secondary coach in 1987-88 before following Schottenheimer to the Kansas City Chiefs in 1989 as defensive coordinator. Career record: 91-64.

Background: Excelled in football, basketball, and track for Carlynton High in Crafton, Pa. Was a three-year starter at linebacker for North Carolina State, serving as captain and earning team MVP honors as a senior. Graduated in 1979 with education degree.

Personal: Born in Pittsburgh, on May 8, 1957. His wife Kaye, also a North Carolina State graduate, played professional basketball for the New York Stars of the Women's Professional Basketball League with twin sister Faye. Bill and Kaye live in Pittsburgh and have three daughters—Meagan Lyn, Lauren Marie, and Lindsay Morgan.

ASSISTANT COACHES

Mike Archer, linebackers; born July 26, 1953, State College, Pa., lives in Pittsburgh. Safety/punter Miami 1972-75. No pro playing experience. College coach: Miami 1978-1983, Louisiana State 1984-1990 (head coach 1987-1990), Virginia 1991-92, Kentucky 1993-95. Pro coach: Joined Steelers in 1996.

Tom Clements, quarterbacks; born June 18, 1953, McKees Rocks, Pa., lives in Pittsburgh. Quarterback Notre Dame 1972-74. Pro quarterback Ottawa Rough Riders (CFL) 1975-78, Hamilton Tiger-Cats (CFL) 1979, 1981-82, Kansas City Chiefs 1980, Winnipeg Blue Bombers (CFL) 1983-87. College coach: Notre Dame 1992-95. Pro coach: New Orleans Saints 1997-99, Kansas City Chiefs 2000, joined Steelers in 2001.

Russ Grimm, offensive line; born May 2, 1959, Scottdale, Pa., lives in Pittsburgh. Center Pittsburgh 1977-1980. Pro guard Washington Redskins 1981-1991. Pro coach: Washington Redskins 1992-2000, joined Steelers in 2001.

Jay Hayes, special teams, born March 3, 1960, South Fayette, Pa., lives in Pittsburgh. Defensive end Idaho 1980-81. Pro defensive end/linebacker Michigan Panthers (USFL) 1984, Memphis Showboats (USFL) 1985. College coach: Notre Dame 1988-1991, California 1992-94, Wisconsin 1995-98. Pro coach: Joined Steelers in 1999.

Dick Hoak, running backs; born December 8, 1939, Jeannette, Pa., lives in Greensburg, Pa. Halfback-quarterback Penn State 1958-1960. Pro running back Pittsburgh Steelers 1961-1970. Pro coach: Joined Steelers in 1972.

Kenny Jackson, wide receivers; born February 15, 1962, Neptune, N.J., lives in Pittsburgh. Wide receiver Penn State 1980-83. Pro wide receiver Philadelphia Eagles 1984-88, 1991-92, Houston Oilers 1989. College coach: Penn State 1993-2000. Pro coach: Joined Steelers in 2001.

Tim Lewis, defensive coordinator; born December 18, 1961, Quakertown, Pa., lives in Pittsburgh. Defensive back Pittsburgh 1979-1982. Pro cornerback Green Bay Packers 1983-86. College coach: Texas A&M 1987-88, Southern Methodist 1989-1992, Pittsburgh 1993-94. Pro coach: Joined Steelers in 1995.

2001 FIRST-YEAR ROSTER

Name	Pos.	Ht.	Wt.	Birthdate	College	Hometown	How Acq.
Almanzar, Luis	DT	6-3	282	12/15/76	Southwest Missouri State	Jersey City, N.J.	FA
Bailey, Rodney	DE	6-3	281	10/7/79	Ohio State	Cleveland, Ohio	D6a
Baker, Tim	WR	6-5	200	10/23/77	Texas Tech	Amarillo, Texas	FA
Bell, Kendrell	LB	6-1	236	7/17/80	Georgia	Augusta, Ga.	D2
Bobo, David	G	6-4	290	10/28/77	Texas Christian	Odessa, Texas	FA
Brown, Demetrius (1)	WR	6-3	209	4/10/75	Wisconsin	Milwaukee, Wis.	FA-'00
Evitts, Chad	LB	6-1	235	6/5/78	Tennessee Tech	Hartsville, Tenn.	FA
Faulkner, Eddie	RB	5-9	195	10/20/77	Wisconsin	Muncie, Ind.	FA
Fehrman, Rob	T	6-6	300	1/3/78	Bowling Green	Byesville, Ohio	FA
Frazier, Rod	FB	5-11	249	2/11/78	Florida	Bradenton, Fla.	FA
Getherall, Joey	WR	5-7	175	11/7/78	Notre Dame	Los Angeles, Calif.	FA
Hampton, Casey	DT	6-1	321	9/3/77	Texas	Galveston, Texas	D1
Hoke, Chris	DT	6-2	295	4/6/76	Brigham Young	Long Beach, Calif.	FA
Knight, Roger	LB	6-1	230	10/11/78	Wisconsin	Queens Village, N.Y.	D6b
Kohl, Andy	P	6-4	220	4/25/79	New Mexico State	Waukesha, Wis.	FA
Kurpeikis, Justin	LB	6-3	254	7/17/77	Penn State	Allison Park, Pa.	FA
Nkwenti, Mathias	T	6-3	300	5/11/78	Temple	Jessup, Md.	D4
Okobi, Chukky	C-G	6-1	315	11/18/78	Purdue	Hamden, Conn	D5
Provitt, Vanness	WR	6-3	205	1/20/77	Ohio State	Warren, Ohio	FA
Sadler, Adrian	CB	5-9	190	3/10/78	Rice	Texarkana, Texas	FA
Sands, Mike (1)	LB	6-4	235	12/16/77	Harvard	Cleveland Heights, Ohio	FA
Sprague, Ryan	TE	6-5	250	11/3/77	Florida State	Augusta, Ga.	FA
Strickland, Timothy (1)	CB	5-9	183	1/13/77	Mississippi	Memphis, Tenn.	FA
Stukes, Dwayne (1)	CB	5-11	185	1/24/77	Virginia	Portsmouth, Va.	FA
Taylor, Chris	WR	5-10	184	4/25/79	Texas A&M	Madisonville, Texas	D7
Tharpe, Nigel	DT	6-3	290	3/24/78	Iowa State	Detroit, Mich.	FA
Turman, Johnny	QB	6-4	220	9/19/77	Pittsburgh	Walnut Creek, Calif.	FA
Vincent, Keydrick	G	6-5	330	4/13/78	Mississippi	Bartow, Fla.	FA
Williams, Payton (1)	DB	5-7	170	11/19/78	Fresno State	Riverside, Calif.	FA-'00

The term NFL Rookie is defined as a player who is in his first season of professional football and has not been on the roster of another professional football team for any regular-season or postseason games. A Rookie is designated by an "R" on NFL rosters. Players who have been active in another professional football league or players who have NFL experience, including either preseason training camp or being on an Active List or Inactive List, or on Reserve/Injured or Reserve/Physically Unable to Perform for fewer than six regular-season games, are termed NFL First-Year Players. An NFL First-Year Player is designated by a "1" on NFL rosters. Thereafter, a player is credited with an additional year of experience for each season in which he accumulates six games on the Active List or Inactive List, or on Reserve/Injured or Reserve/Physically Unable to Perform.

NOTES

John Mitchell, defensive line; born October 14, 1951, Mobile, Ala., lives in Pittsburgh. Defensive end Eastern Arizona J.C. 1969-1970, Alabama 1971-72. No pro playing experience. College coach: Alabama 1973-76, Arkansas 1977-1982, Temple 1986, Louisiana State 1987-1990. Pro coach: Birmingham Stallions (USFL) 1983-85, Cleveland Browns 1991-93, joined Steelers in 1994.

Mike Mularkey, offensive coordinator; born November 19, 1961, Ft. Lauderdale, Fla., lives in Pittsburgh. Tight end Florida 1979-1982. Pro tight end Minnesota Vikings 1983-88, Pittsburgh Steelers 1989-1991. College coach: Concordia 1993. Pro coach: Tampa Bay Buccaneers 1994-95, joined Steelers in 1996.

Willy Robinson, defensive backs; born February 10, 1956, Fort Carson, Colo., lives in Pittsburgh. Defensive back Fresno State 1976-77. No pro playing experience. College coach: San Jose State 1979, Fresno State 1980-1992, Miami 1993-94, Oregon State 1999. Pro coach: Seattle Seahawks 1995-98, joined Steelers in 2000.

Ken Whisenhunt, tight ends; born February 29, 1962, Atlanta, lives in Pittsburgh. Tight end-quarterback Georgia Tech 1980-84. Pro tight end Atlanta Falcons 1985-88, Washington Redskins 1989-1990, New York Jets 1991-93. College coach: Vanderbilt 1995-96. Pro coach: Baltimore Ravens 1997-98, Cleveland Browns 1999, New York Jets 2000, joined Steelers in 2001.

SAN DIEGO CHARGERS

American Football Conference
Western Division
Team Colors: Navy Blue, White, and Gold
Qualcomm Stadium
P.O. Box 609609
San Diego, California 92160-9609
Telephone: (858) 874-4500

CLUB OFFICIALS

Chairman of the Board: Alex G. Spanos
President/CEO: Dean A. Spanos
Executive Vice President: Michael A. Spanos
Executive Vice President & General Manager: John Butler
Executive Vice President for Finance: Jeremiah T. Murphy
Vice President of Football Operations: Ed McGuire
Vice President & Chief Financial Officer: Jeanne M. Bonk
Vice President of Sales and Marketing: John Shean
Assistant General Manager: A.J. Smith
Director of Player Personnel: Buddy Nix
Director of College Scouting: Jimmy Raye
Head Athletic Trainer: James Collins
Director of Video Operations: Brian Duddy
Equipment Manager: Bob Wick
Director of Business & Stadium Operations: John Hinek
Director of Public Relations: Bill Johnston
Director of Public Affairs & Corporate/Community Relations: Kimberley Layton
Director of Security & Player Programs: Dick Lewis
Director of Ticket Sales and Services: Jerry McBurney
Director of Marketing & Events: Sean O'Connor
Controller: Marsha Wells
Stadium: Qualcomm Stadium (built in 1967)
•**Capacity:** 71,000
9449 Friars Road
San Diego, California 92108
Playing Surface: Grass
Training Camp: University of California-San Diego
Third College
La Jolla, California 92037

2001 SCHEDULE

PRESEASON

Aug. 11	**San Francisco**	7:30
Aug. 18	at Miami	7:00
Aug. 25	**St. Louis**	7:00
Aug. 31	at Arizona	7:00

REGULAR SEASON

Sept. 9	**Washington**	1:15
Sept. 16	Open Date	
Sept. 23	at Dallas	12:00
Sept. 30	**Cincinnati**	1:15
Oct. 7	at Cleveland	1:00
Oct. 14	at New England	1:00
Oct. 21	**Denver**	1:05
Oct. 28	**Buffalo**	1:15
Nov. 4	**Kansas City**	1:15
Nov. 11	at Denver	2:05
Nov. 18	at Oakland	1:05
Nov. 25	**Arizona**	1:05
Dec. 2	at Seattle	1:05
Dec. 9	at Philadelphia	1:00
Dec. 15	**Oakland** (Sat.)	2:00
Dec. 23	at Kansas City	12:00
Dec. 30	**Seattle**	1:15

RECORD HOLDERS

INDIVIDUAL RECORDS—CAREER

Category	Name	Performance
Rushing (Yds.)	Paul Lowe, 1960-67	4,963
Passing (Yds.)	Dan Fouts, 1973-1987	43,040
Passing (TDs)	Dan Fouts, 1973-1987	254
Receiving (No.)	Charlie Joiner, 1976-1986	586
Receiving (Yds.)	Lance Alworth, 1962-1970	9,585
Interceptions	Gill Byrd, 1983-1992	42
Punting (Avg.)	Darren Bennett, 1995-2000	44.8
Punt Return (Avg.)	Darrien Gordon, 1993-96	13.6
Kickoff Return (Avg.)	Leslie (Speedy) Duncan, 1964-1970	25.3
Field Goals	John Carney, 1990-2000	261
Touchdowns (Tot.)	Lance Alworth, 1962-1970	83
Points	John Carney, 1990-2000	1,076

INDIVIDUAL RECORDS—SINGLE SEASON

Category	Name	Performance
Rushing (Yds.)	Natrone Means, 1994	1,350
Passing (Yds.)	Dan Fouts, 1981	4,802
Passing (TDs)	Dan Fouts, 1981	33
Receiving (No.)	Tony Martin, 1995	90
Receiving (Yds.)	Lance Alworth, 1965	1,602
Interceptions	Charlie McNeil, 1961	9
Punting (Avg.)	Darren Bennett, 2000	46.2
Punt Return (Avg.)	Leslie (Speedy) Duncan, 1965	15.5
Kickoff Return (Avg.)	Keith Lincoln, 1962	28.4
Field Goals	John Carney, 1994	34
Touchdowns (Tot.)	Chuck Muncie, 1981	19
Points	John Carney, 1994	135

INDIVIDUAL RECORDS—SINGLE GAME

Category	Name	Performance
Rushing (Yds.)	Gary Anderson, 12-18-88	217
Passing (Yds.)	Dan Fouts, 10-19-80, 12-11-82	444
Passing (TDs)	Dan Fouts, 11-22-81	6
Receiving (No.)	Kellen Winslow, 10-7-84	15
Receiving (Yds.)	Wes Chandler, 12-20-82	260
Interceptions	Many times	3
	Last time by Dwayne Harper, 11-27-95	
Field Goals	John Carney, 9-5-93, 9-18-93	6
	Greg Davis, 10-5-97	6
Touchdowns (Tot.)	Kellen Winslow, 11-22-81	5
Points	Kellen Winslow, 11-22-81	30

COACHING HISTORY

Los Angeles 1960
(298-321-11)

1960-69	Sid Gillman*	83-51-6
1969-1970	Charlie Waller	9-7-3
1971	Sid Gillman**	4-6-0
1971-73	Harland Svare***	7-17-2
1973	Ron Waller	1-5-0
1974-78	Tommy Prothro****	21-39-0
1978-1986	Don Coryell#	72-60-0
1986-88	Al Saunders	17-22-0
1989-1991	Dan Henning	16-32-0
1992-96	Bobby Ross	50-36-0
1997-98	Kevin Gilbride##	6-16-0
1998	June Jones	3-7-0
1999-2000	Mike Riley	9-23-0

*Retired after nine games in 1969
**Resigned after 10 games in 1971
***Resigned after eight games in 1973
****Resigned after four games in 1978
#Resigned after eight games in 1986
##Released after six games in 1998

QUALCOMM STADIUM

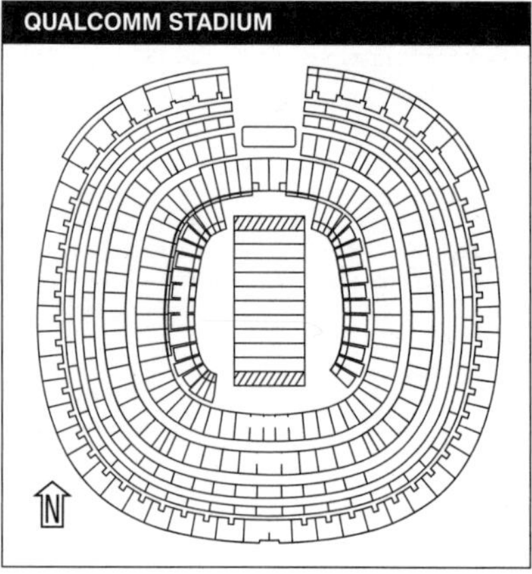

2000 TEAM RECORD

PRESEASON (4-0)

Date	Result		Opponent
8/5	W	23-20	at San Francisco
8/12	W	31-7	Minnesota
8/18	W	28-14	at Atlanta
8/25	W	24-20	Arizona

REGULAR SEASON (1-15)

Date	Result		Opponent	Att.
9/3	L	6-9	at Oakland	56,373
9/10	L	27-28	New Orleans	51,300
9/17	L	10-42	at Kansas City	77,604
9/24	L	12-20	Seattle	47,233
10/1	L	31-57	at St. Louis	66,010
10/8	L	7-21	Denver	56,079
10/15	L	24-27	at Buffalo (OT)	72,351
10/29	L	13-15	Oakland	66,659
11/5	L	15-17	at Seattle	59,884
11/12	L	7-17	Miami	56,896
11/19	L	37-38	at Denver	75,218
11/26	W	17-16	Kansas City	47,228
12/3	L	17-45	San Francisco	57,255
12/10	L	3-24	at Baltimore	68,805
12/17	L	22-30	at Carolina	72,159
12/24	L	21-34	Pittsburgh	50,809

(OT) Overtime

SCORE BY PERIODS

Chargers	58	99	60	52	0	—	269
Opponents	77	128	110	122	3	—	440

ATTENDANCE

Home 539,899 Away 538,300 Total 1,078,199
Single-game home record, 69,288 (11/7/99)
Single-season home record, 546,533 (1999)

2000 TEAM STATISTICS

	Chargers	Opp.
Total First Downs	251	312
Rushing	63	76
Passing	156	195
Penalty	32	41
ThirdDown: Made/Att	72/219	91/242
ThirdDown Pct.	32.9	37.6
Fourth Down: Made/Att	3/14	5/9
Fourth Down Pct.	21.4	55.6
Total Net Yards	4,300	4,959
Avg. Per Game	268.8	309.9
Total Plays	982	1,061
Avg. Per Play	4.4	4.7
Net Yards Rushing	1,062	1,422
Avg. Per Game	66.4	88.9
Total Rushes	351	470
Net Yards Passing	3,238	3,537
Avg. Per Game	202.4	221.1
Sacked/Yards Lost	53/302	39/249
Gross Yards	3,540	3,786
Att./Completions	578/311	552/326
Completion Pct.	53.8	59.1
Had Intercepted	30	16
Punts/Average	92/46.2	91/41.5
Net Punting Avg.	92/36.2	91/36.4
Penalties/Yards	121/1,036	106/851
Fumbles/Ball Lost	38/20	17/6
Touchdowns	31	50
Rushing	7	10
Passing	19	33
Returns	5	7
Avg. Time of Possession	28:08	31:52

2000 INDIVIDUAL STATISTICS

Passing	Att.	Comp.	Yds.	Pct.	TD	Int.	Tkld.	Rate
Leaf	322	161	1,883	50.0	11	18	31/155	56.2
Harbaugh	202	123	1,416	60.9	8	10	14/96	74.6
Moreno	53	27	241	50.9	0	2	8/51	47.8
Chancey	1	0	0	0.0	0	0	0/0	39.6
Chargers	578	311	3,540	53.8	19	30	53/302	61.8
Opponents	552	326	3,786	59.1	33	16	39/249	87.7

SCORING	TD R	TD P	TD Rt	PAT	FG	Saf	PTS
Carney	0	0	0	27/27	18/25	0	81
Conway	0	5	0	0/0	0/0	0	30
F. Jones	0	5	0	0/0	0/0	0	30
Fletcher	3	1	0	0/0	0/0	0	24
J. Graham	0	4	0	0/0	0/0	0	24
Chancey	2	0	0	0/0	0/0	0	12
Fazande	2	0	0	0/0	0/0	0	12
McCrary	0	2	0	0/0	0/0	0	12
Dixon	0	0	1	0/0	0/0	0	6
Dumas	0	0	1	0/0	0/0	0	6
Gaylor	0	1	0	0/0	0/0	0	6
Harrison	0	0	1	0/0	0/0	0	6
Heiden	0	1	0	0/0	0/0	0	6
R. Jenkins	0	0	1	0/0	0/0	0	6
Turner	0	0	1	0/0	0/0	0	6
Fontenot	0	0	0	0/0	0/0	1	2
Chargers	7	19	5	27/27	18/25	1	269
Opponents	10	33	7	46/46	30/34	1	440

2-Pt. Conversions: None.
Chargers 0-4, Opponents 1-4.

RUSHING	Att.	Yds.	Avg.	LG	TD
Fletcher	116	384	3.3	21	3
Fazande	119	368	3.1	26	2
Chancey	42	141	3.4	14	2
Leaf	28	54	1.9	14	0
Conway	3	31	10.3	13	0
Bynum	7	26	3.7	9	0
Harbaugh	16	24	1.5	7	0
Moreno	5	20	4.0	13	0
McCrary	7	8	1.1	4	0
R. Jenkins	8	6	0.8	4	0
Chargers	351	1,062	3.0	26	7
Opponents	470	1,422	3.0	49	10

RECEIVING	No.	Yds.	Avg.	LG	TD
F. Jones	71	766	10.8	44	5
J. Graham	55	907	16.5	83t	4
Conway	53	712	13.4	68t	5
Fletcher	48	355	7.4	26	1
R. Jones	22	253	11.5	34	0
McCrary	18	141	7.8	19	2
Fazande	16	104	6.5	17	0
Gaylor	13	182	14.0	62t	1
Heiden	6	32	5.3	10	1
Ricks	3	35	11.7	23	0
Bynum	2	13	6.5	7	0
Jacquet	1	25	25.0	25	0
Davis	1	8	8.0	8	0
Chancey	1	6	6.0	6	0
R. Jenkins	1	1	1.0	1	0
Chargers	311	3,540	11.4	83t	19
Opponents	326	3,786	11.6	68t	33

INTERCEPTIONS	No.	Yds.	Avg.	LG	TD
Harrison	6	97	16.2	63t	1
Seau	2	2	1.0	2	0
Turner	1	75	75.0	75t	1
Dumas	1	56	56.0	56t	1
Dixon	1	36	36.0	36t	1
Ruff	1	18	18.0	18	0
D. Jenkins	1	16	16.0	16	0
Beckett	1	7	7.0	7	0
Lewis	1	6	6.0	3	0
Brown	1	0	0.0	0	0
Chargers	16	313	19.6	75t	4
Opponents	30	515	17.2	69t	3

PUNTING	No.	Yds.	Avg.	In 20	LG
Bennett	92	4,248	46.2	23	66
Chargers	92	4,248	46.2	23	66
Opponents	91	3,780	41.5	32	68

PUNT RETURNS	No.	FC	Yds.	Avg.	LG	TD
Jacquet	30	8	211	7.0	35	0
R. Jones	9	3	53	5.9	17	0
J. Graham	3	6	7	2.3	7	0
Dumas	1	0	1	1.0	1	0
D. Jenkins	1	0	0	0.0	0	0
Chargers	44	17	272	6.2	35	0
Opponents	51	10	722	14.2	64t	1

KICKOFF RETURNS	No.	Yds.	Avg.	LG	TD
R. Jenkins	67	1,531	22.9	93t	1
Bynum	13	242	18.6	39	0
D. Graham	1	0	0.0	0	0
Jacox	1	8	8.0	8	0
R. Jones	1	11	11.0	11	0
Chargers	83	1,792	21.6	93t	1
Opponents	61	1,471	24.1	98t	1

FIELD GOALS	1-19	20-29	30-39	40-49	50+
Carney	1/1	3/3	5/7	7/10	2/4
Chargers	1/1	3/3	5/7	7/10	2/4
Opponents	1/1	13/13	10/11	4/7	2/2

SACKS	No.
Parrella	7.0
Harrison	6.0
Mickell	6.0
Dixon	5.0
Fontenot	4.0
Seau	3.5
Dingle	2.5
Beckett	1.0
Dumas	1.0
Lewis	1.0
Rusk	1.0
Williams	1.0
Chargers	39.0
Opponents	53.0

2001 DRAFT CHOICES

Round	Name	Pos.	College
1	LaDainian Tomlinson	RB	Texas Christian
2	Drew Brees	QB	Purdue
3	Tay Cody	DB	Florida State
4	Carlos Polk	LB	Nebraska
5	Elliot Silvers	T	Washington
	Zeke Moreno	LB	Southern California
7	Brandon Gorin	T	Purdue
	Robert Carswell	DB	Clemson

SAN DIEGO CHARGERS

2001 VETERAN ROSTER

No.	Name	Pos.	Ht.	Wt.	Birthdate	NFL Exp.	College	Hometown	How Acq.	'00 Games/ Starts
42	Beckett, Rogers	S	6-3	205	1/31/77	2	Marshall	Apopka, Fla.	D2-'00	16/3
2	Bennett, Darren	P	6-5	235	1/9/65	7	No College	Perth, Australia	FA-'95	16/0
50	Binn, David	LS	6-3	250	2/6/72	8	California	San Mateo, Calif.	FA-'94	16/0
24	Brown, Fakhir	CB	5-11	192	9/21/77	3	Grambling State	Mansfield, La.	FA-'99	9/8
96	Carson, Leonardo	DT	6-2	285	2/11/77	2	Auburn	Mobile, Ala.	D4b-'00	4/0
80	Conway, Curtis	WR	6-1	196	1/13/71	9	Southern California	Los Angeles, Calif.	UFA(Chi)-'99	14/14
84	Davis, Reggie	TE	6-3	233	9/3/76	3	Washington	Huntington Beach, Calif.	FA-'99	10/0
90	Dingle, Adrian	DE	6-3	272	6/25/77	3	Clemson	Holly Hill, S.C.	D5a-'99	14/1
51	Dixon, Gerald	LB	6-3	250	6/20/69	9	South Carolina	Rock Hill, S.C.	UFA(Cin)-'98	16/16
85	t- Dwight, Tim	WR	5-8	180	7/13/75	4	Iowa	Iowa City, Iowa	T(Atl)-'01	14/1*
69	Ellis, Ed	T	6-7	325	10/13/75	5	Buffalo	Hamden, Conn.	UFA(Wash)-'01	12/0*
35	Fazande, Jermaine	RB	6-2	255	1/14/75	3	Oklahoma	Marrero, La.	D2-'99	13/7
41	Fletcher, Terrell	RB	5-8	196	9/14/73	7	Wisconsin	St. Louis, Mo.	D2b-'95	16/6
7	Flutie, Doug	QB	5-10	180	10/23/62	8	Boston College	Natick, Mass.	FA-'01	11/5*
95	Fontenot, Al	DE	6-4	287	9/17/70	9	Baylor	Houston, Texas	UFA(Ind)-'99	15/15
67	Fortin, Roman	C-G	6-5	297	2/26/67	12	San Diego State	Ventura, Calif.	FA-'98	16/16
82	Gaylor, Trevor	WR	6-3	195	11/3/77	2	Miami, Ohio	St. Louis, Mo.	D4a-'00	14/2
71	Graham, DeMingo	G-T	6-3	310	9/10/73	3	Hofstra	Newark, N.J.	FA-'98	14/1
81	Graham, Jeff	WR	6-2	206	2/14/69	11	Ohio State	Dayton, Ohio	FA-'99	14/13
37	Harrison, Rodney	S	6-1	207	12/15/72	8	Western Illinois	Chicago Heights, Ill.	D5b-'94	16/16
83	Heiden, Steve	TE	6-5	270	9/21/76	3	South Dakota State	Rushford, Minn.	D3-'99	15/3
53	Humphrey, Deon	LB	6-3	240	5/7/76	2	Florida State	Lake Worth, Fla.	FA-'00	11/0*
64	Jacox, Kendyl	C-G	6-2	330	6/10/75	4	Kansas State	Dallas, Texas	FA-'98	16/3
28	Jenkins, Ronney	RB	5-11	188	5/25/77	2	Northern Arizona	Oxnard, Calif.	FA-'00	16/0
99	Johnson, Raylee	DE	6-3	272	6/1/70	9	Arkansas	Fordyce, Ark.	D4a-'93	0*
88	Jones, Freddie	TE	6-4	255	9/16/74	5	North Carolina	Landover, Md.	D2-'97	16/16
87	Jones, Reggie	WR	6-0	195	5/8/71	2	Louisiana State	Kansas City, Mo.	FA-'00	11/2
44	McCrary, Fred	FB	6-0	235	9/19/72	5	Mississippi State	Naples, Fla.	FA-'99	15/12
77	McIntosh, Damion	T	6-4	325	3/25/77	2	Kansas State	Hollywood, Fla.	D3-'00	3/0
47	McNeil, Ryan	CB	6-2	192	10/4/70	9	Miami	Westwood, Fla.	FA-'01	16/16*
98	Mohring, Michael	DE-DT	6-5	295	3/22/74	5	Pittsburgh	West Chester, Pa.	FA-'97	7/0
25	Molden, Alex	CB	5-10	190	8/4/73	6	Oregon	Colorado Springs, Colo.	UFA(NO)-'01	15/6*
70	Parker, Vaughn	T	6-3	300	6/5/71	8	UCLA	Buffalo, N.Y.	D2b-'94	16/16
97	Parrella, John	DT	6-3	290	11/22/69	9	Nebraska	Topeka, Kan.	FA-'94	16/16
31	Perry, Jason	S	6-0	200	8/1/76	3	North Carolina State	Passaic, N.J.	D4-'99	1/0
91	Pringley, Mike	DE	6-4	277	5/22/76	3	North Carolina	Linden, N.J.	FA-'00	2/0
5	Richey, Wade	K	6-3	205	5/19/76	4	Louisiana State	Lafayette, La.	RFA(SF)-'01	16/0*
59	Rogers, Sam	LB	6-3	245	5/30/70	8	Colorado	Pontiac, Mich.	FA-'01	11/11*
74	Rountree, Raleigh	T	6-4	295	8/31/75	5	South Carolina State	Augusta, Ga.	D4-'97	16/15
56	Ruff, Orlando	LB	6-3	247	9/26/76	3	Furman	Winnsboro, S.C.	FA-'99	16/14
55	Seau, Junior	LB	6-3	250	1/19/69	12	Southern California	Oceanside, Calif.	D1-'90	16/16
94	Taylor, Shannon	LB	6-3	247	2/16/75	2	Virginia	Roanoke, Va.	D6a-'00	11/0
75	Wiley, Marcellus	DE	6-4	275	11/30/74	5	Columbia	Los Angeles, Calif.	UFA(Buff)-'01	16/15*
76	Williams, Jamal	DT	6-3	305	4/28/76	3	Oklahoma State	Washington, D.C.	D2(Supp)-'98	16/16
17	Williams, Rodney	WR	6-1	191	8/15/73	4	Arizona	Palmdale, Calif.	FA-'01	0*

* Dwight played 14 games with Atlanta in '00; Ellis played 12 games with Washington; Flutie played 11 games with Buffalo; Humphrey played 7 games with San Diego and 4 with Carolina; Johnson missed '00 season because of injury; McNeil played 16 games with Dallas; Molden played 15 games with New Orleans; Richey played 16 games with San Francisco; Rogers played 11 games with Buffalo; Wiley played 16 games with Buffalo; R. Williams last active with Oakland in '99.

t- Chargers traded for Dwight (Atl).

Players lost through free agency (2): QB Jim Harbaugh (Det; 7 games in '00), DE Darren Mickell (Oak; 16).

Also played with Chargers in '00—RB Kenny Bynum (14 games), K John Carney (16), RB Robert Chancey (4), G-T Ben Coleman (16), CB Tony Darden (16), CB Tim Denton (5), S Mike Dumas (12), G Kevin Gogan (14), S Armon Hatcher (4), S Greg Jackson (2), CB DeRon Jenkins (15), QB Ryan Leaf (11), CB Darryll Lewis (15), QB Moses Moreno (6), LB John Reeves (9), DB Reggie Rusk (7), DT Antoine Simpson (7), DE Neil Smith (10), LB Steve Tovar (16), CB Scott Turner (16).

COACHING STAFF

Head Coach,
Mike Riley

Pro Career: Mike Riley was named the twelfth head coach in Chargers history on January 10, 1999. In his first season in San Diego, he led the Chargers to a record of 8-8, the team's best record since 1996. The 1999 Chargers had the best intra-division mark in the AFC West at 5-3, including one win each over Denver, Kansas City, and Oakland and a sweep of the two-game series over division champion Seattle. In their second season under Riley, the Chargers earned a record of 1-15. Riley has 26 years of coaching experience. He has spent nine seasons as a head coach, including two on the collegiate level (Oregon State 1997-98), four in the Canadian Football League (Winnipeg 1987-1990) and two in the World League (San Antonio 1991-92). Riley was named the CFL's coach of the year following the 1988 and 1990 seasons, winning the Grey Cup each of those seasons. He also spent three seasons (1983-85) as Winnipeg's secondary coach. Riley led the San Antonio Riders to a record of 11-9 in two World League seasons. His career professional record is 60-64. Career record: 9-23.

Background: Collegiately, Riley won two national championships, one as a player and one as a coach, and three bowl games. In two seasons (1997-98) as the head coach at Oregon State, he led the Beavers to their best record in 27 years. Riley served as an assistant coach at Southern California (1993-96), Northern Colorado (1986), Linfield College (1977-1982), Whitworth College (1976), and California (1975). In college, he played defensive back under Paul (Bear) Bryant at Alabama (1971-74), and won the 1973 national title. Riley graduated from Alabama with a bachelor's degree and earned his master's degree from Whitworth.

Personal: Born July 6, 1953 in Wallace, Idaho. Mike and his wife, Dee, have two children—Matthew and Kate.

ASSISTANT COACHES

Mark Banker, defensive corners; born January 15, 1956, in Plymouth, Mass., lives in San Diego. Running back Springfield College 1975-77. No pro playing experience. College coach: Springfield 1978-1980, Cal State-Northridge 1981-1994, Hawaii 1995, Southern California 1996, Oregon State 1997-98. Pro coach: Joined Chargers in 1999.

Joe Bugel, offensive line; born March 10, 1940, Pittsburgh, lives in San Diego. Guard-linebacker Western Kentucky 1960-63. No pro playing experience. College coach: Western Kentucky 1964-68, Navy 1969-1972, Iowa State 1973, Ohio State 1974. Pro coach: Detroit Lions 1975-76, Houston Oilers 1977-1980, Washington Redskins 1981-89, Phoenix Cardinals 1990-93 (head coach), Oakland Raiders 1995-97 (head coach 1997), joined Chargers in 1998.

Paul Chryst, tight ends; born November 17, 1965, in Madison, Wis., lives in San Diego. Quarterback-linebacker-tight end-holder Wisconsin 1986-88. No pro playing experience. College coach: West Virginia 1989-1990, Wisconsin-Platteville 1993, Illinois State 1995, Oregon State 1997-98. Pro coach: San Antonio Riders (World League) 1991-92, Edmonton Eskimos (CFL) 1993, Ottawa Rough Riders (CFL) 1994, Saskatchewan Roughriders (CFL) 1996, joined Chargers in 1999.

Craig Dickenson, quality control-special teams and offense; born September 4, 1971, Great Falls, Mont., lives in San Diego. Wide receiver-punter-kicker Concordia College 1990, Montana 1991-92. No pro playing experience. College coach: Montana 1993-99, Utah State 2000. Pro coach: Joined Chargers in 2001.

John Hastings, strength and conditioning; born July 5, 1964, in Newport News, Va., lives in San Marcos, Calif. No college or pro playing experience. Pro coach: Joined Chargers in 1990.

Mike Johnson, quarterbacks; born May 2, 1967, in Los Angeles, lives in San Diego. Quarterback Arizona State 1985-86, Akron 1988-89. Pro quarterback Arizona Cardinals 1990, San Antonio Riders (World League) 1991-92, British Columbia Lions (CFL) 1992-93, Shreveport Pirates (CFL) 1994-95. College coach: Oregon State 1997-99. Pro coach: Joined Chargers in 2000.

Andrew McClave, defensive assistant-quality control; born November 1, 1971, in Evanston, Ill., lives in San Diego. Linebacker UCLA 1990-93. No pro playing experience. College coach: Oregon State 1997-99. Pro coach: Joined Chargers in 2000.

Wayne Nunnely, defensive line; born March 29, 1952, Los Angeles, lives in San Diego. Fullback Nevada-Las Vegas 1972-75. No pro playing experience. College coach: Nevada-Las Vegas 1976, 1982-89 (head coach 1986-89), Cal Poly-Pomona 1977-78, Cal State-Fullerton 1979, Pacific 1980-81, Southern California 1991-92, UCLA 1993-94. Pro coach: New Orleans Saints 1995-96, joined Chargers in 1997.

Joe Pascale, defensive coordinator; born April 4, 1946, New York, lives in San Diego. Linebacker Connecticut 1963-66. No pro playing experience. College coach: Connecticut 1967-68, Rhode Island 1969-1973, Idaho State 1974-76 (head coach 1976), Princeton 1977-79. Pro coach: Montreal Alouettes (CFL) 1980-81, Ottawa Rough Riders (CFL) 1982-83, New Jersey Generals (USFL) 1984-85, St. Louis/Phoenix Cardinals 1986-1993, Cincinnati Bengals 1994-96, joined Chargers in 1997.

Rod Perry, secondary; born September 11, 1953, Fresno, Calif., lives in San Diego. Defensive back Colorado 1972-74. Pro cornerback Los Angeles Rams 1975-1982, Cleveland Browns 1983-84. College coach: Columbia 1985, Fresno City College 1986, Fresno State 1987-88. Pro coach: Seattle Seahawks 1989-1991, Los Angeles Rams 1992-94, Houston Oilers 1995-96, joined Chargers in 1997.

Bruce Read, special teams; born January 26, 1962, in Santa Rosa, Calif., lives in San Diego. No college or pro playing experience. College coach: Oregon Institute of Technology 1980, Portland State 1981-84, Montana 1985-1996, Oregon State 1997-98. Pro coach: Joined Chargers in 1999.

Mike Sanford, wide receivers; born April 20, 1955, in Los Altos, Calif., lives in San Diego. Quarterback-safety Southern California 1973-76. No pro playing experience. College coach: Southern California 1977, 1989-1996, San Diego City College 1978, Army 1979-1980, Virginia Military Institute 1981-82, Long Beach State 1983-86, Purdue 1987-88, Notre Dame 1997-98. Pro coach: Joined Chargers in 1999.

Mike Schleelein, asst. strength and conditioning; born January 24, 1974, in Buffalo, lives in San Diego. Tight end Buffalo 1992-96. No pro playing experience. Pro coach: Joined Chargers in 1997.

Norv Turner, offensive coordinator; born May 17, 1952, in LeJeune, N.C., lives in San Diego. Quarterback Oregon 1971-74. No pro playing experience. College coach: Oregon 1975, Southern California 1976-1984. Pro coach: Los Angeles Rams 1985-1990, Dallas 1991-93, Washington 1994-2000 (head coach), joined Chargers in 2001.

Jim Vechiarella, linebackers; born February 20, 1937, Youngstown, Ohio, lives in San Diego. Linebacker Youngstown State 1955-57. No pro playing experience. College coach: Youngstown State 1964-1974, Southern Illinois 1976-77, Tulane 1978-1980. Pro coach: Charlotte (WFL) 1975, Los Angeles Rams 1981-82, Kansas City Chiefs 1983-85, New York Jets 1986-89, 1995-96, Cleveland Browns 1990, Philadelphia Eagles 1991-94, joined Chargers in 1997.

Ollie Wilson, running backs; born March 3, 1951, Worcester, Mass., lives in San Diego. Wide receiver Springfield 1971-73. No pro playing experience. College coach: Springfield 1975, Northeastern 1976-1982, California 1983-1990. Pro coach: Atlanta Falcons 1991-96, joined Chargers in 1997.

2001 FIRST-YEAR ROSTER

Name	Pos.	Ht.	Wt.	Birthdate	College	Hometown	How Acq.
Amman, Justin	G	6-4	305	8/27/78	Florida State	Eustis, Fla.	FA
Batteaux, Patrick (1)	WR	6-0	195	4/18/78	Texas Christian	Missouri City, Texas	FA
Bernard, Walter	CB	6-0	200	5/3/78	New Mexico	Vista, Calif.	FA
Brees, Drew	QB	6-0	213	1/15/79	Purdue	Austin, Texas	D2
Carswell, Robert	S	5-11	215	10/26/78	Clemson	Stone Mountain, Ga.	D7b
Clayton, Carey	C	6-3	285	8/31/77	Texas-El Paso	Southlake, Texas	FA
Cody, Tay	CB	5-9	180	10/6/77	Florida State	Blakely, Ga.	D3
Dickenson, Dave (1)	QB	5-11	185	1/11/73	Montana	Great Falls, Mont.	FA
Ellis, Robert	TE	6-4	263	6/6/78	Boston College	Baytown, Texas	FA
Gilliam, Dondre	WR	6-0	185	2/9/77	Millersville	Aberdeen, Md.	FA
Gorin, Brandon	T	6-6	304	7/17/78	Purdue	Muncie, Ind.	D7a
Grant, Troy	CB	5-9	195	12/5/79	Tennessee Tech	San Antonio, Texas	FA
Guenther, Eric (1)	LB	6-2	240	5/4/77	Illinois	Westlake Village, Calif.	FA
Hatcher, Armon (1)	S	6-0	212	7/15/76	Oregon State	Diamond Bar, Calif.	FA-'00
Hendricks, Bart	QB	6-0	210	8/30/78	Boise State	Reno, Nev.	FA
Hunt, Reggie (1)	S	6-0	210	10/14/77	Texas Christian	Denison, Texas	FA
Johnson, Dirk (1)	P	6-0	233	6/1/75	Northern Colorado	Montrose, Colo.	FA
Keathley, Michael	T	6-4	296	3/9/78	Texas Christian	Glen Rose, Texas	FA
Maurer, Marty	TE	6-4	260	10/23/78	Oregon State	Jacksonville, Ore.	FA
Moore, Keon	CB	5-11	198	4/17/78	Southern Mississippi	Wiggins, Miss.	FA
Moreno, Zeke	LB	6-2	246	10/10/78	Southern California	Chula Vista, Calif.	D5b
Oglesby, Cedric (1)	K	5-10	180	7/26/77	South Carolina State	Decatur, Ga.	FA
Pate, Rob	S	6-3	213	12/21/78	Auburn	Birmingham, Ala.	FA
Pettigrew, Titcus	S	6-0	213	10/23/77	Penn State	Winston-Salem, S.C.	FA
Pitts, DeRonnie	WR	5-11	190	4/5/78	Stanford	Saginaw, Mich.	FA
Polk, Carlos	LB	6-2	250	2/22/77	Nebraska	Rockford, Ill.	D4
Reese, Quinton	DE	6-4	285	8/26/77	Auburn	Birmingham, Ala.	FA
Rekuc, Brad	LB	6-2	240	12/6/77	Weber State	Phoenix, Ariz.	FA
Sanchez, Davis (1)	CB	5-10	180	8/7/74	Oregon	Vancouver, B.C., Canada	FA
Schultz, Scott	DT	6-2	298	4/19/78	North Dakota	Moose Jaw, Saskatchewan, Canada	FA
Scott, Dequincy	DT	6-1	283	3/5/78	Southern Mississippi	Laplace, La.	FA
Sikyala, Mukala	RB	5-9	212	9/20/78	Maryland	Silver Springs, Md.	FA
Silvers, Elliott	T	6-7	348	2/19/78	Washington	Agoura, Calif.	D5a
Stuber, Tim	G	6-5	315	2/2/78	Colorado State	Northglenn, Colo.	FA
Thomas, Jason (1)	G	6-3	300	6/10/77	Hampton	Savannah, Ga.	D7-'00
Tomlinson, LaDainian	RB	5-10	221	6/23/79	Texas Christian	Waco, Texas	D1
Turner, Nate	WR	6-3	200	5/26/78	Nevada-Las Vegas	Compton, Calif.	FA
Witherspoon, Terry	FB	5-11	250	8/22/77	Clemson	Monroe, N.C.	FA

The term NFL Rookie is defined as a player who is in his first season of professional football and has not been on the roster of another professional football team for any regular-season or postseason games. A Rookie is designated by an "R" on NFL rosters. Players who have been active in another professional football league or players who have NFL experience, including either preseason training camp or being on an Active List or Inactive List, or on Reserve/Injured or Reserve/Physically Unable to Perform for fewer than six regular-season games, are termed NFL First-Year Players. An NFL First-Year Player is designated by a "1" on NFL rosters. Thereafter, a player is credited with an additional year of experience for each season in which he accumulates six games on the Active List or Inactive List, or on Reserve/Injured or Reserve/Physically Unable to Perform.

SEATTLE SEAHAWKS

American Football Conference
Western Division
Team Colors: Blue, Green, and Silver
11220 N.E. 53rd Street
Kirkland, Washington 98033
Telephone: (425) 827-9777

CLUB OFFICIALS

Chairman: Paul Allen
President: Bob Whitsitt
Executive VP of Football Operations/
General Manager & Head Coach: Mike Holmgren
Sr. Vice President: Mike Reinfeldt
VP/Community Outreach, I.S., Facilities: Mike Flood
General Counsel: Lance Lopes
Sr. VP/Marketing: Duane McLean
VP/Marketing: Mike Sheehan
VP/Football Operations: Ted Thompson
VP/Corporate Sales: Scott Patrick
VP/Communications: Gary Wright
Director of Player Personnel: John Schneider
Director of College Scouting: Scot McCloughan
Director of Pro Scouting: Will Lewis
Director of Public Relations: Dave Pearson
Asst. Director of Public Relations: Lane Gammel
Director of Community Outreach: Sandy Gregory
Director of Player Programs: Nesby Glasgow
Director of Publications: Vernon Cheek
Director of Broadcasting: Mike Wacker
Director of Vendor Sales: Kevin Williams
Director Ticket Operations/Customer Service:
Chuck Arnold
Director of Football Administration: Gary Reynolds
Football Operations Coordinator/Team Travel:
Bill Nayes
Video Director Football: Thom Fermstad
Head AthleticTrainer: Paul Federici
Equipment Manager: Erik Kennedy
Stadium: Husky Stadium (built in 1920)
•**Capacity:** 68,589
Montlake Boulevard
Seattle, Washington 98195
Playing Surface: Field Turf
Training Camp: Eastern Washington University
Cheney, Washington 99004

2001 SCHEDULE

PRESEASON

Aug. 11	at Indianapolis	5:00
Aug. 18	**Arizona**	6:30
Aug. 25	at San Francisco	6:00
Sept. 1	**New Orleans**	1:00

REGULAR SEASON

Sept. 9	at Cleveland	1:00
Sept. 16	**Kansas City**	1:15
Sept. 23	**Philadelphia**	1:15
Sept. 30	at Oakland	1:15
Oct. 7	**Jacksonville**	1:05
Oct. 14	**Denver**	1:15
Oct. 21	Open Date	
Oct. 28	**Miami**	1:15
Nov. 4	at Washington	4:15
Nov. 11	**Oakland**	5:30
Nov. 18	at Buffalo	1:00
Nov. 25	at Kansas City	12:00
Dec. 2	**San Diego**	1:05
Dec. 9	at Denver	6:30
Dec. 16	**Dallas**	1:15
Dec. 23	at New York Giants	1:00
Dec. 30	at San Diego	1:15

RECORD HOLDERS

INDIVIDUAL RECORDS—CAREER

Category	Name	Performance
Rushing (Yds.)	Chris Warren, 1990-97	6,706
Passing (Yds.)	Dave Krieg, 1980-1991	26,132
Passing (TDs)	Dave Krieg, 1980-1991	195
Receiving (No.)	Steve Largent, 1976-1989	819
Receiving (Yds.)	Steve Largent, 1976-1989	13,089
Interceptions	Dave Brown, 1976-1986	50
Punting (Avg.)	Rick Tuten, 1991-97	43.8
Punt Return (Avg.)	Paul Johns, 1981-84	11.4
Kickoff Return (Avg.)	Steve Broussard, 1995-98	23.2
Field Goals	Norm Johnson, 1982-1990	159
Touchdowns (Tot.)	Steve Largent, 1976-1989	101
Points	Norm Johnson, 1982-1990	810

INDIVIDUAL RECORDS—SINGLE SEASON

Category	Name	Performance
Rushing (Yds.)	Chris Warren, 1994	1,545
Passing (Yds.)	Warren Moon, 1997	3,678
Passing (TDs)	Dave Krieg, 1984	32
Receiving (No.)	Brian Blades, 1994	81
Receiving (Yds.)	Steve Largent, 1985	1,287
Interceptions	John Harris, 1981	10
	Kenny Easley, 1984	10
Punting (Avg.)	Rick Tuten, 1995	45.0
Punt Return (Avg.)	Charlie Rogers, 1999	14.5
Kickoff Return (Avg.)	Charlie Rogers, 2000	24.9
Field Goals	Todd Peterson, 1999	34
Touchdowns (Tot.)	Chris Warren, 1995	16
Points	Todd Peterson, 1999	134

INDIVIDUAL RECORDS—SINGLE GAME

Category	Name	Performance
Rushing (Yds.)	Curt Warner, 11-27-83	207
Passing (Yds.)	Dave Krieg, 11-20-83	418
Passing (TDs)	Dave Krieg, 12-2-84, 9-15-85, 11-28-88	5
	Warren Moon, 10-26-97	5
Receiving (No.)	Steve Largent, 10-18-87	15
Receiving (Yds.)	Steve Largent, 10-18-87	261
Interceptions	Kenny Easley, 9-3-84	3
	Eugene Robinson, 12-6-92	3
	Darryl Williams, 9-21-97	3
Field Goals	Norm Johnson, 9-20-87, 12-18-88	5
Touchdowns (Tot.)	Daryl Turner, 9-15-85	4
	Curt Warner, 12-11-88	4
Points	Daryl Turner, 9-15-85	24
	Curt Warner, 12-11-88	24

COACHING HISTORY

(182-214-0)

1976-1982	Jack Patera*	35-59-0
1982	Mike McCormack	4-3-0
1983-1991	Chuck Knox	83-67-0
1992-94	Tom Flores	14-34-0
1995-98	Dennis Erickson	31-33-0
1999-2000	Mike Holmgren	15-18-0

*Released after two games in 1982

HUSKY STADIUM

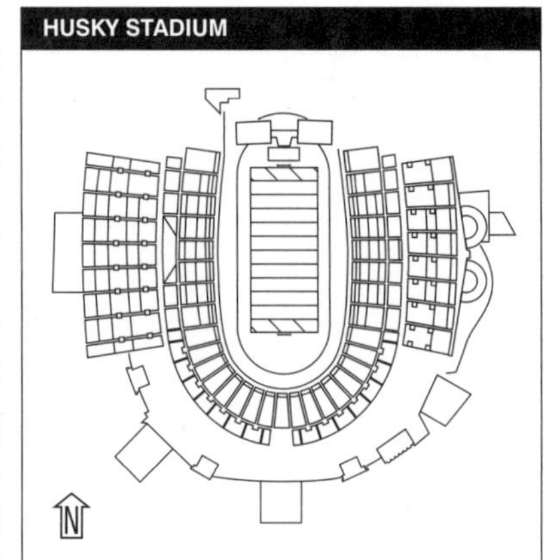

2000 TEAM RECORD

PRESEASON (2-2)

Date	Result		Opponent
8/5	W	28-16	Indianapolis
8/12	L	3-21	at Arizona
8/19	W	25-21	San Francisco
8/24	L	0-20	at Oakland

REGULAR SEASON (6-10)

Date	Result		Opponent	Att.
9/3	L	0-23	at Miami	72,949
9/10	L	34-37	St. Louis	64,869
9/17	W	20-10	New Orleans	59,513
9/24	W	20-12	at San Diego	47,233
10/2	L	17-24	at Kansas City	82,893
10/8	L	3-26	at Carolina	72,192
10/15	L	24-37	Indianapolis	63,593
10/22	L	3-31	at Oakland	57,490
10/29	L	19-24	Kansas City	62,141
11/5	W	17-15	San Diego	59,884
11/12	W	28-21	at Jacksonville	68,063
11/26	L	31-38	Denver	68,661
12/3	W	30-10	at Atlanta	44,680
12/10	L	24-31	at Denver	75,218
12/16	W	27-24	Oakland	68,681
12/23	L	23-42	Buffalo	61,025

SCORE BY PERIODS

Seahawks	70	100	59	91	0	—	320
Opponents	96	140	71	98	0	—	405

ATTENDANCE

Home 498,885 Away 530,616 Total 1,029,501
Single-game home record, 68,681 (12/16/00)
Single-season home record, 522,656 (1999)

2000 TEAM STATISTICS

	Seahawks	Opp.
Total First Downs	281	331
Rushing	98	126
Passing	168	185
Penalty	15	20
Third Down: Made/Att	83/205	89/201
Third Down Pct.	40.5	44.3
Fourth Down: Made/Att	7/14	1/7
Fourth Down Pct.	50.0	14.3
Total Net Yards	4,680	6,391
Avg. Per Game	292.5	399.4
Total Plays	956	1,019
Avg. Per Play	4.9	6.3
Net Yards Rushing	1,720	2,454
Avg. Per Game	107.5	153.4
Total Rushes	403	503
Net Yards Passing	2,960	3,937
Avg. Per Game	185.0	246.1
Sacked/Yards Lost	46/238	27/152
Gross Yards	3,198	4,089
Att./Completions	507/308	489/309
Completion Pct.	60.7	63.2
Had Intercepted	21	17
Punts/Average	75/39.5	62/41.5
Net Punting Avg.	75/36.9	62/33.3
Penalties/Yards	89/728	96/694
Fumbles/Ball Lost	35/17	28/12
Touchdowns	37	46
Rushing	10	20
Passing	21	23
Returns	6	3
Avg. Time of Possession	27:31	32:29

2000 INDIVIDUAL STATISTICS

Passing	Att.	Comp.	Yds.	Pct.	TD	Int.	Tkld.	Rate
Kitna	418	259	2,658	62.0	18	19	33/166	75.6
Huard	87	49	540	56.3	3	2	13/72	76.8
T. Brown	1	0	0	0.0	0	0	0/0	39.6
Feagles	1	0	0	0.0	0	0	0/0	39.6
Seahawks	507	308	3,198	60.7	21	21	46/238	75.5
Opponents	489	309	4,089	63.2	23	17	27/152	90.8

SCORING	TD R	TD P	TD Rt	PAT	FG	Saf	PTS
Lindell	0	0	0	25/25	15/17	0	70
Watters	7	2	0	0/0	0/0	0	54
Jackson	0	6	0	0/0	0/0	0	36
Dawkins	0	5	0	0/0	0/0	0	30
Heppner	0	0	0	8/8	6/9	0	26
Mili	0	3	0	0/0	0/0	0	18
Alexander	2	0	0	0/0	0/0	0	12
Fauria	0	2	0	0/0	0/0	0	12
Bailey	0	1	0	0/0	0/0	0	6
Bellamy	0	0	1	0/0	0/0	0	6
C. Brown	0	0	1	0/0	0/0	0	6
Kitna	1	0	0	0/0	0/0	0	6
Koonce	0	0	1	0/0	0/0	0	6
Mayes	0	1	0	0/0	0/0	0	6
Rogers	0	0	1	0/0	0/0	0	6
Sinclair	0	0	1	0/0	0/0	0	6
Strong	0	1	0	0/0	0/0	0	6
W. Williams	0	0	1	0/0	0/0	0	6
J. Williams	0	0	0	0/0	0/0	1	2
Seahawks	10	21	6	33/33	21/26	1	320
Opponents	20	23	3	45/45	28/33	0	405

2-Pt. Conversions: None.
Seahawks 0-4, Opponents 0-1.

RUSHING	Att.	Yds.	Avg.	LG	TD
Watters	278	1,242	4.5	55	7
Alexander	64	313	4.9	50	2
Kitna	48	127	2.6	13	1
Huard	5	29	5.8	10	0
Strong	3	9	3.0	4	0
R. Brown	3	6	2.0	3	0
Jackson	1	-1	-1.0	-1	0
J. Williams	1	-5	-5.0	-5	0
Seahawks	403	1,720	4.3	55	10
Opponents	503	2,454	4.9	80t	20

RECEIVING	No.	Yds.	Avg.	LG	TD
Dawkins	63	731	11.6	40	5
Watters	63	613	9.7	59	2
Jackson	53	713	13.5	71	6
Mayes	29	264	9.1	40	1
Mili	28	288	10.3	34	3
Fauria	28	237	8.5	16	2
Strong	23	141	6.1	24	1
J. Williams	8	99	12.4	18	0
Bailey	6	62	10.3	22	1
Alexander	5	41	8.2	18	0
R. Brown	2	9	4.5	6	0
Seahawks	308	3,198	10.4	71	21
Opponents	309	4,089	13.2	73	23

INTERCEPTIONS	No.	Yds.	Avg.	LG	TD
Bellamy	4	132	33.0	84t	1
W. Williams	4	74	18.5	69t	1
Simmons	2	15	7.5	8	0
Springs	2	8	4.0	8	0
Bell	1	30	30.0	30	0
Koonce	1	27	27.0	27t	1
Kennedy	1	14	14.0	14	0
C. Brown	1	0	0.0	0	0
Kacyvenski	1	0	0.0	0	0
Seahawks	17	300	17.6	84t	3
Opponents	21	191	9.1	79t	2

PUNTING	No.	Yds.	Avg.	In 20	LG
Feagles	74	2,960	40.0	24	57
Seahawks	75	2,960	39.5	24	57
Opponents	62	2,571	41.5	21	69

PUNT RETURNS	No.	FC	Yds.	Avg.	LG	TD
Rogers	26	12	363	14.0	43	0
Canty	4	1	21	5.3	8	0
Joseph	0	1	0	—	—	0
Seahawks	30	14	384	12.8	43	0
Opponents	32	18	151	4.7	22	0

KICKOFF RETURNS	No.	Yds.	Avg.	LG	TD
Rogers	66	1,629	24.7	81t	1
Bownes	3	83	27.7	38	0
Joseph	3	71	23.7	34	0
J. Williams	3	76	25.3	40	0
R. Brown	2	19	9.5	19	0
Fauria	1	9	9.0	9	0
Mili	1	19	19.0	19	0
Strong	1	26	26.0	26	0
Seahawks	80	1,932	24.2	81t	1
Opponents	64	1,236	19.3	39	0

FIELD GOALS	1-19	20-29	30-39	40-49	50+
Lindell	0/0	4/5	1/1	7/8	3/3
Heppner	1/1	2/2	1/3	2/2	0/1
Seahawks	1/1	6/7	2/4	9/10	3/4
Opponents	1/1	11/12	7/9	9/9	0/2

SACKS	No.
C. Brown	6.0
King	6.0
Simmons	4.0
Sinclair	3.5
Bellamy	2.0
Koonce	1.5
Kennedy	1.0
W. Williams	1.0
Cochran	0.5
LaBounty	0.5
Seahawks	27.0
Opponents	46.0

2001 DRAFT CHOICES

Round	Name	Pos.	College
1	Koren Robinson	WR	North Carolina State
	Steve Hutchinson	G	Michigan
2	Ken Lucas	DB	Mississippi
3	Heath Evans	RB	Auburn
4	Orlando Huff	LB	Fresno State
	Curtis Fuller	DB	Texas Christian
	Floyd Womack	T	Mississippi State
5	Alex Bannister	WR	Eastern Kentucky
6	Josh Booty	QB	Louisiana State
7	Harold Blackmon	DB	Northwestern
	Dennis Norman	T	Princeton
	Kris Kocurek	DT	Texas Tech

SEATTLE SEAHAWKS

2001 VETERAN ROSTER

No.	Name	Pos.	Ht.	Wt.	Birthdate	NFL Exp.	College	Hometown	How Acq.	'00 Games/ Starts
37	Alexander, Shaun	RB	5-11	218	8/30/77	2	Alabama	Florence, Ky.	D1a-'00	16/1
83	Bailey, Karsten	WR	5-10	201	4/26/77	3	Auburn	Newnan, Ga.	D3b-'99	9/0
63	Beede, Frank	G	6-4	296	5/1/73	6	Panhandle State	Antioch, Calif.	FA-'96	7/0
55	Bell, Marcus	LB	6-1	237	7/19/77	2	Arizona	St. John's, Ariz.	D4a-'00	16/0
19	Bownes, Fabien	WR	5-11	189	2/29/72	7	Western Illinois	Aurora, Ill.	W(Chi)-'00	16/0
94	Brown, Chad	LB	6-2	240	7/12/70	9	Colorado	Altadena, Calif.	UFA(Pitt)-'97	16/16
34	Brown, Reggie	RB	6-0	244	6/26/73	6	Fresno State	Detroit, Mich.	D3b-'96	12/1
5	Brown, Travis	QB	6-3	218	7/17/77	2	Northern Arizona	Phoenix, Ariz.	FA-'00	1/0
23	Charlton, Ike	CB	5-11	205	10/6/77	2	Virginia Tech	Orlando, Fla.	D2-'00	16/0
78	Cochran, Antonio	DE	6-4	297	6/21/76	3	Georgia	Montezuma, Ga.	D4-'99	16/0
52	Darche, Jean-Philippe	LS	6-0	242	2/28/75	2	McGill	Montreal, Quebec	FA-'00	16/0
90	Eaton, Chad	DT	6-5	300	4/6/72	6	Washington State	Puyallup, Wash.	UFA(NE)-'01	14/13*
86	Fauria, Christian	TE	6-4	245	9/22/71	7	Colorado	Encino, Calif.	D2-'95	15/10
10	Feagles, Jeff	P	6-1	207	3/7/66	14	Miami	Anaheim, Calif.	UFA(Ariz)-'98	16/0
84	French, Rufus	TE	6-3	257	3/15/78	3	Mississippi	Amory, Miss.	FA-'00	0*
35	Graham, Jay	RB	6-0	224	7/14/75	5	Tennessee	Concord, N.C.	FA-'01	0*
62	Gray, Chris	G-C	6-4	305	6/19/70	9	Auburn	Birmingham, Ala.	UFA(Chi)-'98	16/16
8	t- Hasselbeck, Matt	QB	6-4	220	9/25/75	3	Boston College	Westwood, Mass.	T(GB)-'01	16/0*
85	Hill, James	TE	6-4	246	10/25/74	2	Abilene Christian	Dallas, Texas	FA-'00	10/0
95	Hilliard, John	DE	6-2	294	4/16/76	2	Mississippi State	Houston, Texas	D6c-'00	5/0*
11	Huard, Brock	QB	6-4	228	4/15/76	3	Washington	Puyallup, Wash.	D3a-'99	5/4
82	Jackson, Darrell	WR	6-0	197	12/6/78	2	Florida	Dayton, Ohio	D3-'00	16/10
71	Jones, Walter	T	6-5	300	1/19/74	5	Florida State	Aliceville, Ala.	D1b-'97	16/16
58	Kacyvenski, Isaiah	LB	6-1	250	10/3/77	2	Harvard	Endicott, N.Y.	D4b-'00	16/0
33	Kelly, Maurice	S	6-2	205	10/9/72	2	East Tennessee State	Orangebury, S.C.	FA-'00	16/0
65	King, Eric	T	6-4	305	7/27/75	2	Richmond	Pittsburgh, Pa.	FA-'00	0*
92	King, Lamar	DE	6-3	294	8/10/75	3	Saginaw Valley State	Boston, Mass.	D1-'99	14/14
99	Kirkland, Levon	LB	6-1	270	2/17/69	10	Clemson	Lamar, S.C.	UFA(Pitt)-'01	16/16*
91	LaBounty, Matt	DE	6-4	275	1/3/69	9	Oregon	Novato, Calif.	T(GB)-'96	12/2
9	Lindell, Rian	K	6-3	226	1/20/77	2	Washington State	Vancouver, Wash.	FA-'00	12/0*
75	McIntosh, Chris	T	6-6	315	2/20/77	2	Wisconsin	Pewaukee, Wis.	D1b-'00	14/10
89	Mili, Itula	TE	6-4	265	4/20/73	5	Brigham Young	Laie, Hawaii	D6-'97	16/6
22	Miranda, Paul	CB	5-10	182	5/2/76	3	Central Florida	Thomasville, Ga.	FA-'00	4/0
79	Overhauser, Chad	G	6-4	316	6/17/75	4	UCLA	Sacramento, Calif.	T(Chi)-'00	0*
93	Randle, John	DT	6-1	287	12/12/67	12	Texas A&I	Hearne, Texas	UFA(Minn)-'01	16/16*
31	Robertson, Marcus	S	5-11	205	10/2/69	11	Iowa State	Pasadena, Calif.	UFA(Tenn)-'01	15/15*
20	Rogers, Charlie	RB	5-9	179	6/19/76	3	Georgia Tech	Cliffwood, N.J.	D5b-'99	15/0
46	Settles, Tawambi	S	6-3	199	1/19/76	2	Duke	Jacksonville, Fla.	FA-'01	0*
51	Simmons, Anthony	LB	6-0	230	6/20/76	4	Clemson	Spartanburg, S.C.	D1-'98	16/16
70	Sinclair, Michael	DE	6-4	275	1/31/68	11	Eastern New Mexico	Beaumont, Texas	D6-'91	16/16
24	Springs, Shawn	CB	6-0	195	3/11/75	5	Ohio State	Silver Springs, Md.	D1a-'97	16/16
73	Staat, Jeremy	DT	6-5	300	10/10/76	4	Arizona State	Bakersfield, Calif.	UFA(Pitt)-'01	7/0*
38	Strong, Mack	RB	6-0	235	9/11/71	8	Georgia	Columbus, Ga.	FA-'93	16/12
59	Terry, Tim	LB	6-2	239	7/26/74	3	Temple	Hempstead, N.Y.	FA-'00	6/0
61	Tobeck, Robbie	C-G	6-4	298	3/6/70	8	Washington State	Tarpon Springs, Fla.	UFA(Atl)-'00	4/0
25	Tongue, Reggie	S	6-0	206	4/11/73	6	Oregon State	Fairbanks, Ark.	UFA(KC)-'00	16/6
21	Vinson, Fred	CB	5-11	180	4/2/77	3	Vanderbilt	North Augusta, S.C.	T(GB)-'00	0*
32	Watters, Ricky	RB	6-1	217	4/7/69	11	Notre Dame	Harrisburg, Pa.	UFA(Phil)-'98	16/16
69	Wedderburn, Floyd	T	6-5	333	5/5/76	3	Penn State	Upper Darby, Pa.	D5a-'99	16/16
74	Weiner, Todd	T	6-4	300	9/16/75	4	Kansas State	Coral Springs, Fla.	D2-'98	16/6
88	Williams, James	WR	5-10	180	3/6/78	2	Marshall	Raymond, Miss.	D6a-'00	10/0
27	Williams, Willie	CB	5-9	181	12/26/70	9	Western Carolina	Columbia, S.C.	UFA(Pitt)-'97	16/15
98	Woodard, Cedric	DT	6-2	311	9/5/77	2	Texas	Sweeny, Texas	W(Balt)-'00	0*

* Eaton played 14 games with New England in '00; French, Myles, and Vinson missed '00 season because of injury; Graham last active with Baltimore in '99; Hasselbeck played 16 games with Green Bay; E. King was on the practice squad; Kirkland played 16 games with Pittsburgh; Overhauser was inactive for 13 games; Randle played 16 games with Minnesota; Robertson played 15 games with Tennessee; Settles last active with Jacksonville in '98; Staat played 7 games with Pittsburgh; Woodard was inactive for 16 games.

t- Seahawks traded for Hasselbeck (GB).

Players lost through free agency (4): S Jay Bellamy (NO; 16 games in '00), G Pete Kendall (Ariz; 16), QB Jon Kitna (Cin; 15), DT Riddick Parker (NE; 16)

Also played with Seahawks in '00—CB Chris Canty (12 games), WR Sean Dawkins (16), Kris Heppner (4), S Kerry Joseph (16), DT Cortez Kennedy (16), LB George Koonce (16), LB James Logan (16), QB Matt Lytle (1), WR Derrick Mayes (12).

COACHING STAFF

Executive Vice President of Football Operations/ General Manager & Head Coach, Mike Holmgren

Pro Career: Named to his current position as the Seahawks' executive vice president of football operations/general manager and head coach on January 8, 1999. In addition to his coaching duties, Holmgren oversees all facets of the team's football operations, including scouting, personnel, salary cap, player negotiations, as well as regular coaching responsibilities. In his first season, Holmgren guided the Seahawks to their first postseason appearance since 1988. The Seahawks also won their first AFC West title since 1988, and hosted their first postseason game since 1984. Holmgren took control of the Seahawks following one of the most successful coaching stints in league history as the head coach of the Green Bay Packers (1992-98). By winning at least one game in five consecutive postseasons (1993-97) Holmgren joined John Madden (1973-77) as the only coaches in league history to accomplish that feat. In 15 NFL seasons (1999-2000 head coach, 1992-98 head coach Green Bay, 1986-1991 assistant coach San Francisco) Holmgren's teams have posted a 161-78-1 (.673) record, hit double digits in the victory column 10 times, made the postseason 13 times, won three Super Bowls (XXIII, XXIV, and XXXI), and reached another (Super Bowl XXXII). Career record: 99-60.

Background: Quarterback at Southern California (1966-69) and was drafted by the St. Louis Cardinals in the eighth round of the 1970 NFL draft. He served as an assistant coach at San Francisco State (1981) and Brigham Young (1982-85). Earned his bachelor degree in business finance at Southern California.

Personal: Born June 15, 1948, in San Francisco. He and his wife, Kathy, live in Mercer Island, Wash. and have four daughters—Calla, Jenny, Emily, and Gretchen.

2001 FIRST-YEAR ROSTER

Name	Pos.	Ht.	Wt.	Birthdate	College	Hometown	How Acq.
Bannister, Alex	WR	6-5	201	4/23/79	Eastern Kentucky	Cincinnati, Ohio	D5
Blackmon, Harold	S	5-11	210	5/20/78	Northwestern	Chicago, Ill.	D7a
Booty, Josh	QB	6-2	221	4/29/75	Louisiana State	Shreveport, La.	D6
Brown, Joe	DT	6-6	290	3/5/77	Ohio State	Tucson, Ariz.	FA
Byrd, David (1)	CB	5-11	202	11/15/77	Syracuse	Schenectady, N.Y.	FA
Caldwell, Donnie (1)	S	5-11	179	10/26/77	Western Illinois	Lawton, Okla.	FA
Cook, Kerwin	WR	6-1	178	12/21/79	Tulane	Ferriday, La.	FA
Davis, Wade (1)	CB	5-11	180	4/20/77	Weber State	Aurora, Colo.	FA
Doerr, Kurtis	P	6-1	215	6/25/78	Oregon State	Waterford, Wis.	FA
Dorsey, Jerry	WR	6-1	190	1/18/78	Indiana	Oak Grove, Ky.	FA
Epps, Dwan (1)	LB	6-1	242	1/18/77	Texas Southern	Friendswood, Texas	FA-'00
Evans, Heath	FB	6-0	246	12/30/78	Auburn	West Palm Beach, Fla.	D3
Fuller, Curtis	S	5-10	186	7/25/78	Texas Christian	North Richland Hill, Texas	D4b
Garden, Lloyd	FB	5-10	238	10/29/77	Cincinnati	Akron, Ohio	FA
Graham, Shayne (1)	K	6-0	195	12/9/77	Virginia Tech	Dublin, Va.	FA
Huff, Orlando	LB	6-2	245	8/14/78	Fresno State	Upland, Calif.	D4a
Hutchinson, Steve	G	6-5	306	11/1/77	Michigan	Fort Lauderdale, Fla.	D1b
Jackson, LaDairis	LB	6-2	271	6/16/79	Oregon State	Dallas, Texas	FA
Jones, Dwaune (1)	WR	6-0	191	7/11/77	Richmond	Washington, D.C.	FA-'00
Kocurek, Kris	DT	6-4	296	11/15/78	Texas Tech	Caldwell, Texas	D7c
Lucas, Ken	CB	6-0	200	1/23/79	Mississippi	Cleveland, Miss.	D2
Nelson, Corey	WR	6-1	187	10/9/77	Boise State	Rohnert Park, Calif.	FA
Norman, Dennis	T	6-5	305	1/26/80	Princeton	Marlton, N.J.	D7b
Osborne, Scot (1)	FB-TE	6-4	274	10/30/77	William & Mary	Asheville, N.C.	FA-'00
Phillips, Rodnick (1)	RB	5-11	208	11/17/77	Southern Methodist	Galveston, Texas	FA
Robinson, Koren	WR	6-1	211	3/19/80	North Carolina State	Belmont, N.C.	D1a
Rogers, Chris (1)	CB	5-10	185	1/3/77	Howard	Largo, Md.	FA
Smith, Jermaine (1)	CB	5-11	192	11/10/77	Washington	Simi Valley, Calif.	FA-'00
Stewart, Russell	TE	6-4	251	9/25/77	Stanford	Bellevue, Wash.	FA
Terry, Nate (1)	CB	6-2	180	10/5/76	West Virginia	Homestead, Fla.	FA
Watson, Tim (1)	DT	6-4	290	12/23/74	Rowan	Williamstown, N.J.	D6b-'00
Womack, Floyd	T	6-4	345	11/15/78	Mississippi State	Cleveland, Miss.	D4c
Woodard, Billy (1)	TE	6-5	253	7/15/76	Rutgers	Wilson, N.C.	FA

The term NFL Rookie is defined as a player who is in his first season of professional football and has not been on the roster of another professional football team for any regular-season or postseason games. A Rookie is designated by an "R" on NFL rosters. Players who have been active in another professional football league or players who have NFL experience, including either preseason training camp or being on an Active List or Inactive List, or on Reserve/Injured or Reserve/Physically Unable to Perform for fewer than six regular-season games, are termed NFL First-Year Players. An NFL First-Year Player is designated by a "1" on NFL rosters. Thereafter, a player is credited with an additional year of experience for each season in which he accumulates six games on the Active List or Inactive List, or on Reserve/Injured or Reserve/Physically Unable to Perform

ASSISTANT COACHES

Larry Brooks, defensive line; born June 10, 1950, Prince George, Va., lives in Kirkland, Wash. Defensive lineman Virginia State 1968-1971. Pro defensive tackle Los Angeles Rams 1972-1982. College coach: Virginia State 1992-93. Pro coach: Los Angeles Rams 1983-1990, Green Bay Packers 1994-98, joined Seahawks in 1999.

Jerry Colquitt, offensive quality control; born June 28, 1972, Oak Ridge, Tenn., lives in Kirkland, Wash. Quarterback Tennessee 1991-94. Quarterback Frankfurt Galaxy (NFL Europe) 1997. College coach: Tennessee 1996-98. Pro coach: Joined Seahawks in 1999.

Nolan Cromwell, wide receivers; born January 30, 1955, Smith Center, Kan., lives in Bellevue, Wash. Quarterback-safety Kansas 1973-76. Pro defensive back Los Angeles Rams 1977-1987. Pro coach: Los Angeles Rams 1991, Green Bay Packers 1992-98, joined Seahawks in 1999.

Ken Flajole, defensive backs; born October 4, 1954, Seattle, lives in Kirkland, Wash. Linebacker Wenatchee (Wash.) Valley C.C. 1973-74, Pacific Lutheran 1975-76. No pro playing experience. College coach: Pacific Lutheran 1977-78, Washington 1979, Montana 1980-85, Texas-El Paso 1986-88, Missouri 1989-1993, Richmond 1994, Hawaii 1995, Nevada 1996-97. Pro coach: Green Bay Packers 1998, joined Seahawks in 1999.

Gil Haskell, offensive coordinator; born September 24, 1943, San Francisco, lives in Kirkland. Defensive back San Francisco State 1961, 1963-65. No pro playing experience. College coach: Southern California 1978-1982. Pro coach: Los Angeles Rams 1983-1991, Green Bay Packers 1992-97, Carolina Panthers 1998-99, joined Seahawks in 2000.

Johnny Holland, linebackers; born March 11, 1965, Belleville, Texas, lives in Kirkland. Linebacker Texas A&M 1983-86. Pro linebacker Green Bay Packers 1987-1993. Pro coach: Green Bay Packers 1995-99, joined Seahawks in 2000.

Kent Johnston, strength and conditioning; born February 21, 1956, Mexia, Texas, lives in Bellevue, Wash. Defensive back Stephen F. Austin 1974-77. No pro playing experience. College coach: Northwestern State (La.) 1979, Northeast Louisiana 1980-81, Alabama 1983-86. Pro coach: Tampa Bay Buccaneers 1987-1991, Green Bay Packers 1992-98, joined Seahawks in 1999.

Jim Lind, tight ends; born Novemeber 11, 1947, Isle, Minn., lives in Bellevue, Wash. Linebacker Bethel College 1965-66, defensive back Bemidji State 1971-72. No pro playing experience. College coach: St. Cloud State 1977-78, St. John's (Minn.) 1979-1980, Brigham Young 1981-82, Minnesota-Morris 1983-86 (head coach), Wisconsin-Eau Claire 1987-1991 (head coach). Pro coach: Green Bay Packers 1992-98, joined Seahawks in 1999.

Clayton Lopez, defensive quality control; born May 26, 1971, Los Angeles, lives in Kirkland, Wash. Safety Nevada 1991-94. No pro playing experience. College coach: Nevada 1995-98. Pro coach: Joined Seahawks in 1999.

Tom Lovat, asst. head coach-offensive line; born December 28, 1938, Bingham, Utah, lives in Bellevue, Wash. Guard-linebacker Utah 1958-1960. No pro playing experience. College coach: Utah 1967, 1972-76 (head coach 1974-76), Idaho State 1968-1970, Stanford 1977-79, Wyoming 1989. Pro coach: Saskatchewan Roughriders (CFL) 1971, Green Bay Packers 1980, 1992-98, St. Louis/Phoenix Cardinals 1981-84, 1990-91, Indianapolis Colts 1985-88, joined Seahawks in 1999.

Mark Michaels, asst. special teams; born Aug. 15, 1963, Kingston, Pa., lives in Bothell, Wash. Defensive lineman Connecticut 1983-86. No pro playing experience. College coach: New Haven 1987-1990, Brown 1993-97, Massachusetts 1998. Pro coach: Helsinki Roosters (Finnish Maple League) 1991, Utah Pioneers (Professional Spring Football League) 1992, Cleveland Browns 1999-2000, joined Seahawks in 2001.

Stump Mitchell, running backs; born March 15, 1959, St. Mary's, Ga., lives in Kirkland, Wash. Tailback The Citadel 1977-1980. Running back St. Louis/Phoenix Cardinals 1981-89. College coach: Morgan State 1995-98 (head coach 1996-98). Pro coach: San Antonio Rough Riders (WLAF) 1991, joined Seahawks in 1999.

Pete Rodriguez, special teams coordinator; born July 25, 1940, Chicago, lives in Kirkland, Wash. Guard-linebacker Denver 1959-1960, Western State (Colo.) 1961-63. No pro playing experience. College coach: Western State (Colo.) 1964, Arizona 1968-69, Western Illinois 1970-73, 1979-1982 (head coach), Florida State 1974-75, Iowa State 1976-78, Northern Iowa 1986. Pro coach: Michigan Panthers (USFL) 1983-84, Denver Gold (USFL) 1985, Jacksonville Bulls (USFL) 1986, Ottawa Rough Riders (CFL) 1987, Los Angeles Raiders 1988-89, Phoenix Cardinals 1990-93, Washington Redskins 1994-97, joined Seahawks in 1998.

Zerick Rollins, defensive assistant; born June 20, 1975, Houston, lives in Bothell, Wash. Defensive end Texas A&M 1995-97. No pro playing experience. College coach: Texas A&M 1997-2000. Pro coach: Joined Seahawks in 2001.

Steve Sidwell, defensive coordinator; born August 30, 1944, Winfield, Kan., lives in Kirkland. Linebacker Colorado 1962-65. No pro playing experience. College coach: Colorado 1966-1973, Nevada-Las Vegas 1974-75, Southern Methodist 1976-1981. Pro coach: New England Patriots 1982-84, 1997-99, Indianapolis Colts 1985, New Orleans Saints 1986-1994, Houston Oilers 1995-96, joined Seahawks in 2000.

Rod Springer, asst. strength & conditioning; born September 19, 1960, Oklahoma City, Okla., lives in Kirkland. Attended Tarrleton State. No college or pro playing experience. College coach: Alabama 1985-86. Pro coach: Joined Seahawks in 1999.

Jim Zorn, quarterbacks; born May 10, 1953, Whittier, Calif., lives in Mercer Island, Wash. Quarterback Cal Poly-Pomona 1973-75. Pro quarterback Seattle Seahawks 1975-1984, Green Bay Packers 1985, Winnipeg Blue Bombers (CFL) 1986, Tampa Bay Buccaneers 1987. College coach: Boise State 1989-1991, Utah State 1992-94, Minnesota 1995-96. Pro coach: Seattle Seahawks 1997, Detroit Lions 1998-2000, re-joined Seahawks in 2001.

TENNESSEE TITANS

American Football Conference
Central Division
Team Colors: Navy, Titans Blue, Red, Silver
460 Great Circle Road
Nashville, Tennessee 37228
Telephone: (615) 565-4000

CLUB OFFICIALS

Owner/Chairman of the Board:
K.S. (Bud) Adams, Jr.
Executive Assistant to Owner/
Chairman of the Board: Thomas S. Smith
President/Chief Operating Officer: Jeff Diamond
Executive V.P./General Manager: Floyd Reese
Executive V.P: Don MacLachlan
Vice President/General Counsel: Steve Underwood
Asst. General Counsel: Elza Bullock
Vice President/Finance: Jackie Curley
Vice President/Community Affairs: Bob Hyde
Director of Player Personnel: Rich Snead
Director of Sales and Operations: Stuart Spears
Asst. Dir. of Sales and Operations: Brent Akers
Director of Broadcasting: Mike Keith
Director of Marketing: Ralph Ockenfels
Director of Media Relations: Robbie Bohren
Asst. Dir. of Media Relations: William Bryant
Director of Security: Steve Berk
Director of Ticket Operations: Marty Collins
Director of Player Programs: Al Smith
Director of Cheerleading and Entertainment:
Meeka Gabriel
Director of Stadium Operations: Bill Dickerson
Suite and Club Services Manager: Bill Wainwright
Head Athletic Trainer: Brad Brown
Assistant Athletic Trainers: Don Moseley,
Geoff Kaplan
Equipment Manager: Paul Noska
Video Coordinator: Anthony Pastrana
Stadium: Adelphia Coliseum (built in 1999)
•**Capacity:** 68,498
One Titans Way
Nashville, Tennessee 37213
Playing Surface: Natural Grass
Training Camp: Baptist Sports Park
460 Great Circle Road
Nashville, Tennessee 37228
(615) 565-4000

2001 SCHEDULE

PRESEASON

Aug. 11	**Chicago**	7:00
Aug. 17	at St. Louis	7:00
Aug. 23	**Philadelphia**	7:00
Aug. 30	at Detroit	7:30

REGULAR SEASON

Sept. 9	**Miami**	7:30
Sept. 16	**Cincinnati**	12:00
Sept. 23	at Jacksonville	1:00
Sept. 30	Open Date	
Oct. 7	at Baltimore	1:00
Oct. 14	**Tampa Bay**	12:00
Oct. 21	at Detroit	1:00
Oct. 29	at Pittsburgh (Mon.)	9:00
Nov. 4	**Jacksonville**	12:00
Nov. 12	**Baltimore** (Mon.)	8:00
Nov. 18	at Cincinnati	1:00
Nov. 25	**Pittsburgh**	12:00
Dec. 2	at Cleveland	1:00
Dec. 9	at Minnesota	12:00
Dec. 16	**Green Bay**	3:15
Dec. 22	at Oakland (Sat.)	6:00
Dec. 30	**Cleveland**	12:00

RECORD HOLDERS

INDIVIDUAL RECORDS—CAREER

Category	Name	Performance
Rushing (Yds.)	Earl Campbell, 1978-1984	8,574
Passing (Yds.)	Warren Moon, 1984-1993	33,685
Passing (TDs)	Warren Moon, 1984-1993	196
Receiving (No.)	Ernest Givins, 1986-1994	542
Receiving (Yds.)	Ernest Givins, 1986-1994	7,935
Interceptions	Jim Norton, 1960-68	45
Punting (Avg.)	Greg Montgomery, 1988-1993	43.6
Punt Return (Avg.)	Billy Johnson, 1974-1980	13.2
Kickoff Return (Avg.)	Bobby Jancik, 1962-67	26.5
Field Goals	Al Del Greco, 1991-2000	246
Touchdowns (Tot.)	Earl Campbell, 1978-1984	73
Points	Al Del Greco, 1991-2000	1,060

INDIVIDUAL RECORDS—SINGLE SEASON

Category	Name	Performance
Rushing (Yds.)	Earl Campbell, 1980	1,934
Passing (Yds.)	Warren Moon, 1991	4,690
Passing (TDs)	George Blanda, 1961	36
Receiving (No.)	Charley Hennigan, 1964	101
Receiving (Yds.)	Charley Hennigan, 1961	1,746
Interceptions	Fred Glick, 1963	12
	Mike Reinfeldt, 1979	12
Punting (Avg.)	Craig Hentrich, 1998	47.2
Punt Return (Avg.)	Billy Johnson, 1977	15.4
Kickoff Return (Avg.)	Ken Hall, 1960	31.3
Field Goals	Al Del Greco, 1998	36
Touchdowns (Tot.)	Earl Campbell, 1979	19
Points	Al Del Greco, 1998	136

INDIVIDUAL RECORDS—SINGLE GAME

Category	Name	Performance
Rushing (Yds.)	Billy Cannon, 12-10-61	216
	Eddie George, 8-31-97	216
Passing (Yds.)	Warren Moon, 12-16-90	527
Passing (TDs)	George Blanda, 11-19-61	*7
Receiving (No.)	Charley Hennigan, 10-13-61	13
	Haywood Jeffires, 10-13-91	13
Receiving (Yds.)	Charley Hennigan, 10-13-61	272
Interceptions	Many times.	3
	Last time by Samari Rolle, 12-26-99	
Field Goals	Roy Gerela, 9-28-69	5
	Al Del Greco, 12-3-00	5
Touchdowns (Tot.)	Billy Cannon, 12-10-61	5
Points	Billy Cannon, 12-10-61	30

*NFL Record

ADELPHIA COLISEUM

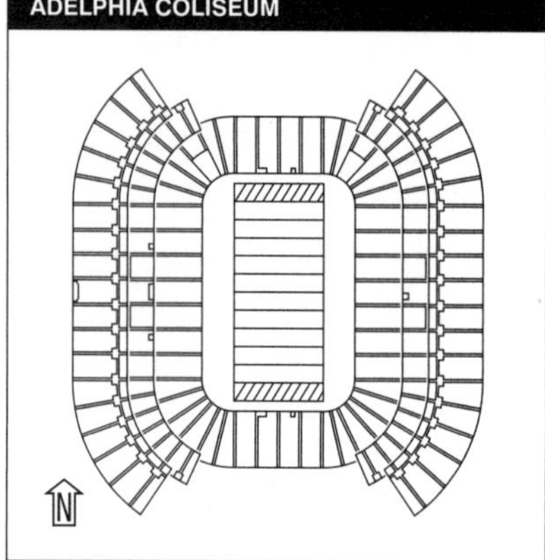

COACHING HISTORY

HOUSTON 1960-1996
(305-328-6)

1960-61	Lou Rymkus*	12-7-1
1961	Wally Lemm	10-0-0
1962-63	Frank (Pop) Ivy	17-12-0
1964	Sammy Baugh	4-10-0
1965	Hugh Taylor	4-10-0
1966-1970	Wally Lemm	28-40-4
1971	Ed Hughes	4-9-1
1972-73	Bill Peterson**	1-18-0
1973-74	Sid Gillman	8-15-0
1975-1980	O.A. (Bum) Phillips	59-38-0
1981-83	Ed Biles***	8-23-0
1983	Chuck Studley	2-8-0
1984-85	Hugh Campbell****	8-22-0
1985-89	Jerry Glanville	35-35-0
1990-94	Jack Pardee#	44-35-0
1994-2000	Jeff Fisher	61-46-0

* Released after five games in 1961
** Released after five games in 1973
*** Resigned after six games in 1983
**** Released after 14 games in 1985
# Released after 10 games in 1994

2000 TEAM RECORD

PRESEASON (3-1)

Date	Result		Opponent
8/5	W	14-10	Kansas City
8/14	W	30-3	St. Louis
8/18	L	32-34	at Philadelphia
8/25	W	34-28	at Chicago

REGULAR SEASON (13-3)

Date	Result		Opponent	Att.
9/3	L	13-16	at Buffalo	77,492
9/10	W	17-14	Kansas City (OT)	68,203
9/24	W	23-20	at Pittsburgh	51,769
10/1	W	28-14	New York Giants	68,341
10/8	W	23-14	at Cincinnati	63,406
10/16	W	27-13	Jacksonville	68,498
10/22	W	14-6	at Baltimore	69,200
10/30	W	27-21	at Washington	83,472
11/5	W	9-7	Pittsburgh	68,498
11/12	L	23-24	Baltimore	68,490
11/19	W	24-10	Cleveland	68,498
11/26	L	13-16	at Jacksonville	65,454
12/3	W	15-13	at Philadelphia	65,639
12/10	W	35-3	Cincinnati	68,498
12/17	W	24-0	at Cleveland	72,318
12/25	W	31-0	Dallas	68,498

(OT) Overtime

POSTSEASON (0-1)

Date	Result		Opponent	Att.
1/7	L	10-24	Baltimore	68,527

SCORE BY PERIODS

Titans	65	111	75	92	3	—	346
Opponents	36	50	30	75	0	—	191

ATTENDANCE

Home 536,723 Away 548,440 Total 1,085,163

Single-game home record, 68,498 (five times: last, 12/25/00)

Single-season home record, 536,723 (2000)

2000 TEAM STATISTICS

	Titans	Opp.
Total First Downs	299	215
Rushing	107	62
Passing	167	134
Penalty	25	19
Third Down: Made/Att	97/228	68/221
Third Down Pct.	42.5	30.8
Fourth Down: Made/Att	4/11	1/12
Fourth Down Pct.	36.4	8.3
Total Net Yards	5,350	3,813
Avg. Per Game	334.4	238.3
Total Plays	1,036	908
Avg. Per Play	5.2	4.2
Net Yards Rushing	2,084	1,390
Avg. Per Game	130.3	86.9
Total Rushes	547	387
Net Yards Passing	3,266	2,423
Avg. Per Game	204.1	151.4
Sacked/Yards Lost	27/164	55/338
Gross Yards	3,430	2,761
Att./Completions	462/286	466/242
Completion Pct.	61.9	51.9
Had Intercepted	16	17
Punts/Average	76/40.8	105/42.7
Net Punting Avg.	76/36.3	105/35.0
Penalties/Yards	107/870	97/778
Fumbles/Ball Lost	24/14	39/13
Touchdowns	38	20
Rushing	14	7
Passing	18	10
Returns	6	3
Avg. Time of Possession	33:48	26:12

2000 INDIVIDUAL STATISTICS

Passing	Att.	Comp.	Yds.	Pct.	TD	Int.	Tkld.	Rate
McNair	396	248	2,847	62.6	15	13	24/141	83.2
O'Donnell	64	36	530	56.3	2	3	3/23	74.3
Wycheck	2	2	53	100.0	1	0	0/0	158.3
Titans	462	286	3,430	61.9	18	16	27/164	83.2
Opponents	466	242	2,761	51.9	10	17	55/338	62.0

SCORING	TD R	TD P	TD Rt	PAT	FG	Saf	PTS
Del Greco	0	0	0	37/38	27/33	0	118
George	14	2	0	0/0	0/0	0	96
Mason	0	5	1	0/0	0/0	0	36
Wycheck	0	4	0	0/0	0/0	0	24
Neal	0	2	0	0/0	0/0	0	12
Thigpen	0	2	0	0/0	0/0	0	12
Bulluck	0	0	1	0/0	0/0	0	6
Dyson	0	1	0	0/0	0/0	0	6
Ford	0	0	1	0/0	0/0	0	6
Godfrey	0	0	1	0/0	0/0	0	6
Kinney	0	1	0	0/0	0/0	0	6
Phenix	0	0	1	0/0	0/0	0	6
Rolle	0	0	1	0/0	0/0	0	6
Thomas	0	1	0	0/0	0/0	0	6
Hentrich	0	0	0	0/0	0/1	0	0
Titans	14	18	6	37/38	27/34	0	346
Opponents	7	10	3	20/20	17/22	0	191

2-Pt. Conversions: None.
Titans 0-0, Opponents 0-0.

RUSHING	Att.	Yds.	Avg.	LG	TD
George	403	1,509	3.7	35t	14
McNair	72	403	5.6	25	0
Thomas	61	175	2.9	20	0
Mason	1	1	1.0	1	0
Neal	1	-2	-2.0	-2	0
O'Donnell	9	-2	-.2	4	0
Titans	547	2,084	3.8	35t	14
Opponents	387	1,390	3.6	80t	7

RECEIVING	No.	Yds.	Avg.	LG	TD
Wycheck	70	636	9.1	26	4
Mason	63	895	14.2	34	5
George	50	453	9.1	24	2
Sanders	33	536	16.2	54	0
Kinney	19	197	10.4	19	1
Thigpen	15	289	19.3	56t	2
Pickens	10	242	24.2	67	0
Neal	9	31	3.4	8	2
Thomas	8	35	4.4	9t	1
Dyson	6	104	17.3	30t	1
Roan	3	12	4.0	6	0
Titans	286	3,430	12.0	67	18
Opponents	242	2,761	11.4	48	10

INTERCEPTIONS	No.	Yds.	Avg.	LG	TD
Rolle	7	140	20.0	81t	1
Sidney	3	19	6.3	19	0
Godfrey	2	25	12.5	24t	1
D. Walker	2	4	2.0	4	0
Phenix	1	87	87.0	87t	1
Bulluck	1	8	8.0	8t	1
Booker	1	2	2.0	2	0
Titans	17	285	16.8	87t	4
Opponents	16	236	14.8	42t	3

PUNTING	No.	Yds.	Avg.	In 20	LG
Hentrich	76	3,101	40.8	33	67
Titans	76	3,101	40.8	33	67
Opponents	105	4,484	42.7	30	64

PUNT RETURNS	No.	FC	Yds.	Avg.	LG	TD
Mason	51	17	662	13.0	69t	1
Thigpen	1	1	9	9.0	9	0
D. Walker	1	0	0	0.0	0	0
Titans	53	18	671	12.7	69t	1
Opponents	28	21	160	5.7	20	0

KICKOFF RETURNS	No.	Yds.	Avg.	LG	TD
Mason	42	1,132	27.0	66	0
Coleman	2	54	27.0	27	0
Leach	1	10	10.0	10	0
Neal	1	15	15.0	15	0
Thornton	1	16	16.0	16	0
Titans	47	1,227	26.1	66	0
Opponents	76	1,587	20.9	38	0

FIELD GOALS	1-19	20-29	30-39	40-49	50+
Del Greco	0/0	13/15	7/8	6/9	1/1
Hentrich	0/0	0/0	0/0	0/0	0/1
Titans	0/0	13/15	7/8	6/9	1/2
Opponents	0/0	5/5	6/8	6/7	0/2

SACKS	No.
Kearse	11.5
Holmes	8.0
Favors	5.5
Robinson	4.0
Salave'a	4.0
Thornton	4.0
Embray	3.5
Godfrey	3.0
Bishop	2.5
Smith	2.5
Fisk	2.0
Ford	2.0
Rolle	1.5
Killens	1.0
Titans	55.0
Opponents	27.0

2001 DRAFT CHOICES

Round	Name	Pos.	College
2	Andre Dyson	DB	Utah
3	Shad Meier	TE	Kansas State
4	Justin McCareins	WR	Northern Illinois
5	Eddie Berlin	WR	Northern Iowa
6	Dan Alexander	RB	Nebraska
	Adam Haayer	T	Minnesota
7	Keith Adams	LB	Clemson

TENNESSEE TITANS

2001 VETERAN ROSTER

No.		Name	Pos.	Ht.	Wt.	Birthdate	NFL Exp.	College	Hometown	How Acq.	'00 Games/ Starts
23		Bishop, Blaine	S	5-9	203	7/24/70	9	Ball State	Indianapolis, Ind.	D8-'93	16/16
33	#	Booker, Michael	CB	6-2	200	4/27/75	5	Nebraska	Oceanside, Calif.	FA-'00	15/0
53		Bulluck, Keith	LB	6-3	232	4/4/77	2	Syracuse	New City, N.Y.	D1-'00	16/1
93	t-	Carter, Kevin	DE	6-5	280	9/21/73	7	Florida	Tallahassee, Fla.	T(StL)-'01	16/13*
57		Chamberlin, Frank	LB	6-1	250	1/2/78	2	Boston College	Mahwah, N.J.	D5b-'00	12/0
80		Coleman, Chris	WR	6-0	202	5/8/77	2	North Carolina State	Murphy, N.C.	FA-'00	13/0
66	†	Dinapoli, Genarro	G	6-3	295	5/25/75	4	Virginia Tech	Manhasset, N.Y.	T(Oak)-'00	0*
87		Dyson, Kevin	WR	6-1	201	6/23/75	4	Utah	Clearfield, Utah	D1-'98	2/2
96		Embray, Keith	DE	6-4	265	11/29/70	2	Utah	San Diego, Calif.	FA-'00	14/0
91		Evans, Josh	DT-DE	6-2	288	9/6/72	6	Alabama-Birmingham	West Shawmut, ALa.	FA-'95	0*
51		Favors, Greg	LB	6-1	244	9/30/74	4	Mississippi State	Atlanta, Ga.	W(KC)-'99	16/16
97		Fisk, Jason	DT	6-3	295	9/4/72	7	Stanford	Davis, Calif.	UFA(Minn)-'99	15/15
92		Ford, Henry	DT	6-3	295	10/30/71	8	Arkansas	Fort Worth, Texas	D1-'94	14/3
99		Frisch, Byron	DE	6-5	267	12/17/76	2	Brigham Young	Bonita, Calif.	D3b-'00	0*
27		George, Eddie	RB	6-3	240	9/24/73	6	Ohio State	Philadelphia, Pa.	D1-'96	16/16
56		Godfrey, Randall	LB	6-2	245	4/6/73	6	Georgia	Valdosta, Ga.	UFA(Dall)-'00	16/16
20		Green, Mike	RB	6-0	249	9/2/76	2	Houston	Houston, Texas	D7a-'00	1/0
15		Hentrich, Craig	P-K	6-3	205	5/18/71	8	Notre Dame	Alton, Ill.	UFA(GB)-'98	16/0
72		Hopkins, Brad	T	6-3	305	9/5/70	9	Illinois	Moline, Ill.	D1-'93	15/15
90		Kearse, Jevon	DE	6-4	265	9/3/76	3	Florida	Fort Myers, Fla.	D1-'99	16/16
88		Kinney, Erron	TE	6-5	272	7/28/77	2	Florida	Ashland, Va.	D3a-'00	16/10
83		Leach, Mike	TE	6-4	238	10/18/76	2	William & Mary	Lake Hopatcong, N.J.	FA-'00	15/0
60	†	Long, Kevin	C	6-5	295	5/2/75	4	Florida State	Summerville, S.C.	D7-'98	16/16
85		Mason, Derrick	WR	5-10	188	1/17/74	5	Michigan State	Detroit, Mich.	D4a-'97	16/12
76		Mathews, Jason	T	6-5	304	2/9/71	8	Texas A&M	Orange, Texas	FA-'98	16/1
74		Matthews, Bruce	G-C	6-5	305	8/8/61	19	Southern California	Arcadia, Calif.	D1-'83	16/16
40		McLemore, Brandon	S	6-3	205	5/2/77	2	Oregon	Torrance, Calif.	FA-'00	0*
9		McNair, Steve	QB	6-2	225	2/14/73	7	Alcorn State	Mt. Olive, Miss.	D1-'95	16/15
71		Miller, Fred	T	6-7	315	2/6/73	6	Baylor	Houston, Texas	UFA(StL)-'00	16/16
30		Mitchell, Donald	CB	5-9	185	12/14/76	3	Southern Methodist	Beaumont, Texas	D4b-'99	0*
28		Morris, Aric	S	5-10	208	7/22/77	2	Michigan State	Oak Park, Mich.	D5a-'00	15/0
32		Myers, Bobby	S	6-1	189	11/10/76	2	Wisconsin	Hamden, Conn.	D4a-'00	16/1
6		Nedney, Joe	K	6-5	220	3/22/73	6	San Jose State	San Jose, Calif.	UFA(Car)-'01	15/0*
14		O'Donnell, Neil	QB	6-3	228	7/3/66	12	Maryland	Madison, N.J.	UFA(Cin)-'99	6/1
75	†	Olson, Benji	G	6-3	315	6/5/75	4	Washington	Port Orchard, Wash.	D5-'98	16/16
35	†	Phenix, Perry	S	5-11	210	11/14/74	4	Southern Mississippi	Dallas, Texas	FA-'98	16/0
69		Piller, Zach	G	6-5	330	5/2/76	3	Florida	Tallahassee, Fla.	D3-'99	16/0
55		Robinson, Eddie	LB	6-1	243	4/13/70	10	Alabama State	New Orleans, La.	FA-'98	16/16
21	†	Rolle, Samari	CB	6-0	175	8/10/76	4	Florida State	Miami, Fla.	D2-'98	15/15
95		Salave'a, Joe	DT	6-3	290	3/23/75	4	Arizona	San Diego, Calif.	D4-'98	15/1
81		Sanders, Chris	WR	6-1	188	5/8/72	7	Ohio State	Denver, Colo.	D3a-'95	16/14
73	#	Sanderson, Scott	G-T	6-6	295	7/25/74	5	Washington State	Concord, Calif.	D3b-'97	9/0
37	†	Sidney, Dainon	CB	6-0	188	5/30/75	4	Alabama-Birmingham	Atlanta, Ga.	D3-'98	11/2
59		Sirmon, Peter	LB	6-2	246	2/18/77	2	Oregon	Walla Walla, Wash.	D4b-'00	5/0
98		Smith, Robaire	DE-DT	6-4	271	11/15/77	2	Michigan State	Flint, Mich.	D6-'00	8/0
78		Thornton, John	DT	6-2	295	10/2/76	3	West Virginia	Philadelphia, Pa.	D2-'99	16/16
12		Volek, Billy	QB	6-2	210	4/28/76	2	Fresno State	Fresno, Calif.	FA-'00	0*
89		Wycheck, Frank	TE	6-3	250	10/14/71	9	Maryland	Philadelphia, Pa.	W(Wash)-'95	16/16

* Carter played 16 games with St. Louis in '00; DiNapoli and Frisch were inactive for 16 games; Evans last active with Tennessee in '99; McLemore and Mitchell missed '00 season because of injury; Nedney played 3 games with Denver and 12 with Carolina; Volek was inactive for 15 games.

† Restricted free agent; subject to developments.

Unrestricted free agent; subject to developments.

t- Titans traded for Carter (St. Louis).

Players lost through free agency (2): DE Kenny Holmes (NYG; 14 games in '00), CB Denard Walker (Den; 15).

Also played with Titans in '00—K Al Del Greco (16 games), CB Ty Howard (1), WR Chris Jackson (1), LB Terry Killens (16), CB George McCullough (10), FB Lorenzo Neal (16), WR Carl Pickens (9), TE Michael Roan (1), S Marcus Robertson (15), WR Yancey Thigpen (12), RB Rodney Thomas (16), WR Bashir Yamini (5).

COACHING STAFF

Head Coach,
Jeff Fisher

Pro Career: Became the franchise's fifteenth head coach on January 5, 1995 after closing his first campaign as head coach/defensive coordinator. He replaced Jack Pardee on November 14, 1994, serving the remaining six games as head coach. Throughout the past two seasons, Fisher has led the Titans to an NFL-best 26-6 regular-season mark, an AFC Championship in 1999, and an AFC Central Division title in 2000. He also owns the franchise record for wins by a head coach (61), surpassing Bum Phillips last season, and is the fourth youngest NFL coach (since 1960) to reach the 50-win plateau. Last season, Fisher became only the fifth coach in NFL history to lead his team to consecutive 13-win seasons, joining Mike Holmgren, George Seifert, Marv Levy, and Mike Ditka. Fisher originally joined the Oilers in 1994 as the defensive coordinator after serving as defensive backs coach for the San Francisco 49ers (1992-93). Prior to heading up the 49ers' secondary, Fisher served as the defensive coordinator for the Los Angeles Rams (1991). He began his coaching career with the Philadelphia Eagles in 1986, where he handled defensive backs until becoming the NFL's youngest defensive coordinator in 1988. Drafted by Chicago in the seventh round in 1981, he spent five seasons as a cornerback and kick returner for the Bears (1981-85). Assisted defensive coordinator Buddy Ryan in Bears' 1985 Super Bowl championship season after being placed on injured reserve with ankle injury. Career record: 61-46.

Background: Played at Southern California (1977-1980) for John Robinson in a star-studded defensive backfield that included Ronnie Lott, Dennis Smith, and Joey Browner. Member of the USC team that won the national championship in 1978. Also served as the Trojans' backup placekicker and was a Pac-10 All-Academic selection in 1980.

Personal: Born February 25, 1958, in Culver City, Calif. Jeff and his wife, Juli, have three children, sons Brandon and Trenton, and daughter Tara. The family resides in Franklin, Tenn.

ASSISTANT COACHES

Chuck Cecil, defensive assistant-quality control; born November 8, 1964, Red Bluff, Calif., lives in Nashville. Defensive back Arizona 1983-87. Pro safety Green Bay Packers 1988-1992, Phoenix Cardinals 1993, Houston Oilers 1995. Pro coach: Joined Titans in 2001.

Gunther Cunningham, asst. head coach-linebackers; born June 19, 1946, Munich, Germany, lives in Nashville. Linebacker-placekicker Oregon 1966-68. No pro playing experience. College coach: Oregon 1969-1971, Arkansas 1972, Stanford 1973, California 1977-1980. Pro coach: Hamilton Tiger-Cats (CFL) 1981, Baltimore-Indianapolis Colts 1982-84, San Diego Chargers 1985-1990, Los Angeles Raiders 1991-94, Kansas City Chiefs 1995-2000 (head coach 1999-2000), joined Titans in 2001.

Mike Heimerdinger, offensive coordinator; born October 13, 1952, DeKalb, Ill., lives in Brentwood, Tenn. Wide receiver Eastern Illinois 1970-74. No pro playing experience. College coach: Florida 1980, Air Force 1981, North Texas State 1982, Florida 1983-87, Cal State-Fullerton 1988, Rice 1989-1993, Duke 1994. Pro coach: Denver Broncos 1995-99, joined Titans in 2000.

George Henshaw, asst. head coach; born January 22, 1948, Richmond, Va., lives in Nashville. Defensive tackle West Virginia 1967-69. No pro playing experience. College coach: West Virginia 1970-75, Florida State 1976-1982, Alabama 1983-86, Tulsa 1987 (head coach). Pro coach: Denver Broncos 1988-1992, New York Giants 1993-96, joined Titans/Oilers in 1997.

Craig Johnson, offensive assistant-quality control; born March 3, 1960, Rome, N.Y., lives in Nashville. Quarterback Wyoming 1978-1982. No pro playing experience. College coach: Wyoming 1983, Arkansas 1984, Army 1985, Rutgers 1986-88, Virginia Military Institute 1989-1991, Northwestern 1992-96, Maryland 1997-99. Pro coach: Joined Titans in 2000.

Alan Lowry, special teams; born November 21, 1950, Miami, Okla., lives in Franklin, Tenn. Defensive back-quarterback Texas 1970-72. No pro playing experience. College coach: Virginia Tech 1974, Wyoming 1975, Texas 1977-1981. Pro coach: Dallas Cowboys 1982-1990, Tampa Bay Buccaneers 1991, San Francisco 49ers 1992-95, joined Titans/Oilers in 1996.

Mike Munchak, offensive line; born March 5, 1960, Scranton, Pa., lives in Brentwood, Tenn. Guard-tackle Penn State 1979-1981. Pro guard Houston Oilers 1982-1993. Pro coach: Joined Titans/Oilers in 1994.

Jim Schwartz, defensive coordinator; born June 2, 1966, Baltimore, lives in Nashville. Linebacker Georgetown 1984-88. No pro playing experience. College coach: Maryland 1989, Minnesota 1990, North Carolina Central 1991, Colgate 1992. Pro coach: Cleveland Browns/Baltimore Ravens 1995-98, joined Titans in 1999.

Sherman Smith, running backs; born November 1, 1954, Youngstown, Ohio, lives in Franklin, Tenn. Quarterback Miami (Ohio) 1972-75. Pro running back Seattle Seahawks 1976-1982, San Diego Chargers 1983-84. College coach: Miami (Ohio) 1990-91, Illinois 1992-94. Pro coach: Joined Titans/Oilers in 1995.

Steve Walters, wide receivers; born June 16, 1948, Jonesboro, Ark., lives in Nashville. Quarterback-defensive back Arkansas 1967-1970. No pro playing experience. College coach: Tampa 1973, Northeastern Louisana 1974-75, Morehead State 1976, Tulsa 1977-78, Memphis State 1979, Southern Methodist 1980-81, Alabama 1985. Pro coach: New England Patriots 1982-84, 1997-98, New Orleans 1986-1996, joined Titans in 1999.

Jim Washburn, defensive line; born December 2, 1949, Shelby, N.C., lives in Nashville. Offensive lineman Gardner-Webb 1969-1973. No pro playing experience. College coach: Southern Methodist 1976, Lees McRae J.C. 1977-78, Livingston 1979, New Mexico 1980-82, South Carolina 1983-88, Purdue 1989, Arkansas 1994-97, Houston 1998. Pro coach: London Monarchs (WLAF) 1991, Charlotte Rage (AFL) 1993, joined Titans in 1999.

Steve Watterson, strength and rehabilitation; born November 27, 1956, Newport, R.I., lives in Brentwood, Tenn. Attended Rhode Island. No college or pro playing experience. Pro coach: Philadelphia Eagles 1984-85, joined Titans/Oilers in 1986.

Everett Withers, defensive backs; born June 15, 1963, Charlotte, lives in Nashville. Defensive back Appalachian State 1981-85. No pro playing experience. College coach: Austin Peay 1988-1990, Tulane 1991, Southern Mississippi 1992-93, Louisville 1995-97, Texas 1998-2000. Pro coach: New Orleans Saints 1994, joined Titans in 2001.

2001 FIRST-YEAR ROSTER

Name	Pos.	Ht.	Wt.	Birthdate	College	Hometown	How Acq.
Adams, Keith	LB	5-11	223	11/22/79	Clemson	College Park, Ga.	D7
Alexander, Dan	RB	6-0	244	3/17/78	Nebraska	Wentzville, Mo.	D6a
Arp, Donovan	DT	6-3	285	1/12/78	Louisville	Salt Lake City, Utah	FA
Barnes, Leo	S	6-0	182	6/2/79	Southern Mississippi	Hattiesburg, Miss.	FA
Bartholomew, Rashad	RB	6-0	215	7/30/78	Yale	Palos Verdes, Calif.	FA
Bennett, Andrew	WR	6-5	203	8/26/78	UCLA	Orinde, Calif.	FA
Berlin, Eddie	WR	5-11	186	1/14/78	Northern Iowa	Urbandale, Iowa	D5
Cheetany, Ray	K-P	5-11	180	12/12/77	Nevada-Las Vegas	Cedar Rapids, Iowa	FA
Chukwuma, Chrys (1)	RB	6-0	232	5/12/78	Arkansas	Montgomery, Ala.	FA
Diehl, Reed	G	6-4	300	9/18/78	California	Irvine, Calif.	FA
Dyson, Andre	CB	5-10	177	5/25/79	Utah	Clearfield, Utah	D2
Haayer, Adam	T	6-6	305	2/22/77	Minnesota	Wyoming, Minn.	D6b
Hall, Barry	T	6-6	315	11/23/77	Middle Tennessee State	Fairmount, Ga.	FA
Johnson, Shawn	LB	6-1	230	9/2/77	Mississippi	Brewton, Ala.	FA
Lorenti, Chris	C	6-5	320	1/11/78	Central Florida	South Daytona, Fla.	FA
Marsh, Dante	CB	5-10	190	2/26/79	Fresno State	Oakland, Calif.	FA
McCareins, Justin	WR	6-2	200	12/11/78	Northern Illinois	Naperville, Ill.	D4
Meier, Shad	TE	6-4	250	6/7/78	Kansas State	Pittsburg, Kan.	D3
Neal, Steve	WR	6-1	188	2/17/77	Western Michigan	Benton Harbor, Mich.	FA
Paul, Larry	DE	6-3	258	2/14/78	North Alabama	Moody, Ala.	FA
Redmond, Jimmy	WR	6-0	188	8/18/77	McNeese State	Kansas City, Mo.	FA
Sanders, Chris	QB	6-1	215	12/22/77	Tennessee-Chattanooga	Flower Mound, Texas	FA
Snelling, Robby	TE	6-2	252	8/14/78	Boise State	Burney, Calif.	FA
Snowden, Michael	WR	6-3	212	11/23/77	Arkansas	Newellton, Calif.	FA
Spencer, Marcus	S	6-1	211	2/15/78	Alabama	Sumter, Ala.	FA
Thomas, Juqua	DE	6-2	249	5/15/78	Oklahoma State	Houston, Texas	FA
Tucker, Marshaun	WR	5-10	184	10/6/79	Oregon	Chula Vista, Calif.	FA
Valletta, Chris	G	6-3	300	3/1/78	Texas A&M	Plano, Texas	FA
Walker, Joe	S	5-10	195	3/19/77	Nebraska	Arlington, Texas	FA
Walker, Rod (1)	DT	6-3	330	2/4/76	Troy State	Milton, Fla.	FA

The term NFL Rookie is defined as a player who is in his first season of professional football and has not been on the roster of another professional football team for any regular-season or postseason games. A Rookie is designated by an "R" on NFL rosters. Players who have been active in another professional football league or players who have NFL experience, including either preseason training camp or being on an Active List or Inactive List, or on Reserve/Injured or Reserve/Physically Unable to Perform for fewer than six regular-season games, are termed NFL First-Year Players. An NFL First-Year Player is designated by a "1" on NFL rosters. Thereafter, a player is credited with an additional year of experience for each season in which he accumulates six games on the Active List or Inactive List, or on Reserve/Injured or Reserve/Physically Unable to Perform.

NOTES

HOUSTON TEXANS

HOUSTON TEXANS

American Football Conference
Team Colors: Battle Red, Deep Steel Blue, and Liberty White
711 Louisiana Street
Suite 3300
Houston, Texas 77002
Telephone: (713) 336-7700

CLUB OFFICIALS

Chairman, President, and CEO: Robert C. McNair
Vice Chairman: Philip Burguieres
Senior Vice President and General Manager, Football Operations: Charley Casserly
Senior Vice President and Chief Development Officer: Steve Patterson
Senior Vice President and Chief Sales & Marketing Officer: Jamey Rootes
Senior Vice President, Treasurer, and Chief Financial Officer: Scott Schwinger
Senior Vice President, General Counsel, and Chief Administrative Officer: Suzie Thomas
Vice President/Corporate Sales: David Peart
Vice President/Communications: Tony Wyllie
Controller: Marilan Logan
Director of Pro Scouting: Chuck Banker
Associate Directors of Pro Scouting: Bobby Grier, Miller McCalmon
Pro Scouting Assistant: Rob Kisiel
Coordinator of College Scouting: Mike Maccagnan
National Scout: George Saimes
College Scouts: Larry Bryan, Don Deisch, Ralph Hawkins, Joel Patten, Pete Russell, Dave Sears
BLESTO Scout: Tom Throckmorton
College Scouting Assistant: Jamaal Stephenson
Director of Operations: Barry Asimos
Director of Marketing: Kim Babiak
Director of Security: Ryan Reichert
Director of Ticket Operations: John Schriever
Director of Corporate Sales: Patrick Streko
Director of Internet Services & Publications: Carter Toole
Human Resources Administrator: Glenda Morrison
Head Athletic Trainer: Kevin Bastin
Equipment Director: Jay Brunetti
Manager of Player Information: Tom Halligan
Stadium: Reliant Stadium (built in 2002)
•**Capacity:** 69,500
Houston, Texas 77054
Playing Surface: Grass
Training Camp: TBA

IMPORTANT DATES

December 15, 2001—Begin signing free agents.
February 18, 2002—Expansion draft.

COACHING STAFF

Head Coach
Dom Capers
Pro Career: The Texans introduced Capers as their first head coach on January 21, 2001. Capers served as the defensive coordinator for the Jacksonville Jaguars the past two seasons. Prior to his stint in Jacksonville, he spent four seasons (1995-98) as head coach of the Carolina Panthers, guiding that expansion franchise from its infancy to a playoff berth in its second season. Capers compiled a 31-35 record in four seasons as the Panthers' head coach. In 1995, the Panthers' 7-9 record set an NFL mark for most victories by an expansion team. Carolina also posted the first four-game winning streak in expansion history, the first winning home record by an expansion club, and the first win over a defending Super Bowl champion (San Francisco) in expansion annals. In 1996, the Panthers shook up the league by winning their final seven regular-season games, resulting in a 12-4 record and the NFC West title. Carolina then defeated defending Super Bowl champion Dallas in the divisional playoffs before losing to Green Bay in the NFC Championship Game at Lambeau Field. Capers was named Coach of the Year by the *Associated Press,* among numerous other honors. The Panthers posted records of 7-9 and 4-12 the next two seasons, resulting in Capers' dismissal. The Jaguars signed him six weeks later, and the hiring paid immediate dividends. Under Capers, the Jaguars improved from twenty-fifth in the NFL in total defense in 1998 to fourth in 1999. Jacksonville also yielded the fewest points (217) in the NFL, an average of 13.6 points per game. Capers cut his NFL teeth in 1984 with current Colts head coach Jim Mora. After winning two USFL titles with the Philadelphia/Baltimore Stars, Mora accepted the Saints' head coaching position in 1986 and brought Capers along with him as defensive backs coach. Capers served in that capacity through the 1991 season, helping the Saints to the first three postseason berths in franchise history. Capers then accepted the defensive coordinator's post with the Pittsburgh Steelers, helping the team win two AFC Central titles. In his three seasons with the Steelers, no team in the NFL yielded fewer points. Capers began his coaching career in 1972 at Kent State, where he was a graduate assistant for three seasons while earning a master's degree in administration. In 1975 he served as a graduate assistant at the University of Washington. Capers became a full-time coach the following year, and then coached with Hawaii, San Jose State, California, Tennessee, and Ohio State. Career record: 31-35.
Background: Capers was a star athlete at Meadowbrook (Ohio) High School. He graduated with a degree in physical education and psychology from Mount Union College in 1972, where he played a combination of safety and linebacker.
Personal: Born August 7, 1950 in Cambridge, Ohio. Capers hosts an annual charity golf tournament in the Buffalo, Ohio, area, which has raised thousands of dollars for the American Heart Association. He and his wife Karen live in Houston.

ASSISTANT COACHES

Chris Palmer, offensive coordinator; born September 23, 1949, Brewster, N.Y., lives in Houston. Quarterback Southern Connecticut State 1968-1971. No pro playing experience. College coach: Connecticut 1972-74, Lehigh 1975, Colgate 1976-1982, New Haven 1986-87 (head coach), Boston 1988-89 (head coach). Pro coach: Montreal Concordes (CFL) 1983, New Jersey Generals (USFL) 1984-85, Houston Oilers 1990-92, New England Patriots 1993-96, Jacksonville Jaguars 1997-98, Cleveland Browns 1999-2000 (head coach), joined Texans in 2001.
Dan Riley, strength and conditioning; born October 19, 1949, Syracuse, N.Y., lives in Pearland, Texas. Attended Keene State. No college or pro playing experience. College coach: Army 1974-77, Penn State 1977-1981. Pro coach: Washington Redskins 1982-2000, joined Texans in 2001.

RELIANT STADIUM

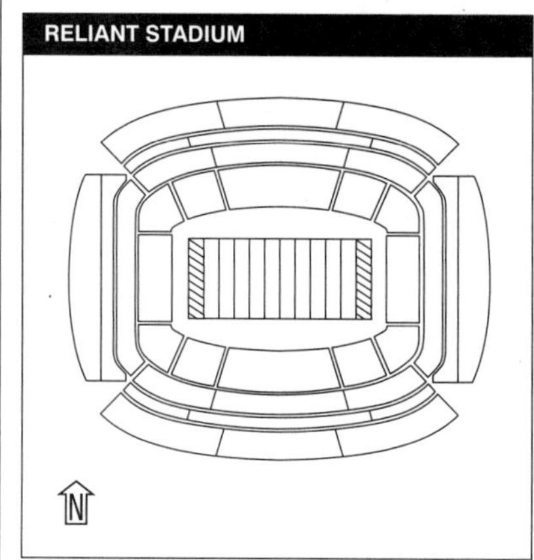

The NFC

ARIZONA CARDINALS

National Football Conference
Eastern Division
Team Colors: Cardinal Red, Black, and White
P.O. Box 888
Phoenix, Arizona 85001-0888
Telephone: (602) 379-0101

CLUB OFFICIALS

President: William V. Bidwill
Vice President: Nancy J. Bidwill
Vice President: Larry Wilson
Vice President: Nicole Bidwill
Vice Chairman: Thomas J. Guilfoil
Treasurer and Chief Financial Officer: Charley Schlegel
Vice President: William V. Bidwill, Jr.
Vice President/General Counsel: Michael Bidwill
Vice President/Sales and Marketing: Ron Minegar
General Manager: Bob Ferguson
Assistant to the President: Rod Graves
Public Relations Director: Paul Jensen
Media Coordinator: Greg Gladysiewski
Publications/Internet Coordinator: Luke Sacks
Director of Players Programs: Anthony Edwards
Director of Community Relations: Luis Zendejas
Director of Marketing and Promotions: Lisa Manning
Director of Corporate Sales: Joe Hickey
Director of Corporate and Broadcast Services: Joe Castor
Business Manager: Steve Walsh
Ticket Manager: Steve Bomar
Trainer: John Omohundro
Assistant Trainers: Jim Shearer, Jeff Herndon
Equipment Manager: Mark Ahlemeier
Assistant Equipment Manager: Steve Christensen
Stadium: Sun Devil Stadium (built in 1958)
•**Capacity:** 73,014
Fifth Street
Tempe, Arizona 85287
Playing Surface: Grass
Training Camp: Northern Arizona University
Flagstaff, Arizona 86011

2001 SCHEDULE

PRESEASON

Aug. 11	**Oakland**	8:00
Aug. 18	at Seattle	6:30
Aug. 25	at Chicago	7:00
Aug. 31	**San Diego**	7:00

REGULAR SEASON

Sept. 9	Open Date	
Sept. 16	at Washington	1:00
Sept. 23	**Denver**	5:30
Sept. 30	**Atlanta**	1:05
Oct. 7	at Philadelphia	1:00
Oct. 14	at Chicago	12:00
Oct. 21	**Kansas City**	1:05
Oct. 28	at Dallas	3:05
Nov. 4	**Philadelphia**	2:05
Nov. 11	**New York Giants**	2:15
Nov. 18	**Detroit**	2:15
Nov. 25	at San Diego	1:05
Dec. 2	at Oakland	1:15
Dec. 9	**Washington**	2:05
Dec. 15	at New York Giants (Sat.)	1:30
Dec. 23	**Dallas**	2:05
Dec. 30	at Carolina	1:00

RECORD HOLDERS

INDIVIDUAL RECORDS—CAREER

Category	Name	Performance
Rushing (Yds.)	Ottis Anderson, 1979-1986	7,999
Passing (Yds.)	Jim Hart, 1966-1983	34,639
Passing (TDs)	Jim Hart, 1966-1983	209
Receiving (No.)	Larry Centers, 1990-98	535
Receiving (Yds.)	Roy Green, 1979-1990	8,497
Interceptions	Larry Wilson, 1960-1972	52
Punting (Avg.)	Jerry Norton, 1959-1961	44.9
Punt Return (Avg.)	Charley Trippi, 1947-1955	13.7
Kickoff Return (Avg.)	Ollie Matson, 1952, 1954-58	28.5
Field Goals	Jim Bakken, 1962-1978	282
Touchdowns (Tot.)	Roy Green, 1979-1990	70
Points	Jim Bakken, 1962-1978	1,380

INDIVIDUAL RECORDS—SINGLE SEASON

Category	Name	Performance
Rushing (Yds.)	Ottis Anderson, 1979	1,605
Passing (Yds.)	Neil Lomax, 1984	4,614
Passing (TDs)	Charley Johnson, 1963	28
	Neil Lomax, 1984	28
Receiving (No.)	Larry Centers, 1995	101
Receiving (Yds.)	Rob Moore, 1997	1,584
Interceptions	Bob Nussbaumer, 1949	12
Punting (Avg.)	Jerry Norton, 1960	45.6
Punt Return (Avg.)	John (Red) Cochran, 1949	20.9
Kickoff Return (Avg.)	Ollie Matson, 1958	35.5
Field Goals	Greg Davis, 1995	30
Touchdowns (Tot.)	John David Crow, 1962	17
Points	Jim Bakken, 1967	117
	Neil O'Donoghue, 1984	117

INDIVIDUAL RECORDS—SINGLE GAME

Category	Name	Performance
Rushing (Yds.)	LeShon Johnson, 9-22-96	214
Passing (Yds.)	Boomer Esiason, 11-10-96 (OT)	522
Passing (TDs)	Jim Hardy, 10-2-50	6
	Charley Johnson, 9-26-65, 11-2-69	6
Receiving (No.)	Sonny Randle, 11-4-62	16
Receiving (Yds.)	Sonny Randle, 11-4-62	256
Interceptions	Bob Nussbaumer, 11-13-49	*4
	Jerry Norton, 11-20-60	*4
	Kwamie Lassiter, 12-27-98	*4
Field Goals	Jim Bakken, 9-24-67	*7
Touchdowns (Tot.)	Ernie Nevers, 11-28-29	*6
Points	Ernie Nevers, 11-28-29	*40

*NFL Record

COACHING HISTORY

Chicago 1920-1959, St. Louis 1960-1987
(428-598-39)

1920-22	John (Paddy) Driscoll	17-8-4
1923-24	Arnold Horween	13-8-1
1925-26	Norman Barry	16-8-2
1927	Guy Chamberlin	3-7-1
1928	Fred Gillies	1-5-0
1929	Dewey Scanlon	6-6-1
1930	Ernie Nevers	5-6-2
1931	LeRoy Andrews*	0-1-0
1931	Ernie Nevers	5-3-0
1932	Jack Chevigny	2-6-2
1933-34	Paul Schissler	6-15-1
1935-38	Milan Creighton	16-26-4
1939	Ernie Nevers	1-10-0
1940-42	Jimmy Conzelman	8-22-3
1943-45	Phil Handler**	1-29-0
1946-48	Jimmy Conzelman	27-10-0
1949	Phil Handler-Buddy Parker***	2-4-0
1949	Raymond (Buddy) Parker	4-1-1
1950-51	Earl (Curly) Lambeau****	7-15-0
1951	Phil Handler-Cecil Isbell#	1-1-0
1952	Joe Kuharich	4-8-0
1953-54	Joe Stydahar	3-20-1
1955-57	Ray Richards	14-21-1
1958-1961	Frank (Pop) Ivy##	17-29-2
1961	Chuck Drulis-Ray Prochaska-Ray Willsey###	2-0-0
1962-65	Wally Lemm	27-26-3
1966-1970	Charley Winner	35-30-5
1971-72	Bob Hollway	8-18-2
1973-77	Don Coryell	42-29-1
1978-79	Bud Wilkinson####	9-20-0
1979	Larry Wilson	2-1-0
1980-85	Jim Hanifan	39-50-1
1986-89	Gene Stallings@	23-34-1
1989	Hank Kuhlmann	0-5-0
1990-93	Joe Bugel	20-44-0
1994-95	Buddy Ryan	12-20-0
1996-2000	Vince Tobin@@	29-44-0
2000	Dave McGinnis	1-8-0

* Resigned after one game in 1931
** Co-coach with Walt Kiesling in Chicago Cardinals-Pittsburgh merger in 1944
*** Co-coaches for first six games in 1949
**** Resigned after 10 games in 1951
# Co-coaches
Resigned after 12 games in 1961
Co-coaches
Released after 13 games in 1979
@ Released after 11 games in 1989
@@ Released after seven games in 2000

SUN DEVIL STADIUM

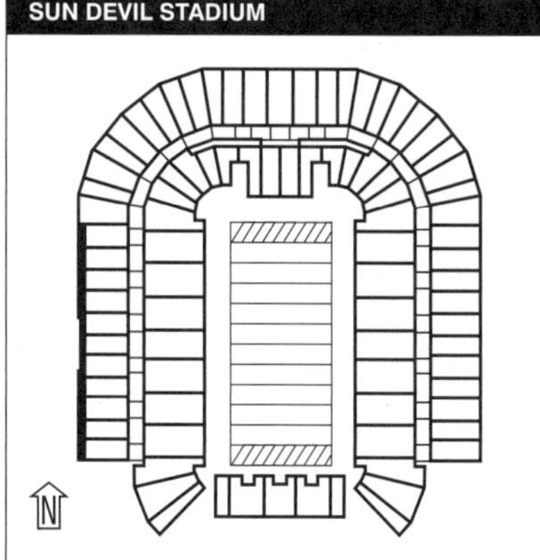

2000 TEAM RECORD

PRESEASON (1-3)

Date	Result		Opponent
8/5	L	17-31	Denver
8/12	W	21-3	Seattle
8/18	L	17-35	at Minnesota
8/25	L	20-24	at San Diego

REGULAR SEASON (3-13)

Date	Result		Opponent	Att.
9/3	L	16-21	at New York Giants	77,434
9/10	W	32-31	Dallas	58,303
9/24	L	3-29	Green Bay	69,568
10/1	L	20-27	at San Francisco	66,985
10/8	W	29-21	Cleveland	39,148
10/15	L	14-33	Philadelphia	36,590
10/22	L	7-48	at Dallas	62,981
10/29	L	10-21	New Orleans	35,016
11/5	W	16-15	Washington	44,723
11/12	L	14-31	at Minnesota	64,223
11/19	L	9-34	at Philadelphia	65,356
11/26	L	7-31	New York Giants	38,909
12/3	L	13-24	at Cincinnati	50,289
12/10	L	10-44	at Jacksonville	53,472
12/17	L	7-13	Baltimore	37,452
12/24	L	3-20	at Washington	65,711

SCORE BY PERIODS

Cardinals	30	48	57	75	0	—	210
Opponents	114	130	95	104	0	—	443

ATTENDANCE

Home 386,724 Away 530,473 Total 917,197
Single-game home record, 73,025 (9/19/93)
Single-season home record, 497,330 (1994)

2000 TEAM STATISTICS

	Cardinals	Opp.
Total First Downs	253	345
Rushing	71	149
Passing	156	175
Penalty	26	21
Third Down: Made/Att	75/199	105/222
Third Down Pct.	37.7	47.3
Fourth Down: Made/Att	8/27	10/15
Fourth Down Pct.	29.6	66.7
Total Net Yards	4,528	5,737
Avg. Per Game	283.0	358.6
Total Plays	932	1,062
Avg. Per Play	4.9	5.4
Net Yards Rushing	1,278	2,609
Avg. Per Game	79.9	163.1
Total Rushes	343	578
Net Yards Passing	3,250	3,128
Avg. Per Game	203.1	195.5
Sacked/Yards Lost	35/228	25/135
Gross Yards	3478	3263
Att./Completions	554/316	459/296
Completion Pct.	57.0	64.5
Had Intercepted	24	10
Punts/Average	65/44.2	59/41.1
Net Punting Avg.	65/37.3	59/35.2
Penalties/Yards	96/785	96/914
Fumbles/Ball Lost	32/20	17/10
Touchdowns	24	52
Rushing	6	29
Passing	16	19
Returns	2	4
Avg. Time of Possession	26:32	33:28

2000 INDIVIDUAL STATISTICS

Passing	Att.	Comp.	Yds.	Pct.	TD	Int.	Tkld.	Rating
Plummer	475	270	2,946	56.8	13	21	22/151	66.0
Da. Brown	69	40	467	58.0	2	3	10/53	70.1
Greisen	10	6	65	60.0	1	0	3/24	112.5
Player	0	0	0	—	—	—	0/0	—
Cardinals	554	316	3,478	57.0	16	24	35/228	67.4
Opponents	459	296	3,263	64.5	19	10	25/135	90.2

SCORING	TD R	TD P	TD Rt	PAT	FG	Saf	PTS
Blanchard	0	0	0	18/19	16/23	0	66
Boston	0	7	0	0/0	0/0	0	42
Pittman	4	2	0	0/0	0/0	0	36
Sanders	0	6	0	0/0	0/0	0	36
Jones	2	0	0	0/0	0/0	0	12
Hardy	0	1	0	0/0	0/0	0	6
Jenkins	0	0	1	0/0	0/0	0	6
A. Williams	0	0	1	0/0	0/0	0	6
Cardinals	6	16	2	18/19	16/23	0	210
Opponents	29	19	4	50/51	27/34	0	443

2-Pt. Conversions: None.
Cardinals 0-5, Opponents 0-1.

RUSHING	Att.	Yds.	Avg.	LG	TD
Pittman	184	719	3.9	29	4
Jones	112	373	3.3	29	2
Plummer	37	183	4.9	24	0
Boston	3	9	3.0	24	0
Makovicka	3	8	2.7	7	0
Greisen	1	1	1.0	1	0
Da. Brown	1	0	0.0	0	0
Jenkins	1	-4	-4.0	-4	0
Player	1	-11	-11.0	-11	0
Cardinals	343	1,278	3.7	29	6
Opponents	578	2,609	4.5	78t	29

RECEIVING	No.	Yds.	Avg.	LG	TD
Pittman	73	579	7.9	36t	2
Boston	71	1,156	16.3	70t	7
Sanders	54	749	13.9	53t	6
Jones	32	208	6.5	20	0
Hardy	27	160	5.9	13	1
Jenkins	17	219	12.9	34	0
Cody	17	212	12.5	24	0
Gedney	10	75	7.5	24	0
Makovicka	6	18	3.0	5	0
Mitchell	5	80	16.0	42	0
McKinley	2	13	6.5	9	0
C. Williams	1	5	5.0	5	0
Tant	1	4	4.0	4	0
Cardinals	316	3,478	11.0	70t	16
Opponents	296	3,263	11.0	65t	19

INTERCEPTIONS	No.	Yds.	Avg.	LG	TD
A. Williams	5	102	20.4	48	0
Tillman	1	30	30.0	27	0
Lassiter	1	11	11.0	11	0
Fredrickson	1	8	8.0	8	0
Chavous	1	0	0.0	0	0
Walz	1	0	0.0	0	0
Cardinals	10	151	15.1	48	0
Opponents	24	383	16.0	45	2

PUNTING	No.	Yds.	Avg.	In 20	LG
Player	65	2,871	44.2	17	55
Cardinals	65	2,871	44.2	17	55
Opponents	59	2,422	41.1	15	61

PUNT RETURNS	No.	FC	Yds.	Avg.	LG	TD
Cody	31	11	222	7.2	25	0
Jenkins	1	0	1	1.0	1	0
Cardinals	32	11	223	7.0	25	0
Opponents	37	18	347	9.4	64t	2

KICKOFF RETURNS	No.	Yds.	Avg.	LG	TD
Jenkins	82	2,186	26.7	98t	1
Bennett	1	17	17.0	17	0
Cody	1	18	18.0	18	0
McKinley	1	20	20.0	20	0
McKinnon	1	9	9.0	9	0
Barrett	0	46	—	41	0
Cardinals	86	2,296	26.7	98t	1
Opponents	46	827	18.0	40	0

FIELD GOALS	1-19	20-29	30-39	40-49	50+
Blanchard	1/1	2/2	9/11	2/5	2/4
Cardinals	1/1	2/2	9/11	2/5	2/4
Opponents	0/0	7/7	10/12	8/12	2/3

SACKS	No.
Rice	7.5
McKinnon	4.0
Smith	3.0
Folston	2.0
Maddox	1.5
Tillman	1.5
Fredrickson	1.0
Issa	1.0
Knight	1.0
Ottis	1.0
Wadsworth	1.0
Davis	0.5
Cardinals	25.0
Opponents	35.0

2001 DRAFT CHOICES

Round	Name	Pos.	College
1	Leonard Davis	T	Texas
2	Kyle Vanden Bosch	DE	Nebraska
	Michael Stone	DB	Memphis
3	Adrian Wilson	DB	North Carolina State
4	Bill Gramatica	K	South Florida
	Marcus Bell	DT	Memphis
5	Mario Fatafehi	DT	Kansas State
6	Bobby Newcombe	WR	Nebraska
7	Renaldo Hill	DB	Michigan State
	Tevita Ofahengaue	TE	Brigham Young

ARIZONA CARDINALS

2001 VETERAN ROSTER

No.	Name	Pos.	Ht.	Wt.	Birthdate	NFL Exp.	College	Hometown	How Acq.	'00 Games/ Starts
36	Barrett, David	CB	5-11	198	12/22/77	2	Arkansas	Osceola, Ark.	D4-'00	16/0
28	Bennett, Tommy	S	6-2	219	2/19/73	6	UCLA	San Diego, Calif.	FA-'96	10/0
15	Blanchard, Cary	K	6-1	232	11/5/68	10	Oklahoma State	Fort Worth, Texas	UFA(NYG)-'00	16/0
89	Boston, David	WR	6-2	210	8/19/78	3	Ohio State	Humble, Texas	D1a-'99	16/16
7	Brown, Dave	QB	6-5	230	2/25/70	10	Duke	Summit, N.J.	UFA(NYG)-'98	3/2
95	Burke, Thomas	DE	6-3	261	10/12/76	3	Wisconsin	Poplar, Wis.	D3-'99	2/0
25	Chavous, Corey	CB	6-0	204	1/15/76	4	Vanderbilt	Aiken, S.C.	D2a-'98	16/1
65	Clement, Anthony	T	6-7	355	4/10/76	4	Southwestern Louisiana	Lafayette, La.	D2b-'98	16/16
12	Cooper, Andre	WR	6-2	210	6/21/75	3	Florida State	Jacksonville, Fla.	FA-'01	0*
64	Davidds-Garrido, Norberto	T	6-5	315	6/11/72	6	Southern California	La Puente, Calif.	UFA(Car)-'00	9/2
98	Davis, Russell	DT	6-4	295	3/28/75	3	North Carolina	Fayetteville, N.C.	W(Chi)-'00	14/9
67	Dishman, Chris	G	6-3	320	2/27/74	5	Nebraska	Cozad, Neb.	D4-'97	13/11
58	Folston, James	LB	6-3	240	8/14/71	8	Northeast Louisiana	Cocoa, Fla.	FA-'99	12/2
59	Fredrickson, Rob	LB	6-4	240	5/13/71	8	Michigan State	St. Joseph, Mich.	UFA(Oak)-'99	12/11
60	Gruttadauria, Mike	C	6-3	297	12/6/72	6	Central Florida	Tarpon Springs, Fla.	UFA(StL)-'00	8/8
80	Hardy, Terry	TE	6-4	266	5/31/76	4	Southern Mississippi	Montgomery, Ala.	D5-'98	16/15
72	Issa, Jabari	DT-DE	6-5	302	4/18/78	2	Washington	Foster City, Calif.	D6-'00	11/0
19	Jenkins, Martay	WR	5-11	193	2/28/75	3	Nebraska-Omaha	Waterloo, Iowa	W(Dall)-'99	16/2
26	Jones, Thomas	RB	5-10	211	8/19/78	2	Virginia	Big Stone Gap, Va.	D1-'00	14/4
86	Junkin, Trey	LS-TE	6-2	258	1/23/61	19	Louisiana Tech	North Little Rock, Ark.	W(Oak)-'96	16/0
9	Keenan, Sean	QB	6-3	209	1/2/77	2	Williams College (Mass.)	Rutland, Vt.	FA-'00	0*
66	Kendall, Pete	G	6-5	292	7/9/73	6	Boston College	Weymouth, Mass.	UFA(Sea)-'01	16/16*
24	Knight, Tom	CB	5-11	196	12/29/74	5	Iowa	Marlton, N.J.	D1-'97	15/14
42	Lassiter, Kwamie	CB-S	6-0	202	12/3/69	7	Kansas	Newport News, Va.	FA-'95	16/16
41	Lucas, Justin	DB	5-10	187	7/15/76	3	Abilene Christian	Victoria, Texas	FA-'99	16/0
34	Makovicka, Joel	FB	5-11	246	10/6/75	3	Nebraska	Brainard, Neb.	D4-'99	14/10
39	McKinley, Dennis	FB	6-2	245	11/3/76	3	Mississippi State	Weir, Miss.	D6b-'99	16/0
57	McKinnon, Ronald	LB	6-0	240	9/20/73	6	North Alabama	Elba, Ala.	FA-'96	16/16
83	Mitchell, Tywan	TE	6-5	245	12/10/75	2	Minnesota State-Mankato	Crete, Ill.	FA-'99	11/1
85	Moore, Rob	WR	6-3	203	9/27/68	11	Syracuse	Hempstead, N.Y.	T(NYJ)-'95	0*
96	Ottis, Brad	DT	6-5	281	8/2/72	7	Wayne State (Neb.)	Fremont, Neb.	FA-'96	15/11
32	Pittman, Michael	RB	6-0	214	8/14/75	4	Fresno State	San Diego, Calif.	D4-'98	16/11
10	Player, Scott	P	6-0	220	12/17/69	4	Florida State	St. Augustine, Fla.	FA-'98	16/0
16	Plummer, Jake	QB	6-2	197	12/19/74	5	Arizona State	Boise, Idaho	D2-'97	14/14
23	Rhinehart, Coby	CB	5-10	186	2/7/77	2	Southern Methodist	Dallas, Texas	D6a-'99	0*
51	Rutledge, Johnny	LB	6-3	242	1/4/77	3	Florida	Belle Glade, Fla.	D2-'99	11/4
81	Sanders, Frank	WR	6-2	197	2/17/73	7	Auburn	Fort Lauderdale, Fla.	D2-'95	16/16
54	Sanyika, Sekou	LB	6-3	240	3/17/78	2	California	Hercules, Calif.	D7-'00	16/0
68	Scott, Yusuf	G	6-3	332	11/30/76	3	Arizona	La Porte, Texas	D5b-'99	9/0
70	Shelton, L.J.	T	6-6	343	3/21/76	3	Eastern Michigan	Rochester Hills, Mich.	D1b-'99	14/14
33	Shields, Paul	RB	6-1	238	1/31/76	3	Arizona	Mesa, Ariz.	FA-'01	10/0*
50	Starkey, Jason	C	6-5	270	7/15/77	2	Marshall	Barboursville, W. Va.	FA-'00	0*
91	Swinger, Rashod	DT	6-2	286	11/27/74	3	Rutgers	Manalapan, N.J.	FA-'97	0*
92	Tanner, Barron	DT	6-3	320	9/14/73	4	Oklahoma	Athens, Texas	FA-'00	4/0
87	Tant, Jay	TE	6-3	254	12/4/77	2	Northwestern	Kettering, Ohio	D5b-'00	5/0
55	Thompson, Ray	LB	6-3	222	11/21/77	2	Tennessee	New Orleans, La.	D2-'00	11/9
40	Tillman, Pat	S	5-11	204	11/6/76	4	Arizona State	San Jose, Calif.	D7c-'98	16/16
78	Tosi, Mao	DT	6-6	305	12/12/76	2	Idaho	Anchorage, Alaska	D5a-'00	116/10
52	Walz, Zack	LB	6-4	228	2/13/76	4	Dartmouth	San Jose, Calif.	D6-'98	6/5
30	Williams, Clarence	RB	5-9	196	5/16/77	2	Michigan	Detroit, Mich.	FA-'99	3/0

* Cooper last active with Denver in '99; Keenan was on practice squad for 14 games; Kendall played 16 games for Seattle in '00; Moore, Rhinehart, and Swinger missed '00 season because of injury; Shields played 10 games with Indianapolis; Starkey did not play in 6 games.

Traded—CB Aeneas Williams (16 games in '00) to St. Louis.

Players lost through free agency (3): T Ethan Brooks (Den; 15 games in '00), DE Simeon Rice (TB; 15), DT Mark Smith (Cle; 14).

Also played with Cardinals in '00—WR Mac Cody (16), TE Chris Gedney (13), G Lester Holmes (13), G Matt Joyce (13), LB Mark Maddox (14), DT Tony McCoy (6), DE Corey Sears (8), DE Andre Wadsworth (9), DT Darwin Walker (1).

COACHING STAFF

Head Coach, Dave McGinnis

Pro Career: Named Arizona Cardinals' thirty-eighth head coach on December 18, 2000 after serving as team's interim head coach for final nine games of 2000 season and as defensive coordinator since 1996. Prior to joining Arizona in 1996, the Snyder, Texas, native spent 10 seasons (1986-1995) as linebackers coach of the Chicago Bears. In his decade with the Bears, Chicago played in nine playoff games and the defense ranked among the top six teams in fewest yards allowed seven times. McGinnis was part of a defensive staff that led the NFL in fewest points allowed in 1986 and 1988 and ranked first or second in total defense from 1986-88. In addition, McGinnis coached Pro Bowl players at all three linebacker positions—outside linebackers Otis Wilson and Wilber Marshall, and middle linebacker Mike Singletary, a 1998 Pro Football Hall of Fame inductee who made the Pro Bowl every season under McGinnis's tutelage. Career record: 1-8.

Background: Prior to joining the Bears, McGinnis spent 13 years coaching at the major college level. His first assignment was as a freshman coach at his alma mater, Texas Christian University, in 1973-74. In 1975 he moved to Missouri to coach the linebackers and secondary. After spending the 1978-1981 seasons at Indiana State as secondary coach, McGinnis returned to TCU in 1982 for one season as defensive backfield coach before joining Kansas State as defensive ends and linebackers coach from 1983-85. McGinnis was a three-time letterman (1970-72) and two-year starter (1971-72) at defensive back at Texas Christian where he earned academic all-Southwest Conference honors twice (1971-72) and earned a bachelor's degree in business administration. His 5 interceptions as a junior tied for the conference lead.

Personal: Born August 7, 1951, in Independence, Kansas. McGinnis attended Snyder High School in west Texas. He resides in Phoenix with his wife, Kim.

2001 FIRST-YEAR ROSTER

Name	Pos.	Ht.	Wt.	Birthdate	College	Hometown	How Acq.
Afualo, Tait	T	6-5	308	2/26/73	East Texas State	Torrance, Calif.	FA
Barrow, Rick	P	6-3	226	9/22/77	Southwest Texas State	San Antonio, Texas	FA
Bell, Marcus	DT	6-1	319	6/1/79	Memphis	Memphis, Tenn.	D4b
Borum, Jarvis	T	6-7	332	9/16/78	North Carolina State	Columbia, S.C.	FA
Bowers, Andy	DE	6-5	283	2/22/76	Utah	Salt Lake City, Utah	FA
Carson, Elliott	TE	6-4	246	6/20/78	Vanderbilt	Lebanon, Tenn.	FA
Claybrooks, Felipe	DE	6-4	260	1/22/78	Georgia Tech	Decatur, Ga.	FA
Cook, Michael	T	6-4	317	6/23/78	Boston College	Walpole, Mass.	FA
Cooper, Deke (1)	S	6-2	215	10/18/77	Notre Dame	Evansville, Ind.	FA
Crume, Corey	RB	5-11	226	11/17/77	Eastern Kentucky	Lebanon, Ky.	FA
Davis, Leonard	G-T	6-6	370	9/5/78	Texas	Wortham, Texas	D1
Davis, Tarius	S	6-0	228	1/8/77	McNeese State	Lake Charles, La.	FA
Eason, Nijrell	S	6-1	201	5/20/79	Arizona State	Long Beach, Calif.	FA
Fatafehi, Mario	DT	6-2	295	1/27/79	Kansas State	Honolulu, Hawaii	D5
Gilmore, Bryan (1)	WR	5-11	180	7/21/78	Midwestern State (Texas)	Lufkin, Texas	FA
Gramatica, Bill	K	5-10	192	7/10/78	South Florida	La Belle, Fla.	D4a
Hill, Renaldo	DB	5-11	178	11/12/78	Michigan State	Detroit, Mich.	D7a
Jackson, Arnold	WR	5-8	167	4/9/77	Louisville	Jacksonville, Fla.	FA
Newcombe, Bobby	WR	5-10	195	8/8/79	Nebraska	Albuquerque, N.M.	D6
Ofahengaue, Tevita	TE	6-2	253	7/9/76	Brigham Young	Laie, Hawaii	D7b
Owen, Marc	G	6-2	316	5/13/78	Kansas	St. Louis, Mo.	FA
Padget, Jason	C	6-2	286	3/23/79	Louisville	Avondale, Ariz.	FA
Payne, Gerald	WR	6-2	184	11/10/78	Harding (Ark.)	Mendenhall, Miss.	FA
Poole, Nathan	WR	6-1	198	2/1/77	Marshall	Danville, Va.	FA
Shipp, Marcel	RB	5-11	222	8/8/78	Massachusetts	Paterson, N.J.	FA
Stensrud, Andy	T	6-7	272	9/26/78	Iowa State	Lake Mills, Iowa	FA
Stone, Michael	CB	5-11	191	2/13/78	Memphis	Southfield, Mich.	D2b
Vanden Bosch, Kyle	DE	6-4	270	11/17/78	Nebraska	Larchwood, Iowa	D2a
Wakefield, Fred	DE	6-7	287	9/17/78	Illinois	Tuscola, Ill.	FA
Walden, David (1)	C	6-5	315	12/11/77	Stephen F. Austin	Joshua, Texas	FA
Wilson, Adrian	DB	6-2	213	10/12/79	North Carolina State	High Point, N.C.	D3
Woods, LeVar	LB	6-2	241	3/15/78	Iowa	Inwood, Iowa	FA
Young, Michael	LB	6-1	223	6/1/78	Illinois	St. Louis, Mo.	FA
Younger, Jordan (1)	CB	5-10	190	1/24/78	Connecticut	Trenton, N.J.	FA

The term NFL Rookie is defined as a player who is in his first season of professional football and has not been on the roster of another professional football team for any regular-season or postseason games. A Rookie is designated by an "R" on NFL rosters. Players who have been active in another professional football league or players who have NFL experience, including either preseason training camp or being on an Active List or Inactive List, or on Reserve/Injured or Reserve/Physically Unable to Perform for fewer than six regular-season games, are termed NFL First-Year Players. An NFL First-Year Player is designated by a "1" on NFL rosters. Thereafter, a player is credited with an additional year of experience for each season in which he accumulates six games on the Active List or Inactive List, or on Reserve/Injured or Reserve/Physically Unable to Perform.

NOTES

ASSISTANT COACHES

Geep Chryst, quarterbacks; born June 25, 1962, Madison, Wis., lives in Phoenix. Linebacker Princeton 1981-84. Pro linebacker Orlando Thunder (World League) 1992. College coach: Wisconsin-Platteville 1987. Pro Coach: Orlando Thunder (World League) 1991, Chicago Bears 1991-95, Arizona Cardinals 1996-98, San Diego Chargers 1999-2000, rejoined Cardinals in 2001.

Mike Devlin, asst. offensive line-offensive quality control; born November 16, 1979, Blacksburg, Va., lives in Phoenix. Center Iowa. Pro center Buffalo Bills 1993-95, Arizona Cardinals 1996-99. Pro coach: Joined Cardinals in 2000.

Jeff FitzGerald, linebackers; born April 18, 1960, Burbank, Calif., lives in Phoenix. Attended Oregon State. No college or pro playing experience. College coach: Cincinnati 1985-86, Alabama 1987-89, San Diego State 1994-97. Pro coach: Tampa Bay Buccaneers 1990-93, Washington Redskins 1998-99, joined Cardinals in 2000.

Joe Greene, defensive line; born September 24, 1946, Temple, Tex., lives in Phoenix. Defensive tackle North Texas State 1966-68. Pro defensive tackle Pittsburgh Steelers 1969-1981. Inducted into Pro Football Hall of Fame in 1987. Pro coach: Pittsburgh Steelers 1987-1991, Miami Dolphins 1992-95, joined Cardinals in 1996.

Pete Hoener, tight ends; born June 14, 1951, Peoria, Ill., lives in Phoenix. Defensive end Bradley 1969-1970. No pro playing experience. College coach: Missouri 1975-76, Illinois State 1977, Indiana State 1978-1984, Illinois 1987-88, Purdue 1989-1991, Texas Christian 1991-97, Iowa State 1998-99, Texas A&M 2000. Pro Coach: St. Louis Cardinals 1985-86; rejoined Cardinals in 2001.

Hank Kuhlmann, special teams; born October 6, 1937, Webster Groves, Mo., lives in Phoenix. Running back Missouri 1956-59. No pro playing experience. College coach: Missouri 1962-1971, Notre Dame 1975-77. Pro coach: Green Bay Packers 1972-74, Chicago Bears 1978-1982, Birmingham Stallions (USFL) 1983-85, St. Louis/Phoenix Cardinals 1986-89, Tampa Bay Buccaneers 1991, Indianapolis Colts 1994-97, rejoined Cardinals in 1998.

Stan Kwan, special teams assistant and defensive quality control; born November 2, 1967, lives in Phoenix. No college or pro playing experience. Pro coach: San Diego Chargers 1991-96, Detroit Lions 1997-2000, joined Cardinals in 2001.

Larry Marmie, defensive coordinator; born October 17, 1942, Barnesville, Ohio, lives in Phoenix. Quarterback Eastern Kentucky 1962-65. No pro playing experience. College coach: Eastern Kentucky 1967-68, 1972-76, Morehead State 1968-1971, Tulsa 1977-78, North Carolina 1979-1982, Tennessee 1983-84, 1992-94, Arizona State 1988-1991 (head coach), UCLA 1995. Pro coach: Joined Cardinals in 1996.

Rich Olson, offensive coordinator; born July 7, 1948, Wilmington, Calif., lives in Phoenix. Quarterback-free safety Washington State 1968-69. No pro playing experience. College coach: Washington State 1970, Fresno State 1976, Southern California 1977, Southern Methodist 1978-1980, Arkansas 1981-83, Fresno State 1984-1991, Miami 1992-94. Pro coach: Seattle Seahawks 1995-98, Washington Redskins 1999-2000, joined Cardinals in 2001.

Kevin Ramsey, defensive backs; born September 5, 1961, St. Louis, lives in Phoenix. Defensive back Indiana State 1979-1983. No pro playing experience. College coach: Kansas State 1986-1990, Northwestern 1990-92, West Virginia 1993-94, Tennessee 1995-98, Georgia 1999-2000. Pro coach: Joined Cardinals in 2001.

Bob Rogucki, strength and conditioning; born September 27, 1953, Clarksburg, W. Va., lives in Phoenix. No college or pro playing experience. College coach: Penn State 1981, Weber State 1982, Army 1983-89. Pro coach: Joined Cardinals in 1990.

Johnny Roland, running backs; born May 21, 1943, Corpus Christi, Texas, lives in Phoenix. Running back Missouri 1961-65. Pro running back St. Louis Cardinals 1966-1972, New York Giants 1973. College coach: Notre Dame 1975. Pro coach: Green Bay Packers 1974, Philadelphia Eagles 1976-78, Chicago Bears 1983-1992, New York Jets 1993-94, St. Louis Rams 1995-96, joined Cardinals in 1997.

Jerry Sullivan, wide receivers; born July 13, 1944, Miami, lives in Phoenix. Quarterback Florida State 1963-64. No pro playing experience. College coach: Kansas State 1971-72, Texas Tech 1973-75, South Carolina 1976-1982, Indiana 1983, Louisiana State 1984-1990, Ohio State 1991. Pro coach: San Diego Chargers 1992-96, Detroit Lions 1997-2000, joined Cardinals in 2001.

George Warhop, offensive line; born September 19, 1961, Riverside, Calif., lives in Phoenix. Guard Mt. San Jacinto (Calif.) J.C. 1979-80. Pro center Cincinnati Bengals 1981-82. College coach: Cincinnati 1983, Kansas 1984-86, Vanderbilt 1987-89, New Mexico 1990, Southern Methodist 1993, Boston College 1994-95. Pro coach: London Monarchs (World League) 1991-92, St. Louis Rams 1996-97, joined Cardinals in 1998.

ATLANTA FALCONS

National Football Conference
Western Division
Team Colors: Black, Red, Silver, and White
4400 Falcon Parkway
Flowery Branch, Georgia 30542
Telephone: (770) 965-3115

CLUB OFFICIALS

President: Taylor Smith
Executive Vice President/Football Operations and Head Coach: Dan Reeves
Executive Vice President of Administration: Jim Hay
Corporate Secretary: John Knox
General Manager: Harold Richardson
Vice President of Football Operations: Ron Hill
Vice President of Corporate Development: Tommy Nobis
Controller: Wallace Norman
Director of Finance: Greg Beadles
Vice President/Marketing and Sales: Rob Jackson
Director of Corporate Development: Mark Fuhrman
Operations/Special Events Coordinator: Spencer Treadwell
Director of Communications: Aaron Salkin
Director of Media Relations: Frank Kleha
Director of Ticket Operations: Jack Ragsdale
Assistant Director of Ticket Operations: Brent Coleman
Executive Director of the Atlanta Falcons Youth Foundation and Community Relations: Carol Breeding
Director of Community Relations: Chris Demos
Player Programs Coordinator: Billy (White Shoes) Johnson
Director of Information Systems: Joseph Miller
Director of Player Personnel/Pro: Chuck Connor
Director of Player Personnel/College: Reed Johnson
Area Scouts: Ken Blair, Billy Campfield, Dick Corrick, Boyd Dowler, Bill Groman, Bob Harrison
National Scout: Mike Hagan
Regional Scout: Jeff Smith
Assistant to Vice President of Football Operations: Les Snead
Head Athletic Trainer: Ron Medlin
Assistant Athletic Trainers: Harold King, Thomas Reed
Video Director: Mike Crews
Assistant Video Director: Jonah Bassett
Equipment Manager: Brian Boigner
Senior Director/Gameday Coordinator: Horace Daniel
Stadium: Georgia Dome (built in 1992)
•**Capacity:** 71,228
One Georgia Dome Drive
Atlanta, Georgia 30313
Playing Surface: Artificial turf
Training Camp: Furman University
3300 Poinsett Highway
Greenville, South Carolina 29613

RECORD HOLDERS

INDIVIDUAL RECORDS—CAREER

Category	Name	Performance
Rushing (Yds.)	Gerald Riggs, 1982-88	6,631
Passing (Yds.)	Steve Bartkowski, 1975-1985	23,468
Passing (TDs)	Steve Bartkowski, 1975-1985	154
Receiving (No.)	Terance Mathis, 1994-2000	522
Receiving (Yds.)	Terance Mathis, 1994-2000	6,785
Interceptions	Rolland Lawrence, 1973-1980	39
Punting (Avg.)	Rick Donnelly, 1985-89	42.6
Punt Return (Avg.)	Al Dodd, 1973-74	11.8
Kickoff Return (Avg.)	Darrick Vaughn, 2000	27.7
Field Goals	Morten Andersen, 1995-2000	139
Touchdowns (Tot.)	Andre Rison, 1990-94	56
Points	Morten Andersen, 1995-2000	620

INDIVIDUAL RECORDS—SINGLE SEASON

Category	Name	Performance
Rushing (Yds.)	Jamal Anderson, 1998	1,846
Passing (Yds.)	Jeff George, 1995	4,143
Passing (TDs)	Steve Bartkowski, 1980	31
Receiving (No.)	Terance Mathis, 1994	111
Receiving (Yds.)	Alfred Jenkins, 1981	1,358
Interceptions	Scott Case, 1988	10
Punting (Avg.)	Billy Lothridge, 1968	44.3
Punt Return (Avg.)	Al Dodd, 1974	12.7
Kickoff Return (Avg.)	Darrick Vaughn, 2000	27.7
Field Goals	Morten Andersen, 1995	31
Touchdowns (Tot.)	Jamal Anderson, 1998	16
Points	Morten Andersen, 1995	122

INDIVIDUAL RECORDS—SINGLE GAME

Category	Name	Performance
Rushing (Yds.)	Gerald Riggs, 9-2-84	202
Passing (Yds.)	Steve Bartkowski, 11-15-81	416
Passing (TDs)	Wade Wilson, 12-13-92	5
Receiving (No.)	William Andrews, 11-15-81	15
Receiving (Yds.)	Terance Mathis, 12-13-98	198
Interceptions	Many times Last time by Ray Buchanan, 10-29-00	2
Field Goals	Norm Johnson, 11-13-94	6
Touchdowns (Tot.)	Many times Last time by Jamal Anderson, 11-1-98	3
Points	Norm Johnson, 11-13-94	20

2001 SCHEDULE

PRESEASON

Aug. 3	**Pittsburgh**	7:30
Aug. 11	at New York Jets	8:00
Aug. 17	at Washington	8:00
Aug. 31	**Tampa Bay**	7:30

REGULAR SEASON

Sept. 9	at San Francisco	1:15
Sept. 16	at St. Louis	3:05
Sept. 23	**Carolina**	1:00
Sept. 30	at Arizona	1:05
Oct. 7	**Chicago**	1:00
Oct. 14	**San Francisco**	1:00
Oct. 21	at New Orleans	12:00
Oct. 28	Open Date	
Nov. 4	**New England**	1:00
Nov. 11	**Dallas**	1:00
Nov. 18	at Green Bay	12:00
Nov. 25	at Carolina	1:00
Dec. 2	**St. Louis**	1:00
Dec. 9	**New Orleans**	1:00
Dec. 16	at Indianapolis	1:00
Dec. 23	**Buffalo**	1:00
Dec. 30	at Miami	1:00

COACHING HISTORY

(209-324-5)

1966-68	Norb Hecker*	4-26-1
1968-1974	Norm Van Brocklin**	37-49-3
1974-76	Marion Campbell***	6-19-0
1976	Pat Peppler	3-6-0
1977-1982	Leeman Bennett	47-44-0
1983-86	Dan Henning	22-41-1
1987-89	Marion Campbell****	11-32-0
1989	Jim Hanifan	0-4-0
1990-93	Jerry Glanville	28-38-0
1994-96	June Jones	19-30-0
1997-2000	Dan Reeves	32-35-0

*Released after three games in 1968
**Released after eight games in 1974
***Released after five games in 1976
****Retired after 12 games in 1989

GEORGIA DOME

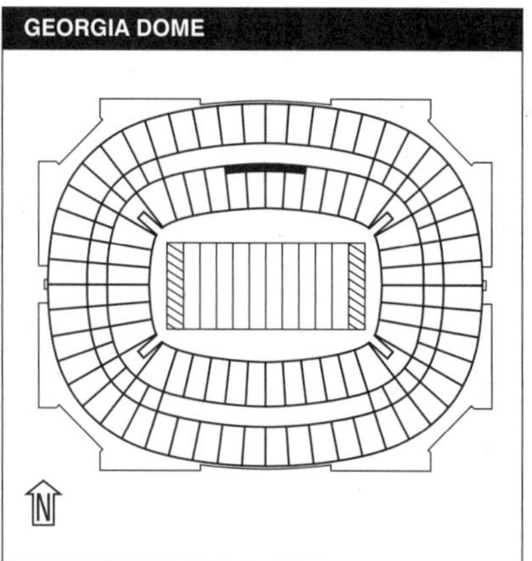

2000 TEAM RECORD

PRESEASON (4-1)

Date	Result		Opponent
7/29	W	20-13	at Indianapolis
8/5	W	20-9	vs. Dallas at Tokyo, Japan
8/11	W	31-16	Cincinnati
8/18	L	14-28	San Diego
8/24	W	31-20	at Jacksonville

REGULAR SEASON (4-12)

Date	Result		Opponent	Att.
9/3	W	36-28	San Francisco	54,626
9/10	L	14-42	at Denver	75,466
9/17	W	15-10	at Carolina	73,025
9/24	L	20-41	St. Louis	58,761
10/1	L	10-38	at Philadelphia	65,424
10/8	L	6-13	New York Giants	50,947
10/15	L	29-45	at St. Louis	66,019
10/22	L	19-21	New Orleans	56,508
10/29	W	13-12	Carolina	46,178
11/5	L	14-27	Tampa Bay	70,097
11/12	L	10-13	at Detroit	74,309
11/19	L	6-16	at San Francisco	67,447
11/26	L	14-41	at Oakland	55,175
12/3	L	10-30	Seattle	44,680
12/17	L	7-23	at New Orleans	64,900
12/24	W	29-13	Kansas City	41,017

SCORE BY PERIODS

Falcons	50	75	57	70	0	—	252
Opponents	97	134	91	91	0	—	413

ATTENDANCE

Home 420,303 Away 537,126 Total 957,429
Single-game home record, 70,097 (11/5/00)
Single-season home record, 553,979 (1992)

2000 TEAM STATISTICS

	Falcons	Opp.
Total First Downs	256	308
Rushing	65	113
Passing	156	175
Penalty	35	20
Third Down: Made/Att	57/197	71/198
Third Down Pct	28.9	35.9
Fourth Down: Made/Att	6/13	11/18
Fourth Down Pct.	46.2	61.1
Total Net Yards	3,994	5,607
Avg. Per Game	249.6	350.4
Total Plays	925	999
Avg. Per Play	4.3	5.6
Net Yards Rushing	1,214	1,983
Avg. Per Game	75.9	123.9
Total Rushes	350	453
Net Yards Passing	2,780	3,624
Avg. Per Game	173.8	226.5
Sacked/Yards Lost	61/386	31/142
Gross Yards	3,166	3,766
Att./Completions	514/285	515/306
Completion Pct.	55.4	59.4
Had Intercepted	20	15
Punts/Average	85/40.6	70/41.9
Net Punting Avg.	85/37.9	70/36.1
Penalties/Yards	97/720	122/1,010
Fumbles/Ball Lost	27/14	18/10
Touchdowns	25	46
Rushing	6	16
Passing	14	23
Returns	5	7
Avg. Time of Possession	29:35	30:25

2000 INDIVIDUAL STATISTICS

Passing	Att.	Comp.	Yds.	Pct.	TD	Int.	Tkld.	Rate
Chandler	331	192	2,236	58.0	10	12	40/251	73.5
Kanell	116	57	524	49.1	2	5	8/60	49.6
Johnson	67	36	406	53.7	2	3	13/75	63.4
Falcons	514	285	3,166	55.4	14	20	61/386	66.8
Opponents	515	306	3,766	59.4	23	15	31/142	84.8

SCORING	TD R	TD P	TD Rt	PAT	FG	Saf	PTS
Andersen	0	0	0	23/23	25/31	0	98
Anderson	6	0	0	0/0	0/0	0	38
Mathis	0	5	0	0/0	0/0	0	30
Dwight	0	3	1	0/0	0/0	0	24
Vaughn	0	0	3	0/0	0/0	0	18
Jefferson	0	2	0	0/0	0/0	0	12
R. Kelly	0	2	0	0/0	0/0	0	12
Kozlowski	0	2	0	0/0	0/0	0	12
Ambrose	0	0	1	0/0	0/0	0	6
Falcons	6	14	5	23/23	25/31	1	252
Opponents	16	23	7	38/38	29/31	0	413

2-Pt. Conversions: Anderson.
Falcons 1-2, Opponents 6-8.

RUSHING	Att.	Yds.	Avg.	LG	TD
Anderson	282	1,024	3.6	42	6
M. Smith	19	69	3.6	16	0
Chandler	21	60	2.9	16	0
Rivers	8	27	3.4	10	0
Christian	9	19	2.1	7	0
Johnson	3	11	3.7	8	0
Dwight	5	8	1.6	5	0
Jefferson	1	1	1.0	1	0
Kanell	1	0	0.0	0	0
Mathis	1	-5	-5.0	-5	0
Falcons	350	1,214	3.5	42	6
Opponents	453	1,983	4.4	85t	16

RECEIVING	No.	Yds.	Avg.	LG	TD
Jefferson	60	822	13.7	49	2
Mathis	57	679	11.9	44t	5
Christian	44	315	7.2	19	0
Anderson	42	382	9.1	55	0
R. Kelly	31	340	11.0	37t	2
Dwight	26	406	15.6	52t	3
Kozlowski	15	151	10.1	30	2
Finneran	7	60	8.6	14	0
German	1	10	10.0	10	0
M. Smith	1	5	5.0	5	0
Chandler	1	-4	-4.0	-4	0
Falcons	285	3,166	11.1	55	14
Opponents	306	3,766	12.3	85t	23

INTERCEPTIONS	No.	Yds.	Avg.	LG	TD
Buchanan	6	114	19.0	60	0
Ambrose	4	139	34.8	42	1
Bradford	3	25	8.3	13	0
Kerney	1	8	8.0	8	0
Williams	1	1	1.0	1	0
Falcons	15	287	19.1	60	1
Opponents	20	271	13.6	70t	3

PUNTING	No.	Yds.	Avg.	In 20	LG
Stryzinski	84	3,447	41.0	27	60
Falcons	85	3,447	40.6	27	60
Opponents	70	2,932	41.9	25	60

PUNT RETURNS	No.	FC	Yds.	Avg.	LG	TD
Dwight	33	17	309	9.4	70t	1
Oliver	4	3	39	9.8	40	0
Falcons	37	20	348	9.4	70t	1
Opponents	29	31	126	4.3	28	0

KICKOFF RETURNS	No.	Yds.	Avg.	LG	TD
Vaughn	39	1,082	27.7	100t	3
Dwight	32	680	21.3	48	0
Kozlowski	7	77	11.0	21	0
Oliver	2	15	7.5	11	0
Williams	2	34	17.0	19	0
Finneran	1	2	2.0	2	0
Falcons	83	1,890	22.8	100t	3
Opponents	50	1,230	24.6	103t	3

FIELD GOALS	1-19	20-29	30-39	40-49	50+
Andersen	0/0	6/6	6/7	11/15	2/3
Falcons	0/0	6/6	6/7	11/15	2/3
Opponents	2/2	8/9	11/11	6/7	2/2

SACKS	No.
Hall	4.5
Bra. Smith	4.5
Wiley	4.0
Jasper	3.5
Kerney	2.5
Carter	2.0
Crockett	2.0
McBurrows	2.0
Swayda	1.5
Brooking	1.0
Draft	1.0
Dronett	1.0
Simoneau	0.5
Falcons	31.0
Opponents	61.0

2001 DRAFT CHOICES

Round	Name	Pos.	College
1	Michael Vick	QB	Virginia Tech
2	Alge Crumpler	TE	North Carolina
4	Roberto Garza	C	Texas A&M-Kingsville
	Matt Stewart	LB	Vanderbilt
5	Vinny Sutherland	WR	Purdue
6	Randy Garner	DE	Arkansas
7	Corey Hall	DB	Appalachian State
	Kynan Forney	T	Hawaii
	Ronald Flemons	DE	Texas A&M
	Quentin McCord	WR	Kentucky

ATLANTA FALCONS

2001 VETERAN ROSTER

No.		Name	Pos.	Ht.	Wt.	Birthdate	NFL Exp.	College	Hometown	How Acq.	'00 Games/ Starts
33		Ambrose, Ashley	CB	5-10	187	9/17/70	10	Mississippi Valley State	New Orleans, La.	UFA(NO)-'00	16/16
5	#	Andersen, Morten	K	6-2	225	8/19/60	20	Michigan State	Struer, Denmark	FA-'95	16/0
32		Anderson, Jamal	RB	5-11	237	9/30/72	8	Utah	Los Angeles, Calif.	D7-'94	16/16
50		Atkins, Corey	LB	6-0	232	11/11/76	2	South Carolina	Greenville, S.C.	FA-'00	12/0
80		Baker, Eugene	WR	6-0	170	3/18/76	2	Kent	Monroeville, Pa.	FA-'99	1/0
76		Banks, Chris	G	6-1	315	4/4/73	4	Kansas	Lexington, Mo.	W(Den)-'00	8/4
23		Bradford, Ronnie	CB-S	5-10	195	10/1/70	9	Colorado	Minot, N.D.	UFA(Ariz)-'97	16/15
56		Brooking, Keith	LB	6-2	245	10/30/75	4	Georgia Tech	Senoia, Ga.	D1-'98	5/5
34		Buchanan, Ray	CB	5-9	186	9/29/71	9	Louisville	Chicago, Ill.	UFA(Ind)-'97	16/16
25		Carter, Marty	S	6-1	213	12/17/69	11	Middle Tennessee State	La Grange, Ga.	UFA(Chi)-'99	16/16
35		Carty, Johndale	S	6-0	196	8/27/77	3	Utah State	Miami, Fla.	D4-'99	15/0
12		Chandler, Chris	QB	6-4	228	10/12/65	14	Washington	Everett, Wash.	T (Hou)-'97	14/13
44		Christian, Bob	FB	5-11	232	11/14/68	9	Northwestern	Florissant, Mo.	UFA(Car)-'97	16/14
71		Claridge, Travis	T-G	6-5	300	3/23/78	2	Southern California	Vancouver, Wash.	D2-'00	16/16
68		Collins, Calvin	G-C	6-2	310	1/5/74	5	Texas A&M	Beaumont, Texas	D6-'97	16/16
45		Downs, Gary	RB	6-1	215	6/6/72	8	North Carolina State	Columbus, Ga.	FA-'97	16/0
54		Draft, Chris	LB	5-11	232	2/26/76	3	Stanford	Anaheim, Calif.	W(SF)-'00	13/8
75		Dronett, Shane	DT	6-6	300	1/12/71	10	Texas	Orange, Texas	FA-'97	3/3
86		Finneran, Brian	WR	6-5	210	1/31/76	2	Villanova	Mission Viejo, Calif.	FA-'00	12/0
87		German, Jammi	WR	6-1	191	7/4/74	4	Miami	Fort Myers, Fla.	FA-'99	9/0
98		Hall, Travis	DT	6-5	295	8/3/72	7	Brigham Young	Kenai, Alaska	D6-'95	16/16
64		Hallen, Bob	C-G	6-4	295	3/9/75	4	Kent State	Cleveland, Ohio	D2-'98	16/5
24		Hamilton, Conrad	CB	5-10	185	11/5/74	4	Eastern New Mexico	Alamogordo, N.M.	FA-'01	0*
47		Hudson, Chris	S	5-10	199	10/6/71	6	Colorado	Houston, Texas	FA-'01	0*
95		Jasper, Ed	DT	6-2	293	1/18/73	5	Texas A&M	Tyler, Texas	FA-'99	15/15
84		Jefferson, Shawn	WR	5-11	185	2/22/69	11	Central Florida	Jacksonville, Fla.	UFA(NE)-'00	16/14
36		Jervey, Travis	RB	6-0	222	5/5/72	7	The Citadel	Columbia, S.C.	FA-'01	8/0*
11		Johnson, Doug	QB	6-2	225	10/27/77	2	Florida	Gainesville, Fla.	FA-'00	4/2
55		Jordan, Antony	LB	6-3	235	12/19/74	3	Vanderbilt	Sewell, N.J.	FA-'00	8/0
13	#	Kanell, Danny	QB	6-3	218	11/21/73	6	Florida State	Ft. Lauderdale, Fla.	FA-'99	5/1
51		Kelly, Jeff	LB	5-11	242	12/13/75	3	Kansas State	La Grange, Texas	D6-'99	12/6
89		Kelly, Reggie	TE	6-3	255	2/22/77	3	Mississippi State	Aberdeen, Miss.	D2-'99	16/16
97		Kerney, Patrick	DE	6-5	273	12/30/76	3	Virginia	Trenton, N.J.	D1-'99	16/16
85		Kozlowski, Brian	TE	6-3	250	10/4/70	8	Connecticut	Rochester, N.Y.	FA-'97	16/3
81		Mathis, Terance	WR	5-10	185	6/7/67	12	New Mexico	Stone Mountain, Ga.	UFA(NYJ)-'94	16/16
22		McBurrows, Gerald	S	5-11	208	10/7/73	7	Kansas	Detroit, Mich.	UFA(StL)-'99	16/4
62		McClure, Todd	C	6-1	286	2/16/77	3	Louisiana State	Baton Rouge, La.	D7-'99	10/7
40		McLeod, Kevin	RB	6-0	250	10/17/74	2	Auburn	Montego Bay, Jamaica	FA-'01	0*
13		Mohr, Chris	P	6-5	215	5/11/66	12	Alabama	Atlanta, Ga.	FA-'01	16/0*
49		Neil, Dallas	TE	6-1	235	9/30/76	2	Montana	Great Falls, Mont.	FA-'00	6/0
59		O'Neal, Matt	C	6-3	285	5/5/77	2	Oklahoma	San Diego, Calif.	FA-'00	0*
63	#	Pilgrim, Evan	G	6-4	298	8/14/72	7	Brigham Young	Antioch, Calif.	FA-'99	7/1
48		Rackley, Derek	TE	6-4	250	7/18/77	2	Minnesota	Apple Valley, Minn.	FA-'00	16/0
61		Redmon, Anthony	G	6-5	305	4/9/71	8	Auburn	Brewton, Ala.	FA-'00	4/4
74	†	Salaam, Ephraim	T	6-7	300	6/19/76	4	San Diego State	Sacramento, Calif.	D7-'98	14/10
53		Simoneau, Mark	LB	6-0	234	1/16/77	2	Kansas State	Smith Center, Kan.	D3-'00	14/4
91		Smith, Brady	DE	6-5	274	6/5/73	6	Colorado State	Barrington, Ill.	UFA(NO)-'00	15/14
43		Smith, Maurice	RB	6-0	235	2/14/77	2	North Carolina A&T	Palmyra, N.C.	FA-'00	10/0
93		Swayda, Shawn	DT	6-5	294	9/4/74	4	Arizona State	Phoenix, Ariz.	FA-'99	16/0
20		Thomas, Rodney	RB	5-10	210	3/30/73	7	Texas A&M	Groveton, Texas	FA-'01	16/0*
66		Thompson, Michael	T	6-4	295	2/11/77	2	Tennessee State	Savannah, Ga.	D4-'00	2/2
58		Tuggle, Jessie	LB	5-11	230	4/4/65	15	Valdosta State	Spalding, Ga.	FA-'87	8/7
94		Ulmer, Artie	LB	6-2	247	7/30/73	4	Valdosta State	Savannah, Ga.	UFA(SF)-'01	12/2*
37		Vaughn, Darrick	CB	5-11	193	10/2/78	2	Southwest Texas	Aldine, Texas	D7-'00	16/0
70		Whitfield, Bob	T	6-5	310	10/18/71	10	Stanford	Carson, Calif.	D1a-'92	15/15
99		Wiley, Chuck	DE	6-5	277	3/6/75	4	Louisiana State	Baton Rouge, La.	W(Car)-'00	16/0
21		Williams, Elijah	CB	5-10	180	8/20/75	4	Florida	Milton, Fla.	D6-'98	15/3
16	t-	Zeier, Eric	QB	6-1	214	9/6/75	7	Georgia	Pensacola, Fla.	T(TB)-'01	3/0*

* Hamilton last active with N.Y. Giants in '99; Hudson last active with Chicago in '99; Jervey played 8 games with San Francisco in '00; McLeod last active with Tampa Bay in '99; Mohr played 16 games with Buffalo; O'Neal missed '00 season because of injury; Thomas played 16 games with Tennessee; Ulmer played 12 games with San Francisco; Zeier played 3 games with Tampa Bay.

† Restricted free agent; subject to developments.

Unrestricted free agent; subject to developments.

t- Falcons traded for Zeier (Tampa Bay).

Traded—WR Tim Dwight (14 games in '00) to San Diego.

Retired—Chris Bordano, 3-year linebacker, 2 games in '00; Pellom McDaniels, 8-year defensive end, last active with Atlanta in '99.

Players lost through free agency (4): LB Henri Crockett (Den; 15 games in '00); DB Terry Cousin (Mia; 15), RB Ron Rivers (Pitt; 6), P Dan Stryzinski (KC; 16).

Also played with Falcons in '00—QB Tony Graziani (1 game), RB Winslow Oliver (12), DT Henry Taylor (5), DE Chris White (5).

COACHING STAFF

Head Coach,
Dan Reeves

Pro Career: Head coach Dan Reeves, the NFL's winningest active coach with 181 career victories, suffered through consecutive losing seasons (5-11 in 1999 and 4-12 in 2000) on the heels of 1998's NFC championship season. Reeves led the Falcons to their first Super Bowl appearance after capturing the NFC championship in 1998, only his second season with Atlanta after taking over on January 20, 1997. Reeves led the Falcons to the NFC West title with a 14-2 record and a franchise-record 442 points. Reeves was named coach of the year in 1998 for the fifth time in his coaching career after the Falcons improved from a 7-9 finish in 1997. Reeves had been the head coach of the New York Giants from 1993-96. Prior to that, he compiled a 117-79-1 record as head coach of the Denver Broncos from 1981-1992, earning NFL coach of the year honors in 1982, 1988, and 1991. He led the Broncos to three Super Bowl berths, four AFC Championship Games, five AFC West Division titles, and eight winning seasons. In his first year in New York, he earned NFL coach of the year honors for a fourth time, taking the Giants from 6-10 to an 11-5 mark and a wild-card playoff victory. Overall, Reeves has accumulated 11 winning seasons as head coach and participated in 48 playoff games and nine Super Bowls as an NFL player, assistant coach, and head coach. Career record: 181-148-1.

Background: Prior to obtaining his first NFL head coaching job in 1981, Reeves had been a member of the Dallas Cowboys' coaching staff since 1970, spending a total of 16 years under Tom Landry as a player and coach. In 1977, he was named offensive coordinator of Landry's staff. Reeves began his pro career as a free agent running back for Dallas in 1965. Prior to that he was a quarterback at South Carolina from 1962-64, passing for 2,561 yards and 16 touchdowns. He totaled 3,376 yards during his career with the Gamecocks, leading to his induction into the school's hall of fame in 1978. Reeves later was inducted into the state of Georgia Sports Hall of Fame.

Personal: Born January 19, 1944, Americus, Ga. Dan and his wife, Pam, live in Atlanta, and have three children—Dana, Laura, and Lee.

ASSISTANT COACHES

Marvin Bass, asst. to head coach-pro personnel; born August 28, 1919, Norfolk, Va., lives in Suwanee, Ga. Tackle William & Mary 1940-42. No pro playing experience. College coach: William & Mary 1944-48, 1950-51 (head coach), North Carolina 1949, 1953-55, South Carolina 1956-59, 1961-65, Georgia Tech 1960, Richmond 1963. Pro coach: Washington Redskins 1952, Montreal Beavers (Continental League) 1966-67, Montreal Alouettes (CFL) 1968, Buffalo Bills 1969-71, Birmingham Americans (WFL) 1974-75, Denver Broncos 1982-92. Joined Falcons in 1997.

Don Blackmon, defensive coordinator; born March 14, 1958, Pompano Beach, Fla., lives in Suwanee, Ga. Linebacker Tulsa 1977-80. Pro linebacker New England Patriots 1981-87. Pro coach: New England Patriots 1988-90, Cleveland Browns 1991-92, New York Giants 1993-96, joined Falcons in 1997.

Greg Brown, secondary; born October 10, 1957, Denver, lives in Suwanee, Ga. Defensive back Texas-El Paso 1980. No pro playing experience. College coach: Wyoming 1987-88, Purdue 1989-1990, Colorado 1991-93. Pro coach: Tampa Bay Buccaneers 1984-86, Atlanta Falcons 1994, San Diego Chargers 1995-96, Tennessee Oilers 1997-98, San Francisco 49ers 1999, rejoined Falcons in 2000.

Jack Burns, quarterbacks; born January 3, 1949, Tampa, Fla., lives in Suwanee, Ga. Safety Florida, 1967-70. No pro playing experience. College coach: Florida 1971-73, 1975, Louisville 1974, 1985-88, Texas 1976, Vanderbilt 1977-78, Auburn 1979-80. Pro coach: Tampa Bay Bandits (USFL) 1983, Washington Redskins 1989-91, Minnesota Vikings 1992-93, joined Falcons in 1997.

Rocky Colburn, asst. strength and conditioning; born May 24, 1963, Dallas, Ore., lives in Lawrenceville, Ga. Safety Alabama 1981-83. No pro playing experience. College coach: Alabama 1984, 1987-1992, Samford 1986. Pro coach: Joined Falcons 1999.

James Daniel, tight ends; born January 17, 1953, Wetumpka, Ala., lives in Suwanee, Ga. Offensive guard Alabama State 1970-73. No pro playing experience. College coach: Auburn 1981-1992. Pro coach: New York Giants 1993-96, joined Falcons in 1997.

Billy Davis, linebackers; born November 5, 1965, Youngstown, Ohio, lives in Suwanee, Ga. Quarterback Cincinnati 1984-88. No pro playing experience. College coach: Michigan State 1990-91. Pro coach: Pittsburgh Steelers 1992-94, Carolina Panthers 1995-98, Cleveland Browns 1999, Green Bay Packers 2000, joined Falcons in 2001.

Joe DeCamillis, special teams; born June 29, 1965, Arvada, Colo., lives in Alpharetta, Ga. No college or pro playing experience. College coach: Wyoming 1988. Pro coach: Denver Broncos 1989, Miami Dolphins 1990, New York Giants 1993-96, joined Falcons in 1997.

Bill Johnson, defensive line; born June 23, 1955, Monroe, Louisiana, lives in Suwanee, Ga. Defensive lineman Northwestern (La.) State 1976-79. No pro playing experience. College coach: Northwestern (La.) State 1980-81, McNeese State 1985-86, Miami 1987, Louisiana Tech 1988-89, Arkansas 1990-91, 2000, Texas A&M 1992-99. Pro coach: Joined Falcons in 2001.

Thom Kaumeyer, defensive quality control; born March 17, 1967, LaJolla, Calif., lives in Suwanee, Ga. Safety Paolmar (Calif.) J.C. 1985-86, Oregon 1987-88. Pro safety Seattle Seahawks 1989-1990, New York Giants 1991-92. College coach: Palomar (Calif.) J.C. 1991, 1993-94, 1997-99. Pro coach: Joined Falcons in 2000.

Pete Mangurian, offensive line; born June 17, 1955, Los Angeles, lives in Alpharetta, Ga. Defensive lineman Louisiana State 1975-78. No pro playing experience. College coach: Southern Methodist 1979-1980, New Mexico State 1981, Stanford 1982-83, Louisiana State 1984-87, Cornell 1998-2000 (head coach). Pro coach: Denver Broncos 1988-1992, New York Giants 1993-96, Atlanta Falcons 1997, rejoined Falcons in 2001.

Al Miller, strength and conditioning; born August 29, 1947, El Dorado, Ark., lives in Alpharetta, Ga. Wide receiver Northeast Louisiana 1965-69. No pro playing experience. College coach: Northwestern State (La.) 1974-78, Mississippi State 1980, Northeast Louisiana 1981, Alabama 1982-84. Pro coach: Denver Broncos 1987-92, New York Giants 1993-96, joined Falcons in 1997.

George Sefcik, offensive coordinator-running backs; born December 27, 1939, Cleveland, Ohio, lives in Suwanee, Ga. Halfback Notre Dame 1959-61. No pro playing experience. College coach: Notre Dame 1963-68, Kentucky 1969-1972. Pro coach: Baltimore Colts 1973-74, Cleveland Browns 1975-77, 1989-90, Cincinnati Bengals 1978-83, Green Bay Packers 1984-87, Kansas City Chiefs 1988, New York Giants 1991-96, joined Falcons in 1997.

Warren (Rennie) Simmons, asst. offensive line; born February 25, 1942, Poughkeepsie, N.Y., lives in Gainesville, Ga. Center San Diego State 1961-65. No pro playing experience. College coach: Cal State-Fullerton 1974-78, Cerritos (Calif.) J.C. 1978-80, Vanderbilt 1995. Pro coach: Washington Redskins 1981-93, Los Angeles Rams 1994, Houston Oilers 1996, joined Falcons in 1997.

Gary Stevens, wide receivers; born March 19, 1943, Cleveland, lives in Suwanee, Ga. Running back John Carroll 1963-65. No pro playing experience. College coach: Louisville 1971-74, Kent State 1975, West Virginia 1976-79, Miami 1980-88. Pro coach: Miami Dolphins 1989-1997, Oakland Raiders 1998-2000, joined Falcons in 2001.

Ed West, offensive quality control; born August 2, 1961, Leighton, Ala., lives in Woodstock, Ga. Tight end Auburn 1980-83. Pro tight end Green Bay Packers 1984-1994, Philadelphia Eagles 1995-96, Atlanta Falcons 1997. Pro coach: Joined Falcons in 1998.

Brian Xanders, director of football systems; born April 10, 1971, East Stroudsburg, Pa., lives in Atlanta. Linebacker Florida State 1989-1992. No pro playing experience. Pro coach: Joined Falcons in 1997.

2001 FIRST-YEAR ROSTER

Name	Pos.	Ht.	Wt.	Birthdate	College	Hometown	How Acq.
Allen, Matt	P	6-4	235	10/23/77	Troy State	Montgomery, Ala.	FA
Arians, Jake (1)	K	5-11	200	1/26/78	Alabama-Birmingham	Blacksburg, Va.	FA-'00
Brown, Corey	WR	6-1	195	8/12/78	Tulsa	Lone Grove, Okla.	FA
Carr, William (1)	DT	6-0	295	1/23/75	Michigan	Dallas, Texas	FA-'00
Clark, Jamara	CB	5-8	175	12/17/77	Georgia Tech	Bradenton, Fla.	FA
Crumpler, Alge	TE	6-2	262	12/23/77	North Carolina	Wilmington, N.C.	D2
Feely, Jay	K	5-10	206	5/23/76	Michigan	Odessa, Fla.	FA
Flemons, Ronald	DE	6-5	265	10/20/79	Texas A&M	San Antonio, Texas	D7c
Forney, Kynan	G	6-2	305	9/8/78	Hawaii	Nacogdoches, Texas	D7b
Garner, Randy	DE	6-3	267	11/28/77	Arkansas	Atlanta, Texas	D6
Garza, Roberto	C	6-2	296	3/2/79	Texas A&M- Kingsville	Rio Hondo, Texas	D4a
Hall, Corey	DB	6-4	203	1/17/79	Appalachian State	Athens, Ga.	D7a
Hawkins, Ahmad	CB	5-10	185	12/10/78	Virginia	Hampton, Va.	FA
Holleman, Chad (1)	K	5-11	200	8/9/76	Georgia	Raliegh, N.C.	FA
Johnson, Jevaris	TE	6-6	254	10/27/77	Georgia	Anniston, Ala.	FA
Kadela, Dave	T	6-6	294	5/6/78	Virginia Tech	Dearborn, Mich.	FA
McCord, Quentin	WR	5-10	188	6/26/78	Kentucky	LaGrange, Ga.	D7d
Merkens, Trey	LB	5-11	235	9/20/78	Texas-El Paso	San Antonio, Texas	FA
Miller, Doug (1)	DT	6-1	281	10/12/75	Howard	Tampa, Fla.	FA
Mills, Shawn	WR	6-1	184	2/10/77	Southern Mississippi	Enid, Okla.	FA
Moore, Ron (1)	DT	6-2	312	8/10/77	Northwestern Oklahoma State	Sanford, Fla.	FA-'00
Philyaw, Mareno (1)	WR	6-2	208	12/19/77	Troy State	Atlanta, Ga.	D6-'00
Popovich, Jeff	DB	5-11	195	10/26/77	Miami	Tucson, Ariz.	FA
Robinson, Ronnie	FB	6-1	235	11/11/77	North Carolina	Atlanta, Ga.	FA
Shivers, Wes (1)	T	6-5	296	3/8/77	Mississippi State	Benton, Miss.	FA-'00
Snellings, Paul (1)	T	6-4	288	11/5/75	Georgia	LaGrange, Ga.	FA
Stewart, Matt	LB	6-3	232	8/31/79	Vanderbilt	Columbus, Ohio	D4b
Sutherland, Vinny	WR	5-8	190	4/22/78	Purdue	West Palm Beach, Fla.	D5
Vick, Michael	QB	6-0	215	6/28/80	Virginia Tech	Newport News, Va.	D1
Zuiderveen, Dave	DE	6-5	260	3/24/78	Ferris State	Kalamazoo, Mich.	FA

The term NFL Rookie is defined as a player who is in his first season of professional football and has not been on the roster of another professional football team for any regular-season or postseason games. A Rookie is designated by an "R" on NFL rosters. Players who have been active in another professional football league or players who have NFL experience, including either preseason training camp or being on an Active List or Inactive List, or on Reserve/Injured or Reserve/Physically Unable to Perform for fewer than six regular-season games, are termed NFL First-Year Players. An NFL First-Year Player is designated by a "1" on NFL rosters. Thereafter, a player is credited with an additional year of experience for each season in which he accumulates six games on the Active List or Inactive List, or on Reserve/Injured or Reserve/Physically Unable to Perform.

CAROLINA PANTHERS

National Football Conference
Western Division
Team Colors: Black, Panther Blue, and Silver
800 South Mint Street
Charlotte, North Carolina 28202-1502
Telephone: (704) 358-7000

CLUB OFFICIALS

Founder/Owner: Jerry Richardson
President Carolina Panthers: Mark Richardson
President Carolinas Stadium Corps.: Jon Richardson
Director of Player Personnel: Jack Bushofsky
Director of Football Operations: Marty Hurney
Director of Marketing and Sponsorships: Charles Waddell
Director of Broadcasting: Linda Ricca
Counsel: Richard Thigpen
Chief Financial Officer: Dave Olsen
Controller: Lisa Garber
Director of Pro Personnel: Mark Koncz
Pro Scouts: Hal Hunter, Ted Plumb, Kenny Roberson
Director of College Scouting: Tony Softli
College Scouts: Hal Athon, Joe Bushofsky, Ryan Cowden, Max McCartney, Jay Mondock, Jeff Morrow
Director of Communications: Charlie Dayton
Communications Assistant: Bruce Speight
Public Relations Assistant: Deedee Thomason
Media Relations Assistant: Ted Crews
Director of Ticket Sales: Phil Youtsey
Director of Player Relations: Donnie Shell
Director of Community Relations/Family Programs: B.J. Harrison Waymer
Director of Entertainment: Leslie Matz
Director of Information Systems: Roger Goss
Football Systems: Rob Rogers
Video Director: Mark Hobbs
Assistant Video Director: Jeff Mueller
Head Trainer: John Kasik
Assistant Trainers: Dan Ruiz, Mike Hooper
Equipment Manager: Jackie Miles
Assistant Equipment Manager: Don Toner
Director of Security: Gene Brown
Director of Stadium Operations: Paul Laky
Stadium Operations Manager: Scott Paul
Head Groundskeeper: Tom Vaughn
Human Resources and Office Manager: Jackie Jeffries
Stadium: Ericsson Stadium (built in 1996)
• **Capacity:** 73,250
Charlotte, North Carolina 28202-1502
Playing Surface: Grass
Training Camp: Wofford College
Spartanburg, South Carolina
29303

RECORD HOLDERS

INDIVIDUAL RECORDS—CAREER

Category	Name	Performance
Rushing (Yds.)	Tshimanga Biakabutuka, 1996-2000	2,300
Passing (Yds.)	Steve Beuerlein, 1996-2000	12,690
Passing (Tds)	Steve Beuerlein, 1996-2000	86
Receiving (No.)	Muhsin Muhammad, 1996-2000	318
Receiving (Yds.)	Muhsin Muhammad, 1996-2000	4,101
Interceptions	Eric Davis, 1996-2000	25
Punting (Avg.)	Ken Walter, 1997-2000	40.4
Punt Return (Avg.)	Winslow Oliver, 1996-98	10.7
Kickoff Return (Avg.)	Michael Bates, 1996-2000	25.7
Field Goals	John Kasay, 1995-2000	126
Touchdowns (Tot.)	Wesley Walls, 1996-2000	35
Points	John Kasay, 1995-2000	532

INDIVIDUAL RECORDS—SINGLE SEASON

Category	Name	Performance
Rushing (Yds.)	Anthony Johnson, 1996	1,120
Passing (Yds.)	Steve Beuerlein, 1999	4,436
Passing (Tds)	Steve Beuerlein, 1999	36
Receiving (No.)	Muhsin Muhammad, 2000	102
Receiving (Yds.)	Muhsin Muhammad, 1999	1,253
Interceptions	Brett Maxie, 1995	6
Punting (Avg.)	Ken Walter, 1997	42.4
Punt Return (Avg.)	Winslow Oliver, 1996	11.5
Kickoff Return (Avg.)	Michael Bates, 1996	30.2
Field Goals	John Kasay, 1996	37
Touchdowns (Tot.)	Wesley Walls, 1999	12
	Patrick Jeffers, 1999	12
Points	John Kasay, 1996	145

INDIVIDUAL RECORDS—SINGLE GAME

Category	Name	Performance
Rushing (Yds.)	Fred Lane, 11-2-97	147
Passing (Yds.)	Steve Beuerlein, 12-12-99	373
Passing (Tds)	Steve Beuerlein, 1-2-00	5
Receiving (No.)	Muhsin Muhammad, 12-18-99, 11-27-00	11
Receiving (Yds.)	Muhsin Muhammad, 9-13-98	192
Interceptions	Many times	2
	Last time by Jimmy Hitchcock, 12-3-00	
Field Goals	John Kasay, 9-1-96, 9-8-96	5
Touchdowns (Tot.)	Fred Lane, 11-2-97	3
	Tshimanga Biakabutuka, 10-3-99	3
	Muhsin Muhammad, 12-18-99	3
Points	Fred Lane, 11-2-97	18
	Tshimanga Biakabutuka, 10-3-99	18
	Muhsin Muhammad, 12-18-99	18

2001 SCHEDULE

PRESEASON

Aug. 10	at Jacksonville	7:30
Aug. 18	**New England**	7:30
Aug. 23	at Baltimore	7:30
Aug. 31	**Cleveland**	8:00

REGULAR SEASON

Sept. 9	at Minnesota	12:00
Sept. 16	**New England**	1:00
Sept. 23	at Atlanta	1:00
Sept. 30	**Green Bay**	1:00
Oct. 7	at San Francisco	5:30
Oct. 14	**New Orleans**	1:00
Oct. 21	at Washington	1:00
Oct. 28	**New York Jets**	1:00
Nov. 4	at Miami	1:00
Nov. 11	at St. Louis	12:00
Nov. 18	**San Francisco**	1:00
Nov. 25	**Atlanta**	1:00
Dec. 2	at New Orleans	12:00
Dec. 9	at Buffalo	1:00
Dec. 16	Open Date	
Dec. 23	**St. Louis**	1:00
Dec. 30	**Arizona**	1:00

ERICSSON STADIUM

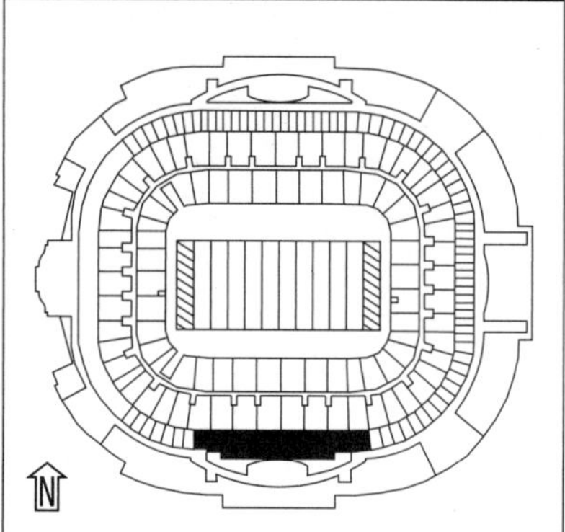

COACHING HISTORY

(46-52-0)

1995-98	Dom Capers	31-35-0
1999-2000	George Seifert	15-17-0

2000 TEAM RECORD

PRESEASON (0-4)

Date	Result		Opponent
8/4	L	14-34	Jacksonville
8/10	L	0-13	at Pittsburgh
8/18	L	13-24	Baltimore
8/24	L	21-29	at New England

REGULAR SEASON (7-9)

Date	Result		Opponent	Att.
9/3	L	17-20	at Washington	80,257
9/10	W	38-22	at San Francisco	66,879
9/17	L	10-15	Atlanta	73,025
10/1	L	13-16	Dallas (OT)	73,310
10/8	W	26-3	Seattle	72,192
10/15	L	6-24	at New Orleans	50,015
10/22	W	34-16	San Francisco	73,169
10/29	L	12-13	at Atlanta	46,178
11/5	W	27-24	at St. Louis	66,048
11/12	L	10-20	New Orleans	72,981
11/19	L	17-31	at Minnesota	64,208
11/27	W	31-14	Green Bay	73,295
12/3	W	16-3	St. Louis	73,358
12/10	L	14-15	at Kansas City	77,481
12/17	W	30-22	San Diego	72,159
12/24	L	9-52	at Oakland	60,637

(OT) Overtime

SCORE BY PERIODS

Panthers	78	106	60	66	0	—	310
Opponents	46	108	70	83	3	—	310

ATTENDANCE

Home 570,035 Away 507,903 Total 1,077,938
Single-game home record, 76,136 (12/10/95)
Single-season home record, 570,035 (2000)

2000 TEAM STATISTICS

	Panthers	Opp.
Total First Downs	304	304
Rushing	63	107
Passing	201	184
Penalty	40	13
Third Down: Made/Att	78/198	90/208
Third Down Pct.	39.4	43.3
Fourth Down: Made/Att	8/14	6/19
Fourth Down Pct.	57.1	31.6
Total Net Yards	4,654	5,656
Avg. Per Game	290.9	353.5
Total Plays	998	1,005
Avg. Per Play	4.7	5.6
Net Yards Rushing	1,186	1,944
Avg. Per Game	74.1	121.5
Total Rushes	363	426
Net Yards Passing	3,468	3,712
Avg. Per Game	216.8	232.0
Sacked/Yards Lost	69/382	27/226
Gross Yards	3,850	3,938
Att./Completions	566/340	552/352
Completion Pct.	60.1	63.8
Had Intercepted	19	17
Punts/Average	66/37.3	58/39.8
Net Punting Avg.	66/33.8	58/32.3
Penalties/Yards	84/683	128/1,073
Fumbles/Ball Lost	25/16	37/21
Touchdowns	31	35
Rushing	7	12
Passing	19	19
Returns	5	4
Avg. Time of Possession	29:54	30:06

2000 INDIVIDUAL STATISTICS

Passing	Att.	Comp.	Yds.	Pct.	TD	Int.	Tkld.	Rate
Beuerlein	533	324	3,730	60.8	19	18	62/331	79.7
Lewis	32	16	120	50.0	0	1	7/51	46.4
Walter	1	0	0	0.0	0	0	0/0	39.6
Panthers	566	340	3,850	60.1	19	19	69/382	77.7
Opponents	552	352	3,938	63.8	19	17	27/226	83.6

SCORING	TD R	TD P	TD Rt	PAT	FG	Saf	PTS
Nedney	0	0	0	20/20	26/28	0	98
Muhammad	0	6	0	0/0	0/0	0	36
Biakabutuka	2	2	0	0/0	0/0	0	24
Cunningham	0	0	0	9/9	5/7	0	24
Hayes	0	3	0	0/0	0/0	0	18
Hetherington	2	1	0	0/0	0/0	0	18
Byrd	0	2	0	0/0	0/0	0	12
Floyd	1	1	0	0/0	0/0	0	12
Walls	0	2	0	0/0	0/0	0	12
Beuerlein	1	0	0	0/0	0/0	0	8
Bates	0	0	1	0/0	0/0	0	6
Crawford	0	1	0	0/0	0/0	0	6
Evans	0	0	1	0/0	0/0	0	6
Hitchcock	0	0	1	0/0	0/0	0	6
Hoover	1	0	0	0/0	0/0	0	6
Mangum	0	1	0	0/0	0/0	0	6
Minter	0	0	1	0/0	0/0	0	6
Uwaezuoke	0	0	1	0/0	0/0	0	6
Panthers	7	19	5	29/29	31/35	0	310
Opponents	12	19	4	30/31	20/30	3	310

2-Pt. Conversions: Beuerlein.
Panthers 1-2, Opponents 2-4.

RUSHING	Att.	Yds.	Avg.	LG	TD
Biakabutuka	173	627	3.6	43	2
Hoover	89	290	3.3	35	1
Beuerlein	44	106	2.4	15	1
Hetherington	23	65	2.8	14	2
Lewis	8	36	4.5	19	0
Floyd	16	33	2.1	8	1
Bates	5	13	2.6	8	0
Muhammad	2	12	6.0	8	0
Craig	2	4	2.0	5	0
Walter	1	0	0.0	0	0
Panthers	363	1,186	3.3	43	7
Opponents	426	1,944	4.6	42	12

RECEIVING	No.	Yds.	Avg.	LG	TD
Muhammad	102	1,183	11.6	36	6
Hayes	66	926	14.0	43t	3
Biakabutuka	34	341	10.0	25	2
Walls	31	422	13.6	54	2
Byrd	22	241	11.0	34t	2
Mangum	19	215	11.3	31	1
Floyd	17	114	6.7	15	1
Hoover	15	112	7.5	16	0
Hetherington	14	116	8.3	19	1
Bates	5	38	7.6	23	0
Crawford	4	47	11.8	16t	1
Uwaezuoke	4	46	11.5	21	0
Hankton	4	38	9.5	14	0
Craig	2	4	2.0	4	0
Kinchen	1	7	7.0	7	0
Panthers	340	3,850	11.3	54	19
Opponents	352	3,938	11.2	62	19

INTERCEPTIONS	No.	Yds.	Avg.	LG	TD
Davis	5	14	2.8	8	0
Hitchcock	3	116	38.7	88t	1
Minter	2	38	19.0	30t	1
Evans	2	17	8.5	17	0
Wells	1	14	14.0	14	0
Gilbert	1	0	0.0	0	0
Navies	1	0	0.0	0	0
Robinson	1	0	0.0	0	0
Woodall	1	0	0.0	0	0
Panthers	17	199	11.7	88t	2
Opponents	19	365	19.2	46	2

PUNTING	No.	Yds.	Avg.	In 20	LG
Walter	64	2,459	38.4	19	66
Panthers	66	2,459	37.3	19	66
Opponents	58	2,311	39.8	13	55

PUNT RETURNS	No.	FC	Yds.	Avg.	LG	TD
Uwaezuoke	10	6	173	17.3	64t	1
Bates	7	3	31	4.4	12	0
Davis	2	2	24	12.0	20	0
Byrd	1	1	10	10.0	10	0
Hitchcock	1	0	0	0.0	0	0
Panthers	21	12	238	11.3	64t	1
Opponents	25	22	187	7.5	36	0

KICKOFF RETURNS	No.	Yds.	Avg.	LG	TD
Bates	42	941	22.4	92t	1
Byrd	9	172	19.1	30	0
Hetherington	2	21	10.5	11	0
Burks	1	25	25.0	25	0
R. Green	1	1	1.0	1	0
Panthers	55	1,160	21.1	92t	1
Opponents	64	1,120	17.5	32	0

FIELD GOALS	1-19	20-29	30-39	40-49	50+
Nedney	1/1	10/10	6/7	7/8	2/2
Cunningham	0/0	3/5	2/2	0/0	0/0
Panthers	1/1	13/15	8/9	7/8	2/2
Opponents	0/0	8/8	7/10	5/9	0/3

SACKS	No.
Williams	6.0
White	5.5
Gilbert	4.0
Rucker	2.5
Minter	2.0
Morabito	2.0
Navies	2.0
Peter	2.0
Swann	1.0
Panthers	27.0
Opponents	69.0

2001 DRAFT CHOICES

Round	Name	Pos.	College
1	Dan Morgan	LB	Miami
2	Kris Jenkins	DT	Maryland
3	Steve Smith	WR	Utah
4	Chris Weinke	QB	Florida State
5	Jarrod Cooper	DB	Kansas State
6	Dee Brown	RB	Syracuse
7	Louis Williams	C	Louisiana State
	Mike Roberg	TE	Idaho

CAROLINA PANTHERS

2001 VETERAN ROSTER

No.	Name	Pos.	Ht.	Wt.	Birthdate	NFL Exp.	College	Hometown	How Acq.	'00 Games/ Starts
46	Anderson, Rashard	S-CB	6-2	204	6/14/77	2	Jackson State	Forest, Miss.	D1-'00	12/0
24	# Bates, Michael	RB	5-10	189	12/19/69	9	Arizona	Tucson, Ariz.	FA-'96	16/0
21	Biakabutuka, Tshimanga	RB	6-0	215	1/24/74	6	Michigan	Lonqueuil, Quebec, Canada	D1-'96	12/11
31	Booth, Tony	S-CB	6-1	195	8/3/75	3	James Madison	Richmond, Va.	D7-'99	0*
3	Brice, Will	P	6-4	235	10/24/74	3	Virginia	Lancaster, S.C.	FA-'01	0*
49	Broughton, Luther	TE	6-2	248	11/30/74	5	Furman	Huger, S.C.	UFA(Phil)-01	15/1*
98	Buckner, Brentson	DT	6-2	305	9/30/71	8	Clemson	Columbus, Ga.	UFA(SF)-'01	16/16*
82	Byrd, Isaac	WR	6-1	188	11/16/74	5	Kansas	St. Louis, Mo.	W(Tenn)-'00	15/3
64	Chester, Larry	DT	6-2	310	10/17/75	4	Temple	Hammond, La.	FA-'01	16/0*
58	Childress, O.J.	LB	6-1	245	12/6/76	2	Clemson	Nashville, Tenn.	FA-'00	0*
2	Craig, Dameyune	QB	6-1	200	4/19/74	3	Auburn	Prichard, Ala.	FA-'98	4/0
84	Crawford, Casey	TE	6-6	255	8/1/77	2	Virginia	Falls Church, Va.	FA-'00	8/0
72	Daniel, Robert	DE	6-6	275	10/19/75	3	Northwestern State (La.)	Dallas, Texas	D6-'99	0*
64	Donnalley, Kevin	G	6-5	310	6/10/68	11	North Carolina	Raleigh, N.C.	UFA(Mia)-'01	16/16*
33	Evans, Doug	CB	6-1	190	5/13/70	9	Louisiana Tech	Haynesville, La.	UFA(GB)-'98	16/16
94	Gilbert, Sean	DT	6-5	318	4/10/70	9	Pittsburgh	Aliquippa, Pa.	FFA(Wash)-'98	15/15
27	Grant, Deon	S	6-2	207	3/14/79	2	Tennessee	Augusta, Ga.	D2-'00	0*
29	Green, Ray	S	6-3	187	3/22/77	2	South Carolina	Charleston, S.C.	FA-'00	16/0
14	Hankton, Karl	WR	6-2	202	7/24/70	3	Trinity College (Ill.)	New Orleans, La.	FA' 00	16/0
28	Harper, Deveron	CB	5-11	187	11/15/77	2	Notre Dame	Orangeburg, S.C.	FA-'00	16/0
81	Hayes, Donald	WR	6-4	208	7/13/75	4	Wisconsin	Madison, Wis.	D4-'98	15/15
44	Hetherington, Chris	FB	6-3	249	11/27/72	6	Yale	North Branford, Conn.	FA-'99	16/5
37	Hitchcock, Jimmy	CB	5-10	187	11/9/70	7	North Carolina	Concord, N.C.	UFA(Minn)-'00	16/2
45	Hoover, Brad	RB	6-2	225	11/11/76	2	Western Carolina	Thomasville, N.C.	FA-'00	16/4
42	Howard, Reggie	CB	6-0	190	5/17/77	2	Memphis State	Memphis, Tenn.	W(NO)-'00	1/0
78	James, Jeno	G	6-3	292	1/12/77	2	Auburn	Montgomery, Ala.	D6-'00	16/4
83	Jeffers, Patrick	WR	6-3	218	2/2/73	6	Virginia	Fort Worth, Texas	RFA(Dall)-'99	0*
75	# Jones, Clarence	T	6-6	300	5/6/68	11	Maryland	Brooklyn, N.Y.	UFA(NO)-'99	11/11
76	Jordan, Leander	G	6-3	333	9/15/77	2	Indiana (Pa.)	Pittsburgh, Pa.	D3-'00	0*
4	Kasay, John	K	5-10	198	10/27/69	11	Georgia	Athens, Ga.	UFA(Sea)-'95	0*
56	Kyle, Jason	LB	6-3	242	5/12/72	7	Arizona State	Tempe, Ariz.	UFA(SF)-'01	2/0*
8	Lewis, Jeff	QB	6-2	211	4/17/73	5	Northern Arizona	Phoenix, Ariz.	T(Den)-'99	5/0
71	Lucas, Al	DT	6-1	294	9/1/78	2	Troy State	Macon, Ga.	FA-'00	13/0
9	Lytle, Matt	QB	6-4	225	9/4/75	2	Pittsburgh	Wyomissing, Pa.	FA-'00	1/0*
86	Mangum, Kris	TE	6-4	249	8/15/73	4	Mississippi	Magee, Miss.	D7-'97	15/6
99	McKinley, Alvin	DT	6-3	292	6/9/78	2	Mississippi State	Weir, Miss.	D4-'00	7/0
52	Minor, Kory	LB	6-1	247	12/14/76	2	Notre Dame	LaPuente, Calif.	FA-'99	15/0
30	Minter, Mike	S	5-10	188	1/15/74	5	Nebraska	Lawton, Okla.	D2-'97	16/16
60	Mitchell, Jeff	C	6-4	300	1/29/74	5	Florida	Dallas, Texas	UFA(Balt)-'01	14/14*
90	Morabito, Tim	DT	6-3	296	10/12/73	6	Boston College	Garnerville, N.Y.	W(Cin)-'97	16/12
87	Muhammad, Muhsin	WR	6-2	217	5/5/73	6	Michigan State	Lansing, Mich.	D2-'96	16/16
29	Murrell, Adrian	RB	5-11	210	10/16/70	9	West Virginia	Wahiawa, Hawaii	UFA(Wash)-'01	15/0*
53	Navies, Hannibal	LB	6-2	240	7/19/77	3	Colorado	Oakland, Calif.	D4-'99	13/1
63	Nesbit, Jamar	C	6-4	330	12/17/76	3	South Carolina	Summerville, S.C.	FA-'99	16/16
26	Perry, Wilmont	RB	6-1	235	2/24/75	3	Livingstone College	Franklinton, N.C.	FA-'00	0*
97	Peter, Jason	DE	6-4	295	9/13/74	4	Nebraska	Locust, N.J.	D1-'98	9/0
54	Reeves, John	LB	6-3	245	2/23/75	3	Purdue	Bradenton, Fla.	FA-'01	9/0*
56	Reid, Spencer	LB	6-1	247	2/8/76	4	Brigham Young	Pago Pago, American Samoa	T(Ind)-'00	0*
39	Richardson, Damien	S	6-1	210	4/3/76	4	Arizona State	Fresno, Calif.	D6-'98	16/1
41	# Robinson, Eugene	S	6-1	200	5/28/63	17	Colgate	Hartford, Conn.	FA-'00	16/16
93	Rucker, Micheal	DE	6-5	258	2/28/75	3	Nebraska	St. Joseph, Mo.	D2b-'99	16/1
10	Sauerbrun, Todd	P	5-10	211	1/4/73	7	West Virginia	Garden City, N.Y.	FA-'01	16/0*
91	Smith, Chuck	DE	6-2	262	12/21/69	10	Tennessee	Athens, Ga.	UFA(Atl)-'00	2/2
75	Steussie, Todd	T	6-6	308	12/1/70	8	California	Aguora, Calif.	FA-'01	16/16*
67	Stoltenberg, Bryan	C	6-1	300	8/25/72	6	Colorado	Sugarland, Texas	FA-'98	8/1
70	Terry, Chris	T	6-5	295	8/8/75	3	Georgia	Jacksonville, Fla.	D2a-'99	16/16
57	Towns, Lester	LB	6-1	252	8/28/77	2	Washington	Pasadena, Calif.	D7-'00	16/14
80	Turner, Jim	WR	6-4	212	11/13/75	4	Syracuse	Jacksonville, Fla.	D7b-'98	0*
73	Tuten, Melvin	T	6-6	305	11/11/71	5	Syracuse	Washington, D.C.	W(Den)-'00	3/0
89	# Uwaezuoke, Iheanyi	WR	6-2	198	7/24/73	6	California	Westlake Village, Calif.	FA-'00	11/1
85	Walls, Wesley	TE	6-5	250	2/26/66	13	Mississippi	Pontotoc, Miss.	UFA(NO)-'96	8/8
95	Wells, Dean	LB	6-3	248	7/20/70	9	Kentucky	Louisville, Ky.	UFA(Sea)-'99	16/14
96	Williams, Jay	DE	6-3	280	10/13/71	6	Wake Forest	Washington, D.C.	UFA(StL)-'00	16/12

* Booth, Daniel, Grant, Jeffers, Kasay, Reid, and Turner missed '00 season because of injury; Brice last active with Cincinnati in '99; Broughton played 15 games with Philadelphia in '00; Buckner played 16 games with San Francisco; Chester played 16 games with Indianapolis; Childress last active with N.Y. Giants in '99; Donnalley played 16 games with Miami; Jordan was inactive for 16 games; Kyle played 2 games with San Francisco; Lytle played 1 game with Seattle; Mitchell played 14 games with Baltimore; Murrell played 15 games with Washington; Perry last active with New Orleans in '99; Reeves played 9 games with San Diego; Sauerbrun played 16 games with Kansas City; Steussie played 16 games with Minnesota.

Unrestricted free agent; subject to developments.

Retired—Eric Swann, 10-year defensive tackle, 16 games in '00; Reggie White, 15-year defensive end, 16 games in '00.

Players lost through free agency (3): G Matt Campbell (Wash; 14 games in '00), C Frank Garcia (StL; 16), K Joe Nedney (Tenn; 12).

Also played with Panthers in '00—QB Steve Beuerlein (16 games), WR Dialleo Burks (1), K Richie Cunningham (4), CB Eric Davis (16), T James Dexter (9), FB William Floyd (10), LB Deon Humphrey (3), TE Brian Kinchen (16), RB Natrone Means (1), P Ken Walter (16), LB Lee Woodall (16).

COACHING STAFF

Head Coach,
George Seifert

Pro Career: Became the second coach in Carolina Panthers history on January 4, 1999. Ranks third all-time among NFL head coaches with a .730 winning percentage (behind Vince Lombardi and John Madden) and reached both 50 and 75 victories faster than any head coach in League history. One of eleven head coaches to win two or more Super Bowls. Coached on all five of San Francisco's Super Bowl championship teams, earning one ring as secondary coach (1981), two as defensive coordinator (1984, 1988), and two as head coach (1989, 1994). Ranks as 49ers' all-time leader with 98 regular-season victories and 108 total wins. Directed 49ers teams that boasted the NFL's best record in 1989, 1990, 1992, and 1994. Guided 49ers to club-record five NFC Championship Game appearances and tied Bill Walsh's club mark with six NFC West titles. Named 49ers head coach in 1989 and became second rookie head coach to win Super Bowl. Appointed San Francisco's defensive coordinator in 1983 after joining 49ers as secondary coach in 1980. No pro playing experience. Career record: 123-52.

Background: Linebacker at University of Utah (1960-62). Served a six-month tour of duty with the U.S. Army following graduation. Returned to Utah as a graduate assistant in 1964. Named head coach at Westminster College in Salt Lake City in 1965. Assistant at Iowa (1966), Oregon (1967-1971), and Stanford (1972-74). Left Stanford to become head coach at Cornell (1975-76). Joined Bill Walsh's staff at Stanford in 1977 and helped the Cardinal to a two-year mark of 17-7, including victories in the Sun and Bluebonnet Bowls. Received bachelor's degree in zoology (1963) and master's degree in physical education (1966) from Utah.

Personal: Born January 22, 1940, in San Francisco. He and his wife, Linda, have two children—Eve and Jason—and live in Los Altos, Calif.

ASSISTANT COACHES

Paul Boudreau, offensive line; born December 30, 1949, Arlington, Mass., lives in Charlotte. Offensive lineman Boston College 1971-73. No pro playing experience. College coach: Boston College 1974-75, Maine 1976-78, Dartmouth 1979-1981, Navy 1982. Pro coach: Edmonton Eskimos (CFL) 1983-86, New Orleans Saints 1987-1993, Detroit Lions 1994-96, New England Patriots 1997-98, Miami Dolphins 1999-2000, joined Panthers in 2001.

Don Breaux, tight ends; born August 3, 1940, Jennings, La., lives in Charlotte. Quarterback McNeese State 1959-1961. Pro quarterback Denver Broncos 1963, San Diego Chargers 1964-65. College coach: Florida State 1966-67, Arkansas 1968-1971, 1977-1980, Florida 1973-74, Texas 1975-76. Pro coach: Houston Oilers 1972, Washington Redskins 1981-1993, New York Jets 1994, joined Panthers in 1995.

Jacob Burney, defensive line; born January 24, 1959, Chattanooga, Tenn., lives in Charlotte. Defensive tackle Tennessee-Chattanooga 1977-1980. No pro playing experience. College coach: New Mexico 1983-86, Tulsa 1987, Mississippi State 1988, Wisconsin 1989, UCLA 1990-92, Tennessee 1993. Pro coach: Cleveland Browns/Baltimore Ravens 1994-98, joined Panthers in 1999.

Chick Harris, running backs; born September 21, 1945, Durham, N.C., lives in Charlotte. Running back Northern Arizona 1966-69. No pro playing experience. College coach: Colorado State 1970-72, Long Beach State 1973-74, Washington 1975-1980. Pro coach: Buffalo Bills 1981-82, Seattle Seahawks 1983-1991, Los Angeles Rams 1992-94, joined Panthers in 1995.

Carlos Mainord, defensive backs, born August 26, 1944, Greenville, Texas, lives in Charlotte, N.C. Linebacker Navarro J.C. (Texas) 1962-63, McMurry College 1964-65. No pro playing experience. College coach: McMurry College 1966-68, Texas Tech 1969, 1983-85, 1987-1992, Ranger J.C. (Texas) 1970-71, 1972-77 (head coach), Rice 1978-1982, Miami 1986. Pro coach: Chicago Bears 1993-98, New Orleans Saints 1999, joined Panthers in 2000.

John Marshall, defensive coordinator-asst. head coach; born October 2, 1945, Arroyo Grande, Calif., lives in Charlotte. Linebacker Washington State 1964. No pro playing experience. College coach: Oregon 1970-76, Southern California 1977-79. Pro coach: Green Bay Packers 1980-82, Atlanta Falcons 1983-85, Indianapolis Colts 1986-88, San Francisco 49ers 1989-1998, joined Panthers in 1999.

Mike McCoy, wide receivers; born April 1, 1972, San Francisco, lives in Charlotte. Quarterback Long Beach State 1990-91, Utah 1992-94. Pro quarterback Amsterdam Admirals (NFL Europe) 1997, Calgary Stampede (CFL) 1999. Pro coach: Joined Panthers in 1999.

Sam Mills, linebackers; born June 3, 1959, Neptune, N.J., lives in Charlotte. Linebacker Montclair State 1977-1980. Pro linebacker Philadelphia/Baltimore Stars (USFL) 1983-85, New Orleans Saints 1986-1994, Carolina Panthers 1995-97. Pro coach: Joined Panthers in 1999.

Scott O'Brien, special teams; born June 25, 1957, Superior, Wis., lives in Charlotte. Defensive end Wisconsin-Superior 1975-78. Pro defensive end Green Bay Packers 1979, Toronto Argonauts (CFL) 1979. College coach: Wisconsin-Superior 1980-82, Nevada-Las Vegas 1983-85, Rice 1986, Pittsburgh 1987-1990. Pro coach: Cleveland Browns/Baltimore Ravens 1991-98, joined Panthers in 1999.

Alvin Reynolds, defensive quality control; born June 24, 1959, Pineville, La., lives in Charlotte. Safety Indiana State 1978-1981. No pro playing experience. College coach: Indiana State 1982-1992. Pro coach: Denver Broncos 1993-95, Baltimore Ravens 1996-98, joined Panthers in 1999.

Greg Roman, offensive quality control; born August 19, 1972, lives in Charlotte. Defensive line-linebacker John Carroll 1990-94. No pro playing experience. Pro coach: Joined Panthers in 1999.

Turk Schonert, quarterbacks; born January 15, 1957, Torrance, Calif., lives in Charlotte. Quarterback Stanford 1975-79. Pro quarterback Cincinnati Bengals 1980-85, Atlanta Falcons 1986, Cincinnati Bengals 1987-89. Pro coach: Tampa Bay Buccaneers 1992-95, Buffalo Bills 1998-2000, joined Panthers in 2001.

Darrin Simmons, special teams quality control-asst. strength and conditioning; born April 9, 1973, Elkhart, Kan., lives in Charlotte. Punter Kansas 1993-95. No pro playing experience. College coach: Kansas 1996, Minnesota 1997. Pro coach: Baltimore Ravens 1998, joined Panthers in 1999.

Jerry Simmons, strength and conditioning; born June 15, 1954, Elkhart, Kan., lives in Charlotte. Linebacker Fort Hays State 1976-77. No pro playing experience. College coach: Fort Hays State 1978, Clemson 1980, Rice 1981-82, Southern California 1983-87. Pro coach: New England Patriots 1988-1990, Cleveland Browns/Baltimore Ravens 1991-98, joined Panthers in 1999.

Richard Williamson, offensive coordinator-asst. head coach offense; born April 13, 1941, Ft. Deposit, Ala., lives in Charlotte. Receiver Alabama 1961-62. No pro playing experience. College coach: Alabama 1963-67, 1970-71, Arkansas 1968-69, 1972-74, Memphis State 1975-1980 (head coach). Pro coach: Kansas City Chiefs 1983-86, Tampa Bay Buccaneers 1987-1991 (interim head coach final three games of 1990, head coach 1991), Cincinnati Bengals 1992-94, joined Panthers in 1995.

2001 FIRST-YEAR ROSTER

Name	Pos.	Ht.	Wt.	Birthdate	College	Hometown	How Acq.
Blackman, Jon (1)	T	6-6	290	10/8/75	Purdue	Yorkville, Ill.	FA
Bowers, R.J.	RB	6-0	241	2/10/74	Grove City College	West Middlesex, Pa.	FA
Brown, Dee	RB	5-10	209	5/12/78	Syracuse	Lake Brantley, Fla.	FA
Buttone, Thadd	FB	6-0	250	5/21/79	Troy State	Atlanta, Ga.	FA
Cabellos, Jimmy	T	6-5	312	4/8/77	Marshall	Alexandria, Va.	FA
Chambers, Derrick	DE	6-4	305	1/28/78	Florida	Lawndale, N.C.	FA
Coffey, Kevin	WR	6-4	200	12/19/77	Virginia	East Cleveland, Ohio	FA
Cooper, Jarrod	S	6-0	210	3/31/78	Kansas State	Pearland, Texas	FA
Crosland, Andy (1)	K	6-0	200	11/17/76	Miami	Dallas, Texas	FA
Daniel, Darryl (1)	WR	5-11	190	1/24/76	Syracuse	Lancaster, Pa.	FA
Deligianis, Harry (1)	DT	6-4	304	8/4/75	Youngstown State	Ashtabula, Ohio	FA
Dukes, Chad (1)	RB	6-0	230	12/29/71	Pittsburgh	Albany, N.Y.	FA
Fritz, Luke	G	6-4	296	8/20/78	Eastern Washington	Osoyoos, B.C., Canada	FA
Goings, Nick	FB	6-0	225	1/26/78	Pittsburgh	Dublin, Ohio	FA
Grant, Kenneth	CB	6-0	205	1/7/79	Kentucky	Austin, Texas	FA
Green, Lamont (1)	LB	6-3	230	7/10/76	Florida State	Miami, Fla.	FA
Hall, Eric	DB	6-0	187	3/28/78	Albany State (Ga.)	Atlanta, Ga.	FA
Hawkes, Michael (1)	LB	6-0	242	4/11/77	Virginia Tech	Blackstone, Va.	FA
Hodel, Nathan	TE	6-2	247	11/12/77	Illinois	Fairview Heights, Ill.	FA
Hood, Kerry (1)	WR	6-0	196	12/16/76	South Carolina	Atlanta, Ga.	FA
Jenkins, Kris	DT	6-4	305	8/3/79	Maryland	Ypsilanti, Mich.	D2
Kelly, Jermale	WR	6-2	200	6/14/77	South Carolina	Greenville, S.C.	FA
Merkerson, Ron (1)	LB	6-2	247	8/30/75	Colorado	Las Vegas, Nev.	FA
Morgan, Dan	LB	6-2	233	12/19/78	Miami	Coral Springs, Fla.	D1
Renfro, Dusty (1)	LB	6-0	239	11/5/76	Texas	Alvarado, Texas	FA
Roberg, Mike	TE	6-4	263	9/18/77	Idaho	Kent, Wash.	D7b
William, Russell	T	6-8	320	3/3/78	West Virginia	Princeton, W. Va.	FA
Shuck, Kofi (1)	WR	6-1	174	5/11/77	Wyoming	Park Forest, Ill.	FA
Smith, Steve (1)	WR	5-9	179	5/12/79	Utah	Lynwood, Calif.	D3
Tanner, Russell	T	6-8	325	3/3/78	West Virginia	Princeton, W. Va.	FA
Thomas, Charles	T	6-4	292	11/26/78	Troy State	Forest Park, Ga.	FA
Washington, T.J. (1)	G-T	6-4	340	7/1/74	Virginia Tech	Onley, Va.	FA
Weinke, Chris	QB	6-4	238	7/1/72	Florida State	St. Paul, Minn.	D4
White, Jerard (1)	DB	6-1	204	10/27/77	Massachusetts	Washington, D.C.	FA
Williams, Louis	T-G	6-4	291	4/11/79	Louisiana State	Fort Walton Beach, Fla.	D7a
Wilson, Gillis (1)	DE	6-2	282	10/15/77	Southern	Patterson, La.	FA

The term NFL Rookie is defined as a player who is in his first season of professional football and has not been on the roster of another professional football team for any regular-season or postseason games. A Rookie is designated by an "R" on NFL rosters. Players who have been active in another professional football league or players who have NFL experience, including either preseason training camp or being on an Active List or Inactive List, or on Reserve/Injured or Reserve/Physically Unable to Perform for fewer than six regular-season games, are termed NFL First-Year Players. An NFL First-Year Player is designated by a "1" on NFL rosters. Thereafter, a player is credited with an additional year of experience for each season in which he accumulates six games on the Active List or Inactive List, or on Reserve/Injured or Reserve/Physically Unable to Perform.

CHICAGO BEARS

National Football Conference
Central Division
Team Colors: Navy Blue, Orange, and White
Halas Hall at Conway Park
1000 Football Drive
Lake Forest, Illinois 60045
Telephone: (847) 295-6600

CLUB OFFICIALS

Chairman Emeritus: Edward W. McCaskey
Chairman of the Board: Michael B. McCaskey
President and CEO: Ted Phillips
Secretary: Virginia H. McCaskey
Vice President: Tim McCaskey
Director of Pro Personnel: Scott Campbell
Director of College Scouting: Bill Rees
Director of Business Operations: Jim Miller
Chief Marketing Officer: Dave Greeley
Director of Administration: Bill McGrane
Director of Business Development: Brian McCaskey
Director of Ticket Operations: George McCaskey
Director of Special Projects: Pat McCaskey
Director of Community Relations: John Bostrom
Director of Public Relations: Scott Hagel
Public Relations Assistant Director: Jim Christman
Public Relations Assistant: Roger Hacker
Director of Player Development: Dwayne Joseph
Controller: Karen Zust
Video Director: Dean Pope
Assistant Video Directors: Dave Hendrickson, Peter Taylor
Head Athletic Trainer: Tim Bream
Assistant Trainers: Chris Hanks, Bobby Slater
Physical Development Coordinator: Russ Riederer
Asst. Physical Development Coordinator: Steve Little
Head Equipment Manager: Tony Medlin
Assistant Equipment Managers: Carl Piekarski, Jamal Nelson
Quality Control: Charlie Coiner, Chuck Bullough
Scouts: Marty Barrett, Glenn Schembechler, George Paton, Jeff Shiver, Pat Roberts, Phil Emery, John Paul Young
Stadium: Soldier Field (built in 1924)
• **Capacity:** 66,944
425 McFetridge Place
Chicago, Illinois 60605
Playing Surface: Grass
Training Camp: University of Wisconsin-Platteville
Platteville, Wisconsin 53818

2001 SCHEDULE

PRESEASON

Aug. 4	**Cincinnati**	7:00
Aug. 11	at Tennessee	7:00
Aug. 18	at Kansas City	7:30
Aug. 25	**Arizona**	7:00

REGULAR SEASON

Sept. 9	at Baltimore	1:00
Sept. 16	**Jacksonville**	3:15
Sept. 23	**Minnesota**	12:00
Sept. 30	Open Date	
Oct. 7	at Atlanta	1:00
Oct. 14	**Arizona**	12:00
Oct. 21	at Cincinnati	1:00
Oct. 28	**San Francisco**	12:00
Nov. 4	**Cleveland**	12:00
Nov. 11	**Green Bay**	12:00
Nov. 18	at Tampa Bay	1:00
Nov. 25	at Minnesota	7:30
Dec. 2	**Detroit**	12:00
Dec. 9	at Green Bay	12:00
Dec. 16	**Tampa Bay**	12:00
Dec. 23	at Washington	1:00
Dec. 30	at Detroit	1:00

RECORD HOLDERS

INDIVIDUAL RECORDS—CAREER

Category	Name	Performance
Rushing (Yds.)	Walter Payton, 1975-1987	*16,726
Passing (Yds.)	Sid Luckman, 1939-1950	14,686
Passing (TDs)	Sid Luckman, 1939-1950	137
Receiving (No.)	Walter Payton, 1975-1987	492
Receiving (Yds.)	Johnny Morris, 1958-1967	5,059
Interceptions	Gary Fencik, 1976-1987	38
Punting (Avg.)	George Gulyanics, 1947-1952	44.5
Punt Return (Avg.)	Ray (Scooter) McLean, 1940-47	14.8
Kickoff Return (Avg.)	Gale Sayers, 1965-1971	*30.6
Field Goals	Kevin Butler, 1985-1995	243
Touchdowns (Tot.)	Walter Payton, 1975-1987	125
Points	Kevin Butler, 1985-1995	1,116

INDIVIDUAL RECORDS—SINGLE SEASON

Category	Name	Performance
Rushing (Yds.)	Walter Payton, 1977	1,852
Passing (Yds.)	Erik Kramer, 1995	3,838
Passing (TDs)	Erik Kramer, 1995	29
Receiving (No.)	Johnny Morris, 1964	93
Receiving (Yds.)	Marcus Robinson, 1999	1,400
Interceptions	Mark Carrier, 1990	10
Punting (Avg.)	Bobby Joe Green, 1963	46.5
Punt Return (Avg.)	Harry Clark, 1943	15.8
Kickoff Return (Avg.)	Gale Sayers, 1967	37.7
Field Goals	Kevin Butler, 1985	31
Touchdowns (Tot.)	Gale Sayers, 1965	22
Points	Kevin Butler, 1985	144

INDIVIDUAL RECORDS—SINGLE GAME

Category	Name	Performance
Rushing (Yds.)	Walter Payton, 11-20-77	275
Passing (Yds.)	Johnny Lujack, 12-11-49	468
Passing (TDs)	Sid Luckman, 11-14-43	*7
Receiving (No.)	Jim Keane, 10-23-49	14
Receiving (Yds.)	Harlon Hill, 10-31-54	214
Interceptions	Many times	3
	Last time by Mark Carrier, 12-9-90	
Field Goals	Roger LeClerc, 12-3-61	5
	Mac Percival, 10-20-68	5
Touchdowns (Tot.)	Gale Sayers, 12-12-65	*6
Points	Gale Sayers, 12-12-65	36

*NFL Record

SOLDIER FIELD

COACHING HISTORY

Decatur Staleys 1920,
Chicago Staleys 1921
(631-453-42)

1920-29	George Halas	84-31-19
1930-32	Ralph Jones	24-10-7
1933-1942	George Halas*	88-24-4
1942-45	Hunk Anderson-Luke Johnsos**	24-12-2
1946-1955	George Halas	76-43-2
1956-57	John (Paddy) Driscoll	14-10-1
1958-1967	George Halas	76-53-6
1968-1971	Jim Dooley	20-36-0
1972-74	Abe Gibron	11-30-1
1975-77	Jack Pardee	20-23-0
1978-1981	Neill Armstrong	30-35-0
1982-1992	Mike Ditka	112-68-0
1993-98	Dave Wannstedt	41-57-0
1999-2000	Dick Jauron	11-21-0

*Retired after five games to enter U.S. Navy
**Co-coaches

2000 TEAM RECORD

PRESEASON (2-2)

Date	Result		Opponent
8/5	W	20-8	at New York Giants
8/12	W	19-6	Cleveland
8/19	L	20-24	at Cincinnati
8/25	L	28-34	Tennessee

REGULAR SEASON (5-11)

Date	Result		Opponent	Att.
9/3	L	27-30	at Minnesota	64,104
9/10	L	0-41	at Tampa Bay	65,569
9/17	L	7-14	New York Giants	66,944
9/24	L	14-21	Detroit	66,944
10/1	W	27-24	at Green Bay	59,869
10/8	L	10-31	New Orleans	66,944
10/15	L	16-28	Minnesota	66,944
10/22	L	9-13	at Philadelphia	65,553
11/5	W	27-24	Indianapolis	66,944
11/12	L	3-20	at Buffalo	72,420
11/19	W	13-10	Tampa Bay	66,944
11/26	L	10-17	at New York Jets	77,354
12/3	L	6-28	Green Bay	66,944
12/10	W	24-17	New England	66,944
12/17	L	0-17	at San Francisco	68,306
12/24	W	23-20	at Detroit	71,957

SCORE BY PERIODS

Bears	46	59	52	59	0	—	216
Opponents	47	117	88	103	0	—	355

ATTENDANCE

Home 526,973 Away 542,056 Total 1,069,029
Single-game home record, 66,900 (9/5/93)
Single-season home record, 527,769 (1999)

2000 TEAM STATISTICS

	Bears	Opp.
Total First Downs	239	297
Rushing	89	106
Passing	143	172
Penalty	7	19
Third Down: Made/Att	67/222	82/223
Third Down Pct.	30.2	36.8
Fourth Down: Made/Att	11/25	12/17
Fourth Down Pct.	44.0	70.6
Total Net Yards	4,541	5,234
Avg. Per Game	283.8	327.1
Total Plays	993	1,035
Avg. Per Play	4.6	5.1
Net Yards Rushing	1,736	1,827
Avg. Per Game	108.5	114.2
Total Rushes	417	469
Net Yards Passing	2,805	3,407
Avg. Per Game	175.3	212.9
Sacked/Yards Lost	34/200	36/230
Gross Yards	3,005	3,637
Att./Completions	542/304	530/332
Completion Pct.	56.1	62.6
Had Intercepted	16	11
Punts/Average	96/37.8	91/39.9
Net Punting Avg.	96/33.7	91/34.7
Penalties/Yards	90/696	78/727
Fumbles/Ball Lost	27/13	20/9
Touchdowns	22	43
Rushing	6	15
Passing	12	25
Returns	4	3
Avg. Time of Possession	28:30	31:30

2000 INDIVIDUAL STATISTICS

Passing	Att.	Comp.	Yds.	Pct.	TD	Int.	Tkld.	Rate
McNown	280	154	1,646	55.0	8	9	27/169	68.5
Matthews	178	102	964	57.3	3	6	5/24	64.0
Miller	82	47	382	57.3	1	1	2/7	68.2
Aguiar	1	1	13	100.0	0	0	0/0	118.8
Hartsell	1	0	0	0.0	0	0	0/0	39.6
Bears	542	304	3,005	56.1	12	16	34/200	67.0
Opponents	530	332	3,637	62.6	25	11	36/230	90.0

SCORING	TD R	TD P	TD Rt	PAT	FG	Saf	PTS
Edinger	0	0	0	21/21	21/27	0	84
M. Robinson	0	5	0	0/0	0/0	0	30
Allen	2	1	0	0/0	0/0	0	18
McNown	3	0	0	0/0	0/0	0	18
Booker	0	2	0	0/0	0/0	0	12
Kennison	0	2	0	0/0	0/0	0	12
Allred	0	1	0	0/0	0/0	0	6
Brown	0	0	1	0/0	0/0	0	6
Enis	1	0	0	0/0	0/0	0	6
W. Harris	0	0	1	0/0	0/0	0	6
McQuarters	0	0	1	0/0	0/0	0	6
Parrish	0	0	1	0/0	0/0	0	6
White	0	1	0	0/0	0/0	0	6
Bears	6	12	4	21/21	21/27	0	216
Opponents	15	25	3	41/41	18/26	0	355

2-Pt. Conversions: None.
Bears 0-1, Opponents 1-2.

RUSHING	Att.	Yds.	Avg.	LG	TD
Allen	290	1,120	3.9	29	2
McNown	50	326	6.5	30	3
Enis	36	84	2.3	11t	1
Barnes	15	81	5.4	20	0
Kennison	3	72	24.0	52	0
Matthews	10	35	3.5	14	0
M. Robinson	1	9	9.0	9	0
Milburn	1	6	6.0	6	0
Miller	7	5	0.7	3	0
Engram	1	1	1.0	1	0
Booker	2	-1	-.5	5	0
Bates	1	-2	-2.0	-2	0
Bears	417	1,736	4.2	52	6
Opponents	469	1,827	3.9	72t	15

RECEIVING	No.	Yds.	Avg.	LG	TD
M. Robinson	55	738	13.4	68t	5
Kennison	55	549	10.0	26	2
Booker	47	490	10.4	41	2
Allen	39	291	7.5	26	1
Brooks	26	216	8.3	27	0
Sinceno	23	206	9.0	28	0
Engram	16	109	6.8	25	0
White	10	87	8.7	25t	1
Allred	9	109	12.1	25	1
Enis	8	68	8.5	18	0
Bates	4	42	10.5	18	0
Mayes	4	40	10.0	19	0
Dragos	4	28	7.0	10	0
Wells	1	13	13.0	13	0
Milburn	1	8	8.0	8	0
Barnes	1	7	7.0	7	0
Lyman	1	4	4.0	4	0
Bears	304	3,005	9.9	68t	12
Opponents	332	3,637	11.0	66	25

INTERCEPTIONS	No.	Yds.	Avg.	LG	TD
Parrish	3	81	27.0	38t	1
W. Harris	2	35	17.5	35t	1
Urlacher	2	19	9.5	19	0
McQuarters	1	61	61.0	61t	1
Brown	1	35	35.0	35t	1
Wells	1	21	21.0	21	0
Azumah	1	2	2.0	2	0
Bears	11	254	23.1	61t	4
Opponents	16	150	9.4	38t	1

PUNTING	No.	Yds.	Avg.	In 20	LG
Aguiar	52	2,017	38.8	8	56
Bartholomew	44	1,607	36.5	12	52
Bears	96	3,624	37.8	20	56
Opponents	91	3,629	39.9	29	59

PUNT RETURNS	No.	FC	Yds.	Avg.	LG	TD
Milburn	35	26	300	8.6	25	0
W. Harris	1	1	14	14.0	14	0
Bears	36	27	314	8.7	25	0
Opponents	36	33	251	7.0	25	0

KICKOFF RETURNS	No.	Yds.	Avg.	LG	TD
Milburn	63	1,468	23.3	38	0
Enis	2	30	15.0	19	0
Sinceno	1	12	12.0	12	0
Tucker	1	0	0.0	0	0
Tuinei	1	2	2.0	2	0
Bears	68	1,512	22.2	38	0
Opponents	51	1,105	21.7	48	0

FIELD GOALS	1-19	20-29	30-39	40-49	50+
Edinger	1/1	5/5	7/9	6/10	2/2
Bears	1/1	5/5	7/9	6/10	2/2
Opponents	1/1	6/6	3/8	7/9	1/2

SACKS	No.
Urlacher	8.0
Daniels	6.0
B. Robinson	4.5
Flanigan	4.0
Colvin	3.0
Parrish	2.0
F. Smith	2.0
Culpepper	1.0
S. Harris	1.0
McQuarters	1.0
Tuinei	1.0
Wells	1.0
Wilson	1.0
Simmons	0.5
Bears	36.0
Opponents	34.0

2001 DRAFT CHOICES

Round	Name	Pos.	College
1	David Terrell	WR	Michigan
2	Anthony Thomas	RB	Michigan
3	Mike Gandy	G	Notre Dame
4	Karon Riley	DE	Minnesota
5	Bernard Robertson	C	Tulane
7	John Capel	WR	Florida

CHICAGO BEARS

2001 VETERAN ROSTER

No.	Name	Pos.	Ht.	Wt.	Birthdate	NFL Exp.	College	Hometown	How Acq.	'00 Games/ Starts
20	Allen, James	RB	5-10	215	3/28/75	4	Oklahoma	Wynnewood, Okla.	FA-'97	16/15
23	Azumah, Jerry	CB	5-10	195	9/1/77	3	New Hampshire	Worcester, Mass.	D5c-'99	14/4
32	Barnes, Marlon	RB	5-9	215	3/13/76	2	Colorado	Memphis, Tenn.	W(Mia)-'00	13/0
12	Bartholomew, Brent	P	6-2	220	10/22/76	3	Ohio State	Apopka, Fla.	T(Mia)-'00	7/0
87	Bates, D'Wayne	WR	6-2	215	12/4/75	3	Northwestern	Aiken, S.C.	D3b-'99	5/0
84	Baxter, Fred	TE	6-3	265	6/14/71	9	Auburn	Brundidge, Ala.	W(NYJ)-'01	9/6*
48	Bell, Shonn	TE	6-4	260	10/25/74	2	Clinch Valley College	Stuarts Draft, Va.	FA-'00	0*
86	Booker, Marty	WR	5-11	215	7/31/76	3	Northeast Louisiana	Jonesboro-Hodge, La.	D3c-'99	15/7
36	Brady, Donny	CB	6-2	195	11/26/73	4	Wisconsin	North Bellmore, N.Y.	FA-'01	0*
78	Brockermeyer, Blake	T	6-4	300	4/11/73	7	Texas	Arlington Heights, Texas	UFA(Car)-'99	15/14
30	Brown, Mike	S	5-10	202	2/13/78	2	Nebraska	Scottsdale, Ariz.	D2-'00	16/16
59	Colvin, Rosevelt	LB	6-3	254	9/5/77	3	Purdue	Indianapolis, Ind.	D4b-'99	13/8
93	Daniels, Phillip	DE	6-5	290	3/4/73	6	Georgia	Donalsonville, Ga.	UFA(Sea)-'00	14/14
45	Dragos, Scott	FB-TE	6-2	245	10/28/75	2	Boston College	Old Rochester, Mass.	W(NYG)-'99	9/2
2	Edinger, Paul	K	5-10	162	1/17/78	2	Michigan State	Lakeland, Fla.	D6b-'00	16/0
81	Engram, Bobby	WR	5-10	185	1/7/73	6	Penn State	Camden, S.C.	D2-'96	3/3
43	Green, Mike	S	6-0	176	12/6/76	2	Northwestern State (La.)	Ruston, La.	D7b-'00	7/0
55	Harris, Sean	LB	6-3	252	2/25/72	7	Arizona	Magnet, Ariz.	D3a-'95	15/13
27	Harris, Walt	CB	5-11	195	8/10/74	6	Mississippi State	La Grange, Ga.	D1-'96	12/12
74	Herndon, Jimmy	T	6-8	318	8/30/73	6	Houston	Baytown, Texas	T(Jax)-'97	10/2
46	Hicks, Skip	RB	6-0	230	10/13/74	4	UCLA	Burkburnett, Texas	FA-'01	10/1*
53	Holdman, Warrick	LB	6-1	246	11/22/75	3	Texas A&M	Alief, Texas	D4a-'99	10/10
95	Jones, Greg	LB	6-4	248	5/22/74	5	Colorado	Denver, Colo.	UFA(Wash)-'01	16/4*
57	Kreutz, Olin	C	6-2	285	6/9/77	4	Washington	Honolulu, Hawaii	D3-'98	7/7
89	Lyman, Dustin	TE	6-4	250	8/5/76	2	Wake Forest	Boulder, Colo.	D3b-'00	14/7
65	Mannelly, Patrick	T-LS	6-5	270	4/18/75	4	Duke	Atlanta, Ga.	D6b-'98	16/0
9	Matthews, Shane	QB	6-3	196	6/1/70	8	Florida	Pascagoula, Miss.	UFA(Car)-'99	6/5
4	Maynard, Brad	P	6-1	190	2/9/74	5	Ball State	Sheridan, Ind.	UFA(NYG)-'01	16/0*
47	McElroy, Ray	S	5-11	196	7/31/72	6	Eastern Illinois	Bellwood, Ill.	FA(Car)-'00	13/0
26	McMillon, Todd	CB	5-10	183	9/26/74	2	Northern Arizona	Bellflower, Calif.	FA-'00	3/0
8	McNown, Cade	QB	6-1	208	1/12/77	3	UCLA	West Linn, Ore.	D1-'99	10/9
21	McQuarters, R.W.	CB	5-9	198	12/21/76	4	Oklahoma State	Tulsa, Okla.	T(SF)-'00	15/2
24	Milburn, Glyn	RB-KR	5-8	176	2/19/71	9	Stanford	Santa Monica, Calif.	T(GB)-'98	16/0
15	Miller, Jim	QB	6-2	215	2/9/71	8	Michigan State	Waterford, Mich.	W(Det)-'98	3/2
62	Newkirk, Robert	DT	6-3	290	3/6/77	2	Michigan State	Bell Glade, Fla.	FA-'00	5/0
37	Parrish, Tony	S	5-10	211	11/23/75	4	Washington	Huntington Beach, Calif.	D2-'98	16/16
72	Powell, Carl	DT	6-2	264	1/4/74	2	Louisville	Louisville, Ky.	W(Balt)-'01	2/0*
98	# Robinson, Bryan	DE	6-4	300	6/22/74	5	Fresno State	Toledo, Ohio	W(StL)-'98	16/16
88	Robinson, Marcus	WR	6-3	215	2/27/75	5	South Carolina	Ft. Valley, Ga.	D4b-'97	11/11
91	Samuel, Khari	LB	6-3	240	10/14/76	3	Massachusetts	Framingham, Mass.	D5b-'99	16/0
31	Shelton, Daimon	FB	6-0	258	9/15/72	5	Sacramento State	Duarte, Calif.	UFA(Jax)-'01	16/9*
96	Simmons, Clyde	DE	6-5	292	8/4/64	16	Western Carolina	Wilmington, N.C.	UFA(Cin)-'99	16/2
85	Sinceno, Kaseem	TE	6-4	255	3/26/76	4	Syracuse	Liberty, N.Y.	W(GB)-'00	11/11
99	Smeenge, Joel	DE	6-6	265	4/1/68	12	Western Michigan	Grand Rapids, Mich.	FA-'01	12/1*
29	Smith, Frankie	S	5-9	194	10/8/68	9	Baylor	Groesbeck, Texas	FA-'98	14/0
25	Smith, Thomas	CB	5-11	190	12/5/70	9	North Carolina	Gates, N.C.	UFA(Buff)-'00	16/16
11	Tolliver, Billy Joe	QB	6-1	217	2/7/66	11	Texas Tech	Boyd, Texas	UFA(NO)-'01	0*
94	Traylor, Keith	DT	6-2	304	9/3/69	10	Central State (Okla.)	Little Rock, Ark.	FA-'01	16/16*
64	Tucker, Rex	G	6-5	315	12/20/76	3	Texas A&M	Midland, Texas	D3a-'99	6/0
90	Tuinei, Van	DT	6-4	290	2/16/71	5	Arizona	Westminster, Calif.	W(Ind)-'99	14/2
54	Urlacher, Brian	LB	6-3	244	5/25/78	2	New Mexico	Lovington, N.M.	D1-'00	16/14
58	Villarrial, Chris	G	6-4	308	6/9/73	6	Indiana (Penn.)	Hershey, Pa.	D5-'96	16/15
73	Wallace, Alonzo	DE	6-5	258	3/25/74	3	Maryland	Delray Beach, Fla.	W(Phil)-'00	0*
92	Washington, Ted	DT	6-5	330	4/13/68	11	Louisville	Tampa, Fla.	FA-'01	16/16*
97	Wells, Mike	DT	6-3	315	1/6/71	9	Iowa	Arnold, Mo.	UFA(Det)-'98	16/14
33	Whigham, Larry	S	6-2	210	6/23/72	8	Northeast Louisiana	Hattiesburg, Miss.	FA-'01	14/4*
80	White, Dez	WR	6-0	219	8/23/79	2	Georgia Tech	Orange Park, Fla.	D3a-'00	15/0
71	Williams, James	T	6-7	331	3/29/68	11	Cheyney State	Allerdice, Pa.	FA-'91	16/16
79	Wisne, Jerry	T	6-6	315	7/28/76	3	Notre Dame	Tulsa, Okla.	D5a-'99	0*
22	Wooden, Shawn	S	5-11	205	10/23/73	6	Notre Dame	Abington, Pa.	UFA(Mia)-'00	11/0

* Baxter played 9 games with N.Y. Jets in '00; Bell last active with San Francisco in '99; Brady last active with Baltimore in '98; Hicks played 10 games with Washington; Jones played 16 games with Washington; Maynard played 16 games with N.Y. Giants; Powell played 2 games with Baltimore; Shelton played 16 games with Jacksonville; Smeenge played 12 games with Jacksonville; Tollliver missed '00 season because of injury with New Orleans; Traylor played 16 games with Denver; Wallace last active with Philadelphia in '98; Washington played 16 games with Buffalo; Whigham played 14 games with New England; Wisne last active with Chicago in '99.

Unrestricted free agent; subject to developments.

Traded—TE Alonzo Mayes (5 games in '00) to Miami.

Players lost through free agency (3): WR Eddie Kennison (Den; 16 games in '00), G Todd Perry (Mia; 16), C Casey Wiegmann (KC; 16).

Also played with Bears in '00—P Louie Aguiar (9 games), TE John Allred (5), WR Macey Brooks (16), RB Curtis Enis (12), DT Jim Flanigan (16), LB Ty Hallock (2), QB Mark Hartsell (1), LB Barry Minter (15), DE Troy Wilson (6).

COACHING STAFF

Head Coach,
Dick Jauron

Pro Career: Named eleventh head coach in franchise history on January 24, 1999. After winning six games in his rookie season of 1999, Jauron became the first Bears coach in history to beat the Packers at Lambeau Field in each of his first two trips with a 27-24 win on October 1, 2000. Guided Chicago to a 4-4 record to close the 2000 season. As Jacksonville's inaugural defensive coordinator, he was instrumental in the success of the Jaguars, which included three playoff berths in the franchise's first four seasons and an appearance in the 1996 AFC Championship Game. Jauron coached defensive backs for nine years in Green Bay (1986-1994) before moving to Jacksonville. His coaching career started in Buffalo in 1985. Jauron played eight years as a defensive back in the NFL with the Detroit Lions and Cincinnati Bengals, earning a trip to the 1975 Pro Bowl. Career record: 11-21.

Background: Played running back at Yale from 1970-72 where he still holds the school's career rushing mark with 2,947 yards. Drafted by the Detroit Lions in the fourth round of the 1973 draft. Played defensive back for Detroit from 1973-77 and was named to the Pro Bowl after the 1974 season. Joined Cincinnati in 1978 and played with the Bengals until retiring in 1980. Spent several years away from NFL before joining the Buffalo Bills' coaching staff in 1985. Moved to Green Bay the following season and served as the defensive backs coach under three different head coaches (Forrest Greg, 1986-87; Lindy Infante, 1988-91; Mike Holmgren, 1992-94). Jauron accepted the defensive coordinator post with the expansion Jacksonville Jaguars in 1995 and helped lead the team to three consecutive playoff berths after their opening season.

Personal: Born October 7, 1950, Peoria, Ill. Dick and his wife Gail live in Lake Forest, Ill. and have two daughters—Kacy and Amy.

ASSISTANT COACHES

Vance Bedford, defensive backs; born August 20, 1958, Houston, Texas. Defensive back Texas 1977-79, 1981. Pro defensive back St. Louis Cardinals 1982, Oklahoma Outlaws (USFL) 1984. College coach: Navarro (Tex.) J.C. 1986, Colorado State 1987-1992, Oklahoma State 1993-94, Michigan 1995-98. Pro coach: Joined Bears in 1999.

Greg Blache, defensive coordinator; born March 9, 1949, New Orleans, lives in Lake Bluff, Ill. Attended Notre Dame. No college or pro playing experience. College coach: Notre Dame 1973-75, 1981-83, Tulane 1976-1980, Southern 1986, Kansas 1987. Pro coach: Jacksonville Bulls (USFL) 1984-85, Green Bay Packers 1988-1993, Indianapolis Colts 1994-98, joined Bears in 1999.

Pete Carmichael, offensive assistant; born March 4, 1941, North Plainfield, N.J., lives in Lake Bluff, Ill. Quarterback Dayton 1961, Montclair State College 1962-63. No pro playing experience. College coach: Virginia Military Institute 1965-66, New Hampshire 1967, Boston College 1968-1972, 1981-1993, Trenton State College 1973 (head coach), Columbia 1974-77, Merchant Marine Academy 1977-1980 (head coach). Pro coach: Jacksonville Jaguars 1995-99, Cleveland Browns 2000, joined Bears in 2001.

Pat Flaherty, tight ends; born April 27, 1956, Hanover, Pa., lives in Waukegan, Ill. Center East Stroudsburg 1976-79. No pro playing experience. College coach: East Stroudsburg 1980-81, Penn State 1982-83, Rutgers 1984-1991, East Carolina 1992, Wake Forest 1993-98, Iowa 1999. Pro coach: Washington Redskins 2000, joined Bears in 2001.

Todd Haley, wide receivers; born February 28, 1967, Atlanta, lives in Waukegan, Ill. Attended Florida and Miami. No college or pro playing experience. Pro coach: New York Jets 1996-2000, joined Bears in 2001.

Dale Lindsey, linebackers; born January 18, 1943, Bedford, Ind., lives in Lake Bluff, Ill. Linebacker Western Kentucky 1961-64. Pro linebacker Cleveland Browns 1965-1973. College coach: Southern Methodist 1988-89. Pro coach: Green Bay Packers 1986-87, New England Patriots 1990, Tampa Bay Buccaneers 1991, San Diego Chargers 1994-96, Washington Redskins 1997-98, joined Bears in 1999.

Earle Mosley, running backs; born December 20, 1946, Darby, Pa., lives in Buffalo Grove, Ill. Defensive back West Chester State 1970-72. No pro playing experience. College coach: West Chester State 1979, Rutgers 1980-83, Northwestern 1984-87, Temple 1988-1991, Notre Dame 1992-96, Stanford 1997-98. Pro coach: Joined Bears in 1999.

Rex Norris, defensive line; born December 10, 1939, Tipton, Ind., lives in Libertyville, Ill. Linebacker San Angelo (Texas) J.C. 1959-1960, East Texas State 1961-62. No pro playing experience. College coach: Navarro (Texas) J.C. 1970-71, Texas A&M 1972, Oklahoma 1973-1983, Arizona State 1984, Florida 1988-89, Tennessee 1990-91, Texas 1992-93. Pro coach: Detroit Lions 1985-87, Denver Broncos 1994, Tennessee Oilers 1995-98, joined Bears in 1999.

John Shoop, offensive coordinator; born August 1, 1969, Pittsburgh, lives in Libertyville, Ill. Quarterback University of the South 1987-1990. No pro playing experience. College coach: Dartmouth 1991, Vanderbilt 1992-94. Pro coach: Carolina Panthers 1995-98, joined Bears in 1999.

Mike Sweatman, special teams; born October 23, 1947, Kansas City, Mo., lives in Lake Bluff, Ill. Linebacker Kansas 1964-67. No pro playing experience. College coach: Kansas 1973-74, 1979-1982, Tulsa 1977-78, Tennessee 1983. Pro coach: Minnesota Vikings 1984, New York Giants 1985-1992, New England Patriots 1993-96, New York Jets 1997-2000, joined Bears in 2001.

Bob Wylie, offensive line; born February 16, 1951, West Warwick, R.I., lives in Lake Bluff, Ill. Linebacker Colorado 1969-1971. No pro playing experience. College coach: Brown 1980-82, Holy Cross 1983-84, Ohio 1985-87, Colorado State 1988-89, Cincinnati 1996. Pro coach: New York Jets 1990-91, Tampa Bay Buccaneers 1992-95, Cincinnati Bengals 1997-98, joined Bears in 1999.

2001 FIRST-YEAR ROSTER

Name	Pos.	Ht.	Wt.	Birthdate	College	Hometown	How Acq.
Austin, Reggie (1)	CB	5-9	173	12/1/77	Wake Forest	Atlanta, Ga.	D4-'00
Boone, Alfonso (1)	DT	6-3	305	1/11/76	Mt. San Antonio (Calif.) J.C.	Saginaw, Mich.	FA-'00
Brown, Chris	T	6-6	315	1/21/78	Georgia Tech	Augusta, Ga.	FA
Capel, John	WR	5-11	163	10/27/78	Florida	Brooksville, Fla.	D7
Coleman, Fred (1)	WR	6-4	190	1/31/75	Washington	Tyler, Texas	FA
Donaldson, Cedric (1)	CB	5-9	176	2/12/76	Louisiana State	Jackson, Miss.	FA-'00
Edwards, Brian (1)	RB	6-1	230	6/6/76	East Tennessee State	Ocala, Fla.	FA-'00
Emmerich, Conrad	FB	6-4	268	4/27/78	Northwestern	Foley, Minn.	FA
Gandy, Mike	G	6-4	313	1/3/79	Notre Dame	Garland, Texas	D3
Gilliam, Rick	G	6-6	330	7/7/77	West Virginia	Newville, Pa.	FA
Howard, Bobbie (1)	LB	5-10	226	6/14/77	Notre Dame	Belle, W. Va.	FA-'00
Johnson, Chris	FB	6-1	255	11/26/76	Kansas State	Chickasha, Okla.	FA
Lemons, Devin	LB	6-3	222	3/20/79	Texas Tech	Pampa, Texas	FA
Maxie, Demetrious (1)	DT	6-2	265	10/18/73	Texas-El Paso	Los Angeles, Calif.	FA
Merritt, Ahmad (1)	WR	5-10	188	2/5/77	Wisconsin	Chicago, Ill.	FA-'00
Mitchell, David	CB	6-1	195	10/18/79	Ohio State	Westerville, Ohio	FA
Pisetsky, Vitaly	K	5-10	219	1/28/78	Wisconsin	New York, N.Y.	FA
Riley, Karon	DE	6-2	251	8/23/78	Minnesota	Detroit, Mich.	D4
Robertson, Bernard	G	6-2	297	6/9/79	Tulane	New Orleans, La.	D5
Sanford, Sulecio (1)	WR	5-10	190	3/23/76	Middle Tennessee State	Milledgeville, Ga.	D7a-'99
Soldano, Garrett	LB	5-11	231	5/26/78	Western Michigan	Onsted, Mich.	FA
Terrell, David	WR	6-3	215	3/13/79	Michigan	Richmond, Va.	D1
Thomas, Anthony	RB	6-1	226	11/11/77	Michigan	Winnfield, La.	D2
Ward, Ryan	T	6-7	310	6/12/77	New Hampshire	Niagara Falls, Ontario, Canada	FA
Williams, Brad (1)	G	6-4	295	3/13/78	Notre Dame	Orange, Calif.	FA-'00
Williams, Gerald (1)	WR	6-3	200	10/7/76	Oklahoma	Tucker, Ga.	FA
Wise, Ty (1)	C	6-2	291	3/9/77	Miami	Pensacola, Fla.	FA-'00
Young, Sam	CB	5-11	180	8/1/78	Illinois State	Chicago, Ill.	FA

The term NFL Rookie is defined as a player who is in his first season of professional football and has not been on the roster of another professional football team for any regular-season or postseason games. A Rookie is designated by an "R" on NFL rosters. Players who have been active in another professional football league or players who have NFL experience, including either preseason training camp or being on an Active List or Inactive List, or on Reserve/Injured or Reserve/Physically Unable to Perform for fewer than six regular-season games, are termed NFL First-Year Players. An NFL First-Year Player is designated by a "1" on NFL rosters. Thereafter, a player is credited with an additional year of experience for each season in which he accumulates six games on the Active List or Inactive List, or on Reserve/Injured or Reserve/Physically Unable to Perform.

NOTES

DALLAS COWBOYS

National Football Conference
Eastern Division
Team Colors: Royal Blue, Metallic Silver Blue, and White
Cowboys Center
One Cowboys Parkway
Irving, Texas 75063
Telephone: (972) 556-9900

CLUB OFFICIALS

Owner/President/General Manager: Jerry Jones
Executive Vice President-Player Personnel: Stephen Jones
Vice President/Marketing: George Hays
Vice President/Director of Charities and Special Events: Charlotte Anderson
Vice President/Legal/Director of Internet: Jerry Jones, Jr.
Public Relations Director: Rich Dalrymple
Assistant Director of Public Relations: Brett Daniels
Director of College and Pro Scouting: Larry Lacewell
Director of Operations: Bruce Mays
Treasurer: Robert Nunez
Ticket Manager: Carol Padgett
Trainer: Jim Maurer
Equipment Manager: Mike McCord
Video Director: Robert Blackwell
Cheerleader Director: Kelli Finglass
Stadium: Texas Stadium (built in 1971)
•**Capacity:** 65,639
2401 E. Airport Freeway
Irving, Texas 75062
Playing Surface: Sportfield Turf
Training Camp: Midwestern State University
Wichita Falls, Texas 76308
(July 21-Aug. 9)
Marriott Residence Inn
Oxnard, Calif. 93030
(Aug. 13-Aug. 25)

2001 SCHEDULE

PRESEASON

Aug. 4	at Oakland	6:00
Aug. 11	**Denver**	8:00
Aug. 18	at New Orleans	7:00
Aug. 27	vs. Oakland at Mexico City	7:00
Aug. 30	**Jacksonville**	7:30

REGULAR SEASON

Sept. 9	**Tampa Bay**	12:00
Sept. 16	at Detroit	1:00
Sept. 23	**San Diego**	12:00
Sept. 30	at Philadelphia	8:30
Oct. 7	Open Date	
Oct. 15	**Washington** (Mon.)	8:00
Oct. 21	at Oakland	1:15
Oct. 28	**Arizona**	3:05
Nov. 4	at New York Giants	1:00
Nov. 11	at Atlanta	1:00
Nov. 18	**Philadelphia**	12:00
Nov. 22	**Denver** (Thurs.)	3:05
Dec. 2	at Washington	4:15
Dec. 9	**New York Giants**	12:00
Dec. 16	at Seattle	1:15
Dec. 23	at Arizona	2:05
Dec. 30	**San Francisco**	12:00

RECORD HOLDERS

INDIVIDUAL RECORDS—CAREER

Category	Name	Performance
Rushing (Yds.)	Emmitt Smith, 1990-2000	15,166
Passing (Yds.)	Troy Aikman, 1989-2000	32,942
Passing (TDs)	Troy Aikman, 1989-2000	165
Receiving (No.)	Michael Irvin, 1988-1999	750
Receiving (Yds.)	Michael Irvin, 1988-1999	11,904
Interceptions	Mel Renfro, 1964-1977	52
Punting (Avg.)	Mike Saxon, 1985-1992	41.5
Punt Return (Avg.)	Deion Sanders, 1995-99	13.3
Kickoff Return (Avg.)	Mel Renfro, 1964-1977	26.4
Field Goals	Rafael Septien, 1978-1986	162
Touchdowns (Tot.)	Emmitt Smith, 1990-2000	156
Points	Emmitt Smith, 1990-2000	938

INDIVIDUAL RECORDS—SINGLE SEASON

Category	Name	Performance
Rushing (Yds.)	Emmitt Smith, 1995	1,773
Passing (Yds.)	Danny White, 1983	3,980
Passing (TDs)	Danny White, 1983	29
Receiving (No.)	Michael Irvin, 1995	111
Receiving (Yds.)	Michael Irvin, 1995	1,603
Interceptions	Everson Walls, 1981	11
Punting (Avg.)	Sam Baker, 1962	45.4
Punt Return (Avg.)	Bob Hayes, 1968	20.8
Kickoff Return (Avg.)	Mel Renfro, 1965	30.0
Field Goals	Richie Cunningham, 1997	34
Touchdowns (Tot.)	Emmitt Smith, 1995	25
Points	Emmitt Smith, 1995	150

INDIVIDUAL RECORDS—SINGLE GAME

Category	Name	Performance
Rushing (Yds.)	Emmitt Smith, 10-31-93	237
Passing (Yds.)	Don Meredith, 11-10-63	460
Passing (TDs)	Many times	5
	Last time by Troy Aikman, 9-12-99	
Receiving (No.)	Lance Rentzel, 11-19-67	13
Receiving (Yds.)	Bob Hayes, 11-13-66	246
Interceptions	Herb Adderley, 9-26-71	3
	Lee Roy Jordan, 11-4-73	3
	Dennis Thurman, 12-13-81	3
Field Goals	Chris Boniol, 11-18-96	*7
Touchdowns (Tot.)	Many times	4
	Last time by Emmitt Smith, 9-4-95	
Points	Many times	24
	Last time by Emmitt Smith, 9-4-95	

*NFL Record

COACHING HISTORY

(389-268-6)

1960-1988	Tom Landry	270-178-6
1989-1993	Jimmy Johnson	51-37-0
1994-97	Barry Switzer	45-26-0
1998-99	Chan Gailey	18-16-0
2000	Dave Campo	5-11-0

TEXAS STADIUM

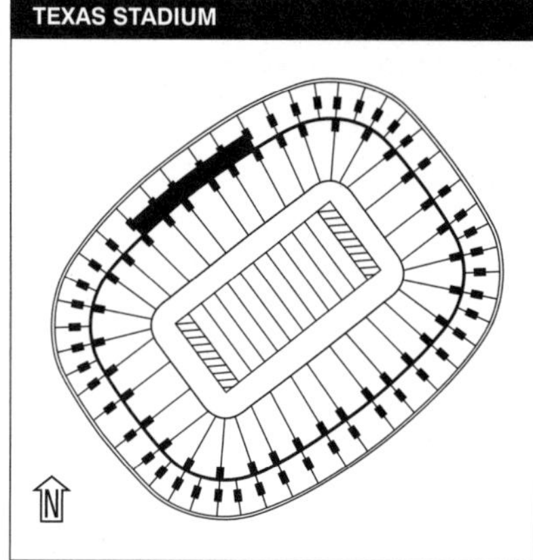

2000 TEAM RECORD

PRESEASON (0-5)

Date	Result		Opponent
7/30	L	10-38	Pittsburgh
8/5	L	9-20	vs. Atlanta at Tokyo, Japan
8/13	L	20-21	Oakland
8/19	L	23-36	at Denver
8/24	L	17-24	St. Louis

REGULAR SEASON (5-11)

Date	Result		Opponent	Att.
9/3	L	14-41	Philadelphia	62,872
9/10	L	31-32	at Arizona	58,303
9/18	W	27-21	at Washington	84,431
9/24	L	24-41	San Francisco	64,127
10/1	W	16-13	at Carolina (OT)	73,310
10/15	L	14-19	at New York Giants	78,189
10/22	W	48-7	Arizona	62,981
10/29	L	17-23	Jacksonville (OT)	63,554
11/5	L	13-16	at Philadelphia (OT)	65,636
11/12	W	23-6	Cincinnati	62,170
11/19	L	0-27	at Baltimore	69,416
11/23	L	15-27	Minnesota	63,878
12/3	L	7-27	at Tampa Bay	65,621
12/10	W	32-13	Washington	63,467
12/17	L	13-17	New York Giants	61,311
12/25	L	0-31	at Tennessee	68,498

(OT) Overtime

SCORE BY PERIODS

Cowboys	51	92	73	75	3	—	294
Opponents	61	101	84	106	9	—	361

ATTENDANCE

Home 489,643 Away 563,305 Total 1,052,948
Single-game home record, 65,180 (11/12/95)
Single-season home record, 518,167 (1995)

2000 TEAM STATISTICS

	Cowboys	Opp.
Total First Downs	276	309
Rushing	116	137
Passing	128	145
Penalty	32	27
Third Down: Made/Att	70/195	84/208
Third Down Pct.	35.9	40.4
Fourth Down: Made/Att	10/18	8/18
Fourth Down Pct.	55.6	44.4
Total Net Yards	4,475	5,329
Avg. Per Game	279.7	333.1
Total Plays	943	1,021
Avg. Per Play	4.7	5.2
Net Yards Rushing	1,953	2,636
Avg. Per Game	122.1	164.8
Total Rushes	463	538
Net Yards Passing	2,522	2,693
Avg. Per Game	157.6	168.3
Sacked/Yards Lost	35/249	25/189
Gross Yards	2,771	2,882
Att./Completions	445/255	458/277
Completion Pct.	57.3	60.5
Had Intercepted	21	16
Punts/Average	68/41.9	70/40.5
Net Punting Avg.	68/35.4	70/33.3
Penalties/Yards	108/963	108/999
Fumbles/Ball Lost	31/18	23/9
Touchdowns	31	41
Rushing	15	17
Passing	14	20
Returns	2	4
Avg. Time of Possession	28:40	31:20

2000 INDIVIDUAL STATISTICS

Passing	Att.	Comp.	Yds.	Pct.	TD	Int.	Tkld.	Rate
Aikman	262	156	1,632	59.5	7	14	13/91	64.3
Cunningham	125	74	849	59.2	6	4	8/45	82.4
Wright	53	22	237	41.5	0	3	12/92	31.7
Stoerner	5	3	53	60.0	1	0	2/21	135.8
Cowboys	445	255	2,771	57.3	14	21	35/249	66.6
Opponents	458	277	2,882	60.5	20	16	25/189	78.7

SCORING	TD R	TD P	TD Rt	PAT	FG	Saf	PTS
Seder	1	0	0	27/27	25/33	0	108
Smith	9	0	0	0/0	0/0	0	54
Harris	0	5	0	0/0	0/0	0	32
McGarity	1	0	2	0/0	0/0	0	18
Warren	2	1	0	0/0	0/0	0	18
McKnight	0	2	0	0/0	0/0	0	12
Thomas	0	2	0	0/0	0/0	0	12
Ismail	0	1	0	0/0	0/0	0	8
Cunningham	1	0	0	0/0	0/0	0	6
Galloway	0	1	0	0/0	0/0	0	6
LaFleur	0	1	0	0/0	0/0	0	6
Tucker	1	0	0	0/0	0/0	0	6
Wiley	0	1	0	0/0	0/0	0	6
Reese	0	0	0	0/0	0/0	1	2
Cowboys	15	14	2	27/27	25/33	1	294
Opponents	17	20	4	37/37	26/31	0	361

2-Pt. Conversions: Harris, Ismail.
Cowboys 2-4, Opponents 0-3.

RUSHING	Att.	Yds.	Avg.	LG	TD
Smith	294	1,203	4.1	52	9
Warren	59	254	4.3	32t	2
Cunningham	23	89	3.9	19	1
Wiley	24	88	3.7	11	0
Ismail	8	73	9.1	37	0
Thomas	15	51	3.4	9	0
McGarity	6	49	8.2	22t	1
Tucker	4	42	10.5	17t	1
Wright	12	36	3.0	19	0
T. Hambrick	6	28	4.7	13	0
Coakley	1	26	26.0	26	0
Aikman	10	13	1.3	5	0
Seder	1	1	1.0	1t	1
Cowboys	463	1,953	4.2	52	15
Opponents	538	2,636	4.9	70t	17

RECEIVING	No.	Yds.	Avg.	LG	TD
McKnight	52	926	17.8	48	2
Harris	39	306	7.8	21	5
Warren	31	302	9.7	76t	1
Ismail	25	350	14.0	44	1
McGarity	25	250	10.0	25	0
Thomas	23	117	5.1	14	2
Wiley	14	72	5.1	15t	1
Tucker	13	126	9.7	18	0
LaFleur	12	109	9.1	19	1
Smith	11	79	7.2	19	0
Galloway	4	62	15.5	22	1
Hodge	4	60	15.0	20	0
Brazzell	2	12	6.0	10	0
Cowboys	255	2,771	10.9	76t	14
Opponents	277	2,882	10.4	68t	20

INTERCEPTIONS	No.	Yds.	Avg.	LG	TD
Sparks	5	59	11.8	43	0
Reese	2	60	30.0	46	0
Nguyen	2	31	15.5	24	0
Woodson	2	12	6.0	12	0
McNeil	2	4	2.0	4	0
Wortham	2	1	0.5	1	0
C. Williams	1	0	0.0	0	0
Cowboys	16	167	10.4	46	0
Opponents	21	179	8.5	42	3

PUNTING	No.	Yds.	Avg.	In 20	LG
Knorr	58	2,485	42.8	12	60
Cantrell	10	367	36.7	3	40
Cowboys	68	2,852	41.9	15	60
Opponents	70	2,838	40.5	22	63

PUNT RETURNS	No.	FC	Yds.	Avg.	LG	TD
McGarity	30	9	353	11.8	64t	2
Tucker	4	5	9	2.3	8	0
Galloway	1	0	2	2.0	2	0
Cowboys	35	14	364	10.4	64t	2
Opponents	29	18	282	9.7	54	0

KICKOFF RETURNS	No.	Yds.	Avg.	LG	TD
Tucker	51	1,099	21.5	90	0
Wiley	13	303	23.3	38	0
LaFleur	2	21	10.5	13	0
Goodrich	1	12	12.0	12	0
Noble	1	8	8.0	8	0
Santiago	1	13	13.0	13	0
Cowboys	69	1,456	21.1	90	0
Opponents	56	1,205	21.5	42	0

FIELD GOALS	1-19	20-29	30-39	40-49	50+
Seder	2/2	5/6	9/11	9/13	0/1
Cowboys	2/2	5/6	9/11	9/13	0/1
Opponents	2/2	9/9	9/9	4/9	2/2

SACKS	No.
Ekuban	6.5
Spellman	5.0
Underwood	4.0
Ellis	3.0
Lett	2.5
Zellner	2.0
D. Hambrick	1.0
Noble	1.0
Cowboys	25.0
Opponents	35.0

2001 DRAFT CHOICES

Round	Name	Pos.	College
2	Quincy Carter	QB	Georgia
	Tony Dixon	DB	Alabama
3	Willie Blade	DT	Mississippi State
4	Markus Steele	LB	Southern California
5	Matt Lehr	C	Virginia Tech
6	Daleroy Stewart	DT	Southern Mississippi
7	Colston Weatherington	DE	Central Missouri
	John Nix	DT	Southern Mississippi
	Char-ron Dorsey	T	Florida State

DALLAS COWBOYS

2001 VETERAN ROSTER

No.	Name	Pos.	Ht.	Wt.	Birthdate	NFL Exp.	College	Hometown	How Acq.	'00 Games/ Starts
76	Adams, Flozell	T	6-7	335	5/18/75	4	Michigan State	Bellwood, Ill.	D2-'98	16/16
73	Allen, Larry	G	6-3	326	11/27/71	8	Sonoma State	Compton, Calif.	D2-'94	16/16
25	Avery, John	RB	5-9	190	1/11/76	3	Mississippi	Ashville, N.C.	FA-'01	0*
3	Banks, Tony	QB	6-4	225	4/5/73	6	Michigan State	San Diego, Calif.	FA-'00	11/8*
58	Bowden, Joe	LB	5-11	235	2/25/70	10	Oklahoma	Mesquite, Texas	FA-'00	16/0
85	Brazzell, Chris	WR	6-2	193	5/22/76	3	Angelo State	Alice, Texas	FA-'99	9/0
52	Coakley, Dexter	LB	5-10	228	10/20/72	5	Appalachian State	Mt. Pleasant, S.C.	D3a-'97	16/16
45	Collins, Ryan	TE	6-6	259	11/1/75	2	St. Thomas	Minneapolis, Minn.	FA-'01	0*
15	Dunn, Damon	WR	5-9	182	3/15/76	2	Stanford	Arlington, Texas	FA-'01	4/0*
27	Edwards, Mario	CB	6-0	191	12/1/75	2	Florida State	Pascagoula, Miss.	D6-'00	11/1
96	Ekuban, Ebenezer	DE	6-3	265	5/29/76	3	North Carolina	Riverdale, Md.	D1-'99	12/2
98	Ellis, Greg	DE	6-6	286	8/14/75	4	North Carolina	Wendell, N.C.	D1-'98	16/16
97	Fields, Aaron	DE	6-4	243	1/9/76	2	Troy State	Notasulga, Ala.	FA-'00	3/0
80	Fontenot, Chris	TE	6-4	250	7/11/74	2	McNeese State	Iota, La.	FA-'00	0*
66	Fricke, Ben	G-C	6-0	295	11/3/75	3	Houston	Austin, Texas	FA-'99	8/5
84	Galloway, Joey	WR	5-11	188	11/20/71	7	Ohio State	Bellaire, Ohio	T(Sea)-'00	1/1
61	Garmon, Kelvin	G	6-2	329	10/26/76	2	Baylor	Haltom, Texas	D7-'99	0*
23	Goodrich, Dwayne	CB	5-11	198	5/29/78	2	Tennessee	Oak Lawn, Ill.	D2-'00	5/0
56	Grant, Orantes	LB	6-0	225	3/18/78	2	Georgia	Atlanta, Ga.	D7-'00	13/0
54	Hambrick, Darren	LB	6-2	227	8/30/75	4	South Carolina	Pasco, Fla.	D5a-'98	16/16
35	Hambrick, Troy	RB	6-1	235	11/6/76	2	Savannah State	Pasco, Fla.	FA-'00	3/0
88	Harris, Jackie	TE	6-4	250	1/4/68	12	Northeast Louisiana	Pine Bluff, Ark.	UFA(Tenn)-'00	16/7
38	Hawthorne, Duane	CB	5-10	175	8/26/76	3	Northern Illinois	St. Louis, Mo.	FA-'99	14/0
16	Hodge, Damon	WR	6-1	192	2/16/77	2	Alabama State	Thomaston, Ala.	FA-'00	9/0
81	Ismail, Raghib	WR	5-11	190	11/18/69	9	Notre Dame	Wilkes Barre, Pa.	UFA(Car)-'99	9/9
71	Jackson, Al	G	6-3	306	5/18/77	2	Louisiana State	Moss Point, Miss.	FA-'00	3/0
40	Key, Sean	S	5-11	185	6/25/77	2	Florida State	Miami, Fla.	FA-'00	0*
4	Knorr, Micah	P	6-2	193	1/9/75	2	Utah State	Orange, Calif.	FA-'00	14/0
89	LaFleur, David	TE	6-7	272	1/29/74	5	Louisiana State	Westlake, La.	D1-'97	15/9
41	Larrimore, Kareem	CB	5-11	190	4/21/76	2	West Texas A&M	Los Angeles, Calif.	D4-'00	15/4
86	Lucky, Mike	TE	6-6	273	11/23/75	3	Arizona	Antioch, Calif.	D7a-'99	0*
83	McGarity, Wane	WR	5-8	197	9/30/76	3	Texas	San Antonio, Texas	D4a-'99	14/0
94	Myers, Michael	DE-DT	6-2	288	1/20/76	4	Alabama	Vicksburg, Miss.	D4-'98	13/7
59	Nguyen, Dat	LB	5-11	231	9/25/75	3	Texas A&M	Rockport, Texas	D3-'99	10/5
75	Noble, Brandon	DT	6-2	285	4/10/74	3	Penn State	Virginia Beach, Va.	FA-'99	16/9
62	Page, Craig	C	6-3	303	1/17/76	2	Georgia Tech	Jupiter, Fla.	FA-'00	2/0
77	Page, Solomon	G	6-4	321	2/27/76	3	West Virginia	Pittsburgh, Pa.	D2-'99	16/16
43	Reese, Izell	S	6-2	190	5/7/74	4	Alabama-Birmingham	Dothan, Ala.	D6-'98	16/7
6	Seder, Tim	K	5-9	180	9/17/74	2	Ashland	Ashland, Ohio	FA-'00	15/0
22	Smith, Emmitt	RB	5-9	209	5/15/69	12	Florida	Escambia, Fla.	D1-'90	16/16
20	Sparks, Phillippi	CB	5-11	195	4/15/69	10	Arizona State	Phoenix, Ariz.	FA-'00	16/12
90	# Spellman, Alonzo	DT-DE	6-4	292	9/27/71	9	Ohio State	Mount Holly, N.J.	FA-'99	16/15
53	Stepnoski, Mark	C	6-2	265	1/20/67	13	Pittsburgh	Erie, Pa.	UFA(Tenn)-'99	11/11
5	Stoerner, Clint	QB	6-2	210	12/29/77	2	Arkansas	Baytown, Texas	FA-'00	2/0
31	Teague, George	S	6-1	196	2/18/71	9	Alabama	Montgomery, Ala.	FA-'98	9/9
44	Thomas, Robert	FB	6-1	252	12/1/74	4	Henderson State	Jacksonville, Ark.	FA-'98	16/16
87	Tucker, Jason	WR	6-1	182	6/24/76	3	Texas Christian	Waco, Texas	FA-'99	16/7
91	Underwood, Dimitrius	DT-DE	6-6	276	3/29/77	2	Michigan State	Fayetteville, N.C.	FA-'00	15/0
46	Whalen, James	TE	6-2	228	12/11/77	2	Kentucky	Portland, Ore.	FA-'00	3/0
92	White, Chris	DE	6-3	285	9/28/76	2	Southern	Shreveport, La.	FA-'00	5/0*
32	Wiley, Michael	RB	5-11	189	1/5/78	2	Ohio State	Spring Valley, Calif.	D5-'00	10/0
95	Williams, Ben	DE	6-2	287	5/28/70	3	Minnesota	Belzoni, Miss.	FA-'01	0*
25	# Williams, Charlie	CB	6-0	204	2/2/72	7	Bowling Green	Detroit, Mich.	D3-'95	11/0
28	Woodson, Darren	S	6-1	219	4/25/69	10	Arizona State	Phoenix, Ariz.	D2b-'92	11/11
57	# Wortham, Barron	LB	5-11	245	11/1/69	8	Texas-El Paso	Everman, Texas	FA-'00	16/11
2	Wright, Anthony	QB	6-1	195	2/14/76	3	South Carolina	Vanceboro, N.C.	FA-'00	4/2
93	Zellner, Peppi	DE	6-5	257	3/14/75	3	Fort Valley State	Forsythe, Ga.	D4b-'99	12/0

* Avery last active with Denver in '99; Banks played 11 games with Baltimore in '00; Collins last active with Baltimore in '99; Dunn played 3 games with Cleveland and 1 game with N.Y. Jets; Fontenot last active with Philadelphia in '98; Garmon was inactive for 15 games; Key and Lucky missed '00 season because of injury; White played 5 games with Atlanta; B. Williams last active with Philadelphia in '99.

\# Unrestricted free agent; subject to developments.

Retired—Troy Aikman, 11-year quarterback, 11 games in '00; Carl Pickens, 9-year wide receiver, 9 games in '00 with Tennessee.

Players lost through free agency (2): DT Leon Lett (Den; 9 games in '00); WR James McKnight (Mia; 16).

Also played with Cowboys in '00—S Chris Akins (8 games), P Barry Cantrell (2), QB Randall Cunningham (6), G Jorge Diaz (9), C Dale Hellestrae (16), DT Chad Hennings (8), CB Ryan McNeil (16), TE O.J. Santiago (11), RB Chris Warren (13), T Erik Williams (16).

COACHING STAFF

Head Coach,
Dave Campo

Pro Career: Dave Campo became the fifth head coach in Cowboys history on January 26, 2000, after eleven seasons as an assistant with the club. In his first season at the helm, the club posted a 5-11 record while struggling through numerous injuries. Campo has participated in three Super Bowls, four NFC Championship Games, and won six division titles. He joins four NFL head coaches who have been a part of three or more Super Bowl titles in their coaching careers. That group includes George Seifert (five times), Mike Shanahan (three), and Mike Holmgren (three). From 1995-99, Campo directed the Dallas defense. Prior to that, Campo served as the Cowboys' secondary coach (1991-94) and was a defensive assistant (1989-1990). Career record: 5-11.

Background: Campo was a defensive back at Central Connecticut State from 1967-1970 and twice earned All-East honors at shortstop. He began his coaching career at Central Connecticut State, coaching linebackers (1971-72). He then moved to Albany State (1973), Bridgeport (1974), Pittsburgh (1975), Washington State (1976), Boise State (1977-79), Oregon State (1980), Weber State (1981-82), Iowa State (1983), Syracuse (1984-86), and Miami (1987-88).

Personal: Born in New London, Conn., on July 18, 1947. Was a standout at Robert E. Fitch High School in Groton, Conn. Dave and his wife, Kay, have six children—Angie, Eric, Becky, Tommy, Shelbie, and Michael.

ASSISTANT COACHES

Joe Avezzano, special teams-tight ends; born November 17, 1943, Yonkers, N.Y., lives in Coppell, Texas. Guard Florida State 1961-65. Pro center Boston Patriots 1966. College coach: Florida State 1968, Iowa State 1969-1972, Pittsburgh 1973-76, Tennessee 1977-79, Oregon State 1980-84 (head coach), Texas 1985-88. Pro coach: Joined Cowboys in 1990.

Bill Bates, defensive nickel package-asst. special teams; born June 6, 1961, Knoxville, Tenn., lives in Plano, Texas. Defensive back Tennessee 1979-1982. Pro defensive back Dallas Cowboys 1983-1997. Pro coach: Joined Cowboys in 1998.

Wes Chandler, wide receivers; born August 22, 1956, New Smyrna Beach, Fla., lives in Grapevine, Texas. Wide receiver Florida 1974-77. Pro wide receiver New Orleans Saints 1978-1981, San Diego Chargers 1981-87, San Francisco 49ers 1988. College coach: Central Florida 1994-95. Pro coach: Orlando Thunder (NFL Europe) 1992, Rhein Fire (NFLE) 1995-97, Frankfurt Galaxy (NFLE) 1998, Berlin Thunder (NFLE) 1999 (head coach), joined Cowboys in 2000.

George Edwards, linebackers; born January 16, 1967, Siler City, N.C., lives in Coppell, Texas. Linebacker Duke 1986-89. No pro playing experience. College coach: Florida 1990-91, Appalachian State 1992-95, Duke 1996, Georgia 1997. Pro coach: Joined Cowboys in 1998.

Steve Hoffman, kickers-quality control; born September 8, 1958, Camden, N.J., lives in Irving, Texas. Quarterback-running back-wide receiver Dickinson College 1979-1982. Pro punter Washington Federals (USFL) 1983. College coach: Miami 1985-87. Pro coach: Joined Cowboys in 1989.

Hudson Houck, offensive line; born January 7, 1943, Los Angeles, lives in Irving, Texas. Center Southern California 1962-64. No pro playing experience. College coach: Southern California 1970-72, 1976-1982, Stanford 1973-75. Pro coach: Los Angeles Rams 1983-1991, Seattle Seahawks 1992, joined Cowboys in 1993.

Jim Jeffcoat, defensive ends; born April 1, 1961, Cliffwood, N.J., lives in Irving, Texas. Defensive end Arizona State 1979-1982. Pro defensive end Dallas Cowboys 1983-1994, Buffalo Bills 1995-97. Pro coach: Joined Cowboys in 1998.

2001 FIRST-YEAR ROSTER

Name	Pos.	Ht.	Wt.	Birthdate	College	Hometown	How Acq.
Alexander, Ronnie	LB	6-2	225	5/6/77	Louisiana State	Bossier City, La.	FA
Anglin, Deneil	CB	5-11	209	6/22/77	Fairmont State	South Holland, Ill.	FA
Bates, Del	CB	5-11	172	1/10/78	Nevada	Sparks, Nev.	FA
Bell, Jason	CB	6-0	179	4/1/78	UCLA	Long Beach, Calif.	FA
Biancamano, Francesco (1)	K	5-8	170	3/12/76	Southern Connecticut	Huntington Station, N.Y.	FA
Blade, Willie	DT	6-3	319	2/7/79	Mississippi State	Warner Robins, Ga.	D3
Burnette, Adrian	WR	5-10	194	6/3/79	Tulane	Bastrop, La.	FA
Carter, Quincy	QB	6-2	225	10/13/77	Georgia	Atlanta, Ga.	D2a
Collins, Dan (1)	G	6-4	300	7/27/76	Boston College	Raynham, Mass.	FA
Collins, Javiar	DT	6-6	314	4/13/78	Northwestern	St. Paul, Minn.	FA
Copeland, Jermaine (1)	WR	6-1	200	2/19/77	Tennessee	Harriman, Tenn.	FA
Dixon, Tony	S	6-1	213	6/18/79	Alabama	Reform, Ala.	D2b
Dorsey, Char-ron	T	6-6	347	11/5/78	Florida State	Jacksonville, Fla.	D7c
Drake, Kevin (1)	WR	6-3	195	1/2/75	Alabama-Birmingham	Gardendale, Ala.	FA
Evans, Demetric	DE	6-3	268	9/3/79	Georgia	Haynesville, La.	FA
Gamble, Jason (1)	G	6-3	307	9/12/75	Clemson	Derby, Kan.	FA
Huggins, Johnny (1)	TE	6-3	245	3/29/76	Alabama State	Zachary, La.	FA
Johnson, Eddie	LB	5-10	229	12/23/75	Cincinnati	Kirkland, Wash.	FA
Jones, J.J.	LB	6-0	231	6/7/78	Arkansas	Magnolia, Ark.	FA
Jones, Jermaine (1)	CB	5-9	182	7/25/76	Northwestern State	Morgan City, La.	FA
Lehr, Matt	G-C	6-2	292	4/25/79	Virginia Tech	Woodbridge, Va.	D5
Manns, Denvis (1)	RB	5-8	200	7/21/76	New Mexico State	Lufkin, Texas	FA
Nix, John	DT	6-1	313	11/24/76	Southern Mississippi	Lucedale, Miss.	D7b
Parmer, Jason (1)	FB	6-2	230	5/16/77	James Madison	Manheim, Pa.	FA
Riley, Earl (1)	S	6-0	208	3/23/77	Washington State	Dos Palos, Calif.	FA
Scarlett, Noel (1)	DT	6-3	320	1/21/74	Langston	Atlanta, Ga.	FA
Scott, Lynn	S	6-0	191	6/23/77	Northwestern Oklahoma State	Turpin, Okla.	FA
Sears, Colin	T	6-3	295	9/25/78	Auburn	Russellville, Ala.	FA
Shaw, Bryant (1)	DE	6-3	287	7/17/78	Mississippi College	Ocean Springs, Miss.	FA
Steele, Markus	LB	6-3	240	7/24/79	Southern California	New Bedford, Ohio	D4
Stewart, Daleroy	DT	6-4	309	11/2/78	Southern Mississippi	Vero Beach, Fla.	D6
Stiggers, Marcus (1)	WR	5-7	183	12/26/77	Colorado	Dallas, Texas	FA
Taylor, Tony	RB	5-9	191	3/9/78	Northwestern Louisiana	Pineville, La.	FA
Tugbenyoh, Mawuko (1)	LB	6-1	245	4/9/78	California	Concord, Calif.	FA
Wagstaff, James	T	6-4	330	2/18/78	North Carolina	Charlotte, N.C.	FA
Weatherington, Colston	DE	6-5	274	10/29/77	Central Missouri State	Graceville, Fla.	D7a
Williamson, Kenny	FB	6-1	260	12/16/77	Mississippi State	Seminary, Miss.	FA
Yamini, Bashir (1)	WR	6-3	190	9/10/77	Iowa	Dolton, Ill.	FA

The term NFL Rookie is defined as a player who is in his first season of professional football and has not been on the roster of another professional football team for any regular-season or postseason games. A Rookie is designated by an "R" on NFL rosters. Players who have been active in another professional football league or players who have NFL experience, including either preseason training camp or being on an Active List or Inactive List, or on Reserve/Injured or Reserve/Physically Unable to Perform for fewer than six regular-season games, are termed NFL First-Year Players. An NFL First-Year Player is designated by a "1" on NFL rosters. Thereafter, a player is credited with an additional year of experience for each season in which he accumulates six games on the Active List or Inactive List, or on Reserve/Injured or Reserve/Physically Unable to Perform.

NOTES

Joe Juraszek, strength and conditioning; born June 8, 1958, Chicago, lives in Coppell, Texas. Linebacker-defensive end New Mexico 1976-1980. No pro playing experience. College coach: Oklahoma 1981-86, 1993-96, Texas Tech 1987-1992. Pro coach: Joined Cowboys in 1997.

Andre Patterson, defensive tackles; born June 12, 1960, Camden, Ark., lives in Grapevine, Texas. Offensive lineman Contra Costa (Calif.) J.C. 1978-1980, Montana 1981. No pro playing experience. College coach: Montana 1982, Weber State 1988, Western Washington 1989, Cornell 1990, Washington State 1992-93, Cal Poly-San Luis Obispo 1994-96 (head coach). Pro coach: New England Patriots 1997, Minnesota Vikings 1998-99, joined Cowboys in 2000.

Clancy Pendergast, secondary; born November 29, 1967, Phoenix, lives in Irving, Texas. No college or pro playing experience. College coach: Mississippi State 1991, Southern California 1992, Oklahoma 1993-94. Pro coach: Houston Oilers 1995, joined Cowboys in 1996.

Jack Reilly, offensive coordinator; born May 22, 1945, Boston, lives in Coppell, Texas. Quarterback Washington State 1963, Santa Monica (Calif.) J.C. 1964, Long Beach State 1965-66. No pro playing experience. College coach: El Camino (Calif.) J.C. 1980-84 (head coach 1981-84), Utah 1985-89. Pro coach: San Diego Chargers 1990-93, Los Angeles Raiders 1994, St. Louis Rams 1995-96, Dallas Cowboys 1997, New England Patriots 1998-99, rejoined Cowboys in 2000.

Clarence Shelmon, running backs; born September 17, 1952, Bossier City, La., lives in Coppell, Texas. Running back Houston 1971-75. No pro playing experience. College coach: Army 1978-1980, Indiana 1981-83, Arizona 1984-86, Southern California 1987-1990. Pro coach: Los Angeles Rams 1991, Seattle Seahawks 1992-97, joined Cowboys in 1998.

Glenn Smith, offensive assistant; born February 8, 1963, Austin, Texas, lives in Irving, Texas. Attended Texas. No college or pro playing experience. College coach: Oklahoma 1988-1991, Northern Illinois 1992-95. Pro coach: Joined Cowboys in 2000.

Wade Wilson, quarterbacks; born February 1, 1959, Commerce, Texas, lives in Irving, Texas. Quarterback East Texas State 1977-1980. Pro quarterback Minnesota Vikings 1981-1991, Atlanta Falcons 1992, New Orleans Saints 1993-94, Dallas Cowboys 1995-97, Oakland Raiders 1998-99. Pro coach: Joined Cowboys in 2000.

Mike Zimmer, defensive coordinator; born June 5, 1956, Peoria, Ill., lives in Colleyville, Texas. Quarterback-linebacker Illinois State 1974-76. No pro playing experience. College coach: Missouri 1979-1980, Weber State 1981-88, Washington State 1989-1993. Pro coach: Joined Cowboys in 1994.

DETROIT LIONS

National Football Conference
Central Division
Team Colors: Honolulu Blue and Silver
Pontiac Silverdome
1200 Featherstone Road
Pontiac, Michigan 48342
Telephone: (248) 335-4131

CLUB OFFICIALS

Chairman and Owner: William Clay Ford
Vice Chairman: William Clay Ford, Jr.
President and CEO: Matt Millen
Senior Vice President: Bill Keenist
Senior Vice President: Kevin Warren
Assistant to President/Finance & Special Projects: Kent Newhart
Vice President of Stadium Development and Salary Cap: Tom Lewand
Executive Director of Player Personnel: Bill Tobin
Vice President of Corporate Sales & Sponsorship: Steve Harms
Vice President of Finance and Chief Financial Officer: Tom Lesnau
Vice President of Ticket Sales/Operations: Jennifer Manzo
Secretary: David Hempstead
Director of Football Administration: Martin Mayhew
Senior Director of Community Affairs: Tim Pendell
Director of Media Relations: Matt Barnhart
Director of Pro Personnel: Sheldon White
Director of College Scouting: Scott McEwen
Scouts: Russ Bollinger, Hessley Hempstead, Chad Henry, Lance Newmark, Charlie Sanders, Dave Uryus
Director of Broadcasting and New Media: Bryan Bender
Director of Ticket Operations: Mark Graham
Head Athletic Trainer: Al Bellamy
Equipment Manager: Mark Glenn
Video Director: Steve Hermans
Stadium: Pontiac Silverdome (built in 1975)
•**Capacity:** 80,311
1200 Featherstone Road
Pontiac, Michigan 48342
Playing Surface: AstroTurf
Training Camp: Saginaw Valley State University
University Center, Michigan 48710

2001 SCHEDULE

PRESEASON

Aug. 10	**Cincinnati**	7:30
Aug. 18	at Indianapolis	7:00
Aug. 25	at Pittsburgh	1:00
Aug. 30	**Tennessee**	7:30

REGULAR SEASON

Sept. 9	at Green Bay	12:00
Sept. 16	**Dallas**	1:00
Sept. 23	at Cleveland	1:00
Sept. 30	Open Date	
Oct. 8	**St. Louis** (Mon.)	9:00
Oct. 14	at Minnesota	12:00
Oct. 21	**Tennessee**	1:00
Oct. 28	**Cincinnati**	1:00
Nov. 4	at San Francisco	1:05
Nov. 11	**Tampa Bay**	1:00
Nov. 18	at Arizona	2:15
Nov. 22	**Green Bay** (Thurs.)	12:30
Dec. 2	at Chicago	12:00
Dec. 9	at Tampa Bay	1:00
Dec. 16	**Minnesota**	1:00
Dec. 23	at Pittsburgh	1:00
Dec. 30	**Chicago**	1:00

RECORD HOLDERS

INDIVIDUAL RECORDS—CAREER

Category	Name	Performance
Rushing (Yds.)	Barry Sanders, 1989-1998	15,269
Passing (Yds.)	Bobby Layne, 1950-58	15,710
Passing (TDs)	Bobby Layne, 1950-58	118
Receiving (No.)	Herman Moore, 1991-2000	666
Receiving (Yds.)	Herman Moore, 1991-2000	9,098
Interceptions	Dick LeBeau, 1959-1972	62
Punting (Avg.)	Yale Lary, 1952-53, 1956-1964	44.3
Punt Return (Avg.)	Jack Christiansen, 1951-58	12.8
Kickoff Return (Avg.)	Pat Studstill, 1961-67	25.7
Field Goals	Eddie Murray, 1980-1991	243
Touchdowns (Tot.)	Barry Sanders, 1989-1998	109
Points	Eddie Murray, 1980-1991	1,113

INDIVIDUAL RECORDS—SINGLE SEASON

Category	Name	Performance
Rushing (Yds.)	Barry Sanders, 1997	2,053
Passing (Yds.)	Scott Mitchell, 1995	4,338
Passing (TDs)	Scott Mitchell, 1995	32
Receiving (No.)	Herman Moore, 1995	*123
Receiving (Yds.)	Herman Moore, 1995	1,686
Interceptions	Don Doll, 1950	12
	Jack Christiansen, 1953	12
Punting (Avg.)	Yale Lary, 1963	48.9
Punt Return (Avg.)	Jack Christiansen, 1952	21.5
Kickoff Return (Avg.)	Tom Watkins, 1965	34.4
Field Goals	Jason Hanson, 1993	34
Touchdowns (Tot.)	Barry Sanders, 1991	17
Points	Jason Hanson, 1995	132

INDIVIDUAL RECORDS—SINGLE GAME

Category	Name	Performance
Rushing (Yds.)	Barry Sanders, 11-13-94	237
Passing (Yds.)	Scott Mitchell, 11-23-95	410
Passing (TDs)	Gary Danielson, 12-9-78	5
Receiving (No.)	Herman Moore, 12-4-95	14
Receiving (Yds.)	Cloyce Box, 12-3-50	302
Interceptions	Don Doll, 10-23-49	*4
Field Goals	Garo Yepremian, 11-13-66	6
	Jason Hanson, 10-17-99	6
Touchdowns (Tot.)	Dutch Clark, 10-22-34	4
	Cloyce Box, 12-3-50	4
	Barry Sanders, 11-24-91	4
Points	Dutch Clark, 10-22-34	24
	Cloyce Box, 12-3-50	24
	Barry Sanders, 11-24-91	24

*NFL Record

COACHING HISTORY

Portsmouth Spartans 1930-33
(464-482-32)

1930	Hal (Tubby) Griffen	5-6-3
1931-36	George (Potsy) Clark	49-20-6
1937-38	Earl (Dutch) Clark	14-8-0
1939	Elmer (Gus) Henderson	6-5-0
1940	George (Potsy) Clark	5-5-1
1941-42	Bill Edwards*	4-9-1
1942	John Karcis	0-8-0
1943-47	Charles (Gus) Dorais	20-31-2
1948-1950	Alvin (Bo) McMillin	12-24-0
1951-56	Raymond (Buddy) Parker	50-24-2
1957-1964	George Wilson	55-45-6
1965-66	Harry Gilmer	10-16-2
1967-1972	Joe Schmidt	43-35-7
1973	Don McCafferty	6-7-1
1974-76	Rick Forzano**	15-17-0
1976-77	Tommy Hudspeth	11-13-0
1978-1984	Monte Clark	43-63-1
1985-88	Darryl Rogers***	18-40-0
1988-1996	Wayne Fontes	67-71-0
1997-2000	Bobby Ross****	27-32-0
2000	Gary Moeller	4-3-0

* Released after three games in 1942
** Resigned after four games in 1976
*** Released after 11 games in 1988
**** Resigned after nine games in 2000

PONTIAC SILVERDOME

N

2000 TEAM RECORD

PRESEASON (2-2)

Date	Result		Opponent
8/4	L	10-13	New England
8/12	W	15-13	Buffalo
8/18	L	17-23	at Oakland
8/25	W	21-13	at Cincinnati

REGULAR SEASON (9-7)

Date	Result		Opponent	Att.
9/3	W	14-10	at New Orleans	64,900
9/10	W	15-10	Washington	74,159
9/17	L	10-31	Tampa Bay	76,928
9/24	W	21-14	at Chicago	66,944
10/1	L	24-31	Minnesota	76,438
10/8	W	31-24	Green Bay	77,549
10/19	W	28-14	at Tampa Bay	65,557
10/29	L	18-30	at Indianapolis	56,971
11/5	L	8-23	Miami	77,813
11/12	W	13-10	Atlanta	74,309
11/19	W	31-21	at New York Giants	77,897
11/23	W	34-9	New England	77,923
11/30	L	17-24	at Minnesota	64,214
12/10	L	13-26	at Green Bay	59,854
12/17	W	10-7	at New York Jets	77,513
12/24	L	20-23	Chicago	71,957

SCORE BY PERIODS

Lions	50	78	52	127	0	—	307
Opponents	81	70	74	82	0	—	307

ATTENDANCE

Home 606,716 Away 523,383 Total 1,130,099
Single-game home record, 80,441 (12/20/81)
Single-season home record, 622,593 (1980)

2000 TEAM STATISTICS

	Lions	Opp.
Total First Downs	264	279
Rushing	101	96
Passing	143	159
Penalty	20	24
Third Down: Made/Att	72/224	80/215
Third Down Pct.	32.1	37.2
Fourth Down: Made/Att	6/13	9/16
Fourth Down Pct.	46.2	56.3
Total Net Yards	4,422	5,033
Avg. Per Game	276.4	314.6
Total Plays	1,004	993
Avg. Per Play	4.4	5.1
Net Yards Rushing	1,747	1,823
Avg. Per Game	109.2	113.9
Total Rushes	448	421
Net Yards Passing	2,675	3,210
Avg. Per Game	167.2	200.6
Sacked/Yards Lost	53/317	28/162
Gross Yards	2,992	3,372
Att./Completions	503/277	544/311
Completion Pct.	55.1	57.2
Had Intercepted	19	25
Punts/Average	95/42.6	84/41.7
Net Punting Avg.	95/34.8	84/33.9
Penalties/Yards	106/805	112/913
Fumbles/Ball Lost	21/12	36/17
Touchdowns	33	32
Rushing	15	14
Passing	14	16
Returns	4	2
Avg. Time of Possession	30:10	29:50

2000 INDIVIDUAL STATISTICS

Passing	Att.	Comp.	Yds.	Pct.	TD	Int.	Tkld.	Rate
Batch	412	221	2,489	53.6	13	15	41/242	67.3
Case	91	56	503	61.5	1	4	12/75	61.7
Lions	503	277	2,992	55.1	14	19	53/317	66.3
Opponents	544	311	3,372	57.2	16	25	28/162	66.2

SCORING	TD R	TD P	TD Rt	PAT	FG	Saf	PTS
Hanson	0	0	0	29/29	24/30	0	101
J. Stewart	10	1	0	0/0	0/0	0	72
Morton	0	3	0	0/0	0/0	0	20
Crowell	0	3	0	0/0	0/0	0	18
Moore	0	3	0	0/0	0/0	0	18
Batch	2	0	0	0/0	0/0	0	12
Bates	2	0	0	0/0	0/0	0	12
Sloan	0	2	0	0/0	0/0	0	12
Campbell	0	0	1	0/0	0/0	0	6
Case	1	0	0	0/0	0/0	0	6
Foster	0	1	0	0/0	0/0	0	6
Hartings	0	0	1	0/0	0/0	0	6
Howard	0	0	1	0/0	0/0	0	6
Rasby	0	1	0	0/0	0/0	0	6
Westbrook	0	0	1	0/0	0/0	0	6
Lions	15	14	4	29/29	24/30	0	307
Opponents	14	16	2	31/31	26/31	2	307

2-Pt. Conversions: J. Stewart 3, Morton.
Lions 4-4, Opponents 1-1.

RUSHING	Att.	Yds.	Avg.	LG	TD
J. Stewart	339	1,184	3.5	34	10
Batch	44	199	4.5	19	2
Bates	31	127	4.1	23	2
Case	16	117	7.3	27	1
Irvin	9	49	5.4	32	0
Foster	2	31	15.5	16	0
Morton	4	25	6.3	27	0
Crowell	1	12	12.0	12	0
Schlesinger	1	3	3.0	3	0
Jett	1	0	0.0	0	0
Lions	448	1,747	3.9	34	15
Opponents	421	1,823	4.3	65t	14

RECEIVING	No.	Yds.	Avg.	LG	TD
Morton	61	788	12.9	42t	3
Moore	40	434	10.9	30t	3
Crowell	34	430	12.6	50t	3
Sloan	32	379	11.8	59	2
J. Stewart	32	287	9.0	32	1
Foster	17	175	10.3	40t	1
Bates	15	109	7.3	17	0
Schlesinger	12	73	6.1	13	0
Rasby	10	78	7.8	17	1
Irvin	8	90	11.3	18	0
Stablein	8	53	6.6	11	0
Olivo	3	50	16.7	19	0
Pupunu	3	32	10.7	17	0
Howard	2	14	7.0	10	0
Lions	277	2,992	10.8	59	14
Opponents	311	3,372	10.8	61t	16

INTERCEPTIONS	No.	Yds.	Avg.	LG	TD
Schulz	7	53	7.6	19	0
Westbrook	6	126	21.0	101t	1
C. Brown	2	12	6.0	12	0
Fair	2	0	0.0	0	0
Pritchett	1	78	78.0	78	0
Campbell	1	42	42.0	42t	1
M. Walker	1	12	12.0	12	0
Rice	1	7	7.0	7	0
D. Walker	1	5	5.0	5	0
Aldridge	1	4	4.0	4	0
Claiborne	1	1	1.0	1	0
Boyd	1	0	0.0	0	0
Lions	25	340	13.6	101t	2
Opponents	19	270	14.2	61t	2

PUNTING	No.	Yds.	Avg.	In 20	LG
Jett	93	4,044	43.5	33	59
Lions	95	4,044	42.6	33	59
Opponents	84	3,501	41.7	16	62

PUNT RETURNS	No.	FC	Yds.	Avg.	LG	TD
Howard	31	24	457	14.7	95t	1
Fair	2	0	15	7.5	11	0
Lions	33	24	472	14.3	95t	1
Opponents	53	14	498	9.4	63	0

KICKOFF RETURNS	No.	Yds.	Avg.	LG	TD
Howard	57	1,401	24.6	70	0
Fair	6	149	24.8	31	0
Olivo	3	25	8.3	13	0
Schlesinger	2	25	12.5	14	0
Beverly	1	0	0.0	0	0
Lions	69	1,600	23.2	70	0
Opponents	59	1,327	22.5	60	0

FIELD GOALS	1-19	20-29	30-39	40-49	50+
Hanson	2/2	6/7	10/12	4/7	2/2
Lions	2/2	6/7	10/12	4/7	2/2
Opponents	0/0	8/8	3/5	10/12	5/6

SACKS	No.
Porcher	8.0
Scroggins	6.5
Elliss	3.0
Jones	3.0
Pritchett	2.5
Aldridge	2.0
Hall	1.0
Boyd	0.5
C. Brown	0.5
Claiborne	0.5
Kirschke	0.5
Lions	28.0
Opponents	53.0

2001 DRAFT CHOICES

Round	Name	Pos.	College
1	Jeff Backus	T	Michigan
2	Dominic Raiola	C	Nebraska
	Shaun Rogers	DT	Texas
5	Scotty Anderson	WR	Grambling State
	Mike McMahon	QB	Rutgers
6	Jason Glenn	LB	Texas A&M

DETROIT LIONS

2001 VETERAN ROSTER

No.	Name	Pos.	Ht.	Wt.	Birthdate	NFL Exp.	College	Hometown	How Acq.	'00 Games/ Starts
55	Aldridge, Allen	LB	6-1	254	5/30/72	8	Houston	Missouri City, Texas	UFA(Den)-'98	16/14
89	Banta, Brad	TE	6-6	255	12/14/70	8	Southern California	Baton Rouge, La.	UFA(NYJ)-'01	16/0*
10	Batch, Charlie	QB	6-2	220	12/5/74	4	Eastern Michigan	Homestead, Pa.	D2b-'98	15/15
79	Beverly, Eric	C	6-3	294	3/28/74	4	Miami (Ohio)	Bedford Heights, Ohio	FA-'97	16/7
65	Blaise, Kerlin	G	6-5	323	12/25/74	4	Miami	Orlando, Fla.	FA-'98	13/0
57	Boyd, Stephen	LB	6-0	242	8/22/72	7	Boston College	Valley Stream, N.Y.	D5a-'95	15/15
39	Campbell, Lamar	CB	5-11	183	8/29/76	4	Wisconsin	Chester, Pa.	FA-'98	16/2
50	Claiborne, Chris	LB	6-3	255	7/26/78	3	Southern California	Riverside, Calif.	D1a-'99	16/14
82	Crowell, Germane	WR	6-3	216	9/13/76	4	Virginia	Winston Salem, N.C.	D2a-'98	9/7
95	DeVries, Jared	DE	6-4	280	6/11/76	3	Iowa	Aplington, Iowa	D3-'99	15/1
21	Droughns, Reuben	RB	5-11	207	8/21/78	2	Oregon	Anaheim, Calif.	D3-'00	0*
94	Elliss, Luther	DT	6-5	305	3/22/73	7	Utah	Mancos, Colo.	D1-'95	16/16
23	Fair, Terry	CB	5-9	184	7/20/76	4	Tennessee	Phoenix, Ariz.	D1-'98	15/15
17	Foster, Larry	WR	5-10	196	11/7/76	2	Louisiana State	Harvey, La.	FA-'00	10/0
71	Gibson, Aaron	T	6-4	380	9/27/77	3	Wisconsin	Indianapolis, Ind.	D1b-'99	10/10
54	Green, Barrett	LB	6-0	217	10/29/77	2	West Virginia	West Palm Beach, Fla.	D2-'00	9/0
96	Hall, James	DE	6-2	271	2/4/77	2	Michigan	New Orleans, La.	FA-'00	5/0
4	Hanson, Jason	K	5-11	182	6/17/70	10	Washington State	Spokane, Wash.	D2b-'92	16/0
9	Harbaugh, Jim	QB	6-3	215	12/23/63	15	Michigan	Ann Arbor, Mich.	UFA(SD)-'01	7/5*
80	Howard, Desmond	WR	5-10	185	5/15/70	10	Michigan	Cleveland, Ohio	FA-'99	15/0
33	Irvin, Sedrick	RB	5-11	226	3/30/78	3	Michigan State	Miami, Fla.	D4-'99	6/0
19	Jett, John	P	6-0	197	11/11/68	9	East Carolina	Reedville, Va.	UFA(Dall)-'97	16/0
98	Jones, James	DT	6-2	295	2/6/69	11	Northern Iowa	Davenport, Iowa	UFA(Balt)-'99	16/16
75	Joyce, Matt	G	6-7	305	3/30/72	7	Richmond	North Little Rock, Ark.	FA-'01	13/3*
67	Kirschke, Travis	DE	6-3	287	9/6/74	5	UCLA	Yorba Linda, Calif.	FA-'97	13/0
52	Kowalkowski, Scott	LB	6-2	220	8/23/68	11	Notre Dame	Orchard Lake, Mich.	FA-'94	16/2
58	Kriewaldt, Clint	LB	6-1	236	3/16/76	3	Wisconsin-Stevens Point	Shiocton, Wis.	D6-'99	13/1
31	Lee, Amp	RB	5-11	200	10/1/71	10	Florida State	Chipley, Fla.	FA-'01	3/0*
24	Lyght, Todd	CB	6-0	190	2/9/69	11	Notre Dame	Flint, Mich.	UFA(StL)-'01	14/12*
73	McDougle, Stockar	T	6-6	350	1/11/77	2	Oklahoma	Deerfield Beach, Fla.	D1-'00	8/8
48	Mitchell, Pete	TE	6-2	248	10/9/71	7	Boston College	Birmingham, Mich.	UFA(NYG)-'01	14/5*
84	Moore, Herman	WR	6-4	224	10/20/69	11	Virginia	Danville, Va.	D1-'91	15/11
87	Morton, Johnnie	WR	6-0	190	10/7/71	8	Southern California	Torrance, Calif.	D1-'94	16/16
26	Olivo, Brock	FB	6-0	232	6/24/76	4	Missouri	Washington, Mo.	FA-'98	13/0
91	Porcher, Robert	DE	6-3	282	7/30/69	10	South Carolina State	Wando, S.C.	D1-'92	16/16
28	Rice, Ron	S	6-1	217	11/9/72	7	Eastern Michigan	Detroit, Mich.	FA-'95	14/14
14	Rone, Andre'	WR	5-10	180	4/14/76	2	Mississippi	Daytona Beach, Fla.	FA-'00	0*
16	Sauter, Cory	QB	6-4	215	11/21/74	3	Minnesota	Hutchinson, Minn.	FA-'99	0*
30	Schlesinger, Cory	FB	6-0	246	6/23/72	7	Nebraska	Duncan, Neb.	D6b-'95	16/8
45	Schulz, Kurt	S	6-1	208	12/12/68	10	Eastern Washington	Yakima, Wash.	UFA(Buff)-'00	11/11
97	Scroggins, Tracy	DE	6-3	273	9/11/69	10	Tulsa	Checotah, Okla.	D2a-'92	16/15
62	# Semple, Tony	G	6-5	303	12/20/70	8	Memphis	Lincoln, Ill.	D5-'94	12/8
86	Sloan, David	TE	6-6	260	6/8/72	7	New Mexico	Tollhouse, Calif.	D3-'95	15/10
83	# Stablein, Brian	WR	6-1	194	4/14/70	8	Ohio State	Erie, Pa.	FA-'98	14/4
66	Stai, Brenden	G	6-4	312	3/30/72	7	Nebraska	Yorba Linda, Calif.	FA-'01	16/16*
34	Stewart, James	RB	6-1	226	12/27/71	7	Tennessee	Morristown, Tenn.	UFA(Jax)-'00	16/16
29	Supernaw, Kywin	S	6-1	207	6/2/75	4	Indiana	Claremore, Okla.	FA-'98	13/3
25	Warren, Lamont	RB	5-11	202	1/4/73	7	Colorado	Los Angeles, Calif.	FA-'01	0*
32	Westbrook, Bryant	CB	6-0	198	12/19/74	5	Texas	Oceanside, Calif.	D1-'97	13/13
35	Wyrick, Jimmy	CB	5-9	179	12/31/76	2	Minnesota	DeSoto, Texas	FA-'00	6/0

* Bailey played 16 games with Baltimore in '00; Banta played 16 games with N.Y. Jets; Droughns missed '00 season because of injury; Harbaugh played 7 games with San Diego; Joyce played 13 games with Arizona; Lee played 3 games with Philadelphia; Lyght played 14 games with St. Louis; Mitchell played 14 games with N.Y. Giants; Rone spent '00 season on practice squad; Sauter was inactive for 15 games; Stai played 16 games with Jacksonville; Warren last active with New England in '99.

\# Unrestricted free agent; subject to developments.

Players lost through free agency (3): C Mike Compton (NE; 16 games in '00), G Jeff Hartings (Pitt; 16), TE Walter Rasby (Wash; 16).

Also played with Lions in '00—T James Atkins (3 games), RB Mario Bates (13), T Barrett Brooks (15), S Corwin Brown (15), CB J.B. Brown (3), QB Stoney Case (5), CB Jeremy Lincoln (3), LB Kevin O'Neill (11), TE Al Pupunu (9), T Ray Roberts (10), S Ryan Stewart (1), CB Darnell Walker (11), CB Marquis Walker (12).

COACHING STAFF

Head Coach,
Marty Mornhinweg

Pro Career: Named Lions' twenty-first head coach January 25, 2001. Joins Lions after spending four years as offensive coordinator for San Francisco 49ers (1997-2000). The 49ers' offense was ranked fourth overall in 2000, accumulating 6,040 total yards, and they led the NFL in rushing two consecutive seasons (1998-99), including a team record 2,544 yards in 1998. Mornhinweg began his pro coaching career with the Green Bay Packers (1995-96). He was the Packers' offensive assistant-quality control coach in 1995 and was the team's quarterbacks coach in 1996 when the team went on to win Super Bowl XXXI. Played quarterback briefly for the Denver Dynamite (Arena Football League) in 1986.

Background: Played quarterback for Montana (1981-84) where he was the school's starter four consecutive seasons and established 15 school passing records. Began coaching career at Montana in 1985. Moved on as an assistant to Texas-El Paso (1986-87), Northern Arizona (1988), Southeast Missouri State (1989-1990), Missouri (1991-93), and Northern Arizona (1994).

Personal: Born March 29, 1962 in Edmond, Okla. Marty and wife, Lindsay, have four children—Madison, Molly Lynn, Skyler, and Bobby Cade—and live in Plymouth, Michigan.

ASSISTANT COACHES

Jason Arapoff, strength and conditioning; born July, 8 1965, Weymouth, Mass., lives in Bloomfield, Mich. Defensive back Springfield College 1985-88. No pro playing experience. Pro coach: Washington Redskins 1992-2000, joined Lions in 2001.

Malcolm Blacken, asst. strength and conditioning; born October 12, 1965, Richmond, Va., lives in Troy, Mich. Running back Virginia Tech 1984-88. No pro playing experience. College coach: South Carolina 1990-91, George Mason 1992-95, Virginia 1995. Pro coach: Washington Redskins 1996-2000, joined Lions in 2001.

Maurice Carthon, running backs; born April 24, 1961, Chicago, lives in Detroit. Running back Arkansas State 1979-1982. Pro running back New Jersey Generals (USFL) 1983-85, New York Giants 1985-1991, Indianapolis Colts 1992. Pro coach: New England Patriots 1994-96, New York Jets 1997-2000, joined Lions in 2001.

Don Clemons, defensive assistant-quality control; born February 15, 1954, Newark, N.J., lives in Rochester Hills, Mich. Defensive end Muhlenberg (Pa.) 1973-76. No pro playing experience. College coach: Kutztown State 1977-78, New Mexico 1979, Arizona State 1980-84. Pro coach: Joined Lions in 1985.

Charles Haley, asst. defensive line-pass rush specialist; born January 6, 1964, Gladys, Va., lives in Auburn Hills, Mich. Defensive end James Madison 1982-85. Pro defensive end San Francisco 49ers 1986-1991, 1998-99, Dallas Cowboys 1992-96. Pro coach: San Francisco 49ers 2000, joined Lions in 2001.

Kevin Higgins, quarterbacks; born December 1, 1955, New York, N.Y., lives in Northville, Mich. Defensive back West Chester (Pa.) 1973-76. No pro playing experience. College coach: Gettysburg College 1981-84, Richmond 1985-87, Lehigh 1988-2000 (head coach 1994-2000). Pro coach: Joined Lions in 2001.

Larry Kirksey, wide receivers; born January 6, 1951, Harlan, Ky., lives in Auburn Hills, Mich. Wide receiver Eastern Kentucky 1969-1972. No pro playing experience. College coach: Miami (Ohio) 1974-76, Kentucky 1977-1981, Kansas 1982, Kentucky State 1983 (head coach), Florida 1984-88, Pittsburgh 1989, Alabama 1990-93, Texas A&M 2000. Pro coach: San Francisco 49ers 1994-99, joined Lions in 2001.

Sean Kugler, tight ends; born August 9, 1966, Lockport, N.Y., lives in Waterford, Mich. Offensive lineman Texas-El Paso 1985-88. Pro offensive lineman Sacramento Surge (WLAF) 1991. College coach: Texas-El Paso 1993-2000. Pro coach: Joined Lions in 2001.

Carl Mauck, offensive line; born July 7, 1947, McLeansboro, Ill., lives in Plymouth, Mich. Linebacker-center Southern Illinois 1966-68. Pro center Baltimore Colts 1969, Miami Dolphins 1970, San Diego Chargers 1971-72, Houston Oilers 1975-1981. Pro coach: New Orleans Saints 1982-85, Kansas City Chiefs 1986-88, Tampa Bay Buccaneers 1991, San Diego Chargers 1992-95, Arizona Cardinals 1996-97, Buffalo Bills 1998-2000, joined Lions in 2001.

Mike McHugh, offensive assistant-quality control; born December 12, 1957, Pottston, Pa., lives in Plymouth, Mich. Attended Findlay. No college or pro playing experience. College coach: Eastern Michigan 1989-1992, Missouri 1993-98, Oregon 1999-2000. Pro coach: Joined Lions in 2001.

Glenn Pires, linebackers; born September 13, 1958, New Bedford, Mass., lives in Novi, Mich. Offensive line Springfield College 1976-79. No pro playing experience. College coach: Syracuse 1983-84, 1989-1994, Dartmouth 1985-88, Michigan State 1995. Pro coach: Arizona Cardinals 1996-2000, joined Lions in 2001.

Chuck Preifer, special teams; born July 26, 1944, Cleveland, lives in Farmington, Mich. Attended John Carroll. No college or pro playing experience. College coach: Miami (Ohio) 1977, North Carolina 1978-1983, Kent State 1986, Georgia Tech 1987-1991. Pro coach: Green Bay Packers 1984-85, San Diego Chargers 1992-96, joined Lions in 1997.

Richard Selcer, defensive backs; born August 22, 1937, Cincinnati, lives in Rochester, Mich. Running back Notre Dame 1955-59. No pro playing experience. College coach: Xavier 1962-64, 1970-71 (head coach 1970-71), Cincinnati 1965-66, Brown 1967-69, Wisconsin 1972-74, Kansas State 1975-77, Southwestern Louisiana 1978-1980. Pro coach: Houston Oilers 1981-83, Cincinnati Bengals 1984-1991, Los Angeles/St. Louis Rams 1992-96, joined Lions in 1997.

Vince Tobin, defensive coordinator; born September 29, 1943, Burlington Junction, Mo., lives in Northville, Mich. Defensive back Missouri 1961-64. No pro playing experience. College coach: Missouri 1965, 1967-1976. Pro coach: British Columbia Lions (CFL) 1977-1982, Philadelphia/Baltimore Stars (USFL) 1983-85, Chicago Bears 1986-1992, Indianapolis Colts 1994-95, Arizona Cardinals 1996-2000 (head coach), joined Lions in 2001.

Bill Young, defensive line; born August 17, 1946, Herford, Texas, lives in Rochester Hills, Mich. Linebacker-defensive tackle Oklahoma State 1965-67. No pro playing experience. College coach: Oklahoma State 1968, 1976-78, Iowa State 1979, Tulsa 1980-84, Arizona State 1985-87, Ohio State 1988-1995, Oklahoma 1996-97, Southern California 1998-2000. Pro coach: Joined Lions in 2001.

2001 FIRST-YEAR ROSTER

Name	Pos.	Ht.	Wt.	Birthdate	College	Hometown	How Acq.
Anderson, Scotty	WR	6-2	184	11/24/79	Grambling State	Jonesboro, La.	D5a
Aoga, Neo	QB	6-3	275	6/19/73	Azusa Pacific	Long Beach, Calif.	FA
Backus, Jeff	T	6-5	308	9/21/77	Michigan	Norcross, Ga.	D1
Bohn, Brad	K	5-9	180	2/12/78	Utah State	Laguna Beach, Calif.	FA
Childers, Matt	DE	5-11	188	10/23/78	Southern California	Castro Valley, Calif.	FA
Clinton, Eugene	S	5-11	187	9/5/76	Mississippi State	Jackson, Miss.	FA
Cottrell, Keith	P	6-4	205	10/23/78	Florida State	Orlando, Fla.	FA
Cuthbert, Will	T	6-5	329	1/31/79	Alabama	Ft. Pierce, Fla.	FA
Douglas, Henry (1)	WR	5-11	167	3/3/77	North Carolina A&T	Southern Pines, N.C.	FA-'00
Gaddis, Versie	WR	5-10	187	5/1/77	Indiana	Atlanta, Ga.	FA
Gibbs, Dennis	CB	5-9	190	12/29/78	Idaho	Lompoc, Calif.	FA
Glenn, Jason	LB	6-0	231	8/20/79	Texas A&M	Houston, Texas	D6
Golliday, Toby	DT	6-1	328	2/18/78	Mississippi State	Cleveland, Miss.	FA
Herron, Anthony	DE	6-3	280	9/24/79	Iowa	Bolingbrook, Ill.	FA
Iwuoma, Chidi	CB	5-8	180	2/19/78	California	Pasadena, Calif.	FA
Jackson, Khary	TE	6-3	256	8/17/77	Oklahoma State	Detroit, Mich.	FA
Jennings, Ligarius	CB	5-8	202	11/3/77	Tennessee State	Birmingham, Ala.	FA
Johnson, Sly	WR	5-10	181	9/15/79	Miami (Ohio)	Miramar, Fla.	FA
Kaiser, Loran	DT	6-4	290	3/22/78	Nebraska	Farwell, Neb.	FA
Kroeker, Dustin	T	6-5	290	10/4/78	Cal Poly	Shafter, Calif.	FA
Lamere, Mark	T	6-5	298	4/27/78	Louisiana-Lafayette	Metairie, La.	FA
Malloy, Donald	S	5-9	181	6/8/77	New Mexico State	Fort Washington, Md.	FA
Mazza, Rich	G	6-2	282	1/5/78	Rutgers	Bethlehem, Pa.	FA
McMahon, Mike	QB	6-2	213	2/8/79	Rutgers	Wexford, Pa.	D5b
Miles, DeWayne	FB	6-0	251	12/11/77	West Texas A&M	Amherst, Texas	FA
Natkin, Brian	TE	6-2	251	1/3/78	Texas-El Paso	San Antonio, Texas	FA
Offing, Andre	LB	6-0	240	9/2/76	South Carolina	Houston, Texas	FA
O'Neill, Joe (1)	LB	6-1	235	12/11/76	Bowling Green	Twinsburg, Ohio	FA-'00
Ordway, Jonathan	CB	5-10	181	10/19/78	Boston College	Seffner, Fla.	FA
Penn, Kawasak	TE	6-4	243	12/1/74	Western Carolina	Winston-Salem, N.C.	FA
Powell, Sean (1)	DT	6-1	292	1/23/74	New Mexico State	Lawndale, Calif.	FA-'00
Raiola, Dominic	C	6-1	303	12/30/78	Nebraska	Honolulu, Hawaii	D2a
Robinson, Darnell	LB	6-0	225	3/16/78	Oregon State	Sacramento, Calif.	FA
Rogers, Shaun	DT	6-4	331	3/12/79	Texas	La Porte, Texas	D2b
Rogers, Wayne	LB	6-1	232	2/10/78	Houston	Waco, Texas	FA
Taupule, Raymond	T	6-4	343	12/3/79	West Texas A&M	Norwalk, Calif.	FA
Trejo, Stephen	FB	6-2	258	11/20/77	Arizona State	Casa Grande, Ariz.	FA
Vincent, Andy (1)	T	6-4	306	6/11/78	Texas A&M	Sulphur, La.	FA-'00
Waerig, John	TE	6-2	264	4/8/76	Maryland	Philadelphia, Pa.	FA
Wilson, Eric	DT	6-3	287	1/30/78	Michigan	Monroe, Mich.	FA

The term NFL Rookie is defined as a player who is in his first season of professional football and has not been on the roster of another professional football team for any regular-season or postseason games. A Rookie is designated by an "R" on NFL rosters. Players who have been active in another professional football league or players who have NFL experience, including either preseason training camp or being on an Active List or Inactive List, or on Reserve/Injured or Reserve/Physically Unable to Perform for fewer than six regular-season games, are termed NFL First-Year Players. An NFL First-Year Player is designated by a "1" on NFL rosters. Thereafter, a player is credited with an additional year of experience for each season in which he accumulates six games on the Active List or Inactive List, or on Reserve/Injured or Reserve/Physically Unable to Perform.

GREEN BAY PACKERS

National Football Conference
Central Division
Team Colors: Dark Green, Gold, and White
1265 Lombardi Avenue
Green Bay, Wisconsin 54304
Telephone: (920) 496-5700

CLUB OFFICIALS

President and CEO: Bob Harlan
Vice President: John Fabry
Secretary: Peter Platten
Treasurer: John Underwood
Exec. V.P./General Manager/Head Coach: Mike Sherman
Senior Vice President of Administration: John Jones
Vice President of Football Operations: Mark Hatley
Director of College Scouting: John Dorsey
Director of Pro Personnel: Reggie McKenzie
Director of Player Finance: Andrew Brandt
Assistant to General Manager/Director of Football Administration: Bruce Warwick
Consultant: Ron Wolf
Exec. Assistant to the President: Phil Pionek
Exec. Director of Public Relations: Lee Remmel
Associate Director of Public Relations: Jeff Blumb
Assistant Director of Public Relations/Travel Coordinator: Aaron Popkey
Public Relations Assistants: Kristin McCormack, Damian Areyan
Director of Player Programs: Edgar Bennett
Director of Family Programs: Sherry Schuldes
Director of Community Relations: Jeanne McKenna
Director of Marketing: Jeff Cieply
Ticket Director: Mark Wagner
Director of Premium Guest Services: Jennifer Ark
Director of Administrative Affairs: Mark Schiefelbein
Director of Finance: Vicki Vannieuwenhoven
Director of Accounting: Duke Copp
Director of Computer Services: Wayne Wichlacz
Corporate Security Officer: Jerry Parins
Staff Counsel: Jason Wied
Pro Personnel Assistant: Marc Lillibridge
Assistant Director of College Scouting: Shaun Herock
College Scouts: Lee Gissendaner, Brian Gutekunst, Alonzo Highsmith, Lenny McGill, Sam Seale, Red Cochran
Scouting Coordinator: Danny Mock
Strength and Conditioning Assistants: Mark Lovat, Vince Workman
Director of Research and Development: Mike Eayrs
Video Director: Bob Eckberg
Head Trainer: Pepper Burruss
Equipment Manager: Gordon (Red) Batty
Stadium Manager: Ted Eisenreich
Fields Supervisor: Allen Johnson
Stadium: Lambeau Field (built in 1957)
•**Capacity:** 60,890
1265 Lombardi Avenue
Green Bay, Wisconsin 54304
Playing Surface: Grass
Training Camp: St. Norbert College
De Pere, Wisconsin 54115

RECORD HOLDERS

INDIVIDUAL RECORDS—CAREER

Category	Name	Performance
Rushing (Yds.)	Jim Taylor, 1958-1966	8,207
Passing (Yds.)	Brett Favre, 1992-2000	34,706
Passing (TDs)	Brett Favre, 1992-2000	255
Receiving (No.)	Sterling Sharpe, 1988-1994	595
Receiving (Yds.)	James Lofton, 1978-1986	9,656
Interceptions	Bobby Dillon, 1952-59	52
Punting (Avg.)	Craig Hentrich, 1994-97	42.8
Punt Return (Avg.)	Desmond Howard, 1996, 1999	13.8
Kickoff Return (Avg.)	Travis Williams, 1967-1970	26.7
Field Goals	Chris Jacke, 1989-1996	173
Touchdowns (Tot.)	Don Hutson, 1935-1945	105
Points	Don Hutson, 1935-1945	823

INDIVIDUAL RECORDS—SINGLE SEASON

Category	Name	Performance
Rushing (Yds.)	Jim Taylor, 1962	1,474
Passing (Yds.)	Lynn Dickey, 1983	4,458
Passing (TDs)	Brett Favre, 1996	39
Receiving (No.)	Sterling Sharpe, 1993	112
Receiving (Yds.)	Robert Brooks, 1995	1,497
Interceptions	Irv Comp, 1943	10
Punting (Avg.)	Craig Hentrich, 1997	45.0
Punt Return (Avg.)	Billy Grimes, 1950	19.1
Kickoff Return (Avg.)	Travis Williams, 1967	*41.1
Field Goals	Chester Marcol, 1972	33
	Ryan Longwell, 2000	33
Touchdowns (Tot.)	Jim Taylor, 1962	19
Points	Paul Hornung, 1960	*176

INDIVIDUAL RECORDS—SINGLE GAME

Category	Name	Performance
Rushing (Yds.)	Dorsey Levens, 11-23-97	190
Passing (Yds.)	Lynn Dickey, 10-12-80	418
Passing (TDs)	Many times. Last time by Brett Favre, 9-27-98	5
Receiving (No.)	Don Hutson, 11-22-42	14
Receiving (Yds.)	Billy Howton, 10-21-56	257
Interceptions	Bobby Dillon, 11-26-53	*4
	Willie Buchanon, 9-24-78	*4
Field Goals	Chris Jacke, 11-11-90, 10-14-96	5
	Ryan Longwell, 9-24-00	5
Touchdowns (Tot.)	Paul Hornung, 12-12-65	5
Points	Paul Hornung, 10-8-61	33

*NFL Record

2001 SCHEDULE

PRESEASON

Aug. 11	at Cleveland	8:00
Aug. 20	**Denver**	7:00
Aug. 25	**Miami**	7:00
Aug. 31	at Oakland	6:00

REGULAR SEASON

Sept. 9	**Detroit**	12:00
Sept. 16	at New York Giants	1:00
Sept. 24	**Washington** (Mon.)	8:00
Sept. 30	at Carolina	1:00
Oct. 7	at Tampa Bay	4:15
Oct. 14	**Baltimore**	12:00
Oct. 21	at Minnesota	3:15
Oct. 28	Open Date	
Nov. 4	**Tampa Bay**	12:00
Nov. 11	at Chicago	12:00
Nov. 18	**Atlanta**	12:00
Nov. 22	at Detroit (Thurs.)	12:30
Dec. 3	at Jacksonville (Mon.)	9:00
Dec. 9	**Chicago**	12:00
Dec. 16	at Tennessee	3:15
Dec. 23	**Cleveland**	12:00
Dec. 30	**Minnesota**	12:00

LAMBEAU FIELD

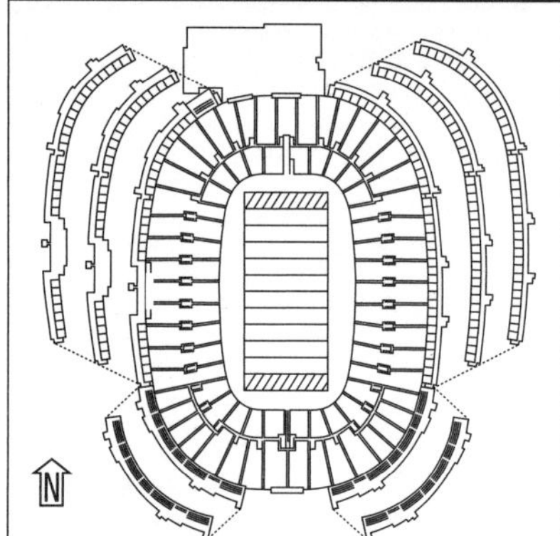

COACHING HISTORY

(590-470-36)

1921-1949	Earl (Curly) Lambeau	212-106-21
1950-53	Gene Ronzani*	14-31-1
1953	Hugh Devore-Ray (Scooter) McLean**	0-2-0
1954-57	Lisle Blackbourn	17-31-0
1958	Ray (Scooter) McLean	1-10-1
1959-1967	Vince Lombardi	98-30-4
1968-1970	Phil Bengtson	20-21-1
1971-74	Dan Devine	25-28-4
1975-1983	Bart Starr	53-77-3
1984-87	Forrest Gregg	25-37-1
1988-1991	Lindy Infante	24-40-0
1992-98	Mike Holmgren	84-42-0
1999	Ray Rhodes	8-8-0
2000	Mike Sherman	9-7-0

*Resigned after 10 games in 1953
**Co-coaches

2000 TEAM RECORD

PRESEASON (2-2)

Date	Result		Opponent
8/4	W	37-24	New York Jets
8/13	L	20-26	at Denver
8/21	L	14-17	at Miami
8/26	W	34-33	Cleveland

REGULAR SEASON (9-7)

Date	Result		Opponent	Att.
9/3	L	16-20	New York Jets	59,870
9/10	L	18-27	at Buffalo	72,722
9/17	W	6-3	Philadelphia	59,869
9/24	W	29-3	at Arizona	69,568
10/1	L	24-27	Chicago	59,869
10/8	L	24-31	at Detroit	77,549
10/15	W	31-28	San Francisco	59,870
10/29	L	20-28	at Miami	73,740
11/6	W	26-20	Minnesota (OT)	59,854
11/12	L	15-20	at Tampa Bay	65,621
11/19	W	26-24	Indianapolis	59,869
11/27	L	14-31	at Carolina	73,295
12/3	W	28-6	at Chicago	66,944
12/10	W	26-13	Detroit	59,854
12/17	W	33-28	at Minnesota	64,183
12/24	W	17-14	Tampa Bay (OT)	59,692

(OT) Overtime

SCORE BY PERIODS

Packers	59	101	83	101	9	—	353
Opponents	51	91	82	99	0	—	323

ATTENDANCE

Home 478,747 Away 560,367 Total 1,039,114
Single-game home record, 60,766 (9/1/97)
Single-season home record, 482,988 (1996)

2000 TEAM STATISTICS

	Packers	Opp.
Total First Downs	315	284
Rushing	88	84
Passing	197	186
Penalty	30	14
Third Down: Made/Att	85/218	82/224
Third Down Pct.	39.0	36.6
Fourth Down: Made/Att	7/12	7/11
Fourth Down Pct.	58.3	63.6
Total Net Yards	5,321	5,069
Avg. Per Game	332.6	316.8
Total Plays	1,038	1,012
Avg. Per Play	5.1	5.0
Net Yards Rushing	1,643	1,618
Avg. Per Game	102.7	101.1
Total Rushes	404	417
Net Yards Passing	3,678	3,451
Avg. Per Game	229.9	215.7
Sacked/Yards Lost	34/238	38/244
Gross Yards	3,916	3,695
Att./Completions	600/348	557/307
Completion Pct.	58.0	55.1
Had Intercepted	16	21
Punts/Average	79/38.4	94/41.4
Net Punting Avg.	79/34.3	94/34.6
Penalties/Yards	88/685	101/992
Fumbles/Ball Lost	30/17	16/7
Touchdowns	36	37
Rushing	13	7
Passing	21	28
Returns	2	2
Avg. Time of Possession	30:45	29:15

2000 INDIVIDUAL STATISTICS

Passing	Att.	Comp.	Yds.	Pct.	TD	Int.	Tkld.	Rate
Favre	580	338	3,812	58.3	20	16	33/236	78.0
Hasselbeck	19	10	104	52.6	1	0	1/2	86.3
Green	1	0	0	0.0	0	0	0/0	39.6
Packers	600	348	3,916	58.0	21	16	34/238	78.2
Opponents	557	307	3,695	55.1	28	21	38/244	76.7

SCORING	TD R	TD P	TD Rt	PAT	FG	Saf	PTS
Longwell	0	0	0	32/32	33/38	0	131
Green	10	3	0	0/0	0/0	0	78
Freeman	0	9	0	0/0	0/0	0	54
Schroeder	0	4	0	0/0	0/0	0	24
Levens	3	0	0	0/0	0/0	0	18
T. Davis	0	2	0	0/0	0/0	0	14
Driver	0	1	0	0/0	0/0	0	8
Franks	0	1	0	0/0	0/0	0	6
Henderson	0	1	0	0/0	0/0	0	6
Rossum	0	0	1	0/0	0/0	0	6
T. Williams	0	0	1	0/0	0/0	0	6
Maryland	0	0	0	0/0	0/0	1	2
Packers	13	21	2	32/32	33/38	1	353
Opponents	7	28	2	36/36	21/25	0	323

2-Pt. Conversions: T. Davis, Driver.
Packers 2-3, Opponents 1-1.

RUSHING	Att.	Yds.	Avg.	LG	TD
Green	263	1,175	4.5	39t	10
Levens	77	224	2.9	17	3
Favre	27	108	4.0	18	0
Parker	18	85	4.7	24	0
Henderson	2	16	8.0	12	0
Rossum	1	16	16.0	16	0
Schroeder	2	11	5.5	12	0
Mitchell	2	8	4.0	4	0
Freeman	2	5	2.5	3	0
Driver	1	4	4.0	4	0
Goodman	3	-2	-.7	3	0
Wuerffel	2	-2	-1.0	-1	0
Hasselbeck	4	-5	-1.3	-1	0
Packers	404	1,643	4.1	39t	13
Opponents	417	1,618	3.9	52	7

RECEIVING	No.	Yds.	Avg.	LG	TD
Green	73	559	7.7	31	3
Schroeder	65	999	15.4	55t	4
Freeman	62	912	14.7	67t	9
Henderson	35	234	6.7	25	1
Franks	34	363	10.7	27t	1
Driver	21	322	15.3	49	1
T. Davis	19	177	9.3	41	2
Levens	16	146	9.1	37	0
Lee	10	134	13.4	38	0
Parker	9	50	5.6	10	0
Wetnight	3	20	6.7	9	0
Goodman	1	0	0.0	0	0
Packers	348	3,916	11.3	67t	21
Opponents	307	3,695	12.0	78t	28

INTERCEPTIONS	No.	Yds.	Avg.	LG	TD
Sharper	9	109	12.1	47	0
T. Williams	4	105	26.3	46	1
McBride	2	43	21.5	43	0
Butler	2	25	12.5	22	0
Edwards	2	4	2.0	4	0
M. McKenzie	1	26	26.0	26	0
Holliday	1	3	3.0	3	0
Packers	21	315	15.0	47	1
Opponents	16	201	12.6	42t	1

PUNTING	No.	Yds.	Avg.	In 20	LG
Bidwell	78	3,003	38.5	22	53
Longwell	1	30	30.0	0	30
Packers	79	3,033	38.4	22	53
Opponents	94	3,888	41.4	25	60

PUNT RETURNS	No.	FC	Yds.	Avg.	LG	TD
Rossum	29	24	248	8.6	43	0
Lee	5	2	52	10.4	16	0
M. McKenzie	1	0	0	0.0	0	0
Packers	35	26	300	8.6	43	0
Opponents	27	27	205	7.6	81t	1

KICKOFF RETURNS	No.	Yds.	Avg.	LG	TD
Rossum	50	1,288	25.8	92t	1
Henderson	5	80	16.0	22	0
Goodman	4	129	32.3	54	0
Berry	1	22	22.0	22	0
Bowens	1	12	12.0	12	0
Mitchell	1	26	26.0	26	0
Morton	1	13	13.0	13	0
Wetnight	1	0	0.0	0	0
Packers	64	1,570	24.5	92t	1
Opponents	76	1,639	21.6	40	0

FIELD GOALS	1-19	20-29	30-39	40-49	50+
Longwell	0/0	7/8	10/10	13/15	3/5
Packers	0/0	7/8	10/10	13/15	3/5
Opponents	1/1	4/4	8/8	6/9	2/3

SACKS	No.
Thierry	6.5
S. Dotson	6.0
Holliday	5.0
Hunt	5.0
Bowens	3.5
Butler	2.0
Harris	2.0
Wayne	2.0
Gbaja-Biamila	1.5
Lyon	1.0
Sharper	1.0
McGarrahan	0.5
B. Williams	0.5
K. Williams	0.5
Packers	38.0
Opponents	34.0

2001 DRAFT CHOICES

Round	Name	Pos.	College
1	Jamal Reynolds	DE	Florida State
2	Robert Ferguson	WR	Texas A&M
3	Bhawoh Jue	DB	Penn State
	Torrance Marshall	LB	Oklahoma
4	Bill Ferrario	G	Wisconsin
6	David Martin	TE	Tennessee

GREEN BAY PACKERS

2001 VETERAN ROSTER

No.	Name	Pos.	Ht.	Wt.	Birthdate	NFL Exp.	College	Hometown	How Acq.	'00 Games/ Starts
31	Akins, Chris	S	5-11	195	11/29/76	3	Arkansas-Pine Bluff	Little Rock, Ark.	W(Dall)-'00	10/0*
9	Bidwell, Josh	P	6-3	222	3/13/76	2	Oregon	Winston, Ore.	D4b-'99	16/0
96	Bowens, David	DE	6-2	261	7/3/77	3	Western Illinois	Orchard Lake, Mich.	T(Den)-'00	14/0
85	† Bradford, Corey	WR	6-1	197	12/8/75	4	Jackson State	Clinton, La.	D5-'98	2/0
93	Brown, Gilbert	DT	6-2	339	2/22/71	8	Kansas	Detroit, Mich.	W(Minn)-'93	0*
36	Butler, LeRoy	S	6-0	203	7/19/68	12	Florida State	Jacksonville, Fla.	D2-'90	16/16
76	Clifton, Chad	T	6-5	325	6/26/76	2	Tennessee	Martin, Tenn.	D2-'00	13/10
61	Curry, Scott	T	6-5	300	12/25/75	3	Montana	Valier, Mont.	D6b-'99	0*
28	Darden, Tony	CB	5-11	193	8/11/75	3	Texas Tech	San Antonio, Texas	W(SD)-'01	16/3*
60	Davis, Rob	LS	6-3	286	12/10/68	6	Shippensburg	Greenbelt, Md.	FA-'97	16/0
81	Davis, Tyrone	TE	6-4	260	6/30/72	6	Virginia	Halifax, Va.	FA-'97	14/9
59	Diggs, Na'il	LB	6-4	234	7/8/78	2	Ohio State	Los Angeles, Calif.	D4a-'00	13/12
72	Dotson, Earl	T	6-4	317	12/17/70	9	Texas A&I	Beaumont, Texas	D3-'93	2/2
71	Dotson, Santana	DT	6-5	285	12/19/69	10	Baylor	Houston, Texas	UFA(TB)-'96	12/12
80	Driver, Donald	WR	6-0	177	2/2/75	3	Alcorn State	Houston, Texas	D7b-'99	16/2
24	Edwards, Antuan	CB-S	6-1	205	5/26/77	3	Clemson	Starkville, Miss.	D1-'99	12/3
4	Favre, Brett	QB	6-2	225	10/10/69	11	Southern Mississippi	Kiln, Miss.	T(Atl)-'92	16/16
58	Flanagan, Mike	C	6-5	297	11/10/73	6	UCLA	Sacramento, Calif.	D3a-'96	16/2
75	Flanigan, Jim	DT	6-2	290	8/27/71	8	Notre Dame	Brussel, Wix.	FA-'01	16/14*
88	Franks, Bubba	TE	6-6	260	1/6/78	2	Miami	Big Spring, Texas	D1-'00	16/13
86	Freeman, Antonio	WR	6-1	198	5/27/72	7	Virginia Tech	Baltimore, Md.	FA-'01	15/15
94	Gbaja-Biamila, Kabeer	DE	6-4	245	9/24/77	2	San Diego State	Los Angeles, Calif.	FA-'00	7/0
57	Gizzi, Chris	LB	6-0	235	3/8/75	2	Air Force	Cleveland, Ohio	FA-'00	11/0
29	Goodman, Herbert	RB	5-11	203	8/31/77	2	Graceland	Homestead, Fla.	FA-'00	5/0
30	Green, Ahman	RB	6-0	217	2/16/77	4	Nebraska	Omaha, Neb.	T(Sea)-'00	16/11
55	Harris, Bernardo	LB	6-2	246	10/15/71	7	North Carolina	Chapel Hill, N.C.	FA-'95	16/16
33	Henderson, William	FB	6-1	253	2/19/71	7	North Carolina	Chester, Va.	D3b-'95	16/6
90	Holliday, Vonnie	DE	6-5	290	12/11/75	4	North Carolina	Camden, S.C.	D1-'98	12/9
97	Hunt, Cletidus	DT	6-4	299	1/2/76	3	Kentucky State	Memphis, Tenn.	D3b-'99	16/11
82	Lee, Charles	WR	6-2	202	11/19/77	2	Central Florida	Homestead, Fla.	D7c-'00	15/1
25	Levens, Dorsey	RB	6-1	230	5/21/70	8	Georgia Tech	Syracuse, N.Y.	D5b-'94	5/5
8	Longwell, Ryan	K	6-0	198	8/16/74	5	California	Bend, Ore.	W(SF)-'97	16/0
87	Lucas, Anthony	WR	6-3	204	11/20/76	2	Arkansas	Tallulah, La.	D4b-'00	0*
98	Lyon, Billy	DE-DT	6-5	295	12/10/73	4	Marshall	Erlanger, Ky.	FA-'98	11/1
67	Maryland, Russell	DT	6-1	308	3/22/69	11	Miami	Chicago, Ill.	FA-'00	16/16
27	McBride, Tod	CB	6-1	207	1/26/76	3	UCLA	Walnut, Calif.	W(Sea)-'99	15/6
43	McGarrahan, Scott	S	6-1	198	2/12/74	4	New Mexico	Arlington, Texas	D6a-'98	16/0
34	McKenzie, Mike	CB	6-0	185	4/26/76	3	Memphis	Miami, Fla.	D3a-'99	10/8
32	Mealey, Rondell	RB	6-0	219	2/24/77	2	Louisiana State	Destrehan, La.	D7e-'00	0*
69	Mercier, Richard	G	6-3	300	5/13/75	2	Miami	Montreal, Quebec, Canada	W(Den)-'00	0*
53	# Morton, Mike	LB	6-4	238	3/28/72	7	North Carolina	Kannaplis, N.C.	UFA(StL)-'00	16/0
22	Parker, De'Mond	RB	5-10	185	12/24/76	3	Oklahoma	Tulsa, Okla.	D5a-'99	8/0
18	Pederson, Doug	QB	6-3	220	1/31/68	9	Northeast Louisiana	Ferndale, Wash.	FA-'01	11/8*
62	Rivera, Marco	G	6-4	310	4/26/72	6	Penn State	Elmont, N.Y.	D6-'96	16/16
20	Rossum, Allen	CB-KR	5-8	178	10/22/75	4	Notre Dame	Dallas, Texas	T(Phil)-'00	16/0
84	Schroeder, Bill	WR	6-3	205	1/9/71	6	Wisconsin-La Crosse	Sheboygan, Wis.	FA-'97	16/16
42	Sharper, Darren	S	6-2	205	11/3/75	5	William & Mary	Richmond, Va.	D2-'97	16/16
44	Snider, Matt	FB	6-2	240	1/26/76	3	Richmond	Wynnewood, Pa.	W(Car)-'99	16/0
79	Stokes, Barry	G-T	6-4	310	12/20/73	4	Eastern Michigan	Davison, Mich.	FA-'00	8/0
65	Tauscher, Mark	T	6-3	313	6/17/77	2	Wisconsin	Auburndale, Wis.	D7a-'00	16/14
91	Thierry, John	DE	6-4	262	9/4/71	8	Alcorn State	Plaisance, La.	UFA(Cle)-'00	16/16
68	Wahle, Mike	T	6-6	310	3/29/77	4	Navy	Lake Arrowhead, Calif.	SD2-'98	16/6
95	Warren, Steve	DT	6-1	298	1/22/78	2	Nebraska	Springfield, Mo.	D3-'00	13/0
54	Wayne, Nate	LB	6-0	230	1/12/75	4	Mississippi	Macon, Miss.	T(Den)-'00	16/13
50	Williams, K.D.	LB	6-0	235	4/22/73	3	Henderson State	Tampa, Fla.	T(NO)-'00	16/3
37	Williams, Tyrone	CB	5-11	193	5/31/73	6	Nebraska	Bradenton, Fla.	D3b-'96	16/16
52	Winters, Frank	C	6-3	305	1/23/64	15	Western Illinois	Union City, N.J.	PB(KC)-'92	14/14

* Akins played 8 games with Dallas and 2 with Green Bay in '00; Brown last active with Green Bay in '99; Curry, Lucas, and Mealey missed '00 season because of injury; Darden played 16 games with San Diego; Flanigan played 16 games with Chicago; Mercier was inactive for 5 games with Denver; Pederson played 11 games with Cleveland.

† Restricted free agent; subject to developments.

Unrestricted free agent; subject to developments.

Traded—QB Matt Hasselbeck (16 games in '00) to Seattle.

Players lost through free agency (1): G Ross Verba (Cle; 16 games in '00).

Also played with Packers in '00—S Gary Berry (4 games), LB Eugene McCaslin (1), G Raleigh McKenzie (3), RB Basil Mitchell (1), CB-S Jason Moore (3), DT Austin Robbins (2), TE Ryan Wetnight (10), LB Brian Williams (4), QB Danny Wuerffel (1).

COACHING STAFF

Executive Vice President/General Manager/ Head Coach, Mike Sherman

Pro Career: Named the thirteenth head coach in Packers history January 18, 2000. Added general manager responsibilities in 2001 following the retirement of Ron Wolf. Guided Packers to a 9-7 record, including a perfect 4-0 December mark, in his initial season as head coach while his team overcame a host of injuries, narrowly missing the playoffs on the final weekend. Joined Pro Football Hall of Fame members Curly Lambeau and Vince Lombardi, along with Mike Holmgren, as the only head coaches in team history to post a winning record in their first seasons. Previously had served as Green Bay's tight ends coach for two seasons (1997-98) before following Holmgren to the Seattle Seahawks in 1999 as offensive coordinator-tight ends coach. Oversaw vast improvement in the Seahawks' offense in his lone season with Seattle as it won the AFC West and made its first playoff appearance since 1988. While a Green Bay assistant coach from 1997-98, he had played a major role in the continued success of Mark Chmura and the emergence of backup tight end Tyrone Davis, who caught 7 touchdown passes in 1998. The Packers participated in the playoffs both years and advanced to Super Bowl XXXII at the end of the 1997 season. Career record: 9-7.
Background: After coaching for three seasons at the high school level, Sherman began a 16-year career in the collegiate ranks in 1981 at Pittsburgh, then went to Tulane in 1983. Subsequently spent four seasons at Holy Cross (1985-88), including the final year as offensive coordinator. Coached at Texas A&M (1989-1993, 1995-96), and UCLA (1994). Played offensive guard and tackle, as well as linebacker, for three seasons (1974, 1976-77) at Central Connecticut State University. Was a prep star at Algonquin Regional High School in Northboro, Mass.
Personal: Born December 19, 1954, in Norwood, Mass., Sherman holds a bachelor's degree in English from Central Connecticut State. He and his wife, Karen, have four children—Sarah, Emily, Matthew, and Benjamin—and live in Green Bay.

ASSISTANT COACHES

Larry Beightol, offensive line; born November 21, 1942, Pittsburgh, lives in Green Bay. Guard-linebacker Catawba College 1960-63. No pro playing experience. College coach: William & Mary 1968-1971, North Carolina State 1972-75, Auburn 1976, Arkansas 1977-78, 1980-82, Louisiana Tech 1979 (head coach), Missouri 1983-84. Pro coach: Atlanta Falcons 1985-86, Tampa Bay Buccaneers 1987-88, San Diego Chargers 1989, New York Jets 1990-94, Houston Oilers 1995, Miami Dolphins 1996-98, joined Packers in 1999.
Darrell Bevell, offensive assistant-quality control; born January 6, 1970, Yuma, Ariz., lives in De Pere, Wis. Quarterback Northern Arizona 1989, Wisconsin 1992-95. No pro playing experience. College coach: Westmar 1996, Iowa State 1997, Connecticut 1998-99. Pro coach: Joined Packers in 2000.
Sylvester Croom, running backs; born September 25, 1954, Tuscaloosa, Ala., lives in Green Bay. Center Alabama 1971-74. Pro center New Orleans Saints 1975. College coach: Alabama 1976-1986. Pro coach: Tampa Bay Buccaneers 1987-1990, Indianapolis Colts 1991, San Diego Chargers 1992-96, Detroit Lions 1997-2000, joined Packers in 2001.
Ed Donatell, defensive coordinator; born February 4, 1957, Akron, Ohio, lives in Green Bay. Defensive back Glenville State 1975-78. No pro playing experience. College coach: Kent State 1979-1980, Washington 1981-82, Pacific 1983-85, Idaho 1986-88, Cal State-Fullerton 1989. Pro coach: New York Jets 1990-94, Denver Broncos 1995-99, joined Packers in 2000.
Stan Drayton, quality control-special teams/offense; born March 11, 1971, Cleveland, lives in Green Bay. Running back Allegheny 1990-92. No pro playing experience. College coach: Allegheny 1993, Eastern Michigan 1994, Pennsylvania 1995, Villanova 1996-2000. Pro coach: Joined Packers in 2001.

2001 FIRST-YEAR ROSTER

Name	Pos.	Ht.	Wt.	Birthdate	College	Hometown	How Acq.
Beasley, Jonathan	QB	6-0	227	4/20/78	Kansas State	Glendale, Ariz.	FA
Bradley, Carl (1)	DT	6-1	288	2/22/79	Virginia Tech	Lynchburg, Va.	FA
Brown, Roosevelt	DT	6-2	311	5/10/78	Texas A&M-Kingsville	Pensacola, Fla.	FA
Burris, Henry (1)	QB	6-1	195	6/4/75	Temple	Spiro, Okla.	FA
Claybrooks, DeVone	DT	6-3	292	9/15/77	East Carolina	Bassett, Va.	FA
Coutain, Kenny (1)	WR	6-2	205	3/12/77	Memphis	Miami, Fla.	FA
Curry, Donte'	LB	6-1	223	7/22/78	Morris Brown	Savannah, Ga.	FA
Demps, Damian	S	6-1	191	8/6/79	Central Florida	Miami, Fla.	FA
Dunlap, London (1)	LB	6-3	235	7/10/77	Texas Christian	Houston, Texas	FA
Ferguson, Robert	WR	6-1	209	12/17/79	Texas A&M	Houston, Texas	D2
Ferrario, Bill	G	6-2	313	9/22/78	Wisconsin	Scranton, Pa.	D4
Franklin, Jason	WR	6-0	207	4/29/79	Delta State	Meridian, Miss.	FA
Freeman, Jason (1)	TE	6-3	245	11/14/76	Oklahoma	Muskogee, Okla.	FA
Gall, Chris (1)	FB	6-0	231	4/4/76	Indiana	Oak Park, Ill.	FA
Horacek, Mike (1)	WR	6-1	204	7/6/73	Iowa State	Omaha, Neb.	W(Jax)
Jordan, Kevin	T	6-5	308	11/7/78	Fresno State	Harbor City, Calif.	FA
Joseph, Gana (1)	S	6-0	212	4/20/77	Oklahoma	Miami, Fla.	FA
Jue, Bhawoh	CB	6-0	197	5/24/79	Penn State	Chantilly, Va.	D3a
Kaesviharn, Kevin (1)	CB	6-1	193	8/29/76	Augustana (S.D.)	Lakeville, Minn.	FA
Kehl, Ed (1)	G	6-4	310	8/3/72	Brigham Young	Sandy, Utah	FA
Lenon, Paris (1)	LB	6-1	233	11/26/77	Richmond	Lynchburg, Va.	FA
Lloyd, DeAngelo	DE	6-5	262	2/9/78	Tennessee	Charlotte, N.C.	FA
Marshall, Torrance	LB	6-2	245	6/12/77	Oklahoma	Miami, Fla.	D3b
Martin, David	TE	6-4	242	3/13/79	Tennessee	Norfolk, Va.	D6
McCaslin, Eugene (1)	LB	6-1	226	7/12/77	Florida	Tampa, Fla.	FA-'00
McFadden, Marques	G-T	6-5	329	9/12/78	Arizona	Boise, Idaho	FA
Newman, Adam (1)	TE	6-5	248	12/8/77	Boston College	Westwood, Mass.	FA
Reynolds, Jamal	DE	6-3	266	2/20/79	Florida State	Aiken, S.C.	D1
Rountree, Glenn (1)	G	6-3	300	11/24/73	Clemson	Suffolk, Va.	FA
Schau, Tom (1)	C	6-4	285	12/30/75	Illinois	Bloomington, Ill.	FA
Stemke, Kevin	P	6-3	189	11/23/78	Wisconsin	Green Bay, Wis.	FA
Sterba, Brett	K	5-10	184	5/4/78	William & Mary	Cleveland, Ohio	FA
Tarver, Hurley (1)	CB	6-0	180	11/30/75	Central Oklahoma	Fort Worth, Texas	FA

The term NFL Rookie is defined as a player who is in his first season of professional football and has not been on the roster of another professional football team for any regular-season or postseason games. A Rookie is designated by an "R" on NFL rosters. Players who have been active in another professional football league or players who have NFL experience, including either preseason training camp or being on an Active List or Inactive List, or on Reserve/Injured or Reserve/Physically Unable to Perform for fewer than six regular-season games, are termed NFL First-Year Players. An NFL First-Year Player is designated by a "1" on NFL rosters. Thereafter, a player is credited with an additional year of experience for each season in which he accumulates six games on the Active List or Inactive List, or on Reserve/Injured or Reserve/Physically Unable to Perform.

Jethro Franklin, defensive line; born October 25, 1965, St. Lazaire, France, lives in De Pere, Wis. Defensive end San Jose (Calif.) C.C. 1984-85, Fresno State 1986-87. Pro defensive end Seattle Seahawks 1989. College coach: Fresno State 1991-98, UCLA 1999. Pro coach: Joined Packers in 2000.
Jeff Jagodzinski, tight ends; born October 12, 1963, Milwaukee, Wis., lives in Green Bay. Running back Wisconsin-Whitewater 1981-84. No pro playing experience. College coach: Wisconsin-Whitewater 1985, Northern Illinois 1986, Louisiana State 1987-88, East Carolina 1989-1996, Boston College 1997-98. Pro coach: Joined Packers in 1999.
Brad Miller, defensive assistant-quality control; born May 30, 1963, Pasadena, Calif., lives in Green Bay. Tight end-safety Oregon State 1981-84. No pro playing experience. College coach: Riverside (Calif.) C.C. 1986-1993, Portland State 1994. Pro coach: Birmingham Barracudas (CFL) 1995, Edmonton Eskimos (CFL) 1996-2000, joined Packers in 2001.
Frank Novak, special teams; born May 18, 1938, Leominster, Mass., lives in De Pere, Wis. Quarterback Northern Michigan 1959-1961. No pro playing experience. College coach: Northern Michigan 1966-1972, East Carolina 1973, Virginia 1974-75, Western Illinois 1976-77, Holy Cross 1978-1983, Missouri 1988. Pro coach: Oklahoma Outlaws (USFL) 1984, Birmingham Stallions (USFL) 1985, Houston Oilers 1989-1994, Detroit Lions 1995-96, San Diego Chargers 1997-98, joined Packers in 2000.
Bo Pelini, linebackers; born December 13, 1967, Youngstown, Ohio, lives in Green Bay. Defensive back Ohio State 1987-1990. No pro playing experience. College coach: Iowa 1991-92. Pro coach: San Francisco 49ers 1994-96, New England Patriots 1997-99, joined Packers in 2000.
Tom Rossley, offensive coordinator; born August 9, 1946, Painesville, Ohio, lives in De Pere, Wis. Wide receiver Cincinnati 1966-68. No pro playing experience. College coach: Arkansas 1972, Rice 1976, 1978-1981, Cincinnati 1977, Holy Cross 1986-87, Southern Methodist 1988-89, 1991-96 (head coach 1991-96). Pro coach: Montreal Concorde (CFL) 1982-84, San Antonio Gunslingers (USFL) 1985, Denver Dynamite (Arena) 1987, Atlanta Falcons 1990, Chicago Bears 1997-98, Kansas City Chiefs 1999, joined Packers in 2000.
Barry Rubin, strength and conditioning; born June 25, 1957, Monroe, La., lives in Green Bay. Running back-punter Louisiana State 1976-77, tight end-punter Northwestern (La.) State 1978-1980. No pro playing experience. College coach: Northeast Louisiana 1981-83, 1987-1990, 1994, Louisiana State 1984-85. Pro coach: Joined Packers in 1995.
Pat Ruel, asst. offensive line; born December 5, 1950, Washington, D.C., lives in Green Bay. Guard Miami 1971-72. No pro playing experience. College coach: Miami 1973-76, Arkansas 1977-78, Washington State 1979-1981, Texas A&M 1982-84, Northern Illinois 1985-87, Kansas 1988-1996, Michigan State 1998-99. Pro coach: Detroit Lions 2000, joined Packers in 2001.
Ray Sherman, wide receivers; born November 27, 1951, Berkeley, Calif., lives in Green Bay. Wide receiver Laney (Calif.) J.C. 1969-1970, Fresno State 1971-72. No pro playing experience. College coach: San Jose State 1974, California 1975, 1981, Michigan State 1976-77, Wake Forest 1978-1980, Purdue 1982-85, Georgia 1986-87. Pro coach: Houston Oilers 1988-89, Atlanta Falcons 1990, San Francisco 49ers 1991-93, New York Jets 1994, Minnesota Vikings 1995-97, 1999, Pittsburgh Steelers 1998, joined Packers in 2000.
Bob Slowik, defensive backs; born May 16, 1954, Pittsburgh, lives in Green Bay. Defensive back Delaware 1973-76. No pro playing experience. College coach: Delaware 1977-78, Florida 1979-1982, Drake 1983, Rutgers 1984-89, East Carolina 1990-91. Pro coach: Dallas Cowboys 1992, Chicago Bears 1993-98, Cleveland Browns 1999, joined Packers in 2000.
Lionel Washington, asst. defensive backs; born October 21, 1960, New Orleans, lives in De Pere, Wis. Defensive back Tulane 1979-1982. Pro defensive back St. Louis Cardinals 1983-86, Los Angeles/Oakland Raiders 1987-1994, 1997, Denver Broncos 1995-96. Pro coach: Joined Packers in 1999.

MINNESOTA VIKINGS

National Football Conference
Central Division
Team Colors: Purple, Gold, and White
9520 Viking Drive
Eden Prairie, Minnesota 55344
Telephone: (612) 828-6500

CLUB OFFICIALS

Owners: Red & Charline McCombs
President: Gary Woods
Head Coach & VP of Football Operations: Dennis Green
Executive Vice President: Mike Kelly
Vice President of Player Personnel: Frank Gilliam
Vice President of Football Administration: Rob Brzezinski
Director of Pro Personnel: Richard Solomon
National Scout: Jerry Reichow
Player Personnel Coordinator: Scott Studwell
Vice President of Sales and Marketing: Steve LaCroix
Vice President of Finance: Steve Poppen
Senior Football Analyst: Dave Blando
Director of Public Relations: Bob Hagan
Director of Operations: Breck Spinner
Director of Ticket Sales: Phil Huebner
Equipment Manager: Dennis Ryan
Head Athletic Trainer: Chuck Barta
Coordinator of Medical Services: Fred Zamberletti
Video Director: Larry Kohout
Stadium: Hubert H. Humphrey Metrodome (built in 1982) •**Capacity:** 64,121
500 11th Avenue South
Minneapolis, Minnesota 55415
Playing Surface: AstroTurf
Training Camp: Minnesota State-Mankato
Mankato, Minnesota 56001

2001 SCHEDULE

PRESEASON

Aug. 11	vs. New Orleans at San Antonio, Texas	7:00
Aug. 16	**Pittsburgh**	7:00
Aug. 24	**Indianapolis**	7:00
Aug. 31	at Miami	7:00

REGULAR SEASON

Sept. 9	**Carolina**	12:00
Sept. 17	at Baltimore (Mon.)	9:00
Sept. 23	at Chicago	12:00
Sept. 30	**Tampa Bay**	12:00
Oct. 7	at New Orleans	12:00
Oct. 14	**Detroit**	12:00
Oct. 21	**Green Bay**	3:15
Oct. 28	at Tampa Bay	1:00
Nov. 4	Open Date	
Nov. 11	at Philadelphia	4:15
Nov. 19	**New York Giants** (Mon.)	8:00
Nov. 25	**Chicago**	7:30
Dec. 2	at Pittsburgh	1:00
Dec. 9	**Tennessee**	12:00
Dec. 16	at Detroit	1:00
Dec. 23	**Jacksonville**	3:15
Dec. 30	at Green Bay	12:00

RECORD HOLDERS

INDIVIDUAL RECORDS—CAREER

Category	Name	Performance
Rushing (Yds.)	Robert Smith, 1993-2000	6,818
Passing (Yds.)	Fran Tarkenton, 1961-66, 1972-78	33,098
Passing (TDs)	Fran Tarkenton, 1961-66, 1972-78	239
Receiving (No.)	Cris Carter, 1990-2000	931
Receiving (Yds.)	Cris Carter, 1990-2000	11,512
Interceptions	Paul Krause, 1968-79	53
Punting (Avg.)	Harry Newsome, 1990-93	43.8
Punt Return (Avg.)	David Palmer, 1994-2000	9.4
Kickoff Return (Avg.)	Charlie West, 1968-73	25.5
Field Goals	Fred Cox, 1963-77	282
Touchdowns (Tot.)	Cris Carter, 1990-2000	104
Points	Fred Cox, 1963-77	1,365

INDIVIDUAL RECORDS—SINGLE SEASON

Category	Name	Performance
Rushing (Yds.)	Robert Smith, 2000	1,521
Passing (Yds.)	Warren Moon, 1994	4,264
Passing (TDs)	Randall Cunningham, 1998	34
Receiving (No.)	Cris Carter, 1994, 1995	122
Receiving (Yds.)	Randy Moss, 2000	1,437
Interceptions	Paul Krause, 1975	10
Punting (Avg.)	Bobby Walden, 1964	46.4
Punt Return (Avg.)	David Palmer, 1995	13.2
Kickoff Return (Avg.)	John Gilliam, 1972	26.3
Field Goals	Gary Anderson, 1998	35
Touchdowns (Tot.)	Chuck Foreman, 1975	22
Points	Gary Anderson, 1998	164

INDIVIDUAL RECORDS—SINGLE GAME

Category	Name	Performance
Rushing (Yds.)	Chuck Foreman, 10-24-76	200
Passing (Yds.)	Tommy Kramer, 11-2-86	490
Passing (TDs)	Joe Kapp, 9-28-69	*7
Receiving (No.)	Rickey Young, 12-16-79	15
Receiving (Yds.)	Sammy White, 11-7-76	210
Interceptions	Many Times	3
	Last time by Jack Del Rio, 12-5-93	
Field Goals	Rich Karlis, 11-5-89	*7
Touchdowns (Tot.)	Chuck Foreman, 12-20-75	4
	Ahmad Rashad, 9-2-79	4
Points	Chuck Foreman, 12-20-75	24
	Ahmad Rashad, 9-2-79	24

*NFL Record

VIKINGS COACHING HISTORY

(351-278-9)

1961-66	Norm Van Brocklin	29-51-4
1967-1983	Bud Grant	161-99-5
1984	Les Steckel	3-13-0
1985	Bud Grant	7-9-0
1986-1991	Jerry Burns	55-46-0
1992-2000	Dennis Green	96-60-0

METRODOME

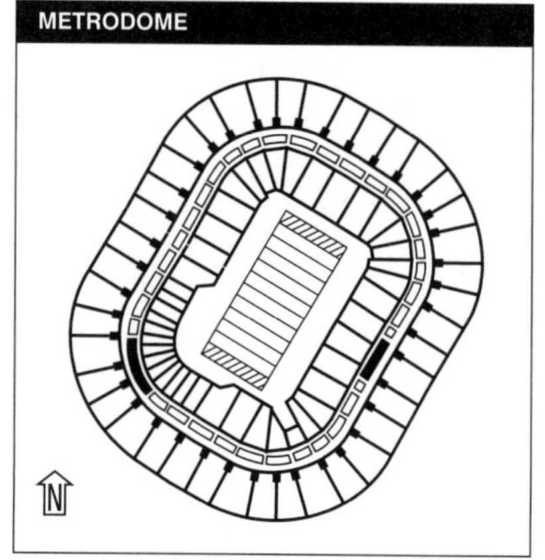

2000 TEAM RECORD

PRESEASON (1-3)

Date	Result		Opponent
8/5	L	24-25	New Orleans
8/12	L	7-31	at San Diego
8/18	W	35-17	Arizona
8/24	L	30-32	at Indianapolis

REGULAR SEASON (11-5)

Date	Result		Opponent	Att.
9/3	W	30-27	Chicago	64,104
9/10	W	13-7	Miami	64,112
9/17	W	21-13	at New England	60,292
10/1	W	31-24	at Detroit	76,438
10/9	W	30-23	Tampa Bay	64,162
10/15	W	28-16	at Chicago	66,944
10/22	W	31-27	Buffalo	64,116
10/29	L	13-41	at Tampa Bay	65,589
11/6	L	20-26	at Green Bay (OT)	59,854
11/12	W	31-14	Arizona	64,223
11/19	W	31-17	Carolina	64,208
11/23	W	27-15	at Dallas	63,878
11/30	W	24-17	Detroit	64,214
12/10	L	29-40	at St. Louis	66,273
12/17	L	28-33	Green Bay	64,183
12/24	L	10-31	at Indianapolis	56,672

(OT) Overtime

POSTSEASON (1-1)

Date	Result		Opponent	Att.
1/6	W	34-16	New Orleans	63,881
1/14	L	0-41	at New York Giants	79,310

SCORE BY PERIODS

Vikings	81	117	90	109	0	— 397
Opponents	96	98	56	115	6	— 371

ATTENDANCE

Home 505,323 Away 506,862 Total 1,012,185
Single-game home record, 64,471 (11/22/98)
Single-season home record, 510,741 (1998)

2000 TEAM STATISTICS

	Vikings	Opp.
Total First Downs	319	344
Rushing	107	110
Passing	193	208
Penalty	19	26
Third Down: Made/Att	86/188	92/202
Third Down Pct.	45.7	45.5
Fourth Down: Made/Att	8/13	4/14
Fourth Down Pct.	61.5	28.6
Total Net Yards	5,961	5,701
Avg. Per Game	372.6	356.3
Total Plays	958	1,011
Avg. Per Play	6.2	5.6
Net Yards Rushing	2,129	1,788
Avg. Per Game	133.1	111.8
Total Rushes	428	396
Net Yards Passing	3,832	3,913
Avg. Per Game	239.5	244.6
Sacked/Yards Lost	35/187	31/214
Gross Yards	4,019	4,127
Att./Completions	495/307	584/369
Completion Pct.	62.0	63.2
Had Intercepted	18	8
Punts/Average	62/44.7	65/39.9
Net Punting Avg.	62/36.2	65/33.7
Penalties/Yards	106/908	104/747
Fumbles/Ball Lost	26/10	17/10
Touchdowns	47	43
Rushing	14	17
Passing	33	23
Returns	0	3
Avg. Time of Possession	29:28	30:32

2000 INDIVIDUAL STATISTICS

Passing	Att.	Comp.	Yds.	Pct.	TD	Int.	Tkld.	Rate
Culpepper	474	297	3,937	62.7	33	16	34/181	98.0
Brister	20	10	82	50.0	0	1	1/6	40.0
Berger	1	0	0	0.0	0	1	0/0	0.0
Vikings	495	307	4,019	62.0	33	18	35/187	94.7
Opponents	584	369	4,127	63.2	23	8	31/214	91.6

SCORING	TD R	TD P	TD Rt	PAT	FG	Saf	PTS
Anderson	0	0	0	45/45	22/23	0	111
Moss	0	15	0	0/0	0/0	0	92
R. Smith	7	3	0	0/0	0/0	0	60
C. Carter	0	9	0	0/0	0/0	0	54
Culpepper	7	0	0	0/0	0/0	0	42
McWilliams	0	3	0	0/0	0/0	0	18
Hatchette	0	2	0	0/0	0/0	0	12
Davis	0	1	0	0/0	0/0	0	6
M. Williams	0	0	0	0/0	0/0	0	2
Vikings	14	33	0	45/45	22/23	0	397
Opponents	17	23	3	38/38	25/29	0	371

2-Pt. Conversions: Moss, M. Williams.
Vikings 2-2, Opponents 0-4.

RUSHING	Att.	Yds.	Avg.	LG	TD
R. Smith	295	1,521	5.2	72t	7
Culpepper	89	470	5.3	27t	7
M. Williams	23	67	2.9	10	0
Kleinsasser	12	43	3.6	7	0
Brister	5	20	4.0	12	0
Moss	3	5	1.7	9	0
Walters	1	3	3.0	3	0
Vikings	428	2,129	5.0	72t	14
Opponents	396	1,788	4.5	52	17

RECEIVING	No.	Yds.	Avg.	LG	TD
C. Carter	96	1,274	13.3	53	9
Moss	77	1,437	18.7	78t	15
R. Smith	36	348	9.7	53t	3
McWilliams	22	180	8.2	26	3
Walsh	18	191	10.6	21	0
Davis	17	202	11.9	37	1
Hatchette	16	190	11.9	39t	2
Kleinsasser	10	98	9.8	21	0
Jordan	8	63	7.9	12	0
M. Williams	4	31	7.8	12	0
Walters	1	5	5.0	5	0
Morrow	1	2	2.0	2	0
D. Palmer	1	-2	-2.0	-2	0
Vikings	307	4,019	13.1	78t	33
Opponents	369	4,127	11.2	52t	23

INTERCEPTIONS	No.	Yds.	Avg.	LG	TD
Wong	2	28	14.0	14	0
Tate	2	12	6.0	12	0
Griffith	1	25	25.0	25	0
Dishman	1	0	0.0	0	0
Thibodeaux	1	0	0.0	0	0
Thomas	1	0	0.0	0	0
Vikings	8	65	8.1	25	0
Opponents	18	181	10.1	47	1

PUNTING	No.	Yds.	Avg.	In 20	LG
Berger	62	2,773	44.7	16	60
Vikings	62	2,773	44.7	16	60
Opponents	65	2,593	39.9	22	65

PUNT RETURNS	No.	FC	Yds.	Avg.	LG	TD
Walters	15	16	217	14.5	63	0
D. Palmer	10	12	33	3.3	16	0
Walsh	1	0	11	11.0	11	0
Vikings	26	28	261	10.0	63	0
Opponents	32	10	310	9.7	35	0

KICKOFF RETURNS	No.	Yds.	Avg.	LG	TD
Walters	30	692	23.1	38	0
T. Carter	17	389	22.9	38	0
M. Williams	10	214	21.4	34	0
D. Palmer	6	120	20.0	24	0
Walsh	2	9	4.5	6	0
Morrow	1	17	17.0	17	0
Thomas	1	15	15.0	15	0
Vikings	67	1,456	21.7	38	0
Opponents	69	1,519	22.0	98t	1

FIELD GOALS	1-19	20-29	30-39	40-49	50+
Anderson	1/1	5/5	9/9	7/7	0/1
Vikings	1/1	5/5	9/9	7/7	0/1
Opponents	1/1	10/11	8/8	5/7	1/2

SACKS	No.
Randle	8.0
Sawyer	6.0
T. Williams	4.0
Burrough	2.0
Hovan	2.0
McDaniel	2.0
Paup	2.0
Wong	2.0
Griffith	1.0
Robbins	1.0
Thomas	1.0
Vikings	31.0
Opponents	35.0

2001 DRAFT CHOICES

Round	Name	Pos.	College
1	Michael Bennett	RB	Wisconsin
2	Willie Howard	DE	Stanford
3	Eric Kelly	DB	Kentucky
4	Shawn Worthen	DT	Texas Christian
	Cedric James	WR	Texas Christian
5	Patrick Chukwurah	LB	Wyoming
6	Carey Scott	DB	Kentucky State
7	Brian Crawford	T	Western Oregon

MINNESOTA VIKINGS

2001 VETERAN ROSTER

No.	Name	Pos.	Ht.	Wt.	Birthdate	NFL Exp.	College	Hometown	How Acq.	'00 Games/ Starts
1	Anderson, Gary	K	5-11	184	7/16/59	20	Syracuse	Durban, South Africa	UFA(SF)-'98	16/0
74	Badger, Brad	T	6-4	312	1/11/75	5	Stanford	Corvallis, Ore.	RFA(Wash)-'00	16/0
17	Berger, Mitch	P	6-4	228	6/24/72	6	Colorado	Vancouver, B.C., Canada	FA-'96	16/0
78	Birk, Matt	C	6-4	316	7/23/76	4	Harvard	St. Paul, Minn.	D6-'98	16/16
96	Boireau, Michael	DE	6-4	265	7/24/78	2	Miami	N. Miami Beach, Fla.	D2b-'00	0*
8	Bouman, Todd	QB	6-2	231	8/1/72	4	St. Cloud State	Ruthton, Minn.	FA-'97	0*
80	Carter, Cris	WR	6-3	208	11/25/65	15	Ohio State	Middletown, Ohio.	W(Phil)-'90	16/16
22	Carter, Tyrone	S	5-8	186	3/31/76	2	Minnesota	Pompano Beach, Fla.	D4b-'00	15/7
87	Chamberlain, Bryon	TE	6-1	242	10/17/71	6	Wayne State	Fort Worth, Texas	UFA(Den)-'01	15/0*
34	Chapman, Doug	RB	5-10	211	8/22/77	2	Marshall	Chesterfield, Va.	D3-'00	0*
11	Culpepper, Daunte	QB	6-4	266	1/28/77	3	Central Florida	Ocala, Fla.	D1a-'99	16/16
89	Davis, John	TE	6-4	271	5/14/73	5	Emporia State	Jasper, Texas	FA-'01	15/9
71	Dixon, David	G	6-5	358	1/5/69	7	Arizona State	Auckland, New Zealand	FA-'94	16/16
24	Griffith, Robert	S	5-11	199	11/30/70	8	San Diego State	Sacramento, Calif.	FA-'94	16/16
55	Hall, Lemanski	LB	6-0	241	11/24/70	7	Alabama	Flint, Mich.	UFA(Dall)-'00	15/1
99	Hovan, Chris	DT	6-2	305	5/12/78	2	Boston College	Warren, Ohio	D1-'00	16/13
67	Humphrey, Jay	T	6-6	314	6/20/76	2	Texas	Harrisburg, Pa.	D4b-'99	0*
83	Jacquet, Nate	WR	6-0	185	9/2/75	4	San Diego State	Inglewood, Calif.	FA-'01	1/0
51	Johnstone, Lance	DE	6-4	250	6/11/73	6	Temple	Crowley, La.	FA-'01	14/9*
85	Jordan, Andrew	TE	6-6	263	6/21/72	8	Western	College Station, Texas	FA-'01	16/4
61	Kelly, Lewis	T	6-4	292	4/21/77	2	South Carolina	Galveston, Texas	D7c-'00	0*
19	Kent, Joey	WR	6-1	191	4/23/74	4	Tennessee	San Diego, Calif.	FA-'01	0*
46	Kidd, Carl	CB	6-1	205	6/14/73	3	Arkansas	Escondido, Calif.	FA-'01	0*
40	Kleinsasser, Jim	FB	6-3	279	1/31/77	3	North Dakota	Columbus, Ga.	D2-'99	14/8
76	Liwienski, Chris	G	6-5	332	8/2/75	3	Indiana	Dallas, Texas	FA-'99	14/1
69	Malano, Mike	C	6-2	304	10/16/76	2	San Diego State	Spokane, Wash	D7a-'00	0*
58	McDaniel, Ed	LB	5-11	230	2/23/69	10	Clemson	Eugene, Ore.	D5-'92	15/16
33	Morrow, Harold	FB	5-11	229	2/24/73	6	Auburn	Harvey, Ill.	W(Dall)-'96	16/0
84	Moss, Randy	WR	6-4	198	2/13/77	4	Marshall	San Diego, Calif.	D1-'98	16/16
56	Nelson, Jim	LB	6-1	238	4/16/75	3	Penn State	Valley, Ala.	W(GB)-'00	16/0
90	Northern, Gabe	LB	6-3	262	6/8/74	6	Louisiana State	Rocky River, Ohio	FA-'00	9/2
57	Palmer, Mitch	LS	6-4	259	9/2/73	4	Colorado State	Richardson, Texas	FA-'01	16/0
86	Reed, Jake	WR	6-3	216	9/28/67	11	Grambling State	Duarte, Calif.	FA-'01	6/6*
98	Robbins, Fred	DT	6-4	310	3/25/77	2	Wake Forest	Germantown, Pa.	D2a-'00	8/0
59	Sauer, Craig	LB	6-1	241	12/13/72	6	Minnesota	Charlotte, N.C.	UFA(Atl)-'00	9/0
97	Sawyer, Talance	DE	6-2	268	6/14/76	3	Nevada-Las Vegas	Lithonia, Ga.	D6a-'99	16/16
29	Serwanga, Wasswa	CB	5-11	190	7/23/76	3	UCLA	Huntsville, Ala.	W(KC)-'00	7/2
92	Smith, Fernando	DE	6-6	286	8/2/71	7	Jackson State	Pine Bluff, Ark.	FA-'01	1/0
77	Stringer, Korey	T	6-4	346	5/8/74	7	Ohio State	Carrington, N.D.	D1b-'95	16/16
28	Tate, Robert	CB	5-10	192	10/19/73	5	Cincinnati	Sterling Heights, Mich.	D6-'97	16/16
42	Thomas, Orlando	S	6-1	222	10/21/72	7	Southwestern Louisiana	Scottsdale, Ariz.	D2a-'95	9/9
82	Walters, Troy	WR	5-7	174	12/15/76	2	Stanford	Batesburg, S.C.	D5-'00	12/0
21	Williams, Moe	RB	6-1	203	7/26/74	6	Kentucky	Rand, W. Va.	D3-'96	16/0
54	Wilson, Antonio	LB	6-2	247	12/29/77	2	Texas A&M-Commerce	Waldorf, Md.	D4a-'00	1/0
60	Withrow, Cory	C	6-2	288	4/5/75	2	Washington State	Baton Rouge, La.	FA-'99	12/0
52	Wong, Kailee	LB	6-2	247	5/23/76	4	Stanford	Poway, Calif.	D2-'98	16/16
20	Wright, Kenny	CB	6-1	205	9/14/77	3	Northwestern State (La.)	Covington, Ga.	D4a-'99	16/6

* Boireau was inactive for 4 games and on Injured Reserve for 12 games in '00; Bouman and Chapman were inactive for 16 games; Chamberlain played 15 games with Denver; Humphrey was on practice squad for 16 games; Johnstone played 14 games with Oakland; Kelly and Malano missed '00 season because of injury; Kent last active with Tennessee in '99; Kidd last active with Oakland in '96; Reed played 6 games with New Orleans.

Retired—Robert Smith, 8-year running back, 16 games in '00.

Players lost through free agency (4): WR Matthew Hatchette (NYJ; 14 games in '00), TE Johnny McWilliams (NE; 15), LB Dwayne Rudd (Cle; 14), DT Tony Williams (Cin; 14).

Also played with Vikings in '00—S Antonio Banks (14 games), DE Roy Barker (4), LB Pete Bercich (2), QB Bubby Brister (2), DE John Burrough (14), CB Cris Dishman (11), G Corbin Lacina (15), RB David Palmer (6), DE Bryce Paup (10), DE John Randle (16), T Todd Steussie (16), CB Keith Thibodeaux (16), WR Chris Walsh (16).

COACHING STAFF

Head Coach,
Dennis Green

Pro Career: Named the fifth head coach in Vikings history on January 10, 1992, Green is one of only seven people in the history of the league to lead his team to the playoffs in each of his first three seasons as an NFL head coach. Among active coaches, Green has guided his team longer than any other coach in the NFL and has led the Vikings to playoffs eight of his nine seasons at the helm, including four NFC Central titles. During the last three seasons, Green has led the Vikings to more wins, 36, than any team in the NFL. Green guided the 2000 team to an NFC Central Division title, posting an 11-5 record, as well as leading them to the NFC Championship Game. In 1998, Green led the Vikings to their best regular-season record (15-1) in franchise history and a trip to the NFC Championship game. Green also was named *Maxwell Club* and *Sports Illustrated* Coach of the Year (tie) following the 1998 season. In 1997, Green became the second winningest coach in franchise history. He also led Minnesota to its biggest come-from-behind playoff win, 23-22 over the Giants on December 27, 1997. In 1994, NFL Commissioner Paul Tagliabue appointed Green to the league's Competition Committee. He earned NFL Coach of the Year honors from the Washington Touchdown Club and NFC Coach of the Year honors from *United Press International* and *College and Pro Football Newsweekly*. Green's first pro coaching opportunity came as special teams coach for the 49ers in 1979. Green briefly played defensive back with the British Columbia Lions (CFL) in 1971. Career record: 96-60.

Background: A running back at Iowa from 1968-70, Green began his coaching career as a graduate assistant for Iowa in 1972. He coached running backs and receivers at Dayton in 1973, then running backs and receivers at Iowa from 1974-76. Green worked with running backs at Stanford in 1977-78. He returned to Stanford as offensive coordinator in 1980, then was head coach at Northwestern from 1981-85. Green was named Big Ten coach of the year in 1982. As head coach at Stanford from 1989-91, he led the Cardinal to the 1991 Aloha Bowl, its first bowl game since 1986.

Personal: Born February 17, 1949 in Harrisburg, Pa., Green earned his degree in recreation from Iowa. He and his wife, Marie, live in Minneapolis, with their daughter Vanessa and son Zachary. Green also has a daughter, Patti, and a son Jeremy.

ASSISTANT COACHES

Charlie Baggett, wide receivers; born January 21, 1953, Fayetteville, N.C., lives in Eden Prairie, Minn. Quarterback Michigan State 1972-75. No pro playing experience. College coach: Bowling Green 1977-1980, Minnesota 1981-82, Michigan State 1983-1992, 1995-98. Pro coach: Houston Oilers 1993-94, Green Bay Packers 1999, joined Vikings in 2000.

Brian Baker, defensive line; born June 20, 1962, Baltimore, lives in Eden Prairie, Minn. Linebacker Maryland 1980-83. No pro playing experience. College coach: Maryland 1984-85, Army 1986, Georgia Tech 1987-1995. Pro coach: San Diego Chargers 1996, Detroit Lions 1997-2000, joined Vikings in 2001.

Dean Dalton, asst. offensive line-quality control; born July 27, 1963, Platteville, Wis., lives in Eden Prairie, Minn. Defensive back Air Force Academy 1981-82, Western Illinois 1983-84. No pro playing experience. College coach: Western Illinois 1984-85, Wisconsin 1986-87, Texas Southern 1988-89, Purdue 1990. Pro coach: Joined Vikings in 1999.

Carl Hargrave, running backs; born November 8, 1954, Frankfurt, Germany, lives in Eden Prairie, Minn. Defensive back Upper Iowa 1972-75. No pro playing experience. College coach: Upper Iowa 1977-1980, Northwestern 1981-85, Pittsburgh 1986, Houston 1987-1991, Iowa 1992-93. Pro coach: Joined Vikings in 1994.

2001 FIRST-YEAR ROSTER

Name	Pos.	Ht.	Wt.	Birthdate	College	Hometown	How Acq.
Bennett, Michael	RB	5-9	210	8/13/78	Wisconsin	Milwaukee, Wis.	D1
Cercone, Matt (1)	TE	6-5	261	11/30/75	Arizona State	Bakersfield, Calif.	FA
Chukwurah, Patrick	LB	6-1	238	3/1/79	Wyoming	Irving, Texas	D5
Clark, Kenny	WR	6-1	210	5/14/78	Central Florida	Ocala, Fla.	FA
Cockerham, Billy (1)	QB	6-1	209	3/18/77	Minnesota	Clayton, Calif.	FA
Comeaux, Oscar	G-T	6-4	300	11/23/77	Northwestern State (La.)	Houston, Texas	FA
Crawford, Brian	T	6-8	315	9/27/77	Western Oregon	Lake Oswego, Ore.	D7
Engelhardt, Tim (1)	DT	6-2	279	5/12/78	New Mexico State	Alamorgordo, N.M.	FA
Garnett, Winfield (1)	DT	6-6	320	7/24/76	Ohio State	Harvey, Ill.	FA
Hazuga, Jeff	DE	6-5	270	4/29/78	Wisconsin-Stout	Thorp, Wis.	FA
Hines, Wes	G-T	6-3	313	12/14/77	McNeese State	Baytown, Texas	FA
Howard, Willie	DT	6-3	295	12/26/77	Stanford	Mountain View, Calif.	D2
James, Cedric	WR	6-1	193	3/19/79	Texas Christian	Kennedale, Texas	D4b
Kelly, Eric	CB	5-1	198	1/15/77	Kentucky	Panama, Fla.	D3
Kostrewa, Jeff	TE	6-5	255	11/21/78	Wisconsin-La Crosse	Kenosha, Wis.	FA
Matich, John	K	6-2	208	10/15/77	Boston College	San Diego, Calif.	FA
Miller, Romaro	QB	6-1	195	9/12/78	Mississippi	Shannon, Miss.	FA
Mitchell, Lonny (1)	WR	6-2	205	1/14/77	San Diego State	San Diego, Calif.	FA
Morgan, Don (1)	S	5-1	198	9/18/75	Nevada	Stockton, Calif.	FA
Morton, Brian	P	6-6	227	9/23/78	Duke	Auburndale, Fla.	FA
Paga, Shaun	LB	6-1	240	11/16/77	California	Atherton, Calif.	FA
Russell, Brian	S	6-2	205	2/5/78	San Diego State	West Covina, Calif.	FA
Scott, Carey	CB	5-1	208	8/11/78	Kentucky State	Savannah, Ga.	D6
Solwold, Mike	LS	6-6	236	9/30/77	Wisconsin	Heartland, Wis.	FA
Waddell, Bennitte	G-T	6-5	312	5/26/77	Tuskegee	Sanford, N.C.	FA
Wickman, Ryland (1)	LB	5-1	225	10/30/75	Cal State-Sacramento	San Diego, Calif.	FA
Wofford, James	RB	6-0	200	6/6/78	Nevada-Las Vegas	Bakersfield, Calif.	FA
Worthen, Shawn	DT	6-0	306	9/12/78	Texas Christian	San Antonio, Texas	D4a
Young, Antwone (1)	DE	6-2	270	1/28/77	San Diego State	Inglewood, Calif.	FA

The term NFL Rookie is defined as a player who is in his first season of professional football and has not been on the roster of another professional football team for any regular-season or postseason games. A Rookie is designated by an "R" on NFL rosters. Players who have been active in another professional football league or players who have NFL experience, including either preseason training camp or being on an Active List or Inactive List, or on Reserve/Injured or Reserve/Physically Unable to Perform for fewer than six regular-season games, are termed NFL First-Year Players. An NFL First-Year Player is designated by a "1" on NFL rosters. Thereafter, a player is credited with an additional year of experience for each season in which he accumulates six games on the Active List or Inactive List, or on Reserve/Injured or Reserve/Physically Unable to Perform.

Chuck Knox, Jr., outside linebackers; born February 19, 1965, Englewood, N.J., lives in Eden Prairie, Minn. Running back Arizona 1984-88. No pro playing experience. Pro coach: Los Angeles Rams 1993-94, Philadelphia Eagles 1995-98, Green Bay Packers 1999, joined Vikings in 2000.

Daryl Lawrence, asst. strength and conditioning; born October 20, 1965, Chicago Heights, Ill., lives in Shakopee, Minn. Attended Illinois State. No college or pro playing experience. College coach: Illinois State 1995-96, Army 1998-99. Pro coach: Minnesota Vikings 1997, rejoined Vikings in 2000.

Sherman Lewis, offensive coordinator; born June 29, 1942, Louisville, Ky., lives in Eden Prairie, Minn. Running back Michigan State 1960-63. Pro running back Toronto Argonauts (CFL) 1964-65, New York Jets 1966. College coach: Michigan State 1969-1982. Pro coach: San Francisco 49ers 1983-1991, Green Bay Packers 1992-99, joined Vikings in 2000.

Willie Shaw, asst. head coach-defensive backs; born January 11, 1944, Glenmora, La., lives in Eden Prairie, Minn. Cornerback New Mexico 1966-68. No pro playing experience. College coach: San Diego (Calif.) C.C. 1970-73, Stanford 1974-76, 1989-1991, Long Beach State 1977-78, Oregon 1979, Arizona State 1980-84. Pro coach: Detroit Lions 1985-88, Minnesota Vikings 1992-93, San Diego Chargers 1994, St. Louis Rams 1995-96, New Orleans Saints 1997, Oakland Raiders 1998-99, Kansas City Chiefs 2000, rejoined Vikings in 2001.

Richard Solomon, inside linebackers; born December 8, 1949, New Orleans, lives in Eden Prairie, Minn. Running back-defensive back Iowa 1970-73. No pro playing experience. College coach: Dubuque 1973-75, Southern Illinois 1976, Iowa 1977-78, Syracuse 1979, Illinois 1980-86. Pro coach: New York Giants 1987-1991 (scout), joined Vikings in 1992.

Emmitt Thomas, defensive coordinator; born June 3, 1943, Angleton, Texas, lives in Eden Prairie, Minn. Quarterback-receiver Bishop (Texas) College 1963-65. Pro defensive back Kansas City Chiefs 1966-1978. College coach: Central Missouri State 1979-1980. Pro coach: St. Louis Cardinals 1981-85, Washington Redskins 1986-1994, Philadelphia Eagles 1995-98, Green Bay Packers 1999, joined Vikings in 2000.

John Tice, tight ends; born June 22, 1960, Bayshore, N.Y., lives in Eden Prairie, Minn. Tight end Maryland 1978-1982. Pro tight end New Orleans Saints 1983-1992. Pro coach: Joined Vikings in 1999.

Mike Tice, asst. head coach-offensive line; born February 2, 1959, Bayshore, N.Y., lives in Eden Prairie, Minn. Quarterback Maryland 1977-1980. Pro tight end Seattle Seahawks 1981-88, 1990-91, Washington Redskins 1989, Minnesota Vikings 1992-93, 1995. Pro coach: Joined Vikings in 1996.

Trent Walters, defensive assistant; born November 20, 1943, Knoxville, Tenn., lives in Eden Prairie, Minn. Defensive back Indiana 1963-65. Pro defensive back Edmonton Eskimos (CFL) 1966-67. College coach: Indiana 1968-1971, Louisville 1972, 1986-1990, Indiana 1973-1980, Washington 1981-83, Pittsburgh 1985, Texas A&M 1991-93. Pro coach: Cincinnati Bengals 1984, joined Vikings in 1994.

Steve Wetzel, strength and conditioning; born May 11, 1963, Washington, D.C., lives in Eden Prairie, Minn. Attended Slippery Rock. No college or pro playing experience. College coach: Maryland 1985-89, George Mason 1990. Pro coach: Washington Redskins 1990-91, joined Vikings in 1992.

Alex Wood, quarterbacks; born March 14, 1955, Massillon, Ohio, lives in Eden Prarie, Minn. Running back Iowa 1974-77. No pro playing experience. College coach: Iowa 1978, Kent 1979-1980, Southern Illinois 1981, Southern 1982-84, Wyoming 1985-86, Washington State 1987-88, Miami 1989-1992, Wake Forest 1993-94, James Madison (head coach) 1995-98. Pro coach: Joined Vikings in 1999.

Gary Zauner, special teams coordinator; born November 2, 1950, Milwaukee, Wis., lives in Eden Prairie, Minn. Kicker Wisconsin-LaCrosse 1968-1972. No pro playing experience. College coach: Brigham Young 1979-1980, San Diego State 1981-86, New Mexico 1987-88, Long Beach State 1990-91. Pro coach: Joined Vikings in 1994.

NEW ORLEANS SAINTS

National Football Conference
Western Division
Team Colors: Old Gold, Black, and White
5800 Airline Drive
Metairie, Louisiana 70003
Telephone: (504) 733-0255

CLUB OFFICIALS

Owner: Tom Benson
General Manager of Football Operations: Randy Mueller
Director of Administration: Arnold D. Fielkow
Assistant General Manager of Football Operations: Charles Bailey
Director of Football Administration: Mickey Loomis
Director of Player Personnel: Rick Mueller
College Scouting Coordinator: Rick Thompson
Scouting Supervisor: Pat Mondock
Pro Scouts: Mike Baugh, Bill Quinter
Area Scouts: Cornell Gowdy, Tim Heffelfinger, Mark Sadowski, James Jefferson
Combine Scout: Andy Weidl
Player Personnel Assistant: Grant Neill
Equipment Manager: Dan Simmons
Head Athletic Trainer: Scottie B. Patton
Video Director: Joe Malota
Director of Player Development & Community Relations: Ricky Porter
Director of Media & Public Relations: Greg Bensel
Media & Public Relations Managers: Chris Pika, Justin Macione, Paul Corliss
New Media Manager: Ricky Zeller
Director of Photography: Michael C. Hebert
Football Operations Assistants: John "Chip" Beake, T.D. Cox, Barrett Wiley
Chief Financial Officer: Dennis Lauscha
Director of Sales & Marketing: Wayne Hodes
Director of Regional Sales & Marketing: Mike Feder
Manager of Ticket Sales & Services: Mike Stanfield
Director of Team Logistics & Box Office Manager: James Nagaoka
Stadium Operations Manager: Robert Sergent
Information Services Manager: Jay Romig
Facility Manager: Terry Ashburn
Stadium: Louisiana Superdome (built in 1975)
•**Capacity:** 65,900
1500 Poydras Street
New Orleans, Louisiana 70112
Playing Surface: AstroTurf
Training Camp: Nicholls State University
Thibodaux, LA 70310

2001 SCHEDULE

PRESEASON

Aug. 11	vs. Minnesota at San Antonio, Texas ...7:00
Aug. 18	**Dallas** ...7:00
Aug. 25	at Denver...7:00
Sept. 1	at Seattle...1:00

REGULAR SEASON

Sept. 9	at Buffalo...1:00
Sept. 16	**San Francisco**...12:00
Sept. 23	Open Date
Sept. 30	at New York Giants ...1:00
Oct. 7	**Minnesota** ...12:00
Oct. 14	at Carolina...1:00
Oct. 21	**Atlanta** ...12:00
Oct. 28	at St. Louis ...12:00
Nov. 4	**New York Jets**...7:30
Nov. 11	at San Francisco ...1:15
Nov. 18	**Indianapolis**...12:00
Nov. 25	at New England ...4:05
Dec. 2	**Carolina**...12:00
Dec. 9	at Atlanta ...1:00
Dec. 17	**St. Louis** (Mon.) ...8:00
Dec. 23	at Tampa Bay ...1:00
Dec. 30	**Washington**...7:30

RECORD HOLDERS

INDIVIDUAL RECORDS—CAREER

Category	Name	Performance
Rushing (Yds.)	George Rogers, 1981-84	4,267
Passing (Yds.)	Archie Manning, 1971-1982	21,734
Passing (TDs)	Archie Manning, 1971-1982	115
Receiving (No.)	Eric Martin, 1985-1993	532
Receiving (Yds.)	Eric Martin, 1985-1993	7,854
Interceptions	Dave Waymer, 1980-89	37
Punting (Avg.)	Mark Royals, 1997-98	45.7
Punt Return (Avg.)	Mel Gray, 1986-88	13.4
Kickoff Return (Avg.)	Walter Roberts, 1967	26.3
Field Goals	Morten Andersen, 1982-1994	302
Touchdowns (Tot.)	Dalton Hilliard, 1986-1993	53
Points	Morten Andersen, 1982-1994	1,318

INDIVIDUAL RECORDS—SINGLE SEASON

Category	Name	Performance
Rushing (Yds.)	George Rogers, 1981	1,674
Passing (Yds.)	Jim Everett, 1995	3,970
Passing (TDs)	Jim Everett, 1995	26
Receiving (No.)	Joe Horn, 2000	94
Receiving (Yds.)	Joe Horn, 2000	1,340
Interceptions	Dave Whitsell, 1967	10
Punting (Avg.)	Mark Royals, 1997	45.9
Punt Return (Avg.)	Mel Gray, 1987	14.7
Kickoff Return (Avg.)	Don Shy, 1969	27.9
	Mel Gray, 1986	27.9
Field Goals	Morten Andersen, 1985	31
Touchdowns (Tot.)	Dalton Hilliard, 1989	18
Points	Morten Andersen, 1987	121

INDIVIDUAL RECORDS—SINGLE GAME

Category	Name	Performance
Rushing (Yds.)	George Rogers, 9-4-83	206
Passing (Yds.)	Aaron Brooks, 12-3-00	441
Passing (TDs)	Billy Kilmer, 11-2-69	6
Receiving (No.)	Tony Galbreath, 9-10-78	14
Receiving (Yds.)	Wes Chandler, 9-2-79	205
Interceptions	Tommy Myers, 9-3-78	3
	Dave Waymer, 10-6-85	3
	Reggie Sutton, 10-18-87	3
	Gene Atkins, 12-22-91	3
Field Goals	Many times	5
	Last time by Morten Andersen, 12-11-94	
Touchdowns (Tot.)	Many times	3
	Last time by Ricky Williams, 10-22-00	
Points	Many times	18
	Last time by Ricky Williams, 10-22-00	

COACHING HISTORY

(203-312-5)

1967-70	Tom Fears*	13-34-2
1970-72	J.D. Roberts	7-25-3
1973-75	John North**	11-23-0
1975	Ernie Hefferle	1-7-0
1976-77	Hank Stram	7-21-0
1978-80	Dick Nolan***	15-29-0
1980	Dick Stanfel	1-3-0
1981-85	O.A. (Bum) Phillips****	27-42-0
1985	Wade Phillips	1-3-0
1986-96	Jim Mora#	93-78-0
1996	Rick Venturi	1-7-0
1997-99	Mike Ditka	15-33-0
2000	Jim Haslett	11-7-0

*Released after seven games in 1970
**Released after six games in 1975
***Released after 12 games in 1980
****Resigned after 12 games in 1985
#Resigned after eight games in 1996

LOUISIANA SUPERDOME

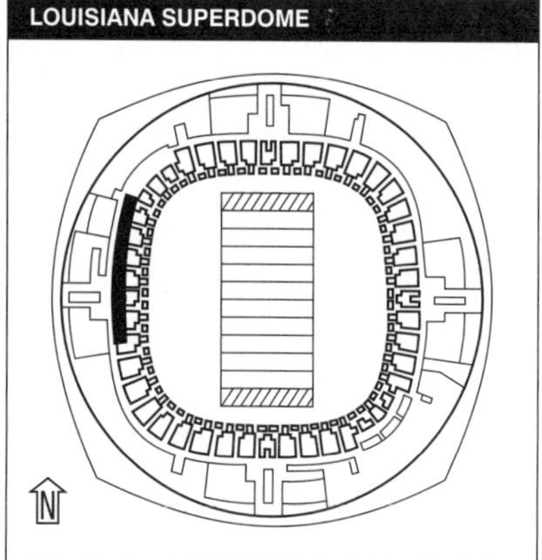

2000 TEAM RECORD

PRESEASON (1-3)

Date	Result		Opponent
7/29	L	20-24	at New York Jets
8/5	W	25-24	at Minnesota
8/12	L	0-17	vs. Indianapolis, at West Lafayette, Ind.
8/25	L	17-22	Miami

REGULAR SEASON (10-6)

Date	Result		Opponent	Att.
9/3	L	10-14	Detroit	64,900
9/10	W	28-27	at San Diego	51,300
9/17	L	10-20	at Seattle	59,513
9/24	L	7-21	Philadelphia	64,900
10/8	W	31-10	at Chicago	66,944
10/15	W	24-6	Carolina	50,015
10/22	W	21-19	at Atlanta	56,508
10/29	W	21-10	at Arizona	35,016
11/5	W	31-15	San Francisco	64,900
11/12	W	20-10	at Carolina	72,981
11/19	L	22-31	Oakland	64,900
11/26	W	31-24	at St. Louis	66,064
12/3	L	23-38	Denver	64,900
12/10	W	31-27	at San Francisco	67,892
12/17	W	23-7	Atlanta	64,900
12/24	L	21-26	St. Louis	64,900

POSTSEASON (1-1)

Date	Result		Opponent	Att.
12/30	W	31-28	St. Louis	64,900
1/6	L	16-34	at Minnesota	63,881

SCORE BY PERIODS

Saints	66	111	67	110	0	—	354
Opponents	58	111	51	85	0	—	305

ATTENDANCE

Home 502,303 Away 487,080 Total 989,383

Single-game home record, 70,940 (9/2/79)

Single-season home record, 548,728 (1992)

2000 TEAM STATISTICS

	Saints	Opp.
Total First Downs	312	279
Rushing	117	95
Passing	169	159
Penalty	26	25
Third Down: Made/Att	97/227	80/204
Third Down Pct.	42.7	39.2
Fourth Down: Made/Att	10/17	4/14
Fourth Down Pct.	58.8	28.6
Total Net Yards	5,397	4,743
Avg. Per Game	337.3	296.4
Total Plays	1,041	949
Avg. Per Play	5.2	5.0
Net Yards Rushing	2,068	1,672
Avg. Per Game	129.3	104.5
Total Rushes	505	395
Net Yards Passing	3,329	3,071
Avg. Per Game	208.1	191.9
Sacked/Yards Lost	39/244	66/378
Gross Yards	3573	3449
Att./Completions	497/298	488/285
Completion Pct.	60.0	58.4
Had Intercepted	15	20
Punts/Average	74/41.1	74/40.9
Net Punting Avg.	74/32.3	74/35.7
Penalties/Yards	124/1,024	105/837
Fumbles/Ball Lost	26/11	24/15
Touchdowns	41	36
Rushing	14	14
Passing	22	17
Returns	5	5
Avg. Time of Possession	31:27	28:33

2000 INDIVIDUAL STATISTICS

Passing	Att.	Comp.	Yds.	Pct.	TD	Int.	Tkld.	Rate
Blake	302	184	2,025	60.9	13	9	24/150	82.7
Brooks	194	113	1,514	58.2	9	6	15/94	85.7
R. Williams	1	1	34	100.0	0	0	0/0	118.8
Saints	497	298	3,573	60.0	22	15	39/244	84.2
Opponents	488	285	3,449	58.4	17	20	66/378	74.7

SCORING	TD R	TD P	TD Rt	PAT	FG	Saf	PTS
Brien	0	0	0	37/37	23/29	0	106
R. Williams	8	1	0	0/0	0/0	0	54
Horn	0	8	0	0/0	0/0	0	48
Jackson	0	6	0	0/0	0/0	0	36
A. Glover	0	4	0	0/0	0/0	0	24
Allen	2	0	0	0/0	0/0	0	14
Brooks	2	0	0	0/0	0/0	0	12
Knight	0	0	2	0/0	0/0	0	12
Mitchell	0	0	2	0/0	0/0	0	12
Blake	1	0	0	0/0	0/0	0	6
Hall	0	1	0	0/0	0/0	0	6
Milne	0	1	0	0/0	0/0	0	6
Moore	1	0	0	0/0	0/0	0	6
Poole	0	1	0	0/0	0/0	0	6
D. Smith	0	0	1	0/0	0/0	0	6
Saints	14	22	5	37/37	23/29	0	354
Opponents	14	17	5	31/31	18/24	0	305

2-Pt. Conversions: Allen.
Saints 1-4, Opponents 2-5.

RUSHING	Att.	Yds.	Avg.	LG	TD
R. Williams	248	1,000	4.0	26t	8
Blake	57	243	4.3	20	1
Allen	46	179	3.9	18	2
Brooks	41	170	4.1	29	2
Moore	37	156	4.2	40	1
Morton	36	136	3.8	16	0
T. Smith	29	131	4.5	16	0
McAfee	2	37	18.5	40	0
Horn	6	10	1.7	16	0
Gowin	1	5	5.0	5	0
Milne	2	1	0.5	1	0
Saints	505	2,068	4.1	40	14
Opponents	395	1,672	4.2	47	14

RECEIVING	No.	Yds.	Avg.	LG	TD
Horn	94	1,340	14.3	52	8
R. Williams	44	409	9.3	24	1
Jackson	37	523	14.1	53t	6
Morton	30	213	7.1	35	0
Poole	21	293	14.0	49t	1
A. Glover	21	281	13.4	39	4
Reed	16	206	12.9	22	0
T. Smith	12	65	5.4	10	0
Wilson	11	154	14.0	30	0
Hall	5	33	6.6	13	1
Milne	5	33	6.6	15	1
Turley	1	16	16.0	16	0
Allen	1	7	7.0	7	0
Saints	298	3,573	12.0	53t	22
Opponents	285	3,449	12.1	69t	17

INTERCEPTIONS	No.	Yds.	Avg.	LG	TD
Knight	5	68	13.6	37t	2
Molden	3	24	8.0	24	0
Perry	3	3	1.0	3	0
D. Smith	2	56	28.0	41t	1
Weary	2	27	13.5	27	0
Oldham	2	0	0.0	0	0
D. Howard	1	46	46.0	46	0
Mitchell	1	40	40.0	40t	1
Mathis	1	0	0.0	0	0
Saints	20	264	13.2	46	4
Opponents	15	125	8.3	35t	1

PUNTING	No.	Yds.	Avg.	In 20	LG
Gowin	74	3,043	41.1	22	58
Saints	74	3,043	41.1	22	58
Opponents	74	3,024	40.9	19	62

PUNT RETURNS	No.	FC	Yds.	Avg.	LG	TD
Morton	30	14	278	9.3	51	0
Canty	9	2	45	5.0	13	0
Mathis	1	1	5	5.0	5	0
Wilson	0	0	11	—	11	0
Saints	40	17	339	8.5	51	0
Opponents	37	17	494	13.4	95t	2

KICKOFF RETURNS	No.	Yds.	Avg.	LG	TD
Morton	44	1,029	23.4	68	0
McAfee	10	251	25.1	52	0
Mathis	8	187	23.4	40	0
Allen	0	6	—	6	0
Saints	62	1,473	23.8	68	0
Opponents	71	1,743	24.5	93t	2

FIELD GOALS	1-19	20-29	30-39	40-49	50+
Brien	1/1	6/6	4/5	12/15	0/2
Saints	1/1	6/6	4/5	12/15	0/2
Opponents	1/1	3/3	6/11	6/7	2/2

SACKS	No.
L. Glover	17.0
Johnson	12.0
D. Howard	11.0
Mitchell	6.5
Whitehead	5.5
Hand	3.0
Fields	2.0
Knight	2.0
Oldham	2.0
D. Smith	2.0
Weary	2.0
Clarke	1.0
Saints	66.0
Opponents	39.0

2001 DRAFT CHOICE

Round	Name	Pos.	College
1	Deuce McAllister	RB	Mississippi
3	Sedrick Hodge	LB	North Carolina
	Kenny Smith	DT	Alabama
4	Moran Norris	RB	Kansas
5	Onome Ojo	WR	California-Davis
6	Mitch White	T	Oregon State
7	Ennis Davis	DT	Southern California

NEW ORLEANS SAINTS

2001 VETERAN ROSTER

No.	Name	Pos.	Ht.	Wt.	Birthdate	NFL Exp.	College	Hometown	How Acq.	'00 Games/ Starts
69	Ackerman, Tom	C-G	6-3	296	9/6/72	6	Eastern Washington	Nooksack, Wash.	D5b-'96	15/0
20	Bellamy, Jay	S	5-11	200	7/8/72	8	Rutgers	Aberdeen, N.J.	UFA(Sea)-'01	16/16*
18	Blake, Jeff	QB	6-0	210	12/4/70	10	East Carolina	Sanford, Fla.	UFA(Cin)-'00	11/11
2	Brooks, Aaron	QB	6-4	205	3/24/76	3	Virginia	Newport News, Va.	T(GB)-'00	8/5
92	Chase, Martin	DT	6-2	310	12/19/74	4	Oklahoma	Lawton, Okla.	W(Balt)-'00	9/0
51	Clarke, Phil	LB	6-0	241	1/19/77	3	Pittsburgh	Miami, Fla.	FA-'99	14/4
85	Cleeland, Cameron	TE	6-4	272	8/15/75	4	Washington	Sedro Woolley, Wash.	D2-'98	0*
56	Clemons, Charlie	LB	6-2	250	7/4/72	5	Georgia	Griffin, Ga.	RFA(StL)-'00	0*
83	Connell, Albert	WR	6-0	190	5/13/74	5	Texas A&M	Fort Lauderdale, Fla.	UFA(Wash)-'01	16/13*
12	Delhomme, Jake	QB	6-2	205	1/10/75	3	Louisiana-Lafayette	Lafayette, La.	FA-'99	0*
95	Douglas, Marques	DE	6-2	270	3/5/77	2	Howard	Greensboro, N.C.	FA-'00	1/0
62	Fontenot, Jerry	C	6-3	300	11/21/66	13	Texas A&M	Lafayette, La.	UFA(Chi)-'97	16/16
97	Glover, La'Roi	DT	6-2	285	7/4/74	6	San Diego State	San Diego, Calif.	W(Oak)-'97	16/16
4	Gowin, Toby	P	5-10	167	3/30/75	5	North Texas	Jacksonville, Texas	RFA(Dall)-'00	16/0
81	Hall, Lamont	TE	6-4	260	11/16/74	3	Clemson	Clover, S.C.	T(GB)-'00	16/5
99	Hand, Norman	DT	6-3	310	9/4/72	7	Mississippi	Walterboro, S.C.	UFA(SD)-'00	15/15
32	Harris, Derrick	FB	6-0	252	9/18/72	4	Miami	Sugar Land, Texas	FA-'01	0*
36	Hawthorne, Michael	CB	6-3	200	1/26/77	2	Purdue	Sarasota, Fla.	D6b-'00	11/1
87	Horn, Joe	WR	6-1	206	1/16/72	6	Itawamba (Miss.) J.C.	New Haven, Conn.	UFA(KC)-'00	16/16
47	Houser, Kevin	FB	6-2	250	8/23/77	2	Ohio State	Westlake, Ohio	D7-'00	16/0
93	Howard, Darren	DE	6-3	281	11/19/76	2	Kansas State	St. Petersburg, Fla.	D2-'00	16/16
21	Israel, Steve	CB	5-11	197	3/16/69	10	Pittsburgh	Haddon Heights, N.J.	UFA(NE)-'00	0*
88	Jackson, Willie	WR	6-1	212	8/16/71	8	Florida	Gainesville, Fla.	UFA(Cin)-'00	15/7
94	Johnson, Joe	DE	6-4	270	7/11/72	8	Louisville	St. Louis, Mo.	D1-'94	16/15
29	Knight, Sammy	S	6-0	215	9/10/75	5	Southern California	Riverside, Calif.	FA-'97	16/16
23	Mathis, Kevin	CB	5-9	181	4/29/74	5	Texas A&M-Commerce	Gainesville, Texas	T(Dall)-'00	16/16
25	McAfee, Fred	RB	5-10	193	6/20/68	10	Mississippi College	Philadelphia, Miss.	UFA(TB)-'00	12/0
82	Mitchell, Johnny	TE	6-3	241	1/20/71	5	Nebraska	Chicago, Ill.	FA-'01	0*
59	Mitchell, Keith	LB	6-2	245	7/24/74	5	Texas A&M	Garland, Texas	FA-'97	16/16
30	Morton, Chad	RB	5-8	186	4/4/77	2	Southern California	Torrance, Calif.	D5c-'00	16/3
65	Naeole, Chris	G	6-3	313	12/25/74	5	Colorado	Kaaawa, Hawaii	D1-'97	16/16
28	Oldham, Chris	S	5-9	200	10/26/68	11	Oregon	Sacramento, Calif.	UFA(Pitt)-'00	13/1
70	Price, Marcus	T	6-6	321	3/3/72	4	Louisiana State	Port Arthur, Texas	FA-'00	7/0
76	Reyes, Tutan	T	6-3	299	10/28/77	2	Mississippi	Queens, N.Y.	D5a-'00	0*
77	Roaf, William	T	6-5	312	4/18/70	9	Louisiana Tech	Pine Bluff, Ark.	D1a-'93	16/16
54	Smith, Darrin	LB	6-1	230	4/15/70	9	Miami	Miami, Fla.	UFA(Sea)-'00	16/11
44	Smith, Terrelle	FB	6-0	246	3/12/78	2	Arizona State	Mareno Valley, Calif.	D4-'00	14/9
89	Stachelski, Dave	TE	6-3	245	3/1/77	2	Boise State	Chicago, Ill.	FA-'00	4/0
78	Terrell, Daryl	T	6-5	296	1/25/75	3	Southern Mississippi	Vossburg, Miss.	FA-'98	16/0
50	Terry, Corey	LB	6-3	243	3/6/76	3	Tennessee	Warrenton, N.C.	FA-'00	7/0
22	Thomas, Fred	CB	5-9	172	9/11/73	6	Tennessee-Martin	Bruce, Miss.	UFA(Sea)-'00	11/0
50	Tolbert, Brandon	LB	6-3	230	4/6/75	3	Georgia	Villa Rica, Ga.	FA-'01	0*
68	Turley, Kyle	T	6-5	300	9/24/75	4	San Diego State	Moreno Valley, Calif.	D1-'98	16/16
24	Weary, Fred	CB	5-10	181	4/12/74	4	Florida	Jacksonville, Fla.	D4a-'98	12/12
84	Wheatley, Austin	TE	6-3	254	11/16/77	2	Iowa	Milan, Ill.	D5b-'00	4/0
98	Whitehead, Willie	DE	6-3	285	1/26/73	3	Auburn	Tuskegee, Ala.	FA-'99	16/2
34	Williams, Ricky	RB	5-10	236	5/21/77	3	Texas	San Diego, Calif.	D1-'99	10/10
63	Williams, Wally	G-C	6-2	321	2/20/71	9	Florida A&M	Tallahassee, Fla.	UFA(Balt)-'99	16/16
80	Wilson, Robert	WR	5-11	176	6/23/74	3	Florida A&M	Monticello, Fla.	FA-'00	15/0

* Bellamy played 16 games with Seattle in '00; Cleeland, Clemons, Israel, and Tolbert missed '00 season because of injury; Connell played 16 games with Washington; Delhomme was inactive for 10 games; Harris was inactive for 1 game with San Diego; Mitchell last active with Dallas in '96; Reyes was inactive for 16 games.

Players lost through free agency (2): CB Alex Molden (SD, 15 games in '00), QB Billy Joe Tolliver (Chi; 0).

Also played with Saints in '00—RB Terry Allen (4 games), K Doug Brien (16), CB Chris Canty (3), LB Mark Fields (16), S Todd Franz (5), TE Andrew Glover (16), CB Corey Harris (3), CB Reggie Howard (1), LB Donta Jones (12), S Rob Kelly (12), FB Brian Milne (16), RB Jerald Moore (11), S Darren Perry (16), WR Keith Poole (15). WR Jake Reed (7), DE Jared Tomich (15), LB Phillip Ward (2).

COACHING STAFF

Head Coach,
Jim Haslett

Pro Career: Named the thirteenth head coach in Saints history on February 3, 2000. Enters his second season as head coach of the Saints. In 2000, led the Saints to a 10-6 record, the franchise's second NFC West title, and first-ever playoff victory. He was selected coach of the year by several media outlets, including the Associated Press and the Pro Football Writers Association as the Saints became the eighteenth team in NFL history to finish in first place in their division the season after finishing last. He joined the Saints following three seasons (1997-99) as defensive coordinator of the Pittsburgh Steelers. He first held the position of defensive coordinator with the New Orleans Saints (1996), while previously serving as the Saints' linebackers coach in 1995 after two seasons (1993-94) in the same capacity with the Los Angeles Raiders. From 1991-92, Haslett was defensive coordinator for the Sacramento Surge, who won a World League title in 1992. Haslett was a second-round draft choice of the Buffalo Bills in 1979, when he was named all-rookie and captured *Associated Press* defensive rookie of the year honors. His playing career spanned nine seasons, including his first eight with the Bills. He concluded his playing career with the New York Jets in 1987. A year later, Haslett assumed his initial coaching post, handling the linebackers at the University of Buffalo. He was promoted to defensive coordinator (1989-1990). Career record: 11-7.

Background: Haslett was a three-time All-America at defensive end at Indiana University of Pennsylvania (1975-78), graduating with a bachelor's degree in elementary education.

Personal: Born December 9, 1955 in Pittsburgh. Haslett and his wife Beth, have two daughters, Kelsey and Elizabeth, and a son, Chase.

ASSISTANT COACHES

Hubbard Alexander, wide receivers; born February 14, 1939, Winston-Salem, N.C., lives in Metairie, La. Center Tennessee State 1958-1961. No pro playing experience. College coach: Tennessee State 1962-63, Vanderbilt 1974-78, Miami 1979-1988. Pro coach: Dallas Cowboys 1989-1997, Minnesota Vikings 1998-99, joined Saints in 2000.

Dave Atkins, running backs; born May 18, 1949, Victoria, Texas, lives in Destrehan, La. Running back Texas-El Paso 1970-72. Pro running back San Francisco 49ers 1973, Honolulu Hawaiians (WFL) 1974, San Diego Chargers 1975. College coach: Texas El-Paso 1979-1980, San Diego State 1981-85. Pro coach: Philadelphia Eagles 1986-1992, New England Patriots 1993, Arizona Cardinals 1994-95, New Orleans Saints 1996, Minnesota Vikings 1997-99, rejoined Saints in 2000.

Joe Baker, secondary-special teams assistant; born June 29, 1969, Glen Ridge, N.J., lives in New Orleans. Wide receiver Princeton 1987-1990. No pro playing experience. College coach: East Stroudsburg 1991, Samford 1993, Wisconsin 1999. Pro coach: Birmingham Fire (WFL) 1992, Jacksonville Jaguars 1994-98, joined Saints in 2000.

Frank Cignetti, Jr., quarterbacks; born October 4, 1965, Pittsburgh, lives in Destrehan, La. Defensive back Indiana (Penn.) 1984-87. No pro playing experience. College coach: Pittsburgh 1989, Indiana (Penn.) 1990-98. Pro coach: Kansas City Chiefs 1999, joined Saints in 2000.

Sam Clancy, defensive line; born May 29, 1958, Pittsburgh, lives in Destrehan, La. No college playing experience. Pro defensive lineman Seattle Seahawks 1982-83, Pittsburgh Maulers (USFL) 1984-85, Cleveland Browns 1985-88, Indianapolis Colts 1989-1993. Pro coach: Barcelona Dragons (NFLE) 1995-99, joined Saints in 2000.

Al Everest, special teams; born August 22, 1950, Santa Barbara, Calif., lives in Destrehan, La. Safety Southern Methodist 1970-71. No pro playing experience. College coach: Southern Methodist 1972, North Texas State 1973-74, Cameron (Okla.) 1974-75, U.S. International 1981-87. Pro coach: Arkansas Miners (PSFL) 1991-92, Birmingham Barracudas (CFL) 1995, Arizona Cardinals 1996-99, joined Saints in 2000.

Rock Gullickson, strength and conditioning; born April 11, 1955, Moorhead, Minn., lives in Destrehan, La. Guard Moorhead (Minn.) State 1973-76. College coach: Moorhead State 1978, Mayville (N.D.) State 1979-1980, South Dakota State 1981, Montana State 1982-89, Rutgers 1990-92, Texas 1993-97, Louisville 1998-99. Pro coach: Joined Saints in 2000.

Jack Henry, offensive line; born March 14, 1946, Wilmerding, Pa., lives in Destrehan, La. Linebacker Penn State 1964-65, guard Indiana (Penn.) 1967-68. No pro playing experience. College coach: West Virginia 1970, 1978-79, Edinboro 1973, Louisville 1974, Millersville 1975-76, Southern Illinois 1977, Appalachian State 1980, Wake Forest 1981-85, Indiana (Penn.) 1986-89, Pittsburgh 1993-95. Pro coach: Pittsburgh Steelers 1990-91, San Diego Chargers 1996, Detroit Lions 1997-99, joined Saints in 2000.

Jim Hostler, offensive assistant; born November 11, 1966, Pittsburgh, lives in Destrehan, La. Defensive back Indiana (Penn.) 1986-89. No pro playing experience. College coach: Indiana (Penn.) 1990-92, 1994-99, Juniata (Penn.) 1993. Pro coach: Kansas City Chiefs 2000, joined Saints in 2001.

Evan Marcus, asst. strength and conditioning; born January 2, 1968, Cranford, N.J., lives in River Ridge, La. Tackle Ithaca College 1986-1990. No pro playing experience. College coach: Arizona State 1990-91, Rutgers 1993, Maryland 1994, Texas 1995-97, Louisville 1998-99. Pro coach: Joined Saints in 2000.

Mike McCarthy, offensive coordinator; born November 10, 1963, Pittsburgh, lives in Destrehan, La. Tight end Baker 1985-86. No pro playing experience. College coach: Fort Hays State 1987-88, Pittsburgh 1989-1992. Pro coach: Kansas City Chiefs 1993-98, Green Bay Packers 1999, joined Saints in 2000.

Winston Moss, linebackers; born December 24, 1965, Miami, lives in Kenner, La. Linebacker Miami 1983-86. Pro linebacker Tampa Bay Buccaneers 1987-1990, Los Angeles Raiders 1991-94, Seattle Seahawks 1995-97. Pro coach: Seattle Seahawks 1998, joined Saints in 2000.

Bob Palcic, tight ends; born July 2, 1948, Gownada, N.Y., lives in Destrehan, La. Linebacker Dayton 1968-1970. No pro playing experience. College coach: Dayton 1974-75, Ball State 1976-77, Wisconsin 1978-1981, Arizona 1984-85, Ohio State 1986-1991, Southern California 1992, UCLA 1993. Pro coach: Atlanta Falcons 1994-96, Detroit Lions 1997-98, Cleveland Browns 1999, joined Saints in 2000.

Rick Venturi, asst. head coach–secondary; born February 23, 1946, Taylorville, Ill., lives in Destrehan, La. Quarterback-defensive back Northwestern 1965-67. No pro playing experience. College coach: Northwestern 1968-1972, 1978-1980 (head coach), Purdue 1973-76, Illinois 1977. Pro coach: Hamilton Tiger-Cats (CFL) 1981, Indianapolis Colts 1982-1993 (interim head coach for final 11 games of 1991), Cleveland Browns 1994-95, joined Saints in 1996 (interim head coach for final eight games of 1996).

Mike Woodford, defensive assistant; born September 4, 1959, Niles, Ohio, lives in Destrehan, La. Defensive back Arizona 1978-1981. No pro playing experience. College coach: Arizona 1982, Arkansas 1983, Rhodes (Tenn.) College 1984, Middle Tennessee State 1985, 1999-2000, Akron 1986-1991, Walsh (Ohio) 1994-98. Pro coach: Joined Saints in 2001.

Ron Zook, defensive coordinator; born April 28, 1954, Ashland, Ohio, lives in Destrehan, La. Defensive back Miami (Ohio) 1972-75. No pro playing experience. College coach: Murray State 1978-1980, Cincinnati 1981-82, Kansas 1983, Tennessee 1984-86, Virginia Tech 1987, Ohio State 1988-1990, Florida 1991-95. Pro coach: Pittsburgh Steelers 1996-98, Kansas City Chiefs 1999, joined Saints in 2000.

2001 FIRST-YEAR ROSTER

Name	Pos.	Ht.	Wt.	Birthdate	College	Hometown	How Acq.
Arnaud, Robert (1)	RB	5-11	210	10/3/76	Georgia	Morrow, Ga.	FA
Atkins, Ron	S	5-11	206	6/19/79	James Madison	Sylmar, Calif.	FA
Carter, Tim	CB	6-0	183	7/15/78	Tulane	Tallahassee, Fla.	FA
Chew, Eric (1)	WR	6-1	185	10/20/75	McNeese State	Alexandria, La.	FA
Collins, Anthony	WR	6-1	208	9/3/78	Morgan State	Baton Rouge, La.	FA
Connell, Kurth	T	6-5	300	12/11/76	Washington	Seattle, Wash.	FA
Davis, Ennis	DT	6-4	308	12/2/77	Southern California	Reseda, Calif.	D7
Dorris, Derek	WR	6-2	196	12/1/78	Texas Tech	Azle, Texas	FA
Fenderson, James	FB	5-9	188	10/24/76	Hawaii	Mililani, Hawaii	FA
Fitzpatrick, Larry (1)	DE	6-4	275	8/17/76	Illinois State	Detroit, Mich.	FA
Garner, Jeff	C	6-4	307	2/8/78	Texas Christian	Decatur, Texas	FA
Gleason, Steve (1)	S	5-11	215	3/19/77	Washington State	Spokane, Wash.	FA-'00
Goodspeed, Joey (1)	FB	6-1	242	2/22/78	Notre Dame	Oswego, Ill.	FA
Guy, Daniel	WR	6-2	211	12/11/77	Jackson State	Memphis, Tenn.	FA
Hall, Jeff (1)	K	6-0	190	7/30/76	Tennessee	Winchester, Tenn.	FA
Henley, Jahi	CB	5-9	192	12/15/78	Tennessee Tech	Nashville, Tenn.	FA
Hilbert, Jon (1)	K	6-2	220	7/15/75	Louisville	Boonville, Ind.	FA
Hodge, Sedrick	LB	6-4	244	9/13/78	North Carolina	Atlanta, Ga.	D3a
Jackson, Jonathan (1)	LB	6-2	248	9/2/77	Oregon State	Las Vegas, Nev.	FA
Kelsey, Keith (1)	LB	6-2	260	7/10/76	Florida	Newberry, Fla.	FA
Lafleur, Bill (1)	P	6-0	205	2/25/76	Nebraska	Norfolk, Neb.	FA
Lewis, Michael (1)	WR	5-8	165	11/14/71	No College	New Orleans, La.	FA-'00
Lewis, Milo	CB	5-11	183	12/3/77	Alabama	Mountain View, Calif.	FA
Livingston, Frank	T	6-4	297	6/29/77	Grambling	Little Rock, Ark.	FA
McAllister, Deuce	RB	6-1	221	12/27/78	Mississippi	Lena, Miss.	D1
Miles, Jermaine (1)	DE	6-4	270	8/16/74	Georgia Tech	Brooklyn, N.Y.	FA
Nevadomsky, Jason (1)	FB	6-2	240	11/8/75	UCLA	Fullerton, Calif.	FA
Newsome, Richard	S	5-11	202	12/6/77	Michigan State	Fostoria, Ohio	FA
Norris, Moran	FB	6-1	250	6/16/78	Kansas	Houston, Texas	D4
O'Brien, Nick (1)	G	6-1	330	11/19/72	Texas A&M-Kingsville	Pine Hill, N.J.	FA
Ojo, Onome	WR	6-4	205	6/3/77	California-Davis	San Francisco, Calif.	D5
Ray, Bryan	LB	6-3	272	3/9/78	Wake Forest	Wheaton, Md.	FA
Reese, Ed	LB	6-0	242	5/1/78	Jackson State	Chunchula, Ala.	FA
Robinson, Jimmy	WR	6-1	201	10/22/76	Kentucky	Stone Mountain, Ga.	FA
Saipaia, Blane (1)	G	6-2	310	8/25/78	Colorado State	Oxnard, Calif.	FA-'00
Seals, Richard (1)	DT	6-3	305	3/18/76	Utah	Houston, Texas	FA
Setzer, Bobby (1)	DE	6-4	280	6/16/76	Boise State	Kelso, Wash.	FA-'00
Smith, Kenny	DT	6-4	295	9/877	Alabama	Meridian, Miss.	D3b
Stambaugh, Phil (1)	QB	6-3	218	8/10/78	Lehigh	Roseto, Pa.	FA
Stockton, Kris	K	5-9	200	2/25/78	Texas	Katy, Texas	FA
Traylor, Albert	G	6-2	305	6/4/78	Northwestern State	Dallas, Texas	FA
Vaughn, Gerald (1)	DB	6-2	205	4/8/70	Mississippi	Oxford, Miss.	FA
Waller, Trayvon	CB	6-0	172	5/26/79	Illinois	Los Angeles, Calif.	FA
White, Mitch	T	6-4	311	3/25/78	Oregon State	San Diego, Calif.	D6
Williams, Eddie	TE	6-4	235	6/22/79	Arkansas	Tallahassee, Fla.	FA
Williams, Richard	WR	5-11	168	4/16/77	Arizona State	Miami, Fla.	FA

The term NFL Rookie is defined as a player who is in his first season of professional football and has not been on the roster of another professional football team for any regular-season or postseason games. A Rookie is designated by an "R" on NFL rosters. Players who have been active in another professional football league or players who have NFL experience, including either preseason training camp or being on an Active List or Inactive List, or on Reserve/Injured or Reserve/Physically Unable to Perform for fewer than six regular-season games, are termed NFL First-Year Players. An NFL First-Year Player is designated by a "1" on NFL rosters. Thereafter, a player is credited with an additional year of experience for each season in which he accumulates six games on the Active List or Inactive List, or on Reserve/Injured or Reserve/Physically Unable to Perform.

NEW YORK GIANTS

National Football Conference
Eastern Division
Team Colors: Blue, Red, and White
Giants Stadium
East Rutherford, New Jersey 07073
Telephone: (201) 935-8111

CLUB OFFICIALS

President/Co-CEO: Wellington T. Mara
Chairman/Co-CEO: Preston Robert Tisch
Executive Vice President/General Counsel: John K. Mara, Esq.
Treasurer: Jonathan Tisch
Vice President-General Manager: Ernie Accorsi
Vice President-Marketing: Rusty Hawley
Vice President-Communications: Pat Hanlon
Assistant General Manager: Rick Donohue
Director of Player Personnel: Marv Sunderland
Director of Pro Personnel: David Gettleman
Assistant Director of Pro Personnel: Jerry Reese
Director of College Scouting: Jerry Shay
Director of Research and Development: Raymond J. Walsh, Jr.
Director of Player Development: Greg Gabriel
Pro Personnel Assistant: Geoff Mazza
Director of Promotion: Frank Mara
Ticket Manager: John Gorman
Director of Administration: Jim Phelan
Controller: Christine Procops
Director of Community Relations: Allison Stangeby
Director of Sales: Dan Lynch
Director of Corporate Sponsorship: Bill Smith
Director of Creative Services: Doug Murphy
Director of Public Relations: Peter John-Baptiste
Assistant Director of Communications: Avis Roper
Head Athletic Trainer: Ronnie Barnes
Assistant Athletic Trainers: John Johnson, Steve Kennelly, Byron Hansen
Equipment Manager: Ed Wagner, Jr.
Stadium: Giants Stadium (built in 1976)
•**Capacity:** 79,469
East Rutherford, New Jersey 07073
Playing Surface: Natural Grass
Training Camp: University at Albany
1400 Washington Avenue
Albany, N.Y. 12222

2001 SCHEDULE

PRESEASON

Aug. 10	at New England	8:00
Aug. 16	**Jacksonville**	8:00
Aug. 25	**New York Jets**	8:00
Aug. 31	at Baltimore	12:00

REGULAR SEASON

Sept. 10	at Denver (Mon.)	7:00
Sept. 16	**Green Bay**	1:00
Sept. 23	at Kansas City	12:00
Sept. 30	**New Orleans**	1:00
Oct. 7	**Washington**	1:00
Oct. 14	at St. Louis	12:00
Oct. 22	**Philadelphia** (Mon.)	9:00
Oct. 28	at Washington	8:30
Nov. 4	**Dallas**	1:00
Nov. 11	at Arizona	2:15
Nov. 19	at Minnesota (Mon.)	8:00
Nov. 25	**Oakland**	4:15
Dec. 2	Open Date	
Dec. 9	at Dallas	12:00
Dec. 15	**Arizona** (Sat.)	1:30
Dec. 23	**Seattle**	1:00
Dec. 30	at Philadelphia	4:05

RECORD HOLDERS

INDIVIDUAL RECORDS—CAREER

Category	Name	Performance
Rushing (Yds.)	Rodney Hampton, 1990-97	6,897
Passing (Yds.)	Phil Simms, 1979-1993	33,462
Passing (TDs)	Phil Simms, 1979-1993	199
Receiving (No.)	Joe Morrison, 1959-1972	395
Receiving (Yds.)	Frank Gifford, 1952-1960, 1962-64	5,434
Interceptions	Emlen Tunnell, 1948-1958	74
Punting (Avg.)	Don Chandler, 1956-1964	43.8
Punt Return (Avg.)	Ward Cuff, 1941-45	12.5
Kickoff Return (Avg.)	Rocky Thompson, 1971-72	27.2
Field Goals	Pete Gogolak, 1966-1974	126
Touchdowns (Tot.)	Frank Gifford, 1952-1960, 1964	78
Points	Pete Gogolak, 1966-1974	646

INDIVIDUAL RECORDS—SINGLE SEASON

Category	Name	Performance
Rushing (Yds.)	Joe Morris, 1986	1,516
Passing (Yds.)	Phil Simms, 1984	4,044
Passing (TDs)	Y.A. Tittle, 1963	36
Receiving (No.)	Amani Toomer, 1999	79
Receiving (Yds.)	Homer Jones, 1967	1,209
Interceptions	Otto Schnellbacher, 1951	11
	Jim Patton, 1958	11
Punting (Avg.)	Don Chandler, 1959	46.6
Punt Return (Avg.)	Amani Toomer, 1996	16.6
Kickoff Return (Avg.)	John Salscheider, 1949	31.6
Field Goals	Ali Haji-Sheikh, 1983	35
Touchdowns (Tot.)	Joe Morris, 1985	21
Points	Ali Haji-Sheikh, 1983	127

INDIVIDUAL RECORDS—SINGLE GAME

Category	Name	Performance
Rushing (Yds.)	Gene Roberts, 11-12-50	218
Passing (Yds.)	Phil Simms, 10-13-85	513
Passing (TDs)	Y.A. Tittle, 10-28-62	*7
Receiving (No.)	Tiki Barber, 1-2-00	13
Receiving (Yds.)	Del Shofner, 10-28-62	269
Interceptions	Many times	3
	Last time by Terry Kinard, 9-27-87	
Field Goals	Joe Danelo, 10-18-81	6
Touchdowns (Tot.)	Ron Johnson, 10-2-72	4
	Earnest Gray, 9-7-80	4
	Rodney Hampton, 9-24-95	4
Points	Ron Johnson, 10-2-72	24
	Earnest Gray, 9-7-80	24
	Rodney Hampton, 9-24-95	24

*NFL Record

COACHING HISTORY

(566-470-33)

1925	Bob Folwell	8-4-0
1926	Joe Alexander	8-4-1
1927-28	Earl Potteiger	15-8-3
1929-1930	LeRoy Andrews*	24-5-1
1930	Benny Friedman-Steve Owen	2-0-0
1931-1953	Steve Owen	153-108-17
1954-1960	Jim Lee Howell	55-29-4
1961-68	Allie Sherman	57-54-4
1969-1973	Alex Webster	29-40-1
1974-76	Bill Arnsparger**	7-28-0
1976-78	John McVay	14-23-0
1979-1982	Ray Perkins	24-35-0
1983-1990	Bill Parcells	85-52-1
1991-92	Ray Handley	14-18-0
1993-96	Dan Reeves	32-34-0
1997-2000	Jim Fassel	39-28-1

*Released after 15 games in 1930
**Released after games in 1976

GIANTS STADIUM

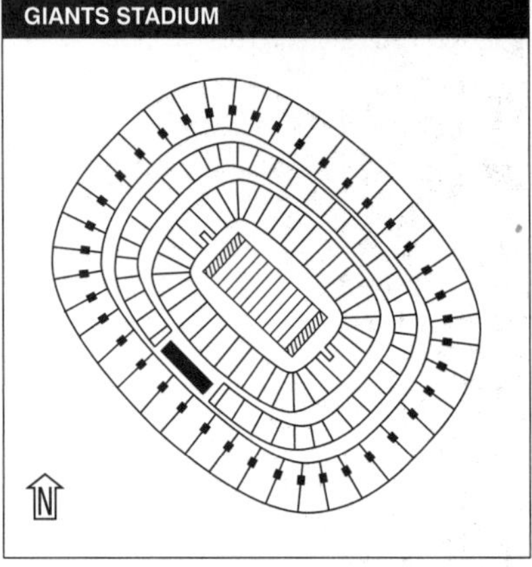

2000 TEAM RECORD

PRESEASON (2-2)

Date	Result		Opponent
8/5	L	8-20	Chicago
8/11	L	13-16	at Jacksonville
8/18	L	24-27	at New York Jets
8/25	L	17-24	Baltimore

REGULAR SEASON (12-4)

Date	Result		Opponent	Att.
9/3	W	21-16	Arizona	77,434
9/10	W	33-18	at Philadelphia	65,530
9/17	W	14-7	at Chicago	66,944
9/24	L	6-16	Washington	78,216
10/1	L	14-28	at Tennessee	68,341
10/8	W	13-6	at Atlanta	50,947
10/15	W	19-14	Dallas	78,189
10/29	W	24-7	Philadelphia	78,087
11/5	W	24-3	at Cleveland	72,718
11/12	L	24-38	St. Louis	78,174
11/19	L	21-31	Detroit	77,897
11/26	W	31-7	at Arizona	38,909
12/3	W	9-7	at Washington	83,485
12/10	W	30-10	Pittsburgh	78,164
12/17	W	17-13	at Dallas	61,311
12/23	W	28-25	Jacksonville	77,924

POSTSEASON (2-1)

Date	Result		Opponent	Att.
1/7	W	20-10	Philadelphia	78,765
1/14	W	41-0	Minnesota	79,310
1/28	L	7-34	vs. Baltimore, at Tampa	62,784

SCORE BY PERIODS

Giants	51	81	82	114	0	—	328
Opponents	31	88	62	65	0	—	246

ATTENDANCE

Home 624,085 Away 504,597 Total 1,128,682
Single-game home record, 78,216 (9/24/00)
Single-season home record, 624,085 (2000)

2000 TEAM STATISTICS

	Giants	Opp.
Total First Downs	310	274
Rushing	100	62
Passing	195	181
Penalty	15	31
Third Down: Made/Att	92/229	78/219
Third Down Pct.	40.2	35.6
Fourth Down: Made/Att	7/15	2/18
Fourth Down Pct.	46.7	11.1
Total Net Yards	5,376	4,546
Avg. Per Game	336.0	284.1
Total Plays	1,064	988
Avg. Per Play	5.1	4.6
Net Yards Rushing	2,009	1,156
Avg. Per Game	125.6	72.3
Total Rushes	507	359
Net Yards Passing	3,367	3,390
Avg. Per Game	210.4	211.9
Sacked/Yards Lost	28/243	44/279
Gross Yards	3,610	3,669
Att./Completions	529/311	585/327
Completion Pct.	58.8	55.9
Had Intercepted	13	20
Punts/Average	80/40.1	86/41.5
Net Punting Avg.	80/33.7	86/37.0
Penalties/Yards	91/839	80/728
Fumbles/Ball Lost	25/11	17/11
Touchdowns	39	30
Rushing	16	7
Passing	22	23
Returns	1	0
Avg. Time of Possession	31:39	28:21

2000 INDIVIDUAL STATISTICS

Passing	Att.	Comp.	Yds.	Pct.	TD	Int.	Tkld.	Rate
Collins	529	311	3,610	58.8	22	13	28/243	83.1
Giants	529	311	3,610	58.8	22	13	28/243	83.1
Opponents	585	327	3,669	55.9	23	20	44/279	73.7

SCORING	TD R	TD P	TD Rt	PAT	FG	Saf	PTS
Daluiso	0	0	0	34/34	17/23	0	85
Barber	8	1	0	0/0	0/0	0	54
Hilliard	0	8	0	0/0	0/0	0	48
Toomer	1	7	0	0/0	0/0	0	48
Dayne	5	0	0	0/0	0/0	0	30
Campbell	0	3	0	0/0	0/0	0	18
Holmes	0	0	0	3/3	2/2	0	9
Collins	1	0	0	0/0	0/0	0	6
Dixon	0	1	0	0/0	0/0	0	6
Jurevicius	0	1	0	0/0	0/0	0	6
Mitchell	0	1	0	0/0	0/0	0	6
Montgomery	1	0	0	0/0	0/0	0	6
Sehorn	0	0	1	0/0	0/0	0	6
Giants	16	22	1	37/37	19/25	0	328
Opponents	7	23	0	25/27	13/24	0	246

2-Pt. Conversions: None.
Giants 0-2, Opponents 1-3.

RUSHING	Att.	Yds.	Avg.	LG	TD
Barber	213	1,006	4.7	78t	8
Dayne	228	770	3.4	50	5
Toomer	5	91	18.2	28	1
Collins	41	65	1.6	15	1
Comella	10	45	4.5	16	0
Hilliard	3	19	6.3	17	0
Dixon	2	13	6.5	12	0
Montgomery	1	4	4.0	4t	1
Garrett	4	-4	-1.0	-1	0
Giants	507	2,009	4.0	78t	16
Opponents	359	1,156	3.2	44t	7

RECEIVING	No.	Yds.	Avg.	LG	TD
Toomer	78	1,094	14.0	54t	7
Barber	70	719	10.3	36	1
Hilliard	55	787	14.3	59	8
Comella	36	274	7.6	25	0
Mitchell	25	245	9.8	22	1
Jurevicius	24	272	11.3	43	1
Campbell	8	46	5.8	13	3
Dixon	6	92	15.3	34t	1
Cross	4	30	7.5	18	0
Dayne	3	11	3.7	12	0
Davis	2	40	20.0	27	0
Giants	311	3,610	11.6	59	22
Opponents	327	3,669	11.2	53	23

INTERCEPTIONS	No.	Yds.	Avg.	LG	TD
McDaniel	6	30	5.0	17	0
S. Williams	3	52	17.3	40	0
Stephens	3	4	1.3	4	0
Sehorn	2	32	16.0	32	0
Phillips	2	22	11.0	12	0
Barrow	1	7	7.0	7	0
Garnes	1	4	4.0	4	0
Thomas	1	0	0.0	0	0
Armstead	1	-2	-2.0	-2	0
Giants	20	149	7.5	40	0
Opponents	13	172	13.2	41	0

PUNTING	No.	Yds.	Avg.	In 20	LG
Maynard	79	3,210	40.6	26	64
Giants	80	3,210	40.1	26	64
Opponents	86	3,570	41.5	28	63

PUNT RETURNS	No.	FC	Yds.	Avg.	LG	TD
Barber	39	20	332	8.5	31	0
Comella	1	0	0	0.0	0	0
Giants	40	20	332	8.3	31	0
Opponents	28	17	353	12.6	50	0

KICKOFF RETURNS	No.	Yds.	Avg.	LG	TD
Dixon	31	658	21.2	44	0
Levingston	7	153	21.9	43	0
Stoutmire	6	140	23.3	47	0
Stephens	3	69	23.0	40	0
Comella	2	20	10.0	11	0
Sehorn	2	31	15.5	38t	1
Barber	1	28	28.0	28	0
Jurevicius	1	3	3.0	3	0
Giants	53	1,102	20.8	47	1
Opponents	67	1,509	22.5	90	0

FIELD GOALS	1-19	20-29	30-39	40-49	50+
Daluiso	0/0	8/8	5/8	4/7	0/0
Holmes	0/0	1/1	1/1	0/0	0/0
Giants	0/0	9/9	6/9	4/7	0/0
Opponents	2/2	3/3	4/7	3/11	1/1

SACKS	No.
Hamilton	10.0
Strahan	9.5
Armstead	5.0
Griffin	5.0
Barrow	3.5
C. Jones	3.5
Monty	2.0
Phillips	1.5
Garnes	1.0
McDaniel	1.0
Peter	1.0
Giants	44.0
Opponents	28.0

2001 DRAFT CHOICES

Round	Name	Pos.	College
1	Will Allen	DB	Syracuse
3	William Peterson	DB	Western Illinois
4	Cedric Scott	DE	Southern Mississippi
	Jesse Palmer	QB	Florida
5	John Markham	K	Vanderbilt
	Jonathan Carter	WR	Troy State
7	Ross Kolodziej	DT	Wisconsin

NEW YORK GIANTS

2001 VETERAN ROSTER

No.	Name	Pos.	Ht.	Wt.	Birthdate	NFL Exp.	College	Hometown	How Acq.	'00 Games/ Starts
98	Armstead, Jessie	LB	6-1	240	10/26/70	9	Miami	Dallas, Texas	D8-'93	16/16
21	Barber, Tiki	RB	5-10	200	4/7/75	5	Virginia	Roanoke, Va.	D2-'97	16/12
58	Barrow, Mike	LB	6-2	240	4/19/70	9	Miami	Homestead, Fla.	FA-'00	15/15
44	Bennett, Sean	RB	6-1	230	11/9/75	2	Northwestern	Evansville, Ind.	D4-'99	0*
67	Bober, Chris	T	6-5	305	12/24/76	2	Nebraska-Omaha	Omaha, Neb.	FA-'00	0*
76	Brown, Lomas	T	6-4	280	3/30/63	17	Florida	Miami, Fla.	UFA(Cle)-'00	16/16
22	Brown, Ralph	CB	5-10	185	9/9/78	2	Nebraska	Hacienda Heights, Calif.	D5-'00	2/0
89	Campbell, Dan	TE	6-5	260	4/13/76	3	Texas A&M	Glen Rose, Texas	D3-'99	16/5
5	Collins, Kerry	QB	6-5	245	12/30/72	7	Penn State	Lebanon, Pa.	UFA(NO)-'99	16/16
34	Comella, Greg	FB	6-1	248	7/29/75	4	Stanford	Wellesley, Mass.	FA-'98	16/12
87	Cross, Howard	TE	6-5	270	8/8/67	13	Alabama	Huntsville, Ala.	D6-'89	16/11
82	Davis, Thabiti	WR	6-2	205	3/24/75	2	Wake Forest	Charlotte, N.C.	FA-'00	13/0
27	Dayne, Ron	RB	5-10	253	3/14/78	2	Wisconsin	Berlin, N.J.	D1-'00	16/4
86	Dixon, Ron	WR	6-0	190	5/28/76	2	Lambuth	Wildwood, Fla.	D3-'00	12/0
20	Garnes, Sam	S	6-3	225	7/12/74	5	Cincinnati	Bronx, N.Y.	D5-'97	15/15
17	Garrett, Jason	QB	6-2	200	3/28/66	9	Princeton	Chagrin, Ohio	UFA(Dall)-'00	2/0
90	Golden, Jack	LB	6-1	240	1/28/77	2	Oklahoma State	Harvey, Ill.	FA-'00	16/0
97	Griffin, Cornelius	DT	6-3	300	12/3/76	2	Alabama	Brundidge, Ala.	D2-'00	15/0
93	Hale, Ryan	DT	6-4	300	7/10/75	3	Arkansas	Rodgers, Ark.	D7a-'99	16/0
75	Hamilton, Keith	DT	6-6	295	5/25/71	10	Pittsburgh	Lynchburg, Va.	D4-'92	16/16
88	Hilliard, Ike	WR	5-11	195	4/5/76	5	Florida	Patterson, La.	D1-'97	14/14
2	Holmes, Jaret	K	6-0	203	3/3/76	3	Auburn	Clinton, Miss.	FA-'00	3/0
90	Holmes, Kenny	DE	6-4	270	10/24/73	7	Miami	Vero Beach, Fla.	UFA(Tenn)-'01	14/13*
55	Jones, Dhani	LB	6-1	240	2/22/78	2	Michigan	Patomac, Md.	D6-'00	0*
84	Jurevicius, Joe	WR	6-5	230	12/23/74	4	Penn State	Chardon, Ohio	D2-'98	15/3
59	Lewis, Kevin	LB	6-1	230	10/6/78	2	Duke	Orlando, Fla.	FA-'00	7/0
26	McDaniel, Emmanuel	CB	5-9	180	7/27/72	6	East Carolina	Griffin, Ga.	FA-'99	16/3
33	Montgomery, Joe	RB	5-10	230	6/8/76	3	Ohio State	Robbins, Ill.	D2-'99	3/0
62	Parker, Glenn	G	6-5	312	4/22/66	12	Arizona	Huntington Beach, Calif.	FA-'00	13/13
77	Petitgout, Luke	T	6-6	310	6/16/76	3	Notre Dame	Georgetown, Del.	D1-'99	16/16
78	Rosenthal, Mike	G	6-7	315	6/10/77	3	Notre Dame	Granger, Ind.	D5-'99	8/2
31	Sehorn, Jason	CB	6-2	215	4/15/71	8	Southern California	Mt. Shasta, Calif.	D2-'94	14/14
53	Short, Brandon	LB	6-3	255	7/11/77	2	Penn State	McKeesport, Pa.	D4-'00	11/0
65	Stone, Ron	G	6-5	320	7/20/71	9	Boston College	Roxbury, Mass.	RFA(Dall)-'96	15/15
23	Stoutmire, Omar	S	5-11	198	7/9/74	5	Fresno State	Long Beach, Calif.	FA-'00	15/0
92	Strahan, Michael	DE	6-5	275	11/21/71	9	Texas Southern	Westbury, Texas	D2-'93	16/16
41	Thomas, Dave	CB	6-3	218	8/25/68	9	Tennessee	Miami, Fla.	FA-'00	16/16
81	Toomer, Amani	WR	6-3	208	9/8/74	6	Michigan	Berkeley, Calif.	D2-'96	16/15
29	Washington, Damon	RB	5-11	193	2/20/77	2	Colorado State	San Diego, Calif.	FA-'00	3/0
66	Whittle, Jason	G	6-4	305	3/7/75	3	Southwest Missouri State	Springfield, Mo.	FA-'98	16/2
36	Williams, Shaun	S	6-2	215	10/10/76	4	UCLA	Encino, Calif.	D1-'98	16/16
52	Zeigler, Dusty	C	6-5	305	9/27/73	6	Notre Dame	Rincon, Ga.	UFA(Buff)-'00	16/16
74	Ziemann, Chris	T	6-7	315	9/20/76	2	Michigan	Aurora, Ill.	FA-'00	8/0

* Bennett and Jones missed '00 season because of injury; Bober was active for 3 games, but did not play in '00; Cherry was inactive for 16 games; Holmes played 14 games with Tennessee.

Players lost to free agency (5): DE Cedric Jones (StL; 16 games in '00), P Brad Maynard (Chi; 16), TE Pete Mitchell (Det; 14), DT Christian Peter (Ind; 16), LB Ryan Phillips (Oak; 16).

Also played with Giants in '00—K Brad Daluiso (14 games), C Derek Engler (8), CB Bashir Levingston (2), CB Ramos McDonald (3), LB Pete Monty (16), DE Jeremiah Parker (4), CB Reggie Stephens (15), FB Craig Walendy (12), S Lyle West (16), DT George Williams (13).

COACHING STAFF

Head Coach,
Jim Fassel

Pro Career: Was named the fifteenth head coach in Giants history on January 15, 1997. Enters his fifth season as head coach of the Giants. Last season, the Giants won their last five regular-season games en route to the best record in the NFC and the franchise's first Super Bowl appearance in 10 seasons. In 1998, the Giants finished 8-8 by winning five of their last six games. In 1997, Fassel led his squad to a 10-5-1 record and a berth in the playoffs while capturing the NFC East title. He was named coach of the year by 11 media outlets as the Giants became the fifteenth team in NFL history to finish in first place in their division the season after finishing last. Fassel entered the NFL with the Giants in 1991 as quarterbacks coach, then as offensive coordinator in 1992. Fassel spent two campaigns as assistant head coach/offensive coordinator for the Denver Broncos (1993 and 1994), the 1995 season as quarterbacks coach for the Oakland Raiders, and was the offensive coordinator and quarterbacks coach for the Arizona Cardinals in 1996. Fassel has been credited with an ability to develop quarterbacks, including John Elway, Kent Graham, and Boomer Esiason. Career record: 39-28-1.

Background: Fassel began coaching in 1973 at his alma mater, Fullerton College, then was a player-coach for the Hawaii Hawaiians of the World Football League in 1974. He coached at Utah (1976), Weber State (1977-78), and Stanford (1979-1983). At Stanford, Fassel was credited with recruiting and coaching John Elway. Fassel entered the pro arena in 1984 as offensive coordinator for the New Orleans Breakers of the USFL, then returned to Utah as head coach (1985-89).

Personal: A native of Anaheim, California, Fassel led Fullerton College to the junior college national championship in 1967. He also played collegiately at Southern California with Seattle Seahawks head coach Mike Holmgren and at Long Beach State. He was drafted by the Chicago Bears in the seventh round of the 1972 NFL draft and played briefly with Chicago, the Houston Oilers, and San Diego Chargers. Born August 31, 1949 in Anaheim, Calif. Fassel and his wife, Kitty, have four children—John, Brian, Jana, and Mike.

ASSISTANT COACHES

Dave Brazil, defensive quality control; born March 25, 1936, Detroit, lives in East Rutherford, N.J. No college or pro playing experience. College coach: Holy Cross 1968, Tulsa 1969-1970, Eastern Michigan 1971-73, Boston College 1980, Kent State 1981-82. Pro coach: Detroit Wheels (WFL) 1974, Chicago Wind (WFL) 1975, Kansas City Chiefs 1984-88, Pittsburgh Steelers 1989-1991, joined Giants in 1992.

John Dunn, strength and conditioning; born July 22, 1956, Hillsdale, N.Y., lives in Wayne, N.J. Guard Penn State 1974-77. No pro playing experience. College coach: Penn State 1978. Pro coach: Washington Redskins 1984-86, Los Angeles Raiders 1987-89, San Diego Chargers 1990-96, joined Giants in 1997.

John Fox, defensive coordinator; born February 8, 1955, Virginia Beach, Va., lives in Wayne, N.J. Defensive back San Diego State 1975-77. No pro playing experience. College coach: U.S. International 1979, Boise State 1980, Long Beach State 1981, Utah 1982, Kansas 1983, 1985, Iowa State 1984, Pittsburgh 1986-88. Pro coach: Los Angeles Express (USFL) 1985, Pittsburgh Steelers 1989-1991, San Diego Chargers 1992-93, Los Angeles/Oakland Raiders 1994-95, St. Louis Rams 1996, joined Giants in 1997.

Johnnie Lynn, defensive backs; born December 19, 1956, Los Angeles, lives in Wayne, N.J. Defensive back UCLA 1975-78. Pro defensive back New York Jets 1979-1986. College coach: Arizona 1988-1993. Pro coach: Tampa Bay Buccaneers 1994-95, San Francisco 49ers 1996, joined Giants in 1997.

Denny Marcin, defensive line; born April 24, 1942, Cleveland, lives in Wayne, N.J. Defensive and offensive line Miami (Ohio) 1961-64. No pro playing experience. College coach: Miami (Ohio) 1974-77, North Carolina 1978-1987, Illinois 1988-1996. Pro coach: Joined Giants in 1997.

Jim McNally, offensive line; born December 13, 1943, Buffalo, lives in Cedar Grove, N.J. Guard Buffalo 1961-65. No pro playing experience. College coach: Buffalo 1965-1970, Marshall 1971-74, Boston College 1975-77, Wake Forest 1978-79. Pro coach: Cincinnati Bengals 1980-1994, Carolina Panthers 1995-98, joined Giants in 1999.

Tom Olivadotti, linebackers; born September 22, 1945, Long Beach, N.J., lives in Glen Rock, N.J. Defensive back-wide receiver Upsala 1963-66. No pro playing experience. College coach: Princeton 1975-77, Boston College 1978-79, Miami 1980-83. Pro coach: Miami Federals (USFL) 1984, Cleveland Browns 1985-86, Miami Dolphins 1987-1995, Minnesota Vikings 1996-99, joined Giants in 2000.

Sean Payton, offensive coordinator-quarterbacks; born December 29, 1963, San Mateo, Calif., lives in Wayne, N.J. Quarterback Eastern Illinois 1982-86. Pro quarterback Ottawa Rough Riders (CFL) 1987, Chicago Bears 1987. College coach: San Diego State 1988-89, 1992-93, Indiana State 1990-91, Miami (Ohio) 1994-95, Illinois 1996. Pro coach: Philadelphia Eagles 1997-98, joined Giants in 1999.

Mike Pope, tight ends; born March 15, 1942, Monroe, N.C., lives in Somerset, N.J. Quarterback Lenoir-Rhyne 1962-64. No pro playing experience. College coach: Florida State 1970-74, Texas Tech 1975-77, Mississippi 1978-1982. Pro coach: New York Giants 1983-1991, Cincinnati Bengals 1992-93, New England Patriots 1994-96, Washington Redskins 1997-99, joined Giants in 2000.

Jay Robertson, offensive assistant; born February 20, 1940, Chicago, lives in Wayne, N.J. Center Northwestern 1960-62. No pro playing experience. College coach: Northwestern 1967-1975, Northern Illinois 1976-79, Wisconsin 1980-1981, Notre Dame 1982-1983, West Point 1984-1991. Pro coach: Indianapolis Colts 1992-1993, 1997, joined Giants in 2000.

Jimmy Robinson, wide receivers; born January 3, 1953, Atlanta, lives in Wayne, N.J. Wide receiver Georgia Tech 1972-74. Pro wide receiver Atlanta Falcons 1975, New York Giants 1976-79, San Francisco 49ers 1980, Denver Broncos 1981. College coach: Georgia Tech 1986-89. Pro coach: Memphis Showboats (USFL) 1984-85, Atlanta Falcons 1990-93, Indianapolis Colts 1994-97, joined Giants in 1998.

Craig Stoddard, asst. strength and conditioning; born February 8, 1972, North Tarrytown, N.Y., lives in Hackensack, N.J. Linebacker Springfield College 1990-93. No pro playing experience. College coach: Penn State 1995-96. Pro coach: San Diego Chargers 1994, joined Giants in 1997.

Eric Studesville, running backs; born May 29, 1969, Madison, Wis., lives in Clifton, N.J. Defensive back Wisconsin-Whitewater 1985-88. No pro playing experience. College coach: Wingate 1994, Kent State 1995-96. Pro coach: Chicago Bears 1997-2000, joined Giants in 2001.

Fred von Appen, special teams; born March 22, 1942, Eugene, Ore., lives in Ramsey, N.J. Linebacker guard Linfield College 1961-63. No pro playing experience. College coach: Linfield 1964-1965, Arkansas 1969, UCLA 1970, Virginia Tech 1971, Oregon 1972-76, Stanford 1977-78, Arkansas 1981, Stanford 1982, 1989, 1992, Pittsburgh 1990-1991, Colorado 1995, Hawaii 1996-98 (head coach). Pro coach: Green Bay Packers 1979-1980, San Francisco 49ers 1983-88, Minnesota Vikings 2000, joined Giants in 2001.

2001 FIRST-YEAR ROSTER

Name	Pos.	Ht.	Wt.	Birthdate	College	Hometown	How Acq.
Allen, Will	CB	5-10	192	8/5/78	Syracuse	Syracuse, N.Y.	D1
Carter, Jonathan	WR	5-11	173	3/20/79	Troy State	Lineville, Ala.	D5b
Coleman, Quincy	CB	5-10	182	2/27/77	Jackson State	Birmingham, Ala.	FA
Goff, Jim (1)	T	6-4	300	12/7/77	Lafayette	Hawthorne, N.J.	FA
Green, Anthony	FB	6-2	245	8/13/77	West Virginia	Jersey City, N.J.	FA
Herndon, Kelly	CB	5-10	180	11/3/76	Toledo	Twinsburg, Ohio	FA
Jones, Delvin	S	6-0	196	2/28/79	Minnesota	Miami, Fla.	FA
Kacmarynski, Mark (1)	FB	6-0	229	2/2/74	Central College (Iowa)	Whitesboro, N.J.	FA
Kiernan, Scott (1)	G	6-3	305	8/16/74	Syracuse	Cos Cob, Conn.	FA-'00
Kolodziej, Ross	DT	6-2	287	5/11/78	Wisconsin	Stevens Point, Wis.	D7
Lagree, Lance	DT	6-1	285	12/22/77	Notre Dame	St. Stephens, S.C.	FA
Layow, Matt	DE	6-4	244	3/22/77	Kentucky	Miami, Fla.	FA
Markham, John	K	6-0	212	2/27/79	Vanderbilt	Brentwood, Tenn.	D5a
McDonnell, Brady	TE	6-4	265	7/24/77	Colorado	Quinn, S.D.	FA
Palmer, Jesse	QB	6-2	219	10/5/78	Florida	Toronto, Ontario, Canada	D4b
Patmon Dwayne	S	6-0	190	4/25/79	Michigan	San Diego, Calif.	FA
Peterson, Will	CB	6-0	197	6/15/79	Western Illinois	Uniontown, Pa.	D3
Phillips, Jerry	LB	6-0	232	8/27/78	Tulane	New Orleans, La.	FA
Redziniak, Ray	C-G	6-2	297	12/17/78	Illinois	Clark, N.J.	FA
Rivers, Marcellus	TE	6-4	231	10/26/78	Oklahoma State	Oklahoma City, Okla.	FA
Rollins, Kevin	LB	6-0	231	2/1/78	Toledo	Twinsburg, Ohio	FA
Scott, Cedric	DE	6-5	274	10/19/77	Southern Mississippi	Gulfport, Miss.	D4a
Seubert, Rich	T	6-5	295	3/30/79	Western Illinois	Twinsburg, Ohio	FA
Simonton, Matt (1)	K	5-9	176	11/11/76	Southern Illinois	Ridge, N.Y.	FA
Spotwood, Quinton (1)	WR	5-11	190	12/13/77	Syracuse	Elizabeth, N.J.	FA-'00
Stamer, Josh	LB	6-2	220	10/11/77	South Dakota	Sutherland, Iowa	FA
Sykes, Terrance	T	6-6	270	2/24/79	Louisiana Tech	Grenada, Miss.	FA
Umholtz, Tony (1)	P	6-0	195	12/13/76	South Florida	Largo, Fla.	FA
Warner, Josh	G	6-6	305	5/15/79	Brockport State	Cato, N.Y.	FA
White, Clayton	LB	5-11	225	12/2/77	North Carolina State	Dunn, N.C.	FA
White, Emile	S	6-0	219	10/24/78	Houston	Houston, Texas	FA
Woodcock, Pat	WR	5-9	166	4/27/77	Syracuse	Kanata, Ontario, Canada	FA
Wright, Adam	FB	6-1	230	12/18/77	Nebraska-Omaha	Omaha, Neb.	FA
Young, Adam (1)	TE	6-4	265	4/15/77	Dartmouth	Concord, N.H.	FA-'00

The term NFL Rookie is defined as a player who is in his first season of professional football and has not been on the roster of another professional football team for any regular-season or postseason games. A Rookie is designated by an "R" on NFL rosters. Players who have been active in another professional football league or players who have NFL experience, including either preseason training camp or being on an Active List or Inactive List, or on Reserve/Injured or Reserve/Physically Unable to Perform for fewer than six regular-season games, are termed NFL First-Year Players. An NFL First-Year Player is designated by a "1" on NFL rosters. Thereafter, a player is credited with an additional year of experience for each season in which he accumulates six games on the Active List or Inactive List, or on Reserve/Injured or Reserve/Physically Unable to Perform.

PHILADELPHIA EAGLES

National Football Conference
Eastern Division
Team Colors: Midnight Green, Silver, Black, and White
NovaCare Complex
One NovaCare Way
Philadelphia, Pennsylvania 19145
Telephone: (215) 463-2500

CLUB OFFICIALS

President/Chief Executive Officer: Jeffrey Lurie
Executive Vice President/Chief Operating Officer: Joe Banner
Head Coach/Executive Vice President of Football Operations: Andy Reid
Director of Player Personnel: Tom Heckert
Senior Vice President/Business Operations: Len Komoroski
Senior Vice President/Chief Financial Officer: Don Smolenski
Vice President, Corporate Sales: Dave Rowan
Vice President, Sales: Jason Gonella
Executive Director of Eagles Youth Partnership: Sarah Helfman
Director of Pro Scouting: Scott Cohen
Director of College Scouting: Marc Ross
Coordinator of Football Media Relations: Derek Boyko
Media Relations Assistants: Rich Burg, Bob Lange
Director, Broadcasting/Exec. Producer Eagles Television Network: Rob Alberino
Ticket Manager: Leo Carlin
Director of Merchandise: Steve Strawbridge
Travel Coordinator: Tracey Bucher
Director of Security: Anthony (Butch) Buchanico
Head Athletic Trainer: Rick Burkholder
Asst. Athletic Trainers: Eric Sugarman, Chris Peduzzi
Video Director: Mike Dougherty
Head Equipment Manager: John Hatfield
Stadium: Veterans Stadium (built in 1971)
•**Capacity:** 65,352
3501 South Broad Street
Philadelphia, Pennsylvania 19148
Playing Surface: NexTurf
Training Camp: Lehigh University
Bethlehem, Pennsylvania 18015

2001 SCHEDULE

PRESEASON

Aug. 13	**Baltimore**	7:30
Aug. 18	at Buffalo	7:30
Aug. 23	at Tennessee	7:00
Aug. 30	**New York Jets**	7:30

REGULAR SEASON

Sept. 9	**St. Louis**	4:15
Sept. 16	at Tampa Bay	1:00
Sept. 23	at Seattle	1:15
Sept. 30	**Dallas**	8:30
Oct. 7	**Arizona**	1:00
Oct. 14	Open Date	
Oct. 22	at New York Giants (Mon.)	9:00
Oct. 28	**Oakland**	4:15
Nov. 4	at Arizona	2:05
Nov. 11	**Minnesota**	4:15
Nov. 18	at Dallas	12:00
Nov. 25	**Washington**	1:00
Nov. 29	at Kansas City (Thurs.)	7:30
Dec. 9	**San Diego**	1:00
Dec. 16	at Washington	1:00
Dec. 22	at San Francisco (Sat.)	2:00
Dec. 30	**New York Giants**	4:05

RECORD HOLDERS

INDIVIDUAL RECORDS—CAREER

Category	Name	Performance
Rushing (Yds.)	Wilbert Montgomery, 1977-1984	6,538
Passing (Yds.)	Ron Jaworski, 1977-1986	26,963
Passing (TDs)	Ron Jaworski, 1977-1986	175
Receiving (No.)	Harold Carmichael, 1971-1983	589
Receiving (Yds.)	Harold Carmichael, 1971-1983	8,978
Interceptions	Bill Bradley, 1969-1976	34
	Eric Allen, 1988-1994	34
Punting (Avg.)	Joe Muha, 1946-1950	42.9
Punt Return (Avg.)	Steve Van Buren, 1944-1951	13.9
Kickoff Return (Avg.)	Steve Van Buren, 1944-1951	26.7
Field Goals	Paul McFadden, 1984-87	91
Touchdowns (Tot.)	Harold Carmichael, 1971-1983	79
Points	Bobby Walston, 1951-1962	881

INDIVIDUAL RECORDS—SINGLE SEASON

Category	Name	Performance
Rushing (Yds.)	Wilbert Montgomery, 1979	1,512
Passing (Yds.)	Randall Cunningham, 1988	3,808
Passing (TDs)	Sonny Jurgensen, 1961	32
Receiving (No.)	Irving Fryar, 1996	88
Receiving (Yds.)	Mike Quick, 1983	1,409
Interceptions	Bill Bradley, 1971	11
Punting (Avg.)	Joe Muha, 1948	47.2
Punt Return (Avg.)	Steve Van Buren, 1944	15.3
Kickoff Return (Avg.)	Al Nelson, 1972	29.1
Field Goals	Paul McFadden, 1984	30
Touchdowns (Tot.)	Steve Van Buren, 1945	18
Points	David Akers, 2000	121

INDIVIDUAL RECORDS—SINGLE GAME

Category	Name	Performance
Rushing (Yds.)	Steve Van Buren, 11-27-49	205
Passing (Yds.)	Randall Cunningham, 9-17-89	447
Passing (TDs)	Adrian Burk, 10-17-54	*7
Receiving (No.)	Don Looney, 12-1-40	14
Receiving (Yds.)	Tommy McDonald, 12-10-60	237
Interceptions	Russ Craft, 9-24-50	*4
Field Goals	Tom Dempsey, 11-12-72	6
Touchdowns (Tot.)	Many times	4
	Last time by Irving Fryar, 10-20-96	
Points	Bobby Walston, 10-17-54	25

*NFL Record

VETERANS STADIUM

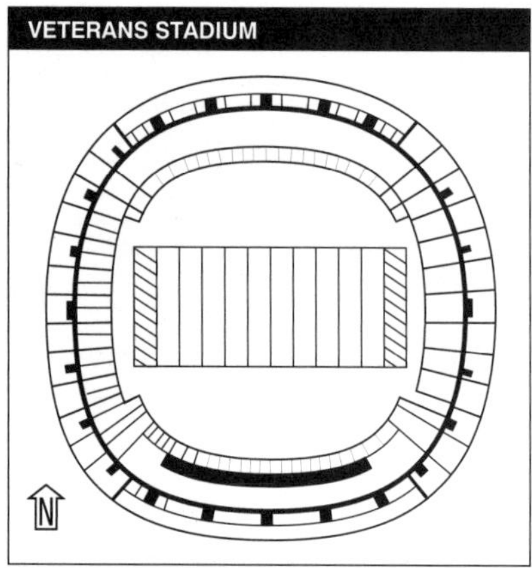

COACHING HISTORY

(417-496-25)

Years	Coach	Record
1933-35	Lud Wray	9-21-1
1936-1940	Bert Bell	10-44-2
1941-1950	Earle (Greasy) Neale*	66-44-5
1951	Alvin (Bo) McMillin**	2-0-0
1951	Wayne Millner	2-8-0
1952-55	Jim Trimble	25-20-3
1956-57	Hugh Devore	7-16-1
1958-1960	Lawrence (Buck) Shaw	20-16-1
1961-63	Nick Skorich	15-24-3
1964-68	Joe Kuharich	28-41-1
1969-1971	Jerry Williams***	7-22-2
1971-72	Ed Khayat	8-15-2
1973-75	Mike McCormack	16-25-1
1976-1982	Dick Vermeil	57-51-0
1983-85	Marion Campbell****	17-29-1
1985	Fred Bruney	1-0-0
1986-1990	Buddy Ryan	43-38-1
1991-94	Rich Kotite	37-29-0
1995-98	Ray Rhodes	30-36-1
1999-2000	Andy Reid	17-17-0

*Co-coach with Walt Kiesling in Philadelphia-Pittsburgh merger in 1943
**Retired after two games in 1951
***Released after three games in 1971
****Released after 15 games in 1985

2000 TEAM RECORD

PRESEASON (1-3)

Date	Result		Opponent
7/30	L	22-33	at Cleveland
8/5	L	13-16	at Baltimore
8/18	W	34-32	Tennessee
8/24	L	12-16	Buffalo

REGULAR SEASON (11-5)

Date	Result		Opponent	Att.
9/3	W	41-14	at Dallas	62,872
9/10	L	18-33	New York Giants	65,530
9/17	L	3-6	at Green Bay	59,869
9/24	W	21-7	at New Orleans	64,900
10/1	W	38-10	Atlanta	65,424
10/8	L	14-17	Washington	65,491
10/15	W	33-14	at Arizona	36,590
10/22	W	13-9	Chicago	65,553
10/29	L	7-24	at New York Giants	78,087
11/5	W	16-13	Dallas (OT)	65,636
11/12	W	26-23	at Pittsburgh (OT)	56,702
11/19	W	34-9	Arizona	65,356
11/26	W	23-20	at Washington	83,284
12/3	L	13-15	Tennessee	65,639
12/10	W	35-24	at Cleveland	72,318
12/24	W	16-7	Cincinnati	64,902

(OT) Overtime

POSTSEASON (1-1)

Date	Result		Opponent	Att.
12/31	W	21-3	Tampa Bay	65,813
1/7	L	10-20	at New York Giants	78,765

SCORE BY PERIODS

Eagles	57	97	71	120	6	—	351
Opponents	34	70	40	101	0	—	245

ATTENDANCE

Home 523,064 Away 512,686 Total 1,035,750
Single-game home record, 72,111 (11/1/81)
Single-season home record, 557,325 (1980)

2000 TEAM STATISTICS

	Eagles	Opp.
Total First Downs	295	295
Rushing	88	105
Passing	182	159
Penalty	25	31
Third Down: Made/Att	90/224	72/221
Third Down Pct.	40.2	32.6
Fourth Down: Made/Att	7/11	14/24
Fourth Down Pct.	63.6	58.3
Total Net Yards	5,006	4,820
Avg. Per Game	312.9	301.3
Total Plays	1,017	1,055
Avg. Per Play	4.9	4.6
Net Yards Rushing	1,882	1,830
Avg. Per Game	117.6	114.4
Total Rushes	397	453
Net Yards Passing	3,124	2,990
Avg. Per Game	195.3	186.9
Sacked/Yards Lost	45/262	50/291
Gross Yards	3,386	3,281
Att./Completions	575/331	552/314
Completion Pct.	57.6	56.9
Had Intercepted	15	19
Punts/Average	86/42.3	87/40.4
Net Punting Avg.	86/36.0	87/35.0
Penalties/Yards	113/980	111/936
Fumbles/Ball Lost	22/14	27/12
Touchdowns	38	23
Rushing	13	10
Passing	21	11
Returns	4	2
Avg. Time of Possession	29:01	30:59

2000 INDIVIDUAL STATISTICS

Passing	Att.	Comp.	Yds.	Pct.	TD	Int.	Tkld.	Rate
McNabb	569	330	3,365	58.0	21	13	45/262	77.8
Mitchell	4	1	21	25.0	0	0	0/0	49.0
Detmer	1	0	0	0.0	0	1	0/0	0.0
Small	1	0	0	0.0	0	1	0/0	0.0
Eagles	575	331	3,386	57.6	21	15	45/262	75.9
Opponents	552	314	3,281	56.9	11	19	50/291	66.6

SCORING	TD R	TD P	TD Rt	PAT	FG	Saf	PTS
Akers	0	0	0	34/36	29/33	0	121
C. Johnson	0	7	0	0/0	0/0	0	42
McNabb	6	0	0	0/0	0/0	0	36
Mitchell	2	1	2	0/0	0/0	0	30
Thomason	0	5	0	0/0	0/0	0	30
Autry	3	1	0	0/0	0/0	0	24
Small	0	3	0	0/0	0/0	0	20
Lewis	0	3	0	0/0	0/0	0	18
Brown	0	1	0	0/0	0/0	0	6
Caldwell	0	0	1	0/0	0/0	0	6
Pritchett	1	0	0	0/0	0/0	0	6
Staley	1	0	0	0/0	0/0	0	6
Trotter	0	0	1	0/0	0/0	0	6
Eagles	13	21	4	34/36	29/33	0	351
Opponents	10	11	2	21/21	28/33	0	245

2-Pt. Conversions: Small.
Eagles 1-2, Opponents 1-2.

RUSHING	Att.	Yds.	Avg.	LG	TD
McNabb	86	629	7.3	54	6
Staley	79	344	4.4	60	1
Autry	112	334	3.0	15	3
Pritchett	58	225	3.9	16	1
Mitchell	25	187	7.5	85t	2
Martin	13	77	5.9	23	0
Warren	15	42	2.8	11	0
C. Johnson	5	18	3.6	15	0
Akers	1	15	15.0	15	0
Detmer	1	8	8.0	8	0
Lee	1	2	2.0	2	0
Small	1	1	1.0	1	0
Eagles	397	1,882	4.7	85t	13
Opponents	453	1,830	4.0	37	10

RECEIVING	No.	Yds.	Avg.	LG	TD
Lewis	69	735	10.7	52	3
C. Johnson	56	642	11.5	59	7
Small	40	569	14.2	70t	3
Martin	31	219	7.1	26	0
Staley	25	201	8.0	26	0
Pritchett	25	193	7.7	17	0
Autry	24	275	11.5	37	1
Mitchell	13	89	6.8	21	1
Broughton	12	104	8.7	21	0
Pinkston	10	181	18.1	45	0
Thomason	10	46	4.6	11	5
Brown	9	80	8.9	18	1
McNabb	2	5	2.5	3	0
Lee	1	20	20.0	20	0
D. Douglas	1	9	9.0	9	0
Miller	1	9	9.0	9	0
Van Dyke	1	8	8.0	8	0
Warren	1	1	1.0	1	0
Eagles	331	3,386	10.2	70t	21
Opponents	314	3,281	10.4	70t	11

INTERCEPTIONS	No.	Yds.	Avg.	LG	TD
Vincent	5	34	6.8	17	0
Dawkins	4	62	15.5	32	0
Taylor	3	64	21.3	38	0
Moore	2	24	12.0	20	0
Emmons	2	8	4.0	8	0
Trotter	1	27	27.0	27t	1
Caldwell	1	26	26.0	26t	1
H. Douglas	1	9	9.0	9	0
Harris	0	1	—	1	0
Eagles	19	255	13.4	38	2
Opponents	15	146	9.7	33	0

PUNTING	No.	Yds.	Avg.	In 20	LG
Landeta	86	3,635	42.3	23	60
Eagles	86	3,635	42.3	23	60
Opponents	87	3,516	40.4	30	52

PUNT RETURNS	No.	FC	Yds.	Avg.	LG	TD
Mitchell	32	33	335	10.5	72t	1
Bostic	1	0	0	0.0	0	0
Eagles	33	33	335	10.2	72t	1
Opponents	47	18	375	8.0	70t	1

KICKOFF RETURNS	No.	Yds.	Avg.	LG	TD
Mitchell	47	1,124	23.9	89t	1
D. Douglas	2	50	25.0	41	0
Broughton	1	20	20.0	20	0
Pritchett	1	15	15.0	15	0
Thomason	1	10	10.0	10	0
Whiting	1	18	18.0	18	0
Eagles	53	1,237	23.3	89t	1
Opponents	72	1,519	21.1	47	0

FIELD GOALS	1-19	20-29	30-39	40-49	50+
Akers	1/1	6/6	14/15	7/10	1/1
Eagles	1/1	6/6	14/15	7/10	1/1
Opponents	0/0	9/9	9/11	8/11	2/2

SACKS	No.
H. Douglas	15.0
Simon	9.5
Mamula	5.5
H. Thomas	4.0
Grasmanis	3.5
Whiting	3.5
Trotter	3.0
Dawkins	2.0
Gardner	1.0
Vincent	1.0
Darling	0.5
Emmons	0.5
Eagles	50.0
Opponents	45.0

2001 DRAFT CHOICES

Round	Name	Pos.	College
1	Freddie Mitchell	WR	UCLA
2	Quinton Caver	LB	Arkansas
3	Derrick Burgess	DE	Mississippi
4	Correll Buckhalter	RB	Nebraska
5	Tony Stewart	TE	Penn State
	A.J. Feeley	QB	Oregon

PHILADELPHIA EAGLES

2001 VETERAN ROSTER

No.	Name	Pos.	Ht.	Wt.	Birthdate	NFL Exp.	College	Hometown	How Acq.	'00 Games/ Starts
2	Akers, David	K	5-10	200	12/9/74	3	Louisville	Lexington, Ky.	FA-'99	16/0
24	Autry, Darnell	RB	5-10	210	6/19/76	3	Northwestern	Tempe, Ariz.	FA-'98	11/7
88	Bartrum, Mike	TE-LS	6-4	245	6/23/70	8	Marshall	Pomeroy, Ohio	FA-'00	16/0
32	Bostic, Jason	S	5-9	181	6/30/76	2	Georgia Tech	Lauderhill, Fla.	FA-'99	16/0
85	Brown, Na	WR	6-0	196	2/22/77	3	North Carolina	Reidsville, N.C.	D4c-'99	14/2
74	Brzezinski, Doug	G	6-4	305	3/11/76	3	Boston College	Detroit, Mich.	D3-'99	16/0
56	Caldwell, Mike	LB	6-2	237	8/31/71	9	Middle Tennessee State	Oak Ridge, Tenn.	FA(Ariz)-'98	16/3
25	# Cherry, Je'Rod	S	6-1	205	5/30/73	6	California	Berkely, Calif.	FA-'00	13/0
42	Cook, Rashard	S	5-11	197	4/18/77	3	Southern California	San Diego, Calif.	W(Chi)-'99	14/0
93	Davis, Pernell	DT	6-2	320	5/19/76	3	Alabama-Birmingham	Birmingham, Ala.	D7b-'99	0*
20	Dawkins, Brian	S	5-11	200	10/13/73	6	Clemson	Jacksonville, Fla.	D2b-'96	13/13
10	Detmer, Koy	QB	6-1	195	7/5/73	5	Colorado	San Antonio, Texas	D7a-'97	16/0
82	Douglas, Dameane	WR	6-0	195	3/15/76	3	California	Hanford, Calif.	W(Oak)-'99	6/0
53	Douglas, Hugh	LB-DE	6-2	280	8/23/71	7	Central State (Ohio)	Mansfield, Ohio	T(NYJ)-'98	16/15
51	Emmons, Carlos	LB	6-5	250	9/3/73	6	Arkansas State	Greenwood, Miss.	FA(Pitt)-'00	16/13
63	Fraley, Hank	C-G	6-2	300	9/21/77	2	Robert Morris	Gaithersburg, Md.	W(Pitt)-'00	0*
52	Gardner, Barry	LB	6-0	248	12/13/76	3	Northwestern	Harvey, Ill.	D2-'99	16/13
96	Grasmanis, Paul	DT	6-3	298	8/2/74	6	Notre Dame	Jenison, Mich.	FA(Den)-'00	16/0
91	Hamiter, Uhuru	DE	6-4	280	3/14/73	4	Delaware State	Philadelphia, Pa.	FA-'00	7/0
31	Harris, Al	CB	6-1	185	12/7/74	4	Texas A&M-Kingsville	Pompano Beach, Fla.	W(TB)98	16/4
45	# Hauck, Tim	S	5-10	187	12/20/66	12	Montana	Big Timber, Mont.	FA-'00	16/3
79	Jefferson, Greg	DE-DT	6-3	280	8/31/71	7	Central Florida	Bartow, Fla.	D3a-'95	0*
62	Johnson, Dwight	DE	6-4	285	1/30/77	2	Baylor	Waco, Texas	FA-'00	4/0
94	Kalu, N.D.	DE	6-3	265	8/3/75	5	Rice	San Antonio, Texas	UFA(Wash)-'01	15/0*
7	Landeta, Sean	P	6-0	215	1/6/62	17	Towson State	Towson, Md.	FA(GB)-'99	16/0
89	Lewis, Chad	TE	6-6	252	10/5/71	4	Brigham Young	Orem, Utah	W(StL)-'99	16/16
38	Martin, Cecil	FB	6-0	235	7/8/75	3	Wisconsin	Evanston, Ill.	D6a-'99	16/9
71	Mayberry, Jermane	G-T	6-4	325	8/29/73	6	Texas A&M-Kingsville	Floresville, Texas	D1-'96	16/16
5	McNabb, Donovan	QB	6-2	226	11/25/76	3	Syracuse	Mt. Carmel, Ill.	D1-'99	16/16
61	Mercer, Giradie	DT	6-2	285	3/19/76	2	Marshall	Washington, D.C.	FA-'00	0*
65	Miller, Bubba	C-G	6-1	305	1/24/73	6	Tennessee	Franklin, Tenn.	FA-'96	16/16
30	Mitchell, Brian	RB-KR	5-10	221	8/18/68	12	Southwestern Louisiana	Plaquemine, La.	FA-'00	16/1
25	Montgomery, Monty	CB	5-11	197	12/8/73	5	Houston	Gladewater, Texas	UFA(SF)-'01	15/9*
43	Moore, Damon	S	5-11	215	9/15/76	3	Ohio State	Fostoria, Ohio	D4b-'99	16/16
87	Pinkston, Todd	WR	6-2	170	4/23/77	2	Southern Mississippi	Forest, Miss.	D2a-'00	16/1
11	Powlus, Ron	QB	6-1	225	7/16/74	2	Notre Dame	Berwick, Pa.	FA-'00	0*
36	Pritchett, Stanley	RB	6-1	240	12/22/73	6	South Carolina	Atlanta, Ga.	FA(Mia)-'00	16/2
58	Reese, Ike	LB	6-2	222	10/16/73	4	Michigan State	Cincinnati, Ohio	D5-'98	16/0
69	Runyan, Jon	T	6-7	330	11/27/73	6	Michigan	Flint, Mich.	FA(Tenn)-'00	16/16
67	Schau, Ryan	T-G	6-6	300	12/30/75	3	Illinois	Bloomington, Ill.	FA-'99	10/0
86	Scott, Gari	WR	6-0	191	6/2/78	2	Michigan State	Riviera Beach, Fla.	D4-'00	0*
90	Simon, Corey	DT	6-2	293	3/2/77	2	Florida State	Pompano Beach, Fla.	D1-'00	16/16
22	Staley, Duce	RB	5-11	220	2/27/75	5	South Carolina	Columbia, S.C.	D3-'97	5/5
21	Taylor, Bobby	CB	6-3	216	12/28/73	7	Notre Dame	Longview, Texas	D2a-'95	16/15
78	Thomas, Hollis	DT	6-0	306	1/10/74	6	Northern Illinois	St. Louis, Mo.	FA-'96	16/16
72	Thomas, Tra	T	6-7	349	11/20/74	4	Florida State	Deland, Fla.	D1-'98	16/16
83	Thomason, Jeff	TE	6-5	255	12/30/69	9	Oregon	Newport Beach, Calif.	T(GB)-'00	16/5
80	Thrash, James	WR	6-0	200	4/28/75	5	Missouri Southern	Denver, Colo.	UFA(Wash)-'01	16/8*
54	† Trotter, Jeremiah	LB	6-1	261	1/20/77	4	Stephen F. Austin	Hooks, Texas	D3a-'98	16/16
23	Vincent, Troy	CB	6-1	200	6/8/71	10	Wisconsin	Trenton, N.J.	RFA(Mia)-'96	16/16
97	Walker, Darwin	DT	6-3	294	6/15/77	2	Tennessee	Walterboro, S.C.	W(Ariz)-'00	0*
35	# Warren, Chris	RB	6-2	227	1/24/68	12	Ferrum	Burke, Va.	W(Dall)-'00	14/1*
76	Welbourn, John	T-G	6-5	318	3/30/76	3	California	Palos Verdes, Calif.	D4a-'99	16/16
98	Whiting, Brandon	DT-DE	6-3	285	7/30/76	4	California	Long Beach, Calif.	D4a-'98	16/11
66	Williams, Bobbie	G	6-3	320	9/25/76	2	Arkansas	Jefferson, Texas	D2b-'00	0*
	Wong, Joe	T	6-6	315	2/24/76	2	Brigham Young	Honolulu, Hawaii	FA-'01	0*

* Davis, Jefferson, and Mercer missed '00 season because of injury; Fraley, Powlus, and Williams were inactive for 16 games; Kalu played 15 games with Washington in '00; Montgomery played 15 games with San Francisco; Scott was inactive for 15 games; Thrash played 16 games with Washington; Walker was inactive for 13 games; Warren played 13 games with Dallas and 1 game with Philadelphia; Wong last active with Miami in '99.

† Restricted free agent; subject to developments.

\# Unrestricted free agent; subject to developments.

Players lost through free agency (2): TE Luther Broughton (Car; 15 games in '00), LB James Darling (NYJ; 16).

Also played with Eagles in '00—WR Charles Johnson (16 games), RB Amp Lee (3), DE Mike Mamula (15), WR Torrance Small (14), WR Alex Van Dyke (4), DE Tyrone Williams (3).

COACHING STAFF

Head Coach/Executive Vice President of Football Operations, Andy Reid

Pro Career: Andy Reid was named the twentieth head coach in franchise history on January 11, 1999. On May 7, 2001, Reid was given the title of head coach/executive vice president of football operations. After finishing his first season at 5-11, led the Eagles to the greatest turnaround in the team's history, finishing second in the NFC East at 11-5 and earning a trip to the NFC Divisional Playoffs. For his efforts, Reid was named the NFL's Coach of the Year by the Maxwell Football Club, *The Sporting News,* and *Football Digest.* Reid came to the Eagles after spending the previous seven seasons as an assistant coach with the Green Bay Packers under Mike Holmgren. With Green Bay, Reid helped the Packers reach the playoffs six consecutive times from 1993-98. During that span, Green Bay defeated the New England Patriots in Super Bowl XXXI and reached the NFL's title game again the following year. Reid also was instrumental in the development of all-pro quarterback Brett Favre when he served as the Packers quarterbacks coach from 1997-98. Career record: 17-17.

Background: Quality pass-blocking offensive lines, in both the Division I and II ranks, have been Reid's hallmark since launching his coaching career at San Francisco State in 1983. The school led the nation in passing offense and total offense for three consecutive years (1983-85) while he served as the school's offensive coordinator, offensive line coach, and strength coach. Reid moved to Northern Arizona as offensive line coach in 1986, to Texas-El Paso for two seasons (1987-88), and coached at Missouri from 1989-1991. Reid's coaching career began at his alma mater, Brigham Young, as a graduate assistant under LaVell Edwards in 1982. Reid first met Holmgren, who was a member of BYU's coaching staff, when Reid was an offensive tackle and guard on three Cougars Holiday Bowl teams. Reid went on to earn three varsity football letters, graduating with a bachelor's degree in physical education. He also received a master's degree in professional leadership in physical education and athletics.

Personal: Born in Los Angeles on March 19, 1958, Reid and his wife Tammy have five children—Garrett, Britt, Crosby, Drew Ann, and Spencer.

ASSISTANT COACHES

Tommy Brasher, defensive line; born Dec. 30, 1940, El Dorado, Ark., lives in Newtown Square, Pa. Linebacker Arkansas 1962-63. No pro playing experience. College coach: Arkansas 1970, Virginia Tech 1971, Northeast Louisiana 1974, 1976, Southern Methodist 1977-1981. Pro coach: Shreveport Steamer (WFL) 1975, New England Patriots 1982-84, Philadelphia Eagles 1985, Atlanta Falcons 1986-89, Tampa Bay Buccaneers 1990, Seattle Seahawks 1992-98, rejoined Eagles in 1999.

Juan Castillo, offensive line; born October 8, 1959, Port Isabel, Texas, lives in Mount Laurel, N.J. Linebacker Texas A&I (now Texas A&M-Kingsville) 1978-1980. Pro linebacker San Antonio Gunslingers (USFL) 1984-85. College coach: Texas A&M-Kingsville 1982-85, 1990-94. Pro coach: Joined Eagles in 1995.

Brad Childress, quarterbacks; born June 27, 1956, Aurora, Ill., lives in Cinnaminson, N.J. Eastern Illinois 1975-78. No pro playing experience. College coach: Illinois 1978-1984, Northern Arizona 1986-89, Utah 1990, Wisconsin 1991-98. Pro coach: Indianapolis Colts 1985, joined Eagles in 1999.

David Culley, wide receivers; born September 17, 1955, Sparta, Tenn., lives in Sewell, N.J. Quarterback Vanderbilt 1973-77. No pro playing experience. College coach: Austin Peay 1978, Vanderbilt 1979-1981, Middle Tennessee State 1982, Tennessee-Chattanooga 1983, Western Kentucky 1984, Southwestern Louisiana 1985-88, Texas-El Paso 1989-1990, Texas A&M 1991-93. Pro coach: Tampa Bay Buccaneers 1994-95, Pittsburgh Steelers 1996-1998, joined Eagles in 1999.

Rod Dowhower, offensive coordinator; born April 15, 1943, Ord, Neb., lives in Newtown Square, Pa. Quarterback San Diego State 1963-65. No pro playing experience. College coach: San Diego State 1966-1972, UCLA 1974-75, Boise State 1976, Stanford 1977-79 (head coach 1979), Vanderbilt 1995-96 (head coach). Pro coach: St. Louis Cardinals 1973, 1982-84, Denver Broncos 1980-1981, Indianapolis Colts 1985-86 (head coach), Atlanta Falcons 1987-89, Washington Redskins 1990-93, New York Giants 1997-98, joined Eagles in 1999.

Leslie Frazier, defensive backs; born April 3, 1959, Columbus, Miss., lives in Cherry Hill, N.J. Defensive back Alcorn State 1979-1980. Pro defensive back Chicago Bears 1981-86. College coach: Trinity (Ill.) College 1988-1996 (head coach), Illinois 1997-98. Pro coach: Joined Eagles in 1999.

John Harbaugh, special teams; born September 23, 1962, Perrysburg, Ohio, lives in Newtown Square, Pa. Defensive back Miami (Ohio) 1980-83. No pro playing experience. College coach: Western Michigan 1984-86, Pittsburgh 1987, Morehead State 1988, Cincinnati 1989-1996, Indiana 1997. Pro coach: Joined Eagles in 1998.

Jim Johnson, defensive coordinator; born May 26, 1941, Maywood, Ill., lives in Newtown Square, Pa. Quarterback Missouri 1959-1962. Pro tight end Buffalo Bills 1963-64. College coach: Missouri Southern 1967-68 (head coach), Drake 1969-1972, Indiana 1973-76, Notre Dame 1977-1980. Pro coach: Oklahoma Outlaws (USFL) 1984, Jacksonville Bulls (USFL) 1985, Phoenix Cardinals 1986-1993, Indianapolis Colts 1994-97, Seattle Seahawks 1998, joined Eagles in 1999.

Sean McDermott, defense assistant-quality control; born March 21, 1974, Omaha, Neb., lives in Conshohocken, Pa. Safety William & Mary 1994-97. No pro playing experience. College coach: William & Mary 1998. Pro coach: Joined Eagles in 1998.

Tom Melvin, offensive assistant-quality control; born October 1, 1961, Redwood City, Calif., lives in Cinnaminson, N.J. Offensive lineman San Francisco State 1982-83. No pro playing experience. College coach: San Francisco State 1984-85, Northern Arizona 1986-87, California-Santa Barbara 1988-1990, Occidental College 1991-98. Pro coach: Joined Eagles in 1999.

Ron Rivera, linebackers; born January 7, 1962, Fort Ord, Calif., lives in Cherry Hill, N.J. Linebacker California 1980-83. Pro linebacker Chicago Bears 1984-1992. Pro coach: Chicago Bears 1997-98, joined Eagles in 1999.

Pat Shurmur, tight ends-asst. offensive line; born April 14, 1965, Dearborn Heights, Mich., lives in Cinnaminson, N.J. Center Michigan State 1983-87. No pro playing experience. College coach: Michigan State 1988-1997, Stanford 1998. Pro coach: Joined Eagles in 1999.

Steve Spagnuolo, defensive backs; born December 21, 1959, Witinsville, Mass., lives in Haddon Heights, N.J. Wide receiver Springfield College 1979-1981. No pro playing experience. College coach: Massachusetts 1982-83, Lafayette 1984-86, Connecticut 1987-1991, Maine 1993, Rutgers 1994-95, Bowling Green 1996-97. Pro coach: Barcelona Dragons (World League) 1992, Frankfurt Galaxy (NFL Europe) 1998, joined Eagles in 1999.

Dave Toub, special teams quality control; born June 1, 1962, Ossining, N.Y., lives in Philadelphia. Offensive lineman Springfield College 1980-81, Texas-El Paso 1983-84. No pro playing experience. College coach: Texas-El Paso 1987-89, Missouri 1989-2000. Pro coach: Joined Eagles in 2001.

Ted Williams, running backs; born November 17, 1943, Lyons, Texas, lives in Sicklerville, N.J. No college or pro playing experience. College coach: UCLA 1980-89, Washington State 1991-93, Arizona 1994. Pro coach: Joined Eagles in 1995.

Mike Wolf, strength and conditioning; born May 15, 1965, Allentown, Pa., lives in Medford, N.J. Center Penn State 1983-87. No pro playing experience. College coach: Vanderbilt 1988-89, Lehigh 1990, Penn State 1991. Pro coach: Minnesota Vikings 1992-94, joined Eagles in 1995.

2001 FIRST-YEAR ROSTER

Name	Pos.	Ht.	Wt.	Birthdate	College	Hometown	How Acq.
Baker, Jason	P	6-1	195	5/17/78	Iowa	Ft. Wayne, Ind.	FA
Booker, Fred	CB	5-9	188	6/4/78	Louisiana State	Hammond, La.	FA
Bradley, Roylin	LB	6-1	234	6/15/78	Texas A&M	La Marque, Texas	FA
Buckhalter, Correll	RB	6-0	222	10/6/78	Nebraska	Collins, Miss.	D4
Burgess, Derrick	DE	6-2	266	8/12/78	Mississippi	Greenbelt, Md.	D3
Carroll, Terrence	FS	6-0	215	8/18/78	Oregon State	Houston, Texas	FA
Caver, Quinton	LB	6-4	230	8/22/78	Arkansas	Anniston, Ala.	D2
Crutchfield, Darrel	CB	6-0	177	2/26/79	Clemson	Jacksonville, Fla.	FA
Feeley, A.J.	QB	6-3	217	5/16/77	Oregon	Ontario, Ore.	D5b
Frank, John	DE	6-4	280	7/1/74	Utah	Salt Lake City, Utah	D6b-'00
Gray, Anthony (1)	RB	6-0	228	10/1/74	Western New Mexico	Hayward, Calif.	FA
Hamner, Thomas (1)	RB	6-0	197	12/25/76	Minnesota	Hamilton, Ohio	D6a-'00
Hampton, William (1)	CB	5-10	190	3/7/75	Murray State	Little Rock, Ark.	FA-'00
Jones, Julian	S	6-0	190	6/8/77	Missouri	Oklahoma City, Okla.	FA
Keys, Scott	WR	6-1	196	12/11/77	Stephen F. Austin	Houston, Texas	FA
Long, Mel	WR	6-1	187	10/15/77	Toledo	Toledo, Ohio	FA
Malecki, Jason	P	6-2	220	8/15/76	Boston College	Springfield, Va.	FA
McCready, Eric	WR	6-3	214	11/14/77	Colorado	Shawnee Mission, Kan.	FA
Mitchell, Freddie	WR	5-11	184	11/28/78	UCLA	Lakeland, Fla.	D1
Moore, Josh	T	6-4	309	5/25/78	Furman	Cross Hill, S.C.	FA
Nuño, Carlos (1)	TE	6-4	260	10/2/75	Brigham Young	Modesto, Calif.	FA
Ochs, Brennan	FB	6-0	230	3/14/78	Southern California	Rockville, Md.	FA
Parry, Josh	LB	6-1	234	4/5/78	San Jose State	Sonora, Calif.	FA
Reader, Jamie	FB	6-0	238	5/4/74	Akron	Monessen, Pa.	W(NYJ)
Rogers, Kendrick	T	6-5	311	10/10/76	Alabama A&M	Mobile, Ala.	FA
Romero, John (1)	C-G	6-3	326	10/3/76	California	San Leandro, Calif.	D6c-'00
Scott, Sean	WR	6-2	190	9/25/78	Millersville	Philadelphia, Pa.	FA
Skinner, Justin (1)	K	6-2	190	7/31/75	Citadel	Charleston, S.C.	FA
Stewart, Tony	TE	6-5	255	8/9/79	Penn State	Allentown, Pa.	D5a
Thomas, Tarlos	T	6-5	323	8/23/77	Florida State	Monticello, Fla.	FA
Thurmon, Elijah (1)	WR	6-3	206	8/2/78	Howard	Severn, Md.	FA-'00
Vagedes, Steve (1)	WR	6-2	215	9/2/76	Ohio Northern	Coldwater, Ohio	FA
Walker, Derrick	LB	6-2	224	8/13/78	Iowa State	Houston, Texas	FA

The term NFL Rookie is defined as a player who is in his first season of professional football and has not been on the roster of another professional football team for any regular-season or postseason games. A Rookie is designated by an "R" on NFL rosters. Players who have been active in another professional football league or players who have NFL experience, including either preseason training camp or being on an Active List or Inactive List, or on Reserve/Injured or Reserve/Physically Unable to Perform for fewer than six regular-season games, are termed NFL First-Year Players. An NFL First-Year Player is designated by a "1" on NFL rosters. Thereafter, a player is credited with an additional year of experience for each season in which he accumulates six games on the Active List or Inactive List, or on Reserve/Injured or Reserve/Physically Unable to Perform.

ST. LOUIS RAMS

National Football Conference
Western Division
Team Colors: New Century Gold, Millennium Blue, and White
One Rams Way
St. Louis, Missouri 63045
Telephone: (314) 982-7267

CLUB OFFICIALS

Owner/Chairman: Georgia Frontiere
Owner/Vice Chairman: Stan Kroenke
President: John Shaw
President-Football Operations: Jay Zygmunt
Senior Vice President-Administration and General Counsel: Bob Wallace
Treasurer: Jeff Brewer
Vice President-Finance: Adrian Barr-Bracy
General Manager: Charley Armey
Vice President-Sales and Marketing: Phil Thomas
Director-College Scouting: Lawrence McCutcheon
Director-Pro Scouting: Mike Ackerley
Vice President-Ticket Operations: Michael T. Naughton
Director of Operations: John Oswald
Director of Public Relations: Rick Smith
Assistant Director of Public Relations: Duane Lewis
Head Trainer: Jim Anderson
Assistant Trainers: Dake Walden, Ron DuBuque
Equipment Manager: Todd Hewitt
Scouts: Dick Daniels, Mel Foels, Ryan Grigson, Tom Marino, Kevin McCabe, David Razzano
Stadium: Dome at America's Center (built in 1995)
• **Capacity:** 66,000
701 Convention Plaza
St. Louis, Missouri 63101
Playing Surface: AstroTurf
Training Camp: Western Illinois University
Thompson Hall
Macomb, Illinois 61455

2001 SCHEDULE

PRESEASON

Aug. 6	vs. Miami at Canton, Ohio	8:00
Aug. 12	at Buffalo	7:30
Aug. 17	**Tennessee**	7:00
Aug. 25	at San Diego	7:00
Aug. 31	**Kansas City**	7:00

REGULAR SEASON

Sept. 9	at Philadelphia	4:15
Sept. 16	**Atlanta**	3:05
Sept. 23	at San Francisco	1:15
Sept. 30	**Miami**	12:00
Oct. 8	at Detroit (Mon.)	9:00
Oct. 14	**New York Giants**	12:00
Oct. 21	at New York Jets	1:00
Oct. 28	**New Orleans**	12:00
Nov. 4	Open Date	
Nov. 11	**Carolina**	12:00
Nov. 18	at New England	8:30
Nov. 26	**Tampa Bay** (Mon.)	8:00
Dec. 2	at Atlanta	1:00
Dec. 9	**San Francisco**	12:00
Dec. 17	at New Orleans (Mon.)	8:00
Dec. 23	at Carolina	1:00
Dec. 30	**Indianapolis**	12:00

RECORD HOLDERS

INDIVIDUAL RECORDS—CAREER

Category	Name	Performance
Rushing (Yds.)	Eric Dickerson, 1983-87	7,245
Passing (Yds.)	Jim Everett, 1986-1993	23,758
Passing (TDs)	Roman Gabriel, 1962-1972	154
Receiving (No.)	Henry Ellard, 1983-1993	593
Receiving (Yds.)	Henry Ellard, 1983-1993	9,761
Interceptions	Ed Meador, 1959-1970	46
Punting (Avg.)	Danny Villanueva, 1960-64	44.2
Punt Return (Avg.)	Henry Ellard, 1983-1992	11.3
Kickoff Return (Avg.)	Tom Wilson, 1956-1961	27.1
Field Goals	Mike Lansford, 1982-1990	158
Touchdowns (Tot.)	Eric Dickerson, 1983-87	58
Points	Mike Lansford, 1982-1990	789

INDIVIDUAL RECORDS—SINGLE SEASON

Category	Name	Performance
Rushing (Yds.)	Eric Dickerson, 1984	*2,105
Passing (Yds.)	Kurt Warner, 1999	4,353
Passing (TDs)	Kurt Warner, 1999	41
Receiving (No.)	Isaac Bruce, 1995	119
Receiving (Yds.)	Isaac Bruce, 1995	1,781
Interceptions	Dick (Night Train) Lane, 1952	*14
Punting (Avg.)	Danny Villanueva, 1962	45.5
Punt Return (Avg.)	Woodley Lewis, 1952	18.5
Kickoff Return (Avg.)	Verda (Vitamin T) Smith, 1950	33.7
Field Goals	David Ray, 1973	30
Touchdowns (Tot.)	Marshall Faulk, 2000	*26
Points	Marshall Faulk, 2000	160

INDIVIDUAL RECORDS—SINGLE GAME

Category	Name	Performance
Rushing (Yds.)	Willie Ellison, 12-5-71	247
Passing (Yds.)	Norm Van Brocklin, 9-28-51	*554
Passing (TDs)	Many times Last time by Kurt Warner, 10-10-99	5
Receiving (No.)	Tom Fears, 12-3-50	18
Receiving (Yds.)	Willie Anderson, 11-26-89	*336
Interceptions	Many times Last time by Keith Lyle, 12-15-96	3
Field Goals	Bob Waterfield, 12-9-51	5
Touchdowns (Tot.)	Many times last time by Marshall Faulk, 12-18-00	4
Points	Many times last time by Marshall Faulk, 12-18-00	24

*NFL Record

COACHING HISTORY

Cleveland 1937-1945, Los Angeles 1946-1994 (456-421-20)

1937-38	Hugo Bezdek*	1-13-0
1938	Art Lewis	4-4-0
1939-1942	Earl (Dutch) Clark	16-26-2
1944	Aldo (Buff) Donelli	4-6-0
1945-46	Adam Walsh	16-5-1
1947	Bob Snyder	6-6-0
1948-49	Clark Shaughnessy	14-8-3
1950-52	Joe Stydahar**	19-9-0
1952-54	Hamp Pool	23-11-2
1955-59	Sid Gillman	28-32-1
1960-62	Bob Waterfield***	9-24-1
1962-65	Harland Svare	14-31-3
1966-1970	George Allen	49-19-4
1971-72	Tommy Prothro	14-12-2
1973-77	Chuck Knox	57-20-1
1978-1982	Ray Malavasi	43-36-0
1983-1991	John Robinson	79-74-0
1992-94	Chuck Knox	15-33-0
1995-96	Rich Brooks	13-19-0
1997-99	Dick Vermeil	25-26-0
2000	Mike Martz	10-7-0

*Released after three games in 1938
**Resigned after one game in 1952
***Resigned after eight games in 1962

DOME AT AMERICA'S CENTER

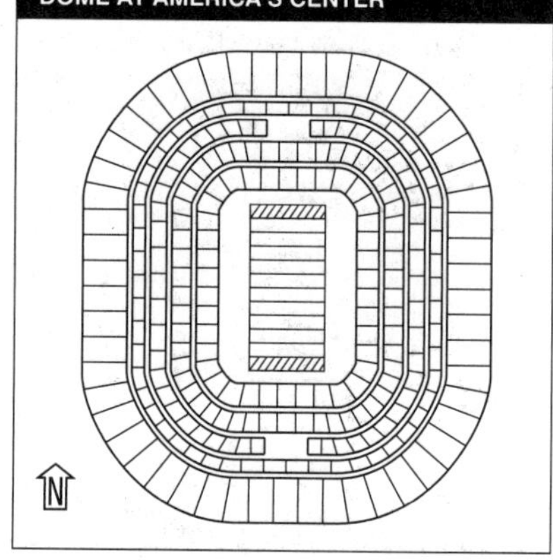

2000 TEAM RECORD

PRESEASON (2-2)

Date	Result		Opponent
8/5	W	31-17	Oakland
8/14	L	3-30	at Tennessee
8/19	L	27-31	Buffalo
8/24	W	24-17	at Dallas

REGULAR SEASON (10-6)

Date	Result		Opponent	Att.
9/4	W	41-36	Denver	65,956
9/10	W	37-34	at Seattle	64,869
9/17	W	41-24	San Francisco	65,945
9/24	W	41-20	at Atlanta	58,761
10/1	W	57-31	San Diego	66,010
10/15	W	45-29	Atlanta	66,019
10/22	L	34-54	at Kansas City	79,142
10/29	W	34-24	at San Francisco	68,109
11/5	L	24-27	Carolina	66,048
11/12	W	38-24	at New York Giants	78,174
11/20	L	20-33	Washington	66,087
11/26	L	24-31	New Orleans	66,064
12/3	L	3-16	at Carolina	73,358
12/10	W	40-29	Minnesota	66,273
12/18	L	35-38	at Tampa Bay	65,653
12/24	W	26-21	at New Orleans	64,900

POSTSEASON (0-1)

Date	Result		Opponent	Att.
12/30	L	28-31	at New Orleans	64,900

SCORE BY PERIODS

Rams	116	147	154	123	0	— 540
Opponents	94	130	103	144	0	— 471

ATTENDANCE

Home 519,269 Away 550,925 Total 1,070,194
Single-game home record, 66,273 (12/10/00)
Single-season home record, 520,926 (1999)

2000 TEAM STATISTICS

	Rams	Opp.
Total First Downs	380	321
Rushing	112	95
Passing	247	195
Penalty	21	31
Third Down: Made/Att	86/181	74/192
Third Down Pct.	47.5	38.5
Fourth Down: Made/Att	8/13	6/12
Fourth Down Pct.	61.5	50.0
Total Net Yards	7,075	5,494
Avg. Per Game	442.2	343.4
Total Plays	1,014	968
Avg. Per Play	7.0	5.7
Net Yards Rushing	1,843	1,697
Avg. Per Game	115.2	106.1
Total Rushes	383	383
Net Yards Passing	5,232	3,797
Avg. Per Game	327.0	237.3
Sacked/Yards Lost	44/260	51/288
Gross Yards	5,492	4,085
Att./Completions	587/380	534/323
Completion Pct.	64.7	60.5
Had Intercepted	23	19
Punts/Average	44/39.5	67/42.2
Net Punting Avg.	44/34.2	67/33.5
Penalties/Yards	111/942	101/747
Fumbles/Ball Lost	24/12	19/6
Touchdowns	67	56
Rushing	26	18
Passing	37	32
Returns	4	6
Avg. Time of Possession	30:54	29:06

2000 INDIVIDUAL STATISTICS

Passing	Att.	Comp.	Yds.	Pct.	TD	Int.	Tkld.	Rate
Warner	347	235	3,429	67.7	21	18	20/115	98.3
Green	240	145	2,063	60.4	16	5	24/145	101.8
Rams	587	380	5,492	64.7	37	23	44/260	99.7
Opponents	534	323	4,085	60.5	32	19	51/288	89.5

SCORING	TD R	TD P	TD Rt	PAT	FG	Saf	PTS
Faulk	18	8	0	0/0	0/0	0	160
Wilkins	0	0	0	38/38	17/17	0	89
Bruce	0	9	0	0/0	0/0	0	54
Holt	0	6	0	0/0	0/0	0	36
Hakim	0	4	1	0/0	0/0	0	30
Holcombe	3	1	0	0/0	0/0	0	24
Proehl	0	4	0	0/0	0/0	0	24
Watson	4	0	0	0/0	0/0	0	24
Hall	0	0	0	9/9	4/5	0	21
Stoyanovich	0	0	0	11/11	3/5	0	20
Williams	0	3	0	0/0	0/0	0	20
Horne	0	2	1	0/0	0/0	0	18
Bush	0	0	1	0/0	0/0	0	6
Green	1	0	0	0/0	0/0	0	6
Lyle	0	0	1	0/0	0/0	0	6
Fletcher	0	0	0	0/0	0/0	0	2
Rams	26	37	4	58/58	24/27	0	540
Opponents	18	32	6	49/50	26/31	1	471

2-Pt. Conversions: Faulk 2, Fletcher, Williams.
Rams 4-9, Opponents 3-6.

RUSHING	Att.	Yds.	Avg.	LG	TD
Faulk	253	1,359	5.4	36	18
Watson	54	249	4.6	49	4
Holcombe	21	70	3.3	11	3
Green	20	69	3.5	18t	1
Conwell	2	23	11.5	17	0
Hakim	5	19	3.8	5	0
Warner	18	17	0.9	11	0
Bruce	1	11	11.0	11	0
Holt	2	7	3.5	7	0
Canidate	3	6	2.0	3	0
Horne	2	6	3.0	9	0
Lyle	1	4	4.0	4	0
Hodgins	1	3	3.0	3	0
Rams	383	1,843	4.8	49	26
Opponents	383	1,697	4.4	69	18

RECEIVING	No.	Yds.	Avg.	LG	TD
Bruce	87	1,471	16.9	78t	9
Holt	82	1,635	19.9	85t	6
Faulk	81	830	10.2	72t	8
Hakim	53	734	13.8	80t	4
Proehl	31	441	14.2	29	4
Williams	11	102	9.3	31t	3
Watson	10	56	5.6	15	0
Holcombe	8	90	11.3	19	1
Robinson	5	52	10.4	27	0
Conwell	5	40	8.0	17	0
Horne	4	32	8.0	18t	2
Hodgins	2	5	2.5	3	0
Canidate	1	4	4.0	4	0
Rams	380	5,492	14.5	85t	37
Opponents	323	4,085	12.6	62t	32

INTERCEPTIONS	No.	Yds.	Avg.	LG	TD
McCleon	8	28	3.5	23	0
Fletcher	4	33	8.3	12	0
Bly	3	44	14.7	22	0
Lyght	2	21	10.5	21	0
Lyle	1	9	9.0	9	0
Shepherd	1	0	0.0	0	0
Rams	19	135	7.1	23	0
Opponents	23	386	16.8	88t	4

PUNTING	No.	Yds.	Avg.	In 20	LG
Baker	43	1,736	40.4	13	59
Rams	44	1,736	39.5	13	59
Opponents	67	2,825	42.2	18	58

PUNT RETURNS	No.	FC	Yds.	Avg.	LG	TD
Hakim	32	17	489	15.3	86t	1
Horne	1	0	16	16.0	16	0
McCleon	1	0	0	0.0	0	0
Bly	0	1	0	—	—	0
Lyght	0	0	16	—	16	0
Rams	34	18	521	15.3	86t	1
Opponents	17	10	132	7.8	19	0

KICKOFF RETURNS	No.	Yds.	Avg.	LG	TD
Horne	57	1,379	24.2	103t	1
Blevins	9	173	19.2	26	0
Bly	9	163	18.1	36	0
Faulk	1	18	18.0	18	0
Fletcher	1	17	17.0	17	0
Hakim	1	2	2.0	2	0
Moran	1	17	17.0	17	0
Proehl	1	2	2.0	2	0
Rams	80	1,771	22.1	103t	1
Opponents	87	2,032	23.4	96t	1

FIELD GOALS	1-19	20-29	30-39	40-49	50+
Wilkins	2/2	5/5	6/6	3/3	1/1
Stoyanovich	0/0	1/1	0/1	2/2	0/1
Hall	0/0	1/1	1/1	1/2	1/1
Rams	2/2	7/7	7/8	6/7	2/3
Opponents	1/1	6/6	12/12	7/11	0/1

SACKS	No.
Wistrom	11.0
Carter	10.5
Fletcher	5.5
Little	5.0
Agnew	4.0
Jones	2.0
McCleon	2.0
Moran	2.0
Zgonina	2.0
Bly	1.0
Bush	1.0
Collins	1.0
Farr	1.0
Hobgood-Chittick	1.0
Lyght	1.0
Styles	1.0
Rams	51.0
Opponents	44.0

2001 DRAFT CHOICES

Round	Name	Pos.	College
1	Damione Lewis	DT	Miami
	Adam Archuleta	DB	Arizona State
	Ryan Pickett	DT	Ohio State
2	Tommy Polley	LB	Florida State
3	Brian Allen	LB	Florida State
4	Milton Wynn	WR	Washington State
	Brandon Manumaleuna	TE	Arizona
5	Jerametrius Butler	DB	Kansas State
6	Francis St. Paul	WR	Northern Arizona

ST. LOUIS RAMS

2001 VETERAN ROSTER

No.	Name	Pos.	Ht.	Wt.	Birthdate	NFL Exp.	College	Hometown	How Acq.	'00 Games/ Starts
99	Agnew, Ray	DT	6-3	305	12/9/67	12	North Carolina State	Winston Salem, N.C.	UFA(NYG)-'98	15/15
4	Baker, John	P	6-3	223	4/22/72	2	North Texas	Beaumont, Texas	T(Ind)-'00	15/0
83	Blevins, Darius	WR	6-2	215	4/21/76	2	Memphis	Morristown, Tenn.	FA-'01	5/0
32	Bly, Dre'	CB	5-9	190	5/22/77	3	North Carolina	Chesapeake, Va.	D2-'99	16/3
27	Bowen, Matt	S	6-1	208	11/12/76	2	Iowa	Glen Ellyn, Ill.	D6-'00	16/2
54	Brigance, O.J.	LB	6-0	236	9/29/69	6	Rice	Sugarland, Texas	UFA(Balt)-'01	16/0*
92	Brown, Jonathan	DE	6-3	270	11/28/75	2	Tennessee	Tulsa, Okla.	FA-'00	0*
80	Bruce, Isaac	WR	6-0	188	11/10/72	8	Memphis	Fort Lauderdale, Fla.	D2A-'94	16/16
23	Bush, Devin	S	6-0	210	7/3/73	7	Florida State	Miami, Fla.	UFA(Atl)-'99	13/12
24	Canidate, Trung	RB	5-11	205	3/3/77	2	Arizona	Phoenix, Ariz.	D1-'00	3/0
38	Coady, Rich	S	6-0	203	1/26/76	3	Texas A&M	Dallas, Texas	D3-'99	12/2
84	Conwell, Ernie	TE	6-1	265	8/17/72	6	Washington	Kent, Wash.	D2B-'96	16/1
36	Crutchfield, Buddy	CB	6-0	200	3/7/76	3	North Carolina Central	Raleigh, N.C.	FA-'01	0*
58	Davis, Don	LB	6-1	234	12/17/72	6	Kansas	Olathe, Kan.	UFA(TB)-'01	16/0*
28	Faulk, Marshall	RB	5-10	211	2/26/73	8	San Diego State	New Orleans, La.	T(Ind)-'99	14/14
55	Fields, Mark	LB	6-2	244	11/9/72	7	Washington	Los Angeles, Calif.	FA-'01	16/14*
59	Fletcher, London	LB	5-10	241	5/19/75	4	John Carroll	Cleveland, Ohio	FA-'98	16/15
9	Germaine, Joe	QB	6-2	220	8/11/75	3	Ohio State	Mesa, Ariz.	D4-'99	0
81	Hakim, Az-Zahir	WR	5-10	182	6/3/77	4	San Diego State	Los Angeles, Calif.	D4A-'98	16/4
20	Herring, Kim	S	6-0	200	9/10/75	5	Penn State	Solon, Ohio	UFA(Balt)-'01	16/16*
42	Hodgins, James	RB	6-1	270	4/30/77	3	San Jose State	San Jose, Calif.	FA-'99	15/2
25	Holcombe, Robert	RB	5-11	225	12/11/75	4	Illinois	Mesa, Ariz.	D2-'98	14/9
88	Holt, Torry	WR	6-0	190	6/5/76	3	North Carolina State	Greensboro, N.C.	D1-'99	16/15
94	Hyder, Gaylon	DT	6-5	317	10/18/74	3	Texas Christian	Longview, Texas	FA-'99	5/1
97	Jackson, Tyoka	DE-DT	6-2	280	11/22/71	7	Penn State	Washington, D.C.	UFA(TB)-'01	16/1*
95	Jones, Cedric	DE	6-4	270	4/30/74	6	Oklahoma	Houston, Texas	UFA(NYG)-'01	16/16*
91	Little, Leonard	LB	6-3	257	10/19/74	4	Tennessee	Asheville, N.C.	D3-'98	14/0
21	McCleon, Dexter	CB	5-10	195	10/9/73	5	Clemson	Meridian, Miss.	D2-'97	16/16
67	McCollum, Andy	G	6-4	300	6/2/70	8	Toledo	Richfield, Ohio	UFA(NO)-'99	16/16
53	Miller, Keith	LB	6-1	238	7/9/76	2	California	San Diego, Calif.	FA-'00	16/0
96	Moran, Sean	DT	6-3	280	6/5/73	6	Colorado State	Aurora, Colo.	UFA(Buff)-'00	15/3
65	Newell, Mike	C	6-4	300	7/22/76	2	Colorado State	Littleton, Colo.	FA-'00	0*
71	Noa, Kaulana	T	6-3	307	12/29/76	2	Hawaii	Honokaa, Hawaii	D4-'00	0*
61	Nütten, Tom	G	6-5	304	6/8/71	5	Western Michigan	Magog, Quebec, Canada	FA-'98	16/16
76	Pace, Orlando	T	6-7	325	11/4/75	5	Ohio State	Sandusky, Ohio	D1-'97	16/16
87	Proehl, Ricky	WR	6-0	190	3/7/68	12	Wake Forest	Hillsborough, N.J.	UFA(Chi)-'98	12/4
45	Robinson, Jeff	TE	6-4	275	2/20/70	9	Idaho	Spokane, Wash.	UFA(Den)-'97	16/2
70	St. Clair, John	T	6-4	315	7/15/77	2	Virginia	Roanoke, Va.	D3-'00	0*
22	Shepherd, Jacoby	CB	6-1	195	8/31/79	2	Oklahoma State	Lufkin, Texas	D2-'00	15/1
73	Spikes, Cameron	DT	6-2	323	11/6/76	3	Texas A&M	Bryan, Texas	D5-'99	9/0
68	Swanson, Pete	G	6-5	315	3/26/74	3	Stanford	San Bernito, Calif.	FA-'00	3/0
62	Timmerman, Adam	G	6-4	300	8/14/71	7	South Dakota State	Cherokee, Iowa	UFA(GB)-'99	16/15
50	Tucker, Ryan	C	6-5	305	6/12/75	5	Texas Christian	Midland, Texas	D4-'97	16/16
44	Walendy, Craig	RB	6-2	228	7/11/77	2	UCLA	Westlake Village, Calif.	FA-'01	12/0*
13	Warner, Kurt	QB	6-2	220	6/22/71	4	Northern Iowa	Burlington, Iowa	FA-'98	11/11
33	Watson, Justin	RB	6-0	230	1/7/75	3	San Diego State	Pasadena, Calif.	FA-'99	14/2
14	Wilkins, Jeff	K	6-2	205	4/19/72	8	Youngstown State	Austintown, Ohio	RFA(SF)-'97	11/0
35	t- Williams, Aeneas	CB	5-11	200	1/28/68	11	Southern	New Orleans, La.	T(Ariz)-'01	16/16*
98	Wistrom, Grant	DE	6-4	272	7/3/76	4	Nebraska	Webb City, Mo.	D1-'98	16/16
66	Young, Brian	DE	6-2	290	7/8/77	2	Texas-El Paso	El Paso, Texas	D5-'00	11/0
90	Zgonina, Jeff	DT	6-2	305	5/24/70	9	Purdue	Mundelein, Ill.	UFA(Ind)-'99	16/10

* Brigance and Herring played 16 games with Baltimore in '00; Brown last active with Green Bay in '98; Crutchfield last active with N.Y. Jets in '99; Davis and Jackson played 16 games with Tampa Bay; Fields played 16 games with New Orleans; Jones played 16 games with N.Y. Giants; Newell last active with Green Bay in '99; Noa missed '00 season because of injury; St. Clair was inactive for 16 games; Walendy played 12 games with N.Y. Giants; Williams played 16 games with Arizona.

t- Rams traded for Williams (Ariz).

Traded—DE Kevin Carter (16 games in '00) to Tennessee, QB Trent Green (8) to Kansas City, TE Roland Williams (16) to Oakland.

Players lost through free agency (5): CB Taje Allen (KC; 11 games in '00), WR Tony Horne (KC; 11), LB Michael Jones (Pitt; 16), CB Todd Lyght (Det; 16), WR Chris Thomas (KC; 16).

Also played with Rams in '00—DE Lionel Barnes (1 game), LB Todd Collins (14), C Steve Everitt (4), DT D'Marco Farr (10), K Jeff Hall (3), DT Nate Hobgood-Chittick (5), S Keith Lyle (16), LB Troy Pelshak (3), DE Fernando Smith (2), K Pete Stoyanovich (3), LB Lorenzo Styles (16).

COACHING STAFF

Head Coach,
Mike Martz

Pro Career: Named twenty-first head coach of the Rams on February 2, 2000. Was fifth head coach to take over a Super Bowl champion, the first since Barry Switzer was named coach of the Dallas Cowboys in 1994. Martz was the mastermind behind one of most explosive offenses in NFL history during the past two seasons, as Rams scored 540 and 526 points in 2000 and 1999, respectively, third and fourth most ever. The Rams are only franchise in NFL history to score at least 500 points in two different seasons, and they have led the NFL in total offense each of the past two seasons. The Rams set league record for consecutive games scoring at least 20 points (28), and 30 points (14), yards gained in a season (7,075), and passing yards gained in a season (5,232) while producing the last two league most valuable players (Marshall Faulk, 2000; Kurt Warner 1999). Rejoined Rams in 1999 after two seasons as quarterbacks coach of Washington Redskins, as he began NFL career with Rams in 1992 as offensive assistant. Coached tight ends, receivers, and quarterbacks through 1996 season. Career record: 10-7.

Background: Played tight end at Fresno State 1972 after transferring from the University of California-Santa Barbara, which dropped football a season earlier. Began coaching career in 1973 at Bullard High School in Fresno, California, before moving to the collegiate ranks as an assistant at San Diego Mesa C.C. (1974, 1976-77), San Jose State (1975), and Santa Ana College (1978) before returning to his alma mater in 1979. Served as assistant at University of Pacific (1980-81) and Minnesota (1982) before moving to Arizona State, where he coached quarterbacks and receivers from 1983-87, and was offensive coordinator from 1987-1991.

Personal: Born May 13, 1951 in Sioux Falls, S.D. Graduated summa cum laude at Fresno State in 1973. Lives with wife Julie in Chesterfield, Mo., and has three sons and one daughter.

ASSISTANT COACHES

Bobby April, special teams; born April 15, 1953, New Orleans, lives in St. Louis. Linebacker-defensive end Nicholls State 1972-75. No pro playing experience. College coach: Southern Mississippi 1978, Tulane 1979, Arizona 1980-86, Southern California 1987-1990. Pro coach: Atlanta Falcons 1991-93, Pittsburgh Steelers 1994-95, New Orleans Saints 1996-99, joined Rams in 2001.

Chris Clausen, strength and conditioning coordinator; born February 21, 1958, Evergreen Park, Ill., lives in St. Louis. Cornerback Indiana 1976-79. No pro playing experience. College coach: San Diego State 1987-88. Pro coach: San Diego Chargers 1989-1991, joined Rams in 1992.

Henry Ellard, offensive assistant; born July 21, 1961, Fresno, Calif., lives in St. Louis. Wide receiver Fresno State 1979-1982. Pro wide receiver-punt returner Los Angeles Rams 1983-1993, Washington Redskins 1994-97, New England Patriots 1998, Washington Redskins 1998. College coach: Fresno State 2000. Pro coach: Joined Rams in 2001.

Mike Haluchak, linebackers; born November 28, 1949, Concord, Calif., lives in St. Louis. Linebacker Southern California 1967-1970. No pro playing experience. College coach: Southern California 1976-77, Cal State-Fullerton 1978, Pacific 1979-1980, California 1981, North Carolina State 1982. Pro coach: Oakland Invaders (USFL) 1983-85, San Diego Chargers 1986-1991, Cincinnati Bengals 1992-93, Washington Redskins 1994-96, New York Giants 1997-99, joined Rams in 2000.

Jim Hanifan, offensive line; born September 21, 1933, Compton, Calif., lives in St. Charles, Mo. Tight end California 1952-54. Pro tight end Toronto Argonauts (USFL) 1955. College coach: Yuba City (Calif.) J.C. 1959-1961, Glendale (Calif.) J.C. 1964-65, Utah 1966-69, California 1970-71, San Diego State 1972. Pro coach: St. Louis Cardinals 1973-78, 1980-85 (head coach), San Diego Chargers 1979, Atlanta Falcons 1987-89, Washington Redskins 1990-96, joined Rams in 1997.

Bobby Jackson, associate head coach-offensive coordinator-running backs; born February 16, 1940, Forsyth, Ga., lives in Chesterfield, Mo. Linebacker-running back Samford 1959-1962. No pro playing experience. College coach: Florida State 1965-69, Kansas State 1970-74, Louisville 1975-76, Tennessee 1977-1982. Pro coach: Atlanta Falcons 1983-86, San Diego Chargers 1987-1991, Phoenix Cardinals 1992-93, Washington Redskins 1994-99, joined Rams in 2000.

Bill Kollar, defensive line; born November 27, 1952, Warren, Ohio, lives in St. Louis. Defensive end Montana State 1971-74. Pro defensive end Cincinnati Bengals 1974-76, Tampa Bay Buccaneers 1977-1981. College coach: Illinois 1985-87, Purdue 1988-89. Pro coach: Tampa Bay Buccaneers 1984, Atlanta Falcons 1990-2000, joined Rams in 2001.

Dana LeDuc, strength and conditioning, born March 22, 1953, Tacoma, Wash., lives in St. Charles, Mo. Attended Texas. No college or pro playing experience. College coach: Texas 1977-1992, Miami 1993-94. Pro coach: Seattle Seahawks 1995-98, joined Rams in 1999.

John Matsko, asst. head coach-offensive line; born February 2, 1951, Cleveland, lives in Lake St. Louis, Mo. Fullback Kent State 1970-73. No pro playing experience. College coach Kent State 1973, Miami (Ohio) 1974-75, 1977, North Carolina 1978-1984, Navy 1985, Arizona 1986, Southern California 1987-1991. Pro coach: Phoenix Cardinals 1992-93, New Orleans Saints 1994-96, New York Giants 1997-98, joined Rams in 1999.

Wilbert Montgomery, tight ends; born September 16, 1954, Greenville, Miss., lives in Chesterfield, Mo. Running back Abilene Christian 1973-76. Pro running back Philadelphia Eagles 1977-1984, Detroit Lions 1985-86. Pro coach: Joined Rams in 1997.

John Ramsdell, quarterbacks; born August 16, 1954, Lafayette, Ind., lives in Chesterfield, Mo. Running back Springfield (Mass.) College 1972-75. No pro playing experience. College coach: San Francisco State 1976-77, Long Beach State 1978, Pacific 1979-1982, Oregon 1983-1994. Pro coach: Joined Rams in 1995.

Al Saunders, receivers, born February 1, 1947, London, England, lives in St. Louis. Defensive back San Jose State 1966-68. No pro playing experience. College coach: Southern California 1970-71, Missouri 1972, Utah State 1973-75, California 1976-1981, Tennessee 1982. Pro coach San Diego Chargers 1983-88 (head coach 1986-88), Kansas City Chiefs 1989-1998, joined Rams in 1999.

Matt Sheldon, defensive assistant-quality control; born February 26, 1969, Berwyn, Ill., lives in O'Fallon, Mo. Cornerback Minnesota 1987-1991. No pro playing experience. College coach: Wisconsin 1997-99. Pro coach: Joined Rams in 2001.

Lovie Smith, defensive coordinator; born May 8, 1958, Gladewater, Texas, lives in St. Louis. Linebacker Tulsa 1976-79. No pro playing experience. College coach: Tulsa 1983-86, Wisconsin 1987, Arizona State 1988-1991, Kentucky 1992, Tennessee 1993-94, Ohio State 1995. Pro coach: Tampa Bay Buccaneers 1996-2000, joined Rams in 2001.

Ken Zampese, wide receivers; born July 19, 1967, Santa Maria, Calif., lives in O'Fallon, Mo. Wide receiver San Diego 1985-88. No pro playing experience. College coach: San Diego 1989, Southern California 1990-91, Northern Arizona 1992-95, Miami (Ohio) 1996-97. Pro coach: Philadelphia Eagles 1988, Green Bay Packers 1999, joined Rams in 2000.

2001 FIRST-YEAR ROSTER

Name	Pos.	Ht.	Wt.	Birthdate	College	Hometown	How Acq.
Allen, Brian	LB	6-1	238	4/1/78	Florida State	Lake City, Fla.	D3
Archuleta, Adam	S	6-0	215	11/27/77	Arizona State	Chandler, Ariz.	D1b
Ayi, Kole	LB	6-1	231	9/27/78	Massachusetts	Nashua, N.H.	FA
Bailey, Lavel	WR	5-9	182	12/15/77	Akron	Cleveland, Ohio	FA
Beck, Matt (1)	LB	6-3	241	2/16/77	California	Grass Valley, Calif.	FA
Benoit, Jermaine	DE	6-3	270	7/11/75	Central Florida	Tampa, Fla.	FA
Blackwood, Bryan	TE	6-4	265	11/7/78	Oklahoma State	Tulsa, Okla.	FA
Bulger, Marc (1)	QB	6-3	215	4/5/77	West Virginia	Pittsburgh, Pa.	FA
Butler, Jerametrius	CB	5-10	181	11/28/78	Kansas State	Dallas, Texas	D5
Cason, Aveion	RB	5-9	210	7/12/79	Illinois State	St. Petersburg, Fla.	FA
Cohen, Dustin	LB	6-3	241	12/22/76	Miami (Ohio)	Cincinnati, Ohio	FA
Cole, Giles (1)	TE	6-6	245	2/4/76	Texas A&M-Kingsville	Orange, Texas	FA
Evans, Troy	LB	6-2	239	12/3/77	Cincinnati	West Chester, Ohio	FA
Gary, Willie	S	5-10	195	11/1/78	Kentucky	Valdosta, Ga.	FA
Gideon, Sherrod	WR	5-11	183	2/21/77	Southern Mississippi	Greenwood, Miss.	FA
Lewis, Damione	DT	6-2	301	3/1/78	Miami	Sulphur Springs, Fla.	D1a
Manumaleuna, Brandon	TE	6-2	288	1/4/80	Arizona	Torrance, Calif.	D4b
Marriott, Jeff (1)	G-T	6-5	303	3/3/77	Missouri	Chilecothe, Mo.	FA
Miles, Tony	WR	5-9	181	5/16/78	Northwest Missouri State	Mart, Texas	FA
Pickett, Ryan	DT	6-2	310	10/8/79	Ohio State	Zephyrhills, Fla.	D1c
Polley, Tommy	LB	6-3	240	1/11/78	Florida State	Baltimore, Md.	D2
Rivers, David	QB	6-3	223	9/1/77	Western Carolina	Augusta, Ga.	FA
St. Paul, Francis	WR	5-10	185	4/25/79	Northern Arizona	Los Angeles, Calif.	D6
Smith, Omar	G	6-2	310	9/8/77	Kentucky	Miramar, Fla.	FA
Toliver, Antoine	WR	5-11	186	1/31/77	Bethune-Cookman	Daytona Beach, Fla.	FA
White, Anthony (1)	RB	6-0	195	5/1/77	Kentucky	Twinsburg, Ohio	FA
Wynn, Milton	WR	6-2	207	9/21/78	Washington State	Lancaster, Calif.	D4a

The term NFL Rookie is defined as a player who is in his first season of professional football and has not been on the roster of another professional football team for any regular-season or postseason games. A Rookie is designated by an "R" on NFL rosters. Players who have been active in another professional football league or players who have NFL experience, including either preseason training camp or being on an Active List or Inactive List, or on Reserve/Injured or Reserve/Physically Unable to Perform for fewer than six regular-season games, are termed NFL First-Year Players. An NFL First-Year Player is designated by a "1" on NFL rosters. Thereafter, a player is credited with an additional year of experience for each season in which he accumulates six games on the Active List or Inactive List, or on Reserve/Injured or Reserve/Physically Unable to Perform.

NOTES

SAN FRANCISCO 49ERS

National Football Conference
Western Division
Team Colors: Forty Niners Gold and Cardinal
4949 Centennial Boulevard
Santa Clara, California 95054
Telephone: (408) 562-4949

CLUB OFFICIALS

Owner: Denise DeBartolo York
Director and Owner's Representative: Dr. John York
President/CEO: Peter Harris
General Manager: Terry Donahue
COO: Les Schmidt
Vice President/Director of Football Administration: John McVay
Consultant: Bill Walsh
Pro Personnel Director: Bill McPherson
Vice President/Business Development: David Goldman
Senior Director of Communications: Rodney Knox
Director of Public Relations: Kirk Reynolds
Ticket Manager: Lynn Carrozzi
Director of Stadium Operations: Murlan (Mo) Fowell
Video Director: Robert Yanagi
Trainer: Lindsy McLean
Equipment Manager: Kevin Lartigue
Stadium: 3Com Park (built in 1958)
•**Capacity:** 69,734
San Francisco, California 94124
Playing Surface: Grass
Training Camp: University of the Pacific
Stockton, California 95211

2001 SCHEDULE

PRESEASON

Aug. 11	at San Diego	7:30
Aug. 19	**Oakland**	4:00
Aug. 25	**Seattle**	6:00
Aug. 31	at Denver	7:00

REGULAR SEASON

Sept. 9	**Atlanta**	1:15
Sept. 16	at New Orleans	12:00
Sept. 23	**St. Louis**	1:15
Oct. 1	at New York Jets (Mon.)	9:00
Oct. 7	**Carolina**	5:30
Oct. 14	at Atlanta	1:00
Oct. 21	Open Date	
Oct. 28	at Chicago	12:00
Nov. 4	**Detroit**	1:05
Nov. 11	**New Orleans**	1:15
Nov. 18	at Carolina	1:00
Nov. 25	at Indianapolis	1:00
Dec. 2	**Buffalo**	5:30
Dec. 9	at St. Louis	12:00
Dec. 16	**Miami**	1:05
Dec. 22	**Philadelphia** (Sat.)	2:00
Dec. 30	at Dallas	12:00

RECORD HOLDERS

INDIVIDUAL RECORDS—CAREER

Category	Name	Performance
Rushing (Yds.)	Joe Perry, 1950-1960, 1963	7,344
Passing (Yds.)	Joe Montana, 1979-1992	35,124
Passing (TDs)	Joe Montana, 1979-1992	244
Receiving (No.)	Jerry Rice, 1985-2000	*1,281
Receiving (Yds.)	Jerry Rice, 1985-2000	*19,247
Interceptions	Ronnie Lott, 1981-1990	51
Punting (Avg.)	Tommy Davis, 1959-1969	44.7
Punt Return (Avg.)	Dana McLemore, 1982-87	10.8
Kickoff Return (Avg.)	Abe Woodson, 1958-1964	29.4
Field Goals	Ray Wersching, 1977-1987	190
Touchdowns (Tot.)	Jerry Rice, 1985-2000	*187
Points	Jerry Rice, 1985-2000	1,130

INDIVIDUAL RECORDS—SINGLE SEASON

Category	Name	Performance
Rushing (Yds.)	Garrison Hearst, 1998	1,570
Passing (Yds.)	Jeff Garcia, 2000	4,278
Passing (TDs)	Steve Young, 1998	36
Receiving (No.)	Jerry Rice, 1995	122
Receiving (Yds.)	Jerry Rice, 1995	*1,848
Interceptions	Dave Baker, 1960	10
	Ronnie Lott, 1986	10
Punting (Avg.)	Tommy Davis, 1965	45.8
Punt Return (Avg.)	Dana McLemore, 1982	22.3
Kickoff Return (Avg.)	Joe Arenas, 1953	34.4
Field Goals	Jeff Wilkins, 1996	30
Touchdowns (Tot.)	Jerry Rice, 1987	23
Points	Jerry Rice, 1987	138

INDIVIDUAL RECORDS—SINGLE GAME

Category	Name	Performance
Rushing (Yds.)	Charlie Garner, 9-24-00	201
Passing (Yds.)	Joe Montana, 10-14-90	476
Passing (TDs)	Joe Montana, 10-14-90	6
Receiving (No.)	Terrell Owens, 12-17-00	*20
Receiving (Yds.)	Jerry Rice, 12-18-95	289
Interceptions	Dave Baker, 12-4-60	*4
Field Goals	Ray Wersching, 10-16-83	6
	Jeff Wilkins, 9-29-96	6
Touchdowns (Tot.)	Jerry Rice, 10-14-90	5
Points	Jerry Rice, 10-14-90	30

*NFL Record

COACHING HISTORY

(427-329-13)

1950-54	Lawrence (Buck) Shaw	33-25-2
1955	Norman (Red) Strader	4-8-0
1956-58	Frankie Albert	19-17-1
1959-1963	Howard (Red) Hickey*	27-27-1
1963-67	Jack Christiansen	26-38-3
1968-1975	Dick Nolan	56-56-5
1976	Monte Clark	8-6-0
1977	Ken Meyer	5-9-0
1978	Pete McCulley**	1-8-0
1978	Fred O'Connor	1-6-0
1979-1988	Bill Walsh	102-63-1
1989-1996	George Seifert	108-35-0
1997-2000	Steve Mariucci	37-31-0

*Resigned after three games in 1963
**Released after nine games in 1978

3COM PARK

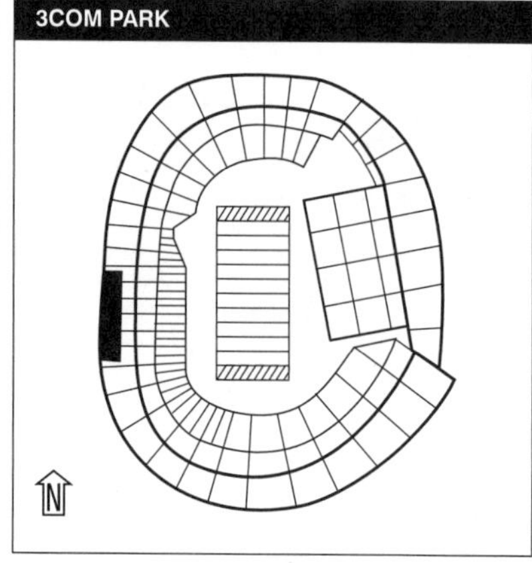

2000 TEAM RECORD

PRESEASON (1-4)

Date	Result		Opponent
7/31	L	0-20	vs. New England at Canton, Ohio
8/5	L	20-23	San Diego
8/13	W	31-10	at Kansas City
8/19	L	21-25	at Seattle
8/25	L	24-28	Denver

REGULAR SEASON (6-10)

Date	Result		Opponent	Att.
9/3	L	28-36	at Atlanta	54,626
9/10	L	22-38	Carolina	66,879
9/17	L	24-41	at St. Louis	65,945
9/24	W	41-24	at Dallas	64,127
10/1	W	27-20	Arizona	66,985
10/8	L	28-34	Oakland (OT)	68,344
10/15	L	28-31	at Green Bay	59,870
10/22	L	16-34	at Carolina	73,169
10/29	L	24-34	St. Louis	68,109
11/5	L	15-31	at New Orleans	64,900
11/12	W	21-7	Kansas City	68,002
11/19	W	16-6	Atlanta	67,447
12/3	W	45-17	at San Diego	57,255
12/10	L	27-31	New Orleans	67,892
12/17	W	17-0	Chicago	68,306
12/23	L	9-38	at Denver	76,098

(OT) Overtime

SCORE BY PERIODS

49ers	48	136	79	125	0	—	388
Opponents	64	142	108	102	6	—	422

ATTENDANCE

Home 541,947 Away 520,253 Total 1,062,200
Single-game home record, 69,014 (11/13/94)
Single-season home record, 544,228 (1999)

2000 TEAM STATISTICS

	49ers	Opp.
Total First Downs	334	347
Rushing	98	110
Passing	211	194
Penalty	25	43
Third Down: Made/Att	84/202	80/204
Third Down Pct.	41.6	39.2
Fourth Down: Made/Att	10/20	12/18
Fourth Down Pct.	50.0	66.7
Total Net Yards	6,040	5,709
Avg. Per Game	377.5	356.8
Total Plays	1,024	1,031
Avg. Per Play	5.9	5.5
Net Yards Rushing	1,801	1,794
Avg. Per Game	112.6	112.1
Total Rushes	416	435
Net Yards Passing	4,239	3,915
Avg. Per Game	264.9	244.7
Sacked/Yards Lost	25/161	38/270
Gross Yards	4,400	4,185
Att./Completions	583/366	558/320
Completion Pct.	62.8	57.3
Had Intercepted	10	13
Punts/Average	70/39.0	65/42.7
Net Punting Avg.	70/32.2	65/36.2
Penalties/Yards	134/1,135	102/857
Fumbles/Ball Lost	22/9	19/8
Touchdowns	49	49
Rushing	15	22
Passing	32	25
Returns	2	2
Avg. Time of Possession	29:38	30:22

2000 INDIVIDUAL STATISTICS

Passing	Att.	Comp.	Yds.	Pct.	TD	Int.	Tkld.	Rate
Garcia	561	355	4,278	63.3	31	10	24/155	97.6
Mirer	20	10	126	50.0	1	0	1/6	86.7
Rattay	1	1	-4	100.0	0	0	0/0	79.2
Rice	1	0	0	0.0	0	0	0/0	39.6
49ers	583	366	4,400	62.8	32	10	25/161	97.0
Opponents	558	320	4,185	57.3	25	13	38/270	86.4

SCORING	TD R	TD P	TD Rt	PAT	FG	Saf	PTS
Richey	0	0	0	43/45	15/22	0	88
Owens	0	13	0	0/0	0/0	0	80
Garner	7	3	0	0/0	0/0	0	60
Rice	0	7	0	0/0	0/0	0	42
Beasley	3	3	0	0/0	0/0	0	36
Garcia	4	0	0	0/0	0/0	0	24
Stokes	0	3	0	0/0	0/0	0	20
Jackson	1	1	0	0/0	0/0	0	14
Clark	0	2	0	0/0	0/0	0	12
Montgomery	0	0	1	0/0	0/0	0	6
Webster	0	0	1	0/0	0/0	0	6
49ers	15	32	2	43/45	15/22	0	388
Opponents	22	25	2	46/46	26/31	0	422

2-Pt. Conversions: Jackson, Owens, Stokes.
49ers 3-4, Opponents 2-2.

RUSHING	Att.	Yds.	Avg.	LG	TD
Garner	258	1,142	4.4	42	7
Garcia	72	414	5.8	33	4
Beasley	50	147	2.9	9	3
Smith	18	72	4.0	14	0
Owens	3	11	3.7	5	0
Jackson	5	6	1.2	3	1
Lewis	1	6	6.0	6	0
Stokes	1	6	6.0	6	0
Jervey	1	0	0.0	0	0
Mirer	3	0	0.0	3	0
Streets	1	0	0.0	0	0
Rattay	2	-1	-.5	0	0
Rice	1	-2	-2.0	-2	0
49ers	416	1,801	4.3	42	15
Opponents	435	1,794	4.1	31	22

RECEIVING	No.	Yds.	Avg.	LG	TD
Owens	97	1,451	15.0	69t	13
Rice	75	805	10.7	68t	7
Garner	68	647	9.5	62	3
Clark	38	342	9.0	34	2
Beasley	31	233	7.5	34	3
Stokes	30	524	17.5	53	3
Streets	19	287	15.1	39	0
Jackson	5	48	9.6	16	1
Smith	2	55	27.5	47	0
Swift	1	8	8.0	8	0
49ers	366	4,400	12.0	69t	32
Opponents	320	4,185	13.1	78t	25

INTERCEPTIONS	No.	Yds.	Avg.	LG	TD
Bronson	3	75	25.0	43	0
Montgomery	3	68	22.7	46t	1
Webster	2	78	39.0	70t	1
Peterson	2	33	16.5	31	0
Prioleau	1	13	13.0	13	0
Tubbs	1	11	11.0	11	0
Keith	1	0	0.0	0	0
49ers	13	278	21.4	70t	2
Opponents	10	94	9.4	36t	2

PUNTING	No.	Yds.	Avg.	In 20	LG
Stanley	69	2,727	39.5	15	56
49ers	70	2,727	39.0	15	56
Opponents	65	2,773	42.7	16	66

PUNT RETURNS	No.	FC	Yds.	Avg.	LG	TD
Williams	26	13	220	8.5	25	0
49ers	26	13	220	8.5	25	0
Opponents	32	20	332	10.4	47	0

KICKOFF RETURNS	No.	Yds.	Avg.	LG	TD
Williams	30	536	17.9	33	0
Lewis	9	168	18.7	26	0
Smith	9	167	18.6	28	0
Jervey	8	209	26.1	68	0
Streets	8	180	22.5	37	0
Jackson	1	9	9.0	9	0
Milem	1	13	13.0	13	0
Okeafor	1	17	17.0	17	0
Plummer	1	0	0.0	0	0
49ers	68	1,299	19.1	68	0
Opponents	63	1,358	21.6	57	0

FIELD GOALS	1-19	20-29	30-39	40-49	50+
Richey	0/0	6/7	6/8	3/6	0/1
49ers	0/0	6/7	6/8	3/6	0/1
Opponents	0/0	8/8	6/8	11/13	1/2

SACKS	No.
Young	9.5
Buckner	7.0
Peterson	4.0
Engelberger	3.0
Killings	3.0
Heard	2.0
Okeafor	2.0
Pleasant	2.0
Tubbs	2.0
Keith	1.0
Ulmer	1.0
Montgomery	0.5
Posey	0.5
Schulters	0.5
49ers	38.0
Opponents	25.0

2001 DRAFT CHOICES

Round	Name	Pos.	College
1	Andre Carter	DE	California
2	Jamie Winborn	LB	Vanderbilt
3	Kevan Barlow	RB	Pittsburgh
6	Cedrick Wilson	WR	Tennessee
	Rashad Holman	DB	Louisville
	Menson Holloway	DE	Texas-El Paso
7	Alex Lincoln	LB	Auburn
	Eric Johnson	TE	Yale

SAN FRANCISCO 49ERS

2001 VETERAN ROSTER

No.		Name	Pos.	Ht.	Wt.	Birthdate	NFL Exp.	College	Hometown	How Acq.	'00 Games/ Starts
40	†	Beasley, Fred	FB	6-0	235	9/18/74	4	Auburn	Montgomery, Ala.	D6-'98	15/15
31		Bronson, Zack	S	6-1	195	1/28/74	5	McNeese State	Jasper, Texas	FA-'97	9/7
65		Brown, Ray	G	6-5	318	12/12/62	16	Arkansas State	Marion, Ark.	UFA(Wash)-'96	16/16
90		Bryant, Junior	DE-DT	6-4	278	1/16/71	7	Notre Dame	Omaha, Neb.	FA-'93	3/3
19		Carmazzi, Giovanni	QB	6-3	224	4/14/77	2	Hofstra	Sacramento, Calif.	D3a-'00	0*
85		Clark, Greg	TE	6-4	251	4/7/72	5	Stanford	Bountiful, Utah	D3-'97	15/15
63		Deese, Derrick	T	6-3	289	5/17/70	10	Southern California	Culver City, Calif.	FA-'92	13/13
95		Engelberger, John	DE	6-4	260	10/18/76	2	Virginia Tech	Blacksburg, Va.	D2a-'00	16/13
74		Fiore, Dave	G	6-4	290	8/10/74	6	Hofstra	Waldwick, N.J.	FA-'98	16/16
5		Garcia, Jeff	QB	6-1	195	2/24/70	3	San Jose State	Gilroy, Calif.	FA-'99	16/16
78		Gragg, Scott	T	6-8	325	2/28/72	7	Montana	Silverton, Ore.	UFA(NYG)-'00	16/16
38		Heard, Ronnie	S	6-2	215	10/5/76	2	Mississippi	Baycity, Texas	FA-'00	13/3
20		Hearst, Garrison	RB	5-11	215	1/4/71	9	Georgia	Lincolnton, Ga.	UFA(Cin)-'97	0*
76	#	Hobgood-Chittick, Nate	DT	6-3	290	11/30/74	4	North Carolina	Allentown, Pa.	FA-'00	5-0
66		Hopson, Tyrone	G	6-2	305	5/28/76	3	Eastern Kentucky	Hopkinsville, Ky.	D5-'99	3/1
22		Jackson, Terry	RB	6-0	232	1/10/76	3	Florida	Gainesville, Fla.	D5-'99	15/1
86		Jennings, Brian	TE-LS	6-5	245	10/14/76	2	Arizona State	Mesa, Ariz.	D7b-'00	16/0
28		Keith, John	S	6-0	207	2/4/77	2	Furman	Newnan, Ga.	D4-'00	6-3
71		Killings, Cedric	DT	6-2	290	12/14/77	2	Carson Newman	Miami, Fla.	FA-'00	14/1
43		Lewis, Jonas	RB	5-9	210	12/27/76	2	San Diego State	San Diego, Calif.	FA-'00	10/0
60		Lynch, Ben	C	6-4	295	11/18/72	3	California	Santa Rosa, Calif.	FA-'99	9/0
92		McGrew, Reggie	DT	6-1	301	12/16/76	3	Florida	Mayo, Fla.	D1-'99	10/0
93		Milem, John	DE	6-7	290	6/9/75	2	Lenoir-Rhyne	Concord, N.C.	D5b-'00	16/0
3		Mirer, Rick	QB	6-3	215	3/19/70	9	Notre Dame	Goshen, Ind.	UFA(NYJ)-'00	1/0
41		Moronkola, Dee	CB	5-9	195	7/1/77	2	Washington State	Richmond, Calif.	FA-'01	0*
62		Newberry, Jeremy	C-G	6-5	315	3/23/76	4	California	Antioch, Calif.	D2-'98	16/16
91		Okeafor, Chike	DE	6-4	248	3/27/76	3	Purdue	West Lafayette, Ind.	D3-'99	15/0
81		Owens, Terrell	WR	6-3	217	12/7/73	6	Tennessee-Chattanooga	Alexander City, Ala.	D3-'96	14/13
26		Parker, Anthony	CB	6-1	200	12/4/75	3	Weber State	Denver, Colo.	D4-'99	16/0
98		Peterson, Julian	LB	6-3	235	7/28/78	2	Michigan State	Hillcrest Heights, Md.	D1a-'00	13/7
29		Plummer, Ahmed	CB	5-11	191	3/26/76	2	Ohio State	Wyoming, Ohio	D1b-'00	16/14
96	#	Posey, Jeff	LB	6-4	240	8/14/75	4	Southern Mississippi	Bassfield, Miss.	FA-'98	16/9
23		Prioleau, Pierson	S	5-10	191	8/6/77	3	Virginia Tech	Charleston, S.C.	D4-'99	14/6
13		Rattay, Tim	QB	6-0	215	3/15/77	2	Louisiana Tech	Elyria, Ohio	D7a-'00	1/0
30	†	Schulters, Lance	S	6-2	195	5/27/75	4	Hofstra	Brooklyn, N.Y.	D4-'98	12/12
50		Smith, Derek	LB	6-2	245	1/18/75	5	Arizona State	American Fork, Utah	UFA(Wash)-'01	16/14*
27		Smith, Paul	RB	5-11	234	1/31/78	2	Texas-El Paso	El Paso, Texas	D5a-'00	10/0
4		Stanley, Chad	P	6-3	205	1/29/76	3	Stephen F. Austin	Pittsburg, Texas	FA-'99	16/0
83		Stokes, J.J.	WR	6-4	217	10/6/72	7	UCLA	San Diego, Calif.	D1-'95	16/3
89		Streets, Tai	WR	6-1	193	4/20/77	3	Michigan	Matteson, Ill.	D6-'99	15/1
88		Swift, Justin	TE	6-3	265	8/14/75	2	Kansas State	Overland Park, Kan.	FA-'99	16/1
53		Ulbrich, Jeff	LB	6-0	249	2/17/77	2	Hawaii	San Jose, Calif.	D3b-'00	4/0
36		Webster, Jason	CB	5-9	180	9/8/77	2	Texas A&M	Houston, Texas	D2b-'00	16/10
77		Willig, Matt	T	6-8	315	1/21/69	10	Southern California	Santa Fe Springs, Calif.	UFA(StL)-'00	16/3
97		Young, Bryant	DT	6-3	291	1/27/72	8	Notre Dame	Chicago Heights, Ill.	D1-'94	15/15

* Carmazzi was inactive for 16 games; Hearst missed '00 season because of injury; Moronkola last active with Jacksonville in '99; D. Smith played 16 games with Washington in '00.

† Restricted free agents; subject to developments.

Unrestricted free agents; subject to developments.

Retired—Chris Dalman, 8-year center, last active with San Francisco in '99.

Players lost through free agency (7): DT Brentson Buckner (Car; 16 games in '00), RB Charlie Garner (Oak; 16), LB Jason Kyle (Car; 2), CB Monty Montgomery (Phil; 15), DE Anthony Pleasant (NE; 16), K Wade Richey (SD; 16), LB Artie Ulmer (Atl; 12).

Also played with 49ers in '00—T Dan Dercher (2 games), RB Travis Jervey (8), T Dwayne Ledford (1), S Jason Moore (5), LB Ken Norton, Jr. (16), G Phil Ostrowski (13), WR Jerry Rice (16), LB Edward Thomas (4), LB Winfred Tubbs (14), WR-KR Kevin Williams (16).

COACHING STAFF

Head Coach,
Steve Mariucci

Pro Career: Became the thirteenth head coach in 49ers history on January 16, 1997. One of thirteen head coaches since the NFL-AFL merger in 1970 to lead his team to a division title in his first season. He established an NFL mark for consecutive wins by a rookie head coach with an 11-game winning streak. He served as quarterbacks coach for the Green Bay Packers (1992-95). His first pro position was in 1985 when he was receivers coach for the USFL's Orlando Renegades. Later that fall, he had a brief stint with the Los Angeles Rams as quality control coach. Career record: 37-31.

Background: Three-time All-America quarterback at Northern Michigan. Began his coaching career at his alma mater (1978-79), and moved to Cal State-Fullerton (1980-82), and Louisville (1983-84). Joined the Southern California staff in 1986, then moved to California in 1987. In 1990-91, he served as the Bears' offensive coordinator. Became the head coach at California in 1996 and guided the squad to a 5-0 start and a berth in the Aloha Bowl.

Personal: Born November 4, 1955, in Iron Mountain, Mich. He and his wife, Gayle, have four children—Tyler, Adam, Stephen, and Brielle—and live in Saratoga, Calif.

ASSISTANT COACHES

Jerry Attaway, physical development; born January 3, 1946, Susanville, Calif., lives in San Jose, Calif. Defensive back Yuba (Calif.) J.C. 1964-65, UC Davis 1967. No pro playing experience. College coach: UC Davis 1970-71, Idaho 1972-74, Utah State 1975-77, Southern California 1978-1982. Pro coach: Joined 49ers in 1983.

Tom Batta, tight ends; born October 6, 1942, in Youngstown, Ohio, lives in Livermore, Calif. Offensive-defensive lineman Kent State 1961-63. No pro playing experience. College coach: Akron 1973, Colorado 1974-78, Kansas 1979-1982, North Carolina State 1983. Pro coach: Minnesota Vikings 1984-1993, Indianapolis Colts 1994-97, Pittsburgh Steelers 1998, joined 49ers in 1999.

Christopher Beake, defensive assistant; born September 10, 1972, Highlands Ranch, Colo., lives in Mountain View, Calif. Quarterback Air Force 1991-92. No pro playing experience. College coach: Air Force 1994-95. Pro coach: Joined 49ers in 1999.

Dwaine Board, defensive line; born November 29, 1956, Rocky Mount, Va., lives in Redwood City, Calif. Defensive lineman North Carolina A&T 1974-77. Pro defensive lineman San Francisco 49ers 1979-1987, New Orleans Saints 1988. Pro coach: Joined 49ers in 1991.

Bruce DeHaven, special teams; born September 6, 1948, Trousdale, Kan., lives in Livermore, Calif. Attended Southwestern (Kan.) College. No college or pro playing experience. College coach: Kansas 1979-1981, New Mexico State 1982. Pro coach: New Jersey Generals (USFL) 1983, Pittsburgh Maulers (USFL) 1984, Orlando Renegades (USFL) 1985, Buffalo Bills 1987-1999, joined 49ers in 2000.

Terrell Jones, strength development; born April 25, 1961, Chicago, lives in San Jose, Calif. Attended San Jose State. No college or pro playing experience. College coach: San Jose (Calif.) C.C. 1998-2000. Pro coach: Joined 49ers in 2000.

Greg Knapp, offensive coordinator; born March 5, 1963, Long Beach, Calif., lives in Los Gatos, Calif. Quarterback Cal State-Sacramento 1982-85. No pro playing experience. College coach: Cal State-Sacramento 1986-1994. Pro coach: Joined 49ers in 1995.

Brett Maxie, asst. secondary; born January 13, 1962, Dallas, lives in Santa Clara, Calif. Safety Texas Southern 1980-84. Pro safety New Orleans Saints 1985-1993, Atlanta Falcons 1994, Carolina Panthers 1995-96, San Francisco 49ers 1997. Pro coach: Carolina Panthers 1998, joined 49ers in 1999.

Jim Mora, defensive coordinator; born November 19, 1961, Los Angeles, lives in Los Gatos, Calif. Defensive back Washington 1980-83. No pro playing experience. College coach: Washington 1984. Pro coach: San Diego Chargers 1985-1991, New Orleans Saints 1992-96, joined 49ers in 1997.

Pat Morris, offensive line; born April 7, 1954, Cleveland, lives in Mountain View, Calif. Offensive lineman Southern California 1972-75. No pro playing experience. College coach: Southern California 1976-77, 1983-86, Northern Arizona 1978, Minnesota 1979-1982, Michigan State 1987-1994, Stanford 1995-96. Pro coach: Joined 49ers in 1997.

Greg Olson, quarterbacks; born March 1, 1963, Richland, Wash., lives in Santa Clara, Calif. Quarterback Central Washington 1983-86. No pro playing experience. College coach: Washington State 1987-89, Central Washington 1990-93, Idaho 1994-96, Purdue 1997-2000. Pro coach: Joined 49ers in 2001.

Dan Quinn, defensive quality control; born September 11, 1970 lives in Santa Clara, Calif. Defensive lineman Salisbury State 1990-93. No pro playing experience. College coach: William & Mary 1994, Virginia Military Institute 1995, Hofstra 1997-2000. Pro coach: Joined 49ers in 2001.

Tom Rathman, running backs; born October 7, 1962, Grand Island, Neb., lives in Redwood City, Calif. Running back Nebraska 1983-85. Pro running back San Francisco 49ers 1986-1993, Los Angeles Raiders 1994. College coach: Menlo College 1996. Pro coach: Joined 49ers in 1997.

Richard Smith, linebackers; born October 17, 1955, Los Angeles, lives in Pleasanton, Calif. Offensive lineman Rio Hondo (Calif.) J.C. 1975-76, Fresno State 1977-78. No pro playing experience. College coach: Rio Hondo J.C. 1979-1980, Cal State-Fullerton 1981-83, California 1984-86, Arizona 1987. Pro coach: Houston Oilers 1988-1992, Denver Broncos 1993-96, joined 49ers in 1997.

George Stewart, wide receivers; born December 29, 1958, Little Rock, Ark., lives in Santa Clara, Calif. Guard Arkansas 1977-1980. No pro playing experience. College coach: Minnesota 1984-85, Notre Dame 1986-88. Pro coach: Pittsburgh Steelers 1989-1991, Tampa Bay Buccaneers 1992-95, joined 49ers in 1996.

Andy Sugarman, offensive assistant; born May 23, 1972, San Francisco, lives in Mountain View, Calif. Attended California. No college or pro playing experience. College coach: California 1990-97. Pro coach: Joined 49ers in 1998.

Jason Tarver, offensive quality control; born August 28, 1974, Stanford, Calif., lives in Santa Clara, Calif. Linebacker West Valley College 1994-95. No pro playing experience. College coach: West Valley College 1996-97, UCLA 1998-2000. Pro coach: Joined 49ers in 2001.

2001 FIRST-YEAR ROSTER

Name	Pos.	Ht.	Wt.	Birthdate	College	Hometown	How Acq.
Alexander, Hilton	WR	6-1	183	6/15/78	Morris Brown	Atlanta, Ga.	FA
Allen, David	RB-KR	5-9	195	2/9/78	Kansas State	Euless, Texas	FA
Allen, Mikki (1)	S	5-11	193	11/15/77	Tennessee	Homestead, Fla.	FA
Ashworth, Tom	T	6-6	290	10/10/77	Colorado	Englewood, Colo.	FA
Banks, Tommy	FB	6-0	270	5/4/78	Louisiana State	West Monroe, La.	FA
Barlow, Kevan	RB	6-1	238	1/7/79	Pittsburgh	Pittsburgh, Pa.	D3
Blades, Al	S	6-2	205	3/19/77	Miami	Plantation, Fla.	FA
Call, Wes	T	6-7	320	10/17/78	Washington	Petaluma, Calif.	FA
Carter, Andre	DE	6-4	265	5/12/79	California	San Jose, Calif.	D1
Carter, Dwight (1)	WR	5-9	185	9/19/77	Hawaii	Los Angeles, Calif.	FA-'00
Casher, Larry	CB	5-10	180	9/2/78	Auburn	Prichard, Ala.	FA
Chatman, Antonio	WR	5-8	186	2/12/79	Cincinnati	Los Angeles, Calif.	FA
Cheek, Stephen	P	6-4	200	4/18/77	Humboldt State	Westfield, N.J.	FA
Cortez, Jose (1)	K	5-11	204	5/27/75	Oregon State	Van Nuys, Calif.	FA
Costa, Dave	G	6-5	305	9/8/78	Wisconsin	Ellwood City, Pa.	FA
Davis, Larry	WR	5-9	185	11/5/77	New Mexico	Houston, Texas	FA
Deckard, Cecil	CB	6-1	205	4/22/78	Southwestern Oklahoma State	Palo Alto, Calif.	FA
Elam, Shane	LB	6-1	240	11/6/77	Mississippi	Covington, Tenn.	FA
Farris, James	WR	5-11	200	4/13/78	Montana	Lewiston, Idaho	FA
Fisher, Stephen (1)	CB	5-10	185	5/20/76	North Carolina	New Bern, Calif.	FA
Godsey, Brandon	CB	6-0	200	9/10/78	Miami (Ohio)	Springfield, Ohio	FA
Goodspeed, Dan (1)	T	6-6	300	5/20/77	Kent State	Cleveland, Ohio	FA
Greer, Daniel (1)	DT	6-2	290	3/2/76	Arizona	Salinas, Calif.	FA
Hay, Shawn	DE	6-4	250	8/8/78	South Florida	Miami, Fla.	FA
Heard, Grant	WR	6-3	200	3/4/78	Mississippi	Clute, Texas	FA
Hill, Marcus (1)	S	6-3	217	6/1/76	Angelo State	Ventura, Calif.	FA
Holloway, Menson	DE	6-2	284	7/12/78	Texas-El Paso	El Paso, Texas	D6c
Holman, Rashad	CB	5-11	191	1/17/78	Louisville	Louisville, Ky.	D6b
Isom, Jasen	FB	5-11	240	1/7/77	Western Illinois	Long Island, N.Y.	FA
Jackson, Steve	WR	5-11	185	6/27/77	Hofstra	Berwyn, Pa.	FA
Johnson, Eric	TE	6-3	256	9/15/79	Yale	Needham, Mass.	D7b
Johnson, Neil	TE	6-4	250	12/18/77	Tennessee	Nashville, Tenn.	FA
Jordan, James	WR	6-1	220	6/11/78	Louisiana Tech	Metairie, La.	FA
Lincoln, Alex	LB	6-0	251	11/17/77	Auburn	Mobile, Ala.	D7a
Mandina, Paul	DT	6-4	300	11/13/77	Indiana	Rochester, N.Y.	FA
McCullough, Saladin (1)	RB	5-9	195	7/17/75	Oregon	Pasadena, Calif.	FA
McCurley, Jeff	C	6-5	290	6/25/79	Pittsburgh	Bessemer, Pa.	FA
Mitchell, Cordell (1)	RB	6-0	208	2/10/77	Penn State	Syracuse, N.Y.	FA
Nofoaiga, Chris	LB	5-10	220	6/28/77	Idaho	Tacoma, Wash.	FA
Ockimey, Ron	S	6-2	208	9/3/78	San Jose State	Philadelphia, Pa.	FA
Rheem, Jamie	K	6-2	210	9/12/77	Kansas State	Wichita, Kan.	FA
Rice, Al (1)	LB	6-2	215	11/6/77	Mississippi	Hattiesburg, Miss.	FA
Schlect, John	DT	6-0	299	5/23/78	Minnesota	St. Paul, Minn.	FA
Smith, Brian	S	6-1	200	7/15/79	Massachusetts	Wilmington, Del.	FA
Steele, Ben	TE	6-5	245	5/27/78	Mesa State	Palisade, Colo.	FA
Stephenson, Milford	T	6-2	300	2/8/77	Kansas State	Houston, Texas	FA
Stewart, Quincy	LB	6-1	227	3/27/78	Louisiana Tech	Tyler, Texas	FA
Stokes, Keith	WR-KR	5-7	177	12/10/78	East Carolina	Dothan, Ala.	FA
Swanson, Brennen (1)	LB	6-2	245	10/18/76	Cal State-Northridge	Santa Barbara, Calif.	FA
Thatcher, J.T.	S	6-0	220	7/12/78	Oklahoma	Norman, Okla.	FA
Tuthill, James (1)	K	6-2	250	3/25/76	Cal Poly	Upland, Calif.	FA
Wiggins, Bruce	C	6-3	285	10/13/77	Arizona	Houston, Texas	FA
Wilson, Cedrick	WR-KR	5-10	179	12/17/78	Tennessee	Memphis, Tenn.	D6a
Winborn, Jamie	LB	5-11	242	5/14/79	Vanderbilt	Wetumpka, Ala.	D2

The term NFL Rookie is defined as a player who is in his first season of professional football and has not been on the roster of another professional football team for any regular-season or postseason games. A Rookie is designated by an "R" on NFL rosters. Players who have been active in another professional football league or players who have NFL experience, including either preseason training camp or being on an Active List or Inactive List, or on Reserve/Injured or Reserve/Physically Unable to Perform for fewer than six regular-season games, are termed NFL First-Year Players. An NFL First-Year Player is designated by a "1" on NFL rosters. Thereafter, a player is credited with an additional year of experience for each season in which he accumulates six games on the Active List or Inactive List, or on Reserve/Injured or Reserve/Physically Unable to Perform.

TAMPA BAY BUCCANEERS

National Football Conference
Central Division
Team Colors: Buccaneer Red, Pewter, Black, and Orange
One Buccaneer Place
Tampa, Florida 33607
Telephone: (813) 870-2700

CLUB OFFICIALS

Owner/President: Malcolm Glazer
Executive Vice President: Bryan Glazer
Executive Vice President: Joel Glazer
Executive Vice President: Edward Glazer
General Manager: Rich McKay
Chief Financial Officer: Tom Alas
Director of Player Personnel: Jerry Angelo
Director of College Scouting: Tim Ruskell
Director of Football Administration: John Idzik
Executive Director of the Glazer Family Foundation: Veronica (Roni) Costello
Director of Communications: Reggie Roberts
Director of Game Day and Video Production: Chris Kartzmark
Director of Human Resources/Sales: Gene Magrini
Director of Marketing: George Woods
Director of Community Relations: Stephanie Waller
Director of Player Development: Cedric Saunders
Director of Special Events: Maury Wilks
Director of Security: Andre Trescastro
Director of Ticketing and Luxury Suite Relations: Mike Newquist
College Scouts: Joe DiMarzo, Jr., Frank Dorazio, Dennis Hickey, Ruston Webster, Mike Yowarsky
Director of Pro Personnel: Mark Dominik
Director of Legal Affairs: Nathan Whitaker
Pro/College Scout: Lloyd Richards, Jr.
Internet Manager: Scott Smith
Communications Manager: Jeff Kamis
Trainer: Todd Toriscelli
Director of Rehabilitation: Jim Whalen
Equipment Manager: Darin Kerns
Assistant Equipment Manager: Mark Meschede
Video Director: Dave Levy
Assistant Video Director: Pat Brazil
Stadium: Raymond James Stadium (built in 1998) •**Capacity:** 65,655 Tampa, Florida 33607
Playing Surface: Grass
Training Camp: University of Tampa Tampa, Florida 33606

2001 SCHEDULE

PRESEASON

Aug. 13	**Miami**	8:00
Aug. 18	at Cleveland	8:00
Aug. 25	**New England**	7:30
Aug. 31	at Atlanta	7:30

REGULAR SEASON

Sept. 9	at Dallas	12:00
Sept. 16	**Philadelphia**	1:00
Sept. 23	Open Date	
Sept. 30	at Minnesota	12:00
Oct. 7	**Green Bay**	4:15
Oct. 14	at Tennessee	12:00
Oct. 21	**Pittsburgh**	1:00
Oct. 28	**Minnesota**	1:00
Nov. 4	at Green Bay	12:00
Nov. 11	at Detroit	1:00
Nov. 18	**Chicago**	1:00
Nov. 26	at St. Louis (Mon.)	8:00
Dec. 2	at Cincinnati	1:00
Dec. 9	**Detroit**	1:00
Dec. 16	at Chicago	12:00
Dec. 23	**New Orleans**	1:00
Dec. 29	**Baltimore** (Sat.)	9:00

RECORD HOLDERS

INDIVIDUAL RECORDS—CAREER

Category	Name	Performance
Rushing (Yds.)	James Wilder, 1981-89	5,957
Passing (Yds.)	Vinny Testaverde, 1987-1992	14,820
Passing (TDs)	Vinny Testaverde, 1987-1992	77
Receiving (No.)	James Wilder, 1981-89	430
Receiving (Yds.)	Mark Carrier, 1987-1992	5,018
Interceptions	Cedric Brown, 1976-1984	29
Punting (Avg.)	Tommy Barnhardt, 1996-98	42.6
Punt Return (Avg.)	Jacquez Green, 1998-2000	12.0
Kickoff Return (Avg.)	Reidel Anthony, 1997-2000	23.5
Field Goals	Michael Husted, 1993-98	117
Touchdowns (Tot.)	James Wilder, 1981-89	46
Points	Michael Husted, 1993-98	502

INDIVIDUAL RECORDS—SINGLE SEASON

Category	Name	Performance
Rushing (Yds.)	James Wilder, 1984	1,544
Passing (Yds.)	Doug Williams, 1981	3,563
Passing (TDs)	Trent Dilfer, 1997, 1998	21
Receiving (No.)	Mark Carrier, 1989	86
Receiving (Yds.)	Mark Carrier, 1989	1,422
Interceptions	Cedric Brown, 1981	9
Punting (Avg.)	Mark Royals, 1999	43.1
Punt Return (Avg.)	Karl Williams, 1996	21.1
Kickoff Return (Avg.)	Karl Williams, 1996	27.4
Field Goals	Martin Gramatica, 2000	28
Touchdowns (Tot.)	James Wilder, 1984	13
Points	Martin Gramatica, 2000	126

INDIVIDUAL RECORDS—SINGLE GAME

Category	Name	Performance
Rushing (Yds.)	James Wilder, 11-6-83	219
Passing (Yds.)	Doug Williams, 11-16-80	486
Passing (TDs)	Steve DeBerg, 9-13-87	5
Receiving (No.)	James Wilder, 9-15-85	13
Receiving (Yds.)	Mark Carrier, 12-6-87	212
Interceptions	Many times	2
	Last time by Donnie Abraham, 11-5-00	
Field Goals	Many times	4
	Last time by Martin Gramatica, 10-19-00	
Touchdowns (Tot.)	Jimmie Giles, 10-20-85	4
Points	Jimmie Giles, 10-20-85	24

COACHING HISTORY

(142-254-1)

1976-1984	John McKay	45-91-1
1985-86	Leeman Bennett	4-28-0
1987-1990	Ray Perkins*	19-41-0
1990-91	Richard Williamson	4-15-0
1992-95	Sam Wyche	23-41-0
1996-2000	Tony Dungy	47-38-0

*Released after 13 games in 1990

RAYMOND JAMES STADIUM

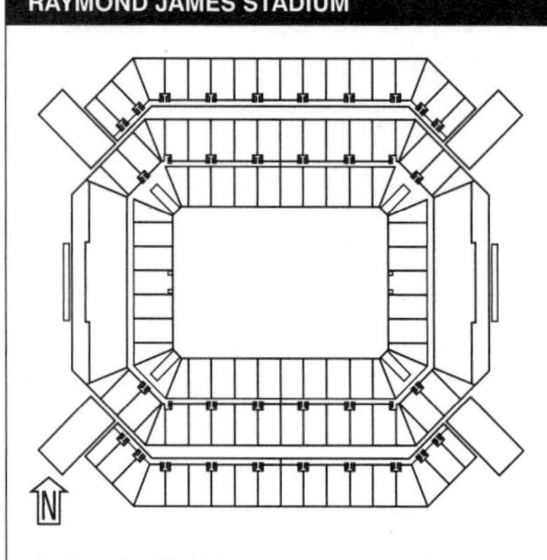

2000 TEAM RECORD

PRESEASON (3-1)

Date	Result		Opponent
8/4	W	13-12	Washington
8/10	L	13-15	at Miami
8/20	W	31-21	at New England
8/25	W	37-14	Kansas City

REGULAR SEASON (10-6)

Date	Result		Opponent	Att.
9/3	W	21-16	at New England	60,292
9/10	W	41-0	Chicago	65,569
9/17	W	31-10	at Detroit	76,928
9/24	L	17-21	New York Jets	65,619
10/1	L	17-20	at Washington (OT)	83,532
10/9	L	23-30	at Minnesota	64,162
10/19	L	14-28	Detroit	65,557
10/29	W	41-13	Minnesota	65,589
11/5	W	27-14	at Atlanta	70,097
11/12	W	20-15	Green Bay	65,621
11/19	L	10-13	at Chicago	66,944
11/26	W	31-17	Buffalo	65,546
12/3	W	27-7	Dallas	65,621
12/10	W	16-13	at Miami	74,307
12/18	W	38-35	St. Louis	65,653
12/24	L	14-17	at Green Bay (OT)	59,692

(OT) Overtime

POSTSEASON (0-1)

Date	Result		Opponent	Att.
12/31	L	3-21	at Philadelphia	65,813

SCORE BY PERIODS

Buccaneers	88	131	60	109	0	—	388
Opponents	39	79	53	92	6	—	269

ATTENDANCE

Home 512,749 Away 550,817 Total 1,063,566
Single-game home record, 73,523 (12/7/97)
Single-season home record, 545,980 (1979)

2000 TEAM STATISTICS

	Buccaneers	Opp.
Total First Downs	275	283
Rushing	111	84
Passing	144	180
Penalty	20	19
Third Down: Made/Att	66/198	74/225
Third Down Pct.	33.3	32.9
Fourth Down: Made/Att	5/12	12/20
Fourth Down Pct.	41.7	60.0
Total Net Yards	4,649	4,800
Avg. Per Game	290.6	300.0
Total Plays	961	1,047
Avg. Per Play	4.8	4.6
Net Yards Rushing	2,066	1,648
Avg. Per Game	129.1	103.0
Total Rushes	490	398
Net Yards Passing	2,583	3,152
Avg. Per Game	161.4	197.0
Sacked/Yards Lost	38/241	55/332
Gross Yards	2,824	3,484
Att./Completions	433/237	594/339
Completion Pct.	54.7	57.1
Had Intercepted	13	25
Punts/Average	85/41.8	89/40.0
Net Punting Avg.	85/35.1	89/33.5
Penalties/Yards	82/702	95/688
Fumbles/Ball Lost	16/11	26/16
Touchdowns	43	29
Rushing	18	12
Passing	18	15
Returns	7	2
Avg. Time of Possession	29:38	30:22

2000 INDIVIDUAL STATISTICS

Passing	Att.	Comp.	Yds.	Pct.	TD	Int.	Tkld.	Rate
King	428	233	2,769	54.4	18	13	37/240	75.8
Zeier	3	3	19	100.0	0	0	0/0	93.1
Alstott	1	0	0	0.0	0	0	0/0	39.6
Royals	1	1	36	100.0	0	0	0/0	118.8
Hamilton	0	0	0	—	0	0	1/1	—
Buccaneers	433	237	2,824	54.7	18	13	38/241	76.2
Opponents	594	339	3,484	57.1	15	25	55/332	65.0

SCORING	TD R	TD P	TD Rt	PAT	FG	Saf	PTS
Gramatica	0	0	0	42/42	28/34	0	126
Dunn	8	1	0	0/0	0/0	0	54
Johnson	0	8	0	0/0	0/0	0	48
King	5	0	0	0/0	0/0	0	32
Alstott	5	0	0	0/0	0/0	0	30
Anthony	0	4	0	0/0	0/0	0	24
Moore	0	3	0	0/0	0/0	0	18
Barber	0	0	2	0/0	0/0	0	12
Abraham	0	0	1	0/0	0/0	0	6
Brooks	0	0	1	0/0	0/0	0	6
Duncan	0	0	1	0/0	0/0	0	6
Green	0	1	0	0/0	0/0	0	6
Kelly	0	0	1	0/0	0/0	0	6
McDaniel	0	1	0	0/0	0/0	0	6
Williams	0	0	1	0/0	0/0	0	6
Buccaneers	18	18	7	42/42	28/34	1	388
Opponents	12	15	2	25/25	22/32	0	269

2-Pt. Conversions: King.
Buccaneers 1-1, Opponents 2-4.

RUSHING	Att.	Yds.	Avg.	LG	TD
Dunn	248	1,133	4.6	70t	8
Alstott	131	465	3.5	20t	5
King	73	353	4.8	19	5
Abdullah	16	70	4.4	19	0
Stecker	12	31	2.6	14	0
Green	5	13	2.6	6	0
Johnson	2	5	2.5	3	0
Hamilton	1	-2	-2.0	-2	0
Zeier	2	-2	-1.0	-1	0
Buccaneers	490	2,066	4.2	70t	18
Opponents	398	1,648	4.1	50t	12

RECEIVING	No.	Yds.	Avg.	LG	TD
Johnson	71	874	12.3	38	8
Green	51	773	15.2	75	1
Dunn	44	422	9.6	45	1
Moore	29	288	9.9	28	3
Anthony	15	232	15.5	46t	4
Alstott	13	93	7.2	21	0
Hape	6	39	6.5	13	0
Williams	2	35	17.5	27	0
Abdullah	2	14	7.0	11	0
Robinson	1	36	36.0	36	0
Stecker	1	15	15.0	15	0
McDaniel	1	2	2.0	2t	1
Yoder	1	1	1.0	1	0
Buccaneers	237	2,824	11.9	75	18
Opponents	339	3,484	10.3	72t	15

INTERCEPTIONS	No.	Yds.	Avg.	LG	TD
Abraham	7	82	11.7	23	0
Robinson	6	1	0.2	1	0
Duncan	4	55	13.8	31t	1
Lynch	3	43	14.3	36	0
Barber	2	46	23.0	37t	1
Brooks	1	34	34.0	34t	1
Kelly	1	9	9.0	9t	1
Quarles	1	5	5.0	5	0
Buccaneers	25	275	11.0	37t	4
Opponents	13	155	11.9	60	1

PUNTING	No.	Yds.	Avg.	In 20	LG
Royals	85	3,551	41.8	17	63
Buccaneers	85	3,551	41.8	17	63
Opponents	89	3,556	40.0	24	64

PUNT RETURNS	No.	FC	Yds.	Avg.	LG	TD
Williams	31	18	286	9.2	73t	1
Hastings	5	1	50	10.0	16	0
Green	2	0	1	0.5	1	0
Yoder	1	0	0	0.0	0	0
Buccaneers	39	19	337	8.6	73t	1
Opponents	41	24	408	10.0	66t	1

KICKOFF RETURNS	No.	Yds.	Avg.	LG	TD
Stecker	29	663	22.9	48	0
Williams	19	453	23.8	41	0
Anthony	3	88	29.3	45	0
Murphy	2	24	12.0	19	0
Abdullah	1	16	16.0	16	0
Green	1	11	11.0	11	0
Buccaneers	55	1,255	22.8	48	0
Opponents	74	1,688	22.8	70	0

FIELD GOALS	1-19	20-29	30-39	40-49	50+
Gramatica	0/0	8/8	8/10	7/9	5/7
Buccaneers	0/0	8/8	8/10	7/9	5/7
Opponents	1/1	6/6	8/12	6/9	1/4

SACKS	No.
Sapp	16.5
Jones	13.0
McFarland	6.5
Barber	5.5
Ahanotu	3.5
Cannida	2.0
T. Jackson	2.0
Quarles	2.0
White	2.0
Brooks	1.0
Lynch	1.0
Buccaneers	55.0
Opponents	38.0

2001 DRAFT CHOICES

Round	Name	Pos.	College
1	Kenyatta Walker	T	Florida
3	Dwight Smith	CB	Akron
4	John Howell	S	Colorado State
5	Russ Hochstein	G	Nebraska
6	Jameel Cook	RB	Illinois
	Ellis Wyms	DT	Mississippi State
7	Dauntae' Finger	TE	North Carolina
	Than Merrill	S	Yale
	Joe Tafoya	DE	Arizona

TAMPA BAY BUCCANEERS

2001 VETERAN ROSTER

No.	Name	Pos.	Ht.	Wt.	Birthdate	NFL Exp.	College	Hometown	How Acq.	'00 Games/ Starts
27	Abdullah, Rabih	RB	6-1	227	4/27/75	4	Lehigh	Roselle, N.J.	FA-'98	12/0
21	Abraham, Donnie	CB	5-10	192	10/8/73	6	East Tennessee State	Orangeburg, S.C.	D3-'96	16/16
40	Alstott, Mike	FB	6-1	248	12/21/73	6	Purdue	Joliet, Ill.	D2-'96	13/13
85	Anthony, Reidel	WR	5-11	180	10/20/76	5	Florida	Glades Central, Fla.	D1b-'97	16/1
20	Barber, Ronde	CB	5-10	184	4/7/75	5	Virginia	Roanoke, Va.	D3b-'97	16/16
55	Brooks, Derrick	LB	6-0	235	4/18/73	7	Florida State	Pensacola, Fla.	D1b-'95	16/16
98	Cannida, James	DT	6-2	291	1/3/75	4	Nevada	Fremont, Calif.	D6a-'98	16/0
62	Christy, Jeff	C	6-2	285	2/3/69	9	Pittsburgh	Freeport, Pa.	UFA(Minn)-'00	16/16
60	Coleman, Cosey	G	6-4	322	10/27/78	2	Tennessee	Clarkston, Ga.	D2-'00	8/0
76	Curry, DeMarcus	T	6-5	332	4/30/75	2	Auburn	Columbus, Ga.	FA-'99	0*
17	Daniels, Chris	WR	6-3	219	3/30/77	2	Purdue	Clearwater, Fla.	FA-'00	0*
65	# Dogins, Kevin	C-G	6-1	301	12/7/72	5	Texas A&M-Kingsville	Eagle Lake, Texas	FA-'96	0*
59	Duncan, Jamie	LB	6-0	242	7/20/75	4	Vanderbilt	Wilmington, Del.	D3-'98	15/15
28	Dunn, Warrick	RB	5-8	180	1/5/75	5	Florida State	Baton Rouge, La.	D1a-'97	16/14
46	Gibson, David	S	6-1	210	11/5/77	2	Southern California	Santa Ana, Calif.	D6-'00	9/0
50	Gooch, Jeff	LB	5-11	225	10/31/74	6	Austin Peay	Nashville, Tenn.	FA-'96	16/0
7	Gramatica, Martin	K	5-8	170	11/27/75	3	Kansas State	LaBelle, Fla.	D3-'99	16/0
81	Green, Jacquez	WR	5-9	168	1/15/76	4	Florida	Fort Valley, Ga.	D2a-'98	16/16
1	Hamilton, Joe	QB	5-10	190	3/13/77	2	Georgia Tech	Alvin, S.C.	D7-'00	1/0
79	Hegamin, George	T	6-7	331	2/14/73	8	North Carolina State	Camden, N.J.	FA-'99	16/1
34	Jackson, Dexter	S	6-0	196	7/28/77	3	Florida State	Quincy, Fla.	D4-'99	13/0
14	Johnson, Brad	QB	6-5	224	9/13/68	10	Florida State	Black Mountain, N.C.	UFA(Wash)-'01	12/11*
19	Johnson, Keyshawn	WR	6-4	212	7/22/72	6	Southern California	Los Angeles, Calif.	T(NYJ)-'00	16/16
78	Jones, Marcus	DE	6-6	278	8/15/73	6	North Carolina	Jacksonville, N.C.	D1b-'96	16/16
25	Kelly, Brian	CB	5-11	193	1/14/76	4	Southern California	Aurora, Colo.	D2b-'98	16/3
10	King, Shaun	QB	6-0	225	5/29/77	3	Tulane	St. Petersburg, Fla.	D2-'99	16/16
48	Kirby, Charles	FB	6-1	249	11/27/74	3	Virginia	South View, N.C.	FA-'00	6/2
16	Leaf, Ryan	QB	6-5	235	5/15/76	4	Washington State	Great Falls, Mont.	W(SD)-'01	11/9*
47	Lynch, John	S	6-2	220	9/25/71	9	Stanford	Solano Beach, Calif.	D3-'93	16/16
64	McDaniel, Randall	G	6-3	287	12/19/64	14	Arizona State	Avondale, Ariz.	FA-'00	16/16
92	McFarland, Anthony	DT	6-0	300	12/18/77	3	Louisiana State	Winnsboro, La.	D1-'99	16/16
95	McLaughlin, John	DE	6-4	247	11/13/75	3	California	Newhall, Calif.	D5-'99	6/0
83	Moore, Dave	TE	6-2	258	11/11/69	9	Pittsburgh	Succasunna, N.J.	FA-'92	16/16
49	Palmer, Randy	TE	6-4	235	11/12/75	2	Texas A&M-Kingsville	Pleasanton, Texas	FA-'01	0*
69	Pierson, Pete	T	6-5	315	2/4/71	7	Washington	Portland, Ore.	D5-'94	15/15
53	Quarles, Shelton	LB	6-1	230	9/11/71	5	Vanderbilt	Whites Creek, Tenn.	FA-'97	14/13
97	Rice, Simeon	DE	6-5	268	2/24/74	6	Illinois	Chicago, Ill.	UFA(Ariz)-'01	15/11*
3	Royals, Mark	P	6-5	215	6/22/65	13	Appalachian State	Mathews, Va.	FA-'99	16/0
99	Sapp, Warren	DT	6-2	303	12/19/72	7	Miami	Apopka, Fla.	D1a-'95	16/15
51	Singleton, Alshermond	LB	6-2	228	8/7/75	5	Temple	Irvington, N.J.	D4-'97	13/1
84	# Spence, Blake	TE	6-4	249	6/20/75	4	Oregon	San Juan Capistrano, Calif.	W(NYJ)-'00	3/0
22	Stecker, Aaron	RB	5-10	205	11/13/75	2	Western Illinois	Green Bay, Wis.	FA-'00	10/0
68	# Unutoa, Morris	C-LS	6-1	284	3/10/71	6	Brigham Young	Carson, Calif.	FA-'99	16/0
33	Vance, Eric	S	6-2	218	7/14/75	4	Vanderbilt	Hurst, Texas	FA-'00	14/0
54	Waddy, Jude	LB	6-2	228	9/12/75	3	William & Mary	Suitland, Md.	FA-'01	0*
93	Warner, Ron	DE	6-2	248	9/26/75	2	Kansas	Independence, Kan.	FA-'01	0*
75	Washington, Todd	C-G	6-3	324	7/19/76	4	Virginia Tech	Melfa, Va.	D4-'98	10/0
52	Webster, Nate	LB	5-11	225	11/29/77	2	Miami	Miami, Fla.	D3-'00	16/0
94	White, Steve	DE	6-2	271	10/25/73	6	Tennessee	Memphis, Tenn.	FA-'96	15/0
86	Williams, Karl	WR	5-10	177	4/10/71	6	Texas A&M-Kingsville	Garland, Texas	FA-'96	13/0
71	Wunsch, Jerry	T	6-6	339	1/21/74	5	Wisconsin	Wausau, Wis.	D2-'97	16/16
80	Yoder, Todd	TE	6-4	234	3/18/78	2	Vanderbilt	New Palestine, Ind.	FA-'00	9/0
31	# Young, Floyd	CB	6-0	179	11/23/75	5	Texas A&M-Kingsville	New Orleans, La.	FA-'97	7/0

* Curry and Dogins were inactive for 15 games; Daniels missed '00 season because of injury; B. Johnson played 12 games with Washington in '00; Leaf played 11 games with San Diego; Palmer last active with Cleveland in '99; Rice played 15 games with Arizona; Waddy last active with Green Bay in '99; Warner last active with New Orleans in '98.

Unrestricted free agent; subject to developments.

Traded—QB Eric Zeier (3 games in '00) to Atlanta.

Retired—Paul Gruber, 12-year tackle, last active with Tampa Bay in '99; Jason Odom, 5-year tackle, last active with Tampa Bay in '99.

Players lost through free agency (5): LB Don Davis (StL; 16 games in '00), TE Patrick Hape (Den; 16), DE-DT Tyoka Jackson (StL; 16), G Frank Middleton (Oak; 16), S Damien Robinson (NYJ; 16).

Also played with Buccaneers in '00—DE Chidi Ahanotu (16 games), WR Andre Hastings (3).

COACHING STAFF

Head Coach,
Tony Dungy

Pro Career: After 15 years as an NFL assistant coach, Dungy was named as the Buccaneers' sixth head coach on January 22, 1996, when he signed a six-year contract. Last season the Buccaneers reached the playoffs for the third time in four seasons and won 10 or more games for the second consecutive year, a first in club history. In 1999, Dungy's Buccaneers set a franchise record with 11 regular-season wins, captured their first NFC Central Division title in 18 years, and advanced to their first NFC Championship Game in 20 years. Tampa Bay also advanced to the playoffs in 1997 under Dungy, posting a 10-6 record and defeating the Detroit Lions in a wild-card game. Dungy is the all-time winningest coach in franchise history with 45 career regular-season victories. Joined Tampa Bay after serving as Minnesota Vikings' defensive coordinator from 1992-95. Prior to going to Vikings, spent 1989-1991 as defensive backs coach for Kansas City Chiefs, and eight years as an assistant coach for the Pittsburgh Steelers under Chuck Noll as a defensive assistant (1981), defensive backs coach (1982-83), and as defensive coordinator (1984-88). At 25, was NFL's youngest assistant coach when hired by Steelers in 1981, then became league's youngest coordinator at age of 28. Began coaching career as defensive backs coach at University of Minnesota in 1980. As an NFL player, signed with Pittsburgh as a free agent in 1977 and played safety for Steelers for two seasons (1977-78). Had 9 interceptions (second in AFC with 6 in 1978) in 30 games for Pittsburgh and played in Super Bowl XIII victory over Dallas Cowboys. Had unusual distinction of making and throwing an interception in same 1977 game against Houston Oilers. Traded to San Francisco 49ers during 1979 training camp and played 15 games for 49ers. Was traded again prior to 1980 season to New York Giants in multi-player deal that sent current Minnesota Vikings defensive coordinator Ray Rhodes to 49ers. Career record: 47-38.

Background: Starred as quarterback at University of Minnesota from 1973-76. Finished career as school's all-time leader in attempts, completions, passing yards, and touchdown passes. Two-time team most valuable player, played in Hula Bowl, East-West Shrine Game, and Japan Bowl. Attended Parkside High School in Jackson, Michigan.

Personal: Born October 6, 1955, in Jackson, Michigan. Tony and his wife, Lauren, have four children including daughter Tiara (15), and sons James (13), Eric (8), and Jordan (1). The family resides in Tampa.

ASSISTANT COACHES

Mark Asanovich, strength and conditioning; born May 20, 1959, Duluth, Minn., lives in Tampa. No college or pro playing experience. College coach: Ohio State 1985, Citadel 1986. Pro coach: Minnesota Vikings 1995, joined Buccaneers in 1996.

Joe Barry, linebackers; born July 5, 1970, Lutz, Fla. lives in Tampa. Linebacker Southern California 1990-93. No pro playing experience. College coach: Southern California 1994-95, Northern Arizona 1996-98, Nevada-Las Vegas 1999. Pro coach: San Francisco 49ers 2000, joined Buccaneers in 2001.

Jim Caldwell, quarterbacks; born January 16, 1955, Beloit, Wis., lives in Tampa. Defensive back Iowa 1973-76. No pro playing experience. College coach: Iowa 1977, Southern Illinois 1978-1980, Northwestern 1981, Colorado 1982-84, Louisville 1985, Penn State 1986-1992, Wake Forest 1993-2000. Pro coach: Joined Buccaneers in 2001.

Clyde Christensen, offensive coordinator; born January 28, 1958, Covina, Calif., lives in Tampa. Quarterback Fresno (Calif.) J.C. 1975, North Carolina 1976-78. No pro playing experience. College coach: East Tennessee State 1980-82, Temple 1983-85, East Carolina 1986-88, Holy Cross 1989-90, South Carolina 1991, Maryland 1992-93, Clemson 1994-95. Pro coach: Joined Buccaneers in 1996.

Les Ebert, asst. strength and conditioning; born October 1, 1972, Brinard, Minn., lives in Tampa. Attended Minnesota-Duluth. No college or pro playing experience. Pro coach: Joined Buccaneers in 1999.

Chris Foerster, offensive line; born October 12, 1961, Milwaukee, Wis., lives in Tampa. Center Colorado State 1979-82. No pro playing experience. College coach: Colorado State 1983-87, Stanford 1988-91, Minnesota 1992. Pro coach: Minnesota Vikings 1993-95, joined Buccaneers in 1996.

Monte Kiffin, defensive coordinator; born February 29, 1940, Lexington, Neb., lives in Tampa. Offensive/defensive tackle Nebraska 1959-63. Pro defensive end Winnipeg Blue Bombers (CFL) 1965. College coach: Nebraska 1966-76, Arkansas 1977-79, North Carolina State 1980-82 (head coach). Pro coach: Green Bay Packers 1983, Buffalo Bills 1984-85, Minnesota Vikings 1986-89, 1991-94, New York Jets 1990, New Orleans Saints 1995, joined Buccaneers in 1996.

Joe Marciano, special teams; born February 10, 1954, Scranton, Pa., lives in Tampa. Quarterback Temple 1972-75. No pro playing experience. College coach: East Stroudsburg 1977, Rhode Island 1978-79, Villanova 1980, Penn State 1981, Temple 1982. Pro coach: Philadelphia/Baltimore Stars (USFL) 1983-85, New Orleans Saints 1986-95, joined Buccaneers in 1996.

Rod Marinelli, defensive line; born July 13, 1949, Rosemead, Calif., lives in Tampa. Offensive/defensive tackle Utah 1968, offensive tackle California Lutheran 1970-72 (military service 1969-70). No pro playing experience. College coach: Utah State 1976-82, California 1983-91, Arizona State 1992-94, Southern California 1995. Pro coach: Joined Buccaneers in 1996.

Tony Nathan, running backs; born December 14, 1956, Birmingham, Ala., lives in Tampa. Running back Alabama 1975-78. Pro running back Miami Dolphins 1979-87. Pro coach: Miami Dolphins 1988-95, joined Buccaneers in 1996.

Kevin O'Dea, offensive assistant; born June 9, 1960, Williamsport, Va., lives in Tampa. Defensive back/wide receiver Lock Haven 1982-85. No pro playing experience. College coach: Lock Haven 1986, Cornell 1987, Virginia 1988-90, Penn State 1991-93. Pro coach: San Diego Chargers 1994-95, joined Buccaneers in 1996.

Ricky Thomas, tight ends; born March 29, 1965, London, England, lives in Tampa. Safety Alabama 1983-86. Pro safety Seattle Seahawks 1987. College coach: Kentucky 1996, Gardner-Webb 1996. Pro coach: Joined Buccaneers in 1997.

Mike Tomlin, defensive backs; born March 15, 1972, Hampton, Va., lives in Tampa. Wide receiver William & Mary 1991-94. No pro playing experience. College coach: Virginia Military Institute 1995, Memphis 1996, Arkansas State 1997-98, Cincinnati 1999-2000. Pro coach: Joined Buccaneers in 2001.

Alan Williams, defensive assistant; born November 4, 1969, Norfolk, Va., lives in Tampa. Running back William & Mary 1988-1991. No pro playing experience. College coach: William & Mary 1996-2000. Pro coach: Joined Buccaneers in 2001.

Charlie Williams, wide receivers; born January 31, 1958, Long Beach, Calif., lives in Tampa. Defensive back Long Beach City College 1977-78, Colorado State 1979-80. No pro playing experience. College coach: Colorado State 1981, Long Beach City College 1984-85, New Mexico State 1986-87, Texas Christian 1988-91, Minnesota 1992, Miami 1993-95. Pro coach: Joined Buccaneers in 1996.

2001 FIRST-YEAR ROSTER

Name	Pos.	Ht.	Wt.	Birthdate	College	Hometown	How Acq.
Aracri, Andy	DT	6-2	285	4/16/78	Miami (Ohio)	Kettering, Ohio	FA
Ardley, Alexander	CB	5-10	170	12/9/78	Clemson	Tallahassee, Fla.	FA
Bayes, Andrew (1)	P	6-2	200	2/11/78	East Carolina	Hyattsville, Md.	FA
Benjamin, Ryan	LS	6-2	240	11/11/77	South Florida	New Port Richey, Fla.	FA
Bonner, Antonious (1)	CB-S	6-1	200	9/3/72	Mississippi	Greenwood, Miss.	FA
Brown, Wilbert (1)	G	6-2	310	5/9/77	Houston	Hooks, Texas	FA
Cerqua, Marq	LB	6-2	223	4/3/77	Carson-Newman	Greenville, S.C.	FA
Chaney, Jeff	RB	6-0	200	11/16/76	Florida State	Lake Wales, Fla.	FA
Cook, Jameel	FB	5-10	227	2/8/79	Illinois	Miami, Fla.	D6a
Darby, Chartric (1)	DT	6-0	270	10/22/75	South Carolina State	North, S.C.	FA-'00
Finger, Dauntae'	TE	6-3	255	4/5/77	North Carolina	Newton, N.C.	D7a
Grice, Shane	G-C	6-1	300	12/20/76	Mississippi	Shannon, Miss.	FA
Gruber, Brian	T	6-7	316	10/10/77	Vanderbilt	Houston, Texas	FA
Hardaway, Eddie (1)	WR	6-1	195	10/7/77	C.W. Post	Amityville, N.Y.	FA
Hires, Leon	G	6-4	285	12/6/77	Florida	Bradenton, Fla.	FA
Hochstein, Russ	G	6-3	288	10/7/77	Nebraska	Hartington, Neb.	D5
Hooks, Margin	WR	6-0	190	2/10/78	Brigham Young	Waco, Texas	FA
Howell, John	S	5-11	196	4/28/78	Colorado State	Mullen, Neb.	D4
Ivy, Khori	WR	6-2	195	3/16/78	West Virginia	Boca Raton, Fla.	FA
Jolly, Terry	DT	6-2	280	12/21/76	Clemson	Fort Valley, Ga.	FA
Kilow, Robert	WR	5-11	167	2/29/76	Arkansas State	Daleville, Ala.	FA
Mack, Kendell (1)	T	6-4	322	7/18/75	Auburn	Pineville, S.C.	FA-'00
Mackenzie, Mike	DT	6-2	269	3/16/78	Colorado State	Miami, Fla.	FA
Merrill, Than	S	6-3	220	12/12/77	Yale	Fresno, Calif.	D7b
Midget, Anthony (1)	CB	5-11	193	2/2/78	Virginia Tech	Clewiston, Fla.	FA-'00
Murphy, Frank (1)	WR	6-0	206	2/11/77	Kansas State	Callahan, Fla.	FA-'00
Newman, David	TE	6-6	245	8/6/78	Louisiana Tech	St. Joseph, La.	FA
Nunnally, Jacquay	WR	5-11	200	1/4/78	Florida A&M	Miami, Fla.	FA
Parrish, Terrance (1)	CB	5-11	190	10/1/76	Southern Mississippi	Theodore, Ala.	FA-'00
Rice, Frank	WR	6-0	175	2/2/78	Colorado State	Gardena, Calif.	FA
Smith, Dwight	CB	5-10	201	8/13/78	Akron	Detroit, Mich.	D3
Sweeney, Matt (1)	DT	6-2	275	5/24/77	Miami	Sussex, N.J.	FA
Tafoya, Joe	DE	6-4	258	9/6/77	Arizona	Pittsburg, Calif.	D7c
Thweatt, Byron	LB	6-2	233	3/21/77	Virginia	Chesterfield, Va.	FA
Vaughn, Damian (1)	TE	6-4	252	6/14/75	Miami (Ohio)	Orrville, Ohio	FA
Walker, Kenyatta	T	6-5	302	2/1/79	Florida	Meridian, Miss.	D1
Willis, Alex	WR	6-0	180	9/2/78	Florida	Jacksonville, Fla.	FA
Wilson, Jamie	RB	6-1	212	1/8/78	East Carolina	Greenville, N.C.	FA
Wyms, Ellis	DE	6-3	279	4/12/79	Mississippi State	Indianola, Miss.	D6b

The term NFL Rookie is defined as a player who is in his first season of professional football and has not been on the roster of another professional football team for any regular-season or postseason games. A Rookie is designated by an "R" on NFL rosters. Players who have been active in another professional football league or players who have NFL experience, including either preseason training camp or being on an Active List or Inactive List, or on Reserve/Injured or Reserve/Physically Unable to Perform for fewer than six regular-season games, are termed NFL First-Year Players. An NFL First-Year Player is designated by a "1" on NFL rosters. Thereafter, a player is credited with an additional year of experience for each season in which he accumulates six games on the Active List or Inactive List, or on Reserve/Injured or Reserve/Physically Unable to Perform.

WASHINGTON REDSKINS

National Football Conference
Eastern Division
Team Colors: Burgundy and Gold
Redskin Park
21300 Redskin Park Drive
Ashburn, Virginia 20147
Telephone: (703) 877-2000

CLUB OFFICIALS

Owner: Daniel M. Snyder
Chief Operating Officer: David Pauken
President: Steve Baldacci
Assistant General Manager: Bobby Mitchell
Senior Vice President: Karl Swanson
Senior Vice President, General Counsel: Robert Gordon
Senior Vice President, Stadium Operations: Michael Dillow
Chief Financial Officer: Jeff Ochs
Vice President, Player Personnel: John Schneider
Vice President, Football Operations: Russ Ball
Manager, Football Operations/Development: John Wuehrmann
Contract Negotiator/Salary Cap: Mark Levin
Salary Cap Assistant: Dustin Nelson
NFC Pro Coordinator: Mel Bratton
AFC Pro Coordinator: Charlie Brown
Director of College Scouting: Mike Faulkiner
College Scouts: Greg Henley, Stacy Harrison, Dan Shonka, Doug Kretz, Ron Nay, Ha'son Graham-BLESTO Scout
Draft Room Coordinator/Scouting Assistant: Mike Szabo
Director of Player Programs: John Jefferson
Director of Public Relations: Michelle Tessier
Director of Publications: Casey Husband
Director, Redskins.com: Jason Gould
Director, Washington Redskins Leadership Council/Community Relations: Alex Hahn
Video Director: Rob Porteus
Assistant Video Director: Mike Bracken
Director of Ticket Operations: Jeff Ritter
Head Trainer: Bubba Tyer
Assistant Trainers: Ryan Vermillion, Eric Steward
Equipment Manager: Brad Berlin
Assistant Equipment Manager: Anders Beutel
Stadium: FedEx Field (built in 1997)
•**Capacity:** 85,407
Landover, Maryland 20785-4236
Playing Surface: Grass
Training Camp: Dickinson College
P.O. Box 1773
Carlislie, Pa. 17013

2001 SCHEDULE

PRESEASON

Aug. 12	at Kansas City	7:30
Aug. 17	**Atlanta**	8:00
Aug. 24	**Cleveland**	8:00
Aug. 30	at New England	8:00

REGULAR SEASON

Sept. 9	at San Diego	1:15
Sept. 16	**Arizona**	1:00
Sept. 24	at Green Bay (Mon.)	8:00
Sept. 30	**Kansas City**	1:00
Oct. 7	at New York Giants	1:00
Oct. 15	at Dallas (Mon.)	8:00
Oct. 21	**Carolina**	1:00
Oct. 28	**New York Giants**	8:30
Nov. 4	**Seattle**	4:15
Nov. 11	Open Date	
Nov. 18	at Denver	2:15
Nov. 25	at Philadelphia	1:00
Dec. 2	**Dallas**	4:15
Dec. 9	at Arizona	2:05
Dec. 16	**Philadelphia**	1:00
Dec. 23	**Chicago**	1:00
Dec. 30	at New Orleans	7:30

RECORD HOLDERS

INDIVIDUAL RECORDS—CAREER

Category	Name	Performance
Rushing (Yds.)	John Riggins, 1976-79, 1981-85	7,472
Passing (Yds.)	Joe Theismann, 1974-1985	25,206
Passing (TDs)	Sammy Baugh, 1937-1952	187
Receiving (No.)	Art Monk, 1980-1993	888
Receiving (Yds.)	Art Monk, 1980-1993	12,028
Interceptions	Darrell Green, 1983-2000	53
Punting (Avg.)	Sammy Baugh, 1937-1952	*45.1
Punt Return (Avg.)	Johnny Williams, 1952-53	12.8
Kickoff Return (Avg.)	Bobby Mitchell, 1962-68	28.5
Field Goals	Mark Moseley, 1974-1986	263
Touchdowns (Tot.)	Charley Taylor, 1964-1977	90
Points	Mark Moseley, 1974-1986	1,206

INDIVIDUAL RECORDS—SINGLE SEASON

Category	Name	Performance
Rushing (Yds.)	Stephen Davis, 1999	1,405
Passing (Yds.)	Jay Schroeder, 1986	4,109
Passing (TDs)	Sonny Jurgensen, 1967	31
Receiving (No.)	Art Monk, 1984	106
Receiving (Yds.)	Bobby Mitchell, 1963	1,436
Interceptions	Dan Sandifer, 1948	13
Punting (Avg.)	Sammy Baugh, 1940	*51.4
Punt Return (Avg.)	Johnny Williams, 1952	15.3
Kickoff Return (Avg.)	Mike Nelms, 1981	29.7
Field Goals	Mark Moseley, 1983	33
Touchdowns (Tot.)	John Riggins, 1983	24
Points	Mark Moseley, 1983	161

INDIVIDUAL RECORDS—SINGLE GAME

Category	Name	Performance
Rushing (Yds.)	Gerald Riggs, 9-17-89	221
Passing (Yds.)	Sammy Baugh, 10-31-43	446
Passing (TDs)	Sammy Baugh, 10-31-43, 11-23-47	6
	Mark Rypien, 11-10-91	6
Receiving (No.)	Art Monk, 12-15-85, 11-4-90	13
	Kelvin Bryant, 12-7-86	13
Receiving (Yds.)	Anthony Allen, 10-4-87	255
Interceptions	Sammy Baugh, 11-14-43	*4
	Dan Sandifer, 10-31-48	*4
Field Goals	Many times	5
	Last time by Chip Lohmiller, 10-25-92	
Touchdowns (Tot.)	Dick James, 12-17-61	4
	Larry Brown, 12-16-73	4
Points	Dick James, 12-17-61	24
	Larry Brown, 12-16-73	24

*NFL Record

COACHING HISTORY

Boston 1932-36
(501-439-27)

1932	Lud Wray	4-4-2
1933-34	William (Lone Star) Dietz	11-11-2
1935	Eddie Casey	2-8-1
1936-1942	Ray Flaherty	56-23-3
1943	Arthur (Dutch) Bergman	7-4-1
1944-45	Dudley DeGroot	14-6-1
1946-48	Glen (Turk) Edwards	16-18-1
1949	John Whelchel*	3-3-1
1949-1951	Herman Ball**	4-16-0
1951	Dick Todd	5-4-0
1952-53	Earl (Curly) Lambeau	10-13-1
1954-58	Joe Kuharich	26-32-2
1959-1960	Mike Nixon	4-18-2
1961-65	Bill McPeak	21-46-3
1966-68	Otto Graham	17-22-3
1969	Vince Lombardi	7-5-2
1970	Bill Austin	6-8-0
1971-77	George Allen	69-35-1
1978-1980	Jack Pardee	24-24-0
1981-1992	Joe Gibbs	140-65-0
1993	Richie Petitbon	4-12-0
1994-2000	Norv Turner***	50-60-1
2000	Terry Robiskie	1-2-0

* Released after seven games in 1949
** Released after three games in 1951
*** Released after 13 games in 2000

FEDEX FIELD

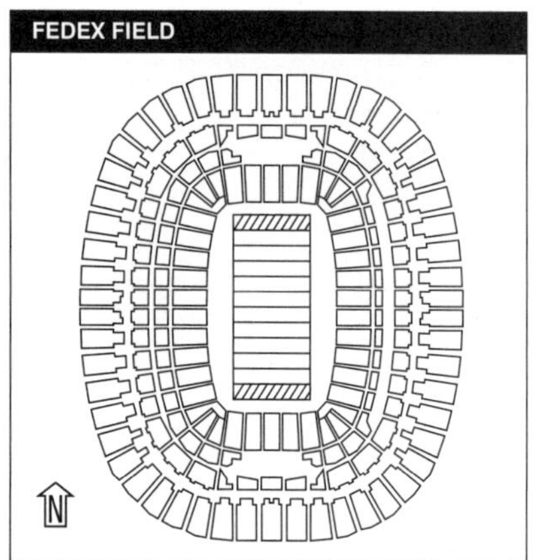

2000 TEAM RECORD

PRESEASON (3-1)

Date	Result		Opponent
8/4	L	12-13	at Tampa Bay
8/11	W	30-20	New England
8/19	W	24-0	at Cleveland
8/25	W	17-10	Pittsburgh

REGULAR SEASON (8-8)

Date	Result		Opponent	Att.
9/3	W	20-17	Carolina	80,257
9/10	L	10-15	at Detroit	74,159
9/18	L	21-27	Dallas	84,431
9/24	W	16-6	at New York Giants	78,216
10/1	W	20-17	Tampa Bay (OT)	83,532
10/8	W	17-14	at Philadelphia	65,491
10/15	W	10-3	Baltimore	83,252
10/22	W	35-16	at Jacksonville	69,061
10/30	L	21-27	Tennessee	83,472
11/5	L	15-16	at Arizona	44,723
11/20	W	33-20	at St. Louis	66,087
11/26	L	20-23	Philadelphia	83,284
12/3	L	7-9	New York Giants	83,485
12/10	L	13-32	at Dallas	63,467
12/16	L	3-24	at Pittsburgh	58,183
12/24	W	20-3	Arizona	65,711

(OT) Overtime

SCORE BY PERIODS

Redskins	65	80	54	79	3	—	281
Opponents	63	91	39	76	0	—	269

ATTENDANCE

Home 656,599 Away 526,253 Total 1,182,852
Single-game home record, 84,431 (9/18/00)
Single-season home record, 656,599 (2000)

2000 TEAM STATISTICS

	Redskins	Opp.
Total First Downs	308	254
Rushing	98	97
Passing	185	134
Penalty	25	23
Third Down: Made/Att	84/213	72/205
Third Down Pct.	39.4	35.1
Fourth Down: Made/Att	4/10	4/10
Fourth Down Pct.	40.0	40.0
Total Net Yards	5,396	4,474
Avg. Per Game	337.3	279.6
Total Plays	1,038	937
Avg. Per Play	5.2	4.8
Net Yards Rushing	1,748	1,853
Avg. Per Game	109.3	115.8
Total Rushes	445	430
Net Yards Passing	3,648	2,621
Avg. Per Game	228.0	163.8
Sacked/Yards Lost	32/244	45/283
Gross Yards	3,892	2,904
Att./Completions	561/343	462/254
Completion Pct.	61.1	55.0
Had Intercepted	21	17
Punts/Average	79/40.0	79/42.9
Net Punting Avg.	79/34.4	79/35.8
Penalties/Yards	115/1,009	106/790
Fumbles/Ball Lost	22/12	28/16
Touchdowns	32	26
Rushing	14	9
Passing	18	12
Returns	0	5
Avg. Time of Possession	31:27	28:33

2000 INDIVIDUAL STATISTICS

Passing	Att.	Comp.	Yds.	Pct.	TD	Int.	Tkld.	Rate
Bra. Johnson	365	228	2,505	62.5	11	15	20/150	75.7
George	194	113	1,389	58.2	7	6	12/94	79.6
Husak	2	2	-2	100.0	0	0	0/0	79.2
Redskins	561	343	3,892	61.1	18	21	32/244	77.0
Opponents	462	254	2,904	55.0	12	17	45/283	67.4

SCORING	TD R	TD P	TD Rt	PAT	FG	Saf	PTS
Davis	11	0	0	0/0	0/0	0	66
Murray	0	0	0	7/8	8/12	0	31
Fryar	0	5	0	0/0	0/0	0	30
Heppner	0	0	0	9/9	4/6	0	21
Husted	0	0	0	8/9	4/8	0	20
Centers	0	3	0	0/0	0/0	0	18
Connell	0	3	0	0/0	0/0	0	18
Alexander	0	2	0	0/0	0/0	0	12
Conway	0	0	0	3/3	3/3	0	12
Sellers	0	2	0	0/0	0/0	0	12
Thrash	0	2	0	0/0	0/0	0	12
Bailey	1	0	0	0/0	0/0	0	6
Hicks	1	0	0	0/0	0/0	0	6
Bra. Johnson	1	0	0	0/0	0/0	0	6
Reed	0	1	0	0/0	0/0	0	6
Bentley	0	0	0	0/0	1/1	0	3
B. Smith	0	0	0	0/0	0/0	1	2
Redskins	14	18	0	27/29	20/30	1	281
Opponents	9	12	5	23/23	30/34	0	269

2-Pt. Conversions: None.
Redskins 0-3, Opponents 0-3.

RUSHING	Att.	Yds.	Avg.	LG	TD
Davis	332	1,318	4.0	50t	11
Centers	19	103	5.4	14	0
Thrash	10	82	8.2	34	0
Hicks	29	78	2.7	12	1
Bra. Johnson	22	58	2.6	21	1
Murrell	20	50	2.5	13	0
George	7	24	3.4	14	0
Fryar	2	16	8.0	15	0
Barnhardt	1	11	11.0	11	0
Bailey	1	7	7.0	7t	1
Sellers	1	2	2.0	2	0
Husak	1	-1	-1.0	-1	0
Redskins	445	1,748	3.9	50t	14
Opponents	430	1,853	4.3	54	9

RECEIVING	No.	Yds.	Avg.	LG	TD
Centers	81	600	7.4	26	3
Thrash	50	653	13.1	50	2
Alexander	47	510	10.9	30	2
Fryar	41	548	13.4	34t	5
Connell	39	762	19.5	77t	3
Davis	33	313	9.5	39	0
Murrell	16	93	5.8	12	0
Reed	10	103	10.3	21t	1
Westbrook	9	103	11.4	21	0
Sellers	8	78	9.8	24	2
Hicks	5	43	8.6	25	0
Bailey	3	78	26.0	42	0
Flemister	1	8	8.0	8	0
Redskins	343	3,892	11.3	77t	18
Opponents	254	2,904	11.4	76t	12

INTERCEPTIONS	No.	Yds.	Avg.	LG	TD
Bailey	5	48	9.6	48	0
Sanders	4	91	22.8	32	0
Green	3	35	11.7	33	0
Shade	2	15	7.5	15	0
Carrier	1	30	30.0	30	0
Mitchell	1	0	0.0	0	0
Stevens	1	0	0.0	0	0
Redskins	17	219	12.9	48	0
Opponents	21	374	17.8	81t	1

PUNTING	No.	Yds.	Avg.	In 20	LG
Barnhardt	79	3,160	40.0	23	53
Redskins	79	3,160	40.0	23	53
Opponents	79	3,386	42.9	23	57

PUNT RETURNS	No.	FC	Yds.	Avg.	LG	TD
Sanders	25	6	185	7.4	57	0
Thrash	10	6	106	10.6	25	0
Bailey	1	1	65	65.0	54	0
Redskins	36	13	356	9.9	57	0
Opponents	33	25	342	10.4	69t	2

KICKOFF RETURNS	No.	Yds.	Avg.	LG	TD
Thrash	45	1,000	22.2	49	0
Murrell	12	214	17.8	30	0
Sellers	3	32	10.7	21	0
Arrington	1	39	39.0	23	0
Hicks	1	17	17.0	17	0
Sanders	1	-1	-1.0	-1	0
Redskins	63	1,301	20.7	49	0
Opponents	60	1,529	25.5	92t	1

FIELD GOALS	1-19	20-29	30-39	40-49	50+
Heppner	0/0	2/2	2/3	0/0	0/1
Murray	0/0	2/2	3/4	3/6	0/0
Husted	0/0	4/4	0/3	0/1	0/0
Conway	0/0	3/3	0/0	0/0	0/0
Bentley	0/0	0/0	0/0	0/0	1/1
Redskins	0/0	11/11	5/10	3/7	1/2
Opponents	1/1	9/10	11/11	6/8	3/4

SACKS	No.
Coleman	12.0
B. Smith	10.0
Arrington	4.0
Wilkinson	3.5
Lang	3.0
Stubblefield	2.5
Barber	2.0
Mason	2.0
N. Harrison	1.0
Jones	1.0
Kalu	1.0
Mitchell	1.0
Shade	1.0
Derek M. Smith	1.0
Redskins	45.0
Opponents	32.0

2001 DRAFT CHOICES

Round	Name	Pos.	College
1	Rod Gardner	WR	Clemson
2	Fred Smoot	DB	Mississippi State
4	Sage Rosenfels	QB	Iowa State
5	Darnerien McCants	WR	Delaware State
6	Mario Monds	DT	Cincinnati

WASHINGTON REDSKINS

2001 VETERAN ROSTER

No.	Name	Pos.	Ht.	Wt.	Birthdate	NFL Exp.	College	Hometown	How Acq.	'00 Games/ Starts
77	Albright, Ethan	LS	6-5	278	5/1/71	8	North Carolina	Greensboro, N.C.	FA-'01	16/0*
80	Alexander, Stephen	TE	6-4	246	11/7/75	4	Oklahoma	Chickasha, Okla.	D2-'98	16/16
56	Arrington, LaVar	LB	6-3	250	6/20/78	2	Penn State	Pittsburgh, Pa.	D1-'00	16/11
24	Bailey, Champ	CB	6-1	184	6/22/78	3	Georgia	Folkston, Ga.	D1-'99	16/16
59	Barber, Shawn	LB	6-2	230	1/14/75	4	Richmond	Heritage, Va.	D4-'98	14/14
4	Barker, Bryan	P	6-1	200	6/28/64	12	Santa Clara	Jacksonville Beach, Fla.	UFA(Jax)-'01	16/0*
32	Bennett, Donnell	FB	6-0	246	9/14/72	8	Miami	Fort Lauderdale, Fla.	UFA(KC)-'01	7/2*
1	Bentley, Scott	K	6-0	203	4/10/74	4	Florida State	Aurora, Colo.	UFA(Den)-'00	6/0
69	Campbell, Matt	G-T	6-4	300	7/14/72	7	South Carolina	Cornelius, N.C.	UFA(Car)-'01	14/14*
99	Coleman, Marco	DE	6-3	267	12/18/69	10	Georgia Tech	Dayton, Ohio	UFA(SD)-'99	16/16
5	Conway, Brett	K	6-2	192	3/8/75	5	Penn State	Lilburn, Ga.	UFA(NYJ)-'01	5/0*
48	Davis, Stephen	RB	6-0	234	3/1/74	6	Auburn	Spartansburg, S.C.	D4-'96	15/15
51	Fischer, Mark	C	6-3	293	7/29/74	4	Purdue	Cincinnati, Ohio	D5-'98	16/16
89	Flemister, Zeron	TE	6-4	249	9/8/76	2	Iowa	Sioux City, Iowa	FA-'00	5/0
63	Fletcher, Derrick	G	6-6	350	9/9/75	3	Baylor	Aldine, Texas	UFA(NO)-'00	1/0
3	George, Jeff	QB	6-4	215	12/8/67	11	Illinois	Indianapolis, Ind.	UFA(Minn)-'00	6/5
28	Green, Darrell	CB	5-8	184	2/15/60	19	Texas A&I	Houston, Texas	D1-'83	13/2
25	Greer, Donovan	CB	5-9	178	9/11/74	5	Texas A&M	Houston, Texas	UFA(Buff)-'01	13/0*
75	Ham, Derrick	DE	6-4	257	3/23/75	2	Miami	Merritt Island, Fla.	FA-'99	1/0
41	Harrison, Lloyd	CB	5-10	190	6/21/77	2	North Carolina State	Floral Park, N.Y.	D3-'00	2/0
8	Husak, Todd	QB	6-3	216	7/6/78	2	Stanford	Long Beach, Calif.	D6-'00	1/0
76	Jansen, Jon	T	6-6	309	1/28/76	3	Michigan	Clawson, Mich.	D2-'99	16/16
90	Lang, Kenard	DE	6-4	277	1/31/75	5	Miami	Orlando, Fla.	D1-'97	16/0
83	Lockett, Kevin	WR	6-0	186	9/8/74	5	Kansas State	Tulsa, Okla.	UFA(KC)-'01	16/2*
53	Mason, Eddie	LB	6-0	236	1/9/72	5	North Carolina	Siler City, N.C.	UFA(Jax)-'99	16/2
55	Mitchell, Kevin	LB	6-1	254	1/1/71	8	Syracuse	Harrisburg, Pa.	UFA(NO)-'00	16/0
66	Moore, Michael	G	6-3	320	11/1/76	2	Troy State	Fayette, Ala.	D4-'00	5/1
86	Rasby, Walter	TE	6-3	256	9/7/72	8	Wake Forest	Charlotte, N.C.	UFA(Det)-'01	16/8*
52	Raymer, Cory	C	6-2	298	3/3/73	7	Wisconsin	Fon du Lac, Wis.	D2-'95	16/8*
60	Samuels, Chris	T	6-5	325	7/28/77	2	Alabama	Mobile, Ala.	D1-'00	16/16
21	Sanders, Deion	CB	6-1	195	8/9/67	13	Florida State	Fort Meyers, Fla.	UFA(Dall)-'00	16/15
29	Shade, Sam	S	6-1	201	6/14/73	7	Alabama	Birmingham, Ala.	UFA(Cin)-'99	16/14
78	Smith, Bruce	DE	6-4	279	6/18/63	17	Virginia Tech	Norfolk, Va.	UFA(Buff)-'00	16/16
31	Terrell, David	CB	6-1	188	7/8/75	3	Texas-El Paso	Sweetwater, Texas	FA-'00	16/0
13	Thompson, Derrius	WR	6-2	215	7/5/77	3	Baylor	Cedar Hill, Texas	FA-'99	4/0
82	Westbrook, Michael	WR	6-3	220	7/7/72	7	Colorado	Detroit, Mich.	D1-'95	2/2
95	Wilkinson, Dan	DT	6-5	313	3/13/73	8	Ohio State	Dayton, Ohio	T(Cin)-'98	16/16

* Albright played 16 games with Buffalo in '00; Barker played 16 games with Jacksonville; Bennett played 7 games with Kansas City; Campbell played 14 games with Carolina; Conway played 2 games with Washington, 2 games with Oakland, and 1 game with N.Y. Jets; Greer played 13 games with Buffalo; Lockett played 16 games with Kansas City; Rasby played 16 games with Detroit; Raymer missed '00 season because of injury.

Players lost through free agency (9): WR Albert Connell (NO; 16 games in '00), T Ed Ellis (SD; 12), QB Brad Johnson (TB; 12), LB Greg Jones (Chi; 16), DE N.D. Kalu (Phil; 15), RB Adrian Murrell (Car; 15), RB Mike Sellers (Cle; 14), LB Derek M. Smith (SF; 16), WR James Thrash (Phil; 16).

Also played with Redskins in '00—P Tommy Barnhardt (16 games), S Mark Carrier (15), RB Larry Centers (15), CB Tyrone Drakeford (9), RB Chad Dukes (1), WR Irving Fryar (14), LB Reggie Givens (9), DE Nolan Harrison (16), K Kris Heppner (4), RB Skip Hicks (10), K Michael Husted (4), G-T Tony Hutson (3), TE James Jenkins (13), G Tré Johnson (4), C Jay Leeuwenburg (16), K Ed Murray (6), WR Andre Reed (13), WR Kenny Shedd (1), G Keith Sims (13), S Matt Stevens (15), DT Dana Stubblefield (15), TE Joe Zelenka (16).

COACHING STAFF

Head Coach,
Marty Schottenheimer

Pro Career: Marty Schottenheimer joined the Washington Redskins as the organization's twenty-second head coach and director of football operations in January 2001. In 14 seasons at the helm of NFL clubs, Schottenheimer has led his teams to 12 winning seasons, accumulating the league's tenth best career winning percentage among coaches with more than 100 career victories (.609). In his 10 years as head coach of the Kansas City Chiefs (1989-1998), he accumulated a 104-65-1 record. Schottenheimer's Chiefs advanced to the playoffs seven times. During his four full seasons with the Cleveland Browns, the team earned four playoff berths and played in two AFC Championship games. Schottenheimer was the consensus AFC Coach of the Year in 1986. He previously coached with the Portland Storm (WFL) in 1974, the New York Giants (1975-77), and Detroit (1978-79), leaving in 1980 to become defensive coordinator with the Cleveland Browns. In 1984 he took over as head coach of the Browns midway through the season. As a seventh-round choice of the Buffalo Bills in 1965, Schottenheimer played linebacker with the Bills until 1968 and finished his pro playing career with the Boston Patriots from 1969-1970. Career record: 150-96-1.

Background: Schottenheimer was an All-America linebacker at the University of Pittsburgh from 1962-64. Before starting his coaching career, he worked as a real estate developer in both Miami and Denver from 1971-74. After leaving the Kansas City Chiefs in 1998, he joined ESPN as a pro football analyst.

Personal: Born September 23, 1943 in Canonsburg, Pa. Marty and his wife Patricia have one daughter, Kristen, and one son, Brian, who is the quarterbacks coach with the Redskins.

ASSISTANT COACHES

Bill Arnsparger, defensive assistant; born December 16, 1926, in Paris, Ky., lives in Herndon, Va. Tackle Miami (Ohio) 1946-49. No pro playing experience. College coach: Miami (Ohio) 1950, Ohio State 1951-53, Kentucky 1954-1961, Tulane 1962-63, Louisiana State 1984-86 (head coach). Pro coach: Baltimore Colts 1964-69, Miami Dolphins 1970-73, 1976-1983, New York Giants 1974-76 (head coach), San Diego Chargers 1992-94, joined Redskins in 2001.

Pete Carmichael Jr., offensive assistant-quality control; born October 6, 1971, Farmingham, Mass., lives in Ashburn, Va. Attended Boston College. No college or pro playing experience. College coach: New Hampshire 1994, Louisiana Tech 1995-99. Pro coach: Cleveland Browns 2000, joined Redskins in 2001.

Jerry Holmes, secondary; born December 22, 1957, Hampton, Va., lives in Sterling, Va. Defensive back Chowon (N.J.) J.C. 1976-77, West Virginia 1978-79. Pro defensive back New York Jets 1980-83, 1986-87, Pittsburgh Maulers (USFL) 1984, New Jersey Generals (USFL) 1985, Detroit Lions 1988-89, Green Bay Packers 1990-91. College coach: Hampton 1992-94, West Virginia 1995-98. Pro coach: Cleveland Browns 1999-2000, joined Redskins in 2001.

Hue Jackson, running backs; born October 22, 1965, Los Angeles, lives in Ashburn, Va. Quarterback Pacific 1985-86. No pro playing experience. College coach: Pacific 1987-89, Cal State-Fullerton 1990, Arizona State 1992-95, California 1996, Southern California 1997-2000. Pro coach: London Monarchs (WFL) 1991, joined Redskins in 2001.

Richard Mann, wide receivers; born April 20, 1947, Aliquippa, Pa., lives in Baltimore. Wide receiver Arizona State 1966-68. No pro playing experience. College coach: Arizona State 1974-79, Louisville 1980-81. Pro coach: Baltimore/Indianapolis Colts 1982-84, Cleveland Browns 1985-1993, New York Jets 1994-96, Baltimore Ravens 1997-98, Kansas City Chiefs 1999-2000, joined Redskins in 2001.

Greg Manusky, linebackers; born August 12, 1966, Wilkes-Barre, Pa., lives in Ashburn, Va. Linebacker Colgate 1983-87. Pro linebacker Washington Redskins 1988-1990, Minnesota Vikings 1991-93, Kansas City Chiefs 1994-99. Pro coach: Joined Redskins in 2001.

Kirk Olivadotti, defensive assistant-quality control; born January 1, 1974, Wilmington, Del., lives in Ashburn, Va. Wide receiver Purdue 1992-96. No pro playing experience. College coach: Maine Maritime Academy 1997, Indiana Sate 1998-99. Pro coach: Joined Redskins in 2000.

Joe Pendry, offensive line; born August 5, 1947, Matheny, W. Va., lives in Ashburn, Va. Tight end West Virginia 1966-67. No pro playing experience. College coach: West Virginia 1967-1974, 1976-77, Kansas State 1975, Pittsburgh 1978-79, Michigan State 1980-81. Pro coach: Philadelphia Stars (USFL) 1983, Pittsburgh Maulers (USFL) 1984 (head coach), Cleveland Browns 1985-88, Kansas City Chiefs 1989-1992, Chicago Bears 1993-94, Carolina Panthers 1995-97, Buffalo Bills 1998-2000, joined Redskins in 2001.

Jimmy Raye, offensive coordinator; born March 26, 1946, Fayetteville, N.C., lives in Leesburg, Va. Quarterback Michigan State 1965-67. Pro defensive back Philadelphia Eagles 1969. College coach: Michigan State 1971-75, Wyoming 1976. Pro coach: San Francisco 49ers 1977, Detroit Lions 1978-79, Atlanta Falcons 1980-82, 1987-89, Los Angeles Rams 1983-84, 1991, Tampa Bay Buccaneers 1985-86, New England Patriots 1990, Kansas City Chiefs 1992-2000, joined Redskins in 2001.

Dave Redding, strength and conditioning; born June 14, 1952, North Platte, Neb., lives in Leesburg, Va. Defensive end Nebraska 1972-75. No pro playing experience. College coach: Nebraska 1976, Washington State 1977, Missouri 1978-1981. Pro coach: Cleveland Browns 1982-88, Kansas City Chiefs 1989-1997, joined Redskins in 2001.

Matt Schiotz, asst. strength and conditioning; born June 8, 1971, Menomonie, Wis., lives in Reston, Va. Attended Wisconsin-La Crosse. No college or pro playing experience. College coach: Kansas 1995-96, Southern California 1998-2000. Pro coach: Kansas City Chiefs 1997, joined Redskins in 2001.

Brian Schottenheimer, quarterbacks; born October 16, 1973, Denver, lives in Reston, Va. Quarterback Kansas 1992, Florida 1993-1996. No pro playing experience. College coach: Syracuse 1999, Southern California 2000. Pro coach: St. Louis Rams 1997, Kansas City Chiefs 1998, joined Redskins in 2001.

Kurt Schottenheimer, defensive coordinator; born October 1, 1949, McDonald, Pa., lives in Ashburn, Va. Defensive back Miami 1969-1970. No pro playing experience. College coach: William Paterson 1974, Michigan State 1978-1982, Tulane 1983, Louisiana State 1984-85, Notre Dame 1986. Pro coach: Cleveland Browns 1987-88, Kansas City Chiefs 1989-2000, joined Redskins in 2001.

Tony Sparano, tight ends; born October 7, 1961, West Haven, Conn., lives in Ashburn, Va. Center New Haven 1978-1981. No pro playing experience. College coach: New Haven 1984-87, 1994-98 (head coach 1994-98), Boston 1988-1993. Pro coach: Cleveland Browns 1999-2000, joined Redskins in 2001.

Mike Stock, special teams; born September 29, 1939, Baberton, Ohio, lives in Leesburg, Va. Fullback Northwestern 1957-1960. Pro running back Saskatchewan Roughriders (CFL) 1961. College coach: Northwestern 1961, Buffalo 1966-67, Navy 1968, Notre Dame 1969-1974, Wisconsin 1975-78, Eastern Michigan 1979-1983 (head coach), Notre Dame 1984-86, Ohio State 1992-94. Pro coach: Cincinnati Bengals 1987-1991, Kansas City Chiefs 1995-2000, joined Redskins in 2001.

Mike Trgovac, defensive line; born February 27, 1959, Youngstown, Ohio, lives in Ashburn, Va. Defensive lineman Michigan 1977-1980. No pro playing experience. College coach: Michigan 1984-85, Ball State 1986-88, Navy 1989, Colorado State 1990-91, Notre Dame 1992-94. Pro coach: Philadelphia Eagles 1995-98, Green Bay Packers 1999, joined Redskins in 2000.

2001 FIRST-YEAR ROSTER

Name	Pos.	Ht.	Wt.	Birthdate	College	Hometown	How Acq.
Anthony, Cornelius	LB	6-0	236	7/3/78	Texas A&M	Pinesville, La.	FA
Brandt, David	T-G	6-4	309	9/25/77	Michigan	Grand Rapids, Mich.	FA
Bryant, Terry	DT	6-4	287	2/5/78	Clemson	Savannah, Ga.	FA
Cerimele, Mike	RB	5-11	237	11/28/77	Penn State	Allentown, Pa.	FA
Cowsette, Delbert (1)	DT	6-1	288	9/3/77	Maryland	Cleveland, Ohio	FA-'00
Dailey, Jauron	LB	6-3	232	5/22/78	Florida A&M	Miami, Fla.	FA
DeLoach, Jerry (1)	DT	6-2	315	7/17/77	California	Elk Grove, Calif.	FA-'00
Dinkins, Jamaal	RB	6-0	230	9/23/78	Mississippi State	Jackson, Miss.	FA
Frantz, Dan	P	6-1	196	7/9/77	Portland State	Vancouver, Wash.	FA
Gardner, Rod	WR	6-2	218	10/26/77	Clemson	Jacksonville, Fla.	D1
Goodson, Tyrone (1)	WR	6-2	180	2/24/74	Auburn	Brooksville, Fla.	FA
Grim, Latef	WR	5-11	190	9/26/78	Pittsburgh	Stockton, Calif.	FA
Harms, Brad	T-G	6-2	295	8/18/77	Northern Iowa	Grundy Center, Iowa	FA
Hopkins, Tam	G-T	6-4	315	3/22/78	Ohio State	Winter Park, Fla.	FA
Houston, Martavius (1)	S	6-0	215	3/8/76	Auburn	Fort Lauderdale, Fla.	FA-'00
Johnson, Bryan (1)	FB	6-1	234	1/18/78	Boise State	Pocatello, Idaho	FA-'00
Kalich, Ryan (1)	G	6-2	297	11/21/76	Florida	Houston, Texas	FA-'00
Kelly, Roderick	DE	6-5	255	12/27/78	Northeast Oklahoma	Houston, Texas	FA
Langley, Trey	T-G	6-4	291	11/28/76	Louisiana State	Eunice, La.	FA
McCants, Darnerien	WR	6-3	214	8/1/77	Delaware State	Odenton, Md.	D5
Mercer, Ivan	TE	6-6	227	9/19/75	Miami	Antelope, Calif.	FA
Monds, Mario	DT	6-3	325	11/10/76	Cincinnati	Fort Pierce, Fla.	D6
Morrison, Jake	LB	6-2	227	2/1/78	McNeese State	Nassau Bay, Texas	FA
Murphy, Chaz	LB	6-3	237	3/30/77	Kansas	Galveston, Texas	FA
Nagle, Kevin (1)	LB	6-1	229	4/30/75	East Stroudsburg	Effort, Pa.	FA
Nash, Tommy (1)	WR	6-0	162	3/2/77	Wyoming	Tulsa, Okla.	FA-'00
October, Winston (1)	WR-KR	5-8	165	7/12/76	Richmond	Dale City, Va.	FA
Ohalete, Ifeanyi	DB	6-2	217	5/22/79	Southern California	Springfield, Ill.	FA
Pierce, Antonio	LB	6-1	232	10/26/78	Arizona	Ontario, Calif.	FA
Rosenfels, Sage	QB	6-4	218	3/6/78	Iowa State	Maquoketa, Iowa	D4
Schwab, Jason	T-G	6-1	304	5/12/77	Nebraska	Eagan, Minn.	FA
Sessions, Anthony	LB	6-0	225	2/16/79	Tennessee	Bonaire, Ga.	FA
Sigmund, John	TE	6-4	266	7/2/78	Wisconsin	Sewell, N.J.	FA
Simmons, Terrance (1)	T-G	6-8	310	5/3/76	Alabama State	Prichard, Ala.	FA-'00
Skaggs, Justin	WR	6-2	200	4/22/79	Evangel	Wentzville, Mo.	FA
Smoot, Fred	CB	5-11	172	4/17/79	Mississippi State	Jackson, Miss.	D2
Spencer, Willie (1)	WR	6-2	215	4/4/77	Tiffin	Massillon, Wash.	FA
Stephens, Stanley	HB	6-0	203	3/24/77	South Carolina State	West Palm Beach, Fla.	FA
Stevenson, Eric (1)	DT	6-2	295	9/21/77	Oklahoma State	Crescent, Okla.	FA-'00
Symonette, Joshua (1)	S	5-10	200	5/8/78	Tennessee Tech	Miami, Fla.	FA-'00
Tucker, Ross	G-T	6-4	305	3/2/79	Princeton	Wyomissing, Pa.	FA
Walls, Greg	DB	6-1	187	2/22/79	Texas Christian	Picayune, Miss.	FA
Watkins, Mike	QB	6-4	220	12/10/78	Louisville	Fort Pierce, Fla.	FA
Watson, Kenny	HB	5-11	205	3/13/78	Penn State	Harrisburg, Pa.	FA
Whitfield, Eric (1)	CB	6-0	205	1/17/78	UCLA	Wilmington, Calif.	FA-'00

The term NFL Rookie is defined as a player who is in his first season of professional football and has not been on the roster of another professional football team for any regular-season or postseason games. A Rookie is designated by an "R" on NFL rosters. Players who have been active in another professional football league or players who have NFL experience, including either preseason training camp or being on an Active List or Inactive List, or on Reserve/Injured or Reserve/Physically Unable to Perform for fewer than six regular-season games, are termed NFL First-Year Players. An NFL First-Year Player is designated by a "1" on NFL rosters. Thereafter, a player is credited with an additional year of experience for each season in which he accumulates six games on the Active List or Inactive List, or on Reserve/Injured or Reserve/Physically Unable to Perform.

2000 Season in Review

TRADES

2000 INTERCONFERENCE TRADES

Running back **Fred Lane** from Carolina to Indianapolis for linebacker **Spencer Reid** (4/21).

Wide receiver **Dane Looker** from St. Louis to New England for an unannounced selection in 2002 (8/7).

Linebacker **Nate Wayne** from Denver to Green Bay for the Packers' fourth-round selection in 2001. Denver selected center **Ben Hamilton** (Minnesota) (8/15).

Punter **John Baker** from Indianapolis to St. Louis for an unannounced selection in 2002 (8/22).

Wide receiver **Jeff Ogden** from Dallas to Miami for an unannounced selection in 2002 (8/23).

Defensive tackle **Chuck Osborne** from Oakland to Green Bay for an unannounced selection in 2002 (8/27).

Tight end **Alonzo Mayes** from Chicago to Miami for the Bears' seventh-round selection in 2001. Chicago selected wide receiver **John Capel** (Florida) (10/2).

2000 AFC TRADES

Wide receiver **Nate Jacquet** from Miami to San Diego for the Chargers' sixth-round selection in 2001. Miami selected tackle **Brandon Winey** (Louisiana State) (8/22).

Defensive back **Chris Watson** from Denver to Buffalo for the Bills' fourth-round selection in 2001. Denver traded the selection back to Buffalo as part of April 21, 2001 deal (8/27).

Guard **Gennaro DiNapoli** from Oakland to Tennessee for the Titans' seventh-round selection in 2001. Oakland selected wide receiver **Ken-Yon Rambo** (Ohio State) (8/27).

2000 NFC TRADES

Center **Joe Zelenka** from San Francisco to Washington for the Redskins' seventh-round selection in 2001. San Francisco selected tight end **Eric Johnson** (Yale) (4/17).

Defensive back **Kevin Mathis** from Dallas to New Orleans for linebacker **Chris Bordano** (4/26).

Defensive back **R.W. McQuarters** from San Francisco to Chicago for the Bears' sixth-round selection in 2001. San Francisco selected wide receiver **Cedrick Wilson** (Tennessee) (6/6).

Running back **Marvin Powell** from New Orleans to Green Bay for tight end **Lawrence Hart** (7/11).

Linebacker **K. D. Williams** and the Saints' third-round selection in 2001 from New Orleans to Green Bay for quarterback **Aaron Brooks** and tight end **Lamont Hall.** Green Bay traded selection to San Francisco as part of April 21, 2001 deal (7/31).

Tight end **Lawrence Hart** from New Orleans to Dallas for an unannounced selection in 2002 (8/10).

Defensive back **Allen Rossum** from Philadelphia to Green Bay for the Packers' fifth-round selection in 2001. Philadelphia selected tight end **Tony Stewart** (Penn State) (8/26).

Tight end **O.J. Santiago** from Atlanta to Dallas for the Cowboys' fourth-round selection in 2001 and an unannounced selection in 2002. Atlanta selected linebacker **Matt Stewart** (Vanderbilt) (8/27).

2001 INTERCONFERENCE TRADES

Quarterback **Matt Hasselbeck** and the Packers' first-round selection in 2001 from Green Bay to Seattle for the Seahawks' first- and third-round selections in 2001. Green Bay selected **Jamal Reynolds** (Florida State) and linebacker **Torrance Marshall** (Oklahoma). Seattle selected guard **Steve Hutchinson** (Michigan) (3/5).

Defensive end **Kevin Carter** from St. Louis to Tennessee for the Titans' first-round selection in 2001. St. Louis selected defensive tackle **Ryan Pickett** (Ohio State) (4/4).

Wide receiver **Tim Dwight** and the Falcons' first- and third-round selection in 2001 and second-round selection in 2002 from Atlanta to San Diego for the Chargers' first-round selection in 2001. San Diego selected running back **LaDainian Tomlinson** (Texas Christian) and defensive back **Tay Cody** (Florida State). Atlanta selected quarterback **Michael Vick** (Virginia Tech) (4/20).

Tight end **Roland Williams** from St. Louis to Oakland for the Raiders' fourth-round selection in 2001. Oakland traded the selection to Arizona (4/21).

Quarterback **Trent Green** and the Rams' fifth-round selection in 2001 from St. Louis to Kansas City for the Chiefs' first-round selection in 2001. St. Louis selected defensive tackle **Damione Lewis** (Miami). Kansas City selected running back **Derrick Blaylock** (Stephen F. Austin) (4/21).

San Francisco 49ers trade their first-round selection, the Saints' third-round selection, and the Rams' seventh-round selection in 2001 to Seattle for the Cowboys' first-round selection and the Raiders' sixth-round selection in 2001. San Francisco selected defensive end **Andre Carter** (California) and defensive end **Menson Holloway** (Texas-El Paso). Seattle selected wide receiver **Koren Robinson** (North Carolina State), running back **Heath Evans** (Auburn), and tackle **Dennis Norman** (Princeton) (4/21).

Buffalo Bills trade their first-round selection in 2001 to Tampa Bay for the Buccaneers' first- and second-round selections in 2001. Buffalo selected defensive back **Nate Clements** (Ohio State) and traded the second-round pick to Denver. Tampa Bay selected tackle **Kenyatta Walker** (Florida) (4/21).

Indianapolis Colts trade their first-round selection in 2001 to the New York Giants for the Giants' first-, third-, and sixth-round selections in 2001. Indianapolis selected wide receiver **Reggie Wayne** (Miami), defensive back **Cory Bird** (Virginia Tech), and defensive back **Jason Doering** (Wisconsin). New York Giants selected defensive back **Will Allen** (Syracuse) (4/21).

Dallas Cowboys trade their second-round selection in 2001 to the Indianapolis Colts for the Colts' second- and third-round selections in 2001. Dallas selected traded the picks to Miami and New Orleans. Indianapolis selected defensive back **Idrees Bashir** (Memphis) (4/21).

Detroit Lions trade their second-round selection in 2001 to the New England Patriots for the Steelers' second-round selection and the 49ers' sixth-round selection in 2001. Detroit selected center **Dominic Raiola** (Nebraska) and linebacker **Jason Glenn** (Texas A&M). New England selected guard **Matt Light** (Purdue) (4/21).

Dallas Cowboys trade the Colts' second-round selection in 2001 to Miami for the Dolphins' second- and fourth-round selections in 2001. Dallas selected defensive back **Tony Dixon** (Alabama) and linebacker **Markus Steele** (Southern California). Miami selected wide receiver **Chris Chambers** (Wisconsin) (4/21).

Minnesota Vikings trade their third- and fourth-round selections in 2001 to New England for the Patriots' third-round selection in 2001. Minnesota selected defensive back **Eric Kelly** (Kentucky). New England selected defensive back **Brock Williams** (Notre Dame) and tight end **Jabari Holloway** (Notre Dame) (4/21).

Miami Dolphins trade their second-round selection in 2002 to Philadelphia for the Eagles' third- and sixth-round selections in 2001. Miami selected linebacker **Morlon Greenwood** (Syracuse) and defensive end **Otis Levfrette** (Alabama-Birmingham) (4/21).

Detroit Lions trade their sixth- and seventh-round selections in 2001 to the New England Patriots for the Jets' fifth-round selection in 2001. Detroit selected quarterback **Mike McMahon** (Rutgers). New England selected tight end **Arther Love** (South Carolina State) and kicker **Owen Pochman** (Brigham Young) (4/22).

Atlanta Falcons trade their fourth-round selection in 2002 to the Denver Broncos for the Redskins' seventh-round selection, the Packers' seventh-round selection, and the Broncos' seventh-round selection in 2001. Atlanta selected defensive back **Corey Hall** (Appalachian State), tackle **Kynan Forney** (Hawaii), and defensive end **Ronald Flemons** (Texas A&M) (4/22).

2001 AFC TRADES

New York Jets trade their first-, fourth-, and sixth-round selections in 2001 to Pittsburgh for the Steelers' first-round selection in 2001. New York Jets selected wide receiver **Santana Moss**. Pittsburgh selected defensive tackle **Casey Hampton** (Texas), tackle **Mathia Nkwenti** (Temple), and defensive end **Rodney Bailey** (Ohio State) (4/21).

New England Patriots trade their second-round selection in 2001 to Pittsburgh for the Steelers' second- and fourth-round selections in 2001. New England traded their picks to Detroit and San Diego. Pittsburgh selected linebacker **Kendrell Bell** (Georgia) (4/21).

Buffalo Bills trade the Buccaneers' second-round selection in 2001 to Denver for the Broncos' second-round selection and the Bills' fourth-round selection in 2001. Buffalo selected running back **Travis Henry** (Tennessee) and linebacker **Brandon Spoon** (North Carolina). Denver selected defensive end **Paul Toviessi** (Marshall) (4/21).

New England Patriots trade the Steelers' fourth-round selection and their fifth-round selection in 2001 to San Diego for the Chargers' fourth-round selection in 2001. New England selected guard **Kenyatta Jones** (South Florida). San Diego selected linebacker **Carlos Polk** (Nebraska) and linebacker **Zeke Moreno** (Southern California) (4/22).

Jacksonville Jaguars trade their fifth-round selection in 2002 to New England for the Patriots' sixth-round selection in 2001. Jacksonville selected guard **Chad Ward** (Washington) (4/22).

2001 NFC TRADES

Quarterback **Eric Zeier** from Tampa Bay to Atlanta for the Falcons' seventh-round selection in 2001. Tampa Bay selected tight end **Dauntae' Finger** (North Carolina) (3/6).

Linebacker **Jeff Gooch** from Tampa Bay to St. Louis for the Broncos' fifth-round selection in 2001. Gooch reverted to Tampa Bay, and St. Louis retained Denver's fifth-round selection (3/19).

Green Bay Packers trade their second-, third-, and sixth-round selections in 2001, the Saints' third-round selection in 2001, and the Rams' seventh-round selection in 2001 to San Francisco for the 49ers' second-, third-, and fourth-round selections in 2001. San Francisco selected linebacker **Jamie Winborn** (Vanderbilt), running back **Kevan Barlow** (Pittsburgh), and defensive back **Rashad Holman** (Louisville), and traded the Saints' third-round selection and the Rams' seventh-round selections to Seattle. Green Bay selected wide receiver **Robert Ferguson** (Texas A&M), defensive back **Bhawoh Jue** (Penn State), and guard **Bill Ferrario** (Wisconsin) (4/21).

Defensive back **Aeneas Williams** from Arizona to St. Louis for the Rams' second-round selection and the Raiders' fourth-round selection in 2001. Arizona selected defensive back **Michael Stone** (Memphis) and defensive tackle **Marcus Bell** (Memphis) (4/21).

Dallas Cowboys trade their third-round selection and the Colts' third-round selection in 2001 to New Orleans for the Saints' second-round selection in 2001. Dallas selected quarterback **Quincy Carter** (Georgia). New Orleans selected linebacker **Sedrick Hodge** (North Carolina) and defensive tackle **Kenny Smith** (Alabama) (4/21).

2000 PRESEASON STANDINGS/RESULTS

Detroit Lions trade their third- and fourth-round selections in 2001 to the New York Giants for their second-round selection in 2001. Detroit selected defensive tackle **Shaun Rogers** (Texas). New York Giants selected defensive back **William Peterson** (Western Illinois) and defensive end **Cedric Scott** (Southern Mississippi) (4/21).

St. Louis Rams trade the Broncos' fifth-round selection and their sixth-round selection in 2001 to Washington for the Redskins' fifth-round selection in 2001. St. Louis selected defensive back **Jerametrius Butler** (Kansas State). Washington selected wide receiver **Darnerien McCants** (Delaware State) and defensive tackle **Mario Monds** (Cincinnati) (4/22).

PRESEASON FINAL STANDINGS

AMERICAN FOOTBALL CONFERENCE

Eastern Division

	W	L	T	Pct.	Pts.	OP
Buffalo	3	1	0	.750	81	74
Miami	3	1	0	.750	64	57
Indianapolis	3	2	0	.600	102	101
New England	3	2	0	.600	103	92
N.Y. Jets	2	2	0	.500	75	91

Central Division

	W	L	T	Pct.	Pts.	OP
Baltimore	4	0	0	1.000	74	43
Jacksonville	3	1	0	.750	96	80
Tennessee	3	1	0	.750	110	75
Pittsburgh	3	2	0	.600	97	61
Cincinnati	1	3	0	.250	73	93
Cleveland	1	3	0	.250	72	99

Western Division

	W	L	T	Pct.	Pts.	OP
Denver	4	0	0	1.000	121	84
San Diego	4	0	0	1.000	106	61
Oakland	3	1	0	.750	81	68
Seattle	2	2	0	.500	56	78
Kansas City	0	4	0	.000	56	110

NATIONAL FOOTBALL CONFERENCE

Eastern Division

	W	L	T	Pct.	Pts.	OP
Washington	3	1	0	.750	83	43
Arizona	1	3	0	.250	75	93
Philadelphia	1	3	0	.250	81	97
N.Y. Giants	0	4	0	.000	62	87
Dallas	0	5	0	.000	79	139

Central Division

	W	L	T	Pct.	Pts.	OP
Tampa Bay	3	1	0	.750	94	62
Chicago	2	2	0	.500	87	72
Detroit	2	2	0	.500	63	62
Green Bay	2	2	0	.500	105	100
Minnesota	1	3	0	.250	96	105

Western Division

	W	L	T	Pct.	Pts.	OP
Atlanta	4	1	0	.800	116	86
St. Louis	2	2	0	.500	85	95
New Orleans	1	3	0	.250	62	87
San Francisco	1	4	0	.200	98	106
Carolina	0	4	0	.000	48	100

AFC PRESEASON RECORDS—TEAM BY TEAM

Eastern Division

BUFFALO (3-1)

21	Cincinnati	20
13	at Detroit	15
31	at St. Louis	27
16	at Philadelphia	12
81		74

INDIANAPOLIS (3-2)

13	Atlanta	20
16	at Seattle	28
17	New Orleans (b)	0
24	vs. Pittsburgh (c)	23
32	Minnesota	30
102		101

MIAMI (3-1)

10	at Pittsburgh	13
15	Tampa Bay	13
17	Green Bay	14
22	at New Orleans	17
64		57

NEW ENGLAND (3-2)

20	vs. San Francisco (a)	0
13	at Detroit	10
20	at Washington	30
21	Tampa Bay	31
29	Carolina	21
103		92

N.Y. JETS (2-2)

24	New Orleans	20
24	at Green Bay	37
0	at Baltimore	10
27	N.Y. Giants	24
75		91

Central Division

BALTIMORE (4-0)

16	Philadelphia	13
10	N.Y. Jets	0
24	at Carolina	13
24	at N.Y. Giants	17
74		43

CINCINNATI (1-3)

20	at Buffalo	21
16	at Atlanta	31
24	Chicago	20
13	Detroit	21
73		93

CLEVELAND (1-3)

33	Philadelphia	22
6	at Chicago	19
0	Washington	24
33	at Green Bay	34
72		99

JACKSONVILLE (3-1)

34	at Carolina	14
16	N.Y. Giants	13
26	at Kansas City	22
20	Atlanta	31
96		80

PITTSBURGH (3-2)

38	at Dallas	10
13	Miami	10
13	Carolina	0
23	vs. Indianapolis (c)	24
10	at Washington	17
97		61

TENNESSEE (3-1)

14	Kansas City	10
30	St. Louis	3
32	at Philadelphia	34
34	at Chicago	28
110		75

Western Division

DENVER (4-0)

31	at Arizona	17
26	Green Bay	20
36	Dallas	23
28	at San Francisco	24
121		84

KANSAS CITY (0-4)

10	at Tennessee	14
10	San Francisco	33
22	Jacksonville	26
14	at Tampa Bay	37
56		110

OAKLAND (3-1)

17	at St. Louis	31
21	at Dallas	20
23	Detroit	17
20	Seattle	0
81		68

SAN DIEGO (4-0)

23	at San Francisco	20
31	Minnesota	7
28	at Atlanta	14
24	Arizona	20
106		61

SEATTLE (2-2)

28	Indianapolis	16
3	at Arizona	21
25	San Francisco	21
0	at Oakland	20
56		78

NFC PRESEASON RECORDS—TEAM BY TEAM

Eastern Division

ARIZONA (1-3)

17	Denver	31
21	Seattle	3
17	at Minnesota	35
20	at San Diego	24
75		93

DALLAS (0-5)

10	Pittsburgh	38
9	vs. Atlanta (d)	20
20	Oakland	21
23	at Denver	36
17	St. Louis	24
79		139

N.Y. GIANTS (0-4)

8	Chicago	20
13	at Jacksonville	16
24	at N.Y. Jets	27
17	Baltimore	24
62		87

PHILADELPHIA (1-3)

22	at Cleveland	33
13	at Baltimore	16
34	Tennessee	32
12	Buffalo	16
81		97

WASHINGTON (3-1)

12	at Tampa Bay	13
30	New England	20
24	at Cleveland	0
17	Pittsburgh	10
83		43

Central Division

CHICAGO (2-2)

20	at N.Y. Giants	8
19	Cleveland	6
20	at Cincinnati	24
28	Tennessee	34
87		72

DETROIT (2-2)

10	New England	13
15	Buffalo	13
17	at Oakland	23
21	at Cincinnati	13
63		62

GREEN BAY (2-2)

37	N.Y. Jets	24
20	at Denver	26
14	at Miami	17
34	Cleveland	33
105		100

MINNESOTA (1-3)

24	New Orleans	25
7	at San Diego	31
35	Arizona	17
30	at Indianapolis	32
96		105

TAMPA BAY (3-1)

13	Washington	12
13	at Miami	15
31	at New England	21
37	Kansas City	14
94		62

Western Division

ATLANTA (4-1)

20	at Indianapolis	13
20	vs. Dallas (d)	9
31	Cincinnati	16
14	San Diego	28
31	at Jacksonville	20
116		86

CAROLINA (0-4)

14	Jacksonville	34
0	at Pittsburgh	13
13	Baltimore	24
21	at New England	29
48		100

NEW ORLEANS (1-3)

20	at N.Y. Jets	24
25	at Minnesota	24
0	at Indianapolis (b)	17
17	Miami	22
62		87

ST. LOUIS (2-2)

31	Oakland	17
3	at Tennessee	30
27	Buffalo	31
24	at Dallas	17
85		95

SAN FRANCISCO (1-4)

0	vs. New England (a)	20
20	San Diego	23
33	at Kansas City	10
21	at Seattle	25
24	Denver	28
98		106

(a) Pro Football Hall of Fame Game at Canton, Ohio
(b) at West Lafayette, Indiana
(c) American Bowl at Mexico City, Mexico
(d) American Bowl at Tokyo, Japan

2000 NFL STANDINGS/RESULTS

FINAL STANDINGS

AMERICAN FOOTBALL CONFERENCE

Eastern Division	W	L	T	Pct.	Pts.	OP
Miami	11	5	0	.688	323	226
*Indianapolis	10	6	0	.625	429	326
N.Y. Jets	9	7	0	.563	321	321
Buffalo	8	8	0	.500	315	350
New England	5	11	0	.313	276	338
Central Division						
#Tennessee	13	3	0	.813	346	191
*Baltimore	12	4	0	.750	333	165
Pittsburgh	9	7	0	.563	321	255
Jacksonville	7	9	0	.438	367	327
Cincinnati	4	12	0	.250	185	359
Cleveland	3	13	0	.188	161	419
Western Division						
Oakland	12	4	0	.750	479	299
*Denver	11	5	0	.688	485	369
Kansas City	7	9	0	.438	355	354
Seattle	6	10	0	.375	320	405
San Diego	1	15	0	.063	269	440

NATIONAL FOOTBALL CONFERENCE

Eastern Division	W	L	T	Pct.	Pts.	OP
#N.Y. Giants	12	4	0	.750	328	246
*Philadelphia	11	5	0	.688	351	245
Washington	8	8	0	.500	281	269
Dallas	5	11	0	.313	294	361
Arizona	3	13	0	.188	210	443
Central Division						
Minnesota	11	5	0	.688	397	371
*Tampa Bay	10	6	0	.625	388	269
Green Bay	9	7	0	.563	353	323
Detroit	9	7	0	.563	307	307
Chicago	5	11	0	.313	216	355
Western Division						
New Orleans	10	6	0	.625	354	305
*St. Louis	10	6	0	.625	540	471
Carolina	7	9	0	.438	310	310
San Francisco	6	10	0	.375	388	422
Atlanta	4	12	0	.250	252	413

**Wild-Card qualifier for playoffs; #Top playoff seed in conference*

Green Bay finished ahead of Detroit based on better division record (5-3 to Lions' 3-5). New Orleans finished ahead of St. Louis based on better division record (7-1 to Rams' 5-3). Tampa Bay was second Wild Card based on head-to-head victory over St. Louis (1-0).

WILD CARD PLAYOFFS

AFC

MIAMI 23, Indianapolis 17 (OT)
BALTIMORE 21, Denver 3

NFC

NEW ORLEANS 31, St. Louis 28
PHILADELPHIA 21, Tampa Bay 3

DIVISIONAL PLAYOFFS

AFC

OAKLAND 27, Miami 0
Baltimore 24, TENNESSEE 10

NFC

MINNESOTA 34, New Orleans 16
N.Y. GIANTS 20, Philadelphia 10

CHAMPIONSHIP GAMES

AFC

Baltimore 16, OAKLAND 3

NFC

N.Y. GIANTS 41, Minnesota 0

SUPER BOWL XXXV

Baltimore (AFC) 34, N.Y. Giants (NFC) 7
at Raymond James Stadium, Tampa, Florida

AFC-NFC PRO BOWL

AFC 38, NFC 17, at Aloha Stadium, Honolulu, Hawaii

Home teams in playoff games are indicated in CAPS.

AFC SEASON RECORDS—TEAM BY TEAM

BALTIMORE

16	at Pittsburgh	0
39	JACKSONVILLE	36
6	at Miami	19
37	CINCINNATI	0
12	at Cleveland	0
15	at Jacksonville	10
3	at Washington	10
6	TENNESSEE	14
6	PITTSBURGH	9
27	at Cincinnati	7
24	at Tennessee	23
27	DALLAS	0
44	CLEVELAND	7
24	SAN DIEGO	3
13	at Arizona	7
34	N.Y. JETS	20
333		165

BUFFALO

16	TENNESSEE	13
27	GREEN BAY	18
14	at N.Y. Jets	27
16	INDIANAPOLIS	18
13	at Miami	22
27	SAN DIEGO (OT)	24
27	at Minnesota	31
23	N.Y. JETS	20
16	at New England (OT)	13
20	CHICAGO	3
21	at Kansas City	17
17	at Tampa Bay	31
6	MIAMI	33
20	at Indianapolis	44
10	NEW ENGLAND (OT)	13
42	at Seattle	23
315		350

CINCINNATI

7	CLEVELAND	24
0	at Jacksonville	13
0	at Baltimore	37
16	MIAMI	31
14	TENNESSEE	23
0	at Pittsburgh	15
31	DENVER	21
12	at Cleveland	3
7	BALTIMORE	27
6	at Dallas	23
13	at New England	16
28	PITTSBURGH	48
24	ARIZONA	13
3	at Tennessee	35
17	JACKSONVILLE	14
7	at Philadelphia	16
185		359

CLEVELAND

7	JACKSONVILLE	27
24	at Cincinnati	7
23	PITTSBURGH	20
10	at Oakland	36
0	BALTIMORE	12
21	at Arizona	29
10	at Denver	44
0	at Pittsburgh	22
3	CINCINNATI	12
3	N.Y. GIANTS	24
19	NEW ENGLAND	11
10	at Tennessee	24
7	at Baltimore	44
0	at Jacksonville	48
24	PHILADELPHIA	35
0	TENNESSEE	24
161		419

DENVER

36	at St. Louis	41
42	ATLANTA	14
33	at Oakland	24
22	KANSAS CITY	23
19	NEW ENGLAND	28
21	at San Diego	7
44	CLEVELAND	10
21	at Cincinnati	31
30	at N.Y. Jets	23
27	OAKLAND	24
38	SAN DIEGO	37
38	at Seattle	31
38	at New Orleans	23
31	SEATTLE	24
7	at Kansas City	20
38	SAN FRANCISCO	9
485		369

INDIANAPOLIS

27	at Kansas City	14
31	OAKLAND	38
43	JACKSONVILLE	14
18	at Buffalo	16
16	at New England	24
37	at Seattle	24
30	NEW ENGLAND	23
30	DETROIT	18
24	at Chicago	27
23	N.Y. JETS	15
24	at Green Bay	26
14	MIAMI	17
17	at N.Y. Jets	27
44	BUFFALO	20
20	at Miami	13
31	MINNESOTA	10
429		326

JACKSONVILLE

27	at Cleveland	7
36	at Baltimore	39
13	CINCINNATI	0
14	at Indianapolis	43
13	PITTSBURGH	24
10	BALTIMORE	15
13	at Tennessee	27
16	WASHINGTON	35
23	at Dallas (OT)	17
21	SEATTLE	28
34	at Pittsburgh	24
16	TENNESSEE	13
48	CLEVELAND	0
44	ARIZONA	10
14	at Cincinnati	17
25	at N.Y. Giants	28
367		327

KANSAS CITY

14	INDIANAPOLIS	27
14	at Tennessee (OT)	17
42	SAN DIEGO	10
23	at Denver	22
24	SEATTLE	17
17	OAKLAND	20
54	ST. LOUIS	34
24	at Seattle	19
31	at Oakland	49
7	at San Francisco	21
17	BUFFALO	21
16	at San Diego	17
24	at New England	30
15	CAROLINA	14
20	DENVER	7
13	at Atlanta	29
355		354

MIAMI

23	SEATTLE	0
7	at Minnesota	13
19	BALTIMORE	6
10	NEW ENGLAND	3
31	at Cincinnati	16
22	BUFFALO	13
37	at N.Y. Jets (OT)	40
28	GREEN BAY	20
23	at Detroit	8
17	at San Diego	7
3	N.Y. JETS	20
17	at Indianapolis	14
33	at Buffalo	6
13	TAMPA BAY	16
13	INDIANAPOLIS	20
27	at New England	24
323		226

NEW ENGLAND

16	TAMPA BAY	21
19	at N.Y. Jets	20
13	MINNESOTA	21
3	at Miami	10
28	at Denver	19
24	INDIANAPOLIS	16
17	N.Y. JETS	34
23	at Indianapolis	30
13	BUFFALO (OT)	16
11	at Cleveland	19
16	CINCINNATI	13
9	at Detroit	34
30	KANSAS CITY	24
17	at Chicago	24
13	at Buffalo (OT)	10
24	MIAMI	27
276		338

N.Y. JETS

20	at Green Bay	16
20	NEW ENGLAND	19
27	BUFFALO	14
21	at Tampa Bay	17
3	PITTSBURGH	20
34	at New England	17
40	MIAMI (OT)	37
20	at Buffalo	23
23	DENVER	30
15	at Indianapolis	23
20	at Miami	3
17	CHICAGO	10
27	INDIANAPOLIS	17
7	at Oakland	31
7	DETROIT	10
20	at Baltimore	34
321		321

OAKLAND

9	SAN DIEGO	6
38	at Indianapolis	31
24	DENVER	33
36	CLEVELAND	10
34	at San Francisco (OT)	28
20	at Kansas City	17
31	SEATTLE	3
15	at San Diego	13
49	KANSAS CITY	31
24	at Denver	27
31	at New Orleans	22
41	ATLANTA	14
20	at Pittsburgh	21
31	N.Y. JETS	7
24	at Seattle	27
52	CAROLINA	9
479		299

PITTSBURGH

0	BALTIMORE	16
20	at Cleveland	23
20	TENNESSEE	23
24	at Jacksonville	13
20	at N.Y. Jets	3
15	CINCINNATI	0
22	CLEVELAND	0
9	at Baltimore	6
7	at Tennessee	9
23	PHILADELPHIA (OT)	26
24	JACKSONVILLE	34
48	at Cincinnati	28
21	OAKLAND	20
10	at N.Y. Giants	30
24	WASHINGTON	3
34	at San Diego	21
321		255

SAN DIEGO

6	at Oakland	9
27	NEW ORLEANS	28
10	at Kansas City	42
12	SEATTLE	20
31	at St. Louis	57
7	DENVER	21
24	at Buffalo (OT)	27
13	OAKLAND	15
15	at Seattle	17
7	MIAMI	17
37	at Denver	38
17	KANSAS CITY	16
17	SAN FRANCISCO	45
3	at Baltimore	24
22	at Carolina	30
21	PITTSBURGH	34
269		440

SEATTLE

0	at Miami	23
34	ST. LOUIS	37
20	NEW ORLEANS	10
20	at San Diego	12
17	at Kansas City	24
3	at Carolina	26
24	INDIANAPOLIS	37
3	at Oakland	31
19	KANSAS CITY	24
17	SAN DIEGO	15
28	at Jacksonville	21
31	DENVER	38
30	at Atlanta	10
24	at Denver	31
27	OAKLAND	24
23	BUFFALO	42
320		405

TENNESSEE

13	at Buffalo	16
17	KANSAS CITY (OT)	14
23	at Pittsburgh	20
28	N.Y. GIANTS	14
23	at Cincinnati	14
27	JACKSONVILLE	13
14	at Baltimore	6
27	at Washington	21
9	PITTSBURGH	7
23	BALTIMORE	24
24	CLEVELAND	10
13	at Jacksonville	16
15	at Philadelphia	13
35	CINCINNATI	3
24	at Cleveland	0
31	DALLAS	0
346		191

NFC SEASON RECORDS—TEAM BY TEAM

ARIZONA		
16	at N.Y. Giants	21
32	DALLAS	31
3	GREEN BAY	29
20	at San Francisco	27
29	CLEVELAND	21
14	PHILADELPHIA	33
7	at Dallas	48
10	NEW ORLEANS	21
16	WASHINGTON	15
14	at Minnesota	31
9	at Philadelphia	34
7	N.Y. GIANTS	31
13	at Cincinnati	24
10	at Jacksonville	44
7	BALTIMORE	13
3	at Washington	20
210		443

ATLANTA		
36	SAN FRANCISCO	28
14	at Denver	42
15	at Carolina	10
20	ST. LOUIS	41
10	at Philadelphia	38
6	N.Y. GIANTS	13
29	at St. Louis	45
19	NEW ORLEANS	21
13	CAROLINA	12
14	TAMPA BAY	27
10	at Detroit	13
6	at San Francisco	16
14	at Oakland	41
10	SEATTLE	30
7	at New Orleans	23
29	KANSAS CITY	13
252		413

CAROLINA		
17	at Washington	20
38	at San Francisco	22
10	ATLANTA	15
13	DALLAS (OT)	16
26	SEATTLE	3
6	at New Orleans	24
34	SAN FRANCISCO	16
12	at Atlanta	13
27	at St. Louis	24
10	NEW ORLEANS	20
17	at Minnesota	31
31	GREEN BAY	14
16	ST. LOUIS	3
14	at Kansas City	15
30	SAN DIEGO	22
9	at Oakland	52
310		310

CHICAGO		
27	at Minnesota	30
0	at Tampa Bay	41
7	N.Y. GIANTS	14
14	DETROIT	21
27	at Green Bay	24
10	NEW ORLEANS	31
16	MINNESOTA	28
9	at Philadelphia	13
27	INDIANAPOLIS	24
3	at Buffalo	20
13	TAMPA BAY	10
10	at N.Y. Jets	17
6	GREEN BAY	28
24	NEW ENGLAND	17
0	at San Francisco	17
23	at Detroit	20
216		355

DALLAS		
14	PHILADELPHIA	41
31	at Arizona	32
27	at Washington	21
24	SAN FRANCISCO	41
16	at Carolina (OT)	13
14	at N.Y. Giants	19
48	ARIZONA	7
17	JACKSONVILLE (OT)	23
13	at Philadelphia (OT)	16
23	CINCINNATI	6
0	at Baltimore	27
15	MINNESOTA	27
7	at Tampa Bay	27
32	WASHINGTON	13
13	N.Y. GIANTS	17
0	at Tennessee	31
294		361

DETROIT		
14	at New Orleans	10
15	WASHINGTON	10
10	TAMPA BAY	31
21	at Chicago	14
24	MINNESOTA	31
31	GREEN BAY	24
28	at Tampa Bay	14
18	at Indianapolis	30
8	MIAMI	23
13	ATLANTA	10
31	at N.Y. Giants	21
34	NEW ENGLAND	9
17	at Minnesota	24
13	at Green Bay	26
10	at N.Y. Jets	7
20	CHICAGO	23
307		307

GREEN BAY		
16	N.Y. JETS	20
18	at Buffalo	27
6	PHILADELPHIA	3
29	at Arizona	3
24	CHICAGO	27
24	at Detroit	31
31	SAN FRANCISCO	28
20	at Miami	28
26	MINNESOTA (OT)	20
15	at Tampa Bay	20
26	INDIANAPOLIS	24
14	at Carolina	31
28	at Chicago	6
26	DETROIT	13
33	at Minnesota	28
17	TAMPA BAY (OT)	14
353		323

MINNESOTA		
30	CHICAGO	27
13	MIAMI	7
21	at New England	13
31	at Detroit	24
30	TAMPA BAY	23
28	at Chicago	16
31	BUFFALO	27
13	at Tampa Bay	41
20	at Green Bay (OT)	26
31	ARIZONA	14
31	CAROLINA	17
27	at Dallas	15
24	DETROIT	17
29	at St. Louis	40
28	GREEN BAY	33
10	at Indianapolis	31
397		371

NEW ORLEANS		
10	DETROIT	14
28	at San Diego	27
10	at Seattle	20
7	PHILADELPHIA	21
31	at Chicago	10
24	CAROLINA	6
21	at Atlanta	19
21	at Arizona	10
31	SAN FRANCISCO	15
20	at Carolina	10
22	OAKLAND	31
31	at St. Louis	24
23	DENVER	38
31	at San Francisco	27
23	ATLANTA	7
21	ST. LOUIS	26
354		305

N.Y. GIANTS		
21	ARIZONA	16
33	at Philadelphia	18
14	at Chicago	7
6	WASHINGTON	16
14	at Tennessee	28
13	at Atlanta	6
19	DALLAS	14
24	PHILADELPHIA	7
24	at Cleveland	3
24	ST. LOUIS	38
21	DETROIT	31
31	at Arizona	7
9	at Washington	7
30	PITTSBURGH	10
17	at Dallas	13
28	JACKSONVILLE	25
328		246

PHILADELPHIA		
41	at Dallas	14
18	N.Y. GIANTS	33
3	at Green Bay	6
21	at New Orleans	7
38	ATLANTA	10
14	WASHINGTON	17
33	at Arizona	14
13	CHICAGO	9
7	at N.Y. Giants	24
16	DALLAS (OT)	13
26	at Pittsburgh (OT)	23
34	ARIZONA	9
23	at Washington	20
13	TENNESSEE	15
35	at Cleveland	24
16	CINCINNATI	7
351		245

ST. LOUIS		
41	DENVER	36
37	at Seattle	34
41	SAN FRANCISCO	24
41	at Atlanta	20
57	SAN DIEGO	31
45	ATLANTA	29
34	at Kansas City	54
34	at San Francisco	24
24	CAROLINA	27
38	at N.Y. Giants	24
20	WASHINGTON	33
24	NEW ORLEANS	31
3	at Carolina	16
40	MINNESOTA	29
35	at Tampa Bay	38
26	at New Orleans	21
540		471

SAN FRANCISCO		
28	at Atlanta	36
22	CAROLINA	38
24	at St. Louis	41
41	at Dallas	24
27	ARIZONA	20
28	OAKLAND (OT)	34
28	at Green Bay	31
16	at Carolina	34
24	ST. LOUIS	34
15	at New Orleans	31
21	KANSAS CITY	7
16	ATLANTA	6
45	at San Diego	17
27	NEW ORLEANS	31
17	CHICAGO	0
9	at Denver	38
388		422

TAMPA BAY		
21	at New England	16
41	CHICAGO	0
31	at Detroit	10
17	N.Y. JETS	21
17	at Washington (OT)	20
23	at Minnesota	30
14	DETROIT	28
41	MINNESOTA	13
27	at Atlanta	14
20	GREEN BAY	15
10	at Chicago	13
31	BUFFALO	17
27	DALLAS	7
16	at Miami	13
38	ST. LOUIS	35
14	at Green Bay (OT)	17
388		269

WASHINGTON		
20	CAROLINA	17
10	at Detroit	15
21	DALLAS	27
16	at N.Y. Giants	6
20	TAMPA BAY (OT)	17
17	at Philadelphia	14
10	BALTIMORE	3
35	at Jacksonville	16
21	TENNESSEE	27
15	at Arizona	16
33	at St. Louis	20
20	PHILADELPHIA	23
7	N.Y. GIANTS	9
13	at Dallas	32
3	at Pittsburgh	24
20	ARIZONA	3
281		269

2000 WEEK BY WEEK

Attendance figures as they appear in the following, and in the club-by-club sections starting on page 28, are turnstile counts and not paid attendance. Paid attendance totals are on page 242.

FIRST WEEK SUMMARIES

American Football Conference

Eastern Division	W	L	T	Pct.	Pts.	OP
Buffalo	1	0	0	1.000	16	13
Indianapolis	1	0	0	1.000	27	14
Miami	1	0	0	1.000	23	0
N.Y. Jets	1	0	0	1.000	20	16
New England	0	1	0	.000	16	21
Central Division						
Baltimore	1	0	0	1.000	16	0
Jacksonville	1	0	0	1.000	27	7
Cincinnati	0	0	0	.000	0	0
Cleveland	0	1	0	.000	7	27
Pittsburgh	0	1	0	.000	0	16
Tennessee	0	1	0	.000	13	16
Western Division						
Oakland	1	0	0	1.000	9	6
Denver	0	1	0	.000	36	41
Kansas City	0	1	0	.000	14	27
San Diego	0	1	0	.000	6	9
Seattle	0	1	0	.000	0	23

National Football Conference

Eastern Division	W	L	T	Pct.	Pts.	OP
N.Y. Giants	1	0	0	1.000	21	16
Philadelphia	1	0	0	1.000	41	14
Washington	1	0	0	1.000	20	17
Arizona	0	1	0	.000	16	21
Dallas	0	1	0	.000	14	41
Central Division						
Detroit	1	0	0	1.000	14	10
Minnesota	1	0	0	1.000	30	27
Tampa Bay	1	0	0	1.000	21	16
Chicago	0	1	0	.000	27	30
Green Bay	0	1	0	.000	16	20
Western Division						
Atlanta	1	0	0	1.000	36	28
St. Louis	1	0	0	1.000	41	36
Carolina	0	1	0	.000	17	20
New Orleans	0	1	0	.000	10	14
San Francisco	0	1	0	.000	28	36

SUNDAY, SEPTEMBER 3

N.Y. GIANTS 21, ARIZONA 16—at Giants Stadium, attendance 77,434. Tiki Barber rushed for a career-high 144 yards and 2 touchdowns as the Giants defeated the Cardinals in a game that was highlighted by a 23-minute lightning delay during the third quarter. Barber's 18-yard punt return set up his first touchdown, a 10-yard run in which Barber ran a sweep right but cut back and scooted into the front left-corner of the end zone. Just over five minutes later, Barber raced through a hole and down the right sideline for a 78-yard touchdown run, the fourth longest in club history. Rookie Ron Dayne's 7-yard touchdown run capped a 15-play, 82-yard drive midway through the fourth quarter to give the Giants a 21-3 lead. Jake Plummer's 9-yard touchdown pass to David Boston with 1:55 left trimmed the deficit to 21-10 and, following a successful onside kick, the pair connected for a 25-yard touchdown with 32 seconds left. However, Plummer's two-point conversion pass fell incomplete, and the Giants recovered the ensuing onside kick to clinch the victory. Kerry Collins was 17 of 25 for 172 yards, with 1 interception. Plummer was 28 of 49 for 318 yards and 2 touchdowns, with 3 interceptions. Boston had 9 receptions for 128 yards.

Arizona	0	0	3	13	—	16
N.Y. Giants	7	7	0	7	—	21

NYG — Barber 10 run (Daluiso kick)
NYG — Barber 78 run (Daluiso kick)
Ariz — FG Blanchard 32
NYG — Dayne 7 run (Daluiso kick)
Ariz — Boston 9 pass from Plummer (Blanchard kick)
Ariz — Boston 25 pass from Plummer (pass failed)

BALTIMORE 16, PITTSBURGH 0—at Three Rivers Stadium, attendance 55,049. The Ravens' defense limited the Steelers to just 223 yards, and Matt Stover kicked 3 field goals as the Ravens handed Pittsburgh its first shutout loss at home since 1989. Midway through the first quarter, the Ravens took advantage of the game's lone turnover. Sam Adams recovered Kent Graham's fumble at the Steelers' 14, which resulted in Stover's 23-yard field goal. The Ravens then forced a punt, and on the next play, Tony Banks completed a 53-yard scoring bomb to Qadry Ismail. The Ravens then held the ball for the final 6:57 of the first half, with Stover's 26-yard field goal culminating a 66-yard drive to give Baltimore a 13-0 lead. Trailing 16-0 in the fourth quarter, the Steelers had first-and-goal at the Ravens' 1-yard line but failed to score. Banks was 18 of 32 for 199 yards and 1 touchdown. Priest Holmes had 27 carries for 119 yards. Ismail had 7 receptions for 102 yards. Graham was 17 of 38 for 199 yards.

Baltimore	10	3	3	0	—	16
Pittsburgh	0	0	0	0	—	0

Balt — FG Stover 23
Balt — Ismail 53 pass from Banks (Stover kick)
Balt — FG Stover 26
Balt — FG Stover 33

WASHINGTON 20, CAROLINA 17—at FedEx Field, attendance 80,257. Stephen Davis rushed for 133 yards and 1 touchdown as the Redskins held off the Panthers. Davis's 2-yard scoring run capped a game-opening 12-play, 79-yard drive. However, Michael Bates returned the ensuing kickoff 92 yards for a touchdown, and Tshimanga Biakabutuka's 41-yard run moments later set up Richie Cunningham's 29-yard field goal to give the Panthers a 10-7 lead. The Panthers reached the Redskins' 2 and had an opportunity to add to the lead just before halftime, but a 15-yard penalty pushed Carolina back and Cunningham missed a 27-yard field-goal attempt. In the third quarter, Ndukwe Kalu recovered Steve Beuerlein's fumble at the Panthers' 28 to set up Brett Conway's game-tying field goal. The Redskins put together back-to-back scoring drives of approximately six minutes each, capped by Conway's second field goal to take a 20-10 lead with 4:59 left in the game. Beuerlein's 20-yard touchdown pass to Wesley Walls with 1:52 remaining trimmed the deficit to 20-17, but Irving Fryar recovered the onside kick and a 33-yard run by Davis helped run out the clock. Brad Johnson was 25 of 36 for 234 yards. Beuerlein was 17 of 26 for 183 yards and 1 touchdown.

Carolina	10	0	0	7	—	17
Washington	7	0	3	10	—	20

Wash — Davis 2 run (Conway kick)
Car — Bates 92 kickoff return (Cunningham kick)
Car — FG Cunningham 29
Wash — FG Conway 24
Wash — Johnson 1 run (Conway kick)
Wash — FG Conway 21
Car — Walls 20 pass from Beuerlein (Cunningham kick)

MINNESOTA 30, CHICAGO 27—at Metrodome, attendance 64,104. In his first career start, Daunte Culpepper had 3 second-half rushing touchdowns to lead the Vikings to a comeback victory. Culpepper had carries of 21 and 24 yards during the game's first drive to set up Gary Anderson's 35-yard field goal. The Bears responded with a 78-yard drive, including a 10-yard run by Cade McNown on third-and-7, and capped by McNown's 18-yard touchdown pass to John Allred. Paul Edinger's 2 field goals just before halftime and McNown's 48-yard touchdown pass to Marcus Robinson to cap the second half's opening drive gave Chicago a 20-9 lead. Culpepper's 10-yard run on third-and-4 sustained a 72-yard drive, capped by Culpepper's 1-yard run. Early in the fourth quarter, Culpepper's 66-yard pass to Randy Moss preceded his 7-yard scoring run, and on the next possession, Robert Smith's 59-yard run set up Culpepper's 4-yard touchdown run to give Minnesota a 30-20 lead with 4:35 remaining. McNown engineered a 75-yard drive, capped by his 8-yard run with 1:17 left, but Moss recovered the ensuing onside kick to preserve the victory. Culpepper was 13 of 23 for 190 yards, with 1 interception, and rushed 13 times for 73 yards. He became the first Vikings player since 1991 to rush for 3 touchdowns in a game. Smith had 14 carries for 109 yards. McNown was 27 of 41 for 290 yards and 2 touchdowns, and rushed 10 times for 87 yards.

Chicago	7	6	7	7	—	27
Minnesota	6	3	7	14	—	30

Minn — FG Anderson 35
Chi — Allred 18 pass from McNown (Edinger kick)
Minn — FG Anderson 38
Chi — FG Edinger 29
Minn — FG Anderson 45
Chi — FG Edinger 49
Chi — Robinson 48 pass from McNown (Edinger kick)
Minn — Culpepper 1 run (Anderson kick)
Minn — Culpepper 7 run (Anderson kick)
Minn — Culpepper 4 run (Anderson kick)
Chi — McNown 8 run (Edinger kick)

DETROIT 14, NEW ORLEANS 10—at Louisiana Superdome, attendance 64,900. Desmond Howard's 95-yard punt return for a touchdown helped the Lions fight off the Saints. Stoney Case started for the injured Charlie Batch and had an inauspicious beginning when Sammy Knight intercepted his pass and returned it 37 yards for a touchdown. The Lions took advantage of 2 Saints' turnovers, Marquis Walker's fumble recovery at the Lions' 37 and Kurt Schulz's interception in Saints' territory, to set up 2 Jason Hanson field goals just before halftime. Howard's punt return late in the third quarter gave Detroit a 12-7 lead, and James Stewart's two-point conversion run increased the advantage to 14-7. Chad Morton returned the ensuing kickoff 45 yards to set up Doug Brien's 48-yard field goal. Chris Oldham recovered a Sedrick Irvin fumble at the Saints' 39 midway through the fourth quarter, but Brien's 52-yard field-goal attempt was blocked by James Jones. The Saints reached the Lions' 21 in the final minute, but Jeff Blake's fourth-and-2 pass fell incomplete. Case was 13 of 25 for 100 yards, with 1 interception. Blake was 18 of 34 for 169 yards, with 1 interception.

Detroit	0	6	8	0	—	14
New Orleans	7	0	0	3	—	10

NO — Knight 37 interception return (Brien kick)
Det — FG Hanson 24
Det — FG Hanson 30
Det — Howard 95 punt return (Stewart run)
NO — FG Brien 48

INDIANAPOLIS 27, KANSAS CITY 14—at Arrowhead Stadium, attendance 78,357. Edgerrin James rushed for 124 yards and scored 2 touchdowns as the Colts handed the Chiefs their first loss in a home opener since 1988. The Colts moved the ball at will on their first two possesions, but committed turnovers both times. James's 1-yard touchdown run in the first minute of the second quarter capped an 11-play, 92-yard drive, but Elvis Grbac's 11-yard touchdown pass to Tony Richardson sent the teams to the locker room tied at halftime. Peyton Manning beat the Chiefs' blitz by lofting a 27-yard touchdown pass to an open James, but the Chiefs responded with a game-tying 76-yard drive, capped by Grbac's 21-yard touchdown pass to Derrick Alexander. Rookie Payton Williams returned a punt 40 yards to set up Mike Vanderjagt's 23-yard field goal to take a 17-14 lead with 13:37 remaining. Jeff Burris intercepted Grbac less than a minute later and returned it 27 yards for a touchdown. James's 30-yard run on third-and-2 set up Vanderjagt's final field goal. Manning was 22 of 32 for 273 yards and 1 touchdown, with 1 interception. Marvin Harrison had 9 receptions for 115 yards. Grbac was 16 of 37 for 212 yards and 2 touchdowns, with 1 interception.

Indianapolis	0	7	7	13	—	27
Kansas City	0	7	7	0	—	14

Ind — James 1 run (Vanderjagt kick)
KC — Richardson 11 pass from Grbac (Stoyanovich kick)
Ind — James 27 pass from Manning (Vanderjagt kick)
KC — Alexander 21 pass from Grbac (Stoyanovich kick)
Ind — FG Vanderjagt 23
Ind — Burris 27 interception return (Vanderjagt kick)
Ind — FG Vanderjagt 40

JACKSONVILLE 27, CLEVELAND 7—at Cleveland Browns Stadium, attendance 72,418. Mark Brunell passed for 301 yards, and the Jaguars' defense limited the Browns to 9 first downs. Brunell's 2-yard touchdown pass to Jimmy Smith capped a 97-yard drive early in the second quarter, but Tim Couch's 13-yard touchdown pass to JaJuan Dawson tied the game with 3:33 left before halftime. However, Mike Hollis kicked a 50-yard field goal just before halftime, giving Jacksonville a 10-7 lead. The Browns drove deep into Jaguars' territory to begin the third quarter, but Aaron Shea fumbled and Lonnie Marts recovered at the Jaguars' 14 to thwart the drive. Jacksonville took advantage of the miscue, driving 86 yards and taking a 17-7 lead on Stacey Mack's 3-yard scoring run. The Jaguars scored on their next two possessions as well, capped by Chris Howard's 9-yard run, which culminated a 17-play, 68-yard drive that took more than 10 minutes, to take a 27-7 lead with 4:20 remaining. Brunell was 24 of 34 for 301 yards and 1 touchdown. Keenan McCardell had 9 receptions for 115 yards. Couch was 19 of 27 for 160 yards and 1 touchdown.

Jacksonville	0	10	10	7	—	27
Cleveland	0	7	0	0	—	7

Jax — Smith 2 pass from Brunell (Hollis kick)
Cle — J. Dawson 13 pass from Couch (P. Dawson kick)
Jax — FG Hollis 50
Jax — Mack 3 run (Hollis kick)
Jax — FG Hollis 25
Jax — Howard 9 run (Hollis kick)

N.Y. JETS 20, GREEN BAY 16—at Lambeau Field, attendance 59,870. Curtis Martin rushed for 110 yards and scored 2 touchdowns, and Victor Green made a leaping interception with 1:06 remaining to punctuate the Jets' comeback victory. In the game's early moments, Darren Sharper's 29-yard interception return to the Jets' 4 set up Brett Favre's touchdown pass to Tyrone Davis. The Jets responded with a 15-play, 75-yard drive capped by Martin's 2-yard scoring run. Allen Rossum's 43-yard punt return set up Ryan Longwell's 45-yard field goal midway through the second quarter, but John Hall's field goal just before halftime tied the game. In the third quarter, Hall missed his second field goal of the game, and Longwell connected from 42 yards to give Green Bay a 13-10 lead. Vinny Testaverde's 34-yard pass to Richie Anderson early in the fourth quarter led to Hall's game-tying field goal with 8:53 left. Favre responded with a 48-yard pass to Antonio Freeman to set up Longwell's third field goal with 6:38 to play, but the Jets answered with Testaverde's 61-yard pass to Dedric Ward down to the Packers' 2. Testaverde's 3-yard touchdown pass to Martin three plays later gave the Jets a 20-16 lead with 3:30 to play. Favre, who guided the Packers to three comebacks at Lambeau Field in 1999, engineered a drive to the Jets' 35, but Green made an acrobatic interception with 1:06 left to preserve the victory. Testaverde was 23 of 44 for 261 yards and 1 touchdown, with 1 interception. Ward had 5 receptions for 104 yards. Favre was 14 of 34 for 152 yards and 1 touchdown, with 1 interception.

N.Y. Jets	7	3	0	10	—	20
Green Bay	7	3	3	3	—	16

GB — Davis 4 pass from Favre (Longwell kick)
NYJ — Martin 2 run (Hall kick)
GB — FG Longwell 45
NYJ — FG Hall 23
GB — FG Longwell 42
NYJ — FG Hall 39
GB — FG Longwell 42
NYJ — Martin 3 pass from Testaverde (Hall kick)

PHILADELPHIA 41, DALLAS 14—at Texas Stadium, attendance 62,872. Duce Staley rushed for 201 yards as the Eagles handed the Cowboys their worst loss in a home opener since 1963. The Eagles began their season by taking a chance and attempting an onside kick. Dameane Douglas recovered, and Donovan McNabb's 1-yard pass to Jeff Thomason eight plays later gave the Eagles a 7-0 lead. Two possessions later, Staley scored from 1-yard out to cap a 61-yard drive, and less than two minutes later, Jeremiah Trotter intercepted Troy Aikman's pass and returned it 27 yards for a touchdown and a 21-0 lead. Aikman, who was sacked 4 times in the first quarter, suffered a concussion and was removed one possession later, following David Akers's 33-yard field goal which gave the Eagles a 24-0 lead. Interceptions by Izell Reese and Dat Nguyen led to Tim Seder field goals, but the Eagles' rushing attack was too much for Dallas. The Eagles scored on drives of 14 and 9 plays on their first two second-half possessions to take a 34-6 lead, and then Staley's 60-yard run set up Brian Mitchell's 6-yard scoring run to give Philadelphia a 41-6 lead with 12:22 remaining. Joey Galloway caught a fourth-quarter touchdown pass, but later in the quarter, suffered a season-ending knee injury. McNabb was 16 of 28 for 130 yards and 1 touchdown, with 2 interceptions. The Eagles rushed 46 times for 306 yards. Randall Cunningham was 13 of 26 for 135 yards and 1 touchdown, with 1 interception.

Philadelphia	14	10	3	14	—	41
Dallas	0	6	0	8	—	14

Phil — Thomason 1 pass from McNabb (Akers kick)
Phil — Staley 1 run (Akers kick)
Phil — Trotter 27 interception return (Akers kick)
Phil — FG Akers 33
Dall — FG Seder 34
Dall — FG Seder 38
Phil — FG Akers 37
Phil — McNabb 3 run (Akers kick)
Phil — Mitchell 6 run (Akers kick)
Dall — Galloway 4 pass from Cunningham (Ismail pass from Cunningham)

OAKLAND 9, SAN DIEGO 6—at Network Associates Coliseum, attendance 56,373. Rich Gannon's 10-yard touchdown pass to Andre Rison with 2:37 remaining lifted the Raiders past the Chargers. The first half featured 11 punts, with the only real scoring opportunity set up by Charles Woodson's 13-yard interception return to the Chargers' 26 late in the first half. However, Sebastian Janikowski missed a 41-yard field-goal attempt, and the teams went to the locker room scoreless. In the middle of the third quarter, Shane Lechler's punt pinned the Chargers back on their own 2-yard line. After losing a yard on first down, Robert Chancey was tackled in the end zone by Darrell Russell for a safety. The Chargers reached the Raiders' 15 late in the third quarter, but Ryan Leaf was sacked and fumbled, and Regan Upshaw recovered. On their next possession, Leaf engineered a 15-play, 80-yard drive, capped by Chancey's 3-yard scoring run to give the Chargers a 6-2 lead with 9:41 left. After an exchange of punts, the Raiders caught a break when a scrambling Rich Gannon fumbled but had the ball bounce right back to him, and he then gained 14 yards. Gannon's touchdown pass to Rison six plays later gave Oakland a 9-6 lead with 2:37 to play. William Thomas intercepted Leaf's fourth-down pass to preserve the victory. Gannon was 20 of 35 for 176 yards and 1 touchdown. Leaf was 17 of 39 for 180 yards, with 3 interceptions.

San Diego	0	0	0	6	—	6
Oakland	0	0	2	7	—	9

Oak — Safety, Russell tackled Chancey in end zone
SD — Chancey 3 run (pass failed)
Oak — Rison 10 pass from Gannon (Janikowski kick)

ATLANTA 36, SAN FRANCISCO 28—at Georgia Dome, attendance 54,626. Morten Andersen kicked 5 field goals and Jamal Anderson, in his first game back from a 1999 knee injury, rushed for 77 yards as the Falcons downed the 49ers. The 49ers drove 74 yards to begin the game, capped by Jeff Garcia's 4-yard touchdown pass to Fred Beasley. The Falcons responded by scoring on their first seven possessions, capped by Chris Chandler's 48-yard touchdown pass to Shawn Jefferson, to give the Falcons a 29-14 lead less than a minute into the third quarter. The 49ers answered with an 11-play, 80-yard drive culminated by another Garcia-to-Beasley touchdown to trim the deficit to 29-21, and then forced a punt. However, Ashley Ambrose intercepted Garcia's pass and returned it 36 yards for a touchdown and a 36-21 lead. Garcia's third touchdown pass, a 6-yarder to Terrell Owens with 2:50 remaining, pulled the 49ers within eight points, but Anderson helped run out the clock. Chandler was 16 of 31 for 264 yards and 2 touchdowns. Jefferson had 7 receptions for 148 yards. Garcia was 23 of 36 for 253 yards and 3 touchdowns, with 1 interception.

San Francisco	7	7	7	7	—	28
Atlanta	6	16	14	0	—	36

SF — Beasley 4 pass from Garcia (Richey kick)
Atl — FG Andersen 43
Atl — FG Andersen 44
Atl — FG Andersen 24
Atl — FG Andersen 44
Atl — Mathis 44 pass from Chandler (Andersen kick)
SF — Beasley 1 run (Richey kick)
Atl — FG Andersen 44
Atl — Jefferson 48 pass from Chandler (Andersen kick)
SF — Beasley 4 pass from Garcia (Richey kick)
Atl — Ashmore 36 interception return (Andersen kick)
SF — Owens 6 pass from Garcia (Richey kick)

MIAMI 23, SEATTLE 0—at Pro Player Stadium, attendance 72,949. Lamar Smith rushed 27 times for 145 yards and 1 touchdown as the Dolphins' defense forced 5 first-half turnovers to shutout the Seahawks. Smith's 4-yard scoring run capped a 13-play, 70-yard game-opening drive. Two interceptions by Sam Madison led to 2 Olindo Mare field goals to give Miami a 13-0 lead, and Jason Taylor's recovery of Jon Kitna's fumble moments later led to Mare's third field goal. After Kris Heppner missed a 52-yard field-goal attempt for the Seahawks, Jay Fiedler engineered a 58-yard drive, capped by Oronde Gadsden's 16-yard touchdown catch 43 seconds before halftime to give Miami a 23-0 lead. Fiedler, the first quarterback other than Dan Marino to start a season-opening game for the Dolphins since 1983, was 15 of 24 for 134 yards and 1 touchdown. Kitna was 6 of 13 for 54 yards, with 4 interceptions.

Seattle	0	0	0	0	—	0
Miami	10	13	0	0	—	23

Mia — Smith 4 run (Mare kick)
Mia — FG Mare 48
Mia — FG Mare 25
Mia — FG Mare 30
Mia — Gadsden 16 pass from Fiedler (Mare kick)

TAMPA BAY 21, NEW ENGLAND 16—at Foxboro Stadium, attendance 60,006. Mike Alstott rushed for 2 touchdowns, and the Buccaneers' defense recorded 6 sacks to hold off the Patriots. Karl Williams fumbled the game's opening kickoff and Kato Serwanga recovered, which set up Adam Vinatieri's 30-yard field goal. Shaun King's 27-yard pass to Keyshawn Johnson, plus a 15-yard roughing-the-passer penalty, keyed an 80-yard drive capped by Alstott's 5-yard run early in the second quarter. Troy Brown's 66-yard punt return for a touchdown gave New England a brief lead, but King's 33-yard pass to Reidel Anthony on third-and-1 set up the pair's 8-yard touchdown pass play 31 seconds before halftime. Kevin Faulk fumbled late in the third quarter, and John Lynch returned it 8 yards to the Patriots' 24 to set up Alstott's second touchdown. The Patriots' offense found the end zone with Drew Bledsoe's 39-yard touchdown pass to Terry Glenn with 3:01 to play, but Michael Bishop was stopped shy of the end zone on the 2-point conversion attempt. The Patriots' defense forced a punt, and Bledsoe drove the Patriots to the Buccaneers' 22 with 14 seconds left, but a harrassed Bledsoe's final pass fell incomplete as time ran out. King was 12 of 24 for 167 yards and 1 touchdown. Bledsoe was 26 of 39 for 216 yards and 1 touchdown.

Tampa Bay	0	14	7	0	—	21
New England	3	7	0	6	—	16

NE — FG Vinatieri 30
TB — Alstott 5 run (Gramatica kick)
NE — Brown 66 punt return (Vinatieri kick)
TB — Anthony 8 pass from King (Gramatica kick)
TB — Alstott 3 run (Gramatica kick)
NE — Glenn 39 pass from Bledsoe (run failed)

SUNDAY NIGHT, SEPTEMBER 3

BUFFALO 16, TENNESSEE 13—at Ralph Wilson Stadium, attendance 72,492. Steve Christie's 33-yard field goal with 31 seconds remaining helped Buffalo defeat the Titans in the Bills' first game since losing to Tennessee in the "Music City Miracle" in January. Rob Johnson's 15-yard touchdown pass to Peerless Price gave Buffalo a 7-0 lead. Leading 7-3, the Bills reached the Titans' 15, but two penalties and an 8-yard sack of Johnson by Kenny Holmes forced Christie to attempt a 51-yard field goal, which he missed. The Titans countered with Al Del Greco's second field goal just before halftime to trim the deficit to 7-6. Christie added 2 field goals to extend the lead to 13-6 early in the fourth quarter, and the Bills' defense forced Steve McNair's fourth-and-1 pass from the Bills' 9 to fall incomplete with 11:00 remaining. But the Titans forced a punt, and a 41-yard pass interference penalty set up Eddie George's game-tying touchdown run with 8:44 left. With Johnson out of the game with a foot injury and Doug Flutie still hobbled by a preseason groin injury, Alex Van Pelt completed a 36-yard pass to Eric Moulds to the Titans' 20 with 50 seconds left to set up Christie's go-ahead kick. Evoking shades of the playoff game, Derrick Mason returned the ensuing kickoff 52 yards to the Titans' 49. After a short pass play, long field-goal specialist Craig Hentrich's 60-yard attempt hooked left as time expired. Johnson was 9 of 18 for 107 yards and 1 touchdown. McNair was 17 of 31 for 152 yards, with 1 interception.

Tennessee	0	6	0	7	—	13
Buffalo	0	7	3	6	—	16

Buff — Price 15 pass from Johnson (Christie kick)
Tenn — FG Del Greco 38
Tenn — FG Del Greco 27
Buff — FG Christie 42
Buff — FG Christie 41
Tenn — George 2 run (Del Greco kick)
Buff — FG Christie 33

MONDAY NIGHT, SEPTEMBER 4

ST. LOUIS 41, DENVER 36—at Trans World Dome, attendance 65,596. Kurt Warner passed for a career-high 441 yards, and Robert Holcombe scored the go-ahead touchdown with 3:02 remaining as the defending Super Bowl champions defeated the Broncos. The Broncos scored on their first possession, and Al Wilson intercepted a Warner pass at the Broncos' 7 to thwart a scoring chance. But St. Louis tied the game on Az-Zahir Hakim's 86-yard punt return late in the first quarter. After Denver took a 17-14 lead, Warner's 7-yard touchdown pass to Ricky Proehl with 38 seconds left in the half put the Rams ahead, 21-17. Warner's sideline pass to Marshall Faulk turned into a 72-yard touchdown and, after forcing a punt, Warner's quick pass to Hakim was turned into an 80-yard touchdown for a 35-20 lead with 4:02 left in the third quarter. The Broncos responded with Brian Griese's 7-yard touchdown pass to Desmond Clark, and Wilson again thwarted another scoring chance by intercepting Warner in the Broncos' end zone. Olandis Gary had 25- and 13-yard runs to set up Jason Elam's third field goal, and Terrell Buckley intercepted Warner and returned the ball 32 yards for a touchdown two plays later to give the Broncos a 36-35 lead with 6:35 remaining. A 30-yard run by Faulk set up Holcombe's go-ahead touchdown, and the Broncos failed to cross the Rams' 40 on their final possession. Warner was 25 of 35 for 441 yards and 3 touchdowns, with 3 interceptions. Hakim had 5 receptions for 116 yards, and Torry Holt had 6 receptions for 103 yards. Griese was 19 of 29 for 307 yards and 2 touchdowns. Ed McCaffrey had 7 receptions for 115 yards. Gary rushed 13 times for 80 yards despite suffering a season-ending knee injury during the second half.

Denver	7	10	10	9	—	36
St. Louis	7	14	14	6	—	41

Den — Griese 8 run (Elam kick)
StL — Hakim 86 punt return (Wilkins kick)
Den — FG Elam 32
StL — Faulk 5 run (Wilkins kick)
Den — R. Smith 25 pass from Griese (Elam kick)
StL — Proehl 7 pass from Warner (Wilkins kick)
Den — FG Elam 38
StL — Faulk 72 pass from Warner (Wilkins kick)
StL — Hakim 80 pass from Warner (Wilkins kick)
Den — Clark 7 pass from Griese (Elam kick)
Den — FG Elam 36
Den — Buckley 32 interception return (run failed)
StL — Holcombe 1 run (pass failed)

SECOND WEEK SUMMARIES

AMERICAN FOOTBALL CONFERENCE

Eastern Division	W	L	T	Pct.	Pts.	OP
Buffalo	2	0	0	1.000	43	31
N.Y. Jets	2	0	0	1.000	40	35
Indianapolis	1	1	0	.500	58	52
Miami	1	1	0	.500	30	13
New England	0	2	0	.000	35	41
Central Division						
Baltimore	2	0	0	1.000	55	36
Cleveland	1	1	0	1.000	31	34
Jacksonville	1	1	0	1.000	63	46
Tennessee	1	1	0	.000	30	30
Cincinnati	0	1	0	.000	7	24
Pittsburgh	0	1	0	.000	0	16
Western Division						
Oakland	2	0	0	1.000	47	37
Denver	1	1	0	.500	78	55
Kansas City	0	2	0	.000	28	44
San Diego	0	2	0	.000	33	37
Seattle	0	2	0	.000	34	60

NATIONAL FOOTBALL CONFERENCE

Eastern Division	W	L	T	Pct.	Pts.	OP
N.Y. Giants	2	0	0	1.000	54	34
Arizona	1	1	0	.500	48	52
Philadelphia	1	1	0	.500	59	47
Washington	1	1	0	.500	30	32
Dallas	0	2	0	.000	45	73
Central Division						
Detroit	2	0	0	1.000	29	20
Minnesota	2	0	0	1.000	43	34
Tampa Bay	2	0	0	1.000	62	16
Chicago	0	2	0	.000	27	71
Green Bay	0	2	0	.000	34	47
Western Division						
St. Louis	2	0	0	1.000	78	70
Atlanta	1	1	0	.500	50	70
Carolina	1	1	0	.500	55	42
New Orleans	1	1	0	.500	38	41
San Francisco	0	2	0	.000	50	74

SUNDAY, SEPTEMBER 10

DENVER 42, ATLANTA 14—at Mile High Stadium, attendance 73,214. Rookie Mike Anderson, in his first NFL start, rushed for 131 yards and 2 touchdowns as the Broncos defeated Dan Reeves in his return to Mile High Stadium. Anderson, a sixth-round pick who was thrust into the starting lineup because of injuries suffered by Terrell Davis and Olandis Gary, carried the ball 6 times on the opening drive, capped by his 2-yard touchdown run. Ian Gold recovered Tim Dwight's fumble on the ensuing kickoff return, and Jason Elam's 29-yard field goal gave Denver a 10-0 lead less than eight minutes into the game. The Broncos scored on their next three drives as well, to take a 27-0 lead, and Brian Griese's 11-yard touchdown pass to Rod Smith two possessions later put Denver ahead 34-0. Darrick Vaughn's ensuing kickoff return broke the shutout just before halftime, but the Broncos drove 83 yards to open the second half, capped by Griese's 37-yard touchdown pass to Smith. The Broncos were forced to go for 2 points following the touchdown because of a leg injury suffered by Elam during Vaughn's scoring return. Denver had an advantage in first downs (29-12), total yards (407-186), and time of possession (37:03-22:57). Griese was 20 of 33 for 268 yards and 3 touchdowns. Anderson rushed 31 times for 131 yards. Smith had 7 receptions for 117 yards. Chris Chandler was 9 of 22 for 128 yards and 1 touchdown.

Atlanta	0	7	7	0	—	14
Denver	13	21	8	0	—	42

Den — Anderson 2 run (Elam kick)
Den — FG Elam 29
Den — FG Elam 51
Den — Griffith 6 pass from Griese (Elam kick)
Den — Anderson 20 run (Elam kick)
Den — R. Smith 11 pass from Griese (Elam kick)
Atl — Vaughn 100 kickoff return (Andersen kick)
Den — R. Smith 37 pass from Griese (Anderson run)
Atl — Dwight 35 pass from Chandler (Andersen kick)

CAROLINA 38, SAN FRANCISCO 22—at 3Com Park, attendance 66,875. Steve Beuerlein passed for 364 yards and 3 touchdowns as the Panthers gave coach George Seifert a 3-0 record against his former team. The loss marked the first time since 1982 that the 49ers had begun the season 0-2. The Panthers drove 80 yards with each of their first two possessions to take a 14-0 lead, and Beuerlein engineered touchdown drives of 71 and 62 yards in the second quarter to give Carolina a 28-0 halftime lead. The 49ers' pierced the end zone on Terry Jackson's 1-yard run to culminate the opening drive of the second half, but the Panthers responded with a 60-yard drive capped by Beuerlein's 9-yard touchdown pass to ex-49ers' tight end Wesley Walls. Ex-49er Eric Davis's interception a few plays later set up Richie Cunningham's field goal and increased Carolina's lead to 38-7 late in the third quarter. Beuerlein was 24 of 32 for 364 yards and 3 touchdowns, with 1 interception. Muhsin Muhammad had 8 receptions for 108 yards, and Donald Hayes added 6 catches for 115 yards. Jeff Garcia was 12 of 20 for 181 yards, with 1 interception before being replaced by Rick Mirer, who was 10 of 20 for 126 yards and 1 touchdown.

Carolina	14	14	10	0	—	38
San Francisco	0	0	7	15	—	22

Car — Floyd 1 run (Cunningham kick)
Car — Hayes 24 pass from Beuerlein (Cunningham kick)
Car — Muhammad 3 pass from Beuerlein (Cunningham kick)
Car — Biakabutuka 1 run (Cunningham kick)
SF — Jackson 1 run (Richey kick)
Car — Walls 9 pass from Beuerlein (Cunningham kick)
Car — FG Cunningham 24
SF — Stokes 17 pass from Mirer (Richey kick)
SF — Beasley 2 run (Owens pass from Mirer)

TAMPA BAY 41, CHICAGO 0—at Soldier Field, attendance 65,569. The Buccaneers' defense limited the Bears to 9 first downs and helped Tampa Bay score 17 points in an 89-second span en route to the largest margin of victory in club history. Donnie Abraham's interception on the first play of the second quarter led to Martin Gramatica's 23-yard field goal. Gramatica added a 47-yard field goal with 2:46 left in the half to give the Buccaneers a 6-0 lead. Abraham's second interception and 18-yard return to the Bears' 4 two plays later led to Shaun King's 3-yard run. Two plays later, Dez White caught a McNown pass but fumbled. Ronde Barber scooped up the ball and raced 24 yards for a touchdown to give Tampa Bay a 20-0 lead with 1:17 left in the half. The Buccaneers scored 14 points in less than a minute in the third quarter. King's 13-yard touchdown pass to Keyshawn Johnson gave Tampa Bay a 27-0 lead and, one play after the defense forced a punt, King found Jacquez Green for a 58-yard touchdown with 7:33 remaining in the third quarter. King was 10 of 21 for 167 yards and 2 touchdowns. Green had 5 receptions for 104 yards. McNown was 15 of 29 for 96 yards, with 2 interceptions.

Chicago	0	0	0	0	—	0
Tampa Bay	0	20	14	7	—	41

TB — FG Gramatica 23
TB — FG Gramatica 47
TB — King 3 run (Gramatica kick)
TB — Barber 24 fumble return (Gramatica kick)
TB — K. Johnson 13 pass from King (Gramatica kick)
TB — Green 58 pass from King (Gramatica kick)
TB — Alstott 20 run (Gramatica kick)

CLEVELAND 24, CINCINNATI 7—at Paul Brown Stadium, attendance 64,006. Tim Couch passed for 259 yards and 2 touchdowns, and the Browns' defense recorded 7 sacks to defeat the Bengals in the first game at Paul Brown Stadium. Travis Prentice's 16-yard touchdown run capped a 76-yard drive late in the first quarter, but the Bengals responded with a 78-yard drive, highlighted by Akili Smith's 25-yard pass to Craig Yeast on third-and-19, and tied the game on Smith's 4-yard scoring pass to Ron Dugans. The Bengals' defense then forced a punt, but Yeast muffed the punt and Tyrone Rodgers recovered at the Bengals' 16 to set up Couch's 5-yard touchdown pass to Mark Campbell. Undaunted, the Bengals drove to the Browns' 25, but Neil Rackers missed a 42-yard field-goal attempt. In the third quarter, Phil Dawson's field goal capped a 12-play drive and extended Cleveland's lead to 17-7. The Bengals responded with a drive to the Browns' 12, but Smith's second-down pass was intercepted in the end zone by Lewis Sanders and the Browns marched 80 yards and scored on Couch's 5-yard touchdown pass to Marc Edwards. The Bengals drove to the Browns' 18 and 24 in the fourth quarter, but Earl Little's interception and Jamir Miller's fourth-down sack preserved the margin of victory. Keith McKenzie had 3 sacks for Cleveland. Couch was 19 of 31 for 259 yards and 2 touchdowns, with 1 interception. Smith was 15 of 40 for 250 yards and 1 touchdown, with 2 interceptions.

Cleveland	7	7	3	7	—	24
Cincinnati	0	7	0	0	—	7

Cle — Prentice 16 run (Dawson kick)
Cin — Dugans 4 pass from Smith (Rackers kick)

Cle — Campbell 5 pass from Couch (Dawson kick)
Cle — FG Dawson 30
Cle — Edwards 5 pass from Couch (Dawson kick)

BUFFALO 27, GREEN BAY 18—at Ralph Wilson Stadium, attendance 72,722. Rob Johnson passed for 3 touchdowns as the Bills sent the Packers to their first 0-2 start since 1992. The club's exchanged punts until Johnson's 6-yard touchdown pass to Jeremy McDaniel with 44 seconds left in the half gave Buffalo a 7-0 lead. Marcellus Wiley sacked Brett Favre three plays later, and Phil Hansen recovered the ball and returned it 29 yards to set up Steve Christie's field goal as the half expired. The Bills then scored on the opening drive of the second half, thus scoring 17 points in less than four minutes. Favre's 7-yard touchdown pass to Antonio Freeman got the Packers on the board, and then the defense forced a punt. However, Allen Rossum fumbled the punt, and Chad Clifton recovered at the Packers' 23 to set up Christie's second field goal. Vonnie Holliday's interception late in the third quarter gave Green Bay another chance, but the Packers had to settle for Ryan Longwell's field goal and then allowed a 37-yard kickoff return by Chris Watson to set up Johnson's 14-yard touchdown pass to Jay Riemersma with 11:45 remaining to give Buffalo a 27-10 lead. Favre and Freeman connected for a second touchdown pass in the game's final minute. Johnson was 18 of 26 for 259 yards and 3 touchdowns, with 1 interception. Eric Moulds had 7 receptions for 103 yards. Favre was 25 of 35 for 269 yards and 2 touchdowns.

Green Bay	0	0	10	8	—	18
Buffalo	0	10	10	7	—	27

Buff — McDaniel 6 pass from R. Johnson (Christie kick)
Buff — FG Christie 45
Buff — Riemersma 6 pass from R. Johnson (Christie kick)
GB — Freeman 7 pass from Favre (Longwell kick)
Buff — FG Christie 20
GB — FG Longwell 24
Buff — Riemersma 14 pass from R. Johnson (Christie kick)
GB — Freeman 18 pass from Favre (T. Davis pass from Favre)

BALTIMORE 39, JACKSONVILLE 36—at PSINet Stadium, attendance 68,843. Tony Banks passed for 5 touchdowns, including a game-winning 29-yard pass to Shannon Sharpe with 41 seconds left, as the Ravens fought off a fantastic performance by Jimmy Smith to defeat the Jaguars. The Jaguars scored on their first three possessions, the last two on bombs from Mark Brunell to Smith, to take a 17-0 lead less than 13 minutes into the game. Duane Starks recovered Chris Howard's fumble at the Ravens' 14, and Banks fired a touchdown pass to Travis Taylor on the next play to get the Ravens on the scoreboard. However, Mike Hollis added 2 field goals, and the Jaguars had a 23-7 halftime lead. Banks began the second half with a 40-yard pass to Taylor, and the pair followed that three plays later with a 23-yard touchdown to cut the lead to 23-15. Rayna Stewart's interception set up Hollis's 34-yard field goal midway through the third quarter, but the Ravens answered with a 10-play, 76-yard drive, capped by Banks's 5-yard pass to Obafemi Ayanbadejo to cut the deficit to 26-22. Jamie Sharper recovered Stacey Mack's fumble at the Jaguars' 14 early in the fourth quarter to set up Banks's 12-yard touchdown pass to Jermaine Lewis to give Baltimore its first lead, 29-26, with 10:00 left. With the Ravens leading 32-29, the Jaguars forced a punt with 2:53 left, and Brunell hit Smith with a 40-yard touchdown bomb four plays later to give Jacksonville a 36-32 lead with 1:55 left. Banks found Billy Davis for 19- and 15-yard receptions to set up Sharpe's winning catch. Banks was 23 of 40 for 262 yards and 5 touchdowns, with 2 interceptions. Brunell was 28 of 50 for 386 yards and 3 touchdowns, with 2 interceptions. Smith had 15 catches for 291 yards, the fifth-most receiving yards in a game in NFL history.

Jacksonville	17	6	3	10	—	36
Baltimore	0	7	15	17	—	39

Jax — FG Hollis 36
Jax — Smith 45 pass from Brunell (Hollis kick)
Jax — Smith 43 pass from Brunell (Hollis kick)
Balt — Taylor 14 pass from Banks (Stover kick)
Jax — FG Hollis 45
Jax — FG Hollis 48
Balt — Taylor 23 pass from Banks (Coates pass from Banks)
Jax — FG Hollis 34
Balt — Ayanbadejo 5 pass from Banks (Stover kick)
Balt — Lewis 12 pass from Banks (Stover kick)
Balt — FG Stover 44
Jax — FG Hollis 48
Jax — Smith 40 pass from Brunell (Hollis kick)
Balt — Sharpe 29 pass from Banks (Stover kick)

TENNESSEE 17, KANSAS CITY 14 (OT)—at Adelphia Coliseum, attendance 68,203. Neil O'Donnell's last minute touchdown pass sent the game to overtime, and Al Del Greco's 36-yard field goal on the first possession of the extra session allowed the Titans to remain undefeated at Adelphia Coliseum. The Titans' defense had a goal-line stand early in the second quarter, stopping the Chiefs on three consecutive running plays from the 1-yard line, including Mike Cloud on fourth down. Two possessions later, the Titans capped a 91-yard drive by having Steve McNair complete a lateral to Frank Wycheck, who then found Kevin Dyson open in the end zone for a 30-yard touchdown with 1:42 left in the half. The Titans then forced a punt, but Donnie Edwards intercepted McNair's pass three plays later and returned it 42 yards for a touchdown with 12 seconds left in the half to tie the game. Kansas City missed another scoring chance in the third quarter when Pete Stoyanovich missed a 35-yard field-goal attempt, but the Chiefs took the lead on Elvis Grbac's 16-yard touchdown pass to Derrick Alexander on the first play of the fourth quarter. McNair suffered a bruised sternum midway through the fourth quarter, and O'Donnell replaced him. O'Donnell drove Tennessee to the Chiefs' 17, but Duane Clemons sacked O'Donnell on fourth down with 2:59 remaining. The Titans' defense forced a three-and-out, and O'Donnell engineered an 8-play, 56-yard drive capped by an 8-yard touchdown pass to Yancey Thigpen on third-and-goal with 56 seconds left. The Titans won the overtime toss, and Eddie George's 29-yard run to the Chiefs' 18 set up Del Greco's winning kick. McNair was 11 of 18 for 93 yards, with 2 interceptions, and O'Donnell was 11 of 17 for 132 yards and 1 touchdown. Dyson had 6 receptions for 104 yards. Grbac was 13 of 21 for 144 yards and 1 touchdown.

Kansas City	0	7	0	7	0	—	14
Tennessee	0	7	0	7	3	—	17

Tenn — Dyson 30 pass from Wycheck (Del Greco kick)
KC — Edwards 42 interception return (Stoyanovich kick)
KC — Alexander 16 pass from Grbac (Stoyanovich kick)
Tenn — Thigpen 8 pass from O'Donnell (Del Greco kick)
Tenn — FG Del Greco 36

MINNESOTA 13, MIAMI 7—at Metrodome, attendance 64,112. Daunte Culpepper passed for 355 yards and 1 touchdown as the Vikings downed the Dolphins. Gary Anderson's 28-yard field goal on their second possession gave the Vikings a 3-0 lead. The teams began the second half by exchanging interceptions as the defenses continued to dominate. In the fourth quarter, Anderson's 49-yard field goal culminated a 13-play, 63-yard drive to give the Vikings a 6-0 lead with 11:30 left. Culpepper's 32-yard pass to Cris Carter gave the Vikings first-and-goal at the Dolphins' 7 with 4:25 remaining, but Tim Bowens intercepted Culpepper's next pass. However, the Vikings' defense forced a punt, and Culpepper's 15-yard touchdown pass to Randy Moss with 1:56 left gave the Vikings a 13-0 lead. Jay Fiedler's 44-yard pass to Tony Martin set up his short touchdown pass to Thurman Thomas with 1:02 left, but the Vikings recovered the ensuing onside kick. Culpepper was 23 of 37 for 355 yards and 1 touchdown, with 3 interceptions. Carter had 9 receptions for 168 yards. Fiedler was 12 of 31 for 175 yards and 1 touchdown, with 1 interception. Martin had 6 catches for 120 yards.

Miami	0	0	0	7	—	7
Minnesota	3	0	0	10	—	13

Minn — FG Anderson 28
Minn — FG Anderson 49
Minn — Moss 15 pass from Culpepper (Anderson kick)
Mia — Thomas 2 pass from Fiedler (Mare kick)

NEW ORLEANS 28, SAN DIEGO 27—at Qualcomm Stadium, attendance 51,300. Jeff Blake's 8-yard touchdown pass to Joe Horn with 43 seconds remaining gave the Saints a comeback victory and handed the Chargers their first 0-2 start since 1992. Trailing 3-0, Blake engineered an 8-play, 76-yard drive capped by his 6-yard touchdown pass to Horn late in the first quarter. The Chargers scored on two of their next three possessions, keyed by rookie Ronney Jenkins's 46-yard kickoff return and Orlando Ruff's fumble recovery at midfield, to take a 17-7 lead midway through the second quarter. Doug Brien's 20-yard field goal with 1:54 left in the half trimmed the deficit to 17-10, but Jenkins returned the ensuing kickoff 93 yards for his first NFL touchdown. However, the Saints drove 65 yards in the half's final 1:37 and cut the lead to 24-13 with another Brien field goal. Charlie Clemons intercepted a Blake pass in the third quarter and returned it to the Saints' 41. However, Fred Weary intercepted Ryan Leaf on the next play and returned the ball 27 yards to set up Blake's 13-yard touchdown pass to Ricky Williams. The Saints forced a punt and Chad Morton returned it 51 yards to set up Brien's third field goal to trim the deficit to 24-22. The Chargers drove to the Saints' 15 but attempted a halfback option pass on fourth-and-1 with Robert Chancey's pass falling incomplete. Nate Jacquet's 17-yard punt return moments later set up John Carney's 49-yard field goal with 5:08 left. However, the Saints drove 90 yards in 10 plays, including two successful third-and-1 passes, and capped by Horn's 8-yard catch. Alex Molden intercepted Leaf's desperation fourth-and-22 pass in the waning seconds to secure the victory. Blake was 33 of 46 for 259 yards and 3 touchdowns, with 2 interceptions. Horn had 12 receptions for 116 yards. Leaf was 12 of 24 for 134 yards and 1 touchdown, with 2 interceptions.

New Orleans	7	6	6	9	—	28
San Diego	3	21	0	3	—	27

SD — FG Carney 42
NO — Horn 6 pass from Blake (Brien kick)
SD — Chancey 3 run (Carney kick)
SD — Conway 20 pass from Leaf (Carney kick)
NO — FG Brien 20
SD — Jenkins 93 kickoff return (Carney kick)
NO — FG Brien 20
NO — Williams 13 pass from Blake (run failed)
NO — FG Brien 31
SD — FG Carney 49
NO — Horn 8 pass from Blake (run failed)

N.Y. GIANTS 33, PHILADELPHIA 18—at Veterans Stadium, attendance 65,530. Kerry Collins passed for 220 yards and 2 touchdowns and the Giants controlled the ball for more than 38 minutes to defeat the Eagles for the seventh consecutive time. David Akers's 33-yard field goal with 5:22 left in the first half cut the Giants lead to 6-3. However, Ron Dixon returned the ensuing kickoff 44 yards, and Collins completed 4 of 5 passes on an 8-play, 55-yard drive, capped by his 25-yard touchdown pass to Amani Toomer on third-and-8 with 1:00 left in the half. The Giants' defense then forced a three-and-out and Tiki Barber had a 15-yard punt return. Three plays later, Barber burst up the middle on a draw play for a 31-yard touchdown with 14 seconds left in the half to give the Giants a commanding 20-3 lead. The Eagles scored on their first two possessions of the second half, but the Giants scored on their first three possessions to pull away. Collins was 21 of 29 for 220 yards and 2 touchdowns. On offense, the Giants converted 7 of 14 third-down opportunities. Donovan McNabb was 19 of 33 for 214 yards and 1 touchdown.

N.Y. Giants	3	17	7	6	—	33
Philadelphia	0	3	9	6	—	18

NYG — FG Daluiso 32
NYG — FG Daluiso 36
Phil — FG Akers 33
NYG — Toomer 25 pass from Collins (Daluiso kick)
NYG — Barber 31 run (Daluiso kick)
Phil — FG Akers 29
NYG — Hilliard 30 pass from Collins (Daluiso kick)
Phil — McNabb 15 run (kick blocked)
NYG — FG Daluiso 44
NYG — FG Daluiso 23
Phil — Lewis 7 pass from McNabb (pass failed)

OAKLAND 38, INDIANAPOLIS 31—at RCA Dome, attendance 56,769. Rich Gannon rushed for 3 touchdowns as the Raiders scored 31 unanswered points to come from behind and defeat the Colts. The Colts came out in a No-Huddle offense and scored on their first three possessions, taking a 21-0 lead on Peyton Manning's 10-yard touchdown pass to Edgerrin James with 11:28 left in the first half. Mike Vanderjagt missed a 47-yard field-goal attempt on the Colts' fourth possession, snapping a streak of 28 consecutive field goals, and Gannon drove the Raiders 63 yards to cut the lead to 21-7. Vanderjagt added a 31-yard field goal just before halftime to give the Colts a 24-7 lead. The Raiders drove 77 yards to begin the second half, capped by Gannon's 7-yard scoring run. Three plays later, Ken Dilger fumbled and Greg Biekert recovered at the Colts' 15 to set up Sebastian Janikowski's 24-yard field goal. Four plays later, Tory James intercepted Manning's pass and returned it 25 yards to the Colts' 15. Gannon's 6-yard touchdown run three plays later tied the game 24-24 with 3:58 remaining in the third quarter. After a Colts punt and Gannon's 34-yard pass to Andre Rison, Tyrone Wheatley gave the Raiders the lead with a 6-yard touchdown run. After another Colts punt, the Raiders marched 77 yards in 14 plays, including 10 rushes and 2 third-down conversions, and took a 38-24 lead on Wheatley's 1-yard run with 5:39 left. Manning's 50-yard touchdown pass to Marvin Harrison cut the deficit to 38-31 with 4:07 to play, and the Colts' defense forced a three-and-out. Manning drove the Colts to the Raiders' 24, but two penalties and three incompletions forced Manning to throw a desparation pass into the end zone on fourth-and-25, which was picked off by James with 1:00 remaining to preserve the victory. Gannon was 15 of 22 for 207 yards. Manning was 33 of 48 for 367 yards and 3 touchdowns, with 2 interceptions. Harrison had 10 receptions for 141 yards.

Oakland	0	7	24	7	—	38
Indianapolis	14	10	0	7	—	31

Ind — Pollard 13 pass from Manning (Vanderjagt kick)
Ind — James 6 run (Vanderjagt kick)
Ind — James 10 pass from Manning (Vanderjagt kick)
Oak — Gannon 3 run (Janikowski kick)
Ind — FG Vanderjagt 31
Oak — Gannon 7 run (Janikowski kick)
Oak — FG Janikowski 24
Oak — Gannon 6 run (Janikowski kick)
Oak — Wheatley 6 run (Janikowski kick)
Oak — Wheatley 1 run (Janikowski kick)
Ind — Harrison 50 pass from Manning (Vanderjagt kick)

ST. LOUIS 37, SEATTLE 34—at Husky Stadium, attendance 64,869. Kurt Warner passed for 386 yards, including a 41-yard third-down pass to Torry Holt to set up Jeff Wilkins's winning field goal with 23 seconds left, as the Rams defeated the Seahawks and set an NFL record by scoring at least 30 points in their eighth consecutive game. Tied 3-3 in the second quarter, Jay Bellamy thwarted a Rams' drive by intercepting Warner's pass and returning it 84 yards for a touchdown. The Rams responded by scoring on their next two drives, capped by Robert Holcombe's 1-yard run with 17 seconds left in the half, to give the Rams a 13-10 lead. While the Rams scored on their first two possessions of the second half, the Seahawks scored on their first three to tie the game 27-27 on Ricky Watters's 1-yard run with 7:40 to play. The Seahawks' defense then forced a punt, but on the next play Todd Collins sacked Jon Kitna and forced him to fumble. Kevin Carter recovered the ball but then fumbled. Devin Bush scooped up the loose ball and raced 15 yards for the go-ahead touchdown with 5:12 to play. Undaunted, the Seahawks drove 71 yards in 7 plays, capped by Kitna's 34-yard touchdown pass to Darrell Jackson with 2:05 remaining to tie the game. Warner completed a 9-yard pass to Az-Zahir Hakim on third-and-7 with 1:26 left to keep the drive alive and then, faced with third-and-17 from midfield with 32 seconds left, Warner fired a 41-yard strike to Holt to set up Wilkins's winning kick. Warner was 35 of 47 for 386 yards and 1 touchdown, with 1 interception, and completed 16 consecutive passes at one point. Holt had 6 receptions for 101 yards. Kitna was 20 of 31 for 245 yards and 1 touchdown, with 2 interceptions.

St. Louis	3	10	7	17	—	37
Seattle	3	7	10	14	—	34

Sea — FG Heppner 19
StL — FG Wilkins 48
Sea — Bellamy 84 interception return (Heppner kick)
StL — FG Wilkins 48
StL — Holcombe 1 run (Wilkins kick)
Sea — Watters 3 run (Heppner kick)
StL — Faulk 1 run (Wilkins kick)
Sea — FG Heppner 43
StL — Williams 4 pass from Warner (Wilkins kick)
Sea — Watters 1 run (Heppner kick)
StL — Bush 15 fumble return (Wilkins kick)
Sea — Jackson 34 pass from Kitna (Heppner kick)
StL — FG Wilkins 27

DETROIT 15, WASHINGTON 10—at Pontiac Silverdome, attendance 74,159. Jason Hanson kicked 5 field goals, and the Lions' defense intercepted 4 passes as Detroit improved to 2-0 despite not having scored an offensive touchdown. Leading 3-0, Kelvin Pritchett intercepted Brad Johnson's pass and returned it 78 yards to the Redskins' 1. However, the Redskins' defense stopped the Lions and set up Hanson's second field goal. The offense responded with a 13-play, 75-yard drive, which included four third-down conversions, capped by Johnson's 5-yard touchdown pass to Stephen Alexander to give Washington a 7-6 lead. The Lions kicked field goals on three consecutive possessions, the last set up by Kurt Schulz's interception at the Lions' 12, to take a 15-10 lead with 6:24 remaining. The Redskins' last two drives ended with interceptions by Bryant Westbrook and Terry Fair, the latter at the Lions' 20 with 49 seconds remaining, to preserve the victory. Charlie Batch, in his first game back from a preseason broken leg, was 16 of 31 for 194 yards, with 2 interceptions. Johnson was 23 of 35 for 245 yards and 1 touchdown, with 4 interceptions.

Washington	0	7	3	0	—	10
Detroit	3	3	3	6	—	15

Det — FG Hanson 49
Det — FG Hanson 20
Wash — Alexander 5 pass from Johnson (Conway kick)
Det — FG Hanson 54
Wash — FG Conway 26
Det — FG Hanson 37
Det — FG Hanson 35

SUNDAY NIGHT, SEPTEMBER 10

ARIZONA 32, DALLAS 31—at Sun Devil Stadium, attendance 66,009. Jake Plummer's 17-yard touchdown pass to Frank Sanders with 1:54 remaining capped his twelfth career fourth-quarter comeback and gave Dallas its first 0-2 start since 1993. The Cowboys took a 7-3 lead on Wane McGarity's 64-yard punt return for a touchdown. After Michael Pittman's 1-yard scoring run gave the Cardinals a lead, the Cowboys responded with 79- and 54-yard touchdown drives on their next two possessions, capped by Randall Cunningham's 1-yard scoring pass to Jackie Harris, to give the Cowboys a 21-10 lead with 26 seconds left in the half. The Cardinals scored on their next five possessions, beginning with Cary Blanchard's 54-yard field goal as the half expired. Trailing 31-26 with 4:00 remaining, Plummer completed a 63-yard pass to David Boston to set up his scoring pass to Sanders. The Cowboys reached the Cardinals' 43 with 31 seconds left, but four consecutive incompletions preserved the Cardinals' victory. Plummer was 18 of 24 for 243 yards and 2 touchdowns. Boston had 6 catches for 102 yards. Cunningham was 24 of 34 for 243 yards and 3 touchdowns.

Dallas	7	14	3	7	—	31
Arizona	3	10	10	9	—	32

Ariz — FG Blanchard 19
Dall — McGarity 64 punt return (Seder kick)
Ariz — Pittman 1 run (Blanchard kick)
Dall — McKnight 47 pass from Cunningham (Seder kick)
Dall — Harris 1 pass from Cunningham (Seder kick)
Ariz — FG Blanchard 54
Dall — FG Seder 44
Ariz — Sanders 4 pass from Plummer (Blanchard kick)
Ariz — FG Blanchard 35
Dall — Wiley 15 pass from Cunningham (Seder kick)
Ariz — FG Blanchard 51
Ariz — Sanders 17 pass from Plummer (run failed)

MONDAY NIGHT, SEPTEMBER 11

N.Y. JETS 20, NEW ENGLAND 19—at Giants Stadium, attendance 77,687. Vinny Testaverde completed 2 touchdown passes to Wayne Chrebet in the final 6:25 as the Jets rallied to defeat the Patriots. Adam Vinatieri kicked 4 first-half field goals to give the Patriots a 12-7 halftime lead. Vinatieri missed a 29-yard attempt in the third quarter, but it seemed of little consequence when Drew Bledsoe culminated a 14-play, 72-yard drive with a 6-yard touchdown pass to Eric Bjornson with 9:56 remaining to give the Patriots a 19-7 lead. Testaverde's 2-yard scoring pass to Chrebet, which went through the hands of Antonio Langham, with 6:25 left capped an 85-yard drive. After two first downs the Patriots were forced to punt with 2:42 left. Dedric Ward muffed the punt, but Tony Scott recovered at the Jets' 28. Ward redeemed himself on the next play by making a one-handed catch for a 44-yard gain. On the next play, Testaverde fired a strike to Chrebet, who reached the end zone by diving for the pylon. Bledsoe was sacked twice in the Patriots' final possession, including on fourth down. Testaverde was 16 of 37 for 281 yards and 3 touchdowns, with 1 interception. Ward had 4 receptions for 100 yards. Bledsoe was 25 of 43 for 229 yards and 1 touchdown.

New England	3	9	0	7	—	19
N.Y. Jets	7	0	0	13	—	20

NE — FG Vinatieri 32
NYJ — Baxter 4 pass from Testaverde (Hall kick)
NE — FG Vinatieri 35
NE — FG Vinatieri 30
NE — FG Vinatieri 33
NE — Bjornson 6 pass from Bledsoe (Vinatieri kick)
NYJ — Chrebet 2 pass from Testaverde (Hall kick)
NYJ — Chrebet 28 pass from Testaverde (run failed)

THIRD WEEK SUMMARIES

AMERICAN FOOTBALL CONFERENCE

Eastern Division	**W**	**L**	**T**	**Pct.**	**Pts.**	**OP**
N.Y. Jets	3	0	0	1.000	67	49
Buffalo	2	1	0	.667	57	58
Miami	2	1	0	.667	49	19
Indianapolis	1	1	0	.500	58	52
New England	0	3	0	.000	48	62
Central Division						
Baltimore	2	1	0	.667	61	55
Cleveland	2	1	0	.667	54	54
Jacksonville	2	1	0	.667	76	46
Tennessee	1	1	0	.500	30	30
Cincinnati	0	2	0	.000	7	37
Pittsburgh	0	2	0	.000	20	39
Western Division						
Denver	2	1	0	.667	111	79
Oakland	2	1	0	.667	71	70
Kansas City	1	2	0	.333	70	54
Seattle	1	2	0	.333	54	70
San Diego	0	3	0	.000	43	79

NATIONAL FOOTBALL CONFERENCE

Eastern Division	**W**	**L**	**T**	**Pct.**	**Pts.**	**OP**
N.Y. Giants	3	0	0	1.000	68	41
Arizona	1	1	0	.500	48	52
Dallas	1	2	0	.333	72	94
Philadelphia	1	2	0	.333	62	53
Washington	1	2	0	.333	51	59
Central Division						
Minnesota	3	0	0	1.000	64	47
Tampa Bay	3	0	0	1.000	93	26
Detroit	2	1	0	.667	39	51
Green Bay	1	2	0	.333	40	50
Chicago	0	3	0	.000	34	85
Western Division						
St. Louis	3	0	0	1.000	119	94
Atlanta	2	1	0	.667	65	80
Carolina	1	2	0	.333	65	57
New Orleans	1	2	0	.333	48	61
San Francisco	0	3	0	.000	74	115

SUNDAY, SEPTEMBER 17

ATLANTA 15, CAROLINA 10—at Ericsson Stadium, attendance 66,498. A rare safety helped the Falcons improve to 2-1 with a divisional road victory. Ray Buchanan's first-quarter interception led to Morten Andersen's 38-yard field goal. Early in the second quarter, Chris Chandler completed two passes to Shawn Jefferson for first downs, leading to Jamal Anderson's 26-yard touchdown run. The Panthers scored on their last two drives of the half to tie the game 10-10, and Andersen opened the second half by missing his second field-goal attempt of the game. Two possessions later, Lee Woodall recovered Terance Mathis's fumble at the Falcons' 23, but the Panthers were unable to capitalize when holder Ken Walter fumbled the snap on what would have been a 34-yard field-goal attempt. Ashley Ambrose's interception and 37-yard return midway through the fourth quarter set up Andersen's 27-yard field goal with 4:10 remaining. Buchanan recovered Tshimanga Biakabutuka's fumble three plays later at the Falcons' 35. Needing a first down on third-and-3 to run down the clock, Anderson broke free for a 42-yard run. However, Doug Evans knocked the ball from Anderson at the Panthers' 16, scooped it up on the dead run at the Panthers' 3 and carried the ball out of the end zone. Since momentum only affects a defender on an interception, the play was properly ruled a safety, giving Atlanta a 15-10 lead with 2:12 left and allowing them to run out the clock. Chandler was 21 of 27 for 174 yards. Steve Beuerlein was 21 of 37 for 241 yards and 1 touchdown, with 2 interceptions.

Atlanta	3	7	0	5	—	15
Carolina	0	10	0	0	—	10

Atl — FG Andersen 38
Atl — Anderson 26 run (Andersen kick)
Car — FG Cunningham 33
Car — Muhammad 9 pass from Beuerlein (Cunningham kick)
Atl — FG Andersen 27
Atl — Safety, Evans recovered fumble at 3-yard line and ran out of end zone

N.Y. JETS 27, BUFFALO 14—at Giants Stadium, attendance 77,884. Defensive back Marcus Coleman's Hail Mary touchdown catch as the first half expired propelled the Jets to their first 3-0 start since 1966. The Bills drove 80 yards with their first possession, capped by Rob Johnson's 3-yard scoring pass to Eric Moulds. However, Kevin Williams returned the ensuing kickoff 97 yards for a touchdown, and Dedric Ward's 19-yard punt return early in the second quarter led to Curtis Martin's 5-yard touchdown run on a fourth-and-one play. The Bills tied the game with 1:07 left in the half on Johnson's third-and-5 pass to Jeremy McDaniel, who made the reception despite an interception attempt by Coleman, and streaked down the left sideline for a touchdown. Coleman, who at 6-feet 2-inches is at least four inches taller than Wayne Chrebet or Ward, was then inserted for Vinny Testaverde's Hail Mary pass. Coleman outleaped three Bills' defenders in the end zone for his first NFL reception. The deflated Bills missed a field goal in the third quarter, and lost a fumble at the Jets' 13 and had a pass intercepted at the Jets' 24 in the fourth quarter. Testaverde was 16 of 32 for 188 yards and 1 touchdown, with 1 interception. Johnson was 21 of 36 for 291 yards and 2 touchdowns, with 1 interception.

Buffalo	7	7	0	0	—	14
N.Y. Jets	7	14	3	3	—	27

Buff — Moulds 3 pass from Johnson (Christie kick)
NYJ — Williams 97 kickoff return (Hall kick)
NYJ — Martin 5 run (Hall kick)
Buff — McDaniel 74 pass from Johnson (Christie kick)
NYJ — Coleman 45 pass from Testaverde (Hall kick)
NYJ — FG Hall 51
NYJ — FG Hall 27

JACKSONVILLE 13, CINCINNATI 0—at ALLTEL Stadium, attendance 45,603. The Jagauars' defense recorded 5 sacks and forced 4 turnovers en route to the first shutout in club history. The game was played in a steady downpour during a tropical storm warning with Hurricane Gordon approaching Jacksonville. R. Jay Soward's 20-yard reverse set up Mark Brunell's 21-yard touchdown pass to Keenan McCardell in the first quarter. Tremain Mack fumbled the ensuing kickoff, and Kiwaukee Thomas recovered at the Bengals' 17 to set up Steve Lindsey's 30-yard field goal moments later for a 10-0 lead. Neil Rackers missed 2 second-quarter field-goal attempts for the Bengals, but Cincinnati's defense stopped Chad Dukes on fourth-and-1 from the Bengals' 2 late in the half. Aaron Beasley's 39-yard interception return to the Bengals' 16 set up Lindsey's 19-yard field goal with 1:45 left to seal the victory. Brunell was 20 of 32 for 176 yards and 1 touchdown, with 1 interception. McCardell had 10 receptions for 108 yards. Akili Smith was 18 of 41 for 183 yards, with 2 interceptions.

Cincinnati	0	0	0	0	—	0
Jacksonville	10	0	0	3	—	13

Jax — McCardell 21 pass from Brunell (Lindsey kick)
Jax — FG Lindsey 30
Jax — FG Lindsey 19

DENVER 33, OAKLAND 24—at Network Associates Coliseum, attendance 62,078. Mike Anderson rushed for 187 yards, Brian Griese passed for 2 touchdowns, and Joe Nedney kicked 4 field goals against his former team as Mike Shanahan improved his record against the Raiders to 10-1. The Broncos had a 10-play, 69-yard drive, capped by Griese's 10-yard touchdown pass to Ed McCaffrey. The Broncos' defense then forced turnovers on the Raiders' first two plays from scrimmage. First, Kavika Pittman sacked Rich Gannon, forcing him to fumble. Trevor Pryce picked up the ball and rumbled 28 yards for a touchdown. On the Raiders' next play from scrimmage, Eric Brown recovered Tyrone Wheatley's fumble, setting up Nedney's 24-yard field goal to give Denver a 17-0 lead 8:36 into the game. Nedney, waived by Oakland in camp, had been signed prior to the game because of Jason Elam's leg injury. After an exchange of touchdowns, Napoleon Kaufman's 60-yard run set up Sebastian Janikowski's 19-yard field goal, cutting the deficit to 24-10. Two plays later, Regan Upshaw recovered Griese's fumble at the Broncos' 12 setting up Gannon's 9-yard touchdown pass to Tim Brown. The Raiders' defense forced a punt on the Broncos' next possession, and Randy Jordan blocked Tom Rouen's punt and returned it 3 yards for the game-tying touchdown with 7:48 remaining in the half. The Raiders had a chance to score on their opening drive of the second half, but John Mobley intercepted Gannon in the end zone to thwart the opportunity. Mobley's interception sparked a 13-play, 79-yard drive capped by Nedney's go-ahead field goal. Behind the running of Anderson, Nedney kicked field goals on the Broncos' next two drives as well, and Terrell Buckley intercepted Gannon with 4:00 remaining. The Broncos ran out the clock to catch Oakland in the standings. Griese was 21 of 31 for 213 yards and 2 touchdowns. Anderson had 32 carries for 187 yards and helped the Broncos maintain a 37:06-22:54 time of possession advantage. Gannon was 13 of 21 for 159 yards and 2 touchdowns, with 2 interceptions.

Denver	17	7	3	6	—	33
Oakland	7	17	0	0	—	24

Den — McCaffrey 10 pass from Griese (Nedney kick)
Den — Pryce 28 fumble return (Nedney kick)
Den — FG Nedney 24
Oak — Brown 11 pass from Gannon (Janikowski kick)
Den — Griffith 1 pass from Griese (Nedney kick)
Oak — FG Janikowski 19
Oak — Brown 9 pass from Gannon (Janikowski kick)
Oak — Jordan 3 blocked punt return (Janikowski kick)
Den — FG Nedney 32
Den — FG Nedney 22
Den — FG Nedney 21

MINNESOTA 21, NEW ENGLAND 13—at Foxboro Stadium, attendance 59,835. Daunte Culpepper passed for 2 touchdowns, and the Vikings controlled the ball for more than 39 minutes to give the Patriots their first 0-3 start since 1993. The Vikings began the game with a 17-play, 73-yard drive that consumed 8 minutes, 54 seconds, capped by Robert Smith's 4-yard touchdown run to take a 7-0 lead. The Patriots responded with Kevin Faulk's 2-yard scoring run, but the Vikings scored touchdowns on their next two possessions, capped by Culpepper's 39-yard scoring strike to Matthew Hatchette, to take a 21-7 lead with 5:18 left in the half. Lawyer Milloy's interception at the Vikings' 21 gave the Patriots a scoring opportunity, but Orlando Thomas sacked Bledsoe on fourth-and-goal from the Vikings' 3 on the first play of the fourth quarter. The Patriots' defense forced a punt, and Faulk's 19-yard return set up Bledsoe's 8-yard touchdown pass to Terry Glenn with 11:11 left, but Lee Johnson mishandled the extra-point snap. The Patriots drove to the Vikings' 14 in the game's waning seconds, but Bryce Paup sacked Bledsoe on fourth-and-7 to preserve the victory. Culpepper was 19 of 28 for 177 yards and 2 touchdowns, with 1 interception. Bledsoe was 21 of 35 for 190 yards and 1 touchdown, with 1 interception.

Minnesota	7	14	0	0	—	21
New England	7	0	0	6	—	13

Minn — Smith 4 run (Anderson kick)
NE — Faulk 2 run (Vinatieri kick)
Minn — McWilliams 1 pass from Culpepper (Anderson kick)
Minn — Hatchette 39 pass from Culpepper (Anderson kick)
NE — Glenn 8 pass from Bledsoe (mishandled snap)

SEATTLE 20, NEW ORLEANS 10—at Husky Stadium, attendance 59,513. Jon Kitna passed for 193 yards and engineered 2 fourth-quarter scoring drives as the Seahawks recorded their first victory at Husky Stadium. Ricky Watters, making his 100th consecutive start, punctuated the Seahawks' opening possession with a 7-yard touchdown run. The Saints had back-to-back scoring drives of 80 and 66 yards, with a Kris Heppner missed field goal in between, to take a 10-7 lead. The Seahawks scored on three of their first four possessions of the second half on drives of 59, 87, and 47 yards, while the Seahawks' defense limited the Saints to just one first down in their three possessions, to take a 20-10 lead on Heppner's 45-yard field goal with 3:47 remaining. The Saints drove to the Seahawks' 19 in the final minutes, but Jeff Blake's fourth-and-3 pass fell incomplete. Kitna was 22 of 29 for 193 yards and 1 touchdown, with 1 interception. Watters rushed 22 times for 105 yards. Blake was 14 of 24 for 159 yards and 1 touchdown.

New Orleans	7	3	0	0	—	10
Seattle	7	0	3	10	—	20

Sea — Watters 7 run (Heppner kick)
NO — Poole 49 pass from Blake (Brien kick)
NO — FG Brien 23
Sea — FG Heppner 31
Sea — Mili 1 pass from Kitna (Heppner kick)
Sea — FG Heppner 45

N.Y. GIANTS 14, CHICAGO 7—at Soldier Field, attendance 60,599. Tiki Barber and Ron Dayne rushed for a combined 155 yards and gave the Giants a 38:11-21:49 edge in time of possession to improve to 3-0 for the first time since 1993. Kerry Collins's 34-yard touchdown pass to Ron Dixon capped the game's opening drive, but Brad Daluiso missed 2 second-quarter field-goal attempts and Cade McNown engineered a 12-play, 74-yard drive, capped by Eddie Kennison's 2-yard touchdown catch with 14 seconds left in the half to tie the game. Barber and Dayne each had 3 carries on a 6-play, 43-yard drive, capped by Barber's 3-yard touchdown run, to take a 14-7 lead late in the third quarter. The Giants had chances to put the game away, but Barber fumbled at the Bears' 8 and Mike Brown recovered, and Daluiso missed a 31-yard field-goal attempt with 1:08 left. However, the Bears failed to gain a first down, and the Giants were victorious. Collins was 24 of 33 for 249 yards and 1 touchdown. McNown was 23 of 36 for 202 yards and 1 touchdown.

N.Y. Giants	7	0	7	0	—	14
Chicago	0	7	0	0	—	7

NYG — Dixon 34 pass from Collins (Daluiso kick)
Chi — Kennison 2 pass from McNown (Edinger kick)
NYG — Barber 3 run (Daluiso kick)

GREEN BAY 6, PHILADELPHIA 3—at Lambeau Field, attendance 59,869. Ryan Longwell kicked a 38-yard field goal with three seconds remaining to give Mike Sherman his first victory. Two third-down conversions by the Eagles set up David Akers's 43-yard field goal with 2:00 left in the first half. Longwell had an opportunity to tie the game, but missed a 40-yard attempt as the half expired. Longwell's 37-yard field goal capped the opening possession of the second half, a drive aided by 2 defensive holding penalties, to tie the game. Brett Favre was intercepted deep in

Eagles' territory twice early in the fourth quarter, but the Packers' defense continued to force punts. Starting from his own 20 with 5:20 remaining, Favre completed passes of 16, 15, 16, and 12 yards to set up Longwell's winning field goal. Favre was 18 of 33 for 189 yards, with 3 interceptions. Donovan McNabb was 15 of 31 for 118 yards, with 1 interception.

Philadelphia	0	3	0	0	—	3
Green Bay	0	0	3	3	—	6

Phil — FG Akers 43
GB — FG Longwell 37
GB — FG Longwell 38

CLEVELAND 23, PITTSBURGH 20—at Cleveland Browns Stadium, attendance 73,018. Courtney Brown sacked Kent Graham at the Browns' 10 and the Steelers were unable to attempt a field goal before time expired, giving the Browns their second consecutive victory. The Browns drove 62 and 61 yards with their first two possessions, both capped by Tim Couch touchdown passes, to take a 14-0 lead. Jerome Bettis had 7 carries for 46 yards on the ensuing 10-play drive, capped by Richard Huntley's touchdown. Kris Brown added two field goals, the second following Hines Ward's 57-yard kickoff return, to trim the deficit to 14-13 early in the third quarter. David Patten returned the ensuing kickoff 62 yards to set up Phil Dawson's 23-yard field goal, but on the Steelers' next drive, Graham completed a 31-yard pass to Ward and Bettis had 5 carries for 43 yards, including a 10-yard scoring run to give Pittsburgh a 20-17 lead. Dawson tied the game early in the fourth quarter after Couch had completed 36-yard passes to Aaron Shea and Patten on an 87-yard drive. Couch's 79-yard pass to Kevin Johnson on the Browns' next possession gave the Browns an excellent opportunity for a touchdown, but the Steelers' defense stopped Errict Rhett on three consecutive plays from the Steelers' 2, setting up Dawson's go-ahead field goal with 2:45 left. Faced with fourth-and-6 from the Steelers' 35, Graham completed a 29-yard pass to Bobby Shaw. On third-and-goal from the Steelers' 6 with 14 seconds, Brown recorded his third sack of the game. The Steelers' kicking unit raced onto the field, but were unable to snap the ball prior to time expiring. Couch was 23 of 31 for 316 yards and 2 touchdowns. Graham was 15 of 28 for 193 yards. Bettis had 23 carries for 122 yards.

Pittsburgh	0	10	10	0	—	20
Cleveland	14	0	3	6	—	23

Cle — Shea 2 pass from Couch (Dawson kick)
Cle — Edwards 21 pass from Couch (Dawson kick)
Pitt — Huntley 4 run (Brown kick)
Pitt — FG Brown 41
Pitt — FG Brown 31
Cle — FG Dawson 23
Pitt — Bettis 10 run (Brown kick)
Cle — FG Dawson 28
Cle — FG Dawson 29

KANSAS CITY 42, SAN DIEGO 10—at Arrowhead Stadium, attendance 77,604. Elvis Grbac matched Len Dawson's club record by completing 5 touchdown passes en route to the Chiefs' first victory of the year. The Chargers jumped out to a quick 10-0 lead before the Chiefs went airborne. Grbac completed a 17-yard pass to Derrick Alexander before firing a 36-yard touchdown pass to Sylvester Morris early in the second quarter. A 23-yard pass to Morris and 21-yard pass interference penalty set up Grbac's 1-yard touchdown pass to Tony Richardson with 47 seconds left in the half. The Chargers had an opportunity to score on their first possession of the second half, but John Carney missed a 51-yard field-goal attempt. The Chiefs responded with a 59-yard drive, highlighted by Grbac's 33-yard pass to Tony Gonzalez on third-and-8, and capped by Morris's 9-yard scoring catch. Marvcus Patton recovered Moses Moreno's fumble on the Chargers' next play, setting up Grbac's 2-yard touchdown pass to Troy Drayton. Moreno suffered a shoulder injury on the next series, and Ryan Leaf drove the Chargers to the Chiefs' 15, only to have Lew Bush intercept his pass early in the fourth quarter. The Chiefs scored on their next two possessions to pull away. Grbac was 20 of 33 for 255 yards and 5 touchdowns, with 1 interception. Morris had 6 receptions for 112 yards. Moreno was 11 of 22 for 107 yards.

San Diego	10	0	0	0	—	10
Kansas City	0	14	14	14	—	42

SD — Dumas 56 interception return (Carney kick)
SD — FG Carney 54
KC — Morris 36 pass from Grbac (Stoyanovich kick)
KC — Richardson 1 pass from Grbac (Stoyanovich kick)
KC — Morris 9 pass from Grbac (Stoyanovich kick)
KC — Drayton 2 pass from Grbac (Stoyanovich kick)
KC — Morris 20 pass from Grbac (Stoyanovich kick)
KC — Moreau 1 run (Stoyanovich kick)

ST. LOUIS 41, SAN FRANCISCO 24—at Trans World Dome, attendance 65,945. Kurt Warner passed for 394 yards, and Marshall Faulk rushed for 134 yards as the Rams amassed 529 yards of offense to remain undefeated. Winfred Tubbs intercepted Warner's pass on the first play from scrimmage. Jeff Garcia fired a 29-yard touchdown pass to Fred Beasley on the next play to give the 49ers a quick 7-0 lead. The Rams drove 77 yards in 6 plays to tie the game 10-10 with 5:09 left in the first half. The 49ers responded with a 5-play, 74-yard drive to take a 17-10 lead on Garcia's 20-yard touchdown pass to Charlie Garner, but Warner fired a 78-yard touchdown pass to Isaac Bruce on the next play to tie the game. The Rams' offense was unstoppable in the second half, driving 60, 85, 80, and 78 yards to score on all four of their second-half possessions, capped by 2 short touchdown runs by Faulk. Warner was 23 of 34 for 394 yards and 2 touchdowns, with 2 interceptions. Bruce had 8 receptions for 188 yards, and Faulk had 199 combined yards. The Rams tallied 32 first downs. Garcia was 21 of 34 for 290 yards and 3 touchdowns, with 2 interceptions. Terrell Owens had 6 catches for 108 yards.

San Francisco	7	10	0	7	—	24
St. Louis	3	14	7	17	—	41

SF — Beasley 29 pass from Garcia (Richey kick)
StL — FG Wilkins 47
SF — FG Richey 21
StL — Horne 18 pass from Warner (Wilkins kick)
SF — Garner 20 pass from Garcia (Richey kick)
StL — Bruce 78 pass from Warner (Wilkins kick)
StL — Faulk 1 run (Wilkins kick)
StL — FG Wilkins 25
SF — Owens 12 pass from Garcia (Richey kick)
StL — Faulk 4 run (Wilkins kick)
StL — Faulk 1 run (Wilkins kick)

TAMPA BAY 31, DETROIT 10—at Pontiac Silverdome, attendance 76,928. The Buccaneers' defense forced 3 turnovers and recorded 7 sacks as Tampa Bay remained undefeated. Trailing 3-0, the Buccaneers used a 42-yard punt return by Karl Williams to set up Shaun King's touchdown run and a 43-yard pass from King to Jacquez Green prior to Mike Alstott's 4-yard run to take a 14-3 lead. In the second quarter, an 8-play, 60-yard drive, highlighted by King's 38-yard pass to Warrick Dunn on third-and-9, was capped by Randall McDaniel's 2-yard touchdown catch. It was the first regular-season catch of McDaniel's 13-year career. The Lions scored their first offensive touchdown of the season on Charlie Batch's 50-yard Hail Mary pass to Germane Crowell as the half expired. However, the Buccaneers began the third quarter with a 19-play, 75-yard drive that consumed 9 minutes, 31 seconds and was capped by Martin Gramatica's 24-yard field goal. In the fourth quarter, John Lynch's 36-yard interception return to the Lions' 37 started a 5 minute, 27 second drive, culminated by Dunn's 1-yard scoring run with 5:39 remaining. King was 18 of 30 for 211 yards and 1 touchdown. Batch was 26 of 36 for 277 yards and 1 touchdown, with 2 interceptions.

Tampa Bay	14	7	3	7	—	31
Detroit	3	7	0	0	—	10

Det — FG Hanson 38
TB — King 6 run (Gramatica kick)
TB — Alstott 4 run (Gramatica kick)
TB — McDaniel 2 pass from King (Gramatica kick)
Det — Crowell 50 pass from Batch (Hanson kick)
TB — FG Gramatica 24
TB — Dunn 1 run (Gramatica kick)

SUNDAY NIGHT, SEPTEMBER 17

MIAMI 19, BALTIMORE 6—at Pro Player Stadium, attendance 73,464. Lamar Smith rushed for 2 touchdowns in the rain as the Dolphins were victorious on the night Dan Marino's jersey was retired. Olindo Mare field goals finished each of the Dolphins' first two possessions, the second of which was set up by Jeff Ogden's 31-yard punt return, to stake the Dolphins to a 6-0 lead. The Ravens had two opportunities to score before halftime, but Patrick Surtain intercepted Tony Banks's pass at the Dolphins' 4 midway through the quarter, and Matt Stover's 30-yard field-goal attempt at the end of the half was tipped at the line of scrimmage by Kenny Mixon to allow Miami to maintain its 6-0 lead. The Dolphins drove 61 and 80 yards with their first two possessions of the second half to take a 19-3 lead with 13:15 left. The Ravens drove to the Dolphins' 13 in the final moments, but Banks's fourth-and-2 pass fell incomplete. Jay Fiedler was 11 of 16 for 160 yards and 1 touchdown, with 1 interception. Banks was 19 of 31 for 189 yards, with 1 interception.

Baltimore	0	0	3	3	—	6
Miami	3	3	7	6	—	19

Mia — FG Mare 42
Mia — FG Mare 41
Mia — Smith 7 run (Mare kick)
Balt — FG Stover 27
Mia — Smith 8 pass from Fiedler (kick failed)
Balt — FG Stover 33

MONDAY NIGHT, SEPTEMBER 18

DALLAS 27, WASHINGTON 21—at FedEx Field, attendance 84,431. Randall Cunningham, playing for the injured Troy Aikman, passed for 185 yards and 2 touchdowns as the Cowboys defeated the Redskins for the sixth consecutive time. Champ Bailey's 54-yard punt return set up Stephen Davis's first-quarter touchdown run. Late in the quarter, Cunningham fumbled the snap but recovered the ball and then completed a sideline pass to Chris Warren who raced into the end zone for a 76-yard touchdown. Leon Lett sacked Brad Johnson on the first play of the second quarter and forced him to fumble. Greg Ellis recovered, and Emmitt Smith's 3-yard touchdown run eight plays later gave Dallas a 14-7 lead. Tim Seder's 32-yard field goal culminated the opening drive of the second half to increase the lead to 17-7, but Sam Shade intercepted Cunningham's pass on the Cowboys' next possession and Davis scored his second touchdown to trim the deficit to 17-14. Cunningham's 44-yard pass to Raghib Ismail on third-and-6 early in the fourth quarter was followed two plays later by Jackie Harris's 16-yard touchdown catch, which gave Dallas a 24-14 lead. The Redskins responded with a 69-yard drive to cut the deficit to 24-21 on Mike Sellers's 7-yard scoring reception with 5:34 left and then forced a Cowboys punt. However, Izell Reese's 46-yard interception return to the Redskins' 23 set up Seder's 38-yard field goal with 1:46 remaining. Ellis sacked Johnson near midfield on the game's final play. Cunningham was 10 of 23 for 185 yards and 2 touchdowns, with 1 interception. Johnson was 30 of 49 for 241 yards and 1 touchdown, with 1 interception.

Dallas	7	7	3	10	—	27
Washington	7	0	7	7	—	21

Wash — Davis 7 run (Husted kick)
Dall — Warren 76 pass from Cunningham (Seder kick)
Dall — Smith 3 run (Seder kick)
Dall — FG Seder 32
Wash — Davis 1 run (Husted kick)
Dall — Harris 16 pass from Cunningham (Seder kick)
Wash — Sellers 7 pass from Johnson (Husted kick)
Dall — FG Seder 38

FOURTH WEEK SUMMARIES

AMERICAN FOOTBALL CONFERENCE

Eastern Division	W	L	T	Pct.	Pts.	OP
N.Y. Jets	4	0	0	1.000	88	66
Miami	3	1	0	.750	59	22
Buffalo	2	1	0	.667	57	58
Indianapolis	2	1	0	.667	101	66
New England	0	4	0	.000	51	72
Central Division						
Baltimore	3	1	0	.750	98	55
Tennessee	2	1	0	.667	53	50

Cleveland	2	2	0	.500	64	90
Jacksonville	2	2	0	.500	90	89
Cincinnati	0	3	0	.000	7	74
Pittsburgh	0	3	0	.000	40	62
Western Division						
Oakland	3	1	0	.750	107	80
Denver	2	2	0	.500	133	102
Kansas City	2	2	0	.500	93	76
Seattle	2	2	0	.500	74	82
San Diego	0	4	0	.000	55	99
NATIONAL FOOTBALL CONFERENCE						
Eastern Division	**W**	**L**	**T**	**Pct.**	**Pts.**	**OP**
N.Y. Giants	3	1	0	.750	74	57
Philadelphia	2	2	0	.500	83	60
Washington	2	2	0	.500	67	65
Arizona	1	2	0	.333	51	81
Dallas	1	3	0	.000	96	135
Central Division						
Minnesota	3	0	0	1.000	64	47
Detroit	3	1	0	.750	60	65
Tampa Bay	3	1	0	.750	110	47
Green Bay	2	2	0	.500	69	53
Chicago	0	4	0	.000	48	106
Western Division						
St. Louis	4	0	0	1.000	160	114
Atlanta	2	2	0	.500	85	121
Carolina	1	2	0	.333	65	57
New Orleans	1	3	0	.250	55	82
San Francisco	1	3	0	.250	115	139

SUNDAY, SEPTEMBER 24

BALTIMORE 37, CINCINNATI 0—at PSINet Stadium, attendance 68,481. The Ravens' defense permitted just 7 first downs and 94 yards to hand the Bengals their second consecutive shutout. While the Ravens' defense allowed just 1 first-half first down, the Ravens' offense scored on four of their five possessions, the latter two of which were set up by O.J. Brigance's fumble recovery and Rod Woodson's interception, to take a 24-0 halftime lead. The Ravens scored on three of their four second-half possessions as well, highlighted by Obafemi Ayanbadejo's 1-yard touchdown run midway through the fourth quarter. The Ravens had advantages in first downs (27-7), total yards (391-94), and time of possession (38:44-21:16). Tony Banks was 20 of 36 for 196 yards and 2 touchdowns. Jamal Lewis rushed 25 times for 116 yards. Scott Mitchell, who replaced an injured Akili Smith in the first quarter, was 14 of 23 for 97 yards, with 2 interceptions.

Cincinnati	0	0	0	0	—	0
Baltimore	10	14	3	10	—	37

Balt — FG Stover 30
Balt — Taylor 8 pass from Banks (Stover kick)
Balt — Ja. Lewis 11 run (Stover kick)
Balt — Sharpe 1 pass from Banks (Stover kick)
Balt — FG Stover 37
Balt — Ayanbadejo 1 run (Stover kick)
Balt — FG Stover 19

OAKLAND 36, CLEVELAND 10—at Network Associates Coliseum, attendance 45,702. William Thomas intercepted 2 passes late in the first half to help spark the Raiders' to a home victory. The Browns marched 77 yards in 9 plays to open the game, capped by Tim Couch's 15-yard touchdown pass to Darrin Chiaverini. The Raiders countered by recovering a surprise onside kick and scoring on their next two possessions, both culminated by 2-yard Tyrone Wheatley touchdown runs, to take a 14-7 lead. Thomas's 12-yard interception return to the Browns' 37 preceeded Zack Crockett's 2-yard touchdown run with 1:17 left in the half. Thomas's 42-yard interception return for a touchdown 35 seconds later staked the Raiders to a 28-7 halftime lead. Rich Gannon was 14 of 23 for 179 yards. Couch was 16 of 29 for 141 yards and 1 touchdown, with 2 interceptions.

Cleveland	7	0	3	0	—	10
Oakland	7	21	0	8	—	36

Cle — Chiaverini 15 pass from Couch (Dawson kick)
Oak — Wheatley 2 run (Janikowski kick)
Oak — Wheatley 2 run (Janikowski kick)
Oak — Crockett 2 run (Janikowski kick)
Oak — Thomas 42 interception return (Janikowski kick)
Cle — FG Dawson 30
Oak — FG Janikowski 37
Oak — FG Janikowski 31
Oak — Safety, Couch penalized for intentional grounding in end zone

DETROIT 21, CHICAGO 14—at Soldier Field, attendance 56,340. Charlie Batch passed for 2 touchdowns, and Kurt Schulz had 3 interceptions as the Lions were victorious in a NFC Central divisional game. Both of Batch's touchdown passes were in the first half, the latter a 36-yard bomb to Germane Crowell with 18 seconds left, to give the Lions a 14-0 lead. Clint Kriewaldt recovered Marty Booker's fumble at the Bears' 12 early in the second half, but the Lions failed to capitalize as Jason Hanson missed a 32-yard field-goal attempt. The Bears responded with a 78-yard scoring drive, capped by Cade McNown's 55-yard touchdown pass to Marcus Robinson. Brian Urlacher's interception at midfield moments later set up McNown's 14-yard scoring run to tie the game. The Lions countered with a 17-play, 91-yard drive that consumed 8 minutes, 37 seconds and was capped by James Stewart's 1-yard run with 9:36 remaining. The Bears twice moved deep into Lions' territory in the final moments, the latter of which concluded with Tracy Scroggins's sack of McNown on fourth down at the Lions' 33. Batch was 20 of 37 for 207 yards and 2 touchdowns, with 1 interception. McNown was 21 of 35 for 261 yards and 1 touchdown, with 3 interceptions.

Detroit	7	7	0	7	—	21
Chicago	0	0	14	0	—	14

Det — Morton 13 pass from Batch (Hanson kick)
Det — Crowell 36 pass from Batch (Hanson kick)
Chi — Robinson 55 pass from McNown (Edinger kick)
Chi — McNown 14 run (Edinger kick)
Det — Stewart 1 run (Hanson kick)

GREEN BAY 29, ARIZONA 3—at Sun Devil Stadium, attendance 71,801. Ryan Longwell kicked 5 field goals, and the Packers accumulated 455 total yards as the defense did not allow touchdowns in consecutive games for the first time in 64 years. The Packers posted consecutive scoring drives of 80, 85, and 61 yards in the first half to take a 17-3 halftime lead. The Packers scored on their first four possessions of the second half as well, all capped by Longwell field goals. Darren Sharper intercepted Jake Plummer's pass in the end zone with 5:45 remaining to thwart the Cardinals' final scoring opportunity. Brett Favre was 17 of 31 for 277 yards and 1 touchdown. Plummer was 21 of 43 for 189 yards, with 4 interceptions.

Green Bay	7	10	6	6	—	29
Arizona	0	3	0	0	—	3

GB — Green 19 run (Longwell kick)
GB — Schroeder 55 pass from Favre (Longwell kick)
Ariz — FG Blanchard 31
GB — FG Longwell 38
GB — FG Longwell 47
GB — FG Longwell 48
GB — FG Longwell 37
GB — FG Longwell 22

KANSAS CITY 23, DENVER 22—at Mile High Stadium, attendance 74,596. Elvis Grbac passed for 2 touchdowns, including a 22-yard pass to Derrick Alexander with 2:21 remaining, as the Chiefs rallied to defeat Denver. The Chiefs opened the game with an 11-play, 80-yard drive, capped by Tony Richardson's 1-yard scoring run. The Broncos scored the next 19 points, highlighted by Ray Crockett's 26-yard interception return and capped by Mike Anderson's 16-yard touchdown run 3:34 into the second half to take a 19-7 lead. The Broncos led 22-14 in the fourth quarter when Rod Smith fumbled and Eric Hicks recovered the ball at the Broncos' 26. Pete Stoyanovich's 42-yard field goal cut the deficit to 22-17 with 8:19 remaining and, after forcing a punt, the Chiefs needed just 8 plays to drive 80 yards, capped by Grbac's touchdown pass to Alexander, to take a 23-22 lead. Marvcus Patton intercepted Gus Frerotte's pass at the Broncos' 37 with 1:40 remaining to preserve the victory. Grbac was 21 of 33 for 250 yards and 2 touchdowns, with 2 interceptions. Tony Gonzalez had 10 receptions for 127 yards. Frerotte, playing for the injured Brian Griese, was 18 of 31 for 208 yards, with 1 interception. Smith had 8 receptions for 134 yards.

Kansas City	7	0	7	9	—	23
Denver	3	9	10	0	—	22

KC — Richardson 1 run (Stoyanovich kick)
Den — FG Nedney 22
Den — FG Nedney 20
Den — Crockett 26 interception return (pass failed)
Den — Anderson 16 run (Nedney kick)
KC — Gonzalez 15 pass from Grbac (Stoyanovich kick)
Den — FG Nedney 43
KC — FG Stoyanovich 42
KC — Alexander 22 pass from Grbac (pass failed)

MIAMI 10, NEW ENGLAND 3—at Pro Player Stadium, attendance 73,344. For the third time in four games, the Dolphins' defense did not allow a touchdown as Miami kept pace with the Jets in the AFC East. Henry Thomas's 16-yard interception return set up Adam Vinatieri's field goal early in the second quarter. The Dolphins scored the game's lone touchdown six plays later, as Jay Fielder completed a 53-yard scoring bomb to Bert Emanuel. Two scrambles by Fiedler netted first downs late in the half to set up Olindo Mare's 43-yard field goal with three seconds left to give the Dolphins a 10-3 lead. Vinatieri missed a 53-yard field-goal attempt early in the fourth quarter, and the Patriots had fourth-and-2 at the Dolphins' 5 with 1:08 remaining, but Drew Bledsoe's end zone pass fell just out of the reach of Eric Bjornson. Fiedler was 12 of 24 for 153 yards and 1 touchdown, with 2 interceptions. Bledsoe was 16 of 33 for 161 yards, with 1 interception.

New England	0	3	0	0	—	3
Miami	0	10	0	0	—	10

NE — FG Vinatieri 40
Mia — Emanuel 53 pass from Fiedler (Mare kick)
Mia — FG Mare 43

N.Y. JETS 21, TAMPA BAY 17—at Raymond James Stadium, attendance 65,619. Curtis Martin's 18-yard halfback-option touchdown pass to Wayne Chrebet with 52 seconds remaining clinched an improbable comeback by the undefeated Jets. The Buccaneers had scoring drives of 83 and 80 yards on consecutive possessions, highlighted by Shaun King's 75-yard pass to Jacquez Green, to take a 10-3 lead. John Hall's second field goal of the game cut the lead to 10-6, and the Jets had a chance to score again before halftime. However, Damien Robinson intercepted Vinny Testaverde's pass at the Buccaneers' 5 to quell the threat, and Ronde Barber's 37-yard interception return for a touchdown late in the third quarter staked Tampa Bay to a 17-6 lead. Jamie Duncan intercepted Testaverde early in the fourth quarter, and Al Groh put Ray Lucas in at quarterback during the Jets' next possession. Testaverde returned with 5:14 left and engineered an 11-play, 64-yard drive, capped by Testaverde's 6-yard pass to Martin with 1:54 left. Testaverde's 2-point conversion pass to Lavernues Coles cut the lead to 17-14. Two plays later Marvin Jones forced Mike Alstott to fumble, and Victor Green recovered the ball at the Buccaneers' 24. Two plays later, Martin rolled to his right and lofted the winning pass to Chrebet with 52 seconds remaining. John Abraham sacked Shaun King on the Buccaneers' next play and forced him to fumble, with Bryan Cox recovering the ball to clinch the game. Testaverde was 22 of 42 for 181 yards and 1 touchdown, with 3 interceptions. King was 7 of 19 for 135 yards and 1 touchdown, with 2 interceptions.

N.Y. Jets	3	3	0	15	—	21
Tampa Bay	3	7	7	0	—	17

TB — FG Gramatica 22
NYJ — FG Hall 41
TB — Moore 3 pass from King (Gramatica kick)
NYJ — FG Hall 27
TB — Barber 37 interception return (Gramatica kick)
NYJ — Martin 6 pass from Testaverde (Coles pass from Testaverde)
NYJ — Chrebet 18 pass from Martin (Hall kick)

PHILADELPHIA 21, NEW ORLEANS 7—at Louisiana Superdome, attendance 64,900. Donovan McNabb passed for 2 touchdowns in 20 seconds, and Brian Mitchell returned a punt for a touchdown as the Eagles' defense forced 4 turnovers to defeat the Saints. Chris Oldham recovered Jason Bostic's muffed punt at the Eagles' 20 to set up Jeff Blake's 10-yard touchdown run midway through the first quarter. McNabb engineered a 10-play, 88-yard drive capped by his 16-yard touchdown pass to Chad Lewis. Ricky Williams fumbled on the next play from scrimmage and Troy Vincent recovered at the Saints' 21, setting up McNabb's 21-yard touchdown pass to Charles Johnson on the next play. Mitchell, who had a kickoff return for a touchdown in the first half nullified by a penalty, returned a punt 72 yards for a touchdown late in the third quarter. The Saints' best scoring chance of the second half was quelled by Carlos Emmons's recovery of Williams's second fumble at the Eagles' 22. McNabb was 20 of 32 for 222 yards and 2 touchdowns. Blake was 19 of 39 for 168 yards, with 2 interceptions. Williams rushed 20 times for 103 yards.

Philadelphia	0	14	7	0	—	21
New Orleans	7	0	0	0	—	7

NO — Blake 10 run (Brien kick)
Phil — Lewis 16 pass from McNabb (Akers kick)
Phil — C. Johnson 21 pass from McNabb (Akers kick)
Phil — Mitchell 72 punt return (Akers kick)

ST. LOUIS 41, ATLANTA 20—at Georgia Dome, attendance 58,761. Torry Holt established an NFL record by averaging 63.0 yards per reception, and Kurt Warner passed for 4 touchdowns as the Rams improved their scoring average to 40 points a game. Turnovers set up the game's first two scores before the Rams drove 62 yards, capped by Warner's 14-yard touchdown pass to Isaac Bruce, to take a 10-7 lead early in the second quarter. Two plays after Morten Andersen's 37-yard field goal tied the game, Warner hit Holt with an 80-yard touchdown pass. Andersen added a field goal as the half expired, and the Falcons drove to the Rams' 5 to begin the second half. However, Jamal Anderson fumbled and Keith Lyle picked up the ball and raced 94 yards for a touchdown. Chris Thomas recovered Darrick Vaughn's fumble on the ensuing kickoff to set up Jeff Wilkins's second field goal for a 27-13 lead. Holt's 85-yard touchdown catch on third-and-7 early in the fourth quarter extended the lead to 34-13. The Falcons responded with a 4-play, 80-yard drive, but Warner hit Bruce with a 66-yard touchdown pass on the next play from scrimmage to put the game away. Warner was 12 of 19 for 336 yards and 4 touchdowns, with 1 interception. Holt had 3 receptions for 189 yards, breaking the average of 60.7 yards (3 catches, 182 yards) set by Bill Groman in 1960 and matched by Homer Jones in 1965. Chris Chandler was 21 of 35 for 255 yards and 1 touchdown, with 2 interceptions.

St. Louis	3	14	10	14	—	41
Atlanta	7	6	0	7	—	20

Atl — Anderson 3 run (Andersen kick)
StL — FG Wilkins 30
StL — Bruce 14 pass from Warner (Wilkins kick)
Atl — FG Andersen 37
StL — Holt 80 pass from Warner (Wilkins kick)
Atl — FG Andersen 45
StL — Lyle 94 fumble return (Wilkins kick)
StL — FG Wilkins 30
StL — Holt 85 pass from Warner (Wilkins kick)
Atl — Kelly 37 pass from Chandler (Andersen kick)
StL — Bruce 66 pass from Warner (Wilkins kick)

SAN FRANCISCO 41, DALLAS 24—at Texas Stadium, attendance 64,127. Charlie Garner rushed for a club-record 201 yards, and Jeff Garcia passed for 4 touchdowns as the 49ers won their first game. With the score tied 3-3, Garner's 1-yard touchdown run midway through the second quarter capped an 83-yard drive. Julian Peterson intercepted Troy Aikman's pass on the next possession, setting up Garcia's 3-yard touchdown pass to Terrell Owens. Aikman's 34-yard pass to Raghib Ismail set up Emmitt Smith's 1-yard touchdown run to trim the deficit to 17-10 just before halftime, but Garcia completed a 68-yard touchdown pass to Jerry Rice three plays into the second half. Jeff Posey recovered Aikman's fumble moments later to set up Wade Richey's 47-yard field goal and give the 49ers a 27-10 lead. The 49ers followed with long scoring drives of 17 plays, 98 yards and 15 plays, 77 yards to take a 41-17 lead with 4:05 remaining. Garcia was 16 of 26 for 178 yards and 4 touchdowns. Aikman was 15 of 26 for 197 yards and 1 touchdown, with 1 interception. James McKnight had 6 receptions for 129 yards.

San Francisco	3	14	10	14	—	41
Dallas	0	10	0	14	—	24

SF — FG Richey 38
Dall — FG Seder 41
SF — Garner 1 run (Richey kick)
SF — Owens 3 pass from Garcia (Richey kick)
Dall — Smith 1 run (Seder kick)
SF — Rice 68 pass from Garcia (Richey kick)
SF — FG Richey 47
SF — Rice 5 pass from Garcia (Richey kick)
Dall — Harris 11 pass from Aikman (Seder kick)
SF — Owens 1 pass from Garcia (Richey kick)
Dall — Harris 16 pass from Stoerner (Seder kick)

SEATTLE 20, SAN DIEGO 12—at Qualcomm Stadium, attendance 47,233. The Seahawks used big plays by Darrell Jackson and Willie Williams to defeat the Chargers. With the score tied 3-3 in the first quarter, Reggie Rusk recovered Charlie Rogers's fumbled kickoff to set up John Carney's second field goal. The Seahawks countered two plays later with Jon Kitna's 68-yard touchdown pass to Jackson. Rogers muffed a punt in the second quarter to set up Carney's third field goal. Kris Heppner's 26-yard field goal capped a 65-yard drive with 36 seconds left in the half, but Kenny Bynum returned the ensuing kickoff 39 yards and Carney booted a 45-yard field goal as the half expired to trim the deficit to 13-12. Midway through the third quarter, Williams intercepted Ryan Leaf's pass and returned it 69 yards for a touchdown. Heppner missed a fourth-quarter field goal, and Jim Harbaugh, who replaced an injured Leaf, drove the Chargers to the Seahawks' 16, but his fourth-and-3 pass fell incomplete. Kitna was 11 of 21 for 196 yards and 1 touchdown. Leaf was 16 of 26 for 153 yards, with 1 interception, while Harbaugh was 8 of 14 for 67 yards, with 1 interception.

Seattle	10	3	7	0	—	20
San Diego	6	6	0	0	—	12

Sea — FG Heppner 25
SD — FG Carney 41
SD — FG Carney 28
Sea — Jackson 68 pass from Kitna (Heppner kick)
SD — FG Carney 24
Sea — FG Heppner 26
SD — FG Carney 45
Sea — Williams 69 interception return (Heppner kick)

TENNESSEE 23, PITTSBURGH 20—at Three Rivers Stadium, attendance 51,769. An injured Steve McNair came off the bench to complete an 18-yard touchdown pass to Erron Kinney with 1:25 remaining to lift the Titans past the Steelers. The Titans scored on their first two possessions, highlighted by Neil O'Donnell's 67-yard pass to Carl Pickens to set up Eddie George's 20-yard scoring run, to take a 10-3 lead. Chad Scott's 33-yard interception return led to Kris Brown's 32-yard field goal to trim the deficit to 10-6. The Steelers had an opportunity to score just before halftime, but Dainon Sidney recovered Bobby Shaw's fumble at the Titans' 8 to preserve the four-point margin. Trailing 13-6, Kordell Stewart, in the game for goal-line situations, scored on a 1-yard run on the first play of the fourth quarter to tie the game. Following Al Del Greco's 40-yard field goal, Kent Graham completed a 36-yard pass to Cory Geason to set up Jerome Bettis's 5-yard scoring run and give Pittsburgh a 20-16 lead with 7:50 remaining. The Titans got the ball back at their own 37 with 3:11 to play. O'Donnell was forced to leave the game after a hard tackle by Jason Gildon, and McNair, nursing a bruised sternum, entered the game with the Titans facing third-and-11 with 2:35 remaining. McNair promptly completed a 22-yard pass to Chris Sanders, scrambled for 9 yards, and completed a 15-yard pass to Derrick Mason before finding Kinney open in the right corner of the end zone. The Steelers had a chance to tie, but Brown missed a 50-yard field-goal attempt as time expired. O'Donell was 13 of 27 for 237 yards, with 3 interceptions, while McNair was 3 of 3 for 55 yards and 1 touchdown. Graham was 18 of 33 for 254 yards.

Tennessee	10	0	3	10	—	23
Pittsburgh	3	3	0	14	—	20

Tenn — George 20 run (Del Greco kick)
Pitt — FG Brown 32
Tenn — FG Del Greco 24
Pitt — FG Brown 32
Tenn — FG Del Greco 40
Pitt — Stewart 1 run (Brown kick)
Tenn — FG Del Greco 40
Pitt — Bettis 5 run (Brown kick)
Tenn — Kinney 18 pass from McNair (Del Greco kick)

SUNDAY NIGHT, SEPTEMBER 24

WASHINGTON 16, N.Y. GIANTS 6—at Giants Stadium, attendance 78,216. Brad Johnson passed for 2 touchdowns, and the Redskins' defense kept the Giants out of the end zone until the final minutes as Washington handed the Giants their first defeat. Johnson's 46-yard pass to James Thrash set up his 23-yard touchdown pass to Irving Fryar early in the second quarter to give the Redskins a 7-0 lead. On their next possession, Johnson completed a 48-yard pass to Albert Connell to set up Michael Husted's 25-yard field goal. Johnson and Connell hooked up again three plays into the third quarter, this time for 53 yards, and that play was followed by Andre Reed's 21-yard touchdown catch for a 16-0 lead. Deion Sanders's end zone interception of Kerry Collins's pass early in the fourth quarter quelled the Giants' first scoring opportunity. Collins did engineer a 13-play, 86-yard drive capped by Ike Hilliard's 7-yard touchdown catch with 2:25 left, but LaVar Arrington recovered the ensuing onside kick and the Redskins ran out the clock. Johnson was 14 of 20 for 289 yards and 2 touchdowns. Connell had 4 receptions for 122 yards. Collins was 21 of 44 for 210 yards and 1 touchdown, with 1 interception.

Washington	0	10	6	0	—	16
N.Y. Giants	0	0	0	6	—	6

Wash — Fryar 23 pass from Johnson (Husted kick)
Wash — FG Husted 25
Wash — Reed 21 pass from Johnson (kick failed)
NYG — Hilliard 7 pass from Collins (run failed)

MONDAY NIGHT, SEPTEMBER 25

INDIANAPOLIS 43, JACKSONVILLE 14—at RCA Dome, attendance 56,816. Peyton Manning passed for a club-record 440 yards and a career-high 4 touchdowns as the Colts defeated the Jaguars. Manning's 76-yard touchdown pass to Marvin Harrison culminated the Colts' first possession. With the score tied 7-7 in the second quarter, Mike Peterson intercepted Mark Brunell's pass at the Jaguars' 26 to set up Manning's 27-yard touchdown pass to Terrence Wilkins. The Colts' defense then forced a punt, and Manning connected with Jerome Pathon for a 16-yard touchdown and a 21-7 lead. Jimmy Smith's 26-yard touchdown reception 11 seconds before halftime trimmed the deficit to 21-14, but the Colts' defense limited the Jaguars to just 54 second-half yards and Chad Bratzke sacked Brunell in the end zone for a safety. Edgerrin James's 14-yard touchdown run with 5:55 left capped a 17-point fourth quarter. Manning was 23 of 36 for 440 yards and 4 touchdowns. Wilkins had 9 receptions for 148 yards and Harrison had 2 for 103 yards. Brunell was 21 of 36 for 229 yards and 2 touchdowns, with 2 interceptions.

Jacksonville	0	14	0	0	—	14
Indianapolis	7	14	5	17	—	43

Ind — Harrison 76 pass from Manning (Vanderjagt kick)
Jax — Smith 9 pass from Brunell (Lindsey kick)
Ind — Wilkins 27 pass from Manning (Vanderjagt kick)
Ind — Pathon 16 pass from Manning (Vanderjagt kick)
Jax — Smith 26 pass from Brunell (Lindsey kick)
Ind — FG Vanderjagt 41
Ind — Safety, Brunell sacked by Bratzke in end zone
Ind — FG Vanderjagt 22
Ind — Dilger 4 pass from Manning (Vanderjagt kick)
Ind — James 14 run (Vanderjagt kick)

FIFTH WEEK SUMMARIES

AMERICAN FOOTBALL CONFERENCE

Eastern Division	W	L	T	Pct.	Pts.	OP
N.Y. Jets	4	0	0	1.000	88	66
Miami	4	1	0	.800	90	38
Indianapolis	3	1	0	.750	119	82
Buffalo	2	2	0	.500	73	76

	W	L	T	Pct.	Pts.	OP
New England	1	4	0	.200	79	91
Central Division						
Baltimore	4	1	0	.800	110	55
Tennessee	3	1	0	.750	81	64
Cleveland	2	3	0	.400	64	102
Jacksonville	2	3	0	.400	103	113
Pittsburgh	1	3	0	.200	64	75
Cincinnati	0	4	0	.000	23	105
Western Division						
Oakland	3	1	0	.750	107	80
Kansas City	3	2	0	.600	117	93
Denver	2	3	0	.400	152	130
Seattle	2	3	0	.400	91	106
San Diego	0	5	0	.000	86	156
NATIONAL FOOTBALL CONFERENCE						
Eastern Division	**W**	**L**	**T**	**Pct.**	**Pts.**	**OP**
N.Y. Giants	3	2	0	.600	88	85
Philadelphia	3	2	0	.600	121	70
Washington	3	2	0	.600	87	82
Dallas	2	3	0	.400	112	148
Arizona	1	3	0	.250	71	108
Central Division						
Minnesota	4	0	0	1.000	95	71
Detroit	3	2	0	.600	84	96
Tampa Bay	3	2	0	.600	127	67
Green Bay	2	3	0	.400	93	80
Chicago	1	4	0	.200	75	130
Western Division						
St. Louis	5	0	0	1.000	217	145
Atlanta	2	3	0	.400	95	159
San Francisco	2	3	0	.400	142	159
Carolina	1	3	0	.250	78	73
New Orleans	1	3	0	.250	55	82

SUNDAY, OCTOBER 1

SAN FRANCISCO 27, ARIZONA 20—at 3Com Park, attendance 66,985. Charlie Garner rushed for 2 touchdowns as the 49ers won their second consecutive game. The teams scored twice in the first 28 minutes before scoring three times in the half's final two minutes. Wade Richey's 33-yard field goal gave the 49ers a 10-3 lead, and Jonas Lewis recovered MarTay Jenkins's fumble on the ensuing kickoff to set up Garner's 1-yard touchdown run with 49 seconds left in the half. However, Jake Plummer fired a 56-yard touchdown pass to David Boston three plays later to trim the deficit to 17-10 at halftime. The 49ers rushed eight times on an 11-play, 63-yard drive in the third quarter to extend their lead to 24-10. Winfred Tubbs recovered Thomas Jones's fumble late in the third quarter to set up Richey's 29-yard field goal for a 27-10 lead. The Cardinals scored on consecutive fourth-quarter possessions, capped by Jones's 4-yard touchdown run with 2:15 remaining, but the Cardinals' got the ball at their own 9 with 16 seconds left and were unable to drive. Garcia was 22 of 33 for 220 yards and 1 touchdown. Plummer was 24 of 41 for 239 yards and 1 touchdown.

Arizona	0	10	0	10	—	20
San Francisco	7	10	7	3	—	27

SF — Rice 5 pass from Garcia (Richey kick)
Ariz — FG Blanchard 32
SF — FG Richey 33
SF — Garner 1 run (Richey kick)
Ariz — Boston 56 pass from Plummer (Blanchard kick)
SF — Garner 1 run (Richey kick)
SF — FG Richey 29
Ariz — FG Blanchard 27
Ariz — Jones 4 run (Blanchard kick)

BALTIMORE 12, CLEVELAND 0—at Cleveland Browns Stadium, attendance 73,018. Matt Stover kicked 4 field goals, and the Ravens' defense recorded its second consecutive shutout en route to victory. The Ravens capitalized on drives of 23 and 50 yards, following punts, for Stover's first two field goals. Duane Starks's interception at the Browns' 32 early in the second quarter led to Stover's 44-yard field goal and a 9-0 lead with 8:12 left in the first half. Late in the half, Tim Couch completed a 38-yard pass to David Patten to the Ravens' 8, but Marc Edwards fumbled two plays later and Rod Woodson recovered in the end zone for a touchback. A 19-play, 76-yard drive that consumed 10:04 to begin the second half was capped by Stover's fourth field goal. The Browns had two more scoring opportunities, but Ray Lewis's interception at the Browns' 15 stopped one drive and Travis Prentice was tackled at the Ravens' 4 on fourth-and-goal with 8:14 remaining. The Ravens then ran out the rest of the clock. Tony Banks was 18 of 34 for 169 yards, with 1 interception. Couch was 20 of 35 for 203 yards, with 3 interceptions. Patten had 7 receptions for 113 yards.

Baltimore	3	6	3	0	—	12
Cleveland	0	0	0	0	—	0

Balt — FG Stover 45
Balt — FG Stover 30
Balt — FG Stover 44
Balt — FG Stover 22

CHICAGO 27, GREEN BAY 24—at Lambeau Field, attendance 59,869. Cade McNown passed for 2 touchdowns and ran for another as the Bears won their first game of the season. Tony Parrish intercepted Brett Favre's pass on the game's first play from scrimmage to set up McNown's 1-yard touchdown run. Eddie Kennison's 52-yard reverse later in the first quarter led to Paul Edinger's 19-yard field goal, and McNown's 68-yard scoring bomb to Marcus Robinson midway through the second quarter staked Chicago to a 17-0 lead. Leading 17-3 but pinned on their own 1 following a Josh Bidwell punt, McNown's 17-yard run to the Bears' 18 sparked a 99-yard drive capped by Robinson's 58-yard touchdown catch to extend Chicago's lead to 24-3. The Packers responded with touchdown drives of 71 and 87 yards, both culminated by Favre touchdown passes, to trim the deficit to 24-17 with 8:44 left. James Allen's 21-yard run set up Edinger's 47-yard field goal with 3:15 remaining, but Favre's 17-yard touchdown pass to Bill Schroeder capped a 6-play drive with 1:58 remaining. The Packers drove to the Bears' 44 with 16 seconds left, but Favre's third- and fourth-down passes fell incomplete. McNown was 11 of 20 for 203 yards and 2 touchdowns. Robinson had 3 receptions for 133 yards. Favre was 31 of 48 for 333 yards and 3 touchdowns, with 1 interception. Schroeder had 8 receptions for 108 yards.

Chicago	10	7	7	3	—	27
Green Bay	0	3	7	14	—	24

Chi — McNown 1 run (Edinger kick)
Chi — FG Edinger 19
Chi — Robinson 68 pass from McNown (Edinger kick)
GB — FG Longwell 42
Chi — Robinson 58 pass from McNown (Edinger kick)
GB — Freeman 14 pass from Favre (Longwell kick)
GB — Schroeder 17 pass from Favre (Longwell kick)
Chi — FG Edinger 47
GB — Schroeder 17 pass from Favre (Longwell kick)

DALLAS 16, CAROLINA 13 (OT)—at Ericsson Stadium, attendance 68,909. Tim Seder's 24-yard field goal capped the first possession of overtime and gave the Cowboys their second consecutive road victory. Carolina led 7-0 when Ken Walter mishandled a punt snap in his end zone and was tackled by Izell Reese for a safety. Emmitt Smith's 8-yard touchdown run, and Troy Aikman's 2-point conversion pass to Jackie Harris, capped the ensuing drive and gave Dallas a 10-0 lead. The Panthers responded with a 10-play drive capped by Richie Cunningham's 39-yard field goal to tie the game at halftime. Seder drilled a 27-yard field goal to culminate a 14-play, 73-yard third-quarter drive, but Cunningham's 23-yard field goal on the ensuing possession tied the game. The Cowboys' defense forced Steve Beuerlein's fourth-and-1 pass from the Cowboys' 30 to fall incomplete with 6:25 remaining. Aikman converted 2 first downs on the ensuing drive, but Seder missed a 45-yard field-goal attempt with 1:07 left in regulation. In overtime, Aikman's 23-yard pass to Chris Warren on third-and-3 to the Panthers' 6 allowed Seder to redeem himself. Aikman was 15 of 23 for 131 yards, with 2 interceptions. Smith rushed 24 times for 132 yards. Beuerlein was 17 of 29 for 161 yards.

Dallas	0	10	3	0	3	—	16
Carolina	0	10	0	3	0	—	13

Car — Biakabutuka 1 run (Cunningham kick)
Dall — Safety, Walter tackled in end zone
Dall — E. Smith 8 run (Harris pass from Aikman)
Car — FG Cunningham 39
Dall — FG Seder 27
Car — FG Cunningham 23
Dall — FG Seder 24

INDIANAPOLIS 18, BUFFALO 16—at Ralph Wilson Stadium, attendance 72,617. Mike Vanderjagt made a 45-yard field goal as time expired as the Colts moved ahead of the Bills in the AFC East standings. Steve Christie field goals capped each of the Bills' first three possessions and gave Buffalo a 9-0 lead midway through the second quarter. However, Peyton Manning engineered a 77-yard drive on the ensuing possession to trim the lead to 9-7, and his 10-yard touchdown pass to Terrence Wilkins two plays into the fourth quarter capped an 80-yard drive and gave the Colts a 15-9 lead. On their own 33 with 1:22 remaining, Rob Johnson completed a 27-yard pass to Jeremy McDaniel and, on the next play, a 40-yard touchdown bomb to Eric Moulds to give the Bills a 16-15 lead. Manning completed 2 passes to Jerome Pathon on the next drive, including an 8-yard pass to the Bills' 27 with six seconds remaining, to set up Vanderjagt's winning kick. Manning was 16 of 27 for 187 yards and 2 touchdowns, with 1 interception. Johnson was 21 of 32 for 246 yards and 1 touchdown.

Indianapolis	0	7	0	11	—	18
Buffalo	3	6	0	7	—	16

Buff — FG Christie 19
Buff — FG Christie 30
Buff — FG Christie 27
Ind — Harrison 14 pass from Manning (Vanderjagt kick)
Ind — Wilkins 10 pass from Manning (James run)
Buff — Moulds 40 pass from R. Johnson (Christie kick)
Ind — FG Vanderjagt 45

MIAMI 31, CINCINNATI 16—at Paul Brown Stadium, attendance 61,535. Jason Taylor's 29-yard fumble return as the first half expired highlighted a 31-0 Dolphins' run to spoil Dick LeBeau's first game as the Bengals' coach. The Bengals, who had scored 7 points in their first three games, scored on their first three possessions, the last of which was set up by John Copeland's recovery of Lamar Smith's fumble at the Dolphins' 28, to take a 13-0 lead. Takeo Spikes thwarted the Dolphins' next drive with an interception in the end zone, but Olindo Mare kicked a 40-yard field goal with 1:01 left in the half. Faced with second-and-5 from their own 37 with 17 seconds left in the half, Akili Smith dropped back to pass. Taylor hit Smith from his blindside, forced him to fumble, and raced 29 yards into the end zone as time expired to cut the deficit to 13-10 and change the game's momentum. The Dolphins drove 70, 54, and 73 yards for touchdowns with their first three possessions of the second half to take a 31-10 lead with 12:26 left. Fiedler was 14 of 21 for 155 yards and 2 touchdowns, with 1 interception. Smith was 20 of 38 for 178 yards and 1 touchdown. Dillon rushed 22 times for 110 yards.

Miami	0	10	14	7	—	31
Cincinnati	10	3	0	3	—	16

Cin — Warrick 9 pass from Smith (Rackers kick)
Cin — FG Rackers 23
Cin — FG Rackers 38
Mia — FG Mare 40
Mia — Taylor 29 fumble return (Mare kick)
Mia — Smith 18 run (Mare kick)
Mia — Gadsden 7 pass from Fiedler (Mare kick)
Mia — Gadsden 21 pass from Fiedler (Mare kick)
Cin — FG Rackers 34

MINNESOTA 31, DETROIT 24—at Pontiac Silverdome, attendance 76,438. Randy Moss had 7 receptions for 168 yards, including 3 touchdowns, as the Vikings remained one of three undefeated teams. The Lions scored on their first possession, but the Vikings countered with Daunte Culpepper's 61-yard touchdown bomb to Moss. Tied late in the third quarter, Culpepper fired a 17-yard touchdown pass to Moss to complete a 65-yard drive and give the Vikings a 17-10 lead. The Lions responded with a 69-yard drive, capped by Charlie Batch's 5-yard run, but the Vikings needed just five plays to retake the lead on Moss's third touchdown catch, a 50-yard bomb, with 8:48 left. The Lions drove to the Vikings' 35, but Batch's fourth-and-8 pass for Germane Crowell fell incomplete, and on the next play Robert Smith raced 65 yards for a touchdown to put the Vikings ahead 31-17. Culpepper was 17 of 29 for 269 yards and 3 touchdowns. Smith had 16 carries for 134 yards. Batch was 25 of 44 for 239 yards and 1 touchdown, with 1 interception.

Minnesota	7	3	7	14	—	31
Detroit	7	3	0	14	—	24

Det — Crowell 9 pass from Batch (Hanson kick)
Minn — Moss 61 pass from Culpepper (Anderson kick)
Det — FG Hanson 21
Minn — FG Anderson 20
Minn — Moss 17 pass from Culpepper (Anderson kick)
Det — Batch 5 run (Hanson kick)
Minn — Moss 50 pass from Culpepper (Anderson kick)
Minn — R. Smith 65 run (Anderson kick)
Det — Bates 1 run (Hanson kick)

NEW ENGLAND 28, DENVER 19—at Mile High Stadium, attendance 72,006. Drew Bledsoe passed for 271 yards and 4 touchdowns to give Bill Belichick his first victory as coach of the Patriots. Willie McGinest sacked Brian Griese, forced him to fumble, and recovered the fumble at the Broncos' 29 four plays into the game to set up Bledsoe's first touchdown pass to Troy Brown. The Patriots' defense then forced a punt, and Bledsoe hit Brown with a 44-yard touchdown pass three plays later to stake the Patriots to a 14-0 lead seven minutes into the game. Bledsoe ran the two-minute drill to perfection, driving the Patriots 80 yards, capped by his 12-yard touchdown pass to J.R. Redmond with 25 seconds left in the half, to take a 21-3 lead. Pinned at their own 1-yard line, punter Lee Johnson intentionally took a safety, but Deltha O'Neal returned the ensuing free kick 87 yards for a touchdown. However, the Patriots responded with a 7-play, 77-yard drive, capped by Bledsoe's 9-yard touchdown pass to Terry Glenn, to take a 28-11 lead. Griese's 43-yard touchdown pass to Travis McGriff with 1:56 remaining gave the Broncos a chance, but Eric Bjornson recovered the onside kick to clinch the victory. Bledsoe was 18 of 26 for 271 yards and 4 touchdowns, with 1 interception. Brown had 6 receptions for 124 yards. Griese was 28 of 47 for 305 yards and 1 touchdown, with 1 interception. Rod Smith had 12 receptions for 153 yards.

New England	14	7	7	0	—	28
Denver	0	3	8	8	—	19

NE — Brown 11 pass from Bledsoe (Vinatieri kick)
NE — Brown 44 pass from Bledsoe (Vinatieri kick)
Den — FG Nedney 20
NE — Redmond 12 pass from Bledsoe (Vinatieri kick)
Den — Safety, Johnson stepped out of end zone
Den — O'Neal 87 kickoff return (run failed)
NE — Glenn 9 pass from Bledsoe (Vinatieri kick)
Den — McGriff 43 pass from Griese (McCaffrey pass from Griese)

TENNESSEE 28, N.Y. GIANTS 14—at Adelphia Coliseum, attendance 68,341. Steve McNair passed for 3 touchdowns as the Titans established an NFL record with their tenth consecutive victory in their new home stadium. The Titans had touchdown drives of 80, 98, and 80 yards in the first half. The 98-yard drive consisted of 19 plays and included 6 third-down conversions en route to a 21-0 lead. Kerry Collins's 14-yard touchdown pass to Ike Hilliard midway through the third quarter cut the deficit to 21-7, but McNair responded by engineering a 14-play, 80-yard drive, capped by his 3-yard touchdown pass to Frank Wycheck with 12:26 remaining. Collins's 1-yard touchdown pass to Dan Campbell trimmed the lead to 28-14 with 7:04 remaining, but interceptions by Denard Walker and Samari Rolle in the final five minutes preserved the victory. McNair was 24 of 35 for 294 yards and 3 touchdowns. Collins was 17 of 36 for 197 yards and 2 touchdowns, with 3 interceptions.

N.Y. Giants	0	0	7	7	—	14
Tennessee	7	14	0	7	—	28

Tenn — Wycheck 14 pass from McNair (Del Greco kick)
Tenn — George 7 run (Del Greco kick)
Tenn — Mason 29 pass from McNair (Del Greco kick)
NYG — Hilliard 14 pass from Collins (Holmes kick)
Tenn — Wycheck 3 pass from McNair (Del Greco kick)
NYG — Campbell 1 pass from Collins (Holmes kick)

PITTSBURGH 24, JACKSONVILLE 13—at ALLTEL Stadium, attendance 64,351. Jerome Bettis rushed for 97 yards and 2 touchdowns, and the Steelers' defense limited the Jaguars to 26 rushing yards and 206 total yards. A blocked punt gave the Jaguars the ball at the Steelers' 4 early in the game, but the Steelers' defense forced Jacksonville to settle for Steve Lindsey's 19-yard field goal. Kordell Stewart, playing for the injured Kent Graham, engineered consecutive 10-play scoring drives to give the Steelers a 10-3 lead, and Lee Flowers's interception at the Jaguars' 24 set up Bettis's 1-yard touchdown run to give the Steelers a 17-3 lead. Bettis's 3-yard scoring run capped a 7-play, 60-yard drive in the third quarter to give Pittsburgh a 24-6 lead. The Jaguars responded by driving inside the Steelers' 15 on their next two possessions, but were stopped on fourth down both times. Reserve Jamie Martin capped a 90-yard drive with an 11-yard touchdown pass to Keenan McCardell with nine seconds left. Stewart was 10 of 16 for 132 yards, with 1 interception. Brunell was 15 of 32 for 137 yards, with 1 interception.

Pittsburgh	7	10	7	0	—	24
Jacksonville	3	3	0	7	—	13

Jax — FG Lindsey 19
Pitt — Fuamatu-Ma'afala 5 run (Brown kick)
Pitt — FG Brown 19
Pitt — Bettis 1 run (Brown kick)
Jax — FG Lindsey 48
Pitt — Bettis 3 run (Brown kick)
Jax — McCardell 11 pass from Martin (Lindsey kick)

ST. LOUIS 57, SAN DIEGO 31—at Trans World Dome, attendance 66,010. Kurt Warner passed for 4 touchdowns as the Rams scored on their first 11 possessions to remain undefeated. The Rams' first 14 plays were passing plays as they built a 17-3 lead. The first half consisted of drives of 42, 71, 29, 71, 83, and 48 yards, none taking more than eight plays, and the Rams led 30-10 halftime. Jim Harbaugh's 3-yard touchdown pass to Fred McCrary on the opening drive of the second half trimmed the deficit to 30-17, but the Rams needed just 10 plays to score 17 points in the next eight minutes. Trent Green's 48-yard touchdown pass to Marshall Faulk gave St. Louis a 47-17 lead with 4:00 left in the third quarter. Justin Watson's 49-yard run in the fourth quarter set up his 12-yard touchdown run with 3:11 remaining to give the Rams a 57-24 lead. Green knelt down three times in the final minute to mark the Rams' lone non-scoring possession of the game. The Rams tallied 29 first downs and 614 total yards. Jeff Wilkins finished with 5 field goals, 4 of which were within 33 yards. Warner was 24 of 30 for 390 yards and 4 touchdowns. Isaac Bruce had 9 receptions for 167 yards and 2 touchdowns, while Faulk had 6 catches for 116 yards and Az-Zahir Hakim had 5 receptions for 104 yards. Watson rushed 14 times for 102 yards. Harbaugh was 27 of 40 for 348 yards and 2 touchdowns, with 1 interception. Jeff Graham had 7 receptions for 107 yards.

San Diego	3	7	7	14	—	31
St. Louis	17	13	17	10	—	57

StL — FG Wilkins 51
StL — Bruce 9 pass from Warner (Wilkins kick)
StL — Faulk 13 pass from Warner (Wilkins kick)
SD — FG Carney 37
StL — FG Wilkins 21
SD — Fazande 2 run (Carney kick)
StL — Holt 7 pass from Warner (Wilkins kick)
StL — FG Wilkins 31
SD — McCrary 3 pass from Harbaugh (Carney kick)
StL — Bruce 12 pass from Warner (Wilkins kick)
StL — FG Wilkins 33
StL — Faulk 48 pass from Green (Wilkins kick)
StL — FG Wilkins 20
SD — Fletcher 6 run (Carney kick)
StL — Watson 12 run (Wilkins kick)
SD — Gaylor 62 pass from Harbaugh (Carney kick)

WASHINGTON 20, TAMPA BAY 17 (OT)—at FedEx Field, attendance 83,532. Deion Sanders's 57-yard punt return in overtime set up Michael Husted's game-winning field goal as the Redskins won their second consecutive game. Damien Robinson's recovery of Brad Johnson's first-quarter fumble at the Redskins' 25 led to Mike Alstott's 2-yard touchdown run. The Redskins had trouble moving the ball until Stephen Davis broke free for a 50-yard touchdown run late in the second quarter. The Redskins' 58-yard drive to open the second half netted a Husted field goal to give Washington a 10-7 lead. Martin Gramatica missed a 40-yard field-goal attempt early in the fourth quarter, and Sam Shade recovered Keyshawn Johnson's fumble at the Buccaneers' 26 midway through the fourth quarter to set up Johnson's 8-yard touchdown pass to Larry Centers and give Washington a 17-7 lead with 3:57 remaining. Shaun King's 46-yard touchdown pass to Reidel Anthony with 2:00 left trimmed the lead to 17-14. Irving Fryar recovered the ensuing onside kick, but Husted missed a 35-yard field-goal attempt with 43 seconds left. King completed a 19-yard pass to Johnson to set up Gramatica's game-tying 42-yard field goal at the end of regulation. After each team had a possession in overtime, Sanders fielded Mark Royals's punt at the Redskins' 35, moved to his right, and used a wall of blockers to break free before being tackled by Aaron Stecker at the Buccaneers' 8. After three Davis running plays, Husted redeemed himself with the game-winning field goal 4:09 into overtime. King was 19 of 38 for 202 yards and 1 touchdown, with 1 interception. Johnson was 20 of 32 for 207 yards and 1 touchdown. Davis rushed 28 times for 141 yards.

Tampa Bay	7	0	0	10	0	—	17
Washington	0	7	3	7	3	—	20

TB — Alstott 2 run (Gramatica kick)
Wash — Davis 50 run (Husted kick)
Wash — FG Husted 29
Wash — Centers 8 pass from Johnson (Husted kick)
TB — Anthony 46 pass from King (Gramatica kick)
TB — FG Gramatica 42
Wash — FG Husted 20

SUNDAY NIGHT, OCTOBER 1

PHILADELPHIA 38, ATLANTA 10—at Veterans Stadium, attendance 65,424. Brian Mitchell tied an NFL record with his eleventh career kick return touchdown, and added an 85-yard touchdown run, as the Eagles defeated the Falcons. Leading 6-0 in the third quarter, Donovan McNabb completed a 70-yard touchdown pass to Torrance Small. The Falcons got on the scoreboard with Tim Dwight's 70-yard punt return for a touchdown, but Dameane Douglas returned the ensuing kickoff 41 yards to set up David Akers's third field goal and a 17-7 lead. Following a Falcons' punt, McNabb capped an 85-yard drive with an 11-yard touchdown pass to Charles Johnson with 8:39 remaining. Morten Andersen's 48-yard field goal trimmed the deficit to 24-10, but Mitchell returned the ensuing kickoff 89 yards for a touchdown. After the Eagles' defense forced Chris Chandler's fourth-and-7 pass to fall incomplete, Mitchell rushed 85 yards for a touchdown on the next play to give the Eagles a 38-10 lead with 1:52 remaining. McNabb completed 30 of 44 passes for a career-high 311 yards and 2 touchdowns, with 2 interceptions. Chandler was 14 of 34 for 151 yards, with 1 interception.

Atlanta	0	0	7	3	—	10
Philadelphia	3	3	11	21	—	38

Phil — FG Akers 39
Phil — FG Akers 38
Phil — Small 70 pass from McNabb (Small pass from McNabb)
Atl — Dwight 70 punt return (Andersen kick)
Phil — FG Akers 19
Phil — C. Johnson 11 pass from McNabb (Akers kick)
Atl — FG Andersen 48
Phil — Mitchell 89 kickoff return (Akers kick)
Phil — Mitchell 85 run (Akers kick)

MONDAY NIGHT, OCTOBER 2

KANSAS CITY 24, SEATTLE 17—at Arrowhead Stadium, attendance 78,502. Mike Cloud's 15-yard touchdown run with 4:26 remaining allowed the Chiefs to overcome a 10-point second-half deficit to defeat the Seahawks. The Seahawks strung together drives of 72 and 75 yards en route to a 14-7 halftime lead. In the third quarter, Jon Kitna completed a 23-yard pass to Darrell Jackson on third-and-9, and Ricky Watters had a 32-yard run moments later, to key a 63-yard drive capped by Rian Lindell's 27-yard field goal and increase Seattle's lead to 17-7. An exchange of punts pinned the Chiefs back on their own 5-yard line with 3:27 left in the third quarter, but Elvis Grbac responded with a 73-yard pass to Derrick Alexander. Two plays later, the pair teamed for a 17-yard touchdown to trim the lead to 17-14. The Chiefs' defense then forced a punt, and Pete Stoyanovich tied the game with a 27-yard field goal with 11:42 to play. Dante Hall's 22-yard punt return and Grbac's 20-yard pass to Alexander set up Cloud's winning touchdown run. Jerome Woods intercepted Kitna's Hail Mary pass at the Chiefs' 11 in the waning seconds to preserve the comeback. Kitna was 17 of 28 for 140 yards and 1 touchdown, with 1 interception. Grbac was 16 of 27 for 256 yards and 2 touchdowns. Alexander had 5 receptions for 153 yards.

Seattle	7	7	3	0	—	17
Kansas City	0	7	7	10	—	24

Sea — Mili 1 pass from Kitna (Lindell kick)
KC — Gonzalez 15 pass from Grbac (Stoyanovich kick)
Sea — Alexander 7 run (Lindell kick)
Sea — FG Lindell 27
KC — Alexander 17 pass from Grbac (Stoyanovich kick)
KC — FG Stoyanovich 27
KC — Cloud 15 run (Stoyanovich kick)

SIXTH WEEK SUMMARIES

AMERICAN FOOTBALL CONFERENCE

Eastern Division	W	L	T	Pct.	Pts.	OP
Miami	5	1	0	.833	112	51
N.Y. Jets	4	1	0	.800	91	86
Indianapolis	3	2	0	.600	135	106
Buffalo	2	3	0	.400	86	98
New England	2	4	0	.333	103	107
Central Division						
Baltimore	5	1	0	.833	125	65
Tennessee	4	1	0	.800	104	78
Pittsburgh	2	3	0	.400	84	78
Cleveland	2	4	0	.333	85	131
Jacksonville	2	4	0	.333	113	128
Cincinnati	0	5	0	.000	37	128
Western Division						
Oakland	4	1	0	.800	141	108
Kansas City	3	2	0	.600	117	93
Denver	3	3	0	.500	173	137
Seattle	2	4	0	.333	94	132
San Diego	0	6	0	.000	93	177

NATIONAL FOOTBALL CONFERENCE

Eastern Division	W	L	T	Pct.	Pts.	OP
N.Y. Giants	4	2	0	.667	101	91
Washington	4	2	0	.667	104	96
Philadelphia	3	3	0	.500	135	87
Arizona	2	3	0	.400	100	129
Dallas	2	3	0	.400	112	148
Central Division						
Minnesota	5	0	0	1.000	125	94
Detroit	4	2	0	.667	115	120
Tampa Bay	3	3	0	.500	150	97
Green Bay	2	4	0	.333	117	111
Chicago	1	5	0	.167	85	161
Western Division						
St. Louis	5	0	0	1.000	217	145
Carolina	2	3	0	.400	104	76
New Orleans	2	3	0	.400	86	92
Atlanta	2	4	0	.333	101	172
San Francisco	2	4	0	.333	170	193

SUNDAY, OCTOBER 8

MIAMI 22, BUFFALO 13—at Pro Player Stadium, attendance 73,901. Sam Madison's 20-yard fumble return for a touchdown capped a 9-point, 6-sack effort by the Dolphins' defense as Miami won its fourth consecutive game. The Dolphins led 6-3 late in the first half when Jay Fiedler connected with Bert Emanuel on a 35-yard third-down pass to set up his 20-yard scoring pass to Leslie Shepherd. In the third quarter, Matt Turk's 41-yard punt to the Bills' 1 was followed two plays later by Jermaine Haley's tackle of Jonathan Linton in the end zone for a safety and a 15-3 lead. Trailing 15-6 in the fourth quarter, Rob Johnson's 41-yard pass to Peerless Price and a 24-yard pass interference penalty led to Sammy Morris's 3-yard touchdown run that cut the deficit to 15-13 with 8:34 left. The Bills forced a punt, but Morris fumbled on the next play. Madison caught the ball out of the air and scampered 20 yards for the game-deciding points. Both teams finished with 15 first downs and 254 total yards. Fiedler was 14 of 24 for 142 yards and 1 touchdown, with 1 interception. Johnson was 11 of 26 for 178 yards.

Buffalo	3	0	0	10	—	13
Miami	3	10	2	7	—	22

Mia — FG Mare 30
Buff — FG Christie 35
Mia — FG Mare 33
Mia — Shepherd 20 pass from Fiedler (Mare kick)
Mia — Safety, Linton tackled by Haley in end zone
Buff — FG Christie 23
Buff — Morris 3 run (Christie kick)
Mia — Madison 20 fumble return (Mare kick)

ARIZONA 29, CLEVELAND 21—at Sun Devil Stadium, attendance 44,296. Michael Pittman, in his second start of the season, rushed for 107 yards, and Jake Plummer passed for 2 touchdowns as the Cardinals downed the Browns. Rookie Travis Prentice, making his first start for the Browns, scored 2 touchdowns to give Cleveland a 14-0 lead. The Cardinals responded by scoring on their next five possessions, including 2 touchdown passes from Plummer to Frank Sanders, to take a 26-14 lead late in the third quarter. Lenoy Jones recovered Mac Cody's fumbled punt at the Cardinals' 24 early in the fourth quarter to set up Prentice's third scoring run, but Cary Blanchard added his third field goal and Cleveland failed to gain a first down on its final two possessions. Plummer was 17 of 30 for 171 yards and 2 touchdowns. Tim Couch was 16 of 22 for 138 yards.

Cleveland	7	7	0	7	—	21
Arizona	0	16	10	3	—	29

Cle — Prentice 1 run (Dawson kick)
Cle — Prentice 1 run (Dawson kick)
Ariz — Jones 10 run (Blanchard kick)
Ariz — Sanders 53 pass from Plummer (dropped hold)
Ariz — FG Blanchard 36
Ariz — FG Blanchard 47
Ariz — Sanders 5 pass from Plummer (Blanchard kick)
Cle — Prentice 6 run (Dawson kick)
Ariz — FG Blanchard 28

DENVER 21, SAN DIEGO 7—at Qualcomm Stadium, attendance 56,079. Brian Griese passed for 3 touchdowns, including 2 to Ed McCaffrey, as the Broncos outlasted the Chargers. Billy Jenkins's 17-yard interception return to the Chargers' 24 led to Griese's first touchdown pass to McCaffrey just 6:03 into the game. Jim Harbaugh engineered two long drives in the second quarter, the first of which resulted in a missed 35-yard John Carney field goal but the second resulted in a game-tying 26-yard touchdown pass to Freddie Jones to cap an 88-yard drive in the half's final minute. Terrell Buckley's 31-yard interception return in the third quarter was followed four plays later by Griese's second touchdown pass to McCaffrey. The Chargers reached the Broncos' 5 with 6:32 remaining in the game, but Harbaugh's fourth-down pass was intercepted by Buckley. The Chargers punted with 1:48 remaining, hoping to get the ball back for one last shot, but Deltha O'Neal spoiled their efforts with a 64-yard return to the Chargers' 14. Two plays later, Griese found Dwayne Carswell for the game-clinching touchdown. Griese was 27 of 40 for 235 yards and 3 touchdowns. McCaffrey had 10 receptions for 71 yards. Harbaugh was 18 of 43 for 237 yards and 1 touchdown, with 3 interceptions.

Denver	7	0	7	7	—	21
San Diego	0	7	0	0	—	7

Den — McCaffrey 2 pass from Griese (Elam kick)
SD — F. Jones 26 pass from Harbaugh (Carney kick)
Den — McCaffrey 5 pass from Griese (Elam kick)
Den — Carswell 14 pass from Griese (Elam kick)

DETROIT 31, GREEN BAY 24—at Pontiac Silverdome, attendance 77,549. Lamar Campbell's 42-yard interception return for a touchdown was one of 5 turnovers forced by the Lions' defense as Detroit moved into second place in the NFC Central. Luther Elliss recovered Brett Favre's fumble at the Packers' 21 in the opening moments to set up Jason Hanson's 30-yard field goal. The Lions received another break early in the second quarter when Josh Bidwell's 9-yard punt gave Detroit the ball at the Packers' 25. Charlie Batch completed a 13-yard touchdown pass to James Stewart four plays later, and Campbell's interception return late in the half gave Detroit a 24-3 lead. Batch's 30-yard scoring strike to Herman Moore with 4:39 in the third quarter staked Detroit to a 31-9 lead, but Favre completed 2 touchdown passes to trim the deficit to 31-24 with 7:15 remaining. However, Favre was intercepted twice in the final six minutes, with Kurt Schulz's NFL-high sixth interception with 1:51 left dashing the Packers' hopes. Batch was 13 of 26 for 199 yards and 3 touchdowns, with 1 interception. Favre was 27 of 43 for 293 yards and 2 touchdowns, with 3 interceptions.

Green Bay	0	6	11	7	—	24
Detroit	10	14	7	0	—	31

Det — FG Hanson 30
Det — Morton 42 pass from Batch (Hanson kick)
GB — FG Longwell 44
Det — Stewart 13 pass from Batch (Hanson kick)
Det — Campbell 42 interception return (Hanson kick)
GB — FG Longwell 51
GB — FG Longwell 31
Det — Moore 30 pass from Batch (Hanson kick)
GB — Freeman 5 pass from Favre (Driver pass from Favre)
GB — Henderson 7 pass from Favre (Longwell kick)

NEW ENGLAND 24, INDIANAPOLIS 16—at Foxboro Stadium, attendance 60,001. Tony Simmons caught a 44-yard Hail Mary touchdown pass just before halftime, and Drew Bledsoe passed for 2 fourth-quarter touchdowns as the Patriots defeated the Colts for the fifth consecutive time in Foxboro. The Colts scored on consecutive possessions in the second quarter to take a 10-3 lead with 10 seconds left. After Simmons returned the ensuing kickoff 39 yards, Michael Bishop's first NFL pass was a high, floating Hail Mary into the end zone as the half expired. Simmons came down with the ball to tie the game. The Colts engineered a 22-play, 65-yard drive that lasted more than 10 minutes to open the third quarter and retake the lead 13-10. However, Bledsoe engineered an 11-play, 77-yard drive, capped by Eric Bjornson's 2-yard touchdown catch. Ty Law's interception at the Patriots' 39 stalled the Colts' next drive, and Bledsoe's touchdown pass to Terry Glenn eight plays later staked the Patriots to a 24-13 lead with 7:26 left. Peyton Manning was intercepted 2 more times in the fourth quarter, and Mike Vanderjagt's field goal came with just 36 seconds remaining. Bjornson recovered the onside kick to clinch the victory. Bledsoe was 15 of 23 for 142 yards and 2 touchdowns. Manning was 31 of 54 for 334 yards and 1 touchdown, with 3 interceptions. Marvin Harrison had 13 receptions for 159 yards.

Indianapolis	0	10	3	3	—	16
New England	3	7	0	14	—	24

NE — FG Vinatieri 21
Ind — Harrison 17 pass from Manning (Vanderjagt kick)
Ind — FG Vanderjagt 33
NE — Simmons 44 pass from Bishop (Vinatieri kick)
Ind — FG Vanderjagt 33
NE — Bjornson 2 pass from Bledsoe (Vinatieri kick)
NE — Glenn 4 pass from Bledsoe (Vinatieri kick)
Ind — FG Vanderjagt 34

NEW ORLEANS 31, CHICAGO 10—at Soldier Field, attendance 54,477. Jeff Blake passed for 3 touchdowns, and Ricky Williams had his third consecutive 100-yard rushing game as the Saints defeated the Bears. Snow and freezing rain the previous evening caused the tarp to stick to the field, which led to imperfect conditions. Rookie Mike Brown's interception and 35-yard touchdown return less than five minutes into the game gave the Bears a 7-0 lead. Chicago's Paul Edinger missed a 30-yard field-goal attempt late in the first quarter, and the Saints responded by scoring on their next three possessions, highlighted by Blake's 47-yard scoring pass to Joe Horn, to take a 17-7 halftime lead. After Edinger's 38-yard field goal trimmed the deficit to 24-10 with 13:23 remaining, Blake engineered an 11-play, 90-yard drive, capped by Andrew

Glover's 29-yard touchdown catch with 7:51 remaining to extend the lead to 31-10. The Saints' top-ranked defense limited the Bears to 245 yards, 83 of which came on the final drive. La'Roi Glover posted 3 sacks. Blake was 18 of 25 for 232 yards and 3 touchdowns, with 1 interception. Williams had 30 carries for 128 yards. Cade McNown was 18 of 37 for 202 yards, with 3 intercpetions.

New Orleans	0	17	7	7	—	31
Chicago	7	0	0	3	—	10

Chi — Brown 35 interception return (Edinger kick)
NO — Horn 4 pass from Blake (Brien kick)
NO — Horn 47 pass from Blake (Brien kick)
NO — FG Brien 44
NO — Williams 2 run (Brien kick)
Chi — FG Edinger 38
NO — Glover 29 pass from Blake (Brien kick)

N.Y. GIANTS 13, ATLANTA 6—at Georgia Dome, attendance 50,947. The Giants' defense recorded 4 sacks and forced 3 turnovers, which led to 10 points, and limited the Falcons to a franchise-low 13 rushing yards as New York kept pace with Washington in the NFC East. Lyle West's recovery of Winslow Oliver's fumbled punt return in the opening moments gave the Giants the ball at the Falcons' 34. Jaret Holmes kicked a 32-yard field goal, but Travis Hall was penalized for using another player as leverage. The Giants took the points off the board, and Ron Dayne scored the game's lone touchdown a few plays later. Jason Sehorn's 32-yard interception return late in the first quarter set up Holmes's 34-yard field goal. The Giants led 13-3 at halftime. Danny Kanell, who had replaced an injured Chris Chandler in the second quarter, completed a 35-yard pass to Shawn Jefferson to set up Morten Andersen's 28-yard field goal to cap the second half's opening drive. However, the Falcons struggled until the final moments, when they drove to the Giants' 10 only to have Kanell's fourth-and-goal desperation heave fall incomplete. Kerry Collins was 14 of 25 for 151 yards, with 2 interceptions. Kanell was 15 of 36 for 166 yards, with 1 interception. Chandler was 8 of 12 for 89 yards, with 1 interception.

N.Y. Giants	10	3	0	0	—	13
Atlanta	0	3	3	0	—	6

NYG — Dayne 2 run (Holmes kick)
NYG — FG Holmes 34
Atl — FG Andersen 42
NYG — FG Holmes 27
Atl — FG Andersen 28

OAKLAND 34, SAN FRANCISCO 28 (OT)—at 3Com Park, attendance 68,344. Rich Gannon's 31-yard touchdown pass to Tim Brown in overtime culminated the first Bay Bridge game since 1979. Trailing 6-0 in the second quarter, the 49ers mounted 76- and 89-yard scoring drives, capped by Jeff Garcia touchdown passes, to give San Francisco a 14-6 halftime lead. The Raiders scored on three consecutive possessions, capped by Rich Gannon's 13-yard touchdown scramble, to give Oakland a 28-14 lead with 14:48 to play. Garcia's 31-yard touchdown pass finished the next drive, cutting the deficit to 28-21, and Pierson Prioleau's 13-yard interception to the Raiders' 13 three plays later set up Garcia's 6-yard touchdown pass to Charlie Garner. Sebastian Janikowski missed a 41-yard field-goal attempt late in regulation and a 35-yard attempt early in overtime, both wide left, as the game remained tied. Following Janikowski's second miss, the 49ers drove to the Raiders' 12 only to have Anthony Dorsett block Wade Richey's 29-yard field-goal attempt. The Raiders needed just five plays to cover 84 yards, with Gannon's pass finding an open Brown at the 49ers' 15 from where he beat everyone to the end zone 10:15 into overtime. Gannon was 21 of 43 for 310 yards and 2 touchdowns, with 1 interception. Brown had 7 receptions for 172 yards. Garcia was 28 of 41 for 336 yards and 4 touchdowns. Terrell Owens had 12 receptions for 176 yards, and Garner rushed 24 times for 109 yards.

Oakland	3	3	15	7	6	—	34
San Francisco	0	14	0	14	0	—	28

Oak — FG Janikowski 23
Oak — FG Janikowski 35
SF — Owens 4 pass from Garcia (Richey kick)
SF — Rice 5 pass from Garcia (Richey kick)
Oak — Wheatley 1 run (Gannon run)
Oak — Brown 30 pass from Gannon (Janikowski kick)
Oak — Gannon 13 run (Janikowski kick)
SF — Owens 31 pass from Garcia (Richey kick)
SF — Garner 6 pass from Garcia (Richey kick)
Oak — Brown 31 pass from Gannon

PITTSBURGH 20, N.Y. JETS 3—at Giants Stadium, attendance 78,441. Jerome Bettis rushed for 107 yards and 1 touchdown as the Steelers stopped the Jets' NFL-high eight-game winning streak. Vinny Testaverde pinched a nerve in the back of his left shoulder when he was hit by Jason Gildon as he attempted his first pass of the game. Testaverde did not play the rest of the day, and the Steelers' defense limited the Jets to just 12 first downs and 206 total yards. Dewayne Washington's 31-yard interception return set up Kris Brown's 43-yard field goal. Bettis's 12-yard second-quarter touchdown run capped a 13-play, 94-yard drive. Kordell Stewart engineered a 13-play, 87-yard drive in the second half, capped by his 10-yard touchdown pass to Bobby Shaw to take a 17-3 lead. Brown's final field goal capped a 13-play drive that began when Kevin Henry recovered Ray Lucas's fumble at the Steelers' 35. Stewart was 17 of 26 for 140 yards and 1 touchdown. Lucas was 13 of 25 for 99 yards, with 2 interceptions.

Pittsburgh	3	7	0	10	—	20
N.Y. Jets	0	3	0	0	—	3

Pitt — FG Brown 43
Pitt — Bettis 12 run (Brown kick)
NYJ — FG Hall 40
Pitt — Shaw 10 pass from Stewart (Brown kick)
Pitt — FG Brown 29

CAROLINA 26, SEATTLE 3—at Ericsson Stadium, attendance 57,090. Steve Beuerlein passed for 2 touchdowns, and the Panthers had more than twice as many first downs (26-10) and total yards (447-209), as Carolina improved to 1-2 at home. Consecutive 70-yard drives culminated with Beuerlein touchdown passes to give the Panthers a quick 14-0 lead. Joe Nedney, in his first game as the Panthers' kicker, added 3 field goals in a 13-minute span to stake Carolina to a 23-0 lead. His fourth field goal midway through the fourth quarter completed the scoring. The Panthers' defense held the Seahawks to an 0-for-11 third-down conversion rate. Beuerlein was 27 of 39 for 332 yards and 2 touchdowns, with 1 interception. Wesley Walls had 7 receptions for 102 yards. Brock Huard, making his first NFL start, was 19 of 34 for 172 yards.

Seattle	0	0	3	0	—	3
Carolina	7	13	3	3	—	26

Car — Hayes 43 pass from Beuerlein (Nedney kick)
Car — Floyd 5 pass from Beuerlein (Nedney kick)
Car — FG Nedney 44
Car — FG Nedney 42
Car — FG Nedney 22
Sea — FG Lindell 42
Car — FG Nedney 29

TENNESSEE 23, CINCINNATI 14—at Paul Brown Stadium, attendance 63,406. Eddie George posted 181 rushing yards and 1 touchdown on a career-high 36 carries as the Titans won their fourth consecutive game. An 80-yard touchdown run by Corey Dillon gave the Bengals a 7-3 second-quarter lead, but the Titans responded with a 14-play, 74-yard drive, which included Steve McNair's 4-yard pass to George on fourth-and-1, and was capped by Derrick Mason's 19-yard scoring catch. Moments later, however, Darryl Williams stepped in front of McNair's short pass and returned it 36 yards for a touchdown to give the Bengals a 14-10 halftime lead. Tennessee did score on its first two possessions of the second half, but the Bengals gained possession with 4:41 left and trailed just 20-14. However, Kenny Holmes sacked Akili Smith and forced him to fumble. John Thornton recovered, and Al Del Greco converted a 34-yard field goal with 2:06 left to clinch the victory. McNair was 19 of 31 for 230 yards and 1 touchdown, with 1 interception. Smith was 10 of 23 for 85 yards. The Titans had the ball for 41 minutes, 22 seconds, and outgained the Bengals 417-213.

Tennessee	3	7	10	3	—	23
Cincinnati	0	14	0	0	—	14

Tenn — FG Del Greco 22
Cin — Dillon 80 run (Rackers kick)
Tenn — Mason 19 pass from McNair (Del Greco kick)
Cin — Williams 36 interception return (Rackers kick)
Tenn — George 5 run (Del Greco kick)
Tenn — FG Del Greco 41
Tenn — FG Del Greco 34

WASHINGTON 17, PHILADELPHIA 14—at Veterans Stadium, attendance 65,491. Michael Husted's 24-yard field goal with two seconds remaining lifted the Redskins past the Eagles. Stephen Davis's 12-yard touchdown run capped the Redskins' opening possession. The Eagles responded with a 6-play, 92-yard drive in the second quarter that concluded with Donovan McNabb's 30-yard touchdown pass to Charles Johnson. McNabb's 22-yard run on third-and-10 set up his 8-yard touchdown pass to Na Brown on the first play of the fourth quarter. The Redskins drove to the Eagles' 25, but Damon Moore intercepted Brad Johnson's pass at the Redskins' 7. However, Moore fumbled during the return, and James Thrash recovered the ball at the Eagles' 15. Skip Hicks scored two plays later to tie the game with 10:15 remaining. After an exchange of punts, the Eagles had the ball at their own 21 with 36 seconds remaining. McNabb rolled right and threw a pass downfield that was intercepted by Darrell Green, who returned it 34 yards to the Eagles' 19. Husted's field goal two plays later sealed the victory. Johnson was 25 of 36 for 289 yards, with 1 interception. McNabb was 17 of 34 for 186 yards and 2 touchdowns, with 2 interceptions.

Washington	7	0	0	10	—	17
Philadelphia	0	7	0	7	—	14

Wash — Davis 12 run (Husted kick)
Phil — C. Johnson 30 pass from McNabb (Akers kick)
Phil — Brown 8 pass from McNabb (Akers kick)
Wash — Hicks 3 run (Husted kick)
Wash — FG Husted 24

SUNDAY NIGHT, OCTOBER 8

BALTIMORE 15, JACKSONVILLE 10—at ALLTEL Stadium, attendance 65,194. Matt Stover kicked 5 field goals, and the Ravens' defense forced 8 fumbles and 6 turnovers as Baltimore won its third consecutive game. Three of Stover's 5 field goals were set up by Jaguars' turnovers, and the Ravens actually lost yards on two of the possessions prior to Stover's field goal. The Jaguars botched 4 center-to-quarterback snap exchanges but trailed just 9-3 in the third quarter when Tony Brackens intercepted Tony Banks's pass at the Ravens' 2. Brackens attempted to score but fumbled, and the Ravens recovered in the end zone. Trailing 15-3, Jamie Martin replaced Mark Brunell in the fourth quarter and engineered a 13-play, 75-yard scoring drive capped by Fred Taylor's 1-yard scoring run with 4:04 left. However, Kim Herring intercepted Martin on the Jaguars' final possession to clinch the victory. The Jaguars' defense limited the Ravens to just 10 first downs and 194 total yards. Banks was 17 of 39 for 154 yards. Brunell was 18 of 28 for 167 yards, with 2 interceptions, and Martin was 11 of 15 for 93 yards, with 1 interception.

Baltimore	3	3	3	6	—	15
Jacksonville	3	0	0	7	—	10

Jax — FG Lindsey 49
Balt — FG Stover 47
Balt — FG Stover 32
Balt — FG Stover 43
Balt — FG Stover 21
Balt — FG Stover 24
Jax — Taylor 1 run (Lindsey kick)

MONDAY NIGHT, OCTOBER 9

MINNESOTA 30, TAMPA BAY 23—at Metrodome, attendance 64,162. Daunte Culpepper passed for 2 touchdowns and rushed for another as the Vikings improved to 5-0. Culpepper's 27-yard touchdown scramble just 24 seconds into the game followed Orlando Thomas's fumble recovery and gave the Vikings a quick 7-0 lead. John Lynch recovered a Culpepper fumble at the Buccaneers' 26 later in the quarter, and Shaun King capped the ensuing drive with a game-tying 11-yard scoring run. Moe Williams's recovery of Aaron Stecker's fumbled punt led to Culpepper's 26-yard touchdown pass to John Davis early in the second quarter. The Vikings led 20-10 in the third quarter when Martin Gramatica ended successive drives with field goals to trim the deficit to 20-16. Gary Anderson attempted to extend the Vikings' lead, but Warren Sapp blocked Anderson's 51-yard attempt and Donnie Abraham raced 53 yards untouched for a go-ahead touchdown with 12:13 remaining. However, the Vikings needed just 6 plays to take the lead back as Randy Moss made a one-handed 42-yard catch to give Minnesota a 27-23 lead. The Buccaneers drove to the Vikings' 47 on the next possession, but Mike Alstott's halfback option pass on fourth-and-1 sailed over the head of wide-open rookie tight end Todd Yoder. Anderson added a 19-yard field goal with 59 seconds remaining, and the Buccaneers reached the Vikings' 36 in the final seconds, but King's Hail Mary pass fell incomplete in the end zone as time expired. Culpepper was 15 of 19 for 231 yards and 2 touchdowns, with 1 interception. Moss had 5 receptions for 118 yards. King was 26 of 40 for 295 yards. Jacquez Green had 11 receptions for 131 yards.

Tampa Bay	7	3	6	7	—	23
Minnesota	7	10	3	10	—	30

Minn — Culpepper 27 run (Anderson kick)
TB — King 11 run (Gramatica kick)
Minn — FG Anderson 37
Minn — Davis 26 pass from Culpepper (Gramatica kick)
TB — FG Gramatica 23
Minn — FG Anderson 42
TB — FG Gramatica 33
TB — FG Gramatica 35
TB — Abraham 53 return of blocked field goal (Gramatica kick)
Minn — Moss 42 pass from Culpepper (Anderson kick)
Minn — FG Anderson 19

SEVENTH WEEK SUMMARIES

AMERICAN FOOTBALL CONFERENCE

Eastern Division	W	L	T	Pct.	Pts.	OP
Miami	5	1	0	.833	112	51
N.Y. Jets	5	1	0	.833	125	103
Indianapolis	4	2	0	.667	172	130
Buffalo	3	3	0	.500	113	122
New England	2	5	0	.286	120	141
Central Division						
Tennessee	5	1	0	.833	131	91
Baltimore	5	2	0	.714	128	75
Pittsburgh	3	3	0	.500	99	78
Cleveland	2	5	0	.286	95	175
Jacksonville	2	5	0	.286	126	155
Cincinnati	0	6	0	.000	37	143
Western Division						
Oakland	5	1	0	.833	161	125
Denver	4	3	0	.571	217	147
Kansas City	3	3	0	.500	134	113
Seattle	2	5	0	.286	118	169
San Diego	0	7	0	.000	117	204

NATIONAL FOOTBALL CONFERENCE

Eastern Division	W	L	T	Pct.	Pts.	OP
N.Y. Giants	5	2	0	.714	120	105
Washington	5	2	0	.714	114	99
Philadelphia	4	3	0	.571	168	101
Arizona	2	4	0	.333	114	162
Dallas	2	4	0	.333	126	167
Central Division						
Minnesota	6	0	0	1.000	153	110
Detroit	4	2	0	.667	115	120
Tampa Bay	3	3	0	.500	150	97
Green Bay	3	4	0	.429	148	139
Chicago	1	6	0	.143	101	189
Western Division						
St. Louis	6	0	0	1.000	262	174
New Orleans	3	3	0	.500	110	98
Carolina	2	4	0	.333	110	100
Atlanta	2	5	0	.286	130	217
San Francisco	2	5	0	.286	198	224

SUNDAY, OCTOBER 15

ST. LOUIS 45, ATLANTA 29—at Trans World Dome, attendance 66,019. Marshall Faulk rushed for a career-high 208 yards, and the Rams set an NFL record with 4 two-point conversions en route to remaining undefeated. Darrick Vaughn returned the game's opening kickoff 96 yards for a touchdown, but Tony Horne responded with a 103-yard kickoff return for a score. It marked the first time in NFL history a game had begun with back-to-back kickoff returns for touchdowns. Jeff Wilkins re-injured his right quadricep muscle on the second kickoff, thus forcing the Rams to implement the two-point conversion following each touchdown and enlist wide reciever Chris Thomas to kickoff. Kurt Warner's 3-yard touchdown pass to Horne capped a 95-yard drive, and holder Keith Lyle completed a pass to London Fletcher for the conversion. Dexter McCleon's interception at the Rams' 3 on the next possession sparked a 12-play, 97-yard drive, capped by Justin Watson's touchdown run. Jamal Anderson's 4-yard scoring run on the ensuing possession tied the game, but the Rams responded with a 10-play, 75-yard drive, capped by Warner's 30-yard touchdown pass to Az-Zahir Hakim with three seconds left in the half, and Faulk's conversion run, to take a 29-21 lead. Another conversion run by Faulk followed Robert Holcombe's touchdown catch in the third quarter, but the Falcons cut the lead to 37-29 with 4:27 remaining on Chris Chandler's 16-yard touchdown pass to Tim Dwight and Anderson's conversion run. The Rams' offense responded with an 8-play, 79-yard drive, culminated by Faulk's 3-yard touchdown run with 1:09 left. Warner's pass to Roland Williams was the Rams' record-breaking fourth two-point conversion of the game, and along with Anderson's conversion, the two teams combined to set a single-game record. Warner was 24 of 40 for 313 yards and 3 touchdowns, with 1 interception. Faulk rushed 25 times for 208 yards and added 3 receptions for 78 yards. Chandler was 18 of 30 for 220 yards and 2 touchdowns, with 1 interception.

Atlanta	14	7	0	8	—	29
St. Louis	7	22	8	8	—	45

Atl — Vaughn 96 kickoff return (Andersen kick)
StL — Horne 103 kickoff return (Wilkins kick)
Atl — Mathis 16 pass from Chandler (Andersen kick)
StL — Horne 3 pass from Warner (Fletcher pass from Lyle)
StL — Watson 2 run (run failed)
Atl — Anderson 4 run (Andersen kick)
StL — Hakim 30 pass from Warner (Faulk run)
StL — Holcombe 12 pass from Warner (Faulk run)
Atl — Dwight 16 pass from Chandler (Anderson run)
StL — Faulk 3 run (Williams pass from Warner)

WASHINGTON 10, BALTIMORE 3—at FedEx Field, attendance 83,252. Stephen Davis's 33-yard touchdown run early in the fourth quarter lifted the Redskins past the Ravens in an intrastate game. In a defensive battle, neither team crossed midfield until the Redskins had an 11-play, 45-yard drive, capped by Kris Heppner's 37-yard field goal midway through the second quarter. The Ravens responded with their best drive of the half, with Matt Stover's 51-yard field goal tying the game. Davis fumbled on the next play, and Chris McAlister recovered at the Redskins' 42. A defensive pass interference penalty gave the Ravens the ball at the Redskins' 1 with 15 seconds left in the half, but Kevin Mitchell intercepted Tony Banks's pass in the end zone for a touchback. Duane Starks intercepted Brad Johnson's pass at the Ravens' 6 to thwart the Redskins' opening drive of the second half, but Davis broke free for a 33-yard touchdown in the opening minute of the fourth quarter. The Redskins converted 3 third-down opportunities in the final five minutes, capped by Davis's 3-yard run on third-and-one, to maintain possession and preserve the victory. Banks was 16 of 27 for 135 yards, with 1 interception. Johnson was 18 of 27 for 158 yards, with 1 interception.

Baltimore	0	3	0	0	—	3
Washington	0	3	0	7	—	10

Wash — FG Heppner 37
Balt — FG Stover 51
Wash — Davis 33 run (Heppner kick)

NEW ORLEANS 24, CAROLINA 6—at Louisiana Superdome, attendance 50,015. Ricky Williams rushed 38 times for 144 yards and 2 touchdowns, and the Saints' defense permitted just 141 yards to move into second place in the NFC West. Jeff Blake lost 2 fumbles deep in Panthers' territory in the first six minutes, and Doug Brien missed a 51-yard field-goal attempt later in the first quarter to keep the game scoreless. Williams had carries of 18 and 8 yards to set up his 2-yard touchdown run early in the second quarter. Kevin Mathis's interception at the Saints' 10 thwarted a Panthers' scoring opportunity, but the Panthers got 2 Joe Nedney field goals, with Brien's 29-yard field goal sandwiched between, to trim the deficit to 10-6 at halftime. Williams had 6 carries and 1 reception on a 10-play, 74-yard drive, capped by Williams's 1-yard touchdown run with 5:16 remaining to take a 17-6 lead. Blake's 29-yard touchdown pass to Joe Horn on third-and-8 with 3:10 left put the game out of reach. Blake was 11 of 23 of 161 yards and 1 touchdown. The Saints' defense limited the Panthers to just 8 first downs, none rushing. Beuerlein was 15 of 28 for 172 yards, with 1 interception.

Carolina	0	6	0	0	—	6
New Orleans	0	10	0	14	—	24

NO — Williams 2 run (Brien kick)
Car — FG Nedney 52
NO — FG Brien 29
Car — FG Nedney 46
NO — Williams 1 run (Brien kick)
NO — Horn 29 pass from Blake (Brien kick)

PITTSBURGH 15, CINCINNATI 0—at Three Rivers Stadium, attendance 54,238. Kent Graham's touchdown pass to Hines Ward two plays into the game was enough to propel the Steelers to their third consecutive victory and post their first shutout in 37 games. Ward caught a 27-yard pass and shook Cory Hall's tackle to race into the end zone. Peter Warrick's 46-yard reverse early in the second quarter gave the Bengals excellent field position, but on fourth-and-3 from the Steelers' 16, Cincinnati attempted a fake field goal and kicker Neil Rackers was tackled for a 5-yard loss. Joey Porter sacked Akili Smith later in the second quarter and forced him to fumble. Jason Gildon recovered the ball at the Bengals' 43 to set up Kris Brown's 36-yard field goal. Scott Mitchell replaced Smith in the third quarter, but Dewayne Washington's interception at the Bengals' 14 led to Brown's second field goal, and Porter sacked Mitchell for a safety in the fourth quarter to complete the scoring. Graham was 13 of 33 for 173 yards and 1 touchdown. Jerome Bettis had 29 carries for 101 yards. Smith was 10 of 20 for 97 yards, while Mitchell was 4 of 16 for 39 yards, with 2 interceptions.

Cincinnati	0	0	0	0	—	0
Pittsburgh	7	3	3	2	—	15

Pitt — Ward 77 pass from Graham (Brown kick)
Pitt — FG Brown 36
Pitt — FG Brown 28
Pitt — Safety, Mitchell sacked by Porter in end zone

DENVER 44, CLEVELAND 10—at Mile High Stadium, attendance 72,791. Brian Griese passed for 336 yards and 3 touchdowns, all to Rod Smith, as the Broncos handed the Browns their fourth consecutive defeat. Griese completed a 61-yard pass to Ed McCaffrey two plays into the game, but the Browns' defense stiffened and Jason Elam made a 22-yard field goal. Tim Couch's 37-yard pass to Aaron Shea led to Phil Dawson's game-tying field goal late in the first quarter. The Broncos scored on their last three possessions of the first half, highlighted by 2 Griese-to-Smith touchdowns, to take a 20-3 halftime lead. Couch's 37-yard pass to Dennis Northcutt set up Travis Prentice's 3-yard touchdown catch to open the third quarter, but Deltha O'Neal returned the ensuing kickoff 62 yards to set up Mike Anderson's 26-yard touchdown run. The Broncos' defense forced a punt, and Griese completed a 32-yard touchdown pass to Smith four plays later to give Denver a 34-10 lead with 4:48 left in the third quarter. The defense took over from there as Billy Jenkins returned an interception for a touchdown and Ray Crockett's interception at the Browns' 30 moments later led to Elam's final field goal. Griese was 19 of 34 for 336 yards and 3 touchdowns. Anderson had 20 carries for 103 yards. McCaffrey had 5 receptions for 129 yards, and Smith added 5 catches for 111 yards. Couch was 24 of 40 for 266 yards and 1 touchdown, with 3 interceptions.

Cleveland	3	0	7	0	—	10
Denver	3	17	14	10	—	44

Den — FG Elam 22
Cle — FG Dawson 45
Den — R. Smith 22 pass from Griese (Elam kick)
Den — R. Smith 17 pass from Griese (Elam kick)
Den — FG Elam 45
Cle — Prentice 3 pass from Couch (Dawson kick)
Den — Anderson 26 run (Elam kick)
Den — R. Smith 32 pass from Griese (Elam kick)
Den — Jenkins 36 interception return (Elam kick)
Den — FG Elam 46

2000 WEEK BY WEEK

N.Y. GIANTS 19, DALLAS 14—at Giants Stadium, attendance 78,189. Ron Dayne rushed for 108 yards, including the winning touchdown, and the Giants' defense intercepted 5 passes to maintain pace with the Redskins in the NFC East. Shaun Williams intercepted Troy Aikman's pass in the end zone early in the second quarter to stop either team's first scoring opportunity. On the Cowboys' next possession Aikman was intercepted again, by Dave Thomas at the Cowboys' 21, to set up Kerry Collins's 1-yard fourth-down touchdown pass to Pete Mitchell. Brad Daluiso's 24-yard field goal began the third quarter, but Jason Tucker returned the ensuing kickoff 90 yards to set up Robert Thomas's 1-yard touchdown catch. The Giants once again drove inside the Cowboys' 10 but had to settle for a Daluiso field goal, and Emmitt Smith's 3-yard touchdown run on the ensuing possession staked the Cowboys to a 14-13 lead. Michael Barrow's interception and 7-yard return to the Cowboys' 31 early in the fourth quarter led to Dayne's second touchdown with 10:00 left. The Cowboys drove to the Giants' 14 with 11 seconds remaining, but Cedric Jones sacked Aikman for an 8-yard loss and, after spiking the ball, Aikman's pass into the end zone was broken up as time expired. Collins was 14 of 25 for 119 yards and 1 touchdown. Dayne had 21 carries for 108 yards. Aikman was 22 of 42 for 211 yards and 1 touchdown, with a career-high 5 interceptions.

Dallas	0	0	14	0	—	14
N.Y. Giants	0	7	6	6	—	19

NYG — Mitchell 1 pass from Collins (Daluiso kick)
NYG — FG Daluiso 24
Dall — Thomas 1 pass from Aikman (Seder kick)
NYG — FG Daluiso 20
Dall — E. Smith 3 run (Seder kick)
NYG — Dayne 3 run (run failed)

INDIANAPOLIS 37, SEATTLE 24—at Husky Stadium, attendance 63,593. Edgerrin James rushed for a club-record 219 yards and added 3 touchdowns, as the Colts outlasted the Seahawks. The Colts scored on their first three possessions, highlighted by 2 touchdown runs by James, to take a 17-7 lead. Willie Williams recovered Terrence Wilkins's fumble at the Colts' 34 to set up Brock Huard's 7-yard touchdown pass to Itula Mili with 1:56 left in the half. The Colts responded with Mike Vanderjagt's 38-yard field goal with 23 seconds left in the half, but Huard completed 2 passes to set up Rian Lindell's 51-yard field goal as the half expired, trimming the deficit to 20-17. Charlie Rogers returned the second half's opening kickoff 81 yards, but Ricky Watters fumbled on the next play and Cornelius Bennett recovered. The Colts drove 76 yards, keyed by Peyton Manning's 6-yard pass to Wilkins on fourth-and-3 to the Seahawks' 28, and capped by Manning's touchdown pass to Ken Dilger. Manning's 39-yard pass to Marvin Harrison on the Colts' next drive led to James's 2-yard touchdown run to take a 34-17 lead. Trailing 37-24 with 5:12 remaining, the Seahawks recovered their own onside kick, but Chad Cota intercepted Huard's pass two plays later. On the Seahawks' final possession, Chad Bratzke recovered a fumble with 2:00 left to seal the victory. Manning was 20 of 30 for 281 yards and 1 touchdown. James had 38 carries for 219 yards. Harrison had 7 receptions for 134 yards. Huard was 19 of 26 for 226 yards and 3 touchdowns, with 1 interception. Sean Dawkins had 6 receptions for 118 yards.

Indianapolis	7	13	14	3	—	37
Seattle	0	17	0	7	—	24

Ind — James 26 run (Vanderjagt kick)
Ind — FG Vanderjagt 23
Sea — Jackson 8 pass from Huard (Lindell kick)
Ind — James 3 run (Vanderjagt kick)
Sea — Mili 7 pass from Huard (Lindell kick)
Ind — FG Vanderjagt 38
Sea — FG Lindell 51
Ind — Dilger 17 pass from Manning (Vanderjagt kick)
Ind — James 2 run (Vanderjagt kick)
Ind — FG Vanderjagt 40
Sea — Bailey 6 pass from Huard (Lindell kick)

N.Y. JETS 34, NEW ENGLAND 17—at Foxboro Stadium, attendance 60,018. Curtis Martin rushed for 143 yards and 3 touchdowns, and the Jets' defense forced 6 turnovers to defeat the Patriots. Bryan Cox recovered Kevin Faulk's fumble three plays into the game to set up Martin's 2-yard touchdown run. Two plays later, Victor Green intercepted Drew Bledsoe's pass and returned it 21 yards for a touchdown and a 14-0 lead with 7:34 left in the first quarter. Bledsoe's 46-yard pass to Tony Simmons set up Faulk's 9-yard touchdown run midway through the second quarter to cut the deficit to 14-10, but the Jets scored 10 points in the final 2:11 of the half, keyed by Shaun Ellis's recovery of Bledsoe's fumble at the Patriots' 43 to set up John Hall's 38-yard field goal, to take a 24-10 halftime lead. Leading 31-17, Mo Lewis intercepted Bledsoe's pass to set up Hall's final field goal with 3:56 remaining to help the Jets preserve the lead. Vinny Testaverde was 15 of 23 for 139 yards. Martin had 34 carries for 143 yards. Bledsoe was 16 of 35 for 208 yards, with 3 interceptions.

N.Y. Jets	14	10	7	3	—	34
New England	3	7	0	7	—	17

NYJ — Martin 2 run (Hall kick)
NYJ — Green 21 interception return (Hall kick)
NE — FG Vinatieri 23
NE — Faulk 9 run (Vinatieri kick)
NYJ — Martin 4 run (Hall kick)
NYJ — FG Hall 38
NYJ — Martin 2 run (Hall kick)
NE — Bledsoe 13 run (Vinatieri kick)
NYJ — FG Hall 27

OAKLAND 20, KANSAS CITY 17—at Arrowhead Stadium, attendance 79,025. Sebastian Janikowski's 43-yard field goal with 25 seconds remaining capped the Raiders' comeback from a 10-point halftime deficit to defeat the Chiefs. The Raiders drove 80 yards in 14 plays on their first possession, culminated by Rich Gannon's 4-yard touchdown pass to Napoleon Kaufman. The Chiefs scored on three consecutive possessions, the last of which was set up by John Browning's recovery of Gannon's fumble at the Chiefs' 40, to take a 17-7 halftime lead. Janikowski, who missed 47- and 59-yard field-goal attempts in the first half, connected from 47 yards to cap the Raiders' opening drive of the second half. The Raiders tied the game on a 14-play, 80-yard drive, capped by Gannon's 7-yard touchdown pass to Tyrone Wheatley with 9:25 remaining. The Chiefs quickly drove downfield, but Sylvester Morris fumbled and Charles Woodson recovered at the Raiders' 12-yard line. After an exchange of punts, Gannon completed 5 passes to four different receivers to set up Janikowski's game-winning 43-yard field goal. Gannon was 28 of 33 for 244 yards and 2 touchdowns. Elvis Grbac was 23 of 40 for 288 yards and 2 touchdowns. Tony Gonzalez had 7 receptions for 100 yards.

Oakland	7	0	3	10	—	20
Kansas City	0	17	0	0	—	17

Oak — Kaufman 4 pass from Gannon (Janikowski kick)
KC — FG Peterson 27
KC — Gonzalez 14 pass from Grbac (Peterson kick)
KC — Richardson 15 pass from Grbac (Peterson kick)
Oak — FG Janikowski 47
Oak — Wheatley 7 pass from Gannon (Janikowski kick)
Oak — FG Janikowski 43

PHILADELPHIA 33, ARIZONA 14—at Sun Devil Stadium, attendance 38,293. Donovan McNabb passed for 226 yards and 1 touchdown, and ran for another, as the Eagles improved to 3-1 on the road. The Cardinals drove to the Eagles' 28 to open the game, but David Boston fumbled while running an end-around and Corey Simon recovered. McNabb's 27-yard run to the Cardinals' 1 keyed the ensuing 10-play drive, capped by Stanley Pritchett's touchdown run. The Eagles used drives of 14, 17, and 10 plays on their next three possessions to score as well, highlighted by McNabb's 3-yard touchdown run 25 seconds before halftime and capped by his 9-yard touchdown pass to Chad Lewis on the second half's opening drive, to take a 24-0 lead. The Cardinals scored on consecutive possessions to close the gap to 24-14 and had the Eagles facing a third-and-10 situation from their own 40 with 6:00 remaining. However, McNabb completed a 59-yard bomb to Charles Johnson to set up Darnell Autry's 1-yard run with 5:28 left. McNabb was 24 of 34 for 226 yards and 1 touchdown. Plummer was 18 of 30 for 213 yards and 2 touchdowns, with 2 interceptions. David Boston had 6 receptions for 123 yards.

Philadelphia	7	10	7	9	—	33
Arizona	0	0	7	7	—	14

Phil — Pritchett 1 run (Akers kick)
Phil — FG Akers 31
Phil — McNabb 3 run (Akers kick)
Phil — Lewis 9 pass from McNabb (Akers kick)
Ariz — Boston 70 pass from Plummer (Blanchard kick)
Ariz — Pittman 10 pass from Plummer (Blanchard kick)
Phil — Autry 1 run (kick failed)
Phil — FG Akers 29

BUFFALO 27, SAN DIEGO 24 (OT)—at Ralph Wilson Stadium, attendance 72,351. Henry Jones's interception in overtime set up Steve Christie's game-winning 46-yard field goal as the Bills overcame a 10-point fourth-quarter deficit to defeat the Chargers. Trailing 3-0 in the second quarter, Pat Williams and Sam Cowart recovered fumbles to set up Buffalo touchdowns. On the second touchdown, Jonathan Linton ran 2 yards to the Chargers' 1, then fumbled into the end zone where center Jerry Ostroski recovered the ball for a Bills touchdown. Jim Harbaugh's 60-yard touchdown pass to Curtis Conway three plays later sparked the Chargers, and Rodeny Harrison's interception in the end zone just before halftime kept Buffalo's lead at 14-10. Darryll Lewis's 29-yard return of Rob Johnson's fumble to the Bills' 17 early in the second half led to Jermaine Fazande's 2-yard touchdown run. The Chargers' defense then forced a punt, and Harbaugh connected with Jeff Graham on a 52-yard touchdown two plays later to take a 24-14 lead. A Darren Bennett punt pinned the Bills back on their own 1, but Buffalo responded with an 11-play, 99-yard drive, highlighted by Johnson's 11-yard pass to Peerless Price on fourth-and-1, and capped by Johnson's 11-yard touchdown pass to Shawn Bryson with 13:48 remaining, to cut the deficit to 24-21. The Bills' defense forced 3 punts in the fourth quarter, and the offense capitalized with a 12-play, 69-yard drive, including two 17-yard passes from Johnson to Eric Moulds, to set up Christie's game-tying 29-yard field goal with seven seconds left in regulation. The Chargers won the coin toss, but were forced to punt. After being forced to punt, the Bills' defense once again rose to the occasion, as Jones intercepted Harbaugh's pass at the Bills' 41. Subbing for Johnson, Doug Flutie's 21-yard pass to Moulds to the Chargers' 25 set up Christie's winning kick 8:26 into overtime. Johnson was 29 of 47 for 321 yards and 1 touchdown, with 1 interception. Moulds had 11 receptions for 170 yards. Harbaugh was 21 of 33 for 287 yards and 2 touchdowns, with 2 interceptions. Conway had 7 catches for 143 yards, and Graham added 9 catches for 113 yards.

San Diego	3	7	14	0	0	—	24
Buffalo	0	14	0	10	3	—	27

SD — FG Carney 36
Buff — Morris 32 run (Christie kick)
Buff — Ostroski recovered fumble in end zone (Christie kick)
SD — Conway 60 pass from Harbaugh (Carney kick)
SD — Fazande 2 run (Carney kick)
SD — Graham 52 pass from Harbaugh (Carney kick)
Buff — Bryson 11 pass from Johnson (Christie kick)
Buff — FG Christie 29
Buff — FG Christie 46

GREEN BAY 31, SAN FRANCISCO 28—at Lambeau Field, attendance 59,870. Brett Favre passed for 266 yards and 1 touchdown and engineered a game-winning drive in the final moments as the Packers defeated the 49ers. Trailing 7-0, the 49ers scored on Jeff Garcia's 39-yard touchdown pass to Charlie Garner. The Packers responded with a 10-play, 74-yard drive, capped by Ahman Green's 2-yard touchdown run 51 seconds before halftime, and opened the second half with an 80-yard drive to take a 21-7 lead. The 49ers drove 77 and 71 yards on their next two possessions to tie the game on Garcia's 16-yard touchdown pass to Terrell Owens with 11:36 remaining. Favre responded with a 37-yard pass to Dorsey Levens to spark a 75-yard drive, capped by Green's 1-yard scoring run, to retake the lead with 8:01 left. Undaunted, the 49ers needed just five plays to tie the game

28-28 on Garcia's 37-yard bomb to Owens with 5:30 left. Allen Rossum returned the ensuing kickoff 32 yards, and Favre completed all 3 of his pass attempts to set up Ryan Longwell's 35-yard field goal with 54 seconds remaining. Garcia completed 3 passes in the final minute, but the 49ers were unable to get into field-goal range. Favre was 20 of 27 for 266 yards and 1 touchdown. Antonio Freeman had 6 catches for 116 yards. Garcia was 27 of 42 for 336 yards and 4 touchdowns.

San Francisco	0	7	7	14	—	28
Green Bay	7	7	7	10	—	31

GB — Freeman 67 pass from Favre (Longwell kick)
SF — Garner 39 pass from Garcia (Richey kick)
GB — Green 2 run (Longwell kick)
GB — Levens 1 run (Longwell kick)
SF — Stokes 23 pass from Garcia (Richey kick)
SF — Owens 16 pass from Garcia (Richey kick)
GB — Green 1 run (Longwell kick)
SF — Owens 37 pass from Garcia (Richey kick)
GB — FG Longwell 35

SUNDAY NIGHT, OCTOBER 15

MINNESOTA 28, CHICAGO 16—at Soldier Field, attendance 58,170. The Bears used consecutive drives of 63 and 76 yards to take a 9-0 lead. However, Robert Smith had a 72-yard touchdown run on the next play from scrimmage; the Vikings' defense then forced a punt that Troy Walters returned 25 yards; and Daunte Culpepper fired a 24-yard touchdown pass to Cris Carter four plays later to stake the Vikings to a 14-9 lead. Culpepper's 24-yard touchdown pass to Matthew Hatchette early in the second half increased the lead, but Cade McNown engineered a 9-play, 74-yard drive to cut the deficit to 21-16 with 14:56 remaining. But Walters returned the ensuing kickoff 35 yards, and Culpepper's 7-yard touchdown pass to Randy Moss nine plays later gave Minnesota a 28-16 lead. Ray McElroy recovered Walters muffed punt at the Vikings' 16 midway through the fourth quarter, but McNown's fourth-down pass fell incomplete. Culpepper was 15 of 26 for 198 yards and 3 touchdowns. Smith rushed 23 times for 170 yards, and Carter had 7 catches for 111 yards. McNown was 19 of 33 for 210 yards and 1 touchdown.

Minnesota	0	14	7	7	—	28
Chicago	6	3	0	7	—	16

Chi — White 25 pass from McNown (mishandled snap)
Chi — FG Edinger 22
Minn — Smith 72 run (Anderson kick)
Minn — Carter 24 pass from Culpepper (Anderson kick)
Minn — Hatchette 24 pass from Culpepper (Anderson kick)
Chi — Allen 6 run (Edinger kick)
Minn — Moss 7 pass from Culpepper (Anderson kick)

MONDAY NIGHT, OCTOBER 16

TENNESSEE 27, JACKSONVILLE 13—at Adelphia Coliseum, attendance 68,498. Eddie George rushed 30 times for 165 yards and 1 touchdown, and Steve McNair passed for 2 touchdowns, as Jeff Fisher became the fourth-youngest coach in NFL history to win 50 games. Fred Taylor's 71-yard run midway through the first quarter led to Mike Hollis's 23-yard field goal, but the Titans scored on their next three possessions. Samari Rolle recovered Mark Brunell's fumble at the Titans' 20 just before halftime to preserve a 17-3 lead. The Titans scored on their first possession of the second half to take a 24-6 lead, and used a 12-play, 72-yard drive that consumed more than six minutes in the fourth quarter to set up Al Del Greco's 28-yard field goal with 3:37 left for a 27-6 lead. McNair was 13 of 21 for 234 yards and 2 touchdowns. Brunell was 18 of 27 for 196 yards. Taylor had 20 carries for 112 yards.

Jacksonville	3	0	0	10	—	13
Tennessee	7	10	7	3	—	27

Jax — FG Hollis 23
Tenn — Wycheck 4 pass from McNair (Del Greco kick)
Tenn — Mason 22 pass from McNair (Del Greco kick)
Tenn — FG Del Greco 26
Tenn — George 19 run (Del Greco kick)
Jax — FG Hollis 45
Tenn — FG Del Greco 28
Jax — Johnson 2 run (Hollis kick)

EIGHTH WEEK SUMMARIES

AMERICAN FOOTBALL CONFERENCE

Eastern Division	**W**	**L**	**T**	**Pct.**	**Pts.**	**OP**
N.Y. Jets	6	1	0	.857	165	140
Indianapolis	5	2	0	.714	202	153
Miami	5	2	0	.714	149	91
Buffalo	3	4	0	.429	140	153
New England	2	6	0	.250	143	171
Central Division						
Tennessee	6	1	0	.857	145	97
Baltimore	5	3	0	.625	134	89
Pittsburgh	4	3	0	.571	121	78
Cleveland	2	6	0	.250	95	197
Jacksonville	2	6	0	.250	142	190
Cincinnati	1	6	0	.143	68	164
Western Division						
Oakland	6	1	0	.857	192	128
Kansas City	4	3	0	.571	188	147
Denver	4	4	0	.500	238	178
Seattle	2	6	0	.250	121	200
San Diego	0	7	0	.000	117	204

NATIONAL FOOTBALL CONFERENCE

Eastern Division	**W**	**L**	**T**	**Pct.**	**Pts.**	**OP**
Washington	6	2	0	.750	149	115
N.Y. Giants	5	2	0	.714	120	105
Philadelphia	5	3	0	.625	181	110
Dallas	3	4	0	.429	174	174
Arizona	2	6	0	.286	121	210
Central Division						
Minnesota	7	0	0	1.000	184	137
Detroit	5	2	0	.714	143	134
Green Bay	3	4	0	.429	148	139
Tampa Bay	3	4	0	.429	164	125
Chicago	1	7	0	.125	110	202
Western Division						
St. Louis	6	1	0	.857	296	228
New Orleans	4	3	0	.571	131	117
Carolina	3	4	0	.429	144	116
Atlanta	2	6	0	.250	149	238
San Francisco	2	6	0	.250	214	258

THURSDAY NIGHT, OCTOBER 19

DETROIT 28, TAMPA BAY 14—at Raymond James Stadium, attendance 65,557. James Stewart rushed for 3 touchdowns, and Detroit's defense forced 4 turnovers as the Lions rallied to defeat the Buccaneers. Tampa Bay led 6-0 early in the second quarter when Nate Webster blocked John Jett's punt. The ball rolled into the end zone, but Ronde Barber was unable to land on it for a touchdown. Instead, Ron Rice fell on the ball for a safety, and Mike Alstott fumbled on the first play following the free kick to set up Jason Hanson's 32-yard field goal. Following Martin Gramatica's third field goal of the half, the Lions mounted a 12-play, 70-yard drive capped by Stewart's 4-yard touchdown run, and his subsequent 2-point conversion run, to tie the game 11-11. Bryant Westbrook's 16-yard interception return early in the third quarter led to Jason Hanson's 47-yard field goal. Marcus Jones, who had 4 sacks on the night, blocked Hanson's 41-yard field-goal attempt late in the third quarter to set up Gramatica's game-tying field goal with 13:10 left. Chris Claiborne's interception near midfield sparked an 8-play, 54-yard drive capped by Stewart's 1-yard touchdown to take a 21-14 lead with 4:28 remaining. The Lions' defense stopped Tampa Bay on downs, and Stewart rumbled 34 yards to the Buccaneers' 3 to set up his third touchdown with 1:53 left. Charlie Batch was 13 of 31 for 144 yards. Stewart had 29 carries for 116 yards. Shaun King was 17 of 34 for 149 yards, with 3 interceptions.

Detroit	0	11	3	14	—	28
Tampa Bay	6	5	0	3	—	14

TB — FG Gramatica 27
TB — FG Gramatica 43
TB — Safety, Rice recovered Lions' blocked punt in end zone
Det — FG Hanson 32
TB — FG Gramatica 50
Det — Stewart 4 run (Stewart run)
Det — FG Hanson 47
TB — FG Gramatica 55
Det — Stewart 4 run (Hanson kick)
Det — Stewart 1 run (Hanson kick)

SUNDAY, OCTOBER 22

DALLAS 48, ARIZONA 7—at Texas Stadium, attendance 62,981. Emmitt Smith rushed for 112 yards, and the Cowboys' defense contributed to 20 Dallas points to defeat the Cardinals. Phillippi Sparks's interception at the Cardinals' 16 late in the first quarter led to Smith's 1-yard touchdown run. Moments later, Wane McGarity returned Scott Player's punt 59 yards for a touchdown and a 14-0 lead. Chris Warren's 32-yard touchdown run on the Cowboys' next possession staked Dallas to a 21-0 lead with 10:52 left in the second quarter. The Cowboys' defense stopped Arizona on downs near midfield to set up Tim Seder's 32-yard field goal with 1:30 remaining in the half. Charlie Williams intercepted Jake Plummer's pass on the next play from scrimmage to set up Seder's 23-yard field goal as the half expired. The Cowboys drove 82 yards for a touchdown on their first possession of the second half and scored again less than three minutes later following Darren Woodson's interception at the Cardinals' 25. Troy Aikman's 2-yard touchdown pass to Robert Thomas capped a 69-yard drive on their next possession to take a 48-0 lead with 12:21 remaining. Aikman was 9 of 15 for 154 yards and 2 touchdowns. Plummer was 20 of 31 for 180 yards, with 3 interceptions.

Arizona	0	0	0	7	—	7
Dallas	14	13	14	7	—	48

Dall — Smith 1 run (Seder kick)
Dall — McGarity 59 punt return (Seder kick)
Dall — Warren 32 run (Seder kick)
Dall — FG Seder 32
Dall — FG Seder 23
Dall — Ismail 24 pass from Aikman (Seder kick)
Dall — Warren 10 run (Seder kick)
Dall — Thomas 2 pass from Aikman (Seder kick)
Ariz — Pittman 1 run (Blanchard kick)

MINNESOTA 31, BUFFALO 27—at Metrodome, attendance 64,116. Gary Anderson became the NFL's all-time leading scorer, and Daunte Culpepper passed for 3 second-half touchdowns as the Vikings overcame an 11-point fourth-quarter deficit to defeat the Bills. Anderson's field goal with 1:04 remaining allowed him to break the record of 2,002 career points held by George Blanda. The Bills led 7-3 when Doug Flutie engineered a 21-play, 80-yard drive that knocked nearly 11 minutes off the clock and was culminated by Steve Christie's 26-yard field goal with 54 seconds left in the half. Culpepper responded by completing 28-yard passes to Randy Moss and Cris Carter to set up Anderson's 20-yard field goal as the half expired to cut the deficit to 10-6. Culpepper's 2-yard touchdown pass to Carter capped the opening drive of the second half and gave the Vikings a 13-10 lead, but the Bills scored on their next two possessions, the second set up by Sam Rogers's 10-yard interception return to the Vikings' 34, to take a 24-13 lead with 14:19 remaining. The Vikings responded with a 69-yard touchdown drive to trim the lead to 24-21, but Chris Watson returned the ensuing kickoff 33 yards to set up Christie's 48-yard field goal with 6:39 left. Following an exchange of punts, the latter of which Troy Walters returned 28 yards, Culpepper fired a 39-yard scoring bomb to Moss to take a 28-27 lead with 3:42 left. Orlando Thomas recovered Peerless Price's fumble on the ensuing possession to set up Anderson's historic 21-yard field goal with 1:04 remaining. The Bills reached the Vikings' 43 with five seconds left, but Flutie's Hail Mary pass fell incomplete. Culpepper, who became just the third quarterback, along with Dieter Brock and Mike Tomczak, to win his first seven NFL starts, was 17 of 29 for 251 yards and 3 touchdowns, with 1 interception. Moss had 5 receptions for 110 yards, and Carter had 7 catches for 107 yards. Flutie was 28 of 43 for 294 yards. Eric Moulds had 12 receptions for 135 yards.

Buffalo	0	10	7	10	—	27
Minnesota	3	3	7	18	—	31

Minn — FG Anderson 38
Buff — Moulds 25 pass from Flutie (Christie kick)
Buff — FG Christie 26
Minn — FG Anderson 20
Minn — Carter 2 pass from Culpepper (Anderson kick)
Buff — Morris 1 run (Christie kick)
Buff — Morris 18 pass from Flutie (Christie kick)

Minn — Carter 11 pass from Culpepper (Williams pass from Culpepper)
Buff — FG Christie 48
Minn — Moss 39 pass from Culpepper (Anderson kick)
Minn — FG Anderson 21

PHILADELPHIA 13, CHICAGO 9—at Veterans Stadium, attendance 65,553. Donovan McNabb passed for 1 touchdown, and the Eagles matched last year's win total by holding off a fourth-quarter rally by the Bears. McNabb's 8-yard run on third-and-13 set up David Akers's 51-yard field goal late in the first quarter. The Eagles scored on their last possession of the first half and first drive of the second half to take a 13-0 lead with 6:35 left in the third quarter. Jim Miller, who replaced an injured Cade McNown in the second quarter, highlighted a 51-yard drive with a successful fourth-down quarterback sneak, to trim the deficit to 13-3 with 12:36 remaining. The Bears drove inside the Eagles' 25 on their next two possessions as well, and Paul Edinger's 40-yard field goal with 4:10 left brought the Bears within four points. The Bears forced a punt with 1:04 remaining, but were unable to cross midfield before time expired. McNabb was 22 of 35 for 207 yards and 1 touchdown. Miller was 14 of 34 for 128 yards, with 1 interception.

Chicago	0	0	0	9	—	9
Philadelphia	3	7	3	0	—	13

Phil — FG Akers 51
Phil — Thomason 3 pass from McNabb (Akers kick)
Phil — FG Akers 29
Chi — FG Edinger 25
Chi — FG Edinger 33
Chi — FG Edinger 40

PITTSBURGH 22, CLEVELAND 0—at Three Rivers Stadium, attendance 57,659. The Steelers' defense permitted just 5 first downs and 104 total yards as Pittsburgh won its fourth consecutive game. Levon Kirkland's interception at the Browns' 36 late in the first quarter led to the first of Kris Brown's career-high 5 field goals. Hank Poteat's 54-yard punt return in the second quarter led to Jerome Bettis's 1-yard touchdown run, and Chad Scott's interception at the Browns' 45 two plays later led to Brown's 20-yard field goal and a 13-0 halftime lead. Brent Alexander's interception at the Browns' 33 led to Brown's 26-yard third-quarter field goal. Trailing 19-0 in the fourth quarter, Jamel White's 36-yard kickoff return and an ensuing 15-yard penalty gave the Browns the ball at the Steelers' 32 for their best scoring opportunity, but Cleveland gained just 7 yards and Phil Dawson missed a 42-yard field goal. Kordell Stewart replaced Kent Graham midway through the second quarter and was 7 of 13 for 74 yards. Bettis rushed 33 times for 105 yards. Doug Pederson, playing in place of Tim Couch, who suffered a season-ending thumb injury in practice during the week, was 9 of 20 for 61 yards, with 3 interceptions.

Cleveland	0	0	0	0	—	0
Pittsburgh	3	10	3	6	—	22

Pitt — FG Brown 44
Pitt — Bettis 2 run (Brown kick)
Pitt — FG Brown 20
Pitt — FG Brown 31
Pitt — FG Brown 26
Pitt — FG Brown 33

CINCINNATI 31, DENVER 21—at Paul Brown Stadium, attendance 61,603. Corey Dillon rushed for an NFL-record 278 yards as the Bengals won their first game of the season. Trailing 7-0, Dillon had a 31-yard run, and Akili Smith passed for the Bengals' lone 2 completions of the day to set up Neil Rackers's 24-yard field goal. After a 68-yard touchdown drive by Denver, Peter Warrick took a handoff on a reverse on the next play from scrimmage. Warrick ran to the right sideline before darting across field for a spectacular 77-yard touchdown run. Jason Elam missed a 48-yard field goal just before halftime, but Denver led 14-10. In the third quarter, Chris Carter recovered Mike Anderson's third-quarter fumble near midfield, and Dillon had a 30-yard run to set up Brandon Bennett's 19-yard touchdown run. The Broncos had two scoring chances early in the fourth quarter, but Elam missed another 48-yard field-goal attempt and Reinard Wilson recovered Brian Griese's fumble at the Bengals' 36 with 5:51 remaining. Two plays after Wilson's recovery, Dillon broke free for a 65-yard touchdown run for a 24-14 lead. It took Denver just three plays to respond, capped by Griese's 28-yard touchdown pass to Rod Smith with 3:43 remaining. But on second-and-8 from the Broncos' 41, Dillon raced down the left sideline for a game-clinching touchdown run with 1:49 to play. Dillon needed just 22 carries to break Walter Payton's record 275-yard rushing game in 1977. Dillon had carries of 26, 21, 31, 37, 30, 65, and 41 yards during the game. The Bengals, who had scored a combined 37 points in their first six games, rushed for 407 of their 421 total yards. Smith was 2 for 9 for 34 yards before being injured on the first series of the second half. His replacement, Scott Mitchell, was 0 for 5. Griese was 30 of 45 for 365 yards and 2 touchdowns, with 1 interception. Ed McCaffrey had 10 receptions for 136 yards, and Smith added 7 catches for 110 yards.

Denver	7	7	0	7	—	21
Cincinnati	0	10	7	14	—	31

Den — D. Smith 1 pass from Griese (Elam kick)
Cin — FG Rackers 24
Den — Anderson 3 run (Elam kick)
Cin — Warrick 77 run (Rackers kick)
Cin — Bennett 19 run (Rackers kick)
Cin — Dillon 65 run (Rackers kick)
Den — R. Smith 28 pass from Griese (Elam kick)
Cin — Dillon 41 run (Rackers kick)

INDIANAPOLIS 30, NEW ENGLAND 23—at RCA Dome, attendance 56,828. Edgerrin James rushed for 124 yards and scored 2 fourth-quarter touchdowns to catapult the Colts past the Patriots. The Patriots scored on their first five possessions on drives of 89, 71, 77, 73, and 80 yards, to take a 23-14 lead with 2:27 left in the third quarter. The Colts' defense forced the Patriots' first punt with 10:11 remaining in the game, and the Colts' offense embarked on an 8-play, 65-yard drive capped by Manning's 1-yard touchdown pass to James to cut the deficit to 23-21 with 6:16 left. The Patriots had a second-and-1 situation, but J.R. Redmond and Kevin Faulk combined to lose a yard on the next two plays and New England punted with 4:42 remaining. James had carries of 16, 13, and 26 yards before scoring on a 3-yard run with 2:09 left to cap a 6-play, 66-yard drive and take a 27-23 lead. The Patriots failed to gain a first down on their next possession, and Mike Vanderjagt's 36-yard field goal with 18 seconds left secured the victory. Manning was 16 of 20 for 268 yards and 2 touchdowns. James had 20 carries for 124 yards. Marvin Harrison had 5 receptions for 156 yards. Drew Bledsoe was 23 of 34 for 231 yards and 1 touchdown.

New England	7	6	10	0	—	23
Indianapolis	7	0	7	16	—	30

NE — Redmond 19 pass from Bledsoe (Vinatieri kick)
Ind — Harrison 51 pass from Manning (Vanderjagt kick)
NE — FG Vinatieri 27
NE — FG Vinatieri 26
NE — FG Vinatieri 28
Ind — Harrison 78 pass from Manning (Vanderjagt kick)
NE — Bledsoe 1 run (Vinatieri kick)
Ind — James 1 pass from Manning (Vanderjagt kick)
Ind — James 3 run (pass failed)
Ind — FG Vanderjagt 36

NEW ORLEANS 21, ATLANTA 19—at Georgia Dome, attendance 56,508. Ricky Williams had his fifth consecutive 100-yard rushing game and scored 3 touchdowns as the Saints snapped a 10-game losing streak to the Falcons. Williams's 12-yard touchdown run capped the Saints' first possession and gave New Orleans a 7-3 lead. Ronnie Bradford's 13-yard interception return to the Saints' 20 midway through the second quarter led to Morten Andersen's 44-yard field goal, and Chris Chandler's 52-yard touchdown pass to Tim Dwight on Atlanta's next possession staked the Falcons to a 13-7 halftime lead. The third quarter became a defensive struggle for field position. The Saints pinned the Falcons back to their own 5-yard line, and Chad Morton returned the ensuing punt 13 yards to set up Williams's 26-yard touchdown burst for a 14-13 lead. Williams's 1-yard touchdown run capped a 15-play, 92-yard drive to give New Orleans a 21-13 lead with 4:10 left. The Falcons needed just three plays to cut the deficit to 21-19 on Chandler's touchdown pass to Terance Mathis with 2:58 remaining, but Chandler's 2-point conversion pass attempt to Reggie Kelly was knocked down by Sammy Knight. The Falcons opted to kick deep, but Jeff Blake passes to Lamont Hall and Joe Horn netted first downs to allow the Saints to run out the clock. Blake was 19 of 31 for 209 yards, with 1 interception. Williams had 29 carries for 156 yards. Chandler was 15 of 20 for 240 yards and 2 touchdowns.

New Orleans	7	0	7	7	—	21
Atlanta	3	10	0	6	—	19

Atl — FG Andersen 50
NO — Williams 12 run (Brien kick)
Atl — FG Andersen 44
Atl — Dwight 52 pass from Chandler (Andersen kick)
NO — Williams 26 run (Brien kick)
NO — Williams 1 run (Brien kick)
Atl — Mathis 33 pass from Chandler (pass failed)

KANSAS CITY 54, ST. LOUIS 34—at Arrowhead Stadium, attendance 79,142. Kimble Anders rushed for 102 yards and 2 touchdowns as the Chiefs jumped out to a 20-0 lead en route to handing the Rams their first defeat of the season. The Rams not only lost the game, but Kurt Warner suffered a broken pinkie finger on his throwing hand in the second quarter and missed the next five games. James Hasty intercepted Warner's pass two plays into the game to set up Frank Moreau's touchdown run. A Rams punt and John Browning's interception at the Rams' 37 set up 2 Todd Peterson field goals, and on the ensuing possession Bracey Walker blocked John Baker's punt and Mike Cloud returned the loose ball 6 yards for a touchdown and a 20-0 lead slightly more than 12 minutes into the game. The Rams scored on their next two drives, but Elvis Grbac completed a 9-yard scoring pass to Tony Gonzalez in between Rams' touchdowns to maintain a 27-14 lead. The Rams drove to the Chiefs' 8 just before halftime, but Warner fumbled the snap and Donnie Edwards recovered, with Warner being injured on the play. Each team scored on their first possession of the second half, and the Rams were driving when Greg Wesley intercepted Trent Green's pass at the Chiefs' 20 and returned it 28 yards. Anders scored six plays later, but Tony Horne's 66-yard kickoff return set up Green's 22-yard touchdown pass to Isaac Bruce to cut the deficit to 40-28 after three quarters. However, Warren Moon replaced an injured Grbac and completed 31- and 39-yard passes before Anders's 4-yard scoring run increased the lead to 47-28. Anders's 69-yard run on the Chiefs' next possession set up Moon's 8-yard touchdown pass to Troy Drayton for a 54-28 lead with 5:27 remaining. Grbac was 18 of 30 for 266 yards and 2 touchdowns. Anders had 13 carries for 102 yards. Derrick Alexander and Tony Gonzalez each had 5 receptions for 117 yards. Warner was 15 of 25 for 185 yards and 1 touchdown, with 2 interceptions, while Green was 15 of 21 for 205 yards and 3 touchdowns, with 1 interception. Bruce had 8 receptions for 129 yards.

St. Louis	0	14	14	6	—	34
Kansas City	20	7	13	14	—	54

KC — Moreau 2 run (Peterson kick)
KC — FG Peterson 34
KC — FG Peterson 20
KC — Cloud 6 return of blocked punt (Peterson kick)
StL — Faulk 1 run (Stoyanovich kick)
KC — Gonzalez 9 pass from Grbac (Peterson kick)
StL — Holt 18 pass from Warner (Stoyanovich kick)
KC — Alexander 30 pass from Grbac (Peterson kick)
StL — Williams 31 pass from Green (Stoyanovich kick)
KC — Anders 6 run (pass failed)
StL — Bruce 22 pass from Green (Stoyanovich kick)
KC — Anders 4 run (Peterson kick)
KC — Drayton 8 pass from Moon (Peterson kick)
StL — Bruce 4 pass from Green (pass failed)

CAROLINA 34, SAN FRANCISCO 16—at Ericsson Stadium, attendance 61,350. Steve Beuerlein passed for 309 yards and 3 touchdowns as George Seifert improved his record against his former team to 4-0. Beuerlein's 3-yard touchdown pass to Isaac Byrd capped a game-opening 16-play, 80-yard drive. The 49ers drove to the Panthers' 9, but Terrell Owens fumbled and Lester Towns recovered.

However, the 49ers' defense forced a punt, and Jeff Garcia fired a 32-yard touchdown pass to Owens six plays later to tie the game. The Panthers responded with a 12-play, 80-yard touchdown drive and scored again 19 seconds later on Mike Minter's 30-yard interception return for a touchdown and a 20-7 lead. Garcia promptly engineered another touchdown drive, but the Panthers responded with Joe Nedney's field goal just before halftime. Beuerlein's touchdown pass to Tshimanga Biakabutuka early in the second half staked the Panthers to a 31-13 lead. The Panthers' defense stopped the 49ers twice on fourth down inside Carolina territory in the fourth quarter. Beuerlein was 28 of 44 for 309 yards and 3 touchdowns. Muhsin Muhammad had 9 receptions for 127 yards. Garcia was 25 of 39 for 307 yards and 2 touchdowns, with 1 interception. Charlie Garner had 7 receptions for 112 yards.

San Francisco	0	13	3	0	—	16
Carolina	7	17	7	3	—	34

Car — Byrd 3 pass from Beuerlein (Nedney kick)
SF — Owens 32 pass from Garcia (kick failed)
Car — Biakabutuka 2 pass from Beuerlein (Nedney kick)
Car — Minter 30 interception return (Nedney kick)
SF — Rice 16 pass from Garcia (Richey kick)
Car — FG Nedney 30
Car — Biakabutuka 8 pass from Beuerlein (Nedney kick)
SF — FG Richey 38
Car — FG Nedney 38

OAKLAND 31, SEATTLE 3—at Network Associates Coliseum, attendance 57,490. Rich Gannon passed for 3 touchdowns as the Raiders won their fourth consecutive game. Brock Huard's 45-yard pass to Ricky Watters during the game's opening possession set up Rian Lindell's 41-yard field goal, but Eric Allen intercepted Huard's pass at the Seahawks' 21 on their next possession to lead to Gannon's 16-yard touchdown pass to Tim Brown. After Huard's fourth-and-11 pass from the Raiders' 30 fell incomplete, Oakland embarked upon a 70-yard drive, capped by Brown's 9-yard touchdown catch for a 14-3 lead. The Raiders' defense forced a punt, and Tyrone Wheatley raced 80 yards off left tackle for a touchdown and a 21-3 lead midway through the second quarter. Jon Kitna replaced an injured Huard and drove the Seahawks into Raiders' territory, but Lindell missed a 43-yard field-goal attempt just before halftime. Greg Biekert recovered Kitna's fumbled snap at the Seahawks' 15 late in the third quarter to set up Sebastian Janikowski's field goal, and Gannon's 23-yard touchdown pass to James Jett midway through the final quarter completed the scoring. Gannon was 15 of 22 for 176 yards and 3 touchdowns, with 1 interception. Wheatley had 15 carries for 156 yards. Kitna was 11 of 18 for 85 yards.

Seattle	3	0	0	0	—	3
Oakland	7	14	0	10	—	31

Sea — FG Lindell 41
Oak — Brown 16 pass from Gannon (Janikowski kick)
Oak — Brown 9 pass from Gannon (Janikowski kick)
Oak — Wheatley 80 run (Janikowski kick)
Oak — FG Janikowski 32
Oak — Jett 23 pass from Gannon (Janikowski kick)

TENNESSEE 14, BALTIMORE 6—at PSINet Stadium, attendance 69,200. Without the services of Eddie George, the Titans' offense had just 7 first downs, but their defense recorded 4 second-half interceptions as Tennessee won its sixth consecutive game. George was injured on his first carry of the game, and two plays later Rodney Thomas was tackled for no gain on fourth-and-1 from the Ravens' 40. Baltimore capitalized by setting up Matt Stover's 21-yard field goal. Stover's 38-yard field goal on the Ravens' next possession capped a 15-play, 77-yard drive and gave Baltimore a 6-0 lead. Derrick Mason's 29-yard punt return and a 15-yard run by Thomas set up Steve McNair's 9-yard touchdown pass to Thomas 44 seconds before halftime. On the Ravens' first play of the second half, Randall Godfrey intercepted Tony Banks's pass and returned it 24 yards for a touchdown and a 14-6 lead. Banks was intercepted 2 more times in the third quarter before being replaced by Trent Dilfer. Dilfer drove the Ravens into Titans' territory twice in the fourth quarter, but Michael Booker's interception at the Titans' 22 with 8:00 left ended one drive and, on fourth down from the Titans' 33 with under two minutes remaining, Qadry Ismail's feet landed out of bounds just beyond the end zone to quell the Ravens' final threat. McNair was 11 of 21 for 101 yards and 1 touchdown, with 1 interception. Banks was 17 of 32 for 229 yards, with 3 interceptions. The Ravens lost despite substantial advantages in first downs (24-7), total yards (368-191), and time of possession (36:01-23:59).

Tennessee	0	7	7	0	—	14
Baltimore	3	3	0	0	—	6

Balt — FG Stover 21
Balt — FG Stover 38
Tenn — Thomas 9 pass from McNair (Del Greco kick)
Tenn — Godfrey 24 interception return (Del Greco kick)

WASHINGTON 35, JACKSONVILLE 16—at ALLTEL Stadium, attendance 69,061. Albert Connell had 7 receptions for 211 yards and 3 touchdowns as the Redskins won their fifth consecutive game. Deion Sanders's 21-yard interception return to the Jaguars' 38 set up Stephen Davis's 1-yard touchdown run five minutes into the game. The Jaguars responded by scoring on their next two possessions, capped by R. Jay Soward's 33-yard touchdown catch, to take a 10-7 lead. However, Soward muffed a punt moments later to set up Connell's first touchdown catch. After the Redskins' defense forced a punt, Brad Johnson fired a 49-yard touchdown pass to Connell two plays later to stake the Redskins to a 21-10 lead with 5:39 remaining in the half. The Jaguars added 2 Mike Hollis field goals just before halftime, but Johnson's 77-yard scoring bomb to Connell early in the third quarter extended the lead to 28-16. The Redskins' defense did not allow the Jaguars inside the Redskins' 39 in the second half, and Davis's 16-yard touchdown run with 4:32 remaining clinched the victory. Johnson was 16 of 24 for 269 yards and 3 touchdowns, with 1 interception. Davis had 24 carries for 114 yards. Mark Brunell was 21 of 42 for 271 yards and 1 touchdown, with 2 interceptions. Fred Taylor had 22 carries for 124 yards. Kyle Brady had 8 receptions for 111 yards.

Washington	7	14	7	7	—	35
Jacksonville	3	13	0	0	—	16

Wash — Davis 1 run (Heppner kick)
Jax — FG Hollis 23
Jax — Soward 33 pass from Brunell (Hollis kick)
Wash — Connell 11 pass from Johnson (Heppner kick)
Wash — Connell 49 pass from Johnson (Heppner kick)
Jax — FG Hollis 33
Jax — FG Hollis 51
Wash — Connell 77 pass from Johnson (Heppner kick)
Wash — Davis 16 run (Heppner kick)

MONDAY NIGHT, OCTOBER 23

N.Y. JETS 40, MIAMI 37 (OT)—at Giants Stadium, attendance 78,389. The Jets scored 30 fourth-quarter points to overcome a 23-point fourth-quarter deficit to shock the Dolphins in overtime. The Dolphins scored on their first four possessions, highlighted by Lamar Smith's 68-yard touchdown run, to take a 20-0 lead. Vinny Testaverde engineered the two-minute offense to perfection, capped by his 10-yard touchdown pass to Wayne Chrebet.53 seconds before halftime, but Olindo Mare's 44-yard field goal just before the half staked Miami to a 23-7 lead. The Dolphins' defense, which entered the game allowing just 8.5 points per game, stopped Richie Anderson for no gain on fourth-and-1 at the Jets' 35. Smith's second touchdown run moments later gave Miami a 30-7 lead with 12 seconds left in the third quarter. The Jets went to a no-huddle offense and needed just 4 plays and 71 seconds to drive 75 yards, capped by Testaverde's 30-yard touchdown pass to Laveranues Coles. Testaverde's pass bounced off the hands of a Dolphins' defender before settling in Coles's hands. The Jets went for two points and missed, but the defense did not allow a first down and forced a punt. Testaverde's 1-yard touchdown pass to Jermaine Wiggins seven plays later cut the deficit to 30-20 with 9:51 remaining. The Jets' defense again forced a three-and-out, and the offense drove 64 yards in less than two minutes, capped by John Hall's 34-yard field goal, to pull within 30-23 with 5:43 left. Another three-and-out and a 33-yard punt to the Dolphins' 39 set up Testaverde's 24-yard touchdown pass to Wayne Chrebet to tie the game with 3:55 remaining. Brock Marion returned the ensuing kickoff 47 yards, and Jay Fiedler's 46-yard touchdown bomb to Leslie Shepherd on the next play allowed the Dolphins to regain the lead with 3:33 left. Kevin Williams's 37-yard kickoff return sparked a 9-play, 57-yard drive. Faced with fourth-and-1 from the Dolphins' 4, Testaverde completed a 2-yard pass to Anderson. Two plays later, Testaverde lofted a pass to tackle Jumbo Elliott, who bobbled the ball but held on for his first NFL catch to tie the game 37-37 with 42 seconds left. Marion returned the ensuing kickoff 37 yards to the Dolphins' 49, but Miami was forced to punt as time expired. Marcus Coleman intercepted Fiedler's pass three plays into overtime but fumbled during his return, and Oronde Gadsden recovered at the Dolphins' 34. Undaunted, Coleman intercepted Fielder again five plays later at the Jets' 34. Testaverde's 28-yard pass to Chrebet on third-and-3 set up Hall's game-winning 40-yard field goal 6:47 into overtime. The Jets' 30 fourth-quarter points were the most by an NFL team in 19 years. The Jets accumulated 20 of their 31 first downs in the fourth quarter. Testaverde was 36 of 59 for 378 yards and 5 touchdowns, with 3 interceptions. Anderson had 12 receptions for 109 yards. Fiedler was 16 of 35 for 250 yards and 2 touchdowns, with 3 interceptions. Smith had 23 carries for 155 yards, and Gadsden had 7 catches for 119 yards.

Miami	17	6	7	7	0	—	37
N.Y. Jets	0	7	0	30	3	—	40

Mia — FG Mare 28
Mia — Shepherd 42 pass from Fiedler (Mare kick)
Mia — Smith 68 run (Mare kick)
Mia — FG Mare 42
NYJ — Chrebet 10 pass from Testaverde (Hall kick)
Mia — FG Mare 44
Mia — Smith 3 run (Mare kick)
NYJ — Coles 30 pass from Testaverde (pass failed)
NYJ — Wiggins 1 pass from Testaverde (Hall kick)
NYJ — FG Hall 34
NYJ — Chrebet 24 pass from Testaverde (Hall kick)
Mia — Shepherd 46 pass from Fiedler (Mare kick)
NYJ — Elliott 3 pass from Testaverde (Hall kick)
NYJ — FG Hall 40

NINTH WEEK SUMMARIES

American Football Conference

Eastern Division	**W**	**L**	**T**	**Pct.**	**Pts.**	**OP**
Indianapolis	6	2	0	.750	232	171
Miami	6	2	0	.750	177	111
N.Y. Jets	6	2	0	.750	185	163
Buffalo	4	4	0	.500	163	173
New England	2	6	0	.250	143	171
Central Division						
Tennessee	7	1	0	.875	172	118
Pittsburgh	5	3	0	.625	130	84
Baltimore	5	4	0	.556	140	98
Jacksonville	3	6	0	.333	165	207
Cincinnati	2	6	0	.250	80	167
Cleveland	2	7	0	.222	98	209
Western Division						
Oakland	7	1	0	.875	207	141
Kansas City	5	3	0	.625	212	166
Denver	4	4	0	.500	238	178
Seattle	2	7	0	.222	140	224
San Diego	0	8	0	.000	130	219

National Football Conference

Eastern Division	**W**	**L**	**T**	**Pct.**	**Pts.**	**OP**
N.Y. Giants	6	2	0	.750	144	112
Washington	6	3	0	.667	170	142
Philadelphia	5	4	0	.556	188	134
Dallas	3	5	0	.375	191	197
Arizona	2	6	0	.250	131	231
Central Division						
Minnesota	7	1	0	.875	197	178
Detroit	5	3	0	.625	161	164
Tampa Bay	4	4	0	.500	205	138
Green Bay	3	5	0	.375	168	167
Chicago	1	7	0	.125	110	202
Western Division						
St. Louis	7	1	0	.875	330	252

New Orleans	5	3	0	.625	152	127
Carolina	3	5	0	.375	156	129
Atlanta	3	6	0	.333	162	250
San Francisco	2	7	0	.222	238	292

SUNDAY, OCTOBER 29

ATLANTA 13, CAROLINA 12—at Georgia Dome, attendance 46,178. The Falcons scored 10 points in a span of 2:11 late in the game to come from behind and snap their five-game losing streak. Joe Nedney's fourth field goal of the game, from 24 yards 2:20 into the final period, gave the Panthers a 12-3 lead. But Atlanta countered with the game's lone touchdown march, a 13-play, 80-yard drive capped by Jamal Anderson's 2-yard touchdown run with 5:04 remaining, to trim the deficit to 12-10. Twenty seconds later, Ray Buchanan intercepted a pass by Steve Beuerlein to position Morten Andersen for a 31-yard field goal with 2:53 to play. The kick held up for the winning points when the Panthers' final two possessions ended in a lost fumble and an interception. Chris Chandler was 19 of 29 for 191 yards, with 2 interceptions. Anderson rushed for 90 yards for the Falcons, who won for the first time since beating Carolina in week 3. Beuerlein was 21 of 41 for 202 yards, with 3 interceptions.

Carolina	3	3	3	3	—	12
Atlanta	3	0	0	10	—	13

Car — FG Nedney 35
Atl — FG Andersen 35
Car — FG Nedney 48
Car — FG Nedney 25
Car — FG Nedney 24
Atl — Anderson 2 run (Andersen kick)
Atl — FG Andersen 31

CINCINNATI 12, CLEVELAND 3—at Cleveland Browns Stadium, attendance 73,118. Corey Dillon rushed for 137 yards and the game's lone touchdown to pace the Bengals to their second consecutive victory. Cincinnati had not scored a point en route to losing its first three road games of the season, but Dillon ended that dubious string when he ran 1 yard for a touchdown 2:46 into the second quarter. Neil Rackers added a 39-yard field goal for a 10-0 lead in the third quarter, and the Bengals' defense took care of the rest, limiting the Browns to only 10 first downs and 182 total yards. Cleveland's lone score came on Phil Dawson's 18-yard field goal late in the third period, but it came after a goal-line stand on which the Bengals held on three consecutive running plays from the 1. Roman Oben was flagged for holding in the end zone midway through the fourth quarter to extend the Bengals' lead to nine points. Akili Smith was 7 of 20 for 84 yards, with 1 interception. Dillon, who carried 27 times, was coming off his NFL-record 278-yard effort against Denver one week earlier. His 415 yards against the Broncos and Browns was the third-most ever recorded in back-to-back games. The Browns managed only 54 yards on the ground the entire game and fared little better through the air as quarterbacks Spergon Wynn and Doug Pederson combined to complete only 13 of 32 passes for 147 yards.

Cincinnati	0	7	3	2	—	12
Cleveland	0	0	3	0	—	3

Cin — Dillon 1 run (Rackers kick)
Cin — FG Rackers 39
Cle — FG Dawson 18
Cin — Safety, Oben called for holding in end zone

INDIANAPOLIS 30, DETROIT 18—at RCA Dome, attendance 56,971. The Colts nearly squandered a 23-point first-half lead, but held off the Lions to win their third consecutive game. Peyton Manning completed 16 of 22 passes for 231 yards in the first half, including touchdown strikes of 31 yards to Marcus Pollard, 3 yards to Marvin Harrison, and 12 yards to Ken Dilger. The Colts also got a safety when defensive end Josh Williams sacked Charlie Batch in the end zone in the second quarter. But the Lions came alive in the third quarter, scoring 11 points on Mario Bates's 9-yard run, a two-point conversion run by James Stewart, and Jason Hanson's 21-yard field goal. And when Batch tossed a 5-yard touchdown pass to Herman Moore with 2:32 left in the game, Detroit trailed just 23-18. The Lions' defense held Indianapolis without a first down on the next possession, and Detroit got the ball back on its 20-yard line with 1:59 to play. But after a penalty moved the ball back to the 15, Batch was intercepted by David Macklin at the 26. Two plays later, Edgerrin James burst 24 yards for the clinching touchdown. Manning was 22 of 33 for 288 yards and 3 touchdowns, with 2 intercepitons. James added 139 yards on 31 carries for the Colts, who amassed 420 total yards. Batch was 18 of 39 for 190 yards. He was intercepted twice, sacked 3 times, and lost a fumble.

Detroit	0	0	11	7	—	18
Indianapolis	7	16	0	7	—	30

Ind — Pollard 31 pass from Manning (Vanderjagt kick)
Ind — Harrison 3 pass from Manning (Vanderjagt kick)
Ind — Safety, J. Williams sacked Batch in end zone
Ind — Dilger 12 pass from Manning (Vanderjagt kick)
Det — Bates 9 run (Stewart run)
Det — FG Hanson 21
Det — Moore 5 pass from Batch (Hanson kick)
Ind — James 24 run (Vanderjagt kick)

MIAMI 28, GREEN BAY 20—at Pro Player Stadium, attendance 73,740. The Dolphins spotted the Packers 17 first-half points, then roared back to win. After giving up 33 points to the Jets in the fourth quarter and overtime the previous Monday night, Miami's previously stingy defense got off to a bad start against Green Bay when Ryan Longwell kicked a 51-yard field goal on the Packers' first possession and Dorsey Levens ran for touchdowns on the next two. But the defense stiffened after that, allowing only a field goal by Longwell in the fourth quarter and giving the Dolphins time to rally. Jay Fiedler ran 1 yard for a touchdown late in the first half to pull Miami within 10 points, and the Dolphins took the lead for good by scoring 3 touchdowns in a span of 7:40 in the third quarter. Fiedler capped Miami's opening drive of the second half with a 15-yard touchdown pass to Oronde Gadsden, and Lamar Smith ran 4 yards for a touchdown and a 21-17 lead the next time the Dolphins had the ball. Green Bay punted on its next possession, and Jeff Ogden returned the kick 81 yards for a touchdown. Fiedler was 16 of 25 for 158 yards and 1 touchdown. He kept alive a streak in which he has thrown at least 1 touchdown pass in every Miami game this season. Brett Favre was 21 of 34 for 194 yards, but was intercepted and lost a fumble on Green Bay's final two possessions. Levens did not play in the second half after spraining his knee.

Green Bay	10	7	0	3	—	20
Miami	0	7	21	0	—	28

GB — FG Longwell 51
GB — Levens 1 run (Longwell kick)
GB — Levens 7 run (Longwell kick)
Mia — Fiedler 1 run (Mare kick)
Mia — Gadsden 15 pass from Fiedler (Mare kick)
Mia — L. Smith 4 run (Mare kick)
Mia — Ogden 81 punt return (Mare kick)
GB — FG Longwell 48

JACKSONVILLE 23, DALLAS 17 (OT)—at Texas Stadium, attendance 63,554. Mark Brunell and Alvis Whitted teamed on a 37-yard touchdown pass 4:44 into overtime to lift the Jaguars to their first victory in six weeks. The touchdown pass was the third of the game for Brunell and the second for Whitted, who saw more playing time than usual because of an injury to starting wide receiver Jimmy Smith. Brunell and Whitted teamed for the first time on a 3-yard touchdown pass nine seconds before halftime to give Jacksonville a 17-7 lead. But the Cowboys pulled within 17-10 on Tim Seder's 19-yard field goal midway through the third quarter, then forced overtime when backup quarterback Randall Cunningham dove 1 yard for the tying touchdown with 1:07 to play in regulation. Cunningham entered the game in the first quarter after starter Troy Aikman, who tossed a 13-yard touchdown pass to Jackie Harris on Dallas's first possession, was forced to leave the game with back spasms. The Jaguars took possession first in the extra session and quickly moved from their 34-yard line to the Cowboys' 37. On second-and-6, Brunell threw a quick out to Whitted, who shed a tackle and raced down the right sideline for the winning score. Brunell was 20 of 24 for 231 yards and 3 touchdowns. Kyle Brady caught 10 passes for 138 yards, while running back Fred Taylor added 107 yards on the ground. Cunningham was 13 of 20 for 177 yards, with 1 interception. Emmitt Smith paced the Cowboys with 102 yards on 24 carries.

Jacksonville	0	17	0	0	6	—	23
Dallas	7	0	3	7	0	—	17

Dall — Harris 13 pass from Aikman (Seder kick)
Jax — FG Hollis 42
Jax — Brady 3 pass from Brunell (Hollis kick)
Jax — Whitted 3 pass from Brunell (Hollis kick)
Dall — FG Seder 19
Dall — Cunningham 1 run (Seder kick)
Jax — Whitted 37 pass from Brunell

KANSAS CITY 24, SEATTLE 19—at Husky Stadium, attendance 62,141. Elvis Grbac passed for 3 touchdowns in the first half, and the Chiefs held off a fourth-quarter rally to deal the Seahawks their fifth consecutive defeat. Grbac teamed with Derrick Alexander for the first of his touchdown passes, a 59-yard strike in the final minute of the first quarter. Then, with Kansas City trailing 10-7 in the second quarter, Grbac completed touchdown passes of 50 yards to Alexander and 34 yards to Kevin Lockett on back-to-back possessions to give the Chiefs a 21-10 halftime lead. Seattle pulled within 21-19 when Rian Lindell kicked a 24-yard field goal and Jon Kitna passed 14 yards to Ricky Watters for a touchdown with 5:53 to go in the game, but the Seahawks' two-point conversion attempt failed. Kitna was intercepted by Pat Dennis on Seattle's next possession, and Kansas City converted the miscue into Todd Peterson's 37-yard field goal with 42 seconds remaining. The Seahawks got no further than their 44-yard line on their final possession. Grbac was 22 of 35 for 342 yards and 3 touchdowns, with 3 interceptions. Alexander had 137 yards on only 4 catches, while tight end Tony Gonzalez recorded his third consecutive 100-yard receiving day when he caught 8 passes for 101 yards. Kitna was 26 of 42 for 224 yards and 2 touchdowns, with 3 interceptions.

Kansas City	7	14	0	3	—	24
Seattle	3	7	0	9	—	19

Sea — FG Lindell 50
KC — Alexander 59 pass from Grbac (Peterson kick)
Sea — Fauria 2 pass from Kitna (Lindell kick)
KC — Alexander 50 pass from Grbac (Peterson kick)
KC — Lockett 34 pass from Grbac (Peterson kick)
Sea — FG Lindell 24
Sea — Watters 14 pass from Kitna (pass failed)
KC — FG Peterson 37

TAMPA BAY 41, MINNESOTA 13—at Raymond James Stadium, attendance 65,589. The Buccaneers snapped a four-game losing streak and ended the Vikings' dream of an undefeated season with a resounding victory. Tampa Bay had been struggling offensively, but scored on its first five possessions to build a 31-13 halftime lead, then coasted to the victory. Shaun King passed for 3 touchdowns in the first half and added another to close the scoring in the fourth quarter. His touchdowns went to four different receivers. The Buccaneers' defense did its part by forcing 3 turnovers, including a 34-yard interception return for a touchdown by Derrick Brooks. Warren Sapp set the tone seven plays into the game when he forced a fumble by Daunte Culpepper that Marcus Jones recovered. Tampa Bay quickly converted that into King's 9-yard touchdown pass to Keyshawn Johnson, and the Buccaneers never looked back. King was 16 of 23 for 267 yards and 4 touchdowns. Johnson had 6 catches for 121 yards, his first 100-yard receiving day since joining the team in an offseason trade with the New York Jets. Culpepper was 29 of 53 for 313 yards and 1 touchdown, with 2 intercepitons. Cris Carter caught 7 passes for 115 yards.

Minnesota	3	10	0	0	—	13
Tampa Bay	14	17	3	7	—	41

TB — Johnson 9 pass from King (Gramatica kick)
Minn — FG Anderson 30
TB — Dunn 23 pass from King (Gramatica kick)
Minn — Moss 7 pass from Culpepper (Anderson kick)
TB — Moore 21 pass from King (Gramatica kick)
TB — Brooks 34 interception return (Gramatica kick)
TB — FG Gramatica 47
Minn — FG Anderson 37
TB — FG Gramatica 37
TB — Anthony 16 pass from King (Gramatica kick)

NEW ORLEANS 21, ARIZONA 10—at Sun Devil Stadium, attendance 35,286. The Saints' defense finally bent, but still came up with the big play to lead New Orleans to its fourth consecutive victory. The Saints had the league's top-ranked defense until the Cardinals amassed 394 total yards, including 289 passing yards by Jake Plummer. But Arizona, playing its first game under interim head coach Dave McGinnis, managed its only touchdown on Plummer's 3-yard pass to Terry Hardy with 12 seconds remaining in the first quarter. It was the first time the Cardinals had scored a touchdown in the opening period in 25 games. Arizona led 10-7 in the third quarter when Keith Mitchell tipped Plummer's pass, gathered it in, and raced 53 yards for the go-ahead score. Ricky Williams's 1-yard touchdown run 4:28 into the fourth quarter provided the final margin of victory. Jeff Blake was 16 of 26 for 167 yards and 1 touchdown, with 1 interception. Williams had his string of five consecutive 100-yard rushing games snapped when he was limited to 54 yards on 21 carries. But he led all pass catchers with 9 receptions for 92 yards. Plummer was 26 of 47 for 289 yards and 1 touchdown, with 2 interceptions.

New Orleans	7	0	7	7	—	21
Arizona	7	3	0	0	—	10

NO — Hall 1 pass from Blake (Brien kick)
Ariz — Hardy 3 pass from Plummer (Blanchard kick)
Ariz — FG Blanchard 34
NO — Mitchell 53 interception return (Brien kick)
NO — R. Williams 1 run (Brien kick)

BUFFALO 23, N.Y. JETS 20—at Ralph Wilson Stadium, attendance 72,861. Steve Christie's 34-yard field goal as time ran out lifted the Bills to victory and foiled another comeback attempt by the Jets. New York, which was coming off a dramatic rally from 23 points down in the fourth quarter against the Dolphins the previous Monday night and had won four games with fourth-quarter comebacks this season, erased a 17-7 deficit in the third quarter when John Hall kicked a 40-yard field goal and Vinny Testaverde tossed a 10-yard touchdown pass to Wayne Chrebet. After the teams traded field goals in the fourth quarter, including Hall's 36-yard kick with 2:20 remaining, Doug Flutie engineered a 57-yard drive to set up the winning field goal. Flutie was 18 of 35 for 253 yards. His prime target was wide receiver Eric Moulds, who caught 6 passes for 137 yards. Testaverde was 28 of 38 for 293 yards and 2 touchdowns, with 2 interceptions. One of the thefts was returned 45 yards for a touchdown by Buffalo's Henry Jones.

N.Y. Jets	7	0	10	3	—	20
Buffalo	7	10	0	6	—	23

Buff — Morris 1 run (Christie kick)
NYJ — Baxter 12 pass from Testaverde (Hall kick)
Buff — FG Christie 20
Buff — H. Jones 45 interception return (Christie kick)
NYJ — FG Hall 40
NYJ — Chrebet 10 pass from Testaverde (Hall kick)
Buff — FG Christie 29
NYJ — FG Hall 36
Buff — FG Christie 34

N.Y. GIANTS 24, PHILADELPHIA 7—at Giants Stadium, attendance 78,087. Ron Dayne rushed for 93 yards and a touchdown, and Kerry Collins passed for a season-high 253 yards and a touchdown to lead the Giants past the Eagles for the second time this season and the eighth consecutive time overall. Collins's 36-yard pass to Tiki Barber was the key play on a 74-yard touchdown drive midway through the first quarter that opened the scoring, a march capped by Dayne's 1-yard burst. Late in the first half, Collins teamed with Amani Toomer on a 27-yard touchdown pass that gave New York a 14-0 lead 1:31 before intermission. The Giants never were seriously threatened in the second half, building a 24-0 advantage and controlling the ball for 24:30 of the game's final 30 minutes. In all, New York had sizeable advantages in first downs (25 to 8), total plays (84 to 46), total yards (384 to 192), and time of possession (43:41 to 16:19). Philadelphia did not score until Donovan McNabb tossed a 25-yard touchdown pass to Charles Johnson with 5:12 to go. Collins was 22 of 37 for 253 yards and 1 touchdown. McNabb was 10 of 31 for 129 yards and 1 touchdown, with 1 interception.

Philadelphia	0	0	0	7	—	7
N.Y. Giants	7	7	0	10	—	24

NYG — Dayne 1 run (Daluiso kick)
NYG — Toomer 27 pass from Collins (Daluiso kick)
NYG — FG Daluiso 31
NYG — Montgomery 4 run (Daluiso kick)
Phil — C. Johnson 25 pass from McNabb (Akers kick)

PITTSBURGH 9, BALTIMORE 6—at PSINet Stadium, attendance 69,405. The Steelers won their fifth in a row while the Ravens failed to score a touchdown for the fifth consecutive game and lost their third consecutive game. Kordell Stewart teamed with Hines Ward on a 45-yard pass for the game's only touchdown, and Kris Brown kicked a tie-breaking, 24-yard field goal in the third quarter for Pittsburgh, which moved past Baltimore and into second place in the AFC Central Division. Baltimore's string of quarters without a touchdown reached 20, just 2 behind the record, established by the Chicago Bears in 1974. Matt Stover kicked field goals of 51 and 49 yards and had scored all 46 of Baltimore's points dating back to week 4. Trent Dilfer got his first start at quarterback for the Ravens but was only 11 of 24 for 152 yards, with 1 interception. He fumbled deep in Steelers' territory on Baltimore's first possession and later was intercepted in the end zone. Stewart was 9 of 18 for 133 yards and 1 touchdown. Pittsburgh's defense did not allow a touchdown for the fourth consecutive game.

Pittsburgh	0	0	9	0	—	9
Baltimore	0	6	0	0	—	6

Balt — FG Stover 51
Balt — FG Stover 49
Pitt — Ward 45 pass from Stewart (kick failed)
Pitt — FG Brown 24

ST. LOUIS 34, SAN FRANCISCO 24—at 3Com Park, attendance 68,109. Marshall Faulk rushed for 2 touchdowns and caught 2 touchdown passes from Trent Green, who won in his first start at quarterback for the Rams. Faulk had a pair of 1-yard touchdown runs in the first half, but the 49ers had a 17-14 edge at intermission. San Francisco still led 24-17 when Green tossed a 19-yard touchdown pass to an uncovered Faulk to tie the game late in the third quarter. The next time the Rams had the ball, the two teamed again on a 16-yard scoring strike that gave St. Louis the lead for good with 10:21 remaining. Pete Stoyanovich's 46-yard field goal with 3:45 left secured the victory. Green, who was slated to become the Rams' starting quarterback in 1999 before missing the season with a torn knee ligament, played in place of Kurt Warner, who had surgery for a broken finger on his passing hand. After a slow start, Green was 22 of 39 for 310 yards and 2 touchdowns, with 1 interception. Faulk, who raised his touchdown total to a league-leading 14, rushed for 83 yards and caught 6 passes for 61 yards. Isaac Bruce caught 8 passes for 129 yards. Jeff Garcia was 26 of 44 for 243 yards and 2 touchdowns to Terrell Owens, who had 8 receptions for 115 yards.

St. Louis	7	7	10	10	—	34
San Francisco	7	10	7	0	—	24

SF — Garner 4 run (Richey kick)
StL — Faulk 1 run (Stoyanovich kick)
SF — FG Richey 44
StL — Faulk 1 run (Stoyanovich kick)
SF — Owens 53 pass from Garcia (Richey kick)
StL — FG Stoyanovich 48
SF — Owens 17 pass from Garcia (Richey kick)
StL — Faulk 19 pass from Green (Stoyanovich kick)
StL — Faulk 16 pass from Green (Stoyanovich kick)
StL — FG Stoyanovich 46

SUNDAY NIGHT, OCTOBER 29

OAKLAND 15, SAN DIEGO 13—at Qualcomm Stadium, attendance 66,659. Sebastian Janikowski kicked 5 field goals, including the game winner from 24 yards out with 13 seconds left, to give the Raiders their fifth consecutive victory and keep the Chargers winless. Janikowski, Oakland's first-round pick in the 2000 draft, made 4 field goals in the first half to stake the Raiders to a 12-0 lead. But San Diego took the second-half kickoff and marched 76 yards, capped by Jim Harbaugh's 8-yard touchdown pass to Freddie Jones. In the fourth quarter, the two teamed again for a 21-yard touchdown pass that gave the Chargers a 13-12 lead with 5:58 remaining. The two-point conversion attempt failed, however, and the Raiders kept the ball for the next 13 plays, driving 58 yards to set up the winning kick. Oakland managed only 228 total yards, but limited San Diego to 224 yards, including just 29 on the ground. Rich Gannon was 16 of 35 for 156 yards, with 1 interception. Harbaugh was 25 of 35 for 222 yards and 2 touchdowns, with 1 interception. Jones had 10 catches for 111 yards for the Chargers.

Oakland	9	3	0	3	—	15
San Diego	0	0	7	6	—	13

Oak — FG Janikowski 40
Oak — FG Janikowski 40
Oak — FG Janikowski 54
Oak — FG Janikowski 29
SD — F. Jones 8 pass from Harbaugh (Carney kick)
SD — F. Jones 21 pass from Harbaugh (pass failed)
Oak — FG Janikowski 24

MONDAY NIGHT, OCTOBER 30

TENNESSEE 27, WASHINGTON 21—at FedEx Field, attendance 83,472. The Titans struggled on offense much of the night, but got touchdowns on defense and special teams to outlast the Redskins and increase their winning streak to seven games. Washington lost for the first time in six weeks. Tennessee, which managed only 191 total yards in a victory over Baltimore in week 8, had just 189 yards against the Redskins, including only 71 in the first half. Still, the Titans went to the locker room at halftime with a 20-7 lead, built largely on the strength of a 69-yard punt return for a touchdown by Derrick Mason and an 81-yard interception return for a touchdown by Samari Rolle. The latter play came on the final snap of the first half. Time expired shortly after Rolle stepped in front of Albert Connell to intercept the pass at Tennessee's 19-yard line, but the cornerback worked his way across and down the field to reach the end zone. In the fourth quarter, the Titans sustained their best drive of the night, a 9-play, 63-yard march aided by two penalties and capped by Steve McNair's 18-yard touchdown pass to Frank Wycheck with 10:12 to go in the game. The touchdown stood up as the game winner, offsetting a pair of Washington touchdowns in the second half, including Brad Johnson's 3-yard touchdown pass to Larry Centers with 6:42 left. Johnson was 21 of 40 passes for 202 yards and 2 touchdowns, but was intercepted 3 times, including twice on the Redskins' final two possessions. McNair was 14 of 18 passes for 96 yards and 1 touchdown.

Tennessee	0	20	0	7	—	27
Washington	7	0	7	7	—	21

Wash — Sellers 5 pass from Johnson (Heppner kick)
Tenn — FG Del Greco 46
Tenn — Mason 69 punt return (Del Greco kick)
Tenn — FG Del Greco 21
Tenn — Rolle 81 interception return (Del Greco kick)
Wash — Davis 1 run (Heppner kick)
Tenn — Wycheck 18 pass from McNair (Del Greco kick)
Wash — Centers 3 pass from Johnson (Heppner kick)

TENTH WEEK SUMMARIES

American Football Conference

Eastern Division	**W**	**L**	**T**	**Pct.**	**Pts.**	**OP**
Miami	7	2	0	.778	200	119
Indianapolis	6	3	0	.667	256	198
N.Y. Jets	6	3	0	.667	208	193
Buffalo	5	4	0	.556	179	186
New England	2	7	0	.222	156	187
Central Division						
Tennessee	8	1	0	.889	181	125
Baltimore	6	4	0	.600	167	105
Pittsburgh	5	4	0	.556	137	93
Jacksonville	3	6	0	.333	165	207
Cincinnati	2	7	0	.222	87	194
Cleveland	2	8	0	.200	101	233
Western Division						
Oakland	8	1	0	.889	256	172
Denver	5	4	0	.556	268	201
Kansas City	5	4	0	.556	243	215

	W	L	T	Pct.	Pts.	OP
Seattle	3	7	0	.300	157	239
San Diego	0	9	0	.000	145	236
National Football Conference						
Eastern Division	**W**	**L**	**T**	**Pct.**	**Pts.**	**OP**
N.Y. Giants	7	2	0	.778	168	115
Philadelphia	6	4	0	.600	204	147
Washington	6	4	0	.600	185	158
Arizona	3	6	0	.333	147	246
Dallas	3	6	0	.333	204	213
Central Division						
Minnesota	7	2	0	.778	217	204
Detroit	5	4	0	.556	169	187
Tampa Bay	5	4	0	.556	232	152
Green Bay	4	5	0	.444	194	187
Chicago	2	7	0	.222	137	226
Western Division						
St. Louis	7	2	0	.778	354	279
New Orleans	6	3	0	.667	183	142
Carolina	4	5	0	.444	183	153
Atlanta	3	7	0	.300	176	277
San Francisco	2	8	0	.200	253	323

SUNDAY, NOVEMBER 5

BALTIMORE 27, CINCINNATI 7—at Paul Brown Stadium, attendance 54,759. Trent Dilfer's 14-yard touchdown pass to Brandon Stokley ended the Ravens' long touchdown drought and sparked Baltimore to the victory. The Ravens had not scored a touchdown since reaching the end zone four times against the Bengals in week 4. The streak reached 21 quarters—falling 1 quarter shy of equaling the 1974 Bears for the longest stretch since the AFL-NFL merger in 1970—before Stokley took a short crossing pattern from Dilfer and raced to the corner of the end zone 53 seconds into the second quarter. Dilfer then passed for touchdowns to Shannon Sharpe on each of Baltimore's next two possessions as the Ravens built a 24-0 halftime lead. Dilfer was 23 of 34 for 244 yards and 3 touchdowns. Rookie Jamal Lewis rushed for 109 yards for Baltimore, which outgained the Bengals 378 to 174. Akili Smith was 15 of 27 for 137 yards. Corey Dillon, who had rushed for 415 yards in victories the previous two weeks, was limited to only 23 yards on 16 carries by the Ravens' top-ranked defense.

Baltimore	3	21	0	3	—	27
Cincinnati	0	0	7	0	—	7

Balt — FG Stover 38
Balt — Stokley 14 pass from Dilfer (Stover kick)
Balt — Sharpe 18 pass from Dilfer (Stover kick)
Balt — Sharpe 19 pass from Dilfer (Stover kick)
Cin — Warrick 4 run (Rackers kick)
Balt — FG Stover 32

BUFFALO 16, NEW ENGLAND 13 (OT)—at Foxboro Stadium, attendance 60,292. Steve Christie tied the game with a 48-yard field goal with eight seconds to play in regulation, then won it for the Bills with a 32-yard kick 4:21 into overtime. The Patriots, with backup quarterback John Friesz in for injured starter Drew Bledsoe, rallied from a 10-0 second-quarter deficit to take the lead for the first time at 13-10 on Adam Vinatieri's 43-yard field goal with 2:03 left in regulation. Buffalo began its next possession at its 24 with 1:57 to go. With quarterback Doug Flutie completing 5 of 8 passes, the Bills marched to New England's 15 with 13 seconds remaining. A delay-of-game penalty and an offensive-pass-interference penalty moved the ball back to the 30, but Christie kicked a low line drive from 48 yards to force overtime. Buffalo held the Patriots without a first down on the first possession of overtime, then began a drive from its 35. A 22-yard pass-interference penalty against Ty Law moved the ball into Patriots' territory, and Shawn Bryson's 15-yard run to the 22 helped set up the winning kick. Both teams struggled on offense on the cold, wet day. Flutie was 18 of 37 for 179 yards and 1 touchdown. Friesz was 11 of 21 for 66 yards, with 1 interception.

Buffalo	3	7	0	3	3	—	16
New England	0	3	0	10	0	—	13

Buff — FG Christie 19
Buff — Riemersma 9 pass from Flutie (Christie kick)
NE — FG Vinatieri 48
NE — Redmond 1 run (Vinatieri kick)
NE — FG Vinatieri 43
Buff — FG Christie 48
Buff — FG Christie 32

PHILADELPHIA 16, DALLAS 13 (OT)—at Veterans Stadium, attendance 65,636. David Akers kicked 3 field goals in the fourth quarter and overtime as the Eagles overcame a 10-point deficit to complete their first season sweep of the Cowboys since 1990. Dallas built a 10-0 lead though three quarters behind Emmitt Smith, who rushed for 134 yards, including a 7-yard touchdown to open the scoring 4:42 into the second quarter. But Akers got Philadelphia on the scoreboard when he capped a 63-yard drive by kicking a 34-yard field goal two minutes into the fourth quarter. The next time the Eagles got the ball, they marched from their 21 to the Cowboys' 46. From there, quarterback Donovan McNabb took over, running for a 23-yard gain, then completing a 23-yard touchdown pass to Darnell Autry to tie the score at 10-10 with 7:22 left in regulation. Neither team managed a first down on its next two possessions until Dallas drove 49 yards to set up Tim Seder's 27-yard field goal with 1:51 remaining, with almost all of the yardage coming on a 46-yard pass-interference penalty against the Eagles. But Philadelphia countered with a 54-yard march, the key play coming on a 19-yard scramble by McNabb, leading to Akers's game-tying 34-yard field goal with 11 seconds to go. In overtime, Tim Hauck recovered a fumble by Robert Thomas at Dallas's 48. Seven plays later and 7:55 into overtime, Akers's 32-yard field goal won it. McNabb, who was 23 of 41 and 1 touchdown with 3 interceptions, accounted for most of Philadelphia's 357 total yards by passing for 228 yards and running for 58. Randall Cunningham, playing in place of injured starter Troy Aikman, returned to the city in which he played for 11 seasons from 1985-1995, but was only 14 of 22 for 109 yards, with 1 interception.

Dallas	0	7	3	3	0	—	13
Philadelphia	0	0	0	13	3	—	16

Dall — Smith 7 run (Seder kick)
Dall — FG Seder 48
Phil — FG Akers 34
Phil — Autry 23 pass from McNabb (Akers kick)
Dall — FG Seder 27
Phil — FG Akers 34
Phil — FG Akers 32

DENVER 30, N.Y. JETS 23—at Giants Stadium, attendance 78,305. Brian Griese passed for 327 yards and 2 touchdowns, and Terrell Davis rushed for 115 yards and a touchdown to carry the Broncos to the victory. Griese, who completed 22 of 35 passes, opened the scoring with a 1-yard touchdown pass to Ed McCaffrey. In the fourth quarter, the two teamed again on a 47-yard touchdown pass that proved to be decisive. In between, Denver gave the ball often to Davis, who was in the lineup for the first time since week 4 because of foot and ankle injuries he suffered in the season opener. Davis carried the ball 33 times en route to his first 100-yard game since Super Bowl XXXIII. His 4-yard touchdown run 9:27 before halftime gave the Broncos a seemingly comfortable 17-0 lead. The Jets, who had trailed in five of their six victories to this point, rallied, pulling even at 20-20 on John Hall's 26-yard field goal with 5:24 remaining in the third quarter. But three plays later, Griese teamed with Rod Smith on a 49-yard pass completion to set up Jason Elam's 23-yard field goal on the final play of the third quarter, giving Denver the lead for good. The next time the Broncos had the ball, Griese's long touchdown pass to McCaffrey built a 10-point lead with nine minutes remaining. New York quickly countered with a 46-yard field goal drive, pulling within seven points on Hall's 28-yard field goal at the 4:45 mark. After forcing a punt, the Jets drove from their 34 to the Broncos' 2 with 49 seconds remaining, but Vinny Testaverde threw incomplete into the end zone on four consecutive passes to end the threat. Testaverde was 21 of 42 for 293 yards and 1 touchdown, with 2 interceptions. Griese was 22 of 35 for 327 yards and 2 touchdowns, with 1 interception. Smith had 5 receptions for 134 yards.

Denver	10	10	3	7	—	30
N.Y. Jets	0	10	10	3	—	23

Den — McCaffrey 1 pass from Griese (Elam kick)
Den — FG Elam 31
Den — Davis 4 run (Elam kick)
NYJ — Martin 1 run (Hall kick)
Den — FG Elam 41
NYJ — FG Hall 45
NYJ — Becht 1 pass from Testaverde (Hall kick)
NYJ — FG Hall 26
Den — FG Elam 23
Den — McCaffrey 47 pass from Griese (Elam kick)
NYJ — FG Hall 28

CHICAGO 27, INDIANAPOLIS 24—at Soldier Field, attendance 66,944. The Bears stunned the Colts, jumping out to a 27-0 lead before hanging on to win at the end. Curtis Enis ran 11 yards for a touchdown, Marcus Robinson caught a 34-yard touchdown pass from Jim Miller, and Paul Edinger kicked 2 field goals to help Chicago forge a 20-0 lead by halftime. And when Walt Harris intercepted Peyton Manning's pass and returned it 35 yards for a touchdown just 78 seconds into the third quarter, the Bears had a seemingly insurmountable 27-point lead. But Indianapolis, whose high-powered offense managed only 2 first downs and 69 yards in the first half, began a drive at its 26 and marched 74 yards in 11 plays, capped by Edgerrin James's 1-yard touchdown run and a two-point conversion pass from Manning to Marcus Pollard. The next time they had the ball, the Colts drove 71 yards in 14 plays to set up Mike Vanderjagt's 19-yard field goal 4:27 into the fourth quarter. The Colts followed with a 6-play, 60-yard march that resulted in Manning's 21-yard touchdown pass to James that trimmed Indianapolis's deficit to 27-17 with 8:21 to play, though the two-point conversion attempt failed. After forcing another punt, the Colts covered 79 yards in only 79 seconds, pulling within 27-24 on Manning's 19-yard touchdown pass to Jerome Pathon at the 1:36 mark. Indianapolis had a chance to win or tie after recovering the ensuing onside kick at its 42, but on second down from the 38, Manning was sacked by Rosevelt Colvin and fumbled. Phillip Daniels recovered to seal the Bears' victory. Miller was 24 of 35 for 214 yards and 1 touchdown. The Bears amassed 273 of their 370 yards in the first two quarters. Manning was 26 of 39 for 302 yards and 3 touchdowns, with 1 interception. James rushed for 68 yards and eclipsed 2,500 career rushing yards in his twenty-fifth game. Only Pro Football Hall of Fame running back Eric Dickerson, who did it in 23 games, reached that plateau faster.

Indianapolis	0	0	8	16	—	24
Chicago	10	10	7	0	—	27

Chi — Enis 11 run (Edinger kick)
Chi — FG Edinger 41
Chi — M. Robinson 34 pass from Miller (Edinger kick)
Chi — FG Edinger 37
Chi — W. Harris 35 interception return (Edinger kick)
Ind — James 1 run (Pollard pass from Manning)
Ind — FG Vanderjagt 19
Ind — James 21 pass from Manning (run failed)
Ind — Pathon 19 pass from Manning (Vanderjagt kick)

OAKLAND 49, KANSAS CITY 31—at Network Associates Coliseum, attendance 62,428. The Raiders swept the season series from their bitter rivals for the first time since 1988 and opened up a three-game lead in the AFC Western Division behind a barrage of touchdowns. Rich Gannon passed for 4 touchdowns, 2 each to Andre Rison and Rickey Dudley; and Zack Crockett, Tyrone Wheatley, and Randy Jordan each ran for touchdowns for Oakland, which built a 14-0 lead on its first two possessions and led by as many as 25 points in the third quarter. The Raiders amassed 473 total yards to help offset a 504-yard passing performance by Elvis Grbac. Gannon completed 20 of 31 for 242 yards and 4 touchdowns, while Wheatley added 112 rushing yards on 20 carries. The Raiders played without rookie kicker Sebastian Janikowski, who developed a bacterial infection in his foot and left the field after pregame warmups. Rookie punter Shane Lechler took over the kicking duties and made all 7 of his extra-point attempts. He missed his only field-goal try from 33 yards. Grbac was 39 of 53 passes and 2 touchdowns, and became only the eighth player in NFL history to surpass 500 yards in a game, but also was intercepted twice. He tried to rally his team by passing for 2 touchdowns and running for another, but could get Kansas City no closer than 11 points in the second half. Derrick Alexander caught 9 passes for 139 yards. Tony Gonzalez became the first tight end in NFL history to surpass 100 yards in four consecutive games when he had 9 receptions for 134 yards. Sylvester Morris also had a 100-yard day, catching 6 passes for 102 yards.

Kansas City	0	10	7	14	—	31
Oakland	14	14	7	14	—	49

Oak — Rison 10 pass from Gannon (Lechler kick)
Oak — Crockett 1 run (Lechler kick)
KC — Richardson 1 run (Peterson kick)
Oak — Rison 6 pass from Gannon (Lechler kick)
Oak — Wheatley 1 run (Lechler kick)
KC — FG Peterson 32
Oak — Dudley 20 pass from Gannon (Lechler kick)
KC — Alexander 9 pass from Grbac (Peterson kick)
KC — Alexander 48 pass from Grbac (Peterson kick)
Oak — Dudley 2 pass from Gannon (Lechler kick)
KC — Grbac 3 run (Peterson kick)
Oak — Jordan 43 run (Lechler kick)

MIAMI 23, DETROIT 8—at Pontiac Silverdome, attendance 77,813. The Dolphins built a 14-0 lead before the Lions' offense ever took the field and never were seriously challenged in Bobby Ross's final game as Detroit's coach. After Autry Denson returned the opening kickoff 56 yards, Lamar Smith raced 46 yards for a touchdown on the first play from scrimmage to give the Dolphins the lead just 21 seconds into the game. Miami then stunned the Lions with a successful onside kick, recovering at its 41. Eight plays later, Smith's 8-yard touchdown run gave the Dolphins a 14-point advantage. Detroit mounted few threats to that lead, punting on 6 of its 10 possessions and turning over the ball on 3 others. The Lions' lone touchdown came on James Stewart's 3-yard run 3:59 into the fourth quarter. Jay Fiedler was 13 of 18 for 112 yards. Smith carried 24 times for 125 yards, and Olindo Mare had 3 field goals for the Dolphins, who moved into first place in the AFC East when the Colts and Jets lost. Charlie Batch and Stoney Case combined to complete 15 of 27 for 169 yards, with 1 interception. Ross resigned as Detroit's coach the next day, even though his team was 5-4 and in the NFC playoff chase.

Miami	14	3	6	0	—	23
Detroit	0	0	0	8	—	8

Mia — L. Smith 46 run (Mare kick)
Mia — L. Smith 8 run (Mare kick)
Mia — FG Mare 40
Mia — FG Mare 38
Mia — FG Mare 41
Det — Stewart 3 run (Morton pass from Case)

N.Y. GIANTS 24, CLEVELAND 3—at Cleveland Browns Stadium, attendance 72,718. Kerry Collins passed for 257 yards and 3 touchdowns to lead the Giants to their fourth consecutive victory. The score was tied 3-3 late in the second quarter when Collins gave New York the lead for good with a 28-yard touchdown strike to Ike Hilliard. In the second half, Collins put the game out of reach with touchdown passes of 17 and 32 yards to Amani Toomer. The Giants' defense did the rest, limiting the Browns to 193 total yards. Cleveland had the ball just four times in the second half, punting three times and turning it over once, while New York controlled possession for 20:36 of the final 30 minutes. Collins was 19 of 31 for 257 yards and 3 touchdowns, and running backs Ron Dayne (64 yards) and Tiki Barber (53) combined for 117 yards. Doug Pederson was 17 of 29 for 176 yards, with 1 interception.

N.Y. Giants	0	10	7	7	—	24
Cleveland	3	0	0	0	—	3

Cle — FG Dawson 19
NYG — FG Daluiso 39
NYG — Hilliard 28 pass from Collins (Daluiso kick)
NYG — Toomer 17 pass from Collins (Daluiso kick)
NYG — Toomer 32 pass from Collins (Daluiso kick)

TENNESSEE 9, PITTSBURGH 7—at Adelphia Coliseum, attendance 68,498. The Titans could not crack the end zone against the Steelers' stingy defense, but pulled out their eighth consecutive victory and snapped Pittsburgh's five-game winning streak when Al Del Greco kicked 3 field goals, including the game winner from 29 yards out with four seconds left. Del Greco kicked field goals of 21 yards and 31 yards to stake Tennessee to a 6-0 lead early in the fourth quarter. But after the second kick, which came with 12:49 to play, the Steelers mounted their lone scoring drive of the day and took the lead on Kordell Stewart's 30-yard touchdown pass to tight end Mark Bruener with 6:33 left. After an exchange of punts, the Titans began the winning march from their 26 with 3:42 to play. Consecutive completions from Steve McNair to Derrick Mason quickly moved the ball into Pittsburgh territory, and on fourth-and-8 from the 42, the pair teamed again on a crucial 17-yard pass at the two-minute warning. Two runs by Eddie George and another by McNair positioned Del Greco for the decisive kick. McNair was 20 of 31 for 227 yards, with 1 interception. George added 98 yards on the ground for Tennessee, which amassed 364 total yards but failed to score a touchdown on five trips inside the red zone. Stewart was 7 of 22 for 112 yards and 1 touchdown, with 1 interception. Pittsburgh did not allow a touchdown for the fifth consecutive game, the longest streak in the NFL since the 1976 Steelers, who also had a five-game string. But Pittsburgh's offense managed only 10 first downs and 167 total yards while maintaining possession for just 20:30 of the game's 60 minutes.

Pittsburgh	0	0	0	7	—	7
Tennessee	0	3	0	6	—	9

Tenn — FG Del Greco 21
Tenn — FG Del Greco 31
Pitt — Bruener 30 pass from Stewart (Brown kick)
Tenn — FG Del Greco 29

SEATTLE 17, SAN DIEGO 15—at Husky Stadium, attendance 59,884. The Seahawks handed the Chargers another crushing defeat when Rian Lindell kicked a 48-yard field goal as time ran out. San Diego fell to 0-9 but didn't go down without a fight. After falling behind 14-0 on 2 second-quarter touchdown passes by Jon Kitna, the Chargers rallied behind 3 field goals by John Carney and Jim Harbaugh's 10-yard touchdown pass to Curtis Conway. Carney's final field goal, from 28 yards with 5:36 to play, gave San Diego the lead for the first time at 15-14. But the Seahawks began their next possession at their 34 and never gave up the ball. They had three third-down conversions, including a crucial third-and-16 from the Chargers' 37, when Kitna completed an 18-yard pass to Darrell Jackson. Seattle got as far as the 14 before a penalty and three consecutive losses on running plays pushed the ball back to the 30 with three seconds left. From there, Lindell made his winning kick. San Diego lost despite enjoying advantages in first downs (22 to 9), total yards (398 to 128), and time of possession (39:51 to 20:09). But the Chargers also had 3 turnovers and 9 penalties en route to their fifth loss by 3 points or less. Kitna was 11 of 19 for 85 yards and 2 touchdowns, with 1 interception. Harbaugh was 22 of 32 for 236 yards and 1 touchdown, with 1 interception.

San Diego	0	3	9	3	—	15
Seattle	0	14	0	3	—	17

Sea — Dawkins 10 pass from Kitna (Lindell kick)
Sea — Fauria 10 pass from Kitna (Lindell kick)
SD — FG Carney 19
SD — FG Carney 41
SD — Conway 10 pass from Harbaugh (run failed)
SD — FG Carney 28
Sea — FG Lindell 48

NEW ORLEANS 31, SAN FRANCISCO 15—at Louisiana Superdome, attendance 64,900. Jeff Blake passed for 3 touchdowns as New Orleans won its fifth consecutive game while handing the 49ers their fifth straight defeat. The Saints wasted little time taking command, scoring touchdowns on all four of their first-half possessions en route to a 28-0 lead at intermission. Blake capped New Orleans's first two drives with short touchdown passes to Andrew Glover and Willie Jackson, then tossed a 43-yard bomb to Joe Horn to break open the game 4:34 before halftime. It was 31-0 before the 49ers scored midway through the third quarter. The Saints were so dominant that they did not punt until early in the fourth quarter. Blake was 20 of 26 for 275 yards and 3 touchdowns. Jeff Garcia was 22 of 36 for 262 yards and 1 touchdown, with 2 interceptions.

San Francisco	0	0	7	8	—	15
New Orleans	7	21	3	0	—	31

NO — Glover 1 pass from Blake (Brien kick)
NO — Jackson 4 pass from Blake (Brien kick)
NO — Horn 43 pass from Blake (Brien kick)
NO — Williams 1 run (Brien kick)
NO — FG Brien 44
SF — Garner 1 run (Richey kick)
SF — Jackson 11 pass from Garcia (Jackson run)

TAMPA BAY 27, ATLANTA 14—at Georgia Dome, attendance 70,097. Shaun King passed for 3 touchdowns as the Buccaneers handed the Falcons their sixth loss in seven games. The Buccaneers' defense and special teams helped set King up for short scoring tosses to Dave Moore and Keyshawn Johnson for a 14-0 lead at halftime. Donnie Abraham intercepted Chris Chandler's pass and returned it 23 yards to the Falcons' 22 to set up the first touchdown, and John McLaughlin's blocked punt, which gave Tampa Bay the ball at Atlanta's 3, led to the second. The Buccaneers took a 24-7 lead in the fourth quarter when King capped an 80-yard drive with a 29-yard touchdown pass to Johnson with 7:59 to play. The Falcons managed a pair of touchdown passes from Danny Kanell to Terance Mathis, the last coming with just three seconds to play. King was 11 of 25 for 110 yards and 3 touchdowns, with 1 interception. Kanell took over for injured starter Chris Chandler, who had to leave the game with a concussion after being sacked on three consecutive plays in the second quarter. Kanell was 26 of 43 for 218 yards and 2 touchdowns, with 2 interceptions.

Tampa Bay	7	7	3	10	—	27
Atlanta	0	0	7	7	—	14

TB — Moore 1 pass from King (Gramatica kick)
TB — Johnson 5 pass from King (Gramatica kick)
Atl — Mathis 19 pass from Kanell (Andersen kick)
TB — FG Gramatica 51
TB — Johnson 29 pass from King (Gramatica kick)
TB — FG Gramatica 34
Atl — Mathis 16 pass from Kanell (Andersen kick)

ARIZONA 16, WASHINGTON 15—at Sun Devil Stadium, attendance 52,244. Aeneas Williams's NFL-record-tying 104-yard fumble return for a touchdown highlighted the Cardinals' upset of the Redskins. Washington took the opening kickoff and quickly marched deep into Arizona territory. On second-and-goal from the 1, Stephen Davis fumbled into the end zone, where Williams picked up the loose ball four yards deep and sprinted all the way down the left sideline for a touchdown. He joined Oakland's Jack Tatum, who returned a fumble 104 yards for a touchdown in a game against Green Bay in 1972, in the record book. Davis later had a 1-yard touchdown run to pull the Redskins within 10-9 midway through the second quarter, but Washington failed to convert the extra point, which would prove costly. Kris Heppner's 28-yard field goal with 1:52 left in the second quarter gave the Redskins the lead at 12-10, but the advantage was short-lived. MarTay Jenkins returned the second-half kickoff 71 yards to Washington's 20, and it took only three plays for the Cardinals to convert that into Michael Pittman's 7-yard touchdown run for a 16-12 lead. Heppner pulled the Redskins within a point with his third field goal, from 29 yards out with 4:43 to go in the third quarter, but missed from 51 and 33 yards on Washington's next two possessions. The Redskins' last chance ended when Jeff George threw four consecutive incompletions from his team's 24-yard line inside of two minutes. Jake Plummer was 12 of 19 for 146 yards, with 1 interception. George, making his first start for Washington in place of injured Brad Johnson, was 20 of 39 for 276 yards, with 2 interceptions. Davis rushed for 124 yards for the Redskins, who outgained Arizona 431 yards to 178 but could not overcome 3 turnovers, 8 penalties, and the missed kicks.

Washington	3	9	3	0	—	15
Arizona	10	0	6	0	—	16

Ariz — Williams 104 fumble return (Blanchard kick)
Ariz — FG Blanchard 30
Wash — FG Heppner 35
Wash — Davis 1 run (kick failed)
Wash — FG Heppner 28
Ariz — Pittman 7 run (pass failed)
Wash — FG Heppner 29

2000 WEEK BY WEEK

SUNDAY NIGHT, NOVEMBER 5

CAROLINA 27, ST. LOUIS 24—at Trans World Dome, attendance 66,048. The Panthers stunned the Rams when Joe Nedney kicked his fourth field goal of the game, from 46 yards out with 40 seconds left. The loss was the second in three games for the defending Super Bowl champions, who had their 13-game home winning streak snapped and failed to score 30 points or more in a game for the first time in 15 regular-season games dating to last year. St. Louis amassed 426 total yards, but stymied itself with 7 penalties, 2 fumbles, and 2 missed field goals. Carolina, meanwhile, was efficient, managing only 268 total yards but scoring on each of its six trips inside Rams' territory. The Panthers trailed 24-16 early in the fourth quarter when Doug Evans recovered a fumble by Isaac Bruce at the Rams' 26. It took Carolina only 10 seconds to convert that into Steve Beuerlein's 13-yard touchdown pass to Donald Hayes. Beuerlein's subsequent two-point conversion run tied the game at 24-24. Trent Green's 79-yard touchdown bomb to Bruce on the next play from scrimmage was nullified by a penalty, and the Panthers eventually got the ball back at their 27 with 6:21 to go. After two first downs, Tshimanga Biakabutuka kept the winning, 13-play drive alive with a key 10-yard run on fourth-and-2 from St. Louis's 42 with two minutes left. Four plays later, Nedney made his winning kick. Beuerlein was 15 of 29 for 214 yards and 2 touchdowns, with 1 interception. Green was 29 of 42 for 431 yards and 2 touchdowns. Az-Zahir Hakim amassed 147 receiving yards on 8 catches, while Torry Holt added 130 yards on only 4 receptions. But St. Louis was hurt by the loss of running back Marshall Faulk, who was a late scratch because of a knee injury (he would have arthroscopic surgery the next day and missed the Rams' next game).

Carolina	6	7	3	11	—	27
St. Louis	7	3	14	0	—	24

Car — FG Nedney 35
StL — Hakim 14 pass from Green (Stoyanovich kick)
Car — FG Nedney 45
StL — FG Stoyanovich 28
Car — Crawford 16 pass from Beuerlein (Nedney kick)
Car — FG Nedney 24
StL — Bruce 4 pass from Green (Stoyanovich kick)
StL — Watson 3 run (Stoyanovich kick)
Car — Hayes 13 pass from Beuerlein (Beuerlein run)
Car — FG Nedney 46

MONDAY NIGHT, NOVEMBER 6

GREEN BAY 26, MINNESOTA 20 (OT)—at Lambeau Field, attendance 59,854. Antonio Freeman's remarkable 43-yard touchdown catch 3:39 into overtime propelled the Packers to victory. After the teams were tied 20-20 at the end of regulation, Green Bay took possession first in the extra session. The Packers marched from their 18 to the Vikings' 43 in six plays before Brett Favre launched a deep pass for Freeman near the right sideline. Cris Dishman appeared to break up the pass near the 15, but the ball fell toward Freeman, who was lying on the turf. He grabbed the ball before it hit the ground and, because he had not been touched, got up and raced into the end zone to complete an unlikely touchdown. It was Green Bay's only lead of the game. Up to that point, the Packers had countered each Minnesota score with one of their own, tying the game for the fourth and final time when Ahman Green ran 2 yards for a touchdown late in the third quarter. The teams played a scoreless fourth quarter, although the Vikings had a chance to win when Gary Anderson lined up for a 32-yard field-goal attempt on the final play of regulation. But with rain coming down, the snap was mishandled by Mitch Berger, whose desperation pass was intercepted by Tyrone Williams at Green Bay's 5-yard line. Favre was 17 of 36 for 235 yards and 3 touchdowns. Daunte Culpepper was 17 of 34 for 276 yards and 2 touchdowns, with 3 interceptions. The Vikings lost their second consecutive game after beginning the season with seven victories. Robert Smith rushed for 122 yards and caught a 45-yard touchdown pass.

Minnesota	3	10	7	0	0	—	20
Green Bay	0	10	10	0	6	—	26

Minn — FG Anderson 30
GB — FG Longwell 24
Minn — Carter 12 pass from Culpepper (Anderson kick)
GB — Green 5 pass from Favre (Longwell kick)
Minn — FG Anderson 48
GB — FG Longwell 41
Minn — Smith 45 pass from Culpepper (Anderson kick)
GB — Green 2 run (Longwell kick)
GB — Freeman 43 pass from Favre

ELEVENTH WEEK SUMMARIES

American Football Conference

Eastern Division	W	L	T	Pct.	Pts.	OP
Miami	8	2	0	.800	217	126
Indianapolis	7	3	0	.700	279	213
Buffalo	6	4	0	.600	199	189
N.Y. Jets	6	4	0	.600	223	216
New England	2	8	0	.200	167	206
Central Division						
Tennessee	8	2	0	.800	204	149
Baltimore	7	4	0	.636	191	128
Pittsburgh	5	5	0	.500	160	119
Jacksonville	3	7	0	.300	186	235
Cleveland	3	8	0	.273	120	244
Cincinnati	2	8	0	.200	93	217
Western Division						
Oakland	8	2	0	.800	280	199
Denver	6	4	0	.600	295	225
Kansas City	5	5	0	.500	250	236
Seattle	4	7	0	.364	185	260
San Diego	0	10	0	.000	152	253

National Football Conference

Eastern Division	W	L	T	Pct.	Pts.	OP
N.Y. Giants	7	3	0	.700	192	153
Philadelphia	7	4	0	.636	230	170
Washington	6	4	0	.600	185	158
Dallas	4	6	0	.400	227	219
Arizona	3	7	0	.300	161	277
Central Division						
Minnesota	8	2	0	.800	248	218
Detroit	6	4	0	.600	182	197
Tampa Bay	6	4	0	.600	252	167
Green Bay	4	6	0	.400	209	207
Chicago	2	8	0	.200	140	246
Western Division						
St. Louis	8	2	0	.800	392	303
New Orleans	7	3	0	.700	203	152
Carolina	4	6	0	.400	193	173
Atlanta	3	8	0	.273	186	290
San Francisco	3	8	0	.273	274	330

SUNDAY, NOVEMBER 12

MINNESOTA 31, ARIZONA 14—at Metrodome, attendance 64,223. Daunte Culpepper passed for 3 touchdowns and ran for another, and the Vikings broke open a close game with 24 unanswered points. The score was tied at 7-7 late in the first half before Minnesota marched 64 yards in the final 2:19 to take a 10-7 lead on Gary Anderson's 33-yard field goal as time ran out. The Vikings then took the second-half kickoff and drove 69 yards in 8 plays, increasing their advantage to 10 points on Culpepper's 4-yard touchdown pass to Randy Moss. Early in the fourth quarter, Robert Tate recovered Michael Pittman's fumble at Minnesota's 45-yard line. Seven plays later, Culpepper bootlegged around left end for a 24-7 lead. His 12-yard touchdown pass to Cris Carter on the Vikings' next possession turned the game into a rout. Culpepper was 25 of 32 for 302 yards and 3 touchdowns, with 1 interception. Carter caught 11 passes for 119 yards, while Moss added 7 receptions for 104. Robert Smith rushed for 117 yards and turned a screen pass into a 33-yard touchdown to open the scoring midway through the first quarter. Jake Plummer was 19 of 28 for 219 yards for the Cardinals, who were outgained 460 yards to 249.

Arizona	7	0	0	7	—	14
Minnesota	7	3	7	14	—	31

Minn — R. Smith 33 pass from Culpepper (Anderson kick)
Ariz — Pittman 1 run (Blanchard kick)
Minn — FG Anderson 33
Minn — Moss 4 pass from Culpepper (Anderson kick)
Minn — Culpepper 3 run (Anderson kick)
Minn — C. Carter 12 pass from Culpepper (Anderson kick)
Ariz — Jenkins 98 kickoff return (Blanchard kick)

DETROIT 13, ATLANTA 10—at Pontiac Silverdome, attendance 74,309. Gary Moeller won his NFL debut as a head coach when Jason Hanson kicked 2 field goals in the fourth quarter, including the game winner from 44 yards out with 1:43 to play. Atlanta, playing without injured quarterback Chris Chandler, relied on the running of Jamal Anderson to take a 10-7 lead into the final period. Detroit marched deep into Falcons' territory, and on fourth-and-goal from the 1 with 5:17 remaining, Moeller, who took over when Bobby Ross resigned earlier in the week, was faced with a crucial decision. He elected to go for a field goal, which Hanson kicked from 18 yards to tie the score. The move paid off when Danny Kanell, Chandler's backup, was intercepted by Corwin Brown, who returned the ball to Atlanta's 29 with 2:13 left. Three runs by James Stewart netted 4 yards and positioned Hanson for his winning kick. Bryant Westbrook intercepted Kanell on the next series to seal the victory. Charlie Batch was 12 of 27 for 128 yards, with 1 interception. Kanell was 14 of 34 for 126 yards, with 2 interceptions. Anderson accounted for most of the Falcons' offense by rushing for 119 yards, including a 14-yard touchdown in the second quarter.

Atlanta	0	7	3	0	—	10
Detroit	7	0	0	6	—	13

Det — Stewart 1 run (Hanson kick)
Atl — Anderson 14 run (Andersen kick)
Atl — FG Andersen 42
Det — FG Hanson 18
Det — FG Hanson 44

BALTIMORE 24, TENNESSEE 23—at Adelphia Coliseum, attendance 68,490. The Ravens became the first visiting team ever to win at Adelphia Coliseum when Trent Dilfer tossed a 2-yard touchdown pass to Patrick Johnson with 25 seconds left, and the Titans' Al Del Greco missed a 43-yard field-goal try on the game's final play. Tennessee, which moved into its new stadium in 1999 and had set an NFL record by winning its first 12 regular-season games there, rallied from a 14-point deficit to take its first lead of the game when Perry Phenix intercepted Dilfer's pass and returned it 87 yards for a touchdown and a 23-17 advantage with 2:30 to play. But the lead remained 6 points when Del Greco's extra-point try bounced off the left upright. It was his first missed conversion in 230 attempts over seven years, but it proved costly when Baltimore marched 70 yards for the go-ahead touchdown. A critical pass-interference penalty on fourth down with less than a minute left gave the Ravens a first down at the Titans' 2, and on third down, Dilfer hit Johnson in the front corner of the end zone for a touchdown. Matt Stover's extra point gave Baltimore a 1-point lead. Still, Tennessee nearly pulled out the victory when Chris Coleman returned the ensuing kickoff to the Titans' 44, and Steve McNair passed 11 yards to Eddie George to move the ball into Ravens' territory with 13 seconds left. McNair scrambled 20 yards on the next play and called time out with three seconds to go. But the normally reliable Del Greco pushed his field-goal attempt to the right as time ran out, and Tennessee lost for the first time since Kickoff Weekend. Dilfer was 23 of 36 for 281 yards and 2 touchdowns, with 1 interception. McNair was 21 of 34 for 228 yards and 2 touchdowns, but Eddie George was limited to only 28 yards on 12 carries by Baltimore's top-ranked defense.

Baltimore	7	10	0	7	—	24
Tennessee	0	14	0	9	—	23

Balt — Ismail 46 pass from Dilfer (Stover kick)
Balt — Ja. Lewis 2 run (Stover kick)
Tenn — Mason 10 pass from McNair (Del Greco kick)
Balt — FG Stover 45
Tenn — Neal 4 pass from McNair (Del Greco kick)
Tenn — FG Del Greco 23
Tenn — Phenix 87 interception return (kick failed)
Balt — P. Johnson 2 pass from Dilfer (Stover kick)

BUFFALO 20, CHICAGO 3—at Ralph Wilson Stadium, attendance 72,420. Doug Flutie's 1-yard touchdown run capped the opening drive of the second half and enabled the Bills to take control of a tight contest. Buffalo's Steve Christie and Chicago's Paul Edinger exchanged field goals in a first half that ended with the Bills holding a 6-3 lead. Buffalo took possession at its 30-yard line to begin the third quarter and marched 70 yards in 13 plays, the key gain coming on Flutie's 21-yard pass to Peerless Price to move the ball into Bears' territory. On fourth-and-goal from the 1, Flutie kept the ball around left end to give the Bills a 10-point lead. Buffalo sealed the outcome when Daryl Porter returned a fumble by teammate Keith Newman 23 yards for a touchdown with 2:40 to go in the game. Newman had recovered a fumble by Chicago quarterback Shane Matthews and returned it 25 yards before fumbling himself. Matthews, who began the season as the Bears' third-string quarterback, was in the game because Jim Miller suffered a season-ending torn Achilles' tendon while scrambling in the second quarter. Miller had been starting in place of injured Cade McNown. Matthews was 11 of 24 for 106 yards and turned over the ball 4 times. Flutie was 16 of 26 for 171 yards, with 1 interception, for the Bills while engineering his third victory in four starts since taking over for injured Rob Johnson. But Johnson played one series in the second quarter and led Buffalo to Christie's 42-yard field goal that broke a 3-3 tie 1:01 before halftime.

Chicago	0	3	0	0	—	3
Buffalo	0	6	7	7	—	20

Buff — FG Christie 27
Chi — FG Edinger 24
Buff — FG Christie 42
Buff — Flutie 1 run (Christie kick)
Buff — Porter 23 fumble return (Christie kick)

DALLAS 23, CINCINNATI 6—at Texas Stadium, attendance 62,170. Troy Aikman passed for 308 yards, but Tim Seder stole the spotlight by scoring 17 points on 3 field goals, 2 extra points, and a touchdown run in the Cowboys' victory. Dallas led 10-6 midway through the third quarter when defensive end Ebenezer Ekuban sacked Akili Smith and recovered Smith's fumble at Cincinnati's 29-yard line. Six plays later, the Cowboys lined up for an apparent field-goal attempt on fourth-and-goal from the 1. But Seder took a handoff from holder Micah Knorr and ran off left tackle untouched into the end zone. Seder kicked the conversion to make it 17-6, then put the game away with field goals on Dallas's next two possessions. Aikman was 24 of 37 for 308 yards and 1 touchdown. His 35-yard touchdown pass to James McKnight midway through the second quarter gave the Cowboys a lead they never relinquished. Smith completed 10 of 25 for 68 yards, with 1 interception. Corey Dillon rushed for 94 yards.

Cincinnati	0	6	0	0	—	6
Dallas	0	7	13	3	—	23

Cin — FG Rackers 22
Dall — McKnight 35 pass from Aikman (Seder kick)
Cin — FG Rackers 37
Dall — FG Seder 43
Dall — Seder 1 run (Seder kick)
Dall — FG Seder 35
Dall — FG Seder 42

TAMPA BAY 20, GREEN BAY 15—at Raymond James Stadium, attendance 65,621. Shaun King passed for 2 touchdowns in the second quarter, and Martin Gramatica kicked a pair of field goals in the fourth period to lift the Buccaneers to their third consecutive victory. King, who passed for 7 touchdowns in the first two victories, teamed with Keyshawn Johnson on a 5-yard touchdown and Reidel Anthony on a 19-yard strike to give the Buccaneers a 14-3 halftime lead. But the Packers battled back, getting field goals from Ryan Longwell on consecutive possessions in the third quarter, then taking the lead 59 seconds into the fourth period when holder Matt Hasselbeck tossed a 27-yard touchdown pass to Bubba Franks out of field-goal formation. The two-point conversion failed, leaving Green Bay's advantage at 15-14. It took Tampa Bay only seven plays to retake the lead, with King's 14-yard run the key gain on a 37-yard drive to Gramatica's 54-yard field goal. Three plays later, Chidi Ahanotu recovered Ahman Green's fumble at the Packers' 38, and Gramatica converted that into a 51-yard field goal with 6:50 remaining. Green Bay could not advance past its 35-yard line on two possessions after that. The Packers played much of the second half without Brett Favre, who sprained his foot when he was sacked by Warren Sapp midway through the third quarter. King was 16 of 27 for 164 yards and 2 touchdowns, with 1 interception. Favre was 14 of 25 for 117 yards before he was forced to leave, and Hasselbeck was 9 of 18 for 93 yards and 1 touchdown.

Green Bay	0	3	6	6	—	15
Tampa Bay	0	14	0	6	—	20

TB — Johnson 5 pass from King (Gramatica kick)
GB — FG Longwell 52
TB — Anthony 19 pass from King (Gramatica kick)
GB — FG Longwell 42
GB — FG Longwell 45
GB — Franks 27 pass from Hasselbeck (pass failed)
TB — FG Gramatica 54
TB — FG Gramatica 51

SAN FRANCISCO 21, KANSAS CITY 7—at 3Com Park, attendance 68,002. The 49ers scored touchdowns on three consecutive possessions in the second quarter and got a lift from their defense to stun the Chiefs. San Francisco entered the game with the poorest-rated defense in the NFL, having allowed a league-high 32.3 points per game, but limited Kansas City to only one touchdown. The 49ers built a 21-0 lead, marching 80, 56, and 65 yards for a pair of short touchdown runs by Jeff Garcia and one by Charlie Garner. Garcia was 20 of 25 for 244 yards, and Garner added 102 yards on the ground for the 49ers, who amassed 389 total yards and maintained possession for 36:10 of the game's 60 minutes. Elvis Grbac was 22 of 40 for 271 yards, with 1 interception, and failed to throw a touchdown pass for the first time this season for the Chiefs, who were making their third consecutive road trip to the West Coast.

Kansas City	0	0	0	7	—	7
San Francisco	0	21	0	0	—	21

SF — Garner 1 run (Richey kick)
SF — Garcia 2 run (Richey kick)
SF — Garcia 1 run (Richey kick)
KC — Bennett 1 run (Peterson kick)

MIAMI 17, SAN DIEGO 7—at Qualcomm Stadium, attendance 56,896. For the second consecutive week, the Dolphins made a big play on the game's first snap, got 2 first-half touchdowns from Lamar Smith, then turned things over to their defense to secure the victory. A week earlier, Smith got things started with a 46-yard touchdown run on the first play against the Lions. This time, quarterback Jay Fiedler teamed with wide receiver Oronde Gadsden on a 61-yard pass completion to the Chargers' 6, and Smith scored from the 2 two plays later. Smith's 6-yard touchdown run capped a 66-yard, 11-play drive and upped Miami's advantage to 14-0. That was more than enough for the Dolphins' defense, which limited San Diego to 238 total yards. The Chargers' lone score came on Ryan Leaf's 8-yard touchdown pass to Fred McCrary on the first play of the fourth quarter. Leaf was in the game because Moses Moreno, who started the game at quarterback, sprained his knee on the first possession of the second half and had to leave the game. Leaf eventually hurt his hamstring and was replaced by Jim Harbaugh, who had started the last five games but was battling an assortment of injuries. Fiedler completed his first 9 attempts and was 13 of 20 for 160 yards. The three Chargers quarterbacks combined to complete only 20 of 47 passes for 178 yards and 1 touchdown, with 4 interceptions.

Miami	7	7	3	0	—	17
San Diego	0	0	0	7	—	7

Mia — L. Smith 2 run (Mare kick)
Mia — L. Smith 6 run (Mare kick)
Mia — FG Mare 35
SD — McCrary 8 pass from Leaf (Carney kick)

CLEVELAND 19, NEW ENGLAND 11—at Cleveland Browns Stadium, attendance 72,618. Doug Pederson passed for a touchdown, and Phil Dawson kicked 4 field goals as the Browns ended a seven-game losing streak and handed the Patriots their fourth consecutive defeat. The game was tied at 3-3 in the second quarter when Darius Holland intercepted a tipped pass at New England's 41-yard line. Eight plays later, Pederson tossed a short pass to rookie Aaron Shea, who bulled his way into the end zone for the Browns' first touchdown since week 7. Dawson, who had a 39-yard field goal in the first quarter, added a 43-yard kick in the final minute of the first half, then made 35-yard field goals in the third and fourth quarters to increase Cleveland's advantage to 19-3. The Patriots pulled within eight points on Drew Bledsoe's 2-yard touchdown pass to Rod Rutledge and a two-point conversion with 5:48 left, but they could not manage a first down on their final possession. The Browns ran out the final 3:09 to seal the victory. Pederson was 20 of 37 for 138 yards and 1 touchdown. Rookie Travis Prentice rushed for 84 yards for Cleveland, which gained a season-high 139 yards on the ground. Bledsoe was 21 of 35 for 212 yards and 1 touchdown, with 1 interception.

New England	3	0	0	8	—	11
Cleveland	3	10	3	3	—	19

Clev — FG Dawson 39
NE — FG Vinatieri 38
Clev — Shea 9 pass from Pedersen (Dawson kick)
Clev — FG Dawson 43
Clev — FG Dawson 35
Clev — FG Dawson 35
NE — Rutledge 2 pass from Bledsoe (Faulk run)

NEW ORLEANS 20, CAROLINA 10—at Ericsson Stadium, attendance 61,473. The Saints' sixth consecutive victory was tempered by the loss of Ricky Williams, who broke his ankle midway through the fourth quarter and missed the rest of the regular season. Jeff Blake's 43-yard touchdown bomb to Joe Horn and a relentless defense that recorded 8 sacks and forced 5 turnovers sparked New Orleans. One of the sacks, by Sammy Knight, forced a fumble by Steve Beuerlein that Keith Mitchell returned 90 yards for a touchdown for a 14-3 lead late in the third quarter. Doug Brien added 2 field goals after that to help keep the game out of Carolina's reach. Blake was 14 of 23 for 179 yards and 1 touchdown, with 1 interception. But Williams, who rushed for 93 yards, was injured on a 2-yard run with less than seven minutes remaining in the game. The gain gave him 1,000 rushing yards for the season. Beuerlein was 24 of 42 for 295 yards and 1 touchdown, with 2 interceptions and 3 lost fumbles.

New Orleans	0	7	7	6	—	20
Carolina	0	3	0	7	—	10

NO — Horn 43 pass from Blake (Brien kick)
Car — FG Nedney 38
NO — Mitchell 90 fumble return (Brien kick)
NO — FG Brien 40
Car — Muhammad 13 pass from Beuerlein (Nedney kick)
NO — FG Brien 42

PHILADELPHIA 26, PITTSBURGH 23 (OT)—at Three Rivers Stadium, attendance 56,702. The Eagles rallied for a dramatic victory by scoring 10 points in the final 2:29 of regulation to tie the game, then winning on David Akers's 42-yard field goal 4:16 into overtime. Joey Porter returned a fumble 32 yards for a touchdown early in the fourth quarter to break a 13-13 tie, and Kris Brown kicked a 40-yard field goal on Pittsburgh's next possession for a 23-13 lead with 3:42 to play. But the Steelers would not get the ball again. Philadelphia, which struggled on offense much of the day, needed only 4 plays and 73 seconds to march 57 yards and pull within three points on Donovan McNabb's 13-yard touchdown pass to Brian Mitchell. The Eagles then successfully executed an onside kick, recovering at their 32. McNabb connected on a pair of third-down conversions with key pass completions, including a 19-yard strike to Torrance Small to move the ball to the Steelers' 31 with 45 seconds left. On third-and-4 from the 25, Mitchell caught a 1-yard pass from McNabb and was tackled in bounds. Philadelphia, which was out of time outs, rushed its field-goal unit onto the field, and Akers made a 42-yard kick to tie the game as time expired. The Eagles won the overtime coin toss and marched from their 37 to the Steelers' 24 in seven plays to position Akers for the winning kick. McNabb was 26 of 55 passes for 213 yards and 2 touchdowns, with 102 yards coming on the final two possessions of regulation and in overtime. Kordell Stewart was 14 of 31 for 159 yards, with 1 interception. Jerome Bettis rushed for 134 yards and a touchdown.

Philadelphia	3	7	3	10	3	—	26
Pittsburgh	0	6	7	10	0	—	23

Phil — FG Akers 26
Phil — Thomason 2 pass from McNabb (Akers kick)
Pitt — FG K. Brown 38
Pitt — FG K. Brown 51
Phil — FG Akers 45
Pitt — Bettis 7 run (K. Brown kick)
Pitt — Porter 32 fumble return (K. Brown kick)
Pitt — FG K. Brown 40
Phil — Mitchell 13 pass from McNabb (Akers kick)
Phil — FG Akers 42
Phil — FG Akers 42

ST. LOUIS 38, N.Y. GIANTS 24—at Giants Stadium, attendance 78,174. Trent Green passed for 4 touchdowns and ran for another to help the Rams halt the Giants' four-game winning streak. New York got off to a bad start, turning over the ball on its first possession when wide receiver Amani Toomer fumbled after catching a pass for an apparent first down. Dexter McCleon picked up the loose ball and returned it 21 yards to the Giants' 1. Green passed to Roland Williams for a touchdown on the next play to give the Rams a 7-0 lead 4:22 into the game. Az-Zahir Hakim's 39-yard punt return late in the first quarter led to Green's 5-yard touchdown pass to Torry Holt, and it was 14-0. New York pulled within 7 points when Kerry Collins teamed with Tiki Barber on a 13-yard touchdown pass, but on the Rams' next two possessions, Green passed 8 yards to Ricky Proehl for a touchdown and scrambled 18 yards for another score to break open the game at 28-7. The Giants tried to rally, cutting the deficit to 11 points with a touchdown and a field goal in the first 3:26 of the second half, but the Rams countered with a 50-yard field goal by Jeff Hall and another touchdown pass by Green, this time a 34-yard bomb to Isaac Bruce, to keep the game out of reach. Green, making his third start in place of injured Kurt Warner, was 27 of 45 for 272 yards and 4 touchdowns, with 1 interception. McCleon had an interception, a fumble recovery, and a sack. Collins was 17 of 34 for 240 yards and 3 touchdowns, with 2 interceptions.

St. Louis	14	14	10	0	—	38
N.Y. Giants	0	7	10	7	—	24

StL — R. Williams 1 pass from Green (Wilkins kick)
StL — Holt 5 pass from Green (Hall kick)
NYG — Barber 13 pass from Collins (Daluiso kick)
StL — Proehl 8 pass from Green (Hall kick)
StL — Green 18 run (Hall kick)
NYG — Hilliard 46 pass from Collins (Daluiso kick)
NYG — FG Daluiso 20
StL — FG Hall 50
StL — Bruce 34 pass from Green (Hall kick)
NYG — Hilliard 34 pass from Collins (Daluiso kick)

SEATTLE 28, JACKSONVILLE 21—at ALLTEL Stadium, attendance 68,063. Jon Kitna threw 3 touchdown passes to rally the Seahawks from a 14-point, first-half deficit. Mark Brunell and Fred Taylor rushed for touchdowns, and Brunell launched a 67-yard bomb to Keenan McCardell as the Jaguars opened up a 21-7 advantage. But Kitna completed 6 of 8 passes, including a 15-yard touchdown strike to Sean Dawkins, on a 67-yard drive that pulled Seattle within 21-14 just 13 seconds before halftime. The Seahawks marched 74 yards on a time-consuming, 14-play drive the first time they had the ball in the second half, tying the score at 21-21 on Kitna's 8-yard touchdown pass to Derrick Mayes. The teams traded possessions after that until Seattle took over at its 33 with 4:23 left in the game. Kitna's 29-yard pass to Dawkins highlighted an 8-play drive capped by Ricky Watters's 4-yard touchdown catch with 2:01 remaining. Jacksonville mounted a final effort, marching from its 26 to the Seahawks' 11 with two seconds to play. Brunell's pass for Kyle Brady in the end zone was incomplete, but Reggie Tongue was whistled for pass interference, giving the Jaguars one last play from the 1 with no time on the clock. But Brunell's pass sailed over the head of Alvis Whitted in the end zone. Kitna was 22 of 33 for 231 yards and 3 touchdowns. Brunell was 24 of 33 for 340 yards and 1 touchdown. Taylor ran for more than 100 yards for the fourth consecutive game, gaining 103 on 21 carries.

Seattle	0	14	7	7	—	28
Jacksonville	7	14	0	0	—	21

Jax — Brunell 2 run (Hollis kick)
Sea — Watters 1 run (Lindell kick)
Jax — Taylor 10 run (Hollis kick)
Jax — McCardell 67 pass from Brunell (Hollis kick)
Sea — Dawkins 15 pass from Kitna (Lindell kick)
Sea — Mayes 8 pass from Kitna (Lindell kick)
Sea — Watters 4 pass from Kitna (Lindell kick)

SUNDAY NIGHT, NOVEMBER 12

INDIANAPOLIS 23, N.Y. JETS 15—at RCA Dome, attendance 56,657. Peyton Manning passed for 1 touchdown, and Edgerrin James ran for another as the Colts built a 20-0 lead, then held off the Jets. Indianapolis dominated the first half, outgaining New York 241 yards to 86 and building a 17-0 lead when the Jets' three possessions resulted in a pair of interceptions and a punt. The Colts increased the advantage to 20-0 when Mike Vanderjagt kicked a 38-yard field goal with four minutes left in the third quarter. But in what had become a weekly occurrence for New York, the Jets rallied. Vinny Testaverde completed all 4 of his passes on a 6-play, 79-yard drive capped by Dedric Ward's 16-yard touchdown catch five seconds before the end of the third quarter to pull New York within 20-7. After Vanderjagt kicked his third field goal of the game, from 35 yards out, and an exchange of punts, the Jets took possession at their 23 with 7:32 to go. They marched to Indianapolis's 38, where Testaverde kept the drive alive with a 29-yard completion to Ward on fourth down. Two plays later, Curtis Martin ran in from 9 yards, and Testaverde completed a 2-point conversion pass to Marcus Coleman to pull New York within 23-15 with 5:11 remaining. The Jets had one more possession and drove from their 25 to Indianapolis's 28 with 1:27 remaining, but Testaverde passes fell incomplete on four consecutive downs to end the threat. Manning was 21 of 35 for 210 yards and 1 touchdown. James rushed for 131 yards on 31 carries. Testaverde was 20 of 38 for 271 yards and 1 touchdown, with 2 interceptions.

N.Y. Jets	0	0	7	8	—	15
Indianapolis	7	10	3	3	—	23

Ind — Harrison 6 pass from Manning (Vanderjagt kick)
Ind — James 2 run (Vanderjagt kick)
Ind — FG Vanderjagt 26
Ind — FG Vanderjagt 38
NYJ — Ward 16 pass from Testaverde (Hall kick)
Ind — FG Vanderjagt 35
NYJ — Martin 9 run (Coleman pass from Testaverde)

MONDAY NIGHT, NOVEMBER 13

DENVER 27, OAKLAND 24—at Mile High Stadium, attendance 75,951. Jason Elam's 41-yard field goal on the final play foiled a dramatic rally by the Raiders and kept the Broncos alive in the AFC West race. Ian Gold's 12-yard return of a blocked punt broke a 10-10 tie in the third quarter, and Brian Griese's 11-yard touchdown pass to Byron Chamberlain gave Denver a 24-10 lead. But Rich Gannon brought Oakland back by completing 4 of 5 passes on a 51-yard drive capped by Zack Crockett's 1-yard touchdown run with 6:30 to play, then connecting on 7 of 10 attempts, including a 22-yard touchdown strike to Tim Brown, on an 11-play, 86-yard march that tied the game with just 1:06 left. Deltha O'Neal returned the ensuing kickoff 23 yards to the Broncos' 33, and on first down, Griese teamed with Rod Smith on a 22-yard completion to move the ball into Raiders' territory with 41 seconds left. Three short completions and Griese's 2-yard keeper positioned Elam for the winning kick. Griese was 25 of 37 for 262 yards and 1 touchdown, with 1 interception, despite playing with a separated shoulder he suffered in the first quarter. The injury sidelined him for the next five weeks. Gannon was 30 of 53 for 382 yards and 1 touchdown, with 2 interceptions. Brown caught 10 passes for 122 yards, and Andre Rison added 117 yards on 6 receptions. Oakland lost for the first time since falling to Denver in week 3. Broncos coach Mike Shanahan improved to 11-1 against the team that fired him as head coach four games into the 1989 season.

Oakland	3	7	0	14	—	24
Denver	7	0	10	10	—	27

Den — Davis 5 run (Elam kick)
Oak — FG Conway 19
Oak — Crockett 1 run (Conway kick)
Den — FG Elam 23
Den — Gold 12 blocked punt return (Elam kick)
Den — Chamberlain 11 pass from Griese (Elam kick)
Oak — Crockett 1 run (Conway kick)
Oak — Brown 22 pass from Gannon (Conway kick)
Den — FG Elam 41

TWELFTH WEEK SUMMARIES

American Football Conference

Eastern Division	**W**	**L**	**T**	**Pct.**	**Pts.**	**OP**
Miami	8	3	0	.727	220	146
Buffalo	7	4	0	.636	220	206
Indianapolis	7	4	0	.636	303	239
N.Y. Jets	7	4	0	.636	243	219
New England	3	8	0	.273	183	219
Central Division						
Tennessee	9	2	0	.818	228	159
Baltimore	8	4	0	.667	218	128
Pittsburgh	5	6	0	.455	184	153
Jacksonville	4	7	0	.364	220	259
Cleveland	3	9	0	.250	130	268
Cincinnati	2	9	0	.182	106	233
Western Division						
Oakland	9	2	0	.818	311	221
Denver	7	4	0	.636	333	262
Kansas City	5	6	0	.455	267	257
Seattle	4	7	0	.364	185	260
San Diego	0	11	0	.000	189	291

National Football Conference

Eastern Division	**W**	**L**	**T**	**Pct.**	**Pts.**	**OP**
Philadelphia	8	4	0	.667	264	179
N.Y. Giants	7	4	0	.636	213	184
Washington	7	4	0	.636	218	178
Dallas	4	7	0	.364	227	246
Arizona	3	8	0	.273	170	311
Central Division						
Minnesota	9	2	0	.818	279	235
Detroit	7	4	0	.636	213	218
Tampa Bay	6	5	0	.545	262	180
Green Bay	5	6	0	.455	235	231
Chicago	3	8	0	.273	153	256
Western Division						
St. Louis	8	3	0	.727	412	336
New Orleans	7	4	0	.636	225	183
Carolina	4	7	0	.364	210	204
San Francisco	4	8	0	.333	290	336
Atlanta	3	9	0	.250	192	306

SUNDAY, NOVEMBER 19

PHILADELPHIA 34, ARIZONA 9—at Veterans Stadium, attendance 65,356. Donovan McNabb passed for 1 touchdown and rushed for another to lead the Eagles into first place in the NFC's Eastern Division. The game was tied at 3-3 in the second quarter before McNabb put his team ahead for good with a 1-yard touchdown pass to Jeff Thomason just 19 seconds before halftime. Philadelphia then took the second-half kickoff and embarked on a 15-play, 65-yard drive that consumed 8:32. McNabb capped the lengthy march with a 7-yard touchdown run, and the Eagles led 17-3. Mike Caldwell's 26-yard interception return for a touchdown and Darnell Autry's 1-yard touchdown run helped turn the game into a rout in the fourth quarter. McNabb was 25 of 34 for 217 yards and 1 touchdown, with 1 interception. Jake Plummer was 8 of 15 for 51 yards before leaving the game early in the fourth quarter with bruised ribs and an injured thumb. Backup Dave Brown was 11 of 13 for 140 yards and 1 touchdown, with 1 interception. The two Cardinals quarterbacks were sacked 8 times, including twice each by Jeremiah Trotter and Brian Dawkins.

Arizona	3	0	0	6	—	9
Philadelphia	0	10	7	17	—	34

Ariz — FG Blanchard 42
Phil — FG Akers 38
Phil — Thomason 1 pass from McNabb (Akers kick)
Phil — McNabb 7 run (Akers kick)
Phil — FG Akers 46
Phil — Caldwell 26 interception return (Akers kick)
Ariz — Boston 44 pass from Brown (pass failed)
Phil — Autry 1 run (Akers kick)

SAN FRANCISCO 16, ATLANTA 6—at 3Com Park, attendance 67,447. Jason Webster returned an interception 70 yards for the game's only touchdown as the 49ers handed the Falcons their eighth loss in nine games. San Francisco entered the game ranked last in the league in total defense but was coming off a strong effort in an upset of the Chiefs in week 11. The 49ers built on that performance by allowing the Falcons only 11 first downs and 211 total yards. Two field goals by Wade Richey staked

San Francisco to a 6-3 lead at halftime, and Webster's interception of Chris Chandler's pass for Jamal Anderson increased the 49ers' advantage to 13-3. Richey's third field goal, from 26 yards out with 10:54 to play, kept the game out of Atlanta's reach. Jeff Garcia was 16 of 31 for 210 yards, and Charlie Garner totaled 135 yards from scrimmage. Chandler was 16 of 33 for 154 yards, with 1 interception.

Atlanta	0	3	3	0	—	6
San Francisco	3	3	7	3	—	16

SF — FG Richey 32
Atl — FG Andersen 21
SF — FG Richey 30
SF — Webster 70 interception return (Richey kick)
Atl — FG Andersen 51
SF — FG Richey 26

BUFFALO 21, KANSAS CITY 17—at Arrowhead Stadium, attendance 78,457. Rob Johnson passed for 2 touchdowns and scrambled for the winning score with 2:58 remaining. The Chiefs led 10-7 before the lead changed hands on three consecutive possessions in a seesaw fourth quarter. First, Johnson capped a 63-yard drive with an 18-yard touchdown pass to Jay Riemersma 1:25 into the final period to put Buffalo ahead 14-10. Then, Kansas City regained the lead by marching 63 yards on a 13-play drive that consumed 5:40 and culminated in Elvis Grbac's second touchdown pass to Tony Gonzalez, a 9-yard strike with 7:55 left. The Bills began their next possession at their 33, and, with Johnson completing 4 of 5 passes for 40 yards, marched to a first-and-goal at the Chiefs' 3. A run lost 4 yards and a sack pushed the ball back to the 12, but Johnson eluded the rush and ran in for the decisive score on third down. Kansas City had two more possessions after that and drove into Buffalo territory each time. But Grbac was intercepted by Keion Carpenter at the 11 with 1:50 left, and his final desperation pass from the 42 was batted away by Bills wide receiver Eric Moulds, who was put into the game for defense. Johnson was 21 of 36 for 196 yards and 2 touchdowns and led Buffalo with 41 rushing yards in his first start since week 7 because of a shoulder injury. Grbac was 28 of 48 for 341 yards and 2 touchdowns, with 1 interception. Derrick Alexander had 146 yards on 7 receptions.

Buffalo	7	0	0	14	—	21
Kansas City	0	3	7	7	—	17

Buff — Moulds 9 pass from Johnson (Christie kick)
KC — FG Peterson 19
KC — Gonzalez 13 pass from Grbac (Peterson kick)
Buff — Riemersma 18 pass from Johnson (Christie kick)
KC — Gonzalez 9 pass from Grbac (Peterson kick)
Buff — Johnson 12 run (Christie kick)

MINNESOTA 31, CAROLINA 17—at Metrodome, attendance 64,208. Daunte Culpepper passed for 357 yards and 3 touchdowns to carry the Vikings past the Panthers. Culpepper, who completed 22 of 29 attempts, spread his touchdowns to each of his three main weapons on offense. He tossed a 36-yard bomb to Randy Moss, teamed with Robert Smith on a 53-yard screen pass in the first quarter, and completed a 15-yard strike to Cris Carter in the third quarter. The latter capped an 81-yard drive that took 11 plays and consumed more than six minutes, and it increased Minnesota's lead to 31-14. Smith, who rushed for 103 yards and caught 3 passes for 70 yards, also had a 3-yard touchdown run to open a 21-7 advantage in the second quarter. Culpepper was 22 of 29 for 357 yards and 3 touchdowns. Carter caught 8 passes for 138 yards, and Moss added 106 yards on 5 receptions for the Vikings, who amassed 446 total yards. Steve Beuerlein was 26 of 44 passes for 272 yards and rushed for a touchdown, but he also was intercepted twice and sacked 5 times.

Carolina	7	7	0	3	—	17
Minnesota	14	10	7	0	—	31

Car — Beuerlein 1 run (Nedney kick)
Minn — Moss 36 pass from Culpepper (Anderson kick)
Minn — R. Smith 53 pass from Culpepper (Anderson kick)
Minn — R. Smith 3 run (Anderson kick)
Car — Hetherington 1 run (Nedney kick)
Minn — FG Anderson 43
Minn — C. Carter 15 pass from Culpepper (Anderson kick)
Car — FG Nedney 28

NEW ENGLAND 16, CINCINNATI 13—at Foxboro Stadium, attendance 60,292. Adam Vinatieri kicked 2 fourth-quarter field goals, including the game winner from 22 yards out with three seconds remaining, to lift the Patriots to the victory. Vinatieri, who also had a 38-yard field goal in the second quarter, tied the game at 13-13 with a 21-yard kick on the first play of the final period. The teams then exchanged punts on the next five possessions until New England took over at its 15-yard line with 3:08 left. The Patriots held the ball for 12 plays, covering 81 yards to set up the winning kick. Drew Bledsoe moved his team into Bengals' territory by completing a 23-yard pass to Troy Brown on third-and-14 from New England's 42, and a pass-interference penalty against Rodney Heath on third-and-7 from the 21 positioned the ball on the 1 with 35 seconds left. Bledsoe, who completed 4 of 6 passes for 65 yards on the decisive march, was 22 of 36 for 258 yards, with 1 interception. Terry Glenn caught 11 passes for 129 yards while Brown had 8 receptions for 110 yards. Scott Mitchell was 20 of 38 for 236 yards and 1 touchdown, with 1 interception.

Cincinnati	0	10	3	0	—	13
New England	7	3	0	6	—	16

NE — Carter 1 run (Vinatieri kick)
Cin — Warrick 13 pass from Mitchell (Rackers kick)
NE — FG Vinatieri 38
Cin — FG Rackers 28
Cin — FG Rackers 45
NE — FG Vinatieri 21
NE — FG Vinatieri 22

TENNESSEE 24, CLEVELAND 10—at Adelphia Coliseum, attendance 68,498. Eddie George rushed for 134 yards and 3 touchdowns, and the AFC Central-leading Titans overcame 7 turnovers to survive a scare from the Browns. Tennessee turned over the ball 5 times on its 6 possessions in the first two quarters—4 times after driving into Cleveland territory—and the game was scoreless at halftime. Just 1:36 into the second half, the Titans turned it over again when Steve McNair was intercepted for the third time, and Percy Ellsworth returned the pick 33 yards for a touchdown. Tennessee needed just 6 plays to counter, with McNair's 28-yard pass to Derrick Mason the key play on a 57-yard drive capped by George's game-tying 4-yard touchdown run. Another lost fumble led to a 38-yard field goal by Phil Dawson that gave Cleveland the lead with 5:17 left in the third quarter, but the Titans dominated after that. They scored on each of their next three possessions while limiting the Browns to only 1 first down the rest of the way. George's 1-yard touchdown run gave Tennessee the lead for good in the final minute of the third quarter, and another 1-yard touchdown run with 2:25 left in the game capped a 14-play, 59-yard drive that took 6:44 off the clock and secured the victory. George carried 36 times and helped the Titans forge sizeable advantages in first downs (23-5), total yards (392-125), and time of possession (38:19-21:41). McNair was 17 of 25 for 222 yards, with 3 interceptions. Doug Pederson was 13 of 20 for 103 yards, with 1 interception.

Cleveland	0	0	10	0	—	10
Tennessee	0	0	14	10	—	24

Cle — Ellsworth 33 interception return (Dawson kick)
Tenn — George 4 run (Del Greco kick)
Cle — FG Dawson 38
Tenn — George 1 run (Del Greco kick)
Tenn — FG Del Greco 22
Tenn — George 1 run (Del Greco kick)

BALTIMORE 27, DALLAS 0—at PSINet Stadium, attendance 69,416. Jamal Lewis rushed for 187 yards, Trent Dilfer passed for 2 touchdowns, and the Ravens' defense turned in another dominating performance in a rout of the Cowboys. Lewis carried 28 times and helped Baltimore accumulate 250 yards on the ground against the league's most porous run defense. Priest Holmes had 64 yards, including a 5-yard touchdown run to cap the scoring in the fourth quarter. Dilfer's 40-yard bomb to Qadry Ismail came just seven plays into the game and gave the Ravens all the points they would need. Baltimore's defense posted its fourth shutout of the season while limiting Dallas to only 9 first downs and 192 total yards. The Cowboys crossed midfield just three times. Troy Aikman was intercepted twice, and Tim Seder missed a 46-yard field goal try on the other. Dilfer was 18 of 24 for 242 yards and 2 touchdowns, with 2 interceptions. Aikman was 19 of 33 for 138 yards, with 3 interceptions.

Dallas	0	0	0	0	—	0
Baltimore	10	7	0	10	—	27

Balt — Ismail 40 pass from Dilfer (Stover kick)
Balt — FG Stover 25
Balt — Sharpe 59 pass from Dilfer (Stover kick)
Balt — FG Stover 19
Balt — Holmes 5 run (Stover kick)

DETROIT 31, N.Y. GIANTS 21—at Giants Stadium, attendance 77,897. Charlie Batch passed for 3 touchdowns as the Lions built a 28-0 lead and coasted to victory over the Giants. Kurt Schulz's interception and Larry Foster's blocked punt set up Batch's first-half touchdown passes of 5 yards to Walter Rasby and 7 yards to Herman Moore. James Stewart added a 1-yard touchdown run in the second quarter, and when Batch capped Detroit's opening drive of the third quarter with a 32-yard touchdown pass to Johnnie Morton, the Lions' lead was 28 points. Batch was 20 of 32 for 225 yards and 3 touchdowns, with 1 interception. Kerry Collins was 29 of 51 for 350 yards and 2 touchdowns, with 1 interception. Amani Toomer caught 8 passes for 108 yards. The Giants amassed 373 total yards but were stymied by 4 turnovers, 4 sacks, and 10 penalties.

Detroit	0	21	7	3	—	31
N.Y. Giants	0	0	14	7	—	21

Det — Rasby 5 pass from Batch (Hanson kick)
Det — Stewart 1 run (Hanson kick)
Det — Moore 7 pass from Batch (Hanson kick)
Det — Morton 32 pass from Batch (Hanson kick)
NYG — Collins 4 run (Daluiso kick)
NYG — Campbell 2 pass from Collins (Daluiso kick)
Det — FG Hanson 19
NYG — Jurevicius 13 pass from Collins (Daluiso kick)

GREEN BAY 26, INDIANAPOLIS 24—at Lambeau Field, attendance 59,869. Brett Favre passed for 301 yards and 2 touchdowns, and the Packers withstood a furious fourth-quarter rally to upend the Colts. Favre, playing despite a sprained left foot, tossed touchdown passes of 1 yard to Tyrone Davis and 17 yards to Antonio Freeman as Green Bay built a 19-0 halftime lead. It was 19-3 in the fourth quarter before Indianapolis covered 70 yards in 9 plays, the last a 34-yard touchdown pass from Peyton Manning to E.G. Green. The next time the Colts had the ball, they drove 83 yards in 12 plays and pulled within two points on Manning's 5-yard touchdown pass to Jim Finn with 4:32 still to play. But the Packers countered when Allen Rossum returned the ensuing kickoff 92 yards for a touchdown to build the lead back to 26-17. Indianapolis scored again on Manning's 11-yard touchdown strike to Jerome Pathon with 2:39 left, but the Colts never got the ball back. Favre completed a 22-yard pass to Bill Schroeder, a pass-interference penalty resulted in another first down, and Ahman Green, who rushed for 153 yards on 24 carries, ran for a pair of first downs to eat up the clock. Favre was 23 of 36 for 301 yards and 2 touchdowns, with 1 interception. Schroeder had 8 catches for 155 yards. Manning was 25 of 44 for 294 yards, including 259 in the second half, and 3 touchdowns, with 1 interception. Edgerrin James totaled 137 yards from scrimmage.

Indianapolis	0	0	3	21	—	24
Green Bay	5	14	0	7	—	26

GB — Safety, Manning recovered fumble in own end zone
GB — FG Longwell 42
GB — T. Davis 1 pass from Favre (Longwell kick)
GB — Freeman 17 pass from Favre (Longwell kick)
Ind — FG Vanderjagt 38
Ind — Green 34 pass from Manning (Vanderjagt kick)
Ind — Finn 5 pass from Manning (Vanderjagt kick)
GB — Rossum 92 kickoff return (Longwell kick)
Ind — Pathon 11 pass from Manning (Vanderjagt kick)

N.Y. JETS 20, MIAMI 3—at Pro Player Stadium, attendance 74,320. Former Dolphins running back Bernie Parmalee, in the game because of an injury to starter Curtis Martin, rushed for 2 fourth-quarter touchdowns to help the Jets end a three-game slide and pull within one game of first place in the crowded AFC Eastern Division. New York led just 6-3 when Tony Scott intercepted Damon Huard's pass at Miami's 27-yard line with 8:18 left. Parmalee carried on the next three plays, the last an 18-yard touchdown burst to increase the Jets' lead to 13-3. Huard was intercepted again two plays later, this time by Shaun Ellis, and Parmalee capped a 25-yard drive with a 7-yard touchdown run to seal the outcome with 3:12 remaining. Parmalee finished with 57 yards on 14 carries after coming into the game in the third quarter for Martin, who suffered a back injury. Testaverde was 13 of 28 for 102 yards, with 2 interceptions. Huard, who was 16 of 29 for 128 yards, with 3 interceptions, was in the game because starter Jay Fiedler was injured. Fiedler pinched a nerve in his neck when he was sacked by Mo Lewis on the game's first play.

N.Y. Jets	3	3	0	14	—	20
Miami	0	3	0	0	—	3

NYJ — FG Hall 39
Mia — FG Mare 47
NYJ — FG Hall 33
NYJ — Parmalee 18 run (Hall kick)
NYJ — Parmalee 7 run (Hall kick)

OAKLAND 31, NEW ORLEANS 22—at Louisiana Superdome, attendance 64,900. Rich Gannon passed for 2 touchdowns and Zack Crockett ran for 2 to lead the Raiders past the Saints. Gannon tossed a 34-yard touchdown to Andre Rison, and Crockett rushed 6 yards for a touchdown as the Raiders built a 17-0 lead midway through the second quarter. New Orleans pulled within 17-13 on Aaron Brooks's 53-yard touchdown pass to Willie Jackson and a pair of third-quarter field goals by Doug Brien before Gannon and Crockett made the plays down the stretch to keep the game out of reach. First, Gannon capped a 73-yard drive with a 21-yard touchdown pass to Tim Brown 2:55 into the fourth quarter. Then, Gannon and Brown teamed on a pair of third-down completions to keep alive a 12-play, 74-yard march that consumed 5:46 the next time Oakland had the ball. Crockett's 6-yard touchdown run with 1:55 left capped the drive. Gannon was 14 of 21 for 168 yards and 2 touchdowns and a team-high 55 rushing yards. Brooks, who replaced injured starter Jeff Blake late in the first quarter, was 14 of 22 for 187 yards and 2 touchdowns, both to Jackson, in the first extended playing time of the quarterback's two-year career. Blake dislocated his foot on a pass play with 1:58 left in the opening period. New Orleans already was playing without starting running back Ricky Williams, who was injured in week 11.

Oakland	3	14	0	14	—	31
New Orleans	0	7	6	9	—	22

Oak — FG Janikowski 49
Oak — Rison 34 pass from Gannon (Janikowski kick)
Oak — Crockett 6 run (Janikowski kick)
NO — Jackson 53 pass from Brooks (Brien kick)
NO — FG Brien 42
NO — FG Brien 40
Oak — Brown 21 pass from Gannon (Janikowski kick)
NO — FG Brien 33
Oak — Crockett 6 run (Janikowski kick)
NO — Jackson 9 pass from Brooks (pass failed)

DENVER 38, SAN DIEGO 37—at Mile High Stadium, attendance 75,218. Backup quarterback Gus Frerotte passed for 5 touchdowns, including the game-winning, 5-yard completion to Ed McCaffrey with 1:33 left, to rally the Broncos past the winless Chargers. Denver trailed by as many as 17 points on two occasions, the last time at 34-17 after Ryan Leaf's 83-yard touchdown bomb to Jeff Graham with eight seconds left in the third quarter. The Broncos countered quickly, marching 65 yards in just 2:08 and pulling within 10 points on Frerotte's 26-yard touchdown pass to Rod Smith. It was 37-24 when Frerotte began a 66-yard march with a 39-yard completion to Smith and ended the drive by passing 10 yards for a touchdown to Desmond Clark to trim Denver's deficit to six points with 4:59 still to play. San Diego's offense could not generate a first down, and Deltha O'Neal's 25-yard punt return positioned the Broncos at the Chargers' 45-yard line with 3:44 to play. Frerotte completed 4 of 5 passes on a 6-play drive, the last the decisive strike to McCaffrey. The Chargers had one final possession beginning at their 16 but could only reach the 22 before Leaf's fourth-down pass for Graham fell incomplete. Frerotte, playing because starter Brian Griese injured his shoulder in a victory over the Raiders in week 11, was 36 of 58 and 5 touchdowns for a club-record 462 yards, with 4 interceptions. Smith caught 11 passes for 187 yards, while McCaffrey had 10 receptions for 148 yards and 2 touchdowns. Leaf was 13 of 27 for 311 yards and 3 touchdowns, with 1 interception. Graham caught 4 passes for 144 yards, including 2 touchdowns, and Curtis Conway caught 4 passes for 118 yards, including a touchdown. Denver amassed 536 total yards; San Diego had 385.

San Diego	3	21	10	3	—	37
Denver	0	10	7	21	—	38

SD — FG Carney 41
Den — McCaffrey 1 pass from Frerotte (Elam kick)
SD — Conway 68 pass from Leaf (Carney kick)
SD — J. Graham 45 pass from Leaf (Carney kick)
SD — Turner 75 interception return (Carney kick)
Den — FG Elam 26
SD — FG Carney 31
Den — Carswell 5 pass from Frerotte (Elam kick)
SD — J. Graham 83 pass from Leaf (Carney kick)
Den — R. Smith 26 pass from Frerotte (Elam kick)
SD — FG Carney 33
Den — Clark 10 pass from Frerotte (Elam kick)
Den — McCaffrey 5 pass from Frerotte (Elam kick)

CHICAGO 13, TAMPA BAY 10—at Soldier Field, attendance 66,944. The Bears took advantage of Buccaneers' miscues to beat Tampa Bay for the first time in seven meetings. Chicago forced 3 turnovers, converting the first 2 into 10 points, then running out the clock after the third. The game was tied at 3-3 in the final minute of the first half when Tony Parrish intercepted Shaun King's pass and returned it 38 yards for a touchdown. King's 9-yard touchdown run on the Buccaneers' first possession of the second half tied the game again, but on Tampa Bay's next drive, Warrick Dunn fumbled, and the ball was recovered by Clyde Simmons at the Bears' 37. Nine plays later, Paul Edinger put Chicago ahead with a 48-yard field goal 4:58 into the fourth period. The kick stood up as the winning points when the Buccaneers could not score on their final two possessions. Their last chance ended when Brian Urlacher intercepted King's pass and returned it 19 yards to the Bears' 40 with 2:00 left. Marlon Barnes ran for a first down three plays later, and Tampa Bay never got the ball back. Shane Matthews, making his first start after injuries to Cade McNown and Jim Miller, was 20 of 34 for 165 yards, with 1 interception. King was 12 of 19 for 91 yards, with 2 interceptions. Tampa Bay, which had its three-game winning streak snapped, fell to 0-18 in franchise history when the temperature at kickoff was less than 40 degrees. It was 37 degrees in Soldier Field.

Tampa Bay	0	3	7	0	—	10
Chicago	3	7	0	3	—	13

Chi — FG Edinger 34
TB — FG Gramatica 33
Chi — Parrish 38 interception return (Edinger kick)
TB — King 9 run (Gramatica kick)
Chi — FG Edinger 48

SUNDAY NIGHT, NOVEMBER 19

JACKSONVILLE 34, PITTSBURGH 24—at Three Rivers Stadium, attendance 50,925. Fred Taylor rushed for a franchise-record 234 yards and scored 4 touchdowns to power the Jaguars past the Steelers. Taylor, who carried 30 times, ran 25 yards for a touchdown to tie the game at 7-7 in the second quarter. The next time Jacksonville had the ball, Taylor accounted for 61 yards on a 65-yard drive capped by his 16-yard touchdown catch to give the Jaguars the lead for good 1:20 before halftime. He added touchdown runs of 2 and 26 yards on back-to-back possessions of the third quarter to help Jacksonville break open the game. Brunell was 17 of 31 for 190 yards and 1 touchdown, with 1 interception. Kordell Stewart was 13 of 27 for 188 yards and 1 touchdown, with 2 interceptions, and ran for 59 yards and 2 scores for the Steelers. Pittsburgh, which had permitted only 3 touchdowns the previous seven games, was singed for 417 total yards on defense while turning over the ball 5 times on offense.

Jacksonville	0	17	17	0	—	34
Pittsburgh	7	3	0	14	—	24

Pitt — Ward 32 pass from K. Stewart (K. Brown kick)
Jax — Taylor 25 run (Hollis kick)
Pitt — FG K. Brown 40
Jax — Taylor 16 pass from Brunell (Hollis kick)
Jax — FG Hollis 36
Jax — FG Hollis 33
Jax — Taylor 2 run (Hollis kick)
Jax — Taylor 26 run (Hollis kick)
Pitt — K. Stewart 2 run (pass failed)
Pitt — K. Stewart 45 run (Huntley run)

MONDAY NIGHT, NOVEMBER 20

WASHINGTON 33, ST. LOUIS 20—at Trans World Dome, attendance 66,087. Jeff George passed for 3 touchdowns, and recently acquired 44-year-old Eddie Murray kicked 4 field goals to pace the Redskins. Washington trailed 13-3 before rallying for a 19-13 advantage when its offense was on the field for 28 of 29 snaps late in the second quarter and early in the third period. First, George capped an 11-play, 70-yard drive with a 19-yard touchdown pass to James Thrash with 1:50 left in the first half. Then, Torry Holt lost a fumble after a 64-yard reception on the next play from scrimmage, leading to Murray's 47-yard field goal as time ran out. The Redskins took the second-half kickoff and drove 58 yards to another touchdown on George's 3-yard pass to Larry Centers, though Murray's extra-point attempt bounced off the upright. After the Rams regained the lead at 20-19, Washington kept its offense on the field again for 15 consecutive plays to score 12 points and take control of the game. George's 34-yard touchdown pass to Irving Fryar gave the Redskins the lead for good in the closing seconds of the third quarter, then kickoff specialist Scott Bentley recovered his own onside kick to give Washington another possession, which they converted into Murray's 41-yard field goal early in the fourth quarter. When Tony Horne lost a fumble on the ensuing kickoff, the Redskins had the ball again. This time, Murray made a 39-yard field goal to increase the lead to 31-20 with 10:38 remaining. A safety with 3:44 left provided the final margin of victory. George was 24 of 34 for 269 yards and 3 touchdowns, with 1 interception, in his second start of the season. Murray and Bentley had been signed after neither Michael Husted nor Kris Heppner was deemed effective in place of Brett Conway, the original starter who was injured early in the season. Trent Green was 23 of 38 for 366 yards and 2 touchdowns, with 1 interception.

Washington	3	10	12	8	—	33
St. Louis	10	3	7	0	—	20

StL — FG Hall 30
StL — Faulk 19 pass from Green (Hall kick)
Wash — FG Murray 37
StL — FG Hall 43
Wash — Thrash 19 pass from George (Murray kick)
Wash — FG Murray 47
Wash — Centers 3 pass from George (kick failed)
StL — Proehl 15 pass from Green (Hall kick)
Wash — Fryar 34 pass from George (pass failed)
Wash — FG Murray 41
Wash — FG Murray 39
Wash — Safety, Smith sacked Green in end zone

THIRTEENTH WEEK SUMMARIES

American Football Conference

Eastern Division	**W**	**L**	**T**	**Pct.**	**Pts.**	**OP**
Miami	9	3	0	.750	237	160
N.Y. Jets	8	4	0	.667	260	229
Buffalo	7	5	0	.583	237	237
Indianapolis	7	5	0	.583	317	256
New England	3	9	0	.250	192	253
Central Division						
Tennessee	9	3	0	.750	241	175
Baltimore	9	4	0	.692	262	135
Pittsburgh	6	6	0	.500	232	181

Jacksonville	5	7	0	.417	236	272
Cleveland	3	10	0	.231	137	312
Cincinnati	2	10	0	.167	134	281
Western Division						
Oakland	10	2	0	.833	352	235
Denver	8	4	0	.667	371	293
Kansas City	5	7	0	.417	283	274
Seattle	4	8	0	.333	216	298
San Diego	1	11	0	.083	206	307
National Football Conference						
Eastern Division	**W**	**L**	**T**	**Pct.**	**Pts.**	**OP**
Philadelphia	9	4	0	.692	287	199
N.Y. Giants	8	4	0	.667	244	191
Washington	7	5	0	.583	238	201
Dallas	4	8	0	.333	242	273
Arizona	3	9	0	.250	177	342
Central Division						
Minnesota	10	2	0	.833	306	250
Detroit	8	4	0	.667	247	227
Tampa Bay	7	5	0	.583	293	197
Green Bay	5	7	0	.417	249	262
Chicago	3	9	0	.250	163	273
Western Division						
New Orleans	8	4	0	.667	256	207
St. Louis	8	4	0	.667	436	367
Carolina	5	7	0	.417	241	218
San Francisco	4	8	0	.333	290	336
Atlanta	3	10	0	.231	206	347

THURSDAY, NOVEMBER 23

MINNESOTA 27, DALLAS 15—at Texas Stadium, attendance 63,878. Randy Moss tormented the Cowboys on Thanksgiving Day for the second time in three years, catching 2 touchdown passes in the Vikings' victory. Moss, who caught 3 touchdowns to beat Dallas on Thanksgiving Day in 1998, his rookie season, had 7 receptions for 144 yards and caught touchdown passes of 7 and 39 yards from Daunte Culpepper in the third quarter, when Minnesota took control of the game by scoring 17 points. His first touchdown catch came on the opening possession of the second half, with the Vikings clinging to a 10-9 lead; the second came with 18 seconds left in the third period and upped the advantage to 27-9. Robert Smith rushed for 148 yards, including a 26-yard touchdown to give the Vikings their first lead and a 39-yard run to set up the first of Moss's touchdowns. Culpepper was 15 of 22 for 202 yards and 2 touchdowns. Troy Aikman was 30 of 43 for 276 yards and 1 touchdown, with 1 interception. Emmitt Smith gained 100 yards on only 12 carries, but left the game with a concussion early in the third quarter.

Minnesota	0	10	17	0	—	27
Dallas	3	6	0	6	—	15

Dall — FG Seder 37
Dall — FG Seder 43
Minn — FG Anderson 49
Minn — R. Smith 26 run (Anderson kick)
Dall — FG Seder 36
Minn — Moss 7 pass from Culpepper (Anderson kick)
Minn — FG Anderson 29
Minn — Moss 39 pass from Culpepper (Anderson kick)
Dall — LaFleur 6 pass from Aikman (run failed)

DETROIT 34, NEW ENGLAND 9—at Pontiac Silverdome, attendance 77,923. Charlie Batch passed for 1 touchdown and ran for another as the Lions broke open a close game with 28 unanswered points in the second half to win on Thanksgiving Day. After Adam Vinatieri's 43-yard field goal capped the opening possession of the second half and gave the Patriots a 9-6 lead, Detroit got its offense going. Desmond Howard returned the ensuing kickoff 39 yards to the Lions' 40, and a penalty moved the ball to New England's 46. On first down, Batch teamed with Johnnie Morton on a 23-yard completion. Seven plays later, Batch found David Sloan in the end zone for the go-ahead touchdown on fourth-and-goal from the 1. The Lions added touchdowns on their next two possessions as well. James Stewart's 1-yard touchdown run ended a 9-play, 70-yard drive early in the fourth quarter, and two plays later Marquis Walker's interception and 12-yard return to the Patriots' 15 set up Batch's 10-yard touchdown scramble for a 27-9 advantage. Bryant Westbrook returned an interception 101 yards for a touchdown with 4:13 left to close the scoring. Batch was 16 of 24 for 194 yards and 1 touchdown despite having to leave the game twice with a rib injury. Drew Bledsoe was 17 of 32 for 148 yards, with 2 interceptions.

New England	6	0	3	0	—	9
Detroit	3	3	7	21	—	34

Det — FG Hanson 31
NE — FG Vinatieri 24
NE — FG Vinatieri 47
Det — FG Hanson 36
NE — FG Vinatieri 43
Det — Sloan 1 pass from Batch (Hanson kick)
Det — Stewart 1 run (Hanson kick)
Det — Batch 10 run (Hanson kick)
Det — Westbrook 101 interception return (Hanson kick)

SUNDAY, NOVEMBER 26

OAKLAND 41, ATLANTA 14—at Network Associates Coliseum, attendance 55,175. Rich Gannon passed for 2 touchdowns, and the Raiders were dominant en route to their tenth victory of the season. Gannon teamed with Tim Brown on a 28-yard touchdown strike and with James Jett on an 84-yard touchdown bomb. Tyrone Wheatley and Zack Crockett added touchdown runs for Oakland, which amassed 492 total yards. The Falcons, meanwhile, managed only 181 yards while losing their fourth consecutive game. Few things went right for Atlanta. Even when the Falcons recovered an onside kick to open the second half, kicker Morten Andersen was called offside. Andersen then kicked deep, and the Raiders' David Dunn returned the ball 87 yards for a touchdown and 31-7 lead. Gannon was 15 of 22 for 231 yards and 2 touchdowns. Chris Chandler was 7 of 12 for 97 yards, with 1 interception and reserve Doug Johnson was 11 of 17 for 85 yards and 1 touchdown.

Atlanta	7	0	0	7	—	14
Oakland	3	21	14	3	—	41

Atl — Anderson 5 run (Andersen kick)
Oak — FG Janikowski 24
Oak — Wheatley 1 run (Janikowski kick)
Oak — Brown 28 pass from Gannon (Janikowski kick)
Oak — Crockett 8 run (Janikowski kick)
Oak — Dunn 87 kickoff return (Janikowski kick)
Oak — Jett 84 pass from Gannon (Janikowski kick)
Atl — Kozlowski 4 pass from D. Johnson (Andersen kick)
Oak — FG Janikowski 35

TAMPA BAY 31, BUFFALO 17—at Raymond James Stadium, attendance 65,546. The Buccaneers ended Buffalo's four-game winning streak when Warrick Dunn rushed for 2 touchdowns in the fourth quarter and Karl Williams returned a punt 73 yards for the back-breaking touchdown. The Bills finished the game with sizeable advantages in first downs (25-13), total yards (433-180), and time of possession (36:17-23:43). Buffalo drove inside Tampa Bay territory eight times, but managed only two touchdowns and a field goal. The Buccaneers, meanwhile, made the most of their best drive of the day. The march came late in the third quarter and early in the fourth, covered 70 yards in 10 plays, and ended with Dunn's 6-yard touchdown run for a 17-7 lead. The Bills pulled close on Rob Johnson's 19-yard touchdown pass to Eric Moulds on the next possession, but Williams upped Tampa Bay's advantage to 10 points when he took Chris Mohr's punt at the Buccaneers' 27-yard line and returned it the distance with 5:34 to play. Dunn added a 39-yard touchdown run with 2:08 left to seal the outcome. He finished with 106 yards on 20 carries, and become the first back to gain more than 100 yards against the Bills' stingy run defense all season. Shaun King was 10 of 18 for 106 yards. Johnson was 24 of 39 for 262 yards and 2 touchdowns. Moulds caught 8 passes for 102 yards.

Buffalo	0	7	0	10	—	17
Tampa Bay	3	7	0	21	—	31

TB — FG Gramatica 45
Buff — Linton 4 pass from R. Johnson (Christie kick)
TB — King 2 run (Gramatica kick)
TB — Dunn 6 run (Gramatica kick)
Buff — Moulds 19 pass from R. Johnson (Christie kick)
TB — K. Williams 73 punt return (Gramatica kick)
Buff — FG Christie 28
TB — Dunn 39 run (Gramatica kick)

N.Y. JETS 17, CHICAGO 10—at Giants Stadium, attendance 77,354. Vinny Testaverde passed for 2 touchdowns in the first half, and the Jets held off the Bears in the second half to win. After Mo Lewis recovered James Allen's fumble in Chicago territory in the first quarter, Testaverde took his team 45 yards for the game's first score, a 2-yard touchdown pass to tight end Anthony Becht. It was 10-0 late in the first half before Testaverde teamed with Richie Anderson on a 15-yard touchdown pass to give the Jets a 17-point advantage just 32 seconds before halftime. New York generated little offense after that, punting on four of its seven second-half possessions. The other drives culminated in an interception, a missed field goal, and the end of the game. The Bears, meanwhile, chipped into their deficit when Paul Edinger kicked a 39-yard field goal in the third quarter and Shane Matthews tossed a 6-yard touchdown pass to Marty Booker with 5:14 to play in the fourth period. But Chicago had the ball just one more time after that and could not manage a first down after taking possession at its 25-yard line. Matthews's pass on fourth down from the 32 was batted down by Shane Burton with 1:41 left. Testaverde was 20 of 34 for 215 yards and 2 touchdowns, with 1 interception. Matthews struggled in wet conditions and was 12 of 32 for 98 yards and 1 touchdown. Allen accounted for the majority of Chicago's 233 total yards by rushing for 122 yards and catching 3 passes for 23 yards, but he lost 3 fumbles.

Chicago	0	0	3	7	—	10
N.Y. Jets	7	10	0	0	—	17

NYJ — Becht 2 pass from Testaverde (Hall kick)
NYJ — FG Hall 20
NYJ — Anderson 15 pass from Testaverde (Hall kick)
Chi — FG Edinger 39
Chi — Booker 6 pass from Matthews (Edinger kick)

BALTIMORE 44, CLEVELAND 7—at PSINet Stadium, attendance 68,361. Rookie Jamal Lewis rushed for 2 touchdowns and Trent Dilfer passed for 2 in the Ravens' rout. Lewis rushed for 170 yards on 30 carries and established a club record for yards in a season (1,095 by game's end). Priest Holmes added 64 yards and a touchdown on the ground for the Ravens, who amassed 25 first downs and 461 total yards. The Browns, on the other hand, were shut down after surprising Baltimore with a 4-play, 86-yard touchdown drive on their first possession, the key blow a 67-yard pass completion from Doug Pederson to Kevin Johnson. Cleveland managed only 3 first downs and 26 total yards after that, and never crossed midfield. Dilfer was 12 of 23 for 169 yards and 2 touchdowns, with 1 inteception. Pederson and Spergon Wynn were a combined 13 of 25 for 138 yards, with 1 interception.

Cleveland	7	0	0	0	—	7
Baltimore	7	24	6	7	—	44

Cle — Prentice 4 run (Dawson kick)
Balt — Ja. Lewis 1 run (Stover kick)
Balt — Gash 2 pass from Dilfer (Stover kick)
Balt — P. Johnson 46 pass from Dilfer (Stover kick)
Balt — FG Stover 39
Balt — Ja. Lewis 36 run (Stover kick)
Balt — FG Stover 26
Balt — FG Stover 38
Balt — Holmes 3 run (Stover kick)

DENVER 38, SEATTLE 31—at Husky Stadium, attendance 68,661. Mike Anderson rushed for 195 yards and 2 touchdowns, including the winning 80-yard dash with 3:34 to play, as the Broncos won their fourth consecutive game. Denver overcame an 11-point, first-half deficit with a number of big plays, including Gus Frerotte's 43-yard touchdown pass to Desmond Clark, Rod Smith's 50-yard touchdown run, and a 21-yard interception return for a touchdown by Jimmy Spencer. Smith, a wide receiver, lined up in the backfield and took a pitchout on his touchdown run to tie the game at 24-24 with 12:37 left. After an exchange of punts, Spencer's interception gave the Broncos the lead with 5:54 to go. The Seahawks rallied by marching 86 yards in just 1:52, tying the game again on Jon Kitna's 8-yard touchdown pass to Sean Dawkins at the 4:02 mark. But Anderson burst around left end on the decisive touchdown run just two plays later. Anderson carried 30 times en route to his career-best rushing effort. He helped Denver amass 301 yards on the ground and 538 in all. Frerotte was 15 of 31 for 244 yards and 1 touchdown, with 2 interceptions. Smith caught 4 passes for 82 yards and set a club record for receiving yards in a season (1,314 at game's end). He also gained 78 yards on 3 runs. Kitna was 20 of 42 for 226 yards and 1 touchdown, with 2 interceptions, in relief of Brock Huard, who left the game with a bruised kidney in the second quarter. Huard had missed the previous three games with a concussion. Ricky Watters rushed for 77 yards and a touchdown and caught 9 passes for 126 yards.

Denver	0	10	7	21	—	38
Seattle	0	14	10	7	—	31

Sea — Sinclair 63 fumble return (Lindell kick)
Den — FG Elam 35
Sea — Watters 1 run (Lindell kick)
Den — Clark 43 pass from Frerotte (Elam kick)
Den — Anderson 15 run (Elam kick)
Sea — C. Brown 10 fumble return (Lindell kick)
Sea — FG Lindell 42
Den — R. Smith 50 run (Elam kick)
Den — Spencer 21 interception return (Elam kick)
Sea — Dawkins 8 pass from Kitna (Lindell kick)
Den — Anderson 80 run (Elam kick)

SAN DIEGO 17, KANSAS CITY 16—at Qualcomm Stadium, attendance 47,228. John Carney's 52-yard field goal with 2:14 remaining gave the Chargers their first victory of the season. San Diego, which lost 6 of its first 11 games by a field goal or less, appeared headed for another close defeat when it trailed 16-14 late in the fourth quarter. But with 3:38 to go, Nate Jacquet returned a punt 35 yards to the Chiefs' 36-yard line. After three plays netted only 3 yards, Carney made the go-ahead kick. Kansas City had one final chance, but Michael Dumas sacked Warren Moon on fourth-and-10 from the Chiefs' 36, sealing the victory with 1:10 left. The 44-year-old Moon, making his first start of the season in place of injured Elvis Grbac, was 12 of 31 for 130 yards, with 1 interception. Ryan Leaf was 17 of 30 for 177 yards, with 2 interceptions, and touchdowns of 20 and 7 yards to tight end Freddie Jones in the first half.

Kansas City	3	3	10	0	—	16
San Diego	7	7	0	3	—	17

KC — FG Peterson 39
SD — F. Jones 20 pass from Leaf (Carney kick)
SD — F. Jones 7 pass from Leaf (Carney kick)
KC — FG Peterson 34
KC — Patton 24 interception return (Peterson kick)
KC — FG Peterson 30
SD — FG Carney 52

MIAMI 17, INDIANAPOLIS 14—at RCA Dome, attendance 56,935. The Dolphins maintained their hold on first place in the AFC East despite playing at Indianapolis without injured starting quarterback Jay Fiedler and injured starting running back Lamar Smith. J.J. Johnson, filling in for Smith, ran 3 yards for a touchdown, and Damon Huard, filling in for Fiedler, tossed a 17-yard touchdown pass to Oronde Gadsden with 1:10 left to engineer the upset. Peyton Manning staked the Colts to a 14-10 lead by passing for 2 touchdowns to Marvin Harrison, including an 8-yard strike early in the fourth quarter. Indianapolis still held that lead when it marched from its 35-yard line to Miami's 30 with 3:07 left. But Manning's pass on third-and-7 was intercepted by safety Brock Marion, and the Dolphins took over possession at their 14 with 2:56 remaining. Huard completed 5 of 6 passes as Miami quickly marched to the Colts' 17, then found Gadsden in the front corner of the end zone for the go-ahead touchdown. Indianapolis drove from its 20 to the Dolphins' 42 in the closing seconds, but Mike Vanderjagt's 59-yard field-goal try on the final play was partially blocked and fell well short. Huard was 22 of 33 for 183 yards and 1 touchdown. Manning was 16 of 34 for 209 yards and 2 touchdowns, with 1 interception. Edgerrin James rushed for 118 yards on 26 carries.

Miami	0	3	7	7	—	17
Indianapolis	7	0	0	7	—	14

Ind — Harrison 27 pass from Manning (Vanderjagt kick)
Mia — FG Mare 28
Mia — J. Johnson 3 run (Mare kick)
Ind — Harrison 8 pass from Manning (Vanderjagt kick)
Mia — Gadsden 17 pass from Huard (Mare kick)

NEW ORLEANS 31, ST. LOUIS 24—at Trans World Dome, attendance 66,064. Aaron Brooks rushed for 2 touchdowns and passed for another in his first career start to lead the Saints over the Rams and into a tie for first place in the NFC West. New Orleans, which lost starting running back Ricky Williams to an injury in week 11 and starting quarterback Jeff Blake to an injury in week 12, pulled even with the defending world champions in the division race when Brooks ran 1 yard for a touchdown to break a 24-24 tie with 3:50 left, and its defense held St. Louis on three possessions after that. The Rams, who lost for the fourth time in six games after a 6-0 start, had rallied from a 24-10 third-quarter deficit to tie the game behind touchdown passes from Trent Green to Az-Zahir Hakim (35 yards) and Ricky Proehl (19 yards). But after the latter, which came with 11:06 to play, the Saints embarked on an 11-play, 85-yard drive that consumed 7:16. New Orleans successfully converted three third downs along the way, and on second-and-goal from the 1, Brooks dove over for the winning score. The Rams did not advance the ball past their 45 after that, turning over the ball on downs and on an interception before time ran out on their last possession with Green sacked at his 40. Brooks was 17 of 29 for 190 yards and 1 touchdown, with 2 interceptions. Saints running backs Jerald Moore (61 yards and a touchdown) and Chad Morton (35 yards) helped make up for the absence of Williams by combining for 96 yards. Green was 20 of 41 for 289 yards and 2 touchdowns, but lost 2 fumbles and was intercepted once. He didn't get any help from St. Louis's ground game, either, which managed only 28 yards on 10 attempts. The teams combined for 31 penalties, including a club-record 17 for New Orleans.

New Orleans	7	14	3	7	—	31
St. Louis	7	3	7	7	—	24

StL — Holcombe 1 run (Hall kick)
NO — Milne 4 pass from Brooks (Brien kick)
NO — Moore 3 run (Brien kick)
NO — Brooks 2 run (Brien kick)
StL — FG Hall 28
NO — FG Brien 30
StL — Hakim 35 pass from Green (Hall kick)
StL — Proehl 19 pass from Green (Hall kick)
NO — Brooks 1 run (Brien kick)

PHILADELPHIA 23, WASHINGTON 20—at FedEx Field, attendance 83,284. The Eagles held off the Redskins when David Akers kicked a 30-yard field goal with 3:00 remaining and Eddie Murray missed a potential tying try from 44 yards with 1:16 to go. With first place in the NFC East at stake, Philadelphia relied heavily on second-year quarterback Donovan McNabb. He passed 3 yards to tight end Jeff Thomason for a touchdown in the first quarter, scrambled 26 yards to set up a field goal in the second quarter, and ran 21 yards for a touchdown 5:57 into the third quarter to give the Eagles a 17-14 lead. Murray and Akers traded field goals on the next four possessions. Akers's third field goal of the game came four plays after McNabb's 54-yard scramble and gave Philadelphia the lead in the closing minutes. The Redskins began their final drive at their 27-yard line, and on third-and-21 from the 16, Jeff George teamed with James Thrash on a 50-yard completion to move into Eagles' territory. The drive stalled at the 26, and the 44-year-old Murray, who was signed less than two weeks earlier to stabilize Washington's underachieving kicking game, was short against the wind on his attempt to tie. McNabb was 19 of 30 for 137 yards and 1 touchdown, with 1 interception, and rushed 11 times for 125 yards and another score. George was 25 of 43 for 288 yards and 2 touchdowns.

Philadelphia	7	3	7	6	—	23
Washington	7	7	3	3	—	20

Wash — Thrash 36 pass from George (Murray kick)
Phil — Thomason 3 pass from McNabb (Akers kick)
Phil — FG Akers 27
Wash — Alexander 19 pass from George (Murray kick)
Phil — McNabb 21 run (Akers kick)
Wash — FG Murray 26
Phil — FG Akers 33
Wash — FG Murray 20
Phil — FG Akers 30

PITTSBURGH 48, CINCINNATI 28—at Paul Brown Stadium, attendance 63,925. Kordell Stewart accounted for 4 touchdowns, and the Steelers converted 3 fumble recoveries into 21 points to pull away from the Bengals. Stewart equaled his career best with 3 touchdown passes and also ran for a touchdown. He capped Pittsburgh's first possession with a 34-yard touchdown pass to Hines Ward and ended its second with a 1-yard touchdown dive for a 14-7 lead. It was 14-14 early in the second quarter when the Steelers took advantage of the first of Cincinnati's miscues to go ahead for good. Punt returner Craig Yeast fumbled when hit by Amos Zereoue, and Mike Vrabel recovered at Cincinnati's 30-yard line. Six plays later, Stewart teamed with Mark Bruener on an 11-yard touchdown pass. Pittsburgh led 31-21 late in the third period before putting the game away with 2 touchdowns in 91 seconds. First, Jason Gildon sacked Akili Smith, forcing a fumble that led to Jerome Bettis's 7-yard touchdown run. Then, Gildon recovered an errant Shotgun snap and returned it 22 yards for a touchdown on the final play of the quarter for an insurmountable 45-21 lead. Stewart, who sat out the final quarter, was 11 of 20 for 182 yards and 3 touchdowns. Akili Smith was 10 of 20 for 129 yards and 1 touchdown. Corey Dillon rushed for 128 yards and 2 scores.

Pittsburgh	14	10	21	3	—	48
Cincinnati	7	7	7	7	—	28

Pitt — Ward 34 pass from Stewart (Brown kick)
Cin — Bennett 37 run (Rackers kick)
Pitt — Stewart 1 run (Brown kick)
Cin — Dillon 20 run (Rackers kick)
Pitt — Bruener 11 pass from Stewart (Brown kick)
Pitt — FG Brown 44
Cin — Dillon 4 run (Rackers kick)
Pitt — Shaw 45 pass from Stewart (Brown kick)
Pitt — Bettis 7 run (Brown kick)
Pitt — Gildon 22 fumble return (Brown kick)
Cin — Warrick 5 pass from Smith (Rackers kick)
Pitt — FG Brown 28

JACKSONVILLE 16, TENNESSEE 13—at ALLTEL Stadium, attendance 65,454. Mike Hollis kicked a 38-yard field goal as time ran out to give the Jaguars an upset victory over their nemesis in the AFC Central. The game was tied at 13-13 midway through the fourth quarter when the Titans took possession for the final time at their 44-yard line. Eddie George rushed for 21 yards and caught a pass for 21 yards on a drive that reached Jacksonville's 10 with 3:13 remaining, but Al Del Greco pulled a 28-yard field goal wide left. The Jaguars took over on their 20, and on third down from there, Mark Brunell teamed with Keenan McCardell on a 30-yard completion to midfield. Brunell then completed a pair of 15-yard passes to Jimmy Smith to position Hollis for his winning kick. Brunell was 15 of 25 for 237 yards and 1 touchdown, with 2 interceptions. Fred Taylor ran for 104 yards (his sixth consecutive 100-yard game) and had a 10-yard touchdown catch in the first quarter. George rushed for 69 yards and a touchdown and caught 7 passes for 109 yards. The victory was a bit of redemption for the struggling Jaguars, who won 15 of 18 games (including playoffs) in 1999, but failed to reach the Super Bowl as all three defeats came against the Titans.

Tennessee	7	3	0	3	—	13
Jacksonville	10	0	3	3	—	16

Jax — FG Hollis 27
Tenn — George 7 run (Del Greco kick)
Jax — Taylor 10 pass from Brunell (Hollis kick)
Tenn — FG Del Greco 30
Jax — FG Hollis 20
Tenn — FG Del Greco 38
Jax — FG Hollis 38

SUNDAY NIGHT, NOVEMBER 26

N.Y. GIANTS 31, ARIZONA 7—at Sun Devil Stadium, attendance 42,094. The Giants snapped a two-game losing streak and remained within a half-game of the lead in the NFC East with an easy victory over the Cardinals. New York marched 65 yards on its first possession, took the lead on Kerry Collins's 5-yard touchdown pass to Mark Campbell, and never was challenged. The Cardinals failed to generate a first down on any of their first four possessions, then lost a fumble after driving into Giants' territory on their fifth. By that time, New York led 14-0, an advantage that grew to 21 points when Tiki Barber ran 23 yards for a touchdown midway through the third quarter. Arizona, which lost for the sixth time in seven weeks, managed its lone touchdown in the third quarter, when Michael Pittman turned a screen pass from Dave Brown into a 36-yard scoring play. Collins was 20 of 30 for 232 yards and 1 touchdown. Brown, playing in place of the injured Jake Plummer, was 18 of 36 passes for 192 yards and 1 touchdown, with 1 interception, in his first start of the season.

N.Y. Giants	7	7	7	10	—	31
Arizona	0	0	7	0	—	7

NYG — Campbell 5 pass from Collins (Daluiso kick)
NYG — Dayne 1 run (Daluiso kick)
NYG — Barber 23 run (Daluiso kick)
Ariz — Pittman 36 pass from Brown (Blanchard kick)
NYG — Toomer 19 run (Daluiso kick)
NYG — FG Daluiso 25

MONDAY NIGHT, NOVEMBER 27

CAROLINA 31, GREEN BAY 14—at Ericsson Stadium, attendance 62,518. Steve Beuerlein passed for 3 touchdowns, and unheralded running backs Brad Hoover and Chris Hetherington scored touchdowns to pace the Panthers to the victory. Beuerlein wasted little time staking Carolina to a 14-0 lead, capping the Panthers' first two drives with touchdown passes of 3 yards to Hetherington and 12 yards to Muhsin Muhammad. The Packers rallied to tie the game at 14-14 in the second quarter by converting Beuerlein's fumble and an interception into touchdowns, but Carolina regained the lead for good when Joe Nedney kicked a 26-yard field goal 1:01 before halftime. In the second half, the Panthers scored 14 points following Packers' turnovers to seal the outcome. Three plays into the third quarter, Eugene Robinson recovered a fumble by Antonio Freeman and returned it 22 yards to Green Bay's 5-yard line, setting up Beuerlein's 3-yard touchdown pass to Muhammad for a 24-14 advantage. And early in the fourth quarter, Eric Davis intercepted Brett Favre's pass and returned it 8 yards to the Packers' 12. Three plays later, Hoover ran 1 yard for a touchdown. Beuerlein was 22 of 37 for 243 yards and 3 touchdowns, with 1 interception. Hoover, an undrafted free agent starting in place of the injured Tshimanga Biakabutuka, rushed for 117 yards on 24 carries. His touchdown was the first of his career, while Hetherington scored only the second touchdown of his five-year career. Muhammad caught 11 passes for 131 yards. Favre was 31 of 51 for 267 yards and 1 touchdown, with 3 interceptions.

Green Bay	0	14	0	0	—	14
Carolina	14	3	7	7	—	31

Car — Hetherington 3 pass from Beuerlein (Nedney kick)
Car — Muhammad 12 pass from Beuerlein (Nedney kick)
GB — Green 26 run (Longwell kick)
GB — Driver 32 pass from Favre (Longwell kick)
Car — FG Nedney 26
Car — Muhammad 3 pass from Beuerlein (Nedney kick)
Car — Hoover 1 run (Nedney kick)

FOURTEENTH WEEK SUMMARIES

American Football Conference

Eastern Division	**W**	**L**	**T**	**Pct.**	**Pts.**	**OP**
Miami	10	3	0	.769	270	166
N.Y. Jets	9	4	0	.692	287	246
Buffalo	7	6	0	.538	243	270
Indianapolis	7	6	0	.538	334	283
New England	4	9	0	.308	222	277
Central Division						
Tennessee	10	3	0	.769	256	188
Baltimore	9	4	0	.692	262	135
Pittsburgh	7	6	0	.538	253	201
Jacksonville	6	7	0	.462	284	272
Cincinnati	3	10	0	.231	158	294
Cleveland	3	11	0	.214	137	360
Western Division						
Oakland	10	3	0	.769	372	256
Denver	9	4	0	.692	409	316
Kansas City	5	8	0	.385	307	304
Seattle	5	8	0	.385	246	308
San Diego	1	12	0	.077	223	352

National Football Conference

Eastern Division	**W**	**L**	**T**	**Pct.**	**Pts.**	**OP**
N.Y. Giants	9	4	0	.692	253	198
Philadelphia	9	5	0	.643	300	214
Washington	7	6	0	.538	245	210
Dallas	4	9	0	.308	249	300
Arizona	3	10	0	.231	190	366
Central Division						
Minnesota#	11	2	0	.846	330	267
Detroit	8	5	0	.615	264	251
Tampa Bay	8	5	0	.615	320	204
Green Bay	6	7	0	.462	277	268
Chicago	3	10	0	.231	169	301
Western Division						
New Orleans	8	5	0	.615	279	245
St. Louis	8	5	0	.615	439	383
Carolina	6	7	0	.462	257	221
San Francisco	5	8	0	.385	335	353
Atlanta	3	11	0	.214	216	377

#Clinched playoff berth

THURSDAY, NOVEMBER 30

MINNESOTA 24, DETROIT 17—at Metrodome, attendance 64,214. The Vikings built a 14-point lead, then held off the Lions in a Thursday night game to become the first team this season to clinch a playoff berth. Troy Walters returned a punt 63 yards to set up Robert Smith's 1-yard touchdown run on Minnesota's first possession, and Daunte Culpepper tossed a 4-yard touchdown pass to Cris Carter on the first play of the second quarter to cap the Vikings' second drive for a 14-0 lead. It was 17-3 at halftime, but the Lions pulled within a touchdown early in the fourth quarter, converting Allen Aldridge's interception into a 3-yard touchdown run by James Stewart. Detroit had the ball twice after that with a chance to draw even, but Minnesota's defense stiffened after the Lions reached the Vikings' 38-yard line on one possession and midfield on the next. Smith then put the game out of reach when he ran 43 yards for a touchdown with 3:04 left. He finished the game with 115 yards on 17 carries. Culpepper was 19 of 32 for 160 yards and 1 touchdown, with 2 interceptions. Carter's touchdown came on the 1,000th reception of his career, a mark previously reached only by the 49ers' Jerry Rice. Stoney Case was 23 of 33 for 230 yards and 1 touchdown, with 1 interception. Case relieved starting quarterback Charlie Batch in the second quarter with Batch still ailing from the sore ribs he suffered in the victory over New England on Thanksgiving Day a week earlier.

Detroit	0	3	0	14	—	17
Minnesota	7	10	0	7	—	24

Minn — Smith 1 run (Anderson kick)
Minn — Carter 4 pass from Culpepper (Anderson kick)
Det — FG Hanson 52
Minn — FG Anderson 40
Det — Stewart 3 run (Hanson kick)
Minn — Smith 43 run (Anderson kick)
Det — Foster 40 pass from Case (Hanson kick)

SUNDAY, DECEMBER 3

CINCINNATI 24, ARIZONA 13—at Paul Brown Stadium, attendance 50,289. Corey Dillon ran for 216 yards and a touchdown as the Bengals snapped a four-game losing streak. Dillon, who rushed for a league-record 278 yards in Cincinnati's victory over Denver in week 8, carried the ball 35 times and was one of four NFL running backs to surpass the 200-yard mark in week 14. No more than two players ever had reached that figure in one weekend before. Dillon set the tone early, running 57 yards on the Bengals' second play to set up Scott Mitchell's 2-yard touchdown pass to Tony McGee 4:14 into the game. By halftime, Dillon had 134 yards and Cincinnati had a 14-0 lead. It was 21-0 in the third quarter before the Cardinals rallied behind 2 touchdown passes from Jake Plummer to David Boston, but Dillon and Brandon Bennett each carried 7 times on a 17-play, 69-yard drive that consumed 7:25 of the fourth quarter and led to Neil Rackers' clinching 32-yard field goal with 1:02 left. Scott Mitchell was 11 of 23 for 103 yards and 1 touchdown, with 1 interception. Cincinnati ran the ball 54 times on 78 offensive plays and gained 292 of its 398 yards on the ground. Plummer was 22 of 44 for 278 yards and 2 touchdowns, with 1 interception. Boston had 9 receptions for 184 yards.

Arizona	0	0	7	6	—	13
Cincinnati	7	7	7	3	—	24

Cin — McGee 2 pass from Mitchell (Rackers kick)
Cin — Dillon 1 run (Rackers kick)
Cin — Bennett 7 run (Rackers kick)
Ariz — Boston 38 pass from Plummer (Blanchard kick)
Ariz — Boston 15 pass from Plummer (kick failed)
Cin — FG Rackers 32

JACKSONVILLE 48, CLEVELAND 0—at ALLTEL Stadium, attendance 51,262. The Jaguars never were challenged en route to their third consecutive victory. Fred Taylor rushed for 181 yards and 3 touchdowns, Mark Brunell passed for 1 touchdown and ran for another, and Jacksonville's defense suffocated the Browns, who lost for the tenth time in 11 games. Cleveland managed only 2 first downs and 53 total yards, and never crossed midfield. Jacksonville, meanwhile, amassed 28 first downs and 449 total yards while maintaining possession for 37:11 of the game's 60 minutes. Brunell was 15 of 31 for 165 yards and 1 touchdown. Jimmy Smith had 6 receptions for 104 yards. Spergon Wynn made his first career start for the Browns but was only 5 of 16 for 17 yards. Cleveland equaled the largest margin of defeat in franchise history.

Cleveland	0	0	0	0	—	0
Jacksonville	3	17	21	7	—	48

Jax — FG Hollis 40
Jax — Taylor 3 run (Hollis kick)
Jax — FG Hollis 24
Jax — McCardell 14 pass from Brunell (Hollis kick)
Jax — Taylor 2 run (Hollis kick)
Jax — Brunell 8 run (Hollis kick)
Jax — Taylor 1 run (Hollis kick)
Jax — Stith 3 run (Hollis kick)

TAMPA BAY 27, DALLAS 7—at Raymond James Stadium, attendance 65,621. Warrick Dunn rushed for a career-high 210 yards and scored 2 touchdowns to lead the Buccaneers over the Cowboys for the first time in franchise history. Tampa Bay was in control from the start, converting Jason Tucker's muff on the opening kickoff into a short field goal by Martin Gramatica just 1:10 into the game, then opening a 10-0 lead when Dunn raced 70 yards for a touchdown on the first play of the Buccaneers' next series. Late in the first quarter, Troy Aikman's pass from deep in Dallas territory bounced off the hands of Chris Warren and into the arms of Brian Kelly, who returned the pick 9 yards for a touchdown and a 17-0 lead. Dunn, who added a 4-yard scoring run midway through the fourth quarter, became the third running back this year to amass more than 200 yards against the Cowboys' defense. It had happened only two times in the first 40 seasons in Dallas's history. The Buccaneers amassed 250 of their 301 total yards on the ground. Tampa Bay's victory was its first ever against Dallas, after having lost the first eight games between the two franchises. Shaun King was 9 of 15 for 65 yards. Aikman was 16 of 30 for 158 yards, with 1 interception.

Dallas	0	0	7	0	—	7
Tampa Bay	17	3	0	7	—	27

TB — FG Gramatica 28
TB — Dunn 70 run (Gramatica kick)
TB — Kelly 9 interception return (Gramatica kick)
TB — FG Gramatica 25
Dall — Smith 4 run (Seder kick)
TB — Dunn 4 run (Gramatica kick)

DENVER 38, NEW ORLEANS 23—at Louisiana Superdome, attendance 64,900. Mike Anderson rushed for an NFL-rookie-record 251 yards and scored 4 touchdowns to lead the Broncos to their fifth consecutive victory. The Saints entered the game with the NFL's fourth-ranked defense (the third best against the run), but could not contain Anderson, who was coming off a 195-yard, 2-touchdown effort against Seattle. A sixth-round draft pick out of Utah, Anderson began the season as Denver's third-string back, but moved into the starting lineup after injuries to Terrell Davis and Olandis Gary. Anderson opened the scoring with a 13-yard touchdown run in the first quarter, then put the Broncos ahead for good with a 5-yard touchdown run 5:15 into the second quarter. He added scoring bursts of 7 and 2 yards to keep the game out of New Orleans's reach. The Saints tried to rally behind the passing of Aaron Brooks, but got no closer than 15 points in the second half. Gus Frerotte was 11 of 16 for 201 yards and 1 touchdown, a 43-yard touchdown strike to Dwayne Carswell. Anderson's rushing total of 446 yards in weeks 13 and 14 surpassed Corey Dillon's 415 yards in weeks 8 and 9 as the NFL's third-best ever in back-to-back games. Brooks was 30 of 48 for a club-record 441 yards and 2 touchdowns, with 2 interceptions in just his second career start. Joe Horn had 10 receptions for 170 yards, and Robert Wilson added 8 catches for 122 yards.

Denver	7	21	3	7	—	38
New Orleans	7	6	3	7	—	23

Den — Anderson 13 run (Elam kick)
NO — Glover 19 pass from Brooks (Brien kick)
Den — Anderson 5 run (Elam kick)
NO — FG Brien 30
Den — Carswell 43 pass from Frerotte (Elam kick)
Den — Anderson 7 run (Elam kick)
NO — FG Brien 19
Den — FG Elam 22
NO — FG Brien 42
Den — Anderson 2 run (Elam kick)
NO — Jackson 28 pass from Brooks (Brien kick)

N.Y. JETS 27, INDIANAPOLIS 17—at Giants Stadium, attendance 78,138. Curtis Martin rushed for a club-record 203 yards to carry the Jets to their third victory in a row and hand the Colts their third consecutive defeat. New York took the opening kickoff and held the ball for 6:13, marching 78 yards in 12 plays and taking a 7-0 lead on Vinny Testaverde's 11-yard touchdown pass to Wayne Chrebet. Indianapolis went three-and-out on its first possession, then the Jets started another touchdown march from their 30. Martin's 36-yard run was the key play on the drive, which was capped by Testaverde's 13-yard touchdown pass to Dedric Ward. Two field goals by John Hall upped the Jets' advantage to 20-0 before Indianapolis got on track. Mike Vanderjagt's 32-yard field goal and touchdown passes from Peyton Manning to Marvin Harrison (17 yards) and Terrence Wilkins (43 yards) pulled the Colts within three points in the fourth quarter. Indianapolis then forced a punt and took over possession at its 20-yard line with 5:01 to play. But on first down, a botched snap was recovered by Bryan Cox. Four plays later, Martin ran in from the 2 for the clinching touchdown with 3:17 remaining. Testaverde was 26 of 41 for 295 yards and 2 touchdowns, with 1 interception. Martin, who carried 30 times, surpassed 1,000 yards for the season and joined Barry Sanders and Eric Dickerson as the only players in NFL history to reach that plateau in each of their first six years. Manning was 27 of 51 for 339 yards and 2 touchdowns, with 2 interceptions. Edgerrin James, who entered the game as the league's leading rusher, was limited to 49 yards on 11 carries.

Indianapolis	0	0	10	7	—	17
N.Y. Jets	14	6	0	7	—	27

NYJ — Chrebet 11 pass from Testaverde (Hall kick)
NYJ — Ward 13 pass from Testaverde (Hall kick)
NYJ — FG Hall 45
NYJ — FG Hall 21
Ind — FG Vanderjagt 32
Ind — Harrison 17 pass from Manning (Vanderjagt kick)
Ind — Wilkins 43 pass from Manning (Vanderjagt kick)
NYJ — Martin 2 run (Hall kick)

MIAMI 33, BUFFALO 6—at Ralph Wilson Stadium, attendance 73,002. Lamar Smith rushed for 100 yards and scored a touchdown to pace the visiting Dolphins to an easy victory in a game played in 27-degree weather. Smith, who missed Miami's victory over Indianapolis in week 13 with a hamstring injury, returned to the lineup and carried the ball on each of the Dolphins' first five plays, then capped the opening 9-play, 64-yard march by taking Jay Fiedler's short pass and turning it into a 6-yard touchdown 4:22 into the game. Fiedler, who also was back after missing one game to injury, added touchdown passes of 6 yards to Oronde Gadsden and 14 yards to Leslie Shepherd as Miami built a 24-0 halftime lead. Olindo Mare, who had a 32-yard field goal in the second quarter, kicked second-half field goals of 31, 20, and 26 yards. Buffalo averted a shutout by converting a fumble by Fiedler into a 2-yard touchdown run by Antowain Smith on the first play of the fourth quarter. Fiedler was 13 of 21 for 214 yards and 3 touchdowns. Rob Johnson was 6 of 18 for 44 yards, with 2 interceptions before being pulled in favor of Doug Flutie late in the third quarter. By then the score was 30-0, and Flutie fared no better, going 2 of 9 for 31 yards, with 1 interception.

Miami	7	17	6	3	—	33
Buffalo	0	0	0	6	—	6

Mia — Smith 6 pass from Fiedler (Mare kick)
Mia — Gadsden 6 pass from Fiedler (Mare kick)
Mia — FG Mare 32
Mia — Shepherd 14 pass from Fiedler (Mare kick)
Mia — FG Mare 31
Mia — FG Mare 20
Buff — Smith 1 run (run failed)
Mia — FG Mare 26

N.Y. GIANTS 9, WASHINGTON 7—at FedEx Field, attendance 83,485. Three field goals by Brad Daluiso were enough for the Giants to fend off the Redskins and move into first place in the NFC East. Daluiso made kicks of 46, 27, and 28 yards as New York built a 9-0 lead through three quarters. But midway through the fourth quarter, Jeff George replaced an ineffective Brad Johnson at quarterback and led Washington on a 10-play, 97-yard drive capped by a 5-yard touchdown pass to Irving Fryar, pulling the Redskins within two points with 4:48 to go. After forcing a punt, Washington took over possession at its 14 with 2:39 left. George quickly marched the Redskins into Giants' territory, but the drive stalled at New York's 30. With 56 seconds left, Eddie Murray attempted a 49-yard field goal. The kick was on target but short, and it sailed under the crossbar. It was the second time in as many weeks that the 44-year-old kicker narrowly missed a an important kick at the end of the game. He also had a 39-yard try bounce off the upright in the second quarter. New York moved one-half game ahead of Philadelphia in the division race. Washington lost for the fourth time in five games and fell to the brink of elimination from the playoffs. Head coach Norv Turner was fired the next day and replaced by Terry Robiskie, the team's wide receivers coach and passing game coordinator. Johnson, making his first start after missing three games with a knee injury, was 14 of 29 for 126 yards, with 2 interceptions. George was 10 of 18 for 143 yards and 1 touchdown in his short stint. Kerry Collins was 18 of 29 for 164 yards, with 1 interception.

N.Y. Giants	0	6	3	0	—	9
Washington	0	0	0	7	—	7

NYG — FG Daluiso 46
NYG — FG Daluiso 27
NYG — FG Daluiso 28
Wash — Fryar 5 pass from George (Murray kick)

PITTSBURGH 21, OAKLAND 20—at Three Rivers Stadium, attendance 55,811. Kordell Stewart left the game with a knee injury in the first half but returned in the second to ignite a comeback by the Steelers. Stewart's 19-yard touchdown pass to Bobby Shaw gave Pittsburgh a 7-0 lead on its first possession. But Stewart gave way to backup Kent Graham after spraining his knee late in the opening period. Graham's first pass was intercepted by Eric Allen, who returned it 27 yards for a touchdown to give the Raiders a 10-7 lead 1:06 into the second quarter. Rich Gannon's 21-yard touchdown pass to Randy Jordan late in the first half upped Oakland's advantage to 17-7. But Stewart returned to the game after the second-half kickoff, and the Steelers maintained possession for 9:10 on a 16-play, 91-yard march capped by his 6-yard touchdown pass to Mark Bruener. On the second play of the fourth quarter, Stewart dashed 17 yards for a touchdown and a 21-17 lead. The Raiders trimmed their deficit to 1 point when Sebastian Janikowski kicked a 42-yard field goal on the next possession, then had the ball two more times after that. But Janikowski missed a 44-yard field goal try with 3:59 left, and Gannon lost track of downs on the final possession, misfiring on a fourth-and-1 toss from Pittsburgh's 41 in the closing seconds when he thought it was third down. Stewart was 14 of 23 for 136 yards and 2 touchdowns. Jerome Bettis added 128 yards on the ground, including a 30-yard run to set up Stewart's winning score. Gannon was 21 of 40 for 273 yards and 1 touchdown.

Oakland	0	17	0	3	—	20
Pittsburgh	7	0	7	7	—	21

Pitt — Shaw 19 pass from Stewart (Brown kick)
Oak — FG Janikowski 40
Oak — Allen 27 interception return (Janikowski kick)
Oak — Jordan 21 pass from Gannon (Janikowski kick)
Pitt — Bruener 6 pass from Stewart (Brown kick)
Pitt — Stewart 17 run (Brown kick)
Oak — FG Janikowski 42

CAROLINA 16, ST. LOUIS 3—at Ericsson Stadium, attendance 46,659. Kurt Warner returned to the lineup for the defending Super Bowl-champion Rams, but it was the Panthers' defense that stole the show with a dominating effort. Carolina completely shut down St. Louis's high-powered attack, forcing 7 turnovers and limiting the Rams to only a field goal on the game's opening possession. The Panthers' defense also scored the game's lone touchdown when Jimmy Hitchcock intercepted Warner's pass and returned it 88 yards for a touchdown with 5:19 left in the third quarter. That play gave Carolina a 7-3 lead, and the Panthers sealed the victory with field goals on three consecutive possessions in the fourth quarter, the first two following interceptions of Warner. The 1999 NFL MVP was rusty after missing five weeks with a broken finger. Steve Beuerlein was 20 of 30 for 195 yards, with 2 interceptions. Carolina did little on offense, managing only 237 total yards. But with the aid of the turnovers, Carolina controlled the ball for 37:55 of the game's 60 minutes. Warner was 18 of 36 for 189 yards, with 4 interceptions. The Rams also hurt themselves with 3 lost fumbles and 9 penalties.

St. Louis	3	0	0	0	—	3
Carolina	0	0	7	9	—	16

StL — FG Wilkins 38
Car — Hitchcock 88 interception return (Nedney kick)
Car — FG Nedney 20
Car — FG Nedney 23
Car — FG Nedney 37

SAN FRANCISCO 45, SAN DIEGO 17—at Qualcomm Stadium, attendance 57,255. Jeff Garcia and Jerry Rice teamed on a pair of touchdown passes as the 49ers blasted the Chargers to win their third consecutive game. San Francisco led 10-7 late in the first half before Garcia began a 74-yard drive with a 28-yard completion to Rice. Five plays later, Rice caught a 1-yard touchdown pass from Garcia to up the 49ers' advantage to 10 points 1:10 before halftime. Midway through the fourth quarter, the two teamed again on a 12-yard touchdown pass to put the 49ers ahead 38-17. The Chargers had the ball four times after Leaf's 17-yard touchdown pass to Curtis Conway pulled them within 27-17 with 12:47 to play. But Leaf was intercepted on each possession, and the 49ers converted the miscues into 17 points, including Monty Montgomery's 46-yard interception return for a touchdown with 1:39 to play. Garcia was 18 of 32 for 323 yards and 2 touchdowns. Leaf was 24 of 47 for 266 yards and 1 touchdown, with 4 interceptions.

San Francisco	0	17	10	18	—	45
San Diego	7	3	0	7	—	17

SD — Fletcher 7 run (Carney kick)
SF — FG Richey 22
SF — Beasley 1 run (Richey kick)
SF — Rice 1 pass from Garcia (Richey kick)
SD — FG Carney 34
SF — FG Richey 28
SF — Garner 4 run (Richey kick)
SD — Conway 17 pass from Leaf (Carney kick)
SF — FG Richey 38
SF — Rice 12 pass from Garcia (Stokes pass from Garcia)
SF — Montgomery 46 interception return (Richey kick)

SEATTLE 30, ATLANTA 10—at Georgia Dome, attendance 44,680. Jon Kitna passed for 252 yards and a touchdown, and the Seahawks sent the Falcons to their fifth consecutive defeat. Seattle was in control from the start, taking the opening kickoff and marching 82 yards in eight plays for a touchdown. Kitna completed all 5 of his passes on the drive, including a 38-yard pass to Ricky Watters and a 6-yard strike to Darrell Jackson for a touchdown 3:42 into the game. Two plays later, George Koonce intercepted Doug Johnson's pass and returned it 27 yards for a touchdown and a 14-0 lead. Seattle eventually led by as many as 27 points. Kitna was 25 of 34 for 252 yards and 1 touchdown. Watters had 137 yards from scrimmage and scored a touchdown. Johnson, a rookie free agent making his first start for Atlanta, was 17 of 33 for 233 yards and 1 touchdown, with 2 interceptions, sacked 4 times, and lost 2 fumbles.

Seattle	17	7	6	0	—	30
Atlanta	0	3	0	7	—	10

Sea — Jackson 6 pass from Kitna (Lindell kick)
Sea — Koonce 27 interception return (Lindell kick)
Sea — FG Lindell 46
Atl — FG Andersen 36
Sea — Watters 1 run (Lindell kick)
Sea — FG Lindell 45
Sea — FG Lindell 29
Atl — Kelly 19 pass from Johnson (Andersen kick)

TENNESSEE 15, PHILADELPHIA 13—at Veterans Stadium, attendance 65,639. Al Del Greco accounted for all of the Titans' points with 5 field goals, including the game winner from 50 yards out as time ran out. Del Greco, whose missed kicks were pivotal in Tennessee's losses two of the previous three weeks, redeemed himself and kept the Titans in first place in the AFC Central, ahead of idle Baltimore. He made field goals of 26, 42, 22, and 44 yards as Tennessee forged a 12-6 lead in the fourth quarter. But after the latter, which came with 5:23 to play, the Eagles embarked on the game's lone touchdown drive, a 77-yard march in 8 plays. Donovan McNabb completed passes of 45 yards to Todd Pinkston and 18 yards to Charles Johnson, then scored from 2 yards out to give Philadelphia a 13-12 advantage at the 3:11 mark. After an exchange of punts, the Titans began the winning drive from their 36 with no time outs and 1:43 to play. Steve McNair teamed with Derrick Mason on a 13-yard pass, then completed successive short tosses of 6, 1, 4, 8, and 5 yards to move the ball to the Eagles' 32 with six seconds to go. From there, Del Greco made his winning kick. McNair, who had to leave the game briefly in the third quarter with knee and ankle injuries, was 23 of 37 for 210 yards. Eddie George added 101 yards on the ground for Tennessee, which controlled the ball for 38:42 of the game's 60 minutes. McNabb was 18 of 31 for 239 yards and rushed for 39. Minus the 33 yards he lost when sacked, he accounted for all but 17 of the Eagles' 262 total yards.

Tennessee	0	6	3	6	—	15
Philadelphia	3	3	0	7	—	13

Phil — FG Akers 23
Tenn — FG Del Greco 26
Tenn — FG Del Greco 42
Phil — FG Akers 40
Tenn — FG Del Greco 22
Tenn — FG Del Greco 44
Phil — McNabb 2 run (Akers kick)
Tenn — FG Del Greco 50

SUNDAY NIGHT, DECEMBER 3

GREEN BAY 28, CHICAGO 6—at Soldier Field, attendance 56,146. Ahman Green rushed for 2 touchdowns and Brett Favre passed for another as the Packers won in Chicago for the seventh consecutive year. Green, who rushed for 69 yards, had a 2-yard touchdown run on the first play of the second quarter to open the scoring. His 8-yard touchdown run midway through the third quarter capped an 81-yard drive and gave the Packers a 21-3 advantage. Tyrone Williams's 38-yard interception return for a touchdown one minute into the fourth quarter ended any doubts about the game's outcome. Favre was 19 of 31 for 225 yards and 1 touchdown. He surpassed 3,000 yards passing for the ninth consecutive season, equaling Dan Marino's NFL record. Shane Matthews was 22 of 43 for 233 yards, with 2 interceptions.

Green Bay	0	14	7	7	—	28
Chicago	0	3	0	3	—	6

GB — Green 2 run (Longwell kick)
Chi — FG Edinger 32
GB — Freeman 5 pass from Favre (Longwell kick)
GB — Green 8 run (Longwell kick)
GB — T. Williams 38 interception return (Longwell kick)
Chi — FG Edinger 46

MONDAY NIGHT, DECEMBER 4

NEW ENGLAND 30, KANSAS CITY 24—at Foxboro Stadium, attendance 50,328. Drew Bledsoe passed for 282 yards and 2 touchdowns as the Patriots sent the Chiefs reeling to their fifth consecutive defeat. Bledsoe had touchdown passes of 17 yards to Troy Brown and 1 yard to Jermaine Wiggins to help New England forge a 27-10 lead entering the final period. But Kansas City rallied behind quarterback Elvis Grbac, who tossed scoring strikes of 4 yards to Tony Gonzalez and 19 yards to Kevin Lockett, the latter pulling the Chiefs within six points with 3:58 left. Kansas City had one more possession after that, taking over at its 26-yard with no time outs and 1:02 remaining. Grbac completed passes of 29 and 23 yards to Gonzalez as the Chiefs marched to the Patriots' 12 with 11 seconds to go. Grbac found Gonzalez again on the next play, but the tight end was tackled inbounds at the 7 and time ran out. Bledsoe was 33 of 48 for 282 yards and 2 touchdowns. Brown had 12 catches for 119 yards. Grbac was 25 of 46 for 350 yards and 3 touchdowns, with 1 interception. Gonzalez caught 11 passes for 147 yards, while Derrick Alexander added 116 yards on 5 receptions, including an 81-yard touchdown in the second quarter.

Kansas City	3	7	0	14	—	24
New England	10	10	7	3	—	30

NE — FG Vinatieri 48
KC — FG Peterson 42
NE — Faulk 1 run (Vinatieri kick)
KC — Alexander 81 pass from Grbac (Peterson kick)
NE — Brown 17 pass from Bledsoe (Vinatieri kick)
NE — FG Vinatieri 53
NE — Wiggins 1 pass from Bledsoe (Vinatieri kick)
KC — Gonzalez 4 pass from Grbac (Peterson kick)
NE — FG Vinatieri 27
KC — Lockett 19 pass from Grbac (Peterson kick)

FIFTEENTH WEEK SUMMARIES

American Football Conference

Eastern Division	**W**	**L**	**T**	**Pct.**	**Pts.**	**OP**
Miami	10	4	0	.714	283	182
N.Y. Jets	9	5	0	.643	294	277
Indianapolis	8	6	0	.571	378	303
Buffalo	7	7	0	.500	263	314
New England	4	10	0	.286	239	301
Central Division						
Tennessee#	11	3	0	.786	291	191
Baltimore#	10	4	0	.714	286	138
Jacksonville	7	7	0	.500	328	282
Pittsburgh	7	7	0	.500	263	231
Cincinnati	3	11	0	.214	161	329
Cleveland	3	12	0	.200	161	395
Western Division						
Oakland#	11	3	0	.786	403	263
Denver#	10	4	0	.714	440	340
Kansas City	6	8	0	.429	322	318
Seattle	5	9	0	.357	270	339
San Diego	1	13	0	.071	226	376

National Football Conference

Eastern Division	**W**	**L**	**T**	**Pct.**	**Pts.**	**OP**
N.Y. Giants	10	4	0	.714	283	208
Philadelphia#	10	5	0	.667	335	238
Washington	7	7	0	.500	258	242
Dallas	5	9	0	.357	281	313
Arizona	3	11	0	.214	200	410
Central Division						
Minnesota#	11	3	0	.786	359	307
Tampa Bay	9	5	0	.643	336	217
Detroit	8	6	0	.571	277	277
Green Bay	7	7	0	.500	303	281
Chicago	4	10	0	.286	193	318
Western Division						
New Orleans	9	5	0	.643	310	272
St. Louis	9	5	0	.643	479	412
Carolina	6	8	0	.429	271	236
San Francisco	5	9	0	.357	362	384
Atlanta	3	11	0	.214	216	377

#Clinched playoff spot

SUNDAY, DECEMBER 10

JACKSONVILLE 44, ARIZONA 10—at ALLTEL Stadium, attendance 53,472. Fred Taylor ran for 2 touchdowns, and Mark Brunell passed for 2 as the Jaguars continued their late-season surge with a rout of the Cardinals. Jacksonville won its fourth in a row and improved to 7-7, though it was too late to make the playoffs for one of the preseason favorites in the AFC. The Jaguars scored on their first seven possessions and built leads of 24-0 and 44-3. Taylor rushed for 137 yards on 23 carries, eclipsing the 100-yard mark for the eighth consecutive game. Only Barry Sanders (14 games), Marcus Allen (11), and Walter Payton (9) have had longer streaks. Brunell was 13 of 18 for 182 yards and 2 touchdowns as Jacksonville amassed 469 total yards. Jimmy Smith caught 8 passes for 147 yards, including a 65-yard touchdown from backup Jamie Martin in the fourth quarter. Dave Brown was 11 of 19 for 135 yards, with 1 interception.

Arizona	0	3	0	7	—	10
Jacksonville	10	17	10	7	—	44

Jax — FG Hollis 36
Jax — Taylor 1 run (Hollis kick)
Jax — Brady 8 pass from Brunell (Hollis kick)
Jax — Taylor 4 run (Hollis kick)
Ariz — FG Blanchard 32
Jax — FG Hollis 50
Jax — FG Hollis 40
Jax — McCardell 25 pass from Brunell (Hollis kick)
Jax — J. Smith 65 pass from Martin (Hollis kick)
Ariz — Sanders 26 pass from Griesen (Blanchard kick)

CHICAGO 24, NEW ENGLAND 17—at Soldier Field, attendance 66,944. Shane Matthews passed for 2 touchdowns, and James Allen scored twice to lead the Bears to the victory. The game was tied 10-10 at halftime before Chicago took the lead for good on the opening possession of the second half. Beginning from their own 36-yard line, the Bears marched 64 yards in 7 plays, with Matthews completing 2 passes to Eddie Kennison for 26 yards and Allen rushing 5 times for 38 yards, including a 16-yard touchdown run 4:08 into the half. On the first play of the fourth quarter, Matthews and Allen teamed on a 6-yard touchdown pass, and Chicago's lead was 24-10. New England pulled within 7 points when Drew Bledsoe passed 7 yards for a touchdown to Troy Brown on the next drive, but the Patriots could not score on their final three possessions. Their last chance ended when Bledsoe completed a 10-yard pass to Brown to the Bears' 21-yard line with 10 seconds left. But the play was nullified by a penalty against New England for illegal motion. By rule, 10 seconds were wiped off the clock, ending the game. Bledsoe was 25 of 46 for 225 yards and 2 touchdowns, but was supported by only 38 yards from the ground game. Matthews completed a club-record 15 consecutive passes en route to a 22-of-27, 239-yard, 2-touchdown performance. Kennison had 100 yards and a touchdown on 8 catches, and Allen had 97 rushing yards.

New England	0	10	0	7	—	17
Chicago	3	7	7	7	—	24

Chi — FG Edinger 24
NE — Glenn 12 pass from Bledsoe (Vinatieri kick)
NE — FG Vinatieri 40
Chi — Kennison 9 pass from Matthews (Edinger kick)
Chi — Allen 16 run (Edinger kick)
Chi — Allen 6 pass from Matthews (Edinger kick)
NE — T. Brown 7 pass from Bledsoe (Vinatieri kick)

DALLAS 32, WASHINGTON 13—at Texas Stadium, attendance 63,467. Emmitt Smith became the third player in NFL history with 15,000 career rushing yards and keyed the Cowboys' rout in Terry Robiskie's debut as the Redskins' coach. Smith rushed for 150 yards and a touchdown and surpassed the 1,000-yard mark for a record-tying tenth consecutive season. He finished the game with 15,100 yards, third only to Walter Payton (16,726) and Barry Sanders (15,269). Smith carried 23 times as Dallas kept the ball on the ground for 43 of its 54 plays and gained 242 of its 314 total yards by rushing. Wane McGarity and Jason Tucker contributed to the ground attack by scoring touchdowns on reverses. McGarity's came from 22 yards and gave the Cowboys a 12-7 lead 5:42 before halftime. Dallas would not relinquish the lead, and when Tucker ran 17 yards for his touchdown midway through the fourth quarter, the Cowboys had their biggest lead at 29-7. The lone disappointment for Dallas as it completed a season sweep of its division rival was a concussion suffered by quarterback Troy Aikman in the first quarter. Aikman gave way to untested Anthony Wright, who was called on to attempt only 5 passes. He completed 3 for 73 yards. Jeff

George was 19 of 33 for 235 yards and 1 touchdown, with 1 interception. Washington, which hoped to get a spark when offensive assistant Robiskie was named to replace the fired Norv Turner earlier in the week, lost for the fifth time in six games and fell to 7-7.

Washington	0	7	0	6	—	13
Dallas	6	6	10	10	—	32

Dall — FG Seder 33
Dall — FG Seder 19
Wash — Davis 1 run (Murray kick)
Dall — McGarity 22 run (run failed)
Dall — E. Smith 2 run (Seder kick)
Dall — FG Seder 20
Dall — Tucker 17 run (Seder kick)
Wash — Fryar 32 pass from George (pass failed)
Dall — FG Seder 43

N.Y. GIANTS 30, PITTSBURGH 10—at Giants Stadium, attendance 78,164. Kerry Collins passed for 2 touchdowns, and the Giants moved a step closer to the playoffs with an easy victory. New York was in command from the start, with its defense forcing the Steelers to punt on their first three possessions while its offense was building a 13-0 lead on the strength of 2 field goals by Brad Daluiso and Tiki Barber's 3-yard touchdown run. After Pittsburgh closed within 13-3 at halftime, the Giants broke open the game by scoring on each of their three possessions in the second half (excluding a kneeldown to end the game). Most of the damage was done through the air, with Collins passing seven times on a 10-play, 74-yard drive capped by his 9-yard touchdown toss to Ike Hilliard for a 20-3 advantage with 5:24 left in the third quarter. On the final play of the period, Collins and Hilliard teamed again on a 59-yard completion to the Steelers' 7-yard line, positioning Daluiso for a 21-yard field goal 1:33 into the fourth quarter. Collins's 2-yard touchdown pass to Amani Toomer ended an 11-play, 80-yard drive and made it 30-3 in the final minutes. With the victory, the Giants remained atop the NFC East, a half game ahead of Philadelphia, and needing only one victory in their final two games to assure themselves of the division title. Collins was 24 of 35 for 333 yards and 2 touchdowns in leading the Giants to their third consecutive victory. Toomer caught 9 passes for 136 yards. Kordell Stewart was 10 of 34 for 224 yards and 1 touchdown, with 1 interception.

Pittsburgh	0	3	0	7	—	10
N.Y. Giants	3	10	7	10	—	30

NYG — FG Daluiso 38
NYG — FG Daluiso 40
NYG — Barber 3 run (Daluiso kick)
Pitt — FG Brown 32
NYG — Hilliard 9 pass from Collins (Daluiso kick)
NYG — FG Daluiso 21
NYG — Toomer 2 pass from Collins (Daluiso kick)
Pitt — Shaw 5 pass from Stewart (Brown kick)

TAMPA BAY 16, MIAMI 13—at Pro Player Stadium, attendance 74,307. Martin Gramatica kicked 2 field goals in a span of 2:24 of the fourth quarter to lift the Buccaneers to victory. Olindo Mare's 23-yard field goal and Lamar Smith's 1-yard touchdown run rallied the Dolphins from a 10-3 halftime deficit to take a 13-10 lead late in the third quarter. But Tampa Bay then embarked on its only drive that produced a first down in the second half, much of which was played in a torrential downpour. The Buccaneers marched 77 yards in 13 plays and 7:42, tying the game on Gramatica's 30-yard field goal with 10:36 remaining. On the next play from scrimmage, Jay Fiedler couldn't handle the snap in the wet conditions, and Jamie Duncan pounced on the ball at the Dolphins' 30-yard line. After three plays netted only 3 yards, Gramatica made the go-ahead field goal from 46 yards with 8:12 to go. Miami's next two possessions resulted in an interception and a punt, and the Dolphins took over for the last time at midfield with 1:57 remaining. Two penalties helped move the ball to Tampa Bay's 19 with 39 seconds remaining, but on first down from there, Fielder was called for intentional grounding, pushing the ball back to the 30. On the next play, he was intercepted by Damien Robinson. It was the Buccaneers' fourth interception of the game, 1 of which was returned 31 yards by Duncan for a touchdown in the second quarter. The combination of the rain and stingy defenses limited the offensive output of both teams. Shaun King was 11 of 15 for 147 yards, with 1 interception. Fiedler was 13 of 28 for 175 yards, with 4 interceptions.

Tampa Bay	0	10	0	6	—	16
Miami	3	0	10	0	—	13

Mia — FG Mare 35
TB — Duncan 31 interception return (Gramatica kick)
TB — FG Gramatica 38
Mia — FG Mare 23
Mia — L. Smith 1 run (Mare kick)
TB — FG Gramatica 30
TB — FG Gramatica 46

TENNESSEE 35, CINCINNATI 3—at Adelphia Coliseum, attendance 68,498. Steve McNair emerged from a slump by passing for 3 touchdowns to key the Titans' rout. The defending AFC champions, who secured a playoff berth with the victory, scored touchdowns on three consecutive possessions and never were challenged. McNair, who had not thrown a touchdown pass in his past three starts, completed scoring passes with Yancey Thigpen (56 yards) and Eddie George (7 and 3 yards). McNair was 16 of 26 for 229 yards and 3 touchdowns. Backup Neil O'-Donnell played much of the fourth quarter and completed all 6 of his passes for 93 yards for the Titans, who amassed 443 total yards. The Bengals, meanwhile, generated only 171 total yards. Scott Mitchell was 12 of 26 for 131 yards. Corey Dillon, who rushed for 344 yards the previous two weeks, was limited to 42 yards on 18 carries.

Cincinnati	0	3	0	0	—	3
Tennessee	14	7	7	7	—	35

Tenn — Thigpen 56 pass from McNair (Del Greco kick)
Tenn — George 5 run (Del Greco kick)
Cin — FG Rackers 45
Tenn — George 7 pass from McNair (Del Greco kick)
Tenn — George 3 pass from McNair (Del Greco kick)
Tenn — Neal 1 pass from O'Donnell (Del Greco kick)

BALTIMORE 24, SAN DIEGO 3—at PSINet Stadium, attendance 68,805. The Ravens won their fifth consecutive game and clinched a playoff berth for the first time in the franchise's history. Trent Dilfer passed for 2 touchdowns, Jamal Lewis ran for 1, and Baltimore's defense feasted on the Chargers' turnover-prone offense. San Diego lost 4 fumbles and an interception, managed only 9 first downs and 128 total yards, and maintained possession for just 22:24 of the game's 60 minutes. The Chargers' lone score came when Rodney Harrison's interception and 19-yard return led to a 14-yard drive that resulted in John Carney's 47-yard field goal in the final minute of the first half. Carney's kick pulled San Diego within 10-3, but the Ravens put the game away by converting a pair of Chargers' miscues into touchdowns in the third quarter. First, Rob Burnett recovered a fumble by Terrell Fletcher at San Diego's 3-yard line, leading to Lewis's 1-yard run 4:13 into the second half. Then, when DeRon Jenkins muffed a punt return 4:02 later, Brad Jackson recovered at San Diego's 17. On third down from the 22, Dilfer threw a strike to Brandon Stokley for the touchdown. Dilfer was 16 of 24 for 187 yards and 2 touchdowns, with 2 interceptions. Ryan Leaf was 9 of 23 for 78 yards, with 1 interception.

San Diego	0	3	0	0	—	3
Baltimore	3	7	14	0	—	24

Balt — FG Stover 32
Balt — Ismail 28 pass from Dilfer (Stover kick)
SD — FG Carney 47
Balt — Ja. Lewis 1 run (Stover kick)
Balt — Stokley 22 pass from Dilfer (Stover kick)

DENVER 31, SEATTLE 24—at Mile High Stadium, attendance 75,218. Mike Anderson rushed for 131 yards and 2 touchdowns, and the Broncos withstood a second-half comeback to defeat the Seahawks. Denver led 14-3 at halftime, then took the second-half kickoff and held the ball for 7:09, marching 85 yards in 13 plays and increasing its advantage to 18 points when Anderson ran 1 yard for a touchdown. He had 52 yards on 8 carries on the drive. Charlie Rogers fumbled on the ensuing kickoff, and Keith Burns recovered at Seattle's 27-yard line. Three plays later, Jason Elam's 38-yard field goal made it 24-3. The Seahawks rallied, scoring touchdowns on their next two possessions on passes from Jon Kitna to Sean Dawkins (4 yards) and to Darrell Jackson (9 yards) to pull within 24-17 with 9:21 to play. But Denver answered the threat when Gus Frerotte's 41-yard pass to Ed McCaffrey set up Anderson's 6-yard touchdown run with 5:57 to play. Kitna's 22-yard touchdown pass to Dawkins narrowed Seattle's deficit to seven points with 2:28 to play, but McCaffrey recovered an onside kick attempt and the Broncos ran out the clock. Frerotte was 14 of 25 for 201 yards and 1 touchdown, with 1 interception. McCaffrey caught 8 passes for 112 yards. Kitna was 26 of 41 for 298 yards and 3 touchdowns, with 3 interceptions, 1 of which was returned 79 yards for a touchdown by Jimmy Spencer. The victory, coupled with Indianapolis's victory over the Bills on Monday night, assured the Broncos of at least a wild-card berth in the playoffs.

Seattle	3	0	7	14	—	24
Denver	7	7	10	7	—	31

Sea — FG Lindell 23
Den — McCaffrey 5 pass from Frerotte (Elam kick)
Den — Spencer 79 interception return (Elam kick)
Den — Anderson 1 run (Elam kick)
Den — FG Elam 38
Sea — Dawkins 4 pass from Kitna (Lindell kick)
Sea — Jackson 9 pass from Kitna (Lindell kick)
Den — Anderson 6 run (Elam kick)
Sea — Dawkins 22 pass from Kitna (Lindell kick)

PHILADELPHIA 35, CLEVELAND 24—at Cleveland Browns Stadium, attendance 72,318. Donovan McNabb passed for 390 yards and 4 touchdowns to carry the Eagles past the Browns and into the playoffs for the first time in four years. Cleveland, which had mustered little offense while losing its previous three games, jumped to a 14-7 lead in the second quarter before McNabb took control. He completed passes of 42 yards to Todd Pinkston and 11 yards to Stanley Pritchett before capping a 4-play, 66-yard drive with a 24-yard touchdown pass to Torrance Small 8:06 before halftime. McNabb and Small teamed again on an 8-yard strike at the 1:04 mark to give Philadelphia the lead for good. The Eagles opened the second half with a 68-yard drive capped by McNabb's 11-yard touchdown pass to Charles Johnson, then put the game away later in the third quarter with a 9-play, 98-yard march on which McNabb and Johnson teamed for a 38-yard touchdown. Philadelphia also had a 98-yard drive capped by the game's initial touchdown on Darnell Autry's 3-yard run. McNabb was 23 of 36 for 390 yards and 4 touchdowns. Chad Lewis had 100 yards on 5 receptions. Doug Pederson was 29 of 40 for 309 yards and 1 touchdown, with 2 interceptions. Cleveland, which had been decimated by injuries on offense, often lined up wide receivers Dennis Northcutt and Kevin Johnson at quarterback. Northcutt had 7 carries for 37 yards out of the Shotgun formation. Johnson completed 1 of 3 passes for 23 yards. Travis Prentice had a pair of 1-yard touchdown runs.

Philadelphia	7	14	14	0	—	35
Cleveland	0	14	0	10	—	24

Phil — Autry 3 run (Akers kick)
Cle — Patten 9 pass from Pederson (Dawson kick)
Cle — Prentice 1 run (Dawson kick)
Phil — Small 24 pass from McNabb (Akers kick)
Phil — Small 8 pass from McNabb (Akers kick)
Phil — C. Johnson 11 pass from McNabb (Akers kick)
Phil — C. Johnson 38 pass from McNabb (Akers kick)
Cle — FG Dawson 29
Cle — Prentice 1 run (Dawson kick)

KANSAS CITY 15, CAROLINA 14—at Arrowhead Stadium, attendance 77,481. The Chiefs snapped a five-game losing streak when Todd Peterson kicked 3 field goals, including the game winner from 33 yards out with 3:51 left. Chris Hetherington's 1-yard touchdown run and Steve Beuerlein's 15-yard touchdown pass to Kris Mangum helped stake the Panthers to a 14-3 lead midway through the third quarter. But Peterson's 24-yard field goal with 3:46 left in the period narrowed the deficit to 8 points. The next time the Chiefs had the ball, they held it for 12 plays, driving 85 yards to score when Elvis Grbac's pass for Derrick Alexander in the end zone was tipped into the hands of Tony Gonzalez for a 6-yard touchdown. A two-point conversion attempt failed, but Kansas City was within 14-12 with 12:31 still to play. After Carolina's next drive stalled near midfield, the Chiefs took possession at their 42-yard line with 7:11 left. Eight plays and 43 yards later, Peterson made his go-ahead kick. Carolina had one last chance to win after driving from its 28 to Kansas City's 30, but Joe Nedney's 48-yard field-goal try sailed wide right with 1:35 remaining. It was Nedney's first miss in 19 attempts. Grbac was 31 of 44 for 315 yards and 1 touchdown, with 2 interceptions. Gonzalez caught 10 passes for 96 yards, and Tony Richardson had 145 yards from scrimmage in his first start at halfback since Kickoff Weekend. Beuerlein was 23 of 31 for 252 yards and 1 touchdown, with 1 interception.

Carolina	0	7	7	0	—	14
Kansas City	0	3	3	9	—	15

Car — Hetherington 1 run (Nedney kick)
KC — FG Peterson 35
Car — Mangum 15 pass from Beuerlein (Nedney kick)
KC — FG Peterson 24
KC — Gonzalez 6 pass from Grbac (pass failed)
KC — FG Peterson 33

GREEN BAY 26, DETROIT 13—at Lambeau Field, attendance 58,854. Ahman Green scored 2 touchdowns in the fourth quarter as the Packers dealt the Lions' playoff hopes a blow. Ryan Longwell kicked 4 field goals to help Green Bay build a 12-3 lead entering the final period before Detroit pulled within 12-10 when James Stewart ran for a touchdown on fourth-and-goal from the 1 with 7:04 to play. But the Packers quickly regained a 9-point advantage by marching 80 yards in only 6 plays. Brett Favre completed passes of 29 yards to Antonio Freeman and 45 yards to Bill Schroeder to position Green for a 3-yard touchdown pass with 4:25 left. Jason Hanson countered with a 36-yard field goal for the Lions at the 2:17 mark, but after a failed onside kick, Green put the game out of reach by racing 39 yards for a touchdown with 1:54 remaining. Favre was 15 of 36 for 208 yards and 1 touchdown. Green finished with 118 yards on 27 carries. Charlie Batch was 17 of 33 for 190 yards , with 3 interceptions.

Detroit	0	0	3	10	—	13
Green Bay	6	0	3	17	—	26

GB — FG Longwell 23
GB — FG Longwell 27
Det — FG Hanson 26
GB — FG Longwell 26
GB — FG Longwell 45
Det — Stewart 1 run (Hanson kick)
GB — Green 3 pass from Favre (Longwell kick)
Det — FG Hanson 36
GB — Green 39 run (Longwell kick)

NEW ORLEANS 31, SAN FRANCISCO 27—at 3Com Park, attendance 67,892. The Saints survived a scare and remained tied atop the NFC West standings when recently acquired Terry Allen ran 1 yard for a touchdown with 46 seconds remaining in the game. Jeff Garcia ran for 2 touchdowns and passed for 2, including a 69-yard strike to Terrell Owens that gave the 49ers a 27-17 lead with 8:27 left in the game. But New Orleans took only 5 plays to counter, marching 69 yards and pulling within 27-24 on Aaron Brooks's 22-yard touchdown pass to Willie Jackson with 5:46 to go. After forcing a punt, the Saints began their last possession at their 32-yard line with 4:00 left. On fourth-and-4 from the 38, Brooks made a critical play when it appeared he would be sacked for a big loss, scrambling for 10 yards and a first down. Six plays later, Chad Morton ran 11 yards to the 1. Terrelle Smith fumbled on the next play, but New Orleans recovered, then Allen scored the winning touchdown. Allen, a 10-year veteran who last played for the Patriots in 1999, was signed only two weeks earlier to help make up for the loss of Ricky Williams. Brooks was 12 of 29 for 203 yards and 2 touchdowns. He also ran for 108 yards. Allen rushed for 80 yards on 18 carries in his first extensive action with his new team. Garcia was 25 of 38 for 305 yards and 2 touchdowns, with 2 interceptions. Owens caught 6 passes for 129 yards.

New Orleans	3	0	11	17	—	31
San Francisco	7	7	0	13	—	27

SF — Garcia 8 run (Richey kick)
NO — FG Brien 40
SF — Garcia 1 run (Richey kick)
NO — FG Brien 41
NO — A. Glover 15 pass from Brooks (Allen run)
SF — Clark 4 pass from Garcia (Richey kick)
NO — FG Brien 28
SF — Owens 69 pass from Garcia (run failed)
NO — W. Jackson 22 pass from Brooks (Brien kick)
NO — Allen 1 run (Brien kick)

ST. LOUIS 40, MINNESOTA 29—at Trans World Dome, attendance 66,273. Kurt Warner nearly was flawless while passing for 346 yards, and Marshall Faulk rushed for 4 touchdowns as the Rams ended their three-game losing streak. Though he didn't throw a touchdown pass for the second consecutive game since returning to the lineup from a broken finger, Warner completed 27 of 32 passes against the Vikings. He was 9 of 9 on St. Louis's first two drives, each of which Faulk capped with 1-yard touchdown runs, as the Rams jumped out to a 14-0 lead. After Minnesota pulled within 20-14 early in the second half, Warner completed strikes of 21 and 22 yards to Torry Holt as St. Louis countered with a 79-yard drive that ended with Faulk's 5-yard touchdown run with 8:09 left in the third quarter. On the Rams' next possesion, Warner and Holt teamed on a 36-yard completion to ignite a 73-yard drive capped by Faulk's 1-yard touchdown run for a 33-14 lead. Warner was 27 of 32 for 346 yards. Faulk finished with 135 yards on 25 carries and 43 yards on 6 catches. Holt had 9 receptions for 172 yards for St. Louis, which amassed 32 first downs and 508 total yards. Daunte Culpepper was 21 of 33 for 221 yards and 3 touchdowns and ran for a touchdown. Minnesota gained 312 total yards, its twenty-ninth consecutive game with more than 300. That equaled the longest streak in NFL history, established by the Rams of 1949-1951.

Minnesota	0	7	14	8	—	29
St. Louis	14	6	13	7	—	40

StL — Faulk 1 run (Wilkins kick)
StL — Faulk 1 run (Wilkins kick)
StL — FG Wilkins 26
Minn — McWilliams 22 pass from Culpepper (Anderson kick)
StL — FG Wilkins 19
Minn — Culpepper 8 run (Anderson kick)
StL — Faulk 5 run (pass failed)
StL — Faulk 1 run (Wilkins kick)
Minn — C. Carter 2 pass from Culpepper (Anderson kick)
StL — Watson 6 run (Wilkins kick)
Minn — Moss 32 pass from Culpepper (Moss pass from Culpepper)

SUNDAY NIGHT, DECEMBER 10

OAKLAND 31, N.Y. JETS 7—at Network Associates Coliseum, attendance 62,632. Rich Gannon passed for 2 touchdowns and the Raiders held New York scoreless until the final minute to clinch their first playoff berth since 1993. The game was scoreless until Eric Allen intercepted Vinny Testaverde's tipped pass and returned it 50 yards for a touchdown 2:29 into the second quarter. That opened the flood gates for the Raiders, who added touchdowns on Gannon's 7-yard pass to Andre Rison and Tyrone Wheatley's 1-yard run for a 21-0 lead at intermission. Gannon's second touchdown pass, to Tim Brown 44 seconds into the fourth quarter, increased the lead to 28 points. It was 31-0 before the Jets averted a shutout when rookie Chad Pennington tossed a 5-yard touchdown pass to Wayne Chrebet with 24 seconds to play. Pennington was the third quarterback New York utilized. Gannon was 11 of 23 for 161 yards and 2 touchdowns, with 1 interception. Allen and William Thomas each had 2 interceptions for the Raiders' defense, which limited Curtis Martin to 11 yards on 17 carries. Martin was coming off a 203-yard rushing effort against the Colts the previous week. Testaverde completed 14 of 25 passes for 149 yards in the first half, but had to leave the game with a groin injury suffered on a second-quarter sack. Backup Ray Lucas was just 6 of 14 for 99 yards, with 2 interceptions before giving way to Pennington, who engineered a 69-yard drive in the final two minutes. The crowd of 62,632 was a Network Associates Coliseum record.

N.Y. Jets	0	0	0	7	—	7
Oakland	0	21	0	10	—	31

Oak — Allen 50 interception return (Janikowski kick)
Oak — Rison 7 pass from Gannon (Janikowski kick)
Oak — Wheatley 1 run (Janikowski kick)
Oak — T. Brown 4 pass from Gannon (Janikowski kick)
Oak — FG Janikowski 32
NYJ — Chrebet 5 pass from Pennington (Hall kick)

MONDAY NIGHT, DECEMBER 11

INDIANAPOLIS 44, BUFFALO 20—at RCA Dome, attendance 56,671. The Colts exploded for 35 points in the second half to put an end to their three-game losing streak and remain alive in the AFC playoff chase. The Bills dropped their third consecutive game and, with it, any chance to reach the postseason. Indianapolis led just 9-6 at halftime in a battle of field goals before taking control in the third quarter after big plays by its special teams and defense. After Mark Thomas recorded 1 of the Colts' 9 sacks to force a punt on the opening possession of the second half, Paul Shields blocked Chris Mohr's kick to set up Indianapolis at the Bills' 25-yard line. Edgerrin James ran the ball on four consecutive plays, the last for a 1-yard touchdown to give Indianapolis a 16-6 lead. The teams exchanged punts, then the Colts opened up a 23-6 advantage when Jeff Burris sacked Rob Johnson, forcing a fumble that Bernard Holsey scooped up and returned 48 yards for a touchdown with 3:58 left in the third period. James added 2 more touchdown runs in the fourth quarter, and Mustafah Muhammad returned an interception 40 yards for a touchdown. James finished with 111 yards on 27 carries. Peyton Manning was 13 of 24 for 132 yards and did not throw a touchdown pass for the first time all season. Johnson was 12 of 22 for 188 yards, with 2 interceptions and gave way to Doug Flutie in the fourth quarter. Flutie was 6 of 12 for 82 yards, including a 29-yard touchdown to Peerless Price. Cornelius Bennett and Brad Scioli each had 2 sacks for Indianapolis.

Buffalo	3	3	6	8	—	20
Indianapolis	3	6	14	21	—	44

Buff — FG Christie 29
Ind — FG Vanderjagt 37
Ind — FG Vanderjagt 23
Buff — FG Christie 46
Ind — FG Vanderjagt 39
Ind — James 1 run (Vanderjagt kick)
Ind — Holsey 48 fumble return (Vanderjagt kick)
Buff — Morris 1 run (kick failed)
Ind — James 1 run (Vanderjagt kick)
Ind — Muhammad 40 interception return (Vanderjagt kick)
Buff — Price 29 pass from Flutie (Bryson run)
Ind — James 13 run (Vanderjagt kick)

SIXTEENTH WEEK SUMMARIES

American Football Conference

Eastern Division	**W**	**L**	**T**	**Pct.**	**Pts.**	**OP**
Miami	10	5	0	.667	296	202
Indianapolis	9	6	0	.600	398	316
N.Y. Jets	9	6	0	.600	301	287
Buffalo	7	8	0	.467	273	327
New England	5	10	0	.333	252	311
Central Division						
Tennessee#	12	3	0	.800	315	191
Baltimore#	11	4	0	.733	299	145
Pittsburgh	8	7	0	.533	287	234
Jacksonville	7	8	0	.467	342	299
Cincinnati	4	11	0	.267	178	343
Cleveland	3	13	0	.188	161	419
Western Division						
Oakland#	11	4	0	.733	427	290
Denver#	10	5	0	.667	447	360
Kansas City	7	8	0	.467	342	325
Seattle	6	9	0	.400	297	363
San Diego	1	14	0	.067	248	406

National Football Conference

Eastern Division	**W**	**L**	**T**	**Pct.**	**Pts.**	**OP**
N.Y. Giants*	11	4	0	.733	300	221
Philadelphia#	10	5	0	.667	335	238
Washington	7	8	0	.467	261	266
Dallas	5	10	0	.333	294	330
Arizona	3	12	0	.200	207	423
Central Division						
Minnesota#	11	4	0	.733	387	340
Tampa Bay#	10	5	0	.667	374	252
Detroit	9	6	0	.600	287	284
Green Bay	8	7	0	.533	336	309
Chicago	4	11	0	.267	193	335
Western Division						
New Orleans*	10	5	0	.667	333	279
St. Louis	9	6	0	.600	514	450

Carolina	7	8	0	.467	301	258
San Francisco	6	9	0	.400	379	384
Atlanta	3	12	0	.200	223	400

**Clinched division title*
#Clinched playoff berth

SATURDAY, DECEMBER 16

SEATTLE 27, OAKLAND 24—at Husky Stadium, attendance 68,681. A bizarre safety and Jon Kitna's touchdown pass to Darrell Jackson in the final minute helped lift the Seahawks to a dramatic come-from-behind victory over the Raiders. Seattle trailed by 11 points early in the fourth quarter before pulling within 24-19 on Shaun Alexander's 4-yard touchdown run with 5:16 left. The next time the Seahawks had the ball, Ricky Watters took a handoff at his 19-yard line and appeared to be on his way to a long touchdown run. But after 53 yards, he was chased down by Charles Woodson, who knocked the ball loose and sent it bouncing toward the end zone. Marquez Pope fell on the ball at the 2, but slid into the end zone on a slippery turf wet with rain. When James Williams fell on him there, it was ruled a safety that trimmed the Seahawks' deficit to three points with 2:24 remaining. Seattle took possession at its 39 following the ensuing free kick and covered the remaining 61 yards in 9 plays. Kitna converted a third-and-1 at Oakland's 16 with a 2-yard sneak with 45 seconds left, then teamed with Jackson on the winning 9-yard pass with 28 seconds to go. Willie Williams sealed the victory 16 seconds later with an interception at the Seahawks' 28. Kitna was 19 of 30 for 177 yards and 2 touchdowns, with 1 interception. Watters rushed for 168 yards. Gannon was 5 of 17 for 136 yards and 1 touchdown, with 3 interceptions. Tyrone Wheatley rushed for 146 yards, and Randy Jordan had 2 touchdown runs.

Oakland	7	3	7	7	—	24
Seattle	10	3	0	14	—	27

Sea — Strong 13 pass from Kitna (Lindell kick)
Oak — Rison 14 pass from Gannon (Janikowski kick)
Sea — FG Lindell 40
Oak — FG Janikowski 25
Sea — FG Lindell 52
Oak — Jordan 6 run (Janikowski kick)
Oak — Jordan 7 run (Janikowski kick)
Sea — Alexander 4 run (pass failed)
Sea — Safety, Williams tackled Pope in end zone
Sea — Jackson 9 pass from Kitna (run failed)

PITTSBURGH 24, WASHINGTON 3—at Three Rivers Stadium, attendance 58,183. With many Steelers greats from the past three decades in attendance, Pittsburgh relied on a couple of staples from that era—a stalwart defense and a devastating rushing attack—to close Three Rivers Stadium with a rout of the Redskins. Jerome Bettis rushed for 104 yards, and backfield mate Richard Huntley had touchdown runs of 3 and 30 yards to key the victory. Hank Poteat returned a punt 53 yards for a touchdown. The Steelers gained 190 of their 364 yards on the ground and limited Washington to just a first-quarter field goal while forcing 5 turnovers. Pittsburgh won four Super Bowls in its 31 seasons in Three Rivers. The Steelers will move into a new facility adjacent to it for the 2001 season. Washington, which led the NFC East after eight weeks, lost for the sixth time in seven games and officially fell out of postseason contention. Kordell Stewart was 11 of 21 for 175 yards. Jeff George was 15 of 27 for 178 yards, with 2 interceptions.

Washington	3	0	0	0	—	3
Pittsburgh	0	17	0	7	—	24

Wash — FG Murray 32
Pitt — FG Brown 28
Pitt — Poteat 53 punt return (Brown kick)
Pitt — Huntley 3 run (Brown kick)
Pitt — Huntley 30 run (Brown kick)

SUNDAY, DECEMBER 17

NEW ORLEANS 23, ATLANTA 7—at Louisiana Superdome, attendance 64,900. Aaron Brooks passed for 285 yards, Terry Allen rushed for 82 yards, and the Saints were in the playoffs for only the fifth time in franchise history by the end of week 16. New Orleans was in command from the start but did not score until Doug Brien kicked a 20-yard field goal in the second quarter. Three plays later, Doug Johnson's pass was intercepted by Sammy Knight, who returned it 31 yards for a touchdown and a 10-0 lead. It was 13-0 before the Falcons trimmed their deficit to 6 points when Darrick Vaughn returned the second-half kickoff 88 yards for a touchdown. But New Orleans countered by driving 75 yards in 9 plays and opening a 20-7 lead on Allen's 2-yard touchdown run 5:15 into the third quarter. Atlanta drove into Saints' territory on its next two possessions but turned the ball over on an interception and a fumble, then never advanced past its 28-yard line after that. Brooks was 24 of 35 for 285 yards, and Joe Horn caught 7 passes for 116 yards for New Orleans, which had a sizeable 373 to 163 advantage in total yards. Johnson completed only 5 of 10 passes for 45 yards, with 1 interception, before being lifted in favor of Chris Chandler in the second half. Chandler was 4 of 10 for 81 yards, with 1 interception.

Atlanta	0	0	7	0	—	7
New Orleans	0	13	7	3	—	23

NO — FG Brien 20
NO — Knight 31 interception return (Brien kick)
NO — FG Brien 46
Atl — Vaughn 88 kickoff return (Andersen kick)
NO — Allen 2 run (Brien kick)
NO — FG Brien 47

BALTIMORE 13, ARIZONA 7—at Sun Devil Stadium, attendance 37,452. The visiting Ravens overcame a sloppy performance to win their sixth in a row and hand the Cardinals their sixth consecutive defeat. Jamal Lewis rushed for 126 yards and a touchdown, but Baltimore generated little offense otherwise. But the Cardinals managed only 1 touchdown on 6 trips inside Baltimore territory. Their last two possessions ended when tight end Terry Hardy fumbled at the Ravens' 10 and when Jake Plummer's fourth-down pass from Baltimore's 12 was knocked down by linebacker Ray Lewis with 1:57 to play. Jamal Lewis carried on five consecutive plays after that and generated 2 first downs to help run out the clock. Trent Dilfer was 12 of 22 for 70 yards, with 1 interception, and was sacked 4 times for 33 yards. Plummer was 23 of 43 for 266 yards and 1 touchdown, with 2 interceptions.

Baltimore	3	0	10	0	—	13
Arizona	0	0	7	0	—	7

Balt — FG Stover 42
Ariz — Sanders 27 pass from Plummer (Blanchard kick)
Balt — Ja. Lewis 1 run (Stover kick)
Balt — FG Stover 42

SAN FRANCISCO 17, CHICAGO 0—at 3Com Park, attendance 68,306. Terrell Owens caught 20 passes to break an NFL record that stood for half a century and helped carry the 49ers to an easy victory. Owens, who had 283 receiving yards, eclipsed the league mark of 18 receptions set by the Rams' Tom Fears in 1950. Owens had 11 catches in the first half, had a 27-yard touchdown catch on his thirteenth reception in the third quarter, and broke Fears's record with an 11-yard catch with a little more than four minutes remaining in the game. His big day overshadowed Jerry Rice's last home game in a 49ers' uniform. Rice, who was not expected to return to the club in 2001, caught 7 passes for 76 yards. Jeff Garcia was 36 of 44 passes for 402 yards and 2 touchdowns. Chicago never mounted a threat on offense. The Bears did not cross midfield and managed only 8 first downs and 104 total yards. Cade McNown was 9 of 29 for 73 yards, with 1 interception.

Chicago	0	0	0	0	—	0
San Francisco	7	3	7	0	—	17

SF — Clark 1 pass from Garcia (Richey kick)
SF — FG Richey 28
SF — Owens 27 pass from Garcia (Richey kick)

KANSAS CITY 20, DENVER 7—at Arrowhead Stadium, attendance 78,406. Tony Richardson rushed for 156 yards and a touchdown as the Chiefs foiled the Broncos' bid to take control of the AFC West. After front-running Oakland lost to Seattle a day earlier, Denver had a chance to move into a tie for first place in the division and control its own destiny by virtue of its season sweep of the Raiders. But Richardson rushed for more yards than any other Kansas City player in 10 years to key a ground attack that amassed 264 yards. His 23-yard run sparked a 70-yard drive capped by Frank Moreau's 2-yard touchdown run that gave the Chiefs the lead for good 5:37 into the second half. Midway through the fourth quarter, Richardson scored on a 28-yard touchdown burst to open a 10-point advantage. The Broncos' usually potent offense managed only 11 first downs and did not score. Denver's lone points came when a punt bounced off the helmet of Kevin Lockett and into the end zone, where it was recovered by Jason Suttle for a touchdown. Elvis Grbac was 14 of 28 for 160 yards and scrambled for 38 yards. Gus Frerotte was 22 of 34 for 234 yards.

Denver	0	7	0	0	—	7
Kansas City	3	0	7	10	—	20

KC — FG Peterson 40
Den — Suttle fumble recovery in end zone (Elam kick)
KC — Moreau 2 run (Peterson kick)
KC — Richardson 28 run (Peterson kick)
KC — FG Peterson 27

DETROIT 10, N.Y. JETS 7—at Giants Stadium, attendance 77,513. The Lions stayed in contention for a playoff berth when guard Jeff Hartings fell on a fumble in the end zone for the winning touchdown with 5:43 to play. Detroit trailed 7-3 before Stephen Boyd intercepted Vinny Testaverde's pass at the Jets' 46-yard line 4:28 into the fourth quarter. James Stewart carried on five of the next seven plays as the Lions marched to the 1. On third-and-goal, the Lions gave it to Stewart again, but this time he fumbled when hit at the goal line. The ball sailed into the end zone, where Hartings recovered it for a rare touchdown by an offensive lineman. New York still had two possessions after that. The Jets punted on one, then drove to Detroit's 17-yard line as time wound down. But John Hall hooked a 35-yard field-goal try wide left with nine seconds to play. Hall also had missed a 47-yard attempt near the end of the first half. Stewart rushed for a career-high 164 yards on 37 attempts to carry the Lions on a wet and sloppy field. New York managed just 240 total yards and scored its only touchdown on Curtis Martin's 1-yard run in the first quarter. Victor Green's interception and 27-yard return to the 1 set up that score. Charlie Batch was 8 of 18 for 110 yards, with 1 interception. Testaverde was 21 of 36 for 194 yards, with 1 interception.

Detroit	0	0	3	7	—	10
N.Y. Jets	7	0	0	0	—	7

NYJ — Martin 1 run (Hall kick)
Det — FG Hanson 35
Det — Hartings fumble recovery in end zone (Hanson kick)

GREEN BAY 33, MINNESOTA 28—at Metrodome, attendance 64,183. Brett Favre passed for 3 touchdowns, and Ahman Green rushed for a career-high 161 yards as the Packers handed the NFC Central-leading Vikings their second consecutive defeat. Ryan Longwell added 4 field goals for Green Bay, which won for only the second time in its past nine games in the Metrodome and kept its slim playoff chances alive. Favre helped the Packers open a 10-0 lead when he teamed with Antonio Freeman on an 18-yard touchdown pass late in the first quarter. Each time Minnesota pulled close, Favre countered with another touchdown pass. It was 10-7 in the second quarter before he capped an 80-yard drive with a 6-yard touchdown pass to Green, and it was 23-21 before he ended a 64-yard march with a 3-yard touchdown pass to Bill Schroeder on the first play of the fourth quarter. After the Vikings narrowed their deficit to 33-28 on Daunte Culpepper's 5-yard touchdown pass to Cris Carter with 2:38 left, Green carried on four consecutive plays to help run out the clock. Favre was 26 of 38 for 290 yards and 3 touchdowns. Culpepper was 23 of 38 for 335 yards and 3 touchdowns, with 1 interception. He also ran 3 yards for another score. But the Packers limited Robert Smith, the NFC's leading rusher, to only 26 yards on 10 carries. The Vikings missed a chance to clinch the division title and secure home-field advantage throughout the NFC playoffs.

Green Bay	10	10	3	10	—	33
Minnesota	7	7	7	7	—	28

GB — FG Longwell 34
GB — Freeman 18 pass from Favre (Longwell kick)
Minn — Moss 78 pass from Culpepper (Anderson kick)
GB — Green 6 pass from Favre (Longwell kick)
GB — FG Longwell 35
Minn — Culpepper 3 run (Anderson kick)
GB — FG Longwell 43
Minn — McWilliams 22 pass from Culpepper

(Anderson kick)
GB — Schroeder 3 pass from Favre (Longwell kick)
GB — FG Longwell 36
Minn — C. Carter 5 pass from Culpepper (Anderson kick)

INDIANAPOLIS 20, MIAMI 13—at Pro Player Stadium, attendance 73,884. Peyton Manning passed for 1 touchdown and ran for another as the Colts built a 20-3 lead, then held on to beat the Dolphins. Manning got his team off to a quick start when he teamed with Marcus Pollard on a 50-yard touchdown pass on Indianapolis's fourth play from scrimmage. Late in the first quarter, Jason Belser's fumble recovery led to a 36-yard drive capped by Manning's 4-yard touchdown run 2:38 into the second period for a 14-0 advantage. Mike Vanderjagt kicked 2 field goals to help the Colts increase their advantage to as much as 17 points, but Lamar Smith ran 8 yards for a touchdown and Olindo Mare kicked a 31-yard field goal to pull Miami within 7 points with 3:25 remaining. The Dolphins quickly forced a punt and took over on their 35-yard line with 2:34 to play. But on third down from there, Jeff Burris intercepted Jay Fiedler's pass to seal the victory. Manning was 21 of 28 for 206 yards and 1 touchdown. Edgerrin James rushed for 112 yards on 32 carries for Indianapolis. Fiedler was 12 of 25 for 150 yards, with 1 interception. Smith rushed for 97 yards for Miami, which remained atop the AFC East despite the loss.

Indianapolis	7	10	3	0	—	20
Miami	0	3	7	3	—	13

Ind — Pollard 50 pass from Manning (Vanderjagt kick)
Ind — Manning 4 run (Vanderjagt kick)
Mia — FG Mare 25
Ind — FG Vanderjagt 48
Ind — FG Vanderjagt 31
Mia — L. Smith 8 run (Mare kick)
Mia — FG Mare 31

CINCINNATI 17, JACKSONVILLE 14—at Paul Brown Stadium, attendance 50,469. Neil Rackers kicked a 27-yard field goal as time ran out to lift the Bengals to the victory and snap the Jaguars' four-game winning streak. With a game-time temperature of 9 degrees, Jacksonville led 14-7 and had a chance to extend its advantage to 10 points when Mike Hollis lined up for a 28-yard field-goal attempt with 4:43 to play. But Hollis, who had missed just one try all season, slipped on the icy turf and the kick fell short. Cincinnati then embarked on a game-tying 80-yard touchdown drive. Scott Mitchell completed back-to-back passes of 38 and 22 yards to Danny Farmer to move into Jaguars' territory, and capped the 10-play march by scrambling 12 yards for a touchdown with 1:15 to play. Tremain Mack forced Shyrone Stith to fumble on the ensuing kickoff, and Canute Curtis recovered at Jacksonville's 34. Mitchell's 8-yard pass to Farmer and a penalty on Kevin Hardy for unnecessary roughness helped position Rackers for the winning kick. Mitchell was 10 of 22 for 171 yards, including 93 on the final two drives, with 1 interception. Farmer caught 5 passes for 102 yards. Mark Brunell was 19 of 28 for 170 yards and 1 touchdown. Fred Taylor ran for 110 yards for Jacksonville. It was his ninth consecutive 100-yard rushing effort, equaling the third-longest streak in NFL history.

Jacksonville	0	7	7	0	—	14
Cincinnati	0	0	7	10	—	17

Jax — J. Smith 3 pass from Brunell (Hollis kick)
Cin — Warrick 82 punt return (Rackers kick)
Jax — Taylor 5 run (Hollis kick)
Cin — Mitchell 12 run (Rackers kick)
Cin — FG Rackers 27

NEW ENGLAND 13, BUFFALO 10 (OT)—at Ralph Wilson Stadium, attendance 47,230. Adam Vinatieri's 24-yard field goal into the wind and in the snow lifted the Patriots to the victory just 19 seconds before the end of overtime. New England trailed 10-3 before a short punt led to Kevin Faulk's tying 13-yard touchdown run with 4:45 left in regulation. The Patriots then had a chance to win after driving to the Bills' 10-yard line in the closing seconds, but Vinatieri slipped and missed a 27-yard field-goal try as time ran out. In overtime, Buffalo held the ball for 14 plays and more than six minutes on its only possession, but Steve Christie also had trouble with his footing and his 30-yard field-goal attempt was blocked. The Patriots took over at their 11 and held the ball for 14 plays themselves. A pass-interference penalty on fourth-and-5 from the Bills' 30 kept the march alive, and Drew Bledsoe scrambled 14 yards for a first down on third-and-6 from the 17 to set up the winning kick. Bledsoe was 13 of 26 for 156 yards and was aided by a running game that produced 189 yards from a committee of backs. Doug Flutie was 15 of 25 for 193 yards and 1 touchdown in relief of starter Rob Johnson, who left the game with a concussion in the second quarter.

New England	3	0	0	7	3	—	13
Buffalo	0	3	0	7	0	—	10

NE — FG Vinatieri 22
Buff — FG Christie 25
Buff — S. Jackson 1 pass from Flutie (Christie kick)
NE — Faulk 13 run (Vinatieri kick)
NE — FG Vinatieri 24

CAROLINA 30, SAN DIEGO 22—at Ericsson Stadium, attendance 42,206. The Panthers were dominated statistically but utilized big plays from their special teams to hand the Chargers their fourteenth loss in 15 games. Ryan Leaf passed for 2 touchdowns, and Gerald Dixon returned an interception 36 yards for a touchdown to help San Diego build a 22-14 lead in the third quarter. But Carolina pulled within two points when Iheanyi Uwaezuoke returned a punt 64 yards for a touchdown with 1:52 left in the period, then took the lead after converting Lee Woodall's interception into Joe Nedney's 18-yard field goal 1:20 into the fourth quarter. San Diego quickly marched into field-goal range, but John Carney's 37-yard attempt was blocked by Jay Williams. Doug Evans scooped up the loose ball and returned it 54 yards for a touchdown with 9:33 left. The Chargers had two possessions after that and moved into Panthers' territory both times but could not score. Their last drive reached Carolina's 1-yard line, but a fumbled snap and a penalty pushed the ball back to the 15, and Leaf's fourth-down pass into the end zone was incomplete. Leaf was 23 of 43 for 259 yards and 2 touchdowns, with 1 interception, for San Diego, which outgained Carolina 358 to 169 and maintained possession for 35:08 of the game's 60 minutes. Carolina managed only 11 yards rushing, and Steve Beuerlein was 12 of 27 for 139 yards and 2 touchdowns.

San Diego	2	14	6	0	—	22
Carolina	7	0	13	10	—	30

Car — Muhammad 11 pass from Beuerlein (Nedney kick)
SD — Safety, Fontenot sacked Beuerlein in end zone
SD — Fletcher 25 pass from Leaf (Carney kick)
SD — Dixon 36 interception return (Carney kick)
Car — Byrd 34 pass from Beuerlein (Nedney kick)
SD — Heiden 4 pass from Leaf (run failed)
Car — Uwaezuoke 64 punt return (pass failed)
Car — FG Nedney 18
Car — Evans 54 return of blocked field goal (Nedney kick)

TENNESSEE 24, CLEVELAND 0—at Cleveland Browns Stadium, attendance 72,318. Undaunted by snow and icy winds, Eddie George rushed for 176 yards and 3 touchdowns in the Titans' lopsided victory over the Browns. Eddie Robinson recovered Travis Prentice's fumble at Cleveland's 29-yard line on the game's second play, and the Titans converted the takeaway into Al Del Greco's 33-yard field goal 4:49 into the game. George, who also rushed for 3 touchdowns in a victory over Cleveland in week 12, had scoring runs of 1 and 2 yards before halftime, then added a 35-yard touchdown burst early in the fourth quarter. He carried 34 times in all to help the Titans maintain possession for 38:53 of the game's 60 minutes. The Browns generated little offense en route to losing their fifth consecutive game. They had only 6 first downs and 113 total yards on 49 plays from scrimmage. Steve McNair was 10 of 18 for 79 yards, with 1 interception. Doug Pederson was 13 of 30 for 75 yards.

Tennessee	10	7	0	7	—	24
Cleveland	0	0	0	0	—	0

Tenn — FG Del Greco 33
Tenn — George 1 run (Del Greco kick)
Tenn — George 2 run (Del Greco kick)
Tenn — George 35 run (Del Greco kick)

SUNDAY NIGHT, DECEMBER 17

N.Y. GIANTS 17, DALLAS 13—at Texas Stadium, attendance 61,311. The Giants clinched the NFC East title and positioned themselves for home-field advantage throughout the NFC playoffs by rallying from a 13-point halftime deficit to win. Emmitt Smith's 1-yard touchdown run and Tim Seder's 2 field goals staked the Cowboys to a 13-0 lead. But New York got on the scoreboard late in the third quarter on Kerry Collins's 33-yard touchdown strike to Amani Toomer. Midway through the fourth quarter, Emmanuel McDaniel intercepted Anthony Wright's pass deep in Dallas territory, and Tiki Barber ran 13 yards for a touchdown on the next play to give the Giants the lead at 14-13 with 8:15 left. Brad Daluiso's 44-yard field goal on New York's next possession provided the final margin of victory. Collins was 12 of 26 for 140 yards and 1 touchdown, with 1 interception. New York limited the Cowboys to 145 total yards, including just 27 in the second half. Wright was 13 of 25 for 119 yards, with 1 interception, in his first career start.

N.Y. Giants	0	0	7	10	—	17
Dallas	7	6	0	0	—	13

Dall — E. Smith 1 run (Seder kick)
Dall — FG Seder 47
Dall — FG Seder 43
NYG — Toomer 33 pass from Collins (Daluiso kick)
NYG — Barber 13 run (Daluiso kick)
NYG — FG Daluiso 44

MONDAY NIGHT, DECEMBER 18

TAMPA BAY 38, ST. LOUIS 35—at Raymond James Stadium, attendance 65,653. Warrick Dunn's third touchdown of the game, a 1-yard dive with 48 seconds left, capped a dramatic 80-yard touchdown march and lifted the Buccaneers past the Rams. Tampa Bay clinched a playoff berth with the victory and left the defending Super Bowl champions on the brink of elimination from the playoffs. St. Louis erased a 10-point, fourth-quarter deficit when Marshall Faulk ran 9 yards for a touchdown and Kurt Warner teamed with Torry Holt on a 72-yard touchdown strike with 5:18 left. After an exchange of possessions, the Buccaneers took over on their 20-yard line with 2:22 left. On second-and-10 from the 35, Dunn made the play of the night. After being trapped for a 14-yard loss, he pitched back to Shaun King, who scrambled down the right sideline to midfield. A personal foul against the Rams at the end of play moved the ball to St. Louis's 35, and on fourth-and-4 from the 29, King scrambled again for 6 yards and a first down. Two plays later, his 22-yard completion to Reidel Anthony set up Dunn's go-ahead score. John Lynch's midfield interception with 25 seconds to go sealed the victory. King was 18 of 38 for 256 yards and 2 touchdowns, with 2 interceptions, and ran for 58 yards. Dunn, who also had a 2-yard touchdown run in the second quarter and a 52-yard scoring burst in the third period, finished with 145 yards on 22 carries. He also caught 5 passes for 53 yards. Keyshawn Johnson caught 7 passes for 116 yards and 2 touchdowns. Warner was 20 of 32 for 316 yards and 2 touchdowns, wtih 3 interceptions. Faulk had 132 yards from scrimmage and scored 4 touchdowns for the Rams, and Holt caught 9 passes for 165 yards. The teams combined for 834 yards, including 446 by Tampa Bay, which won its fourth in a row and seventh in eight games.

St. Louis	7	7	7	14	—	35
Tampa Bay	10	14	7	7	—	38

TB — FG Gramatica 35
StL — Faulk 2 run (Wilkins kick)
TB — Dunn 2 run (Gramatica kick)
StL — Faulk 16 run (Wilkins kick)
TB — Johnson 8 pass from King (Gramatica kick)
TB — Johnson 17 pass from King (Gramatica kick)
StL — Faulk 27 pass from Warner (Wilkins kick)
TB — Dunn 52 run (Gramatica kick)
StL — Faulk 9 run (Wilkins kick)
StL — Holt 72 pass from Warner (Wilkins kick)
TB — Dunn 1 run (Gramatica kick)

SEVENTEENTH WEEK SUMMARIES

American Football Conference

Eastern Division	W	L	T	Pct.	Pts.	OP
Miami*	11	5	0	.688	323	226
Indianapolis#	10	6	0	.625	429	326
N.Y. Jets	9	7	0	.563	321	321
Buffalo	8	8	0	.500	315	350
New England	5	11	0	.313	276	338
Central Division						
Tennessee*	13	3	0	.813	346	191
Baltimore#	12	4	0	.750	333	165
Pittsburgh	9	7	0	.563	321	255
Jacksonville	7	9	0	.438	367	327
Cincinnati	4	12	0	.250	185	359
Cleveland	3	13	0	.188	161	419
Western Division						
Oakland*	12	4	0	.750	479	299
Denver#	11	5	0	.688	485	369
Kansas City	7	9	0	.438	355	354
Seattle	6	10	0	.375	320	405
San Diego	1	15	0	.063	269	440

National Football Conference

Eastern Division	W	L	T	Pct.	Pts.	OP
N.Y. Giants*	12	4	0	.750	328	246
Philadelphia#	11	5	0	.688	351	245
Washington	8	8	0	.500	281	269
Dallas	5	11	0	.313	294	361
Arizona	3	13	0	.188	210	443
Central Division						
Minnesota*	11	5	0	.688	397	371
Tampa Bay#	10	6	0	.625	388	269
Green Bay	9	7	0	.563	353	323
Detroit	9	7	0	.563	307	307
Chicago	5	11	0	.313	216	355
Western Division						
New Orleans*	10	6	0	.625	354	305
St. Louis#	10	6	0	.625	540	471
Carolina	7	9	0	.438	310	310
San Francisco	6	10	0	.375	388	422
Atlanta	4	12	0	.250	252	413

**Clinched division title*
#Clinched playoff berth

SATURDAY, DECEMBER 23

N.Y. GIANTS 28, JACKSONVILLE 25—at Giants Stadium, attendance 77,924. The NFC East-champion Giants scored 3 fourth-quarter touchdowns to close the regular season with five consecutive victories and secure home-field advantage throughout the NFC playoffs. New York trailed 10-7 before taking over at its 25-yard line with 14:00 left. On second down from there, Kerry Collins and Amani Toomer teamed on a 42-yard completion to move the ball into Jaguars' territory. Five plays later, Collins's 5-yard touchdown pass to Ike Hilliard gave the Giants the lead for good with 11:11 to play. Collins's 54-yard touchdown strike to Toomer opened a 21-10 advantage at the 3:05 mark. Jacksonville twice pulled within three points after that, but Jason Sehorn sealed the victory by recovering onside kicks each time. He returned the first 38 yards for a touchdown with 1:51 remaining and fell on the second with 19 seconds to go. Collins was 22 of 39 for 321 yards and 2 touchdowns, with 1 interception. Toomer caught 8 passes for 193 yards. Mark Brunell was 23 of 41 for 262 yards and 2 touchdowns, with 1 interception. Keenan McCardell had 11 receptions for 131 yards. Fred Taylor ran 44 yards for a touchdown in the second quarter but finished with just 52 yards after he was forced out of the game with a thigh bruise in the third quarter. His string of consecutive 100-yard rushing games ended at nine, tied for the third-longest in NFL history.

Jacksonville	0	7	3	15	—	25
N.Y. Giants	7	0	0	21	—	28

NYG — Barber 3 run (Daluiso kick)
Jax — Taylor 44 run (Hollis kick)
Jax — FG Hollis 36
NYG — Hilliard 5 pass from Collins (Daluiso kick)
NYG — Toomer 54 pass from Collins (Daluiso kick)
Jax — Brady 5 pass from Brunell (Brady pass from Brunell)
NYG — Sehorn 38 kickoff return (Daluiso kick)
Jax — Whitted 12 pass from Brunell (Hollis kick)

DENVER 38, SAN FRANCISCO 9—at Mile High Stadium, attendance 76,098. The Broncos routed the 49ers in the last game at Mile High Stadium. After a scoreless first period, Denver scored on all six of its possessions in the second and third quarters to build a 38-0 lead. Mike Anderson had 2 short touchdown runs, and Gus Frerotte passed for 1 touchdown and ran for another to fuel the outburst. Anderson ran for 85 yards to finish the season with 1,487 yards. His 15 touchdowns equaled the second-most ever by an NFL rookie. Ed McCaffrey caught 5 passes for 71 yards, including a 25-yard touchdown in the third quarter, and finished the season with a club-record 101 receptions. He and Rod Smith, who caught 8 passes and finished the year with 100, became only the second set of teammates to catch 100 or more passes in the same year. San Francisco, which has not been shut out in a regular-season game since 1977, did not score until Wade Richey kicked a 44-yard field goal with 9:04 remaining. Jeff Garcia added an 8-yard touchdown pass to J.J. Stokes with 39 seconds left. Frerotte completed 18 of 29 passes for 205 yards and 1 touchdown, though Brian Griese started the game at quarterback. Griese, playing for the first time since separating his shoulder against the Raiders in week 11, completed both of his attempts for 14 yards before reinjuring the shoulder. Garcia ended the season with an NFC-best 4,278 passing yards but was just 18 of 40 for 188 yards and 1 touchdown, with 1 interception, against Denver. Mile High was the Broncos' only home since the inception of the franchise in 1960. In 2001, Denver is scheduled to move into a new stadium adjacent to the old one.

San Francisco	0	0	0	9	—	9
Denver	0	17	21	0	—	38

Den — FG Elam 20
Den — Coleman 24 run (Elam kick)
Den — Anderson 1 run (Elam kick)
Den — McCaffrey 25 pass from Frerotte (Elam kick)
Den — Frerotte 13 run (Elam kick)
Den — Anderson 1 run (Elam kick)
SF — FG Richey 44
SF — Stokes 8 pass from Garcia (kick failed)

SATURDAY NIGHT, DECEMBER 23

BUFFALO 42, SEATTLE 23—at Husky Stadium, attendance 61,025. Doug Flutie passed for 3 touchdowns and Antowain Smith rushed for 3 as the Bills snapped a four-game losing streak. Flutie, embroiled in a season-long quarterback controversy with Rob Johnson, got the starting nod after Johnson suffered a concussion in a week-16 loss to New England. Flutie's third touchdown, a 6-yard strike to Jay Riemersma gave Buffalo a 28-14 lead 1:09 before halftime. Smith, who began the season as a starter but fell deep on the depth chart and entered the final game with only 207 rushing yards, gained a career-high 147 yards on 17 carries. He had 99 yards after halftime and scored on runs of 2 and 4 yards to keep the game out of reach. Smith also ran 9 yards for a touchdown late in the first quarter. Buffalo amassed 579 yards against the league's most porous defense and punted just once. Charlie Rogers's 81-yard kickoff return in the first quarter was the highlight of the game for Seattle. Flutie was 20 of 25 for 3 touchdowns and a career-high 366 yards, including scoring passes of 11 yards to Shawn Bryson and 18 yards to Peerless Price to cap the Bills' first two drives. Jon Kitna was 18 of 29 for 195 yards, with 1 interception.

Buffalo	21	7	7	7	—	42
Seattle	7	7	3	6	—	23

Buff — Bryson 11 pass from Flutie (Christie kick)
Buff — P. Price 18 pass from Flutie (Christie kick)
Sea — Rogers 81 kickoff return (Lindell kick)
Buff — A. Smith 9 run (Christie kick)
Sea — Kitna 1 run (Lindell kick)
Buff — Riemersma 6 pass from Flutie (Christie kick)
Sea — FG Lindell 38
Buff — A. Smith 2 run (Christie kick)
Sea — Watters 6 run (pass failed)
Buff — A. Smith 4 run (Christie kick)

SUNDAY, DECEMBER 24

WASHINGTON 20, ARIZONA 3—at FedEx Field, attendance 65,711. The Redskins snapped a four-game losing streak, albeit too late to salvage a playoff berth. They scored touchdowns on their first two possessions and never were challenged. Champ Bailey, normally a cornerback who played wide receiver on occasion in 2000, lined up in the backfield and capped a 65-yard drive after the opening kickoff with a 7-yard touchdown run 4:04 into the game. After recovering a fumble at the Cardinals' 33 on the next play from scrimmage, Washington needed 7 plays to pad its lead on Brad Johnson's 7-yard touchdown pass to Irving Fryar with 6:39 to play in the first quarter. Eddie Murray and Scott Bentley added field goals to make it 20-0 before Arizona registered its lone points on Cary Blanchard's 37-yard field goal 1:06 before halftime. Johnson, the Redskins' deposed starter, played in place of injured Jeff George and was 18 of 31 for 192 yards and 1 touchdown, with 2 interceptions. Stephen Davis rushed for 120 yards on 27 carries. Jake Plummer was 14 of 31 for 144 yards, with 3 interceptions. Washington, which once led the NFC East with a 6-2 record, finished 8-8. The Cardinals went 3-13, their worst season in 41 years.

Arizona	0	3	0	0	—	3
Washington	14	6	0	0	—	20

Wash — Bailey 7 run (Murray kick)
Wash — Fryar 7 pass from Johnson (Murray kick)
Wash — FG Murray 41
Wash — FG Bentley 50
Ariz — FG Blanchard 37

OAKLAND 52, CAROLINA 9—at Network Associates Coliseum, attendance 60,637. Rich Gannon passed for a career-best 5 touchdowns in a rout that gave the Raiders their first AFC Western Division title since 1990. Oakland, which also secured a bye in the first round of the playoffs, was in command from the start. The Raiders took the opening kickoff and held the ball for 6:47, marching 77 yards in 12 plays and taking a 7-0 lead on Gannon's 4-yard touchdown pass to Jeremy Brigham. It was 10-6 in the second quarter when they embarked on another lengthy drive, a 12-play, 82-yard march that consumed 6:59 and culminated with Gannon's 1-yard touchdown pass to Rickey Dudley 3:08 before halftime. Gannon's 9-yard strike to Tim Brown with 19 seconds left in the second quarter broke open the game at 24-6. Gannon added second-half touchdown passes of 21 yards to Dudley and 2 yards to Brigham, and Oakland's scoring barrage did not end until Darrien Gordon returned a fumble 74 yards on the final play, enabling the Raiders to equal the franchise record for points in a game. Gannon was 26 of 32 for 230 yards and 5 touchdowns, spreading his completions to eight different pass catchers. Oakland outgained Carolina 409 yards to 297 and held the ball for 38:24 of the game's 60 minutes. Steve Beuerlein was 12 of 21 for 156 yards, with 1 interception, before being replaced by Jeff Lewis, who was 10 of 16 for 79 yards.

Carolina	3	6	0	0	—	9
Oakland	7	17	14	14	—	52

Oak — Brigham 4 pass from Gannon (Janikowski kick)
Car — FG Nedney 46
Oak — FG Janikowski 42
Car — FG Nedney 21
Oak — Dudley 1 pass from Gannon (Janikowski kick)
Oak — Brown 9 pass from Gannon (Janikowski kick)
Car — FG Nedney 51
Oak — Dudley 21 pass from Gannon (Janikowski kick)
Oak — Allen 37 interception return (Janikowski kick)
Oak — Brigham 2 pass from Gannon (Janikowski kick)
Oak — Gordon 74 fumble return (Janikowski kick)

CHICAGO 23, DETROIT 20—at Pontiac Silverdome, attendance 71,957. Paul Edinger's 54-yard field goal with two seconds left gave the Bears a stunning victory that knocked the Lions from the playoffs. Detroit, needing only a victory over the last-place team in the NFC Central to secure a wild-card berth, took a 17-13 lead when backup Stoney Case ran 13 yards for a touchdown 3:46 into the final period. But Case, who entered the game after starter Charlie Batch aggravated a rib injury late in the first half, was intercepted on the Lions' next possession by R.W. McQuarters, who returned the pick 61 yards for a touchdown with 6:31 left. With 2:22 remaining, James Allen lost a fumble on his 10-yard line. Detroit converted that into Jason Hanson's tying 26-yard field goal with 1:56 to play, then forced a punt and took over at its 39 with 1:29 left. But on second-and-10 from the Bears' 48, Case was sacked by McQuarters and fumbled, and Rosevelt Colvin recovered at Chicago's 45. Cade McNown completed passes of 9 and 10 yards to Allen to position Edinger for the winning kick. McNown passed for 60 yards in relief of starter Shane Matthews, who broke his thumb near the end of the first half. The Bears' victory came just two minutes after the conclusion of the Rams' victory over the Saints in New Orleans and gave St. Louis the opportunity to defend its Super Bowl title as a wild-card entrant. Matthews was 14 of 18 for 123 yards, and McNown was 5 of 11 for 60 yards and 1 touchdown. Batch was 7 of 15 for 81 yards and 1 touchdown, and Case was 12 of 21 for 89 yards, with 1 interception.

Chicago	0	6	7	10	—	23
Detroit	10	0	0	10	—	20

Det — FG Hanson 41
Det — Sloan 9 pass from Batch (Hanson kick)
Chi — FG Edinger 37
Chi — FG Edinger 50
Chi — Booker 27 pass from McNown (Edinger kick)
Det — Case 13 run (Hanson kick)
Chi — McQuarters 61 interception return (Edinger kick)
Det — FG Hanson 26
Chi — FG Edinger 54

PHILADELPHIA 16, CINCINNATI 7—at Veterans Stadium, attendance 64,902. Donovan McNabb's 39-yard touchdown pass to Charles Johnson highlighted the Eagles' sixth victory in seven games, a win that secured Philadelphia a home game in the wild-card round of the playoffs. The Eagles held the ball for 18 plays and 8:12 on their first possession, a drive that ended with David Akers's 32-yard field goal. Three plays later, Bobby Taylor recovered a fumble by Danny Farmer at Cincinnati's 39-yard line. McNabb and Johnson teamed for their touchdown pass on the next play. It was 13-0 in the fourth quarter when the Bengals scored their lone touchdown on a 17-yard pass from Scott Mitchell to Peter Warrick with 3:12 to play. But Philadelphia recovered the ensuing onside kickoff, and Akers kicked his third field goal of the game, from 33 yards with 1:48 remaining, to seal the outcome. McNabb was 23 of 40 for 198 yards and 1 touchdown, with 1 interception for the Eagles, who were heading to the playoffs for the first time since 1996. Mitchell was 18 of 34 for 183 yards and 1 touchdown, with 1 interception.

Cincinnati	0	0	0	7	—	7
Philadelphia	10	3	0	3	—	16

Phil — FG Akers 32
Phil — Johnson 39 pass from McNabb (Akers kick)
Phil — FG Akers 45
Cin — Warrick 17 pass from Mitchell (Rackers kick)
Phil — FG Akers 33

ATLANTA 29, KANSAS CITY 13—at Georgia Dome, attendance 41,017. Chris Chandler passed for 2 touchdowns, and Morten Andersen kicked 5 field goals as the Falcons snapped a six-game losing streak. Chandler, back in the starting lineup after losing his job to Doug Johnson for two games, completed touchdowns of 17 yards to Shawn Jefferson and 6 yards to Brian Kozlowski. Andersen kicked 5 field goals in a game for the first time since a victory over the 49ers on Kickoff Weekend, a game in which Chandler also passed for 2 touchdowns. Chandler was 20 of 29 for 163 yards and 2 touchdowns. Jamal Anderson complemented Chandler's passing by running for 107 yards to eclipse the 1,000-yard mark for the season. Elvis Grbac was 18 of 32 for 230 yards and 1 touchdown. Tony Gonzalez caught 5 passes to finish the season with 93 receptions, the third-highest total ever for an NFL tight end.

Kansas City	7	0	0	6	—	13
Atlanta	7	6	6	10	—	29

Atl — Jefferson 17 pass from Chandler (Andersen kick)
KC — Gonzalez 21 pass from Grbac (Peterson kick)
Atl — FG Andersen 24
Atl — FG Andersen 48
Atl — FG Andersen 42
Atl — FG Andersen 23
Atl — Kozlowski 6 pass from Chandler (Andersen kick)
Atl — FG Andersen 36
KC — Moreau 1 run (pass failed)

MIAMI 27, NEW ENGLAND 24—at Foxboro Stadium, attendance 60,292. Olindo Mare kicked a 49-yard field goal with nine seconds left, and the Dolphins survived a bizarre finish to win the AFC East title. Miami trailed 24-17 before taking possession at its 35-yard line with 9:27 left. After beginning the series with a pair of incompletions, Jay Fiedler completed his next 7 passes to march his team to the Patriots' 1, and Lamar Smith capped the drive by running in from there to tie the game with 4:09 remaining. Two plays later, Zach Thomas intercepted a pass by Drew Bledsoe at Miami's 24, and the Dolphins took 12 plays to drive 45 yards to the winning field goal. The victory apparently was secured when Bledsoe lost a fumble on the next play from scrimmage as time ran out. But with Miami coaches and players celebrating the division title in the locker room, officials ruled that the play should have been ruled an incompletion and that three seconds remained. After a 35-minute delay, New England's offense and Miami's defense took the field again for one final play from the Patriots' 40. Only a handful of fans were left in the stands when strong-armed backup quarterback Michael Bishop launched a desperation pass that fell incomplete. Despite a game-time temperature below freezing, Fielder was 30 of 45 for 264 yards and 1 touchdown. Smith was limited to 26 yards on 20 rushes but scored twice. Bledsoe was 18 of 34 for 312 yards and 2 touchdowns, with 2 interceptions. Troy Brown caught 8 passes for 102 yards.

Miami	3	14	0	10	—	27
New England	7	14	3	0	—	24

Mia — FG Mare 47
NE — Carter 1 run (Vinatieri kick)
NE — Faulk 52 pass from Bledsoe (Vinatieri kick)
Mia — Goodwin 9 pass from Fiedler (Mare kick)
Mia — L. Smith 1 run (Mare kick)
NE — Glenn 16 pass from Bledsoe (Vinatieri kick)
NE — FG Vinatieri 33
Mia — L. Smith 1 run (Mare kick)
Mia — FG Mare 49

INDIANAPOLIS 31, MINNESOTA 10—at RCA Dome, attendance 56,672. Peyton Manning passed for 4 touchdowns, including 3 to Marvin Harrison, as Indianapolis won its third consecutive game and clinched a wild-card playoff spot. The Colts, on the brink of playoff elimination with a 7-6 record through 14 weeks, took the field knowing that a victory over Minnesota would put them in the postseason after the Jets lost at Baltimore in one of the early games. Manning wasted little time getting his team into the end zone, completing 7 of 9 passes on Indianapolis's first possession, including a 4-yard strike to Harrison to cap the 75-yard march 7:28 into the opening period. The Vikings tied the game at 7-7 when Daunte Culpepper teamed with Randy Moss on a 42-yard bomb 4:25 later, but Manning's 52-yard touchdown pass to Edgerrin James put the Colts ahead for good 9:12 before halftime. Culpepper aggravated a sprained ankle so the Vikings turned to Bubby Brister, who could engineer just a field-goal drive the rest of the way. Manning, meanwhile, put the game out of reach with touchdown passes of 15 and 18 yards to Harrison. Manning was 25 of 36 for 283 yards and 4 touchdowns, with 1 interception, and finished the season with a franchise-record 4,413 yards. James rushed for 128 yards and led the league with 1,709 yards for the year. His touchdown was the thirty-fifth of his career; no player ever had as many in his first two NFL seasons. Harrison caught 12 passes for 109 yards. Brister was 9 of 18 for 78 yards, with 1 interception, and Culpepper was 7 of 10 for 97 yards and 1 touchdown. The Vikings managed only 236 total yards. Minnesota had recorded at least 300 yards in 30 consecutive games, the longest such streak in NFL history.

Minnesota	7	3	0	0	—	10
Indianapolis	7	14	7	3	—	31

Ind — Harrison 4 pass from Manning (Vanderjagt kick)
Minn — Moss 42 pass from Culpepper (Anderson kick)
Ind — James 52 pass from Manning (Vanderjagt kick)
Minn — FG Anderson 31
Ind — Harrison 15 pass from Manning (Vanderjagt kick)
Ind — Harrison 18 pass from Manning (Vanderjagt kick)
Ind — FG Vanderjagt 28

BALTIMORE 34, N.Y. JETS 20—at PSINet Stadium, attendance 69,184. After spotting the Jets 14 first-quarter points, the Ravens' record-setting defense shut down New York and sparked a comeback victory. The Jets marched 70 yards on each of their first two possessions, scoring on touchdown bombs from Vinny Testaverde to Dedric Ward (37 yards on a flea-flicker) and Richie Anderson (35 yards). But New York punted 6 times after that, turned the ball over 6 times, and managed only a pair of second-half field goals by Brett Conway, who was signed earlier in the week to replace struggling John Hall. Baltimore pulled within 14-10 on Trent Dilfer's 7-yard touchdown pass to Qadry Ismail and Matt Stover's 42-yard field goal before its defense made the decisive plays. First, Michael McCrary tackled Curtis Martin in the end zone for a safety midway through the second quarter. Then, Chris McAlister stepped in front of Testaverde's pass at the Ravens' 2-yard line and returned it 98 yards for a touchdown to give Baltimore the lead for good just seven seconds before halftime. Jermaine Lewis returned punts 54 and 89 yards for touchdowns in the second half to seal the Ravens' seventh consecutive victory. Baltimore allowed only 165 points for the season, the fewest since the NFL went to a 16-game schedule in 1978 (bettering the old mark of the 1986 Bears by 22 points). Dilfer was 11 of 25 for 99 yards and 1 touchdown, with 2 interceptions. Testaverde was 36 of 69 for 481 yards and 2 touchdowns, but was intercepted 3 times and could not stave off New York's third consecutive defeat when a victory in any of those games would have secured a playoff berth. Anderson caught 11 passes for 139 yards, and Ward had 8 receptions for 147 yards.

N.Y. Jets	14	0	3	3	—	20
Baltimore	0	20	7	7	—	34

NYJ — Ward 37 pass from Testaverde (Conway kick)
NYJ — Anderson 35 pass from Testaverde (Conway kick)
Balt — Ismail 7 pass from Dilfer (Stover kick)
Balt — FG Stover 42
Balt — Safety, McCrary tackled Martin in end zone
Balt — McAlister 98 interception return (Ja. Lewis run)
NYJ — FG Conway 40
Balt — Je. Lewis 54 punt return (Stover kick)
NYJ — FG Conway 19
Balt — Je. Lewis 89 punt return (Stover kick)

PITTSBURGH 34, SAN DIEGO 21—at Qualcomm Stadium, attendance 50,809. Kordell Stewart ran for 2 touchdowns and passed for another to lead the Steelers to the victory. The Chargers led 14-7 after a wild start. Ryan Leaf opened the scoring with a 71-yard touchdown pass to Jeff Graham, Will Blackwell countered with a 98-yard kickoff return for a touchdown, and Rodney Harrison returned an interception 63 yards for a touchdown, all in the first 4:40 of the game. But the Steelers dominated after that, opening a 24-14 halftime advantage largely on the strength of Stewart, who passed 5 yards for a touchdown to Courtney Hawkins and ran 19 yards for a touchdown in the final minute of the second quarter. Stewart, who also ran 1 yard for a touchdown in the final period, was 16 of 32 passes for 190 yards and 1 touchdown, with 2 intercepitons, and led all rushers with 81 yards on 10 carries. Leaf was 15 of 29 for 171 yards and 1 touchdown, with 1 interception, for San Diego, which concluded the worst season in franchise history at 1-15.

Pittsburgh	7	17	0	10	—	34
San Diego	14	0	7	0	—	21

SD — Graham 71 pass from Leaf (Carney kick)
Pitt — Blackwell 98 kickoff return (K. Brown kick)
SD — Harrison 63 interception return (Carney kick)
Pitt — Hawkins 5 pass from Stewart (K. Brown kick)
Pitt — FG K. Brown 32
Pitt — Stewart 19 run (K. Brown kick)
SD — Fletcher 1 run (Carney kick)
Pitt — Stewart 1 run (K. Brown kick)

Pitt — FG K. Brown 28

ST. LOUIS 26, NEW ORLEANS 21—at Louisiana Superdome, attendance 64,900. Marshall Faulk rushed for 220 yards and scored 3 touchdowns to carry the Rams into the playoffs. The defending Super Bowl champions still were celebrating their victory on the floor of the Superdome when they received word that the Bears had upset the Lions, handing St. Louis a wild-card playoff berth. The Rams' reward was a return trip to New Orleans for the opening round of the postseason one week later. Faulk caught a swing pass from Kurt Warner and turned it into a 13-yard touchdown to open the scoring 5:45 into the game. The Rams led 13-7 before Faulk ran 9 yards for a touchdown late in the third quarter, and his 1-yard scoring run with 3:27 left in the game offset a pair of second-half touchdown passes by Aaron Brooks. Faulk's final touchdown was his eleventh during the past three weeks and his twenty-sixth of the season, 1 better than the previous NFL record set by Dallas's Emmitt Smith in 1995. Warner was 12 of 17 for 133 yards and 1 touchdown, with 1 interceptions, before suffering a concussion and giving way to Trent Green early in the third quarter. Green was 6 of 10 for 115 yards and finished the season as the NFC's highest-rated passer, just ahead of Warner. Faulk carried 32 times and caught 7 passes for 41 yards. Torry Holt had 5 receptions for 121 yards. Brooks completed 16 of 31 passes for 208 yards and 2 touchdowns, with 1 interception.

St. Louis	7	3	9	7	—	26
New Orleans	0	7	0	14	—	21

StL — Faulk 13 pass from Warner (Wilkins kick)
NO — D. Smith 41 interception return (Brien kick)
StL — FG Wilkins 19
StL — FG Wilkins 39
StL — Faulk 9 run (run failed)
NO — Jackson 28 pass from Brooks (Brien kick)
StL — Faulk 1 run (Wilkins kick)
NO — Horn 22 pass from Brooks (Brien kick)

GREEN BAY 17, TAMPA BAY 14 (OT)—at Lambeau Field, attendance 59,692. Ryan Longwell's 22-yard field goal 6:31 into overtime lifted the Packers to the victory and ended the Buccaneers' chances of winning the NFC Central. Tampa Bay, which already was in the playoffs but needed to win and have Minnesota lose at Indianapolis later in the day to capture the division crown, rallied from a 14-point, second-half deficit to tie the game on Martin Gramatica's 43-yard field goal with 7:50 left in regulation. The Buccaneers had a chance to win late in the fourth quarter after driving from their 43-yard line to Green Bay's 22 with 13 seconds left, but Gramatica missed a 40-yard field-goal try, and the game went into overtime. The Packers took the kickoff in the extra session and began the winning drive at their 38. On third-and-4 from Tampa Bay's 45, Brett Favre completed a short pass to De'Mond Parker to the 39. Parker then carried on five consecutive plays, the last a 21-yard run to the 4 to position Longwell for the winning kick. Temperature at game time was 15 degrees, with a wind-chill factor of minus-15. Tampa Bay fell to 0-19 in games played in temperatures below 40 degrees, while Favre improved to 27-0 while starting games in temperatures below 34 degrees. Despite winning, the Packers were eliminated from the playoffs when the Rams concluded their victory over New Orleans while the game in Green Bay still was being decided. Favre was 20 of 42 for 196 yards, with 2 interceptions. Ahman Green rushed for 74 yards and 2 touchdowns and caught 9 passes for 78 yards. Shaun King was 21 of 42 for 237 yards, including an 18-yard touchdown to Keyshawn Johnson in the fourth quarter.

Tampa Bay	0	0	3	11	0	—	14
Green Bay	7	0	7	0	3	—	17

GB — Green 3 run (Longwell kick)
GB — Green 2 run (Longwell kick)
TB — FG Gramatica 38
TB — Johnson 18 pass from King (King run)
TB — FG Gramatica 43
GB — FG Longwell 22

MONDAY NIGHT, DECEMBER 25

TENNESSEE 31, DALLAS 0—at Adelphia Coliseum, attendance 68,498. The Titans overwhelmed the Cowboys on Christmas night to win the AFC Central and secure home-field advantage throughout the conference playoffs. Steve McNair's 17-yard touchdown pass to Derrick Mason capped a 74-yard march on Tennessee's first possession and accounted for the lone scoring in the first half. But Tennessee broke open the game by converting 4 turnovers into 24 points in the third quarter. Randall Godfrey and Blaine Bishop set the tone by sacking Anthony Wright on the second play of the half, forcing a fumble that Eddie Robinson recovered at the Cowboys' 11. Eddie George scooted around left end for a touchdown on the next snap. Four plays after that, Godfrey sacked Wright again, forcing another fumble that Henry Ford returned 30 yards for a touchdown and a 21-0 lead. Later in the quarter, Keith Bulluck added an 8-yard interception return for a touchdown, and Godfrey set up Al Del Greco's 21-yard field goal by recovering a fumble by Michael Wiley at the Cowboys' 24. McNair was 17 of 23 for 188 yards and 1 touchdown, with 2 interceptions, before giving way to backup Neil O'Donnell late in the third quarter with the victory secured. George rushed for 83 yards and finished the season with a career-best 1,509 yards. Wright was 5 of 20 passes for 35 yards, with 2 interceptions, in his second career start. Tennessee had 23 first downs to the Cowboys' 6 and 374 total yards to the Cowboys' 95.

Dallas	0	0	0	0	—	0
Tennessee	7	0	24	0	—	31

Tenn — Mason 17 pass from McNair (Del Greco kick)
Tenn — George 11 run (Del Greco kick)
Tenn — Ford 30 fumble return (Del Greco kick)
Tenn — Bulluck 8 interception return (Del Greco kick)
Tenn — FG Del Greco 21

EIGHTEENTH WEEK SUMMARIES
SATURDAY, DECEMBER 30, 2000
AFC WILD CARD PLAYOFF GAME

MIAMI 23, INDIANAPOLIS 17 (OT)—at Pro Player Stadium, attendance 73,193. Lamar Smith's 17-yard touchdown run around right end 11:26 into overtime capped a remarkable performance and lifted the Dolphins to a come-from-behind victory. Smith rushed for 209 yards, the second most in playoff history, on an NFL-postseason record 40 carries to wear down the Colts' defense and give Miami a 43:40-27:46 time of possession advantage. The Colts led 3-0 early in the second quarter when the Dolphins dropped holder Hunter Smith for a 6-yard loss on a fake field-goal attempt. However, the Colts' defense responded with interceptions on the Dolphins' next two possessions, which resulted in 11 points, capped by Peyton Manning's 17-yard pass to Jerome Pathon to take a 14-0 lead. The Dolphins opened the second half with an 11-play, 70-yard drive, which consisted of 7 carries by Smith, and was capped by Smith's 2-yard touchdown run. The teams exchanged field goals, including a 50-yard kick by Mike Vanderjagt with 4:55 remaining, to give the Colts a 17-10 lead. The Dolphins methodically drove down field, keyed by Jay Fiedler's 19- and 13-yard passes to O.J. McDuffie, and tied the game on Fiedler's third-and-goal pass to Jed Weaver from 9 yards out with 34 seconds remaining. The Colts ran out the clock, and the Dolphins won the overtime coin toss but were forced to punt after gaining one first down. Manning hit Marvin Harrison with a 30-yard pass on the Colts' first play of overtime and the Colts moved the ball into Dolphins' territory. Faced with third-and-12 from the Dolphins' 42, Manning completed an 11-yard pass to Harrison. The Dolphins were offside on the play, but the Colts elected to take the play and allow Vanderjagt to attempt a 49-yard field goal. Vanderjagt's kick missed wide right, and the Dolphins marched 61 yards in 11 plays, capped by Smith dragging Jeff Burris into the end zone on his game-winning run. Fiedler completed 19 of 34 passes for 185 yards and 1 touchdown, with 3 interceptions. Manning was 17 of 32 for 194 yards and 1 touchdown. Edgerrin James had 21 carries for 107 yards.

Indianapolis	3	11	0	3	0	—	17
Miami	0	0	7	10	6	—	23

Ind — FG Vanderjagt 32
Ind — FG Vanderjagt 26
Ind — Pathon 17 pass from Manning (Dilger pass from Manning)
Mia — Smith 2 run (Mare kick)
Mia — FG Mare 38
Ind — FG Vanderjagt 50
Mia — Weaver 9 pass from Fiedler (Mare kick)
Mia — Smith 17 run

NFC WILD CARD PLAYOFF GAME

NEW ORLEANS 31, ST. LOUIS 28—at Louisiana Superdome, attendance 64,900. Aaron Brooks passed for 4 touchdowns and Brian Milne recovered Az-Zahir Hakim's muffed punt return with 1:43 remaining to secure the first playoff victory in Saints history. The defending Super Bowl champion Rams scored on their first possession, driving 68 yards in 11 plays and taking a 7-0 lead on Kurt Warner's 17-yard pass to Isaac Bruce, but were then shut out for the next 40 minutes. The Saints drove 70 yards on their ensuing possession to tie the game on Brooks's 12-yard pass to Robert Wilson, who had not caught a touchdown pass all season. Sammy Knight's 52-yard interception return to the Rams' 20 set up Doug Brien's 33-yard field goal just before halftime, giving New Orleans a 10-7 lead. Chris Oldham's third-quarter interception near midfield led to Brooks's 10-yard touchdown pass to Willie Jackson, and Brooks and Jackson hooked up for 2 more scores within the first 3:03 of the fourth quarter to give the Saints a 31-7 lead with 11:57 remaining. The Rams needed just 4 plays, capped by Warner's 17-yard pass to Ricky Proehl, to cut the deficit to 31-13, and Hakim's 65-yard punt return to the Saints' 9 moments later gave the Rams hope. But Knight intercepted Warner on the next play from scrimmage with 6:28 remaining. However, the Rams' defense forced a punt, and St. Louis needed just 3 plays to drive 62 yards and cut the deficit to 31-20 on Marshall Faulk's 25-yard catch and run. Dre' Bly recovered the ensuing onside kick, and a 38-yard pass to Hakim set up Warner's 5-yard touchdown run. Warner's quick pass to Faulk for the 2-point conversion trimmed the deficit to 31-28 with 2:36 left. Darrin Smith recovered the onside kick for the Saints, but the Rams' defense again forced a punt. Hakim muffed the punt and Milne recovered the ball at the Saints' 11 to seal the victory. Brooks completed 16 of 29 passes for 266 yards and 4 touchdowns, with 1 interception. Jackson had 6 receptions for 142 yards. Warner was 24 of 40 for 365 yards and 3 touchdowns, with 3 interceptions. Bruce had 7 receptions for 127 yards.

St. Louis	7	0	0	21	—	28
New Orleans	0	10	7	14	—	31

StL — Bruce 17 pass from Warner (Wilkins kick)
NO — Wilson 12 pass from Brooks (Brien kick)
NO — FG Brien 33
NO — Jackson 10 pass from Brooks (Brien kick)
NO — Jackson 49 pass from Brooks (Brien kick)
NO — Jackson 16 pass from Brooks (Brien kick)
StL — Proehl 17 pass from Warner (run failed)
StL — Faulk 25 pass from Warner (Wilkins kick)
StL — Warner 5 run (Faulk pass from Warner)

SUNDAY, DECEMBER 31, 2000
AFC WILD CARD PLAYOFF GAME

BALTIMORE 21, DENVER 3—at PSINet Stadium, attendance 69,638. Rookie Jamal Lewis rushed for 110 yards and 2 touchdowns, and the Ravens' defense permitted the Broncos to cross midfield just once, as the city of Baltimore hosted its first NFL playoff game since 1977. Trent Dilfer completed 2 key passes to Qadry Ismail before Lewis scored on a 1-yard run early in the second quarter to give the Ravens a 7-0 lead. The Broncos responded with their lone sustained drive of the day, but Mike Anderson was stopped for no gain on third-and-1 and Denver settled for Jason Elam's 31-yard field goal with 4:31 remaining in the first half. On the Ravens' next play, Dilfer's short pass deflected off the hands of Lewis and Terrell Buckley before being caught by Shannon Sharpe, who eluded two tacklers and raced 58 yards into the end zone to give the Ravens a 14-3 lead. The Broncos never threatened again, and Lewis's 27-yard scoring run in the third quarter capped the Ravens' victory in the franchise's first postseason game. The Ravens' defense limited the Broncos to just 9 first downs and 42 rushing yards. Dilfer completed 9 of 14 passes for 130 yards and 1 touchdown. Gus Frerotte, who played for the injured Brian Griese, was 13 of 28 for 124 yards, with 1 interception.

Denver	0	3	0	0	—	3
Baltimore	0	14	7	0	—	21

Balt — Ja. Lewis 1 run (Stover kick)
Den — FG Elam 31

Balt — Sharpe 58 pass from Dilfer (Stover kick)
Balt — Ja. Lewis 27 run (Stover kick)

NFC WILD CARD PLAYOFF GAME

PHILADELPHIA 21, TAMPA BAY 3—at Veterans Stadium, attendance 65,813. Donovan McNabb passed for 2 touchdowns and ran for another, and the Eagles' defense limited the Buccaneers to just 11 first downs. The Buccaneers dropped to 0-20 when the game-time temperature is below 40 degrees, though Martin Gramatica's 29-yard field goal early in the second quarter staked Tampa Bay to a 3-0 lead. The tide changed a few possessions later when Hugh Douglas sacked Shaun King from behind, forced him to fumble, and Mike Mamula recovered at the Buccaneers' 15. Four plays later, McNabb scrambled 5 yards up the middle for a touchdown with 3:21 left in the half. The Eagles' defense then forced Tampa Bay to punt, and McNabb engineered an 8-play, 69-yard drive, keyed by his 25-yard pass to Charles Johnson. McNabb capped the march with a 5-yard touchdown pass to Na Brown 12 seconds before halftime to take a 14-3 lead. McNabb's 2-yard pass to Jeff Thomason on third-and-goal less than a minute into the fourth quarter finished the scoring. The Buccaneers threatened once in the second half, but King threw consecutive incompletions from the Eagles' 21 with just under four minutes remaining to seal the victory. The Eagles converted 9 of 18 third-down plays, while allowing the Buccaneers to convert just 3 of 13 third-down situations. McNabb completed 24 of 33 passes for 161 yards and 2 touchdowns, with 1 interception. King was 17 of 31 for 171 yards. Keyshawn Johnson had 6 receptions for 106 yards.

Tampa Bay	0	3	0	0	—	3
Philadelphia	0	14	0	7	—	21

TB — FG Gramatica 29
Phil — McNabb 5 run (Akers kick)
Phil — Brown 5 pass from McNabb (Akers kick)
Phil — Thomason 2 pass from McNabb (Akers kick)

NINETEENTH WEEK SUMMARIES

SATURDAY, JANUARY 6, 2001

NFC DIVISIONAL PLAYOFF GAME

MINNESOTA 34, NEW ORLEANS 16—at Metrodome, attendance 63,881. Daunte Culpepper passed for 302 yards and 3 touchdowns as the Vikings defeated the Saints. The Vikings scored on their third play from scrimmage, when Randy Moss caught a short pass and raced untouched 53 yards for a touchdown. The Vikings led 10-3 late in the first half when Culpepper scrambled for 30 yards and, on the next play, fired a 17-yard touchdown pass to Cris Carter. Moss scored on the third play of the second half as well, again taking a quick pass and this time outrunning the Saints 68 yards for a touchdown and a 24-3 lead. Robert Tate's interception at the Saints' 29 late in the third quarter led to Robert Smith's 2-yard touchdown run to give the Vikings a 34-10 lead with 10:46 remaining. Culpepper completed 17 of 31 passes for 302 yards and 3 touchdowns. Moss had 2 catches for 121 yards, and Carter had 8 receptions for 120 yards. Aaron Brooks was 30 of 48 for 295 yards and 2 touchdowns, with 2 interceptions. Chad Morton had 13 catches for 106 yards, and Willie Jackson added 9 receptions for 125 yards.

New Orleans	3	0	7	6	—	16
Minnesota	10	7	10	7	—	34

Minn — Moss 53 pass from Culpepper (Anderson kick)
NO — FG Brien 33
Minn — FG Anderson 24
Minn — Carter 17 pass from Culpepper (Anderson kick)
Minn — Moss 68 pass from Culpepper (Anderson kick)
NO — Stachelski 2 pass from Brooks (Brien kick)
Minn — FG Anderson 44
Minn — Smith 2 run (Anderson kick)
NO — Jackson 48 pass from Brooks (pass failed)

AFC DIVISIONAL PLAYOFF GAME

OAKLAND 27, MIAMI 0—at Network Associates Coliseum, attendance 61,998. The Raiders rushed for 140 yards on offense and forced 4 turnovers on defense to hand the Dolphins their first shutout loss in postseason history. Jeff Ogden's 45-yard punt return gave Miami an excellent scoring opportunity on its first possession. However, Tory James stepped in front of Jay Fiedler's second-down pass and returned it 90 yards for a touchdown. The Raiders added field goals by Sebastian Janikowski on their next two drives to take a 13-0 lead. On the Dolphins' ensuing possession, Charles Woodson recovered Lamar Smith's fumble to set up Rich Gannon's 6-yard touchdown pass to James Jett, which gave Oakland a 20-0 lead. Tyrone Wheatley's 2-yard touchdown run capped a 12-play, 54-yard drive on the Raiders' first possession of the second half for the game's final points. Gannon completed 12 of 18 passes for 143 yards and 1 touchdown. Fiedler was 18 of 37 for 176 yards, with 3 interceptions.

Miami	0	0	0	0	—	0
Oakland	10	10	7	0	—	27

Oak — James 90 interception return (Janikowski kick)
Oak — FG Janikowski 36
Oak — FG Janikowski 33
Oak — Jett 6 pass from Gannon (Janikowski kick)
Oak — Wheatley 2 run (Janikowski kick)

SUNDAY, JANUARY 7, 2001

AFC DIVISIONAL PLAYOFF GAME

BALTIMORE 24, TENNESSEE 10—at Adelphia Coliseum, attendance 68,527. Ray Lewis's 50-yard interception return for a touchdown midway through the fourth quarter iced the Ravens' comeback victory. The Titans drove 68 yards in 11 plays on the game's opening drive, capped by Eddie George's 2-yard touchdown run. It turned out to be the only touchdown allowed by the Ravens' defense in four 2000 postseason games. Trent Dilfer's 56-yard pass to Shannon Sharpe early in the second quarter led to Jamal Lewis's 1-yard scoring run to tie the game. After Al Del Greco's 45-yard field-goal attempt in the second quarter was blocked by Keith Washington, Chris Coleman blocked Kyle Richardson's punt deep in Ravens' territory. However, Del Greco missed a 31-yard attempt just before halftime. Coleman blocked another punt by Richardson two minutes into the second half, but the Titans had to settle for Del Greco's 21-yard field goal and a 10-7 lead. A 15-yard fair-catch interference penalty on Tennessee led to Matt Stover's game-tying field goal late in the third quarter. Early in the fourth quarter, Washington blocked another field-goal attempt by Del Greco. Anthony Mitchell caught the ball and scampered 90 yards down the right sideline for the go-ahead touchdown. Down 17-10, the Titans had the ball at their 47 with 6:55 remaining when Steve McNair's short pass bounced off George's hands to Lewis, who raced 50 yards for the game's final points. Dilfer completed 5 of 16 passes for 117 yards, and the Ravens won despite being held to 6 first downs. McNair was 24 of 46 for 176 yards, with 1 interception.

Baltimore	0	7	3	14	—	24
Tennessee	7	0	3	0	—	10

Tenn — George 2 run (Del Greco kick)
Balt — Ja. Lewis 1 run (Stover kick)
Tenn — FG Del Greco 21
Balt — FG Stover 38
Balt — Mitchell 90 blocked field goal return (Stover kick)
Balt — R. Lewis 50 interception return (Stover kick)

NFC DIVISIONAL PLAYOFF GAME

N.Y. GIANTS 20, PHILADELPHIA 10—at Giants Stadium, attendance 78,765. Ron Dixon returned the opening kickoff 97 yards for a touchdown to spark the Giants to their first playoff victory since 1993. Dixon became the first player to begin a postseason game with a kickoff return for a touchdown since Miami's Nat Moore in 1974. The Giants' defense did not allow a first down during the Eagles' first three possessions, and on their fourth possession Torrance Small fumbled and Dave Thomas recovered to set up Brad Daluiso's 37-yard field goal. Late in the first half, Jason Sehorn made a diving interception, batting the ball in midair with one hand before catching it, got to his feet, and outran the Eagles to the end zone for a 17-0 Giants lead. The Eagles got on the board when David Akers kicked a field goal before halftime, but Akers missed from 30 yards in the third quarter. James Bostic's blocked punt in the final minutes set up Donovan McNabb's 10-yard touchdown pass to Small to close out the scoring. Kerry Collins was 12 of 19 for 125 yards. McNabb completed 20 of 41 passes for 181 yards and 1 touchdown, with 1 interception. The clubs combined for only 423 total yards, but the Giants controlled the clock for 36:09 thanks to 112 rushing yards, including 53 from Ron Dayne and 35 from Tiki Barber despite a broken left forearm.

Philadelphia	0	3	0	7	—	10
N.Y. Giants	7	10	0	3	—	20

NYG — Dixon 97 kickoff return (Daluiso kick)
NYG — FG Daluiso 37
NYG — Sehorn 32 interception return (Daluiso kick)
Phil — FG Akers 28
NYG — FG Daluiso 25
Phil — Small 10 pass from McNabb (Akers kick)

TWENTIETH WEEK SUMMARIES

SUNDAY, JANUARY 14, 2001

NFC CHAMPIONSHIP PLAYOFF GAME

N.Y. GIANTS 41, MINNESOTA 0—at Giants Stadium, attendance 79,310. Kerry Collins passed for 381 yards and 5 touchdowns to lead the Giants to their first Super Bowl berth in 10 years. The Giants' defense forced 5 turnovers and limited the Vikings to 114 yards. Collins needed just 4 plays, and less than two minutes, to score on Ike Hilliard's 46-yard reception. Moe Williams fumbled the ensuing kickoff, and Lyle West recovered at the Vikings' 18. On the next play, Collins lofted a scoring pass to Greg Comella to give the Giants a 14-0 lead 2:13 into the game—before the Vikings had taken a snap. Robert Tate's interception gave Minnesota a scoring opportunity midway through the first quarter, but three plays later Emmanuel McDaniel intercepted Daunte Culpepper's pass in the end zone. The Giants proceeded to score on all four of their second-quarter possessions, including drives of 71, 62, and 77 yards. Collins capped the outburst with a 7-yard scoring pass to Hilliard that gave the Giants a 34-0 halftime lead. Cornelius Griffin recovered Culpepper's fumble at the Vikings' 29 early in the second half, and Collins's 7-yard touchdown pass to Amani Toomer gave the Giants a 41-0 lead with 12:06 left in the third quarter. The Vikings never drove beyond the Giants' 32 the rest of the game, and the Giants used a 19-play drive to run out the final 12:53. Collins completed 28 of 39 passes for 381 yards and 5 touchdowns, with 2 interceptions. Hilliard had 10 receptions for 155 yards. Culpepper was 13 of 28 for 78 yards, with 3 interceptions.

Minnesota	0	0	0	0	—	0
N.Y. Giants	14	20	7	0	—	41

NYG — Hilliard 46 pass from Collins (Daluiso kick)
NYG — Comella 18 pass from Collins (Daluiso kick)
NYG — FG Daluiso 21
NYG — Jurevicius 8 pass from Collins (Daluiso kick)
NYG — FG Daluiso 22
NYG — Hilliard 7 pass from Collins (Daluiso kick)
NYG — Toomer 7 pass from Collins (Daluiso kick)

AFC CHAMPIONSHIP PLAYOFF GAME

BALTIMORE 16, OAKLAND 3—at Network Associates Coliseum, attendance 62,784. Duane Starks intercepted 2 passes and Baltimore's defense forced 5 turnovers as the Ravens earned their first Super Bowl berth. In a battle of field position, the Ravens got the first break when Robert Bailey intercepted Rich Gannon's pass at the Raiders' 19 midway through the first quarter. However, Matt Stover missed a 36-yard field-goal attempt. In the second quarter, the Ravens were pinned on their 4-yard line and faced third-and-18 when Trent Dilfer fired a short pass over the middle to a slanting Shannon Sharpe, who streaked untouched down the middle of the field for a 96-yard touchdown and a 7-0 lead. On the Raiders' next possession, Tony Siragusa knocked down Gannon on a passing play. Gannon left the game with an injured non-throwing shoulder, and Bobby Hoying replaced him. Starks intercepted Hoying's first pass, returning it 9 yards to the Raiders' 20 to set up Stover's 31-yard field goal. Three plays into the second half Johnnie Harris intercepted a pass by Dilfer. Gannon returned for the Raiders and guided the club to first-and-goal at the Ravens' 2. However, Tyrone Wheatley lost a yard, Gannon was sacked by Jamie Sharper, and on third down Gannon's pass fell incomplete, so the Raiders had to settle for Sebastian Janikowski's 24-yard field goal. The Ravens responded with a 9-play, 51-yard drive, capped by Stover's second field goal to take a 13-3 lead.

Early in the fourth quarter, Peter Boulware sacked Gannon and forced him to fumble. Ray Lewis recovered at the Raiders' 7, which set up Stover's third field goal for a 16-3 lead with 7:28 left. Hoying returned for the Raiders and drove Oakland to the Ravens' 5. Hoying's 5-yard touchdown pass to Andre Rison was nullified by offensive pass interference, and Sharper intercepted Hoying two plays later to clinch the victory. Dilfer completed 9 of 18 passes for 190 yards and 1 touchdown, with 1 interception. Gannon was 11 of 21 for 80 yards, with 2 interceptions, while Hoying was 8 of 16 for 107 yards, with 2 interceptions. The Ravens' defense limited the NFL's number-one rushing offense to 24 rushing yards on 17 carries.

Baltimore	0	10	3	3	—	16
Oakland	0	0	3	0	—	3

Balt — Sharpe 96 pass from Dilfer (Stover kick)
Balt — FG Stover 31
Oak — FG Janikowski 24
Balt — FG Stover 28
Balt — FG Stover 21

TWENTY-FIRST WEEK SUMMARY
SUNDAY, JANUARY 28, 2001
SUPER BOWL XXXV

BALTIMORE 34, N.Y. GIANTS 7—at Raymond James Stadium, attendance 71,921. The Ravens' defense completed a dominating season by permitting just 152 yards, forcing 5 turnovers, recording 4 sacks, and not allowing an offensive touchdown en route to the franchise's first Super Bowl victory. Jermaine Lewis's punt return into Giants' territory midway through the first quarter was followed two plays later by Trent Dilfer's 38-yard touchdown pass to Brandon Stokley, which giving the Ravens a 7-0 lead. Early in the second quarter, Jessie Armstead intercepted a short pass by Dilfer and returned it 43 yards for a touchdown, but the play was nullified by a penalty. Dilfer-'s 36-yard pass to Qadry Ismail in the second quarter set up Matt Stover's 47-yard field goal with 1:48 left in the half. Tiki Barber's 27-yard run gave the Giants their deepest penetration of the game, to the Ravens' 29, but Chris McAlister intercepted Kerry Collins's pass on the next play to preserve a 10-0 lead. In the third quarter, Duane Starks stepped in front of Amani Toomer and intercepted Collins's pass. Starks returned it 49 yards untouched for a 17-0 lead. The Giants immediately cut the lead to 10 points when Ron Dixon returned the ensuing kickoff 97 yards for a touchdown. However, Jermaine Lewis then matched Dixon's kickoff return as he cut across the field and raced 84 yards for a 24-7 lead with 3:13 left in the third quarter. The 3 touchdowns in 36 seconds were a Super Bowl record. The Giants gained just 1 first down on their final four possessions. Jamal Lewis's 3-yard touchdown run midway through the fourth quarter gave Baltimore a 31-7 lead, and Robert Bailey recovered Dixon's fumble on the ensuing kickoff return to set up Stover's 34-yard field goal with 5:27 remaining to finish the scoring. Dilfer completed 12 of 25 passes for 153 yards and 1 touchdown. Jamal Lewis had 27 carries for 102 yards. Collins was 15 of 39 for 112 yards, with 4 interceptions. Ray Lewis was named Super Bowl most valuable player.

Baltimore	7	3	14	10	—	34
N.Y. Giants	0	0	7	0	—	7

Balt — Stokley 38 pass from Dilfer (Stover kick)
Balt — FG Stover 47
Balt — Starks 49 interception return (Stover kick)
NYG — Dixon 97 kickoff return (Daluiso kick)
Balt — Je. Lewis 84 kickoff return (Stover kick)
Balt — Ja. Lewis 3 run (Stover kick)
Balt — FG Stover 34

TWENTY-SECOND WEEK SUMMARY
SUNDAY, FEBRUARY 4, 2001
2001 PRO BOWL GAME

AFC 38, NFC 17—at Aloha Stadium, attendance 50,128. Rich Gannon completed 12 of 14 passes for 160 yards during the game's first two possessions to win player of the game honors and lead the AFC to victory. Gannon's touchdown passes capped 87- and 90-yard drives and staked the AFC to a 14-0 lead. Gannon, who was still recovering from a separated non-throwing shoulder suffered in the AFC Championship Game, was replaced by Peyton Manning. The Colts' quarterback engineered a scoring drive, capped by Matt Stover's field goal, to give the AFC a 17-0 lead early in the second quarter. At that point, the AFC had 14 first downs and 231 yards of offense while limiting the NFC to no first downs and 6 yards. Jimmy Smith caught a 2-yard touchdown pass 54 seconds before halftime to give the AFC a 24-3 lead. Third-quarter touchdown passes by Donovan McNabb and Daunte Culpepper trimmed the AFC's lead to 31-17, but Jason Taylor batted down Culpepper's fourth-and-1 pass early in the fourth quarter, and Edgerrin James's 20-yard touchdown run a few plays later iced the game. The NFC attempted a Pro Bowl record 56 pass attempts, and the two teams combined for a Pro Bowl record 98 pass attempts. Tony Gonzalez had 6 receptions for 108 yards, all in the first half, for the AFC. Torry Holt had 7 receptions for 103 yards. Smith's touchdown reception gives him 5 for his career, an AFC-NFC Pro Bowl record.

NFC	0	3	14	0	—	17
AFC	14	10	7	7	—	38

AFC — Gonzalez 8 pass from Gannon (Stover kick)
AFC — Harrison 16 pass from Gannon (Stover kick)
AFC — FG Stover 29
NFC — FG Gramatica 48
AFC — J. Smith 2 pass from Manning (Stover kick)
NFC — Owens 17 pass from McNabb (Gramatica kick)
AFC — Harrison 24 pass from Manning (Stover kick)
NFC — Holt 20 pass from Culpepper (Gramatica kick)
AFC — James 20 run (Stover kick)

2000 PRO FOOTBALL AWARDS

	NFL	AFC	NFC
ASSOCIATED PRESS			
Most Valuable Player	Marshall Faulk		
Offensive Player of the Year	Marshall Faulk		
Defensive Player of the Year	Ray Lewis		
Offensive Rookie of the Year	Mike Anderson		
Defensive Rookie of the Year	Brian Urlacher		
Coach of the Year	Jim Haslett		
Comeback Player of the Year	Joe Johnson		
THE SPORTING NEWS			
Player of the Year	Marshall Faulk		
Rookie of the Year	Brian Urlacher		
Coach of the Year	Andy Reid		
FOOTBALL NEWS			
Player of the Year		Eddie George	Donovan McNabb
Coach of the Year	Jim Haslett		
Rookie of the Year		Jamal Lewis	Brian Urlacher
PRO FOOTBALL WEEKLY/PFWA			
Executive of the Year	Randy Mueller		
Most Valuable Player	Marshall Faulk		
Defensive Most Valuable Player	Ray Lewis		
Offensive Rookie of the Year	Mike Anderson		
Defensive Rookie of the Year	Brian Urlacher		
Coach of the Year	Jim Haslett		
Assistant Coach of the Year	Marvin Lewis		
Golden Toe	Matt Stover		
Comeback Player of the Year	Joe Johnson		
FOOTBALL DIGEST			
Player of the Year	Marshall Faulk		
Defensive Player of the Year	Ray Lewis		
Offensive Rookie of the Year	Mike Anderson		
Defensive Rookie of the Year	Brian Urlacher		
Coach of the Year	Andy Reid		
Comeback Player of the Year	Trent Dilfer		
Most Improved Player of the Year	Jeff Garcia		
Rookie Coach of the Year	Jim Haslett		
Assistant Coach of the Year	Marvin Lewis		
Executive of the Year	Randy Mueller		
SPORTS ILLUSTRATED			
Player of the Year	Marshall Faulk		
Coach of the Year	Jim Haslett		
Rookie of the Year	Brian Urlacher		
USA TODAY			
Coach of the Year		Brian Billick	Jim Haslett
Offensive Rookie of the Year	Jamal Lewis		
Defensive Rookie of the Year	Brian Urlacher		
Assistant Coach of the Year		Marvin Lewis	Mike McCarthy
COLLEGE AND PRO FOOTBALL NEWSWEEKLY			
Offensive Player of the Year	Marshall Faulk		
Defensive Player of the Year	La'Roi Glover		
Coach of the Year	Jim Haslett		
MAXWELL CLUB			
(Bert Bell Trophy)	Rich Gannon		
(Earle "Greasy" Neale Trophy)	Andy Reid		
MILLER LITE PLAYER OF THE YEAR	Marshall Faulk		
WALTER PAYTON NFL MAN OF THE YEAR	(tie) Jim Flanigan and Derrick Brooks		
SUPER BOWL MOST VALUABLE PLAYER (Pete Rozelle Trophy)	Ray Lewis		
AFC-NFC PRO BOWL PLAYER OF THE GAME (Dan McGuire Award)	Rich Gannon		

2000 PLAYERS OF THE WEEK/MONTH

2000 AFC PLAYERS OF THE WEEK

	Offense		Defense		Special Teams	
Week 1	RB	Lamar Smith, Miami	DE	Rob Burnett, Baltimore	K	Steve Christie, Buffalo
Week 2	QB	Tony Banks, Baltimore	DE	Keith McKenzie, Cleveland	KR	Ronney Jenkins, San Diego
Week 3	QB	Elvis Grbac, Kansas City	DE	Courtney Brown, Cleveland	KR	Kevin Williams, New York Jets
Week 4	QB	Peyton Manning, Indianapolis	LB	William Thomas, Oakland	KR	Derrick Mason, Tennessee
Week 5	QB	Drew Bledsoe, New England	S	Rod Woodson, Baltimore	K	Mike Vanderjagt, Indianapolis
Week 6	WR	Tim Brown, Oakland	CB	Terrell Buckley, Denver	K	Matt Stover, Baltimore
Week 7	RB	Edgerrin James, Indianapolis	LB	Mo Lewis, New York Jets	K	Steve Christie, Buffalo
Week 8	RB	Corey Dillon, Cincinnati	LB	Randall Godfrey, Tennessee	K	Kris Brown, Pittsburgh
		QB Vinny Testaverde, New York Jets **(PRIME TIME IV AWARD)**				
Week 9	QB	Mark Brunell, Jacksonville	CB	Samari Rolle, Tennessee	K	Sebastian Janikowski, Oakland
Week 10	QB	Rich Gannon, Oakland	LB	Sam Cowart, Buffalo	K	Steve Christie, Buffalo
Week 11	QB	Jon Kitna, Seattle	S	Brian Walker, Miami	LB	Ian Gold, Denver
Week 12	RB	Fred Taylor, Jacksonville	S	Lawyer Milloy, New England	P	Shane Lechler, Oakland
Week 13	RB	Mike Anderson, Denver	LB	Jason Gildon, Pittsburgh	K	John Carney, San Diego
Week 14	RB	Mike Anderson, Denver	LB	Bryan Cox, New York Jets	K	Al Del Greco, Tennessee
Week 15	RB	Edgerrin James, Indianapolis	CB	Eric Allen, Oakland	P	Shane Lechler, Oakland
Week 16	RB	Eddie George, Tennessee	LB	Jamie Sharper, Baltimore	NT	Chad Eaton, New England
Week 17	QB	Peyton Manning, Indianapolis	LB	Randall Godfrey, Tennessee	KR-PR	Jermaine Lewis, Baltimore

2000 AFC PLAYERS OF THE MONTH

	Offense		Defense		Special Teams	
September	RB	Curtis Martin, New York Jets	DE	Rob Burnett, Baltimore	P	Hunter Smith, Indianapolis
October	RB	Edgerrin James, Indianapolis	LB	Joey Porter, Pittsburgh	KR	Derrick Mason, Tennessee
November	WR	Rod Smith, Denver	LB	Sam Cowart, Buffalo	K	Matt Stover, Baltimore
December	RB	Mike Anderson, Denver	CB	Eric Allen, Oakland	KR-PR	Jermaine Lewis, Baltimore

2000 NFC PLAYERS OF THE WEEK

	Offense		Defense		Special Teams	
Week 1	RB	Duce Staley, Philadelphia	LB	Derrick Brooks, Tampa Bay	K	Morten Andersen, Atlanta
Week 2	QB	Jake Plummer, Arizona	CB	Ronde Barber, Tampa Bay	K	Jason Hanson, Detroit
Week 3	RB	Marshall Faulk, St. Louis	DT	Warren Sapp, Tampa Bay	K	Ryan Longwell, Green Bay
Week 4	RB	Charlie Garner, San Francisco	S	Kurt Schulz, Detroit	PR	Brian Mitchell, Philadelphia
Week 5	QB	Kurt Warner, St. Louis	DE	Marco Coleman, Washington	PR	Deion Sanders, Washington
		RB-PR-KR Brian Mitchell, Philadelphia **(PRIME TIME III AWARD)**				
Week 6	QB	Daunte Culpepper, Minnesota	DT	La'Roi Glover, New Orleans	K	Joe Nedney, Carolina
Week 7	RB	Marshall Faulk, St. Louis	DT	La'Roi Glover, New Orleans	K	David Akers, Philadelphia
Week 8	WR	Albert Connell, Washington	CB	Bryant Westbrook, Detroit	K	Gary Anderson, Minnesota
Week 9	QB	Shaun King, Tampa Bay	LB	Keith Mitchell, New Orleans	PR	Az-Zahir Hakim, St. Louis
Week 10	QB	Jeff Blake, New Orleans	CB	Aeneas Williams, Arizona	K	Joe Nedney Carolina
Week 11	QB	Trent Green, St. Louis	LB	Keith Mitchell, New Orleans	K	David Akers, Philadelphia
Week 12	QB	Daunte Culpepper, Minnesota	DE	Bruce Smith, Washington	KR	Allen Rossum, Green Bay
Week 13	QB	Donovan McNabb, Philadelphia	DT	La'Roi Glover, New Orleans	PR	Karl Williams, Tampa Bay
Week 14	RB	Warrick Dunn, Tampa Bay	CB	Jimmy Hitchcock, Carolina	P	Mitch Berger, Minnesota
Week 15	QB	Donovan McNabb, Philadelphia	LB	London Fletcher, St. Louis	K	Martin Gramatica, Tampa Bay
Week 16	WR	Terrell Owens, San Francisco	DT	Michael Strahan, New York Giants	K	Ryan Longwell, Green Bay
Week 17	RB	Marshall Faulk, St. Louis	CB	R.W. McQuarters, Chicago	K	Paul Edinger, Chicago

2000 NFC PLAYERS OF THE MONTH

	Offense		Defense		Special Teams	
September	QB	Kurt Warner, St. Louis	DE	Hugh Douglas, Philadelphia	KR-PR	Desmond Howard, Detroit
October	RB	Marshall Faulk, St. Louis	DT	La'Roi Glover, New Orleans	K	Martin Gramatica, Tampa Bay
November	RB	Robert Smith, Minnesota	LB	Derrick Brooks, Tampa Bay	K	David Akers, Philadelphia
December	RB	Marshall Faulk, St. Louis	LB	Jeremiah Trotter, Philadelphia	P	Mitch Berger, Minnesota

2000 PLAYOFF PLAYERS OF THE WEEK

	Offense		Defense		Special Teams	
Wild Card	RB	Lamar Smith, Miami	DE	Hugh Douglas, Philadelphia	P	Matt Turk, Miami
Divisional	QB	Daunte Culpepper, Minnesota	CB	Tory James, Oakland	DE	Keith Washington, Baltimore
Championship	QB	Kerry Collins, New York Giants	LB	Ray Lewis, Baltimore	P	Kyle Richardson, Baltimore

2000 ROOKIES OF THE MONTH

	Offense (College)		Defense (College)	
September	RB	Mike Anderson, Denver (Utah)	DE	Darren Howard, New Orleans (Kansas State)
October	T	Chris Samuels, Washington (Alabama)	LB	Brian Urlacher, Chicago (New Mexico)
	T	Todd Wade, Miami (Mississippi)		
November	RB	Jamal Lewis, Baltimore (Tennessee)	DT	Corey Simon, Philadelphia (Florida State)
December	RB	Mike Anderson, Denver (Utah)	DE	Darren Howard, New Orleans (Kansas State)

2000 PFW/PFWA ALL-PRO TEAM

Selected by Pro Football Weekly *and the Professional Football Writers of America*

Offense

Rich Gannon, Oakland	Quarterback
Marshall Faulk, St. Louis	Running Back
Eddie George, Tennessee	Running Back
Randy Moss, Minnesota	Wide Receiver
Marvin Harrison, Indianapolis	Wide Receiver
Tony Gonzalez, Kansas City	Tight End
Jonathan Ogden, Balitmore	Tackle
William Roaf, New Orleans	Tackle
Larry Allen, Dallas	Guard
Bruce Matthews, Tennessee	Guard
Kevin Mawae, New York Jets	Center

Defense

Hugh Douglas, Philadelphia	End
Jason Taylor, Miami	End
Warren Sapp, Tampa Bay	Tackle
La'Roi Glover, New Orleans	Tackle
Derrick Brooks, Tampa Bay	Linebacker
Junior Seau, San Diego	Linebacker
Ray Lewis, Baltimore	Linebacker
Samari Rolle, Tennessee	Cornerback
Sam Madison, Miami	Cornerback
John Lynch, Tampa Bay	Safety
Darren Sharper, Green Bay	Safety

Specialists

Matt Stover, Baltimore	Kicker
Darren Bennett, San Diego	Punter
Derrick Mason, Tennessee	Kick Returner
Az-Zahir Hakim, St. Louis	Punt Returner
Michael Bates, Carolina	Special Teams Player

2000 ASSOCIATED PRESS ALL-PRO TEAM

Selected by the Associated Press

Offense

Rich Gannon, Oakland	Quarterback
Marshall Faulk, St. Louis	Running Back
Eddie George, Tennessee	Running Back
Randy Moss, Minnesota	Wide Receiver
Terrell Owens, San Francisco	Wide Receiver
Tony Gonzalez, Kansas City	Tight End
Jonathan Ogden, Baltimore	Tackle
Kyle Turley, New Orleans	Tackle
Larry Allen, Dallas	Guard
Bruce Matthews, Tennessee	Guard
Tom Nalen, Denver	Center

Defense

Hugh Douglas, Philadelphia	End
Jason Taylor, Miami	End
Warren Sapp, Tampa Bay	Tackle
La'Roi Glover, New Orleans	Tackle
Derrick Brooks, Tampa Bay	Linebacker
Junior Seau, San Diego	Linebacker
Ray Lewis, Baltimore	Linebacker
Jeremiah Trotter, Philadelphia	Linebacker
Sam Madison, Miami	Cornerback
Samari Rolle, Tennessee	Cornerback
John Lynch, Tampa Bay	Safety
Darren Sharper, Green Bay	Safety

Specialists

Matt Stover, Baltimore	Kicker
Derrick Mason, Tennessee	Kick Returner
Shane Lechler, Oakland	Punter

2000 ALL-NFL TEAM

Selected by the Associated Press, Pro Football Weekly, *and the Professional Football Writers of America*

Offense

Randy Moss, Minnesota (AP, PFW)	Wide Receiver
Marvin Harrison, Indianapolis (PFW)	Wide Receiver
Cris Carter, Minnesota (AP)	Wide Receiver
Tony Gonzalez, Kansas City (AP, PFW)	Tight End
William Roaf, New Orleans (AP, PFW)	Tackle
Jonathan Ogden, Baltimore (AP)	Tackle
Kyle Turley, New Orleans (PFW)	Tackle
Larry Allen, Dallas (AP, PFW)	Guard
Bruce Matthews, Tennessee (AP, PFW)	Guard
Tom Nalen, Denver (AP)	Center
Kevin Mawae, New York Jets (PFW)	Center
Rich Gannon, Oakland (AP, PFW)	Quarterback
Marshall Faulk, St. Louis (AP, PFW)	Running Back
Eddie George, Tennessee (AP, PFW)	Running Back

Defense

Hugh Douglas, Philadelphia (AP, PFW)	End
Jason Taylor, Miami (AP, PFW)	End
Warren Sapp, Tampa Bay (AP, PFW)	Tackle
La'Roi Glover, New Orleans (AP, PFW)	Tackle
Derrick Brooks, Tampa Bay (AP, PFW)	Linebacker
Ray Lewis, Baltimore (AP, PFW)	Linebacker
Junior Seau, San Diego (AP, PFW)	Linebacker
Jeremiah Trotter, Philadelphia (AP)	Linebacker
Sam Madison, Miami (AP, PFW)	Cornerback
Samari Rolle, Tennessee (AP, PFW)	Cornerback
John Lynch, Tampa Bay (AP, PFW)	Safety
Darren Sharper, Green Bay (AP, PFW)	Safety

Specialists

Matt Stover, Baltimore (AP, PFW)	Kicker
Darren Bennett, San Diego (PFW)	Punter
Shane Lechler, Oakland (AP)	Punter
Derrick Mason, Tennessee (AP, PFW)	Kick Returner
Az-Zahir Hakim, St. Louis (PFW)	Punt Returner
Michael Bates, Carolina (PFW)	Special Teams Player

2000 ALL-PRO TEAMS

2000 FOOTBALL NEWS ALL-AFC TEAM

Selected by Football News

Offense

Rich Gannon, Oakland	Quarterback
Edgerrin James, Indianapolis	Running Back
Eddie George, Tennessee	Running Back
Rod Smith, Denver	Wide Receiver
Marvin Harrison, Indianapolis	Wide Receiver
Tony Gonzalez, Kansas City	Tight End
Tony Boselli, Jacksonville	Tackle
Jonathan Ogden, Baltimore	Tackle
Bruce Matthews, Tennessee	Guard
Steve Wisniewski, Oakland	Guard
Tom Nalen, Denver	Center

Defense

Jason Taylor, Miami	End
Rob Burnett, Baltimore	End
Trevor Pryce, Denver	Tackle
Sam Adams, Baltimore	Tackle
Junior Seau, San Diego	Linebacker
Mo Lewis, New York Jets	Linebacker
Ray Lewis, Baltimore	Linebacker
Charles Woodson, Oakland	Cornerback
Samari Rolle, Tennessee	Cornerback
Rod Woodson, Baltimore	Safety
Blaine Bishop, Tennessee	Safety

Specialists

Jermaine Lewis, Baltimore	Punt Returner
Chris Gardocki, Cleveland	Punter
Derrick Mason, Tennessee	Kick Returner
Matt Stover, Baltimore	Kicker

2000 FOOTBALL NEWS ALL-NFC TEAM

Selected by Football News

Offense

Donovan McNabb, Philadelphia	Quarterback
Robert Smith, Minnesota	Running Back
Marshall Faulk, St. Louis	Running Back
Randy Moss, Minnesota	Wide Receiver
Terrell Owens, San Francisco	Wide Receiver
Chad Lewis, Philadelphia	Tight End
Orlando Pace, St. Louis	Tackle
Kyle Turley, New Orleans	Tackle
Larry Allen, Dallas	Guard
Ron Stone, New York Giants	Guard
Matt Birk, Minnesota	Center

Defense

Hugh Douglas, Philadelphia	End
Joe Johnson, New Orleans	End
Warren Sapp, Tampa Bay	Tackle
La'Roi Glover, New Orleans	Tackle
Derrick Brooks, Tampa Bay	Linebacker
Jessie Armstead, N.Y. Giants	Linebacker
Stephen Boyd, Detroit	Linebacker
Champ Bailey, Washington	Cornerback
Troy Vincent, Philadelphia	Cornerback
John Lynch, Tampa Bay	Safety
Darren Sharper, Green Bay	Safety

Specialists

Desmond Howard, Detroit	Punt Returner
Scott Player, Arizona	Punter
Darrick Vaughn, Atlanta	Kick Returner
Ryan Longwell, Green Bay	Kicker

2000 PFW/PFWA ALL-ROOKIE TEAM

Selected by Pro Football Weekly *and the Professional Football Writers of America*

Offense

Doug Johnson, Atlanta	Quarterback
Mike Anderson, Denver	Running Back
Jamal Lewis, Baltimore	Running Back
Sylvester Morris, Kansas City	Wide Receiver
Darrell Jackson, Seattle	Wide Receiver
Anthony Becht, New York Jets	Tight End
Chris Samuels, Washington	Tackle
Todd Wade, Miami	Tackle
Brad Meester, Jacksonville	Guard
Jeno James, Carolina	Guard
Jean-Phillipe Darche, Seattle	Center

Defense

Darren Howard, New Orleans	End
Courtney Brown, Cleveland	End
Corey Simon, Philadelphia	Tackle
Chris Hovan, Minnesota	Tackle
Brian Urlacher, Chicago	Linebacker
LaVar Arrington, Washington	Linebacker
Na'il Diggs, Green Bay	Linebacker
Ahmed Plummer, San Francisco	Cornerback
Pat Dennis, Kansas City	Cornerback
Greg Wesley, Kansas City	Safety
Mike Brown, Chicago	Safety

Specialists

Paul Edinger, Chicago	Kicker
Shane Lechler, Oakland	Punter
Darrick Vaughn, Atlanta	Kick Returner
Hank Poteat, Pittsburgh	Punt Returner
Jean-Phillipe Darche, Seattle	Special Teams Player

TEN BEST RUSHING PERFORMANCES, 2000

	Att.	Yards	TD
1. Corey Dillon Cincinnati vs. Denver, Oct. 22	22	278	2
2. Mike Anderson Denver vs. New Orleans, Dec. 3	37	251	4
3. Fred Taylor Jacksonville vs. Pittsburgh, Nov. 19	30	234	3
4. Marshall Faulk St. Louis vs. New Orleans, Dec. 24	32	220	2
5. Edgerrin James Indianapolis vs. Seattle, Oct. 15	38	219	3
6. Corey Dillon Cincinnati vs. Arizona, Dec. 3	35	216	1
7. Warrick Dunn Tampa Bay vs. Dallas, Dec. 3	22	210	2
8. Marshall Faulk St. Louis vs. Atlanta, Oct. 15	25	208	1
9. Curtis Martin New York Jets vs. Indianapolis, Dec. 3	30	203	1
10. Charlie Garner San Francisco vs. Dallas, Sept. 24	36	201	1
Duce Staley Philadelphia vs. Dallas, Sept. 3	26	201	1

100-YARD RUSHING PERFORMANCES, 2000

First Week

Duce Staley, Philadelphia	201 yards vs. Dallas
Lamar Smith, Miami	145 yards vs. Seattle
Tiki Barber, New York Giants	144 yards vs. Arizona
Stephen Davis, Washington	133 yards vs. Carolina
Edgerrin James, Indianapolis	124 yards vs. Kansas City
Priest Holmes, Baltimore	119 yards vs. Pittsburgh
Curtis Martin, New York Jets	110 yards vs. Green Bay
Robert Smith, Minnesota	109 yards vs. Chicago

Second Week

Mike Anderson, Denver	131 yards vs. Atlanta

Third Week

Mike Anderson, Denver	187 yards vs. Oakland
Marshall Faulk, St. Louis	134 yards vs. San Francisco
Jerome Bettis, Pittsburgh	133 yards vs. Cleveland
Ricky Williams, New Orleans	107 yards vs. Seattle
Ricky Watters, Seattle	105 yards vs. New Orleans

Fourth Week

Charlie Garner, San Francisco	201 yards vs. Dallas
Jamal Lewis, Baltimore	116 yards vs. Cincinnati
Ricky Williams, New Orleans	103 yards vs. Philadelphia

Fifth Week

Stephen Davis, Washington	141 yards vs. Tampa Bay
Robert Smith, Minnesota	134 yards vs. Detroit
Emmitt Smith, Dallas	132 yards vs. Carolina
Eddie George, Tennessee	125 yards vs. New York Giants
James Stewart, Detroit	123 yards vs. Minnesota
Corey Dillon, Cincinnati	110 yards vs. Miami
Brian Mitchell, Philadelphia	105 yards vs. Atlanta
Justin Watson, St. Louis	102 yards vs. San Diego

Sixth Week

Eddie George, Tennessee	181 yards vs. Cincinnati
Ricky Williams, New Orleans	128 yards vs. Chicago
Charlie Garner, San Francisco	109 yards vs. Oakland
Jerome Bettis, Pittsburgh	107 yards vs. New York Jets
Michael Pittman, Arizona	107 yards vs. Cleveland
Tshimanga Biakabutuka, Carolina	103 yards vs. Seattle

Seventh Week

Edgerrin James, Indianapolis	219 yards vs. Seattle
Marshall Faulk, St. Louis	208 yards vs. Atlanta
Robert Smith, Minnesota	170 yards vs. Chicago
Eddie George, Tennessee	167 yards vs. Jacksonville
Ricky Williams, New Orleans	144 yards vs. Carolina
Curtis Martin, New York Jets	143 yards vs. New England
Fred Taylor, Jacksonville	112 yards vs. Tennessee
Ron Dayne, New York Giants	108 yards vs. Dallas
Mike Anderson, Denver	103 yards vs. Cleveland
Jerome Bettis, Pittsburgh	101 yards vs. Cincinnati

Eighth Week

Corey Dillon, Cincinnati	278 yards vs. Denver
Tyrone Wheatley, Oakland	156 yards vs. Seattle
Ricky Williams, New Orleans	156 yards vs. Atlanta
Lamar Smith, Miami	155 yards vs. New York Jets
Edgerrin James, Indianapolis	124 yards vs. New England
Fred Taylor, Jacksonville	124 yards vs. Washington
James Stewart, Detroit	116 yards vs. Tampa Bay
Stephen Davis, Washington	114 yards vs. Jacksonville
Emmitt Smith, Dallas	112 yards vs. Arizona
Jerome Bettis, Pittsburgh	105 yards vs. Cleveland
Kimble Anders, Kansas City	102 yards vs. St. Louis

Ninth Week

Edgerrin James, Indianapolis	139 yards vs. Detroit
Corey Dillon, Cincinnati	137 yards vs. Cleveland
Fred Taylor, Jacksonville	107 yards vs. Dallas
Emmitt Smith, Dallas	102 yards vs. Jacksonville

Tenth Week

Emmitt Smith, Dallas	134 yards vs. Philadelphia
Lamar Smith, Miami	125 yards vs. Detroit
Stephen Davis, Washington	124 yards vs. Arizona
Robert Smith, Minnesota	122 yards vs. Green Bay
Terrell Davis, Denver	115 yards vs. New York Jets
Tyrone Wheatley, Oakland	112 yards vs. Kansas City
Jamal Lewis, Baltimore	109 yards vs. Cincinnati

Eleventh Week

Jerome Bettis, Pittsburgh	134 yards vs. Philadelphia
Edgerrin James, Indianapolis	131 yards vs. New York Jets
Jamal Anderson, Atlanta	119 yards vs. Detroit
Robert Smith, Minnesota	117 yards vs. Arizona
Fred Taylor, Jacksonville	103 yards vs. Seattle
Charlie Garner, San Francisco	102 yards vs. Kansas City

Twelfth Week

Fred Taylor, Jacksonville	234 yards vs. Pittsburgh
Jamal Lewis, Baltimore	187 yards vs. Dallas
Ahman Green, Green Bay	153 yards vs. Indianapolis
Eddie George, Tennessee	134 yards vs. Cleveland
Robert Smith, Minnesota	103 yards vs. Carolina

Thirteenth Week

Mike Anderson, Denver	195 yards vs. Seattle
Jamal Lewis, Baltimore	170 yards vs. Cleveland
Robert Smith, Minnesota	148 yards vs. Dallas
Corey Dillon, Cincinnati	128 yards vs. Pittsburgh
Donovan McNabb, Philadelphia	125 yards vs. Washington
James Allen, Chicago	122 yards vs. New York Jets
Edgerrin James, Indianapolis	118 yards vs. Miami
Brad Hoover, Carolina	117 yards vs. Green Bay
Warrick Dunn, Tampa Bay	106 yards vs. Buffalo
Fred Taylor, Jacksonville	104 yards vs. Tennessee
Emmitt Smith, Dallas	100 yards vs. Minnesota

Fourteenth Week

Mike Anderson, Denver	251 yards vs. New Orleans
Corey Dillon, Cincinnati	216 yards vs. Arizona
Warrick Dunn, Tampa Bay	210 yards vs. Dallas
Curtis Martin, New York Jets	203 yards vs. Indianapolis
Fred Taylor, Jacksonville	181 yards vs. Cleveland
Jerome Bettis, Pittsburgh	128 yards vs. Oakland
Robert Smith, Minnesota	115 yards vs. Detroit

2000 BEST PERFORMANCES

Eddie George, Tennessee 101 yards vs. Philadelphia
Lamar Smith, Miami 100 yards vs. Buffalo

Fifteenth Week

Emmitt Smith, Dallas 150 yards vs. Washington
Fred Taylor, Jacksonville 137 yards vs. Arizona
Marshall Faulk, St. Louis 135 yards vs. Minnesota
Mike Anderson, Denver 131 yards vs. Seattle
Ahman Green, Green Bay 118 yards vs. Detroit
Edgerrin James, Indianapolis 111 yards vs. Buffalo
Aaron Brooks, New Orleans 108 yards vs. San Francisco

Sixteenth Week

Eddie George, Tennessee 176 yards vs. Cleveland
Ricky Watters, Seattle 168 yards vs. Oakland
James Stewart, Detroit 164 yards vs. New York Jets
Ahman Green, Green Bay 161 yards vs. Minnesota
Tony Richardson, Kansas City 156 yards vs. Denver
Tyrone Wheatley, Oakland 146 yards vs. Seattle
Warrick Dunn, Tampa Bay 145 yards vs. St. Louis
Jamal Lewis, Baltimore 126 yards vs. Arizona
Edgerrin James, Indianapolis 112 yards vs. Miami
Fred Taylor, Jacksonville 110 yards vs. Cincinnati
Jerome Bettis, Pittsburgh 104 yards vs. Washington

Seventeenth Week

Marshall Faulk, St. Louis 220 yards vs. New Orleans
Antowain Smith, Buffalo 147 yards vs. Seattle
Edgerrin James, Indianapolis 128 yards vs. Minnesota
Stephen Davis, Washington 120 yards vs. Arizona
Jamal Anderson, Atlanta 107 yards vs. Kansas City

Times 100 or More (117)
James, Taylor, 9; R. Smith, 8; Bettis, 7; M. Anderson, George, E. Smith, 6; S. Davis, Dillon, Lewis, Williams, 5; Faulk, L. Smith, 4; Dunn, Garner, Green, Martin, Stewart, Wheatley, 3; J. Anderson, Watters, 2.

TEN BEST PASSING PERFORMANCES, 2000

		Att.	Comp.	Yards	TD
1.	Elvis Grbac Kansas City vs. Oakland, Nov. 5	53	39	504	2
2.	Vinny Testaverde New York Jets vs. Baltimore, Dec. 24	69	36	481	2
3.	Gus Frerotte Denver vs. San Diego, Nov. 19	58	36	462	5
4.	Aaron Brooks New Orleans vs. Denver, Dec. 3	48	30	441	2
	Kurt Warner St. Louis vs. Denver, Sept. 4	35	25	441	3
6.	Peyton Manning Indianapolis vs. Jacksonville, Sept. 25	36	23	440	4
7.	Trent Green St. Louis vs. Carolina, Nov. 5	42	29	431	2
8.	Jeff Garcia San Francisco vs. Chicago, Dec. 17	44	36	402	2
9.	Kurt Warner St. Louis vs. San Francisco, Sept. 17	34	23	394	2
10.	Donovan McNabb Philadelphia vs. Cleveland, Dec. 10	36	23	390	4
	Kurt Warner St. Louis vs. San Diego, Oct. 1	30	24	390	4

300-YARD PASSING PERFORMANCES, 2000

First Week

Kurt Warner, St. Louis 441 yards vs. Denver
Jake Plummer, Arizona 318 yards vs. New York Giants
Brian Griese, Denver 307 yards vs. St. Louis
Mark Brunell, Jacksonville 301 yards vs. Cleveland

Second Week

Mark Brunell, Jacksonville 386 yards vs. Baltimore
Kurt Warner, St. Louis 386 yards vs. Seattle
Peyton Manning, Indianapolis 367 yards vs. Oakland
Steve Beuerlein, Carolina 364 yards vs. San Francisco
Daunte Culpepper, Minnesota 355 yards vs. Miami

Third Week

Kurt Warner, St. Louis 394 yards vs. San Francisco
Tim Couch, Cleveland 316 yards vs. Pittsburgh

Fourth Week

Peyton Manning, Indianapolis 440 yards vs. Jacksonville
Kurt Warner, St. Louis 336 yards vs. Atlanta

Fifth Week

Kurt Warner, St. Louis 390 yards vs. San Diego
Brian Griese, Denver 361 yards vs. New England
Jim Harbaugh, San Diego 348 yards vs. St. Louis
Brett Favre, Green Bay 333 yards vs. Chicago
Donovan McNabb, Philadelphia 311 yards vs. Atlanta

Sixth Week

Jeff Garcia, San Francisco 336 yards vs. Oakland
Peyton Manning, Indianapolis 334 yards vs. New England
Steve Beuerlein, Carolina 332 yards vs. Seattle
Rich Gannon, Oakland 310 yards vs. San Francisco

Seventh Week

Jeff Garcia, San Francisco 336 yards vs. Green Bay
Brian Griese, Denver 336 yards vs. Cleveland
Rob Johnson, Buffalo 321 yards vs. San Diego
Kurt Warner, St. Louis 313 yards vs. Atlanta

Eighth Week

Vinny Testaverde, New York Jets 378 yards vs. Miami
Brian Griese, Denver 365 yards vs. Cincinnati
Steve Beuerlein, Carolina 309 yards vs. San Francisco
Jeff Garcia, San Francisco 307 yards vs. Carolina

Ninth Week

Elvis Grbac, Kansas City 342 yards vs. Seattle

Daunte Culpepper, Minnesota	313 yards vs. Tampa Bay
Trent Green, St. Louis	310 yards vs. San Francisco
Tenth Week	
Elvis Grbac, Kansas City	504 yards vs. Oakland
Trent Green, St. Louis	431 yards vs. Carolina
Brian Griese, Denver	327 yards vs. New York Jets
Peyton Manning, Indianapolis	302 yards vs. Chicago
Eleventh Week	
Rich Gannon, Oakland	382 yards vs. Denver
Mark Brunell, Jacksonville	340 yards vs. Seattle
Troy Aikman, Dallas	308 yards vs. Cincinnati
Daunte Culpepper, Minnesota	302 yards vs. Arizona
Twelfth Week	
Gus Frerotte, Denver	462 yards vs. San Diego
Trent Green, St. Louis	366 yards vs. Washington
Daunte Culpepper, Minnesota	357 yards vs. Carolina
Kerry Collins, New York Giants	350 yards vs. Detroit
Elvis Grbac, Kansas City	341 yards vs. Buffalo
Ryan Leaf, San Diego	311 yards vs. Denver
Brett Favre, Green Bay	301 yards vs. Indianapolis
Thirteenth Week	
None	
Fourteenth Week	
Aaron Brooks, New Orleans	441 yards vs. Denver
Elvis Grbac, Kansas City	350 yards vs. New England
Peyton Manning, Indianapolis	339 yards vs. New York Jets
Jeff Garcia, San Francisco	323 yards vs. San Diego
Fifteenth Week	
Donovan McNabb, Philadelphia	390 yards vs. Cleveland
Kurt Warner, St. Louis	346 yards vs. Minnesota
Kerry Collins, New York Giants	333 yards vs. Pittsburgh
Elvis Grbac, Kansas City	315 yards vs. Carolina
Doug Pederson, Cleveland	309 yards vs. Philadelphia
Jeff Garcia, San Francisco	305 yards vs. New Orleans
Sixteenth Week	
Jeff Garcia, San Francisco	402 yards vs. Chicago
Daunte Culpepper, Minnesota	335 yards vs. Green Bay
Kurt Warner, St. Louis	316 yards vs. Tampa Bay
Seventeenth Week	
Vinny Testaverde, New York Jets	481 yards vs. Baltimore
Doug Flutie, Buffalo	366 yards vs. Seattle
Kerry Collins, New York Giants	321 yards vs. Jacksonville
Drew Bledsoe, New England	312 yards vs. Miami

Times 300 or more (65)
Warner, 8; Garcia, 6; Culpepper, Grbac, Griese, Manning, 5; Beuerlein, Brunell, Collins, Green, 3; Favre, Gannon, McNabb, Testaverde, 2.

TEN BEST RECEIVING PERFORMANCES, 2000

	No.	Yards	TD
1. Jimmy Smith Jacksonville vs. Baltimore, Sept. 10	15	291	3
2. Terrell Owens San Francisco vs. Chicago, Dec. 17	20	283	1
3. Albert Connell Washington vs. Jacksonville, Oct. 22	7	211	3
4. Amani Toomer New York Giants vs. Jacksonville, Dec. 23	8	193	1
5. Torry Holt St. Louis vs. Atlanta, Sept. 24	3	189	2
6. Isaac Bruce St. Louis vs. San Francisco, Sept. 17	8	188	1
7. Rod Smith Denver vs. San Diego, Nov. 19	11	187	1
8. David Boston Arizona vs. Cincinnati, Dec. 3	9	184	2
9. Joe Horn New Orleans vs. San Francisco, Nov. 5	10	180	1
10. Terrell Owens San Francisco vs. Oakland, Oct. 8	12	176	2

100-YARD RECEIVING PERFORMANCES, 2000

First Week	
Shawn Jefferson, Atlanta	148 yards vs. San Francisco
David Boston, Arizona	128 yards vs. New York Giants
Az-Zahir Hakim, St. Louis	116 yards vs. Denver
Marvin Harrison, Indianapolis	115 yards vs. Kansas City
Ed McCaffrey, Denver	115 yards vs. St. Louis
Keenan McCardell, Jacksonville	115 yards vs. Cleveland
Dedric Ward, New York Jets	104 yards vs. Green Bay
Torry Holt, St. Louis	103 yards vs. Denver
Qadry Ismail, Baltimore	102 yards vs. Pittsburgh
Marshall Faulk, St. Louis	100 yards vs. Denver
Second Week	
Jimmy Smith, Jacksonville	291 yards vs. Baltimore
Cris Carter, Minnesota	168 yards vs. Miami
Marvin Harrison, Indianapolis	141 yards vs. Oakland
Tony Martin, Miami	120 yards vs. Minnesota
Rod Smith, Denver	117 yards vs. Atlanta
Joe Horn, New Orleans	116 yards vs. San Diego
Donald Hayes, Carolina	115 yards vs. San Francisco
Muhsin Muhammad, Carolina	108 yards vs. San Francisco
Kevin Dyson, Tennessee	104 yards vs. Kansas City
Jacquez Green, Tampa Bay	104 yards vs. Chicago
Eric Moulds, Buffalo	103 yards vs. Green Bay
David Boston, Arizona	102 yards vs. Dallas
Torry Holt, St. Louis	101 yards vs. Seattle
Dedric Ward, New York Jets	100 yards vs. New England
Third Week	
Isaac Bruce, St. Louis	188 yards vs. San Francisco
Sylvester Morris, Kansas City	112 yards vs. San Diego
Keenan McCardell, Jacksonville	108 yards vs. Cincinnati
Terrell Owens, San Francisco	108 yards vs. St. Louis
Fourth Week	
Torry Holt, St. Louis	189 yards vs. Atlanta
Terrence Wilkins, Indianapolis	148 yards vs. Jacksonville
Rod Smith, Denver	134 yards vs. Kansas City
Jimmy Smith, Jacksonville	132 yards vs. Indianapolis
James McKnight, Dallas	129 yards vs. San Francisco
Tony Gonzalez, Kansas City	127 yards vs. Denver
Albert Connell, Washington	122 yards vs. New York Giants
Carl Pickens, Tennessee	105 yards vs. Pittsburgh
Marvin Harrison, Indianapolis	103 yards vs. Jacksonville

2000 BEST PERFORMANCES

Fifth Week	
Randy Moss, Minnesota	168 yards vs. Detroit
Isaac Bruce, St. Louis	167 yards vs. San Diego
Rod Smith, Denver	160 yards vs. New England
Derrick Alexander, Kansas City	153 yards vs. Seattle
Keenan McCardell, Jacksonville	137 yards vs. Pittsburgh
Marcus Robinson, Chicago	126 yards vs. Green Bay
Torrance Small, Philadelphia	122 yards vs. Atlanta
Marshall Faulk, St. Louis	116 yards vs. San Diego
David Patten, Cleveland	113 yards vs. Baltimore
Eric Moulds, Buffalo	112 yards vs. Indianapolis
Troy Brown, New England	108 yards vs. Denver
Bill Schroeder, Green Bay	108 yards vs. Chicago
Jeff Graham, San Diego	107 yards vs. St. Louis
Az-Zahir Hakim, St. Louis	104 yards vs. San Diego
Derrick Mason, Tennessee	103 yards vs. New York Giants
Sixth Week	
Terrell Owens, San Francisco	176 yards vs. Oakland
Tim Brown, Oakland	172 yards vs. San Francisco
Marvin Harrison, Indianapolis	159 yards vs. New England
Jacquez Green, Tampa Bay	131 yards vs. Minnesota
Randy Moss, Minnesota	118 yards vs. Tampa Bay
Wesley Walls, Carolina	102 yards vs. Seattle
Reggie Jones, San Diego	101 yards vs. Denver
Seventh Week	
Eric Moulds, Buffalo	170 yards vs. San Diego
Curtis Conway, San Diego	143 yards vs. Buffalo
Marvin Harrison, Indianapolis	134 yards vs. Seattle
Ed McCaffrey, Denver	129 yards vs. Cleveland
David Boston, Arizona	123 yards vs. Philadelphia
Sean Dawkins, Seattle	118 yards vs. Indianapolis
Antonio Freeman, Green Bay	116 yards vs. San Francisco
Jeff Graham, San Diego	113 yards vs. Buffalo
Cris Carter, Minnesota	111 yards vs. Chicago
Rod Smith, Denver	111 yards vs. Cleveland
Tony Gonzalez, Kansas City	100 yards vs. Oakland
Eighth Week	
Albert Connell, Washington	211 yards vs. Jacksonville
Marvin Harrison, Indianapolis	156 yards vs. New England
Ed McCaffrey, Denver	136 yards vs. Cincinnati
Eric Moulds, Buffalo	135 yards vs. Minnesota
Isaac Bruce, St. Louis	129 yards vs. Kansas City
Muhsin Muhammad, Carolina	127 yards vs. San Francisco
Oronde Gadsden, Miami	119 yards vs. New York Jets
Derrick Alexander, Kansas City	117 yards vs. St. Louis
Tony Gonzalez, Kansas City	117 yards vs. St. Louis
Charlie Garner, San Francisco	112 yards vs. Carolina
Kyle Brady, Jacksonville	111 yards vs. Washington
Randy Moss, Minnesota	110 yards vs. Buffalo
Rod Smith, Denver	110 yards vs. Cincinnati
Richie Anderson, New York Jets	109 yards vs. Miami
Cris Carter, Minnesota	107 yards vs. Buffalo
Wayne Chrebet, New York Jets	104 yards vs. Miami
Shannon Sharpe, Baltimore	104 yards vs. Tennessee
Ninth Week	
Kyle Brady, Jacksonville	138 yards vs. Dallas
Derrick Alexander, Kansas City	137 yards vs. Seattle
Eric Moulds, Buffalo	137 yards vs. New York Jets
Laveranues Coles, New York Jets	131 yards vs. Buffalo
Isaac Bruce, St. Louis	129 yards vs. San Francisco
Keyshawn Johnson, Tampa Bay	121 yards vs. Minnesota
Cris Carter, Minnesota	115 yards vs. Tampa Bay
Terrell Owens, San Francisco	115 yards vs. St. Louis
James McKnight, Dallas	113 yards vs. Jacksonville
Freddie Jones, San Diego	111 yards vs. Oakland
Marvin Harrison, Indianapolis	109 yards vs. Detroit
Amani Toomer, New York Giants	108 yards vs. Philadelphia
Kevin Johnson, Cleveland	102 yards vs. Cincinnati
Tony Gonzalez, Kansas City	101 yards vs. Seattle
Tenth Week	
Joe Horn, New Orleans	180 yards vs. San Francisco
Az-Zahir Hakim, St. Louis	147 yards vs. Carolina
Derrick Alexander, Kansas City	139 yards vs. Oakland
Tony Gonzalez, Kansas City	134 yards vs. Oakland
Rod Smith, Denver	134 yards vs. New York Jets
Torry Holt, St. Louis	130 yards vs. Carolina
Randy Moss, Minnesota	130 yards vs. Green Bay
Antonio Freeman, Green Bay	118 yards vs. Minnesota
Sylvester Morris, Kansas City	102 yards vs. Oakland
James Thrash, Washington	102 yards vs. Arizona
Amani Toomer, New York Giants	100 yards vs. Cleveland
Eleventh Week	
James McKnight, Dallas	164 yards vs. Cincinnati
Keenan McCardell, Jacksonville	156 yards vs. Seattle
Wayne Chrebet, New York Jets	140 yards vs. Indianapolis
Tim Brown, Oakland	122 yards vs. Denver
Cris Carter, Minnesota	119 yards vs. Arizona
Andre Rison, Oakland	117 yards vs. Denver
Jimmy Smith, Jacksonville	117 yards vs. Seattle
Ike Hilliard, New York Giants	110 yards vs. St. Louis
Randy Moss, Minnesota	104 yards vs. Arizona
Twelfth Week	
Rod Smith, Denver	187 yards vs. San Diego
Bill Schroeder, Green Bay	155 yards vs. Indianapolis
Ed McCaffrey, Denver	148 yards vs. San Diego
Derrick Alexander, Kansas City	146 yards vs. Buffalo
Jeff Graham, San Diego	144 yards vs. Denver
Cris Carter, Minnesota	138 yards vs. Carolina
Terry Glenn, New England	129 yards vs. Cincinnati
Torry Holt, St. Louis	125 yards vs. Washington
Curtis Conway, San Diego	118 yards vs. Denver
Troy Brown, New England	110 yards vs. Cincinnati
Amani Toomer, New York Giants	108 yards vs. Detroit
Randy Moss, Minnesota	106 yards vs. Carolina
Shannon Sharpe, Baltimore	101 yards vs. Dallas
Thirteenth Week	
Randy Moss, Minnesota	144 yards vs. Dallas
Muhsin Muhammad, Carolina	131 yards vs. Green Bay
Ricky Watters, Seattle	126 yards vs. Denver
James Thrash, Washington	121 yards vs. Philadelphia
Eddie George, Tennessee	109 yards vs. Jacksonville
Shawn Jefferson, Atlanta	109 yards vs. Oakland
Eric Moulds, Buffalo	102 yards vs. Tampa Bay
Fourteenth Week	
David Boston, Arizona	184 yards vs. Cincinnati
Joe Horn, New Orleans	170 yards vs. Denver
Tony Gonzalez, Kansas City	147 yards vs. New England
Robert Wilson, New Orleans	122 yards vs. Denver
Troy Brown, New England	119 yards vs. Kansas City
Bill Schroeder, Green Bay	119 yards vs. Chicago
Derrick Alexander, Kansas City	116 yards vs. New England
Terrence Wilkins, Indianapolis	109 yards vs. New York Jets
Larry Foster, Detroit	106 yards vs. Minnesota
Jimmy Smith, Jacksonville	104 yards vs. Cleveland
Fifteenth Week	
Torry Holt, St. Louis	172 yards vs. Minnesota
Jimmy Smith, Jacksonville	147 yards vs. Arizona
Amani Toomer, New York Giants	136 yards vs. Pittsburgh
Terrell Owens, San Francisco	129 yards vs. New Orleans
Ed McCaffrey, Denver	112 yards vs. Seattle
Joe Horn, New Orleans	105 yards vs. San Francisco
Richie Anderson, New York Jets	103 yards vs. Oakland

David Patten, Cleveland	103 yards vs. Philadelphia
Muhsin Muhammad, Carolina	102 yards vs. Kansas City
Eddie Kennison, Chicago	100 yards vs. New England
Chad Lewis, Philadelphia	100 yards vs. Cleveland
Sixteenth Week	
Terrell Owens, San Francisco	283 yards vs. Chicago
Torry Holt, St. Louis	165 yards vs. Tampa Bay
Randy Moss, Minnesota	136 yards vs. Green Bay
Joe Horn, New Orleans	116 yards vs. Atlanta
Keyshawn Johnson, Tampa Bay	116 yards vs. St. Louis
Danny Farmer, Cincinnati	102 yards vs. Jacksonville
Rod Smith, Denver	101 yards vs. Kansas City
Seventeenth Week	
Amani Toomer, New York Giants	193 yards vs. Jacksonville
Dedric Ward, New York Jets	147 yards vs. Baltimore
Richie Anderson, New York Jets	139 yards vs. Baltimore
Peerless Price, Buffalo	132 yards vs. Seattle
Keenan McCardell, Jacksonville	131 yards vs. New York Giants
Torry Holt, St. Louis	121 yards vs. New Orleans
Muhsin Muhammad, Carolina	114 yards vs. Oakland
Jeff Graham, San Diego	113 yards vs. Pittsburgh
Marvin Harrison, Indianapolis	109 yards vs. Minnesota
Troy Brown, New England	102 yards vs. Miami
Eric Moulds, Buffalo	101 yards vs. Seattle

Times 100 or more (180)
Harrison, Holt, Moss, R. Smith, 8; Moulds, 7; Alexander, Carter, Gonzalez, 6; Horn, McCaffrey, McCardell, Muhammad, Owens, J. Smith, Toomer, 5; Boston, Tr. Brown, Bruce, Graham, 4; Anderson, Hakim, McKnight, Schroeder, Ward, 3; Brady, Ti. Brown, Chrebet, Connell, Conway, Faulk, Freeman, Green, Jefferson, Johnson, Morris, Patten, Sharpe, Thrash, Wilkins, 2.

TOP QUARTERBACK SACK PERFORMANCES, 2000

(2.5 or More Sacks Per Game Needed to Qualify)

First Week	
Trace Armstrong, Miami	2.5 vs. Seattle
Marco Coleman, Washington	2.5 vs. Carolina
Second Week	
Keith McKenzie, Cleveland	3.0 vs. Cincinnati
Ronde Barber, Tampa Bay	2.5 vs. Chicago
Duane Clemons, Kansas City	2.5 vs. Tennessee
Third Week	
Courtney Brown, Cleveland	3.0 vs. Pittsburgh
Warren Sapp, Tampa Bay	3.0 vs. Detroit
Hugh Douglas, Philadelphia	2.5 vs. Green Bay
Anthony McFarland, Tampa Bay	2.5 vs. Detroit
Jason Taylor, Miami	2.5 vs. Baltimore
Fourth Week	
Rob Burnett, Baltimore	2.5 vs. Cincinnati
Grant Wistrom, St. Louis	2.5 vs. Atlanta
Fifth Week	
Marco Coleman, Washington	3.0 vs. Tampa Bay
Eric Hicks, Kansas City	3.0 vs. Seattle
Sixth Week	
Trace Armstrong, Miami	3.5 vs. Buffalo
La'Roi Glover, New Orelans	3.0 vs. Chicago
Trevor Pryce, Denver	3.0 vs. San Diego
Seventh Week	
La'Roi Glover, New Orleans	3.0 vs. Carolina
Joey Porter, Pittsburgh	3.0 vs. Cincinnati
Eighth Week	
Marcus Jones, Tampa Bay	4.0 vs. Detroit
Ninth Week	
None	
Tenth Week	
None	
Eleventh Week	
Joe Johnson, New Orleans	3.0 vs. Carolina
Jevon Kearse, Tennessee	3.0 vs. Baltimore
Twelfth Week	
Robert Porcher, Detroit	3.0 vs. New York Giants
Simeon Rice, Arizona	3.0 vs. Philadelphia
Bruce Smith, Washington	3.0 vs. St. Louis
Thirteenth Week	
La'Roi Glover, New Orleans	3.0 vs. St. Louis
Keith Hamilton, New York Giants	3.0 vs. Arizona
Sam Cowart, Buffalo	2.5 vs. Tampa Bay
Fourteenth Week	
Kevin Carter, St. Louis	3.0 vs. Carolina
Jason Taylor, Miami	3.0 vs. Buffalo
Fifteenth Week	
Bryant Young, San Francisco	2.5 vs. New Orleans
Sixteenth Week	
Michael Strahan, New York Giants	2.5 vs. Dallas
Seventeenth Week	
None	

2000 TEAM STATISTICS

AMERICAN FOOTBALL CONFERENCE OFFENSE

	Balt.	Buff.	Cin.	Cle.	Den.	Ind.	Jax	K.C.	Mia.	N.E.	NYJ	Oak.	Pitt.	S.D.	Sea.	Tenn.
First Downs	288	309	254	176	383	357	318	321	251	283	308	337	283	251	281	299
Rushing	116	111	119	53	124	111	109	84	104	80	84	128	124	63	98	107
Passing	156	174	109	110	223	213	193	207	122	172	192	177	128	156	168	167
Penalty	16	24	26	13	36	33	16	30	25	31	32	32	31	32	15	25
Rushes	511	475	495	336	516	435	481	383	496	424	418	520	527	351	403	547
Net Yds. Gained	2199	1922	2314	1085	2311	1859	2032	1465	1894	1390	1471	2470	2248	1062	1720	2084
Avg. Gain	4.3	4.0	4.7	3.2	4.5	4.3	4.2	3.8	3.8	3.3	3.5	4.8	4.3	3.0	4.3	3.8
Avg. Yds. per Game	137.4	120.1	144.6	67.8	144.4	116.2	127.0	91.6	118.4	86.9	91.9	154.4	140.5	66.4	107.5	130.3
Passes Attempted	504	546	454	483	569	571	545	582	421	565	637	475	439	578	507	462
Completed	287	312	207	278	354	357	333	342	243	328	352	284	217	311	308	286
% Completed	56.9	57.1	45.6	57.6	62.2	62.5	61.1	58.8	57.7	58.1	55.3	59.8	49.4	53.8	60.7	61.9
Total Yds. Gained	3102	3936	2219	2728	4464	4413	3947	4408	2720	3461	4023	3430	2738	3540	3198	3430
Times Sacked	43	59	52	40	30	20	54	34	28	48	20	28	43	53	46	27
Yds. Lost	287	360	273	283	221	131	289	259	153	280	99	124	220	302	238	164
Net Yds. Gained	2815	3576	1946	2445	4243	4282	3658	4149	2567	3181	3924	3306	2518	3238	2960	3266
Avg. Yds. per Game	175.9	223.5	121.6	152.8	265.2	267.6	228.6	259.3	160.4	198.8	245.3	206.6	157.4	202.4	185.0	204.1
Net Yds. per Pass Play	5.15	5.91	3.85	4.67	7.08	7.25	6.11	6.74	5.72	5.19	5.97	6.57	5.22	5.13	5.35	6.68
Yds. Gained per Comp.	10.81	12.62	10.72	9.81	12.61	12.36	11.85	12.89	11.19	10.55	11.43	12.08	12.62	11.38	10.38	11.99
Combined Net Yds. Gained	5014	5498	4260	3530	6554	6141	5690	5614	4461	4571	5395	5776	4766	4300	4680	5350
% Total Yds. Rushing	43.9	35.0	54.3	30.7	35.3	30.3	35.7	26.1	42.5	30.4	27.3	42.8	47.2	24.7	36.8	39.0
% Total Yds. Passing	56.1	65.0	45.7	69.3	64.7	69.7	64.3	73.9	57.5	69.6	72.7	57.2	52.8	75.3	63.2	61.0
Avg. Yds. per Game	313.4	343.6	266.3	220.6	409.6	383.8	355.6	350.9	278.8	285.7	337.2	361.0	297.9	268.8	292.5	334.4
Ball Control Plays	1058	1080	1001	859	1115	1026	1080	999	945	1037	1075	1023	1009	982	956	1036
Avg. Yds. per Play	4.7	5.1	4.3	4.1	5.9	6.0	5.3	5.6	4.7	4.4	5.0	5.6	4.7	4.4	4.9	5.2
Avg. Time of Poss.	33:19	31:25	27:13	25:59	33:15	29:33	31:32	27:36	30:43	28:56	30:20	31:53	31:27	28:08	27:31	33:48
Third Down Efficiency	40.3	37.2	33.9	27.6	44.5	46.8	42.6	36.8	35.0	35.0	38.2	43.2	37.6	32.9	40.5	42.5
Had Intercepted	19	10	14	19	12	15	15	15	17	15	29	11	10	30	21	16
Yds. Opp Returned	234	112	138	228	144	212	168	295	102	208	545	93	150	515	191	236
Ret. by Opp. for TD	2	1	0	2	1	1	0	3	1	2	4	0	2	3	2	3
Punts	86	96	94	108	62	65	79	82	92	90	83	66	91	92	75	76
Yds. Punted	3457	3661	3775	4919	2455	2906	3311	3656	3870	3798	3714	2984	3944	4248	2960	3101
Avg. Yds. per Punt	40.2	38.1	40.2	45.5	39.6	44.7	41.9	44.6	42.1	42.2	44.7	45.2	43.3	46.2	39.5	40.8
Punt Returns	45	38	42	29	36	38	46	37	39	45	38	37	42	44	30	53
Yds. Returned	713	190	357	294	364	352	333	295	518	562	276	357	499	272	384	671
Avg. Yds. per Return	15.8	5.0	8.5	10.1	10.1	9.3	7.2	8.0	13.3	12.5	7.3	9.6	11.9	6.2	12.8	12.7
Returned for TD	2	0	1	0	0	0	0	0	1	1	0	0	1	0	0	1
Kickoff Returns	45	69	77	85	66	58	62	70	51	64	74	56	58	83	80	47
Yds. Returned	1005	1262	1423	1710	1477	1155	1323	1466	1133	1335	1552	1336	1221	1792	1932	1227
Avg. Yds. per Return	22.3	18.3	18.5	20.1	22.4	19.9	21.3	20.9	22.2	20.9	21.0	23.9	21.1	21.6	24.2	26.1
Returned for TD	0	0	0	0	1	0	0	0	0	0	1	1	1	1	1	0
Fumbles	26	28	37	21	26	20	27	23	12	23	18	18	24	38	35	24
Lost	7	13	21	9	13	14	14	11	9	10	11	9	11	20	17	14
Out of Bounds	3	1	3	0	2	2	1	2	2	0	0	1	0	1	1	0
Own Rec. for TD	0	2	0	0	0	0	0	0	0	0	0	0	0	0	0	0
Opp. Rec. by	26	13	12	13	17	8	18	14	13	13	14	16	17	6	10	13
Opp. Rec. for TD	0	0	0	0	2	1	0	0	2	0	0	1	2	0	2	1
Penalties	95	101	99	103	89	89	95	118	115	99	76	118	81	121	89	107
Yds. Penalized	730	913	878	925	792	866	703	848	920	815	626	940	667	1036	728	870
Total Points Scored	333	315	185	161	485	429	367	355	323	276	321	479	321	269	320	346
Total TDs	32	34	21	17	58	50	40	44	34	28	36	58	35	31	37	38
TDs Rushing	9	11	13	7	21	14	18	12	16	9	11	23	19	7	10	14
TDs Passing	20	20	6	9	28	33	22	29	15	18	23	28	12	19	21	18
TDs on Ret. and Rec.	3	3	2	1	9	3	0	3	3	1	2	7	4	5	6	6
Extra Point Kicks	30	31	21	17	53	46	38	40	33	25	32	56	32	27	33	37
Extra Point Kicks Att.	30	31	21	17	53	46	38	40	34	25	32	56	33	27	33	38
2Pt Conversions	2	1	0	0	2	2	1	0	0	1	2	1	1	0	0	0
2Pt Conversions Att.	2	3	0	0	5	4	1	4	0	3	4	1	2	4	4	0
Safeties	1	0	1	0	1	2	0	0	1	0	0	2	1	1	1	0
Field Goals Made	35	26	12	14	26	25	29	17	28	27	23	23	25	18	21	27
Field Goals Attempted	39	35	21	17	34	27	33	24	31	33	34	34	30	25	26	34
% Successful	89.7	74.3	57.1	82.4	76.5	92.6	87.9	70.8	90.3	81.8	67.6	67.6	83.3	72.0	80.8	79.4

AMERICAN FOOTBALL CONFERENCE DEFENSE

	Balt.	Buff.	Cin.	Cle.	Den.	Ind.	Jax	K.C.	Mia.	N.E.	NYJ	Oak.	Pitt.	S.D.	Sea.	Tenn.
First Downs	216	252	307	343	294	310	252	330	289	326	267	320	252	312	331	215
Rushing	59	76	101	147	80	109	85	103	92	108	98	85	82	76	126	62
Passing	135	153	182	169	189	177	144	201	156	184	152	202	153	195	185	134
Penalty	22	23	24	27	25	24	23	26	41	34	17	33	17	41	20	19
Rushes	361	444	504	594	344	446	436	441	417	495	476	383	425	470	503	387
Net Yds. Gained	970	1559	1925	2505	1598	1935	1685	1809	1736	1831	1888	1551	1693	1422	2454	1390
Avg. Gain	2.7	3.5	3.8	4.2	4.6	4.3	3.9	4.1	4.2	3.7	4.0	4.0	4.0	3.0	4.9	3.6
Avg. Yds. per Game	60.6	97.4	120.3	156.6	99.9	120.9	105.3	113.1	108.5	114.4	118.0	96.9	105.8	88.9	153.4	86.9
Passes Attempted	528	480	538	486	574	530	458	549	530	544	517	588	521	552	489	466
Completed	295	283	318	262	310	317	258	358	282	321	265	359	280	326	309	242
% Completed	55.9	59.0	59.1	53.9	54.0	59.8	56.3	65.2	53.2	59.0	51.3	61.1	53.7	59.1	63.2	51.9
Total Yds. Gained	3175	3175	3730	3408	4197	3674	3407	3737	3170	3694	3166	3976	3249	3786	4089	2761
Times Sacked	35	42	26	42	44	42	40	51	48	29	40	43	39	39	27	55
Yds. Lost	178	308	168	270	251	252	247	266	270	172	234	278	229	249	152	338
Net Yds. Gained	2997	2867	3562	3138	3946	3422	3160	3471	2900	3522	2932	3698	3020	3537	3937	2423
Avg. Yds. per Game	187.3	179.2	222.6	196.1	246.6	213.9	197.5	216.9	181.3	220.1	183.3	231.1	188.8	221.1	246.1	151.4
Net Yds. per Pass Play	5.32	5.49	6.32	5.94	6.39	5.98	6.35	5.79	5.02	6.15	5.26	5.86	5.39	5.98	7.63	4.65
Yds. Gained per Comp.	10.76	11.22	11.73	13.01	13.54	11.59	13.21	10.44	11.24	11.51	11.95	11.08	11.60	11.61	13.23	11.41
Combined Net Yds. Gained	3967	4426	5487	5643	5544	5357	4845	5280	4636	5353	4820	5249	4713	4959	6391	3813
% Total Yds. Rushing	24.5	35.2	35.1	44.4	28.8	36.1	34.8	34.3	37.4	34.2	39.2	29.5	35.9	28.7	38.4	36.5
% Total Yds. Passing	75.5	64.8	64.9	55.6	71.2	63.9	65.2	65.7	62.6	65.8	60.8	70.5	64.1	71.3	61.6	63.5
Avg. Yds. per Game	247.9	276.6	342.9	352.7	346.5	334.8	302.8	330.0	289.8	334.6	301.3	328.1	294.6	309.9	399.4	238.3
Ball Control Plays	924	966	1068	1122	962	1018	934	1041	995	1068	1033	1014	985	1061	1019	908
Avg. Yds. per Play	4.3	4.6	5.1	5.0	5.8	5.3	5.2	5.1	4.7	5.0	4.7	5.2	4.8	4.7	6.3	4.2
Avg. Time of Poss.	26:41	28:35	32:47	34:01	26:45	30:27	28:28	32:24	29:17	31:04	29:40	28:07	28:33	31:52	32:29	26:12
Third Down Efficiency	34.1	37.0	42.7	43.2	34.6	38.7	36.5	40.6	33.2	43.5	39.1	39.5	35.1	37.6	44.3	30.8
Intercepted By	23	16	9	12	27	14	12	15	28	10	21	21	17	16	17	17
Yds. Returned By	477	131	107	68	343	125	145	198	311	161	229	323	154	313	300	285
Returned for TD	1	1	1	1	5	2	0	2	0	0	1	4	0	4	3	4
Punts	87	92	80	68	73	82	90	78	87	87	88	79	84	91	62	105
Yds. Punted	3872	3865	3338	2868	3196	3503	3822	3363	3532	3513	3523	3289	3641	3780	2571	4484
Avg. Yds. per Punt	44.5	42.0	41.7	42.2	43.8	42.7	42.5	43.1	40.6	40.4	40.0	41.6	43.3	41.5	41.5	42.7
Punt Returns	41	51	40	69	23	28	38	43	36	43	42	30	44	51	32	28
Yds. Returned	382	544	387	793	270	357	478	559	258	384	660	279	371	722	151	160
Avg. Yds. per Return	9.3	10.7	9.7	11.5	11.7	12.8	12.6	13.0	7.2	8.9	15.7	9.3	8.4	14.2	4.7	5.7
Returned for TD	0	1	0	0	1	0	1	0	0	0	2	0	0	1	0	0
Kickoff Returns	73	70	42	42	90	73	73	70	68	62	62	80	69	61	64	76
Yds. Returned	1558	1524	898	1012	1934	1736	1523	1679	1260	1350	1424	1689	1496	1471	1236	1587
Avg. Yds. per Return	21.3	21.8	21.4	24.1	21.5	23.8	20.9	24.0	18.5	21.8	23.0	21.1	21.7	24.1	19.3	20.9
Returned for TD	0	2	0	0	1	1	1	0	0	1	0	0	0	1	0	0
Fumbles	45	30	22	27	31	16	26	19	30	27	21	29	25	17	28	39
Lost	26	13	12	13	17	8	18	14	13	13	14	16	18	6	12	13
Out of Bounds	0	1	1	0	2	0	1	1	0	0	1	1	1	0	3	2
Own Rec. for TD	0	0	0	0	0	0	0	0	0	0	1	0	0	1	1	0
Opp. Rec. by	7	12	21	9	13	13	14	11	8	10	11	9	11	20	17	14
Opp. Rec. for TD	0	2	2	0	2	0	0	1	0	0	0	1	0	0	0	0
Penalties	84	103	115	71	109	103	96	108	86	95	100	117	105	106	96	97
Yds. Penalized	535	905	924	626	898	820	814	1020	793	897	832	912	876	851	694	778
Total Points Scored	165	350	359	419	369	326	327	354	226	338	321	299	255	440	405	191
Total TDs	18	37	40	46	45	37	39	42	23	38	33	35	24	50	46	20
TDs Rushing	5	13	12	26	13	13	14	13	9	12	9	8	9	10	20	7
TDs Passing	11	18	26	18	26	22	23	25	13	23	17	25	13	33	23	10
TDs on Ret. and Rec.	2	6	2	2	6	2	2	4	1	3	7	2	2	7	3	3
Extra Point Kicks	15	33	39	44	42	33	36	39	20	34	32	30	24	46	45	20
Extra Point Kicks Att.	18	33	40	44	43	33	36	39	20	34	32	30	24	46	45	20
2Pt Conversions	0	3	0	1	0	3	2	0	1	1	1	0	0	1	0	0
2Pt Conversions Att.	0	4	0	2	2	4	3	3	3	4	1	5	0	4	1	0
Safeties	0	1	1	2	0	1	1	0	0	1	1	1	0	1	0	0
Field Goals Made	14	29	26	31	19	21	17	21	22	24	29	19	29	30	28	17
Field Goals Attempted	19	33	36	34	23	28	24	30	30	32	34	25	34	34	33	22
% Successful	73.7	87.9	72.2	91.2	82.6	75.0	70.8	70.0	73.3	75.0	85.3	76.0	85.3	88.2	84.8	77.3

2000 TEAM STATISTICS

NATIONAL FOOTBALL CONFERENCE OFFENSE

	Ariz.	Atl.	Car.	Chi.	Dall.	Det.	G.B.	Minn.	N.O.	NYG	Phil.	St.L.	S.F.	T.B.	Wash.
First Downs	253	256	304	239	276	264	315	319	312	310	295	380	334	275	308
Rushing	71	65	63	89	116	101	88	107	117	100	88	112	98	111	98
Passing	156	156	201	143	128	143	197	193	169	195	182	247	211	144	185
Penalty	26	35	40	7	32	20	30	19	26	15	25	21	25	20	25
Rushes	343	350	363	417	463	448	404	428	505	507	397	383	416	490	445
Net Yds. Gained	1278	1214	1186	1736	1953	1747	1643	2129	2068	2009	1882	1843	1801	2066	1748
Avg. Gain	3.7	3.5	3.3	4.2	4.2	3.9	4.1	5.0	4.1	4.0	4.7	4.8	4.3	4.2	3.9
Avg. Yds. per Game	79.9	75.9	74.1	108.5	122.1	109.2	102.7	133.1	129.3	125.6	117.6	115.2	112.6	129.1	109.3
Passes Attempted	554	514	566	542	445	503	600	495	497	529	575	587	583	433	561
Completed	316	285	340	304	255	277	348	307	298	311	331	380	366	237	343
% Completed	57.0	55.4	60.1	56.1	57.3	55.1	58.0	62.0	60.0	58.8	57.6	64.7	62.8	54.7	61.1
Total Yds. Gained	3478	3166	3850	3005	2771	2992	3916	4019	3573	3610	3386	5492	4400	2824	3892
Times Sacked	35	61	69	34	35	53	34	35	39	28	45	44	25	38	32
Yds. Lost	228	386	382	200	249	317	238	187	244	243	262	260	161	241	244
Net Yds. Gained	3250	2780	3468	2805	2522	2675	3678	3832	3329	3367	3124	5232	4239	2583	3648
Avg. Yds. per Game	203.1	173.8	216.8	175.3	157.6	167.2	229.9	239.5	208.1	210.4	195.3	327.0	264.9	161.4	228.0
Net Yds. per Pass Play	5.52	4.83	5.46	4.87	5.25	4.81	5.80	7.23	6.21	6.04	5.04	8.29	6.97	5.48	6.15
Yds. Gained per Comp.	11.01	11.11	11.32	9.88	10.87	10.80	11.25	13.09	11.99	11.61	10.23	14.45	12.02	11.92	11.35
Combined Net Yds. Gained	4528	3994	4654	4541	4475	4422	5321	5961	5397	5376	5006	7075	6040	4649	5396
% Total Yds. Rushing	28.2	30.4	25.5	38.2	43.6	39.5	30.9	35.7	38.3	37.4	37.6	26.0	29.8	44.4	32.4
% Total Yds. Passing	71.8	69.6	74.5	61.8	56.4	60.5	69.1	64.3	61.7	62.6	62.4	74.0	70.2	55.6	67.6
Avg. Yds. per Game	283.0	249.6	290.9	283.8	279.7	276.4	332.6	372.6	337.3	336.0	312.9	442.2	377.5	290.6	337.3
Ball Control Plays	932	925	998	993	943	1004	1038	958	1041	1064	1017	1014	1024	961	1038
Avg. Yds. per Play	4.9	4.3	4.7	4.6	4.7	4.4	5.1	6.2	5.2	5.1	4.9	7.0	5.9	4.8	5.2
Avg. Time of Poss.	26:32	29:35	29:54	28:30	28:40	30:10	30:45	29:28	31:27	31:39	29:01	30:54	29:38	29:38	31:27
Third Down Efficiency	37.7	28.9	39.4	30.2	35.9	32.1	39.0	45.7	42.7	40.2	40.2	47.5	41.6	33.3	39.4
Had Intercepted	24	20	19	16	21	19	16	18	15	13	15	23	10	13	21
Yds. Opp Returned	383	271	365	150	179	270	201	181	125	172	146	386	94	155	374
Ret. by Opp. for TD	2	3	2	1	3	2	1	1	1	0	0	4	2	1	1
Punts	65	85	66	96	68	95	79	62	74	80	86	44	70	85	79
Yds. Punted	2871	3447	2459	3624	2852	4044	3033	2773	3043	3210	3635	1736	2727	3551	3160
Avg. Yds. per Punt	44.2	40.6	37.3	37.8	41.9	42.6	38.4	44.7	41.1	40.1	42.3	39.5	39.0	41.8	40.0
Punt Returns	32	37	21	36	35	33	35	26	40	40	33	34	26	39	36
Yds. Returned	223	348	238	314	364	472	300	261	339	332	335	521	220	337	356
Avg. Yds. per Return	7.0	9.4	11.3	8.7	10.4	14.3	8.6	10.0	8.5	8.3	10.2	15.3	8.5	8.6	9.9
Returned for TD	0	1	1	0	2	1	0	0	0	0	1	1	0	1	0
Kickoff Returns	86	83	55	68	69	69	64	67	62	53	53	80	68	55	63
Yds. Returned	2296	1890	1160	1512	1456	1600	1570	1456	1473	1102	1237	1771	1299	1255	1301
Avg. Yds. per Return	26.7	22.8	21.1	22.2	21.1	23.2	24.5	21.7	23.8	20.8	23.3	22.1	19.1	22.8	20.7
Returned for TD	1	3	1	0	0	0	1	0	0	1	1	1	0	0	0
Fumbles	32	27	25	27	31	21	30	26	26	25	22	24	22	16	22
Lost	20	14	16	13	18	12	17	10	11	11	14	12	9	11	12
Out of Bounds	1	2	2	1	1	2	1	1	1	2	0	0	2	0	1
Own Rec. for TD	0	0	0	0	0	1	0	0	0	0	0	1	0	0	0
Opp. Rec. by	10	10	20	9	9	16	7	10	15	11	12	6	8	16	16
Opp. Rec. for TD	1	0	0	0	0	0	0	0	1	0	0	1	0	1	0
Penalties	96	97	84	90	108	106	88	106	124	91	113	111	134	82	115
Yds. Penalized	785	720	683	696	963	805	685	908	1024	839	980	942	1135	702	1009
Total Points Scored	210	252	310	216	294	307	353	397	354	328	351	540	388	388	281
Total TDs	24	25	31	22	31	33	36	47	41	39	38	67	49	43	32
TDs Rushing	6	6	7	6	15	15	13	14	14	16	13	26	15	18	14
TDs Passing	16	14	19	12	14	14	21	33	22	22	21	37	32	18	18
TDs on Ret. and Rec.	2	5	5	4	2	4	2	0	5	1	4	4	2	7	0
Extra Point Kicks	18	23	29	21	27	29	32	45	37	37	34	58	43	42	27
Extra Point Kicks Att.	19	23	29	21	27	29	32	45	37	37	36	58	45	42	29
2Pt Conversions	0	1	1	0	2	4	2	2	1	0	1	4	3	1	0
2Pt Conversions Att.	5	2	2	1	4	4	3	2	4	2	2	9	4	1	3
Safeties	0	1	0	0	1	0	1	0	0	0	0	0	0	1	1
Field Goals Made	16	25	31	21	25	24	33	22	23	19	29	24	15	28	20
Field Goals Attempted	23	31	35	27	33	30	38	23	29	25	33	27	22	34	30
% Successful	69.6	80.6	88.6	77.8	75.8	80.0	86.8	95.7	79.3	76.0	87.9	88.9	68.2	82.4	66.7

NATIONAL FOOTBALL CONFERENCE DEFENSE

	Ariz.	Atl.	Car.	Chi.	Dall.	Det.	G.B.	Minn.	N.O.	NYG	Phil.	St.L.	S.F.	T.B.	Wash.
First Downs	345	308	304	297	309	279	284	344	279	274	295	321	347	283	254
Rushing	149	113	107	106	137	96	84	110	95	62	105	95	110	84	97
Passing	175	175	184	172	145	159	186	208	159	181	159	195	194	180	134
Penalty	21	20	13	19	27	24	14	26	25	31	31	31	43	19	23
Rushes	578	453	426	469	538	421	417	396	395	359	453	383	435	398	430
Net Yds. Gained	2609	1983	1944	1827	2636	1823	1618	1788	1672	1156	1830	1697	1794	1648	1853
Avg. Gain	4.5	4.4	4.6	3.9	4.9	4.3	3.9	4.5	4.2	3.2	4.0	4.4	4.1	4.1	4.3
Avg. Yds. per Game	163.1	123.9	121.5	114.2	164.8	113.9	101.1	111.8	104.5	72.3	114.4	106.1	112.1	103.0	115.8
Passes Attempted	459	515	552	530	458	544	557	584	488	585	552	534	558	594	462
Completed	296	306	352	332	277	311	307	369	285	327	314	323	320	339	254
% Completed	64.5	59.4	63.8	62.6	60.5	57.2	55.1	63.2	58.4	55.9	56.9	60.5	57.3	57.1	55.0
Total Yds. Gained	3263	3766	3938	3637	2882	3372	3695	4127	3449	3669	3281	4085	4185	3484	2904
Times Sacked	25	31	27	36	25	28	38	31	66	44	50	51	38	55	45
Yds. Lost	135	142	226	230	189	162	244	214	378	279	291	288	270	332	283
Net Yds. Gained	3128	3624	3712	3407	2693	3210	3451	3913	3071	3390	2990	3797	3915	3152	2621
Avg. Yds. per Game	195.5	226.5	232.0	212.9	168.3	200.6	215.7	244.6	191.9	211.9	186.9	237.3	244.7	197.0	163.8
Net Yds. per Pass Play	6.46	6.64	6.41	6.02	5.58	5.61	5.80	6.36	5.54	5.39	4.97	6.49	6.57	4.86	5.17
Yds. Gained per Comp.	11.02	12.31	11.19	10.95	10.40	10.84	12.04	11.18	12.10	11.22	10.45	12.65	13.08	10.28	11.43
Combined Net Yds. Gained	5737	5607	5656	5234	5329	5033	5069	5701	4743	4546	4820	5494	5709	4800	4474
% Total Yds. Rushing	45.5	35.4	34.4	34.9	49.5	36.2	31.9	31.4	35.3	25.4	38.0	30.9	31.4	34.3	41.4
% Total Yds. Passing	54.5	64.6	65.6	65.1	50.5	63.8	68.1	68.6	64.7	74.6	62.0	69.1	68.6	65.7	58.6
Avg. Yds. per Game	358.6	350.4	353.5	327.1	333.1	314.6	316.8	356.3	296.4	284.1	301.3	343.4	356.8	300.0	279.6
Ball Control Plays	1062	999	1005	1035	1021	993	1012	1011	949	988	1055	968	1031	1047	937
Avg. Yds. per Play	5.4	5.6	5.6	5.1	5.2	5.1	5.0	5.6	5.0	4.6	4.6	5.7	5.5	4.6	4.8
Avg. Time of Poss.	33:28	30:25	30:06	31:30	31:20	29:50	29:15	30:32	28:33	28:21	30:59	29:06	30:22	30:22	28:33
Third Down Efficiency	47.3	35.9	43.3	36.8	40.4	37.2	36.6	45.5	39.2	35.6	32.6	38.5	39.2	32.9	35.1
Intercepted By	10	15	17	11	16	25	21	8	20	20	19	19	13	25	17
Yds. Returned By	151	287	199	254	167	340	315	65	264	149	255	135	278	275	219
Returned for TD	0	1	2	4	0	2	1	0	4	0	2	0	2	4	0

	Ariz.	Atl.	Car.	Chi.	Dall.	Det.	G.B.	Minn.	N.O.	NYG	Phil.	St.L.	S.F.	T.B.	Wash.
Punts	59	70	58	91	70	84	94	65	74	86	87	67	65	89	79
Yds. Punted	2422	2932	2311	3629	2838	3501	3888	2593	3024	3570	3516	2825	2773	3556	3386
Avg. Yds. per Punt	41.1	41.9	39.8	39.9	40.5	41.7	41.4	39.9	40.9	41.5	40.4	42.2	42.7	40.0	42.9
Punt Returns	37	29	25	36	29	53	27	32	37	28	47	17	32	41	33
Yds. Returned	347	126	187	251	282	498	205	310	494	353	375	132	332	408	342
Avg. Yds. per Return	9.4	4.3	7.5	7.0	9.7	9.4	7.6	9.7	13.4	12.6	8.0	7.8	10.4	10.0	10.4
Returned for TD	2	0	0	0	0	0	1	0	2	0	1	0	0	1	2
Kickoff Returns	46	50	64	51	56	59	76	69	71	67	72	87	63	74	60
Yds. Returned	827	1230	1120	1105	1205	1327	1639	1519	1743	1509	1519	2032	1358	1688	1529
Avg. Yds. per Return	18.0	24.6	17.5	21.7	21.5	22.5	21.6	22.0	24.5	22.5	21.1	23.4	21.6	22.8	25.5
Returned for TD	0	3	0	0	0	0	0	1	2	0	0	1	0	0	1
Fumbles	17	18	37	20	23	36	16	17	24	17	27	19	19	26	28
Lost	10	10	21	9	9	17	7	10	15	11	12	6	8	16	16
Out of Bounds	2	2	2	1	2	3	0	1	1	1	3	2	2	0	0
Own Rec. for TD	0	0	0	1	0	0	0	0	0	0	0	0	0	0	0
Opp. Rec. by	20	14	16	13	18	12	17	10	11	11	14	12	8	11	11
Opp. Rec. for TD	0	1	2	1	1	0	0	0	0	0	1	0	0	0	1
Penalties	96	122	128	78	108	112	101	104	105	80	111	101	102	95	106
Yds. Penalized	914	1010	1073	727	999	913	992	747	837	728	936	747	857	688	790
Total Points Scored	443	413	310	355	361	307	323	371	305	246	245	471	422	269	269
Total TDs	52	46	35	43	41	32	37	43	36	30	23	56	49	29	26
TDs Rushing	29	16	12	15	17	14	7	17	14	7	10	18	22	12	9
TDs Passing	19	23	19	25	20	16	28	23	17	23	11	32	25	15	12
TDs on Ret. and Rec.	4	7	4	3	4	2	2	3	5	0	2	6	2	2	5
Extra Point Kicks	50	38	30	41	37	31	36	38	31	25	21	49	46	25	23
Extra Point Kicks Att.	51	38	31	41	37	31	36	38	31	27	21	50	46	25	23
2Pt Conversions	0	6	2	1	0	1	1	0	2	1	1	3	2	2	0
2Pt Conversions Att.	1	8	4	2	3	1	1	4	5	3	2	6	2	4	3
Safeties	0	0	3	0	0	2	0	0	0	0	0	1	0	0	0
Field Goals Made	27	29	20	18	26	26	21	25	18	13	28	26	26	22	30
Field Goals Attempted	34	31	30	26	31	31	25	29	24	24	33	31	31	32	34
% Successful	79.4	93.5	66.7	69.2	83.9	83.9	84.0	86.2	75.0	54.2	84.8	83.9	83.9	68.8	88.2

2000 TEAM STATISTICS

AFC, NFC, AND NFL SUMMARY

	AFC Offense Total	AFC Offense Average	AFC Defense Total	AFC Defense Average	NFC Offense Total	NFC Offense Average	NFC Defense Total	NFC Defense Average	NFL Total	NFL Average
First Downs	4699	293.7	4616	288.5	4440	296.0	4523	301.5	9139	294.8
Rushing	1615	100.9	1489	93.1	1424	94.9	1550	103.3	3039	98.0
Passing	2667	166.7	2711	169.4	2650	176.7	2606	173.7	5317	171.5
Penalty	417	26.1	416	26.0	366	24.4	367	24.5	783	25.3
Rushes	7318	457.4	7126	445.4	6359	423.9	6551	436.7	13677	441.2
Net Yds. Gained	29526	1845.4	27951	1746.9	26303	1753.5	27878	1858.5	55829	1800.9
Avg. Gain	—	4.0	—	3.9	—	4.1	—	4.3	—	4.1
Avg. Yds. per Game	—	115.3	—	109.2	—	109.6	—	116.2	—	112.6
Passes Attempted	8338	521.1	8350	521.9	7984	532.3	7972	531.5	16322	526.5
Completed	4799	299.9	4785	299.1	4698	313.2	4712	314.1	9497	306.4
% Completed	—	57.6	—	57.3	—	58.8	—	59.1	—	58.2
Total Yds. Gained	55757	3484.8	56394	3524.6	54374	3624.9	53737	3582.5	110131	3552.6
Times Sacked	625	39.1	642	40.1	607	40.5	590	39.3	1232	39.7
Yds. Lost	3683	230.2	3862	241.4	3842	256.1	3663	244.2	7525	242.7
Net Yds. Gained	52074	3254.6	52532	3283.3	50532	3368.8	50074	3338.3	102606	3309.9
Avg. Yds. per Game	—	203.4	—	205.2	—	210.6	—	208.6	—	206.9
Net Yds. per Pass Play	—	5.81	—	5.84	—	5.88	—	5.85	—	5.85
Yds. Gained per Comp.	—	11.62	—	11.79	—	11.57	—	11.40	—	11.60
Combined Net Yds. Gained	81600	5100.0	80483	5030.2	76835	5122.3	77952	5196.8	158435	5110.8
% Total Yds. Rushing	—	36.2	—	34.7	—	34.2	—	35.8	—	35.2
% Total Yds. Passing	—	63.8	—	65.3	—	65.8	—	64.2	—	64.8
Avg. Yds. per Game	—	318.8	—	314.4	—	320.1	—	324.8	—	319.4
Ball Control Plays	16281	1017.6	16118	1007.4	14950	996.7	15113	1007.5	31231	1007.5
Avg. Yds. per Play	—	5.0	—	5.0	—	5.1	—	5.2	—	5.1
Third Down Efficiency	—	38.4	—	38.2	—	38.2	—	38.4	—	38.3
Interceptions	268	16.8	275	17.2	263	17.5	256	17.1	531	17.1
Yds. Returned	3571	223.2	3670	229.4	3452	230.1	3353	223.5	7023	226.5
Returned for TD	27	1.7	29	1.8	24	1.6	22	1.5	51	1.6
Punts	1337	83.6	1333	83.3	1134	75.6	1138	75.9	2471	79.7
Yds. Punted	56759	3547.4	56160	3510.0	46165	3077.7	46764	3117.6	102924	3320.1
Avg. Yds. per Punt	—	42.5	—	42.1	—	40.7	—	41.1	—	41.7
Punt Returns	639	39.9	639	39.9	503	33.5	503	33.5	1142	36.8
Yds. Returned	6437	402.3	6755	422.2	4960	330.7	4642	309.5	11397	367.6
Avg. Yds. per Return	—	10.1	—	10.6	—	9.9	—	9.2	—	10.0
Returned for TD	7	0.4	6	0.4	8	0.5	9	0.6	15	0.5
Kickoff Returns	1045	65.3	1075	67.2	995	66.3	965	64.3	2040	65.8
Yds. Returned	22349	1396.8	23377	1461.1	22378	1491.9	21350	1423.3	44727	1442.8
Avg. Yds. per Return	—	21.4	—	21.7	—	22.5	—	22.1	—	21.9
Returned for TD	6	0.4	7	0.4	9	0.6	8	0.5	15	0.5
Fumbles	400	25.0	432	27.0	376	25.1	344	22.9	776	25.0
Lost	203	12.7	226	14.1	200	13.3	177	11.8	403	13.0
Out of Bounds	19	1.2	14	0.9	17	1.1	22	1.5	36	1.2
Own Rec. for TD	2	0.1	3	0.2	2	0.1	1	0.1	4	0.1
Opp. Rec.	223	13.9	200	12.5	175	11.7	198	13.2	398	12.8
Opp. Rec. for TD	11	0.7	8	0.5	4	0.3	7	0.5	15	0.5
Penalties	1595	99.7	1591	99.4	1545	103.0	1549	103.3	3140	101.3
Yds. Penalized	13257	828.6	13175	823.4	12876	858.4	12958	863.9	26133	843.0
Total Points Scored	5285	330.3	5144	321.5	4969	331.3	5110	340.7	10254	330.8
Total TDs	593	37.1	573	35.8	558	37.2	578	38.5	1151	37.1
TDs Rushing	214	13.4	193	12.1	198	13.2	219	14.6	412	13.3
TDs Passing	321	20.1	326	20.4	313	20.9	308	20.5	634	20.5
TDs on Ret. and Rec.	58	3.6	54	3.4	47	3.1	51	3.4	105	3.4
Extra Point Kicks	551	34.4	532	33.3	502	33.5	521	34.7	1053	34.0
Extra Point Kicks Att.	554	34.6	537	33.6	509	33.9	526	35.1	1063	34.3
2Pt Conversions	13	0.8	13	0.8	22	1.5	22	1.5	35	1.1
2Pt Conversions Att.	37	2.3	36	2.3	48	3.2	49	3.3	85	2.7
Safeties	11	0.7	10	0.6	5	0.3	6	0.4	16	0.5
Field Goals Made	376	23.5	376	23.5	355	23.7	355	23.7	731	23.6
Field Goals Attempted	477	29.8	471	29.4	440	29.3	446	29.7	917	29.6
% Successful	—	78.8	—	79.8	—	80.7	—	79.6	—	79.7

CLUB LEADERS

	Offense	Defense
First Downs	Den. 383	Tenn. 215
Rushing	Oak. 128	Balt. 59
Passing	St.L. 247	Tenn. & Wash. 134
Penalty	Car. 40	Car. 13
Rushes	Tenn. 547	Den. 344
Net Yds. Gained	Oak. 2470	Balt. 970
Avg. Gain	Minn. 5.0	Balt. 2.7
Passes Attempted	N.Y.J. 637	Dall. & Jax 458
Completed	St.L. 380	Tenn. 242
% Completed	St.L. 64.7	N.Y.J. 51.3
Total Yds. Gained	St.L. 5492	Tenn. 2761
Times Sacked	Ind. & N.Y.J. 20	N.O. 66
Yds. Lost	N.Y.J. 99	N.O. 378
Net Yds. Gained	St.L. 5232	Tenn. 2423
Net Yds. per Pass Play	St.L. 8.3	Tenn. 4.7
Yds. Gained per Comp.	St.L. 14.5	T.B. 10.3
Combined Net Yds. Gained	St.L. 7075	Tenn. 3813
% Total Yds. Rushing	Cin. 54.3	Balt. 24.5
% Total Yds. Passing	S.D. 75.3	Dall. 50.5
Ball Control Plays	Den. 1115	Tenn. 908
Avg. Yds. per Play	St.L. 7.0	Tenn. 4.2
Avg. Time of Poss.	Tenn. 33.48	—
Third Down Efficiency	St.L. 47.5	Tenn. 30.8
Interceptions	—	Mia. 28
Yds. Returned	—	Balt. 477
Returned for TD	—	Den. 5
Punts	Cle. 108	—
Yds. Punted	Cle. 4919	—
Avg. Yds. per Punt	S.D. 46.2	—
Punt Returns	Tenn. 53	St.L. 17
Yds. Returned	Balt. 713	Atl. 126
Avg. Yds. per Return	Balt. 15.8	Atl. 4.3
Returned for TD	Balt. & Dal. 2	—
Kickoff Returns	Ariz. 86	Cin. & Cle. 42
Yds. Returned	Ariz. 2296	Ariz. 827
Avg. Yds. per Return	Ariz. 26.7	Car. 17.5
Returned for TD	Atl. 3	—
Total Points Scored	St.L. 540	Balt. 165
Total TDs	St.L. 67	Balt. 18
TDs Rushing	St.L. 26	Balt. 5
TDs Passing	St.L. 37	Tenn. 10
TDs on Ret. and Rec.	Den. 9	N.Y.G. 0
Extra Point Kicks	St.L. 58	Balt. 15
2-Point Conversions	Det. & St.L. 4	—
Safeties	Ind. & Oak. 2	—
Field Goals Made	Balt. 35	N.Y.G. 13
Field Goals Attempted	Balt. 39	Balt. 19
% Successful	Minn. 95.7	N.Y.G. 54.2

NFL CLUB RANKINGS BY YARDS

	Offense			Defense		
	Total	Rush	Pass	Total	Rush	Pass
Arizona	24	27	17	30	30	11
Atlanta	30	28	24	25	27	24
Baltimore	16	5	22	2	*1	8
Buffalo	9	13	11	3	6	4
Carolina	20	29	12	27	26	26
Chicago	23	21	23	16	19	17
Cincinnati	29	2	31	22	24	23
Cleveland	31	30	30	26	29	12
Dallas	25	12	28	19	31	3
Denver	2	3	3	24	7	31
Detroit	27	20	25	14	18	15
Green Bay	15	23	8	15	8	19
Indianapolis	3	16	2	21	25	18
Jacksonville	7	10	9	12	11	14
Kansas City	8	25	5	18	17	20
Miami	26	14	27	6	14	5
Minnesota	5	6	7	28	15	28
New England	22	26	19	20	21	21
New Orleans	10	8	14	8	10	10
N.Y. Giants	13	11	13	5	2	16
N.Y. Jets	12	24	6	10T	23	6
Oakland	6	*1	15	17	5	25
Philadelphia	17	15	20	10T	20	7
Pittsburgh	18	4	29	7	12	9
St. Louis	*1	17	*1	23	13	27
San Diego	28	31	18	13	4	22
San Francisco	4	18	4	29	16	29
Seattle	19	22	21	31	28	30
Tampa Bay	21	9	26	9	9	13
Tennessee	14	7	16	*1	3	*1
Washington	11	19	10	4	22	2

T = Tied for position
* = League Leader

AFC TAKEAWAYS/GIVEAWAYS

	Takeaways			Giveaways			Net
	Int	Fum	Total	Int	Fum	Total	Diff.
Baltimore	23	26	49	19	7	26	+23
Denver	27	17	44	12	13	25	+19
Oakland	21	16	37	11	9	20	+17
Miami	28	13	41	17	9	26	+15
Pittsburgh	17	18	35	10	11	21	+14
Buffalo	16	13	29	10	13	23	+6
Kansas City	15	14	29	15	11	26	+3
Jacksonville	12	18	30	15	14	29	+1
Tennessee	17	13	30	16	14	30	0
New England	10	13	23	15	10	25	-2
Cleveland	12	13	25	19	9	28	-3
N.Y. Jets	21	14	35	29	11	40	-5
Indianapolis	14	8	22	15	14	29	-7
Seattle	17	12	29	21	17	38	-9
Cincinnati	9	12	21	14	21	35	-14
San Diego	16	6	22	30	20	50	-28
AFC Totals	275	226	501	268	203	471	+30

NFC TAKEAWAYS/GIVEAWAYS

	Takeaways			Giveaways			Net
	Int	Fum	Total	Int	Fum	Total	Diff.
Tampa Bay	25	16	41	13	11	24	+17
Detroit	25	17	42	19	12	31	+11
New Orleans	20	15	35	15	11	26	+9
N.Y. Giants	20	11	31	13	11	24	+7
Carolina	17	21	38	19	16	35	+3
Philadelphia	19	12	31	15	14	29	+2
San Francisco	13	8	21	10	9	19	+2
Washington	17	16	33	21	12	33	0
Green Bay	21	7	28	16	17	33	-5
Atlanta	15	10	25	20	14	34	-9
Chicago	11	9	20	16	13	29	-9
Minnesota	8	10	18	18	10	28	-10
St. Louis	19	6	25	23	12	35	-10
Dallas	16	9	25	21	18	39	-14
Arizona	10	10	20	24	20	44	-24
NFC Totals	256	177	433	263	200	463	-30

2000 INDIVIDUAL STATISTICS—SCORING

SCORING

Points
NFC: 160—Marshall Faulk, St. Louis
AFC: 135—Matt Stover, Baltimore

Touchdowns
NFC: 26—Marshall Faulk, St. Louis
AFC: 18—Edgerrin James, Indianapolis

Extra Points
AFC: 49—Jason Elam, Denver
NFC: 45—Gary Anderson, Minnesota

Field Goals
AFC: 35—Matt Stover, Baltimore
NFC: 33—Ryan Longwell, Green Bay

Field Goal Attempts
AFC: 39—Matt Stover, Baltimore
NFC: 38—Ryan Longwell, Green Bay

Longest Field Goal
NFC: 55—Martin Gramatica, Tampa Bay vs. Detroit, October 19
AFC: 54—John Carney, San Diego at Kansas City, September 17
54—Sebastian Janikowski, Oakland at San Diego, October 29

Most Points, Game
AFC: 24—Fred Taylor, Jacksonville at Pittsburgh, November 19 (4 TD)
24—Mike Anderson, Denver at New Orleans, December 3 (4 TD)
NFC: 24—Marshall Faulk, St. Louis at San Francisco, October 29 (4 TD)
24—Marshall Faulk, St. Louis vs. Minnesota, December 10 (4 TD)
24—Marshall Faulk, St. Louis at Tampa Bay, December 18 (4 TD)

Team Leaders, Points
AFC: BALTIMORE, 135, Matt Stover; BUFFALO, 109, Steve Christie; CINCINNATI, 57, Neil Rackers; CLEVELAND, 59, Phil Dawson; DENVER, 103, Jason Elam; INDIANAPOLIS, 121, Mike Vanderjagt; JACKSONVILLE, 105, Mike Hollis; KANSAS CITY, 70, Todd Peterson; MIAMI, 117, Olindo Mare; NEW ENGLAND, 106, Adam Vinatieri; N.Y. JETS, 93, John Hall; OAKLAND, 112, Sebastian Janikowski; PITTSBURGH, 107, Kris Brown; SAN DIEGO, 81, John Carney; SEATTLE, 70, Rian Lindell; TENNESSEE, 118, Al Del Greco

NFC: ARIZONA, 66, Cary Blanchard; ATLANTA, 98, Morten Andersen; CAROLINA, 98, Joe Nedney; CHICAGO, 84, Paul Edinger; DALLAS, 108, Tim Seder; DETROIT, 101, Jason Hanson; GREEN BAY, 131, Ryan Longwell; MINNESOTA, 111, Gary Anderson; NEW ORLEANS, 106, Doug Brien; N.Y. GIANTS, 85, Brad Daluiso; PHILADELPHIA, 121, David Akers; ST. LOUIS, 160, Marshall Faulk; SAN FRANCISCO, 88, Wade Richey; TAMPA BAY, 126, Martin Gramatica; WASHINGTON, 66, Stephen Davis

Team Champion
NFC: 540—St. Louis
AFC: 485—Denver

AFC SCORING—TEAM

	TD	TDR	TDP	TDM	Extra Pt. Made	Kicks Att.	2-Point Made	Tries Att.	FG	FGA	SAF	PTS
Denver	58	21	28	9	53	53	2	5	26	34	1	485
Oakland	58	23	28	7	56	56	1	1	23	34	2	479
Indianapolis	50	14	33	3	46	46	2	4	25	27	2	429
Jacksonville	40	18	22	0	38	38	1	1	29	33	0	367
Kansas City	44	12	29	3	40	40	0	4	17	24	0	355
Tennessee	38	14	18	6	37	38	0	0	27	34	0	346
Baltimore	32	9	20	3	30	30	2	2	35	39	1	333
Miami	34	16	15	3	33	34	0	0	28	31	1	323
N.Y. Jets	36	11	23	2	32	32	2	4	23	34	0	321
Pittsburgh	35	19	12	4	32	33	1	2	25	30	1	321
Seattle	37	10	21	6	33	33	0	4	21	26	1	320
Buffalo	34	11	20	3	31	31	1	3	26	35	0	315
New England	28	9	18	1	25	25	1	3	27	33	0	276
San Diego	31	7	19	5	27	27	0	4	18	25	1	269
Cincinnati	21	13	6	2	21	21	0	0	12	21	1	185
Cleveland	17	7	9	1	17	17	0	0	14	17	0	161
AFC Total	593	214	321	58	551	554	13	37	376	477	11	5285
AFC Average	37.1	13.4	20.1	3.6	34.4	34.6	0.8	2.3	23.5	29.8	0.7	330.3

NFC SCORING—TEAM

	TD	TDR	TDP	TDM	Extra Pt. Made	Kicks Att.	2-Point Made	Tries Att.	FG	FGA	SAF	PTS
St. Louis	67	26	37	4	58	58	4	9	24	27	0	540
Minnesota	47	14	33	0	45	45	2	2	22	23	0	397
San Francisco	49	15	32	2	43	45	3	4	15	22	0	388
Tampa Bay	43	18	18	7	42	42	1	1	28	34	1	388
New Orleans	41	14	22	5	37	37	1	4	23	29	0	354
Green Bay	36	13	21	2	32	32	2	3	33	38	1	353
Philadelphia	38	13	21	4	34	36	1	2	29	33	0	351
N.Y. Giants	39	16	22	1	37	37	0	2	19	25	0	328
Carolina	31	7	19	5	29	29	1	2	31	35	0	310
Detroit	33	15	14	4	29	29	4	4	24	30	0	307
Dallas	31	15	14	2	27	27	2	4	25	33	1	294
Washington	32	14	18	0	27	29	0	3	20	30	1	281
Atlanta	25	6	14	5	23	23	1	2	25	31	1	252
Chicago	22	6	12	4	21	21	0	1	21	27	0	216
Arizona	24	6	16	2	18	19	0	5	16	23	0	210
NFC Total	558	198	313	47	502	509	22	48	355	440	5	4969
NFC Average	37.2	13.2	20.9	3.1	33.5	33.9	1.5	3.2	23.7	29.3	0.3	331.3
NFL Total	1151	412	634	105	1053	1063	35	85	731	917	16	10254
NFL Average	37.1	13.3	20.5	3.4	34.0	34.3	1.1	2.7	23.6	29.6	0.5	330.8

NFL TOP TEN SCORERS—NONKICKERS

	TD	TDR	TDP	TDM	2-PT	PTS
Faulk, Marshall, St.L.	26	18	8	0	2	160
James, Edgerrin, Ind.	18	13	5	0	1	110
George, Eddie, Tenn.	16	14	2	0	0	96
Smith, Lamar, Mia.	16	14	2	0	0	96
Anderson, Mike, Den.	15	15	0	0	1	92
Moss, Randy, Minn.	15	0	15	0	1	92
Harrison, Marvin, Ind.	14	0	14	0	0	84
Taylor, Fred, Jax.	14	12	2	0	0	84
Owens, Terrell, S.F.	13	0	13	0	1	80
Green, Ahman, G.B.	13	10	3	0	0	78

NFL TOP TEN SCORERS—KICKERS

	XP	XPA	FG	FGA	PTS
Stover, Matt, Balt.	30	30	35	39	135
Longwell, Ryan, G.B.	32	32	33	38	131
Gramatica, Martin, T.B.	42	42	28	34	126
Nedney, Joe, Den.-Car.	24	24	34	38	126
Akers, David, Phil.	34	36	29	33	121
Vanderjagt, Mike, Ind.	46	46	25	27	121
Del Greco, Al, Tenn.	37	38	27	33	118
Mare, Olindo, Mia.	33	34	28	31	117
Janikowski, Sebastian, Oak.	46	46	22	32	112
Anderson, Gary, Minn.	45	45	22	23	111

AFC SCORERS—INDIVIDUAL

Kickers

	XP	XPA	FG	FGA	PTS
Stover, Matt, Balt.	30	30	35	39	135
Vanderjagt, Mike, Ind.	46	46	25	27	121
Del Greco, Al, Tenn.	37	38	27	33	118
Mare, Olindo, Mia.	33	34	28	31	117
Janikowski, Sebastian, Oak.	46	46	22	32	112
Christie, Steve, Buff.	31	31	26	35	109
Brown, Kris, Pitt.	32	33	25	30	107
Vinatieri, Adam, N.E.	25	25	27	33	106
Hollis, Mike, Jax.	33	33	24	26	105
Elam, Jason, Den.	49	49	18	24	103
Hall, John, NYJ	30	30	21	32	93
Carney, John, S.D.	27	27	18	25	81
Lindell, Rian, Sea.	25	25	15	17	70
Peterson, Todd, K.C.	25	25	15	20	70
Dawson, Phil, Cle.	17	17	14	17	59
Rackers, Neil, Cin.	21	21	12	21	57
Conway, Brett, Wash.-Oak.-NYJ	8	8	6	6	26
Lindsey, Steve, Jax.	5	5	5	7	20
Lechler, Shane, Oak.	7	7	0	1	7
Hentrich, Craig, Tenn.	0	0	0	1	0

Nonkickers

	TD	TDR	TDP	TDM	2-PT	PTS
James, Edgerrin, Ind.	18	13	5	0	1	110
George, Eddie, Tenn.	16	14	2	0	0	96
Smith, Lamar, Mia.	16	14	2	0	0	96
Anderson, Mike, Den.	15	15	0	0	1	92
Harrison, Marvin, Ind.	14	0	14	0	0	84
Taylor, Fred, Jax.	14	12	2	0	0	84
Brown, Tim, Oak.	11	0	11	0	0	66
Martin, Curtis, NYJ	11	9	2	0	0	66
Alexander, Derrick, K.C.	10	0	10	0	0	60
Wheatley, Tyrone, Oak.	10	9	1	0	0	60
McCaffrey, Ed, Den.	9	0	9	0	1	56
Gonzalez, Tony, K.C.	9	0	9	0	0	54
Smith, Rod, Den.	9	1	8	0	0	54
Watters, Ricky, Sea.	9	7	2	0	0	54
Bettis, Jerome, Pitt.	8	8	0	0	0	48
Chrebet, Wayne, NYJ	8	0	8	0	0	48
Prentice, Travis, Cle.	8	7	1	0	0	48
Smith, Jimmy, Jax.	8	0	8	0	0	48
Crockett, Zack, Oak.	7	7	0	0	0	42
Dillon, Corey, Cin.	7	7	0	0	0	42
Stewart, Kordell, Pitt.	7	7	0	0	0	42
Warrick, Peter, Cin.	7	2	4	1	0	42
Lewis, Jamal, Balt.	6	6	0	0	1	38
Gadsden, Oronde, Mia.	6	0	6	0	0	36
Glenn, Terry, N.E.	6	0	6	0	0	36
Jackson, Darrell, Sea.	6	0	6	0	0	36
Mason, Derrick, Tenn.	6	0	5	1	0	36
Morris, Sammy, Buff.	6	5	1	0	0	36
Richardson, Tony, K.C.	6	3	3	0	0	36
Rison, Andre, Oak.	6	0	6	0	0	36
Faulk, Kevin, N.E.	5	4	1	0	1	32
Brown, Troy, N.E.	5	0	4	1	0	30
Conway, Curtis, S.D.	5	0	5	0	0	30
Dawkins, Sean, Sea.	5	0	5	0	0	30
Ismail, Qadry, Balt.	5	0	5	0	0	30
Jones, Freddie, S.D.	5	0	5	0	0	30
Jordan, Randy, Oak.	5	3	1	1	0	30
McCardell, Keenan, Jax.	5	0	5	0	0	30
Moulds, Eric, Buff.	5	0	5	0	0	30
Riemersma, Jay, Buff.	5	0	5	0	0	30
Sharpe, Shannon, Balt.	5	0	5	0	0	30
Gannon, Rich, Oak.	4	4	0	0	1	26
Dudley, Rickey, Oak.	4	0	4	0	0	24
Fletcher, Terrell, S.D.	4	3	1	0	0	24
Graham, Jeff, S.D.	4	0	4	0	0	24
Moreau, Frank, K.C.	4	4	0	0	0	24
Shaw, Bobby, Pitt.	4	0	4	0	0	24
Shepherd, Leslie, Mia.	4	0	4	0	0	24
Smith, Antowain, Buff.	4	4	0	0	0	24
Ward, Hines, Pitt.	4	0	4	0	0	24
Wycheck, Frank, Tenn.	4	0	4	0	0	24
Brady, Kyle, Jax.	3	0	3	0	1	20
Huntley, Richard, Pitt.	3	3	0	0	1	20
Pollard, Marcus, Ind.	3	0	3	0	1	20
Allen, Eric, Oak.	3	0	0	3	0	18
Bennett, Brandon, Cin.	3	3	0	0	0	18
Bruener, Mark, Pitt.	3	0	3	0	0	18
Carswell, Dwayne, Den.	3	0	3	0	0	18
Clark, Desmond, Den.	3	0	3	0	0	18
Dilger, Ken, Ind.	3	0	3	0	0	18
Lewis, Jermaine, Balt.	3	0	1	2	0	18
Mili, Itula, Sea.	3	0	3	0	0	18
Morris, Sylvester, K.C.	3	0	3	0	0	18
Pathon, Jerome, Ind.	3	0	3	0	0	18
Price, Peerless, Buff.	3	0	3	0	0	18
Redmond, J.R., N.E.	3	1	2	0	0	18
Taylor, Travis, Balt.	3	0	3	0	0	18
Ward, Dedric, NYJ	3	0	3	0	0	18
Whitted, Alvis, Jax.	3	0	3	0	0	18
Wilkins, Terrence, Ind.	3	0	3	0	0	18
Bryson, Shawn, Buff.	2	0	2	0	1	14
Alexander, Shaun, Sea.	2	2	0	0	0	12
Anders, Kimble, K.C.	2	2	0	0	0	12
Anderson, Richie, NYJ	2	0	2	0	0	12
Ayanbadejo, Obafemi, Balt.	2	1	1	0	0	12
Baxter, Fred, NYJ	2	0	2	0	0	12
Becht, Anthony, NYJ	2	0	2	0	0	12
Bjornson, Eric, N.E.	2	0	2	0	0	12
Bledsoe, Drew, N.E.	2	2	0	0	0	12
Brigham, Jeremy, Oak.	2	0	2	0	0	12
Brunell, Mark, Jax.	2	2	0	0	0	12
Carter, Tony, N.E.	2	2	0	0	0	12
Chancey, Robert, S.D.	2	2	0	0	0	12
Cloud, Mike, K.C.	2	1	0	1	0	12
Davis, Terrell, Den.	2	2	0	0	0	12
Drayton, Troy, K.C.	2	0	2	0	0	12
Edwards, Marc, Cle.	2	0	2	0	0	12
Fauria, Christian, Sea.	2	0	2	0	0	12
Fazande, Jermaine, S.D.	2	2	0	0	0	12
Griffith, Howard, Den.	2	0	2	0	0	12
Holmes, Priest, Balt.	2	2	0	0	0	12
Jett, James, Oak.	2	0	2	0	0	12
Johnson, Patrick, Balt.	2	0	2	0	0	12
Lockett, Kevin, K.C.	2	0	2	0	0	12
McCrary, Fred, S.D.	2	0	2	0	0	12
McDaniel, Jeremy, Buff.	2	0	2	0	0	12
Neal, Lorenzo, Tenn.	2	0	2	0	0	12
Parmalee, Bernie, NYJ	2	2	0	0	0	12
Shea, Aaron, Cle.	2	0	2	0	0	12
Spencer, Jimmy, Den.	2	0	0	2	0	12
Stokley, Brandon, Balt.	2	0	2	0	0	12
Thigpen, Yancey, Tenn.	2	0	2	0	0	12
Wiggins, Jermaine, NYJ-N.E.	2	0	2	0	0	12
Coleman, Marcus, NYJ	1	0	1	0	1	8
Coles, Laveranues, NYJ	1	0	1	0	1	8
Porter, Joey, Pitt.	1	0	0	1	0	*8
Bailey, Karsten, Sea.	1	0	1	0	0	6
Bellamy, Jay, Sea.	1	0	0	1	0	6
Bennett, Donnell, K.C.	1	1	0	0	0	6
Blackwell, Will, Pitt.	1	0	0	1	0	6
Brown, Chad, Sea.	1	0	0	1	0	6
Buckley, Terrell, Den.	1	0	0	1	0	6
Bulluck, Keith, Tenn.	1	0	0	1	0	6

2000 INDIVIDUAL STATISTICS—SCORING

	TD	TDR	TDP	TDM	2-PT	PTS
Burris, Jeff, Ind.	1	0	0	1	0	6
Campbell, Mark, Cle.	1	0	1	0	0	6
Chamberlain, Byron, Den.	1	0	1	0	0	6
Chiaverini, Darrin, Cle.	1	0	1	0	0	6
Coleman, KaRon, Den.	1	1	0	0	0	6
Crockett, Ray, Den.	1	0	0	1	0	6
Dawson, JaJuan, Cle.	1	0	1	0	0	6
Dixon, Gerald, S.D.	1	0	0	1	0	6
Dugans, Ron, Cin.	1	0	1	0	0	6
Dumas, Mike, S.D.	1	0	0	1	0	6
Dunn, David, Oak.	1	0	0	1	0	6
Dyson, Kevin, Tenn.	1	0	1	0	0	6
Edwards, Donnie, K.C.	1	0	0	1	0	6
Elliott, Jumbo, NYJ	1	0	1	0	0	6
Ellsworth, Percy, Cle.	1	0	0	1	0	6
Emanuel, Bert, Mia.	1	0	1	0	0	6
Fiedler, Jay, Mia.	1	1	0	0	0	6
Finn, Jim, Ind.	1	0	1	0	0	6
Flutie, Doug, Buff.	1	1	0	0	0	6
Ford, Henry, Tenn.	1	0	0	1	0	6
Frerotte, Gus, Den.	1	1	0	0	0	6
Fuamatu-Ma'afala, Chris, Pitt.	1	1	0	0	0	6
Gash, Sam, Balt.	1	0	1	0	0	6
Gaylor, Trevor, S.D.	1	0	1	0	0	6
Gildon, Jason, Pitt.	1	0	0	1	0	6
Godfrey, Randall, Tenn.	1	0	0	1	0	6
Gold, Ian, Den.	1	0	0	1	0	6
Goodwin, Hunter, Mia.	1	0	1	0	0	6
Gordon, Darrien, Oak.	1	0	0	1	0	6
Grbac, Elvis, K.C.	1	1	0	0	0	6
Green, E.G., Ind.	1	0	1	0	0	6
Green, Victor, NYJ	1	0	0	1	0	6
Griese, Brian, Den.	1	1	0	0	0	6
Harrison, Rodney, S.D.	1	0	0	1	0	6
Hawkins, Courtney, Pitt.	1	0	1	0	0	6
Heiden, Steve, S.D.	1	0	1	0	0	6
Holsey, Bernard, Ind.	1	0	0	1	0	6
Howard, Chris, Jax.	1	1	0	0	0	6
Jackson, Sheldon, Buff.	1	0	1	0	0	6
Jenkins, Billy, Den.	1	0	0	1	0	6
Jenkins, Ronney, S.D.	1	0	0	1	0	6
Johnson, Anthony, Jax.	1	1	0	0	0	6
Johnson, J.J., Mia.	1	1	0	0	0	6
Johnson, Rob, Buff.	1	1	0	0	0	6
Jones, Henry, Buff.	1	0	0	1	0	6
Kaufman, Napoleon, Oak.	1	0	1	0	0	6
Kinney, Erron, Tenn.	1	0	1	0	0	6
Kitna, Jon, Sea.	1	1	0	0	0	6
Koonce, George, Sea.	1	0	0	1	0	6
Linton, Jonathan, Buff.	1	0	1	0	0	6
Mack, Stacey, Jax.	1	1	0	0	0	6
Madison, Sam, Mia.	1	0	0	1	0	6
Manning, Peyton, Ind.	1	1	0	0	0	6
Mayes, Derrick, Sea.	1	0	1	0	0	6
McAlister, Chris, Balt.	1	0	0	1	0	6
McGee, Tony, Cin.	1	0	1	0	0	6
McGriff, Travis, Den.	1	0	1	0	0	6
Mitchell, Scott, Cin.	1	1	0	0	0	6
Muhammad, Mustafah, Ind.	1	0	0	1	0	6
Ogden, Jeff, Mia.	1	0	0	1	0	6
O'Neal, Deltha, Den.	1	0	0	1	0	6
Ostroski, Jerry, Buff.	1	0	0	1	0	6
Patten, David, Cle.	1	0	1	0	0	6
Patton, Marvcus, K.C.	1	0	0	1	0	6
Phenix, Perry, Tenn.	1	0	0	1	0	6
Porter, Daryl, Buff.	1	0	0	1	0	6
Poteat, Hank, Pitt.	1	0	0	1	0	6
Pryce, Trevor, Den.	1	0	0	1	0	6
Rogers, Charlie, Sea.	1	0	0	1	0	6
Rolle, Samari, Tenn.	1	0	0	1	0	6
Rutledge, Rod, N.E.	1	0	1	0	0	6
Simmons, Tony, N.E.	1	0	1	0	0	6
Sinclair, Michael, Sea.	1	0	0	1	0	6
Smith, Detron, Den.	1	0	1	0	0	6
Soward, R.Jay, Jax.	1	0	1	0	0	6
Stith, Shyrone, Jax.	1	1	0	0	0	6
Strong, Mack, Sea.	1	0	1	0	0	6
Suttle, Jason, Den.	1	0	0	1	0	6
Taylor, Jason, Mia.	1	0	0	1	0	6
Thomas, Rodney, Tenn.	1	0	1	0	0	6
Thomas, Thurman, Mia.	1	0	1	0	0	6
Thomas, William, Oak.	1	0	0	1	0	6
Turner, Scott, S.D.	1	0	0	1	0	6
Williams, Darryl, Cin.	1	0	0	1	0	6
Williams, Kevin L., NYJ	1	0	0	1	0	6
Williams, Willie, Sea.	1	0	0	1	0	6
Bratzke, Chad, Ind.	0	0	0	0	0	*2
Coates, Ben, Balt.	0	0	0	0	1	2
Fontenot, Albert, S.D.	0	0	0	0	0	*2
Haley, Jermaine, Mia.	0	0	0	0	0	*2
McCrary, Michael, Balt.	0	0	0	0	0	*2
Russell, Darrell, Oak.	0	0	0	0	0	*2
Williams, James, Sea.	0	0	0	0	0	*2
Williams, Josh, Ind.	0	0	0	0	0	*2

** Safety*
Team safety credited to Cincinnati, Denver, and Oakland

NFC SCORERS—INDIVIDUAL

Kickers

	XP	XPA	FG	FGA	PTS
Longwell, Ryan, G.B.	32	32	33	38	131
Gramatica, Martin, T.B.	42	42	28	34	126
Nedney, Joe, Den.-Car.	24	24	34	38	126
Akers, David, Phil.	34	36	29	33	121
Anderson, Gary, Minn.	45	45	22	23	111
Seder, Tim, Dall.	27	27	25	33	#108
Brien, Doug, N.O.	37	37	23	29	106
Hanson, Jason, Det.	29	29	24	30	101
Andersen, Morten, Atl.	23	23	25	31	98
Wilkins, Jeff, St.L.	38	38	17	17	89
Richey, Wade, S.F.	43	45	15	22	88
Daluiso, Brad, NYG	34	34	17	23	85
Edinger, Paul, Chi.	21	21	21	27	84
Blanchard, Cary, Ariz.	18	19	16	23	66
Heppner, Kris, Sea.-Wash.	17	17	10	15	47
Stoyanovich, Pete, K.C.-St.L.	26	26	5	9	41
Murray, Eddie, Wash.	7	8	8	12	31
Cunningham, Richie, Car.	9	9	5	7	24
Hall, Jeff, St.L.	9	9	4	5	21
Husted, Michael, Wash.	8	9	4	8	20
Holmes, Jaret, NYG	3	3	2	2	9
Bentley, Scott, Wash.	0	0	1	1	3

 # Scored touchdown

Nonkickers

	TD	TDR	TDP	TDM	2-PT	PTS
Faulk, Marshall, St.L.	26	18	8	0	2	160
Moss, Randy, Minn.	15	0	15	0	1	92
Owens, Terrell, S.F.	13	0	13	0	1	80
Green, Ahman, G.B.	13	10	3	0	0	78
Stewart, James, Det.	11	10	1	0	3	72
Davis, Stephen, Wash.	11	11	0	0	0	66
Garner, Charlie, S.F.	10	7	3	0	0	60
Smith, Robert, Minn.	10	7	3	0	0	60
Barber, Tiki, NYG	9	8	1	0	0	54
Bruce, Isaac, St.L.	9	0	9	0	0	54
Carter, Cris, Minn.	9	0	9	0	0	54
Dunn, Warrick, T.B.	9	8	1	0	0	54
Freeman, Antonio, G.B.	9	0	9	0	0	54
Smith, Emmitt, Dall.	9	9	0	0	0	54
Williams, Ricky, N.O.	9	8	1	0	0	54
Hilliard, Ike, NYG	8	0	8	0	0	48
Horn, Joe, N.O.	8	0	8	0	0	48
Johnson, Keyshawn, T.B.	8	0	8	0	0	48
Toomer, Amani, NYG	8	1	7	0	0	48
Boston, David, Ariz.	7	0	7	0	0	42
Culpepper, Daunte, Minn.	7	7	0	0	0	42
Johnson, Charles, Phil.	7	0	7	0	0	42
Rice, Jerry, S.F.	7	0	7	0	0	42
Anderson, Jamal, Atl.	6	6	0	0	1	38
Beasley, Fred, S.F.	6	3	3	0	0	36
Holt, Torry, St.L.	6	0	6	0	0	36
Jackson, Willie, N.O.	6	0	6	0	0	36
McNabb, Donovan, Phil.	6	6	0	0	0	36
Muhammad, Muhsin, Car.	6	0	6	0	0	36
Pittman, Michael, Ariz.	6	4	2	0	0	36
Sanders, Frank, Ariz.	6	0	6	0	0	36
Harris, Jackie, Dall.	5	0	5	0	1	32
King, Shaun, T.B.	5	5	0	0	1	32
Alstott, Mike, T.B.	5	5	0	0	0	30
Dayne, Ron, NYG	5	5	0	0	0	30
Fryar, Irving, Wash.	5	0	5	0	0	30

2000 INDIVIDUAL STATISTICS—SCORING

	TD	TDR	TDP	TDM	2-PT	PTS
Hakim, Az-Zahir, St.L.	5	0	4	1	0	30
Mathis, Terance, Atl.	5	0	5	0	0	30
Mitchell, Brian, Phil.	5	2	1	2	0	30
Robinson, Marcus, Chi.	5	0	5	0	0	30
Thomason, Jeff, Phil.	5	0	5	0	0	30
Anthony, Reidel, T.B.	4	0	4	0	0	24
Autry, Darnell, Phil.	4	3	1	0	0	24
Biakabutuka, Tim, Car.	4	2	2	0	0	24
Dwight, Tim, Atl.	4	0	3	1	0	24
Garcia, Jeff, S.F.	4	4	0	0	0	24
Glover, Andrew, N.O.	4	0	4	0	0	24
Holcombe, Robert, St.L.	4	3	1	0	0	24
Proehl, Ricky, St.L.	4	0	4	0	0	24
Schroeder, Bill, G.B.	4	0	4	0	0	24
Watson, Justin, St.L.	4	4	0	0	0	24
Morton, Johnnie, Det.	3	0	3	0	1	20
Small, Torrance, Phil.	3	0	3	0	1	20
Stokes, J.J., S.F.	3	0	3	0	1	20
Williams, Roland, St.L.	3	0	3	0	1	20
Allen, James, Chi.	3	2	1	0	0	18
Campbell, Dan, NYG	3	0	3	0	0	18
Centers, Larry, Wash.	3	0	3	0	0	18
Connell, Albert, Wash.	3	0	3	0	0	18
Crowell, Germane, Det.	3	0	3	0	0	18
Hayes, Donald, Car.	3	0	3	0	0	18
Hetherington, Chris, Car.	3	2	1	0	0	18
Horne, Tony, St.L.	3	0	2	1	0	18
Levens, Dorsey, G.B.	3	3	0	0	0	18
Lewis, Chad, Phil.	3	0	3	0	0	18
McGarity, Wane, Dall.	3	1	0	2	0	18
McNown, Cade, Chi.	3	3	0	0	0	18
McWilliams, Johnny, Minn.	3	0	3	0	0	18
Moore, Dave, T.B.	3	0	3	0	0	18
Moore, Herman, Det.	3	0	3	0	0	18
Vaughn, Darrick, Atl.	3	0	0	3	0	18
Warren, Chris, Dall.	3	2	1	0	0	18
Allen, Terry, N.O.	2	2	0	0	1	14
Davis, Tyrone, G.B.	2	0	2	0	1	14
Jackson, Terry, S.F.	2	1	1	0	1	14
Alexander, Stephen, Wash.	2	0	2	0	0	12
Barber, Ronde, T.B.	2	0	0	2	0	12
Batch, Charlie, Det.	2	2	0	0	0	12
Bates, Mario, Det.	2	2	0	0	0	12
Booker, Marty, Chi.	2	0	2	0	0	12
Brooks, Aaron, N.O.	2	2	0	0	0	12
Byrd, Isaac, Car.	2	0	2	0	0	12
Clark, Greg, S.F.	2	0	2	0	0	12
Floyd, William, Car.	2	1	1	0	0	12
Hatchette, Matt, Minn.	2	0	2	0	0	12
Jefferson, Shawn, Atl.	2	0	2	0	0	12
Jones, Thomas, Ariz.	2	2	0	0	0	12
Kelly, Reggie, Atl.	2	0	2	0	0	12
Kennison, Eddie, Chi.	2	0	2	0	0	12
Knight, Sammy, N.O.	2	0	0	2	0	12
Kozlowski, Brian, Atl.	2	0	2	0	0	12
McKnight, James, Dall.	2	0	2	0	0	12
Mitchell, Keith, N.O.	2	0	0	2	0	12
Sellers, Mike, Wash.	2	0	2	0	0	12
Sloan, David, Det.	2	0	2	0	0	12
Thomas, Robert, Dall.	2	0	2	0	0	12
Thrash, James, Wash.	2	0	2	0	0	12
Walls, Wesley, Car.	2	0	2	0	0	12
Beuerlein, Steve, Car.	1	1	0	0	1	8
Driver, Donald, G.B.	1	0	1	0	1	8
Ismail, Raghib, Dall.	1	0	1	0	1	8
Abraham, Donnie, T.B.	1	0	0	1	0	6
Allred, John, Chi.	1	0	1	0	0	6
Ambrose, Ashley, Atl.	1	0	0	1	0	6
Bailey, Champ, Wash.	1	1	0	0	0	6
Bates, Michael, Car.	1	0	0	1	0	6
Blake, Jeff, N.O.	1	1	0	0	0	6
Brooks, Derrick, T.B.	1	0	0	1	0	6
Brown, Mike, Chi.	1	0	0	1	0	6
Brown, Na, Phil.	1	0	1	0	0	6
Bush, Devin, St.L.	1	0	0	1	0	6
Caldwell, Mike, Phil.	1	0	0	1	0	6
Campbell, Lamar, Det.	1	0	0	1	0	6
Case, Stoney, Det.	1	1	0	0	0	6
Collins, Kerry, NYG	1	1	0	0	0	6
Crawford, Casey, Car.	1	0	1	0	0	6
Cunningham, Randall, Dall.	1	1	0	0	0	6
Davis, John, Minn.	1	0	1	0	0	6

	TD	TDR	TDP	TDM	2-PT	PTS
Dixon, Ron, NYG	1	0	1	0	0	6
Duncan, Jamie, T.B.	1	0	0	1	0	6
Enis, Curtis, Chi.	1	1	0	0	0	6
Evans, Doug, Car.	1	0	0	1	0	6
Foster, Larry, Det.	1	0	1	0	0	6
Franks, Bubba, G.B.	1	0	1	0	0	6
Galloway, Joey, Dall.	1	0	1	0	0	6
Green, Jacquez, T.B.	1	0	1	0	0	6
Green, Trent, St.L.	1	1	0	0	0	6
Hall, Lamont, N.O.	1	0	1	0	0	6
Hardy, Terry, Ariz.	1	0	1	0	0	6
Harris, Walt, Chi.	1	0	0	1	0	6
Hartings, Jeff, Det.	1	0	0	1	0	6
Henderson, William, G.B.	1	0	1	0	0	6
Hicks, Skip, Wash.	1	1	0	0	0	6
Hitchcock, Jimmy, Car.	1	0	0	1	0	6
Hoover, Brad, Car.	1	1	0	0	0	6
Howard, Desmond, Det.	1	0	0	1	0	6
Jenkins, MarTay, Ariz.	1	0	0	1	0	6
Johnson, Brad, Wash.	1	1	0	0	0	6
Jurevicius, Joe, NYG	1	0	1	0	0	6
Kelly, Brian, T.B.	1	0	0	1	0	6
LaFleur, David, Dall.	1	0	1	0	0	6
Lyle, Keith, St.L.	1	0	0	1	0	6
Mangum, Kris, Car.	1	0	1	0	0	6
McDaniel, Randall, T.B.	1	0	1	0	0	6
McQuarters, R.W., Chi.	1	0	0	1	0	6
Milne, Brian, N.O.	1	0	1	0	0	6
Minter, Mike, Car.	1	0	0	1	0	6
Mitchell, Pete, NYG	1	0	1	0	0	6
Montgomery, Joe, NYG	1	1	0	0	0	6
Montgomery, Monty, S.F.	1	0	0	1	0	6
Moore, Jerald, N.O.	1	1	0	0	0	6
Parrish, Tony, Chi.	1	0	0	1	0	6
Poole, Keith, N.O.	1	0	1	0	0	6
Pritchett, Stanley, Phil.	1	1	0	0	0	6
Rasby, Walter, Det.	1	0	1	0	0	6
Reed, Andre, Wash.	1	0	1	0	0	6
Rossum, Allen, G.B.	1	0	0	1	0	6
Sehorn, Jason, NYG	1	0	0	1	0	6
Smith, Darrin, N.O.	1	0	0	1	0	6
Staley, Duce, Phil.	1	1	0	0	0	6
Trotter, Jeremiah, Phil.	1	0	0	1	0	6
Tucker, Jason, Dall.	1	1	0	0	0	6
Uwaezuoke, Iheanyi, Car.	1	0	0	1	0	6
Webster, Jason, S.F.	1	0	0	1	0	6
Westbrook, Bryant, Det.	1	0	0	1	0	6
White, Dez, Chi.	1	0	1	0	0	6
Wiley, Michael, Dall.	1	0	1	0	0	6
Williams, Aeneas, Ariz.	1	0	0	1	0	6
Williams, Karl, T.B.	1	0	0	1	0	6
Williams, U. Tyrone, G.B.	1	0	0	1	0	6
Fletcher, London, St.L.	0	0	0	0	1	2
Maryland, Russell, G.B.	0	0	0	0	0	*2
Reese, Izell, Dall.	0	0	0	0	0	*2
Smith, Bruce, Wash.	0	0	0	0	0	*2
Williams, Moe, Minn.	0	0	0	0	1	2

** Safety*
Team safety credited to Atlanta and Tampa Bay

2000 INDIVIDUAL STATISTICS—FIELD GOALS

FIELD GOALS

Field Goal Percentage

NFC:	1.000	Jeff Wilkins, St. Louis
AFC:	.926	Mike Vanderjagt, Indianapolis

Field Goals

AFC:	35	Matt Stover, Baltimore
NFC:	33	Ryan Longwell, Green Bay

Field Goal Attempts

AFC:	39	Matt Stover, Baltimore
NFC:	38	Ryan Longwell, Green Bay

Longest Field Goal

NFC:	55	Martin Gramatica, Tampa Bay vs. Detroit, October 19
AFC:	54	John Carney, San Diego at Kansas City, September 17
	54	Sebastian Janikowski, Oakland at San Diego, October 29

Average Yards Made

AFC:	40.1	Rian Lindell, Seattle
NFC:	37.8	Ryan Longwell, Green Bay

AFC FIELD GOALS—TEAM

	FG	FGA	Pct.	Long
Indianapolis	25	27	.926	48
Miami	28	31	.903	49
Baltimore	35	39	.897	51
Jacksonville	29	33	.879	51
Pittsburgh	25	30	.833	52
Cleveland	14	17	.824	45
New England	27	33	.818	53
Seattle	21	26	.808	52
Tennessee	27	34	.794	50
Denver	26	34	.765	51
Buffalo	26	35	.743	48
San Diego	18	25	.720	54
Kansas City	17	24	.708	42
N.Y. Jets	23	34	.676	51
Oakland	23	34	.676	54
Cincinnati	12	21	.571	45
AFC Total	376	477	—	54
AFC Average	23.5	29.8	.788	—

NFC FIELD GOALS—TEAM

	FG	FGA	Pct.	Long
Minnesota	22	23	.957	49
St. Louis	24	27	.889	51
Carolina	31	35	.886	52
Philadelphia	29	33	.879	51
Green Bay	33	38	.868	52
Tampa Bay	28	34	.824	55
Atlanta	25	31	.806	51
Detroit	24	30	.800	54
New Orleans	23	29	.793	48
Chicago	21	27	.778	54
N.Y. Giants	19	25	.760	46
Dallas	25	33	.758	48
Arizona	16	23	.696	54
San Francisco	15	22	.682	47
Washington	20	30	.667	50
NFC Total	355	440	—	55
NFC Average	23.7	29.3	.807	—
League Total	731	917	—	55
League Average	23.6	29.6	.797	—

AFC FIELD GOALS—INDIVIDUAL

	1-19 Yards	20-29 Yards	30-39 Yards	40-49 Yards	50 or Longer	Totals	Avg. Yds. Att.	Avg. Yds. Made	Avg. Yds. Miss	Long
Vanderjagt, Mike, Ind.	1-1	6-6	13-13	5-6	0-1	25-27	34.8	33.3	53.0	48
	1.000	1.000	1.000	.833	.000	.926				
Hollis, Mike, Jax.	0-0	6-7	8-8	7-8	3-3	24-26	36.9	36.8	38.5	51
	—	.857	1.000	.875	1.000	.923				
Mare, Olindo, Mia.	0-0	7-8	9-10	12-13	0-0	28-31	35.6	35.5	37.0	49
	—	.875	.900	.923	—	.903				
Stover, Matt, Balt.	2-2	9-9	12-13	10-12	2-3	35-39	35.5	34.6	43.3	51
	1.000	1.000	.923	.833	.667	.897				
Lindell, Rian, Sea.	0-0	4-5	1-1	7-8	3-3	15-17	39.1	40.1	32.0	52
	—	.800	1.000	.875	1.000	.882				
Brown, Kris, Pitt.	1-1	8-8	9-10	6-9	1-2	25-30	34.9	33.2	43.4	52
	1.000	1.000	.900	.667	.500	.833				
Dawson, Phil, Cle.	3-3	4-4	5-5	2-5	0-0	14-17	32.7	30.7	42.0	45
	1.000	1.000	1.000	.400	—	.824				
Del Greco, Al, Tenn.	0-0	13-15	7-8	6-9	1-1	27-33	32.5	31.7	36.3	50
	—	.867	.875	.667	1.000	.818				
Vinatieri, Adam, N.E.	0-0	11-13	8-9	7-8	1-3	27-33	34.6	33.2	40.8	53
	—	.846	.889	.875	.333	.818				
Elam, Jason, Den.	0-0	7-7	6-7	4-9	1-1	18-24	35.8	33.3	43.5	51
	—	1.000	.857	.444	1.000	.750				
Peterson, Todd, K.C.	1-1	5-5	7-9	2-5	0-0	15-20	33.4	31.3	39.6	42
	1.000	1.000	.778	.400	—	.750				
Christie, Steve, Buff.	2-2	11-13	4-6	9-13	0-1	26-35	34.2	32.8	38.3	48
	1.000	.846	.667	.692	.000	.743				
Carney, John, S.D.	1-1	3-3	5-7	7-10	2-4	18-25	39.5	37.9	43.6	54
	1.000	1.000	.714	.700	.500	.720				
Janikowski, Sebastian, Oak.	1-1	6-6	6-7	8-14	1-4	22-32	38.3	34.9	45.8	54
	1.000	1.000	.857	.571	.250	.688				
Hall, John, NYJ	0-0	8-9	6-8	6-12	1-3	21-32	37.6	34.3	43.9	51
	—	.889	.750	.500	.333	.656				
Rackers, Neil, Cin.	0-0	5-5	5-9	2-7	0-0	12-21	35.7	32.8	39.6	45
	—	1.000	.556	.286	—	.571				
(Nonqualifiers)										
Lindsey, Steve, Jax.	2-2	0-0	1-3	2-2	0-0	5-7	32.7	33.0	32.0	49
	1.000	—	.333	1.000	—	.714				
Conway, Brett, Wash.-Oak.-NYJ	2-2	3-3	0-0	1-1	0-0	6-6	24.8	24.8	—	40
	1.000	1.000	—	1.000	—	1.000				
Hentrich, Craig, Tenn.	0-0	0-0	0-0	0-0	0-1	0-1	60.0	—	60.0	0
	—	—	—	—	.000	.000				
Lechler, Shane, Oak.	0-0	0-0	0-1	0-0	0-0	0-1	33.0	—	33.0	0
	—	—	.000	—	—	.000				
AFC Totals	17-17	122-132	114-140	107-156	16-32	376-477	35.5	33.8	41.5	54
	1.000	.924	.814	.686	.500	.788				

Leader based on percentage, minimum 16 field-goal attempts

NFC FIELD GOALS—INDIVIDUAL

	1-19 Yards	20-29 Yards	30-39 Yards	40-49 Yards	50 or Longer	Totals	Avg. Yds. Att.	Avg. Yds. Made	Avg. Yds. Miss	Long
Wilkins, Jeff, St.L.	2-2	5-5	6-6	3-3	1-1	17-17	32.5	32.5	—	51
	1.000	1.000	1.000	1.000	1.000	1.000				
Anderson, Gary, Minn.	1-1	5-5	9-9	7-7	0-1	22-23	35.3	34.6	51.0	49
	1.000	1.000	1.000	1.000	.000	.957				
Nedney, Joe, Den.-Car.	1-1	16-16	7-8	8-10	2-3	34-38	33.5	32.3	43.8	52
	1.000	1.000	.875	.800	.667	.895				
Akers, David, Phil.	1-1	6-6	14-15	7-10	1-1	29-33	35.8	34.9	41.8	51
	1.000	1.000	.933	.700	1.000	.879				
Longwell, Ryan, G.B.	0-0	7-8	10-10	13-15	3-5	33-38	38.6	37.8	43.8	52
	—	.875	1.000	.867	.600	.868				
Gramatica, Martin, T.B.	0-0	8-8	8-10	7-9	5-7	28-34	38.3	37.4	42.5	55
	—	1.000	.800	.778	.714	.824				
Andersen, Morten, Atl.	0-0	6-6	6-7	11-15	2-3	25-31	38.9	37.8	43.8	51
	—	1.000	.857	.733	.667	.806				
Hanson, Jason, Det.	2-2	6-7	10-12	4-7	2-2	24-30	34.1	33.4	37.0	54
	1.000	.857	.833	.571	1.000	.800				
Brien, Doug, N.O.	1-1	6-6	4-5	12-15	0-2	23-29	36.8	34.7	44.7	48
	1.000	1.000	.800	.800	.000	.793				
Edinger, Paul, Chi.	1-1	5-5	7-9	6-10	2-2	21-27	37.6	36.6	41.3	54
	1.000	1.000	.778	.600	1.000	.778				
Seder, Tim, Dall.	2-2	5-6	9-11	9-13	0-1	25-33	36.3	34.7	41.5	48
	1.000	.833	.818	.692	.000	.758				
Daluiso, Brad, NYG	0-0	8-8	5-8	4-7	0-0	17-23	33.4	31.6	38.3	46
	—	1.000	.625	.571	—	.739				
Blanchard, Cary, Ariz.	1-1	2-2	9-11	2-5	2-4	16-23	37.8	35.4	43.3	54
	1.000	1.000	.818	.400	.500	.696				
Richey, Wade, S.F.	0-0	6-7	6-8	3-6	0-1	15-22	35.8	33.2	41.3	47
	—	.857	.750	.500	.000	.682				
(Nonqualifiers)										
Heppner, Kris, Sea.-Wash.	1-1	4-4	3-6	2-2	0-2	10-15	35.0	31.8	41.4	45
	1.000	1.000	.500	1.000	.000	.667				
Murray, Eddie, Wash.	0-0	2-2	3-4	3-6	0-0	8-12	38.2	35.4	43.8	47
	—	1.000	.750	.500	—	.667				
Stoyanovich, Pete, K.C.-St.L.	0-0	2-2	0-3	3-3	0-1	5-9	39.0	38.2	40.0	48
	—	1.000	.000	1.000	.000	.556				
Husted, Michael, Wash.	0-0	4-4	0-3	0-1	0-0	4-8	29.6	24.3	35.0	28
	—	1.000	.000	.000	—	.500				
Cunningham, Richie, Car.	0-0	3-5	2-2	0-0	0-0	5-7	28.6	29.6	26.0	39
	—	.600	1.000	—	—	.714				
Hall, Jeff, St.L.	0-0	1-1	1-1	1-2	1-1	4-5	39.6	37.8	47.0	50
	—	1.000	1.000	.500	1.000	.800				
Holmes, Jaret, NYG	0-0	1-1	1-1	0-0	0-0	2-2	30.5	30.5	—	34
	—	1.000	1.000	—	—	1.000				
Bentley, Scott, Wash.	0-0	0-0	0-0	0-0	1-1	1-1	50.0	50.0	—	50
	—	—	—	—	1.000	1.000				
NFC Totals	12-12	102-108	118-143	101-141	22-36	355-440	36.2	35.0	41.3	55
	1.000	.944	.825	.716	.611	.807				
League Totals	29-29	224-240	232-283	208-297	38-68	731-917	35.8	34.4	41.4	55
	1.000	.933	.820	.700	.559	.797				

Leader based on percentage, minimum 16 field-goal attempts

RUSHING

Yards
AFC: 1709—Edgerrin James, Indianapolis
NFC: 1521—Robert Smith, Minnesota

Yards, Game
AFC: 278—Corey Dillon, Cincinnati vs. Denver, October 22 (22 attempts, 2 TD)
NFC: 220—Marshall Faulk, St. Louis at New Orleans, December 24 (32 attempts, 2 TD)

Longest
NFC: 85—Brian Mitchell, Philadelphia vs. Atlanta, October 1 - TD
AFC: 80—Corey Dillon, Cincinnati vs. Tennessee, October 8 - TD
80—Tyrone Wheatley, Oakland vs. Seattle, October 22 - TD
80—Mike Anderson, Denver at Seattle, November 26 - TD

Attempts
AFC: 403—Eddie George, Tennessee
NFC: 339—James Stewart, Detroit

Attempts, Game
NFC: 38—Ricky Williams, New Orleans vs. Carolina, October 15 (144 yards, 2 TD)
AFC: 38—Edgerrin James, Indianapolis at Seattle, October 15 (219 yards, 3 TD)

Yards Per Attempt
NFC: 5.4—Marshall Faulk, St. Louis
AFC: 5.0—Mike Anderson, Denver

Touchdowns
NFC: 18—Marshall Faulk, St. Louis
AFC: 15—Mike Anderson, Denver

Team Leaders, Yards
AFC: BALTIMORE, 1364, Jamal Lewis; BUFFALO, 591, Shawn Bryson; CINCINNATI, 1435, Corey Dillon; CLEVELAND, 512, Travis Prentice; DENVER, 1487, Mike Anderson; INDIANAPOLIS, 1709, Edgerrin James; JACKSONVILLE, 1399, Fred Taylor; KANSAS CITY, 697, Tony Richardson; MIAMI, 1139, Lamar Smith; NEW ENGLAND, 570, Kevin Faulk; N.Y. JETS, 1204, Curtis Martin; OAKLAND, 1046, Tyrone Wheatley; PITTSBURGH, 1341, Jerome Bettis; SAN DIEGO, 384, Terrell Fletcher; SEATTLE, 1242, Ricky Watters; TENNESSEE, 1509, Eddie George
NFC: ARIZONA, 719, Michael Pittman; ATLANTA, 1024, Jamal Anderson; CAROLINA, 627, Tim Biakabutuka; CHICAGO, 1120, James Allen; DALLAS, 1203, Emmitt Smith; DETROIT, 1184, James Stewart; GREEN BAY, 1175, Ahman Green; MINNESOTA, 1521, Robert Smith; NEW ORLEANS, 1000, Ricky Williams; N.Y. GIANTS, 1006, Tiki Barber; PHILADELPHIA, 629, Donovan McNabb; ST. LOUIS, 1359, Marshall Faulk; SAN FRANCISCO, 1142, Charlie Garner; TAMPA BAY, 1133, Warrick Dunn; WASHINGTON, 1318, Stephen Davis

Team Champion
AFC: 2470—Oakland
NFC: 2129—Minnesota

2000 INDIVIDUAL STATISTICS—RUSHING

AFC RUSHING—TEAM

	Att.	Yards	Avg.	Long	TD
Oakland	520	2470	4.8	80t	23
Cincinnati	495	2314	4.7	80t	13
Denver	516	2311	4.5	80t	21
Pittsburgh	527	2248	4.3	45t	19
Baltimore	511	2199	4.3	45	9
Tennessee	547	2084	3.8	35t	14
Jacksonville	481	2032	4.2	71	18
Buffalo	475	1922	4.0	59	11
Miami	496	1894	3.8	68t	16
Indianapolis	435	1859	4.3	30	14
Seattle	403	1720	4.3	55	10
N.Y. Jets	418	1471	3.5	55	11
Kansas City	383	1465	3.8	69	12
New England	424	1390	3.3	35	9
Cleveland	336	1085	3.2	42	7
San Diego	351	1062	3.0	26	7
AFC Total	7318	29526	4.0	80t	214
AFC Average	457.4	1845.4	4.0	—	13.4

NFC RUSHING—TEAM

	Att.	Yards	Avg.	Long	TD
Minnesota	428	2129	5.0	72t	14
New Orleans	505	2068	4.1	40	14
Tampa Bay	490	2066	4.2	70t	18
N.Y. Giants	507	2009	4.0	78t	16
Dallas	463	1953	4.2	52	15
Philadelphia	397	1882	4.7	85t	13
St. Louis	383	1843	4.8	49	26
San Francisco	416	1801	4.3	42	15
Washington	445	1748	3.9	50t	14
Detroit	448	1747	3.9	34	15
Chicago	417	1736	4.2	52	6
Green Bay	404	1643	4.1	39t	13
Arizona	343	1278	3.7	29	6
Atlanta	350	1214	3.5	42	6
Carolina	363	1186	3.3	43	7
NFC Total	6359	26303	4.1	85t	198
NFC Average	423.9	1753.5	4.1	—	13.2
League Total	13677	55829	—	85t	412
League Average	441.2	1800.9	4.1	—	13.3

NFL TOP TEN RUSHERS

	Att.	Yards	Avg.	Long	TD
James, Edgerrin, Ind.	387	1709	4.4	30	13
Smith, Robert, Minn.	295	1521	5.2	72t	7
George, Eddie, Tenn.	403	1509	3.7	35t	14
Anderson, Mike, Den.	297	1487	5.0	80t	15
Dillon, Corey, Cin.	315	1435	4.6	80t	7
Taylor, Fred, Jax.	292	1399	4.8	71	12
Lewis, Jamal, Balt.	309	1364	4.4	45	6
Faulk, Marshall, St.L.	253	1359	5.4	36	18
Bettis, Jerome, Pitt.	355	1341	3.8	30	8
Davis, Stephen, Wash.	332	1318	4.0	50t	11

AFC RUSHERS—INDIVIDUAL

	Att.	Yards	Avg.	Long	TD
James, Edgerrin, Ind.	387	1709	4.4	30	13
George, Eddie, Tenn.	403	1509	3.7	35t	14
Anderson, Mike, Den.	297	1487	5.0	80t	15
Dillon, Corey, Cin.	315	1435	4.6	80t	7
Taylor, Fred, Jax.	292	1399	4.8	71	12
Lewis, Jamal, Balt.	309	1364	4.4	45	6
Bettis, Jerome, Pitt.	355	1341	3.8	30	8
Watters, Ricky, Sea.	278	1242	4.5	55	7
Martin, Curtis, NYJ	316	1204	3.8	55	9
Smith, Lamar, Mia.	309	1139	3.7	68t	14
Wheatley, Tyrone, Oak.	232	1046	4.5	80t	9
Richardson, Tony, K.C.	147	697	4.7	33	3
Bryson, Shawn, Buff.	161	591	3.7	24	0
Holmes, Priest, Balt.	137	588	4.3	21	2
Faulk, Kevin, N.E.	164	570	3.5	18	4
Gannon, Rich, Oak.	89	529	5.9	23	4
Prentice, Travis, Cle.	173	512	3.0	17	7
Kaufman, Napoleon, Oak.	93	499	5.4	60	0
Stewart, Kordell, Pitt.	78	436	5.6	45t	7
Redmond, J.R., N.E.	125	406	3.2	20	1
McNair, Steve, Tenn.	72	403	5.6	25	0
Fletcher, Terrell, S.D.	116	384	3.3	21	3
Fazande, Jermaine, S.D.	119	368	3.1	26	2
Smith, Antowain, Buff.	101	354	3.5	59	4
Morris, Sammy, Buff.	93	341	3.7	32t	5
Anders, Kimble, K.C.	76	331	4.4	69	2
Bennett, Brandon, Cin.	90	324	3.6	37t	3
Alexander, Shaun, Sea.	64	313	4.9	50	2
Johnson, Rob, Buff.	42	307	7.3	23	1
Davis, Terrell, Den.	78	282	3.6	24	2
Fiedler, Jay, Mia.	54	267	4.9	30	1
Rhett, Errict, Cle.	71	258	3.6	42	0
Brunell, Mark, Jax.	48	236	4.9	16	2
Smith, Akili, Cin.	41	232	5.7	21	0
Huntley, Richard, Pitt.	46	215	4.7	30t	3
Jordan, Randy, Oak.	46	213	4.6	43t	3
Coleman, KaRon, Den.	54	183	3.4	24t	1
Moreau, Frank, K.C.	67	179	2.7	22	4
Thomas, Rodney, Tenn.	61	175	2.9	20	0
Johnson, J.J., Mia.	50	168	3.4	16	1
Flutie, Doug, Buff.	36	161	4.5	32	1
Bledsoe, Drew, N.E.	47	158	3.4	16	2
Fuamatu-Ma'afala, Chris, Pitt.	21	149	7.1	23	1
Warrick, Peter, Cin.	16	148	9.3	77t	2
Mack, Stacey, Jax.	54	145	2.7	14	1
White, Jamel, Cle.	47	145	3.1	14	0
Chancey, Robert, S.D.	42	141	3.4	14	2
Thomas, Thurman, Mia.	28	136	4.9	25	0
Crockett, Zack, Oak.	43	130	3.0	11	7
Kitna, Jon, Sea.	48	127	2.6	13	1
Manning, Peyton, Ind.	37	116	3.1	14	1
Johnson, Anthony, Jax.	28	112	4.0	19	1
Linton, Jonathan, Buff.	38	112	2.9	12	0
Grbac, Elvis, K.C.	30	110	3.7	22	1
Denson, Autry, Mia.	31	108	3.5	12	0
Griese, Brian, Den.	29	102	3.5	18	1
Smith, Rod, Den.	6	99	16.5	50t	1
Carter, Tony, N.E.	37	90	2.4	9	2
Parmalee, Bernie, NYJ	27	87	3.2	18t	2
Cloud, Mike, K.C.	30	84	2.8	15t	1
Gary, Olandis, Den.	13	80	6.2	25	0
Dilfer, Trent, Balt.	20	75	3.8	19	0
Pederson, Doug, Cle.	18	68	3.8	15	0
Frerotte, Gus, Den.	22	64	2.9	13t	1
Anderson, Richie, NYJ	27	63	2.3	9	0
Mitchell, Scott, Cin.	10	61	6.1	12t	1
Pass, Patrick, N.E.	18	58	3.2	11	0
Banks, Tony, Balt.	19	57	3.0	10	0
Stith, Shyrone, Jax.	20	55	2.8	12	1
Leaf, Ryan, S.D.	28	54	1.9	14	0
Williams, Nick, Cin.	10	54	5.4	13	0
Ward, Hines, Pitt.	4	53	13.3	23	0
Howard, Chris, Jax.	21	52	2.5	9t	1
Kirby, Terry, Oak.	11	51	4.6	28	0
Brown, Troy, N.E.	6	46	7.7	35	0
Alexander, Derrick, K.C.	3	45	15.0	26	0
Couch, Tim, Cle.	12	45	3.8	31	0
Lucas, Ray, NYJ	6	42	7.0	17	0
Glenn, Terry, N.E.	4	39	9.8	35	0
Izzo, Larry, Mia.	1	39	39.0	39	0
Konrad, Rob, Mia.	15	39	2.6	5	0
Lewis, Jermaine, Balt.	3	38	12.7	23	0
Ayanbadejo, Obafemi, Balt.	15	37	2.5	8	1
Harris, Raymont, Den.-N.E.	13	36	2.8	7	0
Northcutt, Dennis, Cle.	9	33	3.7	13	0
Price, Peerless, Buff.	2	32	16.0	27	0
Testaverde, Vinny, NYJ	25	32	1.3	15	0
Conway, Curtis, S.D.	3	31	10.3	13	0
Huard, Brock, Sea.	5	29	5.8	10	0
Soward, R.Jay, Jax.	3	28	9.3	20	0
Bynum, Kenny, S.D.	7	26	3.7	9	0
Bennett, Donnell, K.C.	27	24	0.9	6	1
Harbaugh, Jim, S.D.	16	24	1.5	7	0
Keaton, Curtis, Cin.	6	24	4.0	8	0
Kreider, Dan, Pitt.	2	24	12.0	22	0
Moulds, Eric, Buff.	2	24	12.0	20	0
Ward, Dedric, NYJ	4	23	5.8	12	0
Pope, Daniel, Cin.	2	22	11.0	22	0
Johnson, Patrick, Balt.	2	21	10.5	19	0
Moreno, Moses, S.D.	5	20	4.0	13	0
Coles, Laveranues, NYJ	2	15	7.5	8	0

	Att.	Yards	Avg.	Long	TD
Wynn, Spergon, Cle.	3	15	5.0	11	0
Yeast, Craig, Cin.	1	15	15.0	15	0
Zereoue, Amos, Pitt.	6	14	2.3	11	0
Gordon, Lennox, Ind.	4	13	3.3	6	0
Brown, Tim, Oak.	3	12	4.0	7	0
Shaw, Harold, N.E.	9	12	1.3	5	0
Smith, Hunter, Ind.	1	11	11.0	11	0
Taylor, Travis, Balt.	2	11	5.5	12	0
Edwards, Marc, Cle.	2	9	4.5	6	0
Strong, Mack, Sea.	3	9	3.0	4	0
McCrary, Fred, S.D.	7	8	1.1	4	0
Wilkins, Terrence, Ind.	3	8	2.7	6	0
Williams, Jermaine, Jax.	2	8	4.0	4	0
Graham, Kent, Pitt.	8	7	0.9	7	0
Brown, Reggie, Sea.	3	6	2.0	3	0
Jenkins, Ronney, S.D.	8	6	0.8	4	0
Stokley, Brandon, Balt.	1	6	6.0	6	0
Witman, Jon, Pitt.	3	5	1.7	2	0
Edwards, Troy, Pitt.	3	4	1.3	15	0
Griffith, Howard, Den.	5	4	0.8	3	0
Groce, Clif, Cin.	3	4	1.3	5	0
Lewis, Mo, NYJ	1	3	3.0	3	0
Pathon, Jerome, Ind.	1	3	3.0	3	0
Shelton, Daimon, Jax.	2	3	1.5	2	0
Shepherd, Leslie, Mia.	4	3	0.8	14	0
Stone, Dwight, NYJ	3	3	1.0	9	0
Dukes, Chad, Jax.	2	2	1.0	2	0
Gash, Sam, Balt.	2	2	1.0	1	0
Hayes, Windrell, NYJ	1	2	2.0	2	0
Moon, Warren, K.C.	2	2	1.0	2	0
Finn, Jim, Ind.	1	1	1.0	1	0
Mason, Derrick, Tenn.	1	1	1.0	1	0
Miller, Josh, Pitt.	1	0	0.0	0	0
Pennington, Chad, NYJ	1	0	0.0	0	0
Redman, Chris, Balt.	1	0	0.0	0	0
Sowell, Jerald, NYJ	2	0	0.0	1	0
Thompson, Kevin, Cle.	1	0	0.0	0	0
Bishop, Michael, N.E.	7	-1	-0.1	2	0
Floyd, Chris, N.E.	2	-1	-0.5	0	0
Jackson, Darrell, Sea.	1	-1	-1.0	-1	0
Jackson, Jarious, Den.	1	-1	-1.0	-1	0
Johnson, Lee, N.E.	2	-1	-0.5	0	0
al-Jabbar, Abdul-Karim, Ind.	1	-2	-2.0	-2	0
Emanuel, Bert, Mia.	3	-2	-0.7	0	0
Neal, Lorenzo, Tenn.	1	-2	-2.0	-2	0
O'Donnell, Neil, Tenn.	9	-2	-0.2	4	0
Quinn, Jonathan, Jax.	2	-2	-1.0	-1	0
Chrebet, Wayne, NYJ	3	-3	-1.0	8	0
Hoying, Bobby, Oak.	2	-3	-1.5	-1	0
McDuffie, O.J., Mia.	1	-3	-3.0	-3	0
Rackers, Neil, Cin.	1	-5	-5.0	-5	0
Williams, James, Sea.	1	-5	-5.0	-5	0
Martin, Jamie, Jax.	7	-6	-0.9	2	0
Dudley, Rickey, Oak.	1	-7	-7.0	-7	0
Parker, Larry, K.C.	1	-7	-7.0	-7	0
Rouen, Tom, Den.	1	-11	-11.0	-11	0

t = Touchdown
Leader based on most yards gained

NFC RUSHERS—INDIVIDUAL

	Att.	Yards	Avg.	Long	TD
Smith, Robert, Minn.	295	1521	5.2	72t	7
Faulk, Marshall, St.L.	253	1359	5.4	36	18
Davis, Stephen, Wash.	332	1318	4.0	50t	11
Smith, Emmitt, Dall.	294	1203	4.1	52	9
Stewart, James, Det.	339	1184	3.5	34	10
Green, Ahman, G.B.	263	1175	4.5	39t	10
Garner, Charlie, S.F.	258	1142	4.4	42	7
Dunn, Warrick, T.B.	248	1133	4.6	70t	8
Allen, James, Chi.	290	1120	3.9	29	2
Anderson, Jamal, Atl.	282	1024	3.6	42	6
Barber, Tiki, NYG	213	1006	4.7	78t	8
Williams, Ricky, N.O.	248	1000	4.0	26t	8
Dayne, Ron, NYG	228	770	3.4	50	5
Pittman, Michael, Ariz.	184	719	3.9	29	4
McNabb, Donovan, Phil.	86	629	7.3	54	6
Biakabutuka, Tim, Car.	173	627	3.6	43	2
Culpepper, Daunte, Minn.	89	470	5.3	27t	7
Alstott, Mike, T.B.	131	465	3.5	20t	5
Garcia, Jeff, S.F.	72	414	5.8	33	4
Jones, Thomas, Ariz.	112	373	3.3	29	2
King, Shaun, T.B.	73	353	4.8	19	5
Staley, Duce, Phil.	79	344	4.4	60	1
Autry, Darnell, Phil.	112	334	3.0	15	3
McNown, Cade, Chi.	50	326	6.5	30	3
Warren, Chris, Dall.-Phil.	74	296	4.0	32t	2
Hoover, Brad, Car.	89	290	3.3	35	1
Watson, Justin, St.L.	54	249	4.6	49	4
Blake, Jeff, N.O.	57	243	4.3	20	1
Pritchett, Stanley, Phil.	58	225	3.9	16	1
Levens, Dorsey, G.B.	77	224	2.9	17	3
Batch, Charlie, Det.	44	199	4.5	19	2
Mitchell, Brian, Phil.	25	187	7.5	85t	2
Plummer, Jake, Ariz.	37	183	4.9	24	0
Allen, Terry, N.O.	46	179	3.9	18	2
Brooks, Aaron, N.O.	41	170	4.1	29	2
Moore, Jerald, N.O.	37	156	4.2	40	1
Beasley, Fred, S.F.	50	147	2.9	9	3
Morton, Chad, N.O.	36	136	3.8	16	0
Smith, Terrelle, N.O.	29	131	4.5	16	0
Bates, Mario, Det.	31	127	4.1	23	2
Case, Stoney, Det.	16	117	7.3	27	1
Favre, Brett, G.B.	27	108	4.0	18	0
Beuerlein, Steve, Car.	44	106	2.4	15	1
Centers, Larry, Wash.	19	103	5.4	14	0
Toomer, Amani, NYG	5	91	18.2	28	1
Cunningham, Randall, Dall.	23	89	3.9	19	1
Wiley, Michael, Dall.	24	88	3.7	11	0
Parker, De'Mond, G.B.	18	85	4.7	24	0
Enis, Curtis, Chi.	36	84	2.3	11t	1
Thrash, James, Wash.	10	82	8.2	34	0
Barnes, Marlon, Chi.	15	81	5.4	20	0
Hicks, Skip, Wash.	29	78	2.7	12	1
Martin, Cecil, Phil.	13	77	5.9	23	0
Ismail, Raghib, Dall.	8	73	9.1	37	0
Kennison, Eddie, Chi.	3	72	24.0	52	0
Smith, Paul, S.F.	18	72	4.0	14	0
Abdullah, Rabih, T.B.	16	70	4.4	19	0
Holcombe, Robert, St.L.	21	70	3.3	11	3
Green, Trent, St.L.	20	69	3.5	18t	1
Smith, Maurice, Atl.	19	69	3.6	16	0
Williams, Moe, Minn.	23	67	2.9	10	0
Collins, Kerry, NYG	41	65	1.6	15	1
Hetherington, Chris, Car.	23	65	2.8	14	2
Chandler, Chris, Atl.	21	60	2.9	16	0
Johnson, Brad, Wash.	22	58	2.6	21	1
Thomas, Robert, Dall.	15	51	3.4	9	0
Murrell, Adrian, Wash.	20	50	2.5	13	0
Irvin, Sedrick, Det.	9	49	5.4	32	0
McGarity, Wane, Dall.	6	49	8.2	22t	1
Comella, Greg, NYG	10	45	4.5	16	0
Kleinsasser, Jimmy, Minn.	12	43	3.6	7	0
Tucker, Jason, Dall.	4	42	10.5	17t	1
McAfee, Fred, N.O.	2	37	18.5	40	0
Lewis, Jeff, Car.	8	36	4.5	19	0
Wright, Anthony, Dall.	12	36	3.0	19	0
Matthews, Shane, Chi.	10	35	3.5	14	0
Floyd, William, Car.	16	33	2.1	8	1
Foster, Larry, Det.	2	31	15.5	16	0
Stecker, Aaron, T.B.	12	31	2.6	14	0
Hambrick, Troy, Dall.	6	28	4.7	13	0
Rivers, Ron, Atl.	8	27	3.4	10	0
Coakley, Dexter, Dall.	1	26	26.0	26	0
Morton, Johnnie, Det.	4	25	6.3	27	0
George, Jeff, Wash.	7	24	3.4	14	0
Conwell, Ernie, St.L.	2	23	11.5	17	0
Brister, Bubby, Minn.	5	20	4.0	12	0
Christian, Bob, Atl.	9	19	2.1	7	0
Hakim, Az-Zahir, St.L.	5	19	3.8	5	0
Hilliard, Ike, NYG	3	19	6.3	17	0
Johnson, Charles, Phil.	5	18	3.6	15	0
Warner, Kurt, St.L.	18	17	0.9	11	0
Fryar, Irving, Wash.	2	16	8.0	15	0
Henderson, William, G.B.	2	16	8.0	12	0
Rossum, Allen, G.B.	1	16	16.0	16	0
Akers, David, Phil.	1	15	15.0	15	0
Aikman, Troy, Dall.	10	13	1.3	5	0
Bates, Michael, Car.	5	13	2.6	8	0
Dixon, Ron, NYG	2	13	6.5	12	0
Green, Jacquez, T.B.	5	13	2.6	6	0
Crowell, Germane, Det.	1	12	12.0	12	0
Muhammad, Muhsin, Car.	2	12	6.0	8	0
Barnhardt, Tommy, Wash.	1	11	11.0	11	0

2000 INDIVIDUAL STATISTICS—RUSHING/PASSING

	Att.	Yards	Avg.	Long	TD
Bruce, Isaac, St.L.	1	11	11.0	11	0
Johnson, Doug, Atl.	3	11	3.7	8	0
Owens, Terrell, S.F.	3	11	3.7	5	0
Schroeder, Bill, G.B.	2	11	5.5	12	0
Horn, Joe, N.O.	6	10	1.7	16	0
Boston, David, Ariz.	3	9	3.0	24	0
Robinson, Marcus, Chi.	1	9	9.0	9	0
Detmer, Koy, Phil.	1	8	8.0	8	0
Dwight, Tim, Atl.	5	8	1.6	5	0
Makovicka, Joel, Ariz.	3	8	2.7	7	0
Mitchell, Basil, G.B.	2	8	4.0	4	0
Bailey, Champ, Wash.	1	7	7.0	7t	1
Holt, Torry, St.L.	2	7	3.5	7	0
Canidate, Trung, St.L.	3	6	2.0	3	0
Horne, Tony, St.L.	2	6	3.0	9	0
Jackson, Terry, S.F.	5	6	1.2	3	1
Lewis, Jonas, S.F.	1	6	6.0	6	0
Milburn, Glyn, Chi.	1	6	6.0	6	0
Stokes, J.J., S.F.	1	6	6.0	6	0
Freeman, Antonio, G.B.	2	5	2.5	3	0
Gowin, Toby, N.O.	1	5	5.0	5	0
Johnson, Keyshawn, T.B.	2	5	2.5	3	0
Miller, Jim, Chi.	7	5	0.7	3	0
Moss, Randy, Minn.	3	5	1.7	9	0
Craig, Dameyune, Car.	2	4	2.0	5	0
Driver, Donald, G.B.	1	4	4.0	4	0
Lyle, Keith, St.L.	1	4	4.0	4	0
Montgomery, Joe, NYG	1	4	4.0	4t	1
Hodgins, James, St.L.	1	3	3.0	3	0
Schlesinger, Cory, Det.	1	3	3.0	3	0
Walters, Troy, Minn.	1	3	3.0	3	0
Lee, Amp, Phil.	1	2	2.0	2	0

	Att.	Yards	Avg.	Long	TD
Sellers, Mike, Wash.	1	2	2.0	2	0
Engram, Bobby, Chi.	1	1	1.0	1	0
Greisen, Chris, Ariz.	1	1	1.0	1	0
Jefferson, Shawn, Atl.	1	1	1.0	1	0
Milne, Brian, N.O.	2	1	0.5	1	0
Seder, Tim, Dall.	1	1	1.0	1t	1
Small, Torrance, Phil.	1	1	1.0	1	0
Brown, Dave, Ariz.	1	0	0.0	0	0
Jervey, Travis, S.F.	1	0	0.0	0	0
Jett, John, Det.	1	0	0.0	0	0
Kanell, Danny, Atl.	1	0	0.0	0	0
Mirer, Rick, S.F.	3	0	0.0	3	0
Streets, Tai, S.F.	1	0	0.0	0	0
Walter, Ken, Car.	1	0	0.0	0	0
Booker, Marty, Chi.	2	-1	-0.5	5	0
Husak, Todd, Wash.	1	-1	-1.0	-1	0
Rattay, Tim, S.F.	2	-1	-0.5	0	0
Bates, D'Wayne, Chi.	1	-2	-2.0	-2	0
Goodman, Herbert, G.B.	3	-2	-0.7	3	0
Hamilton, Joe, T.B.	1	-2	-2.0	-2	0
Rice, Jerry, S.F.	1	-2	-2.0	-2	0
Wuerffel, Danny, G.B.	2	-2	-1.0	-1	0
Zeier, Eric, T.B.	2	-2	-1.0	-1	0
Garrett, Jason, NYG	4	-4	-1.0	-1	0
Jenkins, MarTay, Ariz.	1	-4	-4.0	-4	0
Hasselbeck, Matt, G.B.	4	-5	-1.3	-1	0
Mathis, Terance, Atl.	1	-5	-5.0	-5	0
Player, Scott, Ariz.	1	-11	-11.0	-11	0

t = Touchdown
Leader based on most yards gained

PASSING

Highest Rating
AFC: 102.9—Brian Griese, Denver
NFC: 101.8—Trent Green, St. Louis

Completion Percentage
NFC: 67.7—Kurt Warner, St. Louis
AFC: 64.3—Brian Griese, Denver

Attempts
AFC: 590—Vinny Testaverde, N.Y. Jets
NFC: 580—Brett Favre, Green Bay

Completions
AFC: 357—Peyton Manning, Indianapolis
NFC: 355—Jeff Garcia, San Francisco

Yards
AFC: 4413—Peyton Manning, Indianapolis
NFC: 4278—Jeff Garcia, San Francisco

Yards, Game
AFC: 504—Elvis Grbac, Kansas City at Oakland, November 5 (39-53, 2 TD)
NFC: 441—Kurt Warner, St. Louis vs. Denver, September 4 (25-35, 3 TD)
441—Aaron Brooks, New Orleans vs. Denver, December 3 (30-48, 2 TD)

Longest
NFC: 85—Kurt Warner (to Torry Holt), St. Louis at Atlanta, September 24 - TD
AFC: 84—Rich Gannon (to James Jett), Oakland vs. Atlanta, November 5 - TD

Yards Per Attempt
NFC: 9.88—Kurt Warner, St. Louis
AFC: 8.00—Brian Griese, Denver

Touchdown Passes
AFC: 33—Peyton Manning, Indianapolis
NFC: 33—Daunte Culpepper, Minnesota

Touchdown Passes, Game
AFC: 5—Tony Banks, Baltimore vs. Jacksonville, September 10 (23-40, 262 yards)
5—Elvis Grbac, Kansas City vs. San Diego, September 17 (20-33, 235 yards)
5—Vinny Testaverde, N.Y. Jets vs. Miami, October 23 (36-59, 378 yards) - OT
5—Gus Frerotte, Denver vs. San Diego, November 19 (36-58, 462 yards)
5—Rich Gannon, Oakland vs. Carolina, December 24 (26-32, 230 yards)
NFC: 4—Many times

Lowest Interception Percentage
AFC: 1.2—Brian Griese, Denver
NFC: 1.8—Jeff Garcia, San Francisco

Team Champion (Most Net Yards)
NFC: 5232—St. Louis
AFC: 4282—Indianapolis

AFC PASSING—TEAM

	Att.	Comp.	Pct. Comp.	Gross Yards	Sacked	Yds. Lost	Net Yards	Yds./ Att.	Yds./ Comp.	TD	Pct. TD	Long	Int.	Pct. Int.
Denver	569	354	62.2	4464	30	221	4243	7.85	12.61	28	4.92	61	12	2.1
Indianapolis	571	357	62.5	4413	20	131	4282	7.73	12.36	33	5.78	78t	15	2.6
Kansas City	582	342	58.8	4408	34	259	4149	7.57	12.89	29	4.98	81t	15	2.6
N.Y. Jets	637	352	55.3	4023	20	99	3924	6.32	11.43	23	3.61	63	29	4.6
Jacksonville	545	333	61.1	3947	54	289	3658	7.24	11.85	22	4.04	67t	15	2.8
Buffalo	546	312	57.1	3936	59	360	3576	7.21	12.62	20	3.66	74t	10	1.8
San Diego	578	311	53.8	3540	53	302	3238	6.12	11.38	19	3.29	83t	30	5.2
New England	565	328	58.1	3461	48	280	3181	6.13	10.55	18	3.19	59	15	2.7
Oakland	475	284	59.8	3430	28	124	3306	7.22	12.08	28	5.89	84t	11	2.3
Tennessee	462	286	61.9	3430	27	164	3266	7.42	11.99	18	3.90	67	16	3.5
Seattle	507	308	60.7	3198	46	238	2960	6.31	10.38	21	4.14	71	21	4.1
Baltimore	504	287	56.9	3102	43	287	2815	6.15	10.81	20	3.97	59t	19	3.8
Pittsburgh	439	217	49.4	2738	43	220	2518	6.24	12.62	12	2.73	77t	10	2.3
Cleveland	483	278	57.6	2728	40	283	2445	5.65	9.81	9	1.86	79	19	3.9
Miami	421	243	57.7	2720	28	153	2567	6.46	11.19	15	3.56	61	17	4.0
Cincinnati	454	207	45.6	2219	52	273	1946	4.89	10.72	6	1.32	46	14	3.1
AFC Total	8338	4799	—	55757	625	3683	52074	—	—	321	—	84t	268	—
AFC Average	521.1	299.9	57.6	3484.8	39.1	230.2	3254.6	6.69	11.62	20.1	3.8	—	16.8	3.2

2000 INDIVIDUAL STATISTICS—PASSING

NFC PASSING—TEAM

	Att.	Comp.	Pct. Comp.	Gross Yards	Sacked	Yds. Lost	Net Yards	Yds./ Att.	Yds./ Comp.	TD	Pct. TD	Long	Int.	Pct. Int.
St. Louis	587	380	64.7	5492	44	260	5232	9.36	14.45	37	6.30	85t	23	3.9
San Francisco	583	366	62.8	4400	25	161	4239	7.55	12.02	32	5.49	69t	10	1.7
Minnesota	495	307	62.0	4019	35	187	3832	8.12	13.09	33	6.67	78t	18	3.6
Green Bay	600	348	58.0	3916	34	238	3678	6.53	11.25	21	3.50	67t	16	2.7
Washington	561	343	61.1	3892	32	244	3648	6.94	11.35	18	3.21	77t	21	3.7
Carolina	566	340	60.1	3850	69	382	3468	6.80	11.32	19	3.36	54	19	3.4
N.Y. Giants	529	311	58.8	3610	28	243	3367	6.82	11.61	22	4.16	59	13	2.5
New Orleans	497	298	60.0	3573	39	244	3329	7.19	11.99	22	4.43	53t	15	3.0
Arizona	554	316	57.0	3478	35	228	3250	6.28	11.01	16	2.89	70t	24	4.3
Philadelphia	575	331	57.6	3386	45	262	3124	5.89	10.23	21	3.65	70t	15	2.6
Atlanta	514	285	55.4	3166	61	386	2780	6.16	11.11	14	2.72	55	20	3.9
Chicago	542	304	56.1	3005	34	200	2805	5.54	9.88	12	2.21	68t	16	3.0
Detroit	503	277	55.1	2992	53	317	2675	5.95	10.80	14	2.78	59	19	3.8
Tampa Bay	433	237	54.7	2824	38	241	2583	6.52	11.92	18	4.16	75	13	3.0
Dallas	445	255	57.3	2771	35	249	2522	6.23	10.87	14	3.15	76t	21	4.7
NFC Total	7984	4698	—	54374	607	3842	50532	—	—	313	—	85t	263	—
NFC Average	532.3	313.2	58.8	3624.9	40.5	256.1	3368.8	6.81	11.57	20.9	3.9	—	17.5	3.3
League Total	16322	9497	—	110131	1232	7525	102606	—	—	634	—	85t	531	—
League Average	526.5	306.4	58.2	3552.6	39.7	242.7	3309.9	6.75	11.60	20.5	3.9	—	17.1	3.3

Leader based on net yards

NFL TOP TEN PASSERS

	Att.	Comp.	Pct. Comp.	Yds.	Avg. Gain	TD	Pct. TD	Long	Int.	Pct. Int.	Sack	Yds. Lost	Rating Points
Griese, Brian, Den.	336	216	64.3	2688	8.00	19	5.7	61	4	1.2	17	139	102.9
Green, Trent, St.L.	240	145	60.4	2063	8.60	16	6.7	64	5	2.1	24	145	101.8
Warner, Kurt, St.L.	347	235	67.7	3429	9.88	21	6.1	85t	18	5.2	20	115	98.3
Culpepper, Daunte, Minn.	474	297	62.7	3937	8.31	33	7.0	78t	16	3.4	34	181	98.0
Garcia, Jeff, S.F.	561	355	63.3	4278	7.63	31	5.5	69t	10	1.8	24	155	97.6
Manning, Peyton, Ind.	571	357	.62.5	4413	7.73	33	5.8	78t	15	2.6	20	131	94.7
Gannon, Rich, Oak.	473	284	60.0	3430	7.25	28	5.9	84t	11	2.3	28	124	92.4
Grbac, Elvis, K.C.	547	326	59.6	4169	7.62	28	5.1	81t	14	2.6	29	213	89.9
Flutie, Doug, Buff.	231	132	57.1	1700	7.36	8	3.5	52	3	1.3	10	68	86.5
Brunell, Mark, Jax.	512	311	60.7	3640	7.11	20	3.9	67t	14	2.7	54	289	84.0

AFC PASSING—INDIVIDUAL

	Att.	Comp.	Pct. Comp.	Yds.	Avg. Gain	TD	Pct. TD	Long	Int.	Pct. Int.	Sack	Yds. Lost	Rating Points
Griese, Brian, Den.	336	216	64.3	2688	8.00	19	5.7	61	4	1.2	17	139	102.9
Manning, Peyton, Ind.	571	357	62.5	4413	7.73	33	5.8	78t	15	2.6	20	131	94.7
Gannon, Rich, Oak.	473	284	60.0	3430	7.25	28	5.9	84t	11	2.3	28	124	92.4
Grbac, Elvis, K.C.	547	326	59.6	4169	7.62	28	5.1	81t	14	2.6	29	213	89.9
Flutie, Doug, Buff.	231	132	57.1	1700	7.36	8	3.5	52	3	1.3	10	68	86.5
Brunell, Mark, Jax.	512	311	60.7	3640	7.11	20	3.9	67t	14	2.7	54	289	84.0
McNair, Steve, Tenn.	396	248	62.6	2847	7.19	15	3.8	56t	13	3.3	24	141	83.2
Johnson, Rob, Buff.	306	175	57.2	2125	6.94	12	3.9	74t	7	2.3	49	292	82.2
Frerotte, Gus, Den.	232	138	59.5	1776	7.66	9	3.9	44	8	3.4	12	77	82.1
Bledsoe, Drew, N.E.	531	312	58.8	3291	6.20	17	3.2	59	13	2.4	45	264	77.3
Dilfer, Trent, Balt.	226	134	59.3	1502	6.65	12	5.3	59t	11	4.9	23	135	76.6
Kitna, Jon, Sea.	418	259	62.0	2658	6.36	18	4.3	71	19	4.5	33	166	75.6
Fiedler, Jay, Mia.	357	204	57.1	2402	6.73	14	3.9	61	14	3.9	23	129	74.5
Stewart, Kordell, Pitt.	289	151	52.2	1860	6.44	11	3.8	45t	8	2.8	30	150	73.6
Banks, Tony, Balt.	274	150	54.7	1578	5.76	8	2.9	53t	8	2.9	20	152	69.3
Testaverde, Vinny, NYJ	590	328	55.6	3732	6.33	21	3.6	63	25	4.2	13	71	69.0
Leaf, Ryan, S.D.	322	161	50.0	1883	5.85	11	3.4	83t	18	5.6	31	155	56.2
Smith, Akili, Cin.	267	118	44.2	1253	4.69	3	1.1	46	6	2.2	36	191	52.8
(Nonqualifiers)													
Martin, Jamie, Jax.	33	22	66.7	307	9.30	2	6.1	65t	1	3.0	0	0	104.0
Couch, Tim, Cle.	215	137	63.7	1483	6.90	7	3.3	79	9	4.2	10	78	77.3
Huard, Brock, Sea.	87	49	56.3	540	6.21	3	3.4	45	2	2.3	13	72	76.8
Harbaugh, Jim, S.D.	202	123	60.9	1416	7.01	8	4.0	62t	10	5.0	14	96	74.6
O'Donnell, Neil, Tenn.	64	36	56.3	530	8.28	2	3.1	67	3	4.7	3	23	74.3
Graham, Kent, Pitt.	148	66	44.6	878	5.93	1	0.7	77t	1	0.7	13	70	63.4
Moon, Warren, K.C.	34	15	44.1	208	6.12	1	2.9	41	1	2.9	5	46	61.9
Huard, Damon, Mia.	63	39	61.9	318	5.05	1	1.6	29	3	4.8	4	22	60.2
Pederson, Doug, Cle.	210	117	55.7	1047	4.99	2	1.0	67	8	3.8	17	116	56.6
Mitchell, Scott, Cin.	187	89	47.6	966	5.17	3	1.6	38	8	4.3	16	82	50.8
Moreno, Moses, S.D.	53	27	50.9	241	4.55	0	0.0	26	2	3.8	8	51	47.8
Wynn, Spergon, Cle.	54	22	40.7	167	3.09	0	0.0	32	1	1.9	13	89	41.2
Friesz, John, N.E.	21	11	52.4	66	3.14	0	0.0	17	1	4.8	3	16	39.0
Lucas, Ray, NYJ	41	21	51.2	206	5.02	0	0.0	30	4	9.8	6	24	26.1
(Fewer than 10 attempts)													
Bettis, Jerome, Pitt.	2	0	0.0	0	0.00	0	0.0	0	1	50.0	0	0	0.0
Bishop, Michael, N.E.	9	3	33.3	80	8.89	1	11.1	44t	1	11.1	0	0	64.4
Brady, Tom, N.E.	3	1	33.3	6	2.00	0	0.0	6	0	0.0	0	0	42.4

2000 INDIVIDUAL STATISTICS—PASSING

	Att.	Comp.	Pct. Comp.	Yds.	Avg. Gain	TD	Pct. TD	Long	Int.	Pct. Int.	Sack	Yds. Lost	Rating Points
Brown, Travis, Sea.	1	0	0.0	0	0.00	0	0.0	0	0	0.0	0	0	39.6
Chancey, Robert, S.D.	1	0	0.0	0	0.00	0	0.0	0	0	0.0	0	0	39.6
Feagles, Jeff, Sea.	1	0	0.0	0	0.00	0	0.0	0	0	0.0	0	0	39.6
Hoying, Bobby, Oak.	2	0	0.0	0	0.00	0	0.0	0	0	0.0	0	0	39.6
Jackson, Jarious, Den.	1	0	0.0	0	0.00	0	0.0	0	0	0.0	1	5	39.6
Johnson, Kevin, Cle.	3	1	33.3	23	7.67	0	0.0	23	1	33.3	0	0	22.2
Johnson, Lee, N.E.	1	1	100.0	18	18.00	0	0.0	18	0	0.0	0	0	118.8
Lewis, Jermaine, Balt.	1	1	100.0	3	3.00	0	0.0	3	0	0.0	0	0	79.2
Martin, Curtis, NYJ	1	1	100.0	18	18.00	1	100.0	18t	0	0.0	0	0	158.3
Mohr, Chris, Buff.	1	1	100.0	44	44.00	0	0.0	44	0	0.0	0	0	118.8
Morris, Sylvester, K.C.	1	1	100.0	31	31.00	0	0.0	31	0	0.0	0	0	118.8
Pennington, Chad, NYJ	5	2	40.0	67	13.40	1	20.0	62	0	0.0	1	4	127.1
Redman, Chris, Balt.	3	2	66.7	19	6.33	0	0.0	12	0	0.0	0	0	84.0
Smith, Lamar, Mia.	1	0	0.0	0	0.00	0	0.0	0	0	0.0	0	0	39.6
Thomas, Thurman, Mia.	0	0	—	0	—	0	—	—	0	—	1	2	—
Thompson, Kevin, Cle.	1	1	100.0	8	8.00	0	0.0	8	0	0.0	0	0	100.0
Van Pelt, Alex, Buff.	8	4	50.0	67	8.38	0	0.0	36	0	0.0	0	0	78.6
Wycheck, Frank, Tenn.	2	2	100.0	53	26.50	1	50.0	30t	0	0.0	0	0	158.3

t = Touchdown
Leader based on rating points, minimum 224 attempts

NFC PASSING—INDIVIDUAL

	Att.	Comp.	Pct. Comp.	Yds.	Avg. Gain	TD	Pct. TD	Long	Int.	Pct. Int.	Sack	Yds. Lost	Rating Points
Green, Trent, St.L.	240	145	60.4	2063	8.60	16	6.7	64	5	2.1	24	145	101.8
Warner, Kurt, St.L.	347	235	67.7	3429	9.88	21	6.1	85t	18	5.2	20	115	98.3
Culpepper, Daunte, Minn.	474	297	62.7	3937	8.31	33	7.0	78t	16	3.4	34	181	98.0
Garcia, Jeff, S.F.	561	355	63.3	4278	7.63	31	5.5	69t	10	1.8	24	155	97.6
Collins, Kerry, NYG	529	311	58.8	3610	6.82	22	4.2	59	13	2.5	28	243	83.1
Blake, Jeff, N.O.	302	184	60.9	2025	6.71	13	4.3	49t	9	3.0	24	150	82.7
Beuerlein, Steve, Car.	533	324	60.8	3730	7.00	19	3.6	54	18	3.4	62	331	79.7
Favre, Brett, G.B.	580	338	58.3	3812	6.57	20	3.4	67t	16	2.8	33	236	78.0
McNabb, Donovan, Phil.	569	330	58.0	3365	5.91	21	3.7	70t	13	2.3	45	262	77.8
King, Shaun, T.B.	428	233	54.4	2769	6.47	18	4.2	75	13	3.0	37	240	75.8
Johnson, Brad, Wash.	365	228	62.5	2505	6.86	11	3.0	77t	15	4.1	20	150	75.7
Chandler, Chris, Atl.	331	192	58.0	2236	6.76	10	3.0	55	12	3.6	40	251	73.5
McNown, Cade, Chi.	280	154	55.0	1646	5.88	8	2.9	68t	9	3.2	27	169	68.5
Batch, Charlie, Det.	412	221	53.6	2489	6.04	13	3.2	59	15	3.6	41	242	67.3
Plummer, Jake, Ariz.	475	270	56.8	2946	6.20	13	2.7	70t	21	4.4	22	151	66.0
Aikman, Troy, Dall.	262	156	59.5	1632	6.23	7	2.7	48	14	5.3	13	91	64.3
(Nonqualifiers)													
Greisen, Chris, Ariz.	10	6	60.0	65	6.50	1	10.0	26t	0	0.0	3	24	112.5
Mirer, Rick, S.F.	20	10	50.0	126	6.30	1	5.0	26	0	0.0	1	6	86.7
Hasselbeck, Matt, G.B.	19	10	52.6	104	5.47	1	5.3	27t	0	0.0	1	2	86.3
Brooks, Aaron, N.O.	194	113	58.2	1514	7.80	9	4.6	53t	6	3.1	15	94	85.7
Cunningham, Randall, Dall.	125	74	59.2	849	6.79	6	4.8	76t	4	3.2	8	45	82.4
George, Jeff, Wash.	194	113	58.2	1389	7.16	7	3.6	50	6	3.1	12	94	79.6
Brown, Dave, Ariz.	69	40	58.0	467	6.77	2	2.9	44t	3	4.3	10	53	70.1
Miller, Jim, Chi.	82	47	57.3	382	4.66	1	1.2	34t	1	1.2	2	7	68.2
Matthews, Shane, Chi.	178	102	57.3	964	5.42	3	1.7	41	6	3.4	5	24	64.0
Johnson, Doug, Atl.	67	36	53.7	406	6.06	2	3.0	26	3	4.5	13	75	63.4
Case, Stoney, Det.	91	56	61.5	503	5.53	1	1.1	40t	4	4.4	12	75	61.7
Kanell, Danny, Atl.	116	57	49.1	524	4.52	2	1.7	35	5	4.3	8	60	49.6
Lewis, Jeff, Car.	32	16	50.0	120	3.75	0	0.0	16	1	3.1	7	51	46.4
Brister, Bubby, Minn.	20	10	50.0	82	4.10	0	0.0	20	1	5.0	1	6	40.0
Wright, Anthony, Dall.	53	22	41.5	237	4.47	0	0.0	46	3	5.7	12	92	31.7
(Fewer than 10 attempts)													
Aguiar, Louie, Chi.	1	1	100.0	13	13.00	0	0.0	13	0	0.0	0	0	118.8
Alstott, Mike, T.B.	1	0	0.0	0	0.00	0	0.0	0	0	0.0	0	0	39.6
Berger, Mitch, Minn.	1	0	0.0	0	0.00	0	0.0	0	1	100.0	0	0	0.0
Detmer, Koy, Phil.	1	0	0.0	0	0.00	0	0.0	0	1	100.0	0	0	0.0
Green, Ahman, G.B.	1	0	0.0	0	0.00	0	0.0	0	0	0.0	0	0	39.6
Hamilton, Joe, T.B.	0	0	—	0	—	0	—	—	0	—	1	1	-1.0
Hartsell, Mark, Chi.	1	0	0.0	0	0.00	0	0.0	0	0	0.0	0	0	39.6
Husak, Todd, Wash.	2	2	100.0	-2	-1.00	0	0.0	6	0	0.0	0	0	79.2
Mitchell, Brian, Phil.	4	1	25.0	21	5.25	0	0.0	21	0	0.0	0	0	49.0
Rattay, Tim, S.F.	1	1	100.0	-4	-4.00	0	0.0	-4	0	0.0	0	0	79.2
Rice, Jerry, S.F.	1	0	0.0	0	0.00	0	0.0	0	0	0.0	0	0	39.6
Royals, Mark, T.B.	1	1	100.0	36	36.00	0	0.0	36	0	0.0	0	0	118.8
Small, Torrance, Phil.	1	0	0.0	0	0.00	0	0.0	0	1	100.0	0	0	0.0
Stoerner, Clint, Dall.	5	3	60.0	53	10.60	1	20.0	29	0	0.0	2	21	135.8
Walter, Ken, Car.	1	0	0.0	0	0.00	0	0.0	0	0	0.0	0	0	39.6
Williams, Ricky, N.O.	1	1	100.0	34	34.00	0	0.0	34	0	0.0	0	0	118.8
Zeier, Eric, T.B.	3	3	100.0	19	6.33	0	0.0	14	0	0.0	0	0	93.1

t = Touchdown
Leader based on rating points, minimum 224 attempts

PASS RECEIVING

Receptions

AFC: 102—Marvin Harrison, Indianapolis
NFC: 102—Muhsin Muhammad, Carolina

Receptions, Game

NFC: 20—Terrell Owens, San Francisco vs. Chicago, December 17 (283 yards, 1 TD)
AFC: 15—Jimmy Smith, Jacksonville at Baltimore, September 10 (291 yards, 3 TD)

Yards

NFC: 1635—Torry Holt, St. Louis
AFC: 1602—Rod Smith, Denver

Yards, Game

AFC: 291—Jimmy Smith, Jacksonville at Baltimore, September 10 (15 receptions, 3 TD)
NFC: 283—Terrell Owens, San Francisco vs. Chicago, December 17 (20 receptions, 1 TD)

Longest

NFC: 85—Torry Holt (from Kurt Warner), St. Louis at Atlanta, September 24 - TD
AFC: 84—James Jett (from Rich Gannon), Oakland vs. Atlanta, November 5 - TD

Yards Per Reception

NFC: 19.9—Torry Holt, St. Louis
AFC: 17.8—Derrick Alexander, Kansas City

Touchdowns

NFC: 15—Randy Moss, Minnesota
AFC: 14—Marvin Harrison, Indianapolis

Team Leaders, Receptions

AFC: BALTIMORE 67, Shannon Sharpe; BUFFALO 94, Eric Moulds; CINCINNATI 51, Peter Warrick; CLEVELAND 57, Kevin Johnson; DENVER 101, Ed McCaffrey; INDIANAPOLIS 102, Marvin Harrison; JACKSONVILLE 94, Keenan McCardell; KANSAS CITY 93, Tony Gonzalez; MIAMI 56, Oronde Gadsden; NEW ENGLAND 83, Troy Brown; N.Y. JETS 88, Richie Anderson; OAKLAND 76, Tim Brown; PITTSBURGH 48, Hines Ward; SAN DIEGO 71, Freddie Jones; SEATTLE 63, Sean Dawkins, Ricky Watters; TENNESSEE 70, Frank Wycheck

NFC: ARIZONA 73, Michael Pittman; ATLANTA 60, Shawn Jefferson; CAROLINA 102, Muhsin Muhammad; CHICAGO 55, Eddie Kennison, Marcus Robinson; DALLAS 52, James McKnight; DETROIT 61, Johnnie Morton; GREEN BAY 73, Ahman Green; MINNESOTA 96, Cris Carter; NEW ORLEANS 94, Joe Horn; N.Y. GIANTS 78, Amani Toomer; PHILADELPHIA 69, Chad Lewis; ST. LOUIS 87, Isaac Bruce; SAN FRANCISCO 97, Terrell Owens; TAMPA BAY 71, Keyshawn Johnson; WASHINGTON 81, Larry Centers

NFL TOP TEN PASS RECEIVERS

	No.	Yards	Avg.	Long	TD
Harrison, Marvin, Ind.	102	1413	13.9	78t	14
Muhammad, Muhsin, Car.	102	1183	11.6	36	6
McCaffrey, Ed, Den.	101	1317	13.0	61	9
Smith, Rod, Den.	100	1602	16.0	49	8
Owens, Terrell, S.F.	97	1451	15.0	69t	13
Carter, Cris, Minn.	96	1274	13.3	53	9
Horn, Joe, N.O.	94	1340	14.3	52	8
Moulds, Eric, Buff.	94	1326	14.1	52	5
McCardell, Keenan, Jax.	94	1207	12.8	67t	5
Gonzalez, Tony, K.C.	93	1203	12.9	39	9

NFL TOP TEN PASS RECEIVERS BY YARDS

	Yards	No.	Avg.	Long	TD
Holt, Torry, St.L.	1635	82	19.9	85t	6
Smith, Rod, Den.	1602	100	16.0	49	8
Bruce, Isaac, St.L.	1471	87	16.9	78t	9
Owens, Terrell, S.F.	1451	97	15.0	69t	13
Moss, Randy, Minn.	1437	77	18.7	78t	15
Harrison, Marvin, Ind.	1413	102	13.9	78t	14
Alexander, Derrick, K.C.	1391	78	17.8	81t	10
Horn, Joe, N.O.	1340	94	14.3	52	8
Moulds, Eric, Buff.	1326	94	14.1	52	5
McCaffrey, Ed, Den.	1317	101	13.0	61	9

AFC RECEIVERS—INDIVIDUAL

	No.	Yards	Avg.	Long	TD
Harrison, Marvin, Ind.	102	1413	13.9	78t	14
McCaffrey, Ed, Den.	101	1317	13.0	61	9
Smith, Rod, Den.	100	1602	16.0	49	8
Moulds, Eric, Buff.	94	1326	14.1	52	5
McCardell, Keenan, Jax.	94	1207	12.8	67t	5
Gonzalez, Tony, K.C.	93	1203	12.9	39	9
Smith, Jimmy, Jax.	91	1213	13.3	65t	8
Anderson, Richie, NYJ	88	853	9.7	41	2
Brown, Troy, N.E.	83	944	11.4	44t	4
Glenn, Terry, N.E.	79	963	12.2	39t	6
Alexander, Derrick, K.C.	78	1391	17.8	81t	10
Brown, Tim, Oak.	76	1128	14.8	45	11
Jones, Freddie, S.D.	71	766	10.8	44	5
Wycheck, Frank, Tenn.	70	636	9.1	26	4
Martin, Curtis, NYJ	70	508	7.3	31	2
Chrebet, Wayne, NYJ	69	937	13.6	50	8
Sharpe, Shannon, Balt.	67	810	12.1	59t	5
Brady, Kyle, Jax.	64	729	11.4	36	3
Mason, Derrick, Tenn.	63	895	14.2	34	5
Dawkins, Sean, Sea.	63	731	11.6	40	5
Watters, Ricky, Sea.	63	613	9.7	59	2
James, Edgerrin, Ind.	63	594	9.4	60	5
Richardson, Tony, K.C.	58	468	8.1	24	3
Johnson, Kevin, Cle.	57	669	11.7	79	0
Gadsden, Oronde, Mia.	56	786	14.0	61	6
Graham, Jeff, S.D.	55	907	16.5	83t	4
Ward, Dedric, NYJ	54	801	14.8	61	3
Jackson, Darrell, Sea.	53	713	13.5	71	6
Conway, Curtis, S.D.	53	712	13.4	68t	5
Price, Peerless, Buff.	52	762	14.7	42	3
Warrick, Peter, Cin.	51	592	11.6	46	4
Faulk, Kevin, N.E.	51	465	9.1	52t	1
Pathon, Jerome, Ind.	50	646	12.9	38	3
George, Eddie, Tenn.	50	453	9.1	24	2
Ismail, Qadry, Balt.	49	655	13.4	53t	5
Carswell, Dwayne, Den.	49	495	10.1	43t	3
Morris, Sylvester, K.C.	48	678	14.1	47	3
Ward, Hines, Pitt.	48	672	14.0	77t	4
Fletcher, Terrell, S.D.	48	355	7.4	26	1
Dilger, Ken, Ind.	47	538	11.4	32	3
McDaniel, Jeremy, Buff.	43	697	16.2	74t	2
Wilkins, Terrence, Ind.	43	569	13.2	43t	3
Rison, Andre, Oak.	41	606	14.8	49	6
Shaw, Bobby, Pitt.	40	672	16.8	45t	4
Northcutt, Dennis, Cle.	39	422	10.8	37	0
Patten, David, Cle.	38	546	14.4	65	1
Morris, Sammy, Buff.	37	268	7.2	24	1
Prentice, Travis, Cle.	37	191	5.2	13	1
Taylor, Fred, Jax.	36	240	6.7	19	2
Shepherd, Leslie, Mia.	35	446	12.7	46t	4
Sanders, Chris, Tenn.	33	536	16.2	54	0
Lockett, Kevin, K.C.	33	422	12.8	34t	2
Bryson, Shawn, Buff.	32	271	8.5	32	2
Holmes, Priest, Balt.	32	221	6.9	27	0
Riemersma, Jay, Buff.	31	372	12.0	35	5
Smith, Lamar, Mia.	31	201	6.5	28	2
Pollard, Marcus, Ind.	30	439	14.6	50t	3
Shea, Aaron, Cle.	30	302	10.1	37	2
Dudley, Rickey, Oak.	29	350	12.1	30	4
Mayes, Derrick, Sea.	29	264	9.1	40	1
Mili, Itula, Sea.	28	288	10.3	34	3
Taylor, Travis, Balt.	28	276	9.9	40	3
Fauria, Christian, Sea.	28	237	8.5	16	2
Clark, Desmond, Den.	27	339	12.6	44	3
Jordan, Randy, Oak.	27	299	11.1	55	1
Lewis, Jamal, Balt.	27	296	11.0	45	0
Martin, Tony, Mia.	26	393	15.1	44	0
McGee, Tony, Cin.	26	309	11.9	39	1
Ritchie, Jon, Oak.	26	173	6.7	17	0
Yeast, Craig, Cin.	24	301	12.5	27	0
Anderson, Mike, Den.	23	169	7.3	18	0
Ayanbadejo, Obafemi, Balt.	23	168	7.3	26	1
Strong, Mack, Sea.	23	141	6.1	24	1
Coles, Laveranues, NYJ	22	370	16.8	63	1
Chamberlain, Byron, Den.	22	283	12.9	38	1
Burress, Plaxico, Pitt.	22	273	12.4	39	0
Jones, Reggie, S.D.	22	253	11.5	34	0
Jett, James, Oak.	20	356	17.8	84t	2
Wheatley, Tyrone, Oak.	20	156	7.8	17	1
Bjornson, Eric, N.E.	20	152	7.6	19	2
Redmond, J.R., N.E.	20	126	6.3	20	2

2000 INDIVIDUAL STATISTICS—PASS RECEIVING

	No.	Yards	Avg.	Long	TD
Farmer, Danny, Cin.	19	268	14.1	38	0
Hawkins, Courtney, Pitt.	19	238	12.5	33	1
Kinney, Erron, Tenn.	19	197	10.4	19	1
Bennett, Brandon, Cin.	19	168	8.8	25	0
Lewis, Jermaine, Balt.	19	161	8.5	26	1
Edwards, Troy, Pitt.	18	215	11.9	27	0
Wiggins, Jermaine, NYJ-N.E.	18	207	11.5	59	2
Green, E.G., Ind.	18	201	11.2	34t	1
Dillon, Corey, Cin.	18	158	8.8	31	0
McCrary, Fred, S.D.	18	141	7.8	19	2
Bruener, Mark, Pitt.	17	192	11.3	30t	3
Becht, Anthony, NYJ	16	144	9.0	30	2
Edwards, Marc, Cle.	16	128	8.0	21t	2
Thomas, Thurman, Mia.	16	117	7.3	15	1
Fazande, Jermaine, S.D.	16	104	6.5	17	0
Griffith, Howard, Den.	16	101	6.3	16	2
Thigpen, Yancey, Tenn.	15	289	19.3	56t	2
Rutledge, Rod, N.E.	15	103	6.9	16	1
Anders, Kimble, K.C.	15	76	5.1	12	0
Simmons, Tony, N.E.	14	231	16.5	46	1
Soward, R.Jay, Jax.	14	154	11.0	45	1
McDuffie, O.J., Mia.	14	143	10.2	24	0
Dugans, Ron, Cin.	14	125	8.9	17	1
Denson, Autry, Mia.	14	105	7.5	28	0
Konrad, Rob, Mia.	14	83	5.9	18	0
Rhett, Errict, Cle.	14	78	5.6	16	0
Gaylor, Trevor, S.D.	13	182	14.0	62t	1
Whitted, Alvis, Jax.	13	137	10.5	37t	3
Kaufman, Napoleon, Oak.	13	127	9.8	25	1
Brigham, Jeremy, Oak.	13	107	8.2	19	2
Battaglia, Marco, Cin.	13	105	8.1	15	0
White, Jamel, Cle.	13	100	7.7	25	0
Bettis, Jerome, Pitt.	13	97	7.5	25	0
Johnson, Patrick, Balt.	12	156	13.0	46t	2
Johnson, Anthony, Jax.	12	153	12.8	48	0
Campbell, Mark, Cle.	12	80	6.7	17	1
Stokley, Brandon, Balt.	11	184	16.7	32	2
Fuamatu-Ma'afala, Chris, Pitt.	11	107	9.7	25	0
Groce, Clif, Cin.	11	45	4.1	14	0
Pickens, Carl, Tenn.	10	242	24.2	67	0
Weaver, Jed, Mia.	10	179	17.9	41	0
Huntley, Richard, Pitt.	10	91	9.1	19	0
Crockett, Zack, Oak.	10	62	6.2	15	0
Johnson, J.J., Mia.	10	61	6.1	11	0
Dawson, JaJuan, Cle.	9	97	10.8	26	1
Coates, Ben, Balt.	9	84	9.3	28	0
Carter, Tony, N.E.	9	73	8.1	21	0
Parmalee, Bernie, NYJ	9	66	7.3	18	0
Neal, Lorenzo, Tenn.	9	31	3.4	8	2
Williams, James, Sea.	8	99	12.4	18	0
Drayton, Troy, K.C.	8	70	8.8	21	2
Chiaverini, Darrin, Cle.	8	68	8.5	18	1
Thomas, Rodney, Tenn.	8	35	4.4	9t	1
Emanuel, Bert, Mia.	7	132	18.9	53t	1
Williams, Nick, Cin.	7	84	12.0	20	0
Hayes, Windrell, NYJ	6	126	21.0	32	0
Dyson, Kevin, Tenn.	6	104	17.3	30t	1
Sowell, Jerald, NYJ	6	84	14.0	62	0
Collins, Bobby, Buff.	6	72	12.0	23	0
Bailey, Karsten, Sea.	6	62	10.3	22	1
Goodwin, Hunter, Mia.	6	36	6.0	9t	1
Heiden, Steve, S.D.	6	32	5.3	10	1
Gash, Sam, Balt.	6	30	5.0	9	1
Calloway, Chris, N.E.	5	95	19.0	28	0
Jackson, Curtis, N.E.	5	44	8.8	13	0
Kreider, Dan, Pitt.	5	42	8.4	14	0
Alexander, Shaun, Sea.	5	41	8.2	18	0
Jackson, Sheldon, Buff.	5	36	7.2	12	1
Witman, Jon, Pitt.	5	33	6.6	11	0
Cavil, Kwame, Buff.	4	66	16.5	39	0
Brisby, Vincent, NYJ	4	60	15.0	19	0
Shelton, Daimon, Jax.	4	48	12.0	16	0
Dunn, David, Oak.	4	33	8.3	14	0
Baxter, Fred, NYJ	4	22	5.5	12t	2
Harris, Raymont, Den.-N.E.	4	20	5.0	16	0
Cushing, Matt, Pitt.	4	17	4.3	5	0
Pass, Patrick, N.E.	4	17	4.3	15	0
Finn, Jim, Ind.	4	13	3.3	6	1
Geason, Cory, Pitt.	3	66	22.0	36	0
Davis, Billy, Balt.	3	62	20.7	28	0
Brooks, Robert, Den.	3	51	17.0	25	0
Parker, Larry, K.C.	3	41	13.7	27	0
Bush, Steve, Cin.	3	39	13.0	18	0
Ricks, Mikhael, S.D.	3	35	11.7	23	0
Howard, Chris, Jax.	3	26	8.7	13	0
Smith, Antowain, Buff.	3	20	6.7	9	0
Kirby, Terry, Oak.	3	19	6.3	9	0
Roan, Michael, Tenn.	3	12	4.0	6	0
Gary, Olandis, Den.	3	10	3.3	7	0
Linton, Jonathan, Buff.	3	8	2.7	4t	1
McGriff, Travis, Den.	2	51	25.5	43t	1
Dunn, Jason, K.C.	2	26	13.0	20	0
Griffin, Damon, Cin.	2	25	12.5	16	0
Ogden, Jeff, Mia.	2	24	12.0	12	0
Blackwell, Will, Pitt.	2	23	11.5	14	0
Bennett, Donnell, K.C.	2	17	8.5	13	0
Cloud, Mike, K.C.	2	16	8.0	13	0
Brown, Bobby, Cle.	2	14	7.0	8	0
Dyer, Deon, Mia.	2	14	7.0	13	0
Bynum, Kenny, S.D.	2	13	6.5	7	0
Davis, Shockmain, N.E.	2	12	6.0	9	0
Shaw, Harold, N.E.	2	11	5.5	8	0
Brown, Reggie, Sea.	2	9	4.5	6	0
Davis, Terrell, Den.	2	4	2.0	5	0
Coleman, Marcus, NYJ	1	45	45.0	45t	1
Porter, Daryl, Buff.	1	44	44.0	44	0
Barlow, Reggie, Jax.	1	28	28.0	28	0
Jacquet, Nate, S.D.	1	25	25.0	25	0
Saleh, Tarek, Cle.	1	22	22.0	22	0
Floyd, Chris, N.E.	1	21	21.0	21	0
Jones, Damon, Jax.	1	12	12.0	12	0
Montgomery, Scottie, Den.	1	10	10.0	10	0
Davis, Reggie, S.D.	1	8	8.0	8	0
Woodson, Charles, Oak.	1	8	8.0	8	0
Miller, Billy, Den.	1	7	7.0	7	0
Chancey, Robert, S.D.	1	6	6.0	6	0
Dunn, Damon, Cle.	1	6	6.0	6	0
Porter, Jerry, Oak.	1	6	6.0	6	0
Coleman, KaRon, Den.	1	5	5.0	5	0
Jackson, Lenzie, Cle.	1	5	5.0	5	0
Elliott, Jumbo, NYJ	1	3	3.0	3t	1
Jenkins, Ronney, S.D.	1	1	1.0	1	0
Smith, Detron, Den.	1	1	1.0	1t	1
Dilfer, Trent, Balt.	1	-1	-1.0	-1	0
Johnson, Rob, Buff.	1	-6	-6.0	-6	0

t = Touchdown
Leader based on receptions

NFC RECEIVERS—INDIVIDUAL

	No.	Yards	Avg.	Long	TD
Muhammad, Muhsin, Car.	102	1183	11.6	36	6
Owens, Terrell, S.F.	97	1451	15.0	69t	13
Carter, Cris, Minn.	96	1274	13.3	53	9
Horn, Joe, N.O.	94	1340	14.3	52	8
Bruce, Isaac, St.L.	87	1471	16.9	78t	9
Holt, Torry, St.L.	82	1635	19.9	85t	6
Faulk, Marshall, St.L.	81	830	10.2	72t	8
Centers, Larry, Wash.	81	600	7.4	26	3
Toomer, Amani, NYG	78	1094	14.0	54t	7
Moss, Randy, Minn.	77	1437	18.7	78t	15
Rice, Jerry, S.F.	75	805	10.7	68t	7
Pittman, Michael, Ariz.	73	579	7.9	36t	2
Green, Ahman, G.B.	73	559	7.7	31	3
Boston, David, Ariz.	71	1156	16.3	70t	7
Johnson, Keyshawn, T.B.	71	874	12.3	38	8
Barber, Tiki, NYG	70	719	10.3	36	1
Lewis, Chad, Phil.	69	735	10.7	52	3
Garner, Charlie, S.F.	68	647	9.5	62	3
Hayes, Donald, Car.	66	926	14.0	43t	3
Schroeder, Bill, G.B.	65	999	15.4	55t	4
Freeman, Antonio, G.B.	62	912	14.7	67t	9
Morton, Johnnie, Det.	61	788	12.9	42t	3
Jefferson, Shawn, Atl.	60	822	13.7	49	2
Mathis, Terance, Atl.	57	679	11.9	44t	5
Johnson, Charles, Phil.	56	642	11.5	59	7
Hilliard, Ike, NYG	55	787	14.3	59	8
Robinson, Marcus, Chi.	55	738	13.4	68t	5
Kennison, Eddie, Chi.	55	549	10.0	26	2
Sanders, Frank, Ariz.	54	749	13.9	53t	6
Hakim, Az-Zahir, St.L.	53	734	13.8	80t	4
McKnight, James, Dall.	52	926	17.8	48	2
Green, Jacquez, T.B.	51	773	15.2	75	1

2000 INDIVIDUAL STATISTICS—PASS RECEIVING

	No.	Yards	Avg.	Long	TD
Thrash, James, Wash.	50	653	13.1	50	2
Alexander, Stephen, Wash.	47	510	10.9	30	2
Booker, Marty, Chi.	47	490	10.4	41	2
Dunn, Warrick, T.B.	44	422	9.6	45	1
Williams, Ricky, N.O.	44	409	9.3	24	1
Christian, Bob, Atl.	44	315	7.2	19	0
Anderson, Jamal, Atl.	42	382	9.1	55	0
Fryar, Irving, Wash.	41	548	13.4	34t	5
Small, Torrance, Phil.	40	569	14.2	70t	3
Moore, Herman, Det.	40	434	10.9	30t	3
Connell, Albert, Wash.	39	762	19.5	77t	3
Harris, Jackie, Dall.	39	306	7.8	21	5
Allen, James, Chi.	39	291	7.5	26	1
Clark, Greg, S.F.	38	342	9.0	34	2
Jackson, Willie, N.O.	37	523	14.1	53t	6
Smith, Robert, Minn.	36	348	9.7	53t	3
Comella, Greg, NYG	36	274	7.6	25	0
Henderson, William, G.B.	35	234	6.7	25	1
Crowell, Germane, Det.	34	430	12.6	50t	3
Franks, Bubba, G.B.	34	363	10.7	27t	1
Biakabutuka, Tim, Car.	34	341	10.0	25	2
Davis, Stephen, Wash.	33	313	9.5	39	0
Sloan, David, Det.	32	379	11.8	59	2
Warren, Chris, Dall.-Phil.	32	303	9.5	76t	1
Stewart, James, Det.	32	287	9.0	32	1
Jones, Thomas, Ariz.	32	208	6.5	20	0
Proehl, Ricky, St.L.	31	441	14.2	29	4
Walls, Wesley, Car.	31	422	13.6	54	2
Kelly, Reggie, Atl.	31	340	11.0	37t	2
Beasley, Fred, S.F.	31	233	7.5	34	3
Martin, Cecil, Phil.	31	219	7.1	26	0
Stokes, J.J., S.F.	30	524	17.5	53	3
Morton, Chad, N.O.	30	213	7.1	35	0
Moore, Dave, T.B.	29	288	9.9	28	3
Hardy, Terry, Ariz.	27	160	5.9	13	1
Dwight, Tim, Atl.	26	406	15.6	52t	3
Brooks, Macey, Chi.	26	216	8.3	27	0
Ismail, Raghib, Dall.	25	350	14.0	44	1
McGarity, Wane, Dall.	25	250	10.0	25	0
Mitchell, Pete, NYG	25	245	9.8	22	1
Staley, Duce, Phil.	25	201	8.0	26	0
Pritchett, Stanley, Phil.	25	193	7.7	17	0
Autry, Darnell, Phil.	24	275	11.5	37	1
Jurevicius, Joe, NYG	24	272	11.3	43	1
Sinceno, Kaseem, Chi.	23	206	9.0	28	0
Thomas, Robert, Dall.	23	117	5.1	14	2
Byrd, Isaac, Car.	22	241	11.0	34t	2
McWilliams, Johnny, Minn.	22	180	8.2	26	3
Driver, Donald, G.B.	21	322	15.3	49	1
Poole, Keith, N.O.	21	293	14.0	49t	1
Glover, Andrew, N.O.	21	281	13.4	39	4
Streets, Tai, S.F.	19	287	15.1	39	0
Mangum, Kris, Car.	19	215	11.3	31	1
Davis, Tyrone, G.B.	19	177	9.3	41	2
Walsh, Chris, Minn.	18	191	10.6	21	0
Jenkins, MarTay, Ariz.	17	219	12.9	34	0
Cody, Mac, Ariz.	17	212	12.5	24	0
Davis, John, Minn.	17	202	11.9	37	1
Foster, Larry, Det.	17	175	10.3	40t	1
Floyd, William, Car.	17	114	6.7	15	1
Reed, Jake, N.O.	16	206	12.9	22	0
Hatchette, Matt, Minn.	16	190	11.9	39t	2
Levens, Dorsey, G.B.	16	146	9.1	37	0
Engram, Bobby, Chi.	16	109	6.8	25	0
Murrell, Adrian, Wash.	16	93	5.8	12	0
Anthony, Reidel, T.B.	15	232	15.5	46t	4
Kozlowski, Brian, Atl.	15	151	10.1	30	2
Hoover, Brad, Car.	15	112	7.5	16	0
Bates, Mario, Det.	15	109	7.3	17	0
Hetherington, Chris, Car.	14	116	8.3	19	1
Wiley, Michael, Dall.	14	72	5.1	15t	1
Tucker, Jason, Dall.	13	126	9.7	18	0
Alstott, Mike, T.B.	13	93	7.2	21	0
Mitchell, Brian, Phil.	13	89	6.8	21	1
LaFleur, David, Dall.	12	109	9.1	19	1
Broughton, Luther, Phil.	12	104	8.7	21	0
Schlesinger, Cory, Det.	12	73	6.1	13	0
Smith, Terrelle, N.O.	12	65	5.4	10	0
Wilson, Robert, N.O.	11	154	14.0	30	0
Williams, Roland, St.L.	11	102	9.3	31t	3
Smith, Emmitt, Dall.	11	79	7.2	19	0
Pinkston, Todd, Phil.	10	181	18.1	45	0

	No.	Yards	Avg.	Long	TD
Lee, Charles, G.B.	10	134	13.4	38	0
Reed, Andre, Wash.	10	103	10.3	21t	1
Kleinsasser, Jimmy, Minn.	10	98	9.8	21	0
White, Dez, Chi.	10	87	8.7	25t	1
Rasby, Walter, Det.	10	78	7.8	17	1
Gedney, Chris, Ariz.	10	75	7.5	24	0
Watson, Justin, St.L.	10	56	5.6	15	0
Thomason, Jeff, Phil.	10	46	4.6	11	5
Allred, John, Chi.	9	109	12.1	25	1
Westbrook, Michael, Wash.	9	103	11.4	21	0
Brown, Na, Phil.	9	80	8.9	18	1
Parker, De'Mond, G.B.	9	50	5.6	10	0
Holcombe, Robert, St.L.	8	90	11.3	19	1
Irvin, Sedrick, Det.	8	90	11.3	18	0
Sellers, Mike, Wash.	8	78	9.8	24	2
Enis, Curtis, Chi.	8	68	8.5	18	0
Jordan, Andrew, Minn.	8	63	7.9	12	0
Stablein, Brian, Det.	8	53	6.6	11	0
Campbell, Dan, NYG	8	46	5.8	13	3
Finneran, Brian, Atl.	7	60	8.6	14	0
Dixon, Ron, NYG	6	92	15.3	34t	1
Hape, Patrick, T.B.	6	39	6.5	13	0
Makovicka, Joel, Ariz.	6	18	3.0	5	0
Mitchell, Tywan, Ariz.	5	80	16.0	42	0
Robinson, Jeff, St.L.	5	52	10.4	27	0
Jackson, Terry, S.F.	5	48	9.6	16	1
Hicks, Skip, Wash.	5	43	8.6	25	0
Conwell, Ernie, St.L.	5	40	8.0	17	0
Bates, Michael, Car.	5	38	7.6	23	0
Hall, Lamont, N.O.	5	33	6.6	13	1
Milne, Brian, N.O.	5	33	6.6	15	1
Galloway, Joey, Dall.	4	62	15.5	22	1
Hodge, Damon, Dall.	4	60	15.0	20	0
Crawford, Casey, Car.	4	47	11.8	16t	1
Uwaezuoke, Iheanyi, Car.	4	46	11.5	21	0
Bates, D'Wayne, Chi.	4	42	10.5	18	0
Mayes, Alonzo, Chi.	4	40	10.0	19	0
Hankton, Karl, Car.	4	38	9.5	14	0
Horne, Tony, St.L.	4	32	8.0	18t	2
Williams, Moe, Minn.	4	31	7.8	12	0
Cross, Howard, NYG	4	30	7.5	18	0
Dragos, Scott, Chi.	4	28	7.0	10	0
Bailey, Champ, Wash.	3	78	26.0	42	0
Olivo, Brock, Det.	3	50	16.7	19	0
Pupunu, Alfred, Det.	3	32	10.7	17	0
Wetnight, Ryan, G.B.	3	20	6.7	9	0
Dayne, Ron, NYG	3	11	3.7	12	0
Smith, Paul, S.F.	2	55	27.5	47	0
Davis, Thabiti, NYG	2	40	20.0	27	0
Williams, Karl, T.B.	2	35	17.5	27	0
Abdullah, Rabih, T.B.	2	14	7.0	11	0
Howard, Desmond, Det.	2	14	7.0	10	0
McKinley, Dennis, Ariz.	2	13	6.5	9	0
Brazzell, Chris, Dall.	2	12	6.0	10	0
Hodgins, James, St.L.	2	5	2.5	3	0
McNabb, Donovan, Phil.	2	5	2.5	3	0
Craig, Dameyune, Car.	2	4	2.0	4	0
Robinson, Damien, T.B.	1	36	36.0	36	0
Lee, Amp, Phil.	1	20	20.0	20	0
Turley, Kyle, N.O.	1	16	16.0	16	0
Stecker, Aaron, T.B.	1	15	15.0	15	0
Wells, Mike, Chi.	1	13	13.0	13	0
German, Jammi, Atl.	1	10	10.0	10	0
Douglas, Dameane, Phil.	1	9	9.0	9	0
Miller, Bubba, Phil.	1	9	9.0	9	0
Flemister, Zeron, Wash.	1	8	8.0	8	0
Milburn, Glyn, Chi.	1	8	8.0	8	0
Swift, Justin, S.F.	1	8	8.0	8	0
Van Dyke, Alex, Phil.	1	8	8.0	8	0
Allen, Terry, N.O.	1	7	7.0	7	0
Barnes, Marlon, Chi.	1	7	7.0	7	0
Kinchen, Brian, Car.	1	7	7.0	7	0
Smith, Maurice, Atl.	1	5	5.0	5	0
Walters, Troy, Minn.	1	5	5.0	5	0
Williams, Clarence, Ariz.	1	5	5.0	5	0
Canidate, Trung, St.L.	1	4	4.0	4	0
Lyman, Dustin, Chi.	1	4	4.0	4	0
Tant, Jay, Ariz.	1	4	4.0	4	0
McDaniel, Randall, T.B.	1	2	2.0	2t	1
Morrow, Harold, Minn.	1	2	2.0	2	0
Yoder, Todd, T.B.	1	1	1.0	1	0
Goodman, Herbert, G.B.	1	0	0.0	0	0

2000 INDIVIDUAL STATISTICS—PASS RECEIVING/INTERCEPTIONS

	No.	Yards	Avg.	Long	TD
Palmer, David, Minn.	1	-2	-2.0	-2	0
Chandler, Chris, Atl.	1	-4	-4.0	-4	0

t = Touchdown
Leader based on receptions

INTERCEPTIONS

Interceptions
NFC: 9—Darren Sharper, Green Bay
AFC: 7—Samari Rolle, Tennessee
7—Brian Walker, Miami

Interceptions, Game
AFC: 3—Marcus Coleman, N.Y. Jets vs. Miami (7 yards, 0 TD) - OT
2—many times
NFC: 3—Kurt Schulz, Detroit at Chicago, September 24 (8 yards, 0 TD)

Yards
AFC: 165—Chris McAlister, Baltimore
NFC: 139—Ashley Ambrose, Atlanta

Longest
NFC: 101—Bryant Westbrook, Detroit vs. New England, November 23 - TD
AFC: 98—Chris McAlister, Baltimore vs. N.Y. Jets, December 24 - TD

Touchdowns
AFC: 3—Eric Allen, Oakland
NFC: 2—Sammy Knight, New Orleans

Team Leaders, Interceptions
AFC: BALTIMORE, 6, Duane Starks; BUFFALO, 5, Keion Carpenter; CINCINNATI, 2, Tom Carter, Takeo Spikes; CLEVELAND, 3, Corey Fuller; DENVER, 6, Terrell Buckley; INDIANAPOLIS, 4, Jeff Burris; JACKSONVILLE, 2, Donovin Darius, Mike Logan, Rayna Stewart; KANSAS CITY, 4, James Hasty; MIAMI, 7, Brian Walker; NEW ENGLAND, 2, Tebucky Jones, Ty Law, Lawyer Milloy; N.Y. JETS, 6, Victor Green; OAKLAND, 6, Eric Allen, William Thomas; PITTSBURGH, 5, Chad Scott, Dewayne Washington; SAN DIEGO, 6, Rodney Harrison; SEATTLE, 4, Jay Bellamy, Willie Williams; TENNESSEE, 7, Samari Rolle
NFC: ARIZONA, 5, Aeneas Williams; ATLANTA, 6, Ray Buchanan; CAROLINA, 5, Eric Davis; CHICAGO, 3, Tony Parrish; DALLAS, 5, Phillippi Sparks; DETROIT, 7, Kurt Schulz; GREEN BAY, 9, Darren Sharper; MINNESOTA, 2, Robert Tate, Kailee Wong; NEW ORLEANS, 5, Sammy Knight; N.Y. GIANTS, 6, Emmanuel McDaniel; PHILADELPHIA, 5, Troy Vincent; ST. LOUIS, 8, Dexter McCleon; SAN FRANCISCO, 3, Zack Bronson, Monty Montgomery; TAMPA BAY, 7, Donnie Abraham; WASHINGTON, 5, Champ Bailey

Team Champion
AFC: 28—Miami
NFC: 25—Detroit
25—Tampa Bay

AFC INTERCEPTIONS—TEAM

	No.	Yards	Avg.	Long	TD
Miami	28	311	11.1	43	0
Denver	27	343	12.7	79t	5
Baltimore	23	477	20.7	98t	1
N.Y. Jets	21	229	10.9	43	1
Oakland	21	323	15.4	50t	4
Pittsburgh	17	154	9.1	33	0
Seattle	17	300	17.6	84t	3
Tennessee	17	285	16.8	87t	4
Buffalo	16	131	8.2	45t	1
San Diego	16	313	19.6	75t	4
Kansas City	15	198	13.2	42t	2
Indianapolis	14	125	8.9	40t	2
Cleveland	12	68	5.7	33t	1
Jacksonville	12	145	12.1	39	0
New England	10	161	16.1	56	0
Cincinnati	9	107	11.9	36t	1
AFC Total	275	3670	13.3	98t	29
AFC Average	17.2	229.4	13.3	—	1.8

NFC INTERCEPTIONS—TEAM

	No.	Yards	Avg.	Long	TD
Detroit	25	340	13.6	101t	2
Tampa Bay	25	275	11.0	37t	4
Green Bay	21	315	15.0	47	1
New Orleans	20	264	13.2	46	4
N.Y. Giants	20	149	7.5	40	0
Philadelphia	19	255	13.4	38	2
St. Louis	19	135	7.1	23	0
Carolina	17	199	11.7	88t	2
Washington	17	219	12.9	48	0
Dallas	16	167	10.4	46	0
Atlanta	15	287	19.1	60	1
San Francisco	13	278	21.4	70t	2
Chicago	11	254	23.1	61t	4
Arizona	10	151	15.1	48	0
Minnesota	8	65	8.1	25	0
NFC Total	256	3353	13.1	101t	22
NFC Average	17.1	223.5	13.1	—	1.5
League Total	531	7023	—	101t	51
League Average	17.1	226.5	13.2	—	1.6

NFL TOP TEN INTERCEPTORS

	No.	Yards	Avg.	Long	TD
Sharper, Darren, G.B.	9	109	12.1	47	0
McCleon, Dexter, St.L.	8	28	3.5	23	0
Rolle, Samari, Tenn.	7	140	20.0	81t	1
Abraham, Donnie, T.B.	7	82	11.7	23	0
Walker, Brian, Mia.	7	80	11.4	31	0
Schulz, Kurt, Det.	7	53	7.6	19	0
Allen, Eric, Oak.	6	145	24.2	50t	3
Green, Victor, NYJ	6	144	24.0	43	1
Westbrook, Bryant, Det.	6	126	21.0	101t	1
Starks, Duane, Balt.	6	125	20.8	64	0
Buchanan, Ray, Atl.	6	114	19.0	60	0
Buckley, Terrell, Den.	6	110	18.3	33	1
Harrison, Rodney, S.D.	6	97	16.2	63t	1
Thomas, William, Oak.	6	68	11.3	46t	1
McDaniel, Emmanuel, NYG	6	30	5.0	17	0
Robinson, Damien, T.B.	6	1	0.2	1	0

AFC INTERCEPTIONS—INDIVIDUAL

	No.	Yards	Avg.	Long	TD
Rolle, Samari, Tenn.	7	140	20.0	81t	1
Walker, Brian, Mia.	7	80	11.4	31	0
Allen, Eric, Oak.	6	145	24.2	50t	3
Green, Victor, NYJ	6	144	24.0	43	1
Starks, Duane, Balt.	6	125	20.8	64	0
Buckley, Terrell, Den.	6	110	18.3	33	1
Harrison, Rodney, S.D.	6	97	16.2	63t	1
Thomas, William, Oak.	6	68	11.3	46t	1
Madison, Sam, Mia.	5	80	16.0	34	0
Marion, Brock, Mia.	5	72	14.4	24	0
Carpenter, Keion, Buff.	5	63	12.6	22	0
Washington, Dewayne, Pitt.	5	59	11.8	31	0
Surtain, Patrick, Mia.	5	55	11.0	43	0
Scott, Chad, Pitt.	5	49	9.8	33	0
McAlister, Chris, Balt.	4	165	41.3	98t	1
Bellamy, Jay, Sea.	4	132	33.0	84t	1
Williams, Willie, Sea.	4	74	18.5	69t	1
Jenkins, Billy, Den.	4	61	15.3	36t	1
Hasty, James, K.C.	4	53	13.3	38	0
Burris, Jeff, Ind.	4	38	9.5	27t	1
Woodson, Charles, Oak.	4	36	9.0	23	0
Glenn, Aaron, NYJ	4	34	8.5	34	0
Crockett, Ray, Den.	4	31	7.8	26t	1
Woodson, Rod, Balt.	4	20	5.0	18	0
Coleman, Marcus, NYJ	4	6	1.5	7	0
Spencer, Jimmy, Den.	3	102	34.0	79t	2
Herring, Kim, Balt.	3	74	24.7	30	0
Alexander, Brent, Pitt.	3	31	10.3	15	0
Wilson, Al, Den.	3	21	7.0	20	0
Sidney, Dainon, Tenn.	3	19	6.3	19	0
Brown, Eric, Den.	3	9	3.0	9	0
Fuller, Corey, Cle.	3	0	0.0	0	0
Edwards, Donnie, K.C.	2	45	22.5	42t	1
Jones, Henry, Buff.	2	45	22.5	45t	1
Harris, Corey, Balt.	2	44	22.0	42	0
Carter, Tom, Cin.	2	40	20.0	30	0
Patton, Marvcus, K.C.	2	39	19.5	24t	1
Stewart, Rayna, Jax.	2	37	18.5	24	0
Macklin, David, Ind.	2	35	17.5	35	0
Law, Ty, N.E.	2	32	16.0	32	0
Wesley, Greg, K.C.	2	28	14.0	28	0
Darius, Donovin, Jax.	2	26	13.0	21	0
Godfrey, Randall, Tenn.	2	25	12.5	24t	1
James, Tory, Oak.	2	25	12.5	25	0
Pope, Marquez, Oak.	2	25	12.5	25	0
Jones, Tebucky, N.E.	2	20	10.0	20	0

2000 INDIVIDUAL STATISTICS—INTERCEPTIONS

	No.	Yards	Avg.	Long	TD
Simmons, Anthony, Sea.	2	15	7.5	8	0
Logan, Mike, Jax.	2	14	7.0	14	0
Spikes, Takeo, Cin.	2	12	6.0	7	0
Peterson, Mike, Ind.	2	8	4.0	5	0
Springs, Shawn, Sea.	2	8	4.0	8	0
Cowart, Sam, Buff.	2	4	2.0	2	0
Walker, Denard, Tenn.	2	4	2.0	4	0
Cota, Chad, Ind.	2	3	1.5	3	0
Milloy, Lawyer, N.E.	2	2	1.0	2	0
Seau, Junior, S.D.	2	2	1.0	2	0
Irvin, Ken, Buff.	2	1	0.5	1	0
Lewis, Ray, Balt.	2	1	0.5	1	0
Romanowski, Bill, Den.	2	0	0.0	3	0
Woods, Jerome, K.C.	2	0	0.0	0	0
Phenix, Perry, Tenn.	1	87	87.0	87t	1
Turner, Scott, S.D.	1	75	75.0	75t	1
Dumas, Mike, S.D.	1	56	56.0	56t	1
Smith, Otis, N.E.	1	56	56.0	56	0
Sharper, Jamie, Balt.	1	45	45.0	45	0
Muhammad, Mustafah, Ind.	1	40	40.0	40t	1
Beasley, Aaron, Jax.	1	39	39.0	39	0
Dixon, Gerald, S.D.	1	36	36.0	36t	1
Williams, Darryl, Cin.	1	36	36.0	36t	1
Bush, Lewis, K.C.	1	33	33.0	33	0
Ellsworth, Percy, Cle.	1	33	33.0	33t	1
Bell, Marcus, Sea.	1	30	30.0	30	0
Koonce, George, Sea.	1	27	27.0	27t	1
Langham, Antonio, N.E.	1	24	24.0	24	0
Taves, Josh, Oak.	1	24	24.0	24	0
Lewis, Mo, NYJ	1	23	23.0	23	0
Ferguson, Nick, NYJ	1	20	20.0	20	0
McCutcheon, Daylon, Cle.	1	20	20.0	20	0
Wilson, Jerry, Mia.	1	19	19.0	19	0
Ruff, Orlando, S.D.	1	18	18.0	18	0
Jenkins, DeRon, S.D.	1	16	16.0	16	0
Thomas, Henry, N.E.	1	16	16.0	16	0
Codie, Nikia, Pitt.	1	14	14.0	14	0
Kennedy, Cortez, Sea.	1	14	14.0	14	0
Boyer, Brant, Jax.	1	12	12.0	12	0
Hall, Cory, Cin.	1	12	12.0	12	0
Harris, Antwan, N.E.	1	11	11.0	11	0
Nickerson, Hardy, Jax.	1	10	10.0	10	0
Rogers, Sam, Buff.	1	10	10.0	10	0
Mobley, John, Den.	1	9	9.0	9	0
Bulluck, Keith, Tenn.	1	8	8.0	8t	1
Winfield, Antoine, Buff.	1	8	8.0	8	0
Beckett, Rogers, S.D.	1	7	7.0	7	0
Brackens, Tony, Jax.	1	7	7.0	7	0
Little, Earl, Cle.	1	7	7.0	7	0
Carter, Chris, Cin.	1	6	6.0	6	0
Lewis, Darryll, S.D.	1	6	6.0	3	0
Rainer, Wali, Cle.	1	5	5.0	5	0
Burnett, Rob, Balt.	1	3	3.0	3	0
Jeffries, Greg, Mia.	1	3	3.0	3	0
Moore, Marty, Cle.	1	3	3.0	3	0
Booker, Michael, Tenn.	1	2	2.0	2	0
Taylor, Jason, Mia.	1	2	2.0	2	0
Ellis, Shaun, NYJ	1	1	1.0	1	0
Foley, Steve, Cin.	1	1	1.0	1	0
Frost, Scott, NYJ	1	1	1.0	1	0
Kirkland, Levon, Pitt.	1	1	1.0	1	0
Poole, Tyrone, Ind.	1	1	1.0	1	0
Washington, Marcus, Ind.	1	1	1.0	1	0
Bean, Robert, Cin.	1	0	0.0	0	0
Bowens, Tim, Mia.	1	0	0.0	0	0
Brown, Chad, Sea.	1	0	0.0	0	0
Brown, Fakhir, S.D.	1	0	0.0	0	0
Browning, John, K.C.	1	0	0.0	0	0
Bryant, Fernando, Jax.	1	0	0.0	0	0
Chapman, Lamar, Cle.	1	0	0.0	0	0
Dennis, Pat, K.C.	1	0	0.0	0	0
Farrior, James, NYJ	1	0	0.0	0	0
Flowers, Erik, Buff.	1	0	0.0	0	0
Flowers, Lethon, Pitt.	1	0	0.0	0	0
Hardy, Kevin, Jax.	1	0	0.0	0	0
Hayes, Chris, NYJ	1	0	0.0	0	0
Holecek, John, Buff.	1	0	0.0	0	0
Holland, Darius, Cle.	1	0	0.0	0	0
Kacyvenski, Isaiah, Sea.	1	0	0.0	0	0
Kennedy, Kenoy, Den.	1	0	0.0	0	0
Miller, Jamir, Cle.	1	0	0.0	0	0
Porter, Daryl, Buff.	1	0	0.0	0	0
Porter, Joey, Pitt.	1	0	0.0	0	0
Sanders, Lewis, Cle.	1	0	0.0	0	0
Scott, Tony, NYJ	1	0	0.0	0	0
Shaw, Terrance, Mia.	1	0	0.0	0	0
Thomas, Zach, Mia.	1	0	0.0	0	0
Johnson, Ellis, Ind.	1	-1	-1.0	-1	0

t = Touchdown
Leader based on interceptions

NFC INTERCEPTIONS—INDIVIDUAL

	No.	Yards	Avg.	Long	TD
Sharper, Darren, G.B.	9	109	12.1	47	0
McCleon, Dexter, St.L.	8	28	3.5	23	0
Abraham, Donnie, T.B.	7	82	11.7	23	0
Schulz, Kurt, Det.	7	53	7.6	19	0
Westbrook, Bryant, Det.	6	126	21.0	101t	1
Buchanan, Ray, Atl.	6	114	19.0	60	0
McDaniel, Emmanuel, NYG	6	30	5.0	17	0
Robinson, Damien, T.B.	6	1	0.2	1	0
Williams, Aeneas, Ariz.	5	102	20.4	48	0
Knight, Sammy, N.O.	5	68	13.6	37t	2
Sparks, Phillippi, Dall.	5	59	11.8	43	0
Bailey, Champ, Wash.	5	48	9.6	48	0
Vincent, Troy, Phil.	5	34	6.8	17	0
Davis, Eric, Car.	5	14	2.8	8	0
Ambrose, Ashley, Atl.	4	139	34.8	42	1
Williams, U. Tyrone, G.B.	4	105	26.3	46	1
Sanders, Deion, Wash.	4	91	22.8	32	0
Dawkins, Brian, Phil.	4	62	15.5	32	0
Duncan, Jamie, T.B.	4	55	13.8	31t	1
Fletcher, London, St.L.	4	33	8.3	12	0
Hitchcock, Jimmy, Car.	3	116	38.7	88t	1
Parrish, Tony, Chi.	3	81	27.0	38t	1
Bronson, Zack, S.F.	3	75	25.0	43	0
Montgomery, Monty, S.F.	3	68	22.7	46t	1
Taylor, Bobby, Phil.	3	64	21.3	38	0
Williams, Shaun, NYG	3	52	17.3	40	0
Bly, Dre', St.L.	3	44	14.7	22	0
Lynch, John, T.B.	3	43	14.3	36	0
Green, Darrell, Wash.	3	35	11.7	33	0
Bradford, Ronnie, Atl.	3	25	8.3	13	0
Molden, Alex, N.O.	3	24	8.0	24	0
Stephens, Reggie, NYG	3	4	1.3	4	0
Perry, Darren, N.O.	3	3	1.0	3	0
Webster, Jason, S.F.	2	78	39.0	70t	1
Reese, Izell, Dall.	2	60	30.0	46	0
Smith, Darrin, N.O.	2	56	28.0	41t	1
Barber, Ronde, T.B.	2	46	23.0	37t	1
McBride, Tod, G.B.	2	43	21.5	43	0
Minter, Mike, Car.	2	38	19.0	30t	1
Harris, Walt, Chi.	2	35	17.5	35t	1
Peterson, Julian, S.F.	2	33	16.5	31	0
Sehorn, Jason, NYG	2	32	16.0	32	0
Nguyen, Dat, Dall.	2	31	15.5	24	0
Wong, Kailee, Minn.	2	28	14.0	14	0
Weary, Fred, N.O.	2	27	13.5	27	0
Butler, LeRoy, G.B.	2	25	12.5	22	0
Moore, Damon, Phil.	2	24	12.0	20	0
Phillips, Ryan, NYG	2	22	11.0	12	0
Lyght, Todd, St.L.	2	21	10.5	21	0
Urlacher, Brian, Chi.	2	19	9.5	19	0
Evans, Doug, Car.	2	17	8.5	17	0
Shade, Sam, Wash.	2	15	7.5	15	0
Brown, Corwin, Det.	2	12	6.0	12	0
Tate, Robert, Minn.	2	12	6.0	12	0
Woodson, Darren, Dall.	2	12	6.0	12	0
Emmons, Carlos, Phil.	2	8	4.0	8	0
Edwards, Antuan, G.B.	2	4	2.0	4	0
McNeil, Ryan, Dall.	2	4	2.0	4	0
Wortham, Barron, Dall.	2	1	0.5	1	0
Fair, Terry, Det.	2	0	0.0	0	0
Oldham, Chris, N.O.	2	0	0.0	0	0
Pritchett, Kelvin, Det.	1	78	78.0	78	0
McQuarters, R.W., Chi.	1	61	61.0	61t	1
Howard, Darren, N.O.	1	46	46.0	46	0
Campbell, Lamar, Det.	1	42	42.0	42t	1
Mitchell, Keith, N.O.	1	40	40.0	40t	1
Brown, Mike, Chi.	1	35	35.0	35t	1
Brooks, Derrick, T.B.	1	34	34.0	34t	1
Carrier, Mark, Wash.	1	30	30.0	30	0
Tillman, Pat, Ariz.	1	30	30.0	27	0

2000 INDIVIDUAL STATISTICS—INTERCEPTIONS/PUNTING

	No.	Yards	Avg.	Long	TD
Trotter, Jeremiah, Phil.	1	27	27.0	27t	1
Caldwell, Mike, Phil.	1	26	26.0	26t	1
McKenzie, Mike, G.B.	1	26	26.0	26	0
Griffith, Robert, Minn.	1	25	25.0	25	0
Wells, Mike, Chi.	1	21	21.0	21	0
Wells, Dean, Car.	1	14	14.0	14	0
Prioleau, Pierson, S.F.	1	13	13.0	13	0
Walker, Marquis, Det.	1	12	12.0	12	0
Lassiter, Kwamie, Ariz.	1	11	11.0	11	0
Tubbs, Winfred, S.F.	1	11	11.0	11	0
Douglas, Hugh, Phil.	1	9	9.0	9	0
Kelly, Brian, T.B.	1	9	9.0	9t	1
Lyle, Keith, St.L.	1	9	9.0	9	0
Fredrickson, Rob, Ariz.	1	8	8.0	8	0
Kerney, Patrick, Atl.	1	8	8.0	8	0
Barrow, Micheal, NYG	1	7	7.0	7	0
Rice, Ron, Det.	1	7	7.0	7	0
Quarles, Shelton, T.B.	1	5	5.0	5	0
Walker, Darnell, Det.	1	5	5.0	5	0
Aldridge, Allen, Det.	1	4	4.0	4	0
Garnes, Sam, NYG	1	4	4.0	4	0
Holliday, Vonnie, G.B.	1	3	3.0	3	0
Azumah, Jerry, Chi.	1	2	2.0	2	0
Claiborne, Chris, Det.	1	1	1.0	1	0
Williams, Elijah, Atl.	1	1	1.0	1	0
Boyd, Stephen, Det.	1	0	0.0	0	0
Chavous, Corey, Ariz.	1	0	0.0	0	0
Dishman, Cris, Minn.	1	0	0.0	0	0
Gilbert, Sean, Car.	1	0	0.0	0	0
Keith, John, S.F.	1	0	0.0	0	0
Mathis, Kevin, N.O.	1	0	0.0	0	0
Mitchell, Kevin, Wash.	1	0	0.0	0	0
Navies, Hannibal, Car.	1	0	0.0	0	0
Robinson, Eugene, Car.	1	0	0.0	0	0
Shepherd, Jacoby, St.L.	1	0	0.0	0	0
Stevens, Matt, Wash.	1	0	0.0	0	0
Thibodeaux, Keith, Minn.	1	0	0.0	0	0
Thomas, Dave, NYG	1	0	0.0	0	0
Thomas, Orlando, Minn.	1	0	0.0	0	0
Walz, Zack, Ariz.	1	0	0.0	0	0
Williams, Charlie, Dall.	1	0	0.0	0	0
Woodall, Lee, Car.	1	0	0.0	0	0
Armstead, Jessie, NYG	1	-2	-2.0	-2	0
Harris, Al, Phil.	0	1	—	1	0

t = Touchdown
Leader based on interceptions

PUNTING

Average Yards Per Punt
AFC: 46.2—Darren Bennett, San Diego
NFC: 44.7—Mitch Berger, Minnesota

Net Average Yards Per Punt
AFC: 38.0—Shane Lechler, Oakland
NFC: 37.9—Dan Stryzinski, Atlanta

Longest
AFC: 70—Tom Tupa, N.Y. Jets vs. Buffalo, September 17
70—Matt Turk, Miami at Cincinnati, October 1
70—Matt Turk, Miami at Indianapolis, November 26
NFC: 66—Ken Walter, Carolina vs. San Diego, December 17

Punts
AFC: 108—Chris Gardocki, Cleveland
NFC: 93—John Jett, Detroit

Punts, Game
AFC: 12—Josh Miller, Pittsburgh vs. Cincinnati, October 15 (526 yards)
12—Chris Gardocki, Cleveland at Jacksonville, December 3 (517 yards)
NFC: 11—Mark Royals, Tampa Bay at Green Bay, December 24 (434 yards) - OT
10—many times

Team Champion
AFC: 46.2—San Diego
NFC: 44.7—Minnesota

AFC PUNTING—TEAM

	Total Punts	Yards	Long	Avg.	TB	Blk.	Opp. Ret.	Ret. Yds.	In 20	Net. Avg.
San Diego	92	4248	66	46.2	10	0	51	722	23	36.2
Cleveland	108	4919	67	45.5	5	0	69	793	25	37.3
Oakland	66	2984	69	45.2	10	1	30	279	24	38.0
N.Y. Jets	83	3714	70	44.7	15	0	42	660	18	33.2
Indianapolis	65	2906	65	44.7	9	0	28	357	20	36.4
Kansas City	82	3656	68	44.6	8	0	43	559	28	35.8
Pittsburgh	91	3944	67	43.3	8	1	44	371	34	37.5
New England	90	3798	62	42.2	5	1	43	384	31	36.8
Miami	92	3870	70	42.1	14	0	36	258	25	36.2
Jacksonville	79	3311	65	41.9	6	0	38	478	29	34.3
Tennessee	76	3101	67	40.8	9	0	28	160	33	36.3
Baltimore	86	3457	55	40.2	8	0	41	382	35	33.9
Cincinnati	94	3775	57	40.2	14	0	40	387	18	33.1
Denver	62	2455	62	39.6	9	1	23	270	18	32.3
Seattle	75	2960	57	39.5	2	1	32	151	24	36.9
Buffalo	96	3661	57	38.1	5	1	51	544	19	31.4
AFC Total	1337	56759	70	—	137	6	639	6755	404	—
AFC Average	83.6	3547.4	—	42.5	8.6	0.4	39.9	422.2	25.3	35.4

NFC PUNTING—TEAM

	Total Punts	Yards	Long	Avg.	TB	Blk.	Opp. Ret.	Ret. Yds.	In 20	Net. Avg.
Minnesota	62	2773	60	44.7	11	0	32	310	16	36.2
Arizona	65	2871	55	44.2	5	0	37	347	17	37.3
Detroit	95	4044	59	42.6	12	2	53	498	33	34.8
Philadelphia	86	3635	60	42.3	8	0	47	375	23	36.0
Dallas	68	2852	60	41.9	8	0	29	282	15	35.4
Tampa Bay	85	3551	63	41.8	8	0	41	408	17	35.1
New Orleans	74	3043	58	41.1	8	0	37	494	22	32.3
Atlanta	85	3447	60	40.6	5	1	29	126	27	37.9
N.Y. Giants	80	3210	64	40.1	8	1	28	353	26	33.7
Washington	79	3160	53	40.0	5	0	33	342	23	34.4
St. Louis	44	1736	59	39.5	5	1	17	132	13	34.2
San Francisco	70	2727	56	39.0	7	1	32	332	15	32.2
Green Bay	79	3033	53	38.4	6	0	27	205	22	34.3
Chicago	96	3624	56	37.8	7	0	36	251	20	33.7
Carolina	66	2459	66	37.3	2	2	25	187	19	33.8
NFC Total	1134	46165	66	—	105	8	503	4642	308	—
NFC Average	75.6	3077.7	—	40.7	7.0	0.5	33.5	309.5	20.5	34.8
League Total	2471	102924	70	—	242	14	1142	11397	712	—
League Average	79.7	3320.1	—	41.7	7.8	0.5	36.8	367.6	23.0	35.1

2000 INDIVIDUAL STATISTICS—PUNTING

NFL TOP TEN PUNTERS

	No.	Yards	Long	Avg.	Total Punts	TB	Blk.	Opp. Ret.	Ret. Yds.	In 20	Net. Avg.
Bennett, Darren, S.D.	92	4248	66	46.2	92	10	0	51	722	23	36.2
Lechler, Shane, Oak.	65	2984	69	45.9	66	10	1	30	279	24	38.0
Gardocki, Chris, Cle.	108	4919	67	45.5	108	5	0	69	793	25	37.3
Tupa, Tom, NYJ	83	3714	70	44.7	83	15	0	42	660	18	33.2
Berger, Mitch, Minn.	62	2773	60	44.7	62	11	0	32	310	16	36.2
Smith, Hunter, Ind.	65	2906	65	44.7	65	9	0	28	357	20	36.4
Sauerbrun, Todd, K.C.	82	3656	68	44.6	82	8	0	43	559	28	35.8
Player, Scott, Ariz.	65	2871	55	44.2	65	5	0	37	347	17	37.3
Miller, Josh, Pitt.	90	3944	67	43.8	91	8	1	44	371	34	37.5
Jett, John, Det.	93	4044	59	43.5	95	12	2	53	498	33	34.8

AFC PUNTERS—INDIVIDUAL

	No.	Yards	Long	Avg.	Total Punts	TB	Blk.	Opp. Ret.	Ret. Yds.	In 20	Net. Avg.
Bennett, Darren, S.D.	92	4248	66	46.2	92	10	0	51	722	23	36.2
Lechler, Shane, Oak.	65	2984	69	45.9	66	10	1	30	279	24	38.0
Gardocki, Chris, Cle.	108	4919	67	45.5	108	5	0	69	793	25	37.3
Tupa, Tom, NYJ	83	3714	70	44.7	83	15	0	42	660	18	33.2
Smith, Hunter, Ind.	65	2906	65	44.7	65	9	0	28	357	20	36.4
Sauerbrun, Todd, K.C.	82	3656	68	44.6	82	8	0	43	559	28	35.8
Miller, Josh, Pitt.	90	3944	67	43.8	91	8	1	44	371	34	37.5
Johnson, Lee, N.E.	89	3798	62	42.7	90	5	1	43	384	31	36.8
Turk, Matt, Mia.	92	3870	70	42.1	92	14	0	36	258	25	36.2
Barker, Bryan, Jax.	76	3194	65	42.0	76	5	0	38	478	29	34.4
Hentrich, Craig, Tenn.	76	3101	67	40.8	76	9	0	28	160	33	36.3
Rouen, Tom, Den.	61	2455	62	40.2	62	9	1	23	270	18	32.3
Richardson, Kyle, Balt.	86	3457	55	40.2	86	8	0	41	382	35	33.9
Pope, Daniel, Cin.	94	3775	57	40.2	94	14	0	40	387	18	33.1
Feagles, Jeff, Sea.	74	2960	57	40.0	75	2	1	32	151	24	36.9
Mohr, Chris, Buff.	95	3661	57	38.5	96	5	1	51	544	19	31.4
(Nonqualifiers)											
Lindsey, Steve, Jax.	3	117	46	39.0	3	1	0	0	0	0	32.3

Leader based on average, minimum 40 punts

NFC PUNTERS—INDIVIDUAL

	No.	Yards	Long	Avg.	Total Punts	TB	Blk.	Opp. Ret.	Ret. Yds.	In 20	Net. Avg.
Berger, Mitch, Minn.	62	2773	60	44.7	62	11	0	32	310	16	36.2
Player, Scott, Ariz.	65	2871	55	44.2	65	5	0	37	347	17	37.3
Jett, John, Det.	93	4044	59	43.5	95	12	2	53	498	33	34.8
Knorr, Micah, Dall.	58	2485	60	42.8	58	8	0	25	248	12	35.8
Landeta, Sean, Phil.	86	3635	60	42.3	86	8	0	47	375	23	36.0
Royals, Mark, T.B.	85	3551	63	41.8	85	8	0	41	408	17	35.1
Gowin, Toby, N.O.	74	3043	58	41.1	74	8	0	37	494	22	32.3
Stryzinski, Dan, Atl.	84	3447	60	41.0	85	5	1	29	126	27	37.9
Maynard, Brad, NYG	79	3210	64	40.6	80	8	1	28	353	26	33.7
Baker, John, St.L.	43	1736	59	40.4	44	5	1	17	132	13	34.2
Barnhardt, Tommy, Wash.	79	3160	53	40.0	79	5	0	33	342	23	34.4
Stanley, Chad, S.F.	69	2727	56	39.5	70	7	1	32	332	15	32.2
Aguiar, Louie, Chi.	52	2017	56	38.8	52	4	0	21	121	8	34.9
Bidwell, Josh, G.B.	78	3003	53	38.5	78	5	0	27	205	22	34.6
Walter, Ken, Car.	64	2459	66	38.4	66	2	2	25	187	19	33.8
Bartholomew, Brent, Chi.	44	1607	52	36.5	44	3	0	15	130	12	32.2
(Nonqualifiers)											
Cantrell, Barry, Dall.	10	367	40	36.7	10	0	0	4	34	3	33.3
Longwell, Ryan, G.B.	1	30	30	30.0	1	1	0	0	0	0	10.0

Leader based on average, minimum 40 punts

2000 INDIVIDUAL STATISTICS—PUNT RETURNS

PUNT RETURNS

Yards Per Return
- **AFC:** 16.1—Jermaine Lewis, Baltimore
- **NFC:** 15.3—Az-Zahir Hakim, St. Louis

Yards
- **AFC:** 662—Derrick Mason, Tennessee
- **NFC:** 489—Az-Zahir Hakim, St. Louis

Yards, Game
- **AFC:** 173—Jermaine Lewis, Baltimore vs. N.Y. Jets, December 24 (4 returns, 2 TD)
- **NFC:** 119—Desmond Howard, Detroit at New Orleans, September 3 (4 returns, 1 TD)

Longest
- **NFC:** 95—Desmond Howard, Detroit at New Orleans, September 3 - TD
- **AFC:** 89—Jermaine Lewis, Baltimore vs. N.Y. Jets, December 24 - TD

Returns
- **AFC:** 51—Derrick Mason, Tennessee
- **NFC:** 39—Tiki Barber, N.Y. Giants

Returns, Game
- **AFC:** 7—Craig Yeast, Cincinnati vs. Cleveland, September 10 (35 yards, 0 TD)
- **NFC:** 8—Tim Dwight, Atlanta at Detroit, November 12 (34 yards, 0 TD)

Fair Catches
- **NFC:** 33—Brian Mitchell, Philadelphia
- **AFC:** 19—Troy Brown, New England
  19—Dedric Ward, N.Y. Jets

Touchdowns
- **AFC:** 2—Jermaine Lewis, Baltimore
- **NFC:** 2—Wane McGarity, Dallas

Team Champion
- **AFC:** 15.8—Baltimore
- **NFC:** 15.3—St. Louis

AFC PUNT RETURNS—TEAM

	No.	FC	Yards	Avg.	Long	TD
Baltimore	45	10	713	15.8	89t	2
Miami	39	19	518	13.3	81t	1
Seattle	30	14	384	12.8	43	0
Tennessee	53	18	671	12.7	69t	1
New England	45	22	562	12.5	66t	1
Pittsburgh	42	20	499	11.9	54	1
Cleveland	29	14	294	10.1	30	0
Denver	36	12	364	10.1	64	0
Oakland	37	13	357	9.6	36	0
Indianapolis	38	14	352	9.3	40	0
Cincinnati	42	15	357	8.5	82t	1
Kansas City	37	12	295	8.0	26	0
N.Y. Jets	38	19	276	7.3	19	0
Jacksonville	46	19	333	7.2	22	0
San Diego	44	17	272	6.2	35	0
Buffalo	38	23	190	5.0	20	0
AFC Total	639	261	6437	10.1	89t	7
AFC Average	39.9	16.3	402.3	10.1	—	0.4

NFC PUNT RETURNS—TEAM

	No.	FC	Yards	Avg.	Long	TD
St. Louis	34	18	521	15.3	86t	1
Detroit	33	24	472	14.3	95t	1
Carolina	21	12	238	11.3	64t	1
Dallas	35	14	364	10.4	64t	2
Philadelphia	33	33	335	10.2	72t	1
Minnesota	26	28	261	10.0	63	0
Washington	36	13	356	9.9	57	0
Atlanta	37	20	348	9.4	70t	1
Chicago	36	27	314	8.7	25	0
Tampa Bay	39	19	337	8.6	73t	1
Green Bay	35	26	300	8.6	43	0
New Orleans	40	17	339	8.5	51	0
San Francisco	26	13	220	8.5	25	0
N.Y. Giants	40	20	332	8.3	31	0
Arizona	32	11	223	7.0	25	0
NFC Total	503	295	4960	9.9	95t	8
NFC Average	33.5	19.7	330.7	9.9	—	0.5
League Total	1142	556	11397	—	95t	15
League Average	36.8	17.9	367.6	10.0	—	0.5

NFL TOP TEN PUNT RETURNERS

	No.	FC	Yards	Avg.	Long	TD
Lewis, Jermaine, Balt.	36	9	578	16.1	89t	2
Hakim, Az-Zahir, St.L.	32	17	489	15.3	86t	1
Howard, Desmond, Det.	31	24	457	14.7	95t	1
Rogers, Charlie, Sea.	26	12	363	14.0	43	0
Mason, Derrick, Tenn.	51	17	662	13.0	69t	1
Poteat, Hank, Pitt.	36	7	467	13.0	54	1
Brown, Troy, N.E.	39	19	504	12.9	66t	1
McGarity, Wane, Dall.	30	9	353	11.8	64t	2
Northcutt, Dennis, Cle.	27	12	289	10.7	30	0
Mitchell, Brian, Phil.	32	33	335	10.5	72t	1

AFC—INDIVIDUAL PUNT RETURNERS

	No.	FC	Yards	Avg.	Long	TD
Lewis, Jermaine, Balt.	36	9	578	16.1	89t	2
Rogers, Charlie, Sea.	26	12	363	14.0	43	0
Mason, Derrick, Tenn.	51	17	662	13.0	69t	1
Poteat, Hank, Pitt.	36	7	467	13.0	54	1
Brown, Troy, N.E.	39	19	504	12.9	66t	1
Northcutt, Dennis, Cle.	27	12	289	10.7	30	0
O'Neal, Deltha, Den.	34	11	354	10.4	64	0
Gordon, Darrien, Oak.	29	10	258	8.9	36	0
Wilkins, Terrence, Ind.	29	13	240	8.3	36	0
Lockett, Kevin, K.C.	26	6	208	8.0	26	0
Ward, Dedric, NYJ	27	19	214	7.9	19	0
Jacquet, Nate, S.D.	30	8	211	7.0	35	0
Barlow, Reggie, Jax.	29	14	200	6.9	21	0
Yeast, Craig, Cin.	34	14	225	6.6	27	0
Watson, Chris, Buff.	33	18	163	4.9	20	0
(Nonqualifiers)						
Ogden, Jeff, Mia.	19	11	323	17.0	81t	1
Shepherd, Leslie, Mia.	15	7	164	10.9	32	0
Soward, R.Jay, Jax.	14	5	108	7.7	18	0
Johnson, Leon, NYJ	10	0	62	6.2	16	0
Starks, Duane, Balt.	9	1	135	15.0	47	0
Jones, Reggie, S.D.	9	3	53	5.9	17	0
Dunn, David, Oak.	8	3	99	12.4	25	0
Warrick, Peter, Cin.	7	1	123	17.6	82t	1
Williams, Payton, Ind.	7	1	108	15.4	40	0
Faulk, Kevin, N.E.	6	3	58	9.7	35	0
Hall, Dante, K.C.	6	5	37	6.2	22	0
Parker, Larry, K.C.	5	1	50	10.0	17	0
Kelly, Ben, Mia.	5	0	31	6.2	10	0
Price, Peerless, Buff.	5	5	27	5.4	12	0
Hawkins, Courtney, Pitt.	4	11	15	3.8	9	0
McCardell, Keenan, Jax.	3	0	25	8.3	22	0
Graham, Jeff, S.D.	3	6	7	2.3	7	0
Shaw, Bobby, Pitt.	2	1	17	8.5	10	0
Buckley, Terrell, Den.	2	1	10	5.0	11	0
Muhammad, Mustafah, Ind.	2	0	4	2.0	4	0
Griffin, Damon, Cin.	1	0	9	9.0	9	0
Thigpen, Yancey, Tenn.	1	1	9	9.0	9	0
Chapman, Lamar, Cle.	1	2	5	5.0	5	0
Dumas, Mike, S.D.	1	0	1	1.0	1	0
Barnes, Rashidi, Cle.	1	0	0	0.0	0	0
Dunn, Damon, NYJ	1	0	0	0.0	0	0

2000 INDIVIDUAL STATISTICS—PUNT RETURNS/KICKOFF RETURNS

	No.	FC	Yards	Avg.	Long	TD
Jenkins, DeRon, S.D.	1	0	0	0.0	0	0
Walker, Denard, Tenn.	1	0	0	0.0	0	0
Edwards, Troy, Pitt.	0	1	0	—	—	0
Joseph, Kerry, Sea.	0	1	0	—	—	0
McDuffie, O.J., Mia.	0	1	0	—	—	0

t = Touchdown
Leader based on average return, minimum 20 returns

NFC—INDIVIDUAL PUNT RETURNERS

	No.	FC	Yards	Avg.	Long	TD
Hakim, Az-Zahir, St.L.	32	17	489	15.3	86t	1
Howard, Desmond, Det.	31	24	457	14.7	95t	1
McGarity, Wane, Dall.	30	9	353	11.8	64t	2
Mitchell, Brian, Phil.	32	33	335	10.5	72t	1
Dwight, Tim, Atl.	33	17	309	9.4	70t	1
Morton, Chad, N.O.	30	14	278	9.3	51	0
Williams, Karl, T.B.	31	18	286	9.2	73t	1
Milburn, Glyn, Chi.	35	26	300	8.6	25	0
Rossum, Allen, G.B.	29	24	248	8.6	43	0
Barber, Tiki, NYG	39	20	332	8.5	31	0
Williams, Kevin R., S.F.	26	13	220	8.5	25	0
Sanders, Deion, Wash.	25	6	185	7.4	57	0
Cody, Mac, Ariz.	31	11	222	7.2	25	0
(Nonqualifiers)						
Walters, Troy, Minn.	15	16	217	14.5	63	0
Canty, Chris, Sea.-N.O.	13	3	66	5.1	13	0
Uwaezuoke, Iheanyi, Car.	10	6	173	17.3	64t	1
Thrash, James, Wash.	10	6	106	10.6	25	0
Palmer, David, Minn.	10	12	33	3.3	16	0
Bates, Michael, Car.	7	3	31	4.4	12	0
Lee, Charles, G.B.	5	2	52	10.4	16	0
Hastings, Andre, T.B.	5	1	50	10.0	16	0
Oliver, Winslow, Atl.	4	3	39	9.8	40	0
Tucker, Jason, Dall.	4	5	9	2.3	8	0
Davis, Eric, Car.	2	2	24	12.0	20	0
Fair, Terry, Det.	2	0	15	7.5	11	0
Green, Jacquez, T.B.	2	0	1	0.5	1	0
Bailey, Champ, Wash.	1	1	65	65.0	54	0
Horne, Tony, St.L.	1	0	16	16.0	16	0
Harris, Walt, Chi.	1	1	14	14.0	14	0
Walsh, Chris, Minn.	1	0	11	11.0	11	0
Byrd, Isaac, Car.	1	1	10	10.0	10	0
Mathis, Kevin, N.O.	1	1	5	5.0	5	0
Galloway, Joey, Dall.	1	0	2	2.0	2	0
Jenkins, MarTay, Ariz.	1	0	1	1.0	1	0
Bostic, Jason, Phil.	1	0	0	0.0	0	0
Comella, Greg, NYG	1	0	0	0.0	0	0
Hitchcock, Jimmy, Car.	1	0	0	0.0	0	0
McCleon, Dexter, St.L.	1	0	0	0.0	0	0
McKenzie, Mike, G.B.	1	0	0	0.0	0	0
Yoder, Todd, T.B.	1	0	0	0.0	0	0
Lyght, Todd, St.L.	0	0	16	—	16	0
Wilson, Robert, N.O.	0	0	11	—	11	0
Bly, Dre', St.L.	0	1	0	—	—	0

t = Touchdown
Leader based on average return, minimum 20 returns

KICKOFF RETURNS

Yards Per Return
NFC: 27.7—Darrick Vaughn, Atlanta
AFC: 27.0—Derrick Mason, Tennessee

Yards
NFC: 2186—MarTay Jenkins, Arizona
AFC: 1629—Charlie Rogers, Seattle

Yards, Game
NFC: 267—Tony Horne, St. Louis at Kansas City, October 22 (8 returns, 0 TD)
AFC: 221—Ronney Jenkins, San Diego vs. New Orleans, September 10 (6 returns, 1 TD)

Longest
NFC: 103—Tony Horne, St. Louis vs. Atlanta, October 15 - TD
AFC: 98—Will Blackwell, Pittsburgh at San Diego, December 24 - TD

Returns
NFC: 82—MarTay Jenkins, Arizona
AFC: 67—Ronney Jenkins, San Diego

Returns, Game
NFC: 8—Tony Horne, St. Louis vs. Denver, September 4 (145 yards, 0 TD)
8—Tony Horne, St. Louis at Kansas City, October 22 (267 yards, 0 TD)
8—MarTay Jenkins, Arizona at Jacksonville, December 10 (193 yards, 0 TD)
8—Troy Walters, Minnesota vs. Green Bay, December 17 (177 yards, 0 TD)
AFC: 8—Ronney Jenkins, San Diego at St. Louis, October 1 (187 yards, 0 TD)
8—Ronney Jenkins, San Diego vs. San Francisco, December 3 (164 yards, 0 TD)

Touchdowns
NFC: 3—Darrick Vaughn, Atlanta
AFC: 1—many players

Team Champion
NFC: 26.7—Arizona
AFC: 26.1—Tennessee

AFC KICKOFF RETURNS—TEAM

	No.	Yards	Avg.	Long	TD
Tennessee	47	1227	26.1	66	0
Seattle	80	1932	24.2	81t	1
Oakland	56	1336	23.9	88t	1
Denver	66	1477	22.4	87t	1
Baltimore	45	1005	22.3	41	0
Miami	51	1133	22.2	56	0
San Diego	83	1792	21.6	93t	1
Jacksonville	62	1323	21.3	47	0
Pittsburgh	58	1221	21.1	98t	1
N.Y. Jets	74	1552	21.0	97t	1
Kansas City	70	1466	20.9	38	0
New England	64	1335	20.9	47	0
Cleveland	85	1710	20.1	62	0
Indianapolis	58	1155	19.9	48	0
Cincinnati	77	1423	18.5	50	0
Buffalo	69	1262	18.3	37	0
AFC Total	1045	22349	21.4	98t	6
AFC Average	65.3	1396.8	21.4	—	0.4

NFC KICKOFF RETURNS—TEAM

	No.	Yards	Avg.	Long	TD
Arizona	86	2296	26.7	98t	1
Green Bay	64	1570	24.5	92t	1
New Orleans	62	1473	23.8	68	0
Philadelphia	53	1237	23.3	89t	1
Detroit	69	1600	23.2	70	0
Tampa Bay	55	1255	22.8	48	0
Atlanta	83	1890	22.8	100t	3
Chicago	68	1512	22.2	38	0
St. Louis	80	1771	22.1	103t	1
Minnesota	67	1456	21.7	38	0
Dallas	69	1456	21.1	90	0
Carolina	55	1160	21.1	92t	1
N.Y. Giants	53	1102	20.8	47	1
Washington	63	1301	20.7	49	0
San Francisco	68	1299	19.1	68	0
NFC Total	995	22378	22.5	103t	9
NFC Average	66.3	1491.9	22.5	—	0.6
League Total	2040	44727	—	103t	15
League Average	65.8	1442.8	21.9	—	0.5

NFL TOP TEN KICKOFF RETURNERS

	No.	Yards	Avg.	Long	TD
Vaughn, Darrick, Atl.	39	1082	27.7	100t	3
Mason, Derrick, Tenn.	42	1132	27.0	66	0
Jenkins, MarTay, Ariz.	82	2186	26.7	98t	1
Rossum, Allen, G.B.	50	1288	25.8	92t	1
Williams, Kevin L., NYJ-Mia.	24	615	25.6	97t	1
Denson, Autry, Mia.	20	495	24.8	56	0
Rogers, Charlie, Sea.	66	1629	24.7	81t	1
Howard, Desmond, Det.	57	1401	24.6	70	0
Dunn, David, Oak.	44	1073	24.4	88t	1
Horne, Tony, St.L.	57	1379	24.2	103t	1

2000 INDIVIDUAL STATISTICS—KICKOFF RETURNS

AFC KICKOFF RETURNERS—INDIVIDUAL

	No.	Yards	Avg.	Long	TD
Mason, Derrick, Tenn.	42	1132	27.0	66	0
Williams, Kevin L., NYJ-Mia.	24	615	25.6	97t	1
Denson, Autry, Mia.	20	495	24.8	56	0
Rogers, Charlie, Sea.	66	1629	24.7	81t	1
Dunn, David, Oak.	44	1073	24.4	88t	1
O'Neal, Deltha, Den.	46	1102	24.0	87t	1
Stith, Shyrone, Jax.	33	785	23.8	47	0
Marion, Brock, Mia.	22	513	23.3	47	0
Harris, Corey, Balt.	39	907	23.3	41	0
Jenkins, Ronney, S.D.	67	1531	22.9	93t	1
Pathon, Jerome, Ind.	26	583	22.4	48	0
Stone, Dwight, NYJ	25	555	22.2	43	0
White, Jamel, Cle.	43	935	21.7	40	0
Cloud, Mike, K.C.	36	779	21.6	38	0
Faulk, Kevin, N.E.	38	816	21.5	40	0
Patten, David, Cle.	22	469	21.3	62	0
Mack, Tremain, Cin.	50	1036	20.7	50	0
Watson, Chris, Buff.	44	894	20.3	37	0
Poteat, Hank, Pitt.	24	465	19.4	31	0
(Nonqualifiers)					
Hall, Dante, K.C.	17	358	21.1	36	0
Edwards, Troy, Pitt.	15	298	19.9	37	0
Wilkins, Terrence, Ind.	15	279	18.6	30	0
Parker, Larry, K.C.	14	279	19.9	27	0
Jackson, Curtis, N.E.	13	323	24.8	47	0
Bynum, Kenny, S.D.	13	242	18.6	39	0
Williams, Payton, Ind.	12	238	19.8	29	0
Cole, Chris, Den.	11	264	24.0	37	0
Barlow, Reggie, Jax.	11	224	20.4	27	0
Coles, Laveranues, NYJ	11	207	18.8	24	0
Blackwell, Will, Pitt.	10	281	28.1	98t	1
Kaufman, Napoleon, Oak.	9	198	22.0	31	0
Jackson, Lenzie, Cle.	9	168	18.7	30	0
Black, Avion, Buff.	9	165	18.3	26	0
Griffin, Damon, Cin.	8	129	16.1	29	0
Bryson, Shawn, Buff.	8	122	15.3	26	0
Ward, Hines, Pitt.	7	186	26.6	57	0
Yeast, Craig, Cin.	7	106	15.1	29	0
Johnson, Leon, NYJ	6	117	19.5	27	0
Mack, Stacey, Jax.	6	104	17.3	35	0
Keaton, Curtis, Cin.	6	100	16.7	25	0
Smith, Detron, Den.	5	73	14.6	17	0
Soward, R.Jay, Jax.	4	93	23.3	28	0
Simmons, Tony, N.E.	4	82	20.5	39	0
Whitted, Alvis, Jax.	4	67	16.8	20	0
Saleh, Tarek, Cle.	4	46	11.5	15	0
Bownes, Fabien, Sea.	3	83	27.7	38	0
Williams, James, Sea.	3	76	25.3	40	0
Joseph, Kerry, Sea.	3	71	23.7	34	0
Glenn, Aaron, NYJ	3	51	17.0	22	0
Linton, Jonathan, Buff.	3	40	13.3	17	0
Campbell, Mark, Cle.	3	30	10.0	13	0
Bush, Steve, Cin.	3	18	6.0	8	0
Coleman, Chris, Tenn.	2	54	27.0	27	0
Ismail, Qadry, Balt.	2	51	25.5	38	0
Williams, Jermaine, Jax.	2	50	25.0	30	0
Branch, Calvin, Oak.	2	48	24.0	24	0
Davis, Shockmain, N.E.	2	45	22.5	32	0
Muhammad, Mustafah, Ind.	2	45	22.5	26	0
Dunn, Damon, NYJ	2	35	17.5	21	0
Johnson, J.J., Mia.	2	26	13.0	26	0
Chamberlain, Byron, Den.	2	25	12.5	13	0
Little, Earl, Cle.	2	20	10.0	12	0
Brown, Reggie, Sea.	2	19	9.5	19	0
Brown, Troy, N.E.	2	15	7.5	9	0
Bruschi, Tedy, N.E.	2	13	6.5	7	0
Williams, Nick, Cin.	2	12	6.0	12	0
Goodwin, Hunter, Mia.	2	6	3.0	6	0
Becht, Anthony, NYJ	2	0	0.0	0	0
Strong, Mack, Sea.	1	26	26.0	26	0
Lockett, Kevin, K.C.	1	25	25.0	25	0
Redmond, J.R., N.E.	1	25	25.0	25	0
Edwards, Marc, Cle.	1	24	24.0	24	0
Lewis, Jermaine, Balt.	1	23	23.0	23	0
Heath, Rodney, Cin.	1	22	22.0	22	0
Foreman, Jay, Buff.	1	19	19.0	19	0
Mili, Itula, Sea.	1	19	19.0	19	0
Burnett, Chester, Cle.	1	18	18.0	18	0
Gordon, Darrien, Oak.	1	17	17.0	17	0
Morris, Sammy, Buff.	1	17	17.0	17	0
Washington, Keith, Balt.	1	17	17.0	17	0
Carter, Tony, N.E.	1	16	16.0	16	0
Thornton, John, Tenn.	1	16	16.0	16	0
Baxter, Fred, NYJ	1	15	15.0	15	0
Neal, Lorenzo, Tenn.	1	15	15.0	15	0
Weaver, Jed, Mia.	1	15	15.0	15	0
Anders, Kimble, K.C.	1	14	14.0	14	0
Shepherd, Leslie, Mia.	1	14	14.0	14	0
Miller, Billy, Den.	1	13	13.0	13	0
Wiggins, Jermaine, NYJ	1	12	12.0	12	0
Jones, Reggie, S.D.	1	11	11.0	11	0
Spears, Marcus, K.C.	1	11	11.0	11	0
Holsey, Bernard, Ind.	1	10	10.0	10	0
Leach, Mike, Tenn.	1	10	10.0	10	0
Fauria, Christian, Sea.	1	9	9.0	9	0
Sowell, Jerald, NYJ	1	9	9.0	9	0
Jacox, Kendyl, S.D.	1	8	8.0	8	0
Holmes, Priest, Balt.	1	7	7.0	7	0
Jones, Henry, Buff.	1	4	4.0	4	0
Cavil, Kwame, Buff.	1	1	1.0	1	0
Brown, Cornell, Balt.	1	0	0.0	0	0
Carswell, Dwayne, Den.	1	0	0.0	0	0
Dilger, Ken, Ind.	1	0	0.0	0	0
Fordham, Todd, Jax.	1	0	0.0	0	0
Graham, DeMingo, S.D.	1	0	0.0	0	0
Hamilton, Bobby, N.E.	1	0	0.0	0	0
Kreider, Dan, Pitt.	1	0	0.0	0	0
Leroy, Emarlos, Jax.	1	0	0.0	0	0
Macklin, David, Ind.	1	0	0.0	0	0
Scott, Tony, NYJ	1	0	0.0	0	0
Smith, Antowain, Buff.	1	0	0.0	0	0
Tuman, Jerame, Pitt.	1	-1	-1.0	-1	0
Battaglia, Marco, Cin.	0f	0	—	—	0
Shaw, Bobby, Pitt.	0	-8	—	-8	0

t = Touchdown
f = Fair Catch
Leader based on average return, minimum 20 returns

NFC KICKOFF RETURNERS—INDIVIDUAL

	No.	Yards	Avg.	Long	TD
Vaughn, Darrick, Atl.	39	1082	27.7	100t	3
Jenkins, MarTay, Ariz.	82	2186	26.7	98t	1
Rossum, Allen, G.B.	50	1288	25.8	92t	1
Howard, Desmond, Det.	57	1401	24.6	70	0
Horne, Tony, St.L.	57	1379	24.2	103t	1
Mitchell, Brian, Phil.	47	1124	23.9	89t	1
Morton, Chad, N.O.	44	1029	23.4	68	0
Milburn, Glyn, Chi.	63	1468	23.3	38	0
Walters, Troy, Minn.	30	692	23.1	38	0
Stecker, Aaron, T.B.	29	663	22.9	48	0
Bates, Michael, Car.	42	941	22.4	92t	1
Thrash, James, Wash.	45	1000	22.2	49	0
Tucker, Jason, Dall.	51	1099	21.5	90	0
Dwight, Tim, Atl.	32	680	21.3	48	0
Dixon, Ron, NYG	31	658	21.2	44	0
Williams, Kevin R., S.F.	30	536	17.9	33	0
(Nonqualifiers)					
Williams, Karl, T.B.	19	453	23.8	41	0
Carter, Tyrone, Minn.	17	389	22.9	38	0
Wiley, Michael, Dall.	13	303	23.3	38	0
Murrell, Adrian, Wash.	12	214	17.8	30	0
McAfee, Fred, N.O.	10	251	25.1	52	0
Williams, Moe, Minn.	10	214	21.4	34	0
Blevins, Darrius, St.L.	9	173	19.2	26	0
Byrd, Isaac, Car.	9	172	19.1	30	0
Lewis, Jonas, S.F.	9	168	18.7	26	0
Smith, Paul, S.F.	9	167	18.6	28	0
Bly, Dre', St.L.	9	163	18.1	36	0
Jervey, Travis, S.F.	8	209	26.1	68	0
Mathis, Kevin, N.O.	8	187	23.4	40	0
Streets, Tai, S.F.	8	180	22.5	37	0
Levingston, Bashir, NYG	7	153	21.9	43	0
Kozlowski, Brian, Atl.	7	77	11.0	21	0
Fair, Terry, Det.	6	149	24.8	31	0
Stoutmire, Omar, NYG	6	140	23.3	47	0
Palmer, David, Minn.	6	120	20.0	24	0
Henderson, William, G.B.	5	80	16.0	22	0
Goodman, Herbert, G.B.	4	129	32.3	54	0
Anthony, Reidel, T.B.	3	88	29.3	45	0
Stephens, Reggie, NYG	3	69	23.0	40	0
Sellers, Mike, Wash.	3	32	10.7	21	0
Olivo, Brock, Det.	3	25	8.3	13	0

2000 INDIVIDUAL STATISTICS—KICKOFF RETURNS/FUMBLES

	No.	Yards	Avg.	Long	TD
Douglas, Dameane, Phil.	2	50	25.0	41	0
Williams, Elijah, Atl.	2	34	17.0	19	0
Sehorn, Jason, NYG	2	31	15.5	38t	1
Enis, Curtis, Chi.	2	30	15.0	19	0
Schlesinger, Cory, Det.	2	25	12.5	14	0
Murphy, Frank, T.B.	2	24	12.0	19	0
Hetherington, Chris, Car.	2	21	10.5	11	0
LaFleur, David, Dall.	2	21	10.5	13	0
Comella, Greg, NYG	2	20	10.0	11	0
Oliver, Winslow, Atl.	2	15	7.5	11	0
Walsh, Chris, Minn.	2	9	4.5	6	0
Arrington, LaVar, Wash.	1	39	39.0	23	0
Barber, Tiki, NYG	1	28	28.0	28	0
Mitchell, Basil, G.B.	1	26	26.0	26	0
Burks, Dialleo, Car.	1	25	25.0	25	0
Berry, Gary, G.B.	1	22	22.0	22	0
Broughton, Luther, Phil.	1	20	20.0	20	0
McKinley, Dennis, Ariz.	1	20	20.0	20	0
Cody, Mac, Ariz.	1	18	18.0	18	0
Faulk, Marshall, St.L.	1	18	18.0	18	0
Whiting, Brandon, Phil.	1	18	18.0	18	0
Bennett, Tommy, Ariz.	1	17	17.0	17	0
Fletcher, London, St.L.	1	17	17.0	17	0
Hicks, Skip, Wash.	1	17	17.0	17	0
Moran, Sean, St.L.	1	17	17.0	17	0
Morrow, Harold, Minn.	1	17	17.0	17	0
Okeafor, Chike, S.F.	1	17	17.0	17	0
Abdullah, Rabih, T.B.	1	16	16.0	16	0
Pritchett, Stanley, Phil.	1	15	15.0	15	0
Thomas, Orlando, Minn.	1	15	15.0	15	0
Milem, John, S.F.	1	13	13.0	13	0
Morton, Mike, G.B.	1	13	13.0	13	0
Santiago, O.J., Dall.	1	13	13.0	13	0
Bowens, David, G.B.	1	12	12.0	12	0
Goodrich, Dwayne, Dall.	1	12	12.0	12	0
Sinceno, Kaseem, Chi.	1	12	12.0	12	0
Green, Jacquez, T.B.	1	11	11.0	11	0
Thomason, Jeff, Phil.	1	10	10.0	10	0
Jackson, Terry, S.F.	1	9	9.0	9	0
McKinnon, Ronald, Ariz.	1	9	9.0	9	0
Noble, Brandon, Dall.	1	8	8.0	8	0
Jurevicius, Joe, NYG	1	3	3.0	3	0
Finneran, Brian, Atl.	1	2	2.0	2	0
Hakim, Az-Zahir, St.L.	1	2	2.0	2	0
Proehl, Ricky, St.L.	1	2	2.0	2	0
Tuinei, Van, Chi.	1	2	2.0	2	0
Green, Ray, Car.	1	1	1.0	1	0
Beverly, Eric, Det.	1	0	0.0	0	0
Plummer, Ahmed, S.F.	1	0	0.0	0	0
Tucker, Rex, Chi.	1	0	0.0	0	0
Wetnight, Ryan, G.B.	1	0	0.0	0	0
Sanders, Deion, Wash.	1	-1	-1.0	-1	0
Barrett, David, Ariz.	0	46	—	41	0
Allen, Terry, N.O.	0	6	—	6	0

t = Touchdown
Leader based on average return, minimum 20 returns

FUMBLES

Most Fumbles
AFC: 17—Jon Kitna, Seattle
NFC: 11—Daunte Culpepper, Minnesota

Most Fumbles, Game
NFC: 4—Cade McNown, Chicago vs. Detroit, September 24
AFC: 4—Jon Kitna, Seattle vs. Buffalo, December 23

Own Fumbles Recovered
AFC: 9—Jon Kitna, Seattle
NFC: 5—Daunte Culpepper, Minnesota
5—Tiki Barber, N.Y. Giants

Most Own Fumbles Recovered, Game
AFC: 3—Jon Kitna, Seattle at Jacksonville, November 12
3—Doug Pederson, Cleveland vs. Philadelphia, December 10
NFC: 3—Tiki Barber, N.Y. Giants vs. Philadelphia, October 29
3—Kyle Turley, New Orleans vs. St. Louis, December 24

Opponents' Fumbles Recovered
AFC: 5—Rob Burnett, Baltimore
5—Marquez Pope, Oakland
NFC: 5—Doug Evans, Carolina

Most Opponents' Fumbles Recovered, Game
AFC: 2—Sam Cowart, Buffalo vs. N.Y. Jets, October 29
2—Lethon Flowers, Pittsburgh vs. Oakland, December 3
2—Michael Sinclair, Seattle at Atlanta, December 3
2—Takeo Spikes, Cincinnati at Philadelphia, December 24
NFC: 2—Doug Evans, Carolina at St. Louis, November 5
2—Keith Mitchell, New Orleans at Carolina, November 12
2—Michael Strahan, N.Y. Giants at Arizona, November 26
2—Shawn Barber, Washington vs. N.Y. Giants, December 3

Yards
NFC: 104—Aeneas Williams, Arizona
AFC: 74—Darrien Gordon, Oakland

Longest
NFC: 104—Aeneas Williams, Arizona vs. Washington, November 5 - TD
AFC: 74—Darrien Gordon, Oakland vs. Carolina, December 24 - TD

AFC FUMBLES—TEAM

	Fum.	Own Rec.	Fum. OB	TD	Opp. Rec.	TD	Fum. Yards	Tot. Rec.
Miami	12	2	2	0	13	2	41	15
N.Y. Jets	18	7	0	0	14	0	1	21
Oakland	18	8	1	0	16	1	88	24
Indianapolis	20	5	2	0	8	1	53	13
Cleveland	21	12	0	0	13	0	38	25
Kansas City	23	10	2	0	14	0	9	24
New England	23	13	0	0	13	0	6	26
Pittsburgh	24	13	0	0	17	2	30	30
Tennessee	24	10	0	0	13	1	-1	23
Baltimore	26	16	3	0	26	0	4	42
Denver	26	11	2	0	17	2	70	28
Jacksonville	27	12	1	0	18	0	80	30
Buffalo	28	15	1	2	13	0	128	28
Seattle	35	17	1	0	10	2	84	27
Cincinnati	37	13	3	0	12	0	-36	25
San Diego	38	17	1	0	6	0	34	23
AFC Total	400	181	19	2	223	11	629	404
AFC Average	25.0	11.3	1.2	0.1	13.9	0.7	39.3	25.3

NFC FUMBLES—TEAM

	Fum.	Own Rec.	Fum. OB	TD	Opp. Rec.	TD	Fum. Yards	Tot. Rec.
Tampa Bay	16	5	0	0	16	1	42	21
Detroit	21	7	2	1	16	0	-2	23
Philadelphia	22	8	0	0	12	0	2	20
San Francisco	22	12	2	0	8	0	11	20
Washington	22	10	1	0	16	0	-29	26
St. Louis	24	12	0	1	6	1	118	18
Carolina	25	7	2	0	20	0	7	27
N.Y. Giants	25	12	2	0	11	0	-5	23
Minnesota	26	15	1	0	10	0	-11	25
New Orleans	26	14	1	0	15	1	80	29
Atlanta	27	11	2	0	10	0	-4	21
Chicago	27	13	1	0	9	0	-2	22
Green Bay	30	12	1	0	7	0	49	19
Dallas	31	12	1	0	9	0	3	21
Arizona	32	11	1	0	10	1	98	21
NFC Total	376	161	17	2	175	4	357	336
NFC Average	25.1	10.7	1.1	0.1	11.7	0.3	23.8	22.4
League Total	776	342	36	4	398	15	986	740
League Average	25.0	11.0	1.2	0.1	12.8	0.5	31.8	23.9

Fum OB = Fumbled out of bounds, includes fumbled through the end zone.

AFC TOUCHDOWNS ON FUMBLE RECOVERIES

1—Brown, Chad, Sea.; 1—Ford, Henry, Tenn.; 1—Gildon, Jason, Pit.; 1—Gordon, Darrien, Oak.; 1—Holsey, Bernard, Ind.; 1—Madison, Sam, Mia.; 1—Ostroski, Jerry, Buff.; 1—Porter, Daryl, Buff.; 1—Porter, Joey, Pitt.; 1—Pryce, Trevor, Den.; 1—Sinclair, Michael, Sea.; 1—Suttle, Jason, Den.; 1—Taylor, Jason, Mia.

NFC TOUCHDOWNS ON FUMBLE RECOVERIES

1—Barber, Ronde, T.B.; 1—Bush, Devin, St.L.; 1—Hartings, Jeff, Det.; 1—Lyle, Keith, St.L.; 1—Mitchell, Keith, N.O.; 1—Williams, Aeneas, Ariz.

2000 INDIVIDUAL STATISTICS—FUMBLES

AFC FUMBLES—INDIVIDUAL

	Fum.	Own Rec.	Opp. Rec.	Yards	Tot. Rec.
Adams, Sam, Balt.	0	0	1	0	1
Albright, Ethan, Buff.	0	0	1	19	1
Alexander, Brent, Pitt.	0	0	1	0	1
Alexander, Shaun, Sea.	2	0	0	0	0
Anders, Kimble, K.C.	1	0	0	0	0
Anderson, Mike, Den.	4	0	0	0	0
Anderson, Richie, NYJ	2	0	0	0	0
Anderson, Willie, Cin.	0	1	0	0	1
Andruzzi, Joe, N.E.	0	1	0	2	1
Atkins, Larry, K.C.	0	0	1	0	1
Bailey, Robert, Balt.	0	0	1	27	1
Banks, Tony, Balt.	5	2	0	-2	2
Barndt, Tom, Cin.	0	0	1	0	1
Battles, Ainsley, Pitt.	1	2	0	-1	2
Baxter, Fred, NYJ	0	1	0	0	1
Beasley, Aaron, Jax.	0	0	1	0	1
Becht, Anthony, NYJ	1	0	0	0	0
Belser, Jason, Ind.	0	0	1	0	1
Bennett, Brandon, Cin.	2	1	0	0	1
Bennett, Cornelius, Ind.	0	0	1	0	1
Bettis, Jerome, Pitt.	1	1	0	1	1
Biekert, Greg, Oak.	0	0	2	0	2
Bjornson, Eric, N.E.	0	1	0	0	1
Bledsoe, Drew, N.E.	9	3	0	-20	3
Blevins, Tony, Ind.	0	0	1	0	1
Brackens, Tony, Jax.	0	0	2	15	2
Braham, Rich, Cin.	1	0	0	-16	0
Branch, Calvin, Oak.	0	1	0	6	1
Bratzke, Chad, Ind.	0	0	1	0	1
Brigance, O.J., Balt.	0	0	1	0	1
Brown, Chad, Sea.	0	0	3	16	3
Brown, Cornell, Balt.	1	0	0	0	0
Brown, Courtney, Cle.	0	0	1	0	1
Brown, Eric, Den.	0	0	3	8	3
Brown, Troy, N.E.	2	0	0	0	0
Browning, John, K.C.	0	0	1	0	1
Brunell, Mark, Jax.	7	3	0	-2	3
Bryant, Fernando, Jax.	0	0	1	5	1
Bryant, Tony, Oak.	0	0	1	3	1
Bryson, Shawn, Buff.	1	0	0	0	0
Bundren, Jim, Cle.	0	1	0	0	1
Burnett, Rob, Balt.	0	0	5	0	5
Burns, Keith, Den.	0	0	1	0	1
Burress, Plaxico, Pitt.	1	0	0	0	0
Burton, Shane, NYJ	0	0	1	4	1
Bush, Lewis, K.C.	0	1	0	0	1
Carter, Chris, Cin.	0	0	1	0	1
Chanoine, Roger, Cle.	0	1	0	0	1
Chapman, Lamar, Cle.	1	0	0	0	0
Chester, Larry, Ind.	0	0	1	0	1
Chiaverini, Darrin, Cle.	1	0	0	0	0
Chrebet, Wayne, NYJ	0	1	0	0	1
Clark, Danny, Jax.	0	0	2	44	2
Clemons, Duane, K.C.	0	0	1	0	1
Coleman, KaRon, Den.	2	1	0	0	1
Coleman, Marcus, NYJ	1	0	0	0	0
Coleman, Roderick, Oak.	0	0	1	0	1
Colinet, Stalin, Cle.	0	0	1	0	1
Copeland, John, Cin.	0	0	1	4	1
Couch, Tim, Cle.	2	0	0	-8	0
Cowart, Sam, Buff.	0	0	2	3	2
Cox, Bryan, NYJ	0	0	2	0	2
Craft, Jason, Jax.	0	1	0	4	1
Crockett, Zack, Oak.	0	0	1	0	1
Curtis, Canute, Cin.	0	0	1	0	1
Dalton, Antico, N.E.	0	1	0	0	1
Davis, Reggie, S.D.	0	1	0	0	1
Davis, Terrell, Den.	1	0	0	0	0
Dennis, Pat, K.C.	0	0	2	-5	2
Denson, Autry, Mia.	1	0	0	0	0
Dilfer, Trent, Balt.	8	1	0	-7	1
Dilger, Ken, Ind.	1	0	0	0	0
Dillon, Corey, Cin.	4	0	0	0	0
Dixon, Gerald, S.D.	0	0	1	0	1
Dudley, Rickey, Oak.	1	1	0	0	1
Duffy, Roger, Pitt.	1	0	0	-10	0
Dunn, Damon, NYJ	1	0	0	0	0
Edwards, Donnie, K.C.	0	0	1	11	1
Edwards, Marc, Cle.	2	1	0	0	1
Edwards, Troy, Pitt.	1	0	0	0	0
Ellis, Shaun, NYJ	0	0	2	2	2
Ellsworth, Percy, Cle.	0	0	1	16	1
Emanuel, Bert, Mia.	1	0	0	0	0
Faneca, Alan, Pitt.	0	1	0	0	1
Farmer, Danny, Cin.	1	0	0	0	0
Farrior, James, NYJ	0	1	0	0	1
Faulk, Kevin, N.E.	6	1	0	0	1
Fauria, Christian, Sea.	1	1	0	0	1
Fazande, Jermaine, S.D.	1	1	0	0	1
Fiedler, Jay, Mia.	2	0	0	-8	0
Fina, John, Buff.	0	1	0	0	1
Finn, Jim, Ind.	1	0	0	0	0
Fletcher, Terrell, S.D.	2	0	0	0	0
Flowers, Lethon, Pitt.	0	0	3	0	3
Flutie, Doug, Buff.	5	2	0	-9	2
Flynn, Mike, Balt.	1	2	0	-18	2
Foley, Steve, Cin.	0	0	1	0	1
Ford, Henry, Tenn.	0	0	1	30	1
Fordham, Todd, Jax.	1	0	0	0	0
Fortin, Roman, S.D.	2	0	0	-1	0
Frerotte, Gus, Den.	5	0	0	0	0
Friedman, Lennie, Den.	0	2	0	0	2
Fuller, Corey, Cle.	0	0	1	0	1
Gadsden, Oronde, Mia.	0	1	1	0	2
Gamble, Trent, Mia.	0	0	1	0	1
Gandy, Wayne, Pitt.	0	1	0	0	1
Gannon, Rich, Oak.	9	2	0	-1	2
Gaylor, Trevor, S.D.	0	1	0	13	1
George, Eddie, Tenn.	5	2	0	0	2
George, Tony, N.E.	0	1	1	24	2
Gildon, Jason, Pitt.	0	0	4	22	4
Godfrey, Randall, Tenn.	0	0	1	0	1
Goff, Mike, Cin.	0	2	0	0	2
Gold, Ian, Den.	0	1	1	0	2
Gonzalez, Tony, K.C.	0	1	0	0	1
Gordon, Darrien, Oak.	2	0	1	74	1
Graham, Jeff, S.D.	1	0	0	0	0
Graham, Kent, Pitt.	1	0	0	0	0
Granville, Billy, Cin.	0	0	1	0	1
Gray, Chris, Sea.	0	1	0	0	1
Grbac, Elvis, K.C.	7	2	0	-6	2
Green, Victor, NYJ	0	0	4	0	4
Greer, Donovan, Buff.	0	0	1	0	1
Griese, Brian, Den.	5	2	0	-8	2
Griffith, Howard, Den.	0	1	0	0	1
Grunhard, Tim, K.C.	0	1	0	0	1
Hall, Dante, K.C.	1	0	0	0	0
Hamilton, Bobby, N.E.	0	0	1	0	1
Hansen, Phil, Buff.	0	0	1	29	1
Harbaugh, Jim, S.D.	5	1	0	-5	1
Hardy, Kevin, Jax.	0	0	2	2	2
Harris, Corey, Balt.	1	0	0	0	0
Harris, Antwan, N.E.	0	1	0	0	1
Harrison, Marvin, Ind.	2	0	0	0	0
Hasty, James, K.C.	0	0	2	0	2
Hawkins, Artrell, Cin.	0	0	1	12	1
Hayes, Chris, NYJ	0	0	1	0	1
Heath, Rodney, Cin.	0	0	1	0	1
Heiden, Steve, S.D.	0	0	1	0	1
Henry, Kevin, Pitt.	0	0	1	0	1
Hicks, Eric, K.C.	0	0	1	0	1
Holmes, Earl, Pitt.	0	0	1	4	1
Holmes, Priest, Balt.	2	1	0	0	1
Holsey, Bernard, Ind.	0	0	1	48	1
Howard, Chris, Jax.	2	0	0	0	0
Huard, Brock, Sea.	2	1	0	0	1
Humphrey, Deon, S.D.	0	1	0	0	1
Huntley, Richard, Pitt.	1	0	0	0	0
Isaia, Sale, N.E.	0	1	0	0	1
Izzo, Larry, Mia.	1	0	0	0	0
Jackson, Brad, Balt.	0	0	2	0	2
Jackson, Curtis, N.E.	1	0	0	0	0
Jackson, Darrell, Sea.	2	1	0	18	1
Jackson, Grady, Oak.	0	0	1	0	1
Jackson, Sheldon, Buff.	0	1	0	0	1
Jacquet, Nate, S.D.	3	2	0	0	2
James, Edgerrin, Ind.	5	0	0	0	0
Jenkins, Billy, Den.	1	1	0	0	1
Jenkins, DeRon, S.D.	1	0	0	0	0
Jenkins, Ronney, S.D.	3	2	0	0	2
Johnson, Garrett, N.E.	0	0	1	0	1

2000 INDIVIDUAL STATISTICS—FUMBLES

	Fum.	Own Rec.	Opp. Rec.	Yards	Tot. Rec.
Johnson, Lee, N.E.	2	1	0	-12	1
Johnson, Rob, Buff.	4	2	0	0	2
Johnson, Ted, N.E.	0	0	3	0	3
Jones, Freddie, S.D.	3	1	0	0	1
Jones, Henry, Buff.	0	0	1	14	1
Jones, Lenoy, Cle.	0	0	1	0	1
Jones, Marvin, NYJ	0	0	1	0	1
Jones, Reggie, S.D.	1	1	0	0	1
Jones, Robert, Mia.	0	1	0	0	1
Jordan, Randy, Oak.	1	0	0	0	0
Kacyvenski, Isaiah, Sea.	0	0	1	0	1
Kaufman, Napoleon, Oak.	1	0	0	0	0
Kendall, Pete, Sea.	0	1	0	0	1
Kennedy, Lincoln, Oak.	0	2	0	0	2
Kinney, Erron, Tenn.	1	1	0	0	1
Kirkland, Levon, Pitt.	0	0	1	0	1
Kitna, Jon, Sea.	17	9	0	-19	9
Koonce, George, Sea.	0	0	1	0	1
Leaf, Ryan, S.D.	12	4	0	-18	4
Lepsis, Matt, Den.	0	1	0	0	1
Lewis, Darryll, S.D.	0	0	1	29	1
Lewis, Jamal, Balt.	6	3	0	0	3
Lewis, Mo, NYJ	0	0	2	0	2
Lewis, Ray, Balt.	0	0	3	0	3
Lindsay, Everett, Cle.	0	1	0	0	1
Linton, Jonathan, Buff.	3	1	0	0	1
Little, Earl, Cle.	1	0	1	0	1
Lockett, Kevin, K.C.	3	1	0	0	1
Logan, Mike, Jax.	0	0	1	3	1
Long, Kevin, Tenn.	0	1	0	0	1
Loverne, David, NYJ	0	1	0	0	1
Lucas, Ray, NYJ	2	1	0	0	1
Mack, Stacey, Jax.	3	1	0	0	1
Mack, Tremain, Cin.	3	1	0	0	1
Madison, Sam, Mia.	1	0	2	20	2
Manning, Peyton, Ind.	5	1	0	-3	1
Marion, Brock, Mia.	0	0	1	0	1
Martin, Curtis, NYJ	2	0	0	0	0
Marts, Lonnie, Jax.	0	0	1	3	1
Maslowski, Mike, K.C.	0	0	1	0	1
Mason, Derrick, Tenn.	1	1	0	0	1
McAlister, Chris, Balt.	0	0	1	0	1
McCardell, Keenan, Jax.	3	1	0	4	1
McCrary, Fred, S.D.	1	0	0	0	0
McCrary, Michael, Balt.	0	0	3	0	3
McGinest, Willie, N.E.	0	0	2	0	2
McGlockton, Chester, K.C.	0	1	0	0	1
McKenzie, Keith, Cle.	0	0	1	29	1
McKinney, Steve, Ind.	0	0	1	0	1
McNair, Steve, Tenn.	12	3	0	-31	3
Meester, Brad, Jax.	0	1	0	0	1
Mili, Itula, Sea.	1	0	0	0	0
Miller, Fred, Tenn.	0	2	0	0	2
Miller, Josh, Pitt.	1	1	0	-18	1
Mitchell, Anthony, Balt.	0	1	0	0	1
Mitchell, Scott, Cin.	4	0	0	-6	0
Mixon, Kenny, Mia.	0	0	1	0	1
Moon, Warren, K.C.	1	1	0	0	1
Moore, Corey, Buff.	0	0	1	0	1
Moore, Larry, Ind.	0	1	0	0	1
Moreau, Frank, K.C.	2	0	0	0	0
Moreno, Moses, S.D.	3	1	0	-1	1
Morris, Aric, Tenn.	0	0	1	0	1
Morris, Sammy, Buff.	2	1	0	0	1
Morris, Sylvester, K.C.	3	0	0	0	0
Moulds, Eric, Buff.	1	1	0	0	1
Muhammad, Mustafah, Ind.	1	0	0	0	0
Mulitalo, Edwin, Balt.	0	2	0	0	2
Myslinski, Tom, Pitt.	0	1	0	0	1
Nails, Jamie, Buff.	0	1	0	5	1
Nalen, Tom, Den.	1	0	0	-2	0
Newman, Keith, Buff.	1	0	1	25	1
Northcutt, Dennis, Cle.	1	0	0	0	0
Ogden, Jeff, Mia.	1	0	0	0	0
Ogden, Jonathan, Balt.	0	2	0	0	2
O'Hara, Shaun, Cle.	1	0	0	-7	0
O'Neal, Deltha, Den.	6	2	1	6	3
Ostroski, Jerry, Buff.	1	1	0	-12	1
Parker, Larry, K.C.	1	0	0	0	0
Parmalee, Bernie, NYJ	0	0	1	0	1
Pass, Patrick, N.E.	0	1	0	0	1
Patten, David, Cle.	2	0	0	0	0
Patton, Marvcus, K.C.	0	0	1	0	1
Pederson, Doug, Cle.	4	3	0	0	3
Phenix, Perry, Tenn.	0	0	1	0	1
Pittman, Kavika, Den.	0	0	1	0	1
Poole, Tyrone, Ind.	0	1	0	8	1
Pope, Daniel, Cin.	1	1	0	-19	1
Pope, Marquez, Oak.	0	0	5	-2	5
Porter, Daryl, Buff.	0	1	1	54	2
Porter, Joey, Pitt.	0	0	1	32	1
Poteat, Hank, Pitt.	3	0	0	0	0
Prentice, Travis, Cle.	2	0	0	0	0
Price, Peerless, Buff.	4	1	0	0	1
Pryce, Trevor, Den.	0	0	1	28	1
Rainer, Wali, Cle.	0	0	1	0	1
Redmond, J.R., N.E.	2	0	0	0	0
Richardson, Tony, K.C.	3	0	0	0	0
Riemersma, Jay, Buff.	1	0	0	0	0
Robertson, Marcus, Tenn.	0	0	1	0	1
Robinson, Eddie, Tenn.	0	0	3	0	3
Rogers, Charlie, Sea.	5	1	0	0	1
Rogers, Sam, Buff.	0	0	1	0	1
Rogers, Tyrone, Cle.	0	0	3	0	3
Rolle, Samari, Tenn.	0	0	1	0	1
Roman, Mark, Cin.	0	2	0	0	2
Romanowski, Bill, Den.	0	0	2	0	2
Roundtree, Raleigh, S.D.	0	1	0	0	1
Roye, Orpheus, Cle.	0	0	1	8	1
Ruff, Orlando, S.D.	0	0	1	0	1
Rusk, Reggie, S.D.	0	0	1	17	1
Russell, Darrell, Oak.	0	0	1	0	1
Russell, Twan, Mia.	0	0	1	0	1
Rutledge, Rod, N.E.	0	1	0	0	1
Saleh, Tarek, Cle.	0	1	0	0	1
Sanders, Chris, Tenn.	1	0	0	0	0
Saturday, Jeff, Ind.	1	1	0	0	1
Scott, Chad, Pitt.	0	1	1	6	2
Scott, Tony, NYJ	0	1	0	0	1
Serwanga, Kato, N.E.	0	0	2	0	2
Sharper, Jamie, Balt.	0	0	2	0	2
Shaw, Bobby, Pitt.	2	0	0	0	0
Shea, Aaron, Cle.	1	0	0	0	0
Shelton, Daimon, Jax.	0	1	1	0	2
Shields, Scott, Pitt.	1	1	1	-5	2
Shields, Will, K.C.	0	1	0	0	1
Sidney, Dainon, Tenn.	0	0	2	0	2
Simpson, Antoine, S.D.	0	0	1	0	1
Sims, Barry, Oak.	0	1	0	0	1
Sinclair, Michael, Sea.	0	0	4	69	4
Siragusa, Tony, Balt.	0	0	1	0	1
Smith, Antowain, Buff.	1	0	0	0	0
Smith, Jeff, Jax.	1	0	0	0	0
Smith, Jimmy, Jax.	1	0	0	0	0
Smith, Akili, Cin.	14	2	0	-14	2
Smith, Lamar, Mia.	3	0	0	0	0
Smith, Larry, Jax.	0	0	3	1	3
Smith, Otis, N.E.	0	0	1	12	1
Smith, Rod, Den.	1	0	0	0	0
Soward, R.Jay, Jax.	3	1	0	0	1
Spencer, Jimmy, Den.	0	0	1	0	1
Spikes, Takeo, Cin.	0	0	3	0	3
Spires, Greg, N.E.	0	0	1	0	1
Spriggs, Marcus, Cle.	0	0	1	0	1
Starks, Duane, Balt.	1	1	1	0	2
Stewart, Kordell, Pitt.	8	3	0	-1	3
Stewart, Rayna, Jax.	0	0	2	2	2
Stills, Gary, K.C.	0	0	1	0	1
Stith, Shyrone, Jax.	1	0	0	0	0
Stone, Dwight, NYJ	1	1	0	0	1
Storz, Erik, Jax.	0	0	1	0	1
Sullivan, Chris, Pitt.	0	0	2	0	2
Surtain, Patrick, Mia.	0	0	1	0	1
Suttle, Jason, Den.	0	0	1	0	1
Swayne, Harry, Balt.	0	1	0	0	1
Tait, John, K.C.	0	1	0	0	1
Tanuvasa, Maa, Den.	0	0	4	38	4
Taylor, Fred, Jax.	4	2	0	-1	2
Taylor, Jason, Mia.	0	0	4	29	4
Taylor, Travis, Balt.	1	0	0	0	0
Testaverde, Vinny, NYJ	7	0	0	-5	0
Thomas, Henry, N.E.	0	0	1	0	1

2000 INDIVIDUAL STATISTICS—FUMBLES

	Fum.	Own Rec.	Opp. Rec.	Yards	Tot. Rec.
Thomas, Kiwaukee, Jax.	0	0	1	0	1
Thomas, Rodney, Tenn.	1	0	1	0	1
Thomas, Thurman, Mia.	1	0	0	0	0
Thomas, Zach, Mia.	0	0	1	0	1
Thompson, Kevin, Cle.	1	1	0	0	1
Thornton, John, Tenn.	0	0	1	0	1
Traylor, Keith, Den.	0	0	1	0	1
Upshaw, Regan, Oak.	0	0	2	8	2
Vrabel, Mike, Pitt.	0	0	1	0	1
Walker, Denard, Tenn.	1	0	0	0	0
Ward, Dedric, NYJ	1	0	0	0	0
Ward, Hines, Pitt.	2	1	0	0	1
Warrick, Peter, Cin.	2	1	0	0	1
Washington, Keith, Balt.	0	0	1	0	1
Watson, Chris, Buff.	4	2	0	0	2
Watters, Ricky, Sea.	5	2	0	0	2
Weaver, Jed, Mia.	1	0	0	0	0
Webster, Larry, Balt.	0	0	1	0	1
Wesley, Greg, K.C.	0	0	1	0	1
Wheatley, Tyrone, Oak.	4	1	0	0	1
Whitted, Alvis, Jax.	1	0	0	0	0
Wiegert, Zach, Jax.	0	1	0	0	1
Wiggins, Jermaine, N.E.	1	0	0	0	0
Wiley, Marcellus, Buff.	0	0	1	0	1
Wilkins, Terrence, Ind.	4	1	0	0	1
Williams, Dan, K.C.	1	0	1	9	1
Williams, Nick, Cin.	2	1	0	0	1
Williams, Josh, Ind.	0	0	1	0	1
Williams, Pat, Buff.	0	0	2	0	2
Williams, Willie, Sea.	0	0	1	0	1
Wilson, Reinard, Cin.	0	0	1	3	1
Woodson, Charles, Oak.	0	0	1	0	1
Woodson, Rod, Balt.	0	0	3	4	3
Wycheck, Frank, Tenn.	2	0	0	0	0
Wynn, Spergon, Cle.	2	0	0	0	0
Yeast, Craig, Cin.	3	1	0	0	1
Zahursky, Steve, Cle.	0	3	0	0	3

Yards includes aborted plays, own recoveries, and opponents' recoveries.

NFC FUMBLES—INDIVIDUAL

	Fum.	Own Rec.	Opp. Rec.	Yards	Tot. Rec.
Ahanotu, Chidi, T.B.	0	0	1	0	1
Aikman, Troy, Dall.	2	0	0	0	0
Aldridge, Allen, Det.	0	0	1	0	1
Alexander, Stephen, Wash.	2	0	0	0	0
Allen, James, Chi.	5	0	0	0	0
Allen, Larry, Dall.	0	2	0	0	2
Alstott, Mike, T.B.	3	1	0	0	1
Anderson, Jamal, Atl.	6	1	0	0	1
Armstead, Jessie, NYG	0	0	1	0	1
Autry, Darnell, Phil.	2	1	0	0	1
Badger, Brad, Minn.	0	1	0	0	1
Bailey, Champ, Wash.	0	0	1	0	1
Barber, Tiki, NYG	9	5	0	0	5
Barber, Ronde, T.B.	0	0	1	24	1
Barber, Shawn, Wash.	0	0	3	0	3
Barnes, Marlon, Chi.	1	0	0	0	0
Barrett, David, Ariz.	0	0	1	0	1
Barrow, Micheal, NYG	0	0	1	0	1
Bartrum, Mike, Phil.	0	0	1	0	1
Batch, Charlie, Det.	6	1	0	-5	1
Bates, Michael, Car.	4	1	0	0	1
Beuerlein, Steve, Car.	9	0	0	-5	0
Biakabutuka, Tim, Car.	4	0	0	0	0
Bidwell, Josh, G.B.	1	1	0	0	1
Birk, Matt, Minn.	1	0	0	0	0
Blake, Jeff, N.O.	7	3	0	-2	3
Bly, Dre', St.L.	1	1	0	0	1
Booker, Marty, Chi.	2	1	0	0	1
Bostic, Jason, Phil.	1	0	0	0	0
Boston, David, Ariz.	2	1	0	0	1
Bowens, David, G.B.	0	0	1	0	1
Boyd, Stephen, Det.	0	0	1	0	1
Brister, Bubby, Minn.	1	1	0	0	1
Brooks, Aaron, N.O.	4	0	0	-4	0
Broughton, Luther, Phil.	1	0	0	0	0
Brown, Dave, Ariz.	2	0	0	-3	0
Brown, Ray, S.F.	0	1	0	0	1
Brown, Lomas, NYG	0	1	0	0	1
Brown, Mike, Chi.	0	0	1	12	1
Bruce, Isaac, St.L.	1	0	0	0	0
Buchanan, Ray, Atl.	0	0	2	1	2
Bush, Devin, St.L.	0	1	0	15	1
Butler, LeRoy, G.B.	0	0	1	0	1
Byrd, Isaac, Car.	0	1	0	0	1
Campbell, Dan, NYG	1	0	0	0	0
Carter, Cris, Minn.	3	2	0	0	2
Carter, Kevin, St.L.	1	0	1	0	1
Carter, Marty, Atl.	0	0	2	0	2
Case, Stoney, Det.	1	0	0	0	0
Centers, Larry, Wash.	1	1	0	0	1
Chandler, Chris, Atl.	7	4	0	-13	4
Cherry, Je'Rod, Phil.	0	0	1	0	1
Christian, Bob, Atl.	0	0	1	10	1
Clark, Greg, S.F.	1	1	0	0	1
Clarke, Phil, N.O.	0	0	1	0	1
Clement, Anthony, Ariz.	0	1	0	0	1
Coakley, Dexter, Dall.	0	0	1	8	1
Cody, Mac, Ariz.	4	1	0	0	1
Collins, Kerry, NYG	7	1	0	-13	1
Colvin, Rosevelt, Chi.	0	0	1	0	1
Comella, Greg, NYG	2	0	0	0	0
Culpepper, Daunte, Minn.	11	5	0	-23	5
Cunningham, Randall, Dall.	4	3	0	-2	3
Daniels, Phillip, Chi.	0	0	1	0	1
Davis, Eric, Car.	1	1	0	0	1
Davis, Rob, G.B.	0	0	1	0	1
Davis, Stephen, Wash.	4	1	0	0	1
Davis, Tyrone, G.B.	2	0	0	0	0
Dawkins, Brian, Phil.	0	1	1	0	2
Dayne, Ron, NYG	1	0	0	0	0
DeVries, Jared, Det.	0	0	1	0	1
Dexter, James, Car.	0	1	0	0	1
Diggs, Na'il, G.B.	0	0	1	52	1
Dishman, Chris, Ariz.	1	1	0	0	1
Dixon, David, Minn.	0	1	0	0	1
Dotson, Earl, G.B.	0	1	0	0	1
Downs, Gary, Atl.	0	0	1	0	1
Driver, Donald, G.B.	0	1	0	0	1
Duncan, Jamie, T.B.	0	0	1	0	1
Dunn, Warrick, T.B.	1	0	0	0	0
Dwight, Tim, Atl.	3	1	0	0	1
Ekuban, Ebenezer, Dall.	0	0	1	0	1
Ellis, Greg, Dall.	0	0	2	0	2
Elliss, Luther, Det.	0	0	2	3	2
Emmons, Carlos, Phil.	0	0	1	2	1
Engram, Bobby, Chi.	1	1	0	0	1
Evans, Doug, Car.	0	0	5	-3	5
Fair, Terry, Det.	1	0	1	2	1
Faulk, Marshall, St.L.	0	2	0	0	2
Favre, Brett, G.B.	9	2	0	-12	2
Fischer, Mark, Wash.	1	0	0	-18	0
Flanigan, Jim, Chi.	0	0	1	0	1
Fontenot, Jerry, N.O.	0	1	0	0	1
Foster, Larry, Det.	2	0	1	0	1
Franks, Bubba, G.B.	1	0	0	0	0
Freeman, Antonio, G.B.	1	0	0	0	0
Fricke, Ben, Dall.	2	0	0	0	0
Garcia, Frank, Car.	0	1	0	0	1
Garcia, Jeff, S.F.	7	4	0	-6	4
Garner, Charlie, S.F.	4	0	0	0	0
George, Jeff, Wash.	3	1	0	-3	1
Gilbert, Sean, Car.	0	0	1	0	1
Glover, La'Roi, N.O.	0	0	1	0	1
Golden, Jack, NYG	0	0	1	0	1
Goodman, Herbert, G.B.	2	0	0	0	0
Gragg, Scott, S.F.	0	1	0	0	1
Grant, Orantes, Dall.	0	0	2	0	2
Green, Ahman, G.B.	6	1	0	0	1
Green, Barrett, Det.	0	0	1	0	1
Green, Trent, St.L.	3	0	0	0	0
Greisen, Chris, Ariz.	1	0	0	0	0
Griffith, Robert, Minn.	0	0	2	0	2
Hakim, Az-Zahir, St.L.	7	1	0	0	1
Hall, Lemanski, Minn.	0	0	1	1	1
Hall, Travis, Atl.	0	0	1	0	1
Hamilton, Joe, T.B.	1	0	0	0	0
Hankton, Karl, Car.	0	0	1	0	1
Hardy, Terry, Ariz.	2	0	0	0	0
Hartings, Jeff, Det.	0	1	0	0	1

2000 INDIVIDUAL STATISTICS—FUMBLES

	Fum.	Own Rec.	Opp. Rec.	Yards	Tot. Rec.
Hastings, Andre, T.B.	1	0	0	0	0
Hauck, Tim, Phil.	0	0	1	0	1
Hawthorne, Michael, N.O.	0	0	1	0	1
Hayes, Donald, Car.	1	0	0	0	0
Heck, Andy, Wash.	0	1	0	0	1
Henderson, William, G.B.	1	1	0	0	1
Hennings, Chad, Dall.	0	0	1	0	1
Hetherington, Chris, Car.	0	0	1	0	1
Hicks, Skip, Wash.	1	0	0	0	0
Hitchcock, Jimmy, Car.	1	0	0	0	0
Hobgood-Chittick, Nate, S.F.	0	0	1	0	1
Hodgins, James, St.L.	0	1	0	0	1
Holt, Torry, St.L.	2	1	0	0	1
Hoover, Brad, Car.	1	0	1	0	1
Horn, Joe, N.O.	1	1	0	0	1
Horne, Tony, St.L.	3	0	1	0	1
Howard, Darren, N.O.	1	0	2	0	2
Howard, Desmond, Det.	2	1	0	0	1
Irvin, Sedrick, Det.	1	0	0	0	0
Ismail, Raghib, Dall.	1	0	0	0	0
Jackson, Dexter, T.B.	0	0	1	0	1
Jackson, Terry, S.F.	0	1	0	0	1
Jackson, Willie, N.O.	2	0	0	0	0
Jefferson, Shawn, Atl.	1	0	0	0	0
Jenkins, MarTay, Ariz.	3	0	0	0	0
Jett, John, Det.	1	1	0	-10	1
Johnson, Doug, Atl.	4	0	0	0	0
Johnson, Brad, Wash.	5	2	0	-14	2
Johnson, Joe, N.O.	0	0	2	0	2
Johnson, Keyshawn, T.B.	2	0	0	0	0
Jones, Greg, Wash.	0	0	1	0	1
Jones, James, Det.	0	0	1	0	1
Jones, Marcus, T.B.	0	0	1	0	1
Jones, Thomas, Ariz.	4	1	0	0	1
Jurevicius, Joe, NYG	1	0	0	0	0
Kalu, Ndukwe, Wash.	0	0	1	4	1
Kanell, Danny, Atl.	2	2	0	-2	2
Kelly, Brian, T.B.	0	0	2	0	2
Kelly, Reggie, Atl.	1	0	0	0	0
Kennison, Eddie, Chi.	1	1	0	0	1
King, Shaun, T.B.	4	3	0	0	3
Kirschke, Travis, Det.	0	0	1	0	1
Kowalkowski, Scott, Det.	0	0	1	2	1
Kozlowski, Brian, Atl.	0	2	0	0	2
Kriewaldt, Clint, Det.	0	0	1	0	1
Lang, Kenard, Wash.	0	0	1	0	1
Lassiter, Kwamie, Ariz.	0	0	1	0	1
Levingston, Bashir, NYG	2	0	0	0	0
Lewis, Jeff, Car.	1	0	0	0	0
Lewis, Jonas, S.F.	0	0	1	0	1
Lincoln, Jeremy, Det.	0	0	1	0	1
Lucas, Al, Car.	0	0	1	0	1
Lyle, Keith, St.L.	0	0	1	94	1
Lynch, John, T.B.	0	0	2	8	2
Maddox, Mark, Ariz.	0	1	0	-2	1
Martin, Cecil, Phil.	1	0	0	0	0
Mathis, Kevin, N.O.	1	0	0	0	0
Mathis, Terance, Atl.	1	0	0	0	0
Matthews, Shane, Chi.	2	1	0	0	1
McAfee, Fred, N.O.	0	0	1	0	1
McBurrows, Gerald, Atl.	0	0	2	0	2
McCleon, Dexter, St.L.	1	0	1	21	1
McCollum, Andy, St.L.	1	0	0	-4	0
McDaniel, Emmanuel, NYG	0	1	0	0	1
McElroy, Ray, Chi.	0	0	1	0	1
McFarland, Anthony, T.B.	0	0	1	0	1
McGarity, Wane, Dall.	2	2	0	0	2
McKenzie, Mike, G.B.	1	0	0	0	0
McKenzie, Raleigh, G.B.	0	1	0	0	1
McKinnon, Ronald, Ariz.	0	0	1	0	1
McKnight, James, Dall.	1	0	0	0	0
McNabb, Donovan, Phil.	7	2	0	-5	2
McNown, Cade, Chi.	8	4	0	-17	4
Milburn, Glyn, Chi.	4	3	0	0	3
Miller, Jim, Chi.	1	0	0	0	0
Miller, Keith, St.L.	0	1	0	0	1
Minter, Mike, Car.	0	0	1	0	1
Mitchell, Basil, G.B.	1	1	0	0	1
Mitchell, Brian, Phil.	3	1	0	0	1
Mitchell, Keith, N.O.	0	0	4	90	4
Mitchell, Pete, NYG	1	1	0	0	1

	Fum.	Own Rec.	Opp. Rec.	Yards	Tot. Rec.
Monty, Pete, NYG	0	1	0	0	1
Moore, Damon, Phil.	1	0	0	0	0
Morabito, Tim, Car.	0	0	1	0	1
Morrow, Harold, Minn.	0	0	1	0	1
Morton, Chad, N.O.	2	1	0	0	1
Morton, Johnnie, Det.	1	0	0	0	0
Moss, Randy, Minn.	2	0	0	0	0
Muhammad, Muhsin, Car.	1	0	1	0	1
Murrell, Adrian, Wash.	1	0	0	0	0
Myers, Michael, Dall.	0	0	1	0	1
Nguyen, Dat, Dall.	0	1	0	0	1
Norton, Ken, S.F.	0	0	1	0	1
Nutten, Tom, St.L.	0	1	0	0	1
Oldham, Chris, N.O.	0	0	2	2	2
Oliver, Winslow, Atl.	1	0	0	0	0
Owens, Terrell, S.F.	3	0	0	0	0
Palmer, David, Minn.	1	0	0	0	0
Petitgout, Luke, NYG	0	1	0	0	1
Pittman, Michael, Ariz.	5	0	0	0	0
Plummer, Jake, Ariz.	8	4	0	-1	4
Poole, Keith, N.O.	1	1	0	0	1
Porcher, Robert, Det.	0	0	1	0	1
Posey, Jeff, S.F.	0	0	1	0	1
Pritchett, Stanley, Phil.	1	0	0	0	0
Quarles, Shelton, T.B.	0	0	2	5	2
Rasby, Walter, Det.	0	1	0	0	1
Redmon, Anthony, Atl.	0	1	0	0	1
Rice, Jerry, S.F.	3	1	0	0	1
Rice, Ron, Det.	0	0	1	6	1
Rice, Simeon, Ariz.	0	0	1	0	1
Robinson, Damien, T.B.	0	0	3	5	3
Robinson, Eugene, Car.	0	0	3	26	3
Robinson, Jeff, St.L.	0	1	0	0	1
Robinson, Marcus, Chi.	1	0	0	0	0
Rossum, Allen, G.B.	4	3	0	0	3
Runyan, Jon, Phil.	0	1	0	0	1
Rutledge, Johnny, Ariz.	0	0	1	0	1
Sanders, Deion, Wash.	3	2	0	0	2
Sapp, Warren, T.B.	0	0	1	0	1
Sawyer, Talance, Minn.	0	0	2	0	2
Schroeder, Bill, G.B.	1	0	0	0	0
Schulters, Lance, S.F.	0	0	1	16	1
Sears, Corey, Ariz.	0	0	1	0	1
Sehorn, Jason, NYG	0	0	1	8	1
Shade, Sam, Wash.	0	0	4	1	4
Shelton, L.J., Ariz.	0	1	0	0	1
Simmons, Clyde, Chi.	0	0	1	0	1
Simon, Corey, Phil.	0	0	1	5	1
Sims, Keith, Wash.	0	1	0	0	1
Smith, Derek M., Wash.	0	0	1	0	1
Smith, Emmitt, Dall.	6	1	0	0	1
Smith, Paul, S.F.	2	2	0	0	2
Smith, Robert, Minn.	4	3	0	0	3
Smith, Terrelle, N.O.	1	0	0	0	0
Smith, Thomas, Chi.	0	0	1	0	1
Stablein, Brian, Det.	1	0	0	0	0
Stachelski, Dave, N.O.	0	0	1	0	1
Staley, Duce, Phil.	3	1	0	0	1
Stecker, Aaron, T.B.	1	0	0	0	0
Stepnoski, Mark, Dall.	1	0	0	0	0
Stevens, Matt, Wash.	0	0	1	1	1
Stewart, James, Det.	4	1	0	0	1
Strahan, Michael, NYG	0	0	4	0	4
Streets, Tai, S.F.	1	0	0	0	0
Stubblefield, Dana, Wash.	0	0	1	0	1
Tate, Robert, Minn.	0	0	1	0	1
Taylor, Bobby, Phil.	0	0	1	0	1
Terrell, David, Wash.	0	1	1	0	2
Thomas, Chris, St.L.	0	0	1	0	1
Thomas, Hollis, Phil.	0	0	1	0	1
Thomas, Orlando, Minn.	0	0	2	0	2
Thomas, Robert, Dall.	2	1	0	0	1
Thrash, James, Wash.	1	0	1	0	1
Tillman, Pat, Ariz.	0	0	2	0	2
Toomer, Amani, NYG	1	1	0	0	1
Towns, Lester, Car.	0	0	2	0	2
Tubbs, Winfred, S.F.	0	0	1	0	1
Tucker, Jason, Dall.	3	0	0	0	0
Turley, Kyle, N.O.	0	4	0	-6	4
Urlacher, Brian, Chi.	0	0	1	0	1
Vaughn, Darrick, Atl.	1	0	1	0	1

2000 INDIVIDUAL STATISTICS—FUMBLES/SACKS

	Fum.	Own Rec.	Opp. Rec.	Yards	Tot. Rec.
Vincent, Troy, Phil.	0	0	2	0	2
Walker, Marquis, Det.	1	1	1	0	2
Walter, Ken, Car.	2	2	0	-11	2
Walters, Troy, Minn.	2	1	0	0	1
Warner, Kurt, St.L.	4	0	0	-8	0
Warren, Chris, Dall.-Phil.	3	0	0	0	0
Wayne, Nate, G.B.	0	0	1	9	1
Webster, Jason, S.F.	0	0	1	1	1
Welbourn, John, Phil.	0	1	0	0	1
West, Lyle, NYG	0	0	1	0	1
White, Dez, Chi.	1	0	0	0	0
White, Reggie, Car.	0	0	1	0	1
Whiting, Brandon, Phil.	0	0	2	0	2
Wiegmann, Casey, Chi.	0	1	0	0	1
Wiley, Michael, Dall.	3	1	0	0	1
Williams, Aeneas, Ariz.	0	0	2	104	2
Williams, Brian, G.B.	0	0	1	0	1
Williams, Ricky, N.O.	6	2	0	0	2
Williams, George, NYG	0	0	1	0	1
Williams, James O., Chi.	0	1	0	0	1
Williams, Karl, T.B.	2	1	0	0	1
Williams, K.D., G.B.	0	0	1	0	1
Williams, Kevin R., S.F.	1	1	0	0	1
Williams, Moe, Minn.	0	0	1	0	1
Williams, Shaun, NYG	0	0	1	0	1
Williams, Wally, N.O.	0	1	0	0	1
Wong, Kailee, Minn.	1	0	0	0	0
Woodall, Lee, Car.	0	0	1	0	1
Wooden, Shawn, Chi.	0	0	1	3	1
Wortham, Barron, Dall.	0	0	1	0	1
Wright, Anthony, Dall.	3	1	0	-3	1
Wright, Kenny, Minn.	0	1	0	11	1
Yoder, Todd, T.B.	1	0	0	0	0
Young, Bryant, S.F.	0	0	1	0	1
Zgonina, Jeff, St.L.	0	2	1	0	3

Yards includes aborted plays, own recoveries, and opponents' recoveries.

SACKS

Most Sacks

NFC: 17.0—La'Roi Glover, New Orleans
AFC: 16.5—Trace Armstrong, Miami

Most Sacks, Game

NFC: 4.0—Marcus Jones, Tampa Bay vs. Detroit, October 19
AFC: 3.5—Trace Armstrong, Miami vs. Buffalo, October 8

Team Champion

NFC: 66—New Orleans
AFC: 55—Tennessee

Team Leaders, Sacks

AFC: BALTIMORE: 10.5, Rob Burnett; BUFFALO: 10.5, Marcellus Wiley; CINCINNATI: 4.0, Steve Foley, Oliver Gibson, Cory Hall; CLEVELAND: 8.0, Keith McKenzie; DENVER: 12.0, Trevor Pryce; INDIANAPOLIS: 7.5, Chad Bratzke; JACKSONVILLE: 7.5, Tony Brackens; KANSAS CITY: 14.0, Eric Hicks; MIAMI: 16.5, Trace Armstrong; NEW ENGLAND: 6.0, Willie McGinest, Greg Spires; N.Y. JETS: 10.0, Mo Lewis; OAKLAND: 8.0, Grady Jackson; PITTSBURGH: 13.5, Jason Gildon; SAN DIEGO: 7.0, John Parrella; SEATTLE: 6.0, Chad Brown, Lamar King; TENNESSEE: 11.5, Jevon Kearse

NFC: ARIZONA: 7.5, Simeon Rice; ATLANTA: 4.5, Travis Hall, Brady Smith; CAROLINA: 6.0, Jay Williams; CHICAGO: 8.0, Brian Urlacher; DALLAS: 6.5, Ebenezer Ekuban; DETROIT: 8.0, Robert Porcher; GREEN BAY: 6.5, John Thierry; MINNESOTA: 8.0, John Randle; NEW ORLEANS: 17.0, La'Roi Glover; N.Y. GIANTS: 10.0, Keith Hamilton; PHILADELPHIA: 15.0, Hugh Douglas; ST. LOUIS: 11.0, Grant Wistrom; SAN FRANCISCO: 9.5, Bryant Young; TAMPA BAY: 16.5, Warren Sapp; WASHINGTON: 12.0, Marco Coleman

AFC SACKS—TEAM

	Sacks	Yards
Tennessee	55	338
Kansas City	51	266
Miami	48	270
Denver	44	251
Oakland	43	278
Buffalo	42	308
Cleveland	42	270
Indianapolis	42	252
Jacksonville	40	247
N.Y. Jets	40	234
Pittsburgh	39	229
San Diego	39	249
Baltimore	35	178
New England	29	172
Seattle	27	152
Cincinnati	26	168
AFC Total	642	3862
AFC Average	40.1	241.4

NFC SACKS—TEAM

	Sacks	Yards
New Orleans	66	378
Tampa Bay	55	332
St. Louis	51	288
Philadelphia	50	291
Washington	45	283
N.Y. Giants	44	279
Green Bay	38	244
San Francisco	38	270
Chicago	36	230
Atlanta	31	142
Minnesota	31	214
Detroit	28	162
Carolina	27	226
Arizona	25	135
Dallas	25	189
NFC Total	590	3663
NFC Average	39.3	244.2
League Total	1232	7525
League Average	39.7	242.7

SACKS—TOP TEN LEADERS

Glover, La' Roi, N.O.	17.0
Armstrong, Trace, Mia.	16.5
Sapp, Warren, T.B.	16.5
Douglas, Hugh, Phil.	15.0
Taylor, Jason, Mia.	14.5
Hicks, Eric, K.C.	14.0
Gildon, Jason, Pitt.	13.5
Jones, Marcus, T.B.	13.0
Coleman, Marco, Wash.	12.0
Johnson, Joe, N.O.	12.0
Pryce, Trevor, Den.	12.0

AFC SACKS—INDIVIDUAL

Armstrong, Trace, Mia.	16.5
Taylor, Jason, Mia.	14.5
Hicks, Eric, K.C.	14.0
Gildon, Jason, Pitt.	13.5
Pryce, Trevor, Den.	12.0
Kearse, Jevon, Tenn.	11.5
Burnett, Rob, Balt.	10.5
Porter, Joey, Pitt.	10.5
Wiley, Marcellus, Buff.	10.5
Lewis, Mo, NYJ	10.0
Ellis, Shaun, NYJ	8.5
Holmes, Kenny, Tenn.	8.0
Jackson, Grady, Oak.	8.0
McKenzie, Keith, Cle.	8.0
Newman, Keith, Buff.	8.0
Brackens, Tony, Jax.	7.5
Bratzke, Chad, Ind.	7.5
Clemons, Duane, K.C.	7.5
Williams, Dan, K.C.	7.5
Boulware, Peter, Balt.	7.0
Parrella, John, S.D.	7.0
Pittman, Kavika, Den.	7.0
McCrary, Michael, Balt.	6.5
Brown, Chad, Sea.	6.0
Browning, John, K.C.	6.0
Coleman, Roderick, Oak.	6.0
Cox, Bryan, NYJ	6.0
Harrison, Rodney, S.D.	6.0
King, Lamar, Sea.	6.0
McGinest, Willie, N.E.	6.0
Mickell, Darren, S.D.	6.0
Smeenge, Joel, Jax.	6.0
Spires, Greg, N.E.	6.0
Upshaw, Regan, Oak.	6.0
Bryant, Tony, Oak.	5.5
Cowart, Sam, Buff.	5.5
Favors, Greg, Tenn.	5.5
Beasley, Aaron, Jax.	5.0
Belser, Jason, Ind.	5.0
Dixon, Gerald, S.D.	5.0
Johnson, Ellis, Ind.	5.0
Miller, Jamir, Cle.	5.0
Rogers, Sam, Buff.	5.0
Thomas, Mark, Ind.	5.0
Walker, Gary, Jax.	5.0
Wilson, Al, Den.	5.0
Abraham, John, NYJ	4.5
Brown, Courtney, Cle.	4.5
McGlockton, Chester, K.C.	4.5
Thomas, Henry, N.E.	4.5
Foley, Steve, Cin.	4.0
Fontenot, Albert, S.D.	4.0
Gibson, Oliver, Cin.	4.0
Hall, Cory, Cin.	4.0
McCutcheon, Daylon, Cle.	4.0
Phifer, Roman, NYJ	4.0
Robinson, Eddie, Tenn.	4.0
Salave'a, Joe, Tenn.	4.0
Simmons, Anthony, Sea.	4.0
Slade, Chris, N.E.	4.0
Smith, Aaron, Pitt.	4.0
Tanuvasa, Maa, Den.	4.0
Thornton, John, Tenn.	4.0
Boyer, Brant, Jax.	3.5
Colinet, Stalin, Cle.	3.5

2000 INDIVIDUAL STATISTICS—SACKS

Embray, Keith, Tenn.	3.5
Johnstone, Lance, Oak.	3.5
Romanowski, Bill, Den.	3.5
Seau, Junior, S.D.	3.5
Sinclair, Michael, Sea.	3.5
Townsend, Deshea, Pitt.	3.5
Wynn, Renaldo, Jax.	3.5
Bennett, Cornelius, Ind.	3.0
Brown, Cornell, Balt.	3.0
Burris, Jeff, Ind.	3.0
Godfrey, Randall, Tenn.	3.0
Hardy, Kevin, Jax.	3.0
Lewis, Ray, Balt.	3.0
Russell, Darrell, Oak.	3.0
Taves, Josh, Oak.	3.0
Williams, Josh, Ind.	3.0
Wilson, Reinard, Cin.	3.0
Bishop, Blaine, Tenn.	2.5
Bowens, Tim, Mia.	2.5
Chester, Larry, Ind.	2.5
Dingle, Adrian, S.D.	2.5
Eaton, Chad, N.E.	2.5
Gardener, Daryl, Mia.	2.5
Hasselbach, Harald, Den.	2.5
Jones, Lenoy, Cle.	2.5
Mixon, Kenny, Mia.	2.5
Smith, Robaire, Tenn.	2.5
Washington, Ted, Buff.	2.5
Williams, Pat, Buff.	2.5
Abdullah, Rahim, Cle.	2.0
Adams, Sam, Balt.	2.0
Alexander, Elijah, Oak.	2.0
Bellamy, Jay, Sea.	2.0
Biekert, Greg, Oak.	2.0
Bromell, Lorenzo, Mia.	2.0
Curtis, Canute, Cin.	2.0
Fisk, Jason, Tenn.	2.0
Flowers, Erik, Buff.	2.0
Ford, Henry, Tenn.	2.0
Gold, Ian, Den.	2.0
Hansen, Phil, Buff.	2.0
Holsey, Bernard, Ind.	2.0
Maslowski, Mike, K.C.	2.0
Mobley, John, Den.	2.0
Payne, Seth, Jax.	2.0
Reagor, Montae, Den.	2.0
Rogers, Tyrone, Cle.	2.0
Roye, Orpheus, Cle.	2.0
Scioli, Brad, Ind.	2.0
Serwanga, Kato, N.E.	2.0
Spikes, Takeo, Cin.	2.0
Spriggs, Marcus, Cle.	2.0
Steele, Glen, Cin.	2.0
Trapp, James, Balt.	2.0
Walker, Brian, Mia.	2.0
Washington, Marcus, Ind.	2.0
Woods, Jerome, K.C.	2.0
Alexander, Brent, Pitt.	1.5
Haley, Jermaine, Mia.	1.5
Hamilton, Bobby, N.E.	1.5
Koonce, George, Sea.	1.5
Miller, Arnold, Cle.	1.5
Rolle, Samari, Tenn.	1.5
Thomas, Zach, Mia.	1.5
Williams, Tyrone M., K.C.	1.5
Allen, Eric, Oak.	1.0
Bartee, William, K.C.	1.0
Battles, Ainsley, Pitt.	1.0
Beckett, Rogers, S.D.	1.0
Brown, Eric, Den.	1.0
Bruschi, Tedy, N.E.	1.0
Burton, Shane, NYJ	1.0
Bush, Lewis, K.C.	1.0
Carter, Chris, Cin.	1.0
Copeland, John, Cin.	1.0
Crockett, Ray, Den.	1.0
Darius, Donovin, Jax.	1.0
Dorsett, Anthony, Oak.	1.0
Dumas, Mike, S.D.	1.0
Edwards, Donnie, K.C.	1.0
Farrior, James, NYJ	1.0
Ferguson, Jason, NYJ	1.0
Flowers, Lethon, Pitt.	1.0
Frost, Scott, NYJ	1.0
Harris, Antwan, N.E.	1.0
Hasty, James, K.C.	1.0
Herring, Kim, Balt.	1.0
Holland, Darius, Cle.	1.0
Hollier, Dwight, Ind.	1.0
Holmes, Earl, Pitt.	1.0
Jones, Fred, Buff.	1.0
Jones, Marvin, NYJ	1.0
Kennedy, Cortez, Sea.	1.0
Killens, Terry, Tenn.	1.0
Larsen, Leif, Buff.	1.0
Lewis, Darryll, S.D.	1.0
Logan, Mike, Jax.	1.0
Lyle, Rick, NYJ	1.0
Moore, Corey, Buff.	1.0
Moore, Marty, Cle.	1.0
Nickerson, Hardy, Jax.	1.0
Patton, Marvcus, K.C.	1.0
Pope, Marquez, Oak.	1.0
Price, Shawn, Buff.	1.0
Rainer, Wali, Cle.	1.0
Ross, Adrian, Cin.	1.0
Rusk, Reggie, S.D.	1.0
Simmons, Brian, Cin.	1.0
Smith, Marquis, Cle.	1.0
Spearman, Armegis, Cin.	1.0
Spencer, Jimmy, Den.	1.0
Spicer, Paul, Jax.	1.0
Surtain, Patrick, Mia.	1.0
Thomas, William, Oak.	1.0
Thompson, Mike, Cle.	1.0
Traylor, Keith, Den.	1.0
von Oelhoffen, Kimo, Pitt.	1.0
Vrabel, Mike, Pitt.	1.0
Wesley, Greg, K.C.	1.0
Whittington, Bernard, Ind.	1.0
Williams, Jamal, S.D.	1.0
Williams, Willie, Sea.	1.0
Wiltz, Jason, NYJ	1.0
Cochran, Antonio, Sea.	0.5
Johnson, Ted, N.E.	0.5
LaBounty, Matt, Sea.	0.5
Meier, Rob, Jax.	0.5
Owens, Rich, Mia.	0.5
Rodgers, Derrick, Mia.	0.5
Wilson, Jerry, Mia.	0.5

NFC SACKS—INDIVIDUAL

Glover, La'Roi, N.O.	17.0
Sapp, Warren, T.B.	16.5
Douglas, Hugh, Phil.	15.0
Jones, Marcus, T.B.	13.0
Coleman, Marco, Wash.	12.0
Johnson, Joe, N.O.	12.0
Howard, Darren, N.O.	11.0
Wistrom, Grant, St.L.	11.0
Carter, Kevin, St.L.	10.5
Hamilton, Keith, NYG	10.0
Smith, Bruce, Wash.	10.0
Simon, Corey, Phil.	9.5
Strahan, Michael, NYG	9.5
Young, Bryant, S.F.	9.5
Porcher, Robert, Det.	8.0
Randle, John, Minn.	8.0
Urlacher, Brian, Chi.	8.0
Rice, Simeon, Ariz.	7.5
Buckner, Brentson, S.F.	7.0
Ekuban, Ebenezer, Dall.	6.5
McFarland, Anthony, T.B.	6.5
Mitchell, Keith, N.O.	6.5
Scroggins, Tracy, Det.	6.5
Thierry, John, G.B.	6.5
Daniels, Phillip, Chi.	6.0
Dotson, Santana, G.B.	6.0
Sawyer, Talance, Minn.	6.0
Williams, Jay, Car.	6.0
Barber, Ronde, T.B.	5.5
Fletcher, London, St.L.	5.5
Mamula, Mike, Phil.	5.5
White, Reggie, Car.	5.5
Whitehead, Willie, N.O.	5.5
Armstead, Jessie, NYG	5.0
Griffin, Cornelius, NYG	5.0
Holliday, Vonnie, G.B.	5.0
Hunt, Cletidus, G.B.	5.0
Little, Leonard, St.L.	5.0
Spellman, Alonzo, Dall.	5.0
Hall, Travis, Atl.	4.5
Robinson, Bryan, Chi.	4.5
Smith, Brady, Atl.	4.5
Agnew, Ray, St.L.	4.0
Arrington, LaVar, Wash.	4.0
Flanigan, Jim, Chi.	4.0
Gilbert, Sean, Car.	4.0
McKinnon, Ronald, Ariz.	4.0
Peterson, Julian, S.F.	4.0
Thomas, Hollis, Phil.	4.0
Underwood, Dimitrius, Dall.	4.0
Wiley, Chuck, Atl.	4.0
Williams, Tony, Minn.	4.0
Ahanotu, Chidi, T.B.	3.5
Barrow, Micheal, NYG	3.5
Bowens, David, G.B.	3.5
Grasmanis, Paul, Phil.	3.5
Jasper, Edward, Atl.	3.5
Jones, Cedric, NYG	3.5
Whiting, Brandon, Phil.	3.5
Wilkinson, Dan, Wash.	3.5
Colvin, Rosevelt, Chi.	3.0
Ellis, Greg, Dall.	3.0
Elliss, Luther, Det.	3.0
Engelberger, John, S.F.	3.0
Hand, Norman, N.O.	3.0
Jones, James, Det.	3.0
Killings, Cedric, S.F.	3.0
Lang, Kenard, Wash.	3.0
Smith, Mark, Ariz.	3.0
Trotter, Jeremiah, Phil.	3.0
Kerney, Patrick, Atl.	2.5
Lett, Leon, Dall.	2.5
Pritchett, Kelvin, Det.	2.5
Rucker, Mike, Car.	2.5
Stubblefield, Dana, Wash.	2.5
Aldridge, Allen, Det.	2.0
Barber, Shawn, Wash.	2.0
Burrough, John, Minn.	2.0
Butler, LeRoy, G.B.	2.0
Cannida, James, T.B.	2.0
Carter, Marty, Atl.	2.0
Crockett, Henri, Atl.	2.0
Dawkins, Brian, Phil.	2.0
Fields, Mark, N.O.	2.0
Folston, James, Ariz.	2.0
Harris, Bernardo, G.B.	2.0
Heard, Ronnie, S.F.	2.0
Hovan, Chris, Minn.	2.0
Jackson, Tyoka, T.B.	2.0
Jones, Mike A., St.L.	2.0
Knight, Sammy, N.O.	2.0
Mason, Eddie, Wash.	2.0
McBurrows, Gerald, Atl.	2.0
McCleon, Dexter, St.L.	2.0
McDaniel, Ed, Minn.	2.0
Minter, Mike, Car.	2.0
Monty, Pete, NYG	2.0
Morabito, Tim, Car.	2.0
Moran, Sean, St.L.	2.0
Navies, Hannibal, Car.	2.0
Okeafor, Chike, S.F.	2.0
Oldham, Chris, N.O.	2.0
Parrish, Tony, Chi.	2.0
Paup, Bryce, Minn.	2.0
Peter, Jason, Car.	2.0
Pleasant, Anthony, S.F.	2.0
Quarles, Shelton, T.B.	2.0
Smith, Darrin, N.O.	2.0
Smith, Frankie, Chi.	2.0
Tubbs, Winfred, S.F.	2.0
Wayne, Nate, G.B.	2.0
Weary, Fred, N.O.	2.0
White, Steve, T.B.	2.0
Wong, Kailee, Minn.	2.0
Zellner, Peppi, Dall.	2.0
Zgonina, Jeff, St.L.	2.0
Gbaja-Biamila, Kabeer, G.B.	1.5
Maddox, Mark, Ariz.	1.5
Phillips, Ryan, NYG	1.5
Swayda, Shawn, Atl.	1.5
Tillman, Pat, Ariz.	1.5
Bly, Dre', St.L.	1.0
Brooking, Keith, Atl.	1.0
Brooks, Derrick, T.B.	1.0
Bush, Devin, St.L.	1.0
Clarke, Phil, N.O.	1.0
Collins, Todd F., St.L.	1.0
Culpepper, Brad, Chi.	1.0
Draft, Chris, Atl.	1.0
Dronett, Shane, Atl.	1.0
Farr, D'Marco, St.L.	1.0
Fredrickson, Rob, Ariz.	1.0
Gardner, Barry, Phil.	1.0
Garnes, Sam, NYG	1.0
Griffith, Robert, Minn.	1.0
Hall, James, Det.	1.0
Hambrick, Darren, Dall.	1.0
Harris, Sean, Chi.	1.0
Harrison, Nolan, Wash.	1.0
Hobgood-Chittick, Nate, St.L.	1.0
Issa, Jabari, Ariz.	1.0
Jones, Greg, Wash.	1.0
Kalu, Ndukwe, Wash.	1.0
Keith, John, S.F.	1.0
Knight, Tom, Ariz.	1.0
Lyght, Todd, St.L.	1.0
Lynch, John, T.B.	1.0
Lyon, Billy, G.B.	1.0
McDaniel, Emmanuel, NYG	1.0
McQuarters, R.W., Chi.	1.0
Mitchell, Kevin, Wash.	1.0
Noble, Brandon, Dall.	1.0
Ottis, Brad, Ariz.	1.0
Peter, Christian, NYG	1.0
Robbins, Fred, Minn.	1.0
Shade, Sam, Wash.	1.0
Sharper, Darren, G.B.	1.0
Smith, Derek M., Wash.	1.0
Styles, Lorenzo, St.L.	1.0
Swann, Eric, Car.	1.0
Thomas, Orlando, Minn.	1.0
Tuinei, Van, Chi.	1.0
Ulmer, Artie, S.F.	1.0
Vincent, Troy, Phil.	1.0
Wadsworth, Andre, Ariz.	1.0
Wells, Mike, Chi.	1.0
Wilson, Troy, Chi.	1.0
Boyd, Stephen, Det.	0.5
Brown, Corwin, Det.	0.5
Claiborne, Chris, Det.	0.5
Darling, James, Phil.	0.5
Davis, Russell, Ariz.	0.5
Emmons, Carlos, Phil.	0.5
Kirschke, Travis, Det.	0.5
McGarrahan, Scott, G.B.	0.5
Montgomery, Monty, S.F.	0.5
Posey, Jeff, S.F.	0.5
Schulters, Lance, S.F.	0.5
Simmons, Clyde, Chi.	0.5
Simoneau, Mark, Atl.	0.5
Williams, Brian, G.B.	0.5
Williams, K.D., G.B.	0.5

2000 ATTENDANCE

2000 NFL PAID ATTENDANCE BREAKDOWN

	Games	Attendance	Average
NFL Preseason Total	65	3,757,231	57,804
NFL Regular-Season Total	248	16,387,289	66,078
NFL Postseason Total	12	809,132	67,428
NFL All Games	325	20,953,652	64,473

1.1-MILLION CLUB

During the 2000 season, seven teams drew more than 1.1 million paid attendance home and away during the regular season. The Washington Redskins drew an NFL leading 1,182,852 fans in 2000, setting a leauge home attendance record of 656,599.

Team	Total Paid Home Attendance	Total Paid Visiting Attendance	Total Paid Attendance
Washington	656,599	526,253	1,182,852
Denver	594,813	543,302	1,138,115
New York Jets	623,948	513,445	1,137,393
Detroit	606,716	523,383	1,130,099
New York Giants	624,085	504,597	1,128,682
Kansas City	627,093	499,064	1,126,157
Miami	589,909	532,673	1,122,582

For complete year-by-year attendance records, see page 391.

Inside the Numbers

RECORDS FOR NFL TEAMS FOR MOST POINTS IN A GAME (REGULAR SEASON ONLY)

Note: *When the record has been achieved more than once, only the most recent game is shown; summaries are listed in alphabetical order by conference. Bold face indicates team holding record.*

BALTIMORE RAVENS

November 26, 2000, at Baltimore

Cleveland .... 7 0 0 0 — 7
Baltimore .... 7 24 6 7 — 44

TD: Balt—Jamal Lewis 2, Sam Gash, Patrick Johnson, Priest Holmes; Cle—Travis Prentice. TD Passes: Balt—Trent Dilfer 2. FG: Balt—Matt Stover 3.

BUFFALO BILLS

September 18, 1966, at Buffalo

Miami .... 3 7 0 14 — 24
Buffalo .... 21 27 3 7 — 58

TD: Buff—Bobby Burnett 2, Butch Byrd 2, Jack Spikes 2, Bobby Crockett, Jack Kemp; Mia—Dave Kocourek, Bo Roberson, John Roderick. TD Passes: Buff—Jack Kemp, Daryle Lamonica; Mia—George Wilson 3. FG: Buff—Booth Lusteg; Mia—Gene Mingo.

CINCINNATI BENGALS

December 17, 1989, at Cincinnati

Houston .... 0 0 0 7 — 7
Cincinnati .... 21 10 21 9 — 61

TD: Cin—Eddie Brown 2, Eric Ball, James Brooks, Ira Hillary, Rodney Holman, Tim McGee, Craig Taylor; Hou—Lorenzo White. TD Passes: Cin—Boomer Esiason 4, Erik Wilhelm. FG: Cin—Jim Breech 2.

CLEVELAND BROWNS

November 7, 1954, at Cleveland

Washington .... 0 3 0 0 — 3
Cleveland .... 13 14 21 14 — 62

TD: Cle—Darrell Brewster 2, Mo Bassett, Ken Gorgal, Otto Graham, Dub Jones, Dante Lavelli, Curley Morrison. TD Passes: Cle—George Ratterman 3, Otto Graham. FG: Cle—Lou Groza 2; Wash—Vic Janowicz.

DENVER BRONCOS

October 6, 1963, at Denver

San Diego .... 13 7 0 14 — 34
Denver .... 3 14 9 24 — 50

TD: Den—Lionel Taylor 2, Goose Gonsoulin, Gene Prebola, Donnie Stone; SD—Keith Lincoln 2, Lance Alworth, Paul Lowe, Jacque MacKinnon. TD Passes: Den—John McCormick 3; SD—Tobin Rote 3, John Hadl 2. FG: Den—Gene Mingo 5.

INDIANAPOLIS COLTS

December 12, 1976, at Baltimore

Buffalo .... 3 3 7 7 — 20
Baltimore Colts .... 7 13 28 10 — 58

TD: Balt—Roger Carr, Raymond Chester, Glenn Doughty, Roosevelt Leaks, Derrel Luce, Lydell Mitchell, Howard Stevens; Buff—Bob Chandler, O.J. Simpson. TD Passes: Balt—Bert Jones 3; Buff—Gary Marangi. FG: Balt—Toni Linhart 3; Buff—George Jakowenko 2.

JACKSONVILLE JAGUARS

December 3, 2000, at Jacksonville

Cleveland .... 0 0 0 0 — 0
Jacksonville .... 3 17 21 7 — 48

TD: Jax—Fred Taylor 3, Keenan McCardell, Mark Brunell, Shyrone Stith. TD Passes: Jax—Mark Brunell. FG: Jax—Mike Hollis 2.

KANSAS CITY CHIEFS

September 7, 1963, at Denver

Kansas City .... 14 14 21 10 — 59
Denver .... 0 7 0 0 — 7

TD: KC—Chris Burford 2, Frank Jackson 2, Dave Grayson, Abner Haynes, Sherrill Headrick, Curtis McClinton; Den—Lionel Taylor. TD Passes: KC—Len Dawson 4, Curtis McClinton; Den—Mickey Slaughter. FG: KC—Tommy Brooker.

MIAMI DOLPHINS

November 24, 1977, at St. Louis

Miami .... 14 14 20 7 — 55
St. Louis Cardinals .... 7 0 0 7 — 14

TD: Mia—Nat Moore 3, Gary Davis, Duriel Harris, Leroy Harris, Benny Malone, Andre Tillman; StL—Ike Harris, Terry Metcalf. TD Passes: Mia—Bob Griese 6; StL—Jim Hart.

NEW ENGLAND PATRIOTS

September 9, 1979, at New England

New York Jets .... 3 0 0 0 — 3
New England .... 14 21 7 14 — 56

TD: NE—Harold Jackson 3, Stanley Morgan 2, Allan Clark, Andy Johnson, Don Westbrook. TD Passes: NE—Steve Grogan 5, Tom Owen. FG: NYJ—Pat Leahy.

NEW YORK JETS

November 17, 1985, at New York

Tampa Bay .... 14 7 7 0 — 28
New York Jets .... 17 24 14 7 — 62

TD: NYJ—Mickey Shuler 3, Johnny Hector 2, Tony Paige, Al Toon, Wesley Walker; TB—James Wilder 2, Kevin House, Calvin Magee. TD Passes: NYJ—Ken O'Brien 5; TB—Steve DeBerg 2. FG: NYJ—Pat Leahy 2.

OAKLAND RAIDERS

December 24, 2000, at Oakland

Carolina .... 3 6 0 0 — 9
Oakland .... 7 17 14 14 — 52

TD: Oak—Jeremy Brigham 2, Rickey Dudley 2, Tim Brown, Eric Allen, Darrien Gordon. TD Passes: Oak—Rich Gannon 5. FG: Oak—Sebastian Janikowski; Car—Joe Nedney 3.

PITTSBURGH STEELERS

November 30, 1952, at Pittsburgh

New York Giants .... 0 0 7 0 — 7
Pittsburgh .... 14 14 7 28 — 63

TD: Pitt—Lynn Chandnois 2, Dick Hensley 2, Jack Butler, George Hays, Ray Mathews, Ed Modzelewski, Elbie Nickel; NYG—Bill Stribling. TD Passes: Pitt—Jim Finks 4, Gary Kerkorian; NYG—Tom Landry.

SAN DIEGO CHARGERS

December 22, 1963, at San Diego

Denver .... 7 10 3 0 — 20
San Diego .... 10 16 10 22 — 58

TD: SD—Paul Lowe 2, Chuck Allen, Bobby Jackson, Dave Kocourek, Keith Lincoln, Jacque MacKinnon; Den—Billy Joe, Donnie Stone. TD Passes: SD—John Hadl, Tobin Rote; Den—Don Breaux. FG: SD—George Blair 3; Den—Gene Mingo 2.

SEATTLE SEAHAWKS

October 30, 1977, at Seattle

Buffalo .... 3 0 7 7 — 17
Seattle .... 14 28 7 7 — 56

TD: Sea—Steve Largent 2, Duke Fergerson, Al Hunter, David Sims, Sherman Smith, Don Testerman, Jim Zorn; Buff—Joe Ferguson, John Kimbrough. TD Passes: Sea—Jim Zorn 4; Buff—Joe Ferguson. FG: Buff—Carson Long.

TENNESSEE TITANS

December 9, 1990, at Houston

Cleveland .... 0 7 7 0 — 14
Houston Oilers .... 14 31 7 6 — 58

TD: Hou—Lorenzo White 4, Ernest Givins, Leonard Harris, Tony Jones, Terry Kinard; Cle—Eric Metcalf 2. TD Passes: Hou—Warren Moon 2, Cody Carlson; Cle—Bernie Kosar. FG: Hou—Teddy Garcia.

ARIZONA CARDINALS

November 13, 1949, at New York

Chicago Cardinals .... 7 31 14 13 — 65
New York Bulldogs .... 7 0 6 7 — 20

TD: Chi—Red Cochran 2, Pat Harder 2, Bill Dewell, Mel Kutner, Bob Ravensburg, Vic Schwall, Charlie Trippi; NY—Joe Golding, Frank Muehlheuser, Johnny Rauch. TD Passes: Chi—Paul Christman 3, Jim Hardy 3; NY—Bobby Layne. FG: Chi—Pat Harder.

ATLANTA FALCONS

September 16, 1973, at New Orleans

Atlanta .... 0 24 21 17 — 62
New Orleans .... 0 0 7 0 — 7

TD: Atl—Ken Burrow 2, Eddie Ray 2, Wes Chesson, Tom Hayes, Art Malone, Joe Profit; NO—Bill Butler. TD Passes: Atl—Dick Shiner 3, Bob Lee; NO—Archie Manning. FG: Atl—Nick Mike-Mayer 2.

CAROLINA PANTHERS

January 2, 2000, at Carolina

New Orleans .... 0 0 0 13 — 13
Carolina .... 10 7 14 14 — 45

TD: Car—Patrick Jeffers 2, Wesley Walls 2, Michael Bates, Muhsin Muhammad; NO—Jake Delhomme, Eddie Kennison. TD Passes: Car—Steve Beuerlein 5; NO—Jake Delhomme. FG: Car—Richie Cunningham.

CHICAGO BEARS

December 7, 1980, at Chicago

Green Bay .... 0 7 0 0 — 7
Chicago .... 0 28 13 20 — 61

TD: Chi—Walter Payton 3, Brian Baschnagel, Robin Earl, Roland Harper, Willie McClendon, Len Walterscheid, Rickey Watts; GB—James Lofton. TD Passes: Chi—Vince Evans 3; GB—Lynn Dickey.

DALLAS COWBOYS

October 12, 1980, at Dallas

San Francisco .... 0 7 0 7 — 14
Dallas .... 14 24 14 7 — 59

TD: Dall—Drew Pearson 3, Ron Springs 2, Tony Dorsett, Billy Joe DuPree, Robert Newhouse; SF—Dwight Clark 2. TD Passes: Dall—Danny White 4; SF—Steve DeBerg 2. FG: Dall—Rafael Septien.

DETROIT LIONS

November 27, 1997, at Detroit

Chicago .... 14 6 0 0 — 20
Detroit .... 3 14 17 21 — 55

TD: Det—Herman Moore, Johnnie Morton, Ron Rivers, Barry Sanders 3, Tracy Scroggins; Chi—Raymont Harris, Ricky Proehl. TD Passes: Det—Scott Mitchell 2; Chi—Erik Kramer. FG: Det—Jason Hanson 2; Chi—Jeff Jaeger 2.

GREEN BAY PACKERS

October 7, 1945, at Milwaukee

Detroit .... 0 7 7 7 — 21
Green Bay .... 0 41 9 7 — 57

TD: GB—Don Hutson 4, Charley Brock, Irv Comp, Ted Fritsch, Clyde Goodnight; Det—Chuck Fenenbock, John Greene, Bob Westfall. TD Passes: GB—Tex McKay 4, Lou Brock, Irv Comp; Det—Dave Ryan.

MINNESOTA VIKINGS

October 18, 1970, at Minnesota

Dallas .... 3 3 0 7 — 13
Minnesota .... 14 20 17 3 — 54

TD: Minn—Clint Jones 2, Ed Sharockman 2, John Beasley, Dave Osborn; Dall—Calvin Hill. TD Pass: Minn—Gary Cuozzo. FG: Minn—Fred Cox 4; Dall—Mike Clark 2.

NEW ORLEANS SAINTS

November 21, 1976, at Seattle

New Orleans .... 3 17 28 3 — 51
Seattle .... 6 0 7 14 — 27

TD: NO—Bobby Douglass 2, Tony Galbreath, Chuck Muncie, Tom Myers, Elex Price; Sea—Sherman Smith 2, Steve Largent, Jim Zorn. TD Pass: Sea—Bill Munson. FG: NO—Rich Szaro 3.

NEW YORK GIANTS

November 26, 1972, at New York

Philadelphia .... 3 7 0 0 — 10
New York Giants .... 14 24 10 14 — 62

TD: NYG—Don Herrmann 2, Ron Johnson 2, Bob Tucker 2, Randy Johnson; Phil—Harold Jackson. TD Passes: NYG—Norm Snead 3, Randy Johnson 2; Phil—John Reaves. FG: NYG—Pete Gogolak 2; Phil—Tom Dempsey.

PHILADELPHIA EAGLES

November 6, 1934, at Philadelphia

Cincinnati Reds .... 0 0 0 0 — 0
Philadelphia .... 26 6 12 20 — 64

TD: Phil—Joe Carter 3, Swede Hanson 3, Marvin Ellstrom, Roger Kirkman, Ed Matesic, Ed Storm. TD Passes: Phil—Ed Matesic 2, Albert Weiner 2, Marvin Elstrom.

ST. LOUIS RAMS

October 22, 1950, at Los Angeles

Baltimore .... 13 0 7 7 — 27
Los Angeles Rams .... 21 14 14 21 — 70

TD: LA—Bob Boyd 2, Vitamin T. Smith 2, Tom Fears,

Elroy (Crazylegs) Hirsch, Dick Hoerner, Ralph Pasquariello, Dan Towler, Bob Waterfield; Balt—Chet Mutryn 2, Adrian Burk, Billy Stone. TD Passes: LA—Norm Van Brocklin 2, Bob Waterfield 2, Glenn Davis; Balt—Adrian Burk 3.

SAN FRANCISCO 49ERS
October 18, 1992, at San Francisco

Atlanta	7	3	0	7	— 17
San Francisco	21	21	14	0	— 56

TD: SF—Jerry Rice 3, Ricky Watters 3, Brent Jones, Tom Rathman; Atl—Michael Haynes, Jason Phillips. TD Passes: SF—Steve Young 3; Atl—Chris Miller, Wade Wilson. FG: Atl—Norm Johnson.

TAMPA BAY BUCCANEERS
September 13, 1987, at Tampa Bay

Atlanta	0	3	0	7	— 10
Tampa Bay	14	13	7	14	— 48

TD: TB—Gerald Carter 2, Cliff Austin, Steve Bartalo, Mark Carrier, Phil Freeman, Calvin Magee; Atl—Stacey Bailey. TD Passes: TB—Steve DeBerg 5; Atl—Scott Campbell. FG: Atl—Mick Luckhurst.

WASHINGTON REDSKINS
November 27, 1966, at Washington

New York Giants	0	14	14	13	— 41
Washington	13	21	14	24	— 72

TD: Wash—A.D. Whitfield 3, Brig Owens 2, Charley Taylor 2, Rickie Harris, Joe Don Looney, Bobby Mitchell; NYG—Allen Jacobs, Homer Jones, Dan Lewis, Joe Morrison, Aaron Thomas, Gary Wood. TD Passes: Wash—Sonny Jurgensen 3; NYG—Gary Wood 2, Tom Kennedy. FG: Wash—Charlie Gogolak.

TEAMS THAT FINISHED IN FIRST PLACE IN THEIR DIVISION THE SEASON AFTER FINISHING IN LAST PLACE

Season	Team	Record	Previous Season
1967	Houston	9-4-1	*3-11-0
1968	Minnesota	8-6-0	3- 8-3
1970	Cincinnati	8-6-0	4- 9-1
1970	San Francisco	10-3-1	4- 8-2
1972	Green Bay	10-4-0	4- 8-2
1975	Baltimore	10-4-0	2-12-0
1979	Tampa Bay	10-6-0	5-11-0
1981	Cincinnati	12-4-0	6-10-0
1987	Indianapolis	9-6-0	3-13-0
1988	Cincinnati	12-4-0	4-11-0
1990	Cincinnati	9-7-0	8- 8-0
1991	Denver	12-4-0	5-11-0
1992	San Diego	11-5-0	4-12-0
1993	Detroit	10-6-0	5-11-0
1997	N.Y. Giants	10-5-1	6-10-0
1999	Indianapolis	13-3-0	3-13-0
1999	St. Louis	13-3-0	*4-12-0
2000	New Orleans	10-6-0	3-13-0

tied for last place

RECORDS OF NFL TEAMS, 1991-2000

AFC	W	L	T	Pct.	Division Titles	Playoff Berths	Postseason Record	Super Bowl Record
Denver	100	60	0	.625	3	6	8-4	2-0
Buffalo	98	62	0	.613	3	7	8-7	0-3
Kansas City	98	62	0	.613	3	6	3-6	0-0
Miami	94	66	0	.588	3	7	5-7	0-0
Jacksonville	56	40	0	.583	2	4	4-4	0-0
Pittsburgh	93	67	0	.581	5	6	5-6	0-1
Tennessee	92	68	0	.575	3	5	4-5	0-1
Oakland	82	78	0	.513	1	3	2-3	0-0
Baltimore	36	43	1	.456	0	1	4-0	1-0
New England	72	88	0	.450	2	4	3-4	0-1
Indianapolis	69	91	0	.431	1	4	2-4	0-0
San Diego	69	91	0	.431	2	3	3-3	0-1
N.Y. Jets	68	92	0	.425	1	2	1-2	0-0
Seattle	67	93	0	.419	1	1	0-1	0-0
Cleveland	41	71	0	.366	0	1	1-1	0-0
Cincinnati	47	113	0	.294	0	0	0-0	0-0

Oakland totals include L.A. Raiders, 1991-94
Tennessee totals include Houston, 1991-96

NFC	W	L	T	Pct.	Division Titles	Playoff Berths	Postseason Record	Super Bowl Record
San Francisco	105	55	0	.656	5	7	8-6	1-0
Minnesota	100	60	0	.625	4	8	4-8	0-0
Dallas	99	61	0	.619	6	8	12-5	3-0
Green Bay	96	64	0	.600	3	6	9-5	1-1
N.Y. Giants	82	77	1	.516	2	3	3-3	0-1
Detroit	82	78	0	.513	2	6	1-6	0-0
Philadelphia	81	78	1	.509	0	4	3-4	0-0
Washington	77	82	1	.484	2	3	5-2	1-0
Carolina	45	51	0	.469	1	1	1-1	0-0
New Orleans	73	87	0	.456	2	3	1-3	0-0
Atlanta	71	89	0	.444	1	3	3-3	0-1
Tampa Bay	71	89	0	.444	1	3	2-3	0-0
Chicago	67	93	0	.419	0	2	1-2	0-0
St. Louis	63	97	0	.394	1	2	3-1	1-0
Arizona	56	104	0	.350	0	1	1-1	0-0

Arizona totals include Phoenix, 1991-93
St. Louis totals include L.A. Rams, 1991-94

HOME RECORDS, 1991-2000

AFC	W-L-T	Pct.	NFC	W-L-T	Pct.
Denver	62-18-0	.775	Green Bay	62-18-0	.775
Kansas City	62-18-0	.775	San Francisco	62-18-0	.775
Buffalo	57-23-0	.713	Dallas	58-22-0	.725
Jacksonville	34-14-0	.708	Minnesota	56-24-0	.700
Pittsburgh	56-24-0	.700	Detroit	53-27-0	.663
Miami	53-27-0	.663	Philadelphia	49-31-0	.613
Tennessee	50-30-0	.625	Atlanta	47-33-0	.588
Oakland	45-35-0	.563	Tampa Bay	47-33-0	.588
Baltimore	21-18-1	.538	Carolina	27-21-0	.563
New England	42-38-0	.525	N.Y. Giants	45-35-0	.563
Indianapolis	40-40-0	.500	Washington	44-35-1	.556
Seattle	40-40-0	.500	Chicago	40-40-0	.500
San Diego	39-41-0	.488	New Orleans	38-42-0	.475
N.Y. Jets	37-43-0	.463	St. Louis	37-43-0	.463
Cincinnati	32-48-0	.400	Arizona	37-43-0	.463
Cleveland	22-34-0	.393			

Arizona totals include Phoenix, 1991-93
Oakland totals include L.A. Raiders, 1991-94
St. Louis totals include L.A. Rams, 1991-94
Tennessee totals include Houston, 1991-96

ROAD RECORDS, 1991-2000

AFC	W-L-T	Pct.	NFC	W-L-T	Pct.
Tennessee	42-38-0	.525	Minnesota	44-36-0	.550
Buffalo	41-39-0	.513	San Francisco	43-37-0	.538
Miami	41-39-0	.513	Dallas	41-39-0	.513
Denver	38-42-0	.475	N.Y. Giants	37-42-1	.469
Oakland	37-43-0	.463	New Orleans	35-45-0	.438
Pittsburgh	37-43-0	.463	Green Bay	34-46-0	.425
Jacksonville	22-26-0	.458	Washington	33-47-0	.413
Kansas City	36-44-0	.450	Philadelphia	32-47-1	.406
N.Y. Jets	31-49-0	.388	Carolina	18-30-0	.375
Baltimore	15-25-0	.375	Detroit	29-51-0	.363
New England	30-50-0	.375	Chicago	27-53-0	.338
San Diego	30-50-0	.375	St. Louis	26-54-0	.325
Indianapolis	29-51-0	.363	Atlanta	24-56-0	.300
Cleveland	19-37-0	.339	Tampa Bay	24-56-0	.300
Seattle	27-53-0	.338	Arizona	19-61-0	.238
Cincinnati	15-65-0	.188			

Arizona totals include Phoenix, 1991-93
Oakland totals include L.A. Raiders, 1991-94
St. Louis totals include L.A. Rams, 1991-94
Tennessee totals include Houston, 1991-96

RECORDS BY MONTHS, 1991-2000

AFC	Sept. W-L-T	Oct. W-L-T	Nov. W-L-T	Dec. W-L-T	Total W-L-T	Pct.
Denver	26-15	23-14	31-10	20-21	100- 60-0	.625
Buffalo	25-11	24-16	29-15	20-20	98- 62-0	.613
Kansas City	29-12	23-14	23-19	23-17	98- 62-0	.613
Miami	26- 9	26-15	24-19	18-23	94- 66-0	.588
Jacksonville	13-11	12-13	16- 7	15- 9	56- 40-0	.583
Pittsburgh	21-17	26-12	26-18	20-20	93- 67-0	.581
Tennessee	19-19	25-13	22-21	26-15	92- 68-0	.575
Oakland	19-22	26-12	19-21	18-23	82- 78-0	.513
Baltimore	11- 9	5-14	9-12-1	11- 8	36- 43-1	.456
New England	16-21	15-26	19-22	22-19	72- 88-0	.450
Indianapolis	13-23	20-21	13-29	23-18	69- 91-0	.431
San Diego	18-22	15-23	17-24	19-22	69- 91-0	.431
N.Y. Jets	15-25	16-22	24-17	13-28	68- 92-0	.425
Seattle	19-22	14-24	19-21	15-26	67- 93-0	.419
Cleveland	14-13	12-16	8-21	7-21	41- 71-0	.366
Cincinnati	7-31	6-33	15-28	19-21	47-113-0	.294

Oakland totals include L.A. Raiders, 1991-94
Tennessee totals include Houston, 1991-96
September totals include August; December totals include January

NFC	Sept. W-L-T	Oct. W-L-T	Nov. W-L-T	Dec. W-L-T	Total W-L-T	Pct.
San Francisco	26-14	24-14	28-13	27-14	105- 55-0	.656
Minnesota	27-13	24-14	25-17	24-16	100- 60-0	.625
Dallas	23-14	27-12	27-18	22-17	99- 61-0	.619

INSIDE THE NUMBERS

	Sept. W-L-T	Oct. W-L-T	Nov. W-L-T	Dec. W-L-T	Total W-L-T	Pct.
Green Bay	24-17	18-16	25-18	29-13	96- 64-0	.600
N.Y. Giants	20-19	21-18	17-24-1	24-16	82- 77-1	.516
Detroit	23-19	18-17	22-23	19-19	82- 78-0	.513
Philadelphia	18-20	23-17	20-22-1	20-19	81- 78-1	.509
Washington	21-18	20-19	15-26-1	21-19	77- 82-1	.484
Carolina	7-14	10-15	14-12	14-10	45- 51-0	.469
New Orleans	18-22	19-19	19-22	17-24	73- 87-0	.456
Atlanta	12-28	16-23	24-17	19-21	71- 89-0	.444
Tampa Bay	17-24	12-24	21-21	21-20	71- 89-0	.444
Chicago	14-27	20-17	18-25	15-24	67- 93-0	.419
St. Louis	22-18	13-24	11-31	17-24	63- 97-0	.394
Arizona	12-26	12-28	18-25	14-25	56-104-0	.350

Arizona totals include Phoenix, 1991-93
St. Louis totals include L.A. Rams, 1991-94
September totals include August; December totals include January

TAKEAWAYS/GIVEAWAYS, 1991-2000

AFC	Takeaways Int.	Fum.	Total	Giveaways Int.	Fum.	Total	Net.Diff.
Kansas City	179	170	349	132	112	244	105
Pittsburgh	194	149	343	158	126	284	59
Jacksonville	84	86	170	82	63	145	25
Denver	178	127	305	150	134	284	21
N.Y. Jets	187	149	336	188	128	316	20
Miami	185	125	310	164	129	293	17
Baltimore	93	60	153	90	63	153	0
Tennessee	172	151	323	171	156	327	-4
Seattle	193	138	331	192	149	341	-10
Buffalo	177	129	306	182	135	317	-11
Cleveland	96	92	188	120	87	207	-19
Oakland	156	128	284	171	134	305	-21
New England	168	134	302	191	135	326	-24
Cincinnati	148	119	267	156	142	298	-31
San Diego	188	107	295	213	123	336	-41
Indianapolis	133	117	250	170	128	298	-48

Oakland totals include L.A. Raiders, 1991-94
Tennessee totals include Houston, 1991-96

NFC	Takeaways Int.	Fum.	Total	Giveaways Int.	Fum.	Total	Net.Diff.
N.Y. Giants	181	117	298	139	110	249	49
San Francisco	189	116	305	136	124	260	45
Minnesota	185	137	322	171	116	287	35
Washington	191	124	315	178	104	282	33
Dallas	164	110	274	125	121	246	28
Detroit	174	126	300	167	112	279	21
Philadelphia	199	145	344	171	154	325	19
Green Bay	189	119	308	178	130	308	0
New Orleans	179	151	330	198	142	340	-10
Carolina	105	92	197	112	97	209	-12
Tampa Bay	151	135	286	189	127	316	-30
Chicago	146	134	280	174	143	317	-37
Atlanta	153	130	283	194	128	322	-39
St. Louis	191	99	290	194	156	350	-60
Arizona	157	144	301	229	152	381	-80

Arizona totals include Phoenix, 1991-93
St. Louis totals include L.A. Rams, 1991-94

BEST TAKEAWAY/GIVEAWAY DIFFERENTIAL, SEASON

+43 Washington, 1983
+26 Kansas City, 1990
+25 N.Y. Giants, 1997

HIGH AND LOW SINGLE-GAME YARDAGE TOTALS, 1991-2000

Most Total Yards, Game
615 Arizona vs. Washington, Nov. 10, 1996 (OT)
614 St. Louis vs. San Diego, Oct. 1, 2000
598 San Francisco vs. Buffalo, Sept. 13, 1992
590 San Francisco vs. Atlanta, Oct. 18, 1992
583 Houston vs. Dallas, Nov. 10, 1991 (OT)

Fewest Total Yards, Game
40 Cleveland vs. Pittsburgh, Sept. 12, 1999
53 Cleveland vs. Jacksonville, Dec. 3, 2000
62 Seattle vs. Dallas, Oct. 11, 1992
82 Denver vs. Philadelphia, Sept. 20, 1992
87 Seattle vs. Philadelphia, Dec. 13, 1992 (OT)

Most Yards Rushing, Game
407 Cincinnati vs. Denver, Oct. 22, 2000
328 San Francisco vs. Detroit, Dec. 14, 1998
315 Buffalo vs. Atlanta, Nov. 22, 1992
306 Philadelphia vs. Dallas, Sept. 3, 2000
302 N.Y. Jets vs. Indianapolis, Sept. 20, 1998

Fewest Yards Rushing, Game
4 Indianapolis vs. Detroit, Sept. 22, 1991
Buffalo vs. Tennessee, Nov. 23, 1997
Cincinnati vs. Baltimore, Sept. 24, 2000
8 Oakland vs. Kansas City, Dec. 3, 1995
Dallas vs. New Orleans, Dec. 6, 1998

Most Yards Passing, Game
507 Arizona vs. Washington, Nov. 10, 1996 (OT)
475 San Francisco vs. L.A. Rams, Nov. 28, 1993
474 Kansas City vs. Oakland, Nov. 5, 2000
473 N.Y. Jets vs. Baltimore, Dec. 24, 2000
456 Miami vs. New England, Sept. 4, 1994

Fewest Yards Passing, Game
-19 San Diego vs. Kansas City, Sept. 20, 1998
-9 Cleveland vs. Jacksonville, Dec. 3, 2000
9 Dallas vs. Tennessee, Dec. 25, 2000
12 Carolina vs. Buffalo, Sept. 10, 1995
Philadelphia vs. Seattle, Sept. 6, 1998

NFL INDIVIDUAL LEADERS, 1991-2000

Points		Touchdowns		Field Goals	
Gary Anderson	1,149	Emmitt Smith	145	Gary Anderson	255
Morten Andersen	1,086	Jerry Rice	104	Morten Andersen	249
Steve Christie	1,078	Cris Carter	101	Steve Christie	249
Al Del Greco	1,060	Ricky Watters	90	Al Del Greco	246
Pete Stoyanovich	1,041	Marshall Faulk	89	John Carney	242

Rushes		Rushing Yards		Rushing TDs	
Emmitt Smith	3,296	Emmitt Smith	14,229	Emmitt Smith	134
Ricky Watters	2,550	Barry Sanders	12,495	Ricky Watters	77
Barry Sanders	2,527	Ricky Watters	10,325	Barry Sanders	72
Jerome Bettis	2,461	Jerome Bettis	9,804	Terry Allen	70
Thurman Thomas	2,101	Thurman Thomas	8,652	Marshall Faulk	67

Pass Attempts		Completions		Passing Yards	
Brett Favre	4,932	Brett Favre	2,997	Brett Favre	34,706
Drew Bledsoe	4,452	Troy Aikman	2,517	Dan Marino	29,945
Dan Marino	4,177	Drew Bledsoe	2,504	Drew Bledsoe	29,257
Troy Aikman	4,023	Dan Marino	2,487	Troy Aikman	28,614
Warren Moon	3,798	Warren Moon	2,287	Steve Young	27,229

TD Passes		Receptions		Reception Yards	
Brett Favre	255	Cris Carter	904	Jerry Rice	11,381
Steve Young	198	Jerry Rice	835	Cris Carter	11,099
Dan Marino	179	Tim Brown	784	Tim Brown	11,074
Vinny Testaverde	171	Larry Centers	685	Michael Irvin	10,459
John Elway	165	Michael Irvin	672	Herman Moore	9,098

Receiving TDs		Interceptions		Sacks	
Cris Carter	101	Aeneas Williams	46	John Randle	113.0
Jerry Rice	97	Rod Woodson	45	Bruce Smith	104.5
Tim Brown	78	Eugene Robinson	40	Reggie White	103.0
Andre Rison	70	Deion Sanders	40	Kevin Greene	100.5
Carl Pickens	63	2 tied	38	Derrick Thomas	96.0

NFL GAMES IN WHICH A TEAM HAS SCORED 60 OR MORE POINTS

(Home team in capitals)

Regular Season
WASHINGTON 72, New York Giants 41 .... November 27, 1966
LOS ANGELES RAMS 70, Baltimore 27 .... October 22, 1950
Chicago Cardinals 65, NEW YORK BULLDOGS 20 .... November 13, 1949
LOS ANGELES RAMS 65, Detroit 24 .... October 29, 1950
PHILADELPHIA 64, Cincinnati 0 .... November 6, 1934
CHICAGO CARDINALS 63, New York Giants 35 .... October 17, 1948
AKRON 62, Oorang 0 .... October 29, 1922
PITTSBURGH 62, New York Giants 7 .... November 30, 1952
CLEVELAND 62, New York Giants 14 .... December 6, 1953
CLEVELAND 62, Washington 3 .... November 7, 1954
NEW YORK GIANTS 62, Philadelphia 10 .... November 26, 1972
Atlanta 62, NEW ORLEANS 7 .... September 16, 1973
NEW YORK JETS 62, Tampa Bay 28 .... November 17, 1985
CHICAGO 61, San Francisco 20 .... December 12, 1965
Cincinnati 61, HOUSTON 17 .... December 17, 1972
CHICAGO 61, Green Bay 7 .... December 7, 1980
CINCINNATI 61, Houston 7 .... December 17, 1989
ROCK ISLAND 60, Evansville 0 .... October 15, 1922
CHICAGO CARDINALS 60, Rochester 0 .... October 7, 1923

Postseason
Chicago Bears 73, WASHINGTON 0 .... December 8, 1940
JACKSONVILLE 62, Miami 7 .... January 15, 2000

YOUNGEST AND OLDEST PLAYERS IN NFL IN 2000

10 Youngest Players	Birthdate	Games	Starts	Position
Jacoby Shepherd, St. Louis	8/31/79	15	1	CB-S
Jamal Lewis, Baltimore	8/29/79	16	13	RB
Dez White, Chicago	8/23/79	15	0	WR
Kwame Cavil, Buffalo	5/3/79	16	0	WR
Darrell Jackson, Seattle	12/6/78	16	9	WR
Payton Williams, Indianapolis	11/19/78	7	0	CB-S
Cosey Coleman, Tampa Bay	10/27/78	8	0	G
Tommy Hendricks, Miami	10/23/78	8	0	LB
Kevin Lewis, N.Y. Giants	10/6/78	7	0	LB
Darrick Vaughn, Atlanta	10/2/78	16	0	CB

10 Oldest Players	Birthdate	Games	Starts	Position
Eddie Murray, Washington	8/29/56	6	0	K
Warren Moon, Kansas City	11/18/56	2	1	QB
Gary Anderson, Minnesota	7/16/59	16	0	K
Darrell Green, Washington	2/15/60	13	2	CB
Morten Andersen, Atlanta	8/19/60	16	0	K
Trey Junkin, Arizona	1/23/61	16	0	TE
Bruce Matthews, Tennessee	8/8/61	16	16	G
Lee Johnson, New England	11/27/61	16	0	P
Reggie White, Carolina	12/19/61	16	16	DE
Sean Landeta, Philadelphia	1/6/62	16	0	P

YOUNGEST AND OLDEST REGULAR STARTERS BY POSITION IN 2000

Minimum: 8 Games Started

	Youngest		Oldest	
QB	5/29/77	Shaun King, T.B.	11/13/63	Vinny Testaverde, N.Y.J.
RB	8/29/79	Jamal Lewis, Balt.	11/17/67	Howard Griffith, Den.
WR	12/6/78	Darrell Jackson, Sea.	10/13/62	Jerry Rice, S.F.
TE	1/6/78	Bubba Franks, G.B.	2/26/66	Wesley Walls, Car.
C	11/3/77	Damien Woody, N.E.	1/23/64	Frank Winters, G.B.
G	3/23/78	Travis Claridge, Atl.	8/8/61	Bruce Matthews, Tenn.
T	8/6/78	Marvel Smith, Pitt.	3/30/63	Lomas Brown, N.Y.G.
DE	2/14/78	Courtney Brown, Cle.	12/19/61	Reggie White, Car.
DT	5/12/78	Chris Hovan, Minn.	10/20/65	Chad Hennings, Dall.
LB	7/26/78	Chris Claiborne, Det.	8/25/65	Cornelius Bennett, Ind.
CB	6/22/78	Champ Bailey, Wash.	5/23/65	James Hasty, K.C.
S	2/13/78	Mike Brown, Chi.	5/28/63	Eugene Robinson, Car.

OLDEST INDIVIDUAL SINGLE-SEASON OR SINGLE-GAME RECORDS IN NFL RECORD & FACT BOOK

Most Points, Game—40, Ernie Nevers, Chi. Cardinals vs. Chi. Bears, Nov. 28, 1929 (6-td, 4-pat)

Most Touchdowns Rushing, Game—6, Ernie Nevers, Chi. Cardinals vs. Chi. Bears, Nov. 28, 1929

Highest Punting Average, Season (Qualifiers)—51.40, Sammy Baugh, Washington, 1940 (35-1,799)

Highest Punting Average, Rookie, Season (Qualifiers)—45.92, Frank Sinkwich, Detroit, 1943 (12-551)

Highest Punting Average, Game (minimum: 4 punts)—61.75, Bob Cifers, Detroit vs. Chi. Bears, Nov. 24, 1946 (4-247)

Highest Average Gain, Pass Receptions, Season (minimum: 24 receptions)—32.58, Don Currivan, Boston, 1947 (24-782)

Highest Average Gain, Passing, Game (minimum: 20 passes)—18.58, Sammy Baugh, Washington vs. Boston, Oct. 31, 1948 (24-446)

Most Touchdowns, Fumble Recoveries, Game—2, Fred (Dippy) Evans, Chi. Bears vs. Washington, Nov. 28, 1948

Most Yards Gained, Intercepted Passes, Rookie, Season—301, Don Doll, Detroit, 1949

Most Passes Had Intercepted, Game—8, Jim Hardy, Chi. Cardinals vs. Philadelphia, Sept. 24, 1950

Highest Average Gain, Rushing, Game (minimum: 10 attempts)—17.09, Marion Motley, Cleveland vs. Pittsburgh, Oct. 29, 1950 (11-188)

Highest Kickoff Return Average, Game (minimum: 3 returns)—73.50, Wally Triplett, Detroit vs. Los Angeles, Oct. 29, 1950 (4-294)

Highest Punt Return Average, Season (Qualifiers)—23.00, Herb Rich, Baltimore, 1950 (12-276)

Highest Punt Return Average, Rookie, Season (Qualifiers)—23.00, Herb Rich, Baltimore, 1950 (12-276)

Most Yards Passing, Game—554, Norm Van Brocklin, Los Angeles vs. N.Y. Yanks, Sept. 28, 1951

Most Touchdowns, Punt Returns, Rookie, Season—4, Jack Christiansen, Detroit, 1951

Most Interceptions By, Season—14, Dick (Night Train) Lane, Los Angeles, 1952

Most Interceptions By, Rookie, Season—14, Dick (Night Train) Lane, Los Angeles, 1952

Highest Average Gain, Passing, Season (Qualifiers)—11.17, Tommy O'Connell, Cleveland, 1957 (110-1,229)

Most Points, Season—176, Paul Hornung, Green Bay, 1960 (15-td, 41-pat,15-fg)

Most Yards Gained, Pass Receptions, Rookie, Season—1,473, Bill Groman, Houston, 1960

RECORDS OF TEAMS ON OPENING DAY, 1933-2000

	W	L	T	Pct.	Longest W Strk.	Longest L Strk.	Current Streak
AFC							
Jacksonville	5	1	0	.833	5	1	W-5
Denver	25	15	1	.625	4	4	L-2
Miami	20	14	1	.588	9	5	W-9
Kansas City	23	18	0	.561	7	4	L-2
San Diego	23	18	0	.561	6	6	L-1
Cleveland	26	22	0	.542	5	5	L-3
Oakland	22	19	0	.537	5	5	W-1
Indianapolis	25	23	1	.521	8	8	W-2
Pittsburgh	32	30	4	.516	4	3	L-1
Tennessee	21	20	0	.512	4	3	L-1
New England	19	22	0	.463	6	3	L-1
Cincinnati	15	18	0	.455	4	4	L-3
Buffalo	17	24	0	.415	6	5	W-1
N.Y. Jets	17	24	0	.415	3	5	W-1
Baltimore	2	3	0	.400	1	3	W-1
Seattle	6	19	0	.240	3	8	L-2
NFC							
Dallas	30	10	1	.750	17	3	L-1
N.Y. Giants	39	25	4	.609	4	3	W-4
Minnesota	23	16	1	.590	5	3	W-5
Chicago	39	28	1	.582	9	6	L-1
St. Louis	35	28	0	.556	5	6	W-2
Green Bay	35	30	3	.538	5	6	L-1
Detroit	35	31	2	.530	7	4	W-2
Atlanta	18	17	0	.514	5	3	W-1
San Francisco	25	25	1	.500	5	3	L-2
Washington	32	32	4	.500	6	5	W-1
Philadelphia	27	39	1	.409	5	9	W-1
Arizona	27	39	1	.409	6	7	L-1
Tampa Bay	10	15	0	.400	3	5	W-1
New Orleans	9	25	0	.265	2	6	L-1
Carolina	1	5	0	.167	1	4	L-4

Kansas City totals include Dallas Texans, 1960-62.
Oakland totals include L.A. Raiders, 1982-94.
San Diego totals include L.A. Chargers, 1960.
Indianapolis totals include Baltimore, 1953-83.
Tennessee totals include Houston, 1960-96.
New England totals include Boston, 1960-70.
St. Louis totals include Cleveland, 1937-42 and 1944-45, and L.A. Rams, 1946-94.
Detroit totals include Portsmouth, 1933.
Arizona totals include Chi. Cardinals, 1933-59, St. Louis, 1960-87, and Phoenix, 1988-93.
NOTE: All tied games occurred prior to 1972, when calculation of ties in percentages as half-win, half-loss was begun.

EMMITT SMITH'S CAREER RUSHING VS. EACH OPPONENT

Opponent	Games	Rushes	Yards	Yards Per Rush	Yards Per Game	TD
Arizona	22	465	1,993	4.3	90.6	25
Atlanta	7	143	695	4.9	99.3	9
Baltimore	1	11	48	4.4	48.0	0
Buffalo	1	15	25	1.7	25.0	1
Carolina	3	47	247	5.3	82.3	2
Chicago	4	67	322	4.8	80.5	1
Cincinnati	4	73	238	3.3	59.5	1
Cleveland	2	58	224	3.9	112.0	1
Denver	3	72	269	3.7	89.7	3
Detroit	3	64	276	4.3	92.0	4
Green Bay	6	139	567	4.1	94.5	6
Indianapolis	3	73	298	4.1	99.3	4
Jacksonville	2	48	177	3.7	88.5	1
Kansas City	3	56	193	3.4	64.3	2
Miami	3	69	228	3.3	76.0	0
Minnesota	5	82	538	6.6	107.6	8
New England	2	46	160	3.5	80.0	0
New Orleans	5	104	387	3.7	77.4	3
N.Y. Giants	21	419	1,796	4.3	85.5	17
N.Y. Jets	3	54	256	4.7	85.3	0
Oakland	3	79	321	4.1	107.0	7
Philadelphia	22	483	2,246	4.7	102.1	13
Pittsburgh	3	89	349	3.9	116.3	2
St. Louis	2	40	134	3.4	67.0	1
San Diego	2	24	70	2.9	35.0	2
San Francisco	7	121	453	3.7	64.7	5
Seattle	2	39	152	3.9	76.0	2
Tampa Bay	3	59	249	4.2	83.0	2
Tennessee	4	61	181	3.0	45.3	1
Washington	20	437	2,074	4.7	103.7	22
Totals	171	3,537	15,166	4.3	88.7	145

Arizona totals include eight games vs. Phoenix
Oakland totals include one game vs. L.A. Raiders
St. Louis totals include two games vs. L.A. Rams
Tennessee totals include two games vs. Houston

INSIDE THE NUMBERS

RICKY WATTERS'S CAREER RUSHING VS. EACH OPPONENT

Opponent	Games	Rushes	Yards	Yards Per Rush	Yards Per Game	TD
Arizona	9	195	723	3.7	80.3	6
Atlanta	8	141	663	4.7	82.9	8
Baltimore	1	11	37	3.4	37.0	0
Buffalo	4	74	276	3.7	69.0	1
Carolina	2	31	96	3.1	48.0	1
Chicago	2	35	112	3.2	56.0	0
Cincinnati	3	64	309	4.8	103.0	5
Cleveland	1	13	83	6.4	83.0	0
Dallas	9	177	733	4.1	81.4	4
Denver	8	126	464	3.7	58.0	6
Detroit	4	59	231	3.9	57.8	2
Green Bay	3	64	244	3.8	81.3	1
Indianapolis	3	47	235	5.0	78.3	1
Jacksonville	2	39	124	3.2	62.0	1
Kansas City	7	139	580	4.2	82.9	4
Miami	2	36	232	6.4	116.0	1
Minnesota	3	29	82	2.8	27.3	1
New England	1	19	104	5.5	104.0	1
New Orleans	8	169	780	4.6	97.5	1
N.Y. Giants	7	149	640	4.3	91.4	5
N.Y. Jets	4	61	244	4.0	61.0	2
Oakland	8	159	636	4.0	79.5	3
Philadelphia	4	39	163	4.2	40.8	1
Pittsburgh	4	80	239	3.0	59.8	0
St. Louis	8	150	583	3.9	72.9	7
San Diego	8	153	481	3.1	60.1	3
San Francisco	1	14	42	3.0	42.0	0
Seattle	1	21	69	3.3	69.0	2
Tampa Bay	5	74	305	4.1	61.0	3
Tennessee	1	14	63	4.5	63.0	0
Washington	8	168	752	4.5	94.0	7
Totals	139	2,550	10,325	4.0	74.3	77

Arizona totals include two games vs. Phoenix
Oakland totals include one game vs. L.A. Raiders
St. Louis totals include six games vs. L.A. Rams

JEROME BETTIS'S CAREER RUSHING VS. EACH OPPONENT

Opponent	Games	Rushes	Yards	Yards Per Rush	Yards Per Game	TD
Arizona	3	73	309	4.2	103.0	4
Atlanta	8	160	686	4.3	85.8	2
Baltimore	9	176	671	3.8	74.6	2
Buffalo	3	34	160	4.7	53.3	3
Carolina	4	81	305	3.8	76.3	3
Chicago	4	90	358	4.0	89.5	2
Cincinnati	11	264	1,125	4.3	102.3	8
Cleveland	5	117	482	4.1	96.4	3
Dallas	1	15	63	4.2	63.0	0
Denver	2	57	216	3.8	108.0	1
Detroit	2	49	180	3.7	90.0	0
Green Bay	4	68	193	2.8	48.3	0
Indianapolis	2	41	195	4.8	97.5	1
Jacksonville	10	208	774	3.7	77.4	3
Kansas City	5	131	520	4.0	104.0	1
Miami	3	46	188	4.1	62.7	0
New England	2	40	128	3.2	64.0	0
New Orleans	5	103	513	5.0	102.6	1
N.Y. Giants	3	56	160	2.9	53.3	0
N.Y. Jets	2	33	119	3.6	59.5	1
Oakland	2	34	141	4.1	70.5	0
Philadelphia	3	60	241	4.0	80.3	1
Pittsburgh	1	16	76	4.8	76.0	1
St. Louis	1	19	129	6.8	129.0	2
San Diego	3	52	160	3.1	53.3	0
San Francisco	8	116	454	3.9	56.8	5
Seattle	2	39	177	4.5	88.5	0
Tampa Bay	2	30	86	2.9	43.0	0
Tennessee	10	162	602	3.7	60.2	3
Washington	5	91	393	4.3	78.6	2
Totals	125	2,461	9,804	4.0	78.4	49

Arizona totals include one game vs. Phoenix
Oakland totals include one game vs. L.A. Raiders
Tennessee totals include three games vs. Houston

MARSHALL FAULK'S CAREER RUSHING VS. EACH OPPONENT

Opponent	Games	Rushes	Yards	Yards Per Rush	Yards Per Game	TD
Arizona	1	12	46	3.8	46.0	0
Atlanta	5	99	648	6.5	129.6	3
Baltimore	3	55	290	5.3	96.7	2
Buffalo	10	194	690	3.6	69.0	5
Carolina	5	91	410	4.5	82.0	1
Chicago	1	10	54	5.4	54.0	0
Cincinnati	6	103	350	3.4	58.3	3
Cleveland	2	38	194	5.1	97.0	2
Denver	1	14	78	5.6	78.0	1
Detroit	2	23	53	2.3	26.5	0
Green Bay	1	17	116	6.8	116.0	0
Jacksonville	1	22	54	2.5	54.0	1
Kansas City	2	37	138	3.7	69.0	1
Miami	9	162	588	3.6	65.3	3
Minnesota	2	48	237	4.9	118.5	6
New England	9	134	454	3.4	50.4	1
New Orleans	6	131	662	5.1	110.3	6
N.Y. Giants	1	16	68	4.3	68.0	0
N.Y. Jets	10	186	710	3.8	71.0	5
Oakland	1	14	41	2.9	41.0	2
Philadelphia	2	22	180	8.2	90.0	3
Pittsburgh	2	35	116	3.3	58.0	0
St. Louis	1	19	177	9.3	177.0	3
San Diego	5	69	201	2.9	40.2	1
San Francisco	6	109	513	4.7	85.5	6
Seattle	5	98	364	3.7	72.8	4
Tampa Bay	3	54	223	4.1	74.3	4
Tennessee	2	39	233	6.0	116.5	3
Washington	3	44	172	3.9	57.3	1
Totals	107	1,895	8,060	4.3	75.3	67

Tennessee totals include one game vs. Houston

VINNY TESTAVERDE'S CAREER PASSING VS. EACH OPPONENT

Opponent	Games	Att.	Cmp.	Pct.	Yards	Avg. Gain	TD	Int.	Sacked
Arizona	7	238	127	53.4	1,487	6.25	9	7	23/179
Atlanta	5	121	62	51.2	939	7.76	4	7	11/73
Baltimore	1	69	36	52.2	481	6.97	2	3	1/8
Buffalo	7	197	113	57.4	1,351	6.86	8	4	9/65
Carolina	2	58	36	62.1	495	8.53	3	2	4/20
Chicago	11	316	155	49.1	1,951	6.17	12	17	27/212
Cincinnati	8	255	144	56.5	1,715	6.73	15	13	6/46
Cleveland	1	50	27	54.0	370	7.40	2	4	2/21
Dallas	3	78	49	62.8	583	7.47	3	3	10/89
Denver	3	101	54	53.5	705	6.98	5	3	4/29
Detroit	12	268	152	56.7	1,835	6.85	10	14	16/154
Green Bay	11	348	206	59.2	2,719	7.81	12	15	29/205
Indianapolis	11	353	183	51.8	2,732	7.74	19	15	22/199
Jacksonville	6	214	131	61.2	1,666	7.79	9	8	13/67
Kansas City	3	82	45	54.9	502	6.12	4	1	2/15
Miami	7	248	145	58.5	1,507	6.08	9	8	9/50
Minnesota	10	247	119	48.2	1,483	6.00	8	13	20/153
New England	9	258	160	62.0	2,038	7.90	19	8	17/92
New Orleans	6	165	82	49.7	1,214	7.36	6	7	14/95
N.Y. Giants	3	100	58	58.0	583	5.83	3	5	9/56
N.Y. Jets	4	137	77	56.2	946	6.91	3	4	5/54
Oakland	3	80	43	53.8	562	7.03	1	3	6/50
Philadelphia	3	95	45	47.4	516	5.43	3	8	6/44
Pittsburgh	10	284	155	54.6	1,883	6.63	12	15	17/97
St. Louis	6	138	86	62.3	1,078	7.81	9	6	12/83
San Diego	3	112	65	58.0	718	6.41	3	3	10/60
San Francisco	3	75	34	45.3	444	5.92	3	2	5/49
Seattle	2	84	58	69.0	646	7.69	4	2	0/0
Tampa Bay	2	69	39	56.5	437	6.33	3	3	1/3
Tennessee	9	304	182	59.9	2,268	7.46	19	11	15/138
Washington	2	59	29	49.2	453	7.68	4	2	4/24
Totals	173	5,203	2,897	55.7	36,307	6.98	226	216	329/2,430

Arizona totals include one game vs. St. Louis, four games vs. Phoenix
Oakland totals include one game vs. L.A. Raiders
St. Louis totals include four games vs. L.A. Rams
Tennessee totals include seven games vs. Houston

BRETT FAVRE'S CAREER PASSING VS. EACH OPPONENT

Opponent	Games	Att.	Cmp.	Pct.	Yards	Avg. Gain	TD	Int.	Sacked
Arizona	2	65	38	58.5	588	9.05	3	1	3/21
Atlanta	2	87	62	71.3	597	6.86	3	2	4/26
Baltimore	1	41	22	53.7	260	6.34	2	2	1/8
Buffalo	3	93	59	63.4	639	6.87	7	1	5/44
Carolina	4	168	102	60.7	1,213	7.22	11	8	10/73
Chicago	18	573	365	63.7	4,244	7.41	36	18	31/191
Cincinnati	3	117	76	65.0	902	7.71	6	2	9/68
Cleveland	2	61	43	70.5	433	7.10	3	0	4/22
Dallas	6	240	138	57.5	1,383	5.76	11	4	12/91
Denver	3	93	47	50.5	635	6.83	5	8	2/12
Detroit	18	648	397	61.3	4,796	7.40	30	26	34/214
Indianapolis	2	61	41	67.2	664	10.89	5	3	5/43
Jacksonville	1	30	20	66.7	202	6.73	2	1	2/9
Kansas City	2	83	47	56.6	527	6.35	3	4	8/50
Miami	3	122	76	62.3	809	6.63	4	2	7/28
Minnesota	17	542	325	60.0	3,619	6.68	26	18	39/257
New England	2	81	48	59.3	533	6.58	4	2	5/42
New Orleans	2	62	39	62.9	458	7.39	5	0	8/39
N.Y. Giants	3	102	62	60.8	687	6.74	4	3	6/37
N.Y. Jets	2	62	34	54.8	335	5.40	3	1	2/14
Oakland	2	75	42	56.0	523	6.97	5	3	5/24
Philadelphia	7	240	133	55.4	1,716	7.15	10	12	16/93
Pittsburgh	3	90	59	65.6	745	8.28	4	1	7/44
St. Louis	7	219	130	59.4	1,471	6.72	10	10	15/124
San Diego	3	78	47	60.3	550	7.05	6	3	5/56
San Francisco	4	151	87	57.6	1,176	7.79	7	5	7/49
Seattle	2	69	34	49.3	389	5.64	5	4	5/28
Tampa Bay	18	622	391	62.9	4,204	6.76	31	10	37/193
Tennessee	2	52	33	63.5	408	7.85	4	1	5/11
Washington	1	5	0	0.0	0	0.00	0	2	1/11
Totals	145	4,932	2,997	60.8	34,706	7.04	255	157	300/1,922

Oakland totals include one game vs. L.A. Raiders
St. Louis totals include four games vs. L.A. Rams
Tennessee totals include one game vs. Houston

DREW BLEDSOE'S CAREER PASSING VS. EACH OPPONENT

Opponent	Games	Att.	Cmp.	Pct.	Yards	Avg. Gain	TD	Int.	Sacked
Arizona	3	74	43	58.1	582	7.86	8	0	9/55
Atlanta	1	34	19	55.9	229	6.74	1	1	5/48
Baltimore	2	64	40	62.5	418	6.53	5	1	2/6
Buffalo	16	504	280	55.6	3,327	6.60	22	10	37/261
Carolina	1	44	22	50.0	228	5.18	0	0	0/0
Chicago	3	121	72	59.5	803	6.64	5	2	7/51
Cincinnati	3	108	63	58.3	729	6.75	2	3	1/6
Cleveland	5	215	119	55.3	1,283	5.97	3	6	11/74
Dallas	2	65	34	52.3	354	5.45	0	5	1/0
Denver	6	219	117	53.4	1,468	6.70	7	3	17/121
Detroit	3	114	66	57.9	638	5.60	2	3	5/19
Green Bay	2	89	49	55.1	602	6.76	3	4	4/35
Indianapolis	15	490	300	61.2	3,487	7.12	25	10	23/168
Jacksonville	2	79	53	67.1	489	6.19	3	1	6/32
Kansas City	4	166	98	59.0	1,079	6.50	9	3	9/61
Miami	16	600	326	54.3	4,208	7.01	21	26	27/168
Minnesota	3	147	93	63.3	929	6.32	6	2	6/46
New Orleans	2	66	39	59.1	514	7.79	1	5	5/32
N.Y. Giants	2	75	51	68.0	534	7.12	2	2	3/29
N.Y. Jets	15	520	277	53.3	3,278	6.30	16	20	36/249
Oakland	1	55	23	41.8	321	5.84	2	3	3/16
Philadelphia	1	49	23	46.9	331	6.76	0	4	6/43
Pittsburgh	4	178	99	55.6	1,170	6.57	8	11	4/37
St. Louis	1	35	11	31.4	176	5.03	1	1	4/30
San Diego	3	104	66	63.5	796	7.65	9	2	3/10
San Francisco	1	51	21	41.2	241	4.73	0	3	4/22
Seattle	1	44	20	45.5	238	5.41	1	2	2/15
Tampa Bay	2	64	39	60.9	333	5.20	1	2	11/84
Tennessee	1	30	18	60.0	250	8.33	1	0	4/22
Washington	1	48	23	47.9	222	4.63	0	1	2/17
Totals	122	4,452	2,504	56.2	29,257	6.57	164	136	257/1,757

Arizona totals include one game vs. Phoenix
Oakland totals include one game vs. L.A. Raiders

JERRY RICE'S CAREER RECEIVING VS. EACH OPPONENT

Opponent	Games	Rec.	Yards	Yds./Rec.	Yds./Game	TD
Arizona	7	35	559	16.0	79.9	7
Atlanta	29	175	2,731	15.6	94.2	25
Baltimore	1	6	58	9.7	58.0	1
Buffalo	4	14	158	11.3	39.5	1
Carolina	10	58	783	13.5	78.3	4
Chicago	6	31	500	16.1	83.3	7
Cincinnati	5	32	508	15.9	101.6	4
Cleveland	3	19	275	14.5	91.7	4
Dallas	8	47	744	15.8	93.0	6
Denver	5	25	367	14.7	73.4	2
Detroit	9	42	559	13.3	62.1	2
Green Bay	8	47	716	15.2	89.5	7
Indianapolis	4	22	414	18.8	103.5	5
Jacksonville	1	2	17	8.5	17.0	0
Kansas City	4	17	209	12.3	52.3	2
Miami	3	18	304	16.9	101.3	5
Minnesota	10	55	919	16.7	91.9	10
New England	5	24	409	17.0	81.8	6
New Orleans	30	147	2,025	13.8	67.5	14
N.Y. Giants	8	37	550	14.9	68.8	5
N.Y. Jets	4	21	351	16.7	87.8	3
Oakland	5	23	408	17.7	81.6	3
Philadelphia	6	31	490	15.8	81.7	5
Pittsburgh	5	29	280	9.7	56.0	4
St. Louis	30	158	2,409	15.2	80.3	20
San Diego	4	30	506	16.9	126.5	6
Seattle	3	14	272	19.4	90.7	4
Tampa Bay	8	47	710	15.1	88.8	10
Tennessee	5	34	330	9.7	66.0	2
Washington	8	41	686	16.7	85.8	2
Totals	238	1,281	19,247	15.0	80.9	176

Arizona totals include one game vs. St. Louis, four games vs. Phoenix
Oakland totals include four games vs. L.A. Raiders
St. Louis totals include 20 games vs. L.A. Rams
Tennessee totals include four games vs. Houston

ANDRE REED'S CAREER RECEIVING VS. EACH OPPONENT

Opponent	Games	Rec.	Yards	Yds./Rec.	Yds./Game	TD
Arizona	4	3	42	14.0	10.5	0
Atlanta	2	9	170	18.9	85.0	1
Baltimore	2	7	76	10.9	38.0	0
Carolina	2	2	17	8.5	8.5	0
Chicago	4	16	185	11.6	46.3	0
Cincinnati	7	24	344	14.3	49.1	2
Cleveland	5	25	347	13.9	69.4	2
Dallas	4	9	79	8.8	19.8	0
Denver	7	34	478	14.1	68.3	3
Detroit	3	15	184	12.3	61.3	2
Green Bay	3	21	249	11.9	83.0	3
Indianapolis	28	128	1,718	13.4	61.4	16
Jacksonville	3	6	57	9.5	19.0	0
Kansas City	7	36	557	15.5	79.6	5
Miami	28	122	1,731	14.2	61.8	10
Minnesota	4	18	247	13.7	61.8	0
New England	26	101	1,610	15.9	61.9	8
New Orleans	3	8	74	9.3	24.7	0
N.Y. Giants	6	19	310	16.3	51.7	3
N.Y. Jets	29	110	1,408	12.8	48.6	12
Oakland	7	35	499	14.3	71.3	1
Philadelphia	7	21	233	11.1	33.3	3
Pittsburgh	10	40	471	11.8	47.1	3
St. Louis	4	14	170	12.1	42.5	2
San Diego	3	16	232	14.5	77.3	2
San Francisco	2	20	259	13.0	129.5	0
Seattle	4	10	154	15.4	38.5	1
Tampa Bay	4	8	119	14.9	29.8	0
Tennessee	11	50	766	15.3	69.6	6
Washington	5	24	412	17.2	82.4	2
Totals	234	951	13,198	13.9	56.4	87

Arizona totals include one game vs. St. Louis, one game vs. Phoenix
Oakland totals include five games vs. L.A. Raiders
St. Louis totals include two games vs. L.A. Rams
Tennessee totals include nine games vs. Houston

CRIS CARTER'S CAREER RECEIVING VS. EACH OPPONENT

Opponent	Games	Rec.	Yards	Yds./Rec.	Yds./Game	TD
Arizona	13	64	893	14.0	68.7	12
Atlanta	4	20	324	16.2	81.0	6
Baltimore	1	11	85	7.7	85.0	1
Buffalo	4	25	349	14.0	87.3	4
Carolina	3	17	246	14.5	82.0	4
Chicago	23	130	1,504	11.6	65.4	9
Cincinnati	4	25	310	12.4	77.5	3
Cleveland	3	12	166	13.8	55.3	0
Dallas	9	40	525	13.1	58.3	7
Denver	6	28	403	14.4	67.2	5
Detroit	22	99	1,070	10.8	48.6	9
Green Bay	21	101	1,212	12.0	57.7	10
Indianapolis	2	9	156	17.3	78.0	3
Jacksonville	1	4	27	6.8	27.0	1
Kansas City	4	15	199	13.3	49.8	3
Miami	3	16	249	15.6	83.0	3
Minnesota	2	5	30	6.0	15.0	1
New England	5	31	343	11.1	68.6	1
New Orleans	7	37	433	11.7	61.9	4
N.Y. Giants	10	24	460	19.2	46.0	3
N.Y. Jets	3	18	219	12.2	73.0	2
Oakland	5	26	327	12.6	65.4	1
Philadelphia	2	11	209	19.0	104.5	3
Pittsburgh	2	9	140	15.6	70.0	2
St. Louis	5	19	231	12.2	46.2	2
San Diego	3	20	258	12.9	86.0	2
San Francisco	8	38	367	9.7	45.9	6
Seattle	3	12	217	18.1	72.3	1
Tampa Bay	23	105	1,299	12.4	56.5	9
Tennessee	4	23	289	12.6	72.3	4
Washington	8	26	422	16.2	52.8	2
Totals	213	1,020	12,962	12.7	60.9	123

Arizona totals include two games vs. St. Louis, six games vs. Phoenix
Oakland totals include three games vs. L.A. Raiders
St. Louis totals include three games vs. L.A. Rams
Tennessee totals include three games vs. Houston

TIM BROWN'S CAREER RECEIVING VS. EACH OPPONENT

Opponent	Games	Rec.	Yards	Yds./Rec.	Yds./Game	TD
Arizona	1	2	13	6.5	13.0	0
Atlanta	5	24	393	16.4	78.6	3
Baltimore	2	9	99	11.0	49.5	2
Buffalo	7	24	536	22.3	76.6	5
Carolina	2	13	181	13.9	90.5	1
Chicago	4	17	192	11.3	48.0	2
Cincinnati	7	24	434	18.1	62.0	6
Cleveland	3	5	83	16.6	27.7	0
Dallas	3	18	224	12.4	74.7	1
Denver	24	112	1,502	13.4	62.6	11
Detroit	2	6	48	8.0	24.0	1
Green Bay	3	13	161	12.4	53.7	0
Indianapolis	3	13	184	14.2	61.3	0
Jacksonville	2	19	224	11.8	112.0	1
Kansas City	23	110	1,586	14.4	69.0	5
Miami	8	43	563	13.1	70.4	5
Minnesota	4	16	175	10.9	43.8	1
New England	1	2	46	23.0	46.0	0
New Orleans	5	20	268	13.4	53.6	3
N.Y. Giants	3	11	254	23.1	84.7	2
N.Y. Jets	6	42	651	15.5	108.5	5
Philadelphia	2	9	115	12.8	57.5	1
Pittsburgh	4	16	181	11.3	45.3	0
St. Louis	4	11	203	18.5	50.8	1
San Diego	25	104	1,365	13.1	54.6	7
San Francisco	4	17	284	16.7	71.0	3
Seattle	24	93	1,458	15.7	60.8	12
Tampa Bay	3	13	180	13.8	60.0	1
Tennessee	5	21	293	14.0	58.6	5
Washington	3	19	176	9.3	58.7	2
Totals	192	846	12,072	14.3	62.9	86

St. Louis totals include three games vs. L.A. Rams
Tennessee totals include three games vs. Houston

MORTEN ANDERSEN'S CAREER KICKING VS. EACH OPPONENT

Opponent	Games	FG	FGA	FG%	Long FG	XP	XPA	Pts.
Arizona	12	21	21	100.0	52	32	33	95
Atlanta	25	40	51	78.4	49	56	58	176
Baltimore	1	2	3	66.7	41	1	1	7
Buffalo	4	7	11	63.6	50	7	7	28
Carolina	12	22	28	78.6	51	23	23	89
Chicago	6	5	8	62.5	60	14	14	29
Cincinnati	5	5	8	62.5	49	17	17	32
Cleveland	4	7	8	87.5	53	7	7	28
Dallas	11	18	25	72.0	54	18	18	72
Denver	5	4	8	50.0	55	16	17	28
Detroit	10	11	17	64.7	50	19	19	52
Green Bay	6	10	11	90.9	52	15	15	45
Indianapolis	3	3	5	60.0	46	11	11	20
Jacksonville	2	1	2	50.0	46	3	3	6
Kansas City	5	9	10	90.0	50	9	9	36
Miami	5	5	7	71.4	35	15	15	30
Minnesota	10	15	19	78.9	47	17	17	62
New England	6	10	12	83.3	54	16	16	46
New Orleans	12	22	28	78.6	55	28	28	94
N.Y. Giants	9	17	20	85.0	45	15	15	66
N.Y. Jets	6	10	11	90.9	53	12	12	42
Oakland	6	7	9	77.8	51	13	13	34
Philadelphia	11	19	23	82.6	56	20	20	77
Pittsburgh	6	7	10	70.0	50	10	10	31
St. Louis	35	53	61	86.9	51	85	87	244
San Diego	4	3	7	42.9	35	9	9	18
San Francisco	37	60	72	83.3	59	59	61	239
Seattle	5	7	8	87.5	47	9	9	30
Tampa Bay	16	24	32	75.0	50	35	35	107
Tennessee	6	9	13	69.2	47	13	13	40
Washington	7	8	14	57.1	45	11	11	35
Totals	292	441	562	78.5	60	615	623	1,938

Arizona totals include five games vs. St. Louis, four games vs. Phoenix
Oakland totals include four games vs. L.A. Raiders
St. Louis totals include 23 games vs. L.A. Rams
Tennessee totals include five games vs. Houston

GARY ANDERSON'S CAREER KICKING VS. EACH OPPONENT

Opponent	Games	FG	FGA	FG%	Long FG	XP	XPA	Pts.
Arizona	8	14	19	73.7	44	22	22	64
Atlanta	7	8	10	80.0	39	26	26	50
Baltimore	1	6	6	100.0	46	2	2	20
Buffalo	10	17	20	85.0	49	21	21	72
Carolina	4	7	8	87.5	48	13	13	34
Chicago	10	16	20	80.0	50	24	24	72
Cincinnati	26	39	48	81.3	52	60	60	177
Cleveland	26	35	52	67.3	49	47	47	152
Dallas	13	22	28	78.6	49	27	27	93
Denver	11	19	23	82.6	42	24	24	81
Detroit	11	17	24	70.8	44	28	28	79
Green Bay	10	14	18	77.8	48	23	24	65
Indianapolis	8	11	13	84.6	53	22	22	55
Jacksonville	1	3	3	100.0	53	5	5	14
Kansas City	10	23	29	79.3	49	24	24	93
Miami	10	16	21	76.2	49	24	24	72
Minnesota	5	3	7	42.9	44	10	10	19
New England	8	10	10	100.0	49	20	20	50
New Orleans	8	20	22	90.9	51	18	18	78
N.Y. Giants	8	10	12	83.3	46	18	18	48
N.Y. Jets	8	13	19	68.4	45	24	24	63
Oakland	5	5	12	41.7	37	8	8	23
Philadelphia	4	5	7	71.4	52	9	9	24
St. Louis	8	9	11	81.8	46	22	22	49
San Diego	14	25	27	92.6	55	41	42	116
San Francisco	5	8	11	72.7	50	12	12	36
Seattle	10	13	15	86.7	43	10	10	49
Tampa Bay	10	14	18	77.8	44	22	22	64
Tennessee	26	47	52	90.4	54	50	52	191
Washington	8	12	13	92.3	49	20	21	56
Totals	293	461	578	79.8	55	676	681	2,059

Arizona totals include one game vs. St. Louis, one game vs. Phoenix
Indianapolis totals include one game vs. Baltimore
Oakland totals include three games vs. L.A. Raiders
Tennessee totals include 25 games vs. Houston
St. Louis totals include three games vs. L.A. Rams

STARTING RECORDS OF ACTIVE NFL QUARTERBACKS

Minimum: 10 starts

	W - L - T	Pct.
Kurt Warner	21 - 6	.778
Daunte Culpepper	11 - 5	.688
Jay Fiedler	11 - 5	.688
Doug Flutie	30 - 14	.682
Shaun King	14 - 7	.667
Brett Favre	91 - 50	.645
Steve McNair	41 - 23	.641
Brad Johnson	32 - 18	.640
Mark Brunell	51 - 33	.607
Randall Cunningham	80 - 52 -1	.605
Donovan McNabb	13 - 9	.591
Mike Tomczak	42 - 31	.575
Elvis Grbac	32 - 24	.571
Rich Gannon	51 - 39	.567
Kordell Stewart	30 - 24	.556
Neil O'Donnell	54 - 44	.551
Jon Kitna	18 - 15	.545
Peyton Manning	26 - 22	.542
Trent Dilfer	45 - 39	.536
Kerry Collins	38 - 34	.528
Drew Bledsoe	63 - 58	.521
Rodney Peete	37 - 35	.514
Charlie Batch	19 - 18	.514
Shane Matthews	6 - 6	.500
Bubby Brister	37 - 38	.493
Brian Griese	11 - 12	.478
Danny Kanell	10 - 11 - 1	.477
Ty Detmer	10 - 11	.476
Rob Johnson	9 - 10	.474
Jim Harbaugh	66 - 74	.471
Steve Beuerlein	45 - 52	.464
Chris Chandler	56 - 67	.455
Scott Mitchell	32 - 39	.451
Kent Graham	17 - 21	.447
Gus Frerotte	25 - 32 - 1	.440
Dave Brown	26 - 34	.433
Vinny Testaverde	69 - 92 - 1	.429
Trent Green	8 - 11	.421
Jeff Blake	32 - 45	.416
Todd Collins	7 - 10	.412
Tony Banks	25 - 36	.410
Jeff George	46 - 76	.377
Rick Mirer	22 - 38	.367
Jake Plummer	18 - 32	.360
John Friesz	13 - 25	.342
Eric Zeier	4 - 8	.333
Billy Joe Tolliver	15 - 32	.319
Jeff Garcia	8 - 18	.308
Paul Justin	3 - 7	.300
Bobby Hoying	3 - 9 - 1	.269
Billy Joe Hobert	4 - 13	.235
Ryan Leaf	4 - 14	.222
Cade McNown	3 - 12	.200
Akili Smith	3 - 12	.200
Tim Couch	4 - 17	.190
Doug Pederson	3 - 14	.176

ALL-TIME RANKINGS OF PLAYERS IN FOUR CATEGORIES THAT DETERMINE NFL PASSER RATING

Minimum: 1,500 Attempts

COMPLETION PERCENTAGE	Pct.	Att.	Comp.
Steve Young	64.28	4,149	2,667
Joe Montana	63.24	5,391	3,409
Brad Johnson	61.83	1,821	1,126
Troy Aikman	61.46	4,715	2,898
Brett Favre	60.77	4,932	2,997
Peyton Manning	60.39	1,679	1,014
Mark Brunell	60.18	2,672	1,608
Jim Kelly	60.14	4,779	2,874
Ken Stabler	59.85	3,793	2,270
Elvis Grbac	59.71	1,978	1,181

AVERAGE YARDS PER PASS	Avg.	Att.	Yards
Otto Graham	8.63	1,565	13,499
Sid Luckman	8.42	1,744	14,686
Norm Van Brocklin	8.16	2,895	23,611
Steve Young	7.98	4,149	33,124
Ed Brown	7.85	1,987	15,600
Bart Starr	7.85	3,149	24,718
Johnny Unitas	7.76	5,186	40,239
Earl Morrall	7.74	2,689	20,809
Dan Fouts	7.68	5,604	43,040
Len Dawson	7.67	3,741	28,711

TOUCHDOWN PERCENTAGE	Pct.	Att.	TD
Sid Luckman	7.86	1,744	137
Frank Ryan	6.99	2,133	149
Len Dawson	6.39	3,741	239
Daryle Lamonica	6.31	2,601	164
Sammy Baugh	6.24	2,995	187
Charley Conerly	6.11	2,833	173
Bob Waterfield	6.00	1,617	97
Earl Morrall	5.99	2,689	161
Sonny Jurgensen	5.98	4,262	255
Norm Van Brocklin	5.98	2,895	173

INTERCEPTION PERCENTAGE	Pct.	Att.	Int.
Neil O'Donnell	2.08	3,121	65
Steve Bono	2.47	1,701	42
Mark Brunell	2.47	2,672	66
Joe Montana	2.58	5,391	139
Steve Young	2.58	4,149	107
Bernie Kosar	2.59	3,365	87
Steve McNair	2.64	1,857	49
Ken O'Brien	2.72	3,602	98
Jeff George	2.80	3,925	110
Jeff Blake	2.84	2,532	72

HIGHEST NFL POSTSEASON PASSER RATINGS (MINIMUM: 150 ATTEMPTS)

	Games	Att.	Comp.	Pct.	Yds.	Avg. Gain	TD	Int.	Rating
Bart Starr	10	213	130	61.0	1,753	8.23	15	3	104.8
Kurt Warner	4	161	101	62.7	1,428	8.87	11	7	96.0
Joe Montana	23	734	460	62.7	5,772	7.86	45	21	95.6
Ken Anderson	6	166	110	66.3	1,321	7.96	9	6	93.5
Joe Theismann	10	211	128	60.7	1,782	8.45	11	7	91.4
Brett Favre	14	449	270	60.1	3,390	7.55	25	12	91.1
Troy Aikman	16	502	320	63.7	3,849	7.67	23	17	88.3
Steve Young	22	471	292	62.0	3,326	7.06	20	13	85.8
Warren Moon	10	403	259	64.3	2,870	7.12	17	14	84.9
Ken Stabler	13	351	203	57.8	2,641	7.52	19	13	84.2

HIGHEST NFL POSTSEASON PASSER RATINGS, ACTIVE PLAYERS (MINIMUM: 150 ATTEMPTS)

	Games	Att.	Comp.	Pct.	Yds.	Avg. Gain	TD	Int.	Rating
Kurt Warner	4	161	101	62.7	1,428	8.87	11	7	96.0
Brett Favre	14	449	270	60.1	3,390	7.55	25	12	91.1
Neil O'Donnell	8	274	159	58.0	1,709	6.23	9	8	75.2
Randall Cunningham	12	365	192	52.6	2,426	6.65	12	9	74.3
Jim Harbaugh	5	163	83	50.9	906	5.56	6	5	67.2
Kerry Collins	5	156	86	55.1	933	5.98	8	9	66.0
Mark Brunell	9	255	127	49.8	1,550	6.08	10	10	65.6
Steve McNair	5	153	86	56.2	690	4.51	1	3	61.7
Drew Bledsoe	6	231	119	51.5	1,233	5.34	5	12	52.8

INSIDE THE NUMBERS

NFL INDIVIDUAL LEADERS OVER RECENT SEASONS

Points

Last 2 Seasons		Last 3 Seasons		Last 4 Seasons	
266	Mike Vanderjagt	378	Gary Anderson	503	Gary Anderson
261	Olindo Mare	372	Ryan Longwell	492	Ryan Longwell
251	Matt Stover	370	Mike Vanderjagt	477	Mike Hollis
244	Ryan Longwell	360	Al Del Greco	477	Olindo Mare
235	Mike Hollis	360	Olindo Mare	473	Al Del Greco

Touchdowns

Last 2 Seasons		Last 3 Seasons		Last 4 Seasons	
38	Marshall Faulk	48	Marshall Faulk	56	Marshall Faulk
35	Edgerrin James	44	Randy Moss	47	Cris Carter
29	Eddie George	37	Emmitt Smith	44	Randy Moss
28	Stephen Davis	37	Fred Taylor	42	Terrell Davis
27	Randy Moss	35	Two tied	42	Eddie George

Field Goals

Last 2 Seasons		Last 3 Seasons		Last 4 Seasons	
67	Olindo Mare	89	Olindo Mare	117	Olindo Mare
63	Matt Stover	87	Ryan Longwell	111	Al Del Greco
59	Mike Vanderjagt	86	Mike Vanderjagt	111	Ryan Longwell
58	Ryan Longwell	84	Four tied	110	Matt Stover
55	Two tied			109	Adam Vinatieri

Rushes

Last 2 Seasons		Last 3 Seasons		Last 4 Seasons	
756	Edgerrin James	1,071	Eddie George	1,428	Eddie George
723	Eddie George	1,052	Curtis Martin	1,345	Jerome Bettis
683	Curtis Martin	970	Jerome Bettis	1,326	Curtis Martin
654	Jerome Bettis	942	Emmitt Smith	1,207	Ricky Watters
623	Emmitt Smith	922	Ricky Watters	1,203	Emmitt Smith

Rushing Yards

Last 2 Seasons		Last 3 Seasons		Last 4 Seasons	
3,262	Edgerrin James	4,107	Eddie George	5,506	Eddie George
2,813	Eddie George	4,059	Marshall Faulk	5,282	Jerome Bettis
2,740	Marshall Faulk	3,955	Curtis Martin	5,115	Curtis Martin
2,723	Stephen Davis	3,932	Emmitt Smith	5,113	Marshall Faulk
2,668	Curtis Martin	3,765	Corey Dillon	5,006	Emmitt Smith

Rushing Touchdowns

Last 2 Seasons		Last 3 Seasons		Last 4 Seasons	
28	Stephen Davis	33	Emmitt Smith	40	Terrell Davis
26	Edgerrin James	32	Fred Taylor	38	Marshall Faulk
25	Marshall Faulk	31	Marshall Faulk	37	Emmitt Smith
23	Eddie George	28	Stephen Davis	34	Eddie George
23	James Stewart	28	Eddie George	33	James Stewart

Passes

Last 2 Seasons		Last 3 Seasons		Last 4 Seasons	
1,175	Brett Favre	1,726	Brett Favre	2,239	Brett Favre
1,104	Steve Beuerlein	1,679	Peyton Manning	2,073	Drew Bledsoe
1,104	Peyton Manning	1,551	Drew Bledsoe	1,742	Mark Brunell
1,070	Drew Bledsoe	1,447	Steve Beuerlein	1,699	Jake Plummer
1,046	Elvis Grbac	1,403	Jake Plummer	1,679	Peyton Manning

Completions

Last 2 Seasons		Last 3 Seasons		Last 4 Seasons	
688	Peyton Manning	1,026	Brett Favre	1,330	Brett Favre
679	Brett Favre	1,014	Peyton Manning	1,194	Drew Bledsoe
667	Steve Beuerlein	883	Steve Beuerlein	1,042	Mark Brunell
620	Elvis Grbac	880	Drew Bledsoe	1,014	Peyton Manning
617	Drew Bledsoe	795	Jake Plummer	972	Steve Beuerlein

Passing Yards

Last 2 Seasons		Last 3 Seasons		Last 4 Seasons	
8,548	Peyton Manning	12,287	Peyton Manning	15,982	Brett Favre
8,166	Steve Beuerlein	12,115	Brett Favre	14,615	Drew Bledsoe
7,903	Brett Favre	10,909	Drew Bledsoe	12,582	Mark Brunell
7,782	Kurt Warner	10,779	Steve Beuerlein	12,287	Peyton Manning
7,558	Elvis Grbac	9,575	Rich Gannon	11,811	Steve Beuerlein

Touchdown Passes

Last 2 Seasons		Last 3 Seasons		Last 4 Seasons	
62	Kurt Warner	85	Peyton Manning	108	Brett Favre
59	Peyton Manning	73	Brett Favre	85	Peyton Manning
55	Steve Beuerlein	72	Steve Beuerlein	84	Drew Bledsoe
52	Rich Gannon	62	Rich Gannon	78	Steve Beuerlein
50	Elvis Grbac	62	Kurt Warner	72	Mark Brunell

Receptions

Last 2 Seasons		Last 3 Seasons		Last 4 Seasons	
217	Marvin Harrison	285	Jimmy Smith	367	Jimmy Smith
207	Jimmy Smith	276	Marvin Harrison	353	Cris Carter
198	Muhsin Muhammad	266	Muhsin Muhammad	351	Tim Brown
186	Cris Carter	265	Rod Smith	349	Marvin Harrison
179	Rod Smith	264	Cris Carter	335	Rod Smith

Reception Yards

Last 2 Seasons		Last 3 Seasons		Last 4 Seasons	
3,076	Marvin Harrison	4,163	Randy Moss	5,355	Jimmy Smith
2,850	Randy Moss	4,031	Jimmy Smith	5,024	Rod Smith
2,849	Jimmy Smith	3,852	Marvin Harrison	4,892	Tim Brown
2,636	Isaac Bruce	3,844	Rod Smith	4,718	Marvin Harrison
2,622	Rod Smith	3,688	Eric Moulds	4,653	Antonio Freeman

Receiving Touchdowns

Last 2 Seasons		Last 3 Seasons		Last 4 Seasons	
26	Marvin Harrison	43	Randy Moss	47	Cris Carter
26	Randy Moss	34	Cris Carter	43	Randy Moss
22	Cris Carter	33	Marvin Harrison	41	Antonio Freeman
21	Isaac Bruce	31	Terrell Owens	39	Marvin Harrison
20	Tony Gonzalez	29	Antonio Freeman	39	Terrell Owens

Interceptions

Last 2 Seasons		Last 3 Seasons		Last 4 Seasons	
14	Donnie Abraham	20	Sam Madison	22	Ray Buchanan
12	Sam Madison	17	Ray Buchanan	21	Terrell Buckley
12	Dexter McCleon	17	Terrell Buckley	21	Sam Madison
12	Darren Sharper	17	Rod Woodson	20	Three tied
12	Troy Vincent	16	Two tied		

Sacks

Last 2 Seasons		Last 3 Seasons		Last 4 Seasons	
29.0	Warren Sapp	39.5	Kevin Carter	47.0	Kevin Carter
27.5	Kevin Carter	36.0	Warren Sapp	47.0	Robert Porcher
26.0	Jevon Kearse	35.5	La'Roi Glover	46.5	Warren Sapp
25.5	La'Roi Glover	34.5	Trace Armstrong	44.0	John Randle
25.0	Trevor Pryce	34.5	Robert Porcher	44.0	Michael Strahan

NFL TEAM LEADERS OVER RECENT SEASONS

Highest Won-Lost Percentage

Last 2 Seasons		Last 3 Seasons		Last 4 Seasons	
.813	Tennessee	.750	Minnesota	.703	Minnesota
.719	Indianapolis	.708	Tennessee	.672	Denver
.719	St. Louis	.667	Jacksonville	.672	Jacksonville
.656	Three tied	.646	Denver	.656	Tennessee
		.625	Miami	.641	Green Bay

Most Points

Last 2 Seasons		Last 3 Seasons		Last 4 Seasons	
1,066	St. Louis	1,352	Minnesota	1,772	Denver
869	Oakland	1,351	St. Louis	1,706	Minnesota
852	Indianapolis	1,300	Denver	1,650	St. Louis
799	Denver	1,162	Indianapolis	1,549	Jacksonville
796	Minnesota	1,162	San Francisco	1,540	Green Bay

Most Total Yards

Last 2 Seasons		Last 3 Seasons		Last 4 Seasons	
13,487	St. Louis	18,220	San Francisco	23,801	Denver
11,867	Indianapolis	18,018	Minnesota	23,372	Minnesota
11,837	Denver	17,959	St. Louis	23,332	San Francisco
11,754	Minnesota	17,929	Denver	22,720	St. Louis
11,469	Oakland	16,983	Indianapolis	21,990	Green Bay

Most Rushing Yards

Last 2 Seasons		Last 3 Seasons		Last 4 Seasons	
4,554	Oakland	6,643	Denver	9,021	Denver
4,365	Cincinnati	6,440	San Francisco	8,752	Pittsburgh
4,239	Pittsburgh	6,281	Oakland	8,409	San Francisco
4,175	Denver	6,273	Pittsburgh	8,279	Tennessee
4,123	Jacksonville	6,225	Jacksonville	7,970	Cincinnati

Most Passing Yards

Last 2 Seasons		Last 3 Seasons		Last 4 Seasons	
9,585	St. Louis	12,672	St. Louis	15,870	St. Louis
8,348	Indianapolis	12,149	Minnesota	15,462	Minnesota
7,821	Minnesota	11,978	Indianapolis	15,393	Green Bay
7,662	Denver	11,780	San Francisco	15,120	Indianapolis
7,629	Carolina	11,688	Green Bay	14,923	San Francisco

***Fewest Turnovers**

Last 2 Seasons		Last 3 Seasons		Last 4 Seasons	
46	Pittsburgh	67	Jacksonville	87	Jacksonville
47	Jacksonville	70	Buffalo	94	Denver
49	Oakland	71	Tennessee	97	Tennessee
50	Buffalo	73	Denver	99	N.Y. Giants
50	Kansas City	77	Dallas	100	Dallas

***Fewest Points Allowed**

Last 2 Seasons		Last 3 Seasons		Last 4 Seasons	
442	Baltimore	777	Baltimore	1,062	Tampa Bay
504	Tampa Bay	799	Tampa Bay	1,122	Baltimore
515	Tennessee	827	Miami	1,145	Tennessee
544	Jacksonville	835	Tennessee	1,154	Miami
562	Miami	878	Pittsburgh	1,178	N.Y. Giants

***Fewest Total Yards Allowed**

8,189	Baltimore	13,162	Buffalo	18,015	Buffalo
8,471	Buffalo	13,425	Tampa Bay	18,053	Tampa Bay
9,040	Miami	13,475	Miami	18,839	Miami
9,058	Tennessee	13,486	Baltimore	18,849	Baltimore
9,080	Tampa Bay	14,072	San Diego	19,238	San Diego

***Fewest Rushing Yards Allowed**

2,201	Baltimore	3,883	San Diego	5,581	San Diego
2,716	N.Y. Giants	3,906	Baltimore	5,596	Baltimore
2,743	San Diego	4,422	Buffalo	6,123	Tennessee
2,886	St. Louis	4,550	Tennessee	6,171	N.Y. Giants
2,929	Buffalo	4,622	Denver	6,214	Buffalo

***Fewest Passing Yards Allowed**

5,542	Buffalo	8,740	Buffalo	11,798	Tampa Bay
5,828	Miami	8,752	Miami	11,801	Buffalo
5,946	Pittsburgh	8,787	Tampa Bay	12,089	Washington
5,988	Baltimore	9,171	Philadelphia	12,094	Philadelphia
6,025	Tampa Bay	9,267	Pittsburgh	12,158	Dallas

Most Opponents' Turnovers

80	Baltimore	107	Kansas City	141	Kansas City
77	Philadelphia	107	Seattle	136	Seattle
74	Detroit	105	Miami	132	Miami
74	Kansas City	105	Oakland	132	New Orleans
72	Tampa Bay	103	Baltimore	131	Two tied

**Cleveland excluded from last three and four seasons' lists.*

LONGEST WINNING STREAKS SINCE 1970

16	Miami, 1971-73	(1 in 1971, 14 in 1972, 1 in 1973)
16	Miami, 1983-84	(5 in 1983, 11 in 1984)
15	San Francisco, 1989-90	(5 in 1989, 10 in 1990)
14	Oakland, 1976-77	(10 in 1976, 4 in 1977)
14	Denver, 1997-98	(1 in 1997, 13 in 1998)
13	Minnesota, 1974-75	(3 in 1974, 10 in 1975)
13	Chicago, 1984-85	(1 in 1984, 12 in 1985)
13	N.Y. Giants, 1989-90	(3 in 1989, 10 in 1990)
12	Washington, 1990-91	(1 in 1990, 11 in 1991)
11	Pittsburgh, 1975	
11	Baltimore, 1975-76	(9 in 1975, 2 in 1976)
11	Chicago, 1986-87	(7 in 1986, 4 in 1987)
11	Houston, 1993	
11	San Francisco, 1997	
11	Jacksonville, 1999	
11	Indianapolis, 1999	
10	Miami, 1973	
10	Pittsburgh, 1976-77	(9 in 1976, 1 in 1977)
10	Denver, 1984	
10	San Francisco, 1994	
10	Minnesota, 1999-00	(3 in 1999, 7 in 2000)

NFL PLAYOFF APPEARANCES BY SEASONS

Team	Number of Seasons in Playoffs
Dallas	26
N.Y. Giants	25
St. Louis	24
Cleveland	23
Minnesota	23
Chicago	21
Miami	20
San Francisco	20
Washington	20
Green Bay	19
Oakland	19
Pittsburgh	19
Buffalo	17
Tennessee	17
Indianapolis	15
Philadelphia	15
Denver	14
Detroit	14
Kansas City	13
San Diego	12
New England	10
N.Y. Jets	8
Cincinnati	7
Arizona	6
Atlanta	6
Tampa Bay	6
New Orleans	5
Seattle	5
Jacksonville	4
Baltimore	1
Carolina	1

TEAMS IN SUPER BOWL CONTENTION, 1978-2000

	With 3 Weeks to Play	With 2 Weeks to Play	With 1 Week to Play
2000	19	17	16
1999	23	20	16
1998	22	19	14
1997	22	18	14
1996	23	21	13
1995	*27	21	*18
1994	25	*22	15
1993	20	18	16
1992	20	16	14
1991	20	18	13
1990	23	20	15
1989	21	18	17
1988	21	18	15
1987	19	19	15
1986	19	17	14
1985	21	18	13
1984	18	14	13
1983	24	19	15
1982	20	17	16
1981	21	20	16
1980	20	14	12
1979	19	15	13
1978	20	17	12

GAMES DECIDED BY 7 POINTS OR LESS AND 3 POINTS OR LESS (1970-2000)

	Games Decided by 7 Points or Less	Games Decided by 3 Points or Less
1970	59 of 182 (32.4%)	34 of 182 (18.7%)
1971	76 of 182 (41.8%)	35 of 182 (19.2%)
1972	71 of 182 (39.0%)	38 of 182 (20.9%)
1973	60 of 182 (32.9%)	28 of 182 (15.4%)
1974	91 of 182 (50.0%)	37 of 182 (20.3%)
1975	62 of 182 (34.1%)	35 of 182 (19.2%)
1976	73 of 196 (37.2%)	38 of 196 (19.4%)
1977	85 of 196 (43.4%)	36 of 196 (18.4%)
1978	108 of 224 (48.2%)	49 of 224 (21.9%)
1979	104 of 224 (46.4%)	51 of 224 (22.8%)
1980	108 of 224 (48.2%)	58 of 224 (25.9%)
1981	91 of 224 (40.6%)	60 of 224 (26.8%)
1982	61 of 126 (48.4%)	33 of 126 (26.2%)
1983	106 of 224 (47.3%)	54 of 224 (24.1%)
1984	95 of 224 (42.4%)	58 of 224 (25.9%)
1985	87 of 224 (38.8%)	38 of 224 (17.0%)
1986	106 of 224 (47.3%)	48 of 224 (21.4%)
1987	99 of 210 (47.1%)	40 of 210 (19.0%)
1988	113 of 224 (50.4%)	62 of 224 (27.7%)
1989	107 of 224 (47.8%)	55 of 224 (24.6%)
1990	97 of 224 (43.3%)	54 of 224 (24.1%)
1991	112 of 224 (50.0%)	57 of 224 (25.4%)
1992	88 of 224 (39.3%)	48 of 224 (21.4%)
1993	*105 of 224 (46.9%)	53 of 224 (23.7%)
1994	115 of 224 (51.3%)	60 of 224 (26.8%)
1995	115 of 240 (47.9%)	61 of 240 (25.4%)
1996	109 of 240 (45.4%)	47 of 240 (19.6%)
1997	111 of 240 (46.3%)	67 of 240 (27.9%)
1998	113 of 240 (47.1%)	50 of 240 (20.8%)
1999	115 of 248 (46.4%)	**64 of 248 (25.8%)
2000	109 of 248 (44.0%)	61 of 248 (24.6%)

*Week record: Dec. 11-13, 1993 (Week 15), 12 of 14 games (86%) decided by 7 points or less.

**Week record: Oct. 10-11, 1999 (Week 5), 10 of 14 games (71%) decided by 3 points or less.

2000 RECORDS OF TEAMS IN CLOSE GAMES

AFC	Overall Record	Decided by 8 Pts. or Less	Decided By 3 Pts. or Less
Baltimore	12-4	4-3	2-1
Buffalo	8-8	5-3	4-2
Cincinnati	4-12	1-1	1-1
Cleveland	3-13	2-1	1-0
Denver	11-5	5-2	2-1
Indianapolis	10-6	4-5	1-3
Jacksonville	7-9	2-5	1-3
Kansas City	7-9	4-5	2-3
Miami	11-5	4-4	2-2
New England	5-11	4-9	2-3
N.Y. Jets	9-7	5-4	2-2
Oakland	12-4	5-3	3-3
Pittsburgh	9-7	2-4	2-4
San Diego	1-15	1-8	1-6
Seattle	6-10	4-5	2-1
Tennessee	13-3	6-3	4-3

NFC	Overall Record	Decided by 8 Pts. or Less	Decided By 3 Pts. or Less
Arizona	3-13	3-3	2-0
Atlanta	4-12	3-3	1-2
Carolina	7-9	2-5	1-4
Chicago	5-11	5-5	4-1
Dallas	5-11	2-5	1-2
Detroit	9-7	6-3	2-1
Green Bay	9-7	6-5	4-1
Minnesota	11-5	7-2	1-0
New Orleans	10-6	4-2	2-0
N.Y. Giants	12-4	7-0	2-0
Philadelphia	11-5	4-3	3-3
St. Louis	10-6	3-3	1-2
San Francisco	6-10	1-4	0-1
Tampa Bay	10-6	4-5	2-3
Washington	8-8	4-6	3-3

SUPER BOWL CHAMPIONS THAT DID NOT MAKE PLAYOFFS THE FOLLOWING YEAR

Denver—Super Bowl XXXIII champions did not make playoffs in the 1999 season.

N.Y. Giants—Super Bowl XXV champions did not make playoffs in the 1991 season.

Washington—Super Bowl XXII champions did not make playoffs in the 1988 season.

N.Y. Giants—Super Bowl XXI champions did not make playoffs in the 1987 season.

San Francisco—Super Bowl XVI champions did not make playoffs in the 1982 season.

Oakland—Super Bowl XV champions did not make playoffs in the 1981 season.

Pittsburgh—Super Bowl XIV champions did not make playoffs in the 1980 season.

Kansas City—Super Bowl IV champions did not make playoffs in the 1970 season.

Green Bay—Super Bowl II champions did not make playoffs in the 1968 season.

NON-DIVISION WINNERS THAT PLAYED IN SUPER BOWL

2000	Baltimore Ravens (Defeated N.Y. Giants, 34-7)	Super Bowl XXXV
1999	Tennessee Titans (Lost to St. Louis, 23-16)	Super Bowl XXXIV
1997	Denver Broncos (Defeated Green Bay, 31-24)	Super Bowl XXXII
1992	Buffalo Bills (Lost to Dallas, 52-17)	Super Bowl XXVII
1985	New England Patriots (Lost to Chicago, 46-10)	Super Bowl XX
1980	Oakland Raiders (Defeated Philadelphia, 27-10)	Super Bowl XV
1975	Dallas Cowboys (Lost to Pittsburgh, 21-17)	Super Bowl X
1969	Kansas City Chiefs (Defeated Minnesota, 23-7)	Super Bowl IV

TEAMS AT OR UNDER .500 IN POSTSEASON PLAY

1999	Dallas Cowboys	8-8
1999	Detroit Lions	8-8
1991	New York Jets	8-8
1990	New Orleans Saints	8-8
1985	Cleveland Browns	8-8
1982	Cleveland Browns	4-5
1982	Detroit Lions	4-5
1969	Houston Oilers	6-6-2

COLDEST NFL GAMES ON RECORD

-13 degrees (-48 degree wind chill)—December 31, 1967, Lambeau Field, Green Bay, Wisconsin, NFL Championship (Green Bay 21, Dallas 17)

-9 degrees (-59 degree wind chill)—January 10, 1982, Riverfront Stadium, Cincinnati, Ohio, AFC Championship (Cincinnati 27, San Diego 7)

0 degrees (-32 degree wind chill)—January 15, 1994, Rich Stadium, Orchard Park, New York, AFC Divisional Playoff (Buffalo 29, Los Angeles Raiders 23)

1 degree (wind chill not recorded)—January 4, 1981, Cleveland Stadium, Cleveland, Ohio, AFC Divisional Playoff (Oakland 14, Cleveland 12)

2000 NFL SCORE BY QUARTERS

AFC Offense	1	2	3	4	OT	PTS
Denver	88	156	121	120	0	485
Oakland	77	179	86	131	6	479
Indianapolis	73	117	84	155	0	429
Jacksonville	69	142	74	76	6	367
Kansas City	50	99	82	124	0	355
Tennessee	65	111	75	92	3	346
Baltimore	62	134	67	70	0	333
Miami	67	109	90	57	0	323
N.Y. Jets	90	69	40	119	3	321
Pittsburgh	58	99	67	97	0	321
Seattle	70	100	59	91	0	320
Buffalo	54	97	40	118	6	315
New England	76	86	30	81	3	276
San Diego	58	99	60	52	0	269
Cincinnati	24	74	41	46	0	185
Cleveland	51	45	32	33	0	161

NFC Offense	1	2	3	4	OT	PTS
St. Louis	116	147	154	123	0	540
Minnesota	81	117	90	109	0	397
San Francisco	48	136	79	125	0	388
Tampa Bay	88	131	60	109	0	388
New Orleans	66	111	67	110	0	354
Green Bay	59	101	83	101	9	353
Philadelphia	57	97	71	120	6	351
N.Y. Giants	51	81	82	114	0	328
Carolina	78	106	60	66	0	310
Detroit	50	78	52	127	0	307
Dallas	51	92	73	75	3	294
Washington	65	80	54	79	3	281
Atlanta	50	75	57	70	0	252
Chicago	46	59	52	59	0	216
Arizona	30	48	57	75	0	210

AFC Defense	1	2	3	4	OT	PTS
Baltimore	44	36	43	42	0	165
Tennessee	36	50	30	75	0	191
Miami	50	57	9	107	3	226
Pittsburgh	67	76	50	59	3	255
Oakland	75	74	43	107	0	299
N.Y. Jets	67	120	46	88	0	321
Indianapolis	52	106	86	82	0	326
Jacksonville	59	88	61	119	0	327
New England	53	122	52	108	3	338
Buffalo	46	93	76	132	3	350
Kansas City	75	123	64	89	3	354
Cincinnati	92	106	91	70	0	359
Denver	57	120	96	96	0	369
Seattle	96	140	71	98	0	405
Cleveland	46	176	115	82	0	419
San Diego	77	128	110	122	3	440

NFC Defense	1	2	3	4	OT	PTS
Philadelphia	34	70	40	101	0	245
N.Y. Giants	31	88	62	65	0	246
Tampa Bay	39	79	53	92	6	269
Washington	63	91	39	76	0	269
New Orleans	58	111	51	85	0	305
Detroit	81	70	74	82	0	307
Carolina	46	108	70	83	3	310
Green Bay	51	91	82	99	0	323
Chicago	47	117	88	103	0	355
Dallas	61	101	84	106	9	361
Minnesota	96	98	56	115	6	371
Atlanta	97	134	91	91	0	413
San Francisco	64	142	108	102	6	422
Arizona	114	130	95	104	0	443
St. Louis	94	130	103	144	0	471
NFL Totals	**1,968**	**3,175**	**2,139**	**2,924**	**48**	**10,254**

TEAM LEADERS

Offense	Most Scored	Fewest Scored
1st Quarter	116 St. Louis	24 Cincinnati
2nd Quarter	179 Oakland	45 Cleveland
3rd Quarter	154 St. Louis	30 New England
4th Quarter	155 Indianapolis	33 Cleveland

Defense	Most Allowed	Fewest Allowed
1st Quarter	114 Arizona	31 N.Y. Giants
2nd Quarter	176 Cleveland	36 Baltimore
3rd Quarter	115 Cleveland	9 Miami
4th Quarter	144 St. Louis	42 Baltimore

LARGEST TRADES IN NFL HISTORY

(Based on number of players or draft choices involved)

18—October 13, 1989—RB Herschel Walker from the Dallas Cowboys to Minnesota. Dallas also traded its third-round choice in 1990, its tenth-round choice in 1990, and its third-round choice in 1991 to Minnesota. Minnesota traded LB Jesse Solomon, LB David Howard, CB Issiac Holt, and DE Alex Stewart along with its first-round choice in 1990, its second-round choice in 1990, its sixth-round choice in 1990, its first-round choice in 1991, its second-round choice in 1991, its first-round choice in 1992, its second-round choice in 1992, and its third-round choice in 1992 to Dallas. Minnesota traded RB Darrin Nelson to Dallas, which traded Nelson to San Diego for the Chargers' fifth-round choice in 1990, which Dallas then sent to Minnesota.

15—March 26, 1953—T Mike McCormack, DT Don Colo, LB Tom Catlin, DB John Petitbon, and G Herschell Forester from Baltimore to Cleveland for DB Don Shula, DB Bert Rechichar, DB Carl Taseff, LB Ed Sharkey, E Gern Nagler, QB Harry Agganis, T Dick Batten, T Stu Sheets, G Art Spinney, and G Elmer Willhoite.

15—January 28, 1971—LB Marlin McKeever, first- and third-round choices in 1971, and third-, fourth-, fifth-, sixth-, and seventh-round choices in 1972 from Washington to the Los Angeles Rams for LB Maxie Baughan, LB Jack Pardee, LB Myron Pottios, RB Jeff Jordan, G John Wilbur, DT Diron Talbert, and a fifth-round choice in 1971.

12—June 13, 1952—Selection rights to Les Richter from the Dallas Texans to the Los Angeles Rams for RB Dick Hoerner, DB Tom Keane, DB George Sims, C Joe Reid, HB Billy Baggett, T Jack Halliday, FB Dick McKissack, LB Vic Vasicek, E Richard Wilkins, C Aubrey Phillips, and RB Dave Anderson.

10—March 23, 1959—HB Ollie Matson from the Chicago Cardinals to the Los Angeles Rams for T Frank Fuller, DE Glenn Holtzman, T Ken Panfil, DT Art Hauser, E John Tracey, FB Larry Hickman, HB Don Brown, the Rams second-round choice in 1960, and a player to be delivered during the 1959 training camp.

10—October 31, 1987—RB Eric Dickerson from the Los Angeles Rams to Indianapolis. The rights to LB Cornelius Bennett from Indianapolis to Buffalo. Indianapolis running back Owen Gill and the Colts' first- and second-round choices in 1988 and second-round choice in 1989, plus Bills running back Greg Bell and Buffalo's first-round choice in 1988 and first- and second-round choices in 1989 to the Rams.

OTHER SIGNIFICANT TRADES

March 21, 1967—QB Fran Tarkenton from Minnesota to the New York Giants for the Giants' first- and second-round selections in 1967, first-round selection in 1968, and second-round selection in 1969.

January 27, 1972—QB Fran Tarkenton from the New York Giants to Minnesota for QB Norm Snead, WR Bob Grim, RB Vince Clements, and the Vikings' first-round selection in 1972 and second-round selection in 1973.

June 8, 1973—QB Roman Gabriel from Los Angeles to Philadelphia for WR Harold Jackson, RB Tony Baker, the Eagles' first-round selection in 1974, and the Eagles' first- and third-round selections in 1975.

October 22, 1974—QB John Hadl from Los Angeles to Green Bay for the Packers' first- and third-round selections in 1975, Baltimore's second-round selection in 1975, and the Packers' first- and second-round selections in 1976.

April 5, 1976—QB Jim Plunkett from New England to San Francisco for the 49ers' first-round selection in 1976, Houston's first-round selection in 1976, the 49ers' first- and second-round selections in 1977, and QB Tom Owen.

April 17, 1999—Washington's first-round selection in 1999 (fifth overall) to New Orleans for the Saints first-round selection in 1999 (12th overall); third-round, fourth-round, fifth-round, sixth-round, and seventh-round selections in 1999; and first-round and third-round selections in 2000. The Saints drafted Texas RB Ricky Williams.

INSIDE THE NUMBERS

RETIRED UNIFORM NUMBERS IN NFL

AFC

Baltimore: None
Buffalo: None
Cincinnati: Bob Johnson 54
Cleveland: Otto Graham 14
Jim Brown 32
Ernie Davis 45
Don Fleming 46
Lou Groza 76
Denver: John Elway 7
Frank Tripucka 18
Floyd Little 44
Indianapolis: Johnny Unitas 19
Buddy Young 22
Lenny Moore 24
Art Donovan 70
Jim Parker 77
Raymond Berry 82
Gino Marchetti 89
Jacksonville None
Kansas City: Jan Stenerud 3
Len Dawson 16
Abner Haynes 28
Stone Johnson 33
Mack Lee Hill 36
Willie Lanier 63
Bobby Bell 78
Buck Buchanan 86
Miami: Bob Griese 12
Dan Marino 13
New England: Gino Cappelletti 20
Mike Haynes 40
Steve Nelson 57
John Hannah 73
Jim Hunt 79
Bob Dee 89
New York Jets: Joe Namath 12
Don Maynard 13
Oakland: None
Pittsburgh: Ernie Stautner 70
San Diego: Dan Fouts 14
Seattle: "Fans/the twelfth man" 12
Steve Largent 80
Tennessee: Earl Campbell 34
Jim Norton 43
Mike Munchak 63
Elvin Bethea 65

NFC

Arizona: Larry Wilson 8
Stan Mauldin 77
J.V. Cain 88
Marshall Goldberg 99
Atlanta: Steve Bartowski 10
William Andrews 31
Jeff Van Note 57
Tommy Nobis 60
Carolina None
Chicago: Bronko Nagurski 3
George McAfee 5
George Halas 7
Willie Galimore 28
Walter Payton 34
Gale Sayers 40
Brian Piccolo 41
Sid Luckman 42
Dick Butkus 51
Bill Hewitt 56
Bill George 61
Bulldog Turner 66
Red Grange 77
Dallas: None
Detroit: Dutch Clark 7
Bobby Layne 22
Doak Walker 37
Joe Schmidt 56
Chuck Hughes 85
Charlie Sanders 88
Green Bay: Tony Canadeo 3
Don Hutson 14
Bart Starr 15
Ray Nitschke 66
Minnesota: Fran Tarkenton 10
Jim Marshall 70
Alan Page 88
New Orleans: Jim Taylor 31
Doug Atkins 81
New York Giants: Ray Flaherty 1
Tuffy Leemans 4
Mel Hein 7
Phil Simms 11
Y.A. Tittle 14
Frank Gifford 16
Al Blozis 32
Joe Morrison 40
Charlie Conerly 42
Ken Strong 50
Lawrence Taylor 56
Philadelphia: Steve Van Buren 15
Tom Brookshier 40
Pete Retzlaff 44
Chuck Bednarik 60
Al Wistert 70
Jerome Brown 99
St. Louis: Bob Waterfield 7
Eric Dickerson 29
Merlin Olsen 74
Jackie Slater 78
Jack Youngblood 85
San Francisco: John Brodie 12
Joe Montana 16
Joe Perry 34
Jimmy Johnson 37
Hugh McElhenny 39
Charlie Krueger 70
Leo Nomellini 73
Dwight Clark 87
Tampa Bay: Lee Roy Selmon 63
Washington: Sammy Baugh 33

2000 TOP 100 TELEVISION MARKETS

(NFL Team Markets in Bold)

	Market	TV HHLD'S	% of U.S. TV HHLD'S	Cable TV HHLD'S	% of Cable Penetration
1	**NEW YORK**	**6,874,990**	**6.820**	**5,069,690**	**74**
2	Los Angeles	5,234,690	5.193	3,392,820	65
3	**CHICAGO**	**3,204,710**	**3.179**	**2,072,800**	**65**
4	**PHILADELPHIA**	**2,670,710**	**2.649**	**2,099,650**	**79**
5	**SAN FRAN. - OAKLAND**	**2,423,120**	**2.404**	**1,747,340**	**72**
6	**BOSTON**	**2,210,580**	**2.193**	**1,766,870**	**80**
7	**DALLAS - FT. WORTH**	**2,018,120**	**2.002**	**1,031,620**	**51**
8	**WASHINGTON, D.C.**	**1,999,870**	**1.984**	**1,398,020**	**70**
9	**DETROIT**	**1,855,500**	**1.841**	**1,260,010**	**68**
10	**ATLANTA**	**1,774,720**	**1.761**	**1,250,690**	**70**
11	Houston	1,712,060	1.698	984,810	58
12	**SEATTLE - TACOMA**	**1,591,100**	**1.578**	**1,175,170**	**74**
13	**TAMPA - ST. PETE**	**1,485,980**	**1.474**	**1,100,610**	**74**
14	**MINNEAPOLIS-ST. PAUL**	**1,481,050**	**1.469**	**796,420**	**54**
15	**CLEVELAND**	**1,479,020**	**1.467**	**1,057,870**	**72**
16	**MIAMI - FT. LAUDERDALE**	**1,441,570**	**1.430**	**1,053,840**	**73**
17	**PHOENIX**	**1,390,750**	**1.380**	**819,470**	**59**
18	**DENVER**	**1,268,230**	**1.258**	**775,840**	**61**
19	Sacramento-Stktn-Modesto	1,159,820	1.151	742,610	64
20	**PITTSBURGH**	**1,135,290**	**1.126**	**900,930**	**79**
21	**ST. LOUIS**	**1,114,370**	**1.106**	**623,180**	**56**
22	Orlando - Daytona Beach	1,101,920	1.093	847,150	77
23	Portland, Ore.	1,004,140	0.966	273,660	62
24	**BALTIMORE**	**999,200**	**0.991**	**677,730**	**68**
25	**SAN DIEGO**	**980,620**	**0.973**	**817,060**	**83**
26	**INDIANAPOLIS**	**963,320**	**0.956**	**627,000**	**65**
27	Hartford & New Haven	915,940	0.909	806,420	88
28	**CHARLOTTE**	**880,570**	**0.874**	**590,060**	**67**
29	Raleigh - Durham	858,490	0.852	536,230	62
30	**NASHVILLE**	**826,090**	**0.820**	**523,800**	**63**
31	**KANSAS CITY**	**820,580**	**0.814**	**535,100**	**65**
32	**CINCINNATI**	**820,000**	**0.813**	**523,540**	**64**
33	Milwaukee	815,640	0.809	510,740	63
34	Columbus, Ohio	757,860	0.752	503,120	66
35	Greenville - Asheville	732,490	0.727	449,540	61
36	Salt Lake City	720,860	0.715	384,840	53
37	San Antonio	684,730	0.679	449,560	66
38	Grand Rapids-Kalmzoo-BtlCrk	671,320	0.666	417,320	62
39	Birmingham	667,650	0.662	463,380	69
40	Memphis	632,110	0.627	401,770	64
41	**NEW ORLEANS**	**629,820**	**0.625**	**475,990**	**76**
42	Norfolk - Newport News	629,100	0.624	480,610	76
43	West Palm Beach - Ft. Pierce	623,760	0.619	527,110	85
44	**BUFFALO**	**621,460**	**0.617**	**476,060**	**77**
45	Oklahoma City	600,240	0.595	380,010	63
46	Harrisburg - Lancaster	599,930	0.595	465,290	78
47	Greensboro - High Point	592,770	0.588	381,590	64
48	Louisville	576,850	0.572	374,260	65
49	Albuquerque - Santa Fe	568,650	0.564	326,890	57
50	Providence - New Bedford	565,230	0.561	447,020	79
51	Wilkes Barre - Scranton	555,400	0.551	456,850	82
52	**JACKSONVILLE**	**540,450**	**0.536**	**394,760**	**73**
53	Las Vegas	521,200	0.517	357,010	68
54	Fresno - Visalia	511,050	0.507	261,820	51
55	Albany - Schenectady - Troy	507,000	0.503	278,210	75
56	Dayton	506,440	0.502	359,980	71
57	Little Rock - Pine Bluff	488,000	0.484	311,180	64
58	Tulsa	482,740	0.479	293,880	61
59	Charleston - Huntington	481,410	0.478	353,960	74
60	Richmond - Petersburg	474,610	0.471	308,270	65
61	Austin	472,780	0.469	315,650	67
62	Mobile - Pensacola	471,920	0.468	347,420	74
63	Knoxville	451,870	0.448	314,390	70
64	Flint - Saginaw - Bay City	444,120	0.441	290,360	65
65	Wichita - Hutchinson	443,690	0.440	305,860	69
66	Lexington	416,200	0.413	287,460	69
67	Toledo	411,450	0.408	284,020	69
68	Roanoke - Lynchburg	403,270	0.400	261,150	65
69	**GREEN BAY - APPLETON**	**392,300**	**0.389**	**234,860**	**60**
70	Des Moines - Ames	387,850	0.385	237,190	61
71	Honolulu	385,790	0.383	343,000	89
72	Tucson (Sierra Vista)	380,900	0.378	228,480	60
73	Omaha	373,320	0.370	263,650	71
74	Paducah-C Gir-Harbg-Mt.Ver	370,900	0.368	219,700	59
75	Shreveport	370,480	0.368	218,440	59
76	Syracuse	369,680	0.367	276,670	75
77	Rochester, N.Y.	366,770	0.364	267,380	73
78	Spokane	366,080	0.363	219,170	60
79	Springfield, Mo.	363,500	0.361	178,660	49
80	Portland - Auburn	355,040	0.352	273,660	77
81	Ft. Myers - Naples	343,550	0.341	275,530	80
82	Huntsville - Decatur, Fla.	342,460	0.340	238,900	70
83	Champaign & Springfield	341,990	0.339	257,990	75
84	Chattanooga	327,310	0.325	231,860	71
85	Madison	322,780	0.320	204,030	63
86	Columbia, S.C.	317,740	0.315	192,500	61
87	South Bend - Elkhart	314,920	0.312	187,610	60
88	Davenport - Rhode Island	308,790	0.306	208,230	67
89	Jackson, Miss.	305,830	0.303	178,610	58
90	Cedar Rapids - Waterloo	303,470	0.301	201,400	66
91	Burlington - Plattsburgh	295,480	0.293	181,880	62
92	Tr-Cities, Tenn. - Va.	293,150	0.291	218,270	74
93	Colorado Springs - Pueblo	290,830	0.289	200,460	69
94	Waco - Temple - Bryan	286,300	0.284	184,800	65
95	Johnstown - Altoona	286,070	0.284	235,250	82
96	El Paso	276,980	0.275	167,530	60
97	Baton Rouge	276,130	0.274	210,240	76
98	Evansville	274,660	0.272	173,510	63
99	Youngstown	272,990	0.271	199,760	73
100	Savannah	261,830	0.260	178,930	68
	TOTAL NFL MARKETS:	**45,894,090**	**45.529**		
	TOTAL TOP 100 MARKETS:	**86,497,060**	**85.779**		

GREATEST COMEBACKS IN NFL HISTORY
(Most Points Overcome To Win Game)

REGULAR SEASON GAMES

FROM 28 POINTS BEHIND TO WIN:
December 7, 1980, at San Francisco

New Orleans	14	21	0	0	0	— 35
San Francisco	0	7	14	14	3	— 38

NO — Harris 33 pass from Manning (Ricardo kick)
NO — Childs 21 pass from Manning (Ricardo kick)
NO — Holmes 1 run (Ricardo kick)
SF — Solomon 57 punt return (Wersching kick)
NO — Holmes 1 run (Ricardo kick)
NO — Harris 41 pass from Manning (Ricardo kick)
SF — Montana 1 run (Wersching kick)
SF — Clark 71 pass from Montana (Wersching kick)
SF — Solomon 14 pass from Montana (Wersching kick)
SF — Elliott 7 run (Wersching kick)
SF — FG Wersching 36

	N.O.	S.F.
First Downs	27	24
Total Yards	519	430
Yards Rushing	143	176
Yards Passing	376	254
Turnovers	3	0

FROM 26 POINTS BEHIND TO WIN:
September 21, 1997, at Buffalo

Indianapolis	14	12	0	9	— 35
Buffalo	0	10	6	21	— 37

Ind — Bailey 10 pass from Harbaugh (Blanchard kick)
Ind — Faulk 10 run (Blanchard kick)
Ind — FG Blanchard 39
Ind — FG Blanchard 36
Ind — FG Blanchard 49
Ind — FG Blanchard 22
Buff — Johnson 16 pass from Collins (Christie kick)
Buff — FG Christie 27
Buff — A. Smith 15 run (2-pt attempt failed)
Ind — FG Blanchard 25
Buff — Early 4 pass from Collins (Christie kick)
Buff — A. Smith 1 run (Christie kick)
Buff — A. Smith 54 run (Christie kick)
Ind — Harrison 2 pass from Justin (2-pt attempt failed)

	Ind.	Buff.
First Downs	17	25
Total Yards	322	393
Yards Rushing	124	163
Yards Passing	198	230
Turnovers	1	5

FROM 25 POINTS BEHIND TO WIN:
November 8, 1987, at St. Louis

Tampa Bay	7	7	14	0	— 28
St. Louis	0	3	0	28	— 31

TB — Carrier 5 pass from DeBerg (Igwebuike kick)
TB — Carter 3 pass from DeBerg (Igwebuike kick)
StL — FG Gallery 31
TB — Smith 34 pass from DeBerg (Igwebuike kick)
TB — Smith 3 run (Igwebuike kick)
StL — Awalt 4 pass from Lomax (Gallery kick)
StL — Noga 23 fumble recovery (Gallery kick)
StL — J. Smith 11 pass from Lomax (Gallery kick)
StL — J. Smith 17 pass from Lomax (Gallery kick)

	T.B.	St.L.
First Downs	26	26
Total Yards	377	415
Yards Rushing	83	137
Yards Passing	294	278
Turnovers	1	2

FROM 24 POINTS BEHIND TO WIN:
October 27, 1946, at Washington

Philadelphia	0	0	14	14	— 28
Washington	10	14	0	0	— 24

Wash — Rosato 2 run (Poillon kick)
Wash — FG Poillon 28
Wash — Rosato 4 run (Poillon kick)
Wash — Lapka recovered fumble in end zone (Poillon kick)
Phil — Steele 1 run (Lio kick)
Phil — Pritchard 45 pass from Thompson (Lio kick)
Phil — Steinke 7 pass from Thompson (Lio kick)
Phil — Ferrante 30 pass from Thompson (Lio kick)

	Phil.	Wash.
First Downs	14	8
Total Yards	262	127
Yards Rushing	34	66
Yards Passing	228	61
Turnovers	6	3

FROM 24 POINTS BEHIND TO WIN:
October 20, 1957, at Detroit

Baltimore	7	14	6	0	— 27
Detroit	0	3	7	21	— 31

Balt — Mutscheller 15 pass from Unitas (Rechichar kick)
Det — FG Martin 47
Balt — Moore 72 pass from Unitas (Rechichar kick)
Balt — Mutscheller 52 pass from Unitas (Rechichar kick)
Balt — Moore 4 pass from Unitas (kick failed)
Det — Junker 14 pass from Rote (Layne kick)
Det — Cassady 26 pass from Layne (Layne kick)
Det — Johnson 1 run (Layne kick)
Det — Cassady 29 pass from Layne (Layne kick)

	Balt.	Det.
First Downs	15	20
Total Yards	322	369
Yards Rushing	117	178
Yards Passing	205	191
Turnovers	6	4

FROM 24 POINTS BEHIND TO WIN:
October 25, 1959, at Minneapolis

Philadelphia	0	0	21	7	— 28
Chicago Cardinals	7	10	7	0	— 24

Cardinals — Crow 10 pass from Roach (Conrad kick)
Cardinals — J. Hill 77 blocked field goal return (Conrad kick)
Cardinals — FG Conrad 15
Cardinals — Lane 37 interception return (Conrad kick)
Phil — Barnes 1 run (Walston kick)
Phil — McDonald 29 pass from Van Brocklin (Walston kick)
Phil — Barnes 2 run (Walston kick)
Phil — McDonald 22 pass from Van Brocklin (Walston kick)

	Phil.	Cardinals
First Downs	22	14
Total Yards	399	313
Yards Rushing	168	163
Yards Passing	231	150
Turnovers	2	6

FROM 24 POINTS BEHIND TO WIN:
October 23, 1960, at Denver

Boston	10	7	7	0	— 24
Denver	0	0	14	17	— 31

Bos — FG Cappelletti 12
Bos — Colclough 10 pass from Songin (Cappelletti kick)
Bos — Wells 6 pass from Songin (Cappelletti kick)
Bos — Miller 47 pass from Songin (Cappelletti kick)
Den — Carmichael 21 pass from Tripucka (Mingo kick)
Den — Jessup 19 pass from Tripucka (Mingo kick)
Den — Carmichael 35 lateral from Taylor, pass from Tripucka (Mingo kick)
Den — Taylor 8 pass from Tripucka (Mingo kick)
Den — FG Mingo 9

	Bos.	Den.
First Downs	19	16
Total Yards	434	326
Yards Rushing	211	65
Yards Passing	223	261
Turnovers	7	4

FROM 24 POINTS BEHIND TO WIN:
December 15, 1974, at Miami

New England	21	3	0	3	— 27
Miami	0	17	7	10	— 34

NE — Hannah recovered fumble in end zone (J. Smith kick)
NE — Sanders 23 interception return (J. Smith kick)
NE — Herron 4 pass from Plunkett (J. Smith kick)
NE — FG J. Smith 46
Mia — Nottingham 1 run (Yepremian kick)
Mia — Baker 37 pass from Morrall (Yepremian kick)
Mia — FG Yepremian 28
Mia — Baker 46 pass from Morrall (Yepremian kick)
NE — FG J. Smith 34
Mia — Nottingham 2 run (Yepremian kick)
Mia — FG Yepremian 40

	N.E.	Mia.
First Downs	18	18
Total Yards	333	333
Yards Rushing	114	61
Yards Passing	219	272
Turnovers	3	4

FROM 24 POINTS BEHIND TO WIN:
December 4, 1977, at Minnesota

San Francisco	0	10	14	3	— 27
Minnesota	0	0	7	21	— 28

SF — Delvin Williams 2 run (Wersching kick)
SF — FG Wersching 31
SF — Dave Williams 80 kickoff return (Wersching kick)
SF — Delvin Williams 5 run (Wersching kick)
Minn— McClanahan 15 pass from Lee (Cox kick)
Minn— Rashad 8 pass from Kramer (Cox kick)
Minn— Tucker 9 pass from Kramer (Cox kick)
SF — FG Wersching 31
Minn— S. White 69 pass from Kramer (Cox kick)

	S.F.	Minn.
First Downs	19	18
Total Yards	243	309
Yards Rushing	196	52
Yards Passing	47	257
Turnovers	2	5

FROM 24 POINTS BEHIND TO WIN:
September 23, 1979, at Denver

Seattle	10	10	14	0	— 34
Denver	0	10	21	6	— 37

Sea — FG Herrera 28
Sea — Doornink 5 run (Herrera kick)
Den — FG Turner 27
Sea — Doornink 5 run (Herrera kick)
Den — Armstrong 2 run (Turner kick)
Sea — FG Herrera 22
Sea — McCullum 13 pass from Zorn (Herrera kick)
Sea — Smith 1 run (Herrera kick)
Den — Studdard 2 pass from Morton (Turner kick)
Den — Moses 11 pass from Morton (Turner kick)
Den — Upchurch 35 pass from Morton (Turner kick)
Den — Lytle 1 run (kick failed)

	Sea.	Den.
First Downs	22	23
Total Yards	350	344
Yards Rushing	153	90
Yards Passing	197	254
Turnovers	4	3

FROM 24 POINTS BEHIND TO WIN:
September 23, 1979, at Cincinnati

Houston	0	10	17	0	3	—30
Cincinnati	14	10	0	3	0	—27

Cin — Johnson 1 run (Bahr kick)
Cin — Alexander 2 run (Bahr kick)
Cin — Johnson 1 run (Bahr kick)
Cin — FG Bahr 52
Hou — Burrough 35 pass from Pastorini (Fritsch kick)
Hou — FG Fritsch 33
Hou — Campbell 8 run (Fritsch kick)
Hou — Caster 22 pass from Pastorini (Fritsch kick)
Hou — FG Fritsch 47
Cin — FG Bahr 55
Hou — FG Fritsch 29

	Hou.	Cin.
First Downs	19	21
Total Yards	361	265
Yards Rushing	177	165
Yards Passing	184	100
Turnovers	3	2

FROM 24 POINTS BEHIND TO WIN:
November 22, 1982, at Los Angeles

San Diego	10	14	0	0	— 24
L.A. Raiders	0	7	14	7	— 28

SD — FG Benirschke 19
SD — Scales 29 pass from Fouts (Benirschke kick)
SD — Muncie 2 run (Benirschke kick)
SD — Muncie 1 run (Benirschke kick)
Raiders — Christensen 1 pass from Plunkett (Bahr kick)
Raiders — Allen 3 run (Bahr kick)
Raiders — Allen 6 run (Bahr kick)
Raiders — Hawkins 1 run (Bahr kick)

	S.D.	Raiders
First Downs	26	23
Total Yards	411	326
Yards Rushing	72	181
Yards Passing	339	145
Turnovers	4	2

FROM 24 POINTS BEHIND TO WIN:
September 26, 1988, at Denver

L.A. Raiders	0	0	14	13	3 — 30
Denver	7	17	0	3	0 — 27

Den — Dorsett 1 run (Karlis kick)
Den — Dorsett 1 run (Karlis kick)
Den — Sewell 7 pass from Elway (Karlis kick)
Den — FG Karlis 39
Raiders — Smith 40 pass from Schroeder (Bahr kick)
Raiders — Smith 42 pass from Schroeder (Bahr kick)
Raiders — FG Bahr 28
Raiders — Allen 4 run (Bahr kick)
Den — FG Karlis 25
Raiders — FG Bahr 44
Raiders — FG Bahr 35

	Raiders	Den.
First Downs	20	23
Total Yards	363	398
Yards Rushing	128	189
Yards Passing	235	209
Turnovers	1	5

FROM 24 POINTS BEHIND TO WIN:
December 6, 1992, at Tampa

L.A. Rams	0	3	21	7	— 31
Tampa Bay	6	21	0	0	— 27

TB — FG Murray 34
TB — FG Murray 47
TB — Armstrong 81 pass from Testaverde (Murray kick)
TB — Jones 26 fumble recovery (Murray kick)
Rams — FG Zendejas 18
TB — Carrier 10 pass from Testaverde (Murray kick)
Rams — Anderson 40 pass from Everett (Zendejas kick)
Rams — Chadwick 27 pass from Everett (Zendejas kick)
Rams — Lang 1 run (Zendejas kick)
Rams — Carter 8 pass from Everett (Zendejas kick)

	Rams	T.B.
First Downs	21	16
Total Yards	405	313
Yards Rushing	63	150
Yards Passing	342	163
Turnovers	3	3

POSTSEASON GAMES

FROM 32 POINTS BEHIND TO WIN:
AFC First-Round Playoff Game
January 3, 1993, at Buffalo

Houston	7	21	7	3	0 — 38
Buffalo	3	0	28	7	3 — 41

Hou — Jeffires 3 pass from Moon (Del Greco kick)
Buff — FG Christie 36
Hou — Slaughter 7 pass from Moon (Del Greco kick)
Hou — Duncan 26 pass from Moon (Del Greco kick)
Hou — Jeffires 27 pass from Moon (Del Greco kick)
Hou — McDowell 58 interception return (Del Greco kick)
Buff — Davis 1 run (Christie kick)
Buff — Beebe 38 pass from Reich (Christie kick)
Buff — Reed 26 pass from Reich (Christie kick)
Buff — Reed 18 pass from Reich (Christie kick)
Buff — Reed 17 pass from Reich (Christie kick)
Hou — FG Del Greco 26
Buff — FG Christie 32

	Hou.	Buff.
First Downs	27	19
Total Yards	429	366
Yards Rushing	82	98
Yards Passing	347	268
Turnovers	2	1

FROM 20 POINTS BEHIND TO WIN:
Western Conference Playoff Game
December 22, 1957, at San Francisco

Detroit	0	7	14	10	— 31
San Francisco	14	10	3	0	— 27

SF — Owens 34 pass from Tittle (Soltau kick)
SF — McElhenny 47 pass from Tittle (Soltau kick)
Det — Junker 4 pass from Rote (Martin kick)
SF — Wilson 12 pass from Tittle (Soltau kick)
SF — FG Soltau 25
SF — FG Soltau 10
Det — Tracy 2 run (Martin kick)
Det — Tracy 58 run (Martin kick)
Det — Gedman 3 run (Martin kick)
Det — FG Martin 14

	Det.	S.F.
First Downs	22	20
Total Yards	324	351
Yards Rushing	129	127
Yards Passing	195	224
Turnovers	5	4

FROM 18 POINTS BEHIND TO WIN:
NFC Divisional Playoff Game
December 23, 1972, at San Francisco

Dallas	3	10	0	17	— 30
San Francisco	7	14	7	0	— 28

SF — Washington 97 kickoff return (Gossett kick)
Dall — FG Fritsch 37
SF — Schreiber 1 run (Gossett kick)
SF — Schreiber 1 run (Gossett kick)
Dall — FG Fritsch 45
Dall — Alworth 28 pass from Morton (Fritsch kick)
SF — Schreiber 1 run (Gossett kick)
Dall — FG Fritsch 27
Dall — Parks 20 pass from Staubach (Fritsch kick)
Dall — Sellers 10 pass from Staubach (Fritsch kick)

	Dall.	S.F.
First Downs	22	13
Total Yards	402	255
Yards Rushing	165	105
Yards Passing	237	150
Turnovers	5	3

FROM 18 POINTS BEHIND TO WIN:
AFC Divisional Playoff Game
January 4, 1986, at Miami

Cleveland	7	7	7	0	— 21
Miami	3	0	14	7	— 24

Mia — FG Reveiz 51
Cle — Newsome 16 pass from Kosar (Bahr kick)
Cle — Byner 21 run (Bahr kick)
Cle — Byner 66 run (Bahr kick)
Mia — Moore 6 pass from Marino (Reveiz kick)
Mia — Davenport 31 run (Reveiz kick)
Mia — Davenport 1 run (Reveiz kick)

	Clev.	Mia.
First Downs	17	20
Total Yards	313	330
Yards Rushing	251	92
Yards Passing	62	238
Turnovers	1	1

RECORDS OF NFL TEAMS SINCE 1970 AFL-NFL MERGER

AFC	W - L - T	Pct.	Division Titles	Playoff Berths	Post-season Record	Super Bowl Record
Miami	304-166-2	.647	12	20	20-18	2-3
Oakland	283-183-6	.607	10	16	19-13	3-0
Pittsburgh	278-193-1	.590	14	18	21-14	4-1
Denver	273-193-6	.585	9	14	16-12	2-4
Jacksonville**	56- 40-0	.583	2	4	4-4	0-0
Kansas City	235-230-7	.505	4	9	3-9	0-0
Buffalo	231-239-2	.492	7	13	12-13	0-4
Tennessee	223-247-2	.474	3	12	10-12	0-1
Cleveland+	199-222-3	.473	6	10	4-10	0-0
Seattle*	179-209-0	.461	2	5	3-5	0-0
New England	217-255-0	.460	4	9	6-9	0-2
Baltimore***	36- 43-1	.456	0	1	4-0	1-0
Cincinnati	211-261-0	.447	5	7	5-7	0-2
San Diego	205-262-5	.439	5	7	6-7	0-1
Indianapolis	203-267-2	.432	6	10	6-9	1-0
N.Y. Jets	200-270-2	.426	1	6	4-6	0-0

NFC	W - L - T	Pct.	Division Titles	Playoff Berths	Post-season Record	Super Bowl Record
Dallas	290-182-0	.614	15	22	31-17	5-3
San Francisco	283-186-3	.603	16	19	24-14	5-0
Minnesota	282-188-2	.600	14	21	15-21	0-3
Washington	275-195-2	.585	6	14	19-11	3-2
St. Louis	252-216-4	.538	9	16	13-15	1-1
Chicago	230-241-1	.488	6	10	7-9	1-0
Green Bay	224-240-8	.483	4	8	10-7	1-1
N.Y. Giants	226-243-3	.482	5	9	12-7	2-1
Philadelphia	223-242-7	.479	2	11	6-11	0-1
Carolina**	45- 51-0	.469	1	1	1-1	0-0
Detroit	215-253-4	.460	3	9	1-9	0-0
Atlanta	193-275-4	.413	2	6	4-6	0-1
Arizona	192-274-6	.413	2	4	1-4	0-0
New Orleans	190-278-4	.406	2	5	1-5	0-0
Tampa Bay*	139-248-1	.360	3	6	3-6	0-0

*Entered NFL in 1976.
**Entered NFL in 1995.
***Entered NFL in 1996.
+ Did not play 1996-98.
Oakland totals include L.A. Raiders, 1982-1994.
Tennessee totals include Houston, 1970-1996.
Indianapolis totals include Baltimore, 1970-1983.
St. Louis totals include L.A. Rams, 1970-1994.
Arizona totals include St. Louis, 1970-1987, and Phoenix, 1988-1993.
Tie games before 1972 are not calculated in won-lost percentage.
In 1982, because of players' strike, the divisional format was abandoned; L.A. Raiders and Washington won regular-season conference titles, not included in "Division Titles" totals listed above. Sixteen teams were awarded playoff berths, included in totals listed above.

ALL-TIME REGULAR-SEASON RECORDS OF CURRENT NFL TEAMS

AFC

BALTIMORE RAVENS

	All Games			Home Games			Road Games		
Season	W	L	T	W	L	T	W	L	T
1996	4	12		4	4		0	8	
1997	6	9	1	3	4	1	3	5	
1998	6	10		4	4		2	6	
1999	8	8		4	4		4	4	
2000	12	4		6	2		6	2	
	36	43	1	21	18	1	15	25	

BUFFALO BILLS

	All Games			Home Games			Road Games		
Season	W	L	T	W	L	T	W	L	T
1960	5	8	1	3	4		2	4	1
1961	6	8		2	5		4	3	
1962	7	6	1	3	3	1	4	3	
1963	7	6	1	4	2	1	3	4	
1964	12	2		6	1		6	1	
1965	10	3	1	5	2		5	1	1
1966	9	4	1	4	2	1	5	2	
1967	4	10		2	5		2	5	
1968	1	12	1	1	6		0	6	1
1969	4	10		4	3		0	7	
1970	3	10	1	1	6		2	4	1
1971	1	13		1	6		0	7	
1972	4	9	1	2	4	1	2	5	
1973	9	5		5	2		4	3	
1974	9	5		5	2		4	3	
1975	8	6		3	4		5	2	
1976	2	12		1	6		1	6	
1977	3	11		1	6		2	5	
1978	5	11		4	4		1	7	
1979	7	9		3	5		4	4	
1980	11	5		6	2		5	3	
1981	10	6		7	1		3	5	
1982	4	5		4	1		0	4	
1983	8	8		3	5		5	3	
1984	2	14		2	6		0	8	
1985	2	14		2	6		0	8	
1986	4	12		3	5		1	7	
1987	7	8		4	4		3	4	
1988	12	4		8	0		4	4	
1989	9	7		6	2		3	5	
1990	13	3		8	0		5	3	
1991	13	3		7	1		6	2	
1992	11	5		6	2		5	3	
1993	12	4		6	2		6	2	
1994	7	9		4	4		3	5	
1995	10	6		6	2		4	4	
1996	10	6		7	1		3	5	
1997	6	10		4	4		2	6	
1998	10	6		6	2		4	4	
1999	11	5		6	2		5	3	
2000	8	8		5	3		3	5	
	296	308	8	170	133	4	126	175	4

CINCINNATI BENGALS

	All Games			Home Games			Road Games		
Season	W	L	T	W	L	T	W	L	T
1968	3	11		2	5		1	6	
1969	4	9	1	4	3		0	6	1
1970	8	6		5	2		3	4	
1971	4	10		3	4		1	6	
1972	8	6		4	3		4	3	
1973	10	4		7	0		3	4	
1974	7	7		4	3		3	4	
1975	11	3		6	1		5	2	
1976	10	4		6	1		4	3	
1977	8	6		5	2		3	4	
1978	4	12		3	5		1	7	
1979	4	12		4	4		0	8	
1980	6	10		3	5		3	5	
1981	12	4		6	2		6	2	
1982	7	2		4	0		3	2	
1983	7	9		4	4		3	5	
1984	8	8		5	3		3	5	
1985	7	9		5	3		2	6	
1986	10	6		6	2		4	4	
1987	4	11		1	7		3	4	
1988	12	4		8	0		4	4	

	All Games			Home Games			Road Games		
Season	W	L	T	W	L	T	W	L	T
1989	8	8		5	3		3	5	
1990	9	7		5	3		4	4	
1991	3	13		3	5		0	8	
1992	5	11		3	5		2	6	
1993	3	13		3	5		0	8	
1994	3	13		2	6		1	7	
1995	7	9		3	5		4	4	
1996	8	8		6	2		2	6	
1997	7	9		6	2		1	7	
1998	3	13		1	7		2	6	
1999	4	12		2	6		2	6	
2000	4	12		3	5		1	7	
	218	281	1	137	113		81	168	1

CLEVELAND BROWNS*

	All Games			Home Games			Road Games		
Season	W	L	T	W	L	T	W	L	T
1950	10	2		5	1		5	1	
1951	11	1		6	0		5	1	
1952	8	4		4	2		4	2	
1953	11	1		6	0		5	1	
1954	9	3		5	1		4	2	
1955	9	2	1	5	1		4	1	1
1956	5	7		1	5		4	2	
1957	9	2	1	6	0		3	2	1
1958	9	3		4	2		5	1	
1959	7	5		3	3		4	2	
1960	8	3	1	4	2		4	1	1
1961	8	5	1	4	3		4	2	1
1962	7	6	1	4	2	1	3	4	
1963	10	4		5	2		5	2	
1964	10	3	1	5	1	1	5	2	
1965	11	3		5	2		6	1	
1966	9	5		5	2		4	3	
1967	9	5		6	1		3	4	
1968	10	4		5	2		5	2	
1969	10	3	1	5	1	1	5	2	
1970	7	7		4	3		3	4	
1971	9	5		4	3		5	2	
1972	10	4		4	3		6	1	
1973	7	5	2	5	1	1	2	4	1
1974	4	10		3	4		1	6	
1975	3	11		3	4		0	7	
1976	9	5		6	1		3	4	
1977	6	8		2	5		4	3	
1978	8	8		5	3		3	5	
1979	9	7		5	3		4	4	
1980	11	5		6	2		5	3	
1981	5	11		3	5		2	6	
1982	4	5		2	2		2	3	
1983	9	7		6	2		3	5	
1984	5	11		2	6		3	5	
1985	8	8		5	3		3	5	
1986	12	4		6	2		6	2	
1987	10	5		5	2		5	3	
1988	10	6		6	2		4	4	
1989	9	6	1	5	2	1	4	4	
1990	3	13		2	6		1	7	
1991	6	10		3	5		3	5	
1992	7	9		4	4		3	5	
1993	7	9		4	4		3	5	
1994	11	5		6	2		5	3	
1995	5	11		3	5		2	6	
1999	2	14		0	8		2	6	
2000	3	13		2	6		1	7	
	379	293	10	204	131	5	175	162	5

Did not play from 1996-98.

DENVER BRONCOS

	All Games			Home Games			Road Games		
Season	W	L	T	W	L	T	W	L	T
1960	4	9	1	2	4	1	2	5	
1961	3	11		2	5		1	6	
1962	7	7		3	4		4	3	
1963	2	11	1	2	5		0	6	1
1964	2	11	1	2	4	1	0	7	
1965	4	10		2	5		2	5	
1966	4	10		3	4		1	6	
1967	3	11		1	6		2	5	
1968	5	9		3	4		2	5	
1969	5	8	1	4	2	1	1	6	

	All Games			Home Games			Road Games		
Season	W	L	T	W	L	T	W	L	T
1970	5	8	1	3	3	1	2	5	
1971	4	9	1	2	4	1	2	5	
1972	5	9		3	4		2	5	
1973	7	5	2	3	3	1	4	2	1
1974	7	6	1	3	3	1	4	3	
1975	6	8		5	2		1	6	
1976	9	5		6	1		3	4	
1977	12	2		6	1		6	1	
1978	10	6		6	2		4	4	
1979	10	6		6	2		4	4	
1980	8	8		4	4		4	4	
1981	10	6		8	0		2	6	
1982	2	7		1	4		1	3	
1983	9	7		6	2		3	5	
1984	13	3		7	1		6	2	
1985	11	5		6	2		5	3	
1986	11	5		7	1		4	4	
1987	10	4	1	7	1		3	3	1
1988	8	8		6	2		2	6	
1989	11	5		6	2		5	3	
1990	5	11		4	4		1	7	
1991	12	4		7	1		5	3	
1992	8	8		7	1		1	7	
1993	9	7		5	3		4	4	
1994	7	9		4	4		3	5	
1995	8	8		6	2		2	6	
1996	13	3		8	0		5	3	
1997	12	4		8	0		4	4	
1998	14	2		8	0		6	2	
1999	6	10		3	5		3	5	
2000	11	5		6	2		5	3	
	312	290	10	191	109	7	121	181	3

INDIANAPOLIS COLTS*

	All Games			Home Games			Road Games		
Season	W	L	T	W	L	T	W	L	T
1953	3	9		2	4		1	5	
1954	3	9		2	4		1	5	
1955	5	6	1	4	1	1	1	5	
1956	5	7		4	2		1	5	
1957	7	5		4	2		3	3	
1958	9	3		6	0		3	3	
1959	9	3		4	2		5	1	
1960	6	6		4	2		2	4	
1961	8	6		5	2		3	4	
1962	7	7		3	4		4	3	
1963	8	6		4	3		4	3	
1964	12	2		7	1		5	1	
1965	10	3	1	5	2		5	1	1
1966	9	5		5	2		4	3	
1967	11	1	2	6	0	1	5	1	1
1968	13	1		6	1		7	0	
1969	8	5	1	4	2	1	4	3	
1970	11	2	1	5	1	1	6	1	
1971	10	4		5	2		5	2	
1972	5	9		2	5		3	4	
1973	4	10		3	4		1	6	
1974	2	12		0	7		2	5	
1975	10	4		5	2		5	2	
1976	11	3		6	1		5	2	
1977	10	4		6	1		4	3	
1978	5	11		2	6		3	5	
1979	5	11		3	5		2	6	
1980	7	9		2	6		5	3	
1981	2	14		1	7		1	7	
1982	0	8	1	0	3	1	0	5	
1983	7	9		3	5		4	4	
1984	4	12		2	6		2	6	
1985	5	11		4	4		1	7	
1986	3	13		1	7		2	6	
1987	9	6		4	4		5	2	
1988	9	7		6	2		3	5	
1989	8	8		6	2		2	6	
1990	7	9		3	5		4	4	
1991	1	15		0	8		1	7	
1992	9	7		4	4		5	3	
1993	4	12		2	6		2	6	
1994	8	8		5	3		3	5	
1995	9	7		5	3		4	4	
1996	9	7		6	2		3	5	
1997	3	13		2	6		1	7	

	All Games			Home Games			Road Games		
Season	W	L	T	W	L	T	W	L	T
1998	3	13		3	5		0	8	
1999	13	3		7	1		6	2	
2000	10	6		6	2		4	4	
	336	351	7	184	159	5	152	192	2

includes Baltimore Colts (1953-1983).

JACKSONVILLE JAGUARS

	All Games			Home Games			Road Games		
Season	W	L	T	W	L	T	W	L	T
1995	4	12		2	6		2	6	
1996	9	7		7	1		2	6	
1997	11	5		7	1		4	4	
1998	11	5		7	1		4	4	
1999	14	2		7	1		7	1	
2000	7	9		4	4		3	5	
	56	40		34	14		22	26	

KANSAS CITY CHIEFS*

	All Games			Home Games			Road Games		
Season	W	L	T	W	L	T	W	L	T
1960	8	6		5	2		3	4	
1961	6	8		4	3		2	5	
1962	11	3		6	1		5	2	
1963	5	7	2	4	3		1	4	2
1964	7	7		4	3		3	4	
1965	7	5	2	5	2		2	3	2
1966	11	2	1	4	2	1	7	0	
1967	9	5		4	3		5	2	
1968	12	2		6	1		6	1	
1969	11	3		6	1		5	2	
1970	7	5	2	4	1	2	3	4	
1971	10	3	1	7	0		3	3	1
1972	8	6		3	4		5	2	
1973	7	5	2	5	1	1	2	4	1
1974	5	9		1	6		4	3	
1975	5	9		3	4		2	5	
1976	5	9		1	6		4	3	
1977	2	12		1	6		1	6	
1978	4	12		3	5		1	7	
1979	7	9		3	5		4	4	
1980	8	8		3	5		5	3	
1981	9	7		5	3		4	4	
1982	3	6		2	2		1	4	
1983	6	10		5	3		1	7	
1984	8	8		5	3		3	5	
1985	6	10		5	3		1	7	
1986	10	6		6	2		4	4	
1987	4	11		3	4		1	7	
1988	4	11	1	4	4		0	7	1
1989	8	7	1	5	3		3	4	1
1990	11	5		6	2		5	3	
1991	10	6		6	2		4	4	
1992	10	6		7	1		3	5	
1993	11	5		7	1		4	4	
1994	9	7		5	3		4	4	
1995	13	3		8	0		5	3	
1996	9	7		5	3		4	4	
1997	13	3		8	0		5	3	
1998	7	9		5	3		2	6	
1999	9	7		6	2		3	5	
2000	7	9		5	3		2	6	
	322	278	12	190	111	4	132	167	8

includes Dallas Texans (1960-62).

MIAMI DOLPHINS

	All Games			Home Games			Road Games		
Season	W	L	T	W	L	T	W	L	T
1966	3	11		2	5		1	6	
1967	4	10		4	3		0	7	
1968	5	8	1	1	5	1	4	3	
1969	3	10	1	2	4	1	1	6	
1970	10	4		6	1		4	3	
1971	10	3	1	6	1		4	2	1
1972	14	0		7	0		7	0	
1973	12	2		7	0		5	2	
1974	11	3		7	0		4	3	
1975	10	4		5	2		5	2	
1976	6	8		3	4		3	4	
1977	10	4		6	1		4	3	
1978	11	5		7	1		4	4	
1979	10	6		6	2		4	4	
1980	8	8		5	3		3	5	

	All Games			Home Games			Road Games		
Season	W	L	T	W	L	T	W	L	T
1981	11	4	1	6	1	1	5	3	
1982	7	2		4	0		3	2	
1983	12	4		7	1		5	3	
1984	14	2		7	1		7	1	
1985	12	4		8	0		4	4	
1986	8	8		4	4		4	4	
1987	8	7		4	3		4	4	
1988	6	10		4	4		2	6	
1989	8	8		4	4		4	4	
1990	12	4		7	1		5	3	
1991	8	8		5	3		3	5	
1992	11	5		6	2		5	3	
1993	9	7		4	4		5	3	
1994	10	6		6	2		4	4	
1995	9	7		5	3		4	4	
1996	8	8		4	4		4	4	
1997	9	7		6	2		3	5	
1998	10	6		7	1		3	5	
1999	9	7		5	3		4	4	
2000	11	5		5	3		6	2	
	319	205	4	182	78	3	137	127	1

NEW ENGLAND PATRIOTS*

	All Games			Home Games			Road Games		
Season	W	L	T	W	L	T	W	L	T
1960	5	9		3	4		2	5	
1961	9	4	1	4	2	1	5	2	
1962	9	4	1	6	1		3	3	1
1963	7	6	1	5	1	1	2	5	
1964	10	3	1	4	2	1	6	1	
1965	4	8	2	1	4	2	3	4	
1966	8	4	2	4	2	1	4	2	1
1967	3	10	1	2	4		1	6	1
1968	4	10		2	5		2	5	
1969	4	10		2	5		2	5	
1970	2	12		1	6		1	6	
1971	6	8		5	2		1	6	
1972	3	11		2	5		1	6	
1973	5	9		3	4		2	5	
1974	7	7		3	4		4	3	
1975	3	11		2	5		1	6	
1976	11	3		6	1		5	2	
1977	9	5		6	1		3	4	
1978	11	5		5	3		6	2	
1979	9	7		6	2		3	5	
1980	10	6		6	2		4	4	
1981	2	14		2	6		0	8	
1982	5	4		3	1		2	3	
1983	8	8		5	3		3	5	
1984	9	7		5	3		4	4	
1985	11	5		7	1		4	4	
1986	11	5		4	4		7	1	
1987	8	7		5	3		3	4	
1988	9	7		7	1		2	6	
1989	5	11		3	5		2	6	
1990	1	15		0	8		1	7	
1991	6	10		4	4		2	6	
1992	2	14		1	7		1	7	
1993	5	11		3	5		2	6	
1994	10	6		5	3		5	3	
1995	6	10		3	5		3	5	
1996	11	5		6	2		5	3	
1997	10	6		6	2		4	4	
1998	9	7		6	2		3	5	
1999	8	8		5	3		3	5	
2000	5	11		3	5		2	6	
	280	323	9	161	138	6	119	185	3

includes Boston Patriots (1960-1970).

NEW YORK JETS*

	All Games			Home Games			Road Games		
Season	W	L	T	W	L	T	W	L	T
1960	7	7		3	4		4	3	
1961	7	7		5	2		2	5	
1962	5	9		2	5		3	4	
1963	5	8	1	4	2	1	1	6	
1964	5	8	1	5	1	1	0	7	
1965	5	8	1	3	3	1	2	5	
1966	6	6	2	4	3		2	3	2
1967	8	5	1	4	2	1	4	3	
1968	11	3		6	1		5	2	
1969	10	4		5	2		5	2	

	All Games			Home Games			Road Games		
Season	W	L	T	W	L	T	W	L	T
1970	4	10		2	5		2	5	
1971	6	8		4	3		2	5	
1972	7	7		4	3		3	4	
1973	4	10		2	4		2	6	
1974	7	7		3	4		4	3	
1975	3	11		1	6		2	5	
1976	3	11		2	5		1	6	
1977	3	11		1	6		2	5	
1978	8	8		4	4		4	4	
1979	8	8		6	2		2	6	
1980	4	12		2	6		2	6	
1981	10	5	1	6	2		4	3	1
1982	6	3		3	1		3	2	
1983	7	9		2	6		5	3	
1984	7	9		3	5		4	4	
1985	11	5		7	1		4	4	
1986	10	6		5	3		5	3	
1987	6	9		4	4		2	5	
1988	8	7	1	5	2	1	3	5	
1989	4	12		1	7		3	5	
1990	6	10		3	5		3	5	
1991	8	8		4	4		4	4	
1992	4	12		3	5		1	7	
1993	8	8		3	5		5	3	
1994	6	10		4	4		2	6	
1995	3	13		2	6		1	7	
1996	1	15		0	8		1	7	
1997	9	7		5	3		4	4	
1998	12	4		7	1		5	3	
1999	8	8		4	4		4	4	
2000	9	7		5	3		4	4	
	269	335	8	148	152	5	121	183	3

includes New York Titans (1960-62).

OAKLAND RAIDERS*

	All Games			Home Games			Road Games		
Season	W	L	T	W	L	T	W	L	T
1960	6	8		3	4		3	4	
1961	2	12		1	6		1	6	
1962	1	13		1	6		0	7	
1963	10	4		6	1		4	3	
1964	5	7	2	5	2		0	5	2
1965	8	5	1	5	2		3	3	1
1966	8	5	1	3	3	1	5	2	
1967	13	1		7	0		6	1	
1968	12	2		6	1		6	1	
1969	12	1	1	7	0		5	1	1
1970	8	4	2	6	1		2	3	2
1971	8	4	2	5	1	1	3	3	1
1972	10	3	1	5	1	1	5	2	
1973	9	4	1	5	2		4	2	1
1974	12	2		6	1		6	1	
1975	11	3		6	1		5	2	
1976	13	1		7	0		6	1	
1977	11	3		6	1		5	2	
1978	9	7		4	4		5	3	
1979	9	7		6	2		3	5	
1980	11	5		6	2		5	3	
1981	7	9		4	4		3	5	
1982	8	1		4	0		4	1	
1983	12	4		6	2		6	2	
1984	11	5		6	2		5	3	
1985	12	4		7	1		5	3	
1986	8	8		3	5		5	3	
1987	5	10		3	5		2	5	
1988	7	9		3	5		4	4	
1989	8	8		7	1		1	7	
1990	12	4		6	2		6	2	
1991	9	7		5	3		4	4	
1992	7	9		5	3		2	6	
1993	10	6		5	3		5	3	
1994	9	7		4	4		5	3	
1995	8	8		4	4		4	4	
1996	7	9		4	4		3	5	
1997	4	12		2	6		2	6	
1998	8	8		4	4		4	4	
1999	8	8		5	3		3	5	
2000	12	4		7	1		5	3	
	360	241	11	200	103	3	160	138	8

includes Los Angeles Raiders (1982-1994).

INSIDE THE NUMBERS

PITTSBURGH STEELERS*

	All Games			Home Games			Road Games		
Season	W	L	T	W	L	T	W	L	T
1933	3	6	2	2	3		1	3	2
1934	2	10		1	5		1	5	
1935	4	8		2	5		2	3	
1936	6	6		4	1		2	5	
1937	4	7		2	4		2	3	
1938	2	9		0	5		2	4	
1939	1	9	1	1	4		0	5	1
1940	2	7	2	1	2	2	1	5	
1941	1	9	1	1	4		0	5	1
1942	7	4		3	2		4	2	
1945	2	8		1	4		1	4	
1946	5	5	1	4	1		1	4	1
1947	8	4		5	1		3	3	
1948	4	8		4	2		0	6	
1949	6	5	1	3	2	1	3	3	
1950	6	6		2	4		4	2	
1951	4	7	1	1	4	1	3	3	
1952	5	7		2	4		3	3	
1953	6	6		3	3		3	3	
1954	5	7		4	2		1	5	
1955	4	8		3	2		1	6	
1956	5	7		3	3		2	4	
1957	6	6		4	2		2	4	
1958	7	4	1	5	1		2	3	1
1959	6	5	1	3	2	1	3	3	
1960	5	6	1	4	2		1	4	1
1961	6	8		4	3		2	5	
1962	9	5		4	3		5	2	
1963	7	4	3	5	0	2	2	4	1
1964	5	9		2	5		3	4	
1965	2	12		1	6		1	6	
1966	5	8	1	3	3	1	2	5	
1967	4	9	1	1	6		3	3	1
1968	2	11	1	1	6		1	5	1
1969	1	13		1	6		0	7	
1970	5	9		4	3		1	6	
1971	6	8		5	2		1	6	
1972	11	3		7	0		4	3	
1973	10	4		7	1		3	3	
1974	10	3	1	5	2		5	1	1
1975	12	2		6	1		6	1	
1976	10	4		6	1		4	3	
1977	9	5		6	1		3	4	
1978	14	2		7	1		7	1	
1979	12	4		8	0		4	4	
1980	9	7		6	2		3	5	
1981	8	8		5	3		3	5	
1982	6	3		4	0		2	3	
1983	10	6		4	4		6	2	
1984	9	7		6	2		3	5	
1985	7	9		5	3		2	6	
1986	6	10		4	4		2	6	
1987	8	7		4	3		4	4	
1988	5	11		4	4		1	7	
1989	9	7		4	4		5	3	
1990	9	7		6	2		3	5	
1991	7	9		5	3		2	6	
1992	11	5		7	1		4	4	
1993	9	7		6	2		3	5	
1994	12	4		7	1		5	3	
1995	11	5		6	2		5	3	
1996	10	6		7	1		3	5	
1997	11	5		7	1		4	4	
1998	7	9		5	3		2	6	
1999	6	10		2	6		4	4	
2000	9	7		4	4		5	3	
	435	446	19	259	179	8	176	267	11

includes Pittsburgh Pirates (1933-1940).

SAN DIEGO CHARGERS*

	All Games			Home Games			Road Games		
Season	W	L	T	W	L	T	W	L	T
1960	10	4		5	2		5	2	
1961	12	2		6	1		6	1	
1962	4	10		3	4		1	6	
1963	11	3		6	1		5	2	
1964	8	5	1	4	3		4	2	1
1965	9	2	3	4	1	2	5	1	1
1966	7	6	1	5	2		2	4	1
1967	8	5	1	5	2	1	3	3	
1968	9	5		4	3		5	2	
1969	8	6		5	2		3	4	
1970	5	6	3	2	3	2	3	3	1
1971	6	8		6	1		0	7	
1972	4	9	1	2	5		2	4	1
1973	2	11	1	2	5		0	6	1
1974	5	9		3	4		2	5	
1975	2	12		1	6		1	6	
1976	6	8		3	4		3	4	
1977	7	7		3	4		4	3	
1978	9	7		5	3		4	4	
1979	12	4		7	1		5	3	
1980	11	5		6	2		5	3	
1981	10	6		5	3		5	3	
1982	6	3		3	1		3	2	
1983	6	10		4	4		2	6	
1984	7	9		4	4		3	5	
1985	8	8		6	2		2	6	
1986	4	12		2	6		2	6	
1987	8	7		4	3		4	4	
1988	6	10		3	5		3	5	
1989	6	10		4	4		2	6	
1990	6	10		3	5		3	5	
1991	4	12		3	5		1	7	
1992	11	5		6	2		5	3	
1993	8	8		4	4		4	4	
1994	11	5		5	3		6	2	
1995	9	7		5	3		4	4	
1996	8	8		5	3		3	5	
1997	4	12		2	6		2	6	
1998	5	11		4	4		1	7	
1999	8	8		4	4		4	4	
2000	1	15		1	7		0	8	
	291	310	11	164	137	5	127	173	6

includes Los Angeles Chargers (1960).

SEATTLE SEAHAWKS

	All Games			Home Games			Road Games		
Season	W	L	T	W	L	T	W	L	T
1976	2	12		1	6		1	6	
1977	5	9		3	4		2	5	
1978	9	7		5	3		4	4	
1979	9	7		5	3		4	4	
1980	4	12		0	8		4	4	
1981	6	10		5	3		1	7	
1982	4	5		3	2		1	3	
1983	9	7		5	3		4	4	
1984	12	4		7	1		5	3	
1985	8	8		5	3		3	5	
1986	10	6		7	1		3	5	
1987	9	6		6	2		3	4	
1988	9	7		5	3		4	4	
1989	7	9		3	5		4	4	
1990	9	7		5	3		4	4	
1991	7	9		5	3		2	6	
1992	2	14		1	7		1	7	
1993	6	10		4	4		2	6	
1994	6	10		3	5		3	5	
1995	8	8		5	3		3	5	
1996	7	9		4	4		3	5	
1997	8	8		4	4		4	4	
1998	8	8		6	2		2	6	
1999	9	7		5	3		4	4	
2000	6	10		3	5		3	5	
	179	209		105	90		74	119	

TENNESSEE TITANS*

	All Games			Home Games			Road Games		
Season	W	L	T	W	L	T	W	L	T
1960	10	4		6	1		4	3	
1961	10	3	1	6	1		4	2	1
1962	11	3		6	1		5	2	
1963	6	8		4	3		2	5	
1964	4	10		3	4		1	6	
1965	4	10		3	4		1	6	
1966	3	11		3	4		0	7	
1967	9	4	1	5	2		4	2	1
1968	7	7		3	4		4	3	
1969	6	6	2	4	2	1	2	4	1
1970	3	10	1	1	6		2	4	1
1971	4	9	1	3	3	1	1	6	
1972	1	13		1	6		0	7	
1973	1	13		0	7		1	6	
1974	7	7		3	4		4	3	
1975	10	4		5	2		5	2	
1976	5	9		3	4		2	5	
1977	8	6		5	2		3	4	
1978	10	6		5	3		5	3	
1979	11	5		6	2		5	3	
1980	11	5		6	2		5	3	
1981	7	9		5	3		2	6	
1982	1	8		1	4		0	4	
1983	2	14		2	6		0	8	
1984	3	13		2	6		1	7	
1985	5	11		4	4		1	7	
1986	5	11		4	4		1	7	
1987	9	6		5	2		4	4	
1988	10	6		7	1		3	5	
1989	9	7		6	2		3	5	
1990	9	7		6	2		3	5	
1991	11	5		7	1		4	4	
1992	10	6		5	3		5	3	
1993	12	4		7	1		5	3	
1994	2	14		2	6		0	8	
1995	7	9		3	5		4	4	
1996	8	8		2	6		6	2	
1997	8	8		6	2		2	6	
1998	8	8		3	5		5	3	
1999	13	3		8	0		5	3	
2000	13	3		7	1		6	2	
	293	313	6	173	131	2	120	182	4

includes Houston Oilers (1960-1996) and Tennessee Oilers (1997-98).

NFC

ARIZONA CARDINALS*

	All Games			Home Games			Road Games		
Season	W	L	T	W	L	T	W	L	T
1920	6	2	2	5	1	1	1	1	1
1921	3	3	2	3	3	1	0	0	1
1922	8	3		8	3		0	0	
1923	8	4		8	3		0	1	
1924	5	4	1	5	3	1	0	1	
1925	11	2	1	11	2		0	0	1
1926	5	6	1	3	3		2	3	1
1927	3	7	1	2	3	1	1	4	
1928	1	5		1	1		0	4	
1929	6	6	1	3	2		3	4	1
1930	5	6	2	3	2		2	4	2
1931	5	4		3	0		2	4	
1932	2	6	2	1	2	1	1	4	1
1933	1	9	1	0	4	1	1	5	
1934	5	6		2	2		3	4	
1935	6	4	2	2	2		4	2	2
1936	3	8	1	3	1	1	0	7	
1937	5	5	1	1	3		4	2	1
1938	2	9		1	4		1	5	
1939	1	10		0	4		1	6	
1940	2	7	2	2	1	1	0	6	1
1941	3	7	1	0	3	1	3	4	
1942	3	8		2	2		1	6	
1943	0	10		0	3		0	7	
1945	1	9		0	3		1	6	
1946	6	5		2	2		4	3	
1947	9	3		5	0		4	3	
1948	11	1		5	1		6	0	
1949	6	5	1	2	3	1	4	2	
1950	5	7		3	3		2	4	
1951	3	9		1	5		2	4	
1952	4	8		2	4		2	4	
1953	1	10	1	0	5	1	1	5	
1954	2	10		2	4		0	6	
1955	4	7	1	3	2	1	1	5	
1956	7	5		4	2		3	3	
1957	3	9		0	6		3	3	
1958	2	9	1	1	4	1	1	5	
1959	2	10		2	4		0	6	
1960	6	5	1	3	2	1	3	3	
1961	7	7		3	4		4	3	
1962	4	9	1	2	4	1	2	5	
1963	9	5		3	4		6	1	
1964	9	3	2	4	1	1	5	2	1

	All Games			Home Games			Road Games		
Season	W	L	T	W	L	T	W	L	T
1965	5	9		2	5		3	4	
1966	8	5	1	5	1	1	3	4	
1967	6	7	1	3	3	1	3	4	
1968	9	4	1	4	2	1	5	2	
1969	4	9	1	3	4		1	5	1
1970	8	5	1	6	1		2	4	1
1971	4	9	1	1	5	1	3	4	
1972	4	9	1	2	5		2	4	1
1973	4	9	1	2	4	1	2	5	
1974	10	4		5	2		5	2	
1975	11	3		6	1		5	2	
1976	10	4		6	1		4	3	
1977	7	7		4	3		3	4	
1978	6	10		3	5		3	5	
1979	5	11		3	5		2	6	
1980	5	11		2	6		3	5	
1981	7	9		5	3		2	6	
1982	5	4		1	3		4	1	
1983	8	7	1	4	3	1	4	4	
1984	9	7		5	3		4	4	
1985	5	11		4	4		1	7	
1986	4	11	1	3	5		1	6	1
1987	7	8		4	3		3	5	
1988	7	9		4	4		3	5	
1989	5	11		2	6		3	5	
1990	5	11		3	5		2	6	
1991	4	12		2	6		2	6	
1992	4	12		3	5		1	7	
1993	7	9		4	4		3	5	
1994	8	8		5	3		3	5	
1995	4	12		3	5		1	7	
1996	7	9		5	3		2	6	
1997	4	12		3	5		1	7	
1998	9	7		5	3		4	4	
1999	6	10		4	4		2	6	
2000	3	13		3	5		0	8	
	424	585	39	245	255	22	179	330	17

*includes Chicago Cardinals (1920-1959), St. Louis Cardinals (1960-1987), and Phoenix Cardinals (1988-1993).

ATLANTA FALCONS

	All Games			Home Games			Road Games		
Season	W	L	T	W	L	T	W	L	T
1966	3	11		1	6		2	5	
1967	1	12	1	1	5	1	0	7	
1968	2	12		1	6		1	6	
1969	6	8		4	3		2	5	
1970	4	8	2	3	4		1	4	2
1971	7	6	1	4	3		3	3	1
1972	7	7		4	3		3	4	
1973	9	5		4	3		5	2	
1974	3	11		2	5		1	6	
1975	4	10		3	4		1	6	
1976	4	10		3	4		1	6	
1977	7	7		4	3		3	4	
1978	9	7		7	1		2	6	
1979	6	10		3	5		3	5	
1980	12	4		6	2		6	2	
1981	7	9		4	4		3	5	
1982	5	4		2	3		3	1	
1983	7	9		4	4		3	5	
1984	4	12		2	6		2	6	
1985	4	12		3	5		1	7	
1986	7	8	1	2	5	1	5	3	
1987	3	12		2	6		1	6	
1988	5	11		2	6		3	5	
1989	3	13		3	5		0	8	
1990	5	11		5	3		0	8	
1991	10	6		6	2		4	4	
1992	6	10		5	3		1	7	
1993	6	10		4	4		2	6	
1994	7	9		5	3		2	6	
1995	9	7		7	1		2	6	
1996	3	13		2	6		1	7	
1997	7	9		3	5		4	4	
1998	14	2		8	0		6	2	
1999	5	11		4	4		1	7	
2000	4	12		3	5		1	7	
	205	318	5	126	137	2	79	181	3

CAROLINA PANTHERS

	All Games			Home Games			Road Games		
Season	W	L	T	W	L	T	W	L	T
1995	7	9		5	3		2	6	
1996	12	4		8	0		4	4	
1997	7	9		2	6		5	3	
1998	4	12		2	6		2	6	
1999	8	8		5	3		3	5	
2000	7	9		5	3		2	6	
	45	51		27	21		18	30	

CHICAGO BEARS*

	All Games			Home Games			Road Games		
Season	W	L	T	W	L	T	W	L	T
1920	10	1	2	6	0	1	4	1	1
1921	9	1	1	9	1	1	0	0	
1922	9	3		7	1		2	2	
1923	9	2	1	7	1	1	2	1	
1924	6	1	4	5	0	3	1	1	1
1925	9	5	3	7	1	1	2	4	2
1926	12	1	3	10	0	2	2	1	1
1927	9	3	2	7	1	1	2	2	1
1928	7	5	1	6	3		1	2	1
1929	4	9	2	1	5	2	3	4	
1930	9	4	1	5	2	1	4	2	
1931	8	5		6	3		2	2	
1932	7	1	6	6	1	1	1	0	5
1933	10	2	1	6	0		4	2	1
1934	13	0		5	0		8	0	
1935	6	4	2	1	2	2	5	2	
1936	9	3		3	1		6	2	
1937	9	1	1	4	1		5	0	1
1938	6	5		2	3		4	2	
1939	8	3		4	1		4	2	
1940	8	3		5	0		3	3	
1941	10	1		5	1		5	0	
1942	11	0		6	0		5	0	
1943	8	1	1	5	0		3	1	1
1944	6	3	1	4	0	1	2	3	
1945	3	7		2	3		1	4	
1946	8	2	1	4	1	1	4	1	
1947	8	4		4	2		4	2	
1948	10	2		5	1		5	1	
1949	9	3		5	1		4	2	
1950	9	3		6	0		3	3	
1951	7	5		3	3		4	2	
1952	5	7		3	3		2	4	
1953	3	8	1	1	4	1	2	4	
1954	8	4		4	2		4	2	
1955	8	4		5	1		3	3	
1956	9	2	1	6	0		3	2	1
1957	5	7		2	4		3	3	
1958	8	4		5	1		3	3	
1959	8	4		4	2		4	2	
1960	5	6	1	4	2		1	4	1
1961	8	6		5	2		3	4	
1962	9	5		4	3		5	2	
1963	11	1	2	6	0	1	5	1	1
1964	5	9		2	5		3	4	
1965	9	5		5	2		4	3	
1966	5	7	2	4	1	2	1	6	
1967	7	6	1	3	3	1	4	3	
1968	7	7		2	5		5	2	
1969	1	13		1	6		0	7	
1970	6	8		3	4		3	4	
1971	6	8		4	3		2	5	
1972	4	9	1	1	5	1	3	4	
1973	3	11		1	6		2	5	
1974	4	10		4	3		0	7	
1975	4	10		3	4		1	6	
1976	7	7		4	3		3	4	
1977	9	5		5	2		4	3	
1978	7	9		4	4		3	5	
1979	10	6		6	2		4	4	
1980	7	9		5	3		2	6	
1981	6	10		4	4		2	6	
1982	3	6		2	2		1	4	
1983	8	8		5	3		3	5	
1984	10	6		6	2		4	4	
1985	15	1		8	0		7	1	
1986	14	2		7	1		7	1	
1987	11	4		6	2		5	2	
1988	12	4		7	1		5	3	
1989	6	10		4	4		2	6	
1990	11	5		7	1		4	4	
1991	11	5		6	2		5	3	
1992	5	11		4	4		1	7	
1993	7	9		3	5		4	4	
1994	9	7		5	3		4	4	
1995	9	7		5	3		4	4	
1996	7	9		6	2		1	7	
1997	4	12		2	6		2	6	
1998	4	12		3	5		1	7	
1999	6	10		3	5		3	5	
2000	5	11		3	5		2	6	
	617	439	42	363	184	24	254	255	18

*includes Decatur Staleys (1920) and Chicago Staleys (1921).

DALLAS COWBOYS

	All Games			Home Games			Road Games		
Season	W	L	T	W	L	T	W	L	T
1960	0	11	1	0	6		0	5	1
1961	4	9	1	2	4	1	2	5	
1962	5	8	1	2	4	1	3	4	
1963	4	10		3	4		1	6	
1964	5	8	1	2	4	1	3	4	
1965	7	7		5	2		2	5	
1966	10	3	1	6	1		4	2	1
1967	9	5		5	2		4	3	
1968	12	2		5	2		7	0	
1969	11	2	1	6	0	1	5	2	
1970	10	4		6	1		4	3	
1971	11	3		6	1		5	2	
1972	10	4		5	2		5	2	
1973	10	4		6	1		4	3	
1974	8	6		5	2		3	4	
1975	10	4		5	2		5	2	
1976	11	3		6	1		5	2	
1977	12	2		6	1		6	1	
1978	12	4		7	1		5	3	
1979	11	5		6	2		5	3	
1980	12	4		8	0		4	4	
1981	12	4		8	0		4	4	
1982	6	3		3	2		3	1	
1983	12	4		6	2		6	2	
1984	9	7		5	3		4	4	
1985	10	6		7	1		3	5	
1986	7	9		3	5		4	4	
1987	7	8		3	4		4	4	
1988	3	13		1	7		2	6	
1989	1	15		0	8		1	7	
1990	7	9		5	3		2	6	
1991	11	5		6	2		5	3	
1992	13	3		7	1		6	2	
1993	12	4		6	2		6	2	
1994	12	4		6	2		6	2	
1995	12	4		6	2		6	2	
1996	10	6		6	2		4	4	
1997	6	10		5	3		1	7	
1998	10	6		6	2		4	4	
1999	8	8		7	1		1	7	
2000	5	11		3	5		2	6	
	357	247	6	201	100	4	156	147	2

DETROIT LIONS*

	All Games			Home Games			Road Games		
Season	W	L	T	W	L	T	W	L	T
1930	5	6	3	5	1	2	0	5	1
1931	11	3		8	0		3	3	
1932	6	2	4	3	0	2	3	2	2
1933	6	5		4	1		2	4	
1934	10	3		6	2		4	1	
1935	7	3	2	5	0	1	2	3	1
1936	8	4		5	1		3	3	
1937	7	4		4	2		3	2	
1938	7	4		4	3		3	1	
1939	6	5		4	2		2	3	
1940	5	5	1	3	3		2	2	1
1941	4	6	1	3	2		1	4	1
1942	0	11		0	7		0	4	
1943	3	6	1	2	2	1	1	4	
1944	6	3	1	4	2		2	1	1
1945	7	3		4	1		3	2	
1946	1	10		1	5		0	5	

INSIDE THE NUMBERS

Season	All Games W	L	T	Home Games W	L	T	Road Games W	L	T
1947	3	9		2	4		1	5	
1948	2	10		2	4		0	6	
1949	4	8		2	4		2	4	
1950	6	6		4	2		2	4	
1951	7	4	1	3	3	1	4	1	
1952	9	3		6	1		3	2	
1953	10	2		5	1		5	1	
1954	9	2	1	5	0	1	4	2	
1955	3	9		3	4		0	5	
1956	9	3		5	1		4	2	
1957	8	4		5	1		3	3	
1958	4	7	1	2	4		2	3	1
1959	3	8	1	2	4		1	4	1
1960	7	5		5	1		2	4	
1961	8	5	1	2	5		6	0	1
1962	11	3		7	0		4	3	
1963	5	8	1	3	3	1	2	5	
1964	7	5	2	3	3	1	4	2	1
1965	6	7	1	2	4	1	4	3	
1966	4	9	1	3	4		1	5	1
1967	5	7	2	3	4		2	3	2
1968	4	8	2	1	4	2	3	4	
1969	9	4	1	5	2		4	2	1
1970	10	4		6	1		4	3	
1971	7	6	1	3	4		4	2	1
1972	8	5	1	5	2		3	3	1
1973	6	7	1	4	3		2	4	1
1974	7	7		5	2		2	5	
1975	7	7		4	3		3	4	
1976	6	8		5	2		1	6	
1977	6	8		5	2		1	6	
1978	7	9		5	3		2	6	
1979	2	14		2	6		0	8	
1980	9	7		6	2		3	5	
1981	8	8		7	1		1	7	
1982	4	5		2	3		2	2	
1983	9	7		6	2		3	5	
1984	4	11	1	2	5	1	2	6	
1985	7	9		6	2		1	7	
1986	5	11		1	7		4	4	
1987	4	11		1	6		3	5	
1988	4	12		2	6		2	6	
1989	7	9		4	4		3	5	
1990	6	10		3	5		3	5	
1991	12	4		8	0		4	4	
1992	5	11		3	5		2	6	
1993	10	6		5	3		5	3	
1994	9	7		6	2		3	5	
1995	10	6		7	1		3	5	
1996	5	11		4	4		1	7	
1997	9	7		6	2		3	5	
1998	5	11		4	4		1	7	
1999	8	8		6	2		2	6	
2000	9	7		4	4		5	3	
	457	472	32	282	195	14	175	277	18

**includes Portsmouth Spartans (1930-33).*

GREEN BAY PACKERS

Season	All Games W	L	T	Home Games W	L	T	Road Games W	L	T
1921	3	2	1	2	1		1	1	1
1922	4	3	3	4	1	1	0	2	2
1923	7	2	1	4	2	1	3	0	
1924	7	4		5	0		2	4	
1925	8	5		6	0		2	5	
1926	7	3	3	4	1	2	3	2	1
1927	7	2	1	6	1		1	1	1
1928	6	4	3	2	2	2	4	2	1
1929	12	0	1	5	0		7	0	1
1930	10	3	1	6	0		4	3	1
1931	12	2		8	0		4	2	
1932	10	3	1	5	0	1	5	3	
1933	5	7	1	3	2	1	2	5	
1934	7	6		4	2		3	4	
1935	8	4		5	2		3	2	
1936	10	1	1	5	1		5	0	1
1937	7	4		3	2		4	2	
1938	8	3		4	2		4	1	
1939	9	2		4	1		5	1	
1940	6	4	1	4	2		2	2	1
1941	10	1		4	1		6	0	
1942	8	2	1	4	1		4	1	1
1943	7	2	1	2	1	1	5	1	
1944	8	2		5	0		3	2	
1945	6	4		4	1		2	3	
1946	6	5		2	3		4	2	
1947	6	5	1	4	2		2	3	1
1948	3	9		2	4		1	5	
1949	2	10		1	5		1	5	
1950	3	9		3	3		0	6	
1951	3	9		2	4		1	5	
1952	6	6		3	3		3	3	
1953	2	9	1	1	5		1	4	1
1954	4	8		2	4		2	4	
1955	6	6		5	1		1	5	
1956	4	8		2	4		2	4	
1957	3	9		1	5		2	4	
1958	1	10	1	1	4	1	0	6	
1959	7	5		4	2		3	3	
1960	8	4		4	2		4	2	
1961	11	3		6	1		5	2	
1962	13	1		7	0		6	1	
1963	11	2	1	6	1		5	1	1
1964	8	5	1	4	3		4	2	1
1965	10	3	1	6	1		4	2	1
1966	12	2		6	1		6	1	
1967	9	4	1	4	2	1	5	2	
1968	6	7	1	2	5		4	2	1
1969	8	6		5	2		3	4	
1970	6	8		4	3		2	5	
1971	4	8	2	3	3	1	1	5	1
1972	10	4		4	3		6	1	
1973	5	7	2	3	2	2	2	5	
1974	6	8		4	3		2	5	
1975	4	10		3	4		1	6	
1976	5	9		4	3		1	6	
1977	4	10		2	5		2	5	
1978	8	7	1	5	2	1	3	5	
1979	5	11		4	4		1	7	
1980	5	10	1	4	4		1	6	1
1981	8	8		4	4		4	4	
1982	5	3	1	3	1		2	2	1
1983	8	8		5	3		3	5	
1984	8	8		5	3		3	5	
1985	8	8		5	3		3	5	
1986	4	12		1	7		3	5	
1987	5	9	1	2	5	1	3	4	
1988	4	12		2	6		2	6	
1989	10	6		6	2		4	4	
1990	6	10		3	5		3	5	
1991	4	12		2	6		2	6	
1992	9	7		6	2		3	5	
1993	9	7		6	2		3	5	
1994	9	7		7	1		2	6	
1995	11	5		7	1		4	4	
1996	13	3		8	0		5	3	
1997	13	3		8	0		5	3	
1998	11	5		7	1		4	4	
1999	8	8		5	3		3	5	
2000	9	7		6	2		3	5	
	568	460	36	329	186	16	239	274	20

MINNESOTA VIKINGS

Season	All Games W	L	T	Home Games W	L	T	Road Games W	L	T
1961	3	11		3	4		0	7	
1962	2	11	1	1	5	1	1	6	
1963	5	8	1	3	4		2	4	1
1964	8	5	1	4	3		4	2	1
1965	7	7		2	5		5	2	
1966	4	9	1	2	5		2	4	1
1967	3	8	3	1	4	2	2	4	1
1968	8	6		4	3		4	3	
1969	12	2		7	0		5	2	
1970	12	2		7	0		5	2	
1971	11	3		5	2		6	1	
1972	7	7		3	4		4	3	
1973	12	2		7	0		5	2	
1974	10	4		4	3		6	1	
1975	12	2		7	0		5	2	
1976	11	2	1	6	0	1	5	2	
1977	9	5		5	2		4	3	
1978	8	7	1	5	3		3	4	1
1979	7	9		5	3		2	6	
1980	9	7		5	3		4	4	
1981	7	9		5	3		2	6	
1982	5	4		4	1		1	3	
1983	8	8		3	5		5	3	
1984	3	13		2	6		1	7	
1985	7	9		4	4		3	5	
1986	9	7		5	3		4	4	
1987	8	7		5	3		3	4	
1988	11	5		7	1		4	4	
1989	10	6		8	0		2	6	
1990	6	10		4	4		2	6	
1991	8	8		4	4		4	4	
1992	11	5		5	3		6	2	
1993	9	7		4	4		5	3	
1994	10	6		6	2		4	4	
1995	8	8		6	2		2	6	
1996	9	7		5	3		4	4	
1997	9	7		5	3		4	4	
1998	15	1		8	0		7	1	
1999	10	6		6	2		4	4	
2000	11	5		7	1		4	4	
	334	255	9	189	107	4	145	148	5

NEW ORLEANS SAINTS

Season	All Games W	L	T	Home Games W	L	T	Road Games W	L	T
1967	3	11		2	5		1	6	
1968	4	9	1	3	4		1	5	1
1969	5	9		3	4		2	5	
1970	2	11	1	2	5		0	6	1
1971	4	8	2	2	4	1	2	4	1
1972	2	11	1	2	5		0	6	1
1973	5	9		5	2		0	7	
1974	5	9		4	3		1	6	
1975	2	12		2	5		0	7	
1976	4	10		2	5		2	5	
1977	3	11		2	5		1	6	
1978	7	9		3	5		4	4	
1979	8	8		3	5		5	3	
1980	1	15		0	8		1	7	
1981	4	12		2	6		2	6	
1982	4	5		2	3		2	2	
1983	8	8		5	3		3	5	
1984	7	9		3	5		4	4	
1985	5	11		3	5		2	6	
1986	7	9		4	4		3	5	
1987	12	3		6	1		6	2	
1988	10	6		5	3		5	3	
1989	9	7		5	3		4	4	
1990	8	8		5	3		3	5	
1991	11	5		6	2		5	3	
1992	12	4		6	2		6	2	
1993	8	8		4	4		4	4	
1994	7	9		3	5		4	4	
1995	7	9		4	4		3	5	
1996	3	13		2	6		1	7	
1997	6	10		3	5		3	5	
1998	6	10		4	4		2	6	
1999	3	13		3	5		0	8	
2000	10	6		3	5		7	1	
	202	307	5	113	143	1	89	164	4

NEW YORK GIANTS

Season	All Games W	L	T	Home Games W	L	T	Road Games W	L	T
1925	8	4		7	2		1	2	
1926	8	4	1	5	2	1	3	2	
1927	11	1	1	7	1		4	0	1
1928	4	7	2	1	2	2	3	5	
1929	13	1	1	7	1		6	0	1
1930	13	4		6	2		7	2	
1931	7	6	1	4	2	1	3	4	
1932	4	6	2	3	2	1	1	4	1
1933	11	3		7	0		4	3	
1934	8	5		5	1		3	4	
1935	9	3		4	2		5	1	
1936	5	6	1	3	3	1	2	3	
1937	6	3	2	4	2	1	2	1	1
1938	8	2	1	6	1		2	1	1

Season	All Games W	L	T	Home Games W	L	T	Road Games W	L	T
1939	9	1	1	6	0		3	1	1
1940	6	4	1	4	3		2	1	1
1941	8	3		5	2		3	1	
1942	5	5	1	3	2	1	2	3	
1943	6	3	1	4	2		2	1	1
1944	8	1	1	5	1		3	0	1
1945	3	6	1	2	4		1	2	1
1946	7	3	1	5	1	1	2	2	
1947	2	8	2	2	3	1	0	5	1
1948	4	8		2	4		2	4	
1949	6	6		2	4		4	2	
1950	10	2		5	1		5	1	
1951	9	2	1	5	1		4	1	1
1952	7	5		2	4		5	1	
1953	3	9		2	4		1	5	
1954	7	5		4	2		3	3	
1955	6	5	1	4	1	1	2	4	
1956	8	3	1	4	1	1	4	2	
1957	7	5		3	3		4	2	
1958	9	3		5	1		4	2	
1959	10	2		5	1		5	1	
1960	6	4	2	1	3	2	5	1	
1961	10	3	1	4	2	1	6	1	
1962	12	2		6	1		6	1	
1963	11	3		5	2		6	1	
1964	2	10	2	2	5		0	5	2
1965	7	7		3	4		4	3	
1966	1	12	1	1	6		0	6	1
1967	7	7		5	2		2	5	
1968	7	7		3	4		4	3	
1969	6	8		5	2		1	6	
1970	9	5		5	2		4	3	
1971	4	10		1	6		3	4	
1972	8	6		4	3		4	3	
1973	2	11	1	2	4	1	0	7	
1974	2	12		0	7		2	5	
1975	5	9		2	5		3	4	
1976	3	11		3	4		0	7	
1977	5	9		3	4		2	5	
1978	6	10		5	3		1	7	
1979	6	10		4	4		2	6	
1980	4	12		2	6		2	6	
1981	9	7		4	4		5	3	
1982	4	5		2	3		2	2	
1983	3	12	1	1	7		2	5	1
1984	9	7		6	2		3	5	
1985	10	6		6	2		4	4	
1986	14	2		8	0		6	2	
1987	6	9		5	3		1	6	
1988	10	6		5	3		5	3	
1989	12	4		7	1		5	3	
1990	13	3		7	1		6	2	
1991	8	8		5	3		3	5	
1992	6	10		4	4		2	6	
1993	11	5		6	2		5	3	
1994	9	7		4	4		5	3	
1995	5	11		3	5		2	6	
1996	6	10		3	5		3	5	
1997	10	5	1	6	2		4	3	1
1998	8	8		5	3		3	5	
1999	7	9		4	4		3	5	
2000	12	4		5	3		7	1	
	550	450	33	310	208	16	240	242	17

PHILADELPHIA EAGLES

Season	All Games W	L	T	Home Games W	L	T	Road Games W	L	T
1933	3	5	1	2	3	1	1	2	
1934	4	7		2	4		2	3	
1935	2	9		0	5		2	4	
1936	1	11		1	6		0	5	
1937	2	8	1	0	5	1	2	3	
1938	5	6		2	3		3	3	
1939	1	9	1	1	3	1	0	6	
1940	1	10		1	4		0	6	
1941	2	8	1	1	4	1	1	4	
1942	2	9		0	5		2	4	
1944	7	1	2	3	1	2	4	0	
1945	7	3		6	0		1	3	
1946	6	5		3	2		3	3	
1947	8	4		6	1		2	3	

Season	All Games W	L	T	Home Games W	L	T	Road Games W	L	T
1948	9	2	1	6	0		3	2	1
1949	11	1		6	0		5	1	
1950	6	6		2	4		4	2	
1951	4	8		1	5		3	3	
1952	7	5		4	2		3	3	
1953	7	4	1	5	0	1	2	4	
1954	7	4	1	5	1		2	3	1
1955	4	7	1	4	2		0	5	1
1956	3	8	1	2	3	1	1	5	
1957	4	8		3	3		1	5	
1958	2	9	1	2	4		0	5	1
1959	7	5		5	1		2	4	
1960	10	2		5	1		5	1	
1961	10	4		5	2		5	2	
1962	3	10	1	2	5		1	5	1
1963	2	10	2	1	5	1	1	5	1
1964	6	8		3	4		3	4	
1965	5	9		2	5		3	4	
1966	9	5		5	2		4	3	
1967	6	7	1	5	2		1	5	1
1968	2	12		1	6		1	6	
1969	4	9	1	2	5		2	4	1
1970	3	10	1	3	3	1	0	7	
1971	6	7	1	3	4		3	3	1
1972	2	11	1	0	6	1	2	5	
1973	5	8	1	4	3		1	5	1
1974	7	7		5	2		2	5	
1975	4	10		2	5		2	5	
1976	4	10		2	5		2	5	
1977	5	9		4	3		1	6	
1978	9	7		5	3		4	4	
1979	11	5		5	3		6	2	
1980	12	4		7	1		5	3	
1981	10	6		6	2		4	4	
1982	3	6		1	4		2	2	
1983	5	11		1	7		4	4	
1984	6	9	1	5	3		1	6	1
1985	7	9		4	4		3	5	
1986	5	10	1	2	5	1	3	5	
1987	7	8		4	4		3	4	
1988	10	6		5	3		5	3	
1989	11	5		6	2		5	3	
1990	10	6		6	2		4	4	
1991	10	6		4	4		6	2	
1992	11	5		8	0		3	5	
1993	8	8		3	5		5	3	
1994	7	9		5	3		2	6	
1995	10	6		6	2		4	4	
1996	10	6		5	3		5	3	
1997	6	9	1	6	2		0	7	1
1998	3	13		3	5		0	8	
1999	5	11		4	4		1	7	
2000	11	5		5	3		6	2	
	402	480	24	233	213	12	169	267	12

ST. LOUIS RAMS*

Season	All Games W	L	T	Home Games W	L	T	Road Games W	L	T
1937	1	10		0	5		1	5	
1938	4	7		2	2		2	5	
1939	5	5	1	3	2	1	2	3	
1940	4	6	1	3	1	1	1	5	
1941	2	9		1	4		1	5	
1942	5	6		3	2		2	4	
1944	4	6		1	2		3	4	
1945	9	1		4	0		5	1	
1946	6	4	1	3	2		3	2	1
1947	6	6		3	3		3	3	
1948	6	5	1	3	2	1	3	3	
1949	8	2	2	5	1		3	1	2
1950	9	3		5	1		4	2	
1951	8	4		5	2		3	2	
1952	9	3		5	1		4	2	
1953	8	3	1	5	1		3	2	1
1954	6	5	1	3	2	1	3	3	
1955	8	3	1	5	1		3	2	1
1956	4	8		4	2		0	6	
1957	6	6		5	1		1	5	
1958	8	4		4	2		4	2	
1959	2	10		0	6		2	4	
1960	4	7	1	2	3	1	2	4	
1961	4	10		4	3		0	7	
1962	1	12	1	0	7		1	5	1
1963	5	9		3	4		2	5	
1964	5	7	2	3	2	2	2	5	
1965	4	10		3	4		1	6	
1966	8	6		5	2		3	4	
1967	11	1	2	5	1	1	6	0	1
1968	10	3	1	5	2		5	1	1
1969	11	3		5	2		6	1	
1970	9	4	1	3	3	1	6	1	
1971	8	5	1	4	2	1	4	3	
1972	6	7	1	4	3		2	4	1
1973	12	2		7	0		5	2	
1974	10	4		6	1		4	3	
1975	12	2		6	1		6	1	
1976	10	3	1	5	2		5	1	1
1977	10	4		7	0		3	4	
1978	12	4		6	2		6	2	
1979	9	7		4	4		5	3	
1980	11	5		6	2		5	3	
1981	6	10		4	4		2	6	
1982	2	7		1	4		1	3	
1983	9	7		5	3		4	4	
1984	10	6		5	3		5	3	
1985	11	5		6	2		5	3	
1986	10	6		6	2		4	4	
1987	6	9		3	4		3	5	
1988	10	6		4	4		6	2	
1989	11	5		6	2		5	3	
1990	5	11		2	6		3	5	
1991	3	13		2	6		1	7	
1992	6	10		4	4		2	6	
1993	5	11		3	5		2	6	
1994	4	12		3	5		1	7	
1995	7	9		4	4		3	5	
1996	6	10		4	4		2	6	
1997	5	11		2	6		3	5	
1998	4	12		2	6		2	6	
1999	13	3		8	0		5	3	
2000	10	6		5	3		5	3	
	443	400	20	244	172	10	199	228	10

includes Cleveland Rams (1937-1942, 1944-45) and Los Angeles Rams (1946-1994).

SAN FRANCISCO 49ERS

Season	All Games W	L	T	Home Games W	L	T	Road Games W	L	T
1950	3	9		3	3		0	6	
1951	7	4	1	5	1		2	3	1
1952	7	5		3	3		4	2	
1953	9	3		5	1		4	2	
1954	7	4	1	4	2		3	2	1
1955	4	8		2	4		2	4	
1956	5	6	1	3	3		2	3	1
1957	8	4		5	1		3	3	
1958	6	6		4	2		2	4	
1959	7	5		4	2		3	3	
1960	7	5		3	3		4	2	
1961	7	6	1	5	1	1	2	5	
1962	6	8		1	6		5	2	
1963	2	12		2	5		0	7	
1964	4	10		3	4		1	6	
1965	7	6	1	4	2	1	3	4	
1966	6	6	2	4	2	1	2	4	1
1967	7	7		3	4		4	3	
1968	7	6	1	3	3	1	4	3	
1969	4	8	2	3	3	1	1	5	1
1970	10	3	1	5	1	1	5	2	
1971	9	5		4	3		5	2	
1972	8	5	1	4	2	1	4	3	
1973	5	9		3	4		2	5	
1974	6	8		3	4		3	4	
1975	5	9		2	5		3	4	
1976	8	6		4	3		4	3	
1977	5	9		3	4		2	5	
1978	2	14		2	6		0	8	
1979	2	14		2	6		0	8	
1980	6	10		4	4		2	6	
1981	13	3		7	1		6	2	
1982	3	6		0	5		3	1	
1983	10	6		4	4		6	2	

Season	All Games W	L	T	Home Games W	L	T	Road Games W	L	T
1984	15	1		7	1		8	0	
1985	10	6		5	3		5	3	
1986	10	5	1	6	2		4	3	1
1987	13	2		6	1		7	1	
1988	10	6		4	4		6	2	
1989	14	2		6	2		8	0	
1990	14	2		6	2		8	0	
1991	10	6		7	1		3	5	
1992	14	2		7	1		7	1	
1993	10	6		6	2		4	4	
1994	13	3		7	1		6	2	
1995	11	5		6	2		5	3	
1996	12	4		6	2		6	2	
1997	13	3		8	0		5	3	
1998	12	4		8	0		4	4	
1999	4	12		3	5		1	7	
2000	6	10		4	4		2	6	
	403	314	13	218	140	7	185	174	6

TAMPA BAY BUCCANEERS

Season	All Games W	L	T	Home Games W	L	T	Road Games W	L	T
1976	0	14		0	7		0	7	
1977	2	12		1	6		1	6	
1978	5	11		3	5		2	6	
1979	10	6		5	3		5	3	
1980	5	10	1	2	5	1	3	5	
1981	9	7		6	2		3	5	
1982	5	4		4	1		1	3	
1983	2	14		1	7		1	7	
1984	6	10		6	2		0	8	
1985	2	14		2	6		0	8	
1986	2	14		1	7		1	7	
1987	4	11		2	5		2	6	
1988	5	11		3	5		2	6	
1989	5	11		2	6		3	5	
1990	6	10		4	4		2	6	
1991	3	13		3	5		0	8	
1992	5	11		3	5		2	6	
1993	5	11		3	5		2	6	
1994	6	10		4	4		2	6	
1995	7	9		5	3		2	6	
1996	6	10		5	3		1	7	
1997	10	6		5	3		5	3	
1998	8	8		6	2		2	6	
1999	11	5		7	1		4	4	
2000	10	6		6	2		4	4	
	139	248	1	89	104	1	50	144	

WASHINGTON REDSKINS*

Season	All Games W	L	T	Home Games W	L	T	Road Games W	L	T
1932	4	4	2	2	3	1	2	1	1
1933	5	5	2	4	2		1	3	2
1934	6	6		4	3		2	3	
1935	2	8	1	2	5		0	3	1
1936	7	5		4	3		3	2	
1937	8	3		4	2		4	1	
1938	6	3	2	3	1	1	3	2	1
1939	8	2	1	5	0	1	3	2	
1940	9	2		6	0		3	2	
1941	6	5		4	2		2	3	
1942	10	1		5	1		5	0	
1943	6	3	1	4	2		2	1	1
1944	6	3	1	4	2		2	1	1
1945	8	2		6	0		2	2	
1946	5	5	1	3	2	1	2	3	
1947	4	8		4	2		0	6	
1948	7	5		4	2		3	3	
1949	4	7	1	3	3		1	4	1
1950	3	9		1	5		2	4	
1951	5	7		2	4		3	3	
1952	4	8		1	5		3	3	
1953	6	5	1	3	3		3	2	1
1954	3	9		3	3		0	6	
1955	8	4		3	3		5	1	
1956	6	6		4	2		2	4	
1957	5	6	1	2	3	1	3	3	
1958	4	7	1	3	2	1	1	5	
1959	3	9		2	4		1	5	
1960	1	9	2	1	4	1	0	5	1
1961	1	12	1	1	6		0	6	1
1962	5	7	2	3	4		2	3	2
1963	3	11		1	6		2	5	
1964	6	8		4	3		2	5	
1965	6	8		3	4		3	4	
1966	7	7		4	3		3	4	
1967	5	6	3	2	4	1	3	2	2
1968	5	9		3	4		2	5	
1969	7	5	2	4	2	1	3	3	1
1970	6	8		4	3		2	5	
1971	9	4	1	4	2	1	5	2	
1972	11	3		6	1		5	2	
1973	10	4		7	0		3	4	
1974	10	4		6	1		4	3	
1975	8	6		5	2		3	4	
1976	10	4		5	2		5	2	
1977	9	5		5	2		4	3	
1978	8	8		5	3		3	5	
1979	10	6		6	2		4	4	
1980	6	10		4	4		2	6	
1981	8	8		5	3		3	5	
1982	8	1		3	1		5	0	
1983	14	2		7	1		7	1	
1984	11	5		7	1		4	4	
1985	10	6		5	3		5	3	
1986	12	4		7	1		5	3	
1987	11	4		6	1		5	3	
1988	7	9		4	4		3	5	
1989	10	6		4	4		6	2	
1990	10	6		7	1		3	5	
1991	14	2		7	1		7	1	
1992	9	7		6	2		3	5	
1993	4	12		3	5		1	7	
1994	3	13		0	8		3	5	
1995	6	10		4	4		2	6	
1996	9	7		5	3		4	4	
1997	8	7	1	5	2	1	3	5	
1998	6	10		4	4		2	6	
1999	10	6		6	2		4	4	
2000	8	8		4	4		4	4	
	479	424	27	277	186	11	202	238	16

**includes Boston Braves (1932) and Boston Redskins (1933-36).*

History

PRO FOOTBALL HALL OF FAME

The Professional Football Hall of Fame is located in Canton, Ohio, site of the organizational meeting on September 17, 1920, from which the National Football League evolved. The NFL recognized Canton as the Hall of Fame site on April 27, 1961. Canton area individuals, foundations, and companies donated almost $400,000 in cash and services to provide funds for the construction of the original two-building complex, which was dedicated on September 7, 1963. Since that time, the Hall added three buildings with major expansion projects in 1971, 1978, and 1995. The Hall's largest-ever expansion, a $9.2 million project, was completed in early fall 1995. With the new fifth building, the Hall's size is now 82,307-square feet, more than four times its original size.

The expanded Hall represents the sport of pro football in many ways—through (1) GameDay Stadium, a dynamic two-part turntable theater featuring NFL action in Cinemascope for the first time, (2) a standard theater showing NFL films hourly, (3) six large exhibition areas where the history of pro football is detailed in memento, picture, and story form, (4) an extensive archive and information center, and (5) a new and enlarged museum store.

In recent years, the Pro Football Hall of Fame has become an extremely popular tourist attraction. At the end of 2000, a total of 6,889,469 fans had visited the Hall of Fame.

New members of the Pro Football Hall of Fame are elected annually by a 38-member National Board of Selectors, made up of media representatives from every league city, six at-large representatives, and a representative of the Pro Football Writers of America. Between four and seven new members are elected each year. An affirmative vote of approximately 80 percent is needed for election.

Any fan may nominate any eligible player or contributor simply by writing to the Pro Football Hall of Fame. Players must be retired five years to be eligible, while a coach need only to be retired with no time limit specified. Contributors (administrators, owners, *et al.*) may be elected while they are still active.

The charter class of 17 enshrinees was elected in 1963 and the honor roll now stands at 211 with the election of a seven-man class in 2001. That class consists of Nick Buoniconti, Marv Levy, Mike Munchak, Jackie Slater, Lynn Swann, Ron Yary, and Jack Youngblood.

ROSTER OF MEMBERS

HERB ADDERLEY
Cornerback. 6-0, 205. Born in Philadelphia, Pennsylvania, June 8, 1939. Michigan State. Inducted in 1980. 1961-69 Green Bay Packers, 1970-72 Dallas Cowboys. **Highlights:** 48 interceptions, 7 touchdowns. Played in four Super Bowls, five Pro Bowls.

LANCE ALWORTH
Wide receiver. 6-0, 184. Born in Houston, Texas, August 3, 1940. Arkansas. Inducted in 1978. 1962-1970 San Diego Chargers, 1971-72 Dallas Cowboys. **Highlights:** 542 receptions for 10,266 yards, 85 touchdowns. All-AFL seven times, seven All-Star games.

DOUG ATKINS
Defensive end. 6-8, 275. Born in Humboldt, Tennessee, May 8, 1930. Tennessee. Inducted in 1982. 1953-54 Cleveland Browns, 1955-1966 Chicago Bears, 1967-69 New Orleans Saints. **Highlights:** Eight Pro Bowls, All-NFL four times. Played for 17 years, 205 games.

MORRIS (RED) BADGRO
End. 6-0, 190. Born in Orillia, Washington, December 1, 1902. Died July 13, 1998. Southern California. Inducted in 1981. 1927 New York Yankees, 1930-35 New York Giants, 1936 Brooklyn Dodgers. **Highlights:** All-NFL four times. Scored first touchdown in NFL Championship Game series.

LEM BARNEY
Cornerback. 6-0, 190. Born in Gulfport, Mississippi, September 8, 1945. Jackson State. Inducted in 1992. 1967-1977 Detroit Lions. **Highlights:** 56 interceptions for 1,077 yards, 11 touchdowns (7 defensive, 4 special teams). Seven Pro Bowls, All-NFL/NFC four times.

CLIFF BATTLES
Halfback. 6-1, 195. Born in Akron, Ohio, May 1, 1910. Died April 28, 1981. West Virginia Wesleyan. Inducted in 1968. 1932 Boston Braves, 1933-36 Boston Redskins, 1937 Washington Redskins. **Highlights:** NFL rushing champion 1932, 1937. First to gain more than 200 yards in a game, 1933.

SAMMY BAUGH
Quarterback. 6-2, 180. Born in Temple, Texas, March 17, 1914. Texas Christian. Inducted in 1963. 1937-1952 Washington Redskins. **Highlights:** Charter enshrinee. Six-time NFL passing leader. NFL passing, punting, interception champ, 1943.

CHUCK BEDNARIK
Center-linebacker. 6-3, 230. Born in Bethlehem, Pennsylvania, May 1, 1925. Pennsylvania. Inducted in 1967. 1949-1962 Philadelphia Eagles. **Highlights:** Eight Pro Bowls. Missed three games in 14 years. Named NFL all-time center, 1969.

BERT BELL
Team owner. Commissioner. Born in Philadelphia, Pennsylvania, February 25, 1895. Died October 11, 1959. Pennsylvania. Inducted in 1963. 1933-1940 Philadelphia Eagles, 1941-42 Pittsburgh Steelers, 1943 Phil-Pitt, 1944 Card-Pitt, 1945-46 Pittsburgh Steelers. Commissioner, 1946-1959. **Highlights:** Charter enshrinee. Built NFL image as commissioner, 1946-1959. Set up long-term television policies.

BOBBY BELL
Linebacker. 6-4, 225. Born in Shelby, North Carolina, June 17, 1940. Minnesota. Inducted in 1983. 1963-1974 Kansas City Chiefs. **Highlights:** 26 interceptions. All-AFL/AFC eight times. Nine career touchdowns, 1 on onside kick return.

RAYMOND BERRY
End. 6-2, 187. Born in Corpus Christi, Texas, February 27, 1933. Southern Methodist. Inducted in 1973. 1955-1967 Baltimore Colts. **Highlights:** 631 receptions for 9,275 yards, 68 touchdowns. Set NFL title game mark with 12 catches for 178 yards, 1958.

CHARLES W. BIDWILL, SR.
Team owner. Born in Chicago, Illinois, September 16, 1895. Died April 19, 1947. Loyola of Chicago. Inducted in 1967. 1933-1943 Chicago Cardinals, 1944 Card-Pitt, 1945-47 Chicago Cardinals. **Highlights:** Guiding light for NFL during depression years. Built famous "Dream Backfield."

FRED BILETNIKOFF
Wide receiver. 6-1, 190. Born in Erie, Pennsylvania, February 23, 1943. Florida State. Inducted in 1988. 1965-1978 Oakland Raiders. **Highlights:** 589 receptions for 8,974 yards, 76 touchdowns. 40 catches 10 straight years. MVP, Super Bowl XI.

GEORGE BLANDA
Quarterback-kicker. 6-2, 215. Born in Youngwood, Pennsylvania, September 17, 1927. Kentucky. Inducted in 1981. 1949-1958 Chicago Bears, 1950 Baltimore Colts, 1960-66 Houston Oilers, 1967-1975 Oakland Raiders. **Highlights:** 2,002 career points. 26-season, 340-game career longest in NFL history.

MEL BLOUNT
Cornerback. 6-3, 205. Born in Vidalia, Georgia, April 10, 1948. Southern University. Inducted in 1989. 1970-1983 Pittsburgh Steelers. **Highlights:** 57 interceptions for 736 yards. NFL defensive MVP, 1975. Played in five Pro Bowls.

TERRY BRADSHAW
Quarterback. 6-3, 210. Born in Shreveport, Louisiana, September 2, 1948. Louisiana Tech. Inducted in 1989. 1970-1983 Pittsburgh Steelers. **Highlights:** 27,989 yards passing, 212 touchdowns. MVP in Super Bowls XIII, XIV.

JIM BROWN
Fullback. 6-2, 228. Born in St. Simons, Georgia, February 17, 1936. Syracuse. Inducted in 1971. 1957-1965 Cleveland Browns. **Highlights:** 12,312 yards rushing, 756 points. Led NFL rushers eight years. Nine consecutive Pro Bowls.

PAUL BROWN
Coach. Born in Norwalk, Ohio, September 7, 1908. Died August 5, 1991. Miami (Ohio). Inducted in 1967. 1946-49 Cleveland Browns (AAFC), 1950-1962 Cleveland Browns. **Highlights:** Built Cleveland dynasty with 167-53-8 record, four AAFC titles, three NFL crowns. Returned to coaching with Cincinnati Bengals after induction, 1968-1975.

ROOSEVELT BROWN
Tackle. 6-3, 255. Born in Charlottesville, Virginia, October 20, 1932. Morgan State. Inducted in 1975. 1953-1965 New York Giants. **Highlights:** All-NFL eight consecutive years, nine Pro Bowls. NFL's lineman of year, 1956.

WILLIE BROWN
Cornerback. 6-1, 210. Born in Yazoo City, Mississippi, December 2, 1940. Grambling. Inducted in 1984. 1963-66 Denver Broncos, 1967-1978 Oakland Raiders. **Highlights:** 54 interceptions for 472 yards. Scored on 75-yard interception in Super Bowl XI.

BUCK BUCHANAN
Defensive tackle. 6-7, 274. Born in Gainesville, Alabama, September 10, 1940. Died July 16, 1992. Grambling. Inducted in 1990. 1963-1975 Kansas City Chiefs. **Highlights:** Led Chiefs defensive efforts in Super Bowl I, IV. Did not miss a game in 13 years.

NICK BUONICONTI
Linebacker. 5-11, 220. Born in Springfield, Massachusetts, December 15, 1940. Notre Dame. Inducted in 2001. 1962-68 Boston Patriots, 1969-1974, 1976 Miami Dolphins. **Highlights:** All-AFL/AFC eight times. Named to AFL's All-Time Team.

DICK BUTKUS
Linebacker. 6-3, 245. Born in Chicago, Illinois, December 9, 1942. Illinois. Inducted in 1979. 1965-1973 Chicago Bears. **Highlights:** All-NFL six years, eight consecutive Pro Bowls. 25 fumble recoveries.

EARL CAMPBELL
Running back. 5-11, 233. Born in Tyler, Texas, March 29, 1955. Texas. Inducted in 1991. 1978-1984 Houston Oilers, 1984-85 New Orleans Saints. **Highlights:** 9,407 yards rushing, 74 touchdowns. 1,934 yards rushing in 1980, including four games with at least 200 yards.

TONY CANADEO
Halfback. 5-11, 195. Born in Chicago, Illinois, May 5, 1919. Gonzaga. Inducted in 1974. 1941-44, 1946-1952 Green Bay Packers. **Highlights:** Two-way player. Third player to rush for 1,000 yards in single season, 1949.

JOE CARR
NFL president. Born in Columbus, Ohio, October 22, 1880. Died May 20, 1939. Did not attend college. Inducted in 1963. President, 1921-1939 National Football League. **Highlights:** Charter enshrinee. NFL co-organizer, 1920. Introduced standard player's contract.

GUY CHAMBERLIN
End. Coach. 6-2, 196. Born in Blue Springs, Nebraska, January 16, 1894. Died April 4, 1967. Nebraska. Inducted in 1965. 1919 Canton Bulldogs, 1920 Decatur Staleys, 1921 Chicago Staleys, player-coach 1922-23 Canton Bulldogs, 1924 Cleveland Bulldogs, 1925-26 Frankford Yellow Jackets, 1927-28 Chicago Cardinals. **Highlights:** Player-coach of four NFL championship teams. Six-year coaching record of 58-16-7.

JACK CHRISTIANSEN
Safety. 6-1, 185. Born in Sublette, Kansas, December 20, 1928. Died June 29, 1986. Colorado State. Inducted in 1970. 1951-58 Detroit Lions. **Highlights:** 46 interceptions. NFL interception leader, 1953, 1957. Eight punt returns for touchdowns.

EARL (DUTCH) CLARK
Quarterback. 6-0, 185. Born in Fowler, Colorado, October 11, 1906. Died August 5, 1978. Colorado College. Inducted in 1963. 1931-32 Portsmouth Spartans, 1934-38 Detroit Lions. **Highlights:** Charter enshrinee. NFL scoring champion three years. Led Lions to 1935 NFL title.

GEORGE CONNOR
Tackle-linebacker. 6-3, 240. Born in Chicago, Illinois, January 21, 1925. Holy Cross, Notre Dame. Inducted in 1975. 1948-1955 Chicago Bears. **Highlights:** All-NFL at three positions—T, DT, LB. All-NFL five years. Played in first four Pro Bowls.

JIMMY CONZELMAN
Quarterback. Coach. Team owner. 6-0, 180. Born in St. Louis, Missouri, March 6, 1898. Died July 31, 1970. Washington of St. Louis. Inducted in 1964. 1920 Decatur Staleys, 1921-22 Rock Island Independents, 1923-24 Milwaukee Badgers; owner-coach 1925-26 Detroit Panthers; player-coach 1927-29, coach 1930 Providence Steam Roller; coach 1940-42, 1946-48 Chicago Cardinals. **Highlights:** Player-coach of four NFL teams in 1920's. Coached Cardinals to 1947 NFL crown.

LOU CREEKMUR
Tackle-guard. 6-4, 255. Born in Hopelawn, New Jersey. January 22, 1927. William & Mary. Inducted in 1996. 1950-59 Detroit Lions. **Highlights:** All-NFL six times, twice at guard and four times at tackle. Selected to eight Pro Bowls and played on three NFL championship teams.

LARRY CSONKA
Running back. 6-3, 235. Born in Stow, Ohio, December 25, 1946. Syracuse. Inducted in 1987. 1968-1974, 1979 Miami Dolphins, 1976-78 New York Giants. **Highlights:** 8,081 yards rushing, 68 touchdowns. MVP Super Bowl VIII. Only 21 fumbles in 1,891 carries and 106 receptions.

AL DAVIS
Team, League Administrator. Born in Brockton, Massachusetts, July 4, 1929. Wittenberg, Syracuse. Inducted in 1992. 1963-1981, 1995-present Oakland Raiders, 1982-1994 Los Angeles Raiders, 1966 American Football League. **Highlights:** Only person to serve in pros as personnel assistant, scout, assistant coach, head coach, general manager, commissioner, team owner/CEO.

WILLIE DAVIS
Defensive end. 6-3, 245. Born in Lisbon, Louisiana, July 24, 1934. Grambling. Inducted in 1981. 1958-59 Cleveland Browns, 1960-69 Green Bay Packers. **Highlights:** All-NFL five seasons, five Pro Bowls. Did not miss game in 12-year career.

LEN DAWSON
Quarterback. 6-0, 190. Born in Alliance, Ohio, June 20, 1935. Purdue. Inducted in 1987. 1957-59 Pittsburgh Steelers, 1960-61 Cleveland Browns, 1962 Dallas Texans, 1963-1975 Kansas City Chiefs. **Highlights:** 28,711 yards passing, 239 touchdowns. Four AFL passing crowns. MVP, Super Bowl IV.

ERIC DICKERSON
Running back. 6-3, 220. Born in Sealy, Texas, September 2, 1960. Southern Methodist. Inducted in 1999. 1983-87 Los Angeles Rams, 1987-1991 Indianapolis Colts, 1992 Los Angeles Raiders, 1993 Atlanta Falcons. **Highlights:** Rushed for 13,259 career yards, including an NFL record 2,105 yards in 1984. All-Pro five times, six Pro Bowls.

DAN DIERDORF
Tackle. 6-3, 290. Born in Canton, Ohio, June 29, 1949. Michigan. Inducted in 1996. 1971-1983 St. Louis Cardinals. **Highlights:** All-Pro five times, played in six Pro Bowls, named NFL's best blocker three times.

MIKE DITKA
Tight end. 6-3, 225. Born in Carnegie, Pennsylvania, October 18, 1939. Pittsburgh. Inducted in 1988. 1961-66 Chicago Bears, 1967-68 Philadelphia Eagles, 1969-1972 Dallas Cowboys. **Highlights:** 427 receptions for 5,812 yards, 43 touchdowns. First tight end selected to Hall of Fame. Five consecutive Pro Bowls.

ART DONOVAN
Defensive tackle. 6-3, 265. Born in Bronx, New York, June 5, 1925. Boston College. Inducted in 1968. 1950 Baltimore Colts, 1951 New York Yanks, 1952 Dallas Texans, 1953-1961 Baltimore Colts. **Highlights:** Five Pro Bowls. Vital part of Baltimore's climb to powerhouse status in 1950s.

TONY DORSETT
Running back. 5-11, 184. Born in Rochester, Pennsylvania, April 7, 1954. Pittsburgh. Inducted in 1994. 1977-1987 Dallas Cowboys, 1988 Denver Broncos. **Highlights:** 12,739 yards rushing, 398 receptions, 91 touchdowns. Ran record 99 yards for touchdown vs. Minnesota, January, 1983.

JOHN (PADDY) DRISCOLL
Quarterback. 5-11, 160. Born in Evanston, Illinois, January 11, 1896. Died June 29, 1968. Northwestern. Inducted in 1965. 1919 Hammond Pros, 1920 Decatur Staleys, 1920-25 Chicago Cardinals, 1926-29 Chicago Bears. **Highlights:** All-NFL seven times. Dropkicked record 4 field goals in one game, 1925.

BILL DUDLEY
Halfback. 5-10, 182. Born in Bluefield, Virginia, December 24, 1921. Virginia. Inducted in 1966. 1942, 1945-46 Pittsburgh Steelers, 1947-49 Detroit Lions, 1950-51, 1953 Washington Redskins. **Highlights:** Won NFL rushing, interception, punt return titles, 1946. All-NFL 1942, 1946, and 1947.

ALBERT GLEN (TURK) EDWARDS
Tackle. 6-2, 260. Born in Mold, Washington, September 28, 1907. Died January 12, 1973. Washington State. Inducted in 1969. 1932 Boston Braves, 1933-36 Boston Redskins, 1937-1940 Washington Redskins. **Highlights:** All-NFL 1932-34, 1936, 1937. Steamrolling blocker, smothering tackler.

WEEB EWBANK
Coach. Born in Richmond, Indiana, May 6, 1907. Died November 17, 1998. Miami (Ohio). Inducted in 1978. 1954-1962 Baltimore Colts, 1963-1973 New York Jets. **Highlights:** Only coach to win championships in both NFL, AFL. Led both Colts (1958) and Jets (1968) to championships.

TOM FEARS
End. 6-2, 215. Born in Guadalajara, Mexico, December 3, 1923. Died January 4, 2000. Santa Clara, UCLA. Inducted in 1970. 1948-1956 Los Angeles Rams. **Highlights:** 400 receptions for 5,397 yards, 38 touchdowns. Led NFL receivers first three seasons. Had then-record 18 receptions in single game.

JIM FINKS
Administrator. Born in St. Louis, Missouri, August 31, 1927. Died May 8, 1994. Tulsa. Inducted 1995. 1964-1973 Minnesota Vikings, 1974-1982 Chicago Bears, 1986-1993 New Orleans Saints. **Highlights:** Developed Vikings, Bears, Saints—all teams with losing records—into winners.

RAY FLAHERTY
Coach. Born in Spokane, Washington, September 1, 1903. Died July 19, 1994. Gonzaga. Inducted in 1976. 1936 Boston Redskins, 1937-1942 Washington Redskins, 1946-48 New York Yankees (AAFC), 1949 Chicago Hornets (AAFC). **Highlights:** 82-41-5 coaching record. Introduced screen pass in 1937 title game and platoon system.

LEN FORD
Defensive end. 6-4, 260. Born in Washington, D.C., February 18, 1926. Died March 14, 1972. Morgan State, Michigan. Inducted in 1976. 1948-49 Los Angeles Dons (AAFC), 1950-57 Cleveland Browns, 1958 Green Bay Packers. **Highlights:** All-NFL five times, four Pro Bowls. Recovered 20 opponents' fumbles.

DAN FORTMANN
Guard. 6-0, 210. Born in Pearl River, New York, April 11, 1916. Died May 23, 1995. Colgate. Inducted in 1965. 1936-1943 Chicago Bears. **Highlights:** At 20, became youngest starter in NFL. All-NFL six consecutive years.

DAN FOUTS
Quarterback. 6-3, 210. Born in San Francisco, California, June 10, 1951. Oregon. Inducted in 1993. 1973-1987 San Diego Chargers. **Highlights:** 43,040 passing yards, 254 touchdowns. Six Pro Bowls, NFL MVP, 1982.

FRANK GATSKI
Center. 6-3, 240. Born in Farmington, West Virginia, March 18, 1922. Marshall, Auburn. Inducted in 1985. 1946-49 Cleveland Browns (AAFC), 1950-56 Cleveland Browns, 1957 Detroit Lions. **Highlights:** Never missed game in high school, college, or pro football. Played 11 championship games, winning eight.

BILL GEORGE
Linebacker. 6-2, 230. Born in Waynesburg, Pennsylvania, October 27, 1930. Died September 30, 1982. Wake Forest. Inducted in 1974. 1952-1965 Chicago Bears, 1966 Los Angeles Rams. **Highlights:** All-NFL eight years, eight consecutive Pro Bowls. 14 years of service, longest of any Bears player.

JOE GIBBS
Coach. Born in Mocksville, North Carolina, November 25, 1940. Cerritos (Calif.) J.C., San Diego State. Inducted in 1996. 1981-1992 Washington Redskins. **Highlights:** 124-60-0 record in regular season, 16-5 in postseason, including four Super Bowl appearances—winning three. Won 10 or more games eight times.

FRANK GIFFORD
Halfback. 6-1, 195. Born in Santa Monica, California, August 16, 1930. Southern California. Inducted in 1977. 1952-1960, 1962-64 New York Giants. **Highlights:** Starred on both offense and defense. Seven Pro Bowls, 1956 NFL player of the year.

SID GILLMAN
Coach. Born in Minneapolis, Minnesota, October 26, 1911. Ohio State. Inducted in 1983. 1955-59 Los Angeles Rams, 1960 Los Angeles Chargers, 1961-69, 1971 San Diego Chargers, 1973-74 Houston Oilers. **Highlights:** 123-104-7 coaching record. First to win division titles in both NFL, AFL.

PRO FOOTBALL HALL OF FAME

OTTO GRAHAM
Quarterback. 6-1, 195. Born in Waukegan, Illinois, December 6, 1921. Northwestern. Inducted in 1965. 1946-49 Cleveland Browns (AAFC), 1950-55 Cleveland Browns. **Highlights:** 23,584 passing yards, 174 touchdowns. Guided Browns to 10 division or league crowns in 10 years.

HAROLD (RED) GRANGE
Halfback. 6-0, 185. Born in Forksville, Pennsylvania, June 13, 1903. Died January 28, 1991. Illinois. Inducted in 1963. 1925 Chicago Bears, 1926 New York Yankees (AFL), 1927 New York Yankees, 1929-1934 Chicago Bears. **Highlights:** Nicknamed "Galloping Ghost." Name produced first huge pro football crowds.

BUD GRANT
Coach. Born in Superior, Wisconsin, May 20, 1927. Minnesota. Inducted in 1994. 1967-1983, 1985 Minnesota Vikings. **Highlights:** 168-108-5 coaching record. Led Vikings to 11 division championships, four Super Bowls.

JOE GREENE
Defensive tackle. 6-4, 260. Born in Temple, Texas, September 24, 1946. North Texas State. Inducted in 1987. 1969-1981 Pittsburgh Steelers. **Highlights:** NFL defensive player of the year, 1972, 1974. Four-time Super Bowl champion, 10 Pro Bowls.

FORREST GREGG
Tackle. 6-4, 250. Born in Birthright, Texas, October 18, 1933. Southern Methodist. Inducted in 1977. 1956, 1958-1970 Green Bay Packers, 1971 Dallas Cowboys. **Highlights:** Played 188 consecutive games. Nine Pro Bowls. Played on six NFL championship teams, three Super Bowl winners.

BOB GRIESE
Quarterback. 6-1, 190. Born in Evansville, Indiana, February 3, 1945. Purdue. Inducted in 1990. 1967-1980 Miami Dolphins. **Highlights:** 25,092 passing yards, 192 touchdowns. Led Miami to three AFC titles, Super Bowl VII, VIII wins.

LOU GROZA
Tackle-kicker. 6-3, 250. Born in Martins Ferry, Ohio, January 25, 1924. Died November 29, 2000. Ohio State. Inducted in 1974. 1946-49 Cleveland Browns (AAFC), 1950-59, 1961-67 Cleveland Browns. **Highlights:** 1,608 points in 21 years. Nine Pro Bowls, All-NFL six years. NFL player of the year, 1954.

JOE GUYON
Halfback. 6-1, 180. Born on White Earth Indian Reservation, Minnesota, November 26, 1892. Died November 27, 1971. Carlisle, Georgia Tech. Inducted in 1966. 1919-1920 Canton Bulldogs, 1921 Cleveland Indians, 1922-23 Oorang Indians, 1924 Rock Island Independents, 1924-25 Kansas City Cowboys, 1927 New York Giants. **Highlights:** Touchdown pass gave Giants victory over Bears to win 1927 championship.

GEORGE HALAS
End. Coach. Team owner. Born in Chicago, Illinois, February 2, 1895. Died October 31, 1983. Illinois. Inducted in 1963. Player-coach 1920 Decatur Staleys, 1921 Chicago Staleys, 1922-29 Chicago Bears; coach 1933-1942, 1946-1955, 1958-1967 Chicago Bears. **Highlights:** Charter enshrinee. 324 coaching wins. Only person associated with NFL throughout first 50 years. Coached Bears 40 seasons, won six NFL titles.

JACK HAM
Linebacker. 6-1, 225. Born in Johnstown, Pennsylvania, December 23, 1948. Penn State. Inducted in 1988. 1971-1982 Pittsburgh Steelers. **Highlights:** Won four Super Bowls, 21 opponents' fumbles recovered, 32 interceptions. Eight consecutive Pro Bowls.

JOHN HANNAH
Guard. 6-3, 265. Born in Canton, Georgia, April 4, 1951. Alabama. Inducted in 1991. 1973-1985 New England Patriots. **Highlights:** Renowned as premier guard of era. All-Pro 10 years, nine Pro Bowls.

FRANCO HARRIS
Running back. 6-2, 225. Born in Fort Dix, New Jersey, March 7, 1950. Penn State. Inducted in 1990. 1972-1983 Pittsburgh Steelers, 1984 Seattle Seahawks. **Highlights:** 12,120 rushing yards, 100 total touchdowns. 1,556 rushing yards in 19 postseason games. MVP in Super Bowl IX.

MIKE HAYNES
Cornerback. 6-2, 195. Born in Denison, Texas, July 1, 1953. Arizona State. Inducted in 1997. 1976-1982 New England Patriots, 1983-89 Los Angeles Raiders. **Highlights:** Defensive rookie of the year. Selected to nine Pro Bowls and intercepted 46 passes, plus one pick in Super Bowl XVIII.

ED HEALEY
Tackle. 6-3, 220. Born in Indian Orchard, Massachusetts, December 28, 1894. Died December 9, 1978. Dartmouth. Inducted in 1964. 1920-22 Rock Island Independents, 1922-27 Chicago Bears. **Highlights:** Two-way star. Perennial all-pro with Bears.

MEL HEIN
Center. 6-2, 225. Born in Redding, California, August 22, 1909. Died January 31, 1992. Washington State. Inducted in 1963. 1931-1945 New York Giants. **Highlights:** Charter enshrinee. 60-minute regular for 15 years. All-NFL eight consecutive years.

TED HENDRICKS
Linebacker. 6-7, 235. Born in Guatemala City, Guatemala, November 1, 1947. Miami. Inducted in 1990. 1969-1973 Baltimore Colts, 1974 Green Bay Packers, 1975-1981 Oakland Raiders, 1982-83 Los Angeles Raiders. **Highlights:** 25 blocked field goals, extra points, and punts, 26 interceptions. Played in 215 consecutive games.

WILBUR (PETE) HENRY
Tackle. 6-0, 250. Born in Mansfield, Ohio, October 31, 1897. Died February 7, 1952. Washington & Jefferson. Inducted in 1963. 1920-23, 1925-26 Canton Bulldogs, 1927 New York Giants, 1927-28 Pottsville Maroons. **Highlights:** Largest player of his time at 250 pounds. Bulwark of Canton's championship lines.

ARNIE HERBER
Quarterback. 6-0, 200. Born in Green Bay, Wisconsin, April 2, 1910. Died October 14, 1969. Wisconsin, Regis College. Inducted in 1966. 1930-1940 Green Bay Packers, 1944-45 New York Giants. **Highlights:** NFL passing leader 1932, 1934, 1936. Came out of retirement to lead 1944 Giants to NFL Eastern crown.

BILL HEWITT
End. 5-11, 191. Born in Bay City, Michigan, October 8, 1909. Died January 14, 1947. Michigan. Inducted in 1971. 1932-36 Chicago Bears, 1937-39 Philadelphia Eagles, 1943 Phil-Pitt. **Highlights:** First to be named all-NFL with two teams—1933, 1934, 1936 Bears; 1937 Eagles.

CLARKE HINKLE
Fullback. 5-11, 201. Born in Toronto, Ohio, April 10, 1909. Died November 9, 1988. Bucknell. Inducted in 1964. 1932-1941 Green Bay Packers. **Highlights:** 3,860 yards rushing, 379 points. Fullback on offense, linebacker on defense.

ELROY (CRAZYLEGS) HIRSCH
Halfback-end. 6-2, 190. Born in Wausau, Wisconsin, June 17, 1923. Wisconsin, Michigan. Inducted in 1968. 1946-48 Chicago Rockets (AAFC), 1949-1957 Los Angeles Rams. **Highlights:** 387 receptions for 7,029 yards, 60 touchdowns. Key part of Rams' revolutionary "three end" offense, 1949.

PAUL HORNUNG
Halfback. 6-2, 220. Born in Louisville, Kentucky, December 23, 1935. Notre Dame. Inducted in 1986. 1957-1962, 1964-66 Green Bay Packers. **Highlights:** 760 points. Led NFL scorers three years, including record 176 points, 1960. Record 19 points scored in 1961 NFL title game.

KEN HOUSTON
Safety. 6-3, 198. Born in Lufkin, Texas, November 12, 1944. Prairie View A&M. Inducted in 1986. 1967-1972 Houston Oilers, 1973-1980 Washington Redskins. **Highlights:** 49 interceptions, 898 yards, 9 touchdowns. NFL's premier strong safety of 1970s. 12 Pro Bowls.

ROBERT (CAL) HUBBARD
Tackle. 6-5, 250. Born in Keytesville, Missouri, October 31, 1900. Died October 17, 1977. Centenary, Geneva. Inducted in 1963. 1927-28 New York Giants, 1929-1933, 1935 Green Bay Packers, 1936 New York Giants, 1936 Pittsburgh Pirates. **Highlights:** Charter enshrinee. Most feared lineman of his time. All-NFL six years, 1927-29, 1931-33.

SAM HUFF
Linebacker. 6-1, 230. Born in Morgantown, West Virginia, October 4, 1934. West Virginia. Inducted in 1982. 1956-1963 New York Giants, 1964-67, 1969 Washington Redskins. **Highlights:** 30 interceptions. Played in six NFL title games, five Pro Bowls. Redskins player-coach, 1969.

LAMAR HUNT
Team owner. Born in El Dorado, Arkansas, August 2, 1932. Southern Methodist. Inducted in 1972. 1960-62 Dallas Texans, 1963-present Kansas City Chiefs. **Highlights:** Driving force behind organization of AFL. Spearheaded merger negotiations with NFL, 1966.

DON HUTSON
End. 6-1, 180. Born in Pine Bluff, Arkansas, January 31, 1913. Died June 26, 1997. Alabama. Inducted in 1963. 1935-1945 Green Bay Packers. **Highlights:** 488 receptions for 7,991 yards, 99 touchdowns. NFL receiving champion eight years. NFL MVP, 1941, 1942.

JIMMY JOHNSON
Cornerback. 6-2, 187. Born in Dallas, Texas, March 31, 1938. UCLA. Inducted in 1994. 1961-1976 San Francisco 49ers. **Highlights:** 47 interceptions for 615 yards. Five Pro Bowls. Opposing passers avoided throwing in his area.

JOHN HENRY JOHNSON
Fullback. 6-2, 225. Born in Waterproof, Louisiana, November 24, 1929. St. Mary's, Arizona State. Inducted in 1987. 1954-56 San Francisco 49ers, 1957-59 Detroit Lions, 1960-65 Pittsburgh Steelers, 1966 Houston Oilers. **Highlights:** 6,803 yards rushing, 55 total touchdowns. Member of San Francisco's "Million-Dollar" backfield.

CHARLIE JOINER
Wide receiver. 5-11, 180. Born in Many, Louisiana, October 14, 1947. Grambling. Inducted in 1996. 1969-1972 Houston Oilers, 1972-75 Cincinnati Bengals, 1976-1986 San Diego Chargers. **Highlights:** 750 receptions for 12,146 yards and 65 touchdowns. Played 18 seasons, 239 games, most ever for wide receiver.

DAVID (DEACON) JONES
Defensive end. 6-5, 260. Born in Eatonville, Florida, December 9, 1938. South Carolina State, Mississippi Vocational. Inducted in 1980. 1961-1971 Los Angeles Rams, 1972-73 San Diego Chargers, 1974 Washington Redskins. **Highlights:** Specialized in quarterback "sacks," a term he invented. Unanimous all-league five consecutive years.

STAN JONES
Guard-defensive tackle. 6-1, 250. Born in Altoona, Pennsylvania, November 24, 1931. Maryland. Inducted in 1991. 1954-1965 Chicago Bears, 1966 Washington Redskins. **Highlights:** Seven consecutive Pro Bowls. First to rely on weightlifting for football preparation.

HENRY JORDAN
Defensive tackle, 6-3, 240. Born in Emporia, Virginia, January 26, 1935. Died February 21, 1977. Virginia. Inducted in 1995. 1957-58 Cleveland Browns, 1959-1969 Green Bay Packers. **Highlights:** Fixture at DT during Packers' dynasty. Played in four Pro Bowls, seven NFL title games, Super Bowls I, II.

SONNY JURGENSEN
Quarterback. 6-0, 203. Born in Wilmington, North Carolina, August 23, 1934. Duke. Inducted in 1983. 1957-1963 Philadelphia Eagles, 1964-1974 Washington Redskins. **Highlights:** 32,224 yards passing, 255 touchdowns, 82.63 passer rating. Surpassed 3,000 yards passing in five seasons.

LEROY KELLY
Running back. 6-0, 205. Born in Philadelphia, Pennsylvania, May 20, 1942. Morgan State. Inducted in 1994. 1964-1973 Cleveland Browns. **Highlights:** 7,274 yards rushing, 90 total touchdowns, 1,000-yard rusher first three years as starter. Punt return champion, 1965.

WALT KIESLING
Guard. Coach. 6-2, 245. Born in St. Paul, Minnesota, March 27, 1903. Died March 2, 1962. St. Thomas (Minnesota). Inducted in 1966. 1926-27 Duluth Eskimos, 1928 Pottsville Maroons, 1929-1933 Chicago Cardinals, 1934 Chicago Bears, 1935-36 Green Bay Packers, 1937-38 Pittsburgh Pirates; coach, 1939 Pittsburgh Pirates, 1940-42 Pittsburgh Steelers; co-coach, 1943 Phil-Pitt, 1944 Card-Pitt; coach, 1954-56 Pittsburgh Steelers. **Highlights:** 34-year career as pro player, assistant coach, head coach. Led Steelers to first winning season, 1942.

FRANK (BRUISER) KINARD
Tackle. 6-1, 210. Born in Pelahatchie, Mississippi, October 23, 1914. Died September 7, 1985. Mississippi. Inducted in 1971. 1938-1943 Brooklyn Dodgers, 1944 Brooklyn Tigers, 1946-47 New York Yankees (AAFC). **Highlights:** First man to earn both All-NFL, All-AAFC honors. Out because of injury only once.

PAUL KRAUSE
Safety. 6-3, 200. Born in Flint, Michigan, February 19, 1942. Iowa. Inducted in 1998. 1964-67 Washington Redskins, 1968-1979 Minnesota Vikings. **Highlights:** NFL all-time leader with 81 interceptions. Played in eight Pro Bowls. Starting safety in four Super Bowls.

EARL (CURLY) LAMBEAU
Coach. Born in Green Bay, Wisconsin, April 9, 1898. Died June 1, 1965. Notre Dame. Inducted in 1963. 1919-1949 Green Bay Packers, 1950-51 Chicago Cardinals, 1952-53 Washington Redskins. **Highlights:** 229-134-22 coaching record with six NFL championships. Founded pre-NFL Packers, 1919.

JACK LAMBERT
Linebacker. 6-4, 220. Born in Mantua, Ohio, July 8, 1952. Kent State. Inducted in 1990. 1974-1984 Pittsburgh Steelers. **Highlights:** Leader of 'Steel Curtain.' NFL defensive player of year in 1976, nine Pro Bowls.

TOM LANDRY
Coach. Born in Mission, Texas, September 11, 1924. Died February 12, 2000. Texas. Inducted in 1990. 1960-1988 Dallas Cowboys. **Highlights:** 270-178-6 coaching record. 20 consecutive winning seasons. Innovator on offense and defense.

DICK (NIGHT TRAIN) LANE
Cornerback. 6-2, 210. Born in Austin, Texas, April 16, 1928. Scottsbluff Junior College. Inducted in 1974. 1952-53 Los Angeles Rams, 1954-59 Chicago Cardinals, 1960-65 Detroit Lions. **Highlights:** 68 interceptions for 1,207 yards, 5 touchdowns. Record 14 interceptions as rookie. Seven Pro Bowls.

JIM LANGER
Center. 6-2, 255. Born in Little Falls, Minnesota, May 16, 1948. South Dakota State. Inducted in 1987. 1970-79 Miami Dolphins, 1980-81 Minnesota Vikings. **Highlights:** Played every offensive down in Dolphins' perfect 1972 season. Six Pro Bowls.

WILLIE LANIER
Linebacker. 6-1, 245. Born in Clover, Virginia, August 21, 1945. Morgan State. Inducted in 1986. 1967-1977 Kansas City Chiefs. **Highlights:** 27 interceptions. Defensive star in Super Bowl IV upset. Nicknamed 'Contact' for ferocious tackling.

STEVE LARGENT
Wide receiver. 5-11, 191. Born in Tulsa, Oklahoma, September 28, 1954, Tulsa. Inducted in 1995. 1976-1989 Seattle Seahawks. **Highlights:** 819 receptions for 13,089 yards, 100 touchdowns. Receptions in 177 consecutive games.

YALE LARY
Defensive back-punter. 5-11, 189. Born in Fort Worth, Texas, November 24, 1930. Texas A&M. Inducted in 1979. 1952-53, 1956-1964 Detroit Lions. **Highlights:** 50 interceptions. Three NFL punting crowns, three touchdowns on punt returns. Nine Pro Bowls.

DANTE LAVELLI
End. 6-0, 199. Born in Hudson, Ohio, February 23, 1923. Ohio State. Inducted in 1975. 1946-49 Cleveland Browns (AAFC), 1950-56 Cleveland Browns. **Highlights:** 386 receptions for 6,488 yards, 62 touchdowns. 24 catches in six NFL title games.

BOBBY LAYNE
Quarterback. 6-2, 190. Born in Santa Ana, Texas, December 19, 1926. Died December 1, 1986. Texas. Inducted in 1967. 1948 Chicago Bears, 1949 New York Bulldogs, 1950-58 Detroit Lions, 1958-1962 Pittsburgh Steelers. **Highlights:** 26,768 yards passing, 196 touchdowns, 2,451 yards rushing. Late touchdown pass won 1953 NFL title game.

ALPHONSE (TUFFY) LEEMANS
Fullback. 6-0, 200. Born in Superior, Wisconsin, November 12, 1912. Died January 19, 1979. Oregon, George Washington. Inducted in 1978. 1936-1943 New York Giants. **Highlights:** 3,132 yards rushing, 2,318 yards passing, 422 yards receiving. Led NFL rushers as rookie, 1936.

MARV LEVY
Coach. Born in Chicago, Illinois, August 3, 1925. Coe College, Harvard. Inducted in 2001. 1978-1982 Kansas City Chiefs, 1986-1997 Buffalo Bills. **Highlights:** Led Bills to unprecedented four consecutive Super Bowls. Had 154-120 record. Coaching victories ranked 10th when retired.

BOB LILLY
Defensive tackle. 6-5, 260. Born in Olney, Texas, July 26, 1939. Texas Christian. Inducted in 1980. 1961-1974 Dallas Cowboys. **Highlights:** Eleven Pro Bowls. Played 196 consecutive games. Foundation of great Dallas defensive units.

LARRY LITTLE
Guard. 6-1, 265. Born in Groveland, Georgia, November 2, 1945. Bethune-Cookman. Inducted in 1993. 1967-68 San Diego Chargers, 1969-1980 Miami Dolphins. **Highlights:** Five Pro Bowls, started in three Super Bowls. Epitome of powerful Dolphins rushing game of 1970s.

VINCE LOMBARDI
Coach. Born in Brooklyn, New York, June 11, 1913. Died September 3, 1970. Fordham. Inducted in 1971. 1959-1967 Green Bay Packers, 1969 Washington Redskins. **Highlights:** 105-35-6 coaching record in 10 years, including five NFL titles and victories in Super Bowls I and II.

HOWIE LONG
Defensive end. 6-5, 268. Born in Somerville, Massachusetts, January 6, 1960. Villanova. Inducted in 2000. 1981-1993 Oakland/Los Angeles Raiders. **Highlights:** All-Pro 1983, 1984, 1985. Named All-AFC four times, 1983-1986. Eight Pro Bowls.

RONNIE LOTT
Cornerback-safety. 6-0, 203. Born in Albuquerque, New Mexico, May 8, 1959. Southern California. Inducted in 2000. 1981-1990 San Francisco 49ers, 1991-92 Los Angeles Raiders, 1993-94 New York Jets. **Highlights:** Ten Pro Bowls, 63 career interceptions, and was named to the NFL's 75th Anniversary Team.

SID LUCKMAN
Quarterback. 6-0, 195. Born in Brooklyn, New York, November 21, 1916. Died July 5, 1998. Columbia. Inducted in 1965. 1939-1950 Chicago Bears. **Highlights:** 137 touchdown passes. All-NFL five times. League MVP in 1943.

WILLIAM ROY (LINK) LYMAN
Tackle. 6-2, 252. Born in Table Rock, Nebraska, November 30, 1898. Died December 28, 1972. Nebraska. Inducted in 1964. 1922-23, 1925 Canton Bulldogs, 1924 Cleveland Bulldogs, 1925 Frankford Yellow Jackets, 1926-28, 1930-31, 1933-34 Chicago Bears. **Highlights:** Played for four NFL champions. In 16 seasons of college and pro football, played on one losing team.

TOM MACK
Guard. 6-3, 250. Born in Cleveland, Ohio, November 1, 1943. Michigan. Inducted in 1999. 1966-1978 Los Angeles Rams. **Highlights:** Never missed a game in entire 184-game career. Elected to 11 Pro Bowls.

JOHN MACKEY
Tight end. 6-2, 224. Born in New York, New York, September 24, 1941. Syracuse. Inducted in 1992. 1963-1971 Baltimore Colts, 1972 San Diego Chargers. **Highlights:** 331 receptions for 5,236 yards, 38 touchdowns. Second tight end to enter Hall of Fame.

TIM MARA
Team owner. Born in New York, New York, July 29, 1887. Died February 17, 1959. Did not attend college. Inducted in 1963. 1925-1959 New York Giants. **Highlights:** Charter enshrinee. Founder of New York Giants. Built team into powerhouse winning four NFL titles, 10 division titles.

WELLINGTON MARA
Team owner. Born in New York, New York, August 14, 1916. Fordham. Inducted in 1997. 1937-present New York Giants. **Highlights:** Lifetime contributor to NFL and New York Giants. Worked as Giants' ballboy, secretary, vice-president, president and co-CEO. NFC president 1984-present.

GINO MARCHETTI
Defensive end. 6-4, 245. Born in Smithers, West Virginia, January 2, 1927. San Francisco. Inducted in 1972. 1952 Dallas Texans, 1953-1964, 1966 Baltimore Colts. **Highlights:** Named top defensive end of NFL's first 50 years. 10 consecutive Pro Bowls. All-NFL seven times.

GEORGE PRESTON MARSHALL
Team owner. Born in Grafton, West Virginia, October 11, 1896. Died August 9, 1969. Randolph-Macon. Inducted in 1963. 1932 Boston Braves, 1933-36 Boston Redskins, 1937-1969 Washington Redskins. **Highlights:** Charter enshrinee. Sponsored progressive rules changes. Organized first team band, pioneered halftime shows.

PRO FOOTBALL HALL OF FAME

OLLIE MATSON
Halfback. 6-2, 220. Born in Trinity, Texas, May 1, 1930. San Francisco. Inducted in 1972. 1952, 1954-58 Chicago Cardinals, 1959-1962 Los Angeles Rams, 1963 Detroit Lions, 1964-66 Philadelphia Eagles. **Highlights:** Nine touchdowns on kickoff, punt returns. Traded for nine players in 1959.

DON MAYNARD
Wide receiver. 6-1, 185. Born in Crosbyton, Texas, January 25, 1935. Texas Western. Inducted in 1987. 1958 New York Giants, 1960-62 New York Titans, 1963-1972 New York Jets, 1973 St. Louis Cardinals. **Highlights:** 633 receptions for 11,834 yards, 88 touchdowns. At least 50 catches and 1,000 yards in five different seasons.

GEORGE McAFEE
Halfback. 6-0, 177. Born in Corbin, Kentucky, March 13, 1918. Duke. Inducted in 1966. 1940-41, 1945-1950 Chicago Bears. **Highlights:** Two-way star. 25 interceptions, 234 points. Career punt-return average of 12.78 yards per return.

MIKE McCORMACK
Tackle. 6-4, 250. Born in Chicago, Illinois, June 21, 1930. Kansas. Inducted in 1984. 1951 New York Yanks, 1954-1962 Cleveland Browns. **Highlights:** Excelled as offensive right tackle for eight years. Six Pro Bowls.

TOMMY McDONALD
Wide receiver. 5-9, 175. Born in Roy, New Mexico, July 26, 1934. Oklahoma. Inducted in 1998. 1957-1963 Philadelphia Eagles, 1964 Dallas Cowboys, 1965-66 Los Angeles Rams, 1967 Atlanta Falcons, 1968 Cleveland Browns. **Highlights:** Recorded 495 receptions for 8,410 yards, 84 touchdowns.

HUGH McELHENNY
Halfback. 6-1, 198. Born in Los Angeles, California, December 31, 1928. Washington. Inducted in 1970. 1952-1960 San Francisco 49ers, 1961-62 Minnesota Vikings, 1963 New York Giants, 1964 Detroit Lions. **Highlights:** 5,281 rushing yards, 360 points. Totaled 11,369 yards rushing, receiving, and returning kicks.

JOHNNY (BLOOD) McNALLY
Halfback. 6-0, 185. Born in New Richmond, Wisconsin, November 27, 1903. Died November 28, 1985. Notre Dame, St. John's (Minnesota). Inducted in 1963. 1925-26 Milwaukee Badgers, 1926-27 Duluth Eskimos, 1928 Pottsville Maroons, 1929-1933, 1935-36 Green Bay Packers, 1934 Pittsburgh Pirates; player-coach, 1937-38 Pittsburgh Pirates. **Highlights:** 49 touchdowns, 296 points in 14 seasons with five teams.

MIKE MICHALSKE
Guard. 6-0, 209. Born in Cleveland, Ohio, April 24, 1903. Died October 26, 1983. Penn State. Inducted in 1964. 1926 New York Yankees (AFL), 1927-28 New York Yankees, 1929-1935, 1937
Green Bay Packers. **Highlights:** Anchored Packers' championship lines, 1929-1931. First guard enshrined in Canton.

WAYNE MILLNER
End. 6-0, 191. Born in Roxbury, Massachusetts, January 31, 1913. Died November 19, 1976. Notre Dame. Inducted in 1968. 1936 Boston Redskins, 1937-1941, 1945 Washington Redskins. **Highlights:** Redskins' all-time leader with 124 catches when retired. 55- and 78-yard touchdown receptions in 1937 NFL Championship Game.

BOBBY MITCHELL
Running back-wide receiver. 6-0, 195. Born in Hot Springs, Arkansas, June 6, 1935. Illinois. Inducted in 1983. 1958-1961 Cleveland Browns, 1962-68 Washington Redskins. **Highlights:** 91 touchdowns, including 8 on kickoff and punt returns. 14,078 combined yards.

RON MIX
Tackle. 6-4, 255. Born in Los Angeles, California, March 10, 1938. Southern California. Inducted in 1979. 1960 Los Angeles Chargers, 1961-69 San Diego Chargers, 1971 Oakland Raiders. **Highlights:** All-AFL nine times. Only two holding penalties in 10 years with the Chargers.

JOE MONTANA
Quarterback. 6-2, 200. Born in New Eagle, Pennsylvania, June, 11, 1956. Notre Dame. Inducted in 2000. 1979-1992 San Francisco 49ers, 1993-94 Kansas City Chiefs. **Highlights:** MVP in Super Bowl's XVI, XIX, and XXIV. Eight Pro Bowls and All-NFL three times.

LENNY MOORE
Flanker-running back. 6-1, 198. Born in Reading, Pennsylvania, November 25, 1933. Penn State. Inducted in 1975. 1956-1967 Baltimore Colts. **Highlights:** From 1963-65, scored touchdowns in record 18 consecutive games. 113 career touchdowns, 12,451 combined net yards.

MARION MOTLEY
Fullback. 6-1, 238. Born in Leesburg, Georgia, June 5, 1920. Died June 27, 1999. South Carolina State, Nevada. Inducted in 1968. 1946-49 Cleveland Browns (AAFC), 1950-53 Cleveland Browns, 1955 Pittsburgh Steelers. **Highlights:** AAFC's all-time rushing champion. Led league in rushing in first NFL season.

MIKE MUNCHAK
Guard. 6-3, 281. Born in Scranton, Pennsylvania, March 5, 1960. Penn State. Inducted in 2001. 1982-1993 Houston Oilers. **Highlights:** Devastating blocker, All-AFC seven times, elected to nine Pro Bowls.

ANTHONY MUÑOZ
Tackle. 6-6, 278. Born in Ontario, California, August 19, 1958. Southern California. Inducted in 1998. 1980-1992 Cincinnati Bengals. **Highlights:** All-Pro choice 11 consecutive years, 1981-1991. Selected to 11 straight Pro Bowls.

GEORGE MUSSO
Guard-tackle. 6-2, 270. Born in Collinsville, Illinois. April 8, 1910. Died September 5, 2000. Millikin. Inducted in 1982. 1933-1944 Chicago Bears. **Highlights:** First player to achieve All-NFL status at two positions—tackle in 1935 and guard in 1937.

BRONKO NAGURSKI
Fullback. 6-2, 225. Born in Rainy River, Ontario, Canada, November 3, 1908. Died January 7, 1990. Minnesota. Inducted in 1963. 1930-37, 1943 Chicago Bears. **Highlights:** Charter enshrinee. 2,778 rushing yards in nine seasons. All-NFL three times.

JOE NAMATH
Quarterback. 6-2, 200. Born in Beaver Falls, Pennsylvania, May 31, 1943. Alabama. Inducted in 1985. 1965-1976 New York Jets, 1977 Los Angeles Rams. **Highlights:** First quarterback to pass for more than 4,000 yards in season, 1967. Guaranteed, delivered victory over Colts in Super Bowl III.

EARLE (GREASY) NEALE
Coach. Born in Parkersburg, West Virginia, November 5, 1891. Died November 2, 1973. West Virginia Wesleyan. Inducted in 1969. 1941-42, 1944-1950 Philadelphia Eagles; co-coach, 1943 Phil-Pitt. **Highlights:** Turned Eagles into winners with three consecutive division crowns, NFL championships in 1948 and 1949.

ERNIE NEVERS
Fullback. 6-1, 205. Born in Willow River, Minnesota, June 11, 1903. Died May 3, 1976. Stanford. Inducted in 1963. 1926-27 Duluth Eskimos, 1929-1931 Chicago Cardinals. **Highlights:** Charter enshrinee. Holds NFL's longest-standing record, 40 points in one game in 1929.

OZZIE NEWSOME
Tight end. 6-2, 232. Born in Muscle Shoals, Alabama, March 16, 1956. Alabama. Inducted in 1999. 1978-1990 Cleveland Browns. **Highlights:** Leading tight end receiver in NFL history with 662 receptions for 7,980 yards.

RAY NITSCHKE
Linebacker. 6-3, 235. Born in Elmwood Park, Illinois, December 29, 1936. Died March 8, 1998. Illinois. Inducted in 1978. 1958-1972 Green Bay Packers. **Highlights:** MVP of 1962 title game. Named NFL's all-time linebacker in 1969.

CHUCK NOLL
Coach. Born in Cleveland, Ohio, January 5, 1932. Dayton. Inducted in 1993. 1969-1991 Pittsburgh Steelers. **Highlights:** Coached for 23 years. Only coach to win four Super Bowl titles (IX, X, XIII, XIV).

LEO NOMELLINI
Defensive tackle. 6-3, 264. Born in Lucca, Italy, June 19, 1924. Died October 17, 2000. Minnesota. Inducted in 1969. 1950-1963 San Francisco 49ers. **Highlights:** Played every 49ers game for 14 seasons. 10 Pro Bowls.

MERLIN OLSEN
Defensive tackle. 6-5, 270. Born in Logan, Utah, September 15, 1940. Utah State. Inducted in 1982. 1962-1976 Los Angeles Rams. **Highlights:** Member of the Fearsome Foursome. Named to 14 consecutive Pro Bowls, Rams' all-time team.

JIM OTTO
Center. 6-2, 255. Born in Wausau, Wisconsin, January 5, 1938. Miami. Inducted in 1980. 1960-1974 Oakland Raiders. **Highlights:** Named AFL's all-time center. Played in 210 games, 12 AFL All-Star Games or Pro Bowls, six AFL/AFC title games.

STEVE OWEN
Tackle. Coach. 6-2, 235. Born in Cleo Springs, Oklahoma, April 21, 1898. Died May 17, 1964. Phillips. Inducted in 1966. 1924-25 Kansas City Cowboys, 1925 Cleveland Bulldogs, 1926-1931, 1933 New York Giants; coach, 1930-1953 New York Giants. **Highlights:** Both player and coach. Coached Giants to record of 155-108-17, eight divisional titles, two NFL championships.

ALAN PAGE
Defensive tackle. 6-4, 225. Born in Canton, Ohio, August 7, 1945. Notre Dame. Inducted in 1988. 1967-1978 Minnesota Vikings, 1978-1981 Chicago Bears. **Highlights:** Dominating defensive tackle played in 218 consecutive games, four Super Bowls. Won league MVP honors in 1971.

CLARENCE (ACE) PARKER
Quarterback. 5-11, 168. Born in Portsmouth, Virginia, May 17, 1912. Duke. Inducted in 1972. 1937-1941 Brooklyn Dodgers, 1945 Boston Yanks, 1946 New York Yankees (AAFC). **Highlights:** Two-way threat. Two-time All-NFL performer, league MVP in 1940.

JIM PARKER
Guard-tackle. 6-3, 273. Born in Macon, Georgia, April 3, 1934. Ohio State. Inducted in 1973. 1957-1967 Baltimore Colts. **Highlights:** First full-time offensive lineman elected to Hall of Fame. All-NFL eight consecutive years, eight Pro Bowls.

WALTER PAYTON
Running back. 5-10, 202. Born in Columbia, Mississippi, July 25, 1954. Died November 1, 1999. Jackson State. Inducted in 1993. 1975-1987 Chicago Bears. **Highlights:** NFL's all-time leading rusher with 16,726 yards and combined net yardage with 21,803.

JOE PERRY
Fullback. 6-0, 200. Born in Stevens, Arkansas, January 22, 1927. Compton Junior College. Inducted in 1969. 1948-49 San Francisco 49ers (AAFC), 1950-1960, 1963 San Francisco 49ers, 1961-62 Baltimore Colts. **Highlights:** First player in NFL history to gain 1,000 yards two consecutive seasons. 12,505 combined yards.

PETE PIHOS
End. 6-1, 210. Born in Orlando, Florida, October 22, 1923. Indiana. Inducted in 1970. 1947-1955 Philadelphia Eagles. **Highlights:** Three-time NFL receiving champion. Caught winning touchdown in 1949 NFL Championship Game.

HUGH (SHORTY) RAY
Supervisor of officials 1938-1952. Born in Highland Park, Illinois, September 21, 1884. Died September 16, 1956. Illinois. Inducted in 1966. **Highlights:** Supervisor of Officials, 1938-1952. Streamlined rules to improve game tempo, player safety.

DAN REEVES
Team owner. Born in New York, New York, June 30, 1912. Died April 15, 1971. Georgetown. Inducted in 1967. 1941-45 Cleveland Rams, 1946-1971 Los Angeles Rams. **Highlights:** Moved Rams to Los Angeles in 1946 and opened up West Coast to pro football. First postwar owner to sign African-American player.

MEL RENFRO
Cornerback-safety. 6-0, 192. Born in Houston, Texas, December 30, 1941. Oregon. Inducted in 1996. 1964-1977 Dallas Cowboys. **Highlights:** 52 interceptions for 626 yards and 3 touchdowns. Also added 842 yards on punt returns, 2,246 yards on kickoff returns. Elected to Pro Bowl first 10 seasons.

JOHN RIGGINS
Running back. 6-2, 240. Born in Seneca, Kansas, August 4, 1949. Kansas. Inducted in 1992. 1971-75 New York Jets, 1976-79, 1981-85 Washington Redskins. **Highlights:** 11,352 rushing yards, 116 total touchdowns. MVP of Super Bowl XVII with 166 rushing yards including game-winning 43-yard touchdown.

JIM RINGO
Center. 6-2, 230. Born in Orange, New Jersey, November 21, 1931. Syracuse. Inducted in 1981. 1953-1963 Green Bay Packers, 1964-67 Philadelphia Eagles. **Highlights:** Ten-time Pro Bowl selection, six-time All-NFL selection. Started in then-record 182 consecutive games.

ANDY ROBUSTELLI
Defensive end. 6-0, 230. Born in Stamford, Connecticut, December 6, 1925. Arnold College. Inducted in 1971. 1951-55 Los Angeles Rams, 1956-1964 New York Giants. **Highlights:** Anchored defense in eight championship games. Named NFL's top player in 1962.

ART ROONEY
Team owner. Born in Coulterville, Pennsylvania, January 27, 1901. Died August 25, 1988. Georgetown, Duquesne. Inducted in 1964. 1933-39 Pittsburgh Pirates, 1940-42, 1945-1988 Pittsburgh Steelers, 1943 Phil-Pitt, 1944 Card-Pitt. **Highlights:** Founded Pittsburgh Pirates in 1933 and renamed them Steelers in 1940. Team won four Super Bowls in 1970s.

DAN ROONEY
Team owner. Born in Pittsburgh, Pennsylvania, July, 20, 1932. Inducted in 2000. 1955-present Pittsburgh Steelers. **Highlights:** Has been on the board of directors for the NFL Trust Fund, NFL Films, and Scheduling Committee. Played a key role in the labor agreement reached in 1993 between the NFL owners and players.

PETE ROZELLE
Commissioner. Born in South Gate, California, March 1, 1926. Died December 6, 1996. Compton Junior College, San Francisco. Inducted in 1985. Commissioner, 1960-1989. **Highlights:** Negotiated first league-wide television contract in 1962. Generally recognized as premiere commissioner in all of sports. Credited with making NFL the nation's most popular sport.

BOB ST. CLAIR
Tackle. 6-9, 265. Born in San Francisco, California, February 18, 1931. San Francisco, Tulsa. Inducted in 1990. 1953-1963 San Francisco 49ers. **Highlights:** Exceptional offensive lineman. Also played goal-line defense and had 10 blocked field goals, 1956.

GALE SAYERS
Running back. 6-0, 200. Born in Wichita, Kansas, May 30, 1943. Kansas. Inducted in 1977. 1965-1971 Chicago Bears. **Highlights:** Broke into league by scoring rookie-record 22 touchdowns. Led league in rushing in 1966, 1969. MVP of three Pro Bowls.

JOE SCHMIDT
Linebacker. 6-0, 222. Born in Pittsburgh, Pennsylvania, January 18, 1932. Pittsburgh. Inducted in 1973. 1953-1965 Detroit Lions. **Highlights:** 24 interceptions. Lions' team captain for nine years. Mastered middle linebacker position that evolved in 1950s.

TEX SCHRAMM
Team president-general manager. Born in San Gabriel, California, June 2, 1920. Texas. Inducted in 1991. 1947-1956 Los Angeles Rams. 1960-1989 Dallas Cowboys. **Highlights:** Played prominent role in AFL-NFL merger. Chairman of Competition Committee from 1966-1988.

LEE ROY SELMON
Defensive end. 6-3, 250. Born in Eufaula, Oklahoma, October 20, 1954. Oklahoma. Inducted in 1995. 1976-1984 Tampa Bay Buccaneers. **Highlights:** 78½ sacks, 380 quarterback pressures, forced 28 fumbles. Six consecutive Pro Bowl selections.

BILLY SHAW
Guard. 6-2, 258. Born in Natchez, Mississippi, December 15, 1938. Georgia Tech. Inducted in 1999. 1961-69 Buffalo Bills. **Highlights:** First player who played entire career in AFL to be elected to Hall of Fame. Named to AFL's all-time team.

ART SHELL
Tackle. 6-5, 285. Born in Charleston, South Carolina, November 26, 1946. Maryland State-Eastern Shore. Inducted in 1989. 1968-1981 Oakland Raiders, 1982 Los Angeles Raiders. **Highlights:** Cornerstone of Raiders' offensive line in 1970s. 207 regular-season games, 24 postseason games, eight Pro Bowls.

DON SHULA
Coach. Born in Grand River, Ohio, January 4, 1930. John Carroll. Inducted in 1997. 1963-69 Baltimore Colts, 1970-1995 Miami Dolphins. **Highlights:** Won more games (347) than any coach in NFL history. Won two Super Bowl titles, including Super Bowl VII when Dolphins recorded NFL's only perfect season (17-0).

O.J. SIMPSON
Running back. 6-1, 212. Born in San Francisco, California, July 9, 1947. City College (San Francisco), Southern California. Inducted in 1985. 1969-1977 Buffalo Bills, 1978-79 San Francisco 49ers. **Highlights:** In 1973, became first player to rush for 2,000 yards in season. Finished career with four rushing titles, 11,236 yards.

MIKE SINGLETARY
Linebacker. 6-0, 230. Born in Houston, Texas, October 9, 1958. Baylor. Inducted in 1998. 1981-1992 Chicago Bears. **Highlights:** All-Pro choice eight times and All-NFC nine consecutive seasons. Selected to 10 Pro Bowls.

JACKIE SLATER
Tackle. 6-4, 277. Born in Jackson, Mississippi, May 27, 1954. Jackson State. Inducted in 2001. 1976-1995 Los Angeles/St. Louis Rams. **Highlights:** Played 20 seasons, 259 games. Blocked for seven different 1,000-yard rushers. Seven Pro Bowls.

JACKIE SMITH
Tight end. 6-4, 232. Born in Columbia, Mississippi, February 23, 1940. Northwestern State (Louisiana). Inducted in 1994. 1963-1977 St. Louis Cardinals, 1978 Dallas Cowboys. **Highlights:** 480 receptions for 7,918 yards, 40 touchdowns. Third tight end to be elected to Hall of Fame.

BART STARR
Quarterback. 6-1, 200. Born in Montgomery, Alabama, January 9, 1934. Alabama. Inducted in 1977. 1956-1971 Green Bay Packers. **Highlights:** Quarterbacked Packers to six division titles, five NFL titles, and first two Super Bowls in which he was MVP.

ROGER STAUBACH
Quarterback. 6-3, 202. Born in Cincinnati, Ohio, February 5, 1942. New Mexico Military Institute, Navy. Inducted in 1985. 1969-1979 Dallas Cowboys. **Highlights:** Led Cowboys to four NFC titles and victories in Super Bowls VI, XII. When retired, 83.4 career passer rating was best of all time.

ERNIE STAUTNER
Defensive tackle. 6-2, 235. Born in Prinzing-by-Cham, Bavaria, April 20, 1925. Boston College. Inducted in 1969. 1950-1963 Pittsburgh Steelers. **Highlights:** Played in nine Pro Bowls and won the best lineman award in 1957. Recorded 3 safeties.

JAN STENERUD
Kicker. 6-2, 190. Born in Fetsund, Norway, November 26, 1942. Montana State. Inducted in 1991. 1967-1979 Kansas City Chiefs, 1980-83 Green Bay Packers, 1984-85 Minnesota Vikings. **Highlights:** 1,699 points on 580 extra points, 373 field goals. First pure placekicker to enter Hall of Fame.

DWIGHT STEPHENSON
Center. 6-2, 255. Born in Murfreesboro, North Carolina, November 20, 1957. Alabama. Inducted in 1998. 1980-87 Miami Dolphins. **Highlights:** Recognized as premier center of his time. All-Pro, All-AFC five straight years. Selected to five Pro Bowls.

KEN STRONG
Halfback. 5-11, 210. Born in West Haven, Connecticut, April 21, 1906. Died October 5, 1979. New York University. Inducted in 1967. 1929-1932 Staten Island Stapletons, 1933-35, 1939, 1944-47 New York Giants, 1936-37 New York Yanks (AFL). **Highlights:** Scored 17 points to lead Giants to victory in 1934 'Sneakers' game, led NFL with 64 points, 1933.

JOE STYDAHAR
Tackle. 6-4, 230. Born in Kaylor, Pennsylvania, March 17, 1912. Died March 23, 1977. West Virginia. Inducted in 1967. 1936-1942, 1945-46 Chicago Bears. **Highlights:** One of stalwarts of Bears' 'Monsters of the Midway.' Played on five divisional, three NFL championship teams.

PRO FOOTBALL HALL OF FAME

LYNN SWANN
Wide receiver. 5-11, 180. Born in Alcoa, Tennessee, March 7, 1952. Southern California. Inducted in 2001. 1974-1982 Pittsburgh Steelers. **Highlights:** All-AFC three times. Selected to three Pro Bowls. MVP, Super Bowl X.

FRAN TARKENTON
Quarterback. 6-0, 185. Born in Richmond, Virginia, February 3, 1940. Georgia. Inducted in 1986. 1961-66, 1972-78 Minnesota Vikings, 1967-1971 New York Giants. **Highlights:** At retirement, held NFL records for attempts (6,467), completions (3,686), yards (47,003), and touchdowns (342). Four touchdowns passes in first NFL game.

CHARLEY TAYLOR
Running back-wide receiver. 6-3, 210. Born in Grand Prairie, Texas, September 28, 1941. Arizona State. Inducted in 1984. 1964-1975, 1977 Washington Redskins. **Highlights:** Won rookie of year honors as running back. Switched to wide receiver and won receiving titles in 1966, 1967.

JIM TAYLOR
Fullback. 6-0, 216. Born in Baton Rouge, Louisiana, September 20, 1935. Louisiana State. Inducted in 1976. 1958-1966 Green Bay Packers, 1967 New Orleans Saints. **Highlights:** 8,597 rushing yards, 558 points. In 1962, led league in rushing and scoring with 19 touchdowns.

LAWRENCE TAYLOR
Linebacker. 6-3, 237. Born in Williamsburg, Virginia, February 4, 1959. North Carolina. Inducted in 1999. 1981-1993 New York Giants. **Highlights:** Redefined the position of outside linebacker. All-Pro nine times, 10 Pro Bowls. NFL MVP in 1986.

JIM THORPE
Halfback. 6-1, 190. Born in Prague, Oklahoma, May 28, 1888. Died March 28, 1953. Carlisle. Inducted in 1963. 1915-17, 1919-1920, 1926 Canton Bulldogs, 1921 Cleveland Indians, 1922-23 Oorang Indians, 1924 Rock Island Independents, 1925 New York Giants, 1928 Chicago Cardinals. **Highlights:** Charter enshrinee. First president of American Professional Football Association, 1920. Played for 12 seasons.

Y.A. TITTLE
Quarterback. 6-0, 200. Born in Marshall, Texas, October 24, 1926. Louisiana State. Inducted in 1971. 1948-49 Baltimore Colts (AAFC), 1950 Baltimore Colts, 1951-1960 San Francisco 49ers, 1961-64 New York Giants. **Highlights:** 33,070 yards, 242 touchdowns. 33 touchdown passes in 1962 and 36 in 1963. Two-time league MVP.

GEORGE TRAFTON
Center. 6-2, 235. Born in Chicago, Illinois, December 6, 1896. Died September 5, 1971. Notre Dame. Inducted in 1964. 1920 Decatur Staleys, 1921 Chicago Staleys, 1922-1932 Chicago Bears. **Highlights:** First center to snap with one hand. Named top NFL center of 1920s.

CHARLEY TRIPPI
Halfback-quarterback. 6-0, 185. Born in Pittston, Pennsylvania, December 14, 1922. Georgia. Inducted in 1968. 1947-1955 Chicago Cardinals. **Highlights:** One of football's most versatile performers. Played halfback five years, quarterback for two, defense for two.

EMLEN TUNNELL
Safety. 6-1, 200. Born in Bryn Mawr, Pennsylvania, March 29, 1925. Died July 22, 1975. Toledo, Iowa. Inducted in 1967. 1948-1958 New York Giants, 1959-1961 Green Bay Packers. **Highlights:** 79 interceptions. Gained more yards on kickoff, punt, and interception returns (924) in 1952 than that season's NFL rushing leader.

CLYDE (BULLDOG) TURNER
Center. 6-2, 235. Born in Plains, Texas, March 10, 1919. Died October 30, 1998. Hardin-Simmons. Inducted in 1966. 1940-1952 Chicago Bears. **Highlights:** Anchored defense for four NFL championship teams, including 4 interceptions in five title games.

JOHNNY UNITAS
Quarterback. 6-1, 195. Born in Pittsburgh, Pennsylvania, May 7, 1933. Louisville. Inducted in 1979. 1956-1972 Baltimore Colts, 1973 San Diego Chargers. **Highlights:** 40,239 passing yards, 290 touchdowns. Led Colts to two NFL championships. Passed for at least one touchdown in 47 consecutive games.

GENE UPSHAW
Guard. 6-5, 255. Born in Robstown, Texas, August 15, 1945. Texas A & I. Inducted in 1987. 1967-1981 Oakland Raiders. **Highlights:** Premier guard of his era played in 10 AFL/AFC Championship Games, three Super Bowls, seven Pro Bowls.

NORM VAN BROCKLIN
Quarterback. 6-1, 190. Born in Eagle Butte, South Dakota, March 15, 1926. Died May 2, 1983. Oregon. Inducted in 1971. 1949-1957 Los Angeles Rams, 1958-1960 Philadelphia Eagles. **Highlights:** NFL-record 554 yards passing in 1951 season opener. Guided Eagles to NFL crown as league MVP in 1960.

STEVE VAN BUREN
Halfback. 6-1, 200. Born in La Ceiba, Honduras, December 28, 1920. Louisiana State. Inducted in 1965. 1944-1951 Philadelphia Eagles. **Highlights:** Four-time rushing champion. Won 1944 punt-return title and was 1945 kickoff-return champion.

DOAK WALKER
Halfback. 5-11, 173. Born in Dallas, Texas, January 1, 1927. Died September 27, 1998. Southern Methodist. Inducted in 1986. 1950-55 Detroit Lions. **Highlights:** 534 points. Won two NFL scoring titles. Had winning 67-yard scoring run in 1952 title game.

BILL WALSH
Coach. Born in Los Angeles, California, November 30, 1931. San Jose State. Inducted in 1993. 1979-1988 San Francisco 49ers. **Highlights:** 102-63-1 coaching record. Guided 49ers to three Super Bowl titles (XVI, XIX, XXIII) in 10 years.

PAUL WARFIELD
Wide receiver. 6-0, 188. Born in Warren, Ohio, November 28, 1942. Ohio State. Inducted in 1983. 1964-69, 1976-77 Cleveland Browns, 1970-74 Miami Dolphins. **Highlights:** 8,565 yards receiving, 85 touchdowns. Eight-time Pro Bowl player. Key to both Cleveland and Miami offenses.

BOB WATERFIELD
Quarterback. 6-2, 200. Born in Elmira, New York, July 26, 1920. Died March 25, 1983. UCLA. Inducted in 1965. 1945 Cleveland Rams, 1946-1952 Los Angeles Rams. **Highlights:** NFL MVP as rookie in 1945 and led Rams to NFL title. Grabbed 20 interceptions in limited defensive duties.

MIKE WEBSTER
Center. 6-2, 260. Born in Tomahawk, Wisconsin, March 18, 1952. Wisconsin. Inducted in 1997. 1974-1988 Pittsburgh Steelers, 1989-1990 Kansas City Chiefs. **Highlights:** Played in 245 games, nine Pro Bowls, and won four Super Bowls during 17-year career.

ARNIE WEINMEISTER
Defensive tackle. 6-4, 235. Born in Rhein, Saskatchewan, Canada, March 23, 1923. Died June 29, 2000. Washington. Inducted in 1984. 1948-49 New York Yankees (AAFC), 1950-53 New York Giants. **Highlights:** Dominant defensive tackle of his time. Four-time All-NFL selection, four Pro Bowls.

RANDY WHITE
Defensive tackle. 6-4, 265. Born in Pittsburgh, Pennsylvania, January 15, 1953. Maryland. Inducted in 1994. 1975-1988 Dallas Cowboys. **Highlights:** Missed only one game in 14 seasons. Co-MVP of Super Bowl XII. Nine-time Pro Bowl selection.

DAVE WILCOX
Linebacker. 6-3, 241. Born in Ontario, Oregon, September, 29, 1942. Boise State, Oregon. Inducted in 2000. 1964-1974 San Francisco 49ers. **Highlights:** Seven Pro Bowls, All-NFL five times. Missed only one game because of injury.

BILL WILLIS
Guard. 6-2, 215. Born in Columbus, Ohio, October 5, 1921. Ohio State. Inducted in 1977. 1946-49 Cleveland Browns (AAFC), 1950-53 Cleveland Browns. **Highlights:** Two-way player who excelled on defense. Four-time All-NFL player, played in three Pro Bowls.

LARRY WILSON
Safety. 6-0, 190. Born in Rigby, Idaho, March 24, 1938. Utah. Inducted in 1978. 1960-1972 St. Louis Cardinals. **Highlights:** 52 interceptions. Had interception in seven consecutive games in 1966. Made "safety blitz" famous.

KELLEN WINSLOW
Tight end. 6-5, 250. Born in St. Louis, Missouri, November 5, 1957. Missouri. Inducted in 1995. 1979-1987 San Diego Chargers **Highlights:** 541 receptions for 6,741 yards, 45 touchdowns. 13 catches, blocked field goal in 1981 playoff win over Miami.

ALEX WOJCIECHOWICZ
Center. 6-0, 235. Born in South River, New Jersey, August 12, 1915. Died July 13, 1992. Fordham. Inducted in 1968. 1938-1946 Detroit Lions, 1946-1950 Philadelphia Eagles. **Highlights:** One of league's first iron men. Played both ways for eight years with Lions.

WILLIE WOOD
Safety. 5-10, 190. Born in Washington, D.C., December 23, 1936. Southern California. Inducted in 1989. 1960-1971 Green Bay Packers. **Highlights:** 48 interceptions. Competed in six NFL Championship Games and Super Bowls I and II.

RON YARY
Tackle. 6-5, 255. Born in Chicago, Illinois, July 16, 1946. Cerritos (Calif.) J.C., Southern California. Inducted in 2001. 1968-1981 Minnesota Vikings, 1982 Los Angeles Rams. **Highlights:** All-Pro six consecutive seasons, All-NFC eight consecutive years. Named to seven Pro Bowls. Started in four Super Bowls and five NFL/NFC Championship Games.

JACK YOUNGBLOOD
Defensive end. 6-4, 247. Born in Jacksonville, Florida, January 26, 1950. Florida. Inducted in 2001. 1971-1984 Los Angeles Rams. **Highlights:** Played in club-record 201 consecutive games. Played in five NFC Championship Games, one Super Bowl. Named All-Pro five times, All-NFC seven times. Elected to seven consecutive Pro Bowls.

ENSHRINEES BY YEAR OF INDUCTION

**Deceased*
(Date of enshrinement in parentheses)

1963 CHARTER CLASS
(September 7, 1963)
Sammy Baugh
Bert Bell*
Joe Carr*
Earl (Dutch) Clark*
Harold (Red) Grange*
George Halas*
Mel Hein*
Wilbur (Pete) Henry*
Robert (Cal) Hubbard*
Don Hutson*
Earl (Curly) Lambeau*
Tim Mara*
George Preston Marshall*
John (Blood) McNally*
Bronko Nagurski*
Ernie Nevers*
Jim Thorpe*

CLASS OF 1964
(September 6, 1964)
Jimmy Conzelman*
Ed Healey*
Clarke Hinkle*
William Roy (Link) Lyman*
Mike Michalske*
Art Rooney*
George Trafton*

CLASS OF 1965
(September 12, 1965)
Guy Chamberlin*
John (Paddy) Driscoll*
Dan Fortmann*
Otto Graham
Sid Luckman*
Steve Van Buren
Bob Waterfield*

CLASS OF 1966
(September 17, 1966)
Bill Dudley
Joe Guyon*
Arnie Herber*
Walt Kiesling*
George McAfee
Steve Owen*
Hugh (Shorty) Ray*
Clyde (Bulldog) Turner*

CLASS OF 1967
(August 5, 1967)
Chuck Bednarik
Charles W. Bidwill, Sr.*
Paul Brown*
Bobby Layne*
Dan Reeves*
Ken Strong*
Joe Stydahar*
Emlen Tunnell*

CLASS OF 1968
(August 3, 1968)
Cliff Battles*
Art Donovan
Elroy (Crazylegs) Hirsch
Wayne Millner*
Marion Motley*
Charley Trippi
Alex Wojciechowicz*

CLASS OF 1969
(September 13, 1969)
Albert Glen (Turk) Edwards*
Earle (Greasy) Neale*
Leo Nomellini*
Joe Perry
Ernie Stautner

CLASS OF 1970
(August 8, 1970)
Jack Christiansen*
Tom Fears*
Hugh McElhenny
Pete Pihos

CLASS OF 1971
(July 31, 1971)
Jim Brown
Bill Hewitt*
Frank (Bruiser) Kinard*
Vince Lombardi*
Andy Robustelli
Y. A. Tittle
Norm Van Brocklin*

CLASS OF 1972
(July 29, 1972)
Lamar Hunt
Gino Marchetti
Ollie Matson
Clarence (Ace) Parker

CLASS OF 1973
(July 28, 1973)
Raymond Berry
Jim Parker
Joe Schmidt

CLASS OF 1974
(July 27, 1974)
Tony Canadeo
Bill George*
Lou Groza*
Dick (Night Train) Lane

CLASS OF 1975
(August 2, 1975)
Roosevelt Brown
George Connor
Dante Lavelli
Lenny Moore

CLASS OF 1976
(July 24, 1976)
Ray Flaherty*
Len Ford*
Jim Taylor

CLASS OF 1977
(July 30, 1977)
Frank Gifford
Forrest Gregg
Gale Sayers
Bart Starr
Bill Willis

CLASS OF 1978
(July 29, 1978)
Lance Alworth
Weeb Ewbank*
Alphonse (Tuffy) Leemans*
Ray Nitschke*
Larry Wilson

CLASS OF 1979
(July 28, 1979)
Dick Butkus
Yale Lary
Ron Mix
Johnny Unitas

CLASS OF 1980
(August 2, 1980)
Herb Adderley
David (Deacon) Jones
Bob Lilly
Jim Otto

CLASS OF 1981
(August 1, 1981)
Morris (Red) Badgro*
George Blanda
Willie Davis
Jim Ringo

CLASS OF 1982
(August 7, 1982)
Doug Atkins
Sam Huff
George Musso*
Merlin Olsen

CLASS OF 1983
(July 30, 1983)
Bobby Bell
Sid Gillman
Sonny Jurgensen
Bobby Mitchell
Paul Warfield

CLASS OF 1984
(July 28, 1984)
Willie Brown
Mike McCormack
Charley Taylor
Arnie Weinmeister*

CLASS OF 1985
(August 3, 1985)
Frank Gatski
Joe Namath
Pete Rozelle*
O. J. Simpson
Roger Staubach

CLASS OF 1986
(August 2, 1986)
Paul Hornung
Ken Houston
Willie Lanier
Fran Tarkenton
Doak Walker*

CLASS OF 1987
(August 8, 1987)
Larry Csonka
Len Dawson
Joe Greene
John Henry Johnson
Jim Langer
Don Maynard
Gene Upshaw

CLASS OF 1988
(July 30, 1988)
Fred Biletnikoff
Mike Ditka
Jack Ham
Alan Page

CLASS OF 1989
(August 5, 1989)
Mel Blount
Terry Bradshaw
Art Shell
Willie Wood

CLASS OF 1990
(August 4, 1990)
Buck Buchanan*
Bob Griese
Franco Harris
Ted Hendricks
Jack Lambert
Tom Landry*
Bob St. Clair

CLASS OF 1991
(July 27, 1991)
Earl Campbell
John Hannah
Stan Jones
Tex Schramm
Jan Stenerud

CLASS OF 1992
(August 1, 1992)
Lem Barney
Al Davis
John Mackey
John Riggins

CLASS OF 1993
(July 31, 1993)
Dan Fouts
Larry Little
Chuck Noll
Walter Payton*
Bill Walsh

CLASS OF 1994
(July 30, 1994)
Tony Dorsett
Bud Grant
Jimmy Johnson
Leroy Kelly
Jackie Smith
Randy White

CLASS OF 1995
(July 29, 1995)
Jim Finks*
Henry Jordan*
Steve Largent
Lee Roy Selmon
Kellen Winslow

CLASS OF 1996
(July 27, 1996)
Lou Creekmur
Dan Dierdorf
Joe Gibbs
Charlie Joiner
Mel Renfro

CLASS OF 1997
(July 26, 1997)
Mike Haynes
Wellington Mara
Don Shula
Mike Webster

CLASS OF 1998
(August 1, 1998)
Paul Krause
Tommy McDonald
Anthony Muñoz
Mike Singletary
Dwight Stephenson

CLASS OF 1999
(August 7, 1999)
Eric Dickerson
Tom Mack
Ozzie Newsome
Billy Shaw
Lawrence Taylor

CLASS OF 2000
(July 29, 2000)
Howie Long
Ronnie Lott
Joe Montana
Dan Rooney
Dave Wilcox

CLASS OF 2001
(August 4, 2001)
Nick Buoniconti
Marv Levy
Mike Munchak
Jackie Slater
Lynn Swann
Ron Yary
Jack Youngblood

CHRONOLOGY OF PROFESSIONAL FOOTBALL

1869
Rutgers and Princeton played a college soccer football game, the first ever, November 6. The game used modified London Football Association rules. During the next seven years, rugby gained favor with the major eastern schools over soccer, and modern football began to develop from rugby.

1876
At the Massasoit convention, the first rules for American football were written. Walter Camp, who would become known as the father of American football, first became involved with the game.

1892
In an era in which football was a major attraction of local athletic clubs, an intense competition between two Pittsburgh-area clubs, the Allegheny Athletic Association (AAA) and the Pittsburgh Athletic Club (PAC), led to the making of the first professional football player. Former Yale All-America guard William (Pudge) Heffelfinger was paid $500 by the AAA to play in a game against the PAC, becoming the first person to be paid to play football, November 12. The AAA won the game 4-0 when Heffelfinger picked up a PAC fumble and ran 35 yards for a touchdown.

1893
The Pittsburgh Athletic Club signed one of its players, probably halfback Grant Dibert, to the first known pro football contract, which covered all of the PAC's games for the year.

1895
John Brallier became the first football player to openly turn pro, accepting $10 and expenses to play for the Latrobe YMCA against the Jeannette Athletic Club.

1896
The Allegheny Athletic Association team fielded the first completely professional team for its abbreviated two-game season.

1897
The Latrobe Athletic Association football team went entirely professional, becoming the first team to play a full season with only professionals.

1898
A touchdown was changed from four points to five.

1899
Chris O'Brien formed a neighborhood team, which played under the name the Morgan Athletic Club, on the south side of Chicago. The team later became known as the Normals, then the Racine (for a street in Chicago) Cardinals, the Chicago Cardinals, the St. Louis Cardinals, the Phoenix Cardinals, and, in 1994, the Arizona Cardinals. The team remains the oldest continuing operation in pro football.

1900
William C. Temple took over the team payments for the Duquesne Country and Athletic Club, becoming the first known individual club owner.

1902
Baseball's Philadelphia Athletics, managed by Connie Mack, and the Philadelphia Phillies formed professional football teams, joining the Pittsburgh Stars in the first attempt at a pro football league, named the National Football League. The Athletics won the first night football game ever played, 39-0 over Kanaweola AC at Elmira, New York, November 21.

All three teams claimed the pro championship for the year, but the league president, Dave Berry, named the Stars the champions. Pitcher Rube Waddell was with the Athletics, and pitcher Christy Mathewson a fullback for Pittsburgh.

The first World Series of pro football, actually a five-team tournament, was played among a team made up of players from both the Athletics and the Phillies, but simply named New York; the New York Knickerbockers; the Syracuse AC; the Warlow AC; and the Orange (New Jersey) AC at New York's original Madison Square Garden. New York and Syracuse played the first indoor football game before 3,000, December 28. Syracuse, with Glen (Pop) Warner at guard, won 6-0 and went on to win the tournament.

1903
The Franklin (Pa.) Athletic Club won the second and last World Series of pro football over the Oreos AC of Asbury Park, New Jersey; the Watertown Red and Blacks; and the Orange AC.

Pro football was popularized in Ohio when the Massillon Tigers, a strong amateur team, hired four Pittsburgh pros to play in the season-ending game against Akron. At the same time, pro football declined in the Pittsburgh area, and the emphasis on the pro game moved west from Pennsylvania to Ohio.

1904
A field goal was changed from five points to four.

Ohio had at least seven pro teams, with Massillon winning the Ohio Independent Championship, that is, the pro title. Talk surfaced about forming a state-wide league to end spiraling salaries brought about by constant bidding for players and to write universal rules for the game. The feeble attempt to start the league failed.

Halfback Charles Follis signed a contract with the Shelby (Ohio) AC, making him the first known black pro football player.

1905
The Canton AC, later to become known as the Bulldogs, became a professional team. Massillon again won the Ohio League championship.

1906
The forward pass was legalized. The first authenticated pass completion in a pro game came on October 27, when George (Peggy) Parratt of Massillon threw a completion to Dan (Bullet) Riley in a victory over a combined Benwood-Moundsville team.

Arch-rivals Canton and Massillon, the two best pro teams in America, played twice, with Canton winning the first game but Massillon winning the second and the Ohio League championship. A betting scandal and the financial disaster wrought upon the two clubs by paying huge salaries caused a temporary decline in interest in pro football in the two cities and, somewhat, throughout Ohio.

1909
A field goal dropped from four points to three.

1912
A touchdown was increased from five points to six.

Jack Cusack revived a strong pro team in Canton.

1913
Jim Thorpe, a former football and track star at the Carlisle Indian School (Pa.) and a double gold medal winner at the 1912 Olympics in Stockholm, played for the Pine Village Pros in Indiana.

1915
Massillon again fielded a major team, reviving the old rivalry with Canton. Cusack signed Thorpe to play for Canton for $250 a game.

1916
With Thorpe and former Carlisle teammate Pete Calac starring, Canton went 9-0-1, won the Ohio League championship, and was acclaimed the pro football champion.

1917
Despite an upset by Massillon, Canton again won the Ohio League championship.

1919
Canton again won the Ohio League championship, despite the team having been turned over from Cusack to Ralph Hay. Thorpe and Calac were joined in the backfield by Joe Guyon.

Earl (Curly) Lambeau and George Calhoun organized the Green Bay Packers. Lambeau's employer at the Indian Packing Company provided $500 for equipment and allowed the team to use the company field for practices. The Packers went 10-1.

1920
Pro football was in a state of confusion due to three major problems: dramatically rising salaries; players continually jumping from one team to another following the highest offer; and the use of college players still enrolled in school. A league in which all the members would follow the same rules seemed the answer. An organizational meeting, at which the Akron Pros, Canton Bulldogs, Cleveland Indians, and Dayton Triangles were represented, was held at the Jordan and Hupmobile auto showroom in Canton, Ohio, August 20. This meeting resulted in the formation of the American Professional Football Conference.

A second organizational meeting was held in Canton, September 17. The teams were from four states—Akron, Canton, Cleveland, and Dayton from Ohio; the Hammond Pros and Muncie Flyers from Indiana; the Rochester Jeffersons from New York; and the Rock Island Independents, Decatur Staleys, and Racine Cardinals from Illinois. The name of the league was changed to the American Professional Football Association. Hoping to capitalize on his fame, the members elected Thorpe president; Stanley Cofall of Cleveland was elected vice president. A membership fee of $100 per team was charged to give an appearance of respectability, but no team ever paid it. Scheduling was left up to the teams, and there were wide variations, both in the overall number of games played and in the number played against APFA member teams.

Four other teams—the Buffalo All-Americans, Chicago Tigers, Columbus Panhandles, and Detroit Heralds—joined the league sometime during the year. On September 26, the first game featuring an APFA team was played at Rock Island's Douglas Park. A crowd of 800 watched the Independents defeat the St. Paul Ideals 48-0. A week later, October 3, the first game matching two APFA teams was held. At Triangle Park, Dayton defeated Columbus 14-0, with Lou Partlow of Dayton scoring the first touchdown in a game between Association teams. The same day, Rock Island defeated Muncie 45-0.

By the beginning of December, most of the teams in the APFA had abandoned their hopes for a championship, and some of them, including the Chicago Tigers and the Detroit Heralds, had finished their seasons, disbanded, and had their franchises canceled by the Association. Four teams—Akron, Buffalo, Canton, and Decatur—still had championship aspirations, but a series of late-season games among them left Akron as the only undefeated team in the Association. At one of these games, Akron sold tackle Bob Nash to Buffalo for $300 and five percent of the gate receipts—the first APFA player deal.

1921
At the league meeting in Akron, April 30, the championship of the 1920 season was awarded to the Akron Pros. The APFA was reorganized, with Joe Carr of the Columbus Panhandles named president and Carl Storck of Dayton secretary-treasurer. Carr moved the Association's headquarters to Columbus, drafted a league constitution and by-laws, gave teams territorial rights, restricted player movements, developed membership criteria for the franchises, and issued standings for the first time, so that the APFA would have a clear champion.

The Association's membership increased to 22 teams, including the Green Bay Packers, who were awarded to John Clair of the Acme Packing Company.

Thorpe moved from Canton to the Cleveland Indians, but he was hurt early in the season and played very little.

A.E. Staley turned the Decatur Staleys over to player-coach George Halas, who moved the team to Cubs Park in Chicago. Staley paid Halas

$5,000 to keep the name Staleys for one more year. Halas made halfback Ed (Dutch) Sternaman his partner.

Player-coach Fritz Pollard of the Akron Pros became the first black head coach.

The Staleys claimed the APFA championship with a 9-1-1 record, as did Buffalo at 9-1-2. Carr ruled in favor of the Staleys, giving Halas his first championship.

1922

After admitting the use of players who had college eligibility remaining during the 1921 season, Clair and the Green Bay management withdrew from the APFA, January 28. Curly Lambeau promised to obey league rules and then used $50 of his own money to buy back the franchise. Bad weather and low attendance plagued the Packers, and Lambeau went broke, but local merchants arranged a $2,500 loan for the club. A public nonprofit corporation was set up to operate the team, with Lambeau as head coach and manager.

The American Professional Football Association changed its name to the National Football League, June 24. The Chicago Staleys became the Chicago Bears.

The NFL fielded 18 teams, including the new Oorang Indians of Marion, Ohio, an all-Indian team featuring Thorpe, Joe Guyon, and Pete Calac, and sponsored by the Oorang dog kennels.

Canton, led by player-coach Guy Chamberlin and tackles Link Lyman and Wilbur (Pete) Henry, emerged as the league's first true powerhouse, going 10-0-2.

1923

For the first time, all of the franchises considered to be part of the NFL fielded teams. Thorpe played his second and final season for the Oorang Indians. Against the Bears, Thorpe fumbled, and Halas picked up the ball and returned it 98 yards for a touchdown, a record that would last until 1972.

Canton had its second consecutive undefeated season, going 11-0-1 for the NFL title.

1924

The league had 18 franchises, including new ones in Kansas City, Kenosha, and Frankford, a section of Philadelphia. League champion Canton, successful on the field but not at the box office, was purchased by the owner of the Cleveland franchise, who kept the Canton franchise inactive, while using the best players for his Cleveland team, which he renamed the Bulldogs. Cleveland won the title with a 7-1-1 record.

1925

Five new franchises were admitted to the NFL—the New York Giants, who were awarded to Tim Mara and Billy Gibson for $500; the Detroit Panthers, featuring Jimmy Conzelman as owner, coach, and tailback; the Providence Steam Roller; a new Canton Bulldogs team; and the Pottsville Maroons, who had been perhaps the most successful independent pro team. The NFL established its first player limit, at 16 players.

Late in the season, the NFL made its greatest coup in gaining national recognition. Shortly after the University of Illinois season ended in November, All-America halfback Harold (Red) Grange signed a contract to play with the Chicago Bears. On Thanksgiving Day, a crowd of 36,000—the largest in pro football history—watched Grange and the Bears play the Chicago Cardinals to a scoreless tie at Wrigley Field. At the beginning of December, the Bears left on a barnstorming tour that saw them play eight games in 12 days, in St. Louis, Philadelphia, New York City, Washington, Boston, Pittsburgh, Detroit, and Chicago. A crowd of 73,000 watched the game against the Giants at the Polo Grounds, helping assure the future of the troubled NFL franchise in New York. The Bears then played nine more games in the South and West, including a game in Los Angeles, in which 75,000 fans watched them defeat the Los Angeles Tigers in the Los Angeles Memorial Coliseum.

Pottsville and the Chicago Cardinals were the top contenders for the league title, with Pottsville winning a late-season meeting 21-7. Pottsville scheduled a game against a team of former Notre Dame players for Shibe Park in Philadelphia. Frankford lodged a protest not only because the game was in Frankford's protected territory, but because it was being played the same day as a Yellow Jackets home game. Carr gave three different notices forbidding Pottsville to play the game, but Pottsville played anyway, December 12. That day, Carr fined the club, suspended it from all rights and privileges (including the right to play for the NFL championship), and returned its franchise to the league. The Cardinals, who ended the season with the best record in the league, were named the 1925 champions.

1926

Grange's manager, C.C. Pyle, told the Bears that Grange wouldn't play for them unless he was paid a five-figure salary and given one-third ownership of the team. The Bears refused. Pyle leased Yankee Stadium in New York City, then petitioned for an NFL franchise. After he was refused, he started the first American Football League. It lasted one season and included Grange's New York Yankees and eight other teams. The AFL champion Philadelphia Quakers played a December game against the New York Giants, seventh in the NFL, and the Giants won 31-0. At the end of the season, the AFL folded.

Halas pushed through a rule that prohibited any team from signing a player whose college class had not graduated.

The NFL grew to 22 teams, including the Duluth Eskimos, who signed All-America fullback Ernie Nevers of Stanford, giving the league a gate attraction to rival Grange. The 15-member Eskimos, dubbed the Iron Men of the North, played 29 exhibition and league games, 28 on the road, and Nevers played in all but 29 minutes of them.

Frankford edged the Bears for the championship, despite Halas having obtained John (Paddy) Driscoll from the Cardinals. On December 4, the Yellow Jackets scored in the final two minutes to defeat the Bears 7-6 and move ahead of them in the standings.

1927

At a special meeting in Cleveland, April 23, Carr decided to secure the NFL's future by eliminating the financially weaker teams and consolidating the quality players onto a limited number of more successful teams. The new-look NFL dropped to 12 teams, and the center of gravity of the league left the Midwest, where the NFL had started, and began to emerge in the large cities of the East. One of the new teams was Grange's New York Yankees, but Grange suffered a knee injury and the Yankees finished in the middle of the pack. The NFL championship was won by the cross-town rival New York Giants, who posted 10 shutouts in 13 games.

1928

Grange and Nevers both retired from pro football, and Duluth disbanded, as the NFL was reduced to only 10 teams. The Providence Steam Roller of Jimmy Conzelman and Pearce Johnson won the championship, playing in the Cycledrome, a 10,000-seat oval that had been built for bicycle races.

1929

Chris O'Brien sold the Chicago Cardinals to David Jones, July 27.

The NFL added a fourth official, the field judge, July 28.

Grange and Nevers returned to the NFL. Nevers scored six rushing touchdowns and four extra points as the Cardinals beat Grange's Bears 40-6, November 28. The 40 points set a record that remains the NFL's oldest.

Providence became the first NFL team to host a game at night under floodlights, against the Cardinals, November 3.

The Packers added back Johnny Blood (McNally), tackle Cal Hubbard, and guard Mike Michalske, and won their first NFL championship, edging the Giants, who featured quarterback Benny Friedman.

1930

Dayton, the last of the NFL's original franchises, was purchased by William B. Dwyer and John C. Depler, moved to Brooklyn, and renamed the Dodgers. The Portsmouth, Ohio, Spartans entered the league.

The Packers edged the Giants for the title, but the most improved team was the Bears. Halas retired as a player and replaced himself as coach of the Bears with Ralph Jones, who refined the T-formation by introducing wide ends and a halfback in motion. Jones also introduced rookie All-America fullback-tackle Bronko Nagurski.

The Giants defeated a team of former Notre Dame players coached by Knute Rockne 22-0 before 55,000 at the Polo Grounds, December 14. The proceeds went to the New York Unemployment Fund to help those suffering because of the Great Depression, and the easy victory helped give the NFL credibility with the press and the public.

1931

The NFL decreased to 10 teams, and halfway through the season the Frankford franchise folded. Carr fined the Bears, Packers, and Portsmouth $1,000 each for using players whose college classes had not graduated.

The Packers won an unprecedented third consecutive title, beating out the Spartans, who were led by rookie backs Earl (Dutch) Clark and Glenn Presnell.

1932

George Preston Marshall, Vincent Bendix, Jay O'Brien, and M. Dorland Doyle were awarded a franchise for Boston, July 9. Despite the presence of two rookies—halfback Cliff Battles and tackle Glen (Turk) Edwards—the new team, named the Braves, lost money and Marshall was left as the sole owner at the end of the year.

NFL membership dropped to eight teams, the lowest in history. Official statistics were kept for the first time. The Bears and the Spartans finished the season in the first-ever tie for first place. After the season finale, the league office arranged for an additional regular-season game to determine the league champion. The game was moved indoors to Chicago Stadium because of bitter cold and heavy snow. The arena allowed only an 80-yard field that came right to the walls. The goal posts were moved from the end lines to the goal lines and, for safety, inbounds lines or hashmarks where the ball would be put in play were drawn 10 yards from the walls that butted against the sidelines. The Bears won 9-0, December 18, scoring the winning touchdown on a two-yard pass from Nagurski to Grange. The Spartans claimed Nagurski's pass was thrown from less than five yards behind the line of scrimmage, violating the existing passing rule, but the play stood.

1933

The NFL, which long had followed the rules of college football, made a number of significant changes from the college game for the first time and began to develop rules serving its needs and the style of play it preferred. The innovations from the 1932 championship game—inbounds line or hashmarks and goal posts on the goal lines—were adopted. Also the forward pass was legalized from anywhere behind the line of scrimmage, February 25.

Marshall and Halas pushed through a proposal that divided the NFL into two divisions, with the winners to meet in an annual championship game, July 8.

Three new franchises joined the league—the Pittsburgh Pirates of Art Rooney, the Philadelphia Eagles of Bert Bell and Lud Wray, and the Cincinnati Reds. The Staten Island Stapletons suspended operations for a year, but never returned to the league.

Halas bought out Sternaman, became sole owner of the Bears, and reinstated himself as head coach. Marshall changed the name of the Boston Braves to the Redskins. David Jones sold the Chicago Cardinals to Charles W. Bidwill.

In the first NFL Championship Game scheduled before the season, the Western Division champion Bears defeated the Eastern Division champion Giants 23-21 at Wrigley Field, December 17.

1934
G.A. (Dick) Richards purchased the Portsmouth Spartans, moved them to Detroit, and renamed them the Lions.

Professional football gained new prestige when the Bears were matched against the best college football players in the first Chicago College All-Star Game, August 31. The game ended in a scoreless tie before 79,432 at Soldier Field.

The Cincinnati Reds lost their first eight games, then were suspended from the league for defaulting on payments. The St. Louis Gunners, an independent team, joined the NFL by buying the Cincinnati franchise and went 1-2 the last three weeks.

Rookie Beattie Feathers of the Bears became the NFL's first 1,000-yard rusher, gaining 1,004 on 101 carries. The Thanksgiving Day game between the Bears and the Lions became the first NFL game broadcast nationally, with Graham McNamee the announcer for NBC radio.

In the championship game, on an extremely cold and icy day at the Polo Grounds, the Giants trailed the Bears 13-3 in the third quarter before changing to basketball shoes for better footing. The Giants won 30-13 in what has come to be known as the Sneakers Game, December 9.

The player waiver rule was adopted, December 10.

1935
The NFL adopted Bert Bell's proposal to hold an annual draft of college players, to begin in 1936, with teams selecting in an inverse order of finish, May 19. The inbounds line or hashmarks were moved nearer the center of the field, 15 yards from the sidelines.

All-America end Don Hutson of Alabama joined Green Bay. The Lions defeated the Giants 26-7 in the NFL Championship Game, December 15.

1936
There were no franchise transactions for the first year since the formation of the NFL. It also was the first year in which all member teams played the same number of games.

The Eagles made University of Chicago halfback and Heisman Trophy winner Jay Berwanger the first player ever selected in the NFL draft, February 8. The Eagles traded his rights to the Bears, but Berwanger never played pro football. The first player selected to actually sign was the number-two pick, Riley Smith of Alabama, who was selected by Boston.

A rival league was formed, and it became the second to call itself the American Football League. The Boston Shamrocks were its champions.

Because of poor attendance, Marshall, the owner of the host team, moved the Championship Game from Boston to the Polo Grounds in New York. Green Bay defeated the Redskins 21-6, December 13.

1937
Homer Marshman was granted a Cleveland franchise, named the Rams, February 12. Marshall moved the Redskins to Washington, D.C., February 13. The Redskins signed TCU All-America tailback Sammy Baugh, who led them to a 28-21 victory over the Bears in the NFL Championship Game, December 12.

The Los Angeles Bulldogs had an 8-0 record to win the AFL title, but then the 2-year-old league folded.

1938
At the suggestion of Halas, Hugh (Shorty) Ray became a technical advisor on rules and officiating to the NFL. A new rule called for a 15-yard penalty for roughing the passer.

Rookie Byron (Whizzer) White of the Pittsburgh Pirates led the NFL in rushing. The Giants defeated the Packers 23-17 for the NFL title, December 11.

Marshall, *Los Angeles Times* sports editor Bill Henry, and promoter Tom Gallery established the Pro Bowl game between the NFL champion and a team of pro all-stars.

1939
The New York Giants defeated the Pro All-Stars 13-10 in the first Pro Bowl, at Wrigley Field, Los Angeles, January 15.

Carr, NFL president since 1921, died in Columbus, May 20. Carl Storck was named acting president, May 25.

An NFL game was televised for the first time when NBC broadcast the Brooklyn Dodgers-Philadelphia Eagles game from Ebbets Field to the approximately 1,000 sets then in New York.

Green Bay defeated New York 27-0 in the NFL Championship Game, December 10 at Milwaukee. NFL attendance exceeded 1 million in a season for the first time, reaching 1,071,200.

1940
A six-team rival league, the third to call itself the American Football League, was formed, and the Columbus Bullies won its championship.

Halas's Bears, with additional coaching by Clark Shaughnessy of Stanford, defeated the Redskins 73-0 in the NFL Championship Game, December 8. The game, which was the most decisive victory in NFL history, popularized the Bears' T-formation with a man-in-motion. It was the first championship carried on network radio, broadcast by Red Barber to 120 stations of the Mutual Broadcasting System, which paid $2,500 for the rights.

Art Rooney sold the Pittsburgh franchise to Alexis Thompson, December 9, then bought part interest in the Philadelphia Eagles.

1941
Elmer Layden was named the first Commissioner of the NFL, March 1; Storck, the acting president, resigned, April 5. NFL headquarters were moved to Chicago.

Bell and Rooney traded the Eagles to Thompson for the Pirates, then re-named their new team the Steelers. Homer Marshman sold the Rams to Daniel F. Reeves and Fred Levy, Jr.

The league by-laws were revised to provide for playoffs in case there were ties in division races, and sudden-death overtimes in case a playoff game was tied after four quarters. An official *NFL Record Manual* was published for the first time.

Columbus again won the championship of the AFL, but the two-year-old league then folded.

The Bears and the Packers finished in a tie for the Western Division championship, setting up the first divisional playoff game in league history. The Bears won 33-14, then defeated the Giants 37-9 for the NFL championship, December 21.

1942
Players departing for service in World War II depleted the rosters of NFL teams. Halas left the Bears in midseason to join the Navy, and Luke Johnsos and Heartley (Hunk) Anderson served as co-coaches as the Bears went 11-0 in the regular season. The Redskins defeated the Bears 14-6 in the NFL Championship Game, December 13.

1943
The Cleveland Rams, with co-owners Reeves and Levy in the service, were granted permission to suspend operations for one season, April 6. Levy transferred his stock in the team to Reeves, April 16.

The NFL adopted free substitution, April 7. The league also made the wearing of helmets mandatory and approved a 10-game schedule for all teams.

Philadelphia and Pittsburgh were granted permission to merge for one season, June 19. The team, known as Phil-Pitt (and called the Steagles by fans), divided home games between the two cities, and Earle (Greasy) Neale of Philadelphia and Walt Kiesling of Pittsburgh served as co-coaches. The merger automatically dissolved the last day of the season, December 5.

Ted Collins was granted a franchise for Boston, to become active in 1944.

Sammy Baugh led the league in passing, punting, and interceptions. He led the Redskins to a tie with the Giants for the Eastern Division title, and then to a 28-0 victory in a divisional playoff game. The Bears beat the Redskins 41-21 in the NFL Championship Game, December 26.

1944
Collins, who had wanted a franchise in Yankee Stadium in New York, named his new team in Boston the Yanks. Cleveland resumed operations. The Brooklyn Dodgers changed their name to the Tigers.

Coaching from the bench was legalized, April 20.

The Cardinals and the Steelers were granted permission to merge for one year under the name Card-Pitt, April 21. Phil Handler of the Cardinals and Walt Kiesling of the Steelers served as co-coaches. The merger automatically dissolved the last day of the season, December 3.

In the NFL Championship Game, Green Bay defeated the New York Giants 14-7, December 17.

1945
The inbounds lines or hashmarks were moved from 15 yards away from the sidelines to nearer the center of the field—20 yards from the sidelines.

Brooklyn and Boston merged into a team that played home games in both cities and was known simply as The Yanks. The team was coached by former Boston head coach Herb Kopf. In December, the Brooklyn franchise withdrew from the NFL to join the new All-America Football Conference; all the players on its active and reserve lists were assigned to The Yanks, who once again became the Boston Yanks.

Halas rejoined the Bears late in the season after service with the U.S. Navy. Although Halas took over much of the coaching duties, Anderson and Johnsos remained the coaches of record throughout the season.

Steve Van Buren of Philadelphia led the NFL in rushing, kickoff returns, and scoring.

After the Japanese surrendered ending World War II, a count showed that the NFL service roster, limited to men who had played in league games, totaled 638, 21 of whom had died in action.

Rookie quarterback Bob Waterfield led Cleveland to a 15-14 victory over Washington in the NFL Championship Game, December 16.

1946
The contract of Commissioner Layden was not renewed, and Bert Bell, the co-owner of the Steelers, replaced him, January 11. Bell moved the league headquarters from Chicago to the Philadelphia suburb of Bala-Cynwyd.

Free substitution was withdrawn and substitutions were limited to no more than three men at a time. Forward passes were made automatically incomplete upon striking the goal posts, January 11.

The NFL took on a truly national appearance for the first time when Reeves was granted permission by the league to move his NFL champion Rams to Los Angeles.

Halfback Kenny Washington (March 21) and end Woody Strode (May 7) signed with the Los Angeles Rams to become the first African-Americans to play in the NFL in the modern era. Guard Bill Willis (August 6) and running back Marion Motley (August 9) joined the AAFC with the Cleveland Browns.

The rival All-America Football Conference began play with eight teams. The Cleveland Browns, coached by Paul Brown, won the AAFC's first championship, defeating the New York Yankees 14-9.

Bill Dudley of the Steelers led the NFL in rushing, interceptions, and punt returns, and won the league's most valuable player award.

Backs Frank Filchock and Merle Hapes of the Giants were questioned about an attempt by a New York man to fix the championship game with the Bears. Bell suspended Hapes but allowed Filchock to play; he played well, but Chicago won 24-14, December 15.

1947
The NFL added a fifth official, the back judge.

A bonus choice was made for the first time in the NFL draft. One team each year would select the special choice before the first round began. The Chicago Bears won a lottery and the rights to the first choice and drafted back Bob Fenimore of Oklahoma A&M.

The Cleveland Browns again won the AAFC title, defeating the New York Yankees 14-3.

Charles Bidwill, Sr., owner of the Cardinals, died April 19, but his wife and sons retained ownership of the team. On December 28, the Cardinals won the NFL Championship Game 28-21 over the Philadelphia Eagles, who had beaten Pittsburgh 21-0 in a playoff.

1948
Plastic helmets were prohibited. A flexible artificial tee was permitted at the kickoff. Officials other than the referee were equipped with whistles, not horns, January 14.

Fred Mandel sold the Detroit Lions to a syndicate headed by D. Lyle Fife, January 15.

Halfback Fred Gehrke of the Los Angeles Rams painted horns on the Rams' helmets, the first modern helmet emblems in pro football.

The Cleveland Browns won their third straight championship in the AAFC, going 14-0 and then defeating the Buffalo Bills 49-7.

In a blizzard, the Eagles defeated the Cardinals 7-0 in the NFL Championship Game, December 19.

1949
Alexis Thompson sold the champion Eagles to a syndicate headed by James P. Clark, January 15. The Boston Yanks became the New York Bulldogs, sharing the Polo Grounds with the Giants.

Free substitution was adopted for one year, January 20.

The NFL had two 1,000-yard rushers in the same season for the first time—Steve Van Buren of Philadelphia and Tony Canadeo of Green Bay.

The AAFC played its season with a one-division, seven-team format. On December 9, Bell announced a merger agreement in which three AAFC franchises—Cleveland, San Francisco, and Baltimore—would join the NFL in 1950. The Browns won their fourth consecutive AAFC title, defeating the 49ers 21-7, December 11.

In a heavy rain, the Eagles defeated the Rams 14-0 in the NFL Championship Game, December 18.

1950
Unlimited free substitution was restored, opening the way for the era of two platoons and specialization in pro football, January 20.

Curly Lambeau, founder of the franchise and Green Bay's head coach since 1921, resigned under fire, February 1.

The name National Football League was restored after about three months as the National-American Football League. The American and National conferences were created to replace the Eastern and Western divisions, March 3.

The New York Bulldogs became the Yanks and divided the players of the former AAFC Yankees with the Giants. A special allocation draft was held in which the 13 teams drafted the remaining AAFC players, with special consideration for Baltimore, which received 15 choices compared to 10 for other teams.

The Los Angeles Rams became the first NFL team to have all of its games—both home and away—televised. The Washington Redskins followed the Rams in arranging to televise their games; other teams made deals to put selected games on television.

In the first game of the season, former AAFC champion Cleveland defeated NFL champion Philadelphia 35-10. For the first time, deadlocks occurred in both conferences and playoffs were necessary. The Browns defeated the Giants in the American and the Rams defeated the Bears in the National. Cleveland defeated Los Angeles 30-28 in the NFL Championship Game, December 24.

1951
The Pro Bowl game, dormant since 1942, was revived under a new format matching the all-stars of each conference at the Los Angeles Memorial Coliseum. The American Conference defeated the National Conference 28-27, January 14.

Abraham Watner returned the Baltimore franchise and its player contracts back to the NFL for $50,000. Baltimore's former players were made available for drafting at the same time as college players, January 18.

A rule was passed that no tackle, guard, or center would be eligible to catch a forward pass, January 18.

The Rams reversed their television policy and televised only road games.

The NFL Championship Game was televised coast-to-coast for the first time, December 23. The DuMont Network paid $75,000 for the rights to the game, in which the Rams defeated the Browns 24-17.

1952
Ted Collins sold the New York Yanks' franchise back to the NFL, January 19. A new franchise was awarded to a group in Dallas after it purchased the assets of the Yanks, January 24. The new Texans went 1-11, with the owners turning the franchise back to the league in midseason. For the last five games of the season, the commissioner's office operated the Texans as a road team, using Hershey, Pennsylvania, as a home base. At the end of the season the franchise was canceled, the last time an NFL team failed.

The Pittsburgh Steelers abandoned the Single-Wing for the T-formation, the last pro team to do so.

The Detroit Lions won their first NFL championship in 17 years, defeating the Browns 17-7 in the title game, December 28.

1953
A Baltimore group headed by Carroll Rosenbloom was granted a franchise and was awarded the holdings of the defunct Dallas organization, January 23. The team, named the Colts, put together the largest trade in league history, acquiring 10 players from Cleveland in exchange for five.

The names of the American and National conferences were changed to the Eastern and Western conferences, January 24.

Jim Thorpe died, March 28.

Mickey McBride, founder of the Cleveland Browns, sold the franchise to a syndicate headed by Dave R. Jones, June 10.

The NFL policy of blacking out home games was upheld by Judge Allan K. Grim of the U.S. District Court in Philadelphia, November 12.

The Lions again defeated the Browns in the NFL Championship Game, winning 17-16, December 27.

1954
The Canadian Football League began a series of raids on NFL teams, signing quarterback Eddie LeBaron and defensive end Gene Brito of Washington and defensive tackle Arnie Weinmeister of the Giants, among others.

Fullback Joe Perry of the 49ers became the first player in league history to gain 1,000 yards rushing in consecutive seasons.

Cleveland defeated Detroit 56-10 in the NFL Championship Game, December 26.

1955
The sudden-death overtime rule was used for the first time in a preseason game between the Rams and Giants at Portland, Oregon, August 28. The Rams won 23-17 three minutes into overtime.

A rule change declared the ball dead immediately if the ball carrier touched the ground with any part of his body except his hands or feet while in the grasp of an opponent.

The Baltimore Colts made an 80-cent phone call to Johnny Unitas and signed him as a free agent. Another quarterback, Otto Graham, played his last game as the Browns defeated the Rams 38-14 in the NFL Championship Game, December 26. Graham had quarterbacked the Browns to 10 championship-game appearances in 10 years.

NBC replaced DuMont as the network for the title game, paying a rights fee of $100,000.

1956
The NFL Players Association was founded.

Grabbing an opponent's facemask (other than the ball carrier) was made illegal. Using radio receivers to communicate with players on the field was prohibited. A natural leather ball with white end stripes replaced the white ball with black stripes for night games.

The Giants moved from the Polo Grounds to Yankee Stadium.

Halas retired as coach of the Bears, and was replaced by Paddy Driscoll.

CBS became the first network to broadcast some NFL regular-season games to selected television markets across the nation.

The Giants routed the Bears 47-7 in the NFL Championship Game, December 30.

1957
Pete Rozelle was named general manager of the Rams. Anthony J. Morabito, founder and co-owner of the 49ers, died of a heart attack during a game against the Bears at Kezar Stadium, October 28. An NFL-record crowd of 102,368 saw the 49ers-Rams game at the Los Angeles Memorial Coliseum, November 10.

The Lions came from 20 points down to post a 31-27 playoff victory over the 49ers, December 22. Detroit defeated Cleveland 59-14 in the NFL Championship Game, December 29.

1958
The bonus selection in the draft was eliminated, January 29. The last selection was quarterback King Hill of Rice by the Chicago Cardinals.

Halas reinstated himself as coach of the Bears.

Jim Brown of Cleveland gained an NFL-record 1,527 yards rushing. In a divisional playoff game, the Giants held Brown to eight yards and defeated Cleveland 10-0.

Baltimore, coached by Weeb Ewbank, defeated the Giants 23-17 in the first sudden-death overtime in an NFL Championship Game, December 28. The game ended when Colts fullback Alan Ameche scored on a one-yard touchdown run after 8:15 of overtime.

1959
Vince Lombardi was named head coach of the Green Bay Packers, January 28. Tim Mara, the co-founder of the Giants, died, February 17.

Lamar Hunt of Dallas announced his intentions to form a second pro football league. The first meeting was held in Chicago, August 14, and consisted of Hunt representing Dallas; Bob Howsam, Denver; K.S. (Bud) Adams, Houston; Barron Hilton, Los Angeles; Max Winter and Bill Boyer, Minneapolis; and Harry Wismer, New York City. They made plans to begin play in 1960.

The new league was named the American Football League, August 22. Buffalo, owned by Ralph Wilson, became the seventh franchise, October 28. Boston, owned by William H. Sullivan, became the eighth team, November 22. The first AFL draft, lasting 33 rounds, was held, November 22. Joe Foss was named AFL Commissioner, November 30. An additional draft of 20 rounds was held by the AFL, December 2.

NFL Commissioner Bert Bell died of a heart attack suffered at Franklin

Field, Philadelphia, during the last two minutes of a game between the Eagles and the Steelers, October 11. Treasurer Austin Gunsel was named president in the office of the commissioner, October 14.

The Colts again defeated the Giants in the NFL Championship Game, 31-16, December 27.

1960

Pete Rozelle was elected NFL Commissioner as a compromise choice on the twenty-third ballot, January 26. Rozelle moved the league offices to New York City.

Hunt was elected AFL president for 1960, January 26. Minneapolis withdrew from the AFL, January 27, and the same ownership was given an NFL franchise for Minnesota (to start in 1961), January 28. Dallas received an NFL franchise for 1960, January 28. Oakland received an AFL franchise, January 30.

The AFL adopted the two-point option on points after touchdown, January 28. A no-tampering verbal pact, relative to players' contracts, was agreed to between the NFL and AFL, February 9.

The NFL owners voted to allow the transfer of the Chicago Cardinals to St. Louis, March 13.

The AFL signed a five-year television contract with ABC, June 9.

The Boston Patriots defeated the Buffalo Bills 28-7 before 16,000 at Buffalo in the first AFL preseason game, July 30. The Denver Broncos defeated the Patriots 13-10 before 21,597 at Boston in the first AFL regular-season game, September 9.

Philadelphia defeated Green Bay 17-13 in the NFL Championship Game, December 26.

1961

The Houston Oilers defeated the Los Angeles Chargers 24-16 before 32,183 in the first AFL Championship Game, January 1.

Detroit defeated Cleveland 17-16 in the first Playoff Bowl, or Bert Bell Benefit Bowl, between second-place teams in each conference in Miami, January 7.

End Willard Dewveall of the Bears played out his option and joined the Oilers, becoming the first player to move deliberately from one league to the other, January 14.

Ed McGah, Wayne Valley, and Robert Osborne bought out their partners in the ownership of the Raiders, January 17. The Chargers were transferred to San Diego, February 10. Dave R. Jones sold the Browns to a group headed by Arthur B. Modell, March 22. The Howsam brothers sold the Broncos to a group headed by Calvin Kunz and Gerry Phipps, May 26.

NBC was awarded a two-year contract for radio and television rights to the NFL Championship Game for $615,000 annually, $300,000 of which was to go directly into the NFL Player Benefit Plan, April 5.

Canton, Ohio, where the league that became the NFL was formed in 1920, was chosen as the site of the Pro Football Hall of Fame, April 27. Dick McCann, a former Redskins executive, was named executive director.

A bill legalizing single-network television contracts by professional sports leagues was introduced in Congress by Representative Emanuel Celler. It passed the House and Senate and was signed into law by President John F. Kennedy, September 30.

Houston defeated San Diego 10-3 for the AFL championship, December 24. Green Bay won its first NFL championship since 1944, defeating the New York Giants 37-0, December 31.

1962

The Western Division defeated the Eastern Division 47-27 in the first AFL All-Star Game, played before 20,973 in San Diego, January 7.

Both leagues prohibited grabbing any player's facemask. The AFL voted to make the scoreboard clock the official timer of the game.

The NFL entered into a single-network agreement with CBS for telecasting all regular-season games for $4.65 million annually, January 10.

Judge Roszel Thompson of the U.S. District Court in Baltimore ruled against the AFL in its antitrust suit against the NFL, May 21. The AFL had charged the NFL with monopoly and conspiracy in areas of expansion, television, and player signings. The case lasted two and a half years, the trial two months.

McGah and Valley acquired controlling interest in the Raiders, May 24. The AFL assumed financial responsibility for the New York Titans, November 8. With Commissioner Rozelle as referee, Daniel F. Reeves regained the ownership of the Rams, outbidding his partners in sealed-envelope bidding for the team, November 27.

The Dallas Texans defeated the Oilers 20-17 for the AFL championship at Houston after 17 minutes, 54 seconds of overtime on a 25-yard field goal by Tommy Brooker, December 23. The game lasted a record 77 minutes, 54 seconds.

Judge Edward Weinfeld of the U.S. District Court in New York City upheld the legality of the NFL's television blackout within a 75-mile radius of home games and denied an injunction that would have forced the championship game between the Giants and the Packers to be televised in the New York City area, December 28. The Packers beat the Giants 16-7 for the NFL title, December 30.

1963

The Dallas Texans transferred to Kansas City, becoming the Chiefs, February 8. The New York Titans were sold to a five-man syndicate headed by David (Sonny) Werblin, March 28. Weeb Ewbank became the Titans' new head coach and the team's name was changed to the Jets, April 15. They began play in Shea Stadium.

NFL Properties, Inc., was founded to serve as the licensing arm of the NFL.

Rozelle indefinitely suspended Green Bay halfback Paul Hornung and Detroit defensive tackle Alex Karras for placing bets on their own teams and on other NFL games; he also fined five other Detroit players $2,000 each for betting on one game in which they did not participate, and the Detroit Lions Football Company $2,000 on each of two counts for failure to report information promptly and for lack of sideline supervision.

Paul Brown, head coach of the Browns since their inception, was fired and replaced by Blanton Collier. Don Shula replaced Weeb Ewbank as head coach of the Colts.

The AFL allowed the Jets and Raiders to select players from other franchises in hopes of giving the league more competitive balance, May 11.

NBC was awarded exclusive network broadcasting rights for the 1963 AFL Championship Game for $926,000, May 23.

The Pro Football Hall of Fame was dedicated at Canton, Ohio, September 7.

The U.S. Fourth Circuit Court of Appeals reaffirmed the lower court's finding for the NFL in the $10-million suit brought by the AFL, ending three and a half years of litigation, November 21.

Jim Brown of Cleveland rushed for an NFL single-season record 1,863 yards.

Boston defeated Buffalo 26-8 in the first divisional playoff game in AFL history, December 28.

The Bears defeated the Giants 14-10 in the NFL Championship Game, a record sixth and last title for Halas in his thirty-sixth season as the Bears' coach, December 29.

1964

The Chargers defeated the Patriots 51-10 in the AFL Championship Game, January 5.

William Clay Ford, the Lions' president since 1961, purchased the team, January 10. A group representing the late James P. Clark sold the Eagles to a group headed by Jerry Wolman, January 21. Carroll Rosenbloom, the majority owner of the Colts since 1953, acquired complete ownership of the team, January 23.

The AFL signed a five-year, $36-million television contract with NBC to begin with the 1965 season, January 29.

Commissioner Rozelle negotiated an agreement on behalf of the NFL clubs to purchase Ed Sabol's Blair Motion Pictures, which was renamed NFL Films, March 5.

Hornung and Karras were reinstated by Rozelle, March 16.

CBS submitted the winning bid of $14.1 million per year for the NFL regular-season television rights for 1964 and 1965, January 24. CBS acquired the rights to the championship games for 1964 and 1965 for $1.8 million per game, April 17.

Pete Gogolak of Cornell signed a contract with Buffalo, becoming the first soccer-style kicker in pro football.

Buffalo defeated San Diego 20-7 in the AFL Championship Game, December 26. Cleveland defeated Baltimore 27-0 in the NFL Championship Game, December 27.

1965

The NFL teams pledged not to sign college seniors until completion of all their games, including bowl games, and empowered the Commissioner to discipline the clubs up to as much as the loss of an entire draft list for a violation of the pledge, February 15.

The NFL added a sixth official, the line judge, February 19. The color of the officials' penalty flags was changed from white to bright gold, April 5.

Atlanta was awarded an NFL franchise for 1966, with Rankin Smith, Sr., as owner, June 30. Miami was awarded an AFL franchise for 1966, with Joe Robbie and Danny Thomas as owners, August 16.

Field Judge Burl Toler became the first black official in NFL history, September 19.

According to a Harris survey, sports fans chose professional football (41 percent) as their favorite sport, overtaking baseball (38 percent) for the first time, October.

Green Bay defeated Baltimore 13-10 in sudden-death overtime in a Western Conference playoff game. Don Chandler kicked a 25-yard field goal for the Packers after 13 minutes, 39 seconds of overtime, December 26. The Packers then defeated the Browns 23-12 in the NFL Championship Game, January 2.

In the AFL Championship Game, the Bills again defeated the Chargers, 23-0, December 26.

CBS acquired the rights to the NFL regular-season games in 1966 and 1967, with an option for 1968, for $18.8 million per year, December 29.

1966

The AFL-NFL war reached its peak, as the leagues spent a combined $7 million to sign their 1966 draft choices. The NFL signed 75 percent of its 232 draftees, the AFL 46 percent of its 181. Of the 111 common draft choices, 79 signed with the NFL, 28 with the AFL, and 4 went unsigned.

Buddy Young became the first African-American to work in the league office when Commissioner Rozelle named him director of player relations, February 1.

The rights to the 1966 and 1967 NFL Championship Games were sold to CBS for $2 million per game, February 14.

Foss resigned as AFL Commissioner, April 7. Al Davis, the head coach and general manager of the Raiders, was named to replace him, April 8.

Goal posts offset from the goal line, painted bright yellow, and with uprights 20 feet above the cross-bar were made standard in the NFL, May 16.

A series of secret meetings regarding a possible AFL-NFL merger were held in the spring between Hunt of Kansas City and Tex Schramm of Dallas. Rozelle announced the merger, June 8. Under the agreement, the two leagues would combine to form an expanded league with 24 teams, to be increased to 26 in 1968 and to 28 by 1970 or soon thereafter. All existing franchises would be retained, and no franchises would be transferred outside their metropolitan areas. While maintaining separate schedules through 1969, the leagues agreed to play an annual AFL-NFL World Championship Game beginning in January, 1967, and to hold a combined draft, also beginning in 1967. Preseason games would be held between teams of each league starting in 1967. Official regular-season play would start in 1970 when the two leagues would officially merge to form one league with two conferences. Rozelle was named Commissioner of the expanded league setup.

Davis rejoined the Raiders, and Milt Woodard was named president of the AFL, July 25.

The St. Louis Cardinals moved into newly constructed Busch Memorial Stadium.

Barron Hilton sold the Chargers to a group headed by Eugene Klein and Sam Schulman, August 25.

Congress approved the AFL-NFL merger, passing legislation exempting the agreement itself from antitrust action, October 21.

New Orleans was awarded an NFL franchise to begin play in 1967, November 1. John Mecom, Jr., of Houston was designated majority stockholder and president of the franchise, December 15.

The NFL was realigned for the 1967-69 seasons into the Capitol and Century Divisions in the Eastern Conference and the Central and Coastal Divisions in the Western Conference, December 2. New Orleans and the New York Giants agreed to switch divisions in 1968 and return to the 1967 alignment in 1969.

The rights to the Super Bowl for four years were sold to CBS and NBC for $9.5 million, December 13.

1967
Green Bay earned the right to represent the NFL in the first AFL-NFL World Championship Game by defeating Dallas 34-27, January 1. The same day, Kansas City defeated Buffalo 31-7 to represent the AFL. The Packers defeated the Chiefs 35-10 before 61,946 fans at the Los Angeles Memorial Coliseum in the first game between AFL and NFL teams, January 15. The winning players' share for the Packers was $15,000 each, and the losing players' share for the Chiefs was $7,500 each. The game was televised by both CBS and NBC.

The "sling-shot" goal post and a six-foot-wide border around the field were made standard in the NFL, February 22.

Baltimore made Bubba Smith, a Michigan State defensive lineman, the first choice in the first combined AFL-NFL draft, March 14.

The AFL awarded a franchise to begin play in 1968 to Cincinnati, May 24. A group with Paul Brown as part owner, general manager, and head coach, was awarded the Cincinnati franchise, September 27.

Arthur B. Modell, the president of the Cleveland Browns, was elected president of the NFL, May 28.

Defensive back Emlen Tunnell of the New York Giants became the first black player to enter the Pro Football Hall of Fame, August 5.

An AFL team defeated an NFL team for the first time, when Denver beat Detroit 13-7 in a preseason game, August 5.

Green Bay defeated Dallas 21-17 for the NFL championship on a last-minute 1-yard quarterback sneak by Bart Starr in 13-below-zero temperature at Green Bay, December 31. The same day, Oakland defeated Houston 40-7 for the AFL championship.

1968
Green Bay defeated Oakland 33-14 in Super Bowl II at Miami, January 14. The game had the first $3-million gate in pro football history.

Vince Lombardi resigned as head coach of the Packers, but remained as general manager, January 28.

Werblin sold his shares in the Jets to his partners Don Lillis, Leon Hess, Townsend Martin, and Phil Iselin, May 21. Lillis assumed the presidency of the club, but then died July 23. Iselin was appointed president, August 6.

Halas retired for the fourth and last time as head coach of the Bears, May 27.

The Oilers left Rice Stadium for the Astrodome and became the first NFL team to play its home games in a domed stadium.

The movie *Heidi* became a footnote in sports history when NBC didn't show the last :50 of the Jets-Raiders game in order to permit the children's special to begin on time. The Raiders scored two touchdowns in the last 42 seconds to win 43-32, November 17.

Ewbank became the first coach to win titles in both the NFL and AFL when his Jets defeated the Raiders 27-23 for the AFL championship, December 29. The same day, Baltimore defeated Cleveland 34-0.

1969
The AFL established a playoff format for the 1969 season, with the winner in one division playing the runner-up in the other, January 11.

An AFL team won the Super Bowl for the first time, as the Jets defeated the Colts 16-7 at Miami, January 12 in Super Bowl III. The title Super Bowl was recognized by the NFL for the first time.

Vince Lombardi became part owner, executive vice-president, and head coach of the Washington Redskins, February 7.

Wolman sold the Eagles to Leonard Tose, May 1.

Baltimore, Cleveland, and Pittsburgh agreed to join the AFL teams to form the 13-team American Football Conference of the NFL in 1970, May 17. The NFL also agreed on a playoff format that would include one "wild-card" team per conference—the second-place team with the best record.

Monday Night Football was signed for 1970. ABC acquired the rights to televise 13 NFL regular-season Monday night games in 1970, 1971, and 1972.

George Preston Marshall, president emeritus of the Redskins, died at 72, August 9.

The NFL marked its fiftieth year by the wearing of a special patch by each of the 16 teams.

1970
Kansas City defeated Minnesota 23-7 in Super Bowl IV at New Orleans, January 11. The gross receipts of approximately $3.8 million were the largest ever for a one-day sports event.

Four-year television contracts, under which CBS would televise all NFC games and NBC all AFC games (except Monday night games) and the two would divide televising the Super Bowl and AFC-NFC Pro Bowl games, were announced, January 26.

Art Modell resigned as president of the NFL, March 12. Milt Woodard resigned as president of the AFL, March 13. Lamar Hunt was elected president of the AFC and George Halas was elected president of the NFC, March 19.

The merged 26-team league adopted rules changes putting names on the backs of players' jerseys, making a point after touchdown worth only one point, and making the scoreboard clock the official timing device of the game, March 18.

The Players Negotiating Committee and the NFL Players Association announced a four-year agreement guaranteeing approximately $4,535,000 annually to player pension and insurance benefits, August 3. The owners also agreed to contribute $250,000 annually to improve or implement items such as disability payments, widows' benefits, maternity benefits, and dental benefits. The agreement also provided for increased preseason game and per diem payments, averaging approximately $2.6 million annually.

The Pittsburgh Steelers moved into Three Rivers Stadium. The Cincinnati Bengals moved to Riverfront Stadium.

Lombardi died of cancer at 57, September 3.

The Super Bowl trophy was renamed the Vince Lombardi trophy, September 10.

Tom Dempsey of New Orleans kicked a game-winning NFL-record 63-yard field goal against Detroit, November 8.

1971
Baltimore defeated Dallas 16-13 on Jim O'Brien's 32-yard field goal with five seconds to go in Super Bowl V at Miami, January 17. The NBC telecast was viewed in an estimated 23,980,000 homes, the largest audience ever for a one-day sports event.

The NFC defeated the AFC 27-6 in the first AFC-NFC Pro Bowl at Los Angeles, January 24.

The Boston Patriots changed their name to the New England Patriots, March 25. Their new stadium, Schaefer Stadium, was dedicated in a 20-14 preseason victory over the Giants.

The Philadelphia Eagles left Franklin Field and played their games at the new Veterans Stadium.

The San Francisco 49ers left Kezar Stadium and moved their games to Candlestick Park.

Daniel F. Reeves, the president and general manager of the Rams, died at 58, April 15.

The Dallas Cowboys moved from the Cotton Bowl into their new home, Texas Stadium, October 24.

Miami defeated Kansas City 27-24 in sudden-death overtime in an AFC Divisional Playoff Game, December 25. Garo Yepremian kicked a 37-yard field goal for the Dolphins after 22 minutes, 40 seconds of overtime, as the game lasted 82 minutes, 40 seconds overall, making it the longest game in history.

1972
Dallas defeated Miami 24-3 in Super Bowl VI at New Orleans, January 16. The CBS telecast was viewed in an estimated 27,450,000 homes, the top-rated one-day telecast ever.

The inbounds lines or hashmarks were moved nearer the center of the field, 23 yards, 1 foot, 9 inches from the sidelines, March 23. The method of determining won-lost percentage in standings changed. Tie games, previously not counted in the standings, were made equal to a half-game won and a half-game lost, May 24.

Robert Irsay purchased the Los Angeles Rams and transferred ownership of the club to Carroll Rosenbloom in exchange for the Baltimore Colts, July 13.

William V. Bidwill purchased the stock of his brother Charles (Stormy) Bidwill to become the sole owner of the St. Louis Cardinals, September 2.

The National District Attorneys Association endorsed the position of professional leagues in opposing proposed legalization of gambling on professional team sports, September 28.

Franco Harris's "Immaculate Reception" gave the Steelers their first postseason win ever, 13-7 over the Raiders, December 23.

1973
Rozelle announced that all Super Bowl VII tickets were sold and that the game would be telecast in Los Angeles, the site of the game, on an experimental basis, January 3.

Miami defeated Washington 14-7 in Super Bowl VII at Los Angeles, completing a 17-0 season, the first perfect-record regular-season and postseason mark in NFL history, January 14. The NBC telecast was viewed by approximately 75 million people.

The AFC defeated the NFC 33-28 in the Pro Bowl in Dallas, the first time since 1942 that the game was played outside Los Angeles, January 21.

A jersey numbering system was adopted, April 5: 1-19 for quarterbacks and specialists, 20-49 for running backs and defensive backs, 50-59 for centers and linebackers, 60-79 for defensive linemen and interior offensive linemen other than centers, and 80-89 for wide receivers and tight ends. Players who had been in the NFL in 1972 could continue to use old numbers.

NFL Charities, a nonprofit organization, was created to derive an income from monies generated from NFL Properties' licensing of NFL trademarks and team names, June 26. NFL Charities was set up to support education and charitable activities and to supply economic support to persons formerly associated with professional football who were no longer able to support themselves.

Congress adopted experimental legislation (for three years) requiring any NFL game that had been declared a sellout 72 hours prior to kickoff to be made available for local televising, September 14. The legislation provided for an annual review to be made by the Federal Communications Commission.

The Buffalo Bills moved their home games from War Memorial Stadium to Rich Stadium in nearby Orchard Park. The Giants tied the Eagles 23-23 in the final game in Yankee Stadium, September 23. The Giants played the rest of their home games at the Yale Bowl in New Haven, Connecticut.

A rival league, the World Football League, was formed and was reported in operation, October 2. It had plans to start play in 1974.

O.J. Simpson of Buffalo became the first player to rush for more than 2,000 yards in a season, gaining 2,003.

1974

Miami defeated Minnesota 24-7 in Super Bowl VIII at Houston, the second consecutive Super Bowl championship for the Dolphins, January 13. The CBS telecast was viewed by approximately 75 million people.

Rozelle was given a 10-year contract effective January 1, 1973, February 27.

Tampa Bay was awarded a franchise to begin operation in 1976, April 24.

Sweeping rules changes were adopted to add action and tempo to games: one sudden-death overtime period was added for preseason and regular-season games; the goal posts were moved from the goal line to the end lines; kickoffs were moved from the 40- to the 35-yard line; after missed field goals from beyond the 20, the ball was to be returned to the line of scrimmage; restrictions were placed on members of the punting team to open up return possibilities; roll-blocking and cutting of wide receivers was eliminated; the extent of downfield contact a defender could have with an eligible receiver was restricted; the penalties for offensive holding, illegal use of the hands, and tripping were reduced from 15 to 10 yards; wide receivers blocking back toward the ball within three yards of the line of scrimmage were prevented from blocking below the waist, April 25.

Seattle was awarded an NFL franchise to begin play in 1976, June 4. Lloyd W. Nordstrom, president of the Seattle Seahawks, and Hugh Culverhouse, president of the Tampa Bay Buccaneers, signed franchise agreements, December 5.

The Birmingham Americans defeated the Florida Blazers 22-21 in the WFL World Bowl, winning the league championship, December 5.

1975

Pittsburgh defeated Minnesota 16-6 in Super Bowl IX at New Orleans, the Steelers' first championship since entering the NFL in 1933. The NBC telecast was viewed by approximately 78 million people.

The Memphis Southmen of the WFL signed Larry Csonka, Jim Kiick, and Paul Warfield of Miami, March 31.

The divisional winners with the highest won-loss percentage were made the home team for the divisional playoffs, and the surviving winners with the highest percentage made home teams for the championship games, June 26.

Referees were equipped with wireless microphones for all preseason, regular-season, and playoff games.

The Lions moved to the new Pontiac Silverdome. The Giants played their home games in Shea Stadium. The Saints moved into the Louisiana Superdome.

The World Football League folded, October 22.

1976

Pittsburgh defeated Dallas 21-17 in Super Bowl X in Miami. The Steelers joined Green Bay and Miami as the only teams to win two Super Bowls; the Cowboys became the first wild-card team to play in the Super Bowl. The CBS telecast was viewed by an estimated 80 million people, the largest television audience in history.

Lloyd Nordstrom, the president of the Seahawks, died at 66, January 20. His brother Elmer succeeded him as majority representative of the team.

The owners awarded Super Bowl XII, to be played on January 15, 1978, to New Orleans. They also adopted the use of two 30-second clocks for all games, visible to both players and fans to note the official time between the ready-for-play signal and snap of the ball, March 16.

A veteran player allocation was held to stock the Seattle and Tampa Bay franchises with 39 players each, March 30-31. In the college draft, Seattle and Tampa Bay each received eight extra choices, April 8-9.

The Giants moved into new Giants Stadium in East Rutherford, New Jersey.

The Steelers defeated the College All-Stars in a storm-shortened Chicago College All-Star Game, the last of the series, July 23. St. Louis defeated San Diego 20-10 in a preseason game before 38,000 in Korakuen Stadium, Tokyo, in the first NFL game outside of North America, August 16.

1977

Oakland defeated Minnesota 32-14 in Super Bowl XI at Pasadena, January 9. The paid attendance was a pro record 103,438. The NBC telecast was viewed by 81.9 million people, the largest ever to view a sports event. The victory was the fifth consecutive for the AFC in the Super Bowl.

The NFL Players Association and the NFL Management Council ratified a collective bargaining agreement extending until 1982, covering five football seasons while continuing the pension plan—including years 1974, 1975, and 1976—with contributions totaling more than $55 million. The total cost of the agreement was estimated at $107 million. The agreement called for a college draft at least through 1986; contained a no-strike, no-suit clause; established a 43-man active player limit; reduced pension vesting to four years; provided for increases in minimum salaries and preseason and postseason pay; improved insurance, medical, and dental benefits; modified previous practices in player movement and control; and reaffirmed the NFL Commissioner's disciplinary authority. Additionally, the agreement called for the NFL member clubs to make payments totaling $16 million the next 10 years to settle various legal disputes, February 25.

The San Francisco 49ers were sold to Edward J. DeBartolo, Jr., March 28.

A 16-game regular season, 4-game preseason was adopted to begin in 1978, March 29. A second wild-card team was adopted for the playoffs beginning in 1978, with the wild-card teams to play each other and the winners advancing to a round of eight postseason series.

The Seahawks were permanently aligned in the AFC Western Division and the Buccaneers in the NFC Central Division, March 31.

The owners awarded Super Bowl XIII, to be played on January 21, 1979, to Miami, to be played in the Orange Bowl; Super Bowl XIV, to be played January 20, 1980, was awarded to Pasadena, to be played in the Rose Bowl, June 14.

Rules changes were adopted to open up the passing game and to cut down on injuries. Defenders were permitted to make contact with eligible receivers only once; the head slap was outlawed; offensive linemen were prohibited from thrusting their hands to an opponent's neck, face, or head; and wide receivers were prohibited from clipping, even in the legal clipping zone.

Rozelle negotiated contracts with the three television networks to televise all NFL regular-season and postseason games, plus selected preseason games, for four years beginning with the 1978 season. ABC was awarded yearly rights to 16 Monday night games, four prime-time games, the AFC-NFC Pro Bowl, and the Hall of Fame games. CBS received the rights to all NFC regular-season and postseason games (except those in the ABC package) and to Super Bowls XIV and XVI. NBC received the rights to all AFC regular-season and postseason games (except those in the ABC package) and to Super Bowls XIII and XV. Industry sources considered it the largest single television package ever negotiated, October 12.

Chicago's Walter Payton set a single-game rushing record with 275 yards (40 carries) against Minnesota, November 20.

1978

Dallas defeated Denver 27-10 in Super Bowl XII, held indoors for the first time, at the Louisiana Superdome in New Orleans, January 15. The CBS telecast was viewed by more than 102 million people, meaning the game was watched by more viewers than any other show of any kind in the history of television. Dallas's victory was the first for the NFC in six years.

According to a Louis Harris Sports Survey, 70 percent of the nation's sports fans said they followed football, compared to 54 percent who followed baseball. Football increased its lead as the country's favorite, 26 percent to 16 percent for baseball, January 19.

A seventh official, the side judge, was added to the officiating crew, March 14.

The NFL continued a trend toward opening up the game. Rules changes permitted a defender to maintain contact with a receiver within five yards of the line of scrimmage, but restricted contact beyond that point. The pass-blocking rule was interpreted to permit the extending of arms and open hands, March 17.

A study on the use of instant replay as an officiating aid was made during seven nationally televised preseason games.

The NFL played for the first time in Mexico City, with the Saints defeating the Eagles 14-7 in a preseason game, August 5.

Bolstered by the expansion of the regular-season schedule from 14 to 16 weeks, NFL paid attendance exceeded 12 million (12,771,800) for the first time. The per-game average of 57,017 was the third-highest in league history and the most since 1973.

1979

Pittsburgh defeated Dallas 35-31 in Super Bowl XIII at Miami to become the first team ever to win three Super Bowls, January 21. The NBC telecast was viewed in 35,090,000 homes, by an estimated 96.6 million fans.

The owners awarded three future Super Bowl sites: Super Bowl XV to the Louisiana Superdome in New Orleans, to be played on January 25, 1981; Super Bowl XVI to the Pontiac Silverdome in Pontiac, Michigan, to be played on January 24, 1982; and Super Bowl XVII to Pasadena's Rose Bowl, to be played on January 30, 1983, March 13.

NFL rules changes emphasized additional player safety. The changes prohibited players on the receiving team from blocking below the waist during kickoffs, punts, and field-goal attempts; prohibited the wearing of torn or altered equipment and exposed pads that could be hazardous; extended the zone in which there could be no crackback blocks; and instructed officials to quickly whistle a play dead when a quarterback was clearly in the grasp of a tackler, March 16.

Rosenbloom, the president of the Rams, drowned at 72, April 2. His widow, Georgia, assumed control of the club.

1980

Pittsburgh defeated the Los Angeles Rams 31-19 in Super Bowl XIV at Pasadena to become the first team to win four Super Bowls, January 20. The game was viewed in a record 35,330,000 homes.

The AFC-NFC Pro Bowl, won 37-27 by the NFC, was played before 48,060 fans at Aloha Stadium in Honolulu, Hawaii. It was the first time in the 30-year history of the Pro Bowl that the game was played in a non-NFL city.

Rules changes placed greater restrictions on contact in the area of the head, neck, and face. Under the heading of "personal foul," players were prohibited from directly striking, swinging, or clubbing on the head, neck, or face. Starting in 1980, a penalty could be called for such contact whether or not the initial contact was made below the neck area.

CBS, with a record bid of $12 million, won the national radio rights to 26 NFL regular-season games, including Monday Night Football, and all 10 postseason games for the 1980-83 seasons.

The Los Angeles Rams moved their home games to Anaheim Stadium in nearby Orange County, California.

The Oakland Raiders joined the Los Angeles Coliseum Commission's antitrust suit against the NFL. The suit contended the league violated antitrust laws in declining to approve a proposed move by the Raiders from Oakland to Los Angeles.

NFL regular-season attendance of nearly 13.4 million set a record for the third year in a row. The average paid attendance for the 224-game 1980 regular season was 59,787, the highest in the league's 61-year history. NFL games in 1980 were played before 92.4 percent of total stadium capacity.

Television ratings in 1980 were the second-best in NFL history, trailing only the combined ratings of the 1976 season. All three networks posted gains, and NBC's 15.0 rating was its best ever. CBS and ABC had their best ratings since 1977, with 15.3 and 20.8 ratings, respectively. CBS Radio reported a record audience of 7 million for Monday night and special games.

1981

Oakland defeated Philadelphia 27-10 in Super Bowl XV at the Louisiana Superdome in New Orleans, to become the first wild-card team to win a Super Bowl, January 25.

Edgar F. Kaiser, Jr., purchased the Denver Broncos from Gerald and Allan Phipps, February 26.

The owners adopted a disaster plan for re-stocking a team should the club be involved in a fatal accident, March 20.

The owners awarded Super Bowl XVIII to Tampa, to be played in Tampa Stadium on January 22, 1984, June 3.

A CBS-New York Times poll showed that 48 percent of sports fans preferred football to 31 percent for baseball.

The NFL teams hosted 167 representatives from 44 predominantly black colleges during training camps for a total of 289 days. The program was adopted for renewal during each training camp period.

NFL regular-season attendance—13.6 million for an average of 60,745—set a record for the fourth year in a row. It also was the first time the per-game average exceeded 60,000. NFL games in 1981 were played before 93.8 percent of total stadium capacity.

ABC and CBS set all-time rating highs. ABC finished with a 21.7 rating and CBS with a 17.5 rating. NBC was down slightly to 13.9.

1982

San Francisco defeated Cincinnati 26-21 in Super Bowl XVI at the Pontiac Silverdome, in the first Super Bowl held in the North, January 24. The CBS telecast achieved the highest rating of any televised sports event ever, 49.1 with a 73.0 share. The game was viewed by a record 110.2 million fans. CBS Radio reported a record 14 million listeners for the game.

The NFL signed a five-year contract with the three television networks (ABC, CBS, and NBC) to televise all NFL regular-season and postseason games starting with the 1982 season.

The owners awarded the 1983, 1984, and 1985 AFC-NFC Pro Bowls to Honolulu's Aloha Stadium.

A jury ruled against the NFL in the antitrust trial brought by the Los Angeles Coliseum Commission and the Oakland Raiders, May 7. The verdict cleared the way for the Raiders to move to Los Angeles, where they defeated Green Bay 24-3 in their first preseason game, August 29.

The 1982 season was reduced from a 16-game schedule to nine as the result of a 57-day players' strike. The strike was called by the NFLPA at midnight on Monday, September 20, following the Green Bay at New York Giants game. Play resumed November 21-22 following ratification of the Collective Bargaining Agreement by NFL owners, November 17 in New York.

Under the Collective Bargaining Agreement, which was to run through the 1986 season, the NFL draft was extended through 1992 and the veteran free-agent system was left basically unchanged. A minimum salary schedule for years of experience was established; training camp and postseason pay were increased; players' medical, insurance, and retirement benefits were increased; and a severance-pay system was introduced to aid in career transition, a first in professional sports.

Despite the players' strike, the average paid attendance in 1982 was 58,472, the fifth-highest in league history.

The owners awarded the sites of two Super Bowls, December 14: Super Bowl XIX, to be played on January 20, 1985, to Stanford University Stadium in Stanford, California, with San Francisco as host team; and Super Bowl XX, to be played on January 26, 1986, to the Louisiana Superdome in New Orleans.

1983

Because of the shortened season, the NFL adopted a format of 16 teams competing in a Super Bowl Tournament for the 1982 playoffs. The NFC's number-one seed, Washington, defeated the AFC's number-two seed, Miami, 27-17 in Super Bowl XVII at the Rose Bowl in Pasadena, January 30.

Super Bowl XVII was the second-highest rated live television program of all time, giving the NFL a sweep of the top 10 live programs in television history. The game was viewed in more than 40 million homes, the largest ever for a live telecast.

George Halas, the owner of the Bears and the last surviving member of the NFL's second organizational meeting, died at 88, October 31.

1984

The Los Angeles Raiders defeated Washington 38-9 in Super Bowl XVIII at Tampa Stadium, January 22. The game achieved a 46.4 rating and 71.0 share.

An 11-man group headed by H.R. (Bum) Bright purchased the Dallas Cowboys from Clint Murchison, Jr., March 20. Club president Tex Schramm was designated as managing general partner.

Wellington Mara was named president of the NFC, March 20.

Patrick Bowlen purchased a majority interest in the Denver Broncos from Edgar Kaiser, Jr., March 21.

The Colts relocated to Indianapolis, March 28. Their new home became the Hoosier Dome.

The owners awarded two Super Bowl sites at their May 23-25 meetings: Super Bowl XXI, to be played on January 25, 1987, to the Rose Bowl in Pasadena; and Super Bowl XXII, to be played on January 31, 1988, to San Diego Jack Murphy Stadium.

The New York Jets moved their home games to Giants Stadium in East Rutherford, New Jersey.

Alex G. Spanos purchased a majority interest in the San Diego Chargers from Eugene V. Klein, August 28.

Houston defeated Pittsburgh 23-20 to mark the one-hundredth overtime game in regular-season play since overtime was adopted in 1974, December 2.

On the field, many all-time records were set: Dan Marino of Miami passed for 5,084 yards and 48 touchdowns; Eric Dickerson of the Los Angeles Rams rushed for 2,105 yards; Art Monk of Washington caught 106 passes; and Walter Payton of Chicago broke Jim Brown's career rushing mark, finishing the season with 13,309 yards.

According to a CBS Sports/*New York Times* survey, 53 percent of the nation's sports fans said they most enjoyed watching football, compared to 18 percent for baseball, December 2-4.

NFL paid attendance exceeded 13 million for the fifth consecutive complete regular season when 13,398,112, an average of 59,813, attended games. The figure was the second-highest in league history. Teams averaged 42.4 points per game, the second-highest total since the 1970 merger.

1985

San Francisco defeated Miami 38-16 in Super Bowl XIX at Stanford Stadium in Stanford, California, January 20. The game was viewed on television by more people than any other live event in history. President Ronald Reagan, who took his second oath of office before tossing the coin for the game, was one of 115,936,000 viewers. The game drew a 46.4 rating and a 63.0 share. In addition, 6 million people watched the Super Bowl in the United Kingdom and a similar number in Italy. Super Bowl XIX had a direct economic impact of $113.5 million on the San Francisco Bay area.

NBC Radio and the NFL entered into a two-year agreement granting NBC the radio rights to a 37-game package in each of the 1985-86 seasons, March 6. The package included 27 regular-season games and 10 postseason games.

The owners awarded two Super Bowl sites at their annual meeting, March 10-15: Super Bowl XXIII, to be played on January 22, 1989, to the proposed Dolphins Stadium in Miami; and Super Bowl XXIV, to be played on January 28, 1990, to the Louisiana Superdome in New Orleans.

Norman Braman, in partnership with Edward Leibowitz, bought the Philadelphia Eagles from Leonard Tose, April 29.

Bruce Smith, a Virginia Tech defensive lineman selected by Buffalo, was the first player chosen in the fiftieth NFL draft, April 30.

A group headed by Tom Benson, Jr., was approved to purchase the New Orleans Saints from John W. Mecom, Jr., June 3.

The NFL owners adopted a resolution calling for a series of overseas preseason games, beginning in 1986, with one game to be played in England/Europe and/or one game in Japan each year. The game would be a fifth preseason game for the clubs involved and all arrangements and selection of the clubs would be under the control of the Commissioner, May 23.

The league-wide conversion to videotape from movie film for coaching study was approved.

Commissioner Rozelle was authorized to extend the commitment to Honolulu's Aloha Stadium for the AFC-NFC Pro Bowl for 1988, 1989, and 1990, October 15.

The NFL set a single-weekend paid attendance record when 902,657 tickets were sold for the weekend of October 27-28.

A Louis Harris poll in December revealed that pro football remained the sport most followed by Americans. Fifty-nine percent of those surveyed followed pro football, compared with 54 percent who followed baseball.

The Chicago-Miami Monday game had the highest rating, 29.6, and share, 46.0, of any prime-time game in NFL history, December 2. The game was viewed in more than 25 million homes.

The NFL showed a ratings increase on all three networks for the season, gaining 4 percent on NBC, 10 on CBS, and 16 on ABC.

1986

Chicago defeated New England 46-10 in Super Bowl XX at the Louisiana Superdome, January 26. The Patriots had earned the right to play the Bears by becoming the first wild-card team to win three consecutive games on the road. The NBC telecast replaced the final episode of *M*A*S*H* as the most-viewed television program in history, with an audience of 127 million viewers, according to A.C. Nielsen figures. In addition to drawing a 48.3 rating and a 70 percent share in the United States, Super Bowl XX was televised to 59 foreign countries and beamed via satellite to the QE II. An estimated 300 million Chinese viewed a tape delay of the game in March. NBC Radio figures indicated an audience of 10 million for the game.

The owners adopted limited use of instant replay as an officiating aid, prohibited players from wearing or otherwise displaying equipment, apparel, or other items that carry commercial names, names of organizations, or personal messages of any type, March 11.

After an 11-week trial, a jury in U.S. District Court in New York awarded the United States Football League one dollar in its $1.7 billion antitrust suit against the NFL. The jury rejected all of the USFL's television-related claims, which were the self-proclaimed heart of the USFL's case. The jury deliberated five days, July 29.

Chicago defeated Dallas 17-6 at Wembley Stadium in London in the first American Bowl. The game drew a sellout crowd of 82,699 and the NBC national telecast in this country produced a 12.4 rating and 36 percent share, making it the highest daytime preseason television audience ever with 10.65-million viewers, August 3.

ABC'S *Monday Night Football,* in its seventeenth season, became the longest-running prime-time series in the history of the network.

1987

The New York Giants defeated Denver 39-20 in Super Bowl XXI and captured their first NFL title since 1956. The game, played in Pasadena's Rose Bowl, drew a sellout crowd of 101,063. According to A.C. Nielsen figures, the CBS broadcast of the game was viewed in the U.S. on television by 122.64-million people, making the telecast the second most-watched television show of all-time behind Super Bowl XX. The game was watched live or on tape in 55 foreign countries and NBC Radio's broadcast of the game was heard by a record 10.1 million people.

New three-year TV contracts with ABC, CBS, and NBC were announced for 1987-89 at the NFL annual meeting in Maui, Hawaii, March 15. Commissioner Rozelle and Broadcast Committee Chairman Art Modell also announced a three-year contract with ESPN to televise 13 prime-time games each season. The ESPN contract was the first with a cable network. However, NFL games on ESPN also were scheduled for regular television in the city of the visiting team and in the home city if the game was sold out 72 hours in advance.

A special payment program was adopted to benefit nearly 1,000 former NFL players who participated in the League before the current Bert Bell NFL Pension Plan was created and made retroactive to the 1959 season. Players covered by the new program spent at least five years in the League and played all or part of their career prior to 1959. Each vested player would receive $60 per month for each year of service in the League for life.

NFL and CBS Radio jointly announced agreement granting CBS the radio rights to a 40-game package in each of the next three NFL seasons, 1987-89, April 7.

NFL owners awarded Super Bowl XXV, to be played on January 27, 1991, to Tampa Stadium, May 20.

Over 400 former NFL players from the pre-1959 era received first payments from NFL owners, July 1.

The NFL's debut on ESPN produced the two highest-rated and most-watched sports programs in basic cable history. The Chicago at Miami game on August 16 drew an 8.9 rating in 3.81 million homes. Those records fell two weeks later when the Los Angeles Raiders at Dallas game achieved a 10.2 cable rating in 4.36 million homes.

The 1987 season was reduced from a 16-game season to 15 as the result of a 24-day players' strike. The strike was called by the NFLPA on Tuesday, September 22, following the New England at New York Jets game. Games scheduled for the third weekend were canceled but the games of weeks four, five, and six were played with replacement teams. Striking players returned for the seventh week of the season, October 25.

In a three-team deal involving 10 players and/or draft choices, the Los Angeles Rams traded running back Eric Dickerson to the Indianapolis Colts for six draft choices and two players. Buffalo obtained the rights to linebacker Cornelius Bennett from Indianapolis, sending Greg Bell and three draft choices to the Rams. The Colts added Owen Gill and three draft choices of their own to complete the deal with the Rams, October 31.

The Chicago at Minnesota game became the highest-rated and most-watched sports program in basic cable history when it drew a 14.4 cable rating in 6.5 million homes, December 6.

1988

Washington defeated Denver 42-10 in Super Bowl XXII to earn its second victory this decade in the NFL Championship Game. The game, played for the first time in San Diego Jack Murphy Stadium, drew a sellout crowd of 73,302. According to A.C. Nielsen figures, the ABC broadcast of the game was viewed in the U.S. on television by 115,000,000 people. The game was seen live or on tape in 60 foreign countries, including the People's Republic of China, and CBS's radio broadcast of the game was heard by 13.7 million people.

In a unanimous 3-0 decision, the 2nd Circuit Court of Appeals in New York upheld the verdict of the jury that in July, 1986, had awarded the United States Football League one dollar in its $1.7 billion antitrust suit against the NFL. In a 91-page opinion, Judge Ralph K. Winter said the USFL sought through court decree the success it failed to gain among football fans, March 10.

By a 23-5 margin, owners voted to continue the instant replay system for the third consecutive season with the Instant Replay Official to be assigned to a regular seven-man, on-the-field crew. At the NFL annual meeting in Phoenix, Arizona, a 45-second clock was also approved to replace the 30-second clock. For a normal sequence of plays, the interval between plays was changed to 45 seconds from the time the ball is signaled dead until it is snapped on the succeeding play.

NFL owners approved the transfer of the Cardinals' franchise from St. Louis to Phoenix; approved two supplemental drafts each year—one prior to training camp and one prior to the regular season; and voted to initiate an annual series of games in Japan/Asia as early as the 1989 preseason, March 14-18.

The NFL Annual Selection Meeting returned to a separate two-day format and for the first time originated on a Sunday. ESPN drew a 3.6 rating during their seven-hour coverage of the draft, which was viewed in 1.6 million homes, April 24-25.

Art Rooney, founder and owner of the Steelers, died at 87, August 25.

Johnny Grier became the first African-American referee in NFL history, September 4.

Commissioner Rozelle announced that two teams would play a preseason game as part of the American Bowl series on August 6, 1989, in the Korakuen Tokyo Dome in Japan, December 16.

1989

San Francisco defeated Cincinnati 20-16 in Super Bowl XXIII. The game, played for the first time at Joe Robbie Stadium in Miami, was attended by a sellout crowd of 75,129. NBC's telecast of the game was watched by an estimated 110,780,000 viewers, according to A.C. Nielsen, making it the sixth most-watched program in television history. The game was seen live or on tape in 60 foreign countries, including an estimated 300 million in China. The CBS Radio broadcast of the game was heard by 11.2 million people.

Commissioner Rozelle announced his retirement, pending the naming of a successor, March 22 at the NFL annual meeting in Palm Desert, California.

Following the announcement, AFC president Lamar Hunt and NFC president Wellington Mara announced the formation of a six-man search committee composed of Art Modell, Robert Parins, Dan Rooney, and Ralph Wilson. Hunt and Mara served as co-chairmen.

By a 24-4 margin, owners voted to continue the instant replay system for the fourth straight season. A strengthened policy regarding anabolic steroids and masking agents was announced by Commissioner Rozelle. NFL clubs called for strong disciplinary measures in cases of feigned injuries and adopted a joint proposal by the Long-Range Planning and Finance committees regarding player personnel rules, March 19-23.

Two hundred twenty-nine unconditional free agents signed with new teams under management's Plan B system, April 1.

Jerry Jones purchased a majority interest in the Dallas Cowboys from H.R. (Bum) Bright, April 18.

Tex Schramm was named president of the new World League of American Football to work with a six-man committee of Dan Rooney, chairman; Norman Braman, Lamar Hunt, Victor Kiam, Mike Lynn, and Bill Walsh, April 18.

NFL and CBS Radio jointly announced agreement extending CBS's radio rights to an annual 40-game package through the 1994 season, April 18.

NFL owners awarded Super Bowl XXVI, to be played on January 26, 1992, to Minneapolis, May 24.

As of opening day, September 10, of the 229 Plan B free agents, 111 were active and 23 others were on teams' reserve lists. Ninety-two others were waived and three retired.

Art Shell was named head coach of the Los Angeles Raiders making him the NFL's first black head coach since Fritz Pollard coached the Akron Pros in 1921, October 3.

The site of the New England Patriots at San Francisco 49ers game scheduled for Candlestick Park on October 22 was switched to Stanford Stadium in the aftermath of the Bay Area Earthquake of October 17. The change was announced on October 19.

Paul Tagliabue became the seventh chief executive of the NFL on October 26 when he was chosen to succeed Commissioner Pete Rozelle on the sixth ballot of a three-day meeting in Cleveland, Ohio.

In all, 12 ballots were required to select Tagliabue. Two were conducted at a meeting in Chicago on July 6, and four at a meeting in Dallas on October 10-11. On the twelfth ballot, with Seattle absent, Tagliabue received more than the 19 affirmative votes required for election from among the 27 clubs present.

The transfer from Commissioner Rozelle to Commissioner Tagliabue took place at 12:01 A.M. on Sunday, November 5.

NFL Charities donated $1 million through United Way to benefit Bay Area earthquake victims, November 6.

NFL paid attendance of 17,399,538 was the highest total in league history. This included a total of 13,625,662 for an average of 60,829—both NFL records—for the 224-game regular season.

1990

San Francisco defeated Denver 55-10 in Super Bowl XXIV at the Louisiana Superdome, January 28. San Francisco joined Pittsburgh as the NFL's only teams to win four Super Bowls.

The NFL announced revisions in its 1990 draft eligibility rules. College juniors became eligible but must renounce their collegiate football eligibility before applying for the NFL Draft, February 16.

Commissioner Tagliabue announced NFL teams will play their 16-game schedule over 17 weeks in 1990 and 1991 and 16 games over 18 weeks in 1992 and 1993, February 27.

The NFL revised its playoff format to include two additional wild-card teams (one per conference), which raised the total to six wild-card teams.

Commissioner Tagliabue and Broadcast Committee Chairman Art Modell announced a four-year contract with Turner Broadcasting to televise nine Sunday-night games.

New four-year TV agreements were ratified for 1990-93 for ABC, CBS, NBC, ESPN, and TNT at the NFL annual meeting in Orlando, Florida, March 12. The contracts totaled $3.6 billion, the largest in TV history.

The NFL announced plans to expand its American Bowl series of preseason games. In addition to games in London and Tokyo, American Bowl games were scheduled for Berlin, Germany, and Montreal, Canada, in 1990.

For the fifth straight year, NFL owners voted to continue a limited system of Instant Replay. Beginning in 1990, the replay official will have a two-minute time limit to make a decision. The vote was 21-7, March 12.

Commissioner Tagliabue announced the formation of a Committee on Expansion and Realignment, March 13. He also named a Player Advisory Council, comprised of 12 former NFL players, March 14.

One-hundred eighty-four Plan B unconditional free agents signed with new teams, April 2.

Commissioner Tagliabue appointed Dr. John Lombardo as the League's Drug Advisor for Anabolic Steroids, April 25 and named Dr. Lawrence Brown as the League's Advisor for Drugs of Abuse, May 17.

NFL owners awarded Super Bowl XXVIII, to be played in 1994, to the proposed Georgia Dome, May 23.

Commissioner Tagliabue named NFL referee Jerry Seeman as NFL Director of Officiating, replacing Art McNally, who announced his retirement after 31 years on the field and at the league office, July 12.

NFL International Week was celebrated with four preseason games in seven days in Tokyo, London, Berlin, and Montreal. More than 200,000 fans on three continents attended the four games, August 4-11.

Commissioner Tagliabue announced the NFL Teacher of the Month program in which the League furnishes grants and scholarships in recognition of teachers who provided a positive influence upon NFL players in elementary and secondary schools, September 20.

For the first time since 1957, every NFL club won at least one of its first four games, October 1.

The Super Bowl Most Valuable Player trophy was renamed the Pete Rozelle trophy, October 8.

NFL total paid attendance of 17,665,671 was the highest total in League history. The regular-season total paid attendance of 13,959,896 and average of 62,321 for 224 games were the highest ever, surpassing the previous records set in the 1989 season.

1991

The New York Giants defeated Buffalo 20-19 in Super Bowl XXV to capture their second title in five years. The game was played before a sellout crowd of 73,813 at Tampa Stadium and became the first Super Bowl decided by one point, January 26. The ABC broadcast of the game was seen by more than 112-million people in the United States and was seen live or taped in 60 other countries.

NFL playoff games earned the top television rating spot of the week for each week of the month-long playoffs, January 29.

New York businessman Robert Tisch purchased a 50 percent interest in the New York Giants from Mrs. Helen Mara Nugent and her children, Tim Mara and Maura Mara Concannon, February 2.

NFL clubs voted to continue a limited system of Instant Replay for the sixth consecutive year. The vote was 21-7, March 19.

The NFL launched the World League of American Football, the first sports league to operate on a weekly basis on two separate continents, March 23.

NFL Charities presented a $250,000 donation to the United Service Organization. The donation was the second largest single grant ever by NFL Charities, April 5.

Commissioner Tagliabue named Harold Henderson as Executive Vice President for Labor Relations and Chairman of the NFL Management Council Executive Committee, April 8.

NFL clubs approved a recommendation by the Expansion and Realignment Committee to add two teams for the 1994 season, resulting in six divisions of five teams each, May 22.

NFL clubs awarded Super Bowl XXIX, to be played on January 29, 1995, to Miami, May 23.

"NFL International Week" featured six 1990 playoff teams playing nationally televised games in London, Berlin, and Tokyo on July 28 and August 3-4. The games drew more than 150,000 fans.

Paul Brown, founder of the Cleveland Browns and Cincinnati Bengals, died at age 82, August 5.

NFL clubs approved a resolution establishing an international division. A three-year financial plan for the World League was approved by NFL clubs at a meeting in Dallas, October 23.

1992

The NFL agreed to provide a minimum of $2.5 million in financial support to the NFL Alumni Association and assistance to NFL Alumni-related programs. The agreement included contributions from NFL Charities to the Pre-59ers and Dire Need Programs for former players, January 25.

The Washington Redskins defeated the Buffalo Bills 37-24 in Super Bowl XXVI to capture their third world championship in 10 years, January 26. The game was played before a sellout crowd of 63,130 at the Hubert H. Humphrey Metrodome in Minneapolis and attracted the second largest television audience in Super Bowl history. The CBS broadcast was seen by more than 123 million people nationally, second only to the 127 million who viewed Super Bowl XX.

The use in officiating of a limited system of Instant Replay was not approved. The vote was 17-11 in favor of approval (21 votes were required). Instant Replay had been used for six consecutive years (1986-1991), March 18.

St. Louis businessman James Orthwein purchased controlling interest in the New England Patriots from Victor Kiam, May 11.

In a Harris Poll taken during the NFL offseason, professional football again was declared the nation's most popular sport. Professional football finished atop similar surveys conducted by Harris in 1985 and 1989, May 23.

NFL clubs accepted the report of the Expansion Committee at a league meeting in Pasadena. The report names five cities as finalists for the two expansion teams—Baltimore, Charlotte, Jacksonville, Memphis, and St. Louis, May 19.

At a league meeting in Dallas, NFL clubs approved a proposal by the World League Board of Directors to restructure the World League and place future emphasis on its international success, September 17.

NFL teams played their 16-game regular-season schedule over 18 weeks for the only time in league history.

1993

The NFL and lawyers for the players announced a settlement of various lawsuits and an agreement on the terms of a seven-year deal that included a new player system to be in place through the 1999 season, January 6.

Commissioner Tagliabue announced the establishment of the "NFL World Partnership Program" to develop amateur football internationally through a series of clinics conducted by former NFL players and coaches, January 14.

As part of Super Bowl XXVII, the NFL announced the creation of the first NFL Youth Education Town, a facility located in south central Los Angeles for inner city youth. January 25.

The Dallas Cowboys defeated the Buffalo Bills 52-17 in Super Bowl XXVII to capture their first NFL title since 1978. The game was played before a crowd of 98,374 at the Rose Bowl in Pasadena, California. The NBC broadcast of the game was the most watched program in television history and was seen by 133,400,000 people in the United States. The rating for the game was 45.1, the tenth highest for any televised sports event. The game also was seen live or taped in 101 other countries, January 31.

NFL clubs awarded Super Bowl XXX to the city of Phoenix, to be played on January 28, 1996, at Sun Devil Stadium, March 23.

The NFL and the NFL Players Association officially signed a 7-year Collective Bargaining Agreement in Washington, D.C., which guarantees more than $1 billion in pension, health, and post-career benefits for current and retired players—the most extensive benefits plan in pro sports. It was the NFL's first CBA since the 1982 agreement expired in 1987, June 29.

NFL Enterprises, a newly formed division of the NFL responsible for NFL Films, home video, and special domestic and international television programming was announced, August 19.

NFL announced plans to allow fans, for the first time ever, to join players and coaches in selecting the annual AFC and NFC Pro Bowl teams, October 12.

NFL clubs unanimously awarded the league's twenty-ninth franchise to the Carolina Panthers at a meeting in Chicago. NFL clubs also awarded Super Bowl XXXI to New Orleans and Super Bowl XXXII to San Diego, October 26.

At the same meeting in Chicago, NFL clubs approved a plan to form a European league with joint venture partners, October 27.

Don Shula became the winningest coach in NFL history when Miami beat Philadelphia to give Shula his 325th victory, one more than George Halas, November 14.

NFL clubs awarded the league's thirtieth franchise to the Jacksonville Jaguars at a meeting in Chicago, November 30.

The NFL announced new 4-year television agreements with ABC, ESPN, TNT, and NFL newcomer FOX, which took over the NFC package from CBS, December 18.

The NFL completed its new TV agreements by announcing that NBC would retain the rights to the AFC package, December 20.

1994

The Dallas Cowboys defeated the Buffalo Bills 30-13 in Super Bowl XXVIII to become the fifth team to win back-to-back Super Bowl titles. The game was viewed by the largest U.S. audience in television history—134.8 million people. The game's 45.5 rating was the highest for a Super Bowl since 1987 and the tenth highest-rated Super Bowl ever, January 30.

NFL clubs unanimously approved the transfer of the New England Patriots from James Orthwein to Robert Kraft at a meeting in Orlando, February 22.

In a move to increase offensive production, NFL clubs at the league's annual meeting in Orlando adopted a package of changes, including modifications in line play, chucking rules, and the roughing-the-passer rule, plus the adoption of the two-point conversion and moving the spot of the kickoff back to the 30-yard line, March 22.

NFL clubs approved the transfer of the majority interest in the Miami Dolphins from the Robbie family to H. Wayne Huizenga, March 23.

The NFL and FOX announced the formation of a joint venture to create a six-team World League to begin play in Europe in April, 1995, March 23.

The Carolina Panthers earned the right to select first in the 1995 NFL draft by winning a coin toss with the Jacksonville Jaguars. The Jaguars received the second selection in the 1995 draft, April 24.

NFL clubs approved the transfer of the Philadelphia Eagles from Norman Braman to Jeffrey Lurie, May 6.

The NFL launched "NFL Sunday Ticket," a new season subscription service for satellite television dish owners, June 1.

An all-time NFL record crowd of

112,376 attended the American Bowl game between Dallas and Houston in Mexico City. It concluded the biggest American Bowl series in NFL history with four games attracting a record 256,666 fans, August 15.

The NFL reached agreement on a new seven-year contract with its game officials, September 22.

The NFL Management Council and the NFL Players Association announced an agreement on the formulation and implementation of the most comprehensive drug and alcohol policy in sports, October 28.

At an NFL meeting in Chicago, Commissioner Tagliabue slotted the two new expansion teams into the AFC Central (Jacksonville Jaguars) and NFC West (Carolina Panthers) for the 1995 season only. He also appointed a special committee on realignment to make recommendations on the 1996 season and beyond, November 2.

1995
The San Francisco 49ers became the first team to win five Super Bowls when they defeated the San Diego Chargers 49-26 in Super Bowl XXIX at Joe Robbie Stadium in Miami, January 29.

Carolina and Jacksonville stocked their expansion rosters with a total of 66 players from other NFL teams in a veteran player allocation draft in New York, February 16.

CBS Radio and the NFL agreed to a new four-year contract for an annual 53-game package of games, continuing a relationship that spanned 15 of the past 17 years, February 22.

NFL clubs approved the transfer of the Tampa Bay Buccaneers from the estate of the late Hugh Culverhouse to South Florida businessman Malcolm Glazer, March 13.

A series of safety-related rules changes were adopted at a league meeting in Phoenix, primarily related to the use of the helmet against defenseless players, March 14.

After a two-year hiatus, the World League of American Football returned to action with six teams in Europe, April 8.

The NFL became the first major sports league to establish a site on the Internet system of on-line computer communication, April 10.

The transfer of the Rams from Los Angeles to St. Louis was approved by a vote of the NFL clubs at a meeting in Dallas, April 12.

ABC's *NFL Monday Night Football* finished the 1994-95 television season as the fifth highest-rated show out of 146 with a 17.8 average rating, the highest finish in the 25-year history of the series, April 18.

In an ABC News Poll taken during the NFL offseason, America's sports fans chose football as their favorite spectator sport by more than a 2-to-1 margin over basketball and baseball (35%-16%-12%), April 26.

The Frankfurt Galaxy defeated the Amsterdam Admirals 26-22 to win the 1995 World Bowl before a crowd of 23,847 in Amsterdam's Olympic Stadium, June 23.

Former NFL quarterback and Rhein Fire general manager Oliver Luck was named President of the World League, July 13.

The transfer of the Raiders from Los Angeles to Oakland was approved by a vote of the NFL clubs at a meeting in Chicago, July 22.

Jacksonville Municipal Stadium opened before a sold-out crowd of more than 70,000 for the first preseason game in Jaguars history, August 18.

NFL Charities and 50 NFL players donated $1 million to the United Negro College Fund in honor of the fiftieth anniversity of the UNCF and the integration of the modern NFL, September 15.

The Pro Football Hall Of Fame in Canton, Ohio, completed an $8.9 million expansion including a $4 million contribution by the NFL clubs, October 14.

The Trans World Dome opened in St. Louis with a sold-out crowd of 65,598 as the Rams defeated the Carolina Panthers 28-17, November 12.

NFL paid attendance totaled 963,521 for 15 games in Week 12, the highest weekend total in the league's 76-year history, November 19-20.

On the field, many significant records and milestones were achieved: Miami's Dan Marino surpassed Pro Football Hall of Famer Fran Tarkenton in four major passing categories—attempts, completions, yards, and touchdowns—to become the NFL's all-time career leader. San Francisco's Jerry Rice became the all-time reception and receiving-yardage leader with career totals of 942 catches and 15,123 yards. Dallas' Emmitt Smith scored 25 touchdowns, breaking the season record of 24 set by Washington's John Riggins in 1983.

1996
The Dallas Cowboys won their third Super Bowl title in four years when they defeated the Pittsburgh Steelers 27-17 in Super Bowl XXX at Sun Devil Stadium in Tempe, Arizona. The game was viewed by the largest audience in U.S. television history—138.5 million people, January 28.

An agreement between the NFL and the city of Cleveland regarding the Cleveland Browns' relocation was approved by a vote of the NFL clubs, February 9. According to the agreement, the city of Cleveland retained the Browns' heritage and records, including the name, logo, colors, history, playing records, trophies, and memorabilia, and committed to building a new 72,000-seat stadium for a reactivated Browns' franchise to begin play there no later than 1999. Art Modell received approval to move his franchise to Baltimore and rename it.

NFL total paid attendance for all 1995 games reached a record level for the seventh consecutive year, exceeding 19 million for the first time (19,202,757), March 7.

The transfer of the Oilers from Houston to Nashville for the 1998 season was approved by a vote of the NFL clubs at a meeting in Atlanta, April 30.

The Scottish Claymores defeated the Frankfurt Galaxy 32-27 to win the 1996 World Bowl in front of 38,982 at Murrayfield Stadium in Edinburgh, Scotland, June 23.

The NFL returned to Baltimore when the new Baltimore Ravens defeated the Philadelphia Eagles 17-9 in a preseason game before a crowd of 63,804 at Memorial Stadium, August 3.

Ericsson Stadium opened in Charlotte, North Carolina with a crowd of 65,350 as the Carolina Panthers defeated the Chicago Bears 30-12 in a preseason game, August 3.

Points scored totaled 762 and NFL paid attendance totaled 964,079 for 15 games in Week 11, the highest weekend totals in either category in the league's 77-year history, November 10-11.

Former NFL Commissioner Pete Rozelle died at his home in Rancho Santa Fe, California. Rozelle, regarded as the premiere commissioner in sports history, led the NFL for 29 years, from 1960-1989, December 6.

1997
Indianapolis Colts owner Robert Irsay died from complications related to a stroke he suffered in 1995. Irsay acquired the club in 1972 when he traded his Los Angeles Rams to Carrol Rosenbloom for the Colts. He later moved the Colts from Baltimore to Indianapolis in 1984, January 14.

The Green Bay Packers won their first NFL title in 29 years by defeating the New England Patriots 35-21 in Super Bowl XXXI at the Louisiana Superdome in New Orleans. The game was viewed by the fourth-largest audience in U.S. television history—128 million people, January 26.

The rules governing cross-ownership were modified, permitting NFL club owners to also own teams in other sports in their home market or markets without NFL teams. The vote was 24-5 (one abstention) in favor of approval, March 11.

Washington Redskins owner Jack Kent Cooke died at his home in Washington, D.C. Cooke became majority owner in 1974 and the Redskins won three Super Bowls under his leadership, April 6.

The Barcelona Dragons defeated the Rhein Fire 38-24 to win the 1997 World Bowl in front of 31,100 fans at Estadi Olimpic de Montjuic in Barcelona, Spain, June 22.

NFL clubs approved the transfer of the Seattle Seahawks from Ken Behring to Paul Allen, August 19.

Jack Kent Cooke Stadium opened in Raljon, Maryland with a crowd of 78,270 as the Washington Redskins defeated the Arizona Cardinals 19-13 in overtime, September 14.

The 10,000th regular-season game in NFL history was played when the Seattle Seahawks defeated the Tennessee Oilers 16-13 at the Kingdome in Seattle, October 5.

Atlanta Falcons owner Rankin Smith died of heart failure three days prior to his seventy-third birthday. Smith was the founder of the Falcons and was instrumental in bringing Super Bowls XXVIII and XXXIV to Atlanta, October 26.

NFL paid attendance totaled 999,778 for 15 games in Week 12, the highest weekend total in league history, November 16-17.

1998
The NFL reached agreement on record eight-year television contracts with four networks. ABC (*Monday Night Football*) and FOX (NFC) retained their previous rights, CBS took over the AFC package from NBC, and ESPN won the right to broadcast the entire Sunday night cable package, January 13.

The World League was renamed the NFL Europe League, January 22.

The Denver Broncos won their first Super Bowl by defeating the defending champion Green Bay Packers 31-24 in Super Bowl XXXII at Qualcomm Stadium in San Diego. The game tied Super Bowl XXVII for the third-largest audience in U.S. television history with 133.4 million viewers, January 25.

The NFL clubs approved a six-year extension of the Collective Bargaining Agreement through 2003. The extended CBA also created a $100 million fund for youth football, March 22.

The NFL clubs unanimously approved an expansion team for Cleveland to fulfill the commitment to return the Browns to the field in 1999, March 23.

A total of $25.1 million, the largest NFL postseason pool ever, was divided among 737 players who participated in the 1997 playoffs, March 24.

The Rhein Fire defeated the Frankfurt Galaxy 34-10 to win the 1998 World Bowl in front of 47,846 fans in Frankfurt's Waldstadion—the biggest crowd to witness a World Bowl since 1991, June 14.

NFL clubs approved the transfer of the Minnesota Vikings from a 10-man ownership group to Red McCombs, July 28.

The NFL Stadium at Camden Yards opened in Baltimore, Maryland before a crowd of 65,938 as the Baltimore Ravens defeated the Chicago Bears 19-14 in a preseason game, August 8.

Raymond James Stadium opened in Tampa, Florida before a crowd of 62,410 as the Tampa Bay Buccaneers defeated the Chicago Bears 27-15, September 20.

NFL paid attendance totaled 997,835 for 15 games in Week 1, the highest opening weekend total in league history and the second-highest total ever. In 1997, paid attendance totaled 999,778 for 15 games in Week 12, September 6-7.

A Harris Poll says 55 percent of adults follow professional football, up 4 percent from 1997 and 6 percent from 1992, October 15.

Tennessee Oilers owner Bud Adams announced the team will change its name to the Tennessee Titans following the 1998 season. The NFL announced that the name Oilers will be retired–a first in league history, November 14.

1999
The Denver Broncos won their second consecutive Super Bowl title by defeating the NFC champion Atlanta Falcons 34-19 in Super Bowl XXXIII at Pro Player Stadium in Miami. The game was viewed by 127.5 million viewers, the sixth most-watched program in U.S. television history, January 31.

Jim Pyne, a center allocated by the Detroit Lions, was the first selection of the Cleveland Browns in the 1999 NFL Expansion Draft. The Browns eventually selected 37 players, February 9.

CBS Radio/Westwood One agreed to a 3-year extension of their exclusive national radio rights to NFL games, March 11.

NFL paid attendance of 19,741,493 for all games played during the 1998 season was the highest in league history, topping the 19,202,757 fans who paid to attend games in 1995. The 1998 regular-season total paid attendance of 15,364,873 for an average of 64,020 were also records, March 15.

By a vote of 28-3, the owners adopted an instant replay system as an officiating aid for the 1999 season, March 17.

New York Jets owner Leon Hess died from complications of a blood disease. Hess had been involved in the ownership of the Jets since 1963 and was sole owner of the club since 1984, May 9.

A group led by Washington area businessman Daniel Snyder is approved by NFL clubs as the new owner of the Washington Redskins at a league meeting in Atlanta, May 25.

The Frankfurt Galaxy became the first team in NFL Europe League history to win a second World Bowl by defeating the Barcelona Dragons 38-24 at Rheinstadion, in Düsseldorf, Germany, June 27.

The Cleveland Browns returned to the field for the first time since 1995 and defeated the Dallas Cowboys 20-17 in overtime in the annual Hall of Fame Game at Canton, Ohio, August 9.

Cleveland Browns Stadium opened in Cleveland, Ohio before a crowd of 71,398 as the Minnesota Vikings defeated the Browns in a preseason game, 24-17, August 21.

Adelphia Coliseum opened in Nashville, Tennessee before a crowd of 65,729 with the Tennessee Titans defeating the Atlanta Falcons 17-3 in a preseason game, August 26.

Houston, Texas and owner Robert McNair were awarded the NFL's thirty-second franchise in a vote of the NFL clubs at a league meeting in Atlanta. The team will begin play in 2002. The NFL clubs also voted to realign into eight divisions of four teams each for the 2002 season, October 6.

Walter Payton, the NFL's all-time leading rusher, died of liver cancer at the age of 45. Payton played for the Chicago Bears from 1975-1987 and rushed for an NFL-record 16,726 yards, November 1.

Former NFL Commissioner Pete Rozelle, who guided a still-developing league to its position today as America's most popular sport, was named by *The Sporting News* as the most powerful person in sports in the 20th Century, December 15.

2000

Johnson & Johnson heir Robert Wood Johnson IV was approved by NFL clubs as the new owner of the New York Jets at a league meeting, January 18.

The St. Louis Rams won their first Super Bowl by defeating the AFC champion Tennessee Titans 23-16 in Super Bowl XXXIV at the Georgia Dome in Atlanta. The game was viewed by 130.7 million viewers, the fifth most-watched program in U.S. television history, January 30.

For the first time in league history, paid attendance topped 16 million for the regular season and more than 65,000 per game, an increase of 1,300 per game over 1998. Paid attendance for all NFL games increased in 1999 for the third year in a row and was the highest ever in the 80-year history of the league. It marked the first time in league history that the 20-million paid attendance mark was reached for all games in a season, March 27.

The Rhein Fire won their second World Bowl in three years, defeating the Scottish Claymores 13-10 to win World Bowl 2000 in front of 35,680 at Frankfurt's Waldstadion, June 25.

More than 100 of the 136 living members of the Pro Football Hall of Fame gathered to celebrate Pro Football's Greatest Reunion in Canton, Ohio, July 28-31.

Paul Brown Stadium opened in Cincinnati, Ohio with a crowd of 56,180 as the Cincinnati Bengals defeated the Chicago Bears 24-20 in a preseason game, August 19.

Cincinnati's Corey Dillon set a single-game rushing record with 278 yards (22 carries) against Denver, breaking the previous record of 275 yards by Chicago's Walter Payton in 1977, October 22.

Minnesota's Gary Anderson converted a 21-yard field goal against Buffalo to pass George Blanda as the NFL's all-time scoring leader with 2,004 points, October 22.

At a league meeting in Atlanta, NFL owners awarded Super Bowl XXXVIII to Houston, Super Bowl XXXIX to Jacksonville and Super Bowl XL to Detroit, November 1.

The NFL Officiating Department named Mike Pereira as Director of Officiating and Larry Upson as Director of Officiating Operations to replace retiring Senior Director of Officiating Jerry Seeman, December 1.

San Francisco's Terrell Owens set a single-game receiving record with 20 receptions (283 yards) against Chicago, surpassing the previous mark of 18 by Tom Fears of the Los Angeles Rams in 1950, December 17.

2001

NFL clubs approved additional league-wide revenue sharing at a special league meeting in Dallas. The teams agreed to pool the visiting team share of gate receipts for all preseason and regular-season games and divide the pool equally starting in 2002, January 17.

The Baltimore Ravens won their first Super Bowl by defeating the NFC champion New York Giants 34-7 in Super Bowl XXXV at Raymond James Stadium in Tampa. The game was witnessed by 131.2 million viewers, the fifth most-watched program in U.S. television history, January 28.

The *Sports Business Daily* named NFL Commissioner Paul Tagliabue the 2000 Sports Industrialist of the Year, February 28.

The NFL set an all-time paid attendance record in 2000 for the third consecutive year, reaching the 20-million paid attendance mark for only the second time in league history. Regular-season paid attendance of 16,387,289 for an average of 66,078 per game also was an all-time record for the third consecutive season. The Washington Redskins set an all-time NFL regular-season home paid attendance record with a total of 656,599 for eight games, breaking the record of 634,204 held by the 1980 Detroit Lions, March 26.

A jury ruled for the NFL in a lawsuit brought against the league by the Oakland Raiders. The state court jury in Los Angeles rejected the Raiders' claims that the NFL destroyed their 1995 Hollywood Park stadium deal and that they own the Los Angeles market, May 21.

NFL owners unanimously approved a realignment plan for the league starting in 2002. With the addition of the Houston Texans, the league's 32 teams will be divided into eight four-team divisions. Seven clubs change divisions, and the Seattle Seahawks change conferences, moving from the AFC to the NFC. A new scheduling format ensures that every team meets every other team in the league at least once every four years, May 22.

NFL COMMISSIONERS AND PRESIDENTS*

1920 ....Jim Thorpe, President
1921-39.................Joe Carr, President
1939-41 ....Carl Storck, President
1941-46 ....Elmer Layden, Commissioner
1946-59 ....Bert Bell, Commissioner
1960-89 ....Pete Rozelle, Commissioner
1989-present..............Paul Tagliabue, Commissioner

**NFL treasurer Austin Gunsel served as president in the office of the commissioner following the death of Bert Bell (Oct. 11, 1959) until the election of Pete Rozelle (Jan. 26, 1960).*

PAST STANDINGS

2000

AMERICAN CONFERENCE

Eastern Division

	W	L	T	Pct.	Pts.	OP
Miami	11	5	0	.688	323	226
Indianapolis*	10	6	0	.625	429	326
N.Y. Jets	9	7	0	.563	321	321
Buffalo	8	8	0	.500	315	350
New England	5	11	0	.313	276	338

Central Division

	W	L	T	Pct.	Pts.	OP
Tennessee#	13	3	0	.813	346	191
Baltimore*	12	4	0	.750	333	165
Pittsburgh	9	7	0	.563	321	255
Jacksonville	7	9	0	.438	367	327
Cincinnati	4	12	0	.250	185	359
Cleveland	3	13	0	.188	161	419

Western Division

	W	L	T	Pct.	Pts.	OP
Oakland	12	4	0	.750	479	299
Denver*	11	5	0	.688	485	369
Kansas City	7	9	0	.438	355	354
Seattle	6	10	0	.375	320	405
San Diego	1	15	0	.063	269	440

NATIONAL CONFERENCE

Eastern Division

	W	L	T	Pct.	Pts.	OP
N.Y. Giants#	12	4	0	.750	328	246
Philadelphia*	11	5	0	.688	351	245
Washington	8	8	0	.500	281	269
Dallas	5	11	0	.313	294	361
Arizona	3	13	0	.188	210	443

Central Division

	W	L	T	Pct.	Pts.	OP
Minnesota	11	5	0	.688	397	371
Tampa Bay*	10	6	0	.625	388	269
Green Bay	9	7	0	.563	353	323
Detroit	9	7	0	.563	307	307
Chicago	5	11	0	.313	216	355

Western Division

	W	L	T	Pct.	Pts.	OP
New Orleans	10	6	0	.625	354	305
St. Louis*	10	6	0	.625	540	471
Carolina	7	9	0	.438	310	310
San Francisco	6	10	0	.375	388	422
Atlanta	4	12	0	.250	252	413

**Wild-Card qualifier for playoffs; #Top playoff seed in conference*

Green Bay finished ahead of Detroit based on better division record (5-3 to Lions' 3-5). New Orleans finished ahead of St. Louis based on better division record (7-1 to Rams' 5-3). Tampa Bay was second Wild Card based on head-to-head victory over St. Louis (1-0).

Wild-Card playoffs: MIAMI 23, Indianapolis 17 (OT); BALTIMORE 21, Denver 3

Divisional playoffs: OAKLAND 27, Miami 0; Baltimore 24, TENNESSEE 10

AFC Championship: Baltimore 16, OAKLAND 3

Wild-Card playoffs: NEW ORLEANS 31, St. Louis 28; PHILADELPHIA 21, Tampa Bay 3

Divisional playoffs: MINNESOTA 34, New Orleans 16; N.Y. GIANTS 20, Philadelphia 10

NFC Championship: N.Y. GIANTS 41, Minnesota 0

Super Bowl XXXV: Baltimore (AFC) 34, N.Y. Giants (NFC) 7
at Raymond James Stadium, Tampa, Florida

In Past Standings section, home teams in playoff games are indicated by capital letters.

1999

AMERICAN CONFERENCE

Eastern Division

	W	L	T	Pct.	Pts.	OP
Indianapolis	13	3	0	.813	423	333
Buffalo*	11	5	0	.688	320	229
Miami*	9	7	0	.563	326	336
N.Y. Jets	8	8	0	.500	308	309
New England	8	8	0	.500	299	284

Central Division

	W	L	T	Pct.	Pts.	OP
Jacksonville#	14	2	0	.875	396	217
Tennessee*	13	3	0	.813	392	324
Baltimore	8	8	0	.500	324	277
Pittsburgh	6	10	0	.375	317	320
Cincinnati	4	12	0	.250	283	460
Cleveland	2	14	0	.125	217	437

Western Division

	W	L	T	Pct.	Pts.	OP
Seattle	9	7	0	.563	338	298
Kansas City	9	7	0	.563	390	322
San Diego	8	8	0	.500	269	316
Oakland	8	8	0	.500	390	329
Denver	6	10	0	.375	314	318

NATIONAL CONFERENCE

Eastern Division

	W	L	T	Pct.	Pts.	OP
Washington	10	6	0	.625	443	377
Dallas*	8	8	0	.500	352	276
N.Y. Giants	7	9	0	.438	299	358
Arizona	6	10	0	.375	245	382
Philadelphia	5	11	0	.313	272	357

Central Division

	W	L	T	Pct.	Pts.	OP
Tampa Bay	11	5	0	.688	270	235
Minnesota*	10	6	0	.625	399	335
Detroit*	8	8	0	.500	322	323
Green Bay	8	8	0	.500	357	341
Chicago	6	10	0	.375	272	341

Western Division

	W	L	T	Pct.	Pts.	OP
St. Louis#	13	3	0	.813	526	242
Carolina	8	8	0	.500	421	381
Atlanta	5	11	0	.313	285	380
San Francisco	4	12	0	.250	295	453
New Orleans	3	13	0	.188	260	434

**Wild-Card qualifier for playoffs; #Top playoff seed in conference*

Miami was third Wild Card ahead of Kansas City based on better record against common opponents (6-1 to Chiefs' 5-3). N.Y. Jets finished ahead of New England based on better division record (4-4 to Patriots' 2-6). Seattle finished ahead of Kansas City based on head-to-head sweep (2-0). San Diego finished ahead of Oakland based on better division record (5-3 to Raiders' 3-5). Dallas was second Wild Card based on better record against common opponents (3-2 to Lions' 3-3) and better conference record than Carolina (7-5 to Panthers' 6-6). Detroit was third Wild Card based on better conference record than Green Bay (7-5 to Packers' 6-6) and better conference record than Carolina (7-5 to Panthers' 6-6).

Wild-Card playoffs: TENNESSEE 22, Buffalo 16; Miami 20, SEATTLE 17

Divisional playoffs: JACKSONVILLE 62, Miami 7; Tennessee 19, INDIANAPOLIS 16

AFC Championship: Tennessee 33, JACKSONVILLE 14

Wild-Card playoffs: WASHINGTON 27, Detroit 13; MINNESOTA 27, Dallas 10

Divisional playoffs: TAMPA BAY 14, Washington 13; ST. LOUIS 49, Minnesota 37

NFC Championship: ST. LOUIS 11, Tampa Bay 6

Super Bowl XXXIV: St. Louis (NFC) 23, Tennessee (AFC) 16
at Georgia Dome, Atlanta, Georgia

1998

AMERICAN CONFERENCE

Eastern Division

	W	L	T	Pct.	Pts.	OP
N.Y. Jets	12	4	0	.750	416	266
Miami*	10	6	0	.625	321	265
Buffalo*	10	6	0	.625	400	333
New England*	9	7	0	.563	337	329
Indianapolis	3	13	0	.188	310	444

Central Division

	W	L	T	Pct.	Pts.	OP
Jacksonville	11	5	0	.688	392	338
Tennessee	8	8	0	.500	330	320
Pittsburgh	7	9	0	.438	263	303
Baltimore	6	10	0	.375	269	335
Cincinnati	3	13	0	.188	268	452

Western Division

	W	L	T	Pct.	Pts.	OP
Denver#	14	2	0	.875	501	309
Oakland	8	8	0	.500	288	356
Seattle	8	8	0	.500	372	310
Kansas City	7	9	0	.438	327	363
San Diego	5	11	0	.313	241	342

NATIONAL CONFERENCE

Eastern Division

	W	L	T	Pct.	Pts.	OP
Dallas	10	6	0	.625	381	275
Arizona*	9	7	0	.563	325	378
N.Y. Giants	8	8	0	.500	287	309
Washington	6	10	0	.375	319	421
Philadelphia	3	13	0	.188	161	344

Central Division

	W	L	T	Pct.	Pts.	OP
Minnesota#	15	1	0	.938	556	296
Green Bay*	11	5	0	.688	408	319
Tampa Bay	8	8	0	.500	314	295
Detroit	5	11	0	.313	306	378
Chicago	4	12	0	.250	276	368

Western Division

	W	L	T	Pct.	Pts.	OP
Atlanta	14	2	0	.875	442	289
San Francisco*	12	4	0	.750	479	328
New Orleans	6	10	0	.375	305	359
Carolina	4	12	0	.250	336	413
St. Louis	4	12	0	.250	285	378

**Wild-Card qualifier for playoffs; #Top playoff seed in conference*

Miami finished ahead of Buffalo based on better net division points (6 to Bills' 0). Oakland finished ahead of Seattle based on head-to-head sweep (2-0). Carolina finished ahead of St. Louis based on head-to-head sweep (2-0).

Wild-Card playoffs: MIAMI 24, Buffalo 17; JACKSONVILLE 25, New England 10

Divisional playoffs: DENVER 38, Miami 3; N.Y. JETS 34, Jacksonville 24

AFC Championship: DENVER 23, N.Y. Jets 10

Wild-Card playoffs: Arizona 20, DALLAS 7; SAN FRANCISCO 30, Green Bay 27

Divisional playoffs: ATLANTA 20, San Francisco 18; MINNESOTA 41, Arizona 21

NFC Championship: Atlanta 30, MINNESOTA 27 (OT)

Super Bowl XXXIII: Denver (AFC) 34, Atlanta (NFC) 19,
at Pro Player Stadium, Miami, Florida

1997

AMERICAN CONFERENCE

Eastern Division

	W	L	T	Pct.	Pts.	OP
New England	10	6	0	.625	369	289
Miami*	9	7	0	.563	339	327
N.Y. Jets	9	7	0	.563	348	287
Buffalo	6	10	0	.375	255	367
Indianapolis	3	13	0	.188	313	401

Central Division

	W	L	T	Pct.	Pts.	OP
Pittsburgh	11	5	0	.688	372	307
Jacksonville*	11	5	0	.688	394	318
Tennessee	8	8	0	.500	333	310
Cincinnati	7	9	0	.438	355	405
Baltimore	6	9	1	.406	326	345

Western Division

	W	L	T	Pct.	Pts.	OP
Kansas City#	13	3	0	.813	375	232
Denver*	12	4	0	.750	472	287
Seattle	8	8	0	.500	365	362
Oakland	4	12	0	.250	324	419
San Diego	4	12	0	.250	266	425

NATIONAL CONFERENCE

Eastern Division

	W	L	T	Pct.	Pts.	OP
N.Y. Giants	10	5	1	.656	307	265
Washington	8	7	1	.531	327	289
Philadelphia	6	9	1	.406	317	372
Dallas	6	10	0	.375	304	314
Arizona	4	12	0	.250	283	379

Central Division

	W	L	T	Pct.	Pts.	OP
Green Bay	13	3	0	.813	422	282
Tampa Bay*	10	6	0	.625	299	263
Detroit*	9	7	0	.563	379	306
Minnesota*	9	7	0	.563	354	359
Chicago	4	12	0	.250	263	421

Western Division

	W	L	T	Pct.	Pts.	OP
San Francisco#	13	3	0	.813	375	265
Carolina	7	9	0	.438	265	314
Atlanta	7	9	0	.438	320	361
New Orleans	6	10	0	.375	237	327
St. Louis	5	11	0	.313	299	359

**Wild-Card qualifier for playoffs; #Top playoff seed in conference*

Miami finished ahead of N.Y. Jets based on head-to-head sweep (2-0). Pittsburgh finished ahead of Jacksonville based on better net division points (78 to Jaguars' 23). Oakland finished ahead of San Diego based on better division record (2-6 to Chargers' 1-7). San Francisco was top playoff seed based on better conference record than Green Bay (11-1 to Packers' 10-2). Detroit finished ahead of Minnesota based on head-to-head sweep (2-0). Carolina finished ahead of Atlanta based on head-to-head sweep (2-0).

Wild-Card playoffs: DENVER 42, Jacksonville 17; NEW ENGLAND 17, Miami 3

Divisional playoffs: PITTSBURGH 7, New England 6; Denver 14, KANSAS CITY 10

AFC Championship: Denver 24, PITTSBURGH 21

Wild-Card playoffs: Minnesota 23, N.Y. GIANTS 22; TAMPA BAY 20, Detroit 10

Divisional playoffs: SAN FRANCISCO 38, Minnesota 22; GREEN BAY 21, Tampa Bay 7

NFC Championship: Green Bay 23, SAN FRANCISCO 10

Super Bowl XXXII: Denver (AFC) 31, Green Bay (NFC) 24, at Qualcomm Stadium,
San Diego, California

1996

AMERICAN CONFERENCE

Eastern Division

	W	L	T	Pct.	Pts.	OP
New England	11	5	0	.688	418	313
Buffalo*	10	6	0	.625	319	266
Indianapolis*	9	7	0	.563	317	334
Miami	8	8	0	.500	339	325
N.Y. Jets	1	15	0	.063	279	454

Central Division

	W	L	T	Pct.	Pts.	OP
Pittsburgh	10	6	0	.625	344	257
Jacksonville*	9	7	0	.563	325	335
Cincinnati	8	8	0	.500	372	369
Houston	8	8	0	.500	345	319
Baltimore	4	12	0	.250	371	441

Western Division

	W	L	T	Pct.	Pts.	OP
Denver#	13	3	0	.813	391	275
Kansas City	9	7	0	.563	297	300
San Diego	8	8	0	.500	310	376
Oakland	7	9	0	.438	340	293
Seattle	7	9	0	.438	317	376

NATIONAL CONFERENCE

Eastern Division

	W	L	T	Pct.	Pts.	OP
Dallas	10	6	0	.625	286	250
Philadelphia*	10	6	0	.625	363	341
Washington	9	7	0	.563	364	312
Arizona	7	9	0	.438	300	397
N.Y. Giants	6	10	0	.375	242	297

Central Division

	W	L	T	Pct.	Pts.	OP
Green Bay#	13	3	0	.813	456	210
Minnesota*	9	7	0	.563	298	315
Chicago	7	9	0	.438	283	305
Tampa Bay	6	10	0	.375	221	293
Detroit	5	11	0	.313	302	368

Western Division

	W	L	T	Pct.	Pts.	OP
Carolina	12	4	0	.750	367	218
San Francisco*	12	4	0	.750	398	257
St. Louis	6	10	0	.375	303	409
Atlanta	3	13	0	.188	309	461
New Orleans	3	13	0	.188	229	339

**Wild-Card qualifier for playoffs; #Top playoff seed in conference*

Jacksonville was second Wild Card ahead of Indianapolis and Kansas City based on better conference record (7-5 to Colts' 6-6 and Chiefs' 5-7). Indianapolis was third Wild Card based on head-to-head victory over Kansas City (1-0). Cincinnati finished ahead of Houston based on better net division points (19 to Oilers' 11). Oakland finished ahead of Seattle based on better division record (3-5 to Seahawks' 2-6). Dallas finished ahead of Philadelphia based on better record against common opponents (8-5 to Eagles' 7-6). Minnesota was third Wild Card based on better conference record than Washington (8-4 to Redskins' 6-6). Carolina finished ahead of San Francisco based on head-to-head sweep (2-0). Atlanta finished ahead of New Orleans based on head-to-head sweep (2-0).

Wild-Card playoffs: Jacksonville 30, BUFFALO 27; PITTSBURGH 42, Indianapolis 14
Divisional playoffs: Jacksonville 30, DENVER 27; NEW ENGLAND 28, Pittsburgh 3
AFC Championship: NEW ENGLAND 20, Jacksonville 6
Wild-Card playoffs: DALLAS 40, Minnesota 15; SAN FRANCISCO 14, Philadelphia 0
Divisional playoffs: GREEN BAY 35, San Francisco 14; CAROLINA 26, Dallas 17
NFC Championship: GREEN BAY 30, Carolina 13
Super Bowl XXXI: Green Bay (NFC) 35, New England (AFC) 21, at Louisiana Superdome, New Orleans, Louisiana

1995

AMERICAN CONFERENCE

Eastern Division

	W	L	T	Pct.	Pts.	OP
Buffalo	10	6	0	.625	350	335
Indianapolis*	9	7	0	.563	331	316
Miami*	9	7	0	.563	398	332
New England	6	10	0	.375	294	377
N.Y. Jets	3	13	0	.188	233	384

Central Division

	W	L	T	Pct.	Pts.	OP
Pittsburgh	11	5	0	.688	407	327
Cincinnati	7	9	0	.438	349	374
Houston	7	9	0	.438	348	324
Cleveland	5	11	0	.313	289	356
Jacksonville	4	12	0	.250	275	404

Western Division

	W	L	T	Pct.	Pts.	OP
Kansas City#	13	3	0	.813	358	241
San Diego*	9	7	0	.563	321	323
Seattle	8	8	0	.500	363	366
Denver	8	8	0	.500	388	345
Oakland	8	8	0	.500	348	332

NATIONAL CONFERENCE

Eastern Division

	W	L	T	Pct.	Pts.	OP
Dallas#	12	4	0	.750	435	291
Philadelphia*	10	6	0	.625	318	338
Washington	6	10	0	.375	326	359
N.Y. Giants	5	11	0	.313	290	340
Arizona	4	12	0	.250	275	422

Central Division

	W	L	T	Pct.	Pts.	OP
Green Bay	11	5	0	.688	404	314
Detroit*	10	6	0	.625	436	336
Chicago	9	7	0	.563	392	360
Minnesota	8	8	0	.500	412	385
Tampa Bay	7	9	0	.438	238	335

Western Division

	W	L	T	Pct.	Pts.	OP
San Francisco	11	5	0	.688	457	258
Atlanta*	9	7	0	.563	362	349
St. Louis	7	9	0	.438	309	418
Carolina	7	9	0	.438	289	325
New Orleans	7	9	0	.438	319	348

**Wild-Card qualifier for playoffs; #Top playoff seed in conference*

Indianapolis finished ahead of Miami based on head-to-head sweep (2-0). San Diego was first Wild Card based on head-to-head victory over Indianapolis (1-0). Cincinnati finished ahead of Houston based on better division record (4-4 to Oilers' 3-5). Seattle finished ahead of Denver and Oakland based on best head-to-head record (3-1 to Broncos' 2-2 and Raiders' 1-3). Denver finished ahead of Oakland based on head-to-head sweep (2-0). Philadelphia was first Wild Card ahead of Detroit based on better conference record (9-3 to Lions' 7-5). San Francisco was second playoff seed ahead of Green Bay based on better conference record (8-4 to Packers' 7-5). Atlanta was third Wild Card ahead of Chicago based on better record against common opponents (4-2 to Bears' 3-3). St. Louis finished ahead of Carolina and New Orleans based on best head-to-head record (3-1 to Panthers' 1-3 and Saints' 2-2). Carolina finished ahead of New Orleans based on better conference record (4-8 to 3-9).

Wild-Card playoffs: BUFFALO 37, Miami 22; Indianapolis 35, SAN DIEGO 20
Divisional playoffs: PITTSBURGH 40, Buffalo 21; Indianapolis 10, KANSAS CITY 7
AFC Championship: PITTSBURGH 20, Indianapolis 16
Wild-Card playoffs: PHILADELPHIA 58, Detroit 37; GREEN BAY 37, Atlanta 20
Divisional playoffs: Green Bay 27, SAN FRANCISCO 17; DALLAS 30, Philadelphia 11
NFC Championship: DALLAS 38, Green Bay 27
Super Bowl XXX: Dallas (NFC) 27, Pittsburgh (AFC)17, at Sun Devil Stadium, Tempe, Arizona

1994

AMERICAN CONFERENCE

Eastern Division

	W	L	T	Pct.	Pts.	OP
Miami	10	6	0	.625	389	327
New England*	10	6	0	.625	351	312
Indianapolis	8	8	0	.500	307	320
Buffalo	7	9	0	.438	340	356
N.Y. Jets	6	10	0	.375	264	320

Central Division

	W	L	T	Pct.	Pts.	OP
Pittsburgh#	12	4	0	.750	316	234
Cleveland*	11	5	0	.688	340	204
Cincinnati	3	13	0	.188	276	406
Houston	2	14	0	.125	226	352

Western Division

	W	L	T	Pct.	Pts.	OP
San Diego	11	5	0	.688	381	306
Kansas City*	9	7	0	.563	319	298
L.A. Raiders	9	7	0	.563	303	327
Denver	7	9	0	.438	347	396
Seattle	6	10	0	.375	287	323

NATIONAL CONFERENCE

Eastern Division

	W	L	T	Pct.	Pts.	OP
Dallas	12	4	0	.750	414	248
N.Y. Giants	9	7	0	.563	279	305
Arizona	8	8	0	.500	235	267
Philadelphia	7	9	0	.438	308	308
Washington	3	13	0	.188	320	412

Central Division

	W	L	T	Pct.	Pts.	OP
Minnesota	10	6	0	.625	356	314
Green Bay*	9	7	0	.563	382	287
Detroit*	9	7	0	.563	357	342
Chicago*	9	7	0	.563	271	307
Tampa Bay	6	10	0	.375	251	351

Western Division

	W	L	T	Pct.	Pts.	OP
San Francisco#	13	3	0	.813	505	296
New Orleans	7	9	0	.438	348	407
Atlanta	7	9	0	.438	317	385
L.A. Rams	4	12	0	.250	286	365

**Wild-Card qualifier for playoffs; #Top playoff seed in conference*

Miami finished ahead of New England based on head-to-head sweep (2-0). Kansas City finished ahead of L.A. Raiders based on head-to-head sweep (2-0). Green Bay was first Wild Card based on best head-to-head record (3-1) vs. Detroit (2-2) and Chicago (1-3) and better conference record (8-4) than N.Y. Giants (6-6). Detroit was second Wild Card based on better division record (4-4) than Chicago (3-5) and head-to-head victory over N.Y. Giants (1-0). Chicago was third Wild Card based on better record against common opponents (4-4) than N.Y. Giants (3-5). New Orleans finished ahead of Atlanta based on head-to-head sweep (2-0).

Wild-Card playoffs: MIAMI 27, Kansas City 17; CLEVELAND 20, New England 13
Divisional playoffs: PITTSBURGH 29, Cleveland 9; SAN DIEGO 22, Miami 21
AFC Championship: San Diego 17, PITTSBURGH 13
Wild-Card playoffs: GREEN BAY 16, Detroit 12; Chicago 35, MINNESOTA 18
Divisional playoffs: SAN FRANCISCO 44, Chicago 15; DALLAS 35, Green Bay 9
NFC Championship: SAN FRANCISCO 38, Dallas 28
Super Bowl XXIX: San Francisco (NFC) 49, San Diego (AFC) 26, at Joe Robbie Stadium, Miami, Florida

1993

AMERICAN CONFERENCE

Eastern Division

	W	L	T	Pct.	Pts.	OP
Buffalo#	12	4	0	.750	329	242
Miami	9	7	0	.563	349	351
N.Y. Jets	8	8	0	.500	270	247
New England	5	11	0	.313	238	286
Indianapolis	4	12	0	.250	189	378

Central Division

	W	L	T	Pct.	Pts.	OP
Houston	12	4	0	.750	368	238
Pittsburgh*	9	7	0	.563	308	281
Cleveland	7	9	0	.438	304	307
Cincinnati	3	13	0	.188	187	319

Western Division

	W	L	T	Pct.	Pts.	OP
Kansas City	11	5	0	.688	328	291
L.A. Raiders*	10	6	0	.625	306	326
Denver*	9	7	0	.563	373	284
San Diego	8	8	0	.500	322	290
Seattle	6	10	0	.375	280	314

NATIONAL CONFERENCE

Eastern Division

	W	L	T	Pct.	Pts.	OP
Dallas#	12	4	0	.750	376	229
N.Y. Giants*	11	5	0	.688	288	205
Philadelphia	8	8	0	.500	293	315
Phoenix	7	9	0	.438	326	269
Washington	4	12	0	.250	230	345

Central Division

	W	L	T	Pct.	Pts.	OP
Detroit	10	6	0	.625	298	292
Minnesota*	9	7	0	.563	277	290
Green Bay*	9	7	0	.563	340	282
Chicago	7	9	0	.438	234	230
Tampa Bay	5	11	0	.313	237	376

Western Division

	W	L	T	Pct.	Pts.	OP
San Francisco	10	6	0	.625	473	295
New Orleans	8	8	0	.500	317	343
Atlanta	6	10	0	.375	316	385
L.A. Rams	5	11	0	.313	221	367

**Wild-Card qualifier for playoffs; #Top playoff seed in conference.*

Buffalo was top playoff seed based on head-to-head victory over Houston (1-0). Denver was second Wild Card, and Pittsburgh was third Wild Card ahead of Miami, based on better conference record (8-4 to Steelers' 7-5 to Dolphins' 6-6). San Francisco was second playoff seed based on head-to-head victory over Detroit (1-0). Minnesota finished ahead of Green Bay based on head-to-head sweep (2-0).

Wild-Card playoffs: KANSAS CITY 27, Pittsburgh 24 (OT); L.A. RAIDERS 42, Denver 24
Divisional playoffs: BUFFALO 29, L.A. Raiders 23; Kansas City 28, HOUSTON 20
AFC Championship: BUFFALO 30, Kansas City 13
Wild-Card playoffs: Green Bay 28, DETROIT 24; N.Y. GIANTS 17, Minnesota 10
Divisional playoffs: SAN FRANCISCO 44, N.Y. Giants 3; DALLAS 27, Green Bay 17
NFC Championship: DALLAS 38, San Francisco 21
Super Bowl XXVIII: Dallas (NFC) 30, Buffalo (AFC) 13, at Georgia Dome, Atlanta, Georgia

PAST STANDINGS

1992

AMERICAN CONFERENCE

Eastern Division

	W	L	T	Pct.	Pts.	OP
Miami	11	5	0	.688	340	281
Buffalo*	11	5	0	.688	381	283
Indianapolis	9	7	0	.563	216	302
N.Y. Jets	4	12	0	.250	220	315
New England	2	14	0	.125	205	363

Central Division

	W	L	T	Pct.	Pts.	OP
Pittsburgh#	11	5	0	.688	299	225
Houston*	10	6	0	.625	352	258
Cleveland	7	9	0	.438	272	275
Cincinnati	5	11	0	.313	274	364

Western Division

	W	L	T	Pct.	Pts.	OP
San Diego	11	5	0	.688	335	241
Kansas City*	10	6	0	.625	348	282
Denver	8	8	0	.500	262	329
L.A. Raiders	7	9	0	.438	249	281
Seattle	2	14	0	.125	140	312

NATIONAL CONFERENCE

Eastern Division

	W	L	T	Pct.	Pts.	OP
Dallas	13	3	0	.813	409	243
Philadelphia*	11	5	0	.688	354	245
Washington*	9	7	0	.563	300	255
N.Y. Giants	6	10	0	.375	306	367
Phoenix	4	12	0	.250	243	332

Central Division

	W	L	T	Pct.	Pts.	OP
Minnesota	11	5	0	.688	374	249
Green Bay	9	7	0	.563	276	296
Tampa Bay	5	11	0	.313	267	365
Chicago	5	11	0	.313	295	361
Detroit	5	11	0	.313	273	332

Western Division

	W	L	T	Pct.	Pts.	OP
San Francisco#	14	2	0	.875	431	236
New Orleans*	12	4	0	.750	330	202
Atlanta	6	10	0	.375	327	414
L.A. Rams	6	10	0	.375	313	383

**Wild-Card qualifier for playoffs; #Top playoff seed in conference*

Pittsburgh was top playoff seed, and Miami was second playoff seed ahead of San Diego, based on conference record (10-2 to Dolphins' 9-3 to Chargers' 9-5). Miami finished ahead of Buffalo based on better conference record (9-3 to Bills' 7-5). Houston was second Wild Card based on head-to-head victory over Kansas City (1-0). Washington was third Wild Card based on better conference record than Green Bay (7-5 to Packers' 6-6). Tampa Bay finished ahead of Chicago and Detroit based on better conference record (5-9 to Bears' 4-8 and Lions' 3-9). Atlanta finished ahead of L.A. Rams based on better record against common opponents (5-7 to Rams' 4-8).

Wild-Card playoffs: SAN DIEGO 17, Kansas City 0; BUFFALO 41, Houston 38 (OT)
Divisional playoffs: Buffalo 24, PITTSBURGH 3; MIAMI 31, San Diego 0
AFC Championship: Buffalo 29, MIAMI 10
Wild-Card playoffs: Washington 24, MINNESOTA 7; Philadelphia 36, NEW ORLEANS 20
Divisional playoffs: SAN FRANCISCO 20, Washington 13; DALLAS 34, Philadelphia 10
NFC Championship: Dallas 30, SAN FRANCISCO 20
Super Bowl XXVII: Dallas (NFC) 52, Buffalo (AFC) 17, at Rose Bowl, Pasadena, California

1991

AMERICAN CONFERENCE

Eastern Division

	W	L	T	Pct.	Pts.	OP
Buffalo#	13	3	0	.813	458	318
N.Y. Jets*	8	8	0	.500	314	293
Miami	8	8	0	.500	343	349
New England	6	10	0	.375	211	305
Indianapolis	1	15	0	.063	143	381

Central Division

	W	L	T	Pct.	Pts.	OP
Houston	11	5	0	.688	386	251
Pittsburgh	7	9	0	.438	292	344
Cleveland	6	10	0	.375	293	298
Cincinnati	3	13	0	.188	263	435

Western Division

	W	L	T	Pct.	Pts.	OP
Denver	12	4	0	.750	304	235
Kansas City*	10	6	0	.625	322	252
L.A. Raiders*	9	7	0	.563	298	297
Seattle	7	9	0	.438	276	261
San Diego	4	12	0	.250	274	342

NATIONAL CONFERENCE

Eastern Division

	W	L	T	Pct.	Pts.	OP
Washington#	14	2	0	.875	485	224
Dallas*	11	5	0	.688	342	310
Philadelphia	10	6	0	.625	285	244
N.Y. Giants	8	8	0	.500	281	297
Phoenix	4	12	0	.250	196	344

Central Division

	W	L	T	Pct.	Pts.	OP
Detroit	12	4	0	.750	339	295
Chicago*	11	5	0	.688	299	269
Minnesota	8	8	0	.500	301	306
Green Bay	4	12	0	.250	273	313
Tampa Bay	3	13	0	.188	199	365

Western Division

	W	L	T	Pct.	Pts.	OP
New Orleans	11	5	0	.688	341	211
Atlanta*	10	6	0	.625	361	338
San Francisco	10	6	0	.625	393	239
L.A. Rams	3	13	0	.188	234	390

**Wild-Card qualifier for playoffs; #Top playoff seed in conference*

N.Y. Jets finished ahead of Miami based on head-to-head sweep (2-0). Chicago was first Wild Card based on better conference record than Dallas (9-3 to Cowboys' 8-4). Atlanta finished ahead of San Francisco based on head-to-head sweep (2-0), and was third Wild Card ahead of Philadelphia based on better conference record (7-5 to Eagles' 6-6).

Wild-Card playoffs: KANSAS CITY 10, L.A. Raiders 6; HOUSTON 17, N.Y. Jets 10
Divisional playoffs: DENVER 26, Houston 24; BUFFALO 37, Kansas City 14
AFC Championship: BUFFALO 10, Denver 7
Wild-Card playoffs: Atlanta 27, NEW ORLEANS 20; Dallas 17, CHICAGO 13
Divisional playoffs: WASHINGTON 24, Atlanta 7; DETROIT 38, Dallas 6
NFC Championship: WASHINGTON 41, Detroit 10
Super Bowl XXVI: Washington (NFC) 37, Buffalo (AFC) 24, at Hubert H. Humphrey Metrodome, Minneapolis, Minnesota

1990

AMERICAN CONFERENCE

Eastern Division

	W	L	T	Pct.	Pts.	OP
Buffalo#	13	3	0	.813	428	263
Miami*	12	4	0	.750	336	242
Indianapolis	7	9	0	.438	281	353
N.Y. Jets	6	10	0	.375	295	345
New England	1	15	0	.063	181	446

Central Division

	W	L	T	Pct.	Pts.	OP
Cincinnati	9	7	0	.563	360	352
Houston*	9	7	0	.563	405	307
Pittsburgh	9	7	0	.563	292	240
Cleveland	3	13	0	.188	228	462

Western Division

	W	L	T	Pct.	Pts.	OP
L.A. Raiders	12	4	0	.750	337	268
Kansas City*	11	5	0	.688	369	257
Seattle	9	7	0	.563	306	286
San Diego	6	10	0	.375	315	281
Denver	5	11	0	.313	331	374

NATIONAL CONFERENCE

Eastern Division

	W	L	T	Pct.	Pts.	OP
N.Y. Giants	13	3	0	.813	335	211
Philadelphia*	10	6	0	.625	396	299
Washington*	10	6	0	.625	381	301
Dallas	7	9	0	.438	244	308
Phoenix	5	11	0	.313	268	396

Central Division

	W	L	T	Pct.	Pts.	OP
Chicago	11	5	0	.688	348	280
Tampa Bay	6	10	0	.375	264	367
Detroit	6	10	0	.375	373	413
Green Bay	6	10	0	.375	271	347
Minnesota	6	10	0	.375	351	326

Western Division

	W	L	T	Pct.	Pts.	OP
San Francisco#	14	2	0	.875	353	239
New Orleans*	8	8	0	.500	274	275
L.A. Rams	5	11	0	.313	345	412
Atlanta	5	11	0	.313	348	365

**Wild-Card qualifier for playoffs; #Top playoff seed in conference*

Cincinnati finished ahead of Houston and Pittsburgh based on best head-to-head record (3-1 to Oilers' 2-2 to Steelers' 1-3). Houston was Wild Card based on better conference record (8-4) than Seattle (7-5) and Pittsburgh (6-6). Philadelphia finished ahead of Washington based on better division record (5-3 to Redskins' 4-4). Tampa Bay was second in NFC Central based on best head-to-head record (5-1) against Detroit (2-4), Green Bay (3-3), and Minnesota (2-4). Detroit finished third based on best net division points (minus 8) against Green Bay (minus 40). Green Bay finished ahead of Minnesota based on better conference record (5-7 to Vikings' 4-8). The L.A. Rams finished ahead of Atlanta based on net points in division (plus 1 to Falcons' minus 31).

Wild-Card playoffs: MIAMI 17, Kansas City 16; CINCINNATI 41, Houston 14
Divisional playoffs: BUFFALO 44, Miami 34; L.A. RAIDERS 20, Cincinnati 10
AFC Championship: BUFFALO 51, L.A. Raiders 3
Wild-Card playoffs: Washington 20, PHILADELPHIA 6; CHICAGO 16, New Orleans 6
Divisional playoffs: SAN FRANCISCO 28, Washington 10; N.Y. GIANTS 31, Chicago 3
NFC Championship: N.Y. Giants 15, SAN FRANCISCO 13
Super Bowl XXV: N.Y. Giants (NFC) 20, Buffalo (AFC) 19, at Tampa Stadium, Tampa, Florida

1989

AMERICAN CONFERENCE

Eastern Division

	W	L	T	Pct.	Pts.	OP
Buffalo	9	7	0	.563	409	317
Indianapolis	8	8	0	.500	298	301
Miami	8	8	0	.500	331	379
New England	5	11	0	.313	297	391
N.Y. Jets	4	12	0	.250	253	411

Central Division

	W	L	T	Pct.	Pts.	OP
Cleveland	9	6	1	.594	334	254
Houston*	9	7	0	.563	365	412
Pittsburgh*	9	7	0	.563	265	326
Cincinnati	8	8	0	.500	404	285

Western Division

	W	L	T	Pct.	Pts.	OP
Denver#	11	5	0	.688	362	226
Kansas City	8	7	1	.531	318	286
L.A. Raiders	8	8	0	.500	315	297
Seattle	7	9	0	.438	241	327
San Diego	6	10	0	.375	266	290

NATIONAL CONFERENCE

Eastern Division

	W	L	T	Pct.	Pts.	OP
N.Y. Giants	12	4	0	.750	348	252
Philadelphia*	11	5	0	.688	342	274
Washington	10	6	0	.625	386	308
Phoenix	5	11	0	.313	258	377
Dallas	1	15	0	.063	204	393

Central Division

	W	L	T	Pct.	Pts.	OP
Minnesota	10	6	0	.625	351	275
Green Bay	10	6	0	.625	362	356
Detroit	7	9	0	.438	312	364
Chicago	6	10	0	.375	358	377
Tampa Bay	5	11	0	.313	320	419

Western Division

	W	L	T	Pct.	Pts.	OP
San Francisco#	14	2	0	.875	442	253
L.A. Rams*	11	5	0	.688	426	344
New Orleans	9	7	0	.563	386	301
Atlanta	3	13	0	.188	279	437

**Wild-Card qualifier for playoffs; #Top playoff seed in conference*

Indianapolis finished ahead of Miami based on better conference record (7-5 vs. Dolphins' 6-8). Houston finished ahead of Pittsburgh based on head-to-head sweep (2-0). The L.A. Rams did not play San Francisco in the divisional playoffs because, from 1970-1989, two teams from the same division could not meet prior to the conference championship game. Philadelphia was first Wild Card ahead of L.A. Rams based on better record against common opponents (6-3 to Rams' 5-4). Minnesota finished ahead of Green Bay based on better division record (6-2 vs. Packers' 5-3).

Wild-Card playoff: Pittsburgh 26, HOUSTON 23 (OT)
Divisional playoffs: CLEVELAND 34, Buffalo 30; DENVER 24, Pittsburgh 23
AFC Championship: DENVER 37, Cleveland 21
Wild-Card playoff: L.A. Rams 21, PHILADELPHIA 7
Divisional playoffs: L.A. Rams 19, N.Y. GIANTS 13 (OT); SAN FRANCISCO 41, Minnesota 13
NFC Championship: SAN FRANCISCO 30, L.A. Rams 3
Super Bowl XXIV: San Francisco (NFC) 55, Denver (AFC) 10, at Louisiana Superdome, New Orleans, Louisiana

1988

AMERICAN CONFERENCE

Eastern Division

	W	L	T	Pct.	Pts.	OP
Buffalo	12	4	0	.750	329	237
Indianapolis	9	7	0	.563	354	315
New England	9	7	0	.563	250	284
N.Y. Jets	8	7	1	.531	372	354
Miami	6	10	0	.375	319	380

Central Division

	W	L	T	Pct.	Pts.	OP
Cincinnati#	12	4	0	.750	448	329
Cleveland*	10	6	0	.625	304	288
Houston*	10	6	0	.625	424	365
Pittsburgh	5	11	0	.313	336	421

Western Division

	W	L	T	Pct.	Pts.	OP
Seattle	9	7	0	.563	339	329
Denver	8	8	0	.500	327	352
L.A. Raiders	7	9	0	.438	325	369
San Diego	6	10	0	.375	231	332
Kansas City	4	11	1	.281	254	320

NATIONAL CONFERENCE

Eastern Division

	W	L	T	Pct.	Pts.	OP
Philadelphia	10	6	0	.625	379	319
N.Y. Giants	10	6	0	.625	359	304
Washington	7	9	0	.438	345	387
Phoenix	7	9	0	.438	344	398
Dallas	3	13	0	.188	265	381

Central Division

	W	L	T	Pct.	Pts.	OP
Chicago#	12	4	0	.750	312	215
Minnesota*	11	5	0	.688	406	233
Tampa Bay	5	11	0	.313	261	350
Detroit	4	12	0	.250	220	313
Green Bay	4	12	0	.250	240	315

Western Division

	W	L	T	Pct.	Pts.	OP
San Francisco	10	6	0	.625	369	294
L.A. Rams*	10	6	0	.625	407	293
New Orleans	10	6	0	.625	312	283
Atlanta	5	11	0	.313	244	315

**Wild-Card qualifier for playoffs; #Top playoff seed in conference*

Cincinnati was top playoff seed ahead of Buffalo based on head-to-head victory (1-0). Indianapolis finished ahead of New England based on better record against common opponents (7-5 to Patriots' 6-6). Cleveland finished ahead of Houston based on better division record (4-2 to Oilers' 3-3). Houston did not play Cincinnati, and Minnesota did not play Chicago in the divisional playoffs because, from 1970-1989, two teams from the same division could not meet prior to the conference championship game. Philadelphia finished first in NFC East based on head-to-head sweep of N.Y. Giants (2-0). Washington finished third in NFC East based on better division record (4-4) than Phoenix (3-5). Detroit finished fourth in NFC Central based on head-to-head sweep of Green Bay (2-0). San Francisco finished first in NFC West based on better head-to-head record (3-1) against L.A. Rams (2-2) and New Orleans (1-3). L.A. Rams finished second in NFC West based on better division record (4-2) than New Orleans (3-3) and earned Wild-Card position based on better conference record (8-4) than N.Y. Giants (9-5) and New Orleans (6-6).

Wild-Card playoff: Houston 24, CLEVELAND 23
Divisional playoffs: CINCINNATI 21, Seattle 13; BUFFALO 17, Houston 10
AFC Championship: CINCINNATI 21, Buffalo 10
Wild-Card playoff: MINNESOTA 28, L.A. Rams 17
Divisional playoffs: CHICAGO 20, Philadelphia 12;
SAN FRANCISCO 34, Minnesota 9
NFC Championship: San Francisco 28, CHICAGO 3
Super Bowl XXIII: San Francisco (NFC) 20, Cincinnati (AFC) 16, at Joe Robbie Stadium, Miami, Florida

1987

AMERICAN CONFERENCE

Eastern Division

	W	L	T	Pct.	Pts.	OP
Indianapolis	9	6	0	.600	300	238
New England	8	7	0	.533	320	293
Miami	8	7	0	.533	362	335
Buffalo	7	8	0	.467	270	305
N.Y. Jets	6	9	0	.400	334	360

Central Division

	W	L	T	Pct.	Pts.	OP
Cleveland	10	5	0	.667	390	239
Houston*	9	6	0	.600	345	349
Pittsburgh	8	7	0	.533	285	299
Cincinnati	4	11	0	.267	285	370

Western Division

	W	L	T	Pct.	Pts.	OP
Denver#	10	4	1	.700	379	288
Seattle*	9	6	0	.600	371	314
San Diego	8	7	0	.533	253	317
L.A. Raiders	5	10	0	.333	301	289
Kansas City	4	11	0	.267	273	388

NATIONAL CONFERENCE

Eastern Division

	W	L	T	Pct.	Pts.	OP
Washington	11	4	0	.733	379	285
Dallas	7	8	0	.467	340	348
St. Louis	7	8	0	.467	362	368
Philadelphia	7	8	0	.467	337	380
N.Y. Giants	6	9	0	.400	280	312

Central Division

	W	L	T	Pct.	Pts.	OP
Chicago	11	4	0	.733	356	282
Minnesota*	8	7	0	.533	336	335
Green Bay	5	9	1	.367	255	300
Tampa Bay	4	11	0	.267	286	360
Detroit	4	11	0	.267	269	384

Western Division

	W	L	T	Pct.	Pts.	OP
San Francisco#	13	2	0	.867	459	253
New Orleans*	12	3	0	.800	422	283
L.A. Rams	6	9	0	.400	317	361
Atlanta	3	12	0	.200	205	436

**Wild-Card qualifier for playoffs; #Top playoff seed in conference*

New England finished ahead of Miami based on head-to-head sweep (2-0). Houston was first Wild Card ahead of Seattle based on better conference record (7-4 to Seahawks' 5-6). Chicago was second playoff seed ahead of Washington based on better conference record (9-2 to Redskins' 9-3). Dallas finished ahead of St. Louis and Philadelphia based on better division record (4-4 to Cardinals' 3-5 and Eagles' 3-5). St. Louis finished ahead of Philadelphia based on better conference record (7-7 to Eagles' 4-7). Tampa Bay finished ahead of Detroit based on better division record (3-4 to Lions' 2-5).

Wild-Card playoff: HOUSTON 23, Seattle 20 (OT)
Divisional playoffs: CLEVELAND 38, Indianapolis 21; DENVER 34, Houston 10
AFC Championship: DENVER 38, Cleveland 33
Wild-Card playoff: Minnesota 44, NEW ORLEANS 10
Divisional playoffs: Minnesota 36, SAN FRANCISCO 24; Washington 21, CHICAGO 17
NFC Championship: WASHINGTON 17, Minnesota 10
Super Bowl XXII: Washington (NFC) 42, Denver (AFC) 10, at San Diego Jack Murphy Stadium, San Diego, California

Note: 1987 regular season was reduced from 16 to 15 games for each team due to players' strike.

1986

AMERICAN CONFERENCE

Eastern Division

	W	L	T	Pct.	Pts.	OP
New England	11	5	0	.688	412	307
N.Y. Jets*	10	6	0	.625	364	386
Miami	8	8	0	.500	430	405
Buffalo	4	12	0	.250	287	348
Indianapolis	3	13	0	.188	229	400

Central Division

	W	L	T	Pct.	Pts.	OP
Cleveland#	12	4	0	.750	391	310
Cincinnati	10	6	0	.625	409	394
Pittsburgh	6	10	0	.375	307	336
Houston	5	11	0	.313	274	329

Western Division

	W	L	T	Pct.	Pts.	OP
Denver	11	5	0	.688	378	327
Kansas City*	10	6	0	.625	358	326
Seattle	10	6	0	.625	366	293
L.A. Raiders	8	8	0	.500	323	346
San Diego	4	12	0	.250	335	396

NATIONAL CONFERENCE

Eastern Division

	W	L	T	Pct.	Pts.	OP
N.Y. Giants#	14	2	0	.875	371	236
Washington*	12	4	0	.750	368	296
Dallas	7	9	0	.438	346	337
Philadelphia	5	10	1	.344	256	312
St. Louis	4	11	1	.281	218	351

Central Division

	W	L	T	Pct.	Pts.	OP
Chicago	14	2	0	.875	352	187
Minnesota	9	7	0	.563	398	273
Detroit	5	11	0	.313	277	326
Green Bay	4	12	0	.250	254	418
Tampa Bay	2	14	0	.125	239	473

Western Division

	W	L	T	Pct.	Pts.	OP
San Francisco	10	5	1	.656	374	247
L.A. Rams*	10	6	0	.625	309	267
Atlanta	7	8	1	.469	280	280
New Orleans	7	9	0	.438	288	287

**Wild-Card qualifier for playoffs; #Top playoff seed in conference*

Denver was second playoff seed ahead of New England based on head-to-head victory (1-0). N.Y. Jets were first Wild Card based on better conference record (8-4) than Kansas City (9-5), Seattle (7-5), and Cincinnati (7-5). Kansas City was second Wild Card based on better conference record (9-5) than Seattle (7-5) and Cincinnati (7-5). N.Y. Giants were top playoff seed based on better conference record than Chicago (11-1 to Bears' 10-2). Washington did not play the N.Y. Giants in the divisional playoffs because, from 1970-1989, two teams from the same division could not meet prior to the conference championship game.

Wild-Card playoff: N.Y. JETS 35, Kansas City 15
Divisional playoffs: CLEVELAND 23, N.Y. Jets 20 (OT);
DENVER 22, New England 17
AFC Championship: Denver 23, CLEVELAND 20 (OT)
Wild-Card playoff: WASHINGTON 19, L.A. Rams 7
Divisional playoffs: Washington 27, CHICAGO 13
N.Y. GIANTS 49, San Francisco 3
NFC Championship: N.Y. GIANTS 17, Washington 0
Super Bowl XXI: N.Y. Giants (NFC) 39, Denver (AFC) 20, at Rose Bowl, Pasadena, California

1985

AMERICAN CONFERENCE

Eastern Division

	W	L	T	Pct.	Pts.	OP
Miami	12	4	0	.750	428	320
N.Y. Jets*	11	5	0	.688	393	264
New England*	11	5	0	.688	362	290
Indianapolis	5	11	0	.313	320	386
Buffalo	2	14	0	.125	200	381

Central Division

	W	L	T	Pct.	Pts.	OP
Cleveland	8	8	0	.500	287	294
Cincinnati	7	9	0	.438	441	437
Pittsburgh	7	9	0	.438	379	355
Houston	5	11	0	.313	284	412

Western Division

	W	L	T	Pct.	Pts.	OP
L.A. Raiders#	12	4	0	.750	354	308
Denver	11	5	0	.688	380	329
Seattle	8	8	0	.500	349	303
San Diego	8	8	0	.500	467	435
Kansas City	6	10	0	.375	317	360

NATIONAL CONFERENCE

Eastern Division

	W	L	T	Pct.	Pts.	OP
Dallas	10	6	0	.625	357	333
N.Y. Giants*	10	6	0	.625	399	283
Washington	10	6	0	.625	297	312
Philadelphia	7	9	0	.438	286	310
St. Louis	5	11	0	.313	278	414

Central Division

	W	L	T	Pct.	Pts.	OP
Chicago#	15	1	0	.938	456	198
Green Bay	8	8	0	.500	337	355
Minnesota	7	9	0	.438	346	359
Detroit	7	9	0	.438	307	366
Tampa Bay	2	14	0	.125	294	448

Western Division

	W	L	T	Pct.	Pts.	OP
L.A. Rams	11	5	0	.688	340	277
San Francisco*	10	6	0	.625	411	263
New Orleans	5	11	0	.313	294	401
Atlanta	4	12	0	.250	282	452

**Wild-Card qualifier for playoffs; #Top playoff seed in conference*

N.Y. Jets were first Wild Card based on better conference record (9-3) than New England (8-4) and Denver (8-4). New England was second Wild Card ahead of Denver based on better record against common opponents (4-2 to Broncos' 3-3). Cincinnati finished ahead of Pittsburgh based on head-to-head sweep (2-0). Seattle finished ahead of San Diego based on head-to-head sweep (2-0). Dallas finished ahead of N.Y. Giants and Washington based on better head-to-head record (4-0 to Giants' 1-3 and Redskins' 1-3). N.Y. Giants were first Wild Card based on better conference record (8-4) than San Francisco (7-5) and Washington (6-6). San Francisco was second Wild Card based on head-to-head victory over Washington (1-0). Minnesota finished ahead of Detroit based on better division record (3-5 to Lions' 2-6).

Wild-Card playoff: New England 26, N.Y. JETS 14
Divisional playoffs: MIAMI 24, Cleveland 21;
New England 27, L.A. RAIDERS 20
AFC Championship: New England 31, MIAMI 14
Wild-Card playoff: N.Y. GIANTS 17, San Francisco 3
Divisional playoffs: L.A. RAMS 20, Dallas 0;
CHICAGO 21, N.Y. Giants 0
NFC Championship: CHICAGO 24, L.A. Rams 0
Super Bowl XX: Chicago (NFC) 46, New England (AFC) 10, at Louisiana Superdome, New Orleans, Louisiana

PAST STANDINGS

1984

AMERICAN CONFERENCE

Eastern Division

	W	L	T	Pct.	Pts.	OP
Miami#	14	2	0	.875	513	298
New England	9	7	0	.563	362	352
N.Y. Jets	7	9	0	.438	332	364
Indianapolis	4	12	0	.250	239	414
Buffalo	2	14	0	.125	250	454

Central Division

	W	L	T	Pct.	Pts.	OP
Pittsburgh	9	7	0	.563	387	310
Cincinnati	8	8	0	.500	339	339
Cleveland	5	11	0	.313	250	297
Houston	3	13	0	.188	240	437

Western Division

	W	L	T	Pct.	Pts.	OP
Denver	13	3	0	.813	353	241
Seattle*	12	4	0	.750	418	282
L.A. Raiders*	11	5	0	.688	368	278
Kansas City	8	8	0	.500	314	324
San Diego	7	9	0	.438	394	413

NATIONAL CONFERENCE

Eastern Division

	W	L	T	Pct.	Pts.	OP
Washington	11	5	0	.688	426	310
N.Y. Giants*	9	7	0	.563	299	301
St. Louis	9	7	0	.563	423	345
Dallas	9	7	0	.563	308	308
Philadelphia	6	9	1	.406	278	320

Central Division

	W	L	T	Pct.	Pts.	OP
Chicago	10	6	0	.625	325	248
Green Bay	8	8	0	.500	390	309
Tampa Bay	6	10	0	.375	335	380
Detroit	4	11	1	.281	283	408
Minnesota	3	13	0	.188	276	484

Western Division

	W	L	T	Pct.	Pts.	OP
San Francisco#	15	1	0	.938	475	227
L.A. Rams*	10	6	0	.625	346	316
New Orleans	7	9	0	.438	298	361
Atlanta	4	12	0	.250	281	382

**Wild-Card qualifier for playoffs; #Top playoff seed in conference*

N.Y. Giants finished ahead of St. Louis and Dallas based on best head-to-head record (3-1 to Cardinals' 2-2 and Cowboys' 1-3). St. Louis finished ahead of Dallas based on better division record (5-3 to Cowboys' 3-5).

Wild-Card playoff: SEATTLE 13, L.A. Raiders 7

Divisional playoffs: MIAMI 31, Seattle 10; Pittsburgh 24, DENVER 17

AFC Championship: MIAMI 45, Pittsburgh 28

Wild-Card playoff: N.Y. Giants 16, L.A. RAMS 13

Divisional playoffs: SAN FRANCISCO 21, N.Y. Giants 10; Chicago 23, WASHINGTON 19

NFC Championship: SAN FRANCISCO 23, Chicago 0

Super Bowl XIX: San Francisco (NFC) 38, Miami (AFC) 16, at Stanford Stadium, Stanford, California

1983

AMERICAN CONFERENCE

Eastern Division

	W	L	T	Pct.	Pts.	OP
Miami	12	4	0	.750	389	250
New England	8	8	0	.500	274	289
Buffalo	8	8	0	.500	283	351
Baltimore	7	9	0	.438	264	354
N.Y. Jets	7	9	0	.438	313	331

Central Division

	W	L	T	Pct.	Pts.	OP
Pittsburgh	10	6	0	.625	355	303
Cleveland	9	7	0	.563	356	342
Cincinnati	7	9	0	.438	346	302
Houston	2	14	0	.125	288	460

Western Division

	W	L	T	Pct.	Pts.	OP
L.A. Raiders#	12	4	0	.750	442	338
Seattle*	9	7	0	.563	403	397
Denver*	9	7	0	.563	302	327
San Diego	6	10	0	.375	358	462
Kansas City	6	10	0	.375	386	367

NATIONAL CONFERENCE

Eastern Division

	W	L	T	Pct.	Pts.	OP
Washington#	14	2	0	.875	541	332
Dallas*	12	4	0	.750	479	360
St. Louis	8	7	1	.531	374	428
Philadelphia	5	11	0	.313	233	322
N.Y. Giants	3	12	1	.219	267	347

Central Division

	W	L	T	Pct.	Pts.	OP
Detroit	9	7	0	.563	347	286
Green Bay	8	8	0	.500	429	439
Chicago	8	8	0	.500	311	301
Minnesota	8	8	0	.500	316	348
Tampa Bay	2	14	0	.125	241	380

Western Division

	W	L	T	Pct.	Pts.	OP
San Francisco	10	6	0	.625	432	293
L.A. Rams*	9	7	0	.563	361	344
New Orleans	8	8	0	.500	319	337
Atlanta	7	9	0	.438	370	389

**Wild-Card qualifier for playoffs; #Top playoff seed in conference*

Seattle was second Wild Card ahead of Denver based on better division record (5-3 to Broncos' 3-5) after Cleveland was eliminated from three-way tie based on head-to-head record (Seattle and Denver 2-1 to Browns' 0-2). Seattle did not play the L.A. Raiders in the divisional playoffs because, from 1970-1989, two teams from the same division could not meet prior to the conference championship game. New England finished ahead of Buffalo based on head-to-head sweep (2-0). Baltimore finished ahead of N.Y. Jets based on better conference record (5-9 to Jets' 4-8). San Diego finished ahead of Kansas City based on head-to-head sweep (2-0). Green Bay finished ahead of Chicago based on better record against common opponents (5-5 to Bears' 4-6) after Minnesota was eliminated from three-way tie based on conference record (Chicago 7-7 and Green Bay 6-6 to Vikings' 4-8).

Wild-Card playoff: SEATTLE 31, Denver 7

Divisional playoffs: Seattle 27, MIAMI 20; L.A. RAIDERS 38, Pittsburgh 10

AFC Championship: L.A. RAIDERS 30, Seattle 14

Wild-Card playoff: L.A. Rams 24, DALLAS 17

Divisional playoffs: SAN FRANCISCO 24, Detroit 23; WASHINGTON 51, L.A. Rams 7

NFC Championship: WASHINGTON 24, San Francisco 21

Super Bowl XVIII: L.A. Raiders (AFC) 38, Washington (NFC) 9, at Tampa Stadium, Tampa, Florida

1982

AMERICAN CONFERENCE

	W	L	T	Pct.	Pts.	OP
L.A. Raiders#	8	1	0	.889	260	200
Miami	7	2	0	.778	198	131
Cincinnati	7	2	0	.778	232	177
Pittsburgh	6	3	0	.667	204	146
San Diego	6	3	0	.667	288	221
N.Y. Jets	6	3	0	.667	245	166
New England	5	4	0	.556	143	157
Cleveland	4	5	0	.444	140	182
Buffalo	4	5	0	.444	150	154
Seattle	4	5	0	.444	127	147
Kansas City	3	6	0	.333	176	184
Denver	2	7	0	.222	148	226
Houston	1	8	0	.111	136	245
Baltimore	0	8	1	.056	113	236

NATIONAL CONFERENCE

	W	L	T	Pct.	Pts.	OP
Washington#	8	1	0	.889	190	128
Dallas	6	3	0	.667	226	145
Green Bay	5	3	1	.611	226	169
Minnesota	5	4	0	.556	187	198
Atlanta	5	4	0	.556	183	199
St. Louis	5	4	0	.556	135	170
Tampa Bay	5	4	0	.556	158	178
Detroit	4	5	0	.444	181	176
New Orleans	4	5	0	.444	129	160
N.Y. Giants	4	5	0	.444	164	160
San Francisco	3	6	0	.333	209	206
Chicago	3	6	0	.333	141	174
Philadelphia	3	6	0	.333	191	195
L.A. Rams	2	7	0	.222	200	250

As the result of a 57-day players' strike, the 1982 NFL regular season schedule was reduced from 16 weeks to 9. At the conclusion of the regular season, the NFL conducted a 16-team postseason Super Bowl Tournament. Eight teams from each conference were seeded 1-8 based on their records during the season.

#Top playoff seed in conference

Miami finished ahead of Cincinnati based on better conference record (6-1 to Bengals' 6-2). Pittsburgh finished ahead of San Diego based on better record against common opponents (3-1 to Chargers' 2-1) after N.Y. Jets were eliminated from three-way tie based on conference record (Pittsburgh and San Diego 5-3 to Jets' 2-3). Cleveland finished ahead of Buffalo and Seattle based on better conference record (4-3 to Bills' 3-3 to Seahawks' 3-5). Buffalo finished ahead of Seattle based on better conference record (3-3 to Seahawks' 3-5). Minnesota (4-1), Atlanta (4-3), St. Louis (5-4), Tampa Bay (3-3) seeds were determined by best won-lost record in conference games. Detroit finished ahead of New Orleans and the N.Y. Giants based on best conference record (4-4 to Saints' 3-5 to Giants' 3-5). San Francisco finished ahead of Chicago, and Chicago finished ahead of Philadelphia, based on conference record (49ers' 2-3 to Bears' 2-5 to Eagles' 1-5).

First round playoff: MIAMI 28, New England 13; L.A. RAIDERS 27, Cleveland 10; N.Y. Jets 44, CINCINNATI 17; San Diego 31, PITTSBURGH 28

Second round playoff: N.Y. Jets 17, L.A. RAIDERS 14; MIAMI 34, San Diego 13

AFC Championship: MIAMI 14, N.Y. Jets 0

First round playoff: WASHINGTON 31, Detroit 7; GREEN BAY 41, St. Louis 16; MINNESOTA 30, Atlanta 24; DALLAS 30, Tampa Bay 17

Second round playoff: WASHINGTON 21, Minnesota 7; DALLAS 37, Green Bay 26

NFC Championship: WASHINGTON 31, Dallas 17

Super Bowl XVII: Washington (NFC) 27, Miami (AFC) 17, at Rose Bowl, Pasadena, California

1981

AMERICAN CONFERENCE

Eastern Division

	W	L	T	Pct.	Pts.	OP
Miami	11	4	1	.719	345	275
N.Y. Jets*	10	5	1	.656	355	287
Buffalo*	10	6	0	.625	311	276
Baltimore	2	14	0	.125	259	533
New England	2	14	0	.125	322	370

Central Division

	W	L	T	Pct.	Pts.	OP
Cincinnati#	12	4	0	.750	421	304
Pittsburgh	8	8	0	.500	356	297
Houston	7	9	0	.438	281	355
Cleveland	5	11	0	.313	276	375

Western Division

	W	L	T	Pct.	Pts.	OP
San Diego	10	6	0	.625	478	390
Denver	10	6	0	.625	321	289
Kansas City	9	7	0	.563	343	290
Oakland	7	9	0	.438	273	343
Seattle	6	10	0	.375	322	388

NATIONAL CONFERENCE

Eastern Division

	W	L	T	Pct.	Pts.	OP
Dallas	12	4	0	.750	367	277
Philadelphia*	10	6	0	.625	368	221
N.Y. Giants*	9	7	0	.563	295	257
Washington	8	8	0	.500	347	349
St. Louis	7	9	0	.438	315	408

Central Division

	W	L	T	Pct.	Pts.	OP
Tampa Bay	9	7	0	.563	315	268
Detroit	8	8	0	.500	397	322
Green Bay	8	8	0	.500	324	361
Minnesota	7	9	0	.438	325	369
Chicago	6	10	0	.375	253	324

Western Division

	W	L	T	Pct.	Pts.	OP
San Francisco#	13	3	0	.813	357	250
Atlanta	7	9	0	.438	426	355
Los Angeles	6	10	0	.375	303	351
New Orleans	4	12	0	.250	207	378

**Wild-Card qualifier for playoffs; #Top playoff seed in conference*

Baltimore finished ahead of New England based on head-to-head sweep (2-0). San Diego finished ahead of Denver based on better division record (6-2 to Broncos' 5-3). Buffalo was second Wild Card based on head-to-head victory over Denver (1-0). Detroit finished ahead of Green Bay based on better record against common opponents (5-5 to Packers' 4-6).

Wild-Card playoff: Buffalo 31, N.Y. JETS 27

Divisional playoffs: San Diego 41, MIAMI 38 (OT); CINCINNATI 28, Buffalo 21

AFC Championship: CINCINNATI 27, San Diego 7

Wild-Card playoff: N.Y. Giants 27, PHILADELPHIA 21

Divisional playoffs: DALLAS 38, Tampa Bay 0; SAN FRANCISCO 38, N.Y. Giants 24

NFC Championship: SAN FRANCISCO 28, Dallas 27

Super Bowl XVI: San Francisco (NFC) 26, Cincinnati (AFC) 21, at Silverdome, Pontiac, Michigan

1980

AMERICAN CONFERENCE

Eastern Division	W	L	T	Pct.	Pts.	OP
Buffalo	11	5	0	.688	320	260
New England	10	6	0	.625	441	325
Miami	8	8	0	.500	266	305
Baltimore	7	9	0	.438	355	387
N.Y. Jets	4	12	0	.250	302	395
Central Division	W	L	T	Pct.	Pts.	OP
Cleveland	11	5	0	.688	357	310
Houston*	11	5	0	.688	295	251
Pittsburgh	9	7	0	.563	352	313
Cincinnati	6	10	0	.375	244	312
Western Division	W	L	T	Pct.	Pts.	OP
San Diego#	11	5	0	.688	418	327
Oakland*	11	5	0	.688	364	306
Kansas City	8	8	0	.500	319	336
Denver	8	8	0	.500	310	323
Seattle	4	12	0	.250	291	408

NATIONAL CONFERENCE

Eastern Division	W	L	T	Pct.	Pts.	OP
Philadelphia	12	4	0	.750	384	222
Dallas*	12	4	0	.750	454	311
Washington	6	10	0	.375	261	293
St. Louis	5	11	0	.313	299	350
N.Y. Giants	4	12	0	.250	249	425
Central Division	W	L	T	Pct.	Pts.	OP
Minnesota	9	7	0	.563	317	308
Detroit	9	7	0	.563	334	272
Chicago	7	9	0	.438	304	264
Tampa Bay	5	10	1	.344	271	341
Green Bay	5	10	1	.344	231	371
Western Division	W	L	T	Pct.	Pts.	OP
Atlanta#	12	4	0	.750	405	272
Los Angeles*	11	5	0	.688	424	289
San Francisco	6	10	0	.375	320	415
New Orleans	1	15	0	.063	291	487

**Wild-Card qualifier for playoffs; #Top playoff seed in conference*

San Diego was top playoff seed based on better conference record than Cleveland and Buffalo (9-3 to Browns' 8-4 and Bills' 8-4). Cleveland was second playoff seed based on better record against common opponents (5-2 to Bills' 5-3). Cleveland finished ahead of Houston based on better conference record (8-4 to Oilers' 7-5). Oakland was first Wild Card based on better conference record than Houston (9-3 to Oilers' 7-5). San Diego finished ahead of Oakland based on better net points in division games (plus 60 net points to Raiders' plus 37). Oakland did not play San Diego in the divisional playoffs because, from 1970-1989, two teams from the same division could not meet prior to the conference championship game. Kansas City finished ahead of Denver based on head-to-head sweep (2-0). Atlanta was top playoff seed based on head-to-head victory over Philadelphia (1-0). Philadelphia finished ahead of Dallas based on better net points in division games (plus 84 net points to Cowboys' plus 50). Minnesota finished ahead of Detroit based on better conference record (8-4 to Lions' 9-5). Tampa Bay finished ahead of Green Bay based on better head-to-head record (1-0-1 to Packers' 0-1-1).

Wild-Card playoff: OAKLAND 27, Houston 7
Divisional playoffs: SAN DIEGO 20, Buffalo 14; Oakland 14, CLEVELAND 12
AFC Championship: Oakland 34, SAN DIEGO 27
Wild-Card playoff: DALLAS 34, Los Angeles 13
Divisional playoffs: PHILADELPHIA 31, Minnesota 16; Dallas 30, ATLANTA 27
NFC Championship: PHILADELPHIA 20, Dallas 7
Super Bowl XV: Oakland (AFC) 27, Philadelphia (NFC) 10, at Louisiana Superdome, New Orleans, Louisiana

1979

AMERICAN CONFERENCE

Eastern Division	W	L	T	Pct.	Pts.	OP
Miami	10	6	0	.625	341	257
New England	9	7	0	.563	411	326
N.Y. Jets	8	8	0	.500	337	383
Buffalo	7	9	0	.438	268	279
Baltimore	5	11	0	.313	271	351
Central Division	W	L	T	Pct.	Pts.	OP
Pittsburgh	12	4	0	.750	416	262
Houston*	11	5	0	.688	362	331
Cleveland	9	7	0	.563	359	352
Cincinnati	4	12	0	.250	337	421
Western Division	W	L	T	Pct.	Pts.	OP
San Diego#	12	4	0	.750	411	246
Denver*	10	6	0	.625	289	262
Seattle	9	7	0	.563	378	372
Oakland	9	7	0	.563	365	337
Kansas City	7	9	0	.438	238	262

NATIONAL CONFERENCE

Eastern Division	W	L	T	Pct.	Pts.	OP
Dallas#	11	5	0	.688	371	313
Philadelphia*	11	5	0	.688	339	282
Washington	10	6	0	.625	348	295
N.Y. Giants	6	10	0	.375	237	323
St. Louis	5	11	0	.313	307	358
Central Division	W	L	T	Pct.	Pts.	OP
Tampa Bay	10	6	0	.625	273	237
Chicago*	10	6	0	.625	306	249
Minnesota	7	9	0	.438	259	337
Green Bay	5	11	0	.313	246	316
Detroit	2	14	0	.125	219	365
Western Division	W	L	T	Pct.	Pts.	OP
Los Angeles	9	7	0	.563	323	309
New Orleans	8	8	0	.500	370	360
Atlanta	6	10	0	.375	300	388
San Francisco	2	14	0	.125	308	416

**Wild-Card qualifier for playoffs; #Top playoff seed in conference*

San Diego was top playoff seed based on head-to-head victory over Pittsburgh (1-0). Seattle finished ahead of Oakland based on head-to-head sweep (2-0). Dallas finished ahead of Philadelphia based on better conference record (10-2 to Eagles' 9-3). Philadelphia did not play Dallas in the divisional playoffs because, from 1970-1989, two teams from the same division could not meet prior to the conference championship game. Tampa Bay finished ahead of Chicago based on a better division record (6-2 to Bears' 5-3). Chicago was second Wild Card ahead of Washington based on better net points in all games (57 to Redskins' 53).

Wild-Card playoff: HOUSTON 13, Denver 7
Divisional playoffs: Houston 17, SAN DIEGO 14; PITTSBURGH 34, Miami 14
AFC Championship: PITTSBURGH 27, Houston 13
Wild-Card playoff: PHILADELPHIA 27, Chicago 17
Divisional playoffs: TAMPA BAY 24, Philadelphia 17; Los Angeles 21, DALLAS 19
NFC Championship: Los Angeles 9, TAMPA BAY 0
Super Bowl XIV: Pittsburgh (AFC) 31, Los Angeles (NFC) 19, at Rose Bowl, Pasadena, California

1978

AMERICAN CONFERENCE

Eastern Division	W	L	T	Pct.	Pts.	OP
New England	11	5	0	.688	358	286
Miami*	11	5	0	.688	372	254
N.Y. Jets	8	8	0	.500	359	364
Buffalo	5	11	0	.313	302	354
Baltimore	5	11	0	.313	239	421
Central Division	W	L	T	Pct.	Pts.	OP
Pittsburgh#	14	2	0	.875	356	195
Houston*	10	6	0	.625	283	298
Cleveland	8	8	0	.500	334	356
Cincinnati	4	12	0	.250	252	284
Western Division	W	L	T	Pct.	Pts.	OP
Denver	10	6	0	.625	282	198
Oakland	9	7	0	.563	311	283
Seattle	9	7	0	.563	345	358
San Diego	9	7	0	.563	355	309
Kansas City	4	12	0	.250	243	327

NATIONAL CONFERENCE

Eastern Division	W	L	T	Pct.	Pts.	OP
Dallas	12	4	0	.750	384	208
Philadelphia*	9	7	0	.563	270	250
Washington	8	8	0	.500	273	283
St. Louis	6	10	0	.375	248	296
N.Y. Giants	6	10	0	.375	264	298
Central Division	W	L	T	Pct.	Pts.	OP
Minnesota	8	7	1	.531	294	306
Green Bay	8	7	1	.531	249	269
Detroit	7	9	0	.438	290	300
Chicago	7	9	0	.438	253	274
Tampa Bay	5	11	0	.313	241	259
Western Division	W	L	T	Pct.	Pts.	OP
Los Angeles#	12	4	0	.750	316	245
Atlanta*	9	7	0	.563	240	290
New Orleans	7	9	0	.438	281	298
San Francisco	2	14	0	.125	219	350

**Wild-Card qualifier for playoffs; #Top playoff seed in conference*

New England finished ahead of Miami based on better division record (6-2 to Dolphins' 5-3). Buffalo finished ahead of Baltimore based on head-to-head sweep (2-0). Oakland finished ahead of Seattle and San Diego based on better record against common opponents (6-2 to Seahawks' 5-3 and Chargers' 4-4). Atlanta was first WIld Card based on better conference record than Philadelphia (8-4 to Eagles' 6-6). Houston did not play Pittsburgh, and Atlanta did not play Los Angeles in the divisional playoffs because, from 1970-1989, two teams from the same division could not meet prior to the conference championship game. St. Louis finished ahead of N.Y. Giants based on better division record (3-5 to Giants' 2-6). Minnesota finished ahead of Green Bay based on better head-to-head record (1-0-1). Detroit finished ahead of Chicago based on better division record (4-4 to Bears' 3-5).

Wild-Card playoff: Houston 17, MIAMI 9
Divisional playoffs: Houston 31, NEW ENGLAND 14; PITTSBURGH 33, Denver 10
AFC Championship: PITTSBURGH 34, Houston 5
Wild-Card playoff: ATLANTA 14, Philadelphia 13
Divisional playoffs: DALLAS 27, Atlanta 20; LOS ANGELES 34, Minnesota 10
NFC Championship: Dallas 28, LOS ANGELES 0
Super Bowl XIII: Pittsburgh (AFC) 35, Dallas (NFC) 31, at Orange Bowl, Miami, Florida

1977

AMERICAN CONFERENCE

Eastern Division	W	L	T	Pct.	Pts.	OP
Baltimore	10	4	0	.714	295	221
Miami	10	4	0	.714	313	197
New England	9	5	0	.643	278	217
Buffalo	3	11	0	.214	160	313
N.Y. Jets	3	11	0	.214	191	300
Central Division	W	L	T	Pct.	Pts.	OP
Pittsburgh	9	5	0	.643	283	243
Cincinnati	8	6	0	.571	238	235
Houston	8	6	0	.571	299	230
Cleveland	6	8	0	.429	269	267
Western Division	W	L	T	Pct.	Pts.	OP
Denver#	12	2	0	.857	274	148
Oakland*	11	3	0	.786	351	230
San Diego	7	7	0	.500	222	205
Seattle	5	9	0	.357	282	373
Kansas City	2	12	0	.143	225	349

NATIONAL CONFERENCE

Eastern Division	W	L	T	Pct.	Pts.	OP
Dallas#	12	2	0	.857	345	212
Washington	9	5	0	.643	196	189
St. Louis	7	7	0	.500	272	287
Philadelphia	5	9	0	.357	220	207
N.Y. Giants	5	9	0	.357	181	265
Central Division	W	L	T	Pct.	Pts.	OP
Minnesota	9	5	0	.643	231	227
Chicago*	9	5	0	.643	255	253
Detroit	6	8	0	.429	183	252
Green Bay	4	10	0	.286	134	219
Tampa Bay	2	12	0	.143	103	223
Western Division	W	L	T	Pct.	Pts.	OP
Los Angeles	10	4	0	.714	302	146
Atlanta	7	7	0	.500	179	129
San Francisco	5	9	0	.357	220	260
New Orleans	3	11	0	.214	232	336

**Wild-Card qualifier for playoffs; #Top playoff seed in conference*

Baltimore finished ahead of Miami based on better conference record (9-3 to Dolphins' 8-4). Buffalo finished ahead of N.Y. Jets based on better strength of schedule (.582 to Jets' .536). Cincinnati finished ahead of Houston based on better division record (6-3 to Oilers' 5-4). Oakland did not play Denver in the divisional playoffs because, from 1970-1989, two teams from the same division could not meet prior to the conference championship game. Minnesota finished ahead of Chicago based on fewer losses by common opponents (11 losses to 14 losses by the Bears' opponents). Chicago won Wild Card ahead of Washington based on better net points in conference games (48 to Redskins' 4). Philadelphia finished ahead of N.Y. Giants based on head-to-head sweep (2-0).

Divisional playoffs: DENVER 34, Pittsburgh 21; Oakland 37, BALTIMORE 31 (OT)
AFC Championship: DENVER 20, Oakland 17
Divisional playoffs: DALLAS 37, Chicago 7; Minnesota 14, LOS ANGELES 7
NFC Championship: DALLAS 23, Minnesota 6
Super Bowl XII: Dallas (NFC) 27, Denver (AFC) 10, at Louisiana Superdome, New Orleans, Louisiana

PAST STANDINGS

1976

AMERICAN CONFERENCE

Eastern Division

	W	L	T	Pct.	Pts.	OP
Baltimore	11	3	0	.786	417	246
New England*	11	3	0	.786	376	236
Miami	6	8	0	.429	263	264
N.Y. Jets	3	11	0	.214	169	383
Buffalo	2	12	0	.143	245	363

Central Division

	W	L	T	Pct.	Pts.	OP
Pittsburgh	10	4	0	.714	342	138
Cincinnati	10	4	0	.714	335	210
Cleveland	9	5	0	.643	267	287
Houston	5	9	0	.357	222	273

Western Division

	W	L	T	Pct.	Pts.	OP
Oakland#	13	1	0	.929	350	237
Denver	9	5	0	.643	315	206
San Diego	6	8	0	.429	248	285
Kansas City	5	9	0	.357	290	376
Tampa Bay	0	14	0	.000	125	412

NATIONAL CONFERENCE

Eastern Division

	W	L	T	Pct.	Pts.	OP
Dallas	11	3	0	.786	296	194
Washington*	10	4	0	.714	291	217
St. Louis	10	4	0	.714	309	267
Philadelphia	4	10	0	.286	165	286
N.Y. Giants	3	11	0	.214	170	250

Central Division

	W	L	T	Pct.	Pts.	OP
Minnesota#	11	2	1	.821	305	176
Chicago	7	7	0	.500	253	216
Detroit	6	8	0	.429	262	220
Green Bay	5	9	0	.357	218	299

Western Division

	W	L	T	Pct.	Pts.	OP
Los Angeles	10	3	1	.750	351	190
San Francisco	8	6	0	.571	270	190
Atlanta	4	10	0	.286	172	312
New Orleans	4	10	0	.286	253	346
Seattle	2	12	0	.143	229	429

**Wild-Card qualifier for playoffs; #Top playoff seed in conference*

Baltimore finished ahead of New England based on better division record (7-1 to Patriots' 6-2). Pittsburgh finished ahead of Cincinnati based on head-to-head sweep (2-0). Washington finished ahead of St. Louis based on head-to-head sweep (2-0). Atlanta finished ahead of New Orleans based on better division record (2-4 to Saints' 1-5).

Divisional playoffs: OAKLAND 24, New England 21; Pittsburgh 40, BALTIMORE 14
AFC Championship: OAKLAND 24, Pittsburgh 7
Divisional playoffs: MINNESOTA 35, Washington 20; Los Angeles 14, DALLAS 12
NFC Championship: MINNESOTA 24, Los Angeles 13
Super Bowl XI: Oakland (AFC) 32, Minnesota (NFC) 14, at Rose Bowl, Pasadena, California

1975

AMERICAN CONFERENCE

Eastern Division

	W	L	T	Pct.	Pts.	OP
Baltimore	10	4	0	.714	395	269
Miami	10	4	0	.714	357	222
Buffalo	8	6	0	.571	420	355
N.Y. Jets	3	11	0	.214	258	433
New England	3	11	0	.214	258	358

Central Division

	W	L	T	Pct.	Pts.	OP
Pittsburgh#	12	2	0	.857	373	162
Cincinnati*	11	3	0	.786	340	246
Houston	10	4	0	.714	293	226
Cleveland	3	11	0	.214	218	372

Western Division

	W	L	T	Pct.	Pts.	OP
Oakland	11	3	0	.786	375	255
Denver	6	8	0	.429	254	307
Kansas City	5	9	0	.357	282	341
San Diego	2	12	0	.143	189	345

NATIONAL CONFERENCE

Eastern Division

	W	L	T	Pct.	Pts.	OP
St. Louis	11	3	0	.786	356	276
Dallas*	10	4	0	.714	350	268
Washington	8	6	0	.571	325	276
N.Y. Giants	5	9	0	.357	216	306
Philadelphia	4	10	0	.286	225	302

Central Division

	W	L	T	Pct.	Pts.	OP
Minnesota	12	2	0	.857	377	180
Detroit	7	7	0	.500	245	262
Chicago	4	10	0	.286	191	379
Green Bay	4	10	0	.286	226	285

Western Division

	W	L	T	Pct.	Pts.	OP
Los Angeles#	12	2	0	.857	312	135
San Francisco	5	9	0	.357	255	286
Atlanta	4	10	0	.286	240	289
New Orleans	2	12	0	.143	165	360

**Wild-Card qualifier for playoffs; #Top playoff seed in conference*

Baltimore finished ahead of Miami based on head-to-head sweep (2-0). Cincinnati did not play Pittsburgh in the divisional playoffs because, from 1970-1989, two teams from the same division could not meet prior to the conference championship game. N.Y. Jets finished ahead of New England based on head-to-head sweep (2-0). Los Angeles was top playoff seed based on better strength of schedule than Minnesota (.383 to Vikings' .332). Chicago finished ahead of Green Bay based on better division record (2-4 to Bears' 1-5).

Divisional playoffs: PITTSBURGH 28, Baltimore 10; OAKLAND 31, Cincinnati 28
AFC Championship: PITTSBURGH 16, Oakland 10
Divisional playoffs: LOS ANGELES 35, St. Louis 23; Dallas 17, MINNESOTA 14
NFC Championship: Dallas 37, LOS ANGELES 7
Super Bowl X: Pittsburgh (AFC) 21, Dallas (NFC) 17, at Orange Bowl, Miami, Florida

From 1933-1974, sites for league/conference championship games alternated by division.

1974

AMERICAN CONFERENCE

Eastern Division

	W	L	T	Pct.	Pts.	OP
Miami	11	3	0	.786	327	216
Buffalo*	9	5	0	.643	264	244
New England	7	7	0	.500	348	289
N.Y. Jets	7	7	0	.500	279	300
Baltimore	2	12	0	.143	190	329

Central Division

	W	L	T	Pct.	Pts.	OP
Pittsburgh	10	3	1	.750	305	189
Houston	7	7	0	.500	236	282
Cincinnati	7	7	0	.500	283	259
Cleveland	4	10	0	.286	251	344

Western Division

	W	L	T	Pct.	Pts.	OP
Oakland	12	2	0	.857	355	228
Denver	7	6	1	.536	302	294
Kansas City	5	9	0	.357	233	293
San Diego	5	9	0	.357	212	285

NATIONAL CONFERENCE

Eastern Division

	W	L	T	Pct.	Pts.	OP
St. Louis	10	4	0	.714	285	218
Washington*	10	4	0	.714	320	196
Dallas	8	6	0	.571	297	235
Philadelphia	7	7	0	.500	242	217
N.Y. Giants	2	12	0	.143	195	299

Central Division

	W	L	T	Pct.	Pts.	OP
Minnesota	10	4	0	.714	310	195
Detroit	7	7	0	.500	256	270
Green Bay	6	8	0	.429	210	206
Chicago	4	10	0	.286	152	279

Western Division

	W	L	T	Pct.	Pts.	OP
Los Angeles	10	4	0	.714	263	181
San Francisco	6	8	0	.429	226	236
New Orleans	5	9	0	.357	166	263
Atlanta	3	11	0	.214	111	271

**Wild-Card qualifier for playoffs*

New England finished ahead of N.Y. Jets based on better record against common opponents (5-4 to Jets' 4-5). Houston finished ahead of Cincinnati based on head-to-head sweep (2-0). Kansas City finished ahead of San Diego based on better record against common opponents (4-6 to Chargers' 3-7). St. Louis finished ahead of Washington based on head-to-head sweep (2-0).

Divisional playoffs: OAKLAND 28, Miami 26; PITTSBURGH 32, Buffalo 14
AFC Championship: Pittsburgh 24, OAKLAND 13
Divisional playoffs: MINNESOTA 30, St. Louis 14; LOS ANGELES 19, Washington 10
NFC Championship: MINNESOTA 14, Los Angeles 10
Super Bowl IX: Pittsburgh (AFC) 16, Minnesota (NFC) 6, at Tulane Stadium, New Orleans, Louisiana

1973

AMERICAN CONFERENCE

Eastern Division

	W	L	T	Pct.	Pts.	OP
Miami	12	2	0	.857	343	150
Buffalo	9	5	0	.643	259	230
New England	5	9	0	.357	258	300
N.Y. Jets	4	10	0	.286	240	306
Baltimore	4	10	0	.286	226	341

Central Division

	W	L	T	Pct.	Pts.	OP
Cincinnati	10	4	0	.714	286	231
Pittsburgh*	10	4	0	.714	347	210
Cleveland	7	5	2	.571	234	255
Houston	1	13	0	.071	199	447

Western Division

	W	L	T	Pct.	Pts.	OP
Oakland	9	4	1	.679	292	175
Kansas City	7	5	2	.571	231	192
Denver	7	5	2	.571	354	296
San Diego	2	11	1	.179	188	386

NATIONAL CONFERENCE

Eastern Division

	W	L	T	Pct.	Pts.	OP
Dallas	10	4	0	.714	382	203
Washington*	10	4	0	.714	325	198
Philadelphia	5	8	1	.393	310	393
St. Louis	4	9	1	.321	286	365
N.Y. Giants	2	11	1	.179	226	362

Central Division

	W	L	T	Pct.	Pts.	OP
Minnesota	12	2	0	.857	296	168
Detroit	6	7	1	.464	271	247
Green Bay	5	7	2	.429	202	259
Chicago	3	11	0	.214	195	334

Western Division

	W	L	T	Pct.	Pts.	OP
Los Angeles	12	2	0	.857	388	178
Atlanta	9	5	0	.643	318	224
San Francisco	5	9	0	.357	262	319
New Orleans	5	9	0	.357	163	312

**Wild-Card qualifier for playoffs*

Cincinnati finished ahead of Pittsburgh based on better conference record (8-3 to Steelers' 7-4). N.Y. Jets finished ahead of Baltimore based on head-to-head sweep (2-0). Kansas City finished ahead of Denver based on better division record (4-2 to Broncos' 3-2-1). Dallas finished ahead of Washington based on better point differential in head-to-head games (13 points). San Francisco finished ahead of New Orleans based on better division record (2-4 to Saints' 1-5).

Divisional playoffs: OAKLAND 33, Pittsburgh 14; MIAMI 34, Cincinnati 16
AFC Championship: MIAMI 27, Oakland 10
Divisional playoffs: MINNESOTA 27, Washington 20; DALLAS 27, Los Angeles 16
NFC Championship: Minnesota 27, DALLAS 10
Super Bowl VIII: Miami (AFC) 24, Minnesota (NFC) 7, at Rice Stadium, Houston, Texas

1972

AMERICAN CONFERENCE

Eastern Division

	W	L	T	Pct.	Pts.	OP
Miami	14	0	0	1.000	385	171
N.Y. Jets	7	7	0	.500	367	324
Baltimore	5	9	0	.357	235	252
Buffalo	4	9	1	.321	257	377
New England	3	11	0	.214	192	446

Central Division

	W	L	T	Pct.	Pts.	OP
Pittsburgh	11	3	0	.786	343	175
Cleveland*	10	4	0	.714	268	249
Cincinnati	8	6	0	.571	299	229
Houston	1	13	0	.071	164	380

Western Division

	W	L	T	Pct.	Pts.	OP
Oakland	10	3	1	.750	365	248
Kansas City	8	6	0	.571	287	254
Denver	5	9	0	.357	325	350
San Diego	4	9	1	.321	264	344

NATIONAL CONFERENCE

Eastern Division

	W	L	T	Pct.	Pts.	OP
Washington	11	3	0	.786	336	218
Dallas*	10	4	0	.714	319	240
N.Y. Giants	8	6	0	.571	331	247
St. Louis	4	9	1	.321	193	303
Philadelphia	2	11	1	.179	145	352

Central Division

	W	L	T	Pct.	Pts.	OP
Green Bay	10	4	0	.714	304	226
Detroit	8	5	1	.607	339	290
Minnesota	7	7	0	.500	301	252
Chicago	4	9	1	.321	225	275

Western Division

	W	L	T	Pct.	Pts.	OP
San Francisco	8	5	1	.607	353	249
Atlanta	7	7	0	.500	269	274
Los Angeles	6	7	1	.464	291	286
New Orleans	2	11	1	.179	215	361

**Wild-Card qualifier for playoffs*

Dallas did not play Washington in the divisional playoffs because, from 1970-1989, two teams from the same division could not meet prior to the conference championship game.

Divisional playoffs: PITTSBURGH 13, Oakland 7; MIAMI 20, Cleveland 14
AFC Championship: Miami 21, PITTSBURGH 17
Divisional playoffs: Dallas 30, SAN FRANCISCO 28; WASHINGTON 16, Green Bay 3
NFC Championship: WASHINGTON 26, Dallas 3
Super Bowl VII: Miami (AFC) 14, Washington (NFC) 7, at Memorial Coliseum, Los Angeles, California

1971

AMERICAN CONFERENCE

Eastern Division

	W	L	T	Pct.	Pts.	OP
Miami	10	3	1	.769	315	174
Baltimore*	10	4	0	.714	313	140
New England	6	8	0	.429	238	325
N.Y. Jets	6	8	0	.429	212	299
Buffalo	1	13	0	.071	184	394

Central Division

	W	L	T	Pct.	Pts.	OP
Cleveland	9	5	0	.643	285	273
Pittsburgh	6	8	0	.429	246	292
Houston	4	9	1	.308	251	330
Cincinnati	4	10	0	.286	284	265

Western Division

	W	L	T	Pct.	Pts.	OP
Kansas City	10	3	1	.769	302	208
Oakland	8	4	2	.667	344	278
San Diego	6	8	0	.429	311	341
Denver	4	9	1	.308	203	275

NATIONAL CONFERENCE

Eastern Division

	W	L	T	Pct.	Pts.	OP
Dallas	11	3	0	.786	406	222
Washington*	9	4	1	.692	276	190
Philadelphia	6	7	1	.462	221	302
St. Louis	4	9	1	.308	231	279
N.Y. Giants	4	10	0	.286	228	362

Central Division

	W	L	T	Pct.	Pts.	OP
Minnesota	11	3	0	.786	245	139
Detroit	7	6	1	.538	341	286
Chicago	6	8	0	.429	185	276
Green Bay	4	8	2	.333	274	298

Western Division

	W	L	T	Pct.	Pts.	OP
San Francisco	9	5	0	.643	300	216
Los Angeles	8	5	1	.615	313	260
Atlanta	7	6	1	.538	274	277
New Orleans	4	8	2	.333	266	347

**Wild-Card qualifier for playoffs*

New England finished ahead of N.Y. Jets based on better strength of schedule (.537 to Jets' .510).

Divisional playoffs: Miami 27, KANSAS CITY 24 (OT); Baltimore 20, CLEVELAND 3
AFC Championship: MIAMI 21, Baltimore 0
Divisional playoffs: Dallas 20, MINNESOTA 12; SAN FRANCISCO 24, Washington 20
NFC Championship: DALLAS 14, San Francisco 3
Super Bowl VI: Dallas (NFC) 24, Miami (AFC) 3, at Tulane Stadium, New Orleans, Louisiana

1970

AMERICAN CONFERENCE

Eastern Division

	W	L	T	Pct.	Pts.	OP
Baltimore	11	2	1	.846	321	234
Miami*	10	4	0	.714	297	228
N.Y. Jets	4	10	0	.286	255	286
Buffalo	3	10	1	.231	204	337
Boston Patriots	2	12	0	.143	149	361

Central Division

	W	L	T	Pct.	Pts.	OP
Cincinnati	8	6	0	.571	312	255
Cleveland	7	7	0	.500	286	265
Pittsburgh	5	9	0	.357	210	272
Houston	3	10	1	.231	217	352

Western Division

	W	L	T	Pct.	Pts.	OP
Oakland	8	4	2	.667	300	293
Kansas City	7	5	2	.583	272	244
San Diego	5	6	3	.455	282	278
Denver	5	8	1	.385	253	264

NATIONAL CONFERENCE

Eastern Division

	W	L	T	Pct.	Pts.	OP
Dallas	10	4	0	.714	299	221
N.Y. Giants	9	5	0	.643	301	270
St. Louis	8	5	1	.615	325	228
Washington	6	8	0	.429	297	314
Philadelphia	3	10	1	.231	241	332

Central Division

	W	L	T	Pct.	Pts.	OP
Minnesota	12	2	0	.857	335	143
Detroit*	10	4	0	.714	347	202
Green Bay	6	8	0	.429	196	293
Chicago	6	8	0	.429	256	261

Western Division

	W	L	T	Pct.	Pts.	OP
San Francisco	10	3	1	.769	352	267
Los Angeles	9	4	1	.692	325	202
Atlanta	4	8	2	.333	206	261
New Orleans	2	11	1	.154	172	347

**Wild-Card qualifier for playoffs*

Miami did not play Baltimore, and Detroit did not play Minnesota, in the divisional playoffs because, from 1970-1989, two teams from the same division could not meet prior to the conference championship game. Green Bay finished ahead of Chicago based on better division record (2-4 to Bears' 1-5).

Divisional playoffs: BALTIMORE 17, Cincinnati 0; OAKLAND 21, Miami 14
AFC Championship: BALTIMORE 27, Oakland 17
Divisional playoffs: DALLAS 5, Detroit 0; San Francisco 17, MINNESOTA 14
NFC Championship: Dallas 17, SAN FRANCISCO 10
Super Bowl V: Baltimore (AFC) 16, Dallas (NFC) 13, at Orange Bowl, Miami, Florida

1969 NFL

EASTERN CONFERENCE

Capitol Division

	W	L	T	Pct.	Pts.	OP
Dallas	11	2	1	.846	369	223
Washington	7	5	2	.583	307	319
New Orleans	5	9	0	.357	311	393
Philadelphia	4	9	1	.308	279	377

Century Division

	W	L	T	Pct.	Pts.	OP
Cleveland	10	3	1	.769	351	300
N.Y. Giants	6	8	0	.429	264	298
St. Louis	4	9	1	.308	314	389
Pittsburgh	1	13	0	.071	218	404

WESTERN CONFERENCE

Coastal Division

	W	L	T	Pct.	Pts.	OP
Los Angeles	11	3	0	.786	320	243
Baltimore	8	5	1	.615	279	268
Atlanta	6	8	0	.429	276	268
San Francisco	4	8	2	.333	277	319

Central Division

	W	L	T	Pct.	Pts.	OP
Minnesota	12	2	0	.857	379	133
Detroit	9	4	1	.692	259	188
Green Bay	8	6	0	.571	269	221
Chicago	1	13	0	.071	210	339

Conference championships: Cleveland 38, DALLAS 14; MINNESOTA 23, Los Angeles 20
NFL championship: MINNESOTA 27, Cleveland 7
Super Bowl IV: Kansas City (AFL) 23, Minnesota (NFL) 7, at Tulane Stadium, New Orleans, Louisiana

1969 AFL

EASTERN DIVISION

	W	L	T	Pct.	Pts.	OP
N.Y. Jets	10	4	0	.714	353	269
Houston	6	6	2	.500	278	279
Boston Patriots	4	10	0	.286	266	316
Buffalo	4	10	0	.286	230	359
Miami	3	10	1	.231	233	332

WESTERN DIVISION

	W	L	T	Pct.	Pts.	OP
Oakland	12	1	1	.923	377	242
Kansas City	11	3	0	.786	359	177
San Diego	8	6	0	.571	288	276
Denver	5	8	1	.385	297	344
Cincinnati	4	9	1	.308	280	367

Divisional playoffs: Kansas City 13, N.Y. JETS 6; OAKLAND 56, Houston 7
AFL championship: Kansas City 17, OAKLAND 7

PAST STANDINGS

1968 NFL

EASTERN CONFERENCE

Capitol Division

	W	L	T	Pct.	Pts.	OP
Dallas	12	2	0	.857	431	186
N.Y. Giants	7	7	0	.500	294	325
Washington	5	9	0	.357	249	358
Philadelphia	2	12	0	.143	202	351

Century Division

	W	L	T	Pct.	Pts.	OP
Cleveland	10	4	0	.714	394	273
St. Louis	9	4	1	.692	325	289
New Orleans	4	9	1	.308	246	327
Pittsburgh	2	11	1	.154	244	397

WESTERN CONFERENCE

Coastal Division

	W	L	T	Pct.	Pts.	OP
Baltimore	13	1	0	.929	402	144
Los Angeles	10	3	1	.769	312	200
San Francisco	7	6	1	.538	303	310
Atlanta	2	12	0	.143	170	389

Central Division

	W	L	T	Pct.	Pts.	OP
Minnesota	8	6	0	.571	282	242
Chicago	7	7	0	.500	250	333
Green Bay	6	7	1	.462	281	227
Detroit	4	8	2	.333	207	241

Conference championships: CLEVELAND 31, Dallas 20; BALTIMORE 24, Minnesota 14
NFL championship: Baltimore 34, CLEVELAND 0
Super Bowl III: N.Y. Jets (AFL) 16, Baltimore (NFL) 7, at Orange Bowl, Miami, Florida

1968 AFL

EASTERN DIVISION

	W	L	T	Pct.	Pts.	OP
N.Y. Jets	11	3	0	.786	419	280
Houston	7	7	0	.500	303	248
Miami	5	8	1	.385	276	355
Boston Patriots	4	10	0	.286	229	406
Buffalo	1	12	1	.077	199	367

WESTERN DIVISION

	W	L	T	Pct.	Pts.	OP
Oakland	12	2	0	.857	453	233
Kansas City	12	2	0	.857	371	170
San Diego	9	5	0	.643	382	310
Denver	5	9	0	.357	255	404
Cincinnati	3	11	0	.214	215	329

Western Division playoff: OAKLAND 41, Kansas City 6
AFL championship: N.Y. JETS 27, Oakland 23

1967 NFL

EASTERN CONFERENCE

Capitol Division

	W	L	T	Pct.	Pts.	OP
Dallas	9	5	0	.643	342	268
Philadelphia	6	7	1	.462	351	409
Washington	5	6	3	.455	347	353
New Orleans	3	11	0	.214	233	379

Century Division

	W	L	T	Pct.	Pts.	OP
Cleveland	9	5	0	.643	334	297
N.Y. Giants	7	7	0	.500	369	379
St. Louis	6	7	1	.462	333	356
Pittsburgh	4	9	1	.308	281	320

WESTERN CONFERENCE

Coastal Division

	W	L	T	Pct.	Pts.	OP
Los Angeles	11	1	2	.917	398	196
Baltimore	11	1	2	.917	394	198
San Francisco	7	7	0	.500	273	337
Atlanta	1	12	1	.077	175	422

Central Division

	W	L	T	Pct.	Pts.	OP
Green Bay	9	4	1	.692	332	209
Chicago	7	6	1	.538	239	218
Detroit	5	7	2	.417	260	259
Minnesota	3	8	3	.273	233	294

Los Angeles finished ahead of Baltimore based on better point differential in head-to-head games (net 24 points).
Conference championships: DALLAS 52, Cleveland 14; GREEN BAY 28, Los Angeles 7
NFL championship: GREEN BAY 21, Dallas 17
Super Bowl II: Green Bay (NFL) 33, Oakland (AFL) 14, at Orange Bowl, Miami, Florida

1967 AFL

EASTERN DIVISION

	W	L	T	Pct.	Pts.	OP
Houston	9	4	1	.692	258	199
N.Y. Jets	8	5	1	.615	371	329
Buffalo	4	10	0	.286	237	285
Miami	4	10	0	.286	219	407
Boston Patriots	3	10	1	.231	280	389

WESTERN DIVISION

	W	L	T	Pct.	Pts.	OP
Oakland	13	1	0	.929	468	233
Kansas City	9	5	0	.643	408	254
San Diego	8	5	1	.615	360	352
Denver	3	11	0	.214	256	409

AFL championship: OAKLAND 40, Houston 7

1966 NFL

EASTERN CONFERENCE

	W	L	T	Pct.	Pts.	OP
Dallas	10	3	1	.769	445	239
Cleveland	9	5	0	.643	403	259
Philadelphia	9	5	0	.643	326	340
St. Louis	8	5	1	.615	264	265
Washington	7	7	0	.500	351	355
Pittsburgh	5	8	1	.385	316	347
Atlanta	3	11	0	.214	204	437
N.Y. Giants	1	12	1	.077	263	501

WESTERN CONFERENCE

	W	L	T	Pct.	Pts.	OP
Green Bay	12	2	0	.857	335	163
Baltimore	9	5	0	.643	314	226
Los Angeles	8	6	0	.571	289	212
San Francisco	6	6	2	.500	320	325
Chicago	5	7	2	.417	234	272
Detroit	4	9	1	.308	206	317
Minnesota	4	9	1	.308	292	304

NFL championship: Green Bay 34, DALLAS 27
Super Bowl I: Green Bay (NFL) 35, Kansas City (AFL) 10, at Memorial Coliseum, Los Angeles, California

1966 AFL

EASTERN DIVISION

	W	L	T	Pct.	Pts.	OP
Buffalo	9	4	1	.692	358	255
Boston Patriots	8	4	2	.677	315	283
N.Y. Jets	6	6	2	.500	322	312
Houston	3	11	0	.214	335	396
Miami	3	11	0	.214	213	362

WESTERN DIVISION

	W	L	T	Pct.	Pts.	OP
Kansas City	11	2	1	.846	448	276
Oakland	8	5	1	.615	315	288
San Diego	7	6	1	.538	335	284
Denver	4	10	0	.286	196	381

AFL championship: Kansas City 31, BUFFALO 7

1965 NFL

EASTERN CONFERENCE

	W	L	T	Pct.	Pts.	OP
Cleveland	11	3	0	.786	363	325
Dallas	7	7	0	.500	325	280
N.Y. Giants	7	7	0	.500	270	338
Washington	6	8	0	.429	257	301
Philadelphia	5	9	0	.357	363	359
St. Louis	5	9	0	.357	296	309
Pittsburgh	2	12	0	.143	202	397

WESTERN CONFERENCE

	W	L	T	Pct.	Pts.	OP
Green Bay	10	3	1	.769	316	224
Baltimore	10	3	1	.769	389	284
Chicago	9	5	0	.643	409	275
San Francisco	7	6	1	.538	421	402
Minnesota	7	7	0	.500	383	403
Detroit	6	7	1	.462	257	295
Los Angeles	4	10	0	.286	269	328

Western Conference playoff: GREEN BAY 13, Baltimore 10 (OT)
NFL championship: GREEN BAY 23, Cleveland 12

1965 AFL

EASTERN DIVISION

	W	L	T	Pct.	Pts.	OP
Buffalo	10	3	1	.769	313	226
N.Y. Jets	5	8	1	.385	285	303
Boston Patriots	4	8	2	.333	244	302
Houston	4	10	0	.286	298	429

WESTERN DIVISION

	W	L	T	Pct.	Pts.	OP
San Diego	9	2	3	.818	340	227
Oakland	8	5	1	.615	298	239
Kansas City	7	5	2	.583	322	285
Denver	4	10	0	.286	303	392

AFL championship: Buffalo 23, SAN DIEGO 0

1964 NFL

EASTERN CONFERENCE

	W	L	T	Pct.	Pts.	OP
Cleveland	10	3	1	.769	415	293
St. Louis	9	3	2	.750	357	331
Philadelphia	6	8	0	.429	312	313
Washington	6	8	0	.429	307	305
Dallas	5	8	1	.385	250	289
Pittsburgh	5	9	0	.357	253	315
N.Y. Giants	2	10	2	.167	241	399

WESTERN CONFERENCE

	W	L	T	Pct.	Pts.	OP
Baltimore	12	2	0	.857	428	225
Green Bay	8	5	1	.615	342	245
Minnesota	8	5	1	.615	355	296
Detroit	7	5	2	.583	280	260
Los Angeles	5	7	2	.417	283	339
Chicago	5	9	0	.357	260	379
San Francisco	4	10	0	.286	236	330

NFL championship: CLEVELAND 27, Baltimore 0

1964 AFL

EASTERN DIVISION

	W	L	T	Pct.	Pts.	OP
Buffalo	12	2	0	.857	400	242
Boston Patriots	10	3	1	.769	365	297
N.Y. Jets	5	8	1	.385	278	315
Houston	4	10	0	.286	310	355

WESTERN DIVISION

	W	L	T	Pct.	Pts.	OP
San Diego	8	5	1	.615	341	300
Kansas City	7	7	0	.500	366	306
Oakland	5	7	2	.417	303	350
Denver	2	11	1	.154	240	438

AFL championship: BUFFALO 20, San Diego 7

1963 NFL

EASTERN CONFERENCE

	W	L	T	Pct.	Pts.	OP
N.Y. Giants	11	3	0	.786	448	280
Cleveland	10	4	0	.714	343	262
St. Louis	9	5	0	.643	341	283
Pittsburgh	7	4	3	.636	321	295
Dallas	4	10	0	.286	305	378
Washington	3	11	0	.214	279	398
Philadelphia	2	10	2	.167	242	381

WESTERN CONFERENCE

	W	L	T	Pct.	Pts.	OP
Chicago	11	1	2	.917	301	144
Green Bay	11	2	1	.846	369	206
Baltimore	8	6	0	.571	316	285
Detroit	5	8	1	.385	326	265
Minnesota	5	8	1	.385	309	390
Los Angeles	5	9	0	.357	210	350
San Francisco	2	12	0	.143	198	391

NFL championship: CHICAGO 14, N.Y. Giants 10

1963 AFL

EASTERN DIVISION

	W	L	T	Pct.	Pts.	OP
Boston Patriots	7	6	1	.538	327	257
Buffalo	7	6	1	.538	304	291
Houston	6	8	0	.429	302	372
N.Y. Jets	5	8	1	.385	249	399

WESTERN DIVISION

	W	L	T	Pct.	Pts.	OP
San Diego	11	3	0	.786	399	255
Oakland	10	4	0	.714	363	282
Kansas City	5	7	2	.417	347	263
Denver	2	11	1	.154	301	473

Eastern Division playoff: Boston 26, BUFFALO 8
AFL championship: SAN DIEGO 51, Boston 10

1962 NFL

EASTERN CONFERENCE

	W	L	T	Pct.	Pts.	OP
N.Y. Giants	12	2	0	.857	398	283
Pittsburgh	9	5	0	.643	312	363
Cleveland	7	6	1	.538	291	257
Washington	5	7	2	.417	305	376
Dallas Cowboys	5	8	1	.385	398	402
St. Louis	4	9	1	.308	287	361
Philadelphia	3	10	1	.231	282	356

WESTERN CONFERENCE

	W	L	T	Pct.	Pts.	OP
Green Bay	13	1	0	.929	415	148
Detroit	11	3	0	.786	315	177
Chicago	9	5	0	.643	321	287
Baltimore	7	7	0	.500	293	288
San Francisco	6	8	0	.429	282	331
Minnesota	2	11	1	.154	254	410
Los Angeles	1	12	1	.077	220	334

NFL championship: Green Bay 16, N.Y. GIANTS 7

1962 AFL

EASTERN DIVISION

	W	L	T	Pct.	Pts.	OP
Houston	11	3	0	.786	387	270
Boston Patriots	9	4	1	.692	346	295
Buffalo	7	6	1	.538	309	272
N.Y. Titans	5	9	0	.357	278	423

WESTERN DIVISION

	W	L	T	Pct.	Pts.	OP
Dallas Texans	11	3	0	.786	389	233
Denver	7	7	0	.500	353	334
San Diego	4	10	0	.286	314	392
Oakland	1	13	0	.071	213	370

AFL championship: Dallas Texans 20, HOUSTON 17 (OT)

1961 NFL

EASTERN CONFERENCE

	W	L	T	Pct.	Pts.	OP
N.Y. Giants	10	3	1	.769	368	220
Philadelphia	10	4	0	.714	361	297
Cleveland	8	5	1	.615	319	270
St. Louis	7	7	0	.500	279	267
Pittsburgh	6	8	0	.429	295	287
Dallas Cowboys	4	9	1	.308	236	380
Washington	1	12	1	.077	174	392

WESTERN CONFERENCE

	W	L	T	Pct.	Pts.	OP
Green Bay	11	3	0	.786	391	223
Detroit	8	5	1	.615	270	258
Baltimore	8	6	0	.571	302	307
Chicago	8	6	0	.571	326	302
San Francisco	7	6	1	.538	346	272
Los Angeles	4	10	0	.286	263	333
Minnesota	3	11	0	.214	285	407

NFL championship: GREEN BAY 37, N.Y. Giants 0

1961 AFL

EASTERN DIVISION

	W	L	T	Pct.	Pts.	OP
Houston	10	3	1	.769	513	242
Boston Patriots	9	4	1	.692	413	313
N.Y. Titans	7	7	0	.500	301	390
Buffalo	6	8	0	.429	294	342

WESTERN DIVISION

	W	L	T	Pct.	Pts.	OP
San Diego	12	2	0	.857	396	219
Dallas Texans	6	8	0	.429	334	343
Denver	3	11	0	.214	251	432
Oakland	2	12	0	.143	237	458

AFL championship: Houston 10, SAN DIEGO 3

1960 NFL

EASTERN CONFERENCE

	W	L	T	Pct.	Pts.	OP
Philadelphia	10	2	0	.833	321	246
Cleveland	8	3	1	.727	362	217
N.Y. Giants	6	4	2	.600	271	261
St. Louis	6	5	1	.545	288	230
Pittsburgh	5	6	1	.455	240	275
Washington	1	9	2	.100	178	309

WESTERN CONFERENCE

	W	L	T	Pct.	Pts.	OP
Green Bay	8	4	0	.667	332	209
Detroit	7	5	0	.583	239	212
San Francisco	7	5	0	.583	208	205
Baltimore	6	6	0	.500	288	234
Chicago	5	6	1	.455	194	299
L.A. Rams	4	7	1	.364	265	297
Dallas Cowboys	0	11	1	.000	177	369

NFL championship: PHILADELPHIA 17, Green Bay 13

1960 AFL

EASTERN CONFERENCE

	W	L	T	Pct.	Pts.	OP
Houston	10	4	0	.714	379	285
N.Y. Titans	7	7	0	.500	382	399
Buffalo	5	8	1	.385	296	303
Boston	5	9	0	.357	286	349

WESTERN CONFERENCE

	W	L	T	Pct.	Pts.	OP
L.A. Chargers	10	4	0	.714	373	336
Dallas Texans	8	6	0	.571	362	253
Oakland	6	8	0	.429	319	388
Denver	4	9	1	.308	309	393

AFL championship: HOUSTON 24, L.A. Chargers 16

1959

EASTERN CONFERENCE

	W	L	T	Pct.	Pts.	OP
N.Y. Giants	10	2	0	.833	284	170
Cleveland	7	5	0	.583	270	214
Philadelphia	7	5	0	.583	268	278
Pittsburgh	6	5	1	.545	257	216
Washington	3	9	0	.250	185	350
Chi. Cardinals	2	10	0	.167	234	324

WESTERN CONFERENCE

	W	L	T	Pct.	Pts.	OP
Baltimore	9	3	0	.750	374	251
Chi. Bears	8	4	0	.667	252	196
Green Bay	7	5	0	.583	248	246
San Francisco	7	5	0	.583	255	237
Detroit	3	8	1	.273	203	275
Los Angeles	2	10	0	.167	242	315

NFL championship: BALTIMORE 31, N.Y. Giants 16

1958

EASTERN CONFERENCE

	W	L	T	Pct.	Pts.	OP
N.Y. Giants	9	3	0	.750	246	183
Cleveland	9	3	0	.750	302	217
Pittsburgh	7	4	1	.636	261	230
Washington	4	7	1	.364	214	268
Chi. Cardinals	2	9	1	.182	261	356
Philadelphia	2	9	1	.182	235	306

WESTERN CONFERENCE

	W	L	T	Pct.	Pts.	OP
Baltimore	9	3	0	.750	381	203
Chi. Bears	8	4	0	.667	298	230
Los Angeles	8	4	0	.667	344	278
San Francisco	6	6	0	.500	257	324
Detroit	4	7	1	.364	261	276
Green Bay	1	10	1	.091	193	382

Eastern Conference playoff: N.Y. GIANTS 10, Cleveland 0

NFL championship: Baltimore 23, N.Y. GIANTS 17 (OT)

1957

EASTERN CONFERENCE

	W	L	T	Pct.	Pts.	OP
Cleveland	9	2	1	.818	269	172
N.Y. Giants	7	5	0	.583	254	211
Pittsburgh	6	6	0	.500	161	178
Washington	5	6	1	.455	251	230
Philadelphia	4	8	0	.333	173	230
Chi. Cardinals	3	9	0	.250	200	299

WESTERN CONFERENCE

	W	L	T	Pct.	Pts.	OP
Detroit	8	4	0	.667	251	231
San Francisco	8	4	0	.667	260	264
Baltimore	7	5	0	.583	303	235
Los Angeles	6	6	0	.500	307	278
Chi. Bears	5	7	0	.417	203	211
Green Bay	3	9	0	.250	218	311

Western Conference playoff: Detroit 31, SAN FRANCISCO 27

NFL championship: DETROIT 59, Cleveland 14

1956

EASTERN CONFERENCE

	W	L	T	Pct.	Pts.	OP
N.Y. Giants	8	3	1	.727	264	197
Chi. Cardinals	7	5	0	.583	240	182
Washington	6	6	0	.500	183	225
Cleveland	5	7	0	.417	167	177
Pittsburgh	5	7	0	.417	217	250
Philadelphia	3	8	1	.273	143	215

WESTERN CONFERENCE

	W	L	T	Pct.	Pts.	OP
Chi. Bears	9	2	1	.818	363	246
Detroit	9	3	0	.750	300	188
San Francisco	5	6	1	.455	233	284
Baltimore	5	7	0	.417	270	322
Green Bay	4	8	0	.333	264	342
Los Angeles	4	8	0	.333	291	307

NFL championship: N.Y. GIANTS 47, Chi. Bears 7

1955

EASTERN CONFERENCE

	W	L	T	Pct.	Pts.	OP
Cleveland	9	2	1	.818	349	218
Washington	8	4	0	.667	246	222
N.Y. Giants	6	5	1	.545	267	223
Chi. Cardinals	4	7	1	.364	224	252
Philadelphia	4	7	1	.364	248	231
Pittsburgh	4	8	0	.333	195	285

WESTERN CONFERENCE

	W	L	T	Pct.	Pts.	OP
Los Angeles	8	3	1	.727	260	231
Chi. Bears	8	4	0	.667	294	251
Green Bay	6	6	0	.500	258	276
Baltimore	5	6	1	.455	214	239
San Francisco	4	8	0	.333	216	298
Detroit	3	9	0	.250	230	275

NFL championship: Cleveland 38, LOS ANGELES 14

1954

EASTERN CONFERENCE

	W	L	T	Pct.	Pts.	OP
Cleveland	9	3	0	.750	336	162
Philadelphia	7	4	1	.636	284	230
N.Y. Giants	7	5	0	.583	293	184
Pittsburgh	5	7	0	.417	219	263
Washington	3	9	0	.250	207	432
Chi. Cardinals	2	10	0	.167	183	347

WESTERN CONFERENCE

	W	L	T	Pct.	Pts.	OP
Detroit	9	2	1	.818	337	189
Chi. Bears	8	4	0	.667	301	279
San Francisco	7	4	1	.636	313	251
Los Angeles	6	5	1	.545	314	285
Green Bay	4	8	0	.333	234	251
Baltimore	3	9	0	.250	131	279

NFL championship: CLEVELAND 56, Detroit 10

1953

EASTERN CONFERENCE

	W	L	T	Pct.	Pts.	OP
Cleveland	11	1	0	.917	348	162
Philadelphia	7	4	1	.636	352	215
Washington	6	5	1	.545	208	215
Pittsburgh	6	6	0	.500	211	263
N.Y. Giants	3	9	0	.250	179	277
Chi. Cardinals	1	10	1	.091	190	337

WESTERN CONFERENCE

	W	L	T	Pct.	Pts.	OP
Detroit	10	2	0	.833	271	205
San Francisco	9	3	0	.750	372	237
Los Angeles	8	3	1	.727	366	236
Chi. Bears	3	8	1	.273	218	262
Baltimore	3	9	0	.250	182	350
Green Bay	2	9	1	.182	200	338

NFL championship: DETROIT 17, Cleveland 16

1952

AMERICAN CONFERENCE

	W	L	T	Pct.	Pts.	OP
Cleveland	8	4	0	.667	310	213
N.Y. Giants	7	5	0	.583	234	231
Philadelphia	7	5	0	.583	252	271
Pittsburgh	5	7	0	.417	300	273
Chi. Cardinals	4	8	0	.333	172	221
Washington	4	8	0	.333	240	287

NATIONAL CONFERENCE

	W	L	T	Pct.	Pts.	OP
Detroit	9	3	0	.750	344	192
Los Angeles	9	3	0	.750	349	234
San Francisco	7	5	0	.583	285	221
Green Bay	6	6	0	.500	295	312
Chi. Bears	5	7	0	.417	245	326
Dallas Texans	1	11	0	.083	182	427

National Conference playoff: DETROIT 31, Los Angeles 21

NFL championship: Detroit 17, CLEVELAND 7

PAST STANDINGS

1951

AMERICAN CONFERENCE

	W	L	T	Pct.	Pts.	OP
Cleveland	11	1	0	.917	331	152
N.Y. Giants	9	2	1	.818	254	161
Washington	5	7	0	.417	183	296
Pittsburgh	4	7	1	.364	183	235
Philadelphia	4	8	0	.333	234	264
Chi. Cardinals	3	9	0	.250	210	287

NATIONAL CONFERENCE

	W	L	T	Pct.	Pts.	OP
Los Angeles	8	4	0	.667	392	261
Detroit	7	4	1	.636	336	259
San Francisco	7	4	1	.636	255	205
Chi. Bears	7	5	0	.583	286	282
Green Bay	3	9	0	.250	254	375
N.Y. Yanks	1	9	2	.100	241	382

NFL championship: LOS ANGELES 24, Cleveland 17

1950

AMERICAN CONFERENCE

	W	L	T	Pct.	Pts.	OP
Cleveland	10	2	0	.833	310	144
N.Y. Giants	10	2	0	.833	268	150
Philadelphia	6	6	0	.500	254	141
Pittsburgh	6	6	0	.500	180	195
Chi. Cardinals	5	7	0	.417	233	287
Washington	3	9	0	.250	232	326

NATIONAL CONFERENCE

	W	L	T	Pct.	Pts.	OP
Los Angeles	9	3	0	.750	466	309
Chi. Bears	9	3	0	.750	279	207
N.Y. Yanks	7	5	0	.583	366	367
Detroit	6	6	0	.500	321	285
Green Bay	3	9	0	.250	244	406
San Francisco	3	9	0	.250	213	300
Baltimore	1	11	0	.083	213	462

American Conference playoff: CLEVELAND 8, N.Y. Giants 3
National Conference playoff: LOS ANGELES 24, Chi. Bears 14
NFL championship: CLEVELAND 30, Los Angeles 28

1949

EASTERN DIVISION

	W	L	T	Pct.	Pts.	OP
Philadelphia	11	1	0	.917	364	134
Pittsburgh	6	5	1	.545	224	214
N.Y. Giants	6	6	0	.500	287	298
Washington	4	7	1	.364	268	339
N.Y. Bulldogs	1	10	1	.091	153	368

WESTERN DIVISION

	W	L	T	Pct.	Pts.	OP
Los Angeles	8	2	2	.800	360	239
Chi. Bears	9	3	0	.750	332	218
Chi. Cardinals	6	5	1	.545	360	301
Detroit	4	8	0	.333	237	259
Green Bay	2	10	0	.167	114	329

NFL championship: Philadelphia 14, LOS ANGELES 0

1948

EASTERN DIVISION

	W	L	T	Pct.	Pts.	OP
Philadelphia	9	2	1	.818	376	156
Washington	7	5	0	.583	291	287
N.Y. Giants	4	8	0	.333	297	388
Pittsburgh	4	8	0	.333	200	243
Boston	3	9	0	.250	174	372

WESTERN DIVISION

	W	L	T	Pct.	Pts.	OP
Chi. Cardinals	11	1	0	.917	395	226
Chi. Bears	10	2	0	.833	375	151
Los Angeles	6	5	1	.545	327	269
Green Bay	3	9	0	.250	154	290
Detroit	2	10	0	.167	200	407

NFL championship: PHILADELPHIA 7, Chi. Cardinals 0

1947

EASTERN DIVISION

	W	L	T	Pct.	Pts.	OP
Philadelphia	8	4	0	.667	308	242
Pittsburgh	8	4	0	.667	240	259
Boston	4	7	1	.364	168	256
Washington	4	8	0	.333	295	367
N.Y. Giants	2	8	2	.200	190	309

WESTERN DIVISION

	W	L	T	Pct.	Pts.	OP
Chi. Cardinals	9	3	0	.750	306	231
Chi. Bears	8	4	0	.667	363	241
Green Bay	6	5	1	.545	274	210
Los Angeles	6	6	0	.500	259	214
Detroit	3	9	0	.250	231	305

Eastern Division playoff: Philadelphia 21, PITTSBURGH 0
NFL championship: CHI. CARDINALS 28, Philadelphia 21

1946

EASTERN DIVISION

	W	L	T	Pct.	Pts.	OP
N.Y. Giants	7	3	1	.700	236	162
Philadelphia	6	5	0	.545	231	220
Washington	5	5	1	.500	171	191
Pittsburgh	5	5	1	.500	136	117
Boston	2	8	1	.200	189	273

WESTERN DIVISION

	W	L	T	Pct.	Pts.	OP
Chi. Bears	8	2	1	.800	289	193
Los Angeles	6	4	1	.600	277	257
Green Bay	6	5	0	.545	148	158
Chi. Cardinals	6	5	0	.545	260	198
Detroit	1	10	0	.091	142	310

NFL championship: Chi. Bears 24, N.Y. GIANTS 14

1945

EASTERN DIVISION

	W	L	T	Pct.	Pts.	OP
Washington	8	2	0	.800	209	121
Philadelphia	7	3	0	.700	272	133
N.Y. Giants	3	6	1	.333	179	198
Boston	3	6	1	.333	123	211
Pittsburgh	2	8	0	.200	79	220

WESTERN DIVISION

	W	L	T	Pct.	Pts.	OP
Cleveland	9	1	0	.900	244	136
Detroit	7	3	0	.700	195	194
Green Bay	6	4	0	.600	258	173
Chi. Bears	3	7	0	.300	192	235
Chi. Cardinals	1	9	0	.100	98	228

NFL championship: CLEVELAND 15, Washington 14

1944

EASTERN DIVISION

	W	L	T	Pct.	Pts.	OP
N.Y. Giants	8	1	1	.889	206	75
Philadelphia	7	1	2	.875	267	131
Washington	6	3	1	.667	169	180
Boston	2	8	0	.200	82	233
Brooklyn	0	10	0	.000	69	166

WESTERN DIVISION

	W	L	T	Pct.	Pts.	OP
Green Bay	8	2	0	.800	238	141
Chi. Bears	6	3	1	.667	258	172
Detroit	6	3	1	.667	216	151
Cleveland	4	6	0	.400	188	224
Card-Pitt	0	10	0	.000	108	328

NFL championship: Green Bay 14, N.Y. GIANTS 7

1943

EASTERN DIVISION

	W	L	T	Pct.	Pts.	OP
Washington	6	3	1	.667	229	137
N.Y. Giants	6	3	1	.667	197	170
Phil-Pitt	5	4	1	.556	225	230
Brooklyn	2	8	0	.200	65	234

WESTERN DIVISION

	W	L	T	Pct.	Pts.	OP
Chi. Bears	8	1	1	.889	303	157
Green Bay	7	2	1	.778	264	172
Detroit	3	6	1	.333	178	218
Chi. Cardinals	0	10	0	.000	95	238

Eastern Division playoff: Washington 28, N.Y. GIANTS 0
NFL championship: CHI. BEARS 41, Washington 21

1942

EASTERN DIVISION

	W	L	T	Pct.	Pts.	OP
Washington	10	1	0	.909	227	102
Pittsburgh	7	4	0	.636	167	119
N.Y. Giants	5	5	1	.500	155	139
Brooklyn	3	8	0	.273	100	168
Philadelphia	2	9	0	.182	134	239

WESTERN DIVISION

	W	L	T	Pct.	Pts.	OP
Chi. Bears	11	0	0	1.000	376	84
Green Bay	8	2	1	.800	300	215
Cleveland	5	6	0	.455	150	207
Chi. Cardinals	3	8	0	.273	98	209
Detroit	0	11	0	.000	38	263

NFL championship: WASHINGTON 14, Chi. Bears 6

1941

EASTERN DIVISION

	W	L	T	Pct.	Pts.	OP
N.Y. Giants	8	3	0	.727	238	114
Brooklyn	7	4	0	.636	158	127
Washington	6	5	0	.545	176	174
Philadelphia	2	8	1	.200	119	218
Pittsburgh	1	9	1	.100	103	276

WESTERN DIVISION

	W	L	T	Pct.	Pts.	OP
Chi. Bears	10	1	0	.909	396	147
Green Bay	10	1	0	.909	258	120
Detroit	4	6	1	.400	121	195
Chi. Cardinals	3	7	1	.300	127	197
Cleveland	2	9	0	.182	116	244

Western Division playoff: CHI. BEARS 33, Green Bay 14
NFL championship: CHI. BEARS 37, N.Y. Giants 9

1940

EASTERN DIVISION

	W	L	T	Pct.	Pts.	OP
Washington	9	2	0	.818	245	142
Brooklyn	8	3	0	.727	186	120
N.Y. Giants	6	4	1	.600	131	133
Pittsburgh	2	7	2	.222	60	178
Philadelphia	1	10	0	.091	111	211

WESTERN DIVISION

	W	L	T	Pct.	Pts.	OP
Chi. Bears	8	3	0	.727	238	152
Green Bay	6	4	1	.600	238	155
Detroit	5	5	1	.500	138	153
Cleveland	4	6	1	.400	171	191
Chi. Cardinals	2	7	2	.222	139	222

NFL championship: Chi. Bears 73, WASHINGTON 0

1939

EASTERN DIVISION

	W	L	T	Pct.	Pts.	OP
N.Y. Giants	9	1	1	.900	168	85
Washington	8	2	1	.800	242	94
Brooklyn	4	6	1	.400	108	219
Philadelphia	1	9	1	.100	105	200
Pittsburgh	1	9	1	.100	114	216

WESTERN DIVISION

	W	L	T	Pct.	Pts.	OP
Green Bay	9	2	0	.818	233	153
Chi. Bears	8	3	0	.727	298	157
Detroit	6	5	0	.545	145	150
Cleveland	5	5	1	.500	195	164
Chi. Cardinals	1	10	0	.091	84	254

NFL championship: GREEN BAY 27, N.Y. Giants 0

1938

EASTERN DIVISION

	W	L	T	Pct.	Pts.	OP
N.Y. Giants	8	2	1	.800	194	79
Washington	6	3	2	.667	148	154
Brooklyn	4	4	3	.500	131	161
Philadelphia	5	6	0	.455	154	164
Pittsburgh	2	9	0	.182	79	169

WESTERN DIVISION

	W	L	T	Pct.	Pts.	OP
Green Bay	8	3	0	.727	223	118
Detroit	7	4	0	.636	119	108
Chi. Bears	6	5	0	.545	194	148
Cleveland	4	7	0	.364	131	215
Chi. Cardinals	2	9	0	.182	111	168

NFL championship: N.Y. GIANTS 23, Green Bay 17

1937

EASTERN DIVISION

	W	L	T	Pct.	Pts.	OP
Washington	8	3	0	.727	195	120
N.Y. Giants	6	3	2	.667	128	109
Pittsburgh	4	7	0	.364	122	145
Brooklyn	3	7	1	.300	82	174
Philadelphia	2	8	1	.200	86	177

WESTERN DIVISION

	W	L	T	Pct.	Pts.	OP
Chi. Bears	9	1	1	.900	201	100
Green Bay	7	4	0	.636	220	122
Detroit	7	4	0	.636	180	105
Chi. Cardinals	5	5	1	.500	135	165
Cleveland	1	10	0	.091	75	207

NFL championship: Washington 28, CHI. BEARS 21

1936

EASTERN DIVISION

	W	L	T	Pct.	Pts.	OP
Boston	7	5	0	.583	149	110
Pittsburgh	6	6	0	.500	98	187
N.Y. Giants	5	6	1	.455	115	163
Brooklyn	3	8	1	.273	92	161
Philadelphia	1	11	0	.083	51	206

WESTERN DIVISION

	W	L	T	Pct.	Pts.	OP
Green Bay	10	1	1	.909	248	118
Chi. Bears	9	3	0	.750	222	94
Detroit	8	4	0	.667	235	102
Chi. Cardinals	3	8	1	.273	74	143

NFL championship: Green Bay 21, Boston 6, at Polo Grounds, N.Y.

1935

EASTERN DIVISION

	W	L	T	Pct.	Pts.	OP
N.Y. Giants	9	3	0	.750	180	96
Brooklyn	5	6	1	.455	90	141
Pittsburgh	4	8	0	.333	100	209
Boston	2	8	1	.200	65	123
Philadelphia	2	9	0	.182	60	179

WESTERN DIVISION

	W	L	T	Pct.	Pts.	OP
Detroit	7	3	2	.700	191	111
Green Bay	8	4	0	.667	181	96
Chi. Bears	6	4	2	.600	192	106
Chi. Cardinals	6	4	2	.600	99	97

NFL championship: DETROIT 26, N.Y. Giants 7

One game between Boston and Philadelphia was canceled.

1934

EASTERN DIVISION

	W	L	T	Pct.	Pts.	OP
N.Y. Giants	8	5	0	.615	147	107
Boston	6	6	0	.500	107	94
Brooklyn	4	7	0	.364	61	153
Philadelphia	4	7	0	.364	127	85
Pittsburgh	2	10	0	.167	51	206

WESTERN DIVISION

	W	L	T	Pct.	Pts.	OP
Chi. Bears	13	0	0	1.000	286	86
Detroit	10	3	0	.769	238	59
Green Bay	7	6	0	.538	156	112
Chi. Cardinals	5	6	0	.455	80	84
St. Louis	1	2	0	.333	27	61
Cincinnati	0	8	0	.000	10	243

NFL championship: N.Y. GIANTS 30, Chi. Bears 13

1933

EASTERN DIVISION

	W	L	T	Pct.	Pts.	OP
N.Y. Giants	11	3	0	.786	244	101
Brooklyn	5	4	1	.556	93	54
Boston	5	5	2	.500	103	97
Philadelphia	3	5	1	.375	77	158
Pittsburgh	3	6	2	.333	67	208

WESTERN DIVISION

	W	L	T	Pct.	Pts.	OP
Chi. Bears	10	2	1	.833	133	82
Portsmouth	6	5	0	.545	128	87
Green Bay	5	7	1	.417	170	107
Cincinnati	3	6	1	.333	38	110
Chi. Cardinals	1	9	1	.100	52	101

NFL championship: CHI. BEARS 23, N.Y. Giants 21

1932

	W	L	T	Pct.
Chicago Bears	7	1	6	.875
Green Bay Packers	10	3	1	.769
Portsmouth Spartans	6	2	4	.750
Boston Braves	4	4	2	.500
New York Giants	4	6	2	.400
Brooklyn Dodgers	3	9	0	.250
Chicago Cardinals	2	6	2	.250
Staten Island Stapletons	2	7	3	.222

Chicago Bears and Portsmouth finished regularly scheduled games tied for first place. Bears won playoff game, which counted in standings, 9-0.

1931

	W	L	T	Pct.
Green Bay Packers	12	2	0	.857
Portsmouth Spartans	11	3	0	.786
Chicago Bears	8	5	0	.615
Chicago Cardinals	5	4	0	.556
New York Giants	7	6	1	.538
Providence Steam Roller	4	4	3	.500
Staten Island Stapletons	4	6	1	.400
Cleveland Indians	2	8	0	.200
Brooklyn Dodgers	2	12	0	.143
Frankford Yellow Jackets	1	6	1	.143

1930

	W	L	T	Pct.
Green Bay Packers	10	3	1	.769
New York Giants	13	4	0	.765
Chicago Bears	9	4	1	.692
Brooklyn Dodgers	7	4	1	.636
Providence Steam Roller	6	4	1	.600
Staten Island Stapletons	5	5	2	.500
Chicago Cardinals	5	6	2	.455
Portsmouth Spartans	5	6	3	.455
Frankford Yellow Jackets	4	13	1	.222
Minneapolis Red Jackets	1	7	1	.125
Newark Tornadoes	1	10	1	.091

1929

	W	L	T	Pct.
Green Bay Packers	12	0	1	1.000
New York Giants	13	1	1	.929
Frankford Yellow Jackets	10	4	5	.714
Chicago Cardinals	6	6	1	.500
Boston Bulldogs	4	4	0	.500
Staten Island Stapletons	3	4	3	.429
Providence Steam Roller	4	6	2	.400
Orange Tornadoes	3	5	4	.375
Chicago Bears	4	9	2	.308
Buffalo Bisons	1	7	1	.125
Minneapolis Red Jackets	1	9	0	.100
Dayton Triangles	0	6	0	.000

1928

	W	L	T	Pct.
Providence Steam Roller	8	1	2	.889
Frankford Yellow Jackets	11	3	2	.786
Detroit Wolverines	7	2	1	.778
Green Bay Packers	6	4	3	.600
Chicago Bears	7	5	1	.583
New York Giants	4	7	2	.364
New York Yankees	4	8	1	.333
Pottsville Maroons	2	8	0	.200
Chicago Cardinals	1	5	0	.167
Dayton Triangles	0	7	0	.000

1927

	W	L	T	Pct.
New York Giants	11	1	1	.917
Green Bay Packers	7	2	1	.778
Chicago Bears	9	3	2	.750
Cleveland Bulldogs	8	4	1	.667
Providence Steam Roller	8	5	1	.615
New York Yankees	7	8	1	.467
Frankford Yellow Jackets	6	9	3	.400
Pottsville Maroons	5	8	0	.385
Chicago Cardinals	3	7	1	.300
Dayton Triangles	1	6	1	.143
Duluth Eskimos	1	8	0	.111
Buffalo Bisons	0	5	0	.000

1926

	W	L	T	Pct.
Frankford Yellow Jackets	14	1	2	.933
Chicago Bears	12	1	3	.923
Pottsville Maroons	10	2	2	.833
Kansas City Cowboys	8	3	0	.727
Green Bay Packers	7	3	3	.700
Los Angeles Buccaneers	6	3	1	.667
New York Giants	8	4	1	.667
Duluth Eskimos	6	5	3	.545
Buffalo Rangers	4	4	2	.500
Chicago Cardinals	5	6	1	.455
Providence Steam Roller	5	7	1	.417
Detroit Panthers	4	6	2	.400
Hartford Blues	3	7	0	.300
Brooklyn Lions	3	8	0	.273
Milwaukee Badgers	2	7	0	.222
Akron Pros	1	4	3	.200
Dayton Triangles	1	4	1	.200
Racine Tornadoes	1	4	0	.200
Columbus Tigers	1	6	0	.143
Canton Bulldogs	1	9	3	.100
Hammond Pros	0	4	0	.000
Louisville Colonels	0	4	0	.000

1925

	W	L	T	Pct.
Chicago Cardinals	11	2	1	.846
Pottsville Maroons	10	2	0	.833
Detroit Panthers	8	2	2	.800
New York Giants	8	4	0	.667
Akron Indians	4	2	2	.667
Frankford Yellow Jackets	13	7	0	.650
Chicago Bears	9	5	3	.643
Rock Island Independents	5	3	3	.625
Green Bay Packers	8	5	0	.615
Providence Steam Roller	6	5	1	.545
Canton Bulldogs	4	4	0	.500
Cleveland Bulldogs	5	8	1	.385
Kansas City Cowboys	2	5	1	.286
Hammond Pros	1	4	0	.200
Buffalo Bisons	1	6	2	.143
Duluth Kelleys	0	3	0	.000
Rochester Jeffersons	0	6	1	.000
Milwaukee Badgers	0	6	0	.000
Dayton Triangles	0	7	1	.000
Columbus Tigers	0	9	0	.000

1924

	W	L	T	Pct.
Cleveland Bulldogs	7	1	1	.875
Chicago Bears	6	1	4	.857
Frankford Yellow Jackets	11	2	1	.846
Duluth Kelleys	5	1	0	.833
Rock Island Independents	5	2	2	.714
Green Bay Packers	7	4	0	.636
Racine Legion	4	3	3	.571
Chicago Cardinals	5	4	1	.556
Buffalo Bisons	6	5	0	.545
Columbus Tigers	4	4	0	.500
Hammond Pros	2	2	1	.500
Milwaukee Badgers	5	8	0	.385
Akron Indians	2	6	0	.250
Dayton Triangles	2	6	0	.250
Kansas City Blues	2	7	0	.222
Kenosha Maroons	0	4	1	.000
Minneapolis Marines	0	6	0	.000
Rochester Jeffersons	0	7	0	.000

1923

	W	L	T	Pct.
Canton Bulldogs	11	0	1	1.000
Chicago Bears	9	2	1	.818
Green Bay Packers	7	2	1	.778
Milwaukee Badgers	7	2	3	.778
Cleveland Indians	3	1	3	.750
Chicago Cardinals	8	4	0	.667
Duluth Kelleys	4	3	0	.571
Buffalo All-Americans	5	4	3	.556
Columbus Tigers	5	4	1	.556
Racine Legion	4	4	2	.500
Toledo Maroons	3	3	2	.500
Rock Island Independents	2	3	3	.400
Minneapolis Marines	2	5	2	.286
St. Louis All-Stars	1	4	2	.200
Hammond Pros	1	5	1	.167
Dayton Triangles	1	6	1	.143
Akron Indians	1	6	0	.143
Oorang Indians	1	10	0	.091
Louisville Brecks	0	3	0	.000
Rochester Jeffersons	0	4	0	.000

1922

	W	L	T	Pct.
Canton Bulldogs	10	0	2	1.000
Chicago Bears	9	3	0	.750
Chicago Cardinals	8	3	0	.727
Toledo Maroons	5	2	2	.714
Rock Island Independents	4	2	1	.667
Racine Legion	6	4	1	.600
Dayton Triangles	4	3	1	.571
Green Bay Packers	4	3	3	.571
Buffalo All-Americans	5	4	1	.556
Akron Pros	3	5	2	.375
Milwaukee Badgers	2	4	3	.333
Oorang Indians	3	6	0	.333
Minneapolis Marines	1	3	0	.250
Louisville Brecks	1	3	0	.250
Evansville Crimson Giants	0	3	0	.000
Rochester Jeffersons	0	4	1	.000
Hammond Pros	0	5	1	.000
Columbus Panhandles	0	8	0	.000

1921

	W	L	T	Pct.
Chicago Staleys	9	1	1	.900
Buffalo All-Americans	9	1	2	.900
Akron Pros	8	3	1	.727
Canton Bulldogs	5	2	3	.714
Rock Island Independents	4	2	1	.667
Evansville Crimson Giants	3	2	0	.600
Green Bay Packers	3	2	1	.600
Dayton Triangles	4	4	1	.500
Chicago Cardinals	3	3	2	.500
Rochester Jeffersons	2	3	0	.400
Cleveland Indians	3	5	0	.375
Washington Senators	1	2	0	.333
Cincinnati Celts	1	3	0	.250
Hammond Pros	1	3	1	.250
Minneapolis Marines	1	3	0	.250
Detroit Heralds	1	5	1	.167
Columbus Panhandles	1	8	0	.111
Tonawanda Kardex	0	1	0	.000
Muncie Flyers	0	2	0	.000
Louisville Brecks	0	2	0	.000
New York Giants	0	2	0	.000

1920*

	W	L	T	Pct.
Akron Pros	8	0	3	1.000
Decatur Staleys	10	1	2	.909
Buffalo All-Americans	9	1	1	.900
Chicago Cardinals	6	2	2	.750
Rock Island Independents	6	2	2	.750
Dayton Triangles	5	2	2	.714
Rochester Jeffersons	6	3	2	.667
Canton Bulldogs	7	4	2	.636
Detroit Heralds	2	3	3	.400
Cleveland Tigers	2	4	2	.333
Chicago Tigers	2	5	1	.286
Hammond Pros	2	5	0	.286
Columbus Panhandles	2	6	2	.250
Muncie Flyers	0	1	0	.000

**No official standings were maintained for the 1920 season, and the championship was awarded to the Akron Pros in a League meeting on April 30, 1921. Clubs played schedules that included games against nonleague opponents.*

ALL-TIME TEAM VS. TEAM RESULTS

RS=REGULAR SEASON
PS=POSTSEASON
***ARIZONA vs. ATLANTA**
RS: Cardinals lead series, 13-7
1966—Falcons, 16-10 (A)
1968—Cardinals, 17-12 (StL)
1971—Cardinals, 26-9 (A)
1973—Cardinals, 32-10 (A)
1975—Cardinals, 23-20 (StL)
1978—Cardinals, 42-21 (StL)
1980—Falcons, 33-27 (StL) OT
1981—Falcons, 41-20 (A)
1982—Cardinals, 23-20 (A)
1986—Falcons, 33-13 (A)
1987—Cardinals, 34-21 (A)
1989—Cardinals, 34-20 (P)
1990—Cardinals, 24-13 (A)
1991—Cardinals, 16-10 (P)
1992—Falcons, 20-17 (A)
1993—Cardinals, 27-10 (A)
1994—Falcons, 10-6 (Atl)
1995—Cardinals, 40-37 (Ariz) OT
1997—Cardinals, 29-26 (Ariz)
1999—Falcons, 37-14 (Atl)
(RS Pts.—Cardinals 474, Falcons 419)
**Franchise known as Phoenix prior to 1994 and in St. Louis prior to 1988*
***ARIZONA vs. BALTIMORE**
RS: Series tied, 1-1
1997—Cardinals, 16-13 (B)
2000—Ravens, 13-7 (B)
(RS Pts.—Ravens 26, Cardinals 23)
***ARIZONA vs. BUFFALO**
RS: Bills lead series, 4-3
1971—Cardinals, 28-23 (B)
1975—Bills, 32-14 (StL)
1981—Cardinals, 24-0 (StL)
1984—Cardinals, 37-7 (StL)
1986—Bills, 17-10 (B)
1990—Bills, 45-14 (B)
1999—Bills, 31-21 (A)
(RS Pts.—Bills 155, Cardinals 148)
**Franchise known as Phoenix prior to 1994 and in St. Louis prior to 1988*
ARIZONA vs. CAROLINA
RS: Panthers lead series, 1-0
1995—Panthers, 27-7 (C)
(RS Pts.—Panthers 27, Cardinals 7)
***ARIZONA vs. **CHICAGO**
RS: Bears lead series, 52-26-6
(NP denotes Normal Park;
Wr denotes Wrigley Field;
Co denotes Comiskey Park;
So denotes Soldier Field;
all Chicago)
1920—Cardinals, 7-6 (NP)
Staleys, 10-0 (Wr)
1921—Tie, 0-0 (Wr)
1922—Cardinals, 6-0 (Co)
Cardinals, 9-0 (Co)
1923—Bears, 3-0 (Wr)
1924—Bears, 6-0 (Wr)
Bears, 21-0 (Co)
1925—Cardinals, 9-0 (Co)
Tie, 0-0 (Wr)
1926—Bears, 16-0 (Wr)
Bears, 10-0 (So)
Tie, 0-0 (Wr)
1927—Bears, 9-0 (NP)
Cardinals, 3-0 (Wr)
1928—Bears, 15-0 (NP)
Bears, 34-0 (Wr)
1929—Tie, 0-0 (Wr)
Cardinals, 40-6 (Co)
1930—Bears, 32-6 (Co)
Bears, 6-0 (Wr)
1931—Bears, 26-13 (Wr)
Bears, 18-7 (Wr)
1932—Tie, 0-0 (Wr)
Bears, 34-0 (Wr)
1933—Bears, 12-9 (Wr)
Bears, 22-6 (Wr)
1934—Bears, 20-0 (Wr)
Bears, 17-6 (Wr)
1935—Tie, 7-7 (Wr)
Bears, 13-0 (Wr)
1936—Bears, 7-3 (Wr)
Cardinals, 14-7 (Wr)
1937—Bears, 16-7 (Wr)
Bears, 42-28 (Wr)
1938—Bears, 16-13 (So)
Bears, 34-28 (Wr)
1939—Bears, 44-7 (Wr)
Bears, 48-7 (Co)
1940—Cardinals, 21-7 (Co)
Bears, 31-23 (Wr)
1941—Bears, 53-7 (Wr)
Bears, 34-24 (Co)
1942—Bears, 41-14 (Wr)
Bears, 21-7 (Co)
1943—Bears, 20-0 (Wr)
Bears, 35-24 (Co)
1945—Cardinals, 16-7 (Wr)
Bears, 28-20 (Co)
1946—Bears, 34-17 (Co)
Cardinals, 35-28 (Wr)
1947—Cardinals, 31-7 (Co)
Cardinals, 30-21 (Wr)
1948—Bears, 28-17 (Co)
Cardinals, 24-21 (Wr)
1949—Bears, 17-7 (Co)
Bears, 52-21 (Wr)
1950—Bears, 27-6 (Wr)
Cardinals, 20-10 (Co)
1951—Cardinals, 28-14 (Co)
Cardinals, 24-14 (Wr)
1952—Cardinals, 21-10 (Co)
Bears, 10-7 (Wr)
1953—Cardinals, 24-17 (Wr)
1954—Bears, 29-7 (Co)
1955—Cardinals, 53-14 (Co)
1956—Bears, 10-3 (Wr)
1957—Bears, 14-6 (Co)
1958—Bears, 30-14 (Wr)
1959—Bears, 31-7 (So)
1965—Bears, 34-13 (Wr)
1966—Cardinals, 24-17 (StL)
1967—Bears, 30-3 (Wr)
1969—Cardinals, 20-17 (StL)
1972—Bears, 27-10 (StL)
1975—Cardinals, 34-20 (So)
1977—Cardinals, 16-13 (StL)
1978—Bears, 17-10 (So)
1979—Bears, 42-6 (So)
1982—Cardinals, 10-7 (So)
1984—Cardinals, 38-21 (StL)
1990—Bears, 31-21 (P)
1994—Bears, 19-16 (A) OT
1998—Cardinals, 20-7 (A)
(RS Pts.—Bears 1,574, Cardinals 1,034)
**Franchise known as Phoenix prior to 1994, in St. Louis prior to 1988, and in Chicago prior to 1960*
***Franchise in Decatur prior to 1921 and known as Staleys prior to 1922*
***ARIZONA vs. CINCINNATI**
RS: Bengals lead series, 5-2
1973—Bengals, 42-24 (C)
1979—Bengals, 34-28 (C)
1985—Cardinals, 41-27 (StL)
1988—Bengals, 21-14 (C)
1994—Cardinals, 28-7 (A)
1997—Bengals, 24-21 (C)
2000—Bengals, 24-13 (C)
(RS Pts.—Bengals 179, Cardinals 169)
**Franchise known as Phoenix prior to 1994 and in St. Louis prior to 1988*
***ARIZONA vs. CLEVELAND**
RS: Browns lead series, 32-11-3
1950—Browns, 34-24 (Cle)
Browns, 10-7 (Chi)
1951—Browns, 34-17 (Chi)
Browns, 49-28 (Cle)
1952—Browns, 28-13 (Cle)
Browns, 10-0 (Chi)
1953—Browns, 27-7 (Chi)
Browns, 27-16 (Cle)
1954—Browns, 31-7 (Cle)
Browns, 35-3 (Chi)
1955—Browns, 26-20 (Chi)
Browns, 35-24 (Cle)
1956—Cardinals, 9-7 (Chi)
Cardinals, 24-7 (Cle)
1957—Browns, 17-7 (Chi)
Browns, 31-0 (Cle)
1958—Browns, 35-28 (Cle)
Browns, 38-24 (Chi)
1959—Browns, 34-7 (Chi)
Browns, 17-7 (Cle)
1960—Browns, 28-27 (Cle)
Tie, 17-17 (StL)
1961—Browns, 20-17 (Cle)
Browns, 21-10 (StL)
1962—Browns, 34-7 (StL)
Browns, 38-14 (Cle)
1963—Cardinals, 20-14 (Cle)
Browns, 24-10 (StL)
1964—Tie, 33-33 (Cle)
Cardinals, 28-19 (StL)
1965—Cardinals, 49-13 (Cle)
Browns, 27-24 (StL)
1966—Cardinals, 34-28 (Cle)
Browns, 38-10 (StL)
1967—Browns, 20-16 (Cle)
Browns, 20-16 (StL)
1968—Cardinals, 27-21 (Cle)
Cardinals, 27-16 (StL)
1969—Tie, 21-21 (Cle)
Browns, 27-21 (StL)
1974—Cardinals, 29-7 (StL)
1979—Browns, 38-20 (StL)
1985—Cardinals, 27-24 (Cle) OT
1988—Browns, 29-21 (P)
1994—Browns, 32-0 (Cle)
2000—Cardinals, 29-21 (A)
(RS Pts.—Browns 1,162, Cardinals 826)
**Franchise known as Phoenix prior to 1994, in St. Louis prior to 1988, and in Chicago prior to 1960*
***ARIZONA vs. DALLAS**
RS: Cowboys lead series, 51-25-1
PS: Cardinals lead series, 1-0
1960—Cardinals, 12-10 (StL)
1961—Cardinals, 31-17 (D)
Cardinals, 31-13 (StL)
1962—Cardinals, 28-24 (D)
Cardinals, 52-20 (StL)
1963—Cardinals, 34-7 (D)
Cowboys, 28-24 (StL)
1964—Cardinals, 16-6 (D)
Cowboys, 31-13 (StL)
1965—Cardinals, 20-13 (StL)
Cowboys, 27-13 (D)
1966—Tie, 10-10 (StL)
Cowboys, 31-17 (D)
1967—Cowboys, 46-21 (D)
1968—Cowboys, 27-10 (StL)
1969—Cowboys, 24-3 (D)
1970—Cardinals, 20-7 (StL)
Cardinals, 38-0 (D)
1971—Cowboys, 16-13 (StL)
Cowboys, 31-12 (D)
1972—Cowboys, 33-24 (D)
Cowboys, 27-6 (StL)
1973—Cowboys, 45-10 (D)
Cowboys, 30-3 (StL)
1974—Cardinals, 31-28 (StL)
Cowboys, 17-14 (D)
1975—Cowboys, 37-31 (D) OT
Cardinals, 31-17 (StL)
1976—Cardinals, 21-17 (StL)
Cowboys, 19-14 (D)
1977—Cowboys, 30-24 (StL)
Cardinals, 24-17 (D)
1978—Cowboys, 21-12 (D)
Cowboys, 24-21 (StL) OT
1979—Cowboys, 22-21 (StL)
Cowboys, 22-13 (D)
1980—Cowboys, 27-24 (StL)
Cowboys, 31-21 (D)
1981—Cowboys, 30-17 (D)
Cardinals, 20-17 (StL)
1982—Cowboys, 24-7 (StL)
1983—Cowboys, 34-17 (StL)
Cowboys, 35-17 (D)
1984—Cardinals, 31-20 (D)
Cowboys, 24-17 (StL)
1985—Cardinals, 21-10 (StL)
Cowboys, 35-17 (D)
1986—Cowboys, 31-7 (StL)
Cowboys, 37-6 (D)
1987—Cardinals, 24-13 (StL)
Cowboys, 21-16 (D)
1988—Cowboys, 17-14 (P)
Cardinals, 16-10 (D)
1989—Cardinals, 19-10 (D)
Cardinals, 24-20 (P)
1990—Cardinals, 20-3 (P)
Cowboys, 41-10 (D)
1991—Cowboys, 17-9 (P)
Cowboys, 27-7 (D)
1992—Cowboys, 31-20 (D)
Cowboys, 16-10 (P)
1993—Cowboys, 17-10 (P)
Cowboys, 20-15 (D)
1994—Cowboys, 38-3 (D)
Cowboys, 28-21 (A)
1995—Cowboys, 34-20 (D)
Cowboys, 37-13 (A)
1996—Cowboys, 17-3 (D)
Cowboys, 10-6 (A)
1997—Cardinals, 25-22 (A) OT
Cowboys, 24-6 (D)
1998—Cowboys, 38-10 (D)
Cowboys, 35-28 (A)
**Cardinals, 20-7 (D)
1999—Cowboys, 35-7 (D)
Cardinals, 13-9 (A)
2000—Cardinals, 32-31 (A)
Cowboys, 48-7 (D)
(RS Pts.—Cowboys 1,818, Cardinals 1,348)
(PS Pts.—Cardinals 20, Cowboys 7)
**Franchise known as Phoenix prior to 1994 and in St. Louis prior to 1988*
***NFC First-Round Playoff*
***ARIZONA vs. DENVER**
RS: Broncos lead series, 4-0-1
1973—Tie, 17-17 (StL)
1977—Broncos, 7-0 (D)
1989—Broncos, 37-0 (P)
1991—Broncos, 24-19 (D)
1995—Broncos, 38-6 (D)
(RS Pts.—Broncos 123, Cardinals 42)
**Franchise known as Phoenix prior to 1994 and in St. Louis prior to 1988*
***ARIZONA vs. **DETROIT**
RS: Lions lead series, 27-19-5
1930—Tie, 0-0 (Port)
Cardinals, 23-0 (C)
1931—Cardinals, 20-19 (C)
1932—Tie, 7-7 (Port)
1933—Spartans, 7-6 (Port)
1934—Lions, 6-0 (D)
Lions, 17-13 (C)
1935—Tie, 10-10 (D)
Lions, 7-6 (C)
1936—Lions, 39-0 (D)
Lions, 14-7 (C)
1937—Lions, 16-7 (C)
Lions, 16-7 (D)
1938—Lions, 10-0 (D)
Lions, 7-3 (C)
1939—Lions, 21-3 (D)
Lions, 17-3 (C)
1940—Tie, 0-0 (Buffalo)
Lions, 43-14 (C)
1941—Tie, 14-14 (C)
Lions, 21-3 (D)
1942—Cardinals, 13-0 (C)
Cardinals, 7-0 (D)
1943—Lions, 35-17 (D)
Lions, 7-0 (Buffalo)

1945—Lions, 10-0 (Milwaukee)
Lions, 26-0 (D)
1946—Cardinals, 34-14 (C)
Cardinals, 36-14 (D)
1947—Cardinals, 45-21 (C)
Cardinals, 17-7 (D)
1948—Cardinals, 56-20 (C)
Cardinals, 28-14 (D)
1949—Lions, 24-7 (C)
Cardinals, 42-19 (D)
1959—Lions, 45-21 (D)
1961—Lions, 45-14 (StL)
1967—Cardinals, 38-28 (StL)
1969—Lions, 20-0 (D)
1970—Lions, 16-3 (D)
1973—Lions, 20-16 (StL)
1975—Cardinals, 24-13 (D)
1978—Cardinals, 21-14 (StL)
1980—Lions, 20-7 (D)
Cardinals, 24-23 (StL)
1989—Cardinals, 16-13 (D)
1993—Lions, 26-20 (D)
Llons, 21-14 (Phx)
1995—Cardinals, 20-17 (D)
1998—Cardinals, 17-15 (D)
1999—Cardinals, 23-19 (A)
(RS Pts.—Lions 857, Cardinals 736)
**Franchise known as Phoenix prior to 1994, in St. Louis prior to 1988, and in Chicago prior to 1960*
***Franchise in Portsmouth prior to 1934 and known as the Spartans*

***ARIZONA vs. GREEN BAY**
RS: Packers lead series, 41-21-4
PS: Packers lead series, 1-0
1921—Tie, 3-3 (C)
1922—Cardinals, 16-3 (C)
1924—Cardinals, 3-0 (C)
1925—Cardinals, 9-6 (C)
1926—Cardinals, 13-7 (GB)
Packers, 3-0 (C)
1927—Packers, 13-0 (GB)
Tie, 6-6 (C)
1928—Packers, 20-0 (GB)
1929—Packers, 9-2 (GB)
Packers, 7-6 (C)
Packers, 12-0 (C)
1930—Packers, 14-0 (GB)
Cardinals, 13-6 (C)
1931—Packers, 26-7 (GB)
Cardinals, 21-13 (C)
1932—Packers, 15-7 (GB)
Packers, 19-9 (C)
1933—Packers, 14-6 (C)
1934—Packers, 15-0 (GB)
Cardinals, 9-0 (Mil)
Cardinals, 6-0 (C)
1935—Cardinals, 7-6 (GB)
Cardinals, 3-0 (Mil)
Cardinals, 9-7 (C)
1936—Packers, 10-7 (GB)
Packers, 24-0 (Mil)
Tie, 0-0 (C)
1937—Cardinals, 14-7 (GB)
Packers, 34-13 (Mil)
1938—Packers, 28-7 (Mil)
Packers, 24-22 (Buffalo)
1939—Packers, 14-10 (GB)
Packers, 27-20 (Mil)
1940—Packers, 31-6 (Mil)
Packers, 28-7 (C)
1941—Packers, 14-13 (Mil)
Packers, 17-9 (GB)
1942—Packers, 17-13 (C)
Packers, 55-24 (GB)
1943—Packers, 28-7 (C)
Packers, 35-14 (Mil)
1945—Packers, 33-14 (GB)
1946—Packers, 19-7 (C)
Cardinals, 24-6 (GB)
1947—Cardinals, 14-10 (GB)
Cardinals, 21-20 (C)
1948—Cardinals, 17-7 (Mil)
Cardinals, 42-7 (C)
1949—Cardinals, 39-17 (Mil)
Cardinals, 41-21 (C)
1955—Packers, 31-14 (GB)
1956—Packers, 24-21 (C)
1962—Packers, 17-0 (Mil)
1963—Packers, 30-7 (StL)
1967—Packers, 31-23 (StL)
1969—Packers, 45-28 (GB)
1971—Tie, 16-16 (StL)
1973—Packers, 25-21 (GB)
1976—Cardinals, 29-0 (StL)
1982—**Packers, 41-16 (GB)
1984—Packers, 24-23 (GB)
1985—Cardinals, 43-28 (StL)
1988—Packers, 26-17 (P)
1990—Packers, 24-21 (P)
1999—Packers, 49-24 (GB)
2000—Packers, 29-3 (A)
(RS Pts.—Packers 1,156, Cardinals 850)
(PS Pts.—Packers 41, Cardinals 16)
**Franchise known as Phoenix prior to 1994, in St. Louis prior to 1988, and in Chicago prior to 1960*
***NFC First-Round Playoff*

***ARIZONA vs. **INDIANAPOLIS**
RS: Series tied, 6-6
1961—Colts, 16-0 (B)
1964—Colts, 47-27 (B)
1968—Colts, 27-0 (B)
1972—Cardinals, 10-3 (B)
1976—Cardinals, 24-17 (StL)
1978—Colts, 30-17 (StL)
1980—Cardinals, 17-10 (B)
1981—Cardinals, 35-24 (B)
1984—Cardinals, 34-33 (I)
1990—Cardinals, 20-17 (P)
1992—Colts, 16-13 (I)
1996—Colts, 20-13 (I)
(RS Pts.—Colts 260, Cardinals 210)
**Franchise known as Phoenix prior to 1994 and in St. Louis prior to 1988*
***Franchise in Baltimore prior to 1984*

ARIZONA vs. JACKSONVILLE
RS: Jaguars lead series, 1-0
2000—Jaguars, 44-10 (J)
(RS Pts.—Jaguars 44, Cardinals 10)

***ARIZONA vs. KANSAS CITY**
RS: Chiefs lead series, 5-1-1
1970—Tie, 6-6 (KC)
1974—Chiefs, 17-13 (StL)
1980—Chiefs, 21-13 (StL)
1983—Chiefs, 38-14 (KC)
1986—Cardinals, 23-14 (StL)
1995—Chiefs, 24-3 (A)
1998—Chiefs, 34-24 (KC)
(RS Pts.—Chiefs 154, Cardinals 96)
**Franchise known as Phoenix prior to 1994 and in St. Louis prior to 1988*

***ARIZONA vs. MIAMI**
RS: Dolphins lead series, 8-0
1972—Dolphins, 31-10 (M)
1977—Dolphins, 55-14 (StL)
1978—Dolphins, 24-10 (M)
1981—Dolphins, 20-7 (StL)
1984—Dolphins, 36-28 (StL)
1990—Dolphins, 23-3 (M)
1996—Dolphins, 38-10 (A)
1999—Dolphins, 19-16 (M)
(RS Pts.—Dolphins 246, Cardinals 98)
**Franchise known as Phoenix prior to 1994 and in St. Louis prior to 1988*

***ARIZONA vs. MINNESOTA**
RS: Series tied, 8-8
PS: Vikings lead series, 2-0
1963—Cardinals, 56-14 (M)
1967—Cardinals, 34-24 (M)
1969—Vikings, 27-10 (StL)
1972—Cardinals, 19-17 (M)
1974—Vikings, 28-24 (StL)
**Vikings, 30-14 (M)
1977—Cardinals, 27-7 (M)
1979—Cardinals, 37-7 (StL)
1981—Cardinals, 30-17 (StL)
1983—Cardinals, 41-31 (StL)
1991—Vikings, 34-7 (M)
Vikings, 28-0 (P)
1994—Cardinals, 17-7 (A)
1995—Vikings, 30-24 (A) OT
1996—Vikings, 41-17 (M)
1997—Vikings, 20-19 (A)
1998—**Vikings, 41-21 (M)
2000—Vikings, 31-14 (M)
(RS Pts.—Cardinals 376, Vikings 363)
(PS Pts.—Vikings 71, Cardinals 35)
**Franchise known as Phoenix prior to 1994 and in St. Louis prior to 1988*
***NFC Divisional Playoff*

***ARIZONA vs. **NEW ENGLAND**
RS: Cardinals lead series, 6-4
1970—Cardinals, 31-0 (StL)
1975—Cardinals, 24-17 (StL)
1978—Patriots, 16-6 (StL)
1981—Cardinals, 27-20 (NE)
1984—Cardinals, 33-10 (NE)
1990—Cardinals, 34-14 (P)
1991—Cardinals, 24-10 (P)
1993—Patriots, 23-21 (P)
1996—Patriots, 31-0 (NE)
1999—Patriots, 27-3 (A)
(RS Pts.—Cardinals 203, Patriots 168)
**Franchise known as Phoenix prior to 1994 and in St. Louis prior to 1988*
***Franchise in Boston prior to 1971*

***ARIZONA vs. NEW ORLEANS**
RS: Cardinals lead series, 12-11
1967—Cardinals, 31-20 (StL)
1968—Cardinals, 21-20 (NO)
Cardinals, 31-17 (StL)
1969—Saints, 51-42 (StL)
1970—Cardinals, 24-17 (StL)
1974—Saints, 14-0 (NO)
1977—Cardinals, 49-31 (StL)
1980—Cardinals, 40-7 (NO)
1981—Cardinals, 30-3 (StL)
1982—Cardinals, 21-7 (NO)
1983—Saints, 28-17 (NO)
1984—Saints, 34-24 (NO)
1985—Cardinals, 28-16 (StL)
1986—Saints, 16-7 (StL)
1987—Cardinals, 24-19 (StL)
1990—Saints, 28-7 (NO)
1991—Saints, 27-3 (P)
1992—Saints, 30-21 (P)
1993—Saints, 20-17 (P)
1996—Cardinals, 28-14 (NO)
1997—Saints, 27-10 (NO)
1998—Cardinals, 19-17 (A)
2000—Saints, 21-10 (A)
(RS Pts.—Cardinals 504, Saints 484)
**Franchise known as Phoenix prior to 1994 and in St. Louis prior to 1988*

***ARIZONA vs. N.Y. GIANTS**
RS: Giants lead series, 75-39-2
1926—Giants, 20-0 (NY)
1927—Giants, 28-7 (NY)
1929—Giants, 24-21 (NY)
1930—Giants, 25-12 (NY)
Giants, 13-7 (C)
1935—Cardinals, 14-13 (NY)
1936—Giants, 14-6 (NY)
1938—Giants, 6-0 (NY)
1939—Giants, 17-7 (NY)
1941—Cardinals, 10-7 (NY)
1942—Giants, 21-7 (NY)
1943—Giants, 24-13 (NY)
1946—Giants, 28-24 (NY)
1947—Giants, 35-31 (NY)
1948—Cardinals, 63-35 (NY)
1949—Giants, 41-38 (C)
1950—Cardinals, 17-3 (C)
Giants, 51-21 (NY)
1951—Giants, 28-17 (NY)
Giants, 10-0 (C)
1952—Cardinals, 24-23 (NY)
Giants, 28-6 (C)
1953—Giants, 21-7 (NY)
Giants, 23-20 (C)
1954—Giants, 41-10 (C)
Giants, 31-17 (NY)
1955—Cardinals, 28-17 (C)
Giants, 10-0 (NY)
1956—Cardinals, 35-27 (C)
Giants, 23-10 (NY)
1957—Giants, 27-14 (NY)
Giants, 28-21 (C)
1958—Giants, 37-7 (Buffalo)
Cardinals, 23-6 (NY)
1959—Giants, 9-3 (NY)
Giants, 30-20 (Minn)
1960—Giants, 35-14 (StL)
Cardinals, 20-13 (NY)
1961—Cardinals, 21-10 (NY)
Giants, 24-9 (StL)
1962—Giants, 31-14 (StL)
Giants, 31-28 (NY)
1963—Giants, 38-21 (StL)
Cardinals, 24-17 (NY)
1964—Giants, 34-17 (NY)
Tie, 10-10 (StL)
1965—Giants, 14-10 (NY)
Giants, 28-15 (StL)
1966—Cardinals, 24-19 (StL)
Cardinals, 20-17 (NY)
1967—Giants, 37-20 (StL)
Giants, 37-14 (NY)
1968—Cardinals, 28-21 (NY)
1969—Cardinals, 42-17 (StL)
Giants, 49-6 (NY)
1970—Giants, 35-17 (NY)
Giants, 34-17 (StL)
1971—Giants, 21-20 (StL)
Cardinals, 24-7 (NY)
1972—Giants, 27-21 (NY)
Giants, 13-7 (StL)
1973—Cardinals, 35-27 (StL)
Giants, 24-13 (New Haven)
1974—Cardinals, 23-21 (New Haven)
Cardinals, 26-14 (StL)
1975—Cardinals, 26-14 (StL)
Cardinals, 20-13 (NY)
1976—Cardinals, 27-21 (StL)
Cardinals, 17-14 (NY)
1977—Cardinals, 28-0 (StL)
Giants, 27-7 (NY)
1978—Cardinals, 20-10 (StL)
Giants, 17-0 (NY)
1979—Cardinals, 27-14 (NY)
Cardinals, 29-20 (StL)
1980—Giants, 41-35 (StL)
Cardinals, 23-7 (NY)
1981—Giants, 34-14 (NY)
Giants, 20-10 (StL)
1982—Cardinals, 24-21 (StL)
1983—Tie, 20-20 (StL) OT
Cardinals, 10-6 (NY)
1984—Giants, 16-10 (NY)
Cardinals, 31-21 (StL)
1985—Giants, 27-17 (NY)
Giants, 34-3 (StL)
1986—Giants, 13-6 (StL)
Giants, 27-7 (NY)
1987—Giants, 30-7 (NY)
Cardinals, 27-24 (StL)
1988—Cardinals, 24-17 (P)
Giants, 44-7 (NY)
1989—Giants, 35-7 (NY)
Giants, 20-13 (P)
1990—Giants, 20-19 (NY)
Giants, 24-21 (P)
1991—Giants, 20-9 (NY)
Giants, 21-14 (P)
1992—Giants, 31-21 (NY)
Cardinals, 19-0 (P)
1993—Giants, 19-17 (NY)
Cardinals, 17-6 (P)
1994—Giants, 20-17 (A)
Cardinals, 10-9 (NY)
1995—Giants, 27-21 (NY) OT

ALL-TIME TEAM VS. TEAM RESULTS

Giants, 10-6 (A)
1996—Giants, 16-8 (NY)
Cardinals, 31-23 (A)
1997—Giants, 27-13 (A)
Giants, 19-10 (NY)
1998—Giants, 34-7 (NY)
Giants, 23-19 (A)
1999—Cardinals, 14-3 (A)
Cardinals, 34-24 (NY)
2000—Giants, 21-16 (NY)
Giants, 31-7 (A)
(RS Pts.—Giants 2,564, Cardinals 1,966)
**Franchise known as Phoenix prior to 1994, in St. Louis prior to 1988, and in Chicago prior to 1960*

***ARIZONA vs. N.Y. JETS**
RS: Jets lead series, 3-2
1971—Cardinals, 17-10 (StL)
1975—Cardinals, 37-6 (NY)
1978—Jets, 23-10 (NY)
1996—Jets, 31-21 (A)
1999—Jets, 12-7 (NY)
(RS Pts.—Cardinals 92, Jets 82)
**Franchise known as Phoenix prior to 1994 and in St. Louis prior to 1988*

***ARIZONA vs. **OAKLAND**
RS: Raiders lead series, 3-1
1973—Raiders, 17-10 (StL)
1983—Cardinals, 34-24 (LA)
1989—Raiders, 16-14 (LA)
1998—Raiders, 23-20 (A)
(RS Pts.—Raiders 80, Cardinals 78)
**Franchise known as Phoenix prior to 1994 and in St. Louis prior to 1988*
***Franchise in Los Angeles from 1982-1994*

***ARIZONA vs. PHILADELPHIA**
RS: Cardinals lead series, 51-50-5
PS: Series tied, 1-1
1935—Cardinals, 12-3 (C)
1936—Cardinals, 13-0 (C)
1937—Tie, 6-6 (P)
1938—Eagles, 7-0 (Erie, Pa.)
1941—Eagles, 21-14 (P)
1945—Eagles, 21-6 (P)
1947—Cardinals, 45-21 (P)
**Cardinals, 28-21 (C)
1948—Cardinals, 21-14 (C)
**Eagles, 7-0 (P)
1949—Eagles, 28-3 (P)
1950—Eagles, 45-7 (C)
Cardinals, 14-10 (P)
1951—Eagles, 17-14 (C)
1952—Eagles, 10-7 (P)
Cardinals, 28-22 (C)
1953—Eagles, 56-17 (C)
Eagles, 38-0 (P)
1954—Eagles, 35-16 (C)
Eagles, 30-14 (P)
1955—Tie, 24-24 (C)
Eagles, 27-3 (P)
1956—Cardinals, 20-6 (P)
Cardinals, 28-17 (C)
1957—Eagles, 38-21 (C)
Cardinals, 31-27 (P)
1958—Tie, 21-21 (C)
Eagles, 49-21 (P)
1959—Eagles, 28-24 (Minn)
Eagles, 27-17 (P)
1960—Eagles, 31-27 (P)
Eagles, 20-6 (StL)
1961—Cardinals, 30-27 (P)
Eagles, 20-7 (StL)
1962—Cardinals, 27-21 (P)
Cardinals, 45-35 (StL)
1963—Cardinals, 28-24 (P)
Cardinals, 38-14 (StL)
1964—Cardinals, 38-13 (P)
Cardinals, 36-34 (StL)
1965—Eagles, 34-27 (P)
Eagles, 28-24 (StL)
1966—Cardinals, 16-13 (StL)
Cardinals, 41-10 (P)
1967—Cardinals, 48-14 (StL)
1968—Cardinals, 45-17 (P)
1969—Eagles, 34-30 (StL)
1970—Cardinals, 35-20 (P)
Cardinals, 23-14 (StL)
1971—Eagles, 37-20 (StL)
Eagles, 19-7 (P)
1972—Tie, 6-6 (P)
Cardinals, 24-23 (StL)
1973—Cardinals, 34-23 (P)
Eagles, 27-24 (StL)
1974—Cardinals, 7-3 (StL)
Cardinals, 13-3 (P)
1975—Cardinals, 31-20 (StL)
Cardinals, 24-23 (P)
1976—Cardinals, 33-14 (StL)
Cardinals, 17-14 (P)
1977—Cardinals, 21-17 (P)
Cardinals, 21-16 (StL)
1978—Cardinals, 16-10 (P)
Eagles, 14-10 (StL)
1979—Eagles, 24-20 (StL)
Eagles, 16-13 (P)
1980—Cardinals, 24-14 (StL)
Eagles, 17-3 (P)
1981—Eagles, 52-10 (StL)
Eagles, 38-0 (P)
1982—Cardinals, 23-20 (P)
1983—Cardinals, 14-11 (P)
Cardinals, 31-7 (StL)
1984—Cardinals, 34-14 (P)
Cardinals, 17-16 (StL)
1985—Eagles, 30-7 (P)
Eagles, 24-14 (StL)
1986—Cardinals, 13-10 (StL)
Tie, 10-10 (P) OT
1987—Eagles, 28-23 (StL)
Cardinals, 31-19 (P)
1988—Eagles, 31-21 (P)
Eagles, 23-17 (Phx)
1989—Eagles, 17-5 (Phx)
Eagles, 31-14 (P)
1990—Cardinals, 23-21 (P)
Eagles, 23-21 (Phx)
1991—Cardinals, 26-10 (P)
Eagles, 34-14 (Phx)
1992—Eagles, 31-14 (Phx)
Eagles, 7-3 (P)
1993—Eagles, 23-17 (P)
Cardinals, 16-3 (Phx)
1994—Eagles, 17-7 (P)
Cardinals, 12-6 (A)
1995—Eagles, 31-19 (A)
Eagles, 21-20 (P)
1996—Cardinals, 36-30 (A)
Eagles, 29-19 (P)
1997—Eagles, 13-10 (P) OT
Cardinals, 31-21 (A)
1998—Cardinals, 17-3 (A)
Cardinals, 20-17 (P) OT
1999—Cardinals, 25-24 (P)
Cardinals, 21-17 (A)
2000—Eagles, 33-14 (A)
Eagles, 34-9 (P)
(RS Pts.—Eagles 2,240, Cardinals 2,064)
(PS Pts.—Eagles 28, Cardinals 28)
**Franchise known as Phoenix prior to 1994, in St. Louis prior to 1988, and in Chicago prior to 1960*
***NFL Championship*

***ARIZONA vs. **PITTSBURGH**
RS: Steelers lead series, 30-22-3
1933—Pirates, 14-13 (C)
1935—Pirates, 17-13 (P)
1936—Cardinals, 14-6 (C)
1937—Cardinals, 13-7 (P)
1939—Cardinals, 10-0 (P)
1940—Tie, 7-7 (P)
1942—Steelers, 19-3 (P)
1945—Steelers, 23-0 (P)
1946—Steelers, 14-7 (P)
1948—Cardinals, 24-7 (P)
1950—Steelers, 28-17 (C)
Steelers, 28-7 (P)
1951—Steelers, 28-14 (C)
1952—Steelers, 34-28 (C)
Steelers, 17-14 (P)
1953—Steelers, 31-28 (P)
Steelers, 21-17 (C)
1954—Cardinals, 17-14 (C)
Steelers, 20-17 (P)
1955—Steelers, 14-7 (P)
Cardinals, 27-13 (C)
1956—Steelers, 14-7 (P)
Cardinals, 38-27 (C)
1957—Steelers, 29-20 (P)
Steelers, 27-2 (C)
1958—Steelers, 27-20 (C)
Steelers, 38-21 (P)
1959—Cardinals, 45-24 (C)
Steelers, 35-20 (P)
1960—Steelers, 27-14 (P)
Cardinals, 38-7 (StL)
1961—Steelers, 30-27 (P)
Cardinals, 20-0 (StL)
1962—Steelers, 26-17 (StL)
Steelers, 19-7 (P)
1963—Steelers, 23-10 (P)
Cardinals, 24-23 (StL)
1964—Cardinals, 34-30 (StL)
Cardinals, 21-20 (P)
1965—Cardinals, 20-7 (P)
Cardinals, 21-17 (StL)
1966—Steelers, 30-9 (P)
Cardinals, 6-3 (StL)
1967—Cardinals, 28-14 (P)
Tie, 14-14 (StL)
1968—Tie, 28-28 (StL)
Cardinals, 20-10 (P)
1969—Cardinals, 27-14 (P)
Cardinals, 47-10 (StL)
1972—Steelers, 25-19 (StL)
1979—Steelers, 24-21 (StL)
1985—Steelers, 23-10 (P)
1988—Cardinals, 31-14 (Phx)
1994—Cardinals, 20-17 (A) OT
1997—Steelers, 26-20 (A) OT
(RS Pts.—Steelers 1,064, Cardinals 1,023)
**Franchise known as Phoenix prior to 1994, in St. Louis prior to 1988, and in Chicago prior to 1960*
***Steelers known as Pirates prior to 1941*

***ARIZONA vs. **ST. LOUIS**
RS: Rams lead series, 23-21-2
PS: Rams lead series, 1-0
1937—Cardinals, 6-0 (Clev)
Cardinals, 13-7 (Chi)
1938—Cardinals, 7-6 (Clev)
Cardinals, 31-17 (Chi)
1939—Rams, 24-0 (Chi)
Rams, 14-0 (Clev)
1940—Rams, 26-14 (Clev)
Cardinals, 17-7 (Chi)
1941—Rams, 10-6 (Clev)
Cardinals, 7-0 (Chi)
1942—Cardinals, 7-0 (Buffalo)
Rams, 7-3 (Clev)
1945—Rams, 21-0 (Clev)
Rams, 35-21 (Chi)
1946—Cardinals, 34-10 (Chi)
Rams, 17-14 (LA)
1947—Rams, 27-7 (LA)
Cardinals, 17-10 (Chi)
1948—Cardinals, 27-22 (LA)
Cardinals, 27-24 (Chi)
1949—Tie, 28-28 (Chi)
Cardinals, 31-27 (LA)
1951—Rams, 45-21 (LA)
1953—Tie, 24-24 (Chi)
1954—Rams, 28-17 (LA)
1958—Rams, 20-14 (Chi)
1960—Cardinals, 43-21 (LA)
1965—Rams, 27-3 (StL)
1968—Rams, 24-13 (StL)
1970—Rams, 34-13 (LA)
1972—Cardinals, 24-14 (StL)
1975—***Rams, 35-23 (LA)
1976—Cardinals, 30-28 (LA)
1979—Rams, 21-0 (LA)
1980—Rams, 21-13 (StL)
1984—Rams, 16-13 (StL)
1985—Rams, 46-14 (LA)
1986—Rams, 16-10 (StL)
1987—Rams, 27-24 (StL)
1988—Cardinals, 41-27 (LA)
1989—Rams, 37-14 (LA)
1991—Cardinals, 24-14 (LA)
1992—Cardinals, 20-14 (LA)
1993—Cardinals, 38-10 (P)
1994—Rams, 14-12 (LA)
1996—Cardinals, 31-28 (A) OT
1998—Cardinals, 20-17 (StL)
(RS Pts.—Rams 912, Cardinals 793)
(PS Pts.—Rams 35, Cardinals 23)
**Franchise known as Phoenix prior to 1994, in St. Louis prior to 1988, and in Chicago prior to 1960*
***Franchise in Los Angeles prior to 1995 and in Cleveland prior to 1946*
****NFC Divisional Playoff*

***ARIZONA vs. SAN DIEGO**
RS: Chargers lead series, 6-2
1971—Chargers, 20-17 (SD)
1976—Chargers, 43-24 (SD)
1983—Cardinals, 44-14 (StL)
1987—Chargers, 28-24 (SD)
1989—Chargers, 24-13 (P)
1992—Chargers, 27-21 (P)
1995—Chargers, 28-25 (SD)
1998—Cardinals, 16-13 (A)
(RS Pts.—Chargers 197, Cardinals 184)
**Franchise known as Phoenix prior to 1994, in St. Louis prior to 1988,*

***ARIZONA vs. SAN FRANCISCO**
RS: 49ers lead series, 12-9
1951—Cardinals, 27-21 (SF)
1957—Cardinals, 20-10 (SF)
1962—49ers, 24-17 (StL)
1964—Cardinals, 23-13 (SF)
1968—49ers, 35-17 (SF)
1971—49ers, 26-14 (StL)
1974—Cardinals, 34-9 (SF)
1976—Cardinals, 23-20 (StL) OT
1978—Cardinals, 16-10 (SF)
1979—Cardinals, 13-10 (StL)
1980—49ers, 24-21 (SF) OT
1982—49ers, 31-20 (StL)
1983—49ers, 42-27 (StL)
1986—49ers, 43-17 (SF)
1987—49ers, 34-28 (SF)
1988—Cardinals, 24-23 (P)
1991—49ers, 14-10 (SF)
1992—Cardinals, 24-14 (P)
1993—49ers, 28-14 (SF)
1999—49ers, 24-10 (A)
2000—49ers, 27-20 (SF)
(RS Pts.—49ers 482, Cardinals 419)
**Franchise known as Phoenix prior to 1994, in St. Louis prior to 1988, and in Chicago prior to 1960*

***ARIZONA vs. SEATTLE**
RS: Cardinals lead series, 5-1
1976—Cardinals, 30-24 (S)
1983—Cardinals, 33-28 (StL)
1989—Cardinals, 34-24 (S)
1993—Cardinals, 30-27 (S) OT
1995—Cardinals, 20-14 (A) OT
1998—Seahawks, 33-14 (S)
(RS Pts.—Cardinals 161, Seahawks 150)
**Franchise known as Phoenix prior to 1994 and in St. Louis prior to 1988*

***ARIZONA vs. TAMPA BAY**
RS: Series tied, 7-7
1977—Buccaneers, 17-7 (TB)
1981—Buccaneers, 20-10 (TB)
1983—Cardinals, 34-27 (TB)
1985—Buccaneers, 16-0 (TB)
1986—Cardinals, 30-19 (TB)
Cardinals, 21-17 (StL)

1987—Cardinals, 31-28 (StL)
Cardinals, 31-14 (TB)
1988—Cardinals, 30-24 (TB)
1989—Buccaneers, 14-13 (P)
1992—Buccaneers, 23-7 (TB)
Buccaneers, 7-3 (P)
1996—Cardinals, 13-9 (A)
1997—Buccaneers, 19-18 (TB)
(RS Pts.—Buccaneers 254, Cardinals 248)
Franchise known as Phoenix prior to 1994 and in St. Louis prior to 1988

***ARIZONA vs. **TENNESSEE**
RS: Cardinals lead series, 4-3
1970—Cardinals, 44-0 (StL)
1974—Cardinals, 31-27 (H)
1979—Cardinals, 24-17 (H)
1985—Oilers, 20-10 (StL)
1988—Oilers, 38-20 (H)
1994—Cardinals, 30-12 (H)
1997—Oilers, 41-14 (A)
(RS Pts.—Cardinals 173, Titans 155)
**Franchise known as Phoenix prior to 1994 and in St. Louis prior to 1988*
***Franchise in Houston prior to 1997; known as Oilers prior to 1999*

***ARIZONA vs. **WASHINGTON**
RS: Redskins lead series, 67-44-2
1932—Cardinals, 9-0 (B)
Braves, 8-6 (C)
1933—Redskins, 10-0 (C)
Tie, 0-0 (B)
1934—Redskins, 9-0 (B)
1935—Cardinals, 6-0 (B)
1936—Redskins, 13-10 (B)
1937—Cardinals, 21-14 (W)
1939—Redskins, 28-7 (W)
1940—Redskins, 28-21 (W)
1942—Redskins, 28-0 (W)
1943—Redskins, 13-7 (W)
1945—Redskins, 24-21 (W)
1947—Redskins, 45-21 (W)
1949—Cardinals, 38-7 (C)
1950—Cardinals, 38-28 (W)
1951—Redskins, 7-3 (C)
Redskins, 20-17 (W)
1952—Redskins, 23-7 (C)
Cardinals, 17-6 (W)
1953—Redskins, 24-13 (C)
Redskins, 28-17 (W)
1954—Cardinals, 38-16 (C)
Redskins, 37-20 (W)
1955—Cardinals, 24-10 (W)
Redskins, 31-0 (C)
1956—Cardinals, 31-3 (W)
Redskins, 17-14 (C)
1957—Redskins, 37-14 (C)
Cardinals, 44-14 (W)
1958—Cardinals, 37-10 (C)
Redskins, 45-31 (W)
1959—Cardinals, 49-21 (C)
Redskins, 23-14 (W)
1960—Cardinals, 44-7 (StL)
Cardinals, 26-14 (W)
1961—Cardinals, 24-0 (W)
Cardinals, 38-24 (StL)
1962—Redskins, 24-14 (W)
Tie, 17-17 (StL)
1963—Cardinals, 21-7 (W)
Cardinals, 24-20 (StL)
1964—Cardinals, 23-17 (W)
Cardinals, 38-24 (StL)
1965—Cardinals, 37-16 (W)
Redskins, 24-20 (StL)
1966—Cardinals, 23-7 (StL)
Redskins, 26-20 (W)
1967—Cardinals, 27-21 (W)
1968—Cardinals, 41-14 (StL)
1969—Redskins, 33-17 (W)
1970—Cardinals, 27-17 (StL)
Redskins, 28-27 (W)
1971—Redskins, 24-17 (StL)
Redskins, 20-0 (W)
1972—Redskins, 24-10 (W)
Redskins, 33-3 (StL)
1973—Cardinals, 34-27 (StL)
Redskins, 31-13 (W)
1974—Cardinals, 17-10 (W)
Cardinals, 23-20 (StL)
1975—Redskins, 27-17 (W)
Cardinals, 20-17 (StL) OT
1976—Redskins, 20-10 (W)
Redskins, 16-10 (StL)
1977—Redskins, 24-14 (W)
Redskins, 26-20 (StL)
1978—Redskins, 28-10 (StL)
Cardinals, 27-17 (W)
1979—Redskins, 17-7 (StL)
Redskins, 30-28 (W)
1980—Redskins, 23-0 (W)
Redskins, 31-7 (StL)
1981—Cardinals, 40-30 (StL)
Redskins, 42-21 (W)
1982—Redskins, 12-7 (StL)
Redskins, 28-0 (W)
1983—Redskins, 38-14 (StL)
Redskins, 45-7 (W)
1984—Cardinals, 26-24 (StL)
Redskins, 29-27 (W)
1985—Redskins, 27-10 (W)
Redskins, 27-16 (StL)
1986—Redskins, 28-21 (W)
Redskins, 20-17 (StL)
1987—Redskins, 28-21 (W)
Redskins, 34-17 (StL)
1988—Cardinals, 30-21 (P)
Redskins, 33-17 (W)
1989—Redskins, 30-28 (W)
Redskins, 29-10 (P)
1990—Redskins, 31-0 (W)
Redskins, 38-10 (P)
1991—Redskins, 34-0 (W)
Redskins, 20-14 (P)
1992—Cardinals, 27-24 (P)
Redskins, 41-3 (W)
1993—Cardinals, 17-10 (W)
Cardinals, 36-6 (P)
1994—Cardinals, 19-16 (W) OT
Cardinals, 17-15 (A)
1995—Redskins, 27-7 (W)
Cardinals, 24-20 (A)
1996—Cardinals, 37-34 (W) OT
Cardinals, 27-26 (A)
1997—Redskins, 19-13 (W) OT
Redskins, 38-28 (A)
1998—Cardinals, 29-27 (A)
Cardinals, 45-42 (W)
1999—Redskins, 24-10 (A)
Redskins, 28-3 (W)
2000—Cardinals, 16-15 (A)
Redskins, 20-3 (W)
(RS Pts.—Redskins 2,512, Cardinals 2,104)
**Franchise known as Phoenix prior to 1994, in St. Louis prior to 1988, and in Chicago prior to 1960*
***Franchise in Boston prior to 1937 and known as Braves prior to 1933*

ATLANTA vs. ARIZONA
RS: Cardinals lead series, 13-7;
See Arizona vs. Atlanta

ATLANTA vs. BALTIMORE
RS: Ravens lead series, 1-0
1999—Ravens, 19-13 (A) OT
(RS Pts.—Ravens 19, Falcons 13)

ATLANTA vs. BUFFALO
RS: Bills lead series, 4-3
1973—Bills, 17-6 (A)
1977—Bills, 3-0 (B)
1980—Falcons, 30-14 (B)
1983—Falcons, 31-14 (A)
1989—Falcons, 30-28 (A)
1992—Bills, 41-14 (B)
1995—Bills, 23-17 (B)
(RS Pts.—Bills 140, Falcons 128)

ATLANTA vs. CAROLINA
RS: Falcons lead series, 7-5
1995—Falcons, 23-20 (A) OT
Panthers, 21-17 (C)
1996—Panthers, 29-6 (C)
Falcons, 20-17 (A)
1997—Panthers, 9-6 (A)
Panthers, 21-12 (C)
1998—Falcons, 19-14 (C)
Falcons, 51-23 (A)
1999—Falcons, 27-20 (A)
Panthers, 34-28 (C)
2000—Falcons, 15-10 (C)
Falcons, 13-12 (A)
(RS Pts.—Falcons 237, Panthers 230)

ATLANTA vs. CHICAGO
RS: Falcons lead series, 10-9
1966—Bears, 23-6 (C)
1967—Bears, 23-14 (A)
1968—Falcons, 16-13 (C)
1969—Falcons, 48-31 (A)
1970—Bears, 23-14 (A)
1972—Falcons, 37-21 (C)
1973—Falcons, 46-6 (A)
1974—Falcons, 13-10 (A)
1976—Falcons, 10-0 (C)
1977—Falcons, 16-10 (C)
1978—Bears, 13-7 (C)
1980—Falcons, 28-17 (A)
1983—Falcons, 20-17 (C)
1985—Bears, 36-0 (C)
1986—Bears, 13-10 (A)
1990—Bears, 30-24 (C)
1992—Bears, 41-31 (C)
1993—Bears, 6-0 (C)
1998—Falcons, 20-13 (A)
(RS Pts.—Falcons 360, Bears 346)

ATLANTA vs. CINCINNATI
RS: Bengals lead series, 7-2
1971—Falcons, 9-6 (C)
1975—Bengals, 21-14 (A)
1978—Bengals, 37-7 (C)
1981—Bengals, 30-28 (A)
1984—Bengals, 35-14 (C)
1987—Bengals, 16-10 (A)
1990—Falcons, 38-17 (A)
1993—Bengals, 21-17 (C)
1996—Bengals, 41-31 (C)
(RS Pts.—Bengals 224, Falcons 168)

ATLANTA vs. CLEVELAND
RS: Browns lead series, 8-2
1966—Browns, 49-17 (A)
1968—Browns, 30-7 (C)
1971—Falcons, 31-14 (C)
1976—Browns, 20-17 (A)
1978—Browns, 24-16 (A)
1981—Browns, 28-17 (C)
1984—Browns, 23-7 (A)
1987—Browns, 38-3 (C)
1990—Browns, 13-10 (C)
1993—Falcons, 17-14 (A)
(RS Pts.—Browns 253, Falcons 142)

ATLANTA vs. DALLAS
RS: Cowboys lead series, 12-6
PS: Cowboys lead series, 2-0
1966—Cowboys, 47-14 (A)
1967—Cowboys, 37-7 (D)
1969—Cowboys, 24-17 (A)
1970—Cowboys, 13-0 (D)
1974—Cowboys, 24-0 (A)
1976—Falcons, 17-10 (A)
1978—*Cowboys, 27-20 (D)
1980—*Cowboys, 30-27 (A)
1985—Cowboys, 24-10 (D)
1986—Falcons, 37-35 (D)
1987—Falcons, 21-10 (D)
1988—Cowboys, 26-20 (D)
1989—Falcons 27-21 (A)
1990—Falcons, 26-7 (A)
1991—Cowboys, 31-27 (D)
1992—Cowboys, 41-17 (A)
1993—Falcons, 27-14 (A)
1995—Cowboys, 28-13 (A)
1996—Cowboys, 32-28 (D)
1999—Cowboys, 24-7 (D)
(RS Pts.—Cowboys 448, Falcons 315)
(PS Pts.—Cowboys 57, Falcons 47)
**NFC Divisional Playoff*

ATLANTA vs. DENVER
RS: Broncos lead series, 7-3
PS: Broncos lead series, 1-0
1970—Broncos, 24-10 (D)
1972—Falcons, 23-20 (A)
1975—Falcons, 35-21 (A)
1979—Broncos, 20-17 (A) OT
1982—Falcons, 34-27 (D)
1985—Broncos, 44-28 (A)
1988—Broncos, 30-14 (D)
1994—Broncos, 32-28 (D)
1997—Broncos, 29-21 (A)
1998—*Broncos, 34-19 (Miami)
2000—Broncos, 42-14 (D)
(RS Pts.—Broncos 289, Falcons 224)
(PS Pts.—Broncos 34, Falcons 19)
**Super Bowl XXXIII*

ATLANTA vs. DETROIT
RS: Lions lead series, 21-7
1966—Lions, 28-10 (D)
1967—Lions, 24-3 (D)
1968—Lions, 24-7 (A)
1969—Lions, 27-21 (D)
1971—Lions, 41-38 (D)
1972—Lions, 26-23 (A)
1973—Lions, 31-6 (D)
1975—Lions, 17-14 (A)
1976—Lions, 24-10 (D)
1977—Falcons, 17-6 (A)
1978—Falcons, 14-0 (A)
1979—Lions, 24-23 (D)
1980—Falcons, 43-28 (A)
1983—Falcons, 30-14 (D)
1984—Lions, 27-24 (A) OT
1985—Lions, 28-27 (A)
1986—Falcons, 20-6 (D)
1987—Lions, 30-13 (A)
1988—Lions, 31-17 (D)
1989—Lions, 31-24 (A)
1990—Lions, 21-14 (D)
1993—Lions, 30-13 (D)
1994—Lions, 31-28 (D) OT
1995—Falcons, 34-22 (A)
1996—Lions, 28-24 (D)
1997—Lions, 28-17 (D)
1998—Falcons, 24-17 (D)
2000—Lions, 13-10 (D)
(RS Pts.—Lions 657, Falcons 548)

ATLANTA vs. GREEN BAY
RS: Packers lead series, 10-9
PS: Packers lead series, 1-0
1966—Packers, 56-3 (Mil)
1967—Packers, 23-0 (Mil)
1968—Packers, 38-7 (A)
1969—Packers, 28-10 (GB)
1970—Packers, 27-24 (GB)
1971—Falcons, 28-21 (A)
1972—Falcons, 10-9 (Mil)
1974—Falcons, 10-3 (A)
1975—Packers, 22-13 (GB)
1976—Packers, 24-20 (A)
1979—Falcons, 25-7 (A)
1981—Falcons, 31-17 (GB)
1982—Packers, 38-7 (A)
1983—Falcons, 47-41 (A) OT
1988—Falcons, 20-0 (A)
1989—Packers, 23-21 (Mil)
1991—Falcons, 35-31 (A)
1992—Falcons, 24-10 (A)
1994—Packers, 21-17 (Mil)
1995—*Packers, 37-20 (GB)
(RS Pts.—Packers 439, Falcons 352)
(PS Pts.—Packers 37, Falcons 20)
**NFC First-Round Playoff*

ATLANTA vs. *INDIANAPOLIS
RS: Colts lead series, 10-1
1966—Colts, 19-7 (A)
1967—Colts, 38-31 (B)

ALL-TIME TEAM VS. TEAM RESULTS

Colts, 49-7 (A)
1968—Colts, 28-20 (A)
Colts, 44-0 (B)
1969—Colts, 21-14 (A)
Colts, 13-6 (B)
1974—Colts, 17-7 (A)
1986—Colts, 28-23 (A)
1989—Colts, 13-9 (I)
1998—Falcons, 28-21 (A)
(RS Pts.—Colts 291, Falcons 152)
Franchise in Baltimore prior to 1984

ATLANTA vs. JACKSONVILLE
RS: Jaguars lead series, 2-0
1996—Jaguars, 19-17 (J)
1999—Jaguars, 30-7 (A)
(RS Pts.—Jaguars 49, Falcons 24)

ATLANTA vs. KANSAS CITY
RS: Chiefs lead series, 4-1
1972—Chiefs, 17-14 (A)
1985—Chiefs, 38-10 (KC)
1991—Chiefs, 14-3 (KC)
1994—Chiefs, 30-10 (A)
2000—Falcons, 29-13 (A)
(RS Pts.—Chiefs 112, Falcons 66)

ATLANTA vs. MIAMI
RS: Dolphins lead series, 6-2
1970—Dolphins, 20-7 (A)
1974—Dolphins, 42-7 (M)
1980—Dolphins, 20-17 (A)
1983—Dolphins, 31-24 (M)
1986—Falcons, 20-14 (M)
1992—Dolphins, 21-17 (M)
1995—Dolphins, 21-20 (M)
1998—Falcons, 38-16 (A)
(RS Pts.—Dolphins 185, Falcons 150)

ATLANTA vs. MINNESOTA
RS: Vikings lead series, 13-6
PS: Series tied, 1-1
1966—Falcons, 20-13 (M)
1967—Falcons, 21-20 (A)
1968—Vikings, 47-7 (M)
1969—Falcons, 10-3 (A)
1970—Vikings, 37-7 (A)
1971—Vikings, 24-7 (M)
1973—Falcons, 20-14 (A)
1974—Vikings, 23-10 (M)
1975—Vikings, 38-0 (M)
1977—Vikings, 14-7 (A)
1980—Vikings, 24-23 (M)
1981—Falcons, 31-30 (A)
1982—*Vikings, 30-24 (M)
1984—Vikings, 27-20 (M)
1985—Falcons, 14-13 (A)
1987—Vikings, 24-13 (M)
1989—Vikings, 43-17 (M)
1991—Vikings, 20-19 (A)
1996—Vikings, 23-17 (A)
1998—**Falcons, 30-27 (M) OT
1999—Vikings, 17-14 (A)
(RS Pts.—Vikings 454, Falcons 277)
(PS Pts.—Vikings 57, Falcons 54)
*NFC First-Round Playoff
**NFC Championship*

ATLANTA vs. NEW ENGLAND
RS: Falcons lead series, 6-3
1972—Patriots, 21-20 (NE)
1977—Patriots, 16-10 (A)
1980—Falcons, 37-21 (NE)
1983—Falcons, 24-13 (A)
1986—Patriots, 25-17 (NE)
1989—Falcons, 16-15 (A)
1992—Falcons, 34-0 (A)
1995—Falcons, 30-17 (A)
1998—Falcons, 41-10 (NE)
(RS Pts.—Falcons 229, Patriots 138)

ATLANTA vs. NEW ORLEANS
RS: Falcons lead series, 37-26
PS: Falcons lead series, 1-0
1967—Saints, 27-24 (NO)
1969—Falcons, 45-17 (A)
1970—Falcons, 14-3 (NO)
Falcons, 32-14 (A)
1971—Falcons, 28-6 (A)
Falcons, 24-20 (NO)
1972—Falcons, 21-14 (NO)
Falcons, 36-20 (A)
1973—Falcons, 62-7 (NO)
Falcons, 14-10 (A)
1974—Saints, 14-13 (NO)
Saints, 13-3 (A)
1975—Falcons, 14-7 (A)
Saints, 23-7 (NO)
1976—Saints, 30-0 (NO)
Falcons, 23-20 (A)
1977—Saints, 21-20 (NO)
Falcons, 35-7 (A)
1978—Falcons, 20-17 (NO)
Falcons, 20-17 (A)
1979—Falcons, 40-34 (NO) OT
Saints, 37-6 (A)
1980—Falcons, 41-14 (NO)
Falcons, 31-13 (A)
1981—Falcons, 27-0 (A)
Falcons, 41-10 (NO)
1982—Falcons, 35-0 (A)
Saints, 35-6 (NO)
1983—Saints, 19-17 (A)
Saints, 27-10 (NO)
1984—Falcons, 36-28 (NO)
Saints, 17-13 (A)
1985—Falcons, 31-24 (A)
Falcons, 16-10 (NO)
1986—Falcons, 31-10 (NO)
Saints, 14-9 (A)
1987—Saints, 38-0 (A)
1988—Saints, 29-21 (A)
Saints, 10-9 (NO)
1989—Saints, 20-13 (NO)
Saints, 26-17 (A)
1990—Falcons, 28-27 (A)
Saints, 10-7 (NO)
1991—Saints, 27-6 (A)
Falcons, 23-20 (NO) OT
*Falcons, 27-20 (NO)
1992—Saints, 10-7 (A)
Saints, 22-14 (NO)
1993—Saints, 34-31 (A)
Falcons, 26-15 (NO)
1994—Saints, 33-32 (NO)
Saints, 29-20 (A)
1995—Falcons, 27-24 (NO) OT
Falcons, 19-14 (A)
1996—Falcons, 17-15 (A)
Falcons, 31-15 (NO)
1997—Falcons, 23-17 (NO)
Falcons, 20-3 (A)
1998—Falcons, 31-23 (A)
Falcons, 27-17 (NO)
1999—Falcons, 20-17 (NO)
Falcons, 35-12 (A)
2000—Saints, 21-19 (A)
Saints, 23-7 (NO)
(RS Pts.—Falcons 1,375, Saints 1,150)
(PS Pts.—Falcons 27, Saints 20)
NFC First-Round Playoff

ATLANTA vs. N.Y. GIANTS
RS: Series tied, 7-7
1966—Falcons, 27-16 (NY)
1968—Falcons, 24-21 (A)
1971—Giants, 21-17 (A)
1974—Falcons, 14-7 (New Haven)
1977—Falcons, 17-3 (A)
1978—Falcons, 23-20 (A)
1979—Giants, 24-3 (NY)
1981—Giants, 27-24 (A) OT
1982—Falcons, 16-14 (NY)
1983—Giants, 16-13 (A) OT
1984—Giants, 19-7 (A)
1988—Giants, 23-16 (A)
1998—Falcons, 34-20 (NY)
2000—Giants, 13-6 (A)
(RS Pts.—Giants 244, Falcons 241)

ATLANTA vs. N.Y. JETS
RS: Series tied, 4-4
1973—Falcons, 28-20 (NY)
1980—Jets, 14-7 (A)
1983—Falcons, 27-21 (NY)
1986—Jets, 28-14 (A)
1989—Jets, 27-7 (NY)
1992—Falcons, 20-17 (A)
1995—Falcons, 13-3 (A)
1998—Jets, 28-3 (NY)
(RS Pts.—Jets 158, Falcons 119)

ATLANTA vs. *OAKLAND
RS: Raiders lead series, 7-3
1971—Falcons, 24-13 (A)
1975—Raiders, 37-34 (O) OT
1979—Raiders, 50-19 (O)
1982—Raiders, 38-14 (A)
1985—Raiders, 34-24 (A)
1988—Falcons, 12-6 (LA)
1991—Falcons, 21-17 (A)
1994—Raiders, 30-17 (LA)
1997—Raiders, 36-31 (A)
2000—Raiders, 41-14 (O)
(RS Pts.—Raiders 302, Falcons 210)
Franchise in Los Angeles from 1982-1994

ATLANTA vs. PHILADELPHIA
RS: Eagles lead series, 10-9-1
PS: Falcons lead series, 1-0
1966—Eagles, 23-10 (P)
1967—Eagles, 38-7 (A)
1969—Falcons, 27-3 (P)
1970—Tie, 13-13 (P)
1973—Falcons, 44-27 (P)
1976—Eagles, 14-13 (A)
1978—*Falcons, 14-13 (A)
1979—Falcons, 14-10 (P)
1980—Falcons, 20-17 (P)
1981—Eagles, 16-13 (P)
1983—Eagles, 28-24 (A)
1984—Falcons, 26-10 (A)
1985—Eagles, 23-17 (P) OT
1986—Eagles, 16-0 (A)
1988—Falcons, 27-24 (P)
1990—Eagles, 24-23 (A)
1994—Falcons, 28-21 (A)
1996—Eagles, 33-18 (A)
1997—Falcons, 20-17 (A)
1998—Falcons, 17-12 (A)
2000—Eagles, 38-10 (P)
(RS Pts.—Eagles 407, Falcons 371)
(PS Pts.—Falcons 14, Eagles 13)
NFC First-Round Playoff

ATLANTA vs. PITTSBURGH
RS: Steelers lead series, 11-1
1966—Steelers, 57-33 (A)
1968—Steelers, 41-21 (A)
1970—Falcons, 27-16 (A)
1974—Steelers, 24-17 (P)
1978—Steelers, 31-7 (P)
1981—Steelers, 34-20 (A)
1984—Steelers, 35-10 (P)
1987—Steelers, 28-12 (A)
1990—Steelers, 21-9 (P)
1993—Steelers, 45-17 (A)
1996—Steelers, 20-17 (A)
1999—Steelers, 13-9 (P)
(RS Pts.—Steelers 365, Falcons 199)

ATLANTA vs. *ST. LOUIS
RS: Rams lead series, 43-23-2
1966—Rams, 19-14 (A)
1967—Rams, 31-3 (A)
Rams, 20-3 (LA)
1968—Rams, 27-14 (LA)
Rams, 17-10 (A)
1969—Rams, 17-7 (LA)
Rams, 38-6 (A)
1970—Tie, 10-10 (LA)
Rams, 17-7 (A)
1971—Tie, 20-20 (LA)
Rams, 24-16 (A)
1972—Falcons, 31-3 (A)
Rams, 20-7 (LA)
1973—Rams, 31-0 (LA)
Falcons, 15-13 (A)
1974—Rams, 21-0 (LA)
Rams, 30-7 (A)
1975—Rams, 22-7 (LA)
Rams, 16-7 (A)
1976—Rams, 30-14 (A)
Rams, 59-0 (LA)
1977—Falcons, 17-6 (A)
Rams, 23-7 (LA)
1978—Rams, 10-0 (LA)
Falcons, 15-7 (A)
1979—Rams, 20-14 (LA)
Rams, 34-13 (A)
1980—Falcons, 13-10 (A)
Rams, 20-17 (LA) OT
1981—Rams, 37-35 (A)
Rams, 21-16 (LA)
1982—Falcons, 34-17 (A)
1983—Rams, 27-21 (LA)
Rams, 36-13 (A)
1984—Falcons, 30-28 (LA)
Rams, 24-10 (A)
1985—Rams, 17-6 (LA)
Falcons, 30-14 (A)
1986—Falcons, 26-14 (A)
Rams, 14-7 (LA)
1987—Falcons, 24-20 (A)
Rams, 33-0 (LA)
1988—Rams, 33-0 (A)
Rams, 22-7 (LA)
1989—Rams, 31-21 (A)
Rams, 26-14 (LA)
1990—Rams, 44-24 (LA)
Falcons, 20-13 (A)
1991—Falcons, 31-14 (A)
Falcons, 31-14 (LA)
1992—Falcons, 30-28 (A)
Rams, 38-27 (LA)
1993—Falcons, 30-24 (A)
Falcons, 13-0 (LA)
1994—Falcons, 31-13 (A)
Falcons, 8-5 (LA)
1995—Rams, 21-19 (StL)
Falcons, 31-6 (A)
1996—Rams, 59-16 (StL)
Rams, 34-27 (A)
1997—Falcons, 34-31 (A)
Falcons, 27-21 (StL)
1998—Falcons, 37-15 (A)
Falcons, 21-10 (StL)
1999—Rams, 35-7 (StL)
Rams, 41-13 (A)
2000—Rams, 41-20 (A)
Rams, 45-29 (StL)
(RS Pts.—Rams 1,581, Falcons 1,114)
Franchise in Los Angeles prior to 1995

ATLANTA vs. SAN DIEGO
RS: Falcons lead series, 5-1
1973—Falcons, 41-0 (SD)
1979—Falcons, 28-26 (SD)
1988—Chargers, 10-7 (A)
1991—Falcons, 13-10 (SD)
1994—Falcons, 10-9 (A)
1997—Falcons, 14-3 (SD)
(RS Pts.—Falcons 113, Chargers 58)

ATLANTA vs. SAN FRANCISCO
RS: 49ers lead series, 42-25-1
PS: Falcons lead series, 1-0
1966—49ers, 44-7 (A)
1967—49ers, 38-7 (SF)
49ers, 34-28 (A)
1968—49ers, 28-13 (SF)
49ers, 14-12 (A)
1969—Falcons, 24-12 (A)
Falcons, 21-7 (SF)
1970—Falcons, 21-20 (A)
49ers, 24-20 (SF)
1971—Falcons, 20-17 (A)
49ers, 24-3 (SF)
1972—49ers, 49-14 (A)
49ers, 20-0 (SF)
1973—49ers, 13-9 (A)
Falcons, 17-3 (SF)
1974—49ers, 16-10 (A)
49ers, 27-0 (SF)
1975—Falcons, 17-3 (SF)

Falcons, 31-9 (A)
1976—49ers, 15-0 (SF)
Falcons, 21-16 (A)
1977—Falcons, 7-0 (SF)
49ers, 10-3 (A)
1978—Falcons, 20-17 (SF)
Falcons, 21-10 (A)
1979—49ers, 20-15 (SF)
Falcons, 31-21 (A)
1980—Falcons, 20-17 (SF)
Falcons, 35-10 (A)
1981—Falcons, 34-17 (A)
49ers, 17-14 (SF)
1982—Falcons, 17-7 (SF)
1983—49ers, 24-20 (SF)
Falcons, 28-24 (A)
1984—49ers, 14-5 (SF)
49ers, 35-17 (A)
1985—49ers, 35-16 (SF)
49ers, 38-17 (A)
1986—Tie, 10-10 (A) OT
49ers, 20-0 (SF)
1987—49ers, 25-17 (A)
49ers, 35-7 (SF)
1988—Falcons, 34-17 (SF)
49ers, 13-3 (A)
1989—49ers, 45-3 (SF)
49ers, 23-10 (A)
1990—49ers, 19-13 (SF)
49ers, 45-35 (A)
1991—Falcons, 39-34 (SF)
Falcons, 17-14 (A)
1992—49ers, 56-17 (SF)
49ers, 41-3 (A)
1993—49ers, 37-30 (SF)
Falcons, 27-24 (A)
1994—49ers, 42-3 (A)
49ers, 50-14 (SF)
1995—49ers, 41-10 (SF)
Falcons, 28-27 (A)
1996—49ers, 39-17 (SF)
49ers, 34-10 (A)
1997—49ers, 34-7 (SF)
49ers, 35-28 (A)
1998—49ers, 31-20 (SF)
Falcons, 31-19 (A)
*Falcons, 20-18 (A)
1999—49ers, 26-7 (SF)
Falcons, 34-29 (A)
2000—Falcons, 36-28 (A)
49ers, 16-6 (SF)
(RS Pts.—49ers 1,658, Falcons 1,131)
(PS Pts.—Falcons 20, 49ers 18)
NFC Divisional Playoff

ATLANTA vs. SEATTLE
RS: Seahawks lead series, 5-2
1976—Seahawks, 30-13 (S)
1979—Seahawks, 31-28 (A)
1985—Seahawks, 30-26 (S)
1988—Seahawks, 31-20 (A)
1991—Falcons, 26-13 (A)
1997—Falcons, 24-17 (S)
2000—Seahawks, 30-10 (A)
(RS Pts.—Seahawks 182, Falcons 147)

ATLANTA vs. TAMPA BAY
RS: Buccaneers lead series, 9-8
1977—Falcons, 17-0 (TB)
1978—Buccaneers, 14-9 (TB)
1979—Falcons, 17-14 (A)
1981—Buccaneers, 24-23 (TB)
1984—Buccaneers, 23-6 (TB)
1986—Falcons, 23-20 (TB) OT
1987—Buccaneers, 48-10 (TB)
1988—Falcons, 17-10 (A)
1990—Buccaneers, 23-17 (TB)
1991—Falcons, 43-7 (A)
1992—Falcons, 35-7 (TB)
1993—Buccaneers, 31-24 (A)
1994—Falcons, 34-13 (A)
1995—Falcons, 24-21 (TB)
1997—Buccaneers, 31-10 (A)
1999—Buccaneers, 19-10 (TB)
2000—Buccaneers, 27-14 (A)
(RS Pts.—Falcons 333, Buccaneers 332)

ATLANTA vs. *TENNESSEE
RS: Series tied, 5-5
1972—Falcons, 20-10 (A)
1976—Oilers, 20-14 (H)
1978—Falcons, 20-14 (A)
1981—Falcons, 31-27 (H)
1984—Falcons, 42-10 (A)
1987—Oilers, 37-33 (H)
1990—Falcons, 47-27 (A)
1993—Oilers, 33-17 (H)
1996—Oilers, 23-13 (A)
1999—Titans, 30-17 (T)
(RS Pts.—Falcons 254, Titans 231)
Franchise in Houston prior to 1997; known as Oilers prior to 1999

ATLANTA vs. WASHINGTON
RS: Redskins lead series, 13-4-1
PS: Redskins lead series, 1-0
1966—Redskins, 33-20 (W)
1967—Tie, 20-20 (A)
1969—Redskins, 27-20 (W)
1972—Redskins, 24-13 (W)
1975—Redskins, 30-27 (A)
1977—Redskins, 10-6 (W)
1978—Falcons, 20-17 (A)
1979—Redskins, 16-7 (A)
1980—Falcons, 10-6 (A)
1983—Redskins, 37-21 (W)
1984—Redskins, 27-14 (W)
1985—Redskins, 44-10 (A)
1987—Falcons, 21-20 (A)
1989—Redskins, 31-30 (A)
1991—Redskins, 56-17 (W)
*Redskins, 24-7 (W)
1992—Redskins, 24-17 (W)
1993—Redskins, 30-17 (W)
1994—Falcons, 27-20 (W)
(RS Pts.—Redskins 472, Falcons 317)
(PS Pts.—Redskins 24, Falcons 7)
NFC Divisional Playoff

BALTIMORE vs. ARIZONA
RS: Series tied, 1-1;
See Arizona vs. Baltimore

BALTIMORE vs. ATLANTA
RS: Ravens lead series, 1-0;
See Atlanta vs. Baltimore

BALTIMORE vs. BUFFALO
RS: Bills lead series, 1-0
1999—Bills, 13-10 (Balt)
(RS Pts.—Bills 13, Ravens 10)

BALTIMORE vs. CAROLINA
RS: Panthers lead series, 1-0
1996—Panthers, 27-16 (C)
(RS Pts.—Panthers 27, Ravens 16)

BALTIMORE vs. CHICAGO
RS: Bears lead series, 1-0
1998—Bears, 24-3 (C)
(RS Pts.—Bears 24, Ravens 3)

BALTIMORE vs. CINCINNATI
RS: Ravens lead series, 7-3
1996—Bengals, 24-21 (B)
Bengals, 21-14 (C)
1997—Ravens, 23-10 (B)
Bengals, 16-14 (C)
1998—Ravens, 31-24 (B)
Ravens, 20-13 (C)
1999—Ravens, 34-31 (C)
Ravens, 22-0 (B)
2000—Ravens, 37-0 (B)
Ravens, 27-7 (C)
(RS Pts.—Ravens 243, Bengals 146)

BALTIMORE vs. CLEVELAND
RS: Ravens lead series, 4-0
1999—Ravens, 17-10 (B)
Ravens, 41-9 (C)
2000—Ravens, 12-0 (C)
Ravens, 44-7 (B)
(RS Pts.—Ravens 114, Browns 26)

BALTIMORE vs. DALLAS
RS: Ravens lead series, 1-0
2000—Ravens, 27-0 (B)
(RS Pts.—Ravens 27, Cowboys 0)

BALTIMORE vs. DENVER
RS: Broncos lead series, 1-0
PS: Ravens lead series, 1-0
1996—Broncos, 45-34 (D)
2000—*Ravens, 21-3 (B)
(RS Pts.—Broncos 45, Ravens 34)
(PS Pts.—Ravens 21, Broncos 3)
AFC First-Round Playoff

BALTIMORE vs. DETROIT
RS: Ravens lead series, 1-0
1998—Ravens, 19-10 (B)
(RS Pts.—Ravens 19, Lions 10)

BALTIMORE vs. GREEN BAY
RS: Packers lead series, 1-0
1998—Packers, 28-10 (GB)
(RS Pts.—Packers 28, Ravens 10)

BALTIMORE vs. INDIANAPOLIS
RS: Series tied, 1-1
1996—Colts, 26-21 (I)
1998—Ravens, 38-31 (B)
(RS Pts.—Ravens 59, Colts 57)

BALTIMORE vs. JACKSONVILLE
RS: Jaguars lead series, 8-2
1996—Jaguars, 30-27 (J)
Jaguars, 28-25 (B) OT
1997—Jaguars, 28-27 (B)
Jaguars, 29-27 (J)
1998—Jaguars, 24-10 (J)
Jaguars, 45-19 (B)
1999—Jaguars, 6-3 (J)
Jaguars, 30-23 (B)
2000—Ravens, 39-36 (B)
Ravens, 15-10 (J)
(RS Pts.—Jaguars 266, Ravens 215)

BALTIMORE vs. KANSAS CITY
RS: Chiefs lead series, 1-0
1999—Chiefs, 35-8 (B)
(RS Pts.—Chiefs 35, Ravens 8)

BALTIMORE vs. MIAMI
RS: Dolphins lead series, 2-0
1997—Dolphins, 24-13 (B)
2000—Dolphins, 19-6 (M)
(RS Pts.—Dolphins 43, Ravens 19)

BALTIMORE vs. MINNESOTA
RS: Vikings lead series, 1-0
1998—Vikings, 38-28 (B)
(RS Pts.—Vikings 38, Ravens 28)

BALTIMORE vs. NEW ENGLAND
RS: Patriots lead series, 2-0
1996—Patriots, 46-38 (B)
1999—Patriots, 20-3 (NE)
(RS Pts.—Patriots 66, Ravens 41)

BALTIMORE vs. NEW ORLEANS
RS: Ravens lead series, 2-0
1996—Ravens, 17-10 (B)
1999—Ravens, 31-8 (B)
(RS Pts.—Ravens 48, Saints 18)

BALTIMORE vs. N.Y. GIANTS
RS: Ravens lead series, 1-0
PS: Ravens lead series, 1-0
1997—Ravens, 24-23 (NY)
2000—*Ravens, 34-7 (Tampa)
(RS Pts.—Ravens 24, Giants 23)
(PS Pts.—Ravens 34, Giants 7)
Super Bowl XXXV

BALTIMORE vs. N.Y. JETS
RS: Ravens lead series, 2-1
1997—Jets, 19-16 (NY) OT
1998—Ravens, 24-10 (NY)
2000—Ravens, 34-20 (B)
(RS Pts.—Ravens 74, Jets 49)

BALTIMORE vs. OAKLAND
RS: Ravens lead series, 2-0
PS: Ravens lead series, 1-0
1996—Ravens, 19-14 (B)
1998—Ravens, 13-10 (B)
2000—*Ravens, 16-3 (O)
(RS Pts.—Ravens 32, Raiders 24)
(PS Pts.—Ravens 16, Raiders 3)
AFC Championship

BALTIMORE vs. PHILADELPHIA
RS: Series tied, 0-0-1
1997—Tie, 10-10 (B) OT
(RS Pts.—Ravens 10, Eagles 10)

BALTIMORE vs. PITTSBURGH
RS: Steelers lead series, 7-3
1996—Steelers, 31-17 (P)
Ravens, 31-17 (B)
1997—Steelers, 42-34 (B)
Steelers, 37-0 (P)
1998—Steelers, 20-13 (B)
Steelers, 16-6 (P)
1999—Steelers, 23-20 (B)
Ravens, 31-24 (P)
2000—Ravens, 16-0 (P)
Steelers, 9-6 (B)
(RS Pts.—Steelers 219, Ravens 174)

BALTIMORE vs. ST. LOUIS
RS: Series tied, 1-1
1996—Ravens, 37-31 (B) OT
1999—Rams, 27-10 (StL)
(RS Pts.—Rams 58, Ravens 47)

BALTIMORE vs. SAN DIEGO
RS: Chargers lead series, 2-1
1997—Chargers, 21-17 (SD)
1998—Chargers, 14-13 (SD)
2000—Ravens, 24-3 (B)
(RS Pts.—Ravens 54, Chargers 38)

BALTIMORE vs. SAN FRANCISCO
RS: 49ers lead series, 1-0
1996—49ers, 38-20 (SF)
(RS Pts.—49ers 38, Ravens 20)

BALTIMORE vs. SEATTLE
RS: Ravens lead series, 1-0
1997—Ravens, 31-24 (B)
(RS Pts.—Ravens 31, Seahawks 24)

BALTIMORE vs. *TENNESSEE
RS: Titans lead series, 6-4
PS: Ravens lead series, 1-0
1996—Oilers, 29-13 (H)
Oilers, 24-21 (B)
1997—Ravens, 36-10 (T)
Ravens, 21-19 (B)
1998—Oilers, 12-8 (B)
Oilers, 16-14 (T)
1999—Titans, 14-11 (T)
Ravens, 41-14 (B)
2000—Titans, 14-6 (B)
Ravens, 24-23 (T)
**Ravens, 24-10 (T)
(RS Pts.—Ravens 195, Titans 175)
(PS Pts.—Ravens 24, Titans 10)
Franchise in Houston prior to 1997; known as Oilers prior to 1999
***AFC Divisional Playoff*

BALTIMORE vs. WASHINGTON
RS: Series tied, 1-1
1997—Ravens, 20-17 (W)
2000—Redskins, 10-3 (W)
(RS Pts.—Redskins 27, Ravens 23)

BUFFALO vs. ARIZONA
RS: Bills lead series, 4-3;
See Arizona vs. Buffalo

BUFFALO vs. ATLANTA
RS: Bills lead series, 4-3;
See Atlanta vs. Buffalo

BUFFALO vs. BALTIMORE
RS: Bills lead series, 1-0;
See Baltimore vs. Buffalo

BUFFALO vs. CAROLINA
RS: Bills lead series, 2-0
1995—Bills, 31-9 (B)
1998—Bills, 30-14 (C)
(RS Pts.—Bills 61, Panthers 23)

BUFFALO vs. CHICAGO
RS: Bears lead series, 5-3
1970—Bears, 31-13 (C)
1974—Bills, 16-6 (B)
1979—Bears, 7-0 (B)
1988—Bears, 24-3 (C)
1991—Bills, 35-20 (B)
1994—Bears, 20-13 (C)
1997—Bears, 20-3 (C)
2000—Bills, 20-3 (B)

ALL-TIME TEAM VS. TEAM RESULTS

(RS Pts.—Bears 131, Bills 103)
BUFFALO vs. CINCINNATI
RS: Series tied, 9-9
PS: Bengals lead series, 2-0
1968—Bengals, 34-23 (C)
1969—Bills, 16-13 (B)
1970—Bengals, 43-14 (B)
1973—Bengals, 16-13 (B)
1975—Bengals, 33-24 (C)
1978—Bills, 5-0 (B)
1979—Bills, 51-24 (B)
1980—Bills, 14-0 (C)
1981—Bengals, 27-24 (C) OT
*Bengals, 28-21 (C)
1983—Bills, 10-6 (C)
1984—Bengals, 52-21 (C)
1985—Bengals, 23-17 (B)
1986—Bengals, 36-33 (C) OT
1988—Bengals, 35-21 (C)
**Bengals, 21-10 (C)
1989—Bills, 24-7 (B)
1991—Bills, 35-16 (B)
1996—Bills, 31-17 (B)
1998—Bills, 33-20 (C)
(RS Pts.—Bills 409, Bengals 402)
(PS Pts.—Bengals 49, Bills 31)
AFC Divisional Playoff
***AFC Championship*
BUFFALO vs. CLEVELAND
RS: Browns lead series, 7-4
PS: Browns lead series, 1-0
1972—Browns, 27-10 (C)
1974—Bills, 15-10 (C)
1977—Browns, 27-16 (B)
1978—Browns, 41-20 (C)
1981—Bills, 22-13 (B)
1984—Browns, 13-10 (B)
1985—Browns, 17-7 (C)
1986—Browns, 21-17 (B)
1987—Browns, 27-21 (C)
1989—*Browns, 34-30 (C)
1990—Bills, 42-0 (C)
1995—Bills, 22-19 (C)
(RS Pts.—Browns 215, Bills 202)
(PS Pts.—Browns 34, Bills 30)
AFC Divisional Playoff
BUFFALO vs. DALLAS
RS: Series tied, 3-3
PS: Cowboys lead series, 2-0
1971—Cowboys, 49-37 (B)
1976—Cowboys, 17-10 (D)
1981—Cowboys, 27-14 (D)
1984—Bills, 14-3 (B)
1992—*Cowboys, 52-17 (Pasadena)
1993—Bills, 13-10 (D)
**Cowboys, 30-13 (Atlanta)
1996—Bills, 10-7 (B)
(RS Pts.—Cowboys 113, Bills 98)
(PS Pts.—Cowboys 82, Bills 30)
Super Bowl XXVII
***Super Bowl XXVIII*
BUFFALO vs. DENVER
RS: Bills lead series, 17-12-1
PS: Bills lead series, 1-0
1960—Broncos, 27-21 (B)
Tie, 38-38 (D)
1961—Broncos, 22-10 (B)
Bills, 23-10 (D)
1962—Broncos, 23-20 (B)
Bills, 45-38 (D)
1963—Bills, 30-28 (D)
Bills, 27-17 (B)
1964—Bills, 30-13 (B)
Bills, 30-19 (D)
1965—Bills, 30-15 (D)
Bills, 31-13 (B)
1966—Bills, 38-21 (B)
1967—Bills, 17-16 (D)
Broncos, 21-20 (B)
1968—Broncos, 34-32 (D)
1969—Bills, 41-28 (B)
1970—Broncos, 25-10 (B)
1975—Bills, 38-14 (B)
1977—Broncos, 26-6 (D)
1979—Broncos, 19-16 (B)
1981—Bills, 9-7 (B)
1984—Broncos, 37-7 (B)
1987—Bills, 21-14 (B)
1989—Broncos, 28-14 (B)
1990—Bills, 29-28 (B)
1991—*Bills, 10-7 (B)
1992—Bills, 27-17 (B)
1994—Bills, 27-20 (B)
1995—Broncos, 22-7 (D)
1997—Broncos, 23-20 (B) OT
(RS Pts.—Bills 714, Broncos 663)
(PS Pts.—Bills 10, Broncos 7)
AFC Championship
BUFFALO vs. DETROIT
RS: Lions lead series, 3-2-1
1972—Tie, 21-21 (B)
1976—Lions, 27-14 (D)
1979—Bills, 20-17 (D)
1991—Lions, 17-14 (B) OT
1994—Lions, 35-21 (D)
1997—Bills, 22-13 (B)
(RS Pts.—Lions 130, Bills 112)
BUFFALO vs. GREEN BAY
RS: Bills lead series, 6-2
1974—Bills, 27-7 (GB)
1979—Bills, 19-12 (B)
1982—Packers, 33-21 (Mil)
1988—Bills, 28-0 (B)
1991—Bills, 34-24 (Mil)
1994—Bills 29-20 (B)
1997—Packers, 31-21 (GB)
2000—Bills 27-18 (B)
(RS Pts.—Bills 206, Packers 145)
BUFFALO vs. *INDIANAPOLIS
RS: Bills lead series, 34-26-1
1970—Tie, 17-17 (Balt)
Colts, 20-14 (Buff)
1971—Colts, 43-0 (Buff)
Colts, 24-0 (Balt)
1972—Colts, 17-0 (Buff)
Colts, 35-7 (Balt)
1973—Bills, 31-13 (Buff)
Bills, 24-17 (Balt)
1974—Bills, 27-14 (Balt)
Bills, 6-0 (Buff)
1975—Bills, 38-31 (Balt)
Colts, 42-35 (Buff)
1976—Colts, 31-13 (Buff)
Colts, 58-20 (Balt)
1977—Colts, 17-14 (Balt)
Colts, 31-13 (Buff)
1978—Bills, 24-17 (Buff)
Bills, 21-14 (Balt)
1979—Bills, 31-13 (Balt)
Colts, 14-13 (Buff)
1980—Colts, 17-12 (Buff)
Colts, 28-24 (Balt)
1981—Bills, 35-3 (Balt)
Bills, 23-17 (Buff)
1982—Bills, 20-0 (Buff)
1983—Bills, 28-23 (Buff)
Bills, 30-7 (Balt)
1984—Colts, 31-17 (I)
Bills, 21-15 (Buff)
1985—Colts, 49-17 (I)
Bills, 21-9 (Buff)
1986—Bills, 24-13 (Buff)
Colts, 24-14 (I)
1987—Colts, 47-6 (Buff)
Bills, 27-3 (I)
1988—Bills, 34-23 (Buff)
Colts, 17-14 (I)
1989—Colts, 37-14 (I)
Bills, 30-7 (Buff)
1990—Bills, 26-10 (Buff)
Bills, 31-7 (I)
1991—Bills, 42-6 (Buff)
Bills, 35-7 (I)
1992—Bills, 38-0 (Buff)
Colts, 16-13 (I) OT
1993—Bills, 23-9 (Buff)
Bills, 30-10 (I)
1994—Colts, 27-17 (Buff)
Colts, 10-9 (I)
1995—Bills, 20-14 (Buff)
Bills, 16-10 (I)
1996—Bills, 16-13 (Buff) OT
Colts, 13-10 (I) OT
1997—Bills, 37-35 (B)
Bills, 9-6 (I)
1998—Bills, 31-24 (I)
Bills, 34-11 (B)
1999—Colts, 31-14 (I)
Bills, 31-6 (B)
2000—Colts, 18-16 (B)
Colts, 44-20 (I)
(RS Pts.—Bills 1,277, Colts 1,165)
Franchise in Baltimore prior to 1984
BUFFALO vs. JACKSONVILLE
RS: Series tied, 1-1
PS: Jaguars lead series, 1-0
1996—*Jaguars, 30-27 (B)
1997—Jaguars, 20-14 (B)
1998—Bills, 17-16 (B)
(RS Pts.—Jaguars 36, Bills 31)
(PS Pts.—Jaguars 30, Bills 27)
AFC First-Round Playoff
BUFFALO vs. *KANSAS CITY
RS: Bills lead series, 18-14-1
PS: Bills lead series, 2-1
1960—Texans, 45-28 (B)
Texans, 24-7 (D)
1961—Bills, 27-24 (B)
Bills, 30-20 (D)
1962—Texans, 41-21 (D)
Bills, 23-14 (B)
1963—Tie, 27-27 (B)
Bills, 35-26 (KC)
1964—Bills, 34-17 (B)
Bills, 35-22 (KC)
1965—Bills, 23-7 (KC)
Bills, 34-25 (B)
1966—Chiefs, 42-20 (B)
Bills, 29-14 (KC)
**Chiefs, 31-7 (B)
1967—Chiefs, 23-13 (KC)
1968—Chiefs, 18-7 (B)
1969—Chiefs, 29-7 (B)
Chiefs, 22-19 (KC)
1971—Chiefs, 22-9 (KC)
1973—Bills, 23-14 (B)
1976—Bills, 50-17 (B)
1978—Bills, 28-13 (B)
Chiefs, 14-10 (KC)
1982—Bills, 14-9 (B)
1983—Bills, 14-9 (KC)
1986—Chiefs, 20-17 (B)
Bills, 17-14 (KC)
1991—Chiefs, 33-6 (KC)
***Bills, 37-14 (B)
1993—Chiefs, 23-7 (KC)
****Bills, 30-13 (B)
1994—Bills, 44-10 (B)
1996—Bills, 20-9 (B)
1997—Chiefs, 22-16 (KC)
2000—Bills, 21-17 (KC)
(RS Pts.—Bills 715, Chiefs 686)
(PS Pts.—Bills 74, Chiefs 58)
Franchise in Dallas prior to 1963 and known as Texans
***AFL Championship*
****AFC Divisional Playoff*
*****AFC Championship*
BUFFALO vs. MIAMI
RS: Dolphins lead series, 44-25-1
PS: Bills lead series, 3-1
1966—Bills, 58-24 (B)
Bills, 29-0 (M)
1967—Bills, 35-13 (B)
Dolphins, 17-14 (M)
1968—Tie, 14-14 (M)
Dolphins, 21-17 (B)
1969—Dolphins, 24-6 (M)
Bills, 28-3 (B)
1970—Dolphins, 33-14 (B)
Dolphins, 45-7 (M)
1971—Dolphins, 29-14 (B)
Dolphins, 34-0 (M)
1972—Dolphins, 24-23 (M)
Dolphins, 30-16 (B)
1973—Dolphins, 27-6 (M)
Dolphins, 17-0 (B)
1974—Dolphins, 24-16 (B)
Dolphins, 35-28 (M)
1975—Dolphins, 35-30 (B)
Dolphins, 31-21 (M)
1976—Dolphins, 30-21 (B)
Dolphins, 45-27 (M)
1977—Dolphins, 13-0 (B)
Dolphins, 31-14 (M)
1978—Dolphins, 31-24 (M)
Dolphins, 25-24 (B)
1979—Dolphins, 9-7 (B)
Dolphins, 17-7 (M)
1980—Bills, 17-7 (B)
Dolphins, 17-14 (M)
1981—Bills, 31-21 (B)
Dolphins, 16-6 (M)
1982—Dolphins, 9-7 (B)
Dolphins, 27-10 (M)
1983—Dolphins, 12-0 (B)
Bills, 38-35 (M) OT
1984—Dolphins, 21-17 (B)
Dolphins, 38-7 (M)
1985—Dolphins, 23-14 (B)
Dolphins, 28-0 (M)
1986—Dolphins, 27-14 (M)
Dolphins, 34-24 (B)
1987—Bills, 34-31 (M) OT
Bills, 27-0 (B)
1988—Bills, 9-6 (B)
Bills, 31-6 (M)
1989—Bills, 27-24 (M)
Bills, 31-17 (B)
1990—Dolphins, 30-7 (M)
Bills, 24-14 (B)
*Bills, 44-34 (B)
1991—Bills, 35-31 (B)
Bills, 41-27 (M)
1992—Dolphins, 37-10 (B)
Bills, 26-20 (M)
**Bills, 29-10 (M)
1993—Dolphins, 22-13 (B)
Bills, 47-34 (M)
1994—Bills, 21-11 (B)
Bills, 42-31 (M)
1995—Dolphins, 23-6 (M)
Bills, 23-20 (B)
***Bills, 37-22 (B)
1996—Dolphins, 21-7 (B)
Dolphins, 16-14 (M)
1997—Bills, 9-6 (B)
Dolphins, 30-13 (M)
1998—Dolphins, 13-7 (M)
Bills, 30-24 (B)
***Dolphins, 24-17 (M)
1999—Bills, 23-18 (M)
Bills, 23-3 (B)
2000—Dolphins, 22-13 (M)
Dolphins, 33-6 (B)
(RS Pts.—Dolphins 1,566, Bills 1,298)
(PS Pts.—Bills 127, Dolphins 90)
AFC Divisional Playoff
***AFC Championship*
****AFC First-Round Playoff*
BUFFALO vs. MINNESOTA
RS: Vikings lead series, 7-2
1971—Vikings, 19-0 (M)
1975—Vikings, 35-13 (B)
1979—Vikings, 10-3 (M)
1982—Bills, 23-22 (B)
1985—Vikings, 27-20 (B)
1988—Bills, 13-10 (B)
1994—Vikings, 21-17 (B)
1997—Vikings, 34-13 (B)
2000—Vikings, 31-27 (M)
(RS Pts.—Vikings 209, Bills 129)

BUFFALO vs. *NEW ENGLAND
RS: Patriots lead series, 41-39-1
PS: Patriots lead series, 1-0
1960—Bills, 13-0 (Bos)
Bills, 38-14 (Buff)
1961—Patriots, 23-21 (Buff)
Patriots, 52-21 (Bos)
1962—Tie, 28-28 (Buff)
Patriots, 21-10 (Bos)
1963—Bills, 28-21 (Buff)
Patriots, 17-7 (Bos)
**Patriots, 26-8 (Buff)
1964—Patriots, 36-28 (Buff)
Bills, 24-14 (Bos)
1965—Bills, 24-7 (Buff)
Bills, 23-7 (Bos)
1966—Patriots, 20-10 (Buff)
Patriots, 14-3 (Bos)
1967—Patriots, 23-0 (Buff)
Bills, 44-16 (Bos)
1968—Patriots, 16-7 (Buff)
Patriots, 23-6 (Bos)
1969—Bills, 23-16 (Buff)
Patriots, 35-21 (Bos)
1970—Bills, 45-10 (Bos)
Patriots, 14-10 (Buff)
1971—Patriots, 38-33 (NE)
Bills, 27-20 (Buff)
1972—Bills, 38-14 (Buff)
Bills, 27-24 (NE)
1973—Bills, 31-13 (NE)
Bills, 37-13 (Buff)
1974—Bills, 30-28 (Buff)
Bills, 29-28 (NE)
1975—Bills, 45-31 (Buff)
Bills, 34-14 (NE)
1976—Patriots, 26-22 (Buff)
Patriots, 20-10 (NE)
1977—Bills, 24-14 (NE)
Patriots, 20-7 (Buff)
1978—Patriots, 14-10 (Buff)
Patriots, 26-24 (NE)
1979—Patriots, 26-6 (Buff)
Bills, 16-13 (NE) OT
1980—Bills, 31-13 (Buff)
Patriots, 24-2 (NE)
1981—Bills, 20-17 (Buff)
Bills, 19-10 (NE)
1982—Patriots, 30-19 (NE)
1983—Patriots, 31-0 (Buff)
Patriots, 21-7 (NE)
1984—Patriots, 21-17 (Buff)
Patriots, 38-10 (NE)
1985—Patriots, 17-14 (Buff)
Patriots, 14-3 (NE)
1986—Patriots, 23-3 (Buff)
Patriots, 22-19 (NE)
1987—Patriots, 14-7 (NE)
Patriots, 13-7 (Buff)
1988—Bills, 16-14 (NE)
Bills, 23-20 (Buff)
1989—Bills, 31-10 (Buff)
Patriots, 33-24 (NE)
1990—Bills, 27-10 (NE)
Bills, 14-0 (Buff)
1991—Bills, 22-17 (Buff)
Patriots, 16-13 (NE)
1992—Bills, 41-7 (NE)
Bills, 16-7 (Buff)
1993—Bills, 38-14 (Buff)
Bills, 13-10 (NE) OT
1994—Bills, 38-35 (NE)
Patriots, 41-17 (Buff)
1995—Patriots, 27-14 (NE)
Patriots, 35-25 (Buff)
1996—Bills, 17-10 (Buff)
Patriots, 28-25 (NE)
1997—Patriots, 33-6 (NE)
Patriots, 31-10 (B)
1998—Bills, 13-10 (B)
Patriots, 25-21 (NE)
1999—Bills, 17-7 (B)
Bills, 13-10 (NE) OT
2000—Bills, 16-13 (NE) OT
Patriots, 13-10 (B) OT
(RS Pts.—Patriots 1,593, Bills 1,582)
(PS Pts.—Patriots 26, Bills 8)
Franchise in Boston prior to 1971
***Division Playoff*

BUFFALO vs. NEW ORLEANS
RS: Bills lead series, 4-2
1973—Saints, 13-0 (NO)
1980—Bills, 35-26 (NO)
1983—Bills, 27-21 (B)
1989—Saints, 22-19 (B)
1992—Bills, 20-16 (NO)
1998—Bills, 45-33 (NO)
(RS Pts.—Bills 146, Saints 131)

BUFFALO vs. N.Y. GIANTS
RS: Bills lead series, 5-3
PS: Giants lead series, 1-0
1970—Giants, 20-6 (NY)
1975—Giants, 17-14 (B)
1978—Bills, 41-17 (B)
1987—Bills, 6-3 (B) OT
1990—Bills, 17-13 (NY)
*Giants, 20-19 (Tampa)
1993—Bills, 17-14 (B)
1996—Bills, 23-20 (NY) OT
1999—Giants, 19-17 (B)
(RS Pts.—Bills 141, Giants 123)
(PS Pts.—Giants 20, Bills 19)
**Super Bowl XXV*

BUFFALO vs. *N.Y. JETS
RS: Bills lead series, 45-35
PS: Bills lead series, 1-0
1960—Titans, 27-3 (NY)
Titans, 17-13 (B)
1961—Bills, 41-31 (B)
Titans, 21-14 (NY)
1962—Titans, 17-6 (B)
Bills, 20-3 (NY)
1963—Bills, 45-14 (B)
Bills, 19-10 (NY)
1964—Bills, 34-24 (B)
Bills, 20-7 (NY)
1965—Bills, 33-21 (B)
Jets, 14-12 (NY)
1966—Bills, 33-23 (NY)
Bills, 14-3 (B)
1967—Bills, 20-17 (B)
Jets, 20-10 (NY)
1968—Bills, 37-35 (B)
Jets, 25-21 (NY)
1969—Jets, 33-19 (B)
Jets, 16-6 (NY)
1970—Bills, 34-31 (B)
Bills, 10-6 (NY)
1971—Jets, 28-17 (NY)
Jets, 20-7 (B)
1972—Jets, 41-24 (B)
Jets, 41-3 (NY)
1973—Bills, 9-7 (B)
Bills, 34-14 (NY)
1974—Bills, 16-12 (B)
Jets, 20-10 (NY)
1975—Bills, 42-14 (B)
Bills, 24-23 (NY)
1976—Jets, 17-14 (NY)
Jets, 19-14 (B)
1977—Jets, 24-19 (B)
Bills, 14-10 (NY)
1978—Jets, 21-20 (B)
Jets, 45-14 (NY)
1979—Bills, 46-31 (B)
Bills, 14-12 (NY)
1980—Bills, 20-10 (B)
Bills, 31-24 (NY)
1981—Bills, 31-0 (B)
Jets, 33-14 (NY)
**Bills, 31-27 (NY)
1983—Jets, 34-10 (B)
Bills, 24-17 (NY)
1984—Jets, 28-26 (B)
Jets, 21-17 (NY)
1985—Jets, 42-3 (NY)
Jets, 27-7 (B)
1986—Jets, 28-24 (B)
Jets, 14-13 (NY)
1987—Jets, 31-28 (B)
Bills, 17-14 (NY)
1988—Bills, 37-14 (NY)
Bills, 9-6 (B) OT
1989—Bills, 34-3 (B)
Bills, 37-0 (NY)
1990—Bills, 30-7 (NY)
Bills, 30-27 (B)
1991—Bills, 23-20 (NY)
Bills, 24-13 (B)
1992—Bills, 24-20 (NY)
Jets, 24-17 (B)
1993—Bills, 19-10 (NY)
Bills, 16-14 (B)
1994—Jets, 23-3 (B)
Jets, 22-17 (NY)
1995—Bills, 29-10 (B)
Bills, 28-26 (NY)
1996—Bills, 25-22 (NY)
Bills, 35-10 (B)
1997—Bills, 28-22 (NY)
Bills, 20-10 (B)
1998—Jets, 34-12 (NY)
Jets, 17-10 (B)
1999—Bills, 17-3 (B)
Jets, 17-7 (NY)
2000—Jets, 27-14 (NY)
Bills, 23-20 (B)
(RS Pts.—Bills 1,638, Jets 1,558)
(PS Pts.—Bills 31, Jets 27)
**Jets known as Titans prior to 1963*
***AFC First-Round Playoff*

BUFFALO vs. *OAKLAND
RS: Raiders lead series, 16-15
PS: Bills lead series, 2-0
1960—Bills, 38-9 (B)
Raiders, 20-7 (O)
1961—Raiders, 31-22 (B)
Bills, 26-21 (O)
1962—Bills, 14-6 (B)
Bills, 10-6 (O)
1963—Raiders, 35-17 (O)
Bills, 12-0 (B)
1964—Bills, 23-20 (B)
Raiders, 16-13 (O)
1965—Bills, 17-12 (B)
Bills, 17-14 (O)
1966—Bills, 31-10 (O)
1967—Raiders, 24-20 (B)
Raiders, 28-21 (O)
1968—Raiders, 48-6 (B)
Raiders, 13-10 (O)
1969—Raiders, 50-21 (O)
1972—Raiders, 28-16 (O)
1974—Bills, 21-20 (B)
1977—Raiders, 34-13 (O)
1980—Bills, 24-7 (B)
1983—Raiders, 27-24 (B)
1987—Raiders, 34-21 (LA)
1988—Bills, 37-21 (B)
1990—Bills, 38-24 (B)
**Bills, 51-3 (B)
1991—Bills, 30-27 (LA) OT
1992—Raiders, 20-3 (LA)
1993—Raiders, 25-24 (B)
***Bills, 29-23 (B)
1998—Bills, 44-21 (B)
1999—Raiders, 20-14 (B)
(RS Pts.—Raiders 671, Bills 634)
(PS Pts.—Bills 80, Raiders 26)
**Franchise in Los Angeles from 1982-1994*
***AFC Championship*
****AFC Divisional Playoff*

BUFFALO vs. PHILADELPHIA
RS: Bills lead series, 5-4
1973—Bills, 27-26 (B)
1981—Eagles, 20-14 (B)
1984—Eagles, 27-17 (B)
1985—Eagles, 21-17 (P)
1987—Eagles, 17-7 (P)
1990—Bills, 30-23 (B)
1993—Bills, 10-7 (P)
1996—Bills, 24-17 (P)
1999—Bills, 26-0 (B)
(RS Pts.—Bills 172, Eagles 158)

BUFFALO vs. PITTSBURGH
RS: Series tied, 8-8
PS: Steelers lead series, 2-1
1970—Steelers, 23-10 (P)
1972—Steelers, 38-21 (B)
1974—*Steelers, 32-14 (P)
1975—Bills, 30-21 (P)
1978—Steelers, 28-17 (B)
1979—Steelers, 28-0 (P)
1980—Bills, 28-13 (B)
1982—Bills, 13-0 (B)
1985—Steelers, 30-24 (P)
1986—Bills, 16-12 (B)
1988—Bills, 36-28 (B)
1991—Bills, 52-34 (B)
1992—Bills, 28-20 (B)
*Bills, 24-3 (P)
1993—Steelers, 23-0 (P)
1994—Steelers, 23-10 (P)
1995—*Steelers, 40-21 (P)
1996—Steelers, 24-6 (P)
1999—Bills, 24-21 (B)
(RS Pts.—Steelers 366, Bills 315)
(PS Pts.—Steelers 75, Bills 59)
**AFC Divisional Playoff*

BUFFALO vs. *ST. LOUIS
RS: Series tied, 4-4
1970—Rams, 19-0 (B)
1974—Rams, 19-14 (LA)
1980—Bills, 10-7 (B) OT
1983—Rams, 41-17 (LA)
1989—Bills, 23-20 (B)
1992—Bills, 40-7 (B)
1995—Bills, 45-27 (StL)
1998—Rams, 34-33 (B)
(RS Pts.—Bills 182, Rams 174)
**Franchise in Los Angeles prior to 1995*

BUFFALO vs. *SAN DIEGO
RS: Chargers lead series, 17-8-2
PS: Bills lead series, 2-1
1960—Chargers, 24-10 (B)
Bills, 32-3 (LA)
1961—Chargers, 19-11 (B)
Chargers, 28-10 (SD)
1962—Bills, 35-10 (B)
Bills, 40-20 (SD)
1963—Chargers, 14-10 (SD)
Chargers, 23-13 (B)
1964—Bills, 30-3 (B)
Bills, 27-24 (SD)
**Bills, 20-7 (B)
1965—Chargers, 34-3 (B)
Tie, 20-20 (SD)
**Bills, 23-0 (SD)
1966—Chargers, 27-7 (SD)
Tie, 17-17 (B)
1967—Chargers, 37-17 (B)
1968—Chargers, 21-6 (B)
1969—Chargers, 45-6 (SD)
1971—Chargers, 20-3 (SD)
1973—Chargers, 34-7 (SD)
1976—Chargers,.34-13 (B)
1979—Chargers, 27-19 (SD)
1980—Bills, 26-24 (SD)
***Chargers, 20-14 (SD)
1981—Bills, 28-27 (SD)
1985—Chargers, 14-9 (B)
Chargers, 40-7 (SD)
1998—Chargers, 16-14 (SD)
2000—Bills, 27-24 (B) OT
(RS Pts.—Chargers 629, Bills 447)
(PS Pts.—Bills 57, Chargers 27)
**Franchise in Los Angeles prior to 1961*
***AFL Championship*
****AFC Divisional Playoff*

BUFFALO vs. SAN FRANCISCO
RS: Bills lead series, 4-3

ALL-TIME TEAM VS. TEAM RESULTS

1972—Bills, 27-20 (B)
1980—Bills, 18-13 (SF)
1983—49ers, 23-10 (B)
1989—49ers, 21-10 (SF)
1992—Bills, 34-31 (SF)
1995—49ers, 27-17 (SF)
1998—Bills, 26-21 (B)
(RS Pts.—49ers 156, Bills 142)

BUFFALO vs. SEATTLE
RS: Seahawks lead series, 5-3
1977—Seahawks, 56-17 (S)
1984—Seahawks, 31-28 (S)
1988—Bills, 13-3 (S)
1989—Seahawks, 17-16 (S)
1995—Bills, 27-21 (B)
1996—Seahawks, 26-18 (S)
1999—Seahawks, 26-16 (S)
2000—Bills, 42-23 (S)
(RS Pts.—Seahawks 203, Bills 177)

BUFFALO vs. TAMPA BAY
RS: Buccaneers lead series, 5-2
1976—Bills, 14-9 (TB)
1978—Buccaneers, 31-10 (TB)
1982—Buccaneers, 24-23 (TB)
1986—Buccaneers, 34-28 (TB)
1988—Buccaneers, 10-5 (TB)
1991—Bills, 17-10 (TB)
2000—Buccaneers, 31-17 (TB)
(RS Pts.—Buccaneers 149, Bills 114)

BUFFALO vs. *TENNESSEE
RS: Titans lead series, 22-14
PS: Bills lead series, 2-1
1960—Bills, 25-24 (B)
Oilers, 31-23 (H)
1961—Bills, 22-12 (H)
Oilers, 28-16 (B)
1962—Oilers, 28-23 (B)
Oilers, 17-14 (H)
1963—Oilers, 31-20 (B)
Oilers, 28-14 (H)
1964—Bills, 48-17 (H)
Bills, 24-10 (B)
1965—Oilers, 19-17 (B)
Bills, 29-18 (H)
1966—Bills, 27-20 (B)
Bills, 42-20 (H)
1967—Oilers, 20-3 (B)
Oilers, 10-3 (H)
1968—Oilers, 30-7 (B)
Oilers, 35-6 (H)
1969—Oilers, 17-3 (B)
Oilers, 28-14 (H)
1971—Oilers, 20-14 (B)
1974—Oilers, 21-9 (B)
1976—Oilers, 13-3 (B)
1978—Oilers, 17-10 (H)
1983—Bills, 30-13 (B)
1985—Bills, 20-0 (B)
1986—Oilers, 16-7 (H)
1987—Bills, 34-30 (B)
1988—**Bills, 17-10 (B)
1989—Bills, 47-41 (H) OT
1990—Oilers, 27-24 (H)
1992—Oilers, 27-3 (H)
***Bills, 41-38 (B) OT
1993—Bills, 35-7 (B)
1994—Bills, 15-7 (H)
1995—Oilers, 28-17 (B)
1997—Oilers, 31-14 (T)
1999—***Titans, 22-16 (T)
2000—Bills, 16-13 (B)
(RS Pts.—Titans 754, Bills 678)
(PS Pts.—Bills 74, Titans 70)
**Franchise in Houston prior to 1997; known as Oilers prior to 1999*
***AFC Divisional Playoff*
****AFC First-Round Playoff*

BUFFALO vs. WASHINGTON
RS: Bills lead series, 5-4
PS: Redskins lead series, 1-0
1972—Bills, 24-17 (W)
1977—Redskins, 10-0 (B)
1981—Bills, 21-14 (B)
1984—Redskins, 41-14 (W)
1987—Redskins, 27-7 (B)
1990—Redskins, 29-14 (W)
1991—*Redskins, 37-24 (Minneapolis)
1993—Bills, 24-10 (B)
1996—Bills, 38-13 (B)
1999—Bills, 34-17 (W)
(RS Pts.—Redskins 178, Bills 176)
(PS Pts.—Redskins 37, Bills 24)
**Super Bowl XXVI*

CAROLINA vs. ARIZONA
RS: Panthers lead series, 1-0;
See Arizona vs. Carolina

CAROLINA vs. ATLANTA
RS: Falcons lead series, 7-5;
See Atlanta vs. Carolina

CAROLINA vs. BALTIMORE
RS: Panthers lead series, 1-0;
See Baltimore vs. Carolina

CAROLINA vs. BUFFALO
RS: Bills lead series, 2-0;
See Buffalo vs. Carolina

CAROLINA vs. CHICAGO
RS: Bears lead series, 1-0
1995—Bears, 31-27 (Chi)
(RS Pts.—Bears 31, Panthers 27)

CAROLINA vs. CINCINNATI
RS: Panthers lead series, 1-0
1999—Panthers, 27-3 (Car)
(RS Pts.—Panthers 27, Bengals 3)

CAROLINA vs. CLEVELAND
RS: Panthers lead series, 1-0
1999—Panthers, 31-17 (Cle)
(RS Pts.—Panthers 31, Browns 17)

CAROLINA vs. DALLAS
RS: Cowboys lead series, 2-1
PS: Panthers lead series, 1-0
1996—*Panthers, 26-17 (C)
1997—Panthers, 23-13 (D)
1998—Cowboys, 27-20 (D)
2000—Cowboys, 16-13 (C) OT
(RS Pts.—Cowboys 56, Panthers 56)
(PS Pts.—Panthers 26, Cowboys 17)
**NFC Divisional Playoff*

CAROLINA vs. DENVER
RS: Broncos lead series, 1-0
1997—Broncos, 34-0 (D)
(RS Pts.—Broncos 34, Panthers 0)

CAROLINA vs. DETROIT
RS: Lions lead series, 1-0
1999—Lions, 24-9 (C)
(RS Pts.—Lions 24, Panthers 9)

CAROLINA vs. GREEN BAY
RS: Series tied, 2-2
PS: Packers lead series, 1-0
1996—*Packers, 30-13 (GB)
1997—Packers, 31-10 (C)
1998—Packers, 37-30 (C)
1999—Panthers, 33-31 (GB)
2000—Panthers, 31-14 (C)
(RS Pts.—Packers 113, Panthers 104)
(PS Pts.—Packers 30, Panthers 13)
**NFC Championship*

CAROLINA vs. INDIANAPOLIS
RS: Panthers lead series, 2-0
1995—Panthers, 13-10 (C)
1998—Panthers, 27-19 (I)
(RS Pts.—Panthers 40, Colts 29)

CAROLINA vs. JACKSONVILLE
RS: Jaguars lead series, 2-0
1996—Jaguars, 24-14 (J)
1999—Jaguars, 22-20 (C)
(RS Pts.—Jaguars 46, Panthers 34)

CAROLINA vs. KANSAS CITY
RS: Chiefs lead series, 2-0
1997—Chiefs, 35-14 (C)
2000—Chiefs, 15-14 (KC)
(RS Pts.—Chiefs 50, Panthers 28)

CAROLINA vs. MIAMI
RS: Dolphins lead series, 1-0
1998—Dolphins, 13-9 (C)
(RS Pts.—Dolphins 13, Panthers 9)

CAROLINA vs. MINNESOTA
RS: Vikings lead series, 3-0
1996—Vikings, 14-12 (M)
1997—Vikings, 21-14 (M)
2000—Vikings, 31-17 (M)
(RS Pts.—Vikings 66, Panthers 43)

CAROLINA vs. NEW ENGLAND
RS: Panthers lead series, 1-0
1995—Panthers, 20-17 (NE) OT
(RS Pts.—Panthers 20, Patriots 17)

CAROLINA vs. NEW ORLEANS
RS: Series tied, 6-6
1995—Panthers, 20-3 (C)
Saints, 34-26 (NO)
1996—Panthers, 22-20 (NO)
Panthers, 19-7 (C)
1997—Panthers, 13-0 (NO)
Saints, 16-13 (C)
1998—Saints, 19-14 (NO)
Panthers, 31-17 (C)
1999—Saints, 19-10 (NO)
Panthers, 45-13 (C)
2000—Saints, 24-6 (NO)
Saints, 20-10 (C)
(RS Pts.—Panthers 229, Saints 192)

CAROLINA vs. N.Y. GIANTS
RS: Panthers lead series, 1-0
1995—Panthers, 27-17 (C)
(RS Pts.—Panthers 27, Giants 17)

CAROLINA vs. N.Y. JETS
RS: Series tied, 1-1
1995—Panthers, 26-15 (C)
1998—Jets, 48-21 (NY)
(RS Pts.—Jets 63, Panthers 47)

CAROLINA vs. OAKLAND
RS: Series tied, 1-1
1997—Panthers, 38-14 (C)
2000—Raiders, 52-9 (O)
(RS Pts.— Raiders 66, Panthers 47)

CAROLINA vs. PHILADELPHIA
RS: Series tied, 1-1
1996—Eagles, 20-9 (P)
1999—Panthers, 33-7 (C)
(RS Pts.—Panthers 42, Eagles 27)

CAROLINA vs. PITTSBURGH
RS: Series tied, 1-1
1996—Panthers, 18-14 (C)
1999—Steelers, 30-20 (P)
(RS Pts.—Steelers 44, Panthers 38)

CAROLINA vs. ST. LOUIS
RS: Panthers lead series, 7-5
1995—Rams, 31-10 (C)
Rams, 28-17 (StL)
1996—Panthers, 45-13 (C)
Panthers, 20-10 (StL)
1997—Panthers, 16-10 (StL)
Rams, 30-18 (C)
1998—Panthers, 24-20 (StL)
Panthers, 20-13 (C)
1999—Rams, 35-10 (StL)
Rams, 34-21 (C)
2000—Panthers, 27-24 (StL)
Panthers, 16-3 (C)
(RS Pts.—Rams 251, Panthers 244)

CAROLINA vs. SAN DIEGO
RS: Panthers lead series, 2-0
1997—Panthers, 26-7 (SD)
2000—Panthers, 30-22 (C)
(RS Pts.—Panthers 56, Chargers 29)

CAROLINA vs. SAN FRANCISCO
RS: Panthers lead series, 7-5
1995—Panthers, 13-7 (SF)
49ers, 31-10 (C)
1996—Panthers, 23-7 (C)
Panthers, 30-24 (SF)
1997—49ers, 34-21 (C)
49ers, 27-19 (SF)
1998—49ers, 25-23 (SF)
49ers, 31-28 (C) OT
1999—Panthers, 31-29 (SF)
Panthers, 41-24 (C)
2000—Panthers, 38-22 (SF)
Panthers, 34-16 (C)
(RS Pts.—Panthers 311, 49ers 277)

CAROLINA vs. SEATTLE
RS: Panthers lead series, 1-0
2000—Panthers, 26-3 (C)
(RS Pts.—Panthers 26, Seahawks 3)

CAROLINA vs. TAMPA BAY
RS: Buccaneers lead series, 2-1
1995—Buccaneers, 20-13 (C)
1996—Panthers, 24-0 (C)
1998—Buccaneers, 16-13 (TB)
(RS Pts.—Panthers 50, Buccaneers 36)

CAROLINA vs. *TENNESSEE
RS: Panthers lead series, 1-0
1996—Panthers, 31-6 (H)
(RS Pts.—Panthers 31, Titans 6)
**Franchise in Houston prior to 1997; known as Oilers prior to 1999*

CAROLINA vs. WASHINGTON
RS: Redskins lead series, 5-0
1995—Redskins, 20-17 (W)
1997—Redskins, 24-10 (C)
1998—Redskins, 28-25 (C)
1999—Redskins, 38-36 (W)
2000—Redskins, 20-17 (W)
(RS Pts.—Redskins 130, Panthers 105)

CHICAGO vs. ARIZONA
RS: Bears lead series, 52-26-6;
See Arizona vs. Chicago

CHICAGO vs. ATLANTA
RS: Falcons lead series, 10-9;
See Atlanta vs. Chicago

CHICAGO vs. BALTIMORE
RS: Bears lead series, 1-0;
See Baltimore vs. Chicago

CHICAGO vs. BUFFALO
RS: Bears lead series, 5-3;
See Buffalo vs. Chicago

CHICAGO vs. CAROLINA
RS: Bears lead series, 1-0;
See Carolina vs. Chicago

CHICAGO vs. CINCINNATI
RS: Bengals lead series, 4-2
1972—Bengals, 13-3 (Chi)
1980—Bengals, 17-14 (Chi) OT
1986—Bears, 44-7 (Cin)
1989—Bears, 17-14 (Chi)
1992—Bengals, 31-28 (Chi) OT
1995—Bengals, 16-10 (Cin)
(RS Pts.—Bears 116, Bengals 98)

CHICAGO vs. CLEVELAND
RS: Browns lead series, 8-3
1951—Browns, 42-21 (Cle)
1954—Browns, 39-10 (Chi)
1960—Browns, 42-0 (Cle)
1961—Bears, 17-14 (Chi)
1967—Browns, 24-0 (Cle)
1969—Browns, 28-24 (Chi)
1972—Bears, 17-0 (Cle)
1980—Browns, 27-21 (Cle)
1986—Bears, 41-31 (Chi)
1989—Browns, 27-7 (Cle)
1992—Browns, 27-14 (Cle)
(RS Pts.—Browns 301, Bears 172)

CHICAGO vs. DALLAS
RS: Cowboys lead series, 9-8
PS: Cowboys lead series, 2-0
1960—Bears, 17-7 (C)
1962—Bears, 34-33 (D)
1964—Cowboys, 24-10 (C)
1968—Cowboys, 34-3 (C)
1971—Bears, 23-19 (C)
1973—Cowboys, 20-17 (C)
1976—Cowboys, 31-21 (D)
1977—*Cowboys, 37-7 (D)
1979—Cowboys, 24-20 (D)
1981—Cowboys, 10-9 (D)
1984—Cowboys, 23-14 (C)
1985—Bears, 44-0 (D)
1986—Bears, 24-10 (D)
1988—Bears, 17-7 (C)
1991—**Cowboys, 17-13 (C)
1992—Cowboys, 27-14 (D)

1996—Bears, 22-6 (C)
1997—Cowboys, 27-3 (D)
1998—Bears, 13-12 (C)
(RS Pts.—Cowboys 314, Bears 305)
(PS Pts.—Cowboys 54, Bears 20)
NFC Divisional Playoff
***NFC First-Round Playoff*

CHICAGO vs. DENVER
RS: Broncos lead series, 6-5
1971—Broncos, 6-3 (D)
1973—Bears, 33-14 (D)
1976—Broncos, 28-14 (C)
1978—Broncos, 16-7 (D)
1981—Bears, 35-24 (C)
1983—Bears, 31-14 (C)
1984—Bears, 27-0 (C)
1987—Broncos, 31-29 (D)
1990—Bears, 16-13 (D) OT
1993—Broncos, 13-3 (C)
1996—Broncos, 17-12 (D)
(RS Pts.—Bears 210, Broncos 176)

CHICAGO vs. *DETROIT
RS: Bears lead series, 79-58-5
1930—Spartans, 7-6 (P)
Bears, 14-6 (C)
1931—Bears, 9-6 (C)
Spartans, 3-0 (P)
1932—Tie, 13-13 (C)
Tie, 7-7 (P)
Bears, 9-0 (C)
1933—Bears, 17-14 (C)
Bears, 17-7 (P)
1934—Bears, 19-16 (D)
Bears, 10-7 (C)
1935—Tie, 20-20 (C)
Lions, 14-2 (D)
1936—Bears, 12-10 (C)
Lions, 13-7 (D)
1937—Bears, 28-20 (C)
Bears, 13-0 (D)
1938—Lions, 13-7 (C)
Lions, 14-7 (D)
1939—Lions, 10-0 (C)
Bears, 23-13 (D)
1940—Bears, 7-0 (C)
Lions, 17-14 (D)
1941—Bears, 49-0 (C)
Bears, 24-7 (D)
1942—Bears, 16-0 (C)
Bears, 42-0 (D)
1943—Bears, 27-21 (D)
Bears, 35-14 (C)
1944—Tie, 21-21 (C)
Lions, 41-21 (D)
1945—Lions, 16-10 (D)
Lions, 35-28 (C)
1946—Bears, 42-6 (C)
Bears, 45-24 (D)
1947—Bears, 33-24 (C)
Bears, 34-14 (D)
1948—Bears, 28-0 (C)
Bears, 42-14 (D)
1949—Bears, 27-24 (C)
Bears, 28-7 (D)
1950—Bears, 35-21 (D)
Bears, 6-3 (C)
1951—Bears, 28-23 (D)
Lions, 41-28 (C)
1952—Bears, 24-23 (C)
Lions, 45-21 (D)
1953—Lions, 20-16 (C)
Lions, 13-7 (D)
1954—Lions, 48-23 (D)
Bears, 28-24 (C)
1955—Bears, 24-14 (D)
Bears, 21-20 (C)
1956—Lions, 42-10 (D)
Bears, 38-21 (C)
1957—Bears, 27-7 (D)
Lions, 21-13 (C)
1958—Bears, 20-7 (D)
Bears, 21-16 (C)
1959—Bears, 24-14 (D)
Bears, 25-14 (C)
1960—Bears, 28-7 (C)
Lions, 36-0 (D)
1961—Bears, 31-17 (D)
Lions, 16-15 (C)
1962—Lions, 11-3 (D)
Bears, 3-0 (C)
1963—Bears, 37-21 (D)
Bears, 24-14 (C)
1964—Lions, 10-0 (C)
Bears, 27-24 (D)
1965—Bears, 38-10 (C)
Bears, 17-10 (D)
1966—Lions, 14-3 (D)
Tie, 10-10 (C)
1967—Bears, 14-3 (C)
Bears, 27-13 (D)
1968—Lions, 42-0 (D)
Lions, 28-10 (C)
1969—Lions, 13-7 (D)
Lions, 20-3 (C)
1970—Lions, 28-14 (D)
Lions, 16-10 (C)
1971—Bears, 28-23 (D)
Lions, 28-3 (C)
1972—Lions, 38-24 (C)
Lions, 14-0 (D)
1973—Lions, 30-7 (C)
Lions, 40-7 (D)
1974—Bears, 17-9 (C)
Lions, 34-17 (D)
1975—Lions, 27-7 (D)
Bears, 25-21 (C)
1976—Bears, 10-3 (C)
Lions, 14-10 (D)
1977—Bears, 30-20 (C)
Bears, 31-14 (D)
1978—Bears, 19-0 (D)
Lions, 21-17 (C)
1979—Bears, 35-7 (C)
Lions, 20-0 (D)
1980—Bears, 24-7 (C)
Bears, 23-17 (D) OT
1981—Lions, 48-17 (D)
Lions, 23-7 (C)
1982—Lions, 17-10 (D)
Bears, 20-17 (C)
1983—Lions, 31-17 (D)
Lions, 38-17 (C)
1984—Bears, 16-14 (C)
Bears, 30-13 (D)
1985—Bears, 24-3 (C)
Bears, 37-17 (D)
1986—Bears, 13-7 (C)
Bears, 16-13 (D)
1987—Bears, 30-10 (C)
1988—Bears, 24-7 (D)
Bears, 13-12 (C)
1989—Bears, 47-27 (D)
Lions, 27-17 (C)
1990—Bears, 23-17 (C) OT
Lions, 38-21 (D)
1991—Bears, 20-10 (C)
Lions, 16-6 (D)
1992—Bears, 27-24 (C)
Lions, 16-3 (D)
1993—Bears, 10-6 (D)
Lions, 20-14 (C)
1994—Lions, 21-16 (D)
Bears, 20-10 (C)
1995—Lions, 24-17 (C)
Lions, 27-7 (D)
1996—Lions, 35-16 (D)
Bears, 31-14 (C)
1997—Lions, 32-7 (C)
Lions, 55-20 (D)
1998—Bears, 31-27 (C)
Lions, 26-3 (D)
1999—Lions, 21-17 (D)
Bears, 28-10 (C)
2000—Lions, 21-14 (C)
Bears, 23-20 (D)
(RS Pts.—Bears 2,636, Lions 2,499)
**Franchise in Portsmouth prior to 1934 and known as the Spartans*

***CHICAGO vs. GREEN BAY**
RS: Bears lead series, 83-71-6
PS: Bears lead series, 1-0
1921—Staleys, 20-0 (C)
1923—Bears, 3-0 (GB)
1924—Bears, 3-0 (C)
1925—Packers, 14-10 (GB)
Bears, 21-0 (C)
1926—Tie, 6-6 (GB)
Bears, 19-13 (C)
Tie, 3-3 (C)
1927—Bears, 7-6 (GB)
Bears, 14-6 (C)
1928—Tie, 12-12 (GB)
Packers, 16-6 (C)
Packers, 6-0 (C)
1929—Packers, 23-0 (GB)
Packers, 14-0 (C)
Packers, 25-0 (C)
1930—Packers, 7-0 (GB)
Packers, 13-12 (C)
Bears, 21-0 (C)
1931—Packers, 7-0 (GB)
Packers, 6-2 (C)
Bears, 7-6 (C)
1932—Tie, 0-0 (GB)
Packers, 2-0 (C)
Bears, 9-0 (C)
1933—Bears, 14-7 (GB)
Bears, 10-7 (C)
Bears, 7-6 (C)
1934—Bears, 24-10 (GB)
Bears, 27-14 (C)
1935—Packers, 7-0 (GB)
Packers, 17-14 (C)
1936—Bears, 30-3 (GB)
Packers, 21-10 (C)
1937—Bears, 14-2 (GB)
Packers, 24-14 (C)
1938—Bears, 2-0 (GB)
Packers, 24-17 (C)
1939—Packers, 21-16 (GB)
Bears, 30-27 (C)
1940—Bears, 41-10 (GB)
Bears, 14-7 (C)
1941—Bears, 25-17 (GB)
Packers, 16-14 (C)
**Bears, 33-14 (C)
1942—Bears, 44-28 (GB)
Bears, 38-7 (C)
1943—Tie, 21-21 (GB)
Bears, 21-7 (C)
1944—Packers, 42-28 (GB)
Bears, 21-0 (C)
1945—Packers, 31-21 (GB)
Bears, 28-24 (C)
1946—Bears, 30-7 (GB)
Bears, 10-7 (C)
1947—Packers, 29-20 (GB)
Bears, 20-17 (C)
1948—Bears, 45-7 (GB)
Bears, 7-6 (C)
1949—Bears, 17-0 (GB)
Bears, 24-3 (C)
1950—Packers, 31-21 (GB)
Bears, 28-14 (C)
1951—Bears, 31-20 (GB)
Bears, 24-13 (C)
1952—Bears, 24-14 (GB)
Packers, 41-28 (C)
1953—Bears, 17-13 (GB)
Tie, 21-21 (C)
1954—Bears, 10-3 (GB)
Bears, 28-23 (C)
1955—Packers, 24-3 (GB)
Bears, 52-31 (C)
1956—Bears, 37-21 (GB)
Bears, 38-14 (C)
1957—Packers, 21-17 (GB)
Bears, 21-14 (C)
1958—Bears, 34-20 (GB)
Bears, 24-10 (C)
1959—Packers, 9-6 (GB)
Bears, 28-17 (C)
1960—Bears, 17-14 (GB)
Packers, 41-13 (C)
1961—Packers, 24-0 (GB)
Packers, 31-28 (C)
1962—Packers, 49-0 (GB)
Packers, 38-7 (C)
1963—Bears, 10-3 (GB)
Bears, 26-7 (C)
1964—Packers, 23-12 (GB)
Packers, 17-3 (C)
1965—Packers, 23-14 (GB)
Bears, 31-10 (C)
1966—Packers, 17-0 (C)
Packers, 13-6 (GB)
1967—Packers, 13-10 (GB)
Packers, 17-13 (C)
1968—Bears, 13-10 (GB)
Packers, 28-27 (C)
1969—Packers, 17-0 (GB)
Packers, 21-3 (C)
1970—Packers, 20-19 (GB)
Bears, 35-17 (C)
1971—Packers, 17-14 (C)
Packers, 31-10 (GB)
1972—Packers, 20-17 (GB)
Packers, 23-17 (C)
1973—Bears, 31-17 (GB)
Packers, 21-0 (C)
1974—Bears, 10-9 (C)
Packers, 20-3 (Mil)
1975—Bears, 27-14 (C)
Packers, 28-7 (GB)
1976—Bears, 24-13 (C)
Bears, 16-10 (GB)
1977—Bears, 26-0 (GB)
Bears, 21-10 (C)
1978—Packers, 24-14 (GB)
Bears, 14-0 (C)
1979—Bears, 6-3 (C)
Bears, 15-14 (GB)
1980—Packers, 12-6 (GB) OT
Bears, 61-7 (C)
1981—Packers, 16-9 (C)
Packers, 21-17 (GB)
1983—Packers, 31-28 (GB)
Bears, 23-21 (C)
1984—Bears, 9-7 (GB)
Packers, 20-14 (C)
1985—Bears, 23-7 (C)
Bears, 16-10 (GB)
1986—Bears, 25-12 (GB)
Bears, 12-10 (C)
1987—Bears, 26-24 (GB)
Bears, 23-10 (C)
1988—Bears, 24-6 (GB)
Bears, 16-0 (C)
1989—Packers, 14-13 (GB)
Packers, 40-28 (C)
1990—Bears, 31-13 (GB)
Bears, 27-13 (C)
1991—Bears, 10-0 (GB)
Bears, 27-13 (C)
1992—Bears, 30-10 (GB)
Packers, 17-3 (C)
1993—Packers, 17-3 (GB)
Bears, 30-17 (C)
1994—Packers, 33-6 (C)
Packers, 40-3 (GB)
1995—Packers, 27-24 (C)
Packers, 35-28 (GB)
1996—Packers, 37-6 (C)
Packers, 28-17 (GB)
1997—Packers, 38-24 (GB)
Packers, 24-23 (C)
1998—Packers, 26-20 (GB)
Packers, 16-13 (C)
1999—Bears, 14-13 (GB)
Packers, 35-19 (C)
2000—Bears, 27-24 (GB)
Packers, 28-6 (C)

(RS Pts.—Bears 2,708, Packers 2,534)
(PS Pts.—Bears 33, Packers 14)
Bears known as Staleys prior to 1922
**Division Playoff*

CHICAGO vs. *INDIANAPOLIS
RS: Colts lead series, 21-17
1953—Colts, 13-9 (B)
Colts, 16-14 (C)
1954—Bears, 28-9 (C)
Bears, 28-13 (B)
1955—Colts, 23-17 (B)
Bears, 38-10 (C)
1956—Colts, 28-21 (B)
Bears, 58-27 (C)
1957—Colts, 21-10 (B)
Colts, 29-14 (C)
1958—Colts, 51-38 (B)
Colts, 17-0 (C)
1959—Bears, 26-21 (B)
Colts, 21-7 (C)
1960—Colts, 42-7 (B)
Colts, 24-20 (C)
1961—Bears, 24-10 (C)
Bears, 21-20 (B)
1962—Bears, 35-15 (C)
Bears, 57-0 (B)
1963—Bears, 10-3 (C)
Bears, 17-7 (B)
1964—Colts, 52-0 (B)
Colts, 40-24 (C)
1965—Colts, 26-21 (C)
Bears, 13-0 (B)
1966—Bears, 27-17 (C)
Colts, 21-16 (B)
1967—Colts, 24-3 (C)
1968—Colts, 28-7 (B)
1969—Colts, 24-21 (C)
1970—Colts, 21-20 (B)
1975—Colts, 35-7 (C)
1983—Colts, 22-19 (B) OT
1985—Bears, 17-10 (C)
1988—Bears, 17-13 (I)
1991—Bears, 31-17 (I)
2000—Bears, 27-24 (C)
(RS Pts.—Colts 794, Bears 769)
Franchise in Baltimore prior to 1984

CHICAGO vs. JACKSONVILLE
RS: Series tied, 1-1
1995—Bears, 30-27 (J)
1998—Jaguars, 24-23 (C)
(RS Pts.—Bears 53, Jaguars 51)

CHICAGO vs. KANSAS CITY
RS: Bears lead series, 5-3
1973—Chiefs, 19-7 (KC)
1977—Bears, 28-27 (C)
1981—Bears, 16-13 (KC) OT
1987—Bears, 31-28 (C)
1990—Chiefs, 21-10 (C)
1993—Bears, 19-17 (KC)
1996—Chiefs, 14-10 (KC)
1999—Bears, 20-17 (C)
(RS Pts.—Chiefs 156, Bears 141)

CHICAGO vs. MIAMI
RS: Dolphins lead series, 5-3
1971—Dolphins, 34-3 (M)
1975—Dolphins, 46-13 (C)
1979—Dolphins, 31-16 (M)
1985—Dolphins, 38-24 (M)
1988—Bears, 34-7 (C)
1991—Dolphins, 16-13 (C) OT
1994—Bears, 17-14 (M)
1997—Bears, 36-33 (M) OT
(RS Pts.—Dolphins 219, Bears 156)

CHICAGO vs. MINNESOTA
RS: Vikings lead series, 44-33-2
PS: Bears lead series, 1-0
1961—Vikings, 37-13 (M)
Bears, 52-35 (C)
1962—Bears, 13-0 (M)
Bears, 31-30 (C)
1963—Bears, 28-7 (M)
Tie, 17-17 (C)
1964—Bears, 34-28 (M)
Vikings, 41-14 (C)
1965—Bears, 45-37 (M)
Vikings, 24-17 (C)
1966—Bears, 13-10 (M)
Bears, 41-28 (C)
1967—Bears, 17-7 (M)
Tie, 10-10 (C)
1968—Bears, 27-17 (M)
Bears, 26-24 (C)
1969—Vikings, 31-0 (C)
Vikings, 31-14 (M)
1970—Vikings, 24-0 (C)
Vikings, 16-13 (M)
1971—Bears, 20-17 (M)
Vikings, 27-10 (C)
1972—Bears, 13-10 (C)
Vikings, 23-10 (M)
1973—Vikings, 22-13 (C)
Vikings, 31-13 (M)
1974—Vikings, 11-7 (M)
Vikings, 17-0 (C)
1975—Vikings, 28-3 (M)
Vikings, 13-9 (C)
1976—Vikings, 20-19 (M)
Bears, 14-13 (C)
1977—Vikings, 22-16 (M) OT
Bears, 10-7 (C)
1978—Vikings, 24-20 (C)
Vikings, 17-14 (M)
1979—Bears, 26-7 (C)
Vikings, 30-27 (M)
1980—Vikings, 34-14 (C)
Vikings, 13-7 (M)
1981—Vikings, 24-21 (M)
Bears, 10-9 (C)
1982—Vikings, 35-7 (M)
1983—Vikings, 23-14 (C)
Bears, 19-13 (M)
1984—Bears, 16-7 (C)
Bears, 34-3 (M)
1985—Bears, 33-24 (M)
Bears, 27-9 (C)
1986—Bears, 23-0 (C)
Vikings, 23-7 (M)
1987—Bears, 27-7 (C)
Bears, 30-24 (M)
1988—Vikings, 31-7 (C)
Vikings, 28-27 (M)
1989—Bears, 38-7 (C)
Vikings, 27-16 (M)
1990—Bears, 19-16 (C)
Vikings, 41-13 (M)
1991—Bears, 10-6 (C)
Bears, 34-17 (M)
1992—Vikings, 21-20 (M)
Vikings, 38-10 (C)
1993—Vikings, 10-7 (M)
Vikings, 19-12 (C)
1994—Vikings, 42-14 (C)
Vikings, 33-27 (M) OT
*Bears, 35-18 (M)
1995—Bears, 31-14 (C)
Bears, 14-6 (M)
1996—Vikings, 20-14 (C)
Bears, 15-13 (M)
1997—Vikings, 27-24 (C)
Vikings, 29-22 (M)
1998—Vikings, 31-28 (C)
Vikings, 48-22 (M)
1999—Bears, 24-22 (M)
Vikings, 27-24 (C) OT
2000—Vikings, 30-27 (M)
Vikings, 28-16 (C)
RS Pts.—Vikings 1,672, Bears 1,473)
(PS Pts.—Bears 35, Vikings 18)
NFC First-Round Playoff

CHICAGO vs. NEW ENGLAND
RS: Patriots lead series, 5-3
PS: Bears lead series, 1-0
1973—Patriots, 13-10 (C)
1979—Patriots, 27-7 (C)
1982—Bears, 26-13 (C)
1985—Bears, 20-7 (C)
*Bears, 46-10 (New Orleans)
1988—Patriots, 30-7 (NE)
1994—Patriots, 13-3 (C)
1997—Patriots, 31-3 (NE)
2000—Bears, 24-17 (C)
(RS Pts.—Patriots 151, Bears 100)
(PS Pts.—Bears 46, Patriots 10)
Super Bowl XX

CHICAGO vs. NEW ORLEANS
RS: Bears lead series, 10-9
PS: Bears lead series, 1-0
1968—Bears, 23-17 (NO)
1970—Bears, 24-3 (NO)
1971—Bears, 35-14 (C)
1973—Saints, 21-16 (NO)
1974—Bears, 24-10 (C)
1975—Bears, 42-17 (NO)
1977—Saints, 42-24 (C)
1980—Bears, 22-3 (C)
1982—Saints, 10-0 (C)
1983—Saints, 34-31 (NO) OT
1984—Bears, 20-7 (C)
1987—Saints, 19-17 (C)
1990—*Bears, 16-6 (C)
1991—Bears, 20-17 (NO)
1992—Saints, 28-6 (NO)
1994—Bears, 17-7 (C)
1996—Saints, 27-24 (NO)
1997—Saints, 20-17 (C)
1999—Bears, 14-10 (C)
2000—Saints, 31-10 (C)
(RS Pts.—Bears 386, Saints 337)
(PS Pts.—Bears 16, Saints 6)
NFC First-Round Playoff

CHICAGO vs. N.Y. GIANTS
RS: Bears lead series, 25-17-2
PS: Bears lead series, 5-3
1925—Bears, 19-7 (NY)
Giants, 9-0 (C)
1926—Bears, 7-0 (C)
1927—Giants, 13-7 (NY)
1928—Bears, 13-0 (C)
1929—Giants, 26-14 (C)
Giants, 34-0 (NY)
Giants, 14-9 (C)
1930—Giants, 12-0 (C)
Bears, 12-0 (NY)
1931—Bears, 6-0 (C)
Bears, 12-6 (NY)
Giants, 25-6 (C)
1932—Bears, 28-8 (NY)
Bears, 6-0 (C)
1933—Bears, 14-10 (C)
Giants, 3-0 (NY)
*Bears, 23-21 (C)
1934—Bears, 27-7 (C)
Bears, 10-9 (NY)
*Giants, 30-13 (NY)
1935—Bears, 20-3 (NY)
Giants, 3-0 (C)
1936—Bears, 25-7 (NY)
1937—Tie, 3-3 (NY)
1939—Giants, 16-13 (NY)
1940—Bears, 37-21 (NY)
1941—*Bears, 37-9 (C)
1942—Bears, 26-7 (NY)
1943—Bears, 56-7 (NY)
1946—Giants, 14-0 (NY)
*Bears, 24-14 (NY)
1948—Bears, 35-14 (C)
1949—Giants, 35-28 (NY)
1956—Tie, 17-17 (NY)
*Giants, 47-7 (NY)
1962—Giants, 26-24 (C)
1963—*Bears, 14-10 (C)
1965—Bears, 35-14 (NY)
1967—Bears, 34-7 (C)
1969—Giants, 28-24 (NY)
1970—Bears, 24-16 (NY)
1974—Bears, 16-13 (C)
1977—Bears, 12-9 (NY) OT
1985—**Bears, 21-0 (C)
1987—Bears, 34-19 (C)
1990—**Giants, 31-3 (NY)
1991—Bears, 20-17 (C)
1992—Giants, 27-14 (C)
1993—Giants, 26-20 (C)
1995—Bears, 27-24 (NY)
2000—Giants, 14-7 (C)
(RS Pts.—Bears 741, Giants 570)
(PS Pts.—Giants 162, Bears 142)
NFL Championship
**NFC Divisional Playoff*

CHICAGO vs. N.Y. JETS
RS: Bears lead series, 4-3
1974—Jets, 23-21 (C)
1979—Bears, 23-13 (C)
1985—Bears, 19-6 (NY)
1991—Bears, 19-13 (C) OT
1994—Bears, 19-7 (NY)
1997—Jets, 23-15 (C)
2000—Jets, 17-10 (NY)
(RS Pts.—Bears 126, Jets 102)

CHICAGO vs. *OAKLAND
RS: Raiders lead series, 6-4
1972—Raiders, 28-21 (O)
1976—Raiders, 28-27 (C)
1978—Raiders, 25-19 (C) OT
1981—Bears, 23-6 (O)
1984—Bears, 17-6 (C)
1987—Bears, 6-3 (LA)
1990—Raiders, 24-10 (LA)
1993—Raiders, 16-14 (C)
1996—Bears, 19-17 (C)
1999—Raiders, 24-17 (O)
(RS Pts.—Raiders 177, Bears 173)
Franchise in Los Angeles from 1982-1994

CHICAGO vs. PHILADELPHIA
RS: Bears lead series, 24-6-1
PS: Series tied, 1-1
1933—Tie, 3-3 (P)
1935—Bears, 39-0 (P)
1936—Bears, 17-0 (P)
Bears, 28-7 (P)
1938—Bears, 28-6 (P)
1939—Bears, 27-14 (C)
1941—Bears, 49-14 (P)
1942—Bears, 45-14 (C)
1944—Bears, 28-7 (P)
1946—Bears, 21-14 (C)
1947—Bears, 40-7 (C)
1948—Eagles, 12-7 (P)
1949—Bears, 38-21 (C)
1955—Bears, 17-10 (C)
1961—Eagles, 16-14 (P)
1963—Bears, 16-7 (C)
1968—Bears, 29-16 (P)
1970—Bears, 20-16 (C)
1972—Bears, 21-12 (P)
1975—Bears, 15-13 (C)
1979—*Eagles, 27-17 (P)
1980—Eagles, 17-14 (P)
1983—Bears, 7-6 (P)
Bears, 17-14 (C)
1986—Bears, 13-10 (C) OT
1987—Bears, 35-3 (P)
1988—**Bears, 20-12 (C)
1989—Bears, 27-13 (C)
1993—Bears, 17-6 (P)
1994—Eagles, 30-22 (P)
1995—Bears, 20-14 (C)
1999—Eagles, 20-16 (C)
2000—Eagles, 13-9 (P)
(RS Pts.—Bears 699, Eagles 355)
(PS Pts.—Eagles 39, Bears 37)
NFC First-Round Playoff
**NFC Divisional Playoff*

CHICAGO vs. *PITTSBURGH
RS: Bears lead series, 16-6-1
1934—Bears, 28-0 (P)
1935—Bears, 23-7 (P)
1936—Bears, 27-9 (P)
Bears, 26-6 (C)
1937—Bears, 7-0 (P)
1939—Bears, 32-0 (P)

1941—Bears, 34-7 (C)
1945—Bears, 28-7 (C)
1947—Bears, 49-7 (C)
1949—Bears, 30-21 (C)
1958—Steelers, 24-10 (P)
1959—Bears, 27-21 (C)
1963—Tie, 17-17 (P)
1967—Steelers, 41-13 (P)
1969—Bears, 38-7 (C)
1971—Bears, 17-15 (C)
1975—Steelers, 34-3 (P)
1980—Steelers, 38-3 (P)
1986—Bears, 13-10 (C) OT
1989—Bears, 20-0 (P)
1992—Bears, 30-6 (C)
1995—Steelers, 37-34 (C) OT
1998—Steelers, 17-12 (P)
(RS Pts.—Bears 521, Steelers 331)
Steelers known as Pirates prior to 1941

CHICAGO vs. *ST. LOUIS
RS: Bears lead series, 47-32-3
PS: Series tied, 1-1
1937—Bears, 20-2 (Clev)
Bears, 15-7 (C)
1938—Rams, 14-7 (C)
Rams, 23-21 (Clev)
1939—Bears, 30-21 (Clev)
Bears, 35-21 (C)
1940—Bears, 21-14 (Clev)
Bears, 47-25 (C)
1941—Bears, 48-21 (Clev)
Bears, 31-13 (C)
1942—Bears, 21-7 (Clev)
Bears, 47-0 (C)
1944—Rams, 19-7 (Clev)
Bears, 28-21 (C)
1945—Rams, 17-0 (Clev)
Rams, 41-21 (C)
1946—Tie, 28-28 (C)
Bears, 27-21 (LA)
1947—Bears, 41-21 (LA)
Rams, 17-14 (C)
1948—Bears, 42-21 (C)
Bears, 21-6 (LA)
1949—Rams, 31-16 (C)
Rams, 27-24 (LA)
1950—Bears, 24-20 (LA)
Bears, 24-14 (C)
**Rams, 24-14 (LA)
1951—Rams, 42-17 (C)
1952—Rams, 31-7 (LA)
Rams, 40-24 (C)
1953—Rams, 38-24 (LA)
Bears, 24-21 (C)
1954—Rams, 42-38 (LA)
Bears, 24-13 (C)
1955—Bears, 31-20 (LA)
Bears, 24-3 (C)
1956—Bears, 35-24 (LA)
Bears, 30-21 (C)
1957—Bears, 34-26 (C)
Bears, 16-10 (LA)
1958—Bears, 31-10 (C)
Rams, 41-35 (LA)
1959—Rams, 28-21 (C)
Bears, 26-21 (LA)
1960—Bears, 34-27 (C)
Tie, 24-24 (LA)
1961—Bears, 21-17 (LA)
Bears, 28-24 (C)
1962—Bears, 27-23 (LA)
Bears, 30-14 (C)
1963—Bears, 52-14 (LA)
Bears, 6-0 (C)
1964—Bears, 38-17 (C)
Bears, 34-24 (LA)
1965—Rams, 30-28 (LA)
Bears, 31-6 (C)
1966—Rams, 31-17 (LA)
Bears, 17-10 (C)
1967—Rams, 28-17 (C)
1968—Bears, 17-16 (LA)
1969—Rams, 9-7 (C)
1971—Rams, 17-3 (LA)
1972—Tie, 13-13 (C)
1973—Rams, 26-0 (C)
1975—Rams, 38-10 (LA)
1976—Rams, 20-12 (LA)
1977—Bears, 24-23 (C)
1979—Bears, 27-23 (C)
1981—Rams, 24-7 (C)
1982—Bears, 34-26 (LA)
1983—Rams, 21-14 (LA)
1984—Rams, 29-13 (LA)
1985—***Bears, 24-0 (C)
1986—Rams, 20-17 (C)
1988—Rams, 23-3 (LA)
1989—Bears, 20-10 (C)
1990—Bears, 38-9 (C)
1993—Rams, 20-6 (LA)
1994—Bears, 27-13 (C)
1995—Rams, 34-28 (StL)
1996—Bears, 35-9 (C)
1997—Bears, 13-10 (StL)
1998—Rams, 20-12 (C)
1999—Rams, 34-12 (StL)
(RS Pts.—Bears 1,897, Rams 1,679)
(PS Pts.—Bears 38, Rams 24)
Franchise in Los Angeles prior to 1995 and in Cleveland prior to 1946
**Conference Playoff*
***NFC Championship*

CHICAGO vs. SAN DIEGO
RS: Series tied, 4-4
1970—Chargers, 20-7 (C)
1974—Chargers, 28-21 (SD)
1978—Chargers, 40-7 (SD)
1981—Bears, 20-17 (C) OT
1984—Chargers, 20-7 (SD)
1993—Bears, 16-13 (SD)
1996—Bears, 27-14 (C)
1999—Bears, 23-20 (SD) OT
(RS Pts.—Chargers 172, Bears 128)

CHICAGO vs. SAN FRANCISCO
RS: 49ers lead series, 26-25-1
PS: 49ers lead series, 3-0
1950—Bears, 32-20 (SF)
Bears, 17-0 (C)
1951—Bears, 13-7 (C)
1952—49ers, 40-16 (C)
Bears, 20-17 (SF)
1953—49ers, 35-28 (C)
49ers, 24-14 (SF)
1954—49ers, 31-24 (C)
Bears, 31-27 (SF)
1955—49ers, 20-19 (C)
Bears, 34-23 (SF)
1956—Bears, 31-7 (C)
Bears, 38-21 (SF)
1957—49ers, 21-17 (C)
49ers, 21-17 (SF)
1958—Bears, 28-6 (C)
Bears, 27-14 (SF)
1959—49ers, 20-17 (SF)
Bears, 14-3 (C)
1960—Bears, 27-10 (C)
49ers, 25-7 (SF)
1961—Bears, 31-0 (C)
49ers, 41-31 (SF)
1962—Bears, 30-14 (SF)
49ers, 34-27 (C)
1963—49ers, 20-14 (SF)
Bears, 27-7 (C)
1964—49ers, 31-21 (SF)
Bears, 23-21 (C)
1965—49ers, 52-24 (SF)
Bears, 61-20 (C)
1966—Tie, 30-30 (C)
49ers, 41-14 (SF)
1967—Bears, 28-14 (SF)
1968—Bears, 27-19 (C)
1969—49ers, 42-21 (SF)
1970—49ers, 37-16 (C)
1971—49ers, 13-0 (SF)
1972—49ers, 34-21 (C)
1974—49ers, 34-0 (C)
1975—49ers, 31-3 (SF)
1976—Bears, 19-12 (SF)
1978—Bears, 16-13 (SF)
1979—Bears, 28-27 (SF)
1981—49ers, 28-17 (SF)
1983—Bears, 13-3 (C)
1984—*49ers, 23-0 (SF)
1985—Bears, 26-10 (SF)
1987—49ers, 41-0 (SF)
1988—Bears, 10-9 (C)
*49ers, 28-3 (C)
1989—49ers, 26-0 (SF)
1991—49ers, 52-14 (SF)
1994—**49ers, 44-15 (SF)
2000—49ers, 17-0 (SF)
(RS Pts.—49ers 1,165, Bears 1,063)
(PS Pts.—49ers 95, Bears 18)
NFC Championship
**NFC Divisional Playoff*

CHICAGO vs. SEATTLE
RS: Seahawks lead series, 5-2
1976—Bears, 34-7 (S)
1978—Seahawks, 31-29 (C)
1982—Seahawks, 20-14 (S)
1984—Seahawks, 38-9 (S)
1987—Seahawks, 34-21 (C)
1990—Bears, 17-0 (C)
1999—Seahawks, 14-13 (C)
(RS Pts.—Seahawks 144, Bears 137)

CHICAGO vs. TAMPA BAY
RS: Bears lead series, 31-15
1977—Bears, 10-0 (TB)
1978—Buccaneers, 33-19 (TB)
Bears, 14-3 (C)
1979—Buccaneers, 17-13 (C)
Bears, 14-0 (TB)
1980—Bears, 23-0 (C)
Bears, 14-13 (TB)
1981—Bears, 28-17 (C)
Buccaneers, 20-10 (TB)
1982—Buccaneers, 26-23 (TB) OT
1983—Bears, 17-10 (C)
Bears, 27-0 (TB)
1984—Bears, 34-14 (C)
Bears, 44-9 (TB)
1985—Bears, 38-28 (C)
Bears, 27-19 (TB)
1986—Bears, 23-3 (TB)
Bears, 48-14 (C)
1987—Bears, 20-3 (C)
Bears, 27-26 (TB)
1988—Bears, 28-10 (C)
Bears, 27-15 (TB)
1989—Buccaneers, 42-35 (TB)
Buccaneers, 32-31 (C)
1990—Bears, 26-6 (TB)
Bears, 27-14 (C)
1991—Bears, 21-20 (TB)
Bears, 27-0 (C)
1992—Bears, 31-14 (C)
Buccaneers, 20-17 (TB)
1993—Bears, 47-17 (C)
Buccaneers, 13-10 (TB)
1994—Bears, 21-9 (C)
Bears, 20-6 (TB)
1995—Bears, 25-6 (TB)
Bears, 31-10 (C)
1996—Bears, 13-10 (C)
Buccaneers, 34-19 (TB)
1997—Bears, 13-7 (C)
Buccaneers, 31-15 (TB)
1998—Buccaneers, 27-15 (TB)
Buccaneers, 31-17 (C)
1999—Buccaneers, 6-3 (TB)
Buccaneers, 20-6 (C)
2000—Buccaneers, 41-0 (TB)
Bears, 13-10 (C)
(RS Pts.—Bears 1,011, Buccaneers 706)

CHICAGO vs. *TENNESSEE
RS: Series tied, 4-4
1973—Bears, 35-14 (C)
1977—Oilers, 47-0 (H)
1980—Oilers, 10-6 (C)
1986—Bears, 20-7 (H)
1989—Oilers, 33-28 (C)
1992—Oilers, 24-7 (H)
1995—Bears, 35-32 (C)
1998—Bears, 23-20 (T)
(RS Pts.—Titans 187, Bears 154)
Franchise in Houston prior to 1997; known as Oilers prior to 1999

CHICAGO vs. *WASHINGTON
RS: Bears lead series, 18-15-1
PS: Redskins lead series, 4-3
1932—Tie, 7-7 (B)
1933—Bears, 7-0 (C)
Redskins, 10-0 (B)
1934—Bears, 21-0 (B)
1935—Bears, 30-14 (B)
1936—Bears, 26-0 (B)
1937—**Redskins, 28-21 (C)
1938—Bears, 31-7 (C)
1940—Redskins, 7-3 (W)
**Bears, 73-0 (W)
1941—Bears, 35-21 (C)
1942—**Redskins, 14-6 (W)
1943—Redskins, 21-7 (W)
**Bears, 41-21 (C)
1945—Redskins, 28-21 (W)
1946—Bears, 24-20 (C)
1947—Bears, 56-20 (W)
1948—Bears, 48-13 (C)
1949—Bears, 31-21 (W)
1951—Bears, 27-0 (W)
1953—Bears, 27-24 (W)
1957—Redskins, 14-3 (C)
1964—Redskins, 27-20 (W)
1968—Redskins, 38-28 (C)
1971—Bears, 16-15 (C)
1974—Redskins, 42-0 (W)
1976—Bears, 33-7 (C)
1978—Bears, 14-10 (W)
1980—Bears, 35-21 (C)
1981—Redskins, 24-7 (C)
1984—***Bears, 23-19 (W)
1985—Bears, 45-10 (C)
1986—***Redskins, 27-13 (C)
1987—***Redskins, 21-17 (C)
1988—Bears, 34-14 (W)
1989—Redskins, 38-14 (W)
1990—Redskins, 10-9 (W)
1991—Redskins, 20-7 (C)
1996—Redskins, 10-3 (W)
1997—Redskins, 31-8 (C)
1999—Redskins, 48-22 (W)
(RS Pts.—Bears 699, Redskins 592)
(PS Pts.—Bears 194, Redskins 130)
Franchise in Boston prior to 1937 and known as Braves prior to 1933
**NFL Championship*
***NFC Divisional Playoff*

CINCINNATI vs. ARIZONA
RS: Bengals lead series, 5-2;
See Arizona vs. Cincinnati

CINCINNATI vs. ATLANTA
RS: Bengals lead series, 7-2;
See Atlanta vs. Cincinnati

CINCINNATI vs. BALTIMORE
RS: Ravens lead series, 7-3;
See Baltimore vs. Cincinnati

CINCINNATI vs. BUFFALO
RS: Series tied, 9-9
PS: Bengals lead series, 2-0;
See Buffalo vs. Cincinnati

CINCINNATI vs. CAROLINA
RS: Panthers lead series, 1-0;
See Carolina vs. Cincinnati

CINCINNATI vs. CHICAGO
RS: Bengals lead series, 4-2;
See Chicago vs. Cincinnati

CINCINNATI vs. CLEVELAND
RS: Browns lead series, 28-27
1970—Browns, 30-27 (Cle)
Bengals, 14-10 (Cin)
1971—Browns, 27-24 (Cin)

ALL-TIME TEAM VS. TEAM RESULTS

Browns, 31-27 (Cle)
1972—Browns, 27-6 (Cle)
Browns, 27-24 (Cin)
1973—Browns, 17-10 (Cle)
Bengals, 34-17 (Cin)
1974—Bengals, 33-7 (Cin)
Bengals, 34-24 (Cle)
1975—Bengals, 24-17 (Cin)
Browns, 35-23 (Cle)
1976—Bengals, 45-24 (Cle)
Bengals, 21-6 (Cin)
1977—Browns, 13-3 (Cin)
Bengals, 10-7 (Cle)
1978—Browns, 13-10 (Cle) OT
Bengals, 48-16 (Cin)
1979—Browns, 28-27 (Cle)
Bengals, 16-12 (Cin)
1980—Browns, 31-7 (Cle)
Browns, 27-24 (Cin)
1981—Browns, 20-17 (Cin)
Bengals, 41-21 (Cle)
1982—Bengals, 23-10 (Cin)
1983—Browns, 17-7 (Cle)
Bengals, 28-21 (Cin)
1984—Bengals, 12-9 (Cin)
Bengals, 20-17 (Cle) OT
1985—Bengals, 27-10 (Cin)
Browns, 24-6 (Cle)
1986—Bengals, 30-13 (Cle)
Browns, 34-3 (Cin)
1987—Browns, 34-0 (Cin)
Browns, 38-24 (Cle)
1988—Bengals, 24-17 (Cin)
Browns, 23-16 (Cle)
1989—Bengals, 21-14 (Cin)
Bengals, 21-0 (Cle)
1990—Bengals, 34-13 (Cle)
Bengals, 21-14 (Cin)
1991—Browns, 14-13 (Cle)
Bengals, 23-21 (Cin)
1992—Bengals, 30-10 (Cin)
Browns, 37-21 (Cle)
1993—Browns, 27-14 (Cle)
Browns, 28-17 (Cin)
1994—Browns, 28-20 (Cin)
Browns, 37-13 (Cle)
1995—Browns, 29-26 (Cin) OT
Browns, 26-10 (Cle)
1999—Bengals, 18-17 (Cle)
Bengals, 44-28 (Cin)
2000—Browns, 24-7 (Cin)
Bengals, 12-3 (Cle)
(RS Pts.—Bengals 1,134, Browns 1,124)

CINCINNATI vs. DALLAS
RS: Cowboys lead series, 5-3
1973—Cowboys, 38-10 (D)
1979—Cowboys, 38-13 (D)
1985—Bengals, 50-24 (C)
1988—Bengals, 38-24 (D)
1991—Cowboys, 35-23 (D)
1994—Cowboys, 23-20 (C)
1997—Bengals, 31-24 (C)
2000—Cowboys, 23-6 (D)
(RS Pts.—Cowboys 229, Bengals 191)

CINCINNATI vs. DENVER
RS: Broncos lead series, 14-7
1968—Bengals, 24-10 (C)
Broncos, 10-7 (D)
1969—Broncos, 30-23 (C)
Broncos, 27-16 (D)
1971—Bengals, 24-10 (D)
1972—Bengals, 21-10 (C)
1973—Broncos, 28-10 (D)
1975—Bengals, 17-16 (D)
1976—Bengals, 17-7 (C)
1977—Broncos, 24-13 (C)
1979—Broncos, 10-0 (D)
1981—Bengals, 38-21 (C)
1983—Broncos, 24-17 (D)
1984—Broncos, 20-17 (D)
1986—Broncos, 34-28 (D)
1991—Broncos, 45-14 (D)
1994—Broncos, 15-13 (D)
1996—Broncos, 14-10 (C)
1997—Broncos, 38-20 (D)
1998—Broncos, 33-26 (C)
2000—Bengals, 31-21 (C)
(RS Pts.—Broncos 447, Bengals 386)

CINCINNATI vs. DETROIT
RS: Bengals lead series, 4-3
1970—Lions, 38-3 (D)
1974—Lions, 23-19 (C)
1983—Bengals, 17-9 (C)
1986—Bengals, 24-17 (D)
1989—Bengals, 42-7 (C)
1992—Lions, 19-13 (C)
1998—Bengals, 34-28 (D) OT
(RS Pts.—Bengals 152, Lions 141)

CINCINNATI vs. GREEN BAY
RS: Packers lead series, 5-4
1971—Packers, 20-17 (GB)
1976—Bengals, 28-7 (C)
1977—Bengals, 17-7 (Mil)
1980—Packers, 14-9 (GB)
1983—Bengals, 34-14 (C)
1986—Bengals, 34-28 (Mil)
1992—Packers, 24-23 (GB)
1995—Packers, 24-10 (GB)
1998—Packers, 13-6 (C)
(RS Pts.—Bengals 178, Packers 151)

CINCINNATI vs. *INDIANAPOLIS
RS: Colts lead series, 11-8
PS: Colts lead series, 1-0
1970—**Colts, 17-0 (B)
1972—Colts, 20-19 (C)
1974—Bengals, 24-14 (B)
1976—Colts, 28-27 (B)
1979—Colts, 38-28 (B)
1980—Bengals, 34-33 (C)
1981—Bengals, 41-19 (B)
1982—Bengals, 20-17 (B)
1983—Colts, 34-31 (C)
1987—Bengals, 23-21 (I)
1989—Colts, 23-12 (C)
1990—Colts, 34-20 (C)
1992—Colts, 21-17 (C)
1993—Colts, 9-6 (C)
1994—Colts, 17-13 (C)
1995—Bengals, 24-21 (I) OT
1996—Bengals, 31-24 (C)
1997—Bengals, 28-13 (I)
1998—Colts, 39-26 (I)
1999—Colts, 31-10 (I)
(RS Pts.—Colts 456, Bengals 434)
(PS Pts.—Colts 17, Bengals 0)
**Franchise in Baltimore prior to 1984*
***AFC Divisional Playoff*

CINCINNATI vs. JACKSONVILLE
RS: Jaguars lead series, 7-5
1995—Bengals, 24-17 (C)
Bengals, 17-13 (J)
1996—Bengals, 28-21 (C)
Jaguars, 30-27 (J)
1997—Jaguars, 21-13 (J)
Bengals, 31-26 (C)
1998—Jaguars, 24-11 (J)
Jaguars, 34-17 (C)
1999—Jaguars, 41-10 (C)
Jaguars, 24-7 (J)
2000—Jaguars, 13-0 (J)
Bengals, 17-14 (C)
(RS Pts.—Jaguars 278, Bengals 202)

CINCINNATI vs. KANSAS CITY
RS: Chiefs lead series, 11-9
1968—Chiefs, 13-3 (KC)
Chiefs, 16-9 (C)
1969—Bengals, 24-19 (C)
Chiefs, 42-22 (KC)
1970—Chiefs, 27-19 (C)
1972—Bengals, 23-16 (KC)
1973—Bengals, 14-6 (C)
1974—Bengals, 33-6 (C)
1976—Bengals, 27-24 (KC)
1977—Bengals, 27-7 (KC)
1978—Chiefs, 24-23 (C)
1979—Chiefs, 10-7 (C)
1980—Bengals, 20-6 (KC)
1983—Chiefs, 20-15 (KC)
1984—Chiefs, 27-22 (C)
1986—Chiefs, 24-14 (KC)
1987—Bengals, 30-27 (C) OT
1988—Chiefs, 31-28 (KC)
1989—Bengals, 21-17 (KC)
1993—Chiefs, 17-15 (KC)
(RS Pts.—Bengals 396, Chiefs 379)

CINCINNATI vs. MIAMI
RS: Dolphins lead series, 12-3
PS: Dolphins lead series, 1-0
1968—Dolphins, 24-22 (C)
Bengals, 38-21 (M)
1969—Bengals, 27-21 (C)
1971—Dolphins, 23-13 (C)
1973—*Dolphins, 34-16 (M)
1974—Dolphins, 24-3 (M)
1977—Bengals, 23-17 (C)
1978—Dolphins, 21-0 (M)
1980—Dolphins, 17-16 (M)
1983—Dolphins, 38-14 (M)
1987—Dolphins, 20-14 (C)
1989—Dolphins, 20-13 (C)
1991—Dolphins, 37-13 (M)
1994—Dolphins, 23-7 (C)
1995—Dolphins, 26-23 (C)
2000—Dolphins, 31-16 (C)
(RS Pts.—Dolphins 363, Bengals 242)
(PS Pts.—Dolphins 34, Bengals 16)
**AFC Divisional Playoff*

CINCINNATI vs. MINNESOTA
RS: Vikings lead series, 5-4
1973—Bengals, 27-0 (C)
1977—Vikings, 42-10 (M)
1980—Bengals, 14-0 (C)
1983—Vikings, 20-14 (M)
1986—Bengals, 24-20 (C)
1989—Vikings, 29-21 (M)
1992—Vikings, 42-7 (C)
1995—Bengals, 27-24 (C)
1998—Vikings, 24-3 (M)
(RS Pts.—Vikings 201, Bengals 147)

CINCINNATI vs. *NEW ENGLAND
RS: Patriots lead series, 10-7
1968—Patriots, 33-14 (B)
1969—Patriots, 25-14 (C)
1970—Bengals, 45-7 (C)
1972—Bengals, 31-7 (NE)
1975—Bengals, 27-10 (C)
1978—Patriots, 10-3 (C)
1979—Patriots, 20-14 (C)
1984—Patriots, 20-14 (NE)
1985—Patriots, 34-23 (NE)
1986—Bengals, 31-7 (NE)
1988—Patriots, 27-21 (NE)
1990—Bengals, 41-7 (C)
1991—Bengals, 29-7 (C)
1992—Bengals, 20-10 (C)
1993—Patriots, 7-2 (NE)
1994—Patriots, 31-28 (C)
2000—Patriots, 16-13 (NE)
(RS Pts.—Bengals 370, Patriots 278)
**Franchise in Boston prior to 1971*

CINCINNATI vs. NEW ORLEANS
RS: Saints lead series, 5-4
1970—Bengals, 26-6 (C)
1975—Bengals, 21-0 (NO)
1978—Saints, 20-18 (C)
1981—Saints, 17-7 (NO)
1984—Bengals, 24-21 (NO)
1987—Saints, 41-24 (C)
1990—Saints, 21-7 (C)
1993—Saints, 20-13 (NO)
1996—Bengals, 30-15 (C))
(RS Pts.—Bengals 170, Saints 161)

CINCINNATI vs. N.Y. GIANTS
RS: Bengals lead series, 4-2
1972—Bengals, 13-10 (C)
1977—Bengals, 30-13 (C)
1985—Bengals, 35-30 (C)
1991—Bengals, 27-24 (C)
1994—Giants, 27-20 (NY)
1997—Giants, 29-27 (NY)
(RS Pts.—Bengals 152, Giants 133)

CINCINNATI vs. N.Y. JETS
RS: Jets lead series, 10-6
PS: Jets lead series, 1-0
1968—Jets, 27-14 (NY)
1969—Jets, 21-7 (C)
Jets, 40-7 (NY)
1971—Jets, 35-21 (NY)
1973—Bengals, 20-14 (C)
1976—Bengals, 42-3 (NY)
1981—Bengals, 31-30 (NY)
1982—*Jets, 44-17 (C)
1984—Jets, 43-23 (NY)
1985—Jets, 29-20 (C)
1986—Bengals, 52-21 (C)
1987—Jets, 27-20 (NY)
1988—Bengals, 36-19 (C)
1990—Bengals, 25-20 (C)
1992—Jets, 17-14 (NY)
1993—Jets, 17-12 (NY)
1997—Jets, 31-14 (C)
(RS Pts.—Jets 394, Bengals 358)
(PS Pts.—Jets 44, Bengals 17)
**AFC First-Round Playoff*

CINCINNATI vs. *OAKLAND
RS: Raiders lead series, 16-7
PS: Raiders lead series, 2-0
1968—Raiders, 31-10 (O)
Raiders, 34-0 (C)
1969—Bengals, 31-17 (C)
Raiders, 37-17 (O)
1970—Bengals, 31-21 (C)
1971—Raiders, 31-27 (O)
1972—Raiders, 20-14 (C)
1974—Raiders, 30-27 (O)
1975—Bengals, 14-10 (C)
**Raiders, 31-28 (O)
1976—Raiders, 35-20 (O)
1978—Raiders, 34-21 (C)
1980—Raiders, 28-17 (O)
1982—Bengals, 31-17 (C)
1983—Raiders, 20-10 (C)
1985—Raiders, 13-6 (LA)
1988—Bengals, 45-21 (LA)
1989—Raiders, 28-7 (LA)
1990—Raiders, 24-7 (LA)
**Raiders, 20-10 (LA)
1991—Raiders, 38-14 (C)
1992—Bengals, 24-21 (C) OT
1993—Bengals, 16-10 (C)
1995—Raiders, 20-17 (C)
1998—Raiders, 27-10 (O)
(RS Pts.—Raiders 567, Bengals 416)
(PS Pts.—Raiders 51, Bengals 38)
**Franchise in Los Angeles from 1982-1994*
***AFC Divisional Playoff*

CINCINNATI vs. PHILADELPHIA
RS: Bengals lead series, 6-3
1971—Bengals, 37-14 (C)
1975—Bengals, 31-0 (P)
1979—Bengals, 37-13 (C)
1982—Bengals, 18-14 (P)
1988—Bengals, 28-24 (P)
1991—Eagles, 17-10 (P)
1994—Bengals, 33-30 (C)
1997—Eagles, 44-42 (P)
2000—Eagles, 16-7 (P)
(RS Pts.—Bengals 243, Eagles 172)

CINCINNATI vs. PITTSBURGH
RS: Steelers lead series, 35-26
1970—Steelers, 21-10 (P)
Bengals, 34-7 (C)
1971—Steelers, 21-10 (P)
Steelers, 21-13 (C)
1972—Bengals, 15-10 (C)
Steelers, 40-17 (P)
1973—Bengals, 19-7 (C)
Steelers, 20-13 (P)
1974—Bengals, 17-10 (C)
Steelers, 27-3 (P)
1975—Steelers, 30-24 (C)

Steelers, 35-14 (P)
1976—Steelers, 23-6 (P)
Steelers, 7-3 (C)
1977—Steelers, 20-14 (P)
Bengals, 17-10 (C)
1978—Steelers, 28-3 (C)
Steelers, 7-6 (P)
1979—Bengals, 34-10 (C)
Steelers, 37-17 (P)
1980—Bengals, 30-28 (C)
Bengals, 17-16 (P)
1981—Bengals, 34-7 (C)
Bengals, 17-10 (P)
1982—Steelers, 26-20 (P) OT
1983—Steelers, 24-14 (C)
Bengals, 23-10 (P)
1984—Steelers, 38-17 (P)
Bengals, 22-20 (C)
1985—Bengals, 37-24 (P)
Bengals, 26-21 (C)
1986—Bengals, 24-22 (C)
Steelers, 30-9 (P)
1987—Steelers, 23-20 (P)
Steelers, 30-16 (C)
1988—Bengals, 17-12 (P)
Bengals, 42-7 (C)
1989—Bengals, 41-10 (C)
Bengals, 26-16 (P)
1990—Bengals, 27-3 (C)
Bengals, 16-12 (P)
1991—Steelers, 33-27 (C) OT
Steelers, 17-10 (P)
1992—Steelers, 20-0 (P)
Steelers, 21-9 (C)
1993—Steelers, 34-7 (P)
Steelers, 24-16 (C)
1994—Steelers, 14-10 (P)
Steelers, 38-15 (C)
1995—Bengals, 27-9 (P)
Steelers, 49-31 (C)
1996—Steelers, 20-10 (P)
Bengals, 34-24 (C)
1997—Steelers, 26-10 (C)
Steelers, 20-3 (P)
1998—Bengals, 25-20 (C)
Bengals, 25-24 (P)
1999—Steelers, 17-3 (C)
Bengals, 27-20 (P)
2000—Steelers, 15-0 (P)
Steelers, 48-28 (C)
(RS Pts.—Steelers 1,273, Bengals 1,101)

CINCINNATI vs. *ST. LOUIS
RS: Bengals lead series, 5-4
1972—Rams, 15-12 (LA)
1976—Bengals, 20-12 (C)
1978—Bengals, 20-19 (LA)
1981—Bengals, 24-10 (C)
1984—Rams, 24-14 (C)
1990—Bengals, 34-31 (LA) OT
1993—Bengals, 15-3 (C)
1996—Rams, 26-16 (StL)
1999—Rams, 38-10 (C)
(RS Pts.—Rams 178, Bengals 165)
Franchise in Los Angeles prior to 1995

CINCINNATI vs. SAN DIEGO
RS: Chargers lead series, 15-9
PS: Bengals lead series, 1-0
1968—Chargers, 29-13 (SD)
Chargers, 31-10 (C)
1969—Bengals, 34-20 (C)
Chargers, 21-14 (SD)
1970—Bengals, 17-14 (SD)
1971—Bengals, 31-0 (C)
1973—Bengals, 20-13 (SD)
1974—Chargers, 20-17 (C)
1975—Bengals, 47-17 (C)
1977—Chargers, 24-3 (SD)
1978—Chargers, 22-13 (SD)
1979—Chargers, 26-24 (C)
1980—Chargers, 31-14 (C)
1981—Bengals, 40-17 (SD)
*Bengals, 27-7 (C)
1982—Chargers, 50-34 (SD)
1985—Chargers, 44-41 (C)
1987—Chargers, 10-9 (C)
1988—Bengals, 27-10 (C)
1990—Bengals, 21-16 (SD)
1992—Chargers, 27-10 (SD)
1994—Chargers, 27-10 (SD)
1996—Chargers, 27-14 (SD)
1997—Bengals, 38-31 (C)
1999—Chargers, 34-7 (C)
(RS Pts.—Chargers 561, Bengals 508)
(PS Pts.—Bengals 27, Chargers 7)
AFC Championship

CINCINNATI vs. SAN FRANCISCO
RS: 49ers lead series, 7-2
PS: 49ers lead series, 2-0
1974—Bengals, 21-3 (SF)
1978—49ers, 28-12 (SF)
1981—49ers, 21-3 (C)
*49ers, 26-21 (Detroit)
1984—49ers, 23-17 (SF)
1987—49ers, 27-26 (C)
1988—**49ers, 20-16 (Miami)
1990—49ers, 20-17 (C) OT
1993—49ers, 21-8 (SF)
1996—49ers, 28-21 (SF)
1999—Bengals, 44-30 (C)
(RS Pts.—49ers 201, Bengals 169)
(PS Pts.—49ers 46, Bengals 37)
Super Bowl XVI
**Super Bowl XXIII*

CINCINNATI vs. SEATTLE
RS: Seahawks lead series, 8-7
PS: Bengals lead series, 1-0
1977—Bengals, 42-20 (C)
1981—Bengals, 27-21 (C)
1982—Bengals, 24-10 (C)
1984—Seahawks, 26-6 (C)
1985—Seahawks, 28-24 (C)
1986—Bengals, 34-7 (C)
1987—Bengals, 17-10 (S)
1988—*Bengals, 21-13 (C)
1989—Seahawks, 24-17 (C)
1990—Seahawks, 31-16 (S)
1991—Seahawks, 13-7 (C)
1992—Bengals, 21-3 (S)
1993—Seahawks, 19-10 (C)
1994—Bengals, 20-17 (S) OT
1995—Seahawks, 24-21 (S)
1999—Seahawks, 37-20 (S)
(RS Pts.—Bengals 306, Seahawks 290)
(PS Pts.—Bengals 21, Seahawks 13)
AFC Divisional Playoff

CINCINNATI vs. TAMPA BAY
RS: Series tied, 3-3
1976—Bengals, 21-0 (C)
1980—Buccaneers, 17-12 (C)
1983—Bengals, 23-17 (TB)
1989—Bengals, 56-23 (C)
1995—Buccaneers, 19-16 (TB)
1998—Buccaneers, 35-0 (C)
(RS Pts.—Bengals 128, Buccaneers 111)

CINCINNATI vs. *TENNESSEE
RS: Titans lead series, 35-28-1
PS: Bengals lead series, 1-0
1968—Oilers, 27-17 (C)
1969—Tie, 31-31 (H)
1970—Oilers, 20-13 (C)
Bengals, 30-20 (H)
1971—Oilers, 10-6 (H)
Bengals, 28-13 (C)
1972—Bengals, 30-7 (C)
Bengals, 61-17 (H)
1973—Bengals, 24-10 (C)
Bengals, 27-24 (H)
1974—Oilers, 34-21 (C)
Oilers, 20-3 (H)
1975—Bengals, 21-19 (H)
Bengals, 23-19 (C)
1976—Bengals, 27-7 (H)
Bengals, 31-27 (C)
1977—Bengals, 13-10 (C) OT
Oilers, 21-16 (H)
1978—Bengals, 28-13 (C)
Oilers, 17-10 (H)
1979—Oilers, 30-27 (C) OT
Oilers, 42-21 (H)
1980—Oilers, 13-10 (C)
Oilers, 23-3 (H)
1981—Oilers, 17-10 (H)
Bengals, 34-21 (C)
1982—Bengals, 27-6 (C)
Bengals, 35-27 (H)
1983—Bengals, 55-14 (H)
Bengals, 38-10 (C)
1984—Bengals, 13-3 (C)
Bengals, 31-13 (H)
1985—Oilers, 44-27 (H)
Bengals, 45-27 (C)
1986—Bengals, 31-28 (C)
Oilers, 32-28 (H)
1987—Oilers, 31-29 (C)
Oilers, 21-17 (H)
1988—Bengals, 44-21 (C)
Oilers, 41-6 (H)
1989—Oilers, 26-24 (H)
Bengals, 61-7 (C)
1990—Oilers, 48-17 (H)
Bengals, 40-20 (C)
**Bengals, 41-14 (C)
1991—Oilers, 30-7 (C)
Oilers, 35-3 (H)
1992—Oilers, 38-24 (C)
Oilers, 26-10 (H)
1993—Oilers, 28-12 (H)
Oilers, 38-3 (C)
1994—Oilers, 20-13 (H)
Bengals, 34-31 (C)
1995—Oilers, 38-28 (C)
Bengals, 32-25 (H)
1996—Oilers, 30-27 (C) OT
Bengals, 21-13 (H)
1997—Oilers, 30-7 (T)
Bengals, 41-14 (C)
1998—Oilers, 23-14 (C)
Oilers, 44-14 (T)
1999—Titans, 36-35 (T)
Titans, 24-14 (C)
2000—Titans, 23-14 (C)
Titans, 35-3 (T)
(RS Pts.—Titans 1,512, Bengals 1,489)
(PS Pts.—Bengals 41, Titans 14)
Franchise in Houston prior to 1997; known as Oilers prior to 1999
**AFC First-Round Playoff*

CINCINNATI vs. WASHINGTON
RS: Redskins lead series, 4-2
1970—Redskins, 20-0 (W)
1974—Bengals, 28-17 (C)
1979—Redskins, 28-14 (W)
1985—Redskins, 27-24 (W)
1988—Bengals, 20-17 (C) OT
1991—Redskins, 34-27 (C)
(RS Pts.—Redskins 143, Bengals 113)

CLEVELAND vs. ARIZONA
RS: Browns lead series, 32-11-3;
See Arizona vs. Cleveland

CLEVELAND vs. ATLANTA
RS: Browns lead series, 8-2;
See Atlanta vs. Cleveland

CLEVELAND vs. BALTIMORE
RS: Ravens lead series, 4-0;
See Baltimore vs. Cleveland

CLEVELAND vs. BUFFALO
RS: Browns lead series, 7-4
PS: Browns lead series, 1-0;
See Buffalo vs. Cleveland

CLEVELAND vs. CAROLINA
RS: Panthers lead series, 1-0;
See Carolina vs. Cleveland

CLEVELAND vs. CINCINNATI
RS: Browns lead series, 28-27;
See Cincinnati vs. Cleveland

CLEVELAND vs. DALLAS
RS: Browns lead series, 15-9
PS: Browns lead series, 2-1
1960—Browns, 48-7 (D)
1961—Browns, 25-7 (C)
Browns, 38-17 (D)
1962—Browns, 19-10 (C)
Cowboys, 45-21 (D)
1963—Browns, 41-24 (D)
Browns, 27-17 (C)
1964—Browns, 27-6 (C)
Browns, 20-16 (D)
1965—Browns, 23-17 (C)
Browns, 24-17 (D)
1966—Browns, 30-21 (C)
Cowboys, 26-14 (D)
1967—Cowboys, 21-14 (C)
*Cowboys, 52-14 (D)
1968—Cowboys, 28-7 (C)
*Browns, 31-20 (C)
1969—Browns, 42-10 (C)
*Browns, 38-14 (D)
1970—Cowboys, 6-2 (C)
1974—Cowboys, 41-17 (D)
1979—Browns, 26-7 (C)
1982—Cowboys, 31-14 (D)
1985—Cowboys, 20-7 (D)
1988—Browns, 24-21 (C)
1991—Cowboys, 26-14 (C)
1994—Browns, 19-14 (D)
(RS Pts.—Browns 543, Cowboys 455)
(PS Pts.—Cowboys 86, Browns 83)
Conference Championship

CLEVELAND vs. DENVER
RS: Broncos lead series, 14-5
PS: Broncos lead series, 3-0
1970—Browns, 27-13 (D)
1971—Broncos, 27-0 (C)
1972—Browns, 27-20 (D)
1974—Browns, 23-21 (C)
1975—Broncos, 16-15 (D)
1976—Broncos, 44-13 (D)
1978—Broncos, 19-7 (C)
1980—Broncos, 19-16 (C)
1981—Broncos, 23-20 (D) OT
1983—Broncos, 27-6 (D)
1984—Broncos, 24-14 (C)
1986—*Broncos, 23-20 (C) OT
1987—*Broncos, 38-33 (D)
1988—Broncos, 30-7 (D)
1989—Browns, 16-13 (C)
*Broncos, 37-21 (D)
1990—Browns, 30-29 (D)
1991—Broncos, 17-7 (C)
1992—Broncos, 12-0 (C)
1993—Broncos, 29-14 (C)
1994—Broncos, 26-14 (D)
2000—Broncos, 44-10 (D)
(RS Pts.—Broncos 453, Browns 266)
(PS Pts.—Broncos 98, Browns 74)
AFC Championship

CLEVELAND vs. DETROIT
RS: Lions lead series, 12-3
PS: Lions lead series, 3-1
1952—Lions, 17-6 (D)
*Lions, 17-7 (C)
1953—*Lions, 17-16 (D)
1954—Lions, 14-10 (C)
*Browns, 56-10 (C)
1957—Lions, 20-7 (D)
*Lions, 59-14 (D)
1958—Lions, 30-10 (C)
1963—Lions, 38-10 (D)
1964—Browns, 37-21 (C)
1967—Lions, 31-14 (D)
1969—Lions, 28-21 (C)
1970—Lions, 41-24 (C)
1975—Lions, 21-10 (D)
1983—Browns, 31-26 (D)
1986—Browns, 24-21 (C)
1989—Lions, 13-10 (D)
1992—Lions, 24-14 (D)
1995—Lions, 38-20 (D)
(RS Pts.—Lions 383, Browns 248)
(PS Pts.—Lions 103, Browns 93)
NFL Championship

ALL-TIME TEAM VS. TEAM RESULTS

CLEVELAND vs. GREEN BAY
RS: Packers lead series, 8-6
PS: Packers lead series, 1-0
1953—Browns, 27-0 (Mil)
1955—Browns, 41-10 (C)
1956—Browns, 24-7 (Mil)
1961—Packers, 49-17 (C)
1964—Packers, 28-21 (Mil)
1965—*Packers, 23-12 (GB)
1966—Packers, 21-20 (C)
1967—Packers, 55-7 (Mil)
1969—Browns, 20-7 (C)
1972—Packers, 26-10 (C)
1980—Browns, 26-21 (C)
1983—Packers, 35-21 (Mil)
1986—Packers, 17-14 (C)
1992—Browns, 17-6 (C)
1995—Packers, 31-20 (C)
(RS Pts.—Packers 313, Browns 285)
(PS Pts.—Packers 23, Browns 12)
NFL Championship

CLEVELAND vs. *INDIANAPOLIS
RS: Browns lead series, 13-8
PS: Series tied, 2-2
1956—Colts, 21-7 (C)
1959—Browns, 38-31 (B)
1962—Colts, 36-14 (C)
1964—**Browns, 27-0 (C)
1968—Browns, 30-20 (B)
**Colts, 34-0 (C)
1971—Browns, 14-13 (B)
***Colts, 20-3 (C)
1973—Browns, 24-14 (C)
1975—Colts, 21-7 (B)
1978—Browns, 45-24 (B)
1979—Browns, 13-10 (C)
1980—Browns, 28-27 (B)
1981—Browns, 42-28 (C)
1983—Browns, 41-23 (C)
1986—Browns, 24-9 (I)
1987—Colts, 9-7 (C)
***Browns, 38-21 (C)
1988—Browns, 23-17 (C)
1989—Colts, 23-17 (I) OT
1991—Browns, 31-0 (I)
1992—Colts, 14-3 (I)
1993—Colts, 23-10 (I)
1994—Browns, 21-14 (I)
1999—Colts, 29-28 (C)
(RS Pts.—Browns 467, Colts 406)
(PS Pts.—Colts 75, Browns 68)
Franchise in Baltimore prior to 1984
***NFL Championship*
****AFC Divisional Playoff*

CLEVELAND vs. JACKSONVILLE
RS: Jaguars lead series, 6-0
1995—Jaguars, 23-15 (C)
Jaguars, 24-21 (J)
1999—Jaguars, 24-7 (J)
Jaguars, 24-14 (C)
2000—Jaguars, 27-7 (C)
Jaguars, 48-0 (J)
(RS Pts.—Jaguars 170, Browns 64)

CLEVELAND vs. KANSAS CITY
RS: Browns lead series, 8-7-2
1971—Chiefs, 13-7 (KC)
1972—Chiefs, 31-7 (C)
1973—Tie, 20-20 (KC)
1975—Browns, 40-14 (C)
1976—Chiefs, 39-14 (KC)
1977—Browns, 44-7 (C)
1978—Chiefs, 17-3 (KC)
1979—Browns, 27-24 (KC)
1980—Browns, 20-13 (C)
1984—Chiefs, 10-6 (KC)
1986—Browns, 20-7 (C)
1988—Browns, 6-3 (KC)
1989—Tie, 10-10 (C) OT
1990—Chiefs, 34-0 (KC)
1991—Browns, 20-15 (C)
1994—Chiefs, 20-13 (KC)
1995—Browns, 35-17 (C)
(RS Pts.—Chiefs 294, Browns 292)

CLEVELAND vs. MIAMI
RS: Dolphins lead series, 6-4
PS: Dolphins lead series, 2-0
1970—Browns, 28-0 (M)
1972—*Dolphins, 20-14 (M)
1973—Dolphins, 17-9 (C)
1976—Browns, 17-13 (C)
1979—Browns, 30-24 (C) OT
1985—*Dolphins, 24-21 (M)
1986—Browns, 26-16 (C)
1988—Dolphins, 38-31 (M)
1989—Dolphins, 13-10 (M) OT
1990—Dolphins, 30-13 (C)
1992—Dolphins, 27-23 (C)
1993—Dolphins, 24-14 (C)
(RS Pts.—Dolphins 202, Browns 201)
(PS Pts.—Dolphins 44, Browns 35)
**AFC Divisional Playoff*

CLEVELAND vs. MINNESOTA
RS: Vikings lead series, 8-3
PS: Vikings lead series, 1-0
1965—Vikings, 27-17 (C)
1967—Browns, 14-10 (C)
1969—Vikings, 51-3 (M)
*Vikings, 27-7 (M)
1973—Vikings, 26-3 (M)
1975—Vikings, 42-10 (C)
1980—Vikings, 28-23 (M)
1983—Vikings, 27-21 (C)
1986—Browns, 23-20 (M)
1989—Browns, 23-17 (C) OT
1992—Vikings, 17-13 (M)
1995—Vikings, 27-11 (M)
(RS Pts.—Vikings 292, Browns 161)
(PS Pts.—Vikings 27, Browns 7)
**NFL Championship*

CLEVELAND vs. NEW ENGLAND
RS: Browns lead series, 11-5
PS: Browns lead series, 1-0
1971—Browns, 27-7 (C)
1974—Browns, 21-14 (NE)
1977—Browns, 30-27 (C) OT
1980—Patriots, 34-17 (NE)
1982—Browns, 10-7 (C)
1983—Browns, 30-0 (NE)
1984—Patriots, 17-16 (C)
1985—Browns, 24-20 (C)
1987—Browns, 20-10 (NE)
1991—Browns, 20-0 (NE)
1992—Browns, 19-17 (NE)
1993—Patriots, 20-17 (C)
1994—Browns, 13-6 (C)
*Browns, 20-13 (C)
1995—Patriots, 17-14 (NE)
1999—Patriots, 19-7 (C)
2000—Browns, 19-11 (C)
(RS Pts.—Browns 304, Patriots 226)
(PS Pts.—Browns 20, Patriots 13)
**AFC First-Round Playoff*

CLEVELAND vs. NEW ORLEANS
RS: Browns lead series, 10-3
1967—Browns, 42-7 (NO)
1968—Browns, 24-10 (NO)
Browns, 35-17 (C)
1969—Browns, 27-17 (NO)
1971—Browns, 21-17 (NO)
1975—Browns, 17-16 (C)
1978—Browns, 24-16 (NO)
1981—Browns, 20-17 (C)
1984—Saints, 16-14 (C)
1987—Saints, 28-21 (NO)
1990—Saints, 25-20 (NO)
1993—Browns, 17-13 (C)
1999—Browns, 21-16 (NO)
(RS Pts.—Browns 303, Saints 215)

CLEVELAND vs. N.Y. GIANTS
RS: Browns lead series, 25-18-2
PS: Series tied, 1-1
1950—Giants, 6-0 (C)
Giants, 17-13 (NY)
*Browns, 8-3 (C)
1951—Browns, 14-13 (C)
Browns, 10-0 (NY)
1952—Giants, 17-9 (C)
Giants, 37-34 (NY)
1953—Browns, 7-0 (NY)
Browns, 62-14 (C)
1954—Browns, 24-14 (C)
Browns, 16-7 (NY)
1955—Browns, 24-14 (C)
Tie, 35-35 (NY)
1956—Giants, 21-9 (C)
Browns, 24-7 (NY)
1957—Browns, 6-3 (C)
Browns, 34-28 (NY)
1958—Giants, 21-17 (C)
Giants, 13-10 (NY)
*Giants, 10-0 (NY)
1959—Giants, 10-6 (C)
Giants, 48-7 (NY)
1960—Giants, 17-13 (C)
Browns, 48-34 (NY)
1961—Giants, 37-21 (C)
Tie, 7-7 (NY)
1962—Browns, 17-7 (C)
Giants, 17-13 (NY)
1963—Browns, 35-24 (NY)
Giants, 33-6 (C)
1964—Browns, 42-20 (C)
Browns, 52-20 (NY)
1965—Browns, 38-14 (NY)
Browns, 34-21 (C)
1966—Browns, 28-7 (NY)
Browns, 49-40 (C)
1967—Giants, 38-34 (NY)
Browns, 24-14 (C)
1968—Browns, 45-10 (C)
1969—Browns, 28-17 (C)
Giants, 27-14 (NY)
1973—Browns, 12-10 (C)
1977—Browns, 21-7 (NY)
1985—Browns, 35-33 (NY)
1991—Giants, 13-10 (NY)
1994—Giants, 16-13 (C)
2000—Giants, 24-3 (C)
(RS Pts.—Browns 1,003, Giants 832)
(PS Pts.—Giants 13, Browns 8)
**Conference Playoff*

CLEVELAND vs. N.Y. JETS
RS: Browns lead series, 9-6
PS: Browns lead series, 1-0
1970—Browns, 31-21 (C)
1972—Browns, 26-10 (NY)
1976—Browns, 38-17 (C)
1978—Browns, 37-34 (C) OT
1979—Browns, 25-22 (NY) OT
1980—Browns, 17-14 (C)
1981—Jets, 14-13 (C)
1983—Browns, 10-7 (C)
1984—Jets, 24-20 (C)
1985—Jets, 37-10 (NY)
1986—*Browns, 23-20 (C) OT
1988—Jets, 23-3 (C)
1989—Browns, 38-24 (C)
1990—Jets, 24-21 (NY)
1991—Jets, 17-14 (C)
1994—Browns, 27-7 (C)
(RS Pts.—Browns 330, Jets 295)
(PS Pts.—Browns 23, Jets 20)
**AFC Divisional Playoff*

CLEVELAND vs. *OAKLAND
RS: Raiders lead series, 9-4
PS: Raiders lead series, 2-0
1970—Raiders, 23-20 (O)
1971—Raiders, 34-20 (C)
1973—Browns, 7-3 (O)
1974—Raiders, 40-24 (C)
1975—Raiders, 38-17 (O)
1977—Raiders, 26-10 (C)
1979—Raiders, 19-14 (O)
1980—**Raiders, 14-12 (C)
1982—***Raiders, 27-10 (LA)
1985—Raiders, 21-20 (C)
1986—Raiders, 27-14 (LA)
1987—Browns, 24-17 (LA)
1992—Browns, 28-16 (LA)
1993—Browns, 19-16 (LA)
2000—Raiders, 36-10 (O)
(RS Pts.—Raiders 316, Browns 227)
(PS Pts.—Raiders 41, Browns 22)
**Franchise in Los Angeles from 1982-1994*
***AFC Divisional Playoff*
****AFC First-Round Playoff*

CLEVELAND vs. PHILADELPHIA
RS: Browns lead series, 31-13-1
1950—Browns, 35-10 (P)
Browns, 13-7 (C)
1951—Browns, 20-17 (C)
Browns, 24-9 (P)
1952—Browns, 49-7 (P)
Eagles, 28-20 (C)
1953—Browns, 37-13 (C)
Eagles, 42-27 (P)
1954—Eagles, 28-10 (P)
Browns, 6-0 (C)
1955—Browns, 21-17 (C)
Eagles, 33-17 (P)
1956—Browns, 16-0 (P)
Browns, 17-14 (C)
1957—Browns, 24-7 (C)
Eagles, 17-7 (P)
1958—Browns, 28-14 (C)
Browns, 21-14 (P)
1959—Browns, 28-7 (C)
Browns, 28-21 (P)
1960—Browns, 41-24 (P)
Eagles, 31-29 (C)
1961—Eagles, 27-20 (P)
Browns, 45-24 (C)
1962—Eagles, 35-7 (P)
Tie, 14-14 (C)
1963—Browns, 37-7 (C)
Browns, 23-17 (P)
1964—Browns, 28-20 (P)
Browns, 38-24 (C)
1965—Browns, 35-17 (P)
Browns, 38-34 (C)
1966—Browns, 27-7 (C)
Eagles, 33-21 (P)
1967—Eagles, 28-24 (P)
1968—Browns, 47-13 (C)
1969—Browns, 27-20 (P)
1972—Browns, 27-17 (P)
1976—Browns, 24-3 (C)
1979—Browns, 24-19 (P)
1982—Eagles, 24-21 (C)
1988—Browns, 19-3 (C)
1991—Eagles, 32-30 (C)
1994—Browns, 26-7 (P)
2000—Eagles, 35-24 (C)
(RS Pts.—Browns 1,144, Eagles 820)

CLEVELAND vs. PITTSBURGH
RS: Browns lead series, 54-42
PS: Steelers lead series, 1-0
1950—Browns, 30-17 (P)
Browns, 45-7 (C)
1951—Browns, 17-0 (C)
Browns, 28-0 (P)
1952—Browns, 21-20 (P)
Browns, 29-28 (C)
1953—Browns, 34-16 (C)
Browns, 20-16 (P)
1954—Steelers, 55-27 (P)
Browns, 42-7 (C)
1955—Browns, 41-14 (C)
Browns, 30-7 (P)
1956—Browns, 14-10 (P)
Steelers, 24-16 (C)
1957—Browns, 23-12 (P)
Browns, 24-0 (C)
1958—Browns, 45-12 (P)
Browns, 27-10 (C)
1959—Steelers, 17-7 (P)
Steelers, 21-20 (C)
1960—Browns, 28-20 (C)
Steelers, 14-10 (P)
1961—Browns, 30-28 (P)
Steelers, 17-13 (C)

1962—Browns, 41-14 (P)
Browns, 35-14 (C)
1963—Browns, 35-23 (C)
Steelers, 9-7 (P)
1964—Steelers, 23-7 (C)
Browns, 30-17 (P)
1965—Browns, 24-19 (C)
Browns, 42-21 (P)
1966—Browns, 41-10 (C)
Steelers, 16-6 (P)
1967—Browns, 21-10 (C)
Browns, 34-14 (P)
1968—Browns, 31-24 (C)
Browns, 45-24 (P)
1969—Browns, 42-31 (C)
Browns, 24-3 (P)
1970—Browns, 15-7 (C)
Steelers, 28-9 (P)
1971—Browns, 27-17 (C)
Steelers, 26-9 (P)
1972—Browns, 26-24 (C)
Steelers, 30-0 (P)
1973—Steelers, 33-6 (P)
Browns, 21-16 (C)
1974—Steelers, 20-16 (P)
Steelers, 26-16 (C)
1975—Steelers, 42-6 (C)
Steelers, 31-17 (P)
1976—Steelers, 31-14 (P)
Browns, 18-16 (C)
1977—Steelers, 28-14 (C)
Steelers, 35-31 (P)
1978—Steelers, 15-9 (P) OT
Steelers, 34-14 (C)
1979—Steelers, 51-35 (C)
Steelers, 33-30 (P) OT
1980—Browns, 27-26 (C)
Steelers, 16-13 (P)
1981—Steelers, 13-7 (P)
Steelers, 32-10 (C)
1982—Browns, 10-9 (C)
Steelers, 37-21 (P)
1983—Steelers, 44-17 (P)
Browns, 30-17 (C)
1984—Browns, 20-10 (C)
Steelers, 23-20 (P)
1985—Browns, 17-7 (C)
Steelers, 10-9 (P)
1986—Browns, 27-24 (P)
Browns, 37-31 (C) OT
1987—Browns, 34-10 (C)
Browns, 19-13 (P)
1988—Browns, 23-9 (P)
Browns, 27-7 (C)
1989—Browns, 51-0 (P)
Steelers, 17-7 (C)
1990—Browns, 13-3 (C)
Steelers, 35-0 (P)
1991—Browns, 17-14 (C)
Steelers, 17-10 (P)
1992—Browns, 17-9 (C)
Steelers, 23-13 (P)
1993—Browns, 28-23 (C)
Steelers, 16-9 (P)
1994—Steelers, 17-10 (C)
Steelers, 17-7 (P)
*Steelers, 29-9 (P)
1995—Steelers, 20-3 (P)
Steelers, 20-17 (C)
1999—Steelers, 43-0 (C)
Browns, 16-15 (P)
2000—Browns, 23-20 (C)
Steelers, 22-0 (P)
(RS Pts.—Browns 2,028, Steelers 1,856)
(PS Pts.—Steelers 29, Browns 9)
AFC Divisional Playoff

CLEVELAND vs. *ST. LOUIS
RS: Series tied, 8-8
PS: Browns lead series, 2-1
1950—**Browns, 30-28 (C)
1951—Browns, 38-23 (LA)
**Rams, 24-17 (LA)
1952—Browns, 37-7 (C)
1955—**Browns, 38-14 (LA)
1957—Browns, 45-31 (C)
1958—Browns, 30-27 (LA)
1963—Browns, 20-6 (C)
1965—Rams, 42-7 (LA)
1968—Rams, 24-6 (C)
1973—Rams, 30-17 (LA)
1977—Rams, 9-0 (C)
1978—Browns, 30-19 (C)
1981—Rams, 27-16 (LA)
1984—Rams, 20-17 (LA)
1987—Browns, 30-17 (C)
1990—Rams, 38-23 (C)
1993—Browns, 42-14 (LA)
1999—Rams, 34-3 (StL)
(RS Pts.—Rams 368, Browns 361)
(PS Pts.—Browns 85, Rams 66)
Franchise in Los Angeles prior to 1995
***NFL Championship*

CLEVELAND vs. SAN DIEGO
RS: Chargers lead series, 10-6-1
1970—Chargers, 27-10 (C)
1972—Browns, 21-17 (SD)
1973—Tie, 16-16 (C)
1974—Chargers, 36-35 (SD)
1976—Browns, 21-17 (C)
1977—Chargers, 37-14 (SD)
1981—Chargers, 44-14 (C)
1982—Chargers, 30-13 (C)
1983—Browns, 30-24 (SD) OT
1985—Browns, 21-7 (SD)
1986—Browns, 47-17 (C)
1987—Chargers, 27-24 (SD) OT
1990—Chargers, 24-14 (C)
1991—Browns, 30-24 (SD) OT
1992—Chargers, 14-13 (C)
1995—Chargers, 31-13 (SD)
1999—Chargers, 23-10 (SD)
(RS Pts.—Chargers 415, Browns 346)

CLEVELAND vs. SAN FRANCISCO
RS: Browns lead series, 9-6
1950—Browns, 34-14 (C)
1951—49ers, 24-10 (SF)
1953—Browns, 23-21 (C)
1955—Browns, 38-3 (SF)
1959—49ers, 21-20 (C)
1962—Browns, 13-10 (SF)
1968—Browns, 33-21 (SF)
1970—49ers, 34-31 (SF)
1974—Browns, 7-0 (C)
1978—Browns, 24-7 (C)
1981—Browns, 15-12 (SF)
1984—49ers, 41-7 (C)
1987—49ers, 38-24 (SF)
1990—49ers, 20-17 (SF)
1993—Browns, 23-13 (C)
(RS Pts.—Browns 319, 49ers 279)

CLEVELAND vs. SEATTLE
RS: Seahawks lead series, 9-4
1977—Seahawks, 20-19 (S)
1978—Seahawks, 47-24 (S)
1979—Seahawks, 29-24 (C)
1980—Browns, 27-3 (S)
1981—Seahawks, 42-21 (S)
1982—Browns, 21-7 (S)
1983—Seahawks, 24-9 (C)
1984—Seahawks, 33-0 (S)
1985—Seahawks, 31-13 (S)
1988—Seahawks, 16-10 (C)
1989—Browns, 17-7 (S)
1993—Seahawks, 22-5 (S)
1994—Browns, 35-9 (C)
(RS Pts.—Seahawks 290, Browns 225)

CLEVELAND vs. TAMPA BAY
RS: Browns lead series, 5-0
1976—Browns, 24-7 (TB)
1980—Browns, 34-27 (TB)
1983—Browns, 20-0 (C)
1989—Browns, 42-31 (TB)
1995—Browns, 22-6 (C)
(RS Pts.—Browns 142, Buccaneers 71)

CLEVELAND vs. *TENNESSEE
RS: Browns lead series, 30-25
PS: Titans lead series, 1-0
1970—Browns, 28-14 (C)
Browns, 21-10 (H)
1971—Browns, 31-0 (C)
Browns, 37-24 (H)
1972—Browns, 23-17 (H)
Browns, 20-0 (C)
1973—Browns, 42-13 (C)
Browns, 23-13 (H)
1974—Browns, 20-7 (C)
Oilers, 28-24 (H)
1975—Oilers, 40-10 (C)
Oilers, 21-10 (H)
1976—Browns, 21-7 (H)
Browns, 13-10 (C)
1977—Browns, 24-23 (H)
Oilers, 19-15 (C)
1978—Oilers, 16-13 (C)
Oilers, 14-10 (H)
1979—Oilers, 31-10 (H)
Browns, 14-7 (C)
1980—Oilers, 16-7 (C)
Browns, 17-14 (H)
1981—Oilers, 9-3 (C)
Oilers, 17-13 (H)
1982—Browns, 20-14 (H)
1983—Browns, 25-19 (C) OT
Oilers, 34-27 (H)
1984—Browns, 27-10 (C)
Browns, 27-20 (H)
1985—Browns, 21-6 (H)
Browns, 28-21 (C)
1986—Browns, 23-20 (H)
Browns, 13-10 (C) OT
1987—Oilers, 15-10 (C)
Browns, 40-7 (H)
1988—Oilers, 24-17 (H)
Browns, 28-23 (C)
**Oilers, 24-23 (C)
1989—Browns, 28-17 (C)
Browns, 24-20 (H)
1990—Oilers, 35-23 (C)
Oilers, 58-14 (H)
1991—Oilers, 28-24 (H)
Oilers, 17-14 (C)
1992—Browns, 24-14 (H)
Oilers, 17-14 (C)
1993—Oilers, 27-20 (C)
Oilers, 19-17 (H)
1994—Browns, 11-8 (H)
Browns, 34-10 (C)
1995—Browns, 14-7 (H)
Oilers, 37-10 (C)
1999—Titans, 26-9 (T)
Titans, 33-21 (C)
2000—Titans, 24-10 (T)
Titans, 24-0 (C)
(RS Pts.—Browns 1,066, Titans 1,014)
(PS Pts.—Titans 24, Browns 23)
Franchise in Houston prior to 1997; known as Oilers prior to 1999
***AFC First-Round Playoff*

CLEVELAND vs. WASHINGTON
RS: Browns lead series, 32-9-1
1950—Browns, 20-14 (C)
Browns, 45-21 (W)
1951—Browns, 45-0 (C)
1952—Browns, 19-15 (C)
Browns, 48-24 (W)
1953—Browns, 30-14 (W)
Browns, 27-3 (C)
1954—Browns, 62-3 (C)
Browns, 34-14 (W)
1955—Redskins, 27-17 (C)
Browns, 24-14 (W)
1956—Redskins, 20-9 (W)
Redskins, 20-17 (C)
1957—Browns, 21-17 (C)
Tie, 30-30 (W)
1958—Browns, 20-10 (W)
Browns, 21-14 (C)
1959—Browns, 34-7 (C)
Browns, 31-17 (W)
1960—Browns, 31-10 (W)
Browns, 27-16 (C)
1961—Browns, 31-7 (C)
Browns, 17-6 (W)
1962—Redskins, 17-16 (C)
Redskins, 17-9 (W)
1963—Browns, 37-14 (C)
Browns, 27-20 (W)
1964—Browns, 27-13 (W)
Browns, 34-24 (C)
1965—Browns, 17-7 (W)
Browns, 24-16 (C)
1966—Browns, 38-14 (W)
Browns, 14-3 (C)
1967—Browns, 42-37 (C)
1968—Browns, 24-21 (W)
1969—Browns, 27-23 (C)
1971—Browns, 20-13 (W)
1975—Redskins, 23-7 (C)
1979—Redskins, 13-9 (C)
1985—Redskins, 14-7 (C)
1988—Browns, 17-13 (W)
1991—Redskins, 42-17 (W)
(RS Pts.—Browns 1,073, Redskins 667)

DALLAS vs. ARIZONA
RS: Cowboys lead series, 51-25-1
PS: Cardinals lead series, 1-0;
See Arizona vs. Dallas

DALLAS vs. ATLANTA
RS: Cowboys lead series, 12-6
PS: Cowboys lead series, 2-0;
See Atlanta vs. Dallas

DALLAS vs. BALTIMORE
RS: Ravens lead series, 1-0;
See Baltimore vs. Dallas

DALLAS vs. BUFFALO
RS: Series tied, 3-3
PS: Cowboys lead series, 2-0;
See Buffalo vs. Dallas

DALLAS vs. CAROLINA
RS: Cowboys lead series, 2-1
PS: Panthers lead series, 1-0;
See Carolina vs. Dallas

DALLAS vs. CHICAGO
RS: Cowboys lead series, 9-8
PS: Cowboys lead series, 2-0;
See Chicago vs. Dallas

DALLAS vs. CINCINNATI
RS: Cowboys lead series, 5-3;
See Cincinnati vs. Dallas

DALLAS vs. CLEVELAND
RS: Browns lead series, 15-9
PS: Browns lead series, 2-1;
See Cleveland vs. Dallas

DALLAS vs. DENVER
RS: Cowboys lead series, 4-3
PS: Cowboys lead series, 1-0
1973—Cowboys, 22-10 (Den)
1977—Cowboys, 14-6 (Dal)
*Cowboys, 27-10 (New Orleans)
1980—Broncos, 41-20 (Den)
1986—Broncos, 29-14 (Den)
1992—Cowboys, 31-27 (Den)
1995—Cowboys, 31-21 (Dal)
1998—Broncos, 42-23 (Den)
(RS Pts.—Broncos 176, Cowboys 155)
(PS Pts.—Cowboys 27, Broncos 10)
Super Bowl XII

DALLAS vs. DETROIT
RS: Cowboys lead series, 7-6
PS: Series tied, 1-1
1960—Lions, 23-14 (Det)
1963—Cowboys, 17-14 (Dal)
1968—Cowboys, 59-13 (Dal)
1970—*Cowboys, 5-0 (Dal)
1972—Cowboys, 28-24 (Dal)
1975—Cowboys, 36-10 (Det)
1977—Cowboys, 37-0 (Dal)
1981—Lions, 27-24 (Det)
1985—Lions, 26-21 (Det)
1986—Cowboys, 31-7 (Det)
1987—Lions, 27-17 (Det)

ALL-TIME TEAM VS. TEAM RESULTS

1991—Lions, 34-10 (Det)
*Lions, 38-6 (Det)
1992—Cowboys, 37-3 (Det)
1994—Lions, 20-17 (Dal) OT
(RS Pts.—Cowboys 348, Lions 228)
(PS Pts.—Lions 38, Cowboys 11)
*NFC Divisional Playoff

DALLAS vs. GREEN BAY
RS: Cowboys lead series, 10-9
PS: Cowboys lead series, 4-2
1960—Packers, 41-7 (GB)
1964—Packers, 45-21 (D)
1965—Packers, 13-3 (Mil)
1966—*Packers, 34-27 (D)
1967—*Packers, 21-17 (GB)
1968—Packers, 28-17 (D)
1970—Cowboys, 16-3 (D)
1972—Packers, 16-13 (Mil)
1975—Packers, 19-17 (D)
1978—Cowboys, 42-14 (Mil)
1980—Cowboys, 28-7 (Mil)
1982—**Cowboys, 37-26 (D)
1984—Cowboys, 20-6 (D)
1989—Packers, 31-13 (GB)
Packers, 20-10 (D)
1991—Cowboys, 20-17 (Mil)
1993—Cowboys, 36-14 (D)
***Cowboys, 27-17 (D)
1994—Cowboys, 42-31 (D)
***Cowboys, 35-9 (D)
1995—Cowboys, 34-24 (D)
****Cowboys, 38-27 (D)
1996—Cowboys, 21-6 (D)
1997—Packers, 45-17 (GB)
1999—Cowboys, 27-13 (D)
(RS Pts.—Cowboys 404, Packers 393)
(PS Pts.—Cowboys 181, Packers 134)
*NFL Championship
**NFC Second-Round Playoff
***NFC Divisional Playoff
****NFC Championship

DALLAS vs. *INDIANAPOLIS
RS: Cowboys lead series, 7-4
PS: Colts lead series, 1-0
1960—Colts, 45-7 (D)
1967—Colts, 23-17 (B)
1969—Cowboys, 27-10 (D)
1970—**Colts, 16-13 (Miami)
1972—Cowboys, 21-0 (B)
1976—Cowboys, 30-27 (D)
1978—Cowboys, 38-0 (D)
1981—Cowboys, 37-13 (B)
1984—Cowboys, 22-3 (D)
1993—Cowboys, 27-3 (I)
1996—Colts, 25-24 (D)
1999—Colts, 34-24 (I)
(RS Pts.—Cowboys 274, Colts 183)
(PS Pts.—Colts 16, Cowboys 13)
*Franchise in Baltimore prior to 1984
**Super Bowl V

DALLAS VS. JACKSONVILLE
RS: Series tied, 1-1
1997—Cowboys, 26-22 (D)
2000—Jaguars, 23-17 (D) OT
(RS Pts.—Jaguars 45, Cowboys 43)

DALLAS vs. KANSAS CITY
RS: Cowboys lead series, 4-3
1970—Cowboys, 27-16 (KC)
1975—Chiefs, 34-31 (D)
1983—Cowboys, 41-21 (D)
1989—Chiefs, 36-28 (KC)
1992—Cowboys, 17-10 (D)
1995—Cowboys, 24-12 (D)
1998—Chiefs, 20-17 (KC)
(RS Pts.—Cowboys 185, Chiefs 149)

DALLAS vs. MIAMI
RS: Dolphins lead series, 6-3
PS: Cowboys lead series, 1-0
1971—*Cowboys, 24-3 (New Orleans)
1973—Dolphins, 14-7 (D)
1978—Dolphins, 23-16 (M)
1981—Cowboys, 28-27 (D)
1984—Dolphins, 28-21 (M)
1987—Dolphins, 20-14 (D)
1989—Dolphins, 17-14 (D)
1993—Dolphins, 16-14 (D)
1996—Cowboys, 29-10 (M)
1999—Cowboys, 20-0 (D)
(RS Pts.—Cowboys 163, Dolphins 155)
(PS Pts.—Cowboys 24, Dolphins 3)
*Super Bowl VI

DALLAS vs. MINNESOTA
RS: Series tied, 9-9
PS: Cowboys lead series, 4-2
1961—Cowboys, 21-7 (D)
Cowboys, 28-0 (M)
1966—Cowboys, 28-17 (D)
1968—Cowboys, 20-7 (M)
1970—Vikings, 54-13 (M)
1971—*Cowboys, 20-12 (M)
1973—**Vikings, 27-10 (D)
1974—Vikings, 23-21 (D)
1975—*Cowboys, 17-14 (M)
1977—Cowboys, 16-10 (M) OT
**Cowboys, 23-6 (D)
1978—Vikings, 21-10 (D)
1979—Cowboys, 36-20 (M)
1982—Vikings, 31-27 (M)
1983—Cowboys, 37-24 (M)
1987—Vikings, 44-38 (D) OT
1988—Vikings, 43-3 (D)
1993—Cowboys, 37-20 (M)
1995—Cowboys, 23-17 (M) OT
1996—***Cowboys, 40-15 (D)
1998—Vikings, 46-36 (D)
1999—Vikings, 27-17 (M)
***Vikings, 27-10 (M)
2000—Vikings, 27-15 (D)
(RS Pts.—Vikings 438, Cowboys 426)
(PS Pts.—Cowboys 120, Vikings 101)
*NFC Divisional Playoff
**NFC Championship
***NFC First-Round Playoff

DALLAS vs. NEW ENGLAND
RS: Cowboys lead series, 7-1
1971—Cowboys, 44-21 (D)
1975—Cowboys, 34-31 (NE)
1978—Cowboys, 17-10 (D)
1981—Cowboys, 35-21 (NE)
1984—Cowboys, 20-17 (D)
1987—Cowboys, 23-17 (NE) OT
1996—Cowboys, 12-6 (D)
1999—Patriots, 13-6 (NE)
(RS Pts.—Cowboys 191, Patriots 136)

DALLAS vs. NEW ORLEANS
RS: Cowboys lead series, 14-5
1967—Cowboys, 14-10 (D)
Cowboys, 27-10 (NO)
1968—Cowboys, 17-3 (NO)
1969—Cowboys, 21-17 (NO)
Cowboys, 33-17 (D)
1971—Saints, 24-14 (NO)
1973—Cowboys, 40-3 (D)
1976—Cowboys, 24-6 (NO)
1978—Cowboys, 27-7 (D)
1982—Cowboys, 21-7 (D)
1983—Cowboys, 21-20 (D)
1984—Cowboys, 30-27 (D) OT
1988—Saints, 20-17 (NO)
1989—Saints, 28-0 (NO)
1990—Cowboys, 17-13 (D)
1991—Cowboys, 23-14 (D)
1994—Cowboys, 24-16 (NO)
1998—Saints, 22-3 (NO)
1999—Saints, 31-24 (NO)
(RS Pts.—Cowboys 397, Saints 295)

DALLAS vs. N.Y. GIANTS
RS: Cowboys lead series, 47-28-2
1960—Tie, 31-31 (NY)
1961—Giants, 31-10 (D)
Cowboys, 17-16 (NY)
1962—Giants, 41-10 (D)
Giants, 41-31 (NY)
1963—Giants, 37-21 (NY)
Giants, 34-27 (D)
1964—Tie, 13-13 (D)
Cowboys, 31-21 (NY)
1965—Cowboys, 31-2 (D)
Cowboys, 38-20 (NY)
1966—Cowboys, 52-7 (D)
Cowboys, 17-7 (NY)
1967—Cowboys, 38-24 (D)
1968—Giants, 27-21 (D)
Cowboys, 28-10 (NY)
1969—Cowboys, 25-3 (D)
1970—Cowboys, 28-10 (D)
Giants, 23-20 (NY)
1971—Cowboys, 20-13 (D)
Cowboys, 42-14 (NY)
1972—Cowboys, 23-14 (NY)
Giants, 23-3 (D)
1973—Cowboys, 45-28 (D)
Cowboys, 23-10 (New Haven)
1974—Giants, 14-6 (D)
Cowboys, 21-7 (New Haven)
1975—Cowboys, 13-7 (NY)
Cowboys, 14-3 (D)
1976—Cowboys, 24-14 (NY)
Cowboys, 9-3 (D)
1977—Cowboys, 41-21 (D)
Cowboys, 24-10 (NY)
1978—Cowboys, 34-24 (NY)
Cowboys, 24-3 (D)
1979—Cowboys, 16-14 (NY)
Cowboys, 28-7 (D)
1980—Cowboys, 24-3 (D)
Giants, 38-35 (NY)
1981—Cowboys, 18-10 (D)
Giants, 13-10 (NY) OT
1983—Cowboys, 28-13 (D)
Cowboys, 38-20 (NY)
1984—Giants, 28-7 (NY)
Giants, 19-7 (D)
1985—Cowboys, 30-29 (NY)
Cowboys, 28-21 (D)
1986—Cowboys, 31-28 (D)
Giants, 17-14 (NY)
1987—Cowboys, 16-14 (NY)
Cowboys, 33-24 (D)
1988—Giants, 12-10 (D)
Giants, 29-21 (NY)
1989—Giants, 30-13 (D)
Giants, 15-0 (NY)
1990—Giants, 28-7 (D)
Giants, 31-17 (NY)
1991—Cowboys, 21-16 (D)
Giants, 22-9 (NY)
1992—Cowboys, 34-28 (NY)
Cowboys, 30-3 (D)
1993—Cowboys, 31-9 (D)
Cowboys, 16-13 (NY) OT
1994—Cowboys, 38-10 (D)
Giants, 15-10 (NY)
1995—Cowboys, 35-0 (NY)
Cowboys, 21-20 (D)
1996—Cowboys, 27-0 (D)
Giants, 20-6 (NY)
1997—Giants, 20-17 (NY)
Giants, 20-7 (D)
1998—Cowboys, 31-7 (NY)
Cowboys, 16-6 (D)
1999—Giants, 13-10 (NY)
Cowboys, 26-18 (D)
2000—Giants, 19-14 (NY)
Giants, 17-13 (D)
(RS Pts.—Cowboys 1,698, Giants 1,325)

DALLAS vs. N.Y. JETS
RS: Cowboys lead series, 5-2
1971—Cowboys, 52-10 (D)
1975—Cowboys, 31-21 (NY)
1978—Cowboys, 30-7 (NY)
1987—Cowboys, 38-24 (NY)
1990—Jets, 24-9 (NY)
1993—Cowboys, 28-7 (NY)
1999—Jets, 22-21 (D)
(RS Pts.—Cowboys 209, Jets 115)

DALLAS vs. *OAKLAND
RS: Raiders lead series, 4-3
1974—Raiders, 27-23 (O)
1980—Cowboys, 19-13 (O)
1983—Raiders, 40-38 (D)
1986—Raiders, 17-13 (D)
1992—Cowboys, 28-13 (LA)
1995—Cowboys, 34-21 (O)
1998—Raiders, 13-12 (D)
(RS Pts.—Cowboys 167, Raiders 144)
*Franchise in Los Angeles from 1982-1994

DALLAS vs. PHILADELPHIA
RS: Cowboys lead series, 48-32
PS: Cowboys lead series, 2-1
1960—Eagles, 27-25 (D)
1961—Eagles, 43-7 (D)
Eagles, 35-13 (P)
1962—Cowboys, 41-19 (D)
Eagles, 28-14 (P)
1963—Eagles, 24-21 (P)
Cowboys, 27-20 (D)
1964—Eagles, 17-14 (D)
Eagles, 24-14 (P)
1965—Eagles, 35-24 (D)
Cowboys, 21-19 (P)
1966—Cowboys, 56-7 (D)
Eagles, 24-23 (P)
1967—Eagles, 21-14 (P)
Cowboys, 38-17 (D)
1968—Cowboys, 45-13 (P)
Cowboys, 34-14 (D)
1969—Cowboys, 38-7 (P)
Cowboys, 49-14 (D)
1970—Cowboys, 17-7 (P)
Cowboys, 21-17 (D)
1971—Cowboys, 42-7 (P)
Cowboys, 20-7 (D)
1972—Cowboys, 28-6 (D)
Cowboys, 28-7 (P)
1973—Eagles, 30-16 (P)
Cowboys, 31-10 (D)
1974—Eagles, 13-10 (P)
Cowboys, 31-24 (D)
1975—Cowboys, 20-17 (P)
Cowboys, 27-17 (D)
1976—Cowboys, 27-7 (D)
Cowboys, 26-7 (P)
1977—Cowboys, 16-10 (P)
Cowboys, 24-14 (D)
1978—Cowboys, 14-7 (D)
Cowboys, 31-13 (P)
1979—Eagles, 31-21 (D)
Cowboys, 24-17 (P)
1980—Eagles, 17-10 (P)
Cowboys, 35-27 (D)
*Eagles, 20-7 (P)
1981—Cowboys, 17-14 (P)
Cowboys, 21-10 (D)
1982—Eagles, 24-20 (D)
1983—Cowboys, 37-7 (D)
Cowboys, 27-20 (P)
1984—Cowboys, 23-17 (D)
Cowboys, 26-10 (P)
1985—Eagles, 16-14 (P)
Cowboys, 34-17 (D)
1986—Cowboys, 17-14 (P)
Eagles, 23-21 (D)
1987—Cowboys, 41-22 (D)
Eagles, 37-20 (P)
1988—Eagles, 24-23 (P)
Eagles, 23-7 (D)
1989—Eagles, 27-0 (D)
Eagles, 20-10 (P)
1990—Eagles, 21-20 (D)
Eagles, 17-3 (P)
1991—Eagles, 24-0 (D)
Cowboys, 25-13 (P)
1992—Eagles, 31-7 (P)
Cowboys, 20-10 (D)
**Cowboys, 34-10 (D)
1993—Cowboys, 23-10 (P)
Cowboys, 23-17 (D)
1994—Cowboys, 24-13 (D)
Cowboys, 31-19 (P)
1995—Cowboys, 34-12 (D)

Eagles, 20-17 (P)
**Cowboys, 30-11 (D)
1996—Cowboys, 23-19 (P)
Eagles, 31-21 (D)
1997—Cowboys, 21-20 (D)
Eagles, 13-12 (P)
1998—Cowboys, 34-0 (P)
Cowboys, 13-9 (D)
1999—Eagles, 13-10 (P)
Cowboys, 20-10 (D)
2000—Eagles, 41-14 (D)
Eagles, 16-13 (P) OT
(RS Pts.—Cowboys 1,803, Eagles 1,424)
(PS Pts.—Cowboys 71, Eagles 41)
NFC Championship
**NFC Divisional Playoff*

DALLAS vs. PITTSBURGH
RS: Cowboys lead series, 14-11
PS: Steelers lead series, 2-1
1960—Steelers, 35-28 (D)
1961—Cowboys, 27-24 (D)
Steelers, 37-7 (P)
1962—Steelers, 30-28 (D)
Cowboys, 42-27 (P)
1963—Steelers, 27-21 (P)
Steelers, 24-19 (D)
1964—Steelers, 23-17 (P)
Cowboys, 17-14 (D)
1965—Steelers, 22-13 (P)
Cowboys, 24-17 (D)
1966—Cowboys, 52-21 (D)
Cowboys, 20-7 (P)
1967—Cowboys, 24-21 (P)
1968—Cowboys, 28-7 (D)
1969—Cowboys, 10-7 (P)
1972—Cowboys, 17-13 (D)
1975—*Steelers, 21-17 (Miami)
1977—Steelers, 28-13 (P)
1978—**Steelers, 35-31 (Miami)
1979—Steelers, 14-3 (P)
1982—Steelers, 36-28 (D)
1985—Cowboys, 27-13 (D)
1988—Steelers, 24-21 (P)
1991—Cowboys, 20-10 (D)
1994—Cowboys, 26-9 (P)
1995—***Cowboys, 27-17 (Tempe)
1997—Cowboys, 37-7 (P)
(RS Pts.—Cowboys 569, Steelers 497)
(PS Pts.—Cowboys 75, Steelers 73)
Super Bowl X
**Super Bowl XIII*
***Super Bowl XXX*

DALLAS vs. *ST. LOUIS
RS: Rams lead series, 9-8
PS: Series tied, 4-4
1960—Rams, 38-13 (D)
1962—Cowboys, 27-17 (LA)
1967—Rams, 35-13 (D)
1969—Rams, 24-23 (LA)
1971—Cowboys, 28-21 (D)
1973—Rams, 37-31 (LA)
**Cowboys, 27-16 (D)
1975—Cowboys, 18-7 (D)
***Cowboys, 37-7 (LA)
1976—**Rams, 14-12 (D)
1978—Rams, 27-14 (LA)
***Cowboys, 28-0 (LA)
1979—Cowboys, 30-6 (D)
**Rams, 21-19 (D)
1980—Rams, 38-14 (LA)
****Cowboys, 34-13 (D)
1981—Cowboys, 29-17 (D)
1983—****Rams, 24-17 (D)
1984—Cowboys, 20-13 (LA)
1985—**Rams, 20-0 (LA)
1986—Rams, 29-10 (LA)
1987—Cowboys, 29-21 (LA)
1989—Rams, 35-31 (D)
1990—Cowboys, 24-21 (LA)
1992—Rams, 27-23 (D)
(RS Pts.—Rams 413, Cowboys 377)
(PS Pts.—Cowboys 174, Rams 115)
Franchise in Los Angeles prior to 1995
**NFC Divisional Playoff*
***NFC Championship*
****NFC First-Round Playoff*

DALLAS vs. SAN DIEGO
RS: Cowboys lead series, 5-1
1972—Cowboys, 34-28 (SD)
1980—Cowboys, 42-31 (D)
1983—Chargers, 24-23 (SD)
1986—Cowboys, 24-21 (SD)
1990—Cowboys, 17-14 (D)
1995—Cowboys, 23-9 (SD)
(RS Pts.—Cowboys 163, Chargers 127)

DALLAS vs. SAN FRANCISCO
RS: 49ers lead series, 13-7-1
PS: Cowboys lead series, 5-2
1960—49ers, 26-14 (D)
1963—49ers, 31-24 (SF)
1965—Cowboys, 39-31 (D)
1967—49ers, 24-16 (SF)
1969—Tie, 24-24 (D)
1970—*Cowboys, 17-10 (SF)
1971—*Cowboys, 14-3 (D)
1972—49ers, 31-10 (D)
**Cowboys, 30-28 (SF)
1974—Cowboys, 20-14 (D)
1977—Cowboys, 42-35 (SF)
1979—Cowboys, 21-13 (SF)
1980—Cowboys, 59-14 (D)
1981—49ers, 45-14 (SF)
*49ers, 28-27 (SF)
1983—49ers, 42-17 (SF)
1985—49ers, 31-16 (SF)
1989—49ers, 31-14 (D)
1990—49ers, 24-6 (D)
1992—*Cowboys, 30-20 (SF)
1993—Cowboys, 26-17 (D)
*Cowboys, 38-21 (D)
1994—49ers, 21-14 (SF)
*49ers, 38-28 (SF)
1995—49ers, 38-20 (D)
1996—Cowboys, 20-17 (SF) OT
1997—49ers, 17-10 (SF)
2000—49ers, 41-24 (D)
(RS Pts.—49ers 567, Cowboys 450)
(PS Pts.—Cowboys 184, 49ers 148)
NFC Championship
**NFC Divisional Playoff*

DALLAS vs. SEATTLE
RS: Cowboys lead series, 5-1
1976—Cowboys, 28-13 (S)
1980—Cowboys, 51-7 (D)
1983—Cowboys, 35-10 (S)
1986—Seahawks, 31-14 (D)
1992—Cowboys, 27-0 (D)
1998—Cowboys, 30-22 (D)
(RS Pts.—Cowboys 185, Seahawks 83)

DALLAS vs. TAMPA BAY
RS: Cowboys lead series, 6-1
PS: Cowboys lead series, 2-0
1977—Cowboys, 23-7 (D)
1980—Cowboys, 28-17 (D)
1981—*Cowboys, 38-0 (D)
1982—Cowboys, 14-9 (D)
**Cowboys, 30-17 (D)
1983—Cowboys, 27-24 (D) OT
1990—Cowboys, 14-10 (D)
Cowboys, 17-13 (TB)
2000—Buccaneers, 27-7 (TB)
(RS Pts.—Cowboys 130, Buccaneers 107)
(PS Pts.—Cowboys 68, Buccaneers 17)
NFC Divisional Playoff
**NFC First-Round Playoff*

DALLAS vs. *TENNESSEE
RS: Series tied, 5-5
1970—Cowboys, 52-10 (D)
1974—Cowboys, 10-0 (H)
1979—Oilers, 30-24 (D)
1982—Cowboys, 37-7 (H)
1985—Cowboys, 17-10 (H)
1988—Oilers, 25-17 (D)
1991—Oilers, 26-23 (H) OT
1994—Cowboys, 20-17 (D)
1997—Oilers, 27-14 (D)
2000—Titans, 31-0 (T)
(RS Pts.—Cowboys 214, Titans 183)
Franchise in Houston prior to 1997; known as Oilers prior to 1999

DALLAS vs. WASHINGTON
RS: Cowboys lead series, 47-31-2
PS: Redskins lead series, 2-0
1960—Redskins, 26-14 (W)
1961—Tie, 28-28 (D)
Redskins, 34-24 (W)
1962—Tie, 35-35 (D)
Cowboys, 38-10 (W)
1963—Redskins, 21-17 (W)
Cowboys, 35-20 (D)
1964—Cowboys, 24-18 (D)
Redskins, 28-16 (W)
1965—Cowboys, 27-7 (D)
Redskins, 34-31 (W)
1966—Cowboys, 31-30 (W)
Redskins, 34-31 (D)
1967—Cowboys, 17-14 (W)
Redskins, 27-20 (D)
1968—Cowboys, 44-24 (W)
Cowboys, 29-20 (D)
1969—Cowboys, 41-28 (W)
Cowboys, 20-10 (D)
1970—Cowboys, 45-21 (W)
Cowboys, 34-0 (D)
1971—Redskins, 20-16 (D)
Cowboys, 13-0 (W)
1972—Redskins, 24-20 (W)
Cowboys, 34-24 (D)
*Redskins, 26-3 (W)
1973—Redskins, 14-7 (W)
Cowboys, 27-7 (D)
1974—Redskins, 28-21 (W)
Cowboys, 24-23 (D)
1975—Redskins, 30-24 (W) OT
Cowboys, 31-10 (D)
1976—Cowboys, 20-7 (W)
Redskins, 27-14 (D)
1977—Cowboys, 34-16 (D)
Cowboys, 14-7 (W)
1978—Redskins, 9-5 (W)
Cowboys, 37-10 (D)
1979—Redskins, 34-20 (W)
Cowboys, 35-34 (D)
1980—Cowboys, 17-3 (W)
Cowboys, 14-10 (D)
1981—Cowboys, 26-10 (W)
Cowboys, 24-10 (D)
1982—Cowboys, 24-10 (W)
*Redskins, 31-17 (W)
1983—Cowboys, 31-30 (W)
Redskins, 31-10 (D)
1984—Redskins, 34-14 (W)
Redskins, 30-28 (D)
1985—Cowboys, 44-14 (D)
Cowboys, 13-7 (W)
1986—Cowboys, 30-6 (D)
Redskins, 41-14 (W)
1987—Redskins, 13-7 (D)
Redskins, 24-20 (W)
1988—Redskins, 35-17 (D)
Cowboys, 24-17 (W)
1989—Redskins, 30-7 (D)
Cowboys, 13-3 (W)
1990—Redskins, 19-15 (W)
Cowboys, 27-17 (D)
1991—Redskins, 33-31 (D)
Cowboys, 24-21 (W)
1992—Cowboys, 23-10 (D)
Redskins, 20-17 (W)
1993—Redskins, 35-16 (W)
Cowboys, 38-3 (D)
1994—Cowboys, 34-7 (W)
Cowboys, 31-7 (D)
1995—Redskins, 27-23 (W)
Redskins, 24-17 (D)
1996—Cowboys, 21-10 (D)
Redskins, 37-10 (W)
1997—Redskins, 21-16 (W)
Cowboys, 17-14 (D)
1998—Cowboys, 31-10 (W)
Cowboys, 23-7 (D)
1999—Cowboys, 41-35 (W) OT
Cowboys, 38-20 (D)
2000—Cowboys, 27-21 (W)
Cowboys, 32-13 (D)
(RS Pts.—Cowboys 1,926, Redskins 1,562)
(PS Pts.—Redskins 57, Cowboys 20)
NFC Championship

DENVER vs. ARIZONA
RS: Broncos lead series, 4-0-1;
See Arizona vs. Denver

DENVER vs. ATLANTA
RS: Broncos lead series, 7-3
PS: Broncos lead series, 1-0;
See Atlanta vs. Denver

DENVER vs. BALTIMORE
RS: Broncos lead series, 1-0
PS: Ravens lead series, 1-0;
See Baltimore vs. Denver

DENVER vs. BUFFALO
RS: Bills lead series, 17-12-1
PS: Bills lead series, 1-0;
See Buffalo vs. Denver

DENVER vs. CAROLINA
RS: Broncos lead series, 1-0;
See Carolina vs. Denver

DENVER vs. CHICAGO
RS: Broncos lead series, 6-5;
See Chicago vs. Denver

DENVER vs. CINCINNATI
RS: Broncos lead series, 14-7;
See Cincinnati vs. Denver

DENVER vs. CLEVELAND
RS: Broncos lead series, 14-5
PS: Broncos lead series, 3-0;
See Cleveland vs. Denver

DENVER vs. DALLAS
RS: Cowboys lead series, 4-3
PS: Cowboys lead series, 1-0;
See Dallas vs. Denver

DENVER vs. DETROIT
RS: Broncos lead series, 5-3
1971—Lions, 24-20 (Den)
1974—Broncos, 31-27 (Det)
1978—Lions, 17-14 (Det)
1981—Broncos, 27-21 (Den)
1984—Broncos, 28-7 (Det)
1987—Broncos, 34-0 (Den)
1990—Lions, 40-27 (Det)
1999—Broncos, 17-7 (Det)
(RS Pts.—Broncos 198, Lions 143)

DENVER vs. GREEN BAY
RS: Broncos lead series, 5-3-1
PS: Broncos lead series, 1-0
1971—Packers, 34-13 (Mil)
1975—Broncos, 23-13 (D)
1978—Broncos, 16-3 (D)
1984—Broncos, 17-14 (D)
1987—Tie, 17-17 (Mil) OT
1990—Broncos, 22-13 (D)
1993—Packers, 30-27 (GB)
1996—Packers, 41-6 (GB)
1997—*Broncos, 31-24 (San Diego)
1999—Broncos, 31-10 (D)
(RS Pts.—Packers 175, Broncos 172)
(PS Pts.—Broncos 31, Packers 24)
Super Bowl XXXII

DENVER vs. *INDIANAPOLIS
RS: Broncos lead series, 9-2
1974—Broncos, 17-6 (B)
1977—Broncos, 27-13 (D)
1978—Colts, 7-6 (B)
1981—Broncos, 28-10 (D)
1983—Broncos, 17-10 (B)
Broncos, 21-19 (D)
1985—Broncos, 15-10 (I)
1988—Colts, 55-23 (I)
1989—Broncos, 14-3 (D)
1990—Broncos, 27-17 (I)
1993—Broncos, 35-13 (D)
(RS Pts.—Broncos 230, Colts 163)

ALL-TIME TEAM VS. TEAM RESULTS

Franchise in Baltimore prior to 1984

DENVER vs. JACKSONVILLE
RS: Broncos lead series, 2-1
PS: Series tied, 1-1
1995—Broncos, 31-23 (D)
1996—*Jaguars, 30-27 (D)
1997—**Broncos, 42-17 (D)
1998—Broncos, 37-24 (D)
1999—Jaguars, 27-24 (J)
(RS Pts.—Broncos 92, Jaguars 74)
(PS Pts.—Broncos 69, Jaguars 47)
**AFC Divisional Playoff*
***AFC First-Round Playoff*

DENVER vs. *KANSAS CITY
RS: Chiefs lead series, 47-34
PS: Broncos lead series, 1-0
1960—Texans, 17-14 (D)
Texans, 34-7 (Dal)
1961—Texans, 19-12 (D)
Texans, 49-21 (Dal)
1962—Texans, 24-3 (D)
Texans, 17-10 (Dal)
1963—Chiefs, 59-7 (D)
Chiefs, 52-21 (KC)
1964—Broncos, 33-27 (D)
Chiefs, 49-39 (KC)
1965—Chiefs, 31-23 (D)
Chiefs, 45-35 (KC)
1966—Chiefs, 37-10 (KC)
Chiefs, 56-10 (D)
1967—Chiefs, 52-9 (KC)
Chiefs, 38-24 (D)
1968—Chiefs, 34-2 (KC)
Chiefs, 30-7 (D)
1969—Chiefs, 26-13 (D)
Chiefs, 31-17 (KC)
1970—Broncos, 26-13 (D)
Chiefs, 16-0 (KC)
1971—Chiefs, 16-3 (D)
Chiefs, 28-10 (KC)
1972—Chiefs, 45-24 (D)
Chiefs, 24-21 (KC)
1973—Chiefs, 16-14 (KC)
Broncos, 14-10 (D)
1974—Broncos, 17-14 (KC)
Chiefs, 42-34 (D)
1975—Broncos, 37-33 (D)
Chiefs, 26-13 (KC)
1976—Broncos, 35-26 (KC)
Broncos, 17-16 (D)
1977—Broncos, 23-7 (D)
Broncos, 14-7 (KC)
1978—Broncos, 23-17 (KC) OT
Broncos, 24-3 (D)
1979—Broncos, 24-10 (KC)
Broncos, 20-3 (D)
1980—Chiefs, 23-17 (D)
Chiefs, 31-14 (KC)
1981—Chiefs, 28-14 (KC)
Broncos, 16-13 (D)
1982—Chiefs, 37-16 (D)
1983—Broncos, 27-24 (D)
Chiefs, 48-17 (KC)
1984—Broncos, 21-0 (D)
Chiefs, 16-13 (KC)
1985—Broncos, 30-10 (KC)
Broncos, 14-13 (D)
1986—Broncos, 38-17 (D)
Chiefs, 37-10 (KC)
1987—Broncos, 26-17 (KC)
Broncos, 20-17 (D)
1988—Chiefs, 20-13 (KC)
Broncos, 17-11 (D)
1989—Broncos, 34-20 (D)
Broncos, 16-13 (KC)
1990—Broncos, 24-23 (D)
Chiefs, 31-20 (KC)
1991—Broncos, 19-16 (D)
Broncos, 24-20 (KC)
1992—Broncos, 20-19 (D)
Chiefs, 42-20 (KC)
1993—Chiefs, 15-7 (KC)
Broncos, 27-21 (D)
1994—Chiefs, 31-28 (D)
Broncos, 20-17 (KC) OT
1995—Chiefs, 21-7 (D)
Chiefs, 20-17 (KC)
1996—Chiefs, 17-14 (KC)
Broncos, 34-7 (D)
1997—Broncos, 19-3 (D)
Chiefs, 24-22 (KC)
**Broncos, 14-10 (KC)
1998—Broncos, 30-7 (KC)
Broncos, 35-31 (D)
1999—Chiefs, 26-10 (KC)
Chiefs, 16-10 (D)
2000—Chiefs, 23-22 (D)
Chiefs, 20-7 (KC)
(RS Pts.—Chiefs 1,944, Broncos 1,519)
(PS Pts.—Broncos 14, Chiefs 10)
**Franchise in Dallas prior to 1963 and known as Texans*
***AFC Divisional Playoff*

DENVER vs. MIAMI
RS: Dolphins lead series, 7-2-1
PS: Broncos lead series, 1-0
1966—Dolphins, 24-7 (M)
Broncos, 17-7 (D)
1967—Dolphins, 35-21 (M)
1968—Broncos, 21-14 (D)
1969—Dolphins, 27-24 (M)
1971—Tie, 10-10 (D)
1975—Dolphins, 14-13 (M)
1985—Dolphins, 30-26 (D)
1998—Dolphins, 31-21 (M)
*Broncos, 38-3 (D)
1999—Dolphins, 38-21 (D)
(RS Pts.—Dolphins 230, Broncos 181)
(PS Pts.—Broncos 38, Dolphins 3)
**AFC Divisonal Playoff*

DENVER vs. MINNESOTA
RS: Vikings lead series, 6-4
1972—Vikings, 23-20 (D)
1978—Vikings, 12-9 (M) OT
1981—Broncos, 19-17 (D)
1984—Broncos, 42-21 (D)
1987—Vikings, 34-27 (M)
1990—Vikings, 27-22 (M)
1991—Broncos, 13-6 (M)
1993—Vikings, 26-23 (D)
1996—Broncos, 21-17 (M)
1999—Vikings, 23-20 (D)
(RS Pts.—Broncos 216, Vikings 206)

DENVER vs. *NEW ENGLAND
RS: Broncos lead series, 20-14
PS: Broncos lead series, 1-0
1960—Broncos, 13-10 (B)
Broncos, 31-24 (D)
1961—Patriots, 45-17 (B)
Patriots, 28-24 (D)
1962—Patriots, 41-16 (B)
Patriots, 33-29 (D)
1963—Broncos, 14-10 (D)
Patriots, 40-21 (B)
1964—Patriots, 39-10 (D)
Patriots, 12-7 (B)
1965—Broncos, 27-10 (B)
Patriots, 28-20 (D)
1966—Patriots, 24-10 (D)
Broncos, 17-10 (B)
1967—Broncos, 26-21 (D)
1968—Patriots, 20-17 (D)
Broncos, 35-14 (B)
1969—Broncos, 35-7 (D)
1972—Broncos, 45-21 (D)
1976—Patriots, 38-14 (NE)
1979—Broncos, 45-10 (D)
1980—Patriots, 23-14 (NE)
1984—Broncos, 26-19 (D)
1986—Broncos, 27-20 (D)
**Broncos, 22-17 (D)
1987—Broncos, 31-20 (D)
1988—Broncos, 21-10 (D)
1991—Broncos, 9-6 (NE)
Broncos, 20-3 (D)
1995—Broncos, 37-3 (NE)
1996—Broncos, 34-8 (NE)
1997—Broncos, 34-13 (D)
1998—Broncos, 27-21 (D)
1999—Patriots, 24-23 (NE)
2000—Patriots, 28-19 (D)
(RS Pts.—Broncos 795, Patriots 683)
(PS Pts.—Broncos 22, Patriots 17)
**Franchise in Boston prior to 1971*
***AFC Divisional Playoff*

DENVER vs. NEW ORLEANS
RS: Broncos lead series, 5-2
1970—Broncos, 31-6 (NO)
1974—Broncos, 33-17 (D)
1979—Broncos, 10-3 (D)
1985—Broncos, 34-23 (D)
1988—Saints, 42-0 (NO)
1994—Saints, 30-28 (D)
2000—Broncos, 38-23 (NO)
(RS Pts.—Broncos 174, Saints 144)

DENVER vs. N.Y. GIANTS
RS: Giants lead series, 4-3
PS: Giants lead series, 1-0
1972—Giants, 29-17 (NY)
1976—Broncos, 14-13 (D)
1980—Broncos, 14-9 (NY)
1986—Giants, 19-16 (NY)
*Giants, 39-20 (Pasadena)
1989—Giants, 14-7 (D)
1992—Broncos, 27-13 (D)
1998—Giants, 20-16 (NY)
(RS Pts.—Giants 117, Broncos 111)
(PS Pts.—Giants 39, Broncos 20)
**Super Bowl XXI*

DENVER vs. *N.Y. JETS
RS: Broncos lead series, 14-13-1
PS: Broncos lead series, 1-0
1960—Titans, 28-24 (NY)
Titans, 30-27 (D)
1961—Titans, 35-28 (NY)
Broncos, 27-10 (D)
1962—Broncos, 32-10 (NY)
Titans, 46-45 (D)
1963—Tie, 35-35 (NY)
Jets, 14-9 (D)
1964—Jets, 30-6 (NY)
Broncos, 20-16 (D)
1965—Broncos, 16-13 (D)
Jets, 45-10 (NY)
1966—Jets, 16-7 (D)
1967—Jets, 38-24 (D)
Broncos, 33-24 (NY)
1968—Broncos, 21-13 (NY)
1969—Broncos, 21-19 (D)
1973—Broncos, 40-28 (NY)
1976—Broncos, 46-3 (D)
1978—Jets, 31-28 (D)
1980—Broncos, 31-24 (D)
1986—Jets, 22-10 (NY)
1992—Broncos, 27-16 (D)
1993—Broncos, 26-20 (NY)
1994—Jets, 25-22 (NY) OT
1996—Broncos, 31-6 (D)
1998—**Broncos, 23-10 (D)
1999—Jets, 21-13 (D)
2000—Broncos, 30-23 (NY)
(RS Pts.—Broncos 689, Jets 641)
(PS Pts.—Broncos 23, Jets 10)
**Jets known as Titans prior to 1963*
***AFC Championship*

DENVER vs. *OAKLAND
RS: Raiders lead series, 49-30-2
PS: Series tied, 1-1
1960—Broncos, 31-14 (D)
Raiders, 48-10 (O)
1961—Raiders, 33-19 (O)
Broncos, 27-24 (D)
1962—Broncos, 44-7 (D)
Broncos, 23-6 (O)
1963—Raiders, 26-10 (D)
Raiders, 35-31 (O)
1964—Raiders, 40-7 (O)
Tie, 20-20 (D)
1965—Raiders, 28-20 (D)
Raiders, 24-13 (O)
1966—Raiders, 17-3 (D)
Raiders, 28-10 (O)
1967—Raiders, 51-0 (O)
Raiders, 21-17 (D)
1968—Raiders, 43-7 (D)
Raiders, 33-27 (O)
1969—Raiders, 24-14 (D)
Raiders, 41-10 (O)
1970—Raiders, 35-23 (O)
Raiders, 24-19 (D)
1971—Raiders, 27-16 (D)
Raiders, 21-13 (O)
1972—Broncos, 30-23 (O)
Raiders, 37-20 (D)
1973—Tie, 23-23 (D)
Raiders, 21-17 (O)
1974—Raiders, 28-17 (D)
Broncos, 20-17 (O)
1975—Raiders, 42-17 (D)
Raiders, 17-10 (O)
1976—Raiders, 17-10 (D)
Raiders, 19-6 (O)
1977—Broncos, 30-7 (O)
Raiders, 24-14 (D)
**Broncos, 20-17 (D)
1978—Broncos, 14-6 (D)
Broncos, 21-6 (O)
1979—Raiders, 27-3 (O)
Raiders, 14-10 (D)
1980—Raiders, 9-3 (O)
Raiders, 24-21 (D)
1981—Broncos, 9-7 (D)
Broncos, 17-0 (O)
1982—Raiders, 27-10 (LA)
1983—Raiders, 22-7 (D)
Raiders, 22-20 (LA)
1984—Broncos, 16-13 (D)
Broncos, 22-19 (LA) OT
1985—Raiders, 31-28 (LA) OT
Raiders, 17-14 (D) OT
1986—Broncos, 38-36 (D)
Broncos, 21-10 (LA)
1987—Broncos, 30-14 (D)
Broncos, 23-17 (LA)
1988—Raiders, 30-27 (D) OT
Raiders, 21-20 (LA)
1989—Broncos, 31-21 (D)
Raiders, 16-13 (LA) OT
1990—Raiders, 14-9 (LA)
Raiders, 23-20 (D)
1991—Raiders, 16-13 (LA)
Raiders, 17-16 (D)
1992—Broncos, 17-13 (D)
Raiders, 24-0 (LA)
1993—Raiders, 23-20 (D)
Raiders, 33-30 (LA) OT
***Raiders, 42-24 (LA)
1994—Raiders, 48-16 (D)
Raiders, 23-13 (LA)
1995—Broncos, 27-0 (D)
Broncos, 31-28 (O)
1996—Broncos, 22-21 (O)
Broncos, 24-19 (D)
1997—Raiders, 28-25 (O)
Broncos, 31-3 (D)
1998—Broncos, 34-17 (O)
Broncos, 40-14 (D)
1999—Broncos, 16-13 (O)
Broncos, 27-21 (D) OT
2000—Broncos, 33-24 (O)
Broncos, 27-24 (D)
(RS Pts.—Raiders 1,800, Broncos 1,537)
(PS Pts.—Raiders 59, Broncos 44)
**Franchise in Los Angeles from 1982-1994*
***AFC Championship*
****AFC First-Round Playoff*

DENVER vs. PHILADELPHIA
RS: Eagles lead series, 6-3
1971—Eagles, 17-16 (P)
1975—Broncos, 25-10 (D)
1980—Eagles, 27-6 (P)

1983—Eagles, 13-10 (D)
1986—Broncos, 33-7 (P)
1989—Eagles, 28-24 (D)
1992—Eagles, 30-0 (P)
1995—Eagles, 31-13 (P)
1998—Broncos, 41-16 (D)
(RS Pts.—Eagles 179, Broncos 168)

DENVER vs. PITTSBURGH
RS: Broncos lead series, 10-6-1
PS: Broncos lead series, 3-2
1970—Broncos, 16-13 (D)
1971—Broncos, 22-10 (P)
1973—Broncos, 23-13 (P)
1974—Tie, 35-35 (D) OT
1975—Steelers, 20-9 (P)
1977—Broncos, 21-7 (D)
*Broncos, 34-21 (D)
1978—Steelers, 21-17 (D)
*Steelers, 33-10 (P)
1979—Steelers, 42-7 (P)
1983—Broncos, 14-10 (P)
1984—*Steelers, 24-17 (D)
1985—Broncos, 31-23 (P)
1986—Broncos, 21-10 (P)
1988—Steelers, 39-21 (P)
1989—Broncos, 34-7 (D)
*Broncos, 24-23 (D)
1990—Steelers, 34-17 (D)
1991—Broncos, 20-13 (D)
1993—Broncos, 37-13 (D)
1997—Steelers, 35-24 (P)
**Broncos, 24-21 (P)
(RS Pts.—Broncos 369, Steelers 345)
(PS Pts.—Steelers 122, Broncos 109)
AFC Divisional Playoff
***AFC Championship*

DENVER vs. *ST. LOUIS
RS: Rams lead series, 5-4
1972—Broncos, 16-10 (LA)
1974—Rams, 17-10 (D)
1979—Rams, 13-9 (D)
1982—Broncos, 27-24 (LA)
1985—Rams, 20-16 (LA)
1988—Broncos, 35-24 (D)
1994—Rams, 27-21 (LA)
1997—Broncos, 35-14 (D)
2000—Rams, 41-36 (StL)
(RS Pts.—Broncos 205, Rams 190)
Franchise in Los Angeles prior to 1995

DENVER vs. *SAN DIEGO
RS: Broncos lead series, 45-36-1
1960—Chargers, 23-19 (D)
Chargers, 41-33 (LA)
1961—Chargers, 37-0 (SD)
Chargers, 19-16 (D)
1962—Broncos, 30-21 (D)
Broncos, 23-20 (SD)
1963—Broncos, 50-34 (D)
Chargers, 58-20 (SD)
1964—Chargers, 42-14 (SD)
Chargers, 31-20 (D)
1965—Chargers, 34-31 (SD)
Chargers, 33-21 (D)
1966—Chargers, 24-17 (SD)
Broncos, 20-17 (D)
1967—Chargers, 38-21 (D)
Chargers, 24-20 (SD)
1968—Chargers, 55-24 (SD)
Chargers, 47-23 (D)
1969—Broncos, 13-0 (D)
Chargers, 45-24 (SD)
1970—Chargers, 24-21 (SD)
Tie, 17-17 (D)
1971—Broncos, 20-16 (D)
Chargers, 45-17 (SD)
1972—Chargers, 37-14 (SD)
Broncos, 38-13 (D)
1973—Broncos, 30-19 (D)
Broncos, 42-28 (SD)
1974—Broncos, 27-7 (D)
Chargers, 17-0 (SD)
1975—Broncos, 27-17 (SD)
Broncos, 13-10 (D) OT
1976—Broncos, 26-0 (D)
Broncos, 17-0 (SD)
1977—Broncos, 17-14 (SD)
Broncos, 17-9 (D)
1978—Broncos, 27-14 (D)
Chargers, 23-0 (SD)
1979—Broncos, 7-0 (D)
Chargers, 17-7 (SD)
1980—Chargers, 30-13 (D)
Broncos, 20-13 (SD)
1981—Broncos, 42-24 (D)
Chargers, 34-17 (SD)
1982—Chargers, 23-3 (D)
Chargers, 30-20 (SD)
1983—Broncos, 14-6 (D)
Chargers, 31-7 (SD)
1984—Broncos, 16-13 (SD)
Broncos, 16-13 (D)
1985—Chargers, 30-10 (SD)
Broncos, 30-24 (D) OT
1986—Broncos, 31-14 (SD)
Chargers, 9-3 (D)
1987—Broncos, 31-17 (SD)
Broncos, 24-0 (D)
1988—Broncos, 34-3 (D)
Broncos, 12-0 (SD)
1989—Broncos, 16-10 (D)
Chargers, 19-16 (SD)
1990—Chargers, 19-7 (SD)
Broncos, 20-10 (D)
1991—Broncos, 27-19 (D)
Broncos, 17-14 (SD)
1992—Broncos, 21-13 (D)
Chargers, 24-21 (SD)
1993—Broncos, 34-17 (D)
Chargers, 13-10 (SD)
1994—Chargers, 37-34 (D)
Broncos, 20-15 (SD)
1995—Chargers, 17-6 (SD)
Broncos, 30-27 (D)
1996—Broncos, 28-17 (D)
Chargers, 16-10 (SD)
1997—Broncos, 38-28 (SD)
Broncos, 38-3 (D)
1998—Broncos, 27-10 (D)
Broncos, 31-16 (SD)
1999—Broncos, 33-17 (SD)
Chargers, 12-6 (D)
2000—Broncos, 21-7 (SD)
Broncos, 38-37 (D)
(RS Pts.—Broncos 1,715, Chargers 1,703)
Franchise in Los Angeles prior to 1961

DENVER vs. SAN FRANCISCO
RS: Broncos lead series, 5-4
PS: 49ers lead series, 1-0
1970—49ers, 19-14 (SF)
1973—49ers, 36-34 (D)
1979—Broncos, 38-28 (SF)
1982—Broncos, 24-21 (D)
1985—Broncos, 17-16 (D)
1988—Broncos, 16-13 (SF) OT
1989—*49ers, 55-10 (New Orleans)
1994—49ers, 42-19 (SF)
1997—49ers, 34-17 (SF)
2000—Broncos, 38-9 (D)
(RS Pts.—49ers 218, Broncos 217)
(PS Pts.—49ers 55, Broncos 10)
Super Bowl XXIV

DENVER vs. SEATTLE
RS: Broncos lead series, 31-16
PS: Seahawks lead series, 1-0
1977—Broncos, 24-13 (S)
1978—Broncos, 28-7 (D)
Broncos, 20-17 (S) OT
1979—Broncos, 37-34 (D)
Seahawks, 28-23 (S)
1980—Broncos, 36-20 (D)
Broncos, 25-17 (S)
1981—Seahawks, 13-10 (S)
Broncos, 23-13 (D)
1982—Seahawks, 17-10 (D)
Seahawks, 13-11 (S)
1983—Seahawks, 27-19 (S)
Broncos, 38-27 (D)
*Seahawks, 31-7 (S)
1984—Seahawks, 27-24 (D)
Broncos, 31-14 (S)
1985—Broncos, 13-10 (D) OT
Broncos, 27-24 (S)
1986—Broncos, 20-13 (D)
Seahawks, 41-16 (S)
1987—Broncos, 40-17 (D)
Seahawks, 28-21 (S)
1988—Seahawks, 21-14 (D)
Seahawks, 42-14 (S)
1989—Broncos, 24-21 (S) OT
Broncos, 41-14 (D)
1990—Broncos, 34-31 (D) OT
Seahawks, 17-12 (S)
1991—Broncos, 16-10 (D)
Seahawks, 13-10 (S)
1992—Seahawks, 16-13 (S) OT
Broncos, 10-6 (D)
1993—Broncos, 28-17 (D)
Broncos, 17-9 (S)
1994—Broncos, 16-9 (S)
Broncos, 17-10 (D)
1995—Seahawks, 27-10 (S)
Seahawks, 31-27 (D)
1996—Broncos, 30-20 (S)
Broncos, 34-7 (D)
1997—Broncos, 35-14 (S)
Broncos, 30-27 (D)
1998—Broncos, 21-16 (S)
Broncos, 28-21 (D)
1999—Seahawks, 20-17 (S)
Broncos, 36-30 (D) OT
2000—Broncos, 38-31 (S)
Broncos, 31-24 (D)
(RS Pts.—Broncos 1,099, Seahawks 924)
(PS Pts.—Seahawks 31, Broncos 7)
AFC First-Round Playoff

DENVER vs. TAMPA BAY
RS: Broncos lead series, 3-2
1976—Broncos, 48-13 (D)
1981—Broncos, 24-7 (TB)
1993—Buccaneers, 17-10 (D)
1996—Broncos, 27-23 (D)
1999—Buccaneers, 13-10 (TB)
(RS Pts.—Broncos 119, Buccaneers 73)

DENVER vs. *TENNESSEE
RS: Titans lead series, 20-11-1
PS: Broncos lead series, 2-1
1960—Oilers, 45-25 (D)
Oilers, 20-10 (H)
1961—Oilers, 55-14 (D)
Oilers, 45-14 (H)
1962—Broncos, 20-10 (D)
Oilers, 34-17 (H)
1963—Oilers, 20-14 (H)
Oilers, 33-24 (D)
1964—Oilers, 38-17 (D)
Oilers, 34-15 (H)
1965—Broncos, 28-17 (D)
Broncos, 31-21 (H)
1966—Oilers, 45-7 (H)
Broncos, 40-38 (D)
1967—Oilers, 10-6 (H)
Oilers, 20-18 (D)
1968—Oilers, 38-17 (H)
1969—Oilers, 24-21 (H)
Tie, 20-20 (D)
1970—Oilers, 31-21 (H)
1972—Broncos, 30-17 (D)
1973—Broncos, 48-20 (H)
1974—Broncos, 37-14 (D)
1976—Oilers, 17-3 (H)
1977—Broncos, 24-14 (H)
1979—**Oilers, 13-7 (H)
1980—Oilers, 20-16 (D)
1983—Broncos, 26-14 (H)
1985—Broncos, 31-20 (D)
1987—Oilers, 40-10 (D)
***Broncos, 34-10 (D)
1991—Oilers, 42-14 (H)
***Broncos, 26-24 (D)
1992—Broncos, 27-21 (D)
1995—Oilers, 42-33 (H)
(RS Pts.—Titans 879, Broncos 678)
(PS Pts.—Broncos 67, Titans 47)
**Franchise in Houston prior to 1997; known as the Oilers prior to 1999*
***AFC First-Round Playoff*
****AFC Divisional Playoff*

DENVER vs. WASHINGTON
RS: Broncos lead series, 5-3
PS: Redskins lead series, 1-0
1970—Redskins, 19-3 (D)
1974—Redskins, 30-3 (W)
1980—Broncos, 20-17 (D)
1986—Broncos, 31-30 (D)
1987—*Redskins, 42-10 (San Diego)
1989—Broncos, 14-10 (W)
1992—Redskins, 34-3 (W)
1995—Broncos, 38-31 (D)
1998—Broncos, 38-16 (W)
(RS Pts.—Redskins 187, Broncos 150)
(PS Pts.—Redskins 42, Broncos 10)
Super Bowl XXII

DETROIT vs. ARIZONA
RS: Lions lead series, 27-19-5;
See Arizona vs. Detroit

DETROIT vs. ATLANTA
RS: Lions lead series, 21-7;
See Atlanta vs. Detroit

DETROIT vs. BALTIMORE
RS: Ravens lead series, 1-0;
See Baltimore vs. Detroit

DETROIT vs. BUFFALO
RS: Lions lead series, 3-2-1;
See Buffalo vs. Detroit

DETROIT vs. CAROLINA
RS: Lions lead series, 1-0;
See Carolina vs. Detroit

DETROIT vs. CHICAGO
RS: Bears lead series, 79-58-5;
See Chicago vs. Detroit

DETROIT vs. CINCINNATI
RS: Bengals lead series, 4-3;
See Cincinnati vs. Detroit

DETROIT vs. CLEVELAND
RS: Lions lead series, 12-3
PS: Lions lead series, 3-1;
See Cleveland vs. Detroit

DETROIT vs. DALLAS
RS: Cowboys lead series, 7-6
PS: Series tied, 1-1;
See Dallas vs. Detroit

DETROIT vs. DENVER
RS: Broncos lead series, 5-3;
See Denver vs. Detroit

***DETROIT vs. GREEN BAY**
RS: Packers lead series, 72-62-7
PS: Packers lead series, 2-0
1930—Packers, 47-13 (GB)
Tie, 6-6 (P)
1932—Packers, 15-10 (GB)
Spartans, 19-0 (P)
1933—Packers, 17-0 (GB)
Spartans, 7-0 (P)
1934—Lions, 3-0 (GB)
Packers, 3-0 (D)
1935—Packers, 13-9 (Mil)
Packers, 31-7 (GB)
Lions, 20-10 (D)
1936—Packers, 20-18 (GB)
Packers, 26-17 (D)
1937—Packers, 26-6 (GB)
Packers, 14-13 (D)
1938—Lions, 17-7 (GB)
Packers, 28-7 (D)
1939—Packers, 26-7 (GB)
Packers, 12-7 (D)
1940—Lions, 23-14 (GB)
Packers, 50-7 (D)
1941—Packers, 23-0 (GB)
Packers, 24-7 (D)
1942—Packers, 38-7 (Mil)

Packers, 28-7 (D)
1943—Packers, 35-14 (GB)
Packers, 27-6 (D)
1944—Packers, 27-6 (Mil)
Packers, 14-0 (D)
1945—Packers, 57-21 (Mil)
Lions, 14-3 (D)
1946—Packers, 10-7 (Mil)
Packers, 9-0 (D)
1947—Packers, 34-17 (GB)
Packers, 35-14 (D)
1948—Packers, 33-21 (GB)
Lions, 24-20 (D)
1949—Packers, 16-14 (Mil)
Lions, 21-7 (D)
1950—Lions, 45-7 (GB)
Lions, 24-21 (D)
1951—Lions, 24-17 (GB)
Lions, 52-35 (D)
1952—Lions, 52-17 (GB)
Lions, 48-24 (D)
1953—Lions, 14-7 (GB)
Lions, 34-15 (D)
1954—Lions, 21-17 (GB)
Lions, 28-24 (D)
1955—Packers, 20-17 (GB)
Lions, 24-10 (D)
1956—Lions, 20-16 (GB)
Packers, 24-20 (D)
1957—Lions, 24-14 (GB)
Lions, 18-6 (D)
1958—Tie, 13-13 (GB)
Lions, 24-14 (D)
1959—Packers, 28-10 (GB)
Packers, 24-17 (D)
1960—Packers, 28-9 (GB)
Lions, 23-10 (D)
1961—Lions, 17-13 (Mil)
Packers, 17-9 (D)
1962—Packers, 9-7 (GB)
Lions, 26-14 (D)
1963—Packers, 31-10 (Mil)
Tie, 13-13 (D)
1964—Packers, 14-10 (D)
Packers, 30-7 (GB)
1965—Packers, 31-21 (D)
Lions, 12-7 (GB)
1966—Packers, 23-14 (GB)
Packers, 31-7 (D)
1967—Tie, 17-17 (GB)
Packers, 27-17 (D)
1968—Lions, 23-17 (GB)
Tie, 14-14 (D)
1969—Packers, 28-17 (D)
Lions, 16-10 (GB)
1970—Lions, 40-0 (GB)
Lions, 20-0 (D)
1971—Lions, 31-28 (D)
Tie, 14-14 (Mil)
1972—Packers, 24-23 (D)
Packers, 33-7 (GB)
1973—Tie, 13-13 (GB)
Lions, 34-0 (D)
1974—Packers, 21-19 (Mil)
Lions, 19-17 (D)
1975—Lions, 30-16 (Mil)
Lions, 13-10 (D)
1976—Packers, 24-14 (GB)
Lions, 27-6 (D)
1977—Lions, 10-6 (D)
Packers, 10-9 (GB)
1978—Packers, 13-7 (D)
Packers, 35-14 (Mil)
1979—Packers, 24-16 (Mil)
Packers, 18-13 (D)
1980—Lions, 29-7 (Mil)
Lions, 24-3 (D)
1981—Lions, 31-27 (D)
Packers, 31-17 (GB)
1982—Lions, 30-10 (GB)
Lions, 27-24 (D)
1983—Lions, 38-14 (D)
Lions, 23-20 (Mil) OT
1984—Packers, 41-9 (GB)
Lions, 31-28 (D)
1985—Packers, 43-10 (GB)
Packers, 26-23 (D)
1986—Lions, 21-14 (GB)
Packers, 44-40 (D)
1987—Lions, 19-16 (GB) OT
Packers, 34-33 (D)
1988—Lions, 19-9 (Mil)
Lions, 30-14 (D)
1989—Packers, 23-20 (Mil) OT
Lions, 31-22 (D)
1990—Packers, 24-21 (D)
Lions, 24-17 (GB)
1991—Lions, 23-14 (D)
Lions, 21-17 (GB)
1992—Packers, 27-13 (D)
Packers, 38-10 (Mil)
1993—Packers, 26-17 (MIl)
Lions, 30-20 (D)
**Packers, 28-24 (D)
1994—Packers, 38-30 (Mil)
Lions, 34-31 (D)
**Packers, 16-12 (GB)
1995—Packers, 30-21 (GB)
Lions, 24-16 (D)
1996—Packers, 28-18 (GB)
Packers, 31-3 (D)
1997—Lions, 26-15 (D)
Packers, 20-10 (GB)
1998—Packers, 38-19 (GB)
Lions, 27-20 (D)
1999—Lions, 23-15 (D)
Packers, 26-17 (GB)
2000—Lions, 31-24 (D)
Packers, 26-13 (GB)
(RS Pts.—Packers 2,845, Lions 2,567)
(PS Pts.—Packers 44, Lions 36)
Franchise in Portsmouth prior to 1934 and known as the Spartans
***NFC First-Round Playoff*

DETROIT vs. *INDIANAPOLIS
RS: Series tied, 18-18-2
1953—Lions, 27-17 (B)
Lions, 17-7 (D)
1954—Lions, 35-0 (D)
Lions, 27-3 (B)
1955—Colts, 28-13 (B)
Lions, 24-14 (D)
1956—Lions, 31-14 (B)
Lions, 27-3 (D)
1957—Colts, 34-14 (B)
Lions, 31-27 (D)
1958—Colts, 28-15 (B)
Colts, 40-14 (D)
1959—Colts, 21-9 (B)
Colts, 31-24 (D)
1960—Lions, 30-17 (D)
Lions, 20-15 (B)
1961—Lions, 16-15 (B)
Colts, 17-14 (D)
1962—Lions, 29-20 (B)
Lions, 21-14 (D)
1963—Colts, 25-21 (D)
Colts, 24-21 (B)
1964—Colts, 34-0 (D)
Lions, 31-14 (B)
1965—Colts, 31-7 (B)
Tie, 24-24 (D)
1966—Colts, 45-14 (B)
Lions, 20-14 (D)
1967—Colts, 41-7 (B)
1968—Colts, 27-10 (D)
1969—Tie, 17-17 (B)
1973—Colts, 29-27 (D)
1977—Lions, 13-10 (B)
1980—Colts, 10-9 (D)
1985—Colts, 14-6 (I)
1991—Lions, 33-24 (I)
1997—Lions, 32-10 (D)
2000—Colts, 30-18 (I)
(RS Pts.—Colts 788, Lions 748)
Franchise in Baltimore prior to 1984

DETROIT vs. JACKSONVILLE
RS: Series tied, 1-1
1995—Lions, 44-0 (D)
1998—Jaguars, 37-22 (J)
(RS Pts.—Lions 66, Jaguars 37)

DETROIT vs. KANSAS CITY
RS: Chiefs lead series, 6-3
1971—Lions, 32-21 (D)
1975—Chiefs, 24-21 (KC) OT
1980—Chiefs, 20-17 (KC)
1981—Lions, 27-10 (D)
1987—Chiefs, 27-20 (D)
1988—Lions, 7-6 (KC)
1990—Chiefs, 43-24 (KC)
1996—Chiefs, 28-24 (D)
1999—Chiefs, 31-21 (KC)
(RS Pts.—Chiefs 210, Lions 193)

DETROIT vs. MIAMI
RS: Dolphins lead series, 5-2
1973—Dolphins, 34-7 (M)
1979—Dolphins, 28-10 (D)
1985—Lions, 31-21 (D)
1991—Lions, 17-13 (D)
1994—Dolphins, 27-20 (M)
1997—Dolphins, 33-30 (M)
2000—Dolphins, 23-8 (D)
(RS Pts.—Dolphins 179, Lions 123)

DETROIT vs. MINNESOTA
RS: Vikings lead series, 49-28-2
1961—Lions, 37-10 (M)
Lions, 13-7 (D)
1962—Lions, 17-6 (M)
Lions, 37-23 (D)
1963—Lions, 28-10 (D)
Vikings, 34-31 (M)
1964—Lions, 24-20 (M)
Tie, 23-23 (D)
1965—Lions, 31-29 (M)
Vikings, 29-7 (D)
1966—Lions, 32-31 (M)
Vikings, 28-16 (D)
1967—Tie, 10-10 (M)
Lions, 14-3 (D)
1968—Vikings, 24-10 (M)
Vikings, 13-6 (D)
1969—Vikings, 24-10 (M)
Vikings, 27-0 (D)
1970—Vikings, 30-17 (D)
Vikings, 24-20 (M)
1971—Vikings, 16-13 (D)
Vikings, 29-10 (M)
1972—Vikings, 34-10 (D)
Vikings, 16-14 (M)
1973—Vikings, 23-9 (D)
Vikings, 28-7 (M)
1974—Vikings, 7-6 (D)
Lions, 20-16 (M)
1975—Vikings, 25-19 (M)
Lions, 17-10 (D)
1976—Vikings, 10-9 (D)
Vikings, 31-23 (M)
1977—Vikings, 14-7 (M)
Vikings, 30-21 (D)
1978—Vikings, 17-7 (M)
Lions, 45-14 (D)
1979—Vikings, 13-10 (D)
Vikings, 14-7 (M)
1980—Lions, 27-7 (D)
Vikings, 34-0 (M)
1981—Vikings, 26-24 (M)
Lions, 45-7 (D)
1982—Vikings, 34-31 (D)
1983—Vikings, 20-17 (M)
Lions, 13-2 (D)
1984—Vikings, 29-28 (D)
Lions, 16-14 (M)
1985—Vikings, 16-13 (M)
Lions, 41-21 (D)
1986—Lions, 13-10 (M)
Vikings, 24-10 (D)
1987—Vikings, 34-19 (M)
Vikings, 17-14 (D)
1988—Vikings, 44-17 (M)
Vikings, 23-0 (D)
1989—Vikings, 24-17 (M)
Vikings, 20-7 (D)
1990—Lions, 34-27 (M)
Vikings, 17-7 (D)
1991—Lions, 24-20 (D)
Lions, 34-14 (M)
1992—Lions, 31-17 (D)
Vikings, 31-14 (M)
1993—Lions, 30-27 (M)
Vikings, 13-0 (D)
1994—Vikings, 10-3 (M)
Lions, 41-19 (D)
1995—Vikings, 20-10 (M)
Lions, 44-38 (D)
1996—Vikings, 17-13 (M)
Vikings, 24-22 (D)
1997—Lions, 38-15 (D)
Lions, 14-13 (M)
1998—Vikings, 29-6 (M)
Vikings, 34-13 (D)
1999—Lions, 25-23 (D)
Vikings, 24-17 (M)
2000—Vikings, 31-24 (D)
Vikings, 24-17 (M)
(RS Pts.—Vikings 1,645, Lions 1,450)

DETROIT vs. NEW ENGLAND
RS: Lions lead series, 4-3
1971—Lions, 34-7 (NE)
1976—Lions, 30-10 (D)
1979—Patriots, 24-17 (NE)
1985—Patriots, 23-6 (NE)
1993—Lions, 19-16 (NE) OT
1994—Patriots, 23-17 (D)
2000—Lions, 34-9 (D)
(RS Pts.—Lions 157, Patriots 112)

DETROIT vs. NEW ORLEANS
RS: Saints lead series, 8-7-1
1968—Tie, 20-20 (D)
1970—Saints, 19-17 (NO)
1972—Lions, 27-14 (D)
1973—Saints, 20-13 (NO)
1974—Lions, 19-14 (D)
1976—Saints, 17-16 (NO)
1977—Lions, 23-19 (D)
1979—Saints, 17-7 (NO)
1980—Lions, 24-13 (D)
1988—Saints, 22-14 (D)
1989—Lions, 21-14 (D)
1990—Lions, 27-10 (NO)
1992—Saints, 13-7 (D)
1993—Saints, 14-3 (NO)
1997—Saints, 35-17 (NO)
2000—Lions, 14-10 (NO)
(RS Pts.—Saints 271, Lions 269)

***DETROIT vs. N.Y. GIANTS**
RS: Lions lead series, 19-17-1
PS: Lions lead series, 1-0
1930—Giants, 19-6 (P)
1931—Spartans, 14-6 (P)
Giants, 14-0 (NY)
1932—Spartans, 7-0 (P)
Spartans, 6-0 (NY)
1933—Spartans, 17-7 (P)
Giants, 13-10 (NY)
1934—Lions, 9-0 (D)
1935—**Lions, 26-7 (D)
1936—Giants, 14-7 (NY)
Lions, 38-0 (D)
1937—Lions, 17-0 (NY)
1939—Lions, 18-14 (D)
1941—Giants, 20-13 (NY)
1943—Tie, 0-0 (D)
1945—Giants, 35-14 (NY)
1947—Lions, 35-7 (D)
1949—Lions, 45-21 (NY)
1953—Lions, 27-16 (NY)
1955—Giants, 24-19 (D)
1958—Giants, 19-17 (D)
1962—Giants, 17-14 (NY)
1964—Lions, 26-3 (D)
1967—Lions, 30-7 (NY)
1969—Lions, 24-0 (D)

1972—Lions, 30-16 (D)
1974—Lions, 20-19 (D)
1976—Giants, 24-10 (NY)
1982—Giants, 13-6 (D)
1983—Lions, 15-9 (D)
1988—Giants, 30-10 (NY)
Giants, 13-10 (D) OT
1989—Giants, 24-14 (NY)
1990—Giants, 20-0 (NY)
1994—Lions, 28-25 (NY) OT
1996—Giants, 35-7 (D)
1997—Giants, 26-20 (D) OT
2000—Lions, 31-21 (NY)
(RS Pts.—Lions 614, Giants 531)
(PS Pts.—Lions 26, Giants 7)
Franchise in Portsmouth prior to 1934 and known as the Spartans
***NFL Championship*

DETROIT vs. N.Y. JETS
RS: Lions lead series, 6-3
1972—Lions, 37-20 (D)
1979—Jets, 31-10 (NY)
1982—Jets, 28-13 (D)
1985—Lions, 31-20 (D)
1988—Jets, 17-10 (D)
1991—Lions, 34-20 (D)
1994—Lions, 18-7 (NY)
1997—Lions, 13-10 (D)
2000—Lions, 10-7 (NY)
(RS Pts.—Lions 176, Jets 160)

DETROIT vs. *OAKLAND
RS: Raiders lead series, 6-2
1970—Lions, 28-14 (D)
1974—Raiders, 35-13 (O)
1978—Raiders, 29-17 (O)
1981—Lions, 16-0 (D)
1984—Raiders, 24-3 (D)
1987—Raiders, 27-7 (LA)
1990—Raiders, 38-31 (D)
1996—Raiders, 37-21 (O)
(RS Pts.—Raiders 204, Lions 136)
**Franchise in Los Angeles from 1982-1994*

***DETROIT vs. PHILADELPHIA**
RS: Lions lead series, 12-11-2
PS: Eagles lead series, 1-0
1933—Spartans, 25-0 (P)
1934—Lions, 10-0 (P)
1935—Lions, 35-0 (D)
1936—Lions, 23-0 (P)
1938—Eagles, 21-7 (D)
1940—Lions, 21-0 (P)
1941—Lions, 21-17 (D)
1945—Lions, 28-24 (D)
1948—Eagles, 45-21 (P)
1949—Eagles, 22-14 (D)
1951—Lions, 28-10 (P)
1954—Tie, 13-13 (D)
1957—Lions, 27-16 (P)
1960—Eagles, 28-10 (P)
1961—Eagles, 27-24 (D)
1965—Lions, 35-28 (P)
1968—Eagles, 12-0 (D)
1971—Eagles, 23-20 (D)
1974—Eagles, 28-17 (P)
1977—Lions, 17-13 (D)
1979—Eagles, 44-7 (P)
1984—Tie, 23-23 (D) OT
1986—Lions, 13-11 (P)
1995—**Eagles, 58-37 (P)
1996—Eagles, 24-17 (P)
1998—Eagles, 10-9 (P)
(RS Pts.—Lions 465, Eagles 439)
(PS Pts.—Eagles 58, Lions 37)
**Franchise in Portsmouth prior to 1934 and known as the Spartans*
***NFC First-Round Playoff*

DETROIT vs. *PITTSBURGH
RS: Lions lead series, 14-12-1
1934—Lions, 40-7 (D)
1936—Lions, 28-3 (D)
1937—Lions, 7-3 (D)
1938—Lions, 16-7 (D)
1940—Pirates, 10-7 (D)
1942—Steelers, 35-7 (D)
1946—Lions, 17-7 (D)
1947—Steelers, 17-10 (P)
1948—Lions, 17-14 (D)
1949—Steelers, 14-7 (P)
1950—Lions, 10-7 (D)
1952—Lions, 31-6 (P)
1953—Lions, 38-21 (D)
1955—Lions, 31-28 (P)
1956—Lions, 45-7 (D)
1959—Tie, 10-10 (P)
1962—Lions, 45-7 (D)
1966—Steelers, 17-3 (P)
1967—Steelers, 24-14 (D)
1969—Steelers, 16-13 (P)
1973—Steelers, 24-10 (P)
1983—Lions, 45-3 (D)
1986—Steelers, 27-17 (P)
1989—Steelers, 23-3 (D)
1992—Steelers, 17-14 (P)
1995—Steelers, 23-20 (P)
1998—Lions, 19-16 (D) OT
(RS Pts.—Lions 524, Steelers 393)
**Steelers known as Pirates prior to 1941*

DETROIT vs. *ST. LOUIS
RS: Rams lead series, 39-36-1
PS: Lions lead series, 1-0
1937—Lions, 28-0 (C)
Lions, 27-7 (D)
1938—Rams, 21-17 (C)
Lions, 6-0 (D)
1939—Lions, 15-7 (D)
Rams, 14-3 (C)
1940—Lions, 6-0 (D)
Rams, 24-0 (C)
1941—Lions, 17-7 (D)
Lions, 14-0 (C)
1942—Rams, 14-0 (D)
Rams, 27-7 (C)
1944—Rams, 20-17 (D)
Lions, 26-14 (C)
1945—Rams, 28-21 (D)
1946—Rams, 35-14 (LA)
Rams, 41-20 (D)
1947—Rams, 27-13 (D)
Rams, 28-17 (LA)
1948—Rams, 44-7 (LA)
Rams, 34-27 (D)
1949—Rams, 27-24 (LA)
Rams, 21-10 (D)
1950—Rams, 30-28 (D)
Rams, 65-24 (LA)
1951—Rams, 27-21 (D)
Lions, 24-22 (LA)
1952—Lions, 17-14 (LA)
Lions, 24-16 (D)
**Lions, 31-21 (D)
1953—Rams, 31-19 (D)
Rams, 37-24 (LA)
1954—Lions, 21-3 (D)
Lions, 27-24 (LA)
1955—Rams, 17-10 (D)
Rams, 24-13 (LA)
1956—Lions, 24-21 (D)
Lions, 16-7 (LA)
1957—Lions, 10-7 (D)
Rams, 35-17 (LA)
1958—Rams, 42-28 (D)
Lions, 41-24 (LA)
1959—Lions, 17-7 (LA)
Lions, 23-17 (D)
1960—Rams, 48-35 (LA)
Lions, 12-10 (D)
1961—Lions, 14-13 (D)
Lions, 28-10 (LA)
1962—Lions, 13-10 (D)
Lions, 12-3 (LA)
1963—Lions, 23-2 (LA)
Rams, 28-21 (D)
1964—Tie, 17-17 (LA)
Lions, 37-17 (D)
1965—Lions, 20-0 (D)
Lions, 31-7 (LA)
1966—Rams, 14-7 (D)
Rams, 23-3 (LA)
1967—Rams, 31-7 (D)
1968—Rams, 10-7 (LA)
1969—Lions, 28-0 (D)
1970—Lions, 28-23 (LA)
1971—Rams, 21-13 (D)
1972—Lions, 34-17 (LA)
1974—Rams, 16-13 (LA)
1975—Rams, 20-0 (D)
1976—Rams, 20-17 (D)
1980—Lions, 41-20 (LA)
1981—Rams, 20-13 (LA)
1982—Lions, 19-14 (LA)
1983—Rams, 21-10 (LA)
1986—Rams, 14-10 (LA)
1987—Rams, 37-16 (D)
1988—Rams, 17-10 (LA)
1991—Lions, 21-10 (D)
1993—Lions, 16-13 (LA)
1999—Lions, 31-27 (D)
(RS Pts.—Rams 1,463, Lions 1,371)
(PS Pts.—Lions 31, Rams 21)
**Franchise in Los Angeles prior to 1995 and in Cleveland prior to 1946*
***Conference Playoff*

DETROIT vs. SAN DIEGO
RS: Chargers lead series, 4-3
1972—Lions, 34-20 (D)
1977—Lions, 20-0 (D)
1978—Lions, 31-14 (D)
1981—Chargers, 28-23 (SD)
1984—Chargers, 27-24 (SD)
1996—Chargers, 27-21 (SD)
1999—Chargers, 20-10 (D)
(RS Pts.—Lions 163, Chargers 136)

DETROIT vs. SAN FRANCISCO
RS: 49ers lead series, 29-26-1
PS: Series tied, 1-1
1950—Lions, 24-7 (D)
49ers, 28-27 (SF)
1951—49ers, 20-10 (D)
49ers, 21-17 (SF)
1952—49ers, 17-3 (SF)
49ers, 28-0 (D)
1953—Lions, 24-21 (D)
Lions, 14-10 (SF)
1954—49ers, 37-31 (SF)
Lions, 48-7 (D)
1955—49ers, 27-24 (D)
49ers, 38-21 (SF)
1956—Lions, 20-17 (D)
Lions, 17-13 (SF)
1957—49ers, 35-31 (SF)
Lions, 31-10 (D)
*Lions, 31-27 (SF)
1958—49ers, 24-21 (SF)
Lions, 35-21 (D)
1959—49ers, 34-13 (D)
49ers, 33-7 (SF)
1960—49ers, 14-10 (D)
Lions, 24-0 (SF)
1961—49ers, 49-0 (D)
Tie, 20-20 (SF)
1962—Lions, 45-24 (D)
Lions, 38-24 (SF)
1963—Lions, 26-3 (D)
Lions, 45-7 (SF)
1964—Lions, 26-17 (SF)
Lions, 24-7 (D)
1965—49ers, 27-21 (D)
49ers, 17-14 (SF)
1966—49ers, 27-24 (SF)
49ers, 41-14 (D)
1967—Lions, 45-3 (SF)
1968—49ers, 14-7 (D)
1969—Lions, 26-14 (SF)
1970—Lions, 28-7 (D)
1971—49ers, 31-27 (SF)
1973—Lions, 30-20 (D)
1974—Lions, 17-13 (D)
1975—Lions, 28-17 (SF)
1977—49ers, 28-7 (SF)
1978—Lions, 33-14 (D)
1980—Lions, 17-13 (D)
1981—Lions, 24-17 (D)
1983—**49ers, 24-23 (SF)
1984—49ers, 30-27 (D)
1985—Lions, 23-21 (D)
1988—49ers, 20-13 (SF)
1991—49ers, 35-3 (SF)
1992—49ers, 24-6 (SF)
1993—49ers, 55-17 (D)
1994—49ers, 27-21 (D)
1995—Lions, 27-24 (D)
1996—49ers, 24-14 (SF)
1998—49ers, 35-13 (SF)
(RS Pts.—49ers 1,211, Lions 1,202)
(PS Pts.—Lions 54, 49ers 51)
**Conference Playoff*
***NFC Divisional Playoff*

DETROIT vs. SEATTLE
RS: Series tied, 4-4
1976—Lions, 41-14 (S)
1978—Seahawks, 28-16 (S)
1984—Seahawks, 38-17 (S)
1987—Seahawks, 37-14 (D)
1990—Seahawks, 30-10 (S)
1993—Lions, 30-10 (D)
1996—Lions, 17-16 (D)
1999—Lions, 28-20 (S)
(RS Pts.—Seahawks 193, Lions 173)

DETROIT vs. TAMPA BAY
RS: Lions lead series, 26-20
PS: Buccaneers lead series, 1-0
1977—Lions, 16-7 (D)
1978—Lions, 15-7 (TB)
Lions, 34-23 (D)
1979—Buccaneers, 31-16 (TB)
Buccaneers, 16-14 (D)
1980—Lions, 24-10 (TB)
Lions, 27-14 (D)
1981—Buccaneers, 28-10 (TB)
Buccaneers, 20-17 (D)
1982—Buccaneers, 23-21 (TB)
1983—Lions, 11-0 (TB)
Lions, 23-20 (D)
1984—Buccaneers, 21-17 (TB)
Lions, 13-7 (D) OT
1985—Lions, 30-9 (D)
Buccaneers, 19-16 (TB) OT
1986—Buccaneers, 24-20 (D)
Lions, 38-17 (TB)
1987—Buccaneers, 31-27 (D)
Lions, 20-10 (TB)
1988—Buccaneers, 23-20 (D)
Buccaneers, 21-10 (TB)
1989—Lions, 17-16 (TB)
Lions, 33-7 (D)
1990—Buccaneers, 38-21 (D)
Buccaneers, 23-20 (TB)
1991—Lions, 31-3 (D)
Buccaneers, 30-21 (TB)
1992—Buccaneers, 27-23 (D)
Lions, 38-7 (TB)
1993—Buccaneers, 27-10 (TB)
Lions, 23-0 (D)
1994—Buccaneers, 24-14 (TB)
Lions, 14-9 (D)
1995—Lions, 27-24 (D)
Lions, 37-10 (TB)
1996—Lions, 21-6 (D)
Lions, 27-0 (TB)
1997—Buccaneers, 24-17 (D)
Lions, 27-9 (TB)
*Buccaneers, 20-10 (TB)
1998—Lions, 27-6 (D)
Lions, 28-25 (TB)
1999—Lions, 20-3 (D)
Buccaneers, 23-16 (TB)
2000—Buccaneers, 31-10 (D)
Lions, 28-14 (TB)
(RS Pts—Lions 989, Buccaneers 767)
(PS Pts.—Buccaneers 20, Lions 10)
**NFC First-Round Playoff*

ALL-TIME TEAM VS. TEAM RESULTS

DETROIT vs. *TENNESSEE
RS: Titans lead series, 4-3
1971—Lions, 31-7 (H)
1975—Oilers, 24-8 (H)
1983—Oilers, 27-17 (H)
1986—Lions, 24-13 (D)
1989—Oilers, 35-31 (H)
1992—Oilers, 24-21 (D)
1995—Lions, 24-17 (H)
(RS Pts.—Lions 156, Titans 147)
**Franchise in Houston prior to 1997; known as Oilers prior to 1999*
***DETROIT vs. **WASHINGTON**
RS: Redskins lead series, 24-10
PS: Redskins lead series, 3-0
1932—Spartans, 10-0 (P)
1933—Spartans, 13-0 (B)
1934—Lions, 24-0 (D)
1935—Lions, 17-7 (B)
Lions, 14-0 (D)
1938—Redskins, 7-5 (D)
1939—Redskins, 31-7 (W)
1940—Redskins, 20-14 (D)
1942—Redskins, 15-3 (D)
1943—Redskins, 42-20 (W)
1946—Redskins, 17-16 (W)
1947—Lions, 38-21 (D)
1948—Redskins, 46-21 (W)
1951—Lions, 35-17 (D)
1956—Redskins, 18-17 (W)
1965—Lions, 14-10 (D)
1968—Redskins, 14-3 (W)
1970—Redskins, 31-10 (W)
1973—Redskins, 20-0 (D)
1976—Redskins, 20-7 (W)
1978—Redskins, 21-19 (D)
1979—Redskins, 27-24 (D)
1981—Redskins, 33-31 (W)
1982—***Redskins, 31-7 (W)
1983—Redskins, 38-17 (W)
1984—Redskins, 28-14 (W)
1985—Redskins, 24-3 (W)
1987—Redskins, 20-13 (W)
1990—Redskins, 41-38 (D) OT
1991—Redskins, 45-0 (W)
****Redskins, 41-10 (W)
1992—Redskins, 13-10 (W)
1995—Redskins, 36-30 (W) OT
1997—Redskins, 30-7 (W)
1999—Lions, 33-17 (D)
***Redskins, 27-13 (W)
2000—Lions, 15-10 (D)
(RS Pts.—Redskins 719, Lions 542)
(PS Pts.—Redskins 99, Lions 30)
**Franchise in Portsmouth prior to 1934 and known as the Spartans.*
***Franchise in Boston prior to 1937*
****NFC First-Round Playoff*
*****NFC Championship*

GREEN BAY vs. ARIZONA
RS: Packers lead series, 41-21-4
PS: Packers lead series, 1-0;
See Arizona vs. Green Bay
GREEN BAY vs. ATLANTA
RS: Packers lead series, 10-9
PS: Packers lead series, 1-0;
See Atlanta vs. Green Bay
GREEN BAY vs. BALTIMORE
RS: Packers lead series, 1-0;
See Baltimore vs. Green Bay
GREEN BAY vs. BUFFALO
RS: Bills lead series, 6-2;
See Buffalo vs. Green Bay
GREEN BAY vs. CAROLINA
RS: Series tied, 2-2
PS: Packers lead series, 1-0;
See Carolina vs. Green Bay
GREEN BAY vs. CHICAGO
RS: Bears lead series, 83-71-6
PS: Bears lead series, 1-0;
See Chicago vs. Green Bay
GREEN BAY vs. CINCINNATI
RS: Packers lead series, 5-4;
See Cincinnati vs. Green Bay
GREEN BAY vs. CLEVELAND
RS: Packers lead series, 8-6
PS: Packers lead series, 1-0;
See Cleveland vs. Green Bay
GREEN BAY vs. DALLAS
RS: Cowboys lead series, 10-9
PS: Cowboys lead series, 4-2;
See Dallas vs. Green Bay
GREEN BAY vs. DENVER
RS: Broncos lead series, 5-3-1
PS: Broncos lead series, 1-0;
See Denver vs. Green Bay
GREEN BAY vs. DETROIT
RS: Packers lead series, 72-62-7
PS: Packers lead series, 2-0;
See Detroit vs. Green Bay
GREEN BAY vs. *INDIANAPOLIS
RS: Series tied, 19-19-1
PS: Packers lead series, 1-0
1953—Packers, 37-14 (GB)
Packers, 35-24 (B)
1954—Packers, 7-6 (B)
Packers, 24-13 (Mil)
1955—Colts, 24-20 (Mil)
Colts, 14-10 (B)
1956—Packers, 38-33 (Mil)
Colts, 28-21 (B)
1957—Colts, 45-17 (Mil)
Packers, 24-21 (B)
1958—Colts, 24-17 (Mil)
Colts, 56-0 (B)
1959—Colts, 38-21 (B)
Colts, 28-24 (Mil)
1960—Packers, 35-21 (GB)
Colts, 38-24 (B)
1961—Packers, 45-7 (GB)
Colts, 45-21 (B)
1962—Packers, 17-6 (B)
Packers, 17-13 (GB)
1963—Packers, 31-20 (GB)
Packers, 34-20 (B)
1964—Colts, 21-20 (GB)
Colts, 24-21 (B)
1965—Packers, 20-17 (Mil)
Packers, 42-27 (B)
**Packers, 13-10 (GB) OT
1966—Packers, 24-3 (Mil)
Packers, 14-10 (B)
1967—Colts, 13-10 (B)
1968—Colts, 16-3 (GB)
1969—Colts, 14-6 (B)
1970—Colts, 13-10 (Mil)
1974—Packers, 20-13 (B)
1982—Tie, 20-20 (B) OT
1985—Colts, 37-10 (I)
1988—Colts, 20-13 (GB)
1991—Packers, 14-10 (Mil)
1997—Colts, 41-38 (I)
2000—Packers, 26-24 (GB)
(RS Pts.—Colts 861, Packers 830)
(PS Pts.—Packers 13, Colts 10)
**Franchise in Baltimore prior to 1984*
***Conference Playoff*
GREEN BAY vs. JACKSONVILLE
RS: Packers lead series, 1-0
1995—Packers, 24-14 (J)
(RS Pts.—Packers 24, Jaguars 14)
GREEN BAY vs. KANSAS CITY
RS: Chiefs lead series, 5-1-1
PS: Packers lead series, 1-0
1966—*Packers, 35-10 (Los Angeles)
1973—Tie, 10-10 (Mil)
1977—Chiefs, 20-10 (KC)
1987—Packers, 23-3 (KC)
1989—Chiefs, 21-3 (GB)
1990—Chiefs, 17-3 (GB)
1993—Chiefs, 23-16 (KC)
1996—Chiefs, 27-20 (KC)
(RS Pts.—Chiefs 121, Packers 85)
(PS Pts.—Packers 35, Chiefs 10)
**Super Bowl I*
GREEN BAY vs. MIAMI
RS: Dolphins lead series, 9-1
1971—Dolphins, 27-6 (Mia)
1975—Dolphins, 31-7 (GB)
1979—Dolphins, 27-7 (Mia)
1985—Dolphins, 34-24 (GB)
1988—Dolphins, 24-17 (Mia)
1989—Dolphins, 23-20 (Mia)
1991—Dolphins, 16-13 (Mia)
1994—Dolphins, 24-14 (Mil)
1997—Packers, 23-18 (GB)
2000—Dolphins, 28-20 (M)
(RS Pts.—Dolphins 252, Packers 151)
GREEN BAY vs. MINNESOTA
RS: Series tied, 39-39-1
1961—Packers, 33-7 (Minn)
Packers, 28-10 (Mil)
1962—Packers, 34-7 (GB)
Packers, 48-21 (Minn)
1963—Packers, 37-28 (Minn)
Packers, 28-7 (GB)
1964—Vikings, 24-23 (GB)
Packers, 42-13 (Minn)
1965—Packers, 38-13 (Minn)
Packers, 24-19 (GB)
1966—Vikings, 20-17 (GB)
Packers, 28-16 (Minn)
1967—Vikings, 10-7 (Mil)
Packers, 30-27 (Minn)
1968—Vikings, 26-13 (Mil)
Vikings, 14-10 (Minn)
1969—Vikings, 19-7 (Minn)
Vikings, 9-7 (Mil)
1970—Packers, 13-10 (Mil)
Vikings, 10-3 (Minn)
1971—Vikings, 24-13 (GB)
Vikings, 3-0 (Minn)
1972—Vikings, 27-13 (GB)
Packers, 23-7 (Minn)
1973—Vikings, 11-3 (Minn)
Vikings, 31-7 (GB)
1974—Vikings, 32-17 (GB)
Packers, 19-7 (Minn)
1975—Vikings, 28-17 (GB)
Vikings, 24-3 (Minn)
1976—Vikings, 17-10 (Mil)
Vikings, 20-9 (Minn)
1977—Vikings, 19-7 (Minn)
Vikings, 13-6 (GB)
1978—Vikings, 21-7 (Minn)
Tie, 10-10 (GB) OT
1979—Vikings, 27-21 (Minn) OT
Packers, 19-7 (Mil)
1980—Packers, 16-3 (GB)
Packers, 25-13 (Minn)
1981—Vikings, 30-13 (Mil)
Packers, 35-23 (Minn)
1982—Packers, 26-7 (Mil)
1983—Vikings, 20-17 (GB) OT
Packers, 29-21 (Minn)
1984—Packers, 45-17 (Mil)
Packers, 38-14 (Minn)
1985—Packers, 20-17 (Mil)
Packers, 27-17 (Minn)
1986—Vikings, 42-7 (Minn)
Vikings, 32-6 (GB)
1987—Packers, 23-16 (Minn)
Packers, 16-10 (Mil)
1988—Packers, 34-14 (Minn)
Packers, 18-6 (GB)
1989—Vikings, 26-14 (Minn)
Packers, 20-19 (Mil)
1990—Packers, 24-10 (Mil)
Vikings, 23-7 (Minn)
1991—Vikings, 35-21 (GB)
Packers, 27-7 (Minn)
1992—Vikings, 23-20 (GB) OT
Vikings, 27-7 (Minn)
1993—Vikings, 15-13 (Minn)
Vikings, 21-17 (Mil)
1994—Packers, 16-10 (GB)
Vikings, 13-10 (M) OT
1995—Packers, 38-21 (GB)
Vikings, 27-24 (M)
1996—Vikings, 30-21 (M)
Packers, 38-10 (GB)
1997—Packers, 38-32 (GB)
Packers, 27-11 (M)
1998—Vikings, 37-24 (GB)
Vikings, 28-14 (M)
1999—Packers, 23-20 (GB)
Vikings, 24-20 (M)
2000—Packers, 26-20 (GB) OT
Packers, 33-28 (M)
(RS Pts.—Packers 1,591, Vikings 1,457)
GREEN BAY vs. NEW ENGLAND
RS: Series tied, 3-3
PS: Packers lead series, 1-0
1973—Patriots, 33-24 (NE)
1979—Packers, 27-14 (GB)
1985—Patriots, 26-20 (NE)
1988—Packers, 45-3 (Mil)
1994—Patriots, 17-16 (NE)
1996—*Packers, 35-21 (New Orleans)
1997—Packers, 28-10 (NE)
(RS Pts.—Packers 160, Patriots 103)
(PS Pts.—Packers 35, Patriots 21)
**Super Bowl XXXI*
GREEN BAY vs. NEW ORLEANS
RS: Packers lead series, 13-4
1968—Packers, 29-7 (Mil)
1971—Saints, 29-21 (Mil)
1972—Packers, 30-20 (NO)
1973—Packers, 30-10 (Mil)
1975—Saints, 20-19 (NO)
1976—Packers, 32-27 (Mil)
1977—Packers, 24-20 (NO)
1978—Packers, 28-17 (Mil)
1979—Packers, 28-19 (Mil)
1981—Packers, 35-7 (NO)
1984—Packers, 23-13 (NO)
1985—Packers, 38-14 (Mil)
1986—Saints, 24-10 (NO)
1987—Saints, 33-24 (NO)
1989—Packers, 35-34 (GB)
1993—Packers, 19-17 (NO)
1995—Packers, 34-23 (NO)
(RS Pts.—Packers 459, Saints 334)
GREEN BAY vs. N.Y. GIANTS
RS: Packers lead series, 23-20-2
PS: Packers lead series, 4-1
1928—Giants, 6-0 (GB)
Packers, 7-0 (NY)
1929—Packers, 20-6 (NY)
1930—Packers, 14-7 (GB)
Giants, 13-6 (NY)
1931—Packers, 27-7 (GB)
Packers, 14-10 (NY)
1932—Packers, 13-0 (GB)
Giants, 6-0 (NY)
1933—Giants, 10-7 (Mil)
Giants, 17-6 (NY)
1934—Packers, 20-6 (Mil)
Giants, 17-3 (NY)
1935—Packers, 16-7 (GB)
1936—Packers, 26-14 (NY)
1937—Giants, 10-0 (NY)
1938—Giants, 15-3 (NY)
*Giants, 23-17 (NY)
1939—*Packers, 27-0 (Mil)
1940—Giants, 7-3 (NY)
1942—Tie, 21-21 (NY)
1943—Packers, 35-21 (NY)
1944—Giants, 24-0 (NY)
*Packers, 14-7 (NY)
1945—Packers, 23-14 (NY)
1947—Tie, 24-24 (NY)
1948—Giants, 49-3 (Mil)
1949—Giants, 30-10 (GB)
1952—Packers, 17-3 (NY)
1957—Giants, 31-17 (GB)
1959—Giants, 20-3 (NY)
1961—Packers, 20-17 (Mil)
*Packers, 37-0 (GB)
1962—*Packers, 16-7 (NY)

1967—Packers, 48-21 (NY)
1969—Packers, 20-10 (Mil)
1971—Giants, 42-40 (GB)
1973—Packers, 16-14 (New Haven)
1975—Packers, 40-14 (Mil)
1980—Giants, 27-21 (NY)
1981—Packers, 27-14 (NY)
Packers, 26-24 (Mil)
1982—Packers, 27-19 (NY)
1983—Giants, 27-3 (NY)
1985—Packers, 23-20 (GB)
1986—Giants, 55-24 (NY)
1987—Giants, 20-10 (NY)
1992—Giants, 27-7 (NY)
1995—Packers, 14-6 (GB)
1998—Packers, 37-3 (NY)
(RS Pts.—Giants 755, Packers 741)
(PS Pts.—Packers 111, Giants 37)
NFL Championship

GREEN BAY vs. N.Y. JETS
RS: Jets lead series, 6-2
1973—Packers, 23-7 (Mil)
1979—Jets, 27-22 (GB)
1981—Jets, 28-3 (NY)
1982—Jets, 15-13 (NY)
1985—Jets, 24-3 (Mil)
1991—Jets, 19-16 (NY) OT
1994—Packers, 17-10 (GB)
2000—Jets, 20-16 (GB)
(RS Pts.—Jets 150, Packers 113)

GREEN BAY vs. *OAKLAND
RS: Raiders lead series, 5-3
PS: Packers lead series, 1-0
1967—**Packers, 33-14 (Miami)
1972—Raiders, 20-14 (GB)
1976—Raiders, 18-14 (O)
1978—Raiders, 28-3 (GB)
1984—Raiders, 28-7 (LA)
1987—Raiders, 20-0 (GB)
1990—Packers, 29-16 (LA)
1993—Packers, 28-0 (GB)
1999—Packers, 28-24 (GB)
(RS Pts.—Raiders 154, Packers 123)
(PS Pts.—Packers 33, Raiders 14)
**Franchise in Los Angeles from 1982-1994*
***Super Bowl II*

GREEN BAY vs. PHILADELPHIA
RS: Packers lead series, 22-9
PS: Eagles lead series, 1-0
1933—Packers, 35-9 (GB)
Packers, 10-0 (P)
1934—Packers, 19-6 (GB)
1935—Packers, 13-6 (P)
1937—Packers, 37-7 (Mil)
1939—Packers, 23-16 (P)
1940—Packers, 27-20 (GB)
1942—Packers, 7-0 (P)
1946—Packers, 19-7 (P)
1947—Eagles, 28-14 (P)
1951—Packers, 37-24 (GB)
1952—Packers, 12-10 (Mil)
1954—Packers, 37-14 (P)
1958—Packers, 38-35 (GB)
1960—*Eagles, 17-13 (P)
1962—Packers, 49-0 (P)
1968—Packers, 30-13 (GB)
1970—Packers, 30-17 (Mil)
1974—Eagles, 36-14 (P)
1976—Packers, 28-13 (GB)
1978—Eagles, 10-3 (P)
1979—Eagles, 21-10 (GB)
1987—Packers, 16-10 (GB) OT
1990—Eagles, 31-0 (P)
1991—Eagles, 20-3 (GB)
1992—Packers, 27-24 (Mil)
1993—Eagles, 20-17 (GB)
1994—Eagles, 13-7 (P)
1996—Packers, 39-13 (GB)
1997—Eagles, 10-9 (P)
1998—Packers, 24-16 (GB)
2000—Packers, 6-3 (GB)
(RS Pts.—Packers 640, Eagles 452)
(PS Pts.—Eagles 17, Packers 13)
**NFL Championship*

GREEN BAY vs. *PITTSBURGH
RS: Packers lead series, 18-12
1933—Packers, 47-0 (GB)
1935—Packers, 27-0 (GB)
Packers, 34-14 (P)
1936—Packers, 42-10 (Mil)
1938—Packers, 20-0 (GB)
1940—Packers, 24-3 (Mil)
1941—Packers, 54-7 (P)
1942—Packers, 24-21 (Mil)
1946—Packers, 17-7 (GB)
1947—Steelers, 18-17 (Mil)
1948—Steelers, 38-7 (P)
1949—Steelers, 30-7 (Mil)
1951—Packers, 35-33 (Mil)
Steelers, 28-7 (P)
1953—Steelers, 31-14 (P)
1954—Steelers, 21-20 (GB)
1957—Packers, 27-10 (P)
1960—Packers, 19-13 (P)
1963—Packers, 33-14 (Mil)
1965—Packers, 41-9 (P)
1967—Steelers, 24-17 (GB)
1969—Packers, 38-34 (P)
1970—Packers, 20-12 (P)
1975—Steelers, 16-13 (Mil)
1980—Steelers, 22-20 (P)
1983—Steelers, 25-21 (GB)
1986—Steelers, 27-3 (P)
1992—Packers, 17-3 (GB)
1995—Packers, 24-19 (GB)
1998—Steelers, 27-20 (P)
(RS Pts.—Packers 709, Steelers 516)
**Steelers known as Pirates prior to 1941*

GREEN BAY vs. *ST. LOUIS
RS: Rams lead series, 43-39-2
PS: Packers lead series, 1-0
1937—Packers, 35-10 (C)
Packers, 35-7 (GB)
1938—Packers, 26-17 (GB)
Packers, 28-7 (C)
1939—Rams, 27-24 (GB)
Packers, 7-6 (C)
1940—Packers, 31-14 (GB)
Tie, 13-13 (C)
1941—Packers, 24-7 (Mil)
Packers, 17-14 (C)
1942—Packers, 45-28 (GB)
Packers, 30-12 (C)
1944—Packers, 30-21 (GB)
Packers, 42-7 (C)
1945—Rams, 27-14 (GB)
Rams, 20-7 (C)
1946—Rams, 21-17 (Mil)
Rams, 38-17 (LA)
1947—Packers, 17-14 (Mil)
Packers, 30-10 (LA)
1948—Packers, 16-0 (GB)
Rams, 24-10 (LA)
1949—Rams, 48-7 (GB)
Rams, 35-7 (LA)
1950—Rams, 45-14 (Mil)
Rams, 51-14 (LA)
1951—Rams, 28-0 (Mil)
Rams, 42-14 (LA)
1952—Rams, 30-28 (Mil)
Rams, 45-27 (LA)
1953—Rams, 38-20 (Mil)
Rams, 33-17 (LA)
1954—Packers, 35-17 (Mil)
Rams, 35-27 (LA)
1955—Packers, 30-28 (Mil)
Rams, 31-17 (LA)
1956—Packers, 42-17 (Mil)
Rams, 49-21 (LA)
1957—Rams, 31-27 (Mil)
Rams, 42-17 (LA)
1958—Rams, 20-7 (GB)
Rams, 34-20 (LA)
1959—Rams, 45-6 (Mil)
Packers, 38-20 (LA)
1960—Rams, 33-31 (Mil)
Packers, 35-21 (LA)
1961—Packers, 35-17 (GB)
Packers, 24-17 (LA)
1962—Packers, 41-10 (Mil)
Packers, 20-17 (LA)
1963—Packers, 42-10 (GB)
Packers, 31-14 (LA)
1964—Rams, 27-17 (Mil)
Tie, 24-24 (LA)
1965—Packers, 6-3 (Mil)
Rams, 21-10 (LA)
1966—Packers, 24-13 (GB)
Packers, 27-23 (LA)
1967—Rams, 27-24 (LA)
**Packers, 28-7 (Mil)
1968—Rams, 16-14 (Mil)
1969—Rams, 34-21 (LA)
1970—Rams, 31-21 (GB)
1971—Rams, 30-13 (LA)
1973—Rams, 24-7 (LA)
1974—Packers, 17-6 (Mil)
1975—Rams, 22-5 (LA)
1977—Rams, 24-6 (Mil)
1978—Rams, 31-14 (LA)
1980—Rams, 51-21 (LA)
1981—Rams, 35-23 (LA)
1982—Packers, 35-23 (Mil)
1983—Packers, 27-24 (Mil)
1984—Packers, 31-6 (Mil)
1985—Rams, 34-17 (LA)
1988—Rams, 34-7 (GB)
1989—Rams, 41-38 (LA)
1990—Packers, 36-24 (GB)
1991—Rams, 23-21 (LA)
1992—Packers, 28-13 (GB)
1993—Packers, 36-6 (Mil)
1994—Packers, 24-17 (GB)
1995—Rams, 17-14 (GB)
1996—Packers, 24-9 (StL)
1997—Packers, 17-7 (GB)
(RS Pts.—Rams 1,967, Packers 1,858)
(PS Pts.—Packers 28, Rams 7)
**Franchise in Los Angeles prior to 1995 and in Cleveland prior to 1946*
***Conference Championship*

GREEN BAY vs. SAN DIEGO
RS: Packers lead series, 6-1
1970—Packers, 22-20 (SD)
1974—Packers, 34-0 (GB)
1978—Packers, 24-3 (SD)
1984—Chargers, 34-28 (GB)
1993—Packers, 20-13 (SD)
1996—Packers, 42-10 (GB)
1999—Packers, 31-3 (SD)
(RS Pts.—Packers 201, Chargers 83)

GREEN BAY vs. SAN FRANCISCO
RS: Series tied, 25-25-1
PS: Packers lead series, 3-1
1950—Packers, 25-21 (GB)
49ers, 30-14 (SF)
1951—49ers, 31-19 (SF)
1952—49ers, 24-14 (SF)
1953—49ers, 37-7 (Mil)
49ers, 48-14 (SF)
1954—49ers, 23-17 (Mil)
49ers, 35-0 (SF)
1955—Packers, 27-21 (Mil)
Packers, 28-7 (SF)
1956—49ers, 17-16 (GB)
49ers, 38-20 (SF)
1957—49ers, 24-14 (Mil)
49ers, 27-20 (SF)
1958—49ers, 33-12 (Mil)
49ers, 48-21 (SF)
1959—Packers, 21-20 (GB)
Packers, 36-14 (SF)
1960—Packers, 41-14 (Mil)
Packers, 13-0 (SF)
1961—Packers, 30-10 (GB)
49ers, 22-21 (SF)
1962—Packers, 31-13 (Mil)
Packers, 31-21 (SF)
1963—Packers, 28-10 (Mil)
Packers, 21-17 (SF)
1964—Packers, 24-14 (Mil)
49ers, 24-14 (SF)
1965—Packers, 27-10 (GB)
Tie, 24-24 (SF)
1966—49ers, 21-20 (SF)
Packers, 20-7 (Mil)
1967—Packers, 13-0 (GB)
1968—49ers, 27-20 (SF)
1969—Packers, 14-7 (Mil)
1970—49ers, 26-10 (SF)
1972—Packers, 34-24 (Mil)
1973—49ers, 20-6 (SF)
1974—49ers, 7-6 (SF)
1976—49ers, 26-14 (GB)
1977—Packers, 16-14 (Mil)
1980—Packers, 23-16 (Mil)
1981—49ers, 13-3 (Mil)
1986—49ers, 31-17 (Mil)
1987—49ers, 23-12 (GB)
1989—Packers, 21-17 (SF)
1990—49ers, 24-20 (GB)
1995—*Packers, 27-17 (SF)
1996—Packers, 23-20 (GB) OT
*Packers, 35-14 (GB)
1997—**Packers, 23-10 (SF)
1998—Packers, 36-22 (GB)
***49ers, 30-27 (SF)
1999—Packers, 20-3 (SF)
2000—Packers, 31-28 (GB)
(RS Pts.—49ers 1,053, Packers 1,009)
(PS Pts.—Packers 112, 49ers 71)
**NFC Divisional Playoff*
***NFC Championship*
****NFC First-Round Playoff*

GREEN BAY vs. SEATTLE
RS: Series tied, 4-4
1976—Packers, 27-20 (Mil)
1978—Packers, 45-28 (Mil)
1981—Packers, 34-24 (GB)
1984—Seahawks, 30-24 (Mil)
1987—Seahawks, 24-13 (S)
1990—Seahawks, 20-14 (Mil)
1996—Packers, 31-10 (S)
1999—Seahawks, 27-7 (GB)
(RS Pts.—Packers 195, Seahawks 183)

GREEN BAY vs. TAMPA BAY
RS: Packers lead series, 27-16-1
PS: Packers lead series, 1-0
1977—Packers, 13-0 (TB)
1978—Packers, 9-7 (GB)
Packers, 17-7 (TB)
1979—Buccaneers, 21-10 (GB)
Buccaneers, 21-3 (TB)
1980—Tie, 14-14 (TB) OT
Buccaneers, 20-17 (Mil)
1981—Buccaneers, 21-10 (GB)
Buccaneers, 37-3 (TB)
1983—Packers, 55-14 (GB)
Packers, 12-9 (TB) OT
1984—Buccaneers, 30-27 (TB) OT
Packers, 27-14 (GB)
1985—Packers, 21-0 (GB)
Packers, 20-17 (TB)
1986—Packers, 31-7 (Mil)
Packers, 21-7 (TB)
1987—Buccaneers, 23-17 (Mil)
1988—Buccaneers, 13-10 (GB)
Buccaneers, 27-24 (TB)
1989—Buccaneers, 23-21 (GB)
Packers, 17-16 (TB)
1990—Buccaneers, 26-14 (TB)
Packers, 20-10 (Mil)
1991—Packers, 15-13 (GB)
Packers, 27-0 (TB)
1992—Buccaneers, 31-3 (TB)
Packers, 19-14 (Mil)
1993—Packers, 37-14 (TB)
Packers, 13-10 (GB)
1994—Packers, 30-3 (GB)
Packers, 34-19 (TB)
1995—Packers, 35-13 (GB)

ALL-TIME TEAM VS. TEAM RESULTS

Buccaneers, 13-10 (TB) OT
1996—Packers, 34-3 (TB)
Packers, 13-7 (GB)
1997—Packers, 21-16 (GB)
Packers, 17-6 (TB)
*Packers, 21-7 (GB)
1998—Packers, 23-15 (GB)
Buccaneers, 24-22 (TB)
1999—Packers, 26-23 (GB)
Buccaneers, 29-10 (TB)
2000—Buccaneers, 20-15 (TB)
Packers, 17-14 (GB) OT
(RS Pts.—Packers 854, Buccaneers 671)
(PS Pts.—Packers 21, Buccaneers 7)
NFC Divisional Playoff

GREEN BAY vs. *TENNESSEE
RS: Packers lead series, 4-3
1972—Packers, 23-10 (H)
1977—Oilers, 16-10 (GB)
1980—Oilers, 22-3 (GB)
1983—Packers, 41-38 (H) OT
1986—Oilers, 31-3 (GB)
1992—Packers, 16-14 (H)
1998—Packers, 30-22 (GB)
(RS Pts.—Titans 153, Packers 126)
Franchise in Houston prior to 1997; known as Oilers prior to 1999

GREEN BAY vs. *WASHINGTON
RS: Packers lead series, 13-12-1
PS: Series tied, 1-1
1932—Packers, 21-0 (B)
1933—Tie, 7-7 (GB)
Redskins, 20-7 (B)
1934—Packers, 10-0 (B)
1936—Packers, 31-2 (GB)
Packers, 7-3 (B)
**Packers, 21-6 (New York)
1937—Redskins, 14-6 (W)
1939—Packers, 24-14 (Mil)
1941—Packers, 22-17 (W)
1943—Redskins, 33-7 (Mil)
1946—Packers, 20-7 (W)
1947—Packers, 27-10 (Mil)
1948—Redskins, 23-7 (Mil)
1949—Redskins, 30-0 (W)
1950—Packers, 35-21 (Mil)
1952—Packers, 35-20 (Mil)
1958—Redskins, 37-21 (W)
1959—Packers, 21-0 (GB)
1968—Packers, 27-7 (W)
1972—Redskins, 21-16 (W)
***Redskins, 16-3 (W)
1974—Redskins, 17-6 (GB)
1977—Redskins, 10-9 (W)
1979—Redskins, 38-21 (W)
1983—Packers, 48-47 (GB)
1986—Redskins, 16-7 (GB)
1988—Redskins, 20-17 (Mil)
(RS Pts.—Packers 459, Redskins 434)
(PS Pts.—Packers 24, Redskins 22)
Franchise in Boston prior to 1937 and known as Braves prior to 1933
***NFL Championship*
****NFC Divisional Playoff*

INDIANAPOLIS vs. ARIZONA
RS: Series tied, 6-6;
See Arizona vs. Indianapolis

INDIANAPOLIS vs. ATLANTA
RS: Colts lead series, 10-1;
See Atlanta vs. Indianapolis

INDIANAPOLIS vs. BALTIMORE
RS: Series tied, 1-1;
See Baltimore vs. Indianapolis

INDIANAPOLIS vs. BUFFALO
RS: Bills lead series, 34-26-1;
See Buffalo vs. Indianapolis

INDIANAPOLIS vs. CAROLINA
RS: Panthers lead series, 2-0;
See Carolina vs. Indianapolis

INDIANAPOLIS vs. CHICAGO
RS: Colts lead series, 21-17;
See Chicago vs. Indianapolis

INDIANAPOLIS vs. CINCINNATI
RS: Colts lead series, 11-8
PS: Colts lead series, 1-0;
See Cincinnati vs. Indianapolis

INDIANAPOLIS vs. CLEVELAND
RS: Browns lead series, 13-8
PS: Series tied, 2-2;
See Cleveland vs. Indianapolis

INDIANAPOLIS vs. DALLAS
RS: Cowboys lead series, 7-4
PS: Colts lead series, 1-0;
See Dallas vs. Indianapolis

INDIANAPOLIS vs. DENVER
RS: Broncos lead series, 9-2;
See Denver vs. Indianapolis

INDIANAPOLIS vs. DETROIT
RS: Series tied, 18-18-2;
See Detroit vs. Indianapolis

INDIANAPOLIS vs. GREEN BAY
RS: Series tied, 19-19-1
PS: Packers lead series, 1-0;
See Green Bay vs. Indianapolis

INDIANAPOLIS vs. JACKSONVILLE
RS: Colts lead series, 2-0
1995—Colts, 41-31 (J)
2000—Colts, 43-14 (I)
(RS Pts.—Colts 84, Jaguars 45)

***INDIANAPOLIS vs. KANSAS CITY**
RS: Colts lead series, 7-6
PS: Colts lead series, 1-0
1970—Chiefs, 44-24 (B)
1972—Chiefs, 24-10 (KC)
1975—Colts, 28-14 (B)
1977—Colts, 17-6 (KC)
1979—Chiefs, 14-0 (KC)
Chiefs, 10-7 (B)
1980—Colts, 31-24 (KC)
Chiefs, 38-28 (B)
1985—Chiefs, 20-7 (KC)
1990—Colts, 23-19 (I)
1995—**Colts, 10-7 (KC)
1996—Colts, 24-19 (KC)
1999—Colts, 25-17 (I)
2000—Colts, 27-14 (KC)
(RS Pts.—Chiefs 263, Colts 251)
(PS Pts.—Colts 10, Chiefs 7)
Franchise in Baltimore prior to 1984
***AFC Divisional Playoff*

***INDIANAPOLIS vs. MIAMI**
RS: Dolphins lead series, 41-21
PS: Dolphins lead series, 2-0
1970—Colts, 35-0 (B)
Dolphins, 34-17 (M)
1971—Dolphins, 17-14 (M)
Colts, 14-3 (B)
**Dolphins, 21-0 (M)
1972—Dolphins, 23-0 (B)
Dolphins, 16-0 (M)
1973—Dolphins, 44-0 (M)
Colts, 16-3 (B)
1974—Dolphins, 17-7 (M)
Dolphins, 17-16 (B)
1975—Colts, 33-17 (M)
Colts, 10-7 (B) OT
1976—Colts, 28-14 (B)
Colts, 17-16 (M)
1977—Colts, 45-28 (B)
Dolphins, 17-6 (M)
1978—Dolphins, 42-0 (B)
Dolphins, 26-8 (M)
1979—Dolphins, 19-0 (M)
Dolphins, 28-24 (B)
1980—Colts, 30-17 (M)
Dolphins, 24-14 (B)
1981—Dolphins, 31-28 (B)
Dolphins, 27-10 (M)
1982—Dolphins, 24-20 (M)
Dolphins, 34-7 (B)
1983—Dolphins, 21-7 (B)
Dolphins, 37-0 (M)
1984—Dolphins, 44-7 (M)
Dolphins, 35-17 (I)
1985—Dolphins, 30-13 (M)
Dolphins, 34-20 (I)
1986—Dolphins, 30-10 (M)
Dolphins, 17-13 (I)
1987—Dolphins, 23-10 (I)
Colts, 40-21 (M)
1988—Colts, 15-13 (I)
Colts, 31-28 (M)
1989—Dolphins, 19-13 (M)
Colts, 42-13 (I)
1990—Dolphins, 27-7 (I)
Dolphins, 23-17 (M)
1991—Dolphins, 17-6 (M)
Dolphins, 10-6 (I)
1992—Colts, 31-20 (M)
Dolphins, 28-0 (I)
1993—Dolphins, 24-20 (I)
Dolphins, 41-27 (M)
1994—Dolphins, 22-21 (M)
Colts, 10-6 (I)
1995—Colts, 27-24 (M) OT
Colts, 36-28 (I)
1996—Colts, 10-6 (I)
Dolphins, 37-13 (M)
1997—Dolphins, 16-10 (M)
Colts, 41-0 (I)
1998—Dolphins, 24-15 (I)
Dolphins, 27-14 (M)
1999—Dolphins, 34-31 (I)
Colts, 37-34 (M)
2000—Dolphins, 17-14 (I)
Colts, 20-13 (M)
***Dolphins 23-17 (M) OT
(RS Pts.—Dolphins 1,388, Colts 1,050)
(PS Pts.—Dolphins 44, Colts 17)
Franchise in Baltimore prior to 1984
***AFC Championship*
****AFC First-Round Playoff*

***INDIANAPOLIS vs. MINNESOTA**
RS: Colts lead series, 12-7-1
PS: Colts lead series, 1-0
1961—Colts, 34-33 (B)
Vikings, 28-20 (M)
1962—Colts, 34-7 (M)
Colts, 42-17 (B)
1963—Colts, 37-34 (M)
Colts, 41-10 (B)
1964—Vikings, 34-24 (M)
Colts, 17-14 (B)
1965—Colts, 35-16 (B)
Colts, 41-21 (M)
1966—Colts, 38-23 (M)
Colts, 20-17 (B)
1967—Tie, 20-20 (M)
1968—Colts, 21-9 (B)
**Colts, 24-14 (B)
1969—Vikings, 52-14 (M)
1971—Vikings, 10-3 (M)
1982—Vikings, 13-10 (M)
1988—Vikings, 12-3 (M)
1997—Vikings, 39-28 (M)
2000—Colts, 31-10 (I)
(RS Pts.—Colts 513, Vikings 419)
(PS Pts.—Colts 24, Vikings 14)
Franchise in Baltimore prior to 1984
***Conference Championship*

***INDIANAPOLIS vs. **NEW ENGLAND**
RS: Patriots lead series, 37-24
1970—Colts, 14-6 (Bos)
Colts, 27-3 (Balt)
1971—Colts, 23-3 (NE)
Patriots, 21-17 (Balt)
1972—Colts, 24-17 (NE)
Colts, 31-0 (Balt)
1973—Patriots, 24-16 (NE)
Colts, 18-13 (Balt)
1974—Patriots, 42-3 (NE)
Patriots, 27-17 (Balt)
1975—Patriots, 21-10 (NE)
Colts, 34-21 (Balt)
1976—Colts, 27-13 (NE)
Patriots, 21-14 (Balt)
1977—Patriots, 17-3 (NE)
Colts, 30-24 (Balt)
1978—Colts, 34-27 (NE)
Patriots, 35-14 (Balt)
1979—Colts, 31-26 (Balt)
Patriots, 50-21 (NE)
1980—Patriots, 37-21 (Balt)
Patriots, 47-21 (NE)
1981—Colts, 29-28 (NE)
Colts, 23-21 (Balt)
1982—Patriots, 24-13 (Balt)
1983—Colts, 29-23 (NE) OT
Colts, 12-7 (Balt)
1984—Patriots, 50-17 (I)
Patriots, 16-10 (NE)
1985—Patriots, 34-15 (NE)
Patriots, 38-31 (I)
1986—Patriots, 33-3 (NE)
Patriots, 30-21 (I)
1987—Colts, 30-16 (I)
Patriots, 24-0 (NE)
1988—Patriots, 21-17 (NE)
Colts, 24-21 (I)
1989—Patriots, 23-20 (I) OT
Patriots, 22-16 (NE)
1990—Patriots, 16-14 (I)
Colts, 13-10 (NE)
1991—Patriots, 16-7 (I)
Patriots, 23-17 (NE) OT
1992—Patriots, 37-34 (I) OT
Colts, 6-0 (NE)
1993—Colts, 9-6 (I)
Patriots, 38-0 (NE)
1994—Patriots, 12-10 (I)
Patriots, 28-13 (NE)
1995—Colts, 24-10 (NE)
Colts, 10-7 (I)
1996—Patriots, 27-9 (I)
Patriots, 27-13 (NE)
1997—Patriots, 31-6 (I)
Patriots, 20-17 (NE)
1998—Patriots, 29-6 (NE)
Patriots, 21-16 (I)
1999—Patriots, 31-28 (NE)
Colts, 20-15 (I)
2000—Patriots, 24-16 (NE)
Colts, 30-23 (I)
(RS Pts.—Patriots 1,377, Colts 1,078)
Franchise in Baltimore prior to 1984
***Franchise in Boston prior to 1971*

***INDIANAPOLIS vs. NEW ORLEANS**
RS: Saints lead series, 4-3
1967—Colts, 30-10 (B)
1969—Colts, 30-10 (NO)
1973—Colts, 14-10 (B)
1986—Saints, 17-14 (I)
1989—Saints, 41-6 (NO)
1995—Saints, 17-14 (NO)
1998—Saints, 19-13 (I) OT
(RS Pts.—Colts 124, Saints 121)
Franchise in Baltimore prior to 1984

***INDIANAPOLIS vs. N.Y. GIANTS**
RS: Colts lead series, 6-5
PS: Colts lead series, 2-0
1954—Colts, 20-14 (B)
1955—Giants, 17-7 (NY)
1958—Giants, 24-21 (NY)
**Colts, 23-17 (NY) OT
1959—**Colts, 31-16 (B)
1963—Giants, 37-28 (B)
1968—Colts, 26-0 (NY)
1971—Colts, 31-7 (NY)
1975—Colts, 21-0 (NY)
1979—Colts, 31-7 (NY)
1990—Giants, 24-7 (I)
1993—Giants, 20-6 (NY)
1999—Colts, 27-19 (NY)
(RS Pts.—Colts 225, Giants 169)
(PS Pts.—Colts 54, Giants 33)
Franchise in Baltimore prior to 1984
***NFL Championship*

***INDIANAPOLIS vs. N.Y. JETS**
RS: Colts lead series, 37-24
PS: Jets lead series, 1-0
1968—**Jets 16-7 (Miami)

1970—Colts, 29-22 (NY)
Colts, 35-20 (B)
1971—Colts, 22-0 (B)
Colts, 14-13 (NY)
1972—Jets, 44-34 (B)
Jets, 24-20 (NY)
1973—Jets, 34-10 (B)
Jets, 20-17 (NY)
1974—Colts, 35-20 (NY)
Jets, 45-38 (B)
1975—Colts, 45-28 (NY)
Colts, 52-19 (B)
1976—Colts, 20-0 (NY)
Colts, 33-16 (B)
1977—Colts, 20-12 (NY)
Colts, 33-12 (B)
1978—Jets, 33-10 (B)
Jets, 24-16 (NY)
1979—Colts, 10-8 (B)
Jets, 30-17 (NY)
1980—Colts, 17-14 (NY)
Colts, 35-21 (B)
1981—Jets, 41-14 (B)
Jets, 25-0 (NY)
1982—Jets, 37-0 (NY)
1983—Colts, 17-14 (NY)
Jets, 10-6 (B)
1984—Jets, 23-14 (I)
Colts, 9-5 (NY)
1985—Jets, 25-20 (NY)
Jets, 35-17 (I)
1986—Jets, 26-7 (I)
Jets, 31-16 (NY)
1987—Colts, 6-0 (I)
Colts, 19-14 (NY)
1988—Colts, 38-14 (I)
Jets, 34-16 (NY)
1989—Colts, 17-10 (NY)
Colts, 27-10 (I)
1990—Colts, 17-14 (I)
Colts, 29-21 (NY)
1991—Jets, 17-6 (I)
Colts, 28-27 (NY)
1992—Colts, 6-3 (I) OT
Colts, 10-6 (NY)
1993—Jets, 31-17 (I)
Colts, 9-6 (NY)
1994—Jets, 16-6 (NY)
Colts, 28-25 (I)
1995—Colts, 27-24 (NY) OT
Colts, 17-10 (I)
1996—Colts, 21-7 (NY)
Colts, 34-29 (I)
1997—Jets, 16-12 (I)
Colts, 22-14 (NY)
1998—Jets, 44-6 (NY)
Colts, 24-23 (I)
1999—Colts, 16-13 (NY)
Colts, 13-6 (I)
2000—Colts, 23-15 (I)
Jets, 27-17 (NY)
(RS Pts.—Jets 1,207, Colts 1,193)
(PS Pts.—Jets 16, Colts 7)
**Franchise in Baltimore prior to 1984*
***Super Bowl III*

***INDIANAPOLIS vs **OAKLAND**
RS: Raiders lead series, 6-2
PS: Series tied, 1-1
1970—***Colts, 27-17 (B)
1971—Colts, 37-14 (O)
1973—Raiders, 34-21 (B)
1975—Raiders, 31-20 (B)
1977—****Raiders, 37-31 (B) OT
1984—Raiders, 21-7 (LA)
1986—Colts, 30-24 (LA)
1991—Raiders, 16-0 (LA)
1995—Raiders, 30-17 (O)
2000—Raiders, 38-31 (I)
(RS Pts.—Raiders 208, Colts 163)
(PS Pts.—Colts 58, Raiders 54)
**Franchise in Baltimore prior to 1984*
***Franchise in Los Angeles from 1982-1994*
****AFC Championship*
*****AFC Divisional Playoff*

***INDIANAPOLIS vs. PHILADELPHIA**
RS: Colts lead series, 8-6
1953—Eagles, 45-14 (P)
1965—Colts, 34-24 (B)
1967—Colts, 38-6 (P)
1969—Colts, 24-20 (B)
1970—Colts, 29-10 (B)
1974—Eagles, 30-10 (P)
1978—Eagles, 17-14 (B)
1981—Eagles, 38-13 (P)
1983—Colts, 22-21 (P)
1984—Eagles, 16-7 (P)
1990—Colts, 24-23 (P)
1993—Eagles, 20-10 (I)
1996—Colts, 37-10 (I)
1999—Colts, 44-17 (P)
(RS Pts.—Colts 320, Eagles 297)
**Franchise in Baltimore prior to 1984*

***INDIANAPOLIS vs. PITTSBURGH**
RS: Steelers lead series, 12-4
PS: Steelers lead series, 4-0
1957—Steelers, 19-13 (B)
1968—Colts, 41-7 (P)
1971—Colts, 34-21 (B)
1974—Steelers, 30-0 (P)
1975—**Steelers, 28-10 (P)
1976—**Steelers, 40-14 (B)
1977—Colts, 31-21 (B)
1978—Steelers, 35-13 (P)
1979—Steelers, 17-13 (P)
1980—Steelers, 20-17 (B)
1983—Steelers, 24-13 (B)
1984—Colts, 17-16 (I)
1985—Steelers, 45-3 (P)
1987—Steelers, 21-7 (P)
1991—Steelers, 21-3 (I)
1992—Steelers, 30-14 (P)
1994—Steelers, 31-21 (P)
1995—***Steelers, 20-16 (P)
1996—****Steelers, 42-14 (P)
1997—Steelers, 24-22 (P)
(RS Pts.—Steelers 382, Colts 262)
(PS Pts.—Steelers 130, Colts 54)
**Franchise in Baltimore prior to 1984*
***AFC Divisional Playoff*
****AFC Championship*
*****AFC First-Round Playoff*

***INDIANAPOLIS vs. **ST. LOUIS**
RS: Colts lead series, 21-16-2
1953—Rams, 21-13 (B)
Rams, 45-2 (LA)
1954—Rams, 48-0 (B)
Colts, 22-21 (LA)
1955—Tie, 17-17 (B)
Rams, 20-14 (LA)
1956—Colts, 56-21 (B)
Rams, 31-7 (LA)
1957—Colts, 31-14 (B)
Rams, 37-21 (LA)
1958—Colts, 34-7 (B)
Rams, 30-28 (LA)
1959—Colts, 35-21 (B)
Colts, 45-26 (LA)
1960—Colts, 31-17 (B)
Rams, 10-3 (LA)
1961—Colts, 27-24 (B)
Rams, 34-17 (LA)
1962—Colts, 30-27 (B)
Colts, 14-2 (LA)
1963—Rams, 17-16 (LA)
Colts, 19-16 (B)
1964—Colts, 35-20 (B)
Colts, 24-7 (LA)
1965—Colts, 35-20 (B)
Colts, 20-17 (LA)
1966—Colts, 17-3 (LA)
Rams, 23-7 (B)
1967—Tie, 24-24 (B)
Rams, 34-10 (LA)
1968—Colts, 27-10 (B)
Colts, 28-24 (LA)
1969—Rams, 27-20 (B)
Colts, 13-7 (LA)
1971—Colts, 24-17 (B)
1975—Rams, 24-13 (LA)
1986—Rams, 24-7 (I)
1989—Rams, 31-17 (LA)
1995—Colts, 21-18 (I)
(RS Pts.—Rams 836, Colts 824)
**Franchise in Baltimore prior to 1984*
***Franchise in Los Angeles prior to 1995*

***INDIANAPOLIS vs. SAN DIEGO**
RS: Chargers lead series, 12-7
PS: Colts lead series, 1-0
1970—Colts, 16-14 (SD)
1972—Chargers, 23-20 (B)
1976—Colts, 37-21 (SD)
1981—Chargers, 43-14 (B)
1982—Chargers, 44-26 (SD)
1984—Chargers, 38-10 (I)
1986—Chargers, 17-3 (I)
1987—Chargers, 16-13 (I)
Colts, 20-7 (SD)
1988—Colts, 16-0 (SD)
1989—Colts, 10-6 (I)
1992—Chargers, 34-14 (I)
Chargers, 26-0 (SD)
1993—Chargers, 31-0 (I)
1995—Chargers, 27-24 (I)
**Colts, 35-20 (SD)
1996—Chargers, 26-19 (I)
1997—Chargers, 35-19 (SD)
1998—Colts, 17-12 (I)
1999—Colts, 27-19 (SD)
(RS Pts.—Chargers 439, Colts 305)
(PS Pts.—Colts 35, Chargers 20)
**Franchise in Baltimore prior to 1984*
***AFC First-Round Playoff*

***INDIANAPOLIS vs. SAN FRANCISCO**
RS: Colts lead series, 22-17
1953—49ers, 38-21 (B)
49ers, 45-14 (SF)
1954—Colts, 17-13 (B)
49ers, 10-7 (SF)
1955—Colts, 26-14 (B)
49ers, 35-24 (SF)
1956—49ers, 20-17 (B)
49ers, 30-17 (SF)
1957—Colts, 27-21 (B)
49ers, 17-13 (SF)
1958—Colts, 35-27 (B)
49ers, 21-12 (SF)
1959—Colts, 45-14 (B)
Colts, 34-14 (SF)
1960—49ers, 30-22 (B)
49ers, 34-10 (SF)
1961—Colts, 20-17 (B)
Colts, 27-24 (SF)
1962—49ers, 21-13 (B)
Colts, 22-3 (SF)
1963—Colts, 20-14 (SF)
Colts, 20-3 (B)
1964—Colts, 37-7 (B)
Colts, 14-3 (SF)
1965—Colts, 27-24 (B)
Colts, 34-28 (SF)
1966—Colts, 36-14 (B)
Colts, 30-14 (SF)
1967—Colts, 41-7 (B)
Colts, 26-9 (SF)
1968—Colts, 27-10 (B)
Colts, 42-14 (SF)
1969—49ers, 24-21 (B)
49ers, 20-17 (SF)
1972—49ers, 24-21 (SF)
1986—49ers, 35-14 (SF)
1989—49ers, 30-24 (I)
1995—Colts, 18-17 (I)
1998—49ers, 34-31 (SF)
(RS Pts.—Colts 923, 49ers 779)
**Franchise in Baltimore prior to 1984*

***INDIANAPOLIS vs. SEATTLE**
RS: Colts lead series, 5-3
1977—Colts, 29-14 (S)
1978—Colts, 17-14 (S)
1991—Seahawks, 31-3 (S)
1994—Colts, 17-15 (I)
Colts, 31-19 (S)
1997—Seahawks, 31-3 (I)
1998—Seahawks, 27-23 (S)
2000—Colts, 37-24 (S)
(RS Pts.—Seahawks 175, Colts 160)
**Franchise in Baltimore prior to 1984*

***INDIANAPOLIS vs. TAMPA BAY**
RS: Colts lead series, 5-4
1976—Colts, 42-17 (B)
1979—Buccaneers, 29-26 (B) OT
1985—Colts, 31-23 (TB)
1987—Colts, 24-6 (I)
1988—Colts, 35-31 (I)
1991—Buccaneers, 17-3 (TB)
1992—Colts, 24-14 (TB)
1994—Buccaneers, 24-10 (TB)
1997—Buccaneers, 31-28 (I)
(RS Pts.—Colts 223, Buccaneers 192)
**Franchise in Baltimore prior to 1984*

***INDIANAPOLIS vs. **TENNESSEE**
RS: Series tied, 7-7
PS: Titans lead series, 1-0
1970—Colts, 24-20 (H)
1973—Oilers, 31-27 (B)
1976—Colts, 38-14 (B)
1979—Oilers, 28-16 (B)
1980—Oilers, 21-16 (H)
1983—Colts, 20-10 (B)
1984—Colts, 35-21 (H)
1985—Colts, 34-16 (I)
1986—Oilers, 31-17 (H)
1987—Colts, 51-27 (I)
1988—Oilers, 17-14 (I) OT
1990—Oilers, 24-10 (H)
1992—Oilers, 20-10 (I)
1994—Colts, 45-21 (I)
1999—***Titans, 19-16 (I)
(RS Pts.—Colts 357, Titans 301)
(PS Pts.—Titans 19, Colts 16)
**Franchise in Baltimore prior to 1984*
***Franchise in Houston prior to 1997; known as Oilers prior to 1999*
****AFC Divisional Playoff*

***INDIANAPOLIS vs. WASHINGTON**
RS: Colts lead series, 17-9
1953—Colts, 27-17 (B)
1954—Redskins, 24-21 (W)
1955—Redskins, 14-13 (B)
1956—Colts, 19-17 (B)
1957—Colts, 21-17 (W)
1958—Colts, 35-10 (B)
1959—Redskins, 27-24 (W)
1960—Colts, 20-0 (B)
1961—Colts, 27-6 (W)
1962—Colts, 34-21 (B)
1963—Colts, 36-20 (W)
1964—Colts, 45-17 (B)
1965—Colts, 38-7 (W)
1966—Colts, 37-10 (B)
1967—Colts, 17-13 (W)
1969—Colts, 41-17 (B)
1973—Redskins, 22-14 (W)
1977—Colts, 10-3 (B)
1978—Colts, 21-17 (B)
1981—Redskins, 38-14 (W)
1984—Redskins, 35-7 (I)
1990—Colts, 35-28 (I)
1993—Redskins, 30-24 (W)
1994—Redskins, 41-27 (I)
1996—Redskins, 31-16 (W)
1999—Colts, 24-21 (I)
(RS Pts.—Colts 647, Redskins 503)
**Franchise in Baltimore prior to 1984*

JACKSONVILLE vs. ARIZONA
RS: Jaguars lead series, 1-0;
See Arizona vs. Jacksonville

JACKSONVILLE vs. ATLANTA
RS: Jaguars lead series, 2-0;
See Atlanta vs. Jacksonville

ALL-TIME TEAM VS. TEAM RESULTS

JACKSONVILLE vs. BALTIMORE
RS: Jaguars lead series, 8-2;
See Baltimore vs. Jacksonville
JACKSONVILLE vs. BUFFALO
RS: Series tied, 1-1
PS: Jaguars lead series, 1-0;
See Buffalo vs. Jacksonville
JACKSONVILLE vs. CAROLINA
RS: Jaguars lead series, 2-0;
See Carolina vs. Jacksonville
JACKSONVILLE vs. CHICAGO
RS: Series tied, 1-1;
See Chicago vs. Jacksonville
JACKSONVILLE vs. CINCINNATI
RS: Jaguars lead series, 7-5;
See Cincinnati vs. Jacksonville
JACKSONVILLE vs. CLEVELAND
RS: Jaguars lead series, 6-0;
See Cleveland vs. Jacksonville
JACKSONVILLE vs. DALLAS
RS: Series tied, 1-1;
See Dallas vs. Jacksonville
JACKSONVILLE vs. DENVER
RS: Broncos lead series, 2-1
PS: Series tied, 1-1;
See Denver vs. Jacksonville
JACKSONVILLE vs. DETROIT
RS: Series tied, 1-1;
See Detroit vs. Jacksonville
JACKSONVILLE vs. GREEN BAY
RS: Packers lead series, 1-0;
See Green Bay vs. Jacksonville
JACKSONVILLE vs. INDIANAPOLIS
RS: Colts lead series, 2-0;
See Indianapolis vs. Jacksonville
JACKSONVILLE vs. KANSAS CITY
RS: Jaguars lead series, 2-0
1997—Jaguars, 24-10 (J)
1998—Jaguars, 21-16 (J)
(RS Pts.—Jaguars 45, Chiefs 26)
JACKSONVILLE vs. MIAMI
RS: Jaguars lead series, 1-0
PS: Jaguars lead series, 1-0
1998—Jaguars, 28-21 (J)
1999—*Jaguars, 62-7 (J)
(RS Pts.—Jaguars 28, Dolphins 21)
(PS Pts.—Jaguars 62, Dolphins 7)
**AFC Divisional Playoff*
JACKSONVILLE vs. MINNESOTA
RS: Vikings lead series, 1-0
1998—Vikings, 50-10 (M)
(RS Pts.—Vikings 50, Jaguars 10)
JACKSONVILLE vs. NEW ENGLAND
RS: Patriots lead series, 2-0
PS: Series tied, 1-1
1996—Patriots, 28-25 (NE) OT
*Patriots, 20-6 (NE)
1997—Patriots, 26-20 (J)
1998—**Jaguars, 25-10 (J)
(RS Pts.—Patriots 54, Jaguars 45)
(PS Pts.—Jaguars 31, Patriots 30)
**AFC Championship*
***AFC First-Round Playoff*
JACKSONVILLE vs. NEW ORLEANS
RS: Series tied, 1-1
1996—Saints, 17-13 (NO)
1999—Jaguars, 41-23 (J)
(RS Pts.—Jaguars 54, Saints 40)
JACKSONVILLE vs. N.Y. GIANTS
RS: Series tied, 1-1
1997—Jaguars, 40-13 (J)
2000—Giants, 28-25 (NY)
(RS Pts.—Jaguars 65, Giants 41)
JACKSONVILLE vs. N.Y. JETS
RS: Jaguars lead series, 2-1
PS: Jets lead series, 1-0
1995—Jets, 27-10 (NY)
1996—Jaguars, 21-17 (J)
1998—*Jets, 34-24 (NY)
1999—Jaguars, 16-6 (NY)
(RS Pts.—Jets 50, Jaguars 47)
(PS Pts.—Jets 34, Jaguars 24
**AFC Divisional Playoff*

JACKSONVILLE vs. OAKLAND
RS: Series tied, 1-1
1996—Raiders, 17-3 (O)
1997—Jaguars, 20-9 (O)
(RS Pts.—Raiders 26, Jaguars 23)
JACKSONVILLE vs. PHILADELPHIA
RS: Jaguars lead series, 1-0
1997—Jaguars, 38-21 (J)
(RS Pts.—Jaguars 38, Eagles 21)
JACKSONVILLE vs. PITTSBURGH
RS: Jaguars lead series, 7-5
1995—Jaguars, 20-16 (J)
Steelers, 24-7 (P)
1996—Jaguars, 24-9 (J)
Steelers, 28-3 (P)
1997—Jaguars, 30-21 (J)
Steelers, 23-17 (P) OT
1998—Steelers, 30-15 (P)
Jaguars, 21-3 (J)
1999—Jaguars, 17-3 (P)
Jaguars, 20-6 (J)
2000—Steelers, 24-13 (J)
Jaguars, 34-24 (P)
(RS Pts.—Jaguars 221, Steelers 211)
JACKSONVILLE vs. ST. LOUIS
RS: Rams lead series, 1-0
1996—Rams, 17-14 (StL)
(RS Pts.—Rams 17, Jaguars 14)
JACKSONVILLE vs. SAN FRANCISCO
RS: Jaguars lead series, 1-0
1999—Jaguars, 41-3 (J)
(RS Pts.—Jaguars 41, 49ers 3)
JACKSONVILLE vs. SEATTLE
RS: Seahawks lead series, 2-1
1995—Seahawks, 47-30 (J)
1996—Jaguars, 20-13 (J)
2000—Seahawks, 28-21 (J)
(RS Pts.—Seahawks 88, Jaguars 71)
JACKSONVILLE vs. TAMPA BAY
RS: Series tied, 1-1
1995—Buccaneers, 17-16 (TB)
1998—Jaguars, 29-24 (J)
(RS Pts.—Jaguars 45, Buccaneers 41)
JACKSONVILLE vs. *TENNESSEE
RS: Series tied, 6-6
PS: Titans lead, 1-0
1995—Oilers, 10-3 (J)
Jaguars, 17-16 (H)
1996—Oilers, 34-27 (J)
Jaguars, 23-17 (H)
1997—Jaguars, 30-24 (T)
Jaguars, 17-9 (J)
1998—Jaguars, 27-22 (T)
Oilers, 16-13 (J)
1999—Titans, 20-19 (J)
Titans, 41-14 (T)
**Titans, 33-14 (J)
2000—Titans, 27-13 (T)
Jaguars, 16-13 (J)
(RS Pts.—Titans 249, Jaguars 219)
(PS Pts.—Titans 33, Jaguars 14)
**Franchise in Houston prior to 1997; known as Oilers prior to 1999*
***AFC Championship*
JACKSONVILLE vs. WASHINGTON
RS: Redskins lead series, 2-0
1997—Redskins, 24-12 (W)
2000—Redskins, 35-16 (J)
(RS Pts.—Redskins 59, Jaguars 28)

KANSAS CITY vs. ARIZONA
RS: Chiefs lead series, 5-1-1;
See Arizona vs. Kansas City
KANSAS CITY vs. ATLANTA
RS: Chiefs lead series, 4-1;
See Atlanta vs. Kansas City
KANSAS CITY vs. BALTIMORE
RS: Chiefs lead series, 1-0;
See Baltimore vs. Kansas City
KANSAS CITY vs. BUFFALO
RS: Bills lead series, 18-14-1
PS: Bills lead series, 2-1;
See Buffalo vs. Kansas City

KANSAS CITY vs. CARLOINA
RS: Chiefs lead series, 2-0;
See Carolina vs. Kansas City
KANSAS CITY vs. CHICAGO
RS: Bears lead series, 5-3;
See Chicago vs. Kansas City
KANSAS CITY vs. CINCINNATI
RS: Chiefs lead series, 11-9;
See Cincinnati vs. Kansas City
KANSAS CITY vs. CLEVELAND
RS: Browns lead series, 8-7-2;
See Cleveland vs. Kansas City
KANSAS CITY vs. DALLAS
RS: Cowboys lead series, 4-3;
See Dallas vs. Kansas City
KANSAS CITY vs. DENVER
RS: Chiefs lead series, 47-34
PS: Broncos lead series, 1-0;
See Denver vs. Kansas City
KANSAS CITY vs. DETROIT
RS: Chiefs lead series, 6-3;
See Detroit vs. Kansas City
KANSAS CITY vs. GREEN BAY
RS: Chiefs lead series, 5-1-1
PS: Packers lead series, 1-0;
See Green Bay vs. Kansas City
KANSAS CITY vs. INDIANAPOLIS
RS: Colts lead series, 7-6
PS: Colts lead series, 1-0;
See Indianapolis vs. Kansas City
KANSAS CITY vs. JACKSONVILLE
RS: Jaguars lead series, 2-0;
See Jacksonville vs. Kansas City
KANSAS CITY vs. MIAMI
RS: Series tied, 10-10
PS: Dolphins lead series, 3-0
1966—Chiefs, 34-16 (KC)
Chiefs, 19-18 (M)
1967—Chiefs, 24-0 (M)
Chiefs, 41-0 (KC)
1968—Chiefs, 48-3 (M)
1969—Chiefs, 17-10 (KC)
1971—*Dolphins, 27-24 (KC) OT
1972—Dolphins, 20-10 (KC)
1974—Dolphins, 9-3 (M)
1976—Chiefs, 20-17 (M) OT
1981—Dolphins, 17-7 (KC)
1983—Dolphins, 14-6 (M)
1985—Dolphins, 31-0 (M)
1987—Dolphins, 42-0 (M)
1989—Chiefs, 26-21 (KC)
Chiefs, 27-24 (M)
1990—**Dolphins, 17-16 (M)
1991—Chiefs, 42-7 (KC)
1993—Dolphins, 30-10 (M)
1994—Dolphins, 45-28 (M)
**Dolphins, 27-17 (M)
1995—Dolphins, 13-6 (M)
1997—Dolphins, 17-14 (M)
(RS Pts.—Chiefs 382, Dolphins 354)
(PS Pts.—Dolphins 71, Chiefs 57)
**AFC Divisional Playoff*
***AFC First-Round Playoff*
KANSAS CITY vs. MINNESOTA
RS: Chiefs lead series, 4-3
PS: Chiefs lead series, 1-0
1969—*Chiefs, 23-7 (New Orleans)
1970—Vikings, 27-10 (M)
1974—Vikings, 35-15 (KC)
1981—Chiefs, 10-6 (M)
1990—Chiefs, 24-21 (KC)
1993—Vikings, 30-10 (M)
1996—Chiefs, 21-6 (M)
1999—Chiefs, 31-28 (KC)
(RS Pts.—Vikings 153, Chiefs 121)
(PS Pts.—Chiefs 23, Vikings 7)
**Super Bowl IV*
***KANSAS CITY vs. **NEW ENGLAND**
RS: Chiefs lead series, 15-9-3
1960—Patriots, 42-14 (B)
Texans, 34-0 (D)
1961—Patriots, 18-17 (D)
Patriots, 28-21 (B)
1962—Texans, 42-28 (D)
Texans, 27-7 (B)
1963—Tie, 24-24 (B)
Chiefs, 35-3 (KC)
1964—Patriots, 24-7 (B)
Patriots, 31-24 (KC)
1965—Chiefs, 27-17 (KC)
Tie, 10-10 (B)
1966—Chiefs, 43-24 (B)
Tie, 27-27 (KC)
1967—Chiefs, 33-10 (B)
1968—Chiefs, 31-17 (KC)
1969—Chiefs, 31-0 (B)
1970—Chiefs, 23-10 (KC)
1973—Chiefs, 10-7 (NE)
1977—Patriots, 21-17 (NE)
1981—Patriots, 33-17 (NE)
1990—Chiefs, 37-7 (NE)
1992—Chiefs, 27-20 (KC)
1995—Chiefs, 31-26 (KC)
1998—Patriots, 40-10 (NE)
1999—Chiefs, 16-14 (KC)
2000—Patriots, 30-24 (NE)
(RS Pts.—Chiefs 659, Patriots 518)
**Franchise located in Dallas prior to 1963 and known as Texans*
***Franchise in Boston prior to 1971*
KANSAS CITY vs. NEW ORLEANS
RS: Chiefs lead series, 4-3
1972—Chiefs, 20-17 (NO)
1976—Saints, 27-17 (KC)
1982—Saints, 27-17 (NO)
1985—Chiefs, 47-27 (NO)
1991—Saints, 17-10 (KC)
1994—Chiefs, 30-17 (NO)
1997—Chiefs, 25-13 (KC)
(RS Pts.—Chiefs 166, Saints 145)
KANSAS CITY vs. N.Y. GIANTS
RS: Giants lead series, 7-2
1974—Giants, 33-27 (KC)
1978—Giants, 26-10 (NY)
1979—Giants, 21-17 (KC)
1983—Chiefs, 38-17 (KC)
1984—Giants, 28-27 (NY)
1988—Giants, 28-12 (NY)
1992—Giants, 35-21 (NY)
1995—Chiefs, 20-17 (KC) OT
1998—Giants, 28-7 (NY)
(RS Pts.—Giants 233, Chiefs 179)
***KANSAS CITY vs. **N.Y. JETS**
RS: Chiefs lead series, 14-13-1
PS: Series tied, 1-1
1960—Titans, 37-35 (D)
Titans, 41-35 (NY)
1961—Titans, 28-7 (NY)
Texans, 35-24 (D)
1962—Texans, 20-17 (D)
Texans, 52-31 (NY)
1963—Jets, 17-0 (NY)
Chiefs, 48-0 (KC)
1964—Jets, 27-14 (NY)
Chiefs, 24-7 (KC)
1965—Chiefs, 14-10 (NY)
Jets, 13-10 (KC)
1966—Chiefs, 32-24 (NY)
1967—Chiefs, 42-18 (KC)
Chiefs, 21-7 (NY)
1968—Jets, 20-19 (KC)
1969—Chiefs, 34-16 (NY)
***Chiefs, 13-6 (NY)
1971—Jets, 13-10 (NY)
1974—Chiefs, 24-16 (KC)
1975—Jets, 30-24 (KC)
1982—Chiefs, 37-13 (KC)
1984—Jets, 17-16 (KC)
Jets, 28-7 (NY)
1986—****Jets, 35-15 (NY)
1987—Jets, 16-9 (KC)
1988—Tie, 17-17 (NY)
Chiefs, 38-34 (KC)
1992—Chiefs, 23-7 (NY)
1998—Jets, 20-17 (KC)
(RS Pts.—Chiefs 664, Jets 548)

(PS Pts.—Jets 41, Chiefs 28)
*Franchise in Dallas prior to 1963 and known as Texans
**Jets known as Titans prior to 1963
***Inter-Divisional Playoff
****AFC First-Round Playoff

***KANSAS CITY vs. **OAKLAND**
RS: Chiefs lead series, 40-39-2
PS: Chiefs lead series, 2-1
1960—Texans, 34-16 (O)
Raiders, 20-19 (D)
1961—Texans, 42-35 (O)
Texans, 43-11 (D)
1962—Texans, 26-16 (O)
Texans, 35-7 (D)
1963—Raiders, 10-7 (O)
Raiders, 22-7 (KC)
1964—Chiefs, 21-9 (O)
Chiefs, 42-7 (KC)
1965—Raiders, 37-10 (O)
Chiefs, 14-7 (KC)
1966—Chiefs, 32-10 (O)
Raiders, 34-13 (KC)
1967—Raiders, 23-21 (O)
Raiders, 44-22 (KC)
1968—Chiefs, 24-10 (KC)
Raiders, 38-21 (O)
***Raiders, 41-6 (O)
1969—Raiders, 27-24 (KC)
Raiders, 10-6 (O)
****Chiefs, 17-7 (O)
1970—Tie, 17-17 (KC)
Raiders, 20-6 (O)
1971—Tie, 20-20 (O)
Chiefs, 16-14 (KC)
1972—Chiefs, 27-14 (KC)
Raiders, 26-3 (O)
1973—Chiefs, 16-3 (KC)
Raiders, 37-7 (O)
1974—Raiders, 27-7 (O)
Raiders, 7-6 (KC)
1975—Chiefs, 42-10 (KC)
Raiders, 28-20 (O)
1976—Raiders, 24-21 (KC)
Raiders, 21-10 (O)
1977—Raiders, 37-28 (KC)
Raiders, 21-20 (O)
1978—Raiders, 28-6 (O)
Raiders, 20-10 (KC)
1979—Chiefs, 35-7 (KC)
Chiefs, 24-21 (O)
1980—Raiders, 27-14 (KC)
Chiefs, 31-17 (O)
1981—Chiefs, 27-0 (KC)
Chiefs, 28-17 (O)
1982—Raiders, 21-16 (KC)
1983—Raiders, 21-20 (LA)
Raiders, 28-20 (KC)
1984—Raiders, 22-20 (KC)
Raiders, 17-7 (LA)
1985—Chiefs, 36-20 (KC)
Raiders, 19-10 (LA)
1986—Raiders, 24-17 (KC)
Chiefs, 20-17 (LA)
1987—Raiders, 35-17 (LA)
Chiefs, 16-10 (KC)
1988—Raiders, 27-17 (KC)
Raiders, 17-10 (LA)
1989—Chiefs, 24-19 (KC)
Raiders, 20-14 (LA)
1990—Chiefs, 9-7 (KC)
Chiefs, 27-24 (LA)
1991—Chiefs, 24-21 (KC)
Chiefs, 27-21 (LA)
*****Chiefs, 10-6 (KC)
1992—Chiefs, 27-7 (KC)
Raiders, 28-7 (LA)
1993—Chiefs, 24-9 (KC)
Chiefs, 31-20 (LA)
1994—Chiefs, 13-3 (KC)
Chiefs, 19-9 (LA)
1995—Chiefs, 23-17 (KC) OT
Chiefs, 29-23 (O)
1996—Chiefs, 19-3 (KC)
Raiders, 26-7 (O)
1997—Chiefs, 28-27 (O)
Chiefs, 30-0 (KC)
1998—Chiefs, 28-8 (KC)
Chiefs, 31-24 (O)
1999—Chiefs, 37-34 (O)
Raiders, 41-38 (KC) OT
2000—Raiders, 20-17 (KC)
Raiders, 49-31 (O)
(RS Pts.—Chiefs 1,694, Raiders 1,594)
(PS Pts.—Raiders 54, Chiefs 33)
*Franchise in Dallas prior to 1963 and known as Texans
**Franchise in Los Angeles from 1982-1994
***Division Playoff
****AFL Championship
*****AFC First-Round Playoff

KANSAS CITY vs. PHILADELPHIA
RS: Chiefs lead series, 2-1
1972—Eagles, 21-20 (KC)
1992—Chiefs, 24-17 (KC)
1998—Chiefs, 24-21 (P)
(RS Pts.—Chiefs 68, Eagles 59)

KANSAS CITY vs. PITTSBURGH
RS: Steelers lead series, 15-7
PS: Chiefs lead series, 1-0
1970—Chiefs, 31-14 (P)
1971—Chiefs, 38-16 (KC)
1972—Steelers, 16-7 (P)
1974—Steelers, 34-24 (KC)
1975—Steelers, 28-3 (P)
1976—Steelers, 45-0 (KC)
1978—Steelers, 27-24 (P)
1979—Steelers, 30-3 (KC)
1980—Steelers, 21-16 (P)
1981—Chiefs, 37-33 (P)
1982—Steelers, 35-14 (P)
1984—Chiefs, 37-27 (P)
1985—Steelers, 36-28 (KC)
1986—Chiefs, 24-19 (P)
1987—Steelers, 17-16 (KC)
1988—Steelers, 16-10 (P)
1989—Steelers, 23-17 (P)
1992—Steelers, 27-3 (KC)
1993—*Chiefs, 27-24 (KC) OT
1996—Steelers, 17-7 (KC)
1997—Chiefs, 13-10 (KC)
1998—Steelers, 20-13 (KC)
1999—Chiefs, 35-19 (KC)
(RS Pts.—Steelers 530, Chiefs 400)
(PS Pts.—Chiefs 27, Steelers 24)
*AFC First-Round Playoff

KANSAS CITY vs. *ST. LOUIS
RS: Rams lead series, 4-3
1973—Rams, 23-13 (KC)
1982—Rams, 20-14 (LA)
1985—Rams, 16-0 (KC)
1991—Chiefs, 27-20 (LA)
1994—Rams, 16-0 (KC)
1997—Chiefs, 28-20 (StL)
2000—Chiefs, 54-34 (KC)
(RS Pts.—Rams 149, Chiefs 136)
*Franchise in Los Angeles prior to 1995

***KANSAS CITY vs. **SAN DIEGO**
RS: Chiefs lead series, 42-38-1
PS: Chargers lead series, 1-0
1960—Chargers, 21-20 (LA)
Texans, 17-0 (D)
1961—Chargers, 26-10 (D)
Chargers, 24-14 (SD)
1962—Chargers, 32-28 (SD)
Texans, 26-17 (D)
1963—Chargers, 24-10 (SD)
Chargers, 38-17 (KC)
1964—Chargers, 28-14 (KC)
Chiefs, 49-6 (SD)
1965—Tie, 10-10 (SD)
Chiefs, 31-7 (KC)
1966—Chiefs, 24-14 (KC)
Chiefs, 27-17 (SD)
1967—Chargers, 45-31 (SD)
Chargers, 17-16 (KC)
1968—Chiefs, 27-20 (KC)
Chiefs, 40-3 (SD)
1969—Chiefs, 27-9 (SD)
Chiefs, 27-3 (KC)
1970—Chiefs, 26-14 (KC)
Chargers, 31-13 (SD)
1971—Chargers, 21-14 (SD)
Chiefs, 31-10 (KC)
1972—Chiefs, 26-14 (SD)
Chargers, 27-17 (KC)
1973—Chiefs, 19-0 (SD)
Chiefs, 33-6 (KC)
1974—Chiefs, 24-14 (SD)
Chargers, 14-7 (KC)
1975—Chiefs, 12-10 (SD)
Chargers, 28-20 (KC)
1976—Chargers, 30-16 (KC)
Chiefs, 23-20 (SD)
1977—Chargers, 23-7 (KC)
Chiefs, 21-16 (SD)
1978—Chargers, 29-23 (SD) OT
Chiefs, 23-0 (KC)
1979—Chargers, 20-14 (KC)
Chargers, 28-7 (SD)
1980—Chargers, 24-7 (KC)
Chargers, 20-7 (SD)
1981—Chargers, 42-31 (KC)
Chargers, 22-20 (SD)
1982—Chiefs, 19-12 (KC)
1983—Chargers, 17-14 (KC)
Chargers, 41-38 (SD)
1984—Chiefs, 31-13 (KC)
Chiefs, 42-21 (SD)
1985—Chargers, 31-20 (SD)
Chiefs, 38-34 (KC)
1986—Chiefs, 42-41 (KC)
Chiefs, 24-23 (SD)
1987—Chiefs, 20-13 (KC)
Chargers, 42-21 (SD)
1988—Chargers, 24-23 (KC)
Chargers, 24-13 (SD)
1989—Chargers, 21-6 (SD)
Chargers, 20-13 (KC)
1990—Chiefs, 27-10 (KC)
Chiefs, 24-21 (SD)
1991—Chiefs, 14-13 (SD)
Chiefs, 20-17 (KC) OT
1992—Chiefs, 24-10 (SD)
Chiefs, 16-14 (KC)
***Chargers, 17-0 (SD)
1993—Chiefs, 17-14 (SD)
Chiefs, 28-24 (KC)
1994—Chargers, 20-6 (SD)
Chargers, 14-13 (KC)
1995—Chiefs, 29-23 (KC) OT
Chiefs, 22-7 (SD)
1996—Chargers, 22-19 (SD)
Chargers, 28-14 (KC)
1997—Chiefs, 31-3 (KC)
Chiefs, 29-7 (SD)
1998—Chiefs, 23-7 (KC)
Chargers, 38-37 (SD)
1999—Chargers, 21-14 (SD)
Chiefs, 34-0 (KC)
2000—Chiefs, 42-10 (KC)
Chargers, 17-16 (SD)
(RS Pts.—Chiefs 1,769, Chargers 1,541)
(PS Pts.—Chargers 17, Chiefs 0)
*Franchise in Dallas prior to 1963 and known as Texans
**Franchise in Los Angeles prior to 1961
***AFC First-Round Playoff

KANSAS CITY vs. SAN FRANCISCO
RS: 49ers lead series, 5-3
1971—Chiefs, 26-17 (SF)
1975—49ers, 20-3 (KC)
1982—49ers, 26-13 (KC)
1985—49ers, 31-3 (SF)
1991—49ers, 28-14 (SF)
1994—Chiefs, 24-17 (KC)
1997—Chiefs, 44-9 (KC)
2000—49ers, 21-7 (SF)
(PS Pts.—49ers 169, Chiefs 134)

KANSAS CITY vs. SEATTLE
RS: Chiefs lead series, 29-16
1977—Seahawks, 34-31 (KC)
1978—Seahawks, 13-10 (KC)
Seahawks, 23-19 (S)
1979—Chiefs, 24-6 (S)
Chiefs, 37-21 (KC)
1980—Seahawks, 17-16 (KC)
Chiefs, 31-30 (S)
1981—Chiefs, 20-14 (S)
Chiefs, 40-13 (KC)
1983—Chiefs, 17-13 (KC)
Seahawks, 51-48 (S) OT
1984—Seahawks, 45-0 (S)
Chiefs, 34-7 (KC)
1985—Chiefs, 28-7 (KC)
Seahawks, 24-6 (S)
1986—Seahawks, 23-17 (S)
Chiefs, 27-7 (KC)
1987—Seahawks, 43-14 (S)
Chiefs, 41-20 (KC)
1988—Seahawks, 31-10 (S)
Chiefs, 27-24 (KC)
1989—Chiefs, 20-16 (S)
Chiefs, 20-10 (KC)
1990—Seahawks, 19-7 (S)
Seahawks, 17-16 (KC)
1991—Chiefs, 20-13 (KC)
Chiefs, 19-6 (S)
1992—Chiefs, 26-7 (KC)
Chiefs, 24-14 (S)
1993—Chiefs, 31-16 (S)
Chiefs, 34-24 (KC)
1994—Chiefs, 38-23 (KC)
Seahawks, 10-9 (S)
1995—Chiefs, 34-10 (S)
Chiefs, 26-3 (KC)
1996—Chiefs, 35-17 (S)
Chiefs, 34-16 (KC)
1997—Chiefs, 20-17 (KC) OT
Chiefs, 19-14 (S)
1998—Chiefs, 17-6 (KC)
Seahawks, 24-12 (S)
1999—Seahawks, 31-19 (KC)
Seahawks, 23-14 (S)
2000—Chiefs, 24-17 (KC)
Chiefs, 24-19 (S)
(RS Pts.—Chiefs 1,039, Seahawks 838)

KANSAS CITY vs. TAMPA BAY
RS: Chiefs lead series, 5-3
1976—Chiefs, 28-19 (TB)
1978—Buccaneers, 30-13 (KC)
1979—Buccaneers, 3-0 (TB)
1981—Chiefs, 19-10 (KC)
1984—Chiefs, 24-20 (KC)
1986—Chiefs, 27-20 (KC)
1993—Chiefs, 27-3 (TB)
1999—Buccaneers, 17-10 (TB)
(RS Pts.—Chiefs 148, Buccaneers 122)

***KANSAS CITY vs. **TENNESSEE**
RS: Chiefs lead series, 24-18
PS: Chiefs lead series, 2-0
1960—Oilers, 20-10 (H)
Texans, 24-0 (D)
1961—Texans, 26-21 (D)
Oilers, 38-7 (H)
1962—Texans, 31-7 (H)
Oilers, 14-6 (D)
***Texans, 20-17 (H) OT
1963—Chiefs, 28-7 (KC)
Oilers, 28-7 (H)
1964—Chiefs, 28-7 (KC)
Chiefs, 28-19 (H)
1965—Chiefs, 52-21 (KC)
Oilers, 38-36 (H)
1966—Chiefs, 48-23 (KC)
1967—Chiefs, 25-20 (H)
Oilers, 24-19 (KC)
1968—Chiefs, 26-21 (H)
Chiefs, 24-10 (KC)
1969—Chiefs, 24-0 (KC)
1970—Chiefs, 24-9 (KC)

1971—Chiefs, 20-16 (H)
1973—Chiefs, 38-14 (KC)
1974—Chiefs, 17-7 (H)
1975—Oilers, 17-13 (KC)
1977—Oilers, 34-20 (H)
1978—Oilers, 20-17 (KC)
1979—Oilers, 20-6 (H)
1980—Chiefs, 21-20 (KC)
1981—Chiefs, 23-10 (KC)
1983—Chiefs, 13-10 (H) OT
1984—Oilers, 17-16 (KC)
1985—Oilers, 23-20 (H)
1986—Chiefs, 27-13 (KC)
1988—Oilers, 7-6 (H)
1989—Chiefs, 34-0 (KC)
1990—Oilers, 27-10 (KC)
1991—Oilers, 17-7 (H)
1992—Oilers, 23-20 (H) OT
1993—Oilers, 30-0 (H)
****Chiefs, 28-20 (H)
1994—Chiefs, 31-9 (KC)
1995—Chiefs, 20-13 (KC)
1996—Chiefs, 20-19 (H)
2000—Titans, 17-14 (T) OT
(RS Pts.—Chiefs 886, Titans 710)
(PS Pts.—Chiefs 48, Titans 37)
Franchise in Dallas prior to 1963 and known as Texans
**Franchise in Houston prior to 1997; known as Oilers prior to 1999*
***AFL Championship*
****AFC Divisional Playoff*

KANSAS CITY vs. WASHINGTON
RS: Chiefs lead series, 4-1
1971—Chiefs, 27-20 (KC)
1976—Chiefs, 33-30 (W)
1983—Redskins, 27-12 (W)
1992—Chiefs, 35-16 (KC)
1995—Chiefs, 24-3 (KC)
(RS Pts.—Chiefs 131, Redskins 96)

MIAMI vs. ARIZONA
RS: Dolphins lead series, 8-0;
See Arizona vs. Miami

MIAMI vs. ATLANTA
RS: Dolphins lead series, 6-2;
See Atlanta vs. Miami

MIAMI vs. BALTIMORE
RS: Dolphins lead series, 2-0;
See Baltimore vs. Miami

MIAMI vs. BUFFALO
RS: Dolphins lead series, 44-25-1
PS: Bills lead series, 3-1;
See Buffalo vs. Miami

MIAMI vs. CAROLINA
RS: Dolphins lead series, 1-0;
See Carolina vs. Miami

MIAMI vs. CHICAGO
RS: Dolphins lead series, 6-3;
See Chicago vs. Miami

MIAMI vs. CINCINNATI
RS: Dolphins lead series, 12-3
PS: Dolphins lead series, 1-0;
See Cincinnati vs. Miami

MIAMI vs. CLEVELAND
RS: Dolphins lead series, 6-4
PS: Dolphins lead series, 2-0;
See Cleveland vs. Miami

MIAMI vs. DALLAS
RS: Dolphins lead series, 6-3
PS: Cowboys lead series, 1-0;
See Dallas vs. Miami

MIAMI vs. DENVER
RS: Dolphins lead series, 7-2-1
PS: Broncos lead series, 1-0;
See Denver vs. Miami

MIAMI vs. DETROIT
RS: Dolphins lead series, 5-2;
See Detroit vs. Miami

MIAMI vs. GREEN BAY
RS: Dolphins lead series, 9-1;
See Green Bay vs. Miami

MIAMI vs. INDIANAPOLIS
RS: Dolphins lead series, 41-21
PS: Dolphins lead series, 2-0;
See Indianapolis vs. Miami

MIAMI vs. JACKSONVILLE
RS: Jaguars lead series, 1-0
PS: Jaguars lead series, 1-0;
See Jacksonville vs. Miami

MIAMI vs. KANSAS CITY
RS: Series tied, 10-10
PS: Dolphins lead series, 3-0;
See Kansas City vs. Miami

MIAMI vs. MINNESOTA
RS: Dolphins lead series, 4-3
PS: Dolphins lead series, 1-0
1972—Dolphins, 16-14 (Minn)
1973—*Dolphins, 24-7 (Houston)
1976—Vikings, 29-7 (Mia)
1979—Dolphins, 27-12 (Minn)
1982—Dolphins, 22-14 (Mia)
1988—Dolphins, 24-7 (Mia)
1994—Vikings, 38-35 (Minn)
2000—Vikings, 13-7 (Minn)
(RS Pts.—Dolphins 138, Vikings 127)
(PS Pts.—Dolphins 24, Vikings 7)
Super Bowl VIII

MIAMI vs. *NEW ENGLAND
RS: Dolphins lead series, 42-26
PS: Patriots lead series, 2-1
1966—Patriots, 20-14 (M)
1967—Patriots, 41-10 (B)
Dolphins, 41-32 (M)
1968—Dolphins, 34-10 (B)
Dolphins, 38-7 (M)
1969—Dolphins, 17-16 (B)
Patriots, 38-23 (Tampa)
1970—Patriots, 27-14 (B)
Dolphins, 37-20 (M)
1971—Dolphins, 41-3 (M)
Patriots, 34-13 (NE)
1972—Dolphins, 52-0 (M)
Dolphins, 37-21 (NE)
1973—Dolphins, 44-23 (M)
Dolphins, 30-14 (NE)
1974—Patriots, 34-24 (NE)
Dolphins, 34-27 (M)
1975—Dolphins, 22-14 (NE)
Dolphins, 20-7 (M)
1976—Patriots, 30-14 (NE)
Dolphins, 10-3 (M)
1977—Dolphins, 17-5 (M)
Patriots, 14-10 (NE)
1978—Patriots, 33-24 (NE)
Dolphins, 23-3 (M)
1979—Patriots, 28-13 (NE)
Dolphins, 39-24 (M)
1980—Patriots, 34-0 (NE)
Dolphins, 16-13 (M) OT
1981—Dolphins, 30-27 (NE) OT
Dolphins, 24-14 (M)
1982—Patriots, 3-0 (NE)
**Dolphins, 28-13 (M)
1983—Dolphins, 34-24 (M)
Patriots, 17-6 (NE)
1984—Dolphins, 28-7 (M)
Dolphins, 44-24 (NE)
1985—Patriots, 17-13 (NE)
Dolphins, 30-27 (M)
***Patriots, 31-14 (M)
1986—Patriots, 34-7 (NE)
Patriots, 34-27 (M)
1987—Patriots, 28-21 (NE)
Patriots, 24-10 (M)
1988—Patriots, 21-10 (NE)
Patriots, 6-3 (M)
1989—Dolphins, 24-10 (NE)
Dolphins, 31-10 (M)
1990—Dolphins, 27-24 (NE)
Dolphins, 17-10 (M)
1991—Dolphins, 20-10 (NE)
Dolphins, 30-20 (M)
1992—Dolphins, 38-17 (M)
Dolphins, 16-13 (NE) OT
1993—Dolphins, 17-13 (M)
Patriots, 33-27 (NE) OT
1994—Dolphins, 39-35 (M)
Dolphins, 23-3 (NE)
1995—Dolphins, 20-3 (NE)
Patriots, 34-17 (M)
1996—Dolphins, 24-10 (M)
Patriots, 42-23 (NE)
1997—Patriots, 27-24 (NE)
Patriots, 14-12 (M)
**Patriots, 17-3 (NE)
1998—Dolphins, 12-9 (M) OT
Patriots, 26-23 (NE)
1999—Dolphins, 31-30 (NE)
Dolphins, 27-17 (M)
2000—Dolphins, 10-3 (M)
Dolphins, 27-24 (NE)
(RS Pts.—Dolphins 1,557, Patriots 1,319)
(PS Pts.—Patriots 61, Dolphins 45)
Franchise in Boston prior to 1971
**AFC First-Round Playoff*
***AFC Championship*

MIAMI vs. NEW ORLEANS
RS: Dolphins lead series, 5-3
1970—Dolphins, 21-10 (M)
1974—Dolphins, 21-0 (NO)
1980—Dolphins, 21-16 (M)
1983—Saints, 17-7 (NO)
1986—Dolphins, 31-27 (NO)
1992—Saints, 24-13 (NO)
1995—Saints, 33-30 (NO)
1998—Dolphins, 30-10 (M)
(RS Pts.—Dolphins 174, Saints 137)

MIAMI vs. N.Y. GIANTS
RS: Giants lead series, 3-1
1972—Dolphins, 23-13 (NY)
1990—Giants, 20-3 (NY)
1993—Giants, 19-14 (M)
1996—Giants, 17-7 (M)
(RS Pts.—Giants 69, Dolphins 47)

MIAMI vs. N.Y. JETS
RS: Jets lead series, 35-34-1
PS: Dolphins lead series, 1-0
1966—Jets, 19-14 (M)
Jets, 30-13 (NY)
1967—Jets, 29-7 (NY)
Jets, 33-14 (M)
1968—Jets, 35-17 (NY)
Jets, 31-7 (M)
1969—Jets, 34-31 (NY)
Jets, 27-9 (M)
1970—Dolphins, 20-6 (NY)
Dolphins, 16-10 (M)
1971—Jets, 14-10 (M)
Dolphins, 30-14 (NY)
1972—Dolphins, 27-17 (NY)
Dolphins, 28-24 (M)
1973—Dolphins, 31-3 (M)
Dolphins, 24-14 (NY)
1974—Dolphins, 21-17 (M)
Jets, 17-14 (NY)
1975—Dolphins, 43-0 (NY)
Dolphins, 27-7 (M)
1976—Dolphins, 16-0 (M)
Dolphins, 27-7 (NY)
1977—Dolphins, 21-17 (M)
Dolphins, 14-10 (NY)
1978—Jets, 33-20 (NY)
Jets, 24-13 (M)
1979—Jets, 33-27 (NY)
Jets, 27-24 (M)
1980—Jets, 17-14 (NY)
Jets, 24-17 (M)
1981—Tie, 28-28 (M) OT
Jets, 16-15 (NY)
1982—Dolphins, 45-28 (NY)
Dolphins, 20-19 (M)
*Dolphins, 14-0 (M)
1983—Dolphins, 32-14 (NY)
Dolphins, 34-14 (M)
1984—Dolphins, 31-17 (NY)
Dolphins, 28-17 (M)
1985—Jets, 23-7 (NY)
Dolphins, 21-17 (M)
1986—Jets, 51-45 (NY) OT
Dolphins, 45-3 (M)
1987—Jets, 37-31 (NY) OT
Dolphins, 37-28 (M)
1988—Jets, 44-30 (M)
Jets, 38-34 (NY)
1989—Jets, 40-33 (M)
Dolphins, 31-23 (NY)
1990—Dolphins, 20-16 (M)
Dolphins, 17-3 (NY)
1991—Jets, 41-23 (NY)
Jets, 23-20 (M) OT
1992—Jets, 26-14 (NY)
Dolphins, 19-17 (M)
1993—Jets, 24-14 (M)
Jets, 27-10 (NY)
1994—Dolphins, 28-14 (M)
Dolphins, 28-24 (NY)
1995—Dolphins, 52-14 (M)
Jets, 17-16 (NY)
1996—Dolphins, 36-27 (M)
Dolphins, 31-28 (NY)
1997—Dolphins, 31-20 (NY)
Dolphins, 24-17 (M)
1998—Jets, 20-9 (NY)
Jets, 21-16 (M)
1999—Jets, 28-20 (NY)
Jets, 38-31 (M)
2000—Jets, 40-37 (NY) OT
Jets, 20-3 (M)
(RS Pts.—Dolphins 1,642, Jets 1,535)
(PS Pts.—Dolphins 14, Jets 0)
AFC Championship

MIAMI vs. *OAKLAND
RS: Raiders lead series, 15-8-1
PS: Raiders lead series, 3-1
1966—Raiders, 23-14 (M)
Raiders, 21-10 (O)
1967—Raiders, 31-17 (O)
1968—Raiders, 47-21 (M)
1969—Raiders, 20-17 (O)
Tie, 20-20 (M)
1970—Dolphins, 20-13 (M)
**Raiders, 21-14 (O)
1973—Raiders, 12-7 (O)
***Dolphins, 27-10 (M)
1974—**Raiders, 28-26 (O)
1975—Raiders, 31-21 (M)
1978—Dolphins, 23-6 (M)
1979—Raiders, 13-3 (O)
1980—Raiders, 16-10 (O)
1981—Raiders, 33-17 (M)
1983—Raiders, 27-14 (LA)
1984—Raiders, 45-34 (M)
1986—Raiders, 30-28 (M)
1988—Dolphins, 24-14 (LA)
1990—Raiders, 13-10 (M)
1992—Dolphins, 20-7 (M)
1994—Dolphins, 20-17 (M) OT
1996—Raiders, 17-7 (O)
1997—Dolphins, 34-16 (O)
1998—Dolphins, 27-17 (O)
1999—Dolphins, 16-9 (O)
2000—**Raiders, 27-0 (O)
(RS Pts.—Raiders 498, Dolphins 434)
(PS Pts.—Raiders 86, Dolphins 67)
Franchise in Los Angeles from 1982-1994
**AFC Divisional Playoff*
***AFC Championship*

MIAMI vs. PHILADELPHIA
RS: Dolphins lead series, 7-3
1970—Eagles, 24-17 (P)
1975—Dolphins, 24-16 (M)
1978—Eagles, 17-3 (P)
1981—Dolphins, 13-10 (M)
1984—Dolphins, 24-23 (M)
1987—Dolphins, 28-10 (P)
1990—Dolphins, 23-20 (M) OT
1993—Dolphins, 19-14 (P)
1996—Eagles, 35-28 (P)
1999—Dolphins, 16-13 (M)

(RS Pts.—Dolphins 195, Eagles 182)

MIAMI vs. PITTSBURGH
RS: Dolphins lead series, 9-7
PS: Dolphins lead series, 2-1
1971—Dolphins, 24-21 (M)
1972—*Dolphins, 21-17 (P)
1973—Dolphins, 30-26 (M)
1976—Steelers, 14-3 (P)
1979—**Steelers, 34-14 (P)
1980—Steelers, 23-10 (P)
1981—Dolphins, 30-10 (M)
1984—Dolphins, 31-7 (P)
*Dolphins, 45-28 (M)
1985—Dolphins, 24-20 (M)
1987—Dolphins, 35-24 (M)
1988—Steelers, 40-24 (P)
1989—Steelers, 34-14 (M)
1990—Dolphins, 28-6 (P)
1993—Steelers, 21-20 (M)
1994—Steelers, 16-13 (P) OT
1995—Dolphins, 23-10 (M)
1996—Steelers, 24-17 (M)
1998—Dolphins, 21-0 (M)
(RS Pts.—Dolphins 347, Steelers 296)
(PS Pts.—Dolphins 80, Steelers 79)
AFC Championship
***AFC Divisional Playoff*

MIAMI vs. *ST. LOUIS
RS: Dolphins lead series, 7-1
1971—Dolphins, 20-14 (LA)
1976—Rams, 31-28 (M)
1980—Dolphins, 35-14 (LA)
1983—Dolphins, 30-14 (M)
1986—Dolphins, 37-31 (LA) OT
1992—Dolphins, 26-10 (M)
1995—Dolphins, 41-22 (StL)
1998—Dolphins, 14-0 (M)
(RS Pts.—Dolphins 231, Rams 136)
Franchise in Los Angeles prior to 1995

MIAMI vs. SAN DIEGO
RS: Chargers lead series, 10-8
PS: Series tied, 2-2
1966—Chargers, 44-10 (SD)
1967—Chargers, 24-0 (SD)
Dolphins, 41-24 (M)
1968—Chargers, 34-28 (SD)
1969—Chargers, 21-14 (M)
1972—Dolphins, 24-10 (M)
1974—Dolphins, 28-21 (SD)
1977—Chargers, 14-13 (M)
1978—Dolphins, 28-21 (SD)
1980—Chargers, 27-24 (M) OT
1981—*Chargers, 41-38 (M) OT
1982—**Dolphins, 34-13 (M)
1984—Chargers, 34-28 (SD) OT
1986—Chargers, 50-28 (SD)
1988—Dolphins, 31-28 (M)
1991—Chargers, 38-30 (SD)
1992—*Dolphins, 31-0 (M)
1993—Chargers, 45-20 (SD)
1994—*Chargers, 22-21 (SD)
1995—Dolphins, 24-14 (SD)
1999—Dolphins, 12-9 (M)
2000—Dolphins, 17-7 (SD)
(RS Pts.—Chargers 465, Dolphins 400)
(PS Pts.—Dolphins 124, Chargers 76)
AFC Divisional Playoff
***AFC Second-Round Playoff*

MIAMI vs. SAN FRANCISCO
RS: Dolphins lead series, 4-3
PS: 49ers lead series, 1-0
1973—Dolphins, 21-13 (M)
1977—Dolphins, 19-15 (SF)
1980—Dolphins, 17-13 (M)
1983—Dolphins, 20-17 (SF)
1984—*49ers, 38-16 (Stanford)
1986—49ers, 31-16 (M)
1992—49ers, 27-3 (SF)
1995—49ers, 44-20 (M)
(RS Pts.—49ers 160, Dolphins 116)
(PS Pts.—49ers 38, Dolphins 16)
Super Bowl XIX

MIAMI vs. SEATTLE
RS: Dolphins lead series, 5-2
PS: Dolphins lead series, 2-1
1977—Dolphins, 31-13 (M)
1979—Dolphins, 19-10 (M)
1983—*Seahawks, 27-20 (M)
1984—*Dolphins, 31-10 (M)
1987—Seahawks, 24-20 (S)
1990—Dolphins, 24-17 (M)
1992—Dolphins, 19-17 (S)
1996—Seahawks, 22-15 (M)
1999—**Dolphins, 20-17 (S)
2000—Dolphins, 23-0 (M)
(RS Pts.—Dolphins 151, Seahawks 103)
(PS Pts.—Dolphins 71, Seahawks 54)
AFC Divisional Playoff
***AFC First-Round Playoff*

MIAMI vs. TAMPA BAY
RS: Dolphins lead series, 4-3
1976—Dolphins, 23-20 (TB)
1982—Buccaneers, 23-17 (TB)
1985—Dolphins, 41-38 (M)
1988—Dolphins, 17-14 (TB)
1991—Dolphins, 33-14 (M)
1997—Buccaneers, 31-21 (TB)
2000—Buccaneers, 16-13 (M)
(RS Pts.—Dolphins 165, Buccaneers 156)

MIAMI vs. *TENNESSEE
RS: Dolphins lead series, 14-11
PS: Titans lead series, 1-0
1966—Dolphins, 20-13 (H)
Dolphins, 29-28 (M)
1967—Oilers, 17-14 (H)
Oilers, 41-10 (M)
1968—Oilers, 24-10 (M)
Dolphins, 24-7 (H)
1969—Oilers, 22-10 (H)
Oilers, 32-7 (M)
1970—Dolphins, 20-10 (H)
1972—Dolphins, 34-13 (M)
1975—Oilers, 20-19 (H)
1977—Dolphins, 27-7 (M)
1978—Oilers, 35-30 (H)
**Oilers, 17-9 (M)
1979—Oilers, 9-6 (M)
1981—Dolphins, 16-10 (H)
1983—Dolphins, 24-17 (H)
1984—Dolphins, 28-10 (M)
1985—Oilers, 26-23 (H)
1986—Dolphins, 28-7 (M)
1989—Oilers, 39-7 (H)
1991—Oilers, 17-13 (M)
1992—Dolphins, 19-16 (M)
1996—Dolphins, 23-20 (H)
1997—Dolphins, 16-13 (M) OT
1999—Dolphins, 17-0 (M)
(RS Pts.—Dolphins 474, Titans 453)
(PS Pts.—Titans 17, Dolphins 9)
Franchise in Houston prior to 1997; known as Oilers prior to 1999
***AFC First-Round Playoff*

MIAMI vs. WASHINGTON
RS: Dolphins lead series, 5-3
PS: Series tied, 1-1
1972—*Dolphins, 14-7 (Los Angeles)
1974—Redskins, 20-17 (W)
1978—Dolphins, 16-0 (W)
1981—Dolphins, 13-10 (M)
1982—**Redskins, 27-17 (Pasadena)
1984—Dolphins, 35-17 (W)
1987—Dolphins, 23-21 (M)
1990—Redskins, 42-20 (W)
1993—Dolphins, 17-10 (M)
1999—Redskins, 21-10 (W)
(RS Pts.—Dolphins 151, Redskins 141)
(PS Pts.—Redskins 34, Dolphins 31)
Super Bowl VII
***Super Bowl XVII*

MINNESOTA vs. ARIZONA
RS: Series tied, 8-8
PS: Vikings lead series, 2-0;
See Arizona vs. Minnesota

MINNESOTA vs. ATLANTA
RS: Vikings lead series, 13-6
PS: Series tied, 1-1;
See Atlanta vs. Minnesota

MINNESOTA vs. BALTIMORE
RS: Vikings lead series, 1-0;
See Baltimore vs. Minnesota

MINNESOTA vs. BUFFALO
RS: Vikings lead series, 7-2;
See Buffalo vs. Minnesota

MINNESOTA vs. CAROLINA
RS: Vikings lead series, 3-0;
See Carolina vs. Minnesota

MINNESOTA vs. CHICAGO
RS: Vikings lead series, 44-33-2
PS: Bears lead series, 1-0;
See Chicago vs. Minnesota

MINNESOTA vs. CINCINNATI
RS: Vikings lead series, 5-4;
See Cincinnati vs. Minnesota

MINNESOTA vs. CLEVELAND
RS: Vikings lead series, 8-3
PS: Vikings lead series, 1-0;
See Cleveland vs. Minnesota

MINNESOTA vs. DALLAS
RS: Series tied, 9-9
PS: Cowboys lead series, 4-2;
See Dallas vs. Minnesota

MINNESOTA vs. DENVER
RS: Vikings lead series, 6-4;
See Denver vs. Minnesota

MINNESOTA vs. DETROIT
RS: Vikings lead series, 49-28-2;
See Detroit vs. Minnesota

MINNESOTA vs. GREEN BAY
RS: Series tied, 39-39-1;
See Green Bay vs. Minnesota

MINNESOTA vs. INDIANAPOLIS
RS: Colts lead series, 12-7-1
PS: Colts lead series, 1-0;
See Indianapolis vs. Minnesota

MINNESOTA vs. JACKSONVILLE
RS: Vikings lead series, 1-0;
See Jacksonville vs. Minnesota

MINNESOTA vs. KANSAS CITY
RS: Chiefs lead series, 4-3
PS: Chiefs lead series, 1-0;
See Kansas City vs. Minnesota

MINNESOTA vs. MIAMI
RS: Dolphins lead series, 4-3
PS: Dolphins lead series, 1-0;
See Miami vs. Minnesota

MINNESOTA vs. *NEW ENGLAND
RS: Series tied, 4-4
1970—Vikings, 35-14 (B)
1974—Patriots, 17-14 (M)
1979—Patriots, 27-23 (NE)
1988—Vikings, 36-6 (M)
1991—Patriots, 26-23 (NE) OT
1994—Patriots, 26-20 (NE) OT
1997—Vikings, 23-18 (M)
2000—Vikings, 21-13 (NE)
(RS Pts.—Vikings 195, Patriots 147)
Franchise in Boston prior to 1971

MINNESOTA vs. NEW ORLEANS
RS: Vikings lead series, 14-6
PS: Vikings lead series, 2-0
1968—Saints, 20-17 (NO)
1970—Vikings, 26-0 (M)
1971—Vikings, 23-10 (NO)
1972—Vikings, 37-6 (M)
1974—Vikings, 29-9 (M)
1975—Vikings, 20-7 (NO)
1976—Vikings, 40-9 (NO)
1978—Saints, 31-24 (NO)
1980—Vikings, 23-20 (NO)
1981—Vikings, 20-10 (M)
1983—Saints, 17-16 (NO)
1985—Saints, 30-23 (M)
1986—Vikings, 33-17 (M)
1987—*Vikings, 44-10 (NO)
1988—Vikings, 45-3 (M)
1990—Vikings, 32-3 (M)
1991—Saints, 26-0 (NO)
1993—Saints, 17-14 (M)
1994—Vikings, 21-20 (M)
1995—Vikings, 43-24 (M)
1998—Vikings, 31-24 (M)
2000—**Vikings, 34-16 (M)
(RS Pts.—Vikings 517, Saints 303)
(PS Pts.—Vikings 78, Saints 26)
NFC First-Round Playoff
***NFC Divisional Playoff*

MINNESOTA vs. N.Y. GIANTS
RS: Vikings lead series, 8-5
PS: Giants lead series, 2-1
1964—Vikings, 30-21 (NY)
1965—Vikings, 40-14 (M)
1967—Vikings, 27-24 (M)
1969—Giants, 24-23 (NY)
1971—Vikings, 17-10 (NY)
1973—Vikings, 31-7 (New Haven)
1976—Vikings, 24-7 (M)
1986—Giants, 22-20 (M)
1989—Giants, 24-14 (NY)
1990—Giants, 23-15 (NY)
1993—*Giants, 17-10 (NY)
1994—Vikings, 27-10 (NY)
1996—Giants, 15-10 (NY)
1997—*Vikings, 23-22 (NY)
1999—Vikings, 34-17 (NY)
2000—**Giants, 41-0 (NY)
(RS Pts.—Vikings 312, Giants 218)
(PS Pts.—Giants 80, Vikings 33)
NFC First-Round Playoff
***NFC Championship*

MINNESOTA vs. N.Y. JETS
RS: Jets lead series, 5-1
1970—Jets, 20-10 (NY)
1975—Vikings, 29-21 (M)
1979—Jets, 14-7 (NY)
1982—Jets, 42-14 (M)
1994—Jets, 31-21 (M)
1997—Jets, 23-21 (NY)
(RS Pts.—Jets 151, Vikings 102)

MINNESOTA vs. *OAKLAND
RS: Raiders lead series, 7-3
PS: Raiders lead series, 1-0
1973—Vikings, 24-16 (M)
1976—**Raiders, 32-14 (Pasadena)
1977—Raiders, 35-13 (O)
1978—Raiders, 27-20 (O)
1981—Raiders, 36-10 (M)
1984—Raiders, 23-20 (LA)
1987—Vikings, 31-20 (M)
1990—Raiders, 28-24 (M)
1993—Raiders, 24-7 (LA)
1996—Vikings, 16-13 (O) OT
1999—Raiders, 22-17 (M)
(RS Pts.—Raiders 244, Vikings 182)
(PS Pts.—Raiders 32, Vikings 14)
Franchise in Los Angeles from 1982-1994
***Super Bowl XI*

MINNESOTA vs. PHILADELPHIA
RS: Vikings lead series, 11-6
PS: Eagles lead series, 1-0
1962—Vikings, 31-21 (M)
1963—Vikings, 34-13 (P)
1968—Vikings, 24-17 (P)
1971—Vikings, 13-0 (P)
1973—Vikings, 28-21 (M)
1976—Vikings, 31-12 (P)
1978—Vikings, 28-27 (M)
1980—Eagles, 42-7 (M)
*Eagles, 31-16 (P)
1981—Vikings, 35-23 (M)
1984—Eagles, 19-17 (P)
1985—Vikings, 28-23 (P)
Eagles, 37-35 (M)
1988—Vikings, 23-21 (M)
1989—Eagles, 10-9 (P)
1990—Eagles, 32-24 (P)
1992—Eagles, 28-17 (P)
1997—Vikings, 28-19 (M)
(RS Pts.—Vikings 412, Eagles 365)

ALL-TIME TEAM VS. TEAM RESULTS

(PS Pts.—Eagles 31, Vikings 16)
*NFC Divisional Playoff
MINNESOTA vs. PITTSBURGH
RS: Vikings lead series, 8-4
PS: Steelers lead series, 1-0
1962—Steelers, 39-31 (P)
1964—Vikings, 30-10 (M)
1967—Vikings, 41-27 (P)
1969—Vikings, 52-14 (M)
1972—Steelers, 23-10 (P)
1974—*Steelers, 16-6 (New Orleans)
1976—Vikings, 17-6 (M)
1980—Steelers, 23-17 (M)
1983—Vikings, 17-14 (P)
1986—Vikings, 31-7 (M)
1989—Steelers, 27-14 (P)
1992—Vikings, 6-3 (P)
1995—Vikings, 44-24 (P)
(RS Pts.—Vikings 310, Steelers 217)
(PS Pts.—Steelers 16, Vikings 6)
*Super Bowl IX
MINNESOTA vs. *ST. LOUIS
RS: Vikings lead series, 16-12-2
PS: Vikings lead series, 5-2
1961—Rams, 31-17 (LA)
Vikings, 42-21 (M)
1962—Vikings, 38-14 (LA)
Tie, 24-24 (M)
1963—Rams, 27-24 (LA)
Vikings, 21-13 (M)
1964—Rams, 22-13 (LA)
Vikings, 34-13 (M)
1965—Vikings, 38-35 (LA)
Vikings, 24-13 (M)
1966—Vikings, 35-7 (M)
Rams, 21-6 (LA)
1967—Rams, 39-3 (LA)
1968—Rams, 31-3 (M)
1969—Vikings, 20-13 (LA)
**Vikings, 23-20 (M)
1970—Vikings, 13-3 (M)
1972—Vikings, 45-41 (LA)
1973—Vikings, 10-9 (M)
1974—Rams, 20-17 (LA)
***Vikings, 14-10 (M)
1976—Tie, 10-10 (M) OT
***Vikings, 24-13 (M)
1977—Rams, 35-3 (LA)
****Vikings, 14-7 (LA)
1978—Rams, 34-17 (M)
****Rams, 34-10 (LA)
1979—Rams, 27-21 (LA) OT
1985—Rams, 13-10 (LA)
1987—Vikings, 21-16 (LA)
1988—*****Vikings, 28-17 (M)
1989—Vikings, 23-21 (M) OT
1991—Vikings, 20-14 (M)
1992—Vikings, 31-17 (LA)
1998—Vikings, 38-31 (StL)
1999—****Rams, 49-37 (StL)
2000—Rams, 40-29 (StL)
(RS Pts.—Rams 655, Vikings 650)
(PS Pts.—Rams 150, Vikings 150)
*Franchise in Los Angeles prior to 1995
**Conference Championship
***NFC Championship
****NFC Divisional Playoff
*****NFC First-Round Playoff
MINNESOTA vs. SAN DIEGO
RS: Series tied, 4-4
1971—Chargers, 30-14 (SD)
1975—Vikings, 28-13 (M)
1978—Chargers, 13-7 (M)
1981—Vikings, 33-31 (SD)
1984—Chargers, 42-13 (M)
1985—Vikings, 21-17 (M)
1993—Chargers, 30-17 (M)
1999—Vikings, 35-27 (M)
(RS Pts.—Chargers 203, Vikings 168)
MINNESOTA vs. SAN FRANCISCO
RS: Series tied, 17-17-1
PS: 49ers lead series, 4-1
1961—49ers, 38-24 (M)
49ers, 38-28 (SF)
1962—49ers, 21-7 (SF)
49ers, 35-12 (M)
1963—Vikings, 24-20 (SF)
Vikings, 45-14 (M)
1964—Vikings, 27-22 (SF)
Vikings, 24-7 (M)
1965—Vikings, 42-41 (SF)
49ers, 45-24 (M)
1966—Tie, 20-20 (SF)
Vikings, 28-3 (SF)
1967—49ers, 27-21 (M)
1968—Vikings, 30-20 (SF)
1969—Vikings, 10-7 (M)
1970—*49ers, 17-14 (M)
1971—49ers, 13-9 (M)
1972—49ers, 20-17 (SF)
1973—Vikings, 17-13 (SF)
1975—Vikings, 27-17 (M)
1976—49ers, 20-16 (SF)
1977—Vikings, 28-27 (M)
1979—Vikings, 28-22 (M)
1983—49ers, 48-17 (M)
1984—49ers, 51-7 (SF)
1985—Vikings, 28-21 (M)
1986—Vikings, 27-24 (SF) OT
1987—*Vikings, 36-24 (SF)
1988—49ers, 24-21 (SF)
*49ers, 34-9 (SF)
1989—*49ers, 41-13 (SF)
1990—49ers, 20-17 (M)
1991—Vikings, 17-14 (M)
1992—49ers, 20-17 (M)
1993—49ers, 38-19 (SF)
1994—Vikings, 21-14 (M)
1995—49ers, 37-30 (SF)
1997—49ers, 28-17 (SF)
*49ers, 38-22 (SF)
1999—Vikings, 40-16 (M)
(RS Pts.—49ers 845, Vikings 786)
(PS Pts.—49ers 154, Vikings 94)
*NFC Divisional Playoff
MINNESOTA vs. SEATTLE
RS: Seahawks lead series, 4-2
1976—Vikings, 27-21 (M)
1978—Seahawks, 29-28 (S)
1984—Seahawks, 20-12 (M)
1987—Seahawks, 28-17 (S)
1990—Vikings, 24-21 (S)
1996—Seahawks, 42-23 (S)
(RS Pts.—Seahawks 161, Vikings 131)
MINNESOTA vs. TAMPA BAY
RS: Vikings lead series, 30-16
1977—Vikings, 9-3 (TB)
1978—Buccaneers, 16-10 (M)
Vikings, 24-7 (TB)
1979—Buccaneers, 12-10 (M)
Vikings, 23-22 (TB)
1980—Vikings, 38-30 (M)
Vikings, 21-10 (TB)
1981—Buccaneers, 21-13 (TB)
Vikings, 25-10 (M)
1982—Vikings, 17-10 (M)
1983—Vikings, 19-16 (TB) OT
Buccaneers, 17-12 (M)
1984—Buccaneers, 35-31 (TB)
Vikings, 27-24 (M)
1985—Vikings, 31-16 (TB)
Vikings, 26-7 (M)
1986—Vikings, 23-10 (TB)
Vikings, 45-13 (M)
1987—Buccaneers, 20-10 (TB)
Vikings, 23-17 (M)
1988—Vikings, 14-13 (M)
Vikings, 49-20 (TB)
1989—Vikings, 17-3 (M)
Vikings, 24-10 (TB)
1990—Buccaneers, 23-20 (M) OT
Buccaneers, 26-13 (TB)
1991—Vikings, 28-13 (M)
Vikings, 26-24 (TB)
1992—Vikings, 26-20 (M)
Vikings, 35-7 (TB)
1993—Vikings, 15-0 (M)
Buccaneers, 23-10 (TB)
1994—Vikings, 36-13 (TB)
Buccaneers, 20-17 (M) OT
1995—Buccaneers, 20-17 (TB) OT
Vikings, 31-17 (M)
1996—Buccaneers, 24-13 (TB)
Vikings, 21-10 (M)
1997—Buccaneers, 28-14 (M)
Vikings, 10-6 (TB)
1998—Vikings, 31-7 (M)
Buccaneers, 27-24 (TB)
1999—Vikings, 21-14 (M)
Buccaneers, 24-17 (TB)
2000—Vikings, 30-23 (M)
Buccaneers, 41-13 (TB)
(RS Pts.—Vikings 1,009, Buccaneers 772)
MINNESOTA vs. *TENNESSEE
RS: Vikings lead series, 5-3
1974—Vikings, 51-10 (M)
1980—Oilers, 20-16 (H)
1983—Vikings, 34-14 (M)
1986—Oilers, 23-10 (H)
1989—Vikings, 38-7 (M)
1992—Oilers, 17-13 (M)
1995—Vikings, 23-17 (M) OT
1998—Vikings, 26-16 (T)
(RS Pts.—Vikings 211, Titans 124)
*Franchise in Houston prior to 1997; known as Oilers prior to 1999
MINNESOTA vs. WASHINGTON
RS: Redskins lead series, 6-5
PS: Redskins lead series, 3-2
1968—Vikings, 27-14 (M)
1970—Vikings, 19-10 (W)
1972—Redskins, 24-21 (M)
1973—*Vikings, 27-20 (M)
1975—Redskins, 31-30 (W)
1976—*Vikings, 35-20 (M)
1980—Vikings, 39-14 (W)
1982—**Redskins, 21-7 (W)
1984—Redskins, 31-17 (M)
1986—Redskins, 44-38 (W) OT
1987—Redskins, 27-24 (M) OT
***Redskins, 17-10 (W)
1992—Redskins, 15-13 (M)
****Redskins, 24-7 (M)
1993—Vikings, 14-9 (W)
1998—Vikings, 41-7 (M)
(RS Pts.—Vikings 283, Redskins 226)
(PS Pts.—Redskins 102, Vikings 86)
*NFC Divisional Playoff
**NFC Second-Round Playoff
***NFC Championship
****NFC First-Round Playoff

NEW ENGLAND vs. ARIZONA
RS: Cardinals lead series, 6-4;
See Arizona vs. New England
NEW ENGLAND vs. ATLANTA
RS: Falcons lead series, 6-3;
See Atlanta vs. New England
NEW ENGLAND vs. BALTIMORE
RS: Patriots lead series, 2-0;
See Baltimore vs. New England
NEW ENGLAND vs. BUFFALO
RS: Patriots lead series, 41-39-1
PS: Patriots lead series, 1-0;
See Buffalo vs. New England
NEW ENGLAND vs. CAROLINA
RS: Panthers lead series, 1-0;
See Carolina vs. New England
NEW ENGLAND vs. CHICAGO
RS: Patriots lead series, 5-3
PS: Bears lead series, 1-0;
See Chicago vs. New England
NEW ENGLAND vs. CINCINNATI
RS: Patriots lead series, 10-7;
See Cincinnati vs. New England
NEW ENGLAND vs. CLEVELAND
RS: Browns lead series, 11-5
PS: Browns lead series, 1-0;
See Cleveland vs. New England
NEW ENGLAND vs. DALLAS
RS: Cowboys lead series, 7-1;
See Dallas vs. New England
NEW ENGLAND vs. DENVER
RS: Broncos lead series, 20-14
PS: Broncos lead series, 1-0;
See Denver vs. New England
NEW ENGLAND vs. DETROIT
RS: Lions lead series, 4-3;
See Detroit vs. New England
NEW ENGLAND vs. GREEN BAY
RS: Series tied, 3-3
PS: Packers lead series, 1-0;
See Green Bay vs. New England
NEW ENGLAND vs. INDIANAPOLIS
RS: Patriots lead series, 37-24;
See Indianapolis vs. New England
NEW ENGLAND vs. JACKSONVILLE
RS: Patriots lead series, 2-0
PS: Series tied, 1-1;
See Jacksonville vs. New England
NEW ENGLAND vs. KANSAS CITY
RS: Chiefs lead series, 15-9-3;
See Kansas City vs. New England
NEW ENGLAND vs. MIAMI
RS: Dolphins lead series, 42-26
PS: Patriots lead series, 2-1;
See Miami vs. New England
NEW ENGLAND vs. MINNESOTA
RS: Series tied, 4-4;
See Minnesota vs. New England
NEW ENGLAND vs. NEW ORLEANS
RS: Patriots lead series, 6-3
1972—Patriots, 17-10 (NO)
1976—Patriots, 27-6 (NE)
1980—Patriots, 38-27 (NO)
1983—Patriots, 7-0 (NE)
1986—Patriots, 21-20 (NO)
1989—Saints, 28-24 (NE)
1992—Saints, 31-14 (NE)
1995—Saints, 31-17 (NE)
1998—Patriots, 30-27 (NO)
(RS Pts.—Patriots 195, Saints 180)
***NEW ENGLAND vs. N.Y. GIANTS**
RS: Series tied, 3-3
1970—Giants, 16-0 (B)
1974—Patriots, 28-20 (New Haven)
1987—Giants, 17-10 (NY)
1990—Giants, 13-10 (NE)
1996—Patriots, 23-22 (NY)
1999—Patriots, 16-14 (NE)
(RS Pts.—Giants 102, Patriots 87)
*Franchise in Boston prior to 1971
***NEW ENGLAND vs. **N.Y. JETS**
RS: Jets lead series, 45-35-1
PS: Patriots lead series, 1-0
1960—Patriots, 28-24 (NY)
Patriots, 38-21 (B)
1961—Titans, 21-20 (B)
Titans, 37-30 (NY)
1962—Patriots, 43-14 (NY)
Patriots, 24-17 (B)
1963—Patriots, 38-14 (B)
Jets, 31-24 (NY)
1964—Patriots, 26-10 (B)
Jets, 35-14 (NY)
1965—Jets, 30-20 (B)
Patriots, 27-23 (NY)
1966—Tie, 24-24 (B)
Jets, 38-28 (NY)
1967—Jets, 30-23 (NY)
Jets, 29-24 (B)
1968—Jets, 47-31 (Birmingham)
Jets, 48-14 (NY)
1969—Jets, 23-14 (B)
Jets, 23-17 (NY)
1970—Jets, 31-21 (B)
Jets, 17-3 (NY)
1971—Patriots, 20-0 (NE)
Jets, 13-6 (NY)
1972—Jets, 41-13 (NE)
Jets, 34-10 (NY)
1973—Jets, 9-7 (NE)

Jets, 33-13 (NY)
1974—Patriots, 24-0 (NY)
Jets, 21-16 (NE)
1975—Jets, 36-7 (NY)
Jets, 30-28 (NE)
1976—Patriots, 41-7 (NE)
Patriots, 38-24 (NY)
1977—Jets, 30-27 (NY)
Patriots, 24-13 (NE)
1978—Patriots, 55-21 (NE)
Patriots, 19-17 (NY)
1979—Patriots, 56-3 (NE)
Jets, 27-26 (NY)
1980—Patriots, 21-11 (NY)
Patriots, 34-21 (NE)
1981—Jets, 28-24 (NY)
Jets, 17-6 (NE)
1982—Jets, 31-7 (NE)
1983—Patriots, 23-13 (NE)
Jets, 26-3 (NY)
1984—Patriots, 28-21 (NY)
Patriots, 30-20 (NE)
1985—Patriots, 20-13 (NE)
Jets, 16-13 (NY) OT
***Patriots, 26-14 (NY)
1986—Patriots, 20-6 (NY)
Jets, 31-24 (NE)
1987—Jets, 43-24 (NY)
Patriots, 42-20 (NE)
1988—Patriots, 28-3 (NE)
Patriots, 14-13 (NY)
1989—Patriots, 27-24 (NY)
Jets, 27-26 (NE)
1990—Jets, 37-13 (NE)
Jets, 42-7 (NY)
1991—Jets, 28-21 (NE)
Patriots, 6-3 (NY)
1992—Jets, 30-21 (NY)
Patriots, 24-3 (NE)
1993—Jets, 45-7 (NY)
Jets, 6-0 (NE)
1994—Jets, 24-17 (NY)
Patriots, 24-13 (NE)
1995—Patriots, 20-7 (NY)
Patriots, 31-28 (NE)
1996—Patriots, 31-27 (NY)
Patriots, 34-10 (NE)
1997—Patriots, 27-24 (NE) OT
Jets, 24-19 (NY)
1998—Jets, 24-14 (NE)
Jets, 31-10 (NY)
1999—Patriots, 30-28 (NY)
Jets, 24-17 (NE)
2000—Jets, 20-19 (NY)
Jets, 34-17 (NE)
(RS Pts.—Jets 1,842, Patriots 1,784)
(PS Pts.—Patriots 26, Jets 14)
Franchise in Boston prior to 1971
***Jets known as Titans prior to 1963*
****AFC First-Round Playoff*

***NEW ENGLAND vs. **OAKLAND**
RS: Raiders lead series, 13-12-1
PS: Series tied, 1-1
1960—Raiders, 27-14 (O)
Patriots, 34-28 (B)
1961—Patriots, 20-17 (B)
Patriots, 35-21 (O)
1962—Patriots, 26-16 (B)
Raiders, 20-0 (O)
1963—Patriots, 20-14 (O)
Patriots, 20-14 (B)
1964—Patriots, 17-14 (O)
Tie, 43-43 (B)
1965—Raiders, 24-10 (B)
Raiders, 30-21 (O)
1966—Patriots, 24-21 (B)
1967—Raiders, 35-7 (O)
Raiders, 48-14 (B)
1968—Raiders, 41-10 (O)
1969—Raiders, 38-23 (B)
1971—Patriots, 20-6 (NE)
1974—Raiders, 41-26 (O)
1976—Patriots, 48-17 (NE)
***Raiders, 24-21 (O)
1978—Patriots, 21-14 (O)
1981—Raiders, 27-17 (O)
1985—Raiders, 35-20 (NE)
***Patriots, 27-20 (LA)
1987—Patriots, 26-23 (NE)
1989—Raiders, 24-21 (LA)
1994—Raiders, 21-17 (NE)
(RS Pts.—Raiders 659, Patriots 554)
(PS Pts.—Patriots 48, Raiders 44)
Franchise in Boston prior to 1971
***Franchise in Los Angeles from 1982-1994*
****AFC Divisional Playoff*

NEW ENGLAND vs. PHILADELPHIA
RS: Eagles lead series, 6-2
1973—Eagles, 24-23 (P)
1977—Patriots, 14-6 (NE)
1978—Patriots, 24-14 (NE)
1981—Eagles, 13-3 (P)
1984—Eagles, 27-17 (P)
1987—Eagles, 34-31 (NE) OT
1990—Eagles, 48-20 (P)
1999—Eagles, 24-9 (P)
(RS Pts.—Eagles 190, Patriots 141)

NEW ENGLAND vs. PITTSBURGH
RS: Steelers lead series, 11-4
PS: Series tied, 1-1
1972—Steelers, 33-3 (P)
1974—Steelers, 21-17 (NE)
1976—Patriots, 30-27 (P)
1979—Steelers, 16-13 (NE) OT
1981—Steelers, 27-21 (P) OT
1982—Steelers, 37-14 (P)
1983—Patriots, 28-23 (P)
1986—Patriots, 34-0 (P)
1989—Steelers, 28-10 (P)
1990—Steelers, 24-3 (P)
1991—Steelers, 20-6 (P)
1993—Steelers, 17-14 (P)
1995—Steelers, 41-27 (P)
1996—*Patriots, 28-3 (NE)
1997—Steelers, 24-21 (NE) OT
*Steelers, 7-6 (P)
1998—Patriots, 23-9 (P)
(RS Pts.—Steelers 347, Patriots 264)
(PS Pts.—Patriots 34, Steelers 10)
AFC Divisional Playoff

NEW ENGLAND vs. *ST. LOUIS
RS: Rams lead series, 4-3
1974—Patriots, 20-14 (NE)
1980—Rams, 17-14 (NE)
1983—Patriots, 21-7 (LA)
1986—Patriots, 30-28 (LA)
1989—Rams, 24-20 (NE)
1992—Rams, 14-0 (LA)
1998—Rams, 32-18 (StL)
(RS Pts.—Rams 136, Patriots 123)
Franchise in Los Angeles prior to 1995

***NEW ENGLAND vs. **SAN DIEGO**
RS: Patriots lead series, 16-11-2
PS: Chargers lead series, 1-0
1960—Patriots, 35-0 (LA)
Chargers, 45-16 (B)
1961—Chargers, 38-27 (B)
Patriots, 41-0 (SD)
1962—Patriots, 24-20 (B)
Patriots, 20-14 (SD)
1963—Chargers, 17-13 (SD)
Chargers, 7-6 (B)
***Chargers, 51-10 (SD)
1964—Patriots, 33-28 (SD)
Chargers, 26-17 (B)
1965—Tie, 10-10 (B)
Patriots, 22-6 (SD)
1966—Chargers, 24-0 (SD)
Patriots, 35-17 (B)
1967—Chargers, 28-14 (SD)
Tie, 31-31 (SD)
1968—Chargers, 27-17 (B)
1969—Chargers, 13-10 (B)
Chargers, 28-18 (SD)
1970—Chargers, 16-14 (B)
1973—Patriots, 30-14 (NE)
1975—Patriots, 33-19 (SD)
1977—Patriots, 24-20 (SD)
1978—Patriots, 28-23 (NE)
1979—Patriots, 27-21 (NE)
1983—Patriots, 37-21 (NE)
1994—Patriots, 23-17 (NE)
1996—Patriots, 45-7 (SD)
1997—Patriots, 41-7 (NE)
(RS Pts.—Patriots 691, Chargers 544)
(PS Pts.—Chargers 51, Patriots 10)
Franchise in Boston prior to 1971
***Franchise in Los Angeles prior to 1961*
****AFL Championship*

NEW ENGLAND vs. SAN FRANCISCO
RS: 49ers lead series, 7-2
1971—49ers, 27-10 (SF)
1975—Patriots, 24-16 (NE)
1980—49ers, 21-17 (SF)
1983—49ers, 33-13 (NE)
1986—49ers, 29-24 (NE)
1989—49ers, 37-20 (SF)
1992—49ers, 24-12 (NE)
1995—49ers, 28-3 (SF)
1998—Patriots, 24-21 (NE)
(RS Pts.—49ers 236, Patriots 147)

NEW ENGLAND vs. SEATTLE
RS: Seahawks lead series, 7-6
1977—Patriots, 31-0 (NE)
1980—Patriots, 37-31 (S)
1982—Patriots, 16-0 (S)
1983—Seahawks, 24-6 (S)
1984—Patriots, 38-23 (NE)
1985—Patriots, 20-13 (S)
1986—Seahawks, 38-31 (NE)
1988—Patriots, 13-7 (NE)
1989—Seahawks, 24-3 (NE)
1990—Seahawks, 33-20 (NE)
1992—Seahawks, 10-6 (NE)
1993—Seahawks, 17-14 (NE)
Seahawks, 10-9 (S)
(RS Pts.—Patriots 244, Seahawks 230)

NEW ENGLAND vs. TAMPA BAY
RS: Patriots lead series, 3-2
1976—Patriots, 31-14 (TB)
1985—Patriots, 32-14 (TB)
1988—Patriots, 10-7 (NE) OT
1997—Buccaneers, 27-7 (TB)
2000—Buccaneers, 21-16 (NE)
(RS Pts.—Patriots 96, Buccaneers 83)

***NEW ENGLAND vs. **TENNESSEE**
RS: Patriots lead series, 18-14-1
PS: Titans lead series, 1-0
1960—Oilers, 24-10 (B)
Oilers, 37-21 (H)
1961—Tie, 31-31 (B)
Oilers, 27-15 (H)
1962—Patriots, 34-21 (B)
Oilers, 21-17 (H)
1963—Patriots, 45-3 (B)
Patriots, 46-28 (H)
1964—Patriots, 25-24 (B)
Patriots, 34-17 (H)
1965—Oilers, 31-10 (H)
Patriots, 42-14 (B)
1966—Patriots, 27-21 (B)
Patriots, 38-14 (H)
1967—Patriots, 18-7 (B)
Oilers, 27-6 (H)
1968—Oilers, 16-0 (B)
Oilers, 45-17 (H)
1969—Patriots, 24-0 (B)
Oilers, 27-23 (H)
1971—Patriots, 28-20 (NE)
1973—Patriots, 32-0 (H)
1975—Oilers, 7-0 (NE)
1978—Oilers, 26-23 (NE)
***Oilers, 31-14 (NE)
1980—Oilers, 38-34 (H)
1981—Patriots, 38-10 (NE)
1982—Patriots, 29-21 (NE)
1987—Patriots, 21-7 (H)
1988—Oilers, 31-6 (H)
1989—Patriots, 23-13 (NE)
1991—Patriots, 24-20 (NE)
1993—Oilers, 28-14 (NE)
1998—Patriots, 27-16 (NE)
(RS Pts.—Patriots 782, Titans 672)
(PS Pts.—Titans 31, Patriots 14)
Franchise in Boston prior to 1971
***Franchise in Houston prior to 1997; known as Oilers prior to 1999*
****AFC Divisional Playoff*

NEW ENGLAND vs. WASHINGTON
RS: Redskins lead series, 5-1
1972—Patriots, 24-23 (NE)
1978—Redskins, 16-14 (NE)
1981—Redskins, 24-22 (W)
1984—Redskins, 26-10 (NE)
1990—Redskins, 25-10 (NE)
1996—Redskins, 27-22 (NE)
(RS Pts.—Redskins 141, Patriots 102)

NEW ORLEANS vs. ARIZONA
RS: Cardinals lead series, 12-11;
See Arizona vs. New Orleans

NEW ORLEANS vs. ATLANTA
RS: Falcons lead series, 37-26
PS: Falcons lead series, 1-0;
See Atlanta vs. New Orleans

NEW ORLEANS vs. BALTIMORE
RS: Ravens lead series, 2-0;
See Baltimore vs. New Orleans

NEW ORLEANS vs. BUFFALO
RS: Bills lead series, 4-2;
See Buffalo vs. New Orleans

NEW ORLEANS vs. CAROLINA
RS: Series tied, 6-6;
See Carolina vs. New Orleans

NEW ORLEANS vs. CHICAGO
RS: Bears lead series, 10-9
PS: Bears lead series, 1-0;
See Chicago vs. New Orleans

NEW ORLEANS vs. CINCINNATI
RS: Saints lead series, 5-4;
See Cincinnati vs. New Orleans

NEW ORLEANS vs. CLEVELAND
RS: Browns lead series, 10-3;
See Cleveland vs. New Orleans

NEW ORLEANS vs. DALLAS
RS: Cowboys lead series, 14-5;
See Dallas vs. New Orleans

NEW ORLEANS vs. DENVER
RS: Broncos lead series, 5-2;
See Denver vs. New Orleans

NEW ORLEANS vs. DETROIT
RS: Saints lead series, 8-7-1;
See Detroit vs. New Orleans

NEW ORLEANS vs. GREEN BAY
RS: Packers lead series, 13-4;
See Green Bay vs. New Orleans

NEW ORLEANS vs. INDIANAPOLIS
RS: Saints lead series, 4-3;
See Indianapolis vs. New Orleans

NEW ORLEANS vs. JACKSONVILLE
RS: Series tied, 1-1;
See Jacksonville vs. New Orleans

NEW ORLEANS vs. KANSAS CITY
RS: Chiefs lead series, 4-3;
See Kansas City vs. New Orleans

NEW ORLEANS vs. MIAMI
RS: Dolphins lead series, 5-3;
See Miami vs. New Orleans

NEW ORLEANS vs. MINNESOTA
RS: Vikings lead series, 14-6
PS: Vikings lead series, 2-0;
See Minnesota vs. New Orleans

NEW ORLEANS vs. NEW ENGLAND
RS: Patriots lead series, 6-3;
See New England vs. New Orleans

NEW ORLEANS vs. N.Y. GIANTS
RS: Giants lead series, 12-8
1967—Giants, 27-21 (NY)
1968—Giants, 38-21 (NY)
1969—Saints, 25-24 (NY)
1970—Saints, 14-10 (NO)

1972—Giants, 45-21 (NY)
1975—Giants, 28-14 (NY)
1978—Saints, 28-17 (NO)
1979—Saints, 24-14 (NO)
1981—Giants, 20-7 (NY)
1984—Saints, 10-3 (NY)
1985—Giants, 21-13 (NO)
1986—Giants, 20-17 (NY)
1987—Saints, 23-14 (NO)
1988—Giants, 13-12 (NO)
1993—Giants, 24-14 (NO)
1994—Saints, 27-22 (NO)
1995—Giants, 45-29 (NY)
1996—Saints 17-3 (NY)
1997—Giants, 14-9 (NY)
1999—Giants, 31-3 (NY)
(RS Pts.—Giants 433, Saints 349)

NEW ORLEANS vs. N.Y. JETS
RS: Series tied, 4-4
1972—Jets, 18-17 (NY)
1977—Jets, 16-13 (NO)
1980—Saints, 21-20 (NY)
1983—Jets, 31-28 (NO)
1986—Jets, 28-23 (NY)
1989—Saints, 29-14 (NO)
1992—Saints, 20-0 (NY)
1995—Saints, 12-0 (NY)
(RS Pts.—Saints 163, Jets 127)

NEW ORLEANS vs. *OAKLAND
RS: Raiders lead series, 5-3-1
1971—Tie, 21-21 (NO)
1975—Raiders, 48-10 (O)
1979—Raiders, 42-35 (NO)
1985—Raiders, 23-13 (LA)
1988—Saints, 20-6 (NO)
1991—Saints, 27-0 (NO)
1994—Raiders, 24-19 (LA)
1997—Saints, 13-10 (O)
2000—Raiders, 31-22 (NO)
(RS Pts.—Raiders 205, Saints 180)
**Franchise in Los Angeles from 1982-1994*

NEW ORLEANS vs. PHILADELPHIA
RS: Eagles lead series, 13-8
PS: Eagles lead series, 1-0
1967—Saints, 31-24 (NO)
Eagles, 48-21 (P)
1968—Eagles, 29-17 (P)
1969—Eagles, 13-10 (P)
Saints, 26-17 (NO)
1972—Saints, 21-3 (NO)
1974—Saints, 14-10 (NO)
1977—Eagles, 28-7 (P)
1978—Eagles, 24-17 (NO)
1979—Eagles, 26-14 (NO)
1980—Eagles, 34-21 (NO)
1981—Eagles, 31-14 (NO)
1983—Saints, 20-17 (P) OT
1985—Saints, 23-21 (NO)
1987—Eagles, 27-17 (P)
1989—Saints, 30-20 (NO)
1991—Saints, 13-6 (P)
1992—Eagles, 15-13 (P)
*Eagles, 36-20 (NO)
1993—Eagles, 37-26 (P)
1995—Eagles, 15-10 (NO)
2000—Eagles, 21-7 (NO)
(RS Pts.—Eagles 466, Saints 372)
(PS Pts.—Eagles 36, Saints 20)
**NFC First-Round Playoff*

NEW ORLEANS vs. PITTSBURGH
RS: Steelers lead series, 6-5
1967—Steelers, 14-10 (NO)
1968—Saints, 16-12 (P)
Saints, 24-14 (NO)
1969—Saints, 27-24 (NO)
1974—Steelers, 28-7 (NO)
1978—Steelers, 20-14 (P)
1981—Steelers, 20-6 (NO)
1984—Saints, 27-24 (NO)
1987—Saints, 20-16 (P)
1990—Steelers, 9-6 (NO)
1993—Steelers, 37-14 (P)
(RS Pts.—Steelers 218, Saints 171)

NEW ORLEANS vs. *ST. LOUIS
RS: Rams lead series, 35-27
PS: Saints lead series, 1-0
1967—Rams, 27-13 (NO)
1969—Rams, 36-17 (LA)
1970—Rams, 30-17 (NO)
Rams, 34-16 (LA)
1971—Saints, 24-20 (NO)
Rams, 45-28 (LA)
1972—Rams, 34-14 (LA)
Saints, 19-16 (NO)
1973—Rams, 29-7 (LA)
Rams, 24-13 (NO)
1974—Rams, 24-0 (LA)
Saints, 20-7 (NO)
1975—Rams, 38-14 (LA)
Rams, 14-7 (NO)
1976—Rams, 16-10 (NO)
Rams, 33-14 (LA)
1977—Rams, 14-7 (LA)
Saints, 27-26 (NO)
1978—Rams, 26-20 (NO)
Saints, 10-3 (LA)
1979—Rams, 35-17 (NO)
Saints, 29-14 (LA)
1980—Rams, 45-31 (LA)
Rams, 27-7 (NO)
1981—Saints, 23-17 (NO)
Saints, 21-13 (LA)
1983—Rams, 30-27 (LA)
Rams, 26-24 (NO)
1984—Rams, 28-10 (NO)
Rams, 34-21 (LA)
1985—Rams, 28-10 (LA)
Saints, 29-3 (NO)
1986—Saints, 6-0 (NO)
Rams, 26-13 (LA)
1987—Saints, 37-10 (NO)
Saints, 31-14 (LA)
1988—Rams, 12-10 (NO)
Saints, 14-10 (LA)
1989—Saints, 40-21 (LA)
Rams, 20-17 (NO) OT
1990—Saints, 24-20 (LA)
Saints, 20-17 (NO)
1991—Saints, 24-7 (NO)
Saints, 24-17 (LA)
1992—Saints, 13-10 (NO)
Saints, 37-14 (LA)
1993—Saints, 37-6 (LA)
Rams, 23-20 (NO)
1994—Saints, 37-34 (NO)
Saints, 31-15 (LA)
1995—Rams, 17-13 (StL)
Saints, 19-10 (NO)
1996—Rams, 26-10 (NO)
Rams, 14-13 (StL)
1997—Rams, 38-24 (StL)
Rams, 34-27 (NO)
1998—Saints, 24-17 (StL)
Saints, 24-3 (NO)
1999—Rams, 43-12 (StL)
Rams, 30-14 (NO)
2000—Saints, 31-24 (StL)
Rams, 26-21 (NO)
**Saints, 31-28 (NO)
(RS Pts.—Rams 1,354, Saints 1,213)
(PS Pts.—Saints 31, Rams 28)
**Franchise in Los Angeles prior to 1995*
***NFC First-Round Playoff*

NEW ORLEANS vs. SAN DIEGO
RS: Chargers lead series, 6-2
1973—Chargers, 17-14 (SD)
1977—Chargers, 14-0 (NO)
1979—Chargers, 35-0 (NO)
1988—Saints, 23-17 (SD)
1991—Chargers, 24-21 (SD)
1994—Chargers, 36-22 (NO)
1997—Chargers, 20-6 (NO)
2000—Saints, 28-27 (SD)
(RS Pts.—Chargers 190, Saints 114)

NEW ORLEANS vs. SAN FRANCISCO
RS: 49ers lead series, 43-18-2
1967—49ers, 27-13 (SF)
1969—Saints, 43-38 (NO)
1970—Tie, 20-20 (SF)
49ers, 38-27 (NO)
1971—49ers, 38-20 (NO)
Saints, 26-20 (SF)
1972—49ers, 37-2 (NO)
Tie, 20-20 (SF)
1973—49ers, 40-0 (SF)
Saints, 16-10 (NO)
1974—49ers, 17-13 (NO)
49ers, 35-21 (SF)
1975—49ers, 35-21 (SF)
49ers, 16-6 (NO)
1976—49ers, 33-3 (SF)
49ers, 27-7 (NO)
1977—49ers, 10-7 (NO) OT
49ers, 20-17 (SF)
1978—Saints, 14-7 (SF)
Saints, 24-13 (NO)
1979—Saints, 30-21 (SF)
Saints, 31-20 (NO)
1980—49ers, 26-23 (NO)
49ers, 38-35 (SF) OT
1981—49ers, 21-14 (SF)
49ers, 21-17 (NO)
1982—Saints, 23-20 (SF)
1983—49ers, 32-13 (NO)
49ers, 27-0 (SF)
1984—49ers, 30-20 (SF)
49ers, 35-3 (NO)
1985—Saints, 20-17 (SF)
49ers, 31-19 (NO)
1986—49ers, 26-17 (SF)
Saints, 23-10 (NO)
1987—49ers, 24-22 (NO)
Saints, 26-24 (SF)
1988—49ers, 34-33 (NO)
49ers, 30-17 (SF)
1989—49ers, 24-20 (NO)
49ers, 31-13 (SF)
1990—49ers, 13-12 (NO)
Saints, 13-10 (SF)
1991—Saints, 10-3 (NO)
49ers, 38-24 (SF)
1992—49ers, 16-10 (NO)
49ers, 21-20 (SF)
1993—Saints, 16-13 (NO)
49ers, 42-7 (SF)
1994—49ers, 24-13 (SF)
49ers, 35-14 (NO)
1995—49ers, 24-22 (NO)
Saints, 11-7 (SF)
1996—49ers, 27-11 (SF)
49ers, 24-17 (NO)
1997—49ers, 33-7 (SF)
49ers, 23-0 (NO)
1998—49ers, 31-0 (NO)
49ers, 31-20 (SF)
1999—49ers, 28-21 (SF)
Saints, 24-6 (NO)
2000—Saints, 31-15 (NO)
Saints, 31-27 (SF)
(RS Pts.—49ers 1,534, Saints 1,073)

NEW ORLEANS vs. SEATTLE
RS: Saints lead series, 4-3
1976—Saints, 51-27 (S)
1979—Seahawks, 38-24 (S)
1985—Seahawks, 27-3 (NO)
1988—Saints, 20-19 (S)
1991—Saints, 27-24 (NO)
1997—Saints, 20-17 (NO) OT
2000—Seahawks, 20-10 (S)
(RS Pts.—Seahawks 172, Saints 155)

NEW ORLEANS vs. TAMPA BAY
RS: Saints lead series, 13-6
1977—Buccaneers, 33-14 (NO)
1978—Saints, 17-10 (TB)
1979—Saints, 42-14 (TB)
1981—Buccaneers, 31-14 (NO)
1982—Buccaneers, 13-10 (NO)
1983—Saints, 24-21 (TB)
1984—Saints, 17-13 (NO)
1985—Saints, 20-13 (NO)
1986—Saints, 38-7 (NO)
1987—Saints, 44-34 (NO)
1988—Saints, 13-9 (NO)
1989—Buccaneers, 20-10 (TB)
1990—Saints, 35-7 (NO)
1991—Saints, 23-7 (NO)
1992—Saints, 23-21 (NO)
1994—Saints, 9-7 (TB)
1996—Buccaneers, 13-7 (TB)
1998—Saints, 9-3 (NO)
1999—Buccaneers, 31-16 (NO)
(RS Pts.—Saints 385, Buccaneers 307)

NEW ORLEANS vs. *TENNESSEE
RS: Titans lead series, 5-4-1
1971—Tie, 13-13 (H)
1976—Oilers, 31-26 (NO)
1978—Oilers, 17-12 (NO)
1981—Saints, 27-24 (H)
1984—Saints, 27-10 (H)
1987—Saints, 24-10 (NO)
1990—Oilers, 23-10 (H)
1993—Saints, 33-21 (NO)
1996—Oilers, 31-14 (NO)
1999—Titans, 24-21 (NO)
(RS Pts.—Saints 207, Titans 204)
**Franchise in Houston prior to 1997; known as Oilers prior to 1999*

NEW ORLEANS vs. WASHINGTON
RS: Redskins lead series, 12-5
1967—Redskins, 30-10 (NO)
Saints, 30-14 (W)
1968—Saints, 37-17 (NO)
1969—Redskins, 26-20 (NO)
Redskins, 17-14 (W)
1971—Redskins, 24-14 (W)
1973—Saints, 19-3 (NO)
1975—Redskins, 41-3 (W)
1979—Saints, 14-10 (W)
1980—Redskins, 22-14 (W)
1982—Redskins, 27-10 (NO)
1986—Redskins, 14-6 (NO)
1988—Redskins, 27-24 (W)
1989—Redskins, 16-14 (NO)
1990—Redskins, 31-17 (W)
1992—Saints, 20-3 (NO)
1994—Redskins, 38-24 (NO)
(RS Pts.—Redskins 360, Saints 290)

N.Y. GIANTS vs. ARIZONA
RS: Giants lead series, 75-39-2;
See Arizona vs. N.Y. Giants

N.Y. GIANTS vs. ATLANTA
RS: Series tied, 7-7;
See Atlanta vs. N.Y. Giants

N.Y. GIANTS vs. BALTIMORE
RS: Ravens lead series, 1-0
PS: Ravens lead series, 1-0;
See Baltimore vs. N.Y. Giants

N.Y. GIANTS vs. BUFFALO
RS: Bills lead series, 5-3
PS: Giants lead series, 1-0;
See Buffalo vs. N.Y. Giants

N.Y. GIANTS vs. CAROLINA
RS: Panthers lead series, 1-0;
See Carolina vs. N.Y. Giants

N.Y. GIANTS vs. CHICAGO
RS: Bears lead series, 25-17-2
PS: Bears lead series, 5-3;
See Chicago vs. N.Y. Giants

N.Y. GIANTS vs. CINCINNATI
RS: Bengals lead series, 4-2;
See Cincinnati vs. N.Y. Giants

N.Y. GIANTS vs. CLEVELAND
RS: Browns lead series, 25-18-2
PS: Series tied, 1-1;
See Cleveland vs. N.Y. Giants

N.Y. GIANTS vs. DALLAS
RS: Cowboys lead series, 47-28-2;
See Dallas vs. N.Y. Giants

N.Y. GIANTS vs. DENVER
RS: Giants lead series, 4-3
PS: Giants lead series, 1-0;
See Denver vs. N.Y. Giants
N.Y. GIANTS vs. DETROIT
RS: Lions lead series, 19-17-1
PS: Lions lead series, 1-0;
See Detroit vs. N.Y. Giants
N.Y. GIANTS vs. GREEN BAY
RS: Packers lead series, 23-20-2
PS: Packers lead series, 4-1;
See Green Bay vs. N.Y. Giants
N.Y. GIANTS vs. INDIANAPOLIS
RS: Colts lead series, 6-5
PS: Colts lead series, 2-0;
See Indianapolis vs. N.Y. Giants
N.Y. GIANTS vs. JACKSONVILLE
RS: Series tied, 1-1;
See Jacksonville vs. N.Y. Giants
N.Y. GIANTS vs. KANSAS CITY
RS: Giants lead series, 7-2;
See Kansas City vs. N.Y. Giants
N.Y. GIANTS vs. MIAMI
RS: Giants lead series, 3-1;
See Miami vs. N.Y. Giants
N.Y. GIANTS vs. MINNESOTA
RS: Vikings lead series, 8-5
PS: Giants lead series, 2-1;
See Minnesota vs. N.Y. Giants
N.Y. GIANTS vs. NEW ENGLAND
RS: Series tied, 3-3;
See New England vs. N.Y. Giants
N.Y. GIANTS vs. NEW ORLEANS
RS: Giants lead series, 12-8;
See New Orleans vs. N.Y. Giants
N.Y. GIANTS vs. N.Y. JETS
RS: Giants lead series, 5-4
1970—Giants, 22-10 (NYJ)
1974—Jets, 26-20 (New Haven) OT
1981—Jets, 26-7 (NYG)
1984—Giants, 20-10 (NYJ)
1987—Giants, 20-7 (NYG)
1988—Jets, 27-21 (NYJ)
1993—Jets, 10-6 (NYG)
1996—Giants, 13-6 (NYJ)
1999—Giants, 41-28 (NYG)
(RS Pts.—Giants 170, Jets 150)
N.Y. GIANTS vs. *OAKLAND
RS: Raiders lead series, 6-2
1973—Raiders, 42-0 (O)
1980—Raiders, 33-17 (NY)
1983—Raiders, 27-12 (LA)
1986—Giants, 14-9 (LA)
1989—Giants, 34-17 (NY)
1992—Raiders, 13-10 (LA)
1995—Raiders, 17-13 (NY)
1998—Raiders, 20-17 (O)
(RS Pts.—Raiders 178, Giants 117)
**Franchise in Los Angeles from 1982-1994*
N.Y. GIANTS vs. PHILADELPHIA
RS: Giants lead series, 72-58-2
PS: Giants lead series, 2-0
1933—Giants, 56-0 (NY)
Giants, 20-14 (P)
1934—Giants, 17-0 (NY)
Eagles, 6-0 (P)
1935—Giants, 10-0 (NY)
Giants, 21-14 (P)
1936—Eagles, 10-7 (P)
Giants, 21-17 (NY)
1937—Giants, 16-7 (P)
Giants, 21-0 (NY)
1938—Eagles, 14-10 (P)
Giants, 17-7 (NY)
1939—Giants, 13-3 (P)
Giants, 27-10 (NY)
1940—Giants, 20-14 (P)
Giants, 17-7 (NY)
1941—Giants, 24-0 (P)
Giants, 16-0 (NY)
1942—Giants, 35-17 (NY)
Giants, 14-0 (P)
1944—Eagles, 24-17 (NY)
Tie, 21-21 (P)
1945—Eagles, 38-17 (P)
Giants, 28-21 (NY)
1946—Eagles, 24-14 (P)
Giants, 45-17 (NY)
1947—Eagles, 23-0 (P)
Eagles, 41-24 (NY)
1948—Eagles, 45-0 (P)
Eagles, 35-14 (NY)
1949—Eagles, 24-3 (NY)
Eagles, 17-3 (P)
1950—Giants, 7-3 (NY)
Giants, 9-7 (P)
1951—Giants, 26-24 (NY)
Giants, 23-7 (P)
1952—Giants, 31-7 (P)
Eagles, 14-10 (NY)
1953—Eagles, 30-7 (P)
Giants, 37-28 (NY)
1954—Giants, 27-14 (NY)
Eagles, 29-14 (P)
1955—Eagles, 27-17 (P)
Giants, 31-7 (NY)
1956—Giants, 20-3 (NY)
Giants, 21-7 (P)
1957—Giants, 24-20 (P)
Giants, 13-0 (NY)
1958—Eagles, 27-24 (P)
Giants, 24-10 (NY)
1959—Eagles, 49-21 (P)
Giants, 24-7 (NY)
1960—Eagles, 17-10 (NY)
Eagles, 31-23 (P)
1961—Giants, 38-21 (NY)
Giants, 28-24 (P)
1962—Giants, 29-13 (P)
Giants, 19-14 (NY)
1963—Giants, 37-14 (P)
Giants, 42-14 (NY)
1964—Eagles, 38-7 (P)
Eagles, 23-17 (NY)
1965—Giants, 16-14 (P)
Giants, 35-27 (NY)
1966—Eagles, 35-17 (P)
Eagles, 31-3 (NY)
1967—Giants, 44-7 (NY)
1968—Giants, 34-25 (P)
Giants, 7-6 (NY)
1969—Eagles, 23-20 (NY)
1970—Giants, 30-23 (NY)
Eagles, 23-20 (P)
1971—Eagles, 23-7 (P)
Eagles, 41-28 (NY)
1972—Giants, 27-12 (P)
Giants, 62-10 (NY)
1973—Tie, 23-23 (NY)
Eagles, 20-16 (P)
1974—Eagles, 35-7 (P)
Eagles, 20-7 (New Haven)
1975—Giants, 23-14 (P)
Eagles, 13-10 (NY)
1976—Eagles, 20-7 (P)
Eagles, 10-0 (NY)
1977—Eagles, 28-10 (NY)
Eagles, 17-14 (P)
1978—Eagles, 19-17 (NY)
Eagles, 20-3 (P)
1979—Eagles, 23-17 (P)
Eagles, 17-13 (NY)
1980—Eagles, 35-3 (P)
Eagles, 31-16 (NY)
1981—Eagles, 24-10 (NY)
Giants, 20-10 (P)
*Giants, 27-21 (P)
1982—Giants, 23-7 (NY)
Giants, 26-24 (P)
1983—Eagles, 17-13 (NY)
Giants, 23-0 (P)
1984—Giants, 28-27 (NY)
Eagles, 24-10 (P)
1985—Giants, 21-0 (NY)
Giants, 16-10 (P) OT
1986—Giants, 35-3 (NY)
Giants, 17-14 (P)
1987—Giants, 20-17 (P)
Giants, 23-20 (NY) OT
1988—Eagles, 24-13 (P)
Eagles, 23-17 (NY) OT
1989—Eagles, 21-19 (P)
Eagles, 24-17 (NY)
1990—Giants, 27-20 (NY)
Eagles, 31-13 (P)
1991—Eagles, 30-7 (P)
Eagles, 19-14 (NY)
1992—Eagles, 47-34 (NY)
Eagles, 20-10 (P)
1993—Giants, 21-10 (NY)
Giants, 7-3 (P)
1994—Giants, 28-23 (NY)
Giants, 16-13 (P)
1995—Eagles, 17-14 (NY)
Eagles, 28-19 (P)
1996—Eagles, 19-10 (NY)
Eagles, 24-0 (P)
1997—Giants, 31-17 (NY)
Giants, 31-21 (P)
1998—Giants, 20-0 (NY)
Giants, 20-10 (P)
1999—Giants, 16-15 (NY)
Giants, 23-17 (P) OT
2000—Giants, 33-18 (P)
Giants, 24-7 (NY)
**Giants, 20-10 (NY)
(RS Pts.—Giants 2,533, Eagles 2,342)
(PS Pts.—Giants 47, Eagles 31)
**NFC First-Round Playoff*
***NFC Divisional Playoff*
N.Y. GIANTS vs. *PITTSBURGH
RS: Giants lead series, 43-27-3
1933—Giants, 23-2 (P)
Giants, 27-3 (NY)
1934—Giants, 14-12 (P)
Giants, 17-7 (NY)
1935—Giants, 42-7 (P)
Giants, 13-0 (NY)
1936—Pirates, 10-7 (P)
1937—Giants, 10-7 (P)
Giants, 17-0 (NY)
1938—Giants, 27-14 (P)
Pirates, 13-10 (NY)
1939—Giants, 14-7 (P)
Giants, 23-7 (NY)
1940—Tie, 10-10 (P)
Giants, 12-0 (NY)
1941—Giants, 37-10 (P)
Giants, 28-7 (NY)
1942—Steelers, 13-10 (P)
Steelers, 17-9 (NY)
1945—Giants, 34-6 (P)
Steelers, 21-7 (NY)
1946—Giants, 17-14 (P)
Giants, 7-0 (NY)
1947—Steelers, 38-21 (NY)
Steelers, 24-7 (P)
1948—Giants, 34-27 (NY)
Steelers, 38-28 (P)
1949—Steelers, 28-7 (P)
Steelers, 21-17 (NY)
1950—Giants, 18-7 (P)
Steelers, 17-6 (NY)
1951—Tie, 13-13 (P)
Giants, 14-0 (NY)
1952—Steelers, 63-7 (P)
1953—Steelers, 24-14 (P)
Steelers, 14-10 (NY)
1954—Giants, 30-6 (P)
Giants, 24-3 (NY)
1955—Steelers, 30-23 (P)
Steelers, 19-17 (NY)
1956—Giants, 38-10 (NY)
Giants, 17-14 (P)
1957—Giants, 35-0 (NY)
Steelers, 21-10 (P)
1958—Giants, 17-6 (NY)
Steelers, 31-10 (P)
1959—Giants, 21-16 (P)
Steelers, 14-9 (NY)
1960—Giants, 19-17 (P)
Giants, 27-24 (NY)
1961—Giants, 17-14 (P)
Giants, 42-21 (NY)
1962—Giants, 31-27 (P)
Steelers, 20-17 (NY)
1963—Steelers, 31-0 (P)
Giants, 33-17 (NY)
1964—Steelers, 27-24 (P)
Steelers, 44-17 (NY)
1965—Giants, 23-13 (P)
Giants, 35-10 (NY)
1966—Tie, 34-34 (P)
Steelers, 47-28 (NY)
1967—Giants, 27-24 (P)
Giants, 28-20 (NY)
1968—Giants, 34-20 (P)
1969—Giants, 10-7 (NY)
Giants, 21-17 (P)
1971—Steelers, 17-13 (P)
1976—Steelers, 27-0 (NY)
1985—Giants, 28-10 (NY)
1991—Giants, 23-20 (P)
1994—Steelers, 10-6 (NY)
2000—Giants, 30-10 (NY)
(RS Pts.—Giants 1,429, Steelers 1,199)
**Steelers known as Pirates prior to 1941*
N.Y. GIANTS vs. *ST. LOUIS
RS: Rams lead series, 24-9
PS: Series tied, 1-1
1938—Giants, 28-0 (NY)
1940—Rams, 13-0 (NY)
1941—Giants, 49-14 (NY)
1945—Rams, 21-17 (NY)
1946—Rams, 31-21 (NY)
1947—Rams, 34-10 (LA)
1948—Rams, 52-37 (NY)
1953—Rams, 21-7 (LA)
1954—Rams, 17-16 (NY)
1959—Giants, 23-21 (LA)
1961—Giants, 24-14 (NY)
1966—Rams, 55-14 (LA)
1968—Rams, 24-21 (LA)
1970—Rams, 31-3 (NY)
1973—Rams, 40-6 (LA)
1976—Rams, 24-10 (LA)
1978—Rams, 20-17 (NY)
1979—Giants, 20-14 (LA)
1980—Rams, 28-7 (NY)
1981—Giants, 10-7 (NY)
1983—Rams, 16-6 (NY)
1984—Rams, 33-12 (LA)
**Giants, 16-13 (LA)
1985—Giants, 24-19 (NY)
1988—Rams, 45-31 (NY)
1989—Rams, 31-10 (LA)
***Rams, 19-13 (NY) OT
1990—Giants, 31-7 (LA)
1991—Rams, 19-13 (NY)
1992—Rams, 38-17 (LA)
1993—Giants, 20-10 (NY)
1994—Rams, 17-10 (LA)
1997—Rams, 13-3 (StL)
1999—Rams, 31-10 (StL)
2000—Rams, 38-24 (NY)
(RS Pts.—Rams 798, Giants 551)
(PS Pts.—Rams 32, Giants 29)
**Franchise in Los Angeles prior to 1995 and in Cleveland prior to 1946*
***NFC First-Round Playoff*
****NFC Divisional Playoff*
N.Y. GIANTS vs. SAN DIEGO
RS: Giants lead series, 5-3
1971—Giants, 35-17 (NY)
1975—Giants, 35-24 (NY)
1980—Chargers, 44-7 (SD)
1983—Chargers, 41-34 (NY)
1986—Giants, 20-7 (NY)
1989—Giants, 20-13 (SD)
1995—Chargers, 27-17 (NY)
1998—Giants, 34-16 (SD)

ALL-TIME TEAM VS. TEAM RESULTS

(RS Pts.—Giants 202, Chargers 189)
N.Y. GIANTS vs. SAN FRANCISCO
RS: 49ers lead series, 12-11
PS: Series tied, 3-3
1952—Giants, 23-14 (NY)
1956—Giants, 38-21 (SF)
1957—49ers, 27-17 (NY)
1960—Giants, 21-19 (SF)
1963—Giants, 48-14 (NY)
1968—49ers, 26-10 (NY)
1972—Giants, 23-17 (SF)
1975—Giants, 26-23 (SF)
1977—Giants, 20-17 (NY)
1978—Giants, 27-10 (NY)
1979—Giants, 32-16 (NY)
1980—49ers, 12-0 (SF)
1981—49ers, 17-10 (SF)
*49ers, 38-24 (SF)
1984—49ers, 31-10 (NY)
*49ers, 21-10 (SF)
1985—**Giants, 17-3 (NY)
1986—Giants, 21-17 (SF)
*Giants, 49-3 (NY)
1987—49ers, 41-21 (NY)
1988—49ers, 20-17 (NY)
1989—49ers, 34-24 (SF)
1990—49ers, 7-3 (SF)
***Giants, 15-13 (SF)
1991—Giants, 16-14 (NY)
1992—49ers, 31-14 (NY)
1993—*49ers, 44-3 (SF)
1995—49ers, 20-6 (SF)
1998—49ers, 31-7 (SF)
(RS Pts.—49ers 479, Giants 434)
(PS Pts.—49ers 122, Giants 118)
**NFC Divisional Playoff*
***NFC First-Round Playoff*
****NFC Championship*
N.Y. GIANTS vs. SEATTLE
RS: Giants lead series, 5-3
1976—Giants, 28-16 (NY)
1980—Giants, 27-21 (S)
1981—Giants, 32-0 (S)
1983—Seahawks, 17-12 (NY)
1986—Seahawks, 17-12 (S)
1989—Giants, 15-3 (NY)
1992—Giants, 23-10 (NY)
1995—Seahawks, 30-28 (S)
(RS Pts.—Giants 177, Seahawks 114)
N.Y. GIANTS vs. TAMPA BAY
RS: Giants lead series, 9-5
1977—Giants, 10-0 (TB)
1978—Giants, 19-13 (TB)
Giants, 17-14 (NY)
1979—Giants, 17-14 (NY)
Buccaneers, 31-3 (TB)
1980—Buccaneers, 30-13 (TB)
1984—Giants, 17-14 (NY)
Buccaneers, 20-17 (TB)
1985—Giants, 22-20 (NY)
1991—Giants, 21-14 (TB)
1993—Giants, 23-7 (NY)
1997—Buccaneers, 20-8 (NY)
1998—Buccaneers, 20-3 (TB)
1999—Giants, 17-13 (TB)
(RS Pts.—Buccaneers 230, Giants 207)
N.Y. GIANTS vs. *TENNESSEE
RS: Giants lead series, 5-2
1973—Giants, 34-14 (NY)
1982—Giants, 17-14 (NY)
1985—Giants, 35-14 (H)
1991—Giants, 24-20 (NY)
1994—Giants, 13-10 (H)
1997—Oilers, 10-6 (T)
2000—Titans, 28-14 (T)
(RS Pts.—Giants 143, Titans 110)
**Franchise in Houston prior to 1997; known as Oilers prior to 1999*
N.Y. GIANTS vs. *WASHINGTON
RS: Giants lead series, 76-56-4
PS: Series tied, 1-1
1932—Braves, 14-6 (B)
Tie, 0-0 (NY)
1933—Redskins, 21-20 (B)
Giants, 7-0 (NY)
1934—Giants, 16-13 (B)
Giants, 3-0 (NY)
1935—Giants, 20-12 (B)
Giants, 17-6 (NY)
1936—Giants, 7-0 (B)
Redskins, 14-0 (NY)
1937—Redskins, 13-3 (W)
Redskins, 49-14 (NY)
1938—Giants, 10-7 (W)
Giants, 36-0 (NY)
1939—Tie, 0-0 (W)
Giants, 9-7 (NY)
1940—Redskins, 21-7 (W)
Giants, 21-7 (NY)
1941—Giants, 17-10 (W)
Giants, 20-13 (NY)
1942—Giants, 14-7 (W)
Redskins, 14-7 (NY)
1943—Giants, 14-10 (NY)
Giants, 31-7 (W)
**Redskins, 28-0 (NY)
1944—Giants, 16-13 (NY)
Giants, 31-0 (W)
1945—Redskins, 24-14 (NY)
Redskins, 17-0 (W)
1946—Redskins, 24-14 (W)
Giants, 31-0 (NY)
1947—Redskins, 28-20 (W)
Giants, 35-10 (NY)
1948—Redskins, 41-10 (W)
Redskins, 28-21 (NY)
1949—Giants, 45-35 (W)
Giants, 23-7 (NY)
1950—Giants, 21-17 (W)
Giants, 24-21 (NY)
1951—Giants, 35-14 (W)
Giants, 28-14 (NY)
1952—Giants, 14-10 (W)
Redskins, 27-17 (NY)
1953—Redskins, 13-9 (W)
Redskins, 24-21 (NY)
1954—Giants, 51-21 (W)
Giants, 24-7 (NY)
1955—Giants, 35-7 (NY)
Giants, 27-20 (W)
1956—Redskins, 33-7 (W)
Giants, 28-14 (NY)
1957—Giants, 24-20 (W)
Redskins, 31-14 (NY)
1958—Giants, 21-14 (W)
Giants, 30-0 (NY)
1959—Giants, 45-14 (NY)
Giants, 24-10 (W)
1960—Tie, 24-24 (NY)
Giants, 17-3 (W)
1961—Giants, 24-21 (W)
Giants, 53-0 (NY)
1962—Giants, 49-34 (NY)
Giants, 42-24 (W)
1963—Giants, 24-14 (W)
Giants, 44-14 (NY)
1964—Giants, 13-10 (NY)
Redskins, 36-21 (W)
1965—Redskins, 23-7 (NY)
Giants, 27-10 (W)
1966—Giants, 13-10 (NY)
Redskins, 72-41 (W)
1967—Redskins, 38-34 (W)
1968—Giants, 48-21 (NY)
Giants, 13-10 (W)
1969—Redskins, 20-14 (W)
1970—Giants, 35-33 (NY)
Giants, 27-24 (W)
1971—Redskins, 30-3 (NY)
Redskins, 23-7 (W)
1972—Redskins, 23-16 (NY)
Redskins, 27-13 (W)
1973—Redskins, 21-3 (New Haven)
Redskins, 27-24 (W)
1974—Redskins, 13-10 (New Haven)
Redskins, 24-3 (W)
1975—Redskins, 49-13 (W)
Redskins, 21-13 (NY)
1976—Redskins, 19-17 (W)
Giants, 12-9 (NY)
1977—Giants, 20-17 (NY)
Giants, 17-6 (W)
1978—Giants, 17-6 (NY)
Redskins, 16-13 (W) OT
1979—Redskins, 27-0 (W)
Giants, 14-6 (NY)
1980—Redskins, 23-21 (NY)
Redskins, 16-13 (W)
1981—Giants, 17-7 (W)
Redskins, 30-27 (NY) OT
1982—Redskins, 27-17 (NY)
Redskins, 15-14 (W)
1983—Redskins, 33-17 (NY)
Redskins, 31-22 (W)
1984—Redskins, 30-14 (W)
Giants, 37-13 (NY)
1985—Giants, 17-3 (NY)
Redskins, 23-21 (W)
1986—Giants, 27-20 (NY)
Giants, 24-14 (W)
***Giants, 17-0 (NY)
1987—Redskins, 38-12 (NY)
Redskins, 23-19 (W)
1988—Giants, 27-20 (NY)
Giants, 24-23 (W)
1989—Giants, 27-24 (W)
Giants, 20-17 (NY)
1990—Giants, 24-20 (W)
Giants, 21-10 (NY)
1991—Redskins, 17-13 (NY)
Redskins, 34-17 (W)
1992—Giants, 24-7 (W)
Redskins, 28-10 (NY)
1993—Giants, 41-7 (W)
Giants, 20-6 (NY)
1994—Giants, 31-23 (NY)
Giants, 21-19 (W)
1995—Giants, 24-15 (W)
Giants, 20-13 (NY)
1996—Redskins, 31-10 (NY)
Redskins, 31-21 (W)
1997—Tie, 7-7 (W) OT
Giants, 30-10 (NY)
1998—Giants, 31-24 (NY)
Redskins, 21-14 (W)
1999—Redskins, 50-21 (NY)
Redskins, 23-13 (W)
2000—Redskins, 16-6 (NY)
Giants, 9-7 (W)
(RS Pts.—Giants 2,688, Redskins 2,457)
(PS Pts.—Redskins 28, Giants 17)
**Franchise in Boston prior to 1937 and known as Braves prior to 1933*
***Division Playoff*
****NFC Championship*

N.Y. JETS vs. ARIZONA
RS: Jets lead series, 3-2;
See Arizona vs. N.Y. Jets
N.Y. JETS vs. ATLANTA
RS: Series tied, 4-4;
See Atlanta vs. N.Y. Jets
N.Y. JETS vs BALTIMORE
RS: Ravens lead series, 2-1;
See Baltimore vs. N.Y. Jets
N.Y. JETS vs. BUFFALO
RS: Bills lead series, 45-35
PS: Bills lead series, 1-0;
See Buffalo vs. N.Y. Jets
N.Y. JETS vs. CAROLINA
RS: Series tied, 1-1;
See Carolina vs. N.Y. Jets
N.Y. JETS vs. CHICAGO
RS: Bears lead series, 4-3;
See Chicago vs. N.Y. Jets
N.Y. JETS vs. CINCINNATI
RS: Jets lead series, 10-6
PS: Jets lead series, 1-0;
See Cincinnati vs. N.Y. Jets
N.Y. JETS vs. CLEVELAND
RS: Browns lead series, 9-6
PS: Browns lead series, 1-0;
See Cleveland vs. N.Y. Jets
N.Y. JETS vs. DALLAS
RS: Cowboys lead series, 5-2;
See Dallas vs. N.Y. Jets
N.Y. JETS vs. DENVER
RS: Broncos lead series, 14-13-1
PS: Broncos lead series, 1-0;
See Denver vs. N.Y. Jets
N.Y. JETS vs. DETROIT
RS: Lions lead series, 6-3;
See Detroit vs. N.Y. Jets
N.Y. JETS vs. GREEN BAY
RS: Jets lead series, 6-2;
See Green Bay vs. N.Y. Jets
N.Y. JETS vs. INDIANAPOLIS
RS: Colts lead series, 37-24
PS: Jets lead series, 1-0;
See Indianapolis vs. N.Y. Jets
N.Y. JETS vs. JACKSONVILLE
RS: Jaguars lead series, 2-1
PS: Jets lead series, 1-0;
See Jacksonville vs. N.Y. Jets
N.Y. JETS vs. KANSAS CITY
RS: Chiefs lead series, 14-13-1
PS: Series tied, 1-1;
See Kansas City vs. N.Y. Jets
N.Y. JETS vs. MIAMI
RS: Jets lead series, 35-34-1
PS: Dolphins lead series, 1-0;
See Miami vs. N.Y. Jets
N.Y. JETS vs. MINNESOTA
RS: Jets lead series, 5-1;
See Minnesota vs. N.Y. Jets
N.Y. JETS vs. NEW ENGLAND
RS: Jets lead series, 45-35-1
PS: Patriots lead series, 1-0;
See New England vs. N.Y. Jets
N.Y. JETS vs. NEW ORLEANS
RS: Series tied, 4-4;
See New Orleans vs. N.Y. Jets
N.Y. JETS vs. N.Y. GIANTS
RS: Giants lead series, 5-4;
See N.Y. Giants vs. N.Y. Jets
***N.Y. JETS vs. **OAKLAND**
RS: Raiders lead series, 18-10-2
PS: Jets lead series, 2-0
1960—Raiders, 28-27 (NY)
Titans, 31-28 (O)
1961—Titans, 14-6 (O)
Titans, 23-12 (NY)
1962—Titans, 28-17 (O)
Titans, 31-21 (NY)
1963—Jets, 10-7 (NY)
Raiders, 49-26 (O)
1964—Jets, 35-13 (NY)
Raiders, 35-26 (O)
1965—Tie, 24-24 (NY)
Raiders, 24-14 (O)
1966—Raiders, 24-21 (NY)
Tie, 28-28 (O)
1967—Jets, 27-14 (NY)
Raiders, 38-29 (O)
1968—Raiders, 43-32 (O)
***Jets, 27-23 (NY)
1969—Raiders, 27-14 (NY)
1970—Raiders, 14-13 (NY)
1972—Raiders, 24-16 (O)
1977—Raiders, 28-27 (NY)
1979—Jets, 28-19 (NY)
1982—****Jets, 17-14 (LA)
1985—Raiders, 31-0 (LA)
1989—Raiders, 14-7 (NY)
1993—Raiders, 24-20 (LA)
1995—Raiders, 47-10 (NY)
1996—Raiders, 34-13 (NY)
1997—Jets 23-22 (NY)
1999—Raiders, 24-23 (O)
2000—Raiders, 31-7 (O)
(RS Pts.—Raiders 750, Jets 627)
(PS Pts.—Jets 44, Raiders 37)

**Jets known as Titans prior to 1963*
***Franchise in Los Angeles from 1982-1994*
****AFL Championship*
*****AFC Second-Round Playoff*

N.Y. JETS vs. PHILADELPHIA
RS: Eagles lead series, 6-0
1973—Eagles, 24-23 (P)
1977—Eagles, 27-0 (P)
1978—Eagles, 17-9 (P)
1987—Eagles, 38-27 (NY)
1993—Eagles, 35-30 (NY)
1996—Eagles, 21-20 (NY)
(RS Pts.—Eagles 162, Jets 109)

N.Y. JETS vs. PITTSBURGH
RS: Steelers lead series, 13-1
1970—Steelers, 21-17 (P)
1973—Steelers, 26-14 (P)
1975—Steelers, 20-7 (NY)
1977—Steelers, 23-20 (NY)
1978—Steelers, 28-17 (NY)
1981—Steelers, 38-10 (P)
1983—Steelers, 34-7 (NY)
1984—Steelers, 23-17 (NY)
1986—Steelers, 45-24 (NY)
1988—Jets, 24-20 (NY)
1989—Steelers, 13-0 (NY)
1990—Steelers, 24-7 (NY)
1992—Steelers, 27-10 (P)
2000—Steelers, 20-3 (NY)
(RS Pts.—Steelers 362, Jets 177)

N.Y. JETS vs. *ST. LOUIS
RS: Rams lead series, 7-2
1970—Jets, 31-20 (LA)
1974—Rams, 20-13 (NY)
1980—Rams, 38-13 (LA)
1983—Jets, 27-24 (NY) OT
1986—Rams, 17-3 (NY)
1989—Rams, 38-14 (LA)
1992—Rams, 18-10 (LA)
1995—Rams, 23-20 (NY)
1998—Rams, 30-10 (StL)
(RS Pts.—Rams 228, Jets 141)
**Franchise in Los Angeles prior to 1995*

***N.Y. JETS vs. **SAN DIEGO**
RS: Chargers lead series, 17-9-1
1960—Chargers, 21-7 (NY)
Chargers, 50-43 (LA)
1961—Chargers, 25-10 (NY)
Chargers, 48-13 (SD)
1962—Chargers, 40-14 (SD)
Titans, 23-3 (NY)
1963—Chargers, 24-20 (SD)
Chargers, 53-7 (NY)
1964—Tie, 17-17 (NY)
Chargers, 38-3 (SD)
1965—Chargers, 34-9 (NY)
Chargers, 38-7 (SD)
1966—Jets, 17-16 (NY)
Chargers, 42-27 (SD)
1967—Jets, 42-31 (SD)
1968—Jets, 23-20 (NY)
Jets, 37-15 (SD)
1969—Chargers, 34-27 (SD)
1971—Chargers, 49-21 (SD)
1974—Jets, 27-14 (NY)
1975—Chargers, 24-16 (SD)
1983—Jets, 41-29 (SD)
1989—Jets, 20-17 (SD)
1990—Chargers, 39-3 (NY)
Chargers, 38-17 (SD)
1991—Jets, 24-3 (NY)
1994—Chargers, 21-6 (NY)
(RS Pts.—Chargers 783, Jets 521)
**Jets known as Titans prior to 1963*
***Franchise in Los Angeles prior to 1961*

N.Y. JETS vs. SAN FRANCISCO
RS: 49ers lead series, 7-1
1971—49ers, 24-21 (NY)
1976—49ers, 17-6 (SF)
1980—49ers, 37-27 (NY)
1983—Jets, 27-13 (SF)
1986—49ers, 24-10 (SF)
1989—49ers, 23-10 (NY)
1992—49ers, 31-14 (NY)
1998—49ers, 36-30 (SF) OT
(RS Pts.—49ers 205, Jets 145)

N.Y. JETS vs. SEATTLE
RS: Seahawks lead series, 8-7
1977—Seahawks, 17-0 (NY)
1978—Seahawks, 24-17 (NY)
1979—Seahawks, 30-7 (S)
1980—Seahawks, 27-17 (NY)
1981—Seahawks, 19-3 (NY)
Seahawks, 27-23 (S)
1983—Seahawks, 17-10 (NY)
1985—Jets, 17-14 (NY)
1986—Jets, 38-7 (S)
1987—Jets, 30-14 (NY)
1991—Seahawks, 20-13 (S)
1995—Jets, 16-10 (S)
1997—Jets, 41-3 (S)
1998—Jets, 32-31 (NY)
1999—Jets, 19-9 (NY)
(RS Pts.—Jets 283, Seahawks 269)

N.Y. JETS vs. TAMPA BAY
RS: Jets lead series, 7-1
1976—Jets, 34-0 (NY)
1982—Jets, 32-17 (NY)
1984—Buccaneers, 41-21 (TB)
1985—Jets, 62-28 (NY)
1990—Jets, 16-14 (TB)
1991—Jets, 16-13 (NY)
1997—Jets, 31-0 (NY)
2000—Jets, 21-17 (TB)
(RS Pts.—Jets 233, Buccaneers 130)

***N.Y. JETS vs. **TENNESSEE**
RS: Titans lead series, 20-13-1
PS: Titans lead series, 1-0
1960—Oilers, 27-21 (H)
Oilers, 42-28 (NY)
1961—Oilers, 49-13 (H)
Oilers, 48-21 (NY)
1962—Oilers, 56-17 (H)
Oilers, 44-10 (NY)
1963—Jets, 24-17 (NY)
Oilers, 31-27 (H)
1964—Jets, 24-21 (NY)
Oilers, 33-17 (H)
1965—Oilers, 27-21 (H)
Jets, 41-14 (NY)
1966—Jets, 52-13 (NY)
Oilers, 24-0 (H)
1967—Tie, 28-28 (NY)
1968—Jets, 20-14 (H)
Jets, 26-7 (NY)
1969—Jets, 26-17 (NY)
Jets, 34-26 (H)
1972—Oilers, 26-20 (H)
1974—Oilers, 27-22 (NY)
1977—Oilers, 20-0 (H)
1979—Oilers, 27-24 (H) OT
1980—Jets, 31-28 (NY) OT
1981—Jets, 33-17 (NY)
1984—Oilers, 31-20 (H)
1988—Jets, 45-3 (NY)
1990—Jets, 17-12 (H)
1991—Oilers, 23-20 (NY)
***Oilers, 17-10 (H)
1993—Oilers, 24-0 (H)
1994—Oilers, 24-10 (H)
1995—Oilers, 23-6 (H)
1996—Oilers, 35-10 (NY)
1998—Jets, 24-3 (T)
(RS Pts.—Titans 861, Jets 732)
(PS Pts.—Titans 17, Jets 10)
**Jets known as Titans prior to 1963*
***Franchise in Houston prior to 1997; known as Oilers prior to 1999*
****AFC First-Round Playoff*

N.Y. JETS vs. WASHINGTON
RS: Redskins lead series, 6-1
1972—Redskins, 35-17 (NY)
1976—Redskins, 37-16 (NY)
1978—Redskins, 23-3 (W)
1987—Redskins, 17-16 (W)
1993—Jets, 3-0 (W)
1996—Redskins, 31-16 (W)
1999—Redskins, 27-20 (NY)
(RS Pts.—Redskins 170, Jets 91)

OAKLAND vs. ARIZONA
RS: Raiders lead series, 3-1;
See Arizona vs. Oakland

OAKLAND vs. ATLANTA
RS: Raiders lead series, 7-3;
See Atlanta vs. Oakland

OAKLAND vs. BALTIMORE
RS: Ravens lead series, 2-0
PS: Ravens lead series, 1-0;
See Baltimore vs. Oakland

OAKLAND vs. BUFFALO
RS: Raiders lead series, 16-15
PS: Bills lead series, 2-0;
See Buffalo vs. Oakland

OAKLAND vs CAROLINA
RS: Series tied, 1-1;
See Carolina vs Oakland

OAKLAND vs. CHICAGO
RS: Raiders lead series, 6-4;
See Chicago vs. Oakland

OAKLAND vs. CINCINNATI
RS: Raiders lead series, 16-7
PS: Raiders lead series, 2-0;
See Cincinnati vs. Oakland

OAKLAND vs. CLEVELAND
RS: Raiders lead series, 9-4
PS: Raiders lead series, 2-0;
See Cleveland vs. Oakland

OAKLAND vs. DALLAS
RS: Raiders lead series, 4-3;
See Dallas vs. Oakland

OAKLAND vs. DENVER
RS: Raiders lead series, 49-30-2
PS: Series tied, 1-1;
See Denver vs. Oakland

OAKLAND vs. DETROIT
RS: Raiders lead series, 6-2;
See Detroit vs. Oakland

OAKLAND vs. GREEN BAY
RS: Raiders lead series, 5-3
PS: Packers lead series, 1-0;
See Green Bay vs. Oakland

OAKLAND vs. INDIANAPOLIS
RS: Raiders lead series, 6-2
PS: Series tied, 1-1;
See Indianapolis vs. Oakland

OAKLAND vs. JACKSONVILLE
RS: Series tied, 1-1;
See Jacksonville vs. Oakland

OAKLAND vs. KANSAS CITY
RS: Chiefs lead series, 40-39-2
PS: Chiefs lead series, 2-1;
See Kansas City vs. Oakland

OAKLAND vs. MIAMI
RS: Raiders lead series, 15-8-1
PS: Raiders lead series, 3-1;
See Miami vs. Oakland

OAKLAND vs. MINNESOTA
RS: Raiders lead series, 7-3
PS: Raiders lead series, 1-0;
See Minnesota vs. Oakland

OAKLAND vs. NEW ENGLAND
RS: Raiders lead series, 13-12-1
PS: Series tied, 1-1;
See New England vs. Oakland

OAKLAND vs. NEW ORLEANS
RS: Raiders lead series, 5-3-1;
See New Orleans vs. Oakland

OAKLAND vs. N.Y. GIANTS
RS: Raiders lead series, 6-2;
See N.Y. Giants vs. Oakland

OAKLAND vs. N.Y. JETS
RS: Raiders lead series, 18-10-2
PS: Jets lead series, 2-0;
See N.Y. Jets vs. Oakland

***OAKLAND vs. PHILADELPHIA**
RS: Eagles lead series, 4-3
PS: Raiders lead series, 1-0
1971—Raiders, 34-10 (O)
1976—Raiders, 26-7 (P)
1980—Eagles, 10-7 (P)
**Raiders, 27-10 (New Orleans)
1986—Eagles, 33-27 (LA) OT
1989—Eagles, 10-7 (P)
1992—Eagles, 31-10 (P)
1995—Raiders, 48-17 (O)
(RS Pts.—Raiders 159, Eagles 118)
(PS Pts.—Raiders 27, Eagles 10)
**Franchise in Los Angeles from 1982-1994*
***Super Bowl XV*

***OAKLAND vs. PITTSBURGH**
RS: Raiders lead series, 7-6
PS: Series tied, 3-3
1970—Raiders, 31-14 (O)
1972—Steelers, 34-28 (P)
**Steelers, 13-7 (P)
1973—Steelers, 17-9 (O)
**Raiders, 33-14 (O)
1974—Raiders, 17-0 (P)
***Steelers, 24-13 (O)
1975—***Steelers, 16-10 (P)
1976—Raiders, 31-28 (O)
***Raiders, 24-7 (O)
1977—Raiders, 16-7 (P)
1980—Raiders, 45-34 (P)
1981—Raiders, 30-27 (O)
1983—**Raiders, 38-10 (LA)
1984—Steelers, 13-7 (LA)
1990—Raiders, 20-3 (LA)
1994—Steelers, 21-3 (LA)
1995—Steelers, 29-10 (O)
2000—Steelers, 21-20 (P)
(RS Pts.—Raiders 267, Steelers 248)
(PS Pts.—Raiders 125, Steelers 84)
**Franchise in Los Angeles from 1982-1994*
***AFC Divisional Playoff*
****AFC Championship*

***OAKLAND vs. **ST. LOUIS**
RS: Raiders lead series, 7-2
1972—Raiders, 45-17 (O)
1977—Rams, 20-14 (LA)
1979—Raiders, 24-17 (LA)
1982—Raiders, 37-31 (LA Raiders)
1985—Raiders, 16-6 (LA Rams)
1988—Rams, 22-17 (LA Raiders)
1991—Raiders, 20-17 (LA Raiders)
1994—Raiders, 20-17 (LA Rams)
1997—Raiders, 35-17 (O)
(RS Pts.—Raiders 228, Rams 164)
**Franchise in Los Angeles from 1982-1994*
***Franchise in Los Angeles prior to 1995*

***OAKLAND vs. **SAN DIEGO**
RS: Raiders lead series, 50-30-2
PS: Raiders lead series, 1-0
1960—Chargers, 52-28 (LA)
Chargers, 41-17 (O)
1961—Chargers, 44-0 (SD)
Chargers, 41-10 (O)
1962—Chargers, 42-33 (O)
Chargers, 31-21 (SD)
1963—Raiders, 34-33 (SD)
Raiders, 41-27 (O)
1964—Chargers, 31-17 (SD)
Raiders, 21-20 (O)
1965—Chargers, 17-6 (O)
Chargers, 24-14 (SD)
1966—Chargers, 29-20 (O)
Raiders, 41-19 (SD)
1967—Raiders, 51-10 (O)
Raiders, 41-21 (SD)
1968—Chargers, 23-14 (O)
Raiders, 34-27 (SD)
1969—Raiders, 24-12 (SD)
Raiders, 21-16 (O)
1970—Tie, 27-27 (SD)
Raiders, 20-17 (O)

1971—Raiders, 34-0 (SD)
Raiders, 34-33 (O)
1972—Tie, 17-17 (O)
Raiders, 21-19 (SD)
1973—Raiders, 27-17 (SD)
Raiders, 31-3 (O)
1974—Raiders, 14-10 (SD)
Raiders, 17-10 (O)
1975—Raiders, 6-0 (SD)
Raiders, 25-0 (O)
1976—Raiders, 27-17 (SD)
Raiders, 24-0 (O)
1977—Raiders, 24-0 (O)
Chargers, 12-7 (SD)
1978—Raiders, 21-20 (SD)
Chargers, 27-23 (O)
1979—Chargers, 30-10 (SD)
Raiders, 45-22 (O)
1980—Chargers, 30-24 (SD) OT
Raiders, 38-24 (O)
***Raiders, 34-27 (SD)
1981—Chargers, 55-21 (O)
Chargers, 23-10 (SD)
1982—Raiders, 28-24 (LA)
Raiders, 41-34 (SD)
1983—Raiders, 42-10 (SD)
Raiders, 30-14 (LA)
1984—Raiders, 33-30 (LA)
Raiders, 44-37 (SD)
1985—Raiders, 34-21 (LA)
Chargers, 40-34 (SD) OT
1986—Raiders, 17-13 (LA)
Raiders, 37-31 (SD) OT
1987—Chargers, 23-17 (LA)
Chargers, 16-14 (SD)
1988—Raiders, 24-13 (LA)
Raiders, 13-3 (SD)
1989—Raiders, 40-14 (LA)
Chargers, 14-12 (SD)
1990—Raiders, 24-9 (SD)
Raiders, 17-12 (LA)
1991—Chargers, 21-13 (LA)
Raiders, 9-7 (SD)
1992—Chargers, 27-3 (SD)
Chargers, 36-14 (LA)
1993—Chargers, 30-23 (LA)
Raiders, 12-7 (SD)
1994—Chargers, 26-24 (LA)
Raiders, 24-17 (SD)
1995—Raiders, 17-7 (O)
Chargers, 12-6 (SD)
1996—Chargers, 40-34 (O)
Raiders, 23-14 (SD)
1997—Chargers, 25-10 (O)
Raiders, 38-13 (SD)
1998—Raiders, 7-6 (O)
Raiders, 17-10 (SD)
1999—Raiders, 28-9 (O)
Chargers, 23-20 (SD)
2000—Raiders, 9-6 (O)
Raiders, 15-13 (SD)
(RS Pts.—Raiders 1,882, Chargers 1,680)
(PS Pts.—Raiders 34, Chargers 27)
Franchise in Los Angeles from 1982-1994
***Franchise in Los Angeles prior to 1961*
****AFC Championship*

***OAKLAND vs. SAN FRANCISCO**
RS: Raiders lead series, 6-3
1970—49ers, 38-7 (O)
1974—Raiders, 35-24 (SF)
1979—Raiders, 23-10 (O)
1982—Raiders, 23-17 (SF)
1985—49ers, 34-10 (LA)
1988—Raiders, 9-3 (SF)
1991—Raiders, 12-6 (LA)
1994—49ers, 44-14 (SF)
2000—Raiders, 34-28 (SF) OT
(RS Pts.—49ers 204, Raiders 167)
**Franchise in Los Angeles from 1982-1994*

***OAKLAND vs. SEATTLE**
RS: Raiders lead series, 25-21
PS: Series tied, 1-1
1977—Raiders, 44-7 (O)
1978—Seahawks, 27-7 (S)
Seahawks, 17-16 (O)
1979—Seahawks, 27-10 (S)
Seahawks, 29-24 (O)
1980—Raiders, 33-14 (O)
Raiders, 19-17 (S)
1981—Raiders, 20-10 (O)
Raiders, 32-31 (S)
1982—Raiders, 28-23 (LA)
1983—Seahawks, 38-36 (S)
Seahawks, 34-21 (LA)
**Raiders, 30-14 (LA)
1984—Raiders, 28-14 (LA)
Seahawks, 17-14 (S)
***Seahawks, 13-7 (S)
1985—Seahawks, 33-3 (S)
Raiders, 13-3 (LA)
1986—Raiders, 14-10 (LA)
Seahawks, 37-0 (S)
1987—Seahawks, 35-13 (LA)
Raiders, 37-14 (S)
1988—Seahawks, 35-27 (S)
Seahawks, 43-37 (LA)
1989—Seahawks, 24-20 (LA)
Seahawks, 23-17 (S)
1990—Raiders, 17-13 (S)
Raiders, 24-17 (LA)
1991—Raiders, 23-20 (S) OT
Raiders, 31-7 (LA)
1992—Raiders, 19-0 (S)
Raiders, 20-3 (LA)
1993—Raiders, 17-13 (S)
Raiders, 27-23 (LA)
1994—Seahawks, 38-9 (LA)
Raiders, 17-16 (S)
1995—Raiders, 34-14 (O)
Seahawks, 44-10 (S)
1996—Raiders, 27-21 (S)
Seahawks, 28-21 (O)
1997—Seahawks, 45-34 (S)
Seahawks, 22-21 (O)
1998—Raiders, 31-18 (S)
Raiders, 20-17 (O)
1999—Seahawks, 22-21 (S)
Raiders, 30-21 (O)
2000—Raiders, 31-3 (O)
Seahawks, 27-24 (S)
(RS Pts.—Raiders 1,021, Seahawks 994)
(PS Pts.—Raiders 37, Seahawks 27)
**Franchise in Los Angeles from 1982-1994*
***AFC Championship*
****AFC First-Round Playoff*

***OAKLAND vs. TAMPA BAY**
RS: Raiders lead series, 4-1
1976—Raiders, 49-16 (O)
1981—Raiders, 18-16 (O)
1993—Raiders, 27-20 (LA)
1996—Buccaneers, 20-17 (TB) OT
1999—Raiders, 45-0 (O)
(RS Pts.—Raiders 156, Buccaneers 72)
**Franchise in Los Angeles from 1982-1994*

***OAKLAND vs. **TENNESSEE**
RS: Raiders lead series, 20-15
PS: Raiders lead series, 3-0
1960—Oilers, 37-22 (O)
Raiders, 14-13 (H)
1961—Oilers, 55-0 (H)
Oilers, 47-16 (O)
1962—Oilers, 28-20 (O)
Oilers, 32-17 (H)
1963—Raiders, 24-13 (H)
Raiders, 52-49 (O)
1964—Oilers, 42-28 (H)
Raiders, 20-10 (O)
1965—Raiders, 21-17 (O)
Raiders, 33-21 (H)
1966—Oilers, 31-0 (H)
Raiders, 38-23 (O)
1967—Raiders, 19-7 (H)
***Raiders, 40-7 (O)
1968—Raiders, 24-15 (H)
1969—Raiders, 21-17 (O)
****Raiders, 56-7 (O)
1971—Raiders, 41-21 (O)
1972—Raiders, 34-0 (H)
1973—Raiders, 17-6 (H)
1975—Oilers, 27-26 (O)
1976—Raiders, 14-13 (H)
1977—Raiders, 34-29 (O)
1978—Raiders, 21-17 (O)
1979—Oilers, 31-17 (H)
1980—*****Raiders, 27-7 (O)
1981—Oilers, 17-16 (H)
1983—Raiders, 20-6 (LA)
1984—Raiders, 24-14 (H)
1986—Raiders, 28-17 (H)
1988—Oilers, 38-35 (H)
1989—Oilers, 23-7 (H)
1991—Oilers, 47-17 (H)
1994—Raiders, 17-14 (LA)
1997—Oilers, 24-21 (T) OT
1999—Titans, 21-14 (T)
(RS Pts.—Titans 822, Raiders 772)
(PS Pts.—Raiders 123, Titans 21)
**Franchise in Los Angeles from 1982-1994*
***Franchise in Houston prior to 1997; known as Oilers prior to 1999*
****AFL Championship*
*****Inter-Divisional Playoff*
******AFC First-Round Playoff*

***OAKLAND vs. WASHINGTON**
RS: Raiders lead series, 6-3
PS: Raiders lead series, 1-0
1970—Raiders, 34-20 (O)
1975—Raiders, 26-23 (W) OT
1980—Raiders, 24-21 (O)
1983—Redskins, 37-35 (W)
**Raiders, 38-9 (Tampa)
1986—Redskins, 10-6 (W)
1989—Raiders, 37-24 (LA)
1992—Raiders, 21-20 (W)
1995—Raiders, 20-8 (W)
1998—Redskins, 29-19 (O)
(RS Pts.—Raiders 222, Redskins 192)
(PS Pts.—Raiders 38, Redskins 9)
**Franchise in Los Angeles from 1982-1994*
***Super Bowl XVIII*

PHILADELPHIA vs. ARIZONA
RS: Cardinals lead series, 51-50-5
PS: Series tied, 1-1;
See Arizona vs. Philadelphia

PHILADELPHIA vs. ATLANTA
RS: Eagles lead series, 10-9-1
PS: Falcons lead series, 1-0;
See Atlanta vs. Philadelphia

PHILADELPHIA vs. BALTIMORE
RS: Series tied, 0-0-1;
See Baltimore vs. Philadelphia

PHILADELPHIA vs. BUFFALO
RS: Bills lead series, 5-4;
See Buffalo vs. Philadelphia

PHILADELPHIA vs. CAROLINA
RS: Series tied, 1-1;
See Carolina vs. Philadelphia

PHILADELPHIA vs. CHICAGO
RS: Bears lead series, 24-6-1
PS: Series tied, 1-1;
See Chicago vs. Philadelphia

PHILADELPHIA vs. CINCINNATI
RS: Bengals lead series, 6-3;
See Cincinnati vs. Philadelphia

PHILADELPHIA vs. CLEVELAND
RS: Browns lead series, 31-13-1;
See Cleveland vs. Philadelphia

PHILADELPHIA vs. DALLAS
RS: Cowboys lead series, 48-32
PS: Cowboys lead series, 2-1;
See Dallas vs. Philadelphia

PHILADELPHIA vs. DENVER
RS: Eagles lead series, 6-3;
See Denver vs. Philadelphia

PHILADELPHIA vs. DETROIT
RS: Lions lead series, 12-11-2
PS: Eagles lead series, 1-0;
See Detroit vs. Philadelphia

PHILADELPHIA vs. GREEN BAY
RS: Packers lead series, 22-9
PS: Eagles lead series, 1-0;
See Green Bay vs. Philadelphia

PHILADELPHIA vs. INDIANAPOLIS
RS: Colts lead series, 8-6;
See Indianapolis vs. Philadelphia

PHILADELPHIA vs. JACKSONVILLE
RS: Jaguars lead series, 1-0;
See Jacksonville vs. Philadelphia

PHILADELPHIA vs. KANSAS CITY
RS: Chiefs lead series, 2-1;
See Kansas City vs. Philadelphia

PHILADELPHIA vs. MIAMI
RS: Dolphins lead series, 7-3;
See Miami vs. Philadelphia

PHILADELPHIA vs. MINNESOTA
RS: Vikings lead series, 11-6
PS: Eagles lead series, 1-0;
See Minnesota vs. Philadelphia

PHILADELPHIA vs. NEW ENGLAND
RS: Eagles lead series, 6-2;
See New England vs. Philadelphia

PHILADELPHIA vs. NEW ORLEANS
RS: Eagles lead series, 13-8
PS; Eagles lead series, 1-0;
See New Orleans vs. Philadelphia

PHILADELPHIA vs. N.Y. GIANTS
RS: Giants lead series, 72-58-2
PS: Giants lead series, 2-0;
See N.Y. Giants vs. Philadelphia

PHILADELPHIA vs. N.Y. JETS
RS: Eagles lead series, 6-0;
See N.Y. Jets vs. Philadelphia

PHILADELPHIA vs. OAKLAND
RS: Eagles lead series, 4-3
PS: Raiders lead series, 1-0;
See Oakland vs. Philadelphia

PHILADELPHIA vs. *PITTSBURGH
RS: Eagles lead series, 45-26-3
PS: Eagles lead series, 1-0
1933—Eagles, 25-6 (Phila)
1934—Eagles, 17-0 (Pitt)
Pirates, 9-7 (Phila)
1935—Pirates, 17-7 (Phila)
Eagles, 17-6 (Pitt)
1936—Pirates, 17-0 (Pitt)
Pirates, 6-0 (Johnstown, Pa.)
1937—Pirates, 27-14 (Pitt)
Pirates, 16-7 (Pitt)
1938—Eagles, 27-7 (Buffalo)
Eagles, 14-7 (Charleston, W. Va.)
1939—Eagles, 17-14 (Phila)
Pirates, 24-12 (Pitt)
1940—Pirates, 7-3 (Pitt)
Eagles, 7-0 (Phila)
1941—Eagles, 10-7 (Pitt)
Tie, 7-7 (Phila)
1942—Eagles, 24-14 (Pitt)
Steelers, 14-0 (Phila)
1945—Eagles, 45-3 (Pitt)
Eagles, 30-6 (Phila)
1946—Steelers, 10-7 (Pitt)
Eagles, 10-7 (Phila)
1947—Steelers, 35-24 (Pitt)
Eagles, 21-0 (Phila)
**Eagles, 21-0 (Pitt)
1948—Eagles, 34-7 (Pitt)
Eagles, 17-0 (Phila)
1949—Eagles, 38-7 (Pitt)
Eagles, 34-17 (Phila)
1950—Eagles, 17-10 (Pitt)
Steelers, 9-7 (Phila)
1951—Eagles, 34-13 (Pitt)
Steelers, 17-13 (Phila)
1952—Eagles, 31-25 (Pitt)

Eagles, 26-21 (Phila)
1953—Eagles, 23-17 (Phila)
Eagles, 35-7 (Pitt)
1954—Eagles, 24-22 (Phila)
Steelers, 17-7 (Pitt)
1955—Steelers, 13-7 (Pitt)
Eagles, 24-0 (Phila)
1956—Eagles, 35-21 (Pitt)
Eagles, 14-7 (Phila)
1957—Steelers, 6-0 (Pitt)
Eagles, 7-6 (Phila)
1958—Steelers, 24-3 (Pitt)
Steelers, 31-24 (Phila)
1959—Eagles, 28-24 (Phila)
Steelers, 31-0 (Pitt)
1960—Eagles, 34-7 (Phila)
Steelers, 27-21 (Pitt)
1961—Eagles, 21-16 (Phila)
Eagles, 35-24 (Pitt)
1962—Steelers, 13-7 (Pitt)
Steelers, 26-17 (Phila)
1963—Tie, 21-21 (Phila)
Tie, 20-20 (Pitt)
1964—Eagles, 21-7 (Phila)
Eagles, 34-10 (Pitt)
1965—Steelers, 20-14 (Phila)
Eagles, 47-13 (Pitt)
1966—Eagles, 31-14 (Pitt)
Eagles, 27-23 (Phila)
1967—Eagles, 34-24 (Phila)
1968—Steelers, 6-3 (Pitt)
1969—Eagles, 41-27 (Phila)
1970—Eagles, 30-20 (Phila)
1974—Steelers, 27-0 (Pitt)
1979—Eagles, 17-14 (Phila)
1988—Eagles, 27-26 (Pitt)
1991—Eagles, 23-14 (Phila)
1994—Steelers, 14-3 (Pitt)
1997—Eagles, 23-20 (Phila)
2000—Eagles, 26-23 (Pitt) OT
(RS Pts.—Eagles 1,411, Steelers 1,064)
(PS Pts.—Eagles 21, Steelers 0)
Steelers known as Pirates prior to 1941
***Division Playoff*

PHILADELPHIA vs. *ST. LOUIS
RS: Rams lead series, 15-14-1
PS: Series tied, 1-1
1937—Rams, 21-3 (P)
1939—Rams, 35-13 (Colorado Springs)
1940—Rams, 21-13 (C)
1942—Rams, 24-14 (Akron)
1944—Eagles, 26-13 (P)
1945—Eagles, 28-14 (P)
1946—Eagles, 25-14 (LA)
1947—Eagles, 14-7 (P)
1948—Tie, 28-28 (LA)
1949—Eagles, 38-14 (P)
**Eagles, 14-0 (LA)
1950—Eagles, 56-20 (P)
1955—Rams, 23-21 (P)
1956—Rams, 27-7 (LA)
1957—Rams, 17-13 (LA)
1959—Eagles, 23-20 (P)
1964—Rams, 20-10 (LA)
1967—Rams, 33-17 (LA)
1969—Rams, 23-17 (P)
1972—Rams, 34-3 (P)
1975—Rams, 42-3 (P)
1977—Rams, 20-0 (LA)
1978—Rams, 16-14 (P)
1983—Eagles, 13-9 (P)
1985—Rams, 17-6 (P)
1986—Eagles, 34-20 (P)
1988—Eagles, 30-24 (P)
1989—***Rams, 21-7 (P)
1990—Eagles, 27-21 (LA)
1995—Eagles, 20-9 (P)
1998—Eagles, 17-14 (P)
1999—Eagles, 38-31 (P)
(RS Pts.—Rams 631, Eagles 571)
(PS Pts.—Rams 21, Eagles 21)
Franchise in Los Angeles prior to 1995 and in Cleveland prior to 1946
***NFL Championship*
****NFC First-Round Playoff*

PHILADELPHIA vs. SAN DIEGO
RS: Chargers lead series, 5-2
1974—Eagles, 13-7 (SD)
1980—Chargers, 22-21 (SD)
1985—Chargers, 20-14 (SD)
1986—Eagles, 23-7 (P)
1989—Chargers, 20-17 (SD)
1995—Chargers, 27-21 (P)
1998—Chargers, 13-10 (SD)
(RS Pts.—Eagles 119, Chargers 116)

PHILADELPHIA vs. SAN FRANCISCO
RS: 49ers lead series, 14-6-1
PS: 49ers lead series, 1-0
1951—Eagles, 21-14 (P)
1953—49ers, 31-21 (SF)
1956—Tie, 10-10 (P)
1958—49ers, 30-24 (P)
1959—49ers, 24-14 (SF)
1964—49ers, 28-24 (P)
1966—Eagles, 35-34 (SF)
1967—49ers, 28-27 (P)
1969—49ers, 14-13 (SF)
1971—49ers, 31-3 (P)
1973—49ers, 38-28 (SF)
1975—Eagles, 27-17 (P)
1983—Eagles, 22-17 (SF)
1984—49ers, 21-9 (P)
1985—49ers, 24-13 (SF)
1989—49ers, 38-28 (P)
1991—49ers, 23-7 (P)
1992—49ers, 20-14 (SF)
1993—Eagles, 37-34 (SF) OT
1994—Eagles, 40-8 (SF)
1996—*49ers, 14-0 (SF)
1997—49ers, 24-12 (P)
(RS Pts.—49ers 508, Eagles 429)
(PS Pts.—49ers 14, Eagles 0)
**NFC First-Round Playoff*

PHILADELPHIA vs. SEATTLE
RS: Eagles lead series, 4-3
1976—Eagles, 27-10 (P)
1980—Eagles, 27-20 (S)
1986—Seahawks, 24-20 (S)
1989—Eagles, 31-7 (P)
1992—Eagles, 20-17 (S) OT
1995—Seahawks, 26-14 (S)
1998—Seahawks, 38-0 (P)
(RS Pts.—Seahawks 142, Eagles 139)

PHILADELPHIA vs. TAMPA BAY
RS: Series tied, 3-3
PS: Series tied, 1-1
1977—Eagles, 13-3 (P)
1979—*Buccaneers, 24-17 (TB)
1981—Eagles, 20-10 (P)
1988—Eagles, 41-14 (TB)
1991—Buccaneers, 14-13 (TB)
1995—Buccaneers, 21-6 (P)
1999—Buccaneers, 19-5 (P)
2000—**Eagles, 21-3 (P)
(RS Pts.—Eagles 98, Buccaneers 81)
(PS Pts.—Eagles 38, Buccaneers 27)
**NFC Divisional Playoff*
***NFC First-Round Playoff*

PHILADELPHIA vs. *TENNESSEE
RS: Eagles lead series, 6-1
1972—Eagles, 18-17 (H)
1979—Eagles, 26-20 (H)
1982—Eagles, 35-14 (P)
1988—Eagles, 32-23 (P)
1991—Eagles, 13-6 (H)
1994—Eagles, 21-6 (P)
2000—Titans, 15-13 (P)
(RS Pts.—Eagles 158, Titans 101)
Franchise in Houston prior to 1997; known as Oilers prior to 1999

PHILADELPHIA vs. *WASHINGTON
RS: Redskins lead series, 71-55-5
PS: Redskins lead series, 1-0
1934—Redskins, 6-0 (B)
Redskins, 14-7 (P)
1935—Eagles, 7-6 (B)
1936—Redskins, 26-3 (P)
Redskins, 17-7 (B)
1937—Eagles, 14-0 (W)
Redskins, 10-7 (P)
1938—Redskins, 26-23 (P)
Redskins, 20-14 (W)
1939—Redskins, 7-0 (P)
Redskins, 7-6 (W)
1940—Redskins, 34-17 (P)
Redskins, 13-6 (W)
1941—Redskins, 21-17 (P)
Redskins, 20-14 (W)
1942—Redskins, 14-10 (P)
Redskins, 30-27 (W)
1944—Tie, 31-31 (P)
Eagles, 37-7 (W)
1945—Redskins, 24-14 (W)
Eagles, 16-0 (P)
1946—Eagles, 28-24 (W)
Redskins, 27-10 (P)
1947—Eagles, 45-42 (P)
Eagles, 38-14 (W)
1948—Eagles, 45-0 (W)
Eagles, 42-21 (P)
1949—Eagles, 49-14 (P)
Eagles, 44-21 (W)
1950—Eagles, 35-3 (P)
Eagles, 33-0 (W)
1951—Redskins, 27-23 (P)
Eagles, 35-21 (W)
1952—Eagles, 38-20 (P)
Redskins, 27-21 (W)
1953—Tie, 21-21 (P)
Redskins, 10-0 (W)
1954—Eagles, 49-21 (W)
Eagles, 41-33 (P)
1955—Redskins, 31-30 (P)
Redskins, 34-21 (W)
1956—Eagles, 13-9 (P)
Redskins, 19-17 (W)
1957—Eagles, 21-12 (P)
Redskins, 42-7 (W)
1958—Redskins, 24-14 (P)
Redskins, 20-0 (W)
1959—Eagles, 30-23 (P)
Eagles, 34-14 (W)
1960—Eagles, 19-13 (P)
Eagles, 38-28 (W)
1961—Eagles, 14-7 (P)
Eagles, 27-24 (W)
1962—Redskins, 27-21 (P)
Eagles, 37-14 (W)
1963—Eagles, 37-24 (W)
Redskins, 13-10 (P)
1964—Redskins, 35-20 (W)
Redskins, 21-10 (P)
1965—Redskins, 23-21 (W)
Eagles, 21-14 (P)
1966—Redskins, 27-13 (P)
Eagles, 37-28 (W)
1967—Eagles, 35-24 (P)
Tie, 35-35 (W)
1968—Redskins, 17-14 (W)
Redskins, 16-10 (P)
1969—Tie, 28-28 (W)
Redskins, 34-29 (P)
1970—Redskins, 33-21 (P)
Redskins, 24-6 (W)
1971—Tie, 7-7 (W)
Redskins, 20-13 (P)
1972—Redskins, 14-0 (W)
Redskins, 23-7 (P)
1973—Redskins, 28-7 (P)
Redskins, 38-20 (W)
1974—Redskins, 27-20 (P)
Redskins, 26-7 (W)
1975—Eagles, 26-10 (P)
Eagles, 26-3 (W)
1976—Redskins, 20-17 (P) OT
Redskins, 24-0 (W)
1977—Redskins, 23-17 (W)
Redskins, 17-14 (P)
1978—Redskins, 35-30 (W)
Eagles, 17-10 (P)
1979—Eagles, 28-17 (P)
Redskins, 17-7 (W)
1980—Eagles, 24-14 (P)
Eagles, 24-0 (W)
1981—Eagles, 36-13 (P)
Redskins, 15-13 (W)
1982—Redskins, 37-34 (P) OT
Redskins, 13-9 (W)
1983—Redskins, 23-13 (P)
Redskins, 28-24 (W)
1984—Redskins, 20-0 (W)
Eagles, 16-10 (P)
1985—Eagles, 19-6 (W)
Redskins, 17-12 (P)
1986—Redskins, 41-14 (W)
Redskins, 21-14 (P)
1987—Redskins, 34-24 (W)
Eagles, 31-27 (P)
1988—Redskins, 17-10 (W)
Redskins, 20-19 (P)
1989—Eagles, 42-37 (W)
Redskins, 10-3 (P)
1990—Redskins, 13-7 (W)
Eagles, 28-14 (P)
**Redskins, 20-6 (P)
1991—Redskins, 23-0 (W)
Eagles, 24-22 (P)
1992—Redskins, 16-12 (W)
Eagles, 17-13 (P)
1993—Eagles, 34-31 (P)
Eagles, 17-14 (W)
1994—Eagles, 21-17 (P)
Eagles, 31-29 (W)
1995—Eagles, 37-34 (P) (OT)
Eagles, 14-7 (W)
1996—Eagles, 17-14 (W)
Redskins, 26-21 (P)
1997—Eagles, 24-10 (P)
Redskins, 35-32 (W)
1998—Eagles, 17-12 (P)
Redskins, 28-3 (W)
1999—Eagles, 35-28 (P)
Redskins, 20-17 (W) OT
2000—Redskins, 17-14 (P)
Eagles, 23-20 (W)
(RS Pts.—Eagles 2,653, Redskins 2,621)
(PS Pts.—Redskins 20, Eagles 6)
Franchise in Boston prior to 1937
***NFC First-Round Playoff*

PITTSBURGH vs. ARIZONA
RS: Steelers lead series, 30-22-3;
See Arizona vs. Pittsburgh

PITTSBURGH vs. ATLANTA
RS: Steelers lead series, 11-1;
See Atlanta vs. Pittsburgh

PITTSBURGH vs. BALTIMORE
RS: Steelers lead series, 7-3;
See Baltimore vs. Pittsburgh

PITTSBURGH vs. BUFFALO
RS: Series tied, 8-8
PS: Steelers lead series, 2-1;
See Buffalo vs. Pittsburgh

PITTSBURGH vs. CAROLINA
RS: Series tied, 1-1;
See Carolina vs. Pittsburgh

PITTSBURGH vs. CHICAGO
RS: Bears lead series, 16-6-1;
See Chicago vs. Pittsburgh

PITTSBURGH vs. CINCINNATI
RS: Steelers lead series, 35-26;
See Cincinnati vs. Pittsburgh

PITTSBURGH vs. CLEVELAND
RS: Browns lead series, 54-42
PS: Steelers lead series, 1-0;
See Cleveland vs. Pittsburgh

PITTSBURGH vs. DALLAS
RS: Cowboys lead series, 14-11
PS: Steelers lead series, 2-1;
See Dallas vs. Pittsburgh

PITTSBURGH vs. DENVER
RS: Broncos lead series, 10-6-1

ALL-TIME TEAM VS. TEAM RESULTS

PS: Broncos lead series, 3-2;
See Denver vs. Pittsburgh
PITTSBURGH vs. DETROIT
RS: Lions lead series, 14-12-1;
See Detroit vs. Pittsburgh
PITTSBURGH vs. GREEN BAY
RS: Packers lead series, 18-12;
See Green Bay vs. Pittsburgh
PITTSBURGH vs. INDIANAPOLIS
RS: Steelers lead series, 12-4
PS: Steelers lead series, 4-0;
See Indianapolis vs. Pittsburgh
PITTSBURGH vs. JACKSONVILLE
RS: Jaguars lead series, 7-5;
See Jacksonville vs. Pittsburgh
PITTSBURGH vs. KANSAS CITY
RS: Steelers lead series, 15-7
PS: Chiefs lead series, 1-0;
See Kansas City vs. Pittsburgh
PITTSBURGH vs. MIAMI
RS: Dolphins lead series, 9-7
PS: Dolphins lead series, 2-1;
See Miami vs. Pittsburgh
PITTSBURGH vs. MINNESOTA
RS: Vikings lead series, 8-4
PS: Steelers lead series, 1-0;
See Minnesota vs. Pittsburgh
PITTSBURGH vs. NEW ENGLAND
RS: Steelers lead series, 11-4
PS: Series tied, 1-1;
See New England vs. Pittsburgh
PITTSBURGH vs. NEW ORLEANS
RS: Steelers lead series, 6-5;
See New Orleans vs. Pittsburgh
PITTSBURGH vs. N.Y. GIANTS
RS: Giants lead series, 43-27-3;
See N.Y. Giants vs. Pittsburgh
PITTSBURGH vs. N.Y. JETS
RS: Steelers lead series, 13-1;
See N.Y. Jets vs. Pittsburgh
PITTSBURGH vs. OAKLAND
RS: Raiders lead series, 7-6
PS: Series tied, 3-3;
See Oakland vs. Pittsburgh
PITTSBURGH vs. PHILADELPHIA
RS: Eagles lead series, 45-26-3
PS: Eagles lead series, 1-0;
See Philadelphia vs. Pittsburgh
***PITTSBURGH vs. **ST. LOUIS**
RS: Rams lead series, 14-5-2
PS: Steelers lead series, 1-0
1938—Rams, 13-7 (New Orleans)
1939—Tie, 14-14 (C)
1941—Rams, 17-14 (Akron)
1947—Rams, 48-7 (P)
1948—Rams, 31-14 (LA)
1949—Tie, 7-7 (P)
1952—Rams, 28-14 (LA)
1955—Rams, 27-26 (LA)
1956—Steelers, 30-13 (P)
1961—Rams, 24-14 (LA)
1964—Rams, 26-14 (P)
1968—Rams, 45-10 (LA)
1971—Rams, 23-14 (P)
1975—Rams, 10-3 (LA)
1978—Rams, 10-7 (LA)
1979—***Steelers, 31-19 (Pasadena)
1981—Steelers, 24-0 (P)
1984—Steelers, 24-14 (P)
1987—Rams, 31-21 (LA)
1990—Steelers, 41-10 (P)
1993—Rams, 27-0 (LA)
1996—Steelers, 42-6 (P)
(RS Pts.—Rams 424, Steelers 347)
(PS Pts.—Steelers 31, Rams 19)
**Steelers known as Pirates prior to 1941*
***Franchise in Los Angeles prior to 1995 and in Cleveland prior to 1946*
****Super Bowl XIV*
PITTSBURGH vs. SAN DIEGO
RS: Steelers lead series, 17-5
PS: Chargers lead series, 2-0
1971—Steelers, 21-17 (P)
1972—Steelers, 24-2 (SD)
1973—Steelers, 38-21 (P)
1975—Steelers, 37-0 (SD)
1976—Steelers, 23-0 (P)
1977—Steelers, 10-9 (SD)
1979—Chargers, 35-7 (SD)
1980—Chargers, 26-17 (SD)
1982—*Chargers, 31-28 (P)
1983—Steelers, 26-3 (P)
1984—Steelers, 52-24 (P)
1985—Chargers, 54-44 (SD)
1987—Steelers, 20-16 (SD)
1988—Chargers, 20-14 (SD)
1989—Steelers, 20-17 (P)
1990—Steelers, 36-14 (P)
1991—Steelers, 26-20 (P)
1992—Steelers, 23-6 (SD)
1993—Steelers,.16-3 (P)
1994—Chargers, 37-34 (SD)
**Chargers, 17-13 (P)
1995—Steelers, 31-16 (P)
1996—Steelers, 16-3 (P)
2000—Steelers, 34-21 (SD)
(RS Pts.—Steelers 569, Chargers 364)
(PS Pts.—Chargers 48, Steelers 41)
**AFC First-Round Playoff*
***AFC Championship*
PITTSBURGH vs. SAN FRANCISCO
RS: 49ers lead series, 9-8
1951—49ers, 28-24 (P)
1952—Steelers, 24-7 (SF)
1954—49ers, 31-3 (SF)
1958—49ers, 23-20 (SF)
1961—Steelers, 20-10 (P)
1965—49ers, 27-17 (SF)
1968—49ers, 45-28 (P)
1973—Steelers, 37-14 (SF)
1977—Steelers, 27-0 (P)
1978—Steelers, 24-7 (SF)
1981—49ers, 17-14 (P)
1984—Steelers, 20-17 (SF)
1987—Steelers, 30-17 (P)
1990—49ers, 27-7 (SF)
1993—49ers, 24-13 (P)
1996—49ers, 25-15 (P)
1999—Steelers, 27-6 (SF)
(RS Pts.—Steelers 350, 49ers 325)
PITTSBURGH vs. SEATTLE
RS: Seahawks lead series, 7-6
1977—Steelers, 30-20 (P)
1978—Steelers, 21-10 (P)
1981—Seahawks, 24-21 (S)
1982—Seahawks, 16-0 (S)
1983—Steelers, 27-21 (S)
1986—Seahawks, 30-0 (S)
1987—Steelers, 13-9 (P)
1991—Seahawks, 27-7 (P)
1992—Steelers, 20-14 (P)
1993—Seahawks, 16-6 (S)
1994—Seahawks, 30-13 (S)
1998—Steelers, 13-10 (P)
1999—Seahawks, 29-10 (P)
(RS Pts.—Seahawks 256, Steelers 181)
PITTSBURGH vs. TAMPA BAY
RS: Steelers lead series, 4-1
1976—Steelers, 42-0 (P)
1980—Steelers, 24-21 (TB)
1983—Steelers, 17-12 (P)
1989—Steelers, 31-22 (TB)
1998—Buccaneers, 16-3 (TB)
(RS Pts.—Steelers 117, Buccaneers 71)
PITTSBURGH vs. *TENNESSEE
RS: Steelers lead series, 35-26
PS: Steelers lead series, 3-0
1970—Oilers, 19-7 (P)
Steelers, 7-3 (H)
1971—Steelers, 23-16 (P)
Oilers, 29-3 (H)
1972—Steelers, 24-7 (P)
Steelers, 9-3 (H)
1973—Steelers, 36-7 (H)
Steelers, 33-7 (P)
1974—Steelers, 13-7 (H)
Oilers, 13-10 (P)
1975—Steelers, 24-17 (P)
Steelers, 32-9 (H)
1976—Steelers, 32-16 (P)
Steelers, 21-0 (H)
1977—Oilers, 27-10 (H)
Steelers, 27-10 (P)
1978—Oilers, 24-17 (P)
Steelers, 13-3 (H)
**Steelers, 34-5 (P)
1979—Steelers, 38-7 (P)
Oilers, 20-17 (H)
**Steelers, 27-13 (P)
1980—Steelers, 31-17 (P)
Oilers, 6-0 (H)
1981—Steelers, 26-13 (P)
Oilers, 21-20 (H)
1982—Steelers, 24-10 (H)
1983—Steelers, 40-28 (H)
Steelers, 17-10 (P)
1984—Steelers, 35-7 (P)
Oilers, 23-20 (H) OT
1985—Steelers, 20-0 (P)
Steelers, 30-7 (H)
1986—Steelers, 22-16 (H) OT
Steelers, 21-10 (P)
1987—Oilers, 23-3 (P)
Oilers, 24-16 (H)
1988—Oilers, 34-14 (P)
Steelers, 37-34 (H)
1989—Oilers, 27-0 (H)
Oilers, 23-16 (P)
***Steelers, 26-23 (H) OT
1990—Steelers, 20-9 (P)
Oilers, 34-14 (H)
1991—Steelers, 26-14 (P)
Oilers, 31-6 (H)
1992—Steelers, 29-24 (H)
Steelers, 21-20 (P)
1993—Oilers, 23-3 (H)
Oilers, 26-17 (P)
1994—Steelers, 30-14 (P)
Steelers, 12-9 (H) OT
1995—Steelers, 34-17 (H)
Steelers, 21-7 (P)
1996—Steelers, 30-16 (P)
Oilers, 23-13 (H)
1997—Steelers, 37-24 (P)
Oilers, 16-6 (T)
1998—Oilers, 41-31 (P)
Oilers, 23-14 (T)
1999—Titans, 16-10 (T)
Titans, 47-36 (P)
2000—Titans, 23-20 (P)
Titans, 9-7 (T)
(RS Pts.—Steelers 1,225, Titans 1,043)
(PS Pts.—Steelers 87, Titans 41)
**Franchise in Houston prior to 1997; known as Oilers prior to 1999*
***AFC Championship*
****AFC First-Round Playoff*
***PITTSBURGH vs. **WASHINGTON**
RS: Redskins lead series, 42-29-3
1933—Redskins, 21-6 (P)
Pirates, 16-14 (B)
1934—Redskins, 7-0 (P)
Redskins, 39-0 (B)
1935—Pirates, 6-0 (P)
Redskins, 13-3 (B)
1936—Pirates, 10-0 (P)
Redskins, 30-0 (B)
1937—Redskins, 34-20 (W)
Pirates, 21-13 (P)
1938—Redskins, 7-0 (P)
Redskins, 15-0 (W)
1939—Redskins, 44-14 (W)
Redskins, 21-14 (P)
1940—Redskins, 40-10 (P)
Redskins, 37-10 (W)
1941—Redskins, 24-20 (P)
Redskins, 23-3 (W)
1942—Redskins, 28-14 (W)
Redskins, 14-0 (P)
1945—Redskins, 14-0 (P)
Redskins, 24-0 (W)
1946—Tie, 14-14 (W)
Steelers, 14-7 (P)
1947—Redskins, 27-26 (W)
Steelers, 21-14 (P)
1948—Redskins, 17-14 (W)
Steelers, 10-7 (P)
1949—Redskins, 27-14 (P)
Redskins, 27-14 (W)
1950—Steelers, 26-7 (W)
Redskins, 24-7 (P)
1951—Redskins, 22-7 (P)
Steelers, 20-10 (W)
1952—Redskins, 28-24 (P)
Steelers, 24-23 (W)
1953—Redskins, 17-9 (P)
Steelers, 14-13 (W)
1954—Steelers, 37-7 (P)
Redskins, 17-14 (W)
1955—Redskins, 23-14 (P)
Redskins, 28-17 (W)
1956—Steelers, 30-13 (P)
Steelers, 23-0 (W)
1957—Steelers, 28-7 (P)
Redskins, 10-3 (W)
1958—Steelers, 24-16 (P)
Tie, 14-14 (W)
1959—Redskins, 23-17 (P)
Steelers, 27-6 (W)
1960—Tie, 27-27 (W)
Steelers, 22-10 (P)
1961—Steelers, 20-0 (P)
Steelers, 30-14 (W)
1962—Steelers, 23-21 (P)
Steelers, 27-24 (W)
1963—Steelers, 38-27 (P)
Steelers, 34-28 (W)
1964—Redskins, 30-0 (P)
Steelers, 14-7 (W)
1965—Redskins, 31-3 (P)
Redskins, 35-14 (W)
1966—Redskins, 33-27 (P)
Redskins, 24-10 (W)
1967—Redskins, 15-10 (P)
1968—Redskins, 16-13 (W)
1969—Redskins, 14-7 (P)
1973—Steelers, 21-16 (P)
1979—Steelers, 38-7 (P)
1985—Redskins, 30-23 (P)
1988—Redskins, 30-29 (W)
1991—Redskins, 41-14 (P)
1997—Steelers, 14-13 (P)
2000—Steelers, 24-3 (P)
(RS Pts.—Redskins 1,406, Steelers 1,155)
**Steelers known as Pirates prior to 1941*
***Franchise in Boston prior to 1937*

ST. LOUIS vs. ARIZONA
RS: Rams lead series, 23-21-2
PS: Rams lead series, 1-0;
See Arizona vs. St. Louis
ST. LOUIS vs. ATLANTA
RS: Rams lead series, 43-23-2;
See Atlanta vs. St. Louis
ST. LOUIS vs. BALTIMORE
RS: Series tied, 1-1;
See Baltimore vs. St. Louis
ST. LOUIS vs. BUFFALO
RS: Series tied, 4-4;
See Buffalo vs. St. Louis
ST. LOUIS vs. CAROLINA
RS: Panthers lead series, 7-5;
See Carolina vs. St. Louis
ST. LOUIS vs. CHICAGO
RS: Bears lead series, 47-32-3
PS: Series tied, 1-1;
See Chicago vs. St. Louis
ST. LOUIS vs. CINCINNATI
RS: Bengals lead series, 5-4;
See Cincinnati vs. St. Louis
ST. LOUIS vs. CLEVELAND
RS: Series tied, 8-8

PS: Browns lead series, 2-1;
See Cleveland vs. St. Louis
ST. LOUIS vs. DALLAS
RS: Rams lead series, 9-8
PS: Series tied, 4-4;
See Dallas vs. St. Louis
ST. LOUIS vs. DENVER
RS: Rams lead series, 5-4;
See Denver vs. St. Louis
ST. LOUIS vs. DETROIT
RS: Rams lead series, 39-36-1
PS: Lions lead series, 1-0;
See Detroit vs. St. Louis
ST. LOUIS vs. GREEN BAY
RS: Rams lead series, 43-39-2
PS: Packers lead series, 1-0;
See Green Bay vs. St. Louis
ST. LOUIS vs. INDIANAPOLIS
RS: Colts lead series, 21-16-2;
See Indianapolis vs. St. Louis
ST. LOUIS vs. JACKSONVILLE
RS: Rams lead series, 1-0;
See Jacksonville vs. St. Louis
ST. LOUIS vs. KANSAS CITY
RS: Rams lead series, 4-3;
See Kansas City vs. St. Louis
ST. LOUIS vs. MIAMI
RS: Dolphins lead series, 7-1;
See Miami vs. St. Louis
ST. LOUIS vs. MINNESOTA
RS: Vikings lead series, 16-12-2
PS: Vikings lead series, 5-2;
See Minnesota vs. St. Louis
ST. LOUIS vs. NEW ENGLAND
RS: Rams lead series, 4-3;
See New England vs. St. Louis
ST. LOUIS vs. NEW ORLEANS
RS: Rams lead series, 35-27
PS: Saints lead series, 1-0;
See New Orleans vs. St. Louis
ST. LOUIS vs. N.Y. GIANTS
RS: Rams lead series, 24-9
PS: Series tied, 1-1;
See N.Y. Giants vs. St. Louis
ST. LOUIS vs. N.Y. JETS
RS: Rams lead series, 7-2;
See N.Y. Jets vs. St. Louis
ST. LOUIS vs. OAKLAND
RS: Raiders lead series, 7-2;
See Oakland vs. St. Louis
ST. LOUIS vs. PHILADELPHIA
RS: Rams lead series, 15-14-1
PS: Series tied, 1-1;
See Philadelphia vs. St. Louis
ST. LOUIS vs. PITTSBURGH
RS: Rams lead series, 14-5-2
PS: Steelers lead series, 1-0;
See Pittsburgh vs. St. Louis
***ST. LOUIS vs. SAN DIEGO**
RS: Rams lead series, 4-3
1970—Rams, 37-10 (LA)
1975—Rams, 13-10 (SD) OT
1979—Chargers, 40-16 (LA)
1988—Chargers, 38-24 (LA)
1991—Rams, 30-24 (LA)
1994—Chargers, 31-17 (SD)
2000—Rams, 57-31 (StL)
(RS Pts.—Rams 194, Chargers 184)
Franchise in Los Angeles prior to 1995
***ST. LOUIS vs. SAN FRANCISCO**
RS: Rams lead series, 52-48-2
PS: 49ers lead series, 1-0
1950—Rams, 35-14 (SF)
Rams, 28-21 (LA)
1951—49ers, 44-17 (SF)
Rams, 23-16 (LA)
1952—Rams, 35-9 (LA)
Rams, 34-21 (SF)
1953—49ers, 31-30 (SF)
49ers, 31-27 (LA)
1954—Tie, 24-24 (LA)
Rams, 42-34 (SF)
1955—Rams, 23-14 (SF)
Rams, 27-14 (LA)
1956—49ers, 33-30 (SF)
Rams, 30-6 (LA)
1957—49ers, 23-20 (SF)
Rams, 37-24 (LA)
1958—Rams, 33-3 (SF)
Rams, 56-7 (LA)
1959—49ers, 34-0 (SF)
49ers, 24-16 (LA)
1960—49ers, 13-9 (SF)
49ers, 23-7 (LA)
1961—49ers, 35-0 (SF)
Rams, 17-7 (LA)
1962—Rams, 28-14 (SF)
49ers, 24-17 (LA)
1963—Rams, 28-21 (LA)
Rams, 21-17 (SF)
1964—Rams, 42-14 (LA)
49ers, 28-7 (SF)
1965—49ers, 45-21 (LA)
49ers, 30-27 (SF)
1966—Rams, 34-3 (LA)
49ers, 21-13 (SF)
1967—49ers, 27-24 (LA)
Rams, 17-7 (SF)
1968—Rams, 24-10 (LA)
Tie, 20-20 (SF)
1969—Rams, 27-21 (SF)
Rams, 41-30 (LA)
1970—49ers, 20-6 (LA)
Rams, 30-13 (SF)
1971—Rams, 20-13 (SF)
Rams, 17-6 (LA)
1972—Rams, 31-7 (LA)
Rams, 26-16 (SF)
1973—Rams, 40-20 (SF)
Rams, 31-13 (LA)
1974—Rams, 37-14 (LA)
Rams, 15-13 (SF)
1975—Rams, 23-14 (SF)
49ers, 24-23 (LA)
1976—49ers, 16-0 (LA)
Rams, 23-3 (SF)
1977—Rams, 34-14 (LA)
Rams, 23-10 (SF)
1978—Rams, 27-10 (LA)
Rams, 31-28 (SF)
1979—Rams, 27-24 (LA)
Rams, 26-20 (SF)
1980—Rams, 48-26 (LA)
Rams, 31-17 (SF)
1981—49ers, 20-17 (SF)
49ers, 33-31 (LA)
1982—49ers, 30-24 (LA)
Rams, 21-20 (SF)
1983—Rams, 10-7 (SF)
49ers, 45-35 (LA)
1984—49ers, 33-0 (LA)
49ers, 19-16 (SF)
1985—49ers, 28-14 (LA)
Rams, 27-20 (SF)
1986—Rams, 16-13 (LA)
49ers, 24-14 (SF)
1987—49ers, 31-10 (LA)
49ers, 48-0 (SF)
1988—49ers, 24-21 (LA)
Rams, 38-16 (SF)
1989—Rams, 13-12 (SF)
49ers, 30-27 (LA)
**49ers, 30-3 (SF)
1990—Rams, 28-17 (SF)
49ers, 26-10 (LA)
1991—49ers, 27-10 (SF)
49ers, 33-10 (LA)
1992—49ers, 27-24 (SF)
49ers, 27-10 (LA)
1993—49ers, 40-17 (SF)
49ers, 35-10 (LA)
1994—49ers, 34-19 (LA)
49ers, 31-27 (SF)
1995—49ers, 44-10 (StL)
49ers, 41-13 (SF)
1996—49ers, 34-0 (SF)
49ers, 28-11 (StL)
1997—49ers, 15-12 (StL)
49ers, 30-10 (SF)
1998—49ers, 28-10 (StL)
49ers, 38-19 (SF)
1999—Rams, 42-20 (StL)
Rams, 23-7 (SF)
2000—Rams, 41-24 (StL)
Rams, 34-24 (SF)
(RS Pts.—Rams 2,284, 49ers 2,261)
(PS Pts.—49ers 30, Rams 3)
Franchise in Los Angeles prior to 1995
***NFC Championship*
***ST. LOUIS vs. SEATTLE**
RS: Rams lead series, 5-2
1976—Rams, 45-6 (LA)
1979—Rams, 24-0 (S)
1985—Rams, 35-24 (S)
1988—Rams, 31-10 (LA)
1991—Seahawks, 23-9 (S)
1997—Seahawks, 17-9 (StL)
2000—Rams, 37-34 (Sea)
(RS Pts.—Rams 190, Seahawks 114)
Franchise in Los Angeles prior to 1995
***ST. LOUIS vs. TAMPA BAY**
RS: Rams lead series, 8-4
PS: Rams lead series, 2-0
1977—Rams, 31-0 (LA)
1978—Rams, 26-23 (LA)
1979—Buccaneers, 21-6 (TB)
**Rams, 9-0 (TB)
1980—Buccaneers, 10-9 (TB)
1984—Rams, 34-33 (TB)
1985—Rams, 31-27 (TB)
1986—Rams, 26-20 (LA) OT
1987—Rams, 35-3 (LA)
1990—Rams, 35-14 (TB)
1992—Rams, 31-27 (TB)
1994—Buccaneers, 24-14 (TB)
1999—**Rams, 11-6 (StL)
2000—Buccaneers, 38-35 (TB)
(RS Pts.—Rams 313, Buccaneers 240)
(PS Pts.—Rams 20, Buccaneers 6)
Franchise in Los Angeles prior to 1995
***NFC Championship*
***ST. LOUIS vs. **TENNESSEE**
RS: Rams lead series, 5-3
PS: Rams lead series, 1-0
1973—Rams, 31-26 (H)
1978—Rams, 10-6 (H)
1981—Oilers, 27-20 (LA)
1984—Rams, 27-16 (LA)
1987—Oilers, 20-16 (H)
1990—Rams, 17-13 (LA)
1993—Rams, 28-13 (H)
1999—Titans, 24-21 (T)
***Rams, 23-16 (Atlanta)
(RS Pts.—Rams 170, Titans 145)
(PS Pts.—Rams 23, Titans 16)
Franchise in Los Angeles prior to 1995
***Franchise in Houston prior to 1997; known as Oilers prior to 1999*
****Super Bowl XXXIV*
***ST. LOUIS vs. WASHINGTON**
RS: Redskins lead series, 18-6-1
PS: Series tied, 2-2
1937—Redskins, 16-7 (C)
1938—Redskins, 37-13 (W)
1941—Redskins, 17-13 (W)
1942—Redskins, 33-14 (W)
1944—Redskins, 14-10 (W)
1945—**Rams, 15-14 (C)
1948—Rams, 41-13 (W)
1949—Rams, 53-27 (LA)
1951—Redskins, 31-21 (W)
1962—Redskins, 20-14 (W)
1963—Redskins, 37-14 (LA)
1967—Tie, 28-28 (LA)
1969—Rams, 24-13 (W)
1971—Redskins, 38-24 (LA)
1974—Redskins, 23-17 (LA)
***Rams, 19-10 (LA)
1977—Redskins, 17-14 (W)
1981—Redskins, 30-7 (LA)
1983—Redskins, 42-20 (LA)
***Redskins, 51-7 (W)
1986—****Redskins, 19-7 (W)
1987—Rams, 30-26 (W)
1991—Redskins, 27-6 (LA)
1993—Rams, 10-6 (LA)
1994—Redskins, 24-21 (LA)
1995—Redskins, 35-23 (StL)
1996—Redskins, 17-10 (StL)
1997—Rams, 23-20 (W)
2000—Redskins, 33-20 (StL)
(RS Pts.—Redskins 624, Rams 477)
(PS Pts.—Redskins 94, Rams 48)
Franchise in Los Angeles prior to 1995 and in Cleveland prior to 1946
***NFL Championship*
****NFC Divisional Playoff*
*****NFC First-Round Playoff*

SAN DIEGO vs. ARIZONA
RS: Chargers lead series, 6-2;
See Arizona vs. San Diego
SAN DIEGO vs. ATLANTA
RS: Falcons lead series, 5-1;
See Atlanta vs. San Diego
SAN DIEGO vs BALTIMORE
RS: Chargers lead series, 2-1;
See Baltimore vs. San Diego
SAN DIEGO vs. BUFFALO
RS: Chargers lead series, 17-8-2
PS: Bills lead series, 2-1;
See Buffalo vs. San Diego
SAN DIEGO vs. CAROLINA
RS: Panthers lead series, 2-0;
See Carolina vs. San Diego
SAN DIEGO vs. CHICAGO
RS: Series tied, 4-4;
See Chicago vs. San Diego
SAN DIEGO vs. CINCINNATI
RS: Chargers lead series, 15-9
PS: Bengals lead series, 1-0;
See Cincinnati vs. San Diego
SAN DIEGO vs. CLEVELAND
RS: Chargers lead series, 10-6-1;
See Cleveland vs. San Diego
SAN DIEGO vs. DALLAS
RS: Cowboys lead series, 5-1;
See Dallas vs. San Diego
SAN DIEGO vs. DENVER
RS: Broncos lead series, 45-36-1;
See Denver vs. San Diego
SAN DIEGO vs. DETROIT
RS: Chargers lead series, 4-3;
See Detroit vs. San Diego
SAN DIEGO vs. GREEN BAY
RS: Packers lead series, 6-1;
See Green Bay vs. San Diego
SAN DIEGO vs. INDIANAPOLIS
RS: Chargers lead series, 12-7
PS: Colts lead series, 1-0;
See Indianapolis vs. San Diego
SAN DIEGO vs. KANSAS CITY
RS: Chiefs lead series, 42-38-1
PS: Chargers lead series, 1-0;
See Kansas City vs. San Diego
SAN DIEGO vs. MIAMI
RS: Chargers lead series, 10-8
PS: Series tied, 2-2;
See Miami vs. San Diego
SAN DIEGO vs. MINNESOTA
RS: Series tied, 4-4;
See Minnesota vs. San Diego
SAN DIEGO vs. NEW ENGLAND
RS: Patriots lead series, 16-11-2
PS: Chargers lead series, 1-0;
See New England vs. San Diego
SAN DIEGO vs. NEW ORLEANS
RS: Chargers lead series, 6-2;
See New Orleans vs. San Diego
SAN DIEGO vs. N.Y. GIANTS
RS: Giants lead series, 5-3;
See N.Y. Giants vs. San Diego

ALL-TIME TEAM VS. TEAM RESULTS

SAN DIEGO vs. N.Y. JETS
RS: Chargers lead series, 17-9-1;
See N.Y. Jets vs. San Diego
SAN DIEGO vs. OAKLAND
RS: Raiders lead series, 50-30-2
PS: Raiders lead series, 1-0;
See Oakland vs. San Diego
SAN DIEGO vs. PHILADELPHIA
RS: Chargers lead series, 5-2;
See Philadelphia vs. San Diego
SAN DIEGO vs. PITTSBURGH
RS: Steelers lead series, 17-5
PS: Chargers lead series, 2-0;
See Pittsburgh vs. San Diego
SAN DIEGO vs. ST. LOUIS
RS: Rams lead series, 4-3;
See St. Louis vs. San Diego
SAN DIEGO vs. SAN FRANCISCO
RS: 49ers lead series, 6-3
PS: 49ers lead series, 1-0
1972—49ers, 34-3 (SF)
1976—Chargers, 13-7 (SD) OT
1979—Chargers, 31-9 (SD)
1982—Chargers, 41-37 (SF)
1988—49ers, 48-10 (SD)
1991—49ers, 34-14 (SF)
1994—49ers, 38-15 (SD)
*49ers, 49-26 (Miami)
1997—49ers, 17-10 (SF)
2000—49ers, 45-17 (SD)
(RS Pts.—49ers 269, Chargers 154)
(PS Pts.—49ers 49, Chargers 26)
**Super Bowl XXIX*
SAN DIEGO vs. SEATTLE
RS: Series tied, 22-22
1977—Chargers, 30-28 (S)
1978—Chargers, 24-20 (S)
Chargers, 37-10 (SD)
1979—Chargers, 33-16 (S)
Chargers, 20-10 (SD)
1980—Chargers, 34-13 (S)
Chargers, 21-14 (SD)
1981—Chargers, 24-10 (SD)
Seahawks, 44-23 (S)
1983—Seahawks, 34-31 (S)
Chargers, 28-21 (SD)
1984—Seahawks, 31-17 (S)
Seahawks, 24-0 (SD)
1985—Seahawks, 49-35 (SD)
Seahawks, 26-21 (S)
1986—Seahawks, 33-7 (S)
Seahawks, 34-24 (SD)
1987—Seahawks, 34-3 (S)
1988—Chargers, 17-6 (SD)
Seahawks, 17-14 (S)
1989—Seahawks, 17-16 (SD)
Seahawks, 10-7 (S)
1990—Chargers, 31-14 (S)
Seahawks, 13-10 (SD) OT
1991—Seahawks, 20-9 (S)
Chargers, 17-14 (SD)
1992—Chargers, 17-6 (SD)
Chargers, 31-14 (S)
1993—Chargers, 18-12 (SD)
Seahawks, 31-14 (S)
1994—Chargers, 24-10 (S)
Chargers, 35-15 (SD)
1995—Chargers, 14-10 (SD)
Chargers, 35-25 (S)
1996—Chargers, 29-7 (SD)
Seahawks, 32-13 (S)
1997—Seahawks, 26-22 (S)
Seahawks, 37-31 (SD)
1998—Seahawks, 27-20 (SD)
Seahawks, 38-17 (S)
1999—Chargers, 13-10 (SD)
Chargers, 19-16 (S)
2000—Seahawks, 20-12 (SD)
Seahawks, 17-15 (S)
(RS Pts.—Seahawks 915, Chargers 912)
SAN DIEGO vs. TAMPA BAY
RS: Chargers lead series, 6-1
1976—Chargers, 23-0 (TB)
1981—Chargers, 24-23 (TB)
1987—Chargers, 17-13 (TB)
1990—Chargers, 41-10 (SD)
1992—Chargers, 29-14 (SD)
1993—Chargers, 32-17 (TB)
1996—Buccaneers, 25-17 (SD)
(RS Pts.—Chargers 183, Buccaneers 102)
***SAN DIEGO vs. **TENNESSEE**
RS: Chargers lead series, 19-13-1
PS: Titans lead series, 3-0
1960—Oilers, 38-28 (H)
Chargers, 24-21 (LA)
***Oilers, 24-16 (H)
1961—Chargers, 34-24 (SD)
Oilers, 33-13 (H)
***Oilers, 10-3 (SD)
1962—Oilers, 42-17 (SD)
Oilers, 33-27 (H)
1963—Chargers, 27-0 (SD)
Chargers 20-14 (H)
1964—Chargers, 27-21 (SD)
Chargers, 20-17 (H)
1965—Chargers, 31-14 (SD)
Chargers, 37-26 (H)
1966—Chargers, 28-22 (H)
1967—Chargers, 13-3 (SD)
Oilers, 24-17 (H)
1968—Chargers, 30-14 (SD)
1969—Chargers, 21-17 (H)
1970—Tie, 31-31 (SD)
1971—Oilers, 49-33 (H)
1972—Chargers, 34-20 (SD)
1974—Oilers, 21-14 (H)
1975—Oilers, 33-17 (H)
1976—Chargers, 30-27 (SD)
1978—Chargers, 45-24 (H)
1979—****Oilers, 17-14 (SD)
1984—Chargers, 31-14 (SD)
1985—Oilers, 37-35 (H)
1986—Chargers, 27-0 (SD)
1987—Oilers, 33-18 (H)
1989—Oilers, 34-27 (SD)
1990—Oilers, 17-7 (SD)
1992—Oilers, 27-0 (H)
1993—Chargers, 18-17 (SD)
1998—Chargers, 13-7 (T)
(RS Pts.—Chargers 794, Titans 754)
(PS Pts.—Titans 51, Chargers 33)
**Franchise in Los Angeles prior to 1961*
***Franchise in Houston prior to 1997; known as Oilers prior to 1999*
****AFL Championship*
*****AFC Divisional Playoff*
SAN DIEGO vs. WASHINGTON
RS: Redskins lead series, 6-0
1973—Redskins, 38-0 (W)
1980—Redskins, 40-17 (W)
1983—Redskins, 27-24 (SD)
1986—Redskins, 30-27 (SD)
1989—Redskins, 26-21 (W)
1998—Redskins, 24-20 (W)
(RS Pts.—Redskins 185, Chargers 109)

SAN FRANCISCO vs. ARIZONA
RS: 49ers lead series, 12-9;
See Arizona vs. San Francisco
SAN FRANCISCO vs. ATLANTA
RS: 49ers lead series, 42-25-1
PS: Falcons lead series, 1-0;
See Atlanta vs. San Francisco
SAN FRANCISCO vs. BALTIMORE
RS: 49ers lead series, 1-0;
See Baltimore vs. San Francisco
SAN FRANCISCO vs. BUFFALO
RS: Bills lead series, 4-3;
See Buffalo vs. San Francisco
SAN FRANCISCO vs. CAROLINA
RS: Panthers lead series, 7-5;
See Carolina vs. San Francisco
SAN FRANCISCO vs. CHICAGO
RS: 49ers lead series, 26-25-1
PS: 49ers lead series, 3-0;
See Chicago vs. San Francisco
SAN FRANCISCO vs. CINCINNATI
RS: 49ers lead series, 7-2
PS: 49ers lead series, 2-0;
See Cincinnati vs. San Francisco
SAN FRANCISCO vs. CLEVELAND
RS: Browns lead series, 9-6;
See Cleveland vs. San Francisco
SAN FRANCISCO vs. DALLAS
RS: 49ers lead series, 13-7-1
PS: Cowboys lead series, 5-2;
See Dallas vs. San Francisco
SAN FRANCISCO vs. DENVER
RS: Broncos lead series, 5-4
PS: 49ers lead series, 1-0;
See Denver vs. San Francisco
SAN FRANCISCO vs. DETROIT
RS: 49ers lead series, 29-26-1
PS: Series tied, 1-1;
See Detroit vs. San Francisco
SAN FRANCISCO vs. GREEN BAY
RS: Series tied, 25-25-1
PS: Packers lead series, 3-1;
See Green Bay vs. San Francisco
SAN FRANCISCO vs. INDIANAPOLIS
RS: Colts lead series, 22-17;
See Indianapolis vs. San Francisco
SAN FRANCISCO vs. JACKSONVILLE
RS: Jaguars lead series, 1-0;
See Jacksonville vs. San Francisco
SAN FRANCISCO vs. KANSAS CITY
RS: 49ers lead series, 5-3;
See Kansas City vs. San Francisco
SAN FRANCISCO vs. MIAMI
RS: Dolphins lead series, 4-3
PS: 49ers lead series, 1-0;
See Miami vs. San Francisco
SAN FRANCISCO vs. MINNESOTA
RS: Series tied, 17-17-1
PS: 49ers lead series, 4-1;
See Minnesota vs. San Francisco
SAN FRANCISCO vs. NEW ENGLAND
RS: 49ers lead series, 7-2;
See New England vs. San Francisco
SAN FRANCISCO vs. NEW ORLEANS
RS: 49ers lead series, 43-18-2;
See New Orleans vs. San Francisco
SAN FRANCISCO vs. N.Y. GIANTS
RS: 49ers lead series, 12-11
PS: Series tied, 3-3;
See N.Y. Giants vs. San Francisco
SAN FRANCISCO vs. N.Y. JETS
RS: 49ers lead series, 7-1;
See N.Y. Jets vs. San Francisco
SAN FRANCISCO vs. OAKLAND
RS: Raiders lead series, 6-3;
See Oakland vs. San Francisco
SAN FRANCISCO vs. PHILADELPHIA
RS: 49ers lead series, 14-6-1
PS: 49ers lead series, 1-0;
See Philadelphia vs. San Francisco
SAN FRANCISCO vs. PITTSBURGH
RS: 49ers lead series, 9-8;
See Pittsburgh vs. San Francisco
SAN FRANCISCO vs. ST. LOUIS
RS: Rams lead series, 52-48-2
PS: 49ers lead series, 1-0;
See St. Louis vs. San Francisco
SAN FRANCISCO vs. SAN DIEGO
RS: 49ers lead series, 6-3
PS: 49ers lead series, 1-0;
See San Diego vs. San Francisco
SAN FRANCISCO vs. SEATTLE
RS: 49ers lead series, 4-2
1976—49ers, 37-21 (S)
1979—Seahawks, 35-24 (SF)
1985—49ers, 19-6 (SF)
1988—49ers, 38-7 (S)
1991—49ers, 24-22 (S)
1997—Seahawks, 38-9 (S)
(RS Pts.—49ers 151, Seahawks 129)
SAN FRANCISCO vs. TAMPA BAY
RS: 49ers lead series, 12-2
1977—49ers, 20-10 (SF)
1978—49ers, 6-3 (SF)
1979—49ers, 23-7 (SF)
1980—Buccaneers, 24-23 (SF)
1983—49ers, 35-21 (SF)
1984—49ers, 24-17 (SF)
1986—49ers, 31-7 (TB)
1987—49ers, 24-10 (TB)
1989—49ers, 20-16 (TB)
1990—49ers, 31-7 (SF)
1992—49ers, 21-14 (SF)
1993—49ers, 45-21 (TB)
1994—49ers, 41-16 (SF)
1997—Buccaneers, 13-6 (TB)
(RS Pts.—49ers 350, Buccaneers 186)
SAN FRANCISCO vs. *TENNESSEE
RS: 49ers lead series, 7-3
1970—49ers, 30-20 (H)
1975—Oilers, 27-13 (SF)
1978—Oilers, 20-19 (H)
1981—49ers, 28-6 (SF)
1984—49ers, 34-21 (H)
1987—49ers, 27-20 (SF)
1990—49ers, 24-21 (H)
1993—Oilers, 10-7 (SF)
1996—49ers, 10-9 (H)
1999—49ers, 24-22 (SF)
(RS Pts.—49ers 216, Titans 176)
**Franchise in Houston prior to 1997; known as Oilers prior to 1999*
SAN FRANCISCO vs. WASHINGTON
RS: 49ers lead series, 12-7-1
PS: 49ers lead series, 3-1
1952—49ers, 23-17 (W)
1954—49ers, 41-7 (SF)
1955—Redskins, 7-0 (W)
1961—49ers, 35-3 (SF)
1967—Redskins, 31-28 (W)
1969—Tie, 17-17 (SF)
1970—49ers, 26-17 (SF)
1971—*49ers, 24-20 (SF)
1973—Redskins, 33-9 (W)
1976—Redskins, 24-21 (SF)
1978—Redskins, 38-20 (W)
1981—49ers, 30-17 (W)
1983—**Redskins, 24-21 (W)
1984—49ers, 37-31 (SF)
1985—49ers, 35-8 (W)
1986—Redskins, 14-6 (W)
1988—49ers, 37-21 (SF)
1990—49ers, 26-13 (SF)
*49ers, 28-10 (SF)
1992—*49ers, 20-13 (SF)
1994—49ers, 37-22 (W)
1996—49ers, 19-16 (W) OT
1998—49ers, 45-10 (W)
1999—Redskins, 26-20 (SF) OT
(RS Pts.—49ers 512, Redskins 372)
(PS Pts.—49ers 93, Redskins 67)
**NFC Divisional Playoff*
***NFC Championship*

SEATTLE vs. ARIZONA
RS: Cardinals lead series, 5-1;
See Arizona vs. Seattle
SEATTLE vs. ATLANTA
RS: Seahawks lead series, 5-2;
See Atlanta vs. Seattle
SEATTLE vs. BALTIMORE
RS: Ravens lead series, 1-0;
See Baltimore vs. Seattle
SEATTLE vs. BUFFALO
RS: Seahawks lead series, 5-3;
See Buffalo vs. Seattle
SEATTLE vs. CAROLINA
RS: Panthers lead series, 1-0;
See Carolina vs. Seattle
SEATTLE vs. CHICAGO
RS: Seahawks lead series, 5-2;
See Chicago vs. Seattle
SEATTLE vs. CINCINNATI
RS: Seahawks lead series, 8-7
PS: Bengals lead series, 1-0;
See Cincinnati vs. Seattle

SEATTLE vs. CLEVELAND
RS: Seahawks lead series, 9-4;
See Cleveland vs. Seattle
SEATTLE vs. DALLAS
RS: Cowboys lead series, 5-1;
See Dallas vs. Seattle
SEATTLE vs. DENVER
RS: Broncos lead series, 31-16
PS: Seahawks lead series, 1-0;
See Denver vs. Seattle
SEATTLE vs. DETROIT
RS: Series tied, 4-4;
See Detroit vs. Seattle
SEATTLE vs. GREEN BAY
RS: Series tied, 4-4;
See Green Bay vs. Seattle
SEATTLE vs. INDIANAPOLIS
RS: Colts lead series, 5-3;
See Indianapolis vs. Seattle
SEATTLE vs. JACKSONVILLE
RS: Seahawks lead series, 2-1;
See Jacksonville vs. Seattle
SEATTLE vs. KANSAS CITY
RS: Chiefs lead series, 29-16;
See Kansas City vs. Seattle
SEATTLE vs. MIAMI
RS: Dolphins lead series, 5-2
PS: Dolphins lead series, 2-1;
See Miami vs. Seattle
SEATTLE vs. MINNESOTA
RS: Seahawks lead series, 4-2;
See Minnesota vs. Seattle
SEATTLE vs. NEW ENGLAND
RS: Seahawks lead series, 7-6;
See New England vs. Seattle
SEATTLE vs. NEW ORLEANS
RS: Saints lead series, 4-3;
See New Orleans vs. Seattle
SEATTLE vs. N.Y. GIANTS
RS: Giants lead series, 5-3;
See N.Y. Giants vs. Seattle
SEATTLE vs. N.Y. JETS
RS: Seahawks lead series, 8-7;
See N.Y. Jets vs. Seattle
SEATTLE vs. OAKLAND
RS: Raiders lead series, 25-21
PS: Series tied, 1-1;
See Oakland vs. Seattle
SEATTLE vs. PHILADELPHIA
RS: Eagles lead series, 4-3;
See Philadelphia vs. Seattle
SEATTLE vs. PITTSBURGH
RS: Seahawks lead series, 7-6;
See Pittsburgh vs. Seattle
SEATTLE vs. ST. LOUIS
RS: Rams lead series, 5-2;
See St. Louis vs. Seattle
SEATTLE vs. SAN DIEGO
RS: Series tied, 22-22;
See San Diego vs. Seattle
SEATTLE vs. SAN FRANCISCO
RS: 49ers lead series, 4-2;
See San Francisco vs. Seattle
SEATTLE vs. TAMPA BAY
RS: Seahawks lead series, 4-1
1976—Seahawks, 13-10 (TB)
1977—Seahawks, 30-23 (S)
1994—Seahawks, 22-21 (S)
1996—Seahawks, 17-13 (TB)
1999—Buccaneers, 16-3 (S)
(RS Pts.—Seahawks 85, Buccaneers 83)
SEATTLE vs. *TENNESSEE
RS: Seahawks lead series, 8-4
PS: Titans lead series, 1-0
1977—Oilers, 22-10 (S)
1979—Seahawks, 34-14 (S)
1980—Seahawks, 26-7 (H)
1981—Oilers, 35-17 (H)
1982—Oilers, 23-21 (H)
1987—**Oilers, 23-20 (H) OT
1988—Seahawks, 27-24 (S)
1990—Seahawks, 13-10 (S) OT
1993—Oilers, 24-14 (H)
1994—Seahawks, 16-14 (H)
1996—Seahawks, 23-16 (S)
1997—Seahawks, 16-13 (S)
1998—Seahawks, 20-18 (S)
(RS Pts.—Seahawks 237, Titans 220)
(PS Pts.—Titans 23, Seahawks 20)
Franchise in Houston prior to 1997; known as Oilers prior to 1999
***AFC First-Round Playoff*
SEATTLE vs. WASHINGTON
RS: Redskins lead series, 5-4
1976—Redskins, 31-7 (W)
1980—Seahawks, 14-0 (W)
1983—Redskins, 27-17 (S)
1986—Redskins, 19-14 (W)
1989—Redskins, 29-0 (S)
1992—Redskins, 16-3 (S)
1994—Seahawks, 28-7 (W)
1995—Seahawks, 27-20 (W)
1998—Seahawks, 24-14 (S)
(RS Pts.—Redskins 163, Seahawks 134)

TAMPA BAY vs. ARIZONA
RS: Series tied, 7-7;
See Arizona vs. Tampa Bay
TAMPA BAY vs. ATLANTA
RS: Buccaneers lead series, 9-8;
See Atlanta vs. Tampa Bay
TAMPA BAY vs. BUFFALO
RS: Buccaneers lead series, 5-2;
See Buffalo vs. Tampa Bay
TAMPA BAY vs. CAROLINA
RS: Buccaneers lead series, 2-1;
See Carolina vs. Tampa Bay
TAMPA BAY vs. CHICAGO
RS: Bears lead series, 31-15;
See Chicago vs. Tampa Bay
TAMPA BAY vs. CINCINNATI
RS: Series tied, 3-3;
See Cincinnati vs. Tampa Bay
TAMPA BAY vs. CLEVELAND
RS: Browns lead series, 5-0;
See Cleveland vs. Tampa Bay
TAMPA BAY vs. DALLAS
RS: Cowboys lead series, 6-1
PS: Cowboys lead series, 2-0;
See Dallas vs. Tampa Bay
TAMPA BAY vs. DENVER
RS: Broncos lead series, 3-2;
See Denver vs. Tampa Bay
TAMPA BAY vs. DETROIT
RS: Lions lead series, 26-20
PS: Buccaneers lead series, 1-0;
See Detroit vs. Tampa Bay
TAMPA BAY vs. GREEN BAY
RS: Packers lead series, 27-16-1
PS: Packers lead series, 1-1;
See Green Bay vs. Tampa Bay
TAMPA BAY vs. INDIANAPOLIS
RS: Colts lead series, 5-4;
See Indianapolis vs. Tampa Bay
TAMPA BAY vs. JACKSONVILLE
RS: Series tied, 1-1;
See Jacksonville vs. Tampa Bay
TAMPA BAY vs. KANSAS CITY
RS: Chiefs lead series, 5-3;
See Kansas City vs. Tampa Bay
TAMPA BAY vs. MIAMI
RS: Dolphins lead series, 4-3;
See Miami vs. Tampa Bay
TAMPA BAY vs. MINNESOTA
RS: Vikings lead series, 30-16;
See Minnesota vs. Tampa Bay
TAMPA BAY vs. NEW ENGLAND
RS: Patriots lead series, 3-2;
See New England vs. Tampa Bay
TAMPA BAY vs. NEW ORLEANS
RS: Saints lead series, 13-6;
See New Orleans vs. Tampa Bay
TAMPA BAY vs. N.Y. GIANTS
RS: Giants lead series, 9-5;
See N.Y. Giants vs. Tampa Bay
TAMPA BAY vs. N.Y. JETS
RS: Jets lead series, 7-1;
See N.Y. Jets vs. Tampa Bay
TAMPA BAY vs. OAKLAND
RS: Raiders lead series, 4-1;
See Oakland vs. Tampa Bay
TAMPA BAY vs. PHILADELPHIA
RS: Series tied, 3-3
PS: Series tied, 1-1;
See Philadelphia vs. Tampa Bay
TAMPA BAY vs. PITTSBURGH
RS: Steelers lead series, 4-1;
See Pittsburgh vs. Tampa Bay
TAMPA BAY vs. ST. LOUIS
RS: Rams lead series, 8-4
PS: Rams lead series, 2-0;
See St. Louis vs. Tampa Bay
TAMPA BAY vs. SAN DIEGO
RS: Chargers lead series, 6-1;
See San Diego vs. Tampa Bay
TAMPA BAY vs. SAN FRANCISCO
RS: 49ers lead series, 12-2;
See San Francisco vs. Tampa Bay
TAMPA BAY vs. SEATTLE
RS: Seahawks lead series, 4-1;
See Seattle vs. Tampa Bay
TAMPA BAY vs. *TENNESSEE
RS: Titans lead series, 5-1
1976—Oilers, 20-0 (H)
1980—Oilers, 20-14 (H)
1983—Buccaneers, 33-24 (TB)
1989—Oilers, 20-17 (H)
1995—Oilers, 19-7 (H)
1998—Oilers, 31-22 (TB)
(RS Pts.—Titans 134, Buccaneers 93)
Franchise in Houston prior to 1997; known as Oilers prior to 1999
TAMPA BAY vs. WASHINGTON
RS: Redskins lead series, 6-4
PS: Buccaneers lead series, 1-0;
1977—Redskins, 10-0 (TB)
1982—Redskins, 21-13 (TB)
1989—Redskins, 32-28 (W)
1993—Redskins, 23-17 (TB)
1994—Buccaneers, 26-21 (TB)
Buccaneers, 17-14 (W)
1995—Buccaneers, 14-6 (TB)
1996—Buccaneers, 24-10 (TB)
1998—Redskins, 20-16 (W)
1999—*Buccaneers, 14-13 (TB)
2000—Redskins, 20-17 (W) OT
(RS Pts.—Redskins 177, Buccaneers 172)
(PS Pts.—Buccaneers 14, Redskins 13)
NFC Divisional Playoff

TENNESSEE VS. ARIZONA
RS: Cardinals lead series, 4-3;
See Arizona vs. Tennessee
TENNESSEE vs. ATLANTA
RS: Falcons lead series, 5-5;
See Atlanta vs. Tennessee
TENNESSEE vs. BALTIMORE
RS: Titans lead series, 6-4
PS: Ravens lead series, 1-0;
See Baltimore vs. Tennessee
TENNESSEE vs. BUFFALO
RS: Titans lead series, 22-14
PS: Bills lead series, 2-1;
See Buffalo vs. Tennessee
TENNESSEE vs. CAROLINA
RS: Panthers lead series, 1-0;
See Carolina vs. Tennessee
TENNESSEE vs. CHICAGO
RS: Series tied, 4-4;
See Chicago vs. Tennessee
TENNESSEE vs. CINCINNATI
RS: Titans lead series, 35-28-1
PS: Bengals lead series, 1-0;
See Cincinnati vs. Tennessee
TENNESSEE vs. CLEVELAND
RS: Browns lead series, 30-25
PS: Titans lead series, 1-0;
See Cleveland vs. Tennessee
TENNESSEE vs. DALLAS
RS: Series tied, 5-5;
See Dallas vs. Tennessee
TENNESSEE vs. DENVER
RS: Titans lead series, 20-11-1
PS: Broncos lead series, 2-1;
See Denver vs. Tennessee
TENNESSEE vs. DETROIT
RS: Titans lead series, 4-3;
See Detroit vs. Tennessee
TENNESSEE vs. GREEN BAY
RS: Packers lead series, 4-3;
See Green Bay vs. Tennessee
TENNESSEE vs. INDIANAPOLIS
RS: Series tied, 7-7
PS: Titans lead series, 1-0;
See Indianapolis vs. Tennessee
TENNESSEE vs. JACKSONVILLE
RS: Series tied, 6-6
PS: Titans lead series, 1-0;
See Jacksonville vs. Tennessee
TENNESSEE vs. KANSAS CITY
RS: Chiefs lead series, 24-18
PS: Chiefs lead series, 2-0;
See Kansas City vs. Tennessee
TENNESSEE vs. MIAMI
RS: Dolphins lead series, 14-11
PS: Titans lead series, 1-0;
See Miami vs. Tennessee
TENNESSEE vs. MINNESOTA
RS: Vikings lead series, 5-3;
See Minnesota vs. Tennessee
TENNESSEE vs. NEW ENGLAND
RS: Patriots lead series, 18-14-1
PS: Titans lead series, 1-0;
See New England vs. Tennessee
TENNESSEE vs. NEW ORLEANS
RS: Titans lead series, 5-4-1;
See New Orleans vs. Tennessee
TENNESSEE vs. N.Y. GIANTS
RS: Giants lead series, 5-2;
See N.Y. Giants vs. Tennessee
TENNESSEE vs. N.Y. JETS
RS: Titans lead series, 20-13-1
PS: Titans lead series, 1-0;
See N.Y. Jets vs. Tennessee
TENNESSEE vs. OAKLAND
RS: Raiders lead series, 20-15
PS: Raiders lead series, 3-0;
See Oakland vs. Tennessee
TENNESSEE vs. PHILADELPHIA
RS: Eagles lead series, 6-1;
See Philadelphia vs. Tennessee
TENNESSEE vs. PITTSBURGH
RS: Steelers lead series, 35-26
PS: Steelers lead series, 3-0;
See Pittsburgh vs. Tennessee
TENNESSEE vs. ST. LOUIS
RS: Rams lead series, 5-3
PS: Rams lead series, 1-0;
See St. Louis vs. Tennessee
TENNESSEE vs. SAN DIEGO
RS: Chargers lead series, 19-13-1
PS: Titans lead series, 3-0;
See San Diego vs. Tennessee
TENNESSEE vs. SAN FRANCISCO
RS: 49ers lead series, 7-3;
See San Francisco vs. Tennessee
TENNESSEE vs. SEATTLE
RS: Seahawks lead series, 8-4
PS: Titans lead series, 1-0;
See Seattle vs. Tennessee
TENNESSEE vs. TAMPA BAY
RS: Titans lead series, 5-1;
See Tampa Bay vs. Tennessee
***TENNESSEE vs. WASHINGTON**
RS: Titans lead series, 5-3
1971—Redskins, 22-13 (W)
1975—Oilers, 13-10 (H)
1979—Oilers, 29-27 (W)
1985—Redskins, 16-13 (W)
1988—Oilers, 41-17 (H)
1991—Redskins, 16-13 (W) OT

1997—Oilers, 28-14 (T)
2000—Titans, 27-21 (W)
(RS—Titans 177, Redskins 143)
Franchise in Houston prior to 1997; known as Oilers prior to 1999

WASHINGTON vs. ARIZONA
RS: Redskins lead series, 67-44-2;
See Arizona vs. Washington
WASHINGTON vs. ATLANTA
RS: Redskins lead series, 13-4-1
PS: Redskins lead series, 1-0;
See Atlanta vs. Washington
WASHINGTON vs BALTIMORE
RS: Series tied, 1-1;
See Baltimore vs. Washington
WASHINGTON vs. BUFFALO
RS: Bills lead series, 5-4
PS: Redskins lead series, 1-0;
See Buffalo vs. Washington
WASHINGTON vs. CAROLINA
RS: Redskins lead series, 5-0;
See Carolina vs. Washington
WASHINGTON vs. CHICAGO
RS: Bears lead series, 18-15-1
PS: Redskins lead series, 4-3;
See Chicago vs. Washington
WASHINGTON vs. CINCINNATI
RS: Redskins lead series, 4-2;
See Cincinnati vs. Washington
WASHINGTON vs. CLEVELAND
RS: Browns lead series, 32-9-1;
See Cleveland vs. Washington
WASHINGTON vs. DALLAS
RS: Cowboys lead series, 47-31-2
PS: Redskins lead series, 2-0;
See Dallas vs. Washington
WASHINGTON vs. DENVER
RS: Broncos lead series, 5-3
PS: Redskins lead series, 1-0;
See Denver vs. Washington
WASHINGTON vs. DETROIT
RS: Redskins lead series, 24-10
PS: Redskins lead series, 3-0;
See Detroit vs. Washington
WASHINGTON vs. GREEN BAY
RS: Packers lead series, 13-12-1
PS: Series tied, 1-1;
See Green Bay vs. Washington
WASHINGTON vs. INDIANAPOLIS
RS: Colts lead series, 17-9;
See Indianapolis vs. Washington
WASHINGTON vs. JACKSONVILLE
RS: Redskins lead series, 2-0;
See Jacksonville vs. Washington
WASHINGTON vs. KANSAS CITY
RS: Chiefs lead series, 4-1;
See Kansas City vs. Washington
WASHINGTON vs. MIAMI
RS: Dolphins lead series, 5-3
PS: Series tied, 1-1;
See Miami vs. Washington
WASHINGTON vs. MINNESOTA
RS: Redskins lead series, 6-5
PS: Redskins lead series, 3-2;
See Minnesota vs. Washington
WASHINGTON vs. NEW ENGLAND
RS: Redskins lead series, 5-1;
See New England vs. Washington
WASHINGTON vs. NEW ORLEANS
RS: Redskins lead series, 12-5;
See New Orleans vs. Washington
WASHINGTON vs. N.Y. GIANTS
RS: Giants lead series, 76-56-4
PS: Series tied, 1-1;
See N.Y. Giants vs. Washington
WASHINGTON vs. N.Y. JETS
RS: Redskins lead series, 6-1;
See N.Y. Jets vs. Washington
WASHINGTON vs. OAKLAND
RS: Raiders lead series, 6-3
PS: Raiders lead series, 1-0;
See Oakland vs. Washington
WASHINGTON vs. PHILADELPHIA
RS: Redskins lead series, 71-55-5
PS: Redskins lead series, 1-0;
See Philadelphia vs. Washington
WASHINGTON vs. PITTSBURGH
RS: Redskins lead series, 42-29-3;
See Pittsburgh vs. Washington
WASHINGTON vs. ST. LOUIS
RS: Redskins lead series, 18-6-1
PS: Series tied, 2-2;
See St. Louis vs. Washington
WASHINGTON vs. SAN DIEGO
RS: Redskins lead series, 6-0;
See San Diego vs. Washington
WASHINGTON vs. SAN FRANCISCO
RS: 49ers lead series, 12-7-1
PS: 49ers lead series, 3-1;
See San Francisco vs. Washington
WASHINGTON vs. SEATTLE
RS: Redskins lead series, 5-4;
See Seattle vs. Washington
WASHINGTON vs. TAMPA BAY
RS: Redskins lead series, 6-4
PS: Buccaneers lead series, 1-0;
See Tampa Bay vs. Washington
WASHINGTON vs. TENNESSEE
RS: Titans lead series, 5-3;
See Tennessee vs. Washington

RESULTS

Super Bowl	Date	Winner (Share)	Loser (Share)	Score	Site	Attendance
XXXV	1-28-01	Baltimore ($58,000)	N.Y. Giants ($34,500)	34-7	Tampa	71,921
* XXXIV	1-30-00	St. Louis ($58,000)	Tennessee ($33,000)	23-16	Atlanta	72,625
XXXIII	1-31-99	Denver ($53,000)	Atlanta ($32,500)	34-19	Miami	74,803
XXXII	1-25-98	Denver ($48,000)	Green Bay ($29,000)	31-24	San Diego	68,912
XXXI	1-26-97	Green Bay ($48,000)	New England ($29,000)	35-21	New Orleans	72,301
XXX	1-28-96	Dallas ($42,000)	Pittsburgh ($27,000)	27-17	Tempe	76,347
XXIX	1-29-95	San Francisco ($42,000)	San Diego ($26,000)	49-26	Miami	74,107
* XXVIII	1-30-94	Dallas ($38,000)	Buffalo ($23,500)	30-13	Atlanta	72,817
XXVII	1-31-93	Dallas ($36,000)	Buffalo ($18,000)	52-17	Pasadena	98,374
XXVI	1-26-92	Washington ($36,000)	Buffalo ($18,000)	37-24	Minneapolis	63,130
* XXV	1-27-91	N.Y. Giants ($36,000)	Buffalo ($18,000)	20-19	Tampa	73,813
XXIV	1-28-90	San Francisco ($36,000)	Denver ($18,000)	55-10	New Orleans	72,919
XXIII	1-22-89	San Francisco ($36,000)	Cincinnati ($18,000)	20-16	Miami	75,129
XXII	1-31-88	Washington ($36,000)	Denver ($18,000)	42-10	San Diego	73,302
XXI	1-25-87	N.Y. Giants ($36,000)	Denver ($18,000)	39-20	Pasadena	101,063
XX	1-26-86	Chicago ($36,000)	New England ($18,000)	46-10	New Orleans	73,818
XIX	1-20-85	San Francisco ($36,000)	Miami ($18,000)	38-16	Stanford	84,059
XVIII	1-22-84	L.A. Raiders ($36,000)	Washington ($18,000)	38-9	Tampa	72,920
* XVII	1-30-83	Washington ($36,000)	Miami ($18,000)	27-17	Pasadena	103,667
XVI	1-24-82	San Francisco ($18,000)	Cincinnati ($9,000)	26-21	Pontiac	81,270
XV	1-25-81	Oakland ($18,000)	Philadelphia ($9,000)	27-10	New Orleans	76,135
XIV	1-20-80	Pittsburgh ($18,000)	Los Angeles ($9,000)	31-19	Pasadena	103,985
XIII	1-21-79	Pittsburgh ($18,000)	Dallas ($9,000)	35-31	Miami	79,484
XII	1-15-78	Dallas ($18,000)	Denver ($9,000)	27-10	New Orleans	75,583
XI	1-9-77	Oakland ($15,000)	Minnesota ($7,500)	32-14	Pasadena	103,438
X	1-18-76	Pittsburgh ($15,000)	Dallas ($7,500)	21-17	Miami	80,187
IX	1-12-75	Pittsburgh ($15,000)	Minnesota ($7,500)	16-6	New Orleans	80,997
VIII	1-13-74	Miami ($15,000)	Minnesota ($7,500)	24-7	Houston	71,882
VII	1-14-73	Miami ($15,000)	Washington ($7,500)	14-7	Los Angeles	90,182
VI	1-16-72	Dallas ($15,000)	Miami ($7,500)	24-3	New Orleans	81,023
V	1-17-71	Baltimore ($15,000)	Dallas ($7,500)	16-13	Miami	79,204
* IV	1-11-70	Kansas City ($15,000)	Minnesota ($7,500)	23-7	New Orleans	80,562
III	1-12-69	N.Y. Jets ($15,000)	Baltimore ($7,500)	16-7	Miami	75,389
II	1-14-68	Green Bay ($15,000)	Oakland ($7,500)	33-14	Miami	75,546
I	1-15-67	Green Bay ($15,000)	Kansas City ($7,500)	35-10	Los Angeles	61,946

** One week between conference championship games and Super Bowl; all others had two weeks between conference championship games and Super Bowl.*

SUPER BOWL COMPOSITE STANDINGS

	W	L	Pct.	Pts.	OP
San Francisco 49ers	5	0	1.000	188	89
Baltimore Ravens	1	0	1.000	34	7
Chicago Bears	1	0	1.000	46	10
New York Jets	1	0	1.000	16	7
Pittsburgh Steelers	4	1	.800	120	100
Green Bay Packers	3	1	.750	127	76
Oakland/L.A. Raiders	3	1	.750	111	66
New York Giants	2	1	.667	66	73
Dallas Cowboys	5	3	.625	221	132
Washington Redskins	3	2	.600	122	103
Baltimore Colts	1	1	.500	23	29
Kansas City Chiefs	1	1	.500	33	42
St. Louis/L.A. Rams	1	1	.500	42	47
Miami Dolphins	2	3	.400	74	103
Denver Broncos	2	4	.333	115	206
Atlanta Falcons	0	1	.000	19	34
Philadelphia Eagles	0	1	.000	10	27
San Diego Chargers	0	1	.000	26	49
Tennessee Titans	0	1	.000	16	23
Cincinnati Bengals	0	2	.000	37	46
New England Patriots	0	2	.000	31	81
Buffalo Bills	0	4	.000	73	139
Minnesota Vikings	0	4	.000	34	95

SUPER BOWL MOST VALUABLE PLAYERS*

Super Bowl I — QB Bart Starr, Green Bay
Super Bowl II — QB Bart Starr, Green Bay
Super Bowl III — QB Joe Namath, N.Y. Jets
Super Bowl IV — QB Len Dawson, Kansas City
Super Bowl V — LB Chuck Howley, Dallas
Super Bowl VI — QB Roger Staubach, Dallas
Super Bowl VII — S Jake Scott, Miami
Super Bowl VIII — RB Larry Csonka, Miami
Super Bowl IX — RB Franco Harris, Pittsburgh
Super Bowl X — WR Lynn Swann, Pittsburgh
Super Bowl XI — WR Fred Biletnikoff, Oakland
Super Bowl XII — DT Randy White and DE Harvey Martin, Dallas
Super Bowl XIII — QB Terry Bradshaw, Pittsburgh
Super Bowl XIV — QB Terry Bradshaw, Pittsburgh
Super Bowl XV — QB Jim Plunkett, Oakland
Super Bowl XVI — QB Joe Montana, San Francisco
Super Bowl XVII — RB John Riggins, Washington
Super Bowl XVIII — RB Marcus Allen, L.A. Raiders
Super Bowl XIX — QB Joe Montana, San Francisco
Super Bowl XX — DE Richard Dent, Chicago
Super Bowl XXI — QB Phil Simms, N.Y. Giants
Super Bowl XXII — QB Doug Williams, Washington
Super Bowl XXIII — WR Jerry Rice, San Francisco
Super Bowl XXIV — QB Joe Montana, San Francisco
Super Bowl XXV — RB Ottis Anderson, N.Y. Giants
Super Bowl XXVI — QB Mark Rypien, Washington
Super Bowl XXVII — QB Troy Aikman, Dallas
Super Bowl XXVIII — RB Emmitt Smith, Dallas
Super Bowl XXIX — QB Steve Young, San Francisco
Super Bowl XXX — CB Larry Brown, Dallas
Super Bowl XXXI — KR-PR Desmond Howard, Green Bay
Super Bowl XXXII — RB Terrell Davis, Denver
Super Bowl XXXIII — QB John Elway, Denver
Super Bowl XXXIV — QB Kurt Warner, St. Louis
Super Bowl XXXV — LB Ray Lewis, Baltimore

* Award named Pete Rozelle Trophy since Super Bowl XXV.

SUPER BOWL XXXV

Raymond James Stadium, Tampa, Florida
January 28, 2001, Attendance: 71,921

BALTIMORE 34, N.Y. GIANTS 7—The Ravens' defense completed a dominating season by permitting just 152 yards, forcing 5 turnovers, recording 4 sacks, and not allowing an offensive touchdown en route to the franchise's first Super Bowl victory. Jermaine Lewis's punt return into Giants' territory midway through the first quarter was followed two plays later by Trent Dilfer's 38-yard touchdown pass to Brandon Stokley, which gave the Ravens a 7-0 lead. Early in the second quarter, Jessie Armstead intercepted a short pass by Dilfer and returned it 43 yards for a touchdown, but the play was nullified by a penalty. Dilfer's 36-yard pass to Qadry Ismail in the second quarter set up Matt Stover's 47-yard field goal with 1:48 left in the half. Tiki Barber's 27-yard run gave the Giants their deepest penetration of the game, to the Ravens' 29, but Chris McAlister intercepted Kerry Collins's pass on the next play to preserve a 10-0 lead. In the third quarter, Duane Starks stepped in front of Amani Toomer and intercepted Collins's pass. Starks returned it 49 yards untouched for a 17-0 lead. The Giants immediately cut the lead to 10 points when Ron Dixon returned the ensuing kickoff 97 yards for a touchdown. However, Jermaine Lewis then matched Dixon's kickoff return as he cut across the field and raced 84 yards for a 24-7 lead with 3:13 left in the third quarter. The 3 touchdowns in 36 seconds were a Super Bowl record. The Giants gained just 1 first down on their final four possessions. Jamal Lewis's 3-yard touchdown run midway through the fourth quarter gave Baltimore a 31-7 lead, and Robert Bailey recovered Dixon's fumble on the ensuing kickoff return to set up Stover's 34-yard field goal with 5:27 remaining to finish the scoring. Dilfer completed 12 of 25 passes for 153 yards and 1 touchdown. Jamal Lewis had 27 carries for 102 yards. Collins was 15 of 39 for 112 yards, with 4 interceptions. Ray Lewis was named Super Bowl most valuable player.

Baltimore (34)	Offense	N.Y. Giants (7)
Qadry Ismail	WR	Amani Toomer
Jonathan Ogden	LT	Lomas Brown
Edwin Mulitalo	LG	Glenn Parker
Jeff Mitchell	C	Dusty Zeigler
Mike Flynn	RG	Ron Stone
Harry Swayne	RT	Luke Petitgout
Shannon Sharpe	TE-WR	Ike Hilliard
Brandon Stokley	WR	Ron Dixon
Trent Dilfer	QB	Kerry Collins

Sam Gash	FB	Greg Comella
Priest Holmes	RB	Tiki Barber
	Defense	
Rob Burnett	LE	Michael Strahan
Sam Adams	LT	Cornelius Griffin
Tony Siragusa	RT	Keith Hamilton
Michael McCrary	RE	Cedric Jones
Peter Boulware	LLB-MLB	Mike Barrow
Ray Lewis	MLB-OLB	Jessie Armstead
Jamie Sharper	RLB-CB	Emmanuel McDaniel
Duane Starks	LCB	Dave Thomas
Chris McAlister	RCB	Jason Sehorn
Kim Herring	SS	Sam Garnes
Rod Woodson	FS	Shaun Williams

SUBSTITUTIONS

BALTIMORE—Offense: K—Matt Stover. P—Kyle Richardson. QB—Tony Banks. RB—Jamal Lewis. FB—Chuck Evans. WR—Billy Davis, Patrick Johnson, Jermaine Lewis. TE—Ben Coates. G—Kipp Vickers. T—Spencer Folau. C—John Hudson. Defense: DE—Keith Washington. DT—Lional Dalton, Larry Webster. LB—O.J. Brigance, Cornell Brown, Anthony Davis, Brad Jackson. CB—Robert Bailey, James Trapp. S—Corey Harris, Anthony Mitchell. Inactive: QB—Chris Redman. WR—Marcus Nash, Germany Thompson. G—Orlando Bobo. T—Sammy Williams. DE—Adalius Thomas. CB—Clarence Love. S—Anthony Poindexter.

N.Y. GIANTS—Offense: K—Brad Daluiso. P—Brad Maynard. RB—Ron Dayne, Joe Montgomery, Damon Washington. WR—Thabiti Davis, Joe Jurevicius. TE—Dan Campbell, Howard Cross, Pete Mitchell. G—Mike Rosenthal, Jason Whittle. C—Derek Engler. Defense: DT—Ryan Hale, Christian Peter. DE—Ryan Phillips. LB—Jack Golden, Pete Monty, Brandon Short. CB—Ramos McDonald. S—Omar Stoutmire, Lyle West. DNP—Jason Garrett. Inactive: K—Jaret Holmes. QB—Mike Cherry. FB—Craig Walendy. T—Chris Bober. DT—George Williams. DE—Jeremiah Parker. LB—Kevin Lewis. CB—Reggie Stephens.

OFFICIALS

Referee—Gerry Austin. Umpire—Chad Brown. Line Judge—Walt Anderson. Side Judge—Doug Toole. Head Linesman—Tony Veteri. Back Judge—Bill Schmitz. Field Judge—Bill Lovett. Replay Official—Dean Blandino. Video Operator—Ted Campbell.

SCORING

Baltimore	7	3	14	10	—	34
N.Y. Giants	0	0	7	0	—	7

Balt — Stokley 38 pass from Dilfer (Stover kick) (8:10)
Balt — FG Stover 47 (13:19)
Balt — Starks 49 interception return (Stover kick) (11:11)
NYG — Dixon 97 kickoff return (Daluiso kick) (11:29)
Balt — Je. Lewis 84 kickoff return (Stover kick) (11:47)
Balt — Ja. Lewis 3 run (Stover kick) (6:15)
Balt — FG Stover 34 (9:33)

TEAM STATISTICS	BALT.	NYG
Total First Downs	13	11
Rushing	6	2
Passing	6	6
Penalty	1	3
Total Net Yardage	244	152
Total Offensive Plays	62	59
Average Gain Per Offensive Play	3.9	2.6
Rushes	33	16
Yards Gained Rushing (Net)	111	66
Average Yards per Rush	3.4	4.1
Passes Attempted	26	39
Passes Completed	12	15
Had Intercepted	0	4
Tackled Attempting to Pass	3	4
Yards Lost Attempting to Pass	20	26
Yards Gained Passing (Net)	133	86
Punts	10	11
Average Distance	43.0	38.4
Punt Returns	3	5
Punt Return Yardage	34	46
Kickoff Returns	2	7
Kickoff Return Yardage	111	170
Interception Return Yardage	59	0
Total Return Yardage	204	216
Fumbles	2	2
Fumbles Lost	0	1
Own Fumbles Recovered	2	1
Opponent Fumbles Recovered	1	0
Penalties	9	6
Yards Penalized	70	27
Field Goals	2	0
Field Goals Attempted	3	0
Third-Down Efficiency	3/16	2/14
Fourth-Down Efficiency	0/0	1/1
Time of Possession	34:06	25:54

INDIVIDUAL STATISTICS

RUSHING: BALT: Ja. Lewis 27-102-1, Holmes 4-8-0, Je. Lewis 1-1-0, Dilfer 1-0-0. NYG: Barber 11-49-0, Collins 3-12-0, Montgomery 2-5-0.
PASSING: BALT: Dilfer 25-12-153-1-0, Banks 1-0-0-0-0. NYG: Collins 39-15-112-0-4.
RECEIVING: BALT: Stokley 3-52-1, Coates 3-30-0, Ismail 1-44-0, Johnson 1-8-0, Je. Lewis 1-6-0, Sharpe 1-5-0, Ja. Lewis 1-4-0, Holmes 1-4-0. NYG: Barber 6-26-0, Hilliard 3-30-0, Toomer 2-24-0, Dixon 1-16-0, Cross 1-7-0, Mitchell 1-7-0, Comella 1-2-0.
KICKOFF RETURNS: BALT: Je. Lewis 2-111-1. NYG: Dixon 6-153-1, Washington 1-17-0.
PUNT RETURNS: BALT: Je. Lewis 3-34-0. NYG: Hilliard 3-33-0, Barber 2-13-0.
PUNTING: BALT: Richardson 10-430-43.0. NYG: Maynard 11-422-38.4.
INTERCEPTIONS: BALT: Starks 1-49-1, McAlister 1-4-0, Sharper 1-4-0, Herring 1-2-0.
SACKS: BALT: McCrary 2, Burnett, Washington. NYG: Griffin 1.5, Strahan 1.5.

SUPER BOWL XXXIV

Georgia Dome, Atlanta, Georgia
January 30, 2000, Attendance: 72,625

ST. LOUIS 23, TENNESSEE 16—Mike Jones tackled Kevin Dyson at the 1-yard line as time expired, preserving the Rams' first-ever Super Bowl title. The Rams drove inside the Titans' 20 with each of their first six possessions, but compiled just 3 field goals and 1 touchdown to take a 16-0 lead. Holder Mike Horan's bobbled snap averted a 35-yard field-goal attempt to conclude the Rams' first drive. The Titans responded with a 42-yard drive, their longest of the half, but Al Del Greco missed a 47-yard attempt. Jeff Wilkins added 3 field goals and missed a 34-yard attempt while the Titans did not threaten the rest of the half, giving the Rams a 9-0 lead at intermission despite outgaining the Titans in total yards (294-89). Tennessee drove 43 yards with the second half's opening kickoff, but Todd Lyght blocked Del Greco's 47-yard attempt to keep the Titans off the board. Kurt Warner's 31-yard pass to Isaac Bruce keyed the ensuing drive that was capped by Warner's 9-yard touchdown pass to Torry Holt with 7:20 left in the third quarter to give the Rams a 16-0 lead. The Titans responded with touchdown drives in excess of seven minutes on each of their next two possessions. Steve McNair's 23-yard scramble set up Eddie George's 1-yard run in the final minute of the third quarter. McNair's 2-point conversion pass to Frank Wycheck was incomplete, but the Titans' defense forced a punt and the offense drove 79 yards in 13 plays, highlighted by 21-yard passes from McNair to Isaac Byrd and Jackie Harris, and capped by George's 2-yard run to cut the deficit to 16-13 with 7:21 remaining. The Rams once again failed to get a first down, and following a punt, the Titans needed just 28 yards to set up Del Greco's game-tying 43-yard kick with 2:12 left. On the next play from scrimmage, Warner fired a deep pass down the right sideline to Bruce, who caught the ball at the Titans' 38, cut toward the inside, and outran the defense to the end zone to give the Rams a 23-16 lead with 1:54 left. The Titans drove downfield, and McNair avoided a sack and completed a 16-yard pass to Kevin Dyson at the Rams' 10 with six seconds remaining. With no timeouts, McNair attempted a quick pass to a slanting Dyson, who caught the ball in stride at the Rams' 3. However, Jones reacted quickly and stepped up to tackle Dyson at the 1-yard line as time expired. Warner, who was named the game's most valuable player, was 24 of 45 for a Super Bowl-record 414 yards and 2 touchdowns. Bruce had 6 catches for 162 yards, and Holt had 7 for 109 yards. McNair was 22 of 36 for 214 yards. The Titans were the first team in Super Bowl history to come back from a 16-point deficit.

St. Louis (NFC)	3	6	7	7	—	23
Tennessee (AFC)	0	0	6	10	—	16

StL — FG Wilkins 27 (12:00)
StL — FG Wilkins 29 (10:44)
StL — FG Wilkins 28 (14:45)
StL — Holt 9 pass from Warner (Wilkins kick) (11:01)
Tenn — George 1 run (pass failed) (14:46)
Tenn — George 2 run (Del Greco kick) (7:39)
Tenn — FG Del Greco 43 (12:48)
StL — Bruce 73 pass from Warner (Wilkins kick) (13:06)

SUPER BOWL XXXIII

Pro Player Stadium, Miami, Florida
January 31, 1999, Attendance: 74,803

DENVER 34, ATLANTA 19—John Elway, in his last game, passed for 336 yards and ran for a touchdown to earn most valuable player honors as the Broncos became the first AFC team to win consecutive Super Bowls since the Steelers won XIII and XIV. A 25-yard pass interference penalty on Ray Crockett assisted the Falcons' nine-play, 48-yard game-opening drive that was capped by Morten Andersen's 32-yard field goal. Elway's 41-yard pass to Rod Smith kept alive Denver's ensuing drive and led to Howard Griffith's 1-yard touchdown run. Ronnie Bradford's interception and return to the Broncos' 35 late in the first quarter gave Atlanta excellent field position. However, Jamal Anderson was stopped for no gain on third-and-1 and thrown for a 2-yard loss on fourth down. Denver capitalized on its defensive effort with Jason Elam's 26-yard field goal. The Falcons responded by driving to the Broncos' 8, but Andersen's 26-yard field-goal attempt sailed wide right and on the next play, Elway fired an 80-yard touchdown pass to Smith to turn a possible 10-6 game into a 17-3 Broncos lead. Andersen's 28-yard field goal and 2 misses by Elam on the Broncos' first two second-half possessions gave Atlanta an opportunity to climb back into the game. However, Darrien Gordon dashed the Falcons' hopes with interceptions on consecutive possessions inside the Broncos' 20 to stop drives and set up Broncos touchdowns. Gordon returned the first interception, on a tipped pass, 58 yards to the Falcons' 24 to set up Griffith's second touchdown five plays later, and picked the second pass off at the Broncos' 2 and returned it 50 yards. Terrell Davis turned a short pass into a 39-yard gain, and Elway scored two plays later to give Denver a 31-6 lead. Tim Dwight returned the ensuing kickoff for a touchdown, and, after a field goal by Elam, the Falcons' offense scored with 2:04 remaining on Chandler's 3-yard pass to Tony Martin. Byron Chamberlain recovered the ensuing onside kick, but Tyrone Braxton recovered Anderson's fumble at the Falcons' 33 with 1:30 remaining to ice the game. The Falcons drove inside the Broncos' 30 seven times, but tallied just 1 touchdown and 2 field goals, throwing 2 interceptions, missing 1 field goal, and turning the ball over 1 time on downs during the other possessions. Elway was 18 of 29 for 336 yards and 1 touchdown, with 1 interception. Davis had 25 carries for 102 yards. Smith had 5 receptions for 152 yards. Chandler was 19 of 35 for 219 yards and 1 touchdown, with 3 interceptions.

Denver (AFC)	7	10	0	17	—	34
Atlanta (NFC)	3	3	0	13	—	19

Atl — FG Andersen 32 (5:25)
Den — Griffith 1 run (Elam kick) (11:05)
Den — FG Elam 26 (5:43)
Den — R. Smith 80 pass from Elway (Elam kick) (10:06)
Atl — FG Andersen 28 (12:35)
Den — Griffith 1 run (Elam kick) (:04)

Den — Elway 3 run (Elam kick) (3:40)
Atl — Dwight 94 kickoff return (Andersen kick) (3:59)
Den — FG Elam 37 (7:52)
Atl — Mathis 3 pass from Chandler (pass failed) (12:56)

SUPER BOWL XXXII

Qualcomm Stadium, San Diego, California
January 25, 1998, Attendance: 68,912

DENVER 31, GREEN BAY 24—Terrell Davis rushed for 157 yards and a Super Bowl-record 3 touchdowns to lead the Broncos to their first NFL championship and break the NFC's streak of Super Bowl victories at 13. The defending Super Bowl champion Packers took the opening kickoff and marched 76 yards in just over four minutes, scoring the first points on Brett Favre's 22-yard touchdown pass to Antonio Freeman. The Broncos responded with a 10-play, 58-yard drive capped by Davis's 1-yard run to tie the game. Tyrone Braxton intercepted Favre two plays later, and John Elway scored on a third-and-goal play to begin the second quarter. Steve Atwater forced Favre to fumble three plays later, and Neil Smith recovered at the Packers' 33. Jason Elam converted a 51-yard field goal, the second longest in Super Bowl history, to give the Broncos a 17-7 lead with 12:21 left in the half. After an exchange of punts, the Packers produced a 17-play, 95-yard drive that consumed 7:26 and finished with Favre's 6-yard touchdown pass to Mark Chmura on third-and-5 with 12 seconds left in the half. Tyrone Williams forced and recovered Davis's fumble at the Broncos' 26 on the first play from scrimmage in the second half. However, the Broncos' defense kept the Packers out of the end zone as Ryan Longwell's 27-yard field goal tied the game with 11:59 left in the third quarter. After another exchange of punts, Elway's 36-yard pass to Ed McCaffrey keyed a 13-play, 92-yard drive capped by Davis's 1-yard touchdown run with 34 seconds left in the third quarter. Tim McKyer recovered Freeman's fumble at the Packers' 22 on the ensuing kickoff return, giving the Broncos a golden opportunity, but Eugene Robinson intercepted Elway's pass in the end zone on the next play. Sparked by Robinson's play, the Packers took just four plays, three on passes to Freeman, to score the tying touchdown with 13:32 remaining. Each defense stiffened, forcing two punts, but the Broncos got great field position following Craig Hentrich's 39-yard punt to the Packers' 49 with 3:27 left and the score tied 24-24. Davis rushed for 2 yards on the first play, but Darrius Holland's 15-yard facemask penalty moved the ball to the Packers' 32. Elway threw a 23-yard pass to Howard Griffith two plays later, and after a holding penalty, Davis rushed 17 yards to the Packers' 1 with 1:47 left. After a timeout, Davis waltzed into the end zone to give Denver a 31-24 lead with 1:45 remaining. Freeman returned the kickoff 22 yards to the Broncos' 30, and Favre completed 22- and 13-yard screen passes to Dorsey Levens to reach the Broncos' 35 with 1:04 left. But after a 4-yard pass to Levens and incompletions to Freeman and Brooks, John Mobley knocked away Favre's pass to Chmura with 32 seconds left to give the Broncos the Vince Lombardi Trophy. Elway was 12 of 22 for 123 yards, with 1 interception. Favre was 25 of 42 for 256 yards and 1 touchdown, with 1 interception. Freeman had 9 receptions for 126 yards. Davis was named the game's most valuable player.

Green Bay (NFC)	7	7	3	7	—	24
Denver (AFC)	7	10	7	7	—	31

GB — Freeman 22 pass from Favre (Longwell kick) (4:02)
Den — Davis 1 run (Elam kick) (9:21)
Den — Elway 1 run (Elam kick) (:05)
Den — FG Elam 51 (2:39)
GB — Chmura 6 pass from Favre (Longwell kick) (14:48)
GB — FG Longwell 27 (3:01)
Den — Davis 1 run (Elam kick) (14:26)
GB — Freeman 13 pass from Favre (Longwell kick) (1:28)
Den — Davis 1 run (Elam kick) (13:15)

SUPER BOWL XXXI

Louisiana Superdome, New Orleans, Louisiana
January 26, 1997, Attendance: 72,301

GREEN BAY 35, NEW ENGLAND 21— Desmond Howard returned a kickoff 99 yards for a touchdown and Brett Favre passed for 2 touchdowns and ran for a score as the Packers won their first Super Bowl in twenty-nine years. Howard, en route to garnering the MVP trophy, equaled a Super Bowl record with 244 total return yards. It was Favre's arm that struck first, as he hit Andre Rison for a 54-yard touchdown pass on the Packers' second play from scrimmage to take a 7-0 lead. Two plays later Doug Evans made a diving interception of Drew Bledsoe's pass at the 28-yard line, setting up Chris Jacke's field goal and giving the Packers a 10-0 lead just 6:18 into the Super Bowl. The Patriots answered with touchdowns on their next two possessions. Craig Newsome's pass interference penalty set up the first touchdown and a 44-yard completion from Bledsoe to Terry Glenn preceeding Ben Coates's touchdown gave New England its first and only lead. The 24 combined first quarter points were the most in Super Bowl history. Green Bay struck again 56 seconds into the second quarter as Favre hit Antonio Freeman with a Super Bowl-record 81-yard touchdown bomb. Jacke booted his second field goal on Green Bay's next possession. After a Mike Prior interception, Favre orchestrated a 74-yard, nearly 6-minute drive that concluded with a diving Favre touching the ball against the pylon to give Green Bay a 27-14 halftime lead. Curtis Martin brought the Patriots to within a score by running in from 18 yards out with 3:27 left in the third quarter. But Howard broke the Patriots' spirit by returning the ensuing kickoff a Super Bowl-record 99 yards. Favre found Mark Chmura for the 2-point conversion to finish the scoring. Bledsoe was intercepted twice in the fourth quarter as the Patriots never crossed midfield in 4 fourth-quarter possessions. Reggie White set a Super Bowl record with 3 sacks. Favre completed 14 of 27 passes for 246 yards, with no interceptions. Bledsoe completed 11 more passes than Favre, but for just 7 more yards, and threw 4 interceptions.

New England (AFC)	14	0	7	0	—	21
Green Bay (NFC)	10	17	8	0	—	35

GB — Rison 54 pass from Favre (Jacke kick) (3:32)
GB — FG Jacke 37 (6:18)
NE — Byars 1 pass from Bledsoe (Vinatieri kick) (8:25)
NE — Coates 4 pass from Bledsoe (Vinatieri kick) (12:27)
GB — Freeman 81 pass from Favre (Jacke kick) (0:56)
GB — FG Jacke 31 (6:45)
GB — Favre 2 run (Jacke kick) (13:49)
NE — Martin 18 run (Vinatieri kick) (11:33)
GB — Howard 99 kickoff return (Chmura pass from Favre) (11:50)

SUPER BOWL XXX

Sun Devil Stadium, Tempe, Arizona
January 28, 1996, Attendance: 76,347

DALLAS 27, PITTSBURGH 17—Cornerback Larry Brown's 2 interceptions led to 14 second-half points and helped lift the Cowboys to their third Super Bowl victory in the last four seasons and their record-tying fifth title overall. Brown's interceptions foiled the comeback efforts of the Steelers, and earned him the Pete Rozelle Trophy as the game's most valuable player. Dallas scored on each of its first three possessions, taking a 13-0 lead on Troy Aikman's 3-yard touchdown pass to Jay Novacek and a pair of field goals by Chris Boniol. Neil O'Donnell's 6-yard touchdown pass to Yancey Thigpen 13 seconds before halftime pulled Pittsburgh within 6 points, and the Steelers had the ball near midfield midway through the third quarter. But O'Donnell's third-down pass was intercepted by Brown at the Cowboys' 38-yard line, and his 44-yard return carried to Pittsburgh's 18. After Aikman's 17-yard completion to Michael Irvin, Emmitt Smith ran 1 yard for the touchdown that put Dallas ahead again by 13 points. The Steelers rallied, though, behind Norm Johnson's 46-yard field goal, a successful surprise onside kick, and Byron (Bam) Morris's 1-yard touchdown run with 6:36 to play in the game. And when they forced a punt and took possession at their own 32-yard line trailing only 20-17 with 4:15 remaining, it appeared they might have a chance to break the NFC's recent domination in the Super Bowl. But on second down, Brown struck again, intercepting O'Donnell's pass at the 39 and returning it 33 yards to the 6. Two plays later, Smith barreled over from 4 yards out for the clinching touchdown with 3:43 to go. Pittsburgh limited the Cowboys' powerful running game to only 56 yards and enjoyed a whopping 201-61 advantage in total yards in the second half, but could not overcome the 3 interceptions (another came on the game's final play) thrown by O'Donnell, the NFL's career leader for fewest interceptions per pass attempt. In all, O'Donnell completed 28 of 49 passes for 239 yards. Morris rushed for a game-high 73 yards on 19 carries. For Dallas, Aikman completed 15 of 23 pass attempts for 209 yards. The Cowboys' victory was the twelfth in a row for NFC teams over AFC teams in the Super Bowl.

Dallas (NFC)	10	3	7	7	—	27
Pittsburgh (AFC)	0	7	0	10	—	17

Dall — FG Boniol 42 (2:55)
Dall — Novacek 3 pass from Aikman (Boniol kick) (9:37)
Dall — FG Boniol 35 (8:57)
Pitt — Thigpen 6 pass from O'Donnell (N. Johnson kick) (14:47)
Dall — E. Smith 1 run (Boniol kick) (8:18)
Pitt — FG N. Johnson 46 (3:40)
Pitt — Morris 1 run (N. Johnson kick) (8:24)
Dall — E. Smith 4 run (Boniol kick) (11:17)

SUPER BOWL XXIX

Joe Robbie Stadium, Miami, Florida
January 29, 1995, Attendance: 74,107

SAN FRANCISCO 49, SAN DIEGO 26—Steve Young passed for a record 6 touchdowns, and the 49ers became the first team to win five Super Bowls when they routed the Chargers. Young, the game's most valuable player, directed an explosive offense that generated 7 touchdowns, 28 first downs, and 455 total yards. He completed 24 of 36 passes for 325 yards, and broke the record of 5 touchdown passes set by fromer 49ers quarterback Joe Montana in Super Bowl XXIV. San Francisco wasted little time scoring, taking the lead for good on Young's 44-yard touchdown pass to Jerry Rice only three plays and 1:24 into the game. The next time they had the ball, the 49ers marched 79 yards in four plays, taking a 14-0 lead when Young teamed with running back Ricky Watters on a 51-yard touchdown pass with 10:05 still to play in the opening period. San Diego then put together its most impressive possession of the game, a 13-play, 78-yard drive that consumed more than 7 minutes and was capped by Natrone Means's 1-yard touchdown run, to cut its deficit to 14-7 late in the quarter. But San Francisco countered with a 70-yard drive of its own, and Young's 5-yard touchdown pass to fullback William Floyd made it 21-7. Young's fourth touchdown pass of the half, 8 yards to Watters 4:44 before halftime, increased the advantage to 28-7, and the Chargers could get no closer than 18 points after that. Watters, who ran 9 yards for a touchdown in the third quarter, equaled the Super Bowl record with 3 touchdowns. Rice also scored 3 touchdowns (the second time in his career he'd done that in a Super Bowl) while catching 10 passes for 149 yards. He established career records for receptions, yards, and touchdowns in a Super Bowl. Young, who scrambled 21 yards and 15 yards to set up touchdowns in the first half, was the game's leading rusher with 49 yards on 5 carries. San Diego's Means, who rushed for 1,350 yards during the regular season, was limited to 33 yards on 13 attempts. Chargers quarterback Stan Humphries completed 24 of 49 passes for 275 yards. Rookie Andre Coleman became only the third player in Super Bowl history to return a kickoff for a touchdown, going 98 yards in the third quarter. The 75 points scored by the two teams established another record, breaking the previous mark of 69 set in Dallas's 52-17 victory over Buffalo in XXVII. The 49ers' victory was the eleventh straight for NFC teams over AFC teams in the Super Bowl.

San Diego (AFC)	7	3	8	8	—	26
San Francisco (NFC)	14	14	14	7	—	49

SF — Rice 44 pass from S. Young (Brien kick) (1:24)
SF — Watters 51 pass from S. Young (Brien kick) (4:55)
SD — Means 1 run (Carney kick) (12:16)
SF — Floyd 5 pass from S. Young (Brien kick) (1:58)
SF — Watters 8 pass from S. Young (Brien kick) (10:16)
SD — FG Carney 31 (13:16)
SF — Watters 9 run (Brien kick) (5:25)
SF — Rice 15 pass from S. Young (Brien kick) (11:42)
SD — Coleman 98 kickoff return (Seay pass from Humphries) (11:59)
SF — Rice 7 pass from S. Young (Brien kick) (1:11)
SD — Martin 30 pass from Humphries (Pupunu pass from Humphries) (12:35)

SUPER BOWL XXVIII

Georgia Dome, Atlanta, Georgia
January 30, 1994, Attendance: 72,817

DALLAS 30, BUFFALO 13—Emmitt Smith rushed for 132 yards and 2 second-half touchdowns to power the Cowboys to their second consecutive NFL title. By winning, Dallas joined San Francisco and Pittsburgh as the only franchises with four Super Bowl victories. The Bills, meanwhile, extended a dubious string by losing in the Super Bowl for the fourth consecutive year. To win, the Cowboys had to rally from a 13-6 halftime deficit. Buffalo had forged its lead on Thurman Thomas's 4-yard touchdown run and a pair of field goals by Steve Christie, including a 54-yard kick, the longest in Super Bowl history. But just 55 seconds into the second half, Thomas was stripped of the ball by Dallas defensive tackle Leon Lett. Safety James Washington recovered and weaved his way 46 yards for a touchdown to tie the game at 13-13. After forcing the Bills to punt, the Cowboys began their next possession on their 36-yard line and Smith, the game's most valuable player, took over. He carried 7 times for 61 yards on the ensuing 8-play, 64-yard drive, capping the march with a 15-yard touchdown run to give Dallas the lead for good with 8:42 remaining in the third quarter. Early in the fourth quarter, Washington intercepted Jim Kelly's pass and returned it 12 yards to Buffalo's 34. A penalty moved the ball back to the 39, but Smith carried twice for 10 yards and caught a screen pass for 9, and quarterback Troy Aikman completed a 16-yard pass to Alvin Harper to give the Cowboys a first-and-goal at the 6. Smith took it from there, cracking the end zone on fourth-and-goal from the 1 to put Dallas ahead 27-13 with 9:50 remaining. Eddie Murray's third field goal, from 20 yards with 2:50 left, ended any doubt about the game's outcome. Smith had 30 carries in all, with 19 of his attempts and 92 yards coming after intermission. Washington, normally a reserve who played most of the game because the Cowboys used five defensive backs to combat the Bills' No-Huddle offense, had 11 tackles and forced another fumble by Thomas in the first quarter. Aikman completed 19 of 27 passes for 207 yards. Buffalo's Kelly completed a Super Bowl-record 31 passes in 50 attempts for 260 yards. Dallas, the first team in NFL history to begin the regular season 0-2 and go on to win the Super Bowl, also became the fifth to win back-to-back titles, following Green Bay, Miami, Pittsburgh (the Steelers did it twice), and San Francisco. Buffalo became the third team, along with Minnesota and Denver, to lose four Super Bowls. The Cowboys' victory was the tenth in succession for the NFC over the AFC.

Dallas (NFC)	6	0	14	10	—	30
Buffalo (AFC)	3	10	0	0	—	13

Dall — FG Murray 41 (2:19)
Buff — FG Christie 54 (4:41)
Dall — FG Murray 24 (11:05)
Buff — Thomas 4 run (Christie kick) (2:34)
Buff — FG Christie 28 (15:00)
Dall — Washington 46 fumble return (Murray kick) (0:55)
Dall — E. Smith 15 run (Murray kick) (6:18)
Dall — E. Smith 1 run (Murray kick) (5:10)
Dall — FG Murray 20 (12:10)

SUPER BOWL XXVII

Rose Bowl, Pasadena, California
January 31, 1993, Attendance: 98,374

DALLAS 52, BUFFALO 17—Troy Aikman passed for 4 touchdowns, Emmitt Smith rushed for 108 yards, and the Cowboys converted 9 turnovers into 35 points while coasting to the victory. Dallas's win was its third in its record sixth Super Bowl appearance; the Bills became the first team to drop three in succession. Buffalo led 7-0 until the first 2 of its record number of turnovers helped the Cowboys take the lead for good late in the opening quarter. First, Dallas safety James Washington intercepted Jim Kelly's pass and returned it 13 yards to the Bills' 47, setting up Aikman's 23-yard touchdown pass to tight end Jay Novacek with 1:36 remaining in the period. On the next play from scrimmage, Kelly was sacked by Charles Haley and fumbled at the Bills' 2-yard line where the Cowboys' Jimmie Jones picked up the loose ball and ran 2 yards for a touchdown. Dallas, which recovered 5 fumbles and intercepted 4 passes, struck just as quickly late in the first half, when Aikman tossed 19- and 18-yard touchdown passes to Michael Irvin 18 seconds apart to give the Cowboys a 28-10 lead at intermission. The second score was set up when Bills running back Thurman Thomas lost a fumble at his 19-yard line. Buffalo scored for the last time when backup quarterback Frank Reich, playing because Kelly was injured while attempting to pass midway through the second quarter, threw a 40-yard touchdown pass to Don Beebe on the final play of the third period to trim the deficit to 31-17. But Dallas put the game out of reach by scoring three times in a span of 2:33 of the fourth quarter. Aikman, the game's most valuable player, completed 22 of 30 passes for 273 yards. The victory was the ninth in succession for the NFC over the AFC.

Buffalo (AFC)	7	3	7	0	—	17
Dallas (NFC)	14	14	3	21	—	52

Buff — Thomas 2 run (Christie kick) (5:00)
Dall — Novacek 23 pass from Aikman (Elliott kick) (13:24)
Dall — J. Jones 2 fumble recovery return (Elliott kick) (13:39)
Buff — FG Christie 21 (11:36)
Dall — Irvin 19 pass from Aikman (Elliott kick) (13:06)
Dall — Irvin 18 pass from Aikman (Elliott kick) (13:24)
Dall — FG Elliott 20 (6:39)
Buff — Beebe 40 pass from Reich (Christie kick) (15:00)
Dall — Harper 45 pass from Aikman (Elliott kick) (4:56)
Dall — E. Smith 10 run (Elliott kick) (6:48)
Dall — Norton 9 fumble recovery return (Elliott kick) (7:29)

SUPER BOWL XXVI

Metrodome, Minneapolis, Minnesota
January 26, 1992, Attendance: 63,130

WASHINGTON 37, BUFFALO 24—Mark Rypien passed for 292 yards and 2 touchdowns as the Redskins overwhelmed the Bills to win their third Super Bowl in the past 10 years. Rypien, the game's most valuable player, completed 18 of 33 passes, including a 10-yard scoring strike to Earnest Byner and a 30-yard touchdown to Gary Clark. The latter came late in the third quarter after Buffalo had trimmed a 24-0 deficit to 24-10, and effectively put the game out of reach. Washington went on to lead by as much as 37-10 before the Bills made it close wih a pair of touchdowns in the final six minutes. Though the Redskins struggled early, converting their first three drives inside the Bills' 20-yard line into only 3 points, they built a 17-0 halftime lead. And they made it 24-0 just 16 seconds into the second half, after Kurt Gouveia intercepted Buffalo quarterback Jim Kelly's pass on the first play of the third quarter and returned it 23 yards to the Bills' 2. One play later, Gerald Riggs scored his second touchdown of the game to make it 24-0. Kelly, forced to bring Buffalo from behind, completed 28 of a Super Bowl-record 58 passes for 275 yards and 2 touchdowns, but was intercepted 4 times. Bills running back Thurman Thomas, who had an AFC-high 1,407 yards rushing and an NFL-best 2,038 total yards from scrimmage during the regular season, ran for only 13 yards on 10 carries and was limited to 27 yards on 4 receptions. Clark had 7 catches for 114 yards and Art Monk added 7 for 113 for the Redskins, who amassed 417 yards of total offense while limiting the explosive Bills to 283. Washington's Joe Gibbs became only the third head coach to win three Super Bowls.

Washington (NFC)	0	17	14	6	—	37
Buffalo (AFC)	0	0	10	14	—	24

Wash — FG Lohmiller 34 (1:58)
Wash — Byner 10 pass from Rypien (Lohmiller kick) (5:06)
Wash — Riggs 1 run (Lohmiller kick) (7:43)
Wash — Riggs 2 run (Lohmiller kick) (0:16)
Buff — FG Norwood 21 (3:01)
Buff — Thomas 1 run (Norwood kick) (9:02)
Wash — Clark 30 pass from Rypien (Lohmiller kick) (13:36)
Wash — FG Lohmiller 25 (0:06)
Wash — FG Lohmiller 39 (3:24)
Buff — Metzelaars 2 pass from Kelly (Norwood kick) (9:01)
Buff — Beebe 4 pass from Kelly (Norwood kick) (11:05)

SUPER BOWL XXV

Tampa Stadium, Tampa, Florida
January 27, 1991, Attendance: 73,813

NEW YORK GIANTS 20, BUFFALO 19—The NFC champion New York Giants won their second Super Bowl in five years with a 20-19 victory over AFC titlist Buffalo. New York, employing its ball-control offense, had possession for 40 minutes, 33 seconds, a Super Bowl record. The Bills, who scored 95 points in their previous two playoff games leading to Super Bowl XXV, had the ball for less than eight minutes in the second half and just 19:27 for the game. Fourteen of New York's 73 plays came on its initial drive of the third quarter, which covered 75 yards and consumed a Super Bowl-record 9:29 before running back Ottis Anderson ran 1 yard for a touchdown. Giants quarterback Jeff Hostetler kept the long drive going by converting three third-down plays—an 11-yard pass to running back David Meggett on third-and-eight, a 14-yard toss to wide receiver Mark Ingram on third-and-13, and a 9-yard pass to Howard Cross on third-and-four—to give New York a 17-12 lead in the third quarter. Buffalo jumped to a 12-3 lead midway through the second quarter before Hostetler completed a 14-yard scoring strike to wide receiver Stephen Baker to close the score to 12-10 at halftime. Buffalo's Thurman Thomas ran 31 yards for a touchdown on the opening play of the fourth quarter to help Buffalo recapture the lead 19-17. Matt Bahr's 21-yard field goal gave the Giants a 20-19 lead, but Buffalo's Scott Norwood had a chance to win the game with seconds remaining before his 47-yard field-goal attempt sailed wide right. Hostetler completed 20 of 32 passes for 222 yards and 1 touchdown. Anderson rushed 21 times for 102 yards and 1 touchdown to capture most-valuable-player honors. Thomas totaled 190 scrimmage yards, rushing 15 times for 135 yards and catching 5 passes for 55 yards.

Buffalo (AFC)	3	9	0	7	—	19
N.Y. Giants (NFC)	3	7	7	3	—	20

NYG — FG Bahr 28 (7:46)
Buff — FG Norwood 23 (9:09)
Buff — D. Smith 1 run (Norwood kick) (2:30)
Buff — Safety, B. Smith tackled Hostetler in end zone (6:33)
NYG — Baker 14 pass from Hostetler (Bahr kick)

(14:35)
NYG — Anderson 1 run (Bahr kick) (9:29)
Buff — Thomas 31 run (Norwood kick) (0:08)
NYG — FG Bahr 21 (7:40)

SUPER BOWL XXIV

Louisiana Superdome, New Orleans, Louisiana
January 28, 1990, Attendance: 72,919

SAN FRANCISCO 55, DENVER 10—NFC titlist San Francisco won its fourth Super Bowl championship with a 55-10 victory over AFC champion Denver. The 49ers, who also won Super Bowls XVI, XIX, and XXIII, tied the Pittsburgh Steelers for most Super Bowl victories. The Steelers captured Super Bowls IX, X, XIII, and XIV. San Francisco's 55 points broke the previous Super Bowl scoring mark of 46 points by Chicago in Super Bowl XX. San Francisco scored touchdowns on four of its six first-half possessions to hold a 27-3 lead at halftime. Interceptions by Michael Walter and Chet Brooks ended the Broncos' first two possessions of the second half. San Francisco quarterback Joe Montana was named the Super Bowl most valuable player for a record third time. Montana completed 22 of 29 passes for 297 yards and a Super Bowl-record 5 touchdowns. Jerry Rice, Super Bowl XXIII most valuable player, caught 7 passes for 148 yards and 3 touchdowns. The 49ers' domination included first downs (28 to 12), net yards (461 to 167), and time of possession (39:31 to 20:29).

San Francisco (NFC)	13	14	14	14	— 55
Denver (AFC)	3	0	7	0	— 10

SF — Rice 20 pass from Montana (Cofer kick) (4:54)
Den — FG Treadwell 42 (8:13)
SF — Jones 7 pass from Montana (kick failed) (14:57)
SF — Rathman 1 run (Cofer kick) (7:45)
SF — Rice 38 pass from Montana (Cofer kick) (14:26)
SF — Rice 28 pass from Montana (Cofer kick) (2:12)
SF — Taylor 35 pass from Montana (Cofer kick) (5:16)
Den — Elway 3 run (Treadwell kick) (8:07)
SF — Rathman 3 run (Cofer kick) (0:03)
SF — Craig 1 run (Cofer kick) (1:13)

SUPER BOWL XXIII

Joe Robbie Stadium, Miami, Florida
January 22, 1989, Attendance: 75,129

SAN FRANCISCO 20, CINCINNATI 16—NFC champion San Francisco captured its third Super Bowl of the 1980s by defeating AFC champion Cincinnati 20-16. The 49ers, who also won Super Bowls XVI and XIX, became the first NFC team to win three Super Bowls. Pittsburgh, with four Super Bowl titles (IX, X, XIII, and XIV), and the Oakland/Los Angeles Raiders, with three (XI, XV, and XVIII), lead AFC franchises. Even though San Francisco held an advantage in total net yards (453 to 229), the 49ers found themselves trailing the Bengals late in the game. With the score 13-13, Cincinnati took a 16-13 lead on Jim Breech's 40-yard field goal with 3:20 remaining. It was Breech's third field goal of the day, following earlier successes from 34 and 43 yards. The 49ers started their winning drive at their 8-yard line. Over the next 11 plays, San Francisco covered 92 yards with the decisive score coming on a 10-yard pass from quarterback Joe Montana to wide receiver John Taylor with 34 seconds remaining. At halftime, the score was 3-3, the first time in Super Bowl history the game was tied at intermission. After the teams traded third-period field goals, the Bengals jumped ahead 13-6 on Stanford Jennings's 93-yard kickoff return for a touchdown with 34 seconds remaining in the quarter. The 49ers didn't waste any time coming back as they covered 85 yards in four plays, concluding with Montana's 14-yard scoring pass to Jerry Rice 57 seconds into the final stanza. Rice was named the game's most valuable player after compiling 11 catches for a Super Bowl-record 215 yards. Montana completed 23 of 36 passes for a Super Bowl-record 357 yards and 2 touchdowns.

Cincinnati (AFC)	0	3	10	3	— 16
San Francisco (NFC)	3	0	3	14	— 20

SF — FG Cofer 41 (11:46)
Cin — FG Breech 34 (13:45)
Cin — FG Breech 43 (9:21)
SF — FG Cofer 32 (14:10)
Cin — Jennings 93 kickoff return (Breech kick) (14:26)
SF — Rice 14 pass from Montana (Cofer kick) (0:57)
Cin — FG Breech 40 (11:40)
SF — Taylor 10 pass from Montana (Cofer kick) (14:26)

SUPER BOWL XXII

San Diego Jack Murphy Stadium, San Diego, California
January 31, 1988, Attendance: 73,302

WASHINGTON 42, DENVER 10—NFC champion Washington won Super Bowl XXII and its second NFL championship of the 1980s with a 42-10 decision over AFC champion Denver. The Redskins, who also won Super Bowl XVII, enjoyed a record-setting second quarter en route to the victory. The Broncos broke in front 10-0 when quarterback John Elway threw a 56-yard touchdown pass to wide receiver Ricky Nattiel on the Broncos' first play from scrimmage. Following a Washington punt, Denver's Rich Karlis kicked a 24-yard field goal to cap a seven-play, 61-yard scoring drive. The Redskins then erupted for 35 points on five straight possessions in the second period and coasted thereafter. The 35 points established an NFL postseason mark for most points in a period. Redskins quarterback Doug Williams led the second-period explosion by passing for a Super Bowl record-tying 4 touchdowns, including 80- and 50-yard passes to wide receiver Ricky Sanders, a 27-yard toss to wide receiver Gary Clark, and an 8-yard pass to tight end Clint Didier. Washington scored 5 touchdowns in 18 plays with total time of possession of only 5:47. Overall, Williams completed 18 of 29 passes for 340 yards and was named the game's most valuable player. His pass-yardage total eclipsed the Super Bowl record of 331 yards by Joe Montana of San Francisco in Super Bowl XIX. Sanders ended with 193 yards on 8 catches, breaking the previous Super Bowl yardage record of 161 yards by Lynn Swann of Pittsburgh in Game X. Rookie running back Timmy Smith was the game's leading rusher with 22 carries for a Super Bowl-record 204 yards, breaking the previous mark of 191 yards by Marcus Allen of the Raiders in Game XVIII. Smith also scored twice on runs of 58 and 4 yards. Washington's 6 touchdowns and 602 total yards gained also set Super Bowl records. Redskins cornerback Barry Wilburn had 2 of the team's 3 interceptions, and strong safety Alvin Walton had 2 of Washington's 5 sacks.

Washington (NFC)	0	35	0	7	— 42
Denver (AFC)	10	0	0	0	— 10

Den — Nattiel 56 pass from Elway (Karlis kick) (1:57)
Den — FG Karlis 24 (5:51)
Wash — Sanders 80 pass from Williams (Haji-Sheikh kick) (0:53)
Wash — Clark 27 pass from Williams (Haji-Sheikh kick) (4:45)
Wash — Smith 58 run (Haji-Sheikh kick) (8:33)
Wash — Sanders 50 pass from Williams (Haji-Sheikh kick) (11:18)
Wash — Didier 8 pass from Williams (Haji-Sheikh kick) (13:56)
Wash — Smith 4 run (Haji-Sheikh kick) (1:51)

SUPER BOWL XXI

Rose Bowl, Pasadena, California
January 25, 1987, Attendance: 101,063

NEW YORK GIANTS 39, DENVER 20—The NFC champion New York Giants captured their first NFL title since 1956 when they downed the AFC champion Denver Broncos 39-20 in Super Bowl XXI. The victory marked the NFC's fifth NFL title in the past six seasons. The Broncos, behind the passing of quarterback John Elway, who was 13 of 20 for 187 yards in the first half, held a 10-9 lead at intermission, the narrowest halftime margin in Super Bowl history. Denver's Rich Karlis opened the scoring with a Super Bowl record-tying 48-yard field goal. New York drove 78 yards in nine plays on the next series to take a 7-3 lead on quarterback Phil Simms's 6-yard touchdown pass to tight end Zeke Mowatt. The Broncos came right back with a 58-yard scoring drive on six plays capped by Elway's 4-yard touchdown run. The only scoring in the second period was the sack of Elway in the end zone by defensive end George Martin for a New York safety. The Giants produced a key defensive stand early in the second quarter when the Broncos had a first down at the New York 1-yard line, but failed to score on three running plays and Karlis's 23-yard missed field-goal attempt. The Giants took command of the game in the third period en route to a 30-point second half, the most ever scored in one half of Super Bowl play. New York took the lead for good on tight end Mark Bavaro's 13-yard touchdown catch 4:52 into the third period. The nine-play, 63-yard scoring drive included the successful conversion of a fourth-and-1 play on the New York 46-yard line. Denver was limited to only 2 net yards on 10 offensive plays in the third period. Simms set Super Bowl records for most consecutive completions (10) and highest completion percentage (88 percent on 22 completions in 25 attempts). He also passed for 268 yards and 3 touchdowns and was named the game's most valuable player. New York running back Joe Morris was the game's leading rusher with 20 carries for 67 yards. Denver wide receiver Vance Johnson led all receivers with 5 catches for 121 yards.

Denver (AFC)	10	0	0	10	— 20
N.Y. Giants (NFC)	7	2	17	13	— 39

Den — FG Karlis 48 (4:09)
NYG — Mowatt 6 pass from Simms (Allegre kick) (9:33)
Den — Elway 4 run (Karlis kick) (12:54)
NYG — Safety, Martin tackled Elway in end zone (12:14)
NYG — Bavaro 13 pass from Simms (Allegre kick) (4:52)
NYG — FG Allegre 21 (11:06)
NYG — Morris 1 run (Allegre kick) (14:36)
NYG — McConkey 6 pass from Simms (Allegre kick) (4:04)
Den — FG Karlis 28 (8:59)
NYG — Anderson 2 run (kick failed) (10:42)
Den — V. Johnson 47 pass from Elway (Karlis kick) (12:54)

SUPER BOWL XX

Louisiana Superdome, New Orleans, Louisiana
January 26, 1986, Attendance: 73,818

CHICAGO 46, NEW ENGLAND 10—The NFC champion Chicago Bears, seeking their first NFL title since 1963, scored a Super Bowl-record 46 points in downing AFC champion New England 46-10 in Super Bowl XX. The previous record for most points in a Super Bowl was 38, shared by San Francisco in XIX and the Los Angeles Raiders in XVIII. The Bears' league-leading defense tied the Super Bowl record for sacks (7) and limited the Patriots to a record-low 7 rushing yards. New England took the quickest lead in Super Bowl history when Tony Franklin kicked a 36-yard field goal with 1:19 elapsed in the first period. The score came about because of Larry McGrew's fumble recovery at the Chicago 19-yard line. However, the Bears rebounded for a 23-3 first-half lead, while building a yardage advantage of 236 total yards to New England's minus 19. Running back Matt Suhey rushed 8 times for 37 yards, including an 11-yard touchdown run, and caught 1 pass for 24 yards in the first half. After the Patriot's first drive of the second half ended with a punt to the Bears' 4-yard line, Chicago marched 96 yards in nine plays with quarterback Jim McMahon's 1-yard scoring run capping the drive. McMahon became the first quarterback in Super Bowl history to rush for a pair of touchdowns. The Bears completed their scoring via a 28-yard interception return by reserve cornerback Reggie Phillips, a 1-yard run by defensive tackle/fullback William Perry, and a safety when defensive end Henry Waechter tackled Patriots quarterback Steve Grogan in the end zone. Bears defensive end Richard Dent became the fourth defender to be named the game's most valuable player after contributing 1½ sacks. The Bears' victory margin of 36 points was the largest in Super Bowl history, bettering the previous mark of 29 by the Los Angeles Raiders when they topped Washington 38-9 in Game XVIII. McMahon completed 12 of 20 passes for 256 yards before leaving the game in the fourth period with a wrist injury. The NFL's all-time leading rusher, Bears running back Walter Payton, carried 22 times for 61 yards. Wide receiver Willie Gault caught 4 passes for 129 yards, the fourth-most receiving yards in a Super Bowl. Chicago coach Mike Ditka became the second man (Tom Flores of Raiders was the other) to win a Super Bowl ring as a player and as a coach.

Chicago (NFC)	13	10	21	2	— 46
New England (AFC)	3	0	0	7	— 10

NE — FG Franklin 36 (1:19)
Chi — FG Butler 28 (5:40)
Chi — FG Butler 24 (13:34)
Chi — Suhey 11 run (Butler kick) (14:37)
Chi — McMahon 2 run (Butler kick) (7:36)
Chi — FG Butler 24 (15:00)
Chi — McMahon 1 run (Butler kick) (7:38)
Chi — Phillips 28 interception return (Butler kick) (8:44)
Chi — Perry 1 run (Butler kick) (11:38)
NE — Fryar 8 pass from Grogan (Franklin kick) (1:46)
Chi — Safety, Waechter tackled Grogan in end zone (9:24)

SUPER BOWL XIX

Stanford Stadium, Stanford, California
January 20, 1985, Attendance: 84,059

SAN FRANCISCO 38, MIAMI 16—The San Francisco 49ers captured their second Super Bowl title with a dominating offense and a defense that tamed Miami's explosive passing attack. The Dolphins held a 10-7 lead at the end of the first period, which represented the most points scored by two teams in an opening quarter of a Super Bowl. However, the 49ers used excellent field position in the second period to build a 28-16 halftime lead. Running back Roger Craig set a Super Bowl record by scoring 3 touchdowns on pass receptions of 8 and 16 yards and a run of 2 yards. San Francisco's Joe Montana was voted the game's most valuable player. He joined Green Bay's Bart Starr and Pittsburgh's Terry Bradshaw as the only two-time Super Bowl most valuable players. Montana completed 24 of 35 passes for a Super Bowl-record 331 yards and 3 touchdowns, and rushed 5 times for 59 yards, including a 6-yard touchdown. Craig had 58 yards on 15 carries and caught 7 passes for 77 yards. Wendell Tyler rushed 13 times for 65 yards and had 4 catches for 70 yards. Dwight Clark had 6 receptions for 77 yards, while Russ Francis had 5 for 60. San Francisco's 537 total net yards bettered the previous Super Bowl record of 429 yards by Oakland in Super Bowl XI. The 49ers also held a time of possession advantage over the Dolphins of 37:11 to 22:49.

Miami (AFC)	10	6	0	0	— 16
San Francisco (NFC)	7	21	10	0	— 38

Mia — FG von Schamann 37 (7:36)
SF — Monroe 33 pass from Montana (Wersching kick) (11:48)
Mia — D. Johnson 2 pass from Marino (von Schamann kick) (14:15)
SF — Craig 8 pass from Montana (Wersching kick) (3:26)
SF — Montana 6 run (Wersching kick) (8:02)
SF — Craig 2 run (Wersching kick) (12:55)
Mia — FG von Schamann 31 (14:48)
Mia — FG von Schamann 30 (15:00)
SF — FG Wersching 27 (4:48)
SF — Craig 16 pass from Montana (Wersching kick) (8:42)

SUPER BOWL XVIII

Tampa Stadium, Tampa, Florida
January 22, 1984, Attendance: 72,920

LOS ANGELES RAIDERS 38, WASHINGTON 9—The Los Angeles Raiders dominated the Washington Redskins from the beginning in Super Bowl XVIII and achieved the most lopsided victory in Super Bowl history, surpassing Green Bay's 35-10 win over Kansas City in Super Bowl I. The Raiders took a 7-0 lead 4:52 into the game when Derrick Jensen blocked Jeff Hayes's punt and recovered it in the end zone for a touchdown. With 9:14 remaining in the first half, Raiders quarterback Jim Plunkett fired a 12-yard touchdown pass to wide receiver Cliff Branch to complete a three-play, 65-yard drive. Washington cut the Raiders' lead to 14-3 on a 24-yard field goal by Mark Moseley. With seven seconds left in the first half, Raiders linebacker Jack Squirek intercepted Joe Theismann's pass at the Redskins' 5-yard line and ran it in for a touchdown to give Los Angeles a 21-3 halftime lead. In the third period, running back Marcus Allen, who rushed for a Super Bowl-record 191 yards on 20 carries, increased the Raiders' lead to 35-9 on touchdown runs of 5 and 74 yards, the latter erasing the Super Bowl record of 58 yards set by Baltimore's Tom Matte in Game III. Allen was named the game's most valuable player. The victory over Washington raised Raiders coach Tom Flores' playoff record to 8-1, including a 27-10 win against Philadelphia in Super Bowl XV. The 38 points scored by the Raiders were the highest total by a Super Bowl team. The previous high was 35 points by Green Bay in Game I.

Washington (NFC)	0	3	6	0	— 9
L.A. Raiders (AFC)	7	14	14	3	— 38

Raiders — Jensen recovered blocked punt in end zone (Bahr kick) (4:52)
Raiders — Branch 12 pass from Plunkett (Bahr kick) (5:46)
Wash — FG Moseley 24 (11:55)
Raiders — Squirek 5 interception return (Bahr kick) (14:53)
Wash — Riggins 1 run (kick blocked) (4:08)
Raiders — Allen 5 run (Bahr kick) (7:54)
Raiders — Allen 74 run (Bahr kick) (15:00)
Raiders — FG Bahr 21 (12:36)

SUPER BOWL XVII

Rose Bowl, Pasadena, California
January 30, 1983, Attendance: 103,667

WASHINGTON 27, MIAMI 17—Fullback John Riggins ran for a Super Bowl-record 166 yards on 38 carries to spark Washington to a 27-17 victory over AFC champion Miami. It was Riggins's fourth straight 100-yard rushing game during the playoffs, also a record. The win marked Washington's first NFL title since 1942, and was only the second time in Super Bowl history NFL/NFC teams scored consecutive victories (Green Bay did it in Super Bowls I and II and San Francisco won Super Bowl XVI). The Redskins, under second-year head coach Joe Gibbs, used a balanced offense that accounted for 400 total yards (a Super Bowl-record 276 yards rushing and 124 passing), second in Super Bowl history to 429 yards by Oakland in Super Bowl XI. The Dolphins built a 17-10 halftime lead on a 76-yard touchdown pass from quarterback David Woodley to wide receiver Jimmy Cefalo 6:49 into the first period, a 20-yard field goal by Uwe von Schamann with 6:00 left in the half, and a Super Bowl-record 98-yard kickoff return by Fulton Walker with 1:38 remaining. Washington had tied the score at 10-10 with 1:51 left on a 4-yard touchdown pass from Joe Theismann to wide receiver Alvin Garrett. Mark Moseley started the Redskins' scoring with a 31-yard field goal late in the first period, and added a 20-yard kick midway through the third period to cut the Dolphins' lead to 17-13. Riggins, who was voted the game's most valuable player, gave Washington its first lead of the game with 10:01 left when he ran 43 yards off left tackle for a touchdown in a fourth-and-1 situation. Wide receiver Charlie Brown caught a 6-yard scoring pass from Theismann with 1:55 left to complete the scoring. The Dolphins managed only 176 yards (142 in first half). Theismann completed 15 of 23 passes for 143 yards, with 2 touchdowns and 2 interceptions. For Miami, Woodley was 4 of 14 for 97 yards, with 1 touchdown, and 1 interception. Don Strock was 0 for 3 in relief.

Miami (AFC)	7	10	0	0	— 17
Washington (NFC)	0	10	3	14	— 27

Mia — Cefalo 76 pass from Woodley (von Schamann kick) (6:49)
Wash — FG Moseley 31 (0:21)
Mia — FG von Schamann 20 (9:00)
Wash — Garrett 4 pass from Theismann (Moseley kick) (13:09)
Mia — Walker 98 kickoff return (von Schamann kick) (13:22)
Wash — FG Moseley 20 (6:51)
Wash — Riggins 43 run (Moseley kick) (4:59)
Wash — Brown 6 pass from Theismann (Moseley kick) (13:05)

SUPER BOWL XVI

Pontiac Silverdome, Pontiac, Michigan
January 24, 1982, Attendance: 81,270

SAN FRANCISCO 26, CINCINNATI 21—Ray Wersching's Super Bowl record-tying 4 field goals and Joe Montana's controlled passing helped lift the San Francisco 49ers to their first NFL championship with a 26-21 victory over Cincinnati. The 49ers built a game-record 20-0 halftime lead via Montana's 1-yard touchdown run, which capped an 11-play, 68-yard drive; fullback Earl Cooper's 11-yard scoring pass from Montana, which climaxed a Super Bowl record 92-yard drive on 12 plays; and Wersching's 22- and 26-yard field goals. The Bengals rebounded in the second half, closing the gap to 20-14 on quarterback Ken Anderson's 5-yard run and Dan Ross's 4-yard reception from Anderson, who established Super Bowl passing records for completions (25) and completion percentage (73.5 percent on 25 of 34). Wersching added early fourth-period field goals of 40 and 23 yards to increase the 49ers' lead to 26-14. The Bengals managed to score on an Anderson-to-Ross 3-yard pass with only 16 seconds remaining. Ross set a Super Bowl record with 11 receptions for 104 yards. Montana, the game's most valuable player, completed 14 of 22 passes for 157 yards. Cincinnati compiled 356 yards to San Francisco's 275, which marked the first time in Super Bowl history that the team that gained the most yards from scrimmage lost the game.

San Francisco (NFC)	7	13	0	6	— 26
Cincinnati (AFC)	0	0	7	14	— 21

SF — Montana 1 run (Wersching kick) (9:08)
SF — Cooper 11 pass from Montana (Wersching kick) (8:07)
SF — FG Wersching 22 (14:45)
SF — FG Wersching 26 (14:58)
Cin — Anderson 5 run (Breech kick) (3:35)
Cin — Ross 4 pass from Anderson (Breech kick) (4:54)
SF — FG Wersching 40 (9:35)
SF — FG Wersching 23 (13:03)
Cin — Ross 3 pass from Anderson (Breech kick) (14:44)

SUPER BOWL XV

Louisiana Superdome, New Orleans, Louisiana
January 25, 1981, Attendance: 76,135

OAKLAND 27, PHILADELPHIA 10—Jim Plunkett passed for 3 touchdowns, including an 80-yard strike to Kenny King, as the Raiders became the first wild-card team to win the Super Bowl. Plunkett's touchdown bomb to King—the longest play in Super Bowl history—gave Oakland a decisive 14-0 lead with nine seconds left in the first period. Linebacker Rod Martin had set up Oakland's first touchdown, a 2-yard reception by Cliff Branch, with a 17-yard interception return to the Eagles' 30-yard line. The Eagles never recovered from that early deficit, managing only Tony Franklin's field goal (30 yards) and an 8-yard touchdown pass from Ron Jaworski to Keith Krepfle. Plunkett, who became a starter in the sixth game of the season, completed 13 of 21 for 261 yards and was named the game's most valuable player. Oakland won 9 of 11 games with Plunkett starting, but that was good enough only for second place in the AFC West, although they tied division winner San Diego with an 11-5 record. The Raiders, who had previously won Super Bowl XI over Minnesota, had to win three playoff games to get to the championship game. Oakland defeated Houston 27-7 at home followed by road victories over Cleveland (14-12) and San Diego (34-27). Oakland's Mark van Eeghen was the game's leading rusher with 75 yards on 18 carries. Philadelphia's Wilbert Montgomery led all receivers with 6 receptions for 91 yards. Branch had 5 for 67 and Harold Carmichael of Philadelphia 5 for 83. Martin finished the game with 3 interceptions, a Super Bowl record.

Oakland (AFC)	14	0	10	3	— 27
Philadelphia (NFC)	0	3	0	7	— 10

Oak — Branch 2 pass from Plunkett (Bahr kick) (6:04)
Oak — King 80 pass from Plunkett (Bahr kick) (14:51)
Phil — FG Franklin 30 (4:32)
Oak — Branch 29 pass from Plunkett (Bahr kick) (2:36)
Oak — FG Bahr 46 (10:25)
Phil — Krepfle 8 pass from Jaworski (Franklin kick) (1:01)
Oak — FG Bahr 35 (6:31)

SUPER BOWL XIV

Rose Bowl, Pasadena, California
January 20, 1980, Attendance: 103,985

PITTSBURGH 31, LOS ANGELES 19—Terry Bradshaw completed 14 of 21 passes for 309 yards and set two passing records as the Steelers became the first team to win four Super Bowls. Despite 3 interceptions by the Rams, Bradshaw kept his poise and brought the Steelers from behind twice in the second half. Trailing 13-10 at halftime, Pittsburgh went ahead 17-13 when Bradshaw hit Lynn Swann with a 47-yard touchdown pass after 2:48 of the third quarter. On the Rams' next possession Vince Ferragamo, who completed 15 of 25 passes for 212 yards, responded with a 50-yard pass to Billy Waddy that moved Los Angeles from its 26 to the Steelers' 24. On the following play, Lawrence McCutcheon connected with Ron Smith on a halfback option pass that gave the Rams a 19-17 lead. On Pittsburgh's initial possession of the final period, Bradshaw lofted a 73-yard scoring pass to John Stallworth to put the Steelers in front to stay 24-19. Franco Harris scored on a 1-yard run later in the quarter to seal the verdict. A 45-yard pass from Bradshaw to Stallworth was the key play in the drive to Harris's score. Bradshaw, the game's most valuable player for the second straight year, set career Super Bowl records for most touchdown passes (9) and most passing yards (932). Larry Anderson gave the Steelers excellent field position throughout the game with 5 kickoff returns for a record 162 yards.

Los Angeles (NFC)	7	6	6	0	— 19
Pittsburgh (AFC)	3	7	7	14	— 31

Pitt — FG Bahr 41 (7:29)
LA — Bryant 1 run (Corral kick) (12:16)
Pitt — Harris 1 run (Bahr kick) (2:08)
LA — FG Corral 31 (7:39)
LA — FG Corral 45 (14:46)
Pitt — Swann 47 pass from Bradshaw (Bahr kick) (2:48)
LA — Smith 24 pass from McCutcheon (kick failed) (4:45)
Pitt — Stallworth 73 pass from Bradshaw (Bahr kick) (2:56)
Pitt — Harris 1 run (Bahr kick) (13:11)

SUPER BOWL XIII

Orange Bowl, Miami, Florida
January 21, 1979, Attendance: 79,484

PITTSBURGH 35, DALLAS 31—Terry Bradshaw passed for a record 4 touchdowns to lead the Steelers to victory. The Steelers became the first team to win three Super Bowls, mostly because of Bradshaw's accurate arm. Bradshaw, voted the game's most valuable player, completed 17 of 30 passes for 318 yards, a personal high. Four of those passes went for touchdowns—2 to John Stallworth and the third, with 26 seconds remaining in the second period, to Rocky Bleier for a 21-14 halftime lead. The Cowboys scored twice before intermission on Roger Staubach's 39-yard pass to Tony Hill and a 37-yard fumble return by linebacker Mike Hegman, who stole the ball from Bradshaw. The Steelers broke open the contest with 2 touchdowns in a span of 19 seconds midway through the final period. Franco Harris rambled 22 yards up the middle to give the Steelers a 28-17 lead with 7:10 left. Pittsburgh got the ball right back when Randy White fumbled the kickoff and Dennis Winston recovered for the Steelers. On first down, Bradshaw fired his fourth touchdown pass, an 18-yard pass to Lynn Swann to boost the Steelers' lead to 35-17 with 6:51 to play. The Cowboys refused to let the Steelers run away with the contest. Staubach connected with Billy Joe DuPree on a 7-yard scoring pass with 2:23 left. Then the Cowboys recovered an onside kick and Staubach took them in for another score, passing 4 yards to Butch Johnson with 22 seconds remaining. Bleier recovered another onside kick with 17 seconds left to seal the victory for the Steelers.

Pittsburgh (AFC)	7	14	0	14	— 35
Dallas (NFC)	7	7	3	14	— 31

Pitt — Stallworth 28 pass from Bradshaw (Gerela kick) (5:13)
Dall — Hill 39 pass from Staubach (Septien kick) (15:00)
Dall — Hegman 37 fumble recovery return (Septien kick) (2:52)
Pitt — Stallworth 75 pass from Bradshaw (Gerela kick) (4:35)
Pitt — Bleier 7 pass from Bradshaw (Gerela kick) (14:34)
Dall — FG Septien 27 (12:24)
Pitt — Harris 22 run (Gerela kick) (7:50)
Pitt — Swann 18 pass from Bradshaw (Gerela kick) (8:09)
Dall — DuPree 7 pass from Staubach (Septien kick) (12:37)
Dall — B. Johnson 4 pass from Staubach (Septien kick) (14:38)

SUPER BOWL XII

Louisiana Superdome, New Orleans, Louisiana
January 15, 1978, Attendance: 75,583

DALLAS 27, DENVER 10—The Cowboys evened their Super Bowl record at 2-2 by defeating Denver before a sellout crowd plus 102,010,000 television viewers, the largest audience ever to watch a sporting event. Dallas converted 2 interceptions into 10 points and Efren Herrera added a 35-yard field goal for a 13-0 halftime advantage. In the third period Craig Morton engineered a drive to the Cowboys' 30 and Jim Turner's 47-yard field goal made the score 13-3. After an exchange of punts, Butch Johnson made a spectacular diving catch in the end zone to complete a 45-yard pass from Roger Staubach and put the Cowboys ahead 20-3. Following Rick Upchurch's 67-yard kickoff return, Norris Weese guided the Broncos to a touchdown to cut the deficit to 20-10. Dallas clinched the victory when running back Robert Newhouse tossed a 29-yard touchdown pass to Golden Richards with 7:04 left in the game. It was the first pass thrown by Newhouse since 1975. Harvey Martin and Randy White, who were named co-most valuable players, led the Cowboys' defense, which recovered 4 fumbles and intercepted 4 passes.

Dallas (NFC)	10	3	7	7	— 27
Denver (AFC)	0	0	10	0	— 10

Dall — Dorsett 3 run (Herrera kick) (10:31)
Dall — FG Herrera 35 (13:29)
Dall — FG Herrera 43 (3:44)
Den — FG Turner 47 (2:28)
Dall — Johnson 45 pass from Staubach (Herrera kick) (8:01)
Den — Lytle 1 run (Turner kick) (9:21)
Dall — Richards 29 pass from Newhouse (Herrera kick) (7:56)

SUPER BOWL XI

Rose Bowl, Pasadena, California
January 9, 1977, Attendance: 103,438

OAKLAND 32, MINNESOTA 14—The Raiders won their first NFL championship before a record Super Bowl crowd plus 81 million television viewers, the largest audience ever to watch a sporting event. The Raiders gained a record-breaking 429 yards, including running back Clarence Davis's 137 rushing yards. Wide receiver Fred Biletnikoff made 4 key receptions, which earned him the game's most valuable player trophy. Oakland scored on three successive possessions in the second quarter to build a 16-0 halftime lead. Errol Mann's 24-yard field goal opened the scoring, then the AFC champions put together drives of 64 and 35 yards, scoring on a 1-yard pass from Ken Stabler to Dave Casper and a 1-yard run by Pete Banaszak. The Raiders increased their lead to 19-0 on a 40-yard field goal in the third quarter, but Minnesota responded with a 12-play, 58-yard drive late in the period, with Fran Tarkenton passing 8 yards to wide receiver Sammy White to cut the deficit to 19-7. Two fourth-quarter interceptions clinched the title for the Raiders. One set up Banaszak's second touchdown run, the other resulted in cornerback Willie Brown's Super Bowl-record 75-yard interception return.

Oakland (AFC)	0	16	3	13	— 32
Minnesota (NFC)	0	0	7	7	— 14

Oak — FG Mann 24 (0:48)
Oak — Casper 1 pass from Stabler (Mann kick) (7:50)
Oak — Banaszak 1 run (kick failed) (11:27)
Oak — FG Mann 40 (9:44)
Minn — S. White 8 pass from Tarkenton (Cox kick) (14:13)
Oak — Banaszak 2 run (Mann kick) (7:21)
Oak — Brown 75 interception return (kick failed) (9:17)
Minn — Voigt 13 pass from Lee (Cox kick) (14:35)

SUPER BOWL X

Orange Bowl, Miami, Florida
January 18, 1976, Attendance: 80,187

PITTSBURGH 21, DALLAS 17—The Steelers won the Super Bowl for the second year in a row on Terry Bradshaw's 64-yard touchdown pass to Lynn Swann and an aggressive defense that snuffed out a late rally by the Cowboys with an end-zone interception on the final play of the game. In the fourth quarter, Pittsburgh ran on fourth down and gave up the ball on the Cowboys' 39 with 1:22 to play. Roger Staubach ran and passed for 2 first downs but his last desperation pass was picked off by Glen Edwards. Dallas's scoring was the result of 2 touchdown passes by Staubach, one to Drew Pearson for 29 yards and the other to Percy Howard for 34 yards. Toni Fritsch had a 36-yard field goal. The Steelers scored on 2 touchdown passes by Bradshaw, 1 to Randy Grossman for 7 yards and the long bomb to Swann. Roy Gerela had 36- and 18-yard field goals. Reggie Harrison blocked a punt through the end zone for a safety. Swann set a Super Bowl record by gaining 161 yards on his 4 receptions.

Dallas (NFC)	7	3	0	7	— 17
Pittsburgh (AFC)	7	0	0	14	— 21

Dall — D. Pearson 29 pass from Staubach (Fritsch kick) (4:36)
Pitt — Grossman 7 pass from Bradshaw (Gerela kick) (9:03)
Dall — FG Fritsch 36 (0:15)
Pitt — Safety, Harrison blocked Hoopes's punt through end zone (3:32)
Pitt — FG Gerela 36 (6:19)
Pitt — FG Gerela 18 (8:23)
Pitt — Swann 64 pass from Bradshaw (kick failed) (11:58)
Dall — P. Howard 34 pass from Staubach (Fritsch kick) (13:12)

SUPER BOWL SUMMARIES

SUPER BOWL IX

Tulane Stadium, New Orleans, Louisiana
January 12, 1975, Attendance: 80,997

PITTSBURGH 16, MINNESOTA 6—AFC champion Pittsburgh, in its initial Super Bowl appearance, and NFC champion Minnesota, making a third bid for its first Super Bowl title, struggled through a first half in which the only score was produced by the Steelers' defense when Dwight White downed Vikings' quarterback Fran Tarkenton in the end zone for a safety 7:49 into the second period. The Steelers forced another break and took advantage on the second-half kickoff when Minnesota's Bill Brown fumbled and Marv Kellum recovered for Pittsburgh on the Vikings' 30. After Rocky Bleier failed to gain on first down, Franco Harris carried 3 consecutive times for 24 yards, a loss of 3, and a 9-yard touchdown and a 9-0 lead. Though its offense was completely stymied by Pittsburgh's defense, Minnesota managed to move into a threatening position after 4:27 of the final period when Matt Blair blocked Bobby Walden's punt and Terry Brown recovered the ball in the end zone for a touchdown. Fred Cox's kick failed and the Steelers led 9-6. Pittsburgh wasted no time putting the victory away. The Steelers took the ensuing kickoff and marched 66 yards in 11 plays, climaxed by Terry Bradshaw's 4-yard scoring pass to Larry Brown with 3:31 left. Pittsburgh's defense permitted Minnesota only 119 yards total offense, including a Super Bowl low of 17 rushing yards. The Steelers, meanwhile, gained 333 yards, including Harris's record 158 yards on 34 carries.

Pittsburgh (AFC)	0	2	7	7	—	16
Minnesota (NFC)	0	0	0	6	—	6

Pitt — Safety, White downed Tarkenton in end zone (7:49)
Pitt — Harris 9 run (Gerela kick) (1:35)
Minn — T. Brown recovered blocked punt in end zone (kick failed) (4:27)
Pitt — L. Brown 4 pass from Bradshaw (Gerela kick) (11:29)

SUPER BOWL VIII

Rice Stadium, Houston, Texas
January 13, 1974, Attendance: 71,882

MIAMI 24, MINNESOTA 7—The defending NFL champion Dolphins, representing the AFC for the third straight year, scored the first two times they had possession on marches of 62 and 56 yards while the Miami defense limited the Vikings to only seven plays in the first period. Larry Csonka climaxed the initial 10-play drive with a 5-yard touchdown bolt through right guard after 5:27 had elapsed. Four plays later, Miami began another 10-play scoring drive, which ended with Jim Kiick bursting 1 yard through the middle for another touchdown after 13:38 of the period. Garo Yepremian added a 28-yard field goal midway in the second period for a 17-0 Miami lead. Minnesota then drove from its 20 to a second-and-2 situation on the Miami 7 yard line with 1:18 left in the half. But on two plays, Miami limited Oscar Reed to 1 yard. On fourth-and-1 from the 6, Reed went over right tackle, but Dolphins middle linebacker Nick Buoniconti jarred the ball loose and Jake Scott recovered for Miami to halt the Minnesota threat. The Vikings were unable to muster enough offense in the second half to threaten the Dolphins. Csonka rushed 33 times for a Super Bowl-record 145 yards. Bob Griese of Miami completed 6 of 7 passes for 73 yards.

Minnesota (NFC)	0	0	0	7	—	7
Miami (AFC)	14	3	7	0	—	24

Mia — Csonka 5 run (Yepremian kick) (9:33)
Mia — Kiick 1 run (Yepremian kick) (13:38)
Mia — FG Yepremian 28 (8:58)
Mia — Csonka 2 run (Yepremian kick) (6:16)
Minn — Tarkenton 4 run (Cox kick) (1:35)

SUPER BOWL VII

Memorial Coliseum, Los Angeles, California
January 14, 1973, Attendance: 90,182

MIAMI 14, WASHINGTON 7—The Dolphins played virtually perfect football in the first half as their defense permitted the Redskins to cross midfield only once and their offense turned good field position into 2 touchdowns. On its third possession, Miami opened its first scoring drive from the Dolphins' 37 yard line. An 18-yard pass from Bob Griese to Paul Warfield preceded by three plays Griese's 28-yard touchdown pass to Howard Twilley. After Washington moved from its 17 to the Miami 48 with two minutes remaining in the first half, Dolphins linebacker Nick Buoniconti intercepted Billy Kilmer's pass at the Miami 41 and returned it to the Washington 27. Jim Kiick ran for 3 yards, Larry Csonka for 3, Griese passed to Jim Mandich for 19, and Kiick gained 1 to the 1-yard line. With 18 seconds left until intermission, Kiick scored from the 1. Washington's only touchdown came with 2:07 left in the game and resulted from a misplayed field-goal attempt and fumble by Garo Yepremian, with the Redskins' Mike Bass picking the ball out of the air and running 49 yards for the score. Dolphins safety Jake Scott, who had 2 interceptions, including 1 in the end zone to kill a Redskins' drive, was voted the game's most valuable player.

Miami (AFC)	7	7	0	0	—	14
Washington (NFC)	0	0	0	7	—	7

Mia — Twilley 28 pass from Griese (Yepremian kick) (14:59)
Mia — Kiick 1 run (Yepremian kick) (14:42)
Wash — Bass 49 fumble recovery return (Knight kick) (12:53)

SUPER BOWL VI

Tulane Stadium, New Orleans, Louisiana
January 16, 1972, Attendance: 81,023

DALLAS 24, MIAMI 3—The Cowboys rushed for a record 252 yards and their defense limited the Dolphins to a low of 185 yards while not permitting a touchdown for the first time in Super Bowl history. Dallas converted Chuck Howley's recovery of Larry Csonka's first fumble of the season into a 3-0 advantage and led at halftime 10-3. After Dallas received the second-half kickoff, Duane Thomas led a 71-yard march in eight plays for a 17-3 margin. Howley intercepted Bob Griese's pass at the 50 and returned it to the Miami 9 early in the fourth period, and three plays later Roger Staubach passed 7 yards to Mike Ditka for the final touchdown. Thomas rushed for 95 yards and Walt Garrison gained 74. Staubach, voted the game's most valuable player, completed 12 of 19 passes for 119 yards and 2 touchdowns.

Dallas (NFC)	3	7	7	7	—	24
Miami (AFC)	0	3	0	0	—	3

Dall — FG Clark 9 (13:37)
Dall — Alworth 7 pass from Staubach (Clark kick) (13:45)
Mia — FG Yepremian 31 (14:56)
Dall — D. Thomas 3 run (Clark kick) (5:17)
Dall — Ditka 7 pass from Staubach (Clark kick) (3:18)

SUPER BOWL V

Orange Bowl, Miami, Florida
January 17, 1971, Attendance: 79,204

BALTIMORE 16, DALLAS 13—A 32-yard field goal by rookie kicker Jim O'Brien brought the Baltimore Colts a victory over the Dallas Cowboys in the final five seconds of Super Bowl V. The game between the champions of the AFC and NFC was played on artificial turf for the first time. Dallas led 13-6 at the half but interceptions by Rick Volk and Mike Curtis set up a Baltimore touchdown and O'Brien's decisive kick in the fourth period. Earl Morrall relieved an injured Johnny Unitas late in the first half, although Unitas completed the Colts' only scoring pass. It caromed off receiver Eddie Hinton's fingertips, off Dallas defensive back Mel Renfro, and finally settled into the grasp of John Mackey, who went 45 yards to score on a 75-yard play.

Baltimore (AFC)	0	6	0	10	—	16
Dallas (NFC)	3	10	0	0	—	13

Dall — FG Clark 14 (9:28)
Dall — FG Clark 30 (0:08)
Balt — Mackey 75 pass from Unitas (kick blocked) (0:05)
Dall — Thomas 7 pass from Morton (Clark kick) (7:07)
Balt — Nowatzke 2 run (O'Brien kick) (7:25)
Balt — FG O'Brien 32 (14:55)

SUPER BOWL IV

Tulane Stadium, New Orleans, Louisiana
January 11, 1970, Attendance: 80,562

KANSAS CITY 23, MINNESOTA 7—The AFL squared the Super Bowl at two games apiece with the NFL, building a 16-0 halftime lead behind Len Dawson's superb quarterbacking and a powerful defense. Dawson, the fourth consecutive quarterback to be chosen the Super Bowl's top player, called an almost flawless game, completing 12 of 17 passes and hitting Otis Taylor on a 46-yard play for the final Chiefs touchdown. The Kansas City defense limited Minnesota's strong rushing game to 67 yards and had 3 interceptions and 2 fumble recoveries. The crowd of 80,562 set a Super Bowl record, as did the gross receipts of $3,817,872.69.

Minnesota (NFL)	0	0	7	0	—	7
Kansas City (AFL)	3	13	7	0	—	23

KC — FG Stenerud 48 (8:08)
KC — FG Stenerud 32 (1:40)
KC — FG Stenerud 25 (7:08)
KC — Garrett 5 run (Stenerud kick) (9:26)
Minn — Osborn 4 run (Cox kick) (10:28)
KC — Taylor 46 pass from Dawson (Stenerud kick) (13:38)

SUPER BOWL III

Orange Bowl, Miami, Florida
January 12, 1969, Attendance: 75,389

NEW YORK JETS 16, BALTIMORE 7—Jets quarterback Joe Namath "guaranteed" victory on the Thursday before the game, then went out and led the AFL to its first Super Bowl victory over a Baltimore team that had lost only once in 16 games all season. Namath, chosen the outstanding player, completed 17 of 28 passes for 206 yards and directed a steady attack that dominated the NFL champions after the Jets' defense had intercepted Colts quarterback Earl Morrall 3 times in the first half. The Jets had 337 total yards, including 121 rushing yards by Matt Snell. Johnny Unitas, who had missed most of the season with a sore elbow, came off the bench and led Baltimore to its only touchdown late in the fourth quarter after New York led 16-0.

New York Jets (AFL)	0	7	6	3	—	16
Baltimore (NFL)	0	0	0	7	—	7

NYJ — Snell 4 run (Turner kick) (5:57)
NYJ — FG Turner 32 (4:52)
NYJ — FG Turner 30 (11:02)
NYJ — FG Turner 9 (1:34)
Balt — Hill 1 run (Michaels kick) (11:41)

SUPER BOWL II

Orange Bowl, Miami, Florida
January 14, 1968, Attendance: 75,546

GREEN BAY 33, OAKLAND 14—Green Bay, after winning its third consecutive NFL championship, won the Super Bowl title for the second straight year, defeating the AFL champion Raiders in a game that drew the first $3-million gate in football history. Bart Starr again was chosen the game's most valuable player as he completed 13 of 24 passes for 202 yards and 1 touchdown and directed a Packers' attack that was in control all the way after building a 16-7 halftime lead. Don Chandler kicked 4 field goals and all-pro cornerback Herb Adderley capped the Green Bay scoring with a 60-yard interception return. The game marked the last for Vince Lombardi as Packers coach, ending nine years at Green Bay in which he won six Western Conference championships, five NFL championships, and two Super Bowls.

Green Bay (NFL)	3	13	10	7	—	33
Oakland (AFL)	0	7	0	7	—	14

GB — FG Chandler 39 (5:07)
GB — FG Chandler 20 (3:08)
GB — Dowler 62 pass from Starr (Chandler kick) (4:10)
Oak — Miller 23 pass from Lamonica (Blanda kick) (8:45)
GB — FG Chandler 43 (14:59)

GB — Anderson 2 run (Chandler kick) (9:06)
GB — FG Chandler 31 (14:58)
GB — Adderley 60 interception return (Chandler kick) (3:57)
Oak — Miller 23 pass from Lamonica (Blanda kick) (5:47)

SUPER BOWL I

Memorial Coliseum, Los Angeles, California
January 15, 1967, Attendance: 61,946

GREEN BAY 35, KANSAS CITY 10—The Green Bay Packers opened the Super Bowl series by defeating the AFL champion Chiefs behind the passing of Bart Starr, the receiving of Max McGee, and a key interception by all-pro safety Willie Wood. Green Bay broke open the game with 3 second-half touchdowns, the first of which was set up by Wood's 50-yard return of an interception. McGee, filling in for ailing Boyd Dowler after having caught only 4 passes all season, caught 7 from Starr for 138 yards and 2 touchdowns. Elijah Pitts ran for 2 other scores. The Chiefs' 10 points came in the second quarter, the only touchdown on a 7-yard pass from Len Dawson to Curtis McClinton. Starr completed 16 of 23 passes for 250 yards and 2 touchdowns and was chosen the most valuable player. The Packers collected $15,000 per man and the Chiefs $7,500—the largest single-game shares in the history of team sports.

Kansas City (AFL)	0	10	0	0	— 10
Green Bay (NFL)	7	7	14	7	— 35

GB — McGee 37 pass from Starr (Chandler kick) (8:56)
KC — McClinton 7 pass from Dawson (Mercer kick) (4:20)
GB — Taylor 14 run (Chandler kick) (10:23)
KC — FG Mercer 31 (14:06)
GB — Pitts 5 run (Chandler kick) (2:27)
GB — McGee 13 pass from Starr (Chandler kick) (14:09)
GB — Pitts 1 run (Chandler kick) (8:25)

PLAYOFF GAMES SUMMARIES

AFC CHAMPIONSHIP GAME RESULTS

Includes AFL Championship Games (1960-69)

Season	Date	Winner (Share)	Loser (Share)	Score	Site	Attendance
2000	Jan. 14	Baltimore ($34,500)	Oakland ($34,500)	16-3	Oakland	62,784
1999	Jan. 23	Tennessee ($33,000)	Jacksonville ($33,000)	33-14	Jacksonville	75,206
1998	Jan. 17	Denver ($32,500)	N.Y. Jets ($32,500)	23-10	Denver	75,482
1997	Jan. 11	Denver ($30,000)	Pittsburgh ($30,000)	24-21	Pittsburgh	61,382
1996	Jan. 12	New England ($29,000)	Jacksonville ($29,000)	20-6	New England	60,190
1995	Jan. 14	Pittsburgh ($27,000)	Indianapolis ($27,000)	20-16	Pittsburgh	61,062
1994	Jan. 15	San Diego ($26,000)	Pittsburgh ($26,000)	17-13	Pittsburgh	61,545
1993	Jan. 23	Buffalo ($23,500)	Kansas City ($23,500)	30-13	Buffalo	76,642
1992	Jan. 17	Buffalo ($18,000)	Miami ($18,000)	29-10	Miami	72,703
1991	Jan. 12	Buffalo ($18,000)	Denver ($18,000)	10-7	Buffalo	80,272
1990	Jan. 20	Buffalo ($18,000)	L.A. Raiders ($18,000)	51-3	Buffalo	80,325
1989	Jan. 14	Denver ($18,000)	Cleveland ($18,000)	37-21	Denver	76,046
1988	Jan. 8	Cincinnati ($18,000)	Buffalo ($18,000)	21-10	Cincinnati	59,747
1987	Jan. 17	Denver ($18,000)	Cleveland ($18,000)	38-33	Denver	76,197
1986	Jan. 11	Denver ($18,000)	Cleveland ($18,000)	23-20*	Cleveland	79,973
1985	Jan. 12	New England ($18,000)	Miami ($18,000)	31-14	Miami	75,662
1984	Jan. 6	Miami ($18,000)	Pittsburgh ($18,000)	45-28	Miami	76,029
1983	Jan. 8	L.A. Raiders ($18,000)	Seattle ($18,000)	30-14	Los Angeles	91,445
1982	Jan. 23	Miami ($18,000)	N.Y. Jets ($18,000)	14-0	Miami	67,396
1981	Jan. 10	Cincinnati ($9,000)	San Diego ($9,000)	27-7	Cincinnati	46,302
1980	Jan. 11	Oakland ($9,000)	San Diego ($9,000)	34-27	San Diego	52,675
1979	Jan. 6	Pittsburgh ($9,000)	Houston ($9,000)	27-13	Pittsburgh	50,475
1978	Jan. 7	Pittsburgh ($9,000)	Houston ($9,000)	34-5	Pittsburgh	50,725
1977	Jan. 1	Denver ($9,000)	Oakland ($9,000)	20-17	Denver	75,044
1976	Dec. 26	Oakland ($8,500)	Pittsburgh ($5,500)	24-7	Oakland	53,821
1975	Jan. 4	Pittsburgh ($8,500)	Oakland ($5,500)	16-10	Pittsburgh	50,609
1974	Dec. 29	Pittsburgh ($8,500)	Oakland ($5,500)	24-13	Oakland	53,800
1973	Dec. 30	Miami ($8,500)	Oakland ($5,500)	27-10	Miami	79,325
1972	Dec. 31	Miami ($8,500)	Pittsburgh ($5,500)	21-17	Pittsburgh	50,845
1971	Jan. 2	Miami ($8,500)	Baltimore ($5,500)	21-0	Miami	76,622
1970	Jan. 3	Baltimore ($8,500)	Oakland ($5,500)	27-17	Baltimore	54,799
1969	Jan. 4	Kansas City ($7,755)	Oakland ($6,252)	17-7	Oakland	53,564
1968	Dec. 29	N.Y. Jets ($7,007)	Oakland ($5,349)	27-23	New York	62,627
1967	Dec. 31	Oakland ($6,321)	Houston ($4,996)	40-7	Oakland	53,330
1966	Jan. 1	Kansas City ($5,309)	Buffalo ($3,799)	31-7	Buffalo	42,080
1965	Dec. 26	Buffalo ($5,189)	San Diego ($3,447)	23-0	San Diego	30,361
1964	Dec. 26	Buffalo ($2,668)	San Diego ($1,738)	20-7	Buffalo	40,242
1963	Jan. 5	San Diego ($2,498)	Boston ($1,596)	51-10	San Diego	30,127
1962	Dec. 23	Dallas ($2,206)	Houston ($1,471)	20-17*	Houston	37,981
1961	Dec. 24	Houston ($1,792)	San Diego ($1,111)	10-3	San Diego	29,556
1960	Jan. 1	Houston ($1,025)	L.A. Chargers ($718)	24-16	Houston	32,183

**Sudden death overtime*

AFC CHAMPIONSHIP GAME COMPOSITE STANDINGS

	W	L	Pct.	Pts.	OP
Cincinnati Bengals	2	0	1.000	48	17
Baltimore Ravens	1	0	1.000	16	3
Denver Broncos	6	1	.857	172	132
Buffalo Bills	6	2	.750	180	92
Kansas City Chiefs*	3	1	.750	81	61
Miami Dolphins	5	2	.714	152	115
New England Patriots**	2	1	.667	61	71
Pittsburgh Steelers	5	5	.500	207	188
Tennessee Titans##	3	4	.429	109	154
Indianapolis Colts#	1	2	.333	43	58
New York Jets	1	2	.333	37	60
Oakland/L.A. Raiders	4	9	.308	231	280
San Diego Chargers***	2	6	.250	128	161
Seattle Seahawks	0	1	.000	14	30
Jacksonville Jaguars	0	2	.000	20	53
Cleveland Browns	0	3	.000	74	98

**One game played when franchise was in Dallas (Texans) (Won 20-17)*

***One game played when franchise was in Boston.(Lost 51-10)*

****One game played when franchise was in Los Angeles (Lost 24-16)*

#Two games played when franchise was in Baltimore (Won 27-17, lost 21-0)

##Six games played when franchise was in Houston and known as Oilers (Won 2, lost 4)

2000 AFC CHAMPIONSHIP GAME

Network Associates Coliseum, Oakland, California
January 14, 2001, Attendance: 62,784

BALTIMORE 16, OAKLAND 3—Duane Starks intercepted 2 passes and Baltimore's defense forced 5 turnovers as the Ravens earned their first Super Bowl berth. In a battle of field position, the Ravens got the first break when Robert Bailey intercepted Rich Gannon's pass at the Raiders' 19 midway through the first quarter. However, Matt Stover missed a 36-yard field-goal attempt. In the second quarter, the Ravens were pinned on their 4-yard line and faced third-and-18 when Trent Dilfer fired a short pass over the middle to a slanting Shannon Sharpe, who streaked untouched down the middle of the field for a 96-yard touchdown and a 7-0 lead. On the Raiders' next possession, Tony Siragusa knocked down Gannon on a passing play. Gannon left the game with an injured non-throwing shoulder, and Bobby Hoying replaced him. Starks intercepted Hoying's first pass, returning it 9 yards to the Raiders' 20 to set up Stover's 31-yard field goal. Three plays into the second half, Johnnie Harris intercepted a pass by Dilfer. Gannon returned for the Raiders and guided the club to first-and-goal at the Ravens' 2. However, Tyrone Wheatley lost a yard, Gannon was sacked by Jamie Sharper, and on third down Gannon's pass fell incomplete, so the Raiders had to settle for Sebastian Janikowski's 24-yard field goal. The Ravens responded with a 9-play, 51-yard drive, capped by Stover's second field goal to take a 13-3 lead. Early in the fourth quarter, Peter Boulware sacked Gannon and forced him to fumble. Ray Lewis recovered at the Raiders' 7, which set up Stover's third field goal for a 16-3 lead with 7:28 left. Hoying returned for the Raiders and drove Oakland to the Ravens' 5. Hoying's 5-yard touchdown pass to Andre Rison was nullified by offensive pass interference, and Sharper intercepted Hoying two plays later to clinch the victory. Dilfer completed 9 of 18 passes for 190 yards and 1 touchdown, with 1 interception. Gannon was 11 of 21 for 80 yards, with 2 interceptions, while Hoying was 8 of 16 for 107 yards, with 2 interceptions. The Ravens' defense limited the NFL's number-one rushing offense to 24 rushing yards on 17 carries.

Baltimore (16)	Offense	Oakland (3)
Qadry Ismail	WR	Tim Brown
Jonathan Ogden	LT	Barry Sims
Edwin Mulitalo	LG	Steve Wisniewski
Jeff Mitchell	C	Barret Robbins
Mike Flynn	RG	Mo Collins
Harry Swayne	RT	Lincoln Kennedy
Shannon Sharpe	TE	Rickey Dudley
Jermaine Lewis	WR	James Jett
Trent Dilfer	QB	Rich Gannon
Ben Coates	TE-RB	Zack Crockett
Jamal Lewis	RB	Tyrone Wheatley
	Defense	
Rob Burnett	LE	Tony Bryant
Sam Adams	LT	Grady Jackson
Tony Siragusa	RT	Darrell Russell
Michael McCrary	RE	Regan Upshaw
Peter Boulware	LLB	William Thomas
Ray Lewis	MLB	Greg Biekert
Jamie Sharper	RLB	Elijah Alexander
Duane Starks	LCB	Charles Woodson
Chris McAlister	RCB	Eric Allen
Corey Harris	SS	Marquez Pope
Rod Woodson	FS	Anthony Dorsett

SUBSTITUTIONS

Baltimore—Offense: G—Kipp Vickers. T—Spencer Folau. C—John Hudson. WR—Billy Davis, Patrick Johnson, Brandon Stokley. FB—Chuck Evans, Sam Gash. RB—Priest Holmes. P—Kyle Richardson. K—Matt Stover. Defense: DT—Lional Dalton, Larry Webster. DE—Keith Washington, Adalius Thomas. LB—O.J. Brigance, Anthony Davis, Brad Jackson. CB—Robert Bailey, James Trapp. S—Anthony Mitchell, Anthony Poindexter. DNP—Tony Banks.

Oakland—Offense: G—Darryl Ashmore. C—Adam Treu. TE—Jeremy Brigham. WR—David Dunn, Jerry

Porter, Andre Rison. RB—Randy Jordan, Terry Kirby, Jon Ritchie. QB—Bobby Hoying. P—Shane Lechler. K—Sebastian Janikowski. Defense: DT—Roderick Coleman. DE—Lance Johnstone, Josh Taves. LB—Bobby Brooks, Travian Smith. CB—Darrien Gordon, Tory James. S—Calvin Branch, Johnnie Harris, Eric Johnson. DNP—Matt Stinchcomb.

OFFICIALS

Referee—Bill Carollo. Umpire—Jim Quirk. Line Judge—Tom Barnes. Side Judge—Neely Dunn. Head Linesman—Mark Hittner. Back Judge—Kirk Dornan. Field Judge—Peter Morelli. Replay Official—Mark Burns. Video Operator—Danny Louie.

SCORING

Baltimore	0	10	3	3	—	16
Oakland	0	0	3	0	—	3

Balt — Sharpe 96 pass from Dilfer (Stover kick)
Balt — FG Stover 31
Oak — FG Janikowski 24
Balt — FG Stover 28
Balt — FG Stover 21

TEAM STATISTICS	**Balt**	**Oak**
Total First Downs	12	12
Rushing	6	2
Passing	5	8
Penalty	1	2
Total Net Yardage	282	191
Total Offensive Plays	66	58
Average Gain Per Offensive Play	4.3	3.3
Rushes	46	17
Yards Gained Rushing (Net)	110	24
Average Yards per Rush	2.4	1.4
Passes Attempted	18	37
Passes Completed	9	19
Had Intercepted	1	4
Tackled Attempting to Pass	2	4
Yards Lost Attempting to Pass	18	20
Yards Gained Passing (Net)	172	167
Punts	7	7
Average Distance	40.6	45.0
Punt Returns	3	2
Punt Return Yardage	58	9
Kickoff Returns	2	4
Kickoff Return Yardage	45	72
Interception Return Yardage	59	2
Total Return Yardage	162	83
Fumbles	2	2
Fumbles Lost	1	1
Own Fumbles Recovered	1	1
Opponent Fumbles Recovered	1	1
Penalties	10	5
Yards Penalized	95	36
Field Goals	3	1
Field Goals Attempted	4	1
Third-Down Efficiency	6/19	2/14
Fourth-Down Efficiency	0/0	0/0
Time of Possession	34:38	25:22

INDIVIDUAL STATISTICS

RUSHING: BALT: Ja. Lewis 29-79-0, Holmes 9-31-0, Dilfer 7-4-0, Ismail 1-(-4)-0. OAK: Hoying 3-13-0, Wheatley 12-7-0, Gannon 1-2-0, Jordan 1-2-0.

PASSING: BALT: Dilfer 18-9-190-1-1. OAK: Gannon 21-11-80-0-2, Hoying 16-8-107-0-2.

RECEIVING: BALT: Stokley 3-31-0, Ja. Lewis 3-21-0, Sharpe 1-96-1, Coates 1-24-0, Ismail 1-18-0. OAK: Brown 5-48-0, Jett 3-16-0, Kirby 2-41-0, Brigham 2-22-0, Crockett 2-9-0, Porter 1-19-0, Rison 1-16-0, Dudley 1-7-0, Ritchie 1-5-0, Wheatley 1-4-0.

KICKOFF RETURNS: BALT: Je. Lewis 1-29-0, Harris 1-16-0. OAK: Dunn 4-72-0.

PUNT RETURNS: BALT: Je. Lewis 3-58-0. OAK: Gordon 2-9-0.

PUNTING: BALT: Richardson 7-284-40.6. OAK: Lechler 7-315-45.0.

INTERCEPTIONS: BALT: Starks 2-44, Sharper 1-15, Bailey 1-0. OAK: Harris 1-2.

SACKS: BALT: Sharper 2, Boulware, McCrary. OAK: Russell, Thomas.

NFC CHAMPIONSHIP GAME RESULTS

Includes NFL Championship Games (1933-1969)

Season	Date	Winner (Share)	Loser (Share)	Score	Site	Attendance
2000	Jan. 14	N.Y. Giants ($34,500)	Minnesota ($34,500)	41-0	East Rutherford	79,310
1999	Jan. 23	St. Louis ($33,000)	Tampa Bay ($33,000)	11-6	St. Louis	66,396
1998	Jan. 17	Atlanta ($32,500)	Minnesota ($32,500)	30-27*	Minneapolis	64,060
1997	Jan. 11	Green Bay ($30,000)	San Francisco ($30,000)	23-10	San Francisco	68,987
1996	Jan. 12	Green Bay ($29,000)	Carolina ($29,000)	30-13	Green Bay	60,216
1995	Jan. 14	Dallas ($27,000)	Green Bay ($27,000)	38-27	Dallas	65,135
1994	Jan. 15	San Francisco ($26,000)	Dallas ($26,000)	38-28	San Francisco	69,125
1993	Jan. 23	Dallas ($23,500)	San Francisco ($23,500)	38-21	Dallas	64,902
1992	Jan. 17	Dallas ($18,000)	San Francisco ($18,000)	30-20	San Francisco	64,920
1991	Jan. 12	Washington ($18,000)	Detroit ($18,000)	41-10	Washington	55,585
1990	Jan. 20	N.Y. Giants ($18,000)	San Francisco ($18,000)	15-13	San Francisco	65,750
1989	Jan. 14	San Francisco ($18,000)	L.A. Rams ($18,000)	30-3	San Francisco	65,634
1988	Jan. 8	San Francisco ($18,000)	Chicago ($18,000)	28-3	Chicago	66,946
1987	Jan. 17	Washington ($18,000)	Minnesota ($18,000)	17-10	Washington	55,212
1986	Jan. 11	New York Giants ($18,000)	Washington ($18,000)	17-0	East Rutherford	76,891
1985	Jan. 12	Chicago ($18,000)	L.A. Rams ($18,000)	24-0	Chicago	66,030
1984	Jan. 6	San Francisco ($18,000)	Chicago ($18,000)	23-0	San Francisco	61,336
1983	Jan. 8	Washington ($18,000)	San Francisco ($18,000)	24-21	Washington	55,363
1982	Jan. 22	Washington ($18,000)	Dallas ($18,000)	31-17	Washington	55,045
1981	Jan. 10	San Francisco ($9,000)	Dallas ($9,000)	28-27	San Francisco	60,525
1980	Jan. 11	Philadelphia ($9,000)	Dallas ($9,000)	20-7	Philadelphia	71,522
1979	Jan. 6	Los Angeles ($9,000)	Tampa Bay ($9,000)	9-0	Tampa Bay	72,033
1978	Jan. 7	Dallas ($9,000)	Los Angeles ($9,000)	28-0	Los Angeles	71,086
1977	Jan. 1	Dallas ($9,000)	Minnesota ($9,000)	23-6	Dallas	64,293
1976	Dec. 26	Minnesota ($8,500)	Los Angeles ($5,500)	24-13	Minneapolis	48,379
1975	Jan. 4	Dallas ($8,500)	Los Angeles ($5,500)	37-7	Los Angeles	88,919
1974	Dec. 29	Minnesota ($8,500)	Los Angeles ($5,500)	14-10	Minneapolis	48,444
1973	Dec. 30	Minnesota ($8,500)	Dallas ($5,500)	27-10	Dallas	64,422
1972	Dec. 31	Washington ($8,500)	Dallas ($5,500)	26-3	Washington	53,129
1971	Jan. 2	Dallas ($8,500)	San Francisco ($5,500)	14-3	Dallas	63,409
1970	Jan. 3	Dallas ($8,500)	San Francisco ($5,500)	17-10	San Francisco	59,364
1969	Jan. 4	Minnesota ($7,930)	Cleveland ($5,118)	27-7	Minneapolis	46,503
1968	Dec. 29	Baltimore ($9,306)	Cleveland ($5,963)	34-0	Cleveland	78,410
1967	Dec. 31	Green Bay ($7,950)	Dallas ($5,299)	21-17	Green Bay	50,861
1966	Jan. 1	Green Bay ($9,813)	Dallas ($6,527)	34-27	Dallas	74,152
1965	Jan. 2	Green Bay ($7,819)	Cleveland ($5,288)	23-12	Green Bay	50,777
1964	Dec. 27	Cleveland ($8,052)	Baltimore ($5,571)	27-0	Cleveland	79,544
1963	Dec. 29	Chicago ($5,899)	New York ($4,218)	14-10	Chicago	45,801
1962	Dec. 30	Green Bay ($5,888)	New York ($4,166)	16-7	New York	64,892
1961	Dec. 31	Green Bay ($5,195)	New York ($3,339)	37-0	Green Bay	39,029
1960	Dec. 26	Philadelphia ($5,116)	Green Bay ($3,105)	17-13	Philadelphia	67,325
1959	Dec. 27	Baltimore ($4,674)	New York ($3,083)	31-16	Baltimore	57,545
1958	Dec. 28	Baltimore ($4,718)	New York ($3,111)	23-17*	New York	64,185
1957	Dec. 29	Detroit ($4,295)	Cleveland ($2,750)	59-14	Detroit	55,263
1956	Dec. 30	New York ($3,779)	Chi. Bears ($2,485)	47-7	New York	56,836
1955	Dec. 26	Cleveland ($3,508)	Los Angeles ($2,316)	38-14	Los Angeles	85,693
1954	Dec. 26	Cleveland ($2,478)	Detroit ($1,585)	56-10	Cleveland	43,827
1953	Dec. 27	Detroit ($2,424)	Cleveland ($1,654)	17-16	Detroit	54,577
1952	Dec. 28	Detroit ($2,274)	Cleveland ($1,712)	17-7	Cleveland	50,934
1951	Dec. 23	Los Angeles ($2,108)	Cleveland ($1,483)	24-17	Los Angeles	57,522

PLAYOFF GAMES SUMMARIES

Season	Date	Winner (Share)	Loser (Share)	Score	Site	Attendance
1950	Dec. 24	Cleveland ($1,113)	Los Angeles ($686)	30-28	Cleveland	29,751
1949	Dec. 18	Philadelphia ($1,094)	Los Angeles ($739)	14-0	Los Angeles	27,980
1948	Dec. 19	Philadelphia ($1,540)	Chi. Cardinals ($874)	7-0	Philadelphia	36,309
1947	Dec. 28	Chi. Cardinals ($1,132)	Philadelphia ($754)	28-21	Chicago	30,759
1946	Dec. 15	Chi. Bears ($1,975)	New York ($1,295)	24-14	New York	58,346
1945	Dec. 16	Cleveland ($1,469)	Washington ($902)	15-14	Cleveland	32,178
1944	Dec. 17	Green Bay ($1,449)	New York ($814)	14-7	New York	46,016
1943	Dec. 26	Chi. Bears ($1,146)	Washington ($765)	41-21	Chicago	34,320
1942	Dec. 13	Washington ($965)	Chi. Bears ($637)	14-6	Washington	36,006
1941	Dec. 21	Chi. Bears ($430)	New York ($288)	37-9	Chicago	13,341
1940	Dec. 8	Chi. Bears ($873)	Washington ($606)	73-0	Washington	36,034
1939	Dec. 10	Green Bay ($703.97)	New York ($455.57)	27-0	Milwaukee	32,279
1938	Dec. 11	New York ($504.45)	Green Bay ($368.81)	23-17	New York	48,120
1937	Dec. 12	Washington ($225.90)	Chi. Bears ($127.78)	28-21	Chicago	15,870
1936	Dec. 13	Green Bay ($250)	Boston ($180)	21-6	New York	29,545
1935	Dec. 15	Detroit ($313.35)	New York ($200.20)	26-7	Detroit	15,000
1934	Dec. 9	New York ($621)	Chi. Bears ($414.02)	30-13	New York	35,059
1933	Dec. 17	Chi. Bears ($210.34)	New York ($140.22)	23-21	Chicago	26,000

**Sudden death overtime*

NFC CHAMPIONSHIP GAME COMPOSITE STANDINGS

	W	L	Pct.	Pts.	OP
Atlanta Falcons	1	0	1.000	30	27
Philadelphia Eagles	4	1	.800	79	48
Green Bay Packers	10	3	.769	303	177
Baltimore Colts	3	1	.750	88	60
Detroit Lions	4	2	.667	139	141
Washington Redskins*	7	5	.583	222	255
Chicago Bears	7	6	.538	286	245
Dallas Cowboys	8	8	.500	361	319
Minnesota Vikings	4	4	.500	135	151
Arizona Cardinals**	1	1	.500	28	28
San Francisco 49ers	5	7	.417	245	222
Cleveland Browns	4	7	.364	224	253
New York Giants	6	11	.353	281	322
St. Louis Rams***	4	9	.308	134	276
Carolina Panthers	0	1	.000	13	30
Tampa Bay Buccaneers	0	2	.000	6	20

**One game played when franchise was in Boston (Lost 21-6)*

***Both games played when franchise was in Chicago (Won 28-21, lost 7-0)*

****One game played when franchise was in Cleveland (Won 15-14), and 11 games when franchise was in Los Angeles (Won 2, lost 9, scored 108 points, allowed 256 points).*

2000 NFC CHAMPIONSHIP GAME

Giants Stadium, East Rutherford, New Jersey

January 14, 2001, Attendance: 79,310

N.Y. GIANTS 41, MINNESOTA 0—Kerry Collins passed for 381 yards and 5 touchdowns to lead the Giants to their first Super Bowl berth in 10 years. The Giants' defense forced 5 turnovers and limited the Vikings to 114 yards. Collins needed just 4 plays, and less than two minutes, to score on Ike Hilliard's 46-yard reception. Moe Williams fumbled the ensuing kickoff, and Lyle West recovered at the Vikings' 18. On the next play, Collins lofted a scoring pass to Greg Comella to give the Giants a 14-0 lead 2:13 into the game—before the Vikings had taken a snap. Robert Tate's interception gave Minnesota a scoring opportunity midway through the first quarter, but three plays later Emmanuel McDaniel intercepted Daunte Culpepper's pass in the end zone. The Giants proceeded to score on all four of their second-quarter possessions, including drives of 71, 62, and 77 yards. Collins capped the outburst with a 7-yard scoring pass to Hilliard that gave the Giants a 34-0 halftime lead. Cornelius Griffin recovered Culpepper's fumble at the Vikings' 29 early in the second half, and Collins's 7-yard touchdown pass to Amani Toomer gave the Giants a 41-0 lead with 12:06 left in the third quarter. The Vikings never drove beyond the Giants' 32 the rest of the game, and the Giants used a 19-play drive to run out the final 12:53. Collins completed 28 of 39 passes for 381 yards and 5 touchdowns, with 2 interceptions. Hilliard had 10 receptions for 155 yards. Culpepper was 13 of 28 for 78 yards, with 3 interceptions.

Minnesota (0)	Offense	N.Y. Giants (41)
Randy Moss	WR	Amani Toomer
Todd Steussie	LT	Lomas Brown
Corbin Lacina	LG	Glenn Parker
Matt Birk	C	Dusty Zeigler
David Dixon	RG	Ron Stone
Korey Stringer	RT	Luke Petitgout
Johnny McWilliams	TE	Pete Mitchell
Cris Carter	WR	Ike Hilliard
Daunte Culpepper	QB	Kerry Collins
Andrew Jordan	TE-FB	Greg Comella
Robert Smith	RB	Ron Dayne
	Defense	
John Randle	LE	Michael Strahan
Chris Hovan	NT-LT	Christian Peter
Tony Williams	UT-RT	Keith Hamilton
Fernando Smith	RE	Cedric Jones
Dwayne Rudd	SLB-OLB	Ryan Phillips
Kailee Wong	MLB	Mike Barrow
Ed McDaniel	WLB-OLB	Jessie Armstead
Wasswa Serwanga	LCB	Dave Thomas
Robert Tate	RCB	Jason Sehorn
Robert Griffith	SS	Sam Garnes
Tony Carter	FS	Shaun Williams

SUBSTITUTIONS

Minnesota—Offense: G—Chris Liwenski. C—Cory Withrow. LS—Mitch Palmer. TE—John Davis. WR—Matthew Hatchette, Chris Walsh, Troy Walters. FB—Jim Kleinsasser, Harold Morrow. RB—Moe Williams. P—Mitch Berger. Defense: DT—John Burrough. DE—Bryce Paup, Talance Sawyer. LB—Pete Bercich, Lemanski Hall, Jim Nelson. CB—Keith Thibodeaux. S—Anthony Banks, Don Morgan. DNP—Gary Anderson, Brad Badger, Bubby Brister.

N.Y. Giants—Offense: G—Mike Rosenthal, Jason Whittle. C—Derek Engler. TE—Dan Campbell, Howard Cross. WR—Thabiti Davis, Ron Dixon, Joe Jurevicius. QB—Jason Garrett. RB—Tiki Barber, Joe Montgomery, Damon Washington. P—Brad Maynard. K—Brad Daluiso. Defense: DT—Cornelius Griffin. LB—Jack Golden, Pete Monty, Brandon Short. CB—Emmanuel McDaniel, Ramos McDonald. S—Omar Stoutmire, Lyle West. DNP—Ryan Hale.

OFFICIALS

Referee—Tony Corrente. Umpire—Ron Botchan. Line Judge—Jeff Bergman. Side Judge—Terry McAulay. Head Linesman—Mark Baltz. Back Judge—Ron Spitler. Field Judge—Boris Cheek. Replay Official—Jerry Markbreit. Video Operator—Louis Nazzaro.

SCORING

Minnesota	0	0	0	0	— 0
N.Y. Giants	14	20	7	0	— 41

NYG — Hilliard 46 pass from Collins (Daluiso kick)
NYG — Comella 18 pass from Collins (Daluiso kick)
NYG — FG Daluiso 21
NYG — Jurevicius 8 pass from Collins (Daluiso kick)
NYG — FG Daluiso 22
NYG — Hilliard 7 pass from Collins (Daluiso kick)
NYG — Toomer 7 pass from Collins (Daluiso kick)

TEAM STATISTICS	MINN	NYG
Total First Downs	9	31
Rushing	2	10
Passing	6	19
Penalty	1	2
Total Net Yardage	114	518
Total Offensive Plays	41	82
Average Gain Per Offensive Play	2.8	6.3
Rushes	9	41
Yards Gained Rushing (Net)	54	138
Average Yards per Rush	6.0	3.4
Passes Attempted	28	40
Passes Completed	13	29
Had Intercepted	3	2
Tackled Attempting to Pass	4	1
Yards Lost Attempting to Pass	18	5
Yards Gained Passing (Net)	60	380
Punts	6	1
Average Distance	35.0	30.0
Punt Returns	0	2
Punt Return Yardage	0	2
Kickoff Returns	8	1
Kickoff Return Yardage	128	16
Interception Return Yardage	5	13
Total Return Yardage	133	31
Fumbles	2	1
Fumbles Lost	2	0
Own Fumbles Recovered	0	1
Opponent Fumbles Recovered	0	2
Penalties	5	4
Yards Penalized	61	36
Field Goals	0	2
Field Goals Attempted	0	3
Third-Down Efficiency	1/8	8/16
Fourth-Down Efficiency	0/0	1/1
Time of Possession	17:38	42:22

INDIVIDUAL STATISTICS

RUSHING: MINN: Smith 7-44-0, Culpepper 2-10-0. NYG: Barber 12-69-0, Montgomery 16-43-0, Dayne 10-29-0, Garrett 3-(-3)-0.

PASSING: MINN: Culpepper 28-13-78-0-3. NYG: Collins 39-28-381-5-2, Garrett 1-1-4-0-0.

RECEIVING: MINN: Carter 3-24-0, Walsh 3-23-0, Moss 2-18-0, Smith 2-(-2)-0, McWilliams 1-9-0, Jordan 1-4-0, Hatchette 1-2-0. NYG: Hilliard 10-155-2, Toomer 6-88-1, Comella 4-36-1, Barber 4-21-0, Dixon 2-62-0, Jurevicius 2-15-1, Dayne 1-8-0.

KICKOFF RETURNS: MINN: Walters 6-113-0, Williams 2-15-0. NYG: Washington 1-16-0.

PUNT RETURNS: NYG: Hilliard 2-2-0.

PUNTING: MINN: Berger 6-210-35.0. NYG: Maynard 1-30-30.0.

INTERCEPTIONS: MINN: Tate 1-4, Morgan 1-1. NYG: Games 1-13, McDaniel 1-0, Sehorn 1-0

SACKS: MINN: Paup. NYG: Armstead, Barrow, Strahan, Williams.

AFC DIVISIONAL PLAYOFFS RESULTS

Includes Second-Round Playoff Games (1982), AFC Inter-Divisional Games (1969), and special playoff games to break ties for AFL Division Championships (1963, 1968)

Season	Date	Winner (Share)	Loser (Share)	Score	Site	Attendance
2000	Jan. 7	Baltimore ($16,000)	Tennessee ($16,000)	24-10	Nashville	68,527
	Jan. 6	Oakland ($16,000)	Miami ($16,000)	27-0	Oakland	61,998
1999	Jan. 16	Tennessee ($16,000)	Indianapolis ($16,000)	19-16	Indianapolis	57,097
	Jan. 15	Jacksonville ($16,000)	Miami ($16,000)	62-7	Jacksonville	75,173
1998	Jan. 10	N.Y. Jets ($15,000)	Jacksonville ($15,000)	34-24	East Rutherford	78,817
	Jan. 9	Denver ($15,000)	Miami ($15,000)	38-3	Denver	75,729
1997	Jan. 4	Denver ($15,000)	Kansas City ($15,000)	14-10	Kansas City	76,965
	Jan. 3	Pittsburgh ($15,000)	New England ($15,000)	7-6	Pittsburgh	61,228
1996	Jan. 5	New England ($14,000)	Pittsburgh ($14,000)	28-3	New England	60,188
	Jan. 4	Jacksonville ($14,000)	Denver ($14,000)	30-27	Denver	75,678
1995	Jan. 7	Indianapolis ($13,000)	Kansas City ($13,000)	10-7	Kansas City	77,594
	Jan. 6	Pittsburgh ($13,000)	Buffalo ($13,000)	40-21	Pittsburgh	59,072
1994	Jan. 8	San Diego ($12,000)	Miami ($12,000)	22-21	San Diego	63,381
	Jan. 7	Pittsburgh ($12,000)	Cleveland ($12,000)	29-9	Pittsburgh	58,185
1993	Jan. 16	Kansas City ($12,000)	Houston ($12,000)	28-20	Houston	64,011
	Jan. 15	Buffalo ($12,000)	L.A. Raiders ($12,000)	29-23	Buffalo	61,923
1992	Jan. 10	Miami ($10,000)	San Diego ($10,000)	31-0	Miami	71,224
	Jan. 9	Buffalo ($10,000)	Pittsburgh ($10,000)	24-3	Pittsburgh	60,407
1991	Jan. 5	Buffalo ($10,000)	Kansas City ($10,000)	37-14	Buffalo	80,182
	Jan. 4	Denver ($10,000)	Houston ($10,000)	26-24	Denver	75,301
1990	Jan. 13	L.A. Raiders ($10,000)	Cincinnati ($10,000)	20-10	Los Angeles	92,045
	Jan. 12	Buffalo ($10,000)	Miami ($10,000)	44-34	Buffalo	77,087
1989	Jan. 7	Denver ($10,000)	Pittsburgh ($10,000)	24-23	Denver	75,477
	Jan. 6	Cleveland ($10,000)	Buffalo ($10,000)	34-30	Cleveland	78,921
1988	Jan. 1	Buffalo ($10,000)	Houston ($10,000)	17-10	Buffalo	79,532
	Dec. 31	Cincinnati ($10,000)	Seattle ($10,000)	21-13	Cincinnati	58,560
1987	Jan. 10	Denver ($10,000)	Houston ($10,000)	34-10	Denver	75,440
	Jan. 9	Cleveland ($10,000)	Indianapolis ($10,000)	38-21	Cleveland	79,372
1986	Jan. 4	Denver ($10,000)	New England ($10,000)	22-17	Denver	75,262
	Jan. 3	Cleveland ($10,000)	N.Y. Jets ($10,000)	23-20*	Cleveland	79,720
1985	Jan. 5	New England ($10,000)	L.A. Raiders ($10,000)	27-20	Los Angeles	87,163
	Jan. 4	Miami ($10,000)	Cleveland ($10,000)	24-21	Miami	74,667
1984	Dec. 30	Pittsburgh ($10,000)	Denver ($10,000)	24-17	Denver	74,981
	Dec. 29	Miami ($10,000)	Seattle ($10,000)	31-10	Miami	73,469
1983	Jan. 1	L.A. Raiders ($10,000)	Pittsburgh ($10,000)	38-10	Los Angeles	90,380
	Dec. 31	Seattle ($10,000)	Miami ($10,000)	27-20	Miami	74,136
1982	Jan. 16	Miami ($10,000)	San Diego ($10,000)	34-13	Miami	71,383
	Jan. 15	N.Y. Jets ($10,000)	L.A. Raiders ($10,000)	17-14	Los Angeles	90,038
1981	Jan. 3	Cincinnati ($5,000)	Buffalo ($5,000)	28-21	Cincinnati	55,420
	Jan. 2	San Diego ($5,000)	Miami ($5,000)	41-38*	Miami	73,735
1980	Jan. 4	Oakland ($5,000)	Cleveland ($5,000)	14-12	Cleveland	78,245
	Jan. 3	San Diego ($5,000)	Buffalo ($5,000)	20-14	San Diego	52,253
1979	Dec. 30	Pittsburgh ($5,000)	Miami ($5,000)	34-14	Pittsburgh	50,214
	Dec. 29	Houston ($5,000)	San Diego ($5,000)	17-14	San Diego	51,192
1978	Dec. 31	Houston ($5,000)	New England ($5,000)	31-14	New England	60,735
	Dec. 30	Pittsburgh ($5,000)	Denver ($5,000)	33-10	Pittsburgh	50,230
1977	Dec. 24	Oakland ($5,000)	Baltimore ($5,000)	37-31*	Baltimore	59,925
	Dec. 24	Denver ($5,000)	Pittsburgh ($5,000)	34-21	Denver	75,059
1976	Dec. 19	Pittsburgh [$]	Baltimore [$]	40-14	Baltimore	59,296
	Dec. 18	Oakland [$]	New England [$]	24-21	Oakland	53,050
1975	Dec. 28	Oakland [$]	Cincinnati [$]	31-28	Oakland	53,030
	Dec. 27	Pittsburgh [$]	Baltimore [$]	28-10	Pittsburgh	49,557
1974	Dec. 22	Pittsburgh [$]	Buffalo [$]	32-14	Pittsburgh	49,841
	Dec. 21	Oakland [$]	Miami [$]	28-26	Oakland	53,023
1973	Dec. 23	Miami [$]	Cincinnati [$]	34-16	Miami	78,928
	Dec. 22	Oakland [$]	Pittsburgh [$]	33-14	Oakland	52,646
1972	Dec. 24	Miami [$]	Cleveland [$]	20-14	Miami	78,916
	Dec. 23	Pittsburgh [$]	Oakland [$]	13-7	Pittsburgh	50,327
1971	Dec. 26	Baltimore [$]	Cleveland [$]	20-3	Cleveland	70,734
	Dec. 25	Miami [$]	Kansas City [$]	27-24*	Kansas City	50,374
1970	Dec. 27	Oakland [$]	Miami [$]	21-14	Oakland	52,594
	Dec. 26	Baltimore [$]	Cincinnati [$]	17-0	Baltimore	49,694
1969	Dec. 21	Oakland [$]	Houston [$]	56-7	Oakland	53,539
	Dec. 20	Kansas City [$]	N.Y. Jets [$]	13-6	New York	62,977
1968	Dec. 22	Oakland [$]	Kansas City [$]	41-6	Oakland	53,605
1963	Dec. 28	Boston [$]	Buffalo [$]	26-8	Buffalo	33,044

**Sudden death overtime.*

$ Players received 1/14 of annual salary for playoff appearances.

2000 AFC DIVISIONAL PLAYOFF GAMES

Adelphia Coliseum, Nashville, Tennessee
January 7, 2001, Attendance: 68,527

BALTIMORE 24, TENNESSEE 10—Ray Lewis's 50-yard interception return for a touchdown midway through the fourth quarter iced the Ravens' comeback victory. The Titans drove 68 yards in 11 plays on the game's opening drive, capped by Eddie George's 2-yard touchdown run. It turned out to be the only touchdown allowed by the Ravens' defense in four 2000 postseason games. Trent Dilfer's 56-yard pass to Shannon Sharpe early in the second quarter led to Jamal Lewis's 1-yard scoring run to tie the game. After Al Del Greco's 45-yard field-goal attempt in the second quarter was blocked by Keith Washington, Chris Coleman blocked Kyle Richardson's punt deep in Ravens' territory. However, Del Greco missed a 31-yard attempt just before halftime. Coleman blocked another punt by Richardson two minutes into the second half, but the Titans had to settle for Del Greco's 21-yard field goal and a 10-7 lead. A 15-yard fair-catch interference penalty on Tennessee led to Matt Stover's game-tying field goal late in the third quarter.

Early in the fourth quarter, Washington blocked another field-goal attempt by Del Greco. Anthony Mitchell caught the ball and scampered 90 yards down the right sideline for the go-ahead touchdown. Down 17-10, the Titans had the ball at their 47 with 6:55 remaining when Steve McNair's short pass bounced off George's hands to Lewis, who raced 50 yards for the game's final points. Dilfer completed 5 of 16 passes for 117 yards, and the Ravens won despite being held to 6 first downs. McNair was 24 of 46 for 176 yards, with 1 interception.

Baltimore	0	7	3	14	—	24
Tennessee	7	0	3	0	—	10

Tenn — George 2 run (Del Greco kick)
Balt — Ja. Lewis 1 run (Stover kick)
Tenn — FG Del Greco 21
Balt — FG Stover 38
Balt — Mitchell 90 blocked field goal return (Stover kick)
Balt — R. Lewis 50 interception return (Stover kick)

Network Associates Coliseum, Oakland, California
January 6, 2001, Attendance: 61,998

OAKLAND 27, MIAMI 0—The Raiders rushed for 140 yards on offense and forced 4 turnovers on defense to hand the Dolphins their first shutout loss in postseason history. Jeff Ogden's 45-yard punt return gave Miami an excellent scoring opportunity on its first possession. However, Tory James stepped in front of Jay Fiedler's second-down pass and returned it 90 yards for a touchdown. The Raiders added field goals by Sebastian Janikowski on their next two drives to take a 13-0 lead. On the Dolphins' ensuing possession, Charles Woodson recovered Lamar Smith's fumble to set up Rich Gannon's 6-yard touchdown pass to James Jett, which gave Oakland a 20-0 lead. Tyrone Wheatley's 2-yard touchdown run capped a 12-play, 54-yard drive on the Raiders' first possession of the second half for the game's final points. Gannon completed 12 of 18 passes for 143 yards and 1 touchdown. Fiedler was 18 of 37 for 176 yards, with 3 interceptions.

Miami	0	0	0	0	—	0
Oakland	10	10	7	0	—	27

Oak — James 90 interception return (Janikowski kick)
Oak — FG Janikowski 36
Oak — FG Janikowski 33
Oak — Jett 6 pass from Gannon (Janikowski kick)
Oak — Wheatley 2 run (Janikowski kick)

NFC DIVISIONAL PLAYOFFS RESULTS

Includes Second-Round Playoff Games (1982), NFL Conference Championship Games (1967-69), and special playoff games to break ties for NFL Division or Conference Championships (1941, 1943, 1947, 1950, 1952, 1957, 1958, 1965)

Season	Date	Winner (Share)	Loser (Share)	Score	Site	Attendance
2000	Jan. 7	N.Y. Giants ($16,000)	Philadelphia ($16,000)	20-10	East Rutherford	78,765
	Jan. 6	Minnesota ($16,000)	New Orleans ($16,000)	34-16	Minneapolis	63,881
1999	Jan. 16	St. Louis ($16,000)	Minnesota ($16,000)	49-37	St. Louis	66,194
	Jan. 15	Tampa Bay ($16,000)	Washington ($16,000)	14-13	Tampa Bay	65,835
1998	Jan. 10	Minnesota ($15,000)	Arizona ($15,000)	41-21	Minneapolis	63,760
	Jan. 9	Atlanta ($15,000)	San Francisco ($15,000)	20-18	Atlanta	70,262
1997	Jan. 4	Green Bay ($15,000)	Tampa Bay ($15,000)	21-7	Green Bay	60,327
	Jan. 3	San Francisco ($15,000)	Minnesota ($15,000)	38-22	San Francisco	65,018
1996	Jan. 5	Carolina ($14,000)	Dallas ($14,000)	26-17	Carolina	72,808
	Jan. 4	Green Bay ($14,000)	San Francisco ($14,000)	35-14	Green Bay	60,787
1995	Jan. 7	Dallas ($13,000)	Philadelphia ($13,000)	30-11	Dallas	64,371
	Jan. 6	Green Bay ($13,000)	San Francisco ($13,000)	27-17	San Francisco	69,311
1994	Jan. 8	Dallas ($12,000)	Green Bay ($12,000)	35-9	Dallas	64,745
	Jan. 7	San Francisco ($12,000)	Chicago ($12,000)	44-15	San Francisco	64,644
1993	Jan. 16	Dallas ($12,000)	Green Bay ($12,000)	27-17	Dallas	64,790
	Jan. 15	San Francisco ($12,000)	N.Y. Giants ($12,000)	44-3	San Francisco	67,143
1992	Jan. 10	Dallas ($10,000)	Philadelphia ($10,000)	34-10	Dallas	63,721
	Jan. 9	San Francisco ($10,000)	Washington ($10,000)	20-13	San Francisco	64,991
1991	Jan. 5	Detroit ($10,000)	Dallas ($10,000)	38-6	Detroit	78,290
	Jan. 4	Washington ($10,000)	Atlanta ($10,000)	24-7	Washington	55,181
1990	Jan. 13	N.Y. Giants ($10,000)	Chicago ($10,000)	31-3	East Rutherford	77,025
	Jan. 12	San Francisco ($10,000)	Washington ($10,000)	28-10	San Francisco	65,292
1989	Jan. 7	L.A. Rams ($10,000)	N.Y. Giants ($10,000)	19-13*	East Rutherford	76,526
	Jan. 6	San Francisco ($10,000)	Minnesota ($10,000)	41-13	San Francisco	64,918
1988	Jan. 1	San Francisco ($10,000)	Minnesota ($10,000)	34-9	San Francisco	61,848
	Dec. 31	Chicago ($10,000)	Philadelphia ($10,000)	20-12	Chicago	65,534
1987	Jan. 10	Washington ($10,000)	Chicago ($10,000)	21-17	Chicago	65,268
	Jan. 9	Minnesota ($10,000)	San Francisco ($10,000)	36-24	San Francisco	63,008
1986	Jan. 4	N.Y. Giants ($10,000)	San Francisco ($10,000)	49-3	East Rutherford	75,691
	Jan. 3	Washington ($10,000)	Chicago ($10,000)	27-13	Chicago	65,524
1985	Jan. 5	Chicago ($10,000)	N.Y. Giants ($10,000)	21-0	Chicago	65,670
	Jan. 4	L.A. Rams ($10,000)	Dallas ($10,000)	20-0	Anaheim	66,581
1984	Dec. 30	Chicago ($10,000)	Washington ($10,000)	23-19	Washington	55,431
	Dec. 29	San Francisco ($10,000)	N.Y. Giants ($10,000)	21-10	San Francisco	60,303
1983	Jan. 1	Washington ($10,000)	L.A. Rams ($10,000)	51-7	Washington	54,440
	Dec. 31	San Francisco ($10,000)	Detroit ($10,000)	24-23	San Francisco	59,979
1982	Jan. 16	Dallas ($10,000)	Green Bay ($10,000)	37-26	Dallas	63,972
	Jan. 15	Washington ($10,000)	Minnesota ($10,000)	21-7	Washington	54,593
1981	Jan. 3	San Francisco ($5,000)	N.Y. Giants ($5,000)	38-24	San Francisco	58,360
	Jan. 2	Dallas ($5,000)	Tampa Bay ($5,000)	38-0	Dallas	64,848
1980	Jan. 4	Dallas ($5,000)	Atlanta ($5,000)	30-27	Atlanta	59,793
	Jan. 3	Philadelphia ($5,000)	Minnesota ($5,000)	31-16	Philadelphia	70,178
1979	Dec. 30	Los Angeles ($5,000)	Dallas ($5,000)	21-19	Dallas	64,792
	Dec. 29	Tampa Bay ($5,000)	Philadelphia ($5,000)	24-17	Tampa Bay	71,402
1978	Dec. 31	Los Angeles ($5,000)	Minnesota ($5,000)	34-10	Los Angeles	70,436
	Dec. 30	Dallas ($5,000)	Atlanta ($5,000)	27-20	Dallas	63,406
1977	Dec. 26	Dallas ($5,000)	Chicago ($5,000)	37-7	Dallas	63,260
	Dec. 26	Minnesota ($5,000)	Los Angeles ($5,000)	14-7	Los Angeles	70,203
1976	Dec. 19	Los Angeles [$]	Dallas [$]	14-12	Dallas	63,283
	Dec. 18	Minnesota [$]	Washington [$]	35-20	Minneapolis	47,466
1975	Dec. 28	Dallas [$]	Minnesota [$]	17-14	Minneapolis	48,050
	Dec. 27	Los Angeles [$]	St. Louis [$]	35-23	Los Angeles	73,459
1974	Dec. 22	Los Angeles [$]	Washington [$]	19-10	Los Angeles	77,925
	Dec. 21	Minnesota [$]	St. Louis [$]	30-14	Minneapolis	48,150
1973	Dec. 23	Dallas [$]	Los Angeles [$]	27-16	Dallas	63,272
	Dec. 22	Minnesota [$]	Washington [$]	27-20	Minneapolis	48,040
1972	Dec. 24	Washington [$]	Green Bay [$]	16-3	Washington	52,321
	Dec. 23	Dallas [$]	San Francisco [$]	30-28	San Francisco	59,746
1971	Dec. 26	San Francisco [$]	Washington [$]	24-20	San Francisco	45,327
	Dec. 25	Dallas [$]	Minnesota [$]	20-12	Minneapolis	47,307

Season	Date	Winner (Share)	Loser (Share)	Score	Site	Attendance
1970	Dec. 27	San Francisco [$]	Minnesota [$]	17-14	Minneapolis	45,103
	Dec. 26	Dallas [$]	Detroit [$]	5-0	Dallas	69,613
1969	Dec. 28	Cleveland [$]	Dallas [$]	38-14	Dallas	69,321
	Dec. 27	Minnesota [$]	Los Angeles [$]	23-20	Minneapolis	47,900
1968	Dec. 22	Baltimore [$]	Minnesota [$]	24-14	Baltimore	60,238
	Dec. 21	Cleveland [$]	Dallas [$]	31-20	Cleveland	81,497
1967	Dec. 24	Dallas [$]	Cleveland [$]	52-14	Dallas	70,786
	Dec. 23	Green Bay [$]	Los Angeles [$]	28-7	Milwaukee	49,861
1965	Dec. 26	Green Bay [$]	Baltimore [$]	13-10*	Green Bay	50,484
1958	Dec. 21	N.Y. Giants (#)	Cleveland (#)	10-0	New York	61,274
1957	Dec. 22	Detroit (#)	San Francisco (#)	31-27	San Francisco	60,118
1952	Dec. 21	Detroit (#)	Los Angeles (#)	31-21	Detroit	47,645
1950	Dec. 17	Los Angeles (#)	Chicago Bears (#)	24-14	Los Angeles	83,501
	Dec. 17	Cleveland (#)	N.Y. Giants (#)	8-3	Cleveland	33,054
1947	Dec. 21	Philadelphia (#)	Pittsburgh (#)	21-0	Pittsburgh	35,729
1943	Dec. 19	Washington (¢)	N.Y. Giants (¢)	28-0	New York	42,800
1941	Dec. 14	Chicago Bears (¢)	Green Bay (¢)	33-14	Chicago	43,425

** Sudden death overtime*
[$] Players received 1/14 of annual salary for playoff appearances.
 # Players received 1/12 of annual salary for playoff appearances.
¢ Players received 1/10 of annual salary for playoff appearances.

2000 NFC DIVISIONAL PLAYOFF GAMES

Giants Stadium, East Rutherford, New Jersey
January 7, 2001, Attendance: 78,765

N.Y. GIANTS 20, PHILADELPHIA 10—Ron Dixon returned the opening kickoff 97 yards for a touchdown to spark the Giants to their first playoff victory since 1993. Dixon became the first player to begin a postseason game with a kickoff return for a touchdown since Miami's Nat Moore in 1974. The Giants' defense did not allow a first down during the Eagles' first three possessions, and on their fourth possession Torrance Small fumbled and Dave Thomas recovered to set up Brad Daluiso's 37-yard field goal. Late in the first half, Jason Sehorn made a diving interception, batting the ball in midair with one hand before catching it, got to his feet, and outran the Eagles to the end zone for a 17-0 Giants' lead. The Eagles got on the board when David Akers kicked a field goal before halftime, but Akers missed from 30 yards in the third quarter. James Bostic's blocked punt in the final minutes set up Donovan McNabb's 10-yard touchdown pass to Small to close out the scoring. Kerry Collins was 12 of 19 for 125 yards. McNabb completed 20 of 41 passes for 181 yards and 1 touchdown, with 1 interception. The clubs combined for only 423 total yards, but the Giants controlled the clock for 36:09 thanks to 112 rushing yards, including 53 from Ron Dayne and 35 from Tiki Barber, despite a broken left forearm.

Philadelphia	0	3	0	7	—	10
N.Y. Giants	7	10	0	3	—	20

NYG — Dixon 97 kickoff return (Daluiso kick)
NYG — FG Daluiso 37
NYG — Sehorn 32 interception return (Daluiso kick)
Phil — FG Akers 28
NYG — FG Daluiso 25
Phil — Small 10 pass from McNabb (Akers kick)

Metrodome, Minneapolis, Minnesota
January 6, 2001, Attendance: 63,881

MINNESOTA 34, NEW ORLEANS 16—Daunte Culpepper passed for 302 yards and 3 touchdowns as the Vikings defeated the Saints. The Vikings scored on their third play from scrimmage, when Randy Moss caught a short pass and raced untouched 53 yards for a touchdown. The Vikings led 10-3 late in the first half when Culpepper scrambled for 30 yards and, on the next play, fired a 17-yard touchdown pass to Cris Carter. Moss scored on the third play of the second half as well, again taking a quick pass and this time outrunning the Saints 68 yards for a touchdown and a 24-3 lead. Robert Tate's interception at the Saints' 29 late in the third quarter led to Robert Smith's 2-yard touchdown run to give the Vikings a 34-10 lead with 10:46 remaining. Culpepper completed 17 of 31 passes for 302 yards and 3 touchdowns. Moss had 2 catches for 121 yards, and Carter had 8 receptions for 120 yards. Aaron Brooks was 30 of 48 for 295 yards and 2 touchdowns, with 2 interceptions. Chad Morton had 13 catches for 106 yards, and Willie Jackson added 9 receptions for 125 yards.

New Orleans	3	0	7	6	—	16
Minnesota	10	7	10	7	—	34

Minn — Moss 53 pass from Culpepper (Anderson kick)
NO — FG Brien 33
Minn — FG Anderson 24
Minn — Carter 17 pass from Culpepper (Anderson kick)
Minn — Moss 68 pass from Culpepper (Anderson kick)
NO — Stachelski 2 pass from Brooks (Brien kick)
Minn — FG Anderson 44
Minn — Smith 2 run (Anderson kick)
NO — Jackson 48 pass from Brooks (pass failed)

AFC WILD CARD PLAYOFF GAMES RESULTS

Season	Date	Winner (Share)	Loser (Share)	Score	Site	Attendance
2000	Dec. 31	Baltimore (12,500)	Denver ($12,500)	21-3	Baltimore	69,638
	Dec. 30	Miami ($16,000)	Indianapolis ($12,500)	23-17*	Miami	73,193
1999	Jan. 9	Miami ($10,000)	Seattle ($16,000)	20-17	Seattle	66,170
	Jan. 8	Tennessee ($10,000)	Buffalo ($10,000)	22-16	Nashville	66,672
1998	Jan. 3	Jacksonville ($15,000)	New England ($10,000)	25-10	Jacksonville	71,139
	Jan. 2	Miami ($10,000)	Buffalo ($10,000)	24-17	Miami	72,698
1997	Dec. 28	New England ($15,000)	Miami ($10,000)	17-3	New England	60,041
	Dec. 27	Denver ($10,000)	Jacksonville ($10,000)	42-17	Denver	74,481
1996	Dec. 29	Pittsburgh ($14,000)	Indianapolis ($10,000)	42-14	Pittsburgh	58,078
	Dec. 28	Jacksonville ($10,000)	Buffalo ($10,000)	30-27	Buffalo	70,213
1995	Dec. 31	Indianapolis ($7,500)	San Diego ($7,500)	35-20	San Diego	61,182
	Dec. 30	Buffalo ($13,000)	Miami ($7,500)	37-22	Buffalo	73,103
1994	Jan. 1	Cleveland ($7,500)	New England ($7,500)	20-13	Cleveland	77,452
	Dec. 31	Miami ($12,000)	Kansas City ($7,500)	27-17	Miami	67,487
1993	Jan. 9	L.A. Raiders ($7,500)	Denver ($7,500)	42-24	Los Angeles	65,314
	Jan. 8	Kansas City ($12,000)	Pittsburgh ($7,500)	27-24*	Kansas City	74,515
1992	Jan. 3	Buffalo ($6,000)	Houston ($6,000)	41-38*	Buffalo	75,141
	Jan. 2	San Diego ($10,000)	Kansas City ($6,000)	17-0	San Diego	58,278
1991	Dec. 29	Houston ($10,000)	N.Y. Jets ($6,000)	17-10	Houston	61,485
	Dec. 28	Kansas City ($6,000)	L.A. Raiders ($6,000)	10-6	Kansas City	75,827
1990	Jan. 6	Cincinnati ($10,000)	Houston ($6,000)	41-14	Cincinnati	60,012
	Jan. 5	Miami ($6,000)	Kansas City ($6,000)	17-16	Miami	67,276
1989	Dec. 31	Pittsburgh ($6,000)	Houston ($6,000)	26-23*	Houston	59,406
1988	Dec. 26	Houston ($6,000)	Cleveland ($6,000)	24-23	Cleveland	75,896
1987	Jan. 3	Houston ($6,000)	Seattle ($6,000)	23-20*	Houston	50,519
1986	Dec. 28	N.Y. Jets ($6,000)	Kansas City ($6,000)	35-15	East Rutherford	75,210
1985	Dec. 28	New England ($6,000)	N.Y. Jets ($6,000)	26-14	East Rutherford	75,945
1984	Dec. 22	Seattle ($6,000)	L.A. Raiders ($6,000)	13-7	Seattle	62,049
1983	Dec. 24	Seattle ($6,000)	Denver ($6,000)	31-7	Seattle	64,275

PLAYOFF GAMES SUMMARIES

Season	Date	Winner (Share)	Loser (Share)	Score	Site	Attendance
1982	Jan. 9	N.Y. Jets ($6,000)	Cincinnati ($6,000)	44-17	Cincinnati	57,560
	Jan. 9	San Diego ($6,000)	Pittsburgh ($6,000)	31-28	Pittsburgh	53,546
	Jan. 8	L.A. Raiders ($6,000)	Cleveland ($6,000)	27-10	Los Angeles	56,555
	Jan. 8	Miami ($6,000)	New England ($6,000)	28-13	Miami	68,842
1981	Dec. 27	Buffalo ($3,000)	N.Y. Jets ($3,000)	31-27	New York	57,050
1980	Dec. 28	Oakland ($3,000)	Houston ($3,000)	27-7	Oakland	53,333
1979	Dec. 23	Houston ($3,000)	Denver ($3,000)	13-7	Houston	48,776
1978	Dec. 24	Houston ($3,000)	Miami ($3,000)	17-9	Miami	72,445

**Sudden death overtime*

2000 AFC WILD CARD PLAYOFF GAMES

PSINet Stadium, Baltimore, Maryland
December 31, 2000, Attendance: 69,638

BALTIMORE 21, DENVER 3—Rookie Jamal Lewis rushed for 110 yards and 2 touchdowns, and the Ravens' defense permitted the Broncos to cross midfield just once, as the city of Baltimore hosted its first NFL playoff game since 1977. Trent Dilfer completed 2 key passes to Qadry Ismail before Lewis scored on a 1-yard run early in the second quarter to give the Ravens a 7-0 lead. The Broncos responded with their lone sustained drive of the day, but Mike Anderson was stopped for no gain on third-and-1 and Denver settled for Jason Elam's 31-yard field goal with 4:31 remaining in the first half. On the Ravens' next play, Dilfer's short pass deflected off the hands of Lewis and Terrell Buckley before being caught by Shannon Sharpe, who eluded two tacklers and raced 58 yards into the end zone to give the Ravens a 14-3 lead. The Broncos never threatened again, and Lewis's 27-yard scoring run in the third quarter capped the Ravens' victory in the franchise's first postseason game. The Ravens' defense limited the Broncos to just 9 first downs and 42 rushing yards. Dilfer completed 9 of 14 passes for 130 yards and 1 touchdown. Gus Frerotte, who played for the injured Brian Griese, was 13 of 28 for 124 yards, with 1 interception.

Denver	0	3	0	0 —	3
Baltimore	0	14	7	0 —	21

Balt — Ja. Lewis 1 run (Stover kick)
Den — FG Elam 31
Balt — Sharpe 58 pass from Dilfer (Stover kick)
Balt — Ja. Lewis 27 run (Stover kick)

Pro Player Stadium, Miami, Florida
December 30, 2000, Attendance: 73,193

MIAMI 23, INDIANAPOLIS 17 (OT)—Lamar Smith's 17-yard touchdown run around right end 11:26 into overtime capped a remarkable performance and lifted the Dolphins to a come-from-behind victory. Smith rushed for 209 yards, the second most in playoff history, on an NFL-postseason record 40 carries to wear down the Colts' defense and give Miami a 43:40-27:46 time of possession advantage. The Colts led 3-0 early in the second quarter when the Dolphins dropped holder Hunter Smith for a 6-yard loss on a fake field-goal attempt. However, the Colts' defense responded with interceptions on the Dolphins' next two possessions, which resulted in 11 points, capped by Peyton Manning's 17-yard pass to Jerome Pathon to take a 14-0 lead. The Dolphins opened the second half with an 11-play, 70-yard drive, which consisted of 7 carries by Smith, and was capped by Smith's 2-yard touchdown run. The teams exchanged field goals, including a 50-yard kick by Mike Vanderjagt with 4:55 remaining, to give the Colts a 17-10 lead. The Dolphins methodically drove down field, keyed by Jay Fiedler's 19- and 13-yard passes to O.J. McDuffie, and tied the game on Fiedler's third-and-goal pass to Jed Weaver from 9 yards out with 34 seconds remaining. The Colts ran out the clock, and the Dolphins won the overtime coin toss but were forced to punt after gaining one first down. Manning hit Marvin Harrison with a 30-yard pass on the Colts' first play of overtime and the Colts moved the ball into Dolphins' territory. Faced with third-and-12 from the Dolphins' 42, Manning completed an 11-yard pass to Harrison. The Dolphins were offside on the play, but the Colts elected to take the play and allow Vanderjagt to attempt a 49-yard field goal. Vanderjagt's kick missed wide right, and the Dolphins marched 61 yards in 11 plays, capped by Smith dragging Jeff Burris into the end zone on his game-winning run. Fiedler completed 19 of 34 passes for 185 yards and 1 touchdown, with 3 interceptions. Manning was 17 of 32 for 194 yards and 1 touchdown. Edgerrin James had 21 carries for 107 yards.

Indianapolis	3	11	0	3	0 —	17
Miami	0	0	7	10	6 —	23

Ind — FG Vanderjagt 32
Ind — FG Vanderjagt 26
Ind — Pathon 17 pass from Manning (Dilger pass from Manning)
Mia — Smith 2 run (Mare kick)
Mia — FG Mare 38
Ind — FG Vanderjagt 50
Mia — Weaver 9 pass from Fiedler (Mare kick)
Mia — Smith 17 run

NFC WILD CARD PLAYOFF GAMES RESULTS

Season	Date	Winner (Share)	Loser (Share)	Score	Site	Attendance
2000	Dec. 31	Philadelphia ($12,500)	Tampa Bay ($12,500)	21-3	Philadelphia	65,813
	Dec. 30	New Orleans ($16,000)	St. Louis ($12,500)	31-28	New Orleans	64,900
1999	Jan. 9	Minnesota ($10,000)	Dallas ($10,000)	27-10	Minneapolis	64,056
	Jan. 8	Washington ($16,000)	Detroit ($10,000)	27-13	Washington	79,411
1998	Jan. 3	San Francisco ($10,000)	Green Bay ($10,000)	30-27	San Francisco	66,506
	Jan. 2	Arizona ($10,000)	Dallas ($15,000)	20-7	Dallas	62,969
1997	Dec. 28	Tampa Bay ($10,000)	Detroit ($10,000)	20-10	Tampa Bay	73,361
	Dec. 27	Minnesota ($10,000)	N.Y. Giants ($15,000)	23-22	East Rutherford	77,497
1996	Dec. 29	San Francisco ($10,000)	Philadelphia ($10,000)	14-0	San Francisco	56,460
	Dec. 28	Dallas ($14,000)	Minnesota ($10,000)	40-15	Dallas	64,682
1995	Dec. 31	Green Bay ($13,000)	Atlanta ($7,500)	37-20	Green Bay	60,453
	Dec. 30	Philadelphia ($7,500)	Detroit ($7,500)	58-37	Philadelphia	66,099
1994	Jan. 1	Chicago ($7,500)	Minnesota ($12,000)	35-18	Minnesota	60,347
	Dec. 31	Green Bay ($7,500)	Detroit ($7,500)	16-12	Green Bay	58,125
1993	Jan. 9	N.Y. Giants ($7,500)	Minnesota ($7,500)	17-10	East Rutherford	75,089
	Jan. 8	Green Bay ($7,500)	Detroit ($12,000)	28-24	Detroit	68,479
1992	Jan. 3	Philadelphia ($6,000)	New Orleans ($6,000)	36-20	New Orleans	68,893
	Jan. 2	Washington ($6,000)	Minnesota ($10,000)	24-7	Minnesota	57,353
1991	Dec. 29	Dallas ($6,000)	Chicago ($6,000)	17-13	Chicago	62,594
	Dec. 28	Atlanta ($6,000)	New Orleans ($10,000)	27-20	New Orleans	68,794
1990	Jan. 6	Chicago ($10,000)	New Orleans ($6,000)	16-6	Chicago	60,767
	Jan. 5	Washington ($6,000)	Philadelphia ($6,000)	20-6	Philadelphia	65,287
1989	Dec. 31	L.A. Rams ($6,000)	Philadelphia ($6,000)	21-7	Philadelphia	65,479
1988	Dec. 26	Minnesota ($6,000)	L.A. Rams ($6,000)	28-17	Minnesota	61,204
1987	Jan. 3	Minnesota ($6,000)	New Orleans ($6,000)	44-10	New Orleans	68,546
1986	Dec. 28	Washington ($6,000)	L.A. Rams ($6,000)	19-7	Washington	54,567
1985	Dec. 29	N.Y. Giants ($6,000)	San Francisco ($6,000)	17-3	East Rutherford	75,131
1984	Dec. 23	N.Y. Giants ($6,000)	L.A. Rams ($6,000)	16-13	Anaheim	67,037
1983	Dec. 26	L.A. Rams ($6,000)	Dallas ($6,000)	24-17	Dallas	62,118
1982	Jan. 9	Dallas ($6,000)	Tampa Bay ($6,000)	30-17	Dallas	65,042
	Jan. 9	Minnesota ($6,000)	Atlanta ($6,000)	30-24	Minnesota	60,560
	Jan. 8	Green Bay ($6,000)	St. Louis ($6,000)	41-16	Green Bay	54,282
	Jan. 8	Washington ($6,000)	Detroit ($6,000)	31-7	Washington	55,045
1981	Dec. 27	N.Y. Giants ($3,000)	Philadelphia ($3,000)	27-21	Philadelphia	71,611
1980	Dec. 28	Dallas ($3,000)	Los Angeles ($3,000)	34-13	Dallas	63,052
1979	Dec. 23	Philadelphia ($3,000)	Chicago ($3,000)	27-17	Philadelphia	69,397
1978	Dec. 24	Atlanta ($3,000)	Philadelphia ($3,000)	14-13	Atlanta	59,403

2000 NFC WILD CARD PLAYOFF GAMES

Veterans Stadium, Philadelphia, Pennsylvania
December 31, 2000, Attendance: 65,813

PHILADELPHIA 21, TAMPA BAY 3—Donovan McNabb passed for 2 touchdowns and ran for another, and the Eagles' defense limited the Buccaneers to just 11 first downs. The Buccaneers dropped to 0-20 when the game-time temperature is below 40 degrees, though Martin Gramatica's 29-yard field goal early in the second quarter staked Tampa Bay to a 3-0 lead. The tide changed a few possessions later when Hugh Douglas sacked Shaun King from behind, forced him to fumble, and Mike Mamula recovered at the Buccaneers' 15. Four plays later, McNabb scrambled 5 yards up the middle for a touchdown with 3:21 left in the half. The Eagles' defense then forced Tampa Bay to punt, and McNabb engineered an 8-play, 69-yard drive, keyed by his 25-yard pass to Charles Johnson. McNabb capped the march with a 5-yard touchdown pass to Na Brown 12 seconds before halftime to take a 14-3 lead. McNabb's 2-yard pass to Jeff Thomason on third-and-goal less than a minute into the fourth quarter finished the scoring. The Buccaneers threatened once in the second half, but King threw consecutive incompletions from the Eagles' 21 with just under four minutes remaining to seal the victory. The Eagles converted 9 of 18 third-down plays, while allowing the Buccaneers to convert just 3 of 13 third-down situations. McNabb completed 24 of 33 passes for 161 yards and 2 touchdowns, with 1 interception. King was 17 of 31 for 171 yards. Keyshawn Johnson had 6 receptions for 106 yards.

Tampa Bay	0	3	0	0	—	3
Philadelphia	0	14	0	7	—	21

TB — FG Gramatica 29
Phil — McNabb 5 run (Akers kick)
Phil — Brown 5 pass from McNabb (Akers kick)
Phil — Thomason 2 pass from McNabb (Akers kick)

Louisiana Superdome, New Orleans, Lousiana
December 30, 2000, Attendance: 64,900

NEW ORLEANS 31, ST. LOUIS 28—Aaron Brooks passed for 4 touchdowns, and Brian Milne recovered Az-Zahir Hakim's muffed punt return with 1:43 remaining to secure the first playoff victory in Saints' history. The defending Super Bowl champion Rams scored on their first possession, driving 68 yards in 11 plays and taking a 7-0 lead on Kurt Warner's 17-yard pass to Isaac Bruce, but were then shut out for the next 40 minutes. The Saints drove 70 yards on their ensuing possession to tie the game on Brooks's 12-yard pass to Robert Wilson, who had not caught a touchdown pass all season. Sammy Knight's 52-yard interception return to the Rams' 20 set up Doug Brien's 33-yard field goal just before halftime, giving New Orleans a 10-7 lead. Chris Oldham's third-quarter interception near midfield led to Brooks's 10-yard touchdown pass to Willie Jackson, and Brooks and Jackson hooked up for 2 more scores within the first 3:03 of the fourth quarter to give the Saints a 31-7 lead with 11:57 remaining. The Rams needed just 4 plays, capped by Warner's 17-yard pass to Ricky Proehl, to cut the deficit to 31-13, and Hakim's 65-yard punt return to the Saints' 9 moments later gave the Rams hope. But Knight intercepted Warner on the next play from scrimmage with 6:28 remaining. However, the Rams' defense forced a punt, and St. Louis needed just 3 plays to drive 62 yards and cut the deficit to 31-20 on Marshall Faulk's 25-yard catch and run. Dre' Bly recovered the ensuing onside kick, and a 38-yard pass to Hakim set up Warner's 5-yard touchdown run. Warner's quick pass to Faulk for the 2-point conversion trimmed the deficit to 31-28 with 2:36 left. Darrin Smith recovered the onside kick for the Saints, but the Rams' defense again forced a punt. Hakim muffed the punt and Milne recovered the ball at the Saints' 11 to seal the victory. Brooks completed 16 of 29 passes for 266 yards and 4 touchdowns, with 1 interception. Jackson had 6 receptions for 142 yards. Warner was 24 of 40 for 365 yards and 3 touchdowns, with 3 interceptions. Bruce had 7 receptions for 127 yards.

St. Louis	7	0	0	21	—	28
New Orleans	0	10	7	14	—	31

StL — Bruce 17 pass from Warner (Wilkins kick)
NO — Wilson 12 pass from Brooks (Brien kick)
NO — FG Brien 33
NO — Jackson 10 pass from Brooks (Brien kick)
NO — Jackson 49 pass from Brooks (Brien kick)
NO — Jackson 16 pass from Brooks (Brien kick)
StL — Proehl 17 pass from Warner (run failed)
StL — Faulk 25 pass from Warner (Wilkins kick)
StL — Warner 5 run (Faulk pass from Warner)

AFC-NFC PRO BOWL SUMMARIES

AFC-NFC PRO BOWL AT A GLANCE RESULTS (1971-2001)

NFC leads series, 16-15

Year	Date	Winner (Share)	Loser (Share)	Score	Site	Attendance
2001	Feb. 4	AFC ($30,000)	NFC ($15,00)	38-17	Honolulu	50,128
2000	Feb. 6	NFC ($25,000)	AFC ($12,500)	51-31	Honolulu	50,112
1999	Feb. 7	AFC ($25,000)	NFC ($12,500)	23-10	Honolulu	50,075
1998	Feb. 1	AFC ($25,000)	NFC ($12,500)	29-24	Honolulu	49,995
1997	Feb. 2	AFC ($20,000)	NFC ($10,000)	26-23 (OT)	Honolulu	50,031
1996	Feb. 4	NFC ($20,000)	AFC ($10,000)	20-13	Honolulu	50,034
1995	Feb. 5	AFC ($20,000)	NFC ($10,000)	41-13	Honolulu	49,121
1994	Feb. 6	NFC ($20,000)	AFC ($10,000)	17-3	Honolulu	50,026
1993	Feb. 7	AFC ($10,000)	NFC ($5,000)	23-20 (OT)	Honolulu	50,007
1992	Feb. 2	NFC ($10,000)	AFC ($5,000)	21-15	Honolulu	50,209
1991	Feb. 3	AFC ($10,000)	NFC ($5,000)	23-21	Honolulu	50,345
1990	Feb. 4	NFC ($10,000)	AFC ($5,000)	27-21	Honolulu	50,445
1989	Jan. 29	NFC ($10,000)	AFC ($5,000)	34-3	Honolulu	50,113
1988	Feb. 7	AFC ($10,000)	NFC ($5,000)	15-6	Honolulu	50,113
1987	Feb. 1	AFC ($10,000)	NFC ($5,000)	10-6	Honolulu	50,101
1986	Feb. 2	NFC ($10,000)	AFC ($5,000)	28-24	Honolulu	50,101
1985	Jan. 27	AFC ($10,000)	NFC ($5,000)	22-14	Honolulu	50,385
1984	Jan. 29	NFC ($10,000)	AFC ($5,000)	45-3	Honolulu	50,445
1983	Feb. 6	NFC ($10,000)	AFC ($5,000)	20-19	Honolulu	49,883
1982	Jan. 31	AFC ($5,000)	NFC ($2,500)	16-13	Honolulu	50,402
1981	Feb. 1	NFC ($5,000)	AFC ($2,500)	21-7	Honolulu	50,360
1980	Jan. 27	NFC ($5,000)	AFC ($2,500)	37-27	Honolulu	49,800
1979	Jan. 29	NFC ($5,000)	AFC ($2,500)	13-7	Los Angeles	46,281
1978	Jan. 23	NFC ($5,000)	AFC ($2,500)	14-13	Tampa	51,337
1977	Jan. 17	AFC ($2,000)	NFC ($1,500)	24-14	Seattle	64,752
1976	Jan. 26	NFC ($2,000)	AFC ($1,500)	23-20	New Orleans	30,546
1975	Jan. 20	NFC ($2,000)	AFC ($1,500)	17-10	Miami	26,484
1974	Jan. 20	AFC ($2,000)	NFC ($1,500)	15-13	Kansas City	66,918
1973	Jan. 21	AFC ($2,000)	NFC ($1,500)	33-28	Dallas	37,091
1972	Jan. 23	AFC ($2,000)	NFC ($1,500)	26-13	Los Angeles	53,647
1971	Jan. 24	NFC ($2,000)	AFC ($1,500)	27-6	Los Angeles	48,222

2001 AFC-NFC PRO BOWL

Aloha Stadium, Honolulu, Hawaii
February 4, 2001, Attendance: 50,128

AFC 38, NFC 17—Rich Gannon completed 12 of 14 passes for 160 yards during the game's first two possessions to win player of the game honors and lead the AFC to victory. Gannon's touchdown passes capped 87- and 90-yard drives and staked the AFC to a 14-0 lead. Gannon, who was still recovering from a separated non-throwing shoulder suffered in the AFC Championship Game, was replaced by Peyton Manning. The Colts' quarterback engineered a scoring drive, capped by Matt Stover's field goal, to give the AFC a 17-0 lead early in the second quarter. At that point, the AFC had 14 first downs and 231 yards of offense while limiting the NFC to no first downs and 6 yards. Jimmy Smith caught a 2-yard touchdown pass 54 seconds before halftime to give the AFC a 24-3 lead. Third-quarter touchdown passes by Donovan McNabb and Daunte Culpepper trimmed the AFC's lead to 31-17, but Jason Taylor batted down Culpepper's fourth-and-1 pass early in the fourth quarter, and Edgerrin James's 20-yard touchdown run a few plays later iced the game. The NFC attempted a Pro Bowl record 56 pass attempts, and the two teams combined for a Pro Bowl record 98 pass attempts. Tony Gonzalez had 6 receptions for 108 yards, all in the first half, for the AFC. Torry Holt had 7 receptions for 103 yards. Smith's touchdown reception gives him 5 for his career, an AFC-NFC Pro Bowl record.

NFC (17)	Offense	AFC (38)
Cris Carter (Minnesota)	WR	Marvin Harrison (Indianapolis)
Orlando Pace (St. Louis)	LT	Jonathan Ogden (Baltimore)
Randall McDaniel (Tampa Bay)	LG	Ruben Brown (Buffalo)
Jeff Christy (Tampa Bay)	C	Kevin Mawae (N.Y. Jets)
Larry Allen (Dallas)	RG	Steve Wisniewski (Oakland)
William Roaf (New Orleans)	RT	Brad Hopkins (Tennessee)
Chad Lewis (Philadelphia)	TE	Tony Gonzalez (Kansas City)
Torry Holt (St. Louis)	WR	Eric Moulds (Buffalo)
Daunte Culpepper (Minnesota)	QB	Rich Gannon (Oakland)
Mike Alstott (Tampa Bay)	RB	Richie Anderson (N.Y. Jets)
Charlie Garner (San Francisco)	RB	Edgerrin James (Indianapolis)
	Defense	
Hugh Douglas (Philadelphia)	LE	Jason Taylor (Miami)
Warren Sapp (Tampa Bay)	LT	Trevor Pryce (Denver)
La'Roi Glover (New Orleans)	RT	Sam Adams (Baltimore)
Joe Johnson (New Orleans)	RE	Trace Armstrong (Miami)
Derrick Brooks (Tampa Bay)	LOLB	Mo Lewis (N.Y. Jets)
Jeremiah Trotter (Philadelphia)	MLB	Ray Lewis (Baltimore)
Jessie Armstead (N.Y. Giants)	ROLB	Junior Seau (San Diego)
Champ Bailey (Washington)	LCB	Sam Madison (Miami)
Troy Vincent (Philadelphia)	RCB	Samari Rolle (Tennessee)
John Lynch (Tampa Bay)	SS	Blaine Bishop (Tennessee)
Darren Sharper (Green Bay)	FS	Rod Woodson (Baltimore)

SUBSTITUTIONS

NFC—Offense: G—Ron Stone (N.Y. Giants). T—Korey Stringer (Minnesota). C—Matt Birk (Minnesota). TE—Stephen Alexander (Washington). WR—Joe Horn (New Orleans), Terrell Owens (San Francisco). RB—Stephen Davis (Washington), Warrick Dunn (Tampa Bay). QB—Jeff Garcia (San Francisco), Donovan McNabb (Philadelphia). P—Scott Player (Arizona). K—Martin Gramatica (Tampa Bay). KR—Desmond Howard (Detroit). Defense: DT—Luther Elliss (Detroit). DE—Marco Coleman (Washington). LB—Mark Fields (New Orleans), Keith Mitchell (New Orleans), Brian Urlacher (Chicago). DB—Donnie Abraham (Tampa Bay), Robert Griffith (Minnesota). ST—Michael Bates (Carolina).

AFC—Offense: G—Will Shields (Kansas City). T—Lincoln Kennedy (Oakland). C—Tim Ruddy (Miami). TE—Frank Wycheck (Tennessee). WR—Jimmy Smith (Jacksonville), Rod Smith (Denver). RB—Corey Dillon (Cincinnati), Eddie George (Tennessee). QB—Elvis Grbac (Kansas City), Peyton Manning (Indianapolis). P—Darren Bennett (San Diego). K—Matt Stover (Baltimore). KR—Derrick Mason (Tennessee). Defense: DT—Ted Washington (Buffalo). DE—Jevon Kearse (Tennessee). LB—Sam Cowart (Buffalo), Jason Gildon (Pittsburgh), Zach Thomas (Miami). DB—Brock Marion (Miami), Charles Woodson (Oakland). ST—Larry Izzo (Miami).

HEAD COACHES

NFC—Dennis Green (Minnesota)
AFC—Jon Gruden (Oakland)

OFFICIALS

Referee—Bob McElwee. Umpire—Butch Hannah. Side Judge—Rick Patterson. Head Linesman—Paul Weidner. Back Judge—Billy Smith. Field Judge—Tom Sifferman. Line Judge—Tom Stephan.

NFC	0	3	14	0	—	17
AFC	14	10	7	7	—	38

AFC — Gonzalez 8 pass from Gannon (Stover kick)
AFC — Harrison 16 pass from Gannon (Stover kick)
AFC — FG Stover 29
NFC — FG Gramatica 48
AFC — J. Smith 2 pass from Manning (Stover kick)
NFC — Owens 17 pass from McNabb (Gramatica kick)
AFC — Harrison 24 pass from Manning (Stover kick)
NFC — Holt 20 pass from Culpepper (Gramatica kick)
AFC — James 20 run (Stover kick)

TEAM STATISTICS	NFC	AFC
Total First Downs	20	29
Rushing	1	5
Passing	17	23
Penalty	2	1
Total Net Yardage	333	431

Total Offensive Plays	65	69
Average Gain Per Offensive Play	5.1	6.2
Rushes	9	23
Yards Gained Rushing (Net)	36	83
Average Yards per Rush	4.0	3.6
Passes Attempted	56	42
Passes Completed	28	32
Had Intercepted	3	1
Tackled Attempting to Pass	0	4
Yards Lost Attempting to Pass	0	21
Yards Gained Passing (Net)	297	348
Punts	3	3
Average Distance	48.7	39.0
Punt Returns	1	2
Punt Return Yardage	11	33
Kickoff Returns	7	3
Kickoff Return Yardage	187	70
Interception Return Yardage	0	17
Total Return Yardage	198	120
Fumbles	1	1
Fumbles Lost	1	0
Own Fumbles Recovered	0	1
Opponent Fumbles Recovered	0	1
Penalties	1	7
Yards Penalized	17	55
Field Goals	1	1
Field Goals Attempted	1	1
Third-Down Efficiency	7/14	3/9
Fourth-Down Efficiency	1/2	1/1
Time of Possession	25:42	34:18

INDIVIDUAL STATISTICS
RUSHING: NFC: Culpepper 2-16-0, Dunn 2-13-0, Alstott 2-7-0, Garner 2-3-0, Garcia 1-(-3)-0. AFC: George 8-31-0, James 4-26-1, Dillon 5-16-0, Grbac 3-7-0, Anderson 2-4-0, Manning 1-(-1)-0.
PASSING: NFC: Garcia 28-15-144-0-1, Culpepper 21-9-81-1-1, McNabb 7-4-72-1-1. AFC: Manning 22-16-150-2-0, Gannon 14-12-160-2-0, Grbac 6-4-59-0-1.
RECEIVING: NFC: Holt 7-103-1, Dunn 7-69-0, Owens 5-50-1, Carter 5-41-0, Alexander 1-16-0, Lewis 1-11-0, Alstott 1-4-0, Garner 1-3-0. AFC: Harrison 8-84-2, Gonzalez 6-108-1, Moulds 6-65-0, Wycheck 3-23-0, Dillon 2-36-0, J. Smith 2-12-1, Anderson 2-8-0, James 1-15-0, R. Smith 1-12-0, Mason 1-6-0.
KICKOFF RETURNS: NFC: Howard 5-136-0, Bates 1-32-0, Alstott 1-19-0. AFC: Mason 3-70-0.
PUNT RETURNS: NFC: Howard 1-11-0. AFC: Mason 2-33-0.
PUNTING: NFC: Player 3-146-48.7. AFC: Bennett 3-117-39.0.
INTERCEPTIONS: NFC: Bailey 1-0. AFC: M. Lewis 1-16, Rolle 1-1, Marion 1-0.
SACKS: NFC: Coleman, Douglas, Johnson, Sapp.

2000 AFC-NFC PRO BOWL

Aloha Stadium, Honolulu, Hawaii
February 6, 2000, Attendance: 50,112

NFC 51, AFC 31—Randy Moss earned player of the game honors by setting records with 9 receptions for 212 yards as the NFC defeated the AFC in the highest-scoring Pro Bowl ever. Aeneas Williams intercepted Peyton Manning's pass and raced 62 yards down the left sideline to give the NFC an early 7-0 lead. Kurt Warner's 48-yard pass to Moss on the NFC's first possession set up Jason Hanson's first field goal. Mike Alstott and Jimmy Smith each scored twice in the first half, and Michael Bates's 66-yard kickoff return led to Hanson's Pro Bowl-record tying 51-yard field goal as the half expired to give the NFC a 27-21 lead. Alstott's third touchdown increased the NFC's lead to 37-21, and Derrick Brooks's interception of Mark Brunell and 20-yard return staked the NFC to a 44-24 lead with 11:12 left. The AFC responded with Manning's 52-yard touchdown pass to Smith with 6:30 remaining, but Steve Beuerlein found Moss with a 25-yard scoring pass with 1:05 left to finish the scoring. Warner led the three NFC quarterbacks by completing 8 of 11 passes for 123 yards. Alstott led all rushers with 13 carries for 67 yards. The NFC forced 6 turnovers. Manning was 17 of 23 for 270 yards and 2 touchdowns, with 2 interceptions. Smith had 8 receptions for 119 yards. The previous record, 64 points, was set in 1980.

AFC	7	14	0	10	—	31
NFC	10	17	10	14	—	51

NFC — A. Williams 62 interception return (Hanson kick)
NFC — FG Hanson 21
AFC — J. Smith 5 pass from Brunell (Mare kick)
NFC — Alstott 1 run (Hanson kick)
AFC — Gonzalez 10 pass from Gannon (Mare kick)
NFC — Alstott 3 run (Hanson kick)
AFC — J. Smith 21 pass from Manning (Mare kick)
NFC — FG Hanson 51
NFC — Alstott 1 run (Hanson kick)
NFC — FG Hanson 23
AFC — FG Mare 33
NFC — Brooks 20 interception return (Hanson kick)
AFC — J. Smith 52 pass from Manning (Mare kick)
NFC — Moss 25 pass from Beuerlein (Hanson kick)

1999 AFC-NFC PRO BOWL

Aloha Stadium, Honolulu, Hawaii
February 7, 1999, Attendance: 50,075

AFC 23, NFC 10—John Elway, appearing in uniform on a football field for the final time, drove the AFC to its initial touchdown and then watched a strong defensive effort as the AFC won the Pro Bowl for the third consecutive season. Elway capped a game-opening 61-yard drive with a touchdown pass to Sam Gash. The AFC led 10-3 late in the first half when Deion Sanders intercepted a Vinny Testaverde pass at the NFC's 10 and raced downfield, only to be caught by Ed McCaffrey at the AFC 3-yard line as the half expired. The NFC drove into AFC territory early in the second half, but Ty Law thwarted the NFC's spirits with a 67-yard interception return for a touchdown to give the AFC a 17-3 lead with 9:42 left in the third quarter. The NFC reached the end zone three minutes later as Emmitt Smith scored, but the AFC responded with a field goal on its ensuing possession. Jason Elam's third field goal with 1:02 remaining finished the scoring. Elway played just one drive and was 4 of 5 for 55 yards and 1 touchdown. Keyshawn Johnson had 7 catches for 87 yards and shared player of the game honors with Law. Chandler completed 9 of 25 passes for 133 yards en route to leading the NFC to its only touchdown. Randy Moss had 7 catches for 108 yards.

NFC	3	0	7	0	—	10
AFC	7	3	10	3	—	23

AFC — Gash 3 pass from Elway (Elam kick)
NFC — FG Anderson 23
AFC — FG Elam 23
AFC — Law 67 interception return (Elam kick)
NFC — E. Smith 3 run (Anderson kick)
AFC — FG Elam 46
AFC — FG Elam 26

1998 AFC-NFC PRO BOWL

Aloha Stadium, Honolulu, Hawaii
February 1, 1998, Attendance: 49,995

AFC 29, NFC 24—Warren Moon guided the AFC to points on all three of his drives, including the winning touchdown from 1 yard with 1:49 left as the AFC scored the game's final 15 points to beat the NFC. Steve Young threw a 22-yard touchdown pass to Herman Moore to cap the game's opening drive and give the NFC a 7-0 lead. Late in the first quarter, Mark Brunell threw a 17-yard touchdown pass to Andre Rison to tie the game. Both touchdown passes came on third-and-8 plays. The NFC responded with a 7-play, 71-yard drive capped by Young's 36-yard touchdown pass to Rob Moore. Trent Dilfer guided the NFC to its third touchdown, keyed by a 21-yard pass to Irving Fryar and 23-yard pass to Mike Alstott, and capped by Dorsey Levens's 12-yard touchdown run with 1:36 left in the half to give the NFC a 21-7 lead. The NFC had a chance to pad its lead on its first possession of the second half, but Jason Hanson missed a 44-yard field goal. The AFC bounced back with a 10-play, 65-yard drive that culminated with Drew Bledsoe's 14-yard touchdown pass to Jimmy Smith late in the third quarter. After Hanson's 35-yard field goal gave the NFC a 24-14 lead with 13:42 left, Moon entered the game and drove the AFC into field-goal range, where Mike Hollis drilled a 48-yard attempt with 8:51 left. Attempting to grind out the clock, Warrick Dunn fumbled, and Darryl Williams recovered at the AFC's 49 with 3:03 remaining. After a holding penalty moved the AFC back 10 yards, Moon fired a 57-yard pass to Tim Brown to set up Eddie George's 4-yard run with 2:31 left. The AFC went for the lead instead of a tie, but Moon's pass to Rison fell incomplete. However, the AFC got the ball back when Chris Chandler fumbled the snap on the NFC's first play, and Michael Sinclair recovered at the NFC's 16 with 2:19 left. Three runs by George set up Moon's winning sneak with 1:49 remaining. Moon's 2-point conversion pass to Brown was incomplete, keeping the AFC's lead at 29-24. The NFC was unable to move beyond its own 31-yard line in the final moments, and the AFC prevailed. Tim Brown had 5 receptions for 129 yards. Moon, who was 4 of 8 for 89 yards, earned player of the game honors.

AFC	7	0	7	15	—	29
NFC	7	14	0	3	—	24

NFC — H. Moore 22 pass from Young (Hanson kick)
AFC — Rison 17 pass from Brunell (Hollis kick)
NFC — R. Moore 36 pass from Young (Hanson kick)
NFC — Levens 12 run (Hanson kick)
AFC — J. Smith 14 pass from Bledsoe (Hollis kick)
NFC — FG Hanson 35
AFC — FG Hollis 48
AFC — George 4 run (pass failed)
AFC — Moon 1 run (pass failed)

1997 AFC-NFC PRO BOWL

Aloha Stadium, Honolulu, Hawaii
February 2, 1997, Attendance: 50,031

AFC 26, NFC 23 (OT)—Cary Blanchard's 37-yard field goal 8:16 into overtime gave the AFC a 26-23 victory. The field goal was an ironic ending to a game that saw Blanchard and NFC kicker John Kasay, who each broke the previous single-season record of 35 field goals, combine to miss 5 of 8 field-goal attempts. The NFC scored on its first two possessions, with Vikings guard Randall McDaniel, who lined up as a fullback, scoring his first professional touchdown to give the NFC a 9-0 lead. However, the follies of the kicking unit began as holder Matt Turk muffed the snap on the extra point attempt. Blanchard booted a 28-yard field goal with 27 seconds left in the half to cut the NFC's lead to 9-3. In the third quarter, Barry Sanders scored from 6 yards out, but Kerry Collins was sacked on the 2-point attempt. A 41-yard pass from Drew Bledsoe to Tony Martin led to Curtis Martin's 3-yard run, and after Ashley Ambrose ran an interception back 54 yards for a touchdown 11 seconds into the fourth quarter, the AFC found itself with a 16-15 lead. The NFC drove for more than six minutes, only to have Kasay miss a 40-yard field goal attempt. After an AFC punt, Cris Carter caught a 47-yard touchdown bomb from Gus Frerotte to put the NFC ahead 23-16. After each team punted, the AFC got the ball on its own 20-yard line with 55 seconds left. Mark Brunell hit Tim Brown with an 80-yard bomb down the right sideline to tie the game with 44 seconds left. Wesley Walls caught a 33-yard pass to give the NFC a chance to win in regulation, but Kasay missed a 39-yard attempt and the game went to overtime. The AFC won the overtime toss, but Blanchard missed a 41-yard field goal attempt. The NFC had to punt after three plays, and Brunell hit Ben Coates with a 43-yard pass on the AFC's first play. After three running plays failed to gain a first down, Blanchard trotted onto the field and made the game-winning kick. The teams combined for a Pro Bowl record 962 total yards. Brunell, who completed 12 of 22 pass attempts for 236 yards, was selected as the player of the game.

AFC	0	3	7	13	3	— 26
NFC	9	0	6	8	0	— 23

NFC — FG Kasay 20
NFC — R. McDaniel 5 pass from Favre (muffed snap)
AFC — FG Blanchard 28
NFC — Sanders 6 run (pass failed)

AFC — Martin 3 run (Blanchard kick)
AFC — Ambrose 54 interception return (pass failed)
NFC — Carter 53 pass from Frerotte (Walls pass from Frerotte)
AFC — T. Brown 80 pass from Brunell (Blanchard kick)
AFC — FG Blanchard 37

1996 AFC-NFC PRO BOWL

Aloha Stadium, Honolulu, Hawaii
February 4, 1996, Attendance: 50,034

NFC 20, AFC 13—Jerry Rice had 6 receptions for 82 yards and 1 touchdown to earn player of the game honors in the NFC's victory. The 49ers' wide receiver, who was named to the Pro Bowl for the tenth consecutive year, caught a 1-yard touchdown pass from Packers quarterback Brett Favre 1:41 into the second quarter to cap an 80-yard drive and give the NFC the lead for good at 10-7. The AFC had taken a 7-0 lead 2:26 into the game when Bengals quarterback Jeff Blake connected with Steelers wide receiver Yancey Thigpen on a Pro Bowl-record 93-yard touchdown pass. The NFC increased its advantage to 20-7 at halftime on Redskins linebacker Ken Harvey's 36-yard interception return for a touchdown and Falcons kicker Morten Andersen's 24-yard field goal. The AFC trimmed its deficit to 20-13 when Colts quarterback Jim Harbaugh teamed with Patriots running back Curtis Martin on a 17-yard touchdown pass in the final minute of the third quarter, but its bid to win or tie was rebuffed twice in the final minutes of the fourth quarter. First, 49ers safety Tim McDonald intercepted Harbaugh's pass in the end zone with 1:50 remaining. Then, after the AFC forced a punt and got the ball back near midfield, Harbaugh drove his team to the NFC's 9-yard line in the closing seconds. But he spiked the ball once to stop the clock and threw 3 consecutive incompletions as time ran out. The AFC outgained the NFC 390 total yards to 287, but its quarterbacks suffered 4 interceptions, including 3 off Harbaugh, the NFL's leading passer during the regular season. The NFC raised its edge to 15-11 in Pro Bowl games since the AFL-NFL merger in 1970.

NFC	3	17	0	0	—	20
AFC	7	0	6	0	—	13

AFC — Thigpen 93 pass from Blake (Elam kick)
NFC — FG Andersen 36
NFC — Rice 1 pass from Favre (Andersen kick)
NFC — Harvey 36 interception return (Andersen kick)
NFC — FG Andersen 24
AFC — Martin 17 pass from Harbaugh (kick failed)

1995 AFC-NFC PRO BOWL

Aloha Stadium, Honolulu, Hawaii
February 5, 1995, Attendance: 49,121

AFC 41, NFC 13—Colts rookie Marshall Faulk rushed for a Pro Bowl-record 180 yards to key the AFC's rout of the NFC. Faulk, who earned the Dan McGuire Trophy as the player of the game, averaged nearly 14 yards on his 13 carries and shattered the previous rushing mark of 112 yards set by O.J. Simpson in the 1973 game. Faulk's 49-yard touchdown run from punt formation in the fourth quarter was the longest in Pro Bowl history. The Seahawks' Chris Warren added 127 yards on 14 carries as the AFC amassed records for rushing yards (400) and total yards (552). Steelers tight end Eric Green caught 2 touchdown passes for the victors. The NFC managed only 196 total yards, a large chunk coming when 49ers quarterback Steve Young and Vikings wide receiver Cris Carter teamed on a 51-yard touchdown pass in the first quarter. That gave the NFC a 10-0 advantage, but the AFC rallied in the second quarter and took the lead for good when the Browns' Leroy Hoard scored on a 4-yard touchdown run 2:07 before halftime.

AFC	0	17	3	21	—	41
NFC	10	0	3	0	—	13

NFC — FG Reveiz 28
NFC — Carter 51 pass from Young (Reveiz kick)
AFC — Green 22 pass from Elway (Carney kick)
AFC — FG Carney 22
AFC — Hoard 4 run (Carney kick)
NFC — FG Reveiz 49
AFC — FG Carney 23
AFC — Warren 11 run (Carney kick)
AFC — Green 16 pass from Hostetler (Carney kick)
AFC — Faulk 49 run (Carney kick)

1994 AFC-NFC PRO BOWL

Aloha Stadium, Honolulu, Hawaii
February 6, 1994, Attendance: 50,026

NFC 17, AFC 3—The NFC converted a blocked punt and a fumble recovery into touchdowns just 2:20 apart in the second half of its victory over the AFC. With the score tied 3-3 late in the third quarter, Saints linebacker Renaldo Turnbull deflected a punt by the Oilers' Greg Montgomery, and the NFC took possession at the AFC's 48-yard line. A 32-yard pass from Bobby Hebert to Falcons teammate Andre Rison positioned Rams running back Jerome Bettis for a 4-yard touchdown run with 1:27 left in the third quarter. Moments later, Rams defensive tackle Sean Gilbert recovered a fumble by Oilers quarterback Warren Moon at the AFC's 19. Hebert then teamed with the Vikings' Cris Carter on a 15-yard touchdown pass 53 seconds into the fourth period. The NFC kept the AFC out of the end zone by maintaining possession for more than 38 minutes and forcing 6 turnovers. Rison earned the Dan McGuire Trophy as the player of the game by catching 6 passes for 86 yards. The victory was the fourth in the last six years for the NFC, which leads the series 14-10.

NFC	3	0	7	7	—	17
AFC	0	3	0	0	—	3

NFC — FG Johnson 35
AFC — FG Anderson 25
NFC — Bettis 4 run (Johnson kick)
NFC — Carter 15 pass from Hebert (Johnson kick)

1993 AFC-NFC PRO BOWL

Aloha Stadium, Honolulu, Hawaii
February 7, 1993, Attendance: 50,007

AFC 23, NFC 20—Nick Lowery's 33-yard field goal 4:09 into overtime gave the American Conference all-stars an unlikely 23-20 victory over the National Conference. Despite being overwhelmed by the NFC in first downs (30-9), and total yards (471-114), the AFC won because it forced 6 turnovers, blocked a pair of field goals (1 of which was returned for a touchdown), and returned an interception for a score. Special-teams star Steve Tasker of the Bills earned the Dan McGuire Trophy as the player of the game for making 4 tackles, forcing a fumble, and blocking a field goal. The block came with eight minutes left in regulation and the game tied at 13-13. The Raiders' Terry McDaniel picked up the loose ball and ran 28 yards for a touchdown and a 20-13 AFC lead. The NFC rallied behind 49ers quarterback Steve Young, whose fourth-down, 23-yard touchdown pass to Giants running back Rodney Hampton tied the game at 20-20 with 10 seconds left in regulation. Young completed 18 of 32 passes for 196 yards but was intercepted 3 times and lost a fumble when sacked in overtime. Raiders defensive end Howie Long fell on that fumble at the NFC 28-yard line, and five plays later, Lowery converted the winning field goal.

AFC	0	10	3	7	3 — 23
NFC	3	10	0	7	0 — 20

NFC — FG Andersen 27
AFC — Seau 31 interception return (Lowery kick)
NFC — FG Andersen 37
NFC — Irvin 9 pass from Aikman (Andersen kick)
AFC — FG Lowery 42
AFC — FG Lowery 29
AFC — McDaniel 28 blocked field goal return (Lowery kick)
NFC — Hampton 23 pass from Young (Andersen kick)
AFC — FG Lowery 33

1992 AFC-NFC PRO BOWL

Aloha Stadium, Honolulu, Hawaii
February 2, 1992, Attendance: 50,209

NFC 21, AFC 15—Atlanta's Chris Miller threw an 11-yard touchdown pass to San Francisco's Jerry Rice with 4:04 remaining in the game to lift the NFC over the AFC. It was the NFC's thirteenth win in the 22-game series. The AFC had taken a 15-14 lead when the Raiders' Jeff Jaeger kicked a 27-yard field goal 1:49 into the fourth quarter. But the NFC, aided by a key roughing-the-passer penalty on a third-down incompletion from the AFC 24-yard line, drove 85 yards to the winning score. The Cowboys' Michael Irvin, playing in his first Pro Bowl, caught 8 passes for 125 yards, including a 13-yard touchdown in the first quarter, and was named the player of the game. Rice had 7 catches for 77 yards. Mark Rypien of Washington, the Super Bowl most valuable player one week earlier, completed 11 of 18 passes for 165 yards and 2 touchdowns for the NFC, including a 35-yard pass to Redskins teammate Gary Clark just 26 seconds before halftime. Miller completed 7 of his 10 attempts for 85 yards.

NFC	7	7	0	7	—	21
AFC	7	5	0	3	—	15

AFC — Clayton 4 pass from Kelly (Jaeger kick)
NFC — Irvin 13 pass from Rypien (Lohmiller kick)
AFC — Safety, Townsend tackled Byner in end zone
AFC — FG Jaeger 48
NFC — Clark 35 pass from Rypien (Lohmiller kick)
AFC — FG Jaeger 27
NFC — Rice 11 pass from Miller (Lohmiller kick)

1991 AFC-NFC PRO BOWL

Aloha Stadium, Honolulu, Hawaii
February 3, 1991, Attendance: 50,345

AFC 23, NFC 21—Buffalo's Jim Kelly and Houston's Ernest Givins combined for a 13-yard scoring pass late in the fourth quarter to rally the AFC over the NFC. Phoenix rookie Johnny Johnson scored on runs of 1 and 9 yards to put the NFC ahead 14-3 in the third quarter. Buffalo's Andre Reed, who led all receivers with 4 catches for 80 yards, caught a 20-yard scoring reception from Kelly early in the fourth quarter to move the AFC to within 1 point. Barry Sanders ran 22 yards for a touchdown to increase the NFC's lead to 21-13. Miami's Jeff Cross blocked a 46-yard field-goal attempt by New Orleans's Morten Andersen with seven seconds remaining to preserve the win. Buffalo's Bruce Smith recorded 3 sacks and also had a blocked field goal. Kelly, who completed 13 of 19 passes for 210 yards and 2 touchdowns, was presented the Dan McGuire Award as player of the game. The AFC's victory narrowed the NFC's Pro Bowl series lead to 12-9.

AFC	3	0	3	17	—	23
NFC	0	7	7	7	—	21

AFC — FG Lowery 26
NFC — J. Johnson 1 run (Andersen kick)
AFC — FG Lowery 43
NFC — J. Johnson 9 run (Andersen kick)
AFC — Reed 20 pass from Kelly (Lowery kick)
NFC — Sanders 22 run (Andersen kick)
AFC — FG Lowery 34
AFC — Givins 13 pass from Kelly (Lowery kick)

1990 AFC-NFC PRO BOWL

Aloha Stadium, Honolulu, Hawaii
February 4, 1990, Attendance: 50,445

NFC 27, AFC 21—The NFC captured its second straight Pro Bowl as the defense accounted for a pair of touchdowns and forced 5 turnovers before the eleventh consecutive sellout crowd at Aloha Stadium. The AFC held a 7-6 halftime edge on a 1-yard scoring run by Christian Okoye of the Chiefs. The NFC then rallied with 21 unanswered points in the third quarter. David Meggett of the Giants began the comeback with an 11-yard touchdown reception from Philadelphia's Randall Cunningham. The Rams' Jerry Gray followed with a 51-yard interception return for a score and the Vikings' Keith Millard added an 8-yard fumble return for a touchdown four minutes later to give the

NFC a commanding 27-7 lead. Seattle's Dave Krieg rallied the AFC with a 5-yard touchdown pass to Miami's Ferrell Edmunds. Cleveland's Mike Johnson then returned an interception 22 yards for a score to pull the AFC to within 27-21. Gray, who was credited with 7 tackles, was given the Dan McGuire Award as player of the game. Krieg led all quarterbacks by completing 15 of 23 for 148 yards and 1 touchdown. Buffalo's Thurman Thomas topped all receivers with 5 catches for 47 yards, while Indianapolis's Eric Dickerson led all rushers with 46 yards on 15 carries. The win gave the NFC a 12-8 advantage in Pro Bowl games since 1971.

NFC	3	3	21	0	—	27
AFC	0	7	0	14	—	21

NFC — FG Murray 23
NFC — FG Murray 41
AFC — Okoye 1 run (Treadwell kick)
NFC — Meggett 11 pass from Cunningham (Murray kick)
NFC — Gray 51 interception return (Murray kick)
NFC — Millard 8 fumble recovery return (Murray kick)
AFC — Edmunds 5 pass from Krieg (Treadwell kick)
AFC — M. Johnson 22 interception return (Treadwell kick)

1989 AFC-NFC PRO BOWL

Aloha Stadium, Honolulu, Hawaii
January 29, 1989, Attendance: 50,113

NFC 34, AFC 3—The NFC scored 34 unanswered points to snap a two-game losing streak to the AFC before the tenth straight sellout crowd in Honolulu's Aloha Stadium. Bills kicker Scott Norwood provided the AFC's only points on a 38-yard field goal 6:23 into the game. Touchdown runs by Dallas's Herschel Walker (4 yards) and Atlanta's John Settle (1) brought the NFC a 14-3 halftime lead. Walker added a 7-yard scoring run, the Saints' Morten Andersen kicked field goals of 27 and 51 yards, and Los Angeles Rams' wide receiver Henry Ellard caught an 8-yard scoring pass from Minnesota quarterback Wade Wilson in the second half to complete the scoring. Chicago running back Neal Anderson and Philadelphia quarterback Randall Cunningham, who were both appearing in their first Pro Bowl, also played major roles in the NFC's victory. Anderson rushed 13 times for 85 yards and had 2 receptions for 17. Cunningham, who was voted the game's outstanding player, completed 10 of 14 passes for 63 yards and rushed for 49 yards. The NFC, which had 5 takeaways, outgained the AFC 355 yards to 167 and held a time-of-possession advantage of 35:18 to 24:42. Houston quarterback Warren Moon completed 13 of 20 passes for 134 yards for the AFC. The win gave the NFC an 11-8 advantage in Pro Bowl games.

AFC	3	0	0	0	—	3
NFC	7	7	10	10	—	34

AFC — FG Norwood 38
NFC — Walker 4 run (Andersen kick)
NFC — Settle 1 run (Andersen kick)
NFC — FG Andersen 27
NFC — Walker 7 run (Andersen kick)
NFC — FG Andersen 51
NFC — Ellard 8 pass from Wilson (Andersen kick)

1988 AFC-NFC PRO BOWL

Aloha Stadium, Honolulu, Hawaii
February 7, 1988, Attendance: 50,113

AFC 15, NFC 6—Led by a tenacious pass rush, the AFC defeated the NFC for the second consecutive year before the ninth straight sellout crowd in Honolulu's Aloha Stadium. Buffalo quarterback Jim Kelly scored the game's lone touchdown on a 1-yard run for a 7-6 halftime lead. Colts kicker Dean Biasucci added field goals from 37 and 30 yards to complete the AFC's scoring. Saints kicker Morten Andersen had 25- and 36-yard field goals to account for the NFC's points. AFC defenders held the NFC to 213 yards and recorded 8 sacks. Bills defensive end Bruce Smith, who had 2 sacks among his 5 tackles, was voted the game's outstanding player. Oilers running back Mike Rozier led all rushers with 49 yards on 9 carries. Jets wide receiver Al Toon had 5 receptions for 75 yards. The AFC generated 341 yards total offense and held a time-of-possession advantage of 34:14 to 25:46. By winning, the AFC cut the NFC's lead in the Pro Bowl series to 10-8.

NFC	0	6	0	0	—	6
AFC	0	7	6	2	—	15

NFC — FG Andersen 25
AFC — Kelly 1 run (Biasucci kick)
NFC — FG Andersen 36
AFC — FG Biasucci 37
AFC — FG Biasucci 30
AFC — Safety, Montana forced out of end zone

1987 AFC-NFC PRO BOWL

Aloha Stadium, Honolulu, Hawaii
February 1, 1987, Attendance: 50,101

AFC 10, NFC 6—The AFC defeated the NFC in the lowest-scoring game in AFC-NFC Pro Bowl history. The AFC took a 10-0 halftime lead on Broncos quarterback John Elway's 10-yard touchdown pass to Raiders tight end Todd Christensen and Patriots kicker Tony Franklin's 26-yard field goal. The AFC defense made the lead stand by forcing the NFC to settle for a pair of field goals from 38 and 19 yards by Saints kicker Morten Andersen after the NFC had first downs at the AFC 31-, 7-, 16-, 15-, 5-, and 7-yard lines. Both AFC scores were set up by fumble recoveries by Seahawks linebacker Fredd Young and Dolphins linebacker John Offerdahl, respectively. Eagles defensive end Reggie White, who tied a Pro Bowl record with 4 sacks among his 7 solo tackles, was voted the game's outstanding player. The AFC victory cut the NFC's lead in the Pro Bowl series to 10-7.

AFC	7	3	0	0	—	10
NFC	0	0	3	3	—	6

AFC — Christensen 10 pass from Elway (Franklin kick)
AFC — FG Franklin 26
NFC — FG Andersen 38
NFC — FG Andersen 19

1986 AFC-NFC PRO BOWL

Aloha Stadium, Honolulu, Hawaii
February 2, 1986, Attendance: 50,101

NFC 28, AFC 24—New York Giants quarterback Phil Simms brought the NFC back from a 24-7 halftime deficit to defeat the AFC. Simms, who completed 15 of 27 passes for 212 yards and 3 touchdowns, was named the most valuable player of the game. The AFC had taken its first-half lead behind a 2-yard run by Los Angeles Raiders running back Marcus Allen, who also threw a 51-yard scoring pass to San Diego wide receiver Wes Chandler, an 11-yard touchdown catch by Pittsburgh wide receiver Louis Lipps, and a 34-yard field goal by Steelers kicker Gary Anderson. Minnesota's Joey Browner accounted for the NFC's only score before halftime with a 48-yard interception return. After intermission, the NFC blanked the AFC while scoring 3 touchdowns via a 15-yard catch by Washington wide receiver Art Monk, a 2-yard reception by Dallas tight end Doug Cosbie, and a 15-yard catch by Tampa Bay tight end Jimmie Giles with 2:47 remaining in the game. The victory gave the NFC a 10-6 Pro Bowl record against the AFC.

NFC	0	7	7	14	—	28
AFC	7	17	0	0	—	24

AFC — Allen 2 run (Anderson kick)
NFC — Browner 48 interception return (Andersen kick)
AFC — Chandler 51 pass from Allen (Anderson kick)
AFC — FG Anderson 34
AFC — Lipps 11 pass from O'Brien (Anderson kick)
NFC — Monk 15 pass from Simms (Andersen kick)
NFC — Cosbie 2 pass from Simms (Andersen kick)
NFC — Giles 15 pass from Simms (Andersen kick)

1985 AFC-NFC PRO BOWL

Aloha Stadium, Honolulu, Hawaii
January 27, 1985, Attendance: 50,385

AFC 22, NFC 14—Defensive end Art Still of the Kansas City Chiefs recovered a fumble and returned it 83 yards for a touchdown to clinch the AFC's victory over the NFC. Still's touchdown came in the fourth period with the AFC trailing 14-12 and was one of several outstanding defensive plays in a Pro Bowl dominated by two record-breaking defenses. The teams combined for a Pro Bowl-record 17 sacks, including 4 by New York Jets defensive end Mark Gastineau, who was named the game's outstanding player. The AFC's first score came on a safety when Gastineau tackled running back Eric Dickerson of the Los Angeles Rams in the end zone. The AFC's second score, a 6-yard pass from Miami's Dan Marino to Los Angeles Raiders running back Marcus Allen, was set up by a partial block of a punt by Seahawks linebacker Fredd Young. The NFC leads the series 9-6.

AFC	0	9	0	13	—	22
NFC	0	0	7	7	—	14

AFC — Safety, Gastineau tackled Dickerson in end zone
AFC — Allen 6 pass from Marino (Johnson kick)
NFC — Lofton 13 pass from Montana (Stenerud kick)
NFC — Payton 1 run (Stenerud kick)
AFC — FG Johnson 33
AFC — Still 83 fumble recovery return (Johnson kick)
AFC — FG Johnson 22

1984 AFC-NFC PRO BOWL

Aloha Stadium, Honolulu, Hawaii
January 29, 1984, Attendance: 50,445

NFC 45, AFC 3—The NFC won its sixth Pro Bowl in the last seven seasons by routing the AFC. The NFC was led by the passing of most valuable player Joe Theismann of Washington, who completed 21 of 27 passes for 242 yards and 3 touchdowns. Theismann set Pro Bowl records for completions and touchdown passes. The NFC established Pro Bowl marks for most points scored and fewest points allowed. Running back William Andrews of Atlanta had 6 carries for 43 yards and caught 4 passes for 49 yards, including scoring receptions of 16 and 2 yards. Los Angeles Rams rookie Eric Dickerson gained 46 yards on 11 carries, including a 14-yard touchdown run, and had 45 yards on 5 catches. Rams safety Nolan Cromwell had a 44-yard interception return for a touchdown early in the third period to give the NFC a commanding 24-3 lead. Green Bay wide receiver James Lofton caught an 8-yard touchdown pass, while tight end teammate Paul Coffman had a 6-yard scoring catch.

NFC	3	14	14	14	—	45
AFC	0	3	0	0	—	3

NFC — FG Haji-Sheikh 23
NFC — Andrews 16 pass from Theismann (Haji-Sheikh kick)
NFC — Andrews 2 pass from Montana (Haji-Sheikh kick)
AFC — FG Anderson 43
NFC — Cromwell 44 interception return (Haji-Sheikh kick)
NFC — Lofton 8 pass from Theismann (Haji-Sheikh kick)
NFC — Coffman 6 pass from Theismann (Haji-Sheikh kick)
NFC — Dickerson 14 run (Haji-Sheikh kick)

1983 AFC-NFC PRO BOWL

Aloha Stadium, Honolulu, Hawaii
February 6, 1983, Attendance: 49,883

NFC 20, AFC 19—Dallas's Danny White threw an 11-yard touchdown pass to the Packers' John Jefferson with 35 seconds remaining to rally the NFC over the AFC. White, who completed 14 of 26 passes for 162 yards, kept the winning 65-yard drive alive with a 14-yard completion to Jefferson on a fourth-and-7 play at the AFC 25. The AFC was ahead 12-10 at halftime and increased the lead to 19-10 in the third period, when Marcus Allen scored on a 1-yard run. San Diego's Dan Fouts, who attempted 30 passes, set Pro Bowl records for most completions (17) and yards (274). Pittsburgh's John Stallworth was the AFC's leading receiver with 7 catches for 67 yards. William Andrews topped the NFC with 5 receptions for 48 yards. Fouts and Jefferson were co-winners of the player of the game award.

AFC	9	3	7	0	—	19
NFC	0	10	0	10	—	20

AFC — Walker 34 pass from Fouts (Benirschke kick)
AFC — Safety, Still tackled Theismann in end zone
NFC — Andrews 3 run (Moseley kick)
NFC — FG Moseley 35
AFC — FG Benirschke 29
AFC — Allen 1 run (Benirschke kick)
NFC — FG Moseley 41
NFC — Jefferson 11 pass from D. White (Moseley kick)

1982 AFC-NFC PRO BOWL

Aloha Stadium, Honolulu, Hawaii
January 31, 1982, Attendance: 50,402

AFC 16, NFC 13—Nick Lowery of Kansas City kicked a 23-yard field goal with three seconds remaining to give the AFC a last-second victory over the NFC. Lowery's kick climaxed a 69-yard drive directed by quarterback Dan Fouts. The NFC gained a 13-13 tie with 2:43 to go when Dallas's Tony Dorsett ran 4 yards for a touchdown. In the drive to the winning field goal, Fouts completed 3 passes, including a 23-yard toss to San Diego teammate Kellen Winslow that put the ball on the NFC's 5-yard line. Two plays later, Lowery kicked the field goal. Winslow, who caught 6 passes for 86 yards, was named co-player of the game along with Tampa Bay defensive end Lee Roy Selmon.

NFC	0	6	0	7	—	13
AFC	0	0	13	3	—	16

NFC — Giles 4 pass from Montana (kick blocked)
AFC — Muncie 2 run (kick failed)
AFC — Campbell 1 run (Lowery kick)
NFC — Dorsett 4 run (Septien kick)
AFC — FG Lowery 23

1981 AFC-NFC PRO BOWL

Aloha Stadium, Honolulu, Hawaii
February 1, 1981, Attendance: 50,360

NFC 21, AFC 7—Eddie Murray kicked 4 field goals and Steve Bartkowski fired a 55-yard scoring pass to Alfred Jenkins to lead the NFC to its fourth straight victory over the AFC and a 7-4 edge in the series. Murray was named the game's most valuable player and missed tying Garo Yepremian's Pro Bowl record of 5 field goals when a 37-yard attempt hit the crossbar with 22 seconds remaining. The AFC's only score came on a 9-yard pass from Brian Sipe to Stanley Morgan in the second period. Bartkowski completed 9 of 21 passes for 173 yards, while Sipe connected on 10 of 15 for 142 yards. Ottis Anderson led all rushers with 70 yards on 10 carries. Earl Campbell, the NFL's leading rusher in 1980, was limited to 24 yards on 8 attempts.

AFC	0	7	0	0	—	7
NFC	3	6	0	12	—	21

NFC — FG Murray 31
AFC — Morgan 9 pass from Sipe (J. Smith kick)
NFC — FG Murray 31
NFC — FG Murray 34
NFC — Jenkins 55 pass from Bartkowski (Murray kick)
NFC — FG Murray 36
NFC — Safety, Shell called for holding in end zone

1980 AFC-NFC PRO BOWL

Aloha Stadium, Honolulu, Hawaii
January 27, 1980, Attendance: 49,800

NFC 37, AFC 27—Running back Chuck Muncie of New Orleans ran for 2 touchdowns and threw a 25-yard option pass for another score to give the NFC its third consecutive victory over the AFC. Muncie, who was selected the game's most valuable player, snapped a 3-3 tie on a 1-yard touchdown run at 1:41 of the second quarter, then scored on an 11-yard run in the fourth quarter for the NFC's final touchdown. Two scoring records were set in the game— 37 points by the NFC, eclipsing the 33 by the AFC in 1973, and the 64 points by both teams, surpassing the 61 scored in 1973.

NFC	3	20	7	7	—	37
AFC	3	7	10	7	—	27

NFC — FG Moseley 37
AFC — FG Fritsch 19
NFC — Muncie 1 run (Moseley kick)
AFC — Pruitt 1 pass from Bradshaw (Fritsch kick)
NFC — D. Hill 13 pass from Manning (kick failed)
NFC — T. Hill 25 pass from Muncie (Moseley kick)
NFC — Henry 86 punt return (Moseley kick)
AFC — Campbell 2 run (Fritsch kick)
AFC — FG Fritsch 29
NFC — Muncie 11 run (Moseley kick)
AFC — Campbell 1 run (Fritsch kick)

1979 AFC-NFC PRO BOWL

Memorial Coliseum, Los Angeles, California
January 29, 1979, Attendance: 46,281

NFC 13, AFC 7—Roger Staubach completed 9 of 15 passes for 125 yards, including the winning touchdown on a 19-yard strike to Dallas Cowboys teammate Tony Hill in the third period. The winning drive began at the AFC's 45-yard line after a shanked punt. Staubach hit Ahmad Rashad with passes of 15 and 17 yards to set up Hill's decisive catch. The victory gave the NFC a 5-4 advantage in Pro Bowl games. Rashad, who accounted for 89 yards on 5 receptions, was named the player of the game. The AFC led 7-6 at halftime on Bob Griese's 8-yard scoring toss to Steve Largent late in the second quarter. Largent finished the game with 5 receptions for 75 yards. The NFC scored first as Archie Manning marched his team 70 yards in 11 plays, capped by Wilbert Montgomery's 2-yard touchdown run. The AFC's Earl Campbell was the game's leading rusher with 66 yards on 12 carries.

AFC	0	7	0	0	—	7
NFC	0	6	7	0	—	13

NFC — Montgomery 2 run (kick failed)
AFC — Largent 8 pass from Griese (Yepremian kick)
NFC — T. Hill 19 pass from Staubach (Corral kick)

1978 AFC-NFC PRO BOWL

Tampa Stadium, Tampa, Florida
January 23, 1978, Attendance: 51,337

NFC 14, AFC 13—Walter Payton, the NFL's leading rusher in 1977, sparked a second-half comeback to give the NFC the win and tie the series between the two conferences at four victories each. Payton, who was the game's most valuable player, gained 77 yards on 13 carries and scored the tying touchdown on a 1-yard burst with 7:37 left in the game. Efren Herrera kicked the winning extra point. The AFC dominated the first half of the game, taking a 13-0 lead on field goals of 21 and 39 yards by Toni Linhart and a 10-yard touchdown pass from Ken Stabler to Oakland teammate Cliff Branch. On the NFC's first possession of the second half, Pat Haden put together the first touchdown drive after Eddie Brown returned Ray Guy's punt to the AFC 46-yard line. Haden connected on all 4 of his passes on that drive, finally hitting Terry Metcalf with a 4-yard scoring toss. The NFC continued to rally and, with Jim Hart at quarterback, moved 63 yards in 12 plays for the go-ahead score. During the winning drive, Hart completed 5 of 6 passes for 38 yards and Payton picked up 20 more on the ground.

AFC	3	10	0	0	—	13
NFC	0	0	7	7	—	14

AFC — FG Linhart 21
AFC — Branch 10 pass from Stabler (Linhart kick)
AFC — FG Linhart 39
NFC — Metcalf 4 pass from Haden (Herrera kick)
NFC — Payton 1 run (Herrera kick)

1977 AFC-NFC PRO BOWL

Kingdome, Seattle, Washington
January 17, 1977, Attendance: 64,752

AFC 24, NFC 14—O.J. Simpson's 3-yard touchdown burst at 7:03 of the first quarter gave the AFC a lead it would not surrender, breaking a two-game NFC win streak and giving the American Conference stars a 4-3 series lead. The AFC took a 17-7 lead midway through the second period on the first of 2 Ken Anderson touchdown passes, a 12-yard toss to Charlie Joiner. But the NFC mounted a 73-yard drive capped by Lawrence McCutcheon's 1-yard touchdown plunge to pull within 17-14 at the half. Following a scoreless third quarter, player of the game Mel Blount thwarted a possible NFC score when he intercepted Jim Hart's pass in the end zone. Less than three minutes later, Blount again picked off a Hart pass. That set up Anderson's 27-yard touchdown strike to the Raiders' Cliff Branch for the final score.

NFC	0	14	0	0	—	14
AFC	10	7	0	7	—	24

AFC — Simpson 3 run (Linhart kick)
AFC — FG Linhart 31
NFC — Thomas 15 run (Bakken kick)
AFC — Joiner 12 pass from Anderson (Linhart kick)
NFC — McCutcheon 1 run (Bakken kick)
AFC — Branch 27 pass from Anderson (Linhart kick)

1976 AFC-NFC PRO BOWL

Superdome, New Orleans, Louisiana
January 26, 1976, Attendance: 30,546

NFC 23, AFC 20—Mike Boryla, a late substitute who did not enter the game until 5:39 remained, lifted the National Football Conference to the victory over the American Football Conference with 2 touchdown passes in the final minutes. It was the second straight NFC win, squaring the series at 3-3. Until Boryla started firing the ball the AFC was in control, leading 13-0 at the half. Boryla entered the game after Billy Johnson had raced 90 yards with a punt to make the score 20-9 in favor of the AFC. He floated a 14-yard touchdown pass to Terry Metcalf and later fired an 8-yard scoring pass to Mel Gray for the winner.

AFC	0	13	0	7	—	20
NFC	0	0	9	14	—	23

AFC — FG Stenerud 20
AFC — FG Stenerud 35
AFC — Burrough 64 pass from Pastorini (Stenerud kick)
NFC — FG Bakken 42
NFC — Foreman 4 pass from Hart (kick blocked)
AFC — Johnson 90 punt return (Stenerud kick)
NFC — Metcalf 14 pass from Boryla (Bakken kick)
NFC — Gray 8 pass from Boryla (Bakken kick)

1975 AFC-NFC PRO BOWL

Orange Bowl, Miami, Florida
January 20, 1975, Attendance: 26,484

NFC 17, AFC 10—Los Angeles quarterback James Harris, who took over the NFC offense after Jim Hart of St. Louis suffered a laceration above his right eye in the second period, threw 2 touchdown passes early in the fourth period to pace the NFC to its second victory in the five-game Pro Bowl series. The NFC win snapped a three-game AFC victory string. Harris, who was named the player of the game, connected with St. Louis's Mel Gray for an 8-yard touchdown 2:03 into the final period. One minute and 24 seconds later, following a fumble recovery by Washington's Ken Houston, Harris tossed another 8-yard scoring pass to Washington's Charley Taylor for the decisive points.

NFC	0	3	0	14	—	17
AFC	0	0	10	0	—	10

NFC — FG Marcol 33
AFC — Warfield 32 pass from Griese (Gerela kick)
AFC — FG Gerela 33
NFC — Gray 8 pass from J. Harris (Marcol kick)
NFC — Taylor 8 pass from J. Harris (Marcol kick)

1974 AFC-NFC PRO BOWL

Arrowhead Stadium, Kansas City, Missouri
January 20, 1974, Attendance: 66,918

AFC 15, NFC 13—Miami's Garo Yepremian's fifth field goal—a 42-yard kick with 21 seconds remaining—gave the AFC its third straight victory since the NFC won the inaugural game following the 1970 season. The field goal by Yepremian, who was voted the game's outstanding player, offset a 21-yard field goal by Atlanta's Nick Mike-Mayer that had given the NFC a 13-12 advantage with 1:41 remaining. The only touchdown in the game was scored by the NFC on a 14-yard pass from Philadelphia's Roman Gabriel to Lawrence McCutcheon of the Los Angeles Rams.

NFC	0	10	0	3	—	13
AFC	3	3	3	6	—	15

AFC — FG Yepremian 16
NFC — FG Mike-Mayer 27
NFC — McCutcheon 14 pass from Gabriel (Mike-Mayer kick)
AFC — FG Yepremian 37
AFC — FG Yepremian 27
AFC — FG Yepremian 41
NFC — FG Mike-Mayer 21
AFC — FG Yepremian 42

1973 AFC-NFC PRO BOWL

Texas Stadium, Irving, Texas
January 21, 1973, Attendance: 37,091

AFC 33, NFC 28—Paced by the rushing and receiving of player of the game O.J. Simpson, the AFC erased a 14-0 first period deficit and built a commanding 33-14 lead midway through the fourth period before the NFC managed 2 touchdowns in the final minute of play. Simpson rushed for 112 yards and caught 3 passes for 58 more to gain unanimous recognition in the balloting for player of the game. John Brockington scored 3 touchdowns for the NFC.

AFC	0	10	10	13	—	33
NFC	14	0	0	14	—	28

NFC — Brockington 1 run (Marcol kick)
NFC — Brockington 3 pass from Kilmer (Marcol kick)
AFC — Simpson 7 run (Gerela kick)
AFC — FG Gerela 18
AFC — FG Gerela 22
AFC — Hubbard 11 run (Gerela kick)
AFC — O. Taylor 5 pass from Lamonica (kick failed)
AFC — Bell 12 interception return (Gerela kick)
NFC — Brockington 1 run (Marcol kick)
NFC — Kwalick 12 pass from Snead (Marcol kick)

1972 AFC-NFC PRO BOWL

Memorial Coliseum, Los Angeles, California
January 23, 1972, Attendance: 53,647

AFC 26, NFC 13—Kansas City's Jan Stenerud kicked 4 field goals to lead the AFC from a 6-0 deficit to victory. The AFC defense picked off 3 passes. Stenerud was selected as the outstanding offensive player and his Kansas City teammate, linebacker Willie Lanier, was the game's outstanding defensive player.

AFC	0	3	13	10	—	26
NFC	0	6	0	7	—	13

NFC — Grim 50 pass from Landry (kick failed)
AFC — FG Stenerud 25
AFC — FG Stenerud 23
AFC — FG Stenerud 48
AFC — Morin 5 pass from Dawson (Stenerud kick)
AFC — FG Stenerud 42
NFC — V. Washington 2 run (Knight kick)
AFC — F. Little 6 run (Stenerud kick)

1971 AFC-NFC PRO BOWL

Memorial Coliseum, Los Angeles, California
January 24, 1971, Attendance: 48,222

NFC 27, AFC 6—Mel Renfro of Dallas broke open the first meeting between the American Football Conference and National Football Conference all-star teams as he returned a pair of punts 82 and 56 yards for touchdowns in the final period to clinch the NFC victory over the AFC. Renfro was voted the game's outstanding back and linebacker Fred Carr of Green Bay the outstanding lineman.

AFC	0	3	3	0	—	6
NFC	0	3	10	14	—	27

AFC — FG Stenerud 37
NFC — FG Cox 13
NFC — Osborn 23 pass from Brodie (Cox kick)
NFC — FG Cox 35
AFC — FG Stenerud 16
NFC — Renfro 82 punt return (Cox kick)
NFC — Renfro 56 punt return (Cox kick)

PRO BOWL ALL-TIME RESULTS

PRO BOWL ALL-TIME RESULTS

Date	Result	Site (attendance)	Honored players
Jan. 15, 1939	New York Giants 13, Pro All-Stars 10	Wrigley Field, Los Angeles (20,000)	
Jan. 14, 1940	Green Bay 16, NFL All-Stars 7	Gilmore Stadium, Los Angeles (18,000)	
Dec. 29, 1940	Chicago Bears 28, NFL All-Stars 14	Gilmore Stadium, Los Angeles (21,624)	
Jan. 4, 1942	Chicago Bears 35, NFL All-Stars 24	Polo Grounds, New York (17,725)	
Dec. 27, 1942	NFL All-Stars 17, Washington 14	Shibe Park, Philadelphia (18,671)	
Jan. 14, 1951	American Conf. 28, National Conf. 27	Los Angeles Memorial Coliseum (53,676)	Otto Graham, Cleveland, player of the game
Jan. 12, 1952	National Conf. 30, American Conf. 13	Los Angeles Memorial Coliseum (19,400)	Dan Towler, Los Angeles, player of the game
Jan. 10, 1953	National Conf. 27, American Conf. 7	Los Angeles Memorial Coliseum (34,208)	Don Doll, Detroit, player of the game
Jan. 17, 1954	East 20, West 9	Los Angeles Memorial Coliseum (44,214)	Chuck Bednarik, Philadelphia, player of the game
Jan. 16, 1955	West 26, East 19	Los Angeles Memorial Coliseum (43,972)	Billy Wilson, San Francisco, player of the game
Jan. 15, 1956	East 31, West 30	Los Angeles Memorial Coliseum (37,867)	Ollie Matson, Chi. Cardinals, player of the game
Jan. 13, 1957	West 19, East 10	Los Angeles Memorial Coliseum (44,177)	Bert Rechichar, Baltimore, outstanding back Ernie Stautner, Pittsburgh, outstanding lineman
Jan. 12, 1958	West 26, East 7	Los Angeles Memorial Coliseum (66,634)	Hugh McElhenny, San Francisco, outstanding back Gene Brito, Washington, outstanding lineman
Jan. 11, 1959	East 28, West 21	Los Angeles Memorial Coliseum (72,250)	Frank Gifford, N.Y. Giants, outstanding back Doug Atkins, Chi. Bears, outstanding lineman
Jan. 17, 1960	West 38, East 21	Los Angeles Memorial Coliseum (56,876)	Johnny Unitas, Baltimore, outstanding back Gene (Big Daddy) Lipscomb, Baltimore, outstanding lineman
Jan. 15, 1961	West 35, East 31	Los Angeles Memorial Coliseum (62,971)	Johnny Unitas, Baltimore, outstanding back Sam Huff, N.Y. Giants, outstanding lineman
Jan. 7, 1962	AFL West 47, East 27	Balboa Stadium, San Diego (20,973)	Cotton Davidson, Dallas Texans, player of the game
Jan. 14, 1962	NFL West 31, East 30	Los Angeles Memorial Coliseum (57,409)	Jim Brown, Cleveland, outstanding back Henry Jordan, Green Bay, outstanding lineman
Jan. 13, 1963	AFL West 21, East 14	Balboa Stadium, San Diego (27,641)	Curtis McClinton, Dallas Texans, outstanding offensive player Earl Faison, San Diego, outstanding defensive player
Jan. 13, 1963	NFL East 30, West 20	Los Angeles Memorial Coliseum (61,374)	Jim Brown, Cleveland, outstanding back Gene (Big Daddy) Lipscomb, Pittsburgh, outstanding lineman
Jan. 12, 1964	NFL West 31, East 17	Los Angeles Memorial Coliseum (67,242)	Johnny Unitas, Baltimore, player of the game Gino Marchetti, Baltimore, outstanding lineman
Jan. 19, 1964	AFL West 27, East 24	Balboa Stadium, San Diego (20,016)	Keith Lincoln, San Diego, outstanding offensive player Archie Matsos, Oakland, outstanding defensive player
Jan. 10, 1965	NFL West 34, East 14	Los Angeles Memorial Coliseum (60,598)	Fran Tarkenton, Minnesota, outstanding back Terry Barr, Detroit, outstanding lineman
Jan. 16, 1965	AFL West 38, East 14	Jeppesen Stadium, Houston (15,446)	Keith Lincoln, San Diego, outstanding offensive player Willie Brown, Denver, outstanding defensive player
Jan. 15, 1966	AFL All-Stars 30, Buffalo 19	Rice Stadium, Houston (35,572)	Joe Namath, N.Y. Jets, most valuable player, offense Frank Buncom, San Diego, most valuable player, defense
Jan. 15, 1966	NFL East 36, West 7	Los Angeles Memorial Coliseum (60,124)	Jim Brown, Cleveland, outstanding back Dale Meinert, St. Louis, outstanding lineman
Jan. 21, 1967	AFL East 30, West 23	Oakland-Alameda County Coliseum (18,876)	Babe Parilli, Boston, outstanding offensive player Verlon Biggs, N.Y. Jets, outstanding defensive player
Jan. 22, 1967	NFL East 20, West 10	Los Angeles Memorial Coliseum (15,062)	Gale Sayers, Chicago, outstanding back Floyd Peters, Philadelphia, outstanding lineman
Jan. 21, 1968	AFL East 25, West 24	Gator Bowl, Jacksonville, Fla. (40,103)	Joe Namath and Don Maynard, N.Y. Jets, out. off. players Leslie (Speedy) Duncan, San Diego, out. def. player
Jan. 21, 1968	NFL West 38, East 20	Los Angeles Memorial Coliseum (53,289)	Gale Sayers, Chicago, outstanding back Dave Robinson, Green Bay, outstanding lineman
Jan. 19, 1969	AFL West 38, East 25	Gator Bowl, Jacksonville, Fla. (41,058)	Len Dawson, Kansas City, outstanding offensive player George Webster, Houston, outstanding defensive player
Jan. 19, 1969	NFL West 10, East 7	Los Angeles Memorial Coliseum (32,050)	Roman Gabriel, Los Angeles, outstanding back Merlin Olsen, Los Angeles, outstanding lineman
Jan. 17, 1970	AFL West 26, East 3	Astrodome, Houston (30,170)	John Hadl, San Diego, player of the game
Jan. 18, 1970	NFL West 16, East 13	Los Angeles Memorial Coliseum (57,786)	Gale Sayers, Chicago, outstanding back George Andrie, Dallas, outstanding lineman
Jan. 24, 1971	NFC 27, AFC 6	Los Angeles Memorial Coliseum (48,222)	Mel Renfro, Dallas, outstanding back Fred Carr, Green Bay, outstanding lineman
Jan. 23, 1972	AFC 26, NFC 13	Los Angeles Memorial Coliseum (53,647)	Jan Stenerud, Kansas City, outstanding offensive player Willie Lanier, Kansas City, outstanding defensive player
Jan. 21, 1973	AFC 33, NFC 28	Texas Stadium, Irving (37,091)	O.J. Simpson, Buffalo, player of the game
Jan. 20, 1974	AFC 15, NFC 13	Arrowhead Stadium, Kansas City (66,918)	Garo Yepremian, Miami, player of the game
Jan. 20, 1975	NFC 17, AFC 10	Orange Bowl, Miami (26,484)	James Harris, Los Angeles, player of the game
Jan. 26, 1976	NFC 23, AFC 20	Louisiana Superdome, New Orleans (30,546)	Billy Johnson, Houston, player of the game
Jan. 17, 1977	AFC 24, NFC 14	Kingdome, Seattle (64,752)	Mel Blount, Pittsburgh, player of the game
Jan. 23, 1978	NFC 14, AFC 13	Tampa Stadium (51,337)	Walter Payton, Chicago, player of the game
Jan. 29, 1979	NFC 13, AFC 7	Los Angeles Memorial Coliseum (46,281)	Ahmad Rashad, Minnesota, player of the game
Jan. 27, 1980	NFC 37, AFC 27	Aloha Stadium, Honolulu (49,800)	Chuck Muncie, New Orleans, player of the game
Feb. 1, 1981	NFC 21, AFC 7	Aloha Stadium, Honolulu (50,360)	Eddie Murray, Detroit, player of the game
Jan. 31, 1982	AFC 16, NFC 13	Aloha Stadium, Honolulu (50,402)	Kellen Winslow, San Diego, and Lee Roy Selmon, Tampa Bay, players of the game
Feb. 6, 1983	NFC 20, AFC 19	Aloha Stadium, Honolulu (49,883)	Dan Fouts, San Diego, and John Jefferson, Green Bay, players of the game
Jan. 29, 1984	NFC 45, AFC 3	Aloha Stadium, Honolulu (50,445)	Joe Theismann, Washington, player of the game
Jan. 27, 1985	AFC 22, NFC 14	Aloha Stadium, Honolulu (50,385)	Mark Gastineau, N.Y. Jets, player of the game
Feb. 2, 1986	NFC 28, AFC 24	Aloha Stadium, Honolulu (50,101)	Phil Simms, N.Y. Giants, player of the game
Feb. 1, 1987	AFC 10, NFC 6	Aloha Stadium, Honolulu (50,101)	Reggie White, Philadelphia, player of the game
Feb. 7, 1988	AFC 15, NFC 6	Aloha Stadium, Honolulu (50,113)	Bruce Smith, Buffalo, player of the game
Jan. 29, 1989	NFC 34, AFC 3	Aloha Stadium, Honolulu (50,113)	Randall Cunningham, Philadelphia, player of the game
Feb. 4, 1990	NFC 27, AFC 21	Aloha Stadium, Honolulu (50,445)	Jerry Gray, L.A. Rams, player of the game
Feb. 3, 1991	AFC 23, NFC 21	Aloha Stadium, Honolulu (50,345)	Jim Kelly, Buffalo, player of the game
Feb. 2, 1992	NFC 21, AFC 15	Aloha Stadium, Honolulu (50,209)	Michael Irvin, Dallas, player of the game
Feb. 7, 1993	AFC 23, NFC 20 (OT)	Aloha Stadium, Honolulu (50,007)	Steve Tasker, Buffalo, player of the game
Feb. 6, 1994	NFC 17, AFC 3	Aloha Stadium, Honolulu (50,026)	Andre Rison, Atlanta, player of the game
Feb. 5, 1995	AFC 41, NFC 13	Aloha Stadium, Honolulu (49,121)	Marshall Faulk, Indianapolis, player of the game
Feb. 4, 1996	NFC 20, AFC 13	Aloha Stadium, Honolulu (50,034)	Jerry Rice, San Francisco, player of the game
Feb. 2, 1997	AFC 26, NFC 23 (OT)	Aloha Stadium, Honolulu (50,031)	Mark Brunell, Jacksonville, player of the game
Feb. 1, 1998	AFC 29, NFC 24	Aloha Stadium, Honolulu (49,995)	Warren Moon, Seattle, player of the game
Feb. 7, 1999	AFC 23, NFC 10	Aloha Stadium, Honolulu (50,075)	Keyshawn Johnson, N.Y. Jets and Ty Law, New England, co-players of the game
Feb. 6, 2000	NFC 51, AFC 31	Aloha Stadium, Honolulu (50,112)	Randy Moss, Minnesota, player of the game
Feb. 4, 2001	AFC 38, NFC 17	Aloha Stadium, Honolulu (50,128)	Rich Gannon, Oakland, player of the game

PRO FOOTBALL HALL OF FAME GAME (38)

1962	New York Giants 21, St. Louis Cardinals 21
1963	Pittsburgh Steelers 16, Cleveland Browns 7
1964	Baltimore Colts 48, Pittsburgh Steelers 17
1965	Washington Redskins 20, Detroit Lions 3
1966	No game
1967	Philadelphia Eagles 28, Cleveland Browns 13
1968	Chicago Bears 30, Dallas Cowboys 24
1969	Green Bay Packers 38, Atlanta Falcons 24
1970	New Orleans Saints 14, Minnesota Vikings 13
1971	Los Angeles Rams (NFC) 17, Houston Oilers (AFC) 6
1972	Kansas City Chiefs (AFC) 23, New York Giants (NFC) 17
1973	San Francisco 49ers (NFC) 20, New England Patriots (AFC) 7
1974	St. Louis Cardinals (NFC) 21, Buffalo Bills (AFC) 13
1975	Washington Redskins (NFC) 17, Cincinnati Bengals (AFC) 9
1976	Denver Broncos (AFC) 10, Detroit Lions (NFC) 7
1977	Chicago Bears (NFC) 20, New York Jets (AFC) 6
1978	Philadelphia Eagles (NFC) 17, Miami Dolphins (AFC) 3
1979	Oakland Raiders (AFC) 20, Dallas Cowboys (NFC) 13
1980*	San Diego Chargers (AFC) 0, Green Bay Packers (NFC) 0
1981	Cleveland Browns (AFC) 24, Atlanta Falcons (NFC) 10
1982	Minnesota Vikings (NFC) 30, Baltimore Colts (AFC) 14
1983	Pittsburgh Steelers (AFC) 27, New Orleans Saints (NFC) 14
1984	Seattle Seahawks (AFC) 38, Tampa Bay Buccaneers (NFC) 0
1985	New York Giants (NFC) 21, Houston Oilers (AFC) 20
1986	New England Patriots (AFC) 21, St. Louis Cardinals (NFC) 16
1987	San Francisco 49ers (NFC) 20, Kansas City Chiefs (AFC) 7
1988	Cincinnati Bengals (AFC) 14, Los Angeles Rams (NFC) 7
1989	Washington Redskins (NFC) 31, Buffalo Bills (AFC) 6
1990	Chicago Bears (NFC) 13, Cleveland Browns (AFC) 0
1991	Detroit Lions (NFC) 14, Denver Broncos (AFC) 3
1992	New York Jets (AFC) 41, Philadelphia Eagles (NFC) 14
1993	Los Angeles Raiders (AFC) 19, Green Bay Packers (NFC) 3
1994	Atlanta Falcons (NFC) 21, San Diego Chargers (AFC) 17
1995	Carolina Panthers (NFC) 20, Jacksonville Jaguars (AFC) 14
1996	Indianapolis Colts (AFC) 10, New Orleans Saints (NFC) 3
1997	Minnesota Vikings (NFC) 28, Seattle Seahawks (AFC) 26
1998	Tampa Bay Buccaneers (NFC) 30, Pittsburgh Steelers (AFC) 6
1999	Cleveland Browns (AFC) 20, Dallas Cowboys (NFC) 17 (OT)
2000	New England Patriots (AFC) 20, San Francisco 49ers (NFC) 0

Game called with 5:29 remaining because of severe thunder and lightning.

NFL INTERNATIONAL GAMES (52)

Date	Site	Teams
Aug. 12, 1950	Ottawa, Canada	N.Y. Giants 27, Ottawa Rough Riders 6
Aug. 11, 1951	Ottawa, Canada	N.Y. Giants 41, Ottawa Rough Riders 18
Aug. 5, 1959	Toronto, Canada	Chi. Cardinals 55, Tor. Argonauts 26
Aug. 3, 1960	Toronto, Canada	Pittsburgh 43, Toronto Argonauts 16
Aug. 15, 1960	Toronto, Canada	Chicago 16, N.Y. Giants 7
Aug. 2, 1961	Toronto, Canada	St. Louis 36, Toronto Argonauts 7
Aug. 5, 1961	Montreal, Canada	Chicago 34, Montreal Allouettes 16
Aug. 8, 1961	Hamilton, Canada	Hamilton Tiger-Cats 38, Buffalo 21
Sept. 11, 1969	Montreal, Canada	Pittsburgh 17, N.Y. Giants 13
Aug. 25, 1969	Montreal, Canada	Detroit 22, Boston 9
Aug. 16, 1976	Tokyo, Japan	St. Louis 20, San Diego 10
Aug. 5, 1978	Mexico City, Mexico	New Orleans 14, Philadelphia 7
Aug. 6, 1983	London, England	Minnesota 28, St. Louis 10
*Aug. 3, 1986	London, England	Chicago 17, Dallas 6
*Aug. 9, 1987	London, England	L.A. Rams 28, Denver 27
*July 31, 1988	London, England	Miami 27, San Francisco 21
Aug. 14, 1988	Goteborg, Sweden	Minnesota 28, Chicago 21
Aug. 18, 1988	Montreal, Canada	N.Y. Jets 11, Cleveland 7
*Aug. 5, 1989	Tokyo, Japan	L.A. Rams 16, San Francisco 13 (OT)
*Aug. 6, 1989	London, England	Philadelphia 17, Cleveland 13
*Aug. 4, 1990	Tokyo, Japan	Denver 10, Seattle 7
*Aug. 5, 1990	London, England	New Orleans 17, L.A. Raiders 10
*Aug. 9, 1990	Montreal, Canada	Pittsburgh 30, New England 14
*Aug. 11, 1990	Berlin, Germany	L.A. Rams 19, Kansas City 3
*July 28, 1991	London, England	Buffalo 17, Philadelphia 13
*Aug. 3, 1991	Berlin, Germany	San Francisco 21, Chicago 7
*Aug. 3, 1991	Tokyo, Japan	Miami 19, L.A. Raiders 17
*Aug. 1, 1992	Tokyo, Japan	Houston 34, Dallas 23
*Aug. 15, 1992	Berlin, Germany	Miami 31, Denver 27
*Aug. 16, 1992	London, England	San Francisco 17, Washington 15
*July 31, 1993	Tokyo, Japan	New Orleans 28, Philadelphia 16
*Aug. 1, 1993	Barcelona, Spain	San Francisco 21, Pittsburgh 14
*Aug. 7, 1993	Berlin, Germany	Minnesota 20, Buffalo 6
*Aug. 8, 1993	London, England	Dallas 13, Detroit 13 (OT)
Aug. 14, 1993	Toronto, Canada	Cleveland 12, New England 9
*July 31, 1994	Barcelona, Spain	L.A. Raiders 25, Denver 22
*Aug. 6, 1994	Tokyo, Japan	Minnesota 17, Kansas City 9
*Aug. 13, 1994	Berlin, Germany	N.Y. Giants 28, San Diego 20
*Aug. 15, 1994	Mexico City, Mexico	Houston 6, Dallas 0
*Aug. 5, 1995	Tokyo, Japan	Denver 24, San Francisco 10
*Aug. 12, 1995	Toronto, Canada	Buffalo 9, Dallas 7
*July 27, 1996	Tokyo, Japan	San Diego 20, Pittsburgh 10
*Aug. 5, 1996	Monterrey, Mexico	Kansas City 32, Dallas 6
*July 27, 1997	Dublin, Ireland	Pittsburgh 30, Chicago 17
*Aug. 4, 1997	Mexico City, Mexico	Miami 38, Denver 19
*Aug. 16, 1997	Toronto, Canada	Green Bay 35, Buffalo 3
*Aug. 1, 1998	Tokyo, Japan	Green Bay 27, Kansas City 24 (OT)
*Aug. 15, 1998	Vancouver, Canada	San Francisco 24, Seattle 21
*Aug. 17, 1998	Mexico City, Mexico	New England 21, Dallas 3
*Aug. 7, 1999	Sydney, Australia	Denver 20, San Diego 17
*Aug. 5, 2000	Tokyo, Japan	Atlanta 20, Dallas 9
*Aug. 19, 2000	Mexico City, Mexico	Indianapolis 24, Pittsburgh 23

American Bowl Game

CHICAGO ALL-STAR GAME

Pro teams won 31, lost 9, and tied 2. The game was discontinued after 1976.

Year	Date	Winner	Loser	Attendance
1976*	July 23	Pittsburgh 24	All-Stars 0	52,895
1975	Aug. 1	Pittsburgh 21	All-Stars 14	54,103
1974		No game was played		
1973	July 27	Miami 14	All-Stars 3	54,103
1972	July 28	Dallas 20	All-Stars 7	54,162
1971	July 30	Baltimore 24	All-Stars 17	52,289
1970	July 31	Kansas City 24	All-Stars 3	69,940
1969	Aug. 1	N.Y. Jets 26	All-Stars 24	74,208
1968	Aug. 2	Green Bay 34	All-Stars 17	69,917
1967	Aug. 4	Green Bay 27	All-Stars 0	70,934
1966	Aug. 5	Green Bay 38	All-Stars 0	72,000
1965	Aug. 6	Cleveland 24	All-Stars 16	68,000
1964	Aug. 7	Chicago 28	All-Stars 17	65,000
1963	Aug. 2	All-Stars 20	Green Bay 17	65,000
1962	Aug. 3	Green Bay 42	All-Stars 20	65,000
1961	Aug. 4	Philadelphia 28	All-Stars 14	66,000
1960	Aug. 12	Baltimore 32	All-Stars 7	70,000
1959	Aug. 14	Baltimore 29	All-Stars 0	70,000
1958	Aug. 15	All-Stars 35	Detroit 19	70,000
1957	Aug. 9	N.Y. Giants 22	All-Stars 12	75,000
1956	Aug. 10	Cleveland 26	All-Stars 0	75,000
1955	Aug. 12	All-Stars 30	Cleveland 27	75,000
1954	Aug. 13	Detroit 31	All-Stars 6	93,470
1953	Aug. 14	Detroit 24	All-Stars 10	93,818
1952	Aug. 15	Los Angeles 10	All-Stars 7	88,316
1951	Aug. 17	Cleveland 33	All-Stars 0	92,180
1950	Aug. 11	All-Stars 17	Philadelphia 7	88,885
1949	Aug. 12	Philadelphia 38	All-Stars 0	93,780
1948	Aug. 20	Chi. Cardinals 28	All-Stars 0	101,220
1947	Aug. 22	All-Stars 16	Chi. Bears 0	105,840
1946	Aug. 23	All-Stars 16	Los Angeles 0	97,380
1945	Aug. 30	Green Bay 19	All-Stars 7	92,753
1944	Aug. 30	Chi. Bears 24	All-Stars 21	48,769
1943	Aug. 25	All-Stars 27	Washington 7	48,471
1942	Aug. 28	Chi. Bears 21	All-Stars 0	101,100
1941	Aug. 28	Chi. Bears 37	All-Stars 13	98,203
1940	Aug. 29	Green Bay 45	All-Stars 28	84,567
1939	Aug. 30	N.Y. Giants 9	All-Stars 0	81,456
1938	Aug. 31	All-Stars 28	Washington 16	74,250
1937	Sept. 1	All-Stars 6	Green Bay 0	84,560
1936	Sept. 3	Detroit 7	All-Stars 7 (tie)	76,000
1935	Aug. 29	Chi. Bears 5	All-Stars 0	77,450
1934	Aug. 31	Chi. Bears 0	All-Stars 0 (tie)	79,432

Game shortened because of thunderstorms.

NFL PLAYOFF BOWL

Consolation game that matched conference runners-up.
Western Conference won 8, Eastern Conference won 2.
All games played at Miami's Orange Bowl.

1970	Los Angeles Rams 31, Dallas Cowboys 0
1969	Dallas Cowboys 17, Minnesota Vikings 13
1968	Los Angeles Rams 30, Cleveland Browns 6
1967	Baltimore Colts 20, Philadelphia Eagles 14
1966	Baltimore Colts 35, Dallas Cowboys 3
1965	St. Louis Cardinals 24, Green Bay Packers 17
1964	Green Bay Packers 40, Cleveland Browns 23
1963	Detroit Lions 17, Pittsburgh Steelers 10
1962	Detroit Lions 28, Philadelphia Eagles 10
1961	Detroit Lions 17, Cleveland Browns 16

INTERCONFERENCE GAMES

AFC VS. NFC (REGULAR SEASON), 1970-2000

	Balt	Buff	Cin	Cle	Den	Ind	Jax	KC	Mia	NE	NYJ	Oak	Pitt	SD	Sea	Tenn	TB	TOTALS
1970		0-3	1-2	0-3	2-2	3-0		0-2-1	2-1	0-3	2-1	1-2	0-3	1-2		0-3		12-27-1
1971		0-3	1-2	2-1	1-3	2-1		2-1	3-0	0-3	0-3	1-1-1	1-2	2-1		0-2-1		15-23-2
1972		2-0-1	2-1	1-2	1-3	0-3		2-1	3-0	3-0	1-2	3-0	2-1	0-3		0-3		20-19-1
1973		2-1	2-1	1-2	0-3-1	2-1		1-1-1	3-0	2-1	0-3	2-1	3-0	1-2		0-3		19-19-2
1974		2-1	2-1	1-2	2-2	1-2		1-2	2-1	3-0	2-1	3-0	3-0	1-2		0-3		23-17
1975		1-2	3-0	1-3	2-1	2-1		2-1	3-0	1-2	0-3	3-0	2-1	0-3		3-0		23-17
1976		0-2	2-0	2-0	2-0	0-2		1-1	0-2	1-1	0-2	3-0	1-1	2-0		2-0	0-1	16-12
1977		1-1	2-1	1-1	1-1	1-1		1-1	2-0	2-0	1-1	1-1	2-0	1-1	1-0	2-0		19-9
1978		1-1	2-2	4-0	2-2	2-2		0-2	3-1	2-2	1-3	4-0	3-1	2-2	3-1	2-2		31-21
1979		2-2	2-2	3-1	3-1	1-1		0-2	4-0	3-1	3-1	4-0	3-1	3-1	3-1	2-2		36-16
1980		3-1	2-2	3-1	3-1	1-1		2-0	4-0	1-3	1-3	2-2	4-0	2-2	1-3	4-0		33-19
1981		1-3	2-2	3-1	3-1	0-4		2-2	3-1	0-4	2-0	2-2	3-1	2-2	0-2	1-3		24-28
1982		1-2	1-0	0-2	2-1	0-1-1		0-3	1-1	0-1	4-0	3-0	1-0	1-0	1-0	0-3		15-14-1
1983		1-3	3-1	2-2	0-2	2-0		2-2	3-1	2-2	3-1	2-2	2-2	2-2	1-3	1-3		26-26
1984		1-3	2-2	1-3	3-1	0-4		1-1	4-0	0-4	0-2	3-1	3-1	4-0	4-0	0-4		26-26
1985		0-2	2-2	1-3	3-1	3-1		2-2	3-1	3-1	2-2	3-1	1-3	1-1	2-2	1-3		27-25
1986		1-1	3-1	2-2	3-1	1-3		1-1	2-2	3-1	2-2	1-3	2-2	0-4	3-1	2-2		26-26
1987		1-2	1-2	2-2	2-1-1	1-0		1-2	3-0	0-3	0-4	2-2	2-2	2-0	4-0	2-2		23-22-1
1988		2-2	4-0	4-0	3-1	2-2		0-2	3-1	2-2	2-0	1-3	1-3	2-2	1-3	3-1		30-22
1989		1-3	2-2	3-1	2-2	1-3		2-0	2-0	0-4	1-3	2-2	3-1	2-2	0-4	3-1		24-28
1990		3-1	1-3	1-3	1-3	2-2		4-0	2-2	0-4	2-0	3-1	3-1	1-1	2-2	1-3		26-26
1991		3-1	1-3	0-4	2-0	0-4		2-2	3-1	1-1	2-2	2-2	0-4	1-3	1-3	1-3		19-33
1992		4-0	1-3	2-2	1-3	2-0		2-2	2-2	0-4	0-4	2-2	1-3	2-0	0-4	3-1		22-30
1993		4-0	2-2	3-1	1-3	0-4		2-2	3-1	1-1	2-2	3-1	2-2	2-2	0-2	2-2		27-25
1994		1-3	1-3	3-1	1-3	0-2		3-1	2-2	4-0	1-3	3-1	2-2	2-2	2-0	0-4		25-27
1995		3-1	2-2	1-3	2-2	2-2	0-4	3-1	2-2	0-4	0-4	3-1	2-2	3-1	3-1	1-3		27-33
1996	2-2	4-0	2-2		3-1	3-1	2-2	4-0	1-3	2-2	1-3	1-3	2-2	1-3	2-2	2-2		32-28
1997	2-1-1	1-3	2-2		3-1	1-3	2-2	4-0	1-3	1-3	3-1	2-2	2-2	1-3	2-2	4-0		31-28-1
1998	1-3	3-1	1-3		3-1	0-4	3-1	3-1	3-1	2-2	2-2	3-1	2-2	1-3	3-1	1-3		31-29
1999	2-1	3-1	1-2	1-2	2-2	4-0	4-0	2-2	2-2	3-1	2-2	3-1	3-0	1-3	2-2	3-1		38-22
2000	2-1	2-2	1-2	0-3	3-1	2-2	2-2	2-2	2-2	0-4	3-1	4-0	1-2	0-4	2-2	4-0		30-30
Total	9-8-1	54-51-1	56-53	48-51	62-50-2	41-57-1	13-11	54-42-2	76-33	42-64	45-61	75-38-1	62-47	46-57	43-41	50-62-1	0-1	776-727-9

NFC VS. AFC (REGULAR SEASON), 1970-2000

	Ariz	Atl	Car	Chi	Dall	Det	GB	Minn	NO	NYG	Phil	StL	SF	TB	Wash	Sea	TOTALS
1970	2-0-1	1-2		1-2	3-0	3-0	2-1	2-1	0-3	3-0	2-1	2-1	4-0		2-1		27-12-1
1971	2-1	3-0		1-2	3-0	4-0	2-1	2-1	0-1-2	1-2	1-2	1-2	2-1		1-2		23-15-2
1972	1-2	2-2		1-2	3-0	2-0-1	2-1	1-2	0-3	1-2	2-1	1-2	2-1		1-2		19-20-1
1973	0-2-1	2-1		2-2	2-1	0-3	1-1-1	2-1	1-2	1-2	2-1	3-0	1-2		2-1		19-19-2
1974	2-1	0-3		0-3	2-1	1-2	2-1	2-1	0-3	1-2	2-1	3-1	0-3		2-1		17-23
1975	2-1	1-2		0-3	2-1	1-2	0-3	4-0	0-3	2-1	0-3	3-0	1-2		1-2		17-23
1976	1-1	0-2		0-2	2-0	2-0	0-2	2-0	1-2	0-2	0-2	1-1	1-1		1-1	1-0	12-16
1977	0-2	0-2		1-1	1-1	2-0	0-3	1-1	0-2	0-2	1-1	2-0	0-2	0-1	1-1		9-19
1978	0-4	1-3		0-4	3-1	2-2	2-2	1-3	1-3	1-1	3-1	2-2	1-3	2-0	2-2		21-31
1979	1-3	1-3		2-2	1-3	0-4	1-3	1-3	0-4	1-1	2-2	2-2	0-4	2-0	2-2		16-36
1980	1-1	2-2		0-4	3-1	0-2	1-3	1-3	1-3	1-3	3-1	2-2	2-2	1-3	1-3		19-33
1981	3-1	1-3		4-0	4-0	2-2	1-1	1-3	2-2	1-1	3-1	1-3	3-1	0-4	2-2		28-24
1982		1-1		1-1	2-1	0-1	1-1-1	1-3	1-0	1-0	2-1	1-2	1-3	2-1			14-15-1
1983	3-1	3-1		1-1	2-2	1-3	2-2	4-0	1-3	0-4	1-1	1-3	2-2	1-3	4-0		26-26
1984	3-1	1-3		2-2	2-2	0-4	0-4	0-4	3-1	2-0	3-1	3-1	3-1	1-1	3-1		26-26
1985	2-2	0-4		3-1	3-1	2-2	0-4	2-0	0-4	2-2	1-1	3-1	3-1	0-4	4-0		25-27
1986	1-1	1-3		4-0	1-3	1-3	1-3	1-3	1-3	3-1	2-2	2-2	4-0	1-1	3-1		26-26
1987	0-1	0-4		2-2	2-1	0-4	1-2-1	2-1	4-0	2-1	3-1	1-2	3-1	0-2	2-1		22-23-1
1988	1-3	1-3		3-1	0-4	1-1	1-3	2-2	4-0	1-1	2-2	2-2	2-2	1-3	1-3		22-30
1989	1-3	2-2		2-2	0-2	1-3	0-2	2-2	4-0	4-0	3-1	3-1	4-0	0-4	2-2		28-24
1990	2-2	2-2		2-2	1-1	1-3	1-3	2-2	2-2	3-1	1-3	2-2	4-0	0-2	3-1		26-26
1991	1-1	3-1		2-2	3-1	4-0	1-3	0-2	3-1	3-1	4-0	1-3	3-1	1-3	4-0		33-19
1992	0-2	2-2		1-3	4-0	2-2	3-1	3-1	3-1	2-2	3-1	2-2	3-1	0-2	2-2		30-22
1993	1-1	1-3		2-2	2-2	2-0	3-1	2-2	2-2	2-2	2-2	2-2	2-2	1-3	1-3		25-27
1994	3-1	1-3		3-1	3-1	2-2	1-3	2-2	1-3	3-1	1-3	2-2	3-1	1-1	1-1		27-25
1995	1-3	2-2	3-1	2-2	4-0	3-1	4-0	3-1	4-0	0-4	1-3	1-3	3-1	2-2	0-4		33-27
1996	0-4	0-4	3-1	2-2	2-2	1-3	3-1	1-3	1-3	2-2	2-2	2-2	4-0	2-2	3-1		28-32
1997	1-3	2-2	2-2	2-2	2-2	2-2	3-1	3-1	2-2	1-3	2-1-1	0-4	2-2	3-1	1-3		28-31-1
1998	1-3	3-1	1-3	2-2	1-3	1-3	3-1	4-0	1-3	3-1	0-4	3-1	2-2	2-2	2-2		29-31
1999	0-4	0-4	2-2	2-2	1-3	1-3	2-2	2-2	0-4	2-2	1-3	3-1	1-3	3-1	2-2		22-38
2000	1-3	1-3	2-2	2-2	1-3	2-2	1-3	3-1	1-3	3-1	3-1	3-1	2-2	3-1	2-2		30-30
Total	37-58-2	40-73	13-11	52-59	65-43	46-59-1	45-62-3	59-51	44-66-2	52-48	58-50-1	60-53	68-47	29-47	58-49	1-0	727-776-9

INTERCONFERENCE GAMES

2000 INTERCONFERENCE GAMES

(Home Team in capital letters)

AFC 30, NFC 30

AFC Victories

New York Jets 20, GREEN BAY 16
BUFFALO 27, Green Bay 18
DENVER 42, Atlanta 14
SEATTLE 20, New Orleans 10
New York Jets 21, TAMPA BAY 17
TENNESSEE 28, New York Giants 14
Oakland 34, SAN FRANCISCO 28 (OT)
KANSAS CITY 54, St. Louis 34
INDIANAPOLIS 30, Detroit 18
MIAMI 28, Green Bay 20
Jacksonville 23, DALLAS 17 (OT)
Tennessee 27, WASHINGTON 21
Miami 23, DETROIT 8
BUFFALO 20, Chicago 3
Oakland 31, NEW ORLEANS 22
BALTIMORE 27, Dallas 0
NEW YORK JETS 17, Chicago 10
OAKLAND 41, Atlanta 14
CINCINNATI 24, Arizona 13
Denver 38, NEW ORLEANS 23
Seattle 30, ATLANTA 10
Tennessee 15, PHILADELPHIA 13
JACKSONVILLE 44, Arizona 10
KANSAS CITY 15, Carolina 14
PITTSBURGH 24, Washington 3
Baltimore 13, ARIZONA 7
DENVER 38, San Francisco 9
OAKLAND 52, Carolina 9
INDIANAPOLIS 31, Minnesota 10
TENNESSEE 31, Dallas 0

NFC Victories

Tampa Bay 21, NEW ENGLAND 16
ST. LOUIS 41, Denver 36
MINNESOTA 13, Miami 7
New Orleans 28, SAN DIEGO 27
St. Louis 37, SEATTLE 34
Minnesota 21, NEW ENGLAND 13
ST. LOUIS 57, San Diego 31
ARIZONA 29, Cleveland 21
CAROLINA 26, Seattle 3
WASHINGTON 10, Baltimore 3
MINNESOTA 31, Buffalo 27
Washington 35, JACKSONVILLE 16
CHICAGO 27, Indianapolis 24
New York Giants 24, CLEVELAND 3
DALLAS 23, Cincinnati 6
Philadelphia 26, PITTSBURGH 23 (OT)
SAN FRANCISCO 21, Kansas City 7
GREEN BAY 26, Indianapolis 24
DETROIT 34, New England 9
TAMPA BAY 31, Buffalo 17
San Francisco 45, SAN DIEGO 17
CHICAGO 24, New England 17
Philadelphia 35, CLEVELAND 24
NEW YORK GIANTS 30, Pittsburgh 10
Tampa Bay 16, MIAMI 13
Detroit 10, NEW YORK JETS 7
CAROLINA 30, San Diego 22
NEW YORK GIANTS 28, Jacksonville 25
PHILADELPHIA 16, Cincinnati 7
ATLANTA 29, Kansas City 13

REGULAR SEASON INTERCONFERENCE RECORDS, 1970-2000

AMERICAN FOOTBALL CONFERENCE

Eastern Division	W	L	T	Pct.
Miami	76	33	0	.697
Buffalo	54	51	1	.514
New York Jets	45	61	0	.425
Indianapolis	41	57	1	.419
New England	42	64	0	.396
Central Division	**W**	**L**	**T**	**Pct.**
Pittsburgh	62	47	0	.569
Jacksonville	13	11	0	.542
Baltimore	9	8	1	.528
Cincinnati	56	53	0	.514
Cleveland	48	51	0	.485
Tennessee	50	62	1	.447
Western Division	**W**	**L**	**T**	**Pct.**
Oakland	75	38	1	.662
Kansas City	54	42	2	.561
Denver	62	50	2	.553
Seattle*	44	41	0	.518
San Diego	46	57	0	.447

NATIONAL FOOTBALL CONFERENCE

Eastern Division	W	L	T	Pct.
Dallas	65	43	0	.602
Washington	58	49	0	.542
Philadelphia	58	50	1	.537
New York Giants	52	48	0	.520
Arizona	37	58	2	.392
Central Division	**W**	**L**	**T**	**Pct.**
Minnesota	59	51	0	.536
Chicago	52	59	0	.468
Detroit	46	59	1	.439
Green Bay	45	62	3	.423
Tampa Bay*	29	48	0	.377
Western Division	**W**	**L**	**T**	**Pct.**
San Francisco	68	47	0	.591
Carolina	13	11	0	.542
St. Louis	60	53	0	.531
New Orleans	44	66	2	.402
Atlanta	40	73	0	.354

**Records include one game played between Seattle and Tampa Bay, won by the Seahwaks 13-10, in their inaugural season (1976) when Seattle competed in the NFC and Tampa Bay in the AFC.*

INTERCONFERENCE VICTORIES, 1970-2000

REGULAR SEASON

	AFC	NFC	Tie
1970	12	27	1
1971	15	23	2
1972	20	19	1
1973	19	19	2
1974	23	17	0
1975	23	17	0
1976	16	12	0
1977	19	9	0
1978	31	21	0
1979	36	16	0
1980	33	19	0
1981	24	28	0
1982	15	14	1
1983	26	26	0
1984	26	26	0
1985	27	25	0
1986	26	26	0
1987	23	22	1
1988	30	22	0
1989	24	28	0
1990	26	26	0
1991	19	33	0
1992	22	30	0
1993	27	25	0
1994	25	27	0
1995	27	33	0
1996	32	28	0
1997	31	28	1
1998	31	29	0
1999	38	22	0
2000	30	30	0
Total	776	727	9

PRESEASON

	AFC	NFC	Tie
1970	21	28	1
1971	28	28	3
1972	27	25	4
1973	23	35	2
1974	35	25	0
1975	30	26	1
1976	30	31	0
1977	38	25	0
1978	20	19	0
1979	25	18	0
1980	22	20	1
1981	18	19	0
1982	25	16	0
1983	15	24	0
1984	16	19	0
1985	10	22	1
1986	22	17	0
1987	22	22	0
1988	23	16	1
1989	16	27	0
1990	15	29	0
1991	19	27	0
1992	30	22	0
1993	17	22	0
1994	22	16	0
1995	19	26	0
1996	27	19	0
1997	26	17	0
1998	34	16	0
1999	22	25	0
2000	34	17	0
Total	731	698	14

RECORDS AFTER BYE WEEKS, 1990-2000

AFC

Team	Record	Team	Record
Baltimore	2-3	Miami	8-4
Buffalo	9-3	New England	4-8
Cincinnati	3-9	N.Y. Jets	5-7
Cleveland	2-5	Oakland	7-5
Denver	9-3	Pittsburgh	6-6
Indianapolis	5-7	San Diego	5-7
Jacksonville	4-2	Seattle	3-9
Kansas City	8-4	Tennessee	7-5

RECORDS AFTER BYE WEEKS, 1990-2000

NFC

Team	Record	Team	Record
Arizona	5-7	New Orleans	6-6
Atlanta	7-5	N.Y. Giants	3-9
Carolina	2-4	Philadelphia	8-4
Chicago	9-3	St. Louis	6-6
Dallas	9-3	San Francisco	6-6
Detroit	6-6	Tampa Bay	4-8
Green Bay	5-7	Washington	6-6
Minnesota	10-2		

MONDAY NIGHT FOOTBALL, 1970-2000

(Home Team in capitals, games listed in chronological order.)

2000
ST. LOUIS 41, Denver 36
NEW YORK JETS 20, New England 19
Dallas 27, WASHINGTON 21
INDIANAPOLIS 43, Jacksonville 14
KANSAS CITY 24, Seattle 17
MINNESOTA 30, Tampa Bay 23
TENNESSEE 27, Jacksonville 13
NEW YORK JETS 40, Miami 37 (OT)
Tennessee 27, WASHINGTON 21
GREEN BAY 26, Minnesota 20 (OT)
DENVER 27, Oakland 24
Washington 33, ST. LOUIS 20
CAROLINA 31, Green Bay 14
NEW ENGLAND 30, Kansas City 24
INDIANAPOLIS 44, Buffalo 20
TAMPA BAY 38, St. Louis 35
TENNESSEE 31, Dallas 0

1999
Miami 38, DENVER 21
DALLAS 24, Atlanta 7
San Francisco 24, ARIZONA 10
Buffalo 23, MIAMI 18
Jacksonville 16, NEW YORK JETS 6
NEW YORK GIANTS 13, Dallas 10
PITTSBURGH 13, Atlanta 9
Seattle 27, GREEN BAY 7
MINNESOTA 27, Dallas 17
New York Jets 24, NEW ENGLAND 17
DENVER 27, Oakland 21 (OT)
Green Bay 20, SAN FRANCISCO 3
TAMPA BAY 24, Minnesota 17
JACKSONVILLE 27, Denver 24
MINNESOTA 24, Green Bay 20
New York Jets 38, MIAMI 31
ATLANTA 34, San Francisco 29

1998
DENVER 27, New England 21
San Francisco 45, WASHINGTON 10
Dallas 31, NEW YORK GIANTS 7
DETROIT 27, Tampa Bay 6
Minnesota 37, GREEN BAY 24
JACKSONVILLE 28, Miami 21
New York Jets 24, NEW ENGLAND 14
Pittsburgh 20, KANSAS CITY 13
Dallas 34, PHILADELPHIA 0
PITTSBURGH 27, Green Bay 20
Denver 30, KANSAS CITY 7
NEW ENGLAND 26, Miami 23
SAN FRANCISCO 31, New York Giants 7
TAMPA BAY 24, Green Bay 22
SAN FRANCISCO 35, Detroit 13
MIAMI 31, Denver 21
JACKSONVILLE 21, Pittsburgh 3

1997
GREEN BAY 38, Chicago 24
Kansas City 28, OAKLAND 27
DALLAS 21, Philadelphia 20
JACKSONVILLE 30, Pittsburgh 21
San Francisco 34, CAROLINA 21
DENVER 34, New England 13
WASHINGTON 21, Dallas 16
Buffalo 9, INDIANAPOLIS 6
Green Bay 28, NEW ENGLAND 10
Chicago 36, MIAMI 33 (OT)
KANSAS CITY 13, Pittsburgh 10
San Francisco 24, PHILADELPHIA 12
MIAMI 30, Buffalo 13
DENVER 31, Oakland 3
Green Bay 27, MINNESOTA 11
Carolina 23, DALLAS 13
SAN FRANCISCO 34, Denver 17
New England 14, MIAMI 12

1996
CHICAGO 22, Dallas 6
GREEN BAY 39, Philadelphia 13
PITTSBURGH 24, Buffalo 6
INDIANAPOLIS 10, Miami 6
Dallas 23, PHILADELPHIA 19
Pittsburgh 17, KANSAS CITY 7
GREEN BAY 23, San Francisco 20 (OT)
Oakland 23, SAN DIEGO 14
Chicago 15, MINNESOTA 13
Denver 22, OAKLAND 21
SAN DIEGO 27, Detroit 21
DALLAS 21, Green Bay 6
Pittsburgh 24, MIAMI 17
San Francisco 34, ATLANTA 10
OAKLAND 26, Kansas City 7
MIAMI 16, Buffalo 14
SAN FRANCISCO 24, Detroit 14

1995
Dallas 35, NEW YORK GIANTS 0
Green Bay 27, CHICAGO 24
MIAMI 23, Pittsburgh 10
DETROIT 27, San Francisco 24
Buffalo 22, CLEVELAND 19
KANSAS CITY 29, San Diego 23 (OT)
DENVER 27, Oakland 0
NEW ENGLAND 27, Buffalo 14
Chicago 14, MINNESOTA 6
DALLAS 34, Philadelphia 12
PITTSBURGH 20, Cleveland 3
San Francisco 44, MIAMI 20
SAN DIEGO 12, Oakland 6
DETROIT 27, Chicago 7
MIAMI 13, Kansas City 6
SAN FRANCISCO 37, Minnesota 30
Dallas 37, ARIZONA 13

1994
SAN FRANCISCO 44, Los Angeles Raiders 14
PHILADELPHIA 30, Chicago 22
Detroit 20, DALLAS 17 (OT)
BUFFALO 27, Denver 20
PITTSBURGH 30, Houston 14
Minnesota 27, NEW YORK GIANTS 10
Kansas City 31, DENVER 28
PHILADELPHIA 21, Houston 6
Green Bay 33, CHICAGO 6
DALLAS 38, New York Giants 10
PITTSBURGH 23, Buffalo 10
New York Giants 13, HOUSTON 10
San Francisco 35, NEW ORLEANS 14
Los Angeles Raiders 24, SAN DIEGO 17
MIAMI 45, Kansas City 28
Dallas 24, NEW ORLEANS 16
MINNESOTA 21, San Francisco 14

1993
WASHINGTON 35, Dallas 16
CLEVELAND 23, San Francisco 13
KANSAS CITY 15, Denver 7
Pittsburgh 45, ATLANTA 17
MIAMI 17, Washington 10
BUFFALO 35, Houston 7
Los Angeles Raiders 23, DENVER 20
Minnesota 19, CHICAGO 12
BUFFALO 24, Washington 10
KANSAS CITY 23, Green Bay 16
PITTSBURGH 23, Buffalo 0
SAN FRANCISCO 42, New Orleans 7
San Diego 31, INDIANAPOLIS 0
DALLAS 23, Philadelphia 17
Pittsburgh 21, MIAMI 20
New York Giants 24, NEW ORLEANS 14
SAN DIEGO 45, Miami 20
Philadelphia 37, SAN FRANCISCO 34 (OT)

1992
DALLAS 23, Washington 10
Miami 27, CLEVELAND 23
New York Giants 27, CHICAGO 14
KANSAS CITY 27, Los Angeles Raiders 7
PHILADELPHIA 31, Dallas 7
WASHINGTON 34, Denver 3
PITTSBURGH 20, Cincinnati 0
Buffalo 24, NEW YORK JETS 20
Minnesota 38, CHICAGO 10
San Francisco 41, ATLANTA 3
Buffalo 26, MIAMI 20
NEW ORLEANS 20, Washington 3
SEATTLE 16, Denver 13 (OT)
HOUSTON 24, Chicago 7
MIAMI 20, Los Angeles Raiders 7
Dallas 41, ATLANTA 17
SAN FRANCISCO 24, Detroit 6

1991
NEW YORK GIANTS 16, San Francisco 14
Washington 33, DALLAS 31
HOUSTON 17, Kansas City 7
CHICAGO 19, New York Jets 13 (OT)
WASHINGTON 23, Philadelphia 0
KANSAS CITY 33, Buffalo 6
New York Giants 23, PITTSBURGH 20
BUFFALO 35, Cincinnati 16
KANSAS CITY 24, Los Angeles Raiders 21
PHILADELPHIA 30, New York Giants 7
Chicago 34, MINNESOTA 17
Buffalo 41, MIAMI 27
San Francisco 33, LOS ANGELES RAMS 10
Philadelphia 13, HOUSTON 6
MIAMI 37, Cincinnati 13
NEW ORLEANS 27, Los Angeles Raiders 0
SAN FRANCISCO 52, Chicago 14

1990
San Francisco 13, NEW ORLEANS 12
DENVER 24, Kansas City 23
Buffalo 30, NEW YORK JETS 7
SEATTLE 31, Cincinnati 16
Cleveland 30, DENVER 29
PHILADELPHIA 32, Minnesota 24
Cincinnati 34, CLEVELAND 13
PITTSBURGH 41, Los Angeles Rams 10
New York Giants 24, INDIANAPOLIS 7
PHILADELPHIA 28, Washington 14
Los Angeles Raiders 13, MIAMI 10
HOUSTON 27, Buffalo 24
SAN FRANCISCO 7, New York Giants 3
Los Angeles Raiders 38, DETROIT 31
San Francisco 26, LOS ANGELES RAMS 10
NEW ORLEANS 20, Los Angeles Rams 17

1989
New York Giants 27, WASHINGTON 24
Denver 28, BUFFALO 14
CINCINNATI 21, Cleveland 14
CHICAGO 27, Philadelphia 13
Los Angeles Raiders 14, NEW YORK JETS 7
BUFFALO 23, Los Angeles Rams 20
CLEVELAND 27, Chicago 7
NEW YORK GIANTS 24, Minnesota 14
SAN FRANCISCO 31, New Orleans 13
HOUSTON 26, Cincinnati 24
Denver 14, WASHINGTON 10
SAN FRANCISCO 34, New York Giants 24
SEATTLE 17, Buffalo 16
San Francisco 30, LOS ANGELES RAMS 27
NEW ORLEANS 30, Philadelphia 20
MINNESOTA 29, Cincinnati 21

MONDAY NIGHT FOOTBALL

1988
NEW YORK GIANTS 27, Washington 20
Dallas 17, PHOENIX 14
CLEVELAND 23, Indianapolis 17
Los Angeles Raiders 30, DENVER 27 (OT)
NEW ORLEANS 20, Dallas 17
PHILADELPHIA 24, New York Giants 13
Buffalo 37, NEW YORK JETS 14
CHICAGO 10, San Francisco 9
INDIANAPOLIS 55, Denver 23
HOUSTON 24, Cleveland 17
Buffalo 31, MIAMI 6
SAN FRANCISCO 37, Washington 21
SEATTLE 35, Los Angeles Raiders 27
LOS ANGELES RAMS 23, Chicago 3
MIAMI 38, Cleveland 31
MINNESOTA 28, Chicago 27

1987
CHICAGO 34, New York Giants 19
NEW YORK JETS 43, New England 24
San Francisco 41, NEW YORK GIANTS 21
DENVER 30, Los Angeles Raiders 14
Washington 13, DALLAS 7
CLEVELAND 30, Los Angeles Rams 17
MINNESOTA 34, Denver 27
DALLAS 33, New York Giants 24
NEW YORK JETS 30, Seattle 14
DENVER 31, Chicago 29
Los Angeles Rams 30, WASHINGTON 26
Los Angeles Raiders 37, SEATTLE 14
MIAMI 37, New York Jets 28
SAN FRANCISCO 41, Chicago 0
Dallas 29, LOS ANGELES RAMS 21
New England 24, MIAMI 10

1986
DALLAS 31, New York Giants 28
Denver 21, PITTSBURGH 10
Chicago 25, GREEN BAY 12
Dallas 31, ST. LOUIS 7
SEATTLE 33, San Diego 7
CINCINNATI 24, Pittsburgh 22
NEW YORK JETS 22, Denver 10
NEW YORK GIANTS 27, Washington 20
Los Angeles Rams 20, CHICAGO 17
CLEVELAND 26, Miami 16
WASHINGTON 14, San Francisco 6
MIAMI 45, New York Jets 3
New York Giants 21, SAN FRANCISCO 17
SEATTLE 37, Los Angeles Raiders 0
Chicago 16, DETROIT 13
New England 34, MIAMI 27

1985
DALLAS 44, Washington 14
CLEVELAND 17, Pittsburgh 7
Los Angeles Rams 35, SEATTLE 24
Cincinnati 37, PITTSBURGH 24
WASHINGTON 27, St. Louis 10
NEW YORK JETS 23, Miami 7
CHICAGO 23, Green Bay 7
LOS ANGELES RAIDERS 34, San Diego 21
ST. LOUIS 21, Dallas 10
DENVER 17, San Francisco 16
WASHINGTON 23, New York Giants 21
SAN FRANCISCO 19, Seattle 6
MIAMI 38, Chicago 24
Los Angeles Rams 27, SAN FRANCISCO 20
MIAMI 30, New England 27
L.A. Raiders 16, L.A. RAMS 6

1984
Dallas 20, LOS ANGELES RAMS 13
SAN FRANCISCO 37, Washington 31
Miami 21, BUFFALO 17
LOS ANGELES RAIDERS 33, San Diego 30
PITTSBURGH 38, Cincinnati 17
San Francisco 31, NEW YORK GIANTS 10
DENVER 17, Green Bay 14
Los Angeles Rams 24, ATLANTA 10
Seattle 24, SAN DIEGO 0
WASHINGTON 27, Atlanta 14
SEATTLE 17, Los Angeles Raiders 14
NEW ORLEANS 27, Pittsburgh 24
MIAMI 28, New York Jets 17
SAN DIEGO 20, Chicago 7
Los Angeles Raiders 24, DETROIT 3
MIAMI 28, Dallas 21

1983
Dallas 31, WASHINGTON 30
San Diego 17, KANSAS CITY 14
LOS ANGELES RAIDERS 27, Miami 14
NEW YORK GIANTS 27, Green Bay 3
New York Jets 34, BUFFALO 10
Pittsburgh 24, CINCINNATI 14
GREEN BAY 48, Washington 47
ST. LOUIS 20, New York Giants 20 (OT)
Washington 27, SAN DIEGO 24
DETROIT 15, New York Giants 9
Los Angeles Rams 36, ATLANTA 13
New York Jets 31, NEW ORLEANS 28
MIAMI 38, Cincinnati 14
DETROIT 13, Minnesota 2
Green Bay 12, TAMPA BAY 9 (OT)
SAN FRANCISCO 42, Dallas 17

1982
Pittsburgh 36, DALLAS 28
Green Bay 27, NEW YORK GIANTS 19
LOS ANGELES RAIDERS 28, San Diego 24
TAMPA BAY 23, Miami 17
New York Jets 28, DETROIT 13
Dallas 37, HOUSTON 7
SAN DIEGO 50, Cincinnati 34
MIAMI 27, Buffalo 10
MINNESOTA 31, Dallas 27

1981
San Diego 44, CLEVELAND 14
Oakland 36, MINNESOTA 10
Dallas 35, NEW ENGLAND 21
Los Angeles 24, CHICAGO 7
PHILADELPHIA 16, Atlanta 13
BUFFALO 31, Miami 21
DETROIT 48, Chicago 17
PITTSBURGH 26, Houston 13
DENVER 19, Minnesota 17
DALLAS 27, Buffalo 14
SEATTLE 44, San Diego 23
ATLANTA 31, Minnesota 30
MIAMI 13, Philadelphia 10
OAKLAND 30, Pittsburgh 27
LOS ANGELES 21, Atlanta 16
SAN DIEGO 23, Oakland 10

1980
Dallas 17, WASHINGTON 3
Houston 16, CLEVELAND 7
PHILADELPHIA 35, New York Giants 3
NEW ENGLAND 23, Denver 14
CHICAGO 23, Tampa Bay 0
DENVER 20, Washington 17
Oakland 45, PITTSBURGH 34
NEW YORK JETS 17, Miami 14
CLEVELAND 27, Chicago 21
HOUSTON 38, New England 34
Oakland 19, SEATTLE 17
Los Angeles 27, NEW ORLEANS 7
OAKLAND 9, Denver 3
MIAMI 16, New England 13 (OT)
LOS ANGELES 38, Dallas 14
SAN DIEGO 26, Pittsburgh 17

1979
Pittsburgh 16, NEW ENGLAND 13 (OT)
Atlanta 14, PHILADELPHIA 10
WASHINGTON 27, New York Giants 0
CLEVELAND 26, Dallas 7
GREEN BAY 27, New England 14
OAKLAND 13, Miami 3
NEW YORK JETS 14, Minnesota 7
PITTSBURGH 42, Denver 7
Seattle 31, ATLANTA 28
Houston 9, MIAMI 6
Philadelphia 31, DALLAS 21
LOS ANGELES 20, Atlanta 14
SEATTLE 30, New York Jets 7
Oakland 42, NEW ORLEANS 35
HOUSTON 20, Pittsburgh 17
SAN DIEGO 17, Denver 7

1978
DALLAS 38, Baltimore 0
MINNESOTA 12, Denver 9 (OT)
Baltimore 34, NEW ENGLAND 27
Minnesota 24, CHICAGO 20
WASHINGTON 9, Dallas 5
MIAMI 21, Cincinnati 0
DENVER 16, Chicago 7
Houston 24, PITTSBURGH 17
ATLANTA 15, Los Angeles 7
BALTIMORE 21, Washington 17
Oakland 34, CINCINNATI 21
HOUSTON 35, Miami 30
Pittsburgh 24, SAN FRANCISCO 7
SAN DIEGO 40, Chicago 7
Cincinnati 20, LOS ANGELES 19
MIAMI 23, New England 3

1977
PITTSBURGH 27, San Francisco 0
CLEVELAND 30, New England 27 (OT)
Oakland 37, KANSAS CITY 28
CHICAGO 24, Los Angeles 23
PITTSBURGH 20, Cincinnati 14
LOS ANGELES 35, Minnesota 3
ST. LOUIS 28, New York Giants 0
BALTIMORE 10, Washington 3
St. Louis 24, DALLAS 17
WASHINGTON 10, Green Bay 9
OAKLAND 34, Buffalo 13
MIAMI 17, Baltimore 6
Dallas 42, SAN FRANCISCO 35

1976
Miami 30, BUFFALO 21
Oakland 24, KANSAS CITY 21
Washington 20, PHILADELPHIA 17 (OT)
MINNESOTA 17, Pittsburgh 6
San Francisco 16, LOS ANGELES 0
NEW ENGLAND 41, New York Jets 7
WASHINGTON 20, St. Louis 10
BALTIMORE 38, Houston 14
CINCINNATI 20, Los Angeles 12
DALLAS 17, Buffalo 10
Baltimore 17, MIAMI 16
SAN FRANCISCO 20, Minnesota 16
OAKLAND 35, Cincinnati 20

1975
Oakland 31, MIAMI 21
DENVER 23, Green Bay 13
Dallas 36, DETROIT 10
WASHINGTON 27, St. Louis 17
New York Giants 17, BUFFALO 14
Minnesota 13, CHICAGO 9
Los Angeles 42, PHILADELPHIA 3
Kansas City 34, DALLAS 31
CINCINNATI 33, Buffalo 24
Pittsburgh 32, HOUSTON 9
MIAMI 20, New England 7
OAKLAND 17, Denver 10
SAN DIEGO 24, New York Jets 16

1974
BUFFALO 21, Oakland 20
PHILADELPHIA 13, Dallas 10
WASHINGTON 30, Denver 3
MIAMI 21, New York Jets 17
DETROIT 17, San Francisco 13
CHICAGO 10, Green Bay 9
PITTSBURGH 24, Atlanta 17
Los Angeles 15, SAN FRANCISCO 13
Minnesota 28, ST. LOUIS 24
Kansas City 42, DENVER 34
Pittsburgh 28, NEW ORLEANS 7
MIAMI 24, Cincinnati 3
Washington 23, LOS ANGELES 17

1973
GREEN BAY 23, New York Jets 7
DALLAS 40, New Orleans 3
DETROIT 31, Atlanta 6
WASHINGTON 14, Dallas 7
Miami 17, CLEVELAND 9
DENVER 23, Oakland 23
BUFFALO 23, Kansas City 14
PITTSBURGH 21, Washington 16
KANSAS CITY 19, Chicago 7
ATLANTA 20, Minnesota 14
SAN FRANCISCO 20, Green Bay 6
MIAMI 30, Pittsburgh 26
LOS ANGELES 40, New York Giants 6

1972
Washington 24, MINNESOTA 21
Kansas City 20, NEW ORLEANS 17
New York Giants 27, PHILADELPHIA 12
Oakland 34, HOUSTON 0
Green Bay 24, DETROIT 23
CHICAGO 13, Minnesota 10
DALLAS 28, Detroit 24
Baltimore 24, NEW ENGLAND 17
Cleveland 21, SAN DIEGO 17
WASHINGTON 24, Atlanta 13
MIAMI 31, St. Louis 10
Los Angeles 26, SAN FRANCISCO 16
OAKLAND 24, New York Jets 16

1971
Minnesota 16, DETROIT 13
ST. LOUIS 17, New York Jets 10
Oakland 34, CLEVELAND 20
DALLAS 20, New York Giants 13
KANSAS CITY 38, Pittsburgh 16
MINNESOTA 10, Baltimore 3
GREEN BAY 14, Detroit 14
BALTIMORE 24, Los Angeles 17
SAN DIEGO 20, St. Louis 17
ATLANTA 28, Green Bay 21
MIAMI 34, Chicago 3
Kansas City 26, SAN FRANCISCO 17
Washington 38, LOS ANGELES 24

1970
CLEVELAND 31, New York Jets 21
Kansas City 44, BALTIMORE 24
DETROIT 28, Chicago 14
Green Bay 22, SAN DIEGO 20
OAKLAND 34, Washington 20
MINNESOTA 13, Los Angeles 3
PITTSBURGH 21, Cincinnati 10
Baltimore 13, GREEN BAY 10
St. Louis 38, DALLAS 0
PHILADELPHIA 23, New York Giants 20
Miami 20, ATLANTA 7
Cleveland 21, HOUSTON 10
Detroit 28, LOS ANGELES 23

MONDAY NIGHT FOOTBALL

MONDAY NIGHT WON-LOST RECORDS, 1970-2000

AMERICAN FOOTBALL CONFERENCE

	Balt.	Buff.	Cin.	Cle.	Den.	Ind.	Jax.	K.C.	Mia.	N.E.	N.Y.J.	Oak.	Pitt.	S.D.	Sea.	Tenn.
Total	0-0	17-20	7-16	13-11	20-24-1	12-8	5-2	17-13	35-29	8-18	14-17	33-18-1	28-18	14-12	12-6	14-11
2000		0-1			1-1	2-0	0-2	1-1	0-1	1-1	2-0	0-1			0-1	3-0
1999		1-0			1-2		2-0		1-2	0-1	2-1	0-1	1-0		1-0	
1998					2-1		2-0	0-2	1-2	1-2	1-0		2-1			
1997		1-1			2-1	0-1	1-0	2-0	1-2	1-2		0-2	0-2			
1996		0-2			1-0	1-0		0-2	1-2			2-1	3-0	1-1		
1995		1-1		0-2	1-0			1-1	2-1	1-0		0-2	1-1	1-1		
1994		1-1			0-2			1-1	1-0			1-1	2-0	0-1		0-3
1993		2-1		1-0	0-2	0-1		2-0	1-2			1-0	3-0	2-0		0-1
1992		2-0	0-1	0-1	0-2			1-0	2-1		0-1	0-2	1-0		1-0	1-0
1991		2-1	0-2					2-1	1-1		0-1	0-2	0-1			1-1
1990		1-1	1-1	1-1	1-1	0-1		0-1	0-1		0-1	2-0	1-0		1-0	1-0
1989		1-2	1-2	1-1	2-0						0-1	1-0			1-0	1-0
1988		2-0		1-2	0-2	1-1			1-1		0-1	1-1			1-0	1-0
1987				1-0	2-1				1-1	1-1	2-1	1-1			0-2	
1986			1-0	1-0	1-1				1-2	1-0	1-1	0-1	0-2	0-1	2-0	
1985			1-0	1-0	1-0				2-1	0-1	1-0	2-0	0-2	0-1	0-2	
1984		0-1	0-1		1-0				3-0		0-1	2-1	1-1	1-2	2-0	
1983		0-1	0-2					0-1	1-1		2-0	1-0	1-0	1-1		
1982		0-1	0-1		0-1				1-1		1-0	1-0	1-0	1-1		0-1
1981		1-1		0-1	1-0				1-1	0-1		2-1	1-1	2-1	1-0	0-1
1980				1-1	1-2				1-1	1-2	1-0	3-0	0-2	1-0	0-1	2-0
1979				1-0	0-2				0-2	0-2	1-1	2-0	2-1	1-0	2-0	2-0
1978			1-2		1-1	2-1			2-1	0-2		1-0	1-1	1-0		2-0
1977		0-1	0-1	1-0		1-1		0-1	1-0	0-1		2-0	2-0			
1976		0-2	1-1			2-0		0-1	1-1	1-0	0-1	2-0	0-1			0-1
1975		0-2	1-0		1-1			1-0	1-1	0-1	0-1	2-0	1-0	1-0		0-1
1974		1-0	0-1		0-2			1-0	2-0		0-1	0-1	2-0			
1973		1-0		0-1	0-0-1			1-1	2-0		0-1	0-0-1	1-1			
1972				1-0		1-0		1-0	1-0	0-1	0-1	2-0		0-1		0-1
1971				0-1		1-1		2-0	1-0		0-1	1-0	0-1	1-0		
1970			0-1	2-0		1-1		1-0	1-0		0-1	1-0	1-0	0-1		0-1

NATIONAL FOOTBALL CONFERENCE

	Ariz.	Atl.	Car.	Chi.	Dall.	Det.	G.B.	Minn.	N.O.	N.Y.G.	Phil.	St. L.	S.F.	T.B.	Wash.
Total	5-10-1	6-17	2-1	16-28	34-26	11-12-1	16-18-1	20-19	6-12	15-23-1	14-15	18-22	34-20	4-4	24-24
2000			1-0		1-1		1-1	1-1				1-2		1-1	1-2
1999	0-1	1-2			1-2		1-2	2-1		1-0			1-2	1-0	
1998					2-0	1-1	0-3	1-0		0-2	0-1		3-0	1-1	0-1
1997			1-1	1-1	1-2		3-0	0-1			0-2		3-0		1-0
1996		0-1		2-0	2-1	0-2	2-1	0-1			0-2		2-1		
1995	0-1			1-2	3-0	2-0	1-0	0-2		0-1	0-1		2-1		
1994				0-2	2-1	1-0	1-0	2-0	0-2	1-2	2-0		2-1		
1993		0-1		0-1	1-1		0-1	1-0	0-2	1-0	1-1		1-2		1-2
1992		0-2		0-3	2-1	0-1		1-0	1-0	1-0	1-0		2-0		1-2
1991				2-1	0-1			0-1	1-0	2-1	2-1	0-1	2-1		2-0
1990						0-1		0-1	1-1	1-1	2-0	0-3	3-0		0-1
1989				1-1				1-1	1-1	2-1	0-2	0-2	3-0		0-2
1988	0-1			1-2	1-1			1-0	1-0	1-1	1-0	1-0	1-1		0-2
1987				1-2	2-1			1-0		0-3		1-2	2-0		1-1
1986	0-1			2-1	2-0	0-1	0-1			2-1		1-0	0-2		1-1
1985	1-1			1-1	1-1		0-1			0-1		2-1	1-2		2-1
1984		0-2		0-1	1-1	0-1	0-1		1-0	0-1		1-1	2-0		1-1
1983	0-0-1	0-1			1-1	2-0	2-1	0-1	0-1	1-1-1		1-0	1-0	0-1	1-2
1982					1-2	0-1	1-0	1-0		0-1				1-0	
1981		1-2		0-2	2-0	1-0		0-3			1-1	2-0			
1980				1-1	1-1				0-1	0-1	1-0	2-0		0-1	0-2
1979		1-2			0-2		1-0	0-1	0-1	0-1	1-1	1-0			1-0
1978		1-0		0-3	1-1			2-0				0-2	0-1		1-1
1977	2-0			1-0	1-1		0-1	0-1		0-1		1-1	0-2		1-1
1976	0-1				1-0			1-1			0-1	0-2	2-0		2-0
1975	0-1			0-1	1-1	0-1	0-1	1-0		1-0	0-1	1-0			1-0
1974	0-1	0-1		1-0	0-1	1-0	0-1	1-0	0-1		1-0	1-1	0-2		2-0
1973		1-1		0-1	1-1	1-0	1-1	0-1	0-1	0-1		1-0	1-0		1-1
1972	0-1	0-1		1-0	1-0	0-2	1-0	0-2	0-1	1-0	0-1	1-0	0-1		2-0
1971	1-1	1-0		0-1	1-0	0-1-1	0-1-1	2-0		0-1		0-2	0-1		1-0
1970	1-0	0-1		0-1	0-1	2-0	1-1	1-0		0-1	1-0	0-2			0-1

Compiled by Elias Sports Bureau
*Set or tied NFL all-time record.

MONDAY NIGHT RECORDS

SCORING

TOUCHDOWNS

Most Touchdowns, Game

4 Ron Johnson, N.Y. Giants at Philadelphia, Oct. 2, 1972
Earl Campbell, Houston vs. Miami, Nov. 20, 1978
Marcus Allen, L.A. Raiders vs. San Diego, Sept. 24, 1984
Eric Dickerson, Indianapolis vs. Denver, Oct. 31, 1988
Emmitt Smith, Dallas at N.Y. Giants, Sept. 4. 1995
Marshall Faulk, St. Louis at Tampa Bay, Dec. 18, 2000

FIELD GOALS

Most Field Goals, Game

7 Chris Boniol, Dallas vs. Green Bay, Nov. 18, 1996*
5 Tim Mazzetti, Atlanta vs. Los Angeles, Oct. 30, 1978
Roger Ruzek, Dallas at L.A. Rams, Dec. 21, 1987
Rich Karlis, Minnesota vs. Cincinnati, Dec. 25, 1989
Nick Lowery, Kansas City vs. Denver, Sept. 20, 1993
Chris Jacke, Green Bay vs. San Francisco, Oct. 14, 1996 (OT)
Richie Cunningham, Dallas vs. Philadelphia, Sept. 15, 1997

RUSHING

YARDS GAINED

Most Yards Rushing, Game

221 Bo Jackson, L.A. Raiders at Seattle, Nov. 30, 1987
214 Thurman Thomas, Buffalo at N.Y. Jets, Sept. 24, 1990
199 Earl Campbell, Houston vs. Miami, Nov. 20, 1978

Longest Run From Scrimage, Game

99 Tony Dorsett, Dallas at Minnesota, Jan. 3, 1983 (TD)*
91 Bo Jackson, L.A. Raiders at Seattle, Nov. 30, 1987 (TD)
83 James Lofton, Green Bay at N.Y. Giants, Sept. 20, 1982 (TD)

TOUCHDOWNS

Most Rushing Touchdowns, Game

4 Earl Campbell, Houston vs. Miami, Nov. 20, 1978
Eric Dickerson, Indianapolis vs. Denver, Oct. 31, 1988
Emmitt Smith, Dallas at N.Y. Giants, Sept. 4, 1995

PASSING

YARDS GAINED

Most Yards Passing, Game

458 Joe Montana, San Francisco at L.A. Rams, Dec. 11, 1989
447 Ken Anderson, Cincinnati vs. Buffalo, Nov. 17, 1975
445 Charley Johnson, Denver vs. Kansas City, Nov. 18, 1974

Longest Pass Play

99 Brett Favre to Robert Brooks, Green Bay at Chicago, Sept. 11, 1995 (TD)*
97 Bernie Kosar to Webster Slaughter, Cleveland vs. Chicago, Oct. 23, 1989 (TD)
95 Joe Montana to John Taylor, San Francisco at L.A. Rams, Dec. 11, 1989 (TD)

TOUCHDOWNS

Most Touchdown Passes, Game

5 Dave Krieg, Seattle vs. L.A. Raiders, Nov. 28, 1988
Jim Kelly, Buffalo vs. Cincinnati, Oct. 21, 1991
Vinny Testaverde, N.Y. Jets vs. Miami, Oct. 23, 2000 (OT)

PASS RECEIVING

RECEPTIONS

Most Pass Receptions, Game

14 Herman Moore, Detroit vs. Chicago, Dec. 4, 1995
Jerry Rice, San Francisco vs. Minnesota, Dec. 18, 1995
13 Andre Reed, Buffalo vs. Denver, Sept. 18, 1989

YARDS GAINED

Most Yards on Pass Receptions, Game

289 Jerry Rice, San Francisco vs. Minnesota, Dec. 18, 1995
286 John Taylor, San Francisco at L.A. Rams, Dec. 11, 1989
260 Wes Chandler, San Diego vs. Cincinnati, Dec. 20, 1982

TOUCHDOWNS

Most Touchdown Pass Receptions, Game

3 Ron Johnson, N.Y. Giants at Philadelphia, Oct. 2, 1972
Wesley Walker, N.Y. Jets at Detroit, Dec. 6, 1982
Steve Largent, Seattle at San Diego, Oct. 29, 1984
Mark Clayton, Miami vs. Dallas, Dec. 17, 1984
Jerry Rice, San Francisco vs. Chicago, Dec. 14, 1987
Jerry Rice, San Francisco vs. Minnesota, Dec. 18, 1995
Lamar Thomas, Miami vs. Denver, Dec. 21, 1998
Ed McCaffrey, Denver vs. Miami, Sept. 13, 1999

INTERCEPTIONS BY

Most Interceptions, Game

4 Dick Anderson, Miami vs. Pittsburgh, Dec. 3, 1973*
3 Johnny Robinson, Kansas City at Baltimore, Sept. 28, 1970
Charlie Babb, Miami vs. Oakland, Sept. 22, 1975
Charles Phillips, Oakland vs. Denver, Dec. 8, 1975
Mark Murphy, Washington at San Diego, Oct. 31, 1983
Ken Easley, Seattle at San Diego, Oct. 29, 1984
Dwayne Harper, San Diego vs. Oakland, Nov. 27, 1995
Marcus Coleman, N.Y. Jets vs. Miami, Oct. 23, 2000 (OT)

Longest Interception Return

102 Eddie Anderson, L.A. Raiders at Miami, Dec. 14, 1992 (TD)
98 Marcus Coleman, N.Y. Jets vs. Miami, Dec. 27, 1999 (TD)
94 Nolan Cromwell, L.A. Rams vs. Atlanta, Dec. 14, 1981
Walker Lee Ashley, Minnesota vs. Chicago, Dec. 19, 1988 (TD)

PUNTING

Longest Punt

83 Bryan Barker, Jacksonville vs. N.Y. Jets, Oct. 11, 1999
74 Craig Colquitt, Pittsburgh vs. Oakland, Dec. 7, 1981
73 Tom Tupa, New England at Denver, Oct. 6, 1997

PUNT RETURNS

Longest Punt Return

95 John Taylor, San Francisco vs. Washington, Nov. 21, 1988 (TD)
94 Dennis McKinnon, Chicago vs. N.Y. Giants, Sept. 14, 1987 (TD)
91 JoJo Townsell, N.Y. Jets vs. Seattle, Nov. 9, 1987 (TD)

KICKOFF RETURNS

Longest Kickoff Return

105 Terry Fair, Detroit vs. Tampa Bay, Sept. 28, 1998 (TD)
102 Harold Hart, Oakland at Miami, Sept. 22, 1975 (TD)
101 Roell Preston, Green Bay vs. Minnesota, Oct. 5, 1998 (TD)

FUMBLES

Longest Fumble Return

99 Don Griffin, San Francisco vs. Chicago, Dec. 23, 1991 (TD)
96 Joe Lavender, Philadelphia vs. Dallas, Sept. 23, 1974 (TD)
88 Keith McKenzie, Pittsburgh vs. Green Bay, Nov. 9, 1998 (TD)

THANKSGIVING DAY RECORDS

SCORING

Most Touchdowns, Game

6 Ernie Nevers, Chi. Cardinals vs. Chi. Bears, Nov. 28, 1929*
4 Sterling Sharpe, Green Bay at Dallas, Nov. 24, 1994
3 By many players

RUSHING

Most Yards Rushing, Game

273 O.J. Simpson, Buffalo at Detroit, Nov. 25, 1976
198 Bob Hoernschemeyer, Detroit vs. N.Y. Yankees, Nov. 23, 1950
195 Earl Campbell, Houston at Dallas, Nov. 22, 1979

PASSING

Most Yards Passing, Game

455 Troy Aikman, Dallas vs. Minnesota, Nov. 26, 1998
410 Scott Mitchell, Detroit vs. Minnesota, Nov. 23, 1995
384 Warren Moon, Minnesota at Detroit, Nov. 23, 1995

PASS RECEIVING

RECEPTIONS

Most Pass Receptions, Game

12 Brett Perriman, Detroit vs. Minnesota, Nov. 23, 1995
11 Daryl Johnston, Dallas vs. Miami, Nov. 25, 1993
Michael Irvin, Dallas vs Kansas City, Nov. 23, 1995

YARDS GAINED

Most Yards on Pass Receptions, Game

303 Jim Benton, Cleveland at Detroit, Nov. 22, 1945
185 Lance Alworth, San Diego vs. Buffalo, Nov. 26, 1964
184 Anthony Carter, Minnesota at Dallas, Nov. 26, 1987 (OT)

THURSDAY-SUNDAY NIGHT FOOTBALL

THURSDAY-SUNDAY NIGHT FOOTBALL, 1974-2000

(Home Team in capitals, games listed in chronological order.)

2000
BUFFALO 16, Tennessee 13 (Sun.)
ARIZONA 32, Dallas 31 (Sun.)
MIAMI 19, Baltimore 6 (Sun.)
Washington 16, NEW YORK GIANTS 6 (Sun.)
PHILADELPHIA 38, Atlanta 10 (Sun.)
Baltimore 15, JACKSONVILLE 10 (Sun.)
Minnesota 28, CHICAGO 16 (Sun.)
Detroit 28, TAMPA BAY 14 (Thurs.)
Oakland 15, SAN DIEGO 13 (Sun.)
Carolina 27, ST. LOUIS 24 (Sun.)
INDIANAPOLIS 23, New York Jets 15 (Sun.)
Jacksonville 34, PITTSBURGH 24 (Sun.)
New York Giants 31, ARIZONA 7 (Sun.)
MINNESOTA 24, Detroit 17 (Thurs.)
Green Bay 28, CHICAGO 6 (Sun.)
OAKLAND 31, New York Jets 7 (Sun.)
New York Giants 17, DALLAS 13 (Sun.)
Buffalo 42, SEATTLE 23 (Sat.)

1999
Pittsburgh 43, CLEVELAND 0 (Sun.)
BUFFALO 17, N.Y. Jets 3 (Sun.)
NEW ENGLAND 16, N.Y. Giants 14 (Sun.)
SEATTLE 22, Oakland 21 (Sun.)
GREEN BAY 26, Tampa Bay 23 (Sun.)
Washington 24, ARIZONA 10 (Sun.)
Kansas City 35, BALTIMORE 8 (Thurs.)
DETROIT 20, Tampa Bay 3 (Sun.)
MIAMI 17, Tennessee 0 (Sun.)
SEATTLE 20, Denver 17 (Sun.)
JACKSONVILLE 41, New Orleans 23 (Sun.)
CAROLINA 34, Atlanta 28 (Sun.)
JACKSONVILLE 20, Pittsburgh 6 (Thurs.)
NEW ENGLAND 13, Dallas 6 (Sun.)
TENNESSEE 21, Oakland 14 (Thurs.)
KANSAS CITY 31, Minnesota 28 (Sun.)
Buffalo 31, ARIZONA 21 (Sun.)
Washington 26, SAN FRANCISCO 20 (OT) (Sun.)

1998
KANSAS CITY 28, Oakland 8 (Sun.)
NEW ENGLAND 29, Indianapolis 6 (Sun.)
ARIZONA 17, Philadelphia 3 (Sun.)
BALTIMORE 31, Cincinnati 24 (Sun.)
KANSAS CITY 17, Seattle 6 (Sun.)
Atlanta 34, NEW YORK GIANTS 20 (Sun.)
DETROIT 27, Green Bay 20 (Thurs.)
Buffalo 30, CAROLINA 14 (Sun.)
Oakland 31, SEATTLE 18 (Sun.)
Tennessee 31, TAMPA BAY 22 (Sun.)
DETROIT 26, Chicago 3 (Sun.)
SAN FRANCISCO 31, New Orleans 20 (Sun.)
Denver 31, SAN DIEGO 16 (Sun.)
PHILADELPHIA 17, St. Louis 14 (Thurs.)
MINNESOTA 48, Chicago 22 (Sun.)
New York Jets 21, MIAMI 16 (Sun.)
MINNESOTA 50, Jacksonville 10 (Sun.)
Dallas 23, WASHINGTON 7 (Sun.)

1997
Washington 24, CAROLINA 10 (Sun.)
ARIZONA 25, Dallas 22 (OT) (Sun.)
NEW ENGLAND 27, New York Jets 24 (OT) (Sun.)
TAMPA BAY 31, Miami 21 (Sun.)
MINNESOTA 28, Philadelphia 19 (Sun.)
New Orleans 20, CHICAGO 17 (Sun.)
PITTSBURGH 24, Indianapolis 22 (Sun.)
KANSAS CITY 31, San Diego 3 (Thurs.)
CAROLINA 21, Atlanta 12 (Sun.)
GREEN BAY 20, Detroit 10 (Sun.)
PITTSBURGH 37, Baltimore 0 (Sun.)
Oakland 38, SAN DIEGO 13 (Sun.)
WASHINGTON 7, New York Giants 7 (OT) (Sun.)
Denver 38, SAN DIEGO 28 (Sun.)
CINCINNATI 41, Tennessee 14 (Thurs.)
MIAMI 33, Detroit 30 (Sun.)
Chicago 13, ST. LOUIS 10 (Sun.)
SEATTLE 38, San Francisco 9 (Sun.)

1996
Buffalo 23, NEW YORK GIANTS 20 (OT) (Sun.)
Miami 38, ARIZONA 10 (Sun.)
DENVER 27, Tampa Bay 23 (Sun.)
Philadelphia 33, ATLANTA 18 (Sun.)
WASHINGTON 31, New York Jets 16 (Sun.)
Houston 30, CINCINNATI 27 (OT) (Sun.)
INDIANAPOLIS 26, Baltimore 21 (Sun.)
KANSAS CITY 34, Seattle 16 (Thurs.)
NEW ENGLAND 28, Buffalo 25 (Sun.)
San Francisco 24, NEW ORLEANS 17 (Sun.)
CAROLINA 27, New York Giants 17 (Sun.)
Minnesota 16, OAKLAND 13 (OT) (Sun.)
Green Bay 24, ST. LOUIS 9 (Sun.)
New England 45, SAN DIEGO 7 (Sun.)
INDIANAPOLIS 37, Philadelphia 10 (Thurs.)
Minnesota 24, DETROIT 22 (Sun.)
JACKSONVILLE 20, Seattle 13 (Sun.)
SAN DIEGO 16, Denver 10 (Sun.)

1995
DENVER 22, Buffalo 7 (Sun.)
Philadelphia 31, ARIZONA 19 (Sun.)
Dallas 23, MINNESOTA 17 (OT) (Sun.)
Green Bay 24, JACKSONVILLE 14 (Sun.)
Oakland 47, NEW YORK JETS 10 (Sun.)
Denver 37, NEW ENGLAND 3 (Sun.)
ST. LOUIS 21, Atlanta 19 (Thurs.)
Cincinnati 27, PITTSBURGH 9 (Thurs.)
New York Giants 24, WASHINGTON 15 (Sun.)
Miami 24, SAN DIEGO 14 (Sun.)
PHILADELPHIA 31, Denver 13 (Sun.)
KANSAS CITY 20, Houston 13 (Sun.)
NEW ORLEANS 34, Carolina 26 (Sun.)
New York Giants 10, ARIZONA 6 (Thurs.)
SAN FRANCISCO 27, Buffalo 17 (Sun.)
TAMPA BAY 13, Green Bay 10 (OT) (Sun.)
SEATTLE 44, Oakland 10 (Sun.)
INDIANAPOLIS 10, New England 7 (Sat.)

1994
San Diego 17, DENVER 34 (Sun.)
New York Giants 20, ARIZONA 17 (Sun.)
Kansas City 30, ATLANTA 10 (Sun.)
Chicago 19, NEW YORK JETS 7 (Sun.)
Miami 23, CINCINNATI 7 (Sun.)
PHILADELPHIA 21, Washington 17 (Sun.)
Cleveland 11, HOUSTON 8 (Thurs.)
MINNESOTA 13, Green Bay 10 (OT) (Thurs.)
ARIZONA 20, Pittsburgh 17 (OT) (Sun.)
KANSAS CITY 13, Los Angeles Raiders 3 (Sun.)
DETROIT 14, Tampa Bay 9 (Sun.)
SAN FRANCISCO 31, Los Angeles Rams 27 (Sun.)
New England 12, INDIANAPOLIS 10 (Sun.)
MINNESOTA 33, Chicago 27 (OT) (Thurs.)
Buffalo 42, MIAMI 31 (Sun.)
New Orleans 29, ATLANTA 20 (Sun.)
Los Angeles Raiders 17, SEATTLE 16 (Sun.)
MIAMI 27, Detroit 20 (Sun.)

1993
NEW ORLEANS 33, Houston 21 (Sun.)
Los Angeles Raiders 17, SEATTLE 13 (Sun.)
Dallas 17, PHOENIX 10 (Sun.)
NEW YORK JETS 45, New England 7 (Sun.)
BUFFALO 17, New York Giants 14 (Sun.)
GREEN BAY 30, Denver 27 (Sun.)
ATLANTA 30, Los Angeles Rams 24 (Thurs.)
MIAMI 41, Indianapolis 27 (Sun.)
Detroit 30, MINNESOTA 27 (Sun.)
WASHINGTON 30, Indianapolis 24 (Sun.)
Chicago 16, SAN DIEGO 13 (Sun.)
TAMPA BAY 23, Minnesota 10 (Sun.)
HOUSTON 23, Pittsburgh 3 (Sun.)
SAN FRANCISCO 21, Cincinnati 8 (Sun.)
Green Bay 20, SAN DIEGO 13 (Sun.)
Philadelphia 20, INDIANAPOLIS 10 (Sun.)
MINNESOTA 30, Kansas City 10 (Sun.)
HOUSTON 24, New York Jets 0 (Sun.)

1992
DENVER 17, Los Angeles Raiders 13 (Sun.)
Philadelphia 31, PHOENIX 14 (Sun.)
BUFFALO 38, Indianapolis 0 (Sun.)
San Francisco 16, NEW ORLEANS 10 (Sun.)
NEW YORK JETS 30, New England 21 (Sun.)
NEW ORLEANS 13, Los Angeles Rams 10 (Sun.)
MINNESOTA 31, Detroit 14 (Thurs.)
Pittsburgh 27, KANSAS CITY 3 (Sun.)
New York Giants 24, WASHINGTON 7 (Sun.)
Cincinnati 31, CHICAGO 28 (OT) (Sun.)
DENVER 27, New York Giants 13 (Sun.)
Kansas City 24, SEATTLE 14 (Sun.)
SAN DIEGO 27, Los Angeles Raiders 3 (Sun.)
NEW ORLEANS 22, Atlanta 14 (Thurs.)
Los Angeles Rams 31, TAMPA BAY 27 (Sun.)
Green Bay 16, HOUSTON 14 (Sun.)
MIAMI 19, New York Jets 17 (Sun.)
HOUSTON 27, Buffalo 3 (Sun.)

1991
WASHINGTON 45, Detroit 0 (Sun.)
Houston 30, CINCINNATI 7 (Sun.)
NEW ORLEANS 24, Los Angeles Rams 7 (Sun.)
Dallas 17, PHOENIX 9 (Sun.)
Denver 13, MINNESOTA 6 (Sun.)
Pittsburgh 21, INDIANAPOLIS 3 (Sun.)
Los Angeles Raiders 23, SEATTLE 20 (Sun.)
Chicago 10, GREEN BAY 0 (Thurs.)
Washington 17, NEW YORK GIANTS 13 (Sun.)
DENVER 20, Pittsburgh 13 (Sun.)
MIAMI 30, New England 20 (Sun.)
HOUSTON 28, Cleveland 24 (Sun.)
Atlanta 23, NEW ORLEANS 20 (OT) (Sun.)
Los Angeles Raiders 9, SAN DIEGO 7 (Sun.)
Minnesota 26, TAMPA BAY 24 (Sun.)
Buffalo 35, INDIANAPOLIS 7 (Sun.)
SEATTLE 23, Los Angeles Rams 9 (Sun.)

1990
NEW YORK GIANTS 27, Philadelphia 20 (Sun.)
PITTSBURGH 20, Houston 9 (Sun.)
TAMPA BAY 23, Detroit 20 (Sun.)
Washington 38, PHOENIX 10 (Sun.)
BUFFALO 38, Los Angeles Raiders 24 (Sun.)
CHICAGO 38, Los Angeles Rams 9 (Sun.)
MIAMI 17, New England 10 (Thurs.)
ATLANTA 38, Cincinnati 17 (Sun.)
MINNESOTA 27, Denver 22 (Sun.)
San Francisco 24, DALLAS 6 (Sun.)
CINCINNATI 27, Pittsburgh 3 (Sun.)
Seattle 13, SAN DIEGO 10 (Sun.)
MINNESOTA 23, Green Bay 7 (Sun.)
MIAMI 23, Philadelphia 20 (Sun.)
DETROIT 38, Chicago 21 (Sun.)
INDIANAPOLIS 35, Washington 28 (Sat.)
SEATTLE 17, Denver 12 (Sun.)
HOUSTON 34, Pittsburgh 14 (Sun.)

1989
Dallas 13, WASHINGTON 3 (Sun.)
SAN DIEGO 14, Los Angeles Raiders 12 (Sun.)
INDIANAPOLIS 27, New York Jets 10 (Sun.)
Los Angeles Rams 20, NEW ORLEANS 17 (Sun.)
MINNESOTA 27, Chicago 16 (Sun.)
MIAMI 31, New England 10 (Sun.)
SEATTLE 23, Los Angeles Raiders 17 (Sun.)
Cleveland 24, HOUSTON 20 (Sat.)

1988
HOUSTON 41, Washington 17 (Sun.)
Los Angeles Raiders 13, SAN DIEGO 3 (Sun.)
Minnesota 43, DALLAS 3 (Sun.)
New England 6, MIAMI 3 (Sun.)
New York Giants 13, NEW ORLEANS 12 (Sun.)
Pittsburgh 37, HOUSTON 34 (Sun.)
SEATTLE 42, Denver 14 (Sun.)
Los Angeles Rams 38, SAN FRANCISCO 16 (Sun.)

1987
NEW YORK GIANTS 17, New England 10 (Sun.)
SAN DIEGO 16, Los Angeles Raiders 14 (Sun.)
Miami 20, DALLAS 14 (Sun.)
SAN FRANCISCO 38, Cleveland 24 (Sun.)
Chicago 30, MINNESOTA 24 (Sun.)
SEATTLE 28, Denver 21 (Sun.)
MIAMI 23, Washington 21 (Sun.)
SAN FRANCISCO 48, Los Angeles Rams 0 (Sun.)

1986
New England 20, NEW YORK JETS 6 (Thurs.)
Cincinnati 30, CLEVELAND 13 (Thurs.)
Los Angeles Raiders 37, SAN DIEGO 31 (OT) (Thurs.)
LOS ANGELES RAMS 29, Dallas 10 (Sun.)
SAN FRANCISCO 24, Los Angeles Rams 14 (Fri.)

1985
KANSAS CITY 36, Los Angeles Raiders 20 (Thurs.)
Chicago 33, MINNESOTA 24 (Thurs.)
Dallas 30, NEW YORK GIANTS 29 (Sun.)
SAN DIEGO 54, Pittsburgh 44 (Sun.)
Denver 27, SEATTLE 24 (Fri.)

1984
Pittsburgh 23, NEW YORK JETS 17 (Thurs.)
Denver 24, CLEVELAND 14 (Sun.)
DALLAS 30, New Orleans 27 (Sun.)
Washington 31, MINNESOTA 17 (Thurs.)
SAN FRANCISCO 19, Los Angeles Rams 16 (Fri.)

1983
San Francisco 48, MINNESOTA 17 (Thurs.)
CLEVELAND 17, Cincinnati 7 (Thurs.)
Los Angeles Raiders 40, DALLAS 38 (Sun.)
Los Angeles Raiders 42, SAN DIEGO 10 (Thurs.)
MIAMI 34, New York Jets 14 (Fri.)

1982
BUFFALO 23, Minnesota 22 (Thurs.)
SAN FRANCISCO 30, Los Angeles Rams 24 (Thurs.)
ATLANTA 17, San Francisco 7 (Sun.)

1981
MIAMI 30, Pittsburgh 10 (Thurs.)
Philadelphia 20, BUFFALO 14 (Thurs.)
DALLAS 29, Los Angeles 17 (Sun.)
HOUSTON 17, Cleveland 13 (Thurs.)

1980
TAMPA BAY 10, Los Angeles 9 (Thurs.)
DALLAS 42, San Diego 31 (Sun.)
San Diego 27, MIAMI 24 (OT) (Thurs.)
HOUSTON 6, Pittsburgh 0 (Thurs.)

1979
Los Angeles 13, DENVER 9 (Thurs.)
DALLAS 30, Los Angeles 6 (Sun.)
OAKLAND 45, San Diego 22 (Thurs.)
MIAMI 39, New England 24 (Thurs.)

1978
New England 21, OAKLAND 14 (Sun.)
Minnesota 21, DALLAS 10 (Thurs.)
LOS ANGELES 10, Pittsburgh 7 (Sun.)
Denver 21, OAKLAND 6 (Sun.)

1977
Minnesota 30, DETROIT 21 (Sat.)

1976
Los Angeles 20, DETROIT 17 (Sat.)

1975
LOS ANGELES 10, Pittsburgh 3 (Sat.)

1974
OAKLAND 27, Dallas 23 (Sat.)

OVERTIME GAMES

HISTORY OF OVERTIME GAMES

PRESEASON

Aug. 28, 1955	Los Angeles 23, New York Giants 17, at Portland, Oregon
Aug. 24, 1962	Denver 27, Dallas Texans 24, at Fort Worth, Texas
Aug. 10, 1974	San Diego 20, New York Jets 14, at San Diego
Aug. 17, 1974	Pittsburgh 33, Philadelphia 30, at Philadelphia
Aug. 17, 1974	Dallas 19, Houston 13, at Dallas
Aug. 17, 1974	Cincinnati 13, Atlanta 7, at Atlanta
Sept. 6, 1974	Buffalo 23, New York Giants 17, at Buffalo
Aug. 9, 1975	Baltimore 23, Denver 20, at Denver
Aug. 30, 1975	New England 20, Green Bay 17, at Milwaukee
Sept. 13, 1975	Minnesota 14, San Diego 14, at San Diego
Aug. 1, 1976	New England 13, New York Giants 7, at New England
Aug. 2, 1976	Kansas City 9, Houston 3, at Kansas City
Aug. 20, 1976	New Orleans 26, Baltimore 20, at Baltimore
Sept. 4, 1976	Dallas 26, Houston 20, at Dallas
Aug. 13, 1977	Seattle 23, Dallas 17, at Seattle
Aug. 28, 1977	New England 13, Pittsburgh 10, at New England
Aug. 28, 1977	New York Giants 24, Buffalo 21, at East Rutherford, N.J.
Aug. 2, 1979	Seattle 12, Minnesota 9, at Minnesota
Aug. 4, 1979	Los Angeles 20, Oakland 14, at Los Angeles
Aug. 24, 1979	Denver 20, New England 17, at Denver
Aug. 23, 1980	Tampa Bay 20, Cincinnati 14, at Tampa Bay
Aug. 5, 1981	San Francisco 27, Seattle 24, at Seattle
Aug. 29, 1981	New Orleans 20, Detroit 17, at New Orleans
Aug. 28, 1982	Miami 17, Kansas City 17, at Kansas City
Sept. 3, 1982	Miami 16, New York Giants 13, at Miami
Aug. 6, 1983	L.A. Raiders 26, San Francisco 23, at Los Angeles
Aug. 6, 1983	Atlanta 13, Washington 10, at Atlanta
Aug. 13, 1983	St. Louis 27, Chicago 24, at St. Louis
Aug. 18, 1983	New York Jets 20, Cincinnati 17, at Cincinnati
Aug. 27, 1983	Chicago 20, Kansas City 17, at Chicago
Aug. 11, 1984	Pittsburgh 20, Philadelphia 17, at Pittsburgh
Aug. 9, 1985	Buffalo 10, Detroit 10, at Pontiac, Mich.
Aug. 10, 1985	Minnesota 16, Miami 13, at Miami
Aug. 17, 1985	Dallas 27, San Diego 24, at San Diego
Aug. 24, 1985	N.Y. Giants 34, N.Y. Jets 31, at East Rutherford, N.J.
Aug. 15, 1986	Washington 27, Pittsburgh 24, at Washington
Aug. 15, 1986	Detroit 30, Seattle 27, at Detroit
Aug. 23, 1986	Los Angeles Rams 20, San Diego 17, at Anaheim
Aug. 30, 1986	Minnesota 23, Indianapolis 20, at Indianapolis
Aug. 23, 1987	Philadelphia 19, New England 13, at New England
Sept. 5, 1987	Cleveland 30, Green Bay 24, at Milwaukee
Sept. 6, 1987	Kansas City 13, St. Louis 10, at Memphis, Tenn.
Aug. 11, 1988	Seattle 16, Detroit 13, at Detroit
Aug. 19, 1988	Miami 16, Denver 13, at Miami
Aug. 19, 1988	Green Bay 21, Kansas City 21, at Milwaukee
Aug. 20, 1988	Houston 20, Los Angeles Rams 17, at Anaheim
Aug. 21, 1988	Minnesota 19, Phoenix 16, at Phoenix
Aug. 5, 1989	Los Angeles Rams 16, San Francisco 13, at Tokyo, Japan
Aug. 26, 1989	Denver 24, Dallas 21, at Denver
Sept. 1, 1989	N.Y. Jets 15, Kansas City 13, at Kansas City
Aug. 24, 1990	Cincinnati 13, New England 10, at New England
Aug. 16, 1991	Cleveland 24, Washington 21, at Washington
Aug. 17, 1991	Cincinnati 27, Minnesota 24, at Cincinnati
Aug. 23, 1991	Dallas 20, Atlanta 17, at Dallas
Aug. 24, 1991	Cincinnati 19, Green Bay 16, at Green Bay
Aug. 22, 1992	Los Angeles Rams 16, Green Bay 13, at Anaheim
Aug. 8, 1993	Dallas 13, Detroit 13, at London, England
Aug. 12, 1995	Washington 16, Houston 13, at Knoxville, Tenn.
Aug. 19, 1995	Indianapolis 20, Green Bay 17, at Green Bay
Aug. 3, 1996	Minnesota 23, San Diego 20, at Minnesota
Aug. 10, 1996	San Francisco 16, San Diego 13, at San Francisco
Aug. 1, 1998	Green Bay 27, Kansas City 24, at Tokyo, Japan
Aug. 7, 1998	Detroit 13, Arizona 10, at Pontiac, Mich.
Aug. 22, 1998	Minnesota 25, Carolina 22, at Charlotte, N.C.
Aug. 9, 1999	Cleveland 20, Dallas 17, at Canton, Ohio

REGULAR SEASON

Sept. 22, 1974—Pittsburgh 35, Denver 35, at Denver; Steelers win toss. Gilliam's pass intercepted and returned by Rowser to Denver's 42. Turner misses 41-yard field goal. Walden punts and Greer returns to Broncos' 39. Van Heusen punts and Edwards returns to Steelers' 16. Game ends with Steelers on own 26.

Nov. 10, 1974—New York Jets 26, New York Giants 20, at New Haven, Conn.; Giants win toss. Gogolak misses 42-yard field goal. Namath passes to Boozer for five yards and touchdown at 6:53.

Sept. 28, 1975—Dallas 37, St. Louis 31, at Dallas; Cardinals win toss. Hart's pass intercepted and returned by Jordan to Cardinals' 37. Staubach passes to DuPree for three yards and touchdown at 7:53.

Oct. 12, 1975—Los Angeles 13, San Diego 10, at San Diego; Chargers win toss. Partee punts to Rams' 14. Dempsey kicks 22-yard field goal at 9:27.

Nov. 2, 1975—Washington 30, Dallas 24, at Washington; Cowboys win toss. Staubach's pass intercepted and returned by Houston to Cowboys' 35. Kilmer runs one yard for touchdown at 6:34.

Nov. 16, 1975—St. Louis 20, Washington 17, at St. Louis; Cardinals win toss. Bakken kicks 37-yard field goal at 7:00.

Nov. 23, 1975—Kansas City 24, Detroit 21, at Kansas City; Lions win toss. Chiefs take over on downs at own 38. Stenerud kicks 26-yard field goal at 6:44.

Nov. 23, 1975—Oakland 26, Washington 23, at Washington; Redskins win toss. Bragg punts to Raiders' 42. Blanda kicks 27-yard field goal at 7:13.

Nov. 30, 1975—Denver 13, San Diego 10, at Denver; Broncos win toss. Turner kicks 25-yard field goal at 4:13.

Nov. 30, 1975—Oakland 37, Atlanta 34, at Oakland; Falcons win toss. James punts to Raiders' 16. Guy punts and Herron returns to Falcons' 41. Nick Mike-Mayer misses 45-yard field goal. Guy punts into Falcons' end zone. James punts to Raiders' 39. Blanda kicks 36-yard field goal at 15:00.

Dec. 14, 1975—Baltimore 10, Miami 7, at Baltimore; Dolphins win toss. Seiple punts to Colts' 4. Linhart kicks 31-yard field goal at 12:44.

Sept. 19, 1976—Minnesota 10, Los Angeles 10, at Minnesota; Vikings win toss. Tarkenton's pass intercepted by Monte Jackson and returned to Minnesota 16. Allen blocks Dempsey's 30-yard field goal attempt, ball rolls into end zone for touchback. Clabo punts and Scribner returns to Rams' 20. Rusty Jackson punts to Vikings' 35. Tarkenton's pass intercepted by Kay at Rams' 1, no return. Game ends with Rams on own 3.

***Sept. 27, 1976—Washington 20, Philadelphia 17,** at Philadelphia; Eagles win toss. Jones punts and E. Brown loses one yard on return to Redskins' 40. Bragg punts 51 yards into end zone for touchback. Jones punts and E. Brown returns to Redskins' 42. Bragg punts and Marshall returns to Eagles' 41. Boryla's pass intercepted by Dusek at Redskins' 37, no return. Bragg punts and Bradley returns. Philadelphia holding penalty moves ball back to Eagles' 8. Boryla pass intercepted by E. Brown and returned to Eagles' 22. Moseley kicks 29-yard field goal at 12:49.

Oct. 17, 1976—Kansas City 20, Miami 17, at Miami; Chiefs win toss. Wilson punts into end zone for touchback. Bulaich fumbles into Kansas City end zone, Collier recovers for touchback. Stenerud kicks 34-yard field goal at 14:48.

Oct. 31, 1976—St. Louis 23, San Francisco 20, at St. Louis; Cardinals win toss. Joyce punts and Leonard fumbles on return, Jones recovers at 49ers' 43. Bakken kicks 21-yard field goal at 6:42.

Dec. 5, 1976—San Diego 13, San Francisco 7, at San Diego; Chargers win toss. Morris runs 13 yards for touchdown at 5:12.

Sept. 18, 1977—Dallas 16, Minnesota 10, at Minnesota; Vikings win toss. Dallas starts on Vikings' 47 after a punt early in the overtime period. Staubach scores seven plays later on a four-yard run at 6:14.

***Sept. 26, 1977—Cleveland 30, New England 27,** at Cleveland; Browns win toss. Sipe throws a 22-yard pass to Logan at Patriots' 19. Cockroft kicks 35-yard field goal at 4:45.

Oct. 16, 1977—Minnesota 22, Chicago 16, at Minnesota; Bears win toss. Parsons punts 53 yards to Vikings' 18. Minnesota drives to Bears' 11. On a first-and-10, Vikings fake a field goal and holder Krause hits Voigt with a touchdown pass at 6:45.

Oct. 30, 1977—Cincinnati 13, Houston 10, at Cincinnati; Bengals win toss. Bahr kicks a 22-yard field goal at 5:51.

Nov. 13, 1977—San Francisco 10, New Orleans 7, at New Orleans; Saints win toss. Saints fail to move ball and Blanchard punts to 49ers' 41. Wersching kicks a 33-yard field goal at 6:33.

Dec. 18, 1977—Chicago 12, New York Giants 9, at East Rutherford, N.J.; Giants win toss. The ball changes hands eight times before Thomas kicks a 28-yard field goal at 14:51.

Sept. 10, 1978—Cleveland 13, Cincinnati 10, at Cleveland; Browns win toss. Collins returns kickoff 41 yards to Browns' 47. Cockroft kicks 27-yard field goal at 4:30.

***Sept. 11, 1978—Minnesota 12, Denver 9,** at Minnesota; Vikings win toss. Danmeier kicks 44-yard field goal at 2:56.

Sept. 24, 1978—Pittsburgh 15, Cleveland 9, at Pittsburgh; Steelers win toss. Cunningham scores on a 37-yard "gadget" pass from Bradshaw at 3:43. Steelers start winning drive on their 21.

Sept. 24, 1978—Denver 23, Kansas City 17, at Kansas City; Broncos win toss. Dilts punts to Kansas City. Chiefs advance to Broncos' 40 where Reed fails to make first down on fourth-and-one situation. Broncos march downfield. Preston scores two-yard touchdown at 10:28.

Oct. 1, 1978—Oakland 25, Chicago 19, at Chicago; Bears win toss. Both teams punt on first possession. On Chicago's second offensive series, Colzie intercepts Avellini's pass and returns it to Bears' 3. Three plays later, Whittington runs two yards for a touchdown at 5:19.

Oct. 15, 1978—Dallas 24, St. Louis 21, at St. Louis; Cowboys win toss. Dallas drives from its 23 into field goal range. Septien kicks 27-yard field goal at 3:28.

Oct. 29, 1978—Denver 20, Seattle 17, at Seattle; Broncos win toss. Ball changes hands four times before Turner kicks 18-yard field goal at 12:59.

Nov. 12, 1978—San Diego 29, Kansas City 23, at San Diego; Chiefs win toss. Fouts hits Jefferson for decisive 14-yard touchdown pass on the last play (15:00) of overtime period.

Nov. 12, 1978—Washington 16, New York Giants 13, at Washington; Redskins win toss. Moseley kicks winning 45-yard field goal at 8:32 after missing first down field goal attempt of 35 yards at 4:50.

Nov. 26, 1978—Green Bay 10, Minnesota 10, at Green Bay; Packers win toss.

Both teams have possession of the ball four times.

Dec. 9, 1978—Cleveland 37, New York Jets 34, at Cleveland; Browns win toss. Cockroft kicks 22-yard field goal at 3:07.

Sept. 2, 1979—Atlanta 40, New Orleans 34, at New Orleans; Falcons win toss. Bartkowski's pass intercepted by Myers and returned to Falcons' 46. Erxleben punts to Falcons' 4. James punts to Chandler on Saints' 43. Erxleben punts and Ryckman returns to Falcons' 28. James punts and Chandler returns to Saints' 36. Erxleben retrieves punt snap on Saints' 1 and attempts pass. Mayberry intercepts and returns six yards for touchdown at 8:22.

Sept. 2, 1979—Cleveland 25, New York Jets 22, at New York; Jets win toss. Leahy's 43-yard field goal attempt goes wide right at 4:41. Evans's punt blocked by Dykes is recovered by Newton. Ramsey punts into end zone for touchback. Evans punts and Harper returns to Jets' 24. Robinson's pass intercepted by Davis and returned 33 yards to Jets' 31. Cockroft kicks 27-yard field goal at 14:45.

***Sept. 3, 1979—Pittsburgh 16, New England 13,** at Foxboro; Patriots win toss. Hare punts to Swann at Steelers' 31. Bahr kicks 41-yard field goal at 5:10.

Sept. 9, 1979—Tampa Bay 29, Baltimore 26, at Baltimore; Colts win toss. Landry fumbles, recovered by Kollar at Colts' 14. O'Donoghue kicks 31-yard, first-down field goal at 1:41.

Sept. 16, 1979—Denver 20, Atlanta 17, at Atlanta; Broncos win toss. Broncos march 65 yards to Falcons' 7. Turner kicks 24-yard field goal at 6:15.

Sept. 23, 1979—Houston 30, Cincinnati 27, at Cincinnati; Oilers win toss. Parsley punts and Lusby returns to Bengals' 33. Bahr's 32-yard field goal attempt is wide right at 8:05. Parsley's punt downed on Bengals' 5. McInally punts and Ellender returns to Bengals' 42. Fritsch's third down, 29-yard field goal attempt hits left upright and bounces through at 14:28.

Sept. 23, 1979—Minnesota 27, Green Bay 21, at Minnesota; Vikings win toss. Kramer throws 50-yard touchdown pass to Rashad at 3:18.

Oct. 28, 1979—Houston 27, New York Jets 24, at Houston; Oilers win toss. Oilers march 58 yards to Jets' 18. Fritsch kicks 35-yard field goal at 5:10.

Nov. 18, 1979—Cleveland 30, Miami 24, at Cleveland; Browns win toss. Sipe passes 39 yards to Rucker for touchdown at 1:59.

Nov. 25, 1979—Pittsburgh 33, Cleveland 30, at Pittsburgh; Browns win toss. Sipe's pass intercepted by Blount on Steelers' 4. Bradshaw pass intercepted by Bolton on Browns' 12. Evans punts and Bell returns to Steelers' 17. Bahr kicks 37-yard field goal at 14:51.

Nov. 25, 1979—Buffalo 16, New England 13, at Foxboro; Patriots win toss. Hare's punt downed on Bills' 38. Jackson punts and Morgan returns to Patriots' 20. Grogan's pass intercepted by Haslett and returned to Bills' 42. Ferguson's 51-yard pass to Butler sets up N. Mike-Mayer's 29-yard field goal at 9:15.

Dec. 2, 1979—Los Angeles 27, Minnesota 21, at Los Angeles; Rams win toss. Clark punts and Miller returns to Vikings' 25. Kramer's pass intercepted by Brown and returned to Rams' 40. Cromwell, holding for 22-yard field goal attempt, runs around left end untouched for winning score at 6:53.

Sept. 7, 1980—Green Bay 12, Chicago 6, at Green Bay; Bears win toss. Parsons punts and Nixon returns 16 yards. Five plays later, Marcol returns own blocked field goal attempt 24 yards for touchdown at 6:00.

Sept. 14, 1980—San Diego 30, Oakland 24, at San Diego; Raiders win toss. Pastorini's first-down pass intercepted by Edwards. Millen intercepts Fouts' first-down pass and returns to San Diego 46. Bahr's 50-yard field goal attempt partially blocked by Williams and recovered on Chargers' 32. Eight plays later, Fouts throws 24-yard touchdown pass to Jefferson at 8:09.

Sept. 14, 1980—San Francisco 24, St. Louis 21, at San Francisco; Cardinals win toss. Swider punts and Robinson returns to 49ers' 32. San Francisco drives 52 yards to St. Louis 16, where Wersching kicks 33-yard field goal at 4:12.

Oct. 12, 1980—Green Bay 14, Tampa Bay 14, at Tampa Bay; Packers win toss. Teams trade punts twice. Lee returns second Tampa Bay punt to Green Bay 42. Dickey completes three passes to Buccaneers' 18, where Birney's 36-yard field goal attempt is wide right as time expires.

Nov. 9, 1980—Atlanta 33, St. Louis 27, at St. Louis; Falcons win toss. Strong runs 21 yards for touchdown at 4:20.

#Nov. 20, 1980—San Diego 27, Miami 24, at Miami; Chargers win toss. Partridge punts into end zone, Dolphins take over on their own 20. Woodley's pass for Nathan intercepted by Lowe and returned 28 yards to Dolphins' 12. Benirschke kicks 28-yard field goal at 7:14.

Nov. 23, 1980—New York Jets 31, Houston 28, at New York; Jets win toss. Leahy kicks 38-yard field goal at 3:58.

Nov. 27, 1980—Chicago 23, Detroit 17, at Detroit; Bears win toss. Williams returns kickoff 95 yards for touchdown at 0:21.

Dec. 7, 1980—Buffalo 10, Los Angeles 7, at Buffalo; Rams win toss. Corral punts and Hooks returns to Bills' 34. Ferguson's 30-yard pass to Lewis sets up N. Mike-Mayer's 30-yard field goal at 5:14.

Dec. 7, 1980—San Francisco 38, New Orleans 35, at San Francisco; Saints win toss. Erxleben's punt downed by Hardy on 49ers' 27. Wersching kicks 36-yard field goal at 7:40.

***Dec. 8, 1980—Miami 16, New England 13,** at Miami; Dolphins win toss. Von Schamann kicks 23-yard field goal at 3:20.

Dec. 14, 1980—Cincinnati 17, Chicago 14, at Chicago; Bengals win toss. Breech kicks 28-yard field goal at 4:23.

Dec. 21, 1980—Los Angeles 20, Atlanta 17, at Los Angeles; Rams win toss. Corral's punt downed at Rams' 37. James punts into end zone for touchback. Corral's punt downed on Falcons' 17. Bartkowski fumbles when hit by Harris, recovered by Delaney. Corral kicks 23-yard field goal on first play of possession at 7:00.

Sept. 27, 1981—Cincinnati 27, Buffalo 24, at Cincinnati; Bills win toss. Cater punts into end zone for touchback. Bengals drive to the Bills' 10 where Breech kicks 28-yard field goal at 9:33.

Sept. 27, 1981—Pittsburgh 27, New England 21, at Pittsburgh; Patriots win toss. Hubach punts and Smith returns five yards to midfield. Four plays later Bradshaw throws 24-yard touchdown pass to Swann at 3:19.

Oct. 4, 1981—Miami 28, New York Jets 28, at Miami; Jets win toss. Teams trade punts twice. Leahy's 48-yard field goal attempt is wide right as time expires.

Oct. 25, 1981—New York Giants 27, Atlanta 24, at Atlanta; Giants win toss. Jennings' punt goes out of bounds at New York 47. Bright returns Atlanta punt to Giants' 14. Woerner fair catches punt at own 28. Andrews fumbles on first play, recovered by Van Pelt. Danelo kicks 40-yard field goal four plays later at 9:20.

Oct. 25, 1981—Chicago 20, San Diego 17, at Chicago; Bears win toss. Teams trade punts. Bears' second punt returned by Brooks to Chargers' 33. Fouts pass intercepted by Fencik and returned 32 yards to San Diego 27. Roveto kicks 27-yard field goal seven plays later at 9:30.

Nov. 8, 1981—Chicago 16, Kansas City 13, at Kansas City; Bears win toss. Teams trade punts. Kansas City takes over on downs on its own 38. Fuller's fumble recovered by Harris on Chicago 36. Roveto's 37-yard field goal wide, but Chiefs penalized for leverage. Roveto's 22-yard field goal attempt three plays later is good at 13:07.

Nov. 8, 1981—Denver 23, Cleveland 20, at Denver; Browns win toss. D. Smith recovers Hill's fumble at Denver 48. Morton's 33-yard pass to Upchurch and 6-yard run by Preston set up Steinfort's 30-yard field goal at 4:10.

Nov. 8, 1981—Miami 30, New England 27, at New England; Dolphins win toss. Orosz punts and Morgan returns six yards to New England 26. Grogan's pass intercepted by Brudzinski who returns 19 yards to Patriots' 26. Von Schamann kicks 30-yard field goal on first down at 7:09.

Nov. 15, 1981—Washington 30, New York Giants 27, at New York; Giants win toss. Nelms returns Giants' punt 26 yards to New York 47. Five plays later Moseley kicks 48-yard field goal at 3:44.

Dec. 20, 1981—New York Giants 13, Dallas 10, at New York; Cowboys win toss and kick off. Jennings punts to Dallas 40. Taylor recovers Dorsett's fumble on second down. Danelo's 33-yard field goal attempt hits right upright and bounces back. White's pass for Pearson intercepted by Hunt and returned seven yards to Dallas 24. Four plays later Danelo kicks 35-yard field goal at 6:19.

Sept. 12, 1982—Washington 37, Philadelphia 34, at Philadelphia; Redskins win toss. Theismann completes five passes for 63 yards to set up Moseley's 26-yard field goal at 4:47.

Sept. 19, 1982—Pittsburgh 26, Cincinnati 20, at Pittsburgh; Bengals win toss. Anderson's pass intended for Kreider intercepted by Woodruff and returned 30 yards to Cincinnati 2. Bradshaw completes two-yard touchdown pass to Stallworth on first down at 1:08.

Dec. 19, 1982—Baltimore 20, Green Bay 20, at Baltimore; Packers win toss. K. Anderson intercepts Dickey's first-down pass and returns to Packers' 42. Miller's 44-yard field goal attempt blocked by G. Lewis. Teams trade punts before Stenerud's 47-yard field goal attempt is wide right. Teams trade punts again before time expires in Colts possession.

Jan. 2, 1983—Tampa Bay 26, Chicago 23, at Tampa; Bears win toss. Parsons punts to T. Bell at Buccaneers' 40. Capece kicks 33-yard field goal at 3:14.

Sept. 4, 1983—Baltimore 29, New England 23, at New England; Patriots win toss. Cooks runs 52 yards with fumble recovery three plays into overtime at 0:30.

Sept. 4, 1983—Green Bay 41, Houston 38, at Houston; Packers win toss. Stenerud kicks 42-yard field goal at 5:55.

Sept. 11, 1983—New York Giants 16, Atlanta 13, at Atlanta; Giants win toss. Dennis returns kickoff 54 yards to Atlanta 41. Haji-Sheikh kicks 30-yard field goal at 3:38.

Sept. 18, 1983—New Orleans 34, Chicago 31, at New Orleans; Bears win toss. Parsons punts and Groth returns five yards to New Orleans 34. Stabler pass intercepted by Schmidt at Chicago 47. Parsons punt downed by Gentry at New Orleans 2. Stabler gains 36 yards in four passes; Wilson 38 on six carries. Andersen kicks 41-yard field goal at 10:57.

Sept. 18, 1983—Minnesota 19, Tampa Bay 16, at Tampa; Vikings win toss. Coleman punts and Bell returns eight yards to Tampa Bay 47. Capece's 33-yard field goal attempt sails wide at 7:26. Dils and Young combine for 48-yard gain to Tampa Bay 27. Ricardo kicks 42-yard field goal at 9:27.

Sept. 25, 1983—Baltimore 22, Chicago 19, at Baltimore; Colts win toss. Allegre kicks 33-yard field goal nine plays later at 4:51.

Sept. 25, 1983—Cleveland 30, San Diego 24, at San Diego; Browns win toss. Walker returns kickoff 33 yards to Cleveland 37. Sipe completes 48-yard touchdown pass to Holt four plays later at 1:53.

Sept. 25, 1983—New York Jets 27, Los Angeles Rams 24, at New York; Jets win toss. Ramsey punts to Irvin who returns to 25 but penalty puts Rams on own 13. Holmes 30-yard interception return sets up Leahy's 26-yard field goal at 3:22.

Oct. 9, 1983—Buffalo 38, Miami 35, at Miami; Dolphins win toss. Von Schamann's 52-yard field goal attempt goes wide at 12:36. Cater punts to Clayton who loses 11 to own 13. Von Schamann's 43-yard field goal attempt sails wide at 5:15. Danelo kicks 36-yard field goal nine plays later at 13:58.

Oct. 9, 1983—Dallas 27, Tampa Bay 24, at Dallas; Cowboys win toss. Septien's 51-yard field goal attempt goes wide but Buccaneers penalized for roughing kicker. Septien kicks 42-yard field goal at 4:38.

Oct. 23, 1983—Kansas City 13, Houston 10, at Houston; Chiefs win toss. Lowery kicks 41-yard field goal 13 plays later at 7:41.

Oct. 23, 1983—Minnesota 20, Green Bay 17, at Green Bay; Packers win toss. Scribner's punt downed on Vikings' 42. Ricardo kicks 32-yard field goal eight plays later at 5:05.

***Oct. 24, 1983—New York Giants 20, St. Louis 20,** at St. Louis; Cardinals win toss. Teams trade punts before O'Donoghue's 44-yard field goal attempt is wide left. Jennings' punt returned by Bird to St. Louis 21. Lomax pass intercepted by Haynes who loses six yards to New York 33. Jennings' punt downed on St. Louis 17. O'Donoghue's 19-yard field goal attempt is wide right. Rutledge's pass intercepted by L. Washington who returns 25 yards to New York 25. O'Donoghue's 42-yard field goal attempt is wide right. Rutledge's pass intercepted by W. Smith at St. Louis 33 to end game.

Oct. 30, 1983—Cleveland 25, Houston 19, at Cleveland; Oilers win toss. Teams trade punts. Nielsen's pass intercepted by Whitwell who returns to Houston 20. Green runs 20 yards for touchdown on first down at 6:34.

Nov. 20, 1983—Detroit 23, Green Bay 20, at Milwaukee; Packers win toss. Scribner punts and Jenkins returns 14 yards to Green Bay 45. Murray's 33-yard field goal attempt is wide left at 9:32. Whitehurst's pass intercepted by Watkins and returned to Green Bay 27. Murray kicks 37-yard field goal four plays later at 8:30.

Nov. 27, 1983—Atlanta 47, Green Bay 41, at Atlanta; Packers win toss. K. Johnson returns interception 31 yards for touchdown at 2:13.

Nov. 27, 1983—Seattle 51, Kansas City 48, at Seattle; Seahawks win toss. Dixon's 47-yard kickoff return sets up N. Johnson's 42-yard field goal at 1:36.

Dec. 11, 1983—New Orleans 20, Philadelphia 17, at Philadelphia; Eagles win toss. Runager punts to Groth who fair catches on New Orleans 32. Stabler completes two passes for 36 yards to Goodlow to set up Andersen's 50-yard field goal at 5:30.

***Dec. 12, 1983—Green Bay 12, Tampa Bay 9,** at Tampa; Packers win toss. Stenerud kicks 23-yard field goal 11 plays later at 4:07.

Sept. 9, 1984—Detroit 27, Atlanta 24, at Atlanta; Lions win toss. Murray kicks 48-yard field goal nine plays later at 5:06.

Sept. 30, 1984—Tampa Bay 30, Green Bay 27, at Tampa; Packers win toss. Scribner punts 44 yards to Tampa Bay 2. Epps returns Garcia's punt three yards to Green Bay 27. Scribner's punt downed on Buccaneers' 33. Ariri kicks 46-yard field goal 11 plays later at 10:32.

Oct. 14, 1984—Detroit 13, Tampa Bay 7, at Detroit; Buccaneers win toss. Tampa Bay drives to Lions' 39 before Wilder fumbles. Five plays later Danielson hits Thompson with 37-yard touchdown pass at 4:34.

Oct. 21, 1984—Dallas 30, New Orleans 27, at Dallas; Cowboys win toss. Septien kicks 41-yard field goal eight plays later at 3:42.

Oct. 28, 1984—Denver 22, Los Angeles Raiders 19, at Los Angeles; Raiders win toss. Hawkins fumble recovered by Foley at Denver 7. Teams trade punts. Karlis's 42-yard field goal attempt is wide left. Teams trade punts. Wilson pass intercepted by R. Jackson at Los Angeles 45, returned 23 yards to Los Angeles 22. Karlis kicks 35-yard field goal two plays later at 15:00.

Nov. 4, 1984—Philadelphia 23, Detroit 23, at Detroit; Lions win toss. Lions drive to Eagles' 3 in eight plays. Murray's 21-yard field goal attempt hits right upright and bounces back. Jaworski's pass intercepted by Watkins at Detroit 5. Teams trade punts. Cooper returns Black's punt five yards to Eagles' 14. Time expires four plays later with Eagles on own 21.

Nov. 18, 1984—San Diego 34, Miami 28, at San Diego; Chargers win toss. McGee scores eight plays later on a 25-yard run at 3:17.

Dec. 2, 1984—Cincinnati 20, Cleveland 17, at Cleveland; Browns win toss. Simmons returns Cox's punt 30 yards to Cleveland 35. Breech kicks 35-yard field goal seven plays later at 4:34.

Dec. 2, 1984—Houston 23, Pittsburgh 20, at Houston; Oilers win toss. Cooper kicks 30-yard field goal 16 plays later at 5:53.

Sept. 8, 1985—St. Louis 27, Cleveland 24, at Cleveland; Cardinals win toss. O'Donoghue kicks 35-yard field goal nine plays later at 5:27.

Sept. 29, 1985—New York Giants 16, Philadelphia 10, at Philadelphia; Eagles win toss. Jaworski's pass tipped by Quick and intercepted by Patterson who returns 29 yards for touchdown at 0:55.

Oct. 20, 1985—Denver 13, Seattle 10, at Denver; Seahawks win toss. Teams trade punts twice. Krieg's pass intercepted by Hunter and returned to Seahawks' 15. Karlis kicks 24-yard field goal four plays later at 9:19.

Nov. 10, 1985—Philadelphia 23, Atlanta 17, at Philadelphia; Falcons win toss. Donnelly's 62-yard punt goes out of bounds at Eagles' 1. Jaworski completes 99-yard touchdown pass to Quick two plays later at 1:49.

Nov. 10, 1985—San Diego 40, Los Angeles Raiders 34, at San Diego; Chargers win toss. James scores on 17-yard run seven plays later at 3:44.

Nov. 17, 1985—Denver 30, San Diego 24, at Denver; Chargers win toss. Thomas' 40-yard field goal attempt blocked by Smith and returned 60 yards by Wright for touchdown at 4:45.

Nov. 24, 1985—New York Jets 16, New England 13, at New York; Jets win toss. Teams trade punts twice. Patriots' second punt returned 46 yards by Sohn to Patriots' 15. Leahy kicks 32-yard field goal one play later at 10:05.

Nov. 24, 1985—Tampa Bay 19, Detroit 16, at Tampa; Lions win toss. Teams trade punts. Lions' punt downed on Buccaneers' 38. Igwebuike kicks 24-yard field goal 11 plays later at 12:31.

Nov. 24, 1985—Los Angeles Raiders 31, Denver 28, at Los Angeles; Raiders win toss. Bahr kicks 32-yard field goal six plays later at 2:42.

Dec. 8, 1985—Los Angeles Raiders 17, Denver 14, at Denver; Broncos win toss. Teams trade punts twice. Elway's fumble recovered by Townsend at Broncos' 8. Bahr kicks 26-yard field goal one play later at 4:55.

Sept. 14, 1986—Chicago 13, Philadelphia 10, at Chicago; Eagles win toss. Crawford's fumble of kickoff recovered by Jackson at Eagles' 35. Butler kicks 23-yard field goal 10 plays later at 5:56.

Sept. 14, 1986—Cincinnati 36, Buffalo 33, at Cincinnati; Bills win toss. Zander intercepts Kelly's first-down pass and returns it to Bills' 17. Breech kicks 20-yard field goal two plays later at 0:56.

Sept. 21, 1986—New York Jets 51, Miami 45, at New York; Jets win toss. O'Brien completes 43-yard touchdown pass to Walker five plays later at 2:35.

Sept. 28, 1986—Pittsburgh 22, Houston 16, at Houston; Oilers win toss. Johnson's punt returned 41 yards by Woods to Oilers' 15. Abercrombie scores on three-yard run three plays later at 2:35.

Sept. 28, 1986—Atlanta 23, Tampa Bay 20, at Tampa; Falcons win toss. Teams trade punts. Luckhurst kicks 34-yard field goal 10 plays later at 12:35.

Oct. 5, 1986—Los Angeles Rams 26, Tampa Bay 20, at Anaheim; Rams win toss. Dickerson scores four plays later on 42-yard run at 2:16.

Oct. 12, 1986—Minnesota 27, San Francisco 24, at San Francisco; Vikings win toss. C. Nelson kicks 28-yard field goal nine plays later at 4:27.

Oct. 19, 1986—San Francisco 10, Atlanta 10, at Atlanta; Falcons win toss. Teams trade punts twice. Donnelly punts to 49ers' 27. The following play Wilson recovers Rice's fumble at 49ers' 46 as time expires.

Nov. 2, 1986—Washington 44, Minnesota 38, at Washington; Redskins win toss. Schroeder completes 38-yard touchdown pass to Clark four plays later at 1:46.

Nov. 20, 1986—Los Angeles Raiders 37, San Diego 31, at San Diego; Raiders win toss. Teams trade punts. Allen scores five plays later on 28-yard run at 8:33.

Nov. 23, 1986—Cleveland 37, Pittsburgh 31, at Cleveland; Browns win toss. Teams trade punts. Six plays later Kosar hits Slaughter with 36-yard touchdown pass at 6:37.

Nov. 30, 1986—Chicago 13, Pittsburgh 10, at Chicago; Bears win toss and kick off. Newsome's punt returned by Barnes to Chicago 49. Butler kicks 42-yard field goal five plays later at 3:55.

Nov. 30, 1986—Philadelphia 33, Los Angeles Raiders 27, at Los Angeles; Eagles win toss. Teams trade punts. Long recovers Cunningham's fumble at Philadelphia 42. Waters returns Allen's fumble 81 yards to Los Angeles 4. Cunningham scores on one-yard run two plays later at 6:53.

Nov. 30, 1986—Cleveland 13, Houston 10, at Cleveland; Oilers win toss and kick off. Gossett punts to Houston 39. Luck's pass intercepted by Minnifield at Cleveland 21. Gossett punts to Houston 34. Luck's pass intercepted by Minnifield at Cleveland 43 who returns 20 yards to Houston 37. Moseley kicks 29-yard field goal nine plays later at 14:44.

Dec. 7, 1986—St. Louis 10, Philadelphia 10, at Philadelphia; Cardinals win toss. White blocks Schubert's 40-yard field goal attempt. Teams trade punts. McFadden's 43-yard field goal attempt is wide left. Schubert's 37-yard field goal attempt is wide right. Cavanaugh's pass intercepted by Carter and returned to Eagles' 48 to end game.

Dec. 14, 1986—Miami 37, Los Angeles Rams 31, at Anaheim; Dolphins win toss. Marino completes 20-yard touchdown pass to Duper six plays later at 3:04.

Sept. 20, 1987—Denver 17, Green Bay 17, at Milwaukee; Packers win toss. Del Greco's 47-yard field goal attempt is short. Teams trade punts. Elway intercepted by Noble who returns 10 yards to Green Bay 34. Davis fumbles on next play and Smith recovers. Two plays later, Karlis's 40-yard field goal attempt is wide left. Time expires two plays later with Packers on own 23.

Oct. 11, 1987—Detroit 19, Green Bay 16, at Green Bay; Lions win toss. Prindle's 42-yard field goal attempt is wide left. Packers punt downed on Detroit 17. Prindle kicks 31-yard field goal 16 plays later at 12:26.

Oct. 18, 1987—New York Jets 37, Miami 31, at New York; Jets win toss. Teams trade punts. Ryan intercepted by Hooper at Jets' 47 who returns 11 yards. Mackey intercepted by Haslett at Jets' 37 who returns 9 yards. Jets punt. Mackey intercepted by Radachowsky who returns 45 yards to Miami 24. Ryan completes eight-yard touchdown pass to Hunter five plays later at 14:26.

Oct. 18, 1987—Green Bay 16, Philadelphia 10, at Green Bay; Packers win toss. Hargrove scores on seven-yard run 10 plays later at 5:04.

Oct. 18, 1987—Buffalo 6, New York Giants 3, at Buffalo; Bills win toss. Schlopy's 28-yard field goal attempt is wide left. Teams trade punts. Rutledge intercepted by Clark who returns 23 yards to Buffalo 40. Schlopy kicks 27-yard field goal nine plays later at 14:41.

Oct. 25, 1987—Buffalo 34, Miami 31, at Miami; Bills win toss. Norwood kicks 27-yard field goal seven plays later at 4:12.

Nov. 1, 1987—San Diego 27, Cleveland 24, at San Diego; Browns win toss. Kosar intercepted by Glenn who returns 20 yards to Browns' 25. Abbott kicks 33-yard field goal three plays later at 2:16.

Nov. 15, 1987—Dallas 23, New England 17, at New England; Cowboys win toss. Walker scores on 60-yard run four plays later at 1:50.

Nov. 26, 1987—Minnesota 44, Dallas 38, at Dallas; Vikings win toss. Coleman's punt downed by Hilton at Cowboys' 37. White intercepted by Studwell who returns 12 yards to Vikings' 37. D. Nelson scores on 24-yard run seven plays later at 7:51.

Nov. 29, 1987—Philadelphia 34, New England 31, at New England; Patriots win toss. Ramsey intercepted by Joyner who returns 29 yards to Eagles' 32. Fryar fair catches Teltschik's punt at Patriots' 13. Franklin's 46-yard field goal attempt is short. McFadden's 39-yard field goal attempt is wide left. Tatupu fumbles on next play and Cobb recovers. McFadden kicks 38-yard field goal four plays later at 12:16.

Dec. 6, 1987—New York Giants 23, Philadelphia 20, at New York; Giants win toss and kick off. Teams trade punts twice. Teltschik's punt is returned 16 yards by McConkey to Eagles' 33. Three plays later, Allegre's 50-yard field goal attempt is blocked by Joyner and returned 25 yards by Hoage to Eagles' 30. McConkey returns Teltschik's punt four yards to Giants' 44. Allegre kicks 28-yard field goal four plays later at 10:42.

Dec. 6, 1987—Cincinnati 30, Kansas City 27, at Cincinnati; Bengals win toss. Teams trade punts. Breech kicks 32-yard field goal 16 plays later at 9:44.

Dec. 26, 1987—Washington 27, Minnesota 24, at Minnesota; Redskins win toss. Haji-Sheikh kicks 26-yard field goal six plays later at 2:09.

Sept. 4, 1988—Houston 17, Indianapolis 14, at Indianapolis; Colts win toss. Dickerson fumble recovered by Lyles who returns six yards to Colts' 42. Zendejas kicks 35-yard field goal six plays later at 3:51.

***Sept. 26, 1988—Los Angeles Raiders 30, Denver 27,** at Denver; Broncos win toss. Teams trade punts twice. Elway intercepted by Lee who returns 20 yards to Broncos' 31. Bahr kicks 35-yard field goal four plays later at 12:35.

Oct. 2, 1988—New York Jets 17, Kansas City 17, at New York; Chiefs win toss. Chiefs punt goes into end zone for touchback. Leahy's 44-yard field goal attempt is wide right. Chiefs punt is returned by Townsell to Jets' 26. Burruss recovers McNeil's fumble at Chiefs' 11. DeBerg intercepted by Humphery at Jets' 49. Three plays later, time expires.

Oct. 9, 1988—Denver 16, San Francisco 13, at San Francisco; Broncos win toss and kick off. Young intercepted by Haynes at Broncos' 32. Denver punt downed at 49ers' 5. Young intercepted by Wilson who returns seven yards to 49ers' 5. Karlis kicks 22-yard field goal two plays later at 8:11.

Oct. 30, 1988—New York Giants 13, Detroit 10, at Detroit; Lions win toss. James's fumble recovered by Taylor at Lions' 22. Three plays later, McFadden kicks 33-yard field goal at 1:13.

Nov. 20, 1988—Buffalo 9, New York Jets 6, at Buffalo; Jets win toss. Vick's fumble recovered by Bennett at Bills' 32. Norwood kicks 30-yard field goal five plays later at 3:47.

Nov. 20, 1988—Philadelphia 23, New York Giants 17, at New York; Eagles win toss. Philadelphia's punt goes into end zone for touchback. Hostetler intercepted by Hoage who returns 11 yards to Giants' 41. Six plays later, Zendejas's 30-yard field-goal attempt is blocked and ball is recovered behind line of scrimmage by Eagles' Simmons, who runs 15 yards for touchdown at 3:09.

Dec. 11, 1988—New England 10, Tampa Bay 7, at New England; Buccaneers win toss and kick off. Staurovsky kicks 27-yard field goal six plays later at 3:08.

Dec. 17, 1988—Cincinnati 20, Washington 17, at Cincinnati; Bengals win toss. Cincinnati's punt returned by Oliphant to Redskins' 16. Grant recovers Williams's fumble at Redskins' 17. Breech kicks 20-yard field goal three plays later at 7:01.

Sept. 24, 1989—Buffalo 47, Houston 41, at Houston; Oilers win toss. Johnson returns Brady's kickoff 17 yards to Oilers' 19. Oilers drive to Buffalo 25, Zendejas's 37-yard field goal blocked, but Bills offsides and Zendejas's second attempt is wide left. Bills' ball and Kelly completes series of passes, including 28-yard game-winner to Andre Reed, at 8:42.

Oct. 8, 1989—Miami 13, Cleveland 10, at Miami; Browns win toss. Metcalf returns Stoyanovich's kickoff 20 yards to Browns' 28. Browns drive ball 46 yards in eight plays; Bahr wide left on 44-yard field goal attempt. Dolphins ball. Browns called for pass interference on Marino pass to Banks at Cleveland 47. Two plays later, Banks's 20-yard reception at Browns' 23 sets up winning 35-yard field goal by Stoyanovich at 6:23.

Oct. 22, 1989—Denver 24, Seattle 21, at Seattle; Seahawks win toss. Treadwell's 56-yard kickoff returned 18 yards by Jefferson to Seahawks' 27. Seahawks drive to Broncos' 22 in 10 plays, but Johnson's 40-yard field goal attempt wide left. Smith intercepts a Krieg pass and returns it 28 yards to Seahawks' 10. Treadwell kicks winning 27-yard field goal at 7:46.

Oct. 29, 1989—New England 23, Indianapolis 20, at Indianapolis; Patriots win toss. Biasucci kickoff returned 13 yards to Patriots' 23 by Martin. Holding penalty brings ball back to Patriots' 13. After six plays, Feagles punt returned 11 yards by Verdin to Colts' 28. Six plays later, Colts punt to Martin at Patriots' 12. Grogan completes three straight passes to Patriots' 44. Five consecutive runs put New England on Colts' 33. Davis kicks a 51-yard winning field goal for Patriots at 9:46.

Oct. 29, 1989—Green Bay 23, Detroit 20, at Milwaukee; Lions win toss. Sanders touchback on Jacke kickoff. On first play, Murphy intercepts Lions' Peete and returns it three yards to Lions' 26. Fullwood gains five yards on three plays to set up Jacke's 38-yard field goal at 2:14.

Nov. 5, 1989—Minnesota 23, Los Angeles Rams 21, at Minneapolis; Rams win toss. Karlis's kick returned 18 yards by Delpino to Rams' 19. Drive stops at Rams' 28. Merriweather blocks Hatcher's punt at 12. Ball rolls out of end zone for safety.

Nov. 19, 1989—Cleveland 10, Kansas City 10, at Cleveland; Browns win toss. Browns punt three times; Chiefs twice; before Kansas City's Lowery misses 47-yard field goal with 17 seconds remaining in overtime. Kosar's pass intercepted as time expired.

Nov. 26, 1989—Los Angeles Rams 20, New Orleans 17, at New Orleans; Saints win toss. Lansford's kickoff returned 27 yards to Saints' 30. After four plays, Barnhardt punts to Rams' 15. Saints penalized 35 yards for interference to Rams' 43. Three plays later, Everett hits Anderson with 14-yard pass to Saints' 40, then 26-yarder to put Rams in field goal position. Lansford kicks 31-yard field goal at 6:38.

Dec. 3, 1989—Los Angeles Raiders 16, Denver 13, at Los Angeles; Broncos win toss. Bell returns Jaeger kickoff 14 yards to Broncos' 18. Broncos' penalized for illegal block to Broncos' 9. Elway completes three passes for two first downs. On third and eight Elway sacked for 10-yard loss. Horan punts, Adams calls for fair catch at Raiders' 29. Dyal's 26-yard reception moves Raiders to Denver 43. Raiders move ball 34 yards in three plays to set up Jaeger's 26-yard field goal at 7:02.

Dec. 10, 1989—Indianapolis 23, Cleveland 17, at Indianapolis; Browns win toss. Teams trade punts. McNeil returns Colts' punt 42 yards to 42. Seven plays later, Bahr misses 35-yard field goal attempt. Three plays later, Stark punts and McNeil returns ball to 50-yard line. Two plays later, Prior intercepts Kosar's pass at Colts' 42 and returns it 58 yards for touchdown at 10:54.

Dec. 17, 1989—Cleveland 23, Minnesota 17, at Cleveland; Browns win toss. Browns punt to Vikings' 18. Six plays later, Vikings punt to Browns' 22. Nine plays later, Bahr lines up to attempt 31-yard field goal. Holder Pagel takes snap and passes 14 yards to Waiters for touchdown at 9:30.

Sept. 23, 1990—Denver 34, Seattle 31, at Denver; Seahawks win toss. Loville returns kickoff 19 yards to Seahawks' 27. Seahawks drive to Broncos' 26, where Johnson misses 44-yard field goal wide right. Broncos take over and Elway completes series of passes to set up Treadwell's 25-yard field goal at 9:14.

Sept. 30, 1990—Tampa Bay 23, Minnesota 20, at Minnesota; Vikings win toss. Vikings drive to Buccaneers' 31; Igwebuike's 48-yard field goal attempt wide left. Buccaneers drive to Vikings' 43 and punt. Gannon's pass is intercepted at Vikings' 26 by Wayne Haddix. Buccaneers drive to Vikings' 19 to set up Christie's 36-yard field goal at 9:11.

Oct. 7, 1990—Cincinnati 34, Los Angeles Rams 31, at Anaheim; Rams win toss. Berry returns kickoff to Rams' 21. After 3 plays, English punts and Green downs ball at Bengals' 25. After 3 plays, Johnson punts and Sutton downs ball at Rams' 29-yard line. After 3 plays, English punts and Price signals fair catch at Bengals' 47. Esiason completes series of passes to 26-yard line to set up Breech's 44-yard field goal at 11:56.

Nov. 4, 1990—Washington 41, Detroit 38, at Detroit; Redskins win toss. Howard downs kickoff on Redskins' 15. After 3 plays, Mojsiejenko punts to Redskins' 45. After 3 plays, Arnold punts to Redskins' 10. Rutledge completes series of passes to set up Lohmiller's 34-yard field goal at 9:10.

Nov. 18, 1990—Chicago 16, Denver 13, at Denver; Broncos win toss. Ezor returns kickoff to Broncos' 12. Both teams have ball twice and have to punt after each possession. Broncos punt after third possession of overtime and Bailey returns 20 yards to Broncos' 34. Harbaugh completes 10-yard pass to Thornton to set up Butler's 44-yard field goal at 13:14.

Nov. 25, 1990—Seattle 13, San Diego 10, at San Diego; Chargers win toss. Lewis returns kickoff to Chargers' 22. After 2 plays, Cox fumbles and ball is recovered by Porter at Chargers' 23. After two plays, Johnson kicks 40-yard field goal at 3:01.

Dec. 2, 1990—Chicago 23, Detroit 17, at Chicago; Lions win toss. Gray returns kickoff to Lions' 35. After 10 plays, Murray misses 35-yard field goal. Bears take possession at Chicago 20. Harbaugh completes 50-yard game-winning pass to Anderson at 10:57.

Dec. 2, 1990—Seattle 13, Houston 10, at Seattle; Seahawks win toss. Warren returns kickoff to Seahawks' 13. After 5 plays, Donnelly punts to Oilers' 23-yard line. Ford's fumble recovered by Wyman. Seahawks take possession at Oilers' 27. After 2 plays, Johnson kicks 42-yard field goal at 4:25.

Dec. 9, 1990—Miami 23, Philadelphia 20, at Miami; Eagles win toss. After 11 plays, Feagles punts to Dolphins' 26. After 6 plays, Roby punts to Eagles' 14 and Harris returns to 25. After 3 plays, Feagles punts to Dolphins' 43. Marino completes series of passes to Eagles' 22. Stoyanovich kicks 39-yard field goal at 12:32.

Dec. 9, 1990—San Francisco 20, Cincinnati 17, at Cincinnati; 49ers win toss. Carter returns kickoff to 49ers' 19. After 10 plays, Cofer kicks 23-yard field goal at 6:12.

Sept. 23, 1991—Chicago 19, New York Jets 13, at Chicago; Jets win toss. Mathis returns kickoff seven yards to New York's 12. Jets drive to New York 26; Bailey returns punt to Chicago 39. Bears drive to Jets' 44-yard line and punt into the end zone. Jets drive to Bears' 11 where Leahy's 28-yard field goal attempt is wide left. Bears drive from 20 to Jets' 1 where Harbaugh runs for touchdown at 14:42.

Oct. 13, 1991—Los Angeles Raiders 23, Seattle 20, at Seattle. Seahawks win toss. Seahawks begin on 20. After 5 plays, Tuten punts and Brown signals fair catch at Raiders' 24. After 3 plays, Gossett punts and Land downs ball at Seattle 9. After 1 play, Lott intercepts at Seahawks' 19 to set up Jaeger's game-winning 37-yard field goal at 6:37.

Oct. 20, 1991—Cleveland 30, San Diego 24, at San Diego; Chargers win toss. After kickoff, Chargers drive to Browns' 45 and punt to Browns' 6 where Hendrickson downs ball. Browns drive to 38 and punt; Taylor fair catches on Chargers' 14. After 3 plays, Brandon intercepts at Chargers' 30 and scores at 5:58.

Oct. 20, 1991—New England 26, Minnesota 23, at New England; Patriots win toss. Martin returns kickoff 18 yards to New England 22. Patriots drive to Minnesota 19. Staurovsky's 36-yard field goal attempt is wide left. Minnesota drives to the 50 where Newsome punts into end zone. On first play, McMillian intercepts at the 40 for Minnesota. After 2 plays, Marion causes Jordan fumble and Pool recovers at New England 20. New England drives to Minnesota 24 where Staurovsky kicks 42-yard field goal as time expires.

Nov. 3, 1991—New York Jets 19, Green Bay 16, at New York; Packers win toss. Thompson returns kickoff 30 yards to Packers' 39. Green Bay drives to New York 24 where Jacke's 42-yard field goal attempt is wide right. Jets drive to 50. Aguiar's punt is fumbled by Sikahema and recovered by New York at Packers' 23. After 2

OVERTIME GAMES

plays, Leahy kicks 37-yard field goal at 9:40.

Nov. 3, 1991—Washington 16, Houston 13, at Washington; Redskins win toss. Mitchell returns kickoff 9 yards to Washington 14. After 4 plays, Goodburn punts and Givins returns to Houston 31. After 1 play, Moon's pass is intercepted by Green at Oilers' 35. After 3 plays, Lohmiller kicks 41-yard field goal at 4:01.

Nov. 10, 1991—Houston 26, Dallas 23, at Houston; Oilers win toss. Pinkett returns kickoff 20 yards to Houston 24. After 6 plays, Montgomery punts and Martin returns to Dallas 24. Cowboys drive to Oilers' 24 where Smith fumbles and McDowell recovers at Oilers' 15. Houston drives to Dallas 5 where Del Greco kicks 23-yard field goal at 14:31.

Nov. 10, 1991—Pittsburgh 33, Cincinnati 27, at Cincinnati; Pittsburgh wins toss. Woodson downs kickoff for touchback. After 3 plays, Stryzinski punts and Barber returns 7 yards to Cincinnati 38. Bengals drive to Pittsburgh 37 where Woods fumbles and Lloyd returns recovery to Cincinnati 44. After 2 plays, O'Donnell passes to Green for 26-yard touchdown at 6:32.

Nov. 24, 1991—Atlanta 23, New Orleans 20, at New Orleans; Atlanta wins toss. Falcons begin at 20. After 3 plays, Fulhage punts and Fenerty signals fair catch at New Orleans 43. After 3 plays, Barnhardt punts and Thompson downs ball at Atlanta 23. After 3 plays, Fulhage punts and Fenerty fair catches at New Orleans 25. Saints drive to Atlanta 38 where Andersen misses 55-yard field-goal attempt. After 1 play, Rozier fumbles and Martin recovers on 50. Saints drive to Atlanta 38 where Barnhardt punts to Falcons' 2. Atlanta drives to New Orleans 33 where Johnson kicks 50-yard field goal at 13:03.

Nov. 24, 1991—Miami 16, Chicago 13, at Chicago; Miami wins toss. Butler kicks to Miami 20 where Paige returns kickoff 15 yards to 35. Miami drives to Chicago 9 where Stoyanovich kicks 27-yard field goal at 4:11.

Dec. 8, 1991—Buffalo 30, Los Angeles Raiders 27, at Los Angeles; Raiders win toss. Daluiso kicks into end zone for touchback. On third play, Kelso intercepts for Buffalo and returns ball to Bills' 36. Bills drive to Los Angeles 24 where Norwood kicks 42-yard field goal at 2:34.

Dec. 8, 1991—Kansas City 20, San Diego 17, at Kansas City; Chiefs win toss. Carney kicks to Kansas City 10 where Stradford returns 23 yards to 33. After 3 plays, Barker punts to San Diego 4. Chargers drive to 40 where Kidd punts 60 yards into end zone for touchback. Kansas City drives to San Diego 39 where Barker punts 38 yards to 1. After 3 plays, Kidd punts 41 yards to San Diego 42 where Stradford returns 12 yards to 30. Chiefs drive to San Diego 1 where Lowery kicks 18-yard field goal at 11:26.

Dec. 8, 1991—New England 23, Indianapolis 17, at New England; Indianapolis wins toss. Baumann kicks off to Indianapolis 2 where Martin returns 23 yards to 25. After 3 downs, Stark punts to New England 17 where Henderson returns 8 yards to 25. New England drives to 50 where McCarthy punts and Prior signals fair catch at Indianapolis 15. After 3 plays, Stark punts to New England 40 where Henderson returns 7 yards to 47. After 2 plays, Millen passes to Timpson for 45-yard touchdown at 8:55.

Dec. 22, 1991—Detroit 17, Buffalo 14, at Buffalo; Detroit wins toss. Daluiso kicks off to Detroit 20 where Dozier returns 15 yards to Lions 35. Lions drive to Bills' 3 where Murray kicks 21-yard field goal at 4:23.

Dec. 22, 1991—New York Jets 23, Miami 20, at Miami; Jets win toss. Aguiar kicks to Miami's 30 where Logan returns 3 yards to the 33. After 4 downs, Stoyanovich punts to Jets' 15 where Baty returns 8 yards to 23. Jets drive to Miami 12 where Allegre kicks 30-yard field goal at 6:33.

Sept. 6, 1992—Minnesota 23, Green Bay 20, at Green Bay; Vikings win toss. Nelson returns kickoff 14 yards to the Minnesota 23. After 5 plays, Newsome punts 49 yards to Green Bay 21 where Brooks returns 12 yards to the 33. After 2 plays, Glenn intercepts pass at the Vikings' 48. On first play, Allen fumbles and Billups recovers at Green Bay 35. After 3 plays, McJulien punts 33 yards to Vikings' 35. Vikings drive to Minnesota 48; Newsome punts 52 yards for touchback. After 3 plays, McJulien punts and Parker returns 10 yards to Green Bay 48. Vikings drive to Packers' 9 where Reveiz kicks 26-yard field goal at 10:20.

Sept. 13, 1992—Cincinnati 24, Los Angeles Raiders 21, at Cincinnati; Raiders win toss. Land returns kickoff 13 yards but fumbles at Los Angeles's 20; ball recovered by Bengals' Bennett at Raiders' 21. After 1 play, Breech kicks 34-yard field goal at 1:01.

Sept. 20, 1992—Houston 23, Kansas City 20, at Houston; Chiefs win toss. Carter returns kickoff 25 yards to Kansas City 28. On third play of drive, Birden fumbles at Kansas City 34; ball recovered by Houston's D. Smith at Chiefs' 23. After one play, Del Greco kicks 39-yard field goal at 1:55.

Oct. 11, 1992—Indianapolis 6, New York Jets 3, at Indianapolis; Colts win toss. Verdin returns kickoff 33 yards to Colts' 36. Colts drive to Jets' 30 where Biasucci kicks 47-yard field goal at 3:01.

Nov. 8, 1992—Cincinnati 31, Chicago 28, at Chicago; Bears win toss. Lewis returns kickoff 22 yards to Chicago's 29. Bears drive to Chicago's 46 where Gardocki punts; fair catch by Wright at the Cincinnati 17. Bengals drive to Bears' 18 where Breech kicks 36-yard field goal at 8:39.

Nov. 15, 1992—New England 37, Indianapolis 34, at Indianapolis; Colts win toss. Verdin returns kickoff 10 yards to Colts' 20; holding penalty brings ball back to Colts' 10. After two plays, Henderson intercepts pass at Colts' 38 and returns it 9 yards to the 29. In three plays, Patriots drive to 1 where Baumann kicks 18-yard field goal at 3:25.

Nov. 29, 1992—Indianapolis 16, Buffalo 13, at Indianapolis; Colts win toss. Verdin returns kickoff 24 yards to Colts' 22. Colts drive to Buffalo 22 where Biasucci kicks 40-yard field goal at 3:51.

***Nov. 30, 1992—Seattle 16, Denver 13,** at Seattle; Seahawks win toss. Daluiso kicks through end zone for touchback. After three plays, Tuten punts 53 yards to Denver 18 where Marshall returns for no gain. After three plays, Rodriguez punts 29 yards to Seattle 45 where Warren signals fair catch. Seahawks drive to Denver 15 where Kasay's 33-yard field goal attempt misses. Broncos take over at Denver 20. After three plays, Rodriguez punts 43 yards to Seattle 38 where Warren signals for fair catch. After four plays, Tuten punts 39 yards to Denver 4 where Daniels downs punt. After three plays, Rodriguez punts 46 yards to Denver 48 where Warren returns 10 yards to the 38. Seahawks drive to Denver 14 where Kasay kicks 32-yard field goal at 11:10.

Dec. 13, 1992—Philadelphia 20, Seattle 17, at Seattle; Eagles win toss. Sydner returns kick 12 yards to Eagles' 16; illegal block penalty brings ball back to 8. Eagles drive to Philadelphia 45 where Feagles punts for a touchback. After 6 plays, Tuten punts 45 yards to Philadelphia 22 where Sydner returns 7 yards to 29. After 6 plays, Feagles punts 44 yards to Seattle 26 where Warren returns 5 yards to 31. After 5 plays, Tuten punts 32 yards to Philadelphia 20 where Sydner signals for fair catch. Eagles drive to Seattle 27 where Ruzek kicks 44-yard field goal with no time remaining.

Dec. 27, 1992—Miami 16, New England 13, at New England; Patriots win toss. Lockwood returns kickoff 15 yards to Patriots' 21. After three plays, McCarthy punts 39 yards to Miami 33 where Miller returns 2 yards to the 35. Miami drives to New England 18 where Stoyanovich kicks 35-yard field goal at 8:17.

Sept. 12, 1993—Detroit 19, New England 16, at New England; Patriots win toss. Patriots begin at 20. After 3 plays, Saxon punts 42 yards to Detroit 29 where Gray returns 12 yards to the 41. After 3 plays, Arnold punts 41 yards to New England 12 where Brown returns 16 yards to the 28. Patriots drive to Detroit 44 where Saxon punts into the end zone for a touchback. Detroit drives to New England 20 where Hanson kicks 38-yard field goal at 11:04.

Nov. 7, 1993—Buffalo 13, New England 10, at New England; Patriots win toss. T. Brown returns kickoff 27 yards to Patriots 30. Patriots drive to Buffalo 48 where Bills take over on downs. Bills drive to New England 25 where Metzelaars fumbles, and C. Brown recovers. After 3 plays, Saxon punts 46 yards to Buffalo 24 where Copeland returns 11 yards to the 35. Bills drive to New England 14 where Christie kicks 32-yard field goal at 9:22.

Dec. 19, 1993—Phoenix 30, Seattle 27, at Seattle; Cardinals win toss. Bailey returns kickoff 14 yards to Cardinals 20. Cardinals drive to Seattle 23 where Davis kicks 41-yard field goal at 6:45.

Jan. 2, 1994—Dallas 16, New York Giants 13, at New York; Giants win toss. Meggett returns kickoff 19 yards to Giants 19. After 6 plays, Horan punts 45 yards to Cowboys 25 where Widmer downs punt. Cowboys drive to Giants' 23 where Murray kicks 41-yard field goal at 10:44.

Jan. 2, 1994—New England 33, Miami 27, at New England; Dolphins win toss. McDuffie returns kickoff 21 yards to Miami 27. After 3 plays, Hatcher punts 43 yards to New England 29 where Harris returns 6 yards to the 35. After 2 plays, Brown intercepts pass from Bledsoe and returns 3 yards to Miami 49. After 3 plays, Hatcher punts 37 yards to New England 14 where Harris returns 18 yards to the 32. After 2 plays, Bledsoe passes 36 yards to Timpson for touchdown at 4:44.

Jan. 2, 1994—Los Angeles Raiders 33, Denver 30, at Los Angeles; Broncos win toss. Delpino returns kickoff 12 yards to Denver 25. Broncos drive to Los Angeles 22 where Elam's 40-yard field goal attempt is wide left. Raiders drive to Denver 29 where Jaeger kicks 47-yard field goal at 7:10.

***Jan. 3, 1994—Philadelphia 37, San Francisco 34,** at San Francisco; 49ers win toss. Walker returns kickoff, 19 yards to San Francisco 27. 49ers drive to Philadelphia 14 where Cofer misses 32-yard field goal. Eagles start at their 20-yard line, and, after 3 plays, Feagles punts 48 yards to San Francisco 36 where Carter fumbles and 49ers recover. After 7 plays, Wilmsmeyer punts 57 yards to Philadelphia 6 where Sikahema returns 16 yards to the 22. Eagles drive to San Francisco 10 where Ruzek kicks 28-yard field goal with no time remaining.

Sept. 4, 1994—Detroit 31, Atlanta 28, at Detroit; Falcons win toss. Falcons start at their own 16 after holding penalty on kickoff. After 3 plays, Alexander punts 41 yards to Detroit 39 where Clay returns 12 yards to Atlanta 49. Detroit drives to Atlanta 20 where Hanson kicks 37-yard field goal at 5:14.

Sept. 11, 1994—New York Jets 25, Denver 22, at New York; Jets win toss. Murrell returns kickoff 24 yards to New York 33. Jets drive to Denver 22 where Lowery kicks 39-yard field goal at 3:57.

***Sept. 19, 1994—Detroit 20, Dallas 17,** at Dallas; Lions win toss. Gray returns kickoff 24 yards to Detroit 32. Lions drive to Dallas 34 where Hanson's 51-yard field-goal attempt is blocked by Lett. Cowboys take possession at Dallas 42. Cowboys drive to Detroit 37 where Kennard fumbles and Swilling recovers. Lions take possession at Detroit 45. After 6 plays, Montgomery punts 31 yards to Dallas 16. Cowboys drive to Dallas 49 where Aikman fumbles and Thomas recovers at Dallas 43. Lions drive to Dallas 26 where Hanson kicks 44-yard field goal at 14:33.

Oct. 16, 1994—Arizona 19, Washington 16, at Washington; Redskins win toss. Mitchell returns kickoff 27 yards to Washington 41. Redskins drive to Arizona 34 where Lohmiller's 51-yard field-goal attempt is blocked by Joyner and recovered by Williams who returns it to the Washington 37. After 5 plays, Peterson's 45-yard field-goal attempt is wide right. Redskins take possession at the Washington 36. After 3 plays, Roby punts 36 yards to the Arizona 37 where Robinson returns 3 yards to the 40. After 3 plays, Feagles punts 51 yards for a touchback. After 1 play, Shuler's pass is intercepted by Hoage who returns it to the Washington 12. Peterson kicks 29-yard field goal at 10:00.

Oct. 16, 1994—Miami 20, Los Angeles Raiders 17, at Miami; Dolphins win toss. McDuffie returns kickoff 19 yards to Miami 23. Dolphins drive to Los Angeles 12 where Stoyanovich kicks 29-yard field goal at 5:46.

#Oct. 20, 1994—Minnesota 13, Green Bay 10, at Minnesota; Vikings win toss. Ismail returns kickoff 22 yards to Minnesota 29. Vikings drive to Green Bay 9 where Fuad Reveiz kicks 27-yard field goal at 4:26.

Oct. 30, 1994—Detroit 28, New York Giants 25, at New York; Giants win toss. Lewis returns kickoff 16 yards to New York 27. After 3 plays, Horan punts 42 yards to Detroit 24 where Gray calls for fair catch. Detroit drives to New York 6 where Hanson kicks 24-yard field goal at 6:43.

Oct. 30, 1994—Arizona 20, Pittsburgh 17, at Arizona; Steelers win toss. Johnson returns kickoff 24 yards to Pittsburgh 30 where he fumbles and Arizona's Merritt recovers at Pittsburgh 32. After 3 plays, Davis kicks 51-yard field goal at 1:40.

Nov. 6, 1994—Cincinnati 20, Seattle 17, at Seattle; Seahawks win toss. Warren returns kickoff 32 yards to Seattle 33. After 3 plays, Tuten punts 37 yards to Cincinnati 28 where Sawyer calls for fair catch. After 3 plays, Johnson punts 64 yards to Seattle 2 where Truitt downs ball. Seahawks drive to Seattle 38 where Tuten punts 50 yards to Cincinnati 12 and Sawyer returns 5 yards to 17. Blake passes to Scott for 76 yards to Seattle 7. Pelfrey kicks 26-yard field goal at 8:14.

Nov. 6, 1994—Pittsburgh 12, Houston 9, at Houston; Steelers win toss. Stone returns kickoff 15 yards to Pittsburgh 28. After 3 plays, Royals punts 53 yards to Houston 13 where Givins downs ball. After 3 plays, Camarillo punts 57 yards to Pittsburgh 31 where Woodson returns 20 yards to Houston 49. After 3 plays, Royals punts 43 yards to Houston 15 where Coleman returns 3 yards to 18. After 5 plays, Camarillo punts 57 yards to Pittsburgh 12 where Hastings returns 12 yards to 24. Steelers drive to Houston 41 where Royals punts 29 yards to Houston 12, and Coleman calls for fair catch. Brown fumbles on first play and Jones recovers at Houston 22. After 1 play, Anderson kicks 40-yard field goal at 11:24.

Nov. 13, 1994—New England 26, Minnesota 20, at New England; Patriots win toss. Thompson returns kickoff 27 yards to New England 33. Patriots drive to Minnesota 14 where Bledsoe passes 14 yards to Turner for touchdown at 4:10.

Nov. 20, 1994—Pittsburgh 16, Miami 13, at Pittsburgh; Steelers win toss. Stone returns kickoff 15 yards to Pittsburgh 16. Steelers drive to Miami 39 where they lose possession on downs. Dolphins drive to Pittsburgh 47 where Arnold punts 35 yards to Pittsburgh 12 and Oliver downs ball. Steelers drive to Miami 21 where Anderson kicks 39-yard field goal at 10:19.

Nov. 27, 1994—Chicago 19, Arizona 16, at Arizona; Cardinals win toss. Levy returns kickoff 31 yards to Arizona 45. After 5 plays, Feagles punts 38 yards to the end zone for a touchback. Bears drive to Arizona 10 where Butler kicks 27-yard field goal at 8:11.

Nov. 27, 1994—Tampa Bay 20, Minnesota 17, at Minnesota; Buccaneers win toss. Harris returns kickoff 12 yards to Tampa Bay 38. After 6 plays, Stryzinski punts 40 yards to Minnesota 4 where Guliford muffs punt and Buccaneers' Brady recovers. Husted kicks 22-yard field goal at 2:08.

#Dec. 1, 1994—Minnesota 33, Chicago 27, at Minnesota; Bears win toss. Lewis returns kickoff 23 yards to Chicago 33. Bears drive to Minnesota 22 where Butler's 40-yard field goal attempt is wide left. After 1 play, Moon passes 65 yards to Carter for touchdown at 5:46.

Dec. 4, 1994—Denver 20, Kansas City 17, at Kansas City; Broncos win toss. Milburn returns kickoff 24 yards to Denver 29. After 3 plays, Millen fumbles and Phillips recovers at Denver 35. After 4 plays, Allen fumbles and Smith recovers at Denver 27. After 6 plays, Rouen punts 45 yards to Kansas City 25 where Hughes calls for fair catch. After 3 plays, Aguiar punts 33 yards to Denver 42 where Chiefs down ball. Broncos drive to Kansas City 17 where Elam kicks 34-yard field goal at 12:12.

Sept. 3, 1995—Cincinnati 24, Indianapolis 21, at Indianapolis; Bengals win toss. Dunn returns kickoff 15 yards to Bengals' 17. Cincinnati drives to Indianapolis 29 where Pelfrey kicks 47-yard field goal at 2:36.

Sept. 3, 1995—Atlanta 23, Carolina 20, at Atlanta; Panthers win toss. Baldwin downs kickoff for touchback. Panthers drive to Carolina 42 where Reich fumbles and ball is recovered by Archambeau at Carolina 31. Falcons drive to Panthers' 16 where Andersen kicks 35-yard field goal at 6:17.

Sept. 10, 1995—Indianapolis 27, New York Jets 24, at New York; Jets win toss. Carter downs kickoff for touchback. Jets punt downed at Colts' 37. Colts drive to Jets' 35 where Cofer kicks 52-yard field goal at 4:27.

Sept. 10, 1995—Kansas City 20, New York Giants 17, at Kansas City; Chiefs win toss. Vanover returns kickoff 30 yards to Chiefs' 28. Aguiar punts to Giants' 3. Horan punts to Chiefs' 49. Chiefs drive to Giants' 6 where Elliott kicks 23-yard field goal at 7:49.

Sept. 17, 1995—Dallas 23, Minnesota 17, at Minnesota; Cowboys win toss. K. Williams returns kickoff 23 yards to Cowboys' 27. E. Smith scores on 31-yard run at 2:26.

Sept. 17, 1995—Kansas City 23, Oakland 17, at Kansas City; Chiefs win toss. Vanover returns kickoff 28 yards to Chiefs' 41. M. Allen fumbles, ball recovered by Robbins at Raiders' 38. Hasty intercepts pass at Chiefs' 36 and returns it 64 yards for touchdown at 4:27.

Sept. 17, 1995—Atlanta 27, New Orleans 24, at Atlanta; Saints win toss. Hughes returns kickoff 21 yards to Saints' 17. Metcalf returns Wilmsmeyer's punt 18 yards to Saints' 39. Stryzinski punts, fair catch by Hughes at Saints' 14. Wilmsmeyer punt downed at Falcons' 6. Falcons drive to Saints' 3 where Andersen kicks 21-yard field goal at 7:58.

Oct. 8, 1995—Indianapolis 27, Miami 24, at Miami; Colts win toss. Warren returns kickoff 25 yards to Colts' 33. Colts drive to Dolphins' 10 where Blanchard kicks 27-yard field goal at 4:58.

Oct. 8, 1995—New York Giants 27, Arizona 21, at New York; Cardinals win toss. Terry returns kickoff 20 yards to Cardinals' 23. Hamilton recovers Krieg's fumble at Cardinals' 36. Lynch recovers Brown's fumble at Cardinals' 38. Armstead intercepts pass at Giants' 42 and returns it 58 yards for touchdown at 4:05.

Oct. 8, 1995—Minnesota 23, Houston 17, at Minnesota; Vikings win toss. Palmer returns kickoff 10 yards to Vikings' 15. Saxon's punt downed at Oilers' 8. Washington intercepts pass at Vikings' 47 and returns it 25 yards to Oilers' 28. R. Smith scores on 20-yard run at 7:10.

Oct. 8, 1995—Philadelphia 37, Washington 34, at Philadelphia; Redskins win toss. Redskins take possession at their 20 after touchback. Turk punt out of bounds at Eagles' 9. Eagles drive to Redskins' 18 where Anderson kicks 35-yard field goal at 10:06.

***Oct. 9, 1995—Kansas City 29, San Diego 23,** at Kansas City; Chargers win toss. Coleman returns kickoff 24 yards to Chargers' 28. Vanover makes fair catch of Bennett's punt at Chiefs' 15. Coleman makes fair catch of Aguiar's punt at Chargers' 43. Vanover returns Bennett's punt 86 yards for a touchdown at 7:27.

Oct. 15, 1995—Tampa Bay 20, Minnesota 17, at Tampa Bay; Buccaneers win toss. Edmonds returns kickoff 19 yards to Buccaneers' 22. A. Lee returns Roby's punt to Vikings' 48. Vikings drive to Tampa Bays' 35 where Reveiz's 53-yard field-goal attempt is wide right. Buccaneers take over at own 43 and drive to Vikings' 33 where Husted kicks 51-yard field goal at 6:23.

Oct. 22, 1995—Washington 36, Detroit 30, at Washington; Redskins win toss. B. Mitchell returns kickoff 16 yards to Redskins' 27. Turk's punt downed at Lions' 4. D. Green intercepts S. Mitchell's pass and returns it 7 yards for touchdown at 3:41.

Oct. 29, 1995—Carolina 20, New England 17, at New England; Panthers win toss. Baldwin returns kickoff 22 yards to Panthers' 25. Meggett makes fair catch of Barnhardt's punt at Patriots' 9. Guliford returns O'Neill's punt 9 yards to Patriots' 32. Panthers drive to Patriots' 12 where Kasay kicks 29-yard field goal at 7:08.

Oct. 29, 1995—Cleveland 29, Cincinnati 26, at Cincinnati; Browns win toss. Hunter returns kickoff 31 yards to Browns' 31. Bieniemy returns Tupa's punt 9 yards to Bengals' 37. McCardell makes fair catch of Johnson's punt at Browns' 12. Bieniemy returns Tupa's punt 0 yards to Bengals' 38. Hall intercepts Blake's pass and returns it 5 yards to Bengals' 45. Browns drive to Bengals' 11 where Stover kicks 28-yard field goal at 6:30.

Oct. 29, 1995—Arizona 20, Seattle 14, at Arizona; Cardinals win toss. Dowdell returns kickoff 16 yards to Cardinals' 25. Cardinals drive to Seahawks' 10 where G. Davis' 27-yard field goal attempt is blocked. L. Lynch intercepts Friesz's pass at Cardinals' 28 and returns it 72 yards for a touchdown at 11:16.

Nov. 5, 1995—Pittsburgh 37, Chicago 34, at Chicago; Bears win toss. Timpson returns kickoff 23 yards to Bears' 33. Hastings returns Sauerbrun's punt 2 yards to Steelers' 31. Steelers drive to Bears' 6 where N. Johnson kicks 24-yard field goal at 8:19.

Nov. 12, 1995—Minnesota 30, Arizona 24, at Arizona; Vikings win toss. A. Lee returns kickoff 20 yards to Vikings' 25. Moon throws 50-yard touchdown pass to Ismail at 2:16.

Nov. 26, 1995—Arizona 40, Atlanta 37, at Arizona; Falcons win toss. J. Anderson returns kickoff 20 yards to Falcons' 20. Stryzinski fumbles punt snap. Recovered by England at Falcons' 10 where G. Davis kicks 28-yard field goal at 1:43.

Dec. 10, 1995—Tampa Bay 13, Green Bay 10, at Tampa Bay; Buccaneers win toss. Edmonds returns kickoff 24 yards to Buccaneers' 23. Tampa Bay drives to Packers' 29 where Husted kicks 47-yard field goal at 3:46.

Sept. 1, 1996—Buffalo 23, New York Giants 20, at New York; Bills win toss. Daluiso kick is a touchback. Bills drive to Buffalo 46. Toomer returns Mohr's punt to Giants' 16. Dave Brown's fumble recovered by Spielman at Giants' 33. Bills drive to Giants' 16 where Christie kicks 34-yard field goal at 9:08.

Sept. 22, 1996—New England 28, Jacksonville 25, at New England; Patriots win toss. T. Brown returns kickoff 18 yards to Patriots' 29. Patriots drive to Jaguars' 22 where Vinatieri kicks 40-yard field goal at 2:36.

Sept. 29, 1996—Arizona 31, St. Louis 28, at Arizona; Cardinals win toss. Lohmiller kick is a touchback. Cardinals drive to Rams' 7 where G. Davis kicks 24-yard field goal at 1:54.

Oct. 6, 1996—Buffalo 16, Indianapolis 13, at Buffalo; Colts win toss. Christie kick is a touchback. Colts drive to Indianapolis 32. Burris returns Gardocki's punt to Bills' 35. Bills drive to Colts' 48. Mohr punts out of bounds at Colts' 14. Colts drive to Indianapolis 9. Burris returns Gardocki's punt to Colts' 48. Bills drive to Colts' 22 where Christie kicks 39-yard field goal at 9:22.

Oct. 6, 1996—Houston 30, Cincinnati 27, at Cincinnati; Bengals win toss. Dunn returns kickoff 23 yards to Bengals' 34. Bengals drive to Cincinnati 36. Floyd returns L. Johnson's punt to Oilers' 18. Oilers drive to Bengals' 31 where Del Greco kicks 49-yard field goal at 7:07.

***Oct. 14, 1996—Green Bay 23, San Francisco 20,** at Green Bay; 49ers win toss. D. Carter returns kickoff 23 yards to 49ers' 22. 49ers' drive to San Francisco 25. Howard makes fair catch of Thompson's punt at Packers' 44. Packers drive to 49ers' 35 where Jacke kicks 53-yard field goal at 3:41.

Oct. 27, 1996—Baltimore 37, St. Louis 31, at Baltimore; Rams win toss. J. Thomas returns kickoff 17 yard to Rams' 17. Rams drive to Ravens' 15. F. Miller fumble in field goal formation recovered by S. Moore at Ravens' 17. Ravens drive to Baltimore 49 and turn ball over on downs. Rams drive to Ravens' 40 and turn ball over on downs. Testaverde throws 22-yard scoring pass to M. Jackson at 14:50.

OVERTIME GAMES

Nov. 10, 1996—Dallas 20, San Francisco 17, at San Francisco; Cowboys win toss. H. Walker returns kickoff 10 yards to Cowboys' 23. Cowboys drive to 49ers' 11 where Boniol kicks 29-yard field goal at 6:17.
Nov. 10, 1996—Arizona 37, Washington 34, at Washington; Cardinals win toss. Blanton's kickoff is a touchback. Cardinals drive to Redskins' 15 where Butler misses 32-yard field goal. Redskins drive to Cardinals' 43 where Turk punts for touchback. L. Johnson fumble returned by Morrison to Cardinals' 27. Redskins drive to Cardinals' 31 where Blanton misses 48-yard field goal. Cardinals drive to Redskins' 15 where Butler kicks 32-yard field goal at 14:27.
Nov. 10, 1996—Tampa Bay 20, Oakland 17, at Tampa Bay; Buccaneers win toss. M. Marshall returns kickoff 15 yards to Bucs' 17. Bucs drive to Tampa Bay 36. T. Brown returns Barnhardt's punt four yards to Raiders' 22. Raiders drive to Oakland 25. M. Marshall returns Gossett's punt nine yards to Bucs' 39. Bucs drive to Raiders' 4 where Husted kicks 23-yard field goal at 11:56.
Nov. 17, 1996—Minnesota 16, Oakland 13, at Oakland; Raiders win toss. Kaufman returns kickoff 32 yards to Raiders' 27. Raiders drive to Oakland 46 where Gossett punts to Vikings' 17. Vikings drive to Raiders' 12 where Sisson kicks 31-yard field goal at 11:53.
Nov. 24, 1996—Jacksonville 28, Baltimore 25, at Baltimore; Jaguars win toss. Jordon returns kickoff 16 yards to Jaguars' 30. Jaguars drive to Jacksonville 37. Barker's punt is downed at Ravens' 6. Ravens drive to Jaguars' 37 where Pritchett recovers Byner's fumble. Jaguars drive to Ravens' 15 where Hollis kicks 34-yard field goal at 9:06.
Nov. 24, 1996—San Francisco 19, Washington 16, at Washington; 49ers win toss. D. Carter returns kickoff 20 yards to 49ers' 32. 49ers drive to Redskins' 20 where WIlkins kicks 38-yard field goal at 3:24.
Dec. 1, 1996—Indianapolis 13, Buffalo 10, at Indianapolis; Bills win toss. Moulds returns kickoff 26 yards to Bills' 25. Bills drive to Buffalo 49. Stock returns Mohr's punt one yard to Colts' 16. Colts drive to Bills' 32 where Blanchard kicks 49-yard field goal at 10:46.
Aug. 31, 1997—Tennessee 24, Oakland 21, at Tennessee; Oilers win toss. Gray returns kickoff 32 yards to Tennessee 33. Oilers drive to Tennessee 38. Roby's punt is downed at the Oakland 33. Raiders drive to Oakland 32. Gray returns Araguz punt to Tennessee 35. Oilers drive to Oakland 15 where Del Greco kicks 33-yard field goal at 6:57.
Sept. 7, 1997—Miami 16, Tennessee 13, at Miami; Dolphins win toss. Spikes returns kickoff 48 yards to Tennessee 45. Dolphins drive to Tennessee 11 where Mare kicks 29-yard field goal at 2:15.
Sept. 7, 1997— Arizona 25, Dallas 22, at Arizona; Cowboys win toss. Walker returns kickoff 21 yards to Dallas 25. Cowboys drive to Arizona 43. Gowin punts 43 yards for a touchback. Cardinals drive to Dallas 44. Graham fumbles. Cowboys drive to Arizona 42. Williams fumbles. Cardinals drive to Dallas 3 where Butler kicks 20-yard field goal at 8:30.
Sept. 14, 1997—Washington 19, Arizona 13, at Washington; Cardinals win toss. K. Williams returns kickoff 27 yards to Arizona 34. Cardinals drive to Arizona 40. McElroy fumbles. Redskins drive to Arizona 40. Westbrook catches 40-yard touchdown pass from Frerotte at 1:36.
Sept. 14, 1997—New England 27, New York Jets 24, at New England; Patriots win toss. Hall's kickoff is a touchback. Patriots drive to New England 15. Bledsoe pass intercepted by O. Smith. Jets drive to New York 46. Hansen punts 47 yards. Meggett returns to New England 21. Patriots drive to New York 17 where Vinatieri kicks 34-yard field goal at 8:03.
Sept. 28, 1997—Kansas City 20, Seattle 17, at Kansas City; Seahawks win toss. Broussard returns kickoff 12 yards to Seattle 14. Seahawks drive to Seattle 17. Vanover returns Tuten punt 8 yards to Kansas City 26. Chiefs drive to Seattle 44. Aguiar punt downed at Seattle 11. Seahawks drive to Seattle 26. Moon pass intercepted by Woods and returned 13 yards to 50. Chiefs drive to Seattle 23 where Stoyanovich kicks 41-yard field goal at 13:04.
Oct. 19, 1997—Philadelphia 13, Arizona 10, at Philadelphia; Cardinals win toss. K. Williams returns kickoff 28 yards to Arizona 42. Cardinals drive to Philadelphia 48. Feagles punts 48 yards for touchback. Eagles drive to Arizona 7 where Boniol kicks 24-yard field goal at 4:02.
Oct. 19, 1997—New York Giants 26, Detroit 20, at Detroit; Giants win toss. Pegram returns kickoff 16 yards to New York 18. Giants drive to New York 32. Calloway catches 68-yard touchdown pass from Kanell at 1:40.
Oct. 26, 1997—Denver 23, Buffalo 20, at Buffalo; Broncos win toss and elects to kickoff. Holmes returns kickoff 20 yards to Buffalo 25. Bills drive to Buffalo 23. Mohr punt downed at Denver 40. Broncos drive to Buffalo 48. Rouen punt downed at Buffalo 1. Bills drive to Buffalo 20. Gordon returns Mohr punt to Denver 42. Broncos drive to Buffalo 15 where Elam kicks 33-yard field goal at 13:04.
Oct. 26, 1997—Pittsburgh 23, Jacksonville 17, at Pittsburgh; Steelers win toss. Coleman returns kickoff 23 yards to Pittsburgh 23. Steelers drive to Jacksonville 17. Bettis catches 17-yard touchdown pass from Stewart at 3:47.
Oct. 27, 1997—Chicago 36, Miami 33, at Miami; Dolphins win toss. McPhail returns kickoff 23 yards to Miami 27. Dolphins drive to Miami 36. Kidd punts out of bounds at Chicago 10. Bears drive to the Chicago 39. Sauerbrun punt out of bounds at Miami 27. Reeves recovers Marino fumble at Miami 17. Bears drive to Miami 17 where Jaeger kicks 35-yard field goal at 9:25.
Nov. 2, 1997—New York Jets 19, Baltimore 16, at New York; Jets win toss. Stover's kickoff is a touchback. Jets drive to Baltimore 20 where Hall kicks 37-yard field goal at 4:58.
Nov. 16, 1997—Philadelphia 10, Baltimore 10, at Baltimore; Eagles win toss. Stover's kickoff is a touchback. Eagles drive to Philadelphia 19. Hutton punts 36 yards to Baltimore 45. Ravens drive to Baltimore 36 where Eagles take over on downs. Eagles drive to Baltimore 33 where Ravens take over on downs. Ravens drive to Baltimore 37. Montgomery punts 55 yards, and Solomon returns to Philadelphia 22. Eagles drive to Philadelphia 16. Hutton punts 41 yards, and Roe returns to Baltimore 46. Ravens drive to Philadelphia 35 where Stover's 53-yard field-goal attempt is no good. Eagles drive to Baltimore 22 where Boniol's 40-yard field-goal is no good as time expires.
Nov. 16, 1997—New Orleans 20, Seattle 17, at New Orleans; Seahawks win toss. Brien's kickoff is a touchback. Seahawks start at Seattle 20 where Moon's pass intercepted by Tubbs who returns 15 yards to Seattle 20. Saints Brien kicks 38-yard field goal at 17 seconds.
Nov. 23, 1997—New York Giants 7, Washington 7, at Washington; Redskins win toss. Davis returns kickoff 28 yards to Washington 39. Redskins drive to Washington 36 where Hostetler's pass intercepted by Sehorn who returns minus-2 yards before lateralling to Wooten who returns 5 yards to New York 41. Giants drive to New York 26 where Maynard punts 37 yards to Washington 37. Redskins drive to New York 39 where Hostetler fumble is recovered by Harris at New York 40. Giants drive to New York 43 where Maynard punts 57 yards for a touchback. Washington drives to New York 41. Giants take over on downs at New York 40. Giants drive to Washington 36 where Daluiso's 54-yard field-goal attempt is no good. Redskins drive to Washington 45 where Hostetler's pass intercepted by Sparks at New York 49. Giants drive to Washington 36 where Maynard punts 36 yards for a touchback. Redskins drive to New York 36 where Blanton's 54-yard field-goal attempt is no good. Giants drive to New York 45 where Kanell's pass intercepted by Patton who laterals to Pounds who returns 11 yards to Washington 24 as time expires.
Nov. 30, 1997—Pittsburgh 26, Arizona 20, at Arizona; Cardinals win toss. K. Williams returns kickoff 11 yards to Arizona 23. Cardinals drive to Arizona 18 where Feagles punts 43 yards. Hawkins returns punt 9 yards to Pittsburgh 48. Steelers drive to Arizona 10 where Bettis scores on a 10-yard touchdown run at 5:34.
Dec. 13, 1997—Pittsburgh 24, New England 21, at New England; Steelers win toss. Coleman returns kickoff 19 yards to Pittsburgh 26. Steelers drive to New England 13 where Johnson kicks a 31-yard field goal at 4:43.
Sept. 6, 1998—San Francisco 36, New York Jets 30, at San Francisco; Jets win toss. Richey's kickoff is a touchback. Jets drive to New York 11. Gallery punts 48 yards. McQuarters returns to New York 43. 49ers drive to New York 44. Howard punts 23 yards to New York 21. Johnson calls fair catch. Jets drive to New York 47. Gallery's 49-yard punt downed at San Francisco 4. Hearst runs for a 96-yard touchdown at 4:08.
Sept. 13, 1998—Cincinnati 34, Detroit 28, at Detroit; Lions win toss. Johnson's kickoff is a touchback. Lions drive to Detroit 47 where Mitchell's pass is intercepted by Sawyer and returned for a 58-yard touchdown at 2:06.
Sept. 27, 1998—New Orleans 19, Indianapolis 13, at Indianapolis; Saints win toss. Gardocki's kickoff is returned by Ismail to New Orleans 28. Saints drive to New Orleans 30. Royals punts 64 yards. Poole returns to Indianapolis 12. Colts drive to Indianapolis 20. Gardocki punts 58 yards. Hastings returns to New Orleans 29. Saints drive to New Orleans 32. Royals punts 59 yards. Punt downed at Indianapolis 9. Colts drive to Indianapolis 44 where Manning's pass is intercepted by Drakeford and returned to Indianapolis 36. Saints drive to Indianapolis 33. Wuerffel throws 33-yard touchdown pass to Cleeland at 6:10.
Oct. 25, 1998—Miami 12, New England 9, at Miami; Dolphins win toss. Vinatieri's kickoff is returned by Avery to Miami 15. Dolphins drive to New England 26 where Mare kicks 43-yard field goal at 4:36.
Nov. 26, 1998—Detroit 19, Pittsburgh 16, at Detroit; Lions win toss. Johnson's kickoff is returned by Fair to Detroit 35. Lions drive to Pittsburgh 24 where Hanson kicks 42-yard field goal at 2:52.
Dec. 6, 1998—San Francisco 31, Carolina 28, at Carolina; Panthers win toss. Richey's kickoff is returned by Floyd to Carolina 36. Panthers drive to Carolina 38 where Beuerlein's fumble is recovered by Doleman at Carolina 30. 49ers drive to Carolina 5 where Richey kicks 23-yard field goal at 4:16.
Dec. 13, 1998—Arizona 20, Philadelphia 17, at Philadelphia; Cardinals win toss. Boniol's kickoff is returned by Metcalf to Arizona 28. Cardinals drive to Philadelphia 15 where Jacke kicks 32-yard field goal at 4:30.
Sept. 12, 1999—Dallas 41, Washington 35, at Washington; Redskins win toss. Gowin's kickoff is returned by B. Mitchell to Washington 24. Redskins drive to Washington 47. M. Turk punts 48 yards. Punt downed at Dallas 5. Cowboys drive to Dallas 24. Aikman passes 76-yard touchdown to R. Ismail at 4:09.
Oct. 3, 1999—Baltimore 19, Atlanta 13, at Atlanta; Falcons win toss. Stover's kickoff is returned by Oliver to Atlanta 18. Falcons drive to Atlanta 23. Stryzinski punts 41 yards, out of bounds at Baltimore 36. Baltimore drives to Baltimore 46. Case passes 54-yard touchdown to Armour at 2:29.
Oct. 31, 1999—New York Giants 23, Philadelphia 17, at Philadelphia; Giants win toss. Akers' kickoff is returned by Levingston to New York 27. New York drives to Giants 31. Maynard punts 43 yards to Philadelphia 26. Rossum returns to Eagles 28. Pederson drives to New York 45. Pederson's pass is intercepted by Strahan at Philadelphia 44. Giants' Peter batted ball up in the air as Pederson backpedaled. Strahan for 44 yards and touchdown at 4:24.
Nov. 14, 1999—Minnesota 27, Chicago 24, at Chicago; Vikings win toss. Boniol kicks to Minnesota 2, Williams touchback. Minnesota starts from own 20. George's pass is intercepted by Harris at Minnesota 29 for -1 yard. Chicago starts at Minnesota 29 and moves to Minnesota 23. Boniol's 41-yard field goal is no good. Minnesota starts from own 31 and drives to Chicago 20. Anderson

kicks 38-yard field goal at 9:02.

Nov. 21, 1999—Chicago 23, San Diego 20, at San Diego; Bears win toss. Chicago starts from own 22. Miller completes four consecutive passes and Bears drive to San Diego 22. Enis rushes twice to San Diego 19. Boniol kicks 36-yard field goal at 4:58.

***Nov. 22, 1999—Denver 27, Oakland 21,** at Denver; Broncos win toss. Denver starts from own 33 and drives to Broncos' 35. Rouen punts 46 yards to Oakland 19. Oakland starts at own 19 and drives to Raiders' 25. Gannon fumbles and Broncos' Pryce recovers at Oakland 25. Denver running back Gary scores on 24-yard run at 2:40.

Nov. 28, 1999—Washington 20, Philadelphia 17, at Washington; Redskins win toss. Akers' kickoff is returned by Thrash for 48 yards to Philadelphia 46. Johnson completes 20-yard pass to Connell to Philadelphia 26. Johnson completes 9-yard pass to Mitchell to Philadelphia 9. Mitchell runs for seven yards to Philadelphia 2. On third down, Washington attempts field goal from Philadelphia 2. Johnson fumbles and recovers at Philadelphia 9. Conway kicks 27-yard field goal at 4:34.

Dec. 19, 1999—Denver 36, Seattle 30, at Denver; Broncos win toss. Peterson kicks to Denver 8. Watson returns kick to Denver 27 for 19 yards. Broncos do not convert a first down. Rouen punts 46 yards, out of bounds at Seattle 25. Kitna passes to Dawkins for 17 yards at Seattle 47. Watters runs for 6 yards to Denver 47. Kitna sacked for 11-yard loss by Crockett. Kitna fumbles, forced by Crockett, recovered by Cadrez at Seattle 37. Cadrez for 37 yards and touchdown at 2:34.

Dec. 26, 1999—Washington 26, San Francisco 20, at San Francisco; Redskins win toss. Richey kicks to Washington 9, Thrash returns 13 yards to Washington 22. Johnson passes to Hicks for 25 yards to Washington 47. Centers runs for 12 yards to San Francisco 33. Johnson passes to Centers for 33 yards and touchdown at 2:00.

Dec. 26, 1999—Buffalo 13, New England 10, at New England; Patriots win toss. New England's Vinatieri misses 44-yard field goal from Buffalo 26. Buffalo takes over at Bills 34. Flutie passes to Moulds to New England 21 for 17 yards. Moulds fumbles, recovered by Bruschi at Patriots 21. New England drives to own 34. Johnson punts from New England 34 to Buffalo 42. Flutie passes to Price for 7 yards to New England 44. Flutie passes to Moulds for 11 yards to New England 27. Thomas runs for 9 yards to New England 6. Christie kicks 23-yard field goal at 13:12.

Jan. 2, 2000—Oakland 41, Kansas City 38, at Kansas City; Raiders win toss. Baker kicks 69 yards from Kansas City 30 to Oakland 1 and out of bounds. Oakland starts at Raiders 40. Gannon passes to Dudley for 21 yards to Kansas City 40. Gannon passes to Brown at Kansas City 16 for 24 yards. Crockett runs to Kansas City 15 for 1 yard. Nedney kicks 33-yard field goal at 3:13.

Sept. 10, 2000—Tennessee 17, Kansas City 14, at Tennessee; Titans win toss. Mason returns kickoff 28 yards to Tennesse 29. Face-mask penalty on Kansas City, 5 yards, enforced at 29. Titans drive to Kansas City 18 where Del Greco kicks 36-yard field goal at 2:58.

Oct. 1, 2000—Dallas 16, Carolina 13, at Carolina; Cowboys win toss. Tucker returns kickoff 20 yards to Dallas 26. Dallas drives to Carolina 6 where Seder kicks 24-yard field goal at 3:52.

Oct. 1, 2000—Washington 20, Tampa Bay 17, at Washington; Redskins win toss. Thrash returns kickoff 32 yards to Washington 30. Washington gains five yards where Barnhardt punts 52 yards to Tampa Bay 13. Green returns for one yard to Tampa Bay 14. Buccaneers gain one yard to Tampa Bay 15 where Royals punts 50 yards to Washington 35. Sanders returns punt 57 yards to Tampa Bay 8. Davis rushes three times and gets to Tampa Bay 2 where Husted kicks 20-yard field goal at 4:09.

Oct. 8, 2000—Oakland 34, San Francisco 28, at San Francisco; Raiders win toss. Dunn returns kickoff 20 yards to Oakland 19. Raiders drive to San Francisco 17 where Janikowski misses 35-yard field-goal attempt wide right. San Francisco drives to Oakland 11 where Richey's 29-yard field-goal attempt is blocked by Dorsett. Raiders recover at Oakland 16. Oakland drives to San Francisco 31 where Gannon passes to Brown for 31-yard touchdown at 10:15.

Oct. 15, 2000—Buffalo 27, San Diego 24, at Buffalo; Bills win toss. Bills drive to Buffalo 47. Mohr punts 42 yards to San Diego 11. Chargers drive to San Diego 38 where Harbaugh is intercepted at Buffalo 41. Flutie in for injured Johnson. Bills drive to San Diego 28. Christie kicks 46-yard field goal at 8:26.

***Oct. 23, 2000—New York Jets 40, Miami 37,** at New York; Dolphins win toss. Marion returns kickoff 31 yards to Miami 37. Fielder is intercepted at Miami 46 by Coleman, who returns ball to 39 where he fumbles. Gadsden recovers ball for Dolphins and runs out of bounds at Miami 34. Dolphins drive to New York 43 where Fiedler is intercepted again by Coleman at the Jets 34. Jets drive to Miami 23 where Hall kicks 40-yard field goal at 6:47.

Oct. 29, 2000—Jacksonville 23, Dallas 17, at Dallas; Jaguars win toss. Stith returns kickoff 24 yards to Jacksonville 34. Jaguars drive to Dallas 37 where Brunell passes to Whitted for a 37-yard touchdown at 3:02.

Nov. 5, 2000—Buffalo 16, New England 13, at New England; Patriots win toss. Faulk returns kickoff 38 yards to New England 43. Penalty on New England for offensive holding, 10 yards, enforced at New England 33. Patriots lose one yard on three plays. Johnson punts 43 yards to Buffalo 35. Bills drive to New England 13 where Christie kicks 32-yard field goal at 4:21.

Nov. 5, 2000—Philadelphia 16, Dallas 13, at Philadelphia; Eagles win toss. Mitchell returns kickoff 30 yards to Philadelphia 34. Eagles drive to Dallas 36 where McNabb is intercepted by Wortham at Dallas 30. Wortham returns interception to Dallas 31. Cowboys drive to Dallas 48 where Thomas fumbles. Recovered by Hauck at Dallas 48. Eagles drive to Dallas 13 where Akers kicks 32-yard field goal at 7:52.

***Nov. 6, 2000—Green Bay 26, Minnesota 20,** at Green Bay; Packers win toss. Rossum returns kickoff 13 yards to Green Bay 18. Packers drive to Minnesota 43 where Favre passes to Freeman for a 43-yard touchdown at 3:27.

Nov. 12, 2000—Philadelphia 26, Pittsburgh 23, at Pittsburgh; Eagles win toss. Mitchell returns kickoff 24 yards to Philadelphia 37. Eagles drive to Pittsburgh 24 where Akers kicks 42-yard field goal at 4:09.

Dec. 17, 2000—New England 13, Buffalo 10, at Buffalo; Bills win toss and elect to defend the South goal. Patriots elect to receive. Jackson returns kickoff 38 yards to New England 48. Patriots drive to Buffalo 31 where they turn the ball over on downs. Bills drive to New England 12 where Christie's 30-yard field goal attempt is blocked by Eaton. Patriots recover at New England 11. Patriots drive to Buffalo 6 where Vinatieri kicks 24-yard field goal at 14:37.

Dec. 24, 2000—Green Bay 17, Tampa Bay 14, at Green Bay; Packers win toss. Rossum returns kickoff 29 yards to Green Bay 38. Packers drive to Tampa Bay 4 where Longwell kicks 22-yard field goal at 6:28.

**indicates Monday night game*

#indicates Thursday night game

POSTSEASON

Dec. 28, 1958—Baltimore 23, New York Giants 17, at New York in NFL Championship Game; Giants win toss. Maynard returns kickoff to Giants' 20. Chandler punts and Taseff returns one yard to Colts' 20. Colts win at 8:15 on a 1-yard run by Ameche.

Dec. 23, 1962—Dallas Texans 20, Houston Oilers 17, at Houston in AFL Championship Game; Texans win toss and kick off. Jancik returns kickoff to Oilers' 33. Norton punts and Jackson makes fair catch on Texans' 22. Wilson punts and Jancik makes fair catch on Oilers' 45. Robinson intercepts Blanda's pass and returns 13 yards to Oilers' 47. Wilson's punt rolls dead at Oilers' 12. Hull intercepts Blanda's pass and returns 23 yards to midfield. Texans win at 17:54 on a 25-yard field goal by Brooker.

Dec. 26, 1965—Green Bay 13, Baltimore 10, at Green Bay in NFL Divisional Playoff Game; Packers win toss. Moore returns kickoff to Packers' 22. Chandler punts and Haymond returns nine yards to Colts' 41. Gilburg punts and Wood makes fair catch at Packers' 21. Chandler punts and Haymond returns one yard to Colts' 41. Michaels misses 47-yard field goal. Packers win at 13:39 on 25-yard field goal by Chandler.

Dec. 25, 1971—Miami 27, Kansas City 24, at Kansas City in AFC Divisional Playoff Game; Chiefs win toss. Podolak, after a lateral from Buchanan, returns kickoff to Chiefs' 46. Stenerud's 42-yard field goal is blocked. Seiple punts and Podolak makes fair catch at Chiefs' 17. Wilson punts and Scott returns 18 yards to Dolphins' 39. Yepremian misses 62-yard field goal. Scott intercepts Dawson's pass and returns 13 yards to Dolphins' 46. Seiple punts and Podolak loses one yard to Chiefs' 15. Wilson punts and Scott makes fair catch on Dolphins' 30. Dolphins win at 22:40 on a 37-yard field goal by Yepremian.

Dec. 24, 1977—Oakland 37, Baltimore 31, at Baltimore in AFC Divisional Playoff Game; Colts win toss. Raiders start on own 42 following a punt late in the first overtime. Oakland works way into field-goal range on Stabler's 19-yard pass to Branch at Colts' 26. Four plays later, on the second play of the second overtime, Stabler hits Casper with a 10-yard touchdown pass at 15:43.

Jan. 2, 1982—San Diego 41, Miami 38, at Miami in AFC Divisional Playoff Game; Chargers win toss. San Diego drives from its 13 to Miami 8. On second-and-goal, Benirschke misses 27-yard field goal attempt wide left at 9:15. Miami has the ball twice and San Diego twice more before the Dolphins get their third possession. Miami drives from the San Diego 46 to Chargers' 17 and on fourth-and-two, von Schamann's 34-yard field goal attempt is blocked by San Diego's Winslow after 11:27. Fouts then completes four of five passes, including a 39-yarder to Joiner that puts the ball on Dolphins' 10. On first down, Benirschke kicks a 29-yard field goal at 13:52. San Diego's winning drive covered 74 yards in six plays.

Jan. 3, 1987—Cleveland 23, New York Jets 20, at Cleveland in AFC Divisional Playoff Game; Jets win toss. Jets' punt downed at Browns' 26. Moseley's 23-yard field goal attempt is wide right. Teams trade punts. Jets' second punt downed at Browns' 31. First overtime period expires eight plays later with Browns in possession at Jets' 42. Moseley kicks 27-yard field goal four plays into second overtime at 17:02.

Jan. 11, 1987—Denver 23, Cleveland 20, at Cleveland in AFC Championship Game; Browns win toss. Broncos hold Browns on four downs. Browns' punt returned four yards to Denver's 25. Elway completes 22- and 28-yard passes to set up Karlis's 33-yard field goal nine plays into drive at 5:38.

Jan. 3, 1988—Houston 23, Seattle 20, at Houston in AFC Wild Card Game; Seahawks win toss. Rodriguez punts to K. Johnson who returns one yard to Houston 15. Zendejas kicks 32-yard field goal 12 plays later at 8:05.

Dec. 31, 1989—Pittsburgh 26, Houston 23, at Houston in AFC Wild Card Playoff Game; Steelers win toss. Steelers punt to Oilers. Oilers' fumble recovered by Woodson and returned three yards. Four plays and 13 yards later, Anderson kicks a 50-yard field goal at 3:26.

Jan. 7, 1990—Los Angeles Rams 19, New York Giants 13, at New York in NFC Divisional Game; Rams win toss. Everett completes two passes to move ball to Giants' 48. White called for pass interference; ball spotted on Giants' 25. Everett hits Anderson with a 30-yard touchdown pass at 1:06.

OVERTIME GAMES

Jan. 3, 1993—Buffalo 41, Houston 38, at Buffalo in AFC Wild Card Game; Oilers win toss. Oilers begin at 20. After 2 plays, Moon's pass is intercepted by Odomes who returns ball 2 yards to Houston 35. After 2 plays, Christie kicks 32-yard field goal at 3:06.
Jan. 8, 1994—Kansas City 27, Pittsburgh 24, at Kansas City in AFC Wild Card Game; Cheifs win toss. Hughes returns kickoff 20 yards to Kansas City 25. After 3 plays, Barker punts 48 yards to Pittsburgh 18 where Woodson returns 8 yards to the 26. After 6 plays, Royals punts 30 yards to Kansas City 20. Kansas City drives to Pittsburgh 14 where Lowery kicks 32-yard field goal at 11:03.
Jan. 17, 1999—Atlanta 30, Minnesota 27, at Minnesota in NFC Championship Game; Vikings win toss. Palmer returns kickoff 30 yards to Minnesota 29. After four plays, Berger punts 51 yards to Atlanta 7 where Dwight returns 8 yards to Atlanta 15. Falcons drive to Atlanta 36. Stryzinski punts 37 yards to Vikings' 27. Palmer calls fair catch. Vikings drive to Minnesota 39. Berger punts 52 yards to Atlanta 9. Downed by Vikings. Atlanta drives to Minnesota 21 where Andersen kicks 38-yard field goal at 11:52.
Dec. 30, 2000—Miami 23, Indianapolis 17, at Miami in AFC Wild Card Game; Dolphins win toss. Williams returns kickoff 18 yards to Miami 20. Offensive holding penalty on Freeman, 10 yards, ball spotted on Miami 10. Dolphins drive to Miami 29 where Turk punts 53 yards to Indianapolis 18. Colts drive to Miami 31 where Vanderjagt misses 49-yard field-goal attempt wide right. Dolphins drive to Indianapolis 17 where Smith rushes for a 17-yard touchdown at 11:16.

NFL POSTSEASON OVERTIME GAMES
(BY LENGTH OF GAME)

Date	Game	Length
Dec. 25, 1971	Miami 27, KANSAS CITY 24	82:40
Dec. 23, 1962	Dallas Texans 20, HOUSTON 17	77:54
Jan. 3, 1987	CLEVELAND 23, New York Jets 20	77:02
Dec. 24, 1977	Oakland 37, BALTIMORE 31	75:43
Jan. 2, 1982	San Diego 41, MIAMI 38	73:52
Dec. 26, 1965	GREEN BAY 13, Baltimore 10	73:39
Jan. 17, 1999	Atlanta 30, MINNESOTA 27	71:52
Dec. 30, 2000	MIAMI 23, Indianapolis 17	71:16
Jan. 8, 1994	KANSAS CITY 27, Pittsburgh 24	71:03
Dec. 28, 1958	Baltimore 23, N.Y. GIANTS 17	68:15
Jan. 3, 1988	HOUSTON 23, Seattle 20	68:05
Jan. 11, 1987	Denver 23, CLEVELAND 20	65:38
Dec. 31, 1989	Pittsburgh 26, HOUSTON 23	63:26
Jan. 3, 1993	BUFFALO 41, Houston 38	63:06
Jan. 7, 1990	Los Angeles Rams 19, N.Y. GIANTS 13	61:06

Home team in CAPS

There have been 15 overtime postseason games dating back to 1958. In 14 cases, both teams had at least one possession. Last time: 12/30/00, MIAMI 23, Indianapolis 17.

OVERTIME WON-LOST RECORDS, 1974-2000
(REGULAR SEASON)

AFC	W	L	T	Pct.
Baltimore	2	2	1	.500
Buffalo	14	7	0	.667
Cincinnati	13	7	0	.650
Cleveland	12	8	1	.595
Denver	15	9	2	.615
Indianapolis	9	8	1	.528
Jacksonville	2	2	0	.500
Kansas City	8	9	2	.474
Miami	10	15	1	.404
New England	10	18	0	.357
New York Jets	11	9	2	.545
Oakland	12	12	0	.500
Pittsburgh	13	6	1	.675
San Diego	7	12	0	.368
Seattle	4	12	0	.250
Tennessee	9	13	0	.409

NFC	W	L	T	Pct.
Arizona	12	10	2	.542
Atlanta	7	10	1	.417
Carolina	1	3	0	.250
Chicago	12	12	0	.500
Dallas	11	8	0	.579
Detroit	10	10	1	.500
Green Bay	8	10	4	.455
Minnesota	14	13	2	.517
New Orleans	4	7	0	.364
New York Giants	9	10	2	.476
Philadelphia	10	11	3	.479
St. Louis	6	7	1	.464
San Francisco	7	9	1	.441
Tampa Bay	9	9	1	.500
Washington	14	8	1	.630

OVERTIME GAMES BY YEAR
(REGULAR SEASON)

2000-13	1993-7	1986-16	1979-12
1999-11	1992-10	1985-10	1978-11
1998-7	1991-15	1984- 9	1977- 6
1997-17	1990-10	1983-19	1976- 5
1996-14	1989-11	1982- 4	1975- 9
1995-21	1988- 9	1981-10	1974- 2
1994-16	1987-13	1980-13	

OVERTIME GAME SUMMARY—1974-2000

There have been 300 overtime games in regular-season play since the rule was adopted in 1974 (13 in 2000 season). Breakdown follows:

218(7) times both teams had at least one possession (73%)
154(10) times the team which won the toss won the game (51%)
131(3) times the team which lost the toss won the game (44%)
15(0) games ended tied (5%). Last time: Nov. 23, 1997, N.Y. Giants 7, at Washington 7.
82(6) times the team which won the toss drove for winning score (58 FG, 24 TD) (27%)
8(1) times the team which won the toss elected to kick off (4 wins) (3%)
205(10) games were decided by a field goal (68%)
79(3) games were decided by a touchdown (27%)
1(0) games were decided by a safety (.3%)

Note: The number in parentheses represents the 2000 season total in each category.

MOST OVERTIME GAMES, SEASON

5 Green Bay Packers, 1983
4 Denver Broncos, 1985
Cleveland Browns, 1989
Minnesota Vikings, 1994
Arizona Cardinals, 1995
Minnesota Vikings, 1995
Arizona Cardinals, 1997
3 By many teams, last time: Buffalo, 2000

LONGEST CONSECUTIVE GAME STREAKS WITHOUT OVERTIME (Current)

72 St. Louis Rams (last OT game, 10/27/96 vs. Baltimore)
(Record: 110, St. Louis/Phoenix Cardinals, 12/7/86-12/19/93)

SHORTEST OVERTIME GAMES

0:17 New Orleans 20, Seattle 17; 11/16/97
0:21 Chicago 23, Detroit 17; 11/27/80—only kickoff return for TD
0:30 Baltimore 29, New England 23; 9/4/83
0:55 New York Giants 16, Philadelphia 10; 9/29/85

LONGEST OVERTIME GAMES

(ALL POSTSEASON GAMES)

22:40 Miami 27, Kansas City 24; 12/25/71
17:54 Dallas Texans 20, Houston 17; 12/23/62
17:02 Cleveland 23, New York Jets 20; 1/3/87

OVERTIME SCORING SUMMARY

205 were decided by a field goal
36 were decided by a touchdown pass
22 were decided by a touchdown run
11 were decided by interceptions (Atlanta 40, New Orleans 34, 9/2/79; Atlanta 47, Green Bay 41, 11/27/83; New York Giants 16, Philadelphia 10, 9/29/85; Indianapolis 23, Cleveland 17, 12/10/89; Cleveland 30, San Diego 24, 10/20/91; Kansas City 23, Oakland 17, 9/17/95; New York Giants 27, Arizona 21, 10/8/95; Washington 36, Detroit 30, 10/22/95; Arizona 20, Seattle 14, 10/29/95; Cincinnati 34, Detroit 28, 9/13/98; New York Giants 23, Washington 17, 10/31/99)
2 were decided on a fake field goal/touchdown pass (Minnesota 22, Chicago 16, 10/16/77; Cleveland 23, Minnesota 17, 12/17/89)
2 were decided by a fumble recovery (Baltimore 29, New England 23, 9/4/83; Denver 36, Seattle 30, 12/19/99)
1 was decided by a kickoff return (Chicago 23, Detroit 17, 11/27/80)
1 was decided by a punt return (Kansas City 29, San Diego 23, 10/9/95)
1 was decided on a fake field goal/touchdown run (Los Angeles Rams 27, Minnesota 21, 12/2/79)
1 was decided on a blocked field goal (Denver 30, San Diego 24, 11/17/85)
1 was decided on a blocked field goal/recovery by kicker (Green Bay 12, Chicago 6, 9/7/80)
1 was decided on a blocked field goal/recovery by kicking team (Philadelphia 23, New York Giants 17, 11/20/88)
1 was decided by a safety (Minnesota 23, Los Angeles Rams 21, 11/5/89)
15 ended tied

OVERTIME RECORDS

Longest Touchdown Pass

99 Yards — Ron Jaworski to Mike Quick, Philadelphia 23, Atlanta 17 (11/10/85)
76 Yards — Troy Aikman to Raghib Ismail, Dallas 41, Washington 35 (9/12/99)
68 Yards — Danny Kanell to Chris Calloway, New York Giants 26, Detroit 20 (10/20/97)

Longest Touchdown Run

96 Yards — Garrison Hearst, San Francisco 36, N.Y. Jets 30 (9/6/98)
60 Yards — Herschel Walker, Dallas 23, New England 17 (11/15/87)
42 Yards — Eric Dickerson, Los Angeles Rams 26, Tampa Bay 20 (10/5/86)

Longest Field Goal

53 Yards — Chris Jacke, Green Bay 23, San Francisco 20 (10/4/96)
52 Yards — Mike Cofer, Indianapolis 27, N.Y. Jets 24 (9/10/95)
51 Yards — Greg Davis, New England 23, Indianapolis 20 (10/29/89)
Greg Davis, Arizona 20, Pittsburgh 17 (10/30/94)
Michael Husted, Tampa Bay 20, Minnesota 17 (10/15/95)

Longest Touchdown Plays

99 Yards — (Pass) Ron Jaworski to Mike Quick, Philadelphia 23, Atlanta 17 (11/10/85)
96 Yards — (Run) Garrison Hearst, San Francisco 36, N.Y. Jets 30 (9/6/98)
95 Yards — (Kickoff return) Dave Williams, Chicago 23, Detroit 17 (11/27/80)
86 Yards — (Punt return) Tamarick Vanover, Kansas City 29, San Diego 23 (10/9/95)
76 Yards — (Pass) Troy Aikman to Raghib Ismail, Dallas 41, Washington 35 (9/12/99)

ATTENDANCE/TV RATINGS

NFL'S TOP 10 PAID ATTENDANCE WEEKENDS

Weekend	Games	Attendance
November 21-22, 1999	15	1,027,861
November 12-13, 2000	15	1,013,519
November 19-20, 2000	15	1,011,224
September 19-20, 1999	15	1,010,820
December 10-11, 2000	15	1,009,732
September 10-11, 2000	15	1,005,960
November 16-17, 1997	15	999,956
January 2-3, 1999	15	998,656
September 6-7, 1998	15	997,835
November 25, 28-29, 1999	15	995,802

NFL'S 10 HIGHEST SCORING WEEKENDS

Point Total	Date	Weekend
762	November 10-11, 1996	11th
761	October 16-17, 1983	7th
740	November 29-30, 1998	13th
739	November 23, 26-27, 1995	13th
736	October 25-26, 1987	7th
734	November 19-20, 1995	12th
732	November 9-10, 1980	10th
725	November 24, 27-28, 1983	13th
719	November 27, 30-December 1, 1997	14th
714	September 17-18, 1989	2nd

TOP 10 TELEVISED SPORTS EVENTS OF ALL-TIME

(Based on A.C. Nielsen Figures)

Program	Date	Network	Share	Rating
Super Bowl XVI	1/24/82	CBS	73%	49.1
Super Bowl XVII	1/30/83	NBC	69%	48.6
Winter Olympics	2/23/94	CBS	64%	48.5
Super Bowl XX	1/26/86	NBC	70%	48.3
Super Bowl XII	1/15/78	CBS	67%	47.2
Super Bowl XIII	1/21/79	NBC	74%	47.1
Super Bowl XVIII	1/22/84	CBS	71%	46.4
Super Bowl XIX	1/20/85	ABC	63%	46.4
Super Bowl XIV	1/20/80	CBS	67%	46.3
Super Bowl XXX	1/28/96	NBC	68%	46.0

TEN MOST WATCHED TV PROGRAMS & ESTIMATED TOTAL NUMBER OF VIEWERS

(Based on A.C. Nielsen Figures)

Program	Date	Network	*Total Viewers
Super Bowl XXX	Jan. 28, 1996	NBC	138,488,000
Super Bowl XXVIII	Jan. 30, 1994	NBC	134,800,000
Super Bowl XXXII	Jan. 25, 1998	NBC	133,400,000
Super Bowl XXVII	Jan. 31, 1993	NBC	133,400,000
Super Bowl XXXV	Jan. 28, 2001	CBS	131,200,000
Super Bowl XXXIV	Jan. 30, 2000	ABC	130,744,800
Super Bowl XXXI	Jan. 26, 1997	FOX	128,900,000
Super Bowl XXXIII	Jan. 31, 1999	FOX	127,500,000
Super Bowl XX	Jan. 26, 1986	NBC	127,000,000
Winter Olympics	Feb. 23, 1994	CBS	126,686,000

**Watched some portion of the broadcast*

NFL'S TOP 10 TEAM SINGLE-SEASON HOME PAID ATTENDANCE TOTALS

Year	Club	Games	Attendance
2000	Washington Redskins	8	656,599
1980	Detroit Lions	8	634,204
1988	Buffalo Bills	8	631,818
1991	Buffalo Bills	8	631,786
1992	Buffalo Bills	8	630,978
1997	Kansas City Chiefs	8	629,763
1999	Kansas City Chiefs	8	629,569
1998	Kansas City Chiefs	8	629,209
1999	Washington Redskins	8	628,535
1996	Kansas City Chiefs	8	628,460

NFL'S TOP FIVE PAID ATTENDANCE TOTALS FOR ALL GAMES

Year	Preseason	Regular Season	Postseason	All Games
2000	3,757,231	16,387,289	809,132	20,953,652
1999	3,762,331	16,206,640	793,759	20,762,730
1998	3,553,735	15,364,873	822,885	19,741,493
1995	3,368,289	15,043,562	790,906	19,202,757
1997	3,280,693	14,967,314	801,879	19,049,886

TEN HIGHEST-RATED ABC NFL MONDAY NIGHT FOOTBALL GAMES OF ALL-TIME

(Based on A.C. Nielsen Figures)

Game	Date	Share	Rating
Chicago at Miami	12/2/85	46%	29.6
N.Y. Giants at San Francisco	12/3/90	42%	26.9
Dallas at Washington	10/2/78	43%	26.8
Pittsburgh at San Diego	12/22/80	40%	25.3
Philadelphia at Miami	11/30/81	40%	25.3
Pittsburgh at Houston	12/10/79	40%	25.1
Dallas at Miami	12/17/84	40%	25.1
Pittsburgh at Dallas	9/13/82	42%	24.9
Cincinnati at Oakland	12/6/76	40%	24.7
Dallas at Washington	10/8/73	40%	24.6
Minnesota at Atlanta	11/19/73	40%	24.6

NFL'S 10 BIGGEST SINGLE-GAME ATTENDANCE TOTALS

Date	Site	Game	Teams	Attendance
August 15, 1994	Azteca Stadium	American Bowl (Mexico City)	Cowboys vs. Oilers	112,376
August 17, 1998	Azteca Stadium	American Bowl (Mexico City)	Cowboys vs. Patriots	106,424
August 22, 1947	Soldier Field	College All-Star	Bears vs. All-Stars	105,840
August 4, 1997	Estadio Guillermo Canedo	American Bowl (Mexico City)	Broncos vs. Dolphins	104,629
January 20, 1980	Rose Bowl	Super Bowl XIV	Steelers vs. Rams	103,985
January 30, 1983	Rose Bowl	Super Bowl XVII	Redskins vs. Dolphins	103,667
January 9, 1977	Rose Bowl	Super Bowl XI	Raiders vs. Vikings	103,438
November 10, 1957	L.A. Coliseum	Regular Season	49ers at Rams	102,368
January 25, 1987	Rose Bowl	Super Bowl XXI	Giants vs. Broncos	101,643
August 20, 1948	Soldier Field	College All-Star	Cardinals vs. All-Stars	101,220
August 28, 1942	Soldier Field	College All-Star	Bears vs. All-Stars	101,100

NFL PAID ATTENDANCE

For detailed 2000 attendance, see page 244.

Year	Regular Season		Average	Postseason	Total
2000	#16,387,289	(248 games)	#66,078	809,132 (12)	#17,196,421
1999	16,206,640	(248 games)	65,349	793,759 (12)	17,000,399
1998	15,364,873	(240 games)	64,020	822,885 (12)	16,187,758
1997	14,967,314	(240 games)	62,364	801,879 (12)	15,769,193
1996	14,612,417	(240 games)	60,885	769,310 (12)	15,381,727
1995	15,043,562	(240 games)	62,682	790,906 (12)	15,834,468
1994	14,030,435	(224 games)	62,636	779,738 (12)	14,810,173
1993	13,966,843	(224 games)	62,352	814,607 (12)	14,781,450
1992	13,828,887	(224 games)	61,736	815,910 (12)	14,644,797
1991	13,841,459	(224 games)	61,792	813,247 (12)	14,654,706
1990	13,959,896	(224 games)	62,321	847,543 (12)	14,807,439
1989	13,625,662	(224 games)	60,829	685,771 (10)	14,311,433
1988	13,539,848	(224 games)	60,446	658,317 (10)	14,198,165
1987	*11,406,166	(210 games)	54,315	656,977 (10)	12,063,143
1986	13,588,551	(224 games)	60,663	734,002 (10)	14,322,553
1985	13,345,047	(224 games)	59,567	710,768 (10)	14,055,815
1984	13,398,112	(224 games)	59,813	665,194 (10)	14,063,306
1983	13,277,222	(224 games)	59,273	675,513 (10)	13,952,735
1982	**7,367,438	(126 games)	58,472	1,033,153 (16)	8,400,591
1981	13,606,990	(224 games)	60,745	637,763 (10)	14,244,753
1980	13,392,230	(224 games)	59,787	624,430 (10)	14,016,660
1979	13,182,039	(224 games)	58,848	630,326 (10)	13,812,365
1978	12,771,800	(224 games)	57,017	624,388 (10)	13,396,188
1977	11,018,632	(196 games)	56,218	534,925 (8)	11,553,557
1976	11,070,543	(196 games)	56,482	492,884 (8)	11,563,427
1975	10,213,193	(182 games)	56,116	475,919 (8)	10,689,112
1974	10,236,322	(182 games)	56,244	438,664 (8)	10,674,986
1973	10,730,933	(182 games)	58,961	525,433 (8)	11,256,366
1972	10,445,827	(182 games)	57,395	483,345 (8)	10,929,172
1971	10,076,035	(182 games)	55,363	483,891 (8)	10,559,926
1970	9,533,333	(182 games)	52,381	458,493 (8)	9,991,826
1969	6,096,127	(112 games) NFL	54,430	162,279 (3)	6,258,406
	2,843,373	(70 games) AFL	40,620	167,088 (3)	3,010,461
1968	5,882,313	(112 games) NFL	52,521	215,902 (3)	6,098,215
	2,635,004	(70 games) AFL	37,643	114,438 (2)	2,749,442
1967	5,938,924	(112 games) NFL	53,026	166,208 (3)	6,105,132
	2,295,697	(63 games) AFL	36,439	53,330 (1)	2,349,027
1966	5,337,044	(105 games) NFL	50,829	74,152 (1)	5,411,196
	2,160,369	(63 games) AFL	34,291	42,080 (1)	2,202,449
1965	4,634,021	(98 games) NFL	47,286	100,304 (2)	4,734,325
	1,782,384	(56 games) AFL	31,828	30,361 (1)	1,812,745
1964	4,563,049	(98 games) NFL	46,562	79,544 (1)	4,642,593
	1,447,875	(56 games) AFL	25,855	40,242 (1)	1,488,117
1963	4,163,643	(98 games) NFL	42,486	45,801 (1)	4,209,444
	1,208,697	(56 games) AFL	21,584	63,171 (2)	1,271,868
1962	4,003,421	(98 games) NFL	40,851	64,892 (1)	4,068,313
	1,147,302	(56 games) AFL	20,487	37,981 (1)	1,185,283
1961	3,986,159	(98 games) NFL	40,675	39,029 (1)	4,025,188
	1,002,657	(56 games) AFL	17,904	29,556 (1)	1,032,213
1960	3,128,296	(78 games) NFL	40,106	67,325 (1)	3,195,621
	926,156	(56 games) AFL	16,538	32,183 (1)	958,339
1959	3,140,000	(72 games)	43,617	57,545 (1)	3,197,545
1958	3,006,124	(72 games)	41,752	123,659 (2)	3,129,783
1957	2,836,318	(72 games)	39,393	119,579 (2)	2,955,897
1956	2,551,263	(72 games)	35,434	56,836 (1)	2,608,099
1955	2,521,836	(72 games)	35,026	85,693 (1)	2,607,529
1954	2,190,571	(72 games)	30,425	43,827 (1)	2,234,398
1953	2,164,585	(72 games)	30,064	54,577 (1)	2,219,162
1952	2,052,126	(72 games)	28,502	97,507 (2)	2,149,633
1951	1,913,019	(72 games)	26,570	57,522 (1)	1,970,541
1950	1,977,753	(78 games)	25,356	136,647 (3)	2,114,400
1949	1,391,735	(60 games)	23,196	27,980 (1)	1,419,715
1948	1,525,243	(60 games)	25,421	36,309 (1)	1,561,552
1947	1,837,437	(60 games)	30,624	66,268 (2)	1,903,705
1946	1,732,135	(55 games)	31,493	58,346 (1)	1,790,481
1945	1,270,401	(50 games)	25,408	32,178 (1)	1,302,579
1944	1,019,649	(50 games)	20,393	46,016 (1)	1,065,665
1943	969,128	(40 games)	24,228	71,315 (2)	1,040,443
1942	887,920	(55 games)	16,144	36,006 (1)	923,926
1941	1,108,615	(55 games)	20,157	55,870 (2)	1,164,485
1940	1,063,025	(55 games)	19,328	36,034 (1)	1,099,059
1939	1,071,200	(55 games)	19,476	32,279 (1)	1,103,479
1938	937,197	(55 games)	17,040	48,120 (1)	985,317
1937	963,039	(55 games)	17,510	15,878 (1)	978,917
1936	816,007	(54 games)	15,111	29,545 (1)	845,552
1935	638,178	(53 games)	12,041	15,000 (1)	653,178
1934	492,684	(60 games)	8,211	35,059 (1)	527,743

 # Record

**Players' 24-day strike reduced 224-game schedule to 210 games.*

***Players' 57-day strike reduced 224-game schedule to 126 games.*

NUMBER-ONE DRAFT CHOICES

Season	Date	Team	Player	Position	College
2001	April 21-22	Atlanta	Michael Vick	QB	Virginia Tech
2000	April 15-16	Cleveland	Courtney Brown	DE	Penn State
1999	April 17-18	Cleveland	Tim Couch	QB	Kentucky
1998	April 18-19	Indianapolis	Peyton Manning	QB	Tennessee
1997	April 19-20	St. Louis	Orlando Pace	T	Ohio State
1996	April 20-21	New York Jets	Keyshawn Johnson	WR	Southern California
1995	April 22-23	Cincinnati	Ki-Jana Carter	RB	Penn State
1994	April 24-25	Cincinnati	Dan Wilkinson	DT	Ohio State
1993	April 25-26	New England	Drew Bledsoe	QB	Washington State
1992	April 26-27	Indianapolis	Steve Emtman	DT	Washington
1991	April 21-22	Dallas	Russell Maryland	DT	Miami
1990	April 22-23	Indianapolis	Jeff George	QB	Illinois
1989	April 23-24	Dallas	Troy Aikman	QB	UCLA
1988	April 24-25	Atlanta	Aundray Bruce	LB	Auburn
1987	April 28-29	Tampa Bay	Vinny Testaverde	QB	Miami
1986	April 29-30	Tampa Bay	Bo Jackson	RB	Auburn
1985	April 30-May 1	Buffalo	Bruce Smith	DE	Virginia Tech
1984	May 1-2	New England	Irving Fryar	WR	Nebraska
1983	April 26-27	Baltimore	John Elway	QB	Stanford
1982	April 27-28	New England	Kenneth Sims	DT	Texas
1981	April 28-29	New Orleans	George Rogers	RB	South Carolina
1980	April 29-30	Detroit	Billy Sims	RB	Oklahoma
1979	May 3-4	Buffalo	Tom Cousineau	LB	Ohio State
1978	May 2-3	Houston	Earl Campbell	RB	Texas
1977	May 3-4	Tampa Bay	Ricky Bell	RB	Southern California
1976	April 8-9	Tampa Bay	Lee Roy Selmon	DE	Oklahoma
1975	January 28-29	Atlanta	Steve Bartkowski	QB	California
1974	January 29-30	Dallas	Ed Jones	DE	Tennessee State
1973	January 30-31	Houston	John Matuszak	DE	Tampa
1972	February 1-2	Buffalo	Walt Patulski	DE	Notre Dame
1971	January 28-29	New England	Jim Plunkett	QB	Stanford
1970	January 27-28	Pittsburgh	Terry Bradshaw	QB	Louisiana Tech
1969	January 28-29	Buffalo (AFL)	O.J. Simpson	RB	Southern California
1968	January 30-31	Minnesota	Ron Yary	T	Southern California
1967	March 14	Baltimore	Bubba Smith	DT	Michigan State
1966	November 27, 1965	Atlanta	Tommy Nobis	LB	Texas
	November 28, 1965	Miami (AFL)	Jim Grabowski	RB	Illinois
1965	November 28, 1964	New York Giants	Tucker Frederickson	RB	Auburn
	November 28, 1964	Houston (AFL)	Lawrence Elkins	E	Baylor
1964	December 2, 1963	San Francisco	Dave Parks	E	Texas Tech
	November 30, 1963	Boston (AFL)	Jack Concannon	QB	Boston College
1963	December 3, 1962	Los Angeles	Terry Baker	QB	Oregon State
	December 1, 1962	Kansas City (AFL)	Buck Buchanan	DT	Grambling
1962	December 4, 1961	Washington	Ernie Davis	RB	Syracuse
	December 2, 1961	Oakland (AFL)	Roman Gabriel	QB	North Carolina State
1961	December 27-28, 1960	Minnesota	Tommy Mason	RB	Tulane
	November 23, 1960	Buffalo (AFL)	Ken Rice	G	Auburn
1960	Secret Draft	Los Angeles	Billy Cannon	RB	Louisiana State
	November 22, December 2, 1959	(AFL had no formal first pick)			
1959	December 2, 1958	Green Bay	Randy Duncan	QB	Iowa
1958	December 2, 1957	Chicago Cardinals	King Hill	QB	Rice
1957	November 27, 1956	Green Bay	Paul Hornung	HB	Notre Dame
1956	November 29, 1955	Pittsburgh	Gary Glick	DB	Colorado A&M
1955	January 27-28	Baltimore	George Shaw	QB	Oregon
1954	January 28	Cleveland	Bobby Garrett	QB	Stanford
1953	January 22	San Francisco	Harry Babcock	E	Georgia
1952	January 17	Los Angeles	Bill Wade	QB	Vanderbilt
1951	January 18-19	New York Giants	Kyle Rote	HB	Southern Methodist
1950	January 21-22	Detroit	Leon Hart	E	Notre Dame
1949	December 21, 1948	Philadelphia	Chuck Bednarik	C	Pennsylvania
1948	December 19, 1947	Washington	Harry Gilmer	QB	Alabama
1947	December 16, 1946	Chicago Bears	Bob Fenimore	HB	Oklahoma A&M
1946	January 14	Boston	Frank Dancewicz	QB	Notre Dame
1945	April 6	Chicago Cardinals	Charley Trippi	HB	Georgia
1944	April 19	Boston	Angelo Bertelli	QB	Notre Dame
1943	April 8	Detroit	Frank Sinkwich	HB	Georgia
1942	December 22, 1941	Pittsburgh	Bill Dudley	HB	Virginia
1941	December 10, 1940	Chicago Bears	Tom Harmon	HB	Michigan
1940	December 9, 1939	Chicago Cardinals	George Cafego	HB	Tennessee
1939	December 8, 1938	Chicago Cardinals	Ki Aldrich	C	Texas Christian
1938	December 12, 1937	Cleveland	Corbett Davis	FB	Indiana
1937	December 12, 1936	Philadelphia	Sam Francis	FB	Nebraska
1936	February 8	Philadelphia	Jay Berwanger	HB	Chicago

Note: From 1947 through 1958, the first selection in the draft was a Bonus pick, awarded to the winner of a random draw. That club, in turn, forfeited its last-round draft choice. The winner of the Bonus choice was eliminated from future draws. The system was abolished after 1958, by which time all clubs had received a Bonus choice.

FIRST-ROUND SELECTIONS

If club had no first-round selection, first player drafted is listed with round in parentheses.

ARIZONA CARDINALS

Year Player, College, Position

1936 Jim Lawrence, Texas Christian, B
1937 Ray Buivid, Marquette, B
1938 Jack Robbins, Arkansas, B
1939 Charles (Ki) Aldrich, Texas Christian, C
1940 George Cafego, Tennessee, B
1941 John Kimbrough, Texas A&M, B
1942 Steve Lach, Duke, B
1943 Glenn Dobbs, Tulsa, B
1944 Pat Harder, Wisconsin, B
1945 Charley Trippi, Georgia, B
1946 Dub Jones, Louisiana State, B
1947 DeWitt (Tex) Coulter, Army, T
1948 Jim Spavital, Oklahoma A&M, B
1949 Bill Fischer, Notre Dame, G
1950 Jack Jennings, Ohio State, T (2)
1951 Jerry Groom, Notre Dame, C
1952 Ollie Matson, San Francisco, B
1953 Johnny Olszewski, California, B
1954 Lamar McHan, Arkansas, B
1955 Max Boydston, Oklahoma, E
1956 Joe Childress, Auburn, B
1957 Jerry Tubbs, Oklahoma, C
1958 King Hill, Rice, B
John David Crow, Texas A&M, B
1959 Bill Stacy, Mississippi State, B
1960 George Izo, Notre Dame, QB
1961 Ken Rice, Auburn, T
1962 Fate Echols, Northwestern, DT
Irv Goode, Kentucky, C
1963 Jerry Stovall, Louisiana State, S
Don Brumm, Purdue, DE
1964 Ken Kortas, Louisville, DT
1965 Joe Namath, Alabama, QB
1966 Carl McAdams, Oklahoma, LB
1967 Dave Williams, Washington, WR
1968 MacArthur Lane, Utah State, RB
1969 Roger Wehrli, Missouri, DB
1970 Larry Stegent, Texas A&M, RB
1971 Norm Thompson, Utah, CB
1972 Bobby Moore, Oregon, RB-WR
1973 Dave Butz, Purdue, DT
1974 J.V. Cain, Colorado, TE
1975 Tim Gray, Texas A&M, DB
1976 Mike Dawson, Arizona, DT
1977 Steve Pisarkiewicz, Missouri, QB
1978 Steve Little, Arkansas, K
Ken Greene, Washington State, DB
1979 Ottis Anderson, Miami, RB
1980 Curtis Greer, Michigan, DE
1981 E.J. Junior, Alabama, LB
1982 Luis Sharpe, UCLA, T
1983 Leonard Smith, McNeese State, DB
1984 Clyde Duncan, Tennessee, WR
1985 Freddie Joe Nunn, Mississippi, LB
1986 Anthony Bell, Michigan State, LB
1987 Kelly Stouffer, Colorado State, QB
1988 Ken Harvey, California, LB
1989 Eric Hill, Louisiana State, LB
Joe Wolf, Boston College, G
1990 Anthony Thompson, Indiana, RB (2)
1991 Eric Swann, No College, DE
1992 Tony Sacca, Penn State, QB (2)
1993 Garrison Hearst, Georgia, RB
Ernest Dye, South Carolina, T
1994 Jamir Miller, UCLA, LB
1995 Frank Sanders, Auburn, WR (2)
1996 Simeon Rice, Illinois, DE
1997 Tom Knight, Iowa, DB
1998 Andre Wadsworth, Florida State, DE
1999 David Boston, Ohio State, WR
L.J. Shelton, Eastern Michigan, T
2000 Thomas Jones, Virginia, RB
2001 Leonard Davis, Texas, T

ATLANTA FALCONS

Year Player, College, Position

1966 Tommy Nobis, Texas, LB
Randy Johnson, Texas A&I, QB
1967 Leo Carroll, San Diego State, DE (2)
1968 Claude Humphrey, Tennessee State, DE
1969 George Kunz, Notre Dame, T
1970 John Small, Citadel, LB
1971 Joe Profit, Northeast Louisiana, RB
1972 Clarence Ellis, Notre Dame, DB
1973 Greg Marx, Notre Dame, DT (2)
1974 Gerald Tinker, Kent State, WR (2)
1975 Steve Bartkowski, California, QB
1976 Bubba Bean, Texas A&M, RB
1977 Warren Bryant, Kentucky, T
Wilson Faumuina, San Jose State, DT
1978 Mike Kenn, Michigan, T
1979 Don Smith, Miami, DE
1980 Junior Miller, Nebraska, TE
1981 Bobby Butler, Florida State, DB
1982 Gerald Riggs, Arizona State, RB
1983 Mike Pitts, Alabama, DE
1984 Rick Bryan, Oklahoma, DT
1985 Bill Fralic, Pittsburgh, T
1986 Tony Casillas, Oklahoma, NT
Tim Green, Syracuse, LB
1987 Chris Miller, Oregon, QB
1988 Aundray Bruce, Auburn, LB
1989 Deion Sanders, Florida State, DB
Shawn Collins, Northern Arizona, WR
1990 Steve Broussard, Washington State, RB
1991 Bruce Pickens, Nebraska, DB
Mike Pritchard, Colorado, WR
1992 Bob Whitfield, Stanford, T
Tony Smith, Southern Mississippi, RB
1993 Lincoln Kennedy, Washington, T
1994 Bert Emanuel, Rice, WR (2)
1995 Devin Bush, Florida State, DB
1996 Shannon Brown, Alabama, DT (3)
1997 Michael Booker, Nebraska, DB
1998 Keith Brooking, Georgia Tech, LB
1999 Patrick Kerney, Virginia, DE
2000 Travis Claridge, Southern California, T (2)
2001 Michael Vick, Virginia Tech, QB

BALTIMORE RAVENS

Year Player, College, Position

1996 Jonathan Ogden, UCLA, T
Ray Lewis, Miami, LB
1997 Peter Boulware, Florida State, DE
1998 Duane Starks, Miami, DB
1999 Chris McAlister, Arizona, DB
2000 Jamal Lewis, Tennessee, RB
Travis Taylor, Florida, WR
2001 Todd Heap, Arizona State, TE

BUFFALO BILLS

Year Player, College, Position

1960 Richie Lucas, Penn State, QB
1961 Ken Rice, Auburn, T
1962 Ernie Davis, Syracuse, RB
1963 Dave Behrman, Michigan State, C
1964 Carl Eller, Minnesota, DE
1965 Jim Davidson, Ohio State, T
1966 Mike Dennis, Mississippi, RB
1967 John Pitts, Arizona State, S
1968 Haven Moses, San Diego State, WR
1969 O.J. Simpson, Southern California, RB
1970 Al Cowlings, Southern California, DE
1971 J.D. Hill, Arizona State, WR
1972 Walt Patulski, Notre Dame, DE
1973 Paul Seymour, Michigan, TE
Joe DeLamielleure, Michigan State, G
1974 Reuben Gant, Oklahoma State, TE
1975 Tom Ruud, Nebraska, LB
1976 Mario Clark, Oregon, DB
1977 Phil Dokes, Oklahoma State, DT
1978 Terry Miller, Oklahoma State, RB
1979 Tom Cousineau, Ohio State, LB
Jerry Butler, Clemson, WR
1980 Jim Ritcher, North Carolina State, C
1981 Booker Moore, Penn State, RB
1982 Perry Tuttle, Clemson, WR
1983 Tony Hunter, Notre Dame, TE
Jim Kelly, Miami, QB
1984 Greg Bell, Notre Dame, RB
1985 Bruce Smith, Virginia Tech, DE
Derrick Burroughs, Memphis State, DB
1986 Ronnie Harmon, Iowa, RB
Will Wolford, Vanderbilt, T
1987 Shane Conlan, Penn State, LB
1988 Thurman Thomas, Oklahoma State, RB (2)
1989 Don Beebe, Chadron, Neb., WR (3)
1990 James Williams, Fresno State, DB
1991 Henry Jones, Illinois, DB
1992 John Fina, Arizona, T
1993 Thomas Smith, North Carolina, DB
1994 Jeff Burris, Notre Dame, DB
1995 Ruben Brown, Pittsburgh, G
1996 Eric Moulds, Mississippi State, WR
1997 Antowain Smith, Houston, RB
1998 Sam Cowart, Florida State, LB (2)
1999 Antoine Winfield, Ohio State, DB
2000 Erik Flowers, Arizona State, DE
2001 Nate Clements, Ohio State, DB

CAROLINA PANTHERS

Year Player, College, Position

1995 Kerry Collins, Penn State, QB
Tyrone Poole, Ft. Valley State, DB
Blake Brockermeyer, Texas, T
1996 Tim Biakabutuka, Michigan, RB
1997 Rae Carruth, Colorado, WR
1998 Jason Peter, Nebraska, DT
1999 Chris Terry, Georgia, T (2)
2000 Rashard Anderson, Jackson State, DB
2001 Dan Morgan, Miami, LB

CHICAGO BEARS

Year Player, College, Position

1936 Joe Stydahar, West Virginia, T
1937 Les McDonald, Nebraska, E
1938 Joe Gray, Oregon State, B
1939 Sid Luckman, Columbia, QB
Bill Osmanski, Holy Cross, B
1940 Clyde (Bulldog) Turner, Hardin-Simmons, C
1941 Tom Harmon, Michigan, B
Norm Standlee, Stanford, B
Don Scott, Ohio State, B
1942 Frankie Albert, Stanford, B
1943 Bob Steber, Missouri, B
1944 Ray Evans, Kansas, B
1945 Don Lund, Michigan, B
1946 Johnny Lujack, Notre Dame, QB
1947 Bob Fenimore, Oklahoma State, B
Don Kindt, Wisconsin, B
1948 Bobby Layne, Texas, QB
Max Bumgardner, Texas, E
1949 Dick Harris, Texas, C
1950 Chuck Hunsinger, Florida, B
Fred Morrison, Ohio State, B
1951 Bob Williams, Notre Dame, B
Billy Stone, Bradley, B
Gene Schroeder, Virginia, E
1952 Jim Dooley, Miami, B
1953 Billy Anderson, Compton (Calif.) J.C., B
1954 Stan Wallace, Illinois, B
1955 Ron Drzewiecki, Marquette, B
1956 Menan (Tex) Schriewer, Texas, E
1957 Earl Leggett, Louisiana State, T
1958 Chuck Howley, West Virginia, G
1959 Don Clark, Ohio State, B
1960 Roger Davis, Syracuse, G
1961 Mike Ditka, Pittsburgh, E
1962 Ronnie Bull, Baylor, RB
1963 Dave Behrman, Michigan State, C
1964 Dick Evey, Tennessee, DT
1965 Dick Butkus, Illinois, LB
Gale Sayers, Kansas, RB
Steve DeLong, Tennessee, T
1966 George Rice, Louisiana State, DT
1967 Loyd Phillips, Arkansas, DE
1968 Mike Hull, Southern California, RB
1969 Rufus Mayes, Ohio State, T
1970 George Farmer, UCLA, WR (3)
1971 Joe Moore, Missouri, RB
1972 Lionel Antoine, Southern Illinois, T
Craig Clemons, Iowa, DB
1973 Wally Chambers, Eastern Kentucky, DE

FIRST-ROUND SELECTIONS

1974 Waymond Bryant, Tennessee State, LB
Dave Gallagher, Michigan, DT
1975 Walter Payton, Jackson State, RB
1976 Dennis Lick, Wisconsin, T
1977 Ted Albrecht, California, T
1978 Brad Shearer, Texas, DT (3)
1979 Dan Hampton, Arkansas, DT
Al Harris, Arizona State, DE
1980 Otis Wilson, Louisville, LB
1981 Keith Van Horne, Southern California, T
1982 Jim McMahon, Brigham Young, QB
1983 Jim Covert, Pittsburgh, T
Willie Gault, Tennessee, WR
1984 Wilber Marshall, Florida, LB
1985 William Perry, Clemson, DT
1986 Neal Anderson, Florida, RB
1987 Jim Harbaugh, Michigan, QB
1988 Brad Muster, Stanford, RB
Wendell Davis, Louisiana State, WR
1989 Donnell Woolford, Clemson, DB
Trace Armstrong, Florida, DE
1990 Mark Carrier, Southern California, DB
1991 Stan Thomas, Texas, T
1992 Alonzo Spellman, Ohio State, DE
1993 Curtis Conway, Southern California, WR
1994 John Thierry, Alcorn State, DE
1995 Rashaan Salaam, Colorado, RB
1996 Walt Harris, Mississippi State, DB
1997 John Allred, Southern California, TE (2)
1998 Curtis Enis, Penn State, RB
1999 Cade McNown, UCLA, QB
2000 Brian Urlacher, New Mexico, LB
2001 David Terrell, Michigan, WR

CINCINNATI BENGALS

Year Player, College, Position
1968 Bob Johnson, Tennessee, C
1969 Greg Cook, Cincinnati, QB
1970 Mike Reid, Penn State, DT
1971 Vernon Holland, Tennessee State, T
1972 Sherman White, California, DE
1973 Isaac Curtis, San Diego State, WR
1974 Bill Kollar, Montana State, DT
1975 Glenn Cameron, Florida, LB
1976 Billy Brooks, Oklahoma, WR
Archie Griffin, Ohio State, RB
1977 Eddie Edwards, Miami, DT
Wilson Whitley, Houston, DT
Mike Cobb, Michigan State, TE
1978 Ross Browner, Notre Dame, DT
Blair Bush, Washington, C
1979 Jack Thompson, Washington State, QB
Charles Alexander, Louisiana State, RB
1980 Anthony Muñoz, Southern California, T
1981 David Verser, Kansas, WR
1982 Glen Collins, Mississippi State, DE
1983 Dave Rimington, Nebraska, C
1984 Ricky Hunley, Arizona, LB
Pete Koch, Maryland, DE
Brian Blados, North Carolina, T
1985 Eddie Brown, Miami, WR
Emanuel King, Alabama, LB
1986 Joe Kelly, Washington, LB
Tim McGee, Tennessee, WR
1987 Jason Buck, Brigham Young, DE
1988 Rickey Dixon, Oklahoma, DB
1989 Eric Ball, UCLA, RB (2)
1990 James Francis, Baylor, LB
1991 Alfred Williams, Colorado, LB
1992 David Klingler, Houston, QB
Darryl Williams, Miami, DB
1993 John Copeland, Alabama, DE
1994 Dan Wilkinson, Ohio State, DT
1995 Ki-Jana Carter, Penn State, RB
1996 Willie Anderson, Auburn, T
1997 Reinard Wilson, Florida State, LB
1998 Takeo Spikes, Auburn, LB
Brian Simmons, North Carolina, LB
1999 Akili Smith, Oregon, QB
2000 Peter Warrick, Florida State, WR
2001 Justin Smith, Missouri, DE

CLEVELAND BROWNS

Year Player, College, Position
1950 Ken Carpenter, Oregon State, B
1951 Ken Konz, Louisiana State, B
1952 Bert Rechichar, Tennessee, DB
Harry Agganis, Boston U., QB
1953 Doug Atkins, Tennessee, DE
1954 Bobby Garrett, Stanford, QB
John Bauer, Illinois, G
1955 Kurt Burris, Oklahoma, C
1956 Preston Carpenter, Arkansas, B
1957 Jim Brown, Syracuse, RB
1958 Jim Shofner, Texas Christian, DB
1959 Rich Kreitling, Illinois, DE
1960 Jim Houston, Ohio State, DE
1961 Bobby Crespino, Mississippi, TE
1962 Gary Collins, Maryland, WR
Leroy Jackson, Western Illinois, RB
1963 Tom Hutchinson, Kentucky, WR
1964 Paul Warfield, Ohio State, WR
1965 James Garcia, Purdue, T (2)
1966 Milt Morin, Massachusetts, TE
1967 Bob Matheson, Duke, LB
1968 Marvin Upshaw, Trinity, Tex., DT-DE
1969 Ron Johnson, Michigan, RB
1970 Mike Phipps, Purdue, QB
Bob McKay, Texas, T
1971 Clarence Scott, Kansas State, CB
1972 Thom Darden, Michigan, DB
1973 Steve Holden, Arizona State, WR
Pete Adams, Southern California, T
1974 Billy Corbett, Johnson C. Smith, T (2)
1975 Mack Mitchell, Houston, DE
1976 Mike Pruitt, Purdue, RB
1977 Robert Jackson, Texas A&M, LB
1978 Clay Matthews, Southern California, LB
Ozzie Newsome, Alabama, TE
1979 Willis Adams, Houston, WR
1980 Charles White, Southern California, RB
1981 Hanford Dixon, Southern Mississippi, DB
1982 Chip Banks, Southern California, LB
1983 Ron Brown, Arizona State, WR (2)
1984 Don Rogers, UCLA, DB
1985 Greg Allen, Florida State, RB (2)
1986 Webster Slaughter, San Diego State, WR (2)
1987 Mike Junkin, Duke, LB
1988 Clifford Charlton, Florida, LB
1989 Eric Metcalf, Texas, RB
1990 Leroy Hoard, Michigan, RB (2)
1991 Eric Turner, UCLA, DB
1992 Tommy Vardell, Stanford, RB
1993 Steve Everitt, Michigan, C
1994 Antonio Langham, Alabama, DB
Derrick Alexander, Michigan, WR
1995 Craig Powell, Ohio State, LB
1999 Tim Couch, Kentucky, QB
2000 Courtney Brown, Penn State, DE
2001 Gerard Warren, Florida, DT

DALLAS COWBOYS

Year Player, College, Position
1960 None
1961 Bob Lilly, Texas Christian, DT
1962 Sonny Gibbs, Texas Christian, QB (2)
1963 Lee Roy Jordan, Alabama, LB
1964 Scott Appleton, Texas, DT
1965 Craig Morton, California, QB
1966 John Niland, Iowa, G
1967 Phil Clark, Northwestern, DB (3)
1968 Dennis Homan, Alabama, WR
1969 Calvin Hill, Yale, RB
1970 Duane Thomas, West Texas State, RB
1971 Tody Smith, Southern California, DE
1972 Bill Thomas, Boston College, RB
1973 Billy Joe DuPree, Michigan State, TE
1974 Ed (Too Tall) Jones, Tennessee State, DE
Charley Young, North Carolina State, RB
1975 Randy White, Maryland, LB
Thomas Henderson, Langston, LB
1976 Aaron Kyle, Wyoming, DB
1977 Tony Dorsett, Pittsburgh, RB
1978 Larry Bethea, Michigan State, DE
1979 Robert Shaw, Tennessee, C
1980 Bill Roe, Colorado, LB (3)
1981 Howard Richards, Missouri, T
1982 Rod Hill, Kentucky State, DB
1983 Jim Jeffcoat, Arizona State, DE
1984 Billy Cannon, Jr., Texas A&M, LB
1985 Kevin Brooks, Michigan, DE
1986 Mike Sherrard, UCLA, WR
1987 Danny Noonan, Nebraska, DT
1988 Michael Irvin, Miami, WR
1989 Troy Aikman, UCLA, QB
1990 Emmitt Smith, Florida, RB
1991 Russell Maryland, Miami, DT
Alvin Harper, Tennessee, WR
Kelvin Pritchett, Mississippi, DT
1992 Kevin Smith, Texas A&M, DB
Robert Jones, East Carolina, LB
1993 Kevin Williams, Miami, WR (2)
1994 Shante Carver, Arizona State, DE
1995 Sherman Williams, Alabama, RB (2)
1996 Kavika Pittman, McNeese State, DE (2)
1997 David LaFleur, Louisiana State, TE
1998 Greg Ellis, North Carolina, DE
1999 Ebenezer Ekuban, North Carolina, DE
2000 Dwayne Goodrich, Tennessee, DB (2)
2001 Quincy Carter, Georgia, QB (2)

DENVER BRONCOS

Year Player, College, Position
1960 Roger LeClerc, Trinity, Conn., C
1961 Bob Gaiters, New Mexico State, RB
1962 Merlin Olsen, Utah State, DT
1963 Kermit Alexander, UCLA, CB
1964 Bob Brown, Nebraska, T
1965 Dick Butkus, Illinois, LB (2)
1966 Jerry Shay, Purdue, DT
1967 Floyd Little, Syracuse, RB
1968 Curley Culp, Arizona State, DE (2)
1969 Grady Cavness, Texas-El Paso, DB (2)
1970 Bob Anderson, Colorado, RB
1971 Marv Montgomery, Southern California, T
1972 Riley Odoms, Houston, TE
1973 Otis Armstrong, Purdue, RB
1974 Randy Gradishar, Ohio State, LB
1975 Louis Wright, San Jose State, DB
1976 Tom Glassic, Virginia, G
1977 Steve Schindler, Boston College, G
1978 Don Latimer, Miami, DT
1979 Kelvin Clark, Nebraska, T
1980 Rulon Jones, Utah State, DE (2)
1981 Dennis Smith, Southern California, DB
1982 Gerald Willhite, San Jose State, RB
1983 Chris Hinton, Northwestern, G
1984 Andre Townsend, Mississippi, DE (2)
1985 Steve Sewell, Oklahoma, RB
1986 Jim Juriga, Illinois, T (4)
1987 Ricky Nattiel, Florida, WR
1988 Ted Gregory, Syracuse, NT
1989 Steve Atwater, Arkansas, DB
1990 Alton Montgomery, Houston, DB (2)
1991 Mike Croel, Nebraska, LB
1992 Tommy Maddox, UCLA, QB
1993 Dan Williams, Toledo, DE
1994 Allen Aldridge, Houston, LB (2)
1995 Jamie Brown, Florida A&M, T (4)
1996 John Mobley, Kutztown, LB
1997 Trevor Pryce, Clemson, DT
1998 Marcus Nash, Tennessee, WR
1999 Al Wilson, Tennessee, LB
2000 Deltha O'Neal, California, DB
2001 Willie Middlebrooks, Minnesota, DB

DETROIT LIONS

Year Player, College, Position
1936 Sid Wagner, Michigan State, G
1937 Lloyd Cardwell, Nebraska, B
1938 Alex Wojciechowicz, Fordham, C
1939 John Pingel, Michigan State, B
1940 Doyle Nave, Southern California, B
1941 Jim Thomason, Texas A&M, B
1942 Bob Westfall, Michigan, B
1943 Frank Sinkwich, Georgia, B
1944 Otto Graham, Northwestern, B
1945 Frank Szymanski, Notre Dame, C

1946	Bill Dellastatious, Missouri, B
1947	Glenn Davis, Army, B
1948	Y.A. Tittle, Louisiana State, B
1949	John Rauch, Georgia, B
1950	Leon Hart, Notre Dame, E
	Joe Watson, Rice, C
1951	Dick Stanfel, San Francisco, G (2)
1952	Yale Lary, Texas A&M, B (3)
1953	Harley Sewell, Texas, G
1954	Dick Chapman, Rice, T
1955	Dave Middleton, Auburn, B
1956	Hopalong Cassady, Ohio State, B
1957	Bill Glass, Baylor, G
1958	Alex Karras, Iowa, T
1959	Nick Pietrosante, Notre Dame, B
1960	John Robinson, Louisiana State, S
1961	Danny LaRose, Missouri, T (2)
1962	John Hadl, Kansas, QB
1963	Daryl Sanders, Ohio State, T
1964	Pete Beathard, Southern California, QB
1965	Tom Nowatzke, Indiana, RB
1966	Nick Eddy, Notre Dame, RB (2)
1967	Mel Farr, UCLA, RB
1968	Greg Landry, Massachusetts, QB
	Earl McCullouch, Southern California, WR
1969	Altie Taylor, Utah State, RB (2)
1970	Steve Owens, Oklahoma, RB
1971	Bob Bell, Cincinnati, DT
1972	Herb Orvis, Colorado, DE
1973	Ernie Price, Texas A&I, DE
1974	Ed O'Neil, Penn State, LB
1975	Lynn Boden, South Dakota State, G
1976	James Hunter, Grambling, DB
	Lawrence Gaines, Wyoming, RB
1977	Walt Williams, New Mexico State, DB (2)
1978	Luther Bradley, Notre Dame, DB
1979	Keith Dorney, Penn State, T
1980	Billy Sims, Oklahoma, RB
1981	Mark Nichols, San Jose State, WR
1982	Jimmy Williams, Nebraska, LB
1983	James Jones, Florida, RB
1984	David Lewis, California, TE
1985	Lomas Brown, Florida, T
1986	Chuck Long, Iowa, QB
1987	Reggie Rogers, Washington, DE
1988	Bennie Blades, Miami, DB
1989	Barry Sanders, Oklahoma State, RB
1990	Andre Ware, Houston, QB
1991	Herman Moore, Virginia, WR
1992	Robert Porcher, South Carolina State, DE
1993	Ryan McNeil, Miami, DB (2)
1994	Johnnie Morton, Southern California, WR
1995	Luther Elliss, Utah, DT
1996	Reggie Brown, Texas A&M, LB
	Jeff Hartings, Penn State, G
1997	Bryant Westbrook, Texas, DB
1998	Terry Fair, Tennessee, DB
1999	Chris Claiborne, Southern California, LB
	Aaron Gibson, Wisconsin, T
2000	Stockar McDougle, Oklahoma, T
2001	Jeff Backus, Michigan, T

GREEN BAY PACKERS

Year	Player, College, Position
1936	Russ Letlow, San Francisco, G
1937	Eddie Jankowski, Wisconsin, B
1938	Cecil Isbell, Purdue, B
1939	Larry Buhler, Minnesota, B
1940	Harold Van Every, Minnesota, B
1941	George Paskvan, Wisconsin, B
1942	Urban Odson, Minnesota, T
1943	Dick Wildung, Minnesota, T
1944	Merv Pregulman, Michigan, G
1945	Walt Schlinkman, Texas Tech, B
1946	Johnny (Strike) Strzykalski, Marquette, B
1947	Ernie Case, UCLA, B
1948	Earl (Jug) Girard, Wisconsin, B
1949	Stan Heath, Nevada, B
1950	Clayton Tonnemaker, Minnesota, C
1951	Bob Gain, Kentucky, T
1952	Babe Parilli, Kentucky, QB
1953	Al Carmichael, Southern California, B
1954	Art Hunter, Notre Dame, T
	Veryl Switzer, Kansas State, B
1955	Tom Bettis, Purdue, G
1956	Jack Losch, Miami, B
1957	Paul Hornung, Notre Dame, B
	Ron Kramer, Michigan, E
1958	Dan Currie, Michigan State, C
1959	Randy Duncan, Iowa, B
1960	Tom Moore, Vanderbilt, RB
1961	Herb Adderley, Michigan State, CB
1962	Earl Gros, Louisiana State, RB
1963	Dave Robinson, Penn State, LB
1964	Lloyd Voss, Nebraska, DT
1965	Donny Anderson, Texas Tech, RB
	Lawrence Elkins, Baylor, E
1966	Jim Grabowski, Illinois, RB
	Gale Gillingham, Minnesota, T
1967	Bob Hyland, Boston College, C
	Don Horn, San Diego State, QB
1968	Fred Carr, Texas-El Paso, LB
	Bill Lueck, Arizona, G
1969	Rich Moore, Villanova, DT
1970	Mike McCoy, Notre Dame, DT
	Rich McGeorge, Elon, TE
1971	John Brockington, Ohio State, RB
1972	Willie Buchanon, San Diego State, DB
	Jerry Tagge, Nebraska, QB
1973	Barry Smith, Florida State, WR
1974	Barty Smith, Richmond, RB
1975	Bill Bain, Southern California, G (2)
1976	Mark Koncar, Colorado, T
1977	Mike Butler, Kansas, DE
	Ezra Johnson, Morris Brown, DE
1978	James Lofton, Stanford, WR
	John Anderson, Michigan, LB
1979	Eddie Lee Ivery, Georgia Tech, RB
1980	Bruce Clark, Penn State, DE
	George Cumby, Oklahoma, LB
1981	Rich Campbell, California, QB
1982	Ron Hallstrom, Iowa, G
1983	Tim Lewis, Pittsburgh, DB
1984	Alphonso Carreker, Florida State, DE
1985	Ken Ruettgers, Southern California, T
1986	Kenneth Davis, Texas Christian, RB (2)
1987	Brent Fullwood, Auburn, RB
1988	Sterling Sharpe, South Carolina, WR
1989	Tony Mandarich, Michigan State, T
1990	Tony Bennett, Mississippi, LB
	Darrell Thompson, Minnesota, RB
1991	Vinnie Clark, Ohio State, DB
1992	Terrell Buckley, Florida State, DB
1993	Wayne Simmons, Clemson, LB
	George Teague, Alabama, DB
1994	Aaron Taylor, Notre Dame, T
1995	Craig Newsome, Arizona State, DB
1996	John Michels, Southern California, T
1997	Ross Verba, Iowa, T
1998	Vonnie Holliday, North Carolina, DT
1999	Antuan Edwards, Clemson, DB
2000	Bubba Franks, Miami, TE
2001	Jamal Reynolds, Florida State, DE

INDIANAPOLIS COLTS

Year	Player, College, Position
1953	Billy Vessels, Oklahoma, B
1954	Cotton Davidson, Baylor, B
1955	George Shaw, Oregon, B
	Alan Ameche, Wisconsin, FB
1956	Lenny Moore, Penn State, B
1957	Jim Parker, Ohio State, G
1958	Lenny Lyles, Louisville, B
1959	Jackie Burkett, Auburn, C
1960	Ron Mix, Southern California, T
1961	Tom Matte, Ohio State, RB
1962	Wendell Harris, Louisiana State, S
1963	Bob Vogel, Ohio State, T
1964	Marv Woodson, Indiana, CB
1965	Mike Curtis, Duke, LB
1966	Sam Ball, Kentucky, T
1967	Bubba Smith, Michigan State, DT
	Jim Detwiler, Michigan, RB
1968	John Williams, Minnesota, G
1969	Eddie Hinton, Oklahoma, WR
1970	Norman Bulaich, Texas Christian, RB
1971	Don McCauley, North Carolina, RB
	Leonard Dunlap, North Texas State, DB
1972	Tom Drougas, Oregon, T
1973	Bert Jones, Louisiana State, QB
	Joe Ehrmann, Syracuse, DT
1974	John Dutton, Nebraska, DE
	Roger Carr, Louisiana Tech, WR
1975	Ken Huff, North Carolina, G
1976	Ken Novak, Purdue, DT
1977	Randy Burke, Kentucky, WR
1978	Reese McCall, Auburn, TE
1979	Barry Krauss, Alabama, LB
1980	Curtis Dickey, Texas A&M, RB
	Derrick Hatchett, Texas, DB
1981	Randy McMillan, Pittsburgh, RB
	Donnell Thompson, North Carolina, DT
1982	Johnie Cooks, Mississippi State, LB
	Art Schlichter, Ohio State, QB
1983	John Elway, Stanford, QB
1984	Leonard Coleman, Vanderbilt, DB
	Ron Solt, Maryland, G
1985	Duane Bickett, Southern California, LB
1986	Jon Hand, Alabama, DE
1987	Cornelius Bennett, Alabama, LB
1988	Chris Chandler, Washington, QB (3)
1989	Andre Rison, Michigan State, WR
1990	Jeff George, Illinois, QB
1991	Shane Curry, Miami, DE (2)
1992	Steve Emtman, Washington, DT
	Quentin Coryatt, Texas A&M, LB
1993	Sean Dawkins, California, WR
1994	Marshall Faulk, San Diego State, RB
	Trev Alberts, Nebraska, LB
1995	Ellis Johnson, Florida, DT
1996	Marvin Harrison, Syracuse, WR
1997	Tarik Glenn, California, T
1998	Peyton Manning, Tennessee, QB
1999	Edgerrin James, Miami, RB
2000	Rob Morris, Brigham Young, LB
2001	Reggie Wayne, Miami, WR

JACKSONVILLE JAGUARS

Year	Player, College, Position
1995	Tony Boselli, Southern California, T
	James Stewart, Tennessee, RB
1996	Kevin Hardy, Illinois, LB
1997	Renaldo Wynn, Notre Dame, DT
1998	Fred Taylor, Florida, RB
	Donovin Darius, Syracuse, DB
1999	Fernando Bryant, Alabama, DB
2000	R. Jay Soward, Southern California, WR
2001	Marcus Stroud, Georgia, DT

KANSAS CITY CHIEFS

Year	Player, College, Position
1960	Don Meredith, Southern Methodist, QB
1961	E.J. Holub, Texas Tech, C
1962	Ronnie Bull, Baylor, RB
1963	Buck Buchanan, Grambling, DT
	Ed Budde, Michigan State, G
1964	Pete Beathard, Southern California, QB
1965	Gale Sayers, Kansas, RB
1966	Aaron Brown, Minnesota, DE
1967	Gene Trosch, Miami, DE-DT
1968	Mo Moorman, Texas A&M, G
	George Daney, Texas-El Paso, G
1969	Jim Marsalis, Tennessee State, CB
1970	Sid Smith, Southern California, T
1971	Elmo Wright, Houston, WR
1972	Jeff Kinney, Nebraska, RB
1973	Gary Butler, Rice, TE (2)
1974	Woody Green, Arizona State, RB
1975	Elmore Stephens, Kentucky, TE (2)
1976	Rod Walters, Iowa, G
1977	Gary Green, Baylor, DB
1978	Art Still, Kentucky, DE
1979	Mike Bell, Colorado State, DE
	Steve Fuller, Clemson, QB
1980	Brad Budde, Southern California, G
1981	Willie Scott, South Carolina, TE
1982	Anthony Hancock, Tennessee, WR
1983	Todd Blackledge, Penn State, QB
1984	Bill Maas, Pittsburgh, DT

Year	Player, College, Position
	John Alt, Iowa, T
1985	Ethan Horton, North Carolina, RB
1986	Brian Jozwiak, West Virginia, T
1987	Paul Palmer, Temple, RB
1988	Neil Smith, Nebraska, DE
1989	Derrick Thomas, Alabama, LB
1990	Percy Snow, Michigan State, LB
1991	Harvey Williams, Louisiana State, RB
1992	Dale Carter, Tennessee, DB
1993	Will Shields, Nebraska, G (3)
1994	Greg Hill, Texas A&M, RB
1995	Trezelle Jenkins, Michigan, T
1996	Jerome Woods, Memphis, DB
1997	Tony Gonzalez, California, TE
1998	Victor Riley, Auburn, T
1999	John Tait, Brigham Young, T
2000	Sylvester Morris, Jackson State, WR
2001	Eric Downing, Syracuse, DT (3)

MIAMI DOLPHINS

Year	Player, College, Position
1966	Jim Grabowski, Illinois, RB
	Rick Norton, Kentucky, QB
1967	Bob Griese, Purdue, QB
1968	Larry Csonka, Syracuse, RB
	Doug Crusan, Indiana, T
1969	Bill Stanfill, Georgia, DE
1970	Jim Mandich, Michigan, TE (2)
1971	Otto Stowe, Iowa State, WR (2)
1972	Mike Kadish, Notre Dame, DT
1973	Chuck Bradley, Oregon, C (2)
1974	Donald Reese, Jackson State, DE
1975	Darryl Carlton, Tampa, T
1976	Larry Gordon, Arizona State, LB
	Kim Bokamper, San Jose State, LB
1977	A.J. Duhe, Louisiana State, DT
1978	Guy Benjamin, Stanford, QB (2)
1979	Jon Giesler, Michigan, T
1980	Don McNeal, Alabama, DB
1981	David Overstreet, Oklahoma, RB
1982	Roy Foster, Southern California, G
1983	Dan Marino, Pittsburgh, QB
1984	Jackie Shipp, Oklahoma, LB
1985	Lorenzo Hampton, Florida, RB
1986	John Offerdahl, Western Michigan, LB (2)
1987	John Bosa, Boston College, DE
1988	Eric Kumerow, Ohio State, DE
1989	Sammie Smith, Florida State, RB
	Louis Oliver, Florida, DB
1990	Richmond Webb, Texas A&M, T
1991	Randal Hill, Miami, WR
1992	Troy Vincent, Wisconsin, DB
	Marco Coleman, Georgia Tech, LB
1993	O.J. McDuffie, Penn State, WR
1994	Tim Bowens, Mississippi, DT
1995	Billy Milner, Houston, T
1996	Daryl Gardener, Baylor, DT
1997	Yatil Green, Miami, WR
1998	John Avery, Mississippi, RB
1999	James Johnson, Mississippi State, RB (2)
2000	Todd Wade, Mississippi, T (2)
2001	Jamar Fletcher, Wisconsin, DB

MINNESOTA VIKINGS

Year	Player, College, Position
1961	Tommy Mason, Tulane, RB
1962	Bill Miller, Miami, WR (3)
1963	Jim Dunaway, Mississippi, T
1964	Carl Eller, Minnesota, DE
1965	Jack Snow, Notre Dame, WR
1966	Jerry Shay, Purdue, DT
1967	Clint Jones, Michigan State, RB
	Gene Washington, Michigan State, WR
	Alan Page, Notre Dame, DT
1968	Ron Yary, Southern California, T
1969	Ed White, California, G (2)
1970	John Ward, Oklahoma State, DT
1971	Leo Hayden, Ohio State, RB
1972	Jeff Siemon, Stanford, LB
1973	Chuck Foreman, Miami, RB
1974	Fred McNeill, UCLA, LB
	Steve Riley, Southern California, T
1975	Mark Mullaney, Colorado State, DE
1976	James White, Oklahoma State, DT
1977	Tommy Kramer, Rice, QB
1978	Randy Holloway, Pittsburgh, DE
1979	Ted Brown, North Carolina State, RB
1980	Doug Martin, Washington, DT
1981	Mardye McDole, Mississippi State, WR (2)
1982	Darrin Nelson, Stanford, RB
1983	Joey Browner, Southern California, DB
1984	Keith Millard, Washington State, DE
1985	Chris Doleman, Pittsburgh, LB
1986	Gerald Robinson, Auburn, DE
1987	D.J. Dozier, Penn State, RB
1988	Randall McDaniel, Arizona State, G
1989	David Braxton, Wake Forest, LB (2)
1990	Mike Jones, Texas A&M, TE (3)
1991	Carlos Jenkins, Michigan State, LB (3)
1992	Robert Harris, Southern University, DE (2)
1993	Robert Smith, Ohio State, RB
1994	DeWayne Washington, N. Carolina St., DB
	Todd Steussie, California, T
1995	Derrick Alexander, Florida State, DE
	Korey Stringer, Ohio State, T
1996	Duane Clemons, California, DE
1997	Dwayne Rudd, Alabama, LB
1998	Randy Moss, Marshall, WR
1999	Daunte Culpepper, Central Florida, QB
	Dimitrius Underwood, Michigan State, DE
2000	Chris Hovan, Boston College, DT
2001	Michael Bennett, Wisconsin, RB

NEW ENGLAND PATRIOTS

Year	Player, College, Position
1960	Ron Burton, Northwestern, RB
1961	Tommy Mason, Tulane, RB
1962	Gary Collins, Maryland, WR
1963	Art Graham, Boston College, WR
1964	Jack Concannon, Boston College, QB
1965	Jerry Rush, Michigan State, DE
1966	Karl Singer, Purdue, T
1967	John Charles, Purdue, S
1968	Dennis Byrd, North Carolina State, DE
1969	Ron Sellers, Florida State, WR
1970	Phil Olsen, Utah State, DE
1971	Jim Plunkett, Stanford, QB
1972	Tom Reynolds, San Diego State, WR (2)
1973	John Hannah, Alabama, G
	Sam Cunningham, So. California, RB
	Darryl Stingley, Purdue, WR
1974	Steve Corbett, Boston College, G (2)
1975	Russ Francis, Oregon, TE
1976	Mike Haynes, Arizona State, DB
	Pete Brock, Colorado, C
	Tim Fox, Ohio State, DB
1977	Raymond Clayborn, Texas, DB
	Stanley Morgan, Tennessee, WR
1978	Bob Cryder, Alabama, G
1979	Rick Sanford, South Carolina, DB
1980	Roland James, Tennessee, DB
	Vagas Ferguson, Notre Dame, RB
1981	Brian Holloway, Stanford, T
1982	Kenneth Sims, Texas, DT
	Lester Williams, Miami, DT
1983	Tony Eason, Illinois, QB
1984	Irving Fryar, Nebraska, WR
1985	Trevor Matich, Brigham Young, C
1986	Reggie Dupard, Southern Methodist, RB
1987	Bruce Armstrong, Louisville, T
1988	John Stephens, Northwestern St., La., RB
1989	Hart Lee Dykes, Oklahoma State, WR
1990	Chris Singleton, Arizona, LB
	Ray Agnew, North Carolina State, DE
1991	Pat Harlow, Southern California, T
	Leonard Russell, Arizona State, RB
1992	Eugene Chung, Virginia Tech, T
1993	Drew Bledsoe, Washington State, QB
1994	Willie McGinest, Southern California, DE
1995	Ty Law, Michigan, DB
1996	Terry Glenn, Ohio State, WR
1997	Chris Canty, Kansas State, DB
1998	Robert Edwards, Georgia, RB
	Tebucky Jones, Syracuse, DB
1999	Damien Woody, Boston College, C
	Andy Katzenmoyer, Ohio State, LB
2000	Adrian Klemm, Hawaii, T (2)
2001	Richard Seymour, Georgia, DT

NEW ORLEANS SAINTS

Year	Player, College, Position
1967	Les Kelley, Alabama, RB
1968	Kevin Hardy, Notre Dame, DE
1969	John Shinners, Xavier, G
1970	Ken Burrough, Texas Southern, WR
1971	Archie Manning, Mississippi, QB
1972	Royce Smith, Georgia, G
1973	Derland Moore, Oklahoma, DE (2)
1974	Rick Middleton, Ohio State, LB
1975	Larry Burton, Purdue, WR
	Kurt Schumacher, Ohio State, T
1976	Chuck Muncie, California, RB
1977	Joe Campbell, Maryland, DE
1978	Wes Chandler, Florida, WR
1979	Russell Erxleben, Texas, P-K
1980	Stan Brock, Colorado, T
1981	George Rogers, South Carolina, RB
1982	Lindsay Scott, Georgia, WR
1983	Steve Korte, Arkansas, G (2)
1984	James Geathers, Wichita State, DE
1985	Alvin Toles, Tennessee, LB
1986	Jim Dombrowski, Virginia, T
1987	Shawn Knight, Brigham Young, DT
1988	Craig Heyward, Pittsburgh, RB
1989	Wayne Martin, Arkansas, DE
1990	Renaldo Turnbull, West Virginia, DE
1991	Wesley Carroll, Miami, WR (2)
1992	Vaughn Dunbar, Indiana, RB
1993	Willie Roaf, Louisiana Tech, T
	Irv Smith, Notre Dame, TE
1994	Joe Johnson, Louisville, DE
1995	Mark Fields, Washington State, LB
1996	Alex Molden, Oregon, DB
1997	Chris Naeole, Colorado, G
1998	Kyle Turley, San Diego State, T
1999	Ricky Williams, Texas, RB
2000	Darren Howard, Kansas State, DE (2)
2001	Deuce McAllister, Mississippi, RB

NEW YORK GIANTS

Year	Player, College, Position
1936	Art Lewis, Ohio U., T
1937	Ed Widseth, Minnesota, T
1938	George Karamatic, Gonzaga, B
1939	Walt Neilson, Arizona, B
1940	Grenville Lansdell, Southern California, B
1941	George Franck, Minnesota, B
1942	Merle Hapes, Mississippi, B
1943	Steve Filipowicz, Fordham, B
1944	Billy Hillenbrand, Indiana, B
1945	Elmer Barbour, Wake Forest, B
1946	George Connor, Notre Dame, T
1947	Vic Schwall, Northwestern, B
1948	Tony Minisi, Pennsylvania, B
1949	Paul Page, Southern Methodist, B
1950	Travis Tidwell, Auburn, B
1951	Kyle Rote, Southern Methodist, B
	Jim Spavital, Oklahoma A&M, B
1952	Frank Gifford, Southern California, B
1953	Bobby Marlow, Alabama, B
1954	Ken Buck, Pacific, C (2)
1955	Joe Heap, Notre Dame, B
1956	Henry Moore, Arkansas, B (2)
1957	Sam DeLuca, South Carolina, T (2)
1958	Phil King, Vanderbilt, B
1959	Lee Grosscup, Utah, B
1960	Lou Cordileone, Clemson, G
1961	Bruce Tarbox, Syracuse, G (2)
1962	Jerry Hillebrand, Colorado, LB
1963	Frank Lasky, Florida, T (2)
1964	Joe Don Looney, Oklahoma, RB
1965	Tucker Frederickson, Auburn, RB
1966	Francis Peay, Missouri, T
1967	Louis Thompson, Alabama, DT (4)
1968	Dick Buzin, Penn State, T (2)
1969	Fred Dryer, San Diego State, DE
1970	Jim Files, Oklahoma, LB
1971	Rocky Thompson, West Texas State, WR
1972	Eldridge Small, Texas A&I, DB

Year	Player, College, Position
	Larry Jacobson, Nebraska, DE
1973	Brad Van Pelt, Michigan State, LB (2)
1974	John Hicks, Ohio State, G
1975	Al Simpson, Colorado State, T (2)
1976	Troy Archer, Colorado, DE
1977	Gary Jeter, Southern California, DT
1978	Gordon King, Stanford, T
1979	Phil Simms, Morehead State, QB
1980	Mark Haynes, Colorado, DB
1981	Lawrence Taylor, North Carolina, LB
1982	Butch Woolfolk, Michigan, RB
1983	Terry Kinard, Clemson, DB
1984	Carl Banks, Michigan State, LB
	William Roberts, Ohio State, T
1985	George Adams, Kentucky, RB
1986	Eric Dorsey, Notre Dame, DE
1987	Mark Ingram, Michigan State, WR
1988	Eric Moore, Indiana, T
1989	Brian Williams, Minnesota, C-G
1990	Rodney Hampton, Georgia, RB
1991	Jarrod Bunch, Michigan, RB
1992	Derek Brown, Notre Dame, TE
1993	Michael Strahan, Texas Southern, DE (2)
1994	Thomas Lewis, Indiana, WR
1995	Tyrone Wheatley, Michigan, RB
1996	Cedric Jones, Oklahoma, DE
1997	Ike Hilliard, Florida, WR
1998	Shaun Williams, UCLA, DB
1999	Luke Petitgout, Notre Dame, T
2000	Ron Dayne, Wisconsin, RB
2001	Will Allen, Syracuse, DB

NEW YORK JETS

Year	Player, College, Position
1960	George Izo, Notre Dame, QB
1961	Tom Brown, Minnesota, G
1962	Sandy Stephens, Minnesota, QB
1963	Jerry Stovall, Louisiana State, S
1964	Matt Snell, Ohio State, RB
1965	Joe Namath, Alabama, QB
	Tom Nowatzke, Indiana, RB
1966	Bill Yearby, Michigan, DT
1967	Paul Seiler, Notre Dame, T
1968	Lee White, Weber State, RB
1969	Dave Foley, Ohio State, T
1970	Steve Tannen, Florida, CB
1971	John Riggins, Kansas, RB
1972	Jerome Barkum, Jackson State, WR
	Mike Taylor, Michigan, LB
1973	Burgess Owens, Miami, DB
1974	Carl Barzilauskas, Indiana, DT
1975	Anthony Davis, Southern California, RB (2)
1976	Richard Todd, Alabama, QB
1977	Marvin Powell, Southern California, T
1978	Chris Ward, Ohio State, T
1979	Marty Lyons, Alabama, DE
1980	Johnny (Lam) Jones, Texas, WR
1981	Freeman McNeil, UCLA, RB
1982	Bob Crable, Notre Dame, LB
1983	Ken O'Brien, Cal-Davis, QB
1984	Russell Carter, Southern Methodist, DB
	Ron Faurot, Arkansas, DE
1985	Al Toon, Wisconsin, WR
1986	Mike Haight, Iowa, T
1987	Roger Vick, Texas A&M, RB
1988	Dave Cadigan, Southern California, T
1989	Jeff Lageman, Virginia, LB
1990	Blair Thomas, Penn State, RB
1991	Browning Nagle, Louisville, QB (2)
1992	Johnny Mitchell, Nebraska, TE
1993	Marvin Jones, Florida State, LB
1994	Aaron Glenn, Texas A&M, DB
1995	Kyle Brady, Penn State, TE
	Hugh Douglas, Central State, Ohio, DE
1996	Keyshawn Johnson, Southern California, WR
1997	James Farrior, Virginia, LB
1998	Dorian Boose, Washington State, DE (2)
1999	Randy Thomas, Mississippi State, G (2)
2000	Shaun Ellis, Tennessee, DE
	John Abraham, South Carolina, LB
	Chad Pennington, Marshall, QB
	Anthony Becht, West Virginia, TE
2001	Santana Moss, Miami, WR

OAKLAND RAIDERS

Year	Player, College, Position
1960	Dale Hackbart, Wisconsin, CB
1961	Joe Rutgens, Illinois, DT
1962	Roman Gabriel, North Carolina State, QB
1963	George Wilson, Alabama, RB (6)
1964	Tony Lorick, Arizona State, RB
1965	Harry Schuh, Memphis State, T
1966	Rodger Bird, Kentucky, S
1967	Gene Upshaw, Texas A&I, G
1968	Eldridge Dickey, Tennessee State, QB
1969	Art Thoms, Syracuse, DT
1970	Raymond Chester, Morgan State, TE
1971	Jack Tatum, Ohio State, S
1972	Mike Siani, Villanova, WR
1973	Ray Guy, Southern Mississippi, P
1974	Henry Lawrence, Florida A&M, T
1975	Neal Colzie, Ohio State, DB
1976	Charles Philyaw, Texas Southern, DT (2)
1977	Mike Davis, Colorado, DB (2)
1978	Dave Browning, Washington, DE (2)
1979	Willie Jones, Florida State, DE (2)
1980	Marc Wilson, Brigham Young, QB
1981	Ted Watts, Texas Tech, DB
	Curt Marsh, Washington, T
1982	Marcus Allen, Southern California, RB
1983	Don Mosebar, Southern California, T
1984	Sean Jones, Northeastern, DE (2)
1985	Jessie Hester, Florida State, WR
1986	Bob Buczkowski, Pittsburgh, DE
1987	John Clay, Missouri, T
1988	Tim Brown, Notre Dame, WR
	Terry McDaniel, Tennessee, DB
	Scott Davis, Illinois, DE
1989	Jeff Francis, Tennessee, QB (6)
1990	Anthony Smith, Arizona, DE
1991	Todd Marinovich, Southern California, QB
1992	Chester McGlockton, Clemson, DE
1993	Patrick Bates, Texas A&M, DB
1994	Rob Fredrickson, Michigan State, LB
1995	Napoleon Kaufman, Washington, RB
1996	Rickey Dudley, Ohio State, TE
1997	Darrell Russell, Southern California, DT
1998	Charles Woodson, Michigan, DB
	Mo Collins, Florida, T
1999	Matt Stinchcomb, Georgia, T
2000	Sebastian Janikowski, Florida State, K
2001	Derrick Gibson, Florida State, DB

PHILADELPHIA EAGLES

Year	Player, College, Position
1936	Jay Berwanger, Chicago, B
1937	Sam Francis, Nebraska, B
1938	Jim McDonald, Ohio State, B
1939	Davey O'Brien, Texas Christian, B
1940	George McAfee, Duke, B
1941	Art Jones, Richmond, B (2)
1942	Pete Kmetovic, Stanford, B
1943	Joe Muha, Virginia Military, B
1944	Steve Van Buren, Louisiana State, B
1945	John Yonaker, Notre Dame, E
1946	Leo Riggs, Southern California, B
1947	Neill Armstrong, Oklahoma A&M, E
1948	Clyde (Smackover) Scott, Arkansas, B
1949	Chuck Bednarik, Pennsylvania, C
	Frank Tripucka, Notre Dame, B
1950	Harry (Bud) Grant, Minnesota, E
1951	Ebert Van Buren, Louisiana State, B
	Chet Mutryn, Xavier, B
1952	Johnny Bright, Drake, B
1953	Al Conway, Army, B (2)
1954	Neil Worden, Notre Dame, B
1955	Dick Bielski, Maryland, B
1956	Bob Pellegrini, Maryland, C
1957	Clarence Peaks, Michigan State, B
1958	Walt Kowalczyk, Michigan State, B
1959	J.D. Smith, Rice, T (2)
1960	Ron Burton, Northwestern, RB
1961	Art Baker, Syracuse, RB
1962	Pete Case, Georgia, G (2)
1963	Ed Budde, Michigan State, G
1964	Bob Brown, Nebraska, T
1965	Ray Rissmiller, Georgia, T (2)
1966	Randy Beisler, Indiana, DE
1967	Harry Jones, Arkansas, RB
1968	Tim Rossovich, Southern California, DE
1969	Leroy Keyes, Purdue, RB
1970	Steve Zabel, Oklahoma, TE
1971	Richard Harris, Grambling, DE
1972	John Reaves, Florida, QB
1973	Jerry Sisemore, Texas, T
	Charle Young, Southern California, TE
1974	Mitch Sutton, Kansas, DT (3)
1975	Bill Capraun, Miami, T (7)
1976	Mike Smith, Florida, DE (4)
1977	Skip Sharp, Kansas, DB (5)
1978	Reggie Wilkes, Georgia Tech, LB (3)
1979	Jerry Robinson, UCLA, LB
1980	Roynell Young, Alcorn State, DB
1981	Leonard Mitchell, Houston, DE
1982	Mike Quick, North Carolina State, WR
1983	Michael Haddix, Mississippi State, RB
1984	Kenny Jackson, Penn State, WR
1985	Kevin Allen, Indiana, T
1986	Keith Byars, Ohio State, RB
1987	Jerome Brown, Miami, DT
1988	Keith Jackson, Oklahoma, TE
1989	Jessie Small, Eastern Kentucky, LB (2)
1990	Ben Smith, Georgia, DB
1991	Antone Davis, Tennessee, T
1992	Siran Stacy, Alabama, RB (2)
1993	Lester Holmes, Jackson State, T
	Leonard Renfro, Colorado, DT
1994	Bernard Williams, Georgia, T
1995	Mike Mamula, Boston College, DE
1996	Jermane Mayberry, Texas A&M-Kingsville, T
1997	Jon Harris, Virginia, DE
1998	Tra Thomas, Florida State, T
1999	Donovan McNabb, Syracuse, QB
2000	Corey Simon, Florida State, DT
2001	Freddie Mitchell, UCLA, WR

PITTSBURGH STEELERS

Year	Player, College, Position
1936	Bill Shakespeare, Notre Dame, B
1937	Mike Basrak, Duquesne, C
1938	Byron (Whizzer) White, Colorado, B
1939	Bill Patterson, Baylor, B (3)
1940	Kay Eakin, Arkansas, B
1941	Chet Gladchuk, Boston College, C (2)
1942	Bill Dudley, Virginia, B
1943	Bill Daley, Minnesota, B
1944	Johnny Podesto, St. Mary's, Calif., B
1945	Paul Duhart, Florida, B
1946	Felix (Doc) Blanchard, Army, B
1947	Hub Bechtol, Texas, E
1948	Dan Edwards, Georgia, E
1949	Bobby Gage, Clemson, B
1950	Lynn Chandnois, Michigan State, B
1951	Butch Avinger, Alabama, B
1952	Ed Modzelewski, Maryland, B
1953	Ted Marchibroda, St. Bonaventure, B
1954	Johnny Lattner, Notre Dame, B
1955	Frank Varrichione, Notre Dame, T
1956	Gary Glick, Colorado A&M, B
	Art Davis, Mississippi State, B
1957	Len Dawson, Purdue, B
1958	Larry Krutko, West Virginia, B (2)
1959	Tom Barnett, Purdue, B (8)
1960	Jack Spikes, Texas Christian, RB
1961	Myron Pottios, Notre Dame, LB (2)
1962	Bob Ferguson, Ohio State, RB
1963	Frank Atkinson, Stanford, T (8)
1964	Paul Martha, Pittsburgh, S
1965	Roy Jefferson, Utah, WR (2)
1966	Dick Leftridge, West Virginia, RB
1967	Don Shy, San Diego State, RB (2)
1968	Mike Taylor, Southern California, T
1969	Joe Greene, North Texas State, DT
1970	Terry Bradshaw, Louisiana Tech, QB
1971	Frank Lewis, Grambling, WR
1972	Franco Harris, Penn State, RB
1973	J.T. Thomas, Florida State, DB
1974	Lynn Swann, Southern California, WR
1975	Dave Brown, Michigan, DB
1976	Bennie Cunningham, Clemson, TE

1977 Robin Cole, New Mexico, LB
1978 Ron Johnson, Eastern Michigan, DB
1979 Greg Hawthorne, Baylor, RB
1980 Mark Malone, Arizona State, QB
1981 Keith Gary, Oklahoma, DE
1982 Walter Abercrombie, Baylor, RB
1983 Gabriel Rivera, Texas Tech, DT
1984 Louis Lipps, Southern Mississippi, WR
1985 Darryl Sims, Wisconsin, DE
1986 John Rienstra, Temple, G
1987 Rod Woodson, Purdue, DB
1988 Aaron Jones, Eastern Kentucky, DE
1989 Tim Worley, Georgia, RB
Tom Ricketts, Pittsburgh, T
1990 Eric Green, Liberty, TE
1991 Huey Richardson, Florida, DE
1992 Leon Searcy, Miami, T
1993 Deon Figures, Colorado, DB
1994 Charles Johnson, Colorado, WR
1995 Mark Bruener, Washington, TE
1996 Jamain Stephens, North Carolina A&T, T
1997 Chad Scott, Maryland, DB
1998 Alan Faneca, Louisiana State, G
1999 Troy Edwards, Lousiana Tech, WR
2000 Plaxico Burress, Michigan State, WR
2001 Casey Hampton, Texas, DT

ST. LOUIS RAMS

Year Player, College, Position
1937 Johnny Drake, Purdue, B
1938 Corbett Davis, Indiana, B
1939 Parker Hall, Mississippi, B
1940 Ollie Cordill, Rice, B
1941 Rudy Mucha, Washington, C
1942 Jack Wilson, Baylor, B
1943 Mike Holovak, Boston College, B
1944 Tony Butkovich, Illinois, B
1945 Elroy (Crazylegs) Hirsch, Wisconsin, B
1946 Emil Sitko, Notre Dame, B
1947 Herman Wedemeyer, St. Mary's, Calif., B
1948 Tom Keane, West Virginia, B (2)
1949 Bobby Thomason, Virginia Military, B
1950 Ralph Pasquariello, Villanova, B
Stan West, Oklahoma, G
1951 Bud McFadin, Texas, G
1952 Bill Wade, Vanderbilt, QB
Bob Carey, Michigan State, E
1953 Donn Moomaw, UCLA, C
Ed Barker, Washington State, E
1954 Ed Beatty, Cincinnati, C
1955 Larry Morris, Georgia Tech, C
1956 Joe Marconi, West Virginia, B
Charles Horton, Vanderbilt, B
1957 Jon Arnett, Southern California, B
Del Shofner, Baylor, E
1958 Lou Michaels, Kentucky, T
Jim Phillips, Auburn, E
1959 Dick Bass, Pacific, B
Paul Dickson, Baylor, T
1960 Billy Cannon, Louisiana State, RB
1961 Marlin McKeever, Southern California, E-LB
1962 Roman Gabriel, North Carolina State, QB
Merlin Olsen, Utah State, DT
1963 Terry Baker, Oregon State, QB
Rufus Guthrie, Georgia Tech, G
1964 Bill Munson, Utah State, QB
1965 Clancy Williams, Washington State, CB
1966 Tom Mack, Michigan, G
1967 Willie Ellison, Texas Southern, RB (2)
1968 Gary Beban, UCLA, QB (2)
1969 Larry Smith, Florida, RB
Jim Seymour, Notre Dame, WR
Bob Klein, Southern California, TE
1970 Jack Reynolds, Tennessee, LB
1971 Isiah Robertson, Southern, LB
Jack Youngblood, Florida, DE
1972 Jim Bertelsen, Texas, RB (2)
1973 Cullen Bryant, Colorado, DB (2)
1974 John Cappelletti, Penn State, RB
1975 Mike Fanning, Notre Dame, DT
Dennis Harrah, Miami, T
Doug France, Ohio State, T
1976 Kevin McLain, Colorado State, LB
1977 Bob Brudzinski, Ohio State, LB
1978 Elvis Peacock, Oklahoma, RB
1979 George Andrews, Nebraska, LB
Kent Hill, Georgia Tech, T
1980 Johnnie Johnson, Texas, DB
1981 Mel Owens, Michigan, LB
1982 Barry Redden, Richmond, RB
1983 Eric Dickerson, Southern Methodist, RB
1984 Hal Stephens, East Carolina, DE (5)
1985 Jerry Gray, Texas, DB
1986 Mike Schad, Queen's University, Canada, T
1987 Donald Evans, Winston-Salem, DE (2)
1988 Gaston Green, UCLA, RB
Aaron Cox, Arizona State, WR
1989 Bill Hawkins, Miami, DE
Cleveland Gary, Miami, RB
1990 Bern Brostek, Washington, C
1991 Todd Lyght, Notre Dame, DB
1992 Sean Gilbert, Pittsburgh, DE
1993 Jerome Bettis, Notre Dame, RB
1994 Wayne Gandy, Auburn, T
1995 Kevin Carter, Florida, DE
1996 Lawrence Phillips, Nebraska, RB
Eddie Kennison, Louisiana State, WR
1997 Orlando Pace, Ohio State, T
1998 Grant Wistrom, Nebraska, DE
1999 Torry Holt, North Carolina State, WR
2000 Trung Canidate, Arizona, RB
2001 Damione Lewis, Miami, DT
Adam Archuleta, Arizona State, DB
Ryan Pickett, Ohio State, DT

SAN DIEGO CHARGERS

Year Player, College, Position
1960 Monty Stickles, Notre Dame, E
1961 Earl Faison, Indiana, DE
1962 Bob Ferguson, Ohio State, RB
1963 Walt Sweeney, Syracuse, G
1964 Ted Davis, Georgia Tech, LB
1965 Steve DeLong, Tennessee, DE
1966 Don Davis, Cal State-Los Angeles, DT
1967 Ron Billingsley, Wyoming, DE
1968 Russ Washington, Missouri, DT
Jimmy Hill, Texas A&I, DB
1969 Marty Domres, Columbia, QB
Bob Babich, Miami, Ohio, LB
1970 Walker Gillette, Richmond, WR
1971 Leon Burns, Long Beach State, RB
1972 Pete Lazetich, Stanford, DE (2)
1973 Johnny Rodgers, Nebraska, WR
1974 Bo Matthews, Colorado, RB
Don Goode, Kansas, LB
1975 Gary Johnson, Grambling, DT
Mike Williams, Louisiana State, DB
1976 Joe Washington, Oklahoma, RB
1977 Bob Rush, Memphis State, C
1978 John Jefferson, Arizona State, WR
1979 Kellen Winslow, Missouri, TE
1980 Ed Luther, San Jose State, QB (4)
1981 James Brooks, Auburn, RB
1982 Hollis Hall, Clemson, DB (7)
1983 Billy Ray Smith, Arkansas, LB
Gary Anderson, Arkansas, WR
Gill Byrd, San Jose State, DB
1984 Mossy Cade, Texas, DB
1985 Jim Lachey, Ohio State, G
1986 Leslie O'Neal, Oklahoma State, DE
James FitzPatrick, Southern California, T
1987 Rod Bernstine, Texas A&M, TE
1988 Anthony Miller, Tennessee, WR
1989 Burt Grossman, Pittsburgh, DE
1990 Junior Seau, Southern California, LB
1991 Stanley Richard, Texas, DB
1992 Chris Mims, Tennessee, DE
1993 Darrien Gordon, Stanford, DB
1994 Isaac Davis, Arkansas, G (2)
1995 Terrance Shaw, Stephen F. Austin, DB (2)
1996 Bryan Still, Virginia Tech, WR (2)
1997 Freddie Jones, North Carolina, TE (2)
1998 Ryan Leaf, Washington State, QB
1999 Jermaine Fazande, Oklahoma, RB (2)
2000 Rogers Beckett, Marshall, DB (2)
2001 LaDainian Tomlinson, Texas Christian, RB

SAN FRANCISCO 49ERS

Year Player, College, Position
1950 Leo Nomellini, Minnesota, T
1951 Y.A. Tittle, Louisiana State, B
1952 Hugh McElhenny, Washington, B
1953 Harry Babcock, Georgia, E
Tom Stolhandske, Texas, E
1954 Bernie Faloney, Maryland, B
1955 Dickie Moegle, Rice, B
1956 Earl Morrall, Michigan State, B
1957 John Brodie, Stanford, B
1958 Jim Pace, Michigan, B
Charlie Krueger, Texas A&M, T
1959 Dave Baker, Oklahoma, B
Dan James, Ohio State, C
1960 Monty Stickles, Notre Dame, E
1961 Jimmy Johnson, UCLA, CB
Bernie Casey, Bowling Green, WR
Bill Kilmer, UCLA, QB
1962 Lance Alworth, Arkansas, WR
1963 Kermit Alexander, UCLA, CB
1964 Dave Parks, Texas Tech, WR
1965 Ken Willard, North Carolina, RB
George Donnelly, Illinois, DB
1966 Stan Hindman, Mississippi, DE
1967 Steve Spurrier, Florida, QB
Cas Banaszek, Northwestern, T
1968 Forrest Blue, Auburn, C
1969 Ted Kwalick, Penn State, TE
Gene Washington, Stanford, WR
1970 Cedrick Hardman, North Texas State, DE
Bruce Taylor, Boston U., DB
1971 Tim Anderson, Ohio State, DB
1972 Terry Beasley, Auburn, WR
1973 Mike Holmes, Texas Southern, DB
1974 Wilbur Jackson, Alabama, RB
Bill Sandifer, UCLA, DT
1975 Jimmy Webb, Mississippi State, DT
1976 Randy Cross, UCLA, C (2)
1977 Elmo Boyd, Eastern Kentucky, WR (3)
1978 Ken MacAfee, Notre Dame, TE
Dan Bunz, Cal State-Long Beach, LB
1979 James Owens, UCLA, WR (2)
1980 Earl Cooper, Rice, RB
Jim Stuckey, Clemson, DT
1981 Ronnie Lott, Southern California, DB
1982 Bubba Paris, Michigan, T (2)
1983 Roger Craig, Nebraska, RB (2)
1984 Todd Shell, Brigham Young, LB
1985 Jerry Rice, Mississippi Valley State, WR
1986 Larry Roberts, Alabama, DE (2)
1987 Harris Barton, North Carolina, T
Terrence Flagler, Clemson, RB
1988 Danny Stubbs, Miami, DE (2)
1989 Keith DeLong, Tennessee, LB
1990 Dexter Carter, Florida State, RB
1991 Ted Washington, Louisville, DT
1992 Dana Hall, Washington, DB
1993 Dana Stubblefield, Kansas, DT
Todd Kelly, Tennessee, DE
1994 Bryant Young, Notre Dame, DT
William Floyd, Florida State, RB
1995 J.J. Stokes, UCLA, WR
1996 Israel Ifeanyi, Southern California, DE (2)
1997 Jim Druckenmiller, Virginia Tech, QB
1998 R.W. McQuarters, Oklahoma State, DB
1999 Reggie McGrew, Florida, DT
2000 Julian Peterson, Michigan State, LB
Ahmed Plummer, Ohio State, DB
2001 Andre Carter, California, DE

SEATTLE SEAHAWKS

Year Player, College, Position
1976 Steve Niehaus, Notre Dame, DT
1977 Steve August, Tulsa, G
1978 Keith Simpson, Memphis State, DB
1979 Manu Tuiasosopo, UCLA, DT
1980 Jacob Green, Texas A&M, DE
1981 Ken Easley, UCLA, DB
1982 Jeff Bryant, Clemson, DE
1983 Curt Warner, Penn State, RB
1984 Terry Taylor, Southern Illinois, DB
1985 Owen Gill, Iowa, RB (2)

1986 John L. Williams, Florida, RB
1987 Tony Woods, Pittsburgh, LB
1988 Brian Blades, Miami, WR (2)
1989 Andy Heck, Notre Dame, T
1990 Cortez Kennedy, Miami, DT
1991 Dan McGwire, San Diego State, QB
1992 Ray Roberts, Virginia, T
1993 Rick Mirer, Notre Dame, QB
1994 Sam Adams, Texas A&M, DT
1995 Joey Galloway, Ohio State, WR
1996 Pete Kendall, Boston College, T
1997 Shawn Springs, Ohio State, DB
Walter Jones, Florida State, T
1998 Anthony Simmons, Clemson, LB
1999 Lamar King, Saginaw Valley State, DE
2000 Shaun Alexander, Alabama, RB
Chris McIntosh, Wisconsin, T
2001 Koren Robinson, North Carolina State, WR
Steve Hutchinson, Michigan, G

TAMPA BAY BUCCANEERS

Year Player, College, Position
1976 Lee Roy Selmon, Oklahoma, DT
1977 Ricky Bell, Southern California, RB
1978 Doug Williams, Grambling, QB
1979 Greg Roberts, Oklahoma, G (2)
1980 Ray Snell, Wisconsin, G
1981 Hugh Green, Pittsburgh, LB
1982 Sean Farrell, Penn State, G
1983 Randy Grimes, Baylor, C (2)
1984 Keith Browner, Southern California, LB (2)
1985 Ron Holmes, Washington, DE
1986 Bo Jackson, Auburn, RB
Roderick Jones, Southern Methodist, DB
1987 Vinny Testaverde, Miami, QB
1988 Paul Gruber, Wisconsin, T
1989 Broderick Thomas, Nebraska, LB
1990 Keith McCants, Alabama, LB
1991 Charles McRae, Tennessee, T
1992 Courtney Hawkins, Michigan State, WR (2)
1993 Eric Curry, Alabama, DE
1994 Trent Dilfer, Fresno State, QB
1995 Warren Sapp, Miami, DT
Derrick Brooks, Florida State, LB
1996 Regan Upshaw, California, DE
Marcus Jones, North Carolina, DT
1997 Warrick Dunn, Florida State, RB
Reidel Anthony, Florida, WR
1998 Jacquez Green, Florida, WR (2)
1999 Anthony McFarland, Louisiana State, DT
2000 Cosey Coleman, Tennessee, G (2)
2001 Kenyatta Walker, Florida, T

TENNESSEE TITANS

Year Player, College, Position
1960 Billy Cannon, Louisiana State, RB
1961 Mike Ditka, Pittsburgh, E
1962 Ray Jacobs, Howard Payne, DT
1963 Danny Brabham, Arkansas, LB
1964 Scott Appleton, Texas, DT
1965 Lawrence Elkins, Baylor, WR
1966 Tommy Nobis, Texas, LB
1967 George Webster, Michigan State, LB
Tom Regner, Notre Dame, G
1968 Mac Haik, Mississippi, WR (2)
1969 Ron Pritchard, Arizona State, LB
1970 Doug Wilkerson, N. Carolina Central, G
1971 Dan Pastorini, Santa Clara, QB
1972 Greg Sampson, Stanford, DE
1973 John Matuszak, Tampa, DE
George Amundson, Iowa State, RB
1974 Steve Manstedt, Nebraska, LB (4)
1975 Robert Brazile, Jackson State, LB
Don Hardeman, Texas A&I, RB
1976 Mike Barber, Louisiana Tech, TE (2)
1977 Morris Towns, Missouri, T
1978 Earl Campbell, Texas, RB
1979 Mike Stensrud, Iowa State, DE (2)
1980 Angelo Fields, Michigan State, T (2)
1981 Michael Holston, Morgan State, WR (3)
1982 Mike Munchak, Penn State, G
1983 Bruce Matthews, Southern California, T
1984 Dean Steinkuhler, Nebraska, T
1985 Ray Childress, Texas A&M, DE
Richard Johnson, Wisconsin, DB
1986 Jim Everett, Purdue, QB
1987 Alonzo Highsmith, Miami, RB
Haywood Jeffires, North Carolina St., WR
1988 Lorenzo White, Michigan State, RB
1989 David Williams, Florida, T
1990 Lamar Lathon, Houston, LB
1991 Mike Dumas, Indiana, DB (2)
1992 Eddie Robinson, Alabama State, LB (2)
1993 Brad Hopkins, Illinois, T
1994 Henry Ford, Arkansas, DE
1995 Steve McNair, Alcorn State, QB
1996 Eddie George, Ohio State, RB
1997 Kenny Holmes, Miami, DE
1998 Kevin Dyson, Utah, WR
1999 Jevon Kearse, Florida, DE
2000 Keith Bulluck, Syracuse, LB
2001 Andre Dyson, Utah, DB (2)

WASHINGTON REDSKINS

Year Player, College, Position
1936 Riley Smith, Alabama, B
1937 Sammy Baugh, Texas Christian, B
1938 Andy Farkas, Detroit, B
1939 I.B. Hale, Texas Christian, T
1940 Ed Boell, New York U., B
1941 Forest Evashevski, Michigan, B
1942 Orban (Spec) Sanders, Texas, B
1943 Jack Jenkins, Missouri, B
1944 Mike Micka, Colgate, B
1945 Jim Hardy, Southern California, B
1946 Cal Rossi, UCLA, B*
1947 Cal Rossi, UCLA, B
1948 Harry Gilmer, Alabama, B
Lowell Tew, Alabama, B
1949 Rob Goode, Texas A&M, B
1950 George Thomas, Oklahoma, B
1951 Leon Heath, Oklahoma, B
1952 Larry Isbell, Baylor, B
1953 Jack Scarbath, Maryland, B
1954 Steve Meilinger, Kentucky, E
1955 Ralph Guglielmi, Notre Dame, B
1956 Ed Vereb, Maryland, B
1957 Don Bosseler, Miami, B
1958 Mike Sommer, George Washington, B (2)
1959 Don Allard, Boston College, B
1960 Richie Lucas, Penn State, QB
1961 Norman Snead, Wake Forest, QB
Joe Rutgens, Illinois, DT
1962 Ernie Davis, Syracuse, RB
1963 Pat Richter, Wisconsin, TE
1964 Charley Taylor, Arizona State, RB-WR
1965 Bob Breitenstein, Tulsa, T (2)
1966 Charlie Gogolak, Princeton, K
1967 Ray McDonald, Idaho, RB
1968 Jim Smith, Oregon, DB
1969 Eugene Epps, Texas-El Paso, DB (2)
1970 Bill Bundige, Colorado, DT (2)
1971 Cotton Speyrer, Texas, WR (2)
1972 Moses Denson, Maryland State, RB (8)
1973 Charles Cantrell, Lamar, G (5)
1974 Jon Keyworth, Colorado, TE (6)
1975 Mike Thomas, Nevada-Las Vegas, RB (6)
1976 Mike Hughes, Baylor, G (5)
1977 Duncan McColl, Stanford, DE (4)
1978 Tony Green, Florida, RB (6)
1979 Don Warren, San Diego State, TE (4)
1980 Art Monk, Syracuse, WR
1981 Mark May, Pittsburgh, T
1982 Vernon Dean, San Diego State, DB (2)
1983 Darrell Green, Texas A&I, DB
1984 Bob Slater, Oklahoma, DT (2)
1985 Tory Nixon, San Diego State, DB (2)
1986 Markus Koch, Boise State, DE (2)
1987 Brian Davis, Nebraska, DB (2)
1988 Chip Lohmiller, Minnesota, K (2)
1989 Tracy Rocker, Auburn, DT (3)
1990 Andre Collins, Penn State, LB (2)
1991 Bobby Wilson, Michigan State, DT
1992 Desmond Howard, Michigan, WR
1993 Tom Carter, Notre Dame, DB
1994 Heath Shuler, Tennessee, QB
1995 Michael Westbrook, Colorado, WR
1996 Andre Johnson, Penn State, T
1997 Kenard Lang, Miami, DE
1998 Stephen Alexander, Oklahoma, TE (2)
1999 Champ Bailey, Georgia, DB
2000 LaVar Arrington, Penn State, LB
Chris Samuels, Alabama, T
2001 Rod Gardner, Clemson, WR

**Choice lost because of ineligibility*

ASSOCIATED PRESS NFL MOST VALUABLE PLAYERS

NFL MOST VALUABLE PLAYERS NAMED BY *ASSOCIATED PRESS* IN BALLOTING BY A NATIONWIDE PANEL OF MEDIA:

YEAR	PLAYER	POS.	TEAM	ACCOMPLISHMENTS
1957	Jim Brown	RB	Cleveland Browns	Rushed for league-leading 942 yards and added 9 TDs as a rookie.
1958	Gino Marchetti	DE	Baltimore Colts	Leader of defense that permitted league-low 1,291 rushing yards and division-low 203 points.
1959	Charley Conerly	QB	New York Giants	Passed for 14 TDs vs. 4 interceptions. Led offense to division-leading 284 points.
1960	Norm Van Brocklin	QB	Philadelphia Eagles	Guided Eagles to first division title since 1949. Passed for 2,471 yards and 24 TDs.
	Joe Schmidt	LB	Detroit Lions	Team went 7-2 after 0-3 start when he returned from injury. Scored 2 defensive TDs.
1961	Paul Hornung	RB	Green Bay Packers	Led league in scoring for second straight season with 146 points (10 TD, 15 FG, 41 PAT).
1962	Jim Taylor	RB	Green Bay Packers	League rushing champion with 1,474 yards. Scored then all-time record 19 touchdowns.
1963	Y.A. Tittle	QB	New York Giants	Set then all-time season record with 36 TD passes. Guided league's top offense (5,024 yards).
1964	Johnny Unitas	QB	Baltimore Colts	Guided Colts to NFL's best record (12-2) and league's top offensive attack (4,779 yards).
1965	Jim Brown	RB	Cleveland Browns	Leader of NFL's top rushing attack. Led league with 1,544 yards, added 21 total TDs.
1966	Bart Starr	QB	Green Bay Packers	Passed for 14 touchdowns vs. 3 interceptions. Led Packers to league-best 12-2 record.
1967	Johnny Unitas	QB	Baltimore Colts	Passed for 3,428 yards and 20 touchdowns. Led Colts to 11-1-2 record.
1968	Earl Morrall	QB	Baltimore Colts	Guided Colts to NFL-best 13-1 record. Led league with 26 touchdown passes.
1969	Roman Gabriel	QB	Los Angeles Rams	Led NFL with 24 touchdown passes. Guided Rams to 11-3 record.
1970	John Brodie	QB	San Francisco 49ers	Took 49ers to first-ever division title. Threw NFL-best 24 TD passes.
1971	Alan Page	DT	Minnesota Vikings	Led defense that allowed NFL-low 139 points. Vikings won fourth straight NFC Central title.
1972	Larry Brown	RB	Washington Redskins	Led conference with 1,216 rushing yards. Redskins had NFC-best 11-3 record.
1973	O.J. Simpson	RB	Buffalo Bills	Rushed for then all-time record 2,003 yards, including three 200-yard performances.
1974	Ken Stabler	QB	Oakland Raiders	Led league with 26 touchdown passes vs. 12 interceptions. Raiders had NFL-best 12-2 record.
1975	Fran Tarkenton	QB	Minnesota Vikings	Tied for league-best 12-2 record. Led NFC with 91.7 passer rating.
1976	Bert Jones	QB	Baltimore Colts	Threw 24 touchdowns vs. 9 interceptions for 102.5 passer rating.
1977	Walter Payton	RB	Chicago Bears	Rushed for league-leading 1,852 yards and 16 total touchdowns.
1978	Terry Bradshaw	QB	Pittsburgh Steelers	Led Steelers to league-leading 14-2 mark. Set team record with 28 TD passes.
1979	Earl Campbell	RB	Houston Oilers	Led league with 1,697 rushing yards and 19 touchdowns.
1980	Brian Sipe	QB	Cleveland Browns	NFL-best 91.4 passer rating. Set Browns' records with 30 TD passes and 4,132 yards.
1981	Ken Anderson	QB	Cincinnati Bengals	Led Bengals to first division title since 1973. NFL-high 98.5 passer rating.
1982	Mark Moseley	K	Washington Redskins	Converted 20 of 21 FGs. Set then consecutive field-goal record at 23 (including last three in '81).
1983	Joe Theismann	QB	Washington Redskins	Leader of offense that scored then-NFL record 541 points. Redskins had NFL-best 14-2 record.
1984	Dan Marino	QB	Miami Dolphins	Set NFL records with 5,084 yards and 48 TD passes. Led Dolphins to AFC-best 14-2 mark.
1985	Marcus Allen	RB	Los Angeles Raiders	Rushed for league-leading 1,759 yards. Tied for AFC lead with 11 rushing touchdowns.
1986	Lawrence Taylor	LB	New York Giants	Recorded league-high 20.5 sacks, and led Giants' second-ranked defense (297.3).
1987	John Elway	QB	Denver Broncos	In 12 games, passed for 19 TDs and 3,198 yards, including four 300-yard games.
1988	Boomer Esiason	QB	Cincinnati Bengals	Led NFL with 97.4 passer rating. Tied for AFC lead with 28 TD passes.
1989	Joe Montana	QB	San Francisco 49ers	Set then-NFL record with 112.4 passer rating, including 70.2 completion percentage.
1990	Joe Montana	QB	San Francisco 49ers	Led 49ers to league-best 14-2 record. Completed NFC-high 61.7 percent of passes.
1991	Thurman Thomas	RB	Buffalo Bills	Recorded league-high 2,038 yards from scrimmage (1,407 rushing, 631 receiving).
1992	Steve Young	QB	San Francisco 49ers	NFL's top passer with 107.0 rating. Led 49ers to league-best 14-2 record.
1993	Emmitt Smith	RB	Dallas Cowboys	Led league in rushing (1,486 yards) for third straight year despite missing first two games.
1994	Steve Young	QB	San Francisco 49ers	Compiled NFL all-time best 112.8 passer rating. Completed more than 70 percent of his passes.
1995	Brett Favre	QB	Green Bay Packers	Led league with 38 touchdown passes and NFC with 99.5 passer rating.
1996	Brett Favre	QB	Green Bay Packers	Led Packers to top conference record (13-3). Threw NFL-best 39 TD passes.
1997	Brett Favre	QB	Green Bay Packers	Led league with 35 touchdown passes. Led NFC with 3,867 passing yards
	Barry Sanders	RB	Detroit Lions	Rushed for all-time second-best 2,053 yards, including record 14 straight 100-yard games.
1998	Terrell Davis	RB	Denver Broncos	Rushed for 2,008 yards and scored league-best 23 total touchdowns.
1999	Kurt Warner	QB	St. Louis Rams	Became the second QB in history to throw for 40 touchdowns in a season (41).
2000	Marshall Faulk	RB	St. Louis Rams	Set NFL record with 26 touchdowns and led NFC with 2,189 yards from scrimmage.

Total *Associated Press* NFL MVPs: 46
Two-time Winners: Jim Brown, Brett Favre (3), Joe Montana, Johnny Unitas, Steve Young

ASSOCIATED PRESS NFL MVP BY POSITION

Quarterback:	27	**Defensive End:**	1
Running Back:	14	**Defensive Tackle:**	1
Linebacker:	2	**Kicker:**	1

ASSOCIATED PRESS MVPs WHO WON SUPER BOWL/NFL CHAMPIONSHIP IN SAME SEASON: 15

1958	Gino Marchetti	Baltimore Colts
1960	Norm Van Brocklin	Philadelphia Eagles
1961	Paul Hornung	Green Bay Packers
1962	Jim Taylor	Green Bay Packers
1966	Bart Starr	Green Bay Packers
1968	Earl Morrall	Baltimore Colts
1978	Terry Bradshaw	Pittsburgh Steelers
1982	Mark Moseley	Washington Redskins
1986	Lawrence Taylor	New York Giants
1989	Joe Montana	San Francisco 49ers
1993	Emmitt Smith	Dallas Cowboys
1994	Steve Young	San Francisco 49ers
1996	Brett Favre	Green Bay Packers
1998	Terrell Davis	Denver Broncos
1999	Kurt Warner	St. Louis Rams

ASSOCIATED PRESS MVPs BY TEAM

6	Green Bay Packers
5	Baltimore Colts San Francisco 49ers
3	Cleveland Browns New York Giants St. Louis/Los Angeles Rams Washington Redskins
2	Buffalo Bills Cincinnati Bengals Denver Broncos Detroit Lions Minnesota Vikings Oakland/Los Angeles Raiders
1	Chicago Bears Dallas Cowboys Houston Oilers Miami Dolphins Philadelphia Eagles Pittsburgh Steelers

MILLER LITE PLAYERS OF THE YEAR

YEAR	PLAYER	POS.	TEAM
1989	Joe Montana	QB	San Francisco 49ers
1990	Joe Montana	QB	San Francisco 49ers
1991	Thurman Thomas	RB	Buffalo Bills
1992	Steve Young	QB	San Francisco 49ers
1993	Emmitt Smith	RB	Dallas Cowboys
1994	Steve Young	QB	San Francisco 49ers
1995	Brett Favre	QB	Green Bay Packers
1996	Brett Favre	QB	Green Bay Packers
1997	Barry Sanders	RB	Detroit Lions
1998	Randall Cunningham	QB	Minnesota Vikings
1999	Kurt Warner	QB	St. Louis Rams
2000	Marshall Faulk	RB	St. Louis Rams

75TH ANNIVERSARY ALL-TIME TEAM

Chosen by a selection committee of media and league personnel in 1994.

Position	Name	Team(s)	Ht.	Wt.	College
OFFENSE					
QB	Sammy Baugh	Washington Redskins (1937-52)	6-2	180	Texas Christian
QB	Otto Graham	Cleveland Browns (1946-55)	6-1	195	Northwestern
QB	Joe Montana	San Francisco 49ers (1979-92), Kansas City Chiefs (1993-94)	6-2	195	Notre Dame
QB	Johnny Unitas	Baltimore Colts (1956-72), San Diego Chargers (1973)	6-1	195	Louisville
RB	Jim Brown	Cleveland Browns (1957-65)	6-2	232	Syracuse
RB	Marion Motley	Cleveland Browns (1946-53), Pittsburgh Steelers (1955)	6-1	238	Nevada-Reno
RB	Bronko Nagurski	Chicago Bears (1930-37, 1943)	6-2	225	Minnesota
RB	Walter Payton	Chicago Bears (1975-87)	5-10	202	Jackson State
RB	Gale Sayers	Chicago Bears (1965-71)	6-0	200	Kansas
RB	O.J. Simpson	Buffalo Bills (1969-77), San Francisco 49ers (1978-79)	6-1	212	Southern California
RB	Steve Van Buren	Philadelphia Eagles (1944-51)	6-1	200	Louisiana State
WR	Lance Alworth	San Diego Chargers (1962-70), Dallas Cowboys (1971-72)	6-0	184	Arkansas
WR	Raymond Berry	Baltimore Colts (1955-67)	6-2	187	Southern Methodist
WR	Don Hutson	Green Bay Packers (1935-45)	6-1	180	Alabama
WR	Jerry Rice	San Francisco 49ers (1985-present)	6-2	200	Miss. Valley State
TE	Mike Ditka	Chicago Bears (1961-66), Philadelphia Eagles (1967-68), Dallas Cowboys (1969-72)	6-3	225	Pittsburgh
TE	Kellen Winslow	San Diego Chargers (1979-87)	6-5	250	Missouri
T	Roosevelt Brown	New York Giants (1953-65)	6-3	255	Morgan State
T	Forrest Gregg	Green Bay Packers (1956, 1958-70)	6-4	250	Southern Methodist
T	Anthony Muñoz	Cincinnati Bengals (1980-92)	6-6	285	Southern California
G	John Hannah	New England Patriots (1973-85)	6-3	265	Alabama
G	Jim Parker	Baltimore Colts (1957-67)	6-3	273	Ohio State
G	Gene Upshaw	Oakland Raiders (1967-81)	6-5	255	Texas A&I
C	Mel Hein	New York Giants (1931-45)	6-2	225	Washington State
C	Mike Webster	Pittsburgh Steelers (1974-88), Kansas City Chiefs (1989-90)	6-2	250	Wisconsin
DEFENSE					
DE	David (Deacon) Jones	Los Angeles Rams (1961-71), San Diego Chargers (1972-73), Washington Redskins (1974)	6-5	250	Miss. Vocational
DE	Gino Marchetti	Dallas Texans (1952), Baltimore Colts (1953-64,1966)	6-4	245	San Francisco
DE	Reggie White	Philadelphia Eagles (1985-95), Green Bay Packers (1993-present)	6-5	290	Tennessee
DT	Joe Greene	Pittsburgh Steelers (1969-81)	6-4	260	North Texas State
DT	Bob Lilly	Dallas Cowboys (1961-74)	6-5	260	Texas Christian
DT	Merlin Olsen	Los Angeles Rams (1962-76)	6-5	270	Utah State
LB	Dick Butkus	Chicago Bears (1965-73)	6-3	245	Illinois
LB	Jack Ham	Pittsburgh Steelers (1971-82)	6-1	225	Penn State
LB	Ted Hendricks	Baltimore Colts (1969-73), Green Bay Packers (1974), Oakland/L.A. Raiders (1975-83)	6-7	235	Miami
LB	Jack Lambert	Pittsburgh Steelers (1974-84)	6-4	220	Kent State
LB	Willie Lanier	Kansas City Chiefs (1967-77)	6-1	245	Morgan State
LB	Ray Nitschke	Green Bay Packers (1958-72)	6-3	235	Illinois
LB	Lawrence Taylor	New York Giants (1981-93)	6-3	243	North Carolina
CB	Mel Blount	Pittsburgh Steelers (1970-83)	6-3	205	Southern
CB	Mike Haynes	New England Patriots (1976-82), Los Angeles Raiders (1983-89)	6-2	190	Arizona State
CB	Dick (Night Train) Lane	Los Angeles Rams (1952-53), Chicago Cardinals (1954-59), Detroit Lions (1960-65)	6-2	210	Scottsbluff JC
CB	Rod Woodson	Pittsburgh Steelers (1987-96), San Francisco 49ers (1997)	6-0	200	Purdue
S	Ken Houston	Houston Oilers (1967-72), Washington Redskins (1973-80)	6-3	198	Prairie View A&M
S	Ronnie Lott	San Francisco 49ers (1981-90), Los Angeles Raiders (1991-92), New York Jets (1993-94)	6-0	200	Southern California
S	Larry Wilson	St. Louis Cardinals (1960-72)	6-0	190	Utah
SPECIAL TEAMS					
P	Ray Guy	Oakland/L.A. Raiders (1973-86)	6-3	190	Southern Miss.
K	Jan Stenerud	Kansas City Chiefs (1967-79), Green Bay Packers (1980-83), Minnesota Vikings (1984-85)	6-2	190	Montana State
PR	Billy (White Shoes) Johnson	Houston Oilers (1974-80), Atlanta Falcons (1982-87), Washington Redskins (1988)	5-9	170	Widener
KR	Gale Sayers	Chicago Bears (1965-71)	6-0	200	Kansas

ALL-TIME NFL TEAMS

75TH ANNIVERSARY ALL-TWO-WAY TEAM

Positions	
Quarterback, Defensive Halfback, Punter	Sammy Baugh
Center, Linebacker	Chuck Bednarik
Quarterback, Defensive Halfback, Punter	Earl (Dutch) Clark
Tackle, Defensive Tackle	George Connor
Guard, Defensive Tackle	Danny Fortmann
Center, Defensive Tackle	Mel Hein
Tackle, Defensive Tackle, Punter	Wilbur (Pete) Henry
Back, Defensive Halfback	Bill Hewitt
Fullback, Linebacker, Kicker	Clarke Hinkle
Tackle, Defensive Tackle	Cal Hubbard
End, Defensive Halfback	Don Hutson
Back, Defensive Back	George McAfee
Fullback, Linebacker	Marion Motley
Guard-Tackle, Defensive Tackle	George Musso
Fullback, Linebacker	Bronko Nagurski
Halfback, Defensive Halfback	Ernie Nevers
End, Defensive Back	Pete Pihos
Tackle, Defensive Tackle	Joe Stydahar
Running Back, Defensive Back	Steve Van Buren

50TH ANNIVERSARY TEAM

Chosen by the Hall of Fame Selection Committee in 1969.

Offense

Split End	Don Hutson
Tight End	John Mackey
Tackle	Cal Hubbard
Guard	Jerry Kramer
Center	Chuck Bednarik
Flanker	Elroy Hirsch
Quarterback	Johnny Unitas
Halfback	Jim Thorpe
Halfback	Gale Sayers
Fullback	Jim Brown
Kicker	Lou Groza

Defense

End	Gino Marchetti
Tackle	Leo Nomellini
Linebacker	Ray Nitschke
Cornerback	Dick (Night Train) Lane
Safety	Emlen Tunnell

SUPER BOWL SILVER ANNIVERSARY TEAM

Chosen by the fans in 1990 prior to Super Bowl XXV.

Head Coach — Vince Lombardi

Offense

Quarterback	Joe Montana
Running Back	Franco Harris
Running Back	Larry Csonka
Wide Receiver	Lynn Swann
Wide Receiver	Jerry Rice
Tight End	Dave Casper
Tackle	Art Shell
Tackle	Forrest Gregg
Guard	Gene Upshaw
Guard	Jerry Kramer
Center	Mike Webster

Defense

Defensive End	L.C. Greenwood
Defensive End	Ed (Too Tall) Jones
Defensive Tackle	Joe Greene
Defensive Tackle	Randy White
Inside Linebacker	Jack Lambert
Inside Linebacker	Mike Singletary
Outside Linebacker	Jack Ham
Outside Linebacker	Ted Hendricks
Cornerback	Ronnie Lott
Cornerback	Mel Blount
Safety	Donnie Shell
Safety	Willie Wood

Special Teams

Punter	Ray Guy
Kicker	Jan Stenerud
Kick Returner	John Taylor

All-Decade teams chosen by the Hall of Fame Selection Committee Members.

1920s ALL-DECADE TEAM

End	Guy Chamberlin
End	Lavern Dilweg
End	George Halas
Tackle	Ed Healey
Tackle	Wilbur (Pete) Henry
Tackle	Cal Hubbard
Tackle	Steve Owen
Guard	Hunk Anderson
Guard	Walt Kiesling
Guard	Mike Michalske
Center	George Trafton
Quarterback	Jimmy Conzelman
Quarterback	John (Paddy) Driscoll
Halfback	Harold (Red) Grange
Halfback	Joe Guyon
Halfback	Earl (Curly) Lambeau
Halfback	Jim Thorpe
Fullback	Ernie Nevers

1930s ALL-DECADE TEAM

End	Bill Hewitt
End	Don Hutson
End	Wayne Millner
End	Gaynell Tinsley
Tackle	George Christensen
Tackle	Frank Cope
Tackle	Glen (Turk) Edwards
Tackle	Bill Lee
Tackle	Joe Stydahar
Guard	Grover (Ox) Emerson
Guard	Dan Fortmann
Guard	Charles (Buckets) Goldenberg
Guard	Russ Letlow
Center	Mel Hein
Center	George Svendsen
Quarterback	Earl (Dutch) Clark
Quarterback	Arnie Herber
Quarterback	Cecil Isbell
Halfback	Cliff Battles
Halfback	Johnny (Blood) McNally
Halfback	Beattie Feathers
Halfback	Alphonse (Tuffy) Leemans
Halfback	Ken Strong
Fullback	Clarke Hinkle
Fullback	Bronko Nagurski

1940s ALL-DECADE TEAM

End	Jim Benton
End	Jack Ferrante
End	Ken Kavanaugh
End	Dante Lavelli
End	Pete Pihos
End	Mac Speedie
End	Ed Sprinkle
Tackle	Al Blozis
Tackle	George Connor
Tackle	Frank (Bucko) Kilroy
Tackle	Buford (Baby) Ray
Tackle	Vic Sears
Tackle	Al Wistert
Guard	Bruno Banducci
Guard	Bill Edwards
Guard	Garrard (Buster) Ramsey
Guard	Bill Willis
Guard	Len Younce
Center	Charley Brock
Center	Clyde (Bulldog) Turner
Center	Alex Wojciechowicz
Quarterback	Sammy Baugh
Quarterback	Sid Luckman
Quarterback	Bob Waterfield
Halfback	Tony Canadeo
Halfback	Bill Dudley
Halfback	George McAfee
Halfback	Charley Trippi
Halfback	Steve Van Buren
Halfback	Byron (Whizzer) White
Fullback	Pat Harder
Fullback	Marion Motley
Fullback	Bill Osmanski

1950s ALL-DECADE TEAM

Offense

End	Raymond Berry
End	Tom Fears
End	Bobby Walston
Halfback-End	Elroy (Crazylegs) Hirsch
Tackle	Roosevelt Brown
Tackle	Bob St. Clair
Guard	Dick Barwegan
Guard	Jim Parker
Guard	Dick Stanfel
Center	Chuck Bednarik
Quarterback	Otto Graham
Quarterback	Bobby Layne
Quarterback	Norm Van Brocklin
Halfback	Frank Gifford
Halfback	Ollie Matson
Halfback	Hugh McElhenny
Halfback	Lenny Moore
Fullback	Alan Ameche
Fullback	Joe Perry
Kicker	Lou Groza

Defense

End	Len Ford
End	Gino Marchetti
Tackle	Art Donovan
Tackle	Leo Nomellini
Tackle	Ernie Stautner
Linebacker	Joe Fortunato
Linebacker	Bill George
Linebacker	Sam Huff
Linebacker	Joe Schmidt
Halfback	Jack Butler
Halfback	Dick (Night Train) Lane
Safety	Jack Christiansen
Safety	Yale Lary
Safety	Emlen Tunnell

1960s ALL-DECADE TEAM

Offense

Split End	Del Shofner
Split End	Charley Taylor
Flanker	Gary Collins
Flanker	Boyd Dowler
Tight End	John Mackey
Tackle	Bob Brown
Tackle	Forrest Gregg
Tackle	Ralph Neely
Guard	Gene Hickerson
Guard	Jerry Kramer
Guard	Howard Mudd
Center	Jim Ringo
Quarterback	Sonny Jurgensen
Quarterback	Bart Starr
Quarterback	Johnny Unitas
Halfback	John David Crow
Halfback	Paul Hornung
Halfback	Leroy Kelly
Halfback	Gale Sayers
Fullback	Jim Brown
Fullback	Jim Taylor
Kicker	Jim Bakken

Defense

End	Doug Atkins
End	Willie Davis
End	David (Deacon) Jones
Tackle	Alex Karras
Tackle	Bob Lilly
Tackle	Merlin Olsen
Linebacker	Dick Butkus
Linebacker	Larry Morris
Linebacker	Ray Nitschke
Linebacker	Tommy Nobis
Linebacker	Dave Robinson
Cornerback	Herb Adderley
Cornerback	Lem Barney
Cornerback	Bobby Boyd
Safety	Eddie Meador
Safety	Larry Wilson
Safety	Willie Wood
Punter	Don Chandler

ALL-TIME NFL TEAMS

1970s ALL-DECADE TEAM

Offense

Wide Receiver	Harold Carmichael
Wide Receiver	Drew Pearson
Wide Receiver	Lynn Swann
Wide Receiver	Paul Warfield
Tight End	Dave Casper
Tight End	Charlie Sanders
Tackle	Dan Dierdorf
Tackle	Art Shell
Tackle	Rayfield Wright
Tackle	Ron Yary
Guard	Joe DeLamielleure
Guard	John Hannah
Guard	Larry Little
Guard	Gene Upshaw
Center	Jim Langer
Center	Mike Webster
Quarterback	Terry Bradshaw
Quarterback	Ken Stabler
Quarterback	Roger Staubach
Running Back	Earl Campbell
Running Back	Franco Harris
Running Back	Walter Payton
Running Back	O.J. Simpson
Kicker	Garo Yepremian

Defense

End	Carl Eller
End	L.C. Greenwood
End	Harvey Martin
End	Jack Youngblood
Tackle	Joe Greene
Tackle	Bob Lilly
Tackle	Merlin Olsen
Tackle	Alan Page
Linebacker	Bobby Bell
Linebacker	Robert Brazile
Linebacker	Dick Butkus
Linebacker	Jack Ham
Linebacker	Ted Hendricks
Linebacker	Jack Lambert
Cornerback	Willie Brown
Cornerback	Jimmy Johnson
Cornerback	Roger Wehrli
Cornerback	Louis Wright
Safety	Dick Anderson
Safety	Cliff Harris
Safety	Ken Houston
Safety	Larry Wilson
Punter	Ray Guy

1980s ALL-DECADE TEAM

Offense

Wide Receiver	Jerry Rice
Wide Receiver	Steve Largent
Wide Receiver	James Lofton
Wide Receiver	Art Monk
Tight End	Kellen Winslow
Tight End	Ozzie Newsome
Tackle	Anthony Munoz
Tackle	Jim Covert
Tackle	Gary Zimmerman
Tackle	Joe Jacoby
Guard	John Hannah
Guard	Russ Grimm
Guard	Bill Fralic
Guard	Mike Munchak
Center	Dwight Stephenson
Center	Mike Webster
Quarterback	Joe Montana
Quarterback	Dan Fouts
Running Back	Walter Payton
Running Back	Eric Dickerson
Running Back	Roger Craig
Running Back	John Riggins

Defense

End	Reggie White
End	Howie Long
End	Lee Roy Selmon
End	Bruce Smith
Tackle	Randy White
Tackle	Dan Hampton
Tackle	Keith Millard
Tackle	Dave Butz
Linebacker	Mike Singletary
Linebacker	Lawrence Taylor
Linebacker	Ted Hendricks
Linebacker	Jack Lambert
Linebacker	Andre Tippett
Linebacker	John Anderson
Linebacker	Carl Banks
Cornerback	Mike Haynes
Cornerback	Mel Blount
Cornerback	Frank Minnifield
Cornerback	Lester Hayes
Safety	Ronnie Lott
Safety	Kenny Easley
Safety	Deron Cherry
Safety	Joey Browner
Safety	Nolan Cromwell

Specialists

Punter	Sean Landeta
Punter	Reggie Roby
Kicker	Morten Andersen
Kicker	Gary Anderson
Kicker	Eddie Murray
Punt Returner	Billy (White Shoes) Johnson
Punt Returner	John Taylor
Kick Returner	Mike Nelms
Kick Returner	Rick Upchurch
Coach	Bill Walsh
Coach	Chuck Noll

1990s ALL-DECADE TEAM

Offense

Wide Receiver	Cris Carter
Wide Receiver	Jerry Rice
Wide Receiver	Tim Brown
Wide Receiver	Michael Irvin
Tight End	Shannon Sharpe
Tight End	Ben Coates
Tackle	William Roaf
Tackle	Gary Zimmerman
Tackle	Tony Boselli
Tackle	Richmond Webb
Guard	Bruce Matthews
Guard	Randall McDaniel
Guard	Larry Allen
Guard	Steve Wisniewski
Center	Dermontti Dawson
Center	Mark Stepnoski
Quarterback	John Elway
Quarterback	Brett Favre
Running Back	Barry Sanders
Running Back	Emmitt Smith
Running Back	Terrell Davis
Running Back	Thurman Thomas

Defense

End	Bruce Smith
End	Reggie White
End	Chris Doleman
End	Neil Smith
Tackle	Cortez Kennedy
Tackle	John Randle
Tackle	Warren Sapp
Tackle	Bryant Young
Linebacker	Kevin Greene
Linebacker	Junior Seau
Linebacker	Derrick Thomas
Linebacker	Cornelius Bennett
Linebacker	Hardy Nickerson
Linebacker	Levon Kirkland
Cornerback	Deion Sanders
Cornerback	Rod Woodson
Cornerback	Darrell Green
Cornerback	Aeneas Williams
Safety	Steve Atwater
Safety	LeRoy Butler
Safety	Carnell Lake
Safety	Ronnie Lott

Specialists

Punter	Darren Bennett
Punter	Sean Landeta
Kicker	Morten Andersen
Kicker	Gary Anderson
Punt Returner	Deion Sanders
Punt Returner	Mel Gray
Kick Returner	Michael Bates
Kick Returner	Mel Gray
Coach	Bill Parcells
Coach	Marv Levy

ALL-TIME AFL TEAM

Chosen by 1969 AFL Hall of Fame Selection Committee members.

Offense

Flanker	Lance Alworth
End	Don Maynard
Tight End	Fred Arbanas
Tackle	Ron Mix
Tackle	Jim Tyrer
Guard	Ed Budde
Guard	Billy Shaw
Center	Jim Otto
Quarterback	Joe Namath
Running Back	Clem Daniels
Running Back	Paul Lowe

Defense

End	Jerry Mays
End	Gerry Philbin
Tackle	Houston Antwine
Tackle	Tom Sestak
Linebacker	Bobby Bell
Linebacker	George Webster
Linebacker	Nick Buoniconti
Cornerback	Willie Brown
Cornerback	Dave Grayson
Safety	Johnny Robinson
Safety	George Saimes

Special Teams

Kicker	George Blanda
Punter	Jerrel Wilson

ALL-TIME NFL TEAM

Chosen by members of the Hall of Fame Selection Committee in 2000 for the book NFL's Greatest.

Offense

Wide Receiver	Don Hutson
Wide Receiver	Jerry Rice
Tight End	John Mackey
Tackle	Roosevelt Brown
Tackle	Anthony Muñoz
Guard	John Hannah
Guard	Jim Parker
Center	Mike Webster
Quarterback	Johnny Unitas
Running Back	Jim Brown
Running Back	Walter Payton

Defense

End	Deacon Jones
End	Reggie White
Tackle	Joe Greene
Tackle	Bob Lilly
Middle Linebacker	Dick Butkus
Outside Linebacker	Jack Ham
Outside Linebacker	Lawrence Taylor
Cornerback	Mel Blount
Cornerback	Dick (Night Train) Lane
Safety	Ronnie Lott
Safety	Larry Wilson

Special Teams

Kicker	Jan Stenerud
Punter	Ray Guy
Kick Returner	Gale Sayers
Punt Returner	Deion Sanders
Special Teams	Steve Tasker

AFL-NFL 1960-1984 ALL-STAR TEAM

Chosen by the Hall of Fame Selection Committee in 1985.

Offense

Quarterback	Johnny Unitas
Running Back	Jim Brown
Running Back	O.J. Simpson
Wide Receiver	Lance Alworth
Wide Receiver	Raymond Berry
Tight End	Kellen Winslow
Tight End	Forrest Gregg
Tight End	Ron Mix
Guard	Jim Parker
Guard	John Hannah
Center	Jim Otto

Defense

End	Gino Marchetti
End	Willie Davis
Tackle	Bob Lilly
Tackle	Merlin Olsen
Linebacker	Dick Butkus
Linebacker	Jack Lambert
Linebacker	Ray Nitschke
Cornerback	Willie Brown
Cornerback	Dick (Night Train) Lane
Safety	Larry Wilson
Safety	Yale Lary

Special Teams

Punter	Ray Guy
Kicker	Jan Stenerud
Kick Returner	Gale Sayers
Kick Returner	Rick Upchurch
Coach	Don Shula
Coach	Vince Lombardi

Records

ALL-TIME RECORDS

Compiled by Elias Sports Bureau

The following records reflect all available official information on the National Football League from its formation in 1920 to date. Also included are all applicable records from the American Football League, 1960-69.

Individuals eligible for Rookie records are players who were in their first season of professional football and had not been on the roster of another professional football team, including teams in other leagues, for any regular-season or postseason games in a previous season. Eligible players, therefore, include those who were under contract to a National Football League club for a previous season but were terminated prior to their club's first regular-season game and not re-signed, or who were placed on Reserve/Injured (or another category of the Reserve List) prior to their club's first regular-season game and were not activated during the rest of the regular season or postseason.

INDIVIDUAL RECORDS

SERVICE

Most Seasons

26 George Blanda, Chi. Bears, 1949, 1950-58; Baltimore, 1950; Houston, 1960-66; Oakland, 1967-1975
21 Earl Morrall, San Francisco, 1956; Pittsburgh, 1957-58; Detroit, 1958-1964; N.Y. Giants, 1965-67; Baltimore, 1968-1971; Miami, 1972-76
20 Jim Marshall, Cleveland, 1960; Minnesota, 1961-1979
Jackie Slater, L.A. Rams, 1976-1994; St. Louis, 1995

Most Seasons, One Club

20 Jackie Slater, L.A. Rams, 1976-1994; St. Louis, 1995
19 Jim Marshall, Minnesota, 1961-1979
18 Jim Hart, St. Louis, 1966-1983
Jeff Van Note, Atlanta, 1969-1986
Pat Leahy, N.Y. Jets, 1974-1991
Darrell Green, Washington, 1983-2000
Bruce Matthews, Houston, 1983-1996; Tennessee, 1997-2000

Most Games Played, Career

340 George Blanda, Chi. Bears, 1949, 1950-58; Baltimore, 1950; Houston, 1960-66; Oakland, 1967-1975
293 Gary Anderson, Pittsburgh, 1982-1994; Philadelphia, 1995-96; San Francisco, 1997; Minnesota, 1998-2000
292 Morten Andersen, New Orleans, 1982-1994; Atlanta, 1995-2000

Most Consecutive Games Played, Career

282 Jim Marshall, Cleveland, 1960; Minnesota, 1961-1979
240 Mick Tingelhoff, Minnesota, 1962-1978
234 Jim Bakken, St. Louis, 1962-1978

SCORING

Most Seasons Leading League

5 Don Hutson, Green Bay, 1940-44
Gino Cappelletti, Boston, 1961, 1963-66
3 Earl (Dutch) Clark, Portsmouth, 1932; Detroit, 1935-36
Pat Harder, Chi. Cardinals, 1947-49
Paul Hornung, Green Bay, 1959-1961
2 Jack Manders, Chi. Bears, 1934, 1937
Gordy Soltau, San Francisco, 1952-53
Doak Walker, Detroit, 1950, 1955
Gene Mingo, Denver, 1960, 1962
Jim Turner, N.Y. Jets, 1968-69
Fred Cox, Minnesota, 1969-1970
Chester Marcol, Green Bay, 1972, 1974
John Smith, New England, 1979-1980

Most Consecutive Seasons Leading League

5 Don Hutson, Green Bay, 1940-44
4 Gino Cappelletti, Boston, 1963-66
3 Pat Harder, Chi. Cardinals, 1947-49
Paul Hornung, Green Bay, 1959-1961

POINTS

Most Points, Career

2,059 Gary Anderson, Pittsburgh, 1982-1994; Philadelphia, 1995-96; San Francisco, 1997; Minnesota, 1998-2000 (676-pat, 461-fg)
2,002 George Blanda, Chi. Bears, 1949, 1950-58; Baltimore, 1950; Houston, 1960-66; Oakland, 1967-1975 (9-td, 943-pat, 335-fg)
1,938 Morten Andersen, New Orleans, 1982-1994; Atlanta, 1995-2000 (615-pat, 441-fg)

Most Points, Season

176 Paul Hornung, Green Bay, 1960 (15-td, 41-pat, 15-fg)
164 Gary Anderson, Minnesota, 1998 (59-pat, 35-fg)
161 Mark Moseley, Washington, 1983 (62-pat, 33-fg)

Most Points, No Touchdowns, Season

164 Gary Anderson, Minnesota, 1998 (59-pat, 35-fg)
161 Mark Moseley, Washington, 1983 (62-pat, 33-fg)
149 Chip Lohmiller, Washington, 1991 (56-pat, 31-fg)

Most Seasons, 100 or More Points

13 Gary Anderson, Pittsburgh, 1983-85, 1988, 1991-94; Philadelphia, 1996; San Francisco, 1997; Minnesota, 1998-2000
12 Morten Andersen, New Orleans, 1985-89, 1991-94; Atlanta, 1995, 1997-98
11 Nick Lowery, Kansas City, 1981, 1983-86, 1988-1993

Most Points, Rookie, Season

144 Kevin Butler, Chicago, 1985 (51-pat, 31-fg)
132 Gale Sayers, Chicago, 1965 (22-td)
128 Doak Walker, Detroit, 1950 (11-td, 38-pat, 8-fg)
Chester Marcol, Green Bay, 1972 (29-pat, 33-fg)

Most Points, Game

40 Ernie Nevers, Chi. Cardinals vs. Chi. Bears, Nov. 28, 1929 (6-td, 4-pat)
36 Dub Jones, Cleveland vs. Chi. Bears, Nov. 25, 1951 (6-td)
Gale Sayers, Chicago vs. San Francisco, Dec. 12, 1965 (6-td)
33 Paul Hornung, Green Bay vs. Baltimore, Oct. 8, 1961 (4-td, 6-pat, 1-fg)

Most Consecutive Games Scoring

270 Morten Andersen, New Orleans, 1982-1994; Atlanta, 1995-2000 (current)
186 Jim Breech, Oakland, 1979; Cincinnati, 1980-1992
155 Ray Wersching, San Francisco, 1977-1987

TOUCHDOWNS

Most Seasons Leading League

8 Don Hutson, Green Bay, 1935-38, 1941-44
3 Jim Brown, Cleveland, 1958-59, 1963
Lance Alworth, San Diego, 1964-66
Emmitt Smith, Dallas, 1992, 1994-95
2 By many players

Most Consecutive Seasons Leading League

4 Don Hutson, Green Bay, 1935-38, 1941-44
3 Lance Alworth, San Diego, 1964-66
2 By many players

Most Touchdowns, Career

187 Jerry Rice, San Francisco, 1985-2000 (10-r, 176-p, 1-ret)
156 Emmitt Smith, Dallas, 1990-2000 (145-r, 11-p)
145 Marcus Allen, L.A. Raiders, 1982-1992; Kansas City, 1993-97 (123-r, 21-p, 1-ret)

Most Touchdowns, Season

26 Marshall Faulk, St. Louis, 2000 (18-r, 8-p)
25 Emmitt Smith, Dallas, 1995 (25-r)
24 John Riggins, Washington, 1983 (24-r)

Most Touchdowns, Rookie, Season

22 Gale Sayers, Chicago, 1965 (14-r, 6-p, 2-ret)
20 Eric Dickerson, L.A. Rams, 1983 (18-r, 2-p)
17 Randy Moss, Minnesota, 1998 (17-p)
Fred Taylor, Jacksonville, 1998 (14-r, 3-p)
Edgerrin James, Indianapolis, 1999 (13-r, 4-p)

Most Touchdowns, Game

6 Ernie Nevers, Chi. Cardinals vs. Chi. Bears, Nov. 28, 1929 (6-r)
Dub Jones, Cleveland vs. Chi. Bears, Nov. 25, 1951 (4-r, 2-p)
Gale Sayers, Chicago vs. San Francisco, Dec. 12, 1965 (4-r, 1-p, 1-ret)
5 Bob Shaw, Chi. Cardinals vs. Baltimore, Oct. 2, 1950 (5-p)
Jim Brown, Cleveland vs. Baltimore, Nov. 1, 1959 (5-r)
Abner Haynes, Dall. Texans vs. Oakland, Nov. 26, 1961 (4-r, 1-p)
Billy Cannon, Houston vs. N.Y. Titans, Dec. 10, 1961 (3-r, 2-p)
Cookie Gilchrist, Buffalo vs. N.Y. Jets, Dec. 8, 1963 (5-r)
Paul Hornung, Green Bay vs. Baltimore, Dec. 12, 1965 (3-r, 2-p)
Kellen Winslow, San Diego vs. Oakland, Nov. 22, 1981 (5-p)
Jerry Rice, San Francisco vs. Atlanta, Oct. 14, 1990 (5-p)
James Stewart, Jacksonville vs. Philadelphia, Oct. 12, 1997 (5-r)
4 By many players. Last time: Marshall Faulk, St. Louis vs. Tampa Bay, Dec. 18, 2000 (3-r, 1-p)

Most Consecutive Games Scoring Touchdowns

18 Lenny Moore, Baltimore, 1963-65
14 O.J. Simpson, Buffalo, 1975
13 John Riggins, Washington, 1982-83
George Rogers, Washington, 1985-86
Jerry Rice, San Francisco, 1986-87

POINTS AFTER TOUCHDOWN

Most Seasons Leading League

8 George Blanda, Chi. Bears, 1956; Houston, 1961-62; Oakland, 1967-69, 1972, 1974
4 Bob Waterfield, Cleveland, 1945; Los Angeles, 1946, 1950, 1952
3 Earl (Dutch) Clark, Portsmouth, 1932; Detroit, 1935-36
Jack Manders, Chi. Bears, 1933-35
Don Hutson, Green Bay, 1941-42, 1945

Most (Kicking) Points After Touchdown Attempted, Career

959 George Blanda, Chi. Bears, 1949, 1950-58; Baltimore, 1950; Houston, 1960-66; Oakland, 1967-1975
681 Gary Anderson, Pittsburgh, 1982-1994; Philadelphia, 1995-96; San Francisco, 1997; Minnesota, 1998-2000
657 Lou Groza, Cleveland, 1950-59, 1961-67

Most (Kicking) Points After Touchdown Attempted, Season
70 Uwe von Schamann, Miami, 1984
65 George Blanda, Houston, 1961
64 Jeff Wilkins, St. Louis, 1999

Most (Kicking) Points After Touchdown Attempted, Game
10 Charlie Gogolak, Washington vs. N.Y. Giants, Nov. 27, 1966
9 Pat Harder, Chi. Cardinals vs. N.Y. Giants, Oct. 17, 1948; vs. N.Y. Bulldogs, Nov. 13, 1949
Bob Waterfield, Los Angeles vs. Baltimore, Oct. 22, 1950
Bob Thomas, Chicago vs. Green Bay, Dec. 7, 1980
8 By many players

Most (One-Point) Points After Touchdown, Career
943 George Blanda, Chi. Bears, 1949, 1950-58; Baltimore, 1950; Houston, 1960-66; Oakland, 1967-1975
676 Gary Anderson, Pittsburgh, 1982-1994; Philadelphia, 1995-96; San Francisco, 1997; Minnesota, 1998-2000
641 Lou Groza, Cleveland, 1950-59, 1961-67

Most (One-Point) Points After Touchdown, Season
66 Uwe von Schamann, Miami, 1984
64 George Blanda, Houston, 1961
Jeff Wilkins, St. Louis, 1999
62 Mark Moseley, Washington, 1983

Most (One-Point) Points After Touchdown, Game
9 Pat Harder, Chi. Cardinals vs. N.Y. Giants, Oct. 17, 1948
Bob Waterfield, Los Angeles vs. Baltimore, Oct. 22, 1950
Charlie Gogolak, Washington vs. N.Y. Giants, Nov. 27, 1966
8 By many players

Most Consecutive (Kicking) Points After Touchdown
313 Jason Elam, Denver, 1993-2000 (current)
301 Norm Johnson, Atlanta, 1991-94; Pittsburgh, 1995-98; Philadelphia, 1999
250 Eddie Murray, Detroit, 1988-1991; Kansas City, 1992; Tampa Bay, 1992; Dallas, 1993; Philadelphia, 1994; Washington, 1995; Minnesota, 1997

Highest (Kicking) Points After Touchdown Percentage, Career (200 points after touchdown)
100.00 Todd Peterson, Arizona, 1994; Seattle, 1995-99; Kansas City, 2000 (206-206)
99.70 Jason Elam, Denver, 1993-2000 (338-337)
99.53 Mike Hollis, Jacksonville, 1995-2000 (211-210)

Most (Kicking) Points After Touchdown, No Misses, Season
64 Jeff Wilkins, St. Louis, 1999
59 Gary Anderson, Minnesota, 1998
58 Jason Elam, Denver, 1998

Most (Kicking) Points After Touchdown, No Misses, Game
9 Pat Harder, Chi. Cardinals vs. N.Y. Giants, Oct. 17, 1948
Bob Waterfield, Los Angeles vs. Baltimore, Oct. 22, 1950
8 By many players

Most Two-Point Conversions, Career
Two-point conversion records include AFL (1960-69) and NFL (since 1994).
6 Terance Mathis, Atlanta, 1994-2000
5 Cris Carter, Minnesota, 1994-2000
Rob Moore, N.Y. Jets, 1994; Arizona, 1995-99
4 Gino Cappelletti, Boston, 1960-69
Jerry Rice, San Francisco, 1994-2000
Lamar Smith, Seattle, 1994-97; New Orleans, 1998-99; Miami, 2000
Floyd Turner, Indianapolis, 1994-95; Baltimore, 1996, 1998
Marvin Harrison, Indianapolis, 1996-2000
Willie Jackson, Jacksonville, 1995-97; Cincinnati, 1998-99; New Orleans, 2000
Keenan McCardell, Cleveland, 1994-95; Jacksonville, 1996-2000
Jackie Harris, Tampa Bay, 1994-97; Tennessee, 1998-99; Dallas, 2000
Marcus Pollard, Indianapolis, 1995-2000

Most Two-Point Conversions, Season
3 Gino Cappelletti, Boston, 1960
Richie Lucas, Buffalo, 1961
Ronnie Harmon, San Diego, 1994
Haywood Jeffires, Houston, 1994
Tom Tupa, Cleveland, 1994
Terance Mathis, Atlanta, 1995
Lamar Smith, Seattle, 1996
Cris Carter, Minnesota, 1997
Terrell Davis, Denver, 1997
James Stewart, Detroit, 2000
2 By many players

Most Two-Point Conversions, Game
2 Brett Perriman, Detroit vs. Green Bay, Nov. 6, 1994
Michael Jackson, Baltimore vs. New England, Oct. 6, 1996
Terrell Davis, Denver vs. Atlanta, Sept. 28, 1997
Charles Johnson, Pittsburgh vs. Tennessee, Nov. 1, 1998
Marshall Faulk, St. Louis vs. Atlanta, Oct. 15, 2000

FIELD GOALS

Most Seasons Leading League
5 Lou Groza, Cleveland, 1950, 1952-54, 1957
4 Jack Manders, Chi. Bears, 1933-34, 1936-37
Ward Cuff, N.Y. Giants, 1938-39, 1943; Green Bay, 1947
Mark Moseley, Washington, 1976-77, 1979, 1982
3 Bob Waterfield, Los Angeles, 1947, 1949, 1951
Gino Cappelletti, Boston, 1961, 1963-64
Fred Cox, Minnesota, 1965, 1969-1970
Jan Stenerud, Kansas City, 1967, 1970, 1975

Most Consecutive Seasons Leading League
3 Lou Groza, Cleveland, 1952-54
2 Jack Manders, Chi. Bears, 1933-34
Armand Niccolai, Pittsburgh, 1935-36
Jack Manders, Chi. Bears, 1936-37
Ward Cuff, N.Y. Giants, 1938-39
Clark Hinkle, Green Bay, 1940-41
Cliff Patton, Philadelphia, 1948-49
Gino Cappelletti, Boston, 1963-64
Jim Turner, N.Y. Jets, 1968-69
Fred Cox, Minnesota, 1969-1970
Mark Moseley, Washington, 1976-77
Chip Lohmiller, Washington, 1991-92
Pete Stoyanovich, Miami, 1991-92

Most Field Goals Attempted, Career
637 George Blanda, Chi. Bears, 1949, 1950-58; Baltimore, 1950; Houston, 1960-66; Oakland, 1967-1975
578 Gary Anderson, Pittsburgh, 1982-1994; Philadelphia, 1995-96; San Francisco, 1997; Minnesota, 1998-2000
562 Morten Andersen, New Orleans, 1982-1994; Atlanta, 1995-2000

Most Field Goals Attempted, Season
49 Bruce Gossett, Los Angeles, 1966
Curt Knight, Washington, 1971
48 Chester Marcol, Green Bay, 1972
47 Jim Turner, N.Y. Jets, 1969
David Ray, Los Angeles, 1973
Mark Moseley, Washington, 1983

Most Field Goals Attempted, Game
9 Jim Bakken, St. Louis vs. Pittsburgh, Sept. 24, 1967
8 Lou Michaels, Pittsburgh vs. St. Louis, Dec. 2, 1962
Garo Yepremian, Detroit vs. Minnesota, Nov. 13, 1966
Jim Turner, N.Y. Jets vs. Buffalo, Nov. 3, 1968
7 By many players

Most Field Goals, Career
461 Gary Anderson, Pittsburgh, 1982-1994; Philadelphia, 1995-96; San Francisco, 1997; Minnesota, 1998-2000
441 Morten Andersen, New Orleans, 1982-1994; Atlanta, 1995-2000
383 Nick Lowery, New England, 1978; Kansas City, 1980-1993; N.Y. Jets, 1994-1996

Most Field Goals, Season
39 Olindo Mare, Miami, 1999
37 John Kasay, Carolina, 1996
36 Cary Blanchard, Indianapolis, 1996
Al Del Greco, Tennessee, 1998

Most Field Goals, Rookie, Season
35 Ali Haji-Sheikh, N.Y. Giants, 1983
34 Richie Cunningham, Dallas, 1997
33 Chester Marcol, Green Bay, 1972

Most Field Goals, Game
7 Jim Bakken, St. Louis vs. Pittsburgh, Sept. 24, 1967
Rich Karlis, Minnesota vs. L.A. Rams, Nov. 5, 1989 (OT)
Chris Boniol, Dallas vs. Green Bay, Nov. 18, 1996
6 Gino Cappelletti, Boston vs. Denver, Oct. 4, 1964
Garo Yepremian, Detroit vs. Minnesota, Nov. 13, 1966
Jim Turner, N.Y. Jets vs. Buffalo, Nov. 3, 1968
Tom Dempsey, Philadelphia vs. Houston, Nov. 12, 1972
Bobby Howfield, N.Y. Jets vs. New Orleans, Dec. 3, 1972
Jim Bakken, St. Louis vs. Atlanta, Dec. 9, 1973
Joe Danelo, N.Y. Giants vs. Seattle, Oct. 18, 1981
Ray Wersching, San Francisco vs. New Orleans, Oct. 16, 1983
Gary Anderson, Pittsburgh vs. Denver, Oct. 23, 1988
John Carney, San Diego vs. Seattle, Sept. 5, 1993
John Carney, San Diego vs. Houston, Sept. 19, 1993
Doug Pelfrey, Cincinnati vs. Seattle, Nov. 6, 1994 (OT)
Norm Johnson, Atlanta vs. New Orleans, Nov. 13, 1994
Jeff Wilkins, San Francisco vs. Atlanta, Sept. 29, 1996
Steve Christie, Buffalo vs. N.Y. Jets, Oct. 20, 1996
Greg Davis, San Diego vs. Oakland, Oct. 5, 1997
Gary Anderson, Minnesota vs. Baltimore, Dec. 13, 1998
Olindo Mare, Miami vs. New England, Oct. 17, 1999
Jason Hanson, Detroit vs. Minnesota, Oct. 17, 1999
5 By many players

ALL-TIME RECORDS

Most Field Goals, One Quarter

4 Garo Yepremian, Detroit vs. Minnesota, Nov. 13, 1966 (second quarter)
Curt Knight, Washington vs. N.Y. Giants, Nov. 15, 1970 (second quarter)
Roger Ruzek, Dallas vs. N.Y. Giants, Nov. 2, 1987 (fourth quarter)
Cary Blanchard, Indianapolis vs. Buffalo, Sept. 21 1997 (second quarter)
3 By many players

Most Consecutive Games Scoring Field Goals

31 Fred Cox, Minnesota, 1968-1970
28 Jim Turner, N.Y. Jets, 1970; Denver, 1971-72
Chip Lohmiller, Washington, 1988-1990
26 Matt Stover, Baltimore, 1999-2000 (current)

Most Consecutive Field Goals

40 Gary Anderson, San Francisco, 1997; Minnesota, 1998
31 Fuad Reveiz, Minnesota, 1994-95
29 John Carney, San Diego, 1992-93

Longest Field Goal

63 Tom Dempsey, New Orleans vs. Detroit, Nov. 8, 1970
Jason Elam, Denver vs. Jacksonville, Oct. 25, 1998
60 Steve Cox, Cleveland vs. Cincinnati, Oct. 21, 1984
Morten Andersen, New Orleans vs. Chicago, Oct. 27, 1991
59 Tony Franklin, Philadelphia vs. Dallas, Nov. 12, 1979
Pete Stoyanovich, Miami vs. N.Y. Jets, Nov. 12, 1989
Steve Christie, Buffalo vs. Miami, Sept. 26, 1993
Morten Andersen, Atlanta vs. San Francisco, Dec. 24, 1995

Highest Field Goal Percentage, Career (100 field goals)

84.73 Ryan Longwell, Green Bay, 1997-2000 (131-111)
83.57 Olindo Mare, Miami, 1997-2000 (140-117)
83.07 Mike Hollis, Jacksonville, 1995-2000 (189-157)

Highest Field Goal Percentage, Season (Qualifiers)

100.00 Tony Zendejas, L.A. Rams, 1991 (17-17)
Gary Anderson, Minnesota, 1998 (35-35)
Jeff Wilkins, St. Louis, 2000 (17-17)
96.43 Chris Boniol, Dallas, 1995 (28-27)
96.30 Norm Johnson, Atlanta, 1993 (27-26)
Pete Stoyanovich, Kansas City, 1997 (27-26)

Most Field Goals, No Misses, Game

7 Rich Karlis, Minnesota vs. L.A. Rams, Nov. 5, 1989 (OT)
Chris Boniol, Dallas vs. Green Bay, Nov. 18, 1996
6 Gino Cappelletti, Boston vs. Denver, Oct. 4, 1964
Joe Danelo, N.Y. Giants vs. Seattle, Oct. 18, 1981
Ray Wersching, San Francisco vs. New Orleans, Oct. 16, 1983
Gary Anderson, Pittsburgh vs. Denver, Oct. 23, 1988
John Carney, San Diego vs. Seattle, Sept. 5, 1993
John Carney, San Diego vs. Houston, Sept. 19, 1993
Doug Pelfrey, Cincinnati vs. Seattle, Nov. 6, 1994 (OT)
Norm Johnson, Atlanta vs. New Orleans, Nov. 13, 1994
Jeff Wilkins, San Francisco vs. Atlanta, Sept. 29, 1996
Greg Davis, San Diego vs. Oakland, Oct. 5, 1997
Gary Anderson, Minnesota vs. Baltimore, Dec. 13, 1998
Olindo Mare, Miami vs. New England, Oct. 17, 1999
5 By many players

Most Field Goals, 50 or More Yards, Career

37 Morten Andersen, New Orleans, 1982-1994; Atlanta, 1995-2000
23 Jason Elam, Denver, 1993-2000
22 Nick Lowery, New England, 1978; Kansas City, 1980-1993; N.Y. Jets, 1994-96

Most Field Goals, 50 or More Yards, Season

8 Morten Andersen, Atlanta, 1995
6 Dean Biasucci, Indianapolis, 1988
Chris Jacke, Green Bay, 1993
Tony Zendejas, L.A. Rams, 1993
Mike Vanderjagt, Indianapolis, 1998
5 Fred Steinfort, Denver, 1980
Norm Johnson, Seattle, 1986
Kevin Butler, Chicago, 1993
Jason Elam, Denver, 1995
Cary Blanchard, Indianapolis, 1996
Jason Elam, Denver, 1999
Martin Gramatica, Tampa Bay, 2000

Most Field Goals, 50 or More Yards, Game

3 Morten Andersen, Atlanta vs. New Orleans, Dec. 10, 1995
2 By many players. Last time:
Paul Edinger, Chicago vs. Detroit, Dec. 24, 2000

SAFETIES

Most Safeties, Career

4 Ted Hendricks, Baltimore, 1969-1973; Green Bay, 1974; Oakland, 1975-1981; L.A. Raiders, 1982-83
Doug English, Detroit, 1975-79, 1981-85
3 Bill McPeak, Pittsburgh, 1949-1957
Charlie Krueger, San Francisco, 1959-1973
Ernie Stautner, Pittsburgh, 1950-1963
Jim Katcavage, N.Y. Giants, 1956-1968
Roger Brown, Detroit, 1960-66; Los Angeles, 1967-69
Bruce Maher, Detroit, 1960-67; N.Y. Giants, 1968-69
Ron McDole, St. Louis, 1961; Houston, 1962; Buffalo, 1963-1970; Washington, 1971-78
Alan Page, Minnesota, 1967-1978; Chicago, 1979-1981
Lyle Alzado, Denver, 1971-78; Cleveland, 1979-1981; L.A. Raiders, 1982-85
Rulon Jones, Denver, 1980-88
Steve McMichael, New England, 1980; Chicago, 1981-1993; Green Bay, 1994
Kevin Greene, L.A. Rams, 1985-1992; Pittsburgh, 1993-95; Carolina, 1996, 1998-99; San Francisco, 1997
Burt Grossman, San Diego, 1989-1993; Philadelphia, 1994
Eric Swann, Phoenix, 1991-93; Arizona, 1994-99; Carolina, 2000
Dan Saleaumua, Detroit, 1987-88; Kansas City, 1989-1996; Seattle, 1997-98
Derrick Thomas, Kansas City, 1989-1999
Bryant Young, San Francisco, 1994-2000
2 By many players

Most Safeties, Season

2 Tom Nash, Green Bay, 1932
Roger Brown, Detroit, 1962
Ron McDole, Buffalo, 1964
Alan Page, Minnesota, 1971
Fred Dryer, Los Angeles, 1973
Benny Barnes, Dallas, 1973
James Young, Houston, 1977
Doug English, Detroit, 1983
Don Blackmon, New England, 1985
Tim Harris, Green Bay, 1988
Brian Jordan, Atlanta, 1991
Burt Grossman, San Diego, 1992
Rod Stephens, Seattle, 1993
Bryant Young, San Francisco, 1996

Most Safeties, Game

2 Fred Dryer, Los Angeles vs. Green Bay, Oct. 21, 1973

RUSHING

Most Seasons Leading League

8 Jim Brown, Cleveland, 1957-1961, 1963-65
4 Steve Van Buren, Philadelphia, 1945, 1947-49
O.J. Simpson, Buffalo, 1972-73, 1975-76
Eric Dickerson, L.A. Rams, 1983-84, 1986; Indianapolis, 1988
Emmitt Smith, Dallas, 1991-93, 1995
Barry Sanders, Detroit, 1990, 1994, 1996-97
3 Earl Campbell, Houston, 1978-1980

Most Consecutive Seasons Leading League

5 Jim Brown, Cleveland, 1957-1961
3 Steve Van Buren, Philadelphia, 1947-49
Jim Brown, Cleveland, 1963-65
Earl Campbell, Houston, 1978-1980
Emmitt Smith, Dallas, 1991-93
2 Bill Paschal, N.Y. Giants, 1943-44
Joe Perry, San Francisco, 1953-54
Jim Nance, Boston, 1966-67
Leroy Kelly, Cleveland, 1967-68
O.J. Simpson, Buffalo, 1972-73; 1975-76
Eric Dickerson, L.A. Rams, 1983-84
Barry Sanders, Detroit, 1996-97
Edgerrin James, Indianapolis, 1999-2000

ATTEMPTS

Most Seasons Leading League

6 Jim Brown, Cleveland, 1958-59, 1961, 1963-65
4 Steve Van Buren, Philadelphia, 1947-1950
Walter Payton, Chicago, 1976-79
3 Cookie Gilchrist, Buffalo, 1963-64; Denver, 1965
Jim Nance, Boston, 1966-67, 1969
O.J. Simpson, Buffalo, 1973-75
Eric Dickerson, L.A. Rams, 1983, 1986; Indianapolis, 1988
Emmitt Smith, Dallas, 1991, 1994-95

Most Consecutive Seasons Leading League

4 Steve Van Buren, Philadelphia, 1947-1950
Walter Payton, Chicago, 1976-79
3 Jim Brown, Cleveland, 1963-65
Cookie Gilchrist, Buffalo, 1963-64; Denver, 1965
O.J. Simpson, Buffalo, 1973-75
2 By many players

Most Attempts, Career

3,838 Walter Payton, Chicago, 1975-1987
3,537 Emmitt Smith, Dallas, 1990-2000
3,062 Barry Sanders, Detroit, 1989-1998

Most Attempts, Season
410 Jamal Anderson, Atlanta, 1998
407 James Wilder, Tampa Bay, 1984
404 Eric Dickerson, L.A. Rams, 1986

Most Attempts, Rookie, Season
390 Eric Dickerson, L.A. Rams, 1983
378 George Rogers, New Orleans, 1981
369 Edgerrin James, Indianapolis, 1999

Most Attempts, Game
45 Jamie Morris, Washington vs. Cincinnati, Dec. 17, 1988 (OT)
43 Butch Woolfolk, N.Y. Giants vs. Philadelphia, Nov. 20, 1983
James Wilder, Tampa Bay vs. Green Bay, Sept. 30, 1984 (OT)
42 James Wilder, Tampa Bay vs. Pittsburgh, Oct. 30, 1983
Terrell Davis, Denver vs. Buffalo, Oct. 26, 1997 (OT)

YARDS GAINED

Most Yards Gained, Career
16,726 Walter Payton, Chicago, 1975-1987
15,269 Barry Sanders, Detroit, 1989-1998
15,166 Emmitt Smith, Dallas, 1990-2000

Most Seasons, 1,000 or More Yards Rushing
10 Walter Payton, Chicago, 1976-1981, 1983-86
Barry Sanders, Detroit, 1989-1998
Emmitt Smith, Dallas, 1991-2000
8 Franco Harris, Pittsburgh, 1972, 1974-79, 1983
Tony Dorsett, Dallas, 1977-1981, 1983-85
Thurman Thomas, Buffalo, 1989-1996
7 Jim Brown, Cleveland, 1958-1961, 1963-65
Eric Dickerson, L.A. Rams, 1983-86; L.A. Rams-Indianapolis, 1987; Indianapolis, 1988-89
Jerome Bettis, L.A. Rams, 1993-94; Pittsburgh, 1996-2000
Ricky Watters, San Francisco, 1992; Philadelphia 1995-97; Seattle, 1998-2000

Most Consecutive Seasons, 1,000 or More Yards Rushing
10 Barry Sanders, Detroit, 1989-1998
Emmitt Smith, Dallas, 1991-2000 (current)
8 Thurman Thomas, Buffalo, 1989-1996
7 Eric Dickerson, L.A. Rams, 1983-86; L.A. Rams-Indianapolis, 1987; Indianapolis, 1988-89

Most Yards Gained, Season
2,105 Eric Dickerson, L.A. Rams, 1984
2,053 Barry Sanders, Detroit, 1997
2,008 Terrell Davis, Denver, 1998

Most Yards Gained, Rookie, Season
1,808 Eric Dickerson, L.A. Rams, 1983
1,674 George Rogers, New Orleans, 1981
1,605 Ottis Anderson, St. Louis, 1979

Most Yards Gained, Game
278 Corey Dillon, Cincinnati vs. Denver, Oct. 22, 2000
275 Walter Payton, Chicago vs. Minnesota, Nov. 20, 1977
273 O.J. Simpson, Buffalo vs. Detroit, Nov. 25, 1976

Most Games, 200 or More Yards Rushing, Career
6 O.J. Simpson, Buffalo, 1969-1977; San Francisco, 1978-79
4 Jim Brown, Cleveland, 1957-1965
Earl Campbell, Houston, 1978-1984; New Orleans, 1984-85
Barry Sanders, Detroit, 1989-1998
3 Eric Dickerson, L.A. Rams, 1983-87; Indianapolis, 1987-1991; L.A. Raiders, 1992; Atlanta, 1993
Greg Bell, Buffalo, 1984-87; L.A. Rams, 1987-89; L.A. Raiders, 1990
Terrell Davis, Denver, 1995-2000
Corey Dillon, Cincinnati, 1997-2000

Most Games, 200 or More Yards Rushing, Season
4 Earl Campbell, Houston, 1980
3 O.J. Simpson, Buffalo, 1973
2 Jim Brown, Cleveland, 1963
O.J. Simpson, Buffalo, 1976
Walter Payton, Chicago, 1977
Eric Dickerson, L.A. Rams, 1984
Greg Bell, L.A. Rams, 1989
Terrell Davis, Denver, 1997
Barry Sanders, Detroit, 1997
Corey Dillon, Cincinnati, 2000
Marshall Faulk, St. Louis, 2000

Most Consecutive Games, 200 or More Yards Rushing
2 O.J. Simpson, Buffalo, 1973, 1976
Earl Campbell, Houston, 1980

Most Games, 100 or More Yards Rushing, Career
77 Walter Payton, Chicago, 1975-1987
76 Barry Sanders, Detroit, 1989-1998
70 Emmitt Smith, Dallas, 1990-2000

Most Games, 100 or More Yards Rushing, Season
14 Barry Sanders, Detroit, 1997
12 Eric Dickerson, L.A. Rams, 1984
Barry Foster, Pittsburgh, 1992
Jamal Anderson, Atlanta, 1998
11 O.J. Simpson, Buffalo, 1973
Earl Campbell, Houston, 1979
Marcus Allen, L.A. Raiders, 1985
Eric Dickerson, L.A. Rams, 1986
Emmitt Smith, Dallas, 1995
Terrell Davis, Denver, 1998

Most Consecutive Games, 100 or More Yards Rushing
14 Barry Sanders, Detroit, 1997
11 Marcus Allen, L.A. Raiders, 1985-86
9 Walter Payton, Chicago, 1985
Fred Taylor, Jacksonville, 2000

Longest Run From Scrimmage
99 Tony Dorsett, Dallas vs. Minnesota, Jan. 3, 1983 (TD)
97 Andy Uram, Green Bay vs. Chi. Cardinals, Oct. 8, 1939 (TD)
Bob Gage, Pittsburgh vs. Chi. Bears, Dec. 4, 1949 (TD)
96 Jim Spavital, Baltimore vs. Green Bay, Nov. 5, 1950 (TD)
Bob Hoernschemeyer, Detroit vs. N.Y. Yanks, Nov. 23, 1950 (TD)
Garrison Hearst, San Francisco vs. N.Y. Jets, Sept. 6, 1998 (TD)

AVERAGE GAIN

Highest Average Gain, Career (750 attempts)
6.42 Randall Cunningham, Philadelphia, 1985-1995; Minnesota, 1997-99; Dallas, 2000 (761-4,888)
5.22 Jim Brown, Cleveland, 1957-1965 (2,359-12,312)
5.14 Eugene (Mercury) Morris, Miami, 1969-1975; San Diego, 1976 (804-4,133)

Highest Average Gain, Season (Qualifiers)
8.44 Beattie Feathers, Chi. Bears, 1934 (119-1,004)
7.98 Randall Cunningham, Philadelphia 1990 (118-942)
6.87 Bobby Douglass, Chicago, 1972 (141-968)

Highest Average Gain, Game (10 attempts)
17.09 Marion Motley, Cleveland vs. Pittsburgh, Oct. 29, 1950 (11-188)
16.70 Bill Grimes, Green Bay vs. N.Y. Yanks, Oct. 8, 1950 (10-167)
16.57 Bobby Mitchell, Cleveland vs. Washington, Nov. 15, 1959 (14-232)

TOUCHDOWNS

Most Seasons Leading League
5 Jim Brown, Cleveland, 1957-59, 1963, 1965
4 Steve Van Buren, Philadelphia, 1945, 1947-49
3 Abner Haynes, Dall. Texans, 1960-62
Cookie Gilchrist, Buffalo, 1962-64
Paul Lowe, L.A. Chargers, 1960; San Diego, 1961, 1965
Leroy Kelly, Cleveland, 1966-68
Emmitt Smith, Dallas, 1992, 1994-95

Most Consecutive Seasons Leading League
3 Steve Van Buren, Philadelphia, 1947-49
Jim Brown, Cleveland, 1957-59
Abner Haynes, Dall. Texans, 1960-62
Cookie Gilchrist, Buffalo, 1962-64
Leroy Kelly, Cleveland, 1966-68

Most Touchdowns, Career
145 Emmitt Smith, Dallas, 1990-2000
123 Marcus Allen, L.A. Raiders, 1982-1992; Kansas City, 1993-97
110 Walter Payton, Chicago, 1975-1987

Most Touchdowns, Season
25 Emmitt Smith, Dallas, 1995
24 John Riggins, Washington, 1983
21 Joe Morris, N.Y. Giants, 1985
Emmitt Smith, Dallas, 1994
Terry Allen, Washington, 1996
Terrell Davis, Denver, 1998

Most Touchdowns, Rookie, Season
18 Eric Dickerson, L.A. Rams, 1983
15 Ickey Woods, Cincinnati, 1988
Mike Anderson, Denver, 2000
14 Gale Sayers, Chicago, 1965
Barry Sanders, Detroit, 1989
Curtis Martin, New England, 1995
Fred Taylor, Jacksonville, 1998

Most Touchdowns, Game
6 Ernie Nevers, Chi. Cardinals vs. Chi. Bears, Nov. 28, 1929
5 Jim Brown, Cleveland vs. Baltimore, Nov. 1, 1959
Cookie Gilchrist, Buffalo vs. N.Y. Jets, Dec. 8, 1963
James Stewart, Jacksonville vs. Philadelphia, Oct. 12, 1997
4 By many players

Most Consecutive Games Rushing for Touchdowns
13 John Riggins, Washington, 1982-83
George Rogers, Washington, 1985-86
11 Lenny Moore, Baltimore, 1963-64
Emmitt Smith, Dallas, 1994-95
Emmitt Smith, Dallas, 1995

10 Greg Bell, L.A. Rams, 1988-89
Terry Allen, Washington, 1995-96

PASSING

Most Seasons Leading League
6 Sammy Baugh, Washington, 1937, 1940, 1943, 1945, 1947, 1949
Steve Young San Francisco, 1991-94, 1996-97
4 Len Dawson, Dall. Texans; 1962; Kansas City, 1964, 1966, 1968
Roger Staubach, Dallas, 1971, 1973, 1978-79
Ken Anderson, Cincinnati, 1974-75, 1981-82
3 Arnie Herber, Green Bay, 1932, 1934, 1936
Norm Van Brocklin, Los Angeles, 1950, 1952, 1954
Bart Starr, Green Bay, 1962, 1964, 1966

Most Consecutive Seasons Leading League
4 Steve Young, San Francisco, 1991-94
2 Cecil Isbell, Green Bay, 1941-42
Milt Plum, Cleveland, 1960-61
Ken Anderson, Cincinnati, 1974-75, 1981-82
Roger Staubach, Dallas, 1978-79
Steve Young, San Francisco, 1996-97

PASSER RATING

Highest Passer Rating, Career (1,500 attempts)
96.8 Steve Young, Tampa Bay, 1985-86; San Francisco, 1987-1999
92.3 Joe Montana, San Francisco, 1979-1990, 1992; Kansas City, 1993-94
86.4 Dan Marino, Miami, 1983-1999

Highest Passer Rating, Season (Qualifiers)
112.8 Steve Young, San Francisco, 1994
112.4 Joe Montana, San Francisco, 1989
110.4 Milt Plum, Cleveland, 1960

Highest Passer Rating, Rookie, Season (Qualifiers)
96.0 Dan Marino, Miami, 1983
88.2 Greg Cook, Cincinnati, 1969
84.0 Charlie Conerly, N.Y. Giants, 1948

ATTEMPTS

Most Seasons Leading League
5 Dan Marino, Miami, 1984, 1986, 1988, 1992, 1997
4 Sammy Baugh, Washington, 1937, 1943, 1947-48
Johnny Unitas, Baltimore, 1957, 1959-1961
George Blanda, Chi. Bears, 1953; Houston, 1963-65
3 Arnie Herber, Green Bay, 1932, 1934, 1936
Sonny Jurgensen, Washington, 1966-67, 1969
Drew Bledsoe, New England, 1994-96

Most Consecutive Seasons Leading League
3 Johnny Unitas, Baltimore, 1959-1961
George Blanda, Houston, 1963-65
Drew Bledsoe, New England, 1994-96
2 By many players

Most Passes Attempted, Career
8,358 Dan Marino, Miami, 1983-1999
7,250 John Elway, Denver, 1983-1998
6,823 Warren Moon, Houston, 1984-1993; Minnesota, 1994-96; Seattle, 1997-98; Kansas City, 1999-2000

Most Passes Attempted, Season
691 Drew Bledsoe, New England, 1994
655 Warren Moon, Houston, 1991
636 Drew Bledsoe, New England, 1995

Most Passes Attempted, Rookie, Season
575 Peyton Manning, Indianapolis, 1998
486 Rick Mirer, Seattle, 1993
439 Jim Zorn, Seattle, 1976

Most Passes Attempted, Game
70 Drew Bledsoe, New England vs. Minnesota, Nov. 13, 1994 (OT)
69 Vinny Testaverde, N.Y. Jets vs. Baltimore, Dec. 24, 2000
68 George Blanda, Houston vs. Buffalo, Nov. 1, 1964

COMPLETIONS

Most Seasons Leading League
6 Dan Marino, Miami, 1984-86, 1988, 1992, 1997
5 Sammy Baugh, Washington, 1937, 1943, 1945, 1947-48
4 George Blanda, Chi. Bears, 1953; Houston, 1963-65
Sonny Jurgensen, Philadelphia, 1961; Washington, 1966-67, 1969

Most Consecutive Seasons Leading League
3 George Blanda, Houston, 1963-65
Dan Marino, Miami, 1984-86
2 By many players

Most Passes Completed, Career
4,967 Dan Marino, Miami, 1983-1999
4,123 John Elway, Denver, 1983-1998
3,988 Warren Moon, Houston, 1984-1993; Minnesota, 1994-96; Seattle, 1997-98; Kansas City, 1999-2000

Most Passes Completed, Season
404 Warren Moon, Houston, 1991
400 Drew Bledsoe, New England, 1994
385 Dan Marino, Miami, 1994

Most Passes Completed, Rookie, Season
326 Peyton Manning, Indianapolis, 1998
274 Rick Mirer, Seattle, 1993
223 Tim Couch, Cleveland, 1999

Most Passes Completed, Game
45 Drew Bledsoe, New England vs. Minnesota, Nov. 13, 1994 (OT)
42 Richard Todd, N.Y. Jets vs. San Francisco, Sept. 21, 1980
Vinny Testaverde, N.Y. Jets vs. Seattle, Dec. 6, 1998
41 Warren Moon, Houston vs. Dallas, Nov. 10, 1991 (OT)

Most Consecutive Passes Completed
22 Joe Montana, San Francisco vs. Cleveland (5), Nov. 29, 1987; vs. Green Bay (17), Dec. 6, 1987
20 Ken Anderson, Cincinnati vs. Houston, Jan. 2, 1983
Hugh Millen, Denver vs. L.A. Raiders (7), Dec. 11, 1994; vs. San Francisco (13), Dec. 17, 1994
Steve Young, San Francisco vs. Washington, Nov. 24, 1996
18 Steve DeBerg, Denver vs. L.A. Rams (17), Dec. 12, 1982; vs. Kansas City (1), Dec. 19, 1982
Lynn Dickey, Green Bay vs. Houston, Sept. 4, 1983
Joe Montana, San Francisco vs. L.A. Rams (13), Oct. 28, 1984; vs. Cincinnati (5), Nov. 4, 1984
Don Majkowski, Green Bay vs. New Orleans, Sept. 18, 1989
Boomer Esiason, N.Y. Jets vs. Miami (5), Sept. 12, 1993; vs. New England (13), Sept. 26, 1993

COMPLETION PERCENTAGE

Most Seasons Leading League
8 Len Dawson, Dall. Texans, 1962; Kansas City, 1964-69, 1975
7 Sammy Baugh, Washington, 1940, 1942-43, 1945, 1947-49
5 Joe Montana, San Francisco, 1980-81, 1985, 1987, 1989
Steve Young, San Francisco, 1992, 1994-97

Most Consecutive Seasons Leading League
6 Len Dawson, Kansas City, 1964-69
4 Steve Young, San Francisco, 1994-97
3 Sammy Baugh, Washington, 1947-49
Otto Graham, Cleveland, 1953-55
Milt Plum, Cleveland, 1959-1961

Highest Completion Percentage, Career (1,500 attempts)
64.28 Steve Young, Tampa Bay, 1985-86; San Francisco, 1987-1999 (4,149-2,667)
63.24 Joe Montana, San Francisco, 1979-1990, 1992; Kansas City, 1993-94 (5,391-3,409)
61.83 Brad Johnson, Minnesota, 1994-98; Washington, 1999-2000 (1,821-1,126)

Highest Completion Percentage, Season (Qualifiers)
70.55 Ken Anderson, Cincinnati, 1982 (309-218)
70.33 Sammy Baugh, Washington, 1945 (182-128)
70.28 Steve Young, San Francisco, 1994 (461-324)

Highest Completion Percentage, Rookie, Season (Qualifiers)
58.45 Dan Marino, Miami, 1983 (296-173)
57.14 Jim McMahon, Chicago, 1982 (210-120)
57.10 Charlie Batch, Detroit, 1998 (303-173)

Highest Completion Percentage, Game (20 attempts)
91.30 Vinny Testaverde, Cleveland vs. L.A. Rams, Dec. 26, 1993 (23-21)
90.91 Ken Anderson, Cincinnati vs. Pittsburgh, Nov. 10, 1974 (22-20)
90.48 Lynn Dickey, Green Bay vs. New Orleans, Dec. 13, 1981 (21-19)

YARDS GAINED

Most Seasons Leading League
5 Sonny Jurgensen, Philadelphia, 1961-62; Washington, 1966-67, 1969
Dan Marino, Miami, 1984-86, 1988, 1992
4 Sammy Baugh, Washington, 1937, 1940, 1947-48
Johnny Unitas, Baltimore, 1957, 1959-1960, 1963
Dan Fouts, San Diego, 1979-1982
3 Arnie Herber, Green Bay, 1932, 1934, 1936
Sid Luckman, Chi. Bears, 1943, 1945-46
John Brodie, San Francisco, 1965, 1968, 1970
John Hadl, San Diego, 1965, 1968, 1971
Joe Namath, N.Y. Jets, 1966-67, 1972

Most Consecutive Seasons Leading League
4 Dan Fouts, San Diego, 1979-1982
3 Dan Marino, Miami, 1984-86
2 By many players

Most Yards Gained, Career
61,361 Dan Marino, Miami, 1983-1999
51,475 John Elway, Denver, 1983-1998
49,325 Warren Moon, Houston, 1984-1993; Minnesota, 1994-96; Seattle, 1997-98; Kansas City, 1999-2000

Most Seasons, 3,000 or More Yards Passing
13 Dan Marino, Miami, 1984-1992, 1994-95, 1997-98
12 John Elway, Denver, 1985-1991, 1993-97
9 Warren Moon, Houston, 1984, 1986, 1989-1991, 1993; Minnesota, 1994-95; Seattle, 1997
Brett Favre, Green Bay, 1992-2000

Most Yards Gained, Season
5,084 Dan Marino, Miami, 1984
4,802 Dan Fouts, San Diego, 1981
4,746 Dan Marino, Miami, 1986

Most Yards Gained, Rookie, Season
3,739 Peyton Manning, Indianapolis, 1998
2,833 Rick Mirer, Seattle, 1993
2,717 Kerry Collins, Carolina, 1995

Most Yards Gained, Game
554 Norm Van Brocklin, Los Angeles vs. N.Y. Yanks, Sept. 28, 1951
527 Warren Moon, Houston vs. Kansas City, Dec. 16, 1990
522 Boomer Esiason, Arizona vs. Washington, Nov. 10, 1996

Most Games, 400 or More Yards Passing, Career
13 Dan Marino, Miami, 1983-1999
7 Joe Montana, San Francisco, 1979-1990, 1992; Kansas City, 1993-94
Warren Moon, Houston, 1984-1993; Minnesota, 1994-96; Seattle, 1997-98; Kansas City, 1999-2000
6 Dan Fouts, San Diego, 1973-1987

Most Games, 400 or More Yards Passing, Season
4 Dan Marino, Miami, 1984
3 Dan Marino, Miami, 1986
2 By many players

Most Consecutive Games, 400 or More Yards Passing
2 Dan Fouts, San Diego, 1982
Dan Marino, Miami, 1984
Phil Simms, N.Y. Giants, 1985

Most Games, 300 or More Yards Passing, Career
63 Dan Marino, Miami, 1983-1999
51 Dan Fouts, San Diego, 1973-1987
49 Warren Moon, Houston, 1984-1993; Minnesota, 1994-96; Seattle, 1997-98; Kansas City, 1999-2000

Most Games, 300 or More Yards Passing, Season
9 Dan Marino, Miami, 1984
Warren Moon, Houston, 1990
Kurt Warner, St. Louis, 1999
8 Dan Fouts, San Diego, 1980
Kurt Warner, St. Louis, 2000
7 Dan Fouts, San Diego, 1981
Bill Kenney, Kansas City, 1983
Neil Lomax, St. Louis, 1984
Dan Fouts, San Diego, 1985
Brett Favre, Green Bay, 1995
Steve Young, San Francisco, 1998

Most Consecutive Games, 300 or More Yards Passing
6 Steve Young, San Francisco, 1998
Kurt Warner, St. Louis, 2000
5 Joe Montana, San Francisco, 1982
4 Dan Fouts, San Diego, 1979
Dan Fouts, San Diego, 1980-81
Bill Kenney, Kansas City, 1983
Joe Montana, San Francisco, 1985-86
Joe Montana, San Francisco, 1990
Warren Moon, Houston, 1990
Drew Bledsoe, New England, 1993-94
Kurt Warner, St. Louis, 1999

Longest Pass Completion (All TDs except as noted)
99 Frank Filchock (to Farkas), Washington vs. Pittsburgh, Oct. 15, 1939
George Izo (to Mitchell), Washington vs. Cleveland, Sept. 15, 1963
Karl Sweetan (to Studstill), Detroit vs. Baltimore, Oct. 16, 1966
Sonny Jurgensen (to Allen), Washington vs. Chicago, Sept. 15, 1968
Jim Plunkett (to Branch), L.A. Raiders vs. Washington, Oct. 2, 1983
Ron Jaworski (to Quick), Philadelphia vs. Atlanta, Nov. 10, 1985
Stan Humphries (to Martin), San Diego vs. Seattle, Sept. 18, 1994
Brett Favre (to Brooks), Green Bay vs. Chicago, Sept. 11, 1995
98 Doug Russell (to Tinsley), Chi. Cardinals vs. Cleveland, Nov. 27, 1938
Ogden Compton (to Lane), Chi. Cardinals vs. Green Bay, Nov. 13, 1955
Bill Wade (to Farrington), Chicago Bears vs. Detroit, Oct. 8, 1961
Jacky Lee (to Dewveall), Houston vs. San Diego, Nov. 25, 1962
Earl Morrall (to Jones), N.Y. Giants vs. Pittsburgh, Sept. 11, 1966
Jim Hart (to Moore), St. Louis vs. Los Angeles, Dec. 10, 1972 (no TD)
Bobby Hebert (to Haynes), Atlanta vs. New Orleans, Sept. 12, 1993
Charlie Batch (to Morton), Detroit vs. Chicago, Oct. 4, 1998
97 Pat Coffee (to Tinsley), Chi. Cardinals vs. Chi. Bears, Dec. 5, 1937
Bobby Layne (to Box), Detroit vs. Green Bay, Nov. 26, 1953
George Shaw (to Tarr), Denver vs. Boston, Sept. 21, 1962
Bernie Kosar (to Slaughter), Cleveland vs. Chicago, Oct. 23, 1989
Steve Young (to Taylor), San Francisco vs. Atlanta, Nov. 3, 1991

AVERAGE GAIN

Most Seasons Leading League
7 Sid Luckman, Chi. Bears, 1939-1943, 1946-47
5 Steve Young, San Francisco, 1991-94, 1997
3 Arnie Herber, Green Bay, 1932, 1934, 1936
Norm Van Brocklin, Los Angeles, 1950, 1952, 1954
Len Dawson, Dall. Texans, 1962; Kansas City, 1966, 1968
Bart Starr, Green Bay, 1966-68

Most Consecutive Seasons Leading League
5 Sid Luckman, Chi. Bears, 1939-1943
4 Steve Young, San Francisco, 1991-94
3 Bart Starr, Green Bay, 1966-68

Highest Average Gain, Career (1,500 attempts)
8.63 Otto Graham, Cleveland, 1950-55 (1,565-13,499)
8.42 Sid Luckman, Chi. Bears, 1939-1950 (1,744-14,686)
8.16 Norm Van Brocklin, Los Angeles, 1949-1957; Philadelphia, 1958-1960 (2,895-23,611)

Highest Average Gain, Season (Qualifiers)
11.17 Tommy O'Connell, Cleveland, 1957 (110-1,229)
10.86 Sid Luckman, Chi. Bears, 1943 (202-2,194)
10.55 Otto Graham, Cleveland, 1953 (258-2,722)

Highest Average Gain, Rookie, Season (Qualifiers)
9.411 Greg Cook, Cincinnati, 1969 (197-1,854)
9.409 Bob Waterfield, Cleveland, 1945 (171-1,609)
8.36 Zeke Bratkowski, Chi. Bears, 1954 (130-1,087)

Highest Average Gain, Game (20 attempts)
18.58 Sammy Baugh, Washington vs. Boston, Oct. 31, 1948 (24-446)
18.50 Johnny Unitas, Baltimore vs. Atlanta, Nov. 12, 1967 (20-370)
17.71 Joe Namath, N.Y. Jets vs. Baltimore, Sept. 24, 1972 (28-496)

TOUCHDOWNS

Most Seasons Leading League
4 Johnny Unitas, Baltimore, 1957-1960
Len Dawson, Dall. Texans, 1962; Kansas City, 1963, 1965-66
Steve Young, San Francisco, 1992-94, 1998
3 Arnie Herber, Green Bay, 1932, 1934, 1936
Sid Luckman, Chi. Bears, 1943, 1945-46
Y.A. Tittle, San Francisco, 1955; N.Y. Giants, 1962-63
Dan Marino, Miami, 1984-86
Brett Favre, Green Bay, 1995-97
2 By many players

Most Consecutive Seasons Leading League
4 Johnny Unitas, Baltimore, 1957-1960
3 Dan Marino, Miami, 1984-86
Steve Young, San Francisco, 1992-94
Brett Favre, Green Bay, 1995-97
2 By many players

Most Touchdown Passes, Career
420 Dan Marino, Miami, 1983-1999
342 Fran Tarkenton, Minnesota, 1961-66, 1972-78; N.Y. Giants, 1967-1971
300 John Elway, Denver, 1983-1998

Most Touchdown Passes, Season
48 Dan Marino, Miami, 1984
44 Dan Marino, Miami, 1986
41 Kurt Warner, St. Louis, 1999

Most Touchdown Passes, Rookie, Season
26 Peyton Manning, Indianapolis, 1998
22 Charlie Conerly, N.Y. Giants, 1948
20 Dan Marino, Miami, 1983

Most Touchdown Passes, Game
7 Sid Luckman, Chi. Bears vs. N.Y. Giants, Nov. 14, 1943
Adrian Burk, Philadelphia vs. Washington, Oct. 17, 1954
George Blanda, Houston vs. N.Y. Titans, Nov. 19, 1961
Y.A. Tittle, N.Y. Giants vs. Washington, Oct. 28, 1962
Joe Kapp, Minnesota vs. Baltimore, Sept. 28, 1969
6 By many players. Last time:
Mark Rypien, Washington vs. Atlanta, Nov. 10, 1991

Most Games, Four or More Touchdown Passes, Career
21 Dan Marino, Miami, 1983-1999
17 Johnny Unitas, Baltimore, 1956-1972; San Diego, 1973
14 Brett Favre, Atlanta, 1991; Green Bay, 1992-2000

Most Games, Four or More Touchdown Passes, Season
6 Dan Marino, Miami, 1984
5 Dan Marino, Miami, 1986
Brett Favre, Green Bay, 1996
4 George Blanda, Houston, 1961
Vince Ferragamo, Los Angeles, 1980
Steve Young, San Francisco, 1994
Randall Cunningham, Minnesota, 1998

Most Consecutive Games, Four or More Touchdown Passes
4 Dan Marino, Miami, 1984
2 By many players

ALL-TIME RECORDS

Most Consecutive Games, Touchdown Passes
47 Johnny Unitas, Baltimore, 1956-1960
30 Dan Marino, Miami, 1985-87
28 Dave Krieg, Seattle, 1983-85

HAD INTERCEPTED

Most Consecutive Passes Attempted, None Intercepted
308 Bernie Kosar, Cleveland, 1990-91
294 Bart Starr, Green Bay, 1964-65
279 Jeff George, Indianapolis, 1993; Atlanta, 1994

Most Passes Had Intercepted, Career
277 George Blanda, Chi. Bears, 1949, 1950-58; Baltimore, 1950; Houston, 1960-66; Oakland, 1967-1975
268 John Hadl, San Diego, 1962-1972; Los Angeles, 1973-74; Green Bay, 1974-75; Houston, 1976-77
266 Fran Tarkenton, Minnesota, 1961-66, 1972-78; N.Y. Giants, 1967-1971

Most Passes Had Intercepted, Season
42 George Blanda, Houston, 1962
35 Vinny Testaverde, Tampa Bay, 1988
34 Frank Tripucka, Denver, 1960

Most Passes Had Intercepted, Game
8 Jim Hardy, Chi. Cardinals vs. Philadelphia, Sept. 24, 1950
7 Parker Hall, Cleveland vs. Green Bay, Nov. 8, 1942
Frank Sinkwich, Detroit vs. Green Bay, Oct. 24, 1943
Bob Waterfield, Los Angeles vs. Green Bay, Oct. 17, 1948
Zeke Bratkowski, Chicago vs. Baltimore, Oct. 2, 1960
Tommy Wade, Pittsburgh vs. Philadelphia, Dec. 12, 1965
Ken Stabler, Oakland vs. Denver, Oct. 16, 1977
Steve DeBerg, Tampa Bay vs. San Francisco, Sept. 7, 1986
6 By many players

Most Attempts, No Interceptions, Game
70 Drew Bledsoe, New England vs. Minnesota, Nov. 13, 1994 (OT)
63 Rich Gannon, Minnesota vs. New England, Oct. 20, 1991 (OT)
60 Davey O'Brien, Philadelphia vs. Washington, Dec. 1, 1940

LOWEST PERCENTAGE, PASSES HAD INTERCEPTED

Most Seasons Leading League, Lowest Percentage, Passes Had Intercepted
5 Sammy Baugh, Washington, 1940, 1942, 1944-45, 1947
3 Charlie Conerly, N.Y. Giants, 1950, 1956, 1959
Bart Starr, Green Bay, 1962, 1964, 1966
Roger Staubach, Dallas, 1971, 1977, 1979
Ken Anderson, Cincinnati, 1972, 1981-82
Ken O'Brien, N.Y. Jets, 1985, 1987-88
2 By many players

Lowest Percentage, Passes Had Intercepted, Career (1,500 attempts)
2.08 Neil O'Donnell, Pittsburgh, 1991-95; N.Y. Jets, 1996-97; Cincinnati, 1998; Tennessee, 1999-2000 (3,121-65)
2.469 Steve Bono, Minnesota, 1985-86; Pittsburgh, 1987-88; San Francisco, 1989, 1991-93; Kansas City, 1994-96; Green Bay, 1997; St. Louis, 1998; Carolina, 1999 (1,701-42)
2.470 Mark Brunell, Green Bay, 1994; Jacksonville, 1995-2000 (2,672-66)

Lowest Percentage, Passes Had Intercepted, Season (Qualifiers)
0.66 Joe Ferguson, Buffalo, 1976 (151-1)
0.90 Steve DeBerg, Kansas City, 1990 (444-4)
1.16 Steve Bartkowski, Atlanta, 1983 (432-5)

Lowest Percentage, Passes Had Intercepted, Rookie, Season (Qualifiers)
1.98 Charlie Batch, Detroit, 1998 (303-6)
2.03 Dan Marino, Miami, 1983 (296-6)
2.10 Gary Wood, N.Y. Giants, 1964 (143-3)

TIMES SACKED

Times Sacked has been compiled since 1963.

Most Times Sacked, Career
516 John Elway, Denver, 1983-1998
494 Dave Krieg, Seattle, 1980-1991; Kansas City, 1992-93; Detroit, 1994; Arizona, 1995; Chicago, 1996; Tennessee, 1997-98
483 Fran Tarkenton, Minnesota, 1963-66, 1972-78; N.Y. Giants, 1967-1971

Most Times Sacked, Season
72 Randall Cunningham, Philadelphia, 1986
62 Ken O'Brien, N.Y. Jets, 1985
Steve Beuerlein, Carolina, 2000
61 Neil Lomax, St. Louis, 1985

Most Times Sacked, Game
12 Bert Jones, Baltimore vs. St. Louis, Oct. 26, 1980
Warren Moon, Houston vs. Dallas, Sept. 29, 1985
11 Charley Johnson, St. Louis vs. N.Y. Giants, Nov. 1, 1964
Bart Starr, Green Bay vs. Detroit, Nov. 7, 1965
Jack Kemp, Buffalo vs. Oakland, Oct. 15, 1967
Bob Berry, Atlanta vs. St. Louis, Nov. 24, 1968
Greg Landry, Detroit vs. Dallas, Oct. 6, 1975
Ron Jaworski, Philadelphia vs. St. Louis, Dec. 18, 1983
Paul McDonald, Cleveland vs. Kansas City, Sept. 30, 1984
Archie Manning, Minnesota vs. Chicago, Oct. 28, 1984
Steve Pelluer, Dallas vs. San Diego, Nov. 16, 1986
Randall Cunningham, Philadelphia vs. L.A. Raiders, Nov. 30, 1986 (OT)
David Norrie, N.Y. Jets vs. Dallas, Oct. 4, 1987
Troy Aikman, Dallas vs. Philadelphia, Sept. 15, 1991
Bernie Kosar, Cleveland vs. Indianapolis, Sept. 6, 1992
10 By many players

PASS RECEIVING

Most Seasons Leading League
8 Don Hutson, Green Bay, 1936-37, 1939, 1941-45
5 Lionel Taylor, Denver, 1960-63, 1965
3 Tom Fears, Los Angeles, 1948-1950
Pete Pihos, Philadelphia, 1953-55
Billy Wilson, San Francisco, 1954, 1956-57
Raymond Berry, Baltimore, 1958-1960
Lance Alworth, San Diego, 1966, 1968-69
Sterling Sharpe, Green Bay, 1989, 1992-93

Most Consecutive Seasons Leading League
5 Don Hutson, Green Bay, 1941-45
4 Lionel Taylor, Denver, 1960-63
3 Tom Fears, Los Angeles, 1948-1950
Pete Pihos, Philadelphia, 1953-55
Raymond Berry, Baltimore, 1958-1960

Most Pass Receptions, Career
1,281 Jerry Rice, San Francisco, 1985-2000
1,020 Cris Carter, Philadelphia, 1987-89; Minnesota, 1990-2000
951 Andre Reed, Buffalo, 1985-1999; Washington 2000

Most Seasons, 50 or More Pass Receptions
14 Jerry Rice, San Francisco, 1986-1996, 1998-2000
13 Andre Reed, Buffalo, 1986-1994, 1996-99
10 Steve Largent, Seattle, 1976, 1978-1981, 1983-87
Gary Clark, Washington, 1985-1992; Phoenix, 1993; Arizona, 1994
Henry Ellard, L.A. Rams, 1985, 1987-1991, 1993; Washington, 1994-96
Cris Carter, Minnesota, 1991-2000

Most Pass Receptions, Season
123 Herman Moore, Detroit, 1995
122 Cris Carter, Minnesota, 1994
Cris Carter, Minnesota, 1995
Jerry Rice, San Francisco, 1995
119 Isaac Bruce, St. Louis, 1995

Most Pass Receptions, Rookie, Season
90 Terry Glenn, New England, 1996
83 Earl Cooper, San Francisco, 1980
81 Keith Jackson, Philadelphia, 1988

Most Pass Receptions, Game
20 Terrell Owens, San Francisco vs. Chicago, Dec. 17, 2000
18 Tom Fears, Los Angeles vs. Green Bay, Dec. 3, 1950
17 Clark Gaines, N.Y. Jets vs. San Francisco, Sept. 21, 1980

Most Consecutive Games, Pass Receptions
225 Jerry Rice, San Francisco, 1985-2000 (current)
183 Art Monk, Washington, 1983-1993; N.Y. Jets, 1994; Philadelphia, 1995
177 Steve Largent, Seattle, 1977-1989

YARDS GAINED

Most Seasons Leading League
7 Don Hutson, Green Bay, 1936, 1938-39, 1941-44
6 Jerry Rice, San Francisco, 1986, 1989-1990, 1993-95
3 Raymond Berry, Baltimore, 1957, 1959-1960
Lance Alworth, San Diego, 1965-66, 1968

Most Consecutive Seasons Leading League
4 Don Hutson, Green Bay, 1941-44
3 Jerry Rice, San Francisco, 1993-95
2 By many players

Most Yards Gained, Career
19,247 Jerry Rice, San Francisco, 1985-2000
14,004 James Lofton, Green Bay, 1978-1986; L.A. Raiders, 1987-88; Buffalo, 1989-1992; L.A. Rams, 1993; Philadelphia, 1993
13,777 Henry Ellard, L.A. Rams, 1983-1993; Washington, 1994-97; New England-Washington, 1998

Most Seasons, 1,000 or More Yards, Pass Receiving
12 Jerry Rice, San Francisco, 1986-1996, 1998
8 Steve Largent, Seattle, 1978-1981, 1983-86
Tim Brown, L.A. Raiders, 1993-94; Oakland, 1995-2000
Cris Carter, Minnesota, 1993-2000
7 Lance Alworth, San Diego, 1963-69
Henry Ellard, L.A. Rams, 1988-1991; Washington 1994-96
Michael Irvin, Dallas, 1991-95, 1997-98

Most Yards Gained, Season
1,848 Jerry Rice, San Francisco, 1995
1,781 Isaac Bruce, St. Louis, 1995
1,746 Charley Hennigan, Houston, 1961

Most Yards Gained, Rookie, Season
1,473 Bill Groman, Houston, 1960
1,313 Randy Moss, Minnesota, 1998
1,231 Bill Howton, Green Bay, 1952

Most Yards Gained, Game
336 Willie Anderson, L.A. Rams vs. New Orleans, Nov. 26, 1989 (OT)
309 Stephone Paige, Kansas City vs. San Diego, Dec. 22, 1985
303 Jim Benton, Cleveland vs. Detroit, Nov. 22, 1945

Most Games, 200 or More Yards Pass Receiving, Career
5 Lance Alworth, San Diego, 1962-1970; Dallas, 1971-72
4 Don Hutson, Green Bay, 1935-45
Charley Hennigan, Houston, 1960-66
Jerry Rice, San Francisco, 1985-2000
3 Don Maynard, N.Y. Giants, 1958; N.Y. Jets, 1960-1972; St. Louis, 1973
Wes Chandler, New Orleans, 1978-1981; San Diego, 1981-87; San Francisco, 1988
Isaac Bruce, L.A. Rams, 1994; St. Louis, 1995-2000

Most Games, 200 or More Yards Pass Receiving, Season
3 Charley Hennigan, Houston, 1961
2 Don Hutson, Green Bay, 1942
Gene Roberts, N.Y. Giants, 1949
Lance Alworth, San Diego, 1963
Don Maynard, N.Y. Jets, 1968

Most Games, 100 or More Yards Pass Receiving, Career
66 Jerry Rice, San Francisco, 1985-2000
50 Don Maynard, N.Y. Giants, 1958; N.Y. Jets, 1960-1972; St. Louis, 1973
47 Michael Irvin, Dallas, 1988-1999

Most Games, 100 or More Yards Pass Receiving, Season
11 Michael Irvin, Dallas, 1995
10 Charley Hennigan, Houston, 1961
Herman Moore, Detroit, 1995
9 Elroy (Crazylegs) Hirsch, Los Angeles, 1951
Bill Groman, Houston, 1960
Lance Alworth, San Diego, 1965
Don Maynard, N.Y. Jets, 1967
Stanley Morgan, New England, 1986
Mark Carrier, Tampa Bay, 1989
Robert Brooks, Green Bay, 1995
Isaac Bruce, St. Louis, 1995
Jerry Rice, San Francisco, 1995
Marvin Harrison, Indianapolis, 1999
Jimmy Smith, Jacksonville, 1999

Most Consecutive Games, 100 or More Yards Pass Receiving
7 Charley Hennigan, Houston, 1961
Michael Irvin, Dallas, 1995
6 Raymond Berry, Baltimore, 1960
Bill Groman, Houston, 1961
Pat Studstill, Detroit, 1966
Isaac Bruce, St. Louis, 1995
5 Elroy (Crazylegs) Hirsch, Los Angeles, 1951
Bob Boyd, Los Angeles, 1954
Terry Barr, Detroit, 1963
Lance Alworth, San Diego, 1966
Don Maynard, N.Y. Jets, 1968-69
Harold Jackson, Philadelphia, 1971-72
Patrick Jeffers, Carolina, 1999 (current)

Longest Pass Reception (All TDs except as noted)
99 Andy Farkas (from Filchock), Washington vs. Pittsburgh, Oct. 15, 1939
Bobby Mitchell (from Izo), Washington vs. Cleveland, Sept. 15, 1963
Pat Studstill (from Sweetan), Detroit vs. Baltimore, Oct. 16, 1966
Gerry Allen (from Jurgensen), Washington vs. Chicago, Sept. 15, 1968
Cliff Branch (from Plunkett), L.A. Raiders vs. Washington, Oct. 2, 1983
Mike Quick (from Jaworski), Philadelphia vs. Atlanta, Nov. 10, 1985
Tony Martin (from Humphries), San Diego vs. Seattle, Sept. 18, 1994
Robert Brooks (from Favre), Green Bay vs. Chicago, Sept. 11, 1995
98 Gaynell Tinsley (from Russell), Chi. Cardinals vs. Cleveland, Nov. 17, 1938
Dick (Night Train) Lane (from Compton), Chi. Cardinals vs. Green Bay, Nov. 13, 1955
John Farrington (from Wade), Chicago vs. Detroit, Oct. 8, 1961
Willard Dewveall (from Lee), Houston vs. San Diego, Nov. 25, 1962
Homer Jones (from Morrall), N.Y. Giants vs. Pittsburgh, Sept. 11, 1966
Bobby Moore (from Hart), St. Louis vs. Los Angeles, Dec. 10, 1972 (no TD)
Michael Haynes (from Hebert), Atlanta vs. New Orleans, Sept. 12, 1993
Johnnie Morton (from Batch), Detroit vs. Chicago, Oct. 4, 1998
97 Gaynell Tinsley (from Coffee), Chi. Cardinals vs. Chi. Bears, Dec. 5, 1937
Cloyce Box (from Layne), Detroit vs. Green Bay, Nov. 26, 1953
Jerry Tarr (from Shaw), Denver vs. Boston, Sept. 21, 1962
Webster Slaughter (from Kosar), Cleveland vs. Chicago, Oct. 23, 1989
John Taylor (from Young), San Francisco vs. Atlanta, Nov. 3, 1991

AVERAGE GAIN

Highest Average Gain, Career (200 receptions)
22.26 Homer Jones, N.Y. Giants, 1964-69; Cleveland, 1970 (224-4,986)
20.83 Buddy Dial, Pittsburgh, 1959-1963; Dallas, 1964-66 (261-5,436)
20.24 Harlon Hill, Chi. Bears, 1954-1961; Pittsburgh, 1962; Detroit, 1962 (233-4,717)

Highest Average Gain, Season (24 receptions)
32.58 Don Currivan, Boston, 1947 (24-782)
31.44 Bucky Pope, Los Angeles, 1964 (25-786)
28.60 Bobby Duckworth, San Diego, 1984 (25-715)

Highest Average Gain, Game (3 receptions)
63.00 Torry Holt, St. Louis vs. Atlanta, Sept. 24, 2000 (3-189)
60.67 Bill Groman, Houston vs. Denver, Nov. 20, 1960 (3-182)
Homer Jones, N.Y. Giants vs. Washington, Dec. 12, 1965 (3-182)
60.33 Don Currivan, Boston vs. Washington, Nov. 30, 1947 (3-181)

TOUCHDOWNS

Most Seasons Leading League
9 Don Hutson, Green Bay, 1935-38, 1940-44
6 Jerry Rice, San Francisco, 1986-87, 1989-1991, 1993
3 Lance Alworth, San Diego, 1964-66
Cris Carter, Minnesota, 1995, 1997, 1999

Most Consecutive Seasons Leading League
5 Don Hutson, Green Bay, 1940-44
4 Don Hutson, Green Bay, 1935-38
3 Lance Alworth, San Diego, 1964-66
Jerry Rice, San Francisco, 1989-1991

Most Touchdowns, Career
176 Jerry Rice, San Francisco, 1985-2000
123 Cris Carter, Philadelphia, 1987-89; Minnesota, 1990-2000
100 Steve Largent, Seattle, 1976-1989

Most Touchdowns, Season
22 Jerry Rice, San Francisco, 1987
18 Mark Clayton, Miami, 1984
Sterling Sharpe, Green Bay, 1994
17 Don Hutson, Green Bay, 1942
Elroy (Crazylegs) Hirsch, Los Angeles, 1951
Bill Groman, Houston, 1961
Jerry Rice, San Francisco, 1989
Cris Carter, Minnesota, 1995
Carl Pickens, Cincinnati, 1995
Randy Moss, Minnesota, 1998

Most Touchdowns, Rookie, Season
17 Randy Moss, Minnesota, 1998
13 Bill Howton, Green Bay, 1952
John Jefferson, San Diego, 1978
12 Harlon Hill, Chi. Bears, 1954
Bill Groman, Houston, 1960
Mike Ditka, Chicago, 1961
Bob Hayes, Dallas, 1965

Most Touchdowns, Game
5 Bob Shaw, Chi. Cardinals vs. Baltimore, Oct. 2, 1950
Kellen Winslow, San Diego vs. Oakland, Nov. 22, 1981
Jerry Rice, San Francisco vs. Atlanta, Oct. 14, 1990
4 By many players. Last time:
Isaac Bruce, St. Louis vs. San Francisco, Oct. 10, 1999

Most Consecutive Games, Touchdowns
13 Jerry Rice, San Francisco, 1986-87
11 Elroy (Crazylegs) Hirsch, Los Angeles, 1950-51
Buddy Dial, Pittsburgh, 1959-1960
10 Carl Pickens, Cincinnati, 1994-95

INTERCEPTIONS BY

Most Seasons Leading League
3 Everson Walls, Dallas, 1981-82, 1985
2 Dick (Night Train) Lane, Los Angeles, 1952; Chi. Cardinals, 1954
Jack Christiansen, Detroit, 1953, 1957
Milt Davis, Baltimore, 1957, 1959
Dick Lynch, N.Y. Giants, 1961, 1963
Johnny Robinson, Kansas City, 1966, 1970
Bill Bradley, Philadelphia, 1971-72
Emmitt Thomas, Kansas City, 1969, 1974
Ronnie Lott, San Francisco, 1986; L.A. Raiders, 1991

Most Interceptions By, Career
81 Paul Krause, Washington, 1964-67; Minnesota, 1968-1979
79 Emlen Tunnell, N.Y. Giants, 1948-1958; Green Bay, 1959-1961
68 Dick (Night Train) Lane, Los Angeles, 1952-53; Chi. Cardinals, 1954-59; Detroit, 1960-65

ALL-TIME RECORDS

Most Interceptions By, Season
14 Dick (Night Train) Lane, Los Angeles, 1952
13 Dan Sandifer, Washington, 1948
Orban (Spec) Sanders, N.Y. Yanks, 1950
Lester Hayes, Oakland, 1980
12 By nine players

Most Interceptions By, Rookie, Season
14 Dick (Night Train) Lane, Los Angeles, 1952
13 Dan Sandifer, Washington, 1948
12 Woodley Lewis, Los Angeles, 1950
Paul Krause, Washington, 1964

Most Interceptions By, Game
4 Sammy Baugh, Washington vs. Detroit, Nov. 14, 1943
Dan Sandifer, Washington vs. Boston, Oct. 31, 1948
Don Doll, Detroit vs. Chi. Cardinals, Oct. 23, 1949
Bob Nussbaumer, Chi. Cardinals vs. N.Y. Bulldogs, Nov. 13, 1949
Russ Craft, Philadelphia vs. Chi. Cardinals, Sept. 24, 1950
Bobby Dillon, Green Bay vs. Detroit, Nov. 26, 1953
Jack Butler, Pittsburgh vs. Washington, Dec. 13, 1953
Austin (Goose) Gonsoulin, Denver vs. Buffalo, Sept. 18, 1960
Jerry Norton, St. Louis vs. Washington, Nov. 20, 1960; vs. Pittsburgh, Nov. 26, 1961
Dave Baker, San Francisco vs. L.A. Rams, Dec. 4, 1960
Bobby Ply, Dall. Texans vs. San Diego, Dec. 16, 1962
Bobby Hunt, Kansas City vs. Houston, Oct. 4, 1964
Willie Brown, Denver vs. N.Y. Jets, Nov. 15, 1964
Dick Anderson, Miami vs. Pittsburgh, Dec. 3, 1973
Willie Buchanon, Green Bay vs. San Diego, Sept. 24, 1978
Deron Cherry, Kansas City vs. Seattle, Sept. 29, 1985
Kwamie Lassiter, Arizona vs. San Diego, Dec. 27, 1998

Most Consecutive Games, Passes Intercepted By
8 Tom Morrow, Oakland, 1962-63
7 Tom Landry, N.Y. Giants, 1950-51
Paul Krause, Washington, 1964
Larry Wilson, St. Louis, 1966
Ben Davis, Cleveland, 1968
6 By many players. Last time:
Barry Wilburn, Washington, 1987

YARDS GAINED

Most Seasons Leading League
2 Dick (Night Train) Lane, Los Angeles, 1952; Chi. Cardinals, 1954
Herb Adderley, Green Bay, 1965, 1969
Dick Anderson, Miami, 1968, 1970

Most Yards Gained, Career
1,282 Emlen Tunnell, N.Y. Giants, 1948-1958; Green Bay, 1959-1961
1,207 Dick (Night Train) Lane, Los Angeles, 1952-53; Chi. Cardinals, 1954-59; Detroit, 1960-65
1,187 Deion Sanders, Atlanta, 1989-1993; San Francisco, 1994; Dallas, 1995-99; Washington, 2000

Most Yards Gained, Season
349 Charlie McNeil, San Diego, 1961
303 Deion Sanders, San Francisco, 1994
301 Don Doll, Detroit, 1949

Most Yards Gained, Rookie, Season
301 Don Doll, Detroit, 1949
298 Dick (Night Train) Lane, Los Angeles, 1952
275 Woodley Lewis, Los Angeles, 1950

Most Yards Gained, Game
177 Charlie McNeil, San Diego vs. Houston, Sept. 24, 1961
170 Louis Oliver, Miami vs. Buffalo, Oct. 4, 1992
167 Dick Jauron, Detroit vs. Chicago, Nov. 18, 1973

Longest Return (All TDs)
103 Vencie Glenn, San Diego vs. Denver, Nov. 29, 1987
Louis Oliver, Miami vs. Buffalo, Oct. 4, 1992
102 Bob Smith, Detroit vs. Chi. Bears, Nov. 24, 1949
Erich Barnes, N.Y. Giants vs. Dall. Cowboys, Oct. 15, 1961
Gary Barbaro, Kansas City vs. Seattle, Dec. 11, 1977
Louis Breeden, Cincinnati vs. San Diego, Nov. 8, 1981
Eddie Anderson, L.A. Raiders vs. Miami, Dec. 14, 1992
Donald Frank, San Diego vs. L.A. Raiders, Oct. 31, 1993
101 Richie Petitbon, Chicago vs Los Angeles, Dec. 9, 1962
Henry Carr, N.Y. Giants vs. Los Angeles, Nov. 13, 1966
Tony Greene, Buffalo vs. Kansas City, Oct. 3, 1976
Tom Pridemore, Atlanta vs. San Francisco, Sept. 20, 1981
Bryant Westbrook, Detroit vs. New England, Nov. 23, 2000

TOUCHDOWNS

Most Touchdowns, Career
9 Ken Houston, Houston, 1967-1972; Washington, 1973-1980
Rod Woodson, Pittsburgh, 1987-1996; San Francisco, 1997; Baltimore, 1998-2000
8 Deion Sanders, Atlanta, 1989-1993; San Francisco, 1994; Dallas, 1995-99; Washington, 2000
Eric Allen, Philadelphia, 1988-1994; New Orleans, 1995-97; Oakland, 1998-2000
7 Herb Adderley, Green Bay, 1961-69; Dallas, 1970-72
Erich Barnes, Chi. Bears, 1958-1960; N.Y. Giants, 1961-64; Cleveland, 1965-1970
Lem Barney, Detroit, 1967-77

Most Touchdowns, Season
4 Ken Houston, Houston, 1971
Jim Kearney, Kansas City, 1972
Eric Allen, Philadelphia, 1993
3 Dick Harris, San Diego, 1961
Dick Lynch, N.Y. Giants, 1963
Herb Adderley, Green Bay, 1965
Lem Barney, Detroit, 1967
Miller Farr, Houston, 1967
Monte Jackson, Los Angeles, 1976
Rod Perry, Los Angeles, 1978
Ronnie Lott, San Francisco, 1981
Lloyd Burruss, Kansas City, 1986
Wayne Haddix, Tampa Bay, 1990
Robert Massey, Phoenix, 1992
Ray Buchanan, Indianapolis, 1994
Deion Sanders, San Francisco, 1994
Mark McMillian, Kansas City, 1997
Otis Smith, N.Y. Jets, 1997
Jimmy Hitchcock, Minnesota, 1998
Eric Allen, Oakland, 2000
2 By many players

Most Touchdowns, Rookie, Season
3 Lem Barney, Detroit, 1967
Ronnie Lott, San Francisco, 1981
2 By many players

Most Touchdowns, Game
2 Bill Blackburn, Chi. Cardinals vs. Boston, Oct. 24, 1948
Dan Sandifer, Washington vs. Boston, Oct. 31, 1948
Bob Franklin, Cleveland vs. Chicago, Dec. 11, 1960
Bill Stacy, St. Louis vs. Dall. Cowboys, Nov. 5, 1961
Jerry Norton, St. Louis vs. Pittsburgh, Nov. 26, 1961
Miller Farr, Houston vs. Buffalo, Dec. 7, 1968
Ken Houston, Houston vs. San Diego, Dec. 19, 1971
Jim Kearney, Kansas City vs. Denver, Oct. 1, 1972
Lemar Parrish, Cincinnati vs. Houston, Dec. 17, 1972
Dick Anderson, Miami vs. Pittsburgh, Dec. 3, 1973
Prentice McCray, New England vs. N.Y. Jets, Nov. 21, 1976
Kenny Johnson, Atlanta vs. Green Bay, Nov. 27, 1983 (OT)
Mike Kozlowski, Miami vs. N.Y. Jets, Dec. 16, 1983
Dave Brown, Seattle vs. Kansas City, Nov. 4, 1984
Lloyd Burruss, Kansas City vs. San Diego, Oct. 19, 1986
Henry Jones, Buffalo vs. Indianapolis, Sept. 20, 1992
Robert Massey, Phoenix vs. Washington, Oct. 4, 1992
Eric Allen, Philadelphia vs. New Orleans, Dec. 26, 1993
Ken Norton, San Francisco vs. St. Louis, Oct. 22, 1995
Otis Smith, N.Y. Jets vs. Tampa Bay, Dec. 14, 1997
Dewayne Washington, Pittsburgh vs. Jacksonville, Nov. 22, 1998

PUNTING

Most Seasons Leading League
4 Sammy Baugh, Washington, 1940-43
Jerrel Wilson, Kansas City, 1965, 1968, 1972-73
3 Yale Lary, Detroit, 1959, 1961, 1963
Jim Fraser, Denver, 1962-64
Ray Guy, Oakland, 1974-75, 1977
Rohn Stark, Baltimore, 1983; Indianapolis, 1985-86
2 By many players

Most Consecutive Seasons Leading League
4 Sammy Baugh, Washington, 1940-43
3 Jim Fraser, Denver, 1962-64
2 By many players

PUNTS

Most Punts, Career
1,163 Lee Johnson, Houston, 1985-87; Cleveland, 1987-88; Cincinnati, 1988-1998; New England, 1999-2000
1,154 Dave Jennings, N.Y. Giants, 1974-1984; N.Y. Jets, 1985-87
1,141 Rohn Stark, Baltimore, 1982-83; Indianapolis, 1984-1994; Pittsburgh, 1995; Carolina, 1996; Seattle, 1997

Most Punts, Season
114 Bob Parsons, Chicago, 1981
111 Brad Maynard, N.Y. Giants, 1997
109 John James, Atlanta, 1978

Most Punts, Rookie, Season
111 Brad Maynard, N.Y. Giants, 1997
108 John Teltschik, Philadelphia, 1986
101 Daniel Pope, Kansas City, 1999

Most Punts, Game
16 Leo Araguz, Oakland vs. San Diego, Oct. 11, 1998
15 John Teltschik, Philadelphia vs. N.Y. Giants, Dec. 6, 1987 (OT)
14 Dick Nesbitt, Chi. Cardinals vs. Chi. Bears, Nov. 30, 1933
Keith Molesworth, Chi. Bears vs. Green Bay, Dec. 10, 1933
Sammy Baugh, Washington vs. Philadelphia, Nov. 5, 1939
Carl Kinscherf, N.Y. Giants vs. Detroit, Nov. 7, 1943
George Taliaferro, N.Y. Yanks vs. Los Angeles, Sept. 28, 1951

Longest Punt
98 Steve O'Neal, N.Y. Jets vs. Denver, Sept. 21, 1969
94 Joe Lintzenich, Chi. Bears vs. N.Y. Giants, Nov. 16, 1931
93 Shawn McCarthy, New England vs. Buffalo, Nov. 3, 1991

AVERAGE YARDAGE

Highest Average, Punting, Career (250 punts)
45.10 Sammy Baugh, Washington, 1937-1952 (338-15,245)
44.83 Darren Bennett, San Diego, 1995-2000 (524-23,492)
44.68 Tommy Davis, San Francisco, 1959-1969 (511-22,833)

Highest Average, Punting, Season (Qualifiers)
51.40 Sammy Baugh, Washington, 1940 (35-1,799)
48.94 Yale Lary, Detroit, 1963 (35-1,713)
48.73 Sammy Baugh, Washington, 1941 (30-1,462)

Highest Average, Punting, Rookie, Season (Qualifiers)
45.92 Frank Sinkwich, Detroit, 1943 (12-551)
45.91 Shane Lechler, Oakland, 2000 (65-2,984)
45.66 Tommy Davis, San Francisco, 1959 (59-2,694)

Highest Average, Punting, Game (4 punts)
61.75 Bob Cifers, Detroit vs. Chi. Bears, Nov. 24, 1946 (4-247)
61.60 Roy McKay, Green Bay vs. Chi. Cardinals, Oct. 28, 1945 (5-308)
59.50 Darren Bennett, San Diego vs. Pittsburgh, Oct. 1, 1995 (4-238)

PUNTS HAD BLOCKED

Most Consecutive Punts, None Blocked
726 Chris Gardocki, Chicago, 1992-94; Indianapolis, 1995-98; Cleveland, 1999-2000 (current)
623 Dave Jennings, N.Y. Giants, 1976-1983
619 Ray Guy, Oakland, 1979-1981; L.A. Raiders, 1982-86

Most Punts Had Blocked, Career
14 Herman Weaver, Detroit, 1970-76; Seattle, 1977-1980
Harry Newsome, Pittsburgh, 1985-89; Minnesota, 1990-93
12 Jerrel Wilson, Kansas City, 1963-1977; New England, 1978
Tom Blanchard, N.Y. Giants, 1971-73; New Orleans, 1974-78; Tampa Bay, 1979-1981
11 David Lee, Baltimore, 1966-1978

Most Punts Had Blocked, Season
6 Harry Newsome, Pittsburgh, 1988
4 Bryan Wagner, Cleveland, 1990
3 By many players

PUNT RETURNS

Most Seasons Leading League
3 Les (Speedy) Duncan, San Diego, 1965-66; Washington, 1971
Rick Upchurch, Denver, 1976, 1978, 1982
2 Dick Christy, N.Y. Titans, 1961-62
Claude Gibson, Oakland, 1963-64
Billy (White Shoes) Johnson, Houston, 1975, 1977
Mel Gray, New Orleans, 1987; Detroit, 1991
Jermaine Lewis, Baltimore, 1997, 2000

PUNT RETURNS

Most Punt Returns, Career
349 David Meggett, N.Y. Giants, 1989-1994; New England, 1995-97; N.Y. Jets, 1998
Brian Mitchell, Washington, 1990-99; Philadelphia, 2000
315 Eric Metcalf, Cleveland, 1989-1994; Atlanta, 1995-96; San Diego, 1997; Arizona, 1998; Carolina, 1999
304 Tim Brown, L.A. Raiders, 1988-1994; Oakland, 1995-2000

Most Punt Returns, Season
70 Danny Reece, Tampa Bay, 1979
62 Fulton Walker, Miami-L.A. Raiders, 1985
58 J.T. Smith, Kansas City, 1979
Greg Pruitt, L.A. Raiders, 1983
Leo Lewis, Minnesota, 1988
Desmond Howard, Green Bay, 1996

Most Punt Returns, Rookie, Season
57 Lew Barnes, Chicago, 1986
54 James Jones, Dallas, 1980
53 Louis Lipps, Pittsburgh, 1984

Most Punt Returns, Game
11 Eddie Brown, Washington vs. Tampa Bay, Oct. 9, 1977
10 Theo Bell, Pittsburgh vs. Buffalo, Dec. 16, 1979
Mike Nelms, Washington vs. New Orleans, Dec. 26, 1982
Ronnie Harris, New England vs. Pittsburgh, Dec. 5, 1993
9 Rodger Bird, Oakland vs. Denver, Sept. 10, 1967
Ralph McGill, San Francisco vs. Atlanta, Oct. 29, 1972
Ed Podolak, Kansas City vs. San Diego, Nov. 10, 1974
Anthony Leonard, San Francisco vs. New Orleans, Oct. 17, 1976
Butch Johnson, Dallas vs. Buffalo, Nov. 15, 1976
Larry Marshall, Philadelphia vs. Tampa Bay, Sept. 18, 1977
Nesby Glasgow, Baltimore vs. Kansas City, Sept. 2, 1979
Mike Nelms, Washington vs. St. Louis, Dec. 21, 1980
Leon Bright, N.Y. Giants vs. Philadelphia, Dec. 11, 1982
Pete Shaw, N.Y. Giants vs. Philadelphia, Nov. 20, 1983
Cleotha Montgomery, L.A. Raiders vs. Detroit, Dec. 10, 1984
Phil McConkey, N.Y. Giants vs. Philadelphia, Dec. 6, 1987 (OT)
Andre Hastings, Pittsburgh vs. Cleveland, Nov. 13, 1995

FAIR CATCHES

Most Fair Catches, Career
184 Brian Mitchell, Washington, 1990-99; Philadelphia, 2000
137 Glyn Milburn, Denver, 1993-95; Detroit, 1996-97; Chicago, 1998-2000
121 Mel Gray, New Orleans, 1986-88; Detroit, 1989-1994; Houston, 1995-96; Tennessee, 1997; Philadelphia, 1997

Most Fair Catches, Season
33 Brian Mitchell, Philadelphia, 2000
27 Leo Lewis, Minnesota, 1989
26 Eric Guliford, New Orleans, 1997
Glyn Milburn, Detroit, 1997
Glyn Milburn, Chicago, 2000

Most Fair Catches, Game
7 Lem Barney, Detroit vs. Chicago, Nov. 21, 1976
Bobby Morse, Philadelphia vs. Buffalo, Dec. 27, 1987
6 Jake Scott, Miami vs. Buffalo, Dec. 20, 1970
Greg Pruitt, L.A. Raiders vs. Seattle, Oct. 7, 1984
Phil McConkey, San Diego vs. Kansas City, Dec. 17, 1989
Gerald McNeil, Houston vs. Pittsburgh, Sept. 16, 1990
Bobby Engram, Chicago vs. Minnesota, Sept. 15, 1996
Eddie Kennison, New Orleans vs. Baltimore, Dec. 19, 1999
5 By many players

YARDS GAINED

Most Seasons Leading League
3 Alvin Haymond, Baltimore, 1965-66; Los Angeles, 1969
2 Bill Dudley, Pittsburgh, 1942, 1946
Emlen Tunnell, N.Y. Giants, 1951-52
Dick Christy, N.Y. Titans, 1961-62
Claude Gibson, Oakland, 1963-64
Rodger Bird, Oakland, 1966-67
J.T. Smith, Kansas City, 1979-1980
Vai Sikahema, St. Louis, 1986-87
David Meggett, N.Y. Giants, 1989-1990
Tamarick Vanover, Kansas City, 1995, 1999

Most Yards Gained, Career
3,811 Brian Mitchell, Washington, 1990-99; Philadelphia, 2000
3,708 David Meggett, N.Y. Giants, 1989-1994; New England, 1995-97; N.Y. Jets, 1998
3,317 Billy (White Shoes) Johnson, Houston, 1974-1980; Atlanta, 1982-87; Washington, 1988

Most Yards Gained, Season
875 Desmond Howard, Green Bay, 1996
692 Fulton Walker, Miami-L.A. Raiders, 1985
666 Greg Pruitt, L.A. Raiders, 1983

Most Yards Gained, Rookie, Season
656 Louis Lipps, Pittsburgh, 1984
655 Neal Colzie, Oakland, 1975
619 Leon Johnson, N.Y. Jets, 1997

Most Yards Gained, Game
207 LeRoy Irvin, Los Angeles vs. Atlanta, Oct. 11, 1981
205 George Atkinson, Oakland vs. Buffalo, Sept. 15, 1968
184 Tom Watkins, Detroit vs. San Francisco, Oct. 6, 1963
Jermaine Lewis, Baltimore vs. Seattle, Dec. 7, 1997

Longest Punt Return (All TDs)
103 Robert Bailey, L.A. Rams vs. New Orleans, Oct. 23, 1994
98 Gil LeFebvre, Cincinnati vs. Brooklyn, Dec. 3, 1933
Charlie West, Minnesota vs. Washington, Nov. 3, 1968
Dennis Morgan, Dallas vs. St. Louis, Oct. 13, 1974
Terance Mathis, N.Y. Jets vs. Dallas, Nov. 4, 1990
97 Greg Pruitt, L.A. Raiders vs. Washington, Oct. 2, 1983

ALL-TIME RECORDS

AVERAGE YARDAGE

Highest Average, Career (75 returns)

12.78 George McAfee, Chi. Bears, 1940-41, 1945-1950 (112-1,431)
12.75 Jack Christiansen, Detroit, 1951-58 (85-1,084)
12.55 Claude Gibson, San Diego, 1961-62; Oakland, 1963-65 (110-1,381)

Highest Average, Season (Qualifiers)

23.00 Herb Rich, Baltimore, 1950 (12-276)
21.47 Jack Christiansen, Detroit, 1952 (15-322)
21.28 Dick Christy, N.Y. Titans, 1961 (18-383)

Highest Average, Rookie, Season (Qualifiers)

23.00 Herb Rich, Baltimore, 1950 (12-276)
20.88 Jerry Davis, Chi. Cardinals, 1948 (16-334)
20.73 Frank Sinkwich, Detroit, 1943 (11-228)

Highest Average, Game (3 returns)

47.67 Chuck Latourette, St. Louis vs. New Orleans, Sept. 29, 1968 (3-143)
47.33 Johnny Roland, St. Louis vs. Philadelphia, Oct. 2, 1966 (3-142)
45.67 Dick Christy, N.Y. Titans vs. Denver, Sept. 24, 1961 (3-137)

TOUCHDOWNS

Most Touchdowns, Career

9 Eric Metcalf, Cleveland, 1989-1994; Atlanta, 1995-96; San Diego, 1997; Arizona, 1998; Carolina, 1999
8 Jack Christiansen, Detroit, 1951-58
Rick Upchurch, Denver, 1975-1983
Desmond Howard, Washington, 1992-94; Jacksonville, 1995; Green Bay, 1996, 1999; Oakland, 1997-98; Detroit, 1999-2000
Brian Mitchell, Washington, 1990-99; Philadelphia 2000
7 David Meggett, N.Y. Giants, 1989-1994; New England, 1995-97; N.Y. Jets, 1998

Most Touchdowns, Season

4 Jack Christiansen, Detroit, 1951
Rick Upchurch, Denver, 1976
3 Emlen Tunnell, N.Y. Giants, 1951
Billy (White Shoes) Johnson, Houston, 1975
LeRoy Irvin, Los Angeles, 1981
Desmond Howard, Green Bay, 1996
Darrien Gordon, Denver, 1997
Eric Metcalf, San Diego, 1997
2 By many players

Most Touchdowns, Rookie, Season

4 Jack Christiansen, Detroit, 1951
2 By many players

Most Touchdowns, Game

2 Jack Christiansen, Detroit vs. Los Angeles, Oct. 14, 1951; vs. Green Bay, Nov. 22, 1951
Dick Christy, N.Y. Titans vs. Denver, Sept. 24, 1961
Rick Upchurch, Denver vs. Cleveland, Sept. 26, 1976
LeRoy Irvin, Los Angeles vs. Atlanta, Oct. 11, 1981
Vai Sikahema, St. Louis vs. Tampa Bay, Dec. 21, 1986
Todd Kinchen, L.A. Rams vs. Atlanta, Dec. 27, 1992
Eric Metcalf, Cleveland vs. Pittsburgh, Oct. 24, 1993; San Diego vs. Cincinnati, Nov. 2, 1997
Darrien Gordon, Denver vs. Carolina, Nov. 9, 1997
Jermaine Lewis, Baltimore vs. Seattle, Dec. 7, 1997; Baltimore vs. N.Y. Jets, Dec. 24, 2000

KICKOFF RETURNS

Most Seasons Leading League

3 Abe Woodson, San Francisco, 1959, 1962-63
2 Lynn Chandnois, Pittsburgh, 1951-52
Bobby Jancik, Houston, 1962-63
Travis Williams, Green Bay, 1967; Los Angeles, 1971
Mel Gray, Detroit, 1991, 1994
Michael Bates, Carolina, 1996-97

KICKOFF RETURNS

Most Kickoff Returns, Career

468 Brian Mitchell, Washington, 1990-99; Philadelphia 2000
421 Mel Gray, New Orleans, 1986-88; Detroit, 1989-1994; Houston, 1995-96; Tennessee, 1997; Philadelphia, 1997
401 Glyn Milburn, Denver, 1993-95; Detroit, 1996-97; Chicago, 1998-2000

Most Kickoff Returns, Season

82 MarTay Jenkins, Arizona, 2000
70 Tyrone Hughes, New Orleans, 1996
67 Ronney Jenkins, San Diego, 2000

Most Kickoff Returns, Rookie, Season

67 Ronney Jenkins, San Diego, 2000
56 Tony Horne, St. Louis, 1998
55 Stump Mitchell, St. Louis, 1981

Most Kickoff Returns, Game

10 Desmond Howard, Oakland vs. Seattle, Oct. 26, 1997
9 Noland Smith, Kansas City vs. Oakland, Nov. 23, 1967
Dino Hall, Cleveland vs. Pittsburgh, Oct. 7, 1979
Paul Palmer, Kansas City vs. Seattle, Sept. 20, 1987
Eric Metcalf, Atlanta vs. San Francisco, Sept. 29, 1996; vs. St. Louis, Nov. 10, 1996
Michael Bates, Carolina vs. Atlanta, Oct. 4, 1998
8 By many players

YARDS GAINED

Most Seasons Leading League

3 Bruce Harper, N.Y. Jets, 1977-79
Tyrone Hughes, New Orleans, 1994-96
2 Marshall Goldberg, Chi. Cardinals, 1941-42
Woodley Lewis, Los Angeles, 1953-54
Al Carmichael, Green Bay, 1956-57
Timmy Brown, Philadelphia, 1961, 1963
Bobby Jancik, Houston, 1963, 1966
Ron Smith, Atlanta, 1966-67

Most Yards Gained, Career

10,710 Brian Mitchell, Washington, 1990-99; Philadelphia, 2000
10,250 Mel Gray, New Orleans, 1986-88; Detroit, 1989-1994; Houston, 1995-96; Tennessee, 1997; Philadelphia, 1997
9,636 Glyn Milburn, Denver, 1993-95; Detroit, 1996-97; Chicago, 1998-2000

Most Yards Gained, Season

2,186 MarTay Jenkins, Arizona, 2000
1,791 Tyrone Hughes, New Orleans, 1996
1,629 Charlie Rogers, Seattle, 2000

Most Yards Gained, Rookie, Season

1,531 Ronney Jenkins, San Diego, 2000
1,428 Terry Fair, Detroit, 1998
1,345 Buster Rhymes, Minnesota, 1985

Most Yards Gained, Game

304 Tyrone Hughes, New Orleans vs. L.A. Rams, Oct. 23, 1994
294 Wally Triplett, Detroit vs. Los Angeles, Oct. 29, 1950
267 Tony Horne, St. Louis vs. Kansas City, Oct. 22, 2000

Longest Kickoff Return (All TDs)

106 Al Carmichael, Green Bay vs. Chi. Bears, Oct. 7, 1956
Noland Smith, Kansas City vs. Denver, Dec. 17, 1967
Roy Green, St. Louis vs. Dallas, Oct. 21, 1979
105 Frank Seno, Chi. Cardinals vs. N.Y. Giants, Oct. 20, 1946
Ollie Matson, Chi. Cardinals vs. Washington, Oct. 14, 1956
Abe Woodson, San Francisco vs. Los Angeles, Nov. 8, 1959
Timmy Brown, Philadelphia vs. Cleveland, Sept. 17, 1961
Jon Arnett, Los Angeles vs. Detroit, Oct. 29, 1961
Eugene (Mercury) Morris, Miami vs. Cincinnati, Sept. 14, 1969
Travis Williams, Los Angeles vs. New Orleans, Dec. 5, 1971
Terry Fair, Detroit vs. Tampa Bay, Sept. 28, 1998
104 By many players

AVERAGE YARDAGE

Highest Average, Career (75 returns)

30.56 Gale Sayers, Chicago, 1965-1971 (91-2,781)
29.57 Lynn Chandnois, Pittsburgh, 1950-56 (92-2,720)
28.69 Abe Woodson, San Francisco, 1958-1964; St. Louis, 1965-66 (193-5,538)

Highest Average, Season (Qualifiers)

41.06 Travis Williams, Green Bay, 1967 (18-739)
37.69 Gale Sayers, Chicago, 1967 (16-603)
35.50 Ollie Matson, Chi. Cardinals, 1958 (14-497)

Highest Average, Rookie, Season (Qualifiers)

41.06 Travis Williams, Green Bay, 1967 (18-739)
33.08 Tom Moore, Green Bay, 1960 (12-397)
32.88 Duriel Harris, Miami, 1976 (17-559)

Highest Average, Game (3 returns)

73.50 Wally Triplett, Detroit vs. Los Angeles, Oct. 29, 1950 (4-294)
67.33 Lenny Lyles, San Francisco vs. Baltimore, Dec. 18, 1960 (3-202)
65.33 Ken Hall, Houston vs. N.Y. Titans, Oct. 23, 1960 (3-196)

TOUCHDOWNS

Most Touchdowns, Career

6 Ollie Matson, Chi. Cardinals, 1952, 1954-58; L.A. Rams, 1959-1962; Detroit, 1963; Philadelphia, 1964
Gale Sayers, Chicago, 1965-1971
Travis Williams, Green Bay, 1967-1970; Los Angeles, 1971
Mel Gray, New Orleans, 1986-88; Detroit, 1989-1994; Houston, 1995-96; Tennessee, 1997; Philadelphia, 1997
5 Bobby Mitchell, Cleveland, 1958-1961; Washington, 1962-68
Abe Woodson, San Francisco, 1958-1964; St. Louis, 1965-66
Timmy Brown, Green Bay, 1959; Philadelphia, 1960-67; Baltimore, 1968
Michael Bates, Seattle, 1993-94; Cleveland, 1995; Carolina, 1996-2000
4 Cecil Turner, Chicago, 1968-1973
Ron Brown, L.A. Rams, 1984-89, 1991; L.A. Raiders, 1990
Jon Vaughn, New England, 1991-92; Seattle, 1993-94; Kansas City, 1994

Andre Coleman, San Diego, 1994-96; Seattle, 1997; Pittsburgh, 1997-98
Tamarick Vanover, Kansas City, 1995-99
Tony Horne, St. Louis, 1998-2000

Most Touchdowns, Season
4 Travis Williams, Green Bay, 1967
Cecil Turner, Chicago, 1970
3 Verda (Vitamin T) Smith, Los Angeles, 1950
Abe Woodson, San Francisco, 1963
Gale Sayers, Chicago, 1967
Raymond Clayborn, New England, 1977
Ron Brown, L.A. Rams, 1985
Mel Gray, Detroit, 1994
Darrick Vaughn, Atlanta, 2000
2 By many players

Most Touchdowns, Rookie, Season
4 Travis Williams, Green Bay, 1967
3 Raymond Clayborn, New England, 1977
Darrick Vaughn, Atlanta, 2000
2 By many players

Most Touchdowns, Game
2 Timmy Brown, Philadelphia vs. Dallas, Nov. 6, 1966
Travis Williams, Green Bay vs. Cleveland, Nov. 12, 1967
Ron Brown, L.A. Rams vs. Green Bay, Nov. 24, 1985
Tyrone Hughes, New Orleans vs. L.A. Rams, Oct. 23, 1994

COMBINED KICK RETURNS

Most Combined Kick Returns, Career
817 Brian Mitchell, Washington, 1990-99; Philadelphia, 2000 (p-349, k-468)
684 Glyn Milburn, Denver, 1993-95; Detroit, 1996-97; Chicago, 1998-2000 (p-283, k-401)
673 Mel Gray, New Orleans, 1986-88; Detroit, 1989-1994; Houston, 1995-96; Tennessee, 1997; Philadelphia, 1997 (p-252, k-421)

Most Combined Kick Returns, Season
103 Brian Mitchell, Washington, 1998 (p-44; k-59)
102 Glyn Milburn, Detroit, 1997 (p-47, k-55)
101 Roell Preston, Green Bay, 1998 (p-44; k-57)

Most Combined Kick Returns, Game
13 Stump Mitchell, St. Louis vs. Atlanta, Oct. 18, 1981 (p-6, k-7)
Ronnie Harris, New England vs. Pittsburgh, Dec. 5, 1993 (p-10, k-3)
12 Mel Renfro, Dallas vs. Green Bay, Nov. 29, 1964 (p-4, k-8)
Larry Jones, Washington vs. Dallas, Dec. 13, 1975 (p-6, k-6)
Eddie Brown, Washington vs. Tampa Bay, Oct. 9, 1977 (p-11, k-1)
Nesby Glasgow, Baltimore vs. Denver, Sept. 2, 1979 (p-9, k-3)
Tim Dwight, Atlanta vs. Detroit, Nov. 12, 2000 (p-8, k-4)
11 By many players

YARDS GAINED

Most Yards Returned, Career
14,521 Brian Mitchell, Washington, 1990-99; Philadelphia, 2000 (p-3,811; k-10,710)
13,003 Mel Gray, New Orleans, 1986-88; Detroit, 1989-1994; Houston, 1995-96; Tennessee, 1997; Philadelphia, 1997 (p-2,753; k-10,250)
12,448 Glyn Milburn, Denver, 1993-95; Detroit, 1996-97; Chicago, 1998-2000 (p-2,812; k-9,636)

Most Yards Returned, Season
2,187 MarTay Jenkins, Arizona, 2000 (p-1, k-2,186)
1,992 Charlie Rogers, Seattle, 2000 (p-363, k-1,629)
1,943 Tyrone Hughes, New Orleans, 1996 (p-152, k-1,791)

Most Yards Returned, Game
347 Tyrone Hughes, New Orleans vs. L.A. Rams, Oct. 23, 1994 (p-43, k-304)
294 Wally Triplett, Detroit vs. Los Angeles, Oct. 29, 1950 (k-294)
Woodley Lewis, Los Angeles vs. Detroit, Oct. 18, 1953 (p-120, k-174)
289 Eddie Payton, Detroit vs. Minnesota, Dec. 17, 1977 (p-105, k-184)

TOUCHDOWNS

Most Touchdowns, Career
11 Eric Metcalf, Cleveland, 1989-1994; Atlanta, 1995-96; San Diego, 1997; Arizona, 1998; Carolina, 1999 (p-9, k-2)
Brian Mitchell, Washington, 1990-99; Philadelphia, 2000 (p-8, k-3)
9 Ollie Matson, Chi. Cardinals, 1952, 1954-58; Los Angeles, 1959-1962; Detroit, 1963; Philadelphia, 1964-66 (p-3, k-6)
Mel Gray, New Orleans, 1986-88; Detroit, 1989-1994; Houston, 1995-96; Tennessee, 1997; Philadelphia, 1997 (p-3, k-6)
Deion Sanders, Atlanta, 1989-1993; San Francisco, 1994; Dallas, 1995-99; Washington, 2000 (p-6, k-3)
8 Jack Christiansen, Detroit, 1951-58 (p-8)
Bobby Mitchell, Cleveland, 1958-1961; Washington, 1962-68 (p-3, k-5)
Gale Sayers, Chicago, 1965-1971 (p-2, k-6)
Rick Upchurch, Denver, 1975-1983 (p-8)
Billy (White Shoes) Johnson, Houston, 1974-1980; Atlanta, 1982-87; Washington, 1988 (p-6, k-2)
David Meggett, N.Y. Giants, 1989-1994; New England, 1995-97; N.Y. Jets, 1998 (p-7, k-1)
Tamarick Vanover, Kansas City, 1995-99 (p-4, k-4)
Desmond Howard, Washington, 1992-94; Jacksonville, 1995; Green Bay, 1996, 1999; Oakland, 1997-98; Detroit, 1999-2000 (p-8)

Most Touchdowns, Season
4 Jack Christiansen, Detroit, 1951 (p-4)
Emlen Tunnell, N.Y. Giants, 1951 (p-3, k-1)
Gale Sayers, Chicago, 1967 (p-1, k-3)
Travis Williams, Green Bay, 1967 (k-4)
Cecil Turner, Chicago, 1970 (k-4)
Billy Johnson, Houston, 1975 (p-3, k-1)
Rick Upchurch, Denver, 1976 (p-4)
3 Verda (Vitamin T) Smith, Los Angeles, 1950 (k-3)
Abe Woodson, San Francisco, 1963 (k-3)
Raymond Clayborn, New England, 1977 (k-3)
Billy Johnson, Houston, 1977 (p-2, k-1)
LeRoy Irvin, Los Angeles, 1981 (p-3)
Ron Brown, L.A. Rams, 1985 (k-3)
Tyrone Hughes, New Orleans, 1993 (p-2, k-1)
Mel Gray, Detroit, 1994 (k-3)
Andre Coleman, San Diego, 1995 (p-2; k-1)
Tamarick Vanover, Kansas City, 1995 (p-1, k-2)
Desmond Howard, Green Bay, 1996 (p-3)
Darrien Gordon, Denver, 1997 (p-3)
Eric Metcalf, San Diego, 1997 (p-3)
Glyn Milburn, Chicago, 1998 (p-2; k-1)
Roell Preston, Green Bay, 1998 (p-2; k-1)
Darrick Vaughn, Atlanta, 2000 (k-3)
2 By many players

Most Touchdowns, Game
2 Jack Christiansen, Detroit vs. Los Angeles, Oct. 14, 1951 (p-2); vs. Green Bay, Nov. 22, 1951 (p-2)
Jim Patton, N.Y. Giants vs. Washington, Oct. 30, 1955 (p-1, k-1)
Bobby Mitchell, Cleveland vs. Philadelphia, Nov. 23, 1958 (p-1, k-1)
Dick Christy, N.Y. Titans vs. Denver, Sept. 24, 1961 (p-2)
Al Frazier, Denver vs. Boston, Dec. 3, 1961 (p-1, k-1)
Timmy Brown, Philadelphia vs. Dallas, Nov. 6, 1966 (k-2)
Travis Williams, Green Bay vs. Cleveland, Nov. 12, 1967 (k-2); vs. Pittsburgh, Nov. 2, 1969 (p-1, k-1)
Gale Sayers, Chicago vs. San Francisco, Dec. 3, 1967 (p-1, k-1)
Rick Upchurch, Denver vs. Cleveland, Sept. 26, 1976 (p-2)
Eddie Payton, Detroit vs. Minnesota, Dec. 17, 1977 (p-1, k-1)
LeRoy Irvin, Los Angeles vs. Atlanta, Oct. 11, 1981 (p-2)
Ron Brown, L.A. Rams vs. Green Bay, Nov. 24, 1985 (k-2)
Vai Sikahema, St. Louis vs. Tampa Bay, Dec. 21, 1986 (p-2)
Todd Kinchen, L.A. Rams vs. Atlanta, Dec. 27, 1992 (p-2)
Eric Metcalf, Cleveland vs. Pittsburgh, Oct. 24, 1993 (p-2); San Diego vs. Cincinnati, Nov. 2, 1997 (p-2)
Tyrone Hughes, New Orleans vs. L.A. Rams, Oct. 23, 1994 (k-2)
Darrien Gordon, Denver vs. Carolina, Nov. 9, 1997 (p-2)
Jermaine Lewis, Baltimore vs. Seattle, Dec. 7, 1997 (p-2); Baltimore vs. N.Y. Jets, Dec. 24, 2000 (p-2)

FUMBLES

Most Fumbles, Career
161 Warren Moon, Houston, 1984-1993; Minnesota, 1994-96; Seattle, 1997-98; Kansas City, 1999-2000
153 Dave Krieg, Seattle, 1980-1991; Kansas City, 1992-93; Detroit, 1994; Arizona, 1995; Chicago, 1996; Tennessee, 1997-98
137 John Elway, Denver, 1983-1998

Most Fumbles, Season
21 Tony Banks, St. Louis, 1996
18 Dave Krieg, Seattle, 1989
Warren Moon, Houston, 1990
17 Dan Pastorini, Houston, 1973
Warren Moon, Houston, 1984
Randall Cunningham, Philadelphia, 1989
Jon Kitna, Seattle, 2000

Most Fumbles, Game
7 Len Dawson, Kansas City vs. San Diego, Nov. 15, 1964
6 Sam Etcheverry, St. Louis vs. N.Y. Giants, Sept, 17, 1961
Dave Krieg, Seattle vs. Kansas City, Nov. 5, 1989
Brett Favre, Green Bay vs. Tampa Bay, Dec. 7, 1998
5 Paul Christman, Chi. Cardinals vs. Green Bay, Nov. 10, 1946
Charlie Conerly, N.Y. Giants vs. San Francisco, Dec. 1, 1957
Jack Kemp, Buffalo vs. Houston, Oct. 29, 1967
Roman Gabriel, Philadelphia vs. Oakland, Nov. 21, 1976
Randall Cunningham, Philadelphia vs. L.A. Raiders, Nov. 30, 1986 (OT)
Willie Totten, Buffalo vs. Indianapolis, Oct. 4, 1987

Dave Walter, Cincinnati vs. Seattle, Oct. 11, 1987
Dave Krieg, Seattle vs. San Diego, Nov. 25, 1990 (OT)
Andre Ware, Detroit vs. Green Bay, Dec. 6, 1992
Steve Beuerlein, Carolina vs. San Francisco, Nov. 8, 1998

FUMBLES RECOVERED

Most Fumbles Recovered, Career, Own and Opponents'

56 Warren Moon, Houston, 1984-1993; Minnesota, 1994-96; Seattle, 1997-98; Kansas City, 1999-2000 (56 own)
47 Dave Krieg, Seattle, 1980-1991; Kansas City, 1992-93; Detroit, 1994; Arizona, 1995; Chicago, 1996; Tennessee, 1997-98 (47 own)
45 Boomer Esiason, Cincinnati, 1984-1992, 1997; N.Y. Jets, 1993-95; Arizona, 1996 (45 own)

Most Fumbles Recovered, Season, Own and Opponents'

9 Don Hultz, Minnesota, 1963 (9 opp)
Dave Krieg, Seattle, 1989 (9 own)
Brian Griese, Denver, 1999 (9 own)
Jon Kitna, Seattle, 2000 (9 own)
8 Paul Christman, Chi. Cardinals, 1945 (8 own)
Joe Schmidt, Detroit, 1955 (8 opp)
Bill Butler, Minnesota, 1963 (8 own)
Kermit Alexander, San Francisco, 1965 (4 own, 4 opp)
Jack Lambert, Pittsburgh, 1976 (1 own, 7 opp)
Danny White, Dallas, 1981 (8 own)
Dan Marino, Miami, 1988 (7 own, 1 opp)
Tony Banks, St. Louis, 1998 (8 own)
7 By many players

Most Fumbles Recovered, Game, Own and Opponents'

4 Otto Graham, Cleveland vs. N.Y. Giants, Oct. 25, 1953 (4 own)
Sam Etcheverry, St. Louis vs. N.Y. Giants, Sept. 17, 1961 (4 own)
Roman Gabriel, Los Angeles vs. San Francisco, Oct. 12, 1969 (4 own)
Joe Ferguson, Buffalo vs. Miami, Sept. 18, 1977 (4 own)
Randall Cunningham, Philadelphia vs. L.A. Raiders, Nov. 30, 1986 (OT) (4 own)
3 By many players

OWN FUMBLES RECOVERED

Most Own Fumbles Recovered, Career

56 Warren Moon, Houston, 1984-1993; Minnesota, 1994-96; Seattle, 1997-98; Kansas City, 1999-2000
47 Dave Krieg, Seattle, 1980-1991; Kansas City, 1992-93; Detroit, 1994; Arizona, 1995; Chicago, 1996; Tennessee, 1997-98
45 Boomer Esiason, Cincinnati, 1984-1992, 1997; N.Y. Jets, 1993-95; Arizona, 1996

Most Own Fumbles Recovered, Season

9 Dave Krieg, Seattle, 1989
Brian Griese, Denver, 1999
Jon Kitna, Seattle, 2000
8 Paul Christman, Chi. Cardinals, 1945
Bill Butler, Minnesota, 1963
Danny White, Dallas, 1981
Tony Banks, St. Louis, 1998
7 By many players

Most Own Fumbles Recovered, Game

4 Otto Graham, Cleveland vs. N.Y. Giants, Oct. 25, 1953
Sam Etcheverry, St. Louis vs. N.Y. Giants, Sept. 17, 1961
Roman Gabriel, Los Angeles vs. San Francisco, Oct. 12, 1969
Joe Ferguson, Buffalo vs. Miami, Sept. 18, 1977
Randall Cunningham, Philadelphia vs. L.A. Raiders, Nov. 30, 1986 (OT)
3 By many players

OPPONENTS' FUMBLES RECOVERED

Most Opponents' Fumbles Recovered, Career

29 Jim Marshall, Cleveland, 1960; Minnesota, 1961-1979
28 Rickey Jackson, New Orleans, 1981-1993; San Francisco, 1994-95
26 Kevin Greene, L.A. Rams, 1985-1992; Pittsburgh, 1993-95; Carolina, 1996, 1998-99; San Francisco, 1997
Cornelius Bennett, Buffalo, 1987-1995; Atlanta, 1996-98; Indianapolis, 1999-2000

Most Opponents' Fumbles Recovered, Season

9 Don Hultz, Minnesota, 1963
8 Joe Schmidt, Detroit, 1955
7 Alan Page, Minnesota, 1970
Jack Lambert, Pittsburgh, 1976
Ray Childress, Houston, 1988
Rickey Jackson, New Orleans, 1990

Most Opponents' Fumbles Recovered, Game

3 Corwin Clatt, Chi. Cardinals vs. Detroit, Nov. 6, 1949
Vic Sears, Philadelphia vs. Green Bay, Nov. 2, 1952
Ed Beatty, San Francisco vs. Los Angeles, Oct. 7, 1956
Ron Carroll, Houston vs. Cincinnati, Oct. 27, 1974
Maurice Spencer, New Orleans vs. Atlanta, Oct. 10, 1976
Steve Nelson, New England vs. Philadelphia, Oct. 8, 1978
Charles Jackson, Kansas City vs. Pittsburgh, Sept. 6, 1981
Willie Buchanon, San Diego vs. Denver, Sept. 27, 1981
Joey Browner, Minnesota vs. San Francisco, Sept. 8, 1985
Ray Childress, Houston vs. Washington, Oct. 30, 1988
John Thierry, Chicago vs. Houston, Oct. 22, 1995
Stephen Boyd, Detroit vs. Chicago, Oct. 4, 1998
Darryl Williams, Seattle vs. Kansas City, Oct. 4, 1998
2 By many players

YARDS RETURNING FUMBLES

Longest Fumble Run (All TDs)

104 Jack Tatum, Oakland vs. Green Bay, Sept. 24, 1972
Aeneas Williams, Arizona vs. Washington, Nov. 5, 2000
102 Travis Davis, Pittsburgh vs. Carolina, Dec. 26, 1999
100 Chris Martin, Kansas City vs. Miami, Oct. 13, 1991

TOUCHDOWNS

Most Touchdowns, Career (Total)

5 Jessie Tuggle, Atlanta, 1987-2000
4 Bill Thompson, Denver, 1969-1981
Derrick Thomas, Kansas City, 1989-1999
3 By many players

Most Touchdowns, Season (Total)

2 Harold McPhail, Boston, 1934
Harry Ebding, Detroit, 1937
John Morelli, Boston, 1944
Frank Maznicki, Boston, 1947
Fred (Dippy) Evans, Chi. Bears, 1948
Ralph Heywood, Boston, 1948
Art Tait, N.Y. Yanks, 1951
John Dwyer, Los Angeles, 1952
Leo Sugar, Chi. Cardinals, 1957
Doug Cline, Houston, 1961
Jim Bradshaw, Pittsburgh, 1964
Royce Berry, Cincinnati, 1970
Ahmad Rashad, Buffalo, 1974
Tim Gray, Kansas City, 1977
Charles Phillips, Oakland, 1978
Kenny Johnson, Atlanta, 1981
George Martin, N.Y. Giants, 1981
Del Rodgers, Green Bay, 1982
Mike Douglass, Green Bay, 1983
Shelton Robinson, Seattle, 1983
Erik McMillan, N.Y. Jets, 1989
Les Miller, San Diego, 1990
Seth Joyner, Philadelphia, 1991
Robert Goff, New Orleans, 1992
Willie Clay, Detroit, 1993
Tyrone Hughes, New Orleans, 1994
Chad Brown, Seattle, 1997
Marcus Robertson, Tennessee, 1997
Dwayne Rudd, Minnesota, 1998
Keith McKenzie, Green Bay, 1999

Most Touchdowns, Career (Own recovered)

2 Ken Kavanaugh, Chi. Bears, 1940-41, 1945-1950
Mike Ditka, Chicago, 1961-66; Philadelphia, 1967-68; Dallas, 1969-1972
Gail Cogdill, Detroit, 1960-68; Baltimore, 1968; Atlanta, 1969-1970
Ahmad Rashad, St. Louis, 1972-73; Buffalo, 1974; Minnesota, 1976-1982
Jim Mitchell, Atlanta, 1969-1979
Drew Pearson, Dallas, 1973-1983
Del Rodgers, Green Bay, 1982, 1984; San Francisco, 1987-88

Most Touchdowns, Season (Own recovered)

2 Ahmad Rashad, Buffalo, 1974
Del Rodgers, Green Bay, 1982
1 By many players

Most Touchdowns, Career (Opponents' recovered)

5 Jessie Tuggle, Atlanta, 1987-2000
4 Derrick Thomas, Kansas City, 1989-1999
3 By many players

Most Touchdowns, Season (Opponents' recovered)

2 Harold McPhail, Boston, 1934
Harry Ebding, Detroit, 1937
John Morelli, Boston, 1944
Frank Maznicki, Boston, 1947
Fred (Dippy) Evans, Chi. Bears, 1948
Ralph Heywood, Boston, 1948
Art Tait, N.Y. Yanks, 1951
John Dwyer, Los Angeles, 1952
Leo Sugar, Chi. Cardinals, 1957
Doug Cline, Houston, 1961
Jim Bradshaw, Pittsburgh, 1964

Royce Berry, Cincinnati, 1970
Tim Gray, Kansas City, 1977
Charles Phillips, Oakland, 1978
Kenny Johnson, Atlanta, 1981
George Martin, N.Y. Giants, 1981
Mike Douglass, Green Bay, 1983
Shelton Robinson, Seattle, 1983
Erik McMillan, N.Y. Jets, 1989
Les Miller, San Diego, 1990
Seth Joyner, Philadelphia, 1991
Robert Goff, New Orleans, 1992
Willie Clay, Detroit, 1993
Tyrone Hughes, New Orleans, 1994
Chad Brown, Seattle, 1997
Marcus Robertson, Tennessee, 1997
Dwayne Rudd, Minnesota, 1998
Keith McKenzie, Green Bay, 1999

Most Touchdowns, Game (Opponents' recovered)
2 Fred (Dippy) Evans, Chi. Bears vs. Washington, Nov. 28, 1948

COMBINED NET YARDS GAINED

Rushing, receiving, interception returns, punt returns, kickoff returns, and fumble returns

Most Seasons Leading League
5 Jim Brown, Cleveland, 1958-1961, 1964
4 Brian Mitchell, Washington, 1994-96, 1998
3 Cliff Battles, Boston, 1932-33; Washington, 1937
Gale Sayers, Chicago, 1965-67
Eric Dickerson, L.A. Rams, 1983-84, 1986
Thurman Thomas, Buffalo, 1989, 1991-92

Most Consecutive Seasons Leading League
4 Jim Brown, Cleveland, 1958-1961
3 Gale Sayers, Chicago, 1965-67
Brian Mitchell, Washington, 1994-96
2 Cliff Battles, Boston, 1932-33
Charley Trippi, Chi. Cardinals, 1948-49
Timmy Brown, Philadelphia, 1962-63
Floyd Little, Denver, 1967-68
James Brooks, San Diego, 1981-82
Eric Dickerson, L.A. Rams, 1983-84
Thurman Thomas, Buffalo, 1991-92

ATTEMPTS

Most Attempts, Career
4,368 Walter Payton, Chicago, 1975-1987
4,000 Emmitt Smith, Dallas, 1990-2000
3,624 Marcus Allen, L.A. Raiders, 1982-1992; Kansas City, 1993-97

Most Attempts, Season
496 James Wilder, Tampa Bay, 1984
455 Eddie George, Tennessee, 2000
450 Edgerrin James, Indianapolis, 2000

Most Attempts, Rookie, Season
442 Eric Dickerson, L.A. Rams, 1983
433 Edgerrin James, Indianapolis, 1999
401 Curtis Martin, New England, 1995

Most Attempts, Game
48 James Wilder, Tampa Bay vs. Pittsburgh, Oct. 30, 1983
47 James Wilder, Tampa Bay vs. Green Bay, Sept. 30, 1984 (OT)
Terrell Davis, Denver vs. Buffalo, Oct. 26, 1997 (OT)
46 Gerald Riggs, Atlanta vs. L.A. Rams, Nov. 17, 1985

YARDS GAINED

Most Yards Gained, Career
21,803 Walter Payton, Chicago, 1975-1987
19,878 Jerry Rice, San Francisco, 1985-2000
18,640 Brian Mitchell, Washington, 1990-99; Philadelphia, 2000

Most Yards Gained, Season
2,690 Derrick Mason, Tennessee, 2000
2,535 Lionel James, San Diego, 1985
2,477 Brian Mitchell, Washington, 1994

Most Yards Gained, Rookie, Season
2,317 Tim Brown, L.A. Raiders, 1988
2,272 Gale Sayers, Chicago, 1965
2,212 Eric Dickerson, L.A. Rams, 1983

Most Yards Gained, Game
404 Glyn Milburn, Denver vs. Seattle, Dec. 10, 1995
373 Billy Cannon, Houston vs. N.Y. Titans, Dec. 10, 1961
347 Tyrone Hughes, New Orleans vs. L.A. Rams, Oct. 23, 1994

SACKS

Sacks have been compiled since 1982.

Most Seasons Leading League
2 Mark Gastineau, N.Y. Jets, 1983-84
Reggie White, Philadelphia, 1987-88
Kevin Greene, Pittsburgh, 1994; Carolina, 1996

Most Sacks, Career
198.0 Reggie White, Philadelphia, 1985-1992; Green Bay, 1993-98; Carolina, 2000
181.0 Bruce Smith, Buffalo, 1985-1999; Washington, 2000
160.0 Kevin Greene, L.A. Rams, 1985-1992; Pittsburgh, 1993-95; Carolina, 1996, 1998-99; San Francisco, 1997

Most Sacks, Season
22.0 Mark Gastineau, N.Y. Jets, 1984
21.0 Reggie White, Philadelphia, 1987
Chris Doleman, Minnesota, 1989
20.5 Lawrence Taylor, N.Y. Giants, 1986

Most Sacks, Rookie, Season
14.5 Jevon Kearse, Tennessee, 1999
12.5 Leslie O'Neal, San Diego, 1986
Simeon Rice, Arizona, 1996
12.0 Charles Haley, San Francisco, 1986

Most Sacks, Game
7.0 Derrick Thomas, Kansas City vs. Seattle, Nov. 11, 1990
6.0 Fred Dean, San Francisco vs. New Orleans, Nov. 13, 1983
Derrick Thomas, Kansas City vs. Oakland, Sept. 6, 1998
5.5 William Gay, Detroit vs. Tampa Bay, Sept. 4, 1983

Most Seasons, 10 or More Sacks
13 Bruce Smith, Buffalo, 1986-1990, 1992-98; Washington, 2000
12 Reggie White, Philadelphia, 1985-1992; Green Bay, 1993, 1995, 1997-98
10 Kevin Greene, L.A. Rams, 1988-1990, 1992; Pittsburgh, 1993-94; Carolina, 1996, 1998-99; San Francisco, 1997

Most Consecutive Seasons, 10 or More Sacks
9 Reggie White, Philadelphia, 1985-1992; Green Bay, 1993
8 John Randle, Minnesota, 1992-99
7 Lawrence Taylor, N.Y. Giants, 1984-1990
Bruce Smith, Buffalo, 1992-98

Most Consecutive Games, Sack
10 Simon Fletcher, Denver, Nov. 15, 1992-Sept. 20, 1993
9 Bruce Smith, Buffalo, Nov. 16, 1986-Oct. 25, 1987
Kevin Greene, San Francisco-Carolina, Dec. 7, 1997-Oct. 18, 1998
8 By many players

MISCELLANEOUS

Longest Return of Missed Field Goal (All TDs)
104 Aaron Glenn, N.Y. Jets vs. Indianapolis, Nov. 15, 1998
101 Al Nelson, Philadelphia vs. Dallas, Sept. 26, 1971
100 Al Nelson, Philadelphia vs. Cleveland, Dec. 11, 1966
Ken Ellis, Green Bay vs. N.Y. Giants, Sept. 19, 1971

TEAM RECORDS

CHAMPIONSHIPS

Most Seasons League Champion
12 Green Bay, 1929-1931, 1936, 1939, 1944, 1961-62, 1965-67, 1996
9 Chi. Bears, 1921, 1932-33, 1940-41, 1943, 1946, 1963, 1985
6 N.Y. Giants, 1927, 1934, 1938, 1956, 1986, 1990

Most Consecutive Seasons League Champion
3 Green Bay, 1929-1931
Green Bay, 1965-67
2 Canton, 1922-23
Chi. Bears, 1932-33
Chi. Bears, 1940-41
Philadelphia, 1948-49
Detroit, 1952-53
Cleveland, 1954-55
Baltimore, 1958-59
Houston, 1960-61
Green Bay, 1961-62
Buffalo, 1964-65
Miami, 1972-73
Pittsburgh, 1974-75
Pittsburgh, 1978-79
San Francisco, 1988-89
Dallas, 1992-93
Denver, 1997-98

Most Times Finishing First, Regular Season
20 N.Y. Giants, 1927, 1933-35, 1938-39, 1941, 1944, 1946, 1956, 1958-59, 1961-63, 1986, 1989-1990, 1997, 2000
19 Dallas, 1966-1971, 1973, 1976-79, 1981, 1985, 1992-96, 1998
18 Clev. Browns, 1950-55, 1957, 1964-65, 1967-69, 1971, 1980, 1985-87, 1989
Chi. Bears, 1921, 1932-34, 1937, 1940-43, 1946, 1956, 1963, 1984-88, 1990

Most Consecutive Times Finishing First, Regular Season
7 Los Angeles, 1973-79
6 Cleveland, 1950-55

Dallas, 1966-1971
Minnesota, 1973-78
Pittsburgh, 1974-79
5 Oakland, 1972-76
Chicago, 1984-88
San Francisco, 1986-1990
Dallas, 1992-96

GAMES WON

Most Consecutive Games Won
17 Chi. Bears, 1933-34
16 Chi. Bears, 1941-42
Miami, 1971-73
Miami, 1983-84
15 L.A. Chargers/San Diego, 1960-61
San Francisco, 1989-1990

Most Consecutive Games Without Defeat
25 Canton, 1921-23 (won 22, tied 3)
24 Chi. Bears, 1941-43 (won 23, tied 1)
23 Green Bay, 1928-1930 (won 21, tied 2)

Most Games Won, Season
15 San Francisco, 1984
Chicago, 1985
Minnesota, 1998
14 Frankford, 1926
Miami, 1972
Pittsburgh, 1978
Washington, 1983
Miami, 1984
Chicago, 1986
N.Y. Giants, 1986
San Francisco, 1989
San Francisco, 1990
Washington, 1991
San Francisco, 1992
Atlanta, 1998
Denver, 1998
Jacksonville, 1999
13 By many teams

Most Consecutive Games Won, Season
14 Miami, 1972
13 Chi. Bears, 1934
Denver, 1998
12 Minnesota, 1969
Chicago, 1985

Most Consecutive Games Won, Start of Season
14 Miami, 1972, entire season
13 Chi. Bears, 1934, entire season
Denver, 1998
12 Chicago, 1985

Most Consecutive Games Won, End of Season
14 Miami, 1972, entire season
13 Chi. Bears, 1934, entire season
11 Chi. Bears, 1942, entire season
Cleveland, 1951
Houston, 1993

Most Consecutive Games Without Defeat, Season
14 Miami, 1972 (won 14)
13 Chi. Bears, 1926 (won 11, tied 2)
Green Bay, 1929 (won 12, tied 1)
Chi. Bears, 1934 (won 13)
Baltimore, 1967 (won 11, tied 2)
Denver, 1998 (won 13)
12 Canton, 1922 (won 10, tied 2)
Canton, 1923 (won 11, tied 1)
Minnesota, 1969 (won 12)
Chicago, 1985 (won 12)

Most Consecutive Games Without Defeat, Start of Season
14 Miami, 1972 (won 14), entire season
13 Chi. Bears, 1926 (won 11, tied 2)
Green Bay, 1929 (won 12, tied 1), entire season
Chi. Bears, 1934 (won 13), entire season
Baltimore, 1967 (won 11, tied 2)
Denver, 1998 (won 13)
12 Canton, 1922 (won 10, tied 2), entire season
Canton, 1923 (won 11, tied 1), entire season
Chicago, 1985 (won 12)

Most Consecutive Games Without Defeat, End of Season
14 Miami, 1972 (won 14), entire season
13 Green Bay, 1929 (won 12, tied 1), entire season
Chi. Bears, 1934 (won 13), entire season
12 Canton, 1922 (won 10, tied 2), entire season
Canton, 1923 (won 11, tied 1), entire season

Most Consecutive Home Games Won
27 Miami, 1971-74
25 Green Bay, 1995-98
24 Denver, 1996-98

Most Consecutive Home Games Without Defeat
30 Green Bay, 1928-1933 (won 27, tied 3)
27 Miami, 1971-74 (won 27)
25 Chi. Bears, 1923-25 (won 19, tied 6)
Green Bay, 1995-98 (won 25)

Most Consecutive Road Games Won
18 San Francisco, 1988-1990
11 L.A. Chargers/San Diego, 1960-61
San Francisco, 1987-88
10 Chi. Bears, 1941-42
Dallas, 1968-69
New Orleans, 1987-88

Most Consecutive Road Games Without Defeat
18 San Francisco, 1988-1990 (won 18)
13 Chi. Bears, 1941-43 (won 12, tied 1)
12 Green Bay, 1928-1930 (won 10, tied 2)

Most Shutout Games Won or Tied, Season
10 Pottsville, 1926 (won 9, tied 1)
N.Y. Giants, 1927 (won 9, tied 1)
9 Akron, 1921 (won 8, tied 1)
Canton, 1922 (won 7, tied 2)
Frankford, 1926 (won 9)
Frankford, 1929 (won 6, tied 3)
8 By many teams

Most Consecutive Shutout Games Won or Tied
13 Akron, 1920-21 (won 10, tied 3)
7 Pottsville, 1926 (won 6, tied 1)
Detroit, 1934 (won 7)
6 Buffalo, 1920-21 (won 5, tied 1)
Frankford, 1926 (won 6)
Detroit, 1926 (won 4, tied 2)
N.Y. Giants, 1926-27 (won 5, tied 1)

GAMES LOST

Most Consecutive Games Lost
26 Tampa Bay, 1976-1977
19 Chi. Cardinals, 1942-43, 1945
Oakland, 1961-62
18 Houston, 1972-73

Most Consecutive Games Without Victory
26 Tampa Bay, 1976-77 (lost 26)
23 Rochester, 1922-25 (lost 21, tied 2)
Washington, 1960-61 (lost 20, tied 3)
19 Dayton, 1927-29 (lost 18, tied 1)
Chi. Cardinals, 1942-43, 1945 (lost 19)
Oakland, 1961-62 (lost 19)

Most Games Lost, Season
15 New Orleans, 1980
Dallas, 1989
New England, 1990
Indianapolis, 1991
N.Y. Jets, 1996
San Diego, 2000
14 By many teams

Most Consecutive Games Lost, Season
14 Tampa Bay, 1976
New Orleans, 1980
Baltimore, 1981
New England, 1990
13 Oakland, 1962
Pittsburgh, 1969
Indianapolis, 1986
12 Tampa Bay, 1977

Most Consecutive Games Lost, Start of Season
14 Tampa Bay, 1976, entire season
New Orleans, 1980
13 Oakland, 1962
Indianapolis, 1986
12 Tampa Bay, 1977

Most Consecutive Games Lost, End of Season
14 Tampa Bay, 1976, entire season
New England, 1990
13 Pittsburgh, 1969
11 Philadelphia, 1936
Detroit, 1942, entire season
Houston, 1972

Most Consecutive Games Without Victory, Season
14 Tampa Bay, 1976 (lost 14), entire season
New Orleans, 1980 (lost 14)

Baltimore, 1981 (lost 14)
New England, 1990 (lost 14)
13 Washington, 1961 (lost 12, tied 1)
Oakland, 1962 (lost 13)
Pittsburgh, 1969 (lost 13)
Indianapolis, 1986 (lost 13)
12 Dall. Cowboys, 1960 (lost 11, tied 1), entire season
Tampa Bay, 1977 (lost 12)

Most Consecutive Games Without Victory, Start of Season
14 Tampa Bay, 1976 (lost 14), entire season
New Orleans, 1980 (lost 14)
13 Washington, 1961 (lost 12, tied 1)
Oakland, 1962 (lost 13)
Indianapolis, 1986 (lost 13)
12 Dall. Cowboys, 1960 (lost 11, tied 1), entire season
Tampa Bay, 1977 (lost 12)

Most Consecutive Games Without Victory, End of Season
14 Tampa Bay, 1976, (lost 14), entire season
New England, 1990 (lost 14)
13 Pittsburgh, 1969 (lost 13)
12 Dall. Cowboys, 1960 (lost 11, tied 1), entire season

Most Consecutive Home Games Lost
14 Dallas, 1988-89
13 Houston, 1972-73
Tampa Bay, 1976-77
N.Y. Jets, 1995-97
11 Oakland, 1961-62
Los Angeles, 1961-63
Cincinnati, 1998-99

Most Consecutive Home Games Without Victory
14 Dallas, 1988-89 (lost 14)
13 Houston, 1972-73 (lost 13)
Tampa Bay, 1976-77 (lost 13)
N.Y. Jets, 1995-97 (lost 13)
12 Philadelphia, 1936-38 (lost 11, tied 1)

Most Consecutive Road Games Lost
23 Houston, 1981-84
22 Buffalo, 1983-86
19 Tampa Bay, 1983-85
Atlanta, 1988-1991

Most Consecutive Road Games Without Victory
23 Houston, 1981-84 (lost 23)
22 Buffalo, 1983-86 (lost 22)
19 Tampa Bay, 1983-85 (lost 19)
Atlanta, 1988-1991 (lost 19)

Most Shutout Games Lost or Tied, Season
8 Frankford, 1927 (lost 6, tied 2)
Brooklyn, 1931 (lost 8)
7 Dayton, 1925 (lost 6, tied 1)
Orange, 1929 (lost 4, tied 3)
Frankford, 1931 (lost 6, tied 1)
6 By many teams

Most Consecutive Shutout Games Lost or Tied
8 Rochester, 1922-24 (lost 8)
7 Hammond, 1922-23 (lost 6, tied 1)
6 Providence, 1926-27 (lost 5, tied 1)
Brooklyn, 1942-43 (lost 6)

TIE GAMES

Most Tie Games, Season
6 Chi. Bears, 1932
5 Frankford, 1929
4 Chi. Bears, 1924
Orange, 1929
Portsmouth, 1932

Most Consecutive Tie Games
3 Chi. Bears, 1932
2 By many teams

SCORING

Most Seasons Leading League
10 Chi. Bears, 1932, 1934-35, 1939, 1941-43, 1946-47, 1956
9 San Francisco, 1953, 1965, 1970, 1987, 1989, 1992-95
8 L.A./St. Louis Rams, 1950-52, 1957, 1967, 1973, 1999-2000

Most Consecutive Seasons Leading League
4 San Francisco, 1992-1995
3 Green Bay, 1936-38
Chi. Bears, 1941-43
Los Angeles, 1950-52
Oakland, 1967-69
2 By many teams

POINTS

Most Points, Season
556 Minnesota, 1998
541 Washington, 1983
540 St. Louis, 2000

Fewest Points, Season (Since 1932)
37 Cincinnati/St. Louis, 1934
38 Cincinnati, 1933
Detroit, 1942
51 Pittsburgh, 1934
Philadelphia, 1936

Most Points, Game
72 Washington vs. N.Y. Giants, Nov. 27, 1966
70 Los Angeles vs. Baltimore, Oct. 22, 1950
65 Chi. Cardinals vs. N.Y. Bulldogs, Nov. 13, 1949
Los Angeles vs. Detroit, Oct. 29, 1950

Most Points, Both Teams, Game
113 Washington (72) vs. N.Y. Giants (41), Nov. 27, 1966
101 Oakland (52) vs. Houston (49), Dec. 22, 1963
99 Seattle (51) vs. Kansas City (48), Nov. 27, 1983 (OT)

Fewest Points, Both Teams, Game
0 In many games. Last time: N.Y. Giants vs. Detroit, Nov. 7, 1943

Most Points, Shutout Victory, Game
64 Philadelphia vs. Cincinnati, Nov. 6, 1934
62 Akron vs. Oorang, Oct. 29, 1922
60 Rock Island vs. Evansville, Oct. 15, 1922
Chi. Cardinals vs. Rochester, Oct. 7, 1923

Fewest Points, Shutout Victory, Game
2 Green Bay vs. Chi. Bears, Oct. 16, 1932
Chi. Bears vs. Green Bay, Sept. 18, 1938

Most Points Overcome to Win Game
28 San Francisco vs. New Orleans, Dec. 7, 1980 (OT) (trailed 7-35, won 38-35)
26 Buffalo vs. Indianapolis, Sept., 21, 1997 (trailed 0-26, won 37-35)
25 St. Louis vs. Tampa Bay, Nov. 8, 1987 (trailed 3-28, won 31-28)

Most Points Overcome to Tie Game
31 Denver vs. Buffalo, Nov. 27, 1960 (trailed 7-38, tied 38-38)
28 Los Angeles vs. Philadelphia, Oct. 3, 1948 (trailed 0-28, tied 28-28)

Most Points, Each Half
1st: 49 Green Bay vs. Tampa Bay, Oct. 2, 1983
48 Buffalo vs. Miami, Sept. 18, 1966
45 Green Bay vs. Cleveland, Nov. 12, 1967
Indianapolis vs. Denver, Oct. 31, 1988
Houston vs. Cleveland, Dec. 9, 1990
2nd: 49 Chi. Bears vs. Philadelphia, Nov. 30, 1941
48 Chi. Cardinals vs. Baltimore, Oct. 2, 1950
N.Y. Giants vs. Baltimore, Nov. 19, 1950
45 Cincinnati vs. Houston, Dec. 17, 1972

Most Points, Both Teams, Each Half
1st: 70 Houston (35) vs. Oakland (35), Dec. 22, 1963
62 N.Y. Jets (41) vs. Tampa Bay (21), Nov. 17, 1985
59 St. Louis (31) vs. Philadelphia (28), Dec. 16, 1962
2nd: 65 Washington (38) vs. N.Y. Giants (27), Nov. 27, 1966
62 L.A. Raiders (31) vs. San Diego (31), Jan. 2, 1983
58 New England (37) vs. Baltimore (21), Nov. 23, 1980
N.Y. Jets (37) vs. New England (21), Sept. 21, 1987

Most Points, One Quarter
41 Green Bay vs. Detroit, Oct. 7, 1945 (second quarter)
Los Angeles vs. Detroit, Oct. 29, 1950 (third quarter)
37 Los Angeles vs. Green Bay, Sept. 21, 1980 (second quarter)
35 Chi. Cardinals vs. Boston, Oct. 24, 1948 (third quarter)
Green Bay vs. Cleveland, Nov. 12, 1967 (first quarter)
Green Bay vs. Tampa Bay, Oct. 2, 1983 (second quarter)

Most Points, Both Teams, One Quarter
49 Oakland (28) vs. Houston (21), Dec. 22, 1963 (second quarter)
48 Green Bay (41) vs. Detroit (7), Oct. 7, 1945 (second quarter)
Los Angeles (41) vs. Detroit (7), Oct. 29, 1950 (third quarter)
47 St. Louis (27) vs. Philadelphia (20), Dec. 13, 1964 (second quarter)

Most Points, Each Quarter
1st: 35 Green Bay vs. Cleveland, Nov. 12, 1967
31 Buffalo vs. Kansas City, Sept. 13, 1964
28 By eight teams
2nd: 41 Green Bay vs. Detroit, Oct. 7, 1945
37 Los Angeles vs. Green Bay, Sept. 21, 1980
35 Green Bay vs. Tampa Bay, Oct. 2, 1983
3rd: 41 Los Angeles vs. Detroit, Oct. 29, 1950
35 Chi. Cardinals vs. Boston, Oct. 24, 1948
28 By 10 teams
4th: 31 Oakland vs. Denver, Dec. 17, 1960
Oakland vs. San Diego, Dec. 8, 1963
Atlanta vs. Green Bay, Sept. 13, 1981
30 N.Y. Jets vs. Miami, Oct. 23, 2000
28 By many teams

ALL-TIME RECORDS

Most Points, Both Teams, Each Quarter

1st: 42 Green Bay (35) vs. Cleveland (7), Nov. 12, 1967
35 Dall. Texans (21) vs. N.Y. Titans (14), Nov. 11, 1962
Dallas (28) vs. Philadelphia (7), Oct. 19, 1969
Kansas City (21) vs. Seattle (14), Dec. 11, 1977
Detroit (21) vs. L.A. Raiders (14), Dec. 10, 1990
Dallas (21) vs. Atlanta (14), Dec. 22, 1991
34 Los Angeles (21) vs. Baltimore (13), Oct. 22, 1950
Oakland (21) vs. Atlanta (13), Nov. 30, 1975

2nd: 49 Oakland (28) vs. Houston (21), Dec. 22, 1963
48 Green Bay (41) vs. Detroit (7), Oct. 7, 1945
47 St. Louis (27) vs. Philadelphia (20), Dec. 13, 1964

3rd: 48 Los Angeles (41) vs. Detroit (7), Oct. 29, 1950
42 Washington (28) vs. Philadelphia (14), Oct. 1, 1955
41 Green Bay (21) vs. N.Y. Yanks (20), Oct. 8, 1950

4th: 42 Chi. Cardinals (28) vs. Philadelphia (14), Dec. 7, 1947
Green Bay (28) vs. Chi. Bears (14), Nov. 6, 1955
N.Y. Jets (28) vs. Boston (14), Oct. 27, 1968
Pittsburgh (21) vs. Cleveland (21), Oct. 18, 1969
41 Baltimore (27) vs. New England (14), Sept. 18, 1978
New England (27) vs. Baltimore (14), Nov. 23, 1980
40 Chicago (21) vs. Tampa Bay (19), Nov. 19, 1989

Most Consecutive Games Scoring

370 San Francisco, 1977-2000 (current)
274 Cleveland, 1950-1971
218 Dallas, 1970-1985

TOUCHDOWNS

Most Seasons Leading League, Touchdowns

13 Chi. Bears, 1932, 1934-35, 1939, 1941-44, 1946-48, 1956, 1965
7 Dallas, 1966, 1968, 1971, 1973, 1977-78, 1980
San Francisco, 1953, 1970, 1987, 1992-95
6 Oakland, 1967-69, 1972, 1974, 1977
San Diego, 1963, 1965, 1979, 1981-82, 1985
Green Bay, 1932, 1937-38, 1961-62, 1996
L.A./St. Louis Rams, 1949-1952, 1999-2000

Most Consecutive Seasons Leading League, Touchdowns

4 Chi. Bears, 1941-44
Los Angeles, 1949-1952
San Francisco, 1992-95
3 Chi. Bears, 1946-48
Baltimore, 1957-59
Oakland, 1967-69
2 By many teams

Most Touchdowns, Season

70 Miami, 1984
67 St. Louis, 2000
66 Houston, 1961
San Francisco, 1994
St. Louis, 1999

Fewest Touchdowns, Season (Since 1932)

3 Cincinnati, 1933
4 Cincinnati/St. Louis, 1934
5 Detroit, 1942

Most Touchdowns, Game

10 Philadelphia vs. Cincinnati, Nov. 6, 1934
Los Angeles vs. Baltimore, Oct. 22, 1950
Washington vs. N.Y. Giants, Nov. 27, 1966
9 Chi. Cardinals vs. Rochester, Oct. 7, 1923
Chi. Cardinals vs. N.Y. Giants, Oct. 17, 1948
Chi. Cardinals vs. N.Y. Bulldogs, Nov. 13, 1949
Los Angeles vs. Detroit, Oct. 29, 1950
Pittsburgh vs. N.Y. Giants, Nov. 30, 1952
Chicago vs. San Francisco, Dec. 12, 1965
Chicago vs. Green Bay, Dec. 7, 1980
8 By many teams

Most Touchdowns, Both Teams, Game

16 Washington (10) vs. N.Y. Giants (6), Nov. 27, 1966
14 Chi. Cardinals (9) vs. N.Y. Giants (5), Oct. 17, 1948
Los Angeles (10) vs. Baltimore (4), Oct. 22, 1950
Houston (7) vs. Oakland (7), Dec. 22, 1963
13 New Orleans (7) vs. St. Louis (6), Nov. 2, 1969
Kansas City (7) vs. Seattle (6), Nov. 27, 1983 (OT)
San Diego (8) vs. Pittsburgh (5), Dec. 8, 1985
N.Y. Jets (7) vs. Miami (6), Sept. 21, 1986 (OT)

Most Consecutive Games Scoring Touchdowns

166 Cleveland, 1957-1969
97 Oakland, 1966-1973
96 Kansas City, 1963-1970

POINTS AFTER TOUCHDOWN

Most (One-Point) Points After Touchdown, Season

66 Miami, 1984
65 Houston, 1961
64 St. Louis, 1999

Fewest (One-Point) Points After Touchdown, Season

2 Chi. Cardinals, 1933
3 Cincinnati, 1933
Pittsburgh, 1934
4 Cincinnati/St. Louis, 1934

Most (One-Point) Points After Touchdown, Game

10 Los Angeles vs. Baltimore, Oct. 22, 1950
9 Chi. Cardinals vs. N.Y. Giants, Oct. 17, 1948
Pittsburgh vs. N.Y. Giants, Nov. 30, 1952
Washington vs. N.Y. Giants, Nov. 27, 1966
8 By many teams

Most (One-Point) Points After Touchdown, Both Teams, Game

14 Chi. Cardinals (9) vs. N.Y. Giants (5), Oct. 17, 1948
Houston (7) vs. Oakland (7), Dec. 22, 1963
Washington (9) vs. N.Y. Giants (5), Nov. 27, 1966
13 Los Angeles (10) vs. Baltimore (3), Oct. 22, 1950
12 In many games

Most Two-Point Conversions, Season

6 Miami, 1994
Minnesota, 1997
5 Arizona, 1995
Baltimore, 1996
Jacksonville, 1996
Chicago, 1997
San Francisco, 1998
4 By many teams

Most Two-Point Conversions, Game

4 St. Louis vs. Atlanta, Oct. 15, 2000
3 Baltimore vs. New England, Oct. 6, 1996
Pittsburgh vs. Tennessee, Nov. 1, 1998
2 By many teams

Most Two-Point Conversions, Both Teams, Game

5 Baltimore (3) vs. New England (2), Oct. 6, 1996
St. Louis (4) vs. Atlanta (1), Oct. 15, 2000
3 Seattle (2) vs. Kansas City (1), Oct. 23, 1994
Minnesota (2) vs. Seattle (1), Nov. 10, 1996
Pittsburgh (3) vs. Tennessee (0), Nov. 1, 1998
2 In many games

FIELD GOALS

Most Seasons Leading League, Field Goals

11 Green Bay, 1935-36, 1940-43, 1946-47, 1955, 1972, 1974
8 Washington, 1945, 1956, 1971, 1976-77, 1979, 1982, 1992
7 N.Y. Giants, 1933, 1937, 1939, 1941, 1944, 1959, 1983

Most Consecutive Seasons Leading League, Field Goals

4 Green Bay, 1940-43
3 Cleveland, 1952-54
2 By many teams

Most Field Goals Attempted, Season

49 Los Angeles, 1966
Washington, 1971
48 Green Bay, 1972
47 N.Y. Jets, 1969
Los Angeles, 1973
Washington, 1983

Fewest Field Goals Attempted, Season (Since 1938)

0 Chi. Bears, 1944
2 Cleveland, 1939
Card-Pitt, 1944
Boston, 1946
Chi. Bears, 1947
3 Chi. Bears, 1945
Cleveland, 1945

Most Field Goals Attempted, Game

9 St. Louis vs. Pittsburgh, Sept. 24, 1967
8 Pittsburgh vs. St. Louis, Dec. 2, 1962
Detroit vs. Minnesota, Nov. 13, 1966
N.Y. Jets vs. Buffalo, Nov. 3, 1968
7 By many teams

Most Field Goals Attempted, Both Teams, Game

11 St. Louis (6) vs. Pittsburgh (5), Nov. 13, 1966
Washington (6) vs. Chicago (5), Nov. 14, 1971
Green Bay (6) vs. Detroit (5), Sept. 29, 1974
Washington (6) vs. N.Y. Giants (5), Nov. 14, 1976
10 In many games

Most Field Goals, Season

39 Miami, 1999
37 Carolina, 1996
36 Indianapolis, 1996
Tennessee, 1998

Fewest Field Goals, Season (Since 1932)
0 Boston, 1932, 1935
Chi. Cardinals, 1932, 1945
Green Bay, 1932, 1944
N.Y. Giants, 1932
Brooklyn, 1944
Card-Pitt, 1944
Chi. Bears, 1944, 1947
Boston, 1946
Baltimore, 1950
Dallas, 1952

Most Field Goals, Game
7 St. Louis vs. Pittsburgh, Sept. 24, 1967
Minnesota vs. L.A. Rams, Nov. 5, 1989 (OT)
Dallas vs. Green Bay, Nov. 18, 1996
6 Boston vs. Denver, Oct. 4, 1964
Detroit vs. Minnesota, Nov. 13, 1966
N.Y. Jets vs. Buffalo, Nov. 3, 1968
Philadelphia vs. Houston, Nov. 12, 1972
N.Y. Jets vs. New Orleans, Dec. 3, 1972
St. Louis vs. Atlanta, Dec. 9, 1973
N.Y. Giants vs. Seattle, Oct. 18, 1981
San Francisco vs. New Orleans, Oct. 16, 1983
Pittsburgh vs. Denver, Oct. 23, 1988
San Diego vs. Seattle, Sept. 5, 1993
San Diego vs. Houston, Sept. 19, 1993
Cincinnati vs. Seattle, Nov. 6, 1994
Atlanta vs. New Orleans, Nov. 13, 1994
San Francisco vs. Atlanta, Sept. 29, 1996
Buffalo vs. N.Y. Jets, Oct. 20, 1996
San Diego vs. Oakland, Oct. 5, 1997
Minnesota vs. Baltimore, Dec. 13, 1998
Detroit vs. Minnesota, Oct. 17, 1999
Miami vs. New England, Oct. 17, 1999
5 By many teams

Most Field Goals, Both Teams, Game
9 San Diego (5) vs. Kansas City (4), Sept. 29, 1996
Miami (6) vs. New England (3), Oct. 17, 1999
8 Cleveland (4) vs. St. Louis (4), Sept. 20, 1964
Chicago (5) vs. Philadelphia (3), Oct. 20, 1968
Washington (5) vs. Chicago (3), Nov. 14, 1971
Kansas City (5) vs. Buffalo (3), Dec. 19, 1971
Detroit (4) vs. Green Bay (4), Sept. 29, 1974
Cleveland (5) vs. Denver (3), Oct. 19, 1975
New England (4) vs. San Diego (4), Nov. 9, 1975
San Francisco (6) vs. New Orleans (2), Oct. 16, 1983
Seattle (5) vs. L.A. Raiders (3), Dec. 18, 1988
Atlanta (6) vs. New Orleans (2), Nov. 13, 1994
Indianapolis (4) vs. San Diego (4), Nov. 3, 1996
7 In many games

Most Consecutive Games Scoring Field Goals
31 Minnesota, 1968-1970
28 Washington, 1988-1990
26 Baltimore, 1999-2000 (current)

SAFETIES

Most Safeties, Season
4 Cleveland, 1927
Detroit, 1962
Seattle, 1993
San Francisco, 1996
Tennessee, 1999
3 By many teams

Most Safeties, Game
3 L.A. Rams vs. N.Y. Giants, Sept. 30, 1984
2 N.Y. Giants vs. Pottsville, Oct. 30, 1927
Chi. Bears vs. Pottsville, Nov. 13, 1927
Detroit vs. Brooklyn, Dec. 1, 1935
N.Y. Giants vs. Pittsburgh, Sept. 17, 1950
N.Y. Giants vs. Washington, Nov. 5, 1961
Chicago vs. Pittsburgh, Nov. 9, 1969
Dallas vs. Philadelphia, Nov. 19, 1972
Los Angeles vs. Green Bay, Oct. 21, 1973
Oakland vs. San Diego, Oct. 26, 1975
Denver vs. Seattle, Jan. 2, 1983
New Orleans vs. Cleveland, Sept. 13, 1987
Buffalo vs. Denver, Nov. 8, 1987
San Francisco vs. St. Louis, Sept. 8, 1996
Jacksonville vs. Pittsburgh, Oct. 3, 1999

Most Safeties, Both Teams, Game
3 L.A. Rams (3) vs. N.Y. Giants (0), Sept. 30, 1984
2 Chi. Cardinals (1) vs. Frankford (1), Nov. 19, 1927
Chi. Cardinals (1) vs. Cincinnati (1), Nov. 12, 1933
Chi. Bears (1) vs. San Francisco (1), Oct. 19, 1952
Cincinnati (1) vs. Los Angeles (1), Oct. 22, 1972
Chi. Bears (1) vs. San Francisco (1), Sept. 19, 1976
Baltimore (1) vs. Miami (1), Oct. 29, 1978
Atlanta (1) vs. Detroit (1), Oct. 5, 1980
Houston (1) vs. Philadelphia (1), Oct. 2, 1988
Cleveland (1) vs. Seattle (1), Nov. 14, 1993
Arizona (1) vs. Houston (1), Dec. 4, 1994
(Also see previous record)

FIRST DOWNS

Most Seasons Leading League
9 Chi. Bears, 1935, 1939, 1941, 1943, 1945, 1947-49, 1955
7 San Diego, 1965, 1969, 1980-83, 1985
6 L.A. Rams, 1946, 1950-51, 1954, 1957, 1973
San Francisco, 1965, 1987, 1989, 1993-94, 1998

Most Consecutive Seasons Leading League
4 San Diego, 1980-83
3 Chi. Bears, 1947-49
2 By many teams

Most First Downs, Season
387 Miami, 1984
383 Denver, 2000
381 San Francisco, 1998

Fewest First Downs, Season
51 Cincinnati, 1933
64 Pittsburgh, 1935
67 Philadelphia, 1937

Most First Downs, Game
39 N.Y. Jets vs. Miami, Nov. 27, 1988
Washington vs. Detroit, Nov. 4, 1990 (OT)
38 Los Angeles vs. N.Y. Giants, Nov. 13, 1966
37 Green Bay vs. Philadelphia, Nov. 11, 1962

Fewest First Downs, Game
0 N.Y. Giants vs. Green Bay, Oct. 1, 1933
Pittsburgh vs. Boston, Oct. 29, 1933
Philadelphia vs. Detroit, Sept. 20, 1935
N.Y. Giants vs. Washington, Sept. 27, 1942
Denver vs. Houston, Sept. 3, 1966

Most First Downs, Both Teams, Game
62 San Diego (32) vs. Seattle (30), Sept. 15, 1985
Oakland (31) vs. Kansas City (31), Nov. 5, 2000
59 Miami (31) vs. Buffalo (28), Oct. 9, 1983 (OT)
Seattle (33) vs. Kansas City (26), Nov. 27, 1983 (OT)
N.Y. Jets (32) vs. Miami (27), Sept. 21, 1986 (OT)
N.Y. Jets (39) vs. Miami (20), Nov. 27, 1988
Oakland (31) vs. San Francisco (28), Oct. 8, 2000 (OT)
58 Los Angeles (30) vs. Chi. Bears (28), Oct. 24, 1954
Denver (34) vs. Kansas City (24), Nov. 18, 1974
Atlanta (35) vs. New Orleans (23), Sept. 2, 1979 (OT)
Pittsburgh (36) vs. Cleveland (22), Nov. 25, 1979 (OT)
San Diego (34) vs. Miami (24), Nov. 18, 1984 (OT)
Cincinnati (32) vs. San Diego (26), Sept. 22, 1985

Fewest First Downs, Both Teams, Game
7 Chi. Cardinals (2) vs. Detroit (5), Sept. 15, 1940
9 Pittsburgh (1) vs. Boston (8), Oct. 27, 1935
Boston (4) vs. Brooklyn (5), Nov. 24, 1935
N.Y. Giants (3) vs. Detroit (6), Nov. 7, 1943
Pittsburgh (4) vs. Chi. Cardinals (5), Nov. 11, 1945
N.Y. Bulldogs (1) vs. Philadelphia (8), Sept. 22, 1949
10 N.Y. Giants (4) vs. Washington (6), Dec. 11, 1960

Most First Downs, Rushing, Season
181 New England, 1978
177 Los Angeles, 1973
176 Chicago, 1985

Fewest First Downs, Rushing, Season
36 Cleveland, 1942
Boston, 1944
39 Brooklyn, 1943
40 Philadelphia, 1940
Detroit, 1945

Most First Downs, Rushing, Game
25 Philadelphia vs. Washington, Dec. 2, 1951
23 St. Louis vs. New Orleans, Oct. 5, 1980
21 Cleveland vs. Philadelphia, Dec. 13, 1959
Green Bay vs. Philadelphia, Nov. 11, 1962
Los Angeles vs. New Orleans, Nov. 25, 1973
Pittsburgh vs. Kansas City, Nov. 7, 1976
New England vs. Denver, Nov. 28, 1976
Oakland vs. Green Bay, Sept. 17, 1978
Buffalo vs. Washington, Nov. 3, 1996
San Francisco vs. Detroit, Dec. 14, 1998

Fewest First Downs, Rushing, Game
0 By many teams. Last time: Carolina vs. San Diego, Dec. 17, 2000

Most First Downs, Rushing, Both Teams, Game
36 Philadelphia (25) vs. Washington (11), Dec. 2, 1951
31 Detroit (18) vs. Washington (13), Sept. 30, 1951
30 Los Angeles (17) vs. Minnesota (13), Nov. 5, 1961
New Orleans (17) vs. Green Bay (13), Sept. 9, 1979
New Orleans (16) vs. San Francisco (14), Nov. 11, 1979
New England (16) vs. Kansas City (14), Oct. 4, 1981

Fewest First Downs, Rushing, Both Teams, Game
2 Houston (0) vs. Denver (2), Dec. 2, 1962
N.Y. Jets, (1) vs. St. Louis (1), Dec. 3, 1995
Miami (1) vs. San Diego (1), Dec. 19, 1999
New Orleans (0) vs. Baltimore (2), Dec. 19, 1999
3 Philadelphia (1) vs. Pittsburgh (2), Oct. 27, 1957
Boston (1) vs. Buffalo (2), Nov. 15, 1964
Los Angeles (0) vs. San Francisco (3), Dec. 6, 1964
Pittsburgh (1) vs. St. Louis (2), Nov. 13, 1966
Seattle (1) vs. New Orleans (2), Sept. 1, 1991
New Orleans (0) vs. N.Y. Jets (3), Dec. 24, 1995
Philadelphia (1) vs. Carolina (2), Oct. 27, 1996
San Diego (1) vs. New Orleans (2), Sept. 7, 1997
New Orleans (1) vs. Tampa Bay (2), Oct, 25, 1998
New England (1) vs. Miami (2), Oct. 25, 1998 (OT)
Miami (1) vs. New England (2), Nov. 23, 1998
4 In many games

Most First Downs, Passing, Season
259 San Diego, 1985
251 Houston, 1990
250 Miami, 1986

Fewest First Downs, Passing, Season
18 Pittsburgh, 1941
23 Brooklyn, 1942
N.Y. Giants, 1944
24 N.Y. Giants, 1943

Most First Downs, Passing, Game
29 N.Y. Giants vs. Cincinnati, Oct. 13, 1985
27 San Diego vs. Seattle, Sept. 15, 1985
26 Miami vs. Cleveland, Dec. 12, 1988

Fewest First Downs, Passing, Game
0 By many teams. Last time: Cleveland vs. Jacksonville, Dec. 3, 2000

Most First Downs, Passing, Both Teams, Game
43 San Diego (23) vs. Cincinnati (20), Dec. 20, 1982
Miami (24) vs. N.Y. Jets (19), Sept. 21, 1986 (OT)
42 San Francisco (22) vs. San Diego (20), Dec. 11, 1982
41 San Diego (27) vs. Seattle (14), Sept. 15, 1985
Miami (26) vs. Cleveland (15), Dec. 12, 1988
Kansas City (23) vs. Oakland (18), Nov. 5, 2000

Fewest First Downs, Passing, Both Teams, Game
0 Brooklyn vs. Pittsburgh, Nov. 29, 1942
1 Green Bay (0) vs. Cleveland (1), Sept. 21, 1941
Pittsburgh (0) vs. Brooklyn (1), Oct. 11, 1942
N.Y. Giants (0) vs. Detroit (1), Nov. 7, 1943
Pittsburgh (0) vs. Chi. Cardinals (1), Nov. 11, 1945
N.Y. Bulldogs (0) vs. Philadelphia (1), Sept. 22, 1949
Chicago (0) vs. Buffalo (1), Oct. 7, 1979
2 In many games

Most First Downs, Penalty, Season
43 Denver, 1994
42 Chicago, 1987
41 Denver, 1986

Fewest First Downs, Penalty, Season
2 Brooklyn, 1940
4 Chi. Cardinals, 1940
N.Y. Giants, 1942, 1944
Washington, 1944
Cleveland, 1952
Kansas City, 1969
5 Brooklyn, 1939
Chi. Bears, 1939
Detroit, 1953
Los Angeles, 1953
Houston, 1982

Most First Downs, Penalty, Game
11 Denver vs. Houston, Oct. 6, 1985
9 Chi. Bears vs. Cleveland, Nov. 25, 1951
Baltimore vs. Pittsburgh, Oct. 30, 1977
N.Y. Jets vs. Houston, Sept. 18, 1988
8 Philadelphia vs. Detroit, Dec. 2, 1979
Cincinnati vs. N.Y. Jets, Oct. 6, 1985
Buffalo vs. Houston, Sept. 20, 1987
Houston vs. Atlanta, Sept. 9, 1990
Kansas City vs. L.A. Raiders, Oct. 3, 1993
San Francisco vs. New Orleans, Oct. 11, 1998
Oakland vs. San Francisco, Oct. 8, 2000 (OT)

Most First Downs, Penalty, Both Teams, Game
12 Buffalo (7) vs. San Francisco (5), Oct. 4, 1998
11 Chi. Bears (9) vs. Cleveland (2), Nov. 25, 1951
Cincinnati (8) vs. N.Y. Jets (3), Oct. 6, 1985
Denver (11) vs. Houston (0), Oct. 6, 1985
Detroit (6) vs. Dallas (5), Nov. 8, 1987
N.Y. Jets (9) vs. Houston (2), Sept. 18, 1988
Kansas City (8) vs. L.A. Raiders (3), Oct. 3, 1993
Detroit (6) vs. San Diego (5), Nov. 11, 1996
10 In many games

NET YARDS GAINED RUSHING AND PASSING

Most Seasons Leading League
12 Chi. Bears, 1932, 1934-35, 1939, 1941-44, 1947, 1949, 1955-56
8 L.A./St. Louis Rams, 1946, 1950-51, 1954, 1957, 1973, 1999-2000
7 San Diego, 1963, 1965, 1980-83, 1985

Most Consecutive Seasons Leading League
4 Chi. Bears, 1941-44
San Diego, 1980-83
3 Baltimore, 1958-1960
Houston, 1960-62
Oakland, 1968-1970
2 By many teams

Most Yards Gained, Season
7,075 St. Louis, 2000
6,936 Miami, 1984
6,800 San Francisco, 1998

Fewest Yards Gained, Season
1,150 Cincinnati, 1933
1,443 Chi. Cardinals, 1934
1,486 Chi. Cardinals, 1933

Most Yards Gained, Game
735 Los Angeles vs. N.Y. Yanks, Sept. 28, 1951
683 Pittsburgh vs. Chi. Cardinals, Dec. 13, 1958
682 Chi. Bears vs. N.Y. Giants, Nov. 14, 1943

Fewest Yards Gained, Game
–7 Seattle vs. Los Angeles, Nov. 4, 1979
–5 Denver vs. Oakland, Sept. 10, 1967
14 Chi. Cardinals vs. Detroit, Sept. 15, 1940

Most Yards Gained, Both Teams, Game
1,133 Los Angeles (636) vs. N.Y. Yanks (497), Nov. 19, 1950
1,102 San Diego (661) vs. Cincinnati (441), Dec. 20, 1982
1,087 St. Louis (589) vs. Philadelphia (498), Dec. 16, 1962

Fewest Yards Gained, Both Teams, Game
30 Chi. Cardinals (14) vs. Detroit (16), Sept. 15, 1940
136 Chi. Cardinals (50) vs. Green Bay (86), Nov. 18, 1934
154 N.Y. Giants (51) vs. Washington (103), Dec. 11, 1960

Most Consecutive Games, 400 or More Yards Gained
11 San Diego, 1982-83
8 St. Louis, 1999-2000
6 Houston, 1961-62
San Diego, 1981
San Francisco, 1987

Most Consecutive Games, 300 or More Yards Gained
30 Minnesota, 1999-2000
29 Los Angeles, 1949-1951
26 Miami, 1983-85

RUSHING

Most Seasons Leading League
16 Chi. Bears, 1932, 1934-35, 1939-1942, 1951, 1955-56, 1968, 1977, 1983-86
7 Buffalo, 1962, 1964, 1973, 1975, 1982, 1991-92
6 Cleveland, 1958-59, 1963, 1965-67
San Francisco, 1952-54, 1987, 1998-99

Most Consecutive Seasons Leading League
4 Chi. Bears, 1939-1942
Chi. Bears, 1983-86
3 Detroit, 1936-38
San Francisco, 1952-54
Cleveland, 1965-67
2 By many teams

ATTEMPTS

Most Rushing Attempts, Season
681 Oakland, 1977
674 Chicago, 1984
671 New England, 1978

Fewest Rushing Attempts, Season
211 Philadelphia, 1982
219 San Francisco, 1982

225 Houston, 1982

Most Rushing Attempts, Game

72 Chi. Bears vs. Brooklyn, Oct. 20, 1935
70 Chi. Cardinals vs. Green Bay, Dec. 5, 1948
69 Chi. Cardinals vs. Green Bay, Dec. 6, 1936
Kansas City vs. Cincinnati, Sept. 3, 1978

Fewest Rushing Attempts, Game

6 Chi. Cardinals vs. Boston, Oct. 29, 1933
7 Oakland vs. Buffalo, Oct. 15, 1963
Houston vs. N.Y. Giants, Dec. 8, 1985
Seattle vs. L.A. Raiders, Nov. 17, 1991
Green Bay vs. Miami, Sept. 11, 1994
8 Denver vs. Oakland, Dec. 17, 1960
Buffalo vs. St. Louis, Sept. 9, 1984
Detroit vs. San Francisco, Oct. 20, 1991
Atlanta vs. Detroit, Sept. 5, 1993

Most Rushing Attempts, Both Teams, Game

108 Chi. Cardinals (70) vs. Green Bay (38), Dec. 5, 1948
105 Oakland (62) vs. Atlanta (43), Nov. 30, 1975 (OT)
104 Chi. Bears (64) vs. Pittsburgh (40), Oct. 18, 1936

Fewest Rushing Attempts, Both Teams, Game

34 Atlanta (12) vs. Houston (22), Dec. 5, 1993
Atlanta (15) vs. San Francisco (19), Dec. 24, 1995
35 Seattle (15) vs. New Orleans (20), Sept. 1, 1991
36 Houston (15) vs. N.Y. Jets (21), Oct. 13, 1991
St. Louis (16) vs. Detroit (20), Nov. 7, 1999
Detroit (15) vs. Washington (21), Dec. 5, 1999
Tennessee (14) vs. Baltimore (22), Dec. 5, 1999

YARDS GAINED

Most Yards Gained Rushing, Season

3,165 New England, 1978
3,088 Buffalo, 1973
2,986 Kansas City, 1978

Fewest Yards Gained Rushing, Season

298 Philadelphia, 1940
467 Detroit, 1946
471 Boston, 1944

Most Yards Gained Rushing, Game

426 Detroit vs. Pittsburgh, Nov. 4, 1934
423 N.Y. Giants vs. Baltimore, Nov. 19, 1950
420 Boston vs. N.Y. Giants, Oct. 8, 1933

Fewest Yards Gained Rushing, Game

–53 Detroit vs. Chi. Cardinals, Oct. 17, 1943
–36 Philadelphia vs. Chi. Bears, Nov. 19, 1939
–33 Phil-Pitt vs. Brooklyn, Oct. 2, 1943

Most Yards Gained Rushing, Both Teams, Game

595 Los Angeles (371) vs. N.Y. Yanks (224), Nov. 18, 1951
574 Chi. Bears (396) vs. Pittsburgh (178), Oct. 10, 1934
558 Boston (420) vs. N.Y. Giants (138), Oct. 8, 1933

Fewest Yards Gained Rushing, Both Teams, Game

–15 Detroit (–53) vs. Chi. Cardinals (38), Oct. 17, 1943
4 Detroit (–10) vs. Chi. Cardinals (14), Sept. 15, 1940
62 L.A. Rams (15) vs. San Francisco (47), Dec. 6, 1964

AVERAGE GAIN

Highest Average Gain, Rushing, Season

5.74 Cleveland, 1963
5.65 San Francisco, 1954
5.56 San Diego, 1963

Lowest Average Gain, Rushing, Season

0.94 Philadelphia, 1940
1.45 Boston, 1944
1.55 Pittsburgh, 1935

TOUCHDOWNS

Most Touchdowns, Rushing, Season

36 Green Bay, 1962
33 Pittsburgh, 1976
30 Chi. Bears, 1941
New England, 1978
Washington, 1983

Fewest Touchdowns, Rushing, Season

1 Brooklyn, 1934
2 Chi. Cardinals, 1933
Cincinnati, 1933
Pittsburgh, 1934
Philadelphia, 1935
Philadelphia, 1936
Philadelphia, 1937
Philadelphia, 1938
Pittsburgh, 1940
Philadelphia, 1972
N.Y. Jets, 1995
3 By many teams

Most Touchdowns, Rushing, Game

7 Los Angeles vs. Atlanta, Dec. 4, 1976
6 By many teams

Most Touchdowns, Rushing, Both Teams, Game

8 Los Angeles (6) vs. N.Y. Yanks (2), Nov. 18, 1951
Chi. Bears (5) vs. Green Bay (3), Nov. 6, 1955
Cleveland (6) vs. Los Angeles (2), Nov. 24, 1957
7 In many games

PASSING

ATTEMPTS

Most Passes Attempted, Season

709 Minnesota, 1981
699 New England, 1994
686 New England, 1995

Fewest Passes Attempted, Season

102 Cincinnati, 1933
106 Boston, 1933
120 Detroit, 1937

Most Passes Attempted, Game

70 New England vs. Minnesota, Nov. 13, 1994 (OT)
69 N.Y. Jets vs. Baltimore, Dec. 24, 2000
68 Houston vs. Buffalo, Nov 1, 1964

Fewest Passes Attempted, Game

0 Green Bay vs. Portsmouth, Oct. 8, 1933
Detroit vs. Cleveland, Sept. 10, 1937
Pittsburgh vs. Brooklyn, Nov. 16, 1941
Pittsburgh vs. Los Angeles, Nov. 13, 1949
Cleveland vs. Philadelphia, Dec. 3, 1950

Most Passes Attempted, Both Teams, Game

112 New England (70) vs. Minnesota (42), Nov. 13, 1994
104 Miami (55) vs. N.Y. Jets (49), Oct. 18, 1987 (OT)
N.Y. Jets (58) vs. San Francisco (46), Sept. 6, 1998 (OT)
102 San Francisco (57) vs. Atlanta (45), Oct. 6, 1985

Fewest Passes Attempted, Both Teams, Game

4 Chi. Cardinals (1) vs. Detroit (3), Nov. 3, 1935
Detroit (0) vs. Cleveland (4), Sept. 10, 1937
6 Chi. Cardinals (2) vs. Detroit (4), Sept. 15, 1940
8 Brooklyn (2) vs. Philadelphia (6), Oct. 1, 1939

COMPLETIONS

Most Passes Completed, Season

432 San Francisco, 1995
411 Houston, 1991
409 Minnesota, 1994

Fewest Passes Completed, Season

25 Cincinnati, 1933
33 Boston, 1933
34 Chi. Cardinals, 1934
Detroit, 1934

Most Passes Completed, Game

45 New England vs. Minnesota, Nov. 13, 1994 (OT)
43 Washington vs. Detroit, Nov. 4, 1990 (OT)
42 N.Y. Jets vs. San Francisco, Sept. 21, 1980
N.Y. Jets vs. Seattle, Dec. 6, 1998

Fewest Passes Completed, Game

0 By many teams. Last time: Buffalo vs. N.Y. Jets, Sept. 29, 1974

Most Passes Completed, Both Teams, Game

71 New England (45) vs. Minnesota (26), Nov. 13, 1994
68 San Francisco (37) vs. Atlanta (31), Oct. 6, 1985
66 Cincinnati (40) vs. San Diego (26), Dec. 20, 1982

Fewest Passes Completed, Both Teams, Game

1 Chi. Cardinals (0) vs. Philadelphia (1), Nov. 8, 1936
Detroit (0) vs. Cleveland (1), Sept. 10, 1937
Chi. Cardinals (0) vs. Detroit (1), Sept. 15, 1940
Brooklyn (0) vs. Pittsburgh (1), Nov. 29, 1942
2 Chi. Cardinals (0) vs. Detroit (2), Nov. 3, 1935
Buffalo (0) vs. N.Y. Jets (2), Sept. 29, 1974
Chi. Cardinals (0) vs. Green Bay (2), Nov. 18, 1934
3 In seven games

YARDS GAINED

Most Seasons Leading League, Passing Yardage

10 San Diego, 1965, 1968, 1971, 1978-1983, 1985
8 Chi. Bears, 1932, 1939, 1941, 1943, 1945, 1949, 1954, 1964
Washington, 1938, 1940, 1944, 1947-48, 1967, 1974, 1989
7 Houston, 1960-61, 1963-64, 1990-92

Most Consecutive Seasons Leading League, Passing Yardage

6 San Diego, 1978-1983
4 Green Bay, 1934-37
3 Miami, 1986-88

Houston, 1990-92

Most Yards Gained, Passing, Season
5,232 St. Louis, 2000
5,018 Miami, 1984
4,870 San Diego, 1985

Fewest Yards Gained, Passing, Season
302 Chi. Cardinals, 1934
357 Cincinnati, 1933
459 Boston, 1934

Most Yards Gained, Passing, Game
554 Los Angeles vs. N.Y. Yanks, Sept. 28, 1951
530 Minnesota vs. Baltimore, Sept. 28, 1969
521 Miami vs. N.Y. Jets, Oct. 23, 1988

Fewest Yards Gained, Passing, Game
–53 Denver vs. Oakland, Sept. 10, 1967
–52 Cincinnati vs. Houston, Oct. 31, 1971
–39 Atlanta vs. San Francisco, Oct. 23, 1976

Most Yards Gained, Passing, Both Teams, Game
884 N.Y. Jets (449) vs. Miami (435), Sept. 21, 1986 (OT)
883 San Diego (486) vs. Cincinnati (397), Dec. 20, 1982
874 Miami (456) vs. New England (418), Sept. 4, 1994

Fewest Yards Gained, Passing, Both Teams, Game
–11 Green Bay (–10) vs. Dallas (–1), Oct. 24, 1965
1 Chi. Cardinals (0) vs. Philadelphia (1), Nov. 8, 1936
7 Brooklyn (0) vs. Pittsburgh (7), Nov. 29, 1942

TIMES SACKED

Most Seasons Leading League, Fewest Times Sacked
10 Miami, 1973, 1982-1990
5 N.Y. Jets, 1965-66, 1968, 1993, 2000
4 San Diego, 1963-64, 1967-68
San Francisco, 1964-65, 1970-71

Most Consecutive Seasons Leading League, Fewest Times Sacked
9 Miami, 1982-1990
3 St. Louis, 1974-76
2 By many teams

Most Times Sacked, Season
104 Philadelphia, 1986
78 Arizona, 1997
72 Philadelphia, 1987

Fewest Times Sacked, Season
7 Miami, 1988
8 San Francisco, 1970
St. Louis, 1975
9 N.Y. Jets, 1966
Washington, 1991

Most Times Sacked, Game
12 Pittsburgh vs. Dallas, Nov. 20, 1966
Baltimore vs. St. Louis, Oct. 26, 1980
Detroit vs. Chicago, Dec. 16, 1984
Houston vs. Dallas, Sept. 29, 1985
11 St. Louis vs. N.Y. Giants, Nov. 1, 1964
Los Angeles vs. Baltimore, Nov. 22, 1964
Denver vs. Buffalo, Dec. 13, 1964
Green Bay vs. Detroit, Nov. 7, 1965
Buffalo vs. Oakland, Oct. 15, 1967
Denver vs. Oakland, Nov. 5, 1967
Atlanta vs. St. Louis, Nov. 24, 1968
Detroit vs. Dallas, Oct. 6, 1975
Philadelphia vs. St. Louis, Dec. 18, 1983
Cleveland vs. Kansas City, Sept. 30, 1984
Minnesota vs. Chicago, Oct. 28, 1984
Atlanta vs. Cleveland, Nov. 18, 1984
Dallas vs. San Diego, Nov. 16, 1986
Philadelphia vs. Detroit, Nov. 16, 1986
Philadelphia vs. L.A. Raiders, Nov. 30, 1986 (OT)
L.A. Raiders vs. Seattle, Dec. 8, 1986
N.Y. Jets vs. Dallas, Oct. 4, 1987
Philadelphia vs. Chicago, Oct. 4, 1987
Dallas vs. Philadelphia, Sept. 15, 1991
Cleveland vs. Indianapolis, Sept. 6, 1992
10 By many teams

Most Times Sacked, Both Teams, Game
18 Green Bay (10) vs. San Diego (8), Sept. 24, 1978
17 Buffalo (10) vs. N.Y. Titans (7), Nov. 23, 1961
Pittsburgh (12) vs. Dallas (5), Nov. 20, 1966
Atlanta (9) vs. Philadelphia (8), Dec. 16, 1984
Philadelphia (11) vs. L.A. Raiders (6), Nov. 30, 1986 (OT)
16 Los Angeles (11) vs. Baltimore (5), Nov. 22, 1964
Buffalo (11) vs. Oakland (5), Oct. 15, 1967

COMPLETION PERCENTAGE

Most Seasons Leading League, Completion Percentage
14 San Francisco, 1952, 1957-58, 1965, 1981, 1983, 1987, 1989, 1992-97
11 Washington, 1937, 1939-1940, 1942-45, 1947-48, 1969-1970
8 Green Bay, 1936, 1941, 1961-62, 1964, 1966, 1968, 1998

Most Consecutive Seasons Leading League, Completion Percentage
6 San Francisco, 1992-97
4 Washington, 1942-45
Kansas City, 1966-69
3 Cleveland, 1953-55

Highest Completion Percentage, Season
70.65 Cincinnati, 1982 (310-219)
70.25 San Francisco, 1994 (511-359)
70.19 San Francisco, 1989 (483-339)

Lowest Completion Percentage, Season
22.9 Philadelphia, 1936 (170-39)
24.5 Cincinnati, 1933 (102-25)
25.0 Pittsburgh, 1941 (168-42)

TOUCHDOWNS

Most Touchdowns, Passing, Season
49 Miami, 1984
48 Houston, 1961
46 Miami, 1986

Fewest Touchdowns, Passing, Season
0 Cincinnati, 1933
Pittsburgh, 1945
1 Boston, 1932
Boston, 1933
Chi. Cardinals, 1934
Cincinnati/St. Louis, 1934
Detroit, 1942
2 Chi. Cardinals, 1932
Stapleton, 1932
Chi. Cardinals, 1935
Brooklyn, 1936
Pittsburgh, 1942

Most Touchdowns, Passing, Game
7 Chi. Bears vs. N.Y. Giants, Nov. 14, 1943
Philadelphia vs. Washington, Oct. 17, 1954
Houston vs. N.Y. Titans, Nov. 19, 1961
Houston vs. N.Y. Titans, Oct. 14, 1962
N.Y. Giants vs. Washington, Oct. 28, 1962
Minnesota vs. Baltimore, Sept. 28, 1969
San Diego vs. Oakland, Nov. 22, 1981
6 By many teams

Most Touchdowns, Passing, Both Teams, Game
12 New Orleans (6) vs. St. Louis (6), Nov. 2, 1969
11 N.Y. Giants (7) vs. Washington (4), Oct. 28, 1962
Oakland (6) vs. Houston (5), Dec. 22, 1963
10 San Diego (5) vs. Seattle (5), Sept. 15, 1985
Miami (6) vs. N.Y. Jets (4), Sept. 21, 1986 (OT)
San Francisco (6) vs. Atlanta (4), Oct. 14, 1990

PASSES HAD INTERCEPTED

Most Passes Had Intercepted, Season
48 Houston, 1962
45 Denver, 1961
41 Card-Pitt, 1944

Fewest Passes Had Intercepted, Season
5 Cleveland, 1960
Green Bay, 1966
Kansas City, 1990
N.Y. Giants, 1990
6 Green Bay, 1964
St. Louis, 1982
Dallas, 1993
7 Los Angeles, 1969

Most Passes Had Intercepted, Game
9 Detroit vs. Green Bay, Oct. 24, 1943
Pittsburgh vs. Philadelphia, Dec. 12, 1965
8 Green Bay vs. N.Y. Giants, Nov. 21, 1948
Chi. Cardinals vs. Philadelphia, Sept. 24, 1950
N.Y. Yanks vs. N.Y. Giants, Dec. 16, 1951
Denver vs. Houston, Dec. 2, 1962
Chi. Bears vs. Detroit, Sept. 22, 1968
Baltimore vs. N.Y. Jets, Sept. 23, 1973
7 By many teams. Last time:
San Diego vs. Seattle, Dec. 13, 1998

Most Passes Had Intercepted, Both Teams, Game
13 Denver (8) vs. Houston (5), Dec. 2, 1962
11 Philadelphia (7) vs. Boston (4), Nov. 3, 1935

Boston (6) vs. Pittsburgh (5), Dec. 1, 1935
Cleveland (7) vs. Green Bay (4), Oct. 30, 1938
Green Bay (7) vs. Detroit (4), Oct. 20, 1940
Detroit (7) vs. Chi. Bears (4), Nov. 22, 1942
Detroit (7) vs. Cleveland (4), Nov. 26, 1944
Chi. Cardinals (8) vs. Philadelphia (3), Sept. 24, 1950
Washington (7) vs. N.Y. Giants (4), Dec. 8, 1963
Pittsburgh (9) vs. Philadelphia (2), Dec 12, 1965
10 In many games

PUNTING

Most Seasons Leading League (Average Distance)
7 Denver 1962-64, 1966-67, 1982, 1999
6 Washington, 1940-43, 1945, 1958
Kansas City, 1968, 1971-73, 1979, 1984
5 L.A. Rams, 1946, 1949, 1955-56, 1994

Most Consecutive Seasons Leading League (Average Distance)
4 Washington, 1940-43
3 Cleveland, 1950-52
Denver, 1962-64
Kansas City, 1971-73

Most Punts, Season
114 Chicago, 1981
113 Boston, 1934
Brooklyn, 1934
112 Boston, 1935
N.Y. Giants, 1997

Fewest Punts, Season
23 San Diego, 1982
31 Cincinnati, 1982
32 Chi. Bears, 1941

Most Punts, Game
17 Chi. Bears vs. Green Bay, Oct. 22, 1933
Cincinnati vs. Pittsburgh, Oct. 22, 1933
16 Cincinnati vs. Portsmouth, Sept. 17, 1933
Chi. Cardinals vs. Chi. Bears, Nov. 30, 1933
Chi. Cardinals vs. Detroit, Sept. 15, 1940
Oakland vs. San Diego, Oct. 11, 1998
15 N.Y. Giants vs. Chi. Bears, Nov. 17, 1935
Philadelphia vs. N.Y. Giants, Dec. 6, 1987 (OT)

Fewest Punts, Game
0 By many teams. Last time: Kansas City vs. Carolina, Dec. 10, 2000

Most Punts, Both Teams, Game
31 Chi. Bears (17) vs. Green Bay (14), Oct. 22, 1933
Cincinnati (17), vs. Pittsburgh (14), Oct. 22, 1933
29 Chi. Cardinals (15) vs. Cincinnati (14), Nov. 12, 1933
Chi. Cardinals (16) vs. Chi. Bears (13), Nov. 30, 1933
Chi. Cardinals (16) vs. Detroit (13), Sept. 15, 1940
28 Philadelphia (14) vs. Washington (14), Nov. 5, 1939

Fewest Punts, Both Teams, Game
0 Buffalo vs. San Francisco, Sept. 13, 1992
1 Baltimore (0) vs. Cleveland (1), Nov. 1, 1959
Dall. Cowboys (0) vs. Cleveland (1), Dec. 3, 1961
Chicago (0) vs. Detroit (1), Oct. 1, 1972
San Francisco (0) vs. N.Y. Giants (1), Oct. 15, 1972
Green Bay (0) vs. Buffalo (1), Dec. 5, 1982
Miami (0) vs. Buffalo (1), Oct. 12, 1986
Green Bay (0) vs. Chicago (1), Dec. 17, 1989
Oakland (0) vs. Seattle (1), Dec. 5, 1999
Tampa Bay (0) vs. Minnesota (1), Oct. 29, 2000
2 In many games

AVERAGE YARDAGE

Highest Average Distance, Punting, Season
47.6 Detroit, 1961 (56-2,664)
47.2 Tennessee, 1998 (69-3,258)
47.0 Pittsburgh, 1961 (73-3,431)

Lowest Average Distance, Punting, Season
32.7 Card-Pitt, 1944 (60-1,964)
33.8 Cincinnati, 1986 (59-1,996)
33.9 Detroit, 1969 (74-2,510)

PUNT RETURNS

Most Seasons Leading League (Average Return)
9 Detroit, 1943-45, 1951-52, 1962, 1966, 1969, 1991
7 Chi. Cardinals/St. Louis, 1948-49, 1955-56, 1959, 1986-87
6 Green Bay, 1950, 1953-54, 1961, 1972, 1996

Most Consecutive Seasons Leading League (Average Return)
3 Detroit, 1943-45
2 By many teams

Most Punt Returns, Season
71 Pittsburgh, 1976
Tampa Bay, 1979
L.A. Raiders, 1985
67 Pittsburgh, 1974
Los Angeles, 1978
L.A. Raiders, 1984
65 San Francisco, 1976

Fewest Punt Returns, Season
12 Baltimore, 1981
San Diego, 1982
14 Los Angeles, 1961
Philadelphia, 1962
Baltimore, 1982
15 Houston, 1960
Washington, 1960
Oakland, 1961
N.Y. Giants, 1969
Philadelphia, 1973
Kansas City, 1982

Most Punt Returns, Game
12 Philadelphia vs. Cleveland, Dec. 3, 1950
11 Chi. Bears vs. Chi. Cardinals, Oct. 8, 1950
Washington vs. Tampa Bay, Oct. 9, 1977
10 Philadelphia vs. N.Y. Giants, Nov. 26, 1950
Philadelphia vs. Tampa Bay, Sept. 18, 1977
Pittsburgh vs. Buffalo, Dec. 16, 1979
Washington vs. New Orleans, Dec. 26, 1982
Philadelphia vs. Seattle, Dec. 13, 1992 (OT)
New England vs. Pittsburgh, Dec. 5, 1993

Most Punt Returns, Both Teams, Game
17 Philadelphia (12) vs. Cleveland (5), Dec. 3, 1950
16 N.Y. Giants (9) vs. Philadelphia (7), Dec. 12, 1954
Washington (11) vs. Tampa Bay (5), Oct. 9, 1977
Oakland (8) vs. San Diego (8), Oct. 11, 1998
15 Detroit (8) vs. Cleveland (7), Sept. 27, 1942
Los Angeles (8) vs. Baltimore (7), Nov. 27, 1966
Pittsburgh (8) vs. Houston (7), Dec. 1, 1974
Philadelphia (10) vs. Tampa Bay (5), Sept. 18, 1977
Baltimore (9) vs. Kansas City (6), Sept. 2, 1979
Washington (10) vs. New Orleans (5), Dec. 26, 1982
L.A. Raiders (8) vs. Cleveland (7), Nov. 16, 1986

FAIR CATCHES

Most Fair Catches, Season
34 Baltimore, 1971
33 Philadelphia, 2000
32 San Diego, 1969

Fewest Fair Catches, Season
0 San Diego, 1975
New England, 1976
Tampa Bay, 1976
Pittsburgh, 1977
Dallas, 1982
1 Cleveland, 1974
San Francisco, 1975
Kansas City, 1976
St. Louis, 1976
San Diego, 1976
L.A. Rams, 1982
St. Louis, 1982
Tampa Bay, 1982
2 By many teams

Most Fair Catches, Game
7 Minnesota vs. Dallas, Sept. 25, 1966
Detroit vs. Chicago, Nov. 21, 1976
Philadelphia vs. Buffalo, Dec. 27, 1987
6 By many teams

YARDS GAINED

Most Yards, Punt Returns, Season
875 Green Bay, 1996
785 L.A. Raiders, 1985
781 Chi. Bears, 1948

Fewest Yards, Punt Returns, Season
27 St. Louis, 1965
35 N.Y. Giants, 1965
37 New England, 1972

Most Yards, Punt Returns, Game
231 Detroit vs. San Francisco, Oct. 6, 1963
225 Oakland vs. Buffalo, Sept. 15, 1968
219 Los Angeles vs. Atlanta, Oct. 11, 1981

Fewest Yards, Punt Returns, Game
-28 Washington vs. Dallas, Dec. 11, 1966
-23 N.Y. Giants vs. Buffalo, Oct. 20, 1975
Pittsburgh vs. Houston, Sept. 20, 1970

-20 New Orleans vs. Pittsburgh, Oct. 20, 1968

Most Yards, Punt Returns, Both Teams, Game
282 Los Angeles (219) vs. Atlanta (63), Oct. 11, 1981
245 Detroit (231) vs. San Francisco (14), Oct. 6, 1963
244 Oakland (225) vs. Buffalo (19), Sept. 15, 1968

Fewest Yards, Punt Returns, Both Teams, Game
-18 Buffalo (-18) vs. Pittsburgh (0), Oct. 29, 1972
-14 Miami (-14) vs. Boston (0), Nov. 30, 1969
-13 N.Y. Giants (-13) vs. Cleveland (0), Nov. 14, 1965

AVERAGE YARDS RETURNING PUNTS

Highest Average, Punt Returns, Season
20.2 Chi. Bears, 1941 (27-546)
19.1 Chi. Cardinals, 1948 (35-669)
18.2 Chi. Cardinals, 1949 (30-546)

Lowest Average, Punt Returns, Season
1.2 St. Louis, 1965 (23-27)
1.5 N.Y. Giants, 1965 (24-35)
1.7 Washington, 1970 (27-45)

TOUCHDOWNS RETURNING PUNTS

Most Touchdowns, Punt Returns, Season
5 Chi. Cardinals, 1959
4 Chi. Cardinals, 1948
Detroit, 1951
N.Y. Giants, 1951
Denver, 1976
3 Washington, 1941
Detroit, 1952
Pittsburgh, 1952
Houston, 1975
Los Angeles, 1981
Cleveland, 1993
Green Bay, 1996
Denver, 1997
San Diego, 1997

Most Touchdowns, Punt Returns, Game
2 Detroit vs. Los Angeles, Oct. 14, 1951
Detroit vs. Green Bay, Nov. 22, 1951
Chi. Cardinals vs. Pittsburgh, Nov. 1, 1959
Chi. Cardinals vs. N.Y. Giants, Nov. 22, 1959
N.Y. Titans vs. Denver, Sept. 24, 1961
Denver vs. Cleveland, Sept. 26, 1976
Los Angeles vs. Atlanta, Oct. 11, 1981
St. Louis vs. Tampa Bay, Dec. 21, 1986
L.A. Rams vs. Atlanta, Dec. 27, 1992
Cleveland vs. Pittsburgh, Oct. 24, 1993
San Diego vs. Cincinnati, Nov. 2, 1997
Denver vs. Carolina, Nov. 9, 1997
Baltimore vs. Seattle, Dec. 7, 1997
Baltimore vs. N.Y. Jets, Dec. 24, 2000

Most Touchdowns, Punt Returns, Both Teams, Game
2 Philadelphia (1) vs. Washington (1), Nov. 9, 1952
Kansas City (1) vs. Buffalo (1), Sept. 11, 1966
Baltimore (1) vs. New England (1), Nov. 18, 1979
L.A. Raiders (1) vs. Philadelphia (1), Nov. 30, 1986 (OT)
Cincinnati (1) vs. Green Bay (1), Sept. 20, 1992
Oakland (1) vs. Seattle (1), Nov. 15, 1998
(Also see previous record)

KICKOFF RETURNS

Most Seasons Leading League (Average Return)
8 Washington, 1942, 1947, 1962-63, 1973-74, 1981, 1995
6 Chicago Bears, 1943, 1948, 1958, 1966, 1972, 1985
5 N.Y. Giants, 1944, 1946, 1949, 1951, 1953

Most Consecutive Seasons Leading League (Average Return)
3 Denver, 1965-67
2 By many teams

Most Kickoff Returns, Season
89 Cleveland, 1999
88 New Orleans, 1980
87 Atlanta, 1996

Fewest Kickoff Returns, Season
17 N.Y. Giants, 1944
20 N.Y. Giants, 1941, 1943
Chi. Bears, 1942
23 Washington, 1942

Most Kickoff Returns, Game
12 N.Y. Giants vs. Washington, Nov. 27, 1966
10 By many teams

Most Kickoff Returns, Both Teams, Game
19 N.Y. Giants (12) vs. Washington (7), Nov. 27, 1966
18 Houston (10) vs. Oakland (8), Dec. 22, 1963
17 Washington (9) vs. Green Bay (8), Oct. 17, 1983
San Diego (9) vs. Pittsburgh (8), Dec. 8, 1985
Detroit (9) vs. Green Bay (8), Nov. 27, 1986
L.A. Raiders (9) vs. Seattle (8), Dec. 18, 1988
Oakland (10) vs. Seattle (7), Oct. 26, 1997

YARDS GAINED

Most Yards, Kickoff Returns, Season
2,296 Arizona, 2000
2,020 Cincinnati, 1999
1,973 New Orleans, 1980

Fewest Yards, Kickoff Returns, Season
282 N.Y. Giants, 1940
381 Green Bay, 1940
424 Chicago, 1963

Most Yards, Kickoff Returns, Game
367 Baltimore vs. Minnesota, Dec. 13, 1998
362 Detroit vs. Los Angeles, Oct. 29, 1950
304 Chi. Bears vs. Green Bay, Nov. 9, 1952
New Orleans vs. L.A. Rams, Oct. 23, 1994

Most Yards, Kickoff Returns, Both Teams, Game
560 Detroit (362) vs. Los Angeles (198), Oct. 29, 1950
511 Baltimore (367) vs. Minnesota (144), Dec. 13, 1998
501 New Orleans (304) vs. L.A. Rams (197), Oct. 23, 1994

AVERAGE YARDAGE

Highest Average, Kickoff Returns, Season
29.4 Chicago, 1972 (52-1,528)
28.9 Pittsburgh, 1952 (39-1,128)
28.2 Washington, 1962 (61-1,720)

Lowest Average, Kickoff Returns, Season
14.7 N.Y. Jets, 1993 (46-675)
15.8 N.Y. Giants, 1993 (32-507)
15.9 Tampa Bay, 1993 (58-922)

TOUCHDOWNS

Most Touchdowns, Kickoff Returns, Season
4 Green Bay, 1967
Chicago, 1970
Detroit, 1994
3 Los Angeles, 1950
Chi. Cardinals, 1954
San Francisco, 1963
Denver, 1966
Chicago, 1967
New England, 1977
L.A. Rams, 1985
Atlanta, 2000
2 By many teams

Most Touchdowns, Kickoff Returns, Game
2 Chi. Bears vs. Green Bay, Sept. 22, 1940
Chi. Bears vs. Green Bay, Nov. 9, 1952
Philadelphia vs. Dallas, Nov. 6, 1966
Green Bay vs. Cleveland, Nov. 12, 1967
L.A. Rams vs. Green Bay, Nov. 24, 1985
New Orleans vs. L.A. Rams, Oct. 23, 1994
Baltimore vs. Minnesota, Dec. 13, 1998

Most Touchdowns, Kickoff Returns, Both Teams, Game
3 Baltimore (2) vs. Minnesota (1), Dec. 13, 1998
2 In many games

FUMBLES

Most Fumbles, Season
56 Chi. Bears, 1938
San Francisco, 1978
54 Philadelphia, 1946
51 New England, 1973

Fewest Fumbles, Season
8 Cleveland, 1959
10 Indianapolis, 1998
Minnesota, 1998
11 Green Bay, 1944

Most Fumbles, Game
10 Phil-Pitt vs. N.Y. Giants, Oct. 9, 1943
Detroit vs. Minnesota, Nov. 12, 1967
Kansas City vs. Houston, Oct. 12, 1969
San Francisco vs. Detroit, Dec. 17, 1978
9 Philadelphia vs. Green Bay, Oct. 13, 1946
Kansas City vs. San Diego, Nov. 15, 1964
N.Y. Giants vs. Buffalo, Oct. 20, 1975
St. Louis vs. Washington, Oct. 25, 1976
San Diego vs. Green Bay, Sept. 24, 1978
Pittsburgh vs. Cincinnati, Oct. 14, 1979

Cleveland vs. Seattle, Dec. 20, 1981
Cleveland vs. Pittsburgh, Dec. 23, 1990
Oakland vs. Seattle, Dec. 22, 1996
8 By many teams

Most Fumbles, Both Teams, Game
14 Washington (8) vs. Pittsburgh (6), Nov. 14, 1937
Chi. Bears (7) vs. Cleveland (7), Nov. 24, 1940
St. Louis (8) vs. N.Y. Giants (6), Sept. 17, 1961
Kansas City (10) vs. Houston (4), Oct. 12, 1969
13 Washington (8) vs. Pittsburgh (5), Nov. 14, 1937
Philadelphia (7) vs. Boston (6), Dec. 8, 1946
N.Y. Giants (7) vs. Washington (6), Nov. 5, 1950
Kansas City (9) vs. San Diego (4), Nov. 15, 1964
Buffalo (7) vs. Denver (6), Dec. 13, 1964
N.Y. Jets (7) vs. Houston (6), Sept. 12, 1965
Cleveland (7) vs. New Orleans (6), Dec. 12, 1971
Houston (8) vs. Pittsburgh (5), Dec. 9, 1973
St. Louis (9) vs. Washington (4), Oct. 25, 1976
Cleveland (9) vs. Seattle (4), Dec. 20, 1981
Green Bay (7) vs. Detroit (6), Oct. 6, 1985
12 In many games

FUMBLES LOST

Most Fumbles Lost, Season
36 Chi. Cardinals, 1959
31 Green Bay, 1952
29 Chi. Cardinals, 1946
Pittsburgh, 1950
Cleveland, 1978

Fewest Fumbles Lost, Season
3 Philadelphia, 1938
Minnesota, 1980
4 San Francisco, 1960
Kansas City, 1982
Minnesota, 1998
5 Chi. Cardinals, 1943
Detroit, 1943
N.Y. Giants, 1943
Cleveland, 1959
Minnesota, 1982
San Diego, 1993
Detroit, 1996
Indianapolis, 1998

Most Fumbles Lost, Game
8 St. Louis vs. Washington, Oct. 25, 1976
Cleveland vs. Pittsburgh, Dec. 23, 1990
7 Cincinnati vs. Buffalo, Nov. 30, 1969
Pittsburgh vs. Cincinnati, Oct. 14, 1979
Cleveland vs. Seattle, Dec. 20, 1981
6 By many teams

FUMBLES RECOVERED

Most Fumbles Recovered, Season, Own and Opponents'
58 Minnesota, 1963 (27 own, 31 opp)
51 Chi. Bears, 1938 (37 own, 14 opp)
San Francisco, 1978 (24 own, 27 opp)
50 Philadelphia, 1987 (23 own, 27 opp)

Fewest Fumbles Recovered, Season, Own and Opponents'
9 San Francisco, 1982 (5 own, 4 opp)
11 Cincinnati, 1982 (5 own, 6 opp)
12 Washington, 1994 (6 own, 6 opp)
Arizona, 1997 (7 own, 5 opp)

Most Fumbles Recovered, Game, Own and Opponents'
10 Denver vs. Buffalo, Dec. 13, 1964 (5 own, 5 opp)
Pittsburgh vs. Houston, Dec. 9, 1973 (5 own, 5 opp)
Washington vs. St. Louis, Oct. 25, 1976 (2 own, 8 opp)
9 St. Louis vs. N.Y. Giants, Sept. 17, 1961 (6 own, 3 opp)
Houston vs. Cincinnati, Oct. 27, 1974 (4 own, 5 opp)
Kansas City vs. Dallas, Nov. 10, 1975 (4 own, 5 opp)
Green Bay vs. Detroit, Oct. 6, 1985 (5 own, 4 opp)
Pittsburgh vs. Cleveland, Dec. 23, 1990 (1 own, 8 opp)
8 By many teams

Most Own Fumbles Recovered, Season
37 Chi. Bears, 1938
28 Pittsburgh, 1987
27 Philadelphia, 1946
Minnesota, 1963

Fewest Own Fumbles Recovered, Season
2 Washington, 1958
Miami, 2000
3 Detroit, 1956
Cleveland, 1959
Houston, 1982
4 By many teams

Most Opponents' Fumbles Recovered, Season
31 Minnesota, 1963
29 Cleveland, 1951
28 Green Bay, 1946
Houston, 1977
Seattle, 1983

Fewest Opponents' Fumbles Recovered, Season
3 Los Angeles, 1974
Green Bay, 1995
4 Philadelphia, 1944
San Francisco, 1982
5 Baltimore, 1982
Arizona, 1997
Baltimore, 1998

Most Opponents' Fumbles Recovered, Game
8 Washington vs. St. Louis, Oct. 25, 1976
Pittsburgh vs. Cleveland, Dec. 23, 1990
7 Buffalo vs. Cincinnati, Nov. 30, 1969
Cincinnati vs. Pittsburgh, Oct. 14, 1979
Seattle vs. Cleveland, Dec. 20, 1981
6 By many teams

TOUCHDOWNS

Most Touchdowns, Fumbles Recovered, Season, Own and Opponents'
5 Chi. Bears, 1942 (1 own, 4 opp)
Los Angeles, 1952 (1 own, 4 opp)
San Francisco, 1965 (1 own, 4 opp)
Oakland, 1978 (2 own, 3 opp)
4 Chi. Bears, 1948 (1 own, 3 opp)
Boston, 1948 (4 opp)
Denver, 1979 (1 own, 3 opp)
Atlanta, 1981 (1 own, 3 opp)
Denver, 1984 (4 opp)
St. Louis, 1987 (4 opp)
Minnesota, 1989 (4 opp)
Atlanta, 1991 (4 opp)
Philadelphia, 1995 (4 opp)
Atlanta, 1998 (4 opp)
New Orleans, 1998 (4 opp)
Kansas City, 1999 (4 opp)
3 By many teams

Most Touchdowns, Own Fumbles Recovered, Season
2 Chi. Bears, 1953
New England, 1973
Buffalo, 1974
Denver, 1975
Oakland, 1978
Green Bay, 1982
New Orleans, 1983
Cleveland, 1986
Green Bay, 1989
Miami, 1996
Buffalo, 2000

Most Touchdowns, Opponents' Fumbles Recovered, Season
4 Detroit, 1937
Chi. Bears, 1942
Boston, 1948
Los Angeles, 1952
San Francisco, 1965
Denver, 1984
St. Louis, 1987
Minnesota, 1989
Atlanta, 1991
Philadelphia, 1995
Atlanta, 1998
New Orleans, 1998
Kansas City, 1999
3 By many teams

Most Touchdowns, Fumbles Recovered, Game, Own and Opponents'
2 By many teams

Most Touchdowns, Fumbles Recovered, Game, Both Teams, Own and Opponents'
3 Detroit (2) vs. Minnesota (1), Dec. 9, 1962 (2 own, 1 opp)
Green Bay (2) vs. Dallas (1), Nov. 29, 1964 (3 opp)
Oakland (2) vs. Buffalo (1), Dec. 24, 1967 (3 opp)
Oakland (2) vs. Philadelphia (1), Sept. 24, 1995 (3 opp)
Tennessee (2) vs. Pittsburgh (1), Jan. 2, 2000 (3 opp)

Most Touchdowns, Own Fumbles Recovered, Game
2 Miami vs. New England, Sept.1, 1996

Most Touchdowns, Opponents' Fumbles Recovered, Game
2 Many times. Last time: Seattle vs. Denver, Nov. 26, 2000

Most Touchdowns, Opponents' Fumbles Recovered, Game, Both Teams
3 Green Bay (2) vs. Dallas (1), Nov. 29, 1964
Oakland (2) vs. Buffalo (1), Dec. 24, 1967
Oakland (2) vs. Philadelphia (1), Sept. 24, 1995
Tennessee (2) vs. Pittsburgh (1), Jan. 2, 2000

TURNOVERS

(Number of times losing the ball on interceptions and fumbles.)

Most Turnovers, Season
63 San Francisco, 1978
58 Chi. Bears, 1947
Pittsburgh, 1950
N.Y. Giants, 1983
57 Green Bay, 1950
Houston, 1962, 1963
Pittsburgh, 1965

Fewest Turnovers, Season
12 Kansas City, 1982
14 N.Y. Giants, 1943
Cleveland, 1959
N.Y. Giants, 1990
15 Dallas, 1998

Most Turnovers, Game
12 Detroit vs. Chi. Bears, Nov. 22, 1942
Chi. Cardinals vs. Philadelphia, Sept. 24, 1950
Pittsburgh vs. Philadelphia, Dec. 12, 1965
11 San Diego vs. Green Bay, Sept. 24, 1978
10 Washington vs. N.Y. Giants, Dec. 4, 1938
Pittsburgh vs. Green Bay, Nov. 23, 1941
Detroit vs. Green Bay, Oct. 24, 1943
Chi. Cardinals vs. Green Bay, Nov. 10, 1946
Chi. Cardinals vs. N.Y. Giants, Nov. 2, 1952
Minnesota vs. Detroit, Dec. 9, 1962
Houston vs. Oakland, Sept. 7, 1963
Washington vs. N.Y. Giants, Dec. 8, 1963
Chicago vs. Detroit, Sept. 22, 1968
St. Louis vs. Washington, Oct. 25, 1976
N.Y. Jets vs. New England, Nov. 21, 1976
San Francisco vs. Dallas, Oct. 12, 1980
Cleveland vs. Seattle, Dec. 20, 1981
Detroit vs. Denver, Oct. 7, 1984

Most Turnovers, Both Teams, Game
17 Detroit (12) vs. Chi. Bears (5), Nov. 22, 1942
Boston (9) vs. Philadelphia (8), Dec. 8, 1946
16 Chi. Cardinals (12) vs. Philadelphia (4), Sept. 24, 1950
Chi. Cardinals (8) vs. Chi. Bears (8), Dec. 7, 1958
Minnesota (10) vs. Detroit (6), Dec. 9, 1962
Houston (9) vs. Kansas City (7), Oct. 12, 1969
15 Philadelphia (8) vs. Chi. Cardinals (7), Oct. 3, 1954
Denver (9) vs. Houston (6), Dec. 2, 1962
Washington (10) vs. N.Y. Giants (5), Dec. 8, 1963
St. Louis (9) vs. Kansas City (6), Oct. 2, 1983

PENALTIES

Most Seasons Leading League, Fewest Penalties
13 Miami, 1968, 1976-1984, 1986, 1990-91
9 Pittsburgh, 1946-47, 1950-52, 1954, 1963, 1965, 1968
7 Boston/New England, 1962, 1964-65, 1973, 1987, 1989, 1993

Most Consecutive Seasons Leading League, Fewest Penalties
9 Miami, 1976-1984
3 Pittsburgh, 1950-52
2 By many teams

Most Seasons Leading League, Most Penalties
16 Chi. Bears, 1941-44, 1946-49, 1951, 1959-1961, 1963, 1965, 1968, 1976
12 Oakland/L.A. Raiders, 1963, 1966, 1968-69, 1975, 1982, 1984, 1991, 1993-96
7 L.A./St. Louis Rams, 1950, 1952, 1962, 1969, 1978, 1980, 1997

Most Consecutive Seasons Leading League, Most Penalties
4 Chi. Bears, 1941-44, 1946-49
Oakland/L.A. Raiders, 1993-96
3 Chi. Cardinals, 1954-56
Chi. Bears, 1959-1961

Fewest Penalties, Season
19 Detroit, 1937
21 Boston, 1935
24 Philadelphia, 1936

Most Penalties, Season
158 Kansas City, 1998
156 L.A. Raiders, 1994
Oakland, 1996
149 Houston, 1989

Fewest Penalties, Game
0 By many teams. Last time:
Indianapolis vs. Cleveland, Dec. 26, 1999

Most Penalties, Game
22 Brooklyn vs. Green Bay, Sept. 17, 1944
Chi. Bears vs. Philadelphia, Nov. 26, 1944
San Francisco vs. Buffalo, Oct. 4, 1998
21 Cleveland vs. Chi. Bears, Nov. 25, 1951
20 Tampa Bay vs. Seattle, Oct. 17, 1976
Oakland vs. Denver, Dec. 15, 1996

Fewest Penalties, Both Teams, Game
0 Brooklyn vs. Pittsburgh, Oct. 28, 1934
Brooklyn vs. Boston, Sept. 28, 1936
Cleveland vs. Chi. Bears, Oct. 9, 1938
Pittsburgh vs. Philadelphia, Nov. 10, 1940

Most Penalties, Both Teams, Game
37 Cleveland (21) vs. Chi. Bears (16), Nov. 25, 1951
35 Tampa Bay (20) vs. Seattle (15), Oct. 17, 1976
34 San Francisco (22) vs. Buffalo (12), Oct. 4, 1998

YARDS PENALIZED

Most Seasons Leading League, Fewest Yards Penalized
13 Miami, 1967-68, 1973, 1977-1984, 1990-91
10 Boston/Washington, 1935, 1953-54, 1956-58, 1970, 1985, 1995, 1997
7 Pittsburgh, 1946-47, 1950, 1952, 1962, 1965, 1968
Boston/New England, 1962, 1964-66, 1987, 1989, 1993

Most Consecutive Seasons Leading League, Fewest Yards Penalized
8 Miami, 1977-1984
3 Washington, 1956-58
Boston, 1964-66
2 By many teams

Most Seasons Leading League, Most Yards Penalized
15 Chi. Bears, 1935, 1937, 1939-1944, 1946-47, 1949, 1951, 1961-62, 1968
11 Oakland/L.A. Raiders, 1963-64, 1968-69, 1975, 1982, 1984, 1991, 1993-94, 1996
6 Buffalo, 1962, 1967, 1970, 1972, 1981, 1983
Houston, 1961, 1985-86, 1988-1990

Most Consecutive Seasons Leading League, Most Yards Penalized
6 Chi. Bears, 1939-1944
3 Houston, 1988-1990
2 By many teams

Fewest Yards Penalized, Season
139 Detroit, 1937
146 Philadelphia, 1937
159 Philadelphia, 1936

Most Yards Penalized, Season
1,304 Kansas City, 1998
1,274 Oakland, 1969
1,266 Oakland, 1996

Fewest Yards Penalized, Game
0 By many teams. Last time:
Indianapolis vs. Cleveland, Dec. 26, 1999

Most Yards Penalized, Game
212 Tennessee vs. Baltimore, Oct. 10, 1999
209 Cleveland vs. Chi. Bears, Nov. 25, 1951
191 Philadelphia vs. Seattle, Dec. 13, 1992 (OT)

Fewest Yards Penalized, Both Teams, Game
0 Brooklyn vs. Pittsburgh, Oct. 28, 1934
Brooklyn vs. Boston, Sept. 28, 1936
Cleveland vs. Chi. Bears, Oct. 9, 1938
Pittsburgh vs. Philadelphia, Nov. 10, 1940

Most Yards Penalized, Both Teams, Game
374 Cleveland (209) vs. Chi. Bears (165), Nov. 25, 1951
310 Tampa Bay (190) vs. Seattle (120), Oct. 17, 1976
309 Green Bay (184) vs. Boston (125), Oct. 21, 1945

DEFENSE

SCORING

Most Seasons Leading League, Fewest Points Allowed
11 N.Y. Giants, 1927, 1935, 1938-39, 1941, 1944, 1958-59, 1961, 1990, 1993
9 Chi. Bears, 1932, 1936-37, 1942, 1948, 1963, 1985-86, 1988
7 Cleveland, 1951, 1953-57, 1994
Green Bay, 1929, 1935, 1947, 1962, 1965-66, 1996

Most Consecutive Seasons Leading League, Fewest Points Allowed
5 Cleveland, 1953-57
3 Buffalo, 1964-66
Minnesota, 1969-1971
2 By many teams

Fewest Points Allowed, Season (Since 1932)
44 Chi. Bears, 1932

54 Brooklyn, 1933
59 Detroit, 1934

Most Points Allowed, Season
533 Baltimore, 1981
501 N.Y. Giants, 1966
487 New Orleans, 1980

Fewest Touchdowns Allowed, Season (Since 1932)
6 Chi. Bears, 1932
Brooklyn, 1933
7 Detroit, 1934
8 Green Bay, 1932

Most Touchdowns Allowed, Season
68 Baltimore, 1981
66 N.Y. Giants, 1966
63 Baltimore, 1950

FIRST DOWNS

Fewest First Downs Allowed Season
77 Detroit, 1935
79 Boston, 1935
82 Washington, 1937

Most First Downs Allowed, Season
406 Baltimore, 1981
371 Seattle, 1981
368 Cleveland, 1999

Fewest First Downs Allowed, Rushing, Season
35 Chi. Bears, 1942
40 Green Bay, 1939
41 Brooklyn, 1944

Most First Downs Allowed, Rushing, Season
179 Detroit, 1985
178 New Orleans, 1980
175 Seattle, 1981

Fewest First Downs Allowed, Passing, Season
33 Chi. Bears, 1943
34 Pittsburgh, 1941
Washington, 1943
35 Detroit, 1940
Philadelphia, 1940, 1944

Most First Downs Allowed, Passing, Season
230 Atlanta, 1995
218 San Diego, 1985
216 San Diego, 1981
N.Y. Jets, 1986

Fewest First Downs Allowed, Penalty, Season
1 Boston, 1944
3 Philadelphia, 1940
Pittsburgh, 1945
Washington, 1957
4 Cleveland, 1940
Green Bay, 1943
N.Y. Giants, 1943

Most First Downs Allowed, Penalty, Season
56 Kansas City, 1998
48 Houston, 1985
46 Houston, 1986

NET YARDS ALLOWED RUSHING AND PASSING

Most Seasons Leading League, Fewest Yards Allowed
8 Chi. Bears, 1942-43, 1948, 1958, 1963, 1984-86
6 N.Y. Giants, 1938, 1940-41, 1951, 1956, 1959
Philadelphia, 1944-45, 1949, 1953, 1981, 1991
Minnesota, 1969-1970, 1975, 1988-89, 1993
5 Boston/Washington, 1935-37, 1939, 1946

Most Consecutive Seasons Leading League, Fewest Yards Allowed
3 Boston/Washington, 1935-37
Chicago, 1984-86
2 By many teams

Fewest Yards Allowed, Season
1,539 Chi. Cardinals, 1934
1,703 Chi. Bears, 1942
1,789 Brooklyn, 1933

Most Yards Allowed, Season
6,793 Baltimore, 1981
6,403 Green Bay, 1983
6,391 Seattle, 2000

RUSHING

Most Seasons Leading League, Fewest Yards Allowed
10 Chi. Bears, 1937, 1939, 1942, 1946, 1949, 1963, 1984-85, 1987-88
7 Detroit, 1938, 1950, 1952, 1962, 1970, 1980-81
Philadelphia, 1944-45, 1947-48, 1953, 1990-91
Dallas, 1966-69, 1972, 1978, 1992
5 N.Y. Giants, 1940, 1951, 1956, 1959, 1986
L.A./St. Louis Rams, 1964-65, 1973-74, 1999

Most Consecutive Seasons Leading League, Fewest Yards Allowed
4 Dallas, 1966-69
2 By many teams

Fewest Yards Allowed, Rushing, Season
519 Chi. Bears, 1942
558 Philadelphia, 1944
762 Pittsburgh, 1982

Most Yards Allowed, Rushing, Season
3,228 Buffalo, 1978
3,106 New Orleans, 1980
3,010 Baltimore, 1978

Fewest Touchdowns Allowed, Rushing, Season
2 Detroit, 1934
Dallas, 1968
Minnesota, 1971
3 By many teams

Most Touchdowns Allowed, Rushing, Season
36 Oakland, 1961
31 N.Y. Giants, 1980
Tampa Bay, 1986
30 Baltimore, 1981

PASSING

Most Seasons Leading League, Fewest Yards Allowed
9 Green Bay, 1947-48, 1962, 1964-68, 1996
7 Washington, 1939, 1942, 1945, 1952-53, 1980, 1985
Philadelphia 1934, 1936, 1940, 1949, 1981, 1991, 1998
6 Chi. Bears, 1938, 1943-44, 1958, 1960, 1963
Minnesota, 1969-1970, 1972, 1975-76, 1989
Pittsburgh, 1941, 1946, 1951, 1955, 1974, 1990

Most Consecutive Seasons Leading League, Fewest Yards Allowed
5 Green Bay, 1964-68
2 By many teams

Fewest Yards Allowed, Passing, Season
545 Philadelphia, 1934
558 Portsmouth, 1933
585 Chi. Cardinals, 1934

Most Yards Allowed, Passing, Season
4,541 Atlanta, 1995
4,389 N.Y. Jets, 1986
4,311 San Diego, 1981

Fewest Touchdowns Allowed, Passing, Season
1 Portsmouth, 1932
Philadelphia, 1934
2 Brooklyn, 1933
Chi. Bears, 1934
3 Chi. Bears, 1932
Green Bay, 1932
Green Bay, 1934
Chi. Bears, 1936
New York, 1939
New York, 1944

Most Touchdowns Allowed, Passing, Season
40 Denver, 1963
38 St. Louis, 1969
37 Washington, 1961
Baltimore, 1981

SACKS

Most Seasons Leading League
5 Oakland/L.A. Raiders, 1966-68, 1982, 1986
4 New England/Boston, 1961, 1963, 1977, 1979
Dallas, 1966, 1968-69, 1978
Dallas/Kansas City, 1960, 1965, 1969, 1990
L.A./St. Louis Rams, 1968, 1970, 1988, 1999
3 San Francisco, 1967, 1972, 1976
N.Y. Giants, 1963, 1985, 1998
New Orleans, 1992, 1997, 2000

Most Consecutive Seasons Leading League
3 Oakland, 1966-68
2 Dallas, 1968-69

Most Sacks, Season
72 Chicago, 1984
71 Minnesota, 1989
70 Chicago, 1987

Fewest Sacks, Season
11 Baltimore, 1982
12 Buffalo, 1982
13 Baltimore, 1981

Most Sacks, Game
12 Dallas vs. Pittsburgh, Nov. 20, 1966

St. Louis vs. Baltimore, Oct. 26, 1980
Chicago vs. Detroit, Dec. 16, 1984
Dallas vs. Houston, Sept. 29, 1985
11 N.Y. Giants vs. St. Louis, Nov. 1, 1964
Baltimore vs. Los Angeles, Nov. 22, 1964
Buffalo vs. Denver, Dec. 13, 1964
Detroit vs. Green Bay, Nov. 7, 1965
Oakland vs. Buffalo, Oct. 15, 1967
Oakland vs. Denver, Nov. 5, 1967
St. Louis vs. Atlanta, Nov. 24, 1968
Dallas vs. Detroit, Oct. 6, 1975
St. Louis vs. Philadelphia, Dec. 18, 1983
Kansas City vs. Cleveland, Sept. 30, 1984
Chicago vs. Minnesota, Oct. 28, 1984
Cleveland vs. Atlanta, Nov. 18, 1984
Detroit vs. Philadelphia, Nov. 16, 1986
San Diego vs. Dallas, Nov. 16, 1986
L.A. Raiders vs. Philadelphia, Nov. 30, 1986 (OT)
Seattle vs. L.A. Raiders, Dec. 8, 1986
Chicago vs. Philadelphia, Oct. 4, 1987
Dallas vs. N.Y. Jets, Oct. 4, 1987
Philadelphia vs. Dallas, Sept. 15, 1991
Indianapolis vs. Cleveland, Sept. 6, 1992
10 By many teams

Most Opponents Yards Lost Attempting to Pass, Season
666 Oakland, 1967
583 Chicago, 1984
573 San Francisco, 1976

Fewest Opponents Yards Lost Attempting to Pass, Season
72 Jacksonville, 1995
75 Green Bay, 1956
77 N.Y. Bulldogs, 1949

INTERCEPTIONS BY

Most Seasons Leading League
10 N.Y. Giants, 1933, 1937-39, 1944, 1948, 1951, 1954, 1961, 1997
8 Green Bay, 1940, 1942-43, 1947, 1955, 1957, 1962, 1965
Chi. Bears, 1935-36, 1941-42, 1946, 1963, 1985, 1990
6 Kansas City, 1966-1970, 1974

Most Consecutive Seasons Leading League
5 Kansas City, 1966-1970
3 N.Y. Giants, 1937-39
2 By many teams

Most Passes Intercepted By, Season
49 San Diego, 1961
42 Green Bay, 1943
41 N.Y. Giants, 1951

Fewest Passes Intercepted By, Season
3 Houston, 1982
5 Baltimore, 1982
6 Houston, 1972
St. Louis, 1982
Atlanta, 1996

Most Passes Intercepted By, Game
9 Green Bay vs. Detroit, Oct. 24, 1943
Philadelphia vs. Pittsburgh, Dec. 12, 1965
8 N.Y. Giants vs. Green Bay, Nov. 21, 1948
Philadelphia vs. Chi. Cardinals, Sept. 24, 1950
N.Y. Giants vs. N.Y. Yanks, Dec. 16, 1951
Houston vs. Denver, Dec. 2, 1962
Detroit vs. Chicago, Sept. 22, 1968
N.Y. Jets vs. Baltimore, Sept. 23, 1973
7 By many teams. Last time:
Seattle vs. San Diego, Dec. 13, 1998

Most Consecutive Games, One or More Interceptions By
46 L.A. Chargers/San Diego, 1960-63
37 Detroit, 1960-63
36 Boston, 1944-47

Most Yards Returning Interceptions, Season
929 San Diego, 1961
712 Los Angeles, 1952
697 Seattle, 1984

Fewest Yards Returning Interceptions, Season
5 Los Angeles, 1959
37 Dallas, 1989
41 Atlanta, 1996

Most Yards Returning Interceptions, Game
325 Seattle vs. Kansas City, Nov. 4, 1984
314 Los Angeles vs. San Francisco, Oct. 18, 1964
245 Houston vs. N.Y. Jets, Oct. 15, 1967

Most Yards Returning Interceptions, Both Teams, Game
356 Seattle (325) vs. Kansas City (31), Nov. 4, 1984
338 Los Angeles (314) vs. San Francisco (24), Oct. 18, 1964
308 Dallas (182) vs. Los Angeles (126), Nov. 2, 1952

Most Touchdowns, Returning Interceptions, Season
9 San Diego, 1961
8 Seattle, 1998
7 Seattle, 1984
St. Louis, 1999

Most Touchdowns Returning Interceptions, Game
4 Seattle vs. Kansas City, Nov. 4, 1984
3 Baltimore vs. Green Bay, Nov. 5, 1950
Cleveland vs. Chicago, Dec. 11, 1960
Philadelphia vs. Pittsburgh, Dec. 12, 1965
Baltimore vs. Pittsburgh, Sept. 29, 1968
Buffalo vs. N.Y. Jets, Sept. 29, 1968
Houston vs. San Diego, Dec. 19, 1971
Cincinnati vs. Houston, Dec. 17, 1972
Tampa Bay vs. New Orleans, Dec. 11, 1977
2 By many teams

Most Touchdown Returning Interceptions, Both Teams, Game
4 Philadelphia (3) vs. Pittsburgh (1), Dec. 12, 1965
Seattle (4) vs. Kansas City (0), Nov. 4, 1984
3 Los Angeles (2) vs. Detroit (1), Nov. 1, 1953
Cleveland (2) vs. N.Y. Giants (1), Dec. 18, 1960
Pittsburgh (2) vs. Cincinnati (1), Oct. 10, 1983
Kansas City (2) vs. San Diego (1), Oct. 19, 1986
(Also see previous record)

PUNT RETURNS

Fewest Opponents Punt Returns, Season
7 Washington, 1962
San Diego, 1982
10 Buffalo, 1982
11 Boston, 1962

Most Opponents Punt Returns, Season
71 Tampa Bay, 1976, 1977
69 N.Y. Giants, 1953
Cleveland, 2000
68 Cleveland, 1974
Cleveland, 1999

Fewest Yards Allowed, Punt Returns, Season
22 Green Bay, 1967
30 Buffalo, 1982
34 Washington, 1962

Most Yards Allowed, Punt Returns, Season
932 Green Bay, 1949
913 Boston, 1947
906 New Orleans, 1974

Lowest Average Allowed, Punt Returns, Season
1.20 Chi. Cardinals, 1954 (46-55)
1.22 Cleveland, 1959 (32-39)
1.55 Chi. Cardinals, 1953 (44-68)

Highest Average Allowed, Punt Returns, Season
18.6 Green Bay, 1949 (50-932)
18.0 Cleveland, 1977 (31-558)
17.9 Boston, 1960 (20-357)

Most Touchdowns Allowed, Punt Returns, Season
4 New York, 1959
Atlanta, 1992
3 Green Bay, 1949
Chi. Cardinals, 1951
L.A. Rams, 1951, 1994
Washington, 1952
Dallas, 1952
Pittsburgh, 1959, 1993
N.Y. Jets, 1968
Cleveland, 1977
Atlanta, 1986
Tampa Bay, 1986
2 By many teams

KICKOFF RETURNS

Fewest Opponents Kickoff Returns, Season
10 Brooklyn, 1943
13 Denver, 1992
15 Detroit, 1942
Brooklyn, 1944

Most Opponents Kickoff Returns, Season
91 Washington, 1983
90 Denver, 2000
89 New England, 1980
San Francisco, 1994
Denver, 1997
Denver, 1998

Fewest Yards Allowed, Kickoff Returns, Season
225 Brooklyn, 1943
254 Denver, 1992
293 Brooklyn, 1944

Most Yards Allowed, Kickoff Returns, Season
2,115 St. Louis, 1999
2,045 Kansas City, 1966
2,032 St. Louis, 2000

Lowest Average Allowed, Kickoff Returns, Season
14.3 Cleveland, 1980 (71-1,018)
14.9 Indianapolis, 1993 (37-551)
15.0 Seattle, 1982 (24-361)

Highest Average Allowed, Kickoff Returns, Season
29.5 N.Y. Jets, 1972 (47-1,386)
29.4 Los Angeles, 1950 (48-1,411)
29.1 New England, 1971 (49-1,427)

Most Touchdowns Allowed, Kickoff Returns, Season
4 Minnesota, 1998
3 Minnesota, 1963, 1970
Dallas, 1966
Detroit, 1980
Pittsburgh, 1986
Buffalo, 1997
Atlanta, 2000
2 By many teams

FUMBLES

Fewest Opponents Fumbles, Season
11 Cleveland, 1956
Baltimore, 1982
Tennessee, 1998
12 Green Bay, 1995
Cincinnati, 1998
13 Los Angeles, 1956
Chicago, 1960
Cleveland, 1963
Cleveland, 1965
Detroit, 1967
San Diego, 1969

Most Opponents Fumbles, Season
50 Minnesota, 1963
San Francisco, 1978
48 N.Y. Giants, 1980
N.Y. Jets, 1986
47 N.Y. Giants, 1977
Seattle, 1984

TURNOVERS

(Number of times losing the ball on interceptions and fumbles.)

Fewest Opponents Turnovers, Season
11 Baltimore, 1982
13 San Francisco, 1982
15 St. Louis, 1982

Most Opponents Turnovers, Season
66 San Diego, 1961
63 Seattle, 1984
61 Washington, 1983

Most Opponents Turnovers, Game
12 Chi. Bears vs. Detroit, Nov. 22, 1942
Philadelphia vs. Chi. Cardinals, Sept. 24, 1950
Philadelphia vs. Pittsburgh, Dec. 12, 1965
11 Green Bay vs. San Diego, Sept. 24, 1978
10 By 14 teams

OUTSTANDING PERFORMERS

1,000 YARDS RUSHING IN A SEASON

Year	Player, Team	Att.	Yards	Avg.	Long	TD
2000	Edgerrin James, Indianapolis[2]	387	1,709	4.4	30	13
	Robert Smith, Minnesota[4]	295	1,521	5.2	72	7
	Eddie George, Tennessee[5]	403	1,509	3.7	35	14
	*Mike Anderson, Denver	297	1,487	5.0	80	15
	Corey Dillon, Cincinnati[4]	315	1,435	4.6	80	7
	Fred Taylor, Jacksonville[2]	292	1,399	4.8	71	12
	*Jamal Lewis, Baltimore	309	1,364	4.4	45	6
	Marshall Faulk, St. Louis[6]	253	1,359	5.4	36	18
	Jerome Bettis, Pittsburgh[7]	355	1,341	3.8	30	8
	Stephen Davis, Washington[2]	332	1,318	4.0	50	11
	Ricky Watters, Seattle[7]	278	1,242	4.5	55	7
	Curtis Martin, N.Y. Jets[6]	316	1,204	3.8	55	9
	Emmitt Smith, Dallas[10]	294	1,203	4.1	52	9
	James Stewart, Detroit	339	1,184	3.5	34	10
	Ahman Green, Green Bay	263	1,175	4.5	39	10
	Charlie Garner, San Francisco[2]	258	1,142	4.4	42	7
	Lamar Smith, Miami	309	1,139	3.7	68	14
	Warrick Dunn, Tampa Bay[2]	248	1,133	4.6	70	8
	James Allen, Chicago	290	1,120	3.9	29	2
	Tyrone Wheatley, Oakland	232	1,046	4.5	80	9
	Jamal Anderson, Atlanta[4]	282	1,024	3.6	42	6
	Tiki Barber, N.Y. Giants	213	1,006	4.7	78	8
	Ricky Williams, New Orleans	248	1,000	4.0	26	8
1999	*Edgerrin James, Indianapolis	369	1,553	4.2	72	13
	Curtis Martin, N.Y. Jets[5]	367	1,464	4.0	50	5
	Stephen Davis, Washington	290	1,405	4.8	76	17
	Emmitt Smith, Dallas[9]	329	1,397	4.3	63	11
	Marshall Faulk, St. Louis[5]	253	1,381	5.5	58	7
	Eddie George, Tennessee[4]	320	1,304	4.1	40	9
	Duce Staley, Philadelphia[2]	325	1,273	3.9	29	4
	Charlie Garner, San Francisco	241	1,229	5.1	53	4
	Ricky Watters, Seattle[6]	325	1,210	3.7	45	5
	Corey Dillon, Cincinnati[3]	263	1,200	4.6	50	5
	*Olandis Gary, Denver	276	1,159	4.2	71	7
	Jerome Bettis, Pittsburgh[6]	299	1,091	3.7	35	7
	Dorsey Levens, Green Bay[2]	279	1,034	3.7	36	9
	Robert Smith, Minnesota[3]	221	1,015	4.6	70	2
1998	Terrell Davis, Denver[4]	392	2,008	5.1	70	21
	Jamal Anderson, Atlanta[3]	410	1,846	4.5	48	14
	Garrison Hearst, San Francisco[3]	310	1,570	5.1	96	7
	Barry Sanders, Detroit[10]	343	1,491	4.3	73	4
	Emmitt Smith, Dallas[8]	319	1,332	4.2	32	13
	Marshall Faulk, Indianapolis[4]	324	1,319	4.1	68	6
	Eddie George, Tennessee[3]	348	1,294	3.7	37	5
	Curtis Martin, N.Y. Jets[4]	369	1,287	3.5	60	8
	Ricky Watters, Seattle[5]	319	1,239	3.9	39	9
	*Fred Taylor, Jacksonville	264	1,223	4.6	77	14
	Robert Smith, Minnesota[2]	249	1,187	4.8	74	6
	Jerome Bettis, Pittsburgh[5]	316	1,185	3.8	42	3
	Corey Dillon, Cincinnati[2]	262	1,130	4.3	66	4
	Antowain Smith, Buffalo	300	1,124	3.7	30	8
	*Robert Edwards, New England	291	1,115	3.8	53	9
	Duce Staley, Philadelphia	258	1,065	4.1	64	5
	Gary Brown, N.Y. Giants[2]	247	1,063	4.3	45	5
	Adrian Murrell, Arizona[3]	274	1,042	3.8	32	8
	Warrick Dunn, Tampa Bay	245	1,026	4.2	50	2
	Priest Holmes, Baltimore	233	1,008	4.3	56	7
1997	Barry Sanders, Detroit[9]	335	2,053	6.1	82	11
	Terrell Davis, Denver[3]	369	1,750	4.7	50	15
	Jerome Bettis, Pittsburgh[4]	375	1,665	4.4	34	7
	Dorsey Levens, Green Bay	329	1,435	4.4	52	7
	Eddie George, Tennessee[2]	357	1,399	3.9	30	6
	Napoleon Kaufman, Oakland	272	1,294	4.8	83	6
	Robert Smith, Minnesota	232	1,266	5.5	78	6
	Curtis Martin, New England[3]	274	1,160	4.2	70	4
	*Corey Dillon, Cincinnati	233	1,129	4.8	71	10
	Ricky Watters, Philadelphia[4]	285	1,110	3.9	28	7
	Adrian Murrell, N.Y. Jets[2]	300	1,086	3.6	43	7
	Emmitt Smith, Dallas[7]	261	1,074	4.1	44	4
	Marshall Faulk, Indianapolis[3]	264	1,054	4.0	45	7
	Raymont Harris, Chicago	275	1,033	3.8	68	10
	Garrison Hearst, San Francisco[2]	234	1,019	4.4	51	4
	Jamal Anderson, Atlanta[2]	290	1,002	3.5	39	7
1996	Barry Sanders, Detroit[8]	307	1,553	5.1	54	11
	Terrell Davis, Denver[2]	345	1,538	4.5	71	13
	Jerome Bettis, Pittsburgh[3]	320	1,431	4.5	50	11
	Ricky Watters, Philadelphia[3]	353	1,411	4.0	56	13
	*Eddie George, Houston	335	1,368	4.1	76	8
	Terry Allen, Washington[4]	347	1,353	3.9	49	21
	Adrian Murrell, N.Y. Jets	301	1,249	4.1	78	6
	Emmitt Smith, Dallas[6]	327	1,204	3.7	42	12
	Curtis Martin, New England[2]	316	1,152	3.6	57	14
	Anthony Johnson, Carolina	300	1,120	3.7	29	6
	*Karim Abdul-Jabbar, Miami	307	1,116	3.6	29	11
	Jamal Anderson, Atlanta	232	1,055	4.5	32	5
	Thurman Thomas, Buffalo[8]	281	1,033	3.7	36	8
1995	Emmitt Smith, Dallas[5]	377	1,773	4.7	60	25
	Barry Sanders, Detroit[7]	314	1,500	4.8	75	11
	*Curtis Martin, New England	368	1,487	4.0	49	14
	Chris Warren, Seattle[4]	310	1,346	4.3	52	15
	Terry Allen, Washington[3]	338	1,309	3.9	28	10
	Ricky Watters, Philadelphia[2]	337	1,273	3.8	57	11
	Errict Rhett, Tampa Bay[2]	332	1,207	3.6	21	11
	Rodney Hampton, N.Y. Giants[5]	306	1,182	3.9	32	10
	*Terrell Davis, Denver	237	1,117	4.7	60	7
	Harvey Williams, Oakland	255	1,114	4.4	60	9
	Craig Heyward, Atlanta	236	1,083	4.6	31	6
	Marshall Faulk, Indianapolis[2]	289	1,078	3.7	40	11
	*Rashaan Salaam, Chicago	296	1,074	3.6	42	10
	Garrison Hearst, Arizona	284	1,070	3.8	38	1
	Edgar Bennett, Green Bay	316	1,067	3.4	23	3
	Thurman Thomas, Buffalo[7]	267	1,005	3.8	49	6
1994	Barry Sanders, Detroit[6]	331	1,883	5.7	85	7
	Chris Warren, Seattle[3]	333	1,545	4.6	41	9
	Emmitt Smith, Dallas[4]	368	1,484	4.0	46	21
	Natrone Means, San Diego	343	1,350	3.9	25	12
	*Marshall Faulk, Indianapolis	314	1,282	4.1	52	11
	Thurman Thomas, Buffalo[6]	287	1,093	3.8	29	7
	Rodney Hampton, N.Y. Giants[4]	327	1,075	3.3	27	6
	Terry Allen, Minnesota[2]	255	1,031	4.0	45	8
	Jerome Bettis, L.A. Rams[2]	319	1,025	3.2	19	3
	*Errict Rhett, Tampa Bay	284	1,011	3.6	27	7
1993	Emmitt Smith, Dallas[3]	283	1,486	5.3	62	9
	*Jerome Bettis, L.A. Rams	294	1,429	4.9	71	7
	Thurman Thomas, Buffalo[5]	355	1,315	3.7	27	6
	Erric Pegram, Atlanta	292	1,185	4.1	29	3
	Barry Sanders, Detroit[5]	243	1,115	4.6	42	3
	Leonard Russell, New England	300	1,088	3.6	21	7
	Rodney Hampton, N.Y. Giants[3]	292	1,077	3.7	20	5
	Chris Warren, Seattle[2]	273	1,072	3.9	45	7
	*Reggie Brooks, Washington	223	1,063	4.8	85	3
	*Ron Moore, Phoenix	263	1,018	3.9	20	9
	Gary Brown, Houston	195	1,002	5.1	26	6
1992	Emmitt Smith, Dallas[2]	373	1,713	4.6	68	18
	Barry Foster, Pittsburgh	390	1,690	4.3	69	11
	Thurman Thomas, Buffalo[4]	312	1,487	4.8	44	9
	Barry Sanders, Detroit[4]	312	1,352	4.3	55	9
	Lorenzo White, Houston	265	1,226	4.6	44	7
	Terry Allen, Minnesota	266	1,201	4.5	51	13
	Reggie Cobb, Tampa Bay	310	1,171	3.8	25	9
	Harold Green, Cincinnati	265	1,170	4.4	53	2
	Rodney Hampton, N.Y. Giants[2]	257	1,141	4.4	63	14
	Cleveland Gary, L.A. Rams	279	1,125	4.0	63	7
	Herschel Walker, Philadelphia[2]	267	1,070	4.0	38	8
	Chris Warren, Seattle	223	1,017	4.6	52	3
	Ricky Watters, San Francisco	206	1,013	4.9	43	9
1991	Emmitt Smith, Dallas	365	1,563	4.3	75	12
	Barry Sanders, Detroit[3]	342	1,548	4.5	69	16
	Thurman Thomas, Buffalo[3]	288	1,407	4.9	33	7
	Rodney Hampton, N.Y. Giants	256	1,059	4.1	44	10
	Earnest Byner, Washington[3]	274	1,048	3.8	32	5
	Gaston Green, Denver	261	1,037	4.0	63	4
	Christian Okoye, Kansas City[2]	225	1,031	4.6	48	9
1990	Barry Sanders, Detroit[2]	255	1,304	5.1	45	13
	Thurman Thomas, Buffalo[2]	271	1,297	4.8	80	11
	Marion Butts, San Diego	265	1,225	4.6	52	8
	Earnest Byner, Washington[2]	297	1,219	4.1	22	6
	Bobby Humphrey, Denver[2]	288	1,202	4.2	37	7
	Neal Anderson, Chicago[3]	260	1,078	4.1	52	10
	Barry Word, Kansas City	204	1,015	5.0	53	4
	James Brooks, Cincinnati[3]	195	1,004	5.1	56	5
1989	Christian Okoye, Kansas City	370	1,480	4.0	59	12
	*Barry Sanders, Detroit	280	1,470	5.3	34	14
	Eric Dickerson, Indianapolis[7]	314	1,311	4.2	21	7
	Neal Anderson, Chicago[2]	274	1,275	4.7	73	11
	Dalton Hilliard, New Orleans	344	1,262	3.7	40	13
	Thurman Thomas, Buffalo	298	1,244	4.2	38	6
	James Brooks, Cincinnati[2]	221	1,239	5.6	65	7
	*Bobby Humphrey, Denver	294	1,151	3.9	40	7
	Greg Bell, L.A. Rams[3]	272	1,137	4.2	47	15
	Roger Craig, San Francisco[3]	271	1,054	3.9	27	6
	Ottis Anderson, N.Y. Giants[6]	325	1,023	3.1	36	14
1988	Eric Dickerson, Indianapolis[6]	388	1,659	4.3	41	14
	Herschel Walker, Dallas	361	1,514	4.2	38	5

	Roger Craig, San Francisco[2]	310	1,502	4.8	46	9
	Greg Bell, L.A. Rams[2]	288	1,212	4.2	44	16
	*John Stephens, New England	297	1,168	3.9	52	4
	Gary Anderson, San Diego	225	1,119	5.0	36	3
	Neal Anderson, Chicago	249	1,106	4.4	80	12
	Joe Morris, N.Y. Giants[3]	307	1,083	3.5	27	5
	*Ickey Woods, Cincinnati	203	1,066	5.3	56	15
	Curt Warner, Seattle[4]	266	1,025	3.9	29	10
	John Settle, Atlanta	232	1,024	4.4	62	7
	Mike Rozier, Houston	251	1,002	4.0	28	10
1987	Charles White, L.A. Rams	324	1,374	4.2	58	11
	Eric Dickerson, L.A. Rams-Indianapolis[5]	283	1,288	4.6	57	6
1986	Eric Dickerson, L.A. Rams[4]	404	1,821	4.5	42	11
	Joe Morris, N.Y. Giants[2]	341	1,516	4.4	54	14
	Curt Warner, Seattle[3]	319	1,481	4.6	60	13
	*Rueben Mayes, New Orleans	286	1,353	4.7	50	8
	Walter Payton, Chicago[10]	321	1,333	4.2	41	8
	Gerald Riggs, Atlanta[3]	343	1,327	3.9	31	9
	George Rogers, Washington[4]	303	1,203	4.0	42	18
	James Brooks, Cincinnati	205	1,087	5.3	56	5
1985	Marcus Allen, L.A. Raiders[3]	390	1,759	4.6	61	11
	Gerald Riggs, Atlanta[2]	397	1,719	4.3	50	10
	Walter Payton, Chicago[9]	324	1,551	4.8	40	9
	Joe Morris, N.Y. Giants	294	1,336	4.5	65	21
	Freeman McNeil, N.Y. Jets[2]	294	1,331	4.5	69	3
	Tony Dorsett, Dallas[8]	305	1,307	4.3	60	7
	James Wilder, Tampa Bay[2]	365	1,300	3.6	28	10
	Eric Dickerson, L.A. Rams[3]	292	1,234	4.2	43	12
	Craig James, New England	263	1,227	4.7	65	5
	Kevin Mack, Cleveland	222	1,104	5.0	61	7
	Curt Warner, Seattle[2]	291	1,094	3.8	38	8
	George Rogers, Washington[3]	231	1,093	4.7	35	7
	Roger Craig, San Francisco	214	1,050	4.9	62	9
	Earnest Jackson, Philadelphia[2]	282	1,028	3.6	59	5
	Stump Mitchell, St. Louis	183	1,006	5.5	64	7
	Earnest Byner, Cleveland	244	1,002	4.1	36	8
1984	Eric Dickerson, L.A. Rams[2]	379	2,105	5.6	66	14
	Walter Payton, Chicago[8]	381	1,684	4.4	72	11
	James Wilder, Tampa Bay	407	1,544	3.8	37	13
	Gerald Riggs, Atlanta	353	1,486	4.2	57	13
	Wendell Tyler, San Francisco[3]	246	1,262	5.1	40	7
	John Riggins, Washington[5]	327	1,239	3.8	24	14
	Tony Dorsett, Dallas[7]	302	1,189	3.9	31	6
	Earnest Jackson, San Diego	296	1,179	4.0	32	8
	Ottis Anderson, St. Louis[5]	289	1,174	4.1	24	6
	Marcus Allen, L.A. Raiders[2]	275	1,168	4.2	52	13
	Sammy Winder, Denver	296	1,153	3.9	24	4
	*Greg Bell, Buffalo	262	1,100	4.2	85	7
	Freeman McNeil, N.Y. Jets	229	1,070	4.7	53	5
1983	*Eric Dickerson, L.A. Rams	390	1,808	4.6	85	18
	William Andrews, Atlanta[4]	331	1,567	4.7	27	7
	*Curt Warner, Seattle	335	1,449	4.3	60	13
	Walter Payton, Chicago[7]	314	1,421	4.5	49	6
	John Riggins, Washington[4]	375	1,347	3.6	44	24
	Tony Dorsett, Dallas[6]	289	1,321	4.6	77	8
	Earl Campbell, Houston[5]	322	1,301	4.0	42	12
	Ottis Anderson, St. Louis[4]	296	1,270	4.3	43	5
	Mike Pruitt, Cleveland[4]	293	1,184	4.0	27	10
	George Rogers, New Orleans[2]	256	1,144	4.5	76	5
	Joe Cribbs, Buffalo[3]	263	1,131	4.3	45	3
	Curtis Dickey, Baltimore	254	1,122	4.4	56	4
	Tony Collins, New England	219	1,049	4.8	50	10
	Billy Sims, Detroit[3]	220	1,040	4.7	41	7
	Marcus Allen, L.A. Raiders	266	1,014	3.8	19	9
	Franco Harris, Pittsburgh[8]	279	1,007	3.6	19	5
1981	*George Rogers, New Orleans	378	1,674	4.4	79	13
	Tony Dorsett, Dallas[5]	342	1,646	4.8	75	4
	Billy Sims, Detroit[2]	296	1,437	4.9	51	13
	Wilbert Montgomery, Philadelphia[3]	286	1,402	4.9	41	8
	Ottis Anderson, St. Louis[3]	328	1,376	4.2	28	9
	Earl Campbell, Houston[4]	361	1,376	3.8	43	10
	William Andrews, Atlanta[3]	289	1,301	4.5	29	10
	Walter Payton, Chicago[6]	339	1,222	3.6	39	6
	Chuck Muncie, San Diego[2]	251	1,144	4.6	73	19
	*Joe Delaney, Kansas City	234	1,121	4.8	82	3
	Mike Pruitt, Cleveland[3]	247	1,103	4.5	21	7
	Joe Cribbs, Buffalo[2]	257	1,097	4.3	35	3
	Pete Johnson, Cincinnati	274	1,077	3.9	39	12
	Wendell Tyler, Los Angeles[2]	260	1,074	4.1	69	12
	Ted Brown, Minnesota	274	1,063	3.9	34	6
1980	Earl Campbell, Houston[3]	373	1,934	5.2	55	13
	Walter Payton, Chicago[5]	317	1,460	4.6	69	6
	Ottis Anderson, St. Louis[2]	301	1,352	4.5	52	9
	William Andrews, Atlanta[2]	265	1,308	4.9	33	4
	*Billy Sims, Detroit	313	1,303	4.2	52	13
	Tony Dorsett, Dallas[4]	278	1,185	4.3	56	11
	*Joe Cribbs, Buffalo	306	1,185	3.9	48	11
	Mike Pruitt, Cleveland[2]	249	1,034	4.2	56	6
1979	Earl Campbell, Houston[2]	368	1,697	4.6	61	19
	Walter Payton, Chicago[4]	369	1,610	4.4	43	14
	*Ottis Anderson, St. Louis	331	1,605	4.8	76	8
	Wilbert Montgomery, Philadelphia[2]	338	1,512	4.5	62	9
	Mike Pruitt, Cleveland	264	1,294	4.9	77	9
	Ricky Bell, Tampa Bay	283	1,263	4.5	49	7
	Chuck Muncie, New Orleans	238	1,198	5.0	69	11
	Franco Harris, Pittsburgh[7]	267	1,186	4.4	71	11
	John Riggins, Washington[3]	260	1,153	4.4	66	9
	Wendell Tyler, Los Angeles	218	1,109	5.1	63	9
	Tony Dorsett, Dallas[3]	250	1,107	4.4	41	6
	*William Andrews, Atlanta	239	1,023	4.3	23	3
1978	*Earl Campbell, Houston	302	1,450	4.8	81	13
	Walter Payton, Chicago[3]	333	1,395	4.2	76	11
	Tony Dorsett, Dallas[2]	290	1,325	4.6	63	7
	Delvin Williams, Miami[2]	272	1,258	4.6	58	8
	Wilbert Montgomery, Philadelphia	259	1,220	4.7	47	9
	Terdell Middleton, Green Bay	284	1,116	3.9	76	11
	Franco Harris, Pittsburgh[6]	310	1,082	3.5	37	8
	Mark van Eeghen, Oakland[3]	270	1,080	4.0	34	9
	*Terry Miller, Buffalo	238	1,060	4.5	60	7
	Tony Reed, Kansas City	206	1,053	5.1	62	5
	John Riggins, Washington[2]	248	1,014	4.1	31	5
1977	Walter Payton, Chicago[2]	339	1,852	5.5	73	14
	Mark van Eeghen, Oakland[2]	324	1,273	3.9	27	7
	Lawrence McCutcheon, Los Angeles[4]	294	1,238	4.2	48	7
	Franco Harris, Pittsburgh[5]	300	1,162	3.9	61	11
	Lydell Mitchell, Baltimore[3]	301	1,159	3.9	64	3
	Chuck Foreman, Minnesota[3]	270	1,112	4.1	51	6
	Greg Pruitt, Cleveland[3]	236	1,086	4.6	78	3
	Sam Cunningham, New England	270	1,015	3.8	31	4
	*Tony Dorsett, Dallas	208	1,007	4.8	84	12
1976	O.J. Simpson, Buffalo[5]	290	1,503	5.2	75	8
	Walter Payton, Chicago	311	1,390	4.5	60	13
	Delvin Williams, San Francisco	248	1,203	4.9	80	7
	Lydell Mitchell, Baltimore[2]	289	1,200	4.2	43	5
	Lawrence McCutcheon, Los Angeles[3]	291	1,168	4.0	40	9
	Chuck Foreman, Minnesota[2]	278	1,155	4.2	46	13
	Franco Harris, Pittsburgh[4]	289	1,128	3.9	30	14
	Mike Thomas, Washington	254	1,101	4.3	28	5
	Rocky Bleier, Pittsburgh	220	1,036	4.7	28	5
	Mark van Eeghen, Oakland	233	1,012	4.3	21	3
	Otis Armstrong, Denver[2]	247	1,008	4.1	31	5
	Greg Pruitt, Cleveland[2]	209	1,000	4.8	64	4
1975	O.J. Simpson, Buffalo[4]	329	1,817	5.5	88	16
	Franco Harris, Pittsburgh[3]	262	1,246	4.8	36	10
	Lydell Mitchell, Baltimore	289	1,193	4.1	70	11
	Jim Otis, St. Louis	269	1,076	4.0	30	5
	Chuck Foreman, Minnesota	280	1,070	3.8	31	13
	Greg Pruitt, Cleveland	217	1,067	4.9	50	8
	John Riggins, N.Y. Jets	238	1,005	4.2	42	8
	Dave Hampton, Atlanta	250	1,002	4.0	22	5
1974	Otis Armstrong, Denver	263	1,407	5.3	43	9
	*Don Woods, San Diego	227	1,162	5.1	56	7
	O.J. Simpson, Buffalo[3]	270	1,125	4.2	41	3
	Lawrence McCutcheon, Los Angeles[2]	236	1,109	4.7	23	3
	Franco Harris, Pittsburgh[2]	208	1,006	4.8	54	5
1973	O.J. Simpson, Buffalo[2]	332	2,003	6.0	80	12
	John Brockington, Green Bay[3]	265	1,144	4.3	53	3
	Calvin Hill, Dallas[2]	273	1,142	4.2	21	6
	Lawrence McCutcheon, Los Angeles	210	1,097	5.2	37	2
	Larry Csonka, Miami[3]	219	1,003	4.6	25	5
1972	O.J. Simpson, Buffalo	292	1,251	4.3	94	6
	Larry Brown, Washington[2]	285	1,216	4.3	38	8
	Ron Johnson, N.Y. Giants[2]	298	1,182	4.0	35	9
	Larry Csonka, Miami[2]	213	1,117	5.2	45	6
	Marv Hubbard, Oakland	219	1,100	5.0	39	4
	*Franco Harris, Pittsburgh	188	1,055	5.6	75	10
	Calvin Hill, Dallas	245	1,036	4.2	26	6
	Mike Garrett, San Diego[2]	272	1,031	3.8	41	6
	John Brockington, Green Bay[2]	274	1,027	3.7	30	8
	Eugene (Mercury) Morris, Miami	190	1,000	5.3	33	12
1971	Floyd Little, Denver	284	1,133	4.0	40	6
	*John Brockington, Green Bay	216	1,105	5.1	52	4
	Larry Csonka, Miami	195	1,051	5.4	28	7
	Steve Owens, Detroit	246	1,035	4.2	23	8
	Willie Ellison, Los Angeles	211	1,000	4.7	80	4
1970	Larry Brown, Washington	237	1,125	4.7	75	5

OUTSTANDING PERFORMERS

	Ron Johnson, N.Y. Giants	263	1,027	3.9	68	8
1969	Gale Sayers, Chicago[2]	236	1,032	4.4	28	8
1968	Leroy Kelly, Cleveland[3]	248	1,239	5.0	65	16
	*Paul Robinson, Cincinnati	238	1,023	4.3	87	8
1967	Jim Nance, Boston[2]	269	1,216	4.5	53	7
	Leroy Kelly, Cleveland[2]	235	1,205	5.1	42	11
	Hoyle Granger, Houston	236	1,194	5.1	67	6
	Mike Garrett, Kansas City	236	1,087	4.6	58	9
1966	Jim Nance, Boston	299	1,458	4.9	65	11
	Gale Sayers, Chicago	229	1,231	5.4	58	8
	Leroy Kelly, Cleveland	209	1,141	5.5	70	15
	Dick Bass, Los Angeles[2]	248	1,090	4.4	50	8
1965	Jim Brown, Cleveland[7]	289	1,544	5.3	67	17
	Paul Lowe, San Diego[2]	222	1,121	5.0	59	7
1964	Jim Brown, Cleveland[6]	280	1,446	5.2	71	7
	Jim Taylor, Green Bay[5]	235	1,169	5.0	84	12
	John Henry Johnson, Pittsburgh[2]	235	1,048	4.5	45	7
1963	Jim Brown, Cleveland[5]	291	1,863	6.4	80	12
	Clem Daniels, Oakland	215	1,099	5.1	74	3
	Jim Taylor, Green Bay[4]	248	1,018	4.1	40	9
	Paul Lowe, San Diego	177	1,010	5.7	66	8
1962	Jim Taylor, Green Bay[3]	272	1,474	5.4	51	19
	John Henry Johnson, Pittsburgh	251	1,141	4.5	40	7
	Cookie Gilchrist, Buffalo	214	1,096	5.1	44	13
	Abner Haynes, Dall. Texans	221	1,049	4.7	71	13
	Dick Bass, Los Angeles	196	1,033	5.3	57	6
	Charlie Tolar, Houston	244	1,012	4.1	25	7
1961	Jim Brown, Cleveland[4]	305	1,408	4.6	38	8
	Jim Taylor, Green Bay[2]	243	1,307	5.4	53	15
1960	Jim Brown, Cleveland[3]	215	1,257	5.8	71	9
	Jim Taylor, Green Bay	230	1,101	4.8	32	11
	John David Crow, St. Louis	183	1,071	5.9	57	6
1959	Jim Brown, Cleveland[2]	290	1,329	4.6	70	14
	J.D. Smith, San Francisco	207	1,036	5.0	73	10
1958	Jim Brown, Cleveland	257	1,527	5.9	65	17
1956	Rick Casares, Chi. Bears	234	1,126	4.8	68	12
1954	Joe Perry, San Francisco[2]	173	1,049	6.1	58	8
1953	Joe Perry, San Francisco	192	1,018	5.3	51	10
1949	Steve Van Buren, Philadelphia[2]	263	1,146	4.4	41	11
	Tony Canadeo, Green Bay	208	1,052	5.1	54	4
1947	Steve Van Buren, Philadelphia	217	1,008	4.6	45	13
1934	*Beattie Feathers, Chi. Bears	119	1,004	8.4	82	8

**First season of professional football.*

200 YARDS RUSHING IN A GAME

Date	Player, Team, Opponent	Att.	Yards	TD
Dec. 24, 2000	Marshall Faulk, St. Louis vs. New Orleans	32	220	2
Dec. 3, 2000	Corey Dillon, Cincinnati vs. Arizona	35	216	1
Dec. 3, 2000	Warrick Dunn, Tampa Bay vs. Dallas	22	210	2
Dec. 3, 2000	*Mike Anderson, Denver vs. New Orleans	37	251	4
Dec. 3, 2000	Curtis Martin, N.Y. Jets vs. Indianapolis	30	203	1
Nov. 19, 2000	Fred Taylor, Jacksonville vs. Pittsburgh	30	234	3
Oct. 22, 2000	Corey Dillon, Cincinnati vs. Denver	22	278	2
Oct. 15, 2000	Marshall Faulk, St. Louis vs. Atlanta	25	208	1
Oct. 15, 2000	Edgerrin James, Indianapolis vs. Seattle	38	219	3
Sept. 24, 2000	Charlie Garner, San Francisco vs. Dallas	36	201	1
Sept. 3, 2000	Duce Staley, Philadelphia vs. Dallas	26	201	1
Nov. 22, 1998	Priest Holmes, Baltimore vs. Cincinnati	36	227	1
Oct. 11, 1998	Terrell Davis, Denver vs Seattle	30	208	1
Dec. 4, 1997	*Corey Dillon, Cincinnati vs. Tennessee	39	246	4
Nov. 23, 1997	Barry Sanders, Detroit vs. Indianapolis	24	216	2
Oct. 26, 1997	Terrell Davis, Denver vs. Buffalo (OT)	42	207	1
Oct. 19, 1997	Napoleon Kaufman, Oakland vs. Denver	28	227	1
Oct. 12, 1997	Barry Sanders, Detroit vs. Tampa Bay	24	215	2
Sept. 21, 1997	Terrell Davis, Denver vs. Cincinnati	27	215	1
Aug. 31, 1997	Eddie George, Tennessee vs. Oakland (OT)	35	216	1
Sept. 22, 1996	LeShon Johnson, Arizona vs. New Orleans	21	214	2
Nov. 13, 1994	Barry Sanders, Detroit vs. Tampa Bay	26	237	0
Dec. 12, 1993	*Jerome Bettis, L.A. Rams vs. New Orleans	28	212	1
Oct. 31, 1993	Emmitt Smith, Dallas vs. Philadelphia	30	237	1
Nov. 24, 1991	Barry Sanders, Detroit vs. Minnesota	23	220	4
Dec. 23, 1990	James Brooks, Cincinnati vs. Houston	20	201	1
Oct. 14, 1990	Barry Word, Kansas City vs. Detroit	18	200	2
Sept. 24, 1990	Thurman Thomas, Buffalo vs. N.Y. Jets	18	214	0
Dec. 24, 1989	Greg Bell, L.A. Rams vs. New England	26	210	1
Sept. 24, 1989	Greg Bell, L.A. Rams vs. Green Bay	28	221	2
Sept. 17, 1989	Gerald Riggs, Washington vs. Philadelphia	29	221	1
Dec. 18, 1988	Gary Anderson, San Diego vs. Kansas City	34	217	1
Nov. 30, 1987	*Bo Jackson, L.A. Raiders vs. Seattle	18	221	2
Nov. 15, 1987	Charles White, L.A. Rams vs. St. Louis	34	213	1
Dec. 7, 1986	Rueben Mayes, New Orleans vs. Miami	28	203	2
Oct. 5, 1986	Eric Dickerson, L.A. Rams vs. Tampa Bay (OT)	30	207	2
Dec. 21, 1985	George Rogers, Washington vs. St. Louis	34	206	1
Dec. 21, 1985	Joe Morris, N.Y. Giants vs. Pittsburgh	36	202	3
Dec. 9, 1984	Eric Dickerson, L.A. Rams vs. Houston	27	215	2
Nov. 18, 1984	*Greg Bell, Buffalo vs. Dallas	27	206	1
Nov. 4, 1984	Eric Dickerson, L.A. Rams vs. St. Louis	21	208	0
Sept. 2, 1984	Gerald Riggs, Atlanta vs. New Orleans	35	202	2
Nov. 27, 1983	*Curt Warner, Seattle vs. Kansas City (OT)	32	207	3
Nov. 6, 1983	James Wilder, Tampa Bay vs. Minnesota	31	219	1
Sept. 18, 1983	Tony Collins, New England vs. N.Y. Jets	23	212	3
Sept. 4, 1983	George Rogers, New Orleans vs. St. Louis	24	206	2
Dec. 21, 1980	Earl Campbell, Houston vs. Minnesota	29	203	1
Nov. 16, 1980	Earl Campbell, Houston vs. Chicago	31	206	0
Oct. 26, 1980	Earl Campbell, Houston vs. Cincinnati	27	202	2
Oct. 19, 1980	Earl Campbell, Houston vs. Tampa Bay	33	203	0
Nov. 26, 1978	*Terry Miller, Buffalo vs. N.Y. Giants	21	208	2
Dec. 4, 1977	*Tony Dorsett, Dallas vs. Philadelphia	23	206	2
Nov. 20, 1977	Walter Payton, Chicago vs. Minnesota	40	275	1
Oct. 30, 1977	Walter Payton, Chicago vs. Green Bay	23	205	2
Dec. 5, 1976	O.J. Simpson, Buffalo vs. Miami	24	203	1
Nov. 25, 1976	O.J. Simpson, Buffalo vs. Detroit	29	273	2
Oct. 24, 1976	Chuck Foreman, Minnesota vs. Philadelphia	28	200	2
Dec. 14, 1975	Greg Pruitt, Cleveland vs. Kansas City	26	214	3
Sept. 28, 1975	O.J. Simpson, Buffalo vs. Pittsburgh	28	227	1
Dec. 16, 1973	O.J. Simpson, Buffalo vs. N.Y. Jets	34	200	1
Dec. 9, 1973	O.J. Simpson, Buffalo vs. New England	22	219	1
Sept. 16, 1973	O.J. Simpson, Buffalo vs. New England	29	250	2
Dec. 5, 1971	Willie Ellison, Los Angeles vs. New Orleans	26	247	1
Dec. 20, 1970	John (Frenchy) Fuqua, Pittsburgh vs. Philadelphia	20	218	2
Nov. 3, 1968	Gale Sayers, Chicago vs. Green Bay	24	205	0
Oct. 30, 1966	Jim Nance, Boston vs. Oakland	38	208	2
Oct. 10, 1964	John Henry Johnson, Pittsburgh vs. Cleveland	30	200	3
Dec. 8, 1963	Cookie Gilchrist, Buffalo vs. N.Y. Jets	36	243	5
Nov. 3, 1963	Jim Brown, Cleveland vs. Philadelphia	28	223	1
Oct. 20, 1963	Clem Daniels, Oakland vs. N.Y. Jets	27	200	2
Sept. 22, 1963	Jim Brown, Cleveland vs. Dallas	20	232	2
Dec. 10, 1961	Billy Cannon, Houston vs. N.Y. Titans	25	216	3
Nov. 19, 1961	Jim Brown, Cleveland vs. Philadelphia	34	237	4
Dec. 18, 1960	John David Crow, St. Louis vs. Pittsburgh	24	203	0
Nov. 15, 1959	Bobby Mitchell, Cleveland vs. Washington	14	232	3
Nov. 24, 1957	*Jim Brown, Cleveland vs. Los Angeles	31	237	4
Dec. 16, 1956	*Tom Wilson, Los Angeles vs. Green Bay	23	223	0
Nov. 22, 1953	Dan Towler, Los Angeles vs. Baltimore	14	205	1
Nov. 12, 1950	Gene Roberts, N.Y. Giants vs. Chi. Cardinals	26	218	2
Nov. 27, 1949	Steve Van Buren, Philadelphia vs. Pittsburgh	27	205	0
Oct. 8, 1933	Cliff Battles, Boston vs. N.Y. Giants	16	215	1

**First season of professional football.*

TIMES 200 OR MORE

81 times by 55 players...Simpson 6; Brown, Campbell, Sanders 4; Bell, Davis, Dickerson, Dillon 3; Faulk, Payton, Riggs, Rogers 2.

4,000 YARDS PASSING IN A SEASON

Year	Player, Team	Att.	Comp.	Pct.	Yards	TD	Int.
2000	Peyton Manning, Indianapolis[2]	571	357	62.5	4,413	33	15
	Jeff Garcia, San Francisco	561	355	63.3	4,278	31	10
	Elvis Grbac, Kansas City	547	326	59.6	4,169	28	14
1999	Steve Beuerlein, Carolina	571	343	60.1	4,436	36	15
	Kurt Warner, St. Louis	499	325	65.1	4,353	41	13
	Peyton Manning, Indianapolis	533	331	62.1	4,135	26	15
	Brett Favre, Green Bay[3]	595	341	57.3	4,091	22	23
	Brad Johnson, Washington	519	316	60.9	4,005	24	13
1998	Brett Favre, Green Bay[2]	551	347	63.0	4,212	31	23
	Steve Young, San Francisco[2]	517	322	62.3	4,170	36	12
1996	Mark Brunell, Jacksonville	557	353	63.4	4,367	19	20
	Vinny Testaverde, Baltimore	549	325	59.2	4,177	33	19
	Drew Bledsoe, New England[2]	623	373	59.9	4,086	27	15
1995	Brett Favre, Green Bay	570	359	63.0	4,413	38	13
	Scott Mitchell, Detroit	583	346	59.3	4,338	32	12
	Warren Moon, Minnesota[4]	606	377	62.2	4,228	33	14
	Jeff George, Atlanta	557	336	60.3	4,143	24	11
1994	Drew Bledsoe, New England	691	400	57.9	4,555	25	27
	Dan Marino, Miami[6]	615	385	62.6	4,453	30	17
	Warren Moon, Minnesota[3]	601	371	61.7	4,264	18	19
1993	John Elway, Denver	551	348	63.2	4,030	25	10
	Steve Young, San Francisco	462	314	68.0	4,023	29	16
1992	Dan Marino, Miami[5]	554	330	59.6	4,116	24	16
1991	Warren Moon, Houston[2]	655	404	61.7	4,690	23	21
1990	Warren Moon, Houston	584	362	62.0	4,689	33	13
1989	Don Majkowski, Green Bay	599	353	58.9	4,318	27	20
	Jim Everett, L.A. Rams	518	304	58.7	4,310	29	17
1988	Dan Marino, Miami[4]	606	354	58.4	4,434	28	23
1986	Dan Marino, Miami[3]	623	378	60.7	4,746	44	23

	Jay Schroeder, Washington	541	276	51.0	4,109	22	22
1985	Dan Marino, Miami[2]	567	336	59.3	4,137	30	21
1984	Dan Marino, Miami	564	362	64.2	5,084	48	17
	Neil Lomax, St. Louis	560	345	61.6	4,614	28	16
	Phil Simms, N.Y. Giants	533	286	53.7	4,044	22	18
1983	Lynn Dickey, Green Bay	484	289	59.7	4,458	32	29
	Bill Kenney, Kansas City	603	346	57.4	4,348	24	18
1981	Dan Fouts, San Diego[3]	609	360	59.1	4,802	33	17
1980	Dan Fouts, San Diego[2]	589	348	59.1	4,715	30	24
	Brian Sipe, Cleveland	554	337	60.8	4,132	30	14
1979	Dan Fouts, San Diego	530	332	62.6	4,082	24	24
1967	Joe Namath, N.Y. Jets	491	258	52.5	4,007	26	28

400 YARDS PASSING IN A GAME

Date	Player, Team, Opponent	Att.	Comp.	Yards	TD
Dec. 24, 2000	Vinny Testaverde, N.Y. Jets vs. Baltimore	69	36	481	2
Dec. 17, 2000	Jeff Garcia, San Francisco vs. Chicago	44	36	402	2
Dec. 3, 2000	Aaron Brooks, New Orleans vs. Denver	48	30	441	2
Nov. 19, 2000	Gus Frerotte, Denver vs. San Diego	58	36	462	5
Nov. 5, 2000	Elvis Grbac, Kansas City vs. Oakland	53	39	504	2
Nov. 5, 2000	Trent Green, St. Louis vs. Carolina	42	29	431	2
Sept. 25, 2000	Peyton Manning, Indianapolis vs. Jacksonville	36	23	440	4
Sept. 4, 2000	Kurt Warner, St. Louis vs. Denver	35	25	441	3
Dec. 26, 1999	Brad Johnson, Washington vs. San Francisco (OT)	47	32	471	2
Dec. 5, 1999	Jeff Garcia, San Francisco vs. Cincinnati	49	33	437	3
Nov. 28, 1999	Jim Harbaugh, San Diego vs. Minnesota	39	25	404	1
Nov. 14, 1999	Jim Miller, Chicago vs. Minnesota (OT)	48	34	422	3
Sept. 26, 1999	Peyton Manning, Indianapolis vs. San Diego	54	29	404	2
Dec. 6, 1998	Vinny Testaverde, N.Y. Jets vs. Seattle	63	42	418	2
Dec. 6, 1998	John Elway, Denver vs. Kansas City	32	22	400	2
Nov. 26, 1998	Troy Aikman, Dallas vs. Minnesota	57	34	455	1
Nov. 23, 1998	Drew Bledsoe, New England vs. Miami	54	28	423	2
Nov. 15, 1998	Jake Plummer, Arizona vs. Dallas	56	31	465	3
Oct. 5, 1998	Randall Cunningham, Minnesota vs. Green Bay	32	20	442	4
Sept. 6, 1998	Glenn Foley, N.Y. Jets vs. San Francisco (OT)	58	30	415	3
Nov. 2, 1997	Tony Banks, St. Louis vs. Atlanta	34	23	401	2
Oct. 26, 1997	Warren Moon, Seattle vs. Oakland	44	28	409	5
Nov. 10, 1996	Boomer Esiason, Arizona vs. Washington (OT)	59	35	522	3
Nov. 3, 1996	Drew Bledsoe, New England vs. Miami	41	30	419	3
Oct. 27, 1996	Vinny Testaverde, Baltimore vs. St. Louis (OT)	51	31	429	3
Oct. 20, 1996	Mark Brunell, Jacksonville vs. St. Louis	52	37	421	0
Sept. 22, 1996	Mark Brunell, Jacksonville vs. New England (OT)	39	23	432	3
Dec. 18, 1995	Steve Young, San Francisco vs. Minnesota	49	30	425	3
Nov. 26, 1995	Dave Krieg, Arizona vs. Atlanta (OT)	43	27	413	4
Nov. 23, 1995	Scott Mitchell, Detroit vs. Minnesota	45	30	410	4
Oct. 1, 1995	Dan Marino, Miami vs. Cincinnati	48	33	450	2
Nov. 20, 1994	Warren Moon, Minnesota vs. N.Y. Jets	50	33	400	2
Nov. 13, 1994	Drew Bledsoe, New England vs. Minnesota (OT)	70	45	426	3
Nov. 6, 1994	Warren Moon, Minnesota vs. New Orleans	57	33	420	3
Sept. 25, 1994	Dan Marino, Miami vs. Minnesota	54	29	431	3
Sept. 4, 1994	Dan Marino, Miami vs. New England (OT)	42	23	473	5
Sept. 4, 1994	Drew Bledsoe, New England vs. Miami (OT)	51	32	421	4
Dec. 19, 1993	Steve Beuerlein, Phoenix vs. Seattle	53	34	431	3
Dec. 5, 1993	Brett Favre, Green Bay vs. Chicago	54	36	402	2
Nov. 28, 1993	Steve Young, San Francisco vs. L.A. Rams	32	26	462	4
Oct. 31, 1993	Jeff Hostetler, L.A. Raiders vs. San Diego	32	20	424	2
Sept. 13, 1992	Steve Young, San Francisco vs. Buffalo	37	26	449	3
Sept. 13, 1992	Jim Kelly, Buffalo vs. San Francisco	33	22	403	3
Nov. 10, 1991	Warren Moon, Houston vs. Dallas (OT)	56	41	432	0
Nov. 10, 1991	Mark Rypien, Washington vs. Atlanta	31	16	442	6
Oct. 13, 1991	Warren Moon, Houston vs. N.Y. Jets	50	35	423	2
Dec. 16, 1990	Warren Moon, Houston vs. Kansas City	45	27	527	3
Nov. 4, 1990	Joe Montana, San Francisco vs. Green Bay	40	25	411	3
Oct. 14, 1990	Joe Montana, San Francisco vs. Atlanta	49	32	476	6
Oct. 7, 1990	Boomer Esiason, Cincinnati vs. L.A. Rams (OT)	45	31	490	3
Dec. 23, 1989	Warren Moon, Houston vs. Cleveland	51	32	414	2
Dec. 11, 1989	Joe Montana, San Francisco vs. L.A. Rams	42	30	458	3
Nov. 26, 1989	Jim Everett, L.A. Rams vs. New Orleans (OT)	51	29	454	1
Nov. 26, 1989	Mark Rypien, Washington vs. Chicago	47	30	401	4
Oct. 2, 1989	Randall Cunningham, Philadelphia vs. Chicago	62	32	401	1
Sept. 24, 1989	Joe Montana, San Francisco vs. Philadelphia	34	25	428	5
Sept. 24, 1989	Dan Marino, Miami vs. N.Y. Jets	55	33	427	3
Sept. 17, 1989	Randall Cunningham, Phil. vs. Washington	46	34	447	5
Dec. 18, 1988	Dave Krieg, Seattle vs. L.A. Raiders	32	19	410	4
Dec. 12, 1988	Dan Marino, Miami vs. Cleveland	50	30	404	4
Oct. 23, 1988	Dan Marino, Miami vs. N.Y. Jets	60	35	521	3
Oct. 16, 1988	Vinny Testaverde, Tampa Bay vs. Indianapolis	42	25	469	2
Sept. 11, 1988	Doug Williams, Washington vs. Pittsburgh	52	30	430	2
Nov. 29, 1987	Tom Ramsey, New England vs. Philadelphia	53	34	402	3
Nov. 22, 1987	Boomer Esiason, Cincinnati vs. Pittsburgh	53	30	409	0
Sept. 20, 1987	Neil Lomax, St. Louis vs. San Diego	61	32	457	3
Dec. 21, 1986	Boomer Esiason, Cincinnati vs. N.Y. Jets	30	23	425	5
Dec. 14, 1986	Dan Marino, Miami vs. L.A. Rams (OT)	46	29	403	5
Nov. 23, 1986	Bernie Kosar, Cleveland vs. Pittsburgh (OT)	46	28	414	2
Nov. 17, 1986	Joe Montana, San Francisco vs. Washington	60	33	441	0
Nov. 16, 1986	Dan Marino, Miami vs. Buffalo	54	39	404	4
Nov. 10, 1986	Bernie Kosar, Cleveland vs. Miami	50	32	401	0
Nov. 2, 1986	Tommy Kramer, Minnesota vs. Washington (OT)	35	20	490	4
Nov. 2, 1986	Ken O'Brien, N.Y. Jets vs. Seattle	32	26	431	4
Oct. 27, 1986	Jay Schroeder, Washington vs. N.Y. Giants	40	22	420	1
Oct. 12, 1986	Steve Grogan, New England vs. N.Y. Jets	42	23	401	3
Sept. 21, 1986	Ken O'Brien, N.Y. Jets vs. Miami (OT)	43	29	479	4
Sept. 21, 1986	Dan Marino, Miami vs. N.Y. Jets (OT)	50	30	448	6
Sept. 21, 1986	Tony Eason, New England vs. Seattle	45	26	414	3
Dec. 20, 1985	John Elway, Denver vs. Seattle	42	24	432	1
Nov. 10, 1985	Dan Fouts, San Diego vs. L.A. Raiders (OT)	41	26	436	4
Oct. 13, 1985	Phil Simms, N.Y. Giants vs. Cincinnati	62	40	513	1
Oct. 13, 1985	Dave Krieg, Seattle vs. Atlanta	51	33	405	4
Oct. 6, 1985	Phil Simms, N.Y. Giants vs. Dallas	36	18	432	3
Oct. 6, 1985	Joe Montana, San Francisco vs. Atlanta	57	37	429	5
Sept. 19, 1985	Tommy Kramer, Minnesota vs. Chicago	55	28	436	3
Sept. 15, 1985	Dan Fouts, San Diego vs. Seattle	43	29	440	4
Dec. 16, 1984	Neil Lomax, St. Louis vs. Washington	46	37	468	2
Dec. 9, 1984	Dan Marino, Miami vs. Indianapolis	41	29	404	4
Dec. 2, 1984	Dan Marino, Miami vs. L.A. Raiders	57	35	470	4
Nov. 25, 1984	Dave Krieg, Seattle vs. Denver	44	30	406	3
Nov. 4, 1984	Dan Marino, Miami vs. N.Y. Jets	42	23	422	2
Oct. 21, 1984	Dan Fouts, San Diego vs. L.A. Raiders	45	24	410	3
Sept. 30, 1984	Dan Marino, Miami vs. St. Louis	36	24	429	3
Sept. 2, 1984	Phil Simms, N.Y. Giants vs. Philadelphia	30	23	409	4
Dec. 11, 1983	Bill Kenney, Kansas City vs. San Diego	41	31	411	4
Nov. 20, 1983	Dave Krieg, Seattle vs. Denver	42	31	418	3
Oct. 9, 1983	Joe Ferguson, Buffalo vs. Miami (OT)	55	38	419	5
Oct. 2, 1983	Joe Theismann, Washington vs. L.A. Raiders	39	23	417	3
Sept. 25, 1983	Richard Todd, N.Y. Jets vs. L.A. Rams (OT)	50	37	446	2
Dec. 26, 1982	Vince Ferragamo, L.A. Rams vs. Chicago	46	30	509	3
Dec. 20, 1982	Dan Fouts, San Diego vs. Cincinnati	40	25	435	1
Dec. 20, 1982	Ken Anderson, Cincinnati vs. San Diego	56	40	416	2
Dec. 11, 1982	Dan Fouts, San Diego vs. San Francisco	48	33	444	5
Nov. 21, 1982	Joe Montana, San Francisco vs. St. Louis	39	26	408	3
Nov. 15, 1981	Steve Bartkowski, Atlanta vs. Pittsburgh	50	33	416	2
Oct. 25, 1981	Brian Sipe, Cleveland vs. Baltimore	41	30	444	4
Oct. 25, 1981	David Woodley, Miami vs. Dallas	37	21	408	3
Oct. 11, 1981	Tommy Kramer, Minnesota vs. San Diego	43	27	444	4
Dec. 14, 1980	Tommy Kramer, Minnesota vs. Cleveland	49	38	456	4
Nov. 16, 1980	Doug Williams, Tampa Bay vs. Minnesota	55	30	486	4
Oct. 19, 1980	Dan Fouts, San Diego vs. N.Y. Giants	41	26	444	3
Oct. 12, 1980	Lynn Dickey, Green Bay vs. Tampa Bay (OT)	51	35	418	1
Sept. 21, 1980	Richard Todd, N.Y. Jets vs. San Francisco	60	42	447	3
Oct. 3, 1976	James Harris, Los Angeles vs. Miami	29	17	436	2
Nov. 17, 1975	Ken Anderson, Cincinnati vs. Buffalo	46	30	447	2
Nov. 18, 1974	Charley Johnson, Denver vs. Kansas City	42	28	445	2
Dec. 11, 1972	Joe Namath, N.Y. Jets vs. Oakland	46	25	403	1
Sept. 24, 1972	Joe Namath, N.Y. Jets vs. Baltimore	28	15	496	6
Dec. 21, 1969	Don Horn, Green Bay vs. St. Louis	31	22	410	5
Sept. 28, 1969	Joe Kapp, Minnesota vs. Baltimore	43	28	449	7
Sept. 9, 1968	Pete Beathard, Houston vs. Kansas City	48	23	413	2
Nov. 26, 1967	Sonny Jurgensen, Washington vs. Cleveland	50	32	418	3
Oct. 1, 1967	Joe Namath, N.Y. Jets vs. Miami	39	23	415	3
Sept. 17, 1967	Johnny Unitas, Baltimore vs. Atlanta	32	22	401	2
Nov. 13, 1966	Don Meredith, Dallas vs. Washington	29	21	406	2
Nov. 28, 1965	Sonny Jurgensen, Washington vs. Dallas	43	26	411	3
Oct. 24, 1965	Fran Tarkenton, Minnesota vs. San Francisco	35	21	407	3
Nov. 1, 1964	Len Dawson, Kansas City vs. Denver	38	23	435	6
Oct. 25, 1964	Cotton Davidson, Oakland vs. Denver	36	23	427	5
Oct. 16, 1964	Babe Parilli, Boston vs. Oakland	47	25	422	4
Dec. 22, 1963	Tom Flores, Oakland vs. Houston	29	17	407	6
Nov. 17, 1963	Norm Snead, Washington vs. Pittsburgh	40	23	424	2
Nov. 10, 1963	Don Meredith, Dallas vs. San Francisco	48	30	460	3
Oct. 13, 1963	Charley Johnson, St. Louis vs. Pittsburgh	41	20	428	2
Dec. 16, 1962	Sonny Jurgensen, Philadelphia vs. St. Louis	34	15	419	5
Nov. 18, 1962	Bill Wade, Chicago vs. Dall. Cowboys	46	28	466	2
Oct. 28, 1962	Y.A. Tittle, N.Y. Giants vs. Washington	39	27	505	7
Sept. 15, 1962	Frank Tripucka, Denver vs. Buffalo	56	29	447	2
Dec. 17, 1961	Sonny Jurgensen, Philadelphia vs. Detroit	42	27	403	3
Nov. 19, 1961	George Blanda, Houston vs. N.Y. Titans	32	20	418	7
Oct. 29, 1961	George Blanda, Houston vs. Buffalo	32	18	464	4
Oct. 29, 1961	Sonny Jurgensen, Philadelphia vs. Washington	41	27	436	3
Oct. 13, 1961	Jacky Lee, Houston vs. Boston	41	27	457	2
Dec. 13, 1958	Bobby Layne, Pittsburgh vs. Chi. Cardinals	49	23	409	2
Nov. 8, 1953	Bobby Thomason, Philadelphia vs. N.Y. Giants	44	22	437	4
Oct. 4, 1952	Otto Graham, Cleveland vs. Pittsburgh	49	21	401	3
Sept. 28, 1951	Norm Van Brocklin, Los Angeles vs. N.Y. Yanks	41	27	554	5
Dec. 11, 1949	Johnny Lujack, Chi. Bears vs. Chi. Cardinals	39	24	468	6
Oct. 31, 1948	Sammy Baugh, Washington vs. Boston	24	17	446	4
Oct. 31, 1948	Jim Hardy, Los Angeles vs. Chi. Cardinals	53	28	406	3

OUTSTANDING PERFORMERS

Nov. 14, 1943 Sid Luckman, Chi. Bears vs. N.Y. Giants 32 21 433 7

TIMES 400 OR MORE

152 times by 81 players. . .Marino 13; Montana, Moon 7; Fouts 6; Jurgensen, Krieg 5; Bledsoe, Esiason, Kramer, Testaverde 4; Cunningham, Namath, Simms, Young 3; Anderson, Blanda, Brunell, Elway, Garcia, Johnson, Kosar, Lomax, Manning, Meredith, O'Brien, Rypien, Todd, Williams 2.

100 PASS RECEPTIONS IN A SEASON

Year	Player, Team	No.	Yards	Avg.	Long	TD
2000	Marvin Harrison, Indianapolis[2]	102	1,413	13.9	78	14
	Muhsin Muhammad, Carolina	102	1,183	11.6	36	6
	Ed McCaffrey, Denver	101	1,317	13.0	61	9
	Rod Smith, Denver	100	1,602	16.0	49	8
1999	Jimmy Smith, Jacksonville	116	1,636	14.1	62	6
	Marvin Harrison, Indianapolis	115	1,663	14.5	57	12
1997	Tim Brown, Oakland	104	1,408	13.5	59	5
	Herman Moore, Detroit[3]	104	1,293	12.4	79	8
1996	Jerry Rice, San Francisco[4]	108	1,254	11.6	39	8
	Herman Moore, Detroit[2]	106	1,296	12.2	50	9
	Carl Pickens, Cincinnati	100	1,180	11.8	61	12
1995	Herman Moore, Detroit	123	1,686	13.7	69	14
	Jerry Rice, San Francisco[3]	122	1,848	15.1	81	15
	Cris Carter, Minnesota[2]	122	1,371	11.2	60	17
	Isaac Bruce, St. Louis	119	1,781	15.0	72	13
	Michael Irvin, Dallas	111	1,603	14.4	50	10
	Brett Perriman, Detroit	108	1,488	13.8	91	9
	Eric Metcalf, Atlanta	104	1,189	11.4	62	8
	Robert Brooks, Green Bay	102	1,497	14.7	99	13
	Larry Centers, Arizona	101	962	9.5	32	2
1994	Cris Carter, Minnesota	122	1,256	10.3	65	7
	Jerry Rice, San Francisco[2]	112	1,499	13.4	69	13
	Terance Mathis, Atlanta	111	1,342	12.1	81	11
1993	Sterling Sharpe, Green Bay[2]	112	1,274	11.4	54	11
1992	Sterling Sharpe, Green Bay	108	1,461	13.5	76	13
1991	Haywood Jeffires, Houston	100	1,181	11.8	44	7
1990	Jerry Rice, San Francisco	100	1,502	15.0	64	13
1984	Art Monk, Washington	106	1,372	12.9	72	7
1964	Charley Hennigan, Houston	101	1,546	15.3	53	8
1961	Lionel Taylor, Denver	100	1,176	11.8	52	4

1,000 YARDS PASS RECEIVING IN A SEASON

Year	Player, Team	No.	Yards	Avg.	Long	TD
2000	Torry Holt, St. Louis	82	1,635	19.9	85	6
	Rod Smith, Denver[4]	100	1,602	16.0	49	8
	Isaac Bruce, St. Louis[4]	87	1,471	16.9	78	9
	Terrell Owens, San Francisco[2]	97	1,451	15.0	69	13
	Randy Moss, Minnesota[3]	77	1,437	18.7	78	15
	Marvin Harrison, Indianapolis[2]	102	1,413	13.9	78	14
	Derrick Alexander, Kansas City[3]	78	1,391	17.8	81	10
	Joe Horn, New Orleans	94	1,340	14.3	52	8
	Eric Moulds, Buffalo[2]	94	1,326	14.1	52	5
	Ed McCaffrey, Denver[3]	101	1,317	13.0	61	9
	Cris Carter, Minnesota[8]	96	1,274	13.3	53	9
	Jimmy Smith, Jacksonville[5]	91	1,213	13.3	65	8
	Keenan McCardell, Jacksonville[3]	94	1,207	12.8	67	5
	Tony Gonzalez, Kansas City	93	1,203	12.9	39	9
	Muhsin Muhammad, Carolina[2]	102	1,183	11.6	36	6
	David Boston, Arizona	71	1,156	16.3	70	7
	Tim Brown, Oakland[8]	76	1,128	14.8	45	11
	Amani Toomer, N.Y. Giants[2]	78	1,094	14.0	54	7
1999	Marvin Harrison, Indianapolis	115	1,663	14.5	57	12
	Jimmy Smith, Jacksonville[4]	116	1,636	14.1	62	6
	Randy Moss, Minnesota[2]	80	1,413	17.7	67	11
	Marcus Robinson, Chicago	84	1,400	16.7	80	9
	Tim Brown, Oakland[7]	90	1,344	14.9	47	6
	Germane Crowell, Detroit	81	1,338	16.5	77	7
	Muhsin Muhammad, Carolina	96	1,253	13.1	60	8
	Cris Carter, Minnesota[7]	90	1,241	13.8	68	13
	Michael Westbrook, Washington	65	1,191	18.3	65	9
	Amani Toomer, N.Y. Giants	79	1,183	15.0	80	6
	Keyshawn Johnson, N.Y. Jets[2]	89	1,170	13.2	65	8
	Isaac Bruce, St. Louis[3]	77	1,165	15.1	60	12
	Terry Glenn, New England[2]	69	1,147	16.6	67	4
	Albert Connell, Washington	62	1,132	18.3	62	7
	Johnnie Morton, Detroit[3]	80	1,129	14.1	48	5
	Qadry Ismail, Baltimore	68	1,105	16.3	76	6
	Raghib Ismail, Dallas[2]	80	1,097	13.7	76	6
	Patrick Jeffers, Carolina	63	1,082	17.2	88	12
	Antonio Freeman, Green Bay[3]	74	1,074	14.5	51	6
	Bill Schroeder, Green Bay	74	1,051	14.2	51	5
	Marshall Faulk, St. Louis	87	1,048	12.1	57	5
	Tony Martin, Miami[4]	67	1,037	15.5	69	5
	Darnay Scott, Cincinnati	68	1,022	15.0	76	7
	Rod Smith, Denver[3]	79	1,020	12.9	71	4
	Ed McCaffrey, Denver[2]	71	1,018	14.3	78	7
	Terance Mathis, Atlanta[4]	81	1,016	12.5	52	6
1998	Antonio Freeman, Green Bay[2]	84	1,424	17.0	84	14
	Eric Moulds, Buffalo	67	1,368	20.4	84	9
	*Randy Moss, Minnesota	69	1,313	19.0	61	17
	Rod Smith, Denver[2]	86	1,222	14.2	58	6
	Jimmy Smith, Jacksonville[3]	78	1,182	15.2	72	8
	Tony Martin, Atlanta[3]	66	1,181	17.9	62	6
	Jerry Rice, San Francisco[12]	82	1,157	14.1	75	9
	Frank Sanders, Arizona[2]	89	1,145	12.9	42	3
	Terance Mathis, Atlanta[3]	64	1,136	17.8	78	11
	Keyshawn Johnson, N.Y. Jets	83	1,131	13.6	41	10
	Terrell Owens, San Francisco	67	1,097	16.4	79	14
	Wayne Chrebet, N.Y. Jets	75	1,083	14.4	63	8
	Michael Irvin, Dallas[7]	74	1,057	14.3	51	1
	Ed McCaffrey, Denver	64	1,053	16.5	48	10
	O.J. McDuffie, Miami	90	1,050	11.7	61	7
	Joey Galloway, Seattle[3]	65	1,047	16.1	81	10
	Johnnie Morton, Detroit[2]	69	1,028	14.9	98	2
	Raghib Ismail, Carolina	69	1,024	14.8	62	8
	Carl Pickens, Cincinnati[4]	82	1,023	12.5	67	5
	Tim Brown, Oakland[6]	81	1,012	12.5	49	9
	Cris Carter, Minnesota[6]	78	1,011	13.0	54	12
1997	Rob Moore, Arizona[3]	97	1,584	16.3	47	8
	Tim Brown, Oakland[5]	104	1,408	13.5	59	5
	Yancey Thigpen, Pittsburgh[2]	79	1,398	17.7	69	7
	Jimmy Smith, Jacksonville[2]	82	1,324	16.1	75	4
	Irving Fryar, Philadelphia[5]	86	1,316	15.3	72	6
	Herman Moore, Detroit[4]	104	1,293	12.4	79	8
	Antonio Freeman, Green Bay	81	1,243	15.3	58	12
	Michael Irvin, Dallas[6]	75	1,180	15.7	55	9
	Rod Smith, Denver	70	1,180	16.9	78	12
	Keenan McCardell, Jacksonville[2]	85	1,164	13.7	60	5
	Jake Reed, Minnesota[4]	68	1,138	16.7	56	6
	Shannon Sharpe, Denver[3]	72	1,107	15.4	68	3
	Andre Rison, Kansas City[5]	72	1,092	15.2	45	7
	Cris Carter, Minnesota[5]	89	1,069	12.0	43	13
	Johnnie Morton, Detroit	80	1,057	13.2	73	6
	Joey Galloway, Seattle[2]	72	1,049	14.6	53	12
	Frank Sanders, Arizona	75	1,017	13.6	70	4
	Robert Brooks, Green Bay[2]	60	1,010	16.8	48	7
	Derrick Alexander, Baltimore[2]	65	1,009	15.5	92	9
1996	Isaac Bruce, St. Louis[2]	84	1,338	15.9	70	7
	Jake Reed, Minnesota[3]	72	1,320	18.3	82	7
	Herman Moore, Detroit[3]	106	1,296	12.2	50	9
	Jerry Rice, San Francisco[11]	108	1,254	11.6	39	8
	Jimmy Smith, Jacksonville	83	1,244	15.0	62	7
	Michael Jackson, Baltimore	76	1,201	15.8	86	14
	Irving Fryar, Philadelphia[4]	88	1,195	13.6	42	11
	Carl Pickens, Cincinnati[3]	100	1,180	11.8	61	12
	Tony Martin, San Diego[2]	85	1,171	13.8	55	14
	Cris Carter, Minnesota[4]	96	1,163	12.1	43	10
	*Terry Glenn, New England	90	1,132	12.6	37	6
	Keenan McCardell, Jacksonville	85	1,129	13.3	52	3
	Tim Brown, Oakland[4]	90	1,104	12.3	42	9
	Derrick Alexander, Baltimore	62	1,099	17.7	64	9
	Shannon Sharpe, Denver[2]	80	1,062	13.3	51	10
	Curtis Conway, Chicago[2]	81	1,049	13.0	58	7
	Andre Reed, Buffalo[4]	66	1,036	15.7	67	6
	Brett Perriman, Detroit[2]	94	1,021	10.9	44	5
	Rob Moore, Arizona[2]	58	1,016	17.5	69	4
	Henry Ellard, Washington[7]	52	1,014	19.5	51	2
	Charles Johnson, Pittsburgh	60	1,008	16.8	70	3
1995	Jerry Rice, San Francisco[10]	122	1,848	15.1	81	15
	Isaac Bruce, St. Louis	119	1,781	15.0	72	13
	Herman Moore, Detroit[2]	123	1,686	13.7	69	14
	Michael Irvin, Dallas[5]	111	1,603	14.4	50	10
	Robert Brooks, Green Bay	102	1,497	14.7	99	13
	Brett Perriman, Detroit	108	1,488	13.8	91	9
	Cris Carter, Minnesota[3]	122	1,371	11.2	60	17
	Tim Brown, Oakland[3]	89	1,342	15.1	80	10
	Yancey Thigpen, Pittsburgh	85	1,307	15.4	43	5
	Jeff Graham, Chicago	82	1,301	15.9	51	4
	Carl Pickens, Cincinnati[2]	99	1,234	12.5	68	17
	Tony Martin, San Diego	90	1,224	13.6	51	6
	Eric Metcalf, Atlanta	104	1,189	11.4	62	8
	Jake Reed, Minnesota[2]	72	1,167	16.2	55	9
	Quinn Early, New Orleans	81	1,087	13.4	70	8
	Anthony Miller, Denver[5]	59	1,079	18.3	62	14

	Bert Emanuel, Atlanta	74	1,039	14.0	52	5
	*Joey Galloway, Seattle	67	1,039	15.5	59	7
	Terance Mathis, Atlanta[2]	78	1,039	13.3	54	9
	Curtis Conway, Chicago	62	1,037	16.7	76	12
	Henry Ellard, Washington[6]	56	1,005	17.9	59	5
	Mark Carrier, Carolina[2]	66	1,002	15.2	66	3
	Brian Blades, Seattle[4]	77	1,001	13.0	49	4
1994	Jerry Rice, San Francisco[9]	112	1,499	13.4	69	13
	Henry Ellard, Washington[5]	74	1,397	18.9	73	6
	Terance Mathis, Atlanta	111	1,342	12.1	81	11
	Tim Brown, L.A. Raiders[2]	89	1,309	14.7	77	9
	Andre Reed, Buffalo[2]	90	1,303	14.5	83	8
	Irving Fryar, Miami[3]	73	1,270	17.4	54	7
	Cris Carter, Minnesota[2]	122	1,256	10.3	65	7
	Michael Irvin, Dallas[4]	79	1,241	15.7	65	6
	Jake Reed, Minnesota	85	1,175	13.8	59	4
	Ben Coates, New England	96	1,174	12.2	62	7
	Herman Moore, Detroit	72	1,173	16.3	51	11
	Fred Barnett, Philadelphia[2]	78	1,127	14.4	54	5
	Carl Pickens, Cincinnati	71	1,127	15.9	70	11
	Sterling Sharpe, Green Bay[4]	94	1,119	11.9	49	18
	Anthony Miller, Denver[4]	60	1,107	18.5	76	5
	Andre Rison, Atlanta[3]	81	1,088	13.4	69	8
	Brian Blades, Seattle[3]	81	1,088	13.4	45	4
	Rob Moore, N.Y. Jets	78	1,010	12.9	41	6
	Shannon Sharpe, Denver	87	1,010	11.6	44	4
1993	Jerry Rice, San Francisco[8]	98	1,503	15.3	80	15
	Michael Irvin, Dallas[3]	88	1,330	15.1	61	7
	Sterling Sharpe, Green Bay[4]	112	1,274	11.4	54	11
	Andre Rison, Atlanta[3]	86	1,242	14.4	53	15
	Tim Brown, L.A. Raiders	80	1,180	14.8	71	7
	Anthony Miller, San Diego[3]	84	1,162	13.8	66	7
	Cris Carter, Minnesota	86	1,071	12.5	58	9
	Reggie Langhorne, Indianapolis	85	1,038	12.2	72	3
	Irving Fryar, Miami[2]	64	1,010	15.8	65	5
1992	Sterling Sharpe, Green Bay[3]	108	1,461	13.5	76	13
	Michael Irvin, Dallas[2]	78	1,396	17.9	87	7
	Jerry Rice, San Francisco[7]	84	1,201	14.3	80	10
	Andre Rison, Atlanta[2]	93	1,119	12.0	71	11
	Fred Barnett, Philadelphia	67	1,083	16.2	71	6
	Anthony Miller, San Diego[2]	72	1,060	14.7	67	7
	Eric Martin, New Orleans[3]	68	1,041	15.3	52	5
1991	Michael Irvin, Dallas	93	1,523	16.4	66	8
	Gary Clark, Washington[5]	70	1,340	19.1	82	10
	Jerry Rice, San Francisco[6]	80	1,206	15.1	73	14
	Haywood Jeffires, Houston[2]	100	1,181	11.8	44	7
	Michael Haynes, Atlanta	50	1,122	22.4	80	11
	Andre Reed, Buffalo[2]	81	1,113	13.7	55	10
	Drew Hill, Houston[5]	90	1,109	12.3	61	4
	Mark Duper, Miami[4]	70	1,085	15.5	43	5
	James Lofton, Buffalo[6]	57	1,072	18.8	77	8
	Mark Clayton, Miami[5]	70	1,053	15.0	43	12
	Henry Ellard, L.A. Rams[4]	64	1,052	16.4	38	3
	Art Monk, Washington[5]	71	1,049	14.8	64	8
	Irving Fryar, New England	68	1,014	14.9	56	3
	John Taylor, San Francisco[2]	64	1,011	15.8	97	9
	Brian Blades, Seattle[2]	70	1,003	14.3	52	2
1990	Jerry Rice, San Francisco[5]	100	1,502	15.0	64	13
	Henry Ellard, L.A. Rams[3]	76	1,294	17.0	50	4
	Andre Rison, Atlanta	82	1,208	14.7	75	10
	Gary Clark, Washington[4]	75	1,112	14.8	53	8
	Sterling Sharpe, Green Bay[2]	67	1,105	16.5	76	6
	Willie Anderson, L.A. Rams[2]	51	1,097	21.5	55	4
	Haywood Jeffires, Houston	74	1,048	14.2	87	8
	Stephone Paige, Kansas City	65	1,021	15.7	86	5
	Drew Hill, Houston[4]	74	1,019	13.8	57	5
	Anthony Carter, Minnesota[3]	70	1,008	14.4	56	8
1989	Jerry Rice, San Francisco[4]	82	1,483	18.1	68	17
	Sterling Sharpe, Green Bay	90	1,423	15.8	79	12
	Mark Carrier, Tampa Bay	86	1,422	16.5	78	9
	Henry Ellard, L.A. Rams[2]	70	1,382	19.7	53	8
	Andre Reed, Buffalo	88	1,312	14.9	78	9
	Anthony Miller, San Diego	75	1,252	16.7	69	10
	Webster Slaughter, Cleveland	65	1,236	19.0	97	6
	Gary Clark, Washington[3]	79	1,229	15.6	80	9
	Tim McGee, Cincinnati	65	1,211	18.6	74	8
	Art Monk, Washington[4]	86	1,186	13.8	60	8
	Willie Anderson, L.A. Rams	44	1,146	26.0	78	5
	Ricky Sanders, Washington[2]	80	1,138	14.2	68	4
	Vance Johnson, Denver	76	1,095	14.4	69	7
	Richard Johnson, Detroit	70	1,091	15.6	75	8
	Eric Martin, New Orleans[2]	68	1,090	16.0	53	8
	John Taylor, San Francisco	60	1,077	18.0	95	10
	Mervyn Fernandez, L.A. Raiders	57	1,069	18.8	75	9
	Anthony Carter, Minnesota[2]	65	1,066	16.4	50	4
	Brian Blades, Seattle	77	1,063	13.8	60	5
	Mark Clayton, Miami[4]	64	1,011	15.8	78	9
1988	Henry Ellard, L.A. Rams	86	1,414	16.4	68	10
	Jerry Rice, San Francisco[3]	64	1,306	20.4	96	9
	Eddie Brown, Cincinnati	53	1,273	24.0	86	9
	Anthony Carter, Minnesota	72	1,225	17.0	67	6
	Ricky Sanders, Washington	73	1,148	15.7	55	12
	Drew Hill, Houston[3]	72	1,141	15.8	57	10
	Mark Clayton, Miami[3]	86	1,129	13.1	45	14
	Roy Green, Phoenix[3]	68	1,097	16.1	52	7
	Eric Martin, New Orleans	85	1,083	12.7	40	7
	Al Toon, N.Y. Jets[2]	93	1,067	11.5	42	5
	Bruce Hill, Tampa Bay	58	1,040	17.9	42	9
	Lionel Manuel, N.Y. Giants	65	1,029	15.8	46	4
1987	J.T. Smith, St. Louis[2]	91	1,117	12.3	38	8
	Jerry Rice, San Francisco[2]	65	1,078	16.6	57	22
	Gary Clark, Washington[2]	56	1,066	19.0	84	7
	Carlos Carson, Kansas City[3]	55	1,044	19.0	81	7
1986	Jerry Rice, San Francisco	86	1,570	18.3	66	15
	Stanley Morgan, New England[3]	84	1,491	17.8	44	10
	Mark Duper, Miami[3]	67	1,313	19.6	85	11
	Gary Clark, Washington	74	1,265	17.1	55	7
	Al Toon, N.Y. Jets	85	1,176	13.8	62	8
	Todd Christensen, L.A. Raiders[3]	95	1,153	12.1	35	8
	Mark Clayton, Miami[2]	60	1,150	19.2	68	10
	*Bill Brooks, Indianapolis	65	1,131	17.4	84	8
	Drew Hill, Houston[2]	65	1,112	17.1	81	5
	Steve Largent, Seattle[8]	70	1,070	15.3	38	9
	Art Monk, Washington[3]	73	1,068	14.6	69	4
	*Ernest Givins, Houston	61	1,062	17.4	60	3
	Cris Collinsworth, Cincinnati[4]	62	1,024	16.5	46	10
	Wesley Walker, N.Y. Jets[2]	49	1,016	20.7	83	12
	J.T. Smith, St. Louis	80	1,014	12.7	45	6
	Mark Bavaro, N.Y. Giants	66	1,001	15.2	41	4
1985	Steve Largent, Seattle[7]	79	1,287	16.3	43	6
	Mike Quick, Philadelphia[3]	73	1,247	17.1	99	11
	Art Monk, Washington[2]	91	1,226	13.5	53	2
	Wes Chandler, San Diego[4]	67	1,199	17.9	75	10
	Drew Hill, Houston	64	1,169	18.3	57	9
	James Lofton, Green Bay[5]	69	1,153	16.7	56	4
	Louis Lipps, Pittsburgh	59	1,134	19.2	51	12
	Cris Collinsworth, Cincinnati[3]	65	1,125	17.3	71	5
	Tony Hill, Dallas[3]	74	1,113	15.0	53	7
	Lionel James, San Diego	86	1,027	11.9	67	6
	Roger Craig, San Francisco	92	1,016	11.0	73	6
1984	Roy Green, St. Louis[2]	78	1,555	19.9	83	12
	John Stallworth, Pittsburgh[3]	80	1,395	17.4	51	11
	Mark Clayton, Miami	73	1,389	19.0	65	18
	Art Monk, Washington	106	1,372	12.9	72	7
	James Lofton, Green Bay[4]	62	1,361	22.0	79	7
	Mark Duper, Miami[2]	71	1,306	18.4	80	8
	Steve Watson, Denver[3]	69	1,170	17.0	73	7
	Steve Largent, Seattle[6]	74	1,164	15.7	65	12
	Tim Smith, Houston[2]	69	1,141	16.5	75	4
	Stacey Bailey, Atlanta	67	1,138	17.0	61	6
	Carlos Carson, Kansas City[2]	57	1,078	18.9	57	4
	Mike Quick, Philadelphia[2]	61	1,052	17.2	90	9
	Todd Christensen, L.A. Raiders[2]	80	1,007	12.6	38	7
	Kevin House, Tampa Bay[2]	76	1,005	13.2	55	5
	Ozzie Newsome, Cleveland[2]	89	1,001	11.2	52	5
1983	Mike Quick, Philadelphia	69	1,409	20.4	83	13
	Carlos Carson, Kansas City	80	1,351	16.9	50	7
	James Lofton, Green Bay[3]	58	1,300	22.4	74	8
	Todd Christensen, L.A. Raiders	92	1,247	13.6	45	12
	Roy Green, St. Louis	78	1,227	15.7	71	14
	Charlie Brown, Washington	78	1,225	15.7	75	8
	Tim Smith, Houston	83	1,176	14.2	47	6
	Kellen Winslow, San Diego[3]	88	1,172	13.3	46	8
	Earnest Gray, N.Y. Giants	78	1,139	14.6	62	5
	Steve Watson, Denver[2]	59	1,133	19.2	78	5
	Cris Collinsworth, Cincinnati[2]	66	1,130	17.1	63	5
	Steve Largent, Seattle[5]	72	1,074	14.9	46	11
	Mark Duper, Miami	51	1,003	19.7	85	10
1982	Wes Chandler, San Diego[3]	49	1,032	21.1	66	9
1981	Alfred Jenkins, Atlanta[2]	70	1,358	19.4	67	13
	James Lofton, Green Bay[2]	71	1,294	18.2	75	8
	Steve Watson, Denver	60	1,244	20.7	95	13
	Frank Lewis, Buffalo[2]	70	1,244	17.8	33	4
	Steve Largent, Seattle[4]	75	1,224	16.3	57	9
	Charlie Joiner, San Diego[4]	70	1,188	17.0	57	7
	Kevin House, Tampa Bay	56	1,176	21.0	84	9

OUTSTANDING PERFORMERS

Year	Player, Team	No.	Yards	Avg.	Long	TD
	Wes Chandler, N.O.-San Diego[2]	69	1,142	16.6	51	6
	Dwight Clark, San Francisco	85	1,105	13.0	78	4
	John Stallworth, Pittsburgh[2]	63	1,098	17.4	55	5
	Kellen Winslow, San Diego[2]	88	1,075	12.2	67	10
	Pat Tilley, St. Louis	66	1,040	15.8	75	3
	Stanley Morgan, New England[2]	44	1,029	23.4	76	6
	Harold Carmichael, Philadelphia[3]	61	1,028	16.9	85	6
	Freddie Scott, Detroit	53	1,022	19.3	48	5
	*Cris Collinsworth, Cincinnati	67	1,009	15.1	74	8
	Joe Senser, Minnesota	79	1,004	12.7	53	8
	Ozzie Newsome, Cleveland	69	1,002	14.5	62	6
	Sammy White, Minnesota	66	1,001	15.2	53	3
1980	John Jefferson, San Diego[3]	82	1,340	16.3	58	13
	Kellen Winslow, San Diego	89	1,290	14.5	65	9
	James Lofton, Green Bay	71	1,226	17.3	47	4
	Charlie Joiner, San Diego[3]	71	1,132	15.9	51	4
	Ahmad Rashad, Minnesota[2]	69	1,095	15.9	76	5
	Steve Largent, Seattle[3]	66	1,064	16.1	67	6
	Tony Hill, Dallas[2]	60	1,055	17.6	58	8
	Alfred Jenkins, Atlanta	57	1,026	18.0	57	6
1979	Steve Largent, Seattle[2]	66	1,237	18.7	55	9
	John Stallworth, Pittsburgh	70	1,183	16.9	65	8
	Ahmad Rashad, Minnesota	80	1,156	14.5	52	9
	John Jefferson, San Diego[2]	61	1,090	17.9	65	10
	Frank Lewis, Buffalo	54	1,082	20.0	55	2
	Wes Chandler, New Orleans	65	1,069	16.4	85	6
	Tony Hill, Dallas	60	1,062	17.7	75	10
	Drew Pearson, Dallas[2]	55	1,026	18.7	56	8
	Wallace Francis, Atlanta	74	1,013	13.7	42	8
	Harold Jackson, New England[3]	45	1,013	22.5	59	7
	Charlie Joiner, San Diego[2]	72	1,008	14.0	39	4
	Stanley Morgan, New England	44	1,002	22.8	63	12
1978	Wesley Walker, N.Y. Jets	48	1,169	24.4	77	8
	Steve Largent, Seattle	71	1,168	16.5	57	8
	Harold Carmichael, Philadelphia[2]	55	1,072	19.5	56	8
	*John Jefferson, San Diego	56	1,001	17.9	46	13
1976	Roger Carr, Baltimore	43	1,112	25.9	79	11
	Cliff Branch, Oakland[2]	46	1,111	24.2	88	12
	Charlie Joiner, San Diego	50	1,056	21.1	81	7
1975	Ken Burrough, Houston	53	1,063	20.1	77	8
1974	Cliff Branch, Oakland	60	1,092	18.2	67	13
	Drew Pearson, Dallas	62	1,087	17.5	50	2
1973	Harold Carmichael, Philadelphia	67	1,116	16.7	73	9
1972	Harold Jackson, Philadelphia[2]	62	1,048	16.9	77	4
	John Gilliam, Minnesota	47	1,035	22.0	66	7
1971	Otis Taylor, Kansas City[2]	57	1,110	19.5	82	7
1970	Gene Washington, San Francisco	53	1,100	20.8	79	12
	Marlin Briscoe, Buffalo	57	1,036	18.2	48	8
	Dick Gordon, Chicago	71	1,026	14.5	69	13
	Gary Garrison, San Diego[2]	44	1,006	22.9	67	12
1969	Warren Wells, Oakland[2]	47	1,260	26.8	80	14
	Harold Jackson, Philadelphia	65	1,116	17.2	65	9
	Roy Jefferson, Pittsburgh[2]	67	1,079	16.1	63	9
	Dan Abramowicz, New Orleans	73	1,015	13.9	49	7
	Lance Alworth, San Diego[7]	64	1,003	15.7	76	4
1968	Lance Alworth, San Diego[6]	68	1,312	19.3	80	10
	Don Maynard, N.Y. Jets[5]	57	1,297	22.8	87	10
	George Sauer, N.Y. Jets[3]	66	1,141	17.3	43	3
	Warren Wells, Oakland	53	1,137	21.5	94	11
	Gary Garrison, San Diego	52	1,103	21.2	84	10
	Roy Jefferson, Pittsburgh	58	1,074	18.5	62	11
	Paul Warfield, Cleveland	50	1,067	21.3	65	12
	Homer Jones, N.Y. Giants[3]	45	1,057	23.5	84	7
	Fred Biletnikoff, Oakland	61	1,037	17.0	82	6
	Lance Rentzel, Dallas	54	1,009	18.7	65	6
1967	Don Maynard, N.Y. Jets[4]	71	1,434	20.2	75	10
	Ben Hawkins, Philadelphia	59	1,265	21.4	87	10
	Homer Jones, N.Y. Giants[2]	49	1,209	24.7	70	13
	Jackie Smith, St. Louis	56	1,205	21.5	76	9
	George Sauer, N.Y. Jets[2]	75	1,189	15.9	61	6
	Lance Alworth, San Diego[5]	52	1,010	19.4	71	9
1966	Lance Alworth, San Diego[4]	73	1,383	18.9	78	13
	Otis Taylor, Kansas City	58	1,297	22.4	89	8
	Pat Studstill, Detroit	67	1,266	18.9	99	5
	Bob Hayes, Dallas[2]	64	1,232	19.3	95	13
	Charlie Frazier, Houston	57	1,129	19.8	79	12
	Charley Taylor, Washington	72	1,119	15.5	86	12
	George Sauer, N.Y. Jets	63	1,081	17.2	77	5
	Homer Jones, N.Y. Giants	48	1,044	21.8	98	8
	Art Powell, Oakland[5]	53	1,026	19.4	46	11
1965	Lance Alworth, San Diego[3]	69	1,602	23.2	85	14
	Dave Parks, San Francisco	80	1,344	16.8	53	12
	Don Maynard, N.Y. Jets[3]	68	1,218	17.9	56	14
	Pete Retzlaff, Philadelphia	66	1,190	18.0	78	10
	Lionel Taylor, Denver[4]	85	1,131	13.3	63	6
	Tommy McDonald, Los Angeles[3]	67	1,036	15.5	51	9
	*Bob Hayes, Dallas	46	1,003	21.8	82	12
1964	Charley Hennigan, Houston[3]	101	1,546	15.3	53	8
	Art Powell, Oakland[4]	76	1,361	17.9	77	11
	Lance Alworth, San Diego[2]	61	1,235	20.2	82	13
	Johnny Morris, Chicago	93	1,200	12.9	63	10
	Elbert Dubenion, Buffalo	42	1,139	27.1	72	10
	Terry Barr, Detroit[2]	57	1,030	18.1	58	9
1963	Bobby Mitchell, Washington[2]	69	1,436	20.8	99	7
	Art Powell, Oakland[3]	73	1,304	17.9	85	16
	Buddy Dial, Pittsburgh[2]	60	1,295	21.6	83	9
	Lance Alworth, San Diego	61	1,205	19.8	85	11
	Del Shofner, N.Y. Giants[4]	64	1,181	18.5	70	9
	Lionel Taylor, Denver[3]	78	1,101	14.1	72	10
	Terry Barr, Detroit	66	1,086	16.5	75	13
	Charley Hennigan, Houston[2]	61	1,051	17.2	83	10
	Sonny Randle, St. Louis[2]	51	1,014	19.9	68	12
	Bake Turner, N.Y. Jets	71	1,009	14.2	53	6
1962	Bobby Mitchell, Washington	72	1,384	19.2	81	11
	Sonny Randle, St. Louis	63	1,158	18.4	86	7
	Tommy McDonald, Philadelphia[2]	58	1,146	19.8	60	10
	Del Shofner, N.Y. Giants[3]	53	1,133	21.4	69	12
	Art Powell, N.Y. Titans[2]	64	1,130	17.7	80	8
	Frank Clarke, Dall. Cowboys	47	1,043	22.2	66	14
	Don Maynard, N.Y. Titans[2]	56	1,041	18.6	86	8
1961	Charley Hennigan, Houston	82	1,746	21.3	80	12
	Lionel Taylor, Denver[2]	100	1,176	11.8	52	4
	Bill Groman, Houston[2]	50	1,175	23.5	80	17
	Tommy McDonald, Philadelphia	64	1,144	17.9	66	13
	Del Shofner, N.Y. Giants[2]	68	1,125	16.5	46	11
	Jim Phillips, Los Angeles	78	1,092	14.0	69	5
	*Mike Ditka, Chicago	56	1,076	19.2	76	12
	Dave Kocourek, San Diego	55	1,055	19.2	76	4
	Buddy Dial, Pittsburgh	53	1,047	19.8	88	12
	R.C. Owens, San Francisco	55	1,032	18.8	54	5
1960	*Bill Groman, Houston	72	1,473	20.5	92	12
	Raymond Berry, Baltimore	74	1,298	17.5	70	10
	Don Maynard, N.Y. Titans	72	1,265	17.6	65	6
	Lionel Taylor, Denver	92	1,235	13.4	80	12
	Art Powell, N.Y. Titans	69	1,167	16.9	76	14
1958	Del Shofner, Los Angeles	51	1,097	21.5	92	8
1956	Bill Howton, Green Bay[2]	55	1,188	21.6	66	12
	Harlon Hill, Chi. Bears[2]	47	1,128	24.0	79	11
1954	Bob Boyd, Los Angeles	53	1,212	22.9	80	6
	*Harlon Hill, Chi. Bears	45	1,124	25.0	76	12
1953	Pete Pihos, Philadelphia	63	1,049	16.7	59	10
1952	*Bill Howton, Green Bay	53	1,231	23.2	90	13
1951	Elroy (Crazylegs) Hirsch, Los Angeles	66	1,495	22.7	91	17
1950	Tom Fears, Los Angeles[2]	84	1,116	13.3	53	7
	Cloyce Box, Detroit	50	1,009	20.2	82	11
1949	Bob Mann, Detroit	66	1,014	15.4	64	4
	Tom Fears, Los Angeles	77	1,013	13.2	51	9
1945	Jim Benton, Cleveland	45	1,067	23.7	84	8
1942	Don Hutson, Green Bay	74	1,211	16.4	73	17

First season of professional football.

250 YARDS PASS RECEIVING IN A GAME

Date	Player, Team, Opponent	No.	Yards	TD
Dec. 17, 2000	Terrell Owens, San Francisco vs. Chicago	20	283	1
Sept. 10, 2000	Jimmy Smith, Jacksonville vs. Baltimore	15	291	3
Dec. 12, 1999	Qadry Ismail, Baltimore vs. Pittsburgh	6	258	3
Dec. 18, 1995	Jerry Rice, San Francisco vs. Minnesota	14	289	3
Dec. 11, 1989	John Taylor, San Francisco vs. L.A. Rams	11	286	2
Nov. 26, 1989	Willie Anderson, L.A. Rams vs. New Orleans (OT)	15	336	1
Oct. 18, 1987	Steve Largent, Seattle vs. Detroit	15	261	3
Oct. 4, 1987	Anthony Allen, Washington vs. St. Louis	7	255	3
Dec. 22, 1985	Stephone Paige, Kansas City vs. San Diego	8	309	2
Dec. 20, 1982	Wes Chandler, San Diego vs. Cincinnati	10	260	2
Sept. 23, 1979	*Jerry Butler, Buffalo vs. N.Y. Jets	10	255	4
Nov. 4, 1962	Sonny Randle, St. Louis vs. N.Y. Giants	16	256	1
Oct. 28, 1962	Del Shofner, N.Y. Giants vs. Washington	11	269	1
Oct. 13, 1961	Charley Hennigan, Houston vs. Boston	13	272	1
Oct. 21, 1956	Billy Howton, Green Bay vs. Los Angeles	7	257	2
Dec. 3, 1950	Cloyce Box, Detroit vs. Baltimore	12	302	4
Nov. 22, 1945	Jim Benton, Cleveland vs. Detroit	10	303	1

First season of professional football.

2,000 COMBINED NET YARDS GAINED IN A SEASON

Year	Player, Team	Rushing Att.-Yds.	Pass Rec.	Punt Ret.	Kickoff Ret.	Fum. Ret.	Total Yds.
2000	Derrick Mason, Tennessee	1-1	63-895	51-662	42-1,132	1-0	158-2,690

	MarTay Jenkins, Arizona	1-(-4)	17-219	1-1	82-2,186	0-0	101-2,402
	Edgerrin James, Indianapolis	387-1,709	63-594	0-0	0-0	0-0	450-2,303
	Marshall Faulk, St. Louis	253-1,359	81-830	0-0	1-18	2-0	337-2,207
	Tiki Barber, N.Y. Giants	213-1,006	70-719	39-332	1-28	5-0	328-2,085
1999	Marshall Faulk, St. Louis	253-1,381	87-1,048	0-0	0-0	0-0	340-2,429
	*Edgerrin James, Indianapolis	369-1,553	62-586	0-0	0-0	2-0	433-2,139
	*Terrence Wilkins, Indianapolis	1-2	42-565	41-388	51-1,134	1-0	136-2,089
	Glyn Milburn, Chicago	16-102	20-151	30-346	61-1,426	2-0	129-2,025
1998	Brian Mitchell, Washington	39-208	44-306	44-506	59-1,337	0-0	186-2,357
	Marshall Faulk, Indianapolis	324-1,319	86-908	0-0	0-0	2-13	412-2,240
	Terrell Davis, Denver	392-2,008	25-217	0-0	0-0	1-0	418-2,225
	Jamal Anderson, Atlanta	410-1,846	27-319	0-0	0-0	1-0	438-2,165
	Garrison Hearst, San Francisco	310-1,570	39-535	0-0	0-0	1-0	350-2,105
1997	Barry Sanders, Detroit	335-2,053	33-305	0-0	0-0	1-0	369-2,358
	Kevin Williams, Arizona	1-(-2)	20-273	40-462	59-1,458	1-0	121-2,191
	Brian Mitchell, Wash.	23-107	36-438	38-442	47-1,094	0-0	144-2,081
	Terrell Davis, Denver	369-1,750	42-287	0-0	0-0	2-(-7)	413-2,030
	Jermaine Lewis, Balt.	3-35	42-648	28-437	41-905	2-0	116-2,025
1995	Brian Mitchell, Wash.	46-301	38-324	25-315	55-1,408	0-0	164-2,348
	Emmitt Smith, Dallas	377-1,773	62-375	0-0	0-0	0-0	439-2,148
	Glyn Milburn, Denver	49-266	22-191	31-354	47-1,269	0-0	149-2,080
	Ernie Mills, Pittsburgh	5-39	39-679	0-0	54-1,306	0-0	98-2,024
1994	Brian Mitchell, Wash.	78-311	26-236	32-452	58-1,478	0-0	194-2,477
	Barry Sanders, Detroit	331-1,883	44-283	0-0	0-0	0-0	375-2,166
1992	Thurman Thomas, Buffalo	312-1,487	58-626	0-0	0-0	1-0	371-2,113
	Emmitt Smith, Dallas	373-1,713	59-335	0-0	0-0	1-0	433-2,048
	Barry Foster, Pittsburgh	390-1,690	36-344	0-0	0-0	2-(–20)	428-2,014
1991	Thurman Thomas, Buffalo	288-1,407	62-631	0-0	0-0	0-0	350-2,038
1990	Herschel Walker, Minnesota	184-770	35-315	0-0	44-966	4-0	267-2,051
1988	*Tim Brown, L.A. Raiders	14-50	43-725	49-444	41-1,098	7-0	154-2,317
	Roger Craig, San Fran.	310-1,502	76-534	0-0	2-32	2-0	390-2,068
	Eric Dickerson, Indianapolis	388-1,659	36-377	0-0	0-0	1-0	425-2,036
	Herschel Walker, Dallas	361-1,514	53-505	0-0	0-0	3-0	417-2,019
1986	Eric Dickerson, L.A. Rams	404-1,821	26-205	0-0	0-0	2-0	432-2,026
	Gary Anderson, San Diego	127-442	80-871	25-227	24-482	2-0	258-2,022
1985	Lionel James, San Diego	105-516	86-1,027	25-213	36-779	1-0	253-2,535
	Marcus Allen, L.A. Raiders	380-1,759	67-555	0-0	0-0	2-(–6)	449-2,308
	Roger Craig, San Fran.	214-1,050	92-1,016	0-0	0-0	0-0	306-2,066
	Walter Payton, Chicago	324-1,551	49-483	0-0	0-0	1-0	374-2,034
1984	Eric Dickerson, L.A. Rams	379-2,105	21-139	0-0	0-0	4-15	404-2,259
	James Wilder, Tampa Bay	407-1,544	85-685	0-0	0-0	4-0	496-2,229
	Walter Payton, Chicago	381-1,684	45-368	0-0	0-0	1-0	427-2,052
1983	*Eric Dickerson, L.A. Rams	390-1,808	51-404	0-0	0-0	1-0	442-2,212
	William Andrews, Atlanta	331-1,567	59-609	0-0	0-0	2-0	392-2,176
	Walter Payton, Chicago	314-1,421	53-607	0-0	0-0	2-0	369-2,028
1981	*James Brooks, San Diego	109-525	46-329	22-290	40-949	2-0	219-2,093
	William Andrews, Atlanta	289-1,301	81-735	0-0	0-0	0-0	370-2,036
1980	Bruce Harper, N.Y. Jets	45-126	50-634	28-242	49-1,070	3-0	175-2,072
1979	Wilbert Montgomery, Phil.	338-1,512	41-494	0-0	1-6	2-0	382-2,012
1978	Bruce Harper, N.Y. Jets	58-303	13-196	30-378	55-1,280	1-0	157-2,157
1977	Walter Payton, Chicago	339-1,852	27-269	0-0	2-95	5-0	373-2,216
	Terry Metcalf, St. Louis	149-739	34-403	14-108	32-772	1-0	230-2,022
1975	Terry Metcalf, St. Louis	165-816	43-378	23-285	35-960	2-23	268-2,462
	O.J. Simpson, Buffalo	329-1,817	28-426	0-0	0-0	1-0	358-2,243
1974	Mack Herron, New England	231-824	38-474	35-517	28-629	3-0	335-2,444
	Otis Armstrong, Denver	263-1,407	38-405	0-0	16-386	1-0	318-2,198
	Terry Metcalf, St. Louis	152-718	50-377	26-340	20-623	7-0	255-2,058
1973	O.J. Simpson, Buffalo	332-2,003	6-70	0-0	0-0	0-0	338-2,073
1966	Gale Sayers, Chicago	229-1,231	34-447	6-44	23-718	3-0	295-2,440
	Leroy Kelly, Cleveland	209-1,141	32-366	13-104	19-403	0-0	273-2,014
1965	*Gale Sayers, Chicago	166-867	29-507	16-238	21-660	4-0	236-2,272
1963	Timmy Brown, Philadelphia	192-841	36-487	16-152	33-945	2-3	279-2,428
	Jim Brown, Cleveland	291-1,863	24-268	0-0	0-0	0-0	315-2,131
1962	Timmy Brown, Philadelphia	137-545	52-849	6-81	30-831	4-0	229-2,306
	Dick Christy, N.Y. Titans	114-535	62-538	15-250	38-824	2-0	231-2,147
1961	Billy Cannon, Houston	200-948	43-586	9-70	18-439	2-0	272-2,043
1960	*Abner Haynes, Dall. Texans	156-875	55-576	14-215	19-434	4-0	248-2,100

**First season of professional football.*

300 COMBINED NET YARDS GAINED IN A GAME

Date	Player, Team, Opponent	No.	Yards	TD
Dec. 24, 1999	Jason Tucker, Dallas vs. New Orleans	13	331	1
Dec. 7, 1997	Jermaine Lewis, Baltimore vs. Seattle	10	308	3
Dec. 25, 1995	Kevin Williams, Dallas vs. Arizona	16	307	2
Dec. 10, 1995	Glyn Milburn, Denver vs. Seattle	33	404	0
Oct. 23, 1994	Tyrone Hughes, New Orleans vs. L.A. Rams	11	347	2
Dec. 11, 1989	John Taylor, San Francisco vs. L.A. Rams	14	321	2
Nov. 26, 1989	Willie Anderson, L.A. Rams vs. New Orleans (OT)	15	336	1
Nov. 28, 1988	*Tim Brown, L.A. Raiders vs. Seattle	12	308	1
Dec. 22, 1985	Stephone Paige, Kansas City vs. San Diego	8	309	2
Nov. 10, 1985	Lionel James, San Diego vs. L.A. Raiders (OT)	23	345	0
Sept. 22, 1985	Lionel James, San Diego vs. Cincinnati	20	316	2
Dec. 21, 1975	*Walter Payton, Chicago vs. New Orleans	32	300	1
Nov. 23, 1975	Greg Pruitt, Cleveland vs. Cincinnati	28	304	2
Nov. 1, 1970	Eugene (Mercury) Morris, Miami vs. Baltimore	17	302	0
Oct. 4, 1970	O.J. Simpson, Buffalo vs. N.Y. Jets	26	303	2
Dec. 6, 1969	Jerry LeVias, Houston vs. N.Y. Jets	18	329	1
Nov. 2, 1969	Travis Williams, Green Bay vs. Pittsburgh	11	314	3
Dec. 18, 1966	Gale Sayers, Chicago vs. Minnesota	20	339	2
Dec. 12, 1965	*Gale Sayers, Chicago vs. San Francisco	17	336	6
Nov. 17, 1963	Gary Ballman, Pittsburgh vs. Washington	12	320	2
Dec. 16, 1962	Timmy Brown, Philadelphia vs. St. Louis	19	341	2
Dec. 10, 1961	Billy Cannon, Houston vs. N.Y. Titans	32	373	5
Nov. 19, 1961	Jim Brown, Cleveland vs. Philadelphia	38	313	4
Dec. 3, 1950	Cloyce Box, Detroit vs. Baltimore	13	302	4
Oct. 29, 1950	Wally Triplett, Detroit vs. Los Angeles	11	331	1
Nov. 22, 1945	Jim Benton, Cleveland vs. Detroit	10	303	1

**First season of professional football.*

TOP 20 SCORERS

Player	Years	TD	FG	PAT	TP
Gary Anderson	19	0	461	676	2,059
George Blanda	26	9	335	943	2,002
Morten Andersen	19	0	441	615	1,938
Norm Johnson	18	0	366	638	1,736
Nick Lowery	18	0	383	562	1,711
Jan Stenerud	19	0	373	580	1,699
Eddie Murray	19	0	352	538	1,594
Al Del Greco	17	0	347	543	1,584
Pat Leahy	18	0	304	558	1,470
Jim Turner	16	1	304	521	1,439
Matt Bahr	17	0	300	522	1,422
Mark Moseley	16	0	300	482	1,382
Jim Bakken	17	0	282	534	1,380
Fred Cox	15	0	282	519	1,365
Lou Groza	17	1	234	641	1,349
Jim Breech	14	0	243	517	1,246
Pete Stoyanovich	12	0	272	420	1,236
Chris Bahr	14	0	241	490	1,213
Kevin Butler	13	0	265	413	1,208
Steve Christie	11	0	272	358	1,174

TOP 20 TOUCHDOWN SCORERS

Player	Years	Rush	Rec.	Total Returns	TD
Jerry Rice	16	10	176	1	187
Emmitt Smith	11	145	11	0	156
Marcus Allen	16	123	21	1	145
Jim Brown	9	106	20	0	126
Walter Payton	13	110	15	0	125
Cris Carter	14	0	123	1	124
John Riggins	14	104	12	0	116
Lenny Moore	12	63	48	2	113
Barry Sanders	10	99	10	0	109
Don Hutson	11	3	99	3	105
Steve Largent	14	1	100	0	101
Franco Harris	13	91	9	0	100
Eric Dickerson	11	90	6	0	96
Jim Taylor	10	83	10	0	93
Tony Dorsett	12	77	13	1	91
Bobby Mitchell	11	18	65	8	91
Tim Brown	13	1	86	3	90
Leroy Kelly	10	74	13	3	90
Charley Taylor	13	11	79	0	90
Ricky Watters	9	77	13	0	90

TOP 20 RUSHERS

Player	Years	Att.	Yards	Avg.	Long	TD
Walter Payton	13	3,838	16,726	4.4	76	110
Barry Sanders	10	3,062	15,269	5.0	85	99
Emmitt Smith	11	3,537	15,166	4.3	75	145
Eric Dickerson	11	2,996	13,259	4.4	85	90
Tony Dorsett	12	2,936	12,739	4.3	99	77
Jim Brown	9	2,359	12,312	5.2	80	106
Marcus Allen	16	3,022	12,243	4.1	61	123
Franco Harris	13	2,949	12,120	4.1	75	91
Thurman Thomas	13	2,877	12,074	4.2	80	65
John Riggins	14	2,916	11,352	3.9	66	104
O.J. Simpson	11	2,404	11,236	4.7	94	61
Ricky Watters	9	2,550	10,325	4.0	57	77
Ottis Anderson	14	2,562	10,273	4.0	76	81
Jerome Bettis	8	2,461	9,804	4.0	71	49
Earl Campbell	8	2,187	9,407	4.3	81	74
Jim Taylor	10	1,941	8,597	4.4	84	83
Joe Perry	14	1,737	8,378	4.8	78	53
Earnest Byner	14	2,095	8,261	3.9	54	56

Herschel Walker	12	1,954	8,225	4.2	91	61
Roger Craig	11	1,991	8,189	4.1	71	56

TOP 20 COMBINED YARDS GAINED

	Years	Tot.	Rush.	Rec.	Int. Ret.	Punt Ret.	Kickoff Ret.	Fumble Ret.
Walter Payton	13	21,803	16,726	4,538	0	0	539	0
Jerry Rice	16	19,878	625	19,247	0	0	6	0
Brian Mitchell	11	18,640	1,938	2,176	0	3,811	10,710	5
Barry Sanders	10	18,308	15,269	2,921	0	0	118	0
Herschel Walker	12	18,168	8,225	4,859	0	0	5,084	0
Emmitt Smith	11	17,973	15,166	2,807	0	0	0	0
Marcus Allen	16	17,648	12,243	5,411	0	0	0	-6
Eric Metcalf	11	16,727	2,385	5,553	0	3,042	5,747	0
Tim Brown	13	16,548	132	12,072	0	3,106	1,235	3
Thurman Thomas	13	16,532	12,074	4,458	0	0	0	0
Tony Dorsett	12	16,326	12,739	3,554	0	0	0	33
Henry Ellard	16	15,718	50	13,777	0	1,527	364	0
Irving Fryar	17	15,594	242	12,785	0	2,055	505	7
Jim Brown	10	15,459	12,312	2,499	0	0	648	0
Eric Dickerson	11	15,411	13,259	2,137	0	0	0	15
James Brooks	12	14,910	7,962	3,621	0	565	2,762	0
Franco Harris	13	14,622	12,120	2,287	0	0	233	-18
Glyn Milburn	8	14,575	814	1,313	0	2,812	9,636	0
Ricky Watters	9	14,466	10,325	4,141	0	0	0	0
O.J. Simpson	11	14,368	11,236	2,142	0	0	990	0

TOP 20 PASSERS

Player	Years	Att.	Comp.	Pct. Comp.	Yards	Avg. Gain	TD	Pct. TD	Int.	Pct. Int.	Rating
Steve Young	15	4,149	2,667	64.3	33,124	7.98	232	5.6	107	2.6	96.8
Joe Montana	15	5,391	3,409	63.2	40,551	7.52	273	5.1	139	2.6	92.3
Dan Marino	17	8,358	4,967	59.4	61,361	7.34	420	5.0	252	3.0	86.4
Brett Favre	10	4,932	2,997	60.8	34,706	7.04	255	5.2	157	3.2	86.0
Peyton Manning	3	1,679	1,014	60.4	12,287	7.32	85	5.1	58	3.5	85.4
Mark Brunell	7	2,672	1,608	60.2	19,212	7.19	106	4.0	66	2.5	85.1
Brad Johnson	7	1,821	1,126	61.8	12,973	7.12	79	4.3	57	3.1	84.7
Jim Kelly	11	4,779	2,874	60.1	35,467	7.42	237	5.0	175	3.7	84.4
Roger Staubach	11	2,958	1,685	57.0	22,700	7.67	153	5.2	109	3.7	83.4
Neil Lomax	8	3,153	1,817	57.6	22,771	7.22	136	4.3	90	2.9	82.7
Sonny Jurgensen	18	4,262	2,433	57.1	32,224	7.56	255	6.0	189	4.4	82.6
Len Dawson	19	3,741	2,136	57.1	28,711	7.67	239	6.4	183	4.9	82.6
Neil O'Donnell	11	3,121	1,802	57.7	20,938	6.71	116	3.7	65	2.1	81.9
Ken Anderson	16	4,475	2,654	59.3	32,838	7.34	197	4.4	160	3.6	81.9
Bernie Kosar	12	3,365	1,994	59.3	23,301	6.92	124	3.7	87	2.6	81.8
Danny White	13	2,950	1,761	59.7	21,959	7.44	155	5.3	132	4.5	81.7
Elvis Grbac	7	1,978	1,181	59.7	13,741	6.95	84	4.2	63	3.2	81.7
Troy Aikman	12	4,715	2,898	61.5	32,942	6.99	165	3.5	141	3.0	81.6
Dave Krieg	19	5,311	3,105	58.5	38,147	7.18	261	4.9	199	3.7	81.5
Randall Cunningham	15	4,200	2,375	56.6	29,406	7.00	204	4.9	132	3.1	81.5

1,500 or more attempts. The passing ratings are based on performance standards established for completion percentage, interception percentage, touchdown percentage, and average gain. Please consult page 16 for more information.

TOP 20 LEADERS IN PASSES COMPLETED

Dan Marino	4,967
John Elway	4,123
Warren Moon	3,988
Fran Tarkenton	3,686
Joe Montana	3,409
Dan Fouts	3,297
Dave Krieg	3,105
Brett Favre	2,997
Boomer Esiason	2,969
Troy Aikman	2,898
Vinny Testaverde	2,897
Steve DeBerg	2,874
Jim Kelly	2,874
Jim Everett	2,841
Johnny Unitas	2,830
Steve Young	2,667
Ken Anderson	2,654
Jim Hart	2,593
Phil Simms	2,576
Drew Bledsoe	2,504

TOP 20 LEADERS IN PASSING YARDS

Dan Marino	61,361
John Elway	51,475
Warren Moon	49,325
Fran Tarkenton	47,003
Dan Fouts	43,040
Joe Montana	40,551
Johnny Unitas	40,239
Dave Krieg	38,147
Boomer Esiason	37,920
Vinny Testaverde	36,307
Jim Kelly	35,467
Jim Everett	34,837
Brett Favre	34,706
Jim Hart	34,665
Steve DeBerg	34,241
John Hadl	33,503
Phil Simms	33,462
Steve Young	33,124
Troy Aikman	32,942
Ken Anderson	32,838

TOP 20 LEADERS IN TOUCHDOWN PASSES

Dan Marino	420
Fran Tarkenton	342
John Elway	300
Warren Moon	291
Johnny Unitas	290
Joe Montana	273
Dave Krieg	261
Brett Favre	255
Sonny Jurgensen	255
Dan Fouts	254
Boomer Esiason	247
John Hadl	244
Len Dawson	239
Jim Kelly	237
George Blanda	236
Steve Young	232
Vinny Testaverde	226
John Brodie	214
Terry Bradshaw	212
Y.A. Tittle	212

TOP 20 PASS RECEIVERS

Player	Years	No.	Yards	Avg.	Long	TD
Jerry Rice	16	1,281	19,247	15.0	96	176
Cris Carter	14	1,020	12,962	12.7	80	123
Andre Reed	16	951	13,198	13.9	83	87
Art Monk	16	940	12,721	13.5	79	68
Irving Fryar	17	851	12,785	15.0	80	84
Tim Brown	13	846	12,072	14.3	80	86
Steve Largent	14	819	13,089	16.0	74	100
Henry Ellard	16	814	13,777	16.9	81	65
James Lofton	16	764	14,004	18.3	80	75
Michael Irvin	12	750	11,904	15.9	87	65
Charlie Joiner	18	750	12,146	16.2	87	65
Andre Rison	12	743	10,205	13.7	80	84
Gary Clark	11	699	10,856	15.5	84	65
Larry Centers	11	685	5,683	8.3	54	25
Herman Moore	10	666	9,098	13.7	93	62
Ozzie Newsome	13	662	7,980	12.1	74	47
Charley Taylor	13	649	9,110	14.0	88	79
Drew Hill	14	634	9,831	15.5	81	60
Don Maynard	15	633	11,834	18.7	87	88
Raymond Berry	13	631	9,275	14.7	70	68

TOP 20 LEADERS IN RECEPTION YARDS

Jerry Rice	19,247
James Lofton	14,004
Henry Ellard	13,777
Andre Reed	13,198
Steve Largent	13,089
Cris Carter	12,962
Irving Fryar	12,785
Art Monk	12,721
Charlie Joiner	12,146
Tim Brown	12,072
Michael Irvin	11,904
Don Maynard	11,834
Gary Clark	10,856
Stanley Morgan	10,716
Harold Jackson	10,372
Lance Alworth	10,266
Andre Rison	10,205
Drew Hill	9,831
Rob Moore	9,368
Raymond Berry	9,275

TOP 20 INTERCEPTORS

Player	Years	No.	Yards	Avg.	Long	TD
Paul Krause	16	81	1,185	14.6	81	3
Emlen Tunnell	14	79	1,282	16.2	55	4
Dick (Night Train) Lane	14	68	1,207	17.8	80	5
Ken Riley	15	65	596	9.2	66	5
Ronnie Lott	14	63	730	11.6	83	5
Dick LeBeau	14	62	762	12.3	70	3
Dave Brown	15	62	698	11.3	90	5
Rod Woodson	14	58	1,183	20.4	66	9
Emmitt Thomas	13	58	937	16.2	73	5
Bobby Boyd	9	57	994	17.4	74	4
Eugene Robinson	16	57	762	13.4	49	1
Johnny Robinson	12	57	741	13.0	57	1
Mel Blount	14	57	736	12.9	52	2
Everson Walls	13	57	504	8.8	40	1
Lem Barney	11	56	1,077	19.2	71	7
Pat Fischer	17	56	941	16.8	69	4
Willie Brown	16	54	472	8.7	45	2
Eric Allen	13	53	807	15.2	94	8
Darrell Green	18	53	621	11.7	83	6
Bobby Dillon	8	52	976	18.8	61	5
Jack Butler	9	52	827	15.9	52	4
Larry Wilson	13	52	800	15.4	96	5
Jim Patton	12	52	712	13.7	51	2
Mel Renfro	14	52	626	12.0	90	3

TOP 20 PUNTERS

Player	Years	No.	Yards	Avg.	Long	Blk.
Sammy Baugh	16	338	15,245	45.1	85	9
Darren Bennett	6	524	23,492	44.8	66	1
Tommy Davis	11	511	22,833	44.7	82	2
Yale Lary	11	503	22,279	44.3	74	4
Tom Tupa	12	530	23,297	44.0	73	1
Bob Scarpitto	8	283	12,408	43.8	87	4
Horace Gillom	7	385	16,872	43.8	80	5
Jerry Norton	11	358	15,671	43.8	78	2
Tom Rouen	8	531	23,239	43.8	76	4
David Lewis	4	285	12,447	43.7	63	0
Greg Montgomery	9	524	22,831	43.6	77	8
Josh Miller	5	374	16,254	43.5	75	1
Don Chandler	12	660	28,678	43.5	90	4
Rick Tuten	11	741	32,190	43.4	73	2
Matt Turk	6	480	20,851	43.4	70	2
Rohn Stark	16	1,141	49,471	43.4	72	7
Sean Landeta	16	1,119	48,516	43.4	74	6
Reggie Roby	16	992	42,951	43.3	77	5
Mitch Berger	6	364	15,700	43.1	75	2
Chris Gardocki	10	726	31,311	43.1	72	0

250 or more punts.

TOP 20 PUNT RETURNERS

Player	Years	No.	Yards	Avg.	Long	TD
George McAfee	8	112	1,431	12.8	74	2
Jack Christiansen	8	85	1,084	12.8	89	8
Claude Gibson	5	110	1,381	12.6	85	3
Az-Zahir Hakim	3	76	950	12.5	86	2
Desmond Howard	9	213	2,646	12.4	95	8
Bill Dudley	9	124	1,515	12.2	96	3
Rick Upchurch	9	248	3,008	12.1	92	8
Darrien Gordon	7	248	2,984	12.0	94	6
Billy Johnson	14	282	3,317	11.8	87	6
Jermaine Lewis	5	189	2,211	11.7	89	6
Mack Herron	3	84	982	11.7	66	0
Karl Williams	5	120	1,393	11.6	88	3
Billy Thompson	13	157	1,814	11.6	60	0
Henry Ellard	16	135	1,527	11.3	83	4
Rodger Bird	3	94	1,063	11.3	78	0
Bosh Pritchard	6	95	1,072	11.3	81	2
Terry Metcalf	6	84	936	11.1	69	1
Bob Hayes	11	104	1,158	11.1	90	3
Floyd Little	9	81	893	11.0	72	2
Louis Lipps	9	112	1,234	11.0	76	3

75 or more returns.

TOP 20 KICKOFF RETURNERS

Player	Years	No.	Yards	Avg.	Long	TD
Gale Sayers	7	91	2,781	30.6	103	6
Lynn Chandnois	7	92	2,720	29.6	93	3
Abe Woodson	9	193	5,538	28.7	105	5
Claude (Buddy) Young	6	90	2,514	27.9	104	2
Travis Williams	5	102	2,801	27.5	105	6
Joe Arenas	7	139	3,798	27.3	96	1
Clarence Davis	8	79	2,140	27.1	76	0
Steve Van Buren	8	76	2,030	26.7	98	3
Lenny Lyles	12	81	2,161	26.7	103	3
MarTay Jenkins	2	82	2,186	26.7	98	1
Eugene (Mercury) Morris	8	111	2,947	26.5	105	3
Bobby Jancik	6	158	4,185	26.5	61	0
Mel Renfro	14	85	2,246	26.4	100	2
Bobby Mitchell	11	102	2,690	26.4	98	5
Ollie Matson	14	143	3,746	26.2	105	6
Alvin Haymond	10	170	4,438	26.1	98	2
Noland Smith	3	82	2,137	26.1	106	1
Al Nelson	9	101	2,625	26.0	78	0
Timmy Brown	11	184	4,781	26.0	105	5
Vic Washington	6	129	3,341	25.9	98	1

75 or more returns.

TOP 20 LEADERS IN SACKS

Player	*Years	No.
Reggie White	15	198.0
Bruce Smith	16	181.0
Kevin Greene	15	160.0
Chris Doleman	15	150.5
Richard Dent	15	137.5
Leslie O'Neal	13	132.5
Lawrence Taylor	12	132.5
Rickey Jackson	14	128.0
Derrick Thomas	11	126.5
Clyde Simmons	15	121.5
John Randle	11	114.0
Sean Jones	13	113.0
Greg Townsend	13	109.5
Pat Swilling	12	107.5
Neil Smith	13	104.5
Jim Jeffcoat	15	102.5
William Fuller	13	100.5
Charles Haley	12	100.5
Andre Tippett	11	100.0
Trace Armstrong	12	98.5

**Years played since 1982 when sacks became an official statistic.*

POSTSEASON LEADERS

TOP 10 RUSHERS

Player	Att.	Yards	Avg.	Long	TD
Emmitt Smith	349	1,586	4.5	65	19
Franco Harris	400	1,556	3.9	50	16
Thurman Thomas	339	1,442	4.3	40	16
Tony Dorsett	302	1,383	4.6	53	9
Marcus Allen	267	1,347	5.0	74	11
Terrell Davis	204	1,140	5.6	62	12
John Riggins	251	996	4.0	43	12
Larry Csonka	225	891	4.0	49	9
Chuck Foreman	229	860	3.8	62	7
Roger Craig	208	841	4.0	80	7

TOP 10 POSTSEASON PASSERS

Player	Att.	Comp.	Pct. Comp.	Yards	Avg. Gain	TD	Pct. TD	Int.	Pct. Int.	Rating
Bart Starr	213	130	61.0	1,753	8.23	15	7.0	3	1.4	104.8
Kurt Warner	161	101	62.7	1,428	8.87	11	6.8	7	4.3	96.0
Joe Montana	734	460	62.7	5,772	7.86	45	6.1	21	2.9	95.6
Ken Anderson	166	110	66.3	1,321	7.96	9	5.4	6	3.6	93.5
Joe Theismann	211	128	60.7	1,782	8.45	11	5.2	7	3.3	91.4
Brett Favre	449	270	60.1	3,390	7.55	25	5.6	12	2.7	91.1
Troy Aikman	502	320	63.8	3,849	7.67	23	4.6	17	3.4	88.3
Steve Young	471	292	62.0	3,326	7.06	20	4.2	13	2.8	85.8
Warren Moon	403	259	64.3	2,870	7.12	17	4.2	14	3.5	84.9
Ken Stabler	351	203	57.8	2,641	7.52	19	5.4	13	3.7	84.2

150 or more attempts. The passer ratings are based on performance standards established for completion percentage, interception percentage, touchdown percentage, and average gain. Please consult page 16 for more information.

TOP 10 POSTSEASON PASS RECEIVERS

Player	No.	Yards	Avg.	Long	TD
Jerry Rice	124	1,811	14.6	72	19
Michael Irvin	87	1,315	15.1	53	8
Andre Reed	85	1,229	14.5	72	9
Thurman Thomas	76	672	8.8	27	5
Cliff Branch	73	1,289	17.7	72	5
Fred Biletnikoff	70	1,167	16.7	57	10
Art Monk	69	1,062	15.4	48	7
Drew Pearson	67	1,105	16.5	83	8
Tony Nathan	65	649	10.0	39	2
Cris Carter	63	870	13.8	66	8
Roger Craig	63	606	9.6	40	2

OUTSTANDING PERFORMERS

TOP 10 POSTSEASON INTERCEPTION LEADERS

Player	Interceptions
Ronnie Lott	9
Bill Simpson	9
Charlie Waters	9
Lester Hayes	8
Willie Brown	7
Dennis Thurman	7
Bobby Bryant	6
Eric Davis	6
Glen Edwards	6
Darrell Green	6
Cliff Harris	6
Vernon Perry	6

TOP 10 POSTSEASON SACK LEADERS

Player	Sacks
Bruce Smith	14.5
Reggie White	12.0
Charles Haley	11.0
Richard Dent	10.5
Trace Armstrong	10.0
Charles Mann	10.0
Tony Tolbert	10.0
Neil Smith	9.5
Jeff Wright	9.0
Kevin Greene	8.5

ANNUAL SCORING LEADERS

Year	Player, Team	TD	FG	PAT	TP
2000	Marshall Faulk, St. Louis, NFC	26	0	0	##160
	Matt Stover, Baltimore, AFC	0	35	30	135
1999	Mike Vanderjagt, Indianapolis, AFC	0	34	43	145
	Jeff Wilkins, St. Louis, NFC	0	20	64	124
1998	Gary Anderson, Minnesota, NFC	0	35	59	164
	Steve Christie, Buffalo, AFC	0	33	41	140
1997	Mike Hollis, Jacksonville, AFC	0	31	41	134
	Richie Cunningham, Dallas, NFC	0	34	24	126
1996	John Kasay, Carolina, NFC	0	37	34	145
	Cary Blanchard, Indianapolis, AFC	0	36	27	135
1995	Emmitt Smith, Dallas, NFC	25	0	0	150
	Norm Johnson, Pittsburgh, AFC	0	34	39	141
1994	John Carney, San Diego, AFC	0	34	33	135
	Fuad Reveiz, Minnesota, NFC	0	34	30	132
1993	Jeff Jaeger, L.A. Raiders, AFC	0	35	27	132
	Jason Hanson, Detroit, NFC	0	34	28	130
1992	Pete Stoyanovich, Miami, AFC	0	30	34	124
	Morten Andersen, New Orleans, NFC	0	29	33	120
	Chip Lohmiller, Washington, NFC	0	30	30	120
1991	Chip Lohmiller, Washington, NFC	0	31	56	149
	Pete Stoyanovich, Miami, AFC	0	31	28	121
1990	Nick Lowery, Kansas City, AFC	0	34	37	139
	Chip Lohmiller, Washington, NFC	0	30	41	131
1989	Mike Cofer, San Francisco, NFC	0	29	49	136
	*David Treadwell, Denver, AFC	0	27	39	120
1988	Scott Norwood, Buffalo, AFC	0	32	33	129
	Mike Cofer, San Francisco, NFC	0	27	40	121
1987	Jerry Rice, San Francisco, NFC	23	0	0	138
	Jim Breech, Cincinnati, AFC	0	24	25	97
1986	Tony Franklin, New England, AFC	0	32	44	140
	Kevin Butler, Chicago, NFC	0	28	36	120
1985	*Kevin Butler, Chicago, NFC	0	31	51	144
	Gary Anderson, Pittsburgh, AFC	0	33	40	139
1984	Ray Wersching, San Francisco, NFC	0	25	56	131
	Gary Anderson, Pittsburgh, AFC	0	24	45	117
1983	Mark Moseley, Washington, NFC	0	33	62	161
	Gary Anderson, Pittsburgh, AFC	0	27	38	119
1982	*Marcus Allen, L.A. Raiders, AFC	14	0	0	84
	Wendell Tyler, L.A. Rams, NFC	13	0	0	78
1981	Ed Murray, Detroit, NFC	0	25	46	121
	Rafael Septien, Dallas, NFC	0	27	40	121
	Jim Breech, Cincinnati, AFC	0	22	49	115
	Nick Lowery, Kansas City, AFC	0	26	37	115
1980	John Smith, New England, AFC	0	26	51	129
	*Ed Murray, Detroit, NFC	0	27	35	116
1979	John Smith, New England, AFC	0	23	46	115
	Mark Moseley, Washington, NFC	0	25	39	114
1978	*Frank Corral, Los Angeles, NFC	0	29	31	118
	Pat Leahy, N.Y. Jets, AFC	0	22	41	107
1977	Errol Mann, Oakland, AFC	0	20	39	99
	Walter Payton, Chicago, NFC	16	0	0	96
1976	Toni Linhart, Baltimore, AFC	0	20	49	109
	Mark Moseley, Washington, NFC	0	22	31	97
1975	O.J. Simpson, Buffalo, AFC	23	0	0	138
	Chuck Foreman, Minnesota, NFC	22	0	0	132
1974	Chester Marcol, Green Bay, NFC	0	25	19	94
	Roy Gerela, Pittsburgh, AFC	0	20	33	93
1973	David Ray, Los Angeles, NFC	0	30	40	130
	Roy Gerela, Pittsburgh, AFC	0	29	36	123
1972	*Chester Marcol, Green Bay, NFC	0	33	29	128
	Bobby Howfield, N.Y. Jets, AFC	0	27	40	121
1971	Garo Yepremian, Miami, AFC	0	28	33	117
	Curt Knight, Washington, NFC	0	29	27	114
1970	Fred Cox, Minnesota, NFC	0	30	35	125
	Jan Stenerud, Kansas City, AFC	0	30	26	116
1969	Jim Turner, N.Y. Jets, AFL	0	32	33	129
	Fred Cox, Minnesota, NFL	0	26	43	121
1968	Jim Turner, N.Y. Jets, AFL	0	34	43	145
	Leroy Kelly, Cleveland, NFL	20	0	0	120
1967	Jim Bakken, St. Louis, NFL	0	27	36	117
	George Blanda, Oakland, AFL	0	20	56	116
1966	Gino Cappelletti, Boston, AFL	6	16	35	119
	Bruce Gossett, Los Angeles, NFL	0	28	29	113
1965	*Gale Sayers, Chicago, NFL	22	0	0	132
	Gino Cappelletti, Boston, AFL	9	17	27	132
1964	Gino Cappelletti, Boston, AFL	7	25	36	#155
	Lenny Moore, Baltimore, NFL	20	0	0	120
1963	Gino Cappelletti, Boston, AFL	2	22	35	113
	Don Chandler, N.Y. Giants, NFL	0	18	52	106
1962	Gene Mingo, Denver, AFL	4	27	32	137
	Jim Taylor, Green Bay, NFL	19	0	0	114
1961	Gino Cappelletti, Boston, AFL	8	17	48	147
	Paul Hornung, Green Bay, NFL	10	15	41	146
1960	Paul Hornung, Green Bay, NFL	15	15	41	176
	*Gene Mingo, Denver, AFL	6	18	33	123
1959	Paul Hornung, Green Bay	7	7	31	94
1958	Jim Brown, Cleveland	18	0	0	108
1957	Sam Baker, Washington	1	14	29	77
	Lou Groza, Cleveland	0	15	32	77
1956	Bobby Layne, Detroit	5	12	33	99
1955	Doak Walker, Detroit	7	9	27	96
1954	Bobby Walston, Philadelphia	11	4	36	114
1953	Gordy Soltau, San Francisco	6	10	48	114
1952	Gordy Soltau, San Francisco	7	6	34	94
1951	Elroy (Crazylegs) Hirsch, Los Angeles	17	0	0	102
1950	*Doak Walker, Detroit	11	8	38	128
1949	Pat Harder, Chi. Cardinals	8	3	45	102
	Gene Roberts, N.Y. Giants	17	0	0	102
1948	Pat Harder, Chi. Cardinals	6	7	53	110
1947	Pat Harder, Chi. Cardinals	7	7	39	102
1946	Ted Fritsch, Green Bay	10	9	13	100
1945	Steve Van Buren, Philadelphia	18	0	2	110
1944	Don Hutson, Green Bay	9	0	31	85
1943	Don Hutson, Green Bay	12	3	36	117
1942	Don Hutson, Green Bay	17	1	33	138
1941	Don Hutson, Green Bay	12	1	20	95
1940	Don Hutson, Green Bay	7	0	15	57
1939	Andy Farkas, Washington	11	0	2	68
1938	Clarke Hinkle, Green Bay	7	3	7	58
1937	Jack Manders, Chi. Bears	5	8	15	69
1936	Earl (Dutch) Clark, Detroit	7	4	19	73
1935	Earl (Dutch) Clark, Detroit	6	1	16	55
1934	Jack Manders, Chi. Bears	3	10	31	79
1933	Ken Strong, N.Y. Giants	6	5	13	64
	Glenn Presnell, Portsmouth	6	6	10	64
1932	Earl (Dutch) Clark, Portsmouth	6	3	10	55

**First season of professional football.*

#Cappelletti's total includes a two-point conversion.

##Faulk's total includes 2 two-point conversions.

ANNUAL TOUCHDOWN LEADERS

Year	Player, Team	TD	Rush	Pass	Ret.
2000	Marshall Faulk, St. Louis, NFC	26	18	8	0
	Edgerrin James, Indianapolis, AFC	18	13	5	0
1999	Stephen Davis, Washington, NFC	17	17	0	0
	*Edgerrin James, Indianapolis, AFC	17	13	4	0
1998	Terrell Davis, Denver, AFC	23	21	2	0
	*Randy Moss, Minnesota, NFC	17	0	17	0
1997	Karim Abdul-Jabbar, Miami, AFC	16	15	1	0
	Barry Sanders, Detroit, NFC	14	11	3	0
1996	Terry Allen, Washington, NFC	21	21	0	0
	Curtis Martin, New England, AFC	17	14	3	0
1995	Emmitt Smith, Dallas, NFC	25	25	0	0
	Carl Pickens, Cincinnati, AFC	17	0	17	0
1994	Emmitt Smith, Dallas, NFC	22	21	1	0
	*Marshall Faulk, Indianapolis, AFC	12	11	1	0
	Natrone Means, San Diego, AFC	12	12	0	0
1993	Jerry Rice, San Francisco, NFC	16	1	15	0
	Marcus Allen, Kansas City, AFC	15	12	3	0
1992	Emmitt Smith, Dallas, NFC	19	18	1	0
	Thurman Thomas, Buffalo, AFC	12	9	3	0
1991	Barry Sanders, Detroit, NFC	17	16	1	0
	Mark Clayton, Miami, AFC	12	0	12	0
	Thurman Thomas, Buffalo, AFC	12	7	5	0
1990	Barry Sanders, Detroit, NFC	16	13	3	0
	Derrick Fenner, Seattle, AFC	15	14	1	0
1989	Dalton Hilliard, New Orleans, NFC	18	13	5	0
	Christian Okoye, Kansas City, AFC	12	12	0	0
	Thurman Thomas, Buffalo, AFC	12	6	6	0
1988	Greg Bell, L.A. Rams, NFC	18	16	2	0
	Eric Dickerson, Indianapolis, AFC	15	14	1	0
	*Ickey Woods, Cincinnati, AFC	15	15	0	0
1987	Jerry Rice, San Francisco, NFC	23	1	22	0
	Johnny Hector, N.Y. Jets, AFC	11	11	0	0
1986	George Rogers, Washington, NFC	18	18	0	0
	Sammy Winder, Denver, AFC	14	9	5	0
1985	Joe Morris, N.Y. Giants, NFC	21	21	0	0
	Louis Lipps, Pittsburgh, AFC	15	1	12	2
1984	Marcus Allen, L.A. Raiders, AFC	18	13	5	0
	Mark Clayton, Miami, AFC	18	0	18	0
	Eric Dickerson, L.A. Rams, NFC	14	14	0	0
	John Riggins, Washington, NFC	14	14	0	0
1983	John Riggins, Washington, NFC	24	24	0	0
	Pete Johnson, Cincinnati, AFC	14	14	0	0

	*Curt Warner, Seattle, AFC	14	13	1	0
1982	*Marcus Allen, L.A. Raiders, AFC	14	11	3	0
	Wendell Tyler, L.A. Rams, NFC	13	9	4	0
1981	Chuck Muncie, San Diego, AFC	19	19	0	0
	Wendell Tyler, Los Angeles, NFC	17	12	5	0
1980	*Billy Sims, Detroit, NFC	16	13	3	0
	Earl Campbell, Houston, AFC	13	13	0	0
	*Curtis Dickey, Baltimore, AFC	13	11	2	0
	John Jefferson, San Diego, AFC	13	0	13	0
1979	Earl Campbell, Houston, AFC	19	19	0	0
	Walter Payton, Chicago, NFC	16	14	2	0
1978	David Sims, Seattle, AFC	15	14	1	0
	Terdell Middleton, Green Bay, NFC	12	11	1	0
1977	Walter Payton, Chicago, NFC	16	14	2	0
	Nat Moore, Miami, AFC	13	1	12	0
1976	Chuck Foreman, Minnesota, NFC	14	13	1	0
	Franco Harris, Pittsburgh, AFC	14	14	0	0
1975	O.J. Simpson, Buffalo, AFC	23	16	7	0
	Chuck Foreman, Minnesota, NFC	22	13	9	0
1974	Chuck Foreman, Minnesota, NFC	15	9	6	0
	Cliff Branch, Oakland, AFC	13	0	13	0
1973	Larry Brown, Washington, NFC	14	8	6	0
	Floyd Little, Denver, AFC	13	12	1	0
1972	Emerson Boozer, N.Y. Jets, AFC	14	11	3	0
	Ron Johnson, N.Y. Giants, NFC	14	9	5	0
1971	Duane Thomas, Dallas, NFC	13	11	2	0
	Leroy Kelly, Cleveland, AFC	12	10	2	0
1970	Dick Gordon, Chicago, NFC	13	0	13	0
	MacArthur Lane, St. Louis, NFC	13	11	2	0
	Gary Garrison, San Diego, AFC	12	0	12	0
1969	Warren Wells, Oakland, AFL	14	0	14	0
	Tom Matte, Baltimore, NFL	13	11	2	0
	Lance Rentzel, Dallas, NFL	13	0	12	1
1968	Leroy Kelly, Cleveland, NFL	20	16	4	0
	Warren Wells, Oakland, AFL	12	1	11	0
1967	Homer Jones, N.Y. Giants, NFL	14	1	13	0
	Emerson Boozer, N.Y. Jets, AFL	13	10	3	0
1966	Leroy Kelly, Cleveland, NFL	16	15	1	0
	Dan Reeves, Dallas, NFL	16	8	8	0
	Lance Alworth, San Diego, AFL	13	0	13	0
1965	*Gale Sayers, Chicago, NFL	22	14	6	2
	Lance Alworth, San Diego, AFL	14	0	14	0
	Don Maynard, N.Y. Jets, AFL	14	0	14	0
1964	Lenny Moore, Baltimore, NFL	20	16	3	1
	Lance Alworth, San Diego, AFL	15	2	13	0
1963	Art Powell, Oakland, AFL	16	0	16	0
	Jim Brown, Cleveland, NFL	15	12	3	0
1962	Abner Haynes, Dallas, AFL	19	13	6	0
	Jim Taylor, Green Bay, NFL	19	19	0	0
1961	Bill Groman, Houston, AFL	18	1	17	0
	Jim Taylor, Green Bay, NFL	16	15	1	0
1960	Paul Hornung, Green Bay, NFL	15	13	2	0
	Sonny Randle, St. Louis, NFL	15	0	15	0
	Art Powell, N.Y. Titans, AFL	14	0	14	0
1959	Raymond Berry, Baltimore	14	0	14	0
	Jim Brown, Cleveland	14	14	0	0
1958	Jim Brown, Cleveland	18	17	1	0
1957	Lenny Moore, Baltimore	11	3	7	1
1956	Rick Casares, Chi. Bears	14	12	2	0
1955	*Alan Ameche, Baltimore	9	9	0	0
	Harlon Hill, Chi. Bears	9	0	9	0
1954	*Harlon Hill, Chi. Bears	12	0	12	0
1953	Joseph Perry, San Francisco	13	10	3	0
1952	Cloyce Box, Detroit	15	0	15	0
1951	Elroy (Crazylegs) Hirsch, Los Angeles	17	0	17	0
1950	Bob Shaw, Chi. Cardinals	12	0	12	0
1949	Gene Roberts, N.Y. Giants	17	9	8	0
1948	Mal Kutner, Chi. Cardinals	15	1	14	0
1947	Steve Van Buren, Philadelphia	14	13	0	1
1946	Ted Fritsch, Green Bay	10	9	1	0
1945	Steve Van Buren, Philadelphia	18	15	2	1
1944	Don Hutson, Green Bay	9	0	9	0
	Bill Paschal, N.Y. Giants	9	9	0	0
1943	Don Hutson, Green Bay	12	0	11	1
	*Bill Paschal, N.Y. Giants	12	10	2	0
1942	Don Hutson, Green Bay	17	0	17	0
1941	Don Hutson, Green Bay	12	2	10	0
	George McAfee, Chi. Bears	12	6	3	3
1940	John Drake, Cleveland	9	9	0	0
	Richard Todd, Washington	9	4	4	1
1939	Andrew Farkas, Washington	11	5	5	1
1938	Don Hutson, Green Bay	9	0	9	0
1937	Cliff Battles, Washington	7	5	1	1
	Clarke Hinkle, Green Bay	7	5	2	0
	Don Hutson, Green Bay	7	0	7	0
1936	Don Hutson, Green Bay	9	0	8	1
1935	*Don Hutson, Green Bay	7	0	6	1
1934	*Beattie Feathers, Chi. Bears	9	8	1	0
1933	*Charlie (Buckets) Goldenberg, Green Bay	7	4	1	2
	John (Shipwreck) Kelly, Brooklyn	7	2	3	2
	*Elvin (Kink) Richards, N.Y. Giants	7	4	3	0
1932	Earl (Dutch) Clark, Portsmouth	6	3	3	0
	Red Grange, Chi. Bears	6	3	3	0

**First season of professional football.*

ANNUAL LEADERS—MOST FIELD GOALS MADE

Year	Player, Team	Att.	Made	Pct.
2000	Matt Stover, Baltimore, AFC	39	35	89.7
	Ryan Longwell, Green Bay, NFC	38	33	86.8
1999	Olindo Mare, Miami, AFC	46	39	84.8
	*Martin Gramatica, Tampa Bay, NFC	32	27	84.4
1998	Al Del Greco, Tennessee, AFC	39	36	92.3
	Gary Anderson, Minnesota, NFC	35	35	100.0
1997	Richie Cunningham, Dallas, NFC	37	34	91.9
	Cary Blanchard, Indianapolis, AFC	41	32	78.1
1996	John Kasay, Carolina, NFC	45	37	82.2
	Cary Blanchard, Indianapolis, AFC	40	36	90.0
1995	Norm Johnson, Pittsburgh, AFC	41	34	82.9
	Morten Andersen, Atlanta, NFC	37	31	83.8
1994	John Carney, San Diego, AFC	38	34	89.5
	Fuad Reveiz, Minnesota, NFC	39	34	87.2
1993	Jeff Jaeger, L.A. Raiders, AFC	44	35	79.5
	Jason Hanson, Detroit, NFC	43	34	79.1
1992	Pete Stoyanovich, Miami, AFC	37	30	81.1
	Chip Lohmiller, Washington, NFC	40	30	75.0
1991	Pete Stoyanovich, Miami, AFC	37	31	83.8
	Chip Lohmiller, Washington, NFC	43	31	72.1
1990	Nick Lowery, Kansas City, AFC	37	34	91.9
	Chip Lohmiller, Washington, NFC	40	30	75.0
1989	Rich Karlis, Minnesota, NFC	39	31	79.5
	*David Treadwell, Denver, AFC	33	27	81.8
1988	Scott Norwood, Buffalo, AFC	37	32	86.5
	Mike Cofer, San Francisco, NFC	38	27	71.1
1987	Morten Andersen, New Orleans, NFC	36	28	77.8
	Dean Biasucci, Indianpolis, AFC	27	24	88.9
	Jim Breech, Cincinnati, AFC	30	24	80.0
1986	Tony Franklin, New England, AFC	41	32	78.0
	Kevin Butler, Chicago, NFC	41	28	68.3
1985	Gary Anderson, Pittsburgh, AFC	42	33	78.6
	Morten Andersen, New Orleans, NFC	35	31	88.6
	*Kevin Butler, Chicago, NFC	37	31	83.8
1984	*Paul McFadden, Philadelphia, NFC	37	30	81.1
	Gary Anderson, Pittsburgh, AFC	32	24	75.0
	Matt Bahr, Cleveland, AFC	32	24	75.0
1983	*Ali-Haji-Sheikh, N.Y. Giants, NFC	42	35	83.3
	*Raul Allegre, Baltimore, AFC	35	30	85.7
1982	Mark Moseley, Washington, NFC	21	20	95.2
	Nick Lowery, Kansas City, AFC	24	19	79.2
1981	Rafael Septien, Dallas, NFC	35	27	77.1
	Nick Lowery, Kansas City, AFC	36	26	72.2
1980	*Ed Murray, Detroit, NFC	42	27	64.3
	John Smith, New England, AFC	34	26	76.5
	Fred Steinfort, Denver, AFC	34	26	76.5
1979	Mark Moseley, Washington, NFC	33	25	75.8
	John Smith, New England, AFC	33	23	69.7
1978	*Frank Corral, Los Angeles, NFC	43	29	67.4
	Pat Leahy, N.Y. Jets, AFC	30	22	73.3
1977	Mark Moseley, Washington, NFC	37	21	56.8
	Errol Mann, Oakland, AFC	28	20	71.4
1976	Mark Moseley, Washington, NFC	34	22	64.7
	Jan Stenerud, Kansas City, AFC	38	21	55.3
1975	Jan Stenerud, Kansas City, AFC	32	22	68.8
	Toni Fritsch, Dallas, NFC	35	22	62.9
1974	Chester Marcol, Green Bay, NFC	39	25	64.1
	Roy Gerela, Pittsburgh, AFC	29	20	69.0
1973	David Ray, Los Angeles, NFC	47	30	63.8
	Roy Gerela, Pittsburgh, AFC	43	29	67.4
1972	*Chester Marcol, Green Bay, NFC	48	33	68.8
	Roy Gerela, Pittsburgh, AFC	41	28	68.3
1971	Curt Knight, Washington, NFC	49	29	59.2
	Garo Yepremian, Miami, AFC	40	28	70.0
1970	Jan Stenerud, Kansas City, AFC	42	30	71.4
	Fred Cox, Minnesota, NFC	46	30	65.2
1969	Jim Turner, N.Y. Jets, AFL	47	32	68.1
	Fred Cox, Minnesota, NFL	37	26	70.3
1968	Jim Turner, N.Y. Jets, AFL	46	34	73.9

Year	Player, Team			
	Mac Percival, Chicago, NFL	36	25	69.4
1967	Jim Bakken, St. Louis, NFL	39	27	69.2
	Jan Stenerud, Kansas City, AFL	36	21	58.3
1966	Bruce Gossett, Los Angeles, NFL	49	28	57.1
	Mike Mercer, Oakland-Kansas City, AFL	30	21	70.0
1965	Pete Gogolak, Buffalo, AFL	46	28	60.9
	Fred Cox, Minnesota, NFL	35	23	65.7
1964	Jim Bakken, St. Louis, NFL	38	25	65.8
	Gino Cappelletti, Boston, AFL	39	25	64.1
1963	Jim Martin, Baltimore, NFL	39	24	61.5
	Gino Cappelletti, Boston, AFL	38	22	57.9
1962	Gene Mingo, Denver, AFL	39	27	69.2
	Lou Michaels, Pittsburgh, NFL	42	26	61.9
1961	Steve Myhra, Baltimore, NFL	39	21	53.8
	Gino Cappelletti, Boston, AFL	32	17	53.1
1960	Tommy Davis, San Francisco, NFL	32	19	59.4
	*Gene Mingo, Denver, AFL	28	18	64.3
1959	Pat Summerall, N.Y. Giants	29	20	69.0
1958	Paige Cothren, Los Angeles	25	14	56.0
	*Tom Miner, Pittsburgh	28	14	50.0
1957	Lou Groza, Cleveland	22	15	68.2
1956	Sam Baker, Washington	25	17	68.0
1955	Fred Cone, Green Bay	24	16	66.7
1954	Lou Groza, Cleveland	24	16	66.7
1953	Lou Groza, Cleveland	26	23	88.5
1952	Lou Groza, Cleveland	33	19	57.6
1951	Bob Waterfield, Los Angeles	23	13	56.5
1950	Lou Groza, Cleveland	19	13	68.4
1949	Cliff Patton, Philadelphia	18	9	50.0
	Bob Waterfield, Los Angeles	16	9	56.3
1948	Cliff Patton, Philadelphia	12	8	66.7
1947	Ward Cuff, Green Bay	16	7	43.8
	Pat Harder, Chi. Cardinals	10	7	70.0
	Bob Waterfield, Los Angeles	16	7	43.8
1946	Ted Fritsch, Green Bay	17	9	52.9
1945	Joe Aguirre, Washington	13	7	53.8
1944	Ken Strong, N.Y. Giants	12	6	50.0
1943	Ward Cuff, N.Y. Giants	9	3	33.3
	Don Hutson, Green Bay	5	3	60.0
1942	Bill Daddio, Chi. Cardinals	10	5	50.0
1941	Clarke Hinkle, Green Bay	14	6	42.9
1940	Clarke Hinkle, Green Bay	14	9	64.3
1939	Ward Cuff, N.Y. Giants	16	7	43.8
1938	Ward Cuff, N.Y. Giants	9	5	55.6
	Ralph Kercheval, Brooklyn	13	5	38.5
1937	Jack Manders, Chi. Bears		8	
1936	Jack Manders, Chi. Bears		7	
	Armand Niccolai, Pittsburgh		7	
1935	Armand Niccolai, Pittsburgh		6	
	Bill Smith, Chi. Cardinals		6	
1934	Jack Manders, Chi. Bears		10	
1933	*Jack Manders, Chi. Bears		6	
	Glenn Presnell, Portsmouth		6	
1932	Earl (Dutch) Clark, Portsmouth		3	

**First season of professional football.*

ANNUAL RUSHING LEADERS

Year	Player, Team	Att.	Yards	Avg.	TD
2000	Edgerrin James, Indianapolis, AFC	387	1,709	4.4	13
	Robert Smith, Minnesota, NFC	295	1,521	5.2	7
1999	*Edgerrin James, Indianapolis, AFC	369	1,553	4.2	13
	Stephen Davis, Washington, NFC	290	1,405	4.8	17
1998	Terrell Davis, Denver, AFC	392	2,008	5.1	21
	Jamal Anderson, Atlanta, NFC	410	1,846	4.5	14
1997	Barry Sanders, Detroit, NFC	335	2,053	6.1	11
	Terrell Davis, Denver, AFC	369	1,750	4.7	15
1996	Barry Sanders, Detroit, NFC	307	1,553	5.1	11
	Terrell Davis, Denver, AFC	345	1,538	4.5	13
1995	Emmitt Smith, Dallas, NFC	377	1,773	4.7	25
	*Curtis Martin, New England, AFC	368	1,487	4.0	14
1994	Barry Sanders, Detroit, NFC	331	1,883	5.7	7
	Chris Warren, Seattle, AFC	333	1,545	4.6	9
1993	Emmitt Smith, Dallas, NFC	283	1,486	5.3	9
	Thurman Thomas, Buffalo, AFC	355	1,315	3.7	6
1992	Emmitt Smith, Dallas, NFC	373	1,713	4.6	18
	Barry Foster, Pittsburgh, AFC	390	1,690	4.3	11
1991	Emmitt Smith, Dallas, NFC	365	1,563	4.3	12
	Thurman Thomas, Buffalo, AFC	288	1,407	4.9	7
1990	Barry Sanders, Detroit, NFC	255	1,304	5.1	13
	Thurman Thomas, Buffalo, AFC	271	1,297	4.8	11
1989	Christian Okoye, Kansas City, AFC	370	1,480	4.0	12
	*Barry Sanders, Detroit, NFC	280	1,470	5.3	14
1988	Eric Dickerson, Indianapolis, AFC	388	1,659	4.3	14
	Herschel Walker, Dallas, NFC	361	1,514	4.2	5
1987	Charles White, L.A. Rams, NFC	324	1,374	4.2	11
	Eric Dickerson, Indianapolis, AFC	223	1,011	4.5	5
1986	Eric Dickerson, L.A. Rams, NFC	404	1,821	4.5	11
	Curt Warner, Seattle, AFC	319	1,481	4.6	13
1985	Marcus Allen, L.A. Raiders, AFC	380	1,759	4.6	11
	Gerald Riggs, Atlanta, NFC	397	1,719	4.3	10
1984	Eric Dickerson, L.A. Rams, NFC	379	2,105	5.6	14
	Earnest Jackson, San Diego, AFC	296	1,179	4.0	8
1983	*Eric Dickerson, L.A. Rams, NFC	390	1,808	4.6	18
	*Curt Warner, Seattle, AFC	335	1,449	4.3	13
1982	Freeman McNeil, N.Y. Jets, AFC	151	786	5.2	6
	Tony Dorsett, Dallas, NFC	177	745	4.2	5
1981	*George Rogers, New Orleans, NFC	378	1,674	4.4	13
	Earl Campbell, Houston, AFC	361	1,376	3.8	10
1980	Earl Campbell, Houston, AFC	373	1,934	5.2	13
	Walter Payton, Chicago, NFC	317	1,460	4.6	6
1979	Earl Campbell, Houston, AFC	368	1,697	4.6	19
	Walter Payton, Chicago, NFC	369	1,610	4.4	14
1978	*Earl Campbell, Houston, AFC	302	1,450	4.8	13
	Walter Payton, Chicago, NFC	333	1,395	4.2	11
1977	Walter Payton, Chicago, NFC	339	1,852	5.5	14
	Mark van Eeghen, Oakland, AFC	324	1,273	3.9	7
1976	O.J. Simpson, Buffalo, AFC	290	1,503	5.2	8
	Walter Payton, Chicago, NFC	311	1,390	4.5	13
1975	O.J. Simpson, Buffalo, AFC	329	1,817	5.5	16
	Jim Otis, St. Louis, NFC	269	1,076	4.0	5
1974	Otis Armstrong, Denver, AFC	263	1,407	5.3	9
	Lawrence McCutcheon, Los Angeles, NFC	236	1,109	4.7	3
1973	O.J. Simpson, Buffalo, AFC	332	2,003	6.0	12
	John Brockington, Green Bay, NFC	265	1,144	4.3	3
1972	O.J. Simpson, Buffalo, AFC	292	1,251	4.3	6
	Larry Brown, Washington, NFC	285	1,216	4.3	8
1971	Floyd Little, Denver, AFC	284	1,133	4.0	6
	*John Brockington, Green Bay, NFC	216	1,105	5.1	4
1970	Larry Brown, Washington, NFC	237	1,125	4.7	5
	Floyd Little, Denver, AFC	209	901	4.3	3
1969	Gale Sayers, Chicago, NFL	236	1,032	4.4	8
	Dickie Post, San Diego, AFL	182	873	4.8	6
1968	Leroy Kelly, Cleveland, NFL	248	1,239	5.0	16
	*Paul Robinson, Cincinnati, AFL	238	1,023	4.3	8
1967	Jim Nance, Boston, AFL	269	1,216	4.5	7
	Leroy Kelly, Cleveland, NFL	235	1,205	5.1	11
1966	Jim Nance, Boston, AFL	299	1,458	4.9	11
	Gale Sayers, Chicago, NFL	229	1,231	5.4	8
1965	Jim Brown, Cleveland, NFL	289	1,544	5.3	17
	Paul Lowe, San Diego, AFL	222	1,121	5.0	7
1964	Jim Brown, Cleveland, NFL	280	1,446	5.2	7
	Cookie Gilchrist, Buffalo, AFL	230	981	4.3	6
1963	Jim Brown, Cleveland, NFL	291	1,863	6.4	12
	Clem Daniels, Oakland, AFL	215	1,099	5.1	3
1962	Jim Taylor, Green Bay, NFL	272	1,474	5.4	19
	Cookie Gilchrist, Buffalo, AFL	214	1,096	5.1	13
1961	Jim Brown, Cleveland, NFL	305	1,408	4.6	8
	Billy Cannon, Houston, AFL	200	948	4.7	6
1960	Jim Brown, Cleveland, NFL	215	1,257	5.8	9
	*Abner Haynes, Dall. Texans, AFL	156	875	5.6	9
1959	Jim Brown, Cleveland	290	1,329	4.6	14
1958	Jim Brown, Cleveland	257	1,527	5.9	17
1957	*Jim Brown, Cleveland	202	942	4.7	9
1956	Rick Casares, Chi. Bears	234	1,126	4.8	12
1955	*Alan Ameche, Baltimore	213	961	4.5	9
1954	Joe Perry, San Francisco	173	1,049	6.1	8
1953	Joe Perry, San Francisco	192	1,018	5.3	10
1952	Dan Towler, Los Angeles	156	894	5.7	10
1951	Eddie Price, N.Y. Giants	271	971	3.6	7
1950	Marion Motley, Cleveland	140	810	5.8	3
1949	Steve Van Buren, Philadelphia	263	1,146	4.4	11
1948	Steve Van Buren, Philadelphia	201	945	4.7	10
1947	Steve Van Buren, Philadelphia	217	1,008	4.6	13
1946	Bill Dudley, Pittsburgh	146	604	4.1	3
1945	Steve Van Buren, Philadelphia	143	832	5.8	15
1944	Bill Paschal, N.Y. Giants	196	737	3.8	9
1943	*Bill Paschal, N.Y. Giants	147	572	3.9	10
1942	*Bill Dudley, Pittsburgh	162	696	4.3	5
1941	Clarence (Pug) Manders, Brooklyn	111	486	4.4	5
1940	Byron (Whizzer) White, Detroit	146	514	3.5	5
1939	*Bill Osmanski, Chicago	121	699	5.8	7
1938	*Byron (Whizzer) White, Pittsburgh	152	567	3.7	4
1937	Cliff Battles, Washington	216	874	4.0	5
1936	*Alphonse (Tuffy) Leemans, N.Y. Giants	206	830	4.0	2
1935	Doug Russell, Chi. Cardinals	140	499	3.6	0
1934	*Beattie Feathers, Chi. Bears	119	1,004	8.4	8

YEARLY STATISTICAL LEADERS

1933	Jim Musick, Boston	173	809	4.7	5
1932	*Cliff Battles, Boston	148	576	3.9	3

First season of professional football.

ANNUAL PASSING LEADERS

(Current rating system implemented in 1973)

Year	Player, Team	Att.	Comp.	Yards	TD	Int.	Rating
2000	Brian Griese, Denver, AFC	336	216	2,688	19	4	102.9
	Trent Green, St. Louis, NFC	240	145	2,063	16	5	101.8
1999	Kurt Warner, St. Louis, NFC	499	325	4,353	41	13	109.2
	Peyton Manning, Indianapolis, AFC	533	331	4,135	26	15	90.7
1998	Randall Cunningham, Minnesota, NFC	425	259	3,704	34	10	106.0
	Vinny Testaverde, NY Jets, AFC	421	259	3,256	29	7	101.6
1997	Steve Young, San Francisco, NFC	356	241	3,029	19	6	104.7
	Mark Brunell, Jacksonville, AFC	435	264	3,281	18	7	91.2
1996	Steve Young, San Francisco, NFC	316	214	2,410	14	6	97.2
	John Elway, Denver, AFC	466	287	3,328	26	14	89.2
1995	Jim Harbaugh, Indianapolis, AFC	314	200	2,575	17	5	100.7
	Brett Favre, Green Bay, NFC	570	359	4,413	38	13	99.5
1994	Steve Young, San Francisco, NFC	461	324	3,969	35	10	112.8
	Dan Marino, Miami, AFC	615	385	4,453	30	17	89.2
1993	Steve Young, San Francisco, NFC	462	314	4,023	29	16	101.5
	John Elway, Denver, AFC	551	348	4,030	25	10	92.8
1992	Steve Young, San Francisco, NFC	402	268	3,465	25	7	107.0
	Warren Moon, Houston, AFC	346	224	2,521	18	12	89.3
1991	Steve Young, San Francisco, NFC	279	180	2,517	17	8	101.8
	Jim Kelly, Buffalo, AFC	474	304	3,844	33	17	97.6
1990	Jim Kelly, Buffalo, AFC	346	219	2,829	24	9	101.2
	Phil Simms, N.Y. Giants, NFC	311	184	2,284	15	4	92.7
1989	Joe Montana, San Francisco, NFC	386	271	3,521	26	8	112.4
	Boomer Esiason, Cincinnati, AFC	455	258	3,525	28	11	92.1
1988	Boomer Esiason, Cincinnati, AFC	388	223	3,572	28	14	97.4
	Wade Wilson, Minnesota, NFC	332	204	2,746	15	9	91.5
1987	Joe Montana, San Francisco, NFC	398	266	3,054	31	13	102.1
	Bernie Kosar, Cleveland, AFC	389	241	3,033	22	9	95.4
1986	Tommy Kramer, Minnesota, NFC	372	208	3,000	24	10	92.6
	Dan Marino, Miami, AFC	623	378	4,746	44	23	92.5
1985	Ken O'Brien, N.Y. Jets, AFC	488	297	3,888	25	8	96.2
	Joe Montana, San Francisco, NFC	494	303	3,653	27	13	91.3
1984	Dan Marino, Miami, AFC	564	362	5,084	48	17	108.9
	Joe Montana, San Francisco, NFC	432	279	3,630	28	10	102.9
1983	Steve Bartkowski, Atlanta, NFC	432	274	3,167	22	5	97.6
	*Dan Marino, Miami, AFC	296	173	2,210	20	6	96.0
1982	Ken Anderson, Cincinnati, AFC	309	218	2,495	12	9	95.3
	Joe Theismann, Washington, NFC	252	161	2,033	13	9	91.3
1981	Ken Anderson, Cincinnati, AFC	479	300	3,754	29	10	98.4
	Joe Montana, San Francisco, NFC	488	311	3,565	19	12	88.4
1980	Brian Sipe, Cleveland, AFC	554	337	4,132	30	14	91.4
	Ron Jaworski, Philadelphia, NFC	451	257	3,529	27	12	91.0
1979	Roger Staubach, Dallas, NFC	461	267	3,586	27	11	92.3
	Dan Fouts, San Diego, AFC	530	332	4,082	24	24	82.6
1978	Roger Staubach, Dallas, NFC	413	231	3,190	25	16	84.9
	Terry Bradshaw, Pittsburgh, AFC	368	207	2,915	28	20	84.7
1977	Bob Griese, Miami, AFC	307	180	2,252	22	13	87.8
	Roger Staubach, Dallas, NFC	361	210	2,620	18	9	87.0
1976	Ken Stabler, Oakland, AFC	291	194	2,737	27	17	103.4
	James Harris, Los Angeles, NFC	158	91	1,460	8	6	89.6
1975	Ken Anderson, Cincinnati, AFC	377	228	3,169	21	11	93.9
	Fran Tarkenton, Minnesota, NFC	425	273	2,994	25	13	91.8
1974	Ken Anderson, Cincinnati, AFC	328	213	2,667	18	10	95.7
	Sonny Jurgensen, Washington, NFC	167	107	1,185	11	5	94.5
1973	Roger Staubach, Dallas, NFC	286	179	2,428	23	15	94.6
	Ken Stabler, Oakland, AFC	260	163	1,997	14	10	88.3
1972	Norm Snead, N.Y. Giants, NFC	325	196	2,307	17	12	
	Earl Morrall, Miami, AFC	150	83	1,360	11	7	
1971	Roger Staubach, Dallas, NFC	211	126	1,882	15	4	
	Bob Griese, Miami, AFC	263	145	2,089	19	9	
1970	John Brodie, San Francisco, NFC	378	223	2,941	24	10	
	Daryle Lamonica, Oakland, AFC	356	179	2,516	22	15	
1969	Sonny Jurgensen, Washington, NFL	442	274	3,102	22	15	
	*Greg Cook, Cincinnati, AFL	197	106	1,854	15	11	
1968	Len Dawson, Kansas City, AFL	224	131	2,109	17	9	
	Earl Morrall, Baltimore, NFL	317	182	2,909	26	17	
1967	Sonny Jurgensen, Washington, NFL	508	288	3,747	31	16	
	Daryle Lamonica, Oakland, AFL	425	220	3,228	30	20	
1966	Bart Starr, Green Bay, NFL	251	156	2,257	14	3	
	Len Dawson, Kansas City, AFL	284	159	2,527	26	10	
1965	Rudy Bukich, Chicago, NFL	312	176	2,641	20	9	
	John Hadl, San Diego, AFL	348	174	2,798	20	21	
1964	Len Dawson, Kansas City, AFL	354	199	2,879	30	18	
	Bart Starr, Green Bay, NFL	272	163	2,144	15	4	
1963	Y.A. Tittle, N.Y. Giants, NFL	367	221	3,145	36	14	
	Tobin Rote, San Diego, AFL	286	170	2,510	20	17	
1962	Len Dawson, Dall. Texans, AFL	310	189	2,759	29	17	
	Bart Starr, Green Bay, NFL	285	178	2,438	12	9	
1961	George Blanda, Houston, AFL	362	187	3,330	36	22	
	Milt Plum, Cleveland, NFL	302	177	2,416	18	10	
1960	Milt Plum, Cleveland, NFL	250	151	2,297	21	5	
	Jack Kemp, L.A. Chargers, AFL	406	211	3,018	20	25	
1959	Charlie Conerly, N.Y. Giants	194	113	1,706	14	4	
1958	Eddie LeBaron, Washington	145	79	1,365	11	10	
1957	Tommy O'Connell, Cleveland	110	63	1,229	9	8	
1956	Ed Brown, Chi. Bears	168	96	1,667	11	12	
1955	Otto Graham, Cleveland	185	98	1,721	15	8	
1954	Norm Van Brocklin, Los Angeles	260	139	2,637	13	21	
1953	Otto Graham, Cleveland	258	167	2,722	11	9	
1952	Norm Van Brocklin, Los Angeles	205	113	1,736	14	17	
1951	Bob Waterfield, Los Angeles	176	88	1,566	13	10	
1950	Norm Van Brocklin, Los Angeles	233	127	2,061	18	14	
1949	Sammy Baugh, Washington	255	145	1,903	18	14	
1948	Tommy Thompson, Philadelphia	246	141	1,965	25	11	
1947	Sammy Baugh, Washington	354	210	2,938	25	15	
1946	Bob Waterfield, Los Angeles	251	127	1,747	18	17	
1945	Sammy Baugh, Washington	182	128	1,669	11	4	
	Sid Luckman, Chi. Bears	217	117	1,725	14	10	
1944	Frank Filchock, Washington	147	84	1,139	13	9	
1943	Sammy Baugh, Washington	239	133	1,754	23	19	
1942	Cecil Isbell, Green Bay	268	146	2,021	24	14	
1941	Cecil Isbell, Green Bay	206	117	1,479	15	11	
1940	Sammy Baugh, Washington	177	111	1,367	12	10	
1939	*Parker Hall, Cleveland	208	106	1,227	9	13	
1938	Ed Danowski, N.Y. Giants	129	70	848	7	8	
1937	*Sammy Baugh, Washington	171	81	1,127	8	14	
1936	Arnie Herber, Green Bay	173	77	1,239	11	13	
1935	Ed Danowski, N.Y. Giants	113	57	794	10	9	
1934	Arnie Herber, Green Bay	115	42	799	8	12	
1933	*Harry Newman, N.Y. Giants	136	53	973	11	17	
1932	Arnie Herber, Green Bay	101	37	639	9	9	

First season of professional football.

ANNUAL PASSING TOUCHDOWN LEADERS

Year	Player, Team	TD
2000	Daunte Culpepper, Minnesota, NFC	33
	Peyton Manning, Indianapolis, AFC	33
1999	Kurt Warner, St. Louis, NFC	41
	Peyton Manning, Indianapolis, AFC	26
1998	Steve Young, San Francisco, NFC	36
	Vinny Testaverde, N.Y. Jets, AFC	29
1997	Brett Favre, Green Bay, NFC	35
	Jeff George, Oakland, AFC	29
1996	Brett Favre, Green Bay, NFC	39
	Vinny Testaverde, Baltimore, AFC	33
1995	Brett Favre, Green Bay, NFC	38
	Jeff Blake, Cincinnati, AFC	28
1994	Steve Young, San Francisco, NFC	35
	Dan Marino, Miami, AFC	30
1993	Steve Young, San Francisco, NFC	29
	John Elway, Denver, AFC	25
1992	Steve Young, San Francisco, NFC	25
	Dan Marino, Miami, AFC	24
1991	Jim Kelly, Buffalo, AFC	33
	Mark Rypien, Washington, NFC	28
1990	Warren Moon, Houston, AFC	33
	Randall Cunningham, Philadelphia, NFC	30
1989	Jim Everett, L.A. Rams, NFC	29
	Boomer Esiason, Cincinnati, AFC	28
1988	Jim Everett, L.A. Rams, NFC	31
	Boomer Esiason, Cincinnati, AFC	28
	Dan Marino, Miami, AFC	28
1987	Joe Montana, San Francisco, NFC	31
	Dan Marino, Miami, AFC	26
1986	Dan Marino, Miami, AFC	44
	Tommy Kramer, Minnesota, NFC	24
1985	Dan Marino, Miami, AFC	30
	Joe Montana, San Francisco, NFC	27
1984	Dan Marino, Miami, AFC	48
	Neil Lomax, St. Louis, NFC	28
	Joe Montana, San Francisco, NFC	28
1983	Lynn Dickey, Green Bay, NFC	32
	Joe Ferguson, Buffalo, AFC	26
	Brian Sipe, Cleveland, AFC	26
1982	Terry Bradshaw, Pittsburgh, AFC	17
	Dan Fouts, San Diego, AFC	17
	Joe Montana, San Francisco, NFC	17
1981	Dan Fouts, San Diego, AFC	33
	Steve Bartkowski, Atlanta, NFC	30

Year	Player, Team	
1980	Steve Bartkowski, Atlanta, NFC	31
	Dan Fouts, San Diego, AFC	30
	Brian Sipe, Cleveland, AFC	30
1979	Steve Grogan, New England, AFC	28
	Brian Sipe, Cleveland, AFC	28
	Roger Staubach, Dallas, NFC	27
1978	Terry Bradshaw, Pittsburgh, AFC	28
	Roger Staubach, Dallas, NFC	25
	Fran Tarkenton, Minnesota, NFC	25
1977	Bob Griese, Miami, AFC	22
	Ron Jaworski, Philadelphia, NFC	18
	Roger Staubach, Dallas, NFC	18
1976	Ken Stabler, Oakland, AFC	27
	Jim Hart, St. Louis, NFC	18
1975	Joe Ferguson, Buffalo, AFC	25
	Fran Tarkenton, Minnesota, NFC	25
1974	Ken Stabler, Oakland, AFC	26
	Jim Hart, St. Louis, NFC	20
1973	Roman Gabriel, Philadelphia, NFC	23
	Roger Staubach, Dallas, NFC	23
	Charley Johnson, Denver, AFC	20
1972	Billy Kilmer, Washington, NFC	19
	Joe Namath, N.Y. Jets, AFC	19
1971	John Hadl, San Diego, AFC	21
	John Brodie, San Francisco, NFC	18
1970	John Brodie, San Francisco, NFC	24
	John Hadl, San Diego, AFC	22
	Daryle Lamonica, Oakland, AFC	22
1969	Daryle Lamonica, Oakland, AFL	34
	Roman Gabriel, Los Angeles, NFL	24
1968	John Hadl, San Diego, AFL	27
	Earl Morrall, Baltimore, NFL	26
1967	Sonny Jurgensen, Washington, NFL	31
	Daryle Lamonica, Oakland, AFL	30
1966	Frank Ryan, Cleveland, NFL	29
	Len Dawson, Kansas City, AFL	26
1965	John Brodie, San Francisco, NFL	30
	Len Dawson, Kansas City, AFL	21
1964	Babe Parilli, Boston, AFL	31
	Frank Ryan, Cleveland, NFL	25
1963	Y.A. Tittle, N.Y. Giants, NFL	36
	Len Dawson, Kansas City, AFL	26
1962	Y.A. Tittle, N.Y. Giants, NFL	33
	Len Dawson, Dallas, AFL	29
1961	George Blanda, Houston, AFL	36
	Sonny Jurgensen, Philadelphia, NFL	32
1960	Al Dorow, N.Y. Titans, AFL	26
	Johnny Unitas, Baltimore, NFL	25
1959	Johnny Unitas, Baltimore	32
1958	Johnny Unitas, Baltimore	19
1957	Johnny Unitas, Baltimore	24
1956	Tobin Rote, Green Bay	18
1955	Tobin Rote, Green Bay	17
	Y.A. Tittle, San Francisco	17
1954	Adrian Burk, Philadelphia	23
1953	Robert Thomason, Philadelphia	21
1952	Jim Finks, Pittsburgh	20
	Otto Graham, Cleveland	20
1951	Bobby Layne, Detroit	26
1950	George Ratterman, N.Y. Yanks	22
1949	Johnny Lujack, Chi. Bears	23
1948	Tommy Thompson, Philadelphia	25
1947	Sammy Baugh, Washington	25
1946	Sid Luckman, Chi. Bears	17
	Bob Waterfield, Los Angeles	17
1945	Sid Luckman, Chi. Bears	14
	*Bob Waterfield, Cleveland	14
1944	Frank Filchock, Washington	13
1943	Sid Luckman, Chi. Bears	28
1942	Cecil Isbell, Green Bay	24
1941	Cecil Isbell, Green Bay	15
1940	Sammy Baugh, Washington	12
1939	Frank Filchock, Washington	11
1938	Bob Monnett, Green Bay	9
1937	Bernie Masterson, Chi. Bears	9
1936	Arnie Herber, Green Bay	11
1935	Ed Danowski, N.Y. Giants	10
1934	Arnie Herber, Green Bay	8
1933	*Harry Newman, N.Y. Giants	11
1932	Arnie Herber, Green Bay	9

**First season of professional football.*

ANNUAL PASS RECEIVING LEADERS

Year	Player, Team	No.	Yards	Avg.	TD
2000	Marvin Harrison, Indianapolis, AFC	102	1,413	13.9	14
	Muhsin Muhammad, Carolina, NFC	102	1,183	11.6	6
1999	Jimmy Smith, Jacksonville, AFC	116	1,636	14.1	6
	Muhsin Muhammad, Carolina, NFC	96	1,253	13.1	8
1998	O.J. McDuffie, Miami, AFC	90	1,050	11.7	7
	Frank Sanders, Arizona, NFC	89	1,145	12.9	3
1997	Tim Brown, Oakland, AFC	104	1,408	13.5	5
	Herman Moore, Detroit, NFC	104	1,293	12.4	8
1996	Jerry Rice, San Francisco, NFC	108	1,254	11.6	8
	Carl Pickens, Cincinnati, AFC	100	1,180	11.8	12
1995	Herman Moore, Detroit, NFC	123	1,686	13.7	14
	Carl Pickens, Cincinnati, AFC	99	1,234	12.5	17
1994	Cris Carter, Minnesota, NFC	122	1,256	10.3	7
	Ben Coates, New England, AFC	96	1,174	12.2	7
1993	Sterling Sharpe, Green Bay, NFC	112	1,274	11.4	11
	Reggie Langhorne, Indianapolis, AFC	85	1,038	12.2	3
1992	Sterling Sharpe, Green Bay, NFC	108	1,461	13.5	13
	Haywood Jeffires, Houston, AFC	90	913	10.1	9
1991	Haywood Jeffires, Houston, AFC	100	1,181	11.8	7
	Michael Irvin, Dallas, NFC	93	1,523	16.4	8
1990	Jerry Rice, San Francisco, NFC	100	1,502	15.0	13
	Haywood Jeffires, Houston, AFC	74	1,048	14.2	8
	Drew Hill, Houston, AFC	74	1,019	13.8	5
1989	Sterling Sharpe, Green Bay, NFC	90	1,423	15.8	12
	Andre Reed, Buffalo, AFC	88	1,312	14.9	9
1988	Al Toon, N.Y. Jets, AFC	93	1,067	11.5	5
	Henry Ellard, L.A. Rams, NFC	86	1,414	16.4	10
1987	J.T. Smith, St. Louis, NFC	91	1,117	12.3	8
	Al Toon, N.Y. Jets, AFC	68	976	14.4	5
1986	Todd Christensen, L.A. Raiders, AFC	95	1,153	12.1	8
	Jerry Rice, San Francisco, NFC	86	1,570	18.3	15
1985	Roger Craig, San Francisco, NFC	92	1,016	11.0	6
	Lionel James, San Diego, AFC	86	1,027	11.9	6
1984	Art Monk, Washington, NFC	106	1,372	12.9	7
	Ozzie Newsome, Cleveland, AFC	89	1,001	11.2	5
1983	Todd Christensen, L.A. Raiders, AFC	92	1,247	13.6	12
	Roy Green, St. Louis, NFC	78	1,227	15.7	14
	Charlie Brown, Washington, NFC	78	1,225	15.7	8
	Earnest Gray, N.Y. Giants, NFC	78	1,139	14.6	5
1982	Dwight Clark, San Francisco, NFC	60	913	15.2	5
	Kellen Winslow, San Diego, AFC	54	721	13.4	6
1981	Kellen Winslow, San Diego, AFC	88	1,075	12.2	10
	Dwight Clark, San Francisco, NFC	85	1,105	13.0	4
1980	Kellen Winslow, San Diego, AFC	89	1,290	14.5	9
	*Earl Cooper, San Francisco, NFC	83	567	6.8	4
1979	Joe Washington, Baltimore, AFC	82	750	9.1	3
	Ahmad Rashad, Minnesota, NFC	80	1,156	14.5	9
1978	Rickey Young, Minnesota, NFC	88	704	8.0	5
	Steve Largent, Seattle, AFC	71	1,168	16.5	8
1977	Lydell Mitchell, Baltimore, AFC	71	620	8.7	4
	Ahmad Rashad, Minnesota, NFC	51	681	13.4	2
1976	MacArthur Lane, Kansas City, AFC	66	686	10.4	1
	Drew Pearson, Dallas, NFC	58	806	13.9	6
1975	Chuck Foreman, Minnesota, NFC	73	691	9.5	9
	Reggie Rucker, Cleveland, AFC	60	770	12.8	3
	Lydell Mitchell, Baltimore, AFC	60	544	9.1	4
1974	Lydell Mitchell, Baltimore, AFC	72	544	7.6	2
	Charles Young, Philadelphia, NFC	63	696	11.0	3
1973	Harold Carmichael, Philadelphia, NFC	67	1,116	16.7	9
	Fred Willis, Houston, AFC	57	371	6.5	1
1972	Harold Jackson, Philadelphia, NFC	62	1,048	16.9	4
	Fred Biletnikoff, Oakland, AFC	58	802	13.8	7
1971	Fred Biletnikoff, Oakland, AFC	61	929	15.2	9
	Bob Tucker, N.Y. Giants, NFC	59	791	13.4	4
1970	Dick Gordon, Chicago, NFC	71	1,026	14.5	13
	Marlin Briscoe, Buffalo, AFC	57	1,036	18.2	8
1969	Dan Abramowicz, New Orleans, NFL	73	1,015	13.9	7
	Lance Alworth, San Diego, AFL	64	1,003	15.7	4
1968	Clifton McNeil, San Francisco, NFL	71	994	14.0	7
	Lance Alworth, San Diego, AFL	68	1,312	19.3	10
1967	George Sauer, N.Y. Jets, AFL	75	1,189	15.9	6
	Charley Taylor, Washington, NFL	70	990	14.1	9
1966	Lance Alworth, San Diego, AFL	73	1,383	18.9	13
	Charley Taylor, Washington, NFL	72	1,119	15.5	12
1965	Lionel Taylor, Denver, AFL	85	1,131	13.3	6
	Dave Parks, San Francisco, NFL	80	1,344	16.8	12
1964	Charley Hennigan, Houston, AFL	101	1,546	15.3	8
	Johnny Morris, Chicago, NFL	93	1,200	12.9	10
1963	Lionel Taylor, Denver, AFL	78	1,101	14.1	10
	Bobby Joe Conrad, St. Louis, NFL	73	967	13.2	10
1962	Lionel Taylor, Denver, AFL	77	908	11.8	4

Year	Player, Team	No.	Yards	Avg.	TD
	Bobby Mitchell, Washington, NFL	72	1,384	19.2	11
1961	Lionel Taylor, Denver, AFL	100	1,176	11.8	4
	Jim (Red) Phillips, Los Angeles, NFL	78	1,092	14.0	5
1960	Lionel Taylor, Denver, AFL	92	1,235	13.4	12
	Raymond Berry, Baltimore, NFL	74	1,298	17.5	10
1959	Raymond Berry, Baltimore	66	959	14.5	14
1958	Raymond Berry, Baltimore	56	794	14.2	9
	Pete Retzlaff, Philadelphia	56	766	13.7	2
1957	Billy Wilson, San Francisco	52	757	14.6	6
1956	Billy Wilson, San Francisco	60	889	14.8	5
1955	Pete Pihos, Philadelphia	62	864	13.9	7
1954	Pete Pihos, Philadelphia	60	872	14.5	10
	Billy Wilson, San Francisco	60	830	13.8	5
1953	Pete Pihos, Philadelphia	63	1,049	16.7	10
1952	Mac Speedie, Cleveland	62	911	14.7	5
1951	Elroy (Crazylegs) Hirsch, Los Angeles	66	1,495	22.7	17
1950	Tom Fears, Los Angeles	84	1,116	13.3	7
1949	Tom Fears, Los Angeles	77	1,013	13.2	9
1948	*Tom Fears, Los Angeles	51	698	13.7	4
1947	Jim Keane, Chi. Bears	64	910	14.2	10
1946	Jim Benton, Los Angeles	63	981	15.6	6
1945	Don Hutson, Green Bay	47	834	17.7	9
1944	Don Hutson, Green Bay	58	866	14.9	9
1943	Don Hutson, Green Bay	47	776	16.5	11
1942	Don Hutson, Green Bay	74	1,211	16.4	17
1941	Don Hutson, Green Bay	58	738	12.7	10
1940	*Don Looney, Philadelphia	58	707	12.2	4
1939	Don Hutson, Green Bay	34	846	24.9	6
1938	Gaynell Tinsley, Chi. Cardinals	41	516	12.6	1
1937	Don Hutson, Green Bay	41	552	13.5	7
1936	Don Hutson, Green Bay	34	536	15.8	8
1935	*Tod Goodwin, N.Y. Giants	26	432	16.6	4
1934	Joe Carter, Philadelphia	16	238	14.9	4
	Morris (Red) Badgro, N.Y. Giants	16	206	12.9	1
1933	John (Shipwreck) Kelly, Brooklyn	22	246	11.2	3
1932	Ray Flaherty, N.Y. Giants	21	350	16.7	3

First season of professional football.

ANNUAL PASS RECEIVING LEADERS (YARDS)

Year	Player, Team	No.	Yards	Avg.	TD
2000	Torry Holt, St. Louis, NFC	82	1,635	19.9	6
	Rod Smith, Denver, AFC	100	1,602	16.0	8
1999	Marvin Harrison, Indianapolis, AFC	115	1,663	14.5	12
	Randy Moss, Minnesota, NFC	80	1,413	17.7	11
1998	Antonio Freeman, Green Bay, NFC	84	1,424	17.0	14
	Eric Moulds, Buffalo, AFC	67	1,368	20.4	9
1997	Rob Moore, Arizona, NFC	97	1,584	16.3	8
	Tim Brown, Oakland, AFC	104	1,408	13.5	5
1996	Isaac Bruce, St. Louis, NFC	84	1,338	15.9	7
	Jimmy Smith, Jacksonville, AFC	83	1,244	15.0	7
1995	Jerry Rice, San Francisco, NFC	122	1,848	15.1	15
	Tim Brown, Oakland, AFC	89	1,342	15.1	10
1994	Jerry Rice, San Francisco, NFC	112	1,499	13.4	13
	Tim Brown, L.A. Raiders, AFC	89	1,309	14.7	9
1993	Jerry Rice, San Francisco, NFC	98	1,503	15.3	15
	Tim Brown, L.A. Raiders, AFC	80	1,180	14.8	7
1992	Sterling Sharpe, Green Bay, NFC	108	1,461	13.5	13
	Anthony Miller, San Diego, AFC	72	1,060	14.7	7
1991	Michael Irvin, Dallas, NFC	93	1,523	16.4	8
	Haywood Jeffires, Houston, AFC	100	1,181	11.8	7
1990	Jerry Rice, San Francisco, NFC	100	1,502	15.0	13
	Haywood Jeffires, Houston, AFC	74	1,048	14.2	8
1989	Jerry Rice, San Francisco, NFC	82	1,483	18.1	17
	Andre Reed, Buffalo, AFC	88	1,312	14.9	9
1988	Henry Ellard, L.A. Rams, NFC	86	1,414	16.4	10
	Eddie Brown, Cincinnati, AFC	53	1,273	24.0	9
1987	J.T. Smith, St. Louis, NFC	91	1,117	12.3	8
	Carlos Carson, Kansas City, AFC	55	1,044	19.0	7
1986	Jerry Rice, San Francisco, NFC	86	1,570	18.3	15
	Stanley Morgan, New England, AFC	84	1,491	17.8	10
1985	Steve Largent, Seattle, AFC	79	1,287	16.3	6
	Mike Quick, Philadelphia, NFC	73	1,247	17.1	11
1984	Roy Green, St. Louis, NFC	78	1,555	19.9	12
	John Stallworth, Pittsburgh, AFC	80	1,395	17.4	11
1983	Mike Quick, Philadelphia, NFC	69	1,409	20.4	13
	Carlos Carson, Kansas City, AFC	80	1,351	16.9	7
1982	Wes Chandler, San Diego, AFC	49	1,032	21.1	9
	Dwight Clark, San Francisco, NFC	60	913	15.2	5
1981	Alfred Jenkins, Atlanta, NFC	70	1,358	19.4	13
	Frank Lewis, Buffalo, AFC	70	1,244	17.8	4
	Steve Watson, Denver, AFC	60	1,244	20.7	13
1980	John Jefferson, San Diego, AFC	82	1,340	16.3	13
	James Lofton, Green Bay, NFC	71	1,226	17.3	4
1979	Steve Largent, Seattle, AFC	66	1,237	18.7	9
	Ahmad Rashad, Minnesota, NFC	80	1,156	14.5	9
1978	Wesley Walker, N.Y. Jets, AFC	48	1,169	24.4	8
	Harold Carmichael, Philadelphia, NFC	55	1,072	19.5	8
1977	Drew Pearson, Dallas, NFC	48	870	18.1	2
	Ken Burrough, Houston, AFC	43	816	19.0	8
1976	Roger Carr, Baltimore, AFC	43	1,112	25.9	11
	*Sammy White, Minnesota, NFC	51	906	17.8	10
1975	Ken Burrough, Houston, AFC	53	1,063	20.1	8
	Mel Gray, St. Louis, NFC	48	926	19.3	11
1974	Cliff Branch, Oakland, AFC	60	1,092	18.2	13
	Drew Pearson, Dallas, NFC	62	1,087	17.5	2
1973	Harold Carmichael, Philadelphia, NFC	67	1,116	16.7	9
	*Isaac Curtis, Cincinnati, AFC	45	843	18.7	9
1972	Harold Jackson, Philadelphia, NFC	62	1,048	16.9	4
	Rich Caster, N.Y. Jets, AFC	39	833	21.4	10
1971	Otis Taylor, Kansas City, AFC	57	1,110	19.5	7
	Gene Washington, San Francisco, NFC	46	884	19.2	4
1970	Gene Washington, San Francisco, NFC	53	1,100	20.8	12
	Marlin Briscoe, Buffalo, AFC	57	1,036	18.2	8
1969	Warren Wells, Oakland, AFL	47	1,260	26.8	14
	Harold Jackson, Philadelphia, NFL	65	1,116	17.2	9
1968	Lance Alworth, San Diego, AFL	68	1,312	19.3	10
	Roy Jefferson, Pittsburgh, NFL	58	1,074	18.5	11
1967	Don Maynard, N.Y. Jets, AFL	71	1,434	20.3	10
	Ben Hawkins, Philadelphia, NFL	59	1,265	21.4	10
1966	Lance Alworth, San Diego, AFL	73	1,383	18.9	13
	Pat Studstill, Detroit, NFL	67	1,266	18.9	5
1965	Lance Alworth, San Diego, AFL	69	1,602	23.2	14
	Dave Parks, San Francisco, NFL	80	1,344	16.8	12
1964	Charley Hennigan, Houston, AFL	101	1,546	15.3	8
	Johnny Morris, Chicago, NFL	93	1,200	12.9	10
1963	Bobby Mitchell, Washington, NFL	69	1,436	20.8	7
	Art Powell, Oakland, AFL	73	1,304	17.8	16
1962	Bobby Mitchel, Washington, NFL	72	1,384	19.2	11
	Art Powell, N.Y. Titans, AFL	64	1,130	17.6	8
1961	Charley Hennigan, Houston, AFL	82	1,746	21.3	12
	Tommy McDonald, Philadelphia, NFL	64	1,144	17.9	13
1960	*Bill Groman, Houston, AFL	72	1,473	20.5	12
	Raymond Berry, Baltimore, NFL	74	1,298	17.5	10
1959	Raymond Berry, Baltimore	66	959	14.5	14
1958	Del Shofner, Los Angeles	51	1,097	21.5	8
1957	Raymond Berry, Baltimore	47	800	17.0	6
1956	Billy Howton, Green Bay	55	1,188	21.6	12
1955	Pete Pihos, Philadelphia	62	864	13.9	7
1954	Bob Boyd, Los Angeles	53	1,212	22.9	6
1953	Pete Pihos, Philadelphia	63	1,049	16.7	10
1952	*Bill Howton, Green Bay	53	1,231	23.2	13
1951	Elroy (Crazylegs) Hirsch, Los Angeles	66	1,495	22.7	17
1950	Tom Fears, Los Angeles	84	1,116	13.3	7
1949	Bob Mann, Detroit	66	1,014	15.4	4
1948	Mal Kutner, Chi. Cardinals	41	943	23.0	14
1947	Mal Kutner, Chi. Cardinals	43	944	21.9	7
1946	Jim Benton, Los Angeles	63	981	15.5	6
1945	Jim Benton, Cleveland	45	1,067	23.7	8
1944	Don Hutson, Green Bay	58	866	14.6	9
1943	Don Hutson, Green Bay	47	776	16.5	11
1942	Don Hutson, Green Bay	74	1,211	16.4	17
1941	Don Hutson, Green Bay	58	738	12.7	10
1940	*Don Looney, Philadelphia	58	707	12.2	4
1939	Don Hutson, Green Bay	34	846	24.9	6
1938	Don Hutson, Green Bay	32	548	17.1	9
1937	*Gaynell Tinsley, Chi. Cardinals	36	675	18.8	5
1936	Don Hutson, Green Bay	34	526	15.5	8
1935	Charley Malone, Boston	22	433	19.7	2
1934	Harry Ebding, Detroit	9	257	28.6	2
1933	*Paul Moss, Pittsburgh	18	383	21.3	2
1932	Johnny (Blood) McNally, Green Bay	19	326	17.2	3

First season of professional football.

ANNUAL INTERCEPTION LEADERS

Year	Player, Team	No.	Yards	TD
2000	Darren Sharper, Green Bay, NFC	9	109	0
	Samari Rolle, Tennessee, AFC	7	140	1
	Brian Walker, Miami, AFC	7	80	0
1999	Rod Woodson, Baltimore, AFC	7	195	2
	Sam Madison, Miami, AFC	7	164	1
	James Hasty, Kansas City, AFC	7	98	2
	Donnie Abraham, Tampa Bay, NFC	7	115	2
	Troy Vincent, Philadelphia, NFC	7	91	0
1998	Ty Law, New England, AFC	9	133	1
	Kwamie Lassiter, Arizona, NFC	8	80	0
1997	Ryan McNeil, St. Louis, NFC	9	127	1

Year	Player, Team	No.		
	Mark McMillian, Kansas City, AFC	8	274	3
	Darryl Williams, Seattle, AFC	8	172	1
1996	Tyrone Braxton, Denver, AFC	9	128	1
	Keith Lyle, St. Louis, NFC	9	152	0
1995	*Orlando Thomas, Minnesota, NFC	9	108	1
	Willie Williams, Pittsburgh, AFC	7	122	1
1994	Eric Turner, Cleveland, AFC	9	199	1
	Aeneas Williams, Arizona, NFC	9	89	0
1993	Eugene Robinson, Seattle, AFC	9	80	0
	Nate Odomes, Buffalo, AFC	9	65	0
	Deion Sanders, Atlanta, NFC	7	91	0
1992	Henry Jones, Buffalo, AFC	8	263	2
	Audray McMillian, Minnesota, NFC	8	157	2
1991	Ronnie Lott, L.A. Raiders, AFC	8	52	0
	Ray Crockett, Detroit, NFC	6	141	1
	Deion Sanders, Atlanta, NFC	6	119	1
	*Aeneas Williams, Phoenix, NFC	6	60	0
	Tim McKyer, Atlanta, NFC	6	24	0
1990	*Mark Carrier, Chicago, NFC	10	39	0
	Richard Johnson, Houston, AFC	8	100	1
1989	Felix Wright, Cleveland, AFC	9	91	1
	Eric Allen, Philadelphia, NFC	8	38	0
1988	Scott Case, Atlanta, NFC	10	47	0
	Erik McMillan, N.Y. Jets, AFC	8	168	2
1987	Barry Wilburn, Washington, NFC	9	135	1
	Mike Prior, Indianapolis, AFC	6	57	0
	Mark Kelso, Buffalo, AFC	6	25	0
	Keith Bostic, Houston, AFC	6	-14	0
1986	Ronnie Lott, San Francisco, NFC	10	134	1
	Deron Cherry, Kansas City, AFC	9	150	0
1985	Everson Walls, Dallas, NFC	9	31	0
	Albert Lewis, Kansas City, AFC	8	59	0
	Eugene Daniel, Indianapolis, AFC	8	53	0
1984	Ken Easley, Seattle, AFC	10	126	2
	*Tom Flynn, Green Bay, NFC	9	106	0
1983	Mark Murphy, Washington, NFC	9	127	0
	Ken Riley, Cincinnati, AFC	8	89	2
	Vann McElroy, L.A. Raiders, AFC	8	68	0
1982	Everson Walls, Dallas, NFC	7	61	0
	Ken Riley, Cincinnati, AFC	5	88	1
	Bobby Jackson, N.Y Jets, AFC	5	84	1
	Dwayne Woodruff, Pittsburgh, AFC	5	53	0
	Donnie Shell, Pittsburgh, AFC	5	27	0
1981	*Everson Walls, Dallas, NFC	11	133	0
	John Harris, Seattle, AFC	10	155	2
1980	Lester Hayes, Oakland, AFC	13	273	1
	Nolan Cromwell, Los Angeles, NFC	8	140	1
1979	Mike Reinfeldt, Houston, AFC	12	205	0
	Lemar Parrish, Washiongton, NFC	9	65	0
1978	Thom Darden, Cleveland, AFC	10	200	0
	Ken Stone, St. Louis, NFC	9	139	0
	Willie Buchanon, Green Bay, NFC	9	93	1
1977	Lyle Blackwood, Baltimore, AFC	10	163	0
	Rolland Lawrence, Atlanta, NFC	7	138	0
1976	Monte Jackson, Los Angeles, NFC	10	173	3
	Ken Riley, Cincinnati, AFC	9	141	1
1975	Mel Blount, Pittsburgh, AFC	11	121	0
	Paul Krause, Minnesota, NFC	10	201	0
1974	Emmitt Thomas, Kansas City, AFC	12	214	2
	Ray Brown, Atlanta, NFC	8	164	1
1973	Dick Anderson, Miami, AFC	8	163	2
	Mike Wagner, Pittsburgh, AFC	8	134	0
	Bobby Bryant, Minnesota, NFC	7	105	1
1972	Bill Bradley, Philadelphia, NFC	9	73	0
	Mike Sensibaugh, Kansas City, AFC	8	65	0
1971	Bill Bradley, Philadelphia, NFC	11	248	0
	Ken Houston, Houston, AFC	9	220	4
1970	Johnny Robinson, Kansas City, AFC	10	155	0
	Dick LeBeau, Detroit, NFC	9	96	0
1969	Mel Renfro, Dallas, NFL	10	118	0
	Emmitt Thomas, Kansas City, AFL	9	146	1
1968	Dave Grayson, Oakland, AFL	10	195	1
	Willie Williams, N.Y. Giants, NFL	10	103	0
1967	Miller Farr, Houston, AFL	10	264	3
	*Lem Barney, Detroit, NFL	10	232	3
	Tom Janik, Buffalo, AFL	10	222	2
	Dave Whitsell, New Orleans, NFL	10	178	2
	Dick Westmoreland, Miami, AFL	10	127	1
1966	Larry Wilson, St. Louis, NFL	10	180	2
	Johnny Robinson, Kansas City, AFL	10	136	1
	Bobby Hunt, Kansas City, AFL	10	113	0
1965	W.K. Hicks, Houston, AFL	9	156	0
	Bobby Boyd, Baltimore, NFL	9	78	1
1964	Dainard Paulson, N.Y. Jets, AFL	12	157	1
	*Paul Krause, Washington, NFL	12	140	1
1963	Fred Glick, Houston, AFL	12	180	1
	Dick Lynch, N.Y. Giants, NFL	9	251	3
	Roosevelt Taylor, Chicago, NFL	9	172	1
1962	Lee Riley, N.Y. Titans, AFL	11	122	0
	Willie Wood, Green Bay, NFL	9	132	0
1961	Billy Atkins, Buffalo, AFL	10	158	0
	Dick Lynch, N.Y. Giants, NFL	9	60	0
1960	*Austin (Goose) Gonsoulin, Denver, AFL	11	98	0
	Dave Baker, San Francisco, NFL	10	96	0
	Jerry Norton, St. Louis, NFL	10	96	0
1959	Dean Derby, Pittsburgh	7	127	0
	Milt Davis, Baltimore	7	119	1
	Don Shinnick, Baltimore	7	70	0
1958	Jim Patton, N.Y. Giants	11	183	0
1957	Milt Davis, Baltimore	10	219	2
	Jack Christiansen, Detroit	10	137	1
	Jack Butler, Pittsburgh	10	85	0
1956	Linden Crow, Chi. Cardinals	11	170	0
1955	Will Sherman, Los Angeles	11	101	0
1954	Dick (Night Train) Lane, Chi. Cardinals	10	181	0
1953	Jack Christiansen, Detroit	12	238	1
1952	*Dick (Night Train) Lane, Los Angeles	14	298	2
1951	Otto Schnellbacher, N.Y. Giants	11	194	2
1950	Orban (Spec) Sanders, N.Y. Yanks	13	199	0
1949	Bob Nussbaumer, Chi. Cardinals	12	157	0
1948	*Dan Sandifer, Washington	13	258	2
1947	Frank Reagan, N.Y. Giants	10	203	0
	Frank Seno, Boston	10	100	0
1946	Bill Dudley, Pittsburgh	10	242	1
1945	Roy Zimmerman, Philadelphia	7	90	0
1944	*Howard Livingston, N.Y. Giants	9	172	1
1943	Sammy Baugh, Washington	11	112	0
1942	Clyde (Bulldog) Turner, Chi. Bears	8	96	1
1941	Marshall Goldberg, Chi. Cardinals	7	54	0
	*Art Jones, Pittsburgh	7	35	0
1940	Clarence (Ace) Parker, Brooklyn	6	146	1
	Kent Ryan, Detroit	6	65	0
	Don Hutson, Green Bay	6	24	0

**First season of professional football.*

ANNUAL PUNTING LEADERS

Year	Player, Team	No.	Avg.	Long
2000	Darren Bennett, San Diego, AFC	92	46.2	66
	Mitch Berger, Minnesota, NFC	62	44.7	60
1999	Tom Rouen, Denver, AFC	84	46.5	65
	Mitch Berger, Minnesota, NFC	61	45.4	75
1998	Craig Hentrich, Tennessee, AFC	69	47.2	71
	Mark Royals, New Orleans, NFC	88	45.6	64
1997	Mark Royals, New Orleans, NFC	88	45.9	66
	Tom Tupa, New England, AFC	78	45.8	73
1996	John Kidd, Miami, AFC	78	46.3	63
	Matt Turk, Washington, NFC	75	45.1	63
1995	Rick Tuten, Seattle, AFC	83	45.0	73
	Sean Landeta, St. Louis, NFC	83	44.3	63
1994	Sean Landeta, L.A. Rams, NFC	78	44.8	62
	Jeff Gossett, L.A. Raiders, AFC	77	43.9	65
1993	Greg Montgomery, Houston, AFC	54	45.6	77
	Jim Arnold, Detroit, NFC	72	44.5	68
1992	Greg Montgomery, Houston, AFC	53	46.9	66
	Harry Newsome, Minnesota, NFC	72	45.0	84
1991	Reggie Roby, Miami, AFC	54	45.7	64
	Harry Newsome, Minnesota, AFC	68	45.5	65
1990	Mike Horan, Denver, AFC	58	44.4	67
	Sean Landeta, N.Y. Giants, NFC	75	44.1	67
1989	Rich Camarillo, Phoenix, NFC	76	43.4	58
	Greg Montgomery, Hounton, AFC	56	43.3	63
1988	Harry Newsome, Pittsburgh, AFC	65	45.4	62
	Jim Arnold, Detroit, NFC	97	42.4	69
1987	Rick Donnelly, Atlanta, NFC	61	44.0	62
	Ralf Mojsiejenko, San Diego, AFC	67	42.9	57
1986	Rohn Stark, Indianapolis, AFC	76	45.2	63
	Sean Landeta, N.Y. Giants, NFC	79	44.8	61
1985	Rohn Stark, Indianapolis, AFC	78	45.9	68
	*Rick Donnelly, Atlanta, NFC	59	43.6	68
1984	Jim Arnold, Kansas City, AFC	98	44.9	63
	*Brian Hansen, New Orleans, NFC	69	43.8	66
1983	Rohn Stark, Baltimore, AFC	91	45.3	68
	Frank Garcia, Tampa Bay, NFC	95	42.2	64
1982	Luke Prestridge, Denver, AFC	45	45.0	65
	Carl Birdsong, St. Louis, NFC	54	43.8	65
1981	Pat McInally, Cincinnati, AFC	72	45.4	62

Year	Player, Team	No.	Avg.	Long
	Tom Skladany, Detroit, NFC	64	43.5	74
1980	Dave Jennings, N.Y. Giants, NFC	94	44.8	63
	Luke Prestridge, Denver, AFC	70	43.9	57
1979	*Bob Grupp, Kansas City, AFC	89	43.6	74
	Dave Jennings, N.Y. Giants, NFC	104	42.7	72
1978	Pat McInally, Cincinnati, AFC	91	43.1	65
	*Tom Skladany, Detroit, NFC	86	42.5	63
1977	Ray Guy, Oakland, AFC	59	43.3	74
	Tom Blanchard, New Orleans, NFC	82	42.4	66
1976	Marv Bateman, Buffalo, AFC	86	42.8	78
	John James, Atlanta, NFC	101	42.1	67
1975	Ray Guy, Oakland, AFC	68	43.8	64
	Herman Weaver, Detroit, NFC	80	42.0	61
1974	Ray Guy, Oakland, AFC	74	42.2	66
	Tom Blanchard, New Orleans, NFC	88	42.1	71
1973	Jerrel Wilson, Kansas City, AFC	80	45.5	68
	*Tom Wittum, San Francisco, NFC	79	43.7	62
1972	Jerrel Wilson, Kansas City, AFC	66	44.8	69
	Dave Chapple, Los Angeles, NFC	53	44.2	70
1971	Dave Lewis, Cincinnati, AFC	72	44.8	56
	Tom McNeill, Philadelphia, NFC	73	42.0	64
1970	Dave Lewis, Cincinnati, AFC	79	46.2	63
	*Julian Fagan, New Orleans, NFC	77	42.5	64
1969	David Lee, Baltimore, NFL	57	45.3	66
	Dennis Partee, San Diego, AFL	71	44.6	62
1968	Jerrel Wilson, Kansas City, AFL	63	45.1	70
	Billy Lothridge, Atlanta, NFL	75	44.3	70
1967	Bob Scarpitto, Denver, AFL	105	44.9	73
	Billy Lothridge, Atlanta, NFL	87	43.7	62
1966	Bob Scarpitto, Denver, AFL	76	45.8	70
	*David Lee, Baltimore, NFL	49	45.6	64
1965	Gary Collins, Cleveland, NFL	65	46.7	71
	Jerrel Wilson, Kansas City, AFL	69	45.4	64
1964	Bobby Walden, Minnesota, NFL	72	46.4	73
	Jim Fraser, Denver, AFL	73	44.2	67
1963	Yale Lary, Detroit, NFL	35	48.9	73
	Jim Fraser, Denver, AFL	81	44.4	66
1962	Tommy Davis, San Francisco, NFL	48	45.6	82
	Jim Fraser, Denver, AFL	55	43.6	75
1961	Yale Lary, Detroit, NFL	52	48.4	71
	Billy Atkins, Buffalo, AFL	85	44.5	70
1960	Jerry Norton, St. Louis, NFL	39	45.6	62
	*Paul Maguire, L.A. Chargers, AFL	43	40.5	61
1959	Yale Lary, Detroit	45	47.1	67
1958	Sam Baker, Washington	48	45.4	64
1957	Don Chandler, N.Y. Giants	60	44.6	61
1956	Norm Van Brocklin, Los Angeles	48	43.1	72
1955	Norm Van Brocklin, Los Angeles	60	44.6	61
1954	Pat Brady, Pittsburgh	66	43.2	72
1953	Pat Brady, Pittsburgh	80	46.9	64
1952	Horace Gillom, Cleveland	61	45.7	73
1951	Horace Gillom, Cleveland	73	45.5	66
1950	*Fred (Curly) Morrison, Chi. Bears	57	43.3	65
1949	*Mike Boyda, N.Y. Bulldogs	56	44.2	61
1948	Joe Muha, Philadelphia	57	47.3	82
1947	Jack Jacobs, Green Bay	57	43.5	74
1946	Roy McKay, Green Bay	64	42.7	64
1945	Roy McKay, Green Bay	44	41.2	73
1944	Frank Sinkwich, Detroit	45	41.0	73
1943	Sammy Baugh, Washington	50	45.9	81
1942	Sammy Baugh, Washington	37	48.2	74
1941	Sammy Baugh, Washington	30	48.7	75
1940	Sammy Baugh, Washington	35	51.4	85
1939	*Parker Hall, Cleveland	58	40.8	80

**First season of professional football.*

ANNUAL PUNT RETURN LEADERS

Year	Player, Team	No.	Yards	Avg.	Long	TD
2000	Jermaine Lewis, Baltimore, AFC	36	578	16.1	89	2
	Az-Zahir Hakim, St. Louis, NFC	32	489	15.3	86	1
1999	*Charlie Rogers, Seattle, AFC	22	318	14.5	94	1
	*Mac Cody, Arizona, NFC	32	373	11.7	31	0
1998	Deion Sanders, Dallas, NFC	24	375	15.6	69	2
	Reggie Barlow, Jacksonville, AFC	43	555	12.9	85	1
1997	Jermaine Lewis, Baltimore, AFC	28	437	15.6	89	2
	David Palmer, Minnesota, NFC	34	444	13.1	57	0
1996	Desmond Howard, Green Bay, NFC	58	875	15.1	92	3
	Darrien Gordon, San Diego, AFC	36	537	14.9	81	1
1995	David Palmer, Minnesota, NFC	26	342	13.2	74	1
	Andre Coleman, San Diego, AFC	28	326	11.6	88	1
1994	Brian Mitchell, Washington, NFC	32	452	14.1	78	2
	Darrien Gordon, San Diego, AFC	36	475	13.2	90	2
1993	*Tyrone Hughes, New Orleans, NFC	37	503	13.6	83	2
	Eric Metcalf, Cleveland, AFC	36	464	12.9	91	2
1992	Johnny Bailey, Phoenix, NFC	20	263	13.2	65	0
	Rod Woodson, Pittsburgh, AFC	32	364	11.4	80	1
1991	Mel Gray, Detroit, NFC	25	385	15.4	78	1
	Rod Woodson, Pittsburgh, AFC	28	320	11.4	40	0
1990	Clarence Verdin, Indianapolis, AFC	31	396	12.8	36	0
	*Johnny Bailey, Chicago, NFC	36	399	11.1	95	1
1989	Walter Stanley, Detroit, NFC	36	496	13.8	74	0
	Clarence Verdin, Indianapolis, AFC	23	296	12.9	49	1
1988	John Taylor, San Francisco, NFC	44	556	12.6	95	2
	JoJo Townsell, N.Y. Jets, AFC	35	409	11.7	59	1
1987	Mel Gray, New Orleans, NFC	24	352	14.7	80	0
	Bobby Joe Edmonds, Seattle, AFC	20	251	12.6	40	0
1986	*Bobby Joe Edmonds, Seattle, AFC	34	419	12.3	75	1
	*Vai Sikahema, St. Louis, NFC	43	522	12.1	71	2
1985	Irving Fryar, New England, AFC	37	520	14.1	85	2
	Henry Ellard, L.A. Rams, NFC	37	501	13.5	80	1
1984	Mike Martin, Cincinnati, AFC	24	376	15.7	55	0
	Henry Ellard, L.A. Rams, NFC	30	403	13.4	83	2
1983	*Henry Ellard, L.A. Rams, NFC	16	217	13.6	72	1
	Kirk Springs, N.Y. Jets, AFC	23	287	12.5	76	1
1982	Rick Upchurch, Denver, AFC	15	242	16.1	78	2
	Billy Johnson, Atlanta, NFC	24	273	11.4	71	0
1981	LeRoy Irvin, Los Angeles, NFC	46	615	13.4	84	3
	*James Brooks, San Diego, AFC	22	290	13.2	42	0
1980	J.T. Smith, Kansas City, AFC	40	581	14.5	75	2
	*Kenny Johnson, Atlanta, NFC	23	281	12.2	56	0
1979	John Sciarra, Philadelphia, NFC	16	182	11.4	38	0
	*Tony Nathan, Miami, AFC	28	306	10.9	86	1
1978	Rick Upchurch, Denver, AFC	36	493	13.7	75	1
	Jackie Wallace, Los Angeles, NFC	52	618	11.9	58	0
1977	Billy Johnson, Houston, AFC	35	539	15.4	87	2
	Larry Marshall, Philadelphia, NFC	46	489	10.6	48	0
1976	Rick Upchurch, Denver, AFC	39	536	13.7	92	4
	Eddie Brown, Washington, NFC	48	646	13.5	71	1
1975	Billy Johnson, Houston, AFC	40	612	15.3	83	3
	Terry Metcalf, St. Louis, NFC	23	285	12.4	69	1
1974	Lemar Parrish, Cincinnati, AFC	18	338	18.8	90	2
	Dick Jauron, Detroit, NFC	17	286	16.8	58	0
1973	Bruce Taylor, San Francisco, NFC	15	207	13.8	61	0
	Ron Smith, San Diego, AFC	27	352	13.0	84	2
1972	Ken Ellis, Green Bay, NFC	14	215	15.4	80	1
	Chris Farasopoulos, N.Y. Jets, AFC	17	179	10.5	65	1
1971	Les (Speedy) Duncan, Washington, NFC	22	233	10.6	33	0
	Leroy Kelly, Cleveland, AFC	30	292	9.7	74	0
1970	Ed Podolak, Kansas City, AFC	23	311	13.5	60	0
	*Bruce Taylor, San Francisco, NFC	43	516	12.0	76	0
1969	Alvin Haymond, Los Angeles, NFL	33	435	13.2	52	0
	*Bill Thompson, Denver, AFL	25	288	11.5	40	0
1968	Bob Hayes, Dallas, NFL	15	312	20.8	90	2
	Noland Smith, Kansas City, AFL	18	270	15.0	80	1
1967	Floyd Little, Denver, AFL	16	270	16.9	72	1
	Ben Davis, Cleveland, NFL	18	229	12.7	52	1
1966	Les (Speedy) Duncan, San Diego, AFL	18	238	13.2	81	1
	Johnny Roland, St. Louis, NFL	20	221	11.1	86	1
1965	Leroy Kelly, Cleveland, NFL	17	265	15.6	67	2
	Les (Speedy) Duncan, San Diego, AFL	30	464	15.5	66	2
1964	Bobby Jancik, Houston, AFL	12	220	18.3	82	1
	Tommy Watkins, Detroit, NFL	16	238	14.9	68	2
1963	Dick James, Washington, NFL	16	214	13.4	39	0
	Claude (Hoot) Gibson, Oakland, AFL	26	307	11.8	85	2
1962	Dick Christy, N.Y. Titans, AFL	15	250	16.7	73	2
	Pat Studstill, Detroit, NFL	29	457	15.8	44	0
1961	Dick Christy, N.Y. Titans, AFL	18	383	21.3	70	2
	Willie Wood, Green Bay, NFL	14	225	16.1	72	2
1960	*Abner Haynes, Dall. Texans, AFL	14	215	15.4	46	0
	Abe Woodson, San Francisco, NFL	13	174	13.4	48	0
1959	Johnny Morris, Chi. Bears	14	171	12.2	78	1
1958	Jon Arnett, Los Angeles	18	223	12.4	58	0
1957	Bert Zagers, Washington	14	217	15.5	76	2
1956	Ken Konz, Cleveland	13	187	14.4	65	1
1955	Ollie Matson, Chi. Cardinals	13	245	18.8	78	2
1954	*Veryl Switzer, Green Bay	24	306	12.8	93	1
1953	Charley Trippi, Chi. Cardinals	21	239	11.4	38	0
1952	Jack Christiansen, Detroit	15	322	21.5	79	2
1951	Claude (Buddy) Young, N.Y. Yanks	12	231	19.3	79	1
1950	*Herb Rich, Baltimore	12	276	23.0	86	1
1949	Verda (Vitamin T) Smith, Los Angeles	27	427	15.8	85	1
1948	George McAfee, Chi. Bears	30	417	13.9	60	1
1947	*Walt Slater, Pittsburgh	28	435	15.5	33	0
1946	Bill Dudley, Pittsburgh	27	385	14.3	52	0
1945	*Dave Ryan, Detroit	15	220	14.7	56	0
1944	*Steve Van Buren, Philadelphia	15	230	15.3	55	1

Year	Player, Team	No.	Yards	Avg.	Long	TD
1943	Andy Farkas, Washington	15	168	11.2	33	0
1942	Merlyn Condit, Brooklyn	21	210	10.0	23	0
1941	Byron (Whizzer) White, Detroit	19	262	13.8	64	0

First season of professional football.

ANNUAL KICKOFF RETURN LEADERS

Year	Player, Team	No.	Yards	Avg.	Long	TD
2000	*Darrick Vaughn, Atlanta, NFC	39	1,082	27.7	100	3
	Derrick Mason, Tennessee, AFC	42	1,132	27.0	66	0
1999	Tony Horne, St. Louis, NFC	30	892	29.7	101	2
	Tremain Mack, Cincinnati, AFC	51	1,382	27.1	99	1
1998	*Terry Fair, Detroit, NFC	51	1,428	28.0	105	2
	Corey Harris, Baltimore, AFC	35	965	27.6	95	1
1997	Michael Bates, Carolina, NFC	47	1,281	27.3	56	0
	Aaron Glenn, N.Y. Jets, AFC	28	741	26.5	96	1
1996	Michael Bates, Carolina, NFC	33	998	30.2	93	1
	Tamarick Vanover, Kansas City, AFC	33	854	25.9	97	1
1995	Ron Carpenter, N.Y. Jets, AFC	20	553	27.7	58	0
	Brian Mitchell, Washington, NFC	55	1,408	25.6	59	0
1994	Mel Gray, Detroit, NFC	45	1,276	28.4	102	3
	Randy Baldwin, Cleveland, AFC	28	753	26.9	85	1
1993	Robert Brooks, Green Bay, NFC	23	611	26.6	95	1
	*Raghib Ismail, L.A. Raiders, AFC	25	605	24.2	66	0
1992	Jon Vaughn, New England, AFC	20	564	28.2	100	1
	Deion Sanders, Atlanta, NFC	40	1,067	26.7	99	2
1991	Mel Gray, Detroit, NFC	36	929	25.8	71	0
	Nate Lewis, San Diego, AFC	23	578	25.1	95	1
1990	Kevin Clark, Denver, AFC	20	505	25.3	75	0
	David Meggett, N.Y. Giants, NFC	21	492	23.4	58	0
1989	Rod Woodson, Pittsburgh, AFC	36	982	27.3	84	1
	Mel Gray, Detroit, NFC	24	640	26.7	57	0
1988	*Tim Brown, L.A. Raiders, AFC	41	1,098	26.8	97	1
	Donnie Elder, Tampa Bay, NFC	34	772	22.7	51	0
1987	Sylvester Stamps, Atlanta, NFC	24	660	27.5	97	1
	Paul Palmer, Kansas City, AFC	38	923	24.3	95	2
1986	Dennis Gentry, Chicago, NFC	20	576	28.8	91	1
	Lupe Sanchez, Pittsburgh, AFC	25	591	23.6	64	0
1985	Ron Brown, L.A. Rams, NFC	28	918	32.8	98	3
	Glen Young, Cleveland, AFC	35	898	25.7	63	0
1984	*Bobby Humphery, N.Y. Jets, AFC	22	675	30.7	97	1
	Barry Redden, L.A. Rams, NFC	23	530	23.0	40	0
1983	Fulton Walker, Miami, AFC	36	962	26.7	78	0
	Darrin Nelson, Minnesota, NFC	18	445	24.7	50	0
1982	*Mike Mosley, Buffalo, AFC	18	487	27.1	66	0
	Alvin Hall, Detroit, NFC	16	426	26.6	96	1
1981	Mike Nelms, Washington, NFC	37	1,099	29.7	84	0
	Carl Roaches, Houston, AFC	28	769	27.5	96	1
1980	Horace Ivory, New England, AFC	36	992	27.6	98	1
	Rich Mauti, New Orleans, NFC	31	798	25.7	52	0
1979	Larry Brunson, Oakland, AFC	17	441	25.9	89	0
	Jimmy Edwards, Minnesota, NFC	44	1,103	25.1	83	0
1978	Steve Odom, Green Bay, NFC	25	677	27.1	95	1
	*Keith Wright, Cleveland, AFC	30	789	26.3	86	0
1977	*Raymond Clayborn, New England, AFC	28	869	31.0	101	3
	*Wilbert Montgomery, Philadelphia, NFC	23	619	26.9	99	1
1976	*Duriel Harris, Miami, AFC	17	559	32.9	69	0
	Cullen Bryant, Los Angeles, NFC	16	459	28.7	90	1
1975	*Walter Payton, Chicago, NFC	14	444	31.7	70	0
	Harold Hart, Oakland, AFC	17	518	30.5	102	1
1974	Terry Metcalf, St. Louis, NFC	20	623	31.2	94	1
	Greg Pruitt, Cleveland, AFC	22	606	27.5	88	1
1973	Carl Garrett, Chicago, NFC	16	486	30.4	67	0
	*Wallace Francis, Buffalo, AFC	23	687	29.9	101	2
1972	Ron Smith, Chicago, NFC	30	924	30.8	94	1
	*Bruce Laird, Baltimore, AFC	29	843	29.1	73	0
1971	Travis Williams, Los Angeles, NFC	25	743	29.7	105	1
	Eugene (Mercury) Morris, Miami, AFC	15	423	28.2	94	1
1970	Jim Duncan, Baltimore, AFC	20	707	35.4	99	1
	Cecil Turner, Chicago, NFC	23	752	32.7	96	4
1969	Bobby Williams, Detroit, NFL	17	563	33.1	96	1
	*Bill Thompson, Denver, AFL	18	513	28.5	63	0
1968	Preston Pearson, Baltimore, NFL	15	527	35.1	102	2
	*George Atkinson, Oakland, AFL	32	802	25.1	60	0
1967	*Travis Williams, Green Bay, NFL	18	739	41.1	104	4
	*Zeke Moore, Houston, AFL	14	405	28.9	92	1
1966	Gale Sayers, Chicago, NFL	23	718	31.2	93	2
	*Goldie Sellers, Denver, AFL	19	541	28.5	100	2
1965	Tommy Watkins, Detroit, NFL	17	584	34.4	94	0
	Abner Haynes, Denver, AFL	34	901	26.5	60	0
1964	*Clarence Childs, N.Y. Giants, NFL	34	987	29.0	100	1
	Bo Roberson, Oakland, AFL	36	975	27.1	59	0
1963	Abe Woodson, San Francisco, NFL	29	935	32.2	103	3
	Bobby Jancik, Houston, AFL	45	1,317	29.3	53	0
1962	Abe Woodson, San Francisco, NFL	37	1,157	31.3	79	0
	*Bobby Jancik, Houston, AFL	24	826	30.3	61	0
1961	Dick Bass, Los Angeles, NFL	23	698	30.3	64	0
	*Dave Grayson, Dall. Texans, AFL	16	453	28.3	73	0
1960	*Tom Moore, Green Bay, NFL	12	397	33.1	84	0
	Ken Hall, Houston, AFL	19	594	31.3	104	1
1959	Abe Woodson, San Francisco	13	382	29.4	105	1
1958	Ollie Matson, Chi. Cardinals	14	497	35.5	101	2
1957	*Jon Arnett, Los Angeles	18	504	28.0	98	1
1956	*Tom Wilson, Los Angeles	15	477	31.8	103	1
1955	Al Carmichael, Green Bay	14	418	29.9	100	1
1954	Billy Reynolds, Cleveland	14	413	29.5	51	0
1953	Joe Arenas, San Francisco	16	551	34.4	82	0
1952	Lynn Chandnois, Pittsburgh	17	599	35.2	93	2
1951	Lynn Chandnois, Pittsburgh	12	390	32.5	55	0
1950	Verda (Vitamin T) Smith, Los Angeles	22	742	33.7	97	3
1949	*Don Doll, Detroit	21	536	25.5	56	0
1948	*Joe Scott, N.Y. Giants	20	569	28.5	99	1
1947	Eddie Saenz, Washington	29	797	27.5	94	2
1946	Abe Karnofsky, Boston	21	599	28.5	97	1
1945	Steve Van Buren, Philadelphia	13	373	28.7	98	1
1944	Bob Thurbon, Card.-Pitt.	12	291	24.3	55	0
1943	Ken Heineman, Brooklyn	16	444	27.8	69	0
1942	Marshall Goldberg, Chi. Cardinals	15	393	26.2	95	1
1941	Marshall Goldberg, Chi. Cardinals	12	290	24.2	41	0

First season of professional football.

ANNUAL LEADERS IN SACKS (SINCE 1982)

Year	Player, Team	Sacks
2000	La'Roi Glover, New Orleans, NFC	17.0
	Trace Armstrong, Miami, AFC	16.5
1999	Kevin Carter, St. Louis, NFC	17.0
	Jevon Kearse, Tennessee, AFC	14.5
1998	Michael Sinclair, Seattle, AFC	16.5
	Reggie White, Green Bay, NFC	16.0
1997	John Randle, Minnesota, NFC	15.5
	Bruce Smith, Buffalo, AFC	14.0
1996	Kevin Greene, Carolina, NFC	14.5
	Michael McCrary, Seattle, AFC	13.5
	Bruce Smith, Buffalo, AFC	13.5
1995	Bryce Paup, Buffalo, AFC	17.5
	William Fuller, Philadelphia, NFC	13.0
	Wayne Martin, New Orleans, NFC	13.0
1994	Kevin Greene, Pittsburgh, AFC	14.0
	Ken Harvey, Washington, NFC	13.5
	John Randle, Minnesota, NFC	13.5
1993	Neil Smith, Kansas City, AFC	15.0
	Renaldo Turnbull, New Orleans, NFC	13.0
	Reggie White, Green Bay, NFC	13.0
1992	Clyde Simmons, Philadelphia, NFC	19.0
	Leslie O'Neal, San Diego, AFC	17.0
1991	Pat Swilling, New Orleans, NFC	17.0
	William Fuller, Houston, AFC	15.0
1990	Derrick Thomas, Kansas City, AFC	20.0
	Charles Haley, San Francisco, NFC	16.0
1989	Chris Doleman, Minnesota, NFC	21.0
	Lee Williams, San Diego, AFC	14.0
1988	Reggie White, Philadelphia, NFC	18.0
	G. Townsend, L.A. Raiders, AFC	11.5
1987	Reggie White, Philadelphia, NFC	21.0
	Andre Tippett, New England, AFC	12.5
1986	Lawrence Taylor, N.Y. Giants, NFC	20.5
	Sean Jones, L.A. Raiders, AFC	15.5
1985	Richard Dent, Chicago, NFC	17.0
	Andre Tippett, New England, AFC	16.5
1984	Mark Gastineau, N.Y. Jets, AFC	22.0
	Richard Dent, Chicago, NFC	17.5
1983	Mark Gastineau, N.Y. Jets, AFC	19.0
	Fred Dean, San Francisco, NFC	17.5
1982	Doug Martin, Minnesota, NFC	11.5
	Jesse Baker, Houston, AFC	7.5

POINTS SCORED

Year	Team	Points
2000	St. Louis, NFC	540
	Denver, AFC	485
1999	St. Louis, NFC	526
	Indianapolis, AFC	423
1998	Minnesota, NFC	556
	Denver, AFC	501
1997	Denver, AFC	472
	Green Bay, NFC	422
1996	Green Bay, NFC	456
	New England, AFC	418
1995	San Francisco, NFC	457
	Pittsburgh, AFC	407
1994	San Francisco, NFC	505
	Miami, AFC	389
1993	San Francisco, NFC	473
	Denver, AFC	373
1992	San Francisco, NFC	431
	Buffalo, AFC	381
1991	Washington, NFC	485
	Buffalo, AFC	458

YEARLY STATISTICAL LEADERS

Year	Team	Points
1990	Buffalo, AFC	428
	Philadelphia, NFC	396
1989	San Francisco, NFC	442
	Buffalo, AFC	409
1988	Cincinnati, AFC	448
	L.A. Rams, NFC	407
1987	San Francisco, NFC	459
	Cleveland, AFC	390
1986	Miami, AFC	430
	Minnesota, NFC	398
1985	San Diego, AFC	467
	Chicago, NFC	456
1984	Miami, AFC	513
	San Francisco, NFC	475
1983	Washington, NFC	541
	L.A. Raiders, AFC	442
1982	San Diego, AFC	288
	Dallas, NFC	226
	Green Bay, NFC	226
1981	San Diego, AFC	478
	Atlanta, NFC	426
1980	Dallas, NFC	454
	New England, AFC	441
1979	Pittsburgh, AFC	416
	Dallas, NFC	371
1978	Dallas, NFC	384
	Miami, AFC	372
1977	Oakland, AFC	351
	Dallas, NFC	345
1976	Baltimore, AFC	417
	Los Angeles, NFC	351
1975	Buffalo, AFC	420
	Minnesota, NFC	377
1974	Oakland, AFC	355
	Washington, NFC	320
1973	Los Angeles, NFC	388
	Denver, AFC	354
1972	Miami, AFC	385
	San Francisco, NFC	353
1971	Dallas, NFC	406
	Oakland, AFC	344
1970	San Francisco, NFC	352
	Baltimore, AFC	321
1969	Minnesota, NFL	379
	Oakland, AFL	377
1968	Oakland, AFL	453
	Dallas, NFL	431
1967	Oakland, AFL	468
	Los Angeles, NFL	398
1966	Kansas City, AFL	448
	Dallas, NFL	445
1965	San Francisco, NFL	421
	San Diego, AFL	340
1964	Baltimore, NFL	428
	Buffalo, AFL	400
1963	N.Y. Giants, NFL	448
	San Diego, AFL	399
1962	Green Bay, NFL	415
	Dall. Texans, AFL	389
1961	Houston, AFL	513
	Green Bay, NFL	391
1960	N.Y. Titans, AFL	382
	Cleveland, NFL	362
1959	Baltimore	374
1958	Baltimore	381
1957	Los Angeles	307
1956	Chi. Bears	363
1955	Cleveland	349
1954	Detroit	337
1953	San Francisco	372
1952	Los Angeles	349
1951	Los Angeles	392
1950	Los Angeles	466
1949	Philadelphia	364
1948	Chi. Cardinals	395
1947	Chi. Bears	363
1946	Chi. Bears	289
1945	Philadelphia	272
1944	Philadelphia	267
1943	Chi. Bears	303
1942	Chi. Bears	376
1941	Chi. Bears	396
1940	Washington	245
1939	Chi. Bears	298
1938	Green Bay	223
1937	Green Bay	220
1936	Green Bay	248
1935	Chi. Bears	192
1934	Chi. Bears	286
1933	N.Y. Giants	244
1932	Chicago Bears	160

TOTAL YARDS GAINED

Year	Team	Yards
2000	St. Louis, NFC	7,075
	Denver, AFC	6,554
1999	St. Louis, NFC	6,412
	Indianapolis, AFC	5,726
1998	San Francisco, NFC	6,800
	Denver, AFC	6,092
1997	Denver, AFC	5,872
	Detroit, NFC	5,798
1996	Denver, AFC	5,791
	Philadelphia, NFC	5,627
1995	Detroit, NFC	6,113
	Denver, AFC	6,040
1994	Miami, AFC	6,078
	San Francisco, NFC	6,060
1993	San Francisco, NFC	6,435
	Miami, AFC	5,812
1992	San Francisco, NFC	6,195
	Buffalo, AFC	5,893
1991	Buffalo, AFC	6,252
	San Francisco, NFC	5,858
1990	Houston, AFC	6,222
	San Francisco, NFC	5,895
1989	San Francisco, NFC	6,268
	Cincinnati, AFC	6,101
1988	Cincinnati, AFC	6,057
	San Francisco, NFC	5,900
1987	San Francisco, NFC	5,987
	Denver, AFC	5,624
1986	Cincinnati, AFC	6,490
	San Francisco, NFC	6,082
1985	San Diego, AFC	6,535
	San Francisco, NFC	5,920
1984	Miami, AFC	6,936
	San Francisco, NFC	6,366
1983	San Diego, AFC	6,197
	Green Bay, NFC	6,172
1982	San Diego, AFC	4,048
	San Francisco, NFC	3,242
1981	San Diego, AFC	6,744
	Detroit, NFC	5,933
1980	San Diego, AFC	6,410
	Los Angeles, NFC	6,006
1979	Pittsburgh, AFC	6,258
	Dallas, NFC	5,968
1978	New England, AFC	5,965
	Dallas, NFC	5,959
1977	Dallas, NFC	4,812
	Oakland, AFC	4,736
1976	Baltimore, AFC	5,236
	St. Louis, NFC	5,136
1975	Buffalo, AFC	5,467
	Dallas, NFC	5,025
1974	Dallas, NFC	4,983
	Oakland, AFC	4,718
1973	Los Angeles, NFC	4,906
	Oakland, AFC	4,773
1972	Miami, AFC	5,036
	N.Y. Giants, NFC	4,483
1971	Dallas, NFC	5,035
	San Diego, AFC	4,738
1970	Oakland, AFC	4,829
	San Francisco, NFC	4,503
1969	Dallas, NFL	5,122
	Oakland, AFL	5,036
1968	Oakland, AFL	5,696
	Dallas, NFL	5,117
1967	N.Y. Jets, AFL	5,152
	Baltimore, NFL	5,008
1966	Dallas, NFL	5,145
	Kansas City, AFL	5,114
1965	San Francisco, NFL	5,270
	San Diego, AFL	5,188
1964	Buffalo, AFL	5,206
	Baltimore, NFL	4,779
1963	San Diego, AFL	5,153
	N.Y. Giants, NFL	5,024
1962	N.Y. Giants, NFL	5,005
	Houston, AFL	4,971
1961	Houston, AFL	6,288
	Philadelphia, NFL	5,112
1960	Houston, AFL	4,936
	Baltimore, NFL	4,245
1959	Baltimore	4,458
1958	Baltimore	4,539
1957	Los Angeles	4,143
1956	Chi. Bears	4,537
1955	Chi. Bears	4,316
1954	Los Angeles	5,187
1953	Philadelphia	4,811
1952	Cleveland	4,352
1951	Los Angeles	5,506
1950	Los Angeles	5,420
1949	Chi. Bears	4,873
1948	Chi. Cardinals	4,705
1947	Chi. Bears	5,053
1946	Los Angeles	3,793
1945	Washington	3,549
1944	Chi. Bears	3,239
1943	Chi. Bears	4,045
1942	Chi. Bears	3,900
1941	Chi. Bears	4,265
1940	Green Bay	3,400
1939	Chi. Bears	3,988
1938	Green Bay	3,037
1937	Green Bay	3,201
1936	Detroit	3,703
1935	Chi. Bears	3,454
1934	Chi. Bears	3,900
1933	N.Y. Giants	2,973
1932	Chi. Bears	2,755

YARDS RUSHING

Year	Team	Yards
2000	Oakland, AFC	2,470
	Minnesota, NFC	2,129
1999	San Francisco, NFC	2,095
	Jacksonville, AFC	2,091
1998	San Francisco, NFC	2,544
	Denver, AFC	2,468
1997	Pittsburgh, AFC	2,479
	Detroit, NFC	2,464
1996	Denver, AFC	2,362
	Washington, NFC	1,910
1995	Kansas City, AFC	2,222
	Dallas, NFC	2,201
1994	Pittsburgh, AFC	2,180
	Detroit, NFC	2,080
1993	N.Y. Giants, NFC	2,210
	Seattle, AFC	2,015
1992	Buffalo, AFC	2,436
	Philadelphia, NFC	2,388
1991	Buffalo, AFC	2,381
	Minnesota, NFC	2,201
1990	Philadelphia, NFC	2,556
	San Diego, AFC	2,257
1989	Cincinnati, AFC	2,483
	Chicago, NFC	2,287
1988	Cincinnati, AFC	2,710
	San Francisco, NFC	2,523
1987	San Francisco, NFC	2,237
	L.A. Raiders, AFC	2,197
1986	Chicago, NFC	2,700
	Cincinnati, AFC	2,533
1985	Chicago, NFC	2,761
	Indianapolis, AFC	2,439
1984	Chicago, NFC	2,974
	N.Y. Jets, AFC	2,189
1983	Chicago, NFC	2,727
	Baltimore, AFC	2,695
1982	Buffalo, AFC	1,371
	Dallas, NFC	1,313
1981	Detroit, NFC	2,795
	Kansas City, AFC	2,633
1980	Los Angeles, NFC	2,799
	Houston, AFC	2,635
1979	N.Y. Jets, AFC	2,646
	St. Louis, NFC	2,582
1978	New England, AFC	3,165
	Dallas, NFC	2,783
1977	Chicago, NFC	2,811
	Oakland, AFC	2,627
1976	Pittsburgh, AFC	2,971
	Los Angeles, NFC	2,528
1975	Buffalo, AFC	2,974
	Dallas, NFC	2,432
1974	Dallas, NFC	2,454
	Pittsburgh, AFC	2,417
1973	Buffalo, AFC	3,088
	Los Angeles, NFC	2,925
1972	Miami, AFC	2,960
	Chicago, NFC	2,360
1971	Miami, AFC	2,429
	Detroit, NFC	2,376
1970	Dallas, NFC	2,300
	Miami, AFC	2,082
1969	Dallas, NFL	2,276
	Kansas City, AFL	2,220
1968	Chicago, NFL	2,377
	Kansas City, AFL	2,227
1967	Cleveland, NFL	2,139
	Houston, AFL	2,122
1966	Kansas City, AFL	2,274
	Cleveland, NFL	2,166
1965	Cleveland, NFL	2,331
	San Diego, AFL	2,085
1964	Green Bay, NFL	2,276
	Buffalo, AFL	2,040
1963	Cleveland, NFL	2,639
	San Diego, AFL	2,203
1962	Buffalo, AFL	2,480
	Green Bay, NFL	2,460
1961	Green Bay, NFL	2,350
	Dall. Texans, AFL	2,189
1960	St. Louis, NFL	2,356
	Oakland, AFL	2,056
1959	Cleveland	2,149
1958	Cleveland	2,526
1957	Los Angeles	2,142
1956	Chi. Bears	2,468
1955	Chi. Bears	2,388
1954	San Francisco	2,498
1953	San Francisco	2,230
1952	San Francisco	1,905
1951	Chi. Bears	2,408
1950	N.Y. Giants	2,336
1949	Philadelphia	2,607
1948	Chi. Cardinals	2,560
1947	Los Angeles	2,171
1946	Green Bay	1,765
1945	Cleveland	1,714
1944	Philadelphia	1,661
1943	Phil-Pitt	1,730
1942	Chi. Bears	1,881
1941	Chi. Bears	2,263
1940	Chi. Bears	1,818
1939	Chi. Bears	2,043
1938	Detroit	1,893
1937	Detroit	2,074
1936	Detroit	2,885
1935	Chi. Bears	2,096
1934	Chi. Bears	2,847
1933	Boston	2,260
1932	Chi. Bears	1,770

YARDS PASSING

Leadership in this category has been based on net yards since 1952.

Year	Team	Yards
2000	St. Louis, NFC	5,232
	Indianapolis, AFC	4,282
1999	St. Louis, NFC	4,353
	Indianapolis, AFC	4,066
1998	Minnesota, NFC	4,328
	N.Y. Jets, AFC	3,836
1997	Seattle, AFC	3,959
	Green Bay, NFC	3,705
1996	Jacksonville, AFC	4,110
	Philadelphia, NFC	3,745

1995	San Francisco, NFC	4,608
	Miami, AFC	4,210
1994	New England, AFC	4,444
	Minnesota, NFC	4,324
1993	Miami, AFC	4,353
	San Francisco, NFC	4,302
1992	Houston, AFC	4,029
	San Francisco, NFC	3,880
1991	Houston, AFC	4,621
	San Francisco, NFC	3,997
1990	Houston, AFC	4,805
	San Francisco, NFC	4,177
1989	Washington, NFC	4,349
	Miami, AFC	4,216
1988	Miami, AFC	4,516
	Washington, NFC	4,136
1987	Miami, AFC	3,876
	San Francisco, NFC	3,750
1986	Miami, AFC	4,779
	San Francisco, NFC	4,096
1985	San Diego, AFC	4,870
	Dallas, NFC	3,861
1984	Miami, AFC	5,018
	St. Louis, NFC	4,257
1983	San Diego, AFC	4,661
	Green Bay, NFC	4,365
1982	San Diego, AFC	2,927
	San Francisco, NFC	2,502
1981	San Diego, AFC	4,739
	Minnesota, NFC	4,333
1980	San Diego, AFC	4,531
	Minnesota, NFC	3,688
1979	San Diego, AFC	3,915
	San Francisco, NFC	3,641
1978	San Diego, AFC	3,375
	Minnesota, NFC	3,243
1977	Buffalo, AFC	2,530
	St. Louis, NFC	2,499
1976	Baltimore, AFC	2,933
	Minnesota, NFC	2,855
1975	Cincinnati, AFC	3,241
	Washington, NFC	2,917
1974	Washington, NFC	2,978
	Cincinnati, AFC	2,804
1973	Philadelphia, NFC	2,998
	Denver, AFC	2,519
1972	N.Y. Jets, AFC	2,777
	San Francisco, NFC	2,735
1971	San Diego, AFC	3,134
	Dallas, NFC	2,786
1970	San Francisco, NFC	2,923
	Oakland, AFC	2,865
1969	Oakland, AFL	3,271
	San Francisco, NFL	3,158
1968	San Diego, AFL	3,623
	Dallas, NFL	3,026
1967	N.Y. Jets, AFL	3,845
	Washington, NFL	3,730
1966	N.Y. Jets, AFL	3,464
	Dallas, NFL	3,023
1965	San Francisco, NFL	3,487
	San Diego, AFL	3,103
1964	Houston, AFL	3,527
	Chicago, NFL	2,841
1963	Baltimore, NFL	3,296
	Houston, AFL	3,222
1962	Denver, AFL	3,404
	Philadelphia, NFL	3,385
1961	Houston, AFL	4,392
	Philadelphia, NFL	3,605
1960	Houston, AFL	3,203
	Baltimore, NFL	2,956
1959	Baltimore	2,753
1958	Pittsburgh	2,752
1957	Baltimore	2,388
1956	Los Angeles	2,419
1955	Philadelphia	2,472
1954	Chi. Bears	3,104
1953	Philadelphia	3,089
1952	Cleveland	2,566
1951	Los Angeles	3,296
1950	Los Angeles	3,709
1949	Chi. Bears	3,055
1948	Washington	2,861
1947	Washington	3,336
1946	Los Angeles	2,080
1945	Chi. Bears	1,857
1944	Washington	2,021
1943	Chi. Bears	2,310
1942	Green Bay	2,407
1941	Chi. Bears	2,002
1940	Washington	1,887
1939	Chi. Bears	1,965
1938	Washington	1,536
1937	Green Bay	1,398
1936	Green Bay	1,629
1935	Green Bay	1,449
1934	Green Bay	1,165
1933	N.Y. Giants	1,348
1932	Chi. Bears	1,013

FEWEST POINTS ALLOWED

Year	Team	Points
2000	Baltimore, AFC	165
	Philadelphia, NFC	245
1999	Jacksonville, AFC	217
	Tampa Bay, NFC	235
1998	Miami, AFC	265
	Dallas, NFC	275
1997	Kansas City, AFC	232
	Tampa Bay, NFC	263
1996	Green Bay, NFC	210
	Pittsburgh, AFC	257
1995	Kansas City, AFC	241
	San Francisco, NFC	258
1994	Cleveland, AFC	204
	Dallas, NFC	248
1993	N.Y. Giants, NFC	205
	Houston, AFC	238
1992	New Orleans, NFC	202
	Pittsburgh, AFC	225
1991	New Orleans, NFC	211
	Denver, AFC	235
1990	N.Y. Giants, NFC	211
	Pittsburgh, AFC	240
1989	Denver, AFC	226
	N.Y. Giants, NFC	252
1988	Chicago, NFC	215
	Buffalo, AFC	237
1987	Indianapolis, AFC	238
	San Francisco, NFC	253
1986	Chicago, NFC	187
	Seattle, AFC	293
1985	Chicago, NFC	198
	N.Y. Jets, AFC	264
1984	San Francisco, NFC	227
	Denver, AFC	241
1983	Miami, AFC	250
	Detroit, NFC	286
1982	Washington, NFC	128
	Miami, AFC	131
1981	Philadelphia, NFC	221
	Miami, AFC	275
1980	Philadelphia, NFC	222
	Houston, AFC	251
1979	Tampa Bay, NFC	237
	San Diego, AFC	246
1978	Pittsburgh, AFC	195
	Dallas, NFC	208
1977	Atlanta, NFC	129
	Denver, AFC	148
1976	Pittsburgh, AFC	138
	Minnesota, NFC	176
1975	Los Angeles, NFC	135
	Pittsburgh, AFC	162
1974	Los Angeles, NFC	181
	Pittsburgh, AFC	189
1973	Miami, AFC	150
	Minnesota, NFC	168
1972	Miami, AFC	171
	Washington, NFC	218
1971	Minnesota, NFC	139
	Baltimore, AFC	140
1970	Minnesota, NFC	143
	Miami, AFC	228
1969	Minnesota, NFL	133
	Kansas City, AFL	177
1968	Baltimore, NFL	144
	Kansas City, AFL	170
1967	Los Angeles, NFL	196
	Houston, AFL	199
1966	Green Bay, NFL	163
	Buffalo, AFL	255
1965	Green Bay, NFL	224
	Buffalo, AFL	226
1964	Baltimore, NFL	225
	Buffalo, AFL	242
1963	Chicago, NFL	144
	San Diego, AFL	255
1962	Green Bay, NFL	148
	Dall. Texans, AFL	233
1961	San Diego, AFL	219
	N.Y. Giants, NFL	220
1960	San Francisco, NFL	205
	Dall. Texans, AFL	253
1959	N.Y. Giants	170
1958	N.Y. Giants	183
1957	Cleveland	172
1956	Cleveland	177
1955	Cleveland	218
1954	Cleveland	162
1953	Cleveland	162
1952	Detroit	192
1951	Cleveland	152
1950	Philadelphia	141
1949	Philadelphia	134
1948	Chi. Bears	151
1947	Green Bay	210
1946	Pittsburgh	117
1945	Washington	121
1944	N.Y. Giants	75
1943	Washington	137
1942	Chi. Bears	84
1941	N.Y. Giants	114
1940	Brooklyn	120
1939	N.Y. Giants	85
1938	N.Y. Giants	79
1937	Chi. Bears	100
1936	Chi. Bears	94
1935	Green Bay	96
	N.Y. Giants	96
1934	Detroit	59
1933	Brooklyn	54
1932	Chi. Bears	44

FEWEST TOTAL YARDS ALLOWED

Year	Team	Yards
2000	Tennessee, AFC	3,813
	Washington, NFC	4,474
1999	Buffalo, AFC	4,045
	Tampa Bay, NFC	4,280
1998	San Diego, AFC	4,208
	Tampa Bay, NFC	4,345
1997	San Francisco, NFC	4,013
	Denver, AFC	4,671
1996	Green Bay, NFC	4,156
	Pittsburgh, AFC	4,362
1995	San Francisco, NFC	4,398
	Kansas City, AFC	4,549
1994	Dallas, NFC	4,313
	Pittsburgh, AFC	4,326
1993	Minnesota, NFC	4,406
	Pittsburgh, AFC	4,531
1992	Dallas, NFC	3,931
	Houston, AFC	4,211
1991	Philadelphia, NFC	3,549
	Denver, AFC	4,549
1990	Pittsburgh, AFC	4,115
	N.Y. Giants, NFC	4,206
1989	Minnesota, NFC	4,184
	Kansas City, AFC	4,293
1988	Minnesota, NFC	4,091
	Buffalo, AFC	4,578
1987	San Francisco, NFC	4,095
	Cleveland, AFC	4,264
1986	Chicago, NFC	4,130
	L.A. Raiders, AFC	4,804
1985	Chicago, NFC	4,135
	L.A. Raiders, AFC	4,603
1984	Chicago, NFC	3,863
	Cleveland, AFC	4,641
1983	Cincinnati, AFC	4,327
	New Orleans, NFC	4,691
1982	Miami, AFC	2,312
	Tampa Bay, NFC	2,442
1981	Philadelphia, NFC	4,447
	N.Y. Jets, AFC	4,871
1980	Buffalo, AFC	4,101
	Philadelphia, NFC	4,443
1979	Tampa Bay, NFC	3,949
	Pittsburgh, AFC	4,270
1978	Los Angeles, NFC	3,893
	Pittsburgh, AFC	4,168
1977	Dallas, NFC	3,213
	New England, AFC	3,638
1976	Pittsburgh, AFC	3,323
	San Francisco, NFC	3,562
1975	Minnesota, NFC	3,153
	Oakland, AFC	3,629
1974	Pittsburgh, AFC	3,074
	Washington, NFC	3,285
1973	Los Angeles, NFC	2,951
	Oakland, AFC	3,160
1972	Miami, AFC	3,297
	Green Bay, NFC	3,474
1971	Baltimore, AFC	2,852
	Minnesota, NFC	3,406
1970	Minnesota, NFC	2,803
	N.Y. Jets, AFC	3,655
1969	Minnesota, NFL	2,720
	Kansas City, AFL	3,163
1968	Los Angeles, NFL	3,118
	N.Y. Jets, AFL	3,363
1967	Oakland, AFL	3,294
	Green Bay, NFL	3,300
1966	St. Louis, NFL	3,492
	Oakland, AFL	3,910
1965	San Diego, AFL	3,262
	Detroit, NFL	3,557
1964	Green Bay, NFL	3,179
	Buffalo, AFL	3,878
1963	Chicago, NFL	3,176
	Boston, AFL	3,834
1962	Detroit, NFL	3,217
	Dall. Texans, AFL	3,951
1961	San Diego, AFL	3,726
	Baltimore, NFL	3,782
1960	St. Louis, NFL	3,029
	Buffalo, AFL	3,866
1959	N.Y. Giants	2,843
1958	Chi. Bears	3,066
1957	Pittsburgh	2,791
1956	N.Y. Giants	3,081
1955	Cleveland	2,841
1954	Cleveland	2,658
1953	Philadelphia	2,998
1952	Cleveland	3,075
1951	N.Y. Giants	3,250
1950	Cleveland	3,154
1949	Philadelphia	2,831
1948	Chi. Bears	2,931
1947	Green Bay	3,396
1946	Washington	2,451
1945	Philadelphia	2,073
1944	Philadelphia	1,943
1943	Chi. Bears	2,262
1942	Chi. Bears	1,703
1941	N.Y. Giants	2,368
1940	N.Y. Giants	2,219
1939	Washington	2,116
1938	N.Y. Giants	2,029
1937	Washington	2,123
1936	Boston	2,181
1935	Boston	1,996
1934	Chi. Cardinals	1,539
1933	Brooklyn	1,789

YEARLY STATISTICAL LEADERS

FEWEST RUSHING YARDS ALLOWED

Year	Team	Yards
2000	Baltimore, AFC	970
	N.Y. Giants, NFC	1,156
1999	St. Louis, NFC	1,189
	Baltimore, AFC	1,231
1998	San Diego, AFC	1,140
	Atlanta, NFC	1,203
1997	Pittsburgh, AFC	1,318
	San Francisco, NFC	1,366
1996	Denver, AFC	1,331
	Green Bay, NFC	1,416
1995	San Francisco, NFC	1,061
	Pittsburgh, AFC	1,321
1994	Minnesota, NFC	1,090
	San Diego, AFC	1,404
1993	Houston, AFC	1,273
	Minnesota, NFC	1,536
1992	Dallas, NFC	1,244
	Buffalo, AFC	1,395
	San Diego, AFC	1,395
1991	Philadelphia, NFC	1,136
	N.Y. Jets, AFC	1,442
1990	Philadelphia, NFC	1,169
	San Diego, AFC	1,515
1989	New Orleans, NFC	1,326
	Denver, AFC	1,580
1988	Chicago, NFC	1,326
	Houston, AFC	1,592
1987	Chicago, NFC	1,413
	Cleveland, AFC	1,433
1986	N.Y. Giants, NFC	1,284
	Denver, AFC	1,651
1985	Chicago, NFC	1,319
	N.Y. Jets, AFC	1,516
1984	Chicago, NFC	1,377
	Pittsburgh, AFC	1,617
1983	Washington, NFC	1,289
	Cincinnati, AFC	1,499
1982	Pittsburgh, AFC	762
	Detroit, NFC	854
1981	Detroit, NFC	1,623
	Kansas City, AFC	1,747
1980	Detroit, NFC	1,599
	Cincinnati, AFC	1,680
1979	Denver, AFC	1,693
	Tampa Bay, NFC	1,873
1978	Dallas, NFC	1,721
	Pittsburgh, AFC	1,774
1977	Denver, AFC	1,531
	Dallas, NFC	1,651
1976	Pittsburgh, AFC	1,457
	Los Angeles, NFC	1,564
1975	Minnesota, NFC	1,532
	Houston, AFC	1,680
1974	Los Angeles, NFC	1,302
	New England, AFC	1,587
1973	Los Angeles, NFC	1,270
	Oakland, AFC	1,470
1972	Dallas, NFC	1,515
	Miami, AFC	1,548
1971	Baltimore, AFC	1,113
	Dallas, NFC	1,144
1970	Detroit, NFC	1,152
	N.Y. Jets, AFC	1,283
1969	Dallas, NFL	1,050
	Kansas City, AFL	1,091
1968	Dallas, NFL	1,195
	N.Y. Jets, AFL	1,195
1967	Dallas, NFL	1,081
	Oakland, AFL	1,129
1966	Buffalo, AFL	1,051
	Dallas, NFL	1,176
1965	San Diego, AFL	1,094
	Los Angeles, NFL	1,409
1964	Buffalo, AFL	913
	Los Angeles, NFL	1,501
1963	Boston, AFL	1,107
	Chicago, NFL	1,442
1962	Detroit, NFL	1,231
	Dall. Texans, AFL	1,250
1961	Boston, AFL	1,041
	Pittsburgh, NFL	1,463
1960	St. Louis, NFL	1,212
	Dall. Texans, AFL	1,338
1959	N.Y. Giants	1,261
1958	Baltimore	1,291
1957	Baltimore	1,174
1956	N.Y. Giants	1,443
1955	Cleveland	1,189
1954	Cleveland	1,050
1953	Philadelphia	1,117
1952	Detroit	1,145
1951	N.Y. Giants	913
1950	Detroit	1,367
1949	Chi. Bears	1,196
1948	Philadelphia	1,209
1947	Philadelphia	1,329
1946	Chi. Bears	1,060
1945	Philadelphia	817
1944	Philadelphia	558
1943	Phil-Pitt	793
1942	Chi. Bears	519
1941	Washington	1,042
1940	N.Y. Giants	977
1939	Chi. Bears	812
1938	Detroit	1,081
1937	Chi. Bears	933
1936	Boston	1,148
1935	Boston	998
1934	Chi. Cardinals	954
1933	Brooklyn	964

FEWEST PASSING YARDS ALLOWED

Leadership in this category has been based on net yards since 1952.

Year	Team	Yards
2000	Tennessee, AFC	2,423
	Washington, NFC	2,621
1999	Buffalo, AFC	2,675
	Tampa Bay, NFC	2,873
1998	Philadelphia, NFC	2,720
	Oakland, AFC	2,876
1997	Dallas, NFC	2,522
	Indianapolis, AFC	2,820
1996	Green Bay, NFC	2,740
	Pittsburgh, AFC	2,947
1995	N.Y. Jets, AFC	2,740
	Philadelphia, NFC	2,816
1994	Dallas, NFC	2,752
	Houston, AFC	2,795
1993	New Orleans, NFC	2,606
	Cincinnati, AFC	2,798
1992	New Orleans, NFC	2,470
	Kansas City, AFC	2,537
1991	Philadelphia, NFC	2,413
	Denver, AFC	2,755
1990	Pittsburgh, AFC	2,500
	Dallas, NFC	2,639
1989	Minnesota, NFC	2,501
	Kansas City, AFC	2,527
1988	Kansas City, AFC	2,434
	Minnesota, NFC	2,489
1987	San Francisco, NFC	2,484
	L.A. Raiders, AFC	2,727
1986	St. Louis, NFC	2,637
	New England, AFC	2,978
1985	Washington, NFC	2,746
	Pittsburgh, AFC	2,783
1984	New Orleans, NFC	2,453
	Cleveland, AFC	2,696
1983	New Orleans, NFC	2,691
	Cincinnati, AFC	2,828
1982	Miami, AFC	1,027
	Tampa Bay, NFC	1,384
1981	Philadelphia, NFC	2,696
	Buffalo, AFC	2,870
1980	Washington, NFC	2,171
	Buffalo, AFC	2,282
1979	Tampa Bay, NFC	2,076
	Buffalo, AFC	2,530
1978	Buffalo, AFC	1,960
	Los Angeles, NFC	2,048
1977	Atlanta, NFC	1,384
	San Diego, AFC	1,725
1976	Minnesota, NFC	1,575
	Cincinnati, AFC	1,758
1975	Minnesota, NFC	1,621
	Cincinnati, AFC	1,729
1974	Pittsburgh, AFC	1,466
	Atlanta, NFC	1,572
1973	Miami, AFC	1,290
	Atlanta, NFC	1,430
1972	Minnesota, NFC	1,699
	Cleveland, AFC	1,736
1971	Atlanta, NFC	1,638
	Baltimore, AFC	1,739
1970	Minnesota, NFC	1,438
	Kansas City, AFC	2,010
1969	Minnesota, NFL	1,631
	Kansas City, AFL	2,072
1968	Houston, AFL	1,671
	Green Bay, NFL	1,796
1967	Green Bay, NFL	1,377
	Buffalo, AFL	1,825
1966	Green Bay, NFL	1,959
	Oakland, AFL	2,118
1965	Green Bay, NFL	1,981
	San Diego, AFL	2,168
1964	Green Bay, NFL	1,647
	San Diego, AFL	2,518
1963	Chicago, NFL	1,734
	Oakland, AFL	2,589
1962	Green Bay, NFL	1,746
	Oakland, AFL	2,306
1961	Baltimore, NFL	1,913
	San Diego, AFL	2,363
1960	Chicago, NFL	1,388
	Buffalo, AFL	2,124
1959	N.Y. Giants	1,582
1958	Chi. Bears	1,769
1957	Cleveland	1,300
1956	Cleveland	1,103
1955	Pittsburgh	1,295
1954	Cleveland	1,608
1953	Washington	1,751
1952	Washington	1,580
1951	Pittsburgh	1,687
1950	Cleveland	1,581
1949	Philadelphia	1,607
1948	Green Bay	1,626
1947	Green Bay	1,790
1946	Pittsburgh	939
1945	Washington	1,121
1944	Chi. Bears	1,052
1943	Chi. Bears	980
1942	Washington	1,093
1941	Pittsburgh	1,168
1940	Philadelphia	1,012
1939	Washington	1,116
1938	Chi. Bears	897
1937	Detroit	804
1936	Philadelphia	853
1935	Chi. Cardinals	793
1934	Philadelphia	545
1933	Portsmouth	558

Compiled by Elias Sports Bureau

Super Bowl I, 1/15/67
Super Bowl II, 1/14/68
Super Bowl III, 1/12/69
Super Bowl IV, 1/11/70
Super Bowl V, 1/17/71
Super Bowl VI, 1/16/72
Super Bowl VII, 1/14/73
Super Bowl VIII, 1/13/74
Super Bowl IX, 1/12/75
Super Bowl X, 1/18/76
Super Bowl XI, 1/9/77
Super Bowl XII, 1/15/78
Super Bowl XIII, 1/21/79
Super Bowl XIV, 1/20/80
Super Bowl XV, 1/25/81
Super Bowl XVI, 1/24/82
Super Bowl XVII, 1/30/83
Super Bowl XVIII, 1/22/84
Super Bowl XIX, 1/20/85
Super Bowl XX, 1/26/86
Super Bowl XXI, 1/25/87
Super Bowl XXII, 1/31/88
Super Bowl XXIII, 1/22/89
Super Bowl XXIV, 1/28/90
Super Bowl XXV, 1/27/91
Super Bowl XXVI, 1/26/92
Super Bowl XXVII, 1/31/93
Super Bowl XXVIII, 1/30/94
Super Bowl XXIX, 1/29/95
Super Bowl XXX, 1/28/96
Super Bowl XXXI, 1/26/97
Super Bowl XXXII, 1/25/98
Super Bowl XXXIII, 1/31/99
Super Bowl XXXIV, 1/30/00
Super Bowl XXXV, 1/28/01

INDIVIDUAL RECORDS

SERVICE

Most Games

6 Mike Lodish, Buffalo, XXV-XXVIII; Denver, XXXII-XXXIII
5 Marv Fleming, Green Bay, I-II; Miami, VI-VIII
Larry Cole, Dallas, V-VI, X, XII-XIII
Cliff Harris, Dallas, V-VI, X, XII-XIII
Charles Haley, San Francisco, XXIII-XXIV; Dallas, XXVII-XXVIII, XXX
D.D. Lewis, Dallas, V-VI, X, XII-XIII
Preston Pearson, Baltimore, III; Pittsburgh, IX; Dallas, X, XII-XIII
Charlie Waters, Dallas, V-VI, X, XII-XIII
Rayfield Wright, Dallas, V-VI, X, XII-XIII
Cornelius Bennett, Buffalo, XXV-XXVIII; Atlanta, XXXIII
John Elway, Denver, XXI-XXII, XXIV, XXXII-XXXIII
Glenn Parker, Buffalo, XXV-XXVIII; N.Y. Giants, XXXV
4 By many players

Most Games, Winning Team

5 Charles Haley, San Francisco, XXIII-XXIV; Dallas, XXVII-XXVIII, XXX
4 By many players

Most Games, Coach

6 Don Shula, Baltimore, III; Miami, VI-VIII, XVII, XIX
5 Tom Landry, Dallas, V-VI, X, XII-XIII
4 Bud Grant, Minnesota, IV, VIII-IX, XI
Chuck Noll, Pittsburgh, IX-X, XIII-XIV
Joe Gibbs, Washington, XVII-XVIII, XXII, XXVI
Marv Levy, Buffalo, XXV-XXVIII
Dan Reeves, Denver, XXI-XXII, XXIV; Atlanta, XXXIII

Most Games, Winning Team, Coach

4 Chuck Noll, Pittsburgh, IX-X, XIII-XIV
3 Bill Walsh, San Francisco, XVI, XIX, XXIII
Joe Gibbs, Washington, XVII, XXII, XXVI
2 Vince Lombardi, Green Bay, I-II
Tom Landry, Dallas, VI, XII
Don Shula, Miami, VII-VIII
Tom Flores, Oakland, XV; L.A. Raiders, XVIII
Bill Parcells, N.Y. Giants, XXI, XXV
Jimmy Johnson, Dallas, XXVII-XXVIII
George Seifert, San Francisco, XXIV, XXIX
Mike Shanahan, Denver, XXXII-XXXIII

Most Games, Losing Team, Coach

4 Bud Grant, Minnesota, IV, VIII-IX, XI
Don Shula, Baltimore, III; Miami, VI, XVII, XIX
Marv Levy, Buffalo, XXV-XXVIII
Dan Reeves, Denver, XXI-XXII, XXIV; Atlanta, XXXIII
3 Tom Landry, Dallas, V, X, XIII

SCORING

POINTS

Most Points, Career

42 Jerry Rice, San Francisco, 3 games (7-td)
30 Emmitt Smith, Dallas, 3 games (5-td)
24 Franco Harris, Pittsburgh, 4 games (4-td)
Roger Craig, San Francisco, 3 games (4-td)
Thurman Thomas, Buffalo, 4 games (4-td)
John Elway, Denver, 5 games (4-td)

Most Points, Game

18 Roger Craig, San Francisco vs. Miami, XIX (3-td)
Jerry Rice, San Francisco vs. Denver, XXIV (3-td);
vs. San Diego, XXIX (3-td)
Ricky Watters, San Francisco vs. San Diego, XXIX (3-td)
Terrell Davis, Denver vs. Green Bay, XXXII (3-td)
15 Don Chandler, Green Bay vs. Oakland, II (3-pat, 4-fg)
14 Ray Wersching, San Francisco vs. Cincinnati, XVI (2-pat, 4-fg)
Kevin Butler, Chicago vs. New England, XX (5-pat, 3-fg)

TOUCHDOWNS

Most Touchdowns, Career

7 Jerry Rice, San Francisco, 3 games (7-p)
5 Emmitt Smith, Dallas, 3 games (5-r)
4 Franco Harris, Pittsburgh, 4 games (4-r)
Roger Craig, San Francisco, 3 games (2-r, 2-p)
Thurman Thomas, Buffalo, 4 games (4-r)
John Elway, Denver, 5 games (4-r)

Most Touchdowns, Game

3 Roger Craig, San Francisco vs. Miami, XIX (1-r, 2-p)
Jerry Rice, San Francisco. vs. Denver, XXIV (3-p);
vs. San Diego, XXIX (3-p)
Ricky Watters, San Francisco vs. San Diego, XXIX (1-r, 2-p)
Terrell Davis, Denver vs. Green Bay, XXXII (3-r)
2 Max McGee, Green Bay vs. Kansas City, I (2-p)
Elijah Pitts, Green Bay vs. Kansas City, I (2-r)
Bill Miller, Oakland vs. Green Bay, II (2-p)
Larry Csonka, Miami vs. Minnesota, VIII (2-r)
Pete Banaszak, Oakland vs. Minnesota, XI (2-r)
John Stallworth, Pittsburgh vs. Dallas, XIII (2-p)
Franco Harris, Pittsburgh vs. Los Angeles, XIV (2-r)
Cliff Branch, Oakland vs. Philadelphia, XV (2-p)
Dan Ross, Cincinnati vs. San Francisco, XVI (2-p)
Marcus Allen, L.A. Raiders vs. Washington, XVIII (2-r)
Jim McMahon, Chicago vs. New England, XX (2-r)
Ricky Sanders, Washington vs. Denver, XXII (2-p)
Timmy Smith, Washington vs. Denver, XXII (2-r)
Tom Rathman, San Francisco vs. Denver, XXIV (2-r)
Gerald Riggs, Washington vs. Buffalo, XXVI (2-r)
Michael Irvin, Dallas vs. Buffalo, XXVII (2-p)
Emmitt Smith, Dallas vs. Buffalo, XXVIII (2-r)
Emmitt Smith, Dallas vs. Pittsburgh, XXX (2-r)
Antonio Freeman, Green Bay vs. Denver, XXXII (2-p)
Howard Griffith, Denver vs. Atlanta, XXXIII (2-r)
Eddie George, Tennessee vs. St. Louis, XXXIV (2-r)

POINTS AFTER TOUCHDOWN

Most (One-Point) Points After Touchdown, Career

9 Mike Cofer, San Francisco, 2 games (10 att)
8 Don Chandler, Green Bay, 2 games (8 att)
Roy Gerela, Pittsburgh, 3 games (9 att)
Chris Bahr, Oakland-L.A. Raiders, 2 games (8 att)
Jason Elam, Denver, 2 games (8 att)
7 Ray Wersching, San Francisco, 2 games (7 att)
Lin Elliott, Dallas, 1 game (7 att)
Doug Brien, San Francisco, 1 game (7 att)

Most (One-Point) Points After Touchdown, Game

7 Mike Cofer, San Francisco vs. Denver, XXIV (8 att)
Lin Elliott, Dallas vs. Buffalo, XXVII (7 att)
Doug Brien, San Francisco vs. San Diego, XXIX (7 att)
6 Ali Haji-Sheikh, Washington vs. Denver, XXII (6 att)
5 Don Chandler, Green Bay vs. Kansas City, I (5 att)
Roy Gerela, Pittsburgh vs. Dallas, XIII (5 att)
Chris Bahr, L.A. Raiders vs. Washington, XVIII (5 att)
Ray Wersching, San Francisco vs. Miami, XIX (5 att)
Kevin Butler, Chicago vs. New England, XX (5 att)

Most Two-Point Conversions, Game

1 Mark Seay, San Diego vs. San Francisco, XXIX
Alfred Pupunu, San Diego vs. San Francisco, XXIX
Mark Chmura, Green Bay vs. New England, XXXI

FIELD GOALS

Field Goals Attempted, Career

6 Jim Turner, N.Y. Jets-Denver, 2 games
Roy Gerela, Pittsburgh, 3 games
Rich Karlis, Denver, 2 games
5 Efren Herrera, Dallas, 1 game
Ray Wersching, San Francisco, 2 games
Jason Elam, Denver, 2 games

Most Field Goals Attempted, Game

5 Jim Turner, N.Y. Jets vs. Baltimore, III
Efren Herrera, Dallas vs. Denver, XII
4 Don Chandler, Green Bay vs. Oakland, II
Roy Gerela, Pittsburgh vs. Dallas, X
Ray Wersching, San Francisco vs. Cincinnati, XVI
Rich Karlis, Denver vs. N.Y. Giants, XXI
Mike Cofer, San Francisco vs. Cincinnati, XXIII
Jason Elam, Denver vs. Atlanta, XXXIII
Jeff Wilkins, St. Louis vs. Tennessee, XXXIV

SUPER BOWL RECORDS

Most Field Goals, Career
5 Ray Wersching, San Francisco, 2 games (5 att)
4 Don Chandler, Green Bay, 2 games (4 att)
Jim Turner, N.Y. Jets-Denver, 2 games (6 att)
Uwe von Schamann, Miami, 2 games (4 att)
3 Mike Clark, Dallas, 2 games (3 att)
Jan Stenerud, Kansas City, 1 game (3 att)
Chris Bahr, Oakland-L.A. Raiders, 2 games (4 att)
Mark Moseley, Washington, 2 games (4 att)
Kevin Butler, Chicago, 1 game (3 att)
Rich Karlis, Denver, 2 games (6 att)
Jim Breech, Cincinnati, 2 games (3 att)
Matt Bahr, Pittsburgh-N.Y. Giants, 2 games (3 att)
Chip Lohmiller, Washington, 1 game (3 att)
Steve Christie, Buffalo, 2 games (3 att)
Eddie Murray, Dallas, 1 game (3 att)
Jason Elam, Denver, 2 games (5 att)
Jeff Wilkins, St. Louis, 1 game (4 att)

Most Field Goals, Game
4 Don Chandler, Green Bay vs. Oakland, II
Ray Wersching, San Francisco vs. Cincinnati, XVI
3 Jim Turner, N.Y. Jets vs. Baltimore, III
Jan Stenerud, Kansas City vs. Minnesota, IV
Uwe von Schamann, Miami vs. San Francisco, XIX
Kevin Butler, Chicago vs. New England, XX
Jim Breech, Cincinnati vs. San Francisco, XXIII
Chip Lohmiller, Washington vs. Buffalo, XXVI
Eddie Murray, Dallas vs. Buffalo, XXVIII
Jeff Wilkins, St. Louis vs. Tennessee, XXXIV

Longest Field Goal
54 Steve Christie, Buffalo vs. Dallas, XXVIII
51 Jason Elam, Denver vs. Green Bay, XXXII
48 Jan Stenerud, Kansas City vs. Minnesota, IV
Rich Karlis, Denver vs. N.Y. Giants, XXI

SAFETIES
Most Safeties, Game
1 Dwight White, Pittsburgh vs. Minnesota, IX
Reggie Harrison, Pittsburgh vs. Dallas, X
Henry Waechter, Chicago vs. New England, XX
George Martin, N.Y. Giants vs. Denver, XXI
Bruce Smith, Buffalo vs. N.Y. Giants, XXV

RUSHING
ATTEMPTS
Most Attempts, Career
101 Franco Harris, Pittsburgh, 4 games
70 Emmitt Smith, Dallas, 3 games
64 John Riggins, Washington, 2 games

Most Attempts, Game
38 John Riggins, Washington vs. Miami, 1983
34 Franco Harris, Pittsburgh vs. Minnesota, 1975
33 Larry Csonka, Miami vs. Minnesota, 1974

YARDS GAINED
Most Yards Gained, Career
354 Franco Harris, Pittsburgh, 4 games
297 Larry Csonka, Miami, 3 games
289 Emmitt Smith, Dallas, 3 games

Most Yards Gained, Game
204 Timmy Smith, Washington vs. Denver, XXII
191 Marcus Allen, L.A. Raiders vs. Washington, XVIII
166 John Riggins, Washington vs. Miami, XVII

Longest Run From Scrimmage
74 Marcus Allen, L.A. Raiders vs. Washington, XVIII (TD)
58 Tom Matte, Baltimore vs. N.Y. Jets, III
Timmy Smith, Washington vs. Denver, XXII (TD)
49 Larry Csonka, Miami vs. Washington, VII

AVERAGE GAIN
Highest Average Gain, Career (20 attempts)
9.6 Marcus Allen, L.A. Raiders, 1 game (20-191)
9.3 Timmy Smith, Washington, 1 game (22-204)
5.3 Walt Garrison, Dallas, 2 games (26-139)

Highest Average Gain, Game (10 attempts)
10.5 Tom Matte, Baltimore vs. N.Y. Jets, III (11-116)
9.6 Marcus Allen, L.A. Raiders vs. Washington, XVIII (20-191)
9.3 Timmy Smith, Washington vs. Denver, XXII (22-204)

TOUCHDOWNS
Most Touchdowns, Career
5 Emmitt Smith, Dallas, 3 games
4 Franco Harris, Pittsburgh, 4 games
Thurman Thomas, Buffalo, 4 games
John Elway, Denver, 5 games
3 Terrell Davis, Denver, 2 games

Most Touchdowns, Game
3 Terrell Davis, Denver vs. Green Bay, XXXII
2 Elijah Pitts, Green Bay vs. Kansas City, I
Larry Csonka, Miami vs. Minnesota, VIII
Pete Banaszak, Oakland vs. Minnesota, XI
Franco Harris, Pittsburgh vs. Los Angeles, XIV
Marcus Allen, L.A. Raiders vs. Washington, XVIII
Jim McMahon, Chicago vs. New England, XX
Timmy Smith, Washington vs. Denver, XXII
Tom Rathman, San Francisco vs. Denver, XXIV
Gerald Riggs, Washington vs. Buffalo, XXVI
Emmitt Smith, Dallas vs. Buffalo, XXVIII
Emmitt Smith, Dallas vs. Pittsburgh, XXX
Howard Griffith, Denver vs. Atlanta, XXXIII
Eddie George, Tennessee vs. St. Louis, XXXIV

PASSING
PASSER RATING
Highest Passer Rating, Career (40 attempts)
127.8 Joe Montana, San Francisco, 4 games
122.8 Jim Plunkett, Oakland-L.A. Raiders, 2 games
112.8 Terry Bradshaw, Pittsburgh, 4 games

ATTEMPTS
Most Passes Attempted, Career
152 John Elway, Denver, 5 games
145 Jim Kelly, Buffalo, 4 games
122 Joe Montana, San Francisco, 4 games

Most Passes Attempted, Game
58 Jim Kelly, Buffalo vs. Washington, XXVI
50 Dan Marino, Miami vs. San Francisco, XIX
Jim Kelly, Buffalo vs. Dallas, XXVIII
49 Stan Humphries, San Diego vs. San Francisco, XXIX
Neil O'Donnell, Pittsburgh vs. Dallas, XXX

COMPLETIONS
Most Passes Completed, Career
83 Joe Montana, San Francisco, 4 games
81 Jim Kelly, Buffalo, 4 games
76 John Elway, Denver, 5 games

Most Passes Completed, Game
31 Jim Kelly, Buffalo vs. Dallas, XXVIII
29 Dan Marino, Miami vs. San Francisco, XIX
28 Jim Kelly, Buffalo vs. Washington, XXVI
Neil O'Donnell, Pittsburgh vs. Dallas, XXX

Most Consecutive Completions, Game
13 Joe Montana, San Francisco vs. Denver, XXIV
10 Phil Simms, N.Y. Giants vs. Denver, XXI
Troy Aikman, Dallas vs. Pittsburgh, XXX
9 Jim Kelly, Buffalo vs. Dallas, XXVIII
Neil O'Donnell, Pittsburgh vs. Dallas, XXX
Steve McNair, Tennessee vs. St. Louis, XXXIV

COMPLETION PERCENTAGE
Highest Completion Percentage, Career (40 attempts)
70.0 Troy Aikman, Dallas, 3 games, (80-56)
68.0 Joe Montana, San Francisco, 4 games (122-83)
63.6 Len Dawson, Kansas City, 2 games (44-28)

Highest Completion Percentage, Game (20 attempts)
88.0 Phil Simms, N.Y. Giants vs. Denver, XXI (25-22)
75.9 Joe Montana, San Francisco vs. Denver, XXIV (29-22)
73.5 Ken Anderson, Cincinnati vs. San Francisco, XVI (34-25)

YARDS GAINED
Most Yards Gained, Career
1,142 Joe Montana, San Francisco, 4 games
1,128 John Elway, Denver, 5 games
932 Terry Bradshaw, Pittsburgh, 4 games

Most Yards Gained, Game
414 Kurt Warner, St. Louis vs. Tennessee, XXXIV
357 Joe Montana, San Francisco vs. Cincinnati, XXIII
340 Doug Williams, Washington vs. Denver, XXII

Longest Pass Completion
81 Brett Favre (to Freeman), Green Bay vs. New England, XXXI (TD)
80 Jim Plunkett (to King), Oakland vs. Philadelphia, XV (TD)
Doug Williams (to Sanders), Washington vs. Denver, XXII (TD)
John Elway (to R. Smith), Denver vs. Atlanta, XXXIII (TD)
76 David Woodley (to Cefalo), Miami vs. Washington, XVII (TD)

AVERAGE GAIN

Highest Average Gain, Career (40 attempts)

11.10 Terry Bradshaw, Pittsburgh, 4 games (84-932)
9.62 Bart Starr, Green Bay, 2 games (47-452)
9.41 Jim Plunkett, Oakland-L.A. Raiders, 2 games (46-433)

Highest Average Gain, Game (20 attempts)

14.71 Terry Bradshaw, Pittsburgh vs. Los Angeles, XIV (21-309)
12.80 Jim McMahon, Chicago vs. New England, XX (20-256)
12.43 Jim Plunkett, Oakland vs. Philadelphia, XV (21-261)

TOUCHDOWNS

Most Touchdown Passes, Career

11 Joe Montana, San Francisco, 4 games
9 Terry Bradshaw, Pittsburgh, 4 games
8 Roger Staubach, Dallas, 4 games

Most Touchdown Passes, Game

6 Steve Young, San Francisco vs. San Diego, XXIX
5 Joe Montana, San Francisco vs. Denver, XXIV
4 Terry Bradshaw, Pittsburgh vs. Dallas, XIII
Doug Williams, Washington vs. Denver, XXII
Troy Aikman, Dallas vs. Buffalo, XXVII

HAD INTERCEPTED

Lowest Percentage, Passes Had Intercepted, Career (40 attempts)

0.00 Jim Plunkett, Oakland-L.A. Raiders, 2 games (46-0)
Joe Montana, San Francisco, 4 games (122-0)
Kurt Warner, St. Louis, 1 game (45-0)
1.25 Troy Aikman, Dallas, 3 games (80-1)
1.45 Brett Favre, Green Bay, 2 games (69-1)

Most Attempts, Without Interception, Game

45 Kurt Warner, St. Louis vs. Tennessee, XXXIV
36 Joe Montana, San Francisco vs. Cincinnati, XXIII
Steve Young, San Francisco vs. San Diego, XXIX
Steve McNair, Tennessee vs. St. Louis, XXXIV
35 Joe Montana, San Francisco vs. Miami, XIX

Most Passes Had Intercepted, Career

8 John Elway, Denver, 5 games
7 Craig Morton, Dallas-Denver, 2 games
Jim Kelly, Buffalo, 4 games
6 Fran Tarkenton, Minnesota, 3 games

Most Passes Had Intercepted, Game

4 Craig Morton, Denver vs. Dallas, XII
Jim Kelly, Buffalo vs. Washington, XXVI
Drew Bledsoe, New England vs. Green Bay, XXXI
Kerry Collins, N.Y. Giants vs. Baltimore, XXXV
3 By ten players

PASS RECEIVING

RECEPTIONS

Most Receptions, Career

28 Jerry Rice, San Francisco, 3 games
27 Andre Reed, Buffalo, 4 games
20 Roger Craig, San Francisco, 3 games
Thurman Thomas, Buffalo, 4 games

Most Receptions, Game

11 Dan Ross, Cincinnati vs. San Francisco, XVI
Jerry Rice, San Francisco vs. Cincinnati, XXIII
10 Tony Nathan, Miami vs. San Francisco, XIX
Jerry Rice, San Francisco vs. San Diego, XXIX
Andre Hastings, Pittsburgh vs. Dallas, XXX
9 Ricky Sanders, Washington vs. Denver, XXII
Antonio Freeman, Green Bay vs. Denver, XXXII

YARDS GAINED

Most Yards Gained, Career

512 Jerry Rice, San Francisco, 3 games
364 Lynn Swann, Pittsburgh, 4 games
323 Andre Reed, Buffalo, 4 games

Most Yards Gained, Game

215 Jerry Rice, San Francisco vs. Cincinnati, XXIII
193 Ricky Sanders, Washington vs. Denver, XXII
162 Isaac Bruce, St. Louis vs. Tennessee, XXXIV

Longest Reception

81 Antonio Freeman (from Favre), Green Bay vs. New England, XXXI (TD)
80 Kenny King (from Plunkett), Oakland vs. Philadelphia, XV (TD)
Ricky Sanders (from Williams), Washington vs. Denver, XXII (TD)
Rod Smith (from Elway), Denver vs. Atlanta, XXXIII
76 Jimmy Cefalo (from Woodley), Miami vs. Washington, XVII (TD)

AVERAGE GAIN

Highest Average Gain, Career (8 receptions)

24.4 John Stallworth, Pittsburgh, 4 games (11-268)
23.4 Ricky Sanders, Washington, 2 games (10-234)
22.8 Lynn Swann, Pittsburgh, 4 games (16-364)

Highest Average Gain, Game (3 receptions)

40.33 John Stallworth, Pittsburgh vs. Los Angeles, XIV (3-121)
40.25 Lynn Swann, Pittsburgh vs. Dallas, X (4-161)
38.33 John Stallworth, Pittsburgh vs. Dallas, XIII (3-115)

TOUCHDOWNS

Most Touchdowns, Career

7 Jerry Rice, San Francisco, 3 games
3 John Stallworth, Pittsburgh, 4 games
Lynn Swann, Pittsburgh, 4 games
Cliff Branch, Oakland-L.A. Raiders, 3 games
Antonio Freeman, Green Bay, 2 games
2 Max McGee, Green Bay, 2 games
Bill Miller, Oakland, 1 game
Butch Johnson, Dallas, 2 games
Dan Ross, Cincinnati, 1 game
Roger Craig, San Francisco, 3 games
Ricky Sanders, Washington, 2 games
John Taylor, San Francisco, 3 games
Gary Clark, Washington, 2 games
Don Beebe, Buffalo-Green Bay, 4 games
Michael Irvin, Dallas, 3 games
Ricky Watters, San Francisco, 1 game
Jay Novacek, Dallas, 3 games

Most Touchdowns, Game

3 Jerry Rice, San Francisco vs. Denver, XXIV; vs. San Diego, XXIX
2 Max McGee, Green Bay vs. Kansas City, I
Bill Miller, Oakland vs. Green Bay, II
John Stallworth, Pittsburgh vs. Dallas, XIII
Cliff Branch, Oakland vs. Philadelphia, XV
Dan Ross, Cincinnati vs. San Francisco, XVI
Roger Craig, San Francisco vs. Miami, XIX
Ricky Sanders, Washington vs. Denver, XXII
Michael Irvin, Dallas vs. Buffalo, XXVII
Ricky Watters, San Francisco vs. San Diego, XXIX
Antonio Freeman, Green Bay vs. Denver, XXXII

INTERCEPTIONS BY

Most Interceptions By, Career

3 Chuck Howley, Dallas, 2 games
Rod Martin, Oakland-L.A. Raiders, 2 games
Larry Brown, Dallas, 3 games
2 Randy Beverly, N.Y. Jets, 1 game
Jake Scott, Miami, 3 games
Mike Wagner, Pittsburgh, 3 games
Mel Blount, Pittsburgh, 4 games
Eric Wright, San Francisco, 4 games
Barry Wilburn, Washington, 1 game
Brad Edwards, Washington, 1 game
Thomas Everett, Dallas, 2 games
James Washington, Dallas, 2 games
Darrien Gordon, San Diego-Denver, 3 games

Most Interceptions By, Game

3 Rod Martin, Oakland vs. Philadelphia, XV
2 Randy Beverly, N.Y. Jets vs. Baltimore, III
Chuck Howley, Dallas vs. Baltimore, V
Jake Scott, Miami vs. Washington, VII
Barry Wilburn, Washington vs. Denver, XXII
Brad Edwards, Washington vs. Buffalo, XXVI
Thomas Everett, Dallas vs. Buffalo, XXVII
Larry Brown, Dallas vs. Pittsburgh, XXX
Darrien Gordon, Denver vs. Atlanta, XXXIII

YARDS GAINED

Most Yards Gained, Career

108 Darrien Gordon, San Diego-Denver, 3 games
77 Larry Brown, Dallas, 3 games
75 Willie Brown, Oakland, 2 games

Most Yards Gained, Game

108 Darrien Gordon, Denver vs. Atlanta, XXXIII
77 Larry Brown, Dallas vs. Pittsburgh, XXX
75 Willie Brown, Oakland vs. Minnesota, XI

Longest Return

75 Willie Brown, Oakland vs. Minnesota, XI (TD)
60 Herb Adderley, Green Bay vs. Oakland, II (TD)
58 Darrien Gordon, Denver vs. Atlanta, XXXIII

TOUCHDOWNS

Most Touchdowns, Game

1 Herb Adderley, Green Bay vs. Oakland, II
Willie Brown, Oakland vs. Minnesota, XI
Jack Squirek, L.A. Raiders vs. Washington, XVIII

Reggie Phillips, Chicago vs. New England, XX
Duane Starks, Baltimore vs. N.Y. Giants, XXXV

PUNTING

Most Punts, Career

17 Mike Eischeid, Oakland-Minnesota, 3 games
Mike Horan, Denver-St. Louis, 4 games
15 Larry Seiple, Miami, 3 games
14 Ron Widby, Dallas, 2 games
Ray Guy, Oakland-L.A. Raiders, 3 games
Chris Mohr, Buffalo, 3 games
Craig Hentrich, Green Bay-Tennessee, 3 games

Most Punts, Game

11 Brad Maynard, N.Y. Giants vs. Baltimore, XXXV
10 Kyle Richardson, Baltimore vs. N.Y. Giants, XXXV
9 Ron Widby, Dallas vs. Baltimore, V

Longest Punt

63 Lee Johnson, Cincinnati vs. San Francisco, XXIII
62 Rich Camarillo, New England vs. Chicago, XX
61 Jerrel Wilson, Kansas City vs. Green Bay, I

AVERAGE YARDAGE

Highest Average, Punting, Career (10 punts)

46.5 Jerrel Wilson, Kansas City, 2 games (11-511)
43.0 Kyle Richardson, Baltimore, 1 game (10-430)
41.9 Ray Guy, Oakland-L.A. Raiders, 3 games (14-587)

Highest Average, Punting, Game (4 punts)

48.8 Bryan Wagner, San Diego vs. San Francisco, XXIX (4-195)
48.5 Jerrel Wilson, Kansas City vs. Minnesota, IV (4-194)
46.3 Jim Miller, San Francisco vs. Cincinnati, XVI (4-185)

PUNT RETURNS

Most Punt Returns, Career

6 Willie Wood, Green Bay, 2 games
Jake Scott, Miami, 3 games
Theo Bell, Pittsburgh, 2 games
Mike Nelms, Washington, 1 game
John Taylor, San Francisco, 3 games
Desmond Howard, Green Bay, 1 game
David Meggett, N.Y. Giants-New England, 2 games
5 Dana McLemore, San Francisco, 1 game
4 By eight players

Most Punt Returns, Game

6 Mike Nelms, Washington vs. Miami, XVII
Desmond Howard, Green Bay vs. New England, XXXI
5 Willie Wood, Green Bay vs. Oakland, II
Dana McLemore, San Francisco vs. Miami, XIX
4 By seven players

Most Fair Catches, Game

4 Jermaine Lewis, Baltimore vs. N.Y. Giants, XXXV
3 Ron Gardin, Baltimore vs. Dallas, V
Golden Richards, Dallas vs. Pittsburgh, X
Greg Pruitt, L.A. Raiders vs. Washington, XVIII
Al Edwards, Buffalo vs. N.Y. Giants, XXV
David Meggett, N.Y. Giants vs. Buffalo, XXV

YARDS GAINED

Most Yards Gained, Career

94 John Taylor, San Francisco, 3 games
90 Desmond Howard, Green Bay, 1 game
67 David Meggett, N.Y. Giants-New England, 2 games

Most Yards Gained, Game

90 Desmond Howard, Green Bay vs. New England, XXXI
56 John Taylor, San Francisco vs. Cincinnati, XXIII
52 Mike Nelms, Washington vs. Miami, XXII

Longest Return

45 John Taylor, San Francisco vs. Cincinnati, XXIII
34 Darrell Green, Washington vs. L.A. Raiders, XVIII
Desmond Howard, Green Bay vs. New England, XXXI
Jermaine Lewis, Baltimore vs. N.Y. Giants, XXXV
32 Desmond Howard, Green Bay vs. New England, XXXI

AVERAGE YARDAGE

Highest Average, Career (4 returns)

15.7 John Taylor, San Francisco, 3 games (6-94)
15.0 Desmond Howard, Green Bay, 1 game (6-90)
11.2 David Meggett, N.Y. Giants-New England, 2 games (6-67)

Highest Average, Game (3 returns)

18.7 John Taylor, San Francisco vs. Cincinnati, XXIII (3-56)
15.0 Desmond Howard, Green Bay vs. New England, XXXI (6-90)
12.7 John Taylor, San Francisco vs. Denver, XXIV (3-38)

TOUCHDOWNS

Most Touchdowns, Game

None

KICKOFF RETURNS

Most Kickoff Returns, Career

10 Ken Bell, Denver, 3 games
8 Larry Anderson, Pittsburgh, 2 games
Fulton Walker, Miami, 2 games
Andre Coleman, San Diego, 1 game
7 Preston Pearson, Baltimore-Pittsburgh-Dallas, 5 games
Stephen Starring, New England, 1 game
David Meggett, N.Y. Giants-New England, 2 games

Most Kickoff Returns, Game

8 Andre Coleman, San Diego vs. San Francisco, XXIX
7 Stephen Starring, New England vs. Chicago, XX
6 Darren Carrington, Denver vs. San Francisco, XXIV
Antonio Freeman, Green Bay vs. Denver, XXXII
Ron Dixon, N.Y. Giants vs. Baltimore, XXXV

YARDS GAINED

Most Yards Gained, Career

283 Fulton Walker, Miami, 2 games
244 Andre Coleman, San Diego, 1 game
210 Tim Dwight, Atlanta, 1 game

Most Yards Gained, Game

244 Andre Coleman, San Diego vs. San Francisco, XXIX
210 Tim Dwight, Atlanta vs. Denver, XXXIII
190 Fulton Walker, Miami vs. Washington, XVII

Longest Return

99 Desmond Howard, Green Bay vs. New England, XXXI (TD)
98 Fulton Walker, Miami vs. Washington, XVII (TD)
Andre Coleman, San Diego vs. San Francisco, XXIX (TD)
97 Ron Dixon, N.Y. Giants vs. Baltimore, XXXV (TD)

AVERAGE YARDAGE

Highest Average, Career (4 returns)

42.0 Tim Dwight, Atlanta, 1 game (5-210)
38.5 Desmond Howard, Green Bay, 1 game (4-154)
35.4 Fulton Walker, Miami, 2 games (8-283)

Highest Average, Game (3 returns)

47.5 Fulton Walker, Miami vs. Washington, XVII (4-190)
42.0 Tim Dwight, Atlanta vs. Denver, XXXIII (5-210)
38.5 Desmond Howard, Green Bay vs. New England, XXXI (4-154)

TOUCHDOWNS

Most Touchdowns, Game

1 Fulton Walker, Miami vs. Washington, XVII
Stanford Jennings, Cincinnati vs. San Francisco, XXIII
Andre Coleman, San Diego vs. San Francisco, XXIX
Desmond Howard, Green Bay vs. New England, XXXI
Tim Dwight, Atlanta vs. Denver, XXXIII
Ron Dixon, N.Y. Giants vs. Baltimore, XXXV
Jermaine Lewis, Baltimore vs. N.Y. Giants, XXXV

FUMBLES

Most Fumbles, Career

5 Roger Staubach, Dallas, 4 games
4 Jim Kelly, Buffalo, 4 games
3 Franco Harris, Pittsburgh, 4 games
Terry Bradshaw, Pittsburgh, 4 games
John Elway, Denver, 5 games
Frank Reich, Buffalo, 4 games
Thurman Thomas, Buffalo, 4 games

Most Fumbles, Game

3 Roger Staubach, Dallas vs. Pittsburgh, X
Jim Kelly, Buffalo vs. Washington, XXVI
Frank Reich, Buffalo vs. Dallas, XXVII
2 Franco Harris, Pittsburgh vs. Minnesota, IX
Butch Johnson, Dallas vs. Denver, XII
Terry Bradshaw, Pittsburgh vs. Dallas, XIII
Joe Montana, San Francisco vs. Cincinnati, XXIII
John Elway, Denver vs. San Francisco, XXIV
Thurman Thomas, Buffalo vs. Dallas, XXVIII

RECOVERIES

Most Fumbles Recovered, Career

2 Jake Scott, Miami, 3 games (1 own, 1 opp)
Fran Tarkenton, Minnesota, 3 games (2 own)
Franco Harris, Pittsburgh, 4 games (2 own)
Roger Staubach, Dallas, 4 games (2 own)
Bobby Walden, Pittsburgh, 2 games (2 own)
John Fitzgerald, Dallas, 4 games (2 own)

Randy Hughes, Dallas, 3 games (2 opp)
Butch Johnson, Dallas, 2 games (2 own)
Mike Singletary, Chicago, 1 game (2 opp)
John Elway, Denver, 5 games (2 own)
Jimmie Jones, Dallas, 2 games (2 opp)
Kenneth Davis, Buffalo, 4 games (2 own)

Most Fumbles Recovered, Game
2 Jake Scott, Miami vs. Minnesota, VIII (1 own, 1 opp)
Roger Staubach, Dallas vs. Pittsburgh, X (2 own)
Randy Hughes, Dallas vs. Denver, XII (2 opp)
Butch Johnson, Dallas vs. Denver, XII (2 own)
Mike Singletary, Chicago vs. New England, XX (2 opp)
Jimmie Jones, Dallas vs. Buffalo, XXVII (2 opp)

YARDS GAINED

Most Yards Gained, Game
64 Leon Lett, Dallas vs. Buffalo, XXVII (opp)
49 Mike Bass, Washington vs. Miami, VII (opp)
46 James Washington, Dallas vs. Buffalo, XXVIII (opp)

Longest Return
64 Leon Lett, Dallas vs. Buffalo, XXVII
49 Mike Bass, Washington vs. Miami, VII (TD)
46 James Washington, Dallas vs. Buffalo, XXVIII (TD)

TOUCHDOWNS

Most Touchdowns, Game
1 Mike Bass, Washington vs. Miami, VII (opp 49 yds)
Mike Hegman, Dallas vs. Pittsburgh, XIII (opp 37 yds)
Jimmie Jones, Dallas vs. Buffalo, XXVII (opp 2 yds)
Ken Norton, Dallas vs. Buffalo, XXVII (opp 9 yds)
James Washington, Dallas vs. Buffalo, XXVIII (opp 46 yds)

COMBINED NET YARDS GAINED

(Rushing, receiving, interception returns, punt returns, kickoff returns, and fumble returns)

ATTEMPTS

Most Attempts, Career
108 Franco Harris, Pittsburgh, 4 games
81 Emmitt Smith, Dallas, 3 games
72 Roger Craig, San Francisco, 3 games
Thurman Thomas, Buffalo, 4 games

Most Attempts, Game
39 John Riggins, Washington vs. Miami, XVII
35 Franco Harris, Pittsburgh vs. Minnesota, IX
34 Matt Snell, N.Y. Jets vs. Baltimore, III
Emmitt Smith, Dallas vs. Buffalo, XXVIII

YARDS GAINED

Most Yards Gained, Career
527 Jerry Rice, San Francisco, 3 games
468 Franco Harris, Pittsburgh, 4 games
410 Roger Craig, San Francisco, 3 games

Most Yards Gained, Game
244 Andre Coleman, San Diego vs. San Francisco, XXIX
Desmond Howard, Green Bay vs. New England, XXXI
235 Ricky Sanders, Washington vs. Denver, XXII
230 Antonio Freeman, Green Bay vs. Denver, XXXII

SACKS

Sacks have been compiled since XVII.

Most Sacks, Career
4.5 Charles Haley, San Francisco-Dallas, 5 games
3.0 Danny Stubbs, San Francisco, 2 games
Leonard Marshall, N.Y. Giants, 2 games
Jeff Wright, Buffalo, 4 games
Reggie White, Green Bay, 2 games
2.5 Dexter Manley, Washington, 3 games

Most Sacks, Game
3.0 Reggie White, Green Bay vs. New England, XXXI
2.0 Dwaine Board, San Francisco vs. Miami, XIX
Dennis Owens, New England vs. Chicago, XX
Otis Wilson, Chicago vs. New England, XX
Leonard Marshall, N.Y. Giants vs. Denver, XXI
Alvin Walton, Washington vs. Denver, XXII
Charles Haley, San Francisco vs. Cincinnati, XXIII
Danny Stubbs, San Francisco vs. Denver, XXIV
Jeff Wright, Buffalo vs. Dallas, XXVIII
Raylee Johnson, San Diego vs. San Francisco, XXIX
Chad Hennings, Dallas vs. Pittsburgh, XXX
Tedy Bruschi, New England vs. Green Bay, XXXI
Michael McCrary, Baltimore vs. N.Y. Giants, XXXV

TEAM RECORDS

GAMES, VICTORIES, DEFEATS

Most Games
8 Dallas, V-VI, X, XII-XIII, XXVII-XXVIII, XXX
6 Denver, XII, XXI-XXII, XXIV, XXXII-XXXIII
5 Miami, VI-VIII, XVII, XIX
Washington, VII, XVII-XVIII, XXII, XXVI
San Francisco, XVI, XIX, XXIII-XXIV, XXIX
Pittsburgh, IX-X, XIII-XIV, XXX

Most Consecutive Games
4 Buffalo, XXV-XXVIII
3 Miami, VI-VIII
2 Green Bay, I-II; XXXI-XXXII
Dallas, V-VI; XII-XIII; XXVII-XXVIII
Minnesota, VIII-IX
Pittsburgh, IX-X; XIII-XIV
Washington, XVII-XVIII
Denver, XXI-XXII; XXXII-XXXIII
San Francisco XXIII-XXIV

Most Games Won
5 San Francisco, XVI, XIX, XXIII-XXIV, XXIX
Dallas, VI, XII, XXVII-XXVIII, XXX
4 Pittsburgh, IX-X, XIII-XIV
3 Oakland/L.A. Raiders, XI, XV, XVIII
Washington, XVII, XXII, XXVI
Green Bay, I-II, XXXI

Most Consecutive Games Won
2 Green Bay, I-II
Miami, VII-VIII
Pittsburgh, IX-X, XIII-XIV
San Francisco, XXIII-XXIV
Dallas, XXVII-XXVIII
Denver, XXXII-XXXIII

Most Games Lost
4 Minnesota, IV, VIII-IX, XI
Denver, XII, XXI-XXII, XXIV
Buffalo, XXV-XXVIII
3 Dallas, V, X, XIII
Miami, VI, XVII, XIX
2 Washington, VII, XVIII
Cincinnati, XVI, XXIII
New England, XX, XXXI

Most Consecutive Games Lost
4 Buffalo, XXV-XXVIII
2 Minnesota, VIII-IX
Denver, XXI-XXII

SCORING

Most Points, Game
55 San Francisco vs. Denver, XXIV
52 Dallas vs. Buffalo, XXVII
49 San Francisco vs. San Diego, XXIX

Fewest Points, Game
3 Miami vs. Dallas, VI
6 Minnesota vs. Pittsburgh, IX
7 By five teams

Most Points, Both Teams, Game
75 San Francisco (49) vs. San Diego (26), XXIX
69 Dallas (52) vs. Buffalo (17), XXVII
66 Pittsburgh (35) vs. Dallas (31), XIII

Fewest Points, Both Teams, Game
21 Washington (7) vs. Miami (14), VII
22 Minnesota (6) vs. Pittsburgh (16), IX
23 Baltimore (7) vs. N.Y. Jets (16), III

Largest Margin of Victory, Game
45 San Francisco vs. Denver, XXIV (55-10)
36 Chicago vs. New England, XX (46-10)
35 Dallas vs. Buffalo, XXVII (52-17)

Most Points, Each Half
1st: 35 Washington vs. Denver, XXII
2nd: 30 N.Y. Giants vs. Denver, XXI

Most Points, Each Quarter
1st: 14 Miami vs. Minnesota, VIII
Oakland vs. Philadelphia, XV
Dallas vs. Buffalo, XXVII
San Francisco vs. San Diego, XXIX
New England vs. Green Bay, XXXI
2nd: 35 Washington vs. Denver, XXII
3rd: 21 Chicago vs. New England, XX
4th: 21 Dallas vs. Buffalo, XXVII

SUPER BOWL RECORDS

Most Points, Both Teams, Each Half
1st: 45 Washington (35) vs. Denver (10), XXII
2nd: 44 Buffalo (24) vs. Washington (20), XXVI
Fewest Points, Both Teams, Each Half
1st: 2 Minnesota (0) vs. Pittsburgh (2), IX
2nd: 7 Miami (0) vs. Washington (7), VII
Denver (0) vs. Washington (7), XXII
Most Points, Both Teams, Each Quarter
1st: 24 New England (14) vs. Green Bay (10), XXXI
2nd: 35 Washington (35) vs. Denver (0), XXII
3rd: 24 Washington (14) vs. Buffalo (10), XXVI
4th: 30 Denver (17) vs. Atlanta (13), XXXIII

TOUCHDOWNS
Most Touchdowns, Game
8 San Francisco vs. Denver, XXIV
7 Dallas vs. Buffalo, XXVII
San Francisco vs. San Diego, XXIX
6 Washington vs. Denver, XXII
Fewest Touchdowns, Game
0 Miami vs. Dallas, VI
1 By 18 teams
Most Touchdowns, Both Teams, Game
10 San Francisco (7) vs. San Diego (3), XXIX
9 Pittsburgh (5) vs. Dallas (4), XIII
San Francisco (8) vs. Denver (1), XXIV
Dallas (7) vs. Buffalo (2), XXVII
7 N.Y. Giants (5) vs. Denver (2), XXI
Washington (6) vs. Denver (1), XXII
Washington (4) vs. Buffalo (3), XXVI
Green Bay (4) vs. New England (3), XXXI
Denver (4) vs. Green Bay (3), XXXII
Fewest Touchdowns, Both Teams, Game
2 Baltimore (1) vs. N.Y. Jets (1), III
3 In six games

POINTS AFTER TOUCHDOWN
Most (One-Point) Points After Touchdown, Game
7 San Francisco vs. Denver, XXIV
Dallas vs. Buffalo, XXVII
San Francisco vs. San Diego, XXIX
6 Washington vs. Denver, XXII
5 Green Bay vs. Kansas City, I
Pittsburgh vs. Dallas, XIII
L.A. Raiders vs. Washington, XVIII
San Francisco vs. Miami, XIX
Chicago vs. New England, XX
Most (One-Point) Points After Touchdown, Both Teams, Game
9 Pittsburgh (5) vs. Dallas (4), XIII
Dallas (7) vs. Buffalo (2), XXVII
8 San Francisco (7) vs. Denver (1), XXIV
San Francisco (7) vs. San Diego (1), XXIX
7 Washington (6) vs. Denver (1), XXII
Washington (4) vs. Buffalo (3), XXVI
Denver (4) vs. Green Bay (3), XXXII
Fewest (One-Point) Points After Touchdown, Both Teams, Game
2 Baltimore (1) vs. N.Y. Jets (1), III
Baltimore (1) vs. Dallas (1), V
Minnesota (0) vs. Pittsburgh (2), IX
Most Two-Point Conversions, Game
2 San Diego vs. San Francisco, XXIX
Most Two-Point Conversions, Both Teams, Game
2 San Diego (2) vs. San Francisco (0), XXIX

FIELD GOALS
Most Field Goals Attempted, Game
5 N.Y. Jets vs. Baltimore, III
Dallas vs. Denver, XII
4 Green Bay vs. Oakland, II
Pittsburgh vs. Dallas, XX
San Francisco vs. Cincinnati, XVI; XXIII
Denver vs. N.Y. Giants, XXI
Denver vs. Atlanta, XXXIII
St. Louis vs. Tennessee, XXXIV
Most Field Goals Attempted, Both Teams, Game
7 N.Y. Jets (5) vs. Baltimore (2), III
San Francisco (4) vs. Cincinnati (3), XXIII
St. Louis (4) vs. Tennessee (3), XXXIV
Denver (4) vs. Atlanta (3), XXXIII
6 Dallas (5) vs. Denver (1), XII
5 Green Bay (4) vs. Oakland (1), II
Pittsburgh (4) vs. Dallas (1), X
Oakland (3) vs. Philadelphia (2), XV
Denver (4) vs. N.Y. Giants (1), XXI
Dallas (3) vs. Buffalo (2), XXVIII
Fewest Field Goals Attempted, Both Teams, Game
1 Minnesota (0) vs. Miami (1), VIII
San Francisco (0) vs. Denver (1), XXIV
2 Green Bay (0) vs. Kansas City (2), I
Miami (1) vs. Washington (1), VII
Minnesota (1) vs. Pittsburgh (1), IX
Dallas (1) vs. Pittsburgh (1), XIII
Dallas (1) vs. Buffalo (1), XXVII
San Diego (1) vs. San Francisco (1), XXIX
Denver (1) vs. Green Bay (1), XXXII
Most Field Goals, Game
4 Green Bay vs. Oakland, II
San Francisco vs. Cincinnati, XVI
3 N.Y. Jets vs. Baltimore, III
Kansas City vs. Minnesota, IV
Miami vs. San Francisco, XIX
Chicago vs. New England, XX
Cincinnati vs. San Francisco, XXIII
Washington vs. Buffalo, XXVI
Dallas vs. Buffalo, XXVIII
St. Louis vs. Tennessee, XXXIV
Most Field Goals, Both Teams, Game
5 Cincinnati (3) vs. San Francisco (2), XXIII
Dallas (3) vs. Buffalo (2), XXVIII
4 Green Bay (4) vs. Oakland (0), II
San Francisco (4) vs. Cincinnati (0), XVI
Miami (3) vs. San Francisco (1), XIX
Chicago (3) vs. New England (1), XX
Washington (3) vs. Buffalo (1), XXVI
Atlanta (2) vs. Denver (2), XXXIII
St. Louis (3) vs. Tennessee (1), XXXIV
3 In eleven games
Fewest Field Goals, Both Teams, Game
0 Miami vs. Washington, VII
Pittsburgh vs. Minnesota, IX
1 Green Bay (0) vs. Kansas City (1), I
Minnesota (0) vs. Miami (1), VIII
Pittsburgh (0) vs. Dallas (1), XIII
Washington (0) vs. Denver (1), XXII
San Francisco (0) vs. Denver (1), XXIV
San Francisco (0) vs. San Diego (1), XXIX

SAFETIES
Most Safeties, Game
1 Pittsburgh vs. Minnesota, IX; vs. Dallas, X
Chicago vs. New England, XX
N.Y. Giants vs. Denver, XXI
Buffalo vs. N.Y. Giants, XXV

FIRST DOWNS
Most First Downs, Game
31 San Francisco vs. Miami, XIX
28 San Francisco vs. Denver, XXIV
San Francisco vs. San Diego, XXIX
27 Tennessee vs. St. Louis, XXXIV
Fewest First Downs, Game
9 Minnesota vs. Pittsburgh, IX
Miami vs. Washington, XVII
10 Dallas vs. Baltimore, V
Miami vs. Dallas, VI
11 Denver vs. Dallas, XII
N.Y. Giants vs. Baltimore, XXXV
Most First Downs, Both Teams, Game
50 San Francisco (31) vs. Miami (19), XIX
Tennessee (27) vs. St. Louis (23), XXXIV
49 Buffalo (25) vs. Washington (24), XXVI
48 San Francisco (28) vs. San Diego (20), XXIX
Fewest First Downs, Both Teams, Game
24 Dallas (10) vs. Baltimore (14), V
N.Y. Giants (11) vs. Baltimore (13), XXXV
26 Minnesota (9) vs. Pittsburgh (17), IX
27 Pittsburgh (13) vs. Dallas (14), X

RUSHING
Most First Downs, Rushing, Game
16 San Francisco vs. Miami, XIX
15 Dallas vs. Miami, VI
14 Washington vs. Miami, XVII
San Francisco vs. Denver, XXIV
Denver vs. Green Bay, XXXII

Fewest First Downs, Rushing, Game
1 New England vs. Chicago, XX
St. Louis vs. Tennessee, XXXIV
2 Minnesota vs. Kansas City, IV; vs. Pittsburgh, IX; vs. Oakland, XI
Pittsburgh vs. Dallas, XIII
Miami vs. San Francisco, XIX
N.Y. Giants vs. Baltimore, XXXV
3 Miami vs. Dallas, VI
Philadelphia vs. Oakland, XV
New England vs. Green Bay, XXXI

Most First Downs, Rushing, Both Teams, Game
21 Washington (14) vs. Miami (7), XVII
19 Washington (13) vs. Denver (6), XXII
San Francisco (14) vs. Denver (5), XXIV
18 Dallas (15) vs. Miami (3), VI
Miami (13) vs. Minnesota (5), VIII
San Francisco (16) vs. Miami (2), XIX
N.Y. Giants (10) vs. Buffalo (8), XXV
Denver (14) vs. Green Bay (4), XXXII

Fewest First Downs, Rushing, Both Teams, Game
8 Baltimore (4) vs. Dallas (4), V
Pittsburgh (2) vs. Dallas (6), XIII
N.Y. Giants (2) vs. Baltimore (6), XXXV
9 Philadelphia (3) vs. Oakland (6), XV
10 Minnesota (2) vs. Kansas City (8), IV

PASSING

Most First Downs, Passing, Game
18 Buffalo vs. Washington, XXVI
St. Louis vs. Tennessee, XXXIV
17 Miami vs. San Francisco, XIX
San Francisco vs. San Diego, XXIX
16 Denver vs. N.Y. Giants, XXI
San Francisco vs. Cincinnati, XXIII

Fewest First Downs, Passing, Game
1 Denver vs. Dallas, XII
2 Miami vs. Washington, XVII
4 Miami vs. Minnesota, VIII

Most First Downs, Passing, Both Teams, Game
32 Miami (17) vs. San Francisco (15), XIX
31 San Francisco (17) vs. San Diego (14), XXIX
St. Louis (18) vs. Tennessee (13), XXXIV
30 Buffalo (18) vs. Washington (12), XXVI

Fewest First Downs, Passing, Both Teams, Game
9 Denver (1) vs. Dallas (8), XII
10 Minnesota (5) vs. Pittsburgh (5), IX
11 Dallas (5) vs. Baltimore (6), V
Miami (2) vs. Washington (9), XVII

PENALTY

Most First Downs, Penalty, Game
4 Baltimore vs. Dallas, V
Miami vs. Minnesota, VIII
Cincinnati vs. San Francisco, XVI
Buffalo vs. Dallas, XXVII
St. Louis vs. Tennessee, XXXIV
3 Kansas City vs. Minnesota, IV
Minnesota vs. Oakland, XI
Buffalo vs. Washington, XXVI
Green Bay vs. Denver, XXXII
N.Y. Giants vs. Baltimore, XXXV

Most First Downs, Penalty, Both Teams, Game
6 Cincinnati (4) vs. San Francisco (2), XVI
St. Louis (4) vs. Tennessee (2), XXXIV
5 Baltimore (4) vs. Dallas (1), V
Miami (4) vs. Minnesota (1), VIII
Buffalo (3) vs. Washington (2), XXVI
Green Bay (3) vs. Denver (2), XXXII
4 Kansas City (3) vs. Minnesota (1), IV
Buffalo (4) vs. Dallas (0), XXVII
N.Y. Giants (3) vs. Baltimore (1), XXXV

Fewest First Downs, Penalty, Both Teams, Game
0 Dallas vs. Miami, VI
Miami vs. Washington, VII
Dallas vs. Pittsburgh, X
Miami vs. San Francisco, XIX
1 Green Bay (0) vs. Kansas City (1), I
Miami (0) vs. Washington (1), XVII
Cincinnati (0) vs. San Francisco (1), XXIII
San Francisco (0) vs. Denver (1), XXIV
Dallas (0) vs. Buffalo (1), XXVIII
Dallas (0) vs. Pittsburgh (1), XXX
Denver (0) vs. Atlanta (1), XXXIII

NET YARDS GAINED RUSHING AND PASSING

Most Yards Gained, Game
602 Washington vs. Denver, XXII
537 San Francisco vs. Miami, XIX
461 San Francisco vs. Denver, XXIV

Fewest Yards Gained, Game
119 Minnesota vs. Pittsburgh, IXX
123 New England vs. Chicago, XX
152 N.Y. Giants vs. Baltimore, XXXV

Most Yards Gained, Both Teams, Game
929 Washington (602) vs. Denver (327), XII
851 San Francisco (537) vs. Miami (314), XIX
809 San Francisco (455) vs. San Diego (354), XXIX

Fewest Yards Gained, Both Teams, Game
396 N.Y. Giants (152) vs. Baltimore (244), XXXV
452 Minnesota (119) vs. Pittsburgh (333), IX
481 Washington (228) vs. Miami (253), VII
Denver (156) vs. Dallas (325), XII

RUSHING

ATTEMPTS

Most Attempts, Game
57 Pittsburgh vs. Minnesota, IX
53 Miami vs. Minnesota, VIII
52 Oakland vs. Minnesota, XI
Washington vs. Miami, XVII

Fewest Attempts, Game
9 Miami vs. San Francisco, XIX
11 New England vs. Chicago, XX
13 New England vs. Green Bay, XXXI
St. Louis vs. Tennessee, XXXIV

Most Attempts, Both Teams, Game
81 Washington (52) vs. Miami (29), XVII
78 Pittsburgh (57) vs. Minnesota (21), IX
Oakland (52) vs. Minnesota (26), XI
77 Miami (53) vs. Minnesota (24), VIII
Pittsburgh (46) vs. Dallas (31), X

Fewest Attempts, Both Teams, Game
49 Miami (9) vs. San Francisco (40), XIX
New England (13) vs. Green Bay (36), XXXI
St. Louis (13) vs. Tennessee (36), XXXIV
N.Y. Giants (16) vs. Baltimore (33), XXXV
51 San Diego (19) vs. San Francisco (32), XXIX
53 Kansas City (19) vs. Green Bay (34), I

YARDS GAINED

Most Yards Gained, Game
280 Washington vs. Denver, XXII
276 Washington vs. Miami, XVII
266 Oakland vs. Minnesota, XI

Fewest Yards Gained, Game
7 New England vs. Chicago, XX
17 Minnesota vs. Pittsburgh, IX
25 Miami vs. San Francisco, XIX

Most Yards Gained, Both Teams, Game
377 Washington (280) vs. Denver (97), XXII
372 Washington (276) vs. Miami (96), XVII
338 N.Y. Giants (172) vs. Buffalo (166), XXV

Fewest Yards Gained, Both Teams, Game
158 New England (43) vs. Green Bay (115), XXXI
159 Dallas (56) vs. Pittsburgh (103), XXX
168 Buffalo (43) vs. Washington (125), XXVI

AVERAGE GAIN

Highest Average Gain, Game
7.00 L.A. Raiders vs. Washington, XVIII (33-231)
Washington vs. Denver, XXII (40-280)
6.64 Buffalo vs. N.Y. Giants, XXV (25-166)
6.22 Baltimore vs. N.Y. Jets, III (23-143)

Lowest Average Gain, Game
0.64 New England vs. Chicago, XX (11-7)
0.81 Minnesota vs. Pittsburgh, IX (21-17)
2.23 Baltimore vs. Dallas, V (31-69)

TOUCHDOWNS

Most Touchdowns, Game
4 Chicago vs. New England, XX
Denver vs. Green Bay, XXXII
3 Green Bay vs. Kansas City, I
Miami vs. Minnesota, VIII
San Francisco vs. Denver, XXIV
Denver vs. Atlanta, XXXIII
2 Oakland vs. Minnesota, XI

Pittsburgh vs. Los Angeles, XIV
L.A. Raiders vs. Washington, XVIII
San Francisco vs. Miami, XIX
N.Y. Giants vs. Denver, XXI
Washington vs. Denver, XXII; vs. Buffalo, XXVI
Buffalo vs. N.Y. Giants, XXV
Dallas vs. Buffalo, XXVIII; vs. Pittsburgh, XXX
Tennessee vs. St. Louis, XXXIV

Fewest Touchdowns, Game
0 By 22 teams

Most Touchdowns, Both Teams, Game
4 Miami (3) vs. Minnesota (1), VIII
Chicago (4) vs. New England (0), XX
San Francisco (3) vs. Denver (1), XXIV
Denver (4) vs. Green Bay (0), XXXII
3 In nine games

Fewest Touchdowns, Both Teams, Game
0 Pittsburgh vs. Dallas, X
Oakland vs. Philadelphia, XV
Cincinnati vs. San Francisco, XXIII
1 In eight games

PASSING

ATTEMPTS

Most Passes Attempted, Game
59 Buffalo vs. Washington, XXVI
55 San Diego vs. San Francisco, XXIX
50 Miami vs. San Francisco, XIX
Buffalo vs. Dallas, XXVIII

Fewest Passes Attempted, Game
7 Miami vs. Minnesota, VIII
11 Miami vs. Washington, VII
14 Pittsburgh vs. Minnesota, IX

Most Passes Attempted, Both Teams, Game
93 San Diego (55) vs. San Francisco (38), XXIX
92 Buffalo (59) vs. Washington (33), XXVI
85 Miami (50) vs. San Francisco (35), XIX

Fewest Passes Attempted, Both Teams, Game
35 Miami (7) vs. Minnesota (28), VIII
39 Miami (11) vs. Washington (28), VII
40 Pittsburgh (14) vs. Minnesota (26), IX
Miami (17) vs. Washington (23), XVII

COMPLETIONS

Most Passes Completed, Game
31 Buffalo vs. Dallas, XXVIII
29 Miami vs. San Francisco, XIX
Buffalo vs. Washington, XXVI
28 Pittsburgh vs. Dallas, XXX

Fewest Passes Completed, Game
4 Miami vs. Washington, XVII
6 Miami vs. Minnesota, VIII
8 Miami vs. Washington, VII
Denver vs. Dallas, XII

Most Passes Completed, Both Teams, Game
53 Miami (29) vs. San Francisco (24), XIX
52 San Diego (27) vs. San Francisco (25), XXIX
50 Buffalo (31) vs. Dallas (19), XXVIII

Fewest Passes Completed, Both Teams, Game
19 Miami (4) vs. Washington (15), XVII
20 Pittsburgh (9) vs. Minnesota (11), IX
22 Miami (8) vs. Washington (14), VII

COMPLETION PERCENTAGE

Highest Completion Percentage, Game (20 attempts)
88.0 N.Y. Giants vs. Denver, XXI (25-22)
75.0 San Francisco vs. Denver, XXIV (32-24)
73.5 Cincinnati vs. San Francisco, XVI (34-25)

Lowest Completion Percentage, Game (20 attempts)
32.0 Denver vs. Dallas, XII (25-8)
37.9 Denver vs. San Francisco, XXIV (29-11)
38.5 Denver vs. Washington, XXII (39-15)
N.Y. Giants vs. Baltimore, XXXV (39-15)

YARDS GAINED

Most Yards Gained, Game
407 St. Louis vs. Tennessee, XXXIV
341 San Francisco vs. Cincinnati, XXIII
336 Denver vs. Atlanta, XXXIII

Fewest Yards Gained, Game
35 Denver vs. Dallas, XII
63 Miami vs. Minnesota, VIII
69 Miami vs. Washington, VII

Most Yards Gained, Both Teams, Game
615 San Francisco (326) vs. Miami (289), XIX
St. Louis (407) vs. Tennessee (208), XXXIV
603 San Francisco (316) vs. San Diego (287), XXIX
583 Denver (320) vs. N.Y. Giants (263), XXI

Fewest Yards Gained, Both Teams, Game
156 Miami (69) vs. Washington (87), VII
186 Pittsburgh (84) vs. Minnesota (102), IX
204 Miami (80) vs. Washington (124), XVII

TIMES SACKED

Most Times Sacked, Game
7 Dallas vs. Pittsburgh, X
New England vs. Chicago, XX
6 Kansas City vs. Green Bay, I
Washington vs. L.A. Raiders, XVIII
Denver vs. San Francisco, XXIV
5 Dallas vs. Denver, XII; vs. Pittsburgh, XIII
Cincinnati vs. San Francisco, XVI; XXIII
Denver vs. Washington, XXII
Buffalo vs. Washington, XXVI
Green Bay vs. New England, XXXI
New England vs. Green Bay, XXXI

Fewest Times Sacked, Game
0 Baltimore vs. N.Y. Jets, III; vs. Dallas, V
Minnesota vs. Pittsburgh, IX
Pittsburgh vs. Los Angeles, XIV
Philadelphia vs. Oakland, XV
Washington vs. Buffalo, XXVI
Denver vs. Green Bay, XXXII; vs. Atlanta, XXXIII
1 By 13 teams

Most Times Sacked, Both Teams, Game
10 New England (7) vs. Chicago (3), XX
Green Bay (5) vs. New England (5), XXXI
9 Kansas City (6) vs. Green Bay (3), I
Dallas (7) vs. Pittsburgh (2), X
Dallas (5) vs. Denver (4), XII
Dallas (5) vs. Pittsburgh (4), XIII
Cincinnati (5) vs. San Francisco (4), XXIII
8 Washington (6) vs. L.A. Raiders (2), XVIII

Fewest Times Sacked, Both Teams, Game
1 Philadelphia (0) vs. Oakland (1), XV
Denver (0) vs. Green Bay (1), XXXII
2 Baltimore (0) vs. N.Y. Jets (2), III
Baltimore (0) vs. Dallas (2), V
Minnesota (0) vs. Pittsburgh (2), IX
Denver (0) vs. Atlanta (2), XXXIII
3 In five games

TOUCHDOWNS

Most Touchdowns, Game
6 San Francisco vs. San Diego, XXIX
5 San Francisco vs. Denver, XXIV
4 Pittsburgh vs. Dallas, XIII
Washington vs. Denver, XXII
Dallas vs. Buffalo, XXVII

Fewest Touchdowns, Game
0 By 19 teams

Most Touchdowns, Both Teams, Game
7 Pittsburgh (4) vs. Dallas (3), XIII
San Francisco (6) vs. San Diego (1), XXIX
5 Washington (4) vs. Denver (1), XXII
San Francisco (5) vs. Denver (0), XXIV
Dallas (4) vs. Buffalo (1), XXVII
4 Dallas (2) vs. Pittsburgh (2), X
Oakland (3) vs. Philadelphia (1), XV
San Francisco (3) vs. Miami (1), XIX
N.Y. Giants (3) vs. Denver (1), XXI
Washington (2) vs. Buffalo (2), XXVI
Green Bay (2) vs. New England (2), XXXI

Fewest Touchdowns, Both Teams, Game
0 N.Y. Jets vs. Baltimore, III
Miami vs. Minnesota, VIII
Buffalo vs. Dallas, XXVIII
1 In seven games

INTERCEPTIONS BY

Most Interceptions By, Game
4 N.Y. Jets vs. Baltimore, III
Dallas vs. Denver, XII
Washington vs. Buffalo, XXVI
Dallas vs. Buffalo, XXVII
Green Bay vs. New England, XXXI

Baltimore vs. N.Y. Giants, XXXV
3 By 12 teams

Most Interceptions By, Both Teams, Game
6 Baltimore (3) vs. Dallas (3), V
5 Washington (4) vs. Buffalo (1), XXVI
4 In 10 games

Fewest Interceptions By, Both Teams, Game
0 Buffalo vs. N.Y. Giants, XXV
St. Louis vs. Tennessee, XXXIV
1 Oakland (0) vs. Green Bay (1), II
Miami (0) vs. Dallas (1), VI
Minnesota (0) vs. Miami (1), VIII
N.Y. Giants (0) vs. Denver (1), XXI
Cincinnati (0) vs. San Francisco (1), XXIII

YARDS GAINED

Most Yards Gained, Game
136 Denver vs. Atlanta, XXXIII
95 Miami vs. Washington, VII
91 Oakland vs. Minnesota, XI

Most Yards Gained, Both Teams, Game
137 Denver (136) vs. Atlanta (1), XXXIII
95 Miami (95) vs. Washington (0), VII
91 Oakland (91) vs. Minnesota (0), XI

TOUCHDOWNS

Most Touchdowns, Game
1 Green Bay vs. Oakland, II
Oakland vs. Minnesota, XI
L.A. Raiders vs. Washington, XVIII
Chicago vs. New England, XX
Baltimore vs. N.Y. Giants, XXXV

PUNTING

Most Punts, Game
11 N.Y. Giants vs. Baltimore, XXXV
10 Baltimore vs. N.Y. Giants, XXXV
9 Dallas vs. Baltimore, V

Fewest Punts, Game
1 Atlanta vs. Denver, XXXIII
Denver vs. Atlanta, XXXIII
2 Pittsburgh vs. Los Angeles, XIV
Denver vs. N.Y. Giants, XXI
St. Louis vs. Tennessee, XXXIV
3 By 11 teams

Most Punts, Both Teams, Game
21 N.Y. Giants (11) vs. Baltimore (10), XXXV
15 Washington (8) vs. L.A. Raiders (7), XVIII
New England (8) vs. Green Bay (7), XXXI
13 Dallas (9) vs. Baltimore (4), V
Pittsburgh (7) vs. Minnesota (6), IX

Fewest Punts, Both Teams, Game
2 Atlanta (1) vs. Denver (1), XXXIII
5 Denver (2) vs. N.Y. Giants (3), XXI
St. Louis (2) vs. Tennessee (3), XXXIV
6 Oakland (3) vs. Philadelphia (3), XV

AVERAGE YARDAGE

Highest Average, Game (4 punts)
48.75 San Diego vs. San Francisco, XXIX (4-195)
48.50 Kansas City vs. Minnesota, IV (4-194)
46.25 San Francisco vs. Cincinnati, XVI (4-185)

Lowest Average, Game (4 punts)
31.20 Washington vs. Miami, VII (5-156)
32.38 Washington vs. L.A. Raiders, XVIII (8-259)
32.40 Oakland vs. Minnesota, XI (5-162)

PUNT RETURNS

Most Punt Returns, Game
6 Washington vs. Miami, XVII
Green Bay vs. New England, XXXI
5 By six teams

Fewest Punt Returns, Game
0 Minnesota vs. Miami, VIII
Buffalo vs. N.Y. Giants, XXV
Washington vs. Buffalo, XXVI
Denver vs. Green Bay, XXXII
Green Bay vs. Denver, XXXII
Atlanta vs. Denver, XXXIII
Denver vs. Atlanta, XXXIII
1 By 16 teams

Most Punt Returns, Both Teams, Game
10 Green Bay (6) vs. New England (4), XXXI
9 Pittsburgh (5) vs. Minnesota (4), IX
8 Green Bay (5) vs. Oakland (3), II
Baltimore (5) vs. Dallas (3), V
Washington (6) vs. Miami (2), XVII
N.Y. Giants (5) vs. Baltimore (3), XXXV

Fewest Punt Returns, Both Teams, Game
0 Denver vs. Green Bay, XXXII
Atlanta vs. Denver, XXXIII
2 Dallas (1) vs. Miami (1), VI
Denver (1) vs. N.Y. Giants (1), XXI
Buffalo (0) vs. N.Y. Giants (2), XXV
Buffalo (1) vs. Dallas (1), XXVIII
3 Kansas City (1) vs. Minnesota (2), IV
Minnesota (0) vs. Miami (3), VIII
Washington (1) vs. Denver (2), XXII
Washington (0) vs. Buffalo (3), XXVI
Dallas (1) vs. Pittsburgh (2), XXX
Tennessee (1) vs. St. Louis (2), XXXIV

YARDS GAINED

Most Yards Gained, Game
90 Green Bay vs. New England, XXXI
56 San Francisco vs. Cincinnati, XXIII
52 Washington vs. Miami, XVII

Fewest Yards Gained, Game
–1 Dallas vs. Miami, VI
Tennessee vs. St. Louis, XXXIV
0 By 12 teams

Most Yards Gained, Both Teams, Game
120 Green Bay (90) vs. New England (30), XXXI
80 N.Y. Giants (46) vs. Baltimore (34), XXXV
74 Washington (52) vs. Miami (22), XVII

Fewest Yards Gained, Both Teams, Game
0 Denver vs. Green Bay, XXXII
Atlanta vs. Denver, XXXIII
7 Tennessee (-1) vs. St. Louis (8), XXXIV
9 Washington (0) vs. Bufffalo (9), XXVI

AVERAGE RETURN

Highest Average, Game (3 returns)
18.7 San Francisco vs. Cincinnati, XXIII (3-56)
15.0 Green Bay vs. New England, XXXI (6-90)
12.7 San Francisco vs. Denver, XXIV (3-38)

TOUCHDOWNS

Most Touchdowns, Game
None

KICKOFF RETURNS

Most Kickoff Returns, Game
9 Denver vs. San Francisco, XXIV
8 San Diego vs. San Francisco, XXIX
7 By eight teams

Fewest Kickoff Returns, Game
1 N.Y. Jets vs. Baltimore, III
L.A. Raiders vs. Washington, XVIII
Washington vs. Buffalo, XXVI
2 By eight teams

Most Kickoff Returns, Both Teams, Game
12 Denver (9) vs. San Francisco (3), XXIV
San Diego (8) vs. San Francisco (4), XXIX
11 Los Angeles (6) vs. Pittsburgh (5), XIV
Miami (7) vs. San Francisco (4), XIX
New England (7) vs. Chicago (4), XX
Green Bay (6) vs. Denver (5), XXXII
10 Oakland (7) vs. Green Bay (3), II
New England (6) vs. Green Bay (4), XXXI
Atlanta (7) vs. Denver (3), XXXIII

Fewest Kickoff Returns, Both Teams, Game
5 N.Y. Jets (1) vs. Baltimore (4), III
Miami (2) vs. Washington (3), VII
Washington (1) vs. Buffalo (4), XXVI
6 In three games

YARDS GAINED

Most Yards Gained, Game
244 San Diego vs. San Francisco, XXIX
227 Atlanta vs. Denver, XXXIII
222 Miami vs. Washington, XVII

Fewest Yards Gained, Game
16 Washington vs. Buffalo, XXVI
17 L.A. Raiders vs. Washington, XVIII
25 N.Y. Jets vs. Baltimore, III

SUPER BOWL RECORDS

Most Yards Gained, Both Teams, Game
292 San Diego (244) vs. San Francisco (48), XXIX
289 Green Bay (154) vs. New England (135), XXXI
281 N.Y. Giants (170) vs. Baltimore (111), XXXV
Fewest Yards Gained, Both Teams, Game
78 Miami (33) vs. Washington (45), VII
82 Pittsburgh (32) vs. Minnesota (50), IX
92 San Francisco (40) vs. Cincinnati (52), XVI

AVERAGE GAIN
Highest Average, Game (3 returns)
44.0 Cincinnati vs. San Francisco, XXIII (3-132)
38.5 Green Bay vs. New England, XXXI (4-154)
37.0 Miami vs. Washington, XVII (6-222)

TOUCHDOWNS
Most Touchdowns, Game
1 Miami vs. Washington, XVII
Cincinnati vs. San Francisco, XXIII
San Diego vs. San Francisco, XXIX
Green Bay vs. New England, XXXI
Atlanta vs. Denver, XXXIII
Baltimore vs. N.Y. Giants, XXXV
N.Y. Giants vs. Baltimore, XXXV
Most Touchdowns, Both Teams, Game
2 Baltimore (1) vs. N.Y. Giants (1), XXXV

PENALTIES
Most Penalties, Game
12 Dallas vs. Denver, XII
10 Dallas vs. Baltimore, V
9 Dallas vs. Pittsburgh, XIII
Green Bay vs. Denver, XXXII
Baltimore vs. N.Y. Giants, XXXV
Fewest Penalties, Game
0 Miami vs. Dallas, VI
Pittsburgh vs. Dallas, X
Denver vs. San Francisco, XXIV
Atlanta vs. Denver, XXXIII
1 Green Bay vs. Oakland, II
Miami vs. Minnesota, VIII; vs. San Francisco, XIX
Buffalo vs. Dallas, XXVIII
2 By six teams
Most Penalties, Both Teams, Game
20 Dallas (12) vs. Denver (8), XII
16 Cincinnati (8) vs. San Francisco (8), XVI
Green Bay (9) vs. Denver (7), XXXII
15 St. Louis (8) vs. Tennessee (7), XXXIV
Baltimore (9) vs. N.Y. Giants (6), XXXV
Fewest Penalties, Both Teams, Game
2 Pittsburgh (0) vs. Dallas (2), X
3 Miami (0) vs. Dallas (3), VI
Miami (1) vs. San Francisco (2), XIX
4 Denver (0) vs. San Francisco (4), XXIV
Atlanta (0) vs. Denver (4), XXXIII

YARDS PENALIZED
Most Yards Penalized, Game
133 Dallas vs. Baltimore, X
122 Pittsburgh vs. Minnesota, IX
94 Dallas vs. Denver, XII
Fewest Yards Penalized, Game
0 Miami vs. Dallas, VI
Pittsburgh vs. Dallas, X
Denver vs. San Francisco, XXIV
Atlanta vs. Denver, XXXIII
4 Miami vs. Minnesota, VIII
10 Miami vs. San Francisco, XIX
San Francisco vs. Miami, XIX
Buffalo vs. Dallas, XXVIII
Most Yards Penalized, Both Teams, Game
164 Dallas (133) vs. Baltimore (31), V
154 Dallas (94) vs. Denver (60), XII
140 Pittsburgh (122) vs. Minnesota (18), IX
Fewest Yards Penalized, Both Teams, Game
15 Miami (0) vs. Dallas (15), VI
20 Pittsburgh (0) vs. Dallas (20), X
Miami (10) vs. San Francisco (10), XIX
38 Denver (0) vs. San Francisco (38), XXIV

FUMBLES
Most Fumbles, Game
8 Buffalo vs. Dallas, XXVII
6 Dallas vs. Denver, XII
Buffalo vs. Washington, XXVI
5 Baltimore vs. Dallas, V
Fewest Fumbles, Game
0 By 16 teams
Most Fumbles, Both Teams, Game
12 Buffalo (8) vs. Dallas (4), XXVII
10 Dallas (6) vs. Denver (4), XII
8 Dallas (4) vs. Pittsburgh (4), X
Fewest Fumbles, Both Teams, Game
0 Los Angeles vs. Pittsburgh, XIV
Green Bay vs. New England, XXXI
1 Oakland (0) vs. Minnesota (1), XI
Oakland (0) vs. Philadelphia (1), XV
Denver (0) vs. Washington (1), XXII
N.Y. Giants (0) vs. Buffalo (1), XXV
Denver (0) vs. Atlanta (1), XXXIII
2 In five games
Most Fumbles Lost, Game
5 Buffalo vs. Dallas, XXVII
4 Baltimore vs. Dallas, V
Denver vs. Dallas, XII
New England vs. Chicago, XX
2 In many games
Most Fumbles Lost, Both Teams, Game
7 Buffalo (5) vs. Dallas (2), XXVII
6 Denver (4) vs. Dallas (2), XII
New England (4) vs. Chicago (2), XX
5 Baltimore (4) vs. Dallas (1), V
Fewest Fumbles Lost, Both Teams, Game
0 Green Bay vs. Kansas City, I
Dallas vs. Pittsburgh, X
Los Angeles vs. Pittsburgh, XIV
Denver vs. N.Y. Giants, XXI; vs. Washington, XXII
Buffalo vs. N.Y. Giants, XXV
San Diego vs. San Francisco, XXIX
Dallas vs. Pittsburgh, XXX
Green Bay vs. New England, XXXI
St. Louis vs. Tennessee, XXXIV
Most Fumbles Recovered, Game
8 Dallas vs. Denver, XII (4 own, 4 opp.)
6 Dallas vs. Buffalo, XXVII (1 own, 5 opp.)
5 Chicago vs. New England, XX (1 own, 4 opp.)

TURNOVERS
(Number of times losing the ball on interceptions and fumbles.)
Most Turnovers, Game
9 Buffalo vs. Dallas, XXVII
8 Denver vs. Dallas, XII
7 Baltimore vs. Dallas, V
Fewest Turnovers, Game
0 Green Bay vs. Oakland, II
Miami vs. Minnesota, VIII
Pittsburgh vs. Dallas, X
Oakland vs. Minnesota, XI; vs. Philadelphia, XV
N.Y. Giants vs. Denver, XXI; vs. Buffalo, XXV
San Francisco vs. Denver, XXIV; vs. San Diego, XXIX
Buffalo vs. N.Y. Giants, XXV
Dallas vs. Pittsburgh, XXX
Green Bay vs. New England, XXXI
St. Louis vs. Tennessee, XXXIV
Tennessee vs. St. Louis, XXXIV
Baltimore vs. N.Y. Giants, XXXV
1 By many teams
Most Turnovers, Both Teams, Game
11 Baltimore (7) vs. Dallas (4), V
Buffalo (9) vs. Dallas (2), XXVII
10 Denver (8) vs. Dallas (2), XII
8 New England (6) vs. Chicago (2), XX
Fewest Turnovers, Both Teams, Game
0 Buffalo vs. N.Y. Giants, XXV
St. Louis vs. Tennessee, XXXIV
1 N.Y. Giants (0) vs. Denver (1), XXI
2 Green Bay (1) vs. Kansas City (1), I
Miami (0) vs. Minnesota (2), VIII
Cincinnati (1) vs. San Francisco (1), XXIII

Compiled by Elias Sports Bureau

Throughout this all-time postseason record section, the following abbreviations are used to indicate various levels of postseason games:

SB Super Bowl (1966 to date)

AFC AFC Championship Game (1970 to date) or AFL Championship Game (1960-69)

NFC NFC Championship Game (1970 to date) or NFL Championship Game (1933-69)

AFC-D AFC Divisional Playoff Game (1970 to date), AFC Second-Round Playoff Game (1982), AFL Inter-Divisional Playoff Game (1969), or special playoff game to break tie for AFL Division Championship (1963, 1968)

NFC-D NFC Divisional Playoff Game (1970 to date), NFC Second-Round Playoff Game (1982), NFL Conference Championship Game (1967-69), or special playoff game to break tie for NFL Division or Conference Championship (1941, 1943, 1947, 1950, 1952, 1957, 1958, 1965)

AFC-FR AFC First-Round Playoff Game (1978 to date)

NFC-FR NFC First-Round Playoff Game (1978 to date)

Year indicates season in which game took place and does not necessarily reflect calendar year.

POSTSEASON GAME COMPOSITE STANDINGS

	W	L	PCT.	PTS.	OP
Baltimore Ravens	4	0	1.000	95	23
Green Bay Packers	22	10	.688	772	558
San Francisco 49ers	24	15	.615	984	759
Dallas Cowboys	32	21	.604	1,271	979
Washington Redskins*	22	15	.595	778	642
Pittsburgh Steelers	21	15	.583	801	707
Oakland Raiders**	22	16	.579	885	675
Denver Broncos	16	12	.571	616	657
Miami Dolphins	20	18	.526	777	828
Chicago Bears	14	14	.500	579	552
Carolina Panthers	1	1	.500	39	47
Jacksonville Jaguars	4	4	.500	208	200
Buffalo Bills	14	15	.483	681	658
New York Jets	6	7	.462	260	247
Indianapolis Colts***	10	12	.455	393	431
Philadelphia Eagles	10	12	.455	390	392
New York Giants	16	20	.444	609	660
Tennessee Titans†	12	15	.444	471	626
St. Louis Rams††	16	21	.432	612	787
Minnesota Vikings	17	23	.425	779	913
Kansas City Chiefs****	8	11	.421	301	384
Cincinnati Bengals	5	7	.417	246	257
Detroit Lions	7	10	.412	365	404
New England Patriots#	7	10	.412	310	357
Atlanta Falcons	4	6	.400	208	260
San Diego Chargers†††	7	11	.389	332	428
Seattle Seahawks	3	5	.375	145	159
Cleveland Browns	11	19	.367	596	692
Tampa Bay Buccaneers	3	6	.333	91	170
Arizona Cardinals††††	2	5	.286	122	182
New Orleans Saints	1	5	.167	103	185

* *One game played when franchise was in Boston (lost 21-6).*

** *12 games played when franchise was in Los Angeles (won 6, lost 6, 268 points scored, 224 points allowed).*

*** *15 games played when franchise was in Baltimore (won 8, lost 7, 264 points scored, 262 points allowed).*

**** *One game played when franchise was Dallas Texans (won 20-17).*

\# *Two games played when franchise was in Boston (won 26-8, lost 51-10).*

† *22 games played when franchise was in Houston and known as the Oilers (won 9, lost 13, 371 points scored, 533 points allowed).*

†† *One game played when franchise was in Cleveland (won 15-14), 32 games played when franchise was in Los Angeles (won 12, lost 20, 486 points scored, 683 points allowed).*

††† *One game played when franchise was in Los Angeles (lost 24-16).*

†††† *Two games played when franchise was in Chicago (won 28-21, lost 7-0), three games played when franchise was in St. Louis (lost 30-14, lost 35-23, lost 41-16).*

INDIVIDUAL RECORDS

SERVICE

Most Games, Career

27 D.D. Lewis, Dallas (SB 5, NFC 9, NFC-D 12, NFC-FR 1)
26 Larry Cole, Dallas (SB 5, NFC 8, NFC-D 12, NFC-FR 1)
25 Charlie Waters, Dallas (SB 5, NFC 9, NFC-D 10, NFC-FR 1)

Most Games, Head Coach

36 Tom Landry, Dallas
Don Shula, Baltimore-Miami
24 Chuck Noll, Pittsburgh
22 Bud Grant, Minnesota

Most Games Won, Head Coach

20 Tom Landry, Dallas
19 Don Shula, Baltimore-Miami
16 Chuck Noll, Pittsburgh
Joe Gibbs, Washington

Most Games Lost, Head Coach

17 Don Shula, Baltimore-Miami
16 Tom Landry, Dallas
12 Bud Grant, Minnesota

SCORING

POINTS

Most Points, Career

143 Gary Anderson, Pittsburgh-Philadelphia-San Francisco-Minnesota, 20 games (53-pat, 30-fg)
126 Thurman Thomas, Buffalo, 21 games (21-td)
Emmitt Smith, Dallas, 17 games (21-td)
115 George Blanda, Chi. Bears-Houston-Oakland, 19 games (49-pat, 22-fg)

Most Points, Game

30 Ricky Watters, NFC-D:San Francisco vs. N.Y. Giants, 1993 (5-td)
19 Pat Harder, NFC-D: Detroit vs. Los Angeles, 1952 (2-td, 4-pat, 1-fg)
Paul Hornung, NFC: Green Bay vs. N.Y. Giants, 1961 (1-td, 4-pat, 3-fg)
18 By many players

Most Consecutive Games Scoring

19 George Blanda, Chi. Bears-Houston-Oakland, 1956-1975
16 Norm Johnson, Seattle-Atlanta-Pittsburgh, 1983-1997
15 Roy Gerela, Houston-Pittsburgh, 1969-1978

TOUCHDOWNS

Most Touchdowns, Career

21 Thurman Thomas, Buffalo, 21 games (16-r, 5-p)
Emmitt Smith, Dallas, 17 games (19-r, 2-p)
19 Jerry Rice, San Francisco, 23 games (0-r, 19-p)
17 Franco Harris, Pittsburgh, 19 games (16-r, 1-p)

Most Touchdowns, Game

5 Ricky Watters, NFC-D:San Francisco vs. N.Y. Giants, 1993 (5-r)
3 Andy Farkas, NFC-D: Washington vs. N.Y. Giants, 1943 (3-r)
Tom Fears, NFC-D: Los Angeles vs. Chi. Bears, 1950 (3-p)
Otto Graham, NFC: Cleveland vs. Detroit, 1954 (3-r)
Gary Collins, NFC: Cleveland vs. Baltimore, 1964 (3-p)
Craig Baynham, NFC-D: Dallas vs. Cleveland, 1967 (2-r, 1-p)
Fred Biletnikoff, AFC-D: Oakland vs. Kansas City, 1968 (3-p)
Tom Matte, NFC: Baltimore vs. Cleveland, 1968 (3-r)
Larry Schreiber, NFC-D: San Francisco vs. Dallas, 1972 (3-r)
Larry Csonka, AFC: Miami vs. Oakland, 1973 (3-r)
Franco Harris, AFC-D: Pittsburgh vs. Buffalo, 1974 (3-r)
Preston Pearson, NFC: Dallas vs. Los Angeles, 1975 (3-p)
Dave Casper, AFC-D: Oakland vs. Baltimore, 1977 (OT) (3-p)
Alvin Garrett, NFC-FR: Washington vs. Detroit, 1982 (3-p)
John Riggins, NFC-D: Washington vs. L.A. Rams, 1983 (3-r)
Roger Craig, SB: San Francisco vs. Miami, 1984 (1-r, 2-p)
Jerry Rice, NFC-D: San Francisco vs. Minnesota, 1988 (3-p)
Jerry Rice, SB: San Francisco vs. Denver, 1989 (3-p)
Kenneth Davis, AFC: Buffalo vs. L.A. Raiders, 1990 (3-r)
Andre Reed, AFC-FR: Buffalo vs. Houston, 1992 (OT) (3-p)
Sterling Sharpe, NFC-FR: Green Bay vs. Detroit, 1993 (3-p)
Napoleon McCallum, AFC-FR: L.A. Raiders vs. Denver, 1993 (3-r)
Thurman Thomas, AFC: Buffalo vs. Kansas City, 1993 (3-r)
William Floyd, NFC-D: San Francisco vs. Chicago, 1994 (3-r)
Ricky Watters, SB: San Francisco vs. San Diego, 1994 (1-r, 2-p)
Jerry Rice, SB: San Francisco vs. San Diego, 1994 (3-p)
Emmitt Smith, NFC: Dallas vs. Green Bay, 1995 (3-r)
Curtis Martin, AFC-D: New England vs. Pittsburgh, 1996 (3-r)
Terrell Davis, SB: Denver vs. Green Bay, 1997 (3-r)
Mario Bates, NFC-D: Arizona vs. Minnesota, 1998 (3-r)
Leroy Hoard, NFC-D: Minnesota vs. Arizona, 1998 (2-r, 1-p)
Willie Jackson, NFC-FR: New Orleans vs. St. Louis, 2000 (3-p)

Most Consecutive Games Scoring Touchdowns

9 Thurman Thomas, Buffalo, 1992-98
8 John Stallworth, Pittsburgh, 1978-1983
Emmitt Smith, Dallas, 1993-96
7 John Riggins, Washington, 1982-84
Marcus Allen, L.A. Raiders, 1982-85
Terrell Davis, Denver, 1996-98

POINTS AFTER TOUCHDOWN

Most (One-Point) Points After Touchdown, Career

53 Gary Anderson, Pittsburgh-Philadelphia-San Francisco-Minnesota, 20 games (53 att)
49 George Blanda, Chi. Bears-Houston-Oakland, 19 games (49 att)

42 Mike Cofer, San Francisco, 12 games (46 att)

Most (One-Point) Points After Touchdown, Game

8 Lou Groza, NFC: Cleveland vs. Detroit, 1954 (8 att)
Jim Martin, NFC: Detroit vs. Cleveland, 1957 (8 att)
George Blanda, AFC-D: Oakland vs. Houston, 1969 (8 att)
Mike Hollis, AFC-D: Jacksonville vs. Miami, 1999 (8 att)
7 Danny Villanueva, NFC-D: Dallas vs. Cleveland, 1967 (7 att)
Raul Allegre, NFC-D: N.Y. Giants vs. San Francisco, 1986 (7 att)
Mike Cofer, SB: San Francisco vs. Denver, 1989 (8 att)
Lin Elliott, SB: Dallas vs. Buffalo, 1992 (7 att)
Doug Brien, SB: San Francisco vs. San Diego, 1994 (7 att)
Gary Anderson, NFC-FR: Philadelphia vs. Detroit, 1995 (7 att)
Jeff Wilkins, NFC-D: St. Louis vs. Minnesota, 1999 (7 att)
6 George Blair, AFC: San Diego vs. Boston, 1963 (6 att)
Mark Moseley, NFC-D: Washington vs. L.A. Rams, 1983 (6 att)
Uwe von Schamann, AFC: Miami vs. Pittsburgh, 1984 (6 att)
Ali Haji-Sheikh, SB: Washington vs. Denver, 1987 (6 att)
Scott Norwood, AFC: Buffalo vs. L.A. Raiders, 1990 (7 att)
Jeff Jaeger, AFC-FR: L.A. Raiders vs. Denver, 1993 (6 att)
Jason Elam, AFC-FR: Denver vs. Jacksonville, 1997 (6 att)

Most (Kicking) Points After Touchdown, No Misses, Career

53 Gary Anderson, Pittsburgh-Philadelphia-San Francisco-Minnesota, 20 games
49 George Blanda, Chi. Bears-Houston-Oakland, 19 games
41 Rafael Septien, L.A. Rams-Dallas, 15 games

Most Two-Point Conversions, Career

1 By many players

Most Two-Point Conversions, Game

1 By many players

FIELD GOALS

Most Field Goals Attempted, Career

39 George Blanda, Chi. Bears-Houston-Oakland, 19 games
37 Gary Anderson, Pittsburgh-Philadelphia-San Francisco-Minnesota, 20 games
31 Mark Moseley, Washington-Cleveland, 11 games

Most Field Goals Attempted, Game

6 George Blanda, AFC: Oakland vs. Houston, 1967
David Ray, NFC-D: Los Angeles vs. Dallas, 1973
Mark Moseley, AFC-D: Cleveland vs. N.Y. Jets, 1986 (OT)
Matt Bahr, NFC: N.Y. Giants vs. San Francisco, 1990
Steve Christie, AFC: Buffalo vs. Miami, 1992
5 By many players

Most Field Goals, Career

30 Gary Anderson, Pittsburgh-Philadelphia-San Francisco-Minnesota, 20 games
22 George Blanda, Chi. Bears-Houston-Oakland, 19 games
Steve Christie, Buffalo, 12 games
21 Matt Bahr, Pittsburgh-Cleveland-N.Y. Giants-New England, 14 games

Most Field Goals, Game

5 Chuck Nelson, NFC-D: Minnesota vs. San Francisco, 1987
Matt Bahr, NFC: N.Y. Giants vs. San Francisco, 1990
Steve Christie, AFC: Buffalo vs. Miami, 1992
Brad Daluiso, NFC-FR: N.Y. Giants vs. Minnesota, 1997
4 Gino Cappelletti, AFC-D: Boston vs. Buffalo, 1963
George Blanda, AFC: Oakland vs. Houston, 1967
Don Chandler, SB: Green Bay vs. Oakland, 1967
Curt Knight, NFC: Washington vs. Dallas, 1972
George Blanda, AFC-D: Oakland vs. Pittsburgh, 1973
Ray Wersching, SB: San Francisco vs. Cincinnati, 1981
Tony Franklin, AFC-FR: New England vs. N.Y. Jets, 1985
Jess Atkinson, NFC-FR: Washington vs. L.A. Rams, 1986
Luis Zendejas, NFC-D: Philadelphia vs. Chicago, 1988
Gary Anderson, AFC-FR: Pittsburgh vs. Houston, 1989 (OT)
Norm Johnson, AFC-D: Pittsburgh vs. Buffalo, 1995
Chris Boniol, NFC-FR: Dallas vs. Minnesota, 1996
John Kasay, NFC-D: Carolina vs. Dallas, 1996
Mike Hollis, AFC-D: Jacksonville vs. New England, 1998
Al Del Greco, AFC-D: Tennessee vs. Indianapolis, 1999
3 By many players

Most Consecutive Games Scoring Field Goals

13 Toni Fritsch, Dallas-Houston, 1972-79
9 Kevin Butler, Chicago, 1985-1991
Scott Norwood, Buffalo, 1988-1991
Al Del Greco, Houston-Tennessee, 1991-2000 (current)
8 Mark Moseley, Washington-Cleveland, 1982-86
Rich Karlis, Denver-Minnesota, 1984-89
Steve Christie, Buffalo, 1993-95
Gary Anderson, Pittsburgh-Philadelphia, 1989-1995
Morten Andersen, New Orleans-Atlanta, 1987-1998 (current)

Most Consecutive Field Goals

16 Gary Anderson, Pittsburgh-Philadelphia, 1989-1995
15 Rafael Septien, Dallas, 1978-1982
14 Mike Hollis, Jacksonville, 1996-99

Longest Field Goal

58 Pete Stoyanovich, AFC-FR: Miami vs. Kansas City, 1990
54 Ed Murray, NFC-D: Detroit vs. San Francisco, 1983
Steve Christie, SB: Buffalo vs. Dallas, 1993
John Carney, AFC-FR: San Diego vs. Indianapolis, 1995
53 Al Del Greco, AFC-FR: Houston vs. N.Y. Jets, 1991

Highest Field Goal Percentage, Career (10 field goals)

90.9 Chuck Nelson, L.A. Rams-Minnesota, 6 games (11-10)
88.9 Mike Hollis, Jacksonville, 8 games (18-16)
88.0 Steve Christie, Buffalo, 12 games (25-22)

SAFETIES

Most Safeties, Game

1 Bill Willis, NFC-D: Cleveland vs. N.Y. Giants, 1950
Carl Eller, NFC-D: Minnesota vs. Los Angeles, 1969
George Andrie, NFC-D: Dallas vs. Detroit, 1970
Alan Page, NFC-D: Minnesota vs. Dallas, 1971
Dwight White, SB: Pittsburgh vs. Minnesota, 1974
Reggie Harrison, SB: Pittsburgh vs. Dallas, 1975
Jim Jensen, NFC-D: Dallas vs. Los Angeles, 1976
Ted Washington, AFC: Houston vs. Pittsburgh, 1978
Randy White, NFC-D: Dallas vs. Los Angeles, 1979
Henry Waechter, SB: Chicago vs. New England, 1985
Rulon Jones, AFC-FR: Denver vs. New England, 1986
George Martin, SB: N.Y. Giants vs. Denver, 1986
D.D. Hoggard, AFC: Cleveland vs. Denver, 1987
Bruce Smith, SB: Buffalo vs. N.Y. Giants, 1990
Reggie White, NFC-FR: Philadelphia vs. New Orleans, 1992
Willie Clay, NFC-FR: Detroit vs. Green Bay, 1994
Carnell Lake, AFC-D: Pittsburgh vs. Cleveland, 1994
Reuben Davis, AFC-D: San Diego vs. Miami, 1994
Jevon Kearse, AFC-FR: Tennessee vs. Buffalo, 1999

RUSHING

ATTEMPTS

Most Attempts, Career

400 Franco Harris, Pittsburgh, 19 games
349 Emmitt Smith, Dallas, 17 games
339 Thurman Thomas, Buffalo, 21 games

Most Attempts, Game

40 Lamar Smith, AFC-FR: Miami vs. Indianapolis, 2000 (OT)
38 Ricky Bell, NFC-D: Tampa Bay vs. Philadelphia, 1979
John Riggins, SB: Washington vs. Miami, 1982
37 Lawrence McCutcheon, NFC-D: Los Angeles vs. St. Louis, 1975
John Riggins, NFC-D: Washington vs. Minnesota, 1982

YARDS GAINED

Most Yards Gained, Career

1,586 Emmitt Smith, Dallas, 17 games
1,556 Franco Harris, Pittsburgh, 19 games
1,442 Thurman Thomas, Buffalo, 21 games

Most Yards Gained, Game

248 Eric Dickerson, NFC-D: L.A. Rams vs. Dallas, 1985
209 Lamar Smith, AFC-FR: Miami vs. Indianapolis, 2000 (OT)
206 Keith Lincoln, AFC: San Diego vs. Boston, 1963

Most Games, 100 or More Yards Rushing, Career

7 Emmitt Smith, Dallas, 17 games
Terrell Davis, Denver, 8 games
6 John Riggins, Washington, 9 games
Thurman Thomas, Buffalo, 21 games
5 Franco Harris, Pittsburgh, 19 games
Marcus Allen, L.A. Raiders-Kansas City, 16 games

Most Consecutive Games, 100 or More Yards Rushing

7 Terrell Davis, Denver, 1997-98 (current)
6 John Riggins, Washington, 1982-83
4 Thurman Thomas, Buffalo, 1990-91

Longest Run From Scrimmage

90 Fred Taylor, AFC-D: Jacksonville vs. Miami, 1999 (TD)
80 Roger Craig, NFC-D: San Francisco vs. Minnesota, 1988 (TD)
78 Curtis Martin, AFC-D: New England vs. Pittsburgh, 1996 (TD)

AVERAGE GAIN

Highest Average Gain, Career (100 attempts)

5.59 Terrell Davis, Denver, 8 games (204-1,140)
5.04 Marcus Allen, L.A. Raiders-Kansas City, 16 games (267-1,347)
4.89 Eric Dickerson, L.A. Rams-Indianapolis, 7 games (148-724)

Highest Average Gain, Game (10 attempts)

15.90 Elmer Angsman, NFC: Chi. Cardinals vs. Philadelphia, 1947 (10-159)
15.85 Keith Lincoln, AFC: San Diego vs. Boston, 1963 (13-206)
11.31 Zack Crockett, AFC-FR: Indianapolis vs. San Diego, 1995 (13-147)

POSTSEASON GAME RECORDS

TOUCHDOWNS

Most Touchdowns, Career

19 Emmitt Smith, Dallas, 17 games
16 Franco Harris, Pittsburgh, 19 games
Thurman Thomas, Buffalo, 21 games
12 John Riggins, Washington, 9 games
Terrell Davis, Denver, 8 games

Most Touchdowns, Game

5 Ricky Watters, NFC-D: San Francisco vs. N.Y. Giants, 1993
3 Andy Farkas, NFC-D: Washington vs. N.Y. Giants, 1943
Otto Graham, NFC: Cleveland vs. Detroit, 1954
Tom Matte, NFC: Baltimore vs. Cleveland, 1968
Larry Schreiber, NFC-D: San Francisco vs. Dallas, 1972
Larry Csonka, AFC: Miami vs. Oakland, 1973
Franco Harris, AFC-D: Pittsburgh vs. Buffalo, 1974
John Riggins, NFC-D: Washington vs. L.A. Rams, 1983
Kenneth Davis, AFC: Buffalo vs. L.A. Raiders, 1990
Napoleon McCallum, AFC-FR: L.A. Raiders vs. Denver, 1993
Thurman Thomas, AFC: Buffalo vs. Kansas City, 1993
William Floyd, NFC-D: San Francisco vs. Chicago, 1994
Emmitt Smith, NFC: Dallas vs. Green Bay, 1995
Curtis Martin, AFC-D: New England vs. Pittsburgh, 1996
Terrell Davis, SB: Denver vs. Green Bay, 1997
Mario Bates, NFC-D: Arizona vs. Minnesota, 1998

Most Consecutive Games Rushing for Touchdowns

8 Emmitt Smith, Dallas, 1993-96
Thurman Thomas, Buffalo, 1992-98
7 John Riggins, Washington, 1982-84
Terrell Davis, Denver, 1996-98
5 Franco Harris, Pittsburgh, 1974-75
Franco Harris, Pittsburgh, 1977-79
Curtis Martin, New England-N.Y. Jets, 1996-98 (current)

PASSING

PASSER RATING

Highest Passer Rating, Career (150 attempts)

104.8 Bart Starr, Green Bay, 10 games
96.0 Kurt Warner, St. Louis, 4 games
95.6 Joe Montana, San Francisco-Kansas City, 23 games

ATTEMPTS

Most Passes Attempted, Career

734 Joe Montana, San Francisco-Kansas City, 23 games
687 Dan Marino, Miami, 18 games
651 John Elway, Denver, 22 games

Most Passes Attempted, Game

65 Steve Young, NFC-D: San Francisco vs. Green Bay, 1995
64 Bernie Kosar, AFC-D: Cleveland vs. N.Y. Jets, 1986 (OT)
Dan Marino, AFC-FR: Miami vs. Buffalo, 1995
58 Jim Kelly, SB: Buffalo vs. Washington, 1991

COMPLETIONS

Most Passes Completed, Career

460 Joe Montana, San Francisco-Kansas City, 23 games
385 Dan Marino, Miami, 18 games
355 John Elway, Denver, 22 games

Most Passes Completed, Game

36 Warren Moon, AFC-FR: Houston vs. Buffalo, 1992 (OT)
33 Dan Fouts, AFC-D: San Diego vs. Miami, 1981 (OT)
Bernie Kosar, AFC-D: Cleveland vs. N.Y. Jets, 1986 (OT)
Dan Marino, AFC-FR: Miami vs. Buffalo, 1995
32 Neil Lomax, NFC-FR: St. Louis vs. Green Bay, 1982
Danny White, NFC-FR: Dallas vs. L.A. Rams, 1983
Warren Moon, AFC-D: Houston vs. Kansas City, 1993
Neil O'Donnell, AFC: Pittsburgh vs. San Diego, 1994
Steve Young, NFC-D: San Francisco vs. Green Bay, 1995

COMPLETION PERCENTAGE

Highest Completion Percentage, Career (150 attempts)

66.3 Ken Anderson, Cincinnati, 6 games (166-110)
64.3 Warren Moon, Houston-Minnesota, 10 games (403-259)
63.8 Troy Aikman, Dallas, 16 games (502-320)

Highest Completion Percentage, Game (15 completions)

88.0 Phil Simms, SB: N.Y. Giants vs. Denver, 1986 (25-22)
86.7 Joe Montana, NFC: San Francisco vs. L.A. Rams, 1989 (30-26)
84.2 David Woodley, AFC-FR: Miami vs. New England, 1982 (19-16)

YARDS GAINED

Most Yards Gained, Career

5,772 Joe Montana, San Francisco-Kansas City, 23 games
4,964 John Elway, Denver, 22 games
4,510 Dan Marino, Miami, 18 games

Most Yards Gained, Game

489 Bernie Kosar, AFC-D: Cleveland vs. N.Y. Jets, 1986 (OT)
433 Dan Fouts, AFC-D: San Diego vs. Miami, 1981 (OT)
423 Jeff George, NFC-D: Minnesota vs. St. Louis, 1999

Most Games, 300 or More Yards Passing, Career

6 Joe Montana, San Francisco-Kansas City, 23 games
5 Dan Fouts, San Diego, 7 games
4 Warren Moon, Houston-Minnesota, 10 games
Troy Aikman, Dallas, 16 games
Dan Marino, Miami, 18 games
John Elway, Denver, 22 games

Most Consecutive Games, 300 or More Yards Passing

4 Dan Fouts, San Diego, 1979-1981
3 Jim Kelly, Buffalo, 1989-1990
Warren Moon, Houston, 1991-93
2 Daryle Lamonica, Oakland, 1968
Ken Anderson, Cincinnati, 1981-82
Terry Bradshaw, Pittsburgh, 1979-1982
Joe Montana, San Francisco, 1983-84
Dan Marino, Miami, 1984
Troy Aikman, Dallas, 1994
Steve Young, San Francisco, 1994-95
Kurt Warner, St. Louis, 1999-2000 (current)

Longest Pass Completion

96 Trent Dilfer (to Sharpe), AFC: Baltimore vs. Oakland, 2000 (TD)
94 Troy Aikman (to Harper), NFC-D: Dallas vs. Green Bay, 1994 (TD)
93 Daryle Lamonica (to Dubenion), AFC-D: Buffalo vs. Boston, 1963 (TD)

AVERAGE GAIN

Highest Average Gain, Career (150 attempts)

8.87 Kurt Warner, St. Louis, 4 games (161-1,428)
8.45 Joe Theismann, Washington, 10 games (211-1,782)
8.43 Jim Plunkett, Oakland/L.A.Raiders, 10 games (272-2,293)

Highest Average Gain, Game (20 attempts)

14.71 Terry Bradshaw, SB: Pittsburgh vs. Los Angeles, 1979 (21-309)
13.33 Bob Waterfield, NFC-D: Los Angeles vs. Chi. Bears, 1950 (21-280)
13.16 Dan Marino, AFC: Miami vs. Pittsburgh, 1984 (32-421)

TOUCHDOWNS

Most Touchdown Passes, Career

45 Joe Montana, San Francisco-Kansas City, 23 games
32 Dan Marino, Miami, 18 games
30 Terry Bradshaw, Pittsburgh, 19 games

Most Touchdown Passes, Game

6 Daryle Lamonica, AFC-D: Oakland vs. Houston, 1969
Steve Young, SB: San Francisco vs. San Diego, 1994
5 Sid Luckman, NFC: Chi. Bears vs. Washington, 1943
Daryle Lamonica, AFC-D: Oakland vs. Kansas City, 1968
Joe Montana, SB: San Francisco vs. Denver, 1989
Kurt Warner, NFC-D: St. Louis vs. Minnesota, 1999
Kerry Collins, NFC: N.Y. Giants vs. Minnesota, 2000
4 Otto Graham, NFC: Cleveland vs. Los Angeles, 1950
Tobin Rote, NFC: Detroit vs. Cleveland, 1957
Bart Starr, NFC: Green Bay vs. Dallas, 1966
Ken Stabler, AFC-D: Oakland vs. Miami, 1974
Roger Staubach, NFC: Dallas vs. Los Angeles, 1975
Terry Bradshaw, SB: Pittsburgh vs. Dallas, 1978
Don Strock, AFC-D: Miami vs. San Diego, 1981 (OT)
Lynn Dickey, NFC-FR: Green Bay vs. St. Louis, 1982
Dan Marino, AFC: Miami vs. Pittsburgh, 1984
Phil Simms, NFC-D: N.Y. Giants vs. San Francisco, 1986
Doug Williams, SB: Washington vs. Denver, 1987
Jim Kelly, AFC-D: Buffalo vs. Cleveland, 1989
Joe Montana, NFC-D: San Francisco vs. Minnesota, 1989
Warren Moon, AFC-FR: Houston vs. Buffalo, 1992 (OT)
Frank Reich, AFC-FR: Buffalo vs. Houston, 1992 (OT)
Troy Aikman, SB: Dallas vs. Buffalo, 1992
Jeff George, NFC-D: Minnesota vs. St. Louis, 1999
Aaron Brooks, NFC-FR: New Orleans vs. St. Louis, 2000

Most Consecutive Games, Touchdown Passes

13 Dan Marino, Miami, 1983-1995
10 Ken Stabler, Oakland, 1973-77
Joe Montana, San Francisco-Kansas City, 1988-1993
Brett Favre, Green Bay, 1995-98 (current)
9 John Elway, Denver, 1984-89

HAD INTERCEPTED

Lowest Percentage, Passes Had Intercepted, Career (150 attempts)

1.41 Bart Starr, Green Bay, 10 games (213-3)
1.96 Steve McNair, Tennessee, 5 games (153-3)
2.15 Phil Simms, N.Y. Giants, 10 games (279-6)

POSTSEASON GAME RECORDS

Most Attempts Without Interception, Game
54 Neil O'Donnell, AFC: Pittsburgh vs. San Diego, 1994
48 Warren Moon, AFC-FR: Houston vs. Pittsburgh, 1989 (OT)
Randall Cunningham, NFC: Minnesota vs. Atlanta, 1998 (OT)
47 Daryle Lamonica, AFC: Oakland vs. N.Y. Jets, 1968

Most Passes Had Intercepted, Career
28 Jim Kelly, Buffalo, 17 games
26 Terry Bradshaw, Pittsburgh, 19 games
24 Dan Marino, Miami, 18 games

Most Passes Had Intercepted, Game
6 Frank Filchock, NFC: N.Y. Giants vs. Chi. Bears, 1946
Bobby Layne, NFC: Detroit vs. Cleveland, 1954
Norm Van Brocklin, NFC: Los Angeles vs. Cleveland, 1955
5 Frank Filchock, NFC: Washington vs. Chi. Bears, 1940
George Blanda, AFC: Houston vs. San Diego, 1961
George Blanda, AFC: Houston vs. Dall. Texans, 1962 (OT)
Y.A. Tittle, NFC: N.Y. Giants vs. Chicago, 1963
Mike Phipps, AFC-D: Cleveland vs. Miami, 1972
Dan Pastorini, AFC: Houston vs. Pittsburgh, 1978
Dan Fouts, AFC-D: San Diego vs. Houston, 1979
Tommy Kramer, NFC-D: Minnesota vs. Philadelphia, 1980
Dan Fouts, AFC-D: San Diego vs. Miami, 1982
Richard Todd, AFC: N.Y. Jets vs Miami, 1982
Gary Danielson, NFC-D: Detroit vs. San Francisco, 1983
Jay Schroeder, AFC: L.A. Raiders vs. Buffalo, 1990
4 By many players

PASS RECEIVING

RECEPTIONS

Most Receptions, Career
124 Jerry Rice, San Francisco, 23 games
87 Michael Irvin, Dallas, 16 games
85 Andre Reed, Buffalo, 21 games

Most Receptions, Game
13 Kellen Winslow, AFC-D: San Diego vs. Miami, 1981 (OT)
Thurman Thomas, AFC-D: Buffalo vs. Cleveland, 1989
Shannon Sharpe, AFC-FR: Denver vs. L.A. Raiders, 1993
Chad Morton, NFC-D: New Orleans vs. Minnesota, 2000
12 Raymond Berry, NFC: Baltimore vs. N.Y. Giants, 1958
Michael Irvin, NFC: Dallas vs. San Francisco, 1994
11 Dante Lavelli, NFC: Cleveland vs. Los Angeles, 1950
Dan Ross, SB: Cincinnati vs. San Francisco, 1981
Franco Harris, AFC-FR: Pittsburgh vs. San Diego, 1982
Steve Watson, AFC-D: Denver vs. Pittsburgh, 1984
John L. Williams, AFC-D: Seattle vs. Cincinnati, 1988
Jerry Rice, SB: San Francisco vs. Cincinnati, 1988
Ernest Givins, AFC-FR: Houston vs. Pittsburgh, 1989 (OT)
Amp Lee, NFC-D: Minnesota vs. Chicago, 1994
Jay Novacek, NFC-D: Dallas vs. Green Bay, 1994
O.J. McDuffie, AFC-FR: Miami vs. Buffalo, 1995
Jerry Rice, NFC-C: San Francisco vs. Green Bay, 1995

Most Consecutive Games, Pass Receptions
23 Jerry Rice, San Francisco, 1985-1998 (current)
22 Drew Pearson, Dallas, 1973-1983
18 Paul Warfield, Cleveland-Miami, 1964-1974
Cliff Branch, Oakland/L.A. Raiders, 1974-1983
Thurman Thomas, Buffalo, 1989-1998

YARDS GAINED

Most Yards Gained, Career
1,811 Jerry Rice, San Francisco, 23 games
1,315 Michael Irvin, Dallas, 16 games
1,289 Cliff Branch, Oakland/L.A. Raiders, 22 games

Most Yards Gained, Game
240 Eric Moulds, AFC-FR: Buffalo vs. Miami, 1998
227 Anthony Carter, NFC-D: Minnesota vs. San Francisco, 1987
215 Jerry Rice, SB: San Francisco vs. Cincinnati, 1988

Most Games, 100 or More Yards Receiving, Career
7 Jerry Rice, San Francisco, 23 games
6 Michael Irvin, Dallas, 16 games
5 John Stallworth, Pittsburgh, 18 games
Andre Reed, Buffalo, 21 games

Most Consecutive Games, 100 or More Yards Receiving, Career
3 Tom Fears, Los Angeles, 1950-51
Jerry Rice, San Francisco, 1988-89
Randy Moss, Minnesota, 1999-2000
2 By many players

Longest Reception
96 Shannon Sharpe (from Dilfer), AFC: Baltimore vs. Oakland, 2000 (TD)
94 Alvin Harper (from Aikman), NFC-D: Dallas vs. Green Bay, 1994 (TD)
93 Elbert Dubenion (from Lamonica), AFC-D: Buffalo vs. Boston, 1963 (TD)

AVERAGE GAIN

Highest Average Gain, Career (20 receptions)
27.3 Alvin Harper, Dallas, 10 games (24-655)
23.7 Willie Gault, Chicago-L.A. Raiders, 12 games (21-497)
22.8 Harold Jackson, L.A. Rams-New England-Minnesota-Seattle, 14 games (24-548)

Highest Average Gain, Game (3 receptions)
46.3 Harold Jackson, NFC: Los Angeles vs. Minnesota, 1974 (3-139)
42.7 Billy Cannon, AFC: Houston vs. L.A. Chargers, 1960 (3-128)
42.0 Lenny Moore, NFC: Baltimore vs. N.Y. Giants, 1959 (3-126)

TOUCHDOWNS

Most Touchdowns, Career
19 Jerry Rice, San Francisco, 23 games
12 John Stallworth, Pittsburgh, 18 games
10 Fred Biletnikoff, Oakland, 19 games

Most Touchdowns, Game
3 Tom Fears, NFC-D: Los Angeles vs. Chi. Bears, 1950
Gary Collins, NFC: Cleveland vs. Baltimore, 1964
Fred Biletnikoff, AFC-D: Oakland vs. Kansas City, 1968
Preston Pearson, NFC: Dallas vs. Los Angeles, 1975
Dave Casper, AFC-D: Oakland vs. Baltimore, 1977 (OT)
Alvin Garrett, NFC-FR: Washington vs. Detroit, 1982
Jerry Rice, NFC-D: San Francisco vs. Minnesota, 1988
Jerry Rice, SB: San Francisco vs. Denver, 1989
Andre Reed, AFC-FR: Buffalo vs. Houston, 1992 (OT)
Sterling Sharpe, NFC-FR: Green Bay vs. Detroit, 1993
Jerry Rice, SB: San Francisco vs. San Diego, 1994
Willie Jackson, NFC-FR: New Orleans vs. St. Louis, 2000

Most Consecutive Games, Touchdown Passes Caught
8 John Stallworth, Pittsburgh, 1978-1983
5 James Lofton, Green Bay-Buffalo, 1982-1990
Randy Moss, Minnesota, 1998-2000
4 Lynn Swann, Pittsburgh, 1978-79
Harold Carmichael, Philadelphia, 1978-1980
Fred Solomon, San Francisco, 1983-84
Jerry Rice, San Francisco, 1988-89
John Taylor, San Francisco, 1988-89

INTERCEPTIONS BY

Most Interceptions, Career
9 Charlie Waters, Dallas, 25 games
Bill Simpson, Los Angeles-Buffalo, 11 games
Ronnie Lott, San Francisco-L.A. Raiders, 20 games
8 Lester Hayes, Oakland/L.A. Raiders, 13 games
7 Willie Brown, Oakland, 17 games
Dennis Thurman, Dallas, 14 games

Most Interceptions, Game
4 Vernon Perry, AFC-D: Houston vs. San Diego, 1979
3 Joe Laws, NFC: Green Bay vs. N.Y. Giants, 1944
Charlie Waters, NFC-D: Dallas vs. Chicago, 1977
Rod Martin, SB: Oakland vs. Philadelphia, 1980
Dennis Thurman, NFC-D: Dallas vs. Green Bay, 1982
A.J. Duhe, AFC: Miami vs. N.Y. Jets, 1982
2 By many players

Most Consecutive Games, Interceptions
3 Warren Lahr, Cleveland, 1950-51
Ken Gorgal, Cleveland, 1950-53
Joe Schmidt, Detroit, 1954-57
Emmitt Thomas, Kansas City, 1969
Mel Renfro, Dallas, 1970
Rick Volk, Baltimore, 1970-71
Mike Wagner, Pittsburgh, 1975-76
Randy Hughes, Dallas, 1977-78
Vernon Perry, Houston, 1979-1980
Lester Hayes, Oakland, 1980
Gerald Small, Miami, 1982
Lester Hayes, L.A. Raiders, 1982-83
Fred Marion, New England, 1985
John Harris, Seattle-Minnesota, 1984-87
Felix Wright, Cleveland, 1987-88
Kurt Gouveia, Washington, 1991
Eric Davis, San Francisco, 1994
Deion Sanders, San Francisco-Dallas, 1994-95
Craig Newsome, Green Bay, 1996
Eugene Robinson, Green Bay-Atlanta, 1997-98
Jason Sehorn, N.Y. Giants, 1997, 2000

YARDS GAINED
Most Yards Gained, Career
196 Willie Brown, Oakland, 17 games
187 Ronnie Lott, San Francisco-L.A.-Raiders, 20 games
160 George Teague, Green Bay-Dallas-Miami-Dallas, 12 games

Most Yards Gained, Game
108 Darrien Gordon, SB: Denver vs. Atlanta, 1998
101 George Teague, NFC-FR: Green Bay vs. Detroit, 1993
98 Darrol Ray, AFC-FR: N.Y. Jets vs. Cincinnati, 1982
Tory James, AFC-D: Oakland vs. Miami, 2000

Longest Return
101 George Teague, NFC-FR: Green Bay vs. Detroit, 1993 (TD)
98 Darrol Ray, AFC-FR: N.Y. Jets vs. Cincinnati, 1982 (TD)
94 LeRoy Irvin, NFC-FR: L.A. Rams vs. Dallas, 1983

TOUCHDOWNS
Most Touchdowns, Career
3 Willie Brown, Oakland, 17 games
2 Lester Hayes, Oakland/L.A. Raiders, 13 games
Ronnie Lott, San Francisco-L.A. Raiders, 20 games
Darrell Green, Washington, 18 games
Melvin Jenkins, Seattle-Detroit, 5 games
George Teague, Green Bay-Dallas-Miami-Dallas, 12 games

Most Touchdowns, Game
1 By many players

PUNTING
Most Punts, Career
111 Ray Guy, Oakland/L.A. Raiders, 22 games
84 Danny White, Dallas, 18 games
75 Craig Hentrich, Green Bay-Tennessee, 16 games

Most Punts, Game
14 Dave Jennings, AFC-D: N.Y. Jets vs. Cleveland, 1986 (OT)
12 David Lee, AFC-D: Baltimore vs. Oakland, 1977 (OT)
11 Ken Strong, NFC: N.Y. Giants vs. Chi. Bears, 1933
Jim Norton, AFC: Houston vs. Oakland, 1967
Ode Burrell, AFC-D: Houston vs. Oakland, 1969
Dale Hatcher, NFC: L.A. Rams vs. Chicago, 1985
Brad Maynard, SB: N.Y. Giants vs. Baltimore, 2000

Longest Punt
76 Ed Danowski, NFC: N.Y. Giants vs. Detroit, 1935
Mike Horan, AFC: Denver vs. Buffalo, 1991
72 Charlie Conerly, NFC-D: N.Y. Giants vs. Cleveland, 1950
Yale Lary, NFC: Detroit vs. Cleveland, 1953
71 Ray Guy, AFC: Oakland vs. San Diego, 1980

AVERAGE YARDAGE
Highest Average, Career (25 punts)
44.5 Rich Camarillo, New England, 6 games (35-1,559)
44.4 Lee Johnson, Cleveland-Cincinnati, 7 games (28-1,244)
44.3 Jeff Feagles, Philadelphia-Seattle, 4 games (26-1,151)

Highest Average, Game (4 punts)
56.0 Ray Guy, AFC: Oakland vs. San Diego, 1980 (4-224)
52.5 Sammy Baugh, NFC: Washington vs. Chi. Bears, 1942 (6-315)
52.0 Craig Hentrich, AFC-D: Tennessee vs. Indianapolis, 1999 (5-260)

PUNT RETURNS
Most Punt Returns, Career
34 David Meggett, N.Y. Giants-New England-N.Y. Jets, 13 games
25 Theo Bell, Pittsburgh-Tampa Bay, 10 games
22 Brian Mitchell, Washington-Philadelphia, 11 games

Most Punt Returns, Game
7 Ron Gardin, AFC-D: Baltimore vs. Cincinnati, 1970
Carl Roaches, AFC-FR: Houston vs. Oakland, 1980
Gerald McNeil, AFC-D: Cleveland vs. N.Y. Jets, 1986 (OT)
Phil McConkey, NFC-D: N.Y. Giants vs. San Francisco, 1986
David Meggett, AFC-D: New England vs. Pittsburgh, 1996
Reggie Barlow, AFC-FR: Jacksonville vs. New England, 1998
6 George McAfee, NFC-D: Chi. Bears vs. Los Angeles, 1950
Eddie Brown, NFC-D: Washington vs. Minnesota, 1976
Theo Bell, AFC: Pittsburgh vs. Houston, 1978
Eddie Brown, NFC: Los Angeles vs. Tampa Bay, 1979
John Sciarra, NFC: Philadelphia vs. Dallas, 1980
Kurt Sohn, AFC: N.Y. Jets vs. Miami, 1982
Mike Nelms, SB: Washington vs. Miami, 1982
Anthony Carter, NFC-FR: Minnesota vs. New Orleans, 1987
Desmond Howard, SB: Green Bay vs. New England, 1996
Nate Jacquet, AFC-FR: Miami vs. Seattle, 1999
5 By many players

YARDS GAINED
Most Yards Gained, Career
312 David Meggett, N.Y. Giants-New England-N.Y. Jets, 13 games
259 Anthony Carter, Minnesota-Detroit, 9 games
244 Brian Mitchell, Washington-Philadelphia, 11 games

Most Yards Gained, Game
143 Anthony Carter, NFC-FR: Minnesota vs. New Orleans, 1987
141 Bob Hayes, NFC-D: Dallas vs. Cleveland, 1967
117 Desmond Howard, NFC-D: Green Bay vs. San Francisco, 1996

Longest Return
84 Anthony Carter, NFC-FR: Minnesota vs. New Orleans, 1987 (TD)
81 Hugh Gallarneau, NFC-D: Chi. Bears vs. Green Bay, 1941 (TD)
79 Bosh Pritchard, NFC-D: Philadelphia vs. Pittsburgh, 1947 (TD)

AVERAGE YARDAGE
Highest Average, Career (10 returns)
15.3 Robert Brooks, Green Bay, 11 games (14-214)
15.2 Anthony Carter, Minnesota-Detroit, 9 games (17-259)
14.3 Antonio Freeman, Green Bay, 10 games (10-143)

Highest Average Gain, Game (3 returns)
47.0 Bob Hayes, NFC-D: Dallas vs. Cleveland, 1967 (3-141)
29.0 George (Butch) Byrd, AFC: Buffalo vs. San Diego, 1965 (3-87)
25.3 Bosh Pritchard, NFC-D: Philadelphia vs. Pittsburgh, 1947 (4-101)

TOUCHDOWNS
Most Touchdowns
1 Hugh Gallarneau, NFC-D: Chicago Bears vs. Green Bay, 1941
Bosh Pritchard, NFC-D: Philadelphia vs. Pittsburgh, 1947
Charley Trippi, NFC: Chicago Cardinals vs. Philadelphia, 1947
Verda (Vitamin T) Smith, NFC-D: Los Angeles vs. Detroit, 1952
George (Butch) Byrd, AFC: Buffalo vs. San Diego, 1965
Golden Richards, NFC: Dallas vs. Minnesota, 1973
Wes Chandler, AFC-D: San Diego vs. Miami, 1981 (OT)
Shaun Gayle, NFC-D: Chicago vs. N.Y. Giants, 1985
Anthony Carter, NFC-FR: Minnesota vs. New Orleans, 1987
Darrell Green, NFC-D: Washington vs. Chicago, 1987
Antonio Freeman, NFC-FR: Green Bay vs. Atlanta, 1995
Desmond Howard, NFC-D: Green Bay vs. San Francisco, 1996

KICKOFF RETURNS
Most Kickoff Returns, Career
31 Kevin Williams, Dallas-Buffalo, 12 games
29 Fulton Walker, Miami-L.A. Raiders, 10 games
25 David Meggett, N.Y. Giants-New England-N.Y. Jets, 13 games
Eric Metcalf, Cleveland-Atlanta-Arizona, 7 games

Most Kickoff Returns, Game
8 Marc Logan, AFC-D: Miami vs. Buffalo, 1990
Andre Coleman, SB: San Diego vs. San Francisco, 1994
7 Don Bingham, NFC: Chi. Bears vs. N.Y. Giants, 1956
Reggie Brown, NFC-FR: Atlanta vs. Minnesota, 1982
David Verser, AFC-FR: Cincinnati vs. N.Y. Jets, 1982
Del Rodgers, NFC-D: Green Bay vs. Dallas, 1982
Henry Ellard, NFC-D: L.A. Rams vs. Washington, 1983
Stephen Starring, SB: New England vs. Chicago, 1985
Darick Holmes, AFC-D: Buffalo vs. Pittsburgh, 1995
Antonio Freeman, NFC: Green Bay vs. Dallas, 1995
Roell Preston, NFC-FR: Green Bay vs. San Francisco, 1998
Robert Tate, NFC-D: Minnesota vs. St. Louis, 1999
Fred McAfee, NFC-D: New Orleans vs. Minnesota, 2000
6 By many players

YARDS GAINED
Most Yards Gained, Career
677 Fulton Walker, Miami-L.A. Raiders, 10 games
632 Kevin Williams, Dallas-Buffalo, 12 games
565 Eric Metcalf, Cleveland-Atlanta-Arizona, 7 games

Most Yards Gained, Game
244 Andre Coleman, SB: San Diego vs. San Francisco, 1994
210 Tim Dwight, SB: Atlanta vs. Denver, 1998
194 Roell Preston, NFC-FR: Green Bay vs. San Francisco, 1998

Longest Return
100 Brian Mitchell, NFC-D: Washington vs. Tampa Bay, 1999 (TD)
99 Desmond Howard, SB: Green Bay vs. New England, 1996 (TD)
98 Fulton Walker, SB: Miami vs. Washington, 1982 (TD)
Andre Coleman, SB: San Diego vs. San Francisco, 1994 (TD)

AVERAGE YARDAGE
Highest Average, Career (10 returns)
34.3 Tim Dwight, Atlanta, 3 games (10-343)
30.1 Carl Garrett, Oakland, 5 games (16-481)
30.0 Reggie Barlow, Jacksonville, 8 games (12-360)

POSTSEASON GAME RECORDS

Highest Average, Game (3 returns)
56.7 Les (Speedy) Duncan, NFC-D: Washington vs. San Francisco, 1971 (3-170)
51.3 Ed Podolak, AFC-D: Kansas City vs. Miami, 1971 (OT) (3-154)
49.0 Les (Speedy) Duncan, AFC: San Diego vs. Buffalo, 1964 (3-147)

TOUCHDOWNS
Most Touchdowns, Game
1 Vic Washington, NFC-D: San Francisco vs. Dallas, 1972
Nat Moore, AFC-D: Miami vs. Oakland, 1974
Marshall Johnson, AFC-D: Baltimore vs. Oakland, 1977 (OT)
Fulton Walker, SB: Miami vs. Washington, 1982
Stanford Jennings, SB: Cincinnati vs. San Francisco, 1988
Eric Metcalf, AFC-D: Cleveland vs. Buffalo, 1989
Andre Coleman, SB: San Diego vs. San Francisco, 1994
Desmond Howard, SB: Green Bay vs. New England, 1996
Chuck Levy, NFC: San Franisco vs. Green Bay, 1997
Tim Dwight, SB: Atlanta vs. Denver, 1998
Kevin Dyson, AFC-FR: Tennessee vs. Buffalo, 1999
Charlie Rogers, AFC-FR: Seattle vs. Miami, 1999
Brian Mitchell, NFC-D: Washington vs. Tampa Bay, 1999
Tony Horne, NFC-D: St. Louis vs. Minnesota, 1999
Derrick Mason, AFC: Tennessee vs. Jacksonville, 1999
Ron Dixon, NFC-D: N.Y. Giants vs. Philadelphia, 2000;
SB: N.Y. Giants vs. Baltimore, 2000
Jermaine Lewis, SB: Baltimore vs. N.Y. Giants, 2000

FUMBLES
Most Fumbles, Career
16 Warren Moon, Houston-Minnesota, 10 games
14 John Elway, Denver, 22 games
13 Tony Dorsett, Dallas, 17 games
Most Fumbles, Game
5 Warren Moon, AFC-D: Houston vs. Kansas City, 1993
4 Brian Sipe, AFC-D: Cleveland vs. Oakland, 1980
Randall Cunningham, NFC-FR: Minnesota vs. N.Y. Giants, 1997
3 By many players

RECOVERIES
Most Own Fumbles Recovered, Career
8 Warren Moon, Houston-Minnesota, 10 games
7 John Elway, Denver, 22 games
6 Jim Kelly, Buffalo, 17 games
Most Opponents' Fumbles Recovered, Career
4 Cliff Harris, Dallas, 21 games
Harvey Martin, Dallas, 22 games
Ted Hendricks, Baltimore-Oakland/L.A. Raiders, 21 games
Alvin Walton, Washington, 9 games
Monte Coleman, Washington, 21 games
Dave Thomas, Dallas-Jacksonville-N.Y. Giants, 13 games
3 Paul Krause, Minnesota, 19 games
Jack Lambert, Pittsburgh, 18 games
Fred Dryer, Los Angeles, 14 games
Charlie Waters, Dallas, 25 games
Jack Ham, Pittsburgh, 16 games
Mike Hegman, Dallas, 16 games
Tom Jackson, Denver, 10 games
Rich Milot, Washington, 13 games
Mike Singletary, Chicago, 12 games
Darryl Grant, Washington, 16 games
Wes Hopkins, Philadelphia, 3 games
Wilber Marshall, Chicago-Washington, 15 games
Tyrone Braxton, Denver-Miami-Denver, 19 games
Neil Smith, Kansas City-Denver, 16 games
Tony Brackens, Jacksonville, 7 games
Phil Hansen, Buffalo, 14 games
Carnell Lake, Pittsburgh-Jacksonville, 15 games
2 By many players
Most Fumbles Recovered, Game, Own and Opponents'
3 Jack Lambert, AFC: Pittsburgh vs. Oakland, 1975 (3 opp)
Ron Jaworski, NFC-FR: Philadelphia vs. N.Y. Giants, 1981 (3 own)
2 By many players

YARDS GAINED
Longest Return
93 Andy Russell, AFC-D: Pittsburgh vs. Baltimore, 1975 (opp, TD)
79 Neil Smith, AFC-D: Denver vs. Miami, 1998 (opp, TD)
64 Leon Lett, SB: Dallas vs. Buffalo, 1992 (opp)

TOUCHDOWNS
Most Touchdowns
1 By many players

COMBINED NET YARDS GAINED
Rushing, receiving, interception returns, punt returns, kickoff returns, and fumble returns.
ATTEMPTS
Most Attempts, Career
454 Franco Harris, Pittsburgh, 19 games
417 Thurman Thomas, Buffalo, 21 games
397 Emmitt Smith, Dallas, 17 games
Most Attempts, Game
43 Lamar Smith, AFC-FR: Miami vs. Indianapolis, 2000 (OT)
42 Curtis Martin, AFC-D: N.Y. Jets vs. Jacksonville, 1998
40 Lawrence McCutcheon, NFC-D: Los Angeles vs. St. Louis, 1975

YARDS GAINED
Most Yards Gained, Career
2,124 Thurman Thomas, Buffalo, 21 games
2,060 Franco Harris, Pittsburgh, 19 games
1,928 Emmitt Smith, Dallas, 17 games
Most Yards Gained, Game
350 Ed Podolak, AFC-D: Kansas City vs. Miami, 1971 (OT)
329 Keith Lincoln, AFC: San Diego vs. Boston, 1963
285 Bob Hayes, NFC-D: Dallas vs. Cleveland, 1967

SACKS
Sacks have been compiled since 1982.
Most Sacks, Career
14.5 Bruce Smith, Buffalo, 20 games
12.0 Reggie White, Philadelphia-Green Bay, 19 games
11.0 Charles Haley, San Francisco-Dallas-San Francisco, 21 games
Most Sacks, Game
3.5 Rich Milot, NFC-D: Washington vs. Chicago, 1984
Richard Dent, NFC-D: Chicago vs. N.Y. Giants, 1985
3.0 Richard Dent, NFC-D: Chicago vs. Washington, 1984
Garin Veris, AFC-FR: New England vs. N.Y. Jets, 1985
Gary Jeter, NFC-D: L.A. Rams vs. Dallas, 1985
Carl Hairston, AFC-D: Cleveland vs. N.Y. Jets, 1986 (OT)
Charles Mann, NFC-D: Washington vs. Chicago, 1987
Kevin Greene, NFC-FR: L.A. Rams vs. Minnesota, 1988
Greg Townsend, AFC-D: L.A. Raiders vs. Cincinnati, 1990
Wilber Marshall, NFC: Washington vs. Detroit, 1991
Fred Stokes, NFC-FR: Washington vs. Minnesota, 1992
Pierce Holt, NFC-D: San Francisco vs. Washington, 1992
Tony Casillas, NFC: Dallas vs. San Francisco, 1992
Gerald Williams, AFC-FR: Pittsburgh vs. Kansas City, 1993
Chad Brown, AFC-FR: Pittsburgh vs. Indianapolis, 1996
Reggie White, SB: Green Bay vs. New England, 1996
Warren Sapp, NFC-D: Tampa Bay vs. Green Bay, 1997
Trace Armstrong, AFC-FR: Miami vs. Seattle, 1999
Michael McCrary, AFC-FR: Baltimore vs. Denver, 2000
2.5 Lyle Alzado, AFC-D: L.A. Raiders vs. Pittsburgh, 1983
Jacob Green, AFC-FR: Seattle vs. L.A. Raiders, 1984
Larry Roberts, NFC-D: San Francisco vs. Minnesota, 1988
Leslie O'Neal, AFC-FR: San Diego vs. Kansas City, 1992
Bruce Smith, AFC-FR: Buffalo vs. Tennessee, 1999

TEAM RECORDS

GAMES, VICTORIES, DEFEATS
Most Seasons Participating in Postseason Games
26 Dallas, 1966-1973, 1975-1983, 1985, 1991-96, 1998-99
25 N.Y. Giants, 1933-35, 1938-39, 1941, 1943-44, 1946, 1950, 1956, 1958-59, 1961-63, 1981, 1984-86, 1989-1990, 1993, 1997, 2000
24 Cleveland/L.A./St. Louis Rams, 1945, 1949-1952, 1955, 1967, 1969, 1973-1980, 1983-86, 1988-89, 1999-2000
Most Consecutive Seasons Participating in Postseason Games
9 Dallas, 1975-1983
8 Dallas, 1966-1973
Pittsburgh, 1972-79
Los Angeles, 1973-1980
San Francisco, 1983-1990
7 Houston, 1987-1993
San Francisco, 1992-98
Most Games
53 Dallas, 1966-1973, 1975-1983, 1985, 1991-96, 1998-99
40 Minnesota, 1968-1971, 1973-78, 1980, 1982, 1987-89, 1992-94, 1996-2000
39 San Francisco, 1957, 1970-72, 1981, 1983-1990, 1992-98

Most Games Won
32 Dallas, 1967, 1970-73, 1975, 1977-78, 1980-82, 1991-96
24 San Francisco, 1970-71, 1981, 1983-84, 1988-1990, 1992-94, 1996-98
22 Green Bay, 1936, 1939, 1944, 1961-62, 1965-67, 1982, 1993-97
Washington, 1937, 1942-43, 1972, 1982-83, 1986-87, 1990-92, 1999
Oakland/L.A. Raiders, 1967-1970, 1973-77, 1980, 1982-83, 1990, 1993, 2000

Most Consecutive Games Won
9 Green Bay, 1961-62, 1965-67
7 Pittsburgh, 1974-76
San Francisco, 1988-1990
Dallas, 1992-94
Denver, 1997-98
6 Miami, 1972-73
Pittsburgh, 1978-79
Washington, 1982-83

Most Games Lost
23 Minnesota, 1968-1971, 1973-78, 1980, 1982, 1987-89, 1992-94, 1996-2000
21 Dallas, 1966-1970, 1972-73, 1975-76, 1978-1983, 1985, 1991, 1994, 1996, 1998-99
L.A./St. Louis Rams, 1949-1950, 1952, 1955, 1967, 1969, 1973-1980, 1983-86, 1988-89, 2000
20 N.Y. Giants, 1933, 1935, 1939, 1941, 1943-44, 1946, 1950, 1958-59, 1961-63, 1981, 1984-85, 1989, 1993, 1997, 2000

Most Consecutive Games Lost
6 N.Y. Giants, 1939, 1941, 1943-44, 1946, 1950
Cleveland, 1969, 1971-72, 1980, 1982, 1985
Minnesota, 1988-89, 1992-94, 1996
Detroit, 1991, 1993-95, 1997, 1999 (current)
5 N.Y. Giants, 1958-59, 1961-63
Los Angeles, 1952, 1955, 1967, 1969, 1973
Denver, 1977-79, 1983-84
Baltimore/Indianapolis, 1971, 1975-77, 1987
Philadelphia, 1980-81, 1988-1990
4 Washington, 1972-74, 1976
Miami, 1974, 1978-79, 1981
Chi. Cardinals/St. Louis, 1948, 1974-75, 1982
Boston/New England, 1963, 1976, 1978, 1982
New Orleans, 1987, 1990-92
Kansas City, 1993-95, 1997 (current)
Seattle, 1984, 1987-88, 1999 (current)
Buffalo, 1995-96, 1998-99 (current)
Indianapolis, 1995-96, 1999-2000 (current)

SCORING

Most Points, Game
73 NFC: Chi. Bears vs. Washington, 1940
62 AFC-D: Jacksonville vs. Miami, 1999
59 NFC: Detroit vs. Cleveland, 1957

Most Points, Both Teams, Game
95 NFC-FR: Philadelphia (58) vs. Detroit (37), 1995
86 NFC-D: St. Louis (49) vs. Minnesota (37), 1999
79 AFC-D: San Diego (41) vs. Miami (38), 1981 (OT)
AFC-FR: Buffalo (41) vs. Houston (38), 1992 (OT)

Fewest Points, Both Teams, Game
5 NFC-D: Detroit (0) vs. Dallas (5), 1970
7 NFC: Chi. Cardinals (0) vs. Philadelphia (7), 1948
9 NFC: Tampa Bay (0) vs. Los Angeles (9), 1979

Largest Margin of Victory, Game
73 NFC: Chi. Bears vs. Washington, 1940 (73-0)
55 AFC-D: Jacksonville vs. Miami, 1999 (62-7)
49 AFC-D: Oakland vs. Houston, 1969 (56-7)

Most Points, Shutout Victory, Game
73 NFC: Chi. Bears vs. Washington, 1940
41 NFC: N.Y. Giants vs. Minnesota, 2000
38 NFC-D: Dallas vs. Tampa Bay, 1981

Most Points Overcome to Win Game
32 AFC-FR: Buffalo vs. Houston, 1992 (trailed 3-35, won 41-38) (OT)
20 NFC-D: Detroit vs. San Francisco, 1957 (trailed 7-27, won 31-27)
18 NFC-D: Dallas vs. San Francisco, 1972 (trailed 3-21, won 30-28)
AFC-D: Miami vs. Cleveland, 1985 (trailed 3-21, won 24-21)

Most Points, Each Half
1st: 41 AFC: Buffalo vs. L.A. Raiders, 1990
AFC-D: Jacksonville vs. Miami, 1999
38 NFC-D: Washington vs. L.A. Rams, 1983
NFC-FR: Philadelphia vs. Detroit, 1995
35 NFC: Cleveland vs. Detroit, 1954
AFC-D: Oakland vs. Houston, 1969
SB: Washington vs. Denver, 1987
2nd: 45 NFC: Chi. Bears vs. Washington, 1940
35 AFC-FR: Buffalo vs. Houston, 1992
NFC-D: St. Louis vs. Minnesota, 1999
30 SB: N.Y. Giants vs. Denver, 1986
AFC: Cleveland vs. Denver, 1987
NFC-FR: Detroit vs. Philadelphia, 1995

Most Points, Each Quarter
1st: 28 AFC-D: Oakland vs. Houston, 1969
24 AFC-D: San Diego vs. Miami, 1981
AFC-D: Jacksonville vs. Miami, 1999
21 NFC: Chi. Bears vs. Washington, 1940
AFC: San Diego vs. Boston, 1963
AFC-D: Oakland vs. Kansas City, 1968
AFC: Oakland vs. San Diego, 1980
AFC: Buffalo vs. L.A. Raiders, 1990
NFC: San Francisco vs. Dallas, 1994
2nd: 35 SB: Washington vs. Denver, 1987
31 NFC-FR: Philadelphia vs. Detroit, 1995
26 AFC-D: Pittsburgh vs. Buffalo, 1974
3rd: 28 AFC-FR: Buffalo vs. Houston, 1992
26 NFC: Chi. Bears vs. Washington, 1940
21 NFC-D: Dallas vs. Cleveland, 1967
NFC-D: Dallas vs. Tampa Bay, 1981
AFC-D: L.A. Raiders vs. Pittsburgh, 1983
SB: Chicago vs. New England, 1985
NFC-D: N.Y. Giants vs. San Francisco, 1986
AFC: Cleveland vs. Denver, 1987
AFC: Cleveland vs. Denver, 1989
NFC-D: St. Louis vs. Minnesota, 1999
4th: 27 NFC: N.Y. Giants vs. Chi. Bears, 1934
26 NFC-FR: Philadelphia vs. New Orleans, 1992
24 NFC: Baltimore vs. N.Y. Giants, 1959
OT: 6 NFC: Baltimore vs. N.Y. Giants, 1958
AFC-D: Oakland vs. Baltimore, 1977
NFC-D: L.A. Rams vs. N.Y. Giants, 1989
AFC-FR: Miami vs. Indianapolis, 2000

TOUCHDOWNS

Most Touchdowns, Game
11 NFC: Chi. Bears vs. Washington, 1940
8 NFC: Cleveland vs. Detroit, 1954
NFC: Detroit vs. Cleveland, 1957
AFC-D: Oakland vs. Houston, 1969
SB: San Francisco vs. Denver, 1989
AFC-D: Jacksonville vs. Miami, 1999
7 AFC: San Diego vs. Boston, 1963
NFC-D: Dallas vs. Cleveland, 1967
NFC-D: N.Y. Giants vs. San Francisco, 1986
AFC: Buffalo vs. L.A. Raiders, 1990
SB: Dallas vs. Buffalo, 1992
SB: San Francisco vs. San Diego, 1994
NFC-FR: Philadelphia vs. Detroit, 1995
NFC-D: St. Louis vs. Minnesota, 1999

Most Touchdowns, Both Teams, Game
12 NFC-FR: Philadelphia (7) vs. Detroit (5), 1995
NFC-D: St. Louis (7) vs. Minnesota (5), 1999
11 NFC: Chi. Bears (11) vs. Washington (0), 1940
10 NFC: Detroit (8) vs. Cleveland (2), 1957
AFC-D: Miami (5) vs. San Diego (5), 1981 (OT)
AFC: Miami (6) vs. Pittsburgh (4), 1984
AFC-FR: Buffalo (5) vs. Houston (5), 1992 (OT)
SB: San Francisco (7) vs. San Diego (3), 1994

Fewest Touchdowns, Both Teams, Game
0 NFC-D: N.Y. Giants vs. Cleveland, 1950
NFC-D: Dallas vs. Detroit, 1970
NFC: Los Angeles vs. Tampa Bay, 1979
1 NFC: Chi. Cardinals (0) vs. Philadelphia (1), 1948
NFC-D: Cleveland (0) vs. N.Y. Giants (1), 1958
AFC: San Diego (0) vs. Houston (1), 1961
AFC-D: N.Y. Jets (0) vs. Kansas City (1), 1969
NFC-D: Green Bay (0) vs. Washington (1), 1972
NFC-FR: New Orleans (0) vs. Chicago (1), 1990
NFC: N.Y. Giants (0) vs. San Francisco (1), 1990
AFC-FR: L.A. Raiders (0) vs. Kansas City (1), 1991
AFC-D: New England (0) vs. Pittsburgh (1), 1997
NFC: Tampa Bay (0) vs. St. Louis (1), 1999
AFC: Oakland (0) vs. Baltimore (1), 2000
2 In many games

POINTS AFTER TOUCHDOWN

Most (One-Point) Points After Touchdown, Game
8 NFC: Cleveland vs. Detroit, 1954
NFC: Detroit vs. Cleveland, 1957
AFC-D: Oakland vs. Houston, 1969
AFC-D: Jacksonville vs. Miami, 1999
7 NFC: Chi. Bears vs. Washington, 1940

NFC-D: Dallas vs. Cleveland, 1967
NFC-D: N.Y. Giants vs. San Francisco, 1986
SB: San Francisco vs. Denver, 1989
SB: Dallas vs. Buffalo, 1992
SB: San Francisco vs. San Diego, 1994
NFC-FR: Philadelphia vs. Detroit, 1995
NFC-D: St. Louis vs. Minnesota, 1999
6 AFC: San Diego vs. Boston, 1963
NFC-D: Washington vs. L.A. Rams, 1983
AFC: Miami vs. Pittsburgh, 1984
SB: Washington vs. Denver, 1987
AFC: Buffalo vs. L.A. Raiders, 1990
AFC-FR: L.A. Raiders vs. Denver, 1993
AFC-FR: Denver vs. Jacksonville, 1997

Most (One-Point) Points After Touchdown, Both Teams, Game
10 NFC: Detroit (8) vs. Cleveland (2), 1957
AFC-D: Miami (5) vs. San Diego (5), 1981 (OT)
AFC: Miami (6) vs. Pittsburgh (4), 1984
AFC-FR: Buffalo (5) vs. Houston (5), 1992 (OT)
NFC-FR: Philadelphia (7) vs. Detroit (3), 1995
9 In many games

Fewest (One-Point) Points After Touchdown, Both Teams, Game
0 NFC-D: N.Y. Giants vs. Cleveland, 1950
NFC-D: Dallas vs. Detroit, 1970
NFC: Los Angeles vs. Tampa Bay, 1979
NFC: St. Louis vs. Tampa Bay, 1999

Most Two-Point Conversions, Game
2 SB: San Diego vs. San Francisco, 1994
NFC-FR: Detroit vs. Philadelphia, 1995
1 By many teams

FIELD GOALS

Most Field Goals, Game
5 NFC-D: Minnesota vs. San Francisco, 1987
NFC: N.Y. Giants vs. San Francisco, 1990
AFC: Buffalo vs. Miami, 1992
NFC-FR: N.Y. Giants vs. Minnesota, 1997
4 AFC-D: Boston vs. Buffalo, 1963
AFC: Oakland vs. Houston, 1967
SB: Green Bay vs. Oakland, 1967
NFC: Washington vs. Dallas, 1972
AFC-D: Oakland vs. Pittsburgh, 1973
SB: San Francisco vs. Cincinnati, 1981
AFC-FR: New England vs. N.Y. Jets, 1985
NFC-FR: Washington vs. L.A. Rams, 1986
NFC-D: Philadelphia vs. Chicago, 1988
AFC-FR: Pittsburgh vs. Houston, 1989 (OT)
AFC-D: Pittsburgh vs. Buffalo, 1995
NFC-FR: Dallas vs. Minnesota, 1996
NFC-D: Carolina vs. Dallas, 1996
AFC-FR: Jacksonville vs. New England, 1998
AFC-D: Tennessee vs. Indianapolis, 1999
3 By many teams

Most Field Goals, Both Teams, Game
8 NFC-FR: N.Y. Giants (5) vs. Minnesota (3), 1997
7 AFC-FR: Pittsburgh (4) vs. Houston (3), 1989 (OT)
NFC: N.Y. Giants (5) vs. San Francisco (2), 1990
NFC-D: Carolina (4) vs. Dallas (3), 1996
AFC-D: Tennessee (4) vs. Indianapolis (3), 1999
6 NFC-D: Minnesota (5) vs. San Francisco (1), 1987
NFC-D: Philadelphia (4) vs. Chicago (2), 1988
AFC: Buffalo (5) vs. Miami (1), 1992

Most Field Goals Attempted, Game
6 AFC: Oakland vs. Houston, 1967
NFC-D: Los Angeles vs. Dallas, 1973
AFC-D: Cleveland vs. N.Y. Jets, 1986 (OT)
NFC: N.Y. Giants vs. San Francisco, 1990
AFC: Buffalo vs. Miami, 1992
5 By many teams

Most Field Goals Attempted, Both Teams, Game
9 NFC-D: Philadelphia (5) vs. Chicago (4), 1988
NFC-FR: N.Y. Giants (5) vs. Minnesota (4), 1997
8 NFC-D: Los Angeles (6) vs. Dallas (2), 1973
NFC-D: Detroit (5) vs. San Francisco (3), 1983
AFC-D: Cleveland (6) vs. N.Y. Jets (2), 1986 (OT)
NFC-D: Minnesota (5) vs. San Francisco (3), 1987
AFC-FR: Houston (4) vs. Pittsburgh (4), 1989 (OT)
NFC-FR: Chicago (4) vs. New Orleans (4), 1990
NFC: N.Y. Giants (6) vs. San Francisco (2), 1990
7 In many games

SAFETIES

Most Safeties, Game
1 By many teams

Most Safeties, Both Teams, Game
1 In many games

FIRST DOWNS

Most First Downs, Game
34 AFC-D: San Diego vs. Miami, 1981 (OT)
33 AFC-D: Cleveland vs. N.Y. Jets, 1986 (OT)
31 SB: San Francisco vs. Miami, 1984
NFC-D: San Francisco vs. Minnesota, 1997
NFC: N.Y. Giants vs. Minnesota, 2000

Fewest First Downs, Game
6 NFC: N.Y. Giants vs. Green Bay, 1961
AFC-D: Baltimore vs. Tennessee, 2000
7 NFC: Green Bay vs. Boston, 1936
NFC-D: Pittsburgh vs. Philadelphia, 1947
NFC: Chi. Cardinals vs. Philadelphia, 1948
NFC: Los Angeles vs. Philadelphia, 1949
NFC-D: Cleveland vs. N.Y. Giants, 1958
AFC-D: Cincinnati vs. Baltimore, 1970
NFC-D: Detroit vs. Dallas, 1970
NFC: Tampa Bay vs. Los Angeles, 1979
8 By many teams

Most First Downs, Both Teams, Game
59 AFC-D: San Diego (34) vs. Miami (25), 1981 (OT)
55 AFC-FR: San Diego (29) vs. Pittsburgh (26), 1982
54 AFC-FR: Buffalo (28) vs. Miami (26), 1995

Fewest First Downs, Both Teams, Game
15 NFC: Green Bay (7) vs. Boston (8), 1936
19 NFC: N.Y. Giants (9) vs. Green Bay (10), 1939
NFC: Washington (9) vs. Chi. Bears (10), 1942
20 NFC-D: Cleveland (9) vs. N.Y. Giants (11), 1950

RUSHING

Most First Downs, Rushing, Game
19 NFC-FR: Dallas vs. Los Angeles, 1980
18 AFC-D: Miami vs. Cincinnati, 1973
AFC: Miami vs. Oakland, 1973
AFC-D: Pittsburgh vs. Buffalo, 1974
AFC-FR: Buffalo vs. Miami, 1995
AFC-FR: Denver vs. Jacksonville, 1997
17 AFC-D: Cincinnati vs. Seattle, 1988
AFC: Buffalo vs. Kansas City, 1993

Fewest First Downs, Rushing, Game
0 NFC: Los Angeles vs. Philadelphia, 1949
AFC-D: Buffalo vs. Boston, 1963
AFC: Oakland vs. Pittsburgh, 1974
NFC-FR: New Orleans vs. Minnesota, 1987
NFC: L.A. Rams vs. San Francisco, 1989
NFC-D: Chicago vs. N.Y. Giants, 1990
AFC-FR: Indianapolis vs. Pittsburgh, 1996
AFC-FR: Seattle vs. Miami, 1999
AFC-D: Miami vs. Jacksonville, 1999
AFC-D: Miami vs. Oakland, 2000
1 By many teams

Most First Downs, Rushing, Both Teams, Game
26 AFC: Buffalo (14) vs. L.A. Raiders (12), 1990
25 NFC-FR: Dallas (19) vs. Los Angeles (6), 1980
23 NFC: Cleveland (15) vs. Detroit (8), 1952
AFC-D: Miami (18) vs. Cincinnati (5), 1973
AFC-D: Pittsburgh (18) vs. Buffalo (5), 1974
AFC-FR: Buffalo (18) vs. Miami (5), 1995

Fewest First Downs, Rushing, Both Teams, Game
2 NFC-FR: New Orleans (1) vs. St. Louis (1), 2000
5 AFC-D: Buffalo (0) vs. Boston (5), 1963
NFC-D: Washington (1) vs. Tampa Bay (4), 1999
6 NFC: Green Bay (2) vs. Boston (4), 1936
NFC-D: Baltimore (2) vs. Minnesota (4), 1968
AFC-D: Houston (1) vs. Oakland (5), 1969
AFC-FR: N.Y. Jets (1) vs. Houston (5), 1991
AFC-FR: Denver (1) vs. Baltimore (5), 2000

PASSING

Most First Downs, Passing, Game
21 AFC-D: Miami vs. San Diego, 1981 (OT)
AFC-D: San Diego vs. Miami, 1981 (OT)
AFC-D: Cleveland vs. N.Y. Jets, 1986 (OT)
NFC-D: Philadelphia vs. Chicago, 1988
20 NFC-FR: Dallas vs. L.A. Rams, 1983
AFC-D: Buffalo vs. Cleveland, 1989
AFC-FR: Miami vs. Buffalo, 1995

NFC-FR: Detroit vs. Philadelphia, 1995
AFC-FR: San Diego vs. Indianapolis, 1995
NFC-D: Minnesota vs. St. Louis, 1999
19 NFC-FR: St. Louis vs. Green Bay, 1982
NFC-FR: Dallas vs. Tampa Bay, 1982
AFC-FR: Pittsburgh vs. San Diego, 1982
AFC-FR: San Diego vs. Pittsburgh, 1982
NFC: Dallas vs. Washington, 1982
NFC-D: Detroit vs. Dallas, 1991
AFC-FR: Kansas City vs. Pittsburgh, 1993 (OT)
NFC: Minnesota vs. Atlanta, 1998 (OT)
NFC: N.Y. Giants vs. Minnesota, 2000

Fewest First Downs, Passing, Game
0 NFC: Philadelphia vs. Chi. Cardinals, 1948
1 NFC-D: N.Y. Giants vs. Washington, 1943
NFC: Cleveland vs. Detroit, 1953
SB: Denver vs. Dallas, 1977
2 By many teams

Most First Downs, Passing, Both Teams, Game
42 AFC-D: Miami (21) vs. San Diego (21), 1981 (OT)
38 AFC-FR: Pittsburgh (19) vs. San Diego (19), 1982
NFC-D: Minnesota (20) vs. St. Louis (18), 1999
36 NFC: Minnesota (19) vs. Atlanta (17), 1998 (OT)

Fewest First Downs, Passing, Both Teams, Game
2 NFC: Philadelphia (0) vs. Chi. Cardinals (2), 1948
4 NFC-D: Cleveland (2) vs. N.Y. Giants (2), 1950
5 NFC: Detroit (2) vs. N.Y. Giants (3), 1935
NFC: Green Bay (2) vs. N.Y. Giants (3), 1939

PENALTY

Most First Downs, Penalty, Game
7 AFC-D: New England vs. Oakland, 1976
6 AFC-D: Cleveland vs. N.Y. Jets, 1986 (OT)
5 AFC-FR: Cleveland vs. L. A. Raiders, 1982
NFC-D: San Francisco vs. Minnesota, 1997
AFC-FR: Miami vs. Buffalo, 1998
NFC-D: Arizona vs. Minnesota, 1998

Most First Downs, Penalty, Both Teams, Game
9 AFC-D: New England (7) vs. Oakland (2), 1976
8 NFC-FR: Atlanta (4) vs. Minnesota (4), 1982
AFC-FR: Miami (5) vs. Buffalo (3), 1998
7 AFC-D: Baltimore (4) vs. Oakland (3), 1977 (OT)
AFC-FR: Denver (4) vs. L.A. Raiders (3), 1993
NFC-D: Dallas (4) vs. Carolina (3), 1996
AFC-D: Kansas City (4) vs. Denver (3), 1997

NET YARDS GAINED RUSHING AND PASSING

Most Yards Gained, Game
610 AFC: San Diego vs. Boston, 1963
602 SB: Washington vs. Denver, 1987
569 AFC: Miami vs. Pittsburgh, 1984

Fewest Yards Gained, Game
86 NFC-D: Cleveland vs. N.Y. Giants, 1958
99 NFC: Chi. Cardinals vs. Philadelphia, 1948
114 NFC-D: N.Y. Giants vs. Washington, 1943
NFC: Minnesota vs. N.Y. Giants, 2000

Most Yards Gained, Both Teams, Game
1,038 AFC-FR: Buffalo (536) vs. Miami (502), 1995
1,036 AFC-D: San Diego (564) vs. Miami (472), 1981 (OT)
1,024 AFC: Miami (569) vs. Pittsburgh (455), 1984

Fewest Yards Gained, Both Teams, Game
331 NFC: Chi. Cardinals (99) vs. Philadelphia (232), 1948
332 NFC-D: N.Y. Giants (150) vs. Cleveland (182), 1950
336 NFC: Boston (116) vs. Green Bay (220), 1936

RUSHING

ATTEMPTS

Most Attempts, Game
65 NFC: Detroit vs. N.Y. Giants, 1935
61 NFC: Philadelphia vs. Los Angeles, 1949
59 AFC: New England vs. Miami, 1985

Fewest Attempts, Game
8 AFC-D: Miami vs. San Diego, 1994
9 SB: Miami vs. San Francisco, 1984
NFC: Minnesota vs. N.Y. Giants, 2000
10 NFC: L.A. Rams vs. San Francisco, 1989
NFC-FR: Atlanta vs. Green Bay, 1995
NFC-FR: Detroit vs. Washington, 1999

Most Attempts, Both Teams, Game
109 NFC: Detroit (65) vs. N.Y. Giants (44), 1935
97 AFC-D: Baltimore (50) vs. Oakland (47), 1977 (OT)
91 NFC: Philadelphia (57) vs. Chi. Cardinals (34), 1948

Fewest Attempts, Both Teams, Game
32 AFC-D: Houston (14) vs. Kansas City (18), 1993
38 NFC-D: Detroit (16) vs. Dallas (22), 1991
39 NFC-FR: Atlanta (10) vs. Green Bay (29), 1995

YARDS GAINED

Most Yards Gained, Game
382 NFC: Chi. Bears vs. Washington, 1940
341 AFC-FR: Buffalo vs. Miami, 1995
338 NFC-FR: Dallas vs. Los Angeles, 1980

Fewest Yards Gained, Game
–4 NFC-FR: Detroit vs. Green Bay, 1994
7 AFC-D: Buffalo vs. Boston, 1963
SB: New England vs. Chicago, 1985
14 AFC-D: Miami vs. Denver, 1998
AFC: N.Y. Jets vs. Denver, 1998

Most Yards Gained, Both Teams, Game
430 NFC-FR: Dallas (338) vs. Los Angeles (92), 1980
426 NFC: Cleveland (227) vs. Detroit (199), 1952
411 AFC-FR: Buffalo (341) vs. Miami (70), 1995

Fewest Yards Gained, Both Teams, Game
77 NFC-FR: Detroit (–4) vs. Green Bay (81), 1994
84 NFC-FR: St. Louis (34) vs. New Orleans (50), 2000
90 AFC-D: Buffalo (7) vs. Boston (83), 1963
NFC-D: Tampa Bay (44) vs. Washington (46), 1999

AVERAGE GAIN

Highest Average Gain, Game
9.94 AFC: San Diego vs. Boston, 1963 (32-318)
9.29 NFC-D: Green Bay vs. Dallas, 1982 (17-158)
7.35 NFC-FR: Dallas vs. Los Angeles, 1980 (46-338)

Lowest Average Gain, Game
–0.27 NFC-FR: Detroit vs. Green Bay, 1994 (15-(–4))
0.58 AFC-D: Buffalo vs. Boston, 1963 (12-7)
0.64 SB: New England vs. Chicago, 1985 (11-7)

TOUCHDOWNS

Most Touchdowns, Game
7 NFC: Chi. Bears vs. Washington, 1940
6 NFC-D: San Francisco vs. N.Y. Giants, 1993
5 NFC: Cleveland vs. Detroit, 1954
NFC-D: San Francisco vs. Chicago, 1994
AFC-FR: Pittsburgh vs. Indianapolis, 1996
AFC-FR: Denver vs. Jacksonville, 1997

Most Touchdowns, Both Teams, Game
7 NFC: Chi. Bears (7) vs. Washington (0), 1940
6 NFC: Cleveland (5) vs. Detroit (1), 1954
NFC-D: San Francisco (6) vs. N.Y. Giants (0), 1993
NFC-D: San Francisco (5) vs. Chicago (1), 1994
AFC-FR: Denver (5) vs. Jacksonville (1), 1997
5 NFC: Chi. Cardinals (3) vs. Philadelphia (2), 1947
AFC: San Diego (4) vs. Boston (1), 1963
AFC-D: Cincinnati (3) vs. Buffalo (2), 1981
AFC-FR: Pittsburgh (5) vs. Indianapolis (0), 1996
NFC-D: Arizona (3) vs. Minnesota (2), 1998

PASSING

ATTEMPTS

Most Attempts, Game
66 AFC-FR: Miami vs. Buffalo, 1995
65 AFC-D: Cleveland vs. N.Y. Jets, 1986 (OT)
NFC-D: San Francisco vs. Green Bay, 1995
61 NFC-FR: Minnesota vs. Chicago, 1994

Fewest Attempts, Game
5 NFC: Detroit vs. N.Y. Giants, 1935
6 AFC: Miami vs. Oakland, 1973
7 SB: Miami vs. Minnesota, 1973

Most Attempts, Both Teams, Game
102 AFC-D: San Diego (54) vs. Miami (48), 1981 (OT)
96 AFC: N.Y. Jets (49) vs. Oakland (47), 1968
95 AFC-D: Cleveland (65) vs. N.Y. Jets (30), 1986 (OT)

Fewest Attempts, Both Teams, Game
18 NFC: Detroit (5) vs. N.Y. Giants (13), 1935
23 NFC: Chi. Cardinals (11) vs. Philadelphia (12), 1948
24 NFC-D: Cleveland (9) vs. N.Y. Giants (15), 1950

COMPLETIONS

Most Completions, Game
36 AFC-FR: Houston vs. Buffalo, 1992 (OT)
34 AFC-D: Cleveland vs. N.Y. Jets, 1986 (OT)
AFC-FR: Miami vs. Buffalo, 1995
33 AFC-D: San Diego vs. Miami, 1981 (OT)
NFC-FR: Minnesota vs. Chicago, 1994

POSTSEASON GAME RECORDS

Fewest Completions, Game

2 NFC: Detroit vs. N.Y. Giants, 1935
NFC: Philadelphia vs. Chi. Cardinals, 1948
3 NFC: N.Y. Giants vs. Chi. Bears, 1941
NFC: Green Bay vs. N.Y. Giants, 1944
NFC: Chi. Cardinals vs. Philadelphia, 1947
NFC: Chi. Cardinals vs. Philadelphia, 1948
NFC-D: Cleveland vs. N.Y. Giants, 1950
NFC-D: N.Y. Giants vs. Cleveland, 1950
NFC: Cleveland vs. Detroit, 1953
AFC: Miami vs. Oakland, 1973
4 NFC: N.Y. Giants vs. Detroit, 1935
NFC-D: N.Y. Giants vs. Washington, 1943
NFC-D: Pittsburgh vs. Philadelphia, 1947
NFC-D: Dallas vs. Detroit, 1970
AFC: Miami vs. Baltimore, 1971
SB: Miami vs. Washington, 1982
AFC-FR: Seattle vs. L.A. Raiders, 1984

Most Completions, Both Teams, Game

64 AFC-D: San Diego (33) vs. Miami (31), 1981 (OT)
57 AFC-FR: Houston (36) vs. Buffalo (21), 1992 (OT)
56 NFC-D: Dallas (28) vs. Green Bay (28), 1993
NFC: Minnesota (29) vs. Atlanta (27), 1998 (OT)
NFC-D: Minnesota (29) vs. St. Louis (27), 1999

Fewest Completions, Both Teams, Game

5 NFC: Philadelphia (2) vs. Chi. Cardinals (3), 1948
6 NFC: Detroit (2) vs. N.Y. Giants (4), 1935
NFC-D: Cleveland (3) vs. N.Y. Giants (3), 1950
11 NFC: Green Bay (3) vs. N.Y. Giants (8), 1944
NFC-D: Dallas (4) vs. Detroit (7), 1970

COMPLETION PERCENTAGE

Highest Completion Percentage, Game (20 attempts)

88.0 SB: N.Y. Giants vs. Denver, 1986 (25-22)
87.1 NFC: San Francisco vs. L.A. Rams, 1989 (31-27)
81.8 NFC-D: St. Louis vs. Minnesota, 1999 (33-27)

Lowest Completion Percentage, Game (20 attempts)

18.5 NFC: Tampa Bay vs. Los Angeles, 1979 (27-5)
20.0 NFC-D: N.Y. Giants vs. Washington, 1943 (20-4)
25.8 NFC: Chi. Bears vs. Washington, 1937 (31-8)

YARDS GAINED

Most Yards Gained, Game

483 AFC-D: Cleveland vs. N.Y. Jets, 1986 (OT)
435 AFC: Miami vs. Pittsburgh, 1984
432 AFC-FR: Miami vs. Buffalo, 1995

Fewest Yards Gained, Game

3 NFC: Chi. Cardinals vs. Philadelphia, 1948
7 NFC: Philadelphia vs. Chi. Cardinals, 1948
9 NFC-D: N.Y. Giants vs. Cleveland, 1950
NFC: Cleveland vs. Detroit, 1953

Most Yards Gained, Both Teams, Game

809 AFC-D: San Diego (415) vs. Miami (394), 1981 (OT)
762 NFC-D: Minnesota (388) vs. St. Louis (374), 1999
747 AFC: Miami (435) vs. Pittsburgh (312), 1984

Fewest Yards Gained, Both Teams, Game

10 NFC: Chi. Cardinals (3) vs. Philadelphia (7), 1948
38 NFC-D: N.Y. Giants (9) vs. Cleveland (29), 1950
102 NFC-D: Dallas (22) vs. Detroit (80), 1970

TIMES SACKED

Most Times Sacked, Game

9 AFC: Kansas City vs. Buffalo, 1966
NFC: Chicago vs. San Francisco, 1984
AFC-D: N.Y. Jets vs. Cleveland, 1986 (OT)
AFC-D: Houston vs. Kansas City, 1993
8 NFC: Green Bay vs. Dallas, 1967
NFC: Minnesota vs. Washington, 1987
7 NFC-D: Dallas vs. Los Angeles, 1973
SB: Dallas vs. Pittsburgh, 1975
AFC-FR: Houston vs. Oakland, 1980
NFC-D: Washington vs. Chicago, 1984
SB: New England vs. Chicago, 1985
AFC-FR: Kansas City vs. San Diego, 1992
AFC-D: Pittsburgh vs. Buffalo, 1992

Most Times Sacked, Both Teams, Game

13 AFC: Kansas City (9) vs. Buffalo (4), 1966
AFC-D: N.Y. Jets (9) vs. Cleveland (4), 1986 (OT)
12 NFC-D: Dallas (7) vs. Los Angeles (5), 1973
NFC-D: Washington (7) vs. Chicago (5), 1984
NFC: Chicago (9) vs. San Francisco (3), 1984
AFC-FR: Kansas City (7) vs. San Diego (5), 1992
11 AFC-D: Houston (9) vs. Kansas City (2), 1993

Fewest Times Sacked, Both Teams, Game

0 AFC-D: Buffalo vs. Pittsburgh, 1974
AFC-FR: Pittsburgh vs. San Diego, 1982
AFC: Miami vs. Pittsburgh, 1984
AFC-D: Buffalo vs. Miami, 1990
AFC-D: Denver vs. Houston, 1991
AFC-FR: Buffalo vs. Miami, 1995
AFC-D: Indianapolis vs. Tennessee, 1999
1 In many games

TOUCHDOWNS

Most Touchdowns, Game

6 AFC-D: Oakland vs. Houston, 1969
SB: San Francisco vs. San Diego, 1994
5 NFC: Chi. Bears vs. Washington, 1943
NFC: Detroit vs. Cleveland, 1957
AFC-D: Oakland vs. Kansas City, 1968
SB: San Francisco vs. Denver, 1989
NFC-D: St. Louis vs. Minnesota, 1999
NFC: N.Y. Giants vs. Minnesota, 2000
4 By many teams

Most Touchdowns, Both Teams, Game

9 NFC-D: St. Louis (5) vs. Minnesota (4), 1999
8 AFC-FR: Buffalo (4) vs. Houston (4), 1992 (OT)
7 NFC: Chi. Bears (5) vs. Washington (2), 1943
AFC-D: Oakland (6) vs. Houston (1), 1969
SB: Pittsburgh (4) vs. Dallas (3), 1978
AFC-D: Miami (4) vs. San Diego (3), 1981 (OT)
AFC: Miami (4) vs. Pittsburgh (3), 1984
AFC-D: Buffalo (4) vs. Cleveland (3), 1989
SB: San Francisco (6) vs. San Diego (1), 1994
NFC-FR: Detroit (4) vs. Philadelphia (3), 1995
NFC-FR: New Orleans (4) vs. St. Louis (3), 2000

INTERCEPTIONS BY

Most Interceptions By, Game

8 NFC: Chi. Bears vs. Washington, 1940
7 NFC: Cleveland vs. Los Angeles, 1955
6 NFC: Green Bay vs. N.Y. Giants, 1939
NFC: Chi. Bears vs. N.Y. Giants, 1946
NFC: Cleveland vs. Detroit, 1954
AFC: San Diego vs. Houston, 1961
AFC: Buffalo vs. L.A. Raiders, 1990
NFC-FR: Philadelphia vs. Detroit, 1995

Most Interceptions By, Both Teams, Game

10 NFC: Cleveland (7) vs. Los Angeles (3), 1955
AFC: San Diego (6) vs. Houston (4), 1961
9 NFC: Green Bay (6) vs. N.Y. Giants (3), 1939
8 NFC: Chi. Bears (8) vs. Washington (0), 1940
NFC: Chi. Bears (6) vs. N.Y. Giants (2), 1946
NFC: Cleveland (6) vs. Detroit (2), 1954
AFC-FR: Buffalo (4) vs. N.Y. Jets (4), 1981
AFC: Miami (5) vs. N.Y. Jets (3), 1982

YARDS GAINED

Most Yards Gained, Game

138 AFC-FR: N.Y. Jets vs. Cincinnati, 1982
136 AFC: Dall. Texans vs. Houston, 1962 (OT)
SB: Denver vs. Atlanta, 1998
130 NFC-D: Los Angeles vs. St. Louis, 1975

Most Yards Gained, Both Teams, Game

156 NFC: Green Bay (123) vs. N.Y. Giants (33), 1939
149 NFC: Cleveland (103) vs. Los Angeles (46), 1955
141 AFC-FR: Buffalo (79) vs. N.Y. Jets (62), 1981

TOUCHDOWNS

Most Touchdowns, Game

3 NFC: Chi. Bears vs. Washington, 1940
2 NFC-D: Los Angeles vs. St. Louis, 1975
NFC-FR: Philadelphia vs. Detroit, 1995
1 In many games

Most Touchdowns, Both Teams, Game

3 NFC: Chi. Bears (3) vs. Washington (0), 1940
2 NFC-D: Los Angeles (2) vs. St. Louis(0), 1975
NFC-D: Dallas (1) vs. Green Bay (1), 1982
NFC-D: Minnesota (1) vs. San Francisco (1), 1987
NFC-FR: Detroit (1) vs. Green Bay (1), 1993
NFC-FR: Philadelphia (2) vs. Detroit (0), 1995
AFC-FR: Buffalo (1) vs. Jacksonville (1), 1996
1 In many games

PUNTING

Most Punts, Game

14 AFC-D: N.Y. Jets vs. Cleveland, 1986 (OT)
13 NFC: N.Y. Giants vs. Chi. Bears, 1933
AFC-D: Baltimore vs. Oakland, 1977 (OT)
11 AFC: Houston vs. Oakland, 1967
AFC-D: Houston vs. Oakland, 1969
NFC: L.A. Rams vs. Chicago, 1985
SB: N.Y. Giants vs. Baltimore, 2000

Fewest Punts, Game

0 NFC-FR: St. Louis vs. Green Bay, 1982
AFC-FR: N.Y. Jets vs. Cincinnati, 1982
1 By many teams

Most Punts, Both Teams, Game

23 NFC: N.Y. Giants (13) vs. Chi. Bears (10), 1933
22 AFC-D: N.Y. Jets (14) vs. Cleveland (8), 1986 (OT)
21 AFC-D: Baltimore (13) vs. Oakland (8), 1977 (OT)
NFC: L.A. Rams (11) vs. Chicago (10), 1985
SB: N.Y. Giants (11) vs. Baltimore (10), 2000

Fewest Punts, Both Teams, Game

1 NFC-FR: St. Louis (0) vs. Green Bay (1), 1982
2 AFC-FR: N.Y. Jets (0) vs. Cincinnati (2), 1982
SB: Atlanta (1) vs. Denver (1), 1998
3 AFC: Miami (1) vs. Oakland (2), 1973
AFC-FR: San Diego (1) vs. Pittsburgh (2), 1982
AFC-D: Buffalo (1) vs. Miami (2), 1990
AFC-FR: L.A. Raiders (1) vs. Kansas City (2), 1991
AFC-D: Houston (1) vs. Denver (2), 1991
NFC-FR: Dallas (1) vs. Minnesota (2), 1996
AFC-FR: Miami (1) vs. Buffalo (2), 1998
NFC-D: Minnesota (1) vs. Arizona (2), 1998

AVERAGE YARDAGE

Highest Average, Punting, Game (4 punts)

56.0 AFC: Oakland vs. San Diego, 1980
52.5 NFC: Washington vs. Chi. Bears, 1942
52.0 AFC-D: Tennessee vs. Indianapolis, 1999

Lowest Average, Punting, Game (4 punts)

24.9 NFC: Washington vs. Chi. Bears, 1937
25.3 AFC-FR: Pittsburgh vs. Houston, 1989
25.5 NFC: Green Bay vs. N.Y. Giants, 1962

PUNT RETURNS

Most Punt Returns, Game

8 NFC: Green Bay vs. N.Y. Giants, 1944
7 By many teams

Most Punt Returns, Both Teams, Game

13 AFC-FR: Houston (7) vs. Oakland (6), 1980
12 AFC-D: New England (7) vs. Pittsburgh (5), 1996
11 NFC: Green Bay (8) vs. N.Y. Giants (3), 1944
NFC-D: Green Bay (6) vs. Baltimore (5), 1965
AFC-FR: Jacksonville (7) vs. New England (4), 1998

Fewest Punt Returns, Both Teams, Game

0 NFC: Chi. Bears vs. N.Y. Giants, 1941
AFC: Boston vs. San Diego, 1963
NFC-FR: Green Bay vs. St. Louis, 1982
AFC-FR: Houston vs. N.Y. Jets, 1991
AFC-D: Denver vs. Houston, 1991
NFC-D: San Francisco vs. Washington, 1992
SB: Denver vs. Green Bay, 1997
SB: Atlanta vs. Denver, 1998
1 In many games

YARDS GAINED

Most Yards Gained, Game

155 NFC-D: Dallas vs. Cleveland, 1967
150 NFC: Chi. Cardinals vs. Philadelphia, 1947
143 NFC-FR: Minnesota vs. New Orleans, 1987

Fewest Yards Gained, Game

–10 NFC: Green Bay vs. Cleveland, 1965
–9 NFC: Dallas vs. Green Bay, 1966
AFC-D: Kansas City vs. Oakland, 1968
–7 NFC-D: San Francisco vs. Atlanta, 1998

Most Yards Gained, Both Teams, Game

166 NFC-D: Dallas (155) vs. Cleveland (11), 1967
160 NFC: Chi. Cardinals (150) vs. Philadelphia (10), 1947
146 NFC-D: Philadelphia (112) vs. Pittsburgh (34), 1947

Fewest Yards Gained, Both Teams, Game

–9 NFC: Dallas (–9) vs. Green Bay (0), 1966
–6 AFC-D: Miami (–5) vs. Oakland (–1), 1970
–3 NFC-D: San Francisco (–5) vs. Dallas (2), 1972

TOUCHDOWNS

Most Touchdowns, Game

1 By 12 teams

KICKOFF RETURNS

Most Kickoff Returns, Game

10 NFC-D: L.A. Rams vs. Washington, 1983
NFC-FR: Detroit vs. Philadelphia, 1995
9 NFC: Chi. Bears vs. N.Y. Giants, 1956
AFC: Boston vs. San Diego, 1963
AFC: Houston vs. Oakland, 1967
SB: Denver vs. San Francisco, 1989
AFC-D: Miami vs. Buffalo, 1990
AFC: L.A. Raiders vs. Buffalo, 1990
AFC-D: Miami vs. Jacksonville, 1999
8 By many teams

Most Kickoff Returns, Both Teams, Game

15 AFC-D: Miami (9) vs. Buffalo (6), 1990
14 NFC-FR: Detroit (10) vs. Philadelphia (4), 1995
13 NFC-D: Green Bay (7) vs. Dallas (6), 1982
NFC-FR: Green Bay (7) vs. San Francisco (6), 1998

Fewest Kickoff Returns, Both Teams, Game

1 NFC: Green Bay (0) vs. Boston (1), 1936
AFC-FR: San Diego (0) vs. Kansas City (1), 1992
2 NFC-D: Los Angeles (0) vs. Chi. Bears (2), 1950
AFC: Houston (0) vs. San Diego (2), 1961
AFC-D: Oakland (1) vs. Pittsburgh (1), 1972
AFC-D: N.Y. Jets (0) vs. L.A. Raiders (2), 1982
AFC: Miami (1) vs. N.Y. Jets (1), 1982
NFC: N.Y. Giants (0) vs. Washington (2), 1986
3 In many games

YARDS GAINED

Most Yards Gained, Game

244 SB: San Diego vs. San Francisco, 1994
227 SB: Atlanta vs. Denver, 1998
225 NFC: Washington vs. Chi. Bears, 1940

Most Yards Gained, Both Teams, Game

379 AFC-D: Baltimore (193) vs. Oakland (186), 1977 (OT)
348 NFC-D: Minnesota (174) vs. St. Louis (174), 1999
322 NFC-D: Green Bay (194) vs. San Francisco (128), 1998

Fewest Yards Gained, Both Teams, Game

5 AFC-FR: San Diego (0) vs. Kansas City (5), 1992
15 NFC: N.Y. Giants (0) vs. Washington (15), 1986
31 NFC-D: Los Angeles (0) vs. Chi. Bears (31), 1950

TOUCHDOWNS

Most Touchdowns, Game

1 NFC-D: San Francisco vs. Dallas, 1972
AFC-D: Miami vs. Oakland, 1974
AFC-D: Baltimore vs. Oakland, 1977 (OT)
SB: Miami vs. Washington, 1982
SB: Cincinnati vs. San Francisco, 1988
AFC-D: Cleveland vs. Buffalo, 1989
SB: San Diego vs. San Francisco, 1994
SB: Green Bay vs. New England, 1996
NFC: San Francisco vs. Green Bay, 1997
SB: Atlanta vs. Denver, 1998
AFC-FR: Tennessee vs. Buffalo, 1999
AFC-FR: Seattle vs. Miami, 1999
NFC-D: Washington vs. Tampa Bay, 1999
NFC-D: St. Louis vs. Minnesota, 1999
AFC: Tennessee vs. Jacksonville, 1999
NFC-D: N.Y. Giants vs. Philadelphia, 2000
SB: Baltimore vs. N.Y. Giants, 2000
SB: N.Y. Giants vs. Baltimore, 2000

Most Touchdowns, Both Teams, Game

2 SB: Baltimore (1) vs. N.Y. Giants (1), 2000

PENALTIES

Most Penalties, Game

17 AFC-FR: L.A. Raiders vs. Denver, 1993
14 AFC-FR: Oakland vs. Houston, 1980
NFC-D: San Francisco vs. N.Y. Giants, 1981
13 AFC-FR: Houston vs. Cleveland, 1988
AFC-D: Houston vs. Denver, 1991
NFC-D: Arizona vs. Minnesota, 1998

Fewest Penalties, Game

0 NFC: Philadelphia vs. Green Bay, 1960
NFC-D: Detroit vs. Dallas, 1970
AFC-D: Miami vs. Oakland, 1970
SB: Miami vs. Dallas, 1971
NFC-D: Washington vs. Minnesota, 1973
SB: Pittsburgh vs. Dallas, 1975

POSTSEASON GAME RECORDS

NFC: San Francisco vs. Chicago, 1988
SB: Denver vs. San Francisco, 1989
AFC-D: L.A. Raiders vs. Cincinnati, 1990
AFC-D: Miami vs. San Diego, 1992
SB: Atlanta vs. Denver, 1998
1 By many teams

Most Penalties, Both Teams, Game
27 AFC-FR: L.A. Raiders (17) vs. Denver (10), 1993
22 AFC-FR: Oakland (14) vs. Houston (8), 1980
NFC-D: San Francisco (14) vs. N.Y. Giants (8), 1981
AFC-FR: Houston (13) vs. Cleveland (9), 1988
NFC-D: Arizona (13) vs. Minnesota (9), 1998
21 AFC-D: Oakland (11) vs. New England (10), 1976

Fewest Penalties, Both Teams, Game
1 AFC-D: L.A. Raiders (0) vs. Cincinnati (1), 1990
2 NFC: Washington (1) vs. Chi. Bears (1), 1937
NFC-D: Washington (0) vs. Minnesota (2), 1973
SB: Pittsburgh (0) vs. Dallas (2), 1975
3 AFC: Miami (1) vs. Baltimore (2), 1971
NFC: San Francisco (1) vs. Dallas (2), 1971
SB: Miami (0) vs. Dallas (3), 1971
AFC-D: Pittsburgh (1) vs. Oakland (2), 1972
AFC-D: Miami (1) vs. Cincinnati (2), 1973
SB: Miami (1) vs. San Francisco (2), 1984
NFC: San Francisco (0) vs. Chicago (3), 1988

YARDS PENALIZED

Most Yards Penalized, Game
145 NFC-D: San Francisco vs. N.Y. Giants, 1981
133 SB: Dallas vs. Baltimore, 1970
130 AFC-FR: L.A. Raiders vs. Denver, 1993

Fewest Yards Penalized, Game
0 By 11 teams

Most Yards Penalized, Both Teams, Game
227 AFC-FR: L.A. Raiders (130) vs. Denver (97), 1993
206 NFC-D: San Francisco (145) vs. N.Y. Giants (61), 1981
201 NFC-FR: Detroit (126) vs. Washington (75), 1999

Fewest Yards Penalized, Both Teams, Game
5 AFC-D: L.A. Raiders (0) vs. Cincinnati (5), 1990
9 NFC-D: Washington (0) vs. Minnesota (9), 1973
15 SB: Miami (0) vs. Dallas (15), 1971

FUMBLES

Most Fumbles, Game
8 SB: Buffalo vs. Dallas, 1992
7 AFC-D: Houston vs. Kansas City, 1993
6 By 12 teams

Most Fumbles, Both Teams, Game
12 AFC: Houston (6) vs. Pittsburgh (6), 1978
SB: Buffalo (8) vs. Dallas (4), 1992
10 NFC: Chi. Bears (5) vs. N.Y. Giants (5), 1934
SB: Dallas (6) vs. Denver (4), 1977
AFC: Jacksonville (5) vs. Tennessee (5), 1999
9 NFC-D: San Francisco (6) vs. Detroit (3), 1957
NFC-D: San Francisco (5) vs. Dallas (4), 1972
NFC: Dallas (5) vs. Philadelphia (4), 1980

Most Fumbles Lost, Game
5 SB: Buffalo vs. Dallas, 1992
AFC-D: Miami vs. Jacksonville, 1999
4 NFC: N.Y. Giants vs. Baltimore, 1958 (OT)
AFC: Kansas City vs. Oakland, 1969
SB: Baltimore vs. Dallas, 1970
AFC: Pittsburgh vs. Oakland, 1975
SB: Denver vs. Dallas, 1977
AFC: Houston vs. Pittsburgh, 1978
AFC: Miami vs. New England, 1985
SB: New England vs. Chicago, 1985
NFC-FR: L.A. Rams vs. Washington, 1986
NFC-FR: Minnesota vs. Dallas, 1996
AFC-FR: Buffalo vs. Miami, 1998
AFC: N.Y. Jets vs. Denver, 1998
AFC: Jacksonville vs. Tennessee, 1999
3 By many teams

Fewest Fumbles, Both Teams, Game
0 NFC: Green Bay vs. Cleveland, 1965
AFC-D: Houston vs. San Diego, 1979
NFC-D: Dallas vs. Los Angeles, 1979
SB: Los Angeles vs. Pittsburgh, 1979
AFC-D: Buffalo vs. Cincinnati, 1981
NFC: Minnesota vs. Washington, 1987
NFC-D: San Francisco vs. Washington, 1990
NFC: Dallas vs. Green Bay, 1995
AFC-D: New England vs. Pittsburgh, 1996
SB: Green Bay vs. New England, 1996
AFC-FR: Miami vs. Seattle, 1999
AFC-FR: Miami vs. Indianapolis, 2000 (OT)
AFC-D: Baltimore vs. Tennessee, 2000
1 In many games

RECOVERIES

Most Total Fumbles Recovered, Game
8 SB: Dallas vs. Denver, 1977 (4 own, 4 opp)
7 NFC: Chi. Bears vs. N.Y. Giants, 1934 (5 own, 2 opp)
NFC-D: San Francisco vs. Detroit, 1957 (4 own, 3 opp)
NFC-D: San Francisco vs. Dallas, 1972 (4 own, 3 opp)
AFC: Pittsburgh vs. Houston, 1978 (3 own, 4 opp)
6 AFC: Houston vs. San Diego, 1961 (4 own, 2 opp)
AFC-D: Cleveland vs. Baltimore, 1971 (4 own, 2 opp)
AFC-D: Cleveland vs. Oakland, 1980 (5 own, 1 opp)
NFC: Philadelphia vs. Dallas, 1980 (3 own, 3 opp)
SB: Dallas vs. Buffalo, 1992 (1 own, 5 opp)
NFC-D: Green Bay vs. San Francisco, 1996 (4 own, 2 opp)
AFC: Denver vs. N.Y. Jets, 1998 (2 own, 4 opp)
AFC: Tennessee vs. Jacksonville, 1999 (2 own, 4 opp)

Most Own Fumbles Recovered, Game
5 NFC: Chi. Bears vs. N.Y. Giants, 1934
AFC-D: Cleveland vs. Oakland, 1980
4 By many teams

TOUCHDOWNS

Most Touchdowns, Game
2 SB: Dallas vs. Buffalo, 1992

TURNOVERS

Numbers of times losing the ball on interceptions and fumbles.

Most Turnovers, Game
9 NFC: Washington vs. Chi. Bears, 1940
NFC: Detroit vs. Cleveland, 1954
AFC: Houston vs. Pittsburgh, 1978
SB: Buffalo vs. Dallas, 1992
8 NFC: N.Y. Giants vs. Chi. Bears, 1946
NFC: Los Angeles vs. Cleveland, 1955
NFC: Cleveland vs. Detroit, 1957
SB: Denver vs. Dallas, 1977
NFC-D: Minnesota vs. Philadelphia, 1980
7 In many games

Fewest Turnovers, Game
0 By many teams

Most Turnovers, Both Teams, Game
14 AFC: Houston (9) vs. Pittsburgh (5), 1978
13 NFC: Detroit (9) vs. Cleveland (4), 1954
AFC: Houston (7) vs. San Diego (6), 1961
12 AFC: Pittsburgh (7) vs. Oakland (5), 1975

Fewest Turnovers, Both Teams, Game
0 SB: Buffalo vs. N.Y. Giants, 1990
AFC-FR: Kansas City vs Pittsburgh, 1993 (OT)
NFC-FR: Detroit vs. Green Bay, 1994
AFC-FR: Denver vs. Jacksonville, 1996
SB: St. Louis vs. Tennessee, 1999
1 AFC-D: Baltimore (0) vs. Cincinnati (1), 1970
AFC-D: Pittsburgh (0) vs. Buffalo (1), 1974
AFC: Oakland (0) vs. Pittsburgh (1), 1976
NFC-D: Minnesota (0) vs. Washington (1), 1982
NFC-D: Chicago (0) vs. N.Y. Giants (1), 1985
SB: N.Y. Giants (0) vs. Denver (1), 1986
NFC: Washington (0) vs. Minnesota (1), 1987
AFC-D: Cincinnati (0) vs. L.A. Raiders (1), 1990
NFC: N.Y. Giants (0) vs. San Francisco (1), 1990
NFC-FR: N.Y. Giants (0) vs. Minnesota (1), 1993
AFC-FR: L.A. Raiders (0) vs. Denver (1), 1993
NFC: Dallas (0) vs. San Francisco (1), 1993
AFC: Indianapolis (0) vs. Pittsburgh (1), 1995
NFC-D: San Francisco (0) vs. Minnesota (1), 1997
AFC-D: Indianapolis (0) vs. Tennessee (1), 1999
2 In many games

Includes records of AFC-NFC Pro Bowls, 1971-2000
Compiled by Elias Sports Bureau

INDIVIDUAL RECORDS

SERVICE

Most Games

12 Randall McDaniel, Minnesota 1990-2000; Tampa Bay 2001
11 * Reggie White, Philadelphia, 1987-1993; Green Bay, 1994, 1996-97, 1999
10 Lawrence Taylor, N.Y. Giants, 1982-1991
Ronnie Lott, San Francisco, 1982-85, 1987-1991; L.A. Raiders 1992
Mike Singletary, Chicago, 1984-1993
Junior Seau, San Diego, 1992-2001
**Also selected, but did not play, in two additional games*

SCORING

POINTS

Most Points, Career

45 Morten Andersen, New Orleans, 1986-89, 1991, 1993; Atlanta, 1996 (15-pat, 10-fg)
30 Jan Stenerud, Kansas City, 1971-72, 1976; Minnesota, 1985 (6-pat, 8-fg)
Jimmy Smith, Jacksonville, 1998-2001 (5-td)
26 Nick Lowery, Kansas City, 1982, 1991, 1993 (5 pat, 7 fg)

Most Points, Game

18 John Brockington, Green Bay, 1973 (3-td)
Mike Alstott, Tampa Bay, 2000 (3-td)
Jimmy Smith, Jacksonville, 2000 (3-td)
15 Garo Yepremian, Miami, 1974 (5-fg)
Jason Hanson, Detroit, 2000 (6-pat, 3-fg)
14 Jan Stenerud, Kansas City, 1972 (2-pat, 4-fg)

TOUCHDOWNS

Most Touchdowns, Career

5 Jimmy Smith, Jacksonville, 1998-2001 (5-p)
3 John Brockington, Green Bay, 1972-74 (2-r, 1-p)
Earl Campbell, Houston, 1979-1982, 1984 (3-r)
Chuck Muncie, New Orleans, 1980; San Diego, 1982-83 (3-r)
William Andrews, Atlanta, 1981-84 (1-r, 2-p)
Marcus Allen, L.A. Raiders, 1983, 1985-86, 1988; Kansas City, 1994 (2-r, 1-p)
Cris Carter, Minnesota, 1994-2001 (3-p)
Mike Alstott, Tampa Bay, 1998-2001 (3-r)
2 By 19 players

Most Touchdowns, Game

3 John Brockington, Green Bay, 1973 (2-r, 1-p)
Mike Alstott, Tampa Bay, 2000 (3-r)
Jimmy Smith, Jacksonville, 2000 (3-p)
2 Mel Renfro, Dallas, 1971 (2-ret)
Earl Campbell, Houston, 1980 (2-r)
Chuck Muncie, New Orleans, 1980 (2-r)
William Andrews, Atlanta, 1984 (2-p)
Herschel Walker, Dallas, 1989 (2-r)
Johnny Johnson, Phoenix, 1991 (2-r)
Eric Green, Pittsburgh, 1995 (2-p)
Marvin Harrison, Indianapolis, 2001 (2-p)

POINTS AFTER TOUCHDOWN

Most Points After Touchdown, Career

15 Morten Andersen, New Orleans, 1986-89, 1991, 1993; Atlanta, 1996 (15 att)
9 Jason Hanson, Detroit, 1998, 2000 (9 att)
6 Chester Marcol, Green Bay, 1973, 1975 (6 att)
Mark Moseley, Washington, 1980, 1983 (7 att)
Ali Haji-Sheikh, N.Y. Giants, 1984 (6 att)
Jan Stenerud, Kansas City, 1971-72, 1976; Green Bay, 1985 (6 att)

Most Points After Touchdown, Game

6 Ali Haji-Sheikh, N.Y. Giants, 1984 (6 att)
Jason Hanson, Detroit, 2000 (6 att)
5 John Carney, San Diego, 1995 (5 att)
Matt Stover, Baltimore, 2001 (5 att)
4 Chester Marcol, Green Bay, 1973 (4 att)
Mark Moseley, Washington, 1980 (5 att)
Morten Andersen, New Orleans, 1986 (4 att), 1989 (4 att)
Olindo Mare, Miami, 2000 (4 att)

FIELD GOALS

Most Field Goals Attempted, Career

18 Morten Andersen, New Orleans, 1986-89, 1991, 1993; Atlanta, 1996
15 Jan Stenerud, Kansas City, 1971-72, 1976; Minnesota, 1985
10 Nick Lowery, Kansas City, 1982, 1991, 1993

Most Field Goals Attempted, Game

6 Jan Stenerud, Kansas City, 1972
Eddie Murray, Detroit, 1981
Mark Moseley, Washington, 1983
5 Garo Yepremian, Miami, 1974
4 Jan Stenerud, Kansas City, 1976
Nick Lowery, Kansas City, 1991, 1993
Morten Andersen, New Orleans, 1993
Cary Blanchard, Indianapolis, 1997
John Kasay, Carolina, 1997

Most Field Goals, Career

10 Morten Andersen, New Orleans, 1986-89, 1991, 1993; Atlanta, 1996
8 Jan Stenerud, Kansas City, 1971-72, 1976; Minnesota, 1985
7 Nick Lowery, Kansas City, 1982, 1991, 1993

Most Field Goals, Game

5 Garo Yepremian, Miami, 1974 (5 att)
4 Jan Stenerud, Kansas City, 1972 (6 att)
Eddie Murray, Detroit, 1981 (6 att)
3 Nick Lowery, Kansas City, 1991 (4 att)
Nick Lowery, Kansas City, 1993 (4 att)
Jason Elam, Denver, 1999 (3 att)
Jason Hanson, Detroit, 2000 (3 att)

Longest Field Goal

51 Morten Andersen, New Orleans, 1989
Jason Hanson, Detroit, 2000
49 Fuad Reveiz, Minnesota, 1995
48 Jan Stenerud, Kansas City, 1972
Jeff Jaeger, L.A. Raiders, 1992
Mike Hollis, Jacksonville, 1998
Martin Gramatica, Tampa Bay, 2001

SAFETIES

Most Safeties, Game

1 Art Still, Kansas City, 1983
Mark Gastineau, N.Y. Jets, 1985
Greg Townsend, L.A. Raiders, 1992

RUSHING

ATTEMPTS

Most Attempts, Career

81 Walter Payton, Chicago, 1977-1981, 1984-87
68 O.J. Simpson, Buffalo, 1973-77
66 Barry Sanders, Detroit, 1990-93, 1995-98

Most Attempts, Game

19 O.J. Simpson, Buffalo, 1974
17 Marv Hubbard, Oakland, 1974
16 O.J. Simpson, Buffalo, 1973
Marcus Allen, L.A. Raiders, 1986

YARDS GAINED

Most Yards Gained, Career

368 Walter Payton, Chicago, 1977-1981, 1984-87
356 O.J. Simpson, Buffalo, 1973-77
252 Marshall Faulk, Indianapolis, 1995-96, 1999; St. Louis, 2000

Most Yards Gained, Game

180 Marshall Faulk, Indianapolis, 1995
127 Chris Warren, Seattle, 1995
112 O. J. Simpson, Buffalo, 1973

Longest Run From Scrimmage

49 Marshall Faulk, Indianapolis, 1995 (TD)
41 Lawrence McCutcheon, Los Angeles, 1976
Natrone Means, San Diego, 1995
Marshall Faulk, Indianapolis, 1995
39 Chris Warren, Seattle, 1994

AVERAGE GAIN

Highest Average Gain, Career (20 attempts)

9.36 Chris Warren, Seattle, 1994-96, (25-234)
7.64 Marshall Faulk, Indianapolis, 1995-96, 1999; St. Louis, 2000 (33-252)
5.81 Marv Hubbard, Oakland, 1972-74 (36-209)

Highest Average Gain, Game (10 attempts)

13.85 Marshall Faulk, Indianapolis, 1995 (13-180)
9.07 Chris Warren, Seattle, 1995 (14-127)
7.00 O.J. Simpson, Buffalo, 1973 (16-112)
Ottis Anderson, St. Louis, 1981 (10-70)

TOUCHDOWNS

Most Touchdowns, Career

3 Earl Campbell, Houston, 1979-1982, 1984
Chuck Muncie, New Orleans, 1980; San Diego, 1982-83
Mike Alstott, Tampa Bay, 1998-2001
2 John Brockington, Green Bay, 1972-74
O.J. Simpson, Buffalo, 1973-77

Walter Payton, Chicago, 1977-1981, 1984-87
Marcus Allen, L.A. Raiders, 1983, 1985-86, 1988; Kansas City, 1994
Herschel Walker, Dallas, 1988-89
Johnny Johnson, Phoenix, 1991
Barry Sanders, Detroit, 1990-93, 1995-98

Most Touchdowns, Game
3 Mike Alstott, Tampa Bay, 2000
2 John Brockington, Green Bay, 1973
Earl Campbell, Houston, 1980
Chuck Muncie, New Orleans, 1980
Herschel Walker, Dallas, 1989
Johnny Johnson, Phoenix, 1991

PASSING

ATTEMPTS

Most Attempts, Career
120 Dan Fouts, San Diego, 1980-84, 1986
101 Steve Young, San Francisco, 1993-96, 1998-99
90 Warren Moon, Houston, 1989-1994; Minnesota, 1995-96; Seattle 1998

Most Attempts, Game
32 Bill Kenney, Kansas City, 1984
Steve Young, San Francisco, 1993
30 Dan Fouts, San Diego, 1983
28 Jim Hart, St. Louis, 1976
Jeff Garcia, San Francisco, 2001

COMPLETIONS

Most Completions, Career
63 Dan Fouts, San Diego, 1980-84, 1986
48 Steve Young, San Francisco, 1993-96, 1998-99
45 Warren Moon, Houston, 1989-1994; Minnesota, 1995-96; Seattle 1998

Most Completions, Game
21 Joe Theismann, Washington, 1984
18 Steve Young, San Francisco, 1993
17 Dan Fouts, San Diego, 1983
Peyton Manning, Indianapolis, 2000

COMPLETION PERCENTAGE

Highest Completion Percentage, Career (40 attempts)
71.7 Peyton Manning, Indianapolis, 2000-01 (46-33)
68.9 Joe Theismann, Washington, 1983-84 (45-31)
64.4 Jim Kelly, Buffalo, 1988, 1991-92 (45-29)

Highest Completion Percentage, Game (10 attempts)
90.0 Archie Manning, New Orleans, 1980 (10-9)
85.7 Rich Gannon, Oakland, 2001 (14-12)
77.8 Joe Theismann, Washington, 1984 (27-21)

YARDS GAINED

Most Yards Gained, Career
890 Dan Fouts, San Diego, 1980-84, 1986
614 Steve Young, San Francisco, 1993-96, 1998-99
554 Bob Griese, Miami, 1971-72, 1974-75, 1977, 1979

Most Yards Gained, Game
274 Dan Fouts, San Diego, 1983
270 Peyton Manning, Indianapolis, 2000
242 Joe Theismann, Washington, 1984

Longest Completion
93 Jeff Blake, Cincinnati (to Thigpen, Pittsburgh), 1996 (TD)
80 Mark Brunell, Jacksonville (to Brown, Oakland), 1997 (TD)
64 Dan Pastorini, Houston (to Burrough, Houston), 1976 (TD)

AVERAGE GAIN

Highest Average Gain, Career (40 attempts)
9.13 Peyton Manning, Indianapolis, 2000-01 (46-420)
8.12 Brett Favre, Green Bay, 1993-94, 1996-97 (57-463)
8.06 Randall Cunningham, Philadelphia, 1989-1991; Minnesota, 1999 (52-419)

Highest Average Gain, Game (10 attempts)
15.27 Randall Cunningham, Philadelphia, 1991 (11-168)
13.00 Brett Favre, Green Bay, 1997 (11-143)
11.43 Rich Gannon, Oakland, 2001 (14-160)

TOUCHDOWNS

Most Touchdowns, Career
4 Steve Young, San Francisco, 1993-96, 1998-99
Peyton Manning, Indianapolis, 2000-01
3 Joe Theismann, Washington, 1983-84
Joe Montana, San Francisco, 1982, 1984-85, 1988
Phil Simms, N.Y. Giants, 1986
Jim Kelly, Buffalo, 1988, 1991-92
John Elway, Denver, 1987-88, 1994-95, 1999
Mark Brunell, Jacksonville, 1997-98, 2000
Rich Gannon, Oakland, 2000-01
2 James Harris, Los Angeles, 1975
Mike Boryla, Philadelphia, 1976
Ken Anderson, Cincinnati, 1976-77, 1982-83
Bob Griese, Miami, 1971-72, 1974-75, 1977, 1979
Mark Rypien, Washington, 1990, 1992
Brett Favre, Green Bay, 1993-94, 1996-97

Most Touchdowns, Game
3 Joe Theismann, Washington, 1984
Phil Simms, N.Y. Giants, 1986
2 James Harris, Los Angeles, 1975
Mike Boryla, Philadelphia, 1976
Ken Anderson, Cincinnati, 1977
Jim Kelly, Buffalo, 1991
Mark Rypien, Washington, 1992
Steve Young, San Francisco, 1998
Peyton Manning, Indianapolis, 2000
Rich Gannon, Oakland, 2001
Peyton Manning, Indianapolis, 2001

HAD INTERCEPTED

Most Passes Had Intercepted, Career
8 Dan Fouts, San Diego, 1980-84, 1986
6 Jim Hart, St. Louis, 1975-78
5 Ken Stabler, Oakland, 1974-75, 1978

Most Passes Had Intercepted, Game
5 Jim Hart, St. Louis, 1977
4 Ken Stabler, Oakland, 1974
3 Dan Fouts, San Diego, 1986
Mark Rypien, Washington, 1990
Steve Young, San Francisco, 1993
Jim Harbaugh, Indianapolis, 1996
Vinny Testaverde, N.Y. Jets, 1999

Most Attempts, Without Interception, Game
27 Joe Theismann, Washington, 1984
Phil Simms, N.Y. Giants, 1986
26 John Brodie, San Francisco, 1971
Danny White, Dallas, 1983
23 Dave Krieg, Seattle, 1990

PERCENTAGE, PASSES HAD INTERCEPTED

Lowest Percentage, Passes Had Intercepted, Career (40 attempts)
0.00 Joe Theismann, Washington, 1983-84 (45-0)
2.13 Dave Krieg, Seattle, 1985, 1989-1990 (47-1)
2.22 Jim Kelly, Buffalo, 1988, 1991-92 (45-1)

PASS RECEIVING

RECEPTIONS

Most Receptions, Career
33 Jerry Rice, San Francisco, 1987-88, 1990-94, 1996, 1999
27 Cris Carter, Minnesota, 1994-2001
23 Tim Brown, L.A. Raiders, 1989, 1992, 1994-95; Oakland 1996-98

Most Receptions, Game
9 Randy Moss, Minnesota, 2000
8 Steve Largent, Seattle, 1986
Michael Irvin, Dallas, 1992
Andre Rison, Atlanta, 1993
Jimmy Smith, Jacksonville, 2000
Marvin Harrison, Indianapolis, 2001
7 John Stallworth, Pittsburgh, 1983
Jerry Rice, San Francisco, 1992
Isaac Bruce, St. Louis, 1997
Keyshawn Johnson, N.Y. Jets, 1999
Randy Moss, Minnesota, 1999
Warrick Dunn, Tampa Bay, 2001
Torry Holt, St. Louis, 2001

YARDS GAINED

Most Yards Gained, Career
459 Jerry Rice, San Francisco, 1987-88, 1990-94, 1996, 1999
408 Tim Brown, L.A. Raiders, 1989, 1992, 1994-95; Oakland, 1996-98
335 Cris Carter, Minnesota, 1994-2001

Most Yards Gained, Game
212 Randy Moss, Minnesota, 2000
137 Tim Brown, Oakland, 1997
129 Tim Brown, Oakland, 1998

Longest Reception
93 Yancey Thigpen, Pittsburgh (from Blake, Cincinnati), 1996 (TD)
80 Tim Brown, Oakland (from Brunell, Jacksonville), 1997 (TD)
64 Ken Burrough, Houston (from Pastorini, Houston), 1976 (TD)

TOUCHDOWNS

Most Touchdowns, Career

5 Jimmy Smith, Jacksonville, 1998-2001
3 Cris Carter, Minnesota, 1994-2001
2 Mel Gray, St. Louis, 1975-78
Cliff Branch, Oakland, 1975-78
Terry Metcalf, St. Louis, 1975-76, 1978
Tony Hill, Dallas, 1979-1980, 1986
William Andrews, Atlanta, 1981-84
James Lofton, Green Bay, 1979, 1981-86; Buffalo 1992
Jimmie Giles, Tampa Bay, 1981-83, 1986
Michael Irvin, Dallas, 1992-95
Eric Green, Pittsburgh, 1994-95
Jerry Rice, San Francisco, 1987-88, 1990-94, 1996, 1999
Tony Gonzalez, Kansas City, 2000-01
Marvin Harrison, Indianapolis, 2000-01

Most Touchdowns, Game

3 Jimmy Smith, Jacksonville, 2000
2 William Andrews, Atlanta, 1984
Eric Green, Pittsburgh, 1995
Marvin Harrison, Indianapolis, 2001

INTERCEPTIONS BY

Most Interceptions By, Career

4 Everson Walls, Dallas, 1982-84, 1986
Deion Sanders, Atlanta, 1992-94; San Francisco, 1995; Dallas, 1999
3 Ken Houston, Houston, 1971-73; Washington, 1974-79
Jack Lambert, Pittsburgh, 1976-1984
Ted Hendricks, Baltimore, 1972-74; Green Bay, 1975; Oakland, 1981-82; L.A. Raiders, 1983-84
Mike Haynes, New England, 1978-1981, 1983; L.A. Raiders, 1985-87
2 By 13 players

Most Interceptions By, Game

2 Mel Blount, Pittsburgh, 1977
Everson Walls, Dallas, 1982, 1983
LeRoy Irvin, L.A. Rams, 1986
David Fulcher, Cincinnati, 1990
Brian Dawkins, Philadelphia, 2000

YARDS GAINED

Most Yards Gained, Career

103 Deion Sanders, Atlanta, 1992-94; San Francisco, 1995; Dallas, 1999
77 Ted Hendricks, Baltimore, 1972-74; Green Bay, 1975; Oakland, 1981-82; L.A. Raiders, 1983-84
73 Rod Woodson, Pittsburgh, 1990-95, 1997; Baltimore, 2000-01

Most Yards Gained, Game

87 Deion Sanders, Dallas, 1999
73 Rod Woodson, Pittsburgh, 1994
67 Ty Law, New England, 1999

Longest Gain

87 Deion Sanders, Dallas, 1999
73 Rod Woodson, Pittsburgh, 1994 (lateral)
67 Ty Law, New England, 1999 (TD)

TOUCHDOWNS

Most Touchdowns, Game

1 Bobby Bell, Kansas City, 1973
Nolan Cromwell, L.A. Rams, 1984
Joey Browner, Minnesota, 1986
Jerry Gray, L.A. Rams, 1990
Mike Johnson, Cleveland, 1990
Junior Seau, San Diego, 1993
Ken Harvey, Washington, 1996
Ashley Ambrose, Cincinnati, 1997
Ty Law, New England, 1999
Derrick Brooks, Tampa Bay, 2000
Aeneas Williams, Arizona, 2000

PUNTING

Most Punts, Career

33 Ray Guy, Oakland, 1974-79, 1981
23 Rohn Stark, Indianapolis, 1986-87, 1991, 1993
22 Reggie Roby, Miami, 1985, 1990; Washington, 1995

Most Punts, Game

10 Reggie Roby, Miami, 1985
9 Tom Wittum, San Francisco, 1974
Rohn Stark, Indianapolis, 1987
8 Jerrel Wilson, Kansas City, 1971
Tom Skladany, Detroit, 1982
Reggie Roby, Washington, 1995

Longest Punt

64 Tom Wittum, San Francisco, 1974
Darren Bennett, San Diego, 1996
61 Reggie Roby, Miami, 1985
Jeff Feagles, Arizona, 1996
Matt Turk, Washington, 1997
60 Ron Widby, Dallas, 1972
Reggie Roby, Washington, 1995

AVERAGE YARDAGE

Highest Average, Career (10 punts)

46.73 Reggie Roby, Miami, 1985, 1990; Washington, 1995 (22-1,028)
45.27 Matt Turk, Washington, 1997-99 (15-679)
45.25 Jerrel Wilson, Kansas City, 1971-73 (16-724)

Highest Average, Game (4 punts)

55.50 Darren Bennett, San Diego, 1996 (4-222)
52.00 Matt Turk, Washington, 1999 (4-208)
50.13 Reggie Roby, Washington, 1995 (8-401)

PUNT RETURNS

Most Punt Returns, Career

13 Rick Upchurch, Denver, 1977, 1979-1980, 1983
11 Vai Sikahema, St. Louis, 1987-88
Eric Metcalf, Cleveland 1994-95; San Diego 1998
10 Mike Nelms, Washington, 1981-83

Most Punt Returns, Game

7 Vai Sikahema, St. Louis, 1987
6 Henry Ellard, L.A. Rams, 1985
Gerald McNeil, Cleveland, 1988
Eric Metcalf, Cleveland, 1995
5 Rick Upchurch, Denver, 1980
Mike Nelms, Washington, 1981
Carl Roaches, Houston, 1982
Johnny Bailey, Phoenix, 1993

Most Fair Catches, Game

2 Jerry Logan, Baltimore, 1971
Dick Anderson, Miami, 1974
Henry Ellard, L.A. Rams, 1985
Isaac Bruce, St. Louis, 1997
Desmond Howard, Detroit, 2001

YARDS GAINED

Most Yards Gained, Career

183 Billy Johnson, Houston, 1976, 1978; Atlanta, 1984
138 Mel Renfro, Dallas, 1971-72, 1974
Rick Upchurch, Denver, 1977, 1979-1980, 1983
135 Eric Metcalf, Cleveland, 1994-95; San Diego 1998

Most Yards Gained, Game

159 Billy Johnson, Houston, 1976
138 Mel Renfro, Dallas, 1971
117 Wally Henry, Philadelphia, 1980

Longest Punt Return

90 Billy Johnson, Houston, 1976 (TD)
86 Wally Henry, Philadelphia, 1980 (TD)
82 Mel Renfro, Dallas, 1971 (TD)

AVERAGE YARDAGE

Highest Average, Career (4 returns)

22.88 Billy Johnson, Houston, 1976, 1978; Atlanta, 1984 (8-183)
21.50 Tony Green, Washington, 1979 (4-86)
15.67 David Meggett, N.Y. Giants, 1990; New England, 1997

Highest Average, Game (3 returns)

39.75 Billy Johnson, Houston, 1976 (4-159)
39.00 Wally Henry, Philadelphia, 1980 (3-117)
21.50 Tony Green, Washington, 1979 (4-86)

TOUCHDOWNS

Most Touchdowns, Game

2 Mel Renfro, Dallas, 1971
1 Billy Johnson, Houston, 1976
Wally Henry, Philadelphia, 1980

KICKOFF RETURNS

Most Kickoff Returns, Career

17 Michael Bates, Carolina, 1997-2001
14 Mel Gray, Detroit, 1991-92, 1995
11 Eric Metcalf, Cleveland, 1994-95; San Diego, 1998

Most Kickoff Returns, Game

7 Mel Gray, Detroit, 1995
6 Greg Pruitt, L.A. Raiders, 1984
David Meggett, New England, 1997
Michael Bates, Carolina, 1998
5 By seven players

AFC-NFC PRO BOWL RECORDS

YARDS GAINED
Most Yards Gained, Career
488 Michael Bates, Carolina, 1997-2001
309 Greg Pruitt, Cleveland, 1974-75, 1977-78; L.A. Raiders, 1984
294 Mel Gray, Detroit, 1991-92, 1995
Most Yards Gained, Game
192 Greg Pruitt, L.A. Raiders, 1984
175 Les (Speedy) Duncan, Washington, 1972
173 David Meggett, New England, 1997
Longest Kickoff Return
66 Michael Bates, Carolina, 2000
62 Greg Pruitt, L.A. Raiders, 1984
61 Eugene (Mercury) Morris, Miami, 1972

AVERAGE YARDAGE
Highest Average, Career (4 returns)
35.00 Les (Speedy) Duncan, Washington, 1972 (5-175)
31.25 Eugene (Mercury) Morris, Miami, 1972-73 (4-125)
30.90 Greg Pruitt, Cleveland, 1974-75, 1977-78; L.A. Raiders, 1984 (10-309)
Highest Average, Game (3 returns)
42.00 Michael Bates, Carolina, 2000 (4-168)
35.00 Les (Speedy) Duncan, Washington, 1972 (5-175)
32.00 Greg Pruitt, L.A. Raiders, 1984 (6-192)

TOUCHDOWNS
Most Touchdowns, Game
None

FUMBLES

Most Fumbles, Career
6 Dan Fouts, San Diego, 1980-84, 1986
4 Lawrence McCutcheon, Los Angeles, 1974-78
Franco Harris, Pittsburgh, 1973-76, 1978-1981
Jay Schroeder, Washington, 1987
Vai Sikahema, St. Louis, 1987-88
3 O.J. Simpson, Buffalo, 1973-77
William Andrews, Atlanta, 1981-84
Joe Montana, San Francisco, 1982, 1984-85, 1988
Walter Payton, Chicago, 1977-1981, 1984-87
Neil Lomax, St. Louis, 1985, 1988
Jim Kelly, Buffalo, 1988, 1991-92
Chris Chandler, Atlanta, 1998-99
Most Fumbles, Game
4 Jay Schroeder, Washington, 1987
3 Dan Fouts, San Diego, 1982
Vai Sikahema, St. Louis, 1987
2 By 13 players

RECOVERIES
Most Fumbles Recovered, Career
3 Harold Jackson, Philadelphia, 1973; Los Angeles, 1974, 1976, 1978 (3-own)
Dan Fouts, San Diego, 1980-84, 1986 (3-own)
Randy White, Dallas, 1978, 1980-86 (3-opp)
2 By many players
Most Fumbles Recovered, Game
2 Dick Anderson, Miami, 1974 (1-own, 1-opp)
Harold Jackson, Los Angeles, 1974 (2-own)
Dan Fouts, San Diego, 1982 (2-own)
Joey Browner, Minnesota, 1990 (2-opp)
Jessie Armstead, N.Y. Giants, 1999 (1-own, 1-opp)
Steve Beuerlein, Carolina, 2000 (2-own)

YARDAGE
Longest Fumble Return
83 Art Still, Kansas City, 1985 (TD, opp)
51 Phil Villapiano, Oakland, 1974 (opp)
37 Sam Mills, New Orleans, 1988 (opp)

TOUCHDOWNS
Most Touchdowns, Game
1 Art Still, Kansas City, 1985
Keith Millard, Minnesota, 1990

SACKS

Sacks have been compiled since 1983.
Most Sacks, Career
9.5 Reggie White, Philadelphia, 1987-1993; Green Bay, 1994, 1996-97, 1999
9.0 Howie Long, L.A. Raiders, 1984-88, 1990, 1993-1994
7.5 Bruce Smith, Buffalo, 1988-1991, 1995-96, 1998-99
Most Sacks, Game
4.0 Mark Gastineau, N.Y. Jets, 1985
Reggie White, Philadelphia, 1987
3.0 Richard Dent, Chicago, 1985
Bruce Smith, Buffalo, 1991
2.5 Bruce Smith, Buffalo, 1998

TEAM RECORDS

SCORING

Most Points, Game
51 NFC, 2000
Fewest Points, Game
3 AFC, 1984, 1989, 1994
Most Points, Both Teams, Game
82 NFC (51) vs. AFC (31), 2000
Fewest Points, Both Teams, Game
16 NFC (6) vs. AFC (10), 1987

TOUCHDOWNS
Most Touchdowns, Game
6 NFC, 1984, 2000
Fewest Touchdowns, Game
0 AFC, 1971, 1974, 1984, 1989, 1994
NFC, 1987, 1988
Most Touchdowns, Both Teams, Game
10 NFC (6) vs. AFC (4), 2000
Fewest Touchdowns, Both Teams, Game
1 AFC (0) vs. NFC (1), 1974
NFC (0) vs. AFC (1), 1987
NFC (0) vs. AFC (1), 1988

POINTS AFTER TOUCHDOWN
Most Points After Touchdown, Game
6 NFC, 1984, 2000
Most Points After Touchdown, Both Teams, Game
10 NFC (6) vs. AFC (4), 2000

FIELD GOALS
Most Field Goals Attempted, Game
6 AFC, 1972
NFC, 1981, 1983
Most Field Goals Attempted, Both Teams, Game
9 NFC (6) vs. AFC (3), 1983
Most Field Goals, Game
5 AFC, 1974
Most Field Goals, Both Teams, Game
7 AFC (5) vs. NFC (2), 1974

NET YARDS GAINED RUSHING AND PASSING

Most Yards Gained, Game
552 AFC, 1995
Fewest Yards Gained, Game
114 AFC, 1993
Most Yards Gained, Both Teams, Game
962 NFC (496) vs. AFC (466), 1997
Fewest Yards Gained, Both Teams, Game
424 AFC (202) vs. NFC (222), 1987

RUSHING

ATTEMPTS
Most Attempts, Game
50 AFC, 1974
Fewest Attempts, Game
9 NFC, 2001
Most Attempts, Both Teams, Game
80 AFC (50) vs. NFC (30), 1974
Fewest Attempts, Both Teams, Game
32 NFC (9) vs. AFC (23), 2001

YARDS GAINED
Most Yards Gained, Game
400 AFC, 1995
Fewest Yards Gained, Game
28 NFC, 1992
Most Yards Gained, Both Teams, Game
441 AFC (400) vs. NFC (41), 1995
Fewest Yards Gained, Both Teams, Game
119 NFC (36) vs. AFC (83), 2001

TOUCHDOWNS
Most Touchdowns, Game
3 NFC, 1989, 1991, 2000
AFC, 1995
Most Touchdowns, Both Teams, Game
4 AFC (2) vs. NFC (2), 1973
AFC (2) vs. NFC (2), 1980

PASSING

ATTEMPTS
Most Attempts, Game
56 NFC, 2001
Fewest Attempts, Game
17 NFC, 1972
Most Attempts, Both Teams, Game
98 NFC (56) vs. AFC (42), 2001
Fewest Attempts, Both Teams, Game
42 NFC (17) vs. AFC (25), 1972

COMPLETIONS
Most Completions, Game
32 NFC, 1993
AFC, 2001
Fewest Completions, Game
7 NFC, 1972, 1982
Most Completions, Both Teams, Game
60 AFC (32) vs. NFC (28), 2001
Fewest Completions, Both Teams, Game
18 NFC (7) vs. AFC (11), 1972

YARDS GAINED
Most Yards Gained, Game
387 AFC, 1983
Fewest Yards Gained, Game
42 NFC, 1982
Most Yards Gained, Both Teams, Game
735 AFC (369) vs. NFC (366), 1997
Fewest Yards Gained, Both Teams, Game
215 NFC (89) vs. AFC (126), 1972

TIMES SACKED
Most Times Sacked, Game
9 NFC, 1985
Fewest Times Sacked, Game
0 AFC, 1998, 1999, 2000
NFC, 1971, 1997, 2001
Most Times Sacked, Both Teams, Game
17 NFC (9) vs. AFC (8), 1985
Fewest Times Sacked, Both Teams, Game
1 NFC (0) vs. AFC (1), 1997

TOUCHDOWNS
Most Touchdowns, Game
4 NFC, 1984
AFC, 2000, 2001
Most Touchdowns, Both Teams, Game
6 AFC (4) vs. NFC (2), 2001

INTERCEPTIONS BY

Most Interceptions By, Game
6 AFC, 1977
Most Interceptions By, Both Teams, Game
7 AFC (6) vs. NFC (1), 1977

YARDS GAINED
Most Yards Gained, Game
103 AFC, 1994
Most Yards Gained, Both Teams, Game
172 NFC (102) vs. AFC (70), 1999

TOUCHDOWNS
Most Touchdowns, Game
2 NFC, 2000

PUNTING

Most Punts, Game
10 AFC, 1985
Fewest Punts, Game
0 NFC, 1989
Most Punts, Both Teams, Game
16 AFC (10) vs. NFC (6), 1985
Fewest Punts, Both Teams, Game
4 NFC (1) vs. AFC (3), 1992

PUNT RETURNS

Most Punt Returns, Game
7 NFC, 1985, 1987
AFC, 1995
Fewest Punt Returns, Game
0 AFC, 1984, 1989
Most Punt Returns, Both Teams, Game
11 NFC (7) vs. AFC (4), 1985
Fewest Punt Returns, Both Teams, Game
2 AFC (1) vs. NFC (1), 1996

YARDS GAINED
Most Yards Gained, Game
177 AFC, 1976
Fewest Yards Gained, Game
–1 NFC, 1991
Most Yards Gained, Both Teams, Game
263 AFC (177) vs. NFC (86), 1976
Fewest Yards Gained, Both Teams, Game
16 AFC (0) vs. NFC (16), 1984

TOUCHDOWNS
Most Touchdowns, Game
2 NFC, 1971

KICKOFF RETURNS

Most Kickoff Returns, Game
8 NFC, 1995
Fewest Kickoff Returns, Game
1 NFC, 1971, 1984, 1994
AFC, 1988, 1991
Most Kickoff Returns, Both Teams, Game
13 AFC (7) vs. NFC (6), 2000
Fewest Kickoff Returns, Both Teams, Game
5 NFC (2) vs. AFC (3), 1979
AFC (1) vs. NFC (4), 1988
NFC (2) vs. AFC (3), 1992
NFC (1) vs. AFC (4), 1994

YARDS GAINED
Most Yards Gained, Game
232 NFC, 2000
Fewest Yards Gained, Game
6 NFC, 1971
Most Yards Gained, Both Teams, Game
436 NFC (232) vs. AFC (204), 2000
Fewest Yards Gained, Both Teams, Game
99 NFC (48) vs. AFC (51), 1987

TOUCHDOWNS
Most Touchdowns, Game
None

FUMBLES

Most Fumbles, Game
10 NFC, 1974
Most Fumbles, Both Teams, Game
15 NFC (10) vs. AFC (5), 1974

RECOVERIES
Most Fumbles Recovered, Game
10 NFC, 1974 (6 own, 4 opp)
Most Fumbles Lost, Game
4 AFC, 1974, 1988
NFC, 1974

YARDS GAINED
Most Yards Gained, Game
87 AFC, 1985

TOUCHDOWNS
Most Touchdowns, Game
1 AFC, 1985
NFC, 1990

TURNOVERS

(Number of times losing the ball on interceptions and fumbles.)

Most Turnovers, Game

8 AFC, 1974

Fewest Turnovers, Game

0 AFC, 1991, 1997
NFC, 1991, 1995, 1996, 2001

Most Turnovers, Both Teams, Game

12 AFC (8) vs. NFC (4), 1974

Fewest Turnovers, Both Teams, Game

0 AFC vs. NFC, 1991

Rules

OFFICIALS

2001 NFL ROSTER OF OFFICIALS

Mike Pereira, Director of Officiating
Larry Upson, Director of Officiating Operations
Al Hynes, Supervisor of Officials
Jim Daopoulos, Supervisor of Officials
Ron Baynes, Supervisor of Officials
Neely Dunn, Supervisor of Officials

No.	Name	Position	College
81	Anderson, Dave	Line Judge	Salem College
66	Anderson, Walt	Line Judge	Sam Houston State
108	Arthur, Gary	Line Judge	Wright State
34	Austin, Gerald	Referee	Western Carolina
22	Baetz, Paul	Field Judge	Heidelberg
91	Baker, Ken	Side Judge	Eastern Illinois
48	Balliet, Brian	Umpire	Lehigh
26	Baltz, Mark	Head Linesman	Ohio University
55	Barnes, Tom	Line Judge	Minnesota
32	Bergman, Jeff	Line Judge	Robert Morris
7	Blum, Ron	Referee	Marin College
18	Boston, Byron	Line Judge	Austin
110	Botchan, Ron	Umpire	Occidental
31	Brown, Chad	Umpire	East Texas State
134	Camp, Ed	Head Linesman	William Patterson
126	Carey, Don	Back Judge	U.C.-Riverside
94	Carey, Mike	Referee	Santa Clara
39	Carlsen, Don	Side Judge	Cal State-Chico
63	Carollo, Bill	Referee	Wisconsin-Milwaukee
11	Carroll, Duke	Field Judge	Ithaca
41	Cheek, Boris	Field Judge	Morgan State
65	Coleman, Walt	Referee	Arkansas
99	Corrente, Tony	Referee	Cal State-Fullerton
71	Coukart, Ed	Umpire	Northwestern
70	Dawson, Scott	Umpire	Virginia Tech
53	DeFelice, Garth	Umpire	San Diego State
113	Dorkowski, Don	Back Judge	Cal State-Los Angeles
6	Dornan, Kirk	Back Judge	Central Washington
74	Duke, James	Umpire	Howard
3	Edwards, Scott	Field Judge	Alabama
61	Ferguson, Keith	Back Judge	San Jose State
47	Fincken, Tom	Side Judge	Kansas State
111	Frantz, Earnie	Head Linesman	No College
133	Freeman, Steve	Field Judge	Mississippi State
50	Gereb, Neil	Umpire	California
72	Gierke, Terry	Head Linesman	Portland State
19	Green, Scott	Back Judge	Delaware
23	Grier, Johnny	Referee	University of D.C.
104	Hamer, Dale	Head Linesman	California, Pa.
40	Hannah, Charles	Umpire	Middle Tennessee State
105	Hantak, Dick	Referee	Southeast Missouri
125	Hayes, Laird	Side Judge	Princeton
54	Hayward, George	Head Linesman	Missouri Western
97	Hill, Tom	Side Judge	Carson-Newman
28	Hittner, Mark	Head Linesman	Pittsburg State
85	Hochuli, Ed	Referee	Texas-El Paso
82	Horton, Albert	Back Judge	Oregon State
37	Howey, Jim	Back Judge	Erskine College
101	Johnson, Carl	Line Judge	Nicholls State
114	Johnson, Tom	Head Linesman	Miami, Ohio
106	Jury, Al	Field Judge	San Bernardino Valley
86	Kukar, Bernie	Referee	St. John's
120	Lane, Gary	Side Judge	Missouri
17	Lawing, Bob	Back Judge	North Carolina State
127	Leavy, Bill	Referee	San Jose State
130	Lewis, Darryll	Line Judge	Dartmouth
76	Liebsack, Ron	Side Judge	Regis
49	Look, Dean	Side Judge	Michigan State
98	Lovett, Bill	Field Judge	Maryland
59	Luckett, Phil	Back Judge	Texas-El Paso
102	Mack, Keven	Field Judge	Fort Valley State
92	Madsen, Carl	Umpire	Washington
107	Marinucci, Ron	Line Judge	Glassboro State
38	Maurer, Bruce	Line Judge	Ohio State
77	McAulay, Terry	Referee	Louisiana State
95	McElwee, Bob	Referee	Navy
35	McGrath, Bob	Field Judge	Western Kentucky
64	McPeters, Lloyd	Field Judge	Oklahoma State
80	Millis, Timmie	Field Judge	Millsaps
117	Montgomery, Ben	Line Judge	Morehouse
60	Moore, Tommy	Side Judge	Stephen F. Austin
135	Morelli, Peter	Field Judge	St. Mary's College
20	Nemmers, Larry	Referee	Upper Iowa
124	Paganelli, Carl	Umpire	Michigan State
46	Paganelli, Perry	Back Judge	Hope College
132	Parry, John	Side Judge	Purdue
15	Patterson, Rick	Side Judge	Wofford
9	Perlman, Mark	Line Judge	Salem
10	Phares, Ron	Line Judge	Virginia Tech
79	Pointer, Aaron	Head Linesman	Pacific Lutheran
5	Quirk, Jim	Umpire	Delaware
83	Reels, Richard	Back Judge	No College
44	Rice, Jeff	Umpire	Northwestern
121	Rivers, Sanford	Head Linesman	Youngstown State
128	Rose, Larry	Side Judge	Florida
67	Rosenbaum, Doug	Side Judge	Illinois Wesleyan
58	Saracino, Jim	Field Judge	Northern Colorado
21	Schleyer, John	Head Linesman	Millersville
122	Schmitz, Bill	Back Judge	Colorado State
129	Schuster, BIll	Umpire	Alfred
118	Sifferman, Tom	Field Judge	Seattle
73	Skelton, Bobby	Back Judge	Alabama
30	Slaughter, Gary	Head Linesman	East Texas State
2	Smith, Billy	Back Judge	East Carolina
90	Spanier, Michael	Line Judge	St. Cloud State
119	Spitler, Ron	Back Judge	Panhandle State
12	Spyksma, Bill	Side Judge	South Dakota
24	Stabile, Tom	Head Linesman	Slippery Rock
88	Steenson, Scott	Field Judge	North Texas
84	Steinkerchner, Mark	Line Judge	Akron
68	Stephan, Tom	Line Judge	Pittsburg State
112	Steratore, Anthony	Back Judge	California (Penn.)
62	Stewart, Charles	Line Judge	Long Beach State
4	Toole, Doug	Side Judge	Utah State
42	Triplette, Jeff	Referee	Wake Forest
36	Veteri, Tony	Head Linesman	Manhattan College
52	Vinovich, Bill	Side Judge	San Diego
25	Waggoner, Bob	Back Judge	Juniata College
100	Wagner, Bob	Umpire	Penn State
27	Warden, David	Field Judge	Oklahoma State
96	Wash, Undrey	Umpire	Texas-Arlington
87	Weidner, Paul	Head Linesman	Cincinnati
123	White, Tom	Referee	Temple
8	Williams, Dale	Head Linesman	Cal State-Northridge
43	Wilson, James	Head Linesman	Eastern Kentucky
29	Wilson, Steve	Umpire	Whitworth College
14	Winter, Ron	Referee	Michigan State
16	Wyant, David	Side Judge	Virginia
33	Zimmer, Steve	Field Judge	Hofstra

NUMERICAL ROSTER

No.	Name	Position
2	Billy Smith	BJ
3	Scott Edwards	FJ
4	Doug Toole	SJ
5	Jim Quirk	U
6	Kirk Dornan	BJ
7	Ron Blum	R
8	Dale Williams	HL
9	Mark Perlman	LJ
10	Ron Phares	LJ
11	Duke Carroll	FJ
12	Bill Spyksma	SJ
14	Ron Winter	R
15	Rick Patterson	SJ
16	David Wyant	SJ
17	Bob Lawing	BJ
18	Byron Boston	LJ
19	Scott Green	BJ
20	Larry Nemmers	R
21	John Schleyer	HL
22	Paul Baetz	FJ
23	Johnny Grier	R
24	Tom Stabile	HL
25	Bob Waggoner	BJ
26	Mark Baltz	HL
27	David Warden	FJ
28	Mark Hittner	HL
29	Steve Wilson	U
30	Gary Slaughter	HL
31	Chad Brown	U
32	Jeff Bergman	LJ
33	Steve Zimmer	FJ
34	Gerry Austin	R
35	Bob McGrath	FJ
36	Tony Veteri	HL
37	Jim Howey	BJ
38	Bruce Maurer	LJ
39	Don Carlsen	SJ
40	Charles Hannah	U
41	Boris Cheek	FJ
42	Jeff Triplette	R
43	James Wilson	HL
44	Jeff Rice	U
46	Perry Paganelli	BJ
47	Tom Fincken	SJ
48	Brian Balliet	U
49	Dean Look	SJ
50	Neil Gereb	U
52	Bill Vinovich	SJ
53	Garth DeFelice	U
54	George Hayward	HL
55	Tom Barnes	LJ
58	Jim Saracino	FJ
59	Phil Luckett	BJ
60	Tommy Moore	SJ
61	Keith Ferguson	BJ
62	Charles Stewart	LJ
63	Bill Carollo	R
64	Lloyd McPeters	FJ
65	Walt Coleman	R
66	Walt Anderson	LJ
67	Doug Rosenbaum	SJ
68	Tom Stephan	LJ
70	Scott Dawson	U
71	Ed Coukart	U
72	Terry Gierke	HL
73	Bobby Skelton	BJ
74	James Duke	U
76	Ron Liebsack	SJ
77	Terry McAulay	R
79	Aaron Pointer	HL
80	Timmie Millis	FJ
81	Dave Anderson	LJ
82	Albert Horton	BJ
83	Richard Reels	BJ
84	Mark Steinkerchner	LJ
85	Ed Hochuli	R
86	Bernie Kukar	R
87	Paul Weidner	HL
88	Scott Steenson	FJ
90	Michael Spanier	LJ
91	Ken Baker	SJ
92	Carl Madsen	U
94	Mike Carey	R
95	Bob McElwee	R
96	Undrey Wash	U
97	Tom Hill	SJ
98	Bill Lovett	FJ
99	Tony Corrente	R
100	Bob Wagner	U
101	Carl Johnson	LJ
102	Keven Mack	FJ
104	Dale Hamer	HL
105	Dick Hantak	R
106	Al Jury	FJ
107	Ron Marinucci	LJ
108	Gary Arthur	LJ
110	Ron Botchan	U
111	Earnie Frantz	HL
112	Anthony Steratore	BJ
113	Don Dorkowski	BJ
114	Tom Johnson	HL
117	Ben Montgomery	LJ
118	Tom Sifferman	FJ
119	Ron Spitler	BJ
120	Gary Lane	SJ
121	Sanford Rivers	HL
122	Bill Schmitz	BJ
123	Tom White	R
124	Carl Paganelli	U
125	Laird Hayes	SJ
126	Don Carey	BJ
127	Bill Leavy	R
128	Larry Rose	SJ
129	Bill Schuster	U
130	Darryll Lewis	LJ
132	John Parry	SJ
133	Steve Freeman	FJ
134	Ed Camp	HL
135	Peter Morelli	FJ

2001 OFFICIALS AT A GLANCE

REFEREES

Gerry Austin, No. **34,** Western Carolina, president, leadership development group, 20th year.
Ron Blum, No. **7,** Marin College, professional golfer, 17th year.
Mike Carey, No. **94,** Santa Clara, owner, skiing accessories, 12th year.
Bill Carollo, No. **63,** Wisconsin-Milwaukee, marketing executive, 13th year.
Walt Coleman, No. **65,** Arkansas, president, dairy processor, 13th year.
Tony Corrente, No. **99,** Cal State-Fullerton, educator, 7th year.
Johnny Grier, No. **23,** University of D.C., planning engineer, 21st year.
Dick Hantak, No. **105,** Southeast Missouri, educator, 24th year.
Ed Hochuli, No. **85,** Texas-El Paso, attorney, 12th year.
Bernie Kukar, No. **86,** St. John's, sales representative, employees benefit plan, 18th year.
Bill Leavy, No. **127,** San Jose State, supervisor of officials, retired firefighter, 7th year.
Terry McAulay, No. **77,** Louisiana State, senior computer scientist, 4th year.
Bob McElwee, No. **95,** Navy, owner, heavy construction firm, 26th year.
Larry Nemmers, No. **20,** Upper Iowa, motivational speaker, 17th year.
Jeff Triplette, No. **42,** Wake Forest, assistant treasurer, world-wide energy company, 6th year.
Tom White, No. **123,** Temple, president, athletic sportswear, 13th year.
Ron Winter, No. **14,** Michigan State, university professor, 7th year.

UMPIRES

Brian Balliet, No. **48,** Lehigh, sales engineer, 5th year.
Ron Botchan, No. **110,** Occidental, college professor, former AFL player, 22nd year.
Chad Brown, No. **31,** East Texas State, director, intramural/sports clubs, 10th year.
Ed Coukart, No. **71,** Northwestern, vice-president, commercial bank, 13th year.
Scott Dawson, No. **70,** Virginia Tech, president/owner, commercial construction company, 7th year.
Garth Defelice, No. **53,** San Diego State, director of distributing, beverage company, 4th year.
James Duke, No. **74,** Howard, director of volunteer resources boys and girls clubs, 9th year.
Neil Gereb, No. **50,** California, project manager, aircraft company, 21st year.
Charles Hannah, No. **40,** Middle Tennessee State, federal probation officer, 3rd year.
Carl Madsen, No. **92,** Washington, vice president of operations, 5th year.
Carl Paganelli, No. **124,** Michigan State, federal probation officer, 3rd year.
Jim Quirk, No. **5,** Delaware, consultant, 14th year.
Jeff Rice, No. **44,** Northwestern, attorney, 7th year.
Bill Schuster, No. **129,** Alfred College, insurance broker, 2nd year.
Bob Wagner, No. **100,** Penn State, executive director, cardiovascular institute, 17th year.
Undrey Wash, No. **96,** Texas-Arlington, claims manager, 2nd year.
Steve Wilson, No. **29,** Whitworth College, church administrator, 2nd year.

HEAD LINESMEN

Mark Baltz, No. **26,** Ohio University, sales consultant, 12th year.
Ed Camp, No. **134,** William Peterson, teacher, 2nd year.
Earnie Frantz, No. **111,** no college, vice-president and manager, insurance company, 21st year.
Terry Gierke, No. **72,** Portland State, real estate broker, 21st year.
Dale Hamer, No. **104,** California Univ., Pa., consultant, 23rd year.
George Hayward, No. **54,** Missouri Western, vice-president and manager, warehouse company, 11th year.
Mark Hittner, No. **28,** Pittsburg State, insurance sales, 5th year.
Tom Johnson, No. **114,** Miami, Ohio, retired educator, president/owner, security company, 20th year.
Aaron Pointer, No. **79,** Pacific Lutheran, park department administrator, 14th year.
Sanford Rivers, No. **121,** Youngstown State, assistant vice-president, school administration, 13th year.
John Schleyer, No. **21,** Millersville, medical sales, 12th year.
Gary Slaughter, No. **30,** East Texas State, general manager, 6th year.
Tom Stabile, No. **24,** Slippery Rock, secondary educational administrator, 7th year.
Tony Veteri, No. **36,** Manhattan, director of athletics, 10th year.
Paul Weidner, No. **87,** Cincinnati, marketing manager, 16th year.
Dale Williams, No. **8,** Cal State-Northridge, sports official, 22nd year.
James Wilson, No. **43,** Eastern Kentucky, area manager, 4th year.

LINE JUDGES

Dave Anderson, No. **81,** Salem, insurance executive, 18th year.
Walt Anderson, No. **66,** Sam Houston, dentist, orthodontics, 6th year.
Gary Arthur, No. **108,** Wright State, commercial printing sales, 5th year.
Tom Barnes, No. **55,** Minnesota, manufacturing representative, 16th year.
Jeff Bergman, No. **32,** Robert Morris, president and chief executive officer, medical services, 10th year.
Byron Boston, No. **18,** Austin, tax consultant, 7th year.
Carl Johnson, No. **101,** Nicholls State, district sales manager, 1st year.
Darryll Lewis, No. **130,** Dartmouth, associate professor, 3rd year.
Ron Marinucci, No. **107,** Glassboro State, vice president, novelty cone company, 5th year.
Bruce Maurer, No. **38,** Ohio State, administrator/associate director, recreational sports, 15th year.
Ben Montgomery, No. **117,** Morehouse, school administrator, 20th year.
Mark Perlman, No. **9,** Salem, teacher, 2nd year.
Ron Phares, No. **10,** Virginia Tech, president, construction company, 17th year.
Michael Spanier, No. **90,** St. Cloud State, middle-school principal, 3rd year.
Mark Steinkerchner, No. **84,** Akron, vice-president, 8th year.
Tom Stephan, No. **68,** Pittsburg State, business broker, 3rd year.
Charles Stewart, No. **62,** Long Beach State, human services administrator, 9th year.

FIELD JUDGES

Paul Baetz, No. **22,** Heidelberg, financial consultant, 24th year.
Duke Carroll, No. **11,** Ithaca, president, insurance agency, 7th year.
Boris Cheek, No. **41,** Morgan State, director of operations and management, 6th year.
Scott Edwards, No. **3,** Alabama, federal government program analyst, 3rd year.
Steve Freeman, No. **133,** Mississippi State, custom home builder, 1st year.
Al Jury, No. **106,** San Bernardino Valley, state traffic officer, 24th year.
Bill Lovett, No. **98,** Maryland, managing partner, financial sales, 12th year.
Keven Mack, No. **102,** Ft. Valley State, economic development administrator, 5th year.
Bob McGrath, No. **35,** Western Kentucky, sales representative, fund raiser, 9th year.
Lloyd McPeters, No. **64,** Oklahoma State, business insurance sales, 9th year.
Timmie Millis, No. **80,** Millsaps, financial investigative consultant, 13th year.
Pete Morelli, No. **135,** St. Mary's, high school principal, 5th year.
Jim Saracino, No. **58,** Northern Colorado, secondary educator, 7th year.
Tom Sifferman, No. **118,** Seattle, manufacturer's representative, 16th year.
Scott Steenson, No. **88,** North Texas, commercial real estate broker, 11th year.
David Warden, No. **27,** Oklahoma State, dentist, 4th year.
Steven Zimmer, No. **33,** Hofstra, attorney, 5th year.

SIDE JUDGES

Ken Baker, No. **91,** Eastern Illinois, college educator, 11th year.
Don Carlsen, No. **39,** Cal State-Chico, assistant superintendent, county school, 13th year.
Tom Fincken, No. **47,** Emporia State, retired educational administrator, 18th year.
Laird Hayes, No. **125,** Princeton, professor, physical education & athletics, 7th year.
Tom Hill, No. **97,** Erskine College, teacher, 3rd year.
Gary Lane, No. **120,** Missouri, owner hunting resort, former NFL player, 20th year.
Ron Liebsack, No. **76,** Regis, manager, telecommunications, 7th year.
Dean Look, No. **49,** Michigan State, consultant, medical manufacturing, former AFL player, 29th year.
Tommy Moore, No. **60,** Stephen F. Austin, marketing, manufacturing representative, 10th year.
John Parry, No. **132,** Purdue, corporate pilot, 2nd year.
Rick Patterson, No. **15,** Wofford, banker, 6th year.
Larry Rose, No. **128,** Florida, financial planner, 5th year.
Doug Rosenbaum, No. **67,** Illinois Wesleyan, financial consultant, 1st year.
Bill Spyksma, No. **12,** South Dakota, commercial real estate, construction sales, 7th year.
Doug Toole, No. **4,** Utah State, physical therapist, 14th year.
Bill Vinovich, No. **52,** San Diego, certified public accountant, 1st year.
David Wyant, No. **16,** Virginia, systems integration director, 11th year.

BACK JUDGES

Don Carey, No. **126,** California-Riverside, contract manager, 7th year.
Don Dorkowski, No. **113,** Cal State-Los Angeles, work experience coordinator, 16th year.
Kirk Dornan, No. **6,** Central Washington, industrial sales, 8th year.
Keith Ferguson, No. **61,** San Jose State, sales, 2nd year.
Scott Green, No. **19,** Delaware, vice-president, government relations, 11th year.
Buddy Horton, No. **82,** Oregon State, water service worker, 3rd year.
Jim Howey, No. **37,** Erskine College, elemenatry school principal, 3rd year.
Bob Lawing, No. **17,** North Carolina State, real estate management, 5th year.
Phil Luckett, No. **59,** Texas-El Paso, computer program analyst, federal civil services, 11th year.
Perry Paganelli, No. **46,** Hope College, high school administrator, 4th year.
Richard Reels, No. **83,** Chicago State, director of security, court services, 9th year.
Bill Schmitz, No. **122,** Colorado State, general sales manager, 13th year.
Bobby Skelton, No. **73,** Alabama, industrial representative, 17th year.
Billy Smith, No. **2,** East Carolina, federal government, 8th year.
Ron Spitler, No. **119,** Panhandle State, owner, service center, 20th year.
Anthony Steratore, No. **112,** California (Penn.), president, sanitary supply company, 2nd year.
Bob Waggoner, No. **25,** Juniata College, probation officer, 4th year.

OFFICIAL SIGNALS

1

TOUCHDOWN, FIELD GOAL, or SUCCESSFUL TRY
Both arms extended above head.

2

SAFETY
Palms together above head.

3

FIRST DOWN
Arm pointed toward defensive team's goal.

4

CROWD NOISE, DEAD BALL, or NEUTRAL ZONE ESTABLISHED
One arm above head with an open hand.
With fist closed: **Fourth Down.**

5

BALL ILLEGALLY TOUCHED, KICKED, or BATTED
Fingertips tap both shoulders.

6

TIME OUT
Hands crisscrossed above head.

Same signal followed by placing one hand on top of cap: **Referee's Time Out.**

Same signal followed by arm swung at side: **Touchback.**

7

NO TIME OUT or TIME IN WITH WHISTLE
Full arm circled to simulate moving clock.

8

DELAY OF GAME or EXCESS TIME OUT
Folded arms.

9

FALSE START, ILLEGAL FORMATION, or KICKOFF or SAFETY KICK OUT OF BOUNDS or KICKING TEAM PLAYER VOLUNTARILY OUT OF BOUNDS DURING A PUNT
Forearms rotated over and over in front of body.

10

PERSONAL FOUL
One wrist striking the other above head.
Same signal followed by swinging leg: **Roughing the Kicker.**
Same signal followed by raised arm swinging forward: **Roughing the Passer.**
Same signal followed by grasping face mask: **Major Face Mask.**

11

HOLDING
Grasping one wrist, the fist clenched, in front of chest.

12

ILLEGAL USE OF HANDS, ARMS, or BODY
Grasping one wrist, the hand open and facing forward, in front of chest.

13

PENALTY REFUSED, INCOMPLETE PASS, PLAY OVER, or MISSED FIELD GOAL or EXTRA POINT
Hands shifted in horizontal plane.

14

PASS JUGGLED INBOUNDS AND CAUGHT OUT OF BOUNDS
Hands up and down in front of chest (following incomplete pass signal).

15

ILLEGAL FORWARD PASS
One hand waved behind back followed by loss of down signal (23), when appropriate.

16

INTENTIONAL GROUNDING OF PASS
Parallel arms waved in a diagonal plane across body. Followed by loss of down signal (23).

OFFICIAL SIGNALS

17

INTERFERENCE WITH FORWARD PASS or FAIR CATCH
Hands open and extended forward from shoulders with hands vertical.

18

INVALID FAIR-CATCH SIGNAL
One hand waved above head.

19

INELIGIBLE RECEIVER or INELIGIBLE MEMBER OF KICKING TEAM DOWNFIELD
Right hand touching top of cap.

20

ILLEGAL CONTACT
One open hand extended forward.

21

OFFSIDE, ENCROACHMENT, or NEUTRAL ZONE INFRACTION
Hands on hips.

22

ILLEGAL MOTION AT SNAP
Horizontal arc with one hand.

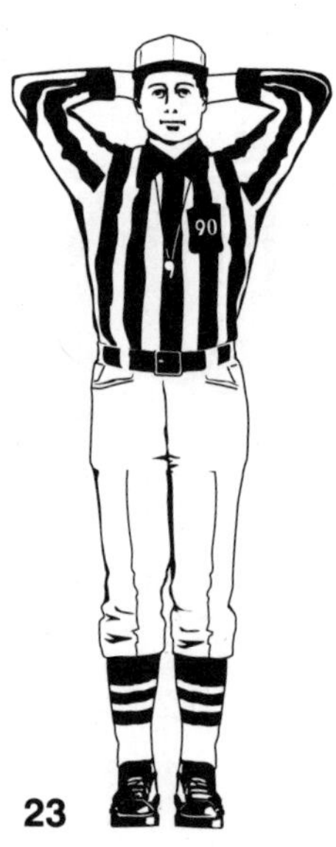

23

LOSS OF DOWN
Both hands held behind head.

24

INTERLOCKING INTERFERENCE, PUSHING, or HELPING RUNNER
Pushing movement of hands to front with arms downward.

25

TOUCHING A FORWARD PASS or SCRIMMAGE KICK
Diagonal motion of one hand across another.

26

UNSPORTSMANLIKE CONDUCT
Arms outstretched, palms down.

27

ILLEGAL CUT
Hand striking front of thigh.
ILLEGAL BLOCK BELOW THE WAIST
One hand striking front of thigh preceded by personal-foul signal (10).
CHOP BLOCK
Both hands striking side of thighs preceded by personal-foul signal (10).
CLIPPING
One hand striking back of calf preceded by personal-foul signal (10).

28

ILLEGAL CRACKBACK
Strike of an open right hand against the right mid-thigh preceded by personal foul signal (10).

29

PLAYER DISQUALIFIED
Ejection signal.

30

TRIPPING
Repeated action of right foot in back of left heel.

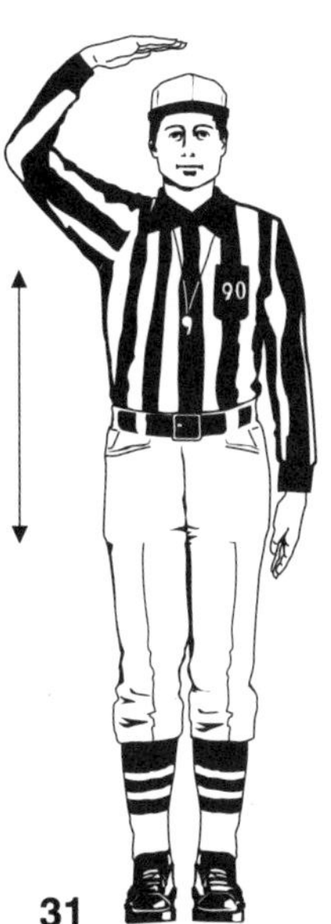

31

UNCATCHABLE FORWARD PASS
Palm of right hand held parallel to ground above head and moved back and forth.

32

TWELVE MEN IN OFFENSIVE HUDDLE or TOO MANY MEN ON THE FIELD
Both hands on top of head.

33

FACE MASK
Grasping face mask with one hand.

34

ILLEGAL SHIFT
Horizontal arcs with two hands.

35

RESET PLAY CLOCK–25 SECONDS
Pump one arm vertically.

36

RESET PLAY CLOCK–40 SECONDS
Pump two arms vertically.

NFL DIGEST OF RULES

This Digest of Rules of the National Football League has been prepared to aid players, fans, and members of the press, radio, and television media in their understanding of the game.

It is not meant to be a substitute for the official rule book. In any case of conflict between these explanations and the official rules, the rules always have precedence.

In order to make it easier to coordinate the information in this digest, the topics discussed generally follow the order of the rule book.

OFFICIALS' JURISDICTIONS, POSITIONS, AND DUTIES

Referee—General oversight and control of game. Gives signals for all fouls and is final authority for rule interpretations. Takes a position in backfield 10 to 12 yards behind line of scrimmage, favors right side (if quarterback is right-handed passer). Determines legality of snap, observes deep back(s) for legal motion. On running play, observes quarterback during and after handoff, remains with him until action has cleared away, then proceeds downfield, checking on runner and contact behind him. When runner is downed, Referee determines forward progress from wing official and, if necessary, adjusts final position of ball.

On pass plays, drops back as quarterback begins to fade back, picks up legality of blocks by near linemen. Changes to complete concentration on quarterback as defenders approach. Primarily responsible to rule on possible roughing action on passer and if ball becomes loose, rules whether ball is free on a fumble or dead on an incomplete pass.

During kicking situations, Referee has primary responsibility to rule on kicker's actions and whether or not any subsequent contact by a defender is legal. The Referee stays wide and parallel on punts and will announce on the microphone when each period has ended.

Umpire—Primary responsibility to rule on players' equipment, as well as their conduct and actions on scrimmage line. Lines up approximately four to five yards downfield, varying position from in front of weakside tackle to strongside guard. Looks for possible false start by offensive linemen. Observes legality of contact by both offensive linemen while blocking and by defensive players while they attempt to ward off blockers. Is prepared to call rule infractions if they occur on offense or defense. Moves forward to line of scrimmage when pass play develops in order to insure that interior linemen do not move illegally downfield. If offensive linemen indicate screen pass is to be attempted, Umpire shifts his attention toward screen side, picks up potential receiver in order to insure that he will legally be permitted to run his pattern and continues to rule on action of blockers. Umpire is to assist in ruling on incomplete or trapped passes when ball is thrown overhead or short. On punt plays, Umpire positions himself opposite Referee in offensive backfield—5 yards from kicker and one yard behind.

Head Linesman—Primarily responsible for ruling on offside, encroachment, and actions pertaining to scrimmage line prior to or at snap. Generally, keys on closest setback on his side of the field. On pass plays, Linesman is responsible to clear his receiver approximately seven yards downfield as he moves to a point five yards beyond the line. Linesman's secondary responsibility is to rule on any illegal action taken by defenders on any delay receiver moving downfield. Has full responsibility for ruling on sideline plays on his side, e.g., pass receiver or runner in or out of bounds. Together with Referee, Linesman is responsible for keeping track of number of downs and is in charge of mechanics of his chain crew in connection with its duties.

Linesman must be prepared to assist in determining forward progress by a runner on play directed toward middle or into his side zone. He, in turn, is to signal Referee or Umpire what forward point ball has reached. Linesman is also responsible to rule on legality of action involving any receiver who approaches his side zone. He is to call pass interference when the infraction occurs and is to rule on legality of blockers and defenders on plays involving ball carriers, whether it is entirely a running play, a combination pass and run, or a play involving a kick. Also assists referee with intentional grounding.

Line Judge—Straddles line of scrimmage on side of field opposite Linesman. Keeps time of game as a backup for clock operator. Along with Linesman is responsible for offside, encroachment, and actions pertaining to scrimmage line prior to or at snap. Line Judge keys on closest setback on his side of field. Line Judge is to observe his receiver until he moves at least seven yards downfield. He then moves toward backfield side, being especially alert to rule on any back in motion and on flight of ball when pass is made (he must rule whether forward or backward). Line Judge has primary responsibility to rule whether or not passer is behind or beyond line of scrimmage when pass is made. He also assists in observing actions by blockers and defenders who are on his side of field. After pass is thrown, Line Judge directs attention toward activities that occur in back of Umpire. During punting situations, Line Judge remains at line of scrimmage to be sure that only the end men move downfield until kick has been made. He also rules whether or not the kick crossed line and then observes action by members of the kicking team who are moving downfield to cover the kick. The Line Judge will advise the Referee when time has expired at the end of each period. Also assists referee with intentional grounding and determines whether pass is forward or backward.

Field Judge—Operates on same side of field as Line Judge, 20 yards deep. Keys on wide receiver on his side. Concentrates on path of end or back, observing legality of his potential block(s) or of actions taken against him. Is prepared to rule from <u>deep</u> position on holding or illegal use of hands by end or back or on defensive infractions committed by player guarding him. Has primary responsibility to make decisions involving sideline on his side of field, e.g., pass receiver or runner in or out of bounds.

Field Judge makes decisions involving catching, recovery, or illegal touching of a loose ball beyond line of scrimmage; rules on plays involving pass receiver, including legality of catch or pass interference; assists in covering actions of runner, including blocks by teammates and that of defenders; calls clipping on punt returns; and, together with Back Judge, rules whether or not field goal attempts are successful.

Side Judge—Operates on same side of field as Linesman, 20 yards deep. Keys on wide receiver on his side. Concentrates on path of end or back, observing legality of his potential block(s) or of actions taken against him. Is prepared to rule from <u>deep</u> position on holding or illegal use of hands by end or back or on defensive infractions committed by player guarding him. Has primary responsibility to make decisions involving sideline on his side of field, e.g., pass receiver or runner in or out of bounds.

Side Judge makes decisions involving catching, recovery, or illegal touching of a loose ball beyond line of scrimmage; rules on plays involving pass receiver, including legality of catch or pass interference; assists in covering actions of runner, including blocks by teammates and that of defenders; and calls clipping on punt returns. On field goals and point after touchdown attempts, he becomes a double umpire.

Back Judge—Takes a position 25 yards downfield. In general, favors the tight end's side of field. Keys on tight end, concentrates on his path and observes legality of tight end's potential block(s) or of actions taken against him. Is prepared to rule from <u>deep</u> position on holding or illegal use of hands by end or back or on defensive infractions committed by player guarding him.

Back Judge times interval between plays on 40/25-second clock plus intermission between two periods of each half; makes decisions involving catching, recovery, or illegal touching of a loose ball beyond line of scrimmage; is responsible to rule on plays involving end line; calls pass interference, fair catch infractions, and clipping on kick returns; together with Field Judge, rules whether or not field goals and conversions are successful; and stays with ball on punts.

DEFINITIONS

1. **Chucking:** Warding off an opponent who is in front of a defender by contacting him with a quick extension of arm or arms, followed by the return of arm(s) to a flexed position, thereby breaking the original contact.
2. **Clipping:** Throwing the body across the back of an opponent's leg or hitting him from the back below the waist while moving up from behind unless the opponent is a runner or the action is in close line play.
3. **Close Line Play:** The area between the positions normally occupied by the offensive tackles, extending three yards on each side of the line of scrimmage. It is legal to clip above the knee.
4. **Crackback:** Eligible receivers who take or move to a position more than two yards outside the tackle may not block an opponent below the waist if they then move back inside to block.
5. **Dead Ball:** Ball not in play.
6. **Double Foul:** A foul by each team during the same down.
7. **Down:** The period of action that starts when the ball is put in play and ends when it is dead.
8. **Encroachment:** When a player enters the neutral zone and makes <u>contact</u> with an opponent before the ball is snapped.
9. **Fair Catch:** An unhindered catch of a kick by a member of the receiving team who must raise one arm a full length above his head and wave his arm from side to side while the kick is in flight.
10. **Foul:** Any violation of a playing rule.
11. **Free Kick:** A kickoff or safety kick. It may be a placekick, dropkick, or punt, except a punt may <u>not</u> be used on a kickoff following a touchdown, successful field goal, or to begin each half or overtime period. A tee cannot be used on a fair-catch or safety kick.
12. **Fumble:** The loss of possession of the ball.
13. **Game Clock:** Scoreboard game clock.
14. **Impetus:** The action of a player that gives momentum to the ball.
15. **Live Ball:** A ball legally free kicked or snapped. It continues in play until the down ends.
16. **Loose Ball:** A live ball not in possession of any player.
17. **Muff:** The touching of a loose ball by a player in an <u>unsuccessful</u> attempt to obtain possession.

18. **Neutral Zone:** The space the length of a ball between the two scrimmage lines. The offensive team and defensive team must remain behind their end of the ball.
 Exception: The offensive player who snaps the ball.
19. **Offside:** A player is offside when any part of his body is beyond his scrimmage or free kick line when the ball is snapped or kicked.
20. **Own Goal:** The goal a team is guarding.
21. **Play Clock:** 40/25 second clock.
22. **Pocket Area:** Applies from a point two yards outside of either offensive tackle and includes the tight end if he drops off the line of scrimmage to pass protect. Pocket extends longitudinally behind the line back to offensive team's own end line.
23. **Possession:** When a player controls the ball throughout the act of clearly touching both feet, or any other part of his body other than his hand(s), to the ground inbounds.
24. **Post-Possession Foul:** A foul by the receiving team that occurs after a ball is legally kicked from scrimmage prior to possession changing. The ball must cross the line of scrimmage and the receiving team must retain possession of the kicked ball.
25. **Punt:** A kick made when a player drops the ball and kicks it while it is in flight.
26. **Safety:** The situation in which the ball is dead on or behind a team's own goal if the impetus comes from a player on that team. Two points are scored for the opposing team.
27. **Shift:** The movement of two or more offensive players at the same time before the snap.
28. **Striking:** The act of swinging, clubbing, or propelling the arm or forearm in contacting an opponent.
29. **Sudden Death:** The continuation of a tied game into sudden death overtime in which the team scoring first (by safety, field goal, or touchdown) wins.
30. **Touchback:** When a ball is dead on or behind a team's own goal line, provided the impetus came from an opponent and provided it is not a touchdown or a missed field goal.
31. **Touchdown:** When any part of the ball, legally in possession of a player inbounds, breaks the plane of the opponent's goal line, provided it is not a touchback.
32. **Unsportsmanlike Conduct:** Any act contrary to the generally understood principles of sportsmanship.

SUMMARY OF PENALTIES

Automatic First Down

1. Awarded to offensive team on all defensive fouls with these exceptions:
 (a) Offside.
 (b) Encroachment.
 (c) Delay of game.
 (d) Illegal substitution.
 (e) Excessive time out(s).
 (f) Incidental grasp of facemask.
 (g) Neutral zone infraction.
 (h) Running into the kicker.
 (i) More than 11 players on the field at the snap.

Five Yards

1. Defensive holding or illegal use of hands (automatic first down).
2. Delay of game on offense or defense.
3. Delay of kickoff.
4. Encroachment.
5. Excessive time out(s).
6. False start.
7. Illegal formation.
8. Illegal shift.
9. Illegal motion.
10. Illegal substitution.
11. First onside kickoff out of bounds between goal lines and untouched or last touched by kicker.
12. Invalid fair catch signal.
13. More than 11 players on the field at snap for either team.
14. Less than seven men on offensive line at snap.
15. Offside.
16. Failure to pause one second after shift or huddle.
17. Running into kicker.
18. More than one man in motion at snap.
19. Grasping facemask of the ball carrier or quarterback.
20. Player out of bounds at snap.
21. Ineligible member(s) of kicking team going beyond line of scrimmage before ball is kicked.
22. Illegal return.
23. Failure to report change of eligibility.
24. Neutral zone infraction.
25. Loss of team time out(s) or five-yard penalty on the defense for excessive crowd noise.
26. Ineligible player downfield during passing down.
27. Second forward pass behind the line.
28. Forward pass is first touched by eligible receiver who has gone out of bounds and returned.
29. Forward pass touches or is caught by an ineligible receiver on or behind line.
30. Forward pass thrown from behind line of scrimmage after ball once crossed the line.
31. Kicking team player voluntarily out of bounds during a punt.
32. Twelve (12) men in the huddle.

10 Yards

1. Offensive pass interference.
2. Holding, illegal use of hands, arms, or body by offense.
3. Tripping by a member of either team.
4. Helping the runner.
5. Deliberately batting or punching a loose ball.
6. Deliberately kicking a loose ball.
7. Illegal block above the waist.

15 Yards

1. Chop block.
2. Clipping below the waist.
3. Fair catch interference.
4. Illegal crackback block by offense.
5. Piling on.
6. Roughing the kicker.
7. Roughing the passer.
8. Twisting, turning, or pulling an opponent by the facemask.
9. Unnecessary roughness.
10. Unsportsmanlike conduct.
11. Delay of game at start of either half.
12. Illegal low block.
13. A tackler using his helmet to butt, spear, or ram an opponent.
14. Any player who uses the top of his helmet unnecessarily.
15. A punter, placekicker, or holder who simulates being roughed by a defensive player.
16. Leaping.
17. Leverage.
18. Any player who removes his helmet after a play while on the field.
19. Taunting.

Five Yards and Loss of Down (Combination Penalty)

1. Forward pass thrown from beyond line of scrimmage.

10 Yards and Loss of Down (Combination Penalty)

1. Intentional grounding of forward pass (safety if passer is in own end zone). If foul occurs more than 10 yards behind line, play results in loss of down at spot of foul.

15 Yards and Loss of Coin Toss Option

1. Team's late arrival on the field prior to scheduled kickoff.
2. Captains not appearing for coin toss.

15 Yards (and disqualification if flagrant)

1. Striking opponent with fist.
2. Kicking or kneeing opponent.
3. Striking opponent on head or neck with forearm, elbow, or hands whether or not the initial contact is made below the neck area.
4. Roughing kicker.
5. Roughing passer.
6. Malicious unnecessary roughness.
7. Unsportsmanlike conduct.
8. Palpably unfair act. (Distance penalty determined by the Referee after consultation with other officials.)

15 Yards and Automatic Disqualification

1. Using a helmet (not worn) as a weapon.
2. Striking or purposely shoving a game official.

Suspension From Game For One Down

1. Illegal equipment. (Player may return after one down when legally equipped.)

Touchdown Awarded (Palpably Unfair Act)

1. When Referee determines a palpably unfair act deprived a team of a touchdown. (Example: Player comes off bench and tackles runner apparently en route to touchdown.)

FIELD

1. Sidelines and end lines are out of bounds. The goal line is actually in the end zone. A player with the ball in his possession scores a touchdown when the

ball is on, above, or over the goal line.

2. The field is rimmed by a white border, six feet wide, along the sidelines. All of this is out of bounds.
3. The hashmarks (inbound lines) are 70 feet, 9 inches from each sideline.
4. Goal posts must be single-standard type, offset from the end line and painted bright gold. The goal posts must be 18 feet, 6 inches wide and the top face of the crossbar must be 10 feet above the ground. Vertical posts extend at least 30 feet above the crossbar. A ribbon 4 inches by 42 inches long is to be attached to the top of each post. The actual goal is the plane extending indefinitely above the crossbar and between the outer edges of the posts.
5. The field is 360 feet long and 160 feet wide. The end zones are 30 feet deep. The line used in try-for-point plays is two yards out from the goal line.
6. Chain crew members and ball boys must be uniformly identifiable.
7. All clubs must use standardized sideline markers. Pylons must be used for goal line and end line markings.
8. End zone markings and club identification at 50 yard line must be approved by the Commissioner to avoid any confusion as to delineation of goal lines, sidelines, and end lines.

BALL

1. The home club shall have 36 balls for outdoor games and 24 for indoor games available for testing with a pressure gauge by the referee two hours prior to the starting time of the game to meet with League requirements. Twelve (12) new footballs, sealed in a special box and shipped by the manufacturer, will be opened in the officials' locker room two hours prior to the starting time of the game. These balls are to be specially marked with the letter "k" and used exclusively for the kicking game.

COIN TOSS

1. The toss of coin will take place within three minutes of kickoff in center of field. The toss will be called by the visiting captain before the coin is flipped. The winner may choose one of two privileges and the loser gets the other:
   (a) Receive or kick
   (b) Goal his team will defend
2. Immediately prior to the start of the second half, the captains of both teams must inform the officials of their respective choices. The loser of the original coin toss gets first choice.

TIMING

1. The stadium game clock is official. In case it stops or is operating incorrectly, the Line Judge takes over the official timing on the field.
2. Each period is 15 minutes. The intermission between the periods is two minutes. Halftime is 12 minutes, unless otherwise specified.
3. On charged team time outs, the Field Judge starts watch and blows whistle after 1 minute 50 seconds, unless television does not utilize the time for commercial. In this case the length of the time out is reduced to 40 seconds.
4. The Referee will allow necessary time to attend to an injured player, or repair a legal player's equipment.
5. Each team is allowed three time outs each half.
6. Time between plays will be 40 seconds from the end of a given play until the snap of the ball for the next play, or a 25-second interval after certain administrative stoppages and game delays.
7. Clock will start running when ball is snapped following all changes of team possession.
8. With the exception of the last two minutes of the first half and the last five minutes of the second half, the game clock will be restarted following a kickoff return, a player going out of bounds on a play from scrimmage, or after declined penalties when appropriate on the referee's signal.
9. Consecutive team time outs can be taken by opposing teams but the length of the second time out will be reduced to 40 seconds.
10. When, in the judgment of the Referee, the level of crowd noise prevents the offense from hearing its signals, he can institute a series of procedures which can result in a loss of team time outs or a five-yard penalty against the defensive team.

SUDDEN DEATH

1. The sudden death system of determining the winner shall prevail when score is tied at the end of the regulation playing time of all NFL games. The team scoring first during overtime play shall be the winner and the game automatically ends upon any score (by safety, field goal, or touchdown) or when a score is awarded by Referee for a palpably unfair act.
2. At the end of regulation time the Referee will immediately toss coin at center of field in accordance with rules pertaining to the usual pregame toss. The captain of the visiting team will call the toss prior to the coin being flipped.
3. Following a three-minute intermission after the end of the regulation game, play will be continued in 15-minute periods or until there is a score. There is a two-minute intermission between subsequent periods. The teams change goals at the start of each period. Each team has three time outs per half and all general timing provisions apply as during a regular game. Disqualified players are not allowed to return.
   Exception: In preseason and regular season games there shall be a maximum of 15 minutes of sudden death with two time outs instead of three. General provisions that apply for the fourth quarter will prevail. Try not attempted if touchdown scored.

TIMING IN FINAL TWO MINUTES OF EACH HALF

1. On kickoff, clock does not start until the ball has been legally touched by player of either team in the field of play. (In all other cases, clock starts with kickoff.)
2. A team cannot buy an excess time out for a penalty. However, a fourth time out is allowed without penalty for an injured player, who must be removed immediately. A fifth time out or more is allowed for an injury and a five-yard penalty is assessed if the clock was running. Additionally, if the clock was running and the score is tied or the team in possession is losing, the ball cannot be put in play for at least 10 seconds on the fourth or more time out. The half or game can end while those 10 seconds are run off on the clock.
3. If the defensive team is behind in the score and commits a foul when it has no time outs left in the final 40 seconds of either half, the offensive team can decline the penalty for the foul and have the time on the clock expire.
4. Fouls that occur in the last five minutes of the fourth quarter as well as the last two minutes of the first half will result in the clock starting on the snap.

TRY

1. After a touchdown, the scoring team is allowed a try during one scrimmage down. The ball may be spotted anywhere between the inbounds lines, two or more yards from the goal line. The successful conversion counts one point by kick; two points for a successful conversion by touchdown; or one point for a safety.
2. The defensive team never can score on a try. As soon as defense gets possession or the kick is blocked or a touchdown is not scored, the try is over.
3. Any distance penalty for fouls committed by the defense that prevent the try from being attempted can be enforced on the succeeding try or succeeding kickoff. Any foul committed on a successful try will result in a distance penalty being assessed on the ensuing kickoff.
4. Only the fumbling player can recover and advance a fumble during a try.

PLAYERS-SUBSTITUTIONS

1. Each team is permitted 11 men on the field at the snap.
2. Unlimited substitution is permitted. However, players may enter the field only when the ball is dead. Players who have been substituted for are not permitted to linger on the field. Such lingering will be interpreted as unsportsmanlike conduct.
3. Players leaving the game must be out of bounds on their own side, clearing the field between the end lines, before a snap or free kick. If player crosses end line leaving field, it is delay of game (five-yard penalty).
4. Offensive substitutes who remain in the game must move onto the field as far as the inside of the field numerals before moving to a wide position.
5. With the exception of the last two minutes of either half, the offensive team, while in the process of substitution or simulated substitution, is prohibited from rushing quickly to the line and snapping the ball with the obvious attempt to cause a defensive foul; i.e., too many men on the field.

KICKOFF

1. The kickoff shall be from the kicking team's 30-yard line at the start of each half and after a field goal and try. A kickoff is one type of free kick.
2. A one-inch tee may be used (no tee permitted for field goal, safety kick, or try attempt) on a kickoff. The ball is put in play by a placekick.
3. A kickoff may not score a field goal.
4. A kickoff is illegal unless it travels 10 yards OR is touched by the receiving team. Once the ball is touched by the receiving team or has gone 10 yards, it is a free ball. Receivers may recover and advance. Kicking team may recover but NOT advance UNLESS receiver had possession and lost the ball.
5. When a kickoff goes out of bounds between the goal lines without being touched by the receiving team, the ball belongs to the receivers 30 yards from the spot of the kick or at the out-of-bounds spot unless the ball went out-of-bounds the first time an onside kick was attempted. In this case, the kicking team is penalized five yards and the ball must be kicked again.
6. When a kickoff goes out of bounds between the goal lines and is touched last

by receiving team, it is receiver's ball at out-of-bounds spot.

7. If the kicking team either illegally kicks off out of bounds or is guilty of a short free kick on two or more consecutive onside kicks, receivers may take possession of the ball at the dead ball spot, out-of-bounds spot, or spot of illegal touch.

SAFETY

1. In addition to a kickoff, the other free kick is a kick after a safety (safety kick). A punt may be used (a punt may not be used on a kickoff).
2. On a safety kick, the team scored upon puts ball in play by a punt, dropkick, or placekick without tee. No score can be made on a free kick following a safety, even if a series of penalties places team in position. (A field goal can be scored only on a play from scrimmage or a free kick after a fair catch.)

FAIR CATCH KICK

1. After a fair catch, the receiving team has the option to put the ball in play by a snap or a fair catch kick (field goal attempt), with fair catch kick lines established ten yards apart. All general rules apply as for a field goal attempt from scrimmage. The clock starts when the ball is kicked. (No tee permitted.)

FIELD GOAL

1. All field goals attempted (kicker) and missed from beyond the 20-yard line will result in the defensive team taking possession of the ball at the spot of the kick. On any field goal attempted and missed where the spot of the kick is on or inside the 20-yard line, ball will revert to defensive team at the 20-yard line.

SAFETY

1. The important factor in a safety is impetus. Two points are scored for the opposing team when the ball is dead on or behind a team's own goal line if the impetus came from a player on that team.

Examples of Safety:

(a) Blocked punt goes out of kicking team's end zone. Impetus was provided by punting team. The block only changes direction of ball, not impetus.
(b) Ball carrier retreats from field of play into his own end zone and is downed. Ball carrier provides impetus.
(c) Offensive team commits a foul and spot of enforcement is behind its own goal line.
(d) Player on receiving team muffs punt and, trying to get ball, forces or illegally kicks (creating new impetus) it into end zone where it goes out of the end zone or is recovered by a member of the receiving team in the end zone.

Examples of Non-Safety:

(a) Player intercepts a pass with both feet inbounds in the field of play and his momentum carries him into his own end zone. Ball is put in play at spot of interception.
(b) Player intercepts a pass in his own end zone and is downed in the end zone, even after recovering in the end zone. Impetus came from passing team, not from defense. (Touchback)
(c) Player passes from behind his own goal line. Opponent bats down ball in end zone. (Incomplete pass)

MEASURING

1. The forward point of the ball is used when measuring.

POSITION OF PLAYERS AT SNAP

1. Offensive team must have at least seven players on line.
2. Offensive players, not on line, must be at least one yard back at snap. **(Exception:** player who takes snap.)
3. No interior lineman may move abruptly after taking or simulating a three-point stance.
4. No player of either team may enter neutral zone before snap.
5. No player of offensive team may charge or move abruptly, after assuming set position, in such manner as to lead defense to believe snap has started. No player of the defensive team within one yard of the line of scrimmage may make an abrupt movement in an attempt to cause the offense to false start.
6. If a player changes his eligibility, the Referee must alert the defensive captain after player has reported to him.
7. All players of offensive team must be stationary at snap, except one back who may be in motion parallel to scrimmage line or backward (not forward).
8. After a shift or huddle all players on offensive team must come to an absolute stop for at least one second with no movement of hands, feet, head, or swaying of body.
9. Quarterbacks can be called for a false start penalty (five yards) if their actions are judged to be an obvious attempt to draw an opponent offside.
10. Offensive linemen are permitted to interlock legs.

USE OF HANDS, ARMS, AND BODY

1. No player on offense may assist a runner except by blocking for him. There shall be no interlocking interference.
2. A runner may ward off opponents with his hands and arms but no other player on offense may use hands or arms to obstruct an opponent by grasping with hands, pushing, or encircling any part of his body during a block. Hands (open or closed) can be thrust forward to initially contact an opponent on or outside the opponent's frame, but the blocker immediately must work to bring his hands on or inside the frame.
Note: Pass blocking: Hand(s) thrust forward that slip outside the body of the defender will be legal if blocker immediately worked to bring them back inside. Hand(s) or arm(s) that encircle a defender—i.e., hook an opponent—are to be considered illegal and officials are to call a foul for holding.
Blocker cannot use his hands or arms to push from behind, hang onto, or encircle an opponent in a manner that restricts his movement as the play develops.
3. Hands cannot be thrust forward above the frame to contact an opponent on the neck, face or head.
Note: The frame is defined as the part of the opponent's body below the neck that is presented to the blocker.
4. A defensive player may not tackle or hold an opponent other than a runner. Otherwise, he may use his hands, arms, or body only:
(a) To defend or protect himself against an obstructing opponent.
Exception: An eligible receiver is considered to be an obstructing opponent ONLY to a point five yards beyond the line of scrimmage unless the player who receives the snap clearly demonstrates no further intention to pass the ball. Within this five-yard zone, a defensive player may chuck an eligible player in front of him. A defensive player is allowed to maintain continuous and unbroken contact within the five-yard zone until a point when the receiver is even with the defender. The defensive player cannot use his hands or arms to push from behind, hang onto, or encircle an eligible receiver in a manner that restricts movement as the play develops. Beyond this five-yard limitation, a defender may use his hands or arms ONLY to defend or protect himself against impending contact caused by a receiver. In such reaction, the defender may not contact a receiver who attempts to take a path to evade him.
(b) To push or pull opponent out of the way on line of scrimmage.
(c) In actual attempt to get at or tackle runner.
(d) To push or pull opponent out of the way in a legal attempt to recover a loose ball.
(e) During a legal block on an opponent who is not an eligible pass receiver.
(f) When legally blocking an eligible pass receiver above the waist.
Exception: Eligible receivers lined up within two yards of the tackle, whether on or immediately behind the line, may be blocked below the waist at or behind the line of scrimmage. NO eligible receiver may be blocked below the waist after he goes beyond the line. (Illegal cut)
Note: Once the quarterback hands off or pitches the ball to a back, or if the quarterback leaves the pocket area, the restrictions (illegal chuck, illegal cut) on the defensive team relative to the offensive receivers will end, provided the ball is not in the air.
5. A defensive player may not contact an opponent above the shoulders with the palm of his hand except to ward him off on the line. This exception is permitted only if it is not a repeated act against the same opponent during any one contact. In all other cases the palms may be used on head, neck, or face only to ward off or push an opponent in legal attempt to get at the ball.
6. Any offensive player who pretends to possess the ball or to whom a teammate pretends to give the ball may be tackled provided he is crossing his scrimmage line between the ends of a normal tight offensive line.
7. An offensive player who lines up more than two yards outside his own tackle or a player who, at the snap, is in a backfield position and subsequently takes a position more than two yards outside a tackle may not clip an opponent anywhere nor may he contact an opponent below the waist if the blocker is moving toward the ball and if contact is made within an area five yards on either side of the line. (crackback)
8. A player of either team may block at any time provided it is not pass interference, fair catch interference, or unnecessary roughness.
9. A player may not bat or punch:
(a) A loose ball (in field of play) toward his opponent's goal line or in any direction in either end zone.
(b) A ball in player possession.
Note: If there is any question as to whether a defender is stripping or batting a ball in player possession, the official(s) will rule the action as a legal

act (stripping the ball).

Exception: A forward or backward pass may be batted, tipped, or deflected in any direction at any time by either the offense or the defense.

Note: A pass in flight that is controlled or caught may only be thrown backward, if it is thrown forward it is considered an illegal bat.

10. No player may deliberately kick any ball except as a punt, dropkick, or placekick.

FORWARD PASS

1. A forward pass may be touched or caught by any eligible receiver. All members of the defensive team are eligible. Eligible receivers on the offensive team are players on either end of line (other than center, guard, or tackle) or players at least one yard behind the line at the snap. A T-formation quarterback is not eligible to receive a forward pass during a play from scrimmage.
   Exception: T-formation quarterback becomes eligible if pass is previously touched by an eligible receiver.
2. An offensive team may make only one forward pass during each play from scrimmage (Loss of 5 yards).
3. The passer must be behind his line of scrimmage (Loss of down and five yards, enforced from the spot of pass).
4. Any eligible offensive player may catch a forward pass. If a pass is touched by one eligible offensive player and touched or caught by a second offensive player, pass completion is legal. Further, all offensive players become eligible once a pass is touched by an eligible receiver or any defensive player.
5. The rules concerning a forward pass and ineligible receivers:
   (a) If ball is touched accidentally by an ineligible receiver on or behind his line: loss of five yards.
   (b) If ineligible receiver is illegally downfield: loss of five yards.
   (c) If touched or caught (intentionally or accidentally) by ineligible receiver beyond the line: loss of 5 yards.
6. The player who first controls and continues to maintain control of a pass will be awarded the ball even though his opponent later establishes joint control of the ball.
7. Any forward pass becomes incomplete and ball is dead if:
   (a) Pass hits the ground or goes out of bounds.
   (b) Pass hits the goal post or the crossbar of either team.
8. A forward pass is complete when a receiver clearly possesses the pass and touches the ground with both feet inbounds while in possession of the ball. If a receiver would have landed inbounds with both feet but is carried or pushed out of bounds while maintaining possession of the ball, pass is complete at the out-of-bounds spot.
9. On a fourth down pass an incomplete pass results in a loss of down at the line of scrimmage.
10. If a personal foul is committed by the defense prior to the completion of a pass, the penalty is 15 yards from the spot where ball becomes dead.
11. If a personal foul is committed by the offense prior to the completion of a pass, the penalty is 15 yards from the previous line of scrimmage.

INTENTIONAL GROUNDING OF FORWARD PASS

1. Intentional grounding of a forward pass is a foul: loss of down and 10 yards from previous spot if passer is in the field of play or loss of down at the spot of the foul if it occurs more than 10 yards behind the line or safety if passer is in his own end zone when ball is released.
2. Intentional grounding will be called when a passer, facing an imminent loss of yardage due to pressure from the defense, throws a forward pass without a realistic chance of completion.
3. Intentional grounding will not be called when a passer, while out of the pocket and facing an imminent loss of yardage, throws a pass that lands at or beyond the line of scrimmage, even if no offensive player(s) have a realistic chance to catch the ball (including if the ball lands out of bounds over the sideline or end line).

PROTECTION OF PASSER

1. By interpretation, a pass begins when the passer—with possession of ball—starts to bring his hand forward. If ball strikes ground after this action has begun, play is ruled an incomplete pass. If passer loses control of ball prior to his bringing his hand forward, play is ruled a fumble.
2. When a passer is holding the ball to pass it forward, any intentional movement forward of his arm starts a forward pass. If a defensive player contacts the passer or the ball after forward movement begins, and the ball leaves the passer's hand, a forward pass is ruled, regardless of where the ball strikes the ground or a player.
3. No defensive player may run into a passer of a legal forward pass after the ball has left his hand (15 yards). The Referee must determine whether opponent had a reasonable chance to stop his momentum during an attempt to block the pass or tackle the passer while he still had the ball.
4. No defensive player who has an unrestricted path to the quarterback may hit him flagrantly in the area of the knee(s) or below when approaching in any direction.
5. Officials are to blow the play dead as soon as the quarterback is clearly in the grasp and control of any tackler, and his safety is in jeopardy.

PASS INTERFERENCE

1. There shall be no interference with a forward pass thrown from behind the line. The restriction for the passing team starts with the snap. The restriction on the defensive team starts when the ball leaves the passer's hand. Both restrictions end when the ball is touched by anyone.
2. The penalty for defensive pass interference is an automatic first down at the spot of the foul. If interference is in the end zone, it is first down for the offense on the defense's 1-yard line. If previous spot was inside the defense's 1-yard line, penalty is half the distance to the goal line.
3. The penalty for offensive pass interference is 10 yards from the previous spot.
4. It is pass interference by either team when any player movement beyond the line of scrimmage significantly hinders the progress of an eligible player of such player's opportunity to catch the ball. Offensive pass interference rules apply from the time the ball is snapped until the ball is touched. Defensive pass interference rules apply from the time the ball is thrown until the ball is touched.
   Actions that constitute defensive pass interference include but are not limited to:
   (a) Contact by a defender who is not playing the ball and such contact restricts the receiver's opportunity to make the catch.
   (b) Playing through the back of a receiver in an attempt to make a play on the ball.
   (c) Grabbing a receiver's arm(s) in such a manner that restricts his opportunity to catch a pass.
   (d) Extending an arm across the body of a receiver thus restricting his ability to catch a pass, regardless of whether the defender is playing the ball.
   (e) Cutting off the path of a receiver by making contact with him without playing the ball.
   (f) Hooking a receiver in an attempt to get to the ball in such a manner that it causes the receiver's body to turn prior to the ball arriving.

   Actions that do not constitute pass interference include but are not limited to:
   (a) Incidental contact by a defender's hands, arms, or body when both players are competing for the ball, or neither player is looking for the ball. If there is any question whether contact is incidental, the ruling shall be no interference.
   (b) Inadvertent tangling of feet when both players are playing the ball or neither player is playing the ball.
   (c) Contact that would normally be considered pass interference, but the pass is clearly uncatchable by the involved players.
   (d) Laying a hand on a receiver that does not restrict the receiver in an attempt to make a play on the ball.
   (e) Contact by a defender who has gained position on a receiver in an attempt to catch the ball.

   Actions that constitute offensive pass interference include but are not limited to:
   (a) Blocking downfield by an offensive player prior to the ball being touched.
   (b) Initiating contact with a defender by shoving or pushing off thus creating a separation in an attempt to catch a pass.
   (c) Driving through a defender who has established a position on the field.

   Actions that do not constitute offensive pass interference include but are not limited to:
   (a) Incidental contact by a receiver's hands, arms, or body when both players are competing for the ball or neither player is looking for the ball.
   (b) Inadvertent touching of feet when both players are playing the ball or neither player is playing the ball.
   (c) Contact that would normally be considered pass interference, but the ball is *clearly* uncatchable by involved players.

Note 1: If there is any question whether player contact is incidental, the ruling should be no interference.

Note 2: Defensive players have as much right to the path of the ball as eligible offensive players.

Note 3: Pass interference for both teams ends when the pass is touched.

Note 4: There can be no pass interference at or behind the line of scrimmage, but defensive actions such as tackling a receiver can still result in a 5-yard penalty for defensive holding, if accepted.

DIGEST OF RULES

Note 5: Whenever a team presents an apparent punting formation, defensive pass interference is not to be called for action on the end man on the line of scrimmage, or an eligible receiver behind the line of scrimmage who is aligned or in motion more than one yard outside the end man on the line. Defensive holding, such as tackling a receiver, still can be called and result in a 5-yard penalty and automatic first down from the previous spot, if accepted. Offensive pass interference rules still apply.

BACKWARD PASS

1. Any pass not forward is regarded as a backward pass. A pass parallel to the line is a backward pass. A runner may pass backward at any time.
2. A backward pass that strikes the ground can be recovered and advanced by either team.
3. A backward pass caught in the air can be advanced by either team.
4. A backward pass in flight may not be batted forward by an offensive player.

FUMBLE

1. The distinction between a fumble and a muff should be kept in mind in considering rules about fumbles. A fumble is the loss of player possession of the ball. A muff is the touching of a loose ball by a player in an unsuccessful attempt to obtain possession.
2. A fumble may be advanced by any player on either team regardless of whether recovered before or after ball hits the ground.
3. A fumble that goes forward and out of bounds will return to the fumbling team at the spot of the fumble unless the ball goes out of bounds in the opponent's end zone. In this case, it is a touchback.
4. On a play from scrimmage, if an offensive player fumbles anywhere on the field during fourth down, only the fumbling player is permitted to recover and/or advance the ball. If any player fumbles after the two-minute warning in a half, only the fumbling player is permitted to recover and/or advance the ball. If recovered by any other offensive player, the ball is dead at the spot of the fumble unless it is recovered behind the spot of the fumble. In that case, the ball is dead at the spot of recovery. Any defensive player may recover and/or advance any fumble at any time.
5. A muffed hand-to-hand snap from center is treated as a fumble.

KICKS FROM SCRIMMAGE

1. Any kick from scrimmage must be made from behind the line to be legal.
2. Any punt or missed field goal that touches a goal post is dead.
3. During a kick from scrimmage, only the end men, as eligible receivers on the line of scrimmage at the time of the snap, are permitted to go beyond the line before the ball is kicked.
   Exception: An eligible receiver who, at the snap, is aligned or in motion behind the line and more than one yard outside the end man on his side of the line, clearly making him the outside receiver, replaces that end man as the player eligible to go downfield after the snap. All other members of the kicking team must remain at the line of scrimmage until the ball has been kicked.
4. Any punt that is blocked and does not cross the line of scrimmage can be recovered and advanced by either team. However, if offensive team recovers it must make the yardage necessary for its first down to retain possession if punt was on fourth down.
5. The kicking team may never advance its own kick even though legal recovery is made beyond the line of scrimmage. Possession only.
6. A member of the receiving team may not run into or rough a kicker who kicks from behind his line unless contact is:
   (a) Incidental to and after he had touched ball in flight.
   (b) Caused by kicker's own motions.
   (c) Occurs during a quick kick, or a kick made after a run behind the line, or after kicker recovers a loose ball on the ground. Ball is loose when kicker muffs snap or snap hits ground.
   (d) Defender is blocked into kicker.
   The penalty for running into the kicker is 5 yards. For roughing the kicker: 15 yards, an automatic first down and disqualification if flagrant.
7. If a member of the kicking team attempting to down the ball on or inside opponent's 5-yard line carries the ball into the end zone, it is a touchback.
8. Fouls during a punt are enforced from the previous spot (line of scrimmage).
   Exception: Illegal touching, fair-catch interference, invalid fair-catch signal, or personal foul (blocking after a fair-catch signal).
9. While the ball is in the air or rolling on the ground following a punt or field-goal attempt and receiving team commits a foul only before or after gaining possession, receiving team will retain possession and will be penalized for its foul.
10. It will be illegal for a defensive player to jump or stand on any player, or be picked up by a teammate or to use a hand or hands on a teammate to gain additional height in an attempt to block a kick (Penalty: 15 yards, unsportsmanlike conduct).
11. A punted ball remains a kicked ball until it is declared dead or in possession of either team.
12. Any member of the punting team may down the ball anywhere in the field of play. However, it is illegal touching (Official's time out and receiver's ball at spot of illegal touching). This foul does not offset any foul by receivers during the down.
13. Defensive team may advance all kicks from scrimmage (including unsuccessful field goal) whether or not ball crosses defensive team's goal line. Rules pertaining to kicks from scrimmage apply until defensive team gains possession.
14. When a team presents a punt formation, defensive pass interference is not to be called for actions on the widest player eligible to go beyond line. Defensive holding may be called.

FAIR CATCH

1. The member of the receiving team must raise one arm a full length above his head and wave it from side to side while kick is in flight. (Failure to give proper sign: receivers' ball five yards behind spot of signal.) **Note:** It is legal for the receiver to shield his eyes from the sun by raising one hand no higher than the helmet.
2. No opponent may interfere with the fair catcher, the ball, or his path to the ball. Penalty: 15 yards from spot of foul and fair catch is awarded.
3. A player who signals for a fair catch is not required to catch the ball. However, if a player signals for a fair catch, he may not block or initiate contact with any player on the kicking team until the ball touches a player. Penalty: snap 15 yards.
4. If ball hits ground or is touched by member of kicking team in flight, fair catch signal is off and all rules for a kicked ball apply.
5. Any undue advance by a fair catch receiver is delay of game. No specific distance is specified for undue advance as ball is dead at spot of catch. If player comes to a reasonable stop, no penalty. For penalty, five yards.
6. If time expires while ball is in play and a fair catch is awarded, receiving team may choose to extend the period with one fair catch kick down. However, placekicker may not use tee.

FOUL ON LAST PLAY OF HALF OR GAME

1. On a foul by defense on last play of half or game, the down is replayed if penalty is accepted.
2. On a foul by the offense on last play of half or game, the down is not replayed and the play in which the foul is committed is nullified.
   Exception: Fair catch interference, foul following change of possession, illegal touching. No score by offense counts.

SPOT OF ENFORCEMENT OF FOUL

1. There are four basic spots at which a penalty for a foul is enforced:
   (a) Spot of foul: The spot where the foul is committed.
   (b) Previous spot: The spot where the ball was put in play.
   (c) Spot of snap, backward pass or fumble: The spot where the foul occurred or the spot where the penalty is to be enforced.
   (d) Succeeding spot: The spot where the ball next would be put in play if no distance penalty were to be enforced.
   Exception: If foul occurs after a touchdown and before the whistle for a try, succeeding spot is spot of next kickoff.
2. All fouls committed by offensive team behind the line of scrimmage (except in the end zone) shall be penalized from the previous spot. If the foul is in the end zone, it is a safety.
3. When spot of enforcement for fouls involving defensive holding or illegal use of hands by the defense is behind the line of scrimmage, any penalty yardage to be assessed on that play shall be measured from the line if the foul occurred beyond the line.

DOUBLE FOUL

1. If there is a double foul during a down in which there is a change of possession, the team last gaining possession may keep the ball unless its foul was committed prior to the change of possession.
2. If double foul occurs after a change of possession, the defensive team retains the ball at the spot of its foul or dead ball spot.
3. If one of the fouls of a double foul involves disqualification, that player must be removed, but no penalty yardage is to be assessed.
4. If the kickers foul during a kickoff, punt, safety kick, or field-goal attempt before possession changes, the receivers will have the option of replaying the down at the previous spot (offsetting fouls), or keeping the ball after enforcement for its fouls.

PENALTY ENFORCED ON FOLLOWING KICKOFF

1. When a team scores by touchdown, field goal, extra point, or safety and either team commits a personal foul, unsportsmanlike conduct, or obvious unfair act during the down, the penalty will be assessed on the following kickoff.

EMERGENCIES AND UNFAIR ACTS

Emergencies—Policy

The National Football League requires all League personnel, including game officials, League office employees, players, coaches, and other club employees to use best effort to see that each game—preseason, regular season, and postseason—is played to its conclusion. The League recognizes, however, that emergencies may arise that make a game's completion impossible or inadvisable. Such circumstances may include, but are not limited to, severely inclement weather, natural or manmade disaster, power failure, and spectator interference. Games should be suspended, cancelled, postponed, or terminated when circumstances exist such that comencement or continuation of play would pose a threat to the safety of participants or spectators.

Authority of Commissioner's Office

1. Authority to cancel, postpone, or terminate games is vested only in the Commissioner and the League President (other League office representatives and referees may suspend play temporarily; see point No. 3 under this section and point No. 1 under "Authority of Referee" below). The following definitions apply:
   - **Cancel.** To cancel a game is to nullify it either before or after it begins and to make no provision for rescheduling it or for including its score or other performance statistics in League records.
   - **Postpone.** To postpone a game is (a) to defer its starting time to a later date, or (b) to suspend it after play has begun and to make provision to resume at a later date with all scores and other performance statistics up to the point of postponement added to those achieved in the resumed portion of the game.
   - **Terminate.** To terminate a game is to end it short of a full 60 minutes of play, to record it officially as a completed game, and to make no provision to resume it at a later date. The Commissioner or League President may terminate a game in an emergency if, in his opinion, it is reasonable to project that its resumption (a) would not change its ultimate result or (b) would not adversely affect any other interteam competitive issue.
   - **Forfeit.** The Commissioner, (except in cases of disciplinary action; see last section on "Removing Team from Field"), League President, and their representatives, including referees, are not authorized unilaterally to declare forfeits. A forfeit occurs only when a game is not played because of the failure or refusal of *one* team to participate. In that event, the other team, if ready and willing to play, is the winner by a score of 2-0.
2. If an emergency arises that may require cancellation, postponement, or termination (see above), the highest ranking representative from the Commissioner's office working the game in a "control" capacity will consult with the Commissioner, League President, or game-day duty officer designated by the League (by telephone, if that person is not in attendance) concerning such decision. If circumstances warrant, the League representative should also attempt to consult with the weather bureau and with appropriate security personnel of the League, club, stadium, and local authorities. If no representative from the Commissioner's office is working the game in a "control" capacity, the referee will be in charge (see "Authority of Referee" below).
3. In circumstances where safety is of immediate concern, the Commissioner's-office representative may, after consulting with the referee, authorize a temporary suspension in play and, if warranted, removal of the participants from the playing field. The representative should be mindful of the safety of spectators, players, game officials, nonplayer personnel in the bench areas, and other field-level personnel such as photographers and cheerleaders.
4. If possible, the League-office representative should consult with authorized representatives of the two participating clubs before any decision involving cancellation, postponement, or termination is made by the Commissioner or League President.
5. If the Commissioner or League President decides to cancel, postpone, or terminate a game, his representative at the game or the game-day duty officer will then determine the method(s) for announcing such decision, e.g., by public-address announcement over referee's wireless microphone, by public-address announcement by home club, or by communication to radio, television, and other news media.

Authority of Referee

1. If a referee determines that an emergency warrants immediate removal of participants from the playing field for safety reasons, he may do so on his own authority. If, however, circumstances allow him the time, he must reach the highest ranking full-time League office representative working at the game in a "control" capacity or the game-day duty officer designated by the League (by telephone, if that person is not in attendance) and discuss the actual or potential emergency with such representative or duty officer. That representative or duty officer then will make the final decision on removal of participants from the field or obtain a decision from the Commissioner or League President.
2. If a referee removes participants from the playing field under No. 1 above, he may order them to their respective bench areas or to their locker rooms, whichever is appropriate in the circumstances.
3. After appropriate consultation under No. 1 above, the referee must advise the two participating head coaches of the nature of the emergency and the action contemplated (if the decision has not yet been reached) or of the final decision.
4. The referee must *not*, before a decision is reached, make an announcement on his microphone concerning the possibility of a cancellation, postponement, or termination unless instructed to do so by an appropriate representative of the Commissioner's office.
5. The referee must *not* discuss a forfeit with head coaches or club personnel and must *not* use that term over the referee's microphone (see definition of *forfeit* under No. 1 of "Authority of Commissioner's Office" above).
6. The referee must *not* assess an unsportsmanlike-conduct penalty on the home team for actions of fans that cause or contribute to an emergency.
7. The referee should be mindful of the safety of not only players and officials, but also of the spectators and other nonparticipants.
8. If an emergency involves spectator interference (for example, nonparticipants on the field or thrown objects), the referee immediately should contact the appropriate club or League representative for additional security assistance, including, if applicable, involvement of the League's security representative(s) assigned to the game.
9. The referee may order the resumption of play when he deems conditions safe for all concerned and, if circumstances warrant, after consultation with appropriate representatives of the Commissioner's office.
10. Under no circumstances is the referee authorized to cancel, postpone, terminate, or declare forfeiture of a game unilaterally.

Procedures for Starting and Resuming Games

Subject to the points of authority listed above, League personnel and referees will be guided by the following procedures for starting and resuming games that are affected by emergencies.

1. If, because of an emergency, a regular-season or postseason game is not started at its scheduled time and cannot be played at any later time that same day, the game nevertheless must be played on a subsequent date to be determined by the Commissioner.
2. If an emergency threatens to occur during the playing of a game (for example, an incoming tropical storm), the starting time of the game will not be moved to an earlier time unless there is clearly sufficient time to make an orderly change.
3. All games that are suspended temporarily and resumed on the same day, and all suspended games that are postponed to a later date, will be resumed at the point of suspension. On suspension, the referee will call timeout and make a record of the following: team possessing the ball, direction in which its offense was headed, position of the ball on the field, down, distance, period, time remaining in the period, and any other pertinent information required for an orderly and equitable resumption of play.
4. For regular-season postponements, the Commissioner will make every effort to set the game for no later than two days after its originally scheduled date and at the same site. If unable to schedule at the same site, he will select an appropriate alternative site. If it is impossible to schedule the game within two days after its original date, the Commissioner will attempt to schedule it on the Tuesday of the next calendar week. The Commissioner will keep in mind the potential for competitive inequities if one or both of the involved clubs has already been scheduled for a game close to the Tuesday of that week (for example, a Thursday game).
5. For postseason postponements, the Commissioner will make every effort to set the game as soon as possible after its originally scheduled date and at the same site. If unable to schedule at the same site, he will select an appropriate alternative site.
6. Whenever postponement is attributable to negligence by a club, the negligent club is responsible for all home club costs and expenses, including, subject to approval by the Commissioner, gate receipts and television-contract income. [See Section 19.11 (C) of the NFL Constitution and Bylaws.]
7. Each home club is strictly responsible for having the playing surface of its stadium well maintained and suitable for NFL play.

UNFAIR ACTS

Commissioner's Authority

The Commissioner has sole authority to investigate and to take appropriate disciplinary or corrective measures if any club action, nonparticipant interference, or emergency occurs in an NFL game which he deems so unfair or outside the accepted tactics encountered in professional football that such action has a major effect on the result of a game.

No Club Protests

The authority and measures provided for in this section (UNFAIR ACTS) do not constitute a protest machinery for NFL clubs to dispute the result of a game. The Commissioner will conduct an investigation under this section only to review an act or occurrence that he deems so unfair that the result of the game in question may be inequitable to one of the participating teams. The Commissioner will not apply his authority under this section when a club registers a complaint concerning judgmental errors or routine errors of omission by game officials. Games involving such complaints will continue to stand as completed.

Penalties for Unfair Acts

The Commissioner's powers under this section (UNFAIR ACTS) include the imposition of monetary fines and draft choice forfeitures, suspension of persons involved, and, if appropriate, the reversal of a game's result or the rescheduling of a game, either from the beginning or from the point at which the extraordinary act occurred. In the event of rescheduling a game, the Commissioner will be guided by the procedures specified above ("Procedures for Starting and Resuming Games" under EMERGENCIES). In all cases, the Commissioner will conduct a full investigation, including the opportunity for hearings, use of game videotape, and any other procedures he deems appropriate.

REMOVING TEAM FROM FIELD

No player, coach, or other person affiliated with a club may remove that club's team from the field during the playing of any game, including preseason, except at the direction of the referee. Any club violating this rule will be subject to disciplinary action by the Commissioner, including possible game forfeiture and sole liability for financial losses suffered by the opposing club and any other affected member clubs of the League. [See Section 9.1 (E) of the NFL Constitution and Bylaws.]

280 Park Avenue, New York, New York 10017 (212) 450-2000

NFL Internet Network: http://NFL.com

Commissioner: Paul Tagliabue

Executive Vice President of Business, Properties & Club Services: Roger Goodell

Executive Vice President-Labor Relations/Chairman NFLMC: Harold Henderson

Executive Vice President, League Counsel & CAO: Jeff Pash

Executive Vice President of New Media/Internet & Enterprises: Tom Spock

Senior Vice President-Football Operations: George Young

NOTES